Liabilities, Preferred Stock and Common Shareholders' Equity

	February 3 1990	January 28 1989
Current Liabilities		
Notes payable to banks—Note C	$ 12,000	$ 34,000
Accounts payable	65,008	52,959
Accrued expenses	13,015	13,710
Federal, state, and local taxes	14,130	10,172
Deferred income taxes	5,204	7,711
Long-term debt and capital lease obligations due within one year	9,767	7,971
Total Current Liabilities	119,124	126,523
Long-Term Debt—due after one year—Note C	167,188	154,267
Capital Lease Obligations—due after one year—Note H	59,179	63,773
Other Liabilities—principally deferred income taxes	37,256	36,755
Preferred Stock—Note E		
$5 Cumulative Preferred Stock, $100 par value, redeemable at $105 a share: authorized 1989—10,230 shares; outstanding—10,217 shares (1988—11,985 shares outstanding)	1,022	1,199
Series Preferred Stock—no par value: authorized—2,000,000 shares; none issued	–0–	–0–
Common Shareholders' Equity—Notes C and F		
Series A Common Stock—par value $1 a share: authorized—20,000,000 shares; issued 1989—5,427,211 shares, 1988—4,966,551 shares	5,427	4,967
Series B Common Stock—par value $1 a share, convertible: authorized—20,000,000 shares; issued 1989—3,051,428 shares, 1988—2,893,347 shares	3,051	2,893
Capital in addition to par value of shares	118,729	97,106
Earnings retained for use in the business	107,570	105,795
Total Common Shareholders' Equity	234,777	210,761
	$618,546	$593,278

See notes to consolidated financial statements in the appendix of this textbook.

INTERMEDIATE ACCOUNTING

FOURTH EDITION

THE DRYDEN/HBJ ACCOUNTING SERIES

Introductory
Bischoff, *Introduction to College Accounting,* Second Edition (Chs. 1–10, 1–14, and 1–28)

Principles
Hillman, Kochanek, and Norgaard, *Principles of Accounting,* Sixth Edition

Walgenbach, Hanson, and Hamre, *Principles of Accounting,* Fifth Edition

Computerized
Brigham and Knechel, *Financial Accounting Using Lotus 1-2-3*

Wanlass, *Computer Resource Guide: Principles of Accounting,* Third Edition

Financial
Backer, Elgers, and Asebrook, *Financial Accounting: Concepts and Practices*

Beirne and Dauderis, *Financial Accounting: An Introduction to Decision Making*

Hoskin and Hughes, *Financial Accounting Cases*

Kochanek, Hillman, and Norgaard, *Financial Accounting,* Second Edition

Stickney, Weil, and Davidson, *Financial Accounting: An Introduction to Concepts, Methods, and Uses,* Sixth Edition

Walgenbach and Hanson, *Financial Accounting,* Sixth Edition

Managerial
Ketz, Campbell, and Baxendale, *Management Accounting*

Maher, Stickney, Weil, and Davidson, *Managerial Accounting: An Introduction to Concepts, Methods, and Uses,* Fourth Edition

Intermediate
Williams, Stanga, and Holder, *Intermediate Accounting,* Fourth Edition

Advanced
Huefner and Largay, *Advanced Financial Accounting,* Third Edition

Pahler and Mori, *Advanced Accounting,* Fourth Edition

Financial Statement Analysis
Stickney, *Financial Statement Analysis: A Strategic Perspective*

Auditing
Guy, Alderman, and Winters, *Auditing,* Second Edition

Governmental and Nonprofit
Douglas, *Government and Nonprofit Accounting*

Ziebell and DeCoster, *Management Control Systems in Nonprofit Organizations*

Theory
Bloom and Elgers, *Accounting Theory and Policy,* Second Edition

Taxation
Everett, Boley, Duncan, and Jamison, *HBJ Federal Tax Course, Vol. I*

Everett, Raabe, and Fortin, *Fundamentals of Taxation*

Sommerfeld, Madeo, and Milliron, *An Introduction to Taxation*

Reference
Miller, *HBJ Miller GAAP Guide,* College Edition

Miller and Bailey, *HBJ Miller GAAS Guide,* College Edition

INTERMEDIATE ACCOUNTING

FOURTH EDITION

Jan R. Williams
The University of Tennessee

Keith G. Stanga
The University of Tennessee

William W. Holder
The University of Southern California

The Dryden Press
Harcourt Brace Jovanovich College Publishers

Fort Worth   Philadelphia   San Diego   New York   Orlando   Austin   San Antonio
Toronto   Montreal   London   Sydney   Tokyo

To Our Families
Elaine, Jennifer, and Julie Williams

Josie, Ben, and Brian Stanga

Carolyn, Mark, and Katie Holder
and Marc Carlson

Acquisitions Editor: Tim Vertovec
Manuscript Editor: Karen Carriere
Production Editor: Michael Ferreira
Designer: Suzanne Montazer
Art Editor: Cindy Robinson
Production Manager: Mary Kay Yearin

Material from Uniform CPA Examination Questions and Unofficial Answers, copyright © 1957 through 1987 by the American Institute of Certified Public Accountants, Inc., is adapted with permission.

Material from the Certificate in Management Accounting Examination, copyright © 1972 through 1984 by the National Association of Accountants, is adapted with permission.

Copyright © 1992, 1989, 1987, 1984 by Harcourt Brace Jovanovich, Inc.

All rights reserved. No part of this publication may be reproduced or transmitted in any form or by any means, electronic or mechanical, including photocopy, recording, or any information storage and retrieval system, without permission in writing from the publisher.

Requests for permission to make copies of any part of the work should be mailed to: Permissions Department, Harcourt Brace Jovanovich, Inc., 8th Floor, Orlando, Florida 32887.

ISBN: 0–15–541314–7

Library of Congress Catalog Card Number: 91–72314

Printed in the United States of America

PREFACE

The primary subject of *Intermediate Accounting* is financial reporting for corporate business enterprises. Financial reporting practices of U.S. corporations involve a complicated but interesting combination of principles and procedures that have emerged over several decades. Many procedures can be explained by several broad accounting principles; others can be justified only by their having gained widespread acceptance in practice over many years.

The Fourth Edition of *Intermediate Accounting* provides the authors an opportunity to refine the approach taken in the previous editions. Specifically, we have attempted to strike a balance between a procedural explanation of currently applied accounting practices and a discussion of the theoretical framework on which those practices are based. Serious accounting students who seek professional success must understand both theory and practice to meet the challenges that will face them in the future.

We have also attempted to strike an appropriate balance between current practice and alternatives to current practice. To understand accounting as it currently exists and as it may evolve in the future, students must understand alternatives to current practice.

ORGANIZATION OF THE TEXT

The text is organized into five major sections:

1. Theoretical Foundation for Financial Reporting (Chapters 1–4)
2. Tools of Accounting (Chapters 5–6)
3. Asset Accounting (Chapters 7–13)
4. Liability and Stockholders' Equity Accounting (Chapters 14–17)
5. Additional Financial Reporting Issues (Chapters 18–26)

In the first section, "Theoretical Foundation for Financial Reporting," we prepare the student for the remainder of the text by providing the conceptual background necessary to understand generally accepted accounting principles and alternatives to those principles. Chapter 1 describes many of the important environmental factors and professional organizations that influence the development of corporate financial reporting. Chapter 2 presents the current conceptual framework of corporate financial reporting. This chapter is important because it explains the broad accounting principles that underlie many specific procedures currently used in the preparation of financial statements. These principles, emphasized in Chapter 2, are then highlighted throughout the text as we illustrate their application to specific reporting practices. Chapter 3 introduces the student to the nature and measurement of the elements of financial statements, stressing alternatives to current practice in a way that is understandable at this early point in the student's study of financial accounting. Chapter 4 reviews the four basic financial statements at the level of understanding that the student should have when entering intermediate accounting. By discussing all of the financial statements in a single chapter, we can stress an important feature of financial statements—*articulation*.

The second section of the text, "Tools of Accounting," covers two major topics. Chapter 5 reviews the accounting cycle and related practices used by business enterprises to keep adequate records efficiently and to prepare effective reports, and Chapter 6 explains compound interest concepts in depth. These tools are used frequently throughout the text.

The third section, "Asset Accounting," includes seven chapters (Chapters 7–13) which deal with the major asset categories typically found on corporate balance sheets: cash, receivables, inventories, investments, plant assets, and intangible assets. Throughout these chapters, material that students have studied in introductory accounting courses is reviewed and new, more advanced aspects of each asset category are discussed. Care has been taken to explain new material thoroughly and extensive use has been made of examples and illustrations to enhance student understanding.

The fourth section, "Liability and Stockholders' Equity Accounting," encompasses four chapters. Chapter 14 addresses current and contingent liabilities. Chapter 15 discusses long-term debt. Chapters 16 and 17 cover a variety of topics related to stockholders' equity. The purpose of this section is to make students aware of the alternative methods of corporate financing and the many accounting principles that are reflected in the liability and stockholders' equity sections of corporate balance sheets.

The fifth section, "Additional Financial Reporting Issues," covers several advanced topics that are new to accounting students or have only been mentioned briefly in other accounting courses. It includes chapters on financial reporting of income taxes (Chapter 18), accounting for changes and error correction (Chapter 19), revenue measurement and income presentation (Chapter 20), earnings per share (Chapter 21), reporting cash flow information (Chapter 22), accounting for leases and retirement benefits (Chapters 23 and 24), additional disclosure issues and financial analysis (Chapter 25), and, finally, financial reporting and changing prices (Chapter 26). These chapters require students to recall, integrate, and apply material from earlier chapters.

Chapter 26 also discusses both constant dollar and current cost approaches to dealing with the need to provide information about the impact of changing prices on a company's financial position and results of operations.

CHANGES IN THE FOURTH EDITION

Several significant changes have been made in the Fourth Edition of *Intermediate Accounting*. Financial accounting is an evolutionary body of knowledge that is constantly changing. This continual change presents both a challenge and an opportunity for authors to write a text that is current and understandable. As this revision goes to press, all authoritative accounting pronouncements that have been issued since the writing of our Third Edition and that affect the content of intermediate accounting have been incorporated. In addition, other important changes have been made in this edition. Some of the most significant of these changes are highlighted below.

Four subjects have received particularly close attention in this revision of Intermediate Accounting: accounting for income taxes (Chapter 18), accounting for leases (Chapter 23), accounting for pensions and other retirement benefits (Chapter 24) and additional disclosure issues and financial analysis (Chapter 25).

Throughout the period of the Third Edition of *Intermediate Accounting,* the FASB has debated the issue of accounting for income taxes and evaluated its positions taken in *SFAS No. 96.* In fact, controversy surrounding that pronouncement has resulted in the deferral of its effective date several times. In this Fourth Edition Chapter 18 has been extensively revised to focus attention on the current controversy surrounding accounting for income taxes with an emphasis on general principles and alternative methods of accounting rather than on the content of any specific authoritative accounting pronouncement. The technical aspects of the current authoritative pronouncements on deferred taxes are explained in a detailed chapter appendix.

One of the most difficult topics for intermediate accounting students is accounting for leases. In an effort to clarify this complex subject, Chapter 23 has been thoroughly revised to reduce technical complexity. It includes a rewrite of the capital lease sections and new, simplified tables.

The scope of Chapter 24 has been broadened from accounting for pensions to accounting for retirement benefits. This chapter is intended to reflect the growing concern and newly-pronounced accounting requirements for retirement benefits other than pensions, including life and health insurance plans for retirees, as well as other retirement benefits. While the primary retirement benefit covered in Chapter 24 continues to be pensions, reasonable attention is given to other benefits in light of the issuance of *SFAS No. 106,* "Employers' Accounting for Postretirement Benefits Other Than Pensions."

Finally, Chapter 25 on the subject of additional disclosure issues and financial analysis has been significantly revised for this Fourth Edition. This revision is not in reaction to changes in authoritative accounting literature. Rather, it is an attempt to strengthen, as well as streamline, the coverage of the dual subjects of financial statement disclosure and financial analysis. Material concerning disclosure issues that overlaps other sections of the text have been eliminated and the financial analysis section has been significantly revised, including analysis of key information from the statement of cash flows.

All of the authors regularly teach intermediate accounting courses at their respective universities. We have listened carefully to our students, colleagues, and faculty members at other colleges and universities and have incorporated many of their suggestions into the Fourth Edition. We have also updated most of the financial statement excerpts to reflect current reporting examples. In most cases, the boxed articles found throughout the text have also been replaced with current readings.

END-OF-CHAPTER MATERIAL

Questions, exercises, problems, cases, and judgment cases appear at the end of each chapter. They offer a variety of opportunities for students to continue the learning process by applying concepts presented in the text.

Questions typically involve short discussions and emphasize the major points of the chapter. Some questions are multiple choice.

Exercises typically involve computations and usually focus on one major point.

Problems require computations and, often, discussion. They usually require the student to apply several major points discussed in the text.

Cases are generally extended discussion questions, often involving in-depth consideration of the issues emerging from topics covered in the chapter. Cases enable students to develop written communication skills in a context similar to what they may encounter in the accounting profession.

Judgment cases are new in the Fourth Edition of *Intermediate Accounting*. They are intended to expose the student to the many uncertainties involved in the financial reporting process and the judgments required by professional accountants. Many require the student to make and support decisions based on logical reasoning, as well as a knowledge of current accounting standards.

Appropriate questions, exercises, problems, and cases have been adapted from CPA and CMA examinations. Exercises, problems, cases, and judgment cases are preceded by a short phrase identifying the major subject of each item.

FEATURES

A brief review of *Intermediate Accounting*, Fourth Edition, reveals many features designed to help students understand the text. Each chapter begins with objectives that preview the chapter and ends with key points that highlight the most important subjects in the chapter.

The basic accounting principles discussed in Chapter 2 are highlighted in the margin throughout the text. This feature is designed to demonstrate how important accounting principles—such as revenue realization, matching, and consistency—are applied in practice.

Throughout the text, short readings are provided to expand the student's understanding of accounting principles and the issues and controversies surrounding those principles. Most readings are taken from business periodicals and provide insight into the importance of corporate financial reporting to investors and creditors.

At appropriate points in the text, diagrams and flowcharts follow discussions and examples to summarize complex procedures—such as accounting for current and noncurrent marketable equity securities, accounting for leases, and preparing earnings-per-share figures for companies with complex capital structures.

End-of-chapter appendixes are designed to present specialized subjects, complex topics and less frequently used accounting methods.

Throughout the text, excerpts from published financial statements of major U.S. corporations illustrate how various accounting principles are applied. These excerpts are usually preceded by a brief description of the company to familiarize the student with the nature of the reporting enterprise.

The 1989 annual report and basic financial statements of Strawbridge & Clothier are reproduced in their entirety and are cited throughout the text. The annual report is presented as an appendix, and three of the financial statements are featured inside the front and back covers.

SUPPLEMENTS

For the Student

- *Study Guide including Lotus® 1-2-3® Applications Manual,* by James M. Reeve, University of Tennessee. Part I of this manual contains a Study Guide, consisting of the following sections for each chapter: Chapter Review, Learning Enrichment, Suggested Readings, Multiple-Choice Questions, Exercises, and Solutions to Questions and Exercises. Part II contains the documentation necessary to build and run Lotus templates. These templates can be used to solve end-of-chapter material designated by the following logo:⬚ . A master disk is available free to instructors.

- *Working Papers* containing the forms necessary to complete all the problems in the text.

- *Practice Set, Classic Toys and Trains,* by Sandra Pelfrey and Gadis J. Dillon (both of Oakland University). This practice set reviews the accounting cycle and is to be used in conjunction with Chapter 5. It can be customized (through random numbers, social security numbers, and so forth) to create an infinite number of data sets.

- *Computerized Practice Set, Classic Toys and Trains,* by Sandra Pelfrey and Gadis J. Dillon (both of Oakland University) and Kent Finkle. A limited, general ledger accounting program is included, allowing students to work the practice set on a computer.

For the Instructor

- *Instructor's Manual,* by Jane Campbell, University of Dayton. Most chapters in the Instructor's Manual contain the following sections: Text Objectives, Teaching Objectives, Major Topics, Chapter/Lecture Outline, Teaching Suggestions, Description of selected text enrichment material, Overview of end-of-chapter material by topic, Overview of end-of-chapter material by item, Suggested end-of-chapter sequences, Correlation chart between the Third and Fourth editions, and Related Readings. In addition, the Instructor's Manual also includes a discussion guide for the judgment cases, a model solution to the practice set, and a reprint of the checklist of key figures.

- *Instructor's Manual on a Disk.* The Instructor's Manual is also available in word processing files on a disk.

- *Solutions Manual,* written by the textbook authors. This manual contains answers to all questions, exercises, problems, and cases.

- *Test Resource Manual,* by Michael Kennelley, Florida State University. Over 1200 questions are included in this manual, and each chapter consists of the following: ten to fifteen true/false questions, five to fifteen conceptual multiple choice, five to ten application multiple choice, six to nine problems, and one to three miscellaneous questions. Suggested examinations and solutions are provided.

- *Computerized Test Bank.* The Test Bank is also available in a computerized format that allows instructors to edit and add questions and generate multiple versions of examinations with answer keys.

- *Transparencies.* Approximately 1000 acetates are available to all adopters. They consist of Solutions Transparencies of all problems and exercises in the text and 2-color Teaching Transparencies of selected exhibits from the textbook.

- *Solutions Template Disk to Practice Set A, Classic Toys and Trains.* This disk allows instructors to generate solutions for any of the infinite data sets that can be created for the Classic Toys and Trains practice set.

- *Instructor's Package to Lotus ® 1-2-3 ® Applications,* by James M. Reeve, University of Tennessee. This package contains the Instructor's Manual, a Master Student Disk, and a Master Instructor's Disk for the electronic spreadsheet templates. Both 5 1/2″ and 3 1/2″ disks are available.

- *Checklist of Key Figures.* This list of principal figures in the textbook is provided free in class quantity.

- *Miller GAAP Guide: College Edition 1992.* All current FASB and AICPA pronouncements are restated and analyzed, cross-referenced, organized by topic, and indexed in this guide.

- *Miller Comprehensive GAAP Guide Update Service.* The update service provides technical analyses of GAAP within weeks of the release of official pronouncements.

ACKNOWLEDGMENTS

Many people have contributed to the writing, review, revision, and publication of *Intermediate Accounting.* The authors recognize the important contributions of these people and deeply appreciate their involvement in the revision.

One of the most useful forms of input concerning a text is the expert evaluation of accounting educators who invest time and effort in reviewing the manuscript at the request of the publisher. We received many thoughtful reviews of our first three editions and gave careful consideration to all suggestions made. We gratefully acknowledge the contributions of the following individuals who were willing to assist us as we sought to improve the overall quality of this text in the current edition: Angela H. Bell, Jacksonville State University; Richard E. Czarnecki, University of Michigan, Dearborn; Bill Faulk, Northwestern Michigan College; Harold Goedde, North Carolina Agricultural and Technical State University; Scott I. Jerris, West Virginia University; Orville Keister, University of Akron; Tim Kelley, University of San Diego; Mike Kennelley, Florida State University; R. David Mautz, Jr., Virginia Polytechnic Institute and State University; Barbara Reider, University of Alaska, Anchorage; Lynn Stephens, Eastern Washington University; Gary L. Waters, University of Texas at Austin; Arlette C. Wilson, Auburn University; and Gail B. Wright, University of Richmond. We also wish to thank the many users of the previous editions who responded to detailed questionnaires or otherwise offered suggestions.

The editorial staff at Harcourt Brace Jovanovich, Inc. has provided guidance, motivation and inspiration to this revision. Kenneth W. Rethmeier, former executive editor, provided broad overall guidance for this revision. As with previous editions, Ken's personal interest in the project and in the authors has been a source of particular encouragement as we have attempted to meet the challenging deadlines required for this revision. Accounting editors Bill Teague and, most recently, Tim Vertovec have skillfully guided the project through its various stages. They, too, have shown great personal interest in the project and have impressed the authors with their understanding of the various components of the textbook and its supplements, as well as the desire of accounting professors for certain changes in the content of the textbook. They have carefully chosen individuals to review the text, yet given the authors relative freedom to interpret those reviews. Finally, manuscript editor Karen Carriere has been a great help on this revision with her careful reading and editing of the manuscript. While the authors are responsible for the technical content of the text, much of its readability is due to Karen's attention to clarity in structure and wording.

Our gratitude also goes to the other members of Harcourt Brace Jovanovich associated with our project, including Ted Barnett, Kevin Cottingim, Alison Howell, Michael Ferreira, Suzanne Montazer, Cindy Robinson, and Mary Kay Yearin.

We want to thank our students and faculty colleagues at the University of Tennessee and the University of Southern California for their advice and counsel. Many useful suggestions from these individuals have been incorporated into this revision. Direct input from those studying the text and those teaching it is invaluable to the authors. Particular mention is due to Lynn Reeves, formerly a Master of Accountancy student and now a lecturer in accounting at the University of Tennessee. She has provided invaluable assistance to the authors in completing this revision.

James Reeve (The University of Tennessee, Knoxville) reviewed the manuscript in early stages of our first edition and assisted in the final revision of several chapters and in the preparation of end-of-chapter material for those chapters. Jim is also the author of the student guide and the computer resource supplement. However, his contribution has extended far beyond these tangible components of this text. He has been and remains a valued consultant who is always willing to share judgments that draw from his outstanding teaching of intermediate accounting.

Jane E. Campbell (University of Dayton), author of the Instructor's Manual for the Fourth Edition, has brought to the project many years of excellence as a teacher of intermediate accounting. We believe she has captured much of her personal teaching style in this significantly revised and expanded manual. Michael D. Kennelley (Florida State University) is author of the revised Test Resource Manual for the Fourth Edition. Adopters will notice a significant increase in the number and variety of examination questions that are now provided. We are very grateful for their work.

Throughout the text, we cite authoritative accounting literature published by the American Institute of Certified Public Accountants (AICPA) and the Financial Accounting Standards Board (FASB). We are grateful for the work done by these organizations. We also acknowledge and thank the AICPA and the Institute of Management Accounting for allowing us to adapt material from past CPA and CMA examinations.

Our text includes many financial reporting examples taken from the published financial statements of U.S. corporations. We have also included several articles from business publications. We appreciate the willingness of these organizations to allow us to use this material, which greatly enriches the learning experience of serious students of this text.

Finally, we wish to acknowledge the contributions of our families during the thirteen-year period required to write and revise this text. Perhaps their greatest contribution has been their patience and understanding during the many hours we were unable to be with them because we were working on the book. We recognize and appreciate their support and feel that much of the credit for this text rightfully belongs to them.

Jan R. Williams
Keith G. Stanga
William W. Holder

BRIEF CONTENTS

CONTENTS

PART 1

THEORETICAL FOUNDATION FOR FINANCIAL REPORTING

CHAPTER 1

The Financial Accounting Environment

OBJECTIVES

1. To introduce and discuss financial accounting.
2. To distinguish clearly between preparers, auditors, and users of financial statements.
3. To introduce the concept of generally accepted accounting principles.
4. To explain how generally accepted accounting principles have been developed.
5. To indicate the major sources of generally accepted accounting principles.
6. To discuss some major issues that are likely to affect the development of generally accepted accounting principles.
7. To introduce the subject of ethics in accounting.

ACCOUNTING AS AN INFORMATION SYSTEM

Accounting **identifies, measures,** and **communicates** information about **economic entities for use** in making **economic decisions.**[1] An accountant's primary task is therefore to supply information to help users, such as stockholders, bankers, and managers, make better decisions. These decisions determine how scarce resources are allocated within and among business enterprises. Accounting information helps society determine what goods and services to produce, as well as how and for whom to produce them. It should come as no surprise, then, that accounting is an exciting, often *controversial* discipline.

Accounting is closely related to several fields of study, including economics, finance, psychology, sociology, communications theory, and political science. By applying psychological principles, for example, accountants learn how people process accounting information and how that information affects their decisions.

INTERNAL AND EXTERNAL USERS

The two types of accounting information users are internal and external. The primary **internal users** are managers, who need accounting information to assist them in basic planning and control. Because of their authority within their companies, managers can usually obtain the internal information they need. When providing information to managers, accountants are not constrained by generally accepted accounting principles, which are principles that have substantial authoritative support. Instead, they prepare whatever information management finds most useful. The branch of accounting concerned with providing information for internal users is called **managerial,** or **management, accounting.** Managerial accounting is the subject of other textbooks and courses.

External users are those outside the business enterprise who have or contemplate having a direct or an indirect interest in the enterprise. They include present and potential owners (stockholders), lenders, suppliers, employees, and customers, as well as financial analysts, stock exchanges, regulatory authorities, and the general public. Compared with management, external users generally have much less authority to request information. When preparing information for external users, accountants follow generally accepted accounting principles presently established by the Financial Accounting Standards Board. The use of such principles enhances the confidence and understanding of users and helps them to make more meaningful comparisons between companies.

Financial accounting is the branch of accounting that measures and reports the financial position of a business enterprise as well as changes in financial position. The main output of the financial accounting process is a set of basic, general purpose financial statements. As illustrated in Chapter 4, the basic financial statements are the balance sheet, the income statement, the statement of cash flows, and the statement of retained earnings or statement of stockholders' equity. Financial accounting information is designed primarily to meet the needs of external users. This textbook deals with financial accounting. In this chapter we discuss the environment of financial accounting.

---

[1]This definition is based on *A Statement of Basic Accounting Theory* (Evanston, Ill.: American Accounting Association, 1966), p. 1, and on *APB Statement No. 4,* "Basic Concepts and Accounting Principles Underlying Financial Statements of Business Enterprises," 1970, par. 40.

BASIC NEEDS OF EXTERNAL USERS

Although there are many types of external users, financial accounting has traditionally focused on meeting the needs of present and potential owners, such as preferred and common stock investors, and creditors, such as bankers and bondholders. Owners and creditors are the most obvious external groups that use financial statements. Moreover, information useful to investors and creditors is likely to be useful to other external users as well.

Fundamentally, investors and creditors want to know how much cash they will receive in return and when they will receive it. Stockholders, for example, typically make decisions **to buy, sell, or hold equity investments.** Before they exchange cash for shares of stock, they seek information that will help them to assess the amounts, timing, and uncertainties of expected cash flows in the form of dividends and appreciated market prices. Similarly, commercial bank loan officers make decisions **to extend or not extend loans.** When making these decisions, bankers want information that will help them to assess their chances of receiving cash via interest and repayment of principal.[2]

Investment and credit decisions involve a comparison of expected cash outflows with expected cash inflows. In most cases, the outflows are known, based on, for example, the market price of the stock on the date of purchase or the amount of the loan requested. But the investor or creditor usually must **predict the amount of cash inflows** and **assess the risk that those inflows will be less than expected.** What an investor or creditor would really like is a knowledge of the future. However, no one can supply such knowledge directly.

The expected cash flows to investors and creditors are related to the expected cash flows to the enterprise to which they have committed their funds. More precisely: "The prospects [of investors and creditors] for those cash receipts are affected by an enterprise's ability to generate enough cash to meet its obligations when due and its other cash operating needs, to reinvest in operations, and to pay cash dividends and may also be affected by perceptions of investors and creditors generally about that ability, which affect market prices of the enterprise's securities."[3]

For an enterprise to generate favorable cash flows over the long run, it must operate profitably and remain solvent. Thus, **profitability** and **solvency** are two basic factors that investors and creditors evaluate based on the information in financial statements. Profitability refers to the ability of an enterprise to generate earnings. Solvency refers to its ability to pay its debts when they come due. A company may be highly profitable yet be on the verge of bankruptcy due to a shortage of liquid assets such as cash and accounts receivable. Investors and creditors must therefore evaluate both aspects of a business enterprise.[4] Furthermore, if a business is to operate profitably and remain solvent, it must be **managed effectively.** Thus, financial statements can also be used to evaluate management's performance.

To summarize, investors and creditors provide cash, and they want to know how much cash they will receive in return and when they will receive it. To help resolve these questions, they use financial statements to

1. Make predictions.
2. Assess risk.

---

[2]*FASB Statement of Financial Accounting Concepts No. 1*, "Objectives of Financial Reporting by Business Enterprises," 1978, par. 25.

[3]*FASB Statement of Financial Accounting Concepts No. 1*, par. 37.

[4]Loyd C. Heath and Paul Rosenfield, "Solvency: The Forgotten Half of Financial Reporting," *Journal of Accountancy* (January 1979), pp. 48–54.

3. Evaluate profitability.
4. Evaluate solvency.
5. Evaluate management's performance.

These uses are interrelated.

GENERAL PURPOSE FINANCIAL STATEMENTS

Even when we narrow the list of external users to owners and creditors, we find that these users make different kinds of decisions under a variety of circumstances. Bankers, for example, make short-term, intermediate-term, and long-term loans to many different types of customers, so their needs for certain items of accounting information may vary. Moreover, users differ in their abilities to read, analyze, and understand accounting information. An unsophisticated stockholder with virtually no understanding of accounting information contrasts with a Chartered Financial Analyst who has met rigorous education, experience, and examination requirements, and who renders professional advice on investment matters.

Clearly, the diversity of users poses a problem. Should accountants prepare "tailor-made" financial statements to meet the needs of a particular user? Or should accountants prepare a single, general purpose set of financial statements to reasonably satisfy the needs of most users? Presently, financial accounting emphasizes general purpose statements because (1) accountants believe that many users need similar information; and (2) general purpose statements are more favorable from a benefit/cost standpoint. As a general rule, **the benefits of information (including financial accounting information) should exceed the costs of providing and using it.** In general purpose financial statements, accountants strive to present information that is "comprehensible to those who have a reasonable understanding of business and economic activities and are willing to study the information with reasonable diligence."[5]

FINANCIAL STATEMENTS AND FINANCIAL REPORTING

The main output of the financial accounting process today is a set of basic, general purpose **financial statements.** These statements are as follows:

1. A **balance sheet,** which summarizes an enterprise's financial position at a particular point in time.
2. An **income statement,** which summarizes an enterprise's income and the components of income over a period of time.
3. A **statement of cash flows,** which summarizes an enterprise's cash receipts and cash payments during a period of time.
4. A **statement of retained earnings,** which describes the changes in an enterprise's retained earnings during a period, or a **statement of stockholders' equity,** which describes the changes in retained earnings as well as in other accounts that compose stockholders' equity.

Actual examples of these financial statements appear in annual reports to shareholders. Companies also present them in other disclosure media such as registration statements and annual reports filed with the Securities and Exchange Commission. This textbook focuses on general purpose financial statements including their related notes (footnotes), which are an integral part of the financial statements. To familiar-

---

[5]*FASB Statement of Financial Accounting Concepts No. 1*, par. 34.

ize you with financial statements, we have reproduced a set of actual financial statements of Strawbridge & Clothier (a retail company that sells general merchandise) on the endpapers (inside the front and back covers). Take a few minutes to review these statements now. We shall refer to them at various times throughout the book. Additionally, the Appendix contains most of the material presented in a recent annual report of Strawbridge & Clothier.

The output of the financial accounting process is not confined to financial statements. **Financial reporting** encompasses not only financial statements but also other means of communicating information that relates directly or indirectly to the financial accounting process. Corporate managers may communicate financial accounting information outside of the financial statements because they are required to do so by rule or custom or because they simply want to do so voluntarily.[6] Annual reports to shareholders, for example, include not only financial statements but also other information such as financial highlights and a multiyear summary of important financial figures. They also include **nonfinancial** information such as a description of major products and a listing of corporate officers and directors.[7]

Financial reporting provides a *major portion, but not all,* of the information needed by external users for making investment, credit, and similar decisions. Professional financial analysts, for example, usually gather and evaluate economic information (such as gross national product and government interest rate figures) and industry information (such as weekly and monthly production figures provided for many industries) before they analyze information about individual companies. Also, many analysts obtain information by talking with representatives of corporate management.

CHARACTERISTICS AND LIMITATIONS OF FINANCIAL STATEMENTS

Some of the more important characteristics and limitations that apply to present-day financial statements are briefly described below:[8]

1. **Financial nature.** The information in financial statements is primarily financial in nature. It is generally expressed in **units of money** regardless of changes in purchasing power.
2. **Business entities.** The information pertains to individual business entities (which may be a group of related companies) rather than to industries or to the entire economy.
3. **Estimates and judgment.** The information reflects estimates and judgment and is therefore inexact. Financial statements look more precise than they really are.
4. **Historical report.** The information reflects the financial effects of transactions and events that have already occurred. Financial statements do not contain future projections.
5. **General purpose.** The information is designed to reasonably meet the needs of many diverse users, particularly present and potential owners and creditors.

[6]*FASB Statement of Financial Accounting Concepts No. 1,* par. 7.
[7]To summarize certain key terms, **financial accounting** is the branch of accounting concerned with measuring and reporting the financial position of a business enterprise and the changes that occur in financial position. **Financial statements** (i.e., balance sheet, income statement, statement of cash flows, and statement of retained earnings or statement of stockholders' equity) represent the main output of the financial accounting process. **Financial reporting** is a broad term that encompasses financial statements as well as other means of communicating information that relates directly or indirectly to the financial accounting process.
[8]*APB Statement No. 4,* par. 35, and *FASB Statement of Financial Accounting Concepts No. 1,* pars. 17–23.

6. **Interrelatedness.**   Financial statements are interrelated because measuring financial position is related to measuring changes in financial position. Thus we say that financial statements **articulate** with one another.

7. **Summarization and classification.**   The information is summarized and classified in a manner designed to help meet users' needs.

8. **Several measurement bases.**   Financial statements reflect several measurement or valuation bases (e.g., accounts receivable are reported at net realizable value, plant assets are usually reported at their original cost less accumulated depreciation).

9. **A single source.**   Financial statements are only one source of the information needed by investors and creditors.

10. **Cost.**   Financial statements involve a cost to provide and use. They can be justified only if the benefits they provide exceed the costs.

OBJECTIVES OF FINANCIAL REPORTING

The objectives of financial reporting are[9]

1. To provide information useful in **investment, credit, and similar decisions.**
2. To provide information useful in **assessing cash flow prospects.**
3. To provide information about **enterprise resources, claims to those resources, and changes in them.**

Notice that the first objective is the most general, while the next two are progressively more specific. Moreover, the third objective flows logically from the second, which in turn flows logically from the first. We explain these objectives more fully in the next chapter.

PREPARERS AND AUDITORS OF FINANCIAL STATEMENTS

Financial statements pertain to an entity such as a corporation. The **management** of that entity has the primary responsibility for preparing and disseminating its financial statements. Financial statements therefore contain **assertions** or **representations made by management,** such as sales, net income, and total assets.

Management's role in the financial reporting process has evolved over many years and is related to the fact that the corporation is the dominant medium for pooling productive resources in our economy. As corporations have grown in size, the separation between those who own the company (stockholders) and those who control it (managers) has widened. As a result, owners have demanded a periodic accounting from those to whom they have entrusted economic resources.

Many critics have charged that management has too much responsibility in the financial reporting process. They claim that since financial statements are reports *on* management's performance, management should have less responsibility for determining their contents. Despite the critics' views, the traditional position of the accounting profession has been that managers, because they are highly familiar with company objectives and operations, are best suited to present pertinent information about the company to external parties.

---

[9]*FASB Statement of Financial Accounting Concepts No. 1*, pars. 34, 37, and 40. For an excellent critical review of these objectives, see Nicholas Dopuch and Shyam Sunder, "FASB's Statements on Objectives and Elements of Financial Accounting: A Review," *Accounting Review* (January 1980), pp. 1–21. Dopuch and Sunder (p. 8) believe that these objectives "are unlikely to help resolve major accounting issues or to set standards of financial reporting as the FASB had expected."

To summarize, management has certain important **accountability** responsibilities to external parties. In discharging these responsibilities, management typically obtains the services of internal and external accountants.

INTERNAL ACCOUNTANTS

Management hires **internal accountants** (commonly called **industrial accountants** or **management accountants**) to work as employees within the company. Internal accountants perform many services, depending on the size and complexity of the enterprise. Perhaps their most distinguishing service is to produce and analyze many kinds of information designed to help management make better planning and control decisions. Should a company buy some new material-handling equipment? What is the optimal quantity of inventory for a company to order? When should a company order inventory? These are only a few of the questions that internal accountants can help to answer.

Internal accountants also design and implement accounting systems. In larger companies, they may serve on an **internal audit staff** that ensures that the company safeguards its assets, produces reliable accounting information, operates efficiently, and adheres to management's policies.

The internal accountant's most important services that relate to financial accounting are **collecting data** and **preparing the financial statements.** Internal accountants must therefore understand and apply the accounting principles we discuss throughout this text.

Some internal accountants have earned the **Certificate in Management Accounting (CMA).** The CMA is the professional designation for management accountants. As you might expect, not all internal accountants have earned the CMA. Moreover, not all persons who have CMAs are internal accountants. Many people with CMAs work in public accounting, colleges and universities, government, and elsewhere. In addition to meeting certain other requirements, a person wishing to earn a CMA must pass a rigorous examination. Several assignment problems in this textbook have been adapted from recent CMA examinations.

EXTERNAL ACCOUNTANTS

Although most managers and internal accountants are both competent and honest, an independent outside party is needed to attest to the fairness of management's financial statements so that users will have more confidence in them. This is the major role of **external** or **public accountants.**

Certified Public Accountant (CPA) is the major professional designation of those who practice public accounting. Not all public accountants are CPAs; not all CPAs practice public accounting. To become a CPA, a person must satisfy certain education and experience requirements and pass a rigorous, uniform examination that the American Institute of Certified Public Accountants (AICPA) prepares and grades. The assignment material in this textbook contains many problems that we have adapted from CPA examinations.

Although CPA firms provide such services as tax advice and management advisory services, their primary service is **auditing** (often called the **attest function**). In an audit, CPAs serve management as independent contractors, but their primary responsibility is to external users of financial statements. Basically, an **audit** consists of an examination of a company's financial statements followed by the issuance of a report which expresses the auditor's opinion about whether the financial statements have been presented fairly in accordance with generally accepted accounting

> **EXHIBIT 1–1**
>
> ### Unqualified Audit Report
>
> **Independent Auditor's Report**
>
> We have audited the accompanying balance sheet of X Company as of December 31, 19XX and the related statements of income, retained earnings, and cash flows for the year then ended. These financial statements are the responsibility of the Company's management. Our responsibility is to express an opinion on these financial statements based on our audit.
>
> We conducted our audit in accordance with generally accepted auditing standards. Those standards require that we plan and perform the audit to obtain reasonable assurance about whether the financial statements are free of material misstatement. An audit includes examining, on a test basis, evidence supporting the amounts and disclosures in the financial statements. An audit also includes assessing the accounting principles used and significant estimates made by management, as well as evaluating the overall financial statement presentation. We believe that our audit provides a reasonable basis for our opinion.
>
> In our opinion, the financial statements referred to above present fairly, in all material respects, the financial position of X Company as of [at] December 31, 19XX, and the results of its operations and its cash flows for the year then ended in conformity with generally accepted accounting principles.
>
> (Date)
>
> SOURCE: *Statement on Auditing Standards No. 58*, "Reports on Audited Financial Statements," 1988, par. 8.

principles. The **audit report** lends credibility to management's financial statements so that users can be more confident that the statements accurately represent what they purport to represent. In other words, an audit adds reliability to financial statements.

The most common type of audit report is one in which the auditor issues an **unqualified opinion,** which means that the auditor believes that the financial statements have been presented fairly in accordance with generally accepted accounting principles. Exhibit 1–1 illustrates a standard audit report in which an unqualified opinion is given. The wording was adopted by the accounting profession in 1988. In the **opening paragraph,** the auditor identifies the financial statements that were audited. The second paragraph, called the **scope paragraph,** describes the nature of an audit. The third paragraph, called the **opinion paragraph,** presents the auditor's opinion on the financial statements.

Auditors may also render qualified opinions, adverse opinions, and disclaimers. A **qualified opinion** is given when the overall financial statements are fairly presented "except for" certain items (which the auditor discloses). An **adverse opinion** means that the financial statements have not been presented fairly in accordance with generally accepted accounting principles. Finally, a **disclaimer of opinion** means that the auditor could not evaluate the fairness of the financial statements and, as a result, expresses no opinion on them.

Publicly owned companies and thousands of nonpublicly owned companies usually issue audited financial statements once each year. The Securities and Exchange Commission and the stock exchanges require that the annual financial statements of companies subject to their jurisdiction be audited by independent CPAs. Bankers often require a company's audited statements before making loans. Even when no one requires audited statements, managers often obtain audits and issue the audited statements.

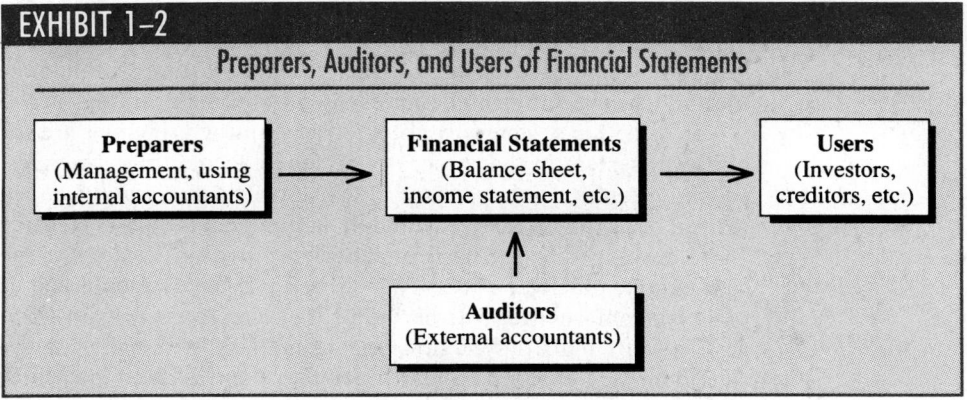

EXHIBIT 1-2

Preparers, Auditors, and Users of Financial Statements

Preparers
(Management, using internal accountants)

Financial Statements
(Balance sheet, income statement, etc.)

Users
(Investors, creditors, etc.)

Auditors
(External accountants)

Auditors must be **competent** and **independent** of any company whose financial statements they audit. To be competent, auditors must have a working knowledge of the generally accepted auditing standards that govern how an audit should be conducted as well as generally accepted accounting principles, many of which we cover in this textbook. To be independent, auditors must be honest and must not have any financial or family interest in the company they are auditing. Auditors must be independent *in fact* and *in appearance*. Users of financial statements simply will not attribute much importance to the auditor's opinion unless they perceive that the auditor is independent of the company being audited.

Exhibit 1–2 provides an overview of the major parties directly involved in the financial reporting process. They include preparers, auditors, and users of financial statements.

GENERALLY ACCEPTED ACCOUNTING PRINCIPLES

Basically, accounting principles are guidelines for gathering and communicating accounting information.[10] Imagine what would happen if companies were free to choose whatever accounting principles they preferred. One company might report its inventory at historical cost (the actual cost to purchase or produce the inventory), while others might use replacement costs, current selling prices, or other measurements. Or one company might publish only an income statement while another might report only a balance sheet. Such a situation could seriously reduce the ability of users to make valid comparisons between companies.

To help overcome this problem, the accounting profession has given some accounting principles the special status of being **generally accepted accounting principles** (commonly called **GAAP**). Generally accepted accounting principles are those that have **substantial authoritative support**.[11] Specifically, they represent "the consensus at any time as to which economic resources and obligations should be recorded as assets and liabilities, which changes in them should be recorded, when these changes should be recorded, how the recorded assets and liabilities and changes in them should be measured, what information should be disclosed and how it should be disclosed, and which financial statements should be prepared."[12] Internal and

---

[10] Accounting principles have also been called standards, concepts, procedures, rules, and practices.

[11] AICPA Special Bulletin, *Disclosure of Departures from Opinions of Accounting Principles Board* (October 1964), par. 3.

[12] *APB Statement No. 4*, par. 27.

external accountants must have a thorough knowledge of generally accepted accounting principles in order to prepare and attest to financial statements. Moreover, users should be familiar with these principles so that they can understand the nature and limitations of the information presented in financial statements.

In some ways, generally accepted accounting principles are similar to laws within our legal system in that generally accepted accounting principles are formulated *by people,* often in an atmosphere in which considerable *political pressures* exist. Thus, instead of having been discovered in nature, generally accepted accounting principles "have developed on the basis of experience, reason, custom, usage, and, to a significant extent, practical necessity."[13] These principles should and do *change* as conditions warrant change. Furthermore, they are often *controversial,* as are laws that govern draft registration, drinking, gambling, and many other areas. Just as laws should be judged based on how much they contribute to the achievement of society's goals, generally accepted accounting principles should be evaluated on the basis of how much they contribute to the **objectives of financial accounting.** Unlike laws, however, generally accepted accounting principles in the United States have largely been determined within the **private sector** rather than the public sector (the government sector) of our economy.

DEVELOPMENT OF GENERALLY ACCEPTED ACCOUNTING PRINCIPLES

Most of the progress made in the development of generally accepted accounting principles (standards) in the United States occurred during and after the 1930s. This progress was spurred by such factors as the growth of the corporate form of business organization in the early 1900s, with its separation of ownership from management; the introduction of income taxation in 1913, which made accounting records necessary for tax purposes; the intense criticism of corporate reporting practices in the financial press during the early part of this century; the stock market crash of 1929 and the depression which followed it; and the passage in 1933–1934 of federal legislation designed to help ensure that investors have adequate information on which to base their investment decisions.

Understanding generally accepted accounting principles requires a knowledge of the various organizations that have influenced their development. Primary among these are the American Institute of Certified Public Accountants, the Financial Accounting Standards Board, and the Securities and Exchange Commission. Publications by these and other organizations assist students of intermediate accounting and more advanced courses in financial accounting.

AMERICAN INSTITUTE OF CERTIFIED PUBLIC ACCOUNTANTS

The **American Institute of Certified Public Accountants (AICPA)** is the national professional organization of CPAs. In addition to many other useful publications, the AICPA publishes a monthly journal, called *The Journal of Accountancy,* that deals primarily with issues that are of concern to practicing accountants.

Committee on Accounting Procedure

The AICPA's first major involvement in developing accounting principles occurred in 1938 when it established the **Committee on Accounting Procedure (CAP).** The CAP was composed of 21 volunteer AICPA members, most of whom were practicing accountants. The CAP's purpose was to further the development of accounting prin-

---

[13] *APB Statement No. 4,* par. 139.

ciples, primarily by reducing the number of alternatives available for a given type of transaction or item.

The CAP issued pronouncements called **Accounting Research Bulletins (ARBs),** which summarized the committee's views concerning the proper accounting treatment for various transactions and items. ARBs were designed to help practicing accountants resolve specific issues, such as depreciation and long-term construction-type contracts.

The assenting votes of two-thirds of the CAP's members were required to issue an ARB, and from 1939 to 1959, the CAP issued 51 ARBs. Although the CAP was dissolved in 1959, those ARBs that have not been superseded by professional pronouncements are still important sources of generally accepted accounting principles.

ARBs were primarily **advisory** in nature. Although accountants generally followed the principles recommended in the ARBs, they were not required to do so. The AICPA could only *encourage* its members to observe the ARBs since it lacked the authority to require compliance. Ultimately, the authority of the ARBs was based on their general acceptance within the financial community.

The CAP authorized the publication of **Accounting Terminology Bulletins.** As the name implies, the purpose of Accounting Terminology Bulletins was to explain and improve accounting terminology. The first eight bulletins were reissued in 1953 as *Accounting Terminology Bulletin No. 1.* Three more bulletins were later published.

Even though the ARBs helped to improve the quality of accounting practice, the CAP was criticized for several reasons. The primary criticism was the committee's failure to develop a coherent framework of objectives and broad principles within which to resolve specific accounting problems. Instead, the CAP followed a more expedient "piecemeal" approach, trying to resolve immediate problems on a case-by-case basis. A result was that the ARBs were sometimes inconsistent with one another. Other major criticisms were that the CAP permitted too many alternative accounting principles to exist, did not move quickly enough, and did not support conclusions with research.

Accounting Principles Board

In 1959 the AICPA replaced the CAP with the **Accounting Principles Board (APB),** which was responsible for developing accounting principles. This new committee consisted of 18–21 volunteer accountants who were drawn from public practice, industry, colleges and universities, and government. The APB issued pronouncements called **Opinions.** These opinions presented the board's views concerning proper accounting in areas such as income taxes, earnings per share, and intangible assets. Issuance of an opinion required a two-thirds vote of the APB's members. From 1959 to 1973 the board issued 31 opinions. Although the APB was replaced in 1973 by the Financial Accounting Standards Board, opinions that have not been superseded are still important sources of generally accepted accounting principles.

In addition to the 31 opinions, the APB issued four **Statements.** Unlike its opinions, the APB felt that its statements contained recommendations rather than requirements. In 1970 the APB issued *Statement No. 4,* entitled "Basic Concepts and Accounting Principles Underlying Financial Statements of Business Enterprises." In this statement, the board identified the broad fundamentals of financial accounting as they were reflected by accounting practice at that time. *Statement No. 4* is a milestone in the accounting profession's search for a coherent theoretical framework, and we cite it frequently in this textbook.

APB Opinions often dealt with complex issues. Thus, the AICPA published a series of **Accounting Interpretations** (of APB Opinions) designed to guide practitioners in applying opinions. Interpretations were not, however, formal pronouncements of the APB.

During the early years of the APB's existence, the AICPA could not require practitioners to comply with APB Opinions. In October 1964, however, the AICPA's governing council adopted a recommendation that AICPA members "should see to it that departures from Opinions of the Accounting Principles Board (as well as effective Accounting Research Bulletins issued by the former Committee on Accounting Procedure) are disclosed, either in footnotes to financial statements or in the audit reports of members in their capacity as independent auditors."[14] In 1972 this recommendation was incorporated in *Rule 203* of the AICPA Code of Professional Conduct. It prohibits an AICPA member from expressing an opinion that financial statements conform with GAAP if the statements contain a material departure from an accounting principle established by the Financial Accounting Standards Board (as well as accounting principles established by effective ARBs and APB Opinions), unless the member can prove that, because of unusual circumstances, following such a principle would result in misleading financial statements.[15]

The AICPA has extended the original scope of *Rule 203* by requiring AICPA members to justify departures from Financial Accounting Standards Board standards that relate to the disclosure of information *outside* of the published financial statements, such as supplementary financial statements adjusted for the effects of inflation.[16] *Rule 203* is very important because it effectively requires that AICPA members either comply with authoritative accounting pronouncements or risk having to defend why they did not do so. Generally, few accountants want to assume such a risk.

When the AICPA established the APB, it also created a separate Accounting Research Division (within the AICPA). Unlike the CAP, the APB emphasis was placed on research. When it established the APB, the AICPA expected that the board's opinions would be influenced by the logical and thorough **Accounting Research Studies** conducted for the Research Division. These studies were designed as a basis for identification and discussion of accounting problems, but the conclusions of the authors did not represent the official position of the AICPA. Fifteen Accounting Research Studies ultimately were published.

The Accounting Research Studies did not have as much impact on the APB's conclusions as was hoped when the Research Division was organized. For example, two of the earliest studies were expected to identify a set of basic postulates (assumptions) and broad principles that would serve as a logical foundation for the APB's Opinions.[17] After these studies were published in 1962, the APB merely acknowledged their contribution to accounting thought. But the board did not accept the studies because it believed that they were too radically different from the generally accepted accounting principles in existence at that time.

Although the APB made significant progress in the development of generally accepted accounting principles, it was criticized for most of the same reasons that the CAP had been criticized earlier. Critics also charged that the views of large public accounting firms and the AICPA had, and were *seen* to have, too much influence on the APB's decisions. Some charged, for example, that public accountants on the board were hard-pressed to criticize poor accounting principles that their own clients were using.

---

[14] AICPA Special Bulletin, *Disclosure of Departures from Opinions of Accounting Principles Board,* par. 1.

[15] *AICPA Professional Standards—Volume 2* (Chicago: Commerce Clearing House), ET Sec. 203.01.

[16] *AICPA Code of Professional Conduct* (New York: AICPA, 1988), p. 11.

[17] These studies are: *Accounting Research Study No. 1,* "The Basic Postulates of Accounting" (New York: AICPA, 1961) by Maurice Moonitz, and *Accounting Research Study No. 3,* "A Tentative Set of Broad Accounting Principles for Business Enterprises" (New York: AICPA, 1962) by Robert T. Sprouse and Maurice Moonitz.

In response to these criticisms, the AICPA appointed a seven-person committee, chaired by Francis M. Wheat, to study the process of establishing accounting principles and to make recommendations for improvement. The Wheat Committee issued its report in March 1972, and this report led to the establishment of the Financial Accounting Standards Board.

FINANCIAL ACCOUNTING STANDARDS BOARD

Since July 1973, the **Financial Accounting Standards Board (FASB)** has been the official private sector body charged with establishing and improving generally accepted accounting principles in the United States.[18] At its outset the board decided that ARBs and APB opinions should remain in force until superseded by an FASB pronouncement.

Like the CAP and the APB, the FASB formulates accounting principles in a committee context. However, the FASB now has several important characteristics that make it different from its predecessors:

1. The FASB consists of only **seven members.** It has considerably fewer members than its predecessors, which tends to reduce the time needed to respond to emerging problems.
2. All FASB members are **fully remunerated** and **serve full time.** Whereas the members of the predecessor committees were part-time volunteers who continued to hold their positions elsewhere, FASB members must sever their ties with former employers before they serve on the board. This feature reduces the possibility of actual or apparent conflicts of interest.
3. FASB members are **not required to be CPAs.** In contrast, members of the predecessor committees were AICPA members and therefore were CPAs. This FASB characteristic reduces the likelihood that FASB pronouncements will reflect only the views of preparers and auditors of financial statements.
4. The FASB is an **independent body.** It is not part of the AICPA, as were its predecessors. This feature reduces the chances that FASB pronouncements will reflect, and be *seen* to reflect, only the views of the AICPA.

The FASB issues three major types of pronouncements:

1. **Statements of Financial Accounting Standards (SFASs).** These establish new or amend existing generally accepted accounting principles.
2. **Interpretations.** These clarify, explain, or elaborate on SFASs, APB Opinions, or ARBs. Interpretations are themselves a part of GAAP.
3. **Statements of Financial Accounting Concepts (SFACs).** These set forth objectives and concepts that the FASB uses as the basis for establishing and improving generally accepted accounting principles. SFACs do not establish generally accepted accounting principles within the scope of *Rule 203*.

In addition, the FASB's staff issues **Technical Bulletins** that are designed to provide guidance on certain financial accounting and reporting problems on a timely basis. Technical Bulletins generally deal with questions about how to implement existing standards in practice. Interested parties are invited to comment on proposed Technical Bulletins, and all Technical Bulletins are considered by the FASB at a public meeting.

---

[18] The Wheat Committee recommended use of the term "standards" instead of "principles" because of confusion over the meaning of "accounting principles." In this textbook we use the terms "principles" and "standards" interchangeably.

In 1984, the FASB established an **Emerging Issues Task Force,** composed of approximately 18 persons who represent CPA firms, major companies, the FASB, and the SEC. This group meets every six weeks to resolve, on a timely basis, accounting problems associated with new types of transactions. The task force publishes *minutes* of its deliberations.

At times, the FASB needs to change accounting principles because of such factors as changing business and economic circumstances, new informational needs of investors and creditors, advances in information technology, and abuses in the application of existing principles. In deciding whether to add a new project to its busy agenda, the FASB considers four criteria: pervasiveness of the accounting issue, availability of alternative solutions, technical feasibility of deriving a solution to the accounting problem, and practical consequences.[19] When the FASB tentatively decides to change accounting principles in a particular area (for example, leases or pensions), people are vitally interested because of the considerable impact that financial statements have on the allocation of wealth in our society. The FASB therefore has an elaborate *due process system* that it follows diligently when developing new accounting principles.

The FASB tries to involve in its standard-setting process everyone who is interested in financial reporting and wants to participate. These people include preparers, auditors, users, and others. FASB members may therefore have backgrounds in financial analysis, industry, government, and academia, as well as in public accounting. FASB meetings are open to the public, and the board keeps a public record. The board's due process system of formulating an SFAS typically involves the following major steps, illustrated in Exhibit 1–3:[20]

1. The board **identifies an accounting problem** (such as accounting for leases or pension plans) and places the problem on its agenda.
2. The board appoints a task force of technical experts which **conducts extensive research** on the problem.
3. The board **issues a Discussion Memorandum,** which summarizes the major issues and possible solutions and serves as the basis for public comment.
4. The board **conducts a public hearing** at which it invites interested parties to present their views.
5. The board **issues an Exposure Draft,** which is a *proposed* SFAS that is distributed for public comment.
6. The board **issues an SFAS** after it has analyzed public responses to the exposure draft. Issuing a pronouncement now requires an affirmative **vote of five of the seven FASB members.**[21]

The **Financial Accounting Foundation** is the independent entity whose board of trustees oversees the basic structure of the standard-setting process. In addition, the trustees appoint members to the FASB and to the FASB's advisory council. They also secure private contributions to fund the FASB's operations. The trustees are appointed by a panel of representatives from several national organizations whose members have a knowledge of and an interest in corporate financial reporting.

---

[19] Dennis R. Beresford, "The 'Balancing Act' in Setting Accounting Standards," *Accounting Horizons* (March 1988), p. 1.

[20] The FASB follows similar steps when issuing Interpretations and SFACs.

[21] The Trustees of the Financial Accounting Foundation recently changed the number of affirmative votes required from four (a simple majority) to five (a supermajority). The requirement for five assenting votes became effective on January 1, 1991. The Trustees made the change to ensure that the FASB would not likely issue a pronouncement when considerable dissent still exists among FASB members.

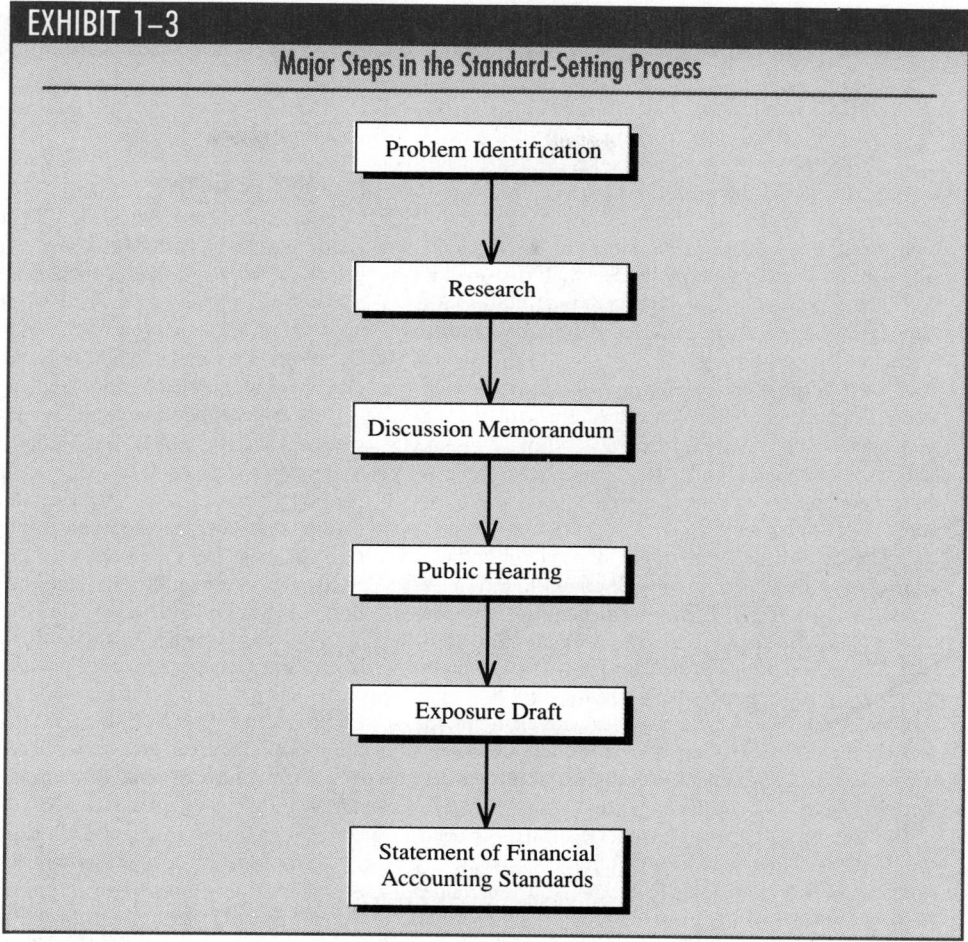

EXHIBIT 1–3

Major Steps in the Standard-Setting Process

Problem Identification

↓

Research

↓

Discussion Memorandum

↓

Public Hearing

↓

Exposure Draft

↓

Statement of Financial Accounting Standards

Financial Accounting Standards Advisory Council helps the FASB to set priorities and to establish ad hoc task forces. Moreover, the advisory council reacts to proposed FASB pronouncements and assists the board in other ways. Often the FASB appoints a task force to help the board resolve a specific problem. Members of the advisory council frequently serve on these task forces. The FASB is also assisted by full-time research and administrative staffs.

Thus far, the FASB has set accounting standards using a case-by-case approach similar to that of its predecessors. But one of the initial tasks undertaken by the FASB was a **Conceptual Framework Project.** The purpose of this project was to develop an authoritative, coherent structure of objectives and broad fundamentals of financial accounting. The FASB calls it a "constitution" that hopefully will lead to better, more consistent standards. This recently completed project will be discussed in more depth later in this chapter.

As you might expect, the existence of the FASB has changed the AICPA's role in the development of accounting principles. Currently, the AICPA has an **Accounting Standards Executive Committee (AcSEC).** This committee issues **Statements of Position (SOPs)** that are intended to influence the development of accounting principles in specialized areas not covered by FASB pronouncements. Currently, the FASB is in the process of developing statements that may designate as standards many of the

FASB FINDS ITSELF UNDER HEAVY ATTACK; ITS NEW RULES ARE CALLED TOO COSTLY

Carl C. Landegger, chairman of Black Clawson Co., is an angry man. "Pain is pain (and) evil is evil," he says. "It cannot be justified or excused by the principle of the greater common good."

Mr. Landegger isn't railing against unjust laws or high taxes. Instead, his ire is aimed at the Financial Accounting Standards Board, the chief rule-making body for accountants, for issuing standards that Mr. Landegger believes can hurt his company, its work force and the economy.

Mr. Landegger's reaction may be somewhat extreme. And accounting isn't a subject that usually triggers such fiery emotions. But accounting standard setters nowadays are under the heaviest fire from industry and others in recent memory. And the blasts aren't likely to let up.

That is because the stakes of accounting rules scheduled to be issued are sharply mounting. For example, a current FASB proposal on post-retirement medical benefits slated to be issued by the FASB next year could chop pretax profits for many big U.S. companies by an average of 10% starting in 1992. And companies complain that a complex rule changing the way companies report their future income-tax liabilities is too costly to implement and that the disclosures it requires aren't worth the expense.

Also, some corporate financial officers and accountants fret that a new FASB project, eventually aimed at forcing companies to set more current values on a myriad of financial instruments including stock options, would penalize corporate earnings, boost accounting costs but yield little useful data for investors.

The FASB, organized in 1973, says its job is to increase financial disclosure, make financial data more comparable among similar companies and require companies in their financial reports to disclose the true costs and risks of doing business.

But many financial executives say that the FASB often chooses the most complicated and burdensome accounting methods to achieve its aims. And they complain that the disclosures aren't worth the often high costs of rejiggering corporate financial reporting systems.

But regulators and legislators, dismayed at the collapse of companies and financial institutions without enough advance warning from financial reports, are pressuring the FASB to set tougher disclosure rules that would alert investors and other financial-statement users to foreseeable problems of businesses.

No Letup in Criticism

Dennis Beresford, chairman of the seven-member FASB, based in Norwalk, Conn., concedes that the barrage from disgruntled companies required to make accounting changes by the FASB doesn't promise to let up. "There aren't many easy issues ahead," says Mr. Beresford. "We make tough decisions, and ours isn't a job where we can keep everyone happy."

Four years ago, corporations leveled some heavy guns against the FASB for forcing the companies to weigh down their balance sheets with heavy unfunded pension liabilities. As it turned out, a healthy stock market that year boosted pension assets and erased many of these liabilities. So when the dust settled, the FASB heaved a sigh of relief, hoping the verbal brickbats being hurled at it would subside.

But they haven't. If anything, the critics may be more vocal. Last month, for example, Colby H. Chandler, chairman and chief executive of Eastman Kodak Co., told a group of 400 financial executives here that the FASB is "a quasi-government agency promulgating mountains of paperwork with little accountability to anyone." Its rules, asserted Mr. Chandler, are "too complex, too theoretical and too expensive."

The FASB proposal that will force companies to accrue or set up a reserve for future medical benefits of retirees is the flash point for the anger of Mr. Landegger. Currently, companies only deduct such benefits from profits as the companies pay for them each year, because unlike pension benefits such costs aren't tax-deductible. Some benefits consultants figure the total unpaid accumulated liability for such benefits at all U.S. companies could reach astronomical heights—more than $200 billion and maybe as much as $1 trillion.

Mr. Landegger says that when the medical-benefits rule is imposed in 1992 for the profit-and-loss statement and for the balance sheet in 1997, it will cause many companies to drop or sharply reduce such benefits. And he says it won't help U.S. companies compete with their overseas rivals, who don't face such medical-benefits accounting rules.

"My company, which makes heavy machinery for the paper, plastics and pipe industry, has about 2,000 employees at four U.S. plants," says Mr. Landegger.

"By 1997, the FASB proposal on medical benefits could reduce the net worth of Black Clawson by half and force us to cut our credit lines substantially. It could also hinder any expansions and reduce our usually heavy research and development outlays," which he says the company needs to keep and expand its market share.

Prudent Management Decisions

As a result, Mr. Landegger says Black Clawson will have to sharply reduce health benefits for new retirees. "The FASB should reconsider this rule," he adds. "The new information it may provide users of financial statements isn't worth all the pain and suffering it will impose."

Responds Mr. Beresford: "Some companies are using the FASB's accounting proposals as an excuse for avoiding prudent management decisions. Many of them should have controlled the costs of medical benefits in the past. Our look at the problem may encourage companies to increase cost control and make wiser decisions in labor negotiations in the future."

Also, the FASB seeks to give investors and other users of financial statements more meaningful and comparable financial data, Mr. Beresford says. When a company has an obligation, accounting rules should make the company own up to such promises, he adds.

Criticism of the FASB is rising at the very time the rule-making body is trying to be more responsive to critics. For example, the FASB has just delayed the effective date of its complex deferred-tax rule another year to give business more time to implement it. The rule would now be effective for 1992 annual financial statements instead of for 1991 reports. And the FASB is mulling ways to simplify the rule to reduce implementation costs.

But some smaller companies say the rule, requiring complicated tax computations, still promises to boost their outside fees with their auditors. "The FASB doesn't realize the impact of its rules on companies our size with limited in-house accounting expertise," says Louise Bierdeman, treasurer and controller of Carrollton Graphics Inc., a closely held printing firm in Carrollton, Ohio, with $21 million in annual sales.

Ms. Bierdeman says to implement deferred-tax accounting treatment will boost the fees of its outside accounting firm by as much as 15%. And she maintains that the increased costs aren't justified by the added financial disclosures, which she says aren't as meaningful for small, non-public companies.

Says Ruth Goertz, the senior tax partner at New Philadelphia, Ohio-based Rea & Associates, Carrollton Graphics' outside accounting firm: "Many FASB rules are totally inappropriate for small non-public companies because they're unreasonably complex and produce little useful information for companies that size."

Value of Hog Pens

As to the FASB's latest project that is moving toward requiring more disclosure about the current risk of all financial instruments and transactions, some bankers say that computing a current market price for every item on their institution's balance sheet is tricky and hardly worth the effort. "Farmers who borrow from us may use the money to build huge concrete hog pens," says John Perry, president of First State Bank of Brazil, Ind. "While these transactions apparently pass the smell test as loans, you'd need a crystal ball to value them every quarter. They aren't highly negotiable and hog pens aren't traded on an exchange."

The pressure by regulators and legislators on the FASB to force greater disclosures of financial risk from financial institutions is growing. Major reasons are the collapse of many thrifts that made too risky real estate, development and acquisition loans and the continuing woes of banks that made loans to troubled nations.

The FASB is permitted to make private-sector accounting rules under the oversight of the Securities and Exchange Commission, which got the job under the 1930s securities laws. And Congress looks over both their shoulders to make sure that both the FASB and the SEC do their jobs.

The FASB's Mr. Beresford says he isn't ignoring "the very real criticisms (by business and others) that have been made (of the FASB), particularly those dealing with implementation overload." But he notes that the FASB also must be responsive to legislators and regulators for improved standard-setting to meet "accelerating changes" in business and on Wall Street.

SOURCE: Lee Berton, "FASB Finds Itself Under Heavy Attack; Its New Rules Are Called Too Costly," *Wall Street Journal,* Tuesday, December 19, 1989, pp. A1, A6. Reprinted by permission of *Wall Street Journal,* © Dow Jones & Company, Inc., 1989. All rights reserved.

specialized accounting and reporting principles contained in the SOPs. In fact, the FASB has already issued several statements based on certain SOPs. Until the FASB's project is complete, the specialized accounting principles contained in the SOPs are considered preferable accounting principles only for purposes of justifying a change in accounting principles.

AcSEC also distributes **Issues Papers** which are designed to identify financial accounting and reporting issues (such as LIFO inventories) that AcSEC believes should be addressed or clarified by the FASB. Issues Papers present neutral discussions of various accounting issues as well as arguments on alternative solutions. Issues Papers normally include advisory conclusions that represent the views of at least a majority of AcSEC members.

In addition to publishing SOPs and Issues Papers, the AICPA also publishes **Industry Audit Guides** and **Industry Accounting Guides.** The guides are prepared by AICPA committees or task forces and usually deal with specialized financial reporting issues that only pertain to a particular industry (e.g., casinos). The guides are normally reviewed by AcSEC and the FASB before being issued. In November, 1987, AcSEC began a series of **Practice Bulletins** which focus on certain narrow accounting issues.

In addition to AcSEC, the AICPA has an **Auditing Standards Board (ASB).** The ASB develops auditing standards and enforces professional ethics.

Since accounting principles help to determine how resources are allocated in our economy, it is not surprising that the FASB, like its predecessor committees, often has had to deal with *political pressures* in addition to having to decide what is theoretically sound accounting. In 1979, for example, the Securities and Exchange Commission, acting under pressure from Congress and the Department of Energy, in effect forced the FASB to change the accounting principles it had developed for oil and gas producing companies. Why did the SEC take this action? One major reason was that many smaller producers claimed that the FASB's principles would force these companies to report lower earnings, thereby making it harder for them to raise capital. According to these smaller producers, this in turn would adversely affect the nation's ability to discover oil and gas. Clearly, the ability of the FASB to survive as a private-sector, standard-setting body will depend to a large extent on how effectively it handles the many conflicting political pressures that are brought on it.

SECURITIES AND EXCHANGE COMMISSION

The level of stock prices in the United States declined dramatically between 1929 and 1933. This occurrence brought considerable public pressure for better disclosure of corporate information. In the midst of this pressure and of a severe depression, Congress enacted legislation that has had a tremendous influence on corporate financial reporting. Basically, Congress passed the **Securities Act of 1933** to improve the disclosures made by companies when they sell a *new* issue of securities to the public. Then it passed the **Securities Exchange Act of 1934** to improve the periodic disclosures made by companies whose shares are publicly traded. The 1934 Act created the **Securities and Exchange Commission (SEC)** as a public sector organization to enforce both of these disclosure statutes.

The SEC does not protect investors from sustaining losses. Instead, its basic purpose is to ensure that companies provide investors with adequate information on which to base their investment decisions. Accordingly, companies under SEC jurisdiction must report to the SEC a substantial quantity of information on a variety of different forms.[22] This information is available for public use. The most important corporate reports required by the SEC are the following:

1. **Registration statement.** This is a detailed report required under the 1933 Act when a company offers publicly its securities. It includes such information as the nature of the company's business, a description of the securities being registered, and audited financial statements.
2. **10-K report.** This is a detailed report that companies file annually under the 1934 Act. It discloses various corporate activities as well as audited financial statements. Companies usually disclose more in their 10-K reports than in their annual reports to shareholders.
3. **10-Q report.** This is a quarterly report filed under the 1934 Act. It is much less detailed than the 10-K. In addition to a description of various activities, the 10-Q report includes financial information that has been reviewed but not audited by an independent CPA.
4. **8-K report.** This report, required under the 1934 Act, explains a material event (such as a major acquisition or a lawsuit) that investors want to know about. An 8-K report usually must be filed within 15 days after a material event has occurred.

These reports reflect the SEC's concern that companies disclose relevant financial and nonfinancial information on a timely basis. The SEC also is concerned about the costs that companies must incur to comply with the various disclosure requirements. Accordingly, the SEC designed an **integrated disclosure system** that allows companies to avoid having to file duplicate copies of certain information that is already publicly available.

The primary sources of the SEC's financial information requirements are

1. **Regulation S-X.** This is the original source which prescribes the form and content of financial statements filed with the SEC. It is revised frequently.
2. **Accounting Series Releases (ASRs).** These are pronouncements which modify the SEC's financial information requirements.
3. **Staff Accounting Bulletins (SABs).** These are interpretations and practices followed by the SEC's staff in administrating the commission's disclosure requirements. SABs are not official rules or interpretations of the SEC itself.
4. **Financial Reporting Releases (FRRs).** These pronouncements were first issued in 1982 and are intended to replace ASRs. The first FRR is a codification of portions of ASRs that were relevant when it was issued.
5. **Accounting and Auditing Enforcement Releases (AAERs).** These pronouncements began in 1982 and deal with enforcement-related matters.

Since its inception, the SEC has had **broad legal authority to establish accounting and reporting standards.** To date, the Commission has largely delegated this authority to private sector organizations (the CAP, APB, and FASB). But the SEC can in effect veto the standards set by these organizations, and it has done so occasionally.[23] The SEC can effectively veto a standard set by the FASB by refusing to

---

[22]In essence, the 1933 Act applies to a company when it makes a public offering of its securities. The 1934 Act applies mainly to companies whose securities are traded on a national securities exchange and to "over-the-counter" companies that have at least $5,000,000 in assets and at least 500 stockholders.

[23]In 1972 an APB member likened the SEC to top management and the APB to lower-level management. See Charles T. Horngren, "Accounting Principles: Public or Private Sector?" *Journal of Accountancy* (May 1972), pp. 37–41.

force companies to apply the standard in reports filed with the Commission. *Remember:* the SEC has statutory authority to prescribe accounting and reporting standards for companies under its jurisdiction.

Generally, the SEC and each of the private sector, standard-setting organizations have cooperated with one another. In *ASR No. 150,* the SEC indicated that it looked to the FASB to provide leadership in establishing and improving accounting principles. The SEC nevertheless has considerable influence on the development of accounting principles. The main ways that the SEC has exerted its influence are by responding to planned and existing pronouncements of the FASB and of its predecessors and by strongly encouraging these organizations to resolve emerging accounting problems.

During the 1970s, the SEC played a more active role in developing accounting principles. Understanding of the significance of the SEC's role is vital to the study of financial accounting.

OTHER INFLUENCES ON ACCOUNTING PRINCIPLES

The AICPA, FASB, and SEC are the organizations that have had the most influence in shaping generally accepted accounting principles as they exist today. However, certain other organizations as well as the income tax law have had an important impact.[24]

Income Tax Law

The **income tax law,** as enacted by Congress, administered by the Internal Revenue Service, and interpreted by the courts, has influenced the development and the implementation of accounting principles. For example, many smaller businesses maintain accounting records primarily for income tax purposes. Moreover, to avoid having to maintain one set of books for financial accounting purposes and a different set for tax purposes, many companies use financial accounting principles that will reduce and postpone their income tax payments. Suppose that a company formed in 1980 plans to use an accelerated depreciation method for tax purposes but has no strong theoretical reason to favor any particular depreciation method for financial reporting purposes. The company may choose the accelerated method for financial reporting purposes (as well as for tax purposes) to avoid the need for two sets of depreciation records.

Finally, the tax law states that if a company uses the last-in, first-out (LIFO) inventory method for tax purposes, it must also use LIFO for financial reporting purposes. We explain this conformity requirement in Chapter 8.

Although tax law has played a role in shaping generally accepted accounting principles, an important point to remember is that **the principles that a company should use for tax purposes are not necessarily the same as those it should use for financial accounting purposes.** Tax accounting focuses on the measurement of taxable income using principles established by tax laws. In contrast, a primary focus

---

[24]Some students who have taken cost accounting may notice that we have not included the **Cost Accounting Standards Board (CASB)** in the following discussion. The CASB is a federal agency initially created by Congress in 1970. It is a public sector body charged with developing cost accounting standards for use by most businesses with large government contracts. The CASB was abolished in 1980 and later re-established in 1988. Overall, it has had a very limited impact on financial accounting.

The **Governmental Accounting Standards Board (GASB)** is also not covered in the following discussion. Recently created by the Financial Accounting Foundation, the GASB formulates accounting principles for municipal and state entities.

Finally, the **International Accounting Standards Committee (IASC)** is not covered in the following discussion. Formed in 1973, this committee has tried to promote more harmonization of accounting standards among countries. IASC pronouncements have had little impact on U.S. accounting standards, but this may change in the future as society develops into a more global economy. In general, many differences currently exist between the accounting principles in various countries. These differences reflect basic historical, philosophical, institutional, legal, and economic differences between countries.

of financial accounting is the measurement of accounting income using generally accepted accounting principles. The objectives of the tax law are to *raise money* for the operation of the government and to achieve certain *social goals*. In contrast, the primary objective of generally accepted accounting principles is to *provide useful information* to investors, creditors, and other users. Since the objectives of tax accounting and financial accounting differ, we find that the principles of tax accounting frequently differ from those of financial accounting.

This textbook deals with financial accounting principles. In Chapter 18, we examine financial accounting issues that relate directly to corporate income taxes.

Interestingly, many accountants feel that income tax law often has played a major role in the "nondevelopment" of GAAP. For example, the use of current value accounting in a company's primary financial statements is not now a generally accepted accounting principle. One reason for the opposition is their fear that such accounting will "create new kinds of income" that the government will want to tax.

American Accounting Association

The **American Accounting Association (AAA)** is dominated by accounting educators, although many practicing accountants are active members. In addition to fostering improvements in accounting education and research, the AAA has helped to develop accounting principles, especially in the area of financial accounting theory.

AAA committees have traditionally followed a broader, more conceptual approach to the development of accounting principles than either the FASB or its predecessors. Publications of the AAA often concentrate on what accounting *should be* rather than on what accounting *is now*.

Unlike the FASB, the AAA is not an organization designed to promulgate accounting principles that practitioners must observe. The AAA has therefore not been highly concerned about whether the work of its committees receives immediate acceptance in practice. AAA publications often affect practice in indirect ways several years after they are published.

Included among many AAA publications are three journals: *The Accounting Review,* which publishes scholarly research in all areas of accounting; *Accounting Horizons,* which publishes applied accounting research; and *Issues in Accounting Education,* which publishes research that pertains to accounting education.

The AAA is actively involved in the work of the FASB. For example, an AAA representative serves on the panel that selects the trustees of the Financial Accounting Foundation, and an AAA committee reacts to FASB pronouncements.

Financial Executives Institute

The **Financial Executives Institute (FEI)** primarily comprises financial executives, such as controllers and treasurers, from large corporations. Members of this organization are an important subset of *preparers* of financial statements. Views expressed by FEI members have played a significant role in the development of generally accepted accounting principles.

The FEI publishes a journal called *Financial Executive,* and it has sponsored several important research studies in financial accounting. Like the AAA, the FEI has been actively involved in the work of the FASB.

National Association of Accountants

The **National Association of Accountants (NAA)** consists largely of industrial accountants. Traditionally, the NAA has focused on cost and managerial accounting. In recent years, however, it has increased its role in the development of financial accounting standards.

The NAA publishes a journal called *Management Accounting*. In addition, it has published several important research studies in financial accounting, and it administers the CMA program. Like the AAA and the FEI, the NAA has been actively involved in the FASB's work.

Financial Analysts Federation

The **Financial Analysts Federation (FAF)**, a national organization of financial analysts, is one of the most knowledgeable and influential groups that *use* accounting information. A **financial analyst** is a person who analyzes information and renders professional advice on investment matters. Many analysts have earned the designation **Chartered Financial Analyst (CFA).** A CFA is an individual who has met certain education and experience requirements and who has passed a rigorous examination on such subjects as accounting, economics, financial analysis, portfolio management, and ethics.

The FAF publishes the *Financial Analysts Journal*. The organization maintains a strong interest in corporate financial reporting, and it plays an active role in the work of the FASB. Financial analysts frequently have served as participants in behavioral studies on the uses of accounting information.

Robert Morris Associates

Robert Morris Associates (RMA) is a national organization of bank loan and credit officers. As *users* of accounting information, commercial bank loan officers have influenced the development of generally accepted accounting principles. Much of this influence occurred around the beginning of this century, when bankers were the dominant external users of accounting information. Like financial analysts, bank loan officers often serve as participants in accounting research studies. RMA publishes *The Journal of Commercial Bank Lending*.

SOURCES OF GENERALLY ACCEPTED ACCOUNTING PRINCIPLES

As stated earlier, generally accepted accounting principles are those that have substantial authoritative support. The accounting profession has never published a complete, official list of such principles. Furthermore, because the profession has not defined precisely what is meant by the phrase "substantial authoritative support," the boundary that separates generally accepted accounting principles from others is sometimes hazy. In practice, therefore, determining whether an accounting principle is generally accepted sometimes requires judgment. Accountants and auditors must be familiar with the sources of generally accepted accounting principles in order to answer difficult measurement and disclosure questions.

Statement on Auditing Standards No. 52 classifies generally accepted accounting principles in the four categories described below.[25] In general, these categories are ranked from the most authoritative sources (Category A) to the least authoritative (Category D).

1. **Category A** contains pronouncements of an authoritative body designated by the AICPA council to establish accounting principles under *Rule 203* of the AICPA Code of Professional Conduct. This category contains the most authoritative sources of GAAP, which are FASB Statements of Financial Accounting Standards, FASB Interpretations, APB Opinions, and Accounting Research Bulletins.
2. **Category B** contains pronouncements of bodies of qualified accountants who follow due process procedures—including broad distribution of proposed accounting

[25]*Statement on Auditing Standards No. 52*, "Omnibus Statement on Auditing Standards—1987," (New York: AICPA, 1988).

principles for public comment—when establishing accounting principles or describing existing practices that are generally accepted. This category includes AICPA Industry Audit Guides, AICPA Industry Accounting Guides, AICPA Statements of Position, and FASB Technical Bulletins.

3. **Category C** contains practices or pronouncements that are widely recognized as being generally accepted because they represent prevalent practice in a particular industry or the knowledgeable application to specific circumstances of pronouncements that are generally accepted. This category includes AICPA Accounting Interpretations and prevalent industry practices.

4. **Category D** contains other accounting literature, which includes APB Statements, AICPA Issues Papers, FASB Statements of Financial Accounting Concepts, other professional pronouncements, and textbooks and journal articles. The isolated appearance of an accounting principle in a textbook or journal article should not be regarded as substantial authoritative support, but a consensus among several authors may be adequate support for an accounting principle not covered elsewhere in the literature.

Accountants should always record transactions in accordance with the *substance* (true nature) of the transactions. If the accounting treatment of a transaction is specified in a Category A pronouncement, then *Rule 203* requires the accountant to adhere to the Category A pronouncement unless unusual circumstances exist. If the accounting treatment is *not* specified in a Category A pronouncement, then the accountant should look for guidance in a source classified in Category B or C. Finally, the accountant should consider using a source in Category D if an accounting treatment is not specified in Categories A, B, or C.

As this textbook goes to press, the Auditing Standards Board is considering a revision to the GAAP hierarchy described above. *If adopted,* the revision would likely leave Category A intact. However, Category B would include FASB Technical Bulletins and, if cleared by the FASB, AICPA Industry Audit and Accounting Guides and AICPA Statements of Position. Category C would include AcSEC Practice Bulletins that have been cleared by the FASB and consensus positions of the FASB Emerging Issues Task Force. Category D would include AICPA accounting interpretations, implementation guides published by the FASB staff, and practices that are widely recognized and prevalent either generally or in the industry. Category D would also include AICPA pronouncements in categories B and C that have not been cleared by the FASB. Finally, a new category (E) would include other accounting literature such as FASB Statements of Financial Accounting Concepts, APB Statements, and so forth.

FUTURE DEVELOPMENT OF GENERALLY ACCEPTED ACCOUNTING PRINCIPLES

Although considerable progress has been made in the development of generally accepted accounting principles, much more work remains to be done. Some of the major issues that are likely to affect progress in this area are briefly discussed below.

CONCEPTUAL FRAMEWORK ISSUE

A project that may ultimately have the greatest overall impact on the accounting standard-setting process is the FASB's Conceptual Framework Project. As stated earlier, this project has sought to develop an authoritative, coherent structure of objectives and broad fundamentals of financial accounting. This structure will be the basis for developing new financial accounting standards and eliminating inconsistencies that exist in current standards. It should provide a strong foundation to help the FASB resolve difficult accounting questions. The FASB also intends that the structure will help everyone who has an interest in financial accounting to better understand the nature and limitations of financial accounting information.

To give you a more concrete idea of what the FASB means by a conceptual framework, here are the major topics that the Conceptual Framework Project comprises:

1. Objectives of financial reporting by business enterprises.
2. Objectives of financial reporting by nonbusiness organizations.
3. Qualitative characteristics of accounting information.
4. Elements of financial statements.
5. Recognition and measurement in financial statements of business enterprises.

The development of an authoritative conceptual framework has taken a lot of time, and there have been no easy, clear-cut answers to the questions that have arisen. The conceptual framework will continue to evolve in the future, but changes in it will not likely occur as fast as changes in accounting standards. In the long run, the FASB's success as a policy-making organization will probably depend heavily on the success of the Conceptual Framework Project. Yet, a conceptual framework is unlikely to be a panacea. Certain factors will limit its usefulness: (1) the accounting policy-making process entails complex social choices; (2) the conceptual framework may not be interpreted uniformly by all FASB members at a given time; and (3) the FASB membership will continue to change over time, thereby possibly altering the board's interpretation of the conceptual framework.[26]

ECONOMIC IMPACT ISSUE

Accounting principles affect the allocation of scarce resources in our society because they determine the content of financial statements that investors, creditors, and others use to make many important decisions. Perhaps less obvious but also very important is the fact that a *manager's behavior,* as reflected in various operating and financial decisions, often is influenced by the manager's knowledge of the information that accounting principles require. Indeed, some of a manager's compensation (i.e., bonus) often is determined by the amount of net income reported in the company's financial statements. Recently, for example, Disney's CEO was awarded a contract that included "an annual cash bonus equal to 2% of Disney's net income in excess of a 9% return on equity. That clause alone resulted in a $6.8 million bonus last year when Disney's ROE hit 25%."[27]

A former chief accountant of the SEC has aptly stated that "the way you keep score determines at least in part the way you play the game."[28] Under current generally accepted accounting principles, for example, a company is not required to include all types of leases among its liabilities. Many people believe that if the FASB required companies to include all leases among their liabilities, companies would engage in fewer leasing transactions. Because of the actions of preparers and users of financial statements, accounting principles have an important *economic impact* on our society. Simply put, they help to determine who gets how much wealth.

In recent years, accounting principles have been directly linked to such issues as health care for retirees, bank lending policies, the merger movement, gross national

---

[26]See Charles T. Horngren, "Uses and Limitations of a Conceptual Framework," *Journal of Accountancy* (April 1981), pp. 86, 88, 90, 92, 94–95.
[27]John A. Byrne, Ronald Grover, and Todd Vogel, "Is the Boss Getting Paid Too Much?" *Business Week* (May 1, 1989), p. 52.
[28]"Why Everybody's Jumping on the Accountants These Days," *Forbes* (March 15, 1977), p. 39.

product, national energy policy, and tax policy designed to encourage business invest-ment. This fact has raised questions about whether and to what extent the FASB should be concerned with the economic impact of the standards that it sets. When the FASB established standards for oil and gas producing companies, to use a recent ex-ample that we mentioned earlier, should the FASB have been concerned only with try-ing to do what it considered correct according to accounting theory, or should it also have been concerned with doing what some energy producers claimed was best for the nation's energy program?

During the 1970s and 1980s, the economic impact issue began to play an increas-ingly important role in the standard-setting process of both the APB and the FASB.[29] An awareness of this role helps to explain some of the generally accepted accounting principles that exist today.

In the future, the FASB is likely to be guided in its decisions primarily by the ac-counting theory that the board has adopted in its Conceptual Framework Project. However, the board will also consider the economic impact of its decisions by assess-ing the economic benefits and costs that its decisions are likely to produce. Doing this will not, of course, be easy.

PUBLIC VERSUS PRIVATE SECTOR ISSUE

As noted earlier, private sector organizations have played the dominant role in shap-ing the development of generally accepted accounting principles in the United States. Nevertheless, the SEC has the legal authority to prescribe accounting principles, and Congress can effectively tell the SEC what to do. Will Congress ever decide that ac-counting principles should be formulated in the public sector?

In the past, Congress has exerted relatively little direct influence on the standard-setting process. The most notable exceptions have been in the areas of LIFO inventory pricing, accounting for the investment tax credit, and accounting for oil and gas pro-ducing companies.

In 1976, however, a report issued by a House of Representatives subcommittee chaired by John E. Moss criticized the lack of uniformity in generally accepted ac-counting principles. Later that year, a Senate subcommittee chaired by Lee Metcalf issued a staff study which recommended that the federal government should establish financial accounting standards for publicly owned corporations. The same Senate subcommittee issued a report in 1977 that was much less critical of the accounting profession and the standard-setting process. In 1984 and 1985, a House of Represen-tatives subcommittee chaired by John D. Dingell held hearings during which many criticisms of accounting standard-setting were expressed. This subcommittee seri-ously questioned whether existing accounting and auditing standards are sufficient to alert investors and creditors to potential business failures.

The accounting profession has responded to these Congressional criticisms in many ways, but presently it appears that Congress does not have a strong interest in creating a federal board to establish financial accounting standards. Nevertheless, the work of the Congressional subcommittees has shown that some elected officials are not pleased with the progress that private sector organizations have made in develop-ing accounting standards.

Most accountants and other business people feel strongly that standard setting should remain in the private sector. A survey of the preferences of 1,329 preparers,

---

[29]See Stephen A. Zeff, "The Rise of 'Economic Consequences,' " *Journal of Accountancy* (December 1978), pp. 56–63.

auditors, and users of financial reports "showed a clear preference for financial accounting reporting standards to be set within the private sector, by a body similar in composition to the current FASB."[30] The reasons for favoring the private sector determination of GAAP appear to be based on such important factors as objectivity, prestige and acceptability, expertise, competence, and image. Expertise is probably the most important of these factors.[31]

In the final analysis, whether or not accounting standard setting remains in the private sector will likely depend on how successful the FASB is in satisfying the various groups who are interested in its decisions, including Congress.

UNIFORMITY VERSUS FLEXIBILITY ISSUE

People can usually think of several ways to account for a given type of transaction. Take depreciation for example. Generally accepted accounting principles support the concept that depreciation is a cost allocation process. But even though most accountants may agree with this concept, several depreciation methods are currently used, such as straight-line, double-declining balance, and sum-of-the-years'-digits. The depreciation method that a company uses will influence the amount of its net income and other financial-statement variables. This fact and the fact that people use financial statements to make *comparisons* between companies are the basis for one of the accounting profession's oldest debates—uniformity versus flexibility of accounting principles.

Proponents of uniformity have argued that company managers have too many accounting options available to them. They believe that these options create confusion and reduce the ability of financial statement users to make meaningful comparisons. On the other side, proponents of flexibility believe that some alternatives should be allowed. These people feel that some flexibility is needed because each company is complex and unique.

Uniformity and flexibility are extremes disliked by most accountants. Strict uniformity would probably result in a "cookbook" prescribing everything from the detailed procedures for gathering data to the precise format to use for financial statements. At the opposite extreme, unlimited flexibility would make it difficult for users to make comparisons and would undermine the integrity of the financial reporting process. The critical issue, therefore, is where on the uniformity/flexibility continuum the accounting profession should be.

One of the major tasks of the FASB and its predecessors has been to eliminate undesirable accounting alternatives. In doing this today, accountants tend to emphasize the goal of **achieving comparability** rather than either uniformity or flexibility. A requirement for financial statements to be comparable is that any differences between the financial statements of different companies should reflect basic differences between the companies themselves and not merely differences between the accounting principles that they use. Achieving comparability requires: "(1) identifying and describing the circumstances that justify or require the use of a particular accounting practice or method, [and] (2) eliminating the use of alternative practices under these circumstances."[32] Accomplishing this goal has not been and will not be easy. History reveals that when the accounting profession's critics feel that it has fallen short of

---

[30]Joshua Ronen and Michael Schiff, "The Setting of Financial Accounting Standards—Private or Public?" *Journal of Accountancy* (March 1978), p. 69.
[31]Ronen and Schiff, pp. 69–70.
[32]*APB Statement No. 4*, par. 102.

achieving comparability, cries for more uniformity tend to become louder. An important determinant of the FASB's success will be the extent to which it contributes to comparability through an acceptable resolution of the uniformity/flexibility debate.

MARKET EFFICIENCY ISSUE

Market efficiency is an issue with important implications for the uniformity/flexibility debate and for other accounting matters. Basically, in an **efficient market** stock prices behave as if they fully reflect publicly available information, including that reported in general purpose financial statements. Although the evidence is not yet conclusive, a large body of empirical literature in accounting and finance suggests that the stock market is highly efficient.

An efficient market reacts to financial statements in a sophisticated manner. It is not fooled when two companies use different accounting methods. Instead, it recognizes that the numbers were generated by different methods. A high degree of market efficiency implies that the market is strongly influenced by the decisions of people who have considerable knowledge of accounting and business. In other words, an efficient market tends to be dominated by *sophisticated* rather than naive users of financial statements.

An efficient market for accounting implies that many financial reporting issues can be resolved by a relatively simple strategy of **adequate disclosure**.[33] Consider the various depreciation methods that we discussed earlier. Those who believe that the market is highly efficient would argue that the reporting of several depreciation figures, each computed according to one of the widely used methods, involves only a small cost. Therefore, a company should use one method in its financial statements but disclose in the footnotes what depreciation would be under the other methods. Users, who are presumed to be highly sophisticated, can then adjust the statements to reflect the other methods if they want to do so.

Efficient-market research has not been fully accepted by all accounting authorities. The research pertains to the market as a whole and not to the behavior of individual investors. Moreover, it says nothing about the information needs of financial statement users, such as bankers, whose decisions do not directly involve publicly traded stocks. Nevertheless, the efficient-markets issue is one that may have an important effect on the course of standard setting in the United States.

BIG GAAP/LITTLE GAAP ISSUE

General purpose financial statements must conform with generally accepted accounting principles. These principles apply to any business regardless of its size or ownership characteristics. But consider a small, closely held business such as a family-owned jewelry store or construction company. Do those who use the financial statements of these kinds of businesses (primarily owners and bankers) really need the same types of information as those who use the financial statements of such companies as Exxon, Chrysler, and Procter & Gamble? Many people say no. And as a result, some have argued that one set of generally accepted accounting principles (which they would call "big GAAP") should apply to larger and/or publicly held companies, while a somewhat different set ("little GAAP") should apply to smaller and/or closely held companies.

---

[33]See William H. Beaver, "What Should Be the FASB's Objectives?" *Journal of Accountancy* (August 1973), pp. 49–56.

Proponents of the big GAAP/little GAAP view believe that general purpose financial statements of smaller companies often are unnecessarily costly because they include information that users really do not want. Proponents also feel that the cost of presenting all this information effectively precludes smaller companies from presenting information that is not required by GAAP but that users would find more useful. As a result, they feel that present accounting standards tend to discriminate against smaller businesses.[34]

The accounting profession has never defined precisely what constitutes a large or a small company. Accountants conveniently use the catchy term "big GAAP/little GAAP" to refer to the broad question of whether differential accounting principles should exist for different types of companies, whether based on size or ownership characteristics, or both.

The number and complexity of pronouncements issued by the APB and the FASB have increased the importance of the big GAAP/little GAAP issue. The FASB is very concerned about this issue and has taken steps to reduce the financial reporting burden of smaller companies. In April 1978, for example, the FASB declared that non-public enterprises no longer are required to report earnings per share and segment information. In the following year, the board made its inflation-accounting requirements applicable only to very large companies. The big GAAP/little GAAP controversy is likely to continue to influence the standard-setting process in the future. The issue is very important because in the U.S. there are about 7,000,000 private businesses compared to only about 10,000 public companies.

ETHICS IN ACCOUNTING

Ethics has been a major news topic during the past several years. Television broadcasts and newspaper articles have bombarded us with stories about such practices as government officials making illegal sales of weapons to foreign countries, corporate officers making money in the stock market by using insider information, and companies profiting from products that are known to cause unreasonable health hazards.

Everyone should behave in a way that is both legally and morally defensible. To behave legally, of course, means to obey laws. Morality provides fundamental guidelines to help people resolve conflicts and live together in groups. Thus, to behave in an ethical (morally defensible) manner, a person must do what is right according to the current values of society.

When applying accounting principles and in other aspects of their professional lives, accountants have a *special* obligation to observe high standards of ethical behavior because of the trust confided in them by the users of financial statements. Investors and creditors must believe in the integrity of financial statements if the statements are to have any value. If accounting is to continue as a useful institution in our society, accountants must have credibility. When an accountant engages in an illegal or unethical act, such as an independent auditor taking a bribe in exchange for allowing management to falsify a company's financial statements, this undermines the integrity of the entire financial reporting process.

If you are an accountant who encounters an ethical dilemma, such as being asked by management to misstate a company's revenues or expenses, you should try to resolve the problem in a calm, reasoned manner. Begin by evaluating all the facts and defining the ethical issues. Identify the parties who would be directly or indirectly

---

[34]See "Report of the Committee on Generally Accepted Accounting Principles for Smaller and/or Closely Held Businesses," *Journal of Accountancy* (October 1976), pp. 116–120.

affected by the ethical decision. Then determine the alternative courses of action and compare the consequences of each response. Next, make a decision that complies with high legal and moral standards of conduct. Finally, you must have the courage and will power to follow through with your ethical decision.

Fortunately, the accounting profession currently enjoys a high degree of moral credibility in the eyes of the general public. A recent news release indicated that in a nationwide survey of business people, accountants were regarded as having the highest business ethics of 16 professions, ranking ahead of dentists and doctors.[35]

CONCLUDING REMARKS

Accounting seeks to identify, measure, and communicate information about economic entities that is useful in making economic decisions. Financial accounting is the branch of accounting that provides information about the financial position of a business enterprise and the changes that occur therein. Its primary focus is meeting the needs of external users such as stockholders and bankers. As you study the remaining chapters, *continually question* whether the accounting principles presented really aid the decision-making processes of external users. Do not assume that an accounting principle is desirable for society just because it is now generally accepted.

General purpose financial statements constitute the main output of financial accounting. Accountants prepare these statements in accordance with generally accepted accounting principles, which are largely determined within the private sector of our economy. Because these principles constantly change, the study of accounting is a lifelong process.

In the following chapters, we examine the hows, whys, and so whats of intermediate accounting. The next chapter focuses on why and deals with the basic theory of general purpose financial statements.

KEY POINTS

1. Accounting seeks to identify, measure, and communicate information about economic entities that is intended to be useful in making economic decisions. (Objective 1)

2. Financial accounting is the branch of accounting that is concerned with measuring and reporting the financial position of a business enterprise and the changes that occur in financial position. Financial accounting information is designed primarily to meet the needs of external users. (Objective 1)

3. External users of financial statements include present and potential owners, lenders, suppliers, employees, and customers, in addition to financial analysts, stock exchanges, regulatory agencies, and the general public. (Objective 2)

4. Investors and creditors use financial statements to make predictions, assess risk, and evaluate profitability, solvency, and management's performance. (Objective 2)

5. The basic financial statements are the balance sheet, income statement, statement of cash flows, and statement of retained earnings or statement of stockholders' equity. (Objective 2)

6. The management of an entity has the primary responsibility for preparing its financial statements. Managers in turn hire internal accountants to collect data and prepare the statements. (Objective 2)

7. Public (external) accountants examine financial statements and express an opinion about whether the statements have been prepared in accordance with generally accepted accounting principles. (Objective 2)

8. Auditors must be competent and independent from the companies they audit. (Objective 2)

---

[35]"Ethics Survey Ranks Accountants First," *Journal of Accountancy* (October 1989), p. 110.

9. Generally accepted accounting principles are those principles that have substantial authoritative support. (Objective 3)

10. The organizations that have had the most influence in developing generally accepted accounting principles are the Committee on Accounting Procedure, the Accounting Principles Board, the Financial Accounting Standards Board, and the Securities and Exchange Commission. (Objective 4)

11. Certain other organizations and the income tax law have also affected the development of generally accepted accounting principles. (Objective 4)

12. Experience, reason, custom, usage, and practical necessity are important factors in developing generally accepted accounting principles. (Objective 4)

13. FASB Statements of Financial Accounting Standards and Interpretations, APB Opinions, and Accounting Research Bulletins are the most authoritative sources of generally accepted accounting principles. (Objective 5)

14. Several important issues are likely to affect the development of generally accepted accounting principles. These include the FASB's Conceptual Framework Project, the economic impact issue, the public versus private sector issue, the uniformity versus flexibility issue, the market efficiency issue, and the big GAAP/little GAAP issue. (Objective 6)

15. Accountants have a special obligation to observe high standards of ethical conduct because of the considerable trust confided in them by the users of financial statements. (Objective 7)

QUESTIONS

1–1   Distinguish between internal and external users of accounting information.

1–2   What is financial accounting?

1–3   What is meant by the term "general purpose financial statements"? Why does the accounting profession emphasize general purpose statements instead of single purpose statements?

1–4   Give three examples of accounting applications that illustrate the following point: "Financial statements are not usually as precise as they appear to be."

1–5   Identify five sources that investors and creditors commonly use to obtain information about specific companies.

1–6   Distinguish between financial statements and financial reporting.

1–7   Briefly explain the role of corporate management in the financial reporting process.

1–8   Briefly explain the professional designations of CMA and CPA.

1–9   What is an audit?

1–10   The following terms relate to audit reports. Briefly explain each one.

[a] Unqualified opinion   [c] Adverse opinion
[b] Qualified opinion   [d] Disclaimer of opinion

1–11   What is meant by the term "generally accepted accounting principles"?

1–12   Distinguish among the following types of pronouncements:

[a] Accounting Research Bulletins
[b] APB Opinions
[c] Statements of Financial Accounting Standards
[d] Statements of Financial Accounting Concepts
[e] FASB Interpretations

1–13   Briefly explain *Rule 203* of the AICPA Code of Professional Conduct. What is the significance of this rule?

1–14   What are the major differences between the FASB and its predecessor standard-setting bodies (the CAP and APB)?

1–15   What major steps does the FASB usually follow when formulating a Statement of Financial Accounting Standards?

1-16 Briefly explain the Securities Act of 1933 and the Securities Exchange Act of 1934.

1-17 What is the SEC's fundamental purpose?

1-18 What is the SEC's role in establishing accounting standards?

1-19 Why do the principles of income tax law often differ from the principles of financial accounting?

1-20 Of what significance are financial analysts and commercial bank loan officers to the accounting profession?

1-21 Explain the various sources of generally accepted accounting principles by going from the most authoritative sources to the least authoritative sources.

1-22 What is the FASB's Conceptual Framework Project?

1-23 Briefly explain how accounting principles affect the manner in which our society allocates its scarce resources.

1-24 Briefly explain the uniformity versus flexibility debate in financial accounting.

1-25 Do generally accepted accounting principles apply only to larger companies? Explain.

1-26 What does "morality" mean and why is it particularly important for accountants to observe high standards of moral behavior?

CASES

1-27 SOURCES OF INFORMATION   Assume that you have recently graduated from college and that your boss asks you to speak to a local civic organization of business people. The topic of your speech is "Sources of Information That May Be Useful in Investment, Credit, and Similar Decisions."

Instructions

Identify the major sources that you should describe in your speech.

1-28 THE ACCOUNTING PROFESSION   A friend of yours majoring in another business field has asked you what, if anything, besides the technical content of accounting courses distinguishes accounting from other business disciplines. He does not understand why accountants can become licensed by the state as certified public accountants and what role such individuals can play in the commercial process.

Instructions

Develop a response to your friend's question. In determining your response, consider the characteristics that distinguish a profession from other business or commercial endeavors. Also be sure to address the role of accounting in the functioning of our capital markets as well as its contribution to the management of business enterprises.

1-29 ACCOUNTING PRINCIPLES   At the completion of the Hardy Department Store audit, the president asks about the meaning of the phrase "in conformity with generally accepted accounting principles" that appears in your audit report on the management's financial statements. He observes that the meaning of the phrase must include more than what he thinks of as "principles."

Instructions

[a] Explain the meaning of the term "accounting principles" as used in the audit report. (Do *not* discuss in this part the significance of "generally accepted.")
[b] The president wants to know how you determine whether or not an accounting principle is generally accepted. Discuss the sources of evidence for determining whether an accounting principle has substantial authoritative support.
[c] The president believes that diversity in accounting practice always will exist among independent entities despite continual improvements in comparability. Develop arguments that *support* his belief.   (AICPA adapted)

1-30 DEPARTURES FROM GAAP   You are preparing the financial statements for your company, a chain of retail clothing stores, when the president calls you in to discuss an accounting problem. The issue involves a transaction that the company has just completed and that has a substantial effect on reported earnings. There is an FASB Statement of Financial Accounting Standards that deals generally with the issue, however, the company's transaction does have a few characteristics that are not considered by the FASB statement. The president wishes to account for the transaction in a way that would depart from the provisions of the FASB statement and you can see some validity to her position. First, the transaction of the company is somewhat different from that contemplated by the FASB statement. While you do not consider the differences to be significant, you do believe that the accounting proposed by the president of your company would better portray the economic substance of the transaction. Nevertheless, you believe that accounting for the transaction in the fashion prescribed by the FASB would also be reasonable. The president concludes the meeting with the following statement: "Study this issue for a while and write a position paper that lets me know your thinking. I know I can count on you to support my efforts to put our best foot forward in the marketplace."

Instructions

Respond to the president's charge. Use the information provided in the case and the material in Chapter 1 to prepare a response that you believe is consistent with the responsibilities of a professional accountant.

1-31 STANDARD-SETTING PROCESS   An article about the FASB on the front page of the *Wall Street Journal* (Apr. 30, 1984) stated that "critics all over the country are bombarding the seven-member board with a cacophony of complaints. Accountants increasingly accuse the FASB of moving too slowly—and of producing little of substance when it finally does act." The article also stated that "by one estimate, it [the FASB] mailed out more than three million documents last year and more than 100,000 letters. It receives up to 600 phone calls daily, many seeking advice on how to interpret its complex rules."

Instructions

[a] Explain why the formulation of accounting policy is considered highly controversial.
[b] Why does the FASB work at a pace that many critics regard as too slow when formulating accounting policy?

1-32 POLITICIZATION IN STANDARD SETTING   Some accountants have said that the development and acceptance of generally accepted accounting principles (i.e., standard setting) is being politicized. Some use the term "politicization" in a narrow sense to mean influence by governmental agencies, particularly the SEC, on the development of generally accepted accounting principles. Others use the term more broadly to mean the compromising that takes place in bodies responsible for developing generally accepted accounting principles because of the influence and pressure of interested groups (e.g., SEC, AAA, NAA, businesses through their various organizations, financial analysts, bankers, and lawyers).

Instructions

[a] The CAP of the AICPA was established in the middle to late 1930s and functioned until 1959, when it was replaced by the APB. In 1973 the FASB was formed and the APB dissolved. Explain how these groups were formed, their methods of operation, and the reasons for the demise of the CAP and the APB. Indicate whether these events show increasing politicization (in the broad sense) of accounting standard setting. Cite specific developments to support your answer.
[b] What arguments support the "politicization" of accounting standard setting?
[c] What arguments can be raised against the "politicization" of accounting standard setting?

(CMA adapted)

1-33 INCOME TAX LAWS   One of your friends is a law school student who recently decided to take an introductory course in financial accounting. After his first day of class, he tells you: "I'm having some trouble understanding what financial accounting is all about. In law school, I learned how to calculate income according to tax laws. Why aren't the tax laws used to calculate income in financial accounting?"

Instructions

[a] Answer your friend's question.
[b] Discuss the significance of income tax law in the development of generally accepted accounting principles.

1–34 STANDARD SETTING FOR LEASES   For many years the accounting profession has debated the merits of two primary methods of accounting for leases by lessees (i.e., companies that lease assets from other enterprises): (1) capitalization of leases, which means that lessees record the present value of expected future lease payments as an asset and liability, treat lease payments as reductions in the liability, and depreciate the recorded asset; and (2) expensing of lease payments as they are made with no initial recording of a lease asset or liability by the lessee.

When the FASB was discussing the issue of accounting for leases, it received a letter from a U.S. senator that read in part as follows:

> *A number of my associates in Congress and I are concerned with the possible effect of lease capitalization upon the financing costs of American industry—which costs enter into the eventual prices to the public of goods and services. In an inflationary period, such suggested accounting practice may have a marked effect upon the prices to the public of transportation, energy, food, and housing. It would be most unfortunate if a theoretical approach to financial disclosure assumed greater importance than the public good especially when effective and more acceptable accounting methods are available for the protection of the investor.*

Instructions

[a] Identify the broad issue in accounting standard setting that underlies the senator's concern.
[b] What effect, if any, do *you* think the points raised in the senator's letter should have on the FASB's deliberations in the matter of accounting for leases?

1–35 DEVELOPMENT STAGE COMPANIES   In 1975 the FASB issued *SFAS No. 7,* "Accounting and Reporting by Development State Enterprises." This pronouncement states that "an enterprise shall be considered to be in the development stage if it is devoting substantially all of its efforts to establishing a new business and either of the following conditions exists:

[a] Planned principal operations have not commenced.
[b] Planned principal operations have commenced but there has been no significant revenue therefrom" (par. 8).

In essence *SFAS No. 7* concluded that development-stage companies must use the same accounting principles as established companies. But when the Exposure Draft that preceded *SFAS No. 7* was issued, "some respondents to the Exposure Draft expressed concern that requiring development stage enterprises to present the same basic financial statements and to apply the same generally accepted accounting principles as established operating enterprises might make it difficult, if not impossible, for development stage enterprises to obtain capital" (par. 48).

Instructions

Identify and explain the broad issue that underlies the concern expressed by the respondents to the Exposure Draft that preceded *SFAS No. 7.*

1–36 GENERAL VERSUS DETAILED STANDARDS   An article in the *Wall Street Journal* (Wednesday, August 3, 1988, p. 6) stated that "John Reed, chairman of Citicorp and chairman of the [Business] Roundtable's accounting principles task force, has been criticizing the FASB in meetings with SEC commissioners and managing partners of major accounting firms . . . According to accountants and businessmen, Roundtable members are telling the SEC that some FASB rules use a 'cookbook' approach and are so narrow and detailed as to make implementation prohibitively costly. They have cited rules on pension costs and deferred taxes."

Instructions

When the FASB publishes an accounting standard, should the standard be written in a manner that is relatively general or relatively detailed in nature? Explain the rationale for your preference.

1–37   EFFECTS OF ACCOUNTING PRINCIPLES   An article in *Forbes* (November 28, 1988, p. 170) stated that "foreign companies have a walloping advantage over U.S. companies in playing the takeover game in this country. The advantage is intangible, but it's a big advantage all the same." The article explains that when a U.S. company acquires another company, generally accepted accounting principles require the U.S. company to amortize any payment that is made for goodwill. The goodwill is amortized over a maximum period of 40 years and causes the acquiring company's net income to be lower by the amount of the amortization. In contrast, British accounting rules provide that when a British company acquires another enterprise, even one located in the U.S., any amount paid for goodwill is immediately written off against stockholders' equity and is therefore never charged against the British company's net income.

Instructions

Do you believe that the British accounting rules for goodwill give British companies an advantage over U.S. companies when acquiring other firms? Present arguments to support your answer.

1–38   MARKET EFFICIENCY ISSUE   At an open meeting in July 1981, it was stated that the SEC "intends to apply the efficient market theory . . . to public offerings by widely-followed companies to take advantage of periodic reports filed under the Securities Exchange Act prior to a new registration statement." (From "The Week in Review," Deloitte Haskins & Sells, July 31, 1981, p. 1.)

Instructions

[a] What is an efficient market?

[b] Briefly indicate how you think the SEC could apply the efficient market theory "to take advantage of periodic reports filed under the Securities Exchange Act prior to a new registration statement."

1–39   BIG GAAP/LITTLE GAAP ISSUE   In an open letter to the FASB, Alexander Grant & Company, a large, international CPA firm, stated "we are genuinely concerned that you are not reacting to a serious problem. A recent exchange of correspondence between the AICPA and the FASB makes it clear to us that the present FASB does not intend to consider relief from onerous accounting and disclosure requirements for the thousands of smaller and/or closely-held businesses across this country" (*Wall Street Journal*, October 25, 1977, p. 24).

Instructions

[a] Take the position that the accounting profession should have one set of generally accepted accounting principles that apply to all companies, regardless of size or ownership characteristics. Develop arguments that support your position.

[b] Take the position that the accounting profession should have one set of generally accepted accounting principles for larger and/or publicly held companies and a somewhat different set for smaller and/or closely held companies. Develop arguments that support your position.

1–40   EXPENSE REIMBURSEMENT   As an accountant for a medium-size company, you have recently returned from a five-day out-of-town assignment and are now completing your expense reimbursement form. Your employer has a written policy allowing you to claim reimbursement for your *actual daily cost of meals* up to a maximum of $30 per day. You are *not* required to provide receipts for the meals that you claim.

While you were on assignment, you ate meals for free at your aunt's home, but no one from your company knows because you worked on the assignment alone. You have learned through informal conversation that some of your fellow employees routinely request reimbursement for the maximum meal allowance of $30, even when the actual cost of their meals is much less.

Instructions

Would you claim reimbursement for the cost of your meals at the maximum daily rate allowed by your company ($30 × 5 days = $150)? Explain your answer.

CHAPTER 2

Financial Accounting Theory

OBJECTIVES

1. To describe financial accounting theory as currently applied. The theory consists of the following elements:
   a. Objectives
   b. Qualitative characteristics
   c. Assumptions
   d. Concepts and elements
   e. Broad principles
   f. Detailed principles
   g. Modifying conventions

O ne author defines accounting theory as "logical reasoning in the form of a set of broad principles that (1) provide a general frame of reference by which accounting practice can be evaluated and (2) guide the development of new practices and procedures."[1] This chapter provides an overview of descriptive financial accounting theory as it pertains to general-purpose external reporting by business enterprises. Note carefully the following words in the preceding sentence:

1. **Overview.** In this chapter we introduce the most important components of financial accounting theory. Entire textbooks have been devoted to explaining these and other components in more depth.
2. **Descriptive.** Descriptive theory refers to the ways in which accounting theory is currently applied. In contrast, normative theory attempts to prescribe how theory ought to be. This chapter is primarily descriptive.
3. **Financial accounting theory.** We present a logical framework that helps to explain why financial accounting is applied the way it is today.
4. **General-purpose external reporting.** The chapter focuses on a theoretical structure for general-purpose (rather than single or limited purpose), external (rather than internal) reporting.

A knowledge of accounting theory should help you to understand and apply generally accepted accounting principles (GAAP) as well as changes in those principles. Because accounting problems often appear to be routine, accountants sometimes bog down in the mechanics of problem solving and lose sight of the theory they seek to apply. For this reason, you should study this chapter carefully. Later, as you study other chapters, reread the appropriate sections of this chapter. Always strive for sound conceptual understanding that can help you to solve most accounting problems, whether you encounter them in a textbook, on an examination, or in the business world.

The accounting profession today does not have a single, comprehensive, generally accepted framework of accounting theory. As we pointed out in Chapter 1, however, the Financial Accounting Standards Board (FASB) has developed a conceptual framework that it hopes will be accepted in the financial community. Recognize, therefore, that accounting is a relatively young and dynamic discipline for which a theoretical structure is still evolving. The theoretical framework presented in this chapter is based on several sources and represents descriptive financial accounting theory today.[2]

A MODEL

Exhibit 2–1 presents the theoretical components discussed in this chapter. These components are **objectives, qualitative characteristics, assumptions, concepts and elements, broad principles, detailed principles,** and **modifying conventions.**[3] A move from the top to the bottom of the exhibit represents a move from the general objectives to detailed principles, which are quite specific. Accountants traditionally have had less difficulty agreeing on the more general components of the model than on the more specific ones. Most accountants agree, for example, that an important accounting objective should be to provide useful information. On the other hand, less

---

[1]Eldon S. Hendricksen, *Accounting Theory,* 4th ed. (Homewood, Ill.: Irwin, 1982), p. 1.
[2]The framework that we present draws heavily from the works published by the FASB in its Conceptual Framework Project.
[3]The labels attached to certain components of the model vary somewhat in practice. Principles, for example, are sometimes called standards, concepts, procedures, rules, and practices.

EXHIBIT 2-1

Financial Accounting Theory: A Model

Most general ↓ *Most specific*

SFAC #1 **Objectives**
1. Financial reporting should provide information useful in investment, credit, and similar decisions.
2. Financial reporting should provide information useful in assessing cash flow prospects.
3. Financial reporting should provide information about enterprise resources, claims to those resources, and changes in them.

↓

Qualitative Characteristics

Relevance	Reliability
Predictive value	Verifiability
Feedback value	Neutrality
Timeliness	Representational faithfulness

↓

Assumptions
Economic entity
Periodicity
Going concern

↓

Concepts and Elements
Financial Position
  Assets
  Liabilities
  Owners' equity
Changes in Financial Position
  Revenues
  Expenses   } 3rd. parties
  Gains
  Losses
  Income
  Investments by owners   } owners
  Distributions to owners

↓

Relates to measurement + disclosure

Broad Principles
Monetary unit
Asset/Liability measurement
Revenue realization
Matching — Expenses
Consistency
Disclosure

↓

Detailed Principles
Covered throughout the text

Constraints to
Modifying Conventions
Materiality
Industry practices
Conservatism
Substance over form

Broad Principles
Detailed Principles

agreement exists about which principles the accounting profession should adopt to achieve the objective of providing useful information.

When studying the model of financial accounting theory, remember that the components are *not all independent of one another.* Many important **interrelationships** exist that are too complex to identify meaningfully in one model. Furthermore, accounting principles have not always developed on the basis of explicit objectives. As we pointed out in Chapter 1, generally accepted accounting principles "have developed on the basis of experience, reason, custom, usage, and, to a significant extent, practical necessity."[4] For this reason some accountants think that certain principles are inconsistent with certain objectives. These components may therefore change as a result of further development of accounting theory. Despite these limitations of the model, we believe that it provides a useful framework in which to study financial accounting.

OBJECTIVES OF FINANCIAL REPORTING

During the 1970s the accounting profession spent considerable time and effort developing a set of objectives for financial accounting. In 1973 the American Institute of Certified Public Accountants (AICPA) published a major study called "Objectives of Financial Statements." This study, commonly called the *Trueblood Report,* set forth several objectives but concluded that "the basic objective of financial statements is to provide information useful for making economic decisions."[5] In 1978 the FASB issued *Statement of Financial Accounting Concepts No. 1,* entitled "Objectives of Financial Reporting by Business Enterprises."[6] This FASB pronouncement was greatly influenced by the *Trueblood Report.*

The objectives outlined in *SFAC No. 1* stem largely from the important needs of external users, who lack the authority to require the information that they want about a given enterprise. Furthermore, the objectives are affected by the economic, legal, political, and social environment in the United States, and as a result, they may change over time. Finally, the objectives are affected by the characteristics and limitations of the information that financial reporting traditionally has provided.

SFAC No. 1 has identified three major objectives of financial reporting, which includes financial statements. These objectives are summarized in Exhibit 2–1. The first objective is the most general, while the next two are progressively more specific.

USEFUL INFORMATION

The initial objective states that "financial reporting should provide information that is useful to present and potential investors and creditors and other users in making rational investment, credit, and similar decisions. The information should be comprehensible to those who have a reasonable understanding of business and economic activities and are willing to study the information with reasonable diligence."[7] This objective underscores the fact that financial reporting is not an end in itself. Instead, the *output* of the financial accounting process should serve as useful *input* for the making of rational investment, credit, and similar decisions in our society.

[4]*APB Statement No. 4,* "Basic Concepts and Accounting Principles Underlying Financial Statements of Business Enterprises," 1970, par. 139.
[5]*Report of the Study Group on the Objectives of Financial Statements,* "Objectives of Financial Statements" (New York: AICPA, 1973), p. 61.
[6]*FASB Statement of Financial Accounting Concepts No. 1,* "Objectives of Financial Reporting by Business Enterprises," 1978.
[7]*FASB Statement of Financial Accounting Concepts No. 1,* p. viii.

Traditionally, anyone proposing usefulness as an accounting objective has had to respond to the important questions, useful to whom? And for what purpose? In stating its initial objective, the FASB's responses to these questions were quite broad. As a result, the scope of financial reporting is not confined to one, or even a few, user groups. Instead, financial reporting attempts to serve many diverse users. These users, however, are expected to understand business affairs and be willing to spend reasonable amounts of time and effort analyzing accounting information. Accountants should always try to produce reports that are understandable to these kinds of users. Naive users of accounting information should consider taking steps to improve their understanding of business matters, or they should rely on professional advisors. **Understandability** to *reasonably informed users* is therefore a desirable quality of useful accounting information.

Although providing useful information is the primary objective of financial reporting, accounting principles do not require companies to report all potentially useful information. Instead, a pervasive constraint stipulates that **accounting information should be provided only when the benefits of the information exceed the costs of providing and using it.** As you might imagine, trying to determine the benefits and costs of accounting information is highly subjective and can lead to honest differences of opinion between competent persons. Benefits of accounting information are enjoyed by preparers (such as improved access to capital markets and favorable impact on the company's public relations), users (better investment and credit decisions, for example), and consumers (steady supply of goods and services, more efficient functioning of the marketplace, and so forth). Most of the costs are initially paid by preparers but are then passed on to users of financial statements and consumers of the company's goods and services.[8]

CASH FLOW PROSPECTS

Rational investment, credit, and similar decisions are made after careful consideration of such factors as expected cost, risk, and return. As noted in Chapter 1, investors and creditors invest and lend cash, and they want to know how much cash they will receive in return and when they will receive it. Information that helps to resolve these uncertainties is surely regarded as useful.

Accordingly, the second objective is that "financial reporting should provide information to help present and potential investors and creditors and other users in assessing the amounts, timing, and uncertainty of prospective cash receipts from dividends or interest and the proceeds from the sale, redemption, or maturity of securities or loans. Since investors' and creditors' cash flows are related to enterprise cash flows, financial reporting should provide information to help investors, creditors, and others assess the amounts, timing, and uncertainty of prospective net cash inflows to the related enterprise."[9] Note that this objective differentiates between cash flows to investors and creditors and cash flows to a given enterprise to which they have committed funds. Chances of investors and creditors receiving cash via dividends, interest, and otherwise depend on the expected cash flows to the enterprise. If the enterprise succeeds in generating favorable cash flows, the probability of investors and creditors receiving favorable cash flows is increased.

---

[8]*FASB Statement of Financial Accounting Concepts No. 2*, "Qualitative Characteristics of Accounting Information," 1980, par. 136.
[9]*FASB Statement of Financial Accounting Concepts No. 1*, p. viii.

ENTERPRISE RESOURCES, CLAIMS, AND CHANGES

What information is helpful to investors, creditors, and other users in assessing prospective cash receipts from a business enterprise? *SFAC No. 1* responds to this question with the third major objective of financial reporting. This objective holds that "financial reporting should provide information about the economic resources of an enterprise, the claims to those resources (obligations of the enterprise to transfer resources to other entities and owners' equity), and the effects of transactions, events, and circumstances that change its resources and claims to those resources."[10]

Some of the most significant transactions and events that change a firm's resources and the claims to those resources are used to measure financial performance. The FASB stated that "the primary focus of financial reporting is information about an enterprise's performance provided by measures of earnings and its components."[11] Thus, investors and creditors may use past measures of earnings to help predict future earnings and, indirectly, to help predict their chances of receiving cash from a given enterprise.

The FASB believes that **accrual accounting** results in better performance measures than does cash basis accounting. However, the board has emphasized that "accrual accounting provides measures of earnings rather than evaluations of management's performance, estimates of 'earning power,' predictions of earnings, assessments of risk, or confirmations or rejections of predictions or assessments. Investors, creditors, and other users of the information do their own evaluating, estimating, predicting, assessing, confirming, or rejecting."[12] Thus, accountants provide useful historical measurements, but they cannot accurately predict the future and they surely do not make decisions for external information users.

While financial reporting focuses primarily on earnings, information about financial position as well as significant changes in financial position (besides earnings) is important when assessing an enterprise's cash flow prospects. Because management knows more about a firm than do outsiders, the usefulness of information often can be enhanced by management's explanation of the financial impact of certain transactions, events, and circumstances.

QUALITATIVE CHARACTERISTICS OF ACCOUNTING INFORMATION

Given that the basic objective of external financial reporting is to provide information that is useful to people making rational economic decisions, a logical question is: What qualitative characteristics determine the usefulness of accounting information? Many studies have addressed this issue and have generally produced similar results.

The FASB believes that **relevance** and **reliability** are the two most fundamental qualitative characteristics of useful accounting information.[13] **Relevance** means "the capacity of information to make a difference in a decision by helping users to form predictions about the outcome of past, present, and future events or to confirm or correct prior expectations."[14] For example, when stockholders decide to buy, sell, or hold equity investments, earnings-per-share information is generally regarded as highly relevant. In contrast, the serial numbers of plant assets, although highly reliable, are irrelevant information.

---

[10]*FASB Statement of Financial Accounting Concepts No. 1*, p. viii.
[11]*FASB Statement of Financial Accounting Concepts No. 1*, par. 43.
[12]*FASB Statement of Financial Accounting Concepts No. 1*, par. 48.
[13]*FASB Statement of Financial Accounting Concepts No. 2*, 1980, p. x.
[14]*FASB Statement of Financial Accounting Concepts No. 2*, p. xvi.

The major characteristics of relevant information are the following.[15]

1. **Predictive value.**   Information has predictive value when it can help users to increase the likelihood of correctly forecasting the outcome of events. For example, if "cash provided by operations" proves valuable in predicting loan default, it is said to have predictive value.

2. **Feedback value.**   Information with feedback value enables users to confirm or correct expectations. A net income measure, for example, has feedback value if it can help stockholders to confirm or revise their expectations about a company's ability to generate earnings.

3. **Timeliness.**   Information is timely when it is available to a decision maker before decisions are made. For example, one of the most important attributes of quarterly financial information is its timeliness.

To be relevant, information must have predictive value *or* feedback value or both, and it must be timely.

Reliability is "the quality of information that assures that information is reasonably free from error and bias and faithfully represents what it purports to represent."[16] In other words, users can trust that reliable measurements will accurately represent the reality that the measurements claim to represent. For example, most people consider the amount of cash that a company has in its bank account to be highly reliable information. However, information about a company's projected earnings per share fifty years from now is usually not very reliable.

Reliable information has three major characteristics:[17]

1. **Verifiability.**   Information is considered verifiable when it is based on reasonable underlying evidence. Such evidence would permit all competent accountants to generate similar measurements under the same circumstances. The amount of a company's cash on hand, for example, usually is highly verifiable because accountants can simply count it.

   Because of the need for verifiability, financial accounting is based primarily on the results of **arm's-length exchange transactions,** in which unrelated parties act in their own best economic interests. Some accountants refer to the verifiability characteristic as objectivity.

2. **Neutrality.**   Information is neutral when it is free of bias toward a desired result or behavior. Accounting information would not be neutral if it systematically produced results that favored one group of users, such as bankers, over another such as labor organizations.

3. **Representational faithfulness.**   Information is representationally faithful when a measure or description agrees with the phenomenon that it claims to represent. A measure of a company's accounts receivable, for example, would have low representational faithfulness if it included a material amount of uncollectible accounts.

To be reliable, information must have all three characteristics described above.

Many accountants have argued that relevance and reliability may require important trade-offs. That is, to increase the relevance of accounting information, accountants may have to sacrifice some reliability, and vice versa. For example, generally accepted accounting principles call for reporting plant assets in the balance sheet at their historical cost. It is possible, however, that the current cost of plant assets is a

---

[15]*FASB Statement of Financial Accounting Concepts No. 2*, pp. xv–xvi.
[16]*FASB Statement of Financial Accounting Concepts No. 2*, p. xvi.
[17]*FASB Statement of Financial Accounting Concepts No. 2*, p. xvi.

more relevant, yet less reliable, measure than the historical cost of these assets. If so, the question then becomes: Which measure of plant assets, historical cost or current cost, results in information that is most useful? One of the great challenges of the accounting profession is to achieve an optimal balance between relevance and reliability to ensure that accounting information will be as useful as possible. Arriving at this balance requires considerable research and is likely to generate many interesting debates in the financial community.

ASSUMPTIONS

To provide information that is both relevant and reliable, and therefore useful, accountants begin by making certain **assumptions**. These assumptions, often called **postulates,** generally relate to things that are taken for granted. By starting with basic assumptions, other components in the theoretical framework may be logically derived.

ECONOMIC ENTITY ASSUMPTION

Applying the principles of accounting requires the identification of specific units of economic activity. Each unit serves as a focal point to guide the accountant's recording and reporting functions. Accordingly, accountants make the **economic entity assumption,** which says that **economic activities can be meaningfully associated with specific entities or units of accountability.** Typical examples of an economic entity are a person (such as a candidate for public office), a sole proprietorship, a partnership, and a corporation. The entity assumed may be somewhat narrow in scope, such as a division of a diversified company, or quite broad, as when consolidated financial statements are prepared for a group of corporations having common ownership. In any case, the name of the entity should appear at the top of the financial statements.

The economic entity assumption requires a careful separation of the financial affairs of a business (the entity) from the affairs of its owners and other businesses. For example, when a building contractor purchases lumber for an addition to his personal residence, this cost should not be included in the financial affairs of his building company.

Accountants sometimes ignore certain legal considerations when complying with the economic entity assumption. For example, the accounting records of a partnership must be kept separate and distinct from the records of the individual partners, even though the partners may be personally liable for partnership debts if liquidation occurs. Similarly, although a parent corporation and one or more subsidiaries constitute separate *legal* entities, accountants often prepare consolidated financial reports depicting the companies as a single *economic* entity.

PERIODICITY ASSUMPTION

The most reliable method of calculating a new firm's income is to wait until the firm is finally liquidated. At that time, lifetime income can be measured as the amount of resources paid by the firm to the owners over the amount paid in by the owners. Of course, measuring income only when a firm is terminated is not a practical way of satisfying the needs of financial statement users. Indeed, for information to be relevant and thereby have an impact on important decisions, it must be timely.

The need for timely dissemination of information has led accountants to make **the periodicity assumption: the economic activities of a firm can be meaningfully related to arbitrary time periods that are shorter than the firm's life.** In practice, annual, quarterly, and monthly time periods are commonly used. An annual period may be a calendar year, ending December 31, or a fiscal year, the end of which often coincides with the lowest point in a firm's business activities.

The economic activities of a typical business are complex and continuous. When a manufacturing firm buys a new machine, for example, the machine will likely last for several accounting periods. During these periods the machine will be used—with raw materials, labor, and other machines—to produce a product that may be sold at some future date for a price that is now uncertain. Given this interaction and uncertainty, no one can precisely determine the benefits of the machine to the firm. Therefore, depreciation expense under accrual accounting cannot be precisely determined for a period shorter than the life of the machine. As this example shows, financial reporting for any brief period requires estimates and professional judgment, and the accountant's measurements are therefore often tentative. In general, as the time period becomes shorter, it becomes increasingly difficult to make meaningful estimates, and the reliability of accounting information is reduced.

GOING-CONCERN (CONTINUITY) ASSUMPTION

The **going-concern assumption** holds that **in the absence of evidence to the contrary, accountants assume that entity operations will continue for a reasonable period of time; that is, the entity will not be liquidated in the near future.** There is no assumption that the entity will exist permanently but simply that it will last at least long enough to fulfill its plans and commitments. This assumption is supported by the fact that most businesses expect to operate for extended periods of time. This expectation is fostered by our relatively stable economic, political, and social environment, in which laws and customs afford certain rights and protections.

The going-concern assumption helps to provide a rationale for several important aspects of accounting. It permits assets to be defined as probable future economic benefits to a firm. Moreover, it supports the historical cost system of measurement, which is based on the premise that historical accounting information can be used to help predict interesting events. If, for example, the firm were expected to liquidate in the immediate future, assets would be better stated at their net realizable values. The going-concern assumption also supports such interperiod allocation procedures as depreciation, amortization, and interperiod tax allocation. It would not make sense, for example, to depreciate a new machine over ten years if the company that owned it was expected to fold next year. Finally, the going-concern assumption serves as a basis for conventional balance sheet classification. Why list certain liabilities as long term, for example, if the firm is expected to go out of business within six months?

The accountant should periodically reevaluate the logic of assuming a going concern for any given enterprise. Perhaps management would like to liquidate in the near future, or perhaps a long period of substantial losses will soon result in a forced liquidation. When evidence indicates that liquidation is imminent, the going-concern assumption should be abandoned in favor of the quitting-concern (i.e., liquidation) assumption, under which assets should be measured at their net realizable values and the priority rights of creditors should be reported. Accounting for companies under the quitting-concern assumption is covered in advanced accounting courses.

CONCEPTS AND ELEMENTS

The economic entity, periodicity, and going-concern assumptions support certain basic **concepts** and **elements.** The concepts are financial position and changes in financial position. The elements that compose financial position are assets, liabilities, and

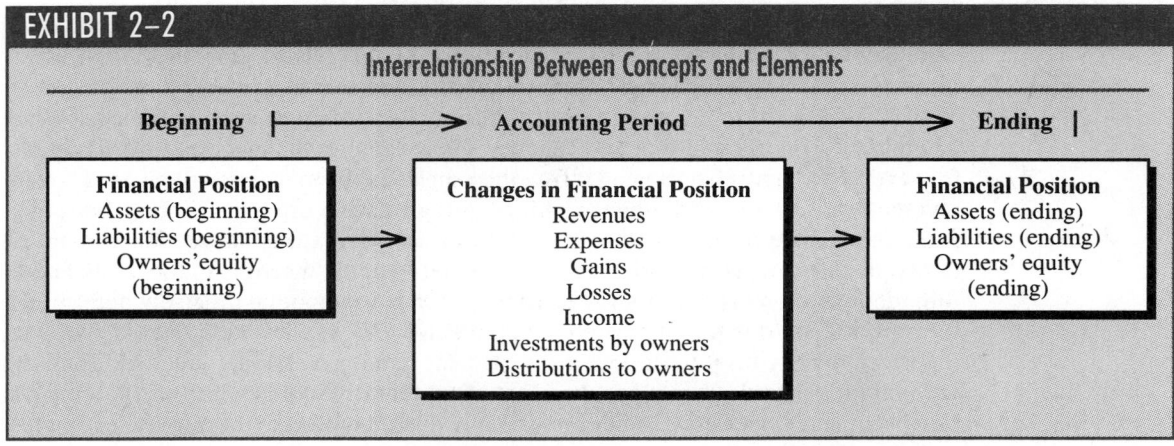

EXHIBIT 2–2

Interrelationship Between Concepts and Elements

Beginning ⊢――――▷ Accounting Period ――――▷ Ending ⊢

Financial Position	Changes in Financial Position	Financial Position
Assets (beginning)	Revenues	Assets (ending)
Liabilities (beginning)	Expenses	Liabilities (ending)
Owners'equity	Gains	Owners' equity
(beginning)	Losses	(ending)
	Income	
	Investments by owners	
	Distributions to owners	

owners' equity; these elements appear on an entity's balance sheet. The major elements that explain the changes in an entity's financial position are revenues, expenses, gains, losses, income, investments by owners, and distributions to owners. Revenues, expenses, gains, losses, and income appear on an entity's income statement, while investments by and distributions to owners are summarized on its statement of stockholders' equity. The relationship of concepts and elements is illustrated in Exhibit 2–2.

FINANCIAL POSITION

The **financial position** of an entity is determined by its economic resources and the claims against those resources **at a particular point in time.**[18]
    Financial position primarily consists of the following:

1. **Assets,** or the probable future economic benefits obtained or controlled by an entity as a result of past transactions or events. Examples are cash, merchandise inventory, and land.
2. **Liabilities,** or the probable future sacrifices of economic benefits arising from present obligations of an entity to transfer assets or provide services to other entities in the future as a result of past transactions or events. Examples are accounts payable, bonds payable, and unearned revenues.
3. **Owners' equity,** which is the residual interest in the assets of an entity that remains after deducting its liabilities. Examples of owners' equity are common stock, paid-in capital in excess of par value, and retained earnings.

CHANGES IN FINANCIAL POSITION

Changes in financial position are the result of certain events that occur **during a period of time.** The key elements that follow account for changes in financial position:[19]

1. **Revenues,** that is, inflows or other enhancements of assets of an entity or settlements of its liabilities (or both) during a period, based on production and delivery

---

[18]The definitions of assets, liabilities, and owners' equity are based on *FASB Statement of Financial Accounting Concepts No. 6,* "Elements of Financial Statements," 1985.
[19]Definitions are based on *FASB Statement of Financial Accounting Standards No. 6,* 1985.

of goods, provision of services, and other activities that constitute the entity's major operations. Examples are sales revenue, interest revenue, and rent revenue.

2. **Expenses,** which include outflows or other use of assets or incurrences of liabilities (or both) during a period as a result of delivering or producing goods, rendering services, or carrying out other activities that constitute the entity's major operations. Examples are cost of goods sold, salaries expense, and advertising expense.

3. **Gains,** or increases in owners' equity (net assets) from peripheral or incidental transactions of an entity and from all other transactions and events affecting the entity during a period, except those that result from revenues or investments by owners. Examples are a gain on the sale of plant assets and a gain on the early retirement of long-term debt.

4. **Losses,** or decreases in owners' equity (net assets) from peripheral or incidental transactions of an entity and from all other transactions and events affecting the entity during a period, except those that result from expenses or distributions to owners. Examples are losses on the sale of investments and on litigation.

5. **Income,** which results from adding all revenues and gains for a period and subtracting all expenses and losses for the period.

6. **Investments by owners** are increases in owners' equity resulting from transfers from other entities of something valuable in exchange for ownership interests. Although assets (typically cash) are usually received as investments by owners, the consideration may also include services or satisfaction of liabilities of the enterprise.

7. **Distributions to owners** are decreases in owners' equity resulting from transferring assets, rendering services, or incurring liabilities to owners. One example is dividends declared.

The elements described above are fairly broad. Although we have defined the term "assets," for example, we have not yet stated what attribute of assets (e.g., historical cost or current value) should be reported on the balance sheet. In order to give the elements a more concrete and practical focus, we must consider broad and detailed principles as well as modifying conventions. Most of the broad and detailed principles enable the accountant to recognize various items in financial statements.

RECOGNITION IN FINANCIAL STATEMENTS

Recognition is the process of including an item in financial statements as an asset, liability, revenue, expense, or the like. A recognized item is represented by both words and numbers (e.g., Accounts receivable $40,000), and the amount is included in the financial statement totals.

For an item to be recognized, the following criteria must be met:

1. **Definitions.** The item must meet the definition of an element of financial statements.

2. **Measurability.** The item must have a relevant attribute measurable with sufficient reliability.

3. **Relevance.** The information about the item must be capable of making a difference in user decisions.

4. **Reliability.** The information must be representationally faithful, verifiable, and neutral.

The above criteria should be applied in the context of a cost-benefit constraint (the benefits of information should exceed the costs of producing it) and a materiality threshold. Note that the recognition criteria are derived from the qualitative characteristics of relevance and reliability and that the criteria help to make the definitions of the elements operational in resolving financial reporting issues.[20]

BROAD PRINCIPLES

To implement the concepts and elements, accountants apply certain generally accepted principles. Broad principles are those that have a pervasive impact on the form and content of financial statements. These principles relate to the basic accounting functions of *measurement* and *disclosure*.

MONETARY UNIT PRINCIPLE

Quantification generally makes information more useful. Although it may be helpful to know that a firm generated net income during a particular period, it would be more helpful to know *how much*. Quantification decreases uncertainty about the firm's performance.

In order to quantify financial position and the changes in it, a measuring unit serves as a common denominator that permits variables (inventories, cost of goods sold, and so on) to be related to one another. It also permits the aggregation of diverse items using basic arithmetic operations (addition, subtraction, and so on). In a barter economy, any valuable resource (for example, cows) could be used as a measuring unit. In a more advanced economy, such as that of the United States, money is a widely accepted medium of exchange. It is a convenient, customary, and understandable way of expressing wealth as well as changes in wealth. The **monetary unit principle** maintains that **accountants should measure in units of money,** that is, **number of dollars,** or **nominal dollars.**

Money measures command over goods and services, just as the mile measures distance and the pound measures weight. Unfortunately, as a measuring unit, money has a major drawback. Most measuring units remain stable over time, but the ability of money to command goods and services (its **general purchasing power,** or **GPP**) usually changes. During a period of inflation (a rise in the overall level of prices), the GPP of money declines. Conversely, during a period of deflation (a decline in the overall level of prices), the GPP of money rises. Clearly, the economic problem of inflation has persisted in the United States for many years. This phenomenon has resulted in financial statements that reflect dollars of *mixed,* rather than uniform, purchasing power. A dollar invested in plant assets thirty years ago, for example, may be combined in financial statements with a dollar that resulted from sales made yesterday. Many observers feel that this tends to distort interperiod and intercompany comparisons and thereby reduces the usefulness of financial statements.

To help make financial statements more useful, some people have proposed that accountants stop measuring in nominal dollars and begin measuring in **constant dollars,** that is, dollars that have *uniform,* rather than mixed, purchasing power. These proposals usually call for companies to issue **constant dollar financial statements,** a topic that we explain in Chapter 26. Current generally accepted accounting principles do not require companies to publish constant dollar financial statements. The prevailing thought in the financial community is that, given the imprecise nature as well as the costs of preparing and interpreting constant dollar finan-

Monetary Unit

---

[20]*FASB Statement of Financial Accounting Concepts No. 5,* "Recognition and Measurement in Financial Statements of Business Enterprises," 1984.

cial statements, the distortive effects of inflation are not now sufficiently material to require a modification of the monetary unit principle. For this reason, we emphasize the monetary unit principle throughout the text.

ASSET/LIABILITY MEASUREMENT PRINCIPLE

Asset/Liability Measurement

The **asset/liability measurement principle** (which we shall sometimes refer to as the **measurement principle**) says that **assets and liabilities currently reported in financial statements are measured by different attributes, depending on the nature of the asset or liability and the relevance and reliability of the attribute measured.**[21] GAAP currently uses five different asset measurement attributes and specifies the circumstances when each is required:

1. **Historical cost** (often simply called "cost") is the cash-equivalent payment actually made to acquire an asset and put the asset to its intended use. The historical cost of a new machine, for example, includes the net invoice price as well as transportation, set-up, and break-in charges. Nonmonetary assets such as inventories, property, plant, and equipment, and intangible assets are ordinarily measured at historical cost.[22]
2. **Current cost** is the cash-equivalent payment that a company would have to make today to acquire the same asset. Accountants measure some inventories at current cost.
3. **Current exit value in orderly liquidation** is the amount of cash an asset could be sold for in an orderly liquidation. Some investments in marketable securities are measured using this attribute.
4. **Expected exit value in due course of business,** often called **net realizable value,** is the amount of cash or cash-equivalent value that a company expects to receive for an asset in the ordinary course of business, less the costs of completing and selling the asset. Accountants use expected exit values to measure accounts receivable and some inventories.
5. **Present value of expected cash flows** is the discounted amount of the net cash inflows that an asset is expected to produce. Accountants use this attribute to measure long-term receivables.

Five similar attributes are used in present practice to measure liabilities. In the next chapter, we further explain and illustrate the various asset and liability measurement attributes.

Each measurement attribute differs conceptually from the others, although different attributes often have the same dollar amounts. For example, the historical cost and current cost of a parcel of land are the same amount on the date that a company acquires the land. After the acquisition date, the two amounts usually differ.

Although current practice uses five different asset attributes, the historical cost attribute tends to dominate because of its wide use in measuring inventories, plant assets, and intangible assets. That is why current GAAP is commonly called **historical cost accounting**

Historical cost is dominant for several reasons. First, people generally perceive it as the most reliable asset measurement attribute. Based on completed, arms'-length transactions, historical costs can be verified. Second, historical costs reliably

---

[21]*FASB Statement of Financial Accounting Concepts No. 5,* par. 66.
[22]Nonmonetary assets are those assets that cannot be expressed in terms of a fixed or predetermined number of dollars to be received by the reporting entity.

measure an asset's current value on the date the asset was acquired. Third, if current values were more widely used, a company would need to revalue its assets and liabilities each time it prepared financial statements (annually, or perhaps even quarterly or monthly). Many people question whether the benefits of the resulting information would exceed the costs of providing it. Finally, government agencies, such as the Internal Revenue Service, require that historical cost measurements be used in reports, such as tax returns, filed with them. These legal requirements have caused the historical cost system of measurement to be widely understood and established in the business community.

Many accountants and financial analysts question the relevance of historical cost measurements. For example, land acquired twenty years ago for $50,000 would be reported on today's balance sheet at its historical cost even though it may now be worth $200,000. Historical cost critics would argue that the $50,000 amount is irrelevant to user decisions. Another limitation of historical cost is that its proper determination is sometimes difficult and often requires estimates, allocations, and judgment. For example, what is the historical cost of a new machine acquired in exchange for an old machine plus a two-year, noninterest-bearing promissory note? We answer this question, and many similar ones, in later chapters.

Recent FASB work in such areas as pension accounting, accounting for income taxes, and financial instruments indicates that the board is becoming increasingly concerned about the proper recognition and measurement of assets and liabilities in corporate balance sheets.

REVENUE REALIZATION PRINCIPLE

Companies engage in many different kinds of earning activities. Generally, these activities include planning, investing cash in productive assets, selling products or services to customers, collecting cash from customers, and providing warranty services. Collectively, a firm's earning activities constitute its earning process, and companies engage in this process with the goal of ultimately receiving more cash (hopefully much more) than they invested in productive assets. Because the goal of the earning process is to receive cash, it is logical for accountants to construct their measure of revenue based on past cash receipts or claims to future cash receipts that result from earning activities during an accounting period.

From a conceptual point of view, a firm generates revenue *continuously* during all phases of its earning process. In theory, therefore, accountants should initially measure revenue when a new product is planned, then measure additional revenue when the product is produced, when it is sold, and when cash is finally collected. As might be expected, measuring revenue during the early stages of an earning process is difficult because of the tremendous uncertainty about the amount of cash that the firm will ultimately receive.

Consequently, despite the theory that revenue is earned continuously, the accounting profession has had to resolve the following practical question: When can revenue be measured in a sufficiently reliable manner to enter it in the accounting records? The profession's answer to this question is found in the **revenue realization principle.** This principle states that **revenue should be recognized (recorded in the accounting records) when (1) the earning process is complete or virtually complete, and (2) the amount and timing of revenue are reasonably determinable.** When these two conditions are met, most of the uncertainty about the existence and amount of revenue has been resolved and revenue can be measured with sufficient reliability.

Revenue
Realization

The two conditions for revenue realization are normally satisfied when a product is sold (when title passes from the seller to the buyer). Thus, an asset such as inventory should generally be carried at historical cost until an increase in its value is verified by a sale transaction. At the time of sale, most of the significant earning activities have been completed, and objective evidence provided by an exchange transaction supports the existence and amount of revenue to be recorded. Furthermore, expenses incurred to produce the revenue are either known or can be estimated with reasonable accuracy. Therefore, the accountant can apply the matching principle to measure periodic income.

The revenue realization principle also governs the recognition of revenue from sources other than product sales. For instance, revenue generated by providing services is recorded when the services have been rendered and are billable. Furthermore, revenue, such as rent revenue and interest revenue, generated by allowing others to use enterprise resources is usually recorded as time passes or as the resources are used.[23]

Because the revenue realization principle usually requires a sale, accountants measure revenue at the fair market value of the consideration received in the exchange transaction or the fair market value of the consideration given up, whichever is more clearly determinable. Moreover, the requirement that the earning process be complete or virtually complete implies that any amount received in advance of providing goods or services must be recorded as a liability, such as unearned subscriptions revenue, until it is earned.

Although the revenue realization principle *normally* requires accountants to record revenue only when a sale occurs, sale is not the only time at which the two revenue realization conditions can be met. Contractors, for example, often engage in construction projects, such as office buildings and dams, that span several accounting periods. Rather than waiting until a contract is completed to measure revenue, contractors may choose to recognize revenue *during production* using the percentage-of-completion method. This method may be used when there is a definite contract price and when reasonable estimates can be made of progress toward project completion. As another example, revenue is sometimes recorded *at the completion of production,* before a sale has occurred. This procedure is appropriate for products, such as certain metals and agricultural commodities, for which a guaranteed market exists in which the firm can sell all that it has produced at a definite price. Finally, the recognition of revenue is sometimes delayed beyond the time of sale to the time *when cash is collected*. This occurs when significant uncertainty exists about the value of the assets received in the sale or the amount of additional expenses that will be incurred in connection with the sale. Under these circumstances, which occasionally pertain to certain kinds of installment sales, either the installment sales method or the cost recovery method may be appropriate for recognizing revenue. The above discussion provides an introductory overview of the revenue realization principle; additional discussion appears in Chapter 20.

MATCHING PRINCIPLE

Today, the income statement is generally regarded as the most important financial statement, and net income is one of the most significant numbers that accountants compute. In measuring periodic income, accountants usually apply the revenue realization principle first to determine when revenue should be recognized. Then they

---
[23]*APB Statement No. 4*, par 151.

Matching

turn to the matching principle to determine when expenses should be recognized. The **matching principle** says that **costs should be recognized as expenses when the goods or services represented by the costs contribute to revenue.** In other words, accountants should attempt to associate (match) the revenues of an accounting period with the expenses incurred to generate those revenues.

From a conceptual point of view, the matching principle implies that the accountant should determine the extent to which the goods and services represented by historical costs have contributed to revenues during the accounting period. Costs that have contributed to revenues should be reported as expenses, and costs that are expected to contribute in the future should be reported as assets. This approach is called **direct matching,** but from a practical standpoint, it can be applied only to certain kinds of costs. For instance, a manufacturing company's costs of direct materials and direct labor can be reasonably identified with the firm's product (inventory). When the product is sold, sales revenue is recognized. Accordingly, because the direct materials and direct labor costs contributed directly to the sales revenue, those costs constitute expenses and should be reflected in the cost of goods sold. As another example, the costs of sales commissions can be directly related to the sales transactions. When sales revenue is recognized, the costs of related commissions should be expensed. Direct matching therefore involves associating expenses with revenues on the basis of a presumed **cause-and-effect relationship.**

Unfortunately, it is virtually impossible to accurately determine the extent to which the goods or services represented by most costs contribute to revenues. For example, when Sears Roebuck & Company purchases a new computer for use in its accounting system, who can precisely determine the pattern of the computer's contribution to revenues? Or when Anheuser Busch incurs advertising costs, who can accurately assess the pattern of future benefits to the company? The lack of answers to these and similar questions often makes direct matching impractical, and accountants must use **indirect matching.** This approach involves estimates, and the accountant may try to match revenues with expenses based on a **systematic and rational allocation** of historical costs, such as depreciation expense or amortization expense. At times, however, the accountant cannot make a systematic and rational allocation, either because of the uncertainty of future revenues or the difficulty of reliably associating certain costs with future revenues. Under these circumstances, costs are reported as expenses in the period in which they are incurred. This is called **immediate recognition** of costs as expenses. Examples of such costs are advertising and research and development. Note that accounting for these kinds of costs reflects the modifying convention of conservatism (discussed later in the chapter), the accountant's general guide for dealing with uncertain situations.

The revenue realization principle and the matching principle are the essence of the **accrual basis of accounting.** Under cash basis accounting, revenue is recorded only when received in cash, and expenses are recorded only when paid in cash. In contrast, accrual basis accounting requires recognition of revenue when earned (according to the revenue realization principle) and recognition of expenses when incurred (according to the matching principle). Differences between cash basis and accrual basis accounting are explained more fully in Chapter 3. To fully implement the accrual basis, the accountant must make certain adjusting entries at the end of every accounting period (as we explain in Chapter 5) so that the accountant can observe the principles of revenue realization and matching.

A final important point is that in conventional accounting, income measurement is closely related to asset and liability measurement. Thus, the balance sheet and the income statement are said to be "fundamentally related." Notice, for example, that measuring depreciation expense, in compliance with the matching principle, directly affects the reported measurement of the asset that is being depreciated. The term **articulation** refers to the fundamental relationship among all financial statements prepared according to GAAP. Because of articulation, an accounting principle designed primarily to match revenues with expenses on the income statement may sometimes have an undesirable effect on asset or liability measurements on the balance sheet. Likewise, an accounting principle designed to better measure assets and liabilities may sometimes have an undesirable effect on matching revenues with expenses. Many accounting principles developed long ago (e.g., inventory accounting, depreciation accounting) appear to have a matching orientation while many principles developed more recently (e.g., pension accounting, income tax accounting) appear to have an asset and liability measurement orientation.

CONSISTENCY PRINCIPLE

To formulate rational investment, credit, and similar decisions, users of accounting information typically make comparisons. Specifically, they compare circumstances of different companies (**intercompany comparisons**) and circumstances of a single company over time (**interperiod comparisons**). **Comparability** is therefore a desirable quality of useful accounting information that allows users to detect similarities in and differences between two underlying sets of objects or events.

Alternative generally accepted accounting principles exist in many areas of accounting. For example, in accounting for depreciation, a company may choose among the double-declining balance method, the sum-of-the-years'-digits method, the straight-line method, and others. Because a company may choose among these alternatives, intercompany comparisons based on financial statements may sometimes be distorted. Nevertheless, these alternatives exist because different companies face substantially different circumstances. The accounting profession recognizes that the validity of intercompany comparisons is enhanced when differences between the financial statements of different companies result from basic differences between the companies themselves or from the nature of their transactions and not merely from differences in accounting principles.[24] For this reason, the FASB and its predecessor committees have sought to eliminate alternative accounting principles that cannot reasonably be justified on the basis of differences in factual circumstances. In the past, for example, some companies capitalized research and development (R & D) costs, while others expensed R & D costs when incurred. The FASB stated that capitalizing most kinds of R & D costs could not be justified, and in 1974 the board issued *Statement of Financial Accounting Standards No. 2*, which basically requires companies to expense R & D costs when incurred. A major aim of this pronouncement was to enable financial statement users to make better comparisons between firms engaged in R & D activities.

Consistency   The accounting profession is also highly concerned with interperiod comparisons, which help users of accounting information discern important trends. Knowing past trends, users can presumably make more accurate predictions about their prospects of receiving cash from an enterprise. To improve the interperiod comparability of accounting information, accountants observe the **consistency principle,** which holds that **accountants must measure and disclose information about an entity in the same manner from one accounting period to the next.** In other words, once a company adopts a certain set of accounting principles, it must observe

---

[24]*APB Statement No. 4*, par. 101.

those principles consistently over time. A company cannot use the first-in, first-out (FIFO) method of inventory cost determination in 1991; the last-in, first-out (LIFO) method in 1992; the average cost method in 1993; and so forth. It should be noted, however, that the consistency principle does not require a company to measure and disclose all information in the same manner in a single accounting period. For example, it does not prohibit a company from using the FIFO method for one part of its inventories and the average cost method for another part.

The consistency principle also does not prohibit a firm from changing from one accounting principle to another if it has a good reason for doing so. *Accounting Principles Board Opinion No. 20* states that "the presumption that an entity should not change an accounting principle may be overcome only if the enterprise justifies the use of an alternative acceptable accounting principle on the basis that it is preferable."[25] The accounting profession has not yet defined precisely what it means by the term "preferable." When a company changes from one accounting principle to another, it must clearly disclose the nature of, reason for, and dollar effects of the change. We cover accounting changes in Chapter 19.

The consistency principle is very important to independent auditors. The standard audit report that was adopted by the accounting profession in 1988 (see Exhibit 1–1 in Chapter 1) implies that the auditor is satisfied that the company has applied accounting principles on a consistent basis over time. On the other hand, if a company makes a change in an accounting principle that has a material effect on the financial statements, then the auditor should refer to an explanatory paragraph of the audit report in the manner shown below:

> *As discussed in Note X to the financial statements, the Company changed its method of computing depreciation in 19X2.*[26]

If the auditor believes that the change in accounting principles has been appropriately accounted for and justified by management, the auditor may issue an unqualified opinion on the financial statements. If the auditor disagrees, however, then the auditor renders a qualified or an adverse opinion.

DISCLOSURE PRINCIPLE

The disclosure principle (often called adequate, fair, or full disclosure) is a significant and far reaching component of accounting theory. In fact, the disclosure principle formed the basis for the securities legislation enacted in the United States in 1933 and 1934. In recognition of the prime importance of adequate disclosure, one of the generally accepted auditing standards of the AICPA holds that "informative disclosures in the financial statements are to be regarded as reasonably adequate unless otherwise stated in the [auditor's] report."[27]

Disclosure   Consistent with the accountant's aim of providing useful information, the **disclosure principle** calls for **revealing information that will be useful in the decision-making processes of reasonably informed users.** To determine an appropriate level of disclosure for a given company, an accountant must apply generally accepted accounting principles to the circumstances involved. This requires considerable professional judgment.

[25]*APB Opinion No. 20*, "Accounting Changes," 1971, par. 16.
[26]*Statement on Auditing Standards No. 58*, "Reports on Audited Financial Statements" (New York: AICPA, 1988), par. 35.
[27]*AICPA Professional Standards—Volume 1*, AU Sec. 430.01.

SOLUTIONS, ANYONE?

If as an investor you're not confused by corporate earnings statements, you ought to be. Consider the 1987 results reported by General Electric, certainly one of our more conservative and straightforward companies:

GE reported net earnings of $2.9 billion, a nice increase over 1986's $2.5 billion. But look above the bottom line. Before various credits from accounting changes, GE's net income fell nearly 15%, to $2.1 billion. Was GE cooking its books? No. Here's what happened:

By recalculating its deferred-tax provision at the new 34% corporate tax rate, GE created a gain of $577 million, thus more than offsetting the drop in operating income. Nothing nefarious here: The company was simply taking some reserves against taxes that were no longer needed as reserves, and swinging them into the profit column. GE also changed its inventory accounting method, thus adding another $281 million to net earnings.

It would be easy to jump to the conclusion that GE was trying to make its operating profits look better than they really were. But that would be a false conclusion. As against these substantial noncash credits to income, there were even larger debits to income—more than $1 billion—for restructuring.

Add it all up and one can only conclude that General Electric did indeed probably make more money from continuing operations in 1987 than in the year before.

The point here is, How is the average investor to make sense out of all these changes? The answers are anything but clear.

In recent years the Financial Accounting Standards Board has issued a bumper crop of accounting changes, each one with a different method of adoption and also a different effective date. "They [the changes] make for confusing financial reporting," frets Coopers & Lybrand partner Clark Chandler.

Consider GE's aforementioned income tax change. It resulted from the FASB's recently introduced Statement of Financial Accounting Standards 96. SFAS 96 can be adopted either in 1987, 1988 or 1989. Moreover, companies have the option to restate past income figures, or post a cumulative catch-up adjustment in the year of adoption.

General Electric decided to adopt SFAS 96 immediately, in 1987, and not restate prior years' results. But many companies—including Du Pont and Citicorp—say they may wait until 1989 to adopt SFAS 96, and will restate prior years' earnings.

Inevitably, the comparability of financial statements suffers. Grumbles Thornton O'glove, publisher of the *Quality of Earnings Report:* "One of the FASB's original missions was to foster more comparability, and they've just made it worse. Nowadays, unless you're a sophisticated portfolio manager, you can just forget about having comparability."

By no means is SFAS 96 the only problem here. The accounting board has also issued such calculator-breaking changes as SFAS 91 on loan origination fees; SFAS 94 on consolidated subsidiaries; and SFAS 95 on cash flow statements.

Some companies have adopted these rules, while others are still weighing the impact of the changes on their bottom line.

Restating prior years' results can really set investors' minds spinning. In 1986, for instance, Tenneco rewrote its past numbers to reflect a change in the accounting method used for oil and gas operations. As a result, Tenneco's 1985 income from continuing operations was cut by $173 million and in 1984 by $262 million. But the company's 1986 net income was boosted by a hefty $1.7 billion.

Herein is a problem that is both easy to describe and difficult to redress. You can't really blame the companies—the accountants, after all, make the rules. And you can't blame the accountants, either, unless you think accountants should stop trying to discover more accurate ways of describing the financial health of a company.

Should the accounting board insist that companies adopt new rules uniformly—all at the same time, all in the same way? That would make financial statements more like apples and apples, but at a cost of imposing rigid rules on a reality that is too complex for straightforward yes or no answers.

Says Peat Marwick Main & Co. partner Walter Schuetze: "We go through a handwringing and soul-searching discussion, and we very seldom come up with two transition and effective dates that are similar."

Comparability of financial statements: a serious problem in search of a solution.

SOURCE: Penelope Wang, "Solutions, Anyone?" *Forbes* (April 18, 1988), p. 72. Reprinted by permission of *Forbes* magazine, April 18, 1988. © Forbes Inc., 1988.

When disclosing information, the accountant must be an effective communicator. A delicate balance must be achieved between completeness and understandability. Although accountants want to issue complete financial reports, the understandability of the reports is impaired by excessive details. The disclosure principle requires that appropriate terminology be used in financial reports. Further, it implies that important information of an unfavorable nature should not be hidden by the use of crafty language, small type, and other means.

Several methods of disclosure are commonly used. The most important information is in the **body of the financial statements.** For example, publicly held companies are required to disclose earnings-per-share information on the face of their income statements. **Notes** (footnotes) are an integral part of the financial statements and may effectively be used to disclose such facts as accounting policies, contractual restrictions, and certain details about leases. In addition, accountants use **schedules** to disclose such items as inventory (i.e., raw materials, work-in-process, and finished goods), operating expenses, and changes in the components of working capital. At times, **supplementary statements,** such as financial statements adjusted for inflation, constitute an effective method of disclosure.

Attempting to comply with the disclosure principle raises many interesting questions. For example, suppose that you are the independent auditor for a paper company. While examining the evidence for the financial statements, you discover that the company has violated an environmental protection statute. If the violation is discovered, the company could be sued for millions of dollars. How would you apply the disclosure principle under these circumstances? Clearly, adequate disclosure will continue to be a challenge in the years ahead.

DETAILED PRINCIPLES

Accountants use **detailed principles** to apply the broad principles. Detailed principles are highly specific, and more than one level of detailed principles may exist in a given area of accounting. Accountants often use the terms "procedures" and "methods" when referring to detailed principles. With plant assets, for example, accountants implement matching (a broad principle) by using depreciation (a detailed principle), which is computed by one of several methods (an even more detailed principle). Like broad principles, detailed principles relate to the basic accounting functions of measurement and disclosure.

Detailed principles are far too numerous to list and explain in this chapter. For this reason they are covered in other chapters of this text and in other financial accounting courses. Accounting Research Bulletins (ARBs), APB Opinions, and FASB Statements of Financial Accounting Standards (SFASs) contain many detailed accounting principles.

MODIFYING CONVENTIONS

To be useful, accounting theory must be applied in the business world by individual accountants, who must use informed judgment to resolve many difficult questions. To help accountants resolve these questions practically and consistently, the accounting profession has adopted conventions (or customs) that modify basic accounting theory.

To a large extent, accountants apply these **modifying conventions** by using generally accepted rules of broad and detailed accounting principles; modifying conventions are therefore technically a part of generally accepted accounting principles. They are usually called modifying conventions, rather than accounting principles, because they cause the accountant to modify the "theoretically ideal" treatment of certain economic things and events. In other words, they enable the accountant in some cases to depart from a rigid interpretation of broad and detailed accounting principles. Modifying conventions may therefore be viewed as exceptions to accounting principles. These exceptions are justified on the grounds that accounting theory:

1. Must yield information for which the benefits exceed the costs.
2. Must be applied in complex business enterprises among which facts and circumstances may differ substantially.
3. Must be applied under conditions of uncertainty.
4. Should focus on the economic substance of business transactions.

MATERIALITY

All FASB Statements of Financial Accounting Standards contain the following appendage: "The provisions of this Statement need not be applied to immaterial items." While *all* transactions must be recorded and their effects ultimately reflected in the financial statements, the requirements of sound theory may be modified somewhat when dealing with immaterial items. For example, current generally accepted accounting principles require that extraordinary items (if material) be presented in a separate section of the income statement. This disclosure principle presumably results in useful information because a knowledge of extraordinary items should assist financial statement users to evaluate enterprise performance and to make important predictions. The question becomes, how large must an extraordinary item be to become material and thereby require separate disclosure? Clearly, a $100 tornado loss sustained by a multimillion dollar company would not require separate disclosure, but would likely be combined with other items in the body of the income statement. Cluttering the financial statements with trivial details would be a disservice to statement
Materiality users and may in some cases make the financial statements misleading. **Materiality,** therefore, refers to **"the magnitude of an omission or misstatement of accounting information that, in the light of surrounding circumstances, makes it probable that the judgment of a reasonable person relying on the information would have been changed or influenced by the omission or misstatement."**[28]

When making materiality decisions accountants must decide whether knowledge of a particular item of information would likely affect a decision made by an informed user of financial statements. The materiality evaluation is complicated by a lack of knowledge about the specific ways in which accounting information influences investment, credit, and similar decisions.

Materiality decisions may involve quantitative as well as qualitative considerations. Quantitative considerations refer to such factors as the effect of the item on the company's earnings trend or its relationship to key financial variables such as assets, liabilities, owners' equity, revenues, expenses, and net income. Qualitative considerations center around the basic nature of the item. Does the item result in a contractual violation? Does the item represent an illegal transaction such as a bribe paid to a foreign official? Does the item represent an insider transaction such as an interest-free loan made to the company president? Affirmative answers to these and similar questions may indicate that the item in question should be disclosed regardless of the dollar magnitudes immediately involved.

Materiality is one of the most complex, pervasive, and elusive components of accounting theory. Making materiality decisions requires considerable *judgment.* Because of differences in circumstances, an item that is judged material for one

---

[28]*FASB Statement of Financial Accounting Concepts No. 2,* p. xv.

company may not necessarily be judged material for another one. To the dismay of some accountants, the accounting profession has not developed a comprehensive set of criteria to evaluate materiality dilemmas. A relatively small number of materiality guidelines are contained in authoritative accounting pronouncements about certain areas (e.g., earnings per share and segment reporting). The FASB's current position, however, is that "no general standards of materiality can be formulated to take into account all the considerations that enter into an experienced human judgment."[29]

INDUSTRY PRACTICES

Generally accepted accounting principles are intended for use in general purpose external financial reporting by business enterprises. Accountants must therefore apply broad and detailed accounting principles to different kinds of companies. In applying these principles, accountants have found that certain industries (groups of similar companies) have peculiar characteristics that sometimes warrant a modification of

Industry Practices

accounting principles. The term **industry practices** pertains to **modifications of accounting principles necessitated by the unusual characteristics of some industries.** Because these modifications presumably enhance the usefulness of accounting information, they have become generally accepted within the accounting profession and are therefore a part of GAAP.

For example, the investment company industry consists of firms that sell their own shares of capital stock to the public and invest most of the proceeds in the securities of other entities. Thus, investment securities comprise most of the assets of a typical investment company. Given the importance of these securities and the fact that accountants can usually determine their market value in a sufficiently reliable manner, generally accepted accounting principles call for reporting the investment securities of investment companies at market value. Notice that this industry practice departs from historical cost measurement. Additionally, it constitutes an exception to the revenue realization principle because the statement of operations (income statement) for an investment company includes unrealized increases and decreases (i.e., not verified by actual sales) in the value of investment securities held.

Industry practices cause many accounting principles to be modified. In fact, these practices have a significant impact on the published financial statements of such companies as banks, savings and loan associations, finance companies, life insurance companies, and public utilities. Knowledgeable preparers and users of external accounting information should be aware of industry practices and their role in the framework of GAAP. AICPA Industry Accounting and Audit Guides are excellent authoritative sources of information about industry practices.

CONSERVATISM

As stated earlier, accountants try to produce reliable measurements. Often these measurements must be made in the presence of significant uncertainties. For example, over what period will a company benefit from research and development costs or from advertising costs? Given the difficult nature of such questions, accountants cannot possibly prepare precise financial statements.

When accountants attempt to resolve measurement uncertainties, they recognize that corporate managers tend to be confident and optimistic (sometimes too optimistic) about their companies. Moreover, many managers desire to maximize their reported earnings each period. From the pragmatic standpoint of avoiding unfavorable legal exposure, it is less risky for the accountant to understate than to overstate net

---

[29]*FASB Statement of Financial Accounting Concepts No. 2*, p. xiii.

income and net assets. Therefore, most accountants adopt a cautious attitude toward the inherent risks and uncertainties of the measurement process. This attitude is reflected in the modifying convention of conservatism.

Conservatism

The **conservatism** convention holds that **when faced with significant uncertainties about the solution to an accounting problem, an accountant should favor the solution that least favorably affects net income and net assets of the current period.** Thus, conservatism is a practical and prudent, yet an imprecise, response to the problem of measurement risk. Implicit in the conservatism convention is the belief that, *when faced with significant uncertainties,* the accountant should observe the following moderating tendencies:

1. Measure revenues and gains lower rather than higher and later rather than earlier.
2. Measure expenses and losses higher rather than lower and earlier rather than later.
3. Measure net income lower rather than higher.
4. Measure assets lower rather than higher.
5. Measure liabilities higher rather than lower.
6. Measure owners' equity lower rather than higher.

Ideally, the accountant's measurements should be neither overstated nor understated. Conservatism is not a license to deliberately understate net income and net assets. If a firm having cash of $100,000 reports only $25,000, this is not conservatism but inaccurate reporting.

Companies are not required to select the most conservative accounting treatment available in every situation. Thus, conservatism is not a basic accounting principle. Instead, it is more appropriately viewed as a modifying convention. For example, the common practice of immediately expensing the costs of major advertising programs is a modification of the matching principle, owing to the uncertainty associated with the existence and timing of future benefits.

Many examples of conservatism are found in accounting practice. These include the lower of cost or market rule for valuing inventories and marketable securities; accelerated depreciation and LIFO; recording goodwill only when purchased in an arm's-length transaction; amortizing organization costs over a relatively brief period even though the life of the firm is benefited; and immediately expensing most R & D and advertising costs even though future periods will likely be benefited.

Many users of financial statements support the conservatism convention. Bankers, for example, recognize that the cost of lending to an applicant who defaults is usually higher than the cost of not lending to a loan applicant who would not have defaulted. Accordingly, bankers tend to support conservatism, including the lower of cost or market rule for inventory valuation. Moreover, most financial analysts evaluate enterprise performance on the basis not only of the quantity but also the quality of reported earnings. An important factor when assessing quality of earnings is the extent to which a firm uses conservative accounting policies. All other things being equal, many analysts tend to look more favorably on a company that adopts conservative accounting policies. Such companies are sometimes said to have "conservative accounting personalities."

SUBSTANCE OVER FORM

Substance over Form

Financial accounting is concerned with the legal as well as the economic effects of accountable events. But **when an apparent conflict exists between the economic substance and the legal form of a business transaction, accountants tend to emphasize economic substance.** To illustrate, computing earnings per share of common stock would appear to involve little more than dividing net income for a period by the average number of common shares outstanding. Certain securities, however, such as bonds that are convertible into common stock, may in substance be equivalent to common stock even though they are not common stock in legal form. *APB Opinion No. 15* therefore requires accountants to include these types of securities in earnings-per-share calculations under certain circumstances. By modifying the way in which accountants had computed earnings-per-share numbers, the APB attempted to put economic substance over legal form.

As another example, accountants sometimes encounter long-term notes that have no stated interest rates. Legally, then, these notes do not bear interest. Nevertheless, the accounting profession recognizes that money has a time value, and as a result, the notes that companies typically issue contain interest even though the interest may not be explicitly stated. Accordingly, even though a long-term note may have no stated interest rate, *APB Opinion No. 21* requires accountants to impute (estimate and record) interest under certain circumstances.

As a final example of putting substance over form, current accounting principles require a lessee to report certain kinds of leases as assets and liabilities even though the lessee does not actually own the leased property. In substance, these leases convey to lessees certain rights that are almost identical to the rights held by companies that purchase rather than lease their property.

CONCLUDING REMARKS

The authors cannot overemphasize the importance of developing a sound conceptual understanding of financial accounting. You should apply this understanding when solving the problems in this book. A procedural approach to solving problems, emphasizing mechanics and memorization, should be avoided. Accounting problems that appear in textbooks, on examinations, and in the business world often are complex and may vary in an endless number of ways. To solve these problems, accountants must have a solid base of theoretical knowledge. In the following chapters, we explain in more detail how theory applies to specific accounting issues, and we highlight in the margin the key elements of accounting theory explained in Chapter 2.

The model presented in this chapter explains most, but not all, of financial accounting as accountants apply it today. In Chapter 1, we explained that because accounting principles help to determine how scarce resources are allocated in our economy, the FASB and its predecessor committees often have had to deal with political pressures in addition to deciding what is theoretically sound accounting. We believe that some accounting principles exist primarily because of political pressures, not because they are consistent with the model. The existence of these principles, however, does not mean that the model is worthless. Instead, it simply reflects the reality that accounting is a pragmatic discipline concerned with producing information that ultimately affects the welfare of people. At appropriate places throughout the text, we point out accounting principles that do not appear to exist primarily because of the model.

In the next chapter we explore certain aspects of descriptive accounting theory in greater depth. We also introduce some proposals that, if adopted, would change the basic information that accountants currently report.

KEY POINTS   1. Financial reporting should (1) provide information useful in investment, credit, and similar decisions; (2) provide information useful in assessing cash flow prospects; and (3) provide information about enterprise resources, claims to those resources, and changes in them. (Objective 1a)

2. Relevance and reliability are the two primary qualities of useful accounting information. (Objective 1b)

3. Financial accounting theory is based on three major assumptions or postulates: (1) economic entity; (2) periodicity; and (3) going concern. (Objective 1c)

4. The assumptions listed above support basic concepts and elements. The first basic concept is financial position, and its elements are assets, liabilities, and owners' equity. The second basic concept is changes in financial position, and its major elements are revenues, expenses, gains, losses, income, investments by owners and distributions to owners. (Objective 1d)

5. Accountants apply certain generally accepted principles in order to implement the concepts and elements. Broad principles have a pervasive impact on the form and content of financial statements. The broad principles of financial accounting are: (1) monetary unit; (2) asset/liability measurement; (3) revenue realization; (4) matching; (5) consistency; and (6) disclosure. (Objective 1e)

6. Detailed principles are the highly specific ones that accountants use to apply the broad principles in practice. Detailed principles are numerous and are covered in later chapters of this text and in other courses. (Objective 1f)

7. Modifying conventions may be viewed as exceptions to accounting principles. These conventions are: (1) materiality; (2) industry practices; (3) conservatism; and (4) substance over form. (Objective 1g)

QUESTIONS

2–1 What is accounting theory?

2–2 What are the objectives of financial reporting? How are these objectives interrelated?

2–3 Why are explicitly stated objectives considered important in the development of a structure of accounting theory?

2–4 In general, how much knowledge does the accounting profession expect of the users of financial statements? Why is it important for the accounting profession to state, at least in general terms, how much knowledge it expects users to have?

2–5 Briefly explain the qualities of relevance and reliability. How do these qualities relate to the basic accounting objective of providing useful information?

2–6 Explain the significance of the contention that relevance and reliability require important trade-offs.

2–7 Should the FASB require companies to report all information that users of financial statements regard as useful? Justify your answer.

2–8 Briefly explain each of the following accounting assumptions: (1) economic entity; (2) periodicity; and (3) going concern.

2–9 Define the concept of financial position and each of the elements that compose it.

2–10 Define the concept of changes in financial position and each of the elements that represent changes in financial position.

2–11 Briefly explain the monetary unit principle. Why is this principle criticized during periods of rapid inflation?

2–12 Briefly explain the asset/liability measurement principle. Why has the accounting profession traditionally preferred historical costs over current costs for measuring nonmonetary assets?

2–13 Briefly explain the revenue realization principle. When are the two conditions for revenue realization normally satisfied? At what times, other than at the time of sale, might it be appropriate under GAAP for a company to recognize revenue?

2–14 Briefly explain the matching principle. Distinguish between direct and indirect matching.

2–15 Distinguish between cash basis and accrual basis accounting.

2–16 Briefly explain the consistency principle. Why is this principle important to the users of financial statements?

2–17   Does the existence of the consistency principle mean that:

[a] A company must use the same depreciation method in a given year to account for all of its depreciable assets?

[b] All companies in the steel industry must use the same inventory cost determination method, such as FIFO or LIFO?

[c] A company can never change from one generally accepted accounting principle to another?

2–18   Briefly explain the disclosure principle. In general, how does an accountant determine an appropriate amount of disclosure for a given company?

2–19   Briefly explain the modifying convention of materiality. Why is materiality regarded as one of the most pervasive aspects of accounting theory?

2–20   Briefly explain the term "industry practices." Cite three industries in which industry practices affect the information reported in corporate financial statements.

2–21   Briefly explain the modifying convention of conservatism. What do financial analysts mean when they say that certain companies have "conservative accounting personalities"?

2–22   Briefly explain the modifying convention of substance over form.

EXERCISES   **2–23**   ASSUMPTIONS, PRINCIPLES, AND CONVENTIONS   Listed below are the assumptions, broad principles, and modifying conventions discussed in Chapter 2:

[a] Economic entity assumption
[b] Periodicity assumption
[c] Going-concern assumption
[d] Monetary unit principle
[e] Asset/liability measurement principle
[f] Revenue realization principle
[g] Matching principle

[h] Consistency principle
[i] Disclosure principle
[j] Materiality
[k] Industry practices
[l] Conservatism
[m] Substance over form

Instructions

Select the letter corresponding to the assumption, broad principle, or modifying convention that best supports each of the following statements. *Do not use any letter more than once.*

[1] A company allocates the cost of its intangible assets to the accounting periods in which the assets help to produce revenue.

[2] A company reports its financial statements in dollars that have mixed, rather than uniform, amounts of purchasing power.

[3] A company records a new computer at the cash-equivalent price paid to purchase it.

[4] A company estimates and records interest expense on a seven-year note payable that has no stated interest rate.

[5] A company reports major details about its leases in the notes to the financial statements.

[6] After adopting the first-in, first-out (FIFO) method of determining inventory costs, a company continues to use this method over time.

[7] A company that is uncertain about what depreciation method to use elects an accelerated method.

[8] The financial statements of an insurance company reflect some noticeable differences from those of most other types of companies.

[9] A small company separates its transactions from those of the owners.

[10] A company decides that whenever an asset costs less than $50, the cost will be charged to an expense account, even though the asset may benefit several accounting periods.

2–24   ASSUMPTIONS, PRINCIPLES, AND CONVENTIONS   Refer to the list presented in 2–23.

Instructions

Select the letter corresponding to the assumption, broad principle, or modifying convention that best supports each of the following statements. *Do not use any letter more than once.*

[1] The balance sheet of a small appraisal firm excludes the owner's personal automobile.

[2] Large companies ordinarily publish a complete set of financial statements at least once a year, regardless of whether the financial results are good or bad.

[3] A company should always report the important details about its long-term liabilities.

[4] When a company prepares financial statements according to GAAP, it ignores changes in the purchasing power of the dollar.

[5] Accounts receivable are reported at their net realizable value.

[6] The cost of a building is charged to expense in the accounting periods in which the building helps to produce revenue.

[7] A company ordinarily does not separately list each account receivable on its balance sheet.

[8] Leases on certain properties are reported as assets by companies that do not own the properties.

[9] Subscriptions received in advance by a magazine publisher are liabilities until the magazines are published.

[10] The amounts reported in financial statements should not ordinarily reflect a liquidation of the business.

2–25 ASSUMPTIONS, PRINCIPLES, AND CONVENTIONS Refer to the list presented in 2–23.

Instructions

Select the letter corresponding to the assumption, broad principle, or modifying convention that best supports each of the following statements. *Do not use any letter more than once.*

[1] Most users of financial statements would not like for companies to record sales before title to the inventory passes from the seller to the buyer.

[2] Most users would not want a company to charge the cost of a new building to expense in the year of acquisition.

[3] Users expect to know certain details about a company's pension plan.

[4] Many users trust the reliability of historical cost valuations of plant assets.

[5] User decisions would not likely be affected if a company listed petty cash separately on the balance sheet.

[6] Many users of financial statements prefer accounting principles such as last-in, first-out (LIFO) and accelerated depreciation that tend to state a company's income on the "low side."

[7] Investors and creditors generally do not want financial statements to reflect a liquidation assumption unless it is likely that the firm will be liquidated in the near future.

[8] Users have trouble making interperiod comparisons when a company changes accounting principles from one year to the next.

[9] Many users believe that when convertible bonds are very similar to common stock, the bonds should be treated as common stock for the purpose of computing earnings per share.

[10] Investors and creditors expect companies to issue financial reports at predetermined time intervals, and not only when the financial results are favorable to the reporting company.

2–26 ASSUMPTIONS, PRINCIPLES, AND CONVENTIONS Refer to the list presented in 2–23.

Instructions

Select the letter corresponding to the assumption, broad principle, or modifying convention that is most clearly *violated* by the accounting practice described in each statement below. *Do not use any letter more than once.*

[1] A company charges the cost of new office equipment to expense in the year of purchase although the equipment is expected to help produce revenue for many years.

[2] A company changes from LIFO to FIFO when accounting for inventories.

[3] A company that has been in business for forty years prepares every financial statement in dollars that have the same amount of purchasing power.

[4] A company records sales after inventory has been produced but before it is sold.

[5] A company decides to publish financial statements only in years when it has good news to report.

[6] A company reports inventories, plant assets, and intangible assets at current cost amounts on the balance sheet date.

[7] An electronics company owned by Mike Hardy reports the cost of Hardy's swimming pool as an asset on the balance sheet.

[8] A company having 150 accounts payable lists each account among the liabilities on the balance sheet.

[9] A company does not report the major details about its stockholders' equity.

[10] A company follows a policy of recording an item as an asset whenever the company is in doubt about whether the item is an asset or an expense of the current period.

2–27   ASSET MEASUREMENT   Mann Company purchased a used delivery truck from Wall Company on July 1, 1993. Wall had acquired the truck new on July 1, 1992, for $25,000 and had taken $5,000 of depreciation for the fiscal year ending June 30, 1993. To acquire the truck, Mann issued to Wall 1,000 shares of Mann's $10 par value common stock. The stock was traded on a national stock exchange, and on July 1, 1993, it had a fair market value of $24 per share. A reputable local mechanic estimated that the truck was worth $21,500 cash on July 1, 1993. Mann had offered Wall this amount, but Wall refused. Immediately after Mann purchased the truck, Jones Company offered to buy it from Mann for $24,700 cash.

Instructions

[a] Record the appropriate journal entry on the books of Mann Company on July 1, 1993.

[b] Explain the rationale for your answer to [a].

2–28   VARIOUS PRINCIPLES   Chase Company recorded the following events as indicated during the current accounting period:

[1] The company purchased equipment on sale for $8,000 cash. The equipment would have cost Chase $10,000 if it had not been on sale.

Equipment	10,000	
Cash		8,000
Revenue		2,000

[2] The company recorded depreciation on its plant assets. The dollar amount was correctly computed according to the straight-line method.

Retained Earnings	25,000	
Accumulated Depreciation		25,000

[3] An appraisal indicated that land acquired for $35,000 at the end of the previous accounting period was worth $40,000 at the end of the current period.

Land	5,000	
Gain from Holding Land		5,000

[4] Because the inflation rate during the current accounting period was 10%, the company reasoned that $40,000 of liabilities held throughout the period could now be paid using "cheaper" dollars.

Liabilities	4,000	
Purchasing Power Gain		4,000

[5] The company purchased a pencil sharpener that was expected to last five years.

Miscellaneous Expense	12	
Cash		12

[6] The company gave its president a new swimming pool for her personal use at home.

Plant Assets	18,000	
Cash		18,000

[7] The company president accepted a three-month loan on the last day of the accounting period.

Accounts Receivable	20,000	
Cash		20,000

Instructions

[a] Using the theoretical model presented in the chapter, comment on the appropriateness of the manner in which Chase Company has recorded each of the above events.
[b] Record the journal entries, if any, that Chase should have made for each of these events.

CASES

2–29 APPLICATION OF ACCOUNTING THEORY   Rex Company has just acquired 100 shares of the outstanding common stock of Luke, Inc., a large company whose stock trades on a major stock exchange. Over the years the accounting profession has discussed three major methods that Rex might use to account for its investment in Luke:

[1] *The cost method*   Here Rex would record the investment at historical cost on the date acquired and continue to report it at cost until sold.
[2] *The lower of cost or market method*   Here Rex would record the investment at historical cost on the date acquired. If, on the balance sheet date, the fair market value of the stock is *less than* historical cost, Rex would report the investment at the lower market value.
[3] *The market value method*   Here Rex would record the investment at historical cost on the date acquired. On the balance sheet date, Rex would report the investment at the market value, regardless of whether the market value was above or below Rex's historical cost.

Instructions

Discuss the major pros and cons of each of these methods within the context of accounting theory. Which method do you feel the FASB should require? Explain the reasoning that supports your answer.

2–30 RELATIONSHIP BETWEEN OBJECTIVES AND A DETAILED PRINCIPLE   A company may occasionally change from one accounting principle to another. For example, it may change from the LIFO method of inventory pricing to the FIFO method and from the double-declining balance method of depreciation to the straight-line method. *APB Opinion No. 20* (par. 17) states that "the nature of and justification for a change in accounting principle and its effect on income should be disclosed in the financial statements of the period in which the change is made." In the context of the theoretical model presented in Chapter 2, this requirement of *Opinion No. 20* is an example of a *detailed principle*.

Instructions

Explain how the detailed principle referred to above logically relates to the objectives of financial reporting.

2–31 ACCRUAL VERSUS CASH BASIS   According to *SFAC No. 1*, a major objective of financial reporting is to provide information that helps stockholders, bankers, and others to assess their chances of receiving *cash* from a given enterprise. Nevertheless, the accounting profession believes that income statements prepared under the *accrual basis* of accounting are more useful than either *cash basis income statements* or *statements of cash receipts and disbursements*.

Instructions

[a] Distinguish clearly between the cash basis and the accrual basis of accounting.
[b] Distinguish clearly between (1) an accrual basis income statement, (2) a cash basis income statement, and (3) a statement of cash receipts and disbursements.
[c] Explain why an accrual basis income statement should be useful to stockholders, bankers, and other users when assessing their chances of receiving cash from a given enterprise.

2–32 INCOME AND VALUE   The general manager of the Michael Manufacturing Company received an income statement from his controller. The statement covered the calendar year 1991.

"Joe," he said to the controller, "this statement indicates that a net income of two million dollars was earned last year. You know the value of the company is not that much more than it was this time last year."

"You're probably right," replied the controller. "You see, there are factors in accounting which sometimes keep reported operating results from reflecting the change in the value of the company."

Instructions

Prepare a detailed explanation of the accounting conventions to which the *controller* referred. Include justification, to the extent possible, for the accounting methods generally used.

(AICPA adapted)

2–33   FAIR PRESENTATION OF INCOME   Section 446 of the 1954 Internal Revenue Code states: "Taxable income shall be computed under the method of accounting on . . . which the taxpayer regularly computes his income in keeping his books"; the method employed shall "clearly reflect income." Among the permissible methods are: "(1) the cash receipts and disbursements method" and "(2) an accrual method."

Instructions

Generally accepted accounting principles normally require the use of accrual accounting to "fairly present" income. If the cash receipts and disbursements method of accounting will "clearly reflect" taxable income, why does this method not usually also "fairly present" income?

(AICPA adapted)

2–34   ASSET MEASUREMENT   In 1965, Hashe Company bought some land in Hawaii for $250,000. Today the land could be sold for $5,000,000.

Instructions

[a] In your opinion, would Hashe Company's financial statements be more useful to investors and creditors if the land were reported at $250,000 or at $5,000,000? Explain your answer.

[b] At what amount would generally accepted accounting principles require the land to be reported? Explain your answer.

2–35   REVENUE REALIZATION   After the presentation of your report on the examination of the financial statements to the board of directors of the Whitman Publishing Company, one of the new directors says he is surprised the income statement assumes that an equal proportion of the revenue is earned with the publication of every issue of the company's magazine. He feels that the "crucial event" in the process of earning revenue in the magazine business is the cash sale of the subscription. He does not understand why—other than for the smoothing of income—most of the revenue cannot be "realized" in the period of the sale.

Instructions

Discuss the propriety of timing the recognition of revenue in the Whitman Publishing Company's accounts with

[a] The cash sale of the magazine subscription.

[b] The publication of the magazine every month.

[c] Both events, by recognizing a portion of the revenue with cash sale of the magazine subscription and a portion of the revenue with the publication of the magazine every month.

(AICPA adapted)

2–36   ECONOMIC VERSUS ACCOUNTING INCOME   On May 5, 1992, Acker Corporation signed a contract with Hyde Associates under which Hyde agreed (1) to construct an office building on land owned by Acker, (2) to accept responsibility for procuring financing for the project and finding tenants, and (3) to manage the property for 50 years. The annual profit from the project, after debt service, was to be divided equally between Acker Corporation and Hyde Associates. Hyde was to accept its share of future profits as full payment for its services in construction, obtaining finances and tenants, and management of the project.

By April 30, 1993, the project was nearly completed and tenants had signed leases to occupy 90% of the available space at annual rentals totaling $2,600,000. It is estimated that, after operating expenses and debt service, the annual profit will amount to $850,000. Hyde Associates believes that the economic benefit derived from the contract should be reflected on its financial statements for the fiscal year ended April 30, 1993. Management has directed that revenue be accrued in an amount equal to the commercial value of the services Hyde rendered during the year, that this amount be carried in contracts receivable, and that all related expenditures be charged against the revenue.

Instructions

[a] Explain the main difference between the economic concept of business income as reflected by Hyde's management and the measurement of income under GAAP.

[b] Discuss the factors to be considered in determining when revenue has been realized for the measurement of periodic income.

[c] Does Hyde's management's measurement of revenue and expense for the year agree with generally accepted accounting principles? Support your opinion by citing the factors to be considered for asset measurement and revenue and expense recognition. (AICPA adapted)

2–37 REVENUE REALIZATION Tinsley Trading Stamps, Inc., was formed early this year to sell trading stamps throughout the Southwest to retailers who distribute the stamps gratuitously to their customers. Books for accumulating the stamps and catalogs illustrating the merchandise for which the stamps may be exchanged are given free to retailers for distribution to stamp recipients. Centers with inventories of merchandise premiums have been established to redeem stamps. Retailers may not return unused stamps to Tinsley.

The following schedule expresses Tinsley's expectations of a "normal month's activity," defined as the level of operations expected when expansion of activities ceases or tapers off to a stable rate. The company expects this level to be attained in the third year, when stamp sales will average $2,000,000 a month.

Month	Actual Stamp Sales	Merchandise Premium Purchases	Stamp Redemptions
6th	30%	40%	10%
12th	60	60	45
18th	80	80	70
24th	90	90	80
30th	100	100	95

Tinsley plans to adopt an annual closing date at the end of each 12-month period.

Instructions

[a] Discuss the factors to be considered in determining when revenue should be recognized in measuring the income of a business enterprise.

[b] Discuss the accounting alternatives that should be considered by Tinsley Trading for the recognition of its revenues and related expenses.

[c] For each accounting alternative discussed in [b], provide a balance sheet account and indicate how each should be classified. (AICPA adapted)

2–38 COST, EXPENSE, AND LOSS You have been asked to deliver your auditor's report to the board of directors of Brewington Manufacturing Corporation and to answer questions about the financial statements. After reading the statements, one director asks: "What are the precise meanings of the terms 'cost', 'expense', and 'loss'? These terms sometimes seem to identify similar items and other times seem to identify dissimilar items."

Instructions

[a] Explain the meanings of these terms and their use in financial reporting under generally accepted accounting principles. Also discuss the distinguishing characteristics of the terms and their similarities and interrelationships.

[b] Classify each of the following items as a cost, expense, loss, or other category and explain how the classification of each item may change:

[1] Cost of goods sold.
[2] Bad debts expense.
[3] Depreciation expense for plant machinery.
[4] Organization costs.
[5] Spoiled goods.

[c] The terms "period cost" and "product cost" describe certain items in financial statements. Define these terms and distinguish between them. To what types of items does each apply?

2–39 MATCHING You are an accountant employed by a large CPA firm. Crestwood Enterprises, one of your clients, is a manufacturer of paper and wood products. The company's president, Martha Dolby, is having trouble understanding her company's most recent income statement, which you audited. "The matching principle of accounting doesn't seem to make sense," Ms. Dolby tells you. "I know the principle says that costs should be recognized as expenses when the goods or services they represent contribute to revenue. The question I have is, how is my company supposed to *know when* the goods and services represented by our costs contribute to revenue? When we purchase a new machine for use in manufacturing, for example, the machine is used along with many other input factors to manufacture our products, which we then sell. Determining exactly how much the new machine contributes to revenues in a particular period is impossible. And I always thought that accountants tried to produce reliable information."

Instructions

[a] Answer the question that Ms. Dolby has raised.
[b] Explain how accountants try to make the matching principle operational.
[c] Describe how the matching principle is applied to account for each of the following types of costs and explain the rationale for each treatment.

[1] Advertising costs.
[2] Raw material costs.
[3] Cost of equipment expected to last five years.
[4] Cost of sales commissions.
[5] Cost of a patent expected to benefit the company for seven years.

2–40 MATCHING Corryton Corporation sells and erects "shell houses." These are frame structures that are completely finished on the outside but are unfinished on the inside except for flooring, partition studding, and ceiling joists. Shell houses are sold chiefly to customers who are handy with tools and who have time to do the interior wiring, plumbing, wall completion and finishing, and other work necessary to make the shell houses livable dwellings.

Corryton buys shell houses from a manufacturer in unassembled packages consisting of all lumber, roofing, doors, windows, and similar materials. Before building in a new area, Corryton buys or leases land for its local warehouse, field office, and display houses. Display houses are erected at a total cost of from $3,000 to $7,000, including the cost of the unassembled packages. The chief cost is the unassembled packages; erection is a short, low-cost operation. Old models are torn down or altered every three to seven years. Sample houses have little salvage value because dismantling and moving costs nearly equal the cost of an unassembled package.

Instructions

[a] A choice must be made between (1) expensing the costs of display houses in the period in which the expenditure is made and (2) spreading the costs over more than one period. Discuss the advantages of each method.
[b] Should Corryton amortize the cost of display houses on the basis of (1) the passage of time or (2) the number of shell houses sold? Explain.   (AICPA adapted)

2–41 MATCHING The general ledger of Good Times, Inc., a corporation engaged in the development and production of television programs for commercial sponsorship, contains the following accounts before amortization at the end of the current year:

Account	Balance (Debit)
Sealing Wax & Kings	$51,000
The Messenger	36,000
The Desperado	17,500
Shin Bone	8,000
Studio Rearrangement	5,000

An examination of contracts and records reveals the following:

[1] The first two accounts listed above represent the total cost of completed programs that were televised during the accounting period just ended. Under the terms of an existing contract, *Sealing Wax & Kings* will be rerun during the next accounting period, at a fee equal to 50% of the fee for the first program televised. The contract for the first run produced $300,000 of revenue. The contract with the sponsor of *The Messenger* provides that he may, at his option, rerun the program during the next season at a fee of 75% of the fee for the first program televised.

[2] The balance in *The Desperado* account is the cost of a new program which has just been completed and is being considered by several companies for commercial sponsorship.

[3] The balance in the *Shin Bone* account represents the cost of a partially completed program for a projected series that has been abandoned.

[4] The balance of the Studio Rearrangement account consists of payments made to a firm of engineers which prepared a report on using studio space and equipment more efficiently.

Instructions

[a] State the general principles of accounting that apply to the first four accounts.

[b] Describe how you would report each of the first four accounts in the financial statements of Good Times, Inc.

[c] In what way, if at all, does the Studio Rearrangement account differ from the first four?

(AICPA adapted)

2–42 CONSISTENCY Everlast Tool Company is a large manufacturing concern that uses the FIFO method of inventory cost determination. The other major companies in Everlast's industry use the LIFO method. At a recent stockholders' meeting, one of Everlast's shareholders made the following statement:

"I'm having a lot of trouble comparing the performance of our company with that of others in the industry because we are the only company that uses FIFO. It seems to me that because of the *consistency principle* of accounting, we should be using LIFO so that our financial results will be consistent with those of our major competitors."

Instructions

Explain the consistency principle and evaluate the stockholder's statement.

2–43 CONSISTENCY AND MATCHING Wyatt Company had used the first-in, first-out (FIFO) method of inventory cost determination from the year the company was organized (1983) until 1988. In 1988, the company changed to the last-in, first-out method (LIFO) method. Management explained that the change was "to achieve a better matching of revenues and expenses." Assume that the current year is 1992 and that Wyatt's management wants to change back to FIFO. The reason management now gives for the change is "to achieve a better matching of revenues and expenses."

Instructions

In your opinion, should generally accepted accounting principles allow Wyatt to change back to FIFO in 1992? (For the purpose of answering this question, ignore the income tax law.) Explain the rationale that supports your opinion.

2–44 MATERIALITY As a recent college graduate, you have been hired as an accountant with the Broadfield Company. Broadfield recently sustained an extraordinary loss due to a flood. In accounting, an extraordinary gain or loss is one that is unusual in nature and not expected to recur in the foreseeable future. Generally accepted accounting principles require companies to disclose extraordinary gains and losses in a specially-labelled section of the income statement *if* they are judged to be material. The reason for special disclosure is to highlight extraordinary items in an effort to permit investors and creditors to make more meaningful evaluations of management's performance and more accurate predictions of future cash flows. If an extraordinary gain or loss is not considered material, it may be combined with other items in the income statement and not reported in a special extraordinary items category.

Broadfield's chief executive officer (CEO) has just entered your office and wants you to explain how the accounting profession would determine whether the extraordinary flood loss is material.

Instructions

Explain to Broadfield's CEO the *general factors* that you believe should be considered in determining whether the flood loss is material. You need not attempt to develop precise, numerical materiality guidelines.

2–45 MATERIALITY Assume that you are the independent auditor of a successful brewing company that has spent approximately 5% of each sales dollar on advertising during each of the past 10 years. The company charges all advertising costs to expense in the period in which the costs are incurred, and in past years, it has separately disclosed the amount of advertising expense in its income statement.

This year management has decided to save money by curtailing its advertising, and advertising expense for the year amounts to only 0.5% of sales. When examining the annual financial statements and the footnotes, you find no mention of advertising expense for the period. Upon asking management about the omission, you are told: "We have not disclosed advertising expense separately in our income statement because the amount clearly is immaterial. We don't want to clutter our financial statements, and thereby confuse our stockholders, by disclosing every minor detail concerning our operations. We have therefore included advertising in the 'other expenses' category of our income statement."

Instructions

[a] Evaluate management's contention that this year's advertising expense is immaterial.
[b] What disclosure relating to the company's advertising do you recommend for this year? Defend your answer from the standpoint of accounting theory.

2–46 CONSERVATISM Brian Langley has recently organized the Langley Company to produce and sell consumer electronic products. As company president, Brian is currently trying to determine the accounting principles that his company should use. He says that "we will need to use LIFO for our inventories and accelerated depreciation for our depreciable assets because these methods produce conservative results and are therefore required by GAAP."

Instructions

Explain to Brian what accountants mean by conservatism. In addition, explain whether conservatism will require Langley Company to use LIFO and accelerated depreciation or whether Brian should use some other criteria in deciding what methods to use.

CHAPTER 3

Nature and Measurement of the Elements of Financial Statements

OBJECTIVES

1. To introduce the measuring units that may be used in financial statements.
2. To discuss the nature and measurement of assets, liabilities, and owners' equity.
3. To discuss the nature, measurement, and components of net income.
4. To discuss the usefulness of accounting net income.
5. To present the arguments favoring and opposing the publication of financial forecasts.

I n this chapter we discuss assets, liabilities, owners' equity, revenues, expenses, gains, losses, and income. Financial forecasts also are discussed so that you may contrast them with the information traditionally reported in financial statements.

Most concepts discussed in this chapter are applied within generally accepted accounting principles (GAAP). Other concepts may be viewed as proposals for changing GAAP. If adopted by the accounting profession, these proposals would alter the present scope of accounting information.

This chapter provides a conceptual foundation that will help explain the strengths and limitations of conventional financial statements (i.e., statements prepared today in accordance with GAAP). The specific content of these statements is covered in Chapter 4. The conceptual foundation will also help you to understand some of the more serious proposals that have been made for changing conventional financial statements. We explain and illustrate these proposals more extensively in other chapters, particularly Chapter 26.

MEASUREMENT IN ACCOUNTING

Accounting is a measurement and disclosure discipline. That is, accountants measure the various elements of a company's financial statements, such as assets, liabilities, and revenues, and disclose their results to users in order to help them make better decisions. The information that accountants choose to measure and disclose should be useful, which means that it should be both relevant and reliable.

The term **measurement** refers to the assignment of numbers to objects, such as inventories and plant assets, and events, such as purchases and sales. Measurement allows us to use numbers to conveniently relate certain objects and events to others. If, for example, we are told that one box weighs 100 pounds and another weighs 200 pounds, we know how heavy the second box is relative to the first without ever having seen or lifted either box. In accounting, the term **valuation** conveys the same meaning as measurement. Accountants often say, for example, that a company's inventories are valued (measured) at a certain amount on the balance sheet.

The elements of financial statements are the subject matter of financial accounting and are the things accountants seek to measure. Users need measurements of assets, liabilities, and other elements to make rational investment, credit, and similar decisions. But in order to measure the elements we must first select a measuring unit and a financial attribute to measure.

Monetary Unit

To illustrate, assume that a company owns some land that we want to measure for financial reporting purposes. The measuring unit could be constant dollars that measure purchasing power as of the balance sheet date, or it could be nominal dollars that reflect the dollar's purchasing power at the time the land was acquired. The monetary unit principle requires the use of nominal dollars in conventional financial statements. The land has several financial attributes, such as how much it actually cost, how much it would cost to replace, and how much it could be sold for. Which one of these financial attributes should we measure? Although historical cost is the financial attribute required in conventional financial statements, other attributes could result in more useful information. Determining which measuring unit and which financial attribute would provide the most useful information are two major challenges that the accounting profession has faced for many years. We explore these issues more fully in later sections of this chapter and in Chapter 26.

THE MEASURING UNIT

Financial statements are expressed in money, which measures command over goods and services in the economy. If the general level of prices of goods and services remained constant over time, money would not be a controversial measuring unit to use in financial statements. Under these circumstances, money received or paid ten years ago could be compared meaningfully with money received or paid today, because both sums would represent the same amount of purchasing power or command over goods and services.

In reality, the general level of prices in the economy usually changes over time. An increase in the general price level means that money's command over goods and services has decreased; this is called **inflation.** Similarly, a decrease in the general price level, known as **deflation,** means that money's command over goods and services has increased. In the United States and in most other countries, inflation has existed for many years and is regarded by many people as simply a way of life. Between 1970 and 1980, for example, inflation in the United States was more than 100%. Persistent inflation has caused accountants to actively debate the pros and cons of the two measuring units that have been suggested for financial statements: **nominal dollars** and **constant dollars.**

A nominal dollar is one that has not been adjusted for inflation (or deflation); a constant dollar is one that has been adjusted. Dollars are adjusted for inflation or deflation by using a **general price-level index,** which is a measure that reveals how much the average price of a given group of goods and services has changed over time. General price-level indexes show the changes that have occurred over time in the overall level of prices in the economy. A general price-level index should be distinguished from a **specific price index,** which is a measure that reveals changes over time in the price of some relatively specific good or service, such as televisions or hospital care. The price of a specific good or service does not necessarily change at the same rate or even in the same direction as do prices in general. In a given year, for example, the inflation rate, which refers to prices in general, might be 10%, while the price of pocket calculators (a specific good) actually falls by 15%.

The most important general price-level indexes are the **Consumer Price Index for All Urban Consumers** and the **Gross National Product Implicit Price Deflator Index.** The federal government derives each index by monitoring the changes over time that occur in the prices of the "market basket." Each index has its own market basket, or predetermined group of goods and services. When constructing an index, a base period is selected and assigned an index number of 100. All other periods are then assigned index numbers that relate to the base. If prices in general rose by 10% in the period immediately following the base, for example, this period would be assigned an index number of 110.

To illustrate the nominal dollar and constant dollar measuring units, suppose that a company acquired land for $10,000 at the beginning of the current year, when the general price-level index was 100. At the end of the year, the general price-level index was 110, which means that the inflation rate during the year was 10%. In an ending balance sheet prepared according to GAAP, we would report the land at $10,000. This amount is simply the historical cost of the land measured in nominal dollars. However, if we wanted to measure the historical cost of the same land using year-end constant dollars, the land would be measured at $11,000 ($10,000 × 110/100). Observe that we measured the *historical cost* of the land in two ways; we did *not* measure the current market value of the land. Using the nominal dollar measuring unit, we measured the historical cost at $10,000. Measured in constant dollars, the historical cost is $11,000. We derived different amounts simply because we used different measuring units. Because of inflation, we would need $11,000 at the end of the year to have the same purchasing power as $10,000 at the beginning.

As another example of nominal versus constant dollar measurement, suppose that a company buys a product costing $200 at the beginning of the year, when the general price-level index is 110, and sells it for $220 at the end of the year, when the general price-level index is 121. How much income did the company earn as a result of these events?

Measured in nominal dollars, as required under GAAP, the income is $20, as shown below:

Sales (measured when the general price-level index was 121)	$220
Less: Cost of product sold (measured when the general price-level index was 110)	200
Nominal-dollar income	$ 20

Observe that the conventional nominal-dollar income of $20 is the result of matching a revenue ($220) and an expense ($200) that are measured in dollars having *different amounts of purchasing power*. In contrast, the income measured in year-end constant dollars is zero, as shown below:

Sales (measured when the general price-level index was 121)	$ 220
Less: Cost of product sold (measured when the general price-level index was 121: $200 × 121/110 = $220)	$ 220
Constant-dollar income	$–0–

Under the nominal dollar approach, the company's income is $20 because the sale allowed the company to recover a larger *number of dollars* than was originally spent to buy the product. In contrast, under the constant dollar approach, income is zero because the sale merely allowed the company to recover the same *amount of purchasing power* that was originally invested in the product.

As a final example contrasting the nominal dollar and constant dollar measuring units, suppose that at the beginning of the current year you invested $1,000 in a savings account that will pay 6% interest on the last day of the year. Ignoring income taxes and assuming that the current annual inflation rate is 12%, how much income will you earn from your savings account during the year? The nominal-dollar income, which ignores inflation, would simply equal the interest of $60 ($1,000 × 6%) to be paid at year-end. This amount suggests that you will be $60 richer at the end of the year. But because of inflation, you were actually better off with $1,000 at the beginning of the year than you will be with $1,060 at year-end. The constant-dollar income for the period would reflect this reality by recognizing a loss of purchasing power as a result of holding cash during a period of inflation. On a constant dollar basis you would actually have a *loss* of $60 for the year, computed as follows:

Interest revenue ($1,000 × .06)	$ 60
Less: Purchasing power loss from holding cash [($1,000 × 1.12) − $1,000]	120
Constant-dollar loss	$(60)

Purchasing power gains and losses exist when the measuring unit is constant dollars, but not when the measuring unit is nominal dollars. These gains and losses occur as a result of holding **monetary assets** (cash or claims to a fixed number of dollars of cash) or **monetary liabilities** (obligations to pay a fixed number of dollars of cash) during periods of inflation or deflation. During a period of inflation, a company gains purchasing power by being in debt because the debt can be paid with dollars having less purchasing power. On the other hand, a company loses purchasing power by holding monetary assets, such as cash, accounts receivable, and notes receivable, during a period of inflation because the assets lose some of their potential for buying goods and services. The opposite results occur in periods of deflation. Purchasing power gains and losses are not presently reported in conventional financial statements because the measuring unit is the nominal dollar.

The desirability of using constant dollars as the measuring unit in financial statements has been one of the most widely discussed topics in financial accounting for several decades. Proponents claim that constant dollar measurements would be useful to users of financial statements by revealing the impact of inflation on business enterprises. Opponents argue that constant dollar measurements are imprecise and costly and that inflation rates in the United States have not been high enough to warrant a departure from nominal dollar accounting. Conventional financial statements are now prepared using nominal dollars, and we emphasize the use of nominal dollars in this textbook. As you read the remaining chapters, however, remember the distinction between nominal dollars and constant dollars and that the use of nominal dollars creates certain distortions in financial statements. You will understand financial statements much better if you are aware of their strengths and their limitations. In Chapter 26 we explain constant dollar accounting in greater depth. We also discuss Financial Accounting Standards Board (FASB) *Statement of Financial Accounting Standards No. 33*, which from 1979 until 1984 required large corporations to report selected constant dollar measurements as supplementary information to their basic financial statements.[1]

Now that we have examined the measuring units available for financial statements, we shall discuss the nature and measurement of the major elements of financial statements.

ASSETS

NATURE OF ASSETS

In Chapter 2 we define **assets** as probable future economic benefits obtained or controlled by an entity as a result of past transactions or events.[2] Assets have three essential characteristics:

1. Assets embody probable future economic benefits.
2. The economic benefits of assets must accrue to a particular entity.
3. Assets are the result of transactions or events that have already occurred.

These characteristics pertain to *all* assets, such as cash, accounts receivable, merchandise inventory, land, and machinery. Historical cost is *not* an essential characteristic. Some assets, such as the land a city donates to attract a company to the area, may be acquired without cost.

---

[1]*FASB Statement of Financial Accounting Standards No. 33*, "Financial Reporting and Changing Prices," 1979.
[2]*FASB Statement of Financial Accounting Concepts No. 6*, "Elements of Financial Statements," 1985, par. 25. The discussion of the nature of assets relies heavily on *SFAC No. 6*.

The most important characteristic of an asset is the probable future economic benefits that usually result in net cash inflows to a company. A company may obtain the future economic benefits by exchanging the asset for something else of value or by using the asset. Two of a tire manufacturer's assets, for example, are the inventory of tires and the machinery used to make tires. The manufacturer usually derives benefits by exchanging the tire inventory for cash or claims to cash and by using the machinery to manufacture tires that can later be sold.

Because the economic benefits of an asset are received in the future, accountants sometimes are uncertain about whether a particular item constitutes an asset. Cash is obviously an asset because it can buy goods and services. Uncollectible accounts receivable are clearly not assets because of the absence of future benefits. But what about a new advertising program that a U.S. automobile manufacturer implements to convince consumers that they should buy American products? When the manufacturer spends money for the advertising, the company hopes to derive future benefits. To an objective observer, however, the future benefits may be too uncertain to acknowledge an asset.

To qualify as an asset, the economic benefits of an item must be controlled by a particular entity. Public highways and public parks are therefore not considered assets of a particular company. Although the company may regularly use the highways to transport goods and the parks to have employee picnics, the company does not have the right to regulate the use of the highways and parks by others. However, private roads and parks that a company has built on its own land are considered assets because the company can regulate access by others.

In accounting we define assets as probable future economic benefits rather than as physical objects. A subtle but important point is that the "bundle" of benefits, and not the physical object itself, is the essence of an asset. A building, for example, is a physical structure that may provide many benefits such as office space and residual value after the building has been used. These *benefits* constitute the asset. At times, two or more entities may share the benefits that a building or other asset provides. In a building that is leased, for example, one party may have the right to use the property while another has the right to receive periodic rents and to realize the residual value of the property when the lease expires. In this case, the building provides economic benefits to both parties to the lease.

Assets result from past transactions or events of a particular entity. A ten-year-old machine becomes an asset to a particular company on the date the company acquires it, not when the machine was manufactured. Similarly, a machine that a company plans to acquire next year will not be an asset to the company until the acquisition occurs.

MEASUREMENT OF ASSETS

Assets have several measurable financial attributes. As discussed in Chapter 2, conventional accounting emphasizes the historical cost attribute. That is why financial statements today are frequently referred to as historical cost financial statements. But as we saw in the previous section, historical cost is not an essential characteristic of an asset. Furthermore, historical cost is not the only attribute that accountants measure. Indeed, the asset measurements reported in financial statements today reflect a *mixture of financial attributes.*

Asset/Liability Measurement

A company operates in both an input market and an output market, and exchange prices exist in both markets. The financial attributes that may be used for asset measurement fall into two general categories that correspond to these markets, as shown below:[3]

Market	Asset Measurement Category	Financial Attribute
Input	Input values	Historical cost
		Current cost
Output	Output values	Current exit value in orderly liquidation
		Expected exit value in due course of business
		Present value of expected cash flows

Fundamentally, an **input market** is one in which a company acquires goods and services from suppliers, employees, and others. An **input value** refers to a measure of the amount a company has to give up to acquire the goods and services. In contrast, an **output market** is one in which a company sells its products to customers. An **output value** refers to a measure of the amount a company will receive in exchange for its product.

As we discuss these financial attributes, remember the following points:

1. Each attribute pertains to an existing asset.
2. Each attribute pertains to an actual transaction (one that has actually occurred), an expected transaction (one that is expected to occur), *or* a hypothetical transaction (one that would occur if certain circumstances existed).
3. Each attribute pertains to the past, the present, *or* the future.
4. Each attribute is used in practice for measuring certain kinds of assets under current GAAP.
5. Asset valuations (and income measurements) may differ significantly depending on which financial attribute is used. Under certain circumstances, the measurement of two or more financial attributes of a given asset may result in the same dollar amounts. Nevertheless, each attribute differs conceptually from the others.

Historical Cost

As we discussed in Chapter 2, the **historical** or **acquisition cost** of an asset is the amount of the cash or cash-equivalent payment actually made to acquire the asset. Historical cost is therefore an input value based on an actual past transaction. In conventional financial statements, historical cost is generally used to measure inventories; property, plant, and equipment; and intangible assets.

Historical costs are based on arm's-length exchange transactions that have actually occurred and can be verified by invoices, canceled checks, and other source documents. The historical cost of an asset equals the market value of the asset at the time the company acquired it. Changes in an asset's market value that occur after acquisition generally are ignored until the company sells the asset.

Proponents of historical cost measurement emphasize that historical costs are objective and reliable. Opponents argue that historical costs lack relevance because they fail to reflect current market values after a company acquires an asset.

Current Cost

The **current cost** of an asset is the amount of cash or cash-equivalent payment that a company would have to make today to acquire the same asset. Like historical cost,

---

[3]The discussion of financial attributes of assets relies heavily on *FASB Discussion Memorandum,* "Conceptual Framework for Financial Accounting and Reporting: Elements of Financial Statements and Their Measurement," 1976, pars. 402–437. The five financial attributes are also discussed in *FASB Statement of Financial Accounting Concepts No. 5,* 1984, pars. 66–70.

current cost is an input value, but unlike historical cost, current cost is based on a hypothetical present transaction. Suppose, for example, that a company owns land that it acquired a year ago for $20,000 (a historical cost). If the company would have to pay $25,000 for the land today, the land has a current cost of $25,000 to the company. Assuming that no inflation occurred during the year, the company has earned a $5,000 **holding gain** simply by holding the land during a time when its market value increased. Holding gains are *not* separately recognized under generally accepted accounting principles, which, as we have stated, are based primarily on historical costs. However, applying the lower of cost or market rule when measuring inventories sometimes results in current cost measurements that appear in conventional financial statements. We explain this rule in detail in Chapter 8.

Various methods can be used to determine the current costs of a company's assets. The current cost of a raw material may be determined by examining the prices listed in the supplier's current catalog. It is often possible to determine the current cost of certain equipment used in operations by applying specific price indexes which measure changes in the price of the equipment over time. Appraisals may be effectively used to determine the current cost of such assets as land and specialized machinery. As we discuss and illustrate in Chapter 26, *SFAS No. 33* required certain large companies to report selected current cost measurements as supplementary information to their conventional financial statements. The major items required by *SFAS No. 33* were inventories, cost of goods sold, plant assets, and depreciation. In essence, *SFAS No. 33* was a large-scale experiment that focused on the preparation and use of current cost and constant dollar measurements. Now this kind of information is encouraged, but not required.

Proponents argue that the use of current cost measurements in financial statements would help users to make more accurate predictions of future cash flows and more meaningful evaluations of a company's financial position and performance. Critics, on the other hand, contend that current cost measurements are generally too subjective and unreliable to be useful in making investment and credit decisions.

Current Exit Value in Orderly Liquidation

The **current exit value** of an asset is the amount of cash the asset could be sold for in an orderly liquidation. In other words, the current exit value of a machine tells us how much cash a company could receive if it were to sell the machine (not the entire business, only the machine) in an orderly manner as opposed to a forced sale. Current exit value is an output value based on a hypothetical present transaction and is used in practice today to measure the securities held by investment companies and certain other entities.

Recall that when an asset is measured at historical cost, changes in the asset's market value are generally ignored until the time of sale. In contrast, when an asset is measured at current exit value, changes in the asset's current exit value are recognized in both the asset valuation and income. Assume, for example, that a company buys an inventory item on December 31, 1992, for $100. Assume further that the current exit value of the item on that date is $140, and the company actually sells the item for $150 on March 3, 1993. Under the historical cost approach, the company would report the asset at $100 at the end of 1992 and would report income of $50 ($150 − $100) in 1993, when the asset is sold. The current exit value approach, in contrast, would require the company to report the asset at $140 at the end of 1992 and to report income of $40 ($140 − $100) during 1992 and $10 ($150 − $140) during 1993.

Proponents argue that current exit values are relevant because they reveal the cash receipts a company can command at the present time. On the other hand critics maintain that companies acquire many assets for use rather than sale and that current exit value measurements of most assets are unreliable. Critics further argue that some intangible assets, work-in-process inventory, and specialized plant assets, such as an oil refinery in a foreign country that has an unstable government, have no current exit values.

Expected Exit Value in Due Course of Business

The **expected exit value** of an asset, often called **net realizable value,** is the amount of cash or cash-equivalent value that a company expects to receive for the asset in the ordinary course of business, minus the costs of completing and selling the asset. Suppose, for example, that a company owns some partially completed inventory that could be sold as is for $6,000. Completing and selling the goods, which the company plans to do, will cost approximately $500, and the company estimates that the completed goods can be sold for $8,000. Under these circumstances, the goods have a current exit value of $6,000. The expected exit value of the goods in due course of business, however, is $7,500 ($8,000 − $500). Expected exit value is therefore an output value based on an expected future transaction. Changes that occur over time in an asset's expected exit value are recognized in both the asset valuation and income. In practice, expected exit values are used to measure accounts receivable and, under certain circumstances, to measure inventories.

An asset's expected exit value is relevant to users because it indicates the net amount of cash the company expects to receive for the asset in the future. Expected exit values, however, are generally subject to the same criticisms as current exit values.

Present Value of Expected Cash Flows

An economic fact universally accepted by rational business people is that money has a time value, commonly called **interest.** Suppose that your neighbor (whom you trust) offers to give you in exchange for cash a written and signed IOU for $112 payable to you one year from now. How much cash would you be willing to pay for the IOU today assuming you want to earn 12% interest on your investment? Clearly you should not pay $112 because you would not earn any interest. The answer of course is $100 ($112 ÷ 1.12). We would say, then, that your neighbor's IOU has a **present value** (that is, a value at the present time) as an asset to you of $100. To determine the present value we **discounted** the amount you would receive at the end of the year ($112) using a 12% discount rate.

Here's the point of the preceding exercise. Ultimately, the value of an asset to a company depends on the asset's ability to generate net cash inflows (cash inflows − cash outflows = net cash inflows) for the company in the future. Inventory, for example, has value because of the net cash inflows that generally result from the future sale. Equipment used in the manufacturing process has value because it is used to produce products that can later be sold to generate cash. The **present value** of an asset is the discounted amount of the net cash inflows that the asset is expected to generate. Present value, then, is an output value based on expected future transactions.

To determine the present value of an asset, we must discount all the expected net cash inflows. This process requires an estimate of (1) the **amount** of net cash inflows that an asset will generate, (2) the **timing** of those cash flows, and (3) the **discount rate.** Changes in an asset's present value are recognized in valuing the asset and in determining income. At this point, you should concentrate on *why* present value is an important financial attribute of assets. Computing present values is not difficult and is explained in Chapter 6.

Present value is widely regarded as the most relevant of the various asset valuation concepts. Assets are essentially expected future economic benefits, and present values tell us how much those benefits are currently worth to the company. The benefits are expressed as the net cash inflows that the company expects the asset to generate in the future. Little doubt exists that investors, creditors, and other users of financial statements would like to know the present values of a company's assets. The problem is that accountants cannot measure present values reliably for most types of assets. For example, a machine used in the manufacturing process is likely to be used with other machines, materials, and labor services to produce a product that the company hopes to sell in the future for some amount of cash. But who knows whether the product will actually sell, how much cash it will sell for, and when the company will receive the cash from the sale? Who knows how much cash is attributable to the machine we are trying to measure, exclusive of the other factors (e.g., materials, labor services, advertising) that are important in producing and selling the product? And what discount rate should we use to compute the present value? The difficulty of answering these kinds of questions is what makes the present value approach impractical for most types of assets. However, the present value approach is used in GAAP today for measuring certain long-term receivables under *Accounting Principles Board Opinion No. 21*.[4] The amount and timing of cash receipts for long-term receivables can usually be estimated with reasonable accuracy, and the discount rate used in practice is one that is reasonable at the time the receivable was created. The FASB is working on a major project that examines accounting measurements based on present value.

Summary

Exhibit 3–1 summarizes the financial attributes we have discussed. Although each attribute is used under GAAP for measuring certain types of assets, the historical cost attribute is presently emphasized. Proponents of historical cost tend to emphasize the reliability of the measurement, while proponents of each alternative to historical cost tend to emphasize the relevance of the measurement to users of a company's financial statements. Recall that relevance and reliability are the most important determinants of the usefulness of information. Assuming that relevance and reliability require important trade-offs, an important question facing the accounting profession is which financial attribute is in fact the most *useful* for decision making. Is it really the historical cost attribute, or is it some other one?

Historical Cost *(margin note)*

LIABILITIES

NATURE OF LIABILITIES

In Chapter 2 we define **liabilities** as probable future sacrifices of economic benefits arising from present obligations of an entity to transfer assets or provide services to other entities in the future as a result of past transactions or events.[5] A liability has three essential characteristics:

1. It embodies a probable future sacrifice of economic benefits.
2. It obligates a particular entity to transfer assets or provide services in the future.
3. It is the result of a transaction or event that has already occurred.

The essential characteristics of a liability are similar to those of an asset, except that an asset entitles an entity to *receive* economic benefits, whereas a liability obli-

---

[4]*APB Opinion No. 21*, "Interest on Receivables and Payables," 1971.
[5]*FASB Statement of Financial Accounting Concepts No. 6*, par. 35. The discussion of the nature of liabilities relies heavily on *SFAC No. 6*.

EXHIBIT 3–1

Financial Attributes of Assets

Financial Attribute	Description	Transaction	Time
Input Values			
Historical cost	Amount of cash or cash-equivalent payment actually made to acquire the asset.	Actual	Past
Current cost	Amount of cash or cash-equivalent payment that a company would have to make today to acquire the same asset.	Hypothetical	Present
Output Values			
Current exit value in orderly liquidation	Amount of cash the asset could be sold for in an orderly liquidation.	Hypothetical	Present
Expected exit value in due course of business	Amount of cash or cash-equivalent value that a company expects to receive for the asset in the ordinary course of business, minus the costs of completing and selling the asset.	Expected	Future
Present value of expected cash flows	Amount of discounted net cash inflows that the asset is expected to generate.	Expected	Future

gates the entity to *pay* economic benefits. Most liabilities, such as accounts payable, are settled by paying cash, but some, such as the liability for magazine subscriptions paid in advance, require settlement in the form of services or assets other than cash. For a liability to exist, it is not necessary to know either the exact amount of the liability or the identity of the parties to whom the entity is obligated. For example, companies report liabilities under product warranties in their financial statements without knowing the identity of the customers whose products will become defective and require servicing. The dollar estimates are based on past experience.

The most significant characteristic of a liability is the duty or requirement to sacrifice economic benefits in the future, either by expending assets or providing services. Liabilities may be payable on demand, on certain maturity dates, or when certain specific events occur. Because a liability entails a probable future sacrifice, uncertainty often exists about whether a particular item qualifies as a liability. For example, accounts payable, interest payable, and wages payable are clearly liabilities because they represent probable future sacrifices. On the other hand, determining that an entity will probably lose a lawsuit and therefore have to pay damages is much more difficult and requires considerable judgment.

Most liabilities, such as bonds payable, are evidenced by contracts or other agreements and by the fact that the entity incurring the liability usually receives proceeds (cash, other assets, or services). However, contracts and the receipt of proceeds are not essential characteristics of a liability. Some liabilities, such as income taxes and lawsuit settlements, result from governmental or legal actions and do not involve proceeds to the entity. Other liabilities, such as donations to charity, result from discretionary actions by an entity's management and the entity does not receive proceeds.

A liability does not have to be legally enforceable, although most liabilities, such as notes payable, are. A liability may exist simply because an entity is bound by custom or tradition to provide money, goods, or services in the future. A liability for year-end bonuses, for example, may exist because a company has always paid such amounts even without a contractual requirement to do so. When an obligation is not legally enforceable, determining whether a liability really exists is often extremely difficult. Under such circumstances, an accountant must apply careful judgment.[6]

Probable future sacrifices alone do not constitute a liability. For a liability to exist, a particular entity must be obligated to transfer assets or provide services to other entities in the future as a result of past transactions or events. A company that has sold all of its inventory has no liability to pay for new inventory until acquired from another entity. Similarly, the amount shown in the next year's budget for labor services is not a liability until the company has received the services.

MEASUREMENT OF LIABILITIES

The five financial attributes discussed earlier for assets also pertain to liabilities.[7] But relative to asset measurement, liability measurement has received much less attention in the accounting literature. The measurement of a liability in practice is often the result of measuring the other side of the transaction that created the liability. When a company acquires an inventory item for $100 on credit, for example, the asset is measured at its historical cost of $100; the liability is also measured at $100, which is the amount the company expects to spend to liquidate the liability. In practice, a variety of financial attributes are used to measure liabilities.

Asset/Liability Measurement

Liabilities enable companies to delay payment. The cost of delaying payment is **interest,** or the time value of money. *Whether interest is explicitly stated or not, it is always inherent in liabilities.* Two issues in liability measurement therefore are (1) whether the interest should be separately recognized, and (2) what rate should be used to recognize the interest.

Each of the following financial attributes pertains to a liability that presently exists. Although each attribute is conceptually unique, the measurement of two or more financial attributes of a given liability may result in the same dollar amount under certain circumstances. Measurements of liabilities and income may differ considerably depending on the financial attribute used.

Present Value of Expected Cash Flows

Conceptually, a liability should be measured on a present-value basis, and many liabilities are currently measured this way. The **present value** of a liability is the discounted amount of the net cash outflows that are expected to be necessary to liquidate the liability. Suppose, for example, that a company has a debt of $1,000 that is payable one year from today. Assuming an interest rate of 12%, the present value of the liability today is $892.86 ($1,000 ÷ 1.12).[8] The $107.14 difference between $1,000 and $892.86 is the interest charge that the company will incur by being indebted during the coming year. Under the present-value approach, the interest would be separately recognized and accounted for.

Present-value measurements reflect the time value of money and are required in current practice when measuring certain long-term payables under *APB Opinion No.*

---

[6]This issue is discussed in more detail in *FASB Statement of Financial Accounting Concepts No. 6,* pars. 40 and 203.

[7]The discussion of financial attributes of liabilities relies heavily on *FASB Discussion Memorandum,* "Conceptual Framework for Financial Accounting and Reporting: Elements of Financial Statements and Their Measurement," 1976, pars. 534–576. The five financial attributes are also discussed in *FASB Statement of Financial Accounting Concepts No. 5,* 1984, pars. 66–70.

[8]Computing present values is discussed more fully in Chapter 6.

21. In practice, accountants apply the present value approach throughout the time a liability exists by using a discount rate equal to the market rate of interest at the time the liability was initially incurred. This discount rate is called the **historical market rate.** Very often the historical market rate is simply the interest rate stated in the loan agreement.

Expected Exit Value in Due Course of Business

The **expected exit value** of a liability is the amount of cash or cash-equivalent value that the company expects to pay to eliminate the liability in the ordinary course of business. The amount of the cash or cash-equivalent payment is not discounted to a present value. Assume that a company acquires some merchandise on credit. The goods cost $5,000, which the company agrees to pay in 60 days. The expected exit value of the liability is $5,000.

Expected exit values show how much cash the company expects to spend to liquidate a liability, but they ignore the time value of money completely. In the example above, the interest on the $5,000 liability for 60 days is not separately considered. To illustrate this point more dramatically, assume that a company currently sells at par value $100,000, 12%, 20-year bonds that the company expects to retire at maturity. The expected exit value of the bonds today would be $340,000 [$100,000 maturity value + $240,000 ($100,000 × .12 × 20) interest]. Recording the bond liability at $340,000 fails to reflect the economic reality that interest of $240,000 will be incurred during the 20-year life of the bonds. Under current GAAP the company would measure the bond liability at $100,000, an amount equal to the present value of the interest and principal payments required to liquidate the bonds.

Expected exit values are used under GAAP for measuring many liabilities. For example, accounts payable to suppliers are usually measured at expected exit values. The interest is ignored because the credit period is usually relatively brief and therefore the interest is immaterial. As another example, liabilities for product warranties are usually measured at their expected exit value. In this case, the interest is ignored because the amount and timing of payment are too uncertain to permit a meaningful estimate of the interest.

Materiality

Historical Proceeds

The **historical proceeds** of a liability is the amount of the cash or cash-equivalent proceeds actually received when the liability was incurred. To illustrate, assume that a company receives $18,000 from magazine subscriptions paid in advance for three years. The company now is obligated to provide the magazines, and it would measure the liability for unearned subscriptions revenue at $18,000, the amount of the cash proceeds received.

Historical proceeds is generally used under GAAP to measure liabilities for products or services that a company has agreed to provide in the future. The time value of money is generally ignored for these types of liabilities because it is considered too impractical to measure.

Current Proceeds

The **current proceeds** of a liability is the amount of cash or cash-equivalent value that a company would receive today by incurring the same liability. The amount changes in response to changes in market interest rates and to changes in the perceived risk of the company that has the liability. As market interest rates rise, the current proceeds of a given liability tend to decrease; similarly, as market interest rates fall, the current proceeds tend to increase.

To illustrate, suppose that on January 1, 1992, a company issues a $10,000, 10%, two-year note payable with interest of $1,000 ($10,000 × 10%) payable at the end of each year. On that date the market rate of interest is 10%, and the company receives proceeds of $10,000, because the present value of the note (including the interest) at the market rate of interest is $10,000. On December 31, 1992, the company pays $1,000 of interest for the year 1992, the current market rate of interest is 12%, and the company's risk level is unchanged from the beginning of the year. Under these circumstances, the current proceeds of the note will be $9,821.43 on December 31, 1992. This amount equals the $10,000 face amount plus $1,000 of interest due at the end of 1993, divided by 1.12 ($11,000 ÷ 1.12 = $9,821.43). We are saying, then, that *if* the company were to issue on December 31, 1992, a $10,000, 10% note with one year remaining to maturity, the company would obtain proceeds of $9,821.43. The reason that the current proceeds are less than $10,000 is because the current market rate of interest (12%) exceeds the interest rate stated in the note (10%). A lender who invested $9,821.43 in the note at the end of 1992 would earn 12% interest (the current market rate) during 1993 [$9,821.43 + ($9,821.43 × 12%) = $11,000]. Notice that $9,821.43 is simply the present value of the note computed using the current market rate of interest (12%) at the end of 1992.

We emphasize that the note payable in the previous example would be reported at $10,000 (not $9,821.43) in conventional financial statements prepared at the end of 1992. This is so because $10,000 is the present value of the note at the end of 1992 computed using the market rate of interest that prevailed when the note was issued ($11,000 ÷ 1.10 = $10,000).

Under the current proceeds approach to liability measurement, the time value of money is measured using a current rather than historical interest rate. Some people believe that the use of current proceeds would enhance the usefulness of financial statements for making predictions of cash flows and evaluations of management. But current proceeds departs from historical cost accounting and is not used for measuring liabilities under GAAP.

Current Exit Value in Orderly Liquidation

The **current exit value** of a liability is the amount a company would have to pay currently to eliminate the liability in an orderly manner. Assume, for example, that a company has $100,000 of bonds payable outstanding and that each of the 100 bonds was originally sold at par value of $1,000. Assume further that market interest rates have fallen since the bonds were issued and that each bond now has a market price of $1,050. In this example the current exit value of the bonds is $105,000 ($1,050 × 100) because this is the amount the company would have to pay currently to retire the bonds by purchasing them in the market.

When a liability requires specified cash payments, such as the bond liability in the example above, the current exit value and current proceeds will usually be the same amount. Nevertheless, current exit value and current proceeds differ conceptually. Current exit value refers to how much a company would have to *pay* to eliminate the liability; current proceeds refers to how much a company would *receive* by incurring the liability. Some people argue that current exit values would be relevant to users when assessing the ability of an entity to adapt to a changing environment. The counterargument is that most companies do not intend to eliminate all of their liabilities currently. Like current proceeds, current exit value measurements represent a departure from historical cost accounting and are not used when measuring liabilities in financial statements prepared in accordance with GAAP.

Summary

The various financial attributes of liabilities are summarized in Exhibit 3–2.

EXHIBIT 3–2

Financial Attributes of Liabilities

Financial Attribute	Description	Transaction	Time
Present value of expected cash flows	Amount of discounted net cash outflows that are expected to be necessary to liquidate the liability.	Expected	Future
Expected exit value in due course of business	Amount of cash or cash-equivalent value that a company expects to pay to eliminate the liability in the ordinary course of business.	Expected	Future
Historical proceeds	Amount of cash or cash-equivalent proceeds actually received when the liability was incurred.	Actual	Past
Current proceeds	Amount of cash or cash-equivalent value that a company would receive today by incurring the same liability.	Hypothetical	Present
Current exit value in orderly liquidation	Amount of cash that a company would have to pay currently to eliminate the liability in an orderly manner.	Hypothetical	Present

OWNERS' EQUITY

NATURE OF OWNERS' EQUITY

Owners' equity is "the residual interest in the assets of an entity that remains after deducting its liabilities."[9] In other words, owners' equity equals net assets, which are assets minus liabilities. Like liabilities, owners' equity represents an interest in the assets of an entity. But liabilities and owners' equity differ in several important aspects:

1. Liabilities represent the interest of creditors in the assets of an entity; owners' equity represents the interest of owners.
2. Liabilities rank ahead of owners' equity when an entity's assets are distributed. A company may not pay dividends to owners until it has made the required interest and principal payments to creditors. Moreover, when a company is liquidated, liabilities must be paid before distributions can be made to owners.
3. The amount of liability payments is usually more certain than is the amount of payments to owners. Oral or written agreements, such as bond contracts, usually specify how much cash a company must pay to liquidate its liabilities. The amount of dividend payments to owners, however, is usually determined at the discretion of a company's board of directors.
4. The timing of liability payments is usually more certain than the timing of payments to owners. Many liabilities have specific maturity dates; owners' equity does not mature.

---

[9]*FASB Statement of Financial Accounting Concepts No. 6*, par. 49. The discussion of the nature of owners' equity relies heavily on *SFAC No. 6*.

Owners' equity represents the interest of parties who stand to lose the largest amount if an entity is unsuccessful and gain the largest amount if it is successful. Owners are the primary beneficiaries of an entity's net income, but they also must bear its losses. Owners' equity is originally created when owners invest cash or other assets in an entity. Subsequently, the interest of owners may be increased by additional investments and net income, and it may be decreased by distributions to owners (dividends) and net losses.

Owners' equity provides an important frame of reference when measuring a company's net income. In the absence of additional investments by owners or distributions to them during a period, net income for the period will equal the increase in owners' equity that occurred during the period.

MEASUREMENT OF OWNERS' EQUITY

Asset/Liability Measurement

As indicated earlier, owners' equity is a **residual figure** derived by deducting liabilities from assets. The measurement of owners' equity is therefore not an independent process. Instead, it depends on the valuations assigned to the individual assets and liabilities. Suppose that a company had only one asset, an account receivable with an expected exit value of $10,000 and no liabilities. Under these circumstances, owners' equity would simply reflect the expected exit value measurement of $10,000 ($10,000 − $0). As we have seen, however, companies actually use a mixture of financial attributes (historical costs, expected exit values, present values, etc.) when measuring their individual assets and liabilities. Owners' equity therefore reflects a mixture of financial attributes. For this reason and because many assets and liabilities are simply too difficult to measure and report at all, owners' equity does not reveal the current market value of the company to its owners.

INCOME

In this section we discuss the nature, measurement, components, and usefulness of net income. Many people feel that net income is the most important single number that appears in the financial statements. Unlike cash on hand, the net income for a typical business cannot be seen or counted. It is not surprising that income concepts have been a highly controversial topic in accounting and economics.

NATURE OF NET INCOME

The famous economist J. R. Hicks defined an individual's income as the maximum amount the person could consume in a period and still be as well off at the end of the period as he/she was at the beginning.[10] This definition can be adapted to a business enterprise: the **net income** of a business is the increase in the net assets (owners' equity) of the firm, assuming no new capital contributions by the owners or dividend distributions by the business.[11] More precisely, the net income for a period equals the ending owners' equity, minus the beginning owners' equity, plus dividends declared during the period, minus additional capital contributions made during the period. To illustrate, assume that during a period a company had ending owners' equity of $25,000, beginning owners' equity of $20,000, dividends declared of $10,000, and additional capital contributions of $3,000. Net income for the period would be $12,000 ($25,000 − $20,000 + $10,000 − $3,000).

---

[10]J. R. Hicks, *Value and Capital* (Oxford: Clarendon Press, 1946), p. 172.
[11]Robert T. Sprouse and Maurice Moonitz, *Accounting Research Study No. 3*, "A Tentative Set of Broad Accounting Principles for Business Enterprises" (New York: AICPA, 1962), p. 54.

Important to the understanding of net income is the distinction between a return *of* capital and a return *on* capital. Stockholders invest in companies to earn a return *on* capital, or an amount in excess of their original investment. A return *of* capital is simply an erosion of the capital invested in the firm. Net income occurs only after the capital used from the beginning of the period is maintained. This concept is known as **capital maintenance.** In the Hicksian sense, the same level of "well-offness" must be maintained before net income can be said to exist. Revenues must be applied to the recovery of the resources used in the business before any net income can result. An important concept is that the capital used in the business does not have to be physically replaced with the exact type of resources consumed. Capital maintenance is a measurement concept, not a statement of how managers should reinvest resources.

To illustrate the concept of capital maintenance, consider a retail store with all its capital invested in an inventory of 800 stereophonic tapes costing $5 each. If the retailer sells 600 tapes at $7 each, the total return is $4,200 (600 × $7). Therefore, at the end of the period, the retailer has 200 tapes and $4,200. To determine net income, we must deduct from $4,200 an amount that represents the capital invested in the 600 tapes that were sold. One way of doing this is to deduct $3,000 (600 × $5) from the $4,200 as a return *of* capital and then consider the remaining $1,200 (600 × $2) as a return *on* capital (i.e., net income). The retailer need not actually replace the 600 tapes that were sold. Our objective in deducting $3,000 is merely to measure the capital consumed by the sale of 600 tapes so that we can determine net income.[12]

Lifetime Net Income

The most definitive measure of net income can be made when a company is liquidated. At that time, the **lifetime net income** of the firm can be determined with certainty. Assuming no additional investments or withdrawals by owners, lifetime net income (or loss) would equal the cash initially invested by owners at the beginning of business, subtracted from the cash remaining for the owners at the end of business—after assets are liquidated and liabilities are satisfied. Over the life of the company, total revenues equal all cash receipts from earning activities (such as sales), and total expenses equal all cash disbursements for earning activities (such as payments to suppliers and employees). Lifetime net income therefore equals lifetime cash receipts from earning activities minus lifetime cash disbursements for earning activities, or net cash inflows from earning activities during the life of the company.

Periodic Net Income

Although the lifetime net income of an enterprise corresponds with its net cash flows from earning activities, this situation does not help the investor or creditor to make *timely* decisions. Investors and creditors are not interested in knowing the net income of a firm after final disposition of assets. Instead, they need periodic disclosures of operating performance in order to assess current investments and loans or to evaluate future capital commitments.

One function of the accountant is to provide statements of periodic net income. This presents a challenge because, in contrast to lifetime net income, periodic net income does not necessarily reflect cash flows for the period. At *some time* during the life of a company, a dollar should be received for every dollar of revenue reported by the company, but the cash receipts do not have to occur in the same period that the

---

[12]Central to the concept of capital maintenance is the accountant's assessment of "well-offness." The accountant's definition of capital has a direct bearing on what is considered as net income. It is beyond the scope of this text to discuss the various concepts of capital. A lucid discussion can be found in Keith Shwayder, "The Capital Maintenance Rule and the Net Asset Valuation Rule," *Accounting Review* (April 1969), pp. 304–316.

EXHIBIT 3-3

Reconciliation Between Cash Flow and Revenue/Expense Recognition

	Cash Precedes Recognition	Cash Follows Recognition
Revenues	**Liability** Example: Unearned Rent Revenue	**Asset** Example: Accrued Interest Receivable
Expenses	**Asset** Example: Prepaid Insurance	**Liability** Example: Accrued Wages Payable

[handwritten annotations: "Cash moves first deferral" above "Cash Precedes Recognition"; "accrual" above "Cash Follows Recognition"]

revenue is recognized. Likewise, at *some time* during the life of a company, a dollar should be spent for every dollar of expense reported by the company, but the cash payments do not have to occur in the same period that the expense is recognized. The accountant attempts to reconcile the recognition of revenues and expenses with the actual cash flows of past, present, and future periods. This reconciliation requires the recognition of certain assets and liabilities, as shown in Exhibit 3–3.

The upper left cell of Exhibit 3–3 illustrates the situation in which cash inflow precedes the recognition of revenue. Consider, for example, a business that rents space in return for a fee received in advance. When the fee is collected, there is no revenue, only the liability to provide rental space. Revenue is recognized only as rental space is provided. Likewise, the lower left cell of Exhibit 3–3 represents the case of cash outflow preceding the recognition of an expense. This occurs when a business pays cash in exchange for future services, such as prepaid insurance. The prepaid insurance represents the right to future protection that is amortized as an expense only as the protection is received.

The upper right cell of the exhibit illustrates transactions in which cash inflow follows revenue recognition. An example is interest on an investment in the bonds of another company. If the interest has been earned as of the end of an accounting period, then the interest must be recognized as a receivable and as revenue, even though the cash associated with the interest will not be received until the next accounting period. The lower right cell concerns transactions in which cash outflow follows expense recognition. Frequently, at the end of a reporting period, an enterprise has received employee services for which it has not yet paid. The labor represents a liability that will later be compensated by actual cash payment.

In each case, revenue and expense recognition for the period do not exactly correspond to cash flows. Although cash flows are reconciled with revenues and expenses over the lifetime of a company, it is unreasonable to postpone income measurement until business is terminated. Instead, methods must be used to measure periodic net income.

THE MEASUREMENT OF PERIODIC NET INCOME

The measurement of periodic net income depends on the valuation of assets and liabilities, since periodic net income is the change in the net assets for the period, assuming no new capital contributions or dividends. At a very simple level, a cash basis system could be used to determine periodic income. Next we compare cash basis accounting and traditional accrual basis accounting.

Cash Basis Accounting Versus Accrual Basis Accounting

Cash basis accounting defines revenues as cash inflows from earning activities, and expenses as cash outflows in earning activities. Frequently, cash inflows and outflows occur in different periods than the related accomplishments and efforts. For example, the purchase of machinery results in an immediate cash outflow but provides useful service over a period of years. **Accrual basis accounting** allows for such cases by recording the results of significant operating events when they occur rather than when cash is received or paid. Under accrual basis accounting, revenues are recognized when earned, regardless of when cash is received, and expenses are recognized when incurred, regardless of when cash is paid.

Because investors and creditors are interested in cash flows (see Chapter 2), wouldn't a simple cash basis income statement be preferable to an accrual basis statement? Most accountants think not. A cash basis system usually fails to provide valuable information about the earning capability of the firm. In addition, cash receipts and disbursements for successive periods are generally unrelated and can produce misleading trends.

Consider a college student who started a business, the Nimble Fingers Typing Service. The following events occurred during the first three months of the academic year.

September

Rented a typewriter for $25 on account.
Purchased paper for $30 on account.
Placed an advertisement in the campus newspaper
    for $40 on account.
Typed several projects and charged customers a total
    fee of $200 on account.

October

Collected $200 in fees from customers.

November

Remitted payments to paper supplier, campus newspaper,
    and office equipment lessor.

Exhibit 3–4 represents the income statement and balance sheet under cash accounting. Close examination of these financial statements reveals some difficulties of cash basis accounting. If we evaluated the performance of Nimble Fingers based on the monthly cash flow figures, our conclusions would change from month to month. For September we might conclude that the business accomplished nothing, because the financial statements contain all zeros. We know, however, that Nimble Fingers provided typing services throughout September.

October appears more promising with a large increase in net income, and we might conclude that the business is proving successful. This, however, is misleading, because we know, as early as the end of September, that of the $200 cash inflow reported in October, only $105 represents a return *on* invested capital, while the remaining $95 is a return *of* capital. This information is known, but the reporting is delayed under cash basis accounting.

The November income statement reports a net loss of $95. This turn of events leaves the outside observer unable to determine what might happen in December. The total net income for all three months is $105 ($0 + $200 − $95), which is accurate. What is not meaningful is the time period in which the $105 was disclosed. Under

EXHIBIT 3–4

Financial Statements for Nimble Fingers Under Cash Basis Accounting

Income Statement (month ending)

	September	October	November
Revenues	$–0–	$200	–0–
Expenses	–0–	–0–	$ 95
Net income (Loss)	$–0–	$200	$(95)

Balance Sheet (last day of the month)

	September	October	November
Total assets (Cash)	$–0–	$200	$105
Owner's capital	$–0–	$200	$105

cash basis accounting we must wait for the final cash payment in November before we have an accurate picture of the events for the first three months. The criticism is that this information was known with reasonable certainty as early as the end of September, but recognition was delayed until cash changed hands.

Accrual accounting alleviates these problems by recording net income when it was *earned* rather than when cash was collected or paid. Exhibit 3–5 presents the Nimble Fingers financial statements under accrual accounting. The information disclosed in September under accrual accounting differs markedly from that under cash accounting. Net income is disclosed in the period in which effort is applied to the typing business, and accomplishments accrue as the jobs are completed. All net income is disclosed in September, when the main activities of the business were completed. After September, all that remains are the incidental activities of collecting customer accounts and satisfying creditor obligations. The income statement reflects this by attributing zero earnings to October and November. The balance sheet includes Accounts Receivable and Accounts Payable among the assets and liabilities in order to reconcile cash flow with revenue and expense recognition (Exhibit 3–3).

In both cash basis and accrual basis accounting the net income for a period equals the change in the net assets, and the lifetime net income is $105. The two methods differ in the assignment of income to periods. Under accrual accounting, revenues and expenses are recorded at the earliest appearance of objective evidence. This frequently precedes cash flow. As a result, accrual accounting assigns income to the period in which it is earned, which is often a more timely measurement than that of cash basis accounting.

Measuring Income Under Accrual Accounting

Asset/Liability Measurement

The methods of measuring income under accrual accounting relate to the financial attributes used in measuring assets and liabilities, as discussed earlier in the chapter. Accrual basis income may be measured under historical cost, current cost, current exit value, expected exit value, and present value methods.

To illustrate the various methods of measuring income under accrual accounting, consider the wholesaler Horizon Sales, Inc. Horizon Sales has only one asset—an in-

EXHIBIT 3–5

Financial Statements for Nimble Fingers
Under Accrual Basis Accounting

Income Statement
(month ending)

	September	October	November
Revenues	$200	$–0–	$–0–
Expenses	95	–0–	–0–
Net income	$105	$–0–	$–0–

Balance Sheet
(last day of the month)

	September	October	November
Cash	–0–	$200	$105
Accounts receivable	$200	–0–	–0–
Total assets	$200	$200	$105
Accounts payable	$ 95	$ 95	–0–
Owner's capital	105	105	$105
Total liabilities and owner's capital	$200	$200	$105

ventory of fur coats purchased on January 1, 1992. Information about the fur coats is as follows.

January 1, 1992
Fur coats are purchased at a cost of $100,000.
December 31, 1992
Current cost to replace the fur coats is $125,000.

Amount of cash that could be received in orderly liquidation (current exit value) of the fur coats is $133,000.

Amount of cash expected to be received for the fur coats after selling costs (expected exit value) is $135,000.
December 31, 1993
Fur coat inventory is sold for $144,000 on account.
January 1, 1994
$144,000 is collected from customers.

Revenue Realization

Historical Cost. If the inventory of fur coats is measured under historical cost, recognition of income is delayed until the sale. This is consistent with the revenue realization principle, which requires that revenue be recorded only when the earning process is complete or virtually complete, and when the amount and timing of revenue are reasonably determinable. The objective evidence provided by the sale is usually necessary to satisfy the criteria for recognizing revenue. Therefore, net income of $44,000 ($144,000 − $100,000) would be recorded for Horizon Sales in 1993.

Current Cost. Although historical cost is consistent with GAAP, it is helpful to understand the alternatives to conventional accounting methods. Under the current cost method, on December 31, 1992, Horizon Sales would write up the inventory to current cost ($125,000). The $25,000 difference between the beginning and ending balance of the inventory is called a **holding gain** (or holding loss if the ending balance was less than the beginning balance). The holding gain would be reported on the 1992 income statement. In 1993 the $19,000 difference between the selling price ($144,000) and the current cost valuation of the inventory on December 31, 1992 ($125,000) would be included in income.[13]

Current Exit Value.   If we assume that the fur coats are reported at their current exit value, the holding gain for 1992 would be $33,000. This is the increase in the current exit value of the inventory from the beginning to the end of the period ($133,000 − $100,000 = $33,000). Horizon's 1993 current exit value income on the sale of the fur coats would be $11,000 ($144,000 − $133,000).

Expected Exit Value.   As discussed previously, current exit value and expected exit value are likely to result in two different valuations of the same item because of the different assumptions used in each method. In the example of Horizon Sales, the holding gain for 1992 would be $35,000 ($135,000 − $100,000), while the expected exit value income recognized in 1993 would be $9,000 ($144,000 − $135,000).

Present Value of Expected Cash Flows.   To illustrate the measurement of earnings under present value, we must first assume that it was *known* when the fur coats were purchased on January 1, 1992, that $144,000 cash would be received for their sale two years later. This is, of course, an unrealistic assumption in the case of an inventory of fur coats.[14] As a result, we illustrate present value income measurement for Horizon Sales, bearing in mind the limitations of this approach to assets and liabilities with uncertain future cash flows.

Horizon Sales invested $100,000 in an asset (fur coats) that will be worth $144,000 in two years. The *annual* rate of growth necessary to increase the inventory from its present value of $100,000 to the future value of $144,000 is 20%.[15] For 1992 the investment is assumed to grow by 20%, or $20,000 ($100,000 × .20). Therefore, the inventory has a value of $120,000 on December 31, 1992. The $20,000, or the difference between the beginning and ending inventory valuation, is the income earned and reported in 1992. For 1993 the investment has a beginning value of $120,000. A 20% annual return on this amount yields $24,000 ($120,000 × .20) and increases the value of the inventory to $144,000. This is not a coincidence. The annual rate of return is determined so that the inventory balance increases to the selling amount of $144,000. The income earned in 1993 would be $24,000, and the increase in the inventory balance would reflect the 20% rate of return.

Summary.   The net income of Horizon Sales under all five methods is summarized in Exhibit 3–6. Clearly, the *total income* on the sale of the fur coats is $44,000. The question is how to assign the $44,000 return on investment to the two periods. Under GAAP (historical cost), the $44,000 is reported in 1993, the year of the sale. Under the four alternatives to historical cost, at least part of the $44,000 is reported in

---

[13]If the current cost valuation of the inventory remained unchanged from December 31, 1992, to December 31, 1993, all of the $19,000 would be considered "current operating profit." If, however, the current cost valuation of the inventory changed during 1993, the $19,000 would be separated into two parts, current operating profit and holding gain. As an example, if the current cost valuation of the inventory was $134,000 on December 31, 1993, then $10,000 ($144,000 − $134,000) would be current operating profit and $9,000 ($134,000 − $125,000) would be a holding gain. We discuss this more fully in Chapter 26.

[14]The assumption of perfect foreknowledge is not so unreasonable in the case of assets and liabilities resulting in fixed cash flows. Examples include notes receivable and payable, which are contracts for certain cash flows in the future. In these cases a present value approach is generally accepted.

[15]The annual rate of return can be determined with the aid of present value interest tables. Use of these tables is discussed in Chapter 6.

EXHIBIT 3-6

Net Income of Horizon Sales for 1992 and 1993
Under Five Asset Valuation Methods

Method	1992	Net Income 1993	Total
Historical cost	–0–	$44,000	$44,000
Current cost	$25,000	19,000	44,000
Current exit value	33,000	11,000	44,000
Expected exit value	35,000	9,000	44,000
Present value of expected cash flows	20,000	24,000	44,000

1992. This points to a frequent criticism of historical cost, namely, the delay in recognizing income. Critics suggest that alternatives are generally more *timely* in the recognition of income and are therefore more relevant to users of financial statements in their attempts to predict future cash flows.

Historical cost proponents counter that the alternatives are too unreliable and also generate income numbers that are less likely to result in cash flows. For example, if the fur coats were sold for only $100,000 on December 31, 1993, the current cost and exit value (current and expected) methods would recognize income in 1992 and a loss in 1993. Supporters of historical cost argue that the reporting of income in 1992 could have harmed users, because that income failed to materialize. The uncertainty of eventual cash realization was too great and resulted in the reversal in 1993 of income recognized in 1992.

COMPONENTS OF NET INCOME

Net income is composed of revenues, expenses, gains, and losses. Each component can be defined according to the asset/liability view or the revenue/expense view. According to the **asset/liability view,** the components of net income are defined by reference to definitions of assets and liabilities. Under the **revenue/expense view,** the components of net income are defined without reference to definitions of assets and liabilities. Both views are used in practice, but the FASB currently favors the asset/liability view implied in the following definitions, which we presented in Chapter 2:

1. **Revenues.**   Inflows or other enhancements of assets of an entity or settlements of its liabilities (or both) during a period, based on production and delivery of goods, provision of services, and other activities that constitute the entity's major operations. Examples are sales revenue, interest revenue, and rent revenue.
2. **Expenses.**   Outflows or other use of assets or incurrences of liabilities (or both) during a period as a result of delivering or producing goods, rendering services, or carrying out other activities that constitute the entity's ongoing major or central operations. Examples are cost of goods sold, salaries expense, and advertising expense.
3. **Gains.**   Increases in owners' equity (net assets) from peripheral or incidental transactions of an entity and from all other transactions and events affecting the entity during a period, except those that result from revenues or investments by owners. Examples are a gain on the sale of plant assets and a gain on the early retirement of long-term debt.

4. Losses.   Decreases in owners' equity (net assets) from peripheral or incidental transactions of an entity and from all other transactions and events affecting the entity during a period, except those that result from expenses or distributions to owners. Examples are losses on the sale of investments and on litigation.

Notice the references to assets, liabilities, and owners' equity (net assets). The components of net income are *not* defined independently of definitions of assets and liabilities. In a sense, the definitions of assets and liabilities are the anchor, or reference point, for the definitions of revenues, expenses, gains, and losses. The FASB calls this the asset/liability view.

According to the alternative conceptual approach—the revenue/expense view—revenues, expenses, gains, and losses are defined without direct reference to definitions of assets and liabilities. Proponents of this view disagree about the correct definition of the components of income, but they generally view revenues as a measure of the operating accomplishments of the enterprise in a particular period and expenses as the efforts necessary to generate the revenues for the period. Fundamental to this

Matching   position is the principle of matching expenses with revenues. Under the revenue/expense view, how we define assets and liabilities is secondary to how we define revenues and expenses. Assets and liabilities are essentially the debits and credits that remain after revenues and expenses are properly matched on the income statement.

Both the asset/liability view and the revenue/expense view are compatible with financial statements that *articulate* with one another. **Articulated financial statements,** which are the kind produced under GAAP, are fundamentally related or tied to one another.

The major issue in the asset/liability and revenue/expense controversy is which definition should take precedence. This is far from a trivial concern. Critics of the revenue/expense view believe that the matching principle lacks objectivity. Furthermore, they believe the income statement may be open to recognition of revenues and expenses that are not changes in enterprise assets or liabilities. It is suggested that such revenues and expenses are meaningless to understanding the change in wealth of a business. Under the revenue/expense view, the balance sheet can become a "dumping ground" for nonresources and nonobligations because of vague definitions of revenues and expenses. Supporters of the asset/liability view impose an objective limit on what will be considered as admissible revenues, expenses, gains, and losses. Only transactions that increase or decrease the assets or liabilities of an enterprise can be considered revenues or expenses.

As indicated earlier, current practice reflects a *combination of both views,* which makes the distinction between them difficult to observe. The FASB has decided to emphasize one view in order to guide future accounting policy decisions. Because the FASB has supported the asset/liability view, we have embraced this view throughout the conceptual discussion in this chapter.

USEFULNESS OF ACCOUNTING NET INCOME

In the mid-1960s many critics of financial reporting argued that the net income number was meaningless. They based their opposition on continued adherence to historical cost, which they thought misrepresented reality. In addition, skeptics denounced the diversity of acceptable accounting methods (e.g., LIFO versus FIFO in inventory costing) for determining net income. They suggested that managers could disclose net income in various ways according to GAAP because of the lack of uniform measurement principles. Indeed, one author showed how identical firms could produce an earnings per share of either $.80 or $1.79, depending on the choice of accounting principles.[16] Critics asserted that such ambiguity reduced the credibility of accounting income numbers as a source of information to statement users. One financial analyst described the situation this way:

Matching

> *The accountant defines it [earnings] as what he gets when he matches costs against revenues, making any necessary allocations of costs to prior periods; or as the change in the equity account over the period. These costs are not economic definitions of earnings but merely descriptions of the motions the accountant goes through to arrive at the earnings number.* [17]

Fortunately, subsequent research on the usefulness of net income disclosures has lessened many of these concerns. One classic study investigated whether knowledge of the next year's net income would be sufficient to earn superior returns in the price of a company's stock.[18] Obviously, if such advance knowledge could not be used in profitable investment strategy, it would be of little value. Results of this study indicated that if just the direction of change in the next year's net income were known for a number of companies, investment decisions would consistently produce better-than-average returns. This suggests that disclosure of net income has value for investors.

Although strong evidence indicates that the net income number is useful for investor decision making, it says nothing about the timeliness of net income disclosures. Such information could have already reached investors in other forms. Investors could use alternative sources of information, such as investment advisory services and government reports, to estimate the current earnings of a company.

A study was conducted to test the timeliness of net income disclosures.[19] This study investigated whether present and potential investors reacted to the initial disclosure of the accounting net income number. Initial disclosure of a corporation's quarterly or annual earnings precedes the dissemination of quarterly or annual reports to shareholders. Major stock exchanges require listed companies to release earnings announcements to the press and wire services as soon as the information becomes available. Most U.S. corporations release earnings data via the Dow-Jones News Service (the Broad Tape), which is a financial-news wire service. The earnings release is then printed in *The Wall Street Journal* the next business day. Exhibit 3–7 shows a typical annual and quarterly earnings announcement. If information in the preliminary earnings release had already reached investors, we would not expect investors to react to the net income disclosure. The study found that the volume of trading increases dramatically in the week the net income disclosure is released publicly, compared to the rest of the year. This finding supports the timeliness of net income disclosure.

Evidence strongly suggests that accounting net income is both useful and timely to investors in their buying and selling decisions. However, the question remains: Why do investors perceive the net income number as relevant information? The significance of net income can be viewed in two interrelated ways. In one sense, net

---

[16]The illustration was provided by Leonard Spacek, "Business Success Requires an Understanding of Unsolved Problems of Accounting and Financial Reporting," in J. Lories and R. Brealey (Eds.), *Modern Developments in Investment Management* (New York: Praeger, 1972), pp. 630–644.
[17]Jack Treynor, "The Trouble with Earnings," *Financial Analysts Journal* (September 1972), p. 41.
[18]Ray Ball and Phillip Brown, "An Empirical Investigation of Accounting Income Numbers," *Journal of Accounting Research* (Autumn 1968), pp. 159–178.
[19]William Beaver, "The Information Content of Annual Earnings Announcements," *Journal of Accounting Research* (Supplement 1968), pp. 67–92.

EXHIBIT 3-7

Preliminary Earnings Announcement

HILTON HOTELS CORP. (N)

	Year Dec 31: 1990	1989
Revenues	$1,124,800,000	$998,200,000
Net income	112,500,000	a110,100,000
Shr earns:		
Net income	2.34	2.27
Quarter:		
Revenues	325,600,000	259,600,000
Net income	27,300,000	26,900,000
Shr earns:		
Net income	.57	.55

a-includes net charge of $2,400,000 related to property transactions.

SOURCE: Hilton Hotels Corporation, 1990 Annual Report.

income is a measure of *past* performance; in another sense, it is an indicator of *future* cash flows. These uses are discussed in the following sections.

Net Income as a Measure of Past Performance

A business enterprise begins operations by obtaining financing from its owners, and possibly from creditors. The cash received is then converted into labor, raw materials, plant, equipment, and other inputs of production. The goal of the organization is to convert these inputs to an output (product) whose value is greater than the sum of the inputs. This is accomplished by adding time, form, and place utility to the inputs. For example, grapes from the Rhine Valley can be pressed into wine; the bottled wine is then aged for several years, after which it may be shipped to The Plaza in New York. The inputs, including vineyard, winepress, storage area, and shipping, combine to produce a fine table wine that can be sold for an amount greater than the sum of the input costs. This is accomplished by adding time (the aging process), form (grapes to wine), and place (Germany to New York) to the product. This process can be characterized as the **earning process** of the firm.

The earning process and financing activities of a firm become interrelated through time. Firms must compete for investment dollars. The amount and cost of funds that a firm can obtain is a function of its earnings performance relative to other companies. Earnings tells owners and creditors how efficiently management converts inputs to outputs. Successful firms, as demonstrated by past earnings activities, enjoy a competitive advantage in the financing markets. In contrast, less successful firms may find their sources of capital diminished or unavailable. The result can be the final liquidation of an inefficient firm.

The earnings of an enterprise can be viewed as a "report card" of management's performance. Did management responsibly utilize the resources entrusted to them? If not, the stockholders have two choices: they can replace existing management, or they can sell their interest in the firm. However, the evaluation of management performance can be very difficult, especially if based solely on net income. Assume, for example, the latest year-to-year net income results of a company show a 10% decrease. From this information alone, we might conclude that past performance is rather poor. However, if we know that during the same period the net income of all firms in the economy decreased by an average of 30%, we might conclude that our company performed rather well. An informed user of financial statements should also recognize that many events affecting a company's performance, such as floods and earthquakes, are beyond management's control.

Net Income as a Predictor of Cash Flows

Net income not only helps investors and creditors to evaluate the past performance of a firm, but also helps them to predict the cash returns they will receive. For stockholders, the value of shares relates to future dividends. For example, the price of a share is generally higher when stockholders expect to receive larger dividends, all else equal. As a result, shareholders want information that helps them predict future dividends. Net income disclosures may be useful in this regard, because future dividends depend on future earnings.

As a first step in predicting cash flow, present earnings should be separated into a transitory component and a permanent component.[20] The **transitory component** of net income is that part which investors do not expect again in the near future. Transitory income can result from unusual or incidental activities of limited duration or in unconventional markets. For example, a publishing company purchases a downtown parking lot as the site of a future office building. Until construction begins, the company operates the parking lot and collects parking fees. The parking fees are income of limited duration (until construction begins), are incidental to the main function of the company (publishing), and are therefore not expected to continue. Transitory income (or loss) can also result from unusual events, such as a casualty loss from an earthquake or an expropriation of plant assets by a foreign country.

The **permanent component** of net income is the part that investors expect to continue. Permanent income results from the primary functions of the enterprise. In the publishing company, permanent income is generated from producing and marketing books. Permanent income is affected by changes in the demand for books, the price of the books, and the cost of making the books.

Predictably, investors focus on permanent earnings, because only they are useful in predicting income. Transitory earnings are not expected to affect future income. Because accounting policy makers, such as the FASB, understand the importance of distinguishing between the two components of net income, various types of transitory earnings must presently be identified. In Chapter 4 we explore the reporting requirements for several of these nonrecurring events. Unfortunately, the financial reporting requirements for net income do not permit these two types of earnings to be clearly distinguished from one another.

Creditors and investors have similar needs. Whereas investors are concerned with the ability of the firm to pay dividends, creditors are interested in the ability of the firm to make interest and principal payments on loans. Both investors and creditors are forward-looking in this regard. As a result, creditors also focus on the permanent component of net income in assessing the future earnings capability of the firm. Future earnings protect interest payments, because interest is paid to creditors before dividends are distributed to stockholders.

As the needs of investors and creditors are satisfied, so too are the needs of other users. Customers, for example, are interested in the longevity of the enterprise, especially if there are warranty contracts or if major support is necessary for the product line (as in the case of computer equipment). Employees are concerned with job

---

[20]A more detailed discussion of these two components of earnings and reporting considerations can be found in *FASB Discussion Memorandum,* "Reporting Earnings" (Stamford, Conn.: FASB, 1979).

INVESTORS NOW CAN GET HELP WITH 'EARNINGS SURPRISES'

You say that stock you bought for $40 a share suddenly slid to $33.50, even though the company reported higher earnings?

Maybe it is because earnings rose only to 70 cents a share when analysts were expecting 90 cents.

If so, you've been slammed by an "earnings surprise."

Fortunately, surprises can also be positive when better-than-expected earnings give a stock a boost.

Taking advantage of earnings surprises—buying stocks that offer pleasant surprises and dumping those that surprise on the downside—can raise an investor's gross return by anywhere from 2.5% to 16% a year, several studies show.

But while professional investors have been making money on surprises for years, many individual investors haven't been so lucky. That is because individuals have lacked the pros' easy access to analysts' earnings estimates.

Starting today, The Wall Street Journal is introducing a new feature designed to help even the odds. The feature is a listing of selected companies that report quarterly earnings substantially different from what stock market analysts have been estimating during the past 30 days and 300 days.

The listing will be published frequently, as warranted by the number of significant surprises. It will accompany the Digest of Earnings, which appears today on Page A8. (Companies in the surprise listing won't necessarily appear in that edition's Digest of Earnings.)

Earnings surprises are perhaps "the most important type of new information" that can quickly change investor expectations about a stock, says Leonard Zacks, president of Zacks Investment Research Inc. The Chicago-based stock-market research firm, which

provides the data for the new feature, follows earnings estimates by some 2,500 analysts at 145 brokerage houses.

Several studies show that earnings surprises tend to push the price of a stock up or down, not only on the day of the announcement, but for days and even weeks afterward. Furthermore, a company with an earnings surprise in one quarter has a better-than-random chance of offering a similar surprise in the next quarter.

Richard J. Rendleman Jr., professor of finance at University of North Carolina at Chapel Hill, was one of the pioneering researchers in the field of earnings surprises. During the 1970s, he says, stocks of companies showing the most extreme surprises outperformed [or underperformed] the market by 3 to 4 percentage points over the 90 days following the earnings announcement.

Interestingly, the same stocks also outperformed [or underperformed] the market by another three to four percentage points during the 20-day period ending with the announcement day. The pre-announcement moves, Mr. Rendleman figures, partly reflect investors' making shrewd guesses about what earnings will be. And in part, he and others say, it probably reflects leakage of information before the earnings announcement.

Even without guessing surprises in advance, however, a person who captures the aftereffect could theoretically make an extra 12% to 16% a year, judging by Mr. Rendleman's figures. Add that to the average 9% return for stocks over the decades, and it looks like an easy way to make 21% to 25% a year.

Unfortunately, Mr. Rendleman hastens to say, it isn't that simple. He suspects that the magnitude of the effect has diminished a bit, now that so many

---

security and compensation. In both cases, the permanent net income can help predict income.

In summary, a firm's earnings have proven useful in the investment decision. Net income reflects past performance and suggests future performance. Net income can tell financial statement users where the firm has been and, to a more limited degree, where it is going.

In present accounting practice, terms such as *net income* and *net earnings* are used interchangeably, and we make no distinction between them in this textbook. The FASB has indicated that in the future, however, it will attempt to enhance the usefulness of the income measurement by distinguishing between an enterprise's **earnings** and **comprehensive income.** Earnings will be considered a measure of an enterprise's performance during a period and will measure the extent to which revenues and gains associated with cash-to-cash cycles substantially completed during a period exceed expenses and losses associated with the same cycles. Comprehensive income investors follow earnings news so closely. And, he cautions, "there are significant transactions costs with a strategy that follows earnings surprises."

Indeed, using earnings surprises as a stock-picking tool raises portfolio turnover "about 2.5 to 3 times," says Jon T. Ender, chief investment officer at Chicago Corp. Turnover in portfolios using the technique averages 100%-125% a year, he says.

For Mr. Ender, whose firm manages $1.2 billion, the additional brokerage commissions generated by all that trading are a nuisance but not a big burden—especially since the trading seems clearly worthwhile. Mr. Ender estimates that buying on positive surprises and selling on negative ones adds about five percentage points a year to the firm's returns.

Frequent trading is more costly for individual investors. Many small investors pay commissions ranging from 1% to 3% of the value of their trades. For them, trading enough to turn the portfolio over once a year could cost 2% to 6% of assets each year.

Nevertheless, even small investors might benefit from paying attention to earnings surprises, professionals say. Besides the short-term performance effect, there is also the chance that one good surprise will lead to another. On Wall Street, it's called the "cockroach effect"—you rarely see just one.

The odds of a repeat surprise were calculated by Melissa Brown, chief quantitative analyst for Prudential-Bache Securities Inc. Over a recent four-year period, she found, 36% of the companies whose earnings were most above analysts' expectations in a given quarter repeated the feat in the subsequent quarter.

Companies with earnings that are a lot worse than expected also tend to give encore performances. After a negative surprise, says Chicago Corp.'s Mr. Ender, "both the company and many of those following the company think these problems are temporary. But often they reflect competitive disadvantages or problems that take many years to fix."

Not everyone is convinced that the surprise effect is long-lasting. That may have once been the case, but it isn't any more, says Pamela Peterson, associate professor of finance at Florida State University. She says that recent research by her and two graduate students, John Alexander and Delbert Goff, found that stocks move significantly only in a short period surrounding an earnings announcement.

Moreover, some successful investors don't care about earnings surprises because they use strategies that aren't earnings-driven. "We're trying to get a dollar's worth of assets for 50 cents," says S. Edward Moore, a principal with the New York money-management firm Moore, Grossman & DeRose Inc. Accordingly, he pays little attention to earnings surprises—and sometimes views a negative surprise as a buying opportunity. "We're happy to pick up the stock if the street is going to throw it away," he says.

Still, most Wall Streeters believe the weight of the evidence says there is money to be made from following surprises. Jack Rivkin, director of research for Shearson Lehman Hutton Inc., says earnings surprises were one of the best predictors of stock gains in 1988, and in most other recent years.

"When we see surprises on earnings, that is very significant," Mr. Rivkin says. "That means something is going on with the company that we didn't understand, or the world didn't understand."

SOURCE: John R. Dorfman, "Investors Now Can Get Help With 'Earnings Surprises'," *Wall Street Journal* (Monday, August 7, 1989), pp. C1, C21. Reprinted by permission of *Wall Street Journal*, 1989. © Dow Jones Inc., 1989.

will be considered a broad measure comprising all recognized changes in owner's equity except those resulting from investments by owners and distributions to owners. Certain transactions and events (e.g., changes in the market values of investments in marketable equity securities classified as noncurrent assets) will be included in the determination of comprehensive income but will be excluded from earnings. The concepts of earnings and comprehensive income will likely evolve gradually over time. We explain the distinction between these concepts more fully in Chapter 20.

FINANCIAL FORECASTS

Thus far in this chapter we have presented information about *past and current measurements*. However, financial statement users want information about the ability of a business to generate income *in the future*. Some observers have suggested that enterprises could provide this information directly to financial statement users in the form of published financial forecasts.

A **financial forecast** is a presentation that shows an enterprise's *expected* future financial position, results of operations and cash flows based on conditions that management expects to exist and actions it expects to take. A financial forecast contrasts with a **financial projection**, which shows future financial position, results of operations, and cash flows that would exist if one or more *hypothetical* (but not expected) assumptions occurred. In other words, forecasts present what management expects to happen, whereas projections present what would happen if certain unexpected events (e.g., a labor strike) occurred. At the present time, neither of these two types of **prospective financial statements** is required by GAAP. However, some companies have in the past voluntarily disclosed financial forecasts, and considerable discussion has taken place about the desirability of requiring the publication of forecasts by all companies as a part of GAAP.

The construction of a financial forecast requires assumptions about the future state of the overall economy and the interaction of the firm with the economy. The accuracy of the forecasts is directly related to the accuracy of these assumptions. As a result, some people have advocated the publication of a range of forecasts during a given period. In this way, financial statement users would be aware of management's range of expectations, from pessimistic to optimistic, and could then select a scenario consistent with their own expectations.

In 1973 the Securities and Exchange Commission (SEC) reversed its long-standing opposition to public disclosure of financial forecasts by issuing guidelines for voluntary disclosures to be filed with the Commission. Since that time there has been a great deal of controversy about mandated public disclosure of financial forecasts. Various surveys have found widespread dissatisfaction with the concept of published financial forecasts.[21] Moreover, very few companies publish financial forecasts. In the rest of this section we briefly discuss the arguments favoring and opposing public disclosure of financial forecasts.

BENEFITS OF PUBLIC DISCLOSURE

The major argument in favor of the required disclosure of financial forecasts is that it would provide useful information to users of financial statements. Proponents of required financial forecasts have argued that forecasts are essential for making more accurate predictions, which lead to informed investment and credit decisions. Investors and creditors could benefit from financial forecasts by learning about management's plans and expectations. Relative to the outside investor, management generally knows more about the firm and at least as much about the impact of the external environment.

Managers could also benefit by the publication of financial forecasts. Financial forecasts put managers' reputations at stake and there is strong incentive to achieve the forecasted figures. Moreover, preparing forecasts for publication forces managers to plan for the future. Such planning may enable managers to take advantage of opportunities and avoid mistakes in judgment.

Some people have argued that reporting forecasts is in the public interest because it reduces the opportunities for privileged insiders to profit from information that is not publicly available. Further, some have argued that certain forecasted information regularly appears in sources such as *The Wall Street Journal,* but the forecasts do not contain management's assumptions and are not subjected to the rigorous standards that would be applied if forecasts were a required part of GAAP.

---

[21]See, for example, *Public Accounting in Transition: A Survey by Opinion Research Corporation* (Chicago: Arthur Andersen & Co., 1974), pp. 106, 107.

COSTS OF PUBLIC DISCLOSURE

The publication of financial forecasts has some serious limitations. A major concern is the possible misinterpretation of the forecasts by financial statement users. Because many investors are untrained in the interpretation of financial forecasts, they are likely to be unaware of the uncertainty of forecasts. Statement users may also have difficulty interpreting the variety of assumptions underlying the forecast. Moreover, across various firms, different forecast assumptions would lead to difficulty in comparing forecasts.

Another possible source of misinterpretation is management's tendency to bias forecasts. Managers may present overly optimistic forecasts to place the firm in the most favorable light. Such forecasts may help the firm obtain bank loans or may raise the stock price, but they may also harm unwary investors as the actual operating results emerge. Likewise, managers may decide to play it safe by issuing overly conservative forecasts that are nearly certain to be attained. If the forecast is exceeded, all the better. Unfortunately, the outside investor may be misled into selling the stock or avoiding its initial purchase, only to find that the company was more prosperous than anticipated.

This limitation can be mitigated by having an independent auditor examine the reasonableness of the assumptions. The auditor's report would state that an examination of the underlying assumptions was made and that they were found reasonable. However, because assumptions can prove faulty, the report is not a guarantee of future performance.

Management has long opposed the publication of financial forecasts because of the possible disclosure of sensitive information, such as major marketing, product, or investment strategies. Competitors could develop counter-strategies to block the firm from realizing its goals. This, of course, would not benefit the forecasting company or its shareholders.

Another serious limitation of financial forecasts is the potential legal liability. What happens if actual results deviate sharply from the forecast? Blaming management for inaccurate forecasts is questionable when there has been an honest attempt to plan properly, make full disclosure, and manage as efficiently as possible. For example, the airlines could not have predicted the effect of the 1973 oil embargo on their operating costs. To hold the airlines responsible for inaccurate forecasts under these circumstances would be inequitable.

Some observers argue further that managers should not engage in the investment function by making financial forecasts. These critics suggest that financial forecasting is largely the domain of investors, who either reap the rewards of accurate forecasting or incur the penalty of inaccurate forecasting. Harvey Kapnick of Arthur Andersen & Co. has stated that "predictions of the future must be the responsibility of the investor. This is the essence of risk taking, and predicting and interpreting the future is the primary function in investment evaluation. No one can take to insure [through lawsuits] the results of future events."[22]

SUMMARY

The issue of mandated disclosure of financial forecasts will be controversial for some time. The SEC and the FASB have been emphasizing disclosures that have a future orientation. In contrast, most managers have opposed the concept for most of the reasons listed above. In terms of the qualitative characteristics we presented in Chapter

---

[22]"Forecasting Earnings," *Forbes* (December 1, 1972), p. 37.

2, proponents of financial forecasts tend to argue that forecasts are relevant while opponents argue that the information lacks sufficient reliability. At this time it is difficult to predict the outcome of this controversy.

CONCLUDING REMARKS

Financial accounting is constantly changing to achieve greater relevance and reliability. It is a discipline that has many interesting, conceptual controversies. An understanding of only the present system of GAAP will not likely be adequate for a person whose future career will be spent preparing or using financial statements. Indeed, the educational process of the professional accountant (and other professional persons) is continuous. You should think of a degree program in business as a foundation on which to build knowledge and skills that will adapt to changing circumstances in an exciting world.

In this chapter, we have presented a conceptual discussion of the nature and measurement of the elements of financial statements. Throughout this discussion we have presented alternatives to the present accounting model to acquaint you with not only what is presently accepted but also what may be generally accepted in the future. An understanding of this chapter should broaden your understanding of accounting and should allow you to accommodate more contemporary accounting ideas. Moreover, this conceptual material should enhance your understanding of present generally accepted accounting principles. Current practice employs, to varying degrees, many of the ideas and valuation methods discussed in this chapter.

In Chapter 26 we use in more practical applications many of the concepts discussed in this chapter. In Chapter 4 we extend our presentation of GAAP for external reporting with an overview of the major financial statements.

KEY POINTS

1. Measurement refers to the assignment of numbers to objects and events. To measure the elements of financial statements, we must select a measuring unit and a financial attribute to measure. (Objective 1)

2. The measuring units that have been suggested for use in financial statements are nominal dollars and constant dollars. A nominal dollar has not been adjusted for inflation or deflation; a constant dollar has been adjusted. Conventional financial statements use nominal dollars. (Objective 1)

3. A general price-level index indicates changes over time in the overall level of prices in the economy. A specific price index indicates changes over time in the price of a specific good or service. (Objective 1)

4. Purchasing power gains and losses are reported when financial statements are presented in constant dollars. These gains and losses result from holding monetary assets or liabilities during periods of inflation or deflation. (Objective 1)

5. Assets are probable future economic benefits that accrue to an entity as a result of past transactions or events. (Objective 2)

6. Financial attributes of assets include historical cost, current cost, current exit value in orderly liquidation, expected exit value in due course of business, and present value of expected cash flows. Conventional financial statements reflect a mixture of these attributes, although historical cost is emphasized. (Objective 2)

7. Liabilities are probable future sacrifices of economic benefits that obligate an entity to transfer assets or perform services in the future as a result of past transactions or events. (Objective 2)

8. Important issues in liability measurement are (1) whether the interest inherent in a liability should be recognized separately, and (2) what interest rate should be used to recognize the interest. (Objective 2)

9. Financial attributes of liabilities include present value of expected cash flows, expected exit value in due course of business, historical proceeds, current proceeds, and current exit value in orderly liquidation. Conceptually, a liability should be measured on a present value basis; many liabilities are measured this way under GAAP. (Objective 2)

10. Owners' equity equals net assets, which are assets minus liabilities. Owners' equity is not measured as an independent element of financial statements. Instead, its valuation depends on the valuations assigned to the individual assets and liabilities. (Objective 2)

11. Net income measures the change in net assets for a period of time, assuming no new capital contributions by the owners or dividend distributions by the business. (Objective 3)

12. Net income should be recognized only after the capital used from the beginning of the period is maintained. (Objective 3)

13. Lifetime net income is the total income of an enterprise from inception to termination. Lifetime revenues of an enterprise equal the total cash received from earning activities, and lifetime expenses equal the total cash disbursed for earning activities. (Objective 3)

14. Periodic net income is the change in the wealth of a business over a short period of time, generally one year. (Objective 3)

15. Accrual basis accounting is generally preferred over cash basis accounting, because earnings disclosures are more timely and less subject to meaningless fluctuations. (Objective 3)

16. Net income measurement under accrual accounting depends on the valuation concepts used to measure assets and liabilities. Unlike lifetime net income, periodic net income is affected by the valuation concepts employed. (Objective 3)

17. Net income is composed of revenues, expenses, gains, and losses. Each component can be defined by the asset/liability or the revenue/expense view. According to the asset/liability view, the components of net income are defined by direct reference to definitions of assets and liabilities. Under the revenue/expense view, the components of net income are defined without reference to definitions of assets and liabilities. Both concepts are used in practice, but the FASB supports the asset/liability view. (Objective 3)

18. Strong evidence supports both the usefulness and timeliness of accounting net income. (Objective 4)

19. Accounting net income can be used to evaluate past performance and predict future earnings. (Objective 4)

20. Financial forecasts represent certain financial expectations of management. Considerable controversy presently exists about the possibility of requiring the publication of financial forecasts. The majority opinion today appears to be that the benefits of providing useful information, of providing certain managerial incentives, reducing insider profits, and of improving the forecast information that is currently published are outweighed by the costs of misinterpretation, biased forecasts, competitive disadvantages, potential legal liability, and the philosophy that future predictions are the responsibility of investors and creditors, not accountants. (Objective 5)

QUESTIONS

3–1 What does "measurement" mean? Why is measurement important in accounting?

3–2 What is the difference between nominal dollars and constant dollars? Which one of these measuring units does GAAP require? Why?

3–3 What is the difference between a general price-level index and a specific price index?

3–4 What are purchasing power gains and losses? Are they reported in conventional financial statements? Explain why or why not.

3–5 Identify three essential characteristics of assets and give ten examples of assets under GAAP.

3–6   Identify and define the financial attributes that may be used when measuring assets.

3–7   Identify three essential characteristics of liabilities and give ten examples of liabilities under GAAP.

3–8   Identify and define the financial attributes that may be used to measure liabilities.

3–9   What does the term "owners' equity" mean? How does owners' equity differ from liabilities? Give five examples of items classified as owners' equity under GAAP.

3–10   How is owners' equity measured in conventional financial statements?

3–11   Provide a conceptual definition of net income.

3–12   Explain the term "capital maintenance." Why is this concept important in determining income for a period?

3–13   What is lifetime net income? What are some distinguishing characteristics of lifetime net income? How does lifetime net income differ from periodic net income?

3–14   Define cash basis accounting. What are some disadvantages of this system?

3–15   Define accrual basis accounting. How can this system produce different periodic net income numbers for the same periods?

3–16   What are the advantages and disadvantages of using historical cost to determine income?

3–17   What are the components of net income? How are they similar?

3–18   How does the revenue/expense view differ from the asset/liability view?

3–19   Is accounting net income a useful number? What are the uses of the accounting net income disclosure?

3–20   What is a financial forecast? What are the major advantages and disadvantages of published forecasts?

PROBLEMS   **3–21**   NOMINAL-DOLLAR VERSUS CONSTANT-DOLLAR MEASUREMENT   Jim Arnold invested $300,000 in a parcel of land on January 1, 1993. He sold the land for $320,000 on December 31, 1993. The Consumer Price Index for All Urban Consumers was 100 on January 1, 1993, and 110 on December 31, 1993.

Instructions

[a] Compute the gain or loss on the sale in accordance with GAAP. Ignore income taxes.
[b] Compute the gain or loss on the sale in constant end-of-1993 dollars. Ignore income taxes.
[c] Based only on the information presented above, was Arnold better or worse off at the end of 1993 than at the beginning? Explain your answer.
[d] In your opinion, should financial statements continue to emphasize the nominal dollar measuring unit, or should they emphasize the constant dollar measuring unit? Present arguments that support your position.

3–22   NOMINAL-DOLLAR VERSUS CONSTANT-DOLLAR MEASUREMENT   At the beginning of 1993, Anne Reed purchased 2,000 shares of Lambert Company's common stock for $50 per share. During 1993 the general price level *declined* by 10%. At the end of 1993 Reed sold the 2,000 shares for $48 per share.

Instructions

[a] Compute the gain or loss on the sale in accordance with GAAP. Ignore income taxes.
[b] Compute the gain or loss on the sale in constant end-of-1993 dollars. Ignore income taxes.
[c] Based only on the information presented above, was Reed better or worse off at the end of 1993 than at the beginning? Explain your answer.
[d] Did Reed have a purchasing power gain during 1993? Did she have a purchasing power loss during 1993? Explain your answers.

3–23   PURCHASING POWER GAINS AND LOSSES   On January 1, 1993, Rice, Inc., sold merchandise to Tully, Inc. for $180,000 on account. Inflation was 10% during 1993, and as of December 31, 1993, Rice had not received the $180,000 payment due from Tully.

Instructions

[a] Calculate the amount of purchasing power gain or loss for Rice and for Tully.

[b] Explain why each company had a purchasing power gain or loss.

[c] Are purchasing power gains and losses reported in conventional financial statements? Why or why not?

3–24   NATURE OF ASSETS   You have been asked to determine whether each of the following items is an asset of Purdy Company.

[1] One hundred shares of IBM's common stock that Purdy has purchased.

[2] A county-owned road constructed on land owned by Purdy.

[3] An order placed by Purdy for merchandise that the supplier has in a warehouse and will ship in 10 days.

[4] A patent, owned by Purdy, to produce a drug that has been linked to cancer and banned by the Food and Drug Administration. The drug will not be sold anywhere in the world.

[5] Ten $1,000, 12%, 20-year bonds of Chrysler Corporation that Purdy has purchased.

[6] The excellent credit reputation that Purdy has earned in the business community.

[7] A note receivable from a debtor who has been declared bankrupt and will not pay the amount owed to Purdy.

[8] A franchise that Purdy has acquired to market a successful product in three states.

[9] An order received from a customer for merchandise that Purdy will ship in five days.

[10] A machine that Purdy has purchased and received from a manufacturer.

[11] Merchandise owned by Jasper Company that Purdy is holding on consignment. (Purdy is the consignee or selling agent and will try to sell the goods for Jasper.)

[12] A noncancelable lease that gives Purdy the right to use a machine owned by Scott Company for five years, which is the estimated economic life of the machine.

[13] Cash received from a customer who has placed a prepaid order for merchandise to be shipped by Purdy in 30 days.

[14] A privately owned park that Purdy has built on its own land and that often is used by the city for sporting events.

[15] A parcel of land that has been given to Purdy by the county.

Instructions

Indicate whether each of the above items is an asset of Purdy Company, according to GAAP. Briefly explain the reason for each decision.

3–25   NATURE OF LIABILITIES   You have been asked to determine whether each of the following items is a liability of Vinci Company on December 31, 1993.

[1] The cash outlay expected to be made on January 7, 1994, to purchase equipment on that date.

[2] The amount expected to be needed to provide warranty services to customers for products sold before the end of 1993.

[3] The expected cash outlay for employee wages that will be earned during 1994.

[4] The obligation to provide future issues of a monthly newsletter for which subscriptions were prepaid during 1993.

[5] The obligation to provide merchandise to a customer who submitted a prepaid order on December 10, 1993.

[6] The obligation to fill orders expected to be made by regular customers during 1994.

[7] An obligation to distribute shares of Vinci's own common stock to Vinci's stockholders as a result of a 10% stock dividend declared on December 15, 1993, and distributable on January 10, 1994.

[8] The obligation that may be required to settle a lawsuit against Vinci Company that is pending on December 31, 1993. Vinci's attorneys expect to win the case.

Bonds Payable

[9] The obligation to retire at maturity $100,000, 12%, 10-year bonds issued at par value on December 31, 1993. (Interest on the bonds is to be paid annually, beginning on December 31, 1994.) _- No_

[10] The obligation to pay $120,000 interest ($100,000 × 12% × 10 years) on the bonds in [9] above.

[11] The burden associated with having earned a poor credit reputation during 1993.

[12] The obligation to provide office space to a tenant who paid six months of rent in advance on December 31, 1993.

Instructions

Indicate whether each of the above items is a liability, according to GAAP, of Vinci Company on December 31, 1993. Briefly explain the reason for each decision.

3–26 CASH VERSUS ACCRUAL MEASUREMENTS Violet Company employs ten people. Salaries are paid biweekly, and certain employees occasionally receive salary advances. The company also owns several warehouses that it leases to various tenants. Some tenants are required to pay rent before using the warehouses while others are allowed to use the warehouses before paying rent.

Violet Company uses the conventional accrual basis of accounting, as required under GAAP. The amount of salaries expense for 1993 was $91,000, and the amount of cash received from warehouse tenants was $137,000. Selected information obtained from the company's comparative balance sheets is shown below:

	Dec. 31, 1992	Dec. 31, 1993
Prepaid salaries	$ 1,000	$ 3,000 _A↑ 2000_
Accrued salaries payable	5,000	2,500 _L ↓ 2500_
Rent receivable	10,000	7,000 _A ↓ 3000_
Unearned rent revenue	18,000	25,000 _↑L 7000_

Instructions

[a] Compute the amount of cash paid for salaries during 1993.

[b] Compute the amount of rent revenue for 1993.

3–27 CASH VERSUS ACCRUAL MEASUREMENTS Raney Company employs several consulting companies. Some consulting companies require payments in advance of performing services while others bill Raney Company after the services are rendered. Raney Company also leases office space to several law firms. Some law firms are required to pay rent in advance of using their offices while others are allowed to use their offices before paying rent.

Raney Company uses the conventional accrual basis of accounting, as required under GAAP. The amount of cash paid to consulting companies during 1993 was $48,000, and the amount of rent revenue earned from leasing office space was $66,000. Selected information obtained from the company's comparative balance sheets is shown below:

	Dec. 31, 1992	Dec. 31, 1993
_CA↑_ Prepaid consulting fees	$ 2,000	$5,000 _↑3000_
_CL↓_ Accrued consulting fees payable	7,000	2,000 _↓5000_
_CA↑_ Rent receivable	6,000	8,000 _↑ 2000_
_CL↓_ Unearned rent revenue	10,000	4,000 _↓ 6000_

Instructions

[a] Compute the amount of consulting expense for 1993.

[b] Compute the amount of cash received from leasing office space during 1993.

3–28 CASH VERSUS ACCRUAL STATEMENTS During the last four months of the academic year, the yearbook committee of Mayfield State University produced and distributed the university's yearbook. The yearbook was published in April at a cost of $15 a copy. The selling price was $22.00 each. If ordered in advance, the yearbook sold for $18.00. The committee estimated that 9,000 yearbooks would be sold for the 1992–93 academic year.

In February the yearbook committee authorized the payment of $1,500, which was the amount left from last year's yearbook sales, to the local newspaper, the campus newspaper, and a local radio station for advertising to be provided in March. In March advance payments for 5,000 yearbooks were received. The printing of 9,000 yearbooks was completed in April and paid for on April 30. The difference between the cash on hand and the printing costs was made up by a short-term loan. In May all advance orders were filled and 3,500 more yearbooks were sold on a cash basis. The short-term loan of April was paid off in May, including an interest charge of $500. The unsold yearbooks were considered worthless and were therefore destroyed.

Instructions

[a] Prepare both cash basis and accrual basis income statements and balance sheets for February, March, April, and May. (The difference between assets and liabilities is termed "fund balance," because the yearbook operation has no owners.)

[b] What is the total income from the yearbook sales for the 1992–93 academic year under each method?

[c] From this problem, what is an obvious limitation of a cash-based system?

3–29 MEASUREMENT OF INCOME Beau Hanna Sales Company, an automobile dealership, started business on January 1, 1992, with $42,900 in cash. Hanna decided to "wait out" the current model year and start purchasing inventory when the 1993 models became available. As a result the Hanna dealership purchased four new 1993 model automobiles on September 1, 1992. The costs of the new 1993 models were as follows:

Model	Cost
Astra	$ 8,800
Blaze	9,900
Cortez Deluxe	11,000
Dynasty Wagon	13,200

On November 1, the dealership sold the Astra for $10,340. On December 30, the manufacturer increased the wholesale price on the 1993 models by 10%. Hanna believed he could sell the Blaze, Cortez, and Dynasty for $12,210, $14,080, and $17,270, respectively, on December 31. The salesmen's commissions were equal to 5% of the sales price. During calendar year 1993 the Blaze was sold for $12,430 and the Cortez for $14,410. Hanna still held the 1993 Dynasty Wagon on the lot as of October 1, 1993. He discounted the vehicle and finally sold it for $14,630 on October 15. On December 31, 1993, Beau Hanna Sales Company ceased operations.

Instructions

[a] Determine the net income for Beau Hanna Sales Company for calendar years 1992 and 1993, assuming the automobile inventory is valued under (1) historical cost, (2) current cost, and (3) current exit value.

[b] What is the lifetime net income of the Hanna dealership under each valuation method?

[c] Which pattern of income flows do you believe is most fair and reasonable?

3–30 MEASUREMENT OF INCOME On January 1, 1992, Belly Beer Company began business with an $880,000 cash investment. The company did not intend to brew beer from raw materials but to use a newly developed aging process on beer purchased wholesale from other producers. After two years of aging by this special process, a top-quality premium beer was to result. One beer distributor was so impressed with the aging process that a contract was made for 20,000 barrels at a price of $60 a barrel, to be delivered and paid for on December 31, 1993.

On January 1, 1992, Belly purchased 20,000 barrels of freshly brewed beer at $20 a barrel in order to start the aging process, which cost $1 per barrel per month. On December 31, 1992, the wholesale price of beer aged one year was $38 a barrel. The company estimated it could sell the beer for $45 a barrel after only one year of aging. On December 31, 1993, the aging process was completed and the beer was delivered to the distributor.

Instructions

[a] Prepare balance sheets for December 31, 1992, for Belly Beer Company under the following four valuation methods: (1) historical cost, (2) current cost, (3) current exit value, and (4) expected exit value.

[b] What is the reported net income for 1992 and 1993 under each valuation method?

[c] Which pattern of income flows do you believe is most fair and reasonable?

3–31   CASH VERSUS ACCRUAL STATEMENTS   Bass State University's 1992–93 basketball season began on December 1, 1992, and will end on March 31, 1993. The BSU basketball arena (fully depreciated) holds 15,000 fans. The *number of home dates* per month are as follows: December, 7; January, 5; February, 5; and March, 5.

Five thousand seats per game are reserved for the BSU students at an admission price of $5 per student per game. The remaining seats are sold to alumni and other fans at a season ticket cost of $308. Season ticket orders are mailed on November 30. Season ticket holders have the choice of paying the $308 as a lump sum by December 6 (the first home date) or using a payment plan of $77 per month with the first payment due by December 7. Forty percent of the season ticket holders choose the payment plan.

The university also operates the concession stands, which cost $3,000 per game and generate $8,000 in cash revenues per game. All concession items are purchased COD seven days before a home date. There is no ending inventory of concession stand items on December 31.

The major cost to the university in managing the arena is the utility bill for heat and lighting. The university receives the utility bill on the fifth of each month for the previous month's usage. The arena uses no heat or lighting in the off season. Monthly usage during the basketball season is $240,000. Arena workers receive wages on a per game basis and are paid on the day following a home date. The payroll cost for a home date is $12,000. In addition, the university insures the arena at a cost of $24,000 per year. The insurance is paid in advance each December 1. The arena had $3,000 cash left from the preceding basketball season.

On December 31, 1992, after a particularly exciting game in which BSU upset their conference rival, the president of the university asks you to prepare financial statements for December. The president noticed that the arena was sold out for each of the home dates in December and, as a result, wants to know how much cash the arena operation is generating.

Instructions

[a] Prepare for the president an income statement for December and a balance sheet on December 31, 1992, under a cash basis assumption. Develop an alternative set of statements under an accrual approach. (Identify the difference between assets and liabilities as "fund balance" rather than owners' equity, because a university does not have shareholders.)

[b] Assuming the arena is used only for basketball, what will the arena operation earn for the period from December 1, 1992, to November 30, 1993?

[c] Show the president the shortcomings of cash basis financial statements in evaluating the arena's operating performance for December.

CASES

3–32   INCOME AND INFLATION   The Whitfield Company was formed on January 1, 1992. On that date, stockholders contributed $100,000 to the company in exchange for 10,000 shares of Whitfield's common stock. The company placed the $100,000 in a noninterest-bearing checking account. For various unforeseen reasons, the company engaged in no further transactions during 1992. On December 31, 1992, the company still had $100,000 in its checking account. Assume the inflation rate during 1992 was 10%.

Instructions

[a] According to GAAP, what is the amount of Whitfield's net income (loss) for 1992? Explain your answer.

[b] In an economic sense, would Whitfield Company generally be considered better off or worse off at the end of 1992 than at the beginning? Explain your answer.

[c] If you were in charge of setting GAAP, how much net income (loss) would you require Whitfield to report for 1992? Explain your answer.

3–33   NATURE OF LIABILITIES   Many companies promise to pay the cost of their employees' health care after they retire. In the past, generally accepted accounting principles have not required companies to include among their liabilities the obligations for postretirement health care benefits. Instead, companies have simply accounted for these costs as expenses when the costs were paid, which of course was after the employees retired. This is sometimes referred to as a "pay as you go" basis of accounting for these costs.

The FASB has recently studied this accounting issue and has argued that companies should be required to account for the cost of postretirement health care benefits during the periods in which the employees work for the company (i.e., before the employees retire). Such accounting would force many companies to report very large expenses and liabilities in their financial statements.

Many corporate managers have objected to the FASB's position, stating that such accounting is too imprecise and would cause many companies to drop or reduce postretirement health care benefits. The managers also claim that the FASB's approach would substantially reduce corporate net income and stockholders' equity and that some companies may even be forced to cut expenses in other vital areas, such as research and development.

In response to the managers' arguments, the FASB has argued that companies should be required to account for all of their obligations. Companies should not be excused from accounting for obligations just because they can only be estimated or because they adversely affect the company's financial statements.

Instructions

[a] Explain the theoretical rationale that supports the FASB's position on the accounting issue described above.

[b] Explain why you agree or disagree with the FASB's position.

[c] What is your opinion of the validity of the arguments that the corporate managers have raised?

3–34 MEASUREMENT OF LIABILITIES On January 1, 1993, Hay Company borrowed $50,000 cash from Culver Company by signing a $50,000, 12%, two-year promissory note calling for interest of $6,000 ($50,000 × 12% = $6,000) to be paid at the end of 1993 and 1994. On that date the market rate of interest for similar notes was 12%.

On December 31, 1993, Hay paid the $6,000 interest for 1993. At that time the market rate of interest for notes similar to the one issued by Hay was 14%.

As the controller for Hay, you are trying to determine the amount the company should report for the note payable on December 31, 1993, in a balance sheet prepared in accordance with GAAP. You are considering the following alternatives:

[1] Report the note payable at $56,000. This amount equals the face amount of the note plus the interest that must be paid at the end of 1994 ($50,000 + $6,000 = $56,000).

[2] Report the note payable at $49,122.81. This amount equals the amount in [1] above, discounted for one year at the current market interest rate of 14% ($56,000 ÷ 1.14 = $49,122.81).

[3] Report the note payable at $50,000. This amount equals the amount in [1] above, discounted for one year at the market interest rate of 12% that was in effect when the note was issued ($56,000 ÷ 1.12 = $50,000).

Instructions

Which of the above alternatives should you select? Explain your answer.

3–35 LIABILITIES VERSUS OWNERS' EQUITY Jane Curren, an accountant employed by Ness Company, has asked for your help in deciding whether each of the items listed below should be reported in Ness Company's balance sheet as a liability or as stockholders' equity:

[1] An issue of subordinated income bonds that mature in 10 years. The bonds provide for interest at an annual rate of 12%, to be paid only in those years during which the company's income is sufficient to cover the interest.

[2] An issue of preferred stock that Ness is required to redeem on specified future dates. The stock confers no voting rights and has a stated cumulative dividend rate of 12%.

[3] An issue of preferred stock that Ness has an option to redeem at any time. The stock confers no voting rights and has a stated cumulative dividend rate of 13%.

Instructions

[a] Explain how the substance over form modifying convention relates to the reporting problem indicated above.

[b] Indicate whether each item listed above should be classified as a liability or as stockholders' equity. Explain your answers.

3–36 MEASUREMENT OF STOCKHOLDERS' EQUITY   On December 31, 1993, Raines Corporation reported total assets of $10,000,000, total liabilities of $4,000,000, and total stockholders' equity of $6,000,000. The stockholders' equity consisted of common stock of $1,000,000 and retained earnings of $5,000,000. Raines had 100,000 shares of $10 par value common stock outstanding on December 31, 1993, and the market price per share on that date was $70.

Instructions

[a] Explain how stockholders' equity is measured in conventional accounting.
[b] Explain why the reported stockholders' equity of $6,000,000 does not equal the ending market price per share multiplied by the shares outstanding ($70 × 100,000 = $7,000,000).

3–37 CASH VERSUS ACCRUAL DISCUSSION   Fishback Foundation is a not-for-profit organization dedicated to the support of the arts in the surrounding communities. The large foundation has investments in real estate, stocks and bonds, and mortgages, as well as unpaid pledges from supporters. The real estate investments have outstanding mortgages. The foundation has been operating its accounting system on a cash basis since its inception in 1956. The trustees have embarked on a program to increase foundation activities, including an aggressive annual fund-raising campaign.

The trustees have decided that the foundation's accounting records should be audited annually and have engaged a CPA firm to conduct the first audit. One of the auditors recommends that the foundation convert its accounting system to an accrual basis from the cash basis. The auditor has stated that accrual accounting is used in profit-making companies but has not been used extensively in governmental or not-for-profit organizations. The auditor believes that accrual accounting has many advantages and would be very useful for Fishback Foundation.

Instructions

[a] Describe how the foundation's statement of financial position and statement of receipts and disbursements prepared on an accrual basis would differ from those prepared on a cash basis.
[b] Identify and briefly explain the advantages accrual accounting provides to profit-making companies that would also be applicable to Fishback Foundation.
[c] Explain how the trustees' ability to evaluate the performance of the foundation's executive director would be improved if the foundation used financial statements prepared on the accrual basis rather than the cash basis method of accounting.   (CMA adapted)

3–38 MEASUREMENT OF INCOME   Larry Jones bought a four-bedroom home on January 1, 1992, for $285,000 cash. After this purchase Jones had only $45,000 cash left in his noninterest-bearing checking account. On December 31, 1992, Jones could sell his house for $360,000 cash. At that time he could engage in one of the following independent transactions:

[1] Sell the house and buy a similar four-bedroom home in the same town for $360,000.
[2] Sell the house and buy a similar four-bedroom home in another region of the country for $285,000.
[3] Sell the house and buy a similar four-bedroom home in another region of the country for $405,000.
[4] Sell the house and buy a six-bedroom home in the same town for $405,000.
[5] Not sell the house.

Instructions

[a] Determine the 1992 income (gain) Jones would record for each of the independent situations above, according to GAAP. Assume no transaction costs or taxes. Also assume that Jones is indifferent about regional location, and that all houses are of similar construction quality.
[b] How well does GAAP capture the economic substance of each transaction above?

3–39 ASSET/LIABILITY VERSUS REVENUE/EXPENSE VIEW   The following definitions of assets and liabilities are given in *Accounting Terminology Bulletin No. 1* (New York: AICPA, 1953), pars. 26 and 27:

Asset—something represented by a debit balance that is or would be properly carried forward upon a closing of books of account according to the rules or principles of accounting.

Liability—something represented by a credit balance that is or would be properly carried forward upon a closing of books of account according to the rules or principles of accounting.

Instructions

Are the above definitions consistent with the asset/liability or the revenue/expense view? What deficiencies can you identify in the above definitions?

3–40   USEFULNESS OF FORECASTS   You and a friend are discussing whether corporate managers should be required to report financial forecasts in their companies' published annual reports. Your friend argues, "forecasts are useful information because investors and creditors want to know as much as possible about the future when they make their decisions. Usefulness is the primary objective of corporate financial reporting. Therefore, if information is useful, then GAAP should require companies to report it."

Instructions

[a] If a certain type of information really is useful, should GAAP require companies to report it?
[b] Summarize the arguments for and against the required disclosure of financial forecasts.
[c] In your opinion, should companies be required to disclose financial forecasts? Defend your answer.

3–41   FORECAST CONSIDERATIONS AND ASSUMPTIONS   Eagle Electronics is a new company in the high-growth electronics field. It produces a unique electronic test package for the defense industry. Eagle Electronics, which has been run very successfully as a private company for two years, will be making its first public offering of common stock within the next month. Naturally, the company wants to obtain the highest-price possible for the new offering. The treasurer of the company, Sam Easton, has suggested that the publication of a three-year earnings forecast may enhance the offering price of the new shares.

Instructions

What factors must Easton consider in the construction of the earnings forecast? What shortcomings in the public disclosure of financial forecasts should Easton be aware of?

3–42   FORECAST CONSIDERATIONS AND ASSUMPTIONS   Hotel management must make many assumptions in constructing financial forecasts. Listed below are some variables management may have to consider in making a financial forecast.

[1] Gasoline prices   [4] Characteristics of automobiles
[2] Aging population   [5] Land values
[3] Financing costs   [6] General economic conditions

The following background information comes from the annual report of Dreamy Inns of America, a fast-growing national motel chain.

> *The market which Dreamy Inns serves is broad and rapidly growing. Responding to today's more demanding traveler, we offer quality lodgings at better prices than our competitors. We cut out such expensive frills as elaborate lobbies, convention space, and meeting halls, and we pass the savings on to our guests. We offer all of the conveniences that travelers appreciate. Each of our strategically located properties provides a cluster of services in one convenient location—lodging, food, gasoline, gifts, and souvenirs.*

Instructions

Explain how each of the above variables may be interpreted by the managers of Dreamy Inns of America in constructing a financial forecast.

CHAPTER 4

Basic Financial Statements

1. To describe the major characteristics of basic financial statements.
2. To discuss and illustrate most major components of the income statement.
3. To discuss and illustrate the statement of retained earnings and the statement of stockholders' equity.
4. To discuss and illustrate the balance sheet, including the major classifications commonly used.
5. To provide a general introduction to the statement of cash flows.
6. To provide a general introduction to certain other topics related to basic financial statements.

CHARACTERISTICS OF BASIC FINANCIAL STATEMENTS

W hat was the net income of Exxon last year? Was this figure large or small in relation to the company's sales and to its stockholders' equity? What was the relationship last year between IBM's dividends and earnings? What proportion of General Motors' assets at the end of last year did the company finance through debt? How did General Electric use its cash last year? These are a few of the many questions that investors, creditors, and other users seek to answer based on information presented in the companies' financial statements.

The basic financial statements are the **balance sheet,** the **income statement,** the **statement of cash flows,** and the **statement of retained earnings** (or **statement of stockholders' equity**). Companies usually present basic financial statements in their annual reports to shareholders and in other disclosure media. The balance sheet summarizes the financial position of an enterprise **at a particular point in time.** The other basic statements summarize various changes in financial position that have occurred **during a period of time.**

Basic financial statements have several important characteristics:

1. They are only a **subset,** although an important subset, of the information needed by users for making rational investment, lending, and similar decisions.
2. They are primarily **historical** in nature.
3. They **summarize** information.
4. They reflect many **estimates.**
5. They are **general-purpose** reports designed to serve the needs of many different users.
6. They **articulate** with one another (i.e., they are **interrelated**).

In this chapter we review the form and content of the basic financial statements. In subsequent chapters we discuss aspects of these statements in greater detail and thereby develop the statements more fully.

This chapter presents the statements in the order in which accountants typically prepare them (i.e., income statement; statement of retained earnings, or statement of stockholders' equity; balance sheet; and statement of cash flows). To emphasize the interrelatedness of basic financial statements, the chapter illustrates a set of statements prepared for the Sunrise Corporation.[1]

INCOME STATEMENT

The **income statement,** generally regarded as the most important financial statement, is used in two major ways:

1. **To predict cash flows.** Users of financial statements typically invest or lend cash, and they want to know *how much* cash they will receive in return and *when* they will receive it. Knowledge of a company's past income and its components helps users to predict more accurately the company's income and to better assess their own chances of receiving cash from the company.

---

[1]A complete set of financial statements of Strawbridge & Clothier (a retail company that sells general merchandise) is presented in the Appendix and inside the front and back covers of this book.

The authors recommend *Accounting Trends and Techniques* for additional examples of disclosures made in financial statements. This annual publication of the American Institute of Certified Public Accountants is based on a survey of the annual reports to shareholders of 600 companies.

2. To evaluate management's performance.   Users regard the income statement as an important indication of management's success. Stockholders typically want to reward good managers and replace poor ones.

From a societal standpoint, measurements reported on the income statement help to ensure that we put our scarce resources to their best uses and that the goods and services we want are available. If a company produces and distributes its products successfully, it should earn income. Moreover, a record of profitable operations should help the company to raise capital and other resources. Generally, resources should flow into companies that have unusually high incomes and out of those that sustain losses.

ELEMENTS OF THE INCOME STATEMENT

Accountants traditionally have measured a company's income by focusing on transactions that caused changes in the company's assets and liabilities during a period of time. These transactions include revenues, expenses, gains, and losses. As you might expect, accountants disagree about the best way to measure these components of a company's income. For example, we could measure expenses using current costs, opportunity costs, or historical costs. Traditionally, accountants have relied primarily on historical costs. Income measurement in conventional accounting involves primarily the **revenue realization, matching,** and **asset/liability measurement** principles, as discussed in Chapter 2.

Revenue Realization

Matching

Asset/Liability Measurement

The fundamental elements of the income statement and their relationships to net income are demonstrated in the following equation:

$$\text{Revenues} - \text{Expenses} + \text{Gains} - \text{Losses} = \text{Net income}$$

A review of several definitions presented in Chapter 2 is appropriate at this point:[2]

1. **Revenues.**   Inflows or other enhancements of assets of an entity or settlements of its liabilities (or both) during a period, based on production and delivery of goods, provision of services, and other activities that constitute the entity's major operations.
2. **Expenses.**   Outflows or other use of assets or incurrences of liabilities (or both) during a period as a result of delivering or producing goods, rendering services, or carrying out other activities that constitute the entity's major operations.
3. **Costs.**   Sacrifices incurred in acquiring resources. We include the term "cost" here so that you can differentiate it from the term "expense." Costs do not enter into the calculation of net income until they expire. An **expense** in conventional accounting is an **expired cost** (more precisely, an **expired historical cost**). In contrast, a **cost that has not yet expired** is reported as an **asset.**
4. **Gains and losses.**   **Gains** are increases in owners' equity (net assets) from peripheral or incidental transactions of an entity and from all other transactions and events affecting the entity during a period, except those resulting from revenues or investments by owners. **Losses** are decreases in owners' equity (net assets) from peripheral or incidental transactions of an entity and from all other events affecting the entity during a period, except those that result from expenses or distributions to owners. Unlike revenues and expenses, which are measured and reported at **gross amounts,** gains and losses are measured and reported at **net amounts.**

[2]These definitions are based largely on *FASB Statement of Financial Accounting Concepts No. 6,* "Elements of Financial Statements," 1985, pars. 78, 80, 82, and 83.

For example, if a company paid $70,000 for land and later sold the land for $100,000, the company would report a $30,000 gain. This gain equals the gross selling price of $100,000, net of the land's cost of $70,000. In practice, gains are sometimes classified broadly as revenues; losses are sometimes classified broadly as expenses.

5. **Net income.**   The net result of adding revenues and gains for a period and deducting expenses and losses for the period. Terms such as **earnings** and **profit** often are used as synonyms for **income.**

Several items that may appear on an income statement are somewhat peculiar and should be explained further at this time. These items include extraordinary gains and losses, unusual or infrequently occurring gains and losses, gains and losses resulting from the disposal of business segments, and the cumulative effect of a change in accounting principles.

Extraordinary Gains and Losses

Materiality

Suppose that a company sustains a loss from an earthquake. Because this kind of loss is rare, users of financial statements could make more accurate predictions and more meaningful evaluations of management's performance if they knew about unusual and nonrecurring gains and losses. As a result, generally accepted accounting principles (GAAP) require companies to report material extraordinary gains and losses in a special section of their income statements.

To be considered an extraordinary gain or loss, an event or transaction must meet *both* of the following criteria:[3]

1. **Unusual nature.**   The underlying event or transaction should be highly unusual and clearly unrelated to, or only incidentally related to, the ordinary activities of the entity, considering the environment in which the entity operates.
2. **Infrequent occurrence.**   The underlying event or transaction should not be expected to recur in the foreseeable future, considering the environment in which the entity operates.

Note that to be considered extraordinary, an item must be both unusual and nonrecurring.[4] The term **extraordinary item** therefore has a technical meaning in accounting that differs from the everyday connotation of items that are simply unusual or peculiar. Furthermore, the criteria require the accountant to consider the specific **characteristics of the company** as well as the **environment in which it operates.** For example, an accountant would be more likely to judge a loss from a hurricane as extraordinary if it were sustained by a company located in Iowa rather than by one located on the Louisiana Gulf Coast.[5]

Accountants must use *judgment* when applying the above criteria, which are inherently very restrictive and are rarely satisfied in practice.[6] In many cases an event or transaction will meet both criteria only as the direct result of a **major casualty** (such

---

[3]*APB Opinion No. 30*, "Reporting the Results of Operations," 1973, par. 20.

[4]As is true of most rules, there are *exceptions* to the criteria for extraordinary items. The exceptions generally require that certain types of gains and losses be classified as extraordinary *regardless of the criteria in APB Opinion No. 30*. Those exceptions that pertain to intermediate accounting will be covered at appropriate places throughout the text. For example, the FASB in *Statement of Financial Accounting Standards No. 4* stated that gains and losses from extinguishment of debt should always be classified as extraordinary. We explain this exception in Chapter 15.

[5]We are referring to a loss in excess of insurance proceeds or a loss not covered at all by insurance.

[6]*Accounting Trends and Techniques,* 44th ed. (New York: AICPA, 1990), p. 291, reveals that only 54 extraordinary items were reported in the 600 annual reports examined. Of the 54 items, 43 were *exceptions* to the criteria for extraordinary items set forth in *APB Opinion No. 30* (see footnote 4).

as an earthquake), an **expropriation** (takeover of property by a government), or a **prohibition** under a newly enacted law. To clarify these restrictions, the Accounting Principles Board (APB) indicated that the following items could be reported as extraordinary *only* if they resulted from a major casualty, expropriation, or prohibition:[7]

Not Extraordinary — unless result from casualty

1. Write-downs or write-offs of receivables, inventories, equipment leased to others, or intangible assets.
2. Gains or losses from foreign currency transactions and translation of foreign currency financial statements.
3. Gains or losses on disposal of a segment of a business.
4. Other gains or losses from sale or abandonment of property, plant, or business equipment.
5. Effects of a strike, including those against competitors and major suppliers.
6. Adjustments of accruals on long-term contracts.

Below are some examples of events or transactions that meet both criteria and should therefore be judged extraordinary:

Are Extraordinary

1. A large portion of a tobacco manufacturer's crops are destroyed by a hailstorm. Severe damage from hailstorms in the locality where the manufacturer grows tobacco is rare.
2. A food canner destroys a large quantity of inventory because of a government ban on canned goods containing cyclamates. Government prohibitions of this kind rarely occur.
3. An earthquake destroys an oil refinery owned by a large multinational oil company. Earthquakes rarely occur in the area where the oil refinery is located.
4. A large company (Johnson & Johnson) incurred substantial costs when it withdrew all Tylenol capsule products from the market as a result of the criminal tampering with Tylenol Extra-Strength Capsules in the Chicago area during the third quarter of 1982. Clearly, the Tylenol case meets the criteria of unusual and nonrecurring.

In contrast, here are some examples of events or transactions that should *not* be judged extraordinary because they do not meet both criteria for extraordinary items:

Not Extraordinary

1. A citrus grower's Florida crop is damaged by frost. Frost damage is normally experienced every three or four years. In this case the criterion of infrequent occurrence is not met.
2. A company which operates a chain of warehouses sells the excess land surrounding one of its warehouses. When the company buys property to establish a new warehouse, it usually buys more land than it will use for the warehouse because it expects the land to appreciate in value. In the past five years, there have been two instances in which the company sold such excess land. Here the criterion of infrequent occurrence has not been met.
3. A large diversified company sells a block of shares from the portfolio of securities it has for investment purposes. This is the first sale from its portfolio. The criterion of unusual nature has not been met in this case because the company owns several securities.
4. A textile manufacturer with only one plant moves to another location. It has not relocated a plant in twenty years and has no plans to do so in the foreseeable fu-

---

[7]*APB Opinion No. 30*, par. 23.

ture. Here the criterion of unusual nature has not been met because, in general, moving from one location to another is a common business occurrence.[8]

Unusual or Infrequently Occurring Items

Materiality

An accountant sometimes encounters a gain or loss that is unusual in nature *or* occurs infrequently, *but not both*. Such a gain or loss is therefore *not* extraordinary. Examples are gains or losses from the sale of plant assets, losses from inventory write-offs, and losses due to a strike. According to *APB Opinion No. 30*, these gains and losses should be reported as separate items in the income statement if they are material. They should *not* be reported in any way which implies that they are extraordinary in nature.

In practice, the distinction between extraordinary items and unusual or infrequently occurring items is sometimes hazy. Accountants should be aware that, because the income statement reports management's performance, many managers want to report gains as nonextraordinary and losses as extraordinary. This tendency should not influence the accountant's judgment about whether a particular event or transaction is extraordinary.

Disposal of a Business Segment

The term **segment of a business** refers to "a component of an entity whose activities represent a separate major line of business or class of customer. A segment may be in the form of a subsidiary, a division, or a department, . . . provided that its assets, results of operations, and activities can be clearly distinguished, physically and operationally and for financial reporting purposes, from the other assets, results of operations, and activities of the entity."[9] A company may **dispose** of a segment of its business. For example, a company that has a furniture division and a clothing division may sell its clothing division.

Gains and losses from disposal of a business segment are *not* extraordinary items. Instead, they must be reported in a special income statement category called **discontinued operations.** In Chapter 20, we discuss in detail the complex requirements for discounted operations and illustrate how to report them in a comprehensive income statement.

Changes in Accounting Principles

A company may occasionally change from one generally accepted accounting principle to another. For example, it may change from the first-in, first-out (FIFO) to the last-in, first-out (LIFO) method of inventory cost determination, or from the sum-of-the-years'-digits method to the straight-line method of computing depreciation. Such changes are called **changes in accounting principles,** and they are permitted under generally accepted accounting principles if the company can establish that the new principle is preferable to the old.

Changes in accounting principles are *not* extraordinary items. Instead, *most* changes in accounting principles are reported in a special income statement category called the **cumulative effect of a change in accounting principles.**[10] Financial reporting requirements for changes in accounting principles are complex. In Chapter 19, we explain the subject of accounting changes. Then in Chapter 20, we illustrate

---

[8]Most of the examples above were taken from *Accounting Interpretations of APB Opinion No. 30,* "Reporting the Results of Operations" (New York: AICPA, 1973).

[9]*APB Opinion No. 30,* par. 13.

[10]*APB Opinion No. 20,* "Accounting Changes," 1971, par. 20.

how to report these changes in a comprehensive income statement. Therefore, this chapter introduces you to the income statement, while Chapter 20 explains additional income statement reporting details at a time when you will be better able to understand their meaning and significance.

INCOME STATEMENT FORMAT

The form and content of the income statement have been greatly affected by recent professional pronouncements relating to such issues as intraperiod income tax allocation, accounting changes, discontinued operations, extraordinary items, and earnings per share. These issues often are complex and require careful study before the implications of income statement reporting can be fully understood. For this reason, we review in this section the fundamental aspects of the income statement format. In Chapter 20 we consider some additional reporting complexities of the income statement.

The accounting profession has not adopted a uniform format for the entire income statement. Instead, it permits some flexibility, and this enables the practicing accountant to structure an income statement that best fits the circumstances of the reporting entity. Nevertheless, many income statement disclosures (such as depreciation expense) are required by GAAP, and we discuss these required disclosures at appropriate places in this book. Accountants traditionally have presented the income statement in either a multiple-step or a single-step form.

Multiple-Step Form

A **multiple-step** income statement presents subtotals for gross margin and operating income before showing net income. Net income is therefore derived in intermediate steps. Exhibit 4–1 illustrates a multiple-step income statement for the Sunrise Corporation. In practice, many details shown in this example may be condensed or may be reported in footnotes or parenthetically. For example, the income statement may begin with net sales if the accountant thinks that the revenue contra account balances

Materiality   are immaterial. Moreover, the accountant may report only the totals for cost of goods sold, selling expenses, and general and administrative expenses. The details may be presented separately in the footnotes.

As Exhibit 4–1 suggests, a multiple-step format calls for deducting cost of goods sold from net sales to measure **gross margin on sales** (often called **gross profit on sales**). Gross margin is an intermediate measure of profitability that indicates the difference between the selling prices and costs of products sold during the accounting period. For example, the gross margin earned by companies that produce cereal products is currently about 50%.

To the extent possible, **operating expenses** usually are divided into two categories: **selling expenses** relate to the sale of the company's products; **general and administrative expenses** relate to the general operations of the business.

Income from operations (also called **operating income**) is a measurement of the company's profitability as a result of its primary business activities. **Other revenues** and **other expenses** are related to the secondary activities of the company; these two sections often are combined. Note that Sunrise Corporation correctly reported an unusual item (loss on sale of long-term investments) as "other expense." As stated earlier, items that are unusual or nonrecurring (but not both) must not be reported as extraordinary items.

EXHIBIT 4–1

Multiple-Step Income Statement

Sunrise Corporation
INCOME STATEMENT
For the Year Ended December 31, 1993

Sales revenue			
Sales			$579,500
Less: Sales returns and allowances ⟩contra accts		$ 18,200	
Sales discounts		11,300	29,500
Net sales			550,000
Cost of goods sold			
Merchandise inventory, Jan. 1, 1993		40,000	
Purchases	$340,000		
Less: Purchase returns and allowances ⟩contra	(20,000)		
Purchase discounts	(6,800)		
Add: Transportation-in – Adjunct	11,800		
Net purchases		325,000	
Cost of goods available for sale		365,000	
Less: Merchandise inventory, Dec. 31, 1993		(35,000)	
Cost of goods sold			330,000
Gross margin on sales			220,000
Operating expenses			
Selling expenses			
Sales salaries	48,000		
Advertising	12,000		
Transportation-out	7,300		
Depreciation of delivery equipment	3,000		
Other selling expenses	2,700	73,000	
General and administrative expenses			
Office salaries	27,100		
Utilities	9,900		
Supplies	7,700		
Insurance	5,800		
Depreciation of building	2,500		
Depreciation of office equipment	2,000		
Amortization	3,200		
Bad debts	4,500		
Other general and administrative expenses	1,800	64,500	
Total operating expenses			137,500
Income from operations			82,500
Other revenues			
Interest		2,100	
Dividends		5,200	
Rent		7,200	
Gain on sale of equipment		6,500	21,000
			103,500
Other expenses			
Interest		14,400	
Unusual item—loss on sale of long-term investments		5,100	19,500
Income before taxes and extraordinary item			84,000
Income tax expense			33,600
Income before extraordinary item			50,400
Extraordinary item—gain from expropriation of land, less applicable income tax expense of $16,000			24,000
Net income			$ 74,400
Per share of common stock			
Income before extraordinary item			$2.32
Extraordinary gain (net of tax)			1.20
Net income			$3.52

(40000 × .40) = 16000   40K – 16K = 24000

Income before taxes and extraordinary item is an intermediate measure of income that would simply be called "income before taxes" if Sunrise Corporation did not have an extraordinary item. **Income tax** is the final expense deducted. The amount is determined by multiplying the income before taxes and extraordinary item by the income tax rate, which we assume is 40%.[11] The amount therefore includes the income tax effect of all income statement items that appear before it. Income tax expense should always be shown separately, not combined with any other expenses.

Income before extraordinary item indicates how profitable the company was without considering the effects of the extraordinary item. Because extraordinary items are unusual *and* nonrecurring, many financial statement users rely heavily on the income before extraordinary item when they make predictions and evaluate management's performance.

The **extraordinary item** is presented next, as required by GAAP. In the exhibit, Sunrise Corporation reported an extraordinary *gain* because the proceeds received from a government expropriation of land exceeded the land's cost. An extraordinary gain or loss is always reported in a special income statement section. Further, the generally accepted accounting principle of **intraperiod tax allocation,** which is discussed in detail in Chapter 18, requires that the gross amount of an extraordinary gain be reduced by the amount of **income tax expense** associated with the gain. Similarly, it requires that the gross amount of an extraordinary loss be reduced by the amount of the **income tax reduction** associated with the loss. Extraordinary gains and losses are therefore always reported **net** of their income tax effects, or on a **net-of-tax basis.** Note in the exhibit that if the extraordinary gain had not been reported on a net of tax basis, the reported income tax expense (associated with income before taxes and extraordinary item) would have been $49,600 ($33,600 + $16,000). Income before extraordinary item would then have been reported as only $34,400 ($84,000 − $49,600). This error could cause some users to evaluate the company in a misleading (and in this case, less favorable) light. Special income statement categories for discontinued operations and the cumulative effect of a change in accounting principles are required by GAAP. In Chapter 20 we present a comprehensive income statement that includes these categories.

Net income includes the effects of all revenues, expenses, gains, and losses. The beneficiaries of net income are the stockholders, both preferred and common.

Earnings per share of common stock is a widely used financial measurement that appears below net income.[12] Its beneficiaries are *common* stockholders. In the simplest case, an accountant calculates earnings per share by dividing net income by the weighted average number of common shares outstanding during the period. Sunrise Corporation had preferred stock outstanding (see Exhibit 4–6). We therefore subtracted preferred dividends from net income when calculating earnings per share of common stock. Note that because Sunrise Corporation had an extraordinary item, it reported *three* per-share numbers: (1) income before extraordinary item; (2) extraordinary gain (net of tax); and (3) net income. Companies report these numbers separately to help users of financial statements make better predictions and more meaningful evaluations of management's performance. Calculating and reporting earnings per share can be extremely complex; we discuss and illustrate these complexities in Chapter 21.

---

[11] So that we can concentrate on the basic form and content of financial statements without being diverted by income tax calculations, we assume a tax rate of 40% for the financial statements presented in this chapter.

[12] Nonpublic enterprises are not required under generally accepted accounting principles to report earnings per share. Unless stated otherwise, you should assume in all end-of-chapter assignments that earnings per share is required.

EXHIBIT 4–2

Single-Step Income Statement
Sunrise Corporation
INCOME STATEMENT
For the Year Ended December 31, 1993

Revenues		
Net sales		$550,000
Other revenues		21,000
Total revenues		571,000
Expenses		
Cost of goods sold	$330,000	
Selling expenses	73,000	
General and administrative expenses	64,500	
Interest	14,400	
Unusual item—loss on sale of long-term investments	5,100	
Total expenses		487,000
Income before taxes and extraordinary item		84,000
Income tax expense		33,600
Income before extraordinary item		50,400
Extraordinary item—gain from expropriation of land, less applicable income tax expense of $16,000		24,000
Net income		$ 74,400
Per share of common stock		
Income before extraordinary item		$2.32
Extraordinary gain (net of tax)		1.20
Net income		$3.52

NOTE TO STUDENTS: With either the multiple-step or the single-step form, generally accepted accounting principles require special income statement categories for discontinued operations and the cumulative effect of a change in accounting principles. In Chapter 20 we discuss and illustrate these categories. We also present a comprehensive income statement that includes these categories.

Single-Step Form

In the **single-step** income statement, the accountant deducts total expenses from total revenues in a single step to measure net income. No separate disclosure is made of gross margin or operating income. Most companies that prepare single-step income statements deduct income tax as a separate, last item.[13] In Exhibit 4–2 we present a somewhat condensed, single-step income statement. Such condensation is not essential. Indeed, **condensed income statements** may be presented in either a multiple-step or a single-step format. A typical annual report contains a condensed income statement. As you can see by comparing Exhibits 4–1 and 4–2, extraordinary items are reported in a special income statement category, regardless of the format used. Moreover, the multiple-step and single-step formats always contain the same information after "income before taxes and extraordinary item."

Multiple-Step Versus Single-Step Form

Many preparers and users of financial statements prefer the multiple-step form because it highlights gross margin and operating income. Others prefer the single-step

---

[13]*Accounting Trends and Techniques,* 1990, p. 213.

EXHIBIT 4–3

Sunrise Corporation
STATEMENT OF RETAINED EARNINGS
For the Year Ended December 31, 1993

Retained earnings, Jan. 1, 1993, as previously reported		$ 45,600
Less: Prior period adjustment–correction of depreciation understatement in 1992 due to error, less applicable income tax effect of $2,000		3,000
Retained earnings, Jan. 1, 1993, as restated		42,600
Add: Net income		74,400
Subtotal		117,000
Less: Dividends declared on preferred stock ($.80 per share)	$ 4,000	
Dividends declared on common stock ($.60 per share)	12,000	16,000
Retained earnings, Dec. 31, 1993		$101,000

form because it often is easier to understand and does not suggest a priority of expenses. In other words, the format does not imply that a company must recover its cost-of-goods-sold expense before it can recover any other expenses. In reality, of course, a company must cover all of its expenses if it is to have net income. Proponents of the single-step form also point out that several terms often used in a multiple-step statement (especially "income from operations") have not been clearly defined by the accounting profession. A survey of the annual reports of 600 companies indicated that in 1989, 232 companies used the single-step form while 368 companies used the multiple-step form.[14]

STATEMENT OF RETAINED EARNINGS

The **statement of retained earnings** describes the changes in a company's retained earnings during a period and relates the income statement to the balance sheet. The retained earnings statement usually is fairly simple and may consist of three sections: (1) **prior period adjustments**; (2) **net income**; and (3) **dividends declared.** Users of financial statements can analyze the statement to determine whether any prior period adjustments exist and what relationship exists between a company's net income and its dividends.

A statement of retained earnings for the Sunrise Corporation is shown in Exhibit 4–3.

PRIOR PERIOD ADJUSTMENTS

Prior period adjustments are charged or credited directly to retained earnings. These items do not appear on the income statement of the period in which they occur.

In 1977 the Financial Accounting Standards Board (FASB) issued *Statement of Financial Accounting Standards No. 16,* which greatly reduced the number of items

[14]*Accounting Trends and Techniques,* 1990, p. 213.

that a company could report as prior period adjustments. In this pronouncement the FASB stated that:

> *Items of profit and loss related to the following shall be accounted for and reported as prior period adjustments and excluded from the determination of net income for the current period:*
>
> **1.** *Correction of an error in the financial statements of a prior period and*
> **2.** *Adjustments that result from realization of income tax benefits of preacquisition operating loss carryforwards of purchased subsidiaries.*[15]

A **correction of an error** that was made in the financial statements of a **prior period** is accounted for in the **current period** as a prior period adjustment.[16] The error may have resulted from mathematical mistakes, errors in selecting or applying accounting principles, or oversight or misuse of facts when the company prepared its erroneous financial statements.[17] Examples of errors are an overstatement of merchandise inventory at the end of the preceding period because of an inaccurate physical count, and an understatement of previously reported depreciation because of an error in computation. A change from an accounting principle that is not generally accepted to one that is generally accepted is considered to be a correction of an error.

In practice, prior period adjustments due to errors are rare, yet they can sometimes have a significant effect on a company's financial statements. In its 1988 annual report American Building Maintenance Industries, Inc. reported a prior period adjustment of $9,397,000. In essence, this company does not carry insurance for property damage and personal liability and worker's compensation coverages. A 1988 analysis of insurance claims showed that in certain prior years the company did not report the effect of claims that had been incurred.

An accountant must carefully distinguish a *correction of an error* from a **change in an accounting estimate.** A change in an accounting estimate is a result from the need for accountants to make many estimates. Changes in these estimates occur when new information or subsequent developments improve the accountant's judgment. Examples include changes in estimates of uncollectible accounts receivable and changes in the estimated service lives or salvage values of plant assets. Changes in accounting estimates are *not* prior period adjustments. These changes should be accounted for in the period of change if the change affects that period only, or in the period of change and future periods if the change affects both.[18] We explain corrections of errors and changes in accounting estimates in Chapter 19.

Prior period adjustments that result from realization of income tax benefits of preacquisition operating loss carryforwards of purchased subsidiaries are not covered extensively in this text. Coverage of this topic is appropriate in advanced accounting courses.

---

[15]*FASB Statement of Financial Accounting Standards No. 16*, "Prior Period Adjustments," 1977, par. 11. This pronouncement did not affect the manner of reporting accounting changes required or permitted by an FASB Statement or Interpretation, or an APB Opinion. We discuss the reporting of accounting changes in Chapter 19, where we see that adjustments to the opening balance of a company's retained earnings need not be confined to prior period adjustments.

[16]Moreover, when comparative statements are reported, erroneous amounts previously reported should be corrected.

[17]*APB Opinion No. 20*, par. 13.

[18]*APB Opinion No. 20*, par. 31.

As shown in Exhibit 4–3, a prior period adjustment is added to or deducted from the previously reported opening balance of retained earnings to derive a **restated (revised) opening balance.** Furthermore, a prior period adjustment is reported **net of its related income tax effect,** like that for extraordinary items. As we discuss in Chapter 18, the principle of intraperiod tax allocation requires that prior period adjustments be reported on a net of tax basis.

NET INCOME AND DIVIDENDS

The **net income** figure on the statement of retained earnings is taken directly from the income statement. When a company sustains a **net loss** during a period, the loss is deducted on the retained earnings statement.

Dividends declared during the period are deducted on the retained earnings statement and dividends per share ordinarily are disclosed. Dividends declared may be in the form of cash, other assets, or the company's own stock. Further, they may relate to both preferred and common stock. Note carefully that dividends declared are deducted on the statement since the declaration represents a reduction in retained earnings. Sometimes a company declares a dividend in one period but does not pay or distribute it until the next. As a result, dividends declared during a period may include an amount paid or distributed during the period and an amount that will be paid or distributed in the next period.

COMBINED STATEMENT OF INCOME AND RETAINED EARNINGS

Exhibit 4–4 illustrates a **combined statement of income and retained earnings.** Some accountants favor a combined statement of income and retained earnings because it integrates important and related information. Opponents claim that it may be too complicated for many users and deemphasizes net income by not placing this item at the bottom of the combined statement.

STATEMENT OF STOCKHOLDERS' EQUITY

Sometimes a company also has changes in other accounts that comprise stockholders' equity. These changes occur as the company sells additional stock, buys and sells treasury stock, or engages in other kinds of capital stock transactions. Such changes

Disclosure   must be disclosed in a separate statement, in the basic statements, or in the notes to the financial statements. Changes in the number of shares outstanding should also be disclosed.[19]

Many companies report all these changes in a separate **statement of stockholders' equity.** This statement combines the retained earnings statement with one that shows changes in all the other components of stockholders' equity. As a result, a company that reports a statement of stockholders' equity need not report a separate retained earnings statement. A statement of stockholders' equity for the Sunrise Corporation appears in Exhibit 4–5.

BALANCE SHEET

The **balance sheet** (sometimes called the **statement of financial position**) shows the financial position of an enterprise at a particular point in time. Investors, creditors, and other users of financial statements analyze an enterprise's balance sheet to evaluate such factors as **liquidity** (how close the assets are to cash realization),

---

[19]*APB Opinion No. 12*, "Omnibus Opinion—1967," 1967, par. 10.

EXHIBIT 4-4

Sunrise Corporation
COMBINED STATEMENT OF INCOME AND RETAINED EARNINGS
For the Year Ended December 31, 1993

Net income*		$ 74,400
Add: Retained earnings, Jan. 1, 1993, as previously reported	$45,600	
Less: Prior period adjustment—correction of depreciation understatement in 1992 due to error, less applicable income tax effect of $2,000	3,000	
Retained earnings, Jan. 1, 1993, as restated		42,600
Subtotal		117,000
Less: Dividends declared on preferred stock ($.80 per share)	4,000	
Dividends declared on common stock ($.60 per share)	12,000	16,000
Retained earnings, Dec. 31, 1993		$101,000
Per share of common stock**		
Income before extraordinary item		$2.32
Extraordinary gain (net of tax)		1.20
Net income		$3.52

* The items shown in Exhibits 4-1 or 4-2 would appear above net income.
**Alternatively, earnings per share may be presented parenthetically in the body of the combined statement of income and retained earnings.

capital structure (what amount of assets has been financed by creditors and what amount by owners), and financial flexibility (the ability of a company to use its financial resources to adapt to change). Generally, companies that lack sufficient liquidity and financial flexibility, perhaps because virtually all of their assets are far removed from cash and a very large proportion of their capital structure consists of debt, are less able than other companies to take advantage of attractive investment opportunities or to absorb adverse changes in operating conditions. Companies without sufficient liquidity and financial flexibility are therefore more likely to fail than are other companies. The 1985 annual report of Texaco, Inc., contains an interesting disclosure that shows how a company's financial flexibility can sometimes be changed drastically. The disclosure says,

> "There was a significant change in Texaco's financial flexibility at December 31, 1985 attributable to the December 10, 1985 judgment of the Texas State District Court against Texaco and for Pennzoil in the amount of $10.5 billion (excluding interest)."

The balance sheet was once regarded as the most important financial statement, but, as stated earlier, most users now regard the income statement as paramount. Nevertheless, the balance sheet may be regaining some attention. For example, a *Business Week* article stated that: "Investors, including the biggest bank trust departments, still look at earnings before they buy a security, but today the deal must also make sense in terms of a company's current ratio, debt/equity ratio, and return on investments. Corporations with balance sheets that cannot pass muster will find themselves closed out

126   4   BASIC FINANCIAL STATEMENTS

EXHIBIT 4-5

Sunrise Corporation
STATEMENT OF STOCKHOLDERS' EQUITY
For the Year Ended December 31, 1993

	Preferred Stock	Common Stock	Paid-In Capital in Excess of Par	Retained Earnings	Total
Balance, Jan. 1, 1993, as previously reported	$50,000	$ 60,000	$25,000	$ 45,600	$180,600
Less: Prior period adjustment—correction of depreciation understatement in 1992 due to error, less applicable income tax effect of $2,000				(3,000)	(3,000)
Balance, Jan. 1, 1993, as restated	50,000	60,000	25,000	42,600	177,600
Add: Net income				74,400	74,400
Less: Dividends declared on preferred stock ($.80 per share)				(4,000)	(4,000)
Dividends declared on common stock ($.60 per share)				(12,000)	(12,000)
Add: Common stock issued on Jan. 2, 1993 (8,000 shares)		40,000	15,000		55,000
Balance, Dec. 31, 1993	$50,000	$100,000	$40,000	$101,000	$291,000

of the marketplace."[20] Moreover, the FASB is clearly giving renewed attention to the balance sheet, as indicated by its asset/liability view of earnings in the Conceptual Framework and its recent standards in such areas as pensions and income taxes.

ELEMENTS OF THE BALANCE SHEET

The following equation presents the three major elements of the balance sheet:

$$Assets = Liabilities + Owners' \ equity$$

In Chapter 2, we defined these elements as follows:[21]

1. **Assets.** Probable future economic benefits obtained or controlled by an entity as a result of past transactions or events.
2. **Liabilities.** Probable future sacrifices of economic benefits arising from present obligations of an entity to transfer assets or provide services to other entities in the future as a result of past transactions or events.
3. **Owners' equity.** The residual interest in the assets of an entity that remains after deducting its liabilities.

BALANCE SHEET CLASSIFICATIONS

Generally accepted accounting principles require a company to report its assets, liabilities, and owners' equity in several classifications or categories. Although some flexibility is permitted in selecting and naming balance sheet categories and in group-

[20]"Focus on Balance Sheet," *Business Week* (June 7, 1976), p. 52.
[21]Based on *FASB Statement of Financial Accounting Concepts No. 6*, pars. 25, 35, and 49.

ing specific items into them, the following categories (in the order shown) are representative of those found in practice:

Assets
Current assets
Investments and funds
Property, plant, and equipment
Intangible assets
Other assets
} Noncurrent assets
Liabilities
Current liabilities
Long-term liabilities
Owners' Equity
Paid-in capital
　Capital stock
　　Preferred stock
　　Common stock
　Paid-in capital in excess of par
Retained earnings

Exhibit 4–6 shows the **account form** of balance sheet for Sunrise Corporation. In this form the liabilities and owners' equity are listed to the right of the assets. The **report form** and the **financial position form** are also acceptable. The report form shows the liabilities and owners' equity directly below the assets. The financial position form shows current liabilities deducted from current assets to determine working capital. Noncurrent assets are then added to working capital and noncurrent liabilities are deducted to arrive at owners' equity.[22]

The following discussion of each classification includes a brief indication of how some of the major items reported in it are valued on the balance sheet. You will see that although balance sheets are based largely on historical costs, they actually reflect several measurement attributes. Many of the remaining chapters in this book are organized within a balance sheet framework, and we explain in detail the nature and valuation of individual assets, liabilities, and owners' equity.

Asset/Liability Measurement

Assets

Current Assets.   Current assets are cash and other assets which are reasonably expected to be realized in cash or sold or consumed during the normal operating cycle of the business or within one year from the balance sheet date, whichever is *longer*.[23] An **operating cycle** for a given enterprise is the *average time* that it takes for the enterprise to spend cash for inventory, sell the inventory in exchange for a receivable, and collect the receivable in cash. The cycle thus progresses from cash, through inventories and receivables, back to cash.

Most companies have operating cycles that are less than one year. Some companies, however, such as those involved in distilling, tobacco, and lumber operations, have longer operating cycles. A balance sheet of one of these companies may therefore contain current assets, such as inventory, for which cash realization is not expected within the next year.

[22]*Accounting Trends and Techniques*, 1990, p. 87, indicates that in 1989, 195 of the 600 companies surveyed used the account form, 404 used the report form, and only 1 used the financial position form.
[23]*Accounting Research Bulletin No. 43*, "Restatement and Revision of Accounting Research Bulletins," 1953, Ch. 3, Sec. A, par. 4.

EXHIBIT 4-6

Sunrise Corporation
BALANCE SHEET
December 31, 1993

Assets

Current Assets			
Cash		$ 22,500	
Marketable securities (at cost; market value $40,700)		40,000	
Accounts receivable	$ 55,000		
Less: Allowance for doubtful accounts	4,500	50,500	
Notes receivable		26,000	
Merchandise inventory (at lower of average cost or market)		35,000	
Prepaid expenses			
Supplies	5,350		
Insurance	4,650	10,000	
Total current assets			$184,000
Investments and Funds			
Investment in Case Company common stock (at cost; market value $46,400)		41,800	
Land held for future plant site		55,000	
Plant expansion fund		48,700	
Total investments and funds			145,500
Property, Plant, and Equipment			
Land		22,000	
Building	100,000		
Less: Accumulated depreciation	30,000	70,000	
Equipment	80,000		
Less: Accumulated depreciation	20,000	60,000	
Total property, plant, and equipment			152,000
Intangible Assets			
Goodwill			38,500
Other Assets			
Bond issue costs			8,000
Total assets			$528,000

Current assets are usually listed in the order of their liquidity. The most common current assets are cash, short-term investments, receivables, inventories, and prepaid expenses.

Cash (on hand and on deposit) is included among current assets only if it is available for current operations. Any cash that has been restricted for other purposes should be reported in the investments and funds section of the balance sheet. Cash is reported at its face amount.

Short-term investments are those that are readily marketable and that management *intends* to convert into cash within the next year or operating cycle, whichever is longer. Often they consist entirely of marketable securities such as stocks or bonds. These securities are normally reported at the lower of their cost or market value.

Liabilities and Stockholders' Equity

Current Liabilities

Accounts payable		$ 47,400	
Notes payable		12,000	
Interest payable		4,200	
Salaries payable		6,400	
Commissions payable		1,000	
Income tax payable		10,000	
Advances from customers		7,200	
Unearned rent revenue		4,800	
Total current liabilities			$ 93,000

Long-Term Liabilities

Bonds payable (10%, due Dec. 31, 2003)		150,000	
Less: Unamortized discount		6,000	144,000
Total liabilities			237,000

Stockholders' Equity

Paid-in capital			
Capital stock			
Preferred stock ($10 par, 8%, cumulative and nonparticipating, 10,000 shares authorized, 5,000 shares issued and outstanding)	$ 50,000		
Common stock ($5 par, 25,000 shares authorized, 20,000 shares issued and outstanding)	100,000	150,000	
Paid-in capital in excess of par		40,000	
Total paid-in capital			190,000
Retained earnings			101,000
Total stockholders' equity			291,000
Total liabilities and stockholders' equity			$528,000

Receivables represent claims to cash. Accounts receivable typically compose the largest dollar value of receivables. An estimated allowance for doubtful accounts should be deducted from the gross amount of accounts receivable so that the accounts are properly reported at their **net realizable value** (estimated amount collectible).

Inventory in a merchandising company normally consists only of merchandise that is ready for sale to customers. On the other hand, the inventories of a manufacturing concern may consist of factory supplies, raw materials, work (goods) in process, and finished goods. Inventories are usually reported at the lower of cost or market value.

Prepaid expenses consist of such items as insurance, rent, advertising, taxes, and operating supplies. These items are not current assets in the sense that they will be converted into cash but rather in the sense that if they had not been paid for in advance, they would require the use of current assets during the next year or operating cycle. A prepaid expense is reported at the amount of its unexpired or unconsumed cost.

In practice, the distinction between current and noncurrent assets is sometimes hazy and is based in part on judgment, custom, and materiality. For example, a company that has a three-month operating cycle may report a two-year prepaid insurance policy as a current asset because the amount involved is immaterial. As another example, companies do not customarily report the following year's depreciation as a current asset, although a portion of plant assets will be consumed in the next year's operations.

Materiality

Investments and Funds.   This category is used to report various types of investments and fund balances that management *intends* to hold for a period longer than the normal operating cycle or one year, whichever is longer, and that are *not* used in the business operations. Assets reported here need not be readily marketable. This category often is called **long-term investments,** or simply, **investments.** Assets commonly included in this category are listed below:

1. Long-term investments in securities of other companies, such as stocks, bonds, and notes.
2. Investments in plant assets that are not currently used in operations, such as land held for a future plant site or for speculation.
3. Special fund balances accumulated for a particular purpose, such as future plant expansion.
4. Cash surrender value of life insurance policies.

The valuation basis used for assets in this category depends on the type of asset. For example, a special fund balance is normally reported at the amount accumulated in the fund, while an investment in bonds is usually reported at face value plus unamortized premium (or face value minus unamortized discount). Long-term equity investments may be valued using the cost, lower of cost or market, or equity method, depending on whether the investment is readily marketable and on the extent of ownership interest held. We discuss the valuation of investments and funds more fully in Chapter 10.

Property, Plant, and Equipment.   This section of the balance sheet reports assets that are tangible (have physical substance) and long-lived, and that are used in the business operations. **Plant assets** is a shorter title that refers to property, plant, and equipment. Examples of plant assets are business sites (the land on which the business is located), buildings, equipment, machinery, furniture, fixtures, tools, containers, and natural resources. Accountants ordinarily record depreciation or depletion on all plant assets except land.

Plant assets are reported on the balance sheet at their historical cost less any accumulated depreciation or depletion. The term **book value** (or **net book value**) refers to the difference between cost and accumulated depreciation or depletion.

Intangible Assets.   Intangible assets are long-lived resources that lack physical substance but convey valuable rights and privileges to the business. Examples include patents, copyrights, goodwill, trademarks, franchises, and organization costs. An accountant usually cannot measure the value of intangible assets with sufficient objectivity to report it in the balance sheet. Therefore, the accountant initially records an intangible asset at cost, based on a completed, arm's-length exchange transaction. The cost is then allocated in a systematic manner over the periods benefited through a process called **amortization.** The balance sheet valuation assigned to an intangible asset is therefore its cost less amortization taken to date. Companies rarely report accumulated amortization in a separate contra account.

Other Assets.   This category includes assets that do not fit conveniently into one of the other four categories. Ideally, accountants should seldom use the other assets category since it is very general and since most assets can be classified in one of the other, more specific categories. Nevertheless, in practice, a wide variety of assets are reported as other assets.

Examples of other assets are machinery rearrangement costs, bond issue costs, long-term rental prepayments, and prepaid income taxes resulting from the application of interperiod tax allocation (a concept we explain in Chapter 18). The valuation reported is usually the unallocated cost. Accountants sometimes use the term **deferred charges** (meaning simply **delayed debits**) to describe certain assets in this category. A deferred charge is essentially a long-term prepayment of an expense. Many accountants avoid this term since, technically speaking, buildings, patents, and similar assets classified elsewhere are also deferred charges.

Liabilities

Current Liabilities.   Current liabilities are "obligations whose liquidation is reasonably expected to require the use of existing resources properly classifiable as current assets or the creation of other current liabilities."[24] Notice that the definition of current liabilities is closely related to that of current assets. That is, if the satisfaction of a liability requires the use of existing current assets or the creation of other current liabilities, then the liability is considered current for accounting purposes. Current liabilities include the following:[25]

1. Payables for items which have entered or relate directly to the operating cycle, such as accounts payable, wages payable, commissions payable, and income taxes payable.
2. Collections received in advance of delivering goods or performing services, such as advances from customers for merchandise ordered or cash received for advance ticket sales.
3. Other obligations that will be liquidated through the use of current assets or the creation of other current liabilities within the next year or operating cycle, whichever is longer. Examples include short-term notes payable resulting from the purchase of equipment and the currently maturing portion of long-term debt. Interest

Not all short-term obligations require the use of current assets or the creation of other current liabilities during the next year or operating cycle. For example, a bond issue that matures during the next year may be paid using cash accumulated in a sinking fund (classified in the investments and funds category), or a short-term note payable may be refinanced on a long-term basis. These obligations should be reported as long-term rather than as current liabilities. Current liabilities are normally listed in the order of their liquidation dates and are usually reported at the amount to be paid.

Working capital (sometimes called **net working capital**) is the difference between total current assets and total current liabilities. Working capital is an approximate measure of the net amount of a company's relatively liquid resources, and many creditors believe that it constitutes a margin of safety for paying short-term debts.[26] Companies without adequate working capital may be more likely than others to have liquidity problems.

[24]*Accounting Research Bulletin No. 43*, Ch. 3, Sec. A, par. 7.
[25]*Accounting Research Bulletin No. 43*, Ch. 3, Sec. A, par. 7.
[26]For an interesting discussion of the limitations of the working capital concept, see Philip Fess, "The Working Capital Concept," *Accounting Review* (April 1966), pp. 266–270.

Because of the emphasis placed by many users of financial statements on working capital and on the size of a company's **current ratio** (current assets *divided by* current liabilities), corporate managers have at times wanted to incorrectly report certain noncurrent assets as current and certain current liabilities as long-term. Accountants and auditors must detect and request that management correct these errors before the financial statements are issued.

Long-Term Liabilities.   Long-term liabilities are obligations that will *not* require the use of current assets or the creation of other current liabilities within the next year or operating cycle, whichever is longer. In other words, this category comprises all liabilities other than those properly classified as current. Examples of long-term liabilities are bonds payable, long-term notes payable, deferred income taxes, long-term obligations under warranty contracts, obligations under capital leases, and pension obligations. Conceptually, a long-term liability should be measured on the date incurred at an amount equal to the present value of the expected future payments.

When bonds payable are reported, any premium associated with the bonds should be added to the face or maturity value; similarly, any discount should be subtracted. An obligation classified as long-term sometimes requires the use of current assets or the creation of other current liabilities within the next year or operating cycle, whichever is longer. Such an obligation, along with any related premium or discount, should be reclassified as a current liability. An example is a five-year note payable that matures within the next year and will be paid using cash that is classified as a current asset.

Some companies use a **deferred credits** category to report certain long-term obligations, such as deferred income taxes and collections received in advance of performing services on a long-term basis. Deferred credits are simply delayed credits which will increase reported income in future periods.

Owners' Equity

Owners' equity is a measure of the owners' interests in the assets of a business. Traditionally, the accountant measures individual assets and liabilities directly. Owners' equity is simply a residual, indirect measurement whose value depends on the values assigned to assets and liabilities.

The three primary forms of business organization are sole proprietorships, partnerships, and corporations. In proprietorships and partnerships, owners' equity is usually summarized in a single capital account for each owner. The balance in a capital account summarizes the owner's investments and withdrawals as well as the owner's share of past net incomes and losses. The balance sheet of a proprietorship or partnership generally does not distinguish between amounts paid into the firm by owners and reinvested earnings, because state laws usually do not restrict the amount of withdrawals that a proprietor or partner can make. Creditors of proprietorships and partnerships are usually more interested in the personal financial conditions of the owners since, in the event of liquidation, owners may be held personally liable for business debts.

Corporations report owners' equity (usually called **stockholders'** or **shareholders' equity**) in two major categories: **paid-in capital** (often called **contributed** or **invested capital**) and **retained earnings**. The use of these categories results in a stockholders' equity that is classified approximately according to *sources* of capital.

Historically, legal considerations have influenced the reporting of stockholders' equity. Because corporate stockholders cannot be held personally liable for company debts, state laws provide that corporations cannot distribute assets to stockholders if so doing would reduce owners' equity below a minimum amount known as **legal** or **stated capital**. The legal capital of a given company depends on the laws of the state in which it is organized.

Paid-In Capital. This category is used to report amounts that stockholders have paid into the company in exchange for shares of stock. It may be divided further into capital stock and additional paid-in capital.

Capital stock includes both preferred and common stock. Here companies report the par or stated value per share multiplied by the number of shares issued. The total amount received is reported for stock that has no par or stated value. If a company has both preferred and common stock outstanding, it should report each type separately.

Materiality

Paid-in capital in excess of par, or **additional paid-in capital,** represents amounts received in excess of the par or stated value of shares sold. Paid-in capital in excess of par may be presented as a single amount, but if several material sources of paid-in capital in excess of par exist, a breakdown by source may be helpful to financial statement users.

Retained Earnings. Retained earnings, which represent a company's accumulated earnings less its dividends, are added to total paid-in capital when determining total stockholders' equity. A negative (debit) balance in retained earnings, called a **deficit**, occurs when a company's losses and dividends have exceeded its earnings. An accountant should simply deduct a deficit from total paid-in capital to arrive at total stockholders' equity.

The retained earnings category is sometimes divided into **appropriated** and **unappropriated** components. Companies may appropriate (or restrict) retained earnings for legal, contractual, or discretionary reasons. The amount appropriated is not available as a basis for declaring dividends during the time of appropriation. Companies usually disclose appropriations of retained earnings in the notes to their financial statements. Occasionally, however, a company may make a formal journal entry for the amount appropriated. This entry involves a debit to retained earnings and a credit to retained earnings appropriated for the designated purpose, such as future plant expansion. These kinds of entries ultimately produce balances in appropriated retained earnings accounts, such as Retained Earnings Appropriated for Future Plant Expansion or Retained Earnings Restricted by the Purchase of Treasury Stock. These accounts and their balances are reported as appropriated retained earnings.

When a company has created accounts for retained earnings appropriations, it reports the amount of its unappropriated retained earnings separate from the amounts appropriated. Unappropriated retained earnings are simply those available for declaring dividends.[27]

Companies sometimes purchase and hold shares of their own stock which they previously sold to investors. These shares constitute **treasury stock**. A company may acquire treasury stock for several reasons. For example, it may want to use the stock to satisfy employee stock option contracts or to effect a merger. Treasury stock is *not* an asset but rather a reduction in stockholders' equity. The vast majority of companies account for treasury stock at cost by debiting a treasury stock account for the cost of the shares purchased. The company later deducts the amount in the treasury stock account as the final account in the stockholders' equity section. Some companies account for treasury stock at par value; under this method treasury stock is deducted in the capital stock subcategory of stockholders' equity. We explain the methods of treasury-stock accounting in Chapter 16.

---

[27]A decision to declare dividends is, of course, influenced by many factors other than retained earnings.

STATEMENT OF CASH FLOWS

A complete set of financial statements includes a **statement of cash flows.**[28] The primary purpose of the statement of cash flows is to report information about a company's cash receipts and payments during a period. If used with the other basic financial statements, the statement of cash flows can help users to assess a company's ability to generate future net cash inflows, assess the company's ability to pay debts and dividends, evaluate the company's needs for external financing, assess the reasons for differences between income and related cash flows, and evaluate both the cash and noncash aspects of the company's investing and financing transactions during the period.

Although the statement of cash flows provides considerable information about a company's current cash receipts and payments, the statement by itself does not provide a sound basis for making predictions about the company's future cash flows. Many current cash receipts result from decisions made in *past* periods (e.g., the decision made in an earlier period to invest in plant assets), and many current decisions involving cash payments are made with the aim of increasing *future* cash receipts (e.g., the decision made in the current period to invest in plant assets). Thus, the statement of cash flows should be used with the other basic financial statements to help investors and creditors assess such important factors as an entity's liquidity, financial flexibility, profitability, and risk.

A statement of cash flows explains the change during the period in a company's cash. If a company invests in highly liquid short-term investments, such as U.S. Treasury bills, then the statement should explain the change during the period in **cash and cash equivalents.**

The statement of cash flows is classified in *three major categories.*

1. **Investing activities** include lending money and collecting loans, acquiring and disposing of securities that are not cash equivalents, and acquiring and selling long-term productive assets.
   a. Investing activities that produce cash *inflows* include:
      (1) Cash receipts from the collection (or sale) of loans made to other enterprises.
      (2) Cash receipts from the sale of assets such as investments in securities (other than cash equivalents) of other companies and property, plant, and equipment.
   b. Investing activities that produce cash *outflows* include:
      (1) Cash outflows to make loans to other enterprises.
      (2) Cash payments to acquire assets such as investments in securities (other than cash equivalents) of other companies and property, plant, and equipment.
2. **Financing activities** include obtaining resources from owners and paying dividends, and obtaining resources from creditors and repaying the amounts borrowed.
   a. Financing activities that produce cash *inflows* include:
      (1) Cash receipts from the issuance of debt securities (short-term or long-term).
      (2) Cash receipts from the issuance of equity securities.

[28]This section is based on *FASB Statement of Financial Accounting Standards No. 95,* "Statement of Cash Flows," 1987.

b. Financing activities that produce cash *outflows* include:
  (1) Repayments of amounts borrowed.
  (2) Cash payments of dividends.
  (3) Cash payments to repurchase the company's own stock (treasury stock).
3. Operating activities include all transactions that are not properly classified as investing or financing activities. Operating activities include producing and selling goods and providing services. Generally, the cash flows from operating activities represent the cash effects of transactions that are reflected in the determination of income.
  a. Operating activities that produce cash *inflows* include:
    (1) Cash receipts from the sale of goods or services to customers.
    (2) Cash receipts from interest, dividends, and other sources that do not represent investing or financing activities.
  b. Operating activities that produce cash *outflows* include:
    (1) Cash payments for the acquisition of inventory.
    (2) Cash payments to employees and other suppliers of goods and services.
    (3) Cash payments for taxes.
    (4) Cash payments for interest.
    (5) Cash payments for other purposes that do not represent investing or financing activities.

Classification according to the three categories described above allows investors and creditors to assess significant relationships within and among a company's major activities—its operating, investing, and financing activities. The classification system provides useful information by linking cash flows that are often considered to be related, such as cash inflows from borrowing money and cash outflows to repay loans.

Exhibit 4–7 shows the statement of cash flows for the Sunrise Corporation. Preparation of such a statement requires comparative balance sheets as well as information that explains changes in the account balances during the period. We have *not* *included* all this information here, because at this point in your study, you should concentrate on the basic form of the statement and the general types of information it conveys. You cannot "verify" all the numbers in Exhibit 4–7, but that is not our purpose at this time. After studying Chapter 4, you should have an introductory understanding of the nature and purpose of the statement of cash flows. In Chapter 22 we discuss the statement in detail and explain how to prepare it.

As Exhibit 4–7 shows, the statement begins with cash flows from operating activities. Remember that operating activities encompass all transactions that are not properly classified as investing or financing activities. Net cash flow from operating activities does *not* include cash flows from certain transactions which are reflected in income but which are investing or financing activities. For example, Sunrise had an unusual loss on the sale of long-term investments during 1993 (as shown in Exhibit 4–1). The sale of long-term investments is really an investing activity, and accordingly, the loss is reflected in the calculation of the proceeds from the sale of long-term investments ($10,900).

Net cash flow from operating activities should be prominently disclosed, because users of financial statements generally are interested in evaluating the ability of a company to generate cash through its operations. Some companies can generate net income but not much cash. Over the long run, a business ordinarily must generate cash through its own operations if it is to survive. A company cannot simply depend on raising cash through such means as borrowing or selling plant assets. In Exhibit

EXHIBIT 4-7

Sunrise Corporation
STATEMENT OF CASH FLOWS
For the Year Ended December 31, 1993

Cash Flows from Operating Activities

Cash received from customers	$538,700	
Interest received	2,100	
Dividends received	5,200	
Rent received	8,400	
Cash provided by operating activities		$554,400
Cash paid to suppliers and employees	455,900	
Interest paid	14,200	
Taxes paid	47,300	
Cash disbursed for operating activities		517,400
Net cash flow from operating activities		37,000

Cash Flows from Investing Activities

Short-term loans made	(18,000)	
Collections on short-term loans	8,000	
Purchases of long-term investments	(14,000)	
Proceeds from sale of long-term investments	10,900	
Purchases of property, plant and equipment	(38,800)	
Proceeds from disposals of property, plant, and equipment	76,400	
Net cash provided by investing activities		24,500

Cash Flows from Financing Activities

Proceeds of short-term debt	23,000	
Payments to settle short-term debt	(25,000)	
Proceeds of long-term debt	50,000	
Payments to settle long-term note	(110,000)	
Proceeds from issuing common stock	55,000	
Dividends paid	(16,000)	
Net cash used by financing activities		(23,000)
Net increase in cash and cash equivalents		38,500
Cash and cash equivalents, Jan. 1, 1993		24,000
Cash and cash equivalents, Dec. 31, 1993		$ 62,500

4-7 we see that Sunrise generated a positive net cash flow of $37,000 as a result of its operating activities during 1993.

Cash flows from investing activities are reported in the next category shown in Exhibit 4-7. Observe how the cash outflows associated with each of the investing activities are deducted from related cash inflows. The statement shows that Sunrise generated $24,500 from its investing activities during 1993, primarily from disposing of certain plant assets.

Cash flows from financing activities are also reported by subtracting cash outflows from related cash inflows, as shown in Exhibit 4-7. The statement shows that Sunrise's major financing activities during 1993 were the issuance of common stock and the settlement of a long-term note payable, thereby increasing the extent to which the firm relies on owner financing. Unlike the operating and investing activities, which *provided* cash during 1993, Sunrise's financing activities *used* cash of $23,000.

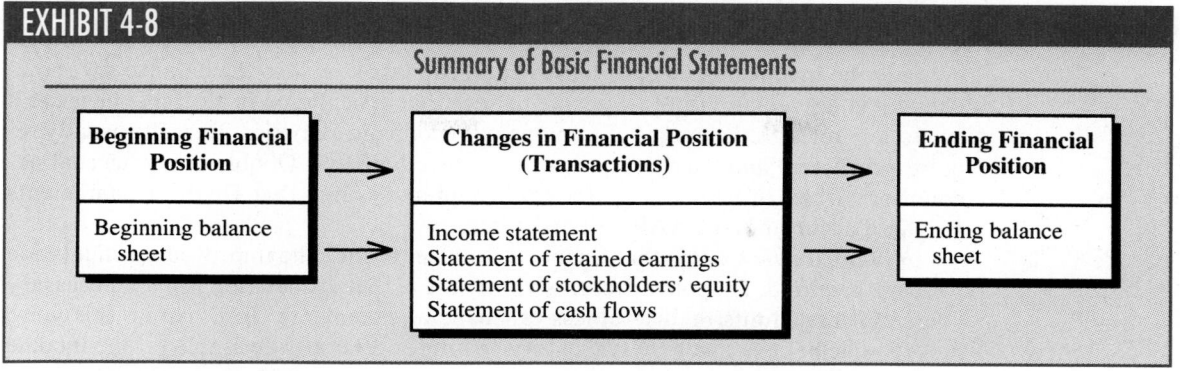

EXHIBIT 4-8

Summary of Basic Financial Statements

Beginning Financial Position		Changes in Financial Position (Transactions)		Ending Financial Position
Beginning balance sheet	→ →	Income statement Statement of retained earnings Statement of stockholders' equity Statement of cash flows	→	Ending balance sheet

Taken together, Sunrise's operating, investing, and financing activities resulted in a net increase in cash and cash equivalents of $38,500. The term "cash and cash equivalents" (as opposed to "cash") is used near the bottom of the statement because Sunrise has marketable securities. These short-term, highly liquid investments are considered to be part of the company's cash management program rather than a part of its operating, investing, or financing activities. Let us now *assume* that Sunrise had cash and cash equivalents of $24,000 at the beginning of 1993. If we add $24,000 to the $38,500 net increase in cash and cash equivalents, we find that Sunrise has cash and cash equivalents of $62,500 at the end of 1993.

Many other issues affect the form and content of the statement of cash flows. For example, when a company reports net cash flow from operating activities in the manner shown in Exhibit 4–7, a reconciliation of net income and net cash flow from operating activities must be provided in a separate schedule. This schedule is explained in Chapter 23.

RELATIONSHIP BETWEEN BASIC FINANCIAL STATEMENTS

As we have stated earlier, the basic financial statements **articulate** with one another. Their relationship is summarized in simplified terms in Exhibit 4–8.

A company's financial position at a particular moment in time is shown on the balance sheet. The other basic financial statements summarize various types of changes in financial position that have occurred during a period of time. The income statement explains the changes in financial position that are the result of earnings activities. The statement of retained earnings (or statement of stockholders' equity) explains certain changes in the equity component of financial position. Finally, the statement of cash flows summarizes all important cash receipts and payments during a period.

The income statement reports the revenues, expenses, gains, losses, and net income for a period. The net income explains a part of the change in retained earnings that is shown on the statement of retained earnings (or statement of stockholders' equity). The statement of cash flows summarizes the major cash-related activities that have occurred during the period. The income statement, statement of retained earnings (or statement of stockholders' equity), and statement of cash flows are tied together by the beginning and ending balance sheets. All of the basic financial statements articulate with one another because of the double-entry system of accounting and because revenues, expenses, gains, losses, investments by owners, and distributions to owners represent flows associated with the economic resources and obligations presented on the balance sheet.

Articulation is an important concept to understand about financial statements. When a company computes depreciation on its plant assets, for example, this affects not only the income statement (depreciation expense) but also the balance sheet (accumulated depreciation). Most people believe that articulation is desirable because it accurately reflects the nature of a company's economic activities. Benefits usually require sacrifices, and sacrifices usually produce benefits. Double entry accrual accounting, which we review in the next chapter, ensures that financial statements prepared according to GAAP will articulate.

A *minority* view holds that financial statements could be improved if articulation were not required. Proponents of this view believe that articulation is an unnecessary constraint that limits the usefulness of financial statements. To illustrate this view, most people believe that LIFO inventory costing is generally desirable for the income statement (because cost of goods sold is measured at recent cost prices) but undesirable for the balance sheet (because inventory is measured at outdated historical costs). In contrast, FIFO is generally viewed as desirable for the balance sheet but undesirable for the income statement. A proponent of nonarticulated financial statements might argue that a company should be allowed to use LIFO on its income statement and FIFO on its balance sheet. Moreover, there is no need for the two statements to articulate. We emphasize that nonarticulated financial statements, although interesting, are *not* generally accepted today.

OTHER FINANCIAL STATEMENT TOPICS

Disclosure   The **disclosure principle** requires an accountant to report information that might affect the decisions made by reasonably informed users of financial statements. To comply with this principle, an accountant usually must report in financial statements considerably more information than we have illustrated thus far in the chapter. Moreover, all of this information must be effectively communicated. In the remaining sections of this chapter, we shall discuss several other topics pertaining to basic financial statements.

To help you understand the kinds of information that companies actually report, we have included a set of financial statements of Strawbridge & Clothier on the endpapers of this book. Look over these statements now and refer to them frequently as you study the remaining chapters. Although the statements contain material that you have not yet encountered, you will understand them much better after you have studied this book.

NOTES TO FINANCIAL STATEMENTS

As illustrated earlier, financial statements are summaries that consist of very few words and dollar amounts. **Notes to financial statements** (often called **footnotes**) are used to report information that does not fit in the body of the statements without reducing the understandability of the statements. **Notes are an integral part of the financial statements and therefore must be prepared and read carefully.** The notes often require several pages.

Five major types of information are commonly disclosed in notes:

1. Information on **accounting policies.** As discussed below, a company must disclose the major accounting policies that it uses in preparing its financial statements.
2. Information on **subsequent events.** As discussed below, companies are required to disclose certain types of events that occur between the date shown on the balance sheet and the date on which the financial statements are issued.

FINANCIAL REPORTING NEEDS MORE THAN THE COMPUTER

The Securities & Exchange Commission is taking its first steps toward an electronic filing and retrieval system that will permit computer access to corporate reports filed with the commission. This is a worthwhile step toward computer technology that will allow for more efficient use of data. But it essentially substitutes access through computers for access through the mail or the SEC's reference room. It does not alter the basic information available, and it barely scratches the surface of the possibilities.

Information technology offers an unprecedented opportunity to effect a dramatic change not only in the way financial reporting is delivered to users but, more important, in its essential character. To appreciate the full potential of technology, consider the current state of corporate reporting.

The Financial Accounting Standards Board has stated that financial reports should provide information to help investors assess the prospective cash flows of reporting companies. At the same time, the board sees the primary focus of financial reporting to be information about earnings and its various components. But this is taking place when share prices do not necessarily follow the pattern of reported earnings. Companies can sustain impressive earnings-per-share growth rates over many years while showing no improvement—or even a decline—in stock prices. Providing financial information to people who wish to estimate company values is consistent with the FASB's objective of corporate financial reporting. Microcomputer technology provides policymakers at the FASB and the SEC with an unprecedented opportunity to accomplish this goal more effectively and at a lower cost to users than has ever been possible before.

Independence. Sophisticated users of financial reports are able to make their own assessments of a company's performance. An accountant's transformation of raw cash-flow data imposes costs on many Wall Street analysts who wish to estimate the company's cash flows before the application of accrual accounting procedures. As the securities market becomes more and more institutionalized, the accountants' contribution should shift from preparing highly structured financial statements to identifying and providing data that the market can then incorporate into its own analysis.

Information technology makes it possible to accommodate this data-base approach to corporate financial reporting. An electronic financial data base containing the data needed to produce conventional financial statements as well as alternative forms of analysis can be developed. Such a data base could make users less dependent on the companies' financial statements. With the data base and a variety of software, users could prepare financial statements under a variety of accounting assumptions. They could compute any number of income figures, or none at all. By merging the data about a specific company with industry and macroeconomic data bases, users could develop better and more comprehensive evaluations.

Regulators are concerned that the lack of uniformity in accounting methods impairs the credibility of financial reporting. This problem could be minimized with the data-base approach because users could choose the methods they prefer.

A shift would occur in the role of accounting standards. Instead of deciding which inventory or depreciation method to permit, the issue for policymakers would be which data to include in the data base and how consistency could be maintained across companies and over time. In brief, there would be less concern with how to calculate the bottom line and more concern with the adequacy and relevance of disclosure.

Judging Management. With the data-base approach, management's performance could be more easily judged by using a variety of measures other than reported earnings. To a large extent, market prices also reflect a comprehensive mix of publicly available information. Management may not always fully recognize this fact. However, if a variety of measures in addition to the official reported net income were readily available, then myopic dependence on a single number would be more difficult to justify.

A major potential benefit from a data-base system would be a shift in management focus. Managers would no longer judge their own performance by short-run reported earnings but by how much they had added to the company's economic value. Such a shift could be reflected in higher market values. In this way it would benefit shareholders, who are among the major users of financial statements.

The cost of implementing this approach will be one problem, of course. But the major obstacle is likely to be a resistance to change. Because the "let the user choose" approach would alter the present corporate reporting system, it no doubt will be vigorously debated. It is already technically feasible. If it does not come to pass, the reason probably will be political, not technological.

SOURCE: William H. Beaver and Alfred Rappaport, "Financial Reporting Needs More Than the Computer," *Business Week*, August 13, 1984, p. 16. Reprinted from the August 13, 1984, issue of *Business Week* by special permission, © 1984 by McGraw-Hill, Inc.

3. Information on **contingencies.** Companies often disclose certain contingencies, which are events, such as pending lawsuits, involving uncertainty about possible gain or loss that will be resolved in the future. We discuss accounting for contingencies in Chapter 14.
4. Information on major **contracts, commitments, and restrictions.** Important details about leases and pension plans, for example, usually are reported in the notes.
5. Information that **amplifies data** presented in the body of the statements. For example, a company may provide a schedule that separates its inventories into raw materials, work in process, and finished goods.

Notes to financial statements should be concise, complete, and easily understood by a reader who has a reasonable understanding of business affairs and is willing to study the financial statements. The precise nature of disclosures required in notes is highly detailed. We discuss these disclosures more fully at appropriate places in most of the remaining chapters.

SUMMARY OF ACCOUNTING POLICIES

Knowledgeable users of financial statements recognize that the numbers reported in a company's financial statements depend on the accounting policies used to generate them. As a result, when analyzing a company's financial statements, users typically want answers to questions such as: What inventory cost determination method (such as FIFO, LIFO, or average cost) does the company use? What depreciation method (such as double-declining balance, sum-of-the-years'-digits, or straight-line) does the company use?

To ensure that users have the information needed to answer these kinds of questions, *APB Opinion No. 22* requires a company to disclose the accounting policies that it uses. The term **accounting policies** refers to the specific principles and methods that a company has adopted for preparing its financial statements. The accounting policies that a company discloses should be those that: (1) involve a selection from existing acceptable alternatives; (2) are peculiar to the reporting company's industry; or (3) are unusual or innovative applications of generally accepted accounting principles.[29]

A company should preferably disclose its accounting policies in a separate **summary of significant accounting policies.** This summary should precede the notes to the financial statements or appear as the first note.[30]

SUBSEQUENT EVENTS

Financial statements seldom are issued on the date shown on the balance sheet. Instead, a period of time usually elapses during which the accountants and auditors complete their work on the statements. During this period, called the **subsequent period,** many important events can occur that have a material effect on the financial statements being prepared.

Materiality

Subsequent events are events that occur during the subsequent period, that is, between the date shown on the balance sheet and the date on which the financial statements are issued. Exhibit 4–9 illustrates the subsequent period, during which subsequent events may occur, in relation to a set of 1993 financial statements. The subsequent period is January 1, 1994, to February 28, 1994.

[29]*APB Opinion No. 22*, "Disclosure of Accounting Policies," 1972, par. 12.
[30]*APB Opinion No. 22*, par. 15.

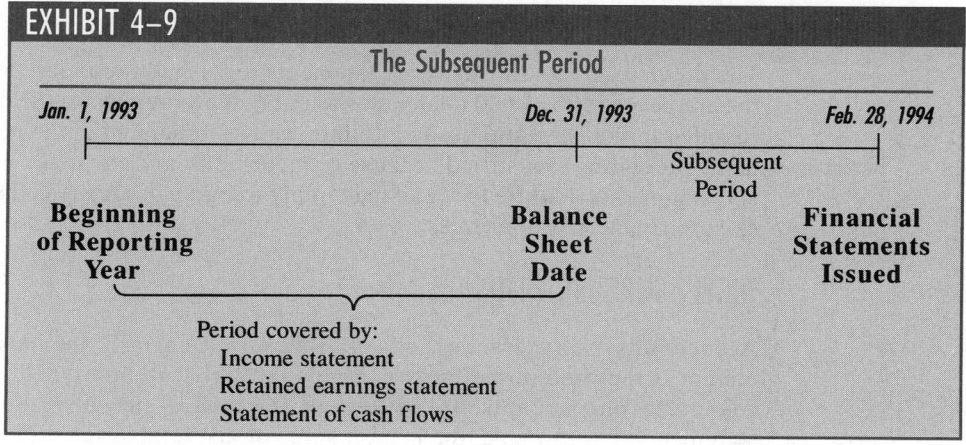

EXHIBIT 4-9

The Subsequent Period

There are two types of subsequent events. The first type consists of events that provide additional evidence about **conditions that existed on the balance sheet date** and that affect the estimates used in preparing the financial statements. The appropriate accounting for this type of subsequent event is to adjust the account balances reported in the financial statements in order to reflect the new information. For example, the bankruptcy of a major customer ten days after the balance sheet date usually reflects a condition (namely, the poor financial health of the customer) that existed on the balance sheet date, and the estimate of bad debts may therefore need to be revised upward to reflect the new information.

The second type of subsequent event is one that provides evidence about **conditions that arose after the balance sheet date.** Events of this type do not result in adjustments of the account balances of the previous period. They may, however, require disclosure in order to prevent the financial statements from being misleading. Examples of subsequent events that require disclosure are the purchase of a business, the loss of inventories or plant assets due to a casualty, and the sale of a bond or capital stock issue.[31]

Obviously, a subsequent event also affects the financial statements of the period in which the event occurs. For example, in the context of Exhibit 4–9, if a material sale of common stock occurred on January 10, 1994, this event should be disclosed in the notes to the 1993 financial statements and recorded as a transaction of 1994. A more thorough treatment of subsequent events usually appears in auditing texts.

COMPARATIVE FINANCIAL STATEMENTS

The financial statements illustrated in this chapter were prepared for one period only. In practice, **comparative financial statements** are ordinarily presented for two or more periods, as shown in the financial statements on the endpapers of this book. Such statements are more useful than single-period statements because they reveal important trends. When comparative financial statements are presented, all elements reported in the current period's statements should be comparable to those reported for the prior period(s). Any exceptions must be clearly explained.

---

[31]*Statement on Auditing Standards No. 1,* "Codification of Auditing Standards and Procedures" (New York: AICPA, 1972), Sec. 560, par. .06.

ROUNDING OF AMOUNTS

Materiality

The dollar amounts in financial statements are usually rounded. A recent survey of the annual reports of 600 companies found that 56 rounded to the nearest dollar, 404 rounded to the nearest thousand dollars, and 140 rounded to the nearest million dollars.[32] Rounding is justified because of materiality and the many estimates in financial statements. Failure to round may imply a degree of precision that simply does not exist in financial statements.

DISCLOSURE METHODS

Accountants use several methods of disclosure. Generally, the most important information is reported in the **body of the financial statements.** In addition to the account titles and amounts, **parenthetical disclosures** may be made in the body of the statements. For example, the market value of marketable securities may be shown in parentheses if it is greater than cost. Or a related asset and liability, such as inventory pledged as collateral on a note payable, may be cross-referenced by a parenthetical remark beside the respective title.

    Notes to the financial statements are used to report details that simply do not fit conveniently in the body of the statements. In addition, accountants often use **schedules** (presented alone or as part of the notes) to report such information as major inventory categories and operating expense details. The use of such schedules is particularly appropriate when a company prepares condensed financial statements. At certain times, accountants may use **supplementary statements** effectively. Such statements may be used, for example, to present financial statements that have been adjusted for inflation.

AMOUNT OF DISCLOSURE

Disclosure

Materiality

An elusive problem that the accountant faces when preparing financial statements is deciding on an appropriate **amount (extent) of disclosure.** Accountants want to prepare financial statements that are reasonably complete, yet understandable. Clearly, to achieve understandability, an accountant must summarize many details. The question is: To what extent can the accountant summarize and still present statements that are sufficiently complete and therefore in compliance with the disclosure principle?

    Deciding on an appropriate amount of disclosure in a given case depends on such related factors as the objectives of the statements, GAAP, the circumstances involved, the modifying convention of materiality, and professional judgment. Statements prepared for bankers, for example, often are fairly detailed in order to satisfy the bankers' needs. Those prepared for publication in annual reports to shareholders often are highly condensed.

    As a general principle, the **offsetting** of assets and liabilities in the balance sheet is improper except when a specific legal right of offset exists. For example, cash in a bond sinking fund should not be offset against the bond liability, even though the company intends to use the cash to pay the bonds.

    As another general principle, material **related-party transactions** should be disclosed. Examples are loans made by the company to its management or to a subsidiary.

---

[32]*Accounting Trends and Techniques,* 1990, p. 26.

TERMINOLOGY

The language of accounting is technical, consisting of some words whose meanings differ from their everyday connotations. To communicate effectively, accountants must select words and phrases that the average user of financial statements can understand.

There is no requirement that the financial statements contain the same account titles that appear in the general ledger. For example, "accounts receivable" in the general ledger is sometimes reported on the balance sheet as "amounts due from customers."

The accounting profession has been very concerned with improving the terminology used in financial statements. *Accounting Terminology Bulletin No. 1,* for example, noted that accountants have used the term "reserve" to describe asset contra accounts, liability accounts, retained earnings appropriations, and loss accounts. To avoid confusion, the bulletin recommended that the use of "reserve" be limited to retained earnings appropriations. The bulletin further recommended that accountants stop using the term "surplus" because it may mislead users by connoting an amount in excess of that needed. Accountants should use "paid-in capital" or "contributed capital" instead of "paid-in surplus" or "capital surplus." Likewise, the use of "retained earnings" is preferable to "earned surplus."[33]

One reason that we mention the terminology recommendations above is that the terms *not* recommended are still sometimes encountered in practice. We emphasize the use of modern, preferred terminology throughout the text. Remember that financial statements will not be useful if they do not communicate effectively.

AUDITOR'S REPORT

As explained in Chapter 1, financial statements often are accompanied by an independent auditor's report. Financial statements contain the representations of management. The functions of an independent auditor are to **examine the statements** and **express an opinion** that lends credibility to management's representations. This enables users to have greater confidence in the statements. Exhibit 1–1 (Chapter 1) illustrates the wording of a standard audit report in which an unqualified opinion was given on the financial statements.

CONCEPTUAL CONSIDERATIONS

The financial statements discussed in this chapter are directly related to the model of financial accounting theory that we explained in Chapter 2 (see Exhibit 2–1). You may wish to review Exhibit 2–1 now and consider the following important points:

1. Financial statements help to accomplish the *objectives* of financial reporting, which are to provide useful information, to provide information helpful in assessing cash flow prospects, and to provide information about enterprise resources, claims to those resources, and changes in them.
2. Financial statements seek to provide information that is both relevant and reliable. Recall that relevance and reliability are the primary *qualitative characteristics* of useful accounting information.

---

[33]*Accounting Terminology Bulletin No. 1,* "Review and Résumé," 1953, pars. 57–70.

3. Financial statements reflect the *assumptions* of economic entity (the entity identified at the top of the financial statements), periodicity (annual periods, quarterly periods, etc.), and going concern.

4. The *concepts* of financial position and changes in financial position are reflected in financial statements. Assets, liabilities, and owners' equity are the *elements* that compose financial position, while revenues, expenses, gains, losses, income, investments by owners and distributions to owners are the major *elements* that compose changes in financial position.

5. The *broad principles* of monetary unit, asset/liability measurement, revenue realization, matching, consistency, and disclosure are all reflected in financial statements.

6. Financial statements also reflect numerous *detailed principles* that we will cover throughout the text.

7. The *modifying conventions* of materiality, industry practices, conservatism, and substance over form also affect financial statements.

CONCLUDING REMARKS

Financial statements are the culmination of an accountant's work. They constitute the *output* of the accounting information system and serve as *input* for investment, credit, and similar decisions that help to determine how resources are allocated in our society.

Financial statements are summaries that are primarily historical. They are interrelated and general purpose, and they reflect many estimates. Underlying the information reported in financial statements are many important measurement and disclosure principles that we discuss throughout the text.

All financial statements bear the name of the reporting entity, the title of the statement, and the date or period of time covered. The balance sheet presents financial position at a particular point in time; the other basic statements present various changes in financial position during a period of time.

The financial statements discussed in this chapter are currently reported under generally accepted accounting principles. To help ensure that companies provide financial statements regularly, accountants follow certain steps during an accounting period. These steps, collectively called the **accounting cycle,** are presented in the next chapter.

KEY POINTS

1. The basic financial statements are the balance sheet, the income statement, the statement of cash flows, and the statement of retained earnings (or statement of stockholders' equity). (Objective 1)

2. Basic financial statements have several important characteristics:

   a. They are only a subset of the information needed by users for making rational investment, lending, and similar decisions.

   b. They are primarily historical in nature.

   c. They summarize information.

   d. They reflect many estimates.

   e. They are general-purpose reports designed to serve the needs of many different users.

   f. They articulate with one another. (Objective 1)

3. Extraordinary gains and losses result from events or transactions that are unusual in nature *and* not expected to recur in the foreseeable future. (Objective 2)

4. A multiple-step income statement presents subtotals for gross margin and operating income; a single-step income statement does not. (Objective 2)

5. Prior period adjustments, such as the correction of an error made in the financial statements of a prior period, should be charged or credited directly to retained earnings. (Objective 3)

6. The major balance sheet categories are:

   a. Assets
   - Current assets
   - Investments and funds
   - Property, plant, and equipment
   - Intangible assets
   - Other assets

   b. Liabilities
   - Current liabilities
   - Long-term liabilities

   c. Owners' equity
   - Paid-in capital
     - Capital stock
       - Preferred stock
       - Common stock
     - Paid-in capital in excess of par
   - Retained earnings   (Objective 4)

7. The statement of cash flows provides information about the cash receipts and cash payments of an entity during a period. (Objective 5)

8. Notes (footnotes) are an integral part of the basic financial statements. (Objective 6)

9. The role of an independent auditor is to examine financial statements and express an opinion on them. (Objective 6)

QUESTIONS

4–1 What are the basic financial statements?

4–2 What are some important characteristics of the basic financial statements?

4–3 What are the criteria used to determine whether a gain or loss is extraordinary?

4–4 Why does the accounting profession require that extraordinary gains and losses be presented in a special section of the income statement?

4–5 Make up three examples of extraordinary items. (Do not use the examples presented in the chapter.)

4–6 May gains and losses from disposal of a business segment and from changes in accounting principles be included in the extraordinary items category? Explain your answer.

4–7 Distinguish clearly between a multiple-step and a single-step income statement.

4–8 What are the advantages of using a multiple-step format for presenting the income statement? What are the advantages of using a single-step format?

4–9 What does the term "prior period adjustments" mean? How should prior period adjustments be reported in the financial statements?

4–10 Suppose that in 1993 a company changes its estimate of the *total* useful life of its 12-year-old building from 30 years to 40 years. For accounting purposes, what kind of an event is this, and how should the event be accounted for?

4–11 Define the term "current assets" and cite five examples of current assets.

4–12 Why are special fund balances and the cash surrender value of life insurance not usually reported among the current assets?

4–13 Define the term "current liabilities" and cite five examples of current liabilities.

4–14   Define the terms "working capital" and "current ratio."

4–15   Explain the various categories that may be used in the stockholders' equity section of the balance sheet.

4–16   What is treasury stock? Is treasury stock an asset? Explain your answer.

4–17   Identify and briefly describe the major categories of a statement of cash flows.

4–18   Distinguish between a cash basis income statement, a statement of cash receipts and disbursements, and a statement of cash flows. Which one is required by GAAP?

4–19   Why are the notes to the financial statements important to users?

4–20   Define the term "subsequent events." Indicate the two types (i.e., categories) of subsequent events and the appropriate accounting treatment for each type in the financial statements of the period preceding the subsequent event.

4–21   What factors should affect an accountant's decision about how detailed a given set of financial statements should be?

4–22   Why is terminology considered an important aspect of accounting?

4–23   What are the roles of management and the independent auditor in relation to a set of financial statements?

EXERCISES

4–24   COST OF GOODS SOLD   The following information pertains to Noe, Inc., for the 1993 accounting period:

Transportation-out	$ 9,500	Transportation-in	$ 7,100
Purchases	150,000	Sales discounts	5,200
Sales returns	11,200	Purchase returns	6,000
Inventory, Dec. 31	25,800	Purchase discounts	3,000
Purchase allowances	2,300	Advertising	28,000
Sales	290,000	Sales allowances	3,600
Inventory, Jan. 1	40,000		

Instructions

[a] Prepare the cost of goods sold section of Noe, Inc.'s income statement for 1993.
[b] Compute the gross margin for 1993.
[c] Indicate how the accounts not used in [a] and [b] should be classified in the income statement for 1993.

4–25   INCOME STATEMENT FORMATS   The following information pertains to the 1993 accounting period of Reams Company:

Cost of goods sold	$160,000
Dividend revenue	6,000
General and administrative expenses	21,000
Interest expense	5,000
Interest revenue	9,000
Net sales	290,000
Selling expenses	29,000
Income tax rate	40%
Number of common shares outstanding	10,000

Instructions

[a] Prepare a multiple-step income statement for 1993.
[b] Prepare a single-step income statement for 1993.

4–26   INCOME STATEMENT SECTIONS   Rao Company has been manufacturing and selling computers, household appliances, and medical supplies since 1981. The following events occurred during the company's 1993 accounting period:

[1] The company sold its computer division.
[2] The company lost one of its manufacturing plants because of an earthquake.
[3] The company lost its inventory held in a Middle Eastern country because of a government expropriation.
[4] The company sold its household appliance division.
[5] The company adopted the FIFO method of inventory cost determination. Prior to 1993, the company used the average cost method.
[6] The company adopted the straight-line method of accounting for all depreciable assets. Prior to 1993, the company used the double-declining balance method.

Instructions

Assume that each of the above events is material and qualifies for reporting in one of the following income statement sections: (1) discontinued operations; (2) extraordinary items; and (3) cumulative effect of a change in accounting principles. In what section should each event be reported?

4–27 RETAINED EARNINGS STATEMENT At the beginning of its 1993 calendar-year accounting period, Reaves, Inc., had retained earnings of $97,000. During 1993 the company earned a net income of $51,000 and declared cash dividends of $25,000 on its common stock. None of these dividends had been paid as of year-end. In addition, the company discovered that because of a mathematical error, depreciation expense had been overstated by $10,000 in 1992.

The company's income tax rate was 40% in 1992 and 1993. The company had 5,000 shares of common stock outstanding throughout 1993.

Instructions

Prepare a statement of retained earnings for Reaves for 1993.

4–28 COMBINED STATEMENT OF INCOME AND RETAINED EARNINGS The following information pertains to the 1993 calendar-year accounting period of Rimmer Corporation:

Number of common shares outstanding throughout the year	10,000
Cost of goods sold	$161,200
Dividends declared	50,000
Loss from earthquake (extraordinary item)	20,000
General and administrative expenses	41,000
Loss due to write-off of worthless equipment (unusual item)	17,000
Net sales	418,000
Selling expenses	48,800

Additional Information

Rimmer Corporation reported retained earnings of $167,000 on December 31, 1992. During 1993 the company discovered that because of a material counting error, ending inventory for 1992 had been overstated by $16,000. The company's income tax rate was 40% in 1992 and 1993.

Instructions

Prepare a combined statement of income and retained earnings for Rimmer Corporation for 1993. Use the single-step format.

4–29 WORKING CAPITAL The following information pertains to Liggett Company on December 31 of the current year:

Equipment	$240,000
Accumulated depreciation—equipment	40,000
Accounts receivable	27,000
Prepaid insurance	3,000
Short-term notes payable	12,000
Cash	40,000
Bonds payable maturing in 20 years	110,000
Total assets	368,000

Land	50,000
Accounts payable	30,000
Allowance for doubtful accounts	2,000
Merchandise inventory	34,000
Short-term investments	16,000
Wages payable	4,000
Total liabilities	171,000
Premium on bonds payable	15,000

Instructions

Compute Liggett Company's working capital on December 31. Show all of your work clearly.

4–30 PROPERTY, PLANT, AND EQUIPMENT AND LONG-TERM LIABILITIES Listed below are some of the account balances of Huskey Oil Company on December 31, 1993, the end of the company's annual accounting period:

Land held for future building site	$ 92,000
Oil deposit	800,000
Term bonds payable (10%, due June 30, 2004)	400,000
Accumulated depreciation—equipment	180,000
Building	250,000
Land on which building is located	55,000
Notes payable (12%, due Apr. 30, 1998)	80,000
Equipment	360,000
Accumulated depletion of oil deposit	150,000
Notes payable (10%, due Aug. 31, 1994)	30,000
Accumulated depreciation—building	75,000
Serial bonds payable (11%, due July 31, 1999 to July 31, 2004, inclusive)	300,000
Unamortized discount on term bonds payable	8,000
Accumulated depreciation—furniture and fixtures	20,000
Bond issue costs	5,000
Furniture and fixtures	50,000

Instructions

[a] Prepare the property, plant, and equipment and long-term liabilities sections of Huskey Oil Company's balance sheet on December 31, 1993.
[b] Indicate how Huskey Oil Company should classify any accounts that you did not use in [a].

4–31 STOCKHOLDERS' EQUITY The following information pertains to Cantey Company on December 31 of the current year:

[1] The company has preferred and common stock outstanding. The preferred stock is $5 par value, 10%, cumulative and nonparticipating. A total of 20,000 shares were authorized, of which 10,000 shares are issued and outstanding on December 31. Cantey sold its preferred stock for $6 per share.
[2] The common stock has a $1 par value. A total of 50,000 shares were authorized, of which 40,000 shares are issued and outstanding on December 31. Cantey sold its common stock for $10 per share.
[3] The company has retained earnings of $1,800,000, of which $320,000 have been appropriated for plant expansion.

Instructions

Prepare the stockholders' equity section of Cantey Company's balance sheet on December 31.

4–32 BALANCE SHEET The following list of accounts and balances pertains to Groves Company on December 31, 1993, the end of the company's annual accounting period:

Accounts payable	$ 28,000
Accounts receivable	37,000
Accumulated depreciation—furniture and fixtures	10,000

Advances from customers (pertaining to goods that Groves Company will supply in 1994)	6,000
Allowance for doubtful accounts	1,800
Bond sinking fund	90,000
Bonds payable (14%, due Jan. 1, 2006)	150,000
Cash	26,000
Common stock ($1 par, 50,000 shares authorized, 30,000 shares issued and outstanding)	30,000
Franchise	86,000
Furniture and fixtures	70,000
Merchandise inventory	48,400
Paid-in capital in excess of par	60,000
Premium on bonds payable	4,000
Prepaid rent (pertains to the first quarter of 1994)	8,400
Retained earnings	?

Instructions

Prepare a balance sheet in good form for Groves Company on December 31, 1993.

4-33 MISSING AMOUNTS IN FINANCIAL STATEMENTS The following *independent* cases pertain to a 1993 calendar-year accounting period:

	Case A	Case B	Case C	Case D
Revenues	$100,000	$200,000	?	?
Expenses	?	?	$ 50,000	$ 70,000
Net income	40,000	?	60,000	?
Retained earnings, Jan. 1	?	300,000	180,000	120,000
Dividends declared	50,000	70,000	?	30,000
Retained earnings, Dec. 31	120,000	310,000	?	?
Current assets, Dec. 31	?	60,000	100,000	?
Noncurrent assets, Dec. 31	420,000	?	580,000	300,000
Total assets, Dec. 31	500,000	?	?	410,000
Current liabilities, Dec. 31	?	30,000	?	20,000
Noncurrent liabilities, Dec. 31	270,000	?	170,000	?
Total liabilities, Dec. 31	?	140,000	?	?
Paid-in capital, Dec. 31	?	520,000	210,000	100,000
Total stockholders' equity, Dec. 31	200,000	?	410,000	210,000

Instructions

Determine the missing amounts.

4-34 INCOME STATEMENT AND BALANCE SHEET CLASSIFICATION Listed below are several categories that may be used in a multiple-step income statement and a balance sheet:

[a] Net sales

[b] Cost of goods sold

[c] Operating expenses

[d] Other revenues

[e] Other expenses

[f] Extraordinary items

[g] Current assets

[h] Investments and funds

[i] Property, plant, and equipment

[j] Intangible assets

[k] Other assets

[l] Current liabilities

[m] Long-term liabilities

[n] Capital stock - *Common, preferred at par*

[o] Paid-in capital in excess of par -

[p] Retained earnings

Instructions

Use the letters above to show where each of the following items should usually be classified.

[1] Goodwill.

[2] Depreciation expense.

[3] Timber stand.

[4] Buildings.

[5] Interest expense.

[6] Accounts payable.

[7] Copyrights.

[8] Bonds payable (due in 20 years).

[9] Advertising.
[10] Investment in subsidiary company.
[11] Patents.
[12] Bond sinking fund.
[13] Sales discounts.
[14] Paid-in capital in excess of par—common stock.

[15] Loss of property in Iowa due to a hurricane.
[16] Write-off of inventories due to obsolescence.
[17] Transportation-out.
[18] Preferred stock.
[19] Accumulated depreciation.
[20] Accounts receivable.

4–35   INCOME STATEMENT AND BALANCE SHEET CLASSIFICATION   Refer to the list of categories ([a] through [p]) in 4–34.

Instructions

Use the appropriate letters to show where each of the following items should usually be classified.

[1] Cash.
[2] Allowance for doubtful accounts.
[3] Common stock dividend distributable.
[4] Merchandise inventory (ending).
[5] Note receivable (due in three months).
[6] Reserve for plant expansion.
[7] Oil deposit.
[8] Premium on bonds that are payable in 10 years.
[9] Transportation-in.
[10] Bond issue costs.

[11] Dividend revenue.
[12] Common stock subscriptions receivable.
[13] Organization costs.
[14] Interest payable.
[15] Sales returns and allowances.
[16] Purchase returns.
[17] Note payable (due in five years).
[18] Wages payable.
[19] Common stock.
[20] Accumulated depletion.

4–36   INCOME STATEMENT AND BALANCE SHEET CLASSIFICATION   Refer to the list of categories ([a] through [p]) in 4–34.

Instructions

Use the appropriate letters to show where each of the following items should usually be classified.

[1] Salaries.
[2] Merchandise inventory (beginning).
[3] Gain from foreign exchange transactions.
[4] Building site.
[5] Pension obligations.
[6] Investment in 100 shares of Exxon's common stock that will likely be sold in three months.
[7] Prepaid insurance.
[8] Bad-debts expense.
[9] Common stock subscribed.
[10] Equipment used in the business.
[11] Purchase allowances.
[12] Building.
[13] Flood loss in an area that floods every two to three years.
[14] Treasury stock.
[15] Pension fund.
[16] Reserve for bond sinking fund.
[17] Cash surrender value of life insurance.
[18] Raw materials.
[19] Premium on preferred stock.
[20] Discount on bonds payable (bonds are payable in 13 years).

4–37   INCOME STATEMENT AND BALANCE SHEET CLASSIFICATION   Refer to the list of categories ([a] through [p]) in 4–34.

Instructions

Use the appropriate letters to indicate where each of the following items should usually be classified. If an item should not be reported on either an income statement or a balance sheet, indicate where the item should be reported.

[1] Trademarks.
[2] Dividends declared.
[3] Purchases.
[4] Correction of an error made last year when computing depreciation expense.
[5] Franchise.
[6] Building that is being constructed for the company's own use.
[7] Small tools used in the business.
[8] Unearned rent revenue (will be earned in the first quarter of the next accounting period).
[9] Returnable containers used in the business.
[10] Machinery rearrangement costs.
[11] Bonds payable (due in six months; payment will be made from current assets).
[12] Equipment held for sale (was previously used in the business).
[13] Dividends payable.
[14] Appropriation for contingencies.
[15] Land held for future plant site.
[16] Deficit.
[17] Loss on sale of land.
[18] Taxes payable.
[19] Work-in-process.
[20] Unusual and nonrecurring loss of inventories due to expropriation by a foreign government.

4–38 STATEMENT OF CASH FLOWS The following information pertains to Cormack Company during 1993:

Dividends paid	$ 10,000
Cash received from customers	120,000
Proceeds from issuing common stock	25,000
Interest received	10,000
Proceeds from sale of long-term investments	6,000
Cash paid to suppliers and employees	95,000
Purchases of long-term investments	18,000
Income taxes paid	15,000

Cormack Company had cash of $51,275 on January 1, 1993.

Instructions

Prepare a statement of cash flows for 1993.

4–39 SUBSEQUENT EVENTS Lauer Company's accounting period ends on December 31, and the company issues its financial statements on the following February 1. Below are some events that occurred during *1994:*

Jan. 4 Sale of common stock. *After UE, at 12/31, no add'l owners yet - only disclose*
7 Write-off of an account receivable because customer was formally declared bankrupt on January 7. The bankruptcy litigation was in process on December 31, 1993. *Made sale before UE*
12 Loss of a material portion of inventories because of a sudden flood.
18 Purchase of a competing business. *Bought this yr.*
21 Purchase of additional inventory. *routine transaction*
27 Write-off of an account receivable because the customer's business was destroyed by an earthquake on January 27. *NO adj. can't foresee natural disaster on 12/31, Assume customer could pay*

Instructions

Indicate the appropriate treatment for each of the above events in Lauer Company's financial statements for *1993.* Assume that each event is material.

PROBLEMS

4–40 INCOME STATEMENT FORMATS The following list of items pertains to the 1993 calendar-year accounting period of Matthews, Inc.:

Advertising expense	$ 19,000
Gain on sale of investments	15,200
Interest expense	7,500

Interest revenue	8,900
Loss of inventory due to flood (considered unusual and nonrecurring)	21,000
Loss on write-off of plant assets due to obsolescence	21,800
Merchandise inventory, Dec. 31	80,000
Merchandise inventory, Jan. 1	62,000
Miscellaneous general and administrative expenses	7,800
Miscellaneous selling expenses	12,000
Office salaries expense	47,500
Office supplies expense	8,100
Purchases	455,000
Purchase discounts	8,700
Purchase returns and allowances	31,000
Sales	911,000
Sales discounts	15,200
Sales returns and allowances	22,800
Sales salaries expense	52,000
Transportation-in	13,700
Utilities expense	10,400

Matthews, Inc., had 10,000 shares of common stock outstanding throughout 1993. The company's income tax rate is 40%.

Instructions

[a] Prepare a detailed, multiple-step income statement for 1993.

[b] Prepare a condensed, single-step income statement for 1993.

[c] Which of the two forms of income statements do you prefer? Explain your answer.

4–41 CORRECTED INCOME STATEMENT AND RETAINED EARNINGS STATEMENT   The accountant for Hardy Company has just handed you the income statement and retained earnings statement that appear below:

Hardy Company
INCOME STATEMENT
As of December 31, 1993

Revenues		
Net sales		$638,000
Extraordinary gain from expropriation of property by a foreign government		50,000
Correction of understatement of 1992 ending inventory due to error		30,000
Rent revenue		11,800
Dividend revenue		7,200
Total revenues		737,000
Expenses		
Cost of goods sold	$328,000	
Selling expenses	109,600	
General and administrative expenses	84,200	
Interest expense	12,200	
Total expenses		534,000
Net income		$203,000

Hardy Company
STATEMENT OF RETAINED EARNINGS
As of December 31, 1993

Retained earnings, Jan. 1		$789,000
Add: Net income		203,000
		992,000
Less: Extraordinary loss of plant assets due to earthquake	$60,000	
Unusual loss on sale of long-term investments	23,000	
Dividends declared	37,000	120,000
Retained earnings, Dec. 31		$872,000

Additional Information

[1] You have determined that the account balances in the above statements are correct. The statements, however, are not presented according to GAAP.

[2] The company had 10,000 shares of common stock outstanding throughout 1993.

[3] The company's income tax rate was 40% in 1992 and 1993.

[4] The company uses a calendar-year accounting period.

Instructions

[a] Prepare a condensed, multiple-step income statement for 1993 that complies with GAAP.

[b] Prepare a condensed, single-step income statement for 1993 that complies with GAAP.

[c] Prepare a statement of retained earnings for 1993 that complies with GAAP.

[d] From the standpoint of user decision making, why should extraordinary gains and losses be presented in a special section of the income statement?

4–42 CORRECTED RETAINED EARNINGS STATEMENT The bookkeeper for Dawson Company recently prepared the following statement of retained earnings:

Dawson Company
STATEMENT OF RETAINED EARNINGS
December 31, 1993

Retained earnings, Jan. 1, 1993			$619,572
Add:	Net income for 1993	$93,477	
	Gain on sale of land	85,420	
	Gain from settlement of litigation that began in 1992	25,000	
	Gain from foreign currency transaction	6,134	210,031
			829,603
Less:	Dividends declared during 1993	20,000	
	Loss of inventory caused by a government prohibition judged to be unusual and nonrecurring	50,000	
	Recognition of salaries expense incurred in 1992 but erroneously not recognized in the 1992 income statement	19,500	
	Loss from write-off of equipment leased to others	12,119	101,619
Retained earnings, Dec. 31, 1993			$727,984

Instructions

[a] Prepare a corrected statement of retained earnings for 1993. Assume an income tax rate of 40% and 10,000 shares of common stock outstanding throughout 1993. (*Note:* The additions and deductions in the statement shown above are *before* income taxes, except for net income.)

[b] Indicate specifically where Dawson Company should report any items that do not belong on the statement of retained earnings.

4–43 COMBINED STATEMENT OF INCOME AND RETAINED EARNINGS The following information pertains to the 1993 calendar-year accounting period of Chun Corporation:

Cost of goods sold	$222,600
Dividend revenue	7,590
Dividends declared	80,000
Gain on sale of investments (not considered unusual or nonrecurring for this company)	89,340
General and administrative expenses	69,587
Interest expense	12,650
Loss from expropriation of properties (considered unusual and nonrecurring)	48,000
Loss from settlement of litigation that began in 1992 (not considered unusual or nonrecurring for this company)	35,000
Loss of warehouse due to hurricane (considered unusual but recurring for this company)	42,150
Net sales	495,554
Selling expenses	63,473
Write-off of inventory due to obsolescence (considered unusual but recurring for this company)	17,024

Additional Information

Chun Corporation reported retained earnings of $187,000 on its balance sheet dated December 31, 1992. During 1993 it was discovered that $60,000 of revenue earned in 1992 had not been reported on the 1992 income statement. The company had 5,000 shares of common stock outstanding throughout 1993.

Instructions

[a] Prepare a combined statement of income and retained earnings for 1993. Use the multiple-step format and assume an income tax rate of 40%.

[b] Do you favor a combined statement of income and retained earnings over separate statements of income and retained earnings? Explain your answer.

4–44 STATEMENT OF STOCKHOLDERS' EQUITY Haven Company reported the following amounts in the stockholders' equity section of its balance sheet dated December 31, 1992:

Preferred stock ($100 par value; 1,000 shares)	$100,000
Common stock ($25 par value; 10,000 shares)	250,000
Paid-in capital in excess of par	300,000
Retained earnings	341,580

On January 3, 1993, the company sold 2,000 additional shares of common stock for $60 per share. During 1993 it was discovered that $25,000 of revenue earned in 1992 had not been reported on the 1992 income statement.

Haven Company reported a net income for 1993 of $55,000. The company declared cash dividends of $2,500 on the preferred stock and $7,500 on the common stock at the end of *each* of the four quarters of 1993. Dividends are paid in cash 30 days after being declared.

Instructions

Prepare a statement of stockholders' equity for the year ended December 31, 1993. Assume an income tax rate of 40%.

4–45 STATEMENT OF STOCKHOLDERS' EQUITY Luther Company reported the following amounts in the stockholders' equity section of its balance sheet dated December 31, 1992:

Preferred stock ($150 par value; 1,000 shares)	$150,000
Common stock ($37.50 par value; 10,000 shares)	375,000
Paid-in capital in excess of par	600,000
Retained earnings	450,400

Additional Information

[1] On January 2, 1993, Luther sold 2,000 additional shares of common stock for $90 per share.

[2] Late in 1993 it was learned that because of a mathematical error, an overstatement of depreciation expense by $37,500 had occurred in 1992.

[3] Luther reported a net income for 1993 of $82,500.

[4] Luther declared cash dividends of $15,000 on the preferred stock and $45,000 on the common stock during 1993.

Instructions

Prepare a statement of stockholders' equity for the year ended December 31, 1993. Assume an income tax rate of 40%.

4–46 BALANCE SHEET The following accounts and balances pertain to Zirkle Corporation on December 31, 1993:

Accounts payable	$ 38,300
Accounts receivable	43,900
Accumulated depletion	165,300
Accumulated depreciation	70,000
Paid-in capital in excess of par	369,000

Advances from customers (advances pertain to goods that Zirkle Corporation will supply in 1994)	4,500
Advances to suppliers (advances pertain to goods that suppliers will provide in 1994)	7,100
Allowance for doubtful accounts	2,600
Appropriation for plant expansion	58,500
Bond issue costs	21,300
Bond sinking fund	190,700
Bonds payable (10%, due July 1, 2004)	500,000
Building	210,000
Cash	21,100
Cash surrender value of life insurance	12,300
Common stock ($1 par, 50,000 shares authorized, 40,000 shares issued and outstanding)	40,000
Common stock subscribed (1,000 shares)	1,000
Franchise	21,840
Interest payable	3,000
Investment in bonds—long term (at cost; market value $72,000)	65,000
Land	99,500
Land held for future plant site	138,000
Marketable securities—short term (at cost which approximates market value)	18,570
Merchandise inventory (at lower of FIFO cost or market)	41,430
Note payable (12%, due Apr. 1, 1997)	25,000
Oil deposit	568,300
Organization costs	10,560
Prepaid insurance	4,300
Salaries payable	6,700
Stock subscriptions receivable (due in 3 months)	10,000
Unamortized discount on bonds payable	11,000
Unappropriated retained earnings	211,000

Instructions

Prepare a balance sheet in good form.

4–47 BALANCE SHEET The following information pertains to Quinn Enterprises on December 31, 1993:

Patents	$160,000
Supplies	20,990
Common stock ($10 par, 20,000 shares authorized, 10,000 shares issued and outstanding)	100,000
Cash	50,000
Land	160,200
Machinery rearrangement costs	48,300
Unappropriated retained earnings	?
Serial 12% debenture bonds, $50,000 installments due annually from June 1, 1994, through June 1, 2003	500,000
Cash surrender value of life insurance	11,400
Trademarks	48,000
Appropriation for contingencies	80,000
Advances from customers (advances pertain to goods that Quinn Enterprises will provide in 1994)	15,875
Allowance for doubtful accounts	3,300
Plant expansion fund	203,100
Accounts payable	31,000
Accumulated depreciation—building	45,000
Investment in land (held for long-term speculative purposes)	196,500
Machinery and equipment	290,800
Unearned rent revenue (Quinn Enterprises will earn this revenue during the first quarter of 1994)	6,125
Paid-in capital in excess of par	400,000
Accumulated depreciation of machinery and equipment	30,000

Building	250,000
Accounts receivable	73,410
Long-term investment in common stock (at cost; market value $98,700)	84,000
Note receivable (due on May 15, 1994)	21,000
Marketable securities (at cost; market value $44,430)	37,000
Notes payable (due in 1994)	40,000
Merchandise inventory (at lower of FIFO cost or market)	58,600

Instructions

[a] Prepare a balance sheet in good form. Compute the missing amount of unappropriated retained earnings.

[b] What are serial 12% debenture bonds? Explain the rationale for the financial reporting treatment of these bonds.

4–48 CORRECTED BALANCE SHEET   The bookkeeper for Totino's Corporation has prepared the following balance sheet:

Totino's Corporation
BALANCE SHEET
For 1993

Debits

Current Debits

Cash	$ 36,000	
Cash surrender value of life insurance	18,000	
Building fund	112,000	
Accounts receivable	58,760	
Merchandise inventory	49,010	
Unamortized discount on bonds payable	12,000	
Total current debits		$ 285,770

Noncurrent Debits

Marketable securities	25,300	
Advances to suppliers	7,500	
Prepaid rent	8,400	
Land held for future plant site	80,000	
Land	125,000	
Building	215,000	
Machinery and equipment	396,000	
Mineral deposit	327,000	
Goodwill	75,700	
Patents	41,300	
Machinery rearrangement costs	51,000	
Total noncurrent debits		1,352,200
Total debits		$1,637,970

Credits

Current Credits

Allowance for doubtful accounts	$ 4,340	
Accounts payable	42,630	
Interest payable	6,000	
Income tax payable	22,500	
Pension obligations	119,000	
Total current credits		$ 194,470

Noncurrent Credits

Accumulated depreciation of building	58,000
Accumulated depreciation of machinery and equipment	66,000
Accumulated depletion of mineral deposit	70,000
Note payable	20,000

Advances from customers	11,000	
Bonds payable	500,000	
Preferred stock	100,000	
Common stock	45,000	
Paid-in capital in excess of par	384,140	
Retained earnings	189,360	
Total noncurrent credits		1,443,500
Total credits		$1,637,970

Additional Information

[1] You have determined that although the *dollar amounts* reported are correct, the balance sheet is not in accordance with GAAP.

[2] Merchandise inventory is reported at the lower of average cost or market value.

[3] The marketable securities, which had a market value of $32,600 on December 31, 1993, are reported at cost. Management plans to sell the securities in 1994.

[4] The advances to suppliers pertain to goods that will be provided during 1994.

[5] The prepaid rent applies to the first quarter of 1994.

[6] The pension obligations will be paid after 2001.

[7] The note payable is due on May 1, 1994.

[8] The advances from customers pertain to goods that Totino's Corporation will provide in 1994.

[9] The bonds payable pay interest of 10% and are due on June 30, 2005.

[10] Relevant details about the preferred and common stock are as follows:
Preferred stock—$10 par value, 8%, cumulative and nonparticipating, 20,000 shares authorized, 10,000 shares issued and outstanding.
Common stock—$1 par value, 50,000 shares authorized, 45,000 shares issued and outstanding.

Instructions

Prepare a balance sheet in good form.

4–49 CORRECTED BALANCE SHEET The bookkeeper for Lenhardt Company prepared the following balance sheet on December 31, 1993:

Lenhardt Company
BALANCE SHEET
December 31, 1993

Assets

Current assets		$ 558,525
Investments and funds		28,520
Property, plant, and equipment		723,600
Intangible assets		80,355
Other assets		98,000
Total assets		$1,489,000

Liabilities and Stockholders' Equity

Current liabilities	$162,000	
Long-term liabilities	562,000	
Total liabilities		$ 724,000
Stockholders' equity		765,000
Total liabilities and stockholders' equity		$1,489,000

Upon inquiry you learn the following additional facts:

[1] Current assets include cash, $83,000; merchandise inventory (at lower of FIFO cost or market), $75,125; note receivable (13%, due June 1, 1996), $100,000; investment in subsidiary (held for control), $215,000; and plant expansion fund, $85,400.

[2] Investments and funds include prepaid insurance (applicable to the first six months of 1994), $12,000; and bond issue costs, $16,520.

[3] Property, plant, and equipment includes land, $167,000; land held for future plant site, $146,600; building, $375,000 less accumulated depreciation, $45,000; and furniture and fixtures, $114,600 less accumulated depreciation, $34,600.

[4] Intangible assets include accounts receivable of $63,000 less an allowance for doubtful accounts of $4,125; and organization costs, $21,480.

[5] Other assets consist of goodwill, $98,000.

[6] Current liabilities include accounts payable, $23,595; interest payable, $8,405; and a note payable (12%, due May 1, 1996), $130,000.

[7] Long-term liabilities include serial 10% debenture bonds, $500,000 ($50,000 installments are payable annually from April 1, 1994, through April 1, 2003); advances from customers (advances pertain to goods that Lenhardt Company will ship in 1994) $12,000; and retained earnings appropriated for bond retirement, $50,000.

[8] Stockholders' equity consists of common stock ($1 par, 50,000 shares authorized, 40,000 shares issued and outstanding), $40,000; paid-in capital in excess of par, $430,000; and unappropriated retained earnings, $295,000.

Instructions

Prepare a balance sheet in good form.

4–50 INCOME STATEMENT, RETAINED EARNINGS STATEMENT, AND BALANCE SHEET The information shown below was obtained from the accounting records of Marshall Company on December 31, 1993, the end of the company's annual accounting period. The account balances shown have been updated through December 31.

Accounts payable	$ 52,500
Accounts receivable	78,000
Accumulated depletion	65,000
Accumulated depreciation	70,000
Advances from customers (advances pertain to goods that Marshall Company will ship in 1994)	18,300
Allowance for doubtful accounts	3,000
Bond issue costs	31,000
Bond sinking fund	115,000
Bonds payable (10%, due June 1, 2006)	400,000
Building	275,000
Cash	41,110
Cash surrender value of life insurance	31,600
Common stock ($10 par, 20,000 shares authorized, 10,000 shares issued and outstanding throughout 1993)	100,000
Cost of goods sold	503,140
Dividend revenue	8,390
Dividends declared	100,000
Gain from expropriation of property by a foreign government (considered unusual and nonrecurring)	100,000
General and administrative expenses	253,430
Goodwill	53,100
Interest expense	50,000
Interest payable	12,500
Investment in common stock—long term (at cost; market value $72,000)	67,000
Land	196,000
Land held for future plant site	140,000
Loss of plant assets due to flood (considered unusual and nonrecurring)	70,000
Loss on sale of long-term investments (considered unusual but not nonrecurring)	10,000
Marketable securities—short term (at cost which approximates market value)	21,890
Merchandise inventory (at lower of FIFO cost or market)	73,500
Mineral deposit	236,400
Net sales	1,482,850
Note payable (12%, due May 1, 1997)	100,000

Paid-in capital in excess of par	236,000
Patents	12,900
Prepaid insurance	8,500
Rent revenue	12,500
Salaries payable	19,700
• Selling expenses	287,170
Unamortized discount on bonds payable	11,000

Additional Information

Marshall Company had retained earnings of $157,000 on January 1, 1993. The company's income tax rate is 40%. Income taxes have already been paid.

Instructions

[a] Prepare an income statement (multiple-step format) for the year ended December 31, 1993.
[b] Prepare a statement of retained earnings for the year ended December 31, 1993.
[c] Prepare a balance sheet as of December 31, 1993.
[d] Provide evidence showing that the financial statements you prepared articulate with each other.

4–51 INCOME STATEMENT, RETAINED EARNINGS STATEMENT, AND BALANCE SHEET   Listed below are account balances of Atino Company on December 31, 1993, the end of the company's annual accounting period. The account balances shown have been updated through December 31.

Paid-in capital in excess of par	$ 361,600
Net sales	1,604,750
Dividends declared	200,000
Cash	118,000
Land	114,000
Franchise	89,900
Note receivable (14%, due July 30, 1998)	50,000
Accounts payable	53,700
Bond issue costs	13,000
Common stock ($10 par, 25,000 shares authorized, 10,000 shares issued and outstanding throughout 1993)	100,000
Note payable (12%, due July 1, 1999)	200,000
Other revenue	45,250
Supplies	12,300
Plant expansion fund	115,000
Accumulated depreciation—furniture and fixtures	37,000
Organization costs	21,700
Serial 10% debenture bonds ($50,000 installments are due annually from June 1, 1994, through June 1, 2001)	400,000
Loss of inventory due to earthquake (considered unusual and nonrecurring)	100,000
Land held for future plant site	90,000
Merchandise inventory (at lower of average cost or market)	87,400
Furniture and fixtures	123,000
Advances from customers (advances pertain to goods that Atino Company will ship in 1994)	25,300
Cost of goods sold	657,500
Loss from write-off of plant assets due to obsolescence (considered unusual but not nonrecurring)	22,000
Investment in subsidiary (held for control)	179,000
Building	375,000
Interest expense	60,000
General and administrative expenses	296,400
Accounts receivable	75,000
Selling expenses	214,100
Allowance for doubtful accounts	3,700
Interest payable	10,000
Accumulated depreciation of building	75,000

Additional Information

Atino Company reported retained earnings of $193,000 on its balance sheet dated December 31, 1992. On July 14, 1993, it was discovered that $40,000 of revenue earned during 1992 had been incorrectly omitted from the 1992 income statement. The company's income tax rate was 40% in 1992 and 1993. Income taxes have already been paid.

Instructions

[a] Prepare an income statement (single-step format) for the year ended December 31, 1993.
[b] Prepare a statement of retained earnings for the year ended December 31, 1993.
[c] Prepare a balance sheet as of December 31, 1993.
[d] Provide evidence showing that the financial statements you prepared articulate with each other.

4–52   STATEMENT OF CASH FLOWS   The following events pertain to the 1993 calendar-year accounting period of Ramsey Company:

[1] Received cash from the following sources:

a. From issuing short-term debt	$ 11,000
b. From issuing long-term debt	25,000
c. From selling land	21,000
d. From selling equipment	30,000
e. From issuing preferred stock	15,000
f. From collecting short-term loans	15,000
g. From dividends received	4,000
h. From customers	300,000
i. From interest received	16,000

[2] Paid cash for the following purposes:

a. To make short-term loans	$ 10,000
b. To purchase land	25,000
c. To liquidate long-term note	32,000
d. To pay dividends	26,000
e. To purchase equipment	44,000
f. To liquidate short-term debt	14,000
g. To pay suppliers and employees	210,000
h. To pay interest	5,000
i. To pay income taxes	25,000

Ramsey Company had cash of $93,000 on January 1, 1993.

Instructions

Prepare a statement of cash flows for 1993.

CASES

4–53   EXTRAORDINARY ITEMS   As an audit partner for Lucke & Lucke, CPAs, you are responsible for many clients. The events listed below occurred during 1993:

[1] Patten Company sustained a loss when it sold its computer division. Patten had been manufacturing computers and household appliances in separate divisions since 1981.
[2] Luce Company lost some uninsured equipment because of an earthquake. This is the first earthquake to occur in the area where the equipment was located, and geologists believe that the area will not experience earthquakes in the future.
[3] Sutch Company changed from the average cost method to the FIFO method of inventory cost determination.
[4] It was discovered that Cloninger Company's bookkeeper forgot to deduct salvage value when computing straight-line depreciation for each of the two preceding years.
[5] Dobbs Corporation wrote off some plant assets because of obsolescence.
[6] Because of an expropriation, Nicley Company lost all of its inventory held in a Middle Eastern country.

[7] Raines Enterprises determined that certain depreciable assets would probably have useful lives 10 years longer than projected when the assets were purchased.

[8] Taft's Children's Wear destroyed a large portion of its inventory because of a government ban on the sale of clothing made of a flameproof fabric that causes skin irritations.

[9] White, Inc., discovered that the ending inventory for the previous year had been misstated because of a counting error.

[10] Keene Company lost some inventory because of a flood. Floods occur every three to five years in the area where the inventory was lost.

[11] Kilby, Inc., lost all of its perishable inventory because its employees went on strike.

[12] International Business Enterprises had a gain from foreign currency transactions.

[13] Maull Corporation realized a gain from an insurance settlement. The settlement pertained to the company's South American plant, which was expropriated in 1993.

[14] Based on recent collection experience, Wertz, Inc., changed the percentage used to estimate bad-debts expense. The percentage was changed from 1% to 1.5% of net sales.

[15] Redmon Company sustained a loss from selling some of the common stock in the company's investment portfolio.

Instructions

Indicate which of the above events should be reported as extraordinary items. If an event should not be reported as an extraordinary item, indicate the appropriate financial statement category in which the event should be reported. Assume a multiple-step format and that all events are material.

4–54 INCOME AND CASH FLOWS As an accountant for Eastpack, Inc., you recently prepared the financial statements for the past year. The statements show that Eastpack had a substantial net income for the year; however, net cash flow from operating activities was a large *negative* amount. After studying the statements carefully, Eastpack's president questions whether the statements are correct. He says, "I thought that net income and net cash flow from operating activities were related concepts. I simply don't understand how we could have a large negative operating cash flow in the same period that we generated such high earnings."

Instructions

Assuming that Eastpack's financial statements are not erroneous, present major reasons that could conceivably explain why the company's net income substantially exceeds its net cash flow from operating activities.

4–55 ESTIMATES IN FINANCIAL STATEMENTS Many companies promise to pay for their active employees' health care after they retire. Two alternative methods of accounting for the cost of medical benefits of retirees have been widely discussed in recent years. Method 1 would treat the costs as expenses when the benefits are ultimately paid to retirees (i.e., after the employees retire). Method 2 would attempt to better comply with the matching principle by *estimating* the future costs of retirees' health care benefits and treating the costs as expenses during the period over which the retirees worked for the company. As the company recognizes the expense, a liability for future medical benefits would also be recognized.

In a *Business Week* article (September 16, 1989, p. 106), a financial analyst arguing in favor of method 1 was quoted as saying that "It is better to be correctly wrong, and have no number in the financial statements, than to be approximately correct and mislead investors."

Instructions

Do you agree or disagree with the financial analyst? Explain the rationale that supports your answer.

4–56 ESTIMATES IN FINANCIAL STATEMENTS Assume that you are a CPA employed by an independent auditing firm. You and an accountant who works for one of your clients (a retail clothing company) are discussing the need to make estimates in the financial statements for the period just ended. The accountant states, "Financial statements presented in conformity with generally accepted accounting principles are described in the authoritative literature of the accounting profession as historical in nature. To me, that means that historical financial statements report transactions and events that have already happened and do not attempt to impound forecasts of future events into the measurements made in the statements. This simplifies the accountant's role and reduces the responsibilities assumed by a preparer of financial statements. I have approached the preparation of our company's financial statements in that manner. In a nutshell, our historical financial statements are just that: a treatise of what has already happened, unaffected by estimates of things that might happen in the future."

Instructions

Do the accountant's assertions accurately describe financial statements as they are presently prepared under GAAP? Explain the rationale that supports your answer.

4–57   FINANCIAL-STATEMENT DEFICIENCIES   The following is the complete set of financial statements prepared by Harton Corporation:

Harton Corporation
STATEMENT OF EARNINGS AND
RETAINED EARNINGS
For the Fiscal Year Ended August 31, 1993

Sales		$3,500,000
Less returns and allowances		35,000
Net sales		3,465,000
Less cost of goods sold		1,039,000
Gross margin		2,426,000
Less:		
Selling expenses	$1,000,000	
General administrative expenses	1,079,000	2,079,000
Operating earnings		347,000
Add other revenue:		
Purchase discounts	10,000	
Gain on increased value of investments		
in real estate	300,000	
Correction of error in last year's statement	90,000	400,000
Ordinary earnings		747,000
Add extraordinary item—gain on sale of		
fixed asset		53,000
Earnings before income tax		800,000
Less income tax expense		380,000
Net earnings		420,000
Add beginning retained earnings		3,258,000
		3,678,000
Less:		
Dividends (12% stock dividend declared		
but not yet issued)		120,000
Contingent liability [Note 2]		808,000
Ending unappropriated retained earnings		$2,750,000

Harton Corporation
STATEMENT OF FINANCIAL POSITION
August 31, 1993
Assets

Current Assets		
Cash	$ 80,000	
Accounts receivable, net	110,000	
Inventory	130,000	
Total current assets		$ 320,000

Other Assets

Land and building, net	4,160,000	
Investments in real estate (current value)	1,508,000	
Goodwill [Note 1]	250,000	
Discount on bonds payable	42,000	
Total other assets		5,960,000
Total assets		$6,280,000

Liabilities and Stockholders' Equity

Current Liabilities

Accounts payable	$ 140,000	
Income taxes payable	320,000	
Stock dividend payable	120,000	
Total current liabilities		$ 580,000

Other Liabilities

Due to Willow, Inc. [Note 2]	808,000	
Bonds payable (including portion due within one year)	1,000,000	
Total other liabilities		1,808,000
Total liabilities		2,388,000

Stockholders' Equity

Common stock	1,000,000	
Paid-in capital in excess of par	142,000	
Unappropriated retained earnings	2,750,000	
Total stockholders' equity		3,892,000
Total liabilities and stockholders' equity		$6,280,000

Notes to the Financial Statements

[1] As required by federal income tax laws, goodwill is not amortized. The goodwill was "acquired" in 1990.

[2] The amount due to Willow, Inc., depends on the outcome of a lawsuit which is currently pending. The amount of loss, if any, is not expected to exceed $808,000.

Instructions

Identify and explain the deficiencies in the presentation of Harton's financial statements. There are *no* arithmetical errors in the statements. Organize your answer as follows:

[a] Deficiencies in the statement of earnings and retained earnings.
[b] Deficiencies in the statement of financial position.
[c] General comments.

If an item appears on both statements, identify the deficiencies for each statement separately.

(AICPA adapted)

4–58 BALANCE SHEET CLASSIFICATION You are the controller for Commerce Lifestyles, Inc. As you plan to prepare the company's most recent financial statements, you identify an important issue that relates to balance sheet classification. During the last year Commerce issued some bonds that are convertible into common stock at the option of the bondholders. The convertible bonds will mature in twenty years if not converted. The convertible bonds do not require the payment of interest unless the company operates profitably. Commerce's president does not want to classify these securities as debt but rather suggests that they be classified as part of stockholders' equity. He notes that they are similar to common stock because they do not require the payment of interest (similar to dividends) unless the company operates profitably. He also asserts that most convertible bond investors have indicated to him that they intend to convert the bonds into stock in the near future.

Instructions

Respond to the president regarding the balance sheet classification issues involved in this case. If you conclude that the president's suggested treatment is inappropriate, be sure to consider whether any compromises are appropriate.

4–59   REPORTING CONTRACTUAL COMMITMENTS   Jones, Inc., a construction contractor, has entered into two contracts during the past few days. Jones' controller has asked your advice as to how the company should report the contracts in the company's financial statements for the year just ended.

The first contract involves a commitment to buy Federal securities (treasury bonds) from a securities dealer in the "when issued" market. The Federal government has indicated that it will issue treasury bonds two weeks after the end of the company's year. Jones, Inc., has committed to buy and pay for $250,000 of those bonds at face amount when they are issued. Since the company entered into the contract, the value of the treasury bonds has increased in the market due to a general decrease in market interest rates. The controller wants to report the gain in value of the treasury bonds but does not wish to report the commitment as a liability and a related asset.

The second contract relates to a commitment of the company to buy a tract of land within the next year. According to the contract terms, Jones, Inc., was required to pay a $25,000 option fee to secure the right to buy the land for $1,000,000 at any time during the next year. The controller asserts that the company intends to buy the land within the option period but wonders how the contract should be reported in the company's financial statements for the year just ended. He wants to report the option fee as an asset called "deposit on land" but does not want to report the remaining amount of the commitment as a liability and a related asset.

The controller does not wish to report the gross amounts of the two contracts as liabilities and assets because of the adverse effects of doing so on the relationships and ratios in the company's financial statements. For example, recording those commitments as liabilities would result in a higher debt/equity ratio, a relationship about which the company's bank has already expressed concern.

Instructions

Evaluate each of the two commitments and determine which, if either, should be reported as a liability and related asset in Jones' financial statements. Also, comment on the propriety of recording and reporting the gain in value on the contract to acquire the treasury bonds in the "when issued" market.

PART 2

—

TOOLS
OF
ACCOUNTING

CHAPTER 5

The Accounting Cycle

OBJECTIVES

To discuss and illustrate the steps in the accounting cycle. These steps are the following:

1. Identify transactions.
2. Analyze transactions.
3. Record transactions in journals.
4. Post to ledger accounts.
5. Prepare an unadjusted trial balance.
6. Prepare adjusting entries.
7. Prepare an adjusted trial balance.
8. Prepare financial statements.
9. Prepare closing entries.
10. Prepare a post-closing trial balance (optional).
11. Prepare reversing entries (optional).

T he primary objective of financial reporting is to provide information useful in making investment, lending, and similar decisions. To provide this information, accountants follow a sequence of steps during an enterprise's accounting period, which is usually one year. This sequence is called the **accounting cycle** or the **accounting process.**

In this chapter we review the steps in the accounting cycle. Most students have been introduced to these steps in previous courses. However, a thorough review of the accounting cycle will solidify the knowledge required to understand the remainder of this text.

The widespread use of electronic computers has had a profound impact on business data processing in recent years. In this chapter, however, we emphasize manual processing methods often used by smaller businesses. Emphasizing a manual system enables us to illustrate the accounting cycle in the simplest, most understandable manner. Fundamentally, the chapter covers the basic accounting functions of recording and summarizing business data. Accountants apply these basic functions regardless of whether a company processes information manually, mechanically, or electronically.

STEPS IN THE ACCOUNTING CYCLE

STEP 1.   IDENTIFY TRANSACTIONS

The initial step in the accounting cycle is transaction identification. Accountants must systematically identify all transactions so that they can be properly recorded. Broadly defined, a **transaction** is an event that (1) changes a firm's financial position *and* (2) can be measured with sufficient objectivity. For example, a cash purchase of supplies is a transaction which changes a firm's financial position by increasing one asset (supplies) and decreasing another (cash). In contrast, employing a new office manager is not presently considered a transaction under generally accepted accounting principles (GAAP). A major reason why hiring activities are not considered accountable events is that the impact on the firm's financial position is too uncertain to measure in a sufficiently reliable manner.

Transactions may be external or internal in nature. **External transactions** are those that involve outside parties. Examples include sales, purchases, and loans. **Internal transactions** are those confined to the accounting entity itself. Examples are depreciation, amortization, and conversion of production costs into inventory.

A firm's accounting system should identify pertinent information about every transaction. When a transaction occurs, a **source document,** often called a **business paper,** is prepared to evidence the transaction. For external transactions, for example, a sales invoice is a source document that supports a sale transaction, a check supports a payment transaction, and a promissory note supports a loan. Depreciation schedules, amortization schedules, and inventory schedules are common examples of source documents for internal transactions. Because entries in accounting records are based on information in the source documents, these documents must be carefully designed, prepared, and controlled. To verify the accuracy of financial statement information, an accountant should be able to trace financial statement numbers to the source documents. This tracing process is important to the auditing function. The term **audit trail** refers to the evidence that links the balances shown in the financial statements with the thousands of transactions that are summarized in those balances.

STEP 2.   ANALYZE TRANSACTIONS

After identifying transactions, the accountant determines their impact on financial position as represented by the basic equation Assets = Liabilities + Owners' Equity. This analysis occurs within the **double-entry system** of accounting. Under this system, which was first described in the fifteenth century by an Italian mathematician named Paciolo, the accountant makes entries in which debits equal credits for every transaction. These entries are made in records called **accounts**; every transaction affects at least two accounts.

There are several forms of accounts. The simplest form, illustrated below, is called a **T account** because it resembles the letter T.

Account Title	
Debits	Credits
(left side)	(right side)

Companies actually use account forms that are more detailed than the T account. Nevertheless, the T account is a convenient and widely used instructional device. We therefore use it throughout the text.

The term **debit** (sometimes called **charge**) refers to the left-hand side of an account; **credit** refers to the right-hand side. When both sides of an account are each totaled and the smaller sum is subtracted from the larger, the difference is called the **balance** of the account. Every account has a **normal balance,** which is simply the balance that one would *ordinarily* find in the account. The normal balance may be either debit or credit, depending on the type of account.

Proper analysis of a transaction requires an understanding of the major types of accounts and the manner in which debit and credit entries affect each, as is summarized below:[1]

Type (Category) of Account	Balance Increased by	Balance Decreased by	Normal Balance
Asset	Debit	Credit	Debit
Liability	Credit	Debit	Credit
Owners' equity	Credit	Debit	Credit
Revenue	Credit	Debit	Credit
Expense	Debit	Credit	Debit

Note that debits and credits affect asset and expense accounts in one way and liability, owners' equity, and revenue accounts in the opposite way. Also note that the normal balance in an account coincides with what is done to increase the balance in the account. For example, we increase the balance in an asset account with a debit; the normal balance in an asset account is therefore debit.

Remember that any transaction affects financial position as represented by the basic equation Assets = Liabilities + Owners' Equity. Revenue and expense accounts are also reflected in this equation because they are **temporary extensions of owners' equity,** as shown in Exhibit 5–1. Companies conveniently use these temporary accounts to determine net income. With these accounts they measure revenue and expense activities in many individual accounts and thereby avoid excessive detail

---

[1]Other types of accounts will be discussed at appropriate places in the text.

in the owners' equity account. At the end of the accounting period, the balances in the revenue and expense accounts are transferred to the owners' equity account via the closing process (explained at Step 9).[2]

STEP 3.   RECORD TRANSACTIONS IN JOURNALS

After the information shown on source documents has been gathered and analyzed, it is entered in chronological order in a journal. Thus, a journal is a chronological record of transactions. The process of recording transactions in a journal is called journalizing. Because this marks the first time that transactions are recorded in the debit-and-credit framework, a journal is often called a book of original entry.

General Journal

The most fundamental journal is the general journal, often called simply the journal. A general journal entry consists of the transaction date, the accounts and amounts to be debited (Dr.), the accounts and amounts to be credited (Cr.), and an explanation of the transaction. A simple journal entry consists of one debit and one credit. A compound journal entry consists of two or more debits or two or more credits. To illustrate, consider the following two transactions of Brookshire Corporation during October:

Oct.   1   Sold merchandise to Johnson Company for $1,200 on account.

       4   Purchased machinery from Roberts Tool Company for $10,000. Paid $2,000 cash and signed a 90-day, 12% promissory note for the remainder of the purchase price.

These transactions would be entered in Brookshire's general journal as follows:

General Journal   Page J7

Date		Description	Post. Ref.	Dr.	Cr.
Oct.	1	Accounts Receivable	111	1,200	
		Sales	401		1,200
		Sold merchandise to Johnson Company on account.			
	4	Machinery	161	10,000	
		Cash	101		2,000
		Notes Payable	211		8,000
		Purchased machinery from Roberts Tool Company. Paid $2,000 cash and signed a 90-day, 12% promissory note.			

As shown above, the account to be debited is customarily listed before the account to be credited. The account credited is also indented to distinguish it clearly from the account debited. The posting reference column contains the identification numbers of the individual ledger accounts to which each part of every journal entry has been posted. These numbers are inserted in the column when posting occurs; they

---

[2]Gain accounts (e.g., Gain on Sale of Land) function in the same way as revenue accounts; loss accounts (e.g., Loss of Building Caused by Fire) function in the same way as expense accounts.

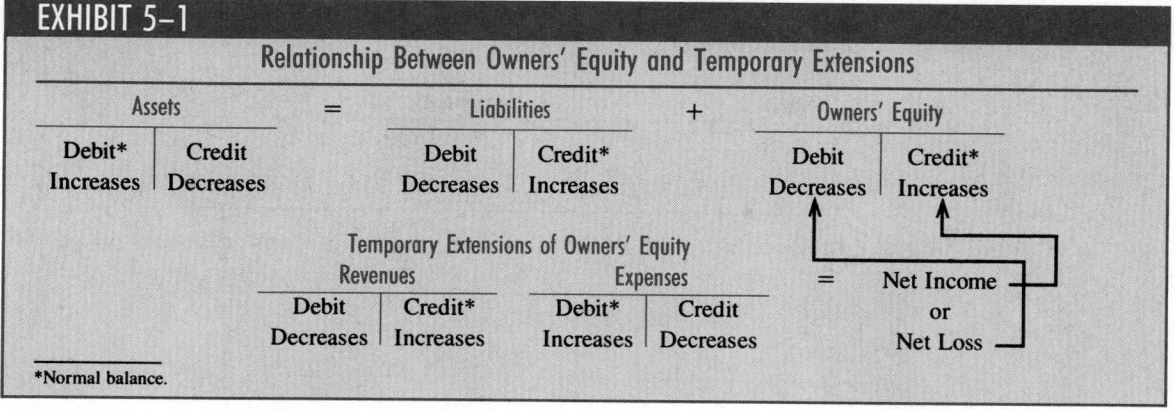

EXHIBIT 5-1

Relationship Between Owners' Equity and Temporary Extensions

permit cross-referencing between the general journal and the ledger accounts. Also, account numbers in the posting reference column verify that journal entries have been posted.

Special Journals

Although all transactions *could* be recorded in a general journal, a business usually has several **special journals** in addition to a general journal in order to facilitate the efficient recording of large numbers of similar transactions. Common types of special journals and the nature of the transactions recorded in each type are listed below:

Type of Special Journal	Nature of Transactions Recorded
Sales journal	Sales of merchandise on credit
Cash receipts journal	Receipts of cash from any source
Purchases journal	Purchases of merchandise on credit[3]
Cash payments journal	Payments of cash for any purpose

The number, purpose, and format of special journals vary considerably. Each business must decide on its special journals based on its needs. The topic of special journals is covered in more depth in Appendix B.

When a company uses special journals, it uses the general journal to record all transactions that do not fit the special journals. The general journal, then, is an integral part of an accounting system whether or not special journals are used. For this reason and because the general journal offers a convenient instructional format, we use it throughout the text to illustrate the application of various accounting concepts and principles.

STEP 4.   POST TO LEDGER ACCOUNTS

General Ledger

After transactions have been journalized, the next step is to transfer the information to accounts in the general ledger. This transfer process is called **posting**. Posting may occur at various times during an accounting period, and it involves reorganizing information from a chronological system to a system of individual accounts. When we post, we bring all like items (e.g., all cash items) together in one place. To illustrate, the

---

[3]Sometimes a purchases journal is expanded to record *all credit purchases,* including merchandise, equipment, and supplies.

journal entries shown earlier for Brookshire Corporation are posted to the general ledger T accounts below:

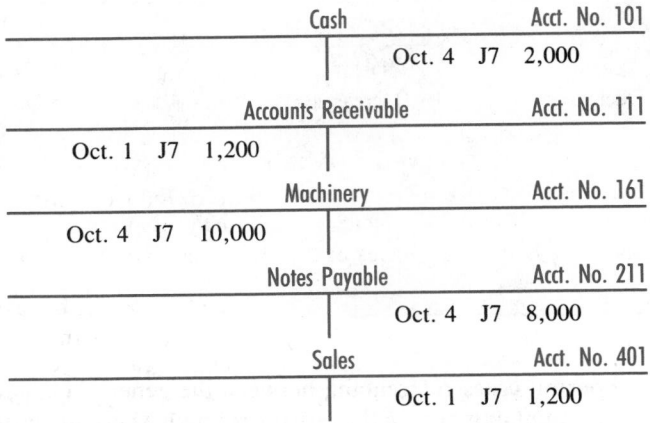

Cash			Acct. No. 101
	Oct. 4	J7	2,000

Accounts Receivable			Acct. No. 111
Oct. 1 J7 1,200			

Machinery			Acct. No. 161
Oct. 4 J7 10,000			

Notes Payable			Acct. No. 211
	Oct. 4	J7	8,000

Sales			Acct. No. 401
	Oct. 1	J7	1,200

As shown above, the accountant must post each part of every general journal entry. The posting process consists of (1) transferring the date and amount to the appropriate side (debit or credit) of the ledger account, (2) inserting the journal page number as a posting reference in the ledger account, and (3) inserting the ledger account number in the posting reference column of the general journal.

The **general ledger,** often called simply the **ledger,** consists of many accounts. Each account is a record of information about a particular asset, such as Cash and Accounts Receivable; liability, such as Accounts Payable and Notes Payable; owners' equity, such as Common Stock and Retained Earnings; revenue, such as Sales and Service Fees Earned; and expense, such as Salaries and Advertising. Based on the scope of its operations and the extent of detail desired for reporting purposes, each business determines the exact nature of its accounts. The **chart of accounts** is a listing of a firm's general ledger accounts. The accounts are usually numbered to permit easy identification and cross-referencing with the journals. Each asset account, for example, might be assigned a code number between 101 and 199; each liability account might be assigned a code number between 201 and 299.

In a computer-based accounting system, the general ledger information is stored on a machine-sensible device such as magnetic tape or disc. In a manual system, the general ledger is often a bound collection of pages. Each page represents an account. Typically, the first group of pages represents the asset accounts, followed by those of the liability, owners' equity, revenue, and expense accounts, in that order.

Certain ledger accounts are called real accounts, whereas others are known as nominal accounts. **Real (or permanent) accounts** remain open. These include asset, liability, and owners' equity accounts. Real accounts measure stocks of things, such as resources or debts, that exist at a certain point in time. **Nominal (or temporary) accounts** are closed at the end of every accounting period. These include revenue and expense accounts. Nominal accounts measure flows, such as sales or cost of goods sold, that occur over time. During an accounting period, **mixed accounts** contain both real and nominal components. At the end of the period, adjusting entries separate mixed accounts into their real and nominal components. For example, before adjusting entries, the Supplies account usually has both consumed (nominal) and unconsumed (real) portions. An adjusting entry places the consumed portion in a nominal account (Supplies Expense) and allows the unconsumed portion to remain in a real account (Supplies). After the accountant makes adjusting entries, all accounts in the ledger are either real or nominal.

The general ledger ordinarily includes certain adjunct and contra accounts. An **adjunct account** is one whose balance is added to the balance in the account to which it relates. For example, Transportation-In is an adjunct account to Purchases, and Premium on Bonds Payable is an adjunct account to Bonds Payable. A **contra** (or **offset**) **account** is one whose balance is subtracted from the balance in the account to which it relates. For instance, Sales Discounts is a contra account to Sales, and Allowance for Doubtful Accounts is a contra account to Accounts Receivable. Adjunct and contra accounts are closed at the end of an accounting period only if the accounts they relate to are also closed.

Subsidiary Ledgers

In addition to a general ledger, most businesses have one or more **subsidiary ledgers.** The purpose of a subsidiary ledger is to store the details of certain general ledger accounts. For example, a company may have thousands of credit customers. While it is certainly necessary to know the total amount that these customers owe the company, it is also essential to know the name and address of each customer and how much each one owes. This information facilitates the billing process and is useful when the company makes credit-granting decisions. Rather than have a separate Accounts Receivable for each customer in the general ledger, firms usually create an Accounts Receivable subsidiary ledger. This ledger is often in the form of a tray of alphabetized cards, each card representing a customer's account. The Accounts Receivable account in the general ledger then becomes a **control** (or **main**) **account** that is supported by many detailed accounts in the subsidiary ledger.

When a subsidiary ledger exists, posting must appear in both the control account and the appropriate subsidiary ledger accounts. The control account is debited for the total debits and credited for the total credits made to the subsidiary ledger accounts. After all accounts have been posted, the balance in the control account should equal the total of the individual account balances in the subsidiary ledger. To assure this equality, the accountant periodically reconciles each control account with its subsidiary ledger accounts.

Why use subsidiary ledgers? One important reason that a company uses them is to reduce the number of accounts in its general ledger. With fewer accounts it is easier to avoid errors and to find them when they occur. Subsidiary ledgers also facilitate the division of labor in an accounting department. Individuals with limited education or experience can often be assigned responsibility for one or more subsidiary ledgers. Work on the various ledgers can thereby proceed simultaneously.

A subsidiary ledger can support any general ledger account. Subsidiary ledgers are often set up for Cash (when a company has several bank accounts), Accounts Receivable, Merchandise Inventory (when a company uses a perpetual inventory system), Plant Assets, Accounts Payable, Capital Stock, Selling Expenses, and Administrative Expenses.

STEP 5. PREPARE AN UNADJUSTED TRIAL BALANCE

A **trial balance** is a list of general ledger accounts and their debit or credit balances. It summarizes, usually on one sheet of paper, information that appears in a company's general ledger. The accountant prepares a trial balance at the end of every accounting period, before making the adjusting entries. Because the account balances do not yet reflect adjustments, the trial balance prepared at this time is often called an **unadjusted trial balance.**

A trial balance serves two main purposes:

1. It provides evidence that total debits in a company's general ledger equal total credits.
2. It provides information that helps the accountant to formulate adjusting entries.

The trial balance is a control device that helps to eliminate accounting errors. When total debits in a company's general ledger do not equal total credits, the trial balance is said to be **out of balance**. This condition alerts the accountant that one or more errors have been made. The accountant must find and correct these errors before preparing financial statements. On the other hand, a trial balance which is **in balance** does not necessarily signify the absence of errors. For example, the trial balance does not indicate the failure to record a transaction or the recording of a transaction in the wrong accounts.

The unadjusted trial balance for Eagle Company at December 31, 1993, is illustrated below. Information pertaining to this company, which uses a calendar-year accounting period, will be used to help explain the subsequent steps in the accounting cycle.

Eagle Company
UNADJUSTED TRIAL BALANCE
December 31, 1993

Account	Dr.	Cr.
Cash	$ 21,079	
Accounts receivable	60,000	
Allowance for doubtful accounts		$ 500
Note receivable	10,000	
Merchandise inventory	57,606	
Prepaid insurance	1,200	
Land	40,000	
Building	100,000	
Accumulated depreciation—building		10,000
Office equipment	120,000	
Accumulated depreciation—office equipment		24,000
Accounts payable		38,405
Unearned rent revenue		4,800
Long-term note payable		72,000
Common stock, $5 par		50,000
Paid-in capital in excess of par value		65,000
Retained earnings		34,215
Sales		523,000
Purchases	187,000	
Purchase returns		2,000
Purchase allowances		2,500
Purchase discounts		3,600
Transportation-in	7,250	
Sales salaries expense	78,000	
Advertising expense	24,000	
Transportation-out	6,000	
Miscellaneous selling expenses	5,141	
Officers' salaries expense	76,000	
Professional services	23,000	
Utilities expense	8,244	
Miscellaneous administrative expenses	5,500	
Totals	$830,020	$830,020

STEP 6.   PREPARE ADJUSTING ENTRIES

Revenue
Realization
Matching

Under the **cash basis of accounting**, revenue is recorded only when received in cash, and expenses are recorded only when paid in cash. In contrast, the **accrual basis of accounting** requires recognition of revenue when it is earned according to the revenue realization principle and recognition of expenses when they are incurred according to the matching principle. Under accrual basis accounting, the cash inflows typically associated with a given period's revenues may occur in past, present, or future periods. Similarly, the cash outflows typically associated with a given period's expenses may occur in past, present, or future periods. Thus, the primary difference between cash basis and accrual basis accounting is the timing of the recognition of revenues and expenses.

Current generally accepted accounting principles require accrual basis accounting, because this system generates measures of performance and financial position that are superior to those of cash basis accounting. To help implement the accrual basis of accounting, the accountant makes certain **adjusting entries** (often called **adjustments**) at the end of every accounting period. Adjusting entries are initially recorded in the general journal, then posted to the appropriate general ledger accounts. If an entry requires an account that is not in the general ledger, the accountant simply creates (opens) a new account.

Purpose of Adjusting Entries

Revenue
Realization
Matching

Adjusting entries permit an accurate measurement of earnings and financial position on the accrual basis. Adjusting entries are based on **revenue realization** and **matching** (see Chapter 2). Every adjusting entry allocates revenues or expenses between current and future periods. Moreover, every adjusting entry affects both a balance sheet account (asset or liability) and an income statement account (revenue or expense).[4]

Accumulating Adjusting Data

An external event such as a purchase or sale signals the accountant to record the transaction. At the end of the accounting period, however, no external events signal the accountant to record adjusting entries. How then does the accountant determine the nature and amounts of adjusting entries to record? Basically, the accountant carefully considers each account in the trial balance and examines certain source documents. Accounts that have mixed balances (i.e., mixed accounts) must be separated into real and nominal components. In addition, certain information not reflected on the trial balance must be entered in the accounting records. For example, the presence of Prepaid Insurance on the trial balance causes the accountant to inquire whether any insurance has expired and therefore should be charged to expense. This inquiry normally involves a review of the company's insurance policies. A Notes Receivable account usually leads the accountant to review the notes to determine whether any interest has been earned. Interest earned should be entered in a revenue account. Because many adjusting entries repeat from one accounting period to the next, accountants can often gain insight into the nature and amounts of this period's adjusting entries by examining the ones that were made at the end of the preceding period.

---

[4]Certain **correcting entries** and **reclassification entries** are sometimes made during the adjustment process. For example, a correcting entry might be made to charge to Advertising Expense an amount that was mistakenly charged to Research and Development Expense during the year. A reclassification entry might be made to reclassify to current liability status the portion of long-term debt that will mature within the next year. As these examples suggest, a correcting or reclassification entry often affects only nominal accounts or only real accounts.

Classification of Adjusting Entries

We shall classify adjusting entries using the following three categories:

1. Accruals
2. Deferrals
3. Special items

Accruals.   Accruals are adjusting entries that normally have *one* of the following characteristics:

1. A revenue is recognized before the related cash receipt, *or*
2. An expense is recognized before the related cash payment.

Accruals are appropriate for revenues and related assets and for expenses and related liabilities that increase or accumulate gradually during the accounting period. Rather than recording these items weekly, daily, or even more frequently, the accountant records them by making adjusting entries at the end of the accounting period.

As an example of **accrued revenues** (accrued assets), on July 1, 1993, Eagle Company acquired a $10,000, one-year, 12% note receivable, with interest payable at maturity. This note represents money loaned by the company and is reflected on its trial balance. The revenue realization principle holds, in part, that revenue generated by allowing others to use enterprise assets, such as money, should be recorded as time passes. Accordingly, the company should make the following adjusting entry on December 31, 1993, the end of the company's annual accounting period:

Revenue Realization

Dec. 31	Interest Receivable	600	
	Interest Revenue		600

To accrue interest for 6 months on note receivable.
Accrued interest is computed as follows:
$10,000 × .12 × 6/12 = $600

Revenue Realization

The adjusting entry assigns the $600 of interest revenue to 1993, the period in which the revenue was earned according to the revenue realization principle. The cash receipt associated with the interest will occur in the next accounting period, specifically on June 30, 1994. Note that the adjusting entry affects both a balance sheet account (Interest Receivable) and an income statement account (Interest Revenue). This journal entry, like all others, must be posted to the general ledger accounts affected.

As an example of **accrued expenses** (accrued liabilities), on October 1, 1993, Eagle Company issued a $72,000, 10-year, 10% note payable with interest payable annually on September 30. September 30, 1994, is therefore the first date that interest will be paid. Nevertheless, the money borrowed was used during the last three months of 1993. Accordingly, the cost of that money (interest) must be reported as an expense in 1993 to comply with the matching principle. The accountant should make the following adjusting entry:

Matching

Dec. 31	Interest Expense	1,800	
	Interest Payable		1,800

To accrue interest for 3 months on note payable.
Accrued interest is computed as follows:
$72,000 × .10 × 3/12 = $1,800

The adjusting entry assigns the $1,800 of interest expense to the current accounting period (1993), the period in which the expense was incurred. The cash payment associated with the accrued interest will occur on September 30 of the next account-

EXHIBIT 5-2

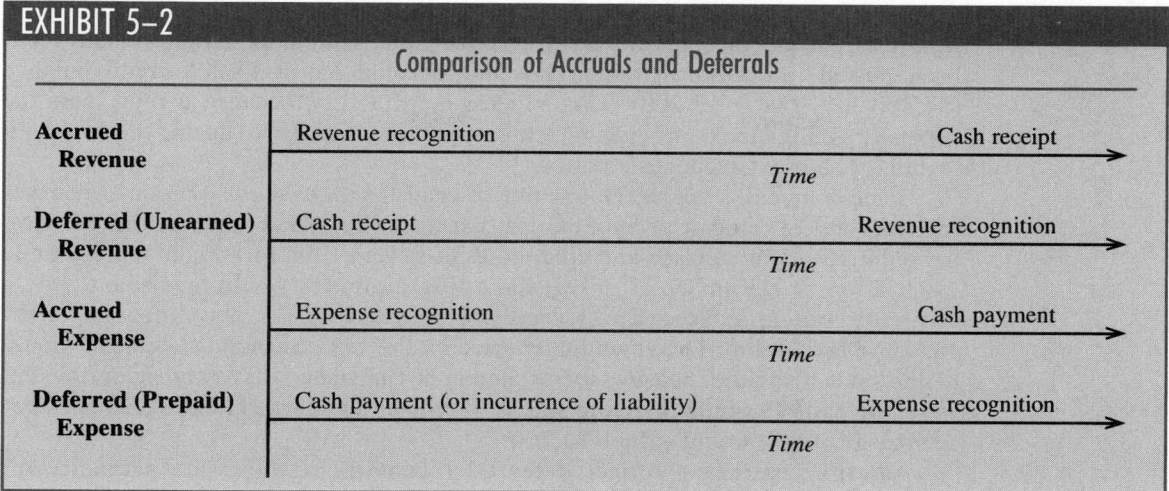

Comparison of Accruals and Deferrals

Accrued Revenue	Revenue recognition	Cash receipt
	Time	
Deferred (Unearned) Revenue	Cash receipt	Revenue recognition
	Time	
Accrued Expense	Expense recognition	Cash payment
	Time	
Deferred (Prepaid) Expense	Cash payment (or incurrence of liability)	Expense recognition
	Time	

ing period. Notice that the adjusting entry affects both a balance sheet account (Interest Payable) and an income statement account (Interest Expense).

Eagle Company must make one other major accrual, that of income tax expense. This is usually the final adjusting entry, because the amount depends on the size of a company's pretax income. We shall therefore make this entry later in the chapter, after we have calculated Eagle's 1993 income before taxes.

Deferrals.   Deferrals are adjusting entries required to separate mixed accounts into their real and nominal components. A deferral-type adjusting entry typically has *one* of the following characteristics:

1. A revenue is recognized after the related cash receipt, *or*
2. An expense is recognized after the related cash payment (or incurrence of a liability).

In Exhibit 5–2 we compare accruals with deferrals.

Adjusting entries to reflect **deferred (unearned) revenues** are necessary for mixed accounts in which a portion of the balance represents revenue that has been earned currently and a portion represents revenue that will be earned in one or more future accounting periods. For example, Eagle Company's trial balance shows Unearned Rent Revenue of $4,800. The lease shows that the $4,800 represents one year's rent received in advance on an office in the company's building. When the amount was received on September 1, 1993, Cash was debited and Unearned Rent Revenue (a liability account) was credited.

Revenue Realization   The revenue realization principle holds, in part, that revenue generated by allowing others to use an enterprise asset, such as an office, is earned as time passes. Accordingly, on December 31, 1993, the following adjusting entry is required to reflect the fact that one-third of the $4,800 has been earned:

Dec. 31	Unearned Rent Revenue	1,600	
	Rent Revenue		1,600
	To record revenue earned on office rented,		
	computed as follows:		
	$4,800 \times \frac{4}{12} = \$1,600$		

As usual, the adjusting entry affects a balance sheet account (Unearned Rent Revenue) and an income statement account (Rent Revenue). After the entry has been posted, the Unearned Rent Revenue account has a $3,200 credit balance ($4,800 − $1,600 = $3,200). This balance is a liability, because it represents the company's obligation to provide the rented asset (i.e., the office) during the first eight months of the next accounting period.

Some companies follow the practice of **crediting a revenue account** whenever revenues are collected in advance of being earned. *If* Eagle had observed this practice, it would have debited Cash and credited Rent Revenue for $4,800 on September 1, 1993. Then on December 31, 1993, the **adjusting entry** would require a **debit to Rent Revenue** to reduce it and a **credit to the liability account Unearned Rent Revenue for $3,200.** The amounts reported on the 1993 financial statements would be the same as before, because the economic circumstances have not changed. Rent Revenue for 1993 would therefore still be $1,600 and Unearned Rent Revenue at December 31, 1993, would still be $3,200.

Adjusting entries to reflect **deferred (prepaid) expenses** are necessary for mixed accounts in which a portion of the balance represents an expense that has been incurred currently and a portion represents an expense that will be incurred in one or more future accounting periods. For example, Eagle Company's trial balance shows Prepaid Insurance of $1,200. The insurance policy shows that this amount represents the cost of fire protection for one year, paid in advance on April 1, 1993. When the original amount was paid, the company debited Prepaid Insurance and credited Cash.

Matching   The matching principle recognizes costs as expenses when the goods or services represented by the costs contribute to revenue. During 1993, three-fourths of the insurance protection has presumably contributed to revenue. The expired portion of the insurance cost must therefore be entered in an expense account. The following adjusting entry is required:

Dec. 31	Insurance Expense	900	
	Prepaid Insurance		900
	To record expired portion of insurance, computed as follows:		
	$1,200 \times \frac{9}{12} = \$900$		

Notice once again that the adjusting entry affects a balance sheet account (Prepaid Insurance) and an income statement account (Insurance Expense). After posting, the Prepaid Insurance account has a $300 debit balance. This balance represents an asset, specifically, the right to receive fire insurance protection during the first three months of the next accounting period.

Some companies follow the practice of **debiting an expense account** for short-term prepayments. *If* Eagle had observed this practice, it would have debited Insurance Expense and credited Cash for $1,200 on April 1, 1993. On December 31, 1993, the **adjusting entry** would require a **debit to Prepaid Insurance** and a **credit to Insurance Expense for $300.** The amounts reported on the 1993 financial statements would be the same as before; Insurance Expense for 1993 would still be $900, and Prepaid Insurance at December 31, 1993, would still be $300.

Matching   The matching principle further requires that Eagle Company record depreciation on its building and office equipment. These assets have contributed to revenues throughout 1993; accordingly, a portion of their cost must be allocated to 1993 expense. Eagle uses the straight-line method to depreciate the building and office equipment over 50 and 10 years, respectively. Furthermore, the company expects each asset to have no salvage value.[5] The adjusting entry appears below:

Dec. 31	Depreciation Expense—Building	2,000	
	Depreciation Expense—Office Equipment	12,000	
	Accumulated Depreciation—Building		2,000
	Accumulated Depreciation—Office Equipment		12,000
	To record depreciation, computed as follows:		

$$\text{Building} \frac{\$100,000 - 0}{50 \text{ years}} = \$2,000$$

$$\text{Office Equipment} \frac{\$120,000 - 0}{10 \text{ years}} = \$12,000$$

Note that a compound entry was made to record depreciation. Two simple entries would also have been appropriate. Once again, the adjusting entry affects a balance sheet account (Accumulated Depreciation) and an income statement account (Depreciation Expense). The credits are made to accumulated depreciation accounts rather than directly to the asset accounts. Accumulated Depreciation is a contra account that permits the balance sheet to show both the cost and the accumulated depreciation of the major types of plant assets. Both pieces of information are generally considered relevant and are required disclosures.[6] The cost of an asset minus its accumulated depreciation is often called the asset's **book value** (or **net book value**).

When a company incurs costs that will likely benefit several accounting periods, such as the cost of buildings and equipment, the normal procedure is to debit an asset account instead of an expense account. Therefore, adjusting entries to record long-term cost allocations, such as depreciation, are usually similar to the one illustrated above.

Special Items.   These are adjusting entries that do not fit neatly into the accrual and deferral categories and are therefore classified separately. Common examples include the adjusting entries for bad debts expense and for cost of goods sold in a company that uses the periodic inventory system.

Companies that sell on credit do not usually expect to collect all of their accounts receivable. Therefore, some portion of credit sales made during a period and some portion of accounts receivable at the end of the period will likely never be collected in cash. To reflect these expectations, companies having credit sales make an adjusting entry to record **estimated bad debts.**

Procedures for estimating bad debts expense are covered in Chapter 7. For now, assume that all of Eagle Company's sales are on credit and that the company expects that 0.5% of its sales will never be collected. The company makes the following adjusting entry:

Dec. 31	Bad Debts Expense	2,615	
	Allowance for Doubtful Accounts		2,615
	To record estimated bad debts, computed as follows: $523,000 × .005 = $2,615		

---

[5]Under the straight-line method, we compute depreciation using the following formula:

$$\text{Annual depreciation} = \frac{\text{Cost} - \text{Salvage value}}{\text{Years of service life}}$$

[6]*APB Opinion No. 12*, "Omnibus Opinion—1967," 1967, par. 5.

The adjusting entry assigns Bad Debts Expense of $2,615 to the current accounting period, where it is matched on the income statement with the revenue from credit sales. Credit sales give rise to the uncollectibles. Bad debts expense is regarded as a cost of making credit sales, and recording it helps implement the matching principle. The credit in the above entry is made to the Allowance for Doubtful Accounts. We do not credit Accounts Receivable because we do not yet know which specific accounts will become uncollectible. The Allowance for Doubtful Accounts is a contra account to Accounts Receivable; we therefore subtract it from Accounts Receivable on the balance sheet. Accounts Receivable minus the Allowance for Doubtful Accounts is often called the **net realizable value** of accounts receivable. The net realizable value of Eagle's accounts receivable at December 31, 1993, is $56,885 [$60,000 − ($500 + $2,615)]. The $500 amount is the balance in the Allowance for Doubtful Accounts before adjustments are made.

An outflow of resources is associated with most expenses. This outflow may occur in past, present, or future periods. In regard to bad debts, however, no such outflow occurs. Instead, there is simply a reduction in the inflow of cash expected. Thus, Bad Debts Expense is somewhat peculiar, and some accountants think it should be treated as a revenue contra account (perhaps called Sales Uncollectible) rather than an expense. We have treated the adjusting entry for bad debts as a special item because of its peculiar nature.

Another special item is the **adjustment for Cost of Goods Sold.** A company using the periodic inventory system debits Purchases whenever it makes a merchandise purchase. Furthermore, the recording of a sale does not involve entries in either Cost of Goods Sold or Merchandise Inventory accounts. As a result, the Merchandise Inventory balance shown on the ending trial balance is the balance that was on hand at the *beginning* of the accounting period.[7] The objectives of the Cost of Goods Sold adjustment are therefore threefold:

1. To enter the ending inventory balance in the Merchandise Inventory account and remove the beginning inventory balance. The ending balance can then be presented on the ending balance sheet.
2. To close all of the accounts included in the calculation of net purchases. These accounts include Purchases, Purchase Returns, Purchase Allowances, Purchase Discounts, and Transportation-In.
3. To enter the Cost of Goods Sold Expense in the accounting records. One computes cost of goods sold using the following formula:

   Cost of Goods Sold = Beginning Inventory + Purchases − Purchase Returns − Purchase Allowances − Purchase Discounts + Transportation-In − Ending Inventory

To illustrate, Eagle Company's physical inventory count at the end of 1993 shows merchandise costing $43,756. The adjusting entry for Cost of Goods Sold appears on page 181.

The adjusting entry accomplishes the three objectives described above. Actually, the entry is nothing more than the implementation of the basic cost of goods sold formula in general journal form. After the entry is posted, the Cost of Goods Sold account will have a $200,000 debit balance. Because Cost of Goods Sold is a nominal account, it must be closed during the closing process.

---

[7]Throughout this chapter we assume that a periodic inventory system is used. In Chapter 8 we review in detail the differences between periodic and perpetual systems.

End

Dec. 31	Merchandise Inventory (Dec. 31)		43,756	
	Purchase Returns		2,000	
	Purchase Allowances		2,500	
	Purchase Discounts		3,600	
	Cost of Goods Sold	*Beg*	200,000	
	Merchandise Inventory (Jan. 1)			57,606
	Purchases			187,000
	Transportation-In			7,250
	To record cost of goods sold and ending inventory.			

The adjusting entry for the Cost of Goods Sold is part adjusting and part closing. Some accountants prefer to treat it as a closing entry. Because it is peculiar, we have classified it as a special item.

STEP 7.   PREPARE AN ADJUSTED TRIAL BALANCE

After journalizing and posting the adjusting entries, the accountant prepares a second trial balance. This is called an **adjusted trial balance** because the account balances listed reflect the company's adjusting entries. An adjusted trial balance serves three major purposes:

1. It provides evidence that, after the adjusting entries have been made, total debits in a company's general ledger equals total credits. It thus helps to control errors made during the adjustment process.
2. It enables the accountant to calculate income before taxes so that the adjusting entry for Income Tax Expense can be made.
3. It provides a convenient listing of account balances for use in the financial statements.

The adjusted trial balance of Eagle Company appears on page 182.

Note that the columns are subtotaled and an informal calculation of income before taxes is made. This calculation may be made on a calculator and need not be shown in detail on the adjusted trial balance. Income before taxes is the difference between the income statement accounts with credit balances and the income statement accounts with debit balances. For Eagle Company, this difference is $80,000.

Income Tax Expense is typically a major expense. Unlike most other expenses, it can be computed only after calculating income before taxes. Eagle Company's income tax rate is 48%.[8] The company therefore records the accrual of its Income Tax Expense as follows:

Dec. 31	Income Tax Expense	38,400	
	Income Tax Payable		38,400
	To accrue income tax expense at a rate of 48%.		

As usual, this adjusting entry is journalized and posted to the affected general ledger accounts listed near the bottom of the adjusted trial balance. The columns are then totaled.

---

[8]In this chapter we review the accounting cycle without being diverted by the mechanics of calculating income taxes. We therefore assume that a tax rate of 48% applies to all income and that no differences exist between the company's pretax-accounting income and its taxable income. In Chapter 18, we discuss and illustrate how to account for income taxes under more complex circumstances.

Eagle Company
ADJUSTED TRIAL BALANCE
December 31, 1993

Account	Dr.	Cr.
Cash	$ 21,079	
Accounts receivable	60,000	
Allowance for doubtful accounts		$ 3,115
Note receivable	10,000	
Interest receivable	600	
Merchandise inventory	43,756	
Prepaid insurance	300	
Land	40,000	
Building	100,000	
Accumulated depreciation—building		12,000
Office equipment	120,000	
Accumulated depreciation—office equipment		36,000
Accounts payable		38,405
Interest payable		1,800
Unearned rent revenue		3,200
Long-term note payable		72,000
Common stock, $5 par		50,000
Paid-in capital in excess of par value		65,000
Retained earnings		34,215
Sales		523,000
Interest revenue		600
Rent revenue		1,600
Cost of goods sold	200,000	
Sales salaries expense	78,000	
Advertising expense	24,000	
Transportation-out	6,000	
Miscellaneous selling expenses	5,141	
Officers' salaries expense	76,000	
Professional services	23,000	
Utilities expense	8,244	
Interest expense	1,800	
Insurance expense	900	
Depreciation expense—building	2,000	
Depreciation expense—office equipment	12,000	
Bad debts expense	2,615	
Miscellaneous administrative expenses	5,500	
Subtotal	840,935	840,935
Income tax expense	38,400	
Income tax payable		38,400
Total	$879,335	$879,335

Income before taxes =
$$\$523,000 + 600 + 1,600 - 200,000 - 78,000 - 24,000$$
$$-6,000 - 5,141 - 76,000 - 23,000 - 8,244 - 1,800$$
$$-900 - 2,000 - 12,000 - 2,615 - 5,500 = \underline{\$80,000}$$

Income tax expense = $\$80,000 \times .48 = \underline{\$38,400}$

STEP 8.   PREPARE FINANCIAL STATEMENTS

Using the information on the adjusted trial balance, the accountant prepares the formal **financial statements**.[9] These important statements are the output of the accounting information system and serve as input for many investment, credit, and similar decisions. Preparing the statements is therefore a crucial step in the accounting cycle.

The accountant ordinarily prepares financial statements in the following order: (1) income statement, (2) statement of retained earnings, (3) balance sheet, and (4) statement of cash flows. These are the basic financial statements explained in Chapter 4. Preparing the statement of cash flows requires more information than appears on the adjusted trial balance. In Chapter 22 we discuss and illustrate how to prepare the statement of cash flows. The income statement, statement of retained earnings, and balance sheet for Eagle Company appear in Exhibit 5–3. We present these statements for illustrative purposes; most accountants would probably combine several of the items shown, based on materiality considerations.

Materiality

STEP 9.   PREPARE CLOSING ENTRIES

After preparing the financial statements, the accountant prepares **closing entries**. These entries are made at the end of the accounting period. They are first recorded in the general journal, then posted to the appropriate ledger accounts.

The accountant closes *only* the nominal accounts. Furthermore, *all* nominal accounts are closed. To **close an account** means to reduce its balance to zero. Closing nominal accounts is logical, because they measure activities or flows that have occurred *during a given period of time*. At the end of the period, nominal accounts have served their purpose. Their balances must therefore be reduced to zero so that the accounts can be used to measure activities in the *next* accounting period. The measurement of any activity, whether it is sales or the 100-meter dash, logically begins at zero.

Because nominal accounts are temporary extensions of owners' equity (see Exhibit 5–1), their balances may be transferred directly to an owners' equity account (Retained Earnings in the case of a corporation) during closing. However, most accountants transfer revenue and expense balances to a clearing account called **Income Summary** (or **Revenue and Expense Summary**). This account merely summarizes the net income or loss for the period, and its balance is closed (i.e., reduced to zero and transferred) to owners' equity.[10] Closing entries are formulated based on the nominal account balances shown on the adjusted trial balance. The closing entries for Eagle Company are presented on page 186.

---

[9]Financial statements may also be prepared using a worksheet, as discussed in Appendix A. A **worksheet** is used to accumulate and organize the information required to prepare financial statements.

[10]Some corporations (especially those that declare dividends quarterly) record the declaration of a dividend by debiting a **Dividends Declared** account, while others charge Retained Earnings directly. Dividends Declared is a nominal account and is presented on the statement of retained earnings. It normally has a debit balance and is closed directly to Retained Earnings at the end of the accounting period:

Dec. 31 Retained Earnings	XXX	
Dividends Declared		XXX
To close the Dividends Declared account.		

In sole proprietorships and partnerships, **Drawing** accounts are used instead of Dividends Declared. Drawing accounts are closed directly to Owners' Capital at the end of the accounting period.

EXHIBIT 5-3

Preparation of Financial Statements

Eagle Company
INCOME STATEMENT
For the Year Ended December 31, 1993

Sales revenue			
Sales			$523,000
Cost of goods sold			
Merchandise inventory, Jan. 1, 1993		$ 57,606	
Purchases	$187,000		
Less: Purchase returns	2,000		
Purchase allowances	2,500		
Purchase discounts	3,600		
Add: Transportation-in	7,250		
Net purchases		186,150	
Cost of goods available for sale		243,756	
Merchandise inventory, Dec. 31, 1993		43,756	
Cost of goods sold			200,000
Gross margin on sales			323,000
Operating expenses			
Selling expenses			
Sales salaries	78,000		
Advertising	24,000		
Transportation-out	6,000		
Miscellaneous	5,141	113,141	
Administrative expenses			
Officers' salaries	76,000		
Professional services	23,000		
Utilities	8,244		
Insurance	900		
Depreciation of building	2,000		
Depreciation of office equipment	12,000		
Bad Debts	2,615		
Miscellaneous	5,500	130,259	
Total operating expenses			243,400
Income from operations			79,600
Other revenues			
Interest		600	
Rent		1,600	2,200
			81,800
Other expense			
Interest			1,800
Income before taxes			80,000
Income tax expense ($80,000 × .48)			38,400
Net income			$ 41,600
Earnings per share ($41,600 ÷ 10,000 shares outstanding)			$4.16

Eagle Company
STATEMENT OF RETAINED EARNINGS*
For the Year Ended December 31, 1993

Retained earnings, Jan. 1, 1993	$ 34,215
Add: Net income	41,600**
Retained earnings, Dec. 31, 1993	$ 75,815

Eagle Company
BALANCE SHEET
December 31, 1993

Assets

Current Assets

Cash		$ 21,079
Accounts receivable	$ 60,000	
Less: Allowance for doubtful accounts	3,115	56,885
Note receivable		10,000
Interest receivable		600
Merchandise inventory		43,756
Prepaid insurance		300
Total current assets		$132,620

Plant Assets

Land		40,000
Building	100,000	
Less: Accumulated depreciation	12,000	88,000
Office equipment	120,000	
Less: Accumulated depreciation	36,000	84,000
Total plant assets		212,000
Total assets		$344,620

Liabilities and Stockholders' Equity

Current Liabilities

Accounts payable	$ 38,405	
Interest payable	1,800	
Income tax payable	38,400	
Unearned rent revenue	3,200	
Total current liabilities		$ 81,805

Long-Term Liabilities

Notes payable		72,000
Total liabilities		153,805

Stockholders' Equity

Paid-in capital		
Common stock, $5 par, 10,000 shares issued and outstanding	$ 50,000	
Paid-in capital in excess of par value	65,000	
Total paid-in capital	115,000	
Retained earnings	75,815†	
Total stockholders' equity		190,815
Total liabilities and stockholders' equity		$344,620

---

*Eagle Company declared no dividends during 1993. If dividends had been declared, they would be subtracted on the retained earnings statement, as discussed and illustrated in Chapter 4.
**This number was obtained from the income statement.
†This number was obtained from the statement of retained earnings.

Dec. 31	Sales	523,000	
	Interest Revenue	600	
	Rent Revenue	1,600	
	Income Summary		525,200
	To close revenue accounts.		
Dec. 31	Income Summary	483,600	
	Cost of Goods Sold		200,000
	Sales Salaries Expense		78,000
	Advertising Expense		24,000
	Transportation-Out		6,000
	Miscellaneous Selling Expenses		5,141
	Officers' Salaries Expense		76,000
	Professional Services		23,000
	Utilities Expense		8,244
	Interest Expense		1,800
	Insurance Expense		900
	Depreciation Expense—Building		2,000
	Depreciation Expense—Office Equipment		12,000
	Bad Debts Expense		2,615
	Miscellaneous Administrative Expenses		5,500
	Income Tax Expense		38,400
	To close expense accounts.		
Dec. 31	Income Summary	41,600	
	Retained Earnings		41,600
	To close the Income Summary account.		

Although compound entries were used to illustrate the closing process, it would also have been appropriate to use a series of simple entries. Note that after closing entries are posted, zero balances will exist in each revenue account, each expense account, and the Income Summary clearing account. Furthermore, the ending balance in the Retained Earnings account is $75,815 ($34,215 + $41,600). Through no coincidence, this is the same figure reported for Retained Earnings on Eagle's balance sheet dated December 31, 1993.

STEP 10.   PREPARE A POST-CLOSING TRIAL BALANCE (OPTIONAL)

After journalizing and posting the closing entries, the accountant usually prepares a **post-closing trial balance**. This is simply a listing of general ledger accounts and their balances after the closing entries have been made. The post-closing trial balance therefore consists entirely of real accounts. Its purpose is to provide evidence that equal debits and credits exist in the general ledger after closing. Thus, it helps to ensure that the closing process has been performed correctly. The post-closing trial balance is not a required step in the accounting cycle, because its purpose is solely error detection.

STEP 11.   PREPARE REVERSING ENTRIES (OPTIONAL)

The final step in the accounting cycle is to journalize and post **reversing entries**. These entries bear the first date of the new accounting period. They are called reversing entries because they are the reverse or opposite of certain adjusting entries made

EXHIBIT 5-4

Effect of Reversing Entries

Event	Accrued Interest Expense Is Reversed		Accrued Interest Expense Is Not Reversed	
	Assumption			

Dec. 31, 1993
Adjusting entry to accrue interest expense
	Interest Expense 1,800
	    Interest Payable
		1,800	Interest Expense 1,800
			    Interest Payable
				1,800

Dec. 31, 1993
Closing entry applicable to accrued interest expense
	Income Summary 1,800
	    Interest Expense
		1,800	Income Summary 1,800
			    Interest Expense
				1,800

Jan. 1, 1994 Reversing entry	Interest Payable 1,800 Interest Expense	1,800	No entry	

Sept. 30, 1994
Payment of Interest
	Interest Expense 7,200
	    Cash
		7,200	Interest Expense 5,400
			Interest Payable 1,800
			    Cash
				7,200

at the end of the preceding period. Reversing entries do not mean that the adjusting entries reversed were unnecessary or inaccurate.

The sole purpose of reversing entries is to **simplify** the subsequent recording of certain kinds of recurring transactions. Because their only purpose is simplification, reversing entries are optional. To illustrate, recall that on December 31, 1993, Eagle Company had outstanding a $72,000, 10-year, 10% note payable with interest payable annually on September 30. In Exhibit 5–4, we summarize selected accounting entries pertaining to the note under alternative assumptions about reversing entries.

Under either assumption the interest expense recorded for the first nine months of 1994 is $5,400. Therefore, either assumption results in the same amounts on the 1994 financial statements. Making the reversing entry on January 1, however, eliminates the need to allocate the September 30 interest payment between the amount currently expensed and the amount previously accrued. This may seem like a trivial simplification for Eagle Company with its single note payable. However, some companies have many notes payable. Moreover, the recording of interest payments is often assigned to a clerical employee who may have had little more than high school bookkeeping courses. Under these circumstances, a qualified accountant may well decide to make reversing entries to simplify the recording of interest payments by the clerical employee. At the end of the period, the accountant can then analyze each note payable and formulate the appropriate adjusting entry for accrued interest.

The following types (i.e., categories) of adjusting entries *may* be reversed: (1) adjusting entries to record accruals (either revenues or expenses), and (2) adjusting entries to record deferrals when the original amount to which the adjusting entry pertains was recorded in a nominal account. For example, an adjusting entry debiting

WESTERN ACCOUNTING ARRIVES IN EASTERN EUROPE

Eastern Europe is hot. The iron curtain is down, markets are opening up and Western companies are rushing in to set up shop. The six largest international accounting firms and a handful of smaller ones are moving in, too, sometimes on the heels of clients, sometimes forging the way and encouraging clients to follow.

Though the Soviet Union and its former satellites are by no means prepared for a capitalist invasion, Western investors can't resist the tempting market of over 300 million new consumers, a continent of raw materials and European know-how offered at Latin American wages. The location isn't bad, either. The European Community is right next door and Europe 1992—the single market initiative—is around the corner.

"This is probably as big as Commodore Perry opening Japan," says Paul Hoffman, a partner and Eastern European liaison in the New York office of Arthur Andersen & Co. "A whole new section of the world is entering the global economy, and the movement is coming on fast."

Arthur Andersen itself came on pretty fast in Moscow, opening an office there in the days of detente, and then closing it in the darker days of the cold war. Today the firm is back again, holding a 70% interest in a joint venture with Promsroy Bank, the Soviet Union's largest industrial bank. In late June the firm announced it would be the first Western accounting firm permitted to perform audits acceptable to the Soviet government. The following day, Ernst & Young announced it, too, would perform official audits. Previously, all certified auditing of transnational joint ventures was carried out by Inaudit, a Soviet agency established for that express purpose.

But business is booming too much for Inaudit. With 1,800 joint ventures taking shape, the Soviet agency simply cannot keep up with the workload. In fact, the agency's situation worsened when Ernst & Young hired Inaudit's second-ranking official and Arthur Andersen took on three others from the agency's staff.

A CPA in the Moscow May Day Parade

All of the six largest accounting firms have or will soon have offices in Moscow, and Ernst & Young already has a second office operating in Kiev. All the firms, however, are experiencing a predictable problem: the conversion of financial information into forms useful to Western companies and investors. The Soviet Union's centrally controlled economy does not deal with such concepts as profitability and stockholder equity. Financial information there is aimed at measuring performance against production goals, not measuring profit and loss.

C. Richard Eigenbrode, senior tax manager at Price Waterhouse, says that when he spoke to a group of upper-level managers at a seminar in Moscow, one of their questions was "What is an operating loss?"

"Even at that upper level," says Eigenbrode, "they're struggling with basic concepts."

To alleviate the accounting education problem and set things in motion for a compatible system of international accounting, the United Nations Center for Transnational Corporations (UNCTC) organized several brainstorming sessions and helped found an ongoing educational program in the Soviet Union. CPAs "donated" by the largest CPA firms are teaching in Soviet universities and institutions, using a special curriculum developed by Dr. Adolf J. H. Enthoven, director of the Center for International Accounting Development at the University of Texas—Dallas. The programs in Moscow, Leningrad and Kiev graduated their first 170 students this June.

Raymon de Reyna, a Deloitte & Touche partner who taught an intensive two-week course at Moscow State University, was invited to march in the famous May Day parade in Red Square, perhaps the first Western CPA to receive such an invitation.

SOURCE: Glenn Alan Cheney, "Western Accounting Arrives in Eastern Europe," *Journal of Accountancy,* September 1990, pp. 40–43.

Prepaid Insurance and crediting Insurance Expense may be reversed because it is a deferral in which the original amount was recorded in a nominal account (i.e., Insurance Expense). In contrast, an adjusting entry debiting Insurance Expense and crediting Prepaid Insurance should not be reversed because, although the adjusting entry is a deferral, the original amount was recorded in a real account (i.e., Prepaid Insurance). Reversing entries should not record the cost of an asset that has expired, nor should they reinstate liabilities that no longer exist.

A company may choose to reverse any number of adjusting entries as long as the entries fall into one of the two categories discussed above. Because reversing entries are optional, companies should not make them unless the benefits exceed the costs.

CONCLUDING REMARKS/CONCEPTUAL CONSIDERATIONS

Of all the steps in the accounting cycle, the preparation of adjusting entries gives typical intermediate accounting students the most trouble. The following broad principles from the theoretical model in Chapter 2 are important to remember when preparing adjusting entries:

Revenue
Realization

1. **Revenue realization.** Under the accrual basis of accounting, certain adjusting entries are necessary to ensure that revenues will be recognized in the period in which they are earned, regardless of when the cash inflows associated with the revenues occur.

Matching

2. **Matching.** Under the accrual basis of accounting, certain adjusting entries are necessary to ensure that expenses will be recognized in the period in which they are incurred, regardless of when the cash outflows associated with the expenses occur.

Together, the revenue realization and matching principles are the essence of the accrual basis of accounting. The need to implement these principles explains why adjusting entries are necessary at the end of every accounting period.

KEY POINTS

1. A transaction is an event that changes a company's financial position and can be measured with sufficient objectivity. (Step 1)

2. Source documents serve as evidence that transactions have occurred. (Step 1)

3. The term "debit" refers to the left-hand side of an account, while "credit" refers to the right-hand side. (Step 2)

4. A journal is a chronological record of transactions. A company should always have a general journal and may have one or more special journals. (Step 3)

5. Posting involves transferring information from journals to accounts in a ledger. A company should always maintain a general ledger and may have one or more subsidiary ledgers. (Step 4)

6. The unadjusted trial balance provides evidence that total debits in a company's general ledger equal total credits. It also provides information that helps the accountant to formulate adjusting entries. (Step 5)

7. Adjusting entries permit accurate measurement of earnings and financial position on the accrual basis. (Step 6)

8. Adjusting entries are based on the revenue realization and matching principles. (Step 6)

9. An adjusted trial balance provides a convenient listing of account balances that may be used to prepare the financial statements. (Step 7)

10. The accountant usually prepares financial statements in the following order (Step 8): **a.** Income statement; **b.** Statement of retained earnings; **c.** Balance sheet; **d.** Statement of cash flows.

11. Closing entries transfer nominal account balances to owners' equity. After closing, all nominal accounts should have zero balances. (Step 9)

12. A post-closing trial balance consists entirely of real accounts. (Step 10)

13. Accountants use reversing entries to simplify the subsequent recording of certain kinds of recurring transactions, such as interest payments. (Step 11)

APPENDIX A: THE WORKSHEET

USING A WORKSHEET TO PREPARE ANNUAL STATEMENTS

A **worksheet** is a multicolumn sheet of paper that the accountant often uses to accumulate and organize the information required to prepare financial statements. Worksheets facilitate the preparation of financial statements by (1) providing a place where adjusting entries can be made informally before they are journalized and posted, (2) providing an orderly means whereby each account can be classified according to the financial statement in which it will appear, and (3) providing a balancing mechanism that helps to uncover accounting errors. Worksheets are never published, because they are not formal financial statements.

In practice, many different worksheet formats exist. The format used in any given case depends on individual or company preferences.

A twelve-column worksheet for Eagle Company is shown in Exhibit 5–5 (pages 192–193). This worksheet includes the same basic data used earlier in the chapter. Eagle Company's worksheet consists of six pairs of amount columns. Sometimes accountants reduce the worksheet's size by eliminating the adjusted trial balance columns or by combining the retained earnings and balance sheet columns. The financial statement balances, of course, are not affected by worksheet size. Eagle Company's worksheet has no columns for the statement of cash flows. Preparing this statement may require a separate worksheet, which we explain later in Chapter 22. The following steps are required to prepare the worksheet:

1. Enter the unadjusted trial balance by using the first pair of amount columns and determine that the columns balance.
2. Enter all adjusting entries, except income taxes, in the adjustments columns. Then subtotal these columns to determine that they balance. The adjusting entries are identified by small letters (a–g) and are presented in the order in which they are discussed in the chapter. Note that when an adjustment requires an account that is not listed in the unadjusted trial balance, a new account is listed below the unadjusted trial balance totals. When a worksheet is used, the adjusting entries are usually made informally in the adjustments columns *before* they are journalized and posted. Errors can then be found and corrected before entering the formal accounting records.
3. Determine the adjusted account balances by combining the unadjusted trial balance amounts with the adjustments amounts. Extend the adjusted balances in the adjusted trial balance columns. Subtotal these columns to determine that they balance.
4. Extend each debit account balance in the adjusted trial balance to the debit column of the financial statement in which the balance will appear. Similarly, extend each credit account balance to the credit column of the financial statement in which the balance will appear.
5. Subtotal the income statement columns. The difference between the columns is the *pretax* income or loss for the period. For Eagle Company the difference is $80,000 ($525,200 − $445,200), and it represents pretax income.
6. Compute the Income Tax Expense by applying the appropriate income tax rate to the pretax income. The Income Tax Expense for Eagle Company is $80,000 × .48 = $38,400.
7. Enter the income tax accrual in the adjustments columns. Then extend the Income Tax Expense balance to the debit column of the adjusted trial balance and of the income statement. Extend the Income Tax Payable balance to the credit column of the adjusted trial balance and of the balance sheet. Total the adjustments columns and the adjusted trial balance columns.
8. Enter net income in the income statement debit column to balance the two income statement columns. The balancing figure is also entered in the Retained Earnings credit column.
9. Subtotal the Retained Earnings columns and enter the balance, which is ending retained earnings, in the Retained Earnings debit column and the balance sheet credit column.
10. Total the balance sheet columns and determine that they balance.

Eagle Company's financial statements may now be prepared directly from the worksheet. These statements would match those illustrated in the chapter. After the statements are prepared, the adjusting entries are journalized and posted on the basis of information shown in the adjustments columns of the worksheet. To complete the accounting cycle, the accountant would close the nominal accounts as illustrated in the chapter. Finally, the accountant *may* prepare a post-closing trial balance and reversing entries.

USING A WORKSHEET TO PREPARE INTERIM STATEMENTS

Most companies formally prepare adjusting and closing entries only at the end of each fiscal year. Nevertheless, companies typically desire interim (e.g., monthly or quarterly) financial statements in addition to annual statements. At the end of each interim period, the accountant enters the necessary adjustments on a worksheet similar to the one for Eagle Company and does not formally record them in journals or ledgers. Adjustments shown on the year-end worksheet then pertain to the entire year;

these amounts are journalized and posted to the accounts in the general ledger.

Because the balance sheet represents financial position at a point in time, the accountant obtains information about assets and equities directly from the balance sheet columns of an interim worksheet. Conversely, revenue and expense amounts on an interim worksheet are cumulative since the beginning of the fiscal year. Therefore, to determine revenues and expenses associated with a particular interim period, the accountant must subtract revenues and expenses attributable to previous interim periods from the corresponding amounts shown on the worksheet. To illustrate, assume that a company closes its books each December 31. To prepare an income statement for March, the accountant must subtract the revenues and expenses for January and February from the corresponding amounts shown on the March 31 worksheet. To prepare an income statement for the second quarter, the accountant must subtract the revenues and expenses for the first quarter from the corresponding amounts shown on the June 30 worksheet. Like the income statement, the retained earnings statement pertains to a certain period of time. It therefore is typically prepared like the income statement.

APPENDIX B: SPECIAL JOURNALS

The general journal format we use throughout this book deemphasizes certain procedural details and enables us to better illustrate how to apply basic accounting concepts and principles. In practice, most businesses have several special journals in addition to a general journal. Special journals typically process most of a company's transactions. This appendix will review some of the more common types of special journals.

A **special journal** is used to initially record a single type of transaction that often recurs. A company may create a special journal to handle virtually any kind of routine transaction. However, a company still needs a general journal to record transactions that do not fit the intended purpose of one of its special journals. Typically, adjusting entries, correcting entries, closing entries, reversing entries (if used), and entries for transactions that occur infrequently, such as the sale of common stock in exchange for land, are recorded in the general journal.

What are the advantages of special journals? First, special journals save time in journalizing and posting transactions. When journalizing, there is no need to rewrite account titles; when posting, transaction *totals* rather than individual amounts may be transferred to general ledger accounts. By simplifying the journalizing and posting requirements for routine transactions, special journals tend to reduce the number of errors made. Moreover, errors are easier to pinpoint once they have occurred.

Another use for special journals is to permit a division of labor within the accounting department. Instead of several people attempting to use the general journal simultaneously, certain individuals can assume responsibility for one or more special journals. This often enables the company to better utilize persons with limited education or experience in bookkeeping or accounting. Such separation of duties also strengthens the company's internal control system.

Each business must determine which types and formats of special journals it needs based on the nature of its transactions. The types and formats presented below are for illustrative purposes only.

SALES JOURNAL

The sales journal is a chronological listing of all *credit* sales of merchandise. For a company that makes five thousand credit sales a month, a sales journal relieves the company of (1) recording five thousand general journal entries debiting Accounts Receivable and crediting Sales, and (2) posting these entries individually to the general ledger. A sales invoice or sales ticket typically initiates an entry in a sales journal.

An abbreviated sales journal of Star-Bright, Inc., is presented in Exhibit 5–6 (page 194). Special journals are normally arranged in columns. Star-Bright's sales journal contains five columns. We assume in the illustration that the company's credit terms are 2/10, n/30.[11] If credit terms varied by customer, a journal column could easily be added to record the terms of each sale.

The process of posting from a sales journal is depicted by the arrows. Individual amounts in the sales journal are posted daily as debits to the appropriate accounts in the accounts receivable subsidiary ledger. Daily posting provides up-to-date credit records, and facilitates the billing process. The check marks in the posting reference column indicate that individual accounts have been posted. At the end of each month, the amount column *total* is posted in the general ledger as a debit to the Accounts Receivable control account and a credit to Sales. The notation (111/401) at the bottom of the amount column indicates that general ledger accounts bearing these numbers have been posted. Note that if each sale were recorded in the general journal instead of the

---

[11]In other words, a customer who pays within 10 days after the invoice date may deduct 2% from the invoice price; a customer who does not pay within the 10-day discount period must pay the gross invoice amount within 30 days after the invoice date.

EXHIBIT 5-5

Eagle Company
WORKSHEET
For the Year Ended December 31, 1993

Accounts	Unadjusted Trial Balance Dr.	Unadjusted Trial Balance Cr.	Adjustments Dr.	Adjustments Cr.	Adjusted Trial Balance Dr.	Adjusted Trial Balance Cr.	Income Statement Dr.	Income Statement Cr.	Retained Earnings Dr.	Retained Earnings Cr.	Balance Sheet Dr.	Balance Sheet Cr.
Cash	21,079				21,079						21,079	
Accounts receivable	60,000				60,000						60,000	
Allowance for doubtful accounts		500		(f) 2,615		3,115						3,115
Note receivable	10,000				10,000						10,000	
Merchandise inventory, Jan. 1, 1993	57,606			(g) 57,606								
Prepaid insurance	1,200			(d) 900	300						300	
Land	40,000				40,000						40,000	
Building	100,000				100,000						100,000	
Accumulated depreciation—building		10,000		(e) 2,000		12,000						12,000
Office equipment	120,000				120,000						120,000	
Accumulated depreciation—office equipment		24,000		(e) 12,000		36,000						36,000
Accounts payable		38,405				38,405						38,405
Unearned rent revenue		4,800	(c) 1,600			3,200						3,200
Long-term note payable		72,000				72,000						72,000
Common stock		50,000				50,000						50,000
Paid-in capital in excess of par value		65,000				65,000						65,000
Retained earnings, Jan. 1, 1993		34,215				34,215				34,215		
Sales		523,000				523,000		523,000				
Purchases	187,000			(g) 187,000								
Purchase returns		2,000	(g) 2,000									
Purchase allowances		2,500	(g) 2,500									
Purchase discounts		3,600	(g) 3,600									

Work Sheet (partial)

Account	Trial Balance Dr	Trial Balance Cr	Adjustments Dr	Adjustments Cr	Adjusted Trial Balance Dr	Adjusted Trial Balance Cr	Income Statement Dr	Income Statement Cr	Retained Earnings Dr	Retained Earnings Cr	Balance Sheet Dr	Balance Sheet Cr
Transportation-in	7,250			(g) 7,250								
Sales salaries expense	78,000				78,000		78,000					
Advertising expense	24,000				24,000		24,000					
Transportation-out	6,000				6,000		6,000					
Miscellaneous selling expenses	5,141				5,141		5,141					
Officers' salaries expense	76,000				76,000		76,000					
Professional services	23,000				23,000		23,000					
Utilities expense	8,244				8,244		8,244					
Miscellaneous administrative expenses	5,500				5,500		5,500					
	830,020	830,020										
Interest receivable			(a) 600		600						600	
Interest revenue				(a) 600		600		600				
Interest expense			(b) 1,800		1,800		1,800					
Interest payable				(b) 1,800		1,800						1,800
Rent revenue				(c) 1,600		1,600		1,600				
Insurance expense			(d) 900		900		900					
Depreciation expense—building			(e) 2,000		2,000		2,000					
Depreciation expense—office equipment			(e) 12,000		12,000		12,000					
Bad-debts expense			(f) 2,615		2,615		2,615					
Merchandise inventory, Dec. 31, 1993			(g) 43,756		43,756						43,756	
Cost of goods sold			(g) 200,000		200,000		200,000					
			273,371	273,371	840,935	840,935	445,200	525,200				
Income tax expense			(h) 38,400		38,400		38,400					
Income tax payable				(h) 38,400		38,400						38,400
			311,771	311,771	879,335	879,335						
Net income							41,600			41,600		
							525,200	525,200				
Retained earnings, Dec. 31, 1993									75,815			75,815
									75,815	75,815	395,735	395,735

EXHIBIT 5-6

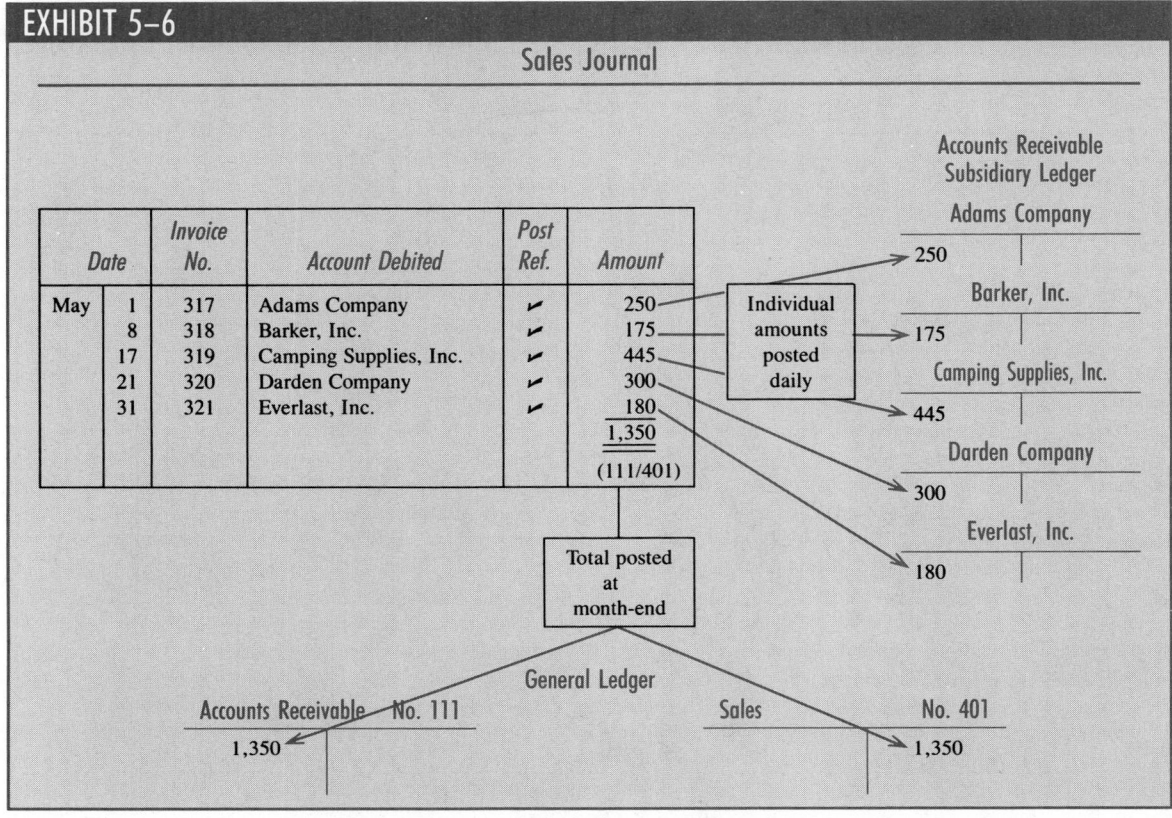

Sales Journal

Date	Invoice No.	Account Debited	Post Ref.	Amount
May 1	317	Adams Company	✔	250
8	318	Barker, Inc.	✔	175
17	319	Camping Supplies, Inc.	✔	445
21	320	Darden Company	✔	300
31	321	Everlast, Inc.	✔	180
				1,350
				(111/401)

Individual amounts posted daily

Accounts Receivable Subsidiary Ledger

Adams Company — 250
Barker, Inc. — 175
Camping Supplies, Inc. — 445
Darden Company — 300
Everlast, Inc. — 180

Total posted at month-end

General Ledger

Accounts Receivable   No. 111   1,350
Sales   No. 401   1,350

sales journal, each debit and credit would have to be separately posted to the general ledger. This would be time-consuming and expensive. As the sales journal illustrates, posting any journal involves making equal debits and credits in the general ledger. Moreover, the sum of the debits (or credits) posted to subsidiary ledger accounts should equal the amount posted as a debit (or credit) to the related control account.

CASH RECEIPTS JOURNAL

The cash receipts journal records all cash receipts, including those resulting from cash sales. Star-Bright's cash receipts journal in Exhibit 5–7 consists of nine columns. Five of these columns are used to record amounts. The following posting features of the cash receipts journal are noteworthy:

1. Column *totals* for cash, sales discounts, and sales are posted at the end of each month. Individual amounts are not posted. The account numbers posted are inserted parenthetically at the bottom of these columns to indicate that posting has occurred.
2. The term "sundry accounts" means various individual accounts. Therefore, sundry accounts are

posted *individually*. Their total is not posted. The account number 211 in the posting reference column indicates that the notes payable account has been posted. The (X) notation at the bottom of the sundry accounts column signifies that the column total is not posted.
3. Amounts in the accounts receivable column are posted *individually and in total*. Individual amounts, referenced by the check marks, are posted daily as credits to the customer accounts in the accounts receivable subsidiary ledger. The column total is posted at the end of the month as a credit to the Accounts Receivable control account in the general ledger. The notation (111) at the bottom of the column indicates that the column total has been posted.

PURCHASES JOURNAL

Some companies use a purchases journal to record *all credit purchases;* others use it to record only *credit purchases of merchandise*. A purchase invoice normally initiates each entry in a purchases journal. Star-Bright's purchases journal in Exhibit 5–8 consists of six columns; its purpose is confined to recording credit acquisitions of

EXHIBIT 5-7

Cash Receipts Journal

Cash Receipts Journal

Date		Account Credited	Explanation	Post. Ref.	Cash Debit	Sales Discounts Debit	Accounts Receivable Credit	Sales Credit	Sundry Accounts Credit
May	3	Sales	Cash sales		500			500	
	11	Adams Company	Payment in full	✔	245	5	250		
	14	Notes Payable	90-day, 10% loan from City National Bank	211	2,000				2,000
	27	Barker, Inc.	Payment in full	✔	175		175		
	31	Darden Company	Payment in full	✔	294	6	300		
					3,214	11	725	500	2,000
					(101)	(402)	(111)	(401)	(X)

Total debits = $3,225   Total credits = $3,225

EXHIBIT 5-8

Purchases Journal

Purchases Journal

Date		Account Credited	Invoice Date	Terms	Post. Ref.	Amount
May	1	Modern Supply Company	Apr. 29	2/10, n/30	✔	200
	16	Dresser, Inc.	May 15	2/10, n/60	✔	550
	18	Office Products Distributors	May 16	n/30	✔	450
	24	Ebenezer, Inc.	May 23	1/10, n/30	✔	196
	31	Wilson Manufacturing Company	May 29	2/10, n/30	✔	254
						1,650
						(501/201)

merchandise. To record all credit acquisitions in its purchases journal, the company would have to add columns to record items such as supplies and equipment.

Individual amounts in the purchases journal are posted daily as credits to the appropriate accounts in the accounts payable subsidiary ledger. The check marks in the posting reference column indicate that individual accounts have been posted. The column *total* is posted in the general ledger at the end of each month as a debit to the Purchases account and a credit to the Accounts Payable control account. The notation (501/201) at the bottom of the amount column signifies a monthly posting.

CASH PAYMENTS JOURNAL

The cash payments journal records all cash payments, including those resulting from cash purchases.

Star-Bright's cash payments journal in Exhibit 5–9 consists of ten columns; five of these are amount columns. Significant posting features in the cash payments journal are described below:

1. Column *totals* for cash, purchase discounts, and purchases are posted at the end of each month. Individual amounts are not posted. The account numbers posted are inserted parenthetically at the bottom of these columns to indicate that posting has occurred.
2. Amounts in the sundry accounts column are posted *individually*. The total of these amounts is not posted. The account numbers 131 and 517 in the posting reference column indicate postings made to the Prepaid Insurance and Advertising Expense accounts, respectively. The (X) notation at the bottom of the sundry accounts column signifies that the column total is not posted.

EXHIBIT 5–9

Cash Payments Journal

Date	Check No.	Account Debited	Explanation	Post. Ref.	Cash Credit	Purchase Discounts Credit	Accounts Payable Debit	Purchases Debit	Sundry Accounts Debit
May 2	477	Purchases	Cash purchases		300			300	
8	478	Modern Supply Company	Payment in full	✔	196	4	200		
12	479	Prepaid Insurance	Fire insurance policy	131	450				450
25	480	Dresser, Inc.	Payment in full	✔	539	11	550		
31	481	Advertising	WACK Radio Station	517	250				250
					1,735	15	750	300	700
					(101)	(502)	(201)	(501)	(X)

Total credits = $1,750   Total debits = $1,750

3. Amounts in the accounts payable column are posted *individually and in total*. Individual amounts, referenced by the check marks, are posted daily as debits to the supplier accounts in the accounts payable subsidiary ledger. The column total is posted at the end of the month as a debit to the Accounts Payable control account in the general ledger. The (201) notation at the bottom of the column indicates that the column total has been posted.

OTHER SPECIAL JOURNALS

To avoid repetition, we have illustrated only the four most common special journals. Remember, however, that companies may use other types.

For example, many companies use a voucher system, in which a voucher is prepared for each transaction that requires a cash payment. A **voucher** is a business paper containing detailed information about a liability and its payment. Each voucher is recorded in a journal called a **voucher register.** This journal is similar to an expanded purchases journal and thus replaces the purchases journal. Checks are drawn only in payment of approved vouchers. A **check register,** which is merely a modified cash payments journal, replaces the cash payments journal in a voucher system.

A **payroll register** is a widely used journal for recording payroll information. A **sales returns and allowances journal** and a **purchases returns and allowances journal** are often used by companies that have many such transactions.

QUESTIONS

5–1   Describe the purpose of the accounting cycle and list in sequence the steps involved.

5–2   Describe the nature of source documents and list five examples.

5–3   State whether the normal balance in each of the following accounts is debit or credit:

[a] Prepaid Insurance D
[b] Wages Expense   D
[c] Sales C
[d] Accounts Payable C
[e] Gain on Sale of Land D
[f] Accumulated Depreciation C

[g] Discount on Bonds Payable
[h] Common Stock C
[i] Dividends
[j] Loss on Sale of Investments
[k] Sales Returns D

5–4   Does a debit increase or decrease the balance in each of the following types of accounts?

[a] Revenue
[b] Liability
[c] Expense
[d] Asset
[e] Owners' Equity

5-5   What is a journal? Why might a company want to use several special journals?

5-6   Give an example of a general journal entry to record each of the following:

[a] An increase in an asset and an increase in a liability.
[b] A decrease in a liability and a decrease in an asset.
[c] An increase in an expense and a decrease in an asset.
[d] An increase in an asset and an increase in a revenue.
[e] An increase in an asset and an increase in owners' equity.

5-7   What is a general ledger? Why is posting to general ledger accounts necessary?

5-8   Distinguish between real, nominal, and mixed accounts.

5-9   What is a subsidiary ledger and a control account? Why might a company want to use several subsidiary ledgers?

5-10   What are the major purposes of an unadjusted trial balance? Does an unadjusted trial balance prove that no errors have been made during an accounting period?

5-11   Distinguish between the cash basis and the accrual basis of accounting.

5-12   What are adjusting entries? Why are they needed?

5-13   A company recently made an adjusting entry to record depreciation and one to record accrued interest on notes receivable. How does each entry relate to an accounting principle?

5-14   Describe how an accountant accumulates the information needed to prepare adjusting entries.

5-15   Distinguish between accruals and deferrals.

5-16   Give two examples of adjusting entries that are based on the revenue realization principle. Give two examples that are based on the matching principle.

5-17   Give an example that illustrates two ways in which an adjusting entry applicable to Prepaid Rent might be recorded.

5-18   Give an example that illustrates two ways in which an adjusting entry applicable to Unearned Subscriptions Revenue might be recorded.

5-19   What are the purposes of the Cost of Goods Sold adjustment assuming the use of a periodic inventory system?

5-20   What are the major purposes of an adjusted trial balance?

5-21   Why is the income tax adjustment usually the final adjusting entry prepared?

5-22   Why are the following statements usually prepared in the sequence indicated?

[a] Income statement   [b] Statement of retained earnings   [c] Balance sheet

5-23   What are closing entries? Why are they needed?

5-24   What types of accounts appear on a postclosing trial balance?

5-25   What are reversing entries? Why are these entries often desirable?

5-26   What is a worksheet? How does a worksheet facilitate the preparation of financial statements?

EXERCISES

5-27   DEBIT/CREDIT RULES   A list of accounts appears below:

[1] Sales.
[2] Common Stock.
[3] Accounts Payable.
[4] Salaries Expense.
[5] Accounts Receivable.
[6] Dividends.
[7] Accumulated Depreciation.
[8] Unearned Subscriptions Revenue.
[9] Dividends Payable.
[10] Premium on Bonds Payable.
[11] Paid-In Capital in Excess of Par Value.
[12] Allowance for Doubtful Accounts.

buy a comp. paid more than market value

[13] Retained Earnings.
[14] Goodwill. *Intangible Asset*
[15] Treasury Stock.
[16] Retained Earnings Appropriated for Plant Expansion. *RE*
[17] Interest Earned. *or Int. Rev.*
[18] Advertising. *Exp*
[19] Sales Returns.
[20] Investment in Bonds.

Appropiation

Instructions

State whether the balance in each account is increased by a debit or a credit.

5–28 JOURNAL ENTRIES During July, Rogoski Company engaged in the transactions listed below. The company uses a periodic inventory system.

July 1   Purchased on account merchandise costing $25,000.
      1   Paid $600 of freight charges in connection with merchandise referred to above.
      6   Purchased land for $10,000.
     10   Sold merchandise for cash of $9,000.
     14   Borrowed $8,000 by signing a 90-day, 10% note.
     16   Sold 1,000 shares of $10 par value common stock for $15,000.
     19   Sold merchandise on account for $6,000.
     23   Sold land that was purchased on July 6. The cash selling price was $11,000.
     27   Received a $1,000, 90-day, 12% note from a customer on account.
     31   Paid July salaries of $5,000.

Instructions

Record the above transactions in general journal form.

5–29 POSTING Ness Inc., recorded the following journal entries during its first month of operations:

Aug. 1	Cash		20,000	
	Common Stock			20,000
3	Prepaid Rent		1,200	
	Cash			1,200
7	Equipment		5,000	
	Cash			5,000
11	Purchases		4,000	
	Accounts Payable			4,000
13	Accounts Receivable		7,000	
	Sales			7,000
24	Cash		2,000	
	Accounts Receivable			2,000
27	Accounts Payable		3,000	
	Cash			3,000
31	Salaries Expense		1,400	
	Advertising Expense		200	
	Utilities Expense		100	
	Cash			1,700

Instructions

[a] Set up a general ledger and post each journal entry to appropriate T accounts.
[b] Prepare an unadjusted trial balance on August 31. *D=C*

5–30 CORRECTING ENTRIES A trial balance for Will Hurt, D.D.S., at the end of his first month in practice is presented below:

Will Hurt, D.D.S.
TRIAL BALANCE
May 31

Account	Dr.	Cr.
Cash	$ 9,560	
Supplies	11,730	
Prepaid rent	6,800	
Equipment	58,000	
Accounts payable		$ 9,640
Will Hurt, capital		75,000
Revenues from patients		5,450
Salaries expense	1,300	
Utilities expense	400	
Miscellaneous office expenses	300	
Will Hurt, drawing	2,000	
	$90,090	$90,090

Additional Information

Upon examining Hurt's books, you discover the following:

[1] Cash of $300 received from a patient had been recorded as $500. (Hurt renders services on a cash basis only.)
[2] A $964 purchase of supplies on account had been recorded as $469.
[3] A $2,000 purchase of equipment had been charged to prepaid rent.
[4] A $677 <u>payment on account</u> had been recorded as $776.

Instructions

[a] Journalize the necessary correcting entries on May 31. (Do not record adjusting entries.)
[b] Prepare a corrected trial balance. Debit = Credit

5-31 ADJUSTING AND REVERSING ENTRIES   The following information pertains to Dano Company for the current year:

[1] On November 1, the company received a $5,000, 90-day, 10% note from a customer.
[2] Accrued wages as of December 31 amount to $2,175.
[3] On September 1, the company received $2,400 for rent paid in advance for eight months on a warehouse that Dano Company leases to Moore Company. Dano Company credited a nominal account.
[4] On October 1, the company paid $1,800 for a two-year fire insurance policy and debited a nominal account.
[5] The company computes $10,000 of depreciation for the year.
[6] The company estimates $2,635 of bad debts for the year.

Instructions

[a] Prepare the necessary adjusting journal entries on <u>December 31</u>, the end of the company's annual accounting period.
[b] Assuming that Dano Company wants to make reversals, prepare the reversing entries that are appropriate on January 1 of the next accounting period.

5-32 ADJUSTING ENTRIES   Amy Wong owns the Wong Hair Styling Center. A trial balance for the business at the end of its first year of operations appears below:

Wong Hair Styling Center
TRIAL BALANCE
December 31

Account	Dr.	Cr.
Cash	$13,000	
Supplies	14,000	
Prepaid rent	12,000	
Equipment	25,000	
Accounts payable		$ 3,000
Note payable		20,000
Wong, capital		7,000
Styling revenues		56,500
Advertising expense	7,000	
Salaries expense	13,000	
Utilities expense	2,500	
	$86,500	$86,500

In addition, the following information applies:

[1] A physical count reveals that supplies costing $1,000 are on hand at year-end.
[2] Rent on the shop was paid in advance for two years on January 1.
[3] The equipment was acquired on January 1. It has an estimated useful life of 10 years and no expected salvage value. Wong elects to use the straight-line depreciation method.
[4] The note payable relates to a one-year, 12% loan obtained from First National Bank on April 1.
[5] Salaries earned by employees but unpaid to them at year-end amount to $1,680.

Instructions

Using the trial balance and the additional information presented above, prepare the necessary adjusting entries in general journal form at December 31.

5–33   COST OF GOODS SOLD AND GROSS MARGIN   Selected account balances for Janzen Company on December 31 are shown below. Each account has a normal balance.

Account	Balance
Transportation-out	$ 12,000
Merchandise inventory, Dec. 31	43,000
Purchase discounts	3,000
Sales returns	11,000
Transportation-in	8,000
Sales discounts	7,000
Merchandise inventory, Jan. 1	30,000
Purchase returns	6,000
Sales allowances	9,000
Purchase allowances	4,000
Purchases	200,000
Sales	370,000

Instructions

[a] Prepare a schedule showing the computation of cost of goods sold.
[b] Calculate the amount of gross margin.

5–34   FINANCIAL STATEMENTS   The adjusted trial balance of Gibney Company on December 31 appears below:

Account	Dr.	Cr.
Cash	$ 27,000	
Accounts receivable	50,000	
Allowance for doubtful accounts		$ 3,000
Note receivable (short-term)	10,000	

Merchandise inventory	20,000	
Prepaid rent (for one year)	6,000	
Equipment	100,000	
Accumulated depreciation		15,000
Accounts payable		23,000
Salaries payable		2,000
Income tax payable		22,000
Common stock ($20 par value; 3,000 shares)		60,000
Paid-in capital in excess of par value		40,000
Retained earnings		50,000
Sales		215,000
Interest revenue		6,000
Cost of goods sold	100,000	
Salaries expense	20,000	
Rent expense	6,000	
Advertising expense	17,000	
Depreciation expense	10,000	
Bad-debts expense	3,000	
Miscellaneous expense	5,000	
Income tax expense	22,000	
Dividends	40,000	
	$436,000	$436,000

Instructions

Prepare an income statement, a statement of retained earnings, and a balance sheet.

5–35 CLOSING ENTRIES   Refer to the information presented for Gibney Company in 5–34.

Instructions

[a] Journalize the closing entries on December 31.
[b] Prepare a post-closing trial balance.

5–36 CLOSING ENTRIES   Listed below are the adjusted account balances of Beli Company on December 31. Each account has a normal balance.

Account	Balance
Accounts payable	$ 40,000
Accounts receivable	37,000
Accumulated depreciation—equipment	20,000
Advertising expense	8,000
Allowance for doubtful accounts	1,000
Bad-debts expense	1,000
Cash	30,000
Common stock	30,000
Cost of goods sold	101,000
Depreciation expense—equipment	10,000
Equipment	100,000
Income tax expense	16,000
Interest expense	6,000
Interest payable	3,000
Merchandise inventory	50,000
Note payable	30,000
Prepaid rent	4,000
Rent expense	12,000
Retained earnings	53,000
Salaries expense	20,000
Sales	236,000
Sales returns	11,000
Transportation-out	5,000
Utilities expense	2,000

Instructions

Prepare closing entries in general journal form at December 31.

5–37   REVERSING ENTRIES   Berger Publishing Company made the following adjusting entries on December 31, 1993:

[1]	Rent Receivable	2,000	
	Rent Revenue		2,000
[2]	Insurance Expense	700	
	Prepaid Insurance		700
[3]	Property Tax Expense	1,200	
	Property Tax Payable		1,200
[4]	Subscriptions Revenue	2,400	
	Unearned Subscriptions Revenue		2,400
[5]	Supplies Expense	850	
	Supplies		850
[6]	Amortization Expense	1,700	
	Copyrights		1,700
[7]	Bad Debts Expense	650	
	Allowance for Doubtful Accounts		650
[8]	Advertising Revenue	3,300	
	Unearned Advertising Revenue		3,300

Instructions

Assuming that the company wants to make reversals, prepare all reversing journal entries that are appropriate on January 1, 1994.

5–38   REVERSING ENTRIES   On November 1, 1993, Moncy Company issued at par value $200,000 of 20-year, 12% bonds with interest payable semiannually on April 30 and October 31. The company uses a calendar-year accounting period.

Instructions

Record all appropriate journal entries using a table similar to the one shown below.

	Assumption	
Event	Moncy Company makes reversing entries for accrued interest.	Moncy Company does not make reversing entries for accrued interest.
12/31/93 adjusting entry to record accrued interest		
12/31/93 entry to close accrued interest		
1/1/94 reversing entry applicable to accrued interest		
4/30/94 entry to record payment of interest		
10/31/94 entry to record payment of interest		

5–39 ACCRUAL ACCOUNTING   A recent comparative balance sheet of Gonzales Inc. showed the following information:

	Balance	
Explanation	12/31/92	12/31/93
Interest receivable	$100	$400
Consulting fees receivable	700	300
Prepaid insurance	500	700
Supplies	400	200
Salaries payable	500	800
Utilities payable	300	200
Unearned subscriptions revenue	600	800
Unearned advertising revenue	600	200

Selected information about the company's 1993 revenues and expenses (accrual basis) appears below:

Revenues		Expenses	
Interest	$1,400	Insurance	$2,200
Consulting fees	5,000	Supplies	1,200
Subscriptions	7,500	Salaries	4,300
Advertising	3,000	Utilities	2,000

Instructions

[a] Compute the amount of 1993 cash receipts from each of the following sources: (1) interest, (2) consulting fees, (3) subscriptions, and (4) advertising.

[b] Compute the amount of 1993 cash payments for each of the following purposes: (1) insurance, (2) supplies, (3) salaries, and (4) utilities.

5–40 ACCRUAL ACCOUNTING   A recent comparative balance sheet of Sims Company revealed the following information:

	Balance	
Explanation	12/31/92	12/31/93
Interest receivable	$200	$300
Consulting fees receivable	800	200
Prepaid insurance	600	800
Supplies	500	100
Salaries payable	600	900
Utilities payable	400	100
Unearned subscriptions revenue	700	900
Unearned advertising revenue	700	400

Selected information about the company's 1993 cash receipts and disbursements appears below:

Explanation	Cash Receipts	Cash Disbursements
Interest	$3,500	
Consulting fees	3,000	
Insurance		$2,900
Supplies		1,200
Salaries		4,400
Utilities		1,000
Subscriptions	7,000	
Advertising	4,200	

Instructions

Compute each of the following income statement amounts for 1993 under the accrual basis of accounting: (1) interest revenue, (2) consulting fees earned, (3) insurance expense, (4) supplies expense, (5) salaries expense, (6) utilities expense, (7) subscriptions revenue, and (8) advertising revenue.

5–41 (Appendix B)   SPECIAL JOURNALS   Maher Company uses the following journals: sales, sales returns and allowances, purchases, purchases returns and allowances, cash receipts, cash payments, and general. The following events occurred during December:

[1]   Borrowed money from bank.
[2]   Purchased merchandise for cash.
[3]   Received defective merchandise from customers and granted credit.
[4]   Discovered that a cash purchase of equipment in October had inadvertently been charged to the Land account at that time.
[5]   Received payments made by customers on account.
[6]   Computed annual depreciation.
[7]   Made cash sales.
[8]   Purchased merchandise on account.
[9]   Paid accounts payable.
[10]   Collected cash from customers on account.
[11]   Made credit sales.
[12]   Issued common stock for legal services received.
[13]   Paid December rent.
[14]   Returned defective merchandise to suppliers and received credit.

Instructions

Indicate the journal in which the company should record each of the above events.

5–42 (Appendix B)   SPECIAL JOURNALS   Presented below are several transactions of Mankel Company that occurred during December 1993. The company uses a periodic inventory system and a calendar-year accounting period.

Dec.   1   Purchased merchandise on account from Marek Company. The cost was $420.
       4   Sold merchandise to Larry Gordon for $205 cash.
       5   Paid Rip Company $440 on account.
       8   Borrowed $10,000 from City & County Bank and signed a one-year, 12% note.
      12   Sold merchandise on account for $1,400 to Hoffmann, Inc.
      13   Signed a two-year, 13% note for $20,000 in exchange for land purchased from Windsor Corporation.
      17   Received $275 on account from Mancini Company.
      20   The company discovered that a $5,000 purchase of equipment on November 14, 1993, had inadvertently been entered in the Land account.
      22   Purchased merchandise from Moore Company for $170 cash.
      30   Paid a utility bill of $235 for services received in December.
      31   Estimated depreciation for the year at $4,000.
      31   Determined that $400 of prepaid insurance had expired during 1993.

Instructions

[a]   Record the above transactions in general journal form.
[b]   Assume that Mankel Company uses the following journals: sales, cash receipts, purchases, cash payments, and general. Indicate where the company should record each transaction.

5–43 (Appendix B)   SALES JOURNAL   Hudgens Company began operations on May 1 and transacted the following credit sales during May:

Date	Customer	Invoice No.	Amount
May 1	Macy Company	101	$550
8	Gresham, Inc.	102	280
16	Epling Enterprises	103	675
21	Davis Company	104	460
31	Cathey, Inc.	105	600

Instructions

[a] Set up a sales journal and record each of the above transactions.
[b] Post the journal entries to appropriate general and subsidiary ledger accounts.

5–44 (Appendix A) WORKSHEET Presented below is the unadjusted trial balance of Meisen-heimer Inc., on December 31, the end of the company's annual accounting period:

Account	Dr.	Cr.
Cash	$ 26,000	
Note receivable	5,000	
Prepaid rent	12,000	
Equipment	100,000	
Accumulated depreciation		$ 20,000
Accounts payable		17,000
Common stock		30,000
Retained earnings		15,000
Consulting revenues		175,000
Salaries expense	90,000	
Travel expense	10,000	
Utilities expense	6,000	
Dividends	8,000	
	$257,000	$257,000

Additional Information

This information is available on December 31:

[1] Accrued interest on note receivable is $250.
[2] Seventy-five percent of the prepaid rent shown above has expired.
[3] Depreciation expense for the year is $12,000.
[4] The December utility bill of $550 has not been paid or recorded.
[5] The income tax rate is 40%.

Instructions

Prepare a twelve-column worksheet (as shown in Appendix A).

PROBLEMS **5–45** JOURNAL ENTRIES AND POSTING Sanchez Company started business on June 1. The company uses a periodic inventory system and records purchases of merchandise at gross amounts. The following transactions occurred during June:

June 1 Issued 1,000 shares of $10 par value common stock for $60,000.
 2 Borrowed $10,000 by signing a one-year, 10% note.
 3 Purchased the following for cash:

	Cost
Land	$10,000
Building	30,000
Equipment	5,000
Total	$45,000

 4 Purchased a three-year fire insurance policy for $4,800. (Debit an asset account.)
 5 Purchased office supplies for $4,000. (Debit an asset account.)
 6 Received merchandise and an invoice dated June 5 from Reath, Inc., for $6,000. Credit terms are 2/10, n/30.
 6 Paid freight of $300 on merchandise received from Reath, Inc.
 8 Sold merchandise on credit to Kerley Company, for $20,000. Terms are n/30.
 10 Purchased merchandise from Kim, Inc., for cash of $6,000.

12   Returned $600 of defective merchandise to Kim, Inc., and received a cash refund.
14   Sold merchandise for cash of $5,000.
15   Paid Reath, Inc., the amount of the June 5 invoice, less the discount.
17   Received merchandise returned by Kerley Company. Granted credit of $1,000.
20   Received one-year's rent of $4,800 in advance on a small office. (Credit a liability account.)
23   Received merchandise and an invoice dated June 21 from Fogle, Inc., for $7,500. Credit terms are 1/10, n/60.
25   Sold merchandise on credit to Corey Company for $3,000. Terms are n/30.
29   Received payment in full from Kerley Company. (See June 8 and June 17 transactions.)
30   Paid the following June expenses:

Salaries	$1,900
Advertising	600
Utilities	500
Total	$3,000

Instructions

[a] Record each of the June transactions in a general journal.
[b] Post each journal entry to appropriate general ledger accounts.
[c] Prepare an unadjusted trial balance on June 30.

5–46   JOURNAL ENTRIES AND POSTING   Presented below is an unadjusted trial balance for Gilhula Company on November 30:

Gilhula Company
UNADJUSTED TRIAL BALANCE
November 30

Account	Dr.	Cr.
Cash	$ 14,000	
Accounts receivable	21,000	
Allowance for doubtful accounts		$ 1,000
Notes receivable	7,000	
Merchandise inventory, Jan. 1	15,000	
Prepaid insurance	3,000	
Prepaid rent	8,000	
Investment in Lee Company stock	20,000	
Equipment	60,000	
Accumulated depreciation		10,000
Accounts payable		11,000
Note payable		5,000
Common stock		40,000
Retained earnings		61,000
Sales		110,000
Sales returns	4,000	
Purchases	55,000	
Purchase returns		2,000
Purchase discounts		1,000
Transportation-in	5,000	
Salaries expense	20,000	
Advertising expense	6,000	
Utilities expense	3,000	
Interest expense	–0–	
	$241,000	$241,000

Additional Information

The following transactions occurred during December:

Dec. 1 Sold the investment in Lee Company stock for $14,000.
   3 Received a $4,000, 90-day, 13% note from a customer on account.
   4 Purchased merchandise for cash of $3,600.
   6 Paid the $5,000 note listed above. The note, which matured on Dec. 6, was for 120 days at 12% interest.
   7 Paid $8,000 of accounts payable. Cash discounts of 2% were taken.
   8 Returned $400 of defective merchandise purchased on Dec. 4 and received a cash refund.
   9 Collected $10,000 from customers on account.
  11 Wrote off uncollectible accounts receivable of $800.
  13 Purchased merchandise on account for $3,000. Terms are n/30.
  13 Paid freight of $200 on merchandise purchased.
  16 Received merchandise returned by a customer. Granted credit of $800.
  18 Sold merchandise on account for $9,000.
  22 Made cash sales of $5,000.
  23 Purchased a one-year insurance policy for $1,900.
  28 Purchased $10,000 of equipment for use in the business. Paid $2,000 cash and signed an $8,000, one-year, 12% note.
  31 Paid the following expenses:

Salaries	$1,800
Advertising	600
Utilities	300
Total	$2,700

Instructions

[a] Record each of the December transactions in a general journal. (Do not record adjusting entries.)

[b] Set up general ledger accounts and enter the opening balances for December. Post each journal entry to appropriate accounts.

[c] Prepare an unadjusted trial balance on December 31.

5–47 ACCOUNTING CYCLE   Coomer Consulting Company began operations on December 1. The following transactions occurred during the first month:

Dec. 1 Sold 500 shares of $100 par value common stock for $50,000 cash.
   1 Purchased equipment for $30,000 cash. (The equipment has an estimated useful life of 10 years and no expected salvage value. The company plans to use straight-line depreciation.)
   1 Purchased a one-year insurance policy for $4,800. (The company records all prepaid amounts in *real,* i.e., balance sheet, accounts.)
   1 Paid $9,600 office rent in advance for one year.
   2 Purchased on account supplies costing $8,000.
  10 Received $2,000 from a client for services rendered.
  16 Borrowed $5,000 from City Bank and signed a 90-day, 12% note.
  30 Paid half of the amount owed for the purchase of supplies on December 2.
  31 Billed clients $6,000 for services rendered during December.
  31 Paid $500 for advertisements run in the local newspaper during December.
  31 Paid the utility bill for $180 for December.
  31 Paid December salaries of $2,500.

Instructions

[a] Record the December transactions in general journal form.

[b] Post the journal entries to general ledger T accounts.

[c] Prepare an unadjusted trial balance at December 31.

[d] Journalize and post all necessary adjusting entries. (A count reveals that supplies costing $7,000 are on hand December 31. The income tax rate is 40%.)

[e] Prepare an adjusted trial balance.

[f] Prepare an income statement, a statement of retained earnings, and a balance sheet for December.

[g] Journalize and post closing entries.

[h] Prepare a post-closing trial balance.

5–48 ACCOUNTING CYCLE   Presented below is the post-closing trial balance of Beal Corporation on December 31, 1992:

Beal Corporation
POST-CLOSING TRIAL BALANCE
December 31, 1992

Account	Dr.	Cr.
Cash	$ 12,000	
Accounts receivable	18,000	
Allowance for doubtful accounts		$ 900
Merchandise inventory	23,000	
Prepaid rent	24,000	
Equipment	50,000	
Accumulated depreciation		10,000
Accounts payable		21,000
Income tax payable		11,000
Common stock		40,000
Retained earnings		44,100
	$127,000	$127,000

Following is a summary of transactions that occurred during 1993:

[1] Purchased merchandise on account for $85,000. (The company uses a periodic inventory system.)
[2] Paid transportation charges of $4,600 on merchandise purchased.
[3] Sold merchandise as follows:

On account	$145,000
For cash	62,900
Total	$207,900

[4] Collected $136,000 of accounts receivable.
[5] Wrote off uncollectible accounts of $850.
[6] Paid the income tax liability that was reported on December 31, 1992.
[7] Paid $78,000 on accounts payable.
[8] Paid the following expenses:

Salaries	$21,000
Advertising	12,000
Utilities	8,000
Telephone and telegraph	4,400
Total	$45,400

[9] Declared dividends of $10,000. The company will pay the dividends early in 1994.

Additional Information

This information is available on December 31, 1993:

[1] The company estimates that 1% of credit sales made during 1993 will never be collected.
[2] A physical count reveals that merchandise costing $19,000 is on hand at year-end.
[3] One-half of the prepaid rent as of December 31, 1992, expired during 1993.
[4] The equipment has an estimated useful life of 10 years and no expected salvage value. The company uses straight-line depreciation.
[5] The income tax rate for 1993 is 40%.

Instructions

[a] Set up general ledger T accounts for the postclosing trial balance accounts and for the following accounts: Dividends Payable, Sales, Cost of Goods Sold, Purchases, Transportation-In, Salaries Expense, Advertising Expense, Utilities Expense, Telephone and Telegraph, Bad

Debts Expense, Rent Expense, Depreciation Expense, Income Tax Expense, Dividends, and Income Summary. Enter the opening balances for 1993 in the ledger T accounts.

[b] Journalize the 1993 transactions in the order in which they are presented above. Use the number at the left of each transaction to indicate the date.

[c] Post the journal entries to the general ledger T accounts.

[d] Prepare an unadjusted trial balance.

[e] Journalize and post adjusting entries.

[f] Prepare an adjusted trial balance.

[g] Prepare an income statement, a statement of retained earnings, and a balance sheet.

[h] Journalize and post closing entries.

[i] Prepare a post-closing trial balance.

5–49 ADJUSTING ENTRIES   The following transactions occurred during the 1993 calendar-year accounting period of Pavaroni Company.

April 1   Paid $4,000 to a local television station for commercial time that will be broadcast evenly over twelve months, beginning in April.

June 1   Received $6,000 from a tenant paying rent in advance for one year.

Sept. 1   Paid $1,200 for a one-year fire insurance policy.

Nov. 1   Received $24,000 from customers for subscriptions paid in advance for one year.

Instructions

[a] Assuming the company has entered the above receipts and payments in *real* (balance sheet) accounts, journalize the adjustments required on December 31, 1993.

[b] Assuming the company has entered the above receipts and payments in *nominal* (income statement) accounts, journalize the adjustments required on December 31, 1993.

[c] Under the assumption in [a], compute the adjusted account balances for the 1993 financial statements for all accounts in your adjusting entries.

[d] Under the assumption in [b], compute the adjusted account balances for the 1993 financial statements for all accounts in your adjusting entries.

5–50 ADJUSTING AND REVERSING ENTRIES   Bower Publishing Company recorded the following transactions during its 1993 calendar-year accounting period:

Mar. 1   Received $18,000 from customers for subscriptions paid in advance for one year.

Apr. 1   Paid $2,400 for a one-year fire insurance policy.

Aug. 1   Received $9,000 from a tenant paying rent in advance for six months.

Oct. 1   Paid $6,000 to a local radio station for advertising time. The station agreed to broadcast two ads each month for 12 months, beginning in October.

Instructions

[a] Journalize the above transactions assuming that the company enters in *real* (balance sheet) accounts the amounts that are received or paid in advance.

[b] Based on [a], journalize the necessary adjustments on December 31, 1993.

[c] Assuming that the company uses reversing entries, journalize the reversals that are appropriate for the adjusting entries in [b].

[d] Journalize the above transactions assuming that the company enters in *nominal* (income statement) accounts the amounts that are received or paid in advance.

[e] Based on [d], journalize the necessary adjustments on December 31, 1993.

[f] Assuming that the company uses reversing entries, journalize the reversals that are appropriate for the adjusting entries in [e].

5–51 ADJUSTING AND REVERSING ENTRIES   The following information pertains to Fred's Laundry Service on June 30, 1993, the end of the company's fiscal year:

[1] On March 1, 1993, the company purchased a three-year fire insurance policy for $3,600. A *real* (balance sheet) account was debited.

[2] The company's estimate of bad debts for the fiscal year is $2,000.

[3] On October 1, 1992, the company received $12,000 for rent received in advance for one year for storage space that it leases to Hall Company. A nominal account was credited.

[4] The company's estimate of depreciation for the year is $12,000.

[5] On April 1, 1993, the company paid $1,800 to the local newspaper for advertising space and debited a nominal account. The newspaper agreed to publish four ads each month for one year, beginning in April.

[6] On May 31, 1993, the company borrowed $10,000 from Citizens' Bank and signed a 120-day, 12% note.

[7] Employees have earned wages of $640 that the company has not paid or recorded as of June 30, 1993.

[8] On December 1, 1992, the company purchased at par value ten $1,000, 12%, 20-year bonds of Hope, Inc. The bonds pay interest semiannually on May 31 and November 30.

[9] On March 1, 1993, the company received $12,000 for laundry service that it will provide for one year, beginning on that date. A *real* (balance sheet) account was credited.

[10] Property taxes owed and unrecorded as of June 30 total $1,300.

Instructions

[a] Prepare adjusting entries in general journal form at June 30, 1993.

[b] Assuming that the company wants to make reversing entries, identify the adjusting entries that it may appropriately reverse.

5-52 ADJUSTING AND REVERSING ENTRIES Presented below is the trial balance of Skinner Company at December 31, 1993, the end of the company's annual accounting period:

Account	Dr.	Cr.
Cash	$ 26,000	
Accounts receivable	25,000	
Allowance for doubtful accounts	150	
Merchandise inventory, Jan. 1	53,000	
Investment in Slaton, Inc., bonds	30,000	
Land	47,000	
Building	200,000	
Accumulated depreciation—building		$ 22,500
Equipment	80,000	
Accumulated depreciation—equipment		24,000
Accounts payable		19,000
Note payable		50,000
Common stock		100,000
Retained earnings, Jan. 1		176,028
Sales		452,000
Interest revenue		2,700
Rent revenue — No unearned Rent Rev. Acct		9,000 — 1½ yrs of rent
Purchases	280,380	
Purchase returns and allowances		11,180
Transportation-in	10,000	
Salaries expense	86,200	
Rent expense	21,000	
Utilities expense	7,678	
	$866,408	$866,408

No P.P. Rent — Only Rent Exp

Additional Information

[1] Eighty percent of 1993 sales were made on credit. The company estimates that 2% of credit sales will never be collected.

[2] A physical count reveals that merchandise costing $50,000 is on hand at year-end.

[3] On March 17, 1992, the company purchased thirty $1,000, 12%, 20-year bonds of Slaton, Inc. The bonds pay interest semiannually on March 31 and September 30.

[4] The company computes annual depreciation as follows:

Building	2.5% of cost
Equipment	5% of cost

[5] The note payable relates to a 90-day, 12% loan obtained from Third National Bank on October 20, 1993.

[6] The company has rented a portion of its building to Purdy's Retail Store since July 1, 1991. The rent is $6,000 per year, payable by Purdy's in advance each July 1.

[7] As of December 31, employees had earned salaries of $5,200 that the company had not paid or recorded.

[8] The company has rented a warehouse from the Suda Storage Company since October 1, 1992. The rent is $12,000 per year, payable by Skinner Company in advance each October 1.

[9] The utility bill for December 1993 is $621. As of December 31, this amount had not been paid or recorded.

[10] The company's income taxes for the year are $27,180 to be paid in 1994.

Instructions

[a] Prepare the adjusting entries in general journal form on December 31, 1993.

[b] Identify the broad accounting principle that underlies each adjusting entry. (*Hint:* Review the principles discussed in Chapter 2.)

[c] Refer to the part of your answer in [b] that pertains to the cost of goods sold adjustment. Explain why the broad accounting principle you identified applies to the cost of goods sold adjustment.

[d] Assuming that Skinner Company wants to make reversing entries, identify the adjusting entries that the company may appropriately reverse.

5–53 ADJUSTING AND REVERSING ENTRIES Presented below is the trial balance of Renfro Corporation at December 31, 1993, the end of the company's annual accounting period:

Renfro Corporation
TRIAL BALANCE
December 31, 1993

Account	Dr.	Cr.
Cash	$ 14,925	
Accounts receivable	24,000	
Allowance for doubtful accounts		$ 300
Note receivable	4,000	
Merchandise inventory, Jan. 1	10,000	
Supplies	1,300	
Prepaid insurance	3,000	
Land	70,000	
Building	60,000	
Accumulated depreciation—building		6,000
Equipment	20,000	
Accumulated depreciation—equipment		4,000
Goodwill	9,375	
Accounts payable		8,600
Unearned rent revenue		7,200
Bonds payable (20-year, 10%)		100,000
Common stock		50,000
Paid-in capital in excess of par value		10,000
Retained earnings, Jan. 1		17,000
Sales		200,000
Purchases	95,000	
Purchase returns		3,000
Transportation-in	8,000	
Salaries expense	30,000	
Travel expense	7,000	
Advertising expense	16,000	
Transportation-out	10,000	
Telephone expense	5,000	
Utilities expense	11,000	
Interest expense	7,500	
	$406,100	$406,100

Additional Information

[1] The company makes all its sales on credit. It estimates that 1.5% of sales made during 1993 will never be collected.

[2] The note receivable is a 90-day, 12% note taken from a customer on December 1, 1993.

[3] A physical inventory indicates that merchandise costing $20,000 is on hand December 31, 1993.

[4] A count reveals that supplies costing $400 are on hand December 31, 1993.

[5] The prepaid insurance account pertains to a three-year fire policy purchased on July 1, 1992, for $3600.

[6] The following information concerns the building and equipment:

	Estimated Useful Life in Years	Estimated Salvage Value	Depreciation Method
Building	40	None	Straight line
Equipment	20	None	Straight line

[7] The company recorded $10,000 of goodwill when it acquired a competing firm on October 1, 1991. Renfro Corporation uses the straight-line method of amortizing goodwill.

[8] On July 1, 1993, the company leased a portion of its building to Kinzer Company and received a check for $7,200 for one year's rent paid in advance.

[9] The company issued the bonds payable at par value on October 1, 1990. The bonds pay interest semiannually on March 31 and September 30.

[10] Salaries earned but unpaid to employees as of year-end totaled $2,700.

[11] On December 17, 1993, the company paid $1,800 for advertising time on a local television show that will be broadcast on January 12, 1994.

[12] A utility bill of $1,340 for December 1993 has been received but not yet recorded or paid.

[13] Property taxes that accrued during 1993 amounted to $3,100.

[14] The company determines that income tax expense for 1993 is $8,900. This amount will be paid in 1994.

Instructions

[a] Prepare adjusting entries in general journal form at December 31, 1993.

[b] Identify the broad accounting principle that underlies each adjusting entry. (*Hint:* Review the principles discussed in Chapter 2.)

[c] Refer to the part of your answer in [b] that pertains to the adjusting entry for the building and equipment (i.e., depreciation). Explain why the broad accounting principle you identified applies to this adjusting entry.

[d] Identify adjusting entries that Renfro Corporation may appropriately reverse, assuming that the company wants to make reversing entries.

5–54 RECONSTRUCTING ADJUSTING ENTRIES Presented below are trial balances of Grayson Company at December 31, 1993:

	Trial Balance Unadjusted Dr.	Cr.	Adjusted Dr.	Cr.
Account				
Cash	$ 14,000		$ 14,000	
Accounts receivable	22,000		22,000	
Allowance for doubtful accounts	56			$ 2,000
Note receivable	10,000		10,000	
Interest receivable			1,000	
Supplies	6,000		3,209	
Merchandise inventory, Jan. 1	20,000			
Merchandise inventory, Dec. 31			25,000	
Prepaid rent	18,000		6,000	

Equipment	120,000		120,000	
Accumulated depreciation—equipment		$ 30,000		40,000
Accounts payable		12,000		12,000
Salaries payable				2,000
Income tax payable				16,000
Common stock		40,000		40,000
Retained earnings		67,265		67,265
Sales		205,631		205,631
Interest revenue				1,000
Cost of goods sold			102,840	
Purchases	107,840			
Salaries expense	29,000		31,000	
Miscellaneous expenses	8,000		8,000	
Supplies expense			2,791	
Rent expense			12,000	
Depreciation expense			10,000	
Bad-debts expense			2,056	
Income tax expense			16,000	
	$354,896	$354,896	$385,896	$385,896

Instructions

Based on the above information, *reconstruct* the adjusting journal entries that Grayson Company made on December 31, 1993.

5–55 EFFECTS OF ADJUSTING ENTRIES At the end of 1993, Coe Company failed to record the adjusting entries indicated below:

[1] Accrued wages owed to employees.
[2] Depreciation of plant assets.
[3] Earned portion on one year's rent that had been received by Coe in advance on July 1, 1993, and recorded in a liability account.
[4] Estimate of bad debts.
[5] Unexpired portion of a one-year fire insurance policy that Coe paid for on September 1, 1993, and charged to a nominal account.
[6] Accrued interest on an investment in bonds.

Instructions

Prepare a table similar to the one shown below and indicate the effect of each error on the 1993 financial statement elements shown. Use the following code in marking your answers: O = overstated, U = understated, and NE = no effect. Assume that each error is independent of the others.

Error	Total Revenues	Total Expenses	Net Income	Total Assets	Total Liabilities	Total Stockholders' Equity
Example: Failed to record accrued interest on note payable.	NE	U	O	NE	U	O
[1]						
[2]						
[3]						
[4]						
[5]						
[6]						

5–56 (Appendix B) GENERAL AND SPECIAL JOURNALS Corkland Company began operations on May 1. The company uses a periodic inventory system. All credit sales are subject to terms of 2/10, n/30. The following transactions occurred during May:

May 1 Issued 10,000 shares of $5 par value common stock for $60,000.
     2 Issued 1,000 shares of $5 par value common stock for land valued at $5,000.
     3 Purchased a building for $30,000. Check no. 101 was issued.
     5 Received merchandise and an invoice dated May 2 from Brown Company for $2,000. Terms are 1/15, n/30.
     7 Sold merchandise on credit to Albert Company for $3,000. Invoice no. 1001 was issued.
     9 Purchased merchandise from Dantley Company for cash of $1,500. Check no. 102 was issued.
    11 Sold merchandise on credit to Hadler Company for $2,500. Invoice no. 1002 was issued.
    12 Received merchandise and an invoice dated May 10 from Gatlin Company for $4,000. Terms are 2/10, n/60.
    13 Sold merchandise to Roundtree Company for cash of $6,300.
    15 Issued check no. 103 for $1,980 to Brown Company in payment of May 2 invoice, less the discount.
    16 Received a check for $2,940 from Albert Company in payment of May 7 invoice, less the discount.
    18 Received a check for $2,450 from Hadler Company in payment of May 11 invoice, less the discount.
    19 Issued check no. 104 for $3,920 to Gatlin Company in payment of May 10 invoice, less the discount.
    24 Received merchandise and an invoice dated May 23 from Early Company for $1,000. Terms are 2/10, n/30.
    25 Sold merchandise on credit to Canton Company for $8,000. Invoice no. 1003 was issued.
    28 Received merchandise and an invoice dated May 26 from Ison Company for $1,800. Terms are 3/15, n/30.
    31 Sold merchandise on credit to Jasper Company for $2,800. Invoice no. 1004 was issued.

Instructions

[a] Record the transactions for May using the following journals (as shown in Appendix B): sales, purchases, cash receipts, cash payments, and general.

[b] Post the appropriate amounts in a general ledger and in accounts receivable and accounts payable subsidiary ledgers. Systematically number all accounts and use posting references.

[c] Prepare a trial balance on May 31.

[d] Reconcile the subsidiary ledgers with the appropriate control accounts.

5-57 (Appendix A) WORKSHEET, FINANCIAL STATEMENTS, ADJUSTING AND CLOSING ENTRIES Defiore Company has adopted a calendar-year accounting period. The company's unadjusted trial balance on December 31, appears below:

Account	Dr.	Cr.
Cash	$ 36,775	
Accounts receivable	30,000	
Allowance for doubtful accounts	225	
Merchandise inventory, Jan. 1	42,000	
Investment in bonds (long-term)	20,000	
Land	52,000	
Building	100,000	
Accumulated depreciation—building		$ 25,000
Equipment	50,000	
Accumulated depreciation—equipment		25,000
Accounts payable		32,000
Common stock ($10 par value, 10,000 shares)		100,000
Retained earnings, Jan. 1		109,500
Sales		475,000
Interest revenue		1,500
Rent revenue		12,000
Purchases	305,000	
Purchase returns		12,000
Salaries expense	88,000	

Advertising expense	22,000	
Utilities expense	6,000	
Supplies expense	30,000	
Dividends	10,000	
	$792,000	$792,000

Additional Information

This information is available on December 31:

[1] The company estimates that bad debts expense for the year is $3,500.
[2] The December 31 merchandise inventory is $50,000.
[3] Unrecorded interest of $500 has accrued on the investment in bonds.
[4] The company estimates depreciation for the year as follows:

Building	$2,500
Equipment	$5,000

[5] One-fourth of the rent revenue shown above has *not* been earned as of December 31.
[6] Employees have earned salaries of $4,000 that the company has not paid or recorded.
[7] The cost of supplies on hand December 31 is $12,000.
[8] The income tax rate is 40%.

Instructions

[a] Enter the unadjusted trial balance on a twelve-column worksheet (as in Appendix A).
[b] Enter the adjusting entries on the worksheet.
[c] Complete the worksheet.
[d] Prepare an income statement, a statement of retained earnings, and a balance sheet.
[e] Record the adjusting and closing entries in the general journal.

5–58 (Appendix A) WORKSHEET, FINANCIAL STATEMENTS, ADJUSTING AND CLOSING ENTRIES   Presented below is the unadjusted trial balance of Gaudet, Inc., on December 31, the end of the company's annual accounting period:

Account	Dr.	Cr.
Cash	$ 4,500	
Accounts receivable	18,000	
Allowance for doubtful accounts		$ 300
Notes receivable (due in six months)	10,000	
Merchandise inventory, Jan. 1	23,000	
Prepaid insurance	4,800	
Land	40,000	
Building	50,000	
Accumulated depreciation—building		20,000
Equipment	20,000	
Accumulated depreciation—equipment		12,000
Accounts payable		21,000
Dividends payable		8,000
Unearned rent revenue		6,000
Common stock ($5 par value, 10,000 shares)		50,000
Retained earnings, Jan. 1		22,000
Sales		225,000
Purchases	123,000	
Transportation-in	7,000	
Salaries expense	34,000	
Advertising expense	8,000	
Utilities expense	4,000	
Dividends	18,000	
	$364,300	$364,300

Additional Information

This information is available on December 31:

[1] Accrued interest on notes receivable totals $500.
[2] Employees have earned salaries of $1,500 that the company has not paid or recorded.
[3] One-half of the unearned rent revenue shown above was earned during the year.
[4] Three-fourths of the prepaid insurance shown above expired during the year.
[5] Depreciation for the year is as follows:

Building	$2,000
Equipment	$4,000

[6] Bad-debts expense for the year is $900.
[7] The inventory on hand December 31 has a cost of $27,000.
[8] The income tax rate is 40%.

Instructions

[a] Enter the unadjusted trial balance on a twelve-column worksheet (as in Appendix A).
[b] Enter the adjusting entries on the worksheet.
[c] Complete the worksheet.
[d] Prepare an income statement, a statement of retained earnings, and a balance sheet.
[e] Record the adjusting and closing entries in the general journal.

CASES

5–59 ACCRUAL ACCOUNTING   Assume that you are working in the office of a small business client of your local CPA firm. The client has always maintained accounting records but has never prepared a set of financial statements completely in accordance with GAAP. Now, however, the client needs a bank loan, and the banker has required a set of financial statements prepared according to GAAP. Your client has asked for your help in understanding the meaning of accrual accounting.

Instructions

[a] How does accrual accounting affect the determination of income? Include in your discussion what constitutes an accrual and a deferral, and give appropriate examples of each.
[b] Compare accrual accounting and cash accounting.   (AICPA adapted)

5–60 PERIODIC FINANCIAL REPORTING   Firms prepare annual financial statements for internal management and for distribution to outside parties. In addition, many firms prepare summary reports or statements quarterly, monthly, and weekly for both internal use and external distribution. The frequency of reporting may affect the preparation cost and the objectivity of the reports or statements.

Instructions

[a] Explain why the accounting period appropriate for internal and external reporting for most firms is one year.
[b] Explain in general terms why summary reports or statements are prepared for reporting periods less than one year. Give an example why (1) internal management and (2) an outside party may want reports or statements which cover a shorter period.
[c] Adjustments to the accounting records are made when summary reports or statements are prepared annually, quarterly, or monthly.
  [1] Explain why these adjustments are needed.
  [2] Cite examples of adjustments that would have to be made to the accounting records.
[d] How is the objectivity of financial information in summary reports or statements affected when more frequent reports are prepared?   (CMA adapted)

CHAPTER 6

Compound Interest Concepts

OBJECTIVES

1. To distinguish clearly between simple and compound interest.
2. To discuss and illustrate the fundamentals of compound interest.
3. To discuss and illustrate how to solve each of the following types of compound interest problems in accounting contexts:
   a. Amount and present value of a single sum.
   b. Amount and present value of an ordinary annuity.
   c. Amount and present value of an annuity due.
   d. Amount and present value of a deferred annuity.

A dollar received today is worth more than a dollar received one year from today. This is true even if we ignore inflation, because the dollar received today can be invested to earn a return. Thus, we could place $1.00 in a 6% savings account today and have $1.06 at the end of one year. Having $1.06 one year hence is obviously better than receiving only $1.00 at that time.

Money has been regarded as a valuable resource ever since scientists first discovered that it doesn't grow on trees. It comes as no surprise, then, that money cannot be used free of charge. Money has a time value, commonly called **interest**, that people must consider when making rational investment and credit decisions.

Interest is the cost of using money over time. From the standpoint of a borrower, interest is the excess money that is paid over the amount that was borrowed. From a lender's point of view, interest is the excess money that is received over the amount that was loaned. Because the value of money changes over time, cash inflows and outflows that occur at different points in time are not directly comparable. Therefore, they should not be lumped together but should be compared as of a common point in time. We may choose to compare cash flows as of some future time. Usually, however, we compare cash flows as of the present time, because the present is the time within which we live and think.

To illustrate, assume that you have just decided to sell your wristwatch. Allen offers you $100, payable immediately, while Baker offers $103, to be paid in one year. Assuming that you can earn a 6% return on your money, which offer should you accept? Clearly, if we compare the alternatives as of one year hence, we find that Allen's offer is worth $106 ($100 × 1.06), whereas Baker's offer is worth only $103. Making the comparison as the present time, we find that Allen's offer is worth $100 while Baker's offer is worth less ($103 ÷ 1.06 = $97.17). In either case, Allen's offer should be accepted. Note that, because money has a time value, we could not meaningfully compare the two offers until we determined the value of each offer as of a common point in time.

In this chapter we explain and illustrate the fundamentals of compound interest. The time value of money has so many applications in business that it often is covered in several college courses, such as accounting, finance, economics, and mathematics. Readers must acquire a working knowledge of compound interest concepts to understand many topics covered in subsequent chapters. Examples are accounting for certain notes receivable and notes payable under *Accounting Principles Board Opinion No. 21*, accounting for bonds as investments and liabilities, accounting for leases under *Financial Accounting Standards Board Statement No. 13*, accounting for pension plans under *FASB Statement No. 87*, accounting for sinking funds, and accounting for installment contracts. That money has a time value is clearly recognized in *APB Opinion No. 21*, a pronouncement that frequently requires accountants to estimate and record interest even though a long-term note may contain no stated interest rate.

In this chapter we are not concerned with changes in general purchasing power of money over time (inflation or deflation). We will compare various sums of money without regard to the ability of those sums to buy goods and services. Assuming a 6% interest rate, for example, the question of whether $1.00 today can buy more or fewer goods and services than can $1.06 one year hence is beyond the scope of this chapter.

SIMPLE VERSUS COMPOUND INTEREST

Interest is earned over a period of time. Therefore, a stated interest rate relates to a particular time period. Because interest is normally stated as an **annual percentage**

rate, such as 8%, 10%, or 12%, we assume throughout the text that a stated interest rate is a rate **per year,** unless indicated otherwise.

There are two types of interest: simple and compound. **Simple interest** is earned only on the principal sum of money invested. The formula for simple interest follows:

$$i = prt$$

where i = simple interest
p = principal sum of money
r = interest rate per unit of time
t = time expressed in units that correspond
     to the rate

If $1,500 is borrowed at 8% for one year, the simple interest is $1,500 × .08 × 1 = $120. If the same amount is borrowed for only six months, simple interest is $1,500 × .08 × $\frac{6}{12}$ = $60. Note that r and t must correspond with one another. If r is an annual rate, t must be expressed in years; if r is a monthly rate, t must be expressed in months; and so forth.

Simple interest is used in many short-term (less than one year) business transactions. Recall that we assumed simple interest in Chapter 5 when we illustrated adjusting entries for the accrual of interest on notes receivable and notes payable.

Compound interest is earned on the principal sum of money invested *and* on the interest accumulated. In other words, the principal earns interest and the accumulated interest earns interest. To illustrate, assume that $1,500 is invested for three years at 8%. A comparison of simple versus compound interest on this investment follows:

Simple Interest					
$i = prt$ = $1,500 × .08 × 3 = $360 Accumulated amount at the end of three years is: $1,500 + $360 = $1,860					
Compound Interest					
(A)	(B)		(C)	(D)	(E)	(F)
Year	Principal		Rate	Time	Compound Interest	Accumulated Amount (B + E)
1	$1,500.00	×	.08	× 1	= $120.00	$1,620.00
2	1,620.00	×	.08	× 1	= 129.60	1,749.60
3	1,749.60	×	.08	× 1	= 139.97	1,889.57
				Total	$389.57	

Notice that with compound interest, the accumulated amount at the end of each year becomes the new principal sum on which interest is earned during the next year. Notice further that $29.57 ($389.57 − $360.00 or $1,889.57 − $1,860.00) of additional interest resulted from compound interest. This is the interest on prior interest accumulations, which can be verified as shown on page 220.

Year	Prior Interest Accumulation		Rate		Time		Interest on Prior Interest Accumulation
1	–0–*	×	.08	×	1	=	–0–
2	$120.00**	×	.08	×	1	=	$ 9.60
3	249.60†	×	.08	×	1	=	19.97
						Total	$29.57

*No interest was accumulated prior to Year 1.
**This is the $120.00 interest for Year 1.
†This is the $120.00 interest for Year 1 plus the $129.60 interest for Year 2.

Compound interest is used in most long-term (beyond one year) business transactions. Although interest is typically stated as an annual percentage rate, when compound interest is assumed, interest may be compounded (calculated and added to principal) for periods of less than one year. For example, interest may be compounded semiannually, quarterly, monthly, daily, or even continuously.[1] To avoid repetition, we make the customary assumption throughout the text that a stated annual interest rate is compounded annually, unless indicated otherwise.

Called the "eighth wonder of the world" by some people, compound interest has impressive power to make a sum of money grow. Francis Baily, a nineteenth century British astronomer, determined that a British penny invested at 5% compound interest at the birth of Christ would have yielded enough gold by the year 1810 to fill 357 million earths. As another example, when Benjamin Franklin died in 1790, he left about $4,600 to the cities of Boston and Philadelphia under the condition that the money not be used for 100 years. By 1890, the $4,600 had grown to $332,000.[2]

BASIC CONCEPTS

The fundamental concepts underlying all compound interest problems are as follows:

1. **Present value (PV).** Present value usually refers to a value at the present time (today). More generally, it refers to a value at the beginning of any time span that is of concern.

2. **Future value (FV).** This usually refers to a value at some time in the future. More generally, future value can refer to a value at the end of any time period that is of concern.

3. **Interest rate (i).** This refers to a rate that corresponds to the length of each compounding period. This rate is computed by dividing the annual interest rate by the number of times a year interest is compounded.[3] For example, if interest is stated

---

[1]Continuous compounding is accomplished using logarithms.
[2]Robert L. Rose, "Compounding: It's Boring but a Wonder," *Wall Street Journal* (June 17, 1985), p. 23.
[3]The interest rate *(i)* is called a **stated**, or **nominal**, **rate**. Furthermore, the term **frequency of compounding** (usually denoted by the letter *m*) refers to the number of times a year interest is compounded.

It is worthwhile to note that whenever *m* is greater than 1, the effective or true rate of interest *(r)* on an investment is greater than the stated annual rate. The **effective rate** is the rate that, when compounded annually, generates the same annual interest as the stated annual rate does when compounded *m* times per year. The effective rate may be calculated using the following formula:

$$r = (1 + i)^m - 1$$

For example, if the stated annual rate is 8% compounded quarterly, the effective annual rate is:

$$r = (1 + i)^m - 1$$
$$= (1 + .02)^4 - 1$$
$$= (1.02)^4 - 1$$
$$= 1.08243 - 1$$
$$= .08243$$
$$= 8.243\%$$

at 8%, compounded annually (once per year), the interest rate is 8% per annual period (8% ÷ 1). If interest is stated at 8%, compounded semiannually (twice per year), the interest rate is 4% per semiannual period (8% ÷ 2). And if interest is stated at 8%, compounded quarterly (four times per year), the interest rate is 2% per quarterly period (8% ÷ 4).

4. **Time periods (*n*).** This refers to the number of compounding periods. It may be computed by multiplying the number of years involved by the number of compounding periods in each year. For example, interest for three years, compounded semiannually, involves 6 (3 × 2) compounding periods. Likewise, interest for three years, compounded quarterly, involves 12 (3 × 4) compounding periods.

Using these four fundamental concepts, we can solve compound interest problems.

Quite often, sketching the known components in the form of a **time diagram** aids in understanding and resolving the compound interest problem. The four concepts discussed above are depicted in the following time diagram:

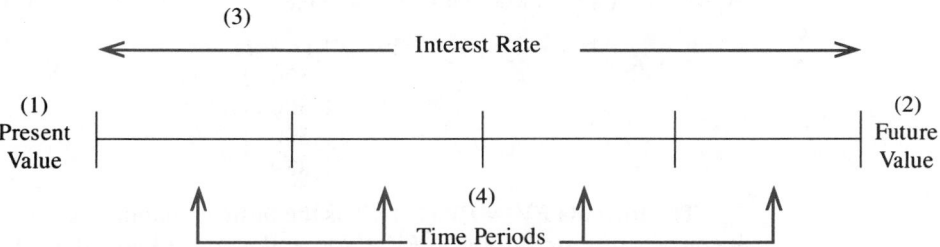

SINGLE SUM PROBLEMS

Single sum problems (sometimes called lump sum problems) involve a single sum of money and generally fall into one of the following two categories:

1. Problems that focus on the future value of a single sum of money that is left on deposit for a certain number of periods at a certain interest rate per period.
2. Problems that focus on the present value of a single sum of money that is discounted for a certain number of periods at a certain interest rate per period.

AMOUNT (FUTURE VALUE) OF A SINGLE SUM

In everyday conversation, "amount" refers to any amount, past, present, or future. In discussions of compound interest, amount refers only to a future value. The amount of a single sum is therefore the future value to which the sum will accumulate if left on deposit for a certain number of periods at a certain interest rate per period. For example, in the earlier discussion of simple and compound interest, $1,889.57 (a future value) is the amount to which $1,500 (a single sum of money) will accumulate if left on deposit for three years at 8% compounded annually. The solution is illustrated in the time diagram in Exhibit 6–1. Note that the arrow points to the right, the direction of the future value.

The period-by-period approach used earlier to calculate future value ($1,889.57) is somewhat cumbersome, and it would be even more so in a problem involving more than three periods. To simplify the calculations, the following formula is often applied:

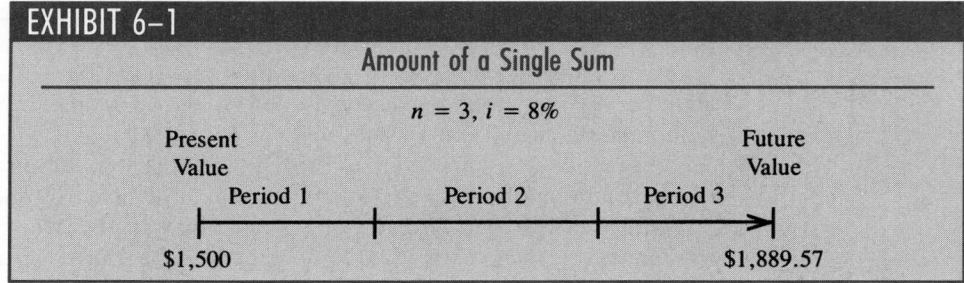

EXHIBIT 6–1

Amount of a Single Sum

$n = 3, i = 8\%$

Present Value

Future Value

Period 1   Period 2   Period 3

$1,500 $1,889.57

$$FV = PV(1 + i)^n$$

where FV = future value of a single sum
PV = present value (principal sum) of a single sum
i = interest rate per compounding period
n = number of compounding periods

Applying this formula, we find that $1,889.57 is indeed the future value:

$$
\begin{aligned}
FV &= PV(1 + i)^n \\
&= \$1,500\,(1 + .08)^3 \\
&= \$1,500\,(1.08)^3 \\
&= \$1,500\,(1.25971) \\
&= \$1,889.57
\end{aligned}
$$

The formula $FV = PV(1 + i)^n$ is the basic compound interest formula. Note that it consists of four variables: FV, PV, i, and n. If we know the values of any three, we can solve for the fourth using algebra.

Focus for a moment on the $(1 + i)^n$ part of the formula. Because of the frequent need to apply compound interest concepts in the business world, tables have been published that provide solutions for $(1 + i)^n$ for many combinations of i and n. We shall refer to each of these solutions as a **future value factor** (*fvf*). Table 6–1 at the end of this chapter contains future value factors for most of the commonly encountered i and n values.[4] It can be used to save time in solving problems that involve the amount of a single sum.

Table 6–1 is entitled "Amount of 1" because it gives the amounts (future values) to which 1 (such as one dollar, one peso, or one mark) will accumulate if left on deposit for n periods at i compound interest. If we know the amount to which 1 will accumulate, we can find the amount to which any single sum will accumulate by simply multiplying the single sum by the amount to which 1 will accumulate. Note that the table consists of rows of compounding periods (n) and columns of interest rates (i). A future value factor is located at the intersection of each row and column.[5] For example, the future value factor of $n = 5$ and $i = 10\%$ is 1.61051. To illustrate finding a table factor, Exhibit 6–2 presents a portion of Table 6–1 with the factor circled for $n = 5$ and $i = 10\%$ (1.61051).

To really understand the solutions to compound interest problems, you should remember how Table 6–1 was constructed—that is, by solving $(1 + i)^n$ for different

---

[4]Table 6–1, as well as the other tables at the end of the chapter, are partial. In practice, more comprehensive tables are widely available. Of course, any compound interest table can be extended by using the formula on which the table is based.

[5]Notice that each table factor is rounded to five decimal places. In practice, tables rounded to ten places are often used when dealing with extremely large numbers in order to minimize the effects of rounding.

EXHIBIT 6-2

Finding the Future Value Factor of $n = 5$, $i = 10\%$ Using Table 6-1 (Amount of 1)

Number of Periods (n)	Interest Rate (i)		
	8%	10%	12%
1	1.08000	1.10000	1.12000
2	1.16640	1.21000	1.25440
3	1.25971	1.33100	1.40493
4	1.36049	1.46410	1.57352
5	1.46933	(1.61051)	1.76234
6	1.58687	1.77156	1.97382

combinations of i and n values. It is no surprise that future value factors increase with each increase in i or n.

Because we know that $FV = PV (1 + i)^n$ and $(1 + i)^n = fvf$, we can now state:

$$FV = PV \cdot fvf_{\overline{n}|\,i} \qquad (6\text{--}1)$$

$$\text{where } \quad FV = \text{future value of a single sum}$$
$$PV = \text{present value (principal sum) of a}$$
$$\text{single sum}$$
$$fvf_{\overline{n}|\,i} = \text{future value factor (from Table}$$
$$6\text{--}1) \text{ for the relevant } n \text{ and } i$$

The expression $fvf_{\overline{n}|\,i}$ is read as "fvf sub n at i" or "fvf angle n at i." When solving a compound interest equation, inserting the values for n and i ensures that you will locate and use the correct table factor.

Recall that we have determined, using both a period-by-period approach and a formula approach, that $1,889.57 is the future value of $1,500 deposited for 3 years at 8% compounded annually. Now we can use Equation 6–1 and Table 6–1 to implement a third approach to solving the problem. This approach is the easiest of all, because some of the calculations have already been performed, and the results appear in Table 6–1. First, note in Table 6–1 that the fvf for $n = 3$ and $i = 8\%$ is 1.25971. Now we can say

$$FV = PV \cdot fvf_{\overline{n}|\,i}$$
$$= \$1{,}500 \cdot fvf_{\overline{3}|\,8\%}$$
$$= \$1{,}500 \,(1.25971)$$
$$= \$1{,}889.57$$

Because of the computational ease and time savings offered by compound interest tables, we emphasize a table-based solution to the problems in this chapter.

Accounting Examples

Problem 1. At the beginning of Year 1, Florida Electric Company deposited $50,000 in a special building fund that earns 8% interest compounded quarterly. How much cash will be in the fund at the end of Year 10?

Solution 1. In this problem we know the present value ($50,000), the interest rate per period (8% ÷ 4 = 2%), and the number of periods (4 × 10 = 40). We are asked to solve for the future value, which we do with Equation 6–1 and Table 6–1:

$$FV = PV \cdot fvf_{\overline{n}|\,i}$$
$$= \$50{,}000 \cdot fvf_{\overline{40}|\,2\%}$$
$$= \$50{,}000\,(2.20804)$$
$$= \$110{,}402$$

Problem 2.   To keep things simple, let's modify Problem 1. Assume that Florida Electric Company wants to accumulate \$110,402 for the purchase of a new building. If at the beginning of Year 1 the company deposited \$50,000 in a special building fund that earns 8% interest compounded quarterly, how many years will it take for the fund to accumulate to \$110,402?

Solution 2.   We know the present value (\$50,000), the future value (\$110,402), and the interest rate per period (8% ÷ 4 = 2%). We are asked to solve for the number of years, which we can easily do using Equation 6–1 and Table 6–1. Since $FV = PV \cdot fvf_{\overline{n}|\,i}$, we can divide both sides of the equation by PV:

$$fvf_{\overline{n}|\,i} = \frac{FV}{PV}$$
$$fvf_{\overline{n}|\,2\%} = \frac{\$110{,}402}{\$50{,}000}$$
$$= 2.20804$$

Now that we know the future value factor and the interest rate per period, we simply run our finger down the 2% column of Table 6–1 until we find 2.20804. Since 2.20804 is found at $n = 40$, we conclude that it will take *10 years* (40 quarterly interest periods ÷ 4) to accumulate \$110,402. If we had not found the number 2.20804 in the 2% column of Table 6–1, we could have approximated our answer using linear interpolation, a procedure explained later in the chapter.

Problem 3.   Suppose that the problem were phrased this way. Florida Electric Company wants to accumulate \$110,402 for the purchase of a new building. If at the beginning of Year 1 the company deposited \$50,000 in a special building fund in which interest is compounded quarterly, what annual rate of interest is required for the \$50,000 deposit to accumulate to \$110,402 at the end of Year 10?

Solution 3.   We follow the same approach taken in Problem 2, except that we look for the future value factor of 2.20804 in Table 6–1 along the row in which $n = 40$ (10 years × 4 compounding periods per year). Because 2.20804 is in the 2% column, we conclude that the required annual rate of interest is 8% (2% × 4).

PRESENT VALUE OF A SINGLE SUM

Determining the present value of a single sum is the inverse of determining the amount of a single sum. Instead of moving forward in time using accumulation to determine a future value, we move backward in time using **discounting** to determine a present value. For example, suppose that we want to know the present value of \$1,889.57 to be received or paid in three years discounted at 8% compounded annually. We could prepare a decumulation table similar to the compound interest accumulation table presented earlier. Instead of going forward in time, we would go backward, and instead of multiplying each year's principal by 1.08, we would multiply by 1/1.08 (which is the same as dividing by 1.08), as shown on page 225 (top).

The time diagram shown in Exhibit 6–3 illustrates the solution to the problem. The arrow in the diagram points to the left, which is the direction of the present value.

That \$1,500 is the present value (the decumulated amount at the beginning of Year 1) is no surprise, because this problem was used earlier to explain the amount of a single sum. Preparing decumulation tables is tedious and time consuming. Fortunately, there are easier ways to solve the problem.

Compound Discount							
(A)	(B)	(C)		(D)		(E)	(F)
		Discount				Decumulated	Compound Discount
Year	Principal	Rate		Time		Amount	(B–E)
3	$1,889.57	×	$\frac{1}{1.08}$	×	1	=	$1,749.60	$139.97
2	1,749.60	×	$\frac{1}{1.08}$	×	1	=	1,620.00	129.60
1	1,620.00	×	$\frac{1}{1.08}$	×	1	=	1,500.00	120.00
						Total	$389.57

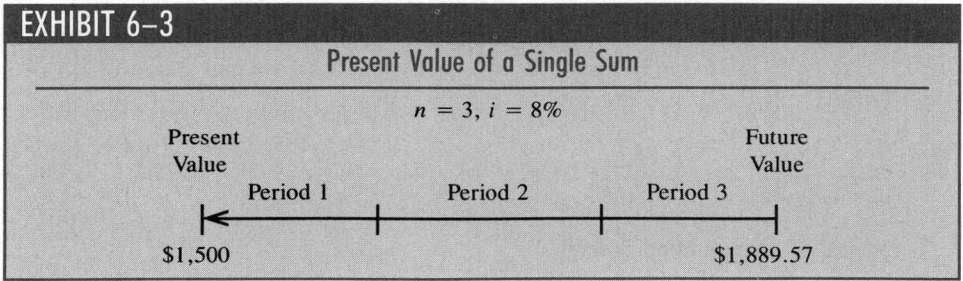

EXHIBIT 6–3

Present Value of a Single Sum

$n = 3$, $i = 8\%$

Present Value ... Future Value

Period 1   Period 2   Period 3

$1,500 $1,889.57

Remember that the basic compound interest formula:

$$FV = PV(1 + i)^n$$

If we divide both sides of this equation by $(1 + i)^n$, we get

$$PV = \frac{FV}{(1 + i)^n}$$

We can now apply this formula to the problem and determine that $1,500 is indeed the present value:

$$PV = \frac{FV}{(1 + i)^n}$$
$$= \frac{\$1,889.57}{(1.08)^3}$$
$$= \frac{\$1,889.57}{1.25971}$$
$$= \$1,500$$

We can easily rewrite the above formula as follows:

$$PV = FV \cdot \frac{1}{(1 + i)^n}$$

The $1/(1 + i)^n$ part of the equation is simply the reciprocal (the inverse) of the formula used to calculate the amount of 1. Tables are widely available that provide solutions for $1/(1 + i)^n$ for combinations of i and n. We shall refer to each of these solutions as a **present value factor** (*pvf*). A present value factor is simply the reciprocal of the future value factor for a given *i* and *n*. Table 6–2 at the end of the chapter contains present value factors for many *i* and *n* combinations. Given the formula used to construct the table, you should not be surprised that present value factors decrease with an increase in *n* or *i*. Note that the table is entitled "Present Value of 1." If we know the present value of 1 for a certain *i* and *n*, we can easily compute the present value of any single sum by multiplying the single sum by the present value of 1.

Because we know that $PV = FV \cdot 1/(1 + i)^n$ and $1/(1 + i)^n = pvf$, we can now state the following:

$$PV = FV \cdot pvf_{\overline{n}|i} \tag{6–2}$$

where PV = present value (principal sum) of
                 a single sum
         FV = future value of a single sum
$pvf_{\overline{n}|i}$ = present value factor (from Table
                 6–2) for the relevant *n* and *i*

Equation 6–2 saves time in solving problems for the present value of a single sum. To illustrate its application to the example problem, we first find in Table 6–2 that the *pvf* for *n* = 3 and *i* = 8% is .79383. Now we can state the following:

$$\begin{aligned} PV &= FV \cdot pvf_{\overline{n}|i} \\ &= \$1,889.57 \cdot pvf_{\overline{3}|8\%} \\ &= \$1,889.57 \,(.79383) \\ &= \$1,500 \end{aligned}$$

Accounting Examples

Problem 4.   What is the value at the beginning of Year 1 of a noninterest-bearing note that has a maturity value of $10,000 at the end of Year 4? Assume that the market rate of interest for similar notes is 8% compounded annually.

Solution 4.   We know the future value (the $10,000 maturity value), the interest rate per period (8%), and the number of periods (4). We can solve for the present value by using Equation 6–2 and Table 6–2:

$$\begin{aligned} PV &= FV \cdot pvf_{\overline{n}|i} \\ &= \$10,000 \cdot pvf_{\overline{4}|8\%} \\ &= \$10,000 \,(.73503) \\ &= \$7,350.30 \end{aligned}$$

In other words, $7,350.30 is the sum that a person would pay today to receive $10,000 at the end of four years, assuming 8% interest compounded annually. That the note could only be sold at a discount ($10,000 − $7,350.30 = $2,649.70) appears reasonable because the note has no stated interest and similar notes yield 8%.

As in the examples concerning the amount of a single sum, we could alter the information in Problem 4 to illustrate solutions for other variables. However, the point should now be clear. That is, we are dealing with one basic equation of four variables. When three of the variables are known, solving for the one unknown is not difficult.

Problem 5.   One of your clients, I. M. Rich, wants to put aside some money to buy his son an $8,000 automobile when his son graduates from college in four years. Assuming that Mr. Rich will earn 6%, compounded annually, on his savings during the first two years and 8%, compounded semiannually, during the last two years, how much should he deposit at the beginning of the four-year period?

Solution 5.   Once again we are seeking the present value of a single sum ($8,000). However, in this case the interest rate and the frequency of compounding change after the second year. We therefore need to break down the problem into two components. First, compute the present value, *as of the beginning of the third year,* of $8,000 to be received at the end of four semiannual periods discounted at 4% per period. (Remember that the 8% interest is compounded semiannually during the last two years.) Second, compute the present value, *as of the beginning of the first year,* of the value calculated in the first step when discounted for 2 years at 6%. Thus, we have

$$\textbf{Step 1.} \quad PV = FV \cdot pvf_{\overline{n}|\,i}$$
$$= \$8,000 \cdot pvf_{\overline{4}|\,4\%}$$
$$= \$8,000\,(.85480)$$
$$= \$6,838.40$$

The value $6,838.40 is the present value as of the beginning of the *third year.* To determine the present value as of the beginning of the *first year,* we must perform Step 2.

$$\textbf{Step 2.} \quad PV = FV \cdot pvf_{\overline{n}|\,i}$$
$$= \$6,838.40 \cdot pvf_{\overline{2}|\,6\%}$$
$$= \$6,838.40\,(.89000)$$
$$= \$6,086.18$$

Mr. Rich should therefore deposit $6,086.18 so that he will have the $8,000 required to purchase the automobile at the end of the four-year period.

Remember from this example that **whenever a compound interest problem appears complex, try to solve the problem by dividing it into its components.**

ANNUITY PROBLEMS

An **annuity** is a series of equal receipts or payments, called **rents,** that occur at uniform intervals at a constant interest rate.[6] This book assumes a standard annuity in which interest is compounded once at the end of each interval. Annuities commonly occur at annual, semiannual, quarterly, or monthly intervals. Lease payments, sinking fund payments, mortgage payments, and retirement payments are only a few examples of annuities that accountants encounter every day.

Annuities may be classified as ordinary annuities or annuities due.[7] The difference lies solely in the timing of the rents. With an **ordinary annuity,** the rents occur at the *end* of each period. With an **annuity due,** the rents occur at the *beginning* of each period. In both kinds of annuities *one* rent occurs during each period, either at the beginning (annuity due) or at the end (ordinary annuity). For this reason the symbol *n* in annuity problems refers to either the number of compounding periods or the number of rents.

As in the single sum problems discussed earlier, annuities involve present and future value concepts. Whereas earlier discussions dealt with the present and future values of a single sum, the following sections concern the present and future values of multiple sums, each of which is equal in size.

AMOUNT (FUTURE VALUE) OF AN ORDINARY ANNUITY

As shown earlier, a single sum of $1,500 left on deposit for three years at 8% will accumulate to $1,889.57. What is the amount (future value) at the end of three years

---

[6]Note that the term **rents** refers to a series of equal receipts or payments of any kind. In compound interest discussions, use of this term is not confined to its everyday connotation of payments on a leased asset.
[7]Ordinary annuities are sometimes called annuities in arrears, while annuities due are sometimes called annuities in advance.

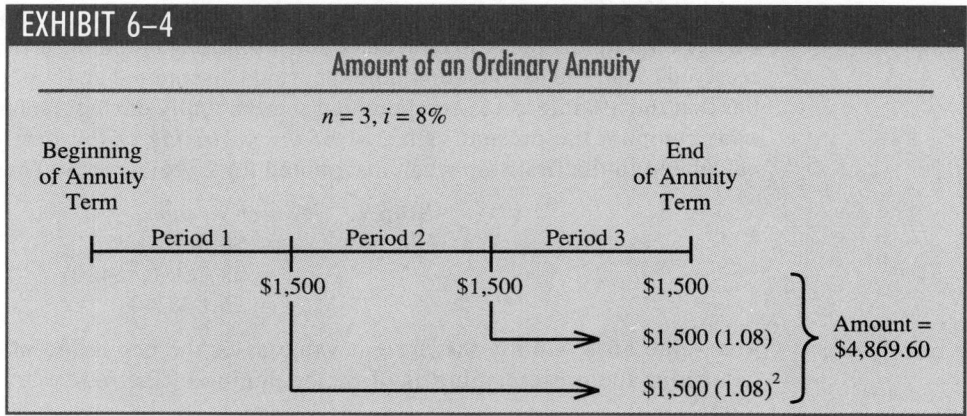

EXHIBIT 6–4

Amount of an Ordinary Annuity

$n = 3, i = 8\%$

Beginning of Annuity Term			End of Annuity Term
Period 1	Period 2	Period 3	

$1,500 $1,500 $1,500

$1,500 (1.08)

$1,500 (1.08)^2

Amount = $4,869.60

of *three periodic rents of $1,500 each* that occur at the end of each year at 8% compounded annually? The question involves the amount of an ordinary annuity.

As the time diagram in Exhibit 6–4 suggests, computing the amount of an ordinary annuity involves nothing more than computing the total amount of a series of single sums.[8] Algebraically, we have

3rd Rent		2nd Rent		1st Rent		Amount of the Ordinary Annuity
$1,500	+	$1,500 (1.08)	+	$1,500 (1.08)^2	=	$4,869.60

Note that although the annuity encompasses three periods, only two rents earn interest. The first rent earns interest during periods two and three; the second rent earns interest during period three only. The third rent earns no interest, because it occurs at the end of the three-year span. In an amount of an ordinary annuity of n rents, only $n - 1$ rents will earn interest, because the last rent occurs at the end of the annuity term and no interest period exists for that rent. **An amount of an ordinary annuity focuses on a future value and the last rent occurs at the end of the annuity term.**

Of course, the $1,500 rent in the preceding equation could be factored out:

$$\$1,500 \ (1 + 1.08 + 1.08^2) = \$4,869.60$$
$$\$1,500 \ (1 + 1.08 + 1.1664) = \$4,869.60$$
$$\$1,500 \ (3.24640) = \$4,869.60$$

Turn to Table 6–3 at the end of the chapter and locate the factor for $n = 3$, $i = 8\%$. You will see that it is 3.24640, the number by which we multiplied $1,500 in the last equation. Note that Table 6–3, entitled "Amount of an Ordinary Annuity of 1," contains factors for many combinations of n and i. Each factor is an **amount of an ordinary annuity factor** (*aoaf*). Each factor could have been determined by the approach used above for $n = 3$ and $i = 8\%$, but the following formula was applied to save time in generating each factor:

---

[8]You may find it helpful to verify this statement by applying Equation 6–1 and Table 6–1 to each of the $1,500 rents. This would give the following results:

1st rent	$1,500	(1.16640) = $1,749.60
2nd rent	1,500	(1.08000) = 1,620.00
3rd rent	1,500	(1.00000) = 1,500.00
	Total	$4,869.60

$$aoaf_{\overline{n}|\,i} = \frac{(1 + i)^n - 1}{i}$$

Each table factor, then, is based on an equation that incorporates values for both n and i.

Using Table 6–3, we can find the amount to which an ordinary annuity of any size rent will accumulate. We simply multiply the size of each rent by the amount to which an ordinary annuity of 1 will accumulate. Expressed algebraically, we have

$$AOA = R \cdot aoaf_{\overline{n}|\,i} \qquad\qquad (6\text{--}3)$$

where AOA = amount (future value) of an ordinary
annuity of n rents at i interest rate
R = size of each periodic rent
$aoaf_{\overline{n}|\,i}$ = amount of an ordinary annuity of
1 factor (from Table 6–3) for the
relevant n and i

Notice that Equation 6–3 contains four variables (AOA, R, n, and i) and if we know the values of any three, we can solve for the fourth using algebra.

Accounting Examples

Problem 6.   On January 1 of the current year, Control Systems Corporation creates a sinking fund to accumulate cash that will be needed to retire a $1,000,000 issue of bonds payable that matures in 10 years. Accordingly, the company decides to make 20 semiannual payments of $30,000 each into a sinking fund. The first payment will be made on June 30 of the current year, and the fund is expected to earn interest at 10% compounded semiannually. How much cash will be in the fund at the end of 10 years?

Solution 6.   The problem clearly involves an annuity, because periodic payments (rents) of $30,000 each will be placed in a sinking fund. Furthermore, it is an ordinary annuity, because the initial rent occurs at the end of the first semiannual period. Because the payments are made semiannually, we know that $n = 10 \times 2 = 20$ and $i = 10\% \div 2 = 5\%$. We must determine the amount of an ordinary annuity of 20 rents of $30,000 each at 5% interest. Using Equation 6–3 and Table 6–3, we have

$$
\begin{aligned}
AOA &= R \cdot aoaf_{\overline{n}|\,i} \\
&= \$30,000 \cdot aoaf_{\overline{20}|\,5\%} \\
&= \$30,000\,(33.06595) \\
&= \$991,978.50
\end{aligned}
$$

Unfortunately, the amount in the sinking fund at the end of 10 years will be $8,021.50 ($1,000,000 − $991,978.50) less than the company needs to retire the bonds.

Problem 7.   Referring to Problem 6, how much would the Control Systems Corporation have to deposit at the end of each semiannual period to accumulate $1,000,000 in the sinking fund at the end of 10 years?

Solution 7.   In Problem 6, semiannual deposits of $30,000 left the company $8,021.50 short of its goal of $1,000,000. Thus, logic dictates that the company will have to deposit somewhat more than $30,000 each period. To find the exact size of each deposit, we refer to Equation 6–3, which states that $AOA = R \cdot aoaf_{\overline{n}|\,i}$. Dividing both sides of the equation by $aoaf_{\overline{n}|\,i}$ and substituting the values of the known variables, we have the following:

$$R = \frac{AOA}{aoaf_{\overline{n}|\,i}}$$

$$= \frac{\$1,000,000}{aoaf_{\overline{20}|\,5\%}}$$

$$= \frac{\$1,000,000}{33.06595}$$

$$= \$30,242.59$$

Control Systems Corporation must therefore deposit $30,242.59 at the end of each semiannual period to accumulate $1,000,000 at the end of 10 years.

Problem 8.   One of your clients, Tom Mack, tells you that he wants to accumulate a $10,000 cash gift for his new baby daughter by depositing $300 at yearly intervals beginning one year from now. The periodic deposits will be placed in a 6% savings account. When Tom accumulates the $10,000, how old will his daughter be?

Solution 8.   We know that this problem involves an ordinary annuity, because the periodic deposits of $300 begin one year from now. Furthermore, we know the desired future amount ($10,000), the size of the periodic rents ($300), and the interest rate per period (6%). The unknown that we seek is the number of periods, which we can determine by rewriting Equation 6–3 and using Table 6–3. Equation 6–3 states that $AOA = R \cdot aoaf_{\overline{n}|\,i}$. Dividing both sides of the equation by R and substituting the known values, we have

$$aoaf_{\overline{n}|\,i} = \frac{AOA}{R}$$

$$aoaf_{\overline{n}|\,6\%} = \frac{\$10,000}{\$300}$$

$$= 33.33333$$

We now search the 6% column of Table 6–3 for the factor 33.33333. We won't find it, but we can determine that it would lie between 30.90565 (the factor for $n = 18$) and 33.75999 (the factor for $n = 19$). Because it is closer to the factor for $n = 19$, we conclude that it will take almost 19 years for Tom Mack to accumulate $10,000. In other words, Tom's daughter will be almost 19 years old when she receives the $10,000 gift from her father.

A closer approximation may be achieved by using linear interpolation. In general, when a factor is computed but does not appear in the pertinent compound interest table, interpolation may be used to find a reasonable approximation of the unknown number of periods (n) or interest rate (i).[9] The smaller the range of interpolation, the smaller the error will be. Interpolation is based on the principle of proportion, as the following format suggests:

		When n is:	The corresponding $aoaf$ is:		
1	x	18	30.90565	2.42768	2.85434
		?	33.33333		
		19	33.75999		

We can set up the following proportion:

$$\frac{x}{1} = \frac{2.42768}{2.85434}$$

---

[9] An exact answer may be determined using logarithms.

Solving for x, we find that it equals .85. Since x is the distance between 18 and n, we conclude that $n = 18 + .85 = 18.85$. Tom's daughter, then, will be approximately 18.85 years old when she receives her gift. Any time you want to interpolate, set up a proportion similar to the one shown above.

Problem 9.   Referring to the information in Problem 8, what interest rate would Tom Mack have to earn on his investment so that he could give his daughter the $10,000 present on her eighteenth birthday?

Solution 9.   Logic dictates that since it would take approximately 18.85 years to accumulate $10,000 at 6% interest, Tom will have to earn more than 6% to accumulate the same amount in less time. Once again, dividing both sides of Equation 6–3 by R, we have

$$aoaf_{\overline{n}|\,i} = \frac{AOA}{R}$$

Therefore, $aoaf_{\overline{18}|\,i} = \$10,000/\$300 = 33.33333$. Looking across the eighteenth row of Table 6–3, we determine that 33.33333 would lie between 30.90565 (the factor for $i = 6\%$) and 37.45024 (the factor for $i = 8\%$). Approximating the answer through interpolation, we have

		When i is:	The corresponding $aoaf$ is:		
2% {	x {	6%	30.90565	} 2.42768	} 6.54459
		?	33.33333		
		8%	37.45024		

Setting up a proportion, we have

$$\frac{x}{2\%} = \frac{2.42768}{6.54459}$$

Solving for x, we find that it equals .74%. Since x is the distance between 6% and i, we conclude that $i = 6\% + .74\% = 6.74\%$. Tom Mack would thus have to earn roughly 6.74%·interest if he wanted to give his daughter $10,000 on her eighteenth birthday.

AMOUNT (FUTURE VALUE) OF AN ANNUITY DUE

Earlier we stated that an annuity due is one in which the rents occur at the *beginning* of each period. Further, we saw that $4,869.60 is the amount of an *ordinary* annuity of three annual rents of $1,500 each at 8%. What is the amount at the end of three years of three annual rents of $1,500 each that occur at the *beginning* of each year at 8% compounded annually?

As the time diagram in Exhibit 6–5 suggests, an annuity due begins with a rent and ends one period *after* the last rent. Thus, if we took the amount of an ordinary annuity of three $1,500 rents at 8% and left all the money on deposit at 8% for one additional period, we would have the amount of an annuity due of three $1,500 rents at 8%. For any given values of n and i, the amount of an annuity due is greater than the amount of an ordinary annuity by the interest on the latter amount for one period. Stated differently, the amount of an annuity due for given values of n and i is equal to the amount of an ordinary annuity of $(n + 1)$ rents at i interest rate, *minus* one rent (the final rent).

An amount of an annuity due focuses on a future value and last rent occurs one period before the end of the annuity term. In an amount of an annuity due of

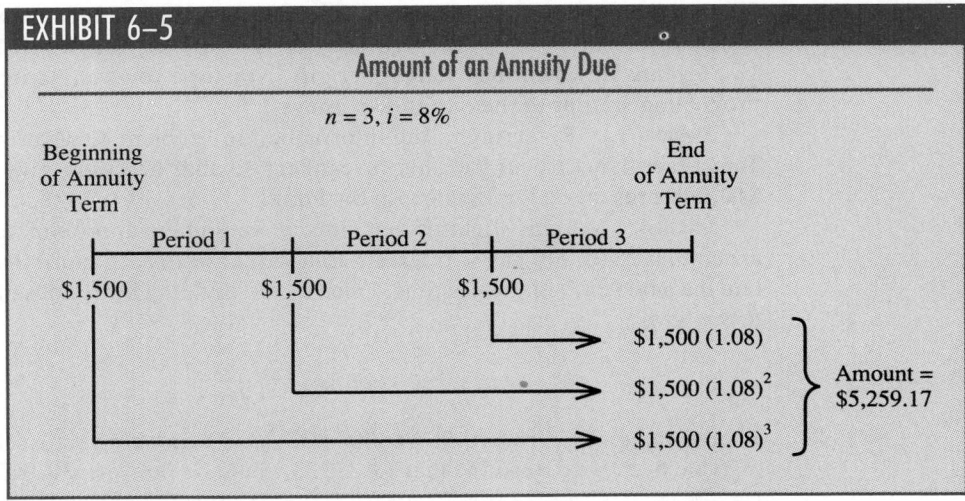

EXHIBIT 6–5

Amount of an Annuity Due

$n = 3, i = 8\%$

Beginning of Annuity Term

End of Annuity Term

Period 1   Period 2   Period 3

$1,500 $1,500 $1,500

$1,500 (1.08)

$1,500 (1.08)^2

$1,500 (1.08)^3

Amount = $5,259.17

n rents, all of the n rents earn interest. Note carefully in Exhibit 6–5 that the third rent earns interest for one period, the second rent earns interest for two periods, and the first rent earns interest for three periods. Algebraically,

$$\$1,500\,(1.08) + \$1,500\,(1.08)^2 + \$1,500\,(1.08)^3 = \$5,259.17$$

Factoring out the $1,500 rent, we have

$$\$1,500\,(1.08 + 1.08^2 + 1.08^3) = \$5,259.17$$
$$\$1,500\,(1.08 + 1.1664 + 1.25971) = \$5,259.17$$
$$\$1,500\,(3.50611) = \$5,259.17$$

In the last equation, 3.50611 is simply a factor for computing the amount of an annuity due (*aadf*) where $n = 3$ and $i = 8\%$. We could construct a table of these factors and call it "Amount of an Annuity Due of 1." However, the relationship between the amount of an ordinary annuity and the amount of an annuity due is so straightforward that a separate table is unnecessary. We can use the "Amount of an Ordinary Annuity of 1" table (Table 6–3) to determine an *aadf* simply by finding the factor for $(n + 1)$ periods and i, and subtracting 1 from the factor we find. Stated algebraically,[10]

$$aadf_{\overline{n}|\,i} = aoaf_{\overline{n+1}|\,i} - 1$$

To illustrate, let's use Table 6–3 to calculate $aadf_{\overline{3}|\,8\%}$. We simply look up the table factor for $n + 1 = 4$ periods and $i = 8\%$, and we find 4.50611. Subtracting 1 from this, we get 3.50611. Now that we know how to derive an *aadf* using Table 6–3, we can state

$$AAD = R \cdot aadf_{\overline{n}|\,i} \qquad\qquad (6\text{–}3A)$$

where AAD = amount of an annuity due of n
rents at i interest rate

R = size of each periodic rent

$aadf_{\overline{n}|\,i}$ = amount of an annuity due of 1 factor
(from Table 6–3, *as adjusted*) for the
relevant n and i

---

[10]A second way to derive $aadf_{\overline{n}|\,i}$ is as follows: $aadf_{\overline{n}|\,i} = aoaf_{\overline{n}|\,i}(1 + i)$. Although this approach is correct, it is more difficult to use when i is the unknown variable.

EXHIBIT 6–6

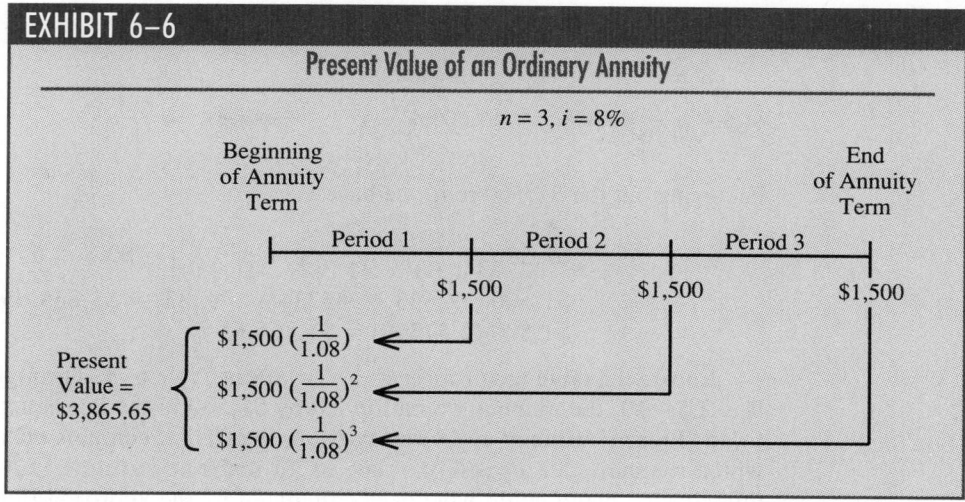

Present Value of an Ordinary Annuity

$$n = 3, i = 8\%$$

Beginning
of Annuity
Term

End
of Annuity
Term

Period 1   Period 2   Period 3

$1,500 $1,500 $1,500

Present
Value =
$3,865.65

$1,500 \left(\dfrac{1}{1.08}\right)$

$1,500 \left(\dfrac{1}{1.08}\right)^2$

$1,500 \left(\dfrac{1}{1.08}\right)^3$

Because the values of n and i determine the value of $aadf_{\overline{n}|\,i}$, Equation 6–3A consists of four variables: AAD, R, n, and i. Remember that if we know the values of any three, we can solve for the fourth using algebra.

Accounting Example

Problem 10.   Warren Wilson has created a fund for his retirement in 35 years. He deposits $3,000 today in a special 8% account, and he plans to make periodic deposits of $3,000 each at annual intervals over the next 34 years. How much cash will be in Wilson's retirement fund when he retires?

Solution 10.   Because the initial rent occurs at the beginning of the first year, we are dealing with an annuity due. Specifically, we are asked to calculate the amount (a future value) of an annuity due of 35 rents of $3,000 at 8%. Using Equation 6–3A and Table 6–3, as adjusted, we have

$$
\begin{aligned}
AAD &= R \cdot aadf_{\overline{n}|\,i} \\
&= \$3{,}000 \cdot aadf_{\overline{35}|\,8\%} \\
&= \$3{,}000 \left(aoaf_{\overline{35+1}|\,8\%} - 1\right) \\
&= \$3{,}000 \left(187.10215 - 1\right) \\
&= \$3{,}000 \left(186.10215\right) \\
&= \$558{,}306.45
\end{aligned}
$$

PRESENT VALUE OF AN ORDINARY ANNUITY

We have seen that the amount of an ordinary annuity of three annual rents of $1,500 each at 8% is $4,869.60. Accountants often must solve problems that are the inverse of this one, for example: What is the present value of an ordinary annuity of three annual rents of $1,500 each discounted at 8%? The time diagram in Exhibit 6–6 illustrates the solution.

A present value of an ordinary annuity focuses on a present value and the first rent occurs one period after the beginning of the annuity term. Note carefully that the initial rent occurs at the end of the first time period, consistent with our definition of an ordinary annuity. When the present value of an ordinary annuity of n rents is computed, each rent is discounted.

In Exhibit 6–6 we compute the present value of an ordinary annuity by computing the present value of each rent and summing the results. Algebraically, we have

	1st Rent		2nd Rent		3rd Rent		Present Value of the Ordinary Annuity
	$1,500 $(\frac{1}{1.08})$	+	$1,500 $(\frac{1}{1.08})^2$	+	$1,500 $(\frac{1}{1.08})^3$	=	$3,865.65

Factoring out the $1,500 rent, we have

$$\$1,500 \, [(\frac{1}{1.08}) + (\frac{1}{1.08})^2 + (\frac{1}{1.08})^3] = \$3,865.65$$
$$\$1,500 \, (.92593 + .85734 + .79383) = \$3,865.65$$
$$\$1,500 \, (2.57710) = \$3,865.65$$

Locate the table factor for $n = 3$, $i = 8\%$ in Table 6–4. Through no coincidence, it is 2.57710, the number we multiplied by $1,500 in the last equation. Table 6–4 is titled "Present Value of an Ordinary Annuity of 1." It contains many factors, each of which we shall call a **present value of an ordinary annuity factor** (*pvoaf*). Although each *pvoaf* could have been calculated by the approach illustrated above for $n = 3$ and $i = 8\%$, the following formula was used to save time:

$$pvoaf_{\overline{n}|\,i} = \frac{1 - \dfrac{1}{(1 + i)^n}}{i}$$

As the title indicates, Table 6–4 includes present value factors assuming an ordinary annuity of 1. For given n and i values, we can easily calculate the present value of an ordinary annuity of any size rent. We simply multiply the size of each rent by the present value of an ordinary annuity of 1.

We can state this algebraically as follows:

$$PVOA = R \cdot pvoaf_{\overline{n}|\,i} \qquad\qquad (6\text{–}4)$$

where $PVOA$ = present value of an ordinary annuity of n rents at i interest rate

R = size of each periodic rent

$pvoaf_{\overline{n}|\,i}$ = present value of an ordinary annuity of 1 factor (from Table 6–4) for the relevant n and i

Of the four variables ($PVOA$, R, n, and i), any three must be known to solve for the fourth.

Accounting Example

Problem 11.   On January 1 of the current year, Allied Steel Company issues $5,000,000 of 8%, 20-year term bonds that pay interest semiannually each June 30 and December 31. How much cash will the bonds sell for if, on January 1, the market rate of interest for bonds similar to those of Allied Steel Company is 10%?

Solution 11.   Note that Allied's bonds have a **coupon interest rate** (often called **nominal rate** or **stated rate**) of 8%. This is simply the annual rate of interest stated in the bond contract. This rate is used to compute the amount of cash that will be paid as interest to bondholders each year. Note also that when the bonds are sold, the **market rate of interest** (often called the **yield rate** or the **effective rate**) for similar bonds is 10%. What would entice bond investors to purchase Allied's 8% bonds when these investors could purchase similar bonds and earn 10%?

Of course, the bonds must sell for a price that is less than their par or face value. In other words, the bonds will sell **at a discount,** the amount necessary to bring the yield rate on Allied's bonds up to the 10% market rate. Logic also dictates that when the coupon rate exceeds the market rate, the bonds will sell **at a premium.** When the two rates are equal, the bonds will sell **at par.**

Now that we have used intuition, let's formulate a more precise solution to the problem. First, recognize that since the bonds pay interest semiannually, they include $20 \times 2 = 40$ periods ($n = 40$), and the stated interest rate per period is $8\% \div 2 = 4\%$. Second, recognize that in addition to paying the $5,000,000 maturity value (a single sum) to bondholders in 20 years, Allied must also pay $200,000 ($4\% \times \$5,000,000$) interest at the end of each semiannual period for 20 years. The interest payments constitute an ordinary annuity. Finally, recognize that to compute the present value of the bonds (the price bondholders would be willing to pay on January 1), we must discount the maturity value and the interest annuity using the market rate of interest per period, so $i = 10\% \div 2 = 5\%$. Now we can determine the present value of Allied's bonds using the following two steps:

Step 1. Compute the present value of the single sum maturity value of $5,000,000 for $n = 40$ and $i = 5\%$. (Use Equation 6–2 and Table 6–2.)

$$
\begin{aligned}
PV &= FV \cdot pvf_{\overline{n}|\,i} \\
&= 5,000,000 \cdot pvf_{\overline{40}|\,5\%} \\
&= \$5,000,000 \, (.14205) \\
&= \$710,250
\end{aligned}
$$

Step 2. Compute the present value of the ordinary interest annuity of $200,000 for $n = 40$ and $i = 5\%$. (Use Equation 6–4 and Table 6–4.)

$$
\begin{aligned}
PVOA &= R \cdot pvoaf_{\overline{n}|\,i} \\
&= \$200,000 \cdot pvoaf_{\overline{40}|\,5\%} \\
&= \$200,000 \, (17.15909) \\
&= \$3,431,818
\end{aligned}
$$

Summing the results of Steps 1 and 2, we get $710,250 + $3,431,818 = $4,142,068, which is the present value of the bonds. Thus, if bondholders pay $4,142,068 for Allied's bonds, they will earn 10%, compounded semiannually, on their investment. Note that our intuition was correct; the bonds sell at a discount of $857,932 ($5,000,000 − $4,142,068). This discount is simply extra interest that Allied must pay. To help implement the matching principle, this discount must be amortized over the life of the bond issue. We discuss discount (and premium) amortization more fully in Chapter 15.

Matching

The bond pricing problem illustrates that **with a seemingly complex problem, it is often helpful to divide it into its components.** As the problem suggests, we sometimes need more than one equation and table. Nevertheless, the same basic compound interest concepts apply.

PRESENT VALUE OF AN ANNUITY DUE

Recall that an annuity due is one in which the rents occur at the beginning of each time period. In the previous section we saw that $3,865.65 is the present value of an ordinary annuity of three rents of $1,500 each discounted at 8%. Now we will simply change the timing of the $1,500 rents and ask this question: What is the present value

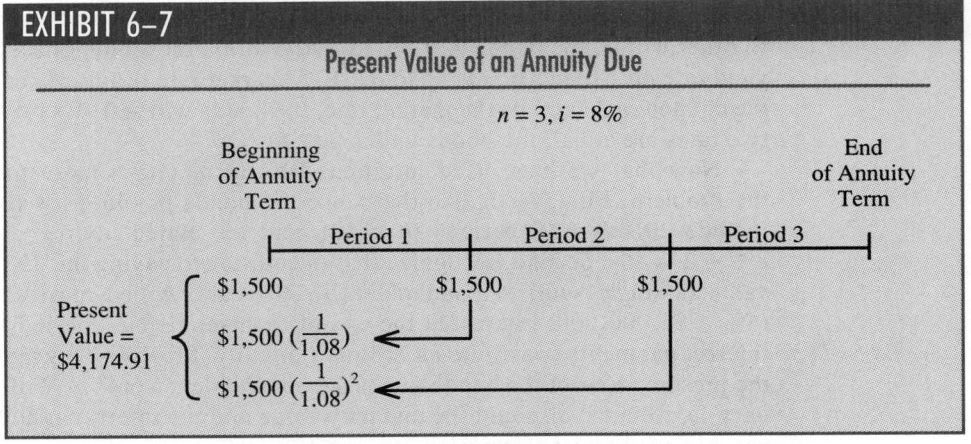

EXHIBIT 6–7

Present Value of an Annuity Due

$n = 3, i = 8\%$

of three annual rents of $1,500 each that occur at the *beginning* of each year (an annuity due) discounted at 8%? Once again a time diagram (Exhibit 6–7) helps us to visualize the solution. Note that the initial rent is not discounted, because it occurs at the beginning of the three-year span. In general, when the present value of an annuity due of *n* rents is computed, only $(n - 1)$ rents will be discounted. **A present value of an annuity due focuses on a present value and the first rent occurs at the beginning of the annuity term.**

As shown in Exhibit 6–7, an annuity due begins with a rent and ends one period *after* the last rent. Therefore, if we computed the present value of an annuity due of three $1,500 rents at 8% and then *discounted* all the money at 8% for one more period, we would have the present value of an ordinary annuity of three $1,500 rents at 8%. Similarly, if we computed the present value of an ordinary annuity of three $1,500 rents at 8% and then *compounded* all the money at 8% for one period into the future, we would have the present value of an annuity due of three rents of $1,500 at 8%. For any given values of *n* and *i,* the present value of an annuity due will be greater than the present value of an ordinary annuity by the interest on the latter amount for one period. Stated somewhat differently, the present value of an annuity due for any given values of *n* and *i* will be equal to the present value of an ordinary annuity of $(n - 1)$ rents at *i* interest rate, *plus* one rent (the initial rent).

As Exhibit 6–7 suggests, we could compute the present value of an annuity due by computing the present value of each rent and summing the results. Expressed algebraically,

$$\$1,500 + \$1,500\left(\frac{1}{1.08}\right) + \$1,500\left(\frac{1}{1.08}\right)^2 = \$4,174.91$$

Factoring out the $1,500 rent, we have

$$\$1,500\left[1 + \frac{1}{1.08} + \left(\frac{1}{1.08}\right)^2\right] = \$4,174.91$$
$$\$1,500\,(1 + .92593 + .85734) = \$4,174.91$$
$$\$1,500\,(2.78327) = \$4,174.91$$

The 2.78327 component in the last equation is simply a factor for computing the present value of an annuity due (*pvadf*) where $n = 3$ and $i = 8\%$. A complete table of these factors would be called a "Present Value of an Annuity Due of 1" table. We have not constructed such a table because we already have Table 6–4 and we know that a relatively simple relationship exists between the present value of an ordinary annuity and the present value of an annuity due. Thus, we can use Table 6–4 to determine a *pvadf* simply by finding the factor for $(n - 1)$ periods and i, and adding 1 to the factor. Stated algebraically,[11]

$$pvadf_{\overline{n}|\,i} = pvoaf_{\overline{n-1}|\,i} + 1.$$

To illustrate, let's use Table 6–4 to calculate $pvadf_{\overline{3}|\,8\%}$. Looking at the table, we find that the factor for $n - 1 = 2$ periods and $i = 8\%$ is 1.78326. Adding 1 to this number, we get 2.78326.

Now that we know how to use Table 6–4 to calculate a *pvadf*, we can state

$$PVAD = R \cdot pvadf_{\overline{n}|\,i} \qquad\qquad (6\text{–}4A)$$

where $PVAD$ = present value of an annuity due
of n rents at i interest rate
R = size of each periodic rent
$pvadf_{\overline{n}|\,i}$ = present value of an annuity due
of 1 factor (from Table 6–4, *as adjusted*) for the relevant n and i

The four variables that make up Equation 6–4A are $PVAD$, R, n, and i. As usual, if we know the values of any three, we can solve for the fourth.

Accounting Examples

Problem 12.   On July 1 of the current year, Rockwell Drilling Company signed a 12-year, noncancelable lease with Equipment Leasing Corporation. The lease gave Rockwell the right to use certain drilling equipment that had a 12-year estimated useful life and no salvage value. In exchange, Rockwell agreed to make 12 annual lease payments of $15,000 each, beginning on July 1. Assuming a relevant interest rate of 10%, what is the present value of the lease on July 1?

Solution 12.   Because the initial lease payment occurs at the beginning of the first interval, the lease payments represent an annuity due. To determine the present value of the lease, we compute the present value of an annuity due of 12 rents ($n = 12$) of $15,000 each at $i = 10\%$. Using Equation 6–4A and Table 6–4, we have

$$
\begin{aligned}
PVAD &= R \cdot pvadf_{\overline{n}|\,i} \\
&= \$15,000 \cdot pvadf_{\overline{12}|\,10\%} \\
&= \$15,000\,(pvoaf_{\overline{12-1}|\,10\%} + 1) \\
&= \$15,000\,(6.49506 + 1) \\
&= \$15,000\,(7.49506) \\
&= \$112,425.90
\end{aligned}
$$

Observe that the *timing* of the lease payments impacts the present value of the lease. **In general, the timing of cash inflows and outflows has an important impact on the valuation of assets and liabilities and on the measurement of revenues and expenses in accounting.**

Problem 13.   Jane Thomas retired today after 40 years with the Stork Candy Company. She has accumulated $187,298.32 in her retirement account, and she wants to withdraw $20,000 annually, beginning today, for as long as her retirement money lasts. Assuming that all money in Jane's account earns 10% interest, how many $20,000 annual withdrawals can she make?

---

[11]A second way to compute $pvadf_{\overline{n}|\,i}$ is as follows: $pvadf_{\overline{n}|\,i} = pvoaf_{\overline{n}|\,i}(1 + i)$. Although this approach is correct, it is more difficult to use when i is the unknown variable.

Solution 13.   We know that $187,298.32 is the present value of an annuity due of n rents of $20,000 each at $i = 10\%$. Dividing both sides of Equation 6–4A by R, we have

$$\frac{PVAD}{R} = pvadf_{\overline{n}|i}$$

$$\text{or } pvadf_{\overline{n}|i} = \frac{PVAD}{R}$$

Substituting the known values for $PVAD$, R, and i, we have

$$pvadf_{\overline{n}|10\%} = \frac{\$187,298.32}{\$20,000}$$

$$pvadf_{\overline{n}|10\%} = 9.36492$$

Of course, we should not look for 9.36492 in Table 6–4, because we have seen that this table assumes an ordinary annuity. However, remember that $pvadf_{\overline{n}|i}$ $= pvoaf_{\overline{n-1}|i} + 1$. Subtracting 1 from both sides of this equation, we have

$$pvadf_{\overline{n}|i} - 1 = pvoaf_{\overline{n-1}|i}$$

Substituting the known values, we have

$$9.36492 - 1 = pvoaf_{\overline{n-1}|10\%}$$

$$\text{or } \quad pvoaf_{\overline{n-1}|10\%} = 8.36492$$

Now we can search the 10% column in Table 6–4 until we find 8.36492. We find it in the row in which $n = 19$; since 19 is the $pvoaf$ for $(n - 1)$ rents, we conclude that Jane Thomas can make *20 withdrawals* (19 + 1 = 20) from her retirement account. If we had not found 8.36492, we could have interpolated to approximate n.

DEFERRED ANNUITIES

In a deferred annuity the initial rent occurs two or more periods in the future. That is, the initial rent does not occur at either the beginning or the end of the first time period but at some later date. For computational convenience, it is customary to treat all deferred annuities as deferred ordinary annuities instead of deferred annuities due. We shall therefore omit the adjective "ordinary" when referring to deferred annuities.

The **deferral period** is the length of time between the present and the *beginning* of the first period in which a rent occurs. Remember, therefore, that the deferral period ends one period *before* the initial rent occurs. Thus, if an annuity begins to produce rents at the end of six periods, we say that it is deferred five periods. Similarly, an annuity which is deferred for nine periods will produce its first rent at the end of ten periods. The time diagram in Exhibit 6–8 illustrates an annuity of three annual rents of $1,500 at 8%, deferred four years.

The deferral period does not affect the calculation of an amount (future value). Because there is nothing on deposit to accumulate interest during the deferral period, the amount of a deferred annuity is the same as the amount of an annuity that is not deferred, assuming that the two annuities have the same values for n, i, and R. In the example above, the amount would be $4,869.60, the same figure computed in the discussion of the amount of an ordinary annuity.

On the other hand, assuming that the two annuities have the same values for n, i, and R, the present value of a deferred annuity is less than the present value of an annuity which is not deferred. The reason is that when we compute a present value, we must discount through the deferral period.

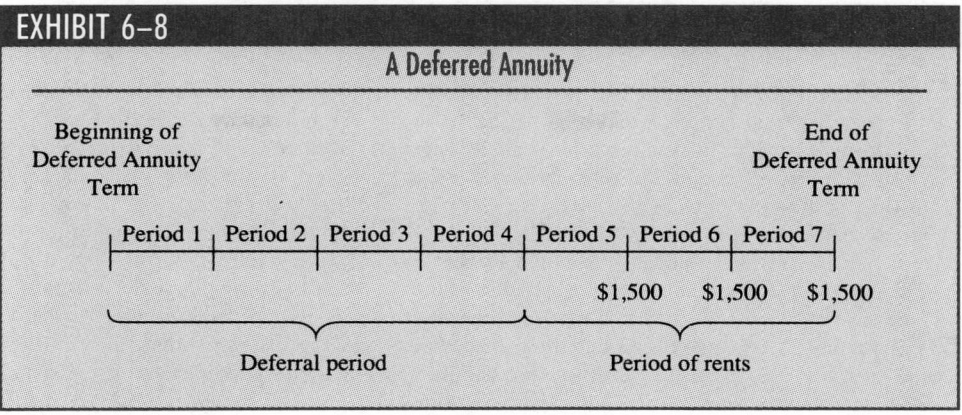

EXHIBIT 6–8

A Deferred Annuity

Beginning of Deferred Annuity Term

End of Deferred Annuity Term

Period 1 | Period 2 | Period 3 | Period 4 | Period 5 | Period 6 | Period 7

$1,500 $1,500 $1,500

Deferral period

Period of rents

The easiest way to compute the present value of a deferred annuity is to find the *pvoaf* for the *total* number of periods involved, that is, the number of periods that the annuity is deferred (k) plus the number of periods in which rents occur (n). Then subtract the *pvoaf* associated with the ordinary annuity that is nonexistent during the deferral period. The resulting factor is then multiplied by the size of the periodic rent. Algebraically, we have:

$$PVDA = R \cdot (pvoaf_{\overline{k+n}|\,i} - pvoaf_{\overline{n}|\,i}) \qquad (6\text{–}5)$$

where $PVDA$ = present value of an ordinary annuity of n rents at i interest rate, *deferred* k periods

R = size of each periodic rent

$pvoaf_{\overline{k+n}|\,i}$ = present value of an ordinary annuity factor for the *total* number of periods involved

$pvoaf_{\overline{n}|\,i}$ = present value of an ordinary annuity factor for the number of periods in which no rents occur

If we want to know the present value of an annuity of three annual rents of $1,500 at 8% deferred four years, we would proceed as follows:

$$\begin{aligned} PVDA &= R \cdot (pvoaf_{\overline{7}|\,8\%} - pvoaf_{\overline{4}|\,8\%}) \\ &= \$1,500\,(5.20637 - 3.31213) \\ &= \$1,500\,(1.89424) \\ &= \$2,841.36 \end{aligned}$$

Another way to compute the present value of a deferred annuity is to first compute the present value of the annuity at the beginning of the first period in which a rent occurs (using Equation 6–4 and Table 6–4) and then discount this single sum to the present (using Equation 6–2 and Table 6–2). Following this approach, we find that the present value of the annuity at the beginning of Period 5 is $3,865.65 ($1,500 × 2.57710). Discounting this single sum to the present, we find that it equals $2,841.37 ($3,865.65 × .73503). The $.01 discrepancy ($2,841.37 − $2,841.36) between answers is the result of rounding.

TIME IS MONEY

It is said that accounting, like law, is a profession that has a rule for every situation. If that's true, then why don't accountants have a consistent standard for when, and under what circumstances, to use one of the most fundamental measurements of finance itself—the time value of money?

As anyone who has bought a bank CD knows, the yield on an investment is basically a function of how much money is invested at what rate of return for how long. In theory, both assets and liabilities of corporations can be measured in the same way. For liabilities: How much money would be needed today to pay for an obligation that does not come due for 5 or 10 years— future health obligations of not-yet-retired workers, say, or the projected pension liabilities of a firm 10 or 20 years in the future? For assets: What is the "present value" of a financial asset—a mortgage, say, or a corporate bond—that is due to mature in the year 2013? In both cases, the solution comes from taking the future value or cost of the asset or liability in question, then using an assumed rate of interest over the period of time involved to "discount" it back to its present value.

Unfortunately, the accountants who actually prepare financial reports have few—and often highly inconsistent rules for when and how to make those calculations in preparing balance sheets. "Financial statements are becoming irrelevant to business decision making," complains G. Michael Crooch, partner at Arthur Andersen. "We are not measuring items according to their economic value because we're ignoring the time value of money."

Now at last the Financial Accounting Standards Board seems willing to face the problem, by adding a discounting project to its agenda. New rules are years away, but they eventually could have a dramatic effect on corporate financials. Depending upon what FASB finally decides, present value accounting could be used for virtually any transaction that involves a long delay before final settlement. Potential targets for discounting include impaired assets, product and manufacturers' warranties, and loss reserves for property-casualty insurers.

Present value accounting could in some ways be quite a boon to corporations, by reducing the liability side of their balance sheets. How? By recognizing that $1 million payable in 1994 is not as effectively large a liability as $1 million payable in 1989. That's common sense. If you were to take $600,000 and invest it at a relatively modest 10%, it would equal $1 million by the time the liability would need to be paid. Thus the effective liability is not $1 million but $600,000.

For example, under current FASB income tax accounting rules, deferred taxes must be booked in full, rather than discounted forward to the time when they are due. Thus, General Electric had a $3.1 billion deferred tax reserve in 1987. "That $3.1 billion is more than we'll really have to pay, considering the interest effect," notes Bernard Doyle, GE's manager of corporate accounting services. We're not talking peanuts. The discounted value of that liability is hundreds of million of dollars less than book value.

In a few cases, present value accounting is already required by FASB. Under a new FASB statement regarding pension accounting, General Electric in 1987 reported only a $15.5 billion liability based on an 8.5% rate of return; without discounting for present value, the liability would have been much greater.

Present value accounting obviously helps a company put its best foot forward, and of course could be abused. How? By making unrealistically high assumptions about interest rates. "Experience has shown that, in many cases, insurers have not been adequately funded in the past," notes Denis Callaghan, analyst at Alex. Brown. "If they were allowed to use discounting, the problem could get worse." Maybe, but any company that overdiscounts the future liability risks having to take major writeoffs as the liabilities come due. All in all, present value accounting has lots to recommend it.

Arthur Wyatt, Arthur Andersen & Co. accounting partner, sums up: "Any company routinely considers present values when doing deals. Why shouldn't investors have that information in the financial statements?"

SOURCE: Penelope Wang, "Time is Money," *Forbes*, January 9, 1989, p. 300. Reprinted by permission of *Forbes* magazine, January 9, 1989. © Forbes Inc., 1989.

Accounting Example

Problem 14.   Sam Sharpe purchases a $50,000 annuity contract that promises a return of 8% compounded annually. Sam shall receive 15 equal annual payments, the first of which is due 10 years from now. How much will each annual payment be?

Solution 14.   Because the annuity begins to produce rents at the end of 10 years, we say that it is deferred 9 years. Therefore, we know that $50,000 is the present value of an ordinary annuity of 15 annual rents at 8%, deferred 9 years. To solve for the size of the periodic rent, we divide both sides of Equation 6–5 by $(pvoaf_{\overline{k+n}|\,i} - pvoaf_{\overline{k}|\,i})$:

$$
\begin{aligned}
R &= \frac{PVDA}{(pvoaf_{\overline{k+n}|\,i} - pvoaf_{\overline{k}|\,i}} \\
&= \frac{\$50,000}{(pvoaf_{\overline{24}|\,8\%} - pvoaf_{\overline{9}|\,8\%})} \\
&= \frac{\$50,000}{10.52876 - 6.24689} \\
&= \frac{\$50,000}{4.28187} \\
&= \$11,677.14
\end{aligned}
$$

CONCLUDING REMARKS

When solving a compound interest problem, you should first determine what type of problem you are being asked to solve. Distinguishing between single sum problems and annuity problems is fairly easy, because periodic rents of equal size clearly indicate an annuity problem.

On the other hand, distinguishing between the following types of annuity problems is often difficult:

1. Amount of an ordinary annuity.
2. Amount of an annuity due.
3. Present value of an ordinary annuity.
4. Present value of an annuity due.

To help you see the differences between these four types of annuity problems, Exhibit 6–9 compares them in one illustration. **When solving an annuity problem that seems difficult, draw a time diagram and remember the following points:**

1. An annuity problem involves a value that represents a single sum of money. This value may occur either before or after the rents. If the value (which may be the unknown variable) occurs *after* the rents, the value is an *amount* (future value). Consequently, we have an amount of an annuity problem. To determine whether the annuity is ordinary or due, note the timing of the *final rent.* If the final rent occurs *at the same time* as the value, we have an amount of an *ordinary* annuity problem. If the final rent occurs *one period before* the value, we have an amount of an annuity *due* problem.
2. If the value (which may be the unknown variable) in the problem occurs *before* the rents, the value is a *present value.* Consequently, we have a present value of an annuity problem. To determine whether the annuity is ordinary or due, observe the timing of the *first rent.* If the first rent occurs *one period after* the value, we have a present value of an *ordinary* annuity problem. If the first rent occurs *at the same time* as the present value, we have a present value of an annuity *due* problem.

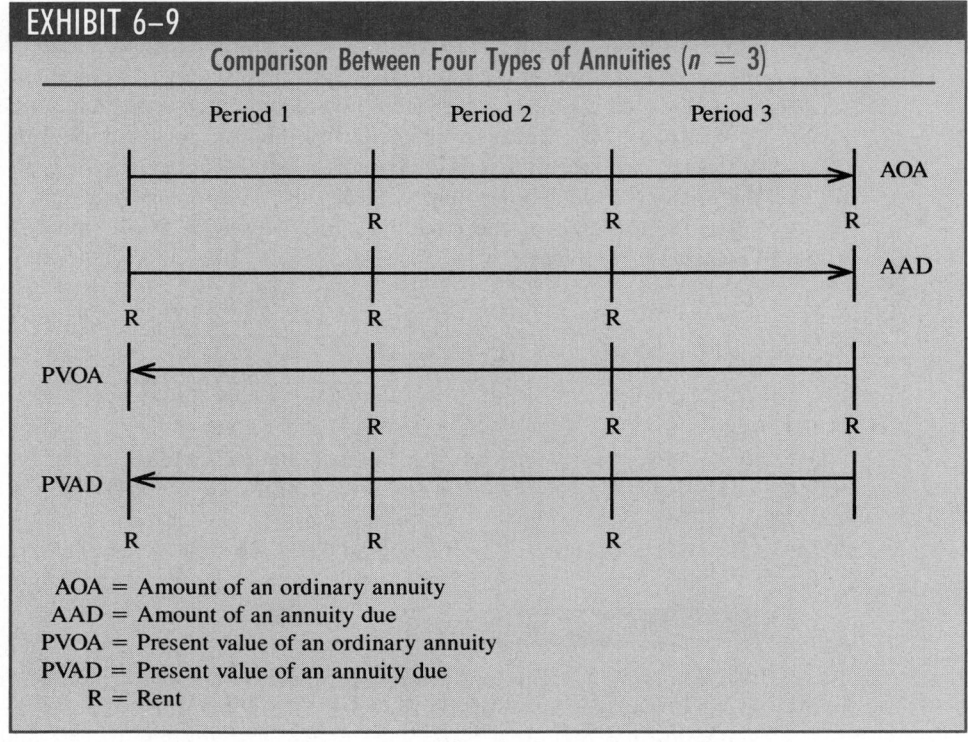

EXHIBIT 6–9

Comparison Between Four Types of Annuities ($n = 3$)

AOA = Amount of an ordinary annuity
AAD = Amount of an annuity due
PVOA = Present value of an ordinary annuity
PVAD = Present value of an annuity due
   R = Rent

A deferred annuity is not difficult to recognize, because the first rent occurs two or more periods after the beginning of the annuity term (see Exhibit 6–8).

Once you have identified the problem, you may solve it using the appropriate equation(s) and table(s). The major equations presented in the chapter are summarized in Exhibit 6–10. After you gain experience working with the equations, you may find that you can simplify the writing of them by omitting the letters that precede the letter f (for factor). For example, equation 6–3 may be concisely written as $AOA = R \cdot f_{\overline{n}|\,i}$. If you simplify the writing of an equation, take care to use the correct type of factor when solving the equation.

Finally, try to form the habit of examining your answers to compound interest problems from a common-sense perspective. We know, for example, that the present value of $1,000 discounted for 2 years at 8% could not possibly be $8,573.40. The actual present value is only $857.34. Obviously, misplacing a decimal can greatly affect the solution to a compound interest problem.

In the remaining chapters of this textbook, you will be asked to apply many of the tools discussed in this chapter and the previous chapters on the accounting cycle. The next chapter, which covers cash and receivables, is the first of a series of seven chapters that explain asset accounting. As we move into our study of various types of assets, you will see the application of these tools.

KEY POINTS

1. Simple interest is earned only on the principal sum of money invested; compound interest is earned not only on the principal but also on the interest accumulated. (Objective 1)

2. Four fundamental concepts underlie all compound interest problems:
   a. present value (PV)   **c.** interest rate (i)
   b. future value (FV)   **d.** time periods (n)   (Objective 2)

EXHIBIT 6-10

Summary of Compound Interest Equations

Equation Number	Equation	Appropriate Table
6-1	$FV = PV \cdot fvf_{\overline{n}|i}$	6-1
6-2	$PV = FV \cdot pvf_{\overline{n}|i}$	6-2
6-3	$AOA = R \cdot aoaf_{\overline{n}|i}$	6-3
6-3A	$AAD = R \cdot aadf_{\overline{n}|i}$	6-3 (adjusted)
6-4	$PVOA = R \cdot pvoaf_{\overline{n}|i}$	6-4
6-4A	$PVAD = R \cdot pvadf_{\overline{n}|i}$	6-4 (adjusted)
6-5	$PVDA = R \cdot (pvoaf_{\overline{k+n}|i} - pvoaf_{\overline{k}|i})$	6-4

3. In a compound interest problem, the values of i and n should reflect the number of times a year that interest is compounded. (Objective 2)

4. An amount of a single sum problem focuses on the future value to which a single sum of money will accumulate if left on deposit for a certain number of periods at a certain interest rate per period. (Objective 3)

5. A present value of a single sum problem focuses on the present value of a single sum of money that is discounted for a certain number of periods at a certain interest rate per period. (Objective 3)

6. An annuity is a series of equal receipts or payments, called rents, that occur at uniform time intervals at a constant interest rate. In an ordinary annuity, the rents occur at the end of each time period; in an annuity due, the rents occur at the beginning of each time period. Present value and future value concepts apply to annuities, just as these concepts apply to single sum problems. (Objective 3)

7. Important characteristics of the major types of annuity problems are summarized in Exhibit 6-11. (Objective 3)

8. A deferred annuity is one in which the initial rent occurs two or more periods in the future. A deferral period does not affect the calculation of an amount, but it does affect the calculation of a present value. (Objective 3)

9. When solving a compound interest problem, you should read the problem carefully to determine the type of problem you are dealing with, solve the problem using the appropriate equations and tables, and make sure your answer seems reasonable. (Objective 3)

10. A complex problem can usually be solved by dividing it into its components. (Objective 3)

EXHIBIT 6-11

Characteristics of Annuity Problems

Type of Annuity Problem	Focus	Rents
Amount of an ordinary annuity	A future value	End of each period. *Final rent occurs at same time as future value.*
Amount of an annuity due	A future value	Beginning of each period. *Final rent occurs one period before future value.*
Present value of an ordinary annuity	A present value	End of each period. *Initial rent occurs one period after the present value.*
Present value of an annuity due	A present value	Beginning of each period. *Initial rent occurs at same time as present value.*

6–1   Explain what is meant by the time value of money.

6–2   Distinguish between simple and compound interest.

6–3   Distinguish between the amount of a single sum and the present value of a single sum.

6–4   What is an annuity?

6–5   Distinguish between an ordinary annuity and an annuity due.

6–6   Distinguish between the amount of an ordinary annuity and the amount of an annuity due.

6–7   Distinguish between the present value of an ordinary annuity and the present value of an annuity due.

6–8   What is a deferred annuity?

6–9   Explain how the factors in each of the following tables were calculated:

   [a] Table 6–1   [b] Table 6–2
   [c] Table 6–3   [d] Table 6–4

6–10   Explain how an Amount of 1 table could be converted to a Present Value of 1 table.

6–11   Explain how an Amount of an Ordinary Annuity of 1 table could be converted to an Amount of an Annuity Due of 1 table.

6–12   Explain how a Present Value of an Ordinary Annuity of 1 table could be converted to a Present Value of an Annuity Due of 1 table.

6–13   Indicate the number of compounding periods (n) and the interest rate per period (i) for each of the following:

   [a] Three years, 12% compounded annually.
   [b] Three years, 12% compounded semiannually.
   [c] Three years, 12% compounded quarterly.
   [d] Three years, 12% compounded monthly.

6–14   Assuming that $n = 15$ and $i = 10\%$, what is

   [a] The amount of 1?
   [b] The present value of 1?
   [c] The amount of an ordinary annuity of 1?
   [d] The amount of an annuity due of 1?
   [e] The present value of an ordinary annuity of 1?
   [f] The present value of an annuity due of 1?

6–15   To what amount will $7,500 accumulate if it is deposited for five years at 10%, assuming
   [a] Simple interest?
   [b] Interest compounded annually?
   [c] Interest compounded semiannually?
   [d] Interest compounded quarterly?

6–16   Assuming an interest rate of 8%, compounded quarterly, how many years will it take for a deposit of $1,800 to accumulate to $2,674.71?

---

*Brief descriptions of the exercises and problems in this chapter are not given so that students may practice learning how to recognize the different types of compound interest problems. As indicated in the chapter, learning to recognize the different types of problems is very important.

6-17   What annual interest rate, when compounded annually, would cause an initial deposit of $6,600 to accumulate to $25,063.50 in 14 years?

6-18   Amy Rooks plans to send each of her two daughters to private universities. For the first daughter, Amy will need $25,000 in 3 years; Amy plans to accumulate this amount by depositing a certain sum today in a 3-year certificate of deposit that pays 6% interest compounded annually. For the second daughter, Amy will need $50,000 in 7 years; Amy plans to accumulate this amount by depositing a certain sum today in a 7-year certificate of deposit that pays 8% interest compounded annually. What is the total amount of cash that Amy needs to deposit today?

6-19   Ray Robusto has deposited $2,000 on the same day of each month for the last two years in an account that pays 12% interest, compounded monthly. He made the last deposit today. How much money does Ray now have in his account?

6-20   Ben Rollo has $30,000 today as a result of having deposited equal amounts of cash in a savings account every six months for 12 years. The account pays interest of 6% compounded semi-annually. Assuming that the last deposit was made today, how much was each deposit?

6-21   As of today, Bill Morie has accumulated $114,550.00 in a retirement account that pays 10% interest compounded annually. He accumulated this sum by depositing $2,000 at annual intervals during each year that he worked in the clothing business. The last deposit was made today. How many deposits did Bill make?

6-22   Jane Harts has $9,433.42 today as a result of having deposited $750 at annual intervals the last 10 years. The last deposit was made today. Assuming annual compounding, what interest rate did Jane earn on her periodic deposits?

6-23   Roger Frankenberg plans to deposit $2,750 in his savings account today and at each of the next 35 monthly intervals, for a total period of 3 years. Assuming that Roger's money earns interest of 12%, compounded monthly, how much money will Roger have in his account at the end of 3 years?

6-24   Helen Freeman wants to accumulate $50,000 at the end of 18 years and will make 18 equal annual deposits into a fund that pays 8% interest, compounded annually. Helen will make the final deposit one year before the $50,000 sum is accumulated. How much will each deposit be?

6-25   When Tom Wilkerson's son was born, Tom deposited $250 in a special savings account that pays interest at 8% compounded annually. Later, Tom deposited $250 on each of his son's birthdays. How old is Tom's son if today is his son's birthday and, just *before* Tom makes his current deposit, the amount accumulated in the account is $7,331.07?

6-26   Paul Rechenbach deposited $1,000 annually in an investment account for five years, ending one year ago. Assuming that interest is compounded annually and that Paul has accumulated $6,715.61 in his account as of today, what stated interest rate did he earn?

6-27   Brenda Schmierbach wants to earn an interest rate of 10%, compounded quarterly. How much money should she pay today to an insurance company for the right to receive $12,000 at quarterly intervals, starting 3 months from now, for the next 8 years?

6-28   Today Harold Reed deposited $18,000 in a savings account that pays 6% interest compounded semiannually. Harold wants to liquidate the balance in his account by making equal semiannual withdrawals, starting 6 months from now, for 4 years. How large will each withdrawal be?

6-29   Doris Boadt has $60,207.90 in a savings account that pays 6% interest compounded annually. How many annual withdrawals of $5,000 each can she make from the account, assuming that she makes the first withdrawal one year from now?

6-30   Paul Yamato buys an automobile having a cash price of $6,473.70 with $1,500 down and payments of $2,000 annually for three years. Assuming annual compounding, what is the stated interest rate in this transaction?

6-31   Assuming that she wants to earn interest of 12%, compounded monthly, how much money should Maria Rucci pay today to an insurance company for the right to receive $5,000 each month for 36 months, with the initial $5,000 to be received today?

6–32   Rita Rogow wants to use all the money in her $30,000 savings account to pay for her college education, which begins today. The account pays 10% interest compounded annually. What constant amount of cash can she withdraw at the beginning of each of her four years in college?

6–33   Fred Granger currently owes a debt of $3,167.46. The debt accrues interest at 10% compounded annually on the unpaid balance. How many annual payments of $500 each will Fred have to make to liquidate the debt and interest, assuming that the first payment is made today?

6–34   Angela Wishart purchased a new video recorder that had a cash price of $526.59. She made an $80 down payment and paid the balance in $80 installments at the end of each year for seven years. What is the stated annual interest rate?

6–35   Assume that it is now the beginning of Year 1. Answer each of the following questions, assuming an interest rate of 6% compounded annually.

[a] What is the amount at the end of Year 10 of ten annual deposits of $7,000 each, the first of which is made at the end of Year 1?

[b] What is the amount at the end of Year 20 of ten annual deposits of $7,000 each, the first of which is made at the end of Year 11?

[c] As of the beginning of Year 11, what is the present value of ten annual receipts of $7,000 each, the first of which is received at the end of Year 11?

[d] As of the beginning of Year 1, what is the present value of ten annual receipts of $7,000 each, the first of which is received at the end of Year 11?

[e] Why are the correct answers to [a] and [b] the same?

[f] Why are the correct answers to [c] and [d] different?

PROBLEMS*   **6–36**   Old Savings and Loan Association, whose slogan is "our interest is more interesting," currently pays interest at a rate of 8%, compounded quarterly. Second Savings and Loan Association, whose slogan is "our interest interests more," pays 8% compounded annually. If you want to deposit $10,000 for five years, what would be the total additional interest that you could earn by depositing the money in Old Savings and Loan rather than Second Savings and Loan?

6–37   McDonald Company deposited $20,000 with each of four investment companies at the following terms:

Investment Company	Annual Rate	Compounded	Investment Term in Years
A	12%	Annually	8
B	10%	Quarterly	6
C	10%	Semiannually	4
D	8%	Quarterly	2

What will be the balance in each investment account at its maturity?

6–38   Joan Ricca was informed by the attorney managing her deceased uncle's estate that the following deposits would be made in her new savings account at the end of each of the following years:

Year	Deposit
1992	$5,000
1993	3,000
1994	4,000
1995	6,000

The account pays 8% interest compounded annually.

---

*Brief descriptions of the exercises and problems in this chapter are not given so that students may practice learning how to recognize the different types of compound interest problems. As indicated in the chapter, learning to recognize the different types of problems is very important.

Instructions

[a] Assuming that Joan makes no additional deposits or withdrawals, what will be the balance in her savings account at the end of 1995, immediately after the last deposit?

[b] What would be the balance in the savings account at the end of 1995 if, instead of the deposits shown above, a deposit of $4,500 was made at the end of each year?

[c] Explain the similarities and differences in the techniques you used to solve [a] and [b].

6–39 Sean Christoff has admired for many years a refurbished Model T automobile owned by his neighbor. Thus, Sean quickly accepted his neighbor's recent offer to sell the car. Which of the following two payment options offered by the neighbor should Sean take?

[1] $4,650 cash payable immediately.

[2] $5,500 cash payable in one sum after two years.

Sean knows that he can earn 8%, compounded annually, on his money.

6–40 Your neighbor has a $7,000 noninterest-bearing note receivable that matures at the end of three years. You recently inherited $20,000, and you know that you could earn 10%, compounded annually, on investments that are similar in risk to your neighbor's note. Your goal is to maximize your income.

Instructions

[a] What is the maximum amount of cash that you would be willing to pay today for your neighbor's note?

[b] What is the maximum amount of cash that you would be willing to pay today if the $7,000 note paid you interest of 3% at the end of each year? (*Hint:* You will receive $7,000 × 3% = $210 at the end of Years 1, 2, and 3 and the $7,000 maturity value at the end of Year 3.)

[c] Explain why the amounts in [a] and [b] are *maximum* amounts.

6–41 On February 1, 1993, Fraser Tool Company leased equipment from French Manufacturing Corporation. The lease term is three years, which equals the estimated economic life of the equipment. The lease requires Fraser to make 36 monthly rental payments of $8,000 each, with the first payment due on February 1, 1993.

Instructions

[a] Assuming a relevant interest rate of 12% compounded monthly, what is the present value of the lease to Fraser Tool Company on February 1, 1993?

[b] Answer [a], assuming that the first of the 36 monthly rental payments is made on March 1, 1993.

6–42 Henry Hudson, a local dentist, opens a tax-deferred retirement account that pays 8% interest compounded annually. He plans to deposit $2,000 at annual intervals for 25 years, with the initial deposit made today.

Instructions

[a] How much cash will Henry have in his account when he retires at the end of 25 years?

[b] How much of the sum that you calculated in [a] is interest?

[c] What equal-size deposits would Henry have to make at the beginning of each year to accumulate $200,000 at the end of 25 years?

6–43 Laura Boley retired from Howden Company today with $165,766.20 in a retirement account that pays 8% interest compounded annually.

Instructions

[a] How many $15,000 annual withdrawals can Laura make from her account if she makes the first withdrawal one year from now?

[b] What equal amount should she withdraw at the end of each year if she wants to make the final withdrawal 25 years from today?

[c] What equal amount should she withdraw annually if she wants to make a total of 15 withdrawals, with the initial withdrawal made today?

[d] What equal amount should she withdraw annually if she wants to make a total of 15 withdrawals, with the initial withdrawal made 5 years from now?

6–44   Pam Bearden plans to retire 20 years from today. She wants to build a tax-deferred retirement account by making 20 annual deposits, with the first deposit made today. Pam wants to make 20 annual withdrawals of $25,000 each from her retirement account, with the initial withdrawal made 20 years from now. The retirement account will earn 12% interest, compounded annually.

Instructions

[a] What equal amounts should Pam deposit in her account?

[b] What is the total amount of interest that Pam will earn on the money in her account?

6–45   Tuff Trucking Company purchased a new truck from Mann Motor Company in exchange for a three-year, noninterest-bearing promissory note with a maturity value of $90,000. The market rate of interest for similar notes is 10% compounded annually.

Instructions

[a] What is the historical cost of the truck to Tuff Trucking Company?

[b] Answer [a], assuming that the $90,000 note paid interest of 2% at the end of each year for three years. (*Hint:* The note pays interest of $90,000 × 2% = $1,800 to the holder at the end of each of the three years, and it pays the maturity value of $90,000 at the end of the third year.)

6–46   Scott Kelso buys a new home today costing $67,736.39. He makes a $10,000 down payment and gets a 10-year mortgage loan for the balance. The mortgage bears interest at 10%, compounded quarterly, and calls for equal quarterly payments, starting 3 months from now.

Instructions

[a] How much will each quarterly payment be?

[b] What is the total sum of cash that Scott will spend on the down payment and the loan?

[c] What is the total amount of interest that Scott will pay on the loan?

[d] What is the total amount of interest that Scott could save if he could get the required loan at 8% compounded quarterly?

6–47   Bryja Company will need $2,500,000 at the end of 20 years to retire a maturing issue of term bonds. To accumulate the desired sum, the company deposits $62,500 at the end of each year in a sinking fund that pays 6% interest compounded annually.

Instructions

[a] Will the fund at the end of 20 years be sufficient to retire the bonds?

[b] If your answer to [a] is no, what equal amount of cash would the company have to deposit at the end of each of the 20 years to accumulate the desired sum?

6–48   Readett Company wants to purchase a new warehouse in 3 years. The company expects the warehouse to cost $525,000 at that time. To accumulate this amount, the company plans to make 12 quarterly deposits of $36,000 each in a special account that pays 10% interest compounded quarterly. The first deposit is made today.

Instructions

[a] Will the amount in the fund at the end of three years be sufficient to purchase the warehouse?

[b] If your answer to [a] is no, what equal amount of cash would the company have to deposit at the beginning of each quarter to accumulate $525,000 at the end of three years?

6–49   Determine the stated annual interest rate in each of the following independent cases (assume annual compounding in each case):

[a] A deposit of $1,300 accumulates to $1,850.30 in 9 years.

[b] A person lends $75,131 today in exchange for $100,000 to be received at the end of 3 years.

[c] Periodic deposits of $1,200 made at the end of each year accumulate to $25,218.08 at the end of 14 years.

[d] Periodic deposits of $2,800 made at the beginning of each year accumulate to $57,075.97 at the end of 11 years.

[e] An annuity contract purchased for $53,373.90 promises to pay $5,000 at the end of each year for the next 25 years.

[f] A person borrows $50,000 in exchange for a written promise to pay $4,821.78 at the beginning of each year for 30 years, with the first payment due now.

6–50 On April 1, 1993, Rechichar Corporation issues 10%, 20-year bonds payable with a total par value of $80,000. Interest is payable semiannually on September 30 and March 31.

Instructions

[a] How much will the bonds sell for if, on April 1, 1993, the market rate of interest for similar bonds is

[1] 8%?   [2] 10%?   [3] 12%?

[b] Make the journal entry for Rechichar Corporation to record the bond issuance under each of the three assumptions in [a].

[c] Explain the meaning and accounting treatment of "Discount on Bonds Payable."

6–51 Stinnette Company has projected substantial growth in sales over the next 5 years. To ensure that sufficient funds are available for capital expansion, Stinnette plans to deposit $75,000 in a building fund at the end of each year for the next 5 years.

Instructions

[a] What will be the balance in the fund at the end of the fifth year if interest is earned at 8% compounded annually?

[b] How many years would it take for the fund to accumulate $348,075 if interest is earned at 10% compounded annually?

[c] What interest rate, compounded annually, would be necessary to accumulate $414,422 by the end of the fifth year?

6–52 How many *years* are involved in each of the following independent situations?

[a] A deposit of $3,600 accumulates to $9,145.26 at 6% compounded annually.

[b] A person lends $22,819.50 today in exchange for $50,000 to be received in the future, which includes interest at 8% compounded semiannually.

[c] Deposits of $300 at the end of each quarter accumulate to $11,115.36 at the end of the final quarter. The interest rate is 8% compounded quarterly.

[d] Deposits of $600 at the beginning of each year accumulate to $14,787.25 at the end of the final year. The interest rate is 4% compounded annually.

[e] A person deposits $1,635.14 today in a savings account that pays interest at 8% compounded quarterly. The account is liquidated by withdrawals of $100 at the end of each quarter, with the initial withdrawals made at the end of the first quarter.

[f] A person deposits $1,777.37 today in a savings account that pays interest at 6% compounded annually. The account is liquidated by annual withdrawals of $200, with the initial withdrawal made today.

6–53 On January 1, 1991, Vicki Wrightson buys new furniture costing $5,000. To pay for it, she signs a promissory note calling for equal monthly payments for three years. The first payment is due in one month. The note bears interest at 12% compounded monthly.

Instructions

[a] How much will each monthly payment be?

[b] How much interest will Vicki pay on the furniture loan in each of the following years:

[1] 1991?   [2] 1992?   [3] 1993?

6–54   Craig Wesson wants to establish a special retirement fund from which he can make five annual withdrawals of $20,000 each, with the first withdrawal to be made on January 1, 2000. Wesson wants to make four equal annual contributions to the retirement fund, beginning January 1, 1993 and ending January 1, 1996. Wesson wants the fund to be exhausted after the final withdrawal on January 1, 2004. The fund will earn 10% interest, compounded annually.

Instructions

[a] What equal annual amount should Wesson contribute to the fund?
[b] What is the total amount of interest that Wesson will earn on the money in his fund?

6–55   Otto Farber wants to establish a college fund for his son, Eddie. Farber estimates that Eddie will require $15,000 per year for four years, beginning September 1, 1999 and ending September 1, 2002. Farber wants to make three equal annual contributions to the college fund, beginning September 1, 1993 and ending September 1, 1995. Farber wants the fund to be exhausted after the final withdrawal on September 1, 2002. The fund will earn 12% interest, compounded annually.

Instructions

[a] What equal annual amount should Farber contribute to the fund?
[b] What is the total amount of interest that Farber will earn on the money in his fund?

6–56   John Lindon wants to buy a log cabin kit from Homely Homes, Inc., for $20,000 cash. The best alternative use of John's money is an investment account that pays 8% interest compounded annually. John expects that it would take him two years working part-time to complete the exterior of the cabin and an additional year to finish the interior. If John decides to buy the kit, he will leave his present part-time job of making Christmas ornaments from pine cones. As a result, he will lose $2,000 cash income at the end of each of the three years that he worked on the cabin.

The cabin would be constructed on a lake in a retirement community. John expects that the annual rent for the first five years after completion would be $2,400 and for the second five years would be $3,600. Rental payments would be due at the beginning of each year. John expects that he would sell the cabin for $26,000 after renting it for 10 years.

Instructions

Using appropriate compound interest concepts, determine whether the log cabin is a sound economic investment for John Lindon. Ignore income taxes.

CASES

6–57   HISTORICAL COST   In Chapter 2 we stated that the historical cost of an asset equals the cash equivalent price of acquiring the asset and putting it to its intended use. Suppose that on July 1, 1993, Dallas Corporation buys 100 shares of common stock of Houston Company as an investment in exchange for a three-year note. The note has a face amount of $14,049.29 and no stated interest rate. Houston Company is a small, closely held enterprise, and the market value of its common stock is not readily determinable. On July 1, 1993, the market rate of interest for notes similar to the one issued by Dallas is 12%.

Instructions

[a] How should Dallas determine the historical cost of its investment in Houston Company.
[b] Justify your answer to [a] from the standpoint of accounting theory.

6–58   REVENUE REALIZATION   On December 31, 1993, Western Galleries, Inc., sold a unique painting to Black Company in exchange for a five-year note receivable. The note had a face amount of $161,051 and no stated interest rate. The market rate of interest for similar notes on December 31, 1993, was 12%. The painting could not be appraised in a reliable manner.

Instructions

Explain how Western Galleries should determine the amount of revenue to recognize on the sale for the period ending December 31, 1993.

6–59 STATE LOTTERY A U.S. state recently ran a full-page advertisement in the state's major newspapers announcing that it was sponsoring a lottery in which "the winner would receive $1,000,000." The fine print near the bottom of the ad indicated that "the $1,000,000 would be paid in $50,000 annual installments over 20 years."

Instructions

Do you feel that the state's ad is fair and reasonable, or is it misleading? Ignoring income taxes, defend your position with appropriate arguments.

TABLE 6-1

Amount of 1

$$fvf_{\overline{n}|\,i} = (1 + i)^n$$

Periods (n)	1%	2%	2.5%	3%	4%	5%
1	1.01000	1.02000	1.02500	1.03000	1.04000	1.05000
2	1.02010	1.04040	1.05062	1.06090	1.08160	1.10250
3	1.03030	1.06121	1.07689	1.09273	1.12486	1.15762
4	1.04060	1.08243	1.10381	1.12551	1.16986	1.21551
5	1.05101	1.10408	1.13141	1.15927	1.21665	1.27628
6	1.06152	1.12616	1.15969	1.19405	1.26532	1.34010
7	1.07214	1.14869	1.18869	1.22987	1.31593	1.40710
8	1.08286	1.17166	1.21840	1.26677	1.36857	1.47746
9	1.09369	1.19509	1.24886	1.30477	1.42331	1.55133
10	1.10462	1.21899	1.28008	1.34392	1.48024	1.62889
11	1.11567	1.24337	1.31209	1.38423	1.53945	1.71034
12	1.12683	1.26824	1.34489	1.42576	1.60103	1.79586
13	1.13809	1.29361	1.37851	1.46853	1.66507	1.88565
14	1.14947	1.31948	1.41297	1.51259	1.73168	1.97993
15	1.16097	1.34587	1.44830	1.55797	1.80094	2.07893
16	1.17258	1.37279	1.48451	1.60471	1.87298	2.18287
17	1.18430	1.40024	1.52162	1.65285	1.94790	2.29202
18	1.19615	1.42825	1.55966	1.70243	2.02582	2.40662
19	1.20811	1.45681	1.59865	1.75351	2.10685	2.52695
20	1.22019	1.48595	1.63862	1.80611	2.19112	2.65330
21	1.23239	1.51567	1.67958	1.86029	2.27877	2.78596
22	1.24472	1.54598	1.72157	1.91610	2.36992	2.92526
23	1.25716	1.57690	1.76461	1.97359	2.46472	3.07152
24	1.26973	1.60844	1.80873	2.03279	2.56330	3.22510
25	1.28243	1.64061	1.85394	2.09378	2.66584	3.38635
26	1.29526	1.67342	1.90029	2.15659	2.77247	3.55567
27	1.30821	1.70689	1.94780	2.22129	2.88337	3.73346
28	1.32129	1.74102	1.99650	2.28793	2.99870	3.92013
29	1.33450	1.77584	2.04641	2.35657	3.11865	4.11614
30	1.34785	1.81136	2.09757	2.42726	3.24340	4.32194
31	1.36133	1.84759	2.15001	2.50008	3.37313	4.53804
32	1.37494	1.88454	2.20376	2.57508	3.50806	4.76494
33	1.38869	1.92223	2.25885	2.65234	3.64838	5.00319
34	1.40258	1.96068	2.31532	2.73191	3.79432	5.25335
35	1.41660	1.99989	2.37321	2.81386	3.94609	5.51602
36	1.43077	2.03989	2.43254	2.89828	4.10393	5.79182
37	1.44508	2.08069	2.49335	2.98523	4.26809	6.08141
38	1.45953	2.12230	2.55568	3.07478	4.43881	6.38548
39	1.47412	2.16474	2.61957	3.16703	4.61637	6.70475
40	1.48886	2.20804	2.68506	3.26204	4.80102	7.03999

TABLE 6–1   253

TABLE 6–1

Amount of 1

6%	8%	10%	12%	16%	20%	24%	Periods (n)
1.06000	1.08000	1.10000	1.12000	1.16000	1.20000	1.24000	1
1.12360	1.16640	1.21000	1.25440	1.34560	1.44000	1.53760	2
1.19102	1.25971	1.33100	1.40493	1.56090	1.72800	1.90662	3
1.26248	1.36049	1.46410	1.57352	1.81064	2.07360	2.36421	4
1.33823	1.46933	1.61051	1.76234	2.10034	2.48832	2.93163	5
1.41852	1.58687	1.77156	1.97382	2.43640	2.98598	3.63522	6
1.50363	1.71382	1.94872	2.21068	2.82622	3.58318	4.50767	7
1.59385	1.85093	2.14359	2.47596	3.27841	4.29982	5.58951	8
1.68948	1.99900	2.35795	2.77308	3.80296	5.15978	6.93099	9
1.79085	2.15892	2.59374	3.10585	4.41144	6.19174	8.59443	10
1.89830	2.33164	2.85312	3.47855	5.11726	7.43008	10.65709	11
2.01220	2.51817	3.13843	3.89598	5.93603	8.91610	13.21479	12
2.13293	2.71962	3.45227	4.36349	6.88579	10.69932	16.38634	13
2.26090	2.93719	3.79750	4.88711	7.98752	12.83918	20.31906	14
2.39656	3.17217	4.17725	5.47357	9.26552	15.40702	25.19563	15
2.54035	3.42594	4.59497	6.13039	10.74800	18.48843	31.24259	16
2.69277	3.70002	5.05447	6.86604	12.46768	22.18611	38.74081	17
2.85434	3.99602	5.55992	7.68997	14.46251	26.62333	48.03860	18
3.02560	4.31570	6.11591	8.61276	16.77652	31.94800	59.56786	19
3.20714	4.66096	6.72750	9.64629	19.46076	38.33760	73.86415	20
3.39956	5.03383	7.40025	10.80385	22.57448	46.00512	91.59155	21
3.60354	5.43654	8.14027	12.10031	26.18640	55.20614	113.57352	22
3.81975	5.87146	8.95430	13.55235	30.37622	66.24737	140.83116	23
4.04893	6.34118	9.84973	15.17863	35.23642	79.49685	174.63064	24
4.29187	6.84848	10.83471	17.00006	40.87424	95.39622	216.54199	25
4.54938	7.39635	11.91818	19.04007	47.41412	114.47546	268.51207	26
4.82235	7.98806	13.10999	21.32488	55.00038	137.37055	332.95497	27
5.11169	8.62711	14.42099	23.88387	63.80044	164.84466	412.86416	28
5.41839	9.31727	15.86309	26.74993	74.00851	197.81359	511.95156	29
5.74349	10.06266	17.44940	29.95992	85.84988	237.37631	634.81993	30
6.08810	10.86767	19.19434	33.55511	99.58586	284.85158	787.17672	31
6.45339	11.73708	21.11378	37.58173	115.51959	341.82189	976.09913	32
6.84059	12.67605	23.22515	42.09153	134.00273	410.18627	1210.36292	33
7.25103	13.69013	25.54767	47.14252	155.44317	492.22352	1500.85002	34
7.68609	14.78534	28.10244	52.79962	180.31407	590.66823	1861.05403	35
8.14725	15.96817	30.91268	59.13557	209.16432	708.80187	2307.70699	36
8.63609	17.24563	34.00395	66.23184	242.63062	850.56225	2861.55667	37
9.15425	18.62528	37.40434	74.17966	281.45151	1020.67470	3548.33027	38
9.70351	20.11530	41.14478	83.08122	326.48376	1224.80964	4399.92954	39
10.28572	21.72452	45.25926	93.05097	378.72116	1469.77157	5455.91262	40

TABLE 6-2

Present Value of 1

$$pvf_{\overline{n}|\,i} = \frac{1}{(1+i)^n}$$

Periods (n)	1%	2%	2.5%	3%	4%	5%
1	.99010	.98039	.97561	.97087	.96154	.95238
2	.98030	.96117	.95181	.94260	.92456	.90703
3	.97059	.94232	.92860	.91514	.88900	.86384
4	.96098	.92385	.90595	.88849	.85480	.82270
5	.95147	.90573	.88385	.86261	.82193	.78353
6	.94205	.88797	.86230	.83748	.79031	.74622
7	.93272	.87056	.84127	.81309	.75992	.71068
8	.92348	.85349	.82075	.78941	.73069	.67684
9	.91434	.83676	.80073	.76642	.70259	.64461
10	.90529	.82035	.78120	.74409	.67556	.61391
11	.89632	.80426	.76214	.72242	.64958	.58468
12	.88745	.78849	.74356	.70138	.62460	.55684
13	.87866	.77303	.72542	.68095	.60057	.53032
14	.86996	.75788	.70773	.66112	.57748	.50507
15	.86135	.74301	.69047	.64186	.55526	.48102
16	.85282	.72845	.67362	.62317	.53391	.45811
17	.84438	.71416	.65720	.60502	.51337	.43630
18	.83602	.70016	.64117	.58739	.49363	.41552
19	.82774	.68643	.62553	.57029	.47464	.39573
20	.81954	.67297	.61027	.55368	.45639	.37689
21	.81143	.65978	.59539	.53755	.43883	.35894
22	.80340	.64684	.58086	.52189	.42196	.34185
23	.79544	.63416	.56670	.50669	.40573	.32557
24	.78757	.62172	.55288	.49193	.39012	.31007
25	.77977	.60953	.53939	.47761	.37512	.29530
26	.77205	.59758	.52623	.46369	.36069	.28124
27	.76440	.58586	.51340	.45019	.34682	.26785
28	.75684	.57437	.50088	.43708	.33348	.25509
29	.74934	.56311	.48866	.42435	.32065	.24295
30	.74192	.55207	.47674	.41199	.30832	.23138
31	.73458	.54125	.46511	.39999	.29646	.22036
32	.72730	.53063	.45377	.38834	.28506	.20987
33	.72010	.52023	.44270	.37703	.27409	.19987
34	.71297	.51003	.43191	.36604	.26355	.19035
35	.70591	.50003	.42137	.35538	.25342	.18129
36	.69892	.49022	.41109	.34503	.24367	.17266
37	.69200	.48061	.40107	.33498	.23430	.16444
38	.68515	.47119	.39128	.32523	.22529	.15661
39	.67837	.46195	.38174	.31575	.21662	.14915
40	.67165	.45289	.37243	.30656	.20829	.14205

TABLE 6–2   255

TABLE 6–2

Present Value of 1

6%	8%	10%	12%	16%	20%	24%	Periods (n)
.94340	.92593	.90909	.89286	.86207	.83333	.80645	1
.89000	.85734	.82645	.79719	.74316	.69444	.65036	2
.83962	.79383	.75131	.71178	.64066	.57870	.52449	3
.79209	.73503	.68301	.63552	.55229	.48225	.42297	4
.74726	.68058	.62092	.56743	.47611	.40188	.34111	5
.70496	.63017	.56447	.50663	.41044	.33490	.27509	6
.66506	.58349	.51316	.45235	.35383	.27908	.22184	7
.62741	.54027	.46651	.40388	.30503	.23257	.17891	8
.59190	.50025	.42410	.36061	.26295	.19381	.14428	9
.55839	.46319	.38554	.32197	.22668	.16151	.11635	10
.52679	.42888	.35049	.28748	.19542	.13459	.09383	11
.49697	.39711	.31863	.25668	.16846	.11216	.07567	12
.46884	.36770	.28966	.22917	.14523	.09346	.06103	13
.44230	.34046	.26333	.20462	.12520	.07789	.04921	14
.41727	.31524	.23939	.18270	.10793	.06491	.03969	15
.39365	.29189	.21763	.16312	.09304	.05409	.03201	16
.37136	.27027	.19784	.14564	.08021	.04507	.02581	17
.35034	.25025	.17986	.13004	.06914	.03756	.02082	18
.33051	.23171	.16351	.11611	.05961	.03130	.01679	19
.31180	.21455	.14864	.10367	.05139	.02608	.01354	20
.29416	.19866	.13513	.09256	.04430	.02174	.01092	21
.27751	.18394	.12285	.08264	.03819	.01811	.00880	22
.26180	.17032	.11168	.07379	.03292	.01509	.00710	23
.24698	.15770	.10153	.06588	.02838	.01258	.00573	24
.23300	.14602	.09230	.05882	.02447	.01048	.00462	25
.21981	.13520	.08391	.05252	.02109	.00874	.00372	26
.20737	.12519	.07628	.04689	.01818	.00728	.00300	27
.19563	.11591	.06934	.04187	.01567	.00607	.00242	28
.18456	.10733	.06304	.03738	.01351	.00506	.00195	29
.17411	.09938	.05731	.03338	.01165	.00421	.00158	30
.16425	.09202	.05210	.02980	.01004	.00351	.00127	31
.15496	.08520	.04736	.02661	.00866	.00293	.00102	32
.14619	.07889	.04306	.02376	.00746	.00244	.00083	33
.13791	.07305	.03914	.02121	.00643	.00203	.00067	34
.13011	.06763	.03558	.01894	.00555	.00169	.00054	35
.12274	.06262	.03235	.01691	.00478	.00141	.00043	36
.11579	.05799	.02941	.01510	.00412	.00118	.00035	37
.10924	.05369	.02673	.01348	.00355	.00098	.00028	38
.10306	.04971	.02430	.01204	.00306	.00082	.00023	39
.09722	.04603	.02209	.01075	.00264	.00068	.00018	40

TABLE 6-3

Amount of an Ordinary Annuity of 1

$$aoaf_{\overline{n}|\,i} = \frac{(1 + i)^n - 1}{i}$$

Periods (n)	1%	2%	2.5%	3%	4%	5%
1	1.00000	1.00000	1.00000	1.00000	1.00000	1.00000
2	2.01000	2.02000	2.02500	2.03000	2.04000	2.05000
3	3.03010	3.06040	3.07562	3.09090	3.12160	3.15250
4	4.06040	4.12161	4.15252	4.18363	4.24646	4.31012
5	5.10101	5.20404	5.25633	5.30914	5.41632	5.52563
6	6.15202	6.30812	6.38774	6.46841	6.63298	6.80191
7	7.21354	7.43428	7.54743	7.66246	7.89829	8.14201
8	8.28567	8.58297	8.73612	8.89234	9.21423	9.54911
9	9.36853	9.75463	9.95452	10.15911	10.58280	11.02656
10	10.46221	10.94972	11.20338	11.46388	12.00611	12.57789
11	11.56683	12.16872	12.48347	12.80780	13.48635	14.20679
12	12.68250	13.41209	13.79555	14.19203	15.02581	15.91713
13	13.80933	14.68033	15.14044	15.61779	16.62684	17.71298
14	14.94742	15.97394	16.51895	17.08632	18.29191	19.59863
15	16.09690	17.29342	17.93193	18.59891	20.02359	21.57856
16	17.25786	18.63929	19.38022	20.15688	21.82453	23.65749
17	18.43044	20.01207	20.86473	21.76159	23.69751	25.84037
18	19.61475	21.41231	22.38635	23.41444	25.64541	28.13238
19	20.81090	22.84056	23.94601	25.11687	27.67123	30.53900
20	22.01900	24.29737	25.54466	26.87037	29.77808	33.06595
21	23.23919	25.78332	27.18327	28.67649	31.96920	35.71925
22	24.47159	27.29898	28.86286	30.53678	34.24797	38.50521
23	25.71630	28.84496	30.58443	32.45288	36.61789	41.43048
24	26.97346	30.42186	32.34904	34.42647	39.08260	44.50200
25	28.24320	32.03030	34.15776	36.45926	41.64591	47.72710
26	29.52563	33.67091	36.01171	38.55304	44.31174	51.11345
27	30.82089	35.34432	37.91200	40.70963	47.08421	54.66913
28	32.12910	37.05121	39.85980	42.93092	49.96758	58.40258
29	33.45039	38.79223	41.85630	45.21885	52.96629	62.32271
30	34.78489	40.56808	43.90270	47.57542	56.08494	66.43885
31	36.13274	42.37944	46.00027	50.00268	59.32834	70.76079
32	37.49407	44.22703	48.15028	52.50276	62.70147	75.29883
33	38.86901	46.11157	50.35403	55.07784	66.20953	80.06377
34	40.25770	48.03380	52.61289	57.73018	69.85791	85.06696
35	41.66028	49.99448	54.92821	60.46208	73.65222	90.32031
36	43.07688	51.99437	57.30141	63.27594	77.59831	95.83632
37	44.50765	54.03425	59.73395	66.17422	81.70225	101.62814
38	45.95272	56.11494	62.22730	69.15945	85.97034	107.70955
39	47.41225	58.23724	64.78298	72.23423	90.40915	114.09502
40	48.88637	60.40198	67.40255	75.40126	95.02552	120.79977

TABLE 6–3   257

TABLE 6–3

Amount of an Ordinary Annuity of 1

6%	8%	10%	12%	16%	20%	24%	Periods (n)
1.00000	1.00000	1.00000	1.00000	1.00000	1.00000	1.00000	1
2.06000	2.08000	2.10000	2.12000	2.16000	2.20000	2.24000	2
3.18360	3.24640	3.31000	3.37440	3.50560	3.64000	3.77760	3
4.37462	4.50611	4.64100	4.77933	5.06650	5.36800	5.68422	4
5.63709	5.86660	6.10510	6.35285	6.87714	7.44160	8.04844	5
6.97532	7.33593	7.71561	8.11519	8.97748	9.92992	10.98006	6
8.39384	8.92280	9.48717	10.08901	11.41387	12.91590	14.61528	7
9.89747	10.63663	11.43589	12.29969	14.24009	16.49908	19.12294	8
11.49132	12.48756	13.57948	14.77566	17.51851	20.79890	24.71245	9
13.18079	14.48656	15.93742	17.54874	21.32147	25.95868	31.64344	10
14.97164	16.64549	18.53117	20.65458	25.73290	32.15042	40.23787	11
16.86994	18.97713	21.38428	24.13313	30.85017	39.58050	50.89495	12
18.88214	21.49530	24.52271	28.02911	36.78620	48.49660	64.10974	13
21.01507	24.21492	27.97498	32.39260	43.67199	59.19592	80.49608	14
23.27597	27.15211	31.77248	37.27971	51.65951	72.03511	100.81514	15
25.67253	30.32428	35.94973	42.75328	60.92503	87.44213	126.01077	16
28.21288	33.75023	40.54470	48.88367	71.67303	105.93056	157.25336	17
30.90565	37.45024	45.59917	55.74971	84.14072	128.11667	195.99416	18
33.75999	41.44626	51.15909	63.43968	98.60323	154.74000	244.03276	19
36.78559	45.76196	57.27500	72.05244	115.37975	186.68800	303.60062	20
39.99273	50.42292	64.00250	81.69874	134.84051	225.02560	377.46477	21
43.39229	55.45676	71.40275	92.50258	157.41499	271.03072	469.05632	22
46.99583	60.89330	79.54302	104.60289	183.60138	326.23686	582.62984	23
50.81558	66.76476	88.49733	118.15524	213.97761	392.48424	723.46100	24
54.86451	73.10594	98.34706	133.33387	249.21402	471.98108	898.09164	25
59.15638	79.95442	109.18177	150.33393	290.08827	567.37730	1114.63363	26
63.70577	87.35077	121.09994	159.37401	337.50239	681.85276	1383.14570	27
68.52811	95.33883	134.20994	190.69889	392.50277	819.22331	1716.10067	28
73.63980	103.96594	148.63093	214.58275	456.30322	984.06797	2128.96483	29
79.05819	113.28321	164.49402	241.33268	530.31173	1181.88157	2640.91639	30
84.80168	123.34587	181.94342	271.29261	616.16161	1419.25788	3275.73632	31
90.88978	134.21354	201.13777	304.84772	715.74746	1704.10946	4062.91304	32
97.34316	145.95062	222.25154	342.42945	831.26706	2045.93135	5039.01217	33
104.18375	158.62667	245.47670	384.52098	965.26979	2456.11762	6249.37509	34
111.43478	172.31680	271.02437	431.66350	1120.71295	2948.34115	7750.22511	35
119.12087	187.10215	299.12681	484.46312	1301.02703	3539.00937	9611.27913	36
127.26812	203.07032	330.03949	543.59869	1510.19135	4247.81125	11918.98612	37
135.90421	220.31595	364.04343	609.83053	1752.82197	5098.37350	14780.54279	38
145.05846	238.94122	401.44778	684.01020	2034.27348	6119.04820	18328.87306	39
154.76197	259.05652	442.59256	767.09142	2360.75724	7343.85784	22728.80260	40

TABLE 6-4

Present Value of an Ordinary Annuity of 1

$$pvoaf_{\overline{n}|\,i} = \frac{1 - \frac{1}{(1 + i)^n}}{i}$$

Periods (n)	1%	2%	2.5%	3%	4%	5%
1	0.99010	0.98039	0.97561	0.97087	0.96154	0.95238
2	1.97040	1.94156	1.92742	1.91347	1.88609	1.85941
3	2.94099	2.88388	2.85602	2.82861	2.77509	2.72325
4	3.90197	3.80773	3.76197	3.71710	3.62990	3.54595
5	4.85343	4.71346	4.64583	4.57971	4.45182	4.32948
6	5.79548	5.60143	5.50813	5.41719	5.24214	5.07569
7	6.72819	6.47199	6.34939	6.23028	6.00205	5.78637
8	7.65168	7.32548	7.17014	7.01969	6.73274	6.46321
9	8.56602	8.16224	7.97087	7.78611	7.43533	7.10782
10	9.47130	8.98259	8.75206	8.53020	8.11090	7.72173
11	10.36763	9.78685	9.51421	9.25262	8.76048	8.30641
12	11.25508	10.57534	10.25776	9.95400	9.38507	8.86325
13	12.13374	11.34837	10.98318	10.63496	9.98565	9.39357
14	13.00370	12.10625	11.69091	11.29607	10.56312	9.89864
15	13.86505	12.84926	12.38138	11.93794	11.11839	10.37966
16	14.71787	13.57771	13.05500	12.56110	11.65230	10.83777
17	15.56225	14.29187	13.71220	13.16612	12.16567	11.27407
18	16.39827	14.99203	14.35336	13.75351	12.65930	11.68959
19	17.22601	15.67846	14.97889	14.32380	13.13394	12.08532
20	18.04555	16.35143	15.58916	14.87747	13.59033	12.46221
21	18.85698	17.01121	16.18455	15.41502	14.02916	12.82115
22	19.66038	17.65805	16.76541	15.93692	14.45112	13.16300
23	20.45582	18.29220	17.33211	16.44361	14.85684	13.48857
24	21.24339	18.91393	17.88499	16.93554	15.24696	13.79864
25	22.02316	19.52346	18.42438	17.41315	15.62208	14.09394
26	22.79520	20.12104	18.95061	17.87684	15.98277	14.37519
27	23.55961	20.70690	19.46401	18.32703	16.32959	14.64303
28	24.31644	21.28127	19.96489	18.76411	16.66306	14.89813
29	25.06579	21.84438	20.45355	19.18845	16.98371	15.14107
30	25.80771	22.39646	20.93029	19.60044	17.29203	15.37245
31	26.54229	22.93770	21.39541	20.00043	17.58849	15.59281
32	27.26959	23.46833	21.84918	20.38877	17.87355	15.80268
33	27.98969	23.98856	22.29188	20.76579	18.14765	16.00255
34	28.70267	24.49859	22.72379	21.13184	18.41120	16.19290
35	29.40858	24.99862	23.14516	21.48722	18.66461	16.37419
36	30.10751	25.48884	23.55625	21.83225	18.90828	16.54685
37	30.79951	25.96945	23.95732	22.16724	19.14258	16.71129
38	31.48466	26.44064	24.34860	22.49246	19.36786	16.86789
39	32.16303	26.90259	24.73034	22.80822	19.58448	17.01704
40	32.83469	27.35548	25.10278	23.11477	19.79277	17.15909

TABLE 6–4   259

TABLE 6–4

Present Value of an Ordinary Annuity of 1

6%	8%	10%	12%	16%	20%	24%	Periods (n)
0.94340	0.92593	0.90909	0.89286	0.86207	0.83333	0.80645	1
1.83339	1.78326	1.73554	1.69005	1.60523	1.52778	1.45682	2
2.67301	2.57710	2.48685	2.40183	2.24589	2.10648	1.98130	3
3.46511	3.31213	3.16987	3.03735	2.79818	2.58873	2.40428	4
4.21236	3.99271	3.79079	3.60478	3.27429	2.99061	2.74538	5
4.91732	4.62288	4.35526	4.11141	3.68474	3.32551	3.02047	6
5.58238	5.20637	4.86842	4.56376	4.03857	3.60459	3.24232	7
6.20979	5.74664	5.33493	4.96764	4.34359	3.83716	3.42122	8
6.80169	6.24689	5.75902	5.32825	4.60654	4.03097	3.56550	9
7.36009	6.71008	6.14457	5.65022	4.83323	4.19247	3.68186	10
7.88687	7.13896	6.49506	5.93770	5.02864	4.32706	3.77569	11
8.38384	7.53608	6.81369	6.19437	5.19711	4.43922	3.85136	12
8.85268	7.90378	7.10336	6.42355	5.34233	4.53268	3.91239	13
9.29498	8.24424	7.36669	6.62817	5.46753	4.61057	3.96160	14
9.71225	8.55948	7.60608	6.81086	5.57546	4.67547	4.00129	15
10.10590	8.85137	7.82371	6.97399	5.66850	4.72956	4.03330	16
10.47726	9.12164	8.02155	7.11963	5.74870	4.77463	4.05911	17
10.82760	9.37189	8.20141	7.24967	5.81785	4.81219	4.07993	18
11.15812	9.60360	8.36492	7.36578	5.87746	4.84350	4.09672	19
11.46992	9.81815	8.51356	7.46944	5.92884	4.86958	4.11026	20
11.76408	10.01680	8.64869	7.56200	5.97314	4.89132	4.12117	21
12.04158	10.20074	8.77154	7.64465	6.01133	4.90943	4.12998	22
12.30338	10.37106	8.88322	7.71843	6.04425	4.92453	4.13708	23
12.55036	10.52876	8.98474	7.78432	6.07263	4.93710	4.14281	24
12.78336	10.67478	9.07704	7.84314	6.09709	4.94759	4.14742	25
13.00317	10.80998	9.16095	7.89566	6.11818	4.95632	4.15115	26
13.21053	10.93516	9.23722	7.94255	6.13636	4.96360	4.15415	27
13.40616	11.05108	9.30657	7.98442	6.15204	4.96967	4.15657	28
13.59072	11.15841	9.36961	8.02181	6.16555	4.97472	4.15853	29
13.76483	11.25778	9.42691	8.05518	6.17720	4.97894	4.16010	30
13.92909	11.34980	9.47901	8.08499	6.18724	4.98245	4.16137	31
14.08404	11.43500	9.52638	8.11159	6.19590	4.98537	4.16240	32
14.23023	11.51389	9.56943	8.13535	6.20336	4.98781	4.16322	33
14.36814	11.58693	9.60857	8.15656	6.20979	4.98984	4.16389	34
14.49825	11.65457	9.64416	8.17550	6.21534	4.99154	4.16443	35
14.62099	11.71719	9.67651	8.19241	6.22012	4.99295	4.16486	36
14.73678	11.77518	9.70592	8.20751	6.22424	4.99412	4.16521	37
14.84602	11.82887	9.73265	8.22099	6.22779	4.99510	4.16549	38
14.94907	11.87858	9.75696	8.23303	6.23086	4.99592	4.16572	39
15.04630	11.92461	9.77905	8.24378	6.23350	4.99660	4.16590	40

PART 3

—

ASSET
ACCOUNTING

CHAPTER 7

Cash and Receivables

OBJECTIVES

1. To discuss and illustrate the financial accounting and reporting requirements for cash and receivables classified as current assets.
2. To explain the accounting for a petty cash fund.
3. To discuss and illustrate the preparation of a bank reconciliation and a proof of cash.
4. To explain the accounting for credit sales.
5. To discuss and illustrate the accounting for uncollectible accounts receivable.
6. To explain certain financing methods under which companies use their accounts receivable to generate cash.
7. To discuss and illustrate the accounting for notes receivable.

I n Part 1 of this book, we discussed the theoretical basis for financial report-ing, and in Part 2 we presented the tools of accounting. In Part 3 our focus shifts to asset accounting. Each of the seven chapters in Part 3 discusses im-portant measurement and disclosure principles that relate to certain assets, and each is related to the theoretical framework presented in Chapter 2. Recall that in Chapter 2 we defined assets as probable future economic benefits obtained or con-trolled by a particular entity as a result of past transactions or events. The Strawbridge & Clothier balance sheet printed on the endpapers shows several of the assets dis-cussed in Part 3.

This chapter focuses on cash and receivables classified as current assets. Cash and receivables classified as noncurrent assets are discussed in Chapter 10. Recall that in Chapter 3 we discussed the nature of asset valuation. Generally, the valuation of cash and short-term receivables is less complex and controversial than the valuation of most other assets.

The assets described in this chapter are highly liquid (i.e., cash or close to cash realization) and are therefore important in assessing a company's overall liquidity. An empirical study provided evidence that users of financial statements are becoming more concerned about liquidity evaluations: "While security analysts used to be con-cerned primarily with earnings per share, they are now devoting increased attention to the balance sheet and cash flow. Liquidity analysis plays a significant part in secu-rity analysts' evaluation of companies."[1]

CASH

COMPOSITION OF CASH

Cash is the standard medium of exchange in business transactions. It includes cur-rency, coins, checks, bank drafts, money orders, and demand deposits (checking ac-counts). Savings accounts are also usually considered cash, because banks generally do not enforce their legal right to demand a notice before the depositor makes a with-drawal. As a result, savings account balances are usually available for immediate ex-penditure.

Most companies maintain several general ledger accounts for cash in order to provide management with adequate details concerning cash balances. For example, a company might establish the following:

1. A **petty cash** account for currency and coins (called a petty cash fund) used to make small disbursements.
2. A **cash on hand** account for undeposited cash receipts.
3. A separate **cash in bank** account for each checking account maintained.

External users of financial statements generally are interested in the total amount of cash that a company has and in the relationship between this amount and other finan-cial statement amounts. That is why companies typically combine the amounts shown in the various cash accounts and report only a single total as "cash" on the balance sheet.

Asset/Liability Measurement   The valuation of cash is not highly controversial. Cash is simply reported at its **face amount.** The classification of cash as current or noncurrent depends on manage-ment's intended use of the cash. To be classified as a current asset, cash must be avail-able for use in current operations. Because it is highly liquid, cash is usually listed

---

[1]Morton Backer and Martin L. Gosman, *Financial Reporting and Business Liquidity* (New York: National Asso-ciation of Accountants, 1978), p. 251.

Materiality   first among the current assets. A material amount of cash that has been restricted or designated for some current purpose, such as the payment of current bond interest, should be reported separately among the current assets. On the other hand, cash that is not available for current purposes, such as cash accumulated in a sinking fund to retire the principal amount of long-term bonds, should be reported in the investments and funds category and not in current assets.

Several noteworthy considerations in accounting for cash are described below.

Not Cash

Cash

1. **Certificates of deposit (CDs)** should normally be included in short-term investments instead of cash, because banks usually impose substantial interest penalties that discourage CD-holders from making withdrawals before the CDs mature.

2. **Postdated checks, NSF checks** (not sufficient funds checks, those that cannot be covered by funds in the debtor's bank account), and **IOUs** should be reported as receivables rather than cash.

3. **Expense advances,** such as advances for employee travel, and **postage stamps** should be reported as prepaid expenses, not cash.

4. A **bank overdraft,** which occurs when a depositor has written checks for a sum greater than that in the depositor's bank account, should be reported as a current liability, except when the depositor has sufficient funds in another account with the *same bank* to cover the account which is overdrawn. Under these circumstances, which may arise when a company maintains a regular operating account and a payroll account with the same bank, the bank will transfer funds to the overdrawn account if the depositor fails to do so. As a result, the depositor may appropriately offset the overdraft against the cash balance and report the net amount of cash among the current assets.

5. **Undelivered checks,** as of the balance sheet date, should be considered part of a debtor's cash. Technically, checks drawn by a company should not be deducted from the company's cash balance until they have been mailed or otherwise delivered. As a result, liabilities that the checks are intended to liquidate still exist and should be reported as current payables.

6. **Compensating balances** are minimum amounts that a company agrees to maintain in a bank checking account as partial consideration for a loan or line of credit. Compensating balances limit the amount of cash that a company can spend in everyday operations. Moreover, compensating balances increase a company's effective interest cost if they are higher than the checking account balances that the company would normally maintain. For these reasons a company should disclose information about compensating balances in the notes to its financial statements. An example of such a note is as follows: "During 1993 informal arrangements were maintained with a number of banks which generally required the Company to maintain compensating cash balances of 8% of the loan commitments plus 8% of the average daily outstanding debt balances. At December 31, 1993, the cash balance includes $9.5 million of such compensating balances."

MANAGEMENT OF CASH

Companies need cash to buy goods and services, to pay off debts, and to make distributions to owners. Because of its critical importance to any business, cash must be managed effectively. As the chief executive of Firestone Tire & Rubber Company has stated: "Cash becomes the final determinant in the way you run a company."[2] Effective cash management involves striking a delicate balance between *risk* and *profitability*. On the one hand, managers try to avoid having too little cash on hand in order

---

[2]Thomas O'Hanlon, "Less Means More at Firestone," *Fortune* (October 20, 1980), p. 116.

to minimize the company's risk of insolvency. On the other hand, they try to avoid excessive cash balances because uninvested cash does not contribute to the company's profits.

Effective cash management requires careful **planning** and **control.** The major aspect of **cash planning** is the **cash budget,** which is an internal statement of projected cash inflows, outflows, and balances. Among other things, the cash budget enables managers to prepare in advance for such activities as the raising of additional cash through borrowing and the investing of idle cash in productive assets. Cash planning is usually covered in managerial accounting and financial management courses.

Cash control is an important part of a firm's **internal control system.** Internal control has been defined as: "The plan of organization and all of the coordinate methods and measures adopted within a business to safeguard its assets, check the accuracy and reliability of its accounting data, promote operational efficiency, and encourage adherence to prescribed managerial policies."[3] Internal control includes **accounting controls,** which relate to the safeguarding of assets and the reliability of financial records, and **administrative controls,** which relate to operational efficiency and adherence to managerial policies. Accountants should have a general awareness of administrative controls, including statistical analyses, time and motion studies, performance reports, employee training programs, and quality controls.[4] In addition, accountants should have a thorough understanding of accounting controls. Several important **principles of internal accounting control** are listed below:

1. Company personnel should be competent and honest, and they should be given specific responsibilities.
2. The responsibility for a series of related events, such as receiving merchandise and paying for it, should be divided between two or more persons.
3. The accounting function should be separated from the custodianship of company assets.
4. Adequate accounting records should be kept at all times.
5. Certain clerical personnel should be rotated among various jobs.
6. Assets should be protected by insurance and by physical safeguards.
7. An internal audit staff should be maintained if management believes the benefits of such a staff exceed the costs.

Maintaining an adequate system of internal accounting control for all assets is important, but it is particularly important for cash. Cash appeals to virtually everyone and is relatively easy to steal if not properly safeguarded. If one person, for example, receives and records a company's cash, that person can easily pocket some of the receipts and fail to record them. The specific features of internal accounting controls over cash vary from company to company. Generally, however, these controls are designed to ensure that

1. Responsibilities are divided between those employees who account for cash and those who have custody of it.
2. All cash receipts are recorded when received and deposited immediately and intact in the bank.
3. All disbursements are made for authorized purposes.
4. All disbursements, except for small ones made from petty cash, are made by check.

---

[3]*AICPA Professional Standards—Volume 1* (Chicago: Commerce Clearing House), AU Sec. 320.09.
[4]*AICPA Professional Standards—Volume 1,* AU Sec. 320.10.

Specific accounting controls for cash are usually covered in more depth in auditing courses. Two important control measures designed to help safeguard a company's cash—the maintenance of a petty cash fund and the periodic reconciliation of the bank statement—are discussed below.

PETTY CASH

A business should generally make all payments by check. But most businesses find it inconvenient or impossible to write checks for such small items as taxi fares, newspaper delivery charges, postage, express charges, and minor supplies. A company usually pays for these kinds of items from a **petty cash fund,** often called an **imprest cash fund.** An imprest fund is established for a fixed amount and allows a company to effectively control small amounts of cash fairly simply.

The following discussion explains how a petty cash fund works.

1. A responsible employee is appointed **petty cashier.** A check drawn payable to petty cash is cashed, and the petty cashier places the money in the petty cash fund (which is often kept in a locked box). The check which establishes the fund is usually for an amount ($300, for example) that the company estimates will last from two to four weeks. The following journal entry is required:

Petty Cash	300	
Cash		300

2. As time passes, the petty cashier disburses money from the fund. To evidence each disbursement, the petty cashier places in the fund a prenumbered receipt, signed by the person who received cash. The amount of petty cash on hand and the amounts shown on the signed receipts should always equal the original amount of the fund ($300 in our example). The company does *not* make journal entries when petty cash is disbursed.

3. When the amount of cash in the fund is low, the petty cashier submits the signed receipts and requests reimbursement from the general cashier for an amount that will increase the cash in the fund to the original amount. At this time, the receipts are canceled so that no one can use them again. In addition, the company records increases in those expenses (or other accounts) that are documented by the receipts.

Now assume that after three weeks only $25 remain in the petty cash fund. The signed receipts show the following petty cash disbursements:

Postage	$ 45
Office supplies	102
Transportation-in	125
Total	$272

Because the fund contains only $25, the general cashier must write a check for $275 ($300 − $25) to restore the fund to its original amount ($300). After the check is written, the company makes the following journal entry:

Postage Expense	45	
Office Supplies Expense	102	
Transportation-In	125	
Cash Short and Over	3	
Cash		275

The check is then cashed and the money is placed in the petty cash fund.

Cash Short and Over is a nominal account that is debited for cash shortages and credited for overages. Such shortages and overages usually result from errors in making change or failure to obtain receipts for very small amounts. A debit balance in the Cash Short and Over account at the end of a period should be reported as a miscellaneous expense and a credit balance as a miscellaneous revenue. However, a material cash shortage resulting from a cause such as theft should be charged to a receivable account if the company expects to recover the amount of the shortage. If recovery is not expected, the company should charge a loss account.

Materiality

Observe that the company debited the Petty Cash account when the fund was established and made no other entries in this account. At the end of an accounting period, therefore, the petty cash fund should ordinarily be replenished. This ensures that all expenses paid with petty cash are recorded and that the petty cash on hand corresponds with the amount shown in the Petty Cash account. If for some reason the fund is not replenished at the end of an accounting period, the company should still debit the appropriate expense accounts, but it should credit the Petty Cash account directly. Over time the pattern of petty cash disbursements may suggest that the original amount of the petty cash fund is either too low or too high. If this occurs, the amount of petty cash and the balance shown in the Petty Cash account should be increased or decreased as appropriate. For example, if the company in the above example increases the fixed amount of the petty cash fund from $300 to $400, the following journal entry would be made:

Petty Cash	100	
Cash		100

CASH IN BANK

The cash that a business has on hand may include petty cash funds, change funds (funds used to make change with customers), and undeposited receipts. As stated earlier, a business normally keeps most of its cash in one or more checking accounts. The checking account gives a company a **double record** of its cash transactions, the company's own record plus that provided by the bank. The bank's record is summarized on a monthly **bank statement.**

An accountant verifies the cash on hand simply by counting it. In contrast, because the cash in a checking account cannot be conveniently counted, accountants verify it by preparing a bank reconciliation.

Bank Reconciliation

When a company receives a bank statement, the company's accountant should immediately prepare a **bank reconciliation.** This schedule explains any differences between a company's book balance of cash and the bank statement balance. A bank reconciliation helps to identify errors made by the depositor or by the bank in recording cash transactions. It also helps in making journal entries to update the depositor's accounting records.

On a depositor's books (accounting records), the cash balance in a bank account is an asset. On the bank's books, the cash in the depositor's account is a liability. Because the depositor and the bank do not simultaneously record all transactions, and because either party can make mistakes, the asset balance on the depositor's books usually does not equal the liability balance on the bank statement. Many factors may explain why the two balances differ:

1. **Deposits in transit.**   These are additions to cash in the bank that the depositor has recorded but do not appear on the bank statement. For example, on the last day

of the month, the depositor may place the day's cash receipts in the bank's night depository, to be recorded by the bank on the next business day. These receipts should appear on the next month's bank statement.

2. **Outstanding checks.** Checks that the depositor has issued and recorded but that have not yet cleared the bank will not yet be deducted on the bank statement.

3. **Bank collections.** Promissory notes are often made payable at the payee's bank. The bank may therefore collect a note for the depositor and credit the proceeds to the depositor's account. Such collections made near the end of a month may appear on the bank statement but not yet appear on the depositor's books because the depositor is not yet aware of the collection.

4. **Bank charges.** The bank often makes various charges that are not yet recorded on the depositor's books, such as charges for bank services, checkbooks, NSF checks, and repayment of depositor loans.

5. **Bank errors.** Occasionally, a bank error might affect the depositor's account. For example, the bank might erroneously charge one company's check to another company's account. The depositor should instruct the bank to correct such errors.

6. **Depositor errors.** Sometimes an error is made in the depositor's accounting records (commonly called a **book error**). For example, the depositor may have written a check for one amount but recorded the check at a different amount. The depositor should promptly correct the accounting records.

An accountant may prepare a bank reconciliation by reconciling from the bank statement balance to the book balance, or vice versa. Accountants prefer, however, to reconcile from both of these balances to the **correct cash balance**. Such a reconciliation is relatively easy to understand, it shows in one place the information needed for making journal entries, and it indicates the correct cash balance that a company can spend from its checking account (the balance after all errors are corrected and all outstanding items clear the bank). A convenient form for this type of bank reconciliation is shown in Exhibit 7–1.

Observe that the bank reconciliation is divided into two sections: "balance per bank statement" and "balance per books." The logic of the additions and deductions in each section is not difficult to understand. Both sections end with the same "correct cash balance." This is the amount of cash that the depositor can spend from the checking account and the amount that should appear on the depositor's balance sheet.

Usually, the depositor must make journal entries after the reconciliation is completed to update the depositor's accounting records. These entries are based on the items added or deducted in the "balance per books" section. Additions and deductions in the other section either have already been recorded by the depositor or represent errors that the bank must correct.

To illustrate, assume that Todd Company keeps all of its cash in a checking account. An examination of the company's accounting records and its bank statement for the month ended May 31, 1993, revealed the following information:

1. The cash balance shown as of May 31 on the bank statement was $17,631.
2. The cash balance shown as of May 31 on the company's books was $15,214.
3. A deposit of $1,500 mailed to the bank on May 31 did not appear on the bank statement.
4. On May 30 the bank collected a note receivable for Todd Company and credited the proceeds of $2,100 to the company's account. The proceeds included $100 of interest, all of which the company earned during 1993. Todd Company has not yet recorded the collection.

EXHIBIT 7–1

Bank Reconciliation Form

Balance per bank statement		$XXX
Add: Deposits in transit	$XX	
Bank errors that understate the balance per bank statement		
(e.g., the bank charges someone else's check to the		
depositor's account)	XX	XX
		XXX
Deduct: Outstanding checks	XX	
Bank errors that overstate the balance per bank statement		
(e.g., the bank charges one of the depositor's checks to		
someone else's account)	XX	XX
Correct cash balance		$XXX
Balance per books		$XXX
Add: Deposits credited by the bank but not yet recorded by the		
depositor (e.g., collection of a promissory note)	$XX	
Book errors that understate the balance per books (e.g.,		
the depositor writes a check for $10 but deducts $100		
on the books)	XX	XX
		XXX
Deduct: Bank charges not yet recorded by the depositor (e.g., bank		
service charges and NSF checks)	XX	
Book errors that overstate the balance per books (e.g., the		
depositor writes a check for $100 but deducts $10 on the		
books)	XX	XX
Correct cash balance		$XXX

5. Outstanding checks as of May 31 were as follows:

No. 902	$ 132
No. 922	870
No. 923	1,645

6. The company discovered that check no. 916, written in May for $527 in payment of an account payable, had been incorrectly recorded as $257.
7. The bank returned a check for $548 that the company deposited on May 29. The check was drawn by a customer who did not have sufficient funds in his bank account to cover the check.
8. The bank statement showed a $12 service charge for May.

    The bank reconciliation for Todd Company is shown in Exhibit 7–2. As stated earlier, the journal entries to update the depositor's accounting records should be based on the items added or deducted in the "balance per books" section.

Cash	2,100	
Notes Receivable		2,000
Interest Revenue		100
(To record collection of note and interest by bank.)		

EXHIBIT 7-2

Todd Company
BANK RECONCILIATION
May 31, 1993

Balance per bank statement		$17,631
Add: Deposit in transit		1,500
		19,131
Deduct: Outstanding checks		
No. 902	$ 132	
No. 922	870	
No. 923	1,645	2,647
Correct cash balance		$16,484
Balance per books		$15,214
Add: Note and interest collected by bank		2,100
		17,314
Deduct: Bank service charge	$ 12	
NSF check received from customer	548	
Error made in recording check no. 916 ($527 − $257)	270	830
Correct cash balance		$16,484

Miscellaneous Expense	12	
Cash		12
(To record bank service charge.)		
Accounts Receivable	548	
Cash		548
(To record NSF check.)		
Accounts Payable	270	
Cash		270
(To correct error made in recording check no. 916.)		

The entries shown above may be combined into a single compound entry. When the entries are posted, Todd Company's cash account will show a balance of $16,484, the correct amount as shown on the bank reconciliation.

An accountant should reconcile the monthly bank statement for each checking account that a company maintains. If a company has more than one checking account, the amount of cash to report on a balance sheet will be the sum of the correct cash balances shown on the bank reconciliations and any cash that the depositor has on hand.

Proof of Cash

Auditors frequently prepare an expanded version of the bank reconciliation known as a **four-column bank reconciliation**, or simply a **proof of cash**. A proof of cash includes four reconciliations:

1. A reconciliation of the bank statement and book balances of cash at the end of the *previous month*.
2. A reconciliation of the cash receipts (deposits) shown on the bank statement with those shown on the books for the *current month*.

3. A reconciliation of the cash payments shown on the bank statement with those shown on the books for the *current month*.

4. A reconciliation of the bank statement and book balances of cash at the end of the *current month*.

The proof of cash is a stronger control measure than the single-column bank reconciliation. Auditors frequently prepare a proof of cash when a company is found to have weak internal control over cash. Because it provides a reconciliation of cash transactions as well as cash balances, the proof of cash makes it easier to pinpoint errors made by the company or the bank. This feature is particularly important when a company has made cash transfers from one bank account to another during the month. If a transfer is shown as a payment from one account but is not shown as a receipt by the other, an accountant or auditor would want to know why. We illustrate how to prepare a proof of cash in the Appendix to this chapter.

RECEIVABLES

Receivables are claims held against others for money, goods, or services. They generally result in an inflow of cash. An enterprise should classify a receivable as a *current asset* only if collection of the receivable is expected within the next year or operating cycle, whichever is longer. Other receivables should be reported in the investments and funds category or in other assets, as we discuss and illustrate in Chapter 10.

Because of the operating cycle concept, current assets include "installment or deferred accounts and notes receivable if they conform generally to normal trade practices and terms within the business."[5] These receivables are often collectible over periods that are longer than one year after the balance sheet date. Accounting for installment receivables is discussed in Chapter 20.

Proper accounting for a receivable requires an assessment of the **amount, timing,** and **uncertainty** associated with its collection. In theory, an accountant should

Asset/Liability Measurement

initially value (measure) a receivable at an amount equal to the present value of the cash that the enterprise expects to collect. Such a valuation reflects the time value of money; an enterprise earns **interest** by waiting to collect money. The amount of interest is the difference between a receivable's maturity value and its present value. In practice, accountants often ignore interest for short-term receivables, because they

Materiality

regard the amount as immaterial.

Receivables may be classified as **trade receivables** or **nontrade receivables,** which are generally reported separately on the balance sheet. **Trade receivables** result from sales of goods or services to customers. They usually compose most of the total dollar value of a company's receivables. All other receivables are **nontrade.** Examples of nontrade receivables are:

1. Receivables from officers or employees.

2. Advances to subsidiaries.

3. Various types of deposits made with other parties.

4. Claims against insurance companies.

5. Receivables from stock subscriptions.

6. Dividends receivable (from other companies).

7. Interest receivable.

---

[5]*Accounting Research Bulletin No. 43,* "Restatement and Revision of Accounting Research Bulletins," 1953, Ch. 3, Sec. A, par. 4.

DESKTOP FORGERY

PAUL SJIEM-FAT, a Netherlands Antilles national living in Boston's North Station neighborhood, claimed on a Bank of Boston credit card application to be an employee of the Dutch consulate. After he defrauded the bank of about $20,000, the bank discovered that his employment claim was a lie, and, since it involved impersonation of a diplomat, the Secret Service was called in, a search warrant was issued and Sjiem-Fat's apartment was raided.

Investigating this seemingly routine case, the Secret Service stumbled upon its first-ever case of computer forgery. It is certainly not going to be the last. While crooks are only just beginning to learn the game, the possibilities are nearly endless: letters of credit, job recommendations, property records, insurance claims, expense account receipts, college transcripts, business licenses. In short, many of the paper credentials on which society relies are henceforward suspect.

What made this Boston case especially alarming was that Sjiem-Fat used no sophisticated equipment. In his apartment police found a personal computer, a laser printer and nine bogus checks totaling $146,500. In a highly original—and perhaps pioneering—way, Sjiem-Fat was using ordinary desktop publishing tools as instruments of crime.

Here is what he apparently did. With the sort of desktop publishing equipment you can buy at any computer retailer, Sjiem-Fat convincingly forged Digital Equipment Corp. letterheads with a phony name, Paul Marques, and a phony vice president title. He also created phony cashier's checks from banks like First American and Chase Manhattan. Stewart Henry, an investigator with the U.S. Secret Service, explains: "He used the official emblems from three different banks and transferred them onto blank check paper with a laser printer. This was the first time we had ever seen anything like this."

According to investigators, Sjiem-Fat used bogus checks to buy computers from various Boston suppliers. After taking delivery of the computers, he sold them for cash to buyers in the Caribbean area.

An isolated case? Not necessarily. Just last month a rash of computer-generated fake checks hit the Phoenix area. "These look like they were done by putting corporate logos onto check paper with a desktop publishing system," says Gail Thackery, an assistant attorney general for Arizona.

Coupled to a good printer and the right software, the personal computer is a powerful publishing device. It can create and store logos as well as type in all sizes and styles. With a scanner, it can read in a document, then modify and reprint it. It is, above all, quite accessible to the amateur. Now you can produce professional-looking brochures and blank business forms without hiring a master printer. You can also, if your taste runs that way, run off a bogus check or two.

The existence of all these potential counterfeiting tools is scary enough, but an unrelated development threatens to turn the situation into a disaster for the banking industry. This other problem is a federal statute compelling banks to give their customers quick access to funds from deposited checks.

The quick-access rule was heralded as a victory for consumers. But it was an even bigger victory for con artists. Why? Today's forger can make crisp and convincing business checks, deposit them into an account opened previously under a fake name, demand cash after waiting as little as three days, and be out of town long before the forgeries are discovered. If the forger has chosen as target a corporation with a large balance and a lot of check volume, it's next to impossible for either the bank or the corporation to detect the scheme without doing a monthly statement reconciliation. And that reconciliation can't possibly take place within three days of when a bogus check is deposited.

In the past, a forger had to have access to professional printing equipment and presses. He either owned a print shop, bribed someone who worked at one, or made do with whatever materials he could copy by hand. The risk of detection was high. Not any longer. The boom in desktop publishing has brought a flood of typesetting products to market, at declining prices and increasing capabilities.

"The market for this equipment has gone wild in the last year," says James Cavuoto, a Torrance, Calif. desktop publishing expert. "It's only a matter of time before the crooks catch on to the opportunity." They clearly already have.

SOURCE: David Churbuck, "Desktop Forgery," *Forbes*, November 27, 1989, pp. 246–253. Excerpted by permission of *Forbes* magazine, November 27, 1989. © Forbes Inc., 1989.

A receivable may be represented by an open account (a nonwritten promise to pay) or by a note (a written promise to pay). Thus, **accounts receivable** and **notes receivable** are reported separately on the balance sheet. They are discussed below.

ACCOUNTS RECEIVABLE

In a broad sense, the term "accounts receivable" includes all receivables not evidenced by written promises to pay. But accountants usually restrict the term to open accounts that have resulted from selling goods or services on credit. Because accounts receivable are very important assets to many companies, they must be managed effectively. Such management involves a trade-off between the revenues generated by credit sales and the costs associated with carrying the resulting accounts receivable.

Asset/Liability Measurement

Materiality

Generally accepted accounting principles (GAAP) require companies to report accounts receivable at **net realizable value.** This is the amount that the company expects to collect, and it equals the face amount of the receivables less an estimated uncollectible amount. Because of materiality, accountants generally ignore the interest inherent in the face amount of accounts receivable.

Recording Credit Sales

Revenue Realization

Recording accounts receivable is closely related to the revenue realization principle (discussed in Chapter 2). That is, a seller should record a receivable that arises from a sale of goods on the date that the sale occurs. This is also when the seller recognizes revenue. Under most circumstances the sales revenue and the related receivable should be recorded at the precise moment that title passes from the seller to the buyer. For practical reasons, however, accounts receivable and related sales revenue are usually recorded when the seller ships the goods.

Trade Discounts.   A trade discount is an amount that a seller deducts from a list price to determine the invoice price of goods sold. List prices are quoted in the seller's catalogs or price lists, while trade discounts usually appear in a separate schedule. A trade discount, then, is merely a convenient device that manufacturers and wholesalers often use to price their goods. The use of trade discounts enables a company to revise its prices periodically without having to reprint its catalogs and to set different prices for different types of customers and for different quantities sold.

Neither sellers nor purchasers should record trade discounts in their accounts. To illustrate, assume that All Star Wholesalers sells 100 footballs to Retail Sports, Inc., for the list price of $30 each, less a trade discount of 40%. The invoice price is therefore $18 ($30 − $12) per football and the total invoice price is $1,800 ($18 × 100). Here is how All Star Wholesalers should record the transaction:

Accounts Receivable	1,800	
Sales		1,800

Many sellers express trade discounts in a series such as 40/20/10. The use of multiple trade discounts allows the seller to conveniently vary the selling price based on such factors as the type of customer or the quantity purchased. If the terms are 40/20/10, a customer may receive a trade discount of (1) 40%; (2) 40% and 20%; *or* (3) 40%, 20%, and 10% depending on the circumstances. Suppose, for example, that MCA, Inc., sells Model 21 television sets for the list price of $100 each, less the following discounts:

EXHIBIT 7–3

Trade Discount

Customer	Quantity Purchased	Applicable Trade Discount	Invoice Price Per Unit	Total Invoice Price
Aim	30	40%	$100 − ($100 × 40%) = $60	$60 × 30 units = $1,800
Bar	60	40% and 20%	$100 − ($100 × 40%) = $60 $60 − ($60 × 20%) = $48	$48 × 60 units = $2,880
Cam	200	40%, 20%, and 10%	$100 − ($100 × 40%) = $60 $60 − ($60 × 20%) = $48 $48 − ($48 × 10%) = $43.20	$43.20 × 200 units = $8,640

40%	If 50 or fewer sets are purchased.
40% and 20%	If more than 50 but fewer than 100 sets are purchased.
40%, 20%, and 10%	If 100 or more sets are purchased.

Assuming that customers Aim, Bar, and Cam purchase 30, 60, and 200 television sets, respectively, Exhibit 7–3 shows how MCA, Inc., would determine the invoice price for each customer.

Cash Discounts.   Companies frequently offer cash discounts to their credit customers. A **cash discount** is a reduction from an invoice price that is offered to buyers to encourage prompt payment. Companies use trade discounts to *establish* an invoice price and cash discounts to *reduce* the invoice price. From the seller's point of view, a cash discount is called a **sales discount**; from the purchaser's point of view, a cash discount is called a **purchase discount**. A cash discount is usually expressed in terms such as 2/10, n/30; or 2/10, EOM (end of month). Terms of 2/10, n/30 mean that the buyer may deduct 2% from the invoice price if payment is made within 10 days after the invoice date. A buyer who does not pay within the 10-day discount period must pay the gross invoice amount within 30 days after the invoice date.

Purchasers generally take cash discounts offered to them because it is usually advantageous to do so. Suppose, for example, that Sim Company sells goods to Burt Company for an invoice price of $1,000, terms 2/10, n/30. Burt Company can liquidate its debt by paying $980 within 10 days after the invoice date. In effect, $980 is the **cash price** of the goods. Instead of paying the $980 by the tenth day, Burt Company may choose to pay a $20 premium in order to keep the $980 for an additional 20 days (30 days − 10 days). This choice will result in an interest rate of 2.04% ($20 ÷ 980) for 20 days. This is equivalent to an effective *annual* rate of 36.7% (2.04% × 360/20). Clearly, most companies try to avoid such a high interest cost.

In theory, an account receivable and the related sales revenue should be measured net of any cash discounts allowable. This is consistent with the **net method** of recording credit sales. In Exhibit 7–4, we compare the net method with the **gross method** of recording credit sales. The net method correctly states the receivable at its realizable value on the date of sale, and correctly states the amount of revenue earned on that date. Under the net method, we record the receivable and the related revenue at an amount that equals the **cash equivalent price** on the date of sale. Remember that sellers offer cash discounts to encourage buyers to pay promptly. A buyer who fails to

EXHIBIT 7–4

Net and Gross Methods of Recording Credit Sales

Transaction	Net Method		Gross Method	
July 1				
Jam Company sells merchandise for $100, terms 2/10, n/30.	Accounts Receivable 98		Accounts Receivable 100	
	Sales	98	Sales	100
Alternative Assumption No. 1				
July 10				
Jam Company receives payment that buyer made within the discount period.	Cash 98		Cash 98	
	Accounts Receivable	98	Sales Discounts 2	
			Accounts Receivable	100
Alternative Assumption No. 2				
July 30				
Jam Company receives payment that buyer made after the discount period.	Cash 100		Cash 100	
	Accounts Receivable	98	Accounts Receivable	100
	Sales Discounts Not Taken	2		

take a cash discount has in effect decided to engage in a deferred payment transaction. The buyer therefore incurs an interest cost, and the seller earns interest revenue. The interest that the seller earns is reflected in the Sales Discounts Not Taken account. The seller should report the balance in this account on the income statement as financial revenue.

Most companies record credit sales at gross amounts by using the gross method. When the seller later receives the buyer's payment, the seller records any cash discounts taken in a Sales Discounts account. The seller later deducts the balance in this account from sales to arrive at net sales. Although the gross method tends to result in an overstatement of accounts receivable and sales revenue, it is practical and convenient, and it enables a company to make a year-end adjusting entry to estimate sales discounts and thereby eliminate material errors from financial statements.

Accounting for Uncollectible Accounts

Companies sell on credit, rather than only for cash, to increase total sales and thereby increase profits. But a company that sells on credit assumes the risk that some customers will not pay their accounts. When an account becomes uncollectible, the company has sustained a **bad-debt loss.** These losses are simply one of the costs of doing business on credit. Accounting for bad-debt losses would be fairly easy if they occurred in the same period as the sale. In reality, bad-debt losses often occur in subsequent periods.

One method of accounting for uncollectible accounts, called the **direct write-off method,** involves debiting Bad Debts Expense and crediting Accounts Receivable in the period in which the company finally determines that the accounts are uncollectible.[6] This method is based on actual rather than estimated bad-debt losses. How-

---

[6]An entry debiting Accounts Receivable and crediting Bad Debts Expense would be made if an account that had been written off was later recovered in the *same* accounting period. If a recovery occurred in a *subsequent* accounting period, Accounts Receivable would be debited and Bad Debts Recovered (a revenue account) would be credited. An entry debiting Cash and crediting Accounts Receivable would be made to record the collection.

Matching ever, the direct write-off method usually violates the matching principle. The reason is that the bad-debts expense is often recognized in a later accounting period than the one in which the related sales revenue was recognized. The result is a mismatching of sales revenue and bad-debts expense. In addition, the direct write-off method leads to the reporting of accounts receivable at an amount greater than their net realizable **Asset/Liability** value (i.e., at an amount greater than the company expects to collect), which violates **Measurement** the asset/liability measurement principle.

Materiality Use of the direct write-off method may be appropriate if a company's bad-debt losses are immaterial or if a company is unable to reasonably estimate its losses from uncollectible receivables.[7] Generally, however, the inability to estimate bad-debt losses suggests that collectibility is so uncertain that the company should defer the recognition of revenue beyond the time of sale. As we explain in Chapter 20, if a company makes a credit sale to a customer who is a relatively poor credit risk, recognition of revenue should occur after the time of sale, and either the installment sales method or the cost recovery method of accounting may be used. Most companies, however, make credit sales only to customers that have a reasonable credit standing, and accordingly, the general rule in accounting is to recognize revenue at the time of sale. Because bad-debt losses usually are material, and because most companies can reasonably estimate their bad-debt losses, based on their own collection experience or that of other similar companies, use of the direct write-off method is discouraged.

Companies that can estimate their uncollectibles use the **allowance method** to account for them.[8] Under this method, a company estimates the total amount of its uncollectible accounts at the end of every accounting period. As we discuss later in the chapter, this estimate may be based on credit sales or on accounts receivable. The company records the estimate in a year-end **adjusting entry** similar to the one shown below (the $5,200 amount is assumed):

Bad Debts Expense	5,200	
Allowance for Doubtful Accounts		5,200

The balance in Bad Debts Expense usually appears as an operating expense on the income statement where the expense is matched with sales revenue.[9] The Allowance for Doubtful Accounts (also called the Allowance for Uncollectible Accounts and the Allowance for Bad Debts) is a contra account to Accounts Receivable. The allowance is therefore deducted from Accounts Receivable on the balance sheet to estimate the net realizable value of the receivables. The use of an allowance account relieves a company of the necessity of crediting individual customer accounts each time it estimates bad debts. Obviously, when a company estimates bad debts and makes an adjusting entry, it does not yet know which accounts will become uncollectible.

The allowance method tends to overcome the matching and asset valuation problems inherent in the direct write-off method. That is why accountants prefer the allowance method, even though it is based on estimated figures.

---

[7] *FASB Statement of Financial Accounting Standards No. 5*, "Accounting for Contingencies," 1975, par. 23.
[8] For income tax purposes, most companies must use the direct write-off method for tax years beginning after 1986.
[9] Because uncollectibles are *expected* when a company makes credit sales, a strong argument can be made that uncollectibles should not be included in revenue. Therefore, the estimated amount of a company's bad debts should be treated as a revenue offset (similar to Sales Returns) rather than an expense. Following this approach, a company should debit Sales—Uncollectibles instead of Bad Debts Expense when it estimates bad debts. The balance in Sales—Uncollectibles would later appear as a deduction from sales on the income statement.
In practice, companies usually debit Bad Debts Expense. The rationale is that even if a receivable proves uncollectible, it existed on the date of sale and revenue was generated for the full amount of the sale.

EXHIBIT 7–5

Downes Company
Facts to Illustrate Allowance Method

Credit sales made during 1993	$210,000
Accounts receivable, 12/31/93	50,000
Allowance for doubtful accounts, 12/31/93,	
before adjustment	400 (credit balance)

Accountants usually consult with a company's credit department personnel to estimate the amount of bad debts. As indicated earlier, the company's collection experience and that of similar companies are usually the most important factors in determining the estimate. These factors should be evaluated in the context of current and projected circumstances that may affect the company's future collection experience. Assessing the collectibility of accounts receivable is a challenging task, particularly in the difficult economic climate that many companies have faced in recent years. When estimating bad debts under the allowance method, accountants may use either an income statement approach or a balance sheet approach.

Income Statement Approach.   Under this approach to the allowance method, an accountant first determines the average percentage relationship between a company's *credit sales* and its actual bad-debt losses. This percentage is then multiplied by credit sales for the current year to estimate bad-debts expense.

The income statement approach is so called because it emphasizes the Bad Debts Expense account rather than the Allowance for Doubtful Accounts. With the income statement approach, credit sales (an income statement number) is multiplied by a percentage to estimate the amount of bad-debts expense (another income statement number) as accurately as possible. This approach emphasizes the matching principle because the bad-debts estimate is based directly on the related sales revenue. Exhibit 7–5 presents facts to illustrate two approaches to the allowance method for Downes Company, an enterprise that uses a calendar-year accounting period.

Matching

To illustrate the income statement approach, let us further assume that in previous years, actual bad-debt losses each year have averaged 1% of credit sales and that the company expects this percentage to continue in the future. Here is the adjusting entry that the company should make on December 31, 1993:

Bad Debts Expense	2,100	
Allowance for Doubtful Accounts		2,100
($210,000 × .01 = $2,100)		

Observe that we made the above entry *without considering* the previous balance ($400 credit) in the Allowance for Doubtful Accounts. The reason is that under the income statement approach, we focus on Bad Debts Expense, not on the Allowance account. After the above entry is posted, Bad Debts Expense will have a balance of $2,100, and the balance in the Allowance account will be $2,500 ($400 + $2,100).

In another variation of the income statement approach, bad-debts expense is based on a percentage of total sales (cash and credit) rather than only credit sales. The use of a percentage based on credit sales is logical, because bad debts arise only from credit sales. Nevertheless, the use of total sales is acceptable since it would produce reasonable results if a company's mix of cash and credit sales is fairly stable over time.

Asset/Liability Measurement

Balance Sheet Approach.   The primary objective of this approach to the allowance method is to report accounts receivable on the balance sheet at net realizable value (and so the name *balance sheet* approach). To accomplish this objective, the balance sheet approach focuses on establishing a **desired balance** in the Allowance for Doubtful Accounts. The desired balance equals the estimated amount of uncollectible accounts receivable. This is the amount that, when subtracted from Accounts Receivable, will reduce the receivables to their net realizable value. Reporting accounts receivable at their net realizable value is consistent with the asset/liability measurement principle.

1. Percentage of Accounts Receivable.   A simple way to implement the balance sheet approach is to multiply the year-end Accounts Receivable balance by a percentage that the company estimates from experience will be uncollectible. The product is the desired balance in the Allowance account. The adjusting entry to estimate bad debts is then recorded for the amount that is necessary to produce the desired balance.

To illustrate, return to Exhibit 7–5. Assume that instead of using the income statement approach, Downes Company elects to use the balance sheet approach and that it estimates that approximately 4% of the accounts receivable balance on December 31, 1993, will be uncollectible. The company should make the following adjusting entry on December 31, 1993:

Bad Debts Expense	1,600	
Allowance for Doubtful Accounts		1,600

Notice carefully that the above entry reflects the amount necessary to produce the desired balance in the Allowance account. The computation is shown below:

Desired balance in Allowance account ($50,000 × .04)	$2,000
Less: Credit balance in Allowance account before adjustment	400
Amount of adjusting entry	$1,600

After the above entry is posted, Bad Debts Expense will have a balance of $1,600; the balance in the Allowance account will be $2,000 ($400 + $1,600).

The Allowance account sometimes has a *debit* balance before adjustment. As we illustrate later in the chapter, a company writes off uncollectible accounts by debiting the Allowance account and crediting Accounts Receivable. A debit balance in the Allowance account therefore occurs when a company has written off a greater amount of accounts receivable than it had previously estimated as uncollectible. A debit balance in the Allowance account before adjustment would simply be *added* to the desired balance in order to determine the amount of the adjusting entry. For example, if Downes Company had a $400 *debit* balance (instead of a $400 *credit* balance) in its Allowance account before adjustment, the company would make the adjusting entry on December 31, 1993, for $2,400 ($2,000 + $400).

2. Aging of Accounts Receivable.   A more accurate way to implement the balance sheet approach is to determine the desired balance in the Allowance account by aging the accounts receivable. Here the accountant groups a company's individual accounts receivable into categories based on how long they have been outstanding. This schedule is called an **aging of accounts receivable.** Next, the total in each category is multiplied by an estimated uncollectible percentage. The accountant then adds the products to derive a total amount that is estimated to be uncollectible. Because this is the desired total in the Allowance account, the adjusting entry to estimate bad debts should be recorded for the amount necessary to produce the desired balance.

EXHIBIT 7-6

Downes Company
AGING OF ACCOUNTS RECEIVABLE
December 31, 1993

| Customer | Accounts Receivable Balance 12/31/93 | Time Outstanding | | | | |
		Under 30 Days	30–60 Days	61–120 Days	121–180 Days	Over 180 Days
Adams Company	$ 1,200	$ 900	$ 300			
Blunt & Company	600			$ 600		
Carver Enterprises	750	600	150			
Dandridge, Inc.	350					$ 350
Zimmerman Company	500				$500	
Total	$50,000	$39,300	$5,600	$3,400	$600	$1,100

The percentages above are based on a company's collection experience and on the advice of its credit department personnel. Higher percentages are usually associated with the higher-age categories because, generally, the longer that an account has been outstanding, the less likely it is to be collected.

To illustrate, refer again to Exhibit 7–5. Assume that Downes Company now elects to estimate its bad debts using the aging form of the balance sheet approach and that it prepares the information shown in Exhibits 7–6 and 7–7. The company should make the following adjusting entry on December 31, 1993:

Bad Debts Expense	1,969	
Allowance for Doubtful Accounts		1,969

Note once again that the above entry is for the amount necessary to produce the desired balance in the allowance account. The computation is shown below:

Desired balance in Allowance account (total estimated amount uncollectible shown in Exhibit 7–7)	$2,369
Less: Credit balance in Allowance account before adjustment	400
Amount of adjusting entry	$1,969

After the above entry is posted, Bad Debts Expense will have a balance of $1,969, and the Allowance balance will be $2,369 ($400 + $1,969). If the Allowance account had a $400 *debit* balance (instead of a $400 *credit* balance) before adjustment, the adjusting entry would have been for $2,769 ($400 + $2,369).

Summary and Evaluation of Approaches.   There are two basic approaches to the allowance method of accounting for uncollectible accounts. Each has two forms or variations:

1. Income statement approach
   a.   Percentage of credit sales
   b.   Percentage of total sales

EXHIBIT 7-7

Downes Company
ESTIMATED AMOUNT UNCOLLECTIBLE BASED ON AGING ANALYSIS
December 31, 1993

Time Outstanding	Amount	Estimated Percentage Uncollectible	Estimated Amount Uncollectible
Under 30 days	$39,300	1%	$ 393
30–60 days	5,600	6%	336
61–120 days	3,400	25%	850
121–180 days	600	40%	240
Over 180 days	1,100	50%	550
Total	$50,000		$2,369

2. Balance sheet approach
   a. Percentage of accounts receivable
   b. Aging of accounts receivable

Matching

Asset/Liability
Measurement

A company may use any form of the allowance method to estimate its bad debts because all are acceptable under GAAP. The income statement approach emphasizes the matching principle, while the balance sheet approach emphasizes the reporting of accounts receivable at their net realizable value. Notice that both approaches demonstrate that financial statements **articulate** with one another. Under the income statement approach, what we do to benefit the income statement directly affects the balance sheet; under the balance sheet approach, what we do to benefit the balance sheet directly affects the income statement.

Remember that all variations of the allowance method are based on **estimates.** A company's actual bad-debt losses will therefore equal its estimates only by chance. Under the income statement approach, the percentage of credit sales usually produces the most accurate results, because bad-debt losses relate only to credit sales. Under the balance sheet approach, an aging of accounts receivable generally produces the most accurate results. In practice, many companies estimate their uncollectible accounts using one approach and then apply another approach to determine if a reasonable result is being obtained. For example, a company might use the percentage of credit sales approach and determine that a bad-debts adjusting entry for $12,000 is necessary. To check the reasonableness of the $12,000 amount, the company might age the accounts receivable and determine that an adjusting entry for only $10,000 is necessary. As a result of applying these two approaches concurrently, the company might finally decide to make the adjusting entry for $11,000.

Over time, a company may determine that its estimates of bad debts were too high or too low, and the company's Allowance balance before year-end adjustment thus contains an excessive credit or debit balance. When this occurs, the company should change the percentage that it uses to estimate bad debts. Such a change is an example of a **change in an accounting estimate,** and as we discussed briefly in Chapter 4 and will discuss in more depth in Chapter 19, the change should be accounted for in current and future periods. In other words, the company should begin using a revised percentage to estimate its bad debts, but should not make a prior period adjustment.

Writing Off Uncollectible Accounts. When all reasonable attempts to collect an account have failed, a company's credit manager should authorize the accounting department to write off the account as uncollectible. Assume that the following balances were taken from the accounting records of Ace Enterprises:

Accounts receivable	$100,000	(Debit)
Allowance for doubtful accounts	1,700	(Credit)

If the company's credit manager decides that an account of $500 from W. Grant is uncollectible, the following entry should be made:

Allowance for Doubtful Accounts	500	
Accounts Receivable		500

The accountant would post the above entry to the appropriate general and subsidiary ledger accounts. After posting, the Accounts Receivable balance will be $99,500 ($100,000 − $500), and the Allowance balance will be $1,200 ($1,700 − $500). Notice that although the write-off reduces Accounts Receivable and the Allowance account, it has no effect on the net realizable value of the receivables. Before the write-off, the net realizable value was $98,300 ($100,000 − $1,700); after the write-off, it is still $98,300 ($99,500 − $1,200).

Collection of Accounts Written Off.   Occasionally, a company collects all or part of an account that it wrote off as uncollectible. When this occurs, the company should first reverse, to the extent of the recovery, the entry that it made to write off the account. Then the company should record the collection in the usual manner. To illustrate, refer to the information presented in the previous section for Ace Enterprises and assume that Ace later collects the account of $500 from W. Grant. Ace should record the following entries:

Accounts Receivable	500	
Allowance for Doubtful Accounts		500
(To reinstate W. Grant's account.)		
Cash	500	
Accounts Receivable		500
(To record the collection.)		

Notice that there are two entries rather than only a single entry debiting Cash and crediting the Allowance account. Making two entries is preferable since this permits Ace Enterprises to accumulate in its accounts receivable subsidiary ledger a complete record of its credit experience with W. Grant.

Other Applications of the Allowance Method

Matching Asset/Liability Measurement

Our discussion of the allowance method has thus far been confined to its use in accounting for uncollectible accounts. We have seen that through the use of estimates, the allowance method enables a company to better match expenses and revenues and to report receivables at their net realizable value. The same logic applies to the use of the allowance method in accounting for other items that affect the cash realization of accounts receivable. For example, a company may use the allowance method to account for:

1. Sales discounts that customers will probably take (assuming that the company records accounts receivable at gross amounts).
2. Anticipated sales returns and allowances.

3. Anticipated collection costs (e.g., attorney's fees) that the company will incur when trying to collect accounts receivable.

4. Anticipated freight costs that customers will be allowed to deduct from their remittances because of the company's shipping terms.

To illustrate, assume that Allen Beam & Company determines from experience that the actual cost of collecting its accounts receivable averages 1% of the year-end accounts receivable balance. If the current year-end accounts receivable balance is $100,000, the company should make the following adjusting entry:

Collection Expense	1,000	
Allowance for Collection Expense		1,000
($100,000 × .01 = $1,000)		

Collection Expense would be reported as an operating expense on the income statement, and the Allowance for Collection Expense would be deducted from Accounts Receivable on the balance sheet. In a subsequent period, the company would charge actual collection costs to the Allowance account, and would credit Cash or other appropriate accounts.

Adjusting entries similar to the one shown above are appropriate to record estimated sales discounts, sales returns and allowances, and freight costs. In each case, a contra-revenue account (e.g., Sales Discounts) or an expense account (e.g., Transportation-Out) is debited and the appropriate Allowance account is credited. The effect of these entries is to reduce current net income and lower the net realizable value of accounts receivable reported on the balance sheet. For example, American Brands, Inc., makers of such diverse products as Master Locks, Titleist golf balls, and Jim Beam bourbon, uses the allowance method to account for sales discounts, uncollectible accounts, and sales returns. In its 1990 Annual Report, the company provided the following information about its accounts receivable:

(In millions)	1990	1989
Accounts receivable, customers	$1,458.8	$1,140.9
Less allowances for discounts,		
doubtful accounts and returns	55.1	47.6
	$1,403.7	$1,093.3

Materiality

Despite the theoretical merits of applying the allowance method to items other than uncollectible accounts, most companies do not do so. Instead of estimating these items in advance, companies usually account for them when they actually occur. This approach, which is required for income tax purposes, is justified under GAAP because of immateriality and because the amounts involved often do not fluctuate significantly from year to year.

Use of an Allowance Account When a Right of Return Exists

Many companies allow customers to return defective merchandise. Some companies, such as those in the newspaper, perishable food, and book publishing industries, permit customers to return merchandise under certain circumstances, even when the merchandise is not defective. These circumstances may include customer dissatisfaction or an inability of the customer to resell the product.

When customers have the right to return products, the seller should recognize revenue at the time of sale only if *all* of the following conditions are met:

1. The seller's price to the buyer is substantially fixed or determinable at the date of sale.

2. The buyer has paid the seller, or the buyer is obligated to pay the seller and the obligation is not contingent on resale of the product.
3. The buyer's obligation to the seller would not be changed in the event of theft or physical destruction or damage of the product.
4. The buyer acquiring the product for resale has economic substance apart from that provided by the seller. (That is, a separate, arm's-length relationship exists between the buyer and seller.)
5. The seller does not have significant obligations for future performance to directly bring about resale of the product by the buyer.
6. The amount of future returns can be reasonably estimated.[10]

Materiality

Further discussion of these conditions appears in Chapter 20. The sixth condition stated above is particularly important for our purposes. In effect, the condition requires that if sales returns are material, companies that sell products with a right of return must use the allowance method of accounting for sales returns to properly recognize revenue at the time of sale.

To illustrate, assume that Averill Company gives customers the right to return products. Recent experience indicates that customers will return approximately 20% of the merchandise Averill Company has sold and that the company can later resell the merchandise for approximately 60% of the original sales price. During the current year, Averill Company made sales of $100,000. Here is the adjusting entry the company should make at year-end, assuming a perpetual inventory system:

Sales Returns	20,000	
Inventory-Estimated Returns	12,000	
Allowance for Sales Returns		20,000
Cost of Goods Sold		12,000

The Inventory-Estimated Returns account is a current asset and shows the net realizable value of inventory that is expected to be returned ($100,000 × 20% × 60% = $12,000). The Allowance for Sales Returns is deducted from Accounts Receivable on the balance sheet. The effect of the above entry is to reduce gross margin and current assets by $8,000.

Suppose now that during the first month of the next accounting period, a customer returns merchandise that had an original sales price of $1,000. Assuming that the customer has not paid for the goods, Averill Company should make the following entry:

Inventory-Returned Goods	600	
Allowance for Sales Returns	1,000	
Inventory-Estimated Returns		600
Accounts Receivable		1,000

Use of Accounts Receivable to Generate Cash

Instead of waiting until customers pay their accounts, companies often want the cash immediately. This is usually accomplished by **pledging, assigning,** or **factoring** the accounts.

The key conceptual issue under each of the three alternatives is whether a **borrowing transaction** or a **sale transaction** has occurred. In a borrowing transaction, the receivables are simply used as collateral to obtain a loan. The borrowing company

---

[10]*FASB Statement of Financial Accounting Standards No. 48,* "Revenue Recognition When Right of Return Exists," 1981, par. 6.

continues to report the receivables as assets and also reports the interest expense and the liability for the loan. In a sale transaction, the selling company receives cash, removes the receivables from the accounting records, and typically recognizes a loss on the receivables sold. The selling company does not recognize a liability because the receivables have actually been sold.

Pledging Accounts Receivable.   Companies sometimes obtain loans by pledging their accounts receivable as collateral. In a pledging arrangement, the borrower agrees to collect its accounts receivable and to use the proceeds to repay the lender. The borrower records the loan and related interest in the usual manner, and the loan balance is reduced as the borrower remits its collections. If the borrower defaults, the lender can recover the amount owed by selling the accounts pledged.

If a company has pledged some or all of its accounts receivable, the company should disclose the amount pledged, either parenthetically or in a note to its financial statements.

Assigning Accounts Receivable.   An assignment of accounts receivable is a more formal type of pledging arrangement. In an assignment, a borrower (called the **assignor**) transfers its rights in some or all of its accounts receivable to a lender (called the **assignee**) in exchange for a loan. The money received from collecting the accounts is later used to pay off the loan.

An assignment is evidenced by a **financing agreement** and a **promissory note,** both of which are signed by the assignor. The financing agreement may indicate that the assignment is on either a **nonnotification** or a **notification** basis. When accounts are assigned on a nonnotification basis, as is usually the case, customers are not informed that their accounts have been assigned. As a result, they continue to make payments to the assignor, who in turn forwards them to the assignee. When accounts are assigned on a notification basis, customers are notified to make their payments directly to the assignee.

The assignor retains ownership of the accounts assigned. As a result, the assignor assumes the risk that accounts receivable will not be realized for their full face amount because of such factors as sales discounts, sales returns and allowances, and bad-debt losses.

Before entering into an assignment, the assignee (usually a bank or a finance company) analyzes the borrower's accounts receivable. The assignee generally refuses to lend money secured by accounts believed to be too risky. Furthermore, the assignee usually lends only a certain percentage (often between 60% and 90%) of the face amount of the accounts that it is willing to lend against. This helps to insulate the assignee from collection losses that the assignor might sustain. As additional protection the assignee frequently requires the assignor to substitute new accounts for ones that become past due or uncollectible. Naturally, the assignee charges **interest** for the loans that it makes. In addition, the assignee usually requires a **service charge** for processing the assignment.

To illustrate, assume that on December 31, 1992, Smith Company assigns $100,000 of accounts receivable to Citibank under a nonnotification arrangement. Citibank advances $80,000 less a service charge of $1,600, and Smith Company signs a promissory note that provides for interest of 1% per month on the unpaid loan balance. Smith Company should make the following entries on December 31:

Assigned Accounts Receivable	100,000	
Accounts Receivable		100,000
Cash	78,400	
Service Charge Expense	1,600	
Notes Payable		80,000

The first entry transfers the assigned accounts to a separate account. The second entry records the receipt of cash on the loan.

To continue the illustration, a series of 1993 transactions and the corresponding journal entries appear below:

1. From January 1 to January 31, Smith Company collected assigned accounts of $60,000, less sales discounts of $700 and sales returns and allowances of $1,300.

Cash	58,000	
Sales Discounts	700	
Sales Returns and Allowances	1,300	
Assigned Accounts Receivable		60,000

2. On January 31, Smith Company remitted the January collections to Citibank.

Notes Payable	57,200	
Interest Expense ($80,000 × .01)	800	
Cash		58,000

3. From February 1 to February 28, Smith Company collected $29,000 of assigned accounts and wrote off as uncollectible $3,000 of assigned accounts.

Cash	29,000	
Allowance for Doubtful Accounts	3,000	
Assigned Accounts Receivable		32,000

4. On February 28, Smith Company paid off the remaining loan balance and transferred the remaining balance in Assigned Accounts Receivable to Accounts Receivable.

Notes Payable ($80,000 − $57,200)	22,800	
Interest Expense ($22,800 × .01)	228	
Cash		23,028
Accounts Receivable	8,000	
Assigned Accounts Receivable		8,000
($100,000 − $60,000 − $32,000)		

Disclosure

Materiality

Smith Company should separately disclose the specifically assigned accounts receivable if they are material. Moreover, Smith should disclose its equity in the assigned accounts, either parenthetically or in a note. A note in the 1992 financial statements, for example, might say that "on December 31, 1992, Smith Company had $20,000 ($100,000 − $80,000) equity in its assigned accounts receivable."

The example shown above provides a general view of accounting for assigned accounts receivable. In practice, the accounting requirements depend in part on the financing agreement. A general description of this agreement should be disclosed in the footnotes to the assignor's financial statements.

Factoring of Accounts Receivable.   In a factoring arrangement, a company (the **seller**) sells its accounts receivable to a financial institution, called a **factor.** In most cases the factor is a bank or a finance company. Factoring differs from an assignment in that the seller actually transfers ownership of its accounts receivable to the factor. Although accounts may be factored **with recourse** (the factor may hold the seller liable if debtors do not pay), accounts are usually factored **without recourse** (the factor

The right to demand pymt.

bears the risk that debtors will not pay). Moreover, accounts are usually factored on a notification basis.

  The details of a factoring arrangement vary and should be spelled out in a factoring contract. A typical factoring arrangement is continuous. The factor maintains a credit department that performs all functions related to the seller's accounts receivable. In addition to deciding to whom the seller may extend credit, the factor assumes responsibility for billing and collecting, and for bad-debt losses. The seller ships merchandise to approved customers and immediately sells the receivables to the factor. Thus, the advantage of factoring to a seller are immediate cash and relief from the burden of carrying accounts receivable. Factoring arrangements are common in the textile, apparel, carpet, and furniture industries. Moreover, the use of credit cards such as American Express, VISA, and MasterCard is in essence a form of factoring.

  When accounts are factored, the factor charges a **factoring fee** for its services of credit approval, billing, collecting, and assuming bad-debt losses. This fee is usually 1% to 3% of the net amount of the receivables factored. The factor then credits the seller's account for the net amount of the receivables factored less the factoring fee. The factor may also withhold some predetermined amount (usually about 10% of the net amount of receivables factored) to protect itself against sales returns and allowances.

  To illustrate, assume that on September 1, 1993, Riley Company factors $20,000 of accounts receivable *without recourse* with First Finance Corporation on a notification basis. First Finance charges a factoring fee of 3% of the amount of receivables factored. In addition, First Finance withholds 10% of the amount of receivables factored to cover sales returns and allowances. Riley would make the following journal entry on September 1:

Cash	17,400	
Receivable from Factor (20,000 × 10%) Sales R/A	2,000	
Loss on Factoring Accounts		
Receivable ($20,000 × 3%) Fee	600	
Accounts Receivable		20,000

Sale →

  Riley Company would classify the Receivable from Factor as a current asset. This account would later be credited when sales returns and allowances occur and when the factor remits the ending balance in Riley's account.

  Notice in the above example that Riley Company factored accounts receivable *without recourse* and accounted for the factoring as a sale. Accordingly, the accounts receivable are removed from the accounting records, and no liability is recorded.

  When receivables are factored *with recourse,* the transfer is recognized as a sale only if all of the following conditions are met:

1. The transferor (i.e., the company selling the accounts) surrenders control of the future economic benefits embodied in the receivables.
2. The transferor's obligation under the recourse provisions can be reasonably estimated.
3. The transferee (i.e., the company buying the accounts) cannot require the transferor to repurchase the receivables except as specified in the recourse provisions.[11]

Substance over Form

  The three conditions help determine whether the transfer of receivables is in substance a sale transaction or a borrowing transaction. If the three conditions are met, then the factoring with recourse is accounted for as a sale, in the same manner as illustrated for Riley Company. On the other hand, if *any* of the three conditions is not met, the

---

[11]*FASB Statement of Financial Accounting Standards No. 77,* "Reporting by Transferors for Transfers of Receivables with Recourse," 1983, par. 5.

amount of the proceeds from the transfer of the receivables should be reported as a liability because the transaction is now regarded as a borrowing, not a sale. Assume that Riley Company factored its receivables *with recourse* and did not satisfy all of the three conditions. Under these circumstances, Riley Company would account for the transfer of receivables as a borrowing and would make the following journal entry on September 1:

Cash	17,400	
Receivable from Factor (20,000 × 10%)	2,000	
Interest Expense ($20,000 × 3%) *Borrowing Trans*	600	
Payable to Factor		20,000

Notice that the accounts receivable of $20,000 that were factored are not removed from Riley's accounting records. These accounts are still considered assets of Riley's, and now Riley has a collateralized loan for which it must account. If the transaction had incorrectly been accounted for as a sale, Riley Company would have been permitted to engage in **off-balance-sheet financing.** That is, the company would have been permitted to borrow money without having to report the liability.

The appropriate accounting practices for a factoring arrangement depend on the specific agreement. If a company has entered into a factoring agreement, the company should briefly describe the agreement in the notes to its financial statements.

NOTES RECEIVABLE

A **promissory note,** often called simply a **note,** is a written promise to pay a certain sum of money at a designated time. The note is signed by the **maker** and is usually made payable to the order of a specified **payee,** who in turn may endorse the note and thereby sell (discount) it to a subsequent holder. From a payee's viewpoint, a note represents a **receivable** and therefore an asset. Notes receivable are more desirable than accounts receivable for the following reasons:

1. Notes are often easier to collect because they represent written claims. Thus, their use may reduce a company's bad-debt losses.
2. Notes can usually be converted into cash by discounting them with a bank or other lender, and this process (which we explain in a subsequent section) is usually quicker and cheaper than assigning or factoring accounts receivable.
3. Notes receivable usually bear a specified rate of interest, while accounts receivable do not.

Companies often acquire notes receivable in exchange for merchandise when customers need credit for a period longer than usual for open accounts. Occasionally, companies acquire notes in exchange for account receivable claims against customers who simply need additional time to pay their accounts. Notes receivable may also result from the sale of other assets and from lending money.

Valuation of Notes Receivable

Asset/Liability Measurement

As indicated earlier in the chapter, notes receivable should be valued initially at an amount equal to the present value of the cash that the company expects to collect. This approach is theoretically sound because it recognizes the time value of money.

If a company can reasonably estimate the amount of its uncollectible notes receivable, the company should establish an allowance for such notes in a manner similar to that used for accounts receivable. Companies that acquire many notes as a result of selling merchandise can usually estimate their uncollectibles with reasonable accuracy.

Because money has a time value, all commercial notes contain interest. Nevertheless, notes are commonly classified as either **interest-bearing** or **noninterest-bearing.** In-

EXHIBIT 7-8

Accounting for Interest-Bearing Notes Receivable

Transaction	Entry		
Oct. 1, 1992			
Sun Company sells merchandise having a sales price of $1,000 to Bin Company in exchange for a one-year *interest-bearing* note. The note has a face amount of $1,000 and a stated interest rate of 12% (equal to the going market rate for similar notes) payable at maturity.	Notes Receivable Sales	1,000	1,000
Dec. 31, 1992			
Sun Company computes accrued interest for three months ($1,000 × .12 × 3/12 = $30).	Interest Receivable Interest Revenue	30	30
Sept. 30, 1993			

Sun Company collects principal and interest at maturity.*	Cash
	    Note Receivable
	    Interest Receivable
	    Interest Revenue
		1,120	1,000
			30
			90

*The illustration assumes that Sun Company does not make reversing entries.

terest-bearing notes specifically state a certain interest rate; noninterest-bearing notes do not. In a noninterest-bearing note, the interest is included in the face amount of the note and is not explicitly stated.

Interest-Bearing Notes Receivable.   Because interest-bearing notes receivable specifically state a certain interest rate, the present value of the note at the time of issuance equals its face amount, assuming that the interest rate is reasonable. Consequently, such notes are initially recorded at their face amount (which equals their present value). Interest revenue is then recognized on the accrual basis as time passes.

To illustrate, assume that on October 1, 1992, Sun Company, which uses a calendar-year accounting period, sells merchandise having a sales price of $1,000 to Bin Company in exchange for a one-year, *interest-bearing* note. The note has a face amount of $1,000 and a stated interest rate of 12% (equal to the going market rate for similar notes) payable at maturity. Sun Company would account for the note as shown in Exhibit 7-8.

Noninterest-Bearing Notes Receivable.   The present value of a noninterest-bearing note receivable is less than its face amount. The reason is that the face amount includes interest even though no interest is specifically stated. Although it is theoretically correct to account for this interest, many companies fail to do so.

To illustrate, let us assume that on October 1, 1992, Sun Company (referred to in the previous section) sells merchandise having a sales price of $1,000 to Bur Company in exchange for a one-year, *noninterest-bearing* note. The note has a face amount of $1,120, and the going market rate for similar notes is 12%. The note therefore has a present value of $1,000, an amount that equals the sales price of the merchandise as well as the face amount of the note ($1,120) divided by 1.12. Sun Company would account for the note using one of the alternative methods shown in Exhibit 7-9.

Under Method 1, the note is initially recorded at its present value of $1,000. This is done by debiting Notes Receivable for the face amount ($1,120) and crediting

EXHIBIT 7-9

Accounting for Noninterest-Bearing Notes Receivable

Transaction	Method 1: Record at Present Value (theoretically correct)		Method 2: Record at Face Amount (theoretically incorrect)	
Oct. 1, 1992				

Sun Company sells merchandise having a sales price of $1,000 to Bur Company in exchange for a one-year, *noninterest-bearing* note. The note has a face amount of $1,120 and the going market rate for similar notes is 12%.	Notes Receivable 1,120
	  Sales
	  Discount on
	    Notes
	    Receivable*
		
		1,000
		
		120
			Notes Receivable 1,120
			  Sales
				
				1,120

Dec. 31, 1992				

Sun Company computes accrued interest for three months ($1,000 × .12 × $^3/_{12}$ = $30).	Discount on Notes
	  Receivable 30
	    Interest Revenue
		
		30
			No entry	

Sept. 30, 1993				

Sun Company collects principal and interest at maturity.**	Cash 1,120
	Discount on Notes
	  Receivable 90
	    Notes Receivable
	    Interest Revenue
		
		1,120
		90
			Cash 1,120
			  Notes Receivable
				
				1,120

*Some firms prefer *not* to use a Discount account. These firms would debit Notes Receivable for $1,000 on October 1 and for $30 on December 31. They would then credit Notes Receivable for $1,030 on September 30, 1993. This approach is an acceptable variation of Method 1 because it produces essentially the same results.
**The illustration assumes that Sun Company does not make reversing entries.

Discount on Notes Receivable for the total amount of interest that the note contains ($120). Notice that the interest equals 12% of the sales price of $1,000 for one year. The balance in the Discount account is deducted from Notes Receivable on the balance sheet. Consequently, if Sun Company prepared a balance sheet on October 1, the company would report a net amount of $1,000, which equals the present value of the note on that date.

Observe that the present value of the Bur Company note ($1,000) is the same as the present value of the Bin Company note recorded in the previous section. The reason is that these are similar one-year notes with maturity values of $1,120. Under Method 1, as shown in Exhibit 7-9, $30 of interest revenue is recorded in 1992 and $90 in 1993. These are the same amounts recorded for the Bin Company note in Exhibit 7-8. Method 1 is theoretically correct because it reflects the economic reality that money has a time value. Method 1 puts substance (i.e., the economic fact that the note contains interest) over form (i.e., the fact that the note has no stated interest rate). Notes receivable, sales, and interest revenue are all correctly reported under Method 1.

Substance over Form

In practice, many companies use Method 2 to record short-term, noninterest-bearing, trade notes receivable. Using this method, these companies initially record such notes at their face amounts, not at their present values. The use of Method 2 leads to several misstatements in the financial statements. In the example shown, sales, net income, assets, and stockholders' equity would each be overstated in 1992, while interest revenue would be understated. In 1993, interest revenue and net income would be understated.

Accounting Principles Board Opinion No. 21, which we explain in Chapter 10, requires companies under certain circumstances to impute (estimate and record) interest in transactions involving receivables and payables for which there is either no stated interest or an unreasonable amount of stated interest. Applying the principles set forth in this pronouncement would produce the results shown under Method 1. However, *APB Opinion No. 21* states that it is not intended to apply to "receivables and payables arising from transactions with customers or suppliers in the normal course of business which are due in customary trade terms not exceeding approximately one year."[12] Consequently, many companies use Method 2 to account for these types of notes receivable. Because the receivables are short-term, an argument can be made that the amount of interest often is not material. In addition, net income may not be significantly distorted if the receivables occur fairly evenly over time.

Materiality

Discounting Notes Receivable

Most notes are **negotiable,** which means that a payee may transfer its rights to collect a note to a subsequent holder. On the maturity date, the holder collects the amount of the note's maturity value from the maker.

When a note is negotiable, therefore, the payee may obtain cash before the maturity date by **discounting** (selling) the note at a bank or other entity. To discount the note, the payee endorses it. In rare cases the endorsement is made **without recourse,** which means that the endorser avoids future liability on the note. Usually, however, banks require that endorsements be made **with recourse,** which means that the endorser agrees to pay the holder if the maker does not. Consequently, endorsers typically remain **contingently liable** on notes receivable that they have discounted.

Contingent liabilities, discussed more fully in Chapter 14, are obligations that must be paid if certain conditions occur. For example, if the maker of a note fails to pay the holder on the maturity date, an endorser (with recourse) must pay. Users of financial statements want to know about a company's contingent obligations. Consequently, the Financial Accounting Standards Board (FASB), in its *Statement of Financial Accounting Standards No. 5*, requires companies to disclose contingent liabilities that relate to notes receivable discounted, even if there is only a remote chance that the company will actually have to pay.[13]

When a company discounts a note at a bank, the company receives cash **proceeds.** These proceeds, which the bank calculates, are equal to the **maturity value** of the note less the bank's **discount.** To calculate the discount, the bank multiplies the **maturity value** of the note by the bank's **discount rate** (the interest rate that the bank charges for discounting the note) and by the **remaining time to maturity.** These calculations are illustrated in the following example.

Suppose that on March 1, 1993, Blue Inc. receives a $10,000, 90-day, 10% note from a customer on account. Thirty days later, on March 31, 1993, Blue Inc.

---

[12]*APB Opinion No. 21*, "Interest on Receivables and Payables," 1971, par. 3.
[13]*FASB Statement of Financial Accounting Standards No. 5*, par. 12.

discounts the note *with recourse* at Park National Bank. The bank's discount rate is 12%, and Blue Inc. receives proceeds of $10,045, computed as follows:

Face amount of note	$10,000
Interest to maturity ($10,000 × .10 × 90/360)	250
Maturity value of note*	10,250
Bank discount ($10,250 × .12 × 60/360)	205
Proceeds	$10,045

*Remember that the maturity value equals the face amount of a noninterest-bearing note.

Substance over Form

How should Blue Inc. account for the note receivable discounted? Similar to the use of accounts receivable to generate cash, the key conceptual issue in accounting for notes receivable discounted is whether a borrowing transaction or a sale transaction has in substance occurred. In practice, most notes receivable are accounted for as sales transactions because most notes are discounted with recourse, and the three conditions for recognizing a transfer of receivables with recourse as a sale usually are satisfied (see page 287). Also, those notes receivable issued without recourse are recognized as sales transactions.

Assuming that the three conditions have been met, and the transfer of receivables with recourse can be recognized as a sale, Blue Inc. should account for the note receivable discounted (with recourse) using one of the two approaches shown in Exhibit 7–10. Because most makers pay their notes at maturity, the **footnote approach** is easier to apply. Under this approach, Notes Receivable is credited when a note is discounted, and the contingent liability is disclosed in a footnote such as: "The company is contingently liable for $10,250 on a note receivable discounted at the bank. It does not expect the maker of the note to default." The company, of course, stops making this disclosure when it is no longer contingently liable on the note. Instead of using a footnote, the company may disclose essentially the same information parenthetically on the balance sheet.

Some accountants prefer the **contra account approach,** under which Notes Receivable Discounted is credited when a company discounts a note. Notes Receivable Discounted is a contra account to Notes Receivable and is deducted from Notes Receivable in the current assets section of the balance sheet in order to disclose the contingent liability. The contra account approach requires slightly more bookkeeping than the footnote approach. Moreover, it fails to disclose the full amount of the contingent liability. Notice in the example that the contingent liability is actually $10,250 (principal + interest). The Notes Receivable Discounted account, however, shows only the face amount of $10,000.

Observe that Interest Revenue is credited for $45 on March 31. Actually, Blue Inc. has earned $83.33 ($10,000 × .10 × 30/360 = $83.33) as a result of holding the note for thirty days. This suggests that on March 31, Blue Inc. should record $83.33 as interest revenue and debit a loss account for $38.33 ($83.33 − $45 = $38.33), as shown below:

Cash	10,045.00	
Loss from Discounting Notes Receivable	38.33	
Notes Receivable (or Notes Receivable		
Discounted)		10,000.00
Interest Revenue		83.33

EXHIBIT 7–10

Accounting for Notes Receivable Discounted

Transaction	Footnote Approach		Contra Account Approach	
Mar. 1, 1993				

Blue Inc. receives a $10,000, 90-day, 10% note from a customer on account.	Notes Receivable 10,000
	  Accounts Receivable
		10,000	Notes Receivable 10,000
			  Accounts Receivable
				10,000

Mar. 31, 1993				

Blue Inc. discounts the note (with recourse) at Park National Bank at a discount rate of 12%.	Cash 10,045
	  Notes Receivable
	  Interest Revenue
		10,000
		45
			Cash 10,045
			  Notes Receivable
			  Discounted
			  Interest Revenue
				10,000
				45

Alternative Assumption No. 1				
May 30, 1993				
The customer pays Park National Bank.	No entry		Notes Receivable Discounted 10,000 Notes Receivable	10,000
Alternative Assumption No. 2				
May 30, 1993				

The customer dishonors the note and the bank charges Blue Inc. with the maturity value plus a protest fee of $25.	Dishonored Notes
	  Receivable 10,275
	  Cash
		10,275	Dishonored Notes
			  Receivable 10,275
			  Cash
			
			Notes Receivable
			Discounted 10,000
			  Notes Receivable
				10,275
				
				10,000

Although this approach is logical, companies rarely use it because of materiality considerations.

When a note has been discounted, the bank will try to collect the maturity value from the maker on the maturity date. If the maker defaults, the bank must promptly notify the endorser. Therefore, the endorser who has not heard from the bank within a few days after the maturity date may generally assume that the maker has paid the note and thereby ended the endorser's contingent liability. If, on the other hand, the maker does not pay the bank, we say that the note has been **dishonored.** In this case, the bank promptly notifies the endorser and holds the endorser liable for the full maturity value plus any **protest fee** (any reasonable cost that the bank incurs in protesting the note). The endorser pays the bank and then has a claim against the maker for the full amount paid. Because the endorser pays the note, the endorser no longer has a contingent liability to the bank.

To illustrate the accounting entries involved, assume that on the maturity date, May 30, 1993, the customer pays Park National Bank the amount owed, thereby ending Blue Inc.'s contingent liability. As shown in Exhibit 7–10, Blue Inc. would not make an entry under the footnote approach but would under the contra account approach. In practice, the entry required under the contra account approach would likely be made a few days after the maturity date, because a company that is contingently liable on a note does not usually know on the maturity date that the maker has paid.

Assume now that instead of paying the note on May 30, 1993, the customer dishonored it and the bank charged Blue Inc. with the maturity value plus a protest fee of $25. Under these circumstances, Blue Inc. should make the appropriate entry or entries shown in Exhibit 7–10.

Dishonored Notes Receivable is a special note receivable account and should be reported separately from Notes Receivable on the balance sheet. This account should be used for all dishonored notes receivable, whether or not they have been discounted. Blue Inc. will earn interest on the amount in this account at the rate allowed by law. The Dishonored Notes Receivable account should be credited if Blue Inc. collects from the maker. If the company cannot collect the dishonored note, it should write off the amount uncollectible to an Allowance for Uncollectible Notes account, assuming that it uses such an account for its notes receivable.

Remember that the above example assumes that Blue Inc. discounted the note receivable on a *with recourse* basis and that the three conditions for recognizing a transfer of receivables with recourse as a sale had been satisfied. If the note had been discounted *without recourse,* Blue Inc. would still account for the discounting as a sale, but *no contingent liability would exist.* On the other hand, if the note had been discounted on a *with recourse* basis and any of the three conditions had *not* been met, Blue would account for the discounting transaction as a borrowing instead of a sale. Accordingly, Blue would make the following journal entry on March 31, when the note was discounted:

Cash	10,045	
Liability for Notes Receivable Discounted		10,000
Interest Revenue		45

Liability for Notes Receivable Discounted is a current liability account. In this case an actual liability, not a contingent liability, would exist. The Notes Receivable account would remain on Blue's books on March 31. If the customer paid Park National Bank on May 30, Blue would make the following entry:

Liability for Notes Receivable Discounted	10,000	
Notes Receivable		10,000

On the other hand, if the customer dishonored the note on May 30, Blue would make the following entries:

Dishonored Notes Receivable	10,275	
Cash		10,275
Liability for Notes Receivable Discounted	10,000	
Notes Receivable		10,000

BALANCE SHEET PRESENTATION OF RECEIVABLES

As stated earlier, an enterprise should classify a receivable as a current asset only if collection is expected within the next year or operating cycle, whichever is longer. Within the current assets category, trade receivables should be reported separately

EXHIBIT 7–11

ONEIDA LTD.
Receivables Disclosure

Receivables

Receivables by major classification are as follows:

	(Thousands)	
	1990	1989
Accounts receivable	$44,445	$49,021
Other accounts and notes receivable	4,282	3,069
Less allowance for doubtful accounts		
and promotional allowances.	(4,878)	(5,378)
Receivables	$43,849	$46,712

SOURCE: Oneida Ltd., 1990 Annual Report.

from nontrade receivables. Moreover, a company should report separately those receivables that reflect **related-party transactions,** such as loans made by the company to officers or to affiliated companies. Accounts and notes receivable should be **Materiality** segregated when the amount of each is material. Exhibit 7–11 shows a receivables disclosure that Oneida Ltd. made in its 1989 Annual Report. Oneida is a well-known manufacturer of dinnerware, china, and crystal.

Cash and receivables are two examples of **financial instruments.** Beginning in **Disclosure** 1990, companies are required by GAAP to disclose information about financial instruments that have off-balance-sheet risk and about financial instruments with concentrations of credit risk. These disclosures are explained in Chapter 25.

CONCEPTUAL CONSIDERATIONS

The following elements of the theoretical model discussed in Chapter 2 are particularly important to the topics that we presented in Chapter 7.

Asset/Liability Measurement
1. **Asset/liability measurement principle.** Cash is measured at its face amount, accounts receivable are measured at net realizable value, and notes receivable are measured at present value on the date received. Also, the balance sheet approach to the allowance method of accounting for uncollectible accounts is consistent with this principle.

Revenue Realization
2. **Revenue realization principle.** A company ordinarily should record revenue and the related receivable that arises from a sale of goods on the date that the sale occurs. Only in exceptional cases does GAAP permit the recognition of revenue either before or after the time of sale.

Matching
3. **Matching.** The income statement approach to the allowance method of accounting for uncollectible accounts helps a company to more accurately match the expense of uncollectible accounts with the sales revenue that is associated with those accounts.

Substance over Form
4. **Substance over form.** When receivables are transferred *with recourse* from one company to another, such as by factoring accounts receivable or discounting a note receivable, the transferor should account for the transfer as a sale of the receivables only if three conditions are met. These conditions help to establish whether the transfer of receivables is in substance a sale of the receivables or whether it is really a borrowing transaction.

When accounting for noninterest-bearing notes receivable, recording the note initially at its present value is theoretically better than recording the note at its face amount because substance is considered more important than form in financial accounting.

CONCLUDING REMARKS

Cash is the standard medium of exchange in business transactions, and receivables are claims held against others which generally result in a future inflow of cash. To be classified as a current asset, cash must be available for use in current operations. Similarly, receivables are properly classified as current assets only when they are collectible within the next year or operating cycle, whichever is longer.

Cash and receivables are two examples of monetary assets because they are fixed or determinable in terms of the number of dollars on hand or to be received, regardless of how prices change. For this reason, the valuation of cash and receivables is less controversial than the valuation of nonmonetary assets. In the next two chapters we focus on accounting for inventory. Inventory is a current asset that is nonmonetary in nature and is considerably more challenging to value than either cash or receivables.

KEY POINTS

1. Cash may include currency, coins, checks, bank drafts, money orders, checking accounts, and savings accounts. (Objective 1)

2. On a balance sheet, cash is valued at face amount and classified as a current asset only if the cash is available for use in current operations. (Objective 1)

3. A petty cash fund is typically used to disburse relatively small amounts of currency and coins for such items as taxi fares, postage, and minor supplies. (Objective 2)

4. A bank reconciliation is a schedule that explains any differences between a company's book balance of cash in a particular bank account and the bank statement balance. (Objective 3)

5. A proof of cash is an expanded, four-column reconciliation that is a stronger control measure than the single-column bank reconciliation. (Objective 3)

6. The preparation of either a bank reconciliation or a proof of cash usually indicates that a company has to make certain adjusting entries to update its accounting records. (Objective 3)

7. Receivables are claims held against others for money, goods, or services. (Objective 1)

8. A receivable should be valued initially at an amount equal to the present value of the cash that the company expects to collect. A receivable should be classified as a current asset only if collection is expected within the next year or operating cycle, whichever is longer. (Objective 1)

9. From the standpoint of accounting theory, the net method of recording credit sales is better than the gross method. But most companies use the gross method because of convenience and materiality. (Objective 4)

10. The allowance method, rather than the direct write-off method, should be used when accounting for uncollectible accounts. (Objective 5)

11. The allowance method requires that bad debts be estimated by an income statement approach or a balance sheet approach. (Objective 5)

12. The income statement approach emphasizes the matching principle and requires that the adjusting entry for bad debts be made without considering the previous balance in the Allowance for Doubtful Accounts. (Objective 5)

13. The balance sheet approach emphasizes the reporting of accounts receivable at net realizable value and requires that the previous balance in the Allowance for Doubtful Accounts be considered in recording the adjusting entry for bad debts. (Objective 5)

14. In addition to its use in accounting for uncollectible accounts, the allowance method can be used in accounting for other items that affect the cash realization of accounts receivable (e.g., sales discounts). (Objective 5)

15. Many companies use accounts receivable to generate cash immediately by pledging, assigning, or factoring the accounts. Each method of accounts receivable financing has important financial statement implications. (Objective 6)

16. Although some notes have no stated interest rates, all commercial notes contain interest, because money has a time value. (Objective 7)

17. To be theoretically correct, we should always account for the interest component of a note receivable, whether or not the interest is explicitly stated. In practice, many companies do not separately account for the interest component of short-term, noninterest-bearing, trade notes receivable because of materiality. (Objective 7)

18. A company may use either a footnote approach or a contra account approach to accounting for certain notes receivable that are discounted. (Objective 7)

APPENDIX A: PREPARING A PROOF OF CASH

As stated earlier in this chapter, auditors often prepare a *four-column bank reconciliation,* also called a *proof of cash.*

To illustrate how to prepare a proof of cash, we shall use the information presented earlier in the chapter when illustrating the preparation of a bank reconciliation for Todd Company for the month ended May 31, 1993. In addition, assume that the following facts pertain to Todd Company during June 1993:

1. The cash receipts (deposits) shown on the June bank statement were $78,839. These receipts included the deposit of $1,500 that was in transit on May 31.
2. The cash receipts shown on the company's books during June were $79,864.
3. The cash payments shown on the June bank statement were $76,188. These payments included the checks of $2,647 that were outstanding on May 31.
4. The cash payments shown on the company's books during June were $77,261.
5. The cash balance shown as of June 30 on the bank statement was $20,282.
6. The cash balance shown as of June 30 on the company's books was $17,817.
7. A deposit of $3,600 mailed to the bank on June 30 did not appear on the June bank statement.
8. On June 30 the bank collected a note receivable for Todd Company and credited the proceeds of $3,175 to the company's account. The proceeds included $175 of interest, all of which the company earned during 1993. Todd Company has not yet recorded the collection.
9. Outstanding checks as of June 30 totaled $2,910.
10. The bank statement showed a $20 service charge for June.

The proof of cash for Todd Company appears in Exhibit 7–12. The form is divided into two sections, like the form in Exhibit 7–1. In the "per bank statement" section, we reconcile from four amounts shown on the bank statement to the correct (true) amounts. In the "per books" section, we reconcile from four amounts shown on the company's books to the same correct amounts that are determined in the "per bank statement" section.

The first column of the proof of cash is simply the single-column bank reconciliation prepared at the end of May (see Exhibit 7–2); the fourth column is a single-column reconciliation for June. The second column reconciles the June receipts, and the third column reconciles the June payments.

To prepare a proof of cash, we may begin by completing the top line in each section. We do this simply by copying the necessary information from the bank statement and the company's books. Next, we copy in the first column the information shown in the fourth column of the proof of cash prepared for the *previous* month. We then prepare in the fourth column a single-column reconciliation for the *current* month. Finally, each reconciling item in one of the two outside columns is ordinarily added or deducted in one of the two inside columns.

A logical analysis of each reconciling item should enable you to determine whether to add or deduct the item. For example:

1. The May 31 deposit in transit of $1,500 is deducted from the June receipts shown on the bank statement. Because this amount is a *May* receipt that is shown as a receipt on the *June* bank statement, we must deduct it in order to derive the *correct amount* of June receipts.

2. The outstanding checks of $2,910 on June 30 are added to the June payments shown on the bank statement. Because these checks are June payments that simply have not cleared the bank as of June 30, we must add them in order to derive the *correct amount* of June payments.

EXHIBIT 7-12

Todd Company
PROOF OF CASH
For June 1993

	May 31 Balance	June Receipts	June Payments	June 30 Balance
Per bank statement	$17,631	$78,839	$76,188	$20,282
Deposits in transit				
May 31	1,500	(1,500)		
June 30		3,600		3,600
Outstanding checks				
May 31	(2,647)		(2,647)	
June 30			2,910	(2,910)
Correct amounts	$16,484	$80,939	$76,451	$20,972
Per books	$15,214	$79,864	$77,261	$17,817
Note and interest collected by bank				
May	2,100	(2,100)		
June		3,175		3,175
Bank service charge				
May	(12)		(12)	
June			20	(20)
NSF check	(548)		(548)	
Error made in recording check no. 916	(270)		(270)	
Correct amounts	$16,484	$80,939	$76,451	$20,972

3. The note and interest collected by the bank in June ($3,175) are added to the June receipts shown on the company's books. Because this amount is a June receipt not yet shown on the company's books, we must add it in order to derive the *correct amount* of June receipts.

4. The bank service charge of $12 for May is deducted from the June payments shown on the company's books. Because this amount is a *May* payment (i.e., the bank charged the company's checking account in May) that the company recorded as a payment in *June,* we must deduct it in order to derive the *correct amount* of June payments.

Remember that a company must usually prepare journal entries based on the information shown on its bank reconciliations. Our illustration assumes that Todd Company prepares such entries near the beginning of the month that follows each reconciliation. In practice, many companies do this because they do not receive their bank statements in the mail on the last day of each month. When a company wants to prepare accurate financial statements (e.g., at year-end), the company should record its journal entries as transactions of the month to which the bank reconciliation pertains.

As with the single-column bank reconciliation, preparation of a proof of cash usually indicates that a company has to make journal entries to update its accounting records. The entries necessary for Todd Company are suggested by the information shown in the "per books" section of the proof of cash:

Cash	3,175	
Notes Receivable		3,000
Interest Revenue		175
(To record collection of note and interest by bank.)		
Miscellaneous Expense	20	
Cash		20
(To record bank service charge.)		

QUESTIONS

7-1   What are the normal components of cash?

7-2   What are the guidelines for the valuation and classification of cash on the balance sheet?

7-3   How should a company report each of the following items?

[a] Bank overdrafts.
[b] Certificates of deposit.
[c] NSF checks received from customers.
[d] Expense advances made to employees.
[e] Postdated checks received from customers.
[f] Postage stamps.
[g] IOUs received from employees.

7–4   What do accountants mean by the term "internal control"?

7–5   Why should a company divide the responsibility for a series of related transactions between two or more persons?

7–6   What is the purpose of a petty cash fund?

7–7   Explain the nature of a Cash Short and Over account.

7–8   What is a bank reconciliation? What purposes does it serve?

7–9   What is a proof of cash? What purposes does it serve?

7–10   What does the term "receivables" mean? How should receivables be classified on the balance sheet?

7–11   How should short-term receivables be valued on the balance sheet?

7–12   What is the difference between a trade discount and a cash discount?

7–13   Explain the distinction between the net method and the gross method of recording credit sales. Which method do companies generally use? Why?

7–14   Briefly compare the direct write-off method and the allowance method of accounting for uncollectible accounts.

7–15   Assume that a company uses the allowance method of accounting for uncollectible accounts. What is the major argument in favor of using the income statement approach? What is the major argument in favor of using the balance sheet approach?

7–16   Why does the Allowance for Doubtful Accounts sometimes have a debit balance?

7–17   What is the theoretical argument for using the allowance method to account for expected sales returns and allowances? (Assume that the expected amount is material.)

7–18   Why is it theoretically correct to account for interest when accounting for a noninterest-bearing note receivable?

7–19   What is the fundamental difference between the footnote approach and the contra account approach to accounting for notes receivable discounted?

EXERCISES

7–20   CASH COMPONENTS   The controller of Wiser Women's Wear is trying to determine the total amount to report as *cash* on a balance sheet dated December 31. The following items are under consideration:

[1] Currency and coins in a change fund (used for making change with customers) on December 31.
[2] NSF checks received during December from customers on account and returned by the bank with the December bank statement.
[3] Certificates of deposit held on December 31.
[4] Checks that the company has drawn payable to suppliers. Checks have been recorded but not mailed as of December 31.
[5] Postage stamps on hand December 31.
[6] Correct cash balance on December 31 in special checking account used for writing payroll checks.
[7] Petty cash on hand December 31.
[8] A check received from a customer and dated January 5 of the following year.
[9] IOUs from company personnel.
[10] Correct cash balance on December 31 in Chemical Bank general checking account.

Instructions

[a] Identify the items that the controller should report as cash on the December 31 balance sheet.

[b] Indicate the proper balance sheet reporting for items that the company should not include as cash.

7–21 CASH COMPONENTS The following information pertains to Weber Company on December 31:

Correct cash balance in general checking account with Third Bank	$ 3,261
Overdraft in special checking account with Second Bank (Weber does not have another account with Second Bank.)	290
Cash accumulated in a special fund that will be used for plant expansion in five years	15,187
Cash surrender value of life insurance	3,265
Cash travel advances in the hands of company salespersons	1,296
Currency and coins in a petty cash fund (The company has not replenished the fund to the imprest amount of $200.)	58

Instructions

[a] Calculate the total amount that Weber company should report as *cash* in the current assets section of the balance sheet dated December 31.

[b] Indicate the proper balance sheet reporting of items that you omitted in [a].

7–22 PETTY CASH On April 1, Dyer Insurance Agency established an imprest petty cash fund for $300 by writing a check on City National Bank. On April 23 the fund contained the following:

Currency and coins	$ 26
Receipts for office supplies expense	84
Receipts for postage expense	167
Receipts for advertising expense	18

On April 26 the agency wrote a check to increase the fund to the imprest amount.

Instructions

Prepare the necessary journal entries to record the petty cash transactions during April.

7–23 CASH BALANCE BEFORE ADJUSTMENTS The following information pertains to Egerton Company as of November 30:

Bank statement balance	$2,148
Bank service charge for November (not previously recorded on Egerton's books)	17
Checks outstanding	215
Interest on bank balance credited by bank during November (not previously recorded on Egerton's books)	37
Deposit in transit	490

Instructions

Based on the above information, compute the general ledger cash balance on November 30 *before* adjustments.

7–24 BANK RECONCILIATION The following information pertains to Ninja, Inc., as of September 30:

Cash balance per general ledger	$2,585
Cash balance per bank statement	2,705
Checks outstanding	350
Bank service charge shown on September bank statement	10
Error made by Ninja, Inc., in recording a check that cleared the bank in September (check was drawn in September for $145 but recorded at $185)	40
Deposit in transit	260

Instructions

Prepare a September bank reconciliation for Ninja.

7–25 CASH TO REPORT   The bookkeeper for Bressler Company recently prepared the following bank reconciliation:

Bressler Company
BANK RECONCILIATION
September 30

Balance per bank statement		$12,642
Add: Deposit in transit	$870	
Checkbook printing charge	21	
Error made in recording check no. 1782 (issued in September to acquire equipment)	160	
NSF check from a customer returned with the bank statement	500	1,551
		14,193
Deduct: Outstanding checks		
No. 1763	$235	
No. 1795	168	
No. 1796	45	448
Note collected by bank (includes $50 interest)	950	1,398
Balance per books		$12,795

Instructions

[a] What amount should Bressler report as *cash* on the balance sheet dated September 30? Assume that the company has $910 cash on hand on September 30.

[b] Prepare the necessary compound journal entry.

7–26 BANK RECONCILIATION   Archer Corporation keeps all its cash in a checking account. An examination of the company's accounting records and bank statement for the month ended June 30 revealed the following information:

[1] The cash balances as of June 30 are:

Bank statement balance	$8,469
Book balance	8,524

[2] A deposit of $950 that was placed in the bank's night depository on June 30 does not appear on the bank statement.

[3] The bank statement shows that on June 30, the bank collected a note for Archer and credited the proceeds of $935 to the company's account. The proceeds included $35 interest, all of which Archer earned during the current accounting period. Archer has not yet recorded the collection.

[4] Checks outstanding on June 30 are:

No. 151	$150
No. 157	48
No. 166	72

[5] Archer discovered that check no. 159, written in June for $183 in payment of an account payable, had been recorded in the company's records as $138.

[6] Included with the June bank statement was an NSF check for $250 that Archer had received from Engin Company on account on June 26. Archer has not yet recorded the returned check.

[7] The bank statement shows a $15 service charge for June.

Instructions

[a] Prepare a June 30 bank reconciliation for Archer.

[b] Prepare the necessary journal entries.

[c] Post the journal entries to Archer's cash account and determine the adjusted cash balance.

7–27   (Appendix A)   PROOF OF CASH   The following information pertains to the cash of Hines Company:

[1]

	July 31	August 31
Balance shown on bank statement	$2,738	$2,696
Balance shown in general ledger before reconciling the bank account	2,578	2,500
Outstanding checks	863	1,015
Deposit in transit	685	1,245

[2]

	For August
Deposits shown on bank statement	$5,588
Charges shown on bank statement	5,630
Cash receipts shown on company's books	5,398
Cash payments shown on company's books	5,476

[3] The bank service charge was $18 in July (recorded by the company during August) and $24 in August (not yet recorded by the company).

[4] Included with the August bank statement was a check for $500 that had been received on August 25 from a customer on account. The returned check, marked "NSF" by the bank, has not yet been recorded on the company's books.

[5] During August the bank collected $750 of bond interest for Hines Company and credited the proceeds to the company's account. The company earned the interest during the current accounting period but has not yet recorded it.

[6] During August the company issued a check for $696 for equipment. The check, which cleared the bank during August, was incorrectly recorded by the company for $896.

Instructions

Prepare a proof of cash for August.

7–28   RECORDING CREDIT SALES   Penato, Inc., engaged in the following transactions during August:

Aug. 1   Sold merchandise to A Company for $5,000; terms 2/10, n/30.
   2   Sold merchandise to B Company for $20,000; terms 2/10, n/30.
  11   Received payment from B Company for the August 2 sale.
  30   Received payment from A Company for the August 1 sale.

Instructions

Prepare general journal entries for the above transactions on Penato's books, using:

[a] The *net method* of recording credit sales.

[b] The *gross method* of recording credit sales.

7–29   BAD DEBTS   The following data pertain to two companies that have calendar-year accounting periods:

	1993 Credit Sales	Accounts Receivable Dec. 31, 1993	Allowance for Doubtful Accounts Dec. 31, 1993 Before Adjustment
Song Company	$200,000	$25,000	$150 credit balance
Wong Company	500,000	60,000	250 debit balance

Instructions

Journalize the necessary adjusting entry on December 31, 1993, based on the following independent assumptions:

[a] For Song Company, assuming the company estimates that 1% of credit sales are uncollectible.

[b] For Song Company, assuming the company estimates that 6% of the accounts receivable balance on December 31, 1993, will be uncollectible.

[c] For Wong Company, assuming the company estimates that 0.5% of credit sales are uncollectible.

[d] For Wong Company, assuming the company estimates that 5% of the accounts receivable balance on December 31, 1993, will be uncollectible.

7–30 BAD DEBTS The following information pertains to Truan Inc.

[1] Sales made during 1993:

Cash	$100,000
Credit	320,000
Total	$420,000

[2] Accounts Receivable classified by age on December 31, 1993:

Age of Accounts	Accounts Receivable Balance		
Under 30 days	$40,000	1%	400
30–60 days	20,000	3%	600
61–120 days	10,000	10%	1000
Over 120 days	5,000	30%	1500
Total	$75,000		3500

Allow / 400

[3] The Allowance for Doubtful Accounts had a $400 credit balance before adjustment on December 31, 1993.

Instructions

Prepare the adjusting entry on December 31, 1993, to record estimated bad debts under each of the following:

[a] The income statement approach, assuming that the uncollectible rate is 1% of *credit* sales.

[b] The income statement approach, assuming that the uncollectible rate is 0.75% of *total* sales.

[c] The balance sheet approach, assuming that the uncollectible rate is 5% of gross accounts receivable.

[d] The balance sheet approach, assuming that the following uncollectible percentages are appropriate: under 30 days, 1%; 30–60 days, 3%; 61–120 days, 10%; over 120 days, 30%.

7–31 AGING SCHEDULE An aging of Sidlowski Company's accounts receivable on December 31, 1993, reveals the following information:

Time Outstanding	Amount of Accounts Receivable		
Under 30 days	$ 80,000	1.5	1200
30–60 days	16,000	3	480
61–120 days	12,000	15	1800
121–180 days	8,000	30	2400
Over 180 days	4,000	60	2400
Total	$120,000		8280

Based on past experience, the company believes that the following uncollectible percentages are appropriate: under 30 days, 1.5%; 30–60 days, 3%; 61–120 days, 15%; 121–180 days, 30%; over 180 days, 60%.

Instructions

Using the aging of accounts receivable variation of the balance sheet approach, prepare the adjusting entry on December 31, 1993 to record estimated bad debts, assuming that the balance in the Allowance for Doubtful Accounts *before adjustment* is:

[a] $440 credit
[b] $560 debit

7–32 ACCOUNTS RECEIVABLE— SELECTED EVENTS Sienknecht, Inc., reported the following information on its balance sheet dated December 31, 1992:

Accounts receivable	$53,800
Less: Allowance for doubtful accounts	2,400
	$51,400

NRV

The following events occurred during 1993:
[1] Made credit sales of $210,000 and cash sales of $56,000.
[2] Collected $201,800 from customers on account.
[3] Wrote off $3,300 of accounts considered to be uncollectible.
[4] Collected $400 from customers whose accounts had been written off as uncollectible.
[5] Estimated that 6% of the accounts receivable balance at year-end would prove to be uncollectible.

Instructions

Prepare journal entries to record the above events.

7–33 ALLOWANCE METHOD FOR SALES RETURNS Levy Company uses the allowance method to account for its sales returns. Based on past experience, Levy estimates that customers will return approximately 10% of the goods that the company sold. The company also estimates that it can resell goods returned by customers for approximately 70% of the original selling price. Levy's sales during the current accounting period were $400,000. The company uses a perpetual inventory system.

Instructions

[a] Prepare an adjusting journal entry to record estimated sales returns for the current accounting period.
[b] Prepare a journal entry to record the return in the next accounting period of goods that Levy sold for $4,000. Assume that the customer had not paid for the goods.

7–34 ASSIGNING ACCOUNTS RECEIVABLE On July 1, Foggin Company assigned $50,000 of accounts receivable to its bank on a nonnotification basis. On that date the bank advanced $40,000, less a service charge of 1% of the total accounts assigned, and Foggin signed a $40,000 note bearing interest of 1% per month on the unpaid loan balance at the beginning of the month.

During July Foggin collected $33,000 on assigned accounts. The company remitted this amount to the bank on July 31.

During August the company collected the remaining balance of assigned accounts. On August 31 the company paid off the remaining loan balance.

Instructions

Record the above events in general journal form.

7–35 FACTORING ACCOUNTS RECEIVABLE On February 1, Fotis Company factored $80,000 of accounts receivable without recourse with Fast Finance Company on a notification basis. Fast Finance charged a factoring fee of 3% of the amount of receivables factored. To cover sales returns and allowances, Fast Finance withheld 5% of the amount of receivables factored.

Instructions

Prepare the necessary journal entry for Fotis on February 1.

7–36 PLEDGING, ASSIGNING, AND FACTORING   On September 30, Hebert Company engaged in the following transactions:

[1] Obtained a $20,000, 30-day, 12% loan from First National Bank. The company pledged $20,000 of accounts receivable as security for the loan.

[2] Assigned $25,000 of accounts receivable on a nonnotification basis to Commerce Bank. The bank advanced $21,000, less a service charge of $420, and Hebert signed a $21,000 note calling for interest of 1% per month on the unpaid loan balance.

[3] Factored $60,000 of accounts receivable without recourse on a notification basis with Quick Finance Company. Quick Finance charged a factoring fee of 2% of the amount of receivables factored and withheld 10% of the amount factored.

Instructions

Journalize each of the above transactions on September 30.

7–37 INTEREST-BEARING NOTES RECEIVABLE   On November 1, 1992, Breece Manufacturing Company sold land in exchange for a $60,000, 12%, 90-day promissory note. The 12% interest rate was the going market rate for similar notes. Breece had paid $22,000 to acquire the land in 1984. When the note matured, Breece collected principal and interest.

Instructions

Prepare all journal entries (including an adjusting entry) required to record the above events on Breece's books in 1992 and 1993. Assume that Breece uses a calendar-year accounting period and does not make reversing entries.

7–38 RECORDING NOTES RECEIVABLE   On October 1, 1992, Bridges, Inc., sold merchandise having a sales price of $5,000 and received a one-year promissory note with a face amount of $5,500. The note had no stated interest rate, although the market rate for similar notes was 10%. When the note matured, Bridges collected the face amount. Bridges, Inc., uses a calendar-year accounting period and does not make reversing entries.   PV < Face Value

Instructions

[a] Prepare all journal entries (including an adjusting entry) required to record the above events on Bridges' books, assuming that the company records the note at present value.

[b] Prepare all journal entries required to record the above events on Bridges' books, assuming that the company records the note at face amount.

[c] From a theoretical standpoint, is it better for Bridges to record the note at present value or at face amount? Explain your answer.

7–39 DISCOUNTING NOTES RECEIVABLE   Aoki Company has the following three notes receivable: Disc on 5/31

Note	Date of Note	Face Amount	Interest Rate	Time of Note
A	April 1, 1993	$30,000	8%	90-day
B	May 1, 1993	40,000	9%	90-day
C	May 16, 1993	60,000	10%	60-day

Instructions

For each note, calculate the proceeds that Aoki would receive by discounting the note on May 31, 1993, at a rate of 12%.

PROBLEMS

7–40 PETTY CASH   The following events pertain to Arp's Supply House:

June 1   Established an imprest petty cash fund for $400 by writing a check on Carter County Bank.

12   Wrote a check to replenish the fund. The fund contained:

Currency and coins	$ 16
Receipts for transportation-in	303
Receipts for postage expense	66

20   Wrote a check to replenish the fund and to increase the imprest amount to $500. The fund contained:

Currency and coins	$ 36
Receipts for transportation-in	277
Receipts for postage expense	70
Receipts for charitable contributions	25

Instructions

Prepare the necessary journal entries to record the petty cash transactions during June.

7–41   BANK RECONCILIATION   Hinson Company keeps all its cash in a checking account. Presented below are the company's bank reconciliation prepared at the end of May, the general ledger account for cash, and a summary of the company's bank statement for June:

Hinson Company
BANK RECONCILIATION
May 31

Balance per bank statement	$6,250
Add: Deposits in transit	225
	6,475
Deduct: Outstanding checks	418
Correct cash balance	$6,057
Balance per books	$6,072
Deduct: Bank service charge	15
Correct cash balance	$6,057

Cash

Balance, June 1	6,057	June disbursements	25,679
June receipts	26,182		

C|B 6560

Summary of Hinson Company's
Bank Statement for June

Balance, June 1	$ 6,250
Deposits shown for June	25,692
Note and interest collected during June	1,575
Checks that cleared during June	(25,707)
June service charge	(17)
Balance, June 30	7,793

Additional Information

90

[1] During June, Hinson incorrectly recorded two checks. Check no. 507 was drawn for $233 but recorded as $323; check no. 521 was drawn for $180 but recorded as $18. Both checks were issued in payment of accounts payable and cleared the bank in June.   162

[2] During June the bank erroneously charged a $210 check of Minson Company to Hinson Company's account.

[3] Of the $1,575 note and interest collected by the bank during June, $75 represents interest, all of which Hinson earned during the current year. The company has not yet recorded the collection.

Instructions

[a] Prepare a June 30 bank reconciliation.
[b] Prepare journal entries to bring Hinson Company's accounting records up to date.
[c] What amount should Hinson report as *cash* on the balance sheet dated June 30?

7–42   **BANK RECONCILIATION**   Witt Company uses a calendar-year accounting period. The following information is available about the company's cash.

Witt Company
BANK RECONCILIATION
April 30

Balance per bank statement		$4,942
Add: Deposit in transit		610
		5,552
Deduct: Outstanding checks		
No. 606	$177	
No. 607	248	425
Correct cash balance		$5,127
Balance per books		$5,139
Deduct: Bank service charge		12
Correct cash balance		$5,127

First National Bank
General Account: Witt Company

Date	Debits		Credits	Balance
4–30				4,942
5–01			610	5,552
5–02	177			5,375
5–04	248	755	1,552	5,924
5–05	437			5,487
5–09	489		3,621	8,619
5–12	705		1,986	9,900
5–20	930			8,970
5–22	423			8,547
5–26			2,549	11,096
5–29	255 NSF			10,841
5–30	20 DM – *error*	5,798	*Note + int.*	5,023
5–31	14 SC ✓		1,290 CM	6,299 *Begr Balance End*
Total debits	**$10,251**		**Total credits**	**$11,608**

Legend: DM: Debit memo   NSF: Not sufficient funds check
CM: Credit memo   SC: Service charge

4906

Witt Company's Cash Account
Taken from General Ledger
Cash

5139
– 5127
12 = April service charge

Balance, April 30	5,139	Cash Payments Journal, May 31	10,816
Cash Receipts Journal, May 31	10,583		

CB 4906

Information Taken from Witt Company

Cash Receipts Journal			Cash Payments Journal		
	Cash				Cash
Date	Debit		Date	Check No.	Credit
5–03	1,552		5–01	608	755
5–08	3,621		5–03	609	473
5–12	1,986		5–06	610	489
5–25	2,549		5–11	611	705
5–31	875 *DIT*		5–16	612	930
	10,583		5–21	613	243
			5–27	614	511 o/s
			5–29	615	5,798
			5–30	616	346 o/s
			5–31	617	566 o/s
					10,816

Additional Information

[1] During May a collection charge of $20 that was applicable to Hitt Company was erroneously deducted by the bank from Witt Company's account.

[2] The credit memo shown on the bank statement relates to a note that the bank collected on Witt's behalf. The note had a face value of $1,200 and Witt earned interest of $90 during the current accounting period. The company has not yet recorded the collection.

[3] Witt failed to record the bank service charge for April (see April reconciliation).

[4] The NSF check shown on the bank statement had been received during May from a customer on account. The return of the check has not yet been recorded by Witt.

[5] Witt made two errors in recording cash payments during May:

Check No.	Actual Amount of Check	Amount Recorded
609	$437	$473
613	423	243

Check no. 609 was for delivery expense; check no. 613 was issued to purchase equipment.

Instructions

[a] Prepare a bank reconciliation dated May 31.
[b] Prepare the necessary journal entries.

7–43 (Appendix A)   PROOF OF CASH   Refer to the information given for Witt Company in 7–42.

Instructions

[a] Prepare a proof of cash for May.
[b] Prepare the necessary journal entries.

7–44   BANK RECONCILIATION   The accounting period of Riblett Company ends on December 31. The following information is available about the company's cash.

Riblett Company
BANK RECONCILIATION
October 31

Balance per bank statement		$18,005
Add: Deposit in transit		1,790
		19,795
Deduct: Outstanding checks		
No. 773	$4,563	
No. 774	2,118	6,681
Correct cash balance		$13,114
Balance per books		$11,534
Add: Note collected by bank		
Principal	1,500	
Interest earned during current accounting period	100	1,600
		13,134
Deduct: Bank service charge		20
Correct cash balance		$13,114

County National Bank
General Account: Riblett Company

Date	Debits		Credits	Balance
10–31				18,005
11–01			1,790	19,795
11–02	4,563			15,232
11–04	2,118	4,567	5,967	14,514
11–05	963			13,551
11–06			3,410	16,961
11–07	2,515			14,446
11–11			1,037	15,483
11–13	2,264			13,219
11–18	3,325			9,894
11–24	964	*not recorded*	4,255	13,185
11–28	619		750 CM	13,316
11–29	3,000	35 DM	500 CM *Error*	10,781
11–30	665 NSF	22 SC		10,094 ← CB
	Total debits $25,620		**Total credits $17,709**	

Legend: DM: Debit memo   NSF: Not sufficient funds check
CM: Credit memo   SC: Service charge

Riblett Company's Cash Account
Taken from General Ledger
Cash

Balance, Oct. 31	11,534	Cash Payments Journal, Nov. 30	21,575
Cash Receipts Journal, Nov. 30	18,269		

CB 8228

Information Taken from Riblett Company

Cash Receipts Journal			Cash Payments Journal		
Date	Cash Debit		Date	Check No.	Cash Credit
11–03	5,967		11–01	775	4,567
11–06	3,410		11–04	776	963
11–11	1,037		11–05	777	2,515
11–23	4,255		11–10	778	3,264
11–30	3,600 DIT		11–17	779	3,325
	18,269		11–22	780	694
			11–27	781	619
			11–28	782	760 ✓ OS
			11–29	783	3,000
			11–30	784	1,868 ✓ O/S
					21,575

Additional Information

[1] After preparing the October 31 reconciliation, Riblett failed to record the necessary journal entries.

[2] The NSF check had been received during November from a customer on account. Riblett has not yet recorded the return of the check.

[3] The credit memos shown on the bank statement pertain to $750 of bond interest that Riblett earned during the current accounting period and that the bank collected on the company's behalf (collection not yet recorded on Riblett's books) and a $500 collection made for Niblett Company that the bank erroneously credited to Riblett's account.

[4] The $35 debit memo shown on the bank statement pertains to the rental of a safe deposit box during November.

[5] Riblett made two errors in recording cash payments during November.

Check No.	Actual Amount of Check	Amount Recorded
778	$2,264	$3,264 *1000*
780	964	694 *270*

Check no. 778 was issued to purchase equipment; check no. 780 was for advertising expense.

Instructions

[a] Prepare a bank reconciliation dated November 30.
[b] Prepare the necessary journal entries.

7–45 (Appendix A)   PROOF OF CASH   Refer to the information given for Riblett Company in 7–44.

Instructions

[a] Prepare a proof of cash for November.
[b] Prepare the necessary journal entries.

7–46   RECORDING CREDIT SALES   Minor, Inc., began operations in 1993. During the year the company sold merchandise with a gross invoice price of $100,000. All sales were subject to credit terms of 3/10, n/60. Of the total sales of $100,000, the company received payments for 50% within the discount period and 30% after the discount period had expired. The company had not collected the other 20% as of year-end.

Instructions

[a] Prepare general journal entries to record the above transactions using: (1) the *net method* of recording credit sales, and (2) the *gross method* of recording credit sales.
[b] What financial statement balances would Minor report on December 31, 1993, for sales, sales discounts not taken, sales discounts, and accounts receivable under (1) the net method, and (2) the gross method?
[c] Which of the above methods of recording credit sales is theoretically superior? Why?

7–47   ACCOUNTS RECEIVABLE—SELECTED EVENTS   Olson Department Store reported the following information on its balance sheet dated December 31, 1992:

Accounts receivable	$138,000
Less: Allowance for doubtful accounts	7,000
	$131,000

The company engaged in the following transactions during 1993:

[1] Made cash sales of $320,000 and credit sales of $670,000.
[2] Collected $650,800 from customers on account.
[3] Wrote off $7,200 of accounts considered to be uncollectible.
[4] Collected $600 from customers whose accounts had been written off as uncollectible.

Instructions

[a] Prepare journal entries to record the above transactions.
[b] Journalize the adjusting entry to record estimated bad debts at the end of 1993 under each of the following *independent* assumptions:

[1] The company estimates that 1.5% of *credit* sales are uncollectible.
[2] The company estimates that 1.0% of *total* sales are uncollectible.
[3] The company estimates that 7% of the accounts receivable balance at the end of 1993 will be uncollectible.
[4] The company estimates that 75% of the year-end balance of accounts receivable has an uncollectible percentage of 3%; the remaining 25% has an uncollectible percentage of 20%.

[c] Assume that the company estimates its bad debts on the basis of assumption [b-1].

[1] Show how accounts receivable would be presented on the balance sheet prepared at the end of 1993.

[2] What is the dollar effect of the year-end bad-debt adjustment on the pretax income for 1993?

[3] What is the dollar effect of the year-end bad-debt adjustment on the working capital (current assets minus current liabilities) reported at the end of 1993?

7–48 AGING SCHEDULE Harding Corporation operates in an industry that has a high rate of bad debts. On December 31, 1993, before any year-end adjustments, Harding's Accounts Receivable balance was $600,000 and its Allowance for Doubtful Accounts balance was $25,000. The year-end balance reported in the statement of financial position for the Allowance for Doubtful Accounts will be based on the aging schedule shown as follows:

Time Outstanding	Amount of Accounts Receivable	Probability of Collection	Uncollectible
Under 15 days	$300,000	.98	6000
16–30 days	200,000	.90	20000
31–45 days	50,000	.80	10000
46–60 days	30,000	.70	9000
61–75 days	10,000	.65	3500
Over 75 days	10,000	.00	10000
			48500 *written off before B/s date*

Instructions

[a] What is the appropriate balance for the Allowance for Doubtful Accounts on December 31, 1993?

[b] Show how Accounts Receivable would be presented on the balance sheet on December 31, 1993.

[c] What is the dollar effect of the year-end bad-debt adjustment on the pretax income for 1993?

(CMA adapted)

7–49 AGING SCHEDULE From inception of operations to December 31, 1992, Dunn Corporation provided for uncollectible accounts receivable under the allowance method: provisions were made monthly at 2% of credit sales; bad debts written off were charged to the Allowance account; recoveries of bad debts previously written off were credited to the Allowance account; and, no year-end adjustments to the Allowance account were made. Dunn's usual credit terms are net 30 days.

The balance in the Allowance for Doubtful Accounts was $130,000 at January 1, 1993. During 1993 credit sales totaled $9,000,000, interim provisions for doubtful accounts were made at 2% of credit sales, $90,000 of bad debts were written off, and recoveries of accounts previously written off amounted to $15,000. Dunn installed a computer facility in November 1993 and an aging of accounts receivable was prepared for the first time as of December 31, 1993. A summary of the aging is as follows:

Classification by Month of Sale	Balance in Each Category	Estimated % Uncollectible	
Nov.–Dec. 1993	$1,140,000	2%	22800
Jul.–Oct.	600,000	10	60000
Jan.–June	400,000	25	100000
Prior to 1/1/93	130,000	75	97500 52500
	$2,270,000		280300 235300

Based on the review of collectibility of the account balances in the "prior to 1/1/93" aging category, additional receivables totaling $60,000 were written off as of December 31, 1993. Effective with the year ended December 31, 1993, Dunn adopted a new accounting method for estimating the Allowance for Doubtful Accounts at the amount indicated by the year-end aging analysis of accounts receivable.

Instructions

[a] Prepare a schedule analyzing the changes in the Allowance for Doubtful Accounts for the year ended December 31, 1993. Show supporting computations in good form.

[b] Prepare the journal entry for the year-end adjustment to the Allowance for Doubtful Accounts balance as of December 31, 1993.

(AICPA adapted)

7–50   AGING SCHEDULE   Keene Company sells office equipment and supplies to many organizations in the city and surrounding area on contract terms of 2/10, n/30. In the past, over 75% of the credit customers have taken advantage of the discount by paying within 10 days of the invoice date.

The number of customers taking the full 30 days to pay has increased within the last year. Current indications are that less than 60% of the customers are now taking the discount. Bad debts as a percentage of gross credit sales have risen from the 1.5% provided in past years to about four percent in the current year.

The controller has responded to a request for more information on the deterioration in collections of accounts receivable with the report reproduced below.

Keene Company
Finance Committee Report
Accounts Receivable Collections
May 31, 1993

The fact that some credit accounts will prove uncollectible is normal. Annual bad debt write-offs have been 1.5% of gross credit sales over the past 5 years. During the last fiscal year, this percentage increased to slightly less than 4%. The current Accounts Receivable balance is $1.2 million. The condition of this balance in terms of age and probability of collection is as follows:

Proportion of Total	Age Categories	Probability of Collection
68%	not yet due	99%
15%	less than 30 days past due	96½%
8%	30 to 60 days past due	95%
5%	61 to 120 days past due	91%
2½%	121 to 180 days past due	60%
1½%	over 180 days past due	10%

The Allowance for Doubtful Accounts had a credit balance of $30,250 on June 1, 1992. Keene has provided for a monthly bad debts expense accrual during the current fiscal year based on the assumption that four percent of gross credit sales will be uncollectible. Total gross credit sales for the 1992–93 fiscal year amounted to $3 million. Write-offs of bad accounts during the year totaled $108,750.

Instructions

[a] Prepare an accounts receivable aging schedule for the Keene Company using the age categories identified in the controller's report to the Finance Committee showing:
   [1] The amount of accounts receivable outstanding for each age category and in total.
   [2] The estimated amount that is uncollectible for each category and in total.
[b] Compute the amount of the year-end adjustment necessary to bring Allowance for Doubtful Accounts to the balance indicated by the age analysis. Then prepare the necessary journal entry to adjust the accounting records.
[c] First assume a recessionary environment with tight credit and high interest rates. Then
   [1] Identify steps Keene Company might consider to improve the accounts receivable situation.
   [2] Evaluate each step identified in terms of the risks and costs involved.   (CMA adapted)

7–51   CHANGING AN ACCOUNTING ESTIMATE OF BAD DEBTS   Provo Company has been in business for five years, but its financial statements have never been audited. Engaged to perform an audit for 1993, you find that the company's balance sheet has no allowance for doubtful accounts. Bad debts have simply been expensed as written-off and recoveries credited to income as collected. The company's policy is to write off at December 31 of each year those accounts on which no collections have been received for three months. The installment contracts are for two years.

Upon your recommendation, the company agrees to revise its accounts for 1993 to reflect the allowance method of accounting for bad debts. The estimate of bad debts is to be based on a percentage of sales that is derived from the experience of prior years.

Statistics for the past five years are as follows:

Year	Charge Sales	Accounts Written Off and Year of Sale			Recoveries and Year of Sale
1989	$100,000	(1989) $ 550			
1990	250,000	(1989) 1,500	(1990) $1,000		(1989) $100
1991	300,000	(1989) 500	(1990) 4,000	(1991) $1,300	(1990) 400
1992	325,000	(1990) 1,200	(1991) 4,500	(1992) 1,500	(1991) 500
1993	275,000	(1991) 2,700	(1992) 5,000	(1993) 1,400	(1992) 600

Accounts receivable at December 31, 1993, were as follows:

1992 sales	$ 15,000
1993 sales	135,000
	$150,000

Instructions

Prepare the adjusting journal entry or entries with appropriate explanations to set up the Allowance for Doubtful Accounts. Support each item with organized computations. Ignore income tax implications.   (AICPA adapted)

7–52 ASSIGNING AND FACTORING ACCOUNTS RECEIVABLE The following information pertains to Carolina Textiles, Inc.:

June 1 Assigned $75,000 of accounts receivable to City Bank on a nonnotification basis. The bank advanced $64,000, less a service charge of $1,600. Carolina signed a $64,000 promissory note bearing interest of 1% per month on the unpaid loan balance.

28 Collected assigned accounts of $50,000, less sales returns and allowances of $1,500.

29 Sold goods on account for $80,000.

30 Remitted the June 28 collection to City Bank.

30 Factored $50,000 of accounts receivable without recourse with Orange Bank on a notification basis. Orange Bank charged a factoring fee of 3% of the amount of receivables factored and withheld 10% of the amount factored to cover sales returns and allowances.

Instructions

[a] Journalize the above events on Carolina's books.

[b] Assume that Carolina wants to prepare a balance sheet dated June 30. Discuss the financial reporting requirements for those receivables that pertain to the assignment and factoring arrangements.

7–53 NOTES RECEIVABLE DISCOUNTED The following events pertain to Troyer Company:

May 1 Troyer receives a $10,000, 90-day, 10% note in satisfaction of West Company's account receivable of $10,000.

31 Troyer discounts the note with recourse at First Bank. The discount rate is 12%. (Relevant circumstances indicate that the discounting should be accounted for as a sale of the note.)

July 30 West Company pays First Bank the total amount owed on the note.

Instructions

[a] Prepare journal entries to record the above events on Troyer books using each of the following approaches to accounting for notes receivable discounted:
  [1] Footnote approach.   [2] Contra account approach.

[b] Assume that instead of paying the note on July 30, West Company dishonors it. First Bank charges Troyer with the maturity value and a $20 protest fee. Journalize the entry or entries required for Troyer on July 30 under the:
  [1] Footnote approach.   [2] Contra account approach.

[c] What is the fundamental difference between these two approaches to accounting for notes receivable discounted?

7–54 NOTES RECEIVABLE   The following events pertain to Rosa Company:

Dec. 1, 1992   Rosa Company sells merchandise to Luna Company. The merchandise has a selling price of $10,000, and Rosa receives a one-year promissory note that has a face amount of $11,000 and no stated interest rate. The market rate for similar notes is 10%.

Dec. 16, 1992   Rosa sells land to Lyons Company in exchange for a $90,000, 10%, 90-day promissory note. The 10% interest rate equals the going market rate for similar notes. The cost of the land to Rosa is $60,000.

Jan. 30, 1993   Rosa discounts the Lyons note with recourse at County Bank. The discount rate is 12%. (Relevant circumstances indicate that Rosa Company should account for the discounting as a sale of the note.)

Mar. 16, 1993   Lyons pays County Bank the full amount owed.

Nov. 30, 1993   Luna pays Rosa the full amount owed.

Rosa Company uses a calendar-year accounting period and does not make reversing entries. The company records notes receivable at present value on the date received, and it uses the footnote approach to accounting for notes receivable discounted.

Instructions

[a] Prepare journal entries (including adjusting entries) to record the above events on Rosa's books.

[b] Should Rosa recognize interest earned on the Luna note? Explain the rationale for your answer.

[c] Assume that the Luna and Lyons notes are dishonored when they mature. County Bank charges Rosa with the maturity value of the Lyons note and a $60 protest fee. Journalize the entry or entries required for Rosa on March 16, 1993, and November 30, 1993.

7–55 NOTES RECEIVABLE   You are examining Nichols Corporation's financial statements for the year ended December 31, 1993. Your analysis of the 1993 entries in the Trade Notes Receivable account was as follows:

Nichols Corporation
ANALYSIS OF TRADE NOTES RECEIVABLE
For the Year Ended December 31, 1993

			Trade Notes Receivable	
Date		Folio	*Debit*	*Credit*
Jan. 1	Balance forward		$118,000	
Feb. 28	Received $25,000 6% note due 10/29/93 from Daley, whose trade account was past due.	MEMO		
28	Discounted Daley note at 6%.	CR		$ 24,960
Mar. 29	Received noninterest-bearing demand note from Edge, the Corporation's treasurer, for a loan.	CD	6,200	
Aug. 30	Received principal and interest due from Allen and, in accordance with agreement, two principal payments in advance.	CR		34,200
Sept. 4	Paid protest fee on note dishonored by Charnes.	CD	5	
Nov. 1	Received check dated 2/1/94 in settlement of Bailey note. The check was included in cash on hand 12/31/93.	CR		8,120

Date	Description		Debit	Credit
Nov. 4	Paid protest fee and maturity value of Daley note to bank. Note discounted 2/28/93 was dishonored.	CD	26,031	
Dec. 27	Accepted furniture and fixtures with a fair market value of $24,000 in full settlement from Daley.	GJ		24,000
31	Received check dated 1/3/94 from Edge in payment of 3/29/93 note. (The check was included in petty cash until 1/2/94, when it was returned to Edge in exchange for a new demand note of the same amount.)	CR		6,200
31	Received principal and interest on Charnes note.	CR		42,437
31	Accrued interest on Allen note.	GJ	1,200	
	Totals		$151,436	$139,917

The following information is available:

[1] Balances at January 1, 1993, were a debit of $1,400 in the Accrued Interest Receivable account and a credit of $400 in the Unearned Interest Income account. The $118,000 debit balance in the Trade Notes Receivable account consisted of the following three notes:

Allen note dated 8/31/89, payable in annual installments of $10,000 principal plus accrued interest at 6% each Aug. 31	$70,000
Bailey note discounted to Nichols at 6% on 11/1/92, due 11/1/93	8,000
Charnes note for $40,000 plus 6% interest dated 12/31/92, due on 9/1/93	40,000

[2] No entries were made during 1993 to the Accrued Interest Receivable account or the Unearned Interest Income account, and only one entry for a credit of $1,200 on December 31 appeared in the Interest Income account.

[3] All notes were from trade customers unless otherwise indicated.

[4] Debits and credits offsetting Trade Notes Receivable debit and credit entries were correctly recorded unless the facts indicate otherwise.

[5] Nichols Corporation uses the contra account approach when accounting for notes receivable discounted. Notes receivable are discounted with recourse and are properly accounted for as sales. The company also follows the practice of debiting Trade Accounts Receivable instead of Dishonored Notes Receivable when a customer's note is dishonored.

Instructions

Prepare a worksheet to adjust each entry to correct or properly reclassify it, if necessary. Enter your adjustments in the proper columns to correspond with the date of each entry. Do not combine related entries for different dates. Your completed worksheet will provide the basis for one compound journal entry to correct all entries to Trade Notes Receivable and related accounts for 1993. Formal journal entries are not required. In addition to the information shown in the above analysis, the following headings are suggested:

Adjustment or Reclassification Required

Trade Notes Receivable	Trade Accounts Receivable	Interest Income	Other Accounts		
				Amount	
Debit (Credit)	Debit (Credit)	Debit (Credit)	Account Title	Debit	Credit

(AICPA adapted)

CASES

7–56   OUTSTANDING CHECKS   You are the controller for Reider, Inc., a company that uses a calendar-year accounting period. Walter Brush, a new person on the accounting staff, has just prepared a bank reconciliation dated December 31, 1993, and has determined that outstanding checks are $14,895. Walter believes that this amount should be classified as liabilities on Reider's year-end balance sheet because the checks have not cleared the bank as of December 31.

Instructions

Explain how Reider, Inc. should account for the outstanding checks on its year-end balance sheet.

7–57   NOTES RECEIVABLE AND BAD DEBTS   Gann Company has significant amounts of trade accounts receivable. Gann uses the allowance method to estimate bad debts instead of the specific write-off method. During the year, some specific accounts were written off as uncollectible, and some that were previously written off as uncollectible were collected.

Gann also has some interest-bearing notes receivable for which the face amount plus interest at the prevailing rate of interest is due at maturity. The notes were received on July 1, 1992, and are due on June 30, 1994.

Instructions

[a] What are the deficiencies of the specific write-off method?
[b] What are the two basic allowance methods used to estimate bad debts, and what is the theoretical justification for each?
[c] How should Gann account for the collection of the specific accounts previously written off as uncollectible?
[d] How should Gann report the effects of the interest-bearing notes receivable on its December 31, 1993, balance sheet and its income statement for the year ended December 31, 1993? Why?

(AICPA adapted)

7–58   NOTES RECEIVABLE AND BAD DEBTS   **Part 1.**   On July 1, 1992, Mayes Company, a calendar-year company, sold special-order merchandise on credit and received in return an interest-bearing note receivable from the customer. Mayes Company will receive interest at the prevailing rate for a note of this type. Both the principal and interest are due in one lump sum on June 30, 1993.

Instructions

[a] When should Mayes Company report interest income from the note receivable? Discuss the rationale for your answer.
[b] Assume that the note receivable was discounted *without recourse* at a bank on December 31, 1992. How would Mayes Company determine the amount of the discount and what is the appropriate accounting for the discounting transaction?

Part 2.   On December 31, 1992, Mayes Company had significant amounts of accounts receivable as a result of credit sales to its customers. Mayes Company uses the allowance method based on credit sales to estimate bad debts. Based on past experience, 1% of credit sales normally will not be collected. This pattern is expected to continue.

Instructions

[a] Discuss the rationale for using the allowance method based on credit sales to estimate bad debts. Contrast this method with the allowance method based on the balance in the trade receivables accounts.
[b] How should Mayes Company report the allowance for bad debts account on its balance sheet at December 31, 1992? Also, describe the alternatives, if any, for presentation of bad debts expense in Mayes Company's 1992 income statement.   (AICPA adapted)

7–59   NOTES RECEIVABLE, ASSIGNING, AND FACTORING   On July 1, 1992, Harris Company sold special-order merchandise on credit and received in return an interest-bearing note receivable from the customer. Harris will receive interest at the prevailing rate for a note of this type. Both the principal and interest are due in one lump sum on June 30, 1993.

On September 1, 1992, Harris sold special-order merchandise on credit and received in return a noninterest-bearing note receivable from the customer. The prevailing rate of interest for a note of this type is determinable. The note receivable is due in one lump sum on August 31, 1994.

Harris also has significant amounts of trade accounts receivable as a result of credit sales to its customers. On October 1, 1992, some trade accounts receivable were assigned to Davidson Finance Company on a with-recourse, nonnotification basis for an advance of 75% of their amount at an interest charge of 20% on the balance outstanding.

On November 1, 1992, other trade accounts receivable were factored on a without-recourse basis. The factor withheld 5% of the trade accounts receivable factored as protection against sales returns and allowances and charged a finance charge of 3%.

Instructions

[a] How should Harris determine the interest revenue for 1992 on the
   1. interest-bearing note receivable? Why?
   2. noninterest-bearing note receivable? Why?

[b] How should Harris report the interest-bearing note receivable and the noninterest-bearing note receivable on its balance sheet at December 31, 1992?

[c] How should Harris account for subsequent collections on the trade accounts receivable assigned on October 1, 1992, and the payments to Davidson Finance? Why?

[d] How should Harris account for the trade accounts receivable factored on November 1, 1992? Why?
                                      (AICPA adapted)

7–60 CREDIT CARD PLAN One of your corporate clients operates a full-line department store that dominates its market area, is easily accessible to public and private transportation, has adequate parking facilities, and is near a large, permanent military base. The president of the company seeks your advice on a proposal he received.

A local bank in which your client has an account recently affiliated with a popular national credit card plan and has invited your client to participate. Under the plan, affiliated banks mail credit card applications to persons in the community who have good credit ratings, regardless of whether they are bank customers. If the recipient wishes to receive a credit card, he completes, signs, and returns the application and installment credit agreement. Card holders may charge merchandise or services at any participating establishment throughout the nation.

The bank guarantees payment to all participating merchants on invoices that have been properly completed, signed, and validated with the impression of credit cards that have not expired or been reported stolen or otherwise canceled. Local merchants, including your client, may turn in all card-validated sales tickets or invoices to their affiliated local bank at any time and receive immediate credits to their checking accounts of 96.5% of the face value of the invoices. If card users pay the bank in full within 30 days for amounts billed, the bank levies no added charges against them. If they elect to make their payments under a deferred payment plan, the bank adds a service charge with an effective annual interest rate of 18% on unpaid balances. Only the local affiliated banks and the franchiser of the credit card plan share in these revenues.

The 18% service charge approximates what your client has been billing customers who pay their accounts over an extended period on a schedule similar to that of the credit card plan. Participation in the plan does not prevent your client from continuing its credit business.

Instructions

[a] What are (1) the positive and (2) the negative financial factors and accounting factors that your client should consider in deciding whether to participate in the credit card plan? Explain.

[b] If your client participates in the plan, which income statement and balance sheet accounts may change materially as the plan becomes fully operative? (Such factors as market position, sales mix, prices, and markup are expected to remain about the same as in the past.) Explain.
                                      (AICPA adapted)

JUDGMENT CASES

7–61 TROUBLED NOTES RECEIVABLE Sam Farmer is the chief financial officer for a small, midwestern company that manufactures farm implements and offers long term credit to buyers. In fulfilling the financing function, the company makes a number of "noninterest bearing" loans.

Under the terms of these loans, the borrower signs a note for an amount greater than the funds actually lent and the interest revenue to the company is implicit in the difference between the amount lent and the amount to be repaid (i.e., the discount on the note receivable). Sam is aware of the provisions of *APB Opinion No. 21,* "Interest on Receivables and Payables" that require the company to amortize the discount on the long term receivables, and the company has consistently recognized interest revenue in this manner.

Recently, Sam read an article in the local newspaper that described the financial implications of a recent drought in the area in which many of the company's best customers operate. While there is no evidence that any financial difficulties are being experienced by the company's customers, the article states that many bankruptcies of farming operations are expected. Sam believes that some of the company's notes receivable may eventually become uncollectible or only partially collectible. He wonders whether his company should continue to recognize interest revenue on those loans that have some uncertainty as to their ultimate collectibility.

Instructions

Help Sam decide what to do. If you believe that additional evidence is necessary before making any decisions, describe the evidence that Sam should obtain in attempting to resolve the problem.

7–62   RECEIVABLE CLASSIFICATION   You are the independent CPA for Enos, Inc., an electronic products' wholesaler. Enos has recently made an important sale to a retail company that is opening several new outlets. Due to the size of the sale, Enos has allowed the retailer to acquire the goods by signing a three-year, interest-bearing note rather than requiring the normal credit terms of 30 days. Enos uses a one-year time period for classifying current assets and liabilities on its balance sheet, and this practice is still appropriate in light of the recent sale to the retailer.

When you explain to Enos' management that the receivable should be classified as noncurrent because of its maturity date, management objects, stating that the company intends to discount the receivable without recourse at a local bank fairly soon after the balance sheet date. Management asserts that although the bank normally used by the company does not engage in such transactions, other banks would be quite willing to do so because they commonly do so for other businesses. Enos' management further objects to classifying the receivable as a noncurrent asset because such a classification would cause the company to violate one of its lending covenants that requires a minimum amount of working capital.

The retailer is a fairly small company that has been a customer of Enos for many years. You recall recently reading a rather negative newspaper article about financial difficulties encountered by the retailer due to keen competition from other large chains of electronics retailers.

Your audit of Enos is now almost completed, and Enos will not accomplish the transfer of the receivable prior to the issuance of the financial statements.

Instructions

Would you accept classifying the receivable as a current asset? Explain your answer. If you believe that additional evidence is needed to resolve the case, be sure to identify the nature of that information as part of your solution.

CHAPTER 8

—

Inventories: Basic Valuation Methods

OBJECTIVES

1. To discuss and illustrate the financial accounting and reporting requirements for inventories.
2. To explain the methods used to determine inventory quantities on hand.
3. To explain the nature of costs that should be included in inventory.
4. To discuss and illustrate various inventory cost flow methods.
5. To discuss and illustrate the valuation of inventory at the lower of cost or market value.
6. To indicate exceptional cases under generally accepted accounting principles of inventory valuation above cost.
7. To indicate effects of inventory errors on financial statements.
8. To explain conceptual considerations in accounting for inventories.

INVENTORIES

I nventories are goods that are held for sale in the ordinary course of business and goods that are in production or that will soon be used in production. A **service business**, such as a legal firm, normally has no inventories. In contrast, inventories are one of the most important assets of **merchandising businesses** and **manufacturing businesses**, which typically derive most of their revenues from sales of inventories. Moreover, cost of goods sold is usually the largest expense of such companies. It is not surprising, then, that the managers of merchandising and manufacturing companies often devote substantial resources to inventory planning and control. Furthermore, users of financial statements regard inventory information as extremely important when they make investment, lending, and similar decisions.

In this chapter and the next, we discuss the accounting valuation of inventories. Inventories are physical resources, and our primary concern is how accountants obtain a financial representation of such resources for external reporting purposes. Most of our discussion focuses on **inventory valuation methods**, often called **inventory pricing methods**, that companies use to prepare their external financial statements in accordance with GAAP. This chapter presents an overview of basic valuation methods; Chapter 9 introduces several additional methods.

ACQUISITION OF INVENTORIES

A merchandising company buys finished inventory and later resells it. In contrast, a manufacturing company produces its inventory. In doing so, a manufacturing company incurs the following **manufacturing** (or **production**) **costs:**

1. **Direct materials.** Raw materials costs that can be traced directly and practically to units of the firm's product. In the case of a manufacturer of wooden desks, for example, the cost of the wood is a direct materials cost.
2. **Direct labor.** Labor costs that can be traced directly and practically to units of the firm's product. For the desk manufacturer, the labor costs of the employees who assemble the desks are direct labor costs.
3. **Manufacturing overhead.** All manufacturing costs, other than direct materials and direct labor, necessary to construct the company's product. For the desk manufacturer, examples are the costs of factory maintenance, the depreciation of factory equipment, and the glue used on certain parts of each desk.

CLASSIFICATION OF INVENTORIES

A merchandising company has one class of inventory, commonly called **merchandise** (or **merchandise inventory**). A manufacturing company, however, may have the following four categories of inventory:

1. **Raw materials.** Goods that can be traced directly to units of the firm's product. An example is the desk manufacturer's inventory of wood.
2. **Factory supplies.** Goods that can be traced only indirectly to units of the firm's product. An example is the desk manufacturer's supply of glue. Generally, it is not practical to trace glue to specific desks. The cost of factory supplies used is an element of overhead that is commonly called **indirect materials.**

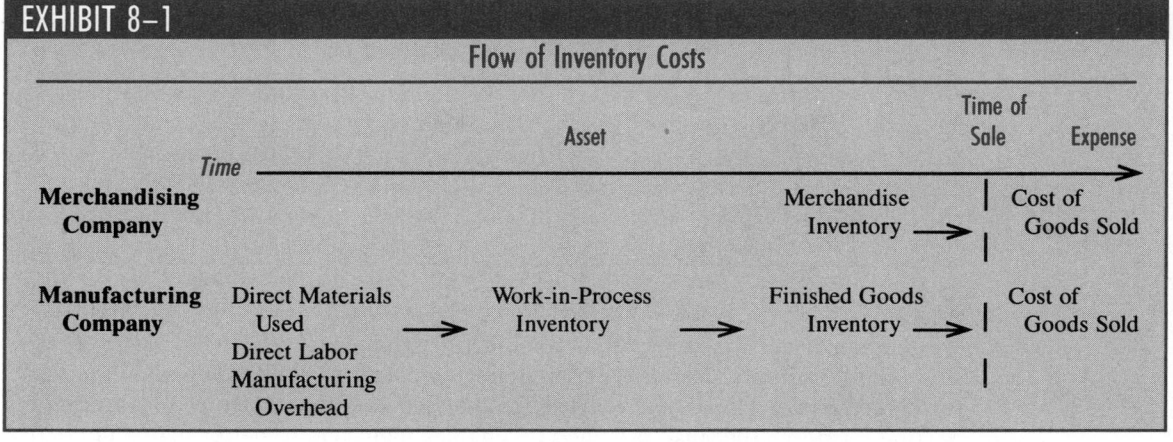

EXHIBIT 8–1

Flow of Inventory Costs

| | | | | Time of Sale | Expense |
| | | | Asset | | |

Time →

Merchandising Company — Merchandise Inventory → | Cost of Goods Sold

Manufacturing Company — Direct Materials Used, Direct Labor, Manufacturing Overhead → Work-in-Process Inventory → Finished Goods Inventory → | Cost of Goods Sold

3. **Work (goods) in process.** Goods that are partially completed. Goods in process have been assigned appropriate manufacturing costs and will remain in production until completed.
4. **Finished goods.** Products that are completed and ready for sale. Finished goods have been assigned their full share of manufacturing costs.

FLOW OF INVENTORY COSTS

Asset/Liability Measurement

Matching

Exhibit 8–1 compares the typical flow of inventory costs in a merchandising company with that in a manufacturing concern. Note that inventory costs are initially accounted for as assets. In other words, a company's inventory is first measured at its historical cost. To implement the matching principle, the costs are expensed in the period when the inventory is sold. In this way the revenue generated by the sale of inventory can be related to the costs incurred to purchase or produce it.

A merchandising company and a manufacturing company calculate cost of goods sold in somewhat different ways. In the comparison shown in Exhibit 8–2, we assume a periodic inventory system.

Note in Exhibit 8–2 that a merchandising company adds the cost of its net purchases to the cost of its beginning inventory to derive the cost of goods available for sale. Because a manufacturing company *produces* (rather than *purchases*) its finished goods inventory, it adds the cost of goods manufactured. We discussed the calculation of net purchases in Chapter 5. The computation of the cost of goods manufactured by Parker Company is shown in Exhibit 8–3 (dollar amounts assumed). The schedule of cost of goods manufactured is generally used for internal purposes and is seldom published.

Observe in Exhibit 8–3 that to calculate cost of goods manufactured, we add the total manufacturing costs incurred during the period to the beginning work-in-process inventory. The total ($257,000) tells us the amount of manufacturing costs that we must account for during the period. From this total we subtract the cost of the ending work-in-process inventory (the partially completed goods on hand at the end of the period) to derive the cost of goods manufactured during the period. As noted in Exhibit 8–2, the cost of goods manufactured is included in the calculation of a manufacturing company's cost of goods sold.

> ### EXHIBIT 8-2
> #### Calculation of Cost of Goods Sold
>
> | Merchandising Company | Manufacturing Company |
> |---|---|
> | Beginning Merchandise Inventory | Beginning Finished Goods Inventory |
> | + Net Purchases | + Cost of Goods Manufactured |
> | = Cost of Goods Available for Sale | = Cost of Goods Available for Sale |
> | − Ending Merchandise Inventory | − Ending Finished Goods Inventory |
> | = Cost of Goods Sold | = Cost of Goods Sold |

As our discussion suggests, a manufacturing company accounts for inventories somewhat differently from a merchandising company. For example, many manufacturing companies use **direct costing** (also called **variable costing**) for internal reporting purposes, because this method enables managers to better plan and control their company's operations. Under direct costing, the accountant classifies all manufacturing costs as either variable or fixed. Variable manufacturing costs are those that vary in total in direct proportion to changes in production volume. They include direct materials, direct labor, and variable overhead. Fixed manufacturing costs, in contrast, are those that remain constant in total as production volume changes over a relevant range of production. Fixed manufacturing costs are confined to such overhead costs as property taxes and depreciation. Under the direct costing method, the accountant records as inventory costs only the variable manufacturing costs. Fixed overhead costs are expensed in the period in which they are incurred, because it is assumed that a company incurs these costs primarily to allow production to occur.

Direct costing contrasts with **absorption costing,** in which fixed overhead costs are treated as a part of the cost of inventory. Proponents of absorption costing point out that because both variable and fixed overhead costs are normally necessary to produce specific goods, both costs should be inventoried. Generally accepted accounting principles require the use of absorption costing for external reporting purposes, because most accountants view fixed overhead as an important component of the historical cost of inventory that is manufactured. Direct costing is not acceptable under GAAP.

Many manufacturing companies use standard costs to account for their inventories. Primarily a management tool, **standard costing** requires a company to accumulate inventory costs using amounts that *should be* incurred to manufacture the inventory rather than actual costs. Standard costing allows a company to detect variances between what it should cost to produce a product and what it actually costs. Standard costs are acceptable for external reporting under GAAP, however, if they reasonably approximate actual costs determined using a recognized cost flow method. Peculiarities in accounting for inventories of manufacturing companies, such as direct costing and standard costing, are covered more extensively in cost accounting courses.

NATURE OF THE INVENTORY VALUATION PROBLEM

Inventory accounting problems would be relatively simple if a company instantaneously sold all the inventory that it purchased or produced. In most cases, however, there is a lag between the time goods are purchased or produced and the time they are sold. As a result, most companies have an inventory of unsold goods on hand at the end of the accounting period, and accountants must then resolve the question of how

EXHIBIT 8-3

Parker Company
SCHEDULE OF COST OF GOODS MANUFACTURED
For the Year Ended December 31

Direct materials used		
Raw materials inventory, Jan. 1	$ 23,000	
Add: Net purchases of raw materials	157,000	
Cost of raw materials available for use	180,000	
Less: Raw materials inventory, Dec. 31	25,000	$155,000
Direct labor		47,000
Manufacturing overhead		
Indirect labor	12,000	
Indirect materials	3,000	
Factory utilities	5,000	
Depreciation of factory building	3,500	
Depreciation of factory equipment	6,000	
Taxes on factory properties	7,000	
Miscellaneous factory expenses	1,500	38,000
Total manufacturing costs incurred during the year		240,000
Add: Work-in-process inventory, Jan. 1		17,000
Total manufacturing costs to account for		257,000
Less: Work-in-process inventory, Dec. 31		15,000
Cost of goods manufactured		$242,000

to allocate the cost of goods available for sale between (1) the goods on hand (ending inventory) and (2) the goods sold.

The accountant may determine cost of goods sold **residually,** that is, by subtracting the cost of the ending inventory from the cost of goods available for sale. To do this, the accountant must value the ending inventory directly, which means resolving the following important questions:

1. What is the physical quantity of goods on hand?
2. What is the accounting valuation of those goods?

DETERMINATION OF INVENTORY QUANTITIES

The method for determining the physical quantity of goods on hand differs depending on whether a company uses a periodic or a perpetual inventory system. Regardless of the system used, the accountant must understand the general principles to determine which goods properly belong in inventory and which goods do not.

PERIODIC VERSUS PERPETUAL INVENTORY SYSTEM

Under a **periodic inventory system**, inventory quantities are *not* maintained on a day-to-day basis in the accounting records. Instead, at the end of each accounting period, the quantity of unsold goods is determined by a physical count. The accountant then determines the inventory's cost by using one of the generally accepted inventory cost flow methods discussed later in the chapter. The inventory cost thus derived is subtracted from the cost of goods available for sale to determine the cost of goods sold. In a periodic system, therefore, cost of goods sold is a residual figure that includes the cost of goods actually sold as well as the cost of those lost by theft, spoilage, and similar causes. Although a periodic system is not ideal for inventory planning and control, it is relatively inexpensive and is often appropriate for products that turn over rapidly and have low unit costs, such as groceries and hardware.

In contrast, a **perpetual inventory system** requires the accountant to maintain continuous records of the quantity of inventory on hand. Under a perpetual system, an account may be established for each product; these accounts are kept in an **inventory subsidiary ledger**. The account for each product shows increases and decreases, as well as the balance on hand. In a complete perpetual system, the subsidiary ledger accounts are maintained in cost dollars as well as in units. Consequently, the balance in the merchandise inventory control account in the general ledger should agree with the total of the individual account balances in the subsidiary ledger.

In a perpetual system it is still desirable to physically count the inventory at least once each year, but the count need not occur at year-end. This count tests the accuracy of the perpetual records. An actual count frequently reveals differences between the records and the physical units on hand. These differences may exist for several reasons, including theft, evaporation, and inaccurate recording. Whenever a careful count indicates differences, the accounting records should be appropriately adjusted. If, for example, the accounting records show inventory on hand costing $10,000 but the physical count indicates only $9,885, the following entry is necessary:

Inventory Shortage	115	
Merchandise Inventory		115
(To record inventory shortage. $10,000 − $9,885 = $115.)		

Materiality The inventory shortage is a loss account that, if material in amount, should be reported separately in the income statement. Many companies simply report inventory shortages as part of cost of goods sold. This practice is justified on the ground that some shortages may be considered a normal cost in the selling process.

Although the perpetual system is more costly than the periodic system to implement, it facilitates better inventory planning and control. In the past, perpetual records were used primarily for low-volume, high-cost items such as jewelry, fur coats, and automobiles. In recent years, however, the widespread use of electronic computers has enabled companies to maintain perpetual records for a greater variety of inventory items. With computers, companies can conveniently store and retrieve large amounts of data in a cost-effective manner. Many companies account for part of their inventories on a periodic basis and the remainder on a perpetual basis.

In a periodic inventory system, merchandise purchases are debited to the Purchases account. Throughout the accounting period, therefore, the Merchandise Inventory account contains only the balance that was on hand at the beginning of the period. At the end of the period, the accountant makes an adjusting entry to record the ending inventory as well as the cost of goods sold for the entire period, as discussed in Chapter 5. In contrast, under a perpetual system, the Merchandise Inventory and Cost of Goods Sold accounts are continually maintained. Merchandise purchases are therefore charged directly to an Inventory account. Moreover, an entry to record a sale is accompanied by an entry that reduces the Inventory account and recognizes an increase in Cost of Goods Sold. At the end of the accounting period, an adjusting entry is not required, because the Inventory account reflects the balance on hand and the Cost of Goods Sold account reflects the expense incurred during the entire period. The proper accounting for selected merchandise transactions under periodic and perpetual inventory systems is shown in Exhibit 8–4.

EXHIBIT 8–4

Accounting Under Periodic and Perpetual Inventory Systems

Transaction	Periodic Inventory System			Perpetual Inventory System		
Purchase merchandise costing $4,000 on account	Purchases	4,000		Merchandise Inventory	4,000	
	Accounts Payable		4,000	Accounts Payable		4,000
Pay freight of $45 on purchase	Transportation-In	45		Merchandise Inventory	45	
	Cash		45	Cash		45
Return defective merchandise costing $250	Accounts Payable	250		Accounts Payable	250	
	Purchase Returns		250	Merchandise Inventory		250
Sell goods costing $3,000 on account for $6,000	Accounts Receivable	6,000		Accounts Receivable	6,000	
	Sales		6,000	Sales		6,000
				Cost of Goods Sold	3,000	
				Merchandise Inventory		3,000

GOODS TO INCLUDE IN INVENTORY

The general rule for determining what items to include in inventory is that goods belong to the entity that has legal title, regardless of where the goods are located. Consequently, when title to goods passes from seller to buyer, the seller should record a sale and exclude the goods from inventory. The buyer in turn should record a purchase and include the goods in inventory.

The Uniform Commercial Code provides that title to goods may pass at any time expressly agreed to by buyer and seller. When the time of title passage is not expressly agreed on, the buyer takes title when goods exist and are identified to the contract, and the seller has completed performance in regard to delivering the goods. If goods are shipped **FOB (free on board) shipping point**, title passes to the buyer when the seller delivers the goods to the carrier. Title to goods shipped **FOB destination** passes when the goods arrive at their ultimate destination. If the buyer agrees to pick up the goods at the seller's place of business, title passes when the seller has completed the goods and identified them to the contract.

Application of the legal title rule may pose problems when a company owns goods that are located elsewhere or when it holds goods that belong to someone else. We discuss these problems in the following sections.

Goods in Transit

During an accounting period, the accountant normally records purchases when goods are received and sales when goods are shipped, regardless of the precise moment at which title passes. This procedure is expedient, and because title usually passes in the same period, no material misstatements occur in the financial statements.

Materiality

On the other hand, the accountant should carefully analyze the invoice terms of goods that are in transit at the end of an accounting period to determine who has legal title. The analysis should encompass goods purchased as well as goods sold. Goods shipped FOB shipping point belong to the buyer; those shipped FOB destination belong to the seller. When analyzing goods in transit, the accountant should examine invoices for several days before and after the end of the accounting period in order to ensure a proper cutoff at year-end.

Consigned Goods

A **consignment** is a method of marketing goods in which the owner (the **consignor**) transfers physical possession of certain goods to an agent (the **consignee**) who sells the goods on the owner's behalf. Goods on consignment should be included in the consignor's inventory and excluded from the consignee's inventory. Similarly, goods in the hands of others for sale, storage, processing, or other reasons should be included in the inventory of the party holding title. Accounting for consignments is covered in advanced accounting courses.

DETERMINATION OF INVENTORY VALUATION AT COST

Asset/Liability Measurement

In accordance with the asset/liability measurement principle, the quantity of inventory on hand should be valued initially at its historical cost. Two questions must be answered when determining an inventory cost valuation:

1. What costs should be included in inventory?
2. What method should be used to associate inventory costs with the physical units on hand?

COSTS TO INCLUDE IN INVENTORY

An accountant must differentiate between product costs and period costs. **Product costs** "attach to" the inventory. These costs are initially capitalized and are regarded as assets (i.e., inventory). When the inventory is later sold, the product costs expire and are therefore charged to expense (cost of goods sold). In contrast, **period costs** are expensed in the period in which they are incurred. In other words, period costs are not inventoried, because their relationship to the product (inventory) is generally considered too difficult to trace. Selling expenses, general and administrative expenses, and income tax expense are examples of period costs.

Product costs are incurred, either directly or indirectly, to purchase or produce inventory as well as to bring the inventory to a condition and location for sale. These costs include direct materials, direct labor, and overhead. They also include the invoice cost of purchased merchandise as well as the costs of inbound transportation, insurance, inspection, handling, warehousing, and purchasing.

The specific content of product costs varies somewhat between companies. Many companies use only the invoice cost plus the cost of inbound transportation to value inventories of purchased goods. Other costs that should in theory be inventoried (such as insurance, handling, and purchasing costs) are treated as period costs. This treatment is justified on the ground that it is often impossible to meaningfully allocate certain indirect costs to inventory. The treatment is considered acceptable if a company applies it *consistently* over time to either a certain portion or to all of its inventories. Inventory costs capitalized for financial reporting purposes may differ from those capitalized for income tax purposes.

Consistency

Materiality

Generally accepted accounting principles do not permit a company to capitalize the interest cost associated with inventories that are routinely manufactured or otherwise produced in large quantities on a repetitive basis. However, interest cost should be capitalized if it is a material part of the cost of acquiring inventory items that are constructed as discrete projects, such as ships.[1] For these items, interest cost represents an important component of historical cost. Companies should also capitalize

---

[1]*FASB Statement of Financial Accounting Standards No. 34*, "Capitalization of Interest Cost," 1979.

EXHIBIT 8–5

Net and Gross Methods of Recording Purchases

Transaction	Net Method		Gross Method	
July 1				
ABC Company purchases merchandise for $100, terms 2/10, n/30.	Purchases*	98	Purchases*	100
	Accounts Payable	98	Accounts Payable	100
Alternative Assumption No. 1				
July 10				
ABC Company pays within the discount period.	Accounts Payable	98	Accounts Payable	100
	Cash	98	Purchase Discounts	2
			Cash	98
Alternative Assumption No. 2				
July 30				
ABC Company pays after the discount period.	Accounts Payable	98	Accounts Payable	100
	Discounts Lost (or		Cash	100
	Interest Expense)	2		
	Cash	100		

*Assuming a periodic inventory system.

interest as part of the historical cost of acquiring certain plant assets. We explain interest capitalization more fully in Chapter 11.

Invoice Cost

The invoice cost itself is the largest component of product cost for purchased inventory. To determine the invoice cost, **trade discounts** are subtracted from the list price and not entered in the accounting records.[2] Theory and practice usually differ about whether the invoice cost component of product cost should also exclude **cash discounts**.[3]

In theory, the cost of purchases (and of inventory) should be measured net of cash discounts allowable. This is known as the **net method** of recording purchases; it is compared with the **gross method** in Exhibit 8–5. The cost measured under the net method represents the cash-equivalent price on the date of purchase and therefore the correct historical cost. Cash discounts encourage early payment. Any discount not taken represents the cost of engaging in a deferred payment transaction. Accordingly, this cost should be shown as a financing expense on the income statement.

In practice, most companies record purchases (and inventory) at gross invoice amounts. Cash discounts taken are recorded in a Purchase Discounts account at the time of payment, and this balance is deducted from purchases when measuring cost of

[2] **A trade discount** is a reduction from a catalog list price granted by manufacturers and wholesalers of certain products. The use of trade discounts enables a company (1) to revise its prices periodically without having to reprint its catalogs, and (2) to set different prices for different types of customers.
[3] **A cash discount** is a reduction from the amount of an invoice that is offered for early payment of cash. The purpose of a cash discount is to encourage early payment. A cash discount is usually expressed in terms such as "2/10, n/30." These terms mean that the purchaser may deduct 2% from the amount of the invoice if payment is made within 10 days of the invoice date. A purchaser who fails to pay within 10 days must pay the entire invoice amount within 30 days of the invoice date. As we explained in Chapter 7, the effective annual interest cost associated with not paying within 10 days is 36.7%. It is usually advantageous for a company to take all available cash discounts, even if the company must borrow money to do so.

goods sold.[4] This procedure is theoretically deficient in two major respects. First, it technically violates the matching principle, because discounts are recorded only when cash is paid rather than when the purchases that give rise to the discounts are made. Second, the procedure does not allocate discounts taken between goods sold and those on hand. This tends to understate cost of goods sold and overstate net income and ending inventory. Despite its theoretical shortcomings, the gross method is supported on the practical grounds that (1) it is more convenient than the net method from a bookkeeping standpoint, and (2) if applied consistently over time, it usually produces no material errors in the financial statements.

Matching

Consistency

Materiality

Transportation Costs

If practical, the costs of inbound transportation should be allocated to specific units of inventory purchased. This procedure, which is facilitated by the use of a perpetual inventory system, permits transportation charges to be appropriately reflected in cost of goods sold as well as in ending inventory. Transportation costs are inventoried because they are an important part of the cost of acquiring goods. In the purchase of coal, for example, rail transportation costs constitute a substantial portion of inventoriable costs.

In a periodic inventory system, inbound transportation charges are usually accumulated in a nominal account entitled Transportation-In or Freight-In. Theoretically, the balance in this account at the end of an accounting period should be allocated in a reasonable manner between cost of goods sold and ending inventory. Instead of implementing this approach, firms often use the more expedient alternative of including all transportation-in costs in the calculation of net purchases. Although the expedient approach tends to overstate cost of goods sold and understate net income and ending inventory, it is often supported on the grounds of conservatism, materiality, and consistency of application.

Conservatism

Materiality

Consistency

INVENTORY COST FLOW METHODS

Inventory costs flow into a business and are treated as assets when goods are purchased or manufactured; they flow out and are charged to expense when goods are sold. The difference between the cost inflows and the cost outflows represents the cost of the inventory on hand.

If inventory unit cost prices remained constant over time, the process of inventory cost determination would be relatively simple. That is, it would simply involve multiplying the quantity of each inventory item on hand by its constant unit cost and summing the results. In reality, of course, unit costs usually fluctuate. With inflation, they tend to rise over time. The reality of fluctuating unit costs underscores the critical importance of the various inventory cost flow methods. When reflecting on these methods, keep the following points in mind:

Asset/Liability Measurement

1. Each method leads to a determination of inventory and cost of goods sold based on historical cost.
2. A company can use one method to account for a certain portion of its inventories (such as raw materials) and other methods to account for different portions (such as finished goods).

Consistency

Disclosure

3. The method(s) adopted should be used consistently over time and should be disclosed in the financial statements.

---

[4]Some companies treat purchase discounts as financial revenue similar to interest. This treatment lacks theoretical support. A purchaser of goods who pays for them within the discount period has not thereby made a loan to the seller. Because no loan has been made, no financial revenue has been realized.

Specific Identification Method

The **specific identification method** requires a company to maintain detailed records which permit the accountant to identify individually the actual unit costs of (1) inventory items on hand and (2) inventory items sold. Each item of inventory is identified (e.g., a code on a sales tag) with its actual unit cost. When an item is sold, the difference between its selling price and its actual cost represents the gross margin.

At first glance this method usually seems appealing. For one thing, the flow of inventory costs corresponds with the physical flow of goods. In addition, the method may be used with either a periodic or a perpetual inventory system.

Despite its appeal, the specific identification method has theoretical and practical shortcomings. On the theoretical side, the method is often criticized because it may permit management to manipulate income. Suppose, for example, that a company offers two identical gold watches for $500 each. Due to recent fluctuations in gold prices, one watch cost $250 and the other $350. Management can earn a gross profit of either $250 or $150 from the sale of one watch simply by choosing which watch to sell. On the practical side, the detailed record keeping requirements usually limit the applicability of the specific identification method to inventories that consist of relatively expensive, slow-moving items such as automobiles, farm equipment, art objects, fur coats, jewelry, and long-term construction projects.

Cost Flow Methods Based on Assumptions

Because it is rarely feasible to specifically identify inventory unit costs, most companies make an **assumption** about the way inventory costs flow through the business. The major cost flow assumptions available under GAAP and the method of implementing each are as follows:

Cost Flow Assumption	Cost Flow Method
1. Cost flow is in the same order in which costs were incurred.	1. First-in, first-out (FIFO).
2. Cost flow is an average of the costs incurred.	2. Average cost.
3. Cost flow is in the reverse order in which costs were incurred.	3. Last-in, first-out (LIFO).

A 1990 survey of the annual reports of 600 companies found a total of 1,015 disclosures of inventory cost flow methods. Some companies obviously use more than one method. The use of FIFO, LIFO, and average cost was reported by 401, 366, and 200 companies, respectively.[5]

In reflecting on the FIFO, average cost, and LIFO methods, bear in mind that each method reflects an **assumed cost flow pattern.** Any method may be used **regardless of the way goods physically flow through the business.** For example, goods may (and usually do) physically flow in the FIFO manner, yet LIFO may be used as the cost flow method.

Jackson Company is a merchandising concern that, for accounting purposes, identifies its inventory items using a combination of numbers and letters. The following inventory data for the company's Product 19-C for the current year will be used to illustrate the application of the FIFO, average cost, and LIFO methods.

---

[5] *Accounting Trends and Techniques*, 44th ed. (New York: AICPA, 1990), p. 105.

Date	Product 19-C	Number of Units	Unit Cost	Total Cost	Sold
Jan. 1	Inventory on hand	300	$5	$ 1,500	1500
Mar. 21	Purchase	900	6	5,400	5400
Aug. 19	Purchase	600	7	4,200 400&7 2800	
Nov. 3	Purchase	200	8	1,600	9700
	Available for sale	2,000		$12,700	

We will assume that 800 units of Product 19-C were sold on May 27 and another 800 units were sold on October 9. A physical count on December 31, indicates that 400 units of Product 19-C are on hand.

First-In, First-Out (FIFO) Method.   The FIFO method is based on the assumption that inventory costs should be matched with sales revenue in the same order in which the costs were incurred. The most recent costs incurred are therefore used in determining the cost of inventory on hand. Assuming a periodic system, the cost of the 400 units of Product 19-C is determined as follows:

Most recent costs (Nov. 3 purchase)	200 units @ $8	$1,600
Next most recent costs (Aug. 19 purchase) units	200 units @ $7	$1,400
Inventory, Dec. 31 left	400	$3,000

Recall that cost of goods sold is a residual figure determined by subtracting the cost of the ending inventory from the cost of goods available for sale. For Product 19-C, cost of goods sold under FIFO is $9,700 ($12,700 − $3,000). Note that under the FIFO method, cost of goods sold consists of the earliest costs incurred [(300 units @ $5) + (900 units @ $6) + (400 units @ $7) = $9,700] sold

The FIFO method produces the same cost figures regardless of whether a company uses a periodic or a perpetual system. For example, if the Jackson Company maintained perpetual records for Product 19-C, the company would use a form similar to the one shown in Exhibit 8–6. Observe in the exhibit that the cost of the ending inventory and the cost of goods sold are still $3,000 and $9,700, respectively.

The FIFO method has been supported on the ground that its assumed cost flow pattern corresponds closely to the physical flow of goods in most businesses. Therefore, when goods physically move in the first-in, first-out manner, the FIFO method approximates specific identification. Unlike specific identification, however, FIFO gives management little opportunity to manipulate income.

In terms of financial statement impact, the use of FIFO produces an ending inventory cost based on the most recent acquisition prices. This cost frequently approximates current replacement cost, a fact often cited in support of FIFO. On the other hand, because the balance sheet and income statement **articulate** with one another, the use of FIFO produces a cost of goods sold figure that is based on the earliest costs incurred. These costs often depart considerably from current replacement costs. The

Matching   failure of FIFO to match current costs with current revenues on the income statement is perhaps the most frequently cited shortcoming of this method.

Average Cost Method.   The average cost method is based on the assumption that a weighted average of all inventory costs should be used to measure inventory cost flow. This average is computed by dividing the total cost of goods available for sale by the total number of units available for sale. Assuming a periodic system, the cost of the 400 units of Product 19-C is determined as follows:

Weighted average unit cost	$12,700 ÷ 2,000 = $6.35
Inventory, Dec. 31	400 units @ $6.35 = $2,540

EXHIBIT 8–6

Perpetual Inventory—FIFO Method

Date	Purchased			Sold			Balance		
	Number of Units	Unit Cost	Total Cost	Number of Units	Unit Cost	Total Cost	Number of Units	Unit Cost	Total Cost
Jan. 1							300	$5	$1,500
Mar. 21	900	$6	$5,400				300	5	1,500
							900	6	5,400
May 27				300	$5	$1,500			
				500	6	3,000	400	6	2,400
Aug. 19	600	7	4,200				400	6	2,400
							600	7	4,200
Oct. 9				400	6	2,400			
				400	7	2,800	200	7	1,400
Nov. 3	200	8	1,600				200	7	1,400 ⎫ Ending
							200	8	1,600 ⎬ inventory =
									⎭ $3,000

Cost of goods sold $9,700

Cost of goods sold is therefore $10,160 ($12,700 − $2,540). We can verify this by multiplying the 1600 units sold by $6.35 (1600 × $6.35 = $10,160). Note that a *weighted average,* rather than a *simple average,* unit cost figure should be used. A weighted average reflects the number of units acquired at each price; a simple average [($5 + $6 + $7 + $8) ÷ 4 = $6.50] does not.

When used with a perpetual inventory system, the average cost method is called the **moving average method.** Under this method, a new weighted average unit cost must be **computed after every purchase;** the average is therefore said to "move." The moving average method for Product 19-C is illustrated in Exhibit 8–7.

Observe carefully that a new weighted average unit cost is computed after each purchase. This is done by dividing the total cost of goods available for sale (immediately after the purchase) by the total number of units available for sale (immediately after the purchase). For example, the weighted average unit cost after the first purchase (March 21) is computed as follows:

Jan. 1	Inventory	300 units @ $5	$1,500
Mar. 21	Purchase	900 units @ $6	$5,400
	Available for sale immediately after		
	Mar. 21 purchase	1,200 units	$6,900

Weighted average unit cost $6,900 ÷ 1,200 = $5.75

The same procedure is used to determine the weighted average unit cost after the August 19 purchase and the November 3 purchase.

Under the average cost method, the cost of the ending inventory usually differs depending on whether a company uses a periodic or a perpetual inventory system. It

EXHIBIT 8-7

Perpetual Inventory—Moving Average Method

	Purchased			Sold			Balance		
Date	Number of Units	Unit Cost	Total Cost	Number of Units	Unit Cost	Total Cost	Number of Units	Unit Cost	Total Cost
Jan. 1							300	$5.00	$1,500
Mar. 21	900	$6	$5,400				1,200	5.75*	6,900
May 27				800	$5.75	$4,600	400	5.75	2,300
Aug. 19	600	7	4,200				1,000	6.50*	6,500
Oct. 9				800	6.50	5,200	200	6.50	1,300
Nov. 3	200	8	1,600				400	7.25*	2,900 } Ending inventory = $2,900

Cost of goods sold $9,800

*Weighted average unit cost is computed after each purchase.

follows that when ending inventories differ, cost of goods sold figures also differ. These differences are shown below for Product 19-C.

Average Cost Method	Ending Inventory	+	Cost of Goods Sold	=	Cost of Goods Available for Sale
Periodic system	$2,540		$10,160		$12,700
Perpetual system	2,900		9,800		12,700

The average cost method is supported on the basis that it generally produces figures for both ending inventory and cost of goods sold that lie between those produced under the FIFO and LIFO methods. The method is essentially a compromise solution to the complex question of how we should assume that inventory costs flow through a business. Furthermore, the method is relatively easy to apply, and it affords management little opportunity to manipulate income.

On the other hand, the weighted average method is not as accurate as FIFO in approximating the current cost of the ending inventory, nor is it as accurate as LIFO in approximating the current cost of goods sold. Furthermore, average cost corresponds with the physical flow of goods only when goods available for sale are sold in essentially a random pattern, which may occur with inventories of liquid products such as chemicals and petroleum.

Last-In, First-Out (LIFO) Method.   The LIFO method assumes that inventory costs should be matched with sales revenue in the reverse order in which the costs were incurred (the opposite of FIFO).[6] Inventory is therefore valued at the earliest costs incurred. Referring to Jackson Company and assuming a *periodic* system, we determine the LIFO cost of the ending inventory of 400 units of Product 19-C as follows:

[6]LIFO is an outgrowth of the base stock method, which some companies in the United States used early in the twentieth century. Because the base stock method is not acceptable for income tax purposes and is not considered an important method for financial reporting purposes, it is not illustrated in this textbook.

EXHIBIT 8-8

Perpetual Inventory—LIFO Method

Date	Purchased Number of Units	Purchased Unit Cost	Purchased Total Cost	Sold Number of Units	Sold Unit Cost	Sold Total Cost	Balance Number of Units	Balance Unit Cost	Balance Total Cost
Jan. 1							300	$5	$1,500
Mar. 21	900	$6	$5,400				300	5	1,500
							900	6	5,400
May 27				800	$6	$4,800	300	5	1,500
							100	6	600
Aug. 19	600	7	4,200				300	5	1,500
							100	6	600
							600	7	4,200
Oct. 9				600	7	4,200			
				100	6	600			
				100	5	500	200	5	1,000
Nov. 3	200	8	1,600				200	5	1,000 ⎫ Ending
							200	8	1,600 ⎬ inventory =
									$2,600 ⎭

Cost of goods sold $10,100

Earliest costs (Jan. 1 inventory)	300 units @ $5	$1,500
Next earliest costs (Mar. 21 purchase)	100 units @ $6	$ 600
Inventory, Dec. 31	400	$2,100

Observe that the ending inventory of 400 units is divided into *two layers* (300 units @ $5 and 100 units @ $6). Cost of goods sold is $10,600 ($12,700 − $2,100) and consists of the most recent costs incurred [(200 units @ $8) + (600 units @ $7) + (800 units @ $6) = $10,600].

The application of LIFO using a *perpetual* system, for Product 19-C is shown in Exhibit 8-8. Under the perpetual system, units sold are costed at the time of sale. Because LIFO is therefore applied currently throughout the period rather than only at the period's end, LIFO results usually differ between a periodic and a perpetual system. These differences are shown below for Product 19-C.

LIFO Method	Ending Inventory	+	Cost of Goods Sold	=	Cost of Goods Available for Sale
Periodic system	$2,100		$10,600		$12,700
Perpetual system	2,600		10,100		12,700

Observe that for Product 19-C, cost of goods sold is higher under the periodic than under the perpetual system. This occurred because of the timing of the purchases and sales and because the unit cost prices of Product 19-C rose steadily during the current year. In our example, the cost of goods sold differences relate to the sale on October 9. Under the perpetual system, the October 9 sale was costed using the most recent cost prices at that time [(600 units @ $7) + (100 units @ $6) + (100 units @ $5) = $5,300]. Under the periodic system, the October 9 sale was costed using the most recent cost prices as of the end of the year [(200 units @ $8) + (600 units @ $7) = $5,800]. Many companies that experience rising inventory costs use LIFO for tax purposes, because it tends to produce a higher cost of goods sold and therefore less income taxes. The tax law states that companies using LIFO for tax purposes must also use it for financial reporting purposes. Consequently, a company that uses LIFO with a perpetual system often restates its cost of goods sold and inventory at year-end to conform with the results that would have occurred under a periodic system. This restatement is done for income tax and external financial reporting purposes.

Most companies that use LIFO for income tax and financial reporting purposes maintain their inventory records throughout the year using a different cost flow method, such as FIFO or average cost, to facilitate the internal reporting preferences of management. At year-end the accountant uses a LIFO Allowance account to adjust the results to a LIFO basis. This account frequently is called a LIFO reserve, although many accountants do not like the term "reserve." As evidence of the significant effect that LIFO can produce over time, the LIFO reserve account of some companies is actually larger than the reported LIFO inventory account.[7]

To illustrate how a LIFO reserve account works, assume that in the current year a company adopts the LIFO method for financial reporting purposes. In the past, the company used the FIFO method, and the company plans to continue to maintain its inventory records on a FIFO basis for internal reporting purposes. If the ending inventory for the year is $56,000 on a FIFO basis and $50,000 on a LIFO basis, the following year-end entry would be appropriate:

Cost of Goods Sold	6,000	
Allowance to Reduce Inventory		
Cost to LIFO Basis		6,000

The balance in the Allowance account would be deducted from the inventory of $56,000 on the balance sheet.

Applying LIFO to each of a company's products, as we have done for Jackson Company's Product 19-C, is called the **specific goods method** of applying LIFO. This method requires that LIFO be applied to *each product* in a company's inventory. In the next chapter, we present other methods of applying LIFO.

1. Major Arguments for LIFO.   LIFO is perhaps the most controversial inventory cost flow method. Nevertheless, certain theoretical and economic arguments support its use. From a theoretical standpoint, the use of LIFO is often said to produce a better matching of cost of goods sold expense (measured using recent cost prices) with sales revenue (measured using recent selling prices). As a result, it is often claimed that LIFO produces a better measure of net income than either FIFO or average cost. When inventory costs are rising, net income normally includes a component called **inventory profits.** These profits equal the difference between the current replacement cost of sales and the cost of sales determined using a generally accepted cost flow method. Inventory profits are illusory, however, because they generally must be used to replace depleted inventories at higher costs. The LIFO method greatly reduces

---

[7]See James M. Reeve and Keith G. Stanga, "Balance Sheet Impact of Using LIFO: An Empirical Study," *Accounting Horizons* (September 1987), pp. 9–15.

inventory profits, thereby causing net income to more accurately reflect an amount that can be distributed to stockholders and still enable the company to replace its inventories. Many financial analysts consider the use of LIFO as a favorable factor when they evaluate the **quality of a company's earnings.** During periods of rising prices, LIFO tends to produce net income and inventory measurements that reflect

Conservatism   conservatism.[8]

LIFO is often supported on the economic ground that, during periods of rising prices, its use tends to lower taxable income and thereby postpone income tax payments until the time, if ever, that inventory unit costs or physical quantities decline. Federal income tax law permits a company to compute taxable income using LIFO only if the company also uses LIFO for financial reporting. This is known as the **LIFO conformity requirement,** and as the name implies, this requirement pertains only to LIFO. Although Congress believed that the conformity requirement was fair and reasonable when LIFO was initially allowed for tax purposes in 1938, many people today argue that the requirement adversely affects GAAP and should be eliminated. With the major exception of LIFO, a company does not have to use the same methods for financial reporting purposes as it uses for income tax purposes, or vice versa.

The LIFO conformity requirement has deterred some companies from adopting LIFO. Nevertheless, occasionally high inflation rates in the United States have made LIFO one of the most popular accounting methods in past years. Hoover Ball & Bearing, for example, changed from FIFO to LIFO in 1974 (a year of high inflation during which many companies switched to LIFO), thereby saving the company $3.3 million in income taxes.[9] One author has estimated that the use of LIFO has permitted General Electric Company to save approximately $1 billion of income taxes during a twenty-five year period ending in 1979.[10] Such tax savings enhance a company's availability of cash. This increased cash flow is in effect an interest-free loan of indefinite and perhaps permanent duration. It reduces borrowing requirements and thereby tends to lower interest costs, which in turn contributes even further toward improving a company's cash flow.

2. Major Arguments Against LIFO.   Despite the theoretical and economic advantages of LIFO, the method has been attacked for several reasons. The major arguments against LIFO are summarized below.

1. LIFO inventories are often valued using outdated cost prices. Some say that LIFO-valued inventories are "unrealistic" because they fail to reflect current costs. When inventory valuations are unrealistic, related measurements such as working capital, the current ratio, and inventory turnover are also distorted.
2. The LIFO cost flow assumption is usually opposite to the physical flow of goods. Only a few types of inventories, such as coal or gravel, physically flow in a LIFO manner.

Matching
3. When a liquidation of LIFO inventory layers occurs, outdated costs tend to be matched with sales revenue, thereby reducing the matching benefits that LIFO generally produces. Matching outdated costs with current revenues is said to produce an "unrealistic" measure of net income. Frequently, the liquidation of LIFO layers is involuntary, as when a strike disrupts production or a supplier fails to

---

[8]Not all companies have experienced a rising trend of inventory costs over time. Some companies in the electronics industry, for example, have experienced declining costs. For these companies, using FIFO is considered more conservative than using LIFO.

[9]"FIFO to LIFO: More and More Companies are Making the Switch," *Barrons* (October 21, 1974), p. 5.

[10]S. Thomas Moser, "LIFO: Inflation Lifeline," *Management Focus* (March–April 1981), p. 24.

Materiality

deliver goods on a timely basis at the end of an accounting period. A LIFO liquidation can sometimes have a material impact on a company's financial statements. For example, in 1980 Bethlehem Steel Corporation had a LIFO liquidation that increased the company's income by 77%. In the same year, a LIFO liquidation by the Firestone Tire & Rubber Company increased the company's income by 65%.[11]

4. The use of LIFO permits income manipulation, such as by making end-of-period purchases designed to preserve existing inventory layers. At times these purchases may not even be in the best economic interests of the company.

5. LIFO generally results in a greater administrative burden than either FIFO or average cost. As stated earlier, most companies that use LIFO for external reporting maintain their records on some other basis (such as FIFO) for internal reporting. Moreover, because LIFO involves many complex tax regulations, its use for tax purposes may cause the Internal Revenue Service (IRS) to take a closer look at a firm's inventory accounting system to determine whether all the tax requirements have been met. A LIFO election can be invalidated because of a technicality.

6. The variations in methods of applying LIFO as well as the fact that most LIFO users have adopted it at different times tend to distort intercompany comparisons, even those made between two LIFO companies in the same industry.

7. During periods of rising inventory costs, the use of LIFO for tax purposes, coupled with the conformity requirement, creates a paradox. That is, it postpones taxes and thereby makes the firm better off economically, yet it lowers reported net income and thereby makes the firm *appear worse* than it would under FIFO or average cost. One study has found that many companies "have voluntarily paid tens of millions of dollars in additional income taxes by continuing to use FIFO rather than switching to LIFO."[12] Many managers are reluctant to adopt LIFO out of fear that the reduced reported earnings will cause investors to penalize the market price of their company's stock. Although the empirical studies in this area have not produced consistent results, research suggests that this fear of managers may be unjustified, because changes to LIFO do not appear to result in unfavorable market reactions.[13] A retired chairman of General Electric Company has speculated that some managers may not want to use LIFO because "most top executive contracts are tied to reported earnings."[14]

Comparison of Results Between FIFO, Average Cost, and LIFO.   Exhibit 8–9 summarizes the financial statement impact of the FIFO, average cost, and LIFO methods of Product 19-C of Jackson Company for the current year. We do not show the results under the specific identification method, because they depend on which units were sold and which are on hand.

As Exhibit 8–9 suggests, certain key financial statement variables for Jackson Company differ depending on which cost flow method the company adopts. These variables include inventory, total current assets, working capital, cost of goods sold, gross margin, and net income. The fact that the various cost flow methods produce different financial statement effects underscores the importance of each company

Disclosure

disclosing the method(s) that it uses.

---

[11]Allen I. Schiff, "The Other Side of LIFO," *Journal of Accountancy,* May 1983, pp. 120–121.

[12]Gary C. Biddle, "Accounting Methods and Management Decisions: The Case of Inventory Costing and Inventory Policy," *Journal of Accounting Research* (Supplement 1980), p. 273.

[13]See, for example, Shyam Sunder, "Stock Price and Risk Related to Accounting Changes in Inventory Valuation," *Accounting Review* (April 1975), pp. 305–315. It is also worth noting that the LIFO conformity requirement does *not* prohibit the disclosure of supplemental non-LIFO income information. This supplemental information, such as the amount of net income that would have been reported if the FIFO method had been used, cannot be presented on the face of the financial statements.

[14]Quotation made by Reginald H. Jones, reprinted in *Journal of Accountancy* (July 1981), p. 28.

EXHIBIT 8–9
Comparison of Results Under FIFO, Average Cost, and LIFO

	FIFO		Average Cost		LIFO	
	Periodic System	Perpetual System	Periodic System	Perpetual System	Periodic System	Perpetual System
Cost of goods available for sale	$12,700	$12,700	$12,700	$12,700	$12,700	$12,700
Cost of ending inventory (Dec. 31)	3,000	3,000	2,540	2,900	2,100	2,600
Cost of goods sold	$ 9,700	$ 9,700	$10,160	$ 9,800	$10,600	$10,100

Because the unit cost of Product 19-C rose steadily during the current year, FIFO produces the lowest cost of goods sold figure, while LIFO used with a periodic system produces the highest. The nature of the differences produced under the various cost flow methods depends primarily on the direction and magnitude of unit cost movements as well as on the length of time that a company has used LIFO.

Strawbridge & Clothier, the company whose financial statements appear on the endpapers and in the appendix to this book, can be used to illustrate the impact of the FIFO and LIFO methods. Strawbridge & Clothier uses LIFO to value its inventories, and for its accounting period that ended on February 3, 1990, the company reported inventories of $139,149,000. Note B to the company's financial statements indicates that if the company had used FIFO, the reported inventories would have been $27,850,000 higher, an increase of about 20%.

Selection of a Cost Flow Method

We have just seen that the various inventory cost flow methods can lead to substantially different financial statement results. We also know that accountants seek to produce information that enables users to make meaningful intercompany comparisons. To help ensure the propriety of these comparisons, differences between the financial statements of different companies should result from basic differences between the companies themselves or from the nature of their transactions and not merely from differences in accounting principles.[15] Given these facts, why does GAAP permit companies to choose among several inventory cost flow methods?

The basic reason is that circumstances may differ substantially between companies. Accountants generally believe that a company should have some leeway in selecting a cost flow method that is most appropriate in light of the circumstances the company faces. The accounting profession has therefore tended to favor **some flexibility,** rather than **strict uniformity,** when formulating accounting principles. Nevertheless, two of the great challenges of the Financial Accounting Standards Board (FASB) and its predecessor committees have been (1) to identify the circumstances that warrant the use of a particular accounting principle and (2) to eliminate alternative principles that are not justified by differences in circumstances.

[15]*APB Statement No. 4,* "Basic Concepts and Accounting Principles Underlying Financial Statements of Business Enterprises," 1970, par. 101.

Given the alternatives currently available under GAAP, what basic criterion should a corporate manager use in selecting an inventory cost flow method? *Accounting Research Bulletin No. 43* states that "the major objective in selecting a method should be to choose the one which, under the circumstances, most clearly reflects periodic income."[16] The phrases "under the circumstances" and "most clearly reflects periodic income" have not been well defined. As a result, they often convey significantly different meanings to different people. The absence of more concrete criteria for selecting a cost flow assumption has *increased the importance of judgment.* In reality many companies appear to select a method based largely on factors such as tax minimization, steady growth in reported earnings, and so forth. Thus, it seems fair to say that financial statements today often reflect certain differences that are unrelated to basic differences between companies or their transactions.

The author of *Accounting Research Study No. 13* concluded that:

> *Specific identification of costs and, if that is not practicable, the FIFO cost flow assumption represent approaches to inventory cost determination which are sound in principle. . . . Enterprises using any cost flow assumption other than specific identification or FIFO should be required to disclose (1) the effect on net income for the period and on the balance sheet inventory amounts of the method used as compared with FIFO and (2) related tax effects.*[17]

These conclusions have not been adopted by the FASB.

Consistency
Disclosure
When a company adopts a cost flow method for a portion or for all of its inventories, the company should use the method consistently over time. As stated earlier, the accountant should disclose the method(s) in the financial statements. When a company changes to another cost flow method, the accountant should disclose the nature of the change, the justification for the change, and the dollar effects of the change on income. We explain accounting changes in Chapter 19.

INVENTORY VALUATION AT THE LOWER OF COST OR MARKET (LCM)

Asset/Liability
Measurement
The accountant initially values inventory items by multiplying quantities on hand by unit costs derived under a cost flow method (specific identification, FIFO, etc.). The resulting valuation is at historical cost. In inventory accounting, GAAP requires a departure from historical cost measurement when the utility of inventory has declined below cost. This departure is known as the **lower of cost or market rule,** or simply the **LCM rule.**[18]

The LCM rule is stated as follows in *Accounting Research Bulletin No. 43:*

> *A departure from the cost basis of pricing the inventory is required when the utility of the goods is no longer as great as its cost. Where there is evidence that the utility of goods, in their disposal in the ordinary course of business, will be less than cost, whether due to physical deterioration, obsolescence, changes in price levels, or other causes, the difference should be*

[16]*Accounting Research Bulletin No. 43*, "Restatement and Revision of Accounting Research Bulletins," Ch. 4, Stmt. 4.
[17]Horace G. Barden, *Accounting Research Study No. 13*, "The Accounting Basis of Inventories" (New York: AICPA, 1973), pp. 12–13.
[18]A company cannot use LCM with LIFO for federal income tax purposes. Generally accepted accounting principles, however, require a company to use LCM with LIFO for financial reporting purposes. Other differences exist between the way in which a company applies LCM for income tax versus financial reporting purposes. Readers interested in the details of how to apply LCM for income tax purposes should consult appropriate tax references.

recognized as a loss of the current period. This is generally accomplished by stating such goods at a lower level commonly designated as market.[19]

A company purchases or manufactures inventory for ultimate sale. The term **utility of goods** thus refers to the ability of the goods to generate revenue via sale. Utility is a very subjective concept, and **market** is used simply as a practical means of measuring it. Therefore, if the market measure of goods on hand at the end of the current period has declined below cost, the accountant should report the difference as a loss of the period in which the decline occurred.

MEANING OF MARKET

What does **market** mean? *Accounting Research Bulletin No. 43* states:

> *As used in the phrase* lower of cost or market *the term market means current replacement cost (by purchase or by reproduction, as the case may be) except that:*
>
> *(1) Market should not exceed the net realizable value (i.e., estimated selling price in the ordinary course of business less reasonably predictable costs of completion and disposal); and*
>
> *(2) Market should not be less than net realizable value reduced by an allowance for an approximately normal profit margin.*[20]

Generally, therefore, market means **current replacement cost** on the balance sheet date. In the case of purchased inventories, this cost includes not only the purchase price that would have to be paid for the quantities usually purchased, but also incidental acquisition costs such as freight and handling. For manufactured inventories, replacement cost is based on current materials prices, prevailing labor rates, and current overhead costs. Note that replacement cost is an **input** (or **entry**) **value**, because it represents an amount that would have to be paid to acquire inventory.

The purpose of using replacement cost to represent market (and therefore utility) is that declines in replacement cost are often associated with declines in selling prices. Selling prices, however, may be influenced by other factors. *Bulletin No. 43* therefore states that in applying the LCM rule, "judgment must always be exercised and no loss should be recognized unless the evidence indicates clearly that a loss has been sustained."[21] To help practicing accountants determine whether or not a loss has been sustained, the bulletin specifies an upper and a lower limit within which market must fall. Each limit is an **output** (or **exit**) **value**, because each is based directly on expected selling prices that the firm will receive for the goods being valued.

The upper limit on market, commonly called the **ceiling,** is **net realizable value.** The lower limit, commonly called the **floor,** is **net realizable value reduced by an allowance for an approximately normal profit margin.** These concepts are illustrated below for one unit of Inventory Item Q.

Estimated selling price in the ordinary course of business	$10
− Reasonably predictable costs of completion and disposal	1
= Net realizable value (ceiling)	9
− Allowance for an approximately normal profit margin (30% of selling price)	3
= Net realizable value less an allowance for an approximately normal profit margin (floor)	$ 6

---

[19]*Accounting Research Bulletin No. 43*, Ch. 4, Stmt. 5.
[20]*Accounting Research Bulletin No. 43*, Ch. 4, Stmt. 6.
[21]*Accounting Research Bulletin No. 43*, Ch. 4, par. 9.

EXHIBIT 8–10

The LCM Rule

Inventory Item		Market Determinants				
	Ceiling[1]	Replacement Cost[2]	Floor[3]	Market[4]	Cost[5]	LCM[6]
A	$7	$6	$5	$6	$3	$3
B	7	8	5	7	9	7
C	7	6	5	6	8	6
D	7	4	5	5	8	5

[1]Net realizable value (the estimated selling price, assumed to be $10, less reasonably predictable costs of completion and disposal, assumed to be $3).
[2]The current replacement cost as of the balance sheet date.
[3]Net realizable value less a normal profit margin. (Normal profit is assumed to be 20% of the $10 selling price).
[4]The middle amount selected from among the ceiling, replacement cost, and floor.
[5]Determined using a cost flow method (specific identification, FIFO, etc.).
[6]Lower of cost or market (the lower amount selected from the cost and market). This amount is used for inventory valuation purposes on the balance sheet.

When applying the LCM rule, **replacement cost is used as market only when it falls between the ceiling and the floor.** On the other hand, **if replacement cost is greater than the ceiling, the ceiling is used as market.** The use of a ceiling is defended on the ground that if inventory were reported at more than its net realizable value, the amount reported would exceed the inventory's utility. This would result in a loss when the inventory is sold. If **replacement cost is less than the floor, the floor is used as market.** Limiting market to the floor is defended on the basis that writing down inventory items below the floor understates the inventory's utility and thereby permits the recognition of an abnormally high profit when the inventory is sold.

From a practical standpoint, the LCM rule requires (1) selecting as market the middle amount from among the ceiling, replacement cost, and floor, and (2) selecting the lower of cost or market to use for inventory valuation purposes. Exhibit 8–10 displays four inventory items. The assumed dollar amounts are on a *per unit basis.*

Observe in Exhibit 8–10 that for each item, market is the middle value selected from among the ceiling, replacement cost, and floor. *After* we have determined market, we compare it with cost. The lower of cost or market is then entered in the LCM column. Unit amounts in the LCM column are the correct ones to use for inventory valuation purposes. Note that these amounts represent the cost for Item A, the ceiling for Item B, the replacement cost for Item C, and the floor for Item D.

The LCM rule applies to goods that a company will sell in the ordinary course of business. At times a company may own damaged, deteriorated, or obsolete goods that it cannot sell in the usual manner. Such goods should be carried in a separate account and, for accounting purposes, should be valued below cost, at their estimated selling prices less disposal costs. The accounting principles that should be used for inventory received in a trade-in are discussed in Chapter 11; accounting for repossessed inventory is presented in Chapter 20.

METHODS OF APPLYING THE LCM RULE

In the preceding example we assumed that the LCM rule was applied to each item in inventory. Actually, a company may choose to apply the rule to (1) each inventory

EXHIBIT 8–11

Methods of Applying the LCM Rule

	Number of Units	Unit Cost	Unit Market	Aggregate Cost	Aggregate Market	LCM Applied to (1) Individual Items	(2) Major Categories	(3) Inventory as a Whole
Category I								
Item A	1,000	$3	$6	$ 3,000	$ 6,000	$ 3,000		
Item B	1,000	9	7	9,000	7,000	7,000		
Subtotal				12,000	13,000		$12,000	
Category II								
Item C	1,000	8	6	8,000	6,000	6,000		
Item D	1,000	8	5	8,000	5,000	5,000		
Subtotal				16,000	11,000		11,000	
Total				$28,000	$24,000			$24,000
Inventory valuation						$21,000	$23,000	$24,000

item, (2) major categories of items, or (3) the inventory as a whole. According to *Bulletin No. 43,* the application method selected should most clearly reflect periodic

Consistency income. Moreover, the method should be applied consistently over time. Most companies use the individual item method.[22] Regardless of what method is used, the quantity of each item should initially be multiplied by (1) unit costs to derive aggregate cost, and (2) unit market values to derive aggregate market.[23] This is shown in Exhibit 8–11, in which we assume the same inventory items (A, B, C, and D) as in Exhibit 8–10. For simplicity, we assume that 1,000 units of each item are on hand.

Observe in Exhibit 8–11 that the final inventory valuation is $21,000, $23,000, or $24,000, depending on how the LCM rule is applied. In certain cases the results under the different methods may be equal. If the results are not equal, applying LCM to individual items produces the lowest inventory valuation; applying it to the inventory as a whole produces the highest.

Once an inventory item has been written down to a value below cost, that value is regarded as its "new cost" for purposes of subsequent accounting. If the market value of an item that has been written down subsequently increases, the increase is *not* reflected in the accounts until a sale occurs.

RECORDING LCM IN THE ACCOUNTS

When application of the LCM rule indicates that inventory should be reported at market, how should this be recorded? Ideally, a loss account should be debited and a valuation allowance account (an inventory *contra* account) should be credited. To illustrate, let's assume the following facts for Bradley Company:

---

[22]Lower of cost or market must be applied to each inventory item for federal income tax purposes.
[23]Multiplying by unit costs overcomes the problem of having to compare more than one unit cost with a single unit market value. Under the FIFO method, for example, more than one unit cost may exist for certain inventory items.

Inventory, Jan. 1, at cost	$ 50,000	
Purchases during the year	200,000	
Inventory, Dec. 31		
At cost	40,000	
At market	33,000	

If the company uses the periodic inventory system, the cost of goods sold adjusting entry would appear as shown below.

Dec. 31	Inventory, Dec. 31	40,000	
	Loss on Reduction of Inventory Cost to Market	7,000	
	Cost of Goods Sold	210,000	
	Inventory, Jan. 1		50,000
	Allowance to Reduce Inventory Cost to		
	Market		7,000
	Purchases		200,000

On the other hand, the following adjusting entry would be made if the company uses a perpetual system.

Dec. 31	Loss on Reduction of Inventory Cost to Market	7,000	
	Allowance to Reduce Inventory		
	Cost to Market		7,000

Under either system, cost of goods sold would be reported at $210,000 and the loss of $7,000 would be shown in the body of the income statement (*not* as an extraordinary item). A clear distinction is therefore made between an *expense* associated with *goods sold* and a *loss* associated with holding *goods on hand*. Separating the expense from the loss is conceptually correct since the two amounts are caused by different factors. Moreover, a separate reporting of the two amounts may help financial statement users to make more accurate predictions of future cash flows.

The Allowance account is deducted from inventory on the balance sheet:

Inventory, at cost	$40,000	
Less: Allowance to reduce inventory		
cost to market	7,000	$33,000

Disclosure Use of the Allowance account facilitates the disclosure of the ending inventory at both cost ($40,000) and market ($33,000).

At the end of the *next* accounting period, the Allowance account should be closed to the Beginning Inventory if a periodic system is used or to Cost of Goods Sold if a perpetual system is used. This avoids overstatement of the beginning inventory and cost of goods sold. If the market value of the ending inventory is below cost, the difference should again be entered in the Loss and the Allowance account.

In practice, a number of acceptable variations of the above procedure are encountered. Conceptually, these variations are less desirable than the procedure described **Materiality** above. They may be supported, however, on the grounds of materiality and practicality. For example, the LCM rule is sometimes applied in the accounts by

1. Debiting Cost of Goods Sold (instead of the Loss account) and crediting the Allowance account.

2. Debiting the Loss account and crediting the Inventory account (instead of the Allowance account).

3. Debiting Cost of Goods Sold (instead of the Loss account) and crediting the Inventory account (instead of the Allowance account).

When an Allowance account is used, some accountants leave it open and merely adjust it upward or downward at year-end so that it agrees with the difference between cost and market. An increase in the Allowance account requires the recognition of a loss. A decrease requires the recognition of a recovery of loss, sometimes called a gain. The balance in the Allowance account is never reduced below zero. In other words, a debit balance should never exist in the Allowance account, because it would cause the carrying value of the inventory to exceed cost.

PROS AND CONS OF LCM

Conservatism   The LCM rule is an example of the conservatism modifying convention. It permits accountants to recognize a loss on inventory, even though evidence of the loss does not result from a sale. The rule has a long history in accounting. Its early use was supported as a means of achieving balance sheet conservatism at a time when creditors were the primary users of external financial statements and the balance sheet was regarded as the most important financial statement. Modern financial reporting emphasizes the income statement, and the LCM rule is now supported on the basis that it produces a conservative income measure in the current period.

Many users of financial statements support the LCM rule because they think it reduces their risk of making poor decisions. In a study involving in-depth interviews of important financial statement users, Backer found that "all but one of the 74 bankers interviewed favored the lower of cost or market rule. . . . The security analysts also overwhelmingly supported the rule. Only four of these 72 analysts interviewed opposed the rule."[24]

Despite the alleged benefits of the LCM rule, it has long been one of the most controversial elements of GAAP. Critics have leveled many arguments against it. Some of the major objections are listed below.

1. The rule requires a write-down to market when cost exceeds market, but it does not permit a write-up to market when market exceeds cost. Some accountants consider this inconsistent and illogical.

2. The rule permits the use of four different inventory measures. Some inventory items may therefore be valued at cost, while others are valued using ceiling, replacement cost, and floor amounts. The existence of these different valuation bases may inhibit the ability of statement users to make valid intercompany and interperiod comparisons.

3. Different methods may be used to apply the LCM rule (i.e., to individual items, major categories, or the inventory as a whole) and to record it in the accounts. As a result, intercompany comparisons may be distorted.

4. Determining a "normal profit" in order to establish a floor is difficult and subjective. These profits vary between inventory items and over time as selling prices and cost prices change.

5. Valuing an inventory item at the floor in order to prevent an abnormally high profit on its sale may be closer to income manipulation than to income measurement.

---

[24]Morton Backer, *Financial Reporting for Security Investment and Credit Decisions* (New York: National Association of Accountants, 1970), p. 102.

COSTLY POSTPONEMENT

In March 1988 investors in General Homes Corp. learned that the Houston-based home builder was marking down the value of its assets, primarily land inventories, by $91 million. Last year came another shocker—a $113 million writedown.

All told, General Homes' losses have exceeded $285 million over the last two years—no small feat for a company that earned $19 million in 1983. Its stock, which traded as high as 21¼, was selling at ⅜ before trading was suspended in April.

What's going on here? Did the assets really decline by almost 40% in just two years? Or should some of those writedowns have come earlier? After all, the Texas real estate market hit bottom in 1987, and yet the company's total chargeoffs between 1984 and 1987 were a mere $8 million.

Was General Homes management deliberately withholding bad news?

Yes it was, according to a class action suit filed in Dallas federal court last year on behalf of the company's bondholders. On top of that, the company filed in mid-August for voluntary Chapter 11 bankruptcy protection after being pressured by bondmailer Stanford N. Phelps (FORBES, *Aug. 6*). He'd sought to force General Homes into involuntary bankruptcy after being refused two board seats.

At issue in the bondholder suit is the use of the concept of net realizable value: the estimated sale price of a piece of real estate, less the estimated costs of completion and disposal.

The Financial Accounting Standards Board, the profession's rulemaking body, says that if you hold real estate for sale or development, you've got to value it at the lower of cost or net realizable value.

An alternative valuation method kicks in when market conditions erode to the point where development is no longer feasible, or when the company doesn't have the money to develop the property. Here, the FASB says you've got to carry the property at the lower of cost or fair market value. In these cases, fair market—or liquidation—value can be significantly lower than cost. And the resulting writeoffs can be substantial.

When General Homes should have owned up to the market realities is at the heart of the bondholder action. Until March 1988 General Homes had carried virtually all its land at the lower of cost or net realizable value, insisting it would develop it all even though real estate in its area was in a tailspin. Most of the land was in economically devastated Texas markets.

Finally, in March 1988, the company changed its accounting method on many of its troubled properties from the "lower of cost or net realizable value" to the "lower of cost or fair market"—resulting in the $91 million hit. It made the same switch last year on just about all of its remaining properties—writing off another $113 million and finally acknowledging that development was impossible.

Given the market context and the fact that General Homes had had negative cash flow since autumn 1986, bondholders argue that General Homes should have made that admission years earlier and that assets and earnings were way overstated in 1986 and 1987. Which in turn kept the company from running afoul of its revolving credit agreement.

Did insiders know the homebuilder was a disaster waiting to happen long before individual investors knew?

One clue surfaced in July 1987, when Montgomery, Ala.-based Kinder-Care, Inc. agreed to buy American Savings & Loan Association (ASLA) of Florida for $145 million. The thrift owned about 43% of General Homes' common shares.

In figuring what to pay for the thrift, Kinder-Care assumed that the General Homes stock was worthless—even though at the time it had a market value of almost $40 million. By the end of the year Kinder-Care had written the stock down to zero.

How does General Homes' auditor, Arthur Andersen, also a defendant, respond? In court papers, Wilber Armatta, the accountant responsible for General Homes from 1983 to August 1987, insists everything was done in accordance with generally accepted accounting principles.

But internal Andersen memos in the court records indicate that the auditors were worried about how to value the properties and felt General Homes' projections of cash flow and home sales were "optimistic." In one memo Armatta wrote that "the NRV [net realizable value] problem casts a shadow on 1986 earnings," because General Homes "still had a lot of property in Houston . . . an economically depressed area."

Yet until March 1988 Arthur Andersen repeatedly backed management on the property valuation question. It was certainly well paid for its amiable attitude: $350,000 a year.

When to impose specific accounting rules is always a judgment call, and this is no exception. But the bottom line is that stock- and bondholders were lulled into a sense of false security by the auditor's failure to insist on earlier writeoffs. And they paid dearly for that false security.

SOURCE: Graham Button, "Costly Postponement," *Forbes*, September 3, 1990, p. 80. Reprinted by permission of *Forbes* magazine, September 3, 1990. © Forbes Inc., 1990.

While management's function is to earn a profit, the accountant's function is to measure and report it.

6. The LCM rule may produce conservative results in the first year of its use. However, when the lower inventory costs are charged to cost of goods sold in a subsequent period, net income tends to be greater and therefore unconservative.

7. The rule is often complicated to apply. Furthermore, there is room to suspect that many preparers and users of financial statements may not adequately understand it.[25]

INVENTORY VALUATION ABOVE COST

Thus far we have discussed the valuation of inventory at cost and at the lower of cost or market. In Chapter 3, we discussed several alternatives to conventional historical cost measurement. These include current cost (replacement cost), current exit value in orderly liquidation, expected exit value in due course of business (net realizable value), and present value of expected cash flows. Many critics of historical cost accounting believe that accounting information would be more useful if inventories were consistently measured using any of the alternatives to conventional historical cost. Some accountants, for example, believe that inventories should be measured and reported at current cost, regardless of whether the current cost measurement is above or below historical cost. Although many theoretical arguments lend support to the valuation of inventory at amounts greater than historical cost, such valuation is permissible under GAAP only in certain exceptional cases.

For example, construction companies often engage in projects that take several years to complete, such as office buildings, ships, and dams. Instead of waiting until the end of a project to recognize income, these companies may, under GAAP, choose to recognize income *during production* using the percentage of completion method. Under this method, an inventory account called "Construction in Progress" consists of **historical costs incurred plus income recognized to date.** The reporting of inventory in this manner is considered appropriate for these companies, given the unusual nature of the construction business. We further explain and illustrate the percentage of completion method in Chapter 20.

The reporting of inventory at **net realizable value,** even though such value may be above cost, is permitted under GAAP in certain exceptional cases. Precious metals that have a fixed monetary value and no substantial marketing costs may be reported at net realizable value. Similarly, certain agricultural and mineral products, units of which are interchangeable, can be sold immediately at quoted market prices, and are difficult to cost appropriately, may be reported at net realizable value.[26] In addition,

Industry Practices

it is customary for companies within certain industries to report inventories at net realizable value, because it is virtually impossible for them to determine costs with sufficient objectivity. A meat packing company, for example, buys its raw material "on the hoof" and divides it into many cuts, such as ribs and chuck. Since any allocation of the cost of the animal to the resulting cuts would be purely arbitrary, these companies value their inventories of cuts at net realizable value.[27]

Revenue Realization

When a company values its inventory above cost, the company is considered to have earned income before the time of sale. Clearly, this is an exceptional treatment, given the revenue realization principle. Financial statements of companies that value inventories above cost should disclose the valuation basis used.

---

[25]Barden, p. 104.
[26]*Accounting Research Bulletin No. 43*, Ch. 4, par. 16.
[27]*Accounting Research Bulletin No. 43*, Ch. 1A, par. 1.

EFFECTS OF INVENTORY ERRORS ON FINANCIAL STATEMENTS

Inventory errors often occur when counting, pricing, or extending inventory amounts. Inventory errors may also arise because certain goods have been either incorrectly included or incorrectly excluded when the inventory was taken. We may better appreciate the importance of accurately accounting for inventories by focusing on the impact of certain inventory errors on financial statements. Several common types of errors made in accounting for merchandise and the effects of each are summarized below.

1. The company's accountant **incorrectly includes** in the ending inventory the cost of certain goods that do not belong to the company.
   a. If the credit purchase of the goods has *not* been recorded, the effects will be an overstatement of ending inventory, an understatement of cost of goods sold, and an overstatement of net income and ending retained earnings.
   b. If the credit purchase of the goods has been recorded, then *two* errors will have occurred (i.e., incorrectly including the goods in inventory *and* incorrectly recording the purchase). The effects will be an overstatement of ending inventory and of accounts payable. Cost of goods sold, net income, and ending retained earnings, however, will be correctly stated, because both purchases and ending inventory are overstated by the same amounts and therefore offset one another in the calculation of cost of goods sold and net income.
2. The company's accountant **incorrectly excludes** from ending inventory the cost of certain goods that belong to the company.
   a. If the credit purchase of the goods has been recorded, the effects will be an understatement of ending inventory, an overstatement of cost of goods sold, and an understatement of net income and ending retained earnings.
   b. If the credit purchase of the goods has *not* been recorded, then *two* errors will have occurred (i.e., incorrectly excluding the goods from inventory *and* incorrectly failing to record the purchase). The effects will be an understatement of ending inventory and of accounts payable. Cost of goods sold, net income, and ending retained earnings, however, will be correctly stated, because both purchases and ending inventory are understated by the same amounts and therefore offset one another in the calculation of cost of goods sold and net income.

When considering the effects that inventory errors have on net income, remembering the following relationships often is helpful. For simplicity, we ignore expenses other than cost of goods sold in the three equations below.

$$S - CGS = NI \tag{1}$$
$$BI + P - EI = CGS \tag{2}$$
$$S - BI - P + EI = NI \tag{3}$$

where
S = Sales (net)
CGS = Cost of goods sold
NI = Net income
BI = Beginning inventory
P = Purchases (net)
EI = Ending inventory

Equation 3 indicates that an overstatement (understatement) of either the beginning inventory or purchases tends to decrease (increase) net income because the beginning inventory and purchases are subtracted when measuring net income. In contrast, an overstatement (understatement) of ending inventory tends to increase (decrease) net income because ending inventory is added when measuring net income.

The types of inventory errors discussed previously relate to purchase transactions. Similar errors may arise in relation to sales transactions. For example, the cost of certain goods that have actually been sold may erroneously be included in the ending inventory.

The various types of inventory errors just discussed affected the current accounting period. Recognize, however, that an error in the ending inventory of the current period has the opposite effect in the next period, because the ending inventory of one period is the beginning inventory of the next. If the error is not corrected in the second period, it will offset the error made in the first period.

Correcting an inventory error requires a logical analysis of the error's effects on the financial statements. The appropriate correction depends in part on when the error is detected. An error in the ending inventory of one period that is discovered near the end of the next, for example, requires a prior period adjustment. Chapter 19 discusses the topic of error correction in greater depth.

CONCLUDING REMARKS/CONCEPTUAL CONSIDERATIONS

Throughout this text we stress the importance of understanding the relationship between the individual topics covered and the theoretical model presented in Chapter 2. The following elements of the model are especially pertinent in inventory accounting.

Asset/Liability Measurement

1. **Asset/liability measurement principle.** The primary basis of accounting for inventories is historical cost. Remember that determining historical cost is not as easy as it may appear. Resolving important issues such as what costs should be inventoried and what cost flow method should be used is a real challenge to the practicing accountant.

Revenue Realization

2. **Revenue realization principle.** When an increase in the value of inventory is verified by a sale, revenue is usually recorded. Only in exceptional cases may accountants properly value inventory above cost and therefore recognize revenue before the time of sale.

Matching

3. **Matching principle.** The cost of the inventory sold must be charged to expense in the period in which the sale occurs. By so doing, the sales revenue is matched with the cost of the goods sold to produce the revenue.

Consistency

4. **Consistency principle.** A company should account for its inventories using the same methods over time. This principle is particularly important in inventory accounting, because several alternative accounting methods exist.

Disclosure

5. **Disclosure principle.** The following disclosure guidelines should be observed when reporting inventories on the balance sheet and in the related notes:
   a. Report inventories in the current assets section.
   b. Disclose separately each major class of inventory, such as raw materials, work-in-process, finished goods, factory supplies, and goods on consignment. Remember to include in inventory only those goods for which the company (i.e., the accounting entity) has legal title on the balance sheet date.
   c. List inventories in order of their liquidity.
   d. Disclose parenthetically, in a footnote, or in a summary of significant accounting policies, the inventory cost flow method used (FIFO, average cost, etc.) as well as basis used in pricing the inventory (cost or LCM). Also disclose any methods used that are peculiar to the firm's industry.
   e. If the company has made a change in its inventory accounting principles, disclose the nature of and justification for the change. The effect of the change

on income should also be disclosed. We explain accounting changes in Chapter 19.

 f. Subtract the amount in an inventory allowance account (such as the Allowance to Reduce Inventory Cost to Market) from the amount in the Inventory account to derive the net amount. Report all three amounts on the balance sheet or in the related notes.

 g. Do *not* offset the cost of inventories pledged as collateral against the loan liability. These inventories are properly reported as assets. However, the nature of the pledge agreement should be disclosed.

 h. Do *not* include in inventories advance payments made to suppliers for goods that the company has ordered but title to which has not been received as of the balance sheet date. These advances should be reported after inventories in an account called "Advances to Suppliers."

Exhibit 8–12 shows recent inventory disclosures of the Goodyear Tire & Rubber Company.

Industry Practices

6. Industry practices.   This modifying convention sometimes requires the reporting of inventories at amounts above cost. Companies in the meat packing industry, for example, typically value their inventories of cuts at net realizable value.

Conservatism

7. Conservatism.   This modifying convention is reflected in the LCM rule. Under this rule a departure from historical cost measurement is required when the utility of inventory has declined below cost.

KEY POINTS

1. Inventories are goods that are held for sale in the ordinary course of business, and goods that are in production or that will soon be used in production. (Objective 1)

2. To value an inventory for financial reporting purposes, an accountant must determine (1) the physical quantity of goods on hand and (2) the accounting valuation that should be associated with those goods. (Objective 1)

3. Inventory quantities are maintained on a day-to-day basis in a perpetual inventory system, but not in a periodic system. (Objective 2)

4. Inventory items should be included in the inventory of the entity that has legal title. Goods in transit at the end of an accounting period that were shipped FOB shipping point belong to the buyer; those shipped FOB destination belong to the seller. Consigned goods belong to the consignor. (Objective 2)

5. To determine the cost of an inventory, an accountant must determine (1) what costs to include in inventory and (2) what method to use in associating inventory costs with the physical units on hand. (Objective 1)

6. Product costs are inventoried; period costs are charged to expense in the period in which they are incurred. (Objective 3)

7. Trade discounts are deducted when determining product costs. In theory, cash discounts should also be deducted, but in practice, most companies account for inventory at gross invoice amounts (i.e., without deducting cash discounts). (Objective 3)

8. Inventory cost flow methods include specific identification, FIFO, average cost, and LIFO. Each method leads to a valuation of inventory and cost of goods sold based on historical cost. (Objective 4)

9. The specific identification method requires that the actual unit costs of goods on hand and goods sold be identified individually. In contrast, the FIFO, average cost, and LIFO methods reflect assumed cost flow patterns. (Objective 4)

10. If a company elects to use LIFO for income tax purposes, it must also use LIFO for financial reporting purposes. The LIFO method is an important exception to the general principle that a

EXHIBIT 8–12

Example Inventory Disclosure

The Goodyear Tire & Rubber Company

Consolidated Balance Sheet

The Goodyear Tire & Rubber Company
and Subsidiaries

	December 31,	
(Dollars in millions)	*1990*	*1989*
Assets		
Current Assets:		
Cash and cash equivalents	$ 220.3	$ 122.5
Short term securities	56.4	92.1
Accounts and notes receivable	1,495.2	1,244.6
Inventories	1,346.0	1,642.0
Prepaid expenses and other current assets	206.3	170.7
Total Current Assets	3,324.2	3,271.9

Accounting Policies

A summary of the significant accounting policies used in the preparation of the accompanying financial statements follows:

Inventory Pricing

Inventories are stated at the lower of cost or market. Cost is determined using the last-in, first-out (LIFO) method for a significant portion of domestic inventories and the first-in, first-out (FIFO) method or average cost method for other inventories.

Inventories

(In millions)	*1990*	*1989*
Raw materials and supplies	$ 234.5	$ 330.5
Work in process	67.5	90.1
Finished product	1,044.0	1,221.4
	$1,346.0	$1,642.0

The cost of inventories using the last-in, first-out (LIFO) method (approximately 38.4% of consolidated inventories in 1990 and 44.7% in 1989) was less than the approximate current cost of inventories by $335.4 million at December 31, 1990 and $330.6 million at December 31, 1989.

SOURCE: The Goodyear Tire & Rubber Company, 1990 Annual Report.

company does not have to use the same methods for financial reporting purposes that it uses for income tax purposes. (Objective 4)

11. A company should select the inventory cost flow method that most clearly reflects its periodic income; once selected, the method should be used consistently over time and disclosed in the financial statements. (Objective 4)

12. Inventory should ordinarily be reported on a balance sheet at the lower of cost or market value. In essence, the term "market" refers to the middle value selected from among the ceiling, replacement cost, and floor amounts. (Objective 5)

13. The lower of cost or market rule may be applied to each inventory item, to major categories of items, or to the inventory as a whole. (Objective 5)

14. The lower of cost or market rule is an exception to historical cost measurement of inventories that is justified on the basis of conservatism. (Objective 5)

15. The valuation of inventory at an amount greater than historical cost is permissible under GAAP only in certain exceptional cases. (Objective 6)

16. Inventory errors can cause several important misstatements to occur in the financial statements. (Objective 7)

17. The following elements of accounting theory are especially important in the area of inventory accounting: asset/liability measurement, revenue realization, matching, consistency, disclosure, industry practices, and conservatism. (Objective 8)

QUESTIONS

8–1 What are the major differences between trading and manufacturing companies regarding the classification of inventories and the calculation of cost of goods sold? Why do these differences exist?

8–2 The primary basis of accounting for inventories under GAAP is historical cost. Identify three inventory valuation methods that are alternatives to historical cost and briefly explain why these methods are not generally accepted today.

8–3 What is a periodic inventory system? What is a perpetual system? What factors should a manager consider when deciding which system the company should use?

8–4 What general rule determines which goods properly belong in a company's inventory? How does the accountant apply this general rule to goods in transit on the balance sheet date and to consigned goods?

8–5 Distinguish between product costs and period costs.

8–6 Why is the net method of recording purchases theoretically superior to the gross method?

8–7 What are the major arguments for and against the specific identification method of inventory cost determination?

8–8 What are the major arguments for and against the FIFO method of inventory cost determination?

8–9 What are the major arguments for and against the average cost method of inventory cost determination?

8–10 What are the major arguments for and against the LIFO method of inventory cost determination?

8–11 What basic problem does the existence within GAAP of several inventory cost flow methods create for external users of financial statements? How does the accounting profession justify these alternative methods?

8–12 What basic criterion should a company manager use in selecting an inventory cost flow method? Why is this criterion difficult to apply?

8–13 What are the major arguments for and against the LCM rule in accounting for inventories?

8–14 What does the term "market" mean in the context of the LCM rule?

8–15 What is the rationale for ceiling and floor limits on market under the LCM rule?

8–16 Under what circumstances, if any, is it appropriate under GAAP to value inventories at amounts greater than historical cost?

8–17 Relate inventory accounting to the asset/liability measurement principle, revenue realization principle, and matching principle.

8–18 Why is the consistency principle especially important in inventory accounting?

8–19 Relate inventory accounting to the conservatism modifying convention.

EXERCISES

8–20 COST OF GOODS SOLD Listed below are selected accounts and their balances that appeared on the *unadjusted* trial balance of Biswal, Inc., at April 30, 1993, the end of the company's annual fiscal period. Each account has a normal balance.

Sales returns	$12,000
Merchandise inventory	35,000
Transportation-out	14,000
Purchase returns	5,000
Sales	300,000
Advertising	15,000
Transportation-in	8,000
Purchases	135,000
Sales discounts	4,000
Sales commissions	12,000
Officers' salaries	40,000

A physical count on April 30 indicates that merchandise costing $28,000 is on hand.

Instructions

[a] Prepare the adjusting journal entry to record cost of goods sold on Biswal's books at April 30, 1993.

[b] What account(s) in [a] will Biswal have to close when it prepares closing entries on April 30, 1993?

[c] Indicate where the accounts you did *not* include in [a] should appear in Biswal's financial statements.

[d] Prepare a schedule of cost of goods sold for Biswal, Inc., for the year ending April 30, 1993.

[e] Calculate the amount of gross margin.

8–21 COST OF GOODS MANUFACTURED Information pertaining to Mapp Manufacturing Corporation for the year ended December 31, 1993, appears as follows:

Indirect labor	$45,000
Salesmen's salaries	42,000
Raw materials inventory, Dec. 31	53,000
Depreciation of factory properties	30,000
Work-in-process, Jan. 1	40,000
Direct labor	110,000
Factory utilities	20,000
Finished goods, Dec. 31	96,000
Work-in-process, Dec. 31	33,000
Advertising expense	25,000
Raw materials inventory, Jan. 1	60,000
Indirect materials	7,000
Purchases of raw materials	400,000
Property taxes on factory	18,000
Finished goods, Jan. 1	68,000
Returned purchases of raw materials	10,000
Net sales	835,000
Miscellaneous factory expenses	4,000

Instructions

[a] Prepare in good form a schedule of cost of goods manufactured for the year ended December 31, 1993.

[b] Calculate the cost of goods sold.

[c] Calculate the amount of gross margin.

8–22 DIRECT VERSUS ABSORPTION COSTING The following information pertains to Newlin Manufacturing Company during its first year of business.

Sales	10,000 units
Production	13,000 units
Cost per unit produced	
Direct materials	$1.00
Direct labor	3.00
Variable overhead	2.50
Fixed overhead	1.50

Instructions

Calculate the cost of the company's year-end inventory, assuming (1) absorption costing and (2) direct costing.

8–23 PERIODIC AND PERPETUAL SYSTEMS   Infantcar, Inc., is a wholesaler of infant car seats. At the beginning of 1993, the company's inventory consisted of 900 car seats priced at $10 each. During 1993 the following events occurred:

[1] Purchased 8,000 car seats on account at $10 each, terms n/30.
[2] Returned 500 defective car seats to supplier and received credit.
[3] Paid for 6,000 of the car seats purchased in [1].
[4] Sold 7,900 car seats on account for $16 each, terms n/30.
[5] Received 200 car seats returned by a customer and gave credit. The goods were in excellent condition and were therefore returned to regular inventory.
[6] Received cash for 6,800 of the car seats sold in item [4].
[7] Physical count at year-end revealed 600 units on hand.

Instructions

[a] Prepare journal entries (including adjusting entries) to record the above events on Infantcar's books, assuming that the company uses (1) a periodic system and (2) a perpetual system.
[b] What is the company's cost of goods sold for 1993 under (1) the periodic system and (2) the perpetual system? Explain any difference you find between the two numbers.

8–24 GOODS IN TRANSIT   Pulley Company had the following purchase and sale transactions near the end of 1993:

No.	Transaction	Terms	Date Merchandise Shipped by Seller	Date Merchandise Received by Buyer
1	Purchase	FOB shipping point yes	12/31/93	1/5/94
2	Purchase	FOB destination NO	12/31/93	1/5/94
3	Sale	FOB shipping point NO	12/31/93	1/5/94
4	Sale	FOB destination yes	12/31/93	1/5/94

Instructions

For each transaction, indicate whether Pulley Company should include the merchandise in its inventory at December 31, 1993. Assume that all dollar amounts are material. Explain your answer in each case.

8–25 GOODS TO INCLUDE IN INVENTORY   As the independent CPA for Qualle Corporation, state whether the goods in each of the following 1993 events should be included in Qualle's inventory for the fiscal year ending June 30, 1993. Explain your answer in each case.

[1] Finished goods pledged as collateral for a 90-day loan from First City Bank were on hand June 30. Incl.
[2] An order, accompanied by cash payment for the total sales price, was received on June 29 for goods that Qualle shipped on July 2. Inc.
[3] Qualle made advance payments of $3,000 to suppliers for goods ordered but not shipped as of June 30. Exc.
[4] On June 30 Qualle shipped goods FOB destination to Shagle Corporation, which received the goods on July 5. Incl.
[5] On June 29 Senape Company shipped goods FOB shipping point to Qualle. Qualle received the goods on July 2. Inc.
[6] Certain raw materials owned by Qualle were at Ramer Company for processing on June 30. Inc.
[7] Qualle had certain goods on hand for which it was acting as a selling agent for Newbrough Company. Excl.
[8] On June 26 Mazzola, Inc., shipped goods FOB destination to Qualle. Qualle received the invoice on June 30 and the goods on July 2. Exc.

[9] On June 29 Harbison Company shipped goods FOB shipping point to Qualle. Qualle received the invoice and the goods on July 2. *Inc,*

[10] On June 30 Qualle sent goods to a consignee and prepaid the freight charges. The consignee received the goods on July 5. *Inc.*

8–26 GOODS TO INCLUDE IN INVENTORY   During an annual audit at December 31, 1993, you find the following transactions:

[1] Merchandise costing $2,116 was received on January 3, 1994, and the related purchase invoice recorded January 5. The invoice showed the shipment was made on December 29, 1993, FOB destination.

[2] Merchandise costing $815 was received on December 28, 1993, and the invoice was not recorded. You located it in the hands of the purchasing agent; it was marked "on consignment."

[3] A packing case containing a product costing $965 was not included in the physical inventory because it was marked "hold for shipping instructions." Your investigation revealed that the customer's order was dated December 18, 1993, but that the case was shipped and the customer billed on January 10, 1994. The product was a stock item of your client.

[4] Merchandise received on January 6, 1994, costing $720 was entered in the purchase register on January 7, 1994. The invoice showed shipment was made FOB supplier's warehouse on December 31, 1993. Because it was not on hand December 31, it was not included in inventory.

[5] A special machine, made to order, was finished and in the shipping room on December 31, 1993. The customer was billed on that date and the machine excluded from inventory although it was shipped on January 4, 1994.

Instructions

Assume that the amount is material in each case. State whether the merchandise should be included in the client's inventory, and explain your decision.   (AICPA adapted)

8–27 NET VERSUS GROSS METHOD   Rao Company, which uses a periodic inventory system, had the following merchandise transactions during December 1993:

Dec. 1 Purchased merchandise from Hall Company for $1,000, terms 2/10, n/30.
  2 Purchased merchandise from Wall Company for $2,000, terms 3/10, n/30.
  11 Paid Wall Company for Dec. 2 purchase.
  30 Paid Hall Company for Dec. 1 purchase.

Instructions

[a] Prepare the general journal entries to record the above transactions on the books of Rao Company using (1) the *net method* of recording purchases and (2) the *gross method* of recording purchases.

[b] Discuss the accounting logic of the net method and the gross method of recording purchases.

8–28 FIFO AND LIFO   Holcomb, Inc., is a wholesaler of footballs. The following information pertains to the company's inventory during July 1993:

Balance, July 1	2,000 units @ $11
Purchase July 12	2,000 units @ $12
Purchase, July 26	2,000 units @ $15
Balance, July 31	2,500 units

Instructions

Assuming that Holcomb uses a periodic inventory system, calculate each of the following amounts for July 1993:

[a] Ending inventory under FIFO.   [c] Ending inventory under LIFO.
[b] Cost of goods sold under LIFO.   [d] Cost of goods sold under FIFO.

8–29 FIFO, LIFO, AND AVERAGE COST   Sweet Food Company sells honey. The following information is available from the company's inventory records for 1993:

	Jars	Cost per Jar	
Inventory, Jan. 1	200	$1.00	2 00
Purchases			
Jan. 16	300	1.50	450
Feb. 22	600	2.00	1200
Mar. 3	500	2.50	1250
Mar. 19	400	3.00	1200 4300

2000

During the first quarter of 1993, the company sold 1,400 jars at $5 each. The company uses a periodic system. A physical inventory on March 31 reveals 600 jars on hand.

Instructions

Prepare a schedule in the form shown below and compute the missing values. Show all supporting computations.

	Inventory Mar. 31, 1993	1st Quarter, 1993		
		Sales	Cost of Goods Sold	Gross Margin
LIFO	$	$	$	$
FIFO				
Average cost				

8–30 FIFO, AVERAGE COST, AND LIFO   Marcee, Inc., uses Raw Material Q in its production process. The following changes occurred in Marcee's inventory of Raw Material Q during October:

Oct.	1	Balance on hand	100 units @ $27	2700
	6	Purchased	300 units @ $25	7500
	14	Purchased	600 units @ $28	16800
	25	Purchased	400 units @ $21	8400
Oct.	9	Issued to production	200 units @ ?	
	28	Issued to production	800 units @ ?	

Instructions

[a] Assuming that Marcee maintains complete *perpetual* records for Raw Material Q, compute the cost of the inventory at October 31 and the cost of materials issued to production during October using the (1) FIFO, (2) average cost, and (3) LIFO methods. (Round unit cost calculation to three places.)

[b] Assuming that Marcee uses a *periodic* system to account for Raw Material Q, compute the cost of the inventory at October 31 and the cost of materials issued to production during October using the (1) FIFO, (2) average cost, and (3) LIFO methods. (Round unit cost calculations to three places.)

8–31 EFFECTS OF LIFO AND FIFO   Neilson Company began operations on January 1, 1990, and adopted the LIFO method of inventory pricing. The following additional facts pertain to the company:

Year	Reported Net Income	Ending Inventory Under LIFO	Ending Inventory That the Company Would Have Reported Under FIFO
1990	$ 60,000	$ 8,000	$15,000
1991	72,000	12,000	22,000
1992	90,000	18,000	12,000
1993	120,000	26,000	17,000

The company's income tax expense has consistently been 40% of income before taxes.

Instructions

Calculate the amount of net income the company would have reported for 1990, 1991, 1992, and 1993 under the FIFO method.

8–32 LOWER OF COST OR MARKET   For each of the following *independent* cases, determine the correct unit value for inventory valuation under the LCM rule:

Case	Historical Cost	Cost to Replace	Ceiling	Floor
A	$50	$48	$60	$53
B	78	76	86	72
C	38	37	48	40
D	80	82	79	71
E	23	21	27	22
F	18	17	20	16
G	60	61	59	50
H	89	84	97	88

8–33 LOWER OF COST OR MARKET   Olinger, Inc., compiled the following inventory information on November 30, 1993, the end of the company's fiscal year:

	Quantity	Unit Cost	Unit Market
Category X			
Product 1	400	$20	$18
Product 2	500	28	32
Category Y			
Product 3	700	17	19
Product 4	600	18	14
Category Z			
Product 5	400	35	39
Product 6	300	31	28

Instructions

Compute Olinger's inventory valuation at November 30, assuming that the company applies the LCM rule to (1) each product, (2) major categories of products, and (3) the inventory as a whole.

8–34 LOWER OF COST OR MARKET   The following information pertains to Loveday, Inc., at December 31, 1993:

Inventory, Jan. 1	$ 75,000
Purchases during 1993	325,000
Inventory, Dec. 31	
Cost	60,000
Market	50,000

Before 1993, application of the LCM rule never produced a need to write down the company's inventory to an amount below cost.

Instructions

Prepare the necessary *adjusting* journal entries to record cost of goods sold and to reflect the application of the LCM rule under each of the following assumptions:

[a] The company uses a *periodic* inventory system and applies the LCM rule using a loss account and a valuation allowance account.

[b] The company uses a *periodic* inventory system and applies the LCM rule using neither a loss account nor a valuation allowance account.

[c] The company uses a *perpetual* inventory system and applies the LCM rule using a loss account and a valuation allowance account.

[d] The company uses a *perpetual* inventory system and applies the LCM rule using neither a loss account nor a valuation allowance account.

8–35 INVENTORY ERRORS   Greene, Inc., began operations on January 1, 1992. The following data pertain to the company's first two years in business:

	Reported Amount	Correct Amount
Inventory		
Dec. 31, 1992	$ 20,000	$40,000
Dec. 31, 1993	35,000	35,000
Net Income		
For 1992	60,000	?
For 1993	66,000	?
Retained earnings		
Dec. 31, 1992	60,000	?
Dec. 31, 1993	126,000	?

During 1992 and 1993 the company's income tax expense rate was 40%, and the company declared no dividends.

Instructions

Compute the correct amount for each of the following variables:

[a] Net income for 1992.
[b] Net income for 1993.
[c] Retained earnings, December 31, 1992.
[d] Retained earnings, December 31, 1993.

8–36   INVENTORY ERRORS   Gresham Company uses a periodic inventory system and sells its merchandise for 100% above cost. The following events occurred near the end of the first year of operations (Year 1): *still have inv., not a sale*

[1] The company recorded a credit sale of goods to which it had not surrendered legal title as of the end of Year 1. These goods were excluded from the company's ending inventory.
[2] The company failed to record the credit sales of goods to which it surrendered legal title during Year 1. The company included the goods in its ending inventory.
[3] The company included certain goods to which it had not yet received legal title in its ending inventory. The company did not record a purchase of these goods.
[4] The company recorded a credit purchase of goods to which it received legal title during Year 1. Although the goods had not been sold by year-end, the company did not include them in its ending inventory.
[5] The company recorded a credit purchase of goods to which it did not receive legal title during Year 1. These goods were included in the company's ending inventory.
[6] The company failed to record the credit purchase of goods to which it received legal title during Year 1. Although the goods had not been sold by year-end, the company did not include them in its ending inventory.

Instructions

Set up a matrix like the one shown below. At the intersection of each row and column, indicate the effect of the event on the financial-statement variable at the end of Year 1, using the following code: O = Overstated, U = Understated, NE = No Effect. Treat each event independently. (*Note:* You should have 36 answers in the completed matrix.)

Event No.	Total Revenues	Total Expenses	Net Income	Total Assets	Total Liabilities	Total Stockholders' Equity
1						
2						
3						
4						
5						
6						

8–37 ACCRUAL BASIS AND CASH FLOWS   The following data were taken from the financial statements of Fishburne, Inc., a calendar-year merchandising corporation:

[1] Balance sheet data:

	Dec. 31, 1992	Dec. 31, 1993
Trade accounts receivable, net	$ 84,000	$ 78,000
Inventory	150,000	140,000
Accounts payable, merchandise (credit)	(95,000)	(98,000)

[2] Total sales were $1,200,000 for 1993 and $1,100,000 for 1992. Cash sales were 20% of total sales each year.

[3] Cost of goods sold was $840,000 for 1993.

[4] Variable general and administrative (G&A) expenses for 1993 were $120,000. They have varied in proportion to sales; 50% have been paid in the year incurred and 50% the following year. Unpaid G&A expenses are *not* included in accounts payable above.

[5] Fixed G&A expenses, including $35,000 depreciation and $5,000 bad-debt expense, totaled $100,000 each year. Eighty percent of fixed G&A expenses involving cash were paid in the year incurred and 20% the following year. Each year there was a $5,000 bad-debt estimate and a $5,000 write-off. Unpaid G&A expenses are *not* included in accounts payable above.

Instructions

[a] Compute the amount of cash collected during 1993 resulting from total sales in 1992 and 1993.

[b] Compute the amount of cash disbursed during 1993 for purchases of merchandise.

[c] Compute the amount of cash disbursed during 1993 for variable and fixed general and administrative expenses.   (AICPA adapted)

8–38 CURRENT VALUE ACCOUNTING   The controller of Connelly Company is discussing a comment you made in the course of presenting your audit report.

"... And frankly," Mr. Colson continues, "I agree that we, too, are responsible for finding ways to produce more relevant financial statements which are as reliable as the ones we now produce. For example, suppose the Company acquired a finished item for inventory for $40 when the general price-level index was 110. And, later, the item was sold for $75 when the general price-level index was 121 and the current replacement cost was $54. We could calculate a 'holding gain.'"

Instructions

[a] Explain to what extent and how current replacement costs already are used in generally accepted accounting principles to value inventories.

[b] Compute the amount of the holding gain in Mr. Colson's example.

[c] Why is the use of current replacement cost for *both* inventories and cost of goods sold preferred by some accounting authorities to the generally accepted use of FIFO or LIFO?

[d] Why do some authorities believe that the present market resale (exit or output) price is a conceptual improvement on current replacement (entry or input) cost for inventory measurement?
                      (AICPA adapted)

PROBLEMS **8–39** GOODS TO INCLUDE IN INVENTORY   Butler, Inc., uses a periodic inventory system and a fiscal year ending September 30. On September 30, 1992, the company correctly reported inventory on hand costing $14,500. During the fiscal year ending September 30, 1993, the company recorded purchases of $45,000. A physical count on September 30, 1993, revealed that goods costing $21,000 were on hand. The following material events occurred between September 23 and October 7, 1993:

[1] Goods costing $3,000 that Butler was holding as a consignee were included in the physical count.

[2] An invoice for goods costing $4,600 was received and entered as a credit purchase on September 29. The goods arrived on October 2. The supplier shipped the goods FOB destination on September 27.

[3] An invoice for goods costing $4,100 was received and entered as a credit purchase on October 3. The goods arrived on that date and were in satisfactory condition. The invoice indicates that the supplier shipped the goods FOB shipping point on September 29.

[4] Goods that Butler specially purchased from an overseas supplier for ultimate sale to Digital Enterprises, Inc., were included in the physical count. A contract between Butler and Digital pertaining to the goods states that "title passes when buyer approves the goods." A representative from Digital Enterprises inspected and approved the goods in Butler's warehouse on September 28. Butler shipped the goods and recorded a sale on October 4. The goods cost $2,500 and were sold on credit for $3,600.

[5] Goods costing $800 and housed in a special storeroom were inadvertently overlooked when the physical count was taken.

[6] An invoice for goods costing $3,100 was received and entered as a credit purchase on September 28. The supplier shipped the goods FOB shipping point on September 26. The receiving report indicates that Butler received the goods on October 1.

Instructions

[a] Make all necessary correcting entries in general journal form for the fiscal year ending September 30, 1993. Assume that the adjusting entry for cost of goods sold has not been made and that the books for the year have not been closed.

[b] Compute the correct inventory amount for Butler's balance sheet dated September 30, 1993.

[c] Make the adjusting journal entry to record the cost of goods sold for the fiscal year ending September 30, 1993.

8–40   GOODS TO INCLUDE IN INVENTORY   Tower Company of New York City uses a periodic inventory system and a fiscal year ending June 30. The company makes all its merchandise purchases and sales on credit. The following information is available from the company's inventory records:

Beginning inventory, July 1, 1992	$20,000
Purchases, July 1, 1992–June 30, 1993	90,000
Purchase returns, July 1, 1992–June 30, 1993	2,000
Ending inventory, June 30, 1993 (per physical count)	16,000

The following events occurred near the end of the fiscal year that ended on June 30, 1993:

[1] Goods costing $4,000 received on June 27 were recorded as a purchase twice.

[2] Goods shipped by rail from New York to a Los Angeles customer were recorded as a sale on June 30. The goods cost $3,600; the selling price was $6,000. The goods were shipped on June 30, FOB Los Angeles. Tower Company did not include these goods in its physical inventory.

[3] Goods costing $3,500 received on June 29 were recorded as a purchase on July 2.

[4] Goods costing $4,500 were recorded as a purchase on July 5. A Seattle supplier shipped the goods to New York by rail, FOB Seattle, on June 30.

[5] Goods costing $5,000 held by Bailey Company on consignment were not counted. Tower Company recorded a sale of $8,000 when it shipped the goods to Bailey on June 23.

[6] Goods costing $3,800 were received on June 18 and returned for credit on June 20 because they were not satisfactory. Tower Company did not record these events.

Instructions

[a] Make all necessary correcting entries in general journal form for the fiscal year ending June 30, 1993. Assume that the adjusting entry for the cost of goods sold has not been made and that the books for the year have not been closed.

[b] Compute the correct inventory amount for Tower Company's balance sheet dated June 30, 1993.

[c] Make the adjusting journal entry to record the cost of goods sold for the fiscal year ending June 30, 1993.

8–41   NET VERSUS GROSS METHOD   Theo, Inc., began operations in 1993. The company maintains complete perpetual records for its merchandise inventory. During 1993 Theo purchased merchandise having a gross invoice cost of $100,000. All purchases were made under the terms 2/10, n/30. Theo paid freight charges of $5,000 for the merchandise.

During the year, Theo paid for 80% of the merchandise within the discount period; it paid for the other 20% after the discount period had expired. Theo sold 70% of the merchandise it acquired for cash of $120,000; the other 30% remains in inventory at year-end.

Instructions

[a] Prepare the general journal entries to record the above transactions on Theo's books using (1) the *net method* of recording purchases and (2) the *gross method* of recording purchases.

[b] What financial statement balances would Theo report at December 31, 1993, for sales, cost of goods sold, gross margin, discounts lost (or interest expense), and ending inventory under (1) the *net method* and (2) the *gross method?*

[c] Which method of recording purchases (net method or gross method) is generally regarded as theoretically superior? Why?

8–42 FIFO, AVERAGE COST, AND LIFO   The following information pertains to Model T calculators of Compu Corporation for the month of June, 1993:

Date	Calculators	Units	Unit Cost	Unit Selling Price
June 1	Beginning inventory	1,000	$52	
7	Purchase	3,000	50	
12	Sale	2,000		$100
17	Purchase	6,000	45	
22	Purchase	2,000	43	
28	Sale	7,000		100
30	Ending inventory	3,000		

52000
150000

270000
86000

558000

Instructions

GA=12000

[a] Assuming that the company uses a *periodic* inventory system, calculate the cost of the ending inventory and the cost of goods sold using (1) the FIFO method, (2) the average cost method, and (3) the LIFO method. (Round unit cost calculations to three places.)

[b] Assuming that the company uses a *perpetual* inventory system, calculate the cost of the ending inventory *and* the cost of goods sold using (1) the FIFO method, (2) the average cost method, and (3) the LIFO method. (Round unit cost calculations to three places.)

[c] Calculate the amount of gross margin in [a-1, 2, 3] and [b-1, 2, 3]. S-CGS = GPM

[d] Assume that the inflation rate (i.e., the increase in the overall level of prices in the economy) was 1% during June 1993. Use your answer to [c] to logically evaluate the claim that the use of LIFO produces lower earnings during inflationary periods.

8–43 FIFO, AVERAGE COST, AND LIFO   The following inventory information pertains to Resting-Boy recliners of Fine Furniture Company for the year ended December 31, 1993:

Date	Recliners	Units	Unit Cost	Total Cost
Jan. 1	Inventory on hand	200	$150	$ 30,000
Apr. 3	Purchase	300	175	52,500
Sept. 28	Purchase	400	200	80,000
	Available for sale	900		$162,500

The company sold 400 recliners on June 25 and 300 on December 10. A physical count on December 31 indicates that 200 recliners are on hand.

Instructions

[a] Assuming that the company uses a *periodic* inventory system, calculate the cost of the ending inventory *and* the cost of goods sold using (1) the FIFO method, (2) the average cost method, and (3) the LIFO method. (Round unit cost calculations to three places.)

[b] Assuming that the company uses a *perpetual* inventory system, calculate the cost of the ending inventory *and* the cost of goods sold using (1) the FIFO method, (2) the average cost method, and (3) the LIFO method. (Round unit cost calculations to three places.)

8–44   EFFECTS OF LIFO AND FIFO   Seminole, Inc., began operations on January 1, 1990, and adopted the LIFO method of inventory pricing. Condensed income statements for Seminole, Inc. for 1990–1993 appear below.

	1990	1991	1992	1993
Net sales	$250,000	$300,000	$400,000	$480,000
Cost of goods sold	125,000	150,000	200,000	240,000
Gross margin	125,000	150,000	200,000	240,000
S&A expenses	75,000	75,000	75,000	75,000
Pretax income	50,000	75,000	125,000	165,000
Income taxes (40%)	20,000	30,000	50,000	66,000
Net income	$ 30,000	$ 45,000	$ 75,000	$ 99,000

Seminole's comparative balance sheets showed the following LIFO inventory amounts at December 31: 1990—$25,000; 1991—$27,000; 1992— $30,000; and 1993—$38,000.

Notes to Seminole's financial statements indicated that if the company had used the FIFO inventory method, December 31 inventories would have been as follows: 1990—$35,000; 1991—$42,000; 1992—$50,000; and 1993—$65,000.

Instructions

[a] Using the condensed format shown above, prepare income statements for Seminole, Inc., for 1990–1993, assuming that the company had used FIFO since its inception.
[b] Explain the underlying factors that cause Seminole's net income under FIFO to differ from its net income under LIFO.

8–45   EFFECT OF CHANGE FROM FIFO TO LIFO   Manford Manufacturing Company manufactures two products: Hoop and Soop. On December 31, 1992, Manford used the FIFO inventory method. On January 1, 1993, Manford changed to the LIFO method. The cumulative effect of this change is not determinable and, as a result, the ending inventory of 1992 under FIFO is also the beginning inventory for 1993 under LIFO. Any layers added during 1993 should be costed by reference to the first acquisitions of 1993, and any layers liquidated during 1993 should be considered a permanent liquidation.

The following information was available from Manford's inventory records for the last two years:

	Hoop		Soop	
	Units	Unit Cost	Units	Unit Cost
1992 Purchases				
Jan. 7	5,000	$4.00	22,000	$2.00
Apr. 16	12,000	4.50		
Nov. 8	17,000	5.00	18,500	2.75
Dec. 13	10,000	6.00		
1993 Purchases				
Feb. 11	3,000	7.00	23,000	3.00
May 20	8,000	7.50		
Oct. 15	20,000	8.00		
Dec. 23			15,500	3.50
Units on Hand				
Dec. 31, 1992	15,000		14,500	
Dec. 31, 1993	16,000		12,000	

Instructions

Compute the effect of the change from the FIFO to the LIFO inventory method on income before income taxes for the year ended December 31, 1993.   (AICPA adapted)

8–46   EFFECTS OF FIFO, LIFO, AND AVERAGE COST   The controller of the Tegano Corporation, a retail company, made three different schedules of gross margin for the first quarter ended September 30, 1993. These schedules appear below.

	Sales ($10 per unit)	Cost of Goods Sold	Gross Margin
Schedule A	$280,000	$118,550	$161,450
Schedule B	280,000	116,900	163,100
Schedule C	280,000	115,750	164,250

The computation of cost of goods sold in each schedule is based on the following data.

	Units	Cost per Unit	Total Cost
Beginning inventory, July 1	10,000	$4.00	$40,000
Purchase, July 25	8,000	4.20	33,600
Purchase, Aug. 15	5,000	4.13	20,650
Purchase, Sept. 5	7,000	4.30	30,100
Purchase, Sept. 25	12,000	4.25	51,000

The president of the corporation cannot understand how three different gross margins can be computed from the same set of data. As controller, you have explained that the three schedules are based on three different assumptions concerning the flow of inventory costs: FIFO, LIFO, and weighted average. Schedules A, B, and C were not necessarily prepared in this sequence of cost flow assumptions.

Instructions

Prepare three separate schedules computing cost of goods sold and supporting schedules. Show the composition of the ending inventory under each of the three cost flow assumptions.

(AICPA adapted)

8–47 LOWER OF COST OR MARKET Yarbro Company manufactures four products and prices its inventory using the lower of average cost or market value. The company maintains a normal profit margin rate of 20% of selling price. Yarbro's accountant gathered the following information, all on a per unit basis, at December 31, 1993:

Product	Historical Cost	Current Replacement Cost	Estimated Selling Price	Estimated Cost to Dispose
A	$24	$23	$30	$ 3
B	28	24	40	5
C	45	48	70	10
D	81	82	90	10

Instructions

[a] Prepare a schedule to determine the correct unit values for the inventory valuation of each product under the LCM rule.

[b] Explain the rationale for the use of selling prices when applying the LCM rule.

8–48 LOWER OF COST OR MARKET Selected items of merchandise information for eight independent cases (1 through 8) appear below. In each case the normal profit margin rate is 30% of selling price.

Instructions

Set up a table similar to the one shown below and compute the missing values.

Case	Estimated Selling Price	Estimated Cost to Dispose	Ceiling	Allowance for Normal Profit Margin	Floor	Replacement Cost	Market	Historical Cost	LCM
1	$60	10	$50	18	32	$52	50	$51	50
2		$5		$15		28		33	
3			18	6			$16		$15
4	30	4						20	18
5	10		9			7		8	
6		6		12		35			32
7			69	24		72		70	
8	70	9				37		42	

8–49 LOWER OF COST OR MARKET The following inventory information pertains to Yokoyama, Inc., at December 31, 1993:

		Per Unit		Ceiling	
	Quantity	Original Cost	Cost to Replace	Net Realizable Value	Floor
Appliances					
Product W	500	$25	$22	$27	$23
Product X	300	31	33	36	29
Sporting Goods					
Product Y	600	14	18	20	13
Product Z	800	21	21	20	15

Instructions

[a] Determine the inventory valuation at December 31, 1993, assuming that the company applies the LCM rule to (1) each product, (2) major categories of products, and (3) the inventory as a whole.

[b] The accountant for Yokoyama is trying to determine which one of the three amounts in [a] she should use in the company's published financial statements. What major factors should the accountant consider?

8–50 INVENTORY ERRORS Condensed income statements for Penner Company for 1988–1993 appear below.

	Year Ending December 31					
	1988	1989	1990	1991	1992	1993
Net sales	$125,000	$132,000	$141,000	$156,000	$163,000	$176,000
Cost of goods sold	75,000	80,000	85,000	94,000	98,000	106,000
Gross margin	50,000	52,000	56,000	62,000	65,000	70,000
Selling and administrative expenses	30,000	31,000	34,000	39,000	41,000	45,000
Pretax income	20,000	21,000	22,000	23,000	24,000	25,000
Income taxes (40%)	8,000	8,400	8,800	9,200	9,600	10,000
Net income	$ 12,000	$ 12,600	$ 13,200	$ 13,800	$ 14,400	$ 15,000

The previous statements were prepared without knowledge of the inventory errors shown below.

Date	Inventory
Dec. 31, 1987	Correctly stated
Dec. 31, 1988	Understated $12,000
Dec. 31, 1989	Overstated $8,000
Dec. 31, 1990	Understated $6,000
Dec. 31, 1991	Correctly stated
Dec. 31, 1992	Overstated $12,000
Dec. 31, 1993	Overstated $6,000

Instructions

[a] Using the condensed format shown above, prepare corrected income statements for Penner Company for 1988–1993.

[b] Describe the overall impact that the correction of the inventory errors in [a] has on the company's earnings trend.

8–51 INVENTORY ERRORS You have been asked to review the records and prepare corrected financial statements for Lufkin Corporation. The books of account are in agreement with the following balance sheet:

Lufkin Corporation
BALANCE SHEET
December 31, 1993

Assets		Liabilities and Capital	
Cash	$ 5,000	Accounts payable	$ 2,000
Accounts receivable	10,000	Notes payable	4,000
Notes receivable	3,000	Capital stock	10,000
Inventory	25,000	Retained earnings	27,000
	$43,000		$43,000

A review of Lufkin's books indicates that the following errors and omissions had *not* been corrected during the applicable years:

Dec. 31	Inventory Overvalued	Inventory Undervalued	Prepaid Expense	Unearned Revenue	Accrued Expense	Accrued Revenue
1990	—	$6,000	$900	—	$200	—
1991	$7,000	—	700	$400	75	$125
1992	8,000	—	500	—	100	—
1993	—	9,000	600	300	50	150

According to the books, profits are $5,500 in 1991, $6,500 in 1992, and $7,500 in 1993. No dividends were declared during these years and no adjustments were made to retained earnings.

Instructions

Prepare a worksheet to develop the correct profits for 1991, 1992, and 1993 and the adjusted balance sheet accounts as of December 31, 1993. (Ignore possible income tax effects.)

(AICPA adapted)

8–52 SALES AND PURCHASES CUTOFF   You have been engaged to audit M Company for the year ended December 31, 1993. M Company, a wholesale chemical business, makes all sales at 25% over cost.

Shown below are portions of M Company's sales and purchases accounts for the calendar year 1993:

Sales

Date	Reference	Amount	Date	Reference	Amount
12/31	Closing entry	700,590	Balance forward		658,320
			12/27	SI#965	5,195
			12/28	SI#966	20,000
			12/28	SI#967	1,302
			12/31	SI#969	5,841
			12/31	SI#970	7,922
			12/31	SI#971	2,010
		700,590			700,590

Purchases

Date	Reference	Amount	Date	Reference	Amount
Balance forward		360,300	12/31	Closing entry	385,346
12/28	RR#1059	3,100			
12/30	RR#1061	8,965			
12/31	RR#1062	4,861			
12/31	RR#1063	8,120			
		385,346			385,346

RR = Receiving report.
SI = Sales invoice.

You observed the physical inventory of goods in the warehouse on December 31, 1993, and were satisfied that it was properly taken. When you conducted a sales and purchases cutoff test (to determine that these transactions are recorded in the proper period), you found that at December 31, 1993, the last receiving report which had been used was no. 1063 and that no shipments had been made on any sales invoices with numbers larger than no. 968. You also obtained the following additional information:

[1] Included in the physical inventory were chemicals which had been purchased and received on receiving report no. 1060 but for which an invoice was not received until 1994. The cost was $4,366.

[2] In the warehouse at December 31, 1993, were goods which had been sold and paid for by the customer but which were not shipped until 1994. They were all sold on sales invoice no. 965 and were not inventoried. (The sales agreement between M Company and this customer provided that title to the goods passes as soon as the customer pays for the goods and the seller processes the customer's order.)

[3] On the evening of December 31, 1993, there were two cars on M Company siding:
   [a] Car #AR38162 was unloaded on January 2, 1994, and received on receiving report no. 1063. The freight was paid by the vendor.
   [b] Car #BAE74123 was loaded and sealed on December 31, 1993, and was switched off the company's siding on January 2, 1994. The sales price was $12,700 and the freight was paid by the customer. This order was sold on sales invoice no. 968.

[4] Two cars of chemicals enroute to Z Pulp and Paper Company were temporarily stranded on December 31, 1993, on a railroad siding. They were sold on sales invoice no. 966 and the terms were FOB destination.

[5] A truckload of material enroute to M Company on December 31, 1993, was received on receiving report no. 1064. The material was shipped FOB destination and freight of $75 was paid by M Company. However, the freight was deducted from the purchase price of $975.

[6] Chemicals exposed to rain in transit and deemed unsalable were included in the physical inventory. Their invoice cost was $1,250 and freight charges of $350 had been paid on the chemicals.

Instructions

[a] Compute the adjustments which should be made to M Company's physical inventory at December 31, 1993.

[b] Prepare the adjusting entries required as of December 31, 1993.   (AICPA adapted)

8–53 INVENTORY RECONCILIATION Hillard Company cans two food commodities which it stores at various warehouses. The company uses a perpetual inventory system under which the finished goods inventory is charged with production and credited for sales at standard cost. The detail of the finished goods inventory is maintained on punched cards by the tabulating department in units and dollars for the various warehouses.

The accounting department receives copies of daily production reports and sales invoices. Units are then extended at standard cost and a summary of the day's activity is posted to the Finished Goods Inventory general ledger control account. Next the sales invoices and production reports are sent to the tabulating department for processing. Every month the control account and detailed tab records are reconciled and adjustments recorded. The last reconciliation and adjustments were made at November 30, 1993.

Your CPA firm observed the taking of the physical inventory at all locations on December 31, 1993. The inventory count began at 4:00 p.m. and was completed at 8:00 p.m. The company's figure for the physical inventory is $342,400. The general ledger control account balance at December 31 was $384,900, and the final "tab run" of the inventory punched cards showed a total of $403,300.

Unit cost data for the company's two products are as follows:

Product	Standard Cost
A	$2
B	3

A review of December transactions disclosed the following:

[1] Sales invoice no. 1301, Dec. 2, was priced at standard cost for $11,700 but was listed on the accounting department's daily summary at $11,200.

[2] A production report for $23,900, Dec. 15, was processed twice in error by the tabulating department.

[3] Sales invoice no. 1423, Dec. 9, for 1,200 units of product A, was priced at a standard cost of $1.50 per unit by the accounting department. The tabulating department corrected the error but did not notify the accounting department of the error.

[4] A shipment of 3,400 units of Product A was invoiced by the billing department as 3,000 units on sales invoice no. 1504, Dec. 27. The error was discovered by your review of transactions.

[5] On December 27 the Memphis warehouse notified the tabulating department to remove 2,200 unsalable units of Product A from the finished goods inventory, which it did without receiving a special invoice from the accounting department. The accounting department received a copy of the Memphis warehouse notification on December 29 and prepared a special invoice which was processed in the normal manner. The units were not included in the physical inventory.

[6] A report for the production on January 3 of 2,500 units of Product B was processed for the Omaha plant as of December 31.

[7] A shipment of 300 units of Product B was made from the Portland warehouse to Ken's Markets, Inc., at 8:30 p.m. on December 31 as an emergency service. The sales invoice was processed as of December 31. Hillard Company prefers to treat the transaction as a sale in 1993.

[8] The working papers of the auditor observing the physical count at the Chicago warehouse revealed that 700 units of Product B were omitted from Hillard's physical count. Hillard concurred that the units were omitted in error.

[9] A sales invoice for 600 units of Product A shipped from the Newark warehouse was mislaid and was not processed until January 5. The units were shipped on December 30.

[10] The physical inventory of the St. Louis warehouse excluded 350 units of Product A marked "reserved." Investigation revealed that this merchandise was being stored as a convenience for Steve's Markets, Inc., a customer. This merchandise, which has not been recorded as a sale, is billed as it is shipped.

[11] A shipment of 10,000 units of Product B was made on December 27 from the Newark warehouse to the Chicago warehouse. The shipment arrived on January 6 but had been excluded from the physical inventories.

Instructions

Prepare a worksheet to reconcile the balances for the physical inventory, Finished Goods Inventory general ledger control account, and tabulating department's detail of finished goods inventory ("tab run"). Use the format shown below.

	Physical Inventory	General Ledger Control Account	Tabulating Department's Detail of Inventory
Balance per client	$342,400	$384,900	$403,300

(AICPA adapted)

8-54 CORRECTED INVENTORY You are auditing Handy Manufacturing Company for the year ended December 31, 1993. To reduce the workload at year-end, the company took its annual physical inventory under your observation on November 30, 1993. The company's Inventory account, which includes raw material and work-in-process, is on a perpetual basis and the FIFO method of pricing is used. There is no finished goods inventory. The company's physical inventory revealed that the book inventory of $58,410 was understated by $3,000. To avoid distorting the interim financial statements, the company decided not to adjust the book inventory, except for obsolete inventory items, until year-end.

Your audit revealed the following information about the November 30 inventory:

[1] Pricing tests showed that the physical inventory was overpriced by $2,200.

[2] Footing and extension errors resulted in a $150 understatement of the physical inventory.

[3] Direct labor included in the physical inventory amounted to $10,000. Overhead was included at the rate of 200% of direct labor. You determined that the amount of direct labor was correct and the overhead rate was proper.

[4] The physical inventory included obsolete materials recorded at $250. During December these obsolete materials were removed from the inventory account and charged to Cost of Sales.

Your audit also disclosed the following information about the December 31 inventory:

[1] Total debits to certain accounts during December are listed below:

Purchases	$24,700
Direct labor	12,100
Manufacturing overhead	25,200
Cost of sales	68,600

[2] The cost of sales of $68,600 included direct labor of $13,800.

[3] Normal scrap loss on established product lines is negligible. However, a special order started and completed during December had excessive scrap loss of $800 which was charged to Manufacturing Overhead.

Instructions

[a] Compute the correct amount of the physical inventory at November 30, 1993.

[b] Without prejudice to your solution to [a], assume that the correct amount of the physical inventory at November 30, 1993, was $55,250. Compute the amount of the inventory at December 31, 1993. (AICPA adapted)

CASES

8–55 LIFO Jack Schaad, president of Pickett, Inc., recently read an article which claimed that at least 100 of the country's largest 500 companies were either adopting or considering adopting the last-in, first-out (LIFO) method for valuing inventories. The article stated that the firms were switching to LIFO to (1) neutralize the effect of inflation in their financial statements, (2) eliminate inventory profits, and (3) reduce income taxes. Schaad wonders if the switch would benefit his company.

Pickett currently uses the first-in, first-out (FIFO) method of inventory valuation in its periodic inventory system. The company has a high inventory turnover rate, and inventories represent a significant proportion of the assets.

In discussing this trend toward LIFO inventory with business friends, Schaad has been told that the LIFO system is more costly to operate and will provide little benefit to companies with high turnover. Schaad intends to use the inventory method that is best for the company in the long run and not to select a method just because it is the current fad.

Instructions

[a] Explain to Mr. Schaad what "inventory profits" are and how the LIFO method of inventory valuation could reduce them.

[b] Explain to Mr. Schaad the conditions that must exist for Pickett to receive tax benefits from the LIFO method. (CMA adapted)

8–56 FIFO AND LIFO Mize Company is considering changing its inventory valuation method from FIFO to LIFO because of the potential tax savings. However, the management wishes to consider all of the effects on the company, including its reported performance, before making the final decision.

The inventory account, currently valued on the FIFO basis, consists of 1,000,000 units at $7 per unit on January 1, 1993. There are 1,000,000 shares of common stock outstanding as of January 1, 1993, and the cash balance is $400,000.

The company has made the following forecasts for the period 1993–1995.

	1993	1994	1995
Unit sales (in millions of units)	1.1	1.0	1.3
Sales price per unit	$10	$10	$12
Unit purchases (in millions of units)	1.0	1.1	1.2
Purchase price per unit	$7	$8	$9
Annual depreciation (in thousands of dollars)	$300	$300	$300
Cash dividends per share	$.15	$.15	$.15
Cash payments for additions to and replacement of plant and equipment (in thousands of dollars)	$350	$350	$350
Income tax rate	40%	40%	40%
Operating expense (exclusive of depreciation) as a percent of sales	15%	15%	15%
Common shares outstanding (in millions)	1	1	1

Instructions

[a] Prepare a schedule that illustrates and compares the following data for Mize Company under the FIFO and the LIFO inventory method for 1993–1995. Assume the company would begin LIFO at the beginning of 1993.

[1] Year-end inventory balances.   [3] Earnings per share.
[2] Annual net income.   [4] Cash balance.

Assume all sales are collected in the year of sale and all purchases, operating expenses, and taxes are paid during the year incurred.

[b] Using the data above, your answer to [a], and any additional issues you believe need to be considered, prepare a report that recommends whether or not Mize Company should change to the LIFO inventory method. Support your conclusions with appropriate arguments.

(CMA adapted)

8–57 INSURANCE COSTS, LCM, AND LIFO Bagchi Company purchased a significant amount of raw materials inventory for a new product that it is manufacturing. Bagchi purchased insurance on these raw materials while they were in transit from the supplier.

Bagchi uses the lower of cost or market rule for these raw materials. The replacement cost of the raw materials is above the net realizable value and both are below the original cost.

Bagchi uses the average cost inventory method for these raw materials. In the last two years, each purchase has been at a lower price than the previous purchase, and the ending inventory quantity for each period has been higher than the beginning inventory quantity for that period.

Instructions

[a] What is the theoretically appropriate method that Bagchi should use to account for the insurance costs on the raw materials while they were in transit from the supplier? Why?

[b] [1] At which amount should Bagchi's raw materials inventory be reported on the balance sheet? Why?

[2] In general, why is the lower of cost or market rule used to report inventory?

[c] What would have been the effect on ending inventory and cost of goods sold had Bagchi used the LIFO inventory method instead of the average cost inventory method for the raw materials? Why?

(AICPA adapted)

JUDGMENT CASES

8–58 RECOGNIZING A SALE You are the controller (head of the accounting department) for Fenwick Corporation, a large, publicly-held manufacturer of electronic products and component parts. The company recognizes sales revenue according to the accrual basis of accounting.

Today's date is *January 20, 1993,* and you have just completed your initial draft of the financial statements for Fenwick's accounting period that ended on December 31, 1992. The income statement shows that the company's earnings per share (EPS) for 1992 are considerably lower than had been previously expected. In fact, the 1992 EPS are lower than EPS for 1991, and this breaks a ten-year trend of rising EPS.

Fenwick's chief executive officer, Jon Weimer, enters your office and lets you know that he is extremely displeased with these earnings results. He is especially concerned about the potential negative effect of the EPS decline on the company's stock price and subsequent shareholder reaction.

Mr. Weimer then brings up the subject of a large order of compact disc players that Fenwick had recently manufactured under a special order placed by Sound Design Corporation, a national retail electronics chain. The contract with Sound Design had provided that the CD players would be manufactured according to Sound Design's precise specifications and that title to the goods would pass "on the date Sound Design approves the goods." Fenwick Corporation produced the goods during 1992, and a Sound Design representative inspected and approved them on January 3, 1993. Fenwick then shipped the goods on January 3.

Mr. Weimer observes that the preliminary 1992 income statement does not reflect the large sale made to Sound Design. He points out that if the income statement could be revised to include the sale, EPS for 1992 would be comfortably higher than for 1991. Fenwick could then continue its string of unbroken EPS increases, and Fenwick's stockholders would be happy. Mr. Weimer tells you that he has a way to convince the independent auditors to go along with the CEO's plan, but he does not explain exactly what he has in mind.

You inform Mr. Weimer that generally accepted accounting principles permit a sale to be recognized only when title to goods in inventory passes from a seller to a buyer, in this case, on January 3, 1993. Mr. Weimer then states that "the goods in question were completed in 1992, and it only seems fair and reasonable to recognize the sales revenue in 1992. The fact that Sound Design did not inspect the goods until January 3, 1993 is trivial."

Mr. Weimer then suggests that you revise the 1992 income statement to reflect a sale of the special-order merchandise to Sound Design. As he leaves your office, Mr. Weimer reminds you of the need for everyone at Fenwick to be a team player.

Instructions

Would you revise the 1992 income statement in accordance with Mr. Weimer's instructions? Explain in detail the rationale that supports your decision. As a *part* of your explanation, include a discussion of the major parties who would be affected by your decision.

8–59   **LOWER OF COST OR MARKET DECISION**   Joy Toys, Inc., typically manufactures most of its product in anticipation of the Christmas season. Sometimes the company will quickly design and manufacture a toy to take advantage of fads (such as Star Wars) that sweep the nation.

During the accounting period that just ended, the company designed and produced a large quantity of a toy called "Sneak Bombers," which the company anticipated rushing to market. The toy emulates a widely-publicized new bomber that the federal government has recently considered funding for the armed forces. Shortly before Joy Toys was set to begin taking customer orders for the toy bombers, the U.S. Congress failed to pass enabling legislation that would fund the real bomber's production. As a result, the news about the bomber has been adverse and interest in it has diminished. Market studies show that if Congress does not fund the bomber's production, little interest in it will exist and the toy bombers probably will not be marketable at a price and volume necessary for Joy Toys to recover its cost of production.

The U.S. president stated at a recent news conference that he intends to fight for the bomber and suggested that he might call Congress back into a special session to reconsider funding for production of the new aircraft. Furthermore, a hostile foreign nation has recently declared war on a U.S. ally, and the president and Congress have expressed outrage. In fact, a number of congressmen who had originally voted against the bomber have said that they are reconsidering their earlier vote in light of the latest world crises.

Joy Toys must file its financial statements for the most recent accounting period with the SEC later this week, and Joy's president does not want to recognize any losses in the value of the inventory of toy bombers. He believes that if Congress provides even limited funding for the bomber's production, the toy will "sell like hotcakes." He believes that the chances of Congress funding the project are "better than 75%," and further observes that "it's an ill wind that blows no good" in regard to the recent outbreak of war between the two foreign countries.

Instructions

Do you believe that Joy Toys should recognize a loss on its inventory of "Sneak Bombers" in the financial statements for the accounting period just ended? Support your answer with careful analysis and reasoning.

8–60 INVENTORY REPORTING   Foliage Partners, Ltd., is a limited partnership formed to fund the cultivation and sale of a variety of tropical plants. The investors provide funding to the limited partnership, which in turn advances monies to a contract grower, Green Top Growers (GTG), Inc., who is then responsible for acquiring the plants and plant materials, planting and cultivating the plants until their maturity, and then selling them on behalf of the limited partnership. GTG, a closely held company whose financial statements are not audited, is involved in a number of such arrangements and also grows plants on its own behalf. GTG has existed for 10 years although it has expanded substantially only in the last two. The types of plants in question take between 18 months and 3 years to grow.

You are the accountant for Foliage Partners and are currently preparing its financial statements for the year just ended. Because the limited partnership has only recently been formed, the project is not very far along at this time. The monies advanced to GTG so far are intended to provide only for the acquisition of the plants and plant materials and their initial planting. GTG is authorized to acquire the plant materials in the form of seeds, seedlings, or cuttings limited only in such a fashion as to meet the projected growing schedules in the partnership agreement.

As of the partnership's balance sheet date, GTG had acquired the required seeds and seedlings and planted them in accordance with the agreement. The cuttings will be made from stock plants owned by GTG and then planted by GTG on behalf of Foliage Partners. On a recent visit to the GTG's facilities, you noticed that none of the cuttings have been made although GTG has a large number of stock plants from which, according to GTG's president, the cuttings will soon be taken.

The general partner of the limited partnership believes that the balance sheet description of the amounts advanced to GTG should be characterized as "plant inventory." She readily agrees to disclosing the fact that the inventory is held and is being cultivated by a contract grower and that the inventory will continue to be cared for by GTG on behalf of the limited partnership. You nevertheless wonder whether calling all of the amounts advanced to GTG "plant inventory" is appropriate in light of the fact that the cuttings have not yet been completed. The president responds to your concerns in the following fashion: "The cuttings exist. They simply have not yet been separated from the stock plants. Moreover, we have paid GTG and they are obligated to perform according to the contract. The plant material exists, is growing at this time, and was growing at the balance sheet date. I believe that those cuttings exist, belong to the limited partnership, and should be so reported. To do otherwise might unduly alarm the investors by causing them to believe that the project is behind schedule or otherwise troubled when, in fact, it is not. We only recently funded the partnership and things are going perfectly. Why plant any seeds of doubt if, in fact, none exist?"

Instructions

What should the amounts advanced to GTG by the partnership be called on the partnership's balance sheet? Do you believe that it would be acceptable to refer to the items as "plant inventory"? Defend your answers with appropriate arguments. Regardless of your answers to these questions, what information do you believe should be disclosed about the state of the inventory and costs paid to the contract grower?

CHAPTER 9

—

Inventories:
Additional
Valuation Methods

The previous chapter provided an overview of basic inventory valuation methods. The objective of this chapter is to explain and illustrate several additional methods of inventory valuation. These methods are dollar-value LIFO, the conventional retail method, retail LIFO, and the gross margin method. Some of these methods may initially appear to be more complex than they really are. However, one reason that companies use them is to simplify the enormous clerical tasks that accounting for inventory can produce.

LIFO APPLICATION METHODS

In Chapter 8 we discussed the **specific goods method** of applying LIFO. According to this method, LIFO is applied to each product in a company's inventory. Although the specific goods method is conceptually simple, its practical application is usually confined to inventories of only a small variety of products. When a company has many kinds of products, the specific goods method can create a large clerical burden. A company that handles hundreds of different goods, for example, usually wants a more efficient method of applying the basic LIFO concept. In this chapter we present the two most commonly used methods of applying LIFO: (1) the dollar-value LIFO method; and (2) the retail LIFO method.[1] Each method is acceptable for income tax purposes and for financial reporting purposes in accordance with GAAP. We present the dollar-value LIFO method below; retail LIFO is presented in a later section on the retail method. Throughout our discussion we shall focus primarily on the general concepts that underlie these methods. In practice, many detailed rules and regulations of the income tax law pertain to the use of LIFO. An accountant who wants to apply the LIFO method must thoroughly understand these rules and regulations and their implications.

As we saw in Chapter 8, the LIFO conformity requirement states that if a company uses LIFO for income tax purposes, the company must also use LIFO for financial reporting purposes. However, income tax regulations allow companies to use **different methods of applying LIFO** for the two purposes as long as the methods used in the financial statements would be acceptable for tax purposes. In practice, the vast majority of LIFO companies use the same methods of applying LIFO for financial reports and income taxes. When deciding how to apply LIFO for financial reporting purposes, a company should be guided by the primary objective of **providing useful information** to investors, creditors, and other users. A company should use different LIFO application methods for financial reporting purposes than used for tax purposes if the expected benefits to users of financial statements exceed the costs to the company of having to administer different LIFO application methods. An excellent discussion of many technical issues that pertain to the implementation of LIFO in practice is contained in an *Issues Paper* published by the AICPA in 1984.[2]

DOLLAR-VALUE LIFO METHOD

Under the specific goods method, LIFO is applied on the basis of changes in the *quantity of physical units of each product* in the inventory. In contrast, the dollar-value

---

[1]Yet another method of applying LIFO is the **specific goods pooling method.** Under this method, a company divides its inventory into **pools,** each of which must consist of **substantially identical goods.** Each pool, rather than each product, then becomes the basis for applying LIFO. The company applies LIFO on the basis of changes in the *quantity of physical units* in the designated inventory pools. The specific goods pooling method is not widely used in practice and, for the sake of brevity, is not illustrated in this book.
[2]Task Force on LIFO Inventory Problems, *Issues Paper,* "Identification and Discussion of Certain Financial Accounting and Reporting Issues Concerning LIFO Inventories" (New York: AICPA, Nov. 30, 1984), File 3175.

LIFO method is applied to goods in **designated pools.** Moreover, it is applied on the basis of **inventory changes measured in cost dollars, not in physical units.**

In 1938, LIFO was initially accepted as a tax method designed to allow companies to charge to expense the higher costs associated with the most recent inventory acquisitions. Dollar-value LIFO was developed during the 1940s as a way to allow companies whose products have style or design changes, such as clothing and automobiles, to obtain the tax benefits of LIFO. If these companies were required to apply LIFO on the basis of specific physical units in inventory, old inventory costs would be expensed whenever the number of physical units of a product declined because of style or design changes. In essence, the dollar-value LIFO method helps companies save taxes by giving them a greater opportunity to preserve old inventory costs while charging the more recent (and presumably higher) costs to expense. This opportunity to preserve old inventory costs exists because dollar-value LIFO is applied on the basis of dollars invested in broadly defined pools of goods. It is not applied to specific physical units of inventory.

A complicating factor when applying dollar-value LIFO is that the cost dollar is seldom a stable device with which to measure inventory changes. Because the ability of a dollar to acquire inventory usually changes over time, we cannot accurately measure inventory changes simply by comparing cost dollars incurred in different time periods. For this reason the dollar-value method requires us to measure all inventory changes in **cost dollars of the same year,** commonly called the **base year.** The term "base-year cost" refers to the total cost, determined as of the *beginning* of the period in which a company adopts the dollar-value LIFO method, of all inventory items in a designated pool. Inland Steel Company, for example, adopted the dollar-value LIFO method in 1950. The company therefore determines its base-year inventory costs as of January 1, 1950.

The accountant uses a year-end **conversion factor** to convert **cost dollars of the current year** to **cost dollars of the base year.** This factor measures changes in the level of inventory cost prices that have occurred since the base period. It is computed as follows:

$$\text{Conversion factor} = \frac{\text{Current year-end specific price index}}{\text{Base-year specific price index}}$$

Note that the conversion factor is derived by using a **specific price index.** A specific rather than a general price index is used because the direction and magnitude of changes in a company's inventory cost prices may differ from those of the overall level of prices in the economy. Methods of determining a specific price index under dollar value LIFO are discussed later in the chapter.

Over time the dollar-value LIFO method may produce several inventory layers, each of which is expressed in **cost dollars rather than physical units.** Therefore, because of changes in the mix of physical units in the inventory, the dollar-value LIFO cost of the ending inventory may exceed that of the beginning inventory even though the total number of physical units in the inventory has declined during the period. The accounting records must permit us to associate each layer with the conversion factor in existence when the layer was constructed.

To implement the dollar-value LIFO method, the accountant must measure in *base-year costs* both the beginning and the ending inventories of the current period. If the ending inventory exceeds the beginning inventory when each is measured in base-year costs, an inventory increment (measured in base-year costs) has occurred. Because the increment occurred in the current year, we price it at current-year costs by multiplying the increment by the current-year conversion factor to obtain a new LIFO inventory layer.[3] We then add this layer to those in existence at the beginning of the current period to get the ending dollar-value LIFO inventory amount.

Conversely, if the ending inventory is less than the beginning inventory when each is measured in base-year costs, a reduction in inventory has occurred in the current period. This reduction requires that we charge previously established LIFO layers to cost of goods sold in a last-in, first-out sequence at amounts that reflect the cost prices in existence when the layers were constructed.

Three major reasons explain why many companies use the dollar-value LIFO method. First, the method greatly eases the clerical burden of applying LIFO to specific goods. Second, because the method maintains inventory layers in cost dollars instead of physical units, it gives a company some room to change the composition of inventory without expensing old (and presumably lower) inventory costs. Finally, dollar-value LIFO permits considerable flexibility when grouping inventory items into pools. Under dollar-value LIFO, pooled goods must only be **similar** in a fairly broad sense. Thus, dollar-value LIFO enables a company to pool a reasonably large number of products. The more items that a company pools, the more room there is for increases in the quantity of certain goods to offset decreases in the quantity of others. As a result, dollar-value LIFO helps to preserve old inventory costs, thereby helping a company to realize more of the tax benefits that it usually seeks from using LIFO. Some companies that use dollar value LIFO are still reporting inventory costs incurred *during the 1940s.*

To illustrate the pooling concept that may be applied under dollar-value LIFO, assume that Brian Enterprises sells ten different models of *each* of the following product lines: sofas, chairs, lamps, tents, exercise bicycles, and canoes. Under the specific goods method of applying LIFO, pools would not exist and the company would therefore apply LIFO to each of its sixty different products ($10 \times 6 = 60$). Under dollar-value LIFO, the company would likely apply LIFO to only two pools: home furniture (sofas, chairs, and lamps) and sporting goods (tents, exercise bicycles, and canoes).

A company may include the entire inventory in a single pool under dollar-value LIFO. In practice, most companies that use LIFO have only a few pools, presumably in an attempt to reduce the chances of LIFO layer liquidations. One empirical study found that the median number of pools used by retailers is six, while the median for nonretailers is three. The most frequently occurring (mode) number of pools is two for retailers and one for nonretailers.[4] A company that has more than one pool must apply the dollar-value method to each pool. The ending dollar-value inventory amounts determined in the various pools are summed to get the overall ending inventory at LIFO cost.

Application Procedures

The following five steps summarize the procedures used to apply the dollar-value LIFO method to a designated pool of goods:

Step 1. Price the ending inventory at the current-year cost. A good measure of this cost is obtained by multiplying the physical quantities on hand by the actual unit costs of the goods most recently purchased or produced.

---

[3]Remember that we derive the current-year's conversion factor by dividing the current *year-end* specific price index by the base-year specific price index. In practice, although a year-end index is most commonly used, the use of a *beginning-of-the-year* index or an *average-for-the-year* index are also considered acceptable.

[4]James M. Reeve and Keith G. Stanga, "The LIFO Pooling Decision: Some Empirical Results from Accounting Practice," *Accounting Horizons* (June 1987), pp. 25–33.

Step 2. Obtain an appropriate year-end conversion factor (as explained later in the chapter) which measures the change in inventory *cost prices* that has occurred since the base period.

Step 3. Restate the ending inventory from current-year cost (as determined in Step 1) to base-year cost by dividing the results in Step 1 by the year-end conversion factor obtained in Step 2.

Step 4. From the ending inventory priced at base-year cost (as determined in Step 3), subtract *the inventory on hand at the beginning of the current period, also priced at base-year cost.*

Step 5. Compute the cost of the ending dollar-value LIFO inventory as follows:

1. If the difference in Step 4 is zero, inventory is unchanged. Thus, the ending dollar-value LIFO inventory valuation is the same as the beginning valuation.

2. If the difference in Step 4 is positive, inventory has increased. Price the increase by multiplying the difference obtained in Step 4 by the year-end conversion factor obtained in Step 2. Then add the result to the beginning dollar-value LIFO inventory valuation to get the correct ending valuation at LIFO cost.

3. If the difference in Step 4 is negative, inventory has decreased. Subtract the decrease from the most recently acquired layer(s) at base-year cost in a last-in, first-out sequence. The correct dollar-value LIFO ending inventory valuation will be the remaining layers multiplied by their respective conversion factors.

Application of these five steps will produce the correct dollar-value LIFO ending inventory amount. One may then determine cost of goods sold residually by subtracting the ending inventory amount from the cost of goods available for sale.

An Illustration

Assume that a company adopts dollar-value LIFO on January 1, 1990. The company's inventory priced at current costs on that date was $10,000, and the specific price index derived internally was 100. This inventory is subsequently regarded as the base LIFO layer from which changes may occur. The current-year cost of the ending inventory, as well as the year-end conversion factor for December 31, 1990, and for each of the succeeding three years, are given below.

Price Index

December 31	Ending Inventory at Current-Year Cost*	Year-End Conversion Factor**
1990	$12,480	1.20
1991	16,950	1.50
1992	14,420	1.40
1993	14,040	1.30

*Obtained by multiplying the physical quantities on hand by the actual unit costs of the goods most recently acquired.
**Obtained by dividing the current year-end specific price index by the base-year specific price index (100). Methods used to determine a specific price index under dollar value LIFO are explained later in the chapter.

The information in Exhibit 9–1 illustrates how to compute the ending dollar-value LIFO inventory amounts. We have keyed the illustration to the five steps presented earlier. Observe carefully the following major points:

EXHIBIT 9–1

Dollar-Value LIFO

December 31	Ending Inventory at Current-Year Cost (Step 1)	Year-End Conversion Factor (Step 2)	Ending Inventory at Base-Year Cost (Step 3)	Ending Minus Beginning Inventory, Both at Base-Year Cost (Step 4)	Cost of Ending Dollar-Value LIFO Inventory (Step 5)
1990	$12,480 ÷	1.20 =	$10,400	$10,400 − $10,000 = $ 400	$10,000 × 1.00 = $10,000 (base layer) 400 × 1.20 = 480 (1990 layer) $10,400 $10,480*
1991	16,950 ÷	1.50 =	11,300	11,300 − 10,400 = 900	$10,000 × 1.00 = $10,000 (base layer) 400 × 1.20 = 480 (1990 layer) 900 × 1.50 = 1,350 (1991 layer) $11,300 $11,830*
1992	14,420 ÷	1.40 =	10,300	10,300 − 11,300 = (1,000)	$10,000 × 1.00 = $10,000 (base layer) 300 × 1.20 = 360 (remaining 1990 layer) $10,300 $10,360*
1993	14,040 ÷	1.30 =	10,800	10,800 − 10,300 = 500	$10,000 × 1.00 = $10,000 (base layer) 300 × 1.20 = 360 (remaining 1990 layer) 500 × 1.30 = 650 (1993 layer) $10,800 $11,010*

*This is the correct amount to report on the ending balance sheet and to subtract from the cost of goods available for sale to measure the cost of goods sold for the year.

1. On December 31, 1990, the application of Step 4 shows an inventory increase of $400 expressed in *base-year costs*. In Step 5 we price this increase using the conversion factor from Step 2 (1.20). The inventory therefore consists of *two layers,* the base plus the 1990 layer, for a total LIFO cost of $10,480.

2. On December 31, 1991, applying Step 4 indicates an inventory increase of $900 expressed in *base-year costs*. Once again, we price the increase using the conversion factor from Step 2 (1.50). The inventory now consists of *three layers,* the base plus the 1990 and 1991 layers, for a total LIFO cost of $11,830.

3. On December 31, 1992, the application of Step 4 shows an inventory *decrease* of $1,000 expressed in *base-year costs*. When a decrease occurs, we must remove it from the existing LIFO inventory layers in a last-in, first-out sequence. In other words we assume that the last layer(s) in is the first to go out. Any layer removed is charged to cost of goods sold at an amount equal to the base-year cost of the layer multiplied by the conversion factor in existence when the layer was created. Expressed in base-year costs, the $1,000 decrease eliminates all of the 1991 layer ($900) and $100 of the 1990 layer. Had the inventory decrease been larger, it could have eliminated the entire 1990 layer and some or all of the base. An inventory layer, once eliminated, cannot subsequently be reconstructed. The inventory at the end of 1992 consists of *two layers,* the base plus three-fourths of the 1990 layer, for a total LIFO cost of $10,360. Note that we do not construct a 1992 layer, because the inventory that year does not increase.

4. On December 31, 1993, applying Step 4 indicates an inventory increase of $500 expressed in *base-year costs*. As usual, we price the increase using the year-end conversion factor (1.30) derived in Step 2. The inventory now consists of *three layers:* the base, the remaining 1990 layer, and the new 1993 layer. Adding these layers produces a total LIFO cost of $11,010. Note that the entire 1991 layer and one-fourth of the 1990 layer are *not* reflected in the 1993 ending inventory; they were eliminated in 1992 and are therefore never added back.

At first glance the dollar-value LIFO method usually appears formidable. In practice, however, many companies find that it is a convenient way to apply LIFO to a large, complex inventory. The financial statement numbers it produces are ordinarily different from those produced by the specific goods method of applying LIFO. Nevertheless, dollar-value LIFO has many practical advantages, and the numbers that it produces are acceptable for financial reporting and income tax purposes. Although a specific price index is used to implement the method, dollar-value LIFO is a **method of determining an inventory's historical cost, not its current value.**

Asset/Liability Measurement

In a survey of 206 companies using LIFO, about 70% were found to use the dollar value method exclusively. Twelve percent use the retail LIFO method (discussed later in the chapter) exclusively. Only 4% use the specific goods method or the specific goods pooling method (see footnote 1) exclusively, while the rest use a combination of methods.[5]

METHODS OF DETERMINING A PRICE INDEX UNDER DOLLAR VALUE LIFO

In practice, a variety of methods are considered acceptable to determine the price index under dollar value LIFO. One widely used method is the **double extension method.** Under this method, which requires a company to construct its own **internal index** at the end of each year, we multiply the actual quantity of each inventory item on hand at year-end by its current-year unit cost. Next, we multiply the actual

---

[5]Keith G. Stanga, "Methods of Applying LIFO in Practice," Working paper, The University of Tennessee, 1985.

PUDDLE MUDDLE

Bone Char . . . that was one of the inventory accounts the Securities & Exchange Commission was concerned about," says Stauffer Chemical's counsel John Ronan. "I mean . . . bone char is not one of our more important products."

Maybe not. But the injunctive action against Connecticut-based Stauffer Chemical for fraudulently overstating its 1982 earnings, settled out of court in August, is one of the SEC's most important actions. The complaint prompted a spate of class action suits against Stauffer, but it also troubles chief finance officers from coast to coast.

Basically the SEC charged the big chemical company with three things: 1) improperly structuring some LIFO "puddles" in its inventory accounting, 2) improperly recognizing inventory profit resulting from intracompany product transfers, and 3) prematurely recognizing sales. As a result, said the commission, Stauffer's 1982 earnings were exaggerated by 25%, or $31.1 million.

This is no arcane bookkeeping hassle. There are "puddles" all over the place in corporate America. If you think of an inventory grouping containing many different products as a "pool," then it follows that a smaller grouping—often containing only one type of product—is a "puddle." Under LIFO accounting, companies assume that the products they are selling today are the newest ones in inventory. That keeps earnings down in periods of high inflation and cuts taxes as a result.

Of course, different products in an inventory pool may fare differently in the marketplace. A sharply lower supply of hot-selling gadgets might force revenues to be compared with lower prior-period costs for the whole pool, not only for gadgets but also for slow-selling widgets, where supply has not changed at all. So puddles, with narrower product ranges, generally produce a more accurate matching of revenues and costs.

The SEC has no objection to puddling. It just didn't like the way Stauffer used the technique. "They required us to take 8 of our 288 inventory puddles— one of them including bone char—and recombine them into other puddles," says Ronan.

Why the nitpicking? One side effect of LIFO is to create sudden surges of earnings when year-end inventory is sharply lower than at the beginning of the year. That's because digging into inventories under LIFO means offsetting today's revenues with unnaturally old, hence low, corporate costs.

The commission alleged that Stauffer was setting up puddles partly in order to hit those lower historic cost figures. It also claimed that Stauffer actually gave "presentations" to its operating people to show them how to set up puddles to maximize LIFO liquidation benefits.

Regulators charged, for example, that inventory had been shipped overseas solely because accounting there was not on a LIFO basis. This created LIFO liquidations, exaggerated by improper puddling, that were not eliminated in consolidation, they said. Earnings without sales, to get right to the point.

It's not hard to guess what triggered the SEC investigation. Look at the first three footnotes of Stauffer's 1982 annual report: The change to puddling increased earnings by $16.5 million. New pesticide sales programs "shifted" $72 million of 1983 sales back to 1982. This boosted earnings by another $18.6 million, much of it because of LIFO liquidations. Significant numbers for a company reporting $124 million in earnings for the year.

To sharp eyes, all this activity seemed suspicious. There was a steep downturn in agricultural chemical demand in 1982. Since Stauffer closed no factories, inventories should have been rising, not falling sharply enough to hit LIFO cushions. And what sort of legitimate marketing scheme would transfer sales from one year to another?

The commission says it found an "Early Order Program" that conveniently boosted profits. To encourage distributors to stock up, Stauffer guaranteed future refunds on unsold product carried at the end of the 1982–83 growing season. It sweetened the package with partial reimbursement of warehouse fees and automatic "redating" of bills until early the following year. In the 1982–83 season almost 40% of Stauffer's agricultural chemical sales were booked this way, according to the SEC.

The SEC attacked all this as "contrary to generally accepted accounting principles." So far, it hasn't lifted a finger against Stauffer's auditors, Deloitte Haskins & Sells, who specifically approved the 1982 change to puddling. Why not? That's what Representative Doug Barnard (D–Ga.), who heads the House Commerce, Consumer & Monetary Affairs Subcommittee, wants to know.

Sometimes, of course, the commission sues auditors separately at a later date. But that's still a good question, Congressman.

SOURCE: Geoffrey Smith, ed. Richard Greene, "Puddle Muddle," *Forbes*, October 8, 1984, p. 92. Reprinted by permission of *Forbes* Magazine. © Forbes Inc., 1984.

EXHIBIT 9-2

Double Extension Method

		Unit Cost		Total Cost	
	Actual				
	Quantity at	*Current*	*Base*	*Current*	*Base*
Item	Year-end	*Year*	*Year*	*Year*	*Year*
A	1,000	$16	$15	$16,000	$15,000
B	2,500	11	10	27,500	25,000
C	500	25	20	12,500	10,000
				$56,000	$50,000

Year-end specific price index   = $56,000 ÷ $50,000 = 112%.

Year-end conversion factor* = $\frac{112}{100}$ = 1.12.

---

*Observe that the base is 100 ($50,000 ÷ $50,000 = 100% or 1.00) when a company develops its own internal index. When the base is 100, the year-end conversion factor is the same as the year-end specific price index (112% = 1.12). If the base is not 100, as is often the case when a company relies on an *external* price index, the year-end conversion factor will differ from the year-end specific price index.

quantity of each item by its base-year unit cost. We now have two columns of extensions, which explains the name "double extension method." We then total the extensions and divide the total current-year cost by the total base-year cost to derive the current year-end specific price index. We illustrate these procedures in Exhibit 9–2 for a simplified inventory of only three items. When applying the double extension method in practice, some companies double extend their entire ending inventory, while others double extend only a representative sample of inventory items.

A significant problem may occur under the double extension method whenever a **new item** (i.e., an item that was not in the base inventory) is added to inventory during a particular year. Under these circumstances, the base-year cost of the new item must be estimated by using published vendor price lists, vendor quotes, or general industry indexes so that the current year's price index can be correctly determined. If a company cannot reasonably estimate the base-year cost of new items, perhaps because the base year has receded far into the past, the price index determined under the double extension method may be significantly distorted.

A second widely used approach for determining a price index under dollar value LIFO is the **link chain method.** Under this method, a company computes an internal price index each year by multiplying the year-end inventory quantities (either the entire inventory or a representative sample) by (1) end-of-the-year unit costs and (2) beginning-of-the-year unit costs. The resulting extensions are totaled, and the totals are divided to determine the current-year price change index. The current-year price change index is then multiplied by the cumulative prior-year's index to determine the current link chain index. We illustrate these procedures in Exhibit 9–3.

Notice in Exhibit 9–3 that in the first year of using the link chain method (1992), there is no cumulative prior-year's index; consequently the price change index for the first year is the link chain index. Note also that in the second year (and subsequent years) of applying the link chain method, base year unit costs (i.e., the beginning-of-year costs for 1992) are no longer used. An advantage of the link chain method over

EXHIBIT 9-3

Link Chain Method

1992—Assumed to be the base year

		Unit Cost		Total Cost	
Item	Actual Quantity at Year-end	End of Year	Beginning of Year*	End of Year	Beginning of Year
X	2,000	$10	$ 9	$ 20,000	$18,000
Y	3,000	22	20	66,000	60,000
Z	1,000	18	15	18,000	15,000
				$104,000	$93,000

*The beginning-of-year unit costs for 1992 are considered to be the base year unit costs.

1992 link chain index = $104,000 ÷ $93,000 = 111.8% (The price change index is the same as the link chain index in 1992 because 1992 is assumed to be the base year.)
1992 year-end conversion factor = 111.8 ÷ 100 = 1.118

1993

		Unit Cost		Total Cost	
Item	Actual Quantity at Year-end	End of Year	Beginning of Year	End of Year	Beginning of Year
X	4,000	$12	$10	$ 48,000	$ 40,000
Y	5,000	25	22	125,000	110,000
Z	3,000	20	18	60,000	54,000
				$233,000	$204,000

1993 price change index = $233,000 ÷ $204,000 = 114.2%
1993 link chain index = 114.2% × 111.8% = 127.7%
1993 year-end conversion factor = 127.7 ÷ 100 = 1.277

the double extension method is that the link chain method does not require a determination of base-year costs for new items.

The price change index computed for the second year (1993) is simply "linked to" the cumulative prior-year's index. Each year's link chain index becomes the cumulative prior-year's index in the next year. In our example, 111.8% is the link chain index for 1992, so it becomes the cumulative prior-year's index in 1993. Moreover, 127.7%, the link chain index for 1993, will become the cumulative prior-year's index in 1994.

Double extension and link chain are methods of deriving an internal price index. If a company can show that an **external index** (a published index) is a suitable measure of the change in cost prices of the specific goods that it actually purchases or produces, the company can use the external index when applying dollar value LIFO. In the survey mentioned earlier of 206 companies that use LIFO, about 54% of the companies that use the dollar value approach reported using the link chain method; 35% use the double extension method; and 7% use the double extension and link chain methods concurrently. Only a small percentage of the companies surveyed use external indexes such as the Producer Price Indexes.

RETAIL INVENTORY METHOD

The **retail inventory method** is a reversed markup procedure of inventory pricing used by many retail businesses, such as department stores. The main advantage of the method is that it produces accounting information and facilitates inventory control at less cost than other methods that could be used in retail concerns. Ending inventory and cost of goods sold figures derived under the retail method are acceptable for financial reporting and income tax purposes.

When applying the retail method, the accountant records the beginning inventory, purchases, and sales in the accounts in the usual manner under a periodic inventory system. Moreover, supplementary records are kept of certain additional information. This information includes the beginning inventory and net purchases, each stated at **retail** (i.e., **selling**) **prices.** The accumulation of supplementary records at retail prices is facilitated by the fact that retail companies usually price their merchandise for sale soon after acquisition. The accountant divides the **cost of goods available for sale** during a period by the **retail value of the same goods** to produce a cost-to-retail percentage that is commonly called the **cost percentage.** This percentage reflects the relationship between cost and retail that prevails in the *current* period. Sales for the period are then deducted from the retail value of goods available for sale to derive an ending inventory valued at *retail prices.* The accountant multiplies the ending inventory at retail by the cost percentage to derive an *estimate* of **Asset/Liability** the **historical cost** of the ending inventory to use for balance sheet reporting pur-**Measurement** poses. Cost of goods sold may then be computed in the usual manner for a periodic system. Alternatively, cost of goods sold may be computed by multiplying the sales for the period by the cost percentage. The following simplified example illustrates the essence of the retail method.

	At Cost	At Retail
Beginning inventory	$ 9,800	$ 14,000
Net purchases	65,200	86,000
Goods available for sale	$75,000	$100,000
Cost percentage ($75,000 ÷ $100,000 = 75%)		
Deduct:		
Sales		80,000
Ending inventory		
At retail		$ 20,000
At cost ($20,000 × 75%)	$15,000	
Cost of goods sold		
($9,800 + $65,200 − $15,000 = $60,000, *or*		
$80,000 × 75% = $60,000)	$60,000	

Observe that the retail method enables us to calculate the cost of the ending inventory without knowing how many physical units are actually on hand. Nevertheless, a company using the retail method **must count its physical inventory at least once each year** for good internal control. Goods counted are extended at retail prices and compared with the inventory at retail value derived under the retail method. Differences may occur for several reasons, including theft, breakage, inaccurate records, and an inaccurate physical count. If the physical count has been performed correctly, the accounting records should be adjusted to agree with it.

The main uses of the retail method are listed below:

1. The retail method enables a company to estimate its inventory at any time without a physical count, because both cost and retail figures are always available. These estimates are used for annual as well as interim reporting purposes.
2. Even when the inventory is counted, the retail method enables a company to take its physical inventory at marked selling prices, thereby expediting the work of personnel since they do not have to refer to purchase invoices.
3. The retail method provides results that are useful when determining insurance coverage and settlements.

The major limitation of the retail method is that the cost percentage is merely an average of all goods reflected in its calculation. The average yields accurate results if the same relationship between cost and selling price exists for all goods or if the mix of goods in ending inventory is the same as that in the goods available for sale. Because some departure from these conditions usually occurs, the retail method produces accounting values of ending inventory and cost of goods sold that are only *approximations*. When the relationship between cost and selling price varies substantially between departments, the accountant should apply the retail method separately to each department, thus improving the accuracy of the method. Ending inventory costs computed in each department are summed to derive the cost for the entire inventory.

A company using the retail method does not have to apply the method to its entire inventory. For example, a large department store may use the retail method when accounting for certain types of merchandise, such as men's clothing, and the specific identification method when accounting for others, such as expensive jewelry.

When applying the retail method, the accountant adds transportation-in and subtracts purchase discounts when computing net purchases in the cost column. These two items are not added or subtracted in the retail column because the original retail price of the inventory is ordinarily set in a manner that reflects them. Purchase returns and purchase allowances are subtracted in the cost and retail columns because these items reduce the amount of goods purchased.

The sales amount that should be subtracted in the retail column should be net of any sales returns and allowances. Sales discounts, however, are not subtracted from sales because they are financial in nature and are not part of the initial markup that is applied to goods purchased. Employee discounts and normal shrinkage (due to damage, theft, etc.) should be subtracted (just as sales are) in the retail column because these items represent normal reductions of the original retail value of goods available for sale during the period.

RETAIL METHOD TERMINOLOGY

The example presented above was simplified in order to introduce the rationale, uses, and limitations of the retail method. To properly handle the complexities encountered in practice, the accountant must understand the meaning of the following important terms used by retailers:

1. **Original retail price.** The price at which merchandise is first marked for sale to customers. This price includes an initial markup equal to the difference between the original retail price and the cost.
2. **Additional markup.** Amount added to the original retail price.

3. **Markup cancellation.** Cancellation, either in part or in total, of an additional markup. A markup cancellation does not reduce the selling price below the original retail price.
4. **Net markup.** Amount of additional markups less markup cancellations.
5. **Markdown.** Amount subtracted from the original retail price.
6. **Markdown cancellation.** Cancellation, either in part or in total, of a markdown. A markdown cancellation does not increase the selling price above the original retail price.
7. **Net markdown.** Amount of markdowns less markdown cancellations.

Assume that a retail concern purchases a new line of summer dresses for $60 each and immediately prices each dress for sale at $100. The *original retail price* is therefore $100. This price, which actually includes an *initial markup* of $40, is now an important point of reference when labeling future changes in selling price. If, in response to great demand for the dresses, the company raises the selling price to $110, we have an *additional markup* of $10. If the price is later lowered from $110 to $106, we have a *markup cancellation* of $4. The *net markup* is now $6. Suppose that near the end of the summer the company lowers its selling price from $106 to $90. This action represents a *markup cancellation* of $6 and a *markdown* of $10. If the company later raises the price from $90 to $92, we have a *markdown cancellation* of $2. The *net markdown* is now $8.

CONVENTIONAL RETAIL METHOD (LOWER OF AVERAGE COST OR MARKET)

The existence of additional markups, markup cancellations, markdowns, and markdown cancellations introduces new complexities to the retail method. First, a company's accounting system must permit an accurate accumulation of each of these items in supplementary records. Second, because these items represent adjustments to the original retail price, they must be included in a logical manner in the basic retail inventory procedures that we illustrated earlier.

The **conventional retail method,** the one most commonly used by retailers, requires (1) including net markups when calculating the cost percentage and (2) subtracting net markdowns along with sales when measuring the ending inventory at retail. In other words, the accountant computes the cost percentage *after* considering net markups but *before* considering net markdowns. These procedures are illustrated in the example on page 383 (top).

The conventional retail method produces an ending inventory that approximates the **lower of average cost or market,** which we will refer to simply as lower of cost or market. Observe in our example that the lower of cost or market valuation is $14,400. *If* we had ignored net markups as well as net markdowns when computing our cost percentage, the cost percentage would have been 74.8% ($57,600 ÷ $77,000). Note that the $77,000 amount equals the retail value of the beginning inventory ($13,000) plus the retail value of the net purchases ($64,000). Ending inventory at cost would then have been $14,960 ($20,000 × 74.8%). *If,* on the other hand, we had included net markups *and* net markdowns when calculating our cost percentage, the cost percentage would have been 75.8% ($57,600 ÷ $76,000). Note that the $76,000 amount equals the retail value of the beginning inventory ($13,000) plus the retail value of the net purchases ($64,000) plus the net markups ($3,000) minus the net markdowns ($4,000). Ending inventory at cost would then have been $15,160 ($20,000 × 75.8%). As these numbers illustrate, the conventional retail method produces the lowest ending inventory valuation when compared with alternative methods of handling net markups and net markdowns.

	At Cost		At Retail
Beginning inventory	$10,000		$ 13,000
Net purchases	47,600		64,000
Additional markups		$ 7,000	
Less: Markup cancellations		4,000	
Net markups			3,000
Goods available for sale	$57,600		80,000
Cost percentage ($57,600 ÷ $80,000 = 72%)			
Deduct:			
Sales			(56,000)
Markdowns		12,000	
Less: Markdown cancellations		8,000	
Net markdowns			(4,000)
Ending inventory			
At retail			$ 20,000
At lower of cost or market ($20,000 × 72%)	$14,400		

Are the results under the conventional retail method simply the most conservative, or do they really approximate those achieved by applying the lower of cost or market rule? Suppose that a company began operations near the end of a year and bought only a single item of merchandise that it was unable to sell. The item cost $100 and was originally priced to sell for $200. The retail price was subsequently raised to $250 (an additional markup of $50). Later the price was lowered to $125 (a markup cancellation of $50 and a markdown of $75). The following illustration shows how to value the ending inventory item using the conventional retail method:

	At Cost		At Retail
Beginning inventory	–0–		–0–
Net purchases	$100.00		$200
Additional markup		$50	
Less: Markup cancellation		50	
Net markup			–0–
Goods available for sale	100.00		200
Cost percentage ($100 ÷ $200 = 50%)			
Deduct:			
Sales			(–0–)
Markdown		75	
Less: Markdown cancellation		–0–	
Net markdown			(75)
Ending inventory			
At retail			$125
At lower of cost or market ($125 × 50%)	$ 62.50		

The lower of cost or market valuation produced by the conventional retail method approximates the inventory's **net realizable value less an allowance for a normal profit margin (i.e., the floor).** In our example, the inventory item which cost $100 was originally priced at $200 to allow a 50% profit margin based on selling price. The sales price of the item was finally reduced to $125. This price indicates that the item's **utility** (its ability to produce future revenue) has declined. Observing the lower of cost or market rule requires that we recognize the decline in the current period, the one in which it occurred. This reflects the conservatism modifying convention. Accordingly, the conventional retail method produces an ending inventory valuation of $62.50, an amount clearly below the historical cost of $100. Note that the lower of cost or market valuation of $62.50 represents the estimated selling price ($125) less an allowance for a normal profit margin of 50% of selling price ($125 × 50% = $62.50).

Conservatism

We emphasize that the conventional retail method only *approximates* an ending inventory valuation at lower of cost or market. The method does *not* measure "market" by comparing ceiling, replacement cost, and floor values. Moreover, accountants apply the method to many inventory items, not simply to a single unit. An averaging effect therefore occurs. The conventional retail method is also limited because it assumes that markdowns apply only to goods sold during a period. This assumption is justified on the ground that goods marked down are more likely than not to have been sold during the period. In reality, however, some of the goods marked down may still be in ending inventory.

RETAIL LIFO METHOD

Many companies adapt the retail method to reflect the LIFO cost flow assumption. This adaptation is called the **retail LIFO method.** Use of this method enables retailers to secure the matching benefits and tax advantages that LIFO usually produces while, at the same time, reducing substantially the clerical burden of applying LIFO.

Matching

Compared with the conventional retail method, the retail LIFO method requires two important changes when calculating the periodic **cost percentage.**

1. The beginning inventory is *excluded* from the calculation. Under retail LIFO the sole purpose of the cost percentage is to price any new LIFO layer that might be added in the current period. Thus, the beginning inventory is excluded to ensure that the resulting cost percentage reflects cost and retail prices of the current period only.
2. Net markups as well as net markdowns are *included* in the calculation. In other words, the accountant computes the cost percentage *after* considering both net markups and net markdowns. The rationale for including both in the cost percentage is that LIFO is a method of arriving at *cost,* not lower of cost or market.

To illustrate the changes described above, assume that the following information pertains to Lite Company for the current year:

	At Cost	At Retail
Inventory, Jan. 1 (base LIFO layer)	$ 19,500	$ 30,000
Net purchases	140,000	208,000
Net markups		7,000
Net markdowns		15,000
Sales		190,000

If we now make the simplifying assumption that the level of specific retail prices remained *constant* during the year, here is how Lite Company would determine the cost percentage and the LIFO cost of the ending inventory.

	At Cost	At Retail
Net purchases	$140,000	$208,000
Net markups		7,000
Net markdowns		(15,000)
Subtotal	$140,000	200,000
Cost percentage ($140,000 ÷ $200,000 = 70%)		
Beginning inventory at retail		30,000
Goods available for sale at retail		230,000
Deduct: Sales		(190,000)
Ending inventory at retail		$ 40,000
Ending inventory at retail		$ 40,000
Less: Beginning inventory at retail		30,000
Inventory increase at retail		$ 10,000
Ending inventory at LIFO cost		
Beginning inventory	$ 19,500	
Add: Inventory increase		
($10,000 × 70%)	7,000	
Ending inventory	$ 26,500	

Note that the beginning inventory was excluded and the net markups and net markdowns were included in the calculation of the cost percentage (70%). The cost percentage was then used to convert the inventory *increase* that occurred during the year from a retail measure ($10,000) to a cost measure ($7,000). The cost of the inventory increase was then added to the cost of the beginning inventory to derive the cost of the ending LIFO inventory ($26,500).

The above example is very simplified; in reality, the retail dollar (like the cost dollar) is rarely a stable device for measuring inventory changes. Indeed, the level of specific retail prices usually fluctuates over time. Therefore the retail LIFO method requires us to measure all inventory changes in **retail dollars of the base year.** The term "base year" refers to the *beginning* of the year in which a company adopts the retail LIFO method. In the remaining discussion of the retail LIFO method, we shall make the realistic assumption that the level of specific retail prices changes over time.

The retail LIFO method is very similar to the dollar-value LIFO method discussed earlier. In fact, the retail LIFO method is sometimes called the **dollar-value retail LIFO method.** Like dollar-value LIFO, retail LIFO is applied to **designated pools** of similar goods. In addition, retail LIFO is applied on the basis of **inventory changes measured in dollars as opposed to physical units.** In contrast with dollar-value LIFO, retail LIFO measures inventory changes in *retail dollars* rather than in cost dollars.

As with the dollar-value LIFO method, retail LIFO requires that we use a conversion factor. Again, we compute this factor by dividing a specific price index for the current year by a specific price index for the base year. However, because the retail method requires a conversion of *retail dollars,* the price index used must measure the change in the level of *retail prices* that has occurred since the base year.

For income tax and financial reporting purposes, most retailers use the Department Store Inventory Price Indexes published monthly by the Bureau of Labor Statistics (BLS). BLS index numbers measure changes in the level of retail prices of goods in twenty department groups, such as infant's wear, men's clothing, housewares, and major appliances. The accountant simply selects the index numbers that are appropriate given the nature of the inventory pool to which retail LIFO is applied. If the BLS indexes are not appropriate for a given retail concern, the company may construct its own *internal* price index using the link chain or double extension methods.

Over time the retail LIFO method may produce several inventory layers. Each layer is expressed in **retail dollars rather than in physical units.** The accounting records must permit us to associate each layer with (1) the year-end conversion factor in existence when the layer was created and (2) the cost percentage for the year the layer was created.

To implement the retail LIFO method, the accountant must measure in *base-year retail prices* both the beginning and the ending inventories of the current period. If the ending inventory exceeds the beginning inventory when each is measured in base-year retail prices, an inventory increment (measured in base-year retail prices) has occurred. Because the increment occurred in the current year, we should price it at current-year costs. To convert the increment from *base-year retail* prices to *current-year cost* prices, we must multiply it by (1) the current year-end conversion factor (this converts the increment from *base-year* retail prices to *current-year* retail prices) and (2) the current-year's cost percentage (this converts the increment from current-year *retail* prices to current-year *cost* prices). The inventory increment so priced forms a layer which is added to those in existence at the beginning of the current period to determine the ending retail LIFO inventory cost.

On the other hand, if the ending inventory is less than the beginning inventory when each is measured at base-year retail prices, a reduction in inventory has occurred. This reduction requires us to charge previously established LIFO layers to cost of goods sold in a last-in, first-out sequence at amounts that reflect the cost prices in existence when the layers were constructed.

Application Procedures

The five steps summarized below are used to apply the retail LIFO method to a designated pool of goods. Note that these steps closely parallel those used to apply the dollar-value LIFO method.

Step 1. Determine the current-year cost percentage and the ending inventory at retail. Again, be sure to (1) exclude the beginning inventory and (2) include net markups and net markdowns when calculating the cost percentage.[6]

Step 2. Obtain an appropriate year-end conversion factor which measures the overall change in inventory *retail prices* that has occurred since the base period. We compute the conversion factor as follows:

$$\text{Conversion factor} = \frac{\text{Current year-end specific price index}}{\text{Base-year specific price index}}$$

Step 3. Restate the ending inventory from current-year retail prices (as determined in Step 1) to base-year retail prices by dividing the results in Step 1 by the year-end conversion factor obtained in Step 2.

Step 4. From the ending inventory priced at base-year retail prices (as determined in Step 3), subtract *the inventory on hand at the beginning of the current period, also priced at base-year retail prices.*

Step 5. Compute the cost of the ending retail LIFO inventory as follows:

---

[6]Actually, calculating the cost percentage is required only when a LIFO layer is added in the current period. Nevertheless, we have included it as a part of Step 1 because it is relatively easy to derive in the process of calculating the ending inventory at retail.

1. If the difference in Step 4 equals zero, inventory is unchanged. Consequently, the ending retail LIFO inventory valuation is the same as the beginning valuation.

2. If the difference in Step 4 is positive, inventory has increased. Price the increase at current-year *cost* by multiplying the difference in Step 4 by (1) the year-end conversion factor obtained in Step 2 *and* (2) the current-year cost percentage obtained in Step 1. Then add the result to the beginning retail LIFO inventory valuation to get the correct ending valuation at LIFO cost.

3. If the difference in Step 4 is negative, inventory has decreased. Subtract the decrease from the most recently acquired layer(s) at base-year retail prices in a last-in, first-out manner. The correct retail LIFO ending inventory valuation will then be the remaining layers multiplied by (1) their respective conversion factors *and* (2) their respective cost percentages.

An Illustration

Let's assume that a retail concern adopts the retail LIFO method on January 1, 1990. On that date the company's inventory at retail prices is $20,000 and its cost percentage is 70%. Furthermore, an appropriate specific retail price index obtained externally is 125. The cost of the inventory on January 1, 1990, is therefore $14,000 ($20,000 × 1.00 × 70%).[7] This inventory layer is regarded in future years as the base. Additional information for 1990, 1991, 1992, and 1993 appears in Exhibit 9–4 (on page 388).

The dollar amounts shown in Exhibit 9–4 for net purchases, net markups, net markdowns, beginning inventory at retail, and sales are obtained from the company's general ledger and supplementary records. Using this information, we *calculated* each year's cost percentage and ending inventory at retail, thereby complying with Step 1 of the basic retail LIFO procedures. Step 2 requires us to obtain an appropriate year-end conversion factor. We computed these factors using the specific price index numbers shown near the bottom of Exhibit 9–4. The index numbers themselves are obtained from an appropriate external source.

Using the information shown in our example, we illustrate in Exhibit 9–5 (on page 389) how to compute each year's ending retail LIFO inventory valuation.

The following points are particularly noteworthy:

1. On December 31, 1990, applying Step 4 reveals an inventory increase of $800 in *base-year retail prices.* In Step 5 we price this increase at *current-year cost* by multiplying it by the year-end conversion factor (1.20) obtained in Step 2 *and* by the current-year cost percentage obtained in Step 1 (72%). The inventory therefore consists of *two layers,* the base plus the 1990 layer, for a total retail LIFO cost of $14,691.

2. On December 31, 1991, applying Step 4 indicates an inventory increase of $2,000 in *base-year retail prices.* Once again, we price the increase at *current-year cost* by multiplying it by the year-end conversion factor from Step 2 (1.40) *and* by the current-year cost percentage from Step 1 (75%). The inventory now consists of *three layers,* the base plus the 1990 and 1991 layers, for a total retail LIFO cost of $16,791.

3. On December 31, 1992, applying Step 4 shows an inventory *decrease* of $2,400 in *base-year retail prices.* When a decrease occurs, we must remove it from the existing

---

[7]125/125 = 1.00.

EXHIBIT 9-4

Information to Illustrate Retail LIFO Method

	1990 At Cost	1990 At Retail	1991 At Cost	1991 At Retail	1992 At Cost	1992 At Retail	1993 At Cost	1993 At Retail
Net purchases	$108,000	$155,000	$120,000	$164,000	$113,150	$159,000	$133,200	$187,000
Net markups		6,000		10,000		4,000		12,000
Net markdowns		(11,000)		(14,000)		(8,000)		(19,000)
Subtotal	$108,000	150,000	$120,000	160,000	$113,150	155,000	$133,200	180,000
Cost percentage								
1990 ($108,000 ÷ $150,000 = 72%)								
1991 (120,000 ÷ 160,000 = 75%)								
1992 (113,150 ÷ 155,000 = 73%)								
1993 (133,200 ÷ 180,000 = 74%)								
Beginning inventory at retail		20,000		24,960		31,920		31,008
Goods available for sale at retail		170,000		184,960		186,920		211,008
Deduct: Sales		145,040		153,040		155,912		181,904
Ending inventory at retail		$ 24,960		$ 31,920		$ 31,008		$ 29,104
Year-end specific retail price index obtained externally		150		175		190		170
Conversion factor		150/125 = 1.20		175/125 = 1.40		190/125 = 1.52		170/125 = 1.36

EXHIBIT 9–5

Retail LIFO

December 31	Current-Year Cost Percentage (Step 1)	Ending Inventory at Current-Year Retail Prices (Step 1)	Year-End Conversion Factor (Step 2)		Ending Inventory at Base-Year Retail Prices (Step 3)	Ending Minus Beginning Inventory, Both at Base-Year Retail Prices (Step 4)	Cost of Ending Retail LIFO Inventory (Step 5)	
1990	72%	$24,960	÷ 1.20	=	$20,800	$20,800 − $20,000 = $ 800	$20,000 × 1.00 × 70% = $14,000	(base layer)
							800 × 1.20 × 72% = 691	(1990 layer)
							$20,800 $14,691*	
1991	75%	31,920	÷ 1.40	=	22,800	22,800 − 20,800 = 2,000	$20,000 × 1.00 × 70% = $14,000	(base layer)
							800 × 1.20 × 72% = 691	(1990 layer)
							2,000 × 1.40 × 75% = 2,100	(1991 layer)
							$22,800 $16,791*	
1992	73%	31,008	÷ 1.52	=	20,400	20,400 − 22,800 = (2,400)	$20,000 × 1.00 × 70% = $14,000	(base layer)
							400 × 1.20 × 72% = 346	(remaining 1990 layer)
							$20,400 $14,346*	
1993	74%	29,104	÷ 1.36	=	21,400	21,400 − 20,400 = 1,000	$20,000 × 1.00 × 70% = $14,000	(base layer)
							400 × 1.20 × 72% = 346	(remaining 1990 layer)
							1,000 × 1.36 × 74% = 1,006	(1993 layer)
							$21,400 $15,352*	

*This is the correct amount to report on the ending balance sheet and to subtract from the cost of goods available for sale to measure the cost of goods sold for the year.

LIFO inventory layers in a last-in, first-out sequence. In other words, we assume that the last layer(s) in is the first to go out. Any layer removed is charged to cost of goods sold at an amount equal to the base-year retail value of the layer multiplied by the conversion factor and by the cost percentage in existence when the layer was created. Expressed in base-year retail prices, the $2,400 decrease eliminates all of the 1991 layer ($2,000) and one-half ($400) of the 1990 layer. Had the inventory decrease been larger, it could have eliminated the entire 1990 layer and some or all of the base. Once eliminated, an inventory layer cannot later be reconstructed. The 1992 ending inventory consists of *two layers,* the base plus one-half of the 1990 layer, for a total retail LIFO cost of $14,346. We do not construct a 1992 layer, because the inventory that year does not increase.

4. On December 31, 1993, applying Step 4 shows an inventory increase of $1,000 expressed in *base-year retail prices.* We therefore price the increase by multiplying it by the year-end conversion factor (from Step 2) *and* by the current-year cost percentage (from Step 1). The inventory now consists of *three layers:* the base, the remaining 1990 layer, and the new 1993 layer. Summing these layers produces a total retail LIFO cost of $15,352. Observe that the entire 1991 layer and one-half of the 1990 layer are *not* reflected in the 1993 ending inventory; they were eliminated forever in 1992.

During past years of relatively high inflation, many companies adopted LIFO. In 1974, for example, the inflation rate exceeded 10%, and many companies adopted LIFO in that year. Many retailers find that the retail LIFO method is a practical means of realizing LIFO's costing benefits. Although the method appears complex, its use can produce substantial clerical savings. The apparent complexity of the method is greatly reduced when we focus on its similarity to the dollar-value LIFO method. This similarity can be seen more clearly in the parallel form of Exhibits 9–1 and 9–5.

GROSS MARGIN METHOD

The **gross margin method** (often called the **gross profit method**) is widely used to obtain the **estimated cost** of an ending inventory. The method requires adding the beginning inventory at cost to the net purchases at cost to produce the cost of goods available for sale during the period. Net sales for the period are then multiplied by a gross margin on sales percentage; the result is subtracted from net sales to produce an estimated cost of goods sold figure. This figure is then subtracted from the cost of goods available for sale to produce an estimate of the cost of the ending inventory, as shown below:

Beginning inventory (measured at cost)		$ 30,000
Net purchases (measured at cost)		150,000
Cost of goods available for sale		180,000
Deduct:		
Net sales (measured at selling prices)	$200,000	
Less: Estimated gross margin		
($200,000 × 20%)	40,000	
Estimated cost of goods sold		160,000
Estimated cost of ending inventory		$ 20,000

Dollar amounts for the beginning inventory, net purchases, and net sales are taken directly from the company's accounting records. The estimated gross margin on sales percentage (20% in this example) is a **historical rate** (not a current rate such as the one we use under the retail method) that reflects recent past experience. Typically, it is an average of the percentages applicable to the past few years.

Notice the similarity between the procedures used in applying the gross margin method and those used in calculating cost of goods sold in a periodic inventory system. In both calculations, we begin by deriving the cost of goods available for sale. Under the gross margin method, we then subtract the estimated cost of goods sold to obtain the estimated cost of the ending inventory. Under the periodic system, we subtract the cost of the ending inventory from the cost of goods available for sale to derive the cost of goods sold.

GROSS MARGIN ON SALES PERCENTAGE

Under the gross margin method, we use a **gross margin on sales percentage** when reducing net sales to an estimated cost basis. Gross margin percentages are usually derived and expressed in relation to selling prices. To illustrate, if a soccer ball costs $8 and sells for $10, the gross margin is $2. The gross margin percentage based on selling price is therefore 20% ($2 ÷ $10 = .20 = 20%). The remaining 80% ($8 ÷ $10 = .80 = 80%) is called the cost of goods sold percentage. The gross margin on sales percentage and the cost of goods sold percentage always sum to 100%.

At times, a gross margin percentage may be based on cost prices instead of selling prices. Using the same basic data shown above for the soccer ball, the gross margin percentage based on cost is 25% ($2 ÷ $8 = .25 = 25%). When we are given a gross margin on cost percentage, we should first convert it to a gross margin on sales percentage in order to correctly apply the gross margin method. The following widely used formulas enable us to convert a gross margin on cost percentage to a gross margin on sales percentage, and vice versa:

$$\text{Gross margin on sales percentage} = \frac{\text{Gross margin on cost percentage}}{100\% + \text{Gross margin on cost percentage}}$$

$$\text{Gross margin on cost percentage} = \frac{\text{Gross margin on sales percentage}}{100\% - \text{Gross margin on sales percentage}}$$

Obviously, only the first formula is required to find an unknown gross margin on sales percentage. Accountants nevertheless should be familiar with both types of conversions.

The following examples illustrate how to apply the formulas:

Gross Margin on Sales Percentage		Gross Margin on Cost Percentage
20% (given)	$\longrightarrow$	$\dfrac{20\%}{100\% - 20\%} = 25\%$
25% (given)	$\longrightarrow$	$\dfrac{25\%}{100\% - 25\%} = 33\tfrac{1}{3}\%$
$\dfrac{50\%}{100\% + 50\%} = 33\tfrac{1}{3}\%$	$\longleftarrow$	50% (given)
$\dfrac{100\%}{100\% + 100\%} = 50\%$	$\longleftarrow$	100% (given)

Because cost prices are less than selling prices, each gross margin on cost percentage is greater than the related percentage based on sales. The gross margin on sales percentage is often called the **markup on sales**; similarly, the gross margin on cost percentage frequently is called the **markup on cost.**

USES OF THE GROSS MARGIN METHOD

Remember that we use an average *historical* (as opposed to a current) gross margin on sales percentage to implement the gross margin method. A major assumption of this method is that this percentage reasonably approximates the rate of gross margin in the current period. Because this rate usually differs to some extent from the average historical rate, the gross margin method yields only an **estimate** of the cost of the ending inventory. This estimate generally approximates the results under whatever inventory cost flow method the company uses (FIFO, average cost, and so forth). An exception may occur when a company using LIFO liquidates layers consisting of outdated costs. In this case the ending inventory estimate under the gross margin method may depart considerably from the actual LIFO cost; we must therefore use caution when interpreting the results produced by the gross margin method.

The estimates produced by the gross margin method are generally considered too imprecise for use in annual financial statements prepared according to GAAP. Nevertheless, many companies use the method when preparing their internal as well as external interim reports (i.e., monthly or quarterly reports). Companies that use the gross margin method in their external interim reports and companies that use other methods than those used for annual reporting purposes "should disclose the method used at the interim date and any significant adjustments that result from reconciliations with the annual physical inventory."[8]

Accountants often use the gross margin method to estimate the cost of an inventory lost by fire or other casualty. The information needed to apply the method may be taken directly from the accounting records. If the records have been lost, the accountant can sometimes construct estimates of the needed information using prior years' financial statements, microfilm copies of bank records showing details of receipts and disbursements, and contact with suppliers and customers. When inventory has been lost, a company may apply the gross margin method to help determine an insurance settlement. We must remember, however, that the method produces an estimate of the *historical cost* of the inventory lost. Insurance coverage and settlements are often based on *replacement costs*. Thus, the results of the gross margin method may need adjusting to an estimated current replacement cost basis.

Materiality — Auditors often use the gross margin method as a rough test of the validity of an inventory's cost determined under either a periodic or a perpetual system. If a material difference exists between the ending inventory cost determined using the gross margin method and that determined under the company's accounting system, the auditor should inquire concerning the reasons for the difference. This inquiry may simply reveal that the gross margin on sales percentage used in the gross margin method does not properly reflect current conditions. On the other hand, the inquiry may reveal errors made when determining cost within the company's accounting system.

GROSS MARGIN METHOD APPLIED TO CLASSES OF GOODS

Gross margin percentages sometimes vary considerably between different classes of goods within a single company. When such variation occurs, the use of a single, company-wide gross margin percentage assumes that goods in the various classes are sold in the same mix each period. This assumption is, of course, seldom valid. As a result, we should apply the gross margin method separately to each class of goods, thereby enhancing the method's accuracy. We can then sum the ending inventory costs determined for each class to produce an overall cost for the company's inventory.

---

[8]*APB Opinion No. 28*, "Interim Financial Reporting," 1973, par. 14a.

CONCLUDING REMARKS

The inventory methods presented in this chapter may at first appear too complex and imprecise. Remember, though, that accountants seek to provide **useful information** for which the **benefits exceed the costs.** Many large companies have tens of thousands, sometimes hundreds of thousands, of products. To account for such large and diverse inventories in a cost effective manner, the methods described in this chapter are often helpful.

Perhaps the most serious adverse consequence of modern inventory accounting is the distorted balance sheet valuations that often result under LIFO. As indicated earlier, some LIFO users are still reporting inventory costs incurred during the 1940s. In the authors' opinion, the future development of GAAP by the FASB should include an attempt to improve the balance sheet valuation of inventory that occurs under LIFO.[9]

The next chapter covers the financial accounting and reporting for investments and funds.

KEY POINTS

1. The dollar-value LIFO method and the retail LIFO method help to simplify the clerical tasks associated with applying LIFO in practice. (Objectives 1 and 3)

2. Dollar-value LIFO is a way of applying LIFO on the basis of changes in base-year cost dollars associated with a pool of similar goods. Under this method, LIFO layers are expressed in cost dollars rather than in physical units. (Objective 1)

3. Dollar-value LIFO gives companies considerable flexibility when grouping their inventory items into pools. The result is that dollar-value LIFO helps to preserve old inventory costs while charging the most recent costs to expense (i.e., cost of goods sold). (Objective 1)

4. Applying dollar-value LIFO requires the use of a specific price index that measures changes in the level of a company's inventory cost prices over time. (Objective 1)

5. The retail inventory method is a reversed markup procedure of inventory pricing used by many retail businesses such as department stores. (Objectives 2 and 3)

6. The conventional retail method requires that we include net markups when calculating the cost percentage and subtract net markdowns along with sales when measuring the ending inventory at retail. The method produces an ending inventory valuation that approximates the lower of cost or market. (Objective 2)

7. The retail LIFO method is an adaptation of the retail method used by many retailers to reflect the LIFO cost flow assumption. Under this method, we apply LIFO on the basis of changes in base-year retail dollars associated with a pool of similar goods. LIFO layers are expressed in retail dollars rather than in physical units; retail LIFO is therefore very similar to dollar-value LIFO. (Objective 3)

8. When calculating the periodic cost percentage under the retail LIFO method, the beginning inventory is excluded, while net markups and net markdowns are included. (Objective 3)

9. Applying retail LIFO requires the use of a specific price index that measures changes in the level of a company's retail prices over time. (Objective 3)

10. The gross margin method is used to estimate the cost of an inventory. The method relies on the use of a historical gross margin on sales percentage. Although the estimate produced by this method is generally considered too imprecise for use in annual financial statements, the

---

[9]One possible solution for the balance sheet problem posed by LIFO is the LIFO/FIFO method, under which a company would use LIFO to measure cost of goods sold on the income statement and FIFO to report inventories on the balance sheet. The LIFO/FIFO method has been considered by the accounting profession but never accepted as GAAP. See Michael P. Bohan and Steven Rubin, "LIFO/FIFO: How Would it Work?" *Journal of Accountancy* (September 1986), pp. 106–110.

method is frequently used for interim reporting purposes, for estimating the cost of an inventory lost by fire or other casualty, and for testing the reasonableness of an inventory cost derived in some other manner. (Objective 4)

11. When we are given a gross margin on cost percentage, we should first convert it to a gross margin on sales percentage in order to correctly apply the gross margin method. (Objective 4)

QUESTIONS

9-1   What are the basic differences between the specific goods method of applying LIFO and the dollar-value LIFO method?

9-2   How is an incremental LIFO inventory layer determined under the specific goods method? How is it determined under dollar-value LIFO?

9-3   Why is it considered appropriate to use a specific price index rather than a general price-level index when implementing the dollar-value LIFO or the retail LIFO method?

9-4   Explain the double extension method and the link chain method of constructing an internal price index.

9-5   Briefly describe the operation of the dollar-value LIFO method.

9-6   Assume that the total number of physical units in a dollar-value LIFO pool has declined from the beginning to the end of a period. Is it possible under this condition for the dollar-value LIFO cost of the ending inventory to exceed that of the beginning inventory? Why?

9-7   Assuming that a company has decided to use LIFO, what are the major advantages of the dollar-value method?

9-8   Briefly describe the general operation of the retail inventory method.

9-9   What are the major uses of the retail method?

9-10   What major assumption about the composition of the ending inventory is inherent in the retail method?

9-11   What is the meaning of each of the following terms?

[a] Original retail price   [e] Markdown
[b] Additional markup   [f] Markdown cancellation
[c] Markup cancellation   [g] Net markdown
[d] Net markup

9-12   Explain why the conventional retail method produces an ending inventory valuation that approximates the lower of cost or market.

9-13   Explain the major differences between the conventional retail method and the retail LIFO method with regard to the manner in which the periodic cost percentage is calculated. Why do these differences exist?

9-14   Briefly describe the operation of the retail LIFO method.

9-15   Briefly describe the operation of the gross margin method.

9-16   Distinguish between a markup on cost and a markup on sales price.

9-17   Should we use a gross margin on cost percentage or a gross margin on sales percentage when applying the gross margin method? Why?

9-18   What are the major uses of the gross margin method?

EXERCISES

9-19   DOUBLE EXTENSION METHOD   Trout Corporation applies the dollar-value LIFO method to each of the five pools into which it has divided its inventory. The following information pertains to Pool No. 1:

Product	Year-End Quantity		Current-Year Unit Cost		Base-Year Unit Cost
	1992	1993	1992	1993	
L	1,000	900	$24	$25	$20
M	1,700	1,800	13	14	10
N	2,100	1,800	32	34	30

Instructions

Compute the year-end specific price index for Pool No. 1 for 1992 and 1993 using the double extension method. (The base-year specific price index is 100.)

9–20 LINK CHAIN METHOD Tunnell Corporation applies the dollar value LIFO method to each of the four pools into which it has divided its inventory. Tunnell adopted dollar value LIFO on January 1, 1992, and the company uses the link chain method in each LIFO pool. The following information pertains to Pool No. 1:

| | Actual Quantity at Year-end | | Unit Cost | | |
Item	1992	1993	1/1/92	12/31/92	12/31/93
X	3,000	4,000	$10	$12	$13
Y	5,000	5,000	16	18	20
Z	4,000	3,000	12	15	17

Instructions

Compute the year-end conversion factor for Pool No. 1 for 1992 and 1993 using the link chain method.

9–21 DOLLAR-VALUE LIFO On January 1, 1991, Patrick, Inc., adopted the dollar-value LIFO method. The company's inventory priced at current costs on that date was $50,000. Additional inventory data are as follows:

Date	Inventory at Year-End Prices	Price Index*
Dec. 31, 1991	$58,300	106
Dec. 31, 1992	59,890	113
Dec. 31, 1993	67,830	119

*Price index at Jan. 1, 1991 = 100.

Instructions

Compute the cost of the company's inventory at December 31, 1991, 1992, and 1993, using the dollar-value LIFO method.

9–22 DOLLAR-VALUE LIFO Jensen Company adopted the dollar-value LIFO method on January 1, 1993. The company's inventory priced at current costs on that date was $100,000. During 1993 the company purchased merchandise costing $900,000. The inventory on December 31, 1993, measured by reference to the actual unit costs of the goods most recently purchased, was $143,000. The specific price index for the company's inventory was 100 on January 1, 1993, and 110 on December 31, 1993.

Instructions

[a] Compute the cost of inventory at December 31, 1993, using the dollar-value LIFO method.
[b] Compute the cost of goods sold for 1993 under the dollar-value LIFO method.

9–23 CONVENTIONAL RETAIL METHOD The following information was taken from the accounting records of Gibbs Department Store for the current year:

	Cost	Retail
Beginning inventory	$15,000	$20,000
Net purchases	60,000	75,000
Net markups		5,000
Net markdowns		6,000
Sales		79,000

Instructions

Calculate the ending inventory using the conventional retail method.

9-24   CONVENTIONAL RETAIL METHOD   The information shown below was taken from the financial records of Harvey's Hardware Store:

Inventory, Jan. 1, 1993	
At cost	$ 6,000
At retail	10,000
Purchases during 1993	
At cost	37,540
At retail	67,000
Purchase returns during 1993	
At cost	1,140
At retail	2,000
Additional markups during 1993, at retail	6,000
Markdowns during 1993, at retail	8,000
Markup cancellations during 1993, at retail	1,000
Markdown cancellations during 1993, at retail	3,000
Transportation-in during 1993, at cost	1,600
Sales during 1993, at retail	65,000

[handwritten annotations: "reductions in inventory"; "↓ Increases the cost only. Orig. MU covered expense"]

Instructions

Calculate the inventory valuation at December 31, 1993, using the conventional retail method.

9-25   CONVENTIONAL RETAIL METHOD   Gwinn Department Store uses the retail inventory method. Information relating to the computation of the inventory at December 31, 1993, appears as follows:

	Cost	Retail
Inventory, Jan. 1, 1993	$ 41,000	$ 96,000
Purchases	387,400	592,000
Freight-in	12,000	
Net markups		46,000
Net markdowns		30,000
Sales		560,000

Estimated normal shrinkage due to breakage and theft is 3% of sales.

Instructions

Calculate the estimated inventory on December 31, 1993, at the lower of cost or market using the retail inventory method.

9-26   CONVENTIONAL RETAIL METHOD   The following data pertain to Canning Company for 1993:

	Cost	Retail
Inventory, Jan. 1	$15,000	$25,000
Net purchases	30,000	65,000
Net markups		10,000
Net markdowns		15,000
Sales		52,520

Instructions

Calculate the estimated ending inventory on the basis of lower of cost or market using the retail method.

9-27   RETAIL LIFO   Using the data presented in 9-26, calculate the cost of the ending inventory using the retail LIFO method. Assume that the inventory on January 1, 1993, is the base LIFO layer and that the retail price index increased by 12% during 1993.

9-28   RETAIL LIFO   The following data pertain to McCammon Supply Company for the current year:

	Cost	Retail
Inventory, Jan. 1		
(base LIFO layer)	$18,250	$ 25,000
Sales		88,700
Net markups		7,000
Net markdowns		10,000
Net purchases	75,000	103,000

Instructions

Calculate the cost of the ending inventory at December 31 using the retail LIFO method. Assume no change in the level of retail prices during the year.

9–29　RETAIL LIFO　Using the data presented in 9–28 and assuming that the retail price index increased by 10% during the year, calculate the cost of the ending inventory at December 31 using the retail LIFO method.

9–30　RETAIL LIFO　Truax Company uses the retail LIFO inventory method. The following information pertains to the company's 1993 accounting period:

	Cost	Retail
Inventory, Jan. 1, 1993	$ 30,000	$ 43,000
Purchases	140,000	180,000
Freight-in	10,000	
Net markups		35,000
Net markdowns		15,000
Sales		180,000

Instructions

Assuming that the inventory on January 1, 1993, is the base inventory and that there was no change in the price index during the year, compute the inventory at December 31, 1993, using the retail LIFO method.

9–31　GROSS MARGIN PERCENTAGES　Prepare a table similar to the one shown below and fill in the missing amount for each case.

Case	Gross Margin on Sales Percentage	Gross Margin on Cost Percentage
1	20%	
2		200%
3	33⅓%	
4		20%
5	75%	
6		66⅔%

9–32　GROSS MARGIN METHOD　On May 2, 1993, a fire destroyed the entire uninsured merchandise inventory of Walter Company. You obtained the following data:

Inventory, Jan. 1, 1993	$10,000
Purchases, Jan. 1 through May 2	70,000
Sales, Jan. 1 through May 2	80,000
Gross margin on sales percentage	25%

Instructions

Calculate the estimated fire loss to report in Walter Company's income statement for 1993.

9–33　GROSS MARGIN METHOD　Drexler Company uses the gross margin method to estimate its inventories for interim reporting purposes. The following data pertain to the company:

Inventory, Jan. 1, 1993	$ 40,000
Purchases, Jan. 1 through Mar. 31, 1993	120,000
Sales, Jan. 1 through Mar. 31, 1993	180,000
Markup on cost	25%

Instructions

Calculate the estimated cost of the inventory at the end of the first quarter of 1993.

9–34   GROSS MARGIN METHOD   You are the independent auditor for Profit's Department Store. Tomorrow is the last day of the current fiscal year. The store will be closed and you will observe the taking of the physical inventory to accurately determine its cost.

Profit's accounting records as of the end of today provide the following data that pertain to the current fiscal year: sales, $446,000; sales returns, $20,000; beginning inventory, $80,000; purchases, $194,000; purchase returns, $4,000; transportation-in, $10,000.

The average rate of gross margin on sales during the last three years is 40%.

Instructions

Calculate an estimate of the cost of the ending inventory.

9–35   GROSS MARGIN METHOD   The following data were obtained from the accounting records of Tully, Inc.:

Inventory, July 1	$12,000
Purchases	
July	60,000
August	70,000
September	79,600
Sales	
July	70,000
August	82,000
September	90,000

The company's markup on cost has averaged 25% during the past few years.

Instructions

Estimate the ending inventory costs for July, August, and September for monthly reporting purposes.

PROBLEMS   **9–36   SPECIFIC GOODS LIFO**   The information shown below pertains to Turley Company, which uses a periodic inventory system.

	Product A		Product B	
	Number of Units	Unit Cost	Number of Units	Unit Cost
Inventory, Jan. 1, 1992	200	$2 400	300	$3 900
Purchases				
1992	300	3 900	600	4 2400
	500	4 2000	600	5 3000
1993	900	5 4500	600	7 4200
	700	6 4200	300	8 2400
Sales				
1992	600		1,300	
1993	1,900		800	

Instructions

[a] Calculate each of the following amounts for Turley Company using the specific goods method of applying LIFO:

[1] Cost of inventory at December 31, 1992.

[2] Cost of goods sold for 1992.

[3] Cost of inventory at December 31, 1993.

[4] Cost of goods sold for 1993.

[b] How is the existence of an incremental LIFO layer determined under the specific goods method?

[c] What are the fundamental differences between the specific goods method and the dollar-value method of applying LIFO?

9–37 DOLLAR VALUE LIFO Tullock Company adopted the dollar-value LIFO inventory method on January 1, 1990. The company's inventory on that date was $10,000, which is considered the base LIFO layer. Additional data about the company appear below.

| | | December 31 Inventory at | Price |
Year	Purchases	Current-Year Prices	Index*
1990	$62,000	$13,200	110
1991	68,000	18,150	121
1992	71,000	14,630	133
1993	82,000	23,200	145

*Price index at Jan. 1, 1990 = 100.

Instructions

[a] Compute the cost of the inventory at December 31, 1990, 1991, 1992, and 1993, using the dollar-value LIFO method.

[b] Compute the cost of goods sold for 1990, 1991, 1992, and 1993, under the dollar-value LIFO method.

9–38 DOLLAR VALUE LIFO Rabinowitz, Inc. sells Products A, B, and C. On January 1, 1991, the company adopted the dollar-value LIFO method. The company's inventory priced at current costs on that date was $200,000. Other data about the company's inventory appear below.

Dec. 31	Quantity			Current-Year Unit Cost			*BY Unit*	
	A	B	C	A	B	C	*A*	*100*
1991	1,000	500	100	$110	$220	$330	*B*	*200*
1992	1,020	510	102	121	242	225	*C*	*300*
1993	350	250	50	140	260	380		

Instructions

Compute the ending inventories for 1991, 1992, and 1993 using the dollar-value LIFO method. The base-year unit costs are $100, $200, and $300 for Products A, B, and C, respectively. Rabinowitz derives a price index using the double extension approach.

9–39 DOLLAR VALUE LIFO Idol, Inc., uses the FIFO inventory method for internal reporting purposes. On January 1, 1990, the company adopted the dollar-value LIFO method for income tax and external reporting purposes. The company's inventory priced at current costs on that date was $20,000. When applying the dollar-value LIFO method, the company relies on an appropriate external price index. Additional data appear below.

Date	Inventory Priced at Current-Year Cost	External Price Index
Dec. 31, 1990	$22,800	132.0
Dec. 31, 1991	34,320	145.2
Dec. 31, 1992	34,650	181.5
Dec. 31, 1993	49,500	217.8

Instructions

[a] Assuming the external price index was 110 on January 1, 1990, compute the cost of the inventory at December 31, 1990, 1991, 1992, and 1993, using dollar-value LIFO.

[b] Explain why a price index is needed to implement the dollar-value LIFO method.

9–40   CONVENTIONAL RETAIL METHOD   The following information pertains to Hutchens Company for the fiscal year ended June 30, 1993:

	Cost	Retail
Inventory, July 1, 1992	$12,600	$20,000
Purchases	46,160	80,500
Purchase returns	1,860	3,000
Purchase allowances	900	1,500
Transportation-in	4,000	
Additional markups		8,000
Markdowns		13,000
Markup cancellations		4,000
Markdown cancellations		8,000
Gross sales		84,000
Sales returns		2,000
Employee discounts granted		1,000
Normal breakage		2,000

Instructions

Calculate the June 30, 1993, inventory at lower of cost or market using the conventional retail method.

9–41   CONVENTIONAL RETAIL METHOD   Brown Store applies the conventional retail method to each of its three departments in order to estimate its monthly inventories for internal reporting purposes. The following information for January 1993 is available from the company's accounting records:

	Department					
	Men's Clothing		Women's Clothing		Infants' Wear	
	Cost	Retail	Cost	Retail	Cost	Retail
Beginning inventory	$1,003	$1,700	$2,040	$ 4,000	$1,176	$2,800
Net purchases	3,797	6,000	5,960	11,500	3,624	8,800
Net markups		300		500		400
Net markdowns		700		900		500
Sales		5,000		10,000		8,000

Instructions

Calculate the estimated January 31 inventory for Brown Store by applying the conventional retail method to each department separately and summing the results.

9–42   CONVENTIONAL RETAIL METHOD   Doucette Department Store, Inc., uses the retail inventory method to estimate ending inventory for its monthly financial statements. The following data pertain to a single department for October 1993.

Inventory, Oct. 1	
At cost	$ 20,000
At retail	30,000
Purchases (exclusive of freight and returns)	
At cost	100,151
At retail	146,495
Freight-in	5,100
Purchase returns	
At cost	2,100
At retail	2,800
Additional markups	2,500
Markup cancellations	265
Markdowns (net)	800
Normal spoilage and breakage	3,600
Sales	134,730

Instructions

[a] Using the conventional retail method, prepare a schedule computing the estimated lower of cost or market inventory on October 31, 1993.

[b] A department store using the conventional retail inventory method estimates the cost of its ending inventory at $29,000. An accurate physical count reveals only $22,000 of inventory at lower of cost or market. List the factors that may have caused the difference between the computed inventory and the physical count. (AICPA adapted)

9–43 RETAIL LIFO The information below pertains to Dow, Inc., which adopted the retail LIFO method Jan. 1, 1990:

Date	Inventory at Retail Prices	Cost Percentage	Retail Price Index
Jan. 1, 1990	$100,000	50%	100
Dec. 31, 1990	123,200	51%	110
Dec. 31, 1991	152,520	55%	124
Dec. 31, 1992	133,280	54%	136
Dec. 31, 1993	163,850	56%	145

Instructions

[a] Calculate the cost of the inventory at December 31, 1990, 1991, 1992, and 1993, using the retail LIFO method.

[b] Explain why a retail price index is needed to implement the retail LIFO method, assuming that the level of retail prices changes over time.

9–44 RETAIL LIFO Hathaway Company adopted the retail LIFO method on January 1, 1991. On that date the company's inventory at retail prices was $50,000, its cost percentage was 45%, and a suitable retail price index was 100. Additional information for 1991, 1992, and 1993, appears below.

	1991	1992	1993
Beginning inventory at retail	$ 50,000	$ 61,040	$ 63,440
Net purchases			
At cost	86,000	101,200	112,800
At retail	205,000	233,000	247,000
Net markups at retail	10,000	7,000	9,000
Net markdowns at retail	15,000	20,000	16,000
Sales at retail	188,960	217,600	225,140
Year-end retail price index	109	122	135

Instructions

[a] Calculate the cost of ending inventory for each year using the retail LIFO method.
[b] Calculate the cost of goods sold for each year under the retail LIFO method.

9–45 RETAIL LIFO Under your guidance Sam's Sporting Goods Store installed the retail method of accounting for its merchandise inventory as of January 1, 1993. When you prepared the store's financial statements on June 30, 1993, the following data were available:

	Cost	Selling Price
Inventory, Jan. 1	$26,900	$ 40,000
Markdowns		10,500
Additional markups		19,500
Markdown cancellations		6,500
Markup cancellations		4,500
Purchases	86,200	111,800
Sales		123,000
Purchase returns and allowances	1,500	1,800
Sales returns and allowances		6,000

Instructions

[a] Prepare a schedule to compute the store's June 30, 1993, inventory under the retail LIFO method. Assume that the level of retail prices has remained constant.

[b] Without prejudice to your solution to [a], assume that you computed the June 30, 1993, inventory to be $45,150 at retail and the cost percentage to be 80%. The level of retail prices has increased from 100 at January 1 to 105 at June 30. Prepare a schedule to compute the June 30, 1993, inventory under the retail LIFO method.   (AICPA adapted)

9–46   CONVENTIONAL RETAIL AND RETAIL LIFO   Conner Corporation, which uses the conventional retail inventory method, wishes to change to the retail LIFO method beginning with the accounting year ending December 31, 1993. Amounts indicated by the firm's accounting records are as follows:

	Cost	Retail
Inventory, Jan. 1, 1993	$ 5,210	$ 15,000
Net purchases in 1993	47,250	100,000
Net markups in 1993		7,000
Net markdowns in 1993		2,000
Sales in 1993		95,000

Assume that all net markups and net markdowns apply to 1993 purchases and that it is appropriate to treat the entire inventory as a single department. Also assume that the level of specific retail prices remained constant in 1993.

Instructions

Compute the inventory valuation at December 31, 1993, using:

[a] The conventional retail method.
[b] The retail LIFO method, effecting the change in method as of January 1, 1993.

                    (AICPA adapted)

9–47   CONVENTIONAL RETAIL AND RETAIL LIFO   Tutterow Department Store converted from the conventional retail method to the retail LIFO method on January 1, 1992. In your examination of the financial statements for the year ended December 31, 1993, management asks that you give a summary of certain computations of inventory costs for the past 3 years.

The following information is available.

[1] The inventory at January 1, 1991, had a retail value of $45,000 and a cost of $27,500, based on the conventional retail method.

[2] Transactions during 1991 were as follows:

	Cost	Retail
Gross purchases	$282,000	$490,000
Purchase returns	6,500	10,000
Purchase discounts	5,000	
Gross sales		492,000
Sales returns		5,000
Employee discounts		3,000
Freight-in	26,500	
Net markups		25,000
Net markdowns		10,000

[3] The retail value of the December 31, 1992, inventory was $56,100; the cost percentage for 1992 under the retail LIFO method was 62%; and the retail price index was 102% of the January 1, 1992, price level.

[4] The retail value of the December 31, 1993, inventory was $48,300; the cost percentage for 1993 under the retail LIFO method was 61%; and the retail price index was 105% of the January 1, 1992, price level.

Instructions

[a] Prepare a schedule showing the computation of the cost of inventory on hand at December 31, 1991, based on the conventional retail method.

[b] Prepare a schedule showing the computation of the cost of inventory on hand at December 31, 1991, based on the retail LIFO method. Tutterow Department Store does not consider beginning inventories in computing its retail LIFO cost percentage. Assume that the retail value of the December 31, 1991, inventory was $50,000.

[c] Without prejudice to your solution to [b], assume that you computed the December 31, 1991, inventory (retail value $50,000) under the retail LIFO method at a cost of $28,000. Prepare a schedule showing the computations of the cost of the store's 1992 and 1993 year-end inventories under the retail LIFO method.   (AICPA adapted)

9–48 GROSS MARGIN METHOD   A major portion of Wadley Company's inventory was stolen on the night of August 16, 1993. A physical count the next day revealed that goods costing $10,000 were still on hand. Your examination of the company's accounting records reveals the following:

Inventory, Jan. 1, 1993	$ 25,000
Transactions, Jan. 1 through Aug. 16, 1993	
Purchases	87,000
Purchase returns	2,500
Transportation-in	5,400
Sales	141,500
Sales returns	5,000

The company began operations early in 1992, and its income statement for that year appears below.

Wadley Company
INCOME STATEMENT
For the Year Ended December 31, 1992

Net sales		$195,000 _100_
Cost of goods sold		117,000 _60_
Gross margin on sales		78,000 _40_
Operating expenses		
Selling expenses	$11,000	
Administrative expenses	17,000	
Total		28,000
Income before income taxes		50,000
Income tax expense		20,000
Net income		$ 30,000

Instructions

Calculate an estimate of the cost of the inventory that was stolen.

9–49 GROSS MARGIN METHOD   On the night of September 30, 1993, a fire destroyed most of the merchandise inventory of Spradlin, Inc. All goods were completely destroyed except for (1) partially damaged goods that normally sell for $10,000 and that had an estimated net realizable value of $2,500 after the fire, and (2) undamaged goods that normally sell for $6,000. _Retail cost = 4500_

The following data are available from the company's accounting records, which were locked in a fireproof safe:

Inventory, Jan. 1, 1993	$ 46,000
Net purchases, Jan. 1 through Sept. 30, 1993	423,750
Net sales, Jan. 1 through Sept. 30, 1993	525,000

Condensed income statement information for the past three years appears below.

	1992	1991	1990
Net sales	$500,000	$300,000	$100,000
Cost of goods sold	384,000	220,000	71,000
Gross margin	116,000	80,000	29,000
Operating expenses	25,000	20,000	9,000
Income before income taxes	91,000	60,000	20,000
Income tax expense	36,400	24,000	8,000
Net income	$ 54,600	$ 36,000	$ 12,000

The company estimates that the rate of gross margin on sales in 1993 is equal to the weighted average rate for the past three years.

Instructions

[a] Estimate the amount of the fire loss, assuming that Spradlin, Inc., does not carry insurance on its inventory.

[b] Assume now that Spradlin does have insurance on the inventory and that you are the adjustor for the insurance company. How might you argue that Spradlin's loss is really smaller than the amount you computed in [a]?

9–50   GROSS MARGIN METHOD   On April 15, 1993, fire damaged the office and warehouse of Yon Wholesale Corporation. The only accounting record saved was the general ledger, from which the following trial balance was prepared.

Yon Wholesale Corporation
TRIAL BALANCE
March 31, 1993

Cash	$ 7,000	
Accounts receivable	27,000	
Inventory, Dec. 31, 1992	50,000	
Land	24,000	
Building and equipment	120,000	
Accumulated depreciation		$ 27,200
Other assets	3,600	
Accounts payable		23,700
Accrued liabilities		7,200
Capital stock		100,000
Retained earnings		47,700
Sales		90,400
Purchases	42,000	
Other expenses	22,600	
	$296,200	$296,200

The following additional information has been gathered:

[1] The fiscal year of the corporation ends on December 31.

[2] An examination of the April bank statement and canceled checks revealed that checks written April 1–15 totaled $11,600: $5,700 for accounts payable as of March 31; $2,000 for April merchandise shipments; and $3,900 for other expenses. Deposits during the same period amounted to $10,650, which consisted of receipts on account from customers, with the exception of a $450 refund from a vendor for merchandise returned in April.

[3] Correspondence with suppliers revealed unrecorded obligations at April 15 of $8,500 for April merchandise shipments, including $1,300 for shipments in transit on that date.

[4] Customers acknowledged indebtedness of $26,400 at April 15, 1993. It was also estimated that customers owe another $5,000 that will never be acknowledged or recovered. Of the acknowledged indebtedness, $600 will probably be uncollectible.

[5] The companies insuring the inventory agreed that the corporation's fire loss claim should be based on the assumption that the overall gross margin on sales percentage for the past two years was in effect during the current year. The corporation's audited financial statements disclosed the following:

	Year Ended December 31	
	1992	1991
Net sales	$400,000	$300,000
Net purchases	226,000	174,000
Beginning inventory	45,000	35,000
Ending inventory	50,000	45,000

[6] Inventory with a cost of $6,500 was salvaged and sold for $1,350. The balance of the inventory was a total loss.

Instructions

Prepare a schedule computing the amount of the inventory fire loss. The supporting schedule of the computation of the gross margin on sales percentage should be in good form.   (AICPA adapted)

9–51 GROSS MARGIN METHOD Reese Corporation is an importer and wholesaler. Its merchandise is purchased from a number of suppliers and is warehoused by Reese until it is sold to customers.

In conducting the audit for the year ended June 30, 1993, the company's CPA determined that the internal control system was good. Accordingly, the physical inventory was observed at an interim date, May 31, 1993, instead of at year-end.

The following information was obtained from the general ledger:

Inventory, July 1, 1992	$ 87,500
Physical inventory, May 31, 1993	95,000
Sales for 11 months ended May 31, 1993	840,000
Sales for year ended June 30, 1993	950,000
Purchases for 11 months ended May 31, 1993	950,000
(before audit adjustments)	675,000
Purchases for year ended June 30, 1993 (before audit adjustments)	790,000

The CPA's audit disclosed the following information:

Shipments received in May and included in the physical inventory but recorded as June purchases	$7,500
Shipments received in unsalable condition and excluded from physical inventory (Credit memos had not been received nor had chargebacks to vendors been recorded.)	
Total at May 31, 1993	1,000
Total at June 30, 1993 (including the May unrecorded chargebacks)	1,500
Deposit made with vendor and charged to purchases in April 1993 (Product was shipped in July 1993.)	2,000
Deposit made with vendor and charged to purchases in May 1993 (Product was shipped, FOB destination, on May 29, 1993, and was included in May 31, 1993, physical inventory as goods in transit.)	5,500

Instructions

In audit engagements in which interim physical inventories are observed, a frequently used auditing procedure is to test the reasonableness of the year-end inventory by the gross margin method. Prepare in good form the following schedules:

[a] Computation of the gross margin on sales percentage for the 11 months ended May 31, 1993.

[b] Computation by the gross margin method of cost of goods sold during June 1993.

[c] Computation by the gross margin method of the June 30, 1993, inventory.   (AICPA adapted)

CASES

9-52   IMPACT OF CHANGING FROM FIFO TO LIFO   Chip Henry, president of Dowling Enterprises, is thinking about changing his company's method of inventory pricing from FIFO to dollar-value LIFO. Dowling Enterprises is a large, publicly-held manufacturer of a wide variety of products whose costs are expected to increase steadily in the near future. Chip has learned that in such an environment, the use of LIFO can result in a material, and sometimes permanent, deferral of income taxes. Chip is concerned, though, that using LIFO could lower his company's net income, stock market price, working capital, and current ratio (current assets divided by current liabilities). He fears that while using LIFO may save income taxes, investors and creditors may not look favorably on the company in the future.

Instructions

Advise Chip as to whether or not Dowling Enterprises should adopt LIFO. Provide rationale for your advice, and be sure to address Chip's concerns about LIFO.

9-53   RETAIL METHOD   Mizysak Paint Company, your client, manufactures paint. The company's president, Mr. Mizysak, has decided to open a retail store to sell Mizysak paint as well as wallpaper and other supplies that would be purchased from other suppliers. He has asked you for information about the retail method of pricing inventories at the retail store.

Instructions

Prepare a report to the president explaining the retail method of pricing inventories. Your report should include the following points:

[a] Description and accounting features of the method.
[b] Conditions that may distort the results under the method.
[c] Advantages of using the method when compared to cost methods of inventory pricing.
[d] Accounting theory underlying the treatment of net markdowns and net markups under the method.   (AICPA adapted)

9-54   INVENTORIES AND CASH BASIS ACCOUNTING   The owner of Lutz's Retail Hardware computes income on a cash basis. At the end of each year, he takes a physical inventory and computes the cost of all merchandise on hand. To this he adds the ending balance of accounts receivable, because he considers this a part of inventory on the cash basis. Using this logic he deducts from this total the ending balance of accounts payable for merchandise and arrives at what he calls inventory (net).

The following information has been taken from Lutz's cash basis income statements:

	1993	1992	1991
Cash received	$173,000	$164,000	$150,000
Cost of goods sold			
Inventory (net), Jan. 1	8,000	11,000	3,000
Total purchases	109,000	102,000	95,000
Goods available for sale	117,000	113,000	98,000
Inventory (net), Dec. 31	1,000	8,000	11,000
Cost of goods sold	116,000	105,000	87,000
Gross margin	$ 57,000	$ 59,000	$ 63,000

The following additional information is available:

	1993	1992	1991
Cash sales	$151,000	$147,000	$141,000
Credit sales	24,000	18,000	14,000
Accounts receivable, Dec. 31	8,000	6,000	5,000
Accounts payable for merchandise, Dec. 31	33,000	20,000	13,000

Instructions

[a] Without reference to the above, discuss the various cash basis concepts of revenue and income and indicate the conceptual merits of each.

[b] Is the gross margin for Lutz's Retail Hardware being computed on a cash basis? Evaluate and explain the approach used with illustrative computations of the cash basis gross margin for 1992.

[c] Explain why the gross margin for Lutz's Retail Hardware shows a decrease while sales and cash receipts are increasing. (AICPA adapted)

JUDGMENT CASES

9–55 LIFO LIQUIDATION You are the chief accountant for the Briggs Company, a large, publicly-held furniture wholesaler that uses the dollar-value LIFO inventory method. Briggs ordinarily buys furniture from a variety of manufacturers and later resells it to numerous retailers throughout the nation. Today's date is *January 10, 1993,* and you are working hard to prepare the financial statements for the accounting period that ended on December 31, 1992. Your LIFO working papers show that Briggs had a LIFO layer liquidation during 1992 because the year-end inventory is less than the beginning inventory when both inventories are priced at base year cost. As a result, 1992 net income will be materially *higher* than it would have been without the liquidation.

The chief executive officer of Briggs Company, Brenda Kerr, enters your office and tells you emphatically that a LIFO layer liquidation is unacceptable. Ms. Kerr is concerned about the incremental income taxes that will have to be paid and about the potentially distortive effects on accounting net income often associated with a LIFO layer liquidation.

Ms. Kerr then reminds you that on December 15, 1992, Briggs placed a large furniture order with Stratford Company, a major supplier, with delivery scheduled for January 15, 1993. Because delivery is now only five days away, Ms. Kerr tells you to call Stratford immediately and ask that Stratford date its sales invoice December 31, 1992. In this way Briggs can assert that it owned the inventory on December 31, 1992, and thereby avoid the 1992 LIFO layer liquidation. Ms. Kerr reminds you about how important it is for everyone at Briggs Company to be a team player.

Instructions

Would you follow Ms. Kerr's instructions by calling Stratford and asking them to predate their sales invoice? Explain in detail the rationale that supports your decision. As a *part* of your explanation, include a discussion of the major parties who would be affected by your decision.

9–56 LIFO LIQUIDATION You are the chief financial officer for the Abacas Company, a manufacturer of small electronic devices that uses dollar-value LIFO to value inventories. In response to heightened competition and new data processing capabilities, the company recently implemented a *just in time* approach to managing inventories. This approach, under which the company tries to manufacture products "just in time" to make sales, has been quite successful. The company has reduced the inventory level it normally carries, resulting in a substantial savings in carrying costs. The end of the year is now approaching and the company's president is meeting with you to plan the preparation of the company's financial statements. You have just pointed out that the new inventory management method will result in reporting a rather large profit during the year due to the liquidation of several LIFO layers that have accumulated over the years.

The president responds that he has been thinking about this issue and does not want to pay the income taxes that will result from the LIFO layer liquidations, nor does he wish to report the higher net income during the current year. He states:

> We have had a really good year without considering the LIFO liquidation, and we don't need to report higher profits at this time. What really concerns me is that we are projecting a slowdown in our business next year due to the recession that many are predicting and I want to "save" those low cost layers of LIFO inventory until we need them. Therefore, I am going to instruct the director of purchasing to acquire additional amounts of inventory necessary to prevent the liquidation of any LIFO layers for bookkeeping purposes this year. If our profits next year are not as high as I want them to be, then we'll just let the liquidation of LIFO layers take care of that problem at that time. By the way, my plan doesn't cause you any problems does it? You aren't going to suggest that we need to provide any financial statement disclosure of our actions and plans to manage our reported income, are you?

Instructions

Should Abacas Company make any disclosures about the president's plans and actions? If so, be specific and describe the nature of the disclosures that you recommend. If not, explain why you believe that disclosures are unnecessary.

9–57   RETAIL METHOD   Katie's Kids Klothes uses the conventional retail method of valuing its inventories. In past years, the company has had a stable cost-to-retail relationship for its inventory due to buying from one manufacturer and marking up the goods by a fixed percentage. Because of excellent sales and a lack of competition, Katie's has not previously needed to mark down any of its goods.

In the current year, however, two national department store chains have opened stores in the small town in which Katie's has its store. Those department stores have provided intense competition and Katie's has found itself buying products from a variety of manufacturers with lower costs, reducing markup on many of its goods, and marking down various items of inventory. Despite these adjustments, Katie's is unable to sell all of certain products.

As an independent CPA, you are beginning the audit of Katie's for the current year and have also been asked to consult on Katie's problems related to the new competition. Of particular concern is determining the value of Katie's ending inventory. In past years you have been able to determine the inventory value at retail by simply counting the items on shelves and extending the quantities of the various items by the retail prices noted on each item. The retail value of the inventory was then reduced to a lower of cost or market valuation by multiplying the retail value by the appropriate cost percentage. You had little concern with obsolete or unsalable goods, because little inventory remained at year-end and what remained was always sold rather quickly after year-end.

At the end of the current year, there is a relatively large amount of inventory on hand because Katie's had bought larger quantities to obtain lower prices and disappointing sales levels had resulted from the increased competition. You are also aware that the stable cost percentage of past years is uncertain today and that the value of some of the inventory may be impaired below its net realizable value less the normal gross margin amount. Katie Helder, the owner of the store has stated, "Let's just get these financial statements out as quickly as possible and turn our attention to solving my business problems. By the way, I don't expect to spend any more money than last year on producing the financial statements. Times are getting real tough here."

Instructions

Describe the methods that you believe should be applied to value Katie's inventory at the end of the current year. Be specific in your answer and identify procedures that you believe should be applied in light of the company's changed conditions. Also comment on the owner's statement about the cost of preparing the financial statements. What should you do in regard to preparing the financial statements and the concerns about your fee?

CHAPTER 10

Investments and Funds

OBJECTIVES

1. To discuss reasons why businesses invest in the securities of other companies.
2. To define the classifications for various types of investments for financial accounting and reporting purposes.
3. To develop the concepts and theories underlying financial accounting and reporting for investments.
4. To describe acceptable accounting practices for the acquisition, holding, and disposal of investments.
5. To illustrate the financial-statement disclosures for investing activities.
6. To introduce market value accounting for investments as an alternative to current practice.

Enterprises invest in income-producing securities issued by other companies for a variety of reasons, including (1) earning a return on otherwise temporarily idle cash; (2) accumulating resources to retire long-term bonds; and (3) acquiring the stock of another enterprise to gain influence, control, or some other business advantage. Pertinent accounting issues concern the classification (current or noncurrent), measurement (valuation basis and cost flow), and disclosure of relevant information, including the accounting methods followed.

This chapter discusses the financial accounting and reporting implications of a variety of investment activities and circumstances. We first consider accounting concepts and practices for short-term or temporary investments. Next, we discuss the issues associated with accounting for long-term or noncurrent investments. Both sections consider investments in both equity and debt securities. Finally we discuss several special problems associated with investments.

TEMPORARY INVESTMENTS

This section deals with accounting measurement and disclosure problems of various investments considered to be current assets. You will recall that **current assets** are defined as cash and other assets that can reasonably be expected to be sold, used up, or converted to cash within one year or one operating cycle, whichever is *longer.*[1]

Cash or investments that may mature or be sold in the near future may be restricted or designated by management for some noncurrent purpose. Even though the asset is highly liquid, it should be classified as noncurrent on the basis of management intent. For example, if a company acquires a short-term treasury bill of the U.S. government to earn a return on otherwise temporarily idle cash, the investment is considered **current.** If the same treasury bill is acquired to provide a fund for the retirement of bonds payable that mature in several years, however, then the investment is considered **noncurrent.** Cash and investments should also be considered noncurrent when held (1) to acquire or construct a noncurrent asset; (2) to acquire influence or control over another business; or (3) to achieve some other continuing business advantage. Thus, the objective of the investment—as well as the marketability of the security held—must be considered in classifying the asset.

Conceptually, we may view the operating cycle of a business as the time and activity required for resources to be productively applied, a product manufactured and sold or service rendered, and cash finally collected (as illustrated in Exhibit 10–1). If there are several operating cycles each year, then a one-year period should be used as the basis for classifying current assets. If the period of time represented by an operating cycle is greater than one year, however, the longer operating cycle is used for purposes of classifying current assets. For example, operating cycles exceed one year in the lumber, tobacco, and distillery businesses. Enterprises that have no clear operating cycle should adopt a one-year period for purposes of distinguishing between current and noncurrent assets.

Therefore, investments classified as current assets should represent securities acquired with temporarily idle cash. The investment is also expected to be liquidated within a year or operating cycle, whichever is longer. Excess cash may be invested in either equity or debt securities. The following paragraphs consider accounting and reporting practices for temporary investments in equity securities.

[1]*Accounting Research Bulletin No. 43*, "Restatement and Revision of Accounting Research Bulletins," 1953, Ch. 3, Sec. A, par. 4.

EXHIBIT 10–1

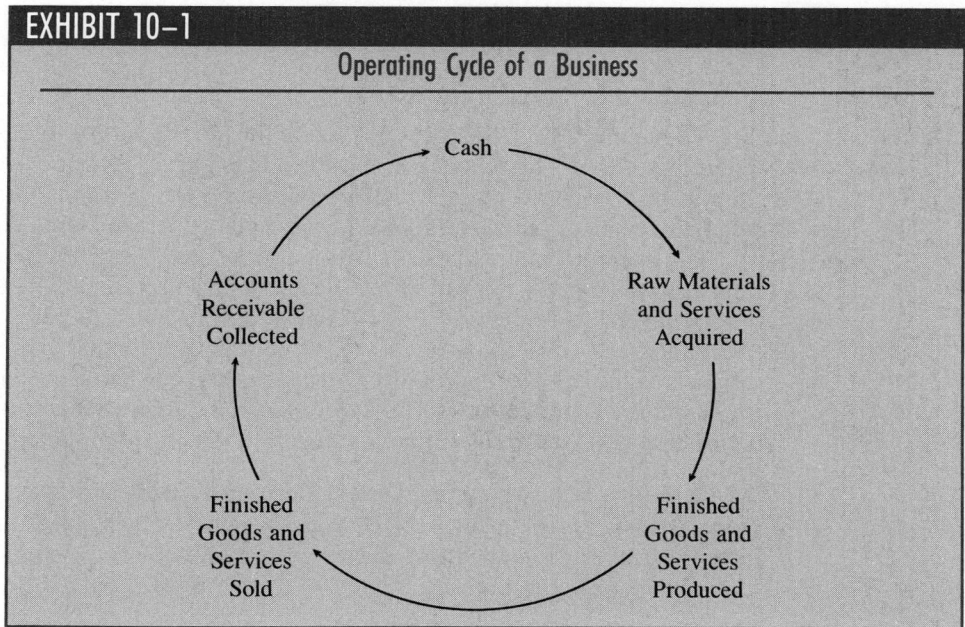

Operating Cycle of a Business

TEMPORARY INVESTMENTS IN EQUITY SECURITIES

The *Financial Accounting Standards Board* (FASB), in its *Statement of Financial Accounting Standards No. 12*, addresses many financial accounting and reporting issues for **marketable equity securities.**[2] *Marketable* identifies securities for which sales prices or bid and ask prices are available from a national securities exchange or in the over-the-counter market. When the sale of stock is restricted by a governmental or contractual requirement, the stock is considered nonmarketable unless the restriction can be removed within one year.[3]

An **equity security** is any instrument representing an ownership interest or the right to acquire or dispose of ownership shares in an enterprise at a fixed or determinable price. Thus, the term includes warrants, common and preferred stock, and certain other ownership instruments. The term does *not* include preferred stock that must be redeemed or is redeemable at the discretion of the investor. For example, if a share of stock can be presented to the issuing corporation and redeemed for cash, an investor should not consider the share an equity security. Rather, such an item is considered a debt of the issuing corporation and a receivable of the investor. Furthermore, equity securities do *not* include treasury stock or convertible bonds. In short, "equity securities" are outstanding stocks and other instruments not subject to a maturity or call date.[4]

Valuation of Marketable Equity Securities

All marketable equity securities owned by an investing company should be recorded at their original cost (or fair market value if donated) and divided into two separate

---

[2]*FASB Statement of Financial Accounting Standards No. 12*, "Accounting for Certain Marketable Securities," 1975.
[3]*FASB Statement of Financial Accounting Standards No. 12*, par. 7.
[4]*FASB Statement of Financial Accounting Standards No. 12*, par. 7.

portfolios: current and noncurrent. Subsequent to acquisition, each portfolio is reported in the financial statements at the lower of cost or market. To apply the lower of cost or market rule, each portfolio should be valued at the lower of *aggregate* cost or market as of the balance sheet date.

Conservatism

Remember that conservatism is one of the modifying conventions of financial accounting theory. The role of conservatism is to ensure that business risks and uncertainties are given adequate consideration in the financial statements and generally requires the recognition of apparent losses and the deferral of all gains until realized.

Accountants value all assets that are to be sold or otherwise converted directly into cash at amounts not exceeding the net realizable value of the assets. Marketable equity securities are valued at the lower of cost or market as are items of inventory. Accounts receivable are also reported at net realizable value, which is the amount of cash expected to be collected after estimating uncollectable accounts. In the case of marketable equity securities, the FASB merely requires a conservative valuation basis consistent with other assets that are held for exchange or collection.

An Illustration of Accounting for Current Marketable Equity Securities

To illustrate, assume that Stable Company acquires 500 shares of Ace Enterprise's common stock at $25 per share as a temporary investment. The following entry would record the stock purchase:

Current Marketable Equity Securities (CMES)	12,500	
Cash		12,500
($25 × 500 shares = $12,500)		

The asset title Current Marketable Equity Securities is used in this entry. Other appropriate titles frequently used are Temporary Investments and Short-Term Investments. In addition to the Ace stock, we shall assume that Stable also holds several other equity securities as temporary investments, all of which were purchased during 1991. Exhibit 10–2 illustrates the determination of the lower of aggregate cost and aggregate market value for the entire current portfolio of marketable equity securities held by Stable Company at December 31, 1991.

Application of the lower of aggregate cost or market rule indicates that the carrying amount of this current portfolio should be $25,800, the aggregate market value of the portfolio, because it is less than the $28,100 aggregate cost. The difference between the two is accounted for as a valuation allowance, and a loss is recognized in the income of the period.

Unrealized Losses.   We recognize the decline in aggregate market value below cost of a current portfolio of securities even if we expect the decline to be short term and it is **unrealized** in that the stock has not yet been sold.

We measure unrealized gains and losses as the difference between the aggregate market value and the aggregate cost of the marketable equity security portfolio at the balance sheet date. The following entry reflects this determination for Stable Company.

Dec. 31, 1991 Loss on Valuation of CMES	2,300	
Allowance to Reduce CMES to Lower of Cost or Market (LCM)		2,300
($28,100 − $25,800 = $2,300)		

EXHIBIT 10-2

Lower of Aggregate Cost or Market Valuation—Current Portfolio
December 31, 1991

Security	(1) Number of Shares	(2) Cost per Share	(3) Market Price per Share	(4) (Col. 1 × Col. 2) Total Cost	(5) (Col. 1 × Col. 3) Total Market Value
Ace Enterprise, common stock	500	$25	$27	$12,500	$13,500
Stress Company, preferred stock	1,000	15	12	15,000	12,000
Stress Company, warrants	300	2	1	600	300
Aggregate totals				$28,100	$25,800

The second account (Allowance to Reduce Current Marketable Equity Securities to Lower of Cost or Market) is a contra asset, or valuation allowance, to the marketable equity securities account. The valuation allowance is subtracted from the aggregate cost of marketable equity securities to arrive at a lower of cost or market valuation of the current equity portfolio for presentation in the balance sheet. Whenever the valuation allowance account has a positive (credit) balance, the current portfolio is valued at market. In contrast, if the valuation allowance account has a zero balance, the current equity portfolio is valued at cost. The valuation allowance cannot have a negative (debit) balance, because the securities cannot be carried in the accounts in excess of their cost.

In the 1991 balance sheet, Stable Company will include current marketable equity securities, less the valuation allowance, among the current assets:

Current Marketable Equity Securities	$28,100
Less: Allowance to reduce current marketable equity securities to lower of cost or market	2,300
	$25,800

The loss account debited in the above entry, Loss on Valuation of Current Marketable Equity Securities, is presented in the 1991 income statement of Stable Company.

Unrealized Loss Recoveries.   If the market value of the portfolio rises in subsequent years, losses already recognized may be partially or fully recovered. Losses that are recovered in future years because of increases in market value are reflected in the financial statements in the period of the recovery. Loss *recoveries* are recognized only to the extent of previously recognized losses. To illustrate, Exhibit 10–3 reflects the December 31, 1992, current marketable equity security portfolio of Stable Company.

The entry to record the change in aggregate market value of the current marketable equity security portfolio during 1992 is:

Dec. 31, 1992	Allowance to Reduce CMES to LCM	2,300
	Loss Recovery on Valuation of CMES	2,300
	(To remove valuation allowance for market recoveries.)	

EXHIBIT 10-3

Lower of Aggregate Cost or Market Valuation—Current Portfolio
December 31, 1992

Security	(1) Number of Shares	(2) Cost per Share	(3) Market Price per Share	(4) (Col. 1 × Col. 2) Total Cost	(5) (Col. 1 × Col. 3) Total Market Value
Ace Enterprise, common stock	500	$25	$32	$12,500	$16,000
Stress Company, preferred stock	1,000	15	12	15,000	12,000
Stress Company, warrants	300	2	1	600	300
Aggregate totals				$28,100	$28,300

Even though the market recovery is so large that it causes the aggregate market value of the entire portfolio to exceed its aggregate cost, the portfolio is written up only to its original cost by bringing the valuation allowance to a zero balance. Therefore, the unrealized loss recovery (gain) to be recognized in the income statement is limited to the previously recognized losses. If the increase in the market value of the portfolio only partially recovers previously recognized losses, then the portfolio is valued at market, and a partial unrealized loss recovery is recognized in income.

As an example, *if* the total market value of Stable's current marketable equity security portfolio was $27,900 (instead of $28,300), the valuation allowance account must have a $200 ($28,100 − $27,900) balance. Since the valuation allowance account has a balance of $2,300 from the previous period, a journal entry to reduce the valuation allowance by $2,100 would be necessary:

Dec. 31, 1992	Allowance to Reduce CMES to LCM	2,100	
	Loss Recovery on		
	Valuation of CMES		2,100

This leaves a $200 credit balance in the valuation allowance, resulting in a portfolio carrying value of $27,900 ($28,100 − $200) in the 1992 balance sheet.

Notice that the credit to the loss recovery account is not the same as a credit to the loss account. The loss of 1991 is a nominal account that has been closed to Retained Earnings. Therefore, an increase in market prices that recovers previously recognized losses cannot be accounted for by credits to the loss account. To do so would result in the reporting of a "negative loss" in the income statement. Such an accounting is unattractive from an informational perspective. Creating a separate Loss Recovery account is more meaningful.

Revenue Realization

Realized Gains and Losses.   *FASB Statement No. 12* defines a **realized gain** or **loss** as the difference between the net proceeds from the sale of a marketable equity security and its cost.[5] Other circumstances giving rise to realized losses are discussed later in this chapter.

When a company disposes of a current marketable equity security by sale or otherwise, accountants generally recognize a realized gain or loss to the extent of the dif-

---

[5]*FASB Statement of Financial Accounting Standards No. 12*, par. 7.

ference between the original cost of the security and the proceeds received from its disposition. The valuation allowance account attaches to the whole portfolio of current marketable equity securities, and not to individual equity securities within the portfolio. As a result, the valuation allowance is not adjusted in any way when various individual securities are sold. The purpose for this procedural approach is to ease the record-keeping burden. Current marketable equity securities are, by their very nature, acquired and disposed of with great regularity. Attaching the valuation allowance to each equity security would add a great burden to the accounting system. A corporation frequently invests in many different marketable equity securities and has a high trading volume. Thus, the method of adjusting the valuation allowance on the complete portfolio at the end of the reporting period is more economical than maintaining subsidiary valuation allowance records for each security.

To illustrate a sale, assume that Stable Company sells all its Ace common stock (Exhibit 10–3) for $20 a share early in 1993. The following entry is necessary to record the sale:

Jan. 15, 1993	Cash	10,000	
	Loss on Disposal of CMES	2,500	
	CMES		12,500
	($20 × 500 shares = $10,000)		

This entry does not affect the valuation allowance in any way, because that account is adjusted only at each balance sheet date. Therefore, if the sale of Ace common stock was the only activity during 1993 and if the market value of the remaining securities remained constant, then the situation at the end of 1993 would be as illustrated in Exhibit 10–4.

Because the aggregate cost of the portfolio exceeds the aggregate market value, a $3,300 entry is necessary to adjust the valuation allowance ($15,600 − $12,300 = $3,300). The difference between the aggregate cost and aggregate market value at the balance sheet date represents what the balance in the valuation allowance account should be. If the valuation allowance contains a balance from the previous year, then an entry is made for the amount of the difference between the current balance of the valuation allowance and the amount that the valuation allowance should contain. In the Stable illustration, the aggregate market value exceeded the aggregate cost of the current marketable equity securities portfolio at December 31, 1992 (Exhibit 10–3),

EXHIBIT 10–4

Lower of Aggregate Cost or Market Valuation—Current Portfolio
December 31, 1993

Security	(1) Number of Shares	(2) Cost per Share	(3) Market Price per Share	(4) (Col. 1 x Col. 2) Total Cost	(5) (Col. 1 x Col. 3) Total Market Value
Stress Company, preferred stock	1,000	$15	$12	$15,000	$12,000
Stress Company, warrants	300	2	1	600	300
Aggregate totals				$15,600	$12,300

and the valuation allowance account was completely eliminated at that date. Therefore, it is necessary to prepare the following entry for the full $3,300 excess of aggre-
gate cost over aggregate market value at December 31, 1993:

Dec. 31, 1993	Loss on Valuation of CMES	3,300	
	Allowance to Reduce CMES to LCM		3,300

This entry is necessary even though there has been *no* change in either the cost or
market values of the securities remaining in the portfolio following the sale of the Ace
common stock. An unrealized loss (due merely to the absence of the Ace stock at December 31, 1993) is reported in the 1993 income statement.

By requiring this treatment, the FASB places a heavy emphasis on distinguishing
between realized gains or losses and unrealized gains or losses. A company may recognize an *unrealized* loss in one period if the market value of a security declines below
cost and a *realized* loss in the following period if the security is sold for less than its
cost. In these circumstances, an unrealized loss recovery may also be recognized in
the period of disposal. To illustrate, assume that Stable Company buys a single share
of Remote, Inc., stock for $100 as a temporary investment on January 10, 1992. As-
sume further that the market value of the Remote stock declines to $80 at December
31, 1992, and that this investment was the only one made by Stable. The following
entries will record the acquisition of the stock and recognize the unrealized loss:

Jan. 10, 1992	CMES	100	
	Cash		100
Dec. 31, 1992	Loss on Valuation of CMES	20	
	Allowance to Reduce CMES to LCM		20

If we now assume that Stable Company sells the share of Remote stock on February 4, 1993, for $80 and makes no further acquisitions of marketable equity securities
during 1993, the following entries are necessary.

Feb. 4, 1993	Loss on Disposal of CMES	20	
	Cash	80	
	CMES		100
	(To report sale of security at loss of $20.)		
Dec. 31, 1993	Allowance to Reduce CMES to LCM	20	
	Loss Recovery on Valuation		
	of CMES		20
	(To remove valuation allowance account.)		

This unusual result of recognizing an unrealized loss in one year and an unrealized loss recovery in the next occurs because the FASB places a high degree of significance on distinguishing between realized and unrealized losses. If the December 31,
1993, adjusting entry had been omitted, then the $20 loss would have been recognized
twice, once as unrealized at the end of 1992 and then again as realized in February
1993. Only the December 31, 1993, adjusting entry eliminates this undesirable effect. The combined income statement effect for 1992 and 1993 properly reflects a $20
loss. In practice, such results are generally not directly observed, because corporations hold many different securities in their portfolios. The impact on the valuation
allowance of transactions such as those illustrated above is combined with the market
value changes of all securities in the portfolio and not recognized separately. Nevertheless, reported results of operations are directly affected in the manner described.

Dividend Revenue.   Dividends on stock investments are ordinarily recorded as revenue when they are received by debiting Cash and crediting Dividend Revenue. Dividends that have been declared by the company issuing the stock but have not been received by the end of the investing company's financial reporting period should be recognized as a receivable and as revenue. Dividend revenue should *not* be anticipated and recognized prior to declaration, however.

Disclosure   **Financial Statement Disclosures.**   The following financial statement disclosures are required for current marketable equity securities:[6]

1. Aggregate cost and market values.
2. As of date of the latest balance sheet, **gross unrealized gains** and **gross unrealized losses.** (Both terms are defined below.)
3. For each period for which an income statement is presented, the net realized gain or loss included in net income and the basis of cost computation (e.g., specific identification, weighted average).

Gross unrealized gains and losses are merely the total gains and total losses that, when combined, represent the net unrealized gain or loss for the aggregate portfolio. In Exhibit 10–2, the gross unrealized gains and losses for Stable Company are determined as follows:

Security	Cost	Market	Gain (Loss)
Stress Company, preferred	$15,000	$12,000	$(3,000)
Stress Company, warrants	600	300	(300)
Gross unrealized losses			(3,300)
Ace Enterprise, common	12,500	13,500	1,000
Net unrealized losses			$(2,300)

Gross losses and gross gains are usually disclosed in a note to the financial statements along with the other required information.

Furthermore, if a company engages in several transactions that involve the same class of security, assumptions concerning the cost flow of the securities may be necessary. In this regard, marketable securities may be viewed in a fashion similar to items of inventory. Because most securities are serially numbered, many companies apply specific identification procedures. Other methods of cost identification, such as first-in, first-out or weighted average, are also commonly encountered. Income tax consequences may also influence the selection of the cost-flow assumptions to be used.

Exhibit 10–5 includes an illustration of the financial statement disclosure of current marketable equity securities for PNC Financial Corp, a multi-bank holding company. Among the types of security investments held, notice the corporate stock marketable equities. Also presented are gross unrealized gains and losses (middle section) and the portion of gains attributable to marketable equity securities (bottom section). Total investments classified as current assets for 1989 are $12,866.6 million, making up approximately 28% of the company's total assets of over $45 million.

A Learning Tool

The learning summary in Exhibit 10–6 displays the significant accounting practices involved in accounting for current marketable equity securities. Although the

---

[6]*FASB Statement of Financial Accounting Standards No. 12*, par. 12.

EXHIBIT 10–5

PNC Financial Corp
Disclosure of Current Marketable Equity Securities

Investment Securities

The carrying and approximate market values of investment securities were as follows:

December 31	1989		1988	
In millions	Carrying Value	Market Value	Carrying Value	Market Value
U.S. Treasury	$ 1,403.6	$ 1,404.7	$ 3,250.9	$ 3,212.0
U.S. Government agencies and corporations	8,655.2	8,626.9	4,335.7	4,104.7
State and municipal	1,038.6	1,042.5	1,102.1	1,073.9
Corporate stocks				
Marketable equities	155.1	221.6	142.7	202.3
Other	23.4	25.0	16.8	20.6
Other	1,590.7	1,588.4	1,975.5	1,955.6
Total	$12,866.6	$12,909.1	$10,823.7	$10,569.1

Data related to marketable equities:

In millions	December 31	1989	1988
Unrealized gains		$ 83.2	$ 81.7
Unrealized losses		(16.7)	(22.1)
Aggregate cost		155.1	142.7
Aggregate market value		$221.6	$202.3

The following table presents the composition of net equity and other security gains:

In millions For the year ended December 31	1989	1988	1987
Net gains on marketable equity securities	$18.6	$21.4	$27.3
Net gains on other securities	1.5	3.6	2.5
Total	$20.1	$25.0	$29.8

SOURCE: PNC Financial Corp, 1989 Annual Report.

---

preceding section discusses and illustrates practices, the flowchart provides a useful summary and review tool to ensure your complete understanding of accounting for current marketable equity securities.

TEMPORARY INVESTMENTS IN DEBT SECURITIES

Debt securities differ from equity securities in several important ways. To the company holding the security as an investment, debt securities represent amounts loaned to the company issuing the security in contrast to the ownership interest represented by equity securities. Return on debt securities, called *interest,* is fixed in amount and timing in comparison with dividends on equity securities, which are declared at the

EXHIBIT 10–6

Current Marketable Equity Securities Portfolio

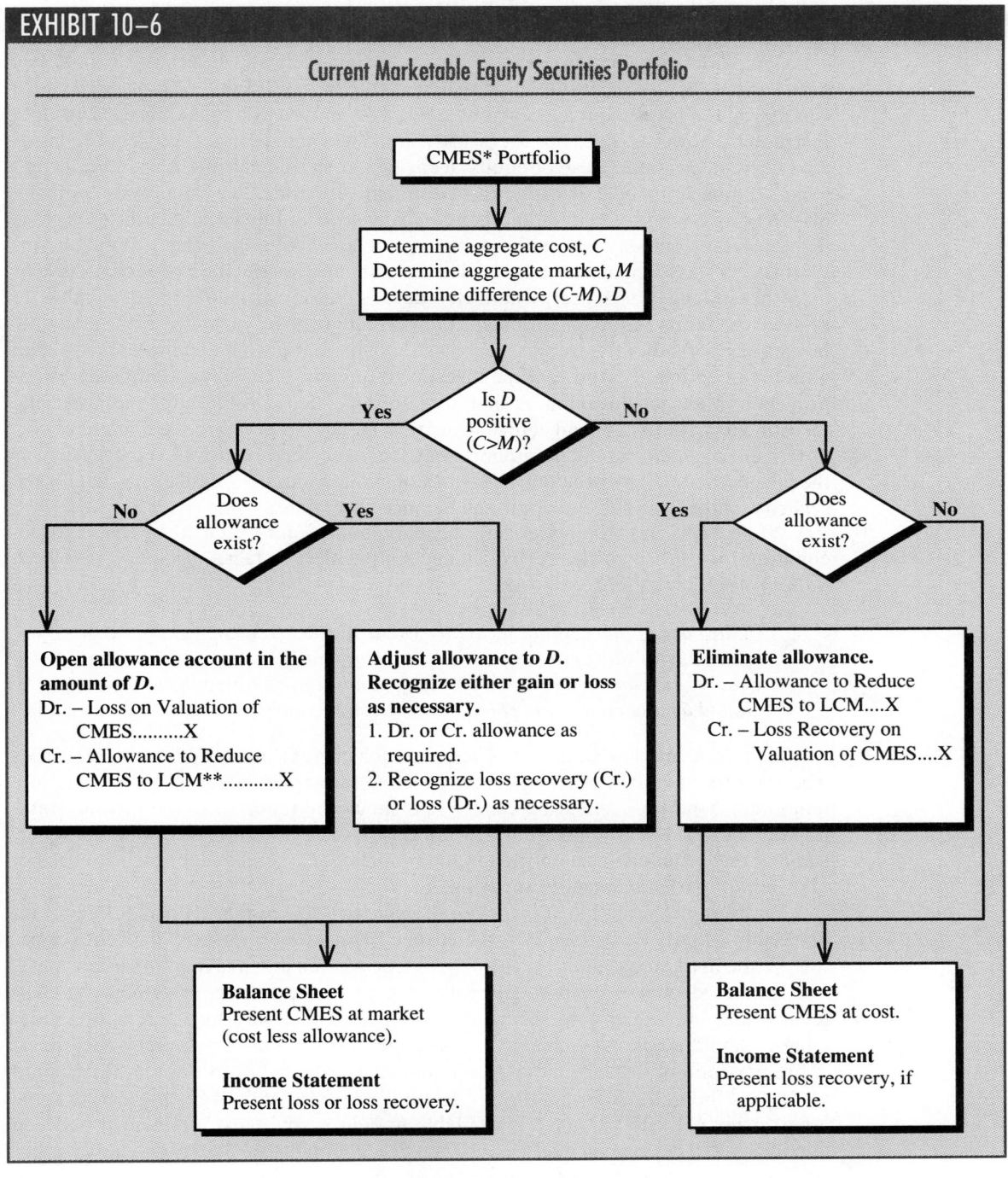

CMES* Portfolio

Determine aggregate cost, C
Determine aggregate market, M
Determine difference $(C\text{-}M)$, D

Is D positive $(C>M)$?

Yes / **No**

Does allowance exist? — **No** / **Yes**

Does allowance exist? — **Yes** / **No**

Open allowance account in the amount of D.
Dr. – Loss on Valuation of
    CMES..........X
Cr. – Allowance to Reduce
    CMES to LCM**...........X

**Adjust allowance to D.
Recognize either gain or loss as necessary.**
1. Dr. or Cr. allowance as required.
2. Recognize loss recovery (Cr.) or loss (Dr.) as necessary.

Eliminate allowance.
Dr. – Allowance to Reduce
    CMES to LCM....X
Cr. – Loss Recovery on
    Valuation of CMES....X

Balance Sheet
Present CMES at market (cost less allowance).

Income Statement
Present loss or loss recovery.

Balance Sheet
Present CMES at cost.

Income Statement
Present loss recovery, if applicable.

discretion of the issuing company. Finally, debt securities have a fixed maturity date while equity securities usually do not.

Companies may acquire debt securities for relatively short periods of time. If a debt security is *not marketable,* a current maturity date is generally necessary for classifying the investment as a current asset. The maturity date of a *marketable* debt instrument, however, does not necessarily indicate whether or not the item is considered current. As in the case of equity securities, management intent is an important consideration in the classification of investment securities. For example, a company may acquire a note or bond of another company with an immediate maturity date. If the acquiring company places the security in a noncurrent investment fund, the investment is classified as noncurrent. The noncurrent classification of such an investment possessing a short-term maturity date is based on management's intent to reinvest the funds at maturity for some noncurrent purpose. In contrast, if a company invests temporarily idle cash in marketable bonds that have a distant maturity date with the intention to dispose of the investment quickly, a current classification is appropriate. Management intent is therefore an important consideration in classifying investments in both debt and equity securities. Of course, the expressed intent of corporate management should be supported by logic and corroborative evidence, such as the purposes of the investment, the history of similar activities, a ready market for the security, and events subsequent to the balance sheet date.

While *SFAS No. 12* applies only to marketable *equity* securities, financial accounting for *debt* securities reflects many similarities. In fact, *Accounting Research Bulletin No. 43* states:

> *In the case of marketable securities where market value is less than cost by a substantial amount and it is evident that the decline in market value is not due to a mere temporary condition, the amount to be included as a current asset should not exceed the market value.*[7]

Therefore, market valuation is required for current marketable debt securities whenever the investment has suffered a decline in market value that is not due to a temporary condition. In such a case, a loss should be reported in the income statement in the period of the investment write-down. Except for this condition, however, some of the latitude in accounting for and reporting marketable debt securities is not allowed for marketable equity securities.

For example, valuation at the lower of *aggregate* cost or market is required for all marketable equity securities, but such a specification does not exist for debt securities. While marketable equity securities must be written down to market for any material market declines, current generally accepted accounting principles (GAAP) require that individual debt securities be written down only for nontemporary declines. Should a company choose to apply the lower of cost or market policy to its entire portfolio of debt securities, no guidance is provided as to whether this should be done at the individual security level, to the portfolio in the aggregate, or in some other manner. Little guidance is available to help accountants distinguish between temporary and permanent declines. Although accountants *may* write down debt securities treated as current assets for *temporary* market declines, such a practice is not mandatory. Finally, *ARB No. 43* does not consider whether or not loss recoveries taking place in later periods may be recognized. Since the practice is not prohibited and, in fact, is required for current marketable equity securities, accountants may logically

---

[7]*Accounting Research Bulletin No. 43*, Ch. 3, par. 9.

EXHIBIT 10-7

Accounting for Short-Term Investments

Issue	Marketable Equity Securities (*SFAS No. 12*)	Marketable Debt Securities (*ARB No. 43*)
Valuation basis	Lower of *aggregate* cost or market.	Cost reduced to market for value declines of individual securities not due to temporary conditions.
Criteria for loss recognition	All market declines recognized in income.	Declines not due to temporary conditions recognized in income.
Loss recoveries	All market recoveries recognized to the extent of previously recognized unrealized losses.	No specification of treatment of market value recoveries.

apply the same practices to debt securities as are applied to current marketable equity securities. Exhibit 10–7 compares current GAAP requirements for each type of current marketable security.

The exhibit shows that the accounting practices specified by the two documents *permit* differences rather than prescribe them. That is, no differences are explicitly established by either of the two statements. Rather, *ARB No. 43* is merely silent about some of the accounting issues addressed by *SFAS No. 12*. As a result, practice varies somewhat in this area; however, logic and consistency support treating current marketable equity and debt securities in a similar fashion. This means that all current marketable securities would be treated in accordance with the more precise requirements of *SFAS No. 12*. The authors support this position.

The following illustration demonstrates acceptable accounting practices for temporary investments in debt securities. Assume Stable Company acquires bonds of Timeless Corporation on March 1, 1992. The bonds are dated January 1, 1992, pay interest semiannually at a stated rate of 12%, mature in 1999, and were acquired by Stable for $10,200 (102% of par) plus accrued interest.

The acquisition or issue price of a bond is frequently stated as a percentage of par or face value. In this case, the bond was acquired at an amount 2% greater than the par amount of the bond or at "102." Furthermore, certain transaction costs, such as broker fees, are frequently incurred in the acquisition of bonds and are considered part of the cost of the bonds. In this simplified example no costs are considered except the direct cost of the bond and related accrued interest. Stable company would make the following journal entry:

Mar. 1, 1992	Short-Term Debt Investment	10,200	
	Interest Receivable	200	
	Cash		10,400
	(To record acquisition of Timeless Corporation bond.)		

The total cash investment is computed as follows:

$10,000 × 102%   = $10,200 Bond price
$10,000 × 12% × 2/12 =   200 Accrued interest
Total cash investment $10,400

The debit of $200 to Interest Receivable could also have been charged to Interest Revenue. In that case, when the semiannual interest is received, the entire cash received ($10,000 × 12% × 6/12 = $600) would be credited directly to the Interest Revenue account. Resuming the example in which Interest Receivable was charged, we find that the following entry would be necessary on June 30, 1992, to record the receipt of the interest payment:

June 30, 1992	Cash	600	
	Interest Revenue		400
	Interest Receivable		200
	(To record semiannual interest payment. $10,000 × 12% × 6/12 = $600, 1/3 of which had previously been recorded as receivable.)		

Note that the $200 amount paid in excess of par value ($10,200 − $10,000 = $200) is not amortized. Accountants usually do not amortize a difference between the purchase price and the par value of a temporary debt investment on the assumption that the investment is short-term and will not be held to maturity. This treatment is consistent with the overall objectives of short-term investments; that is, a temporary productive application of otherwise idle resources.

Finally, if Stable Company sells the bond on November 1, 1992, at 97 plus accrued interest, the following entry is necessary:

Nov. 1, 1992	Cash	10,100	
	Loss on Sale of Debt Investment	500	
	Short-Term Debt Investment		10,200
	Interest Revenue		400
	(To record sale of bond at 97, plus accrued interest for four months. $10,000 × 12% × 4/12 = $400.)		

The cash received is the sum of $9,700 ($10,000 × 97%) plus $400 interest accrued from July 1 ($10,000 × 12% × 4/12). Since the bond cost $10,200 and was sold for $9,700, a loss of $500 is recognized.

NONCURRENT INVESTMENTS

Companies frequently invest in the securities of different enterprises for purposes other than the temporary investment of idle cash. These investments are excluded from current assets and reported as noncurrent investments in the investing company's balance sheet.

In addition to the reasons mentioned earlier, such as accumulating funds for the retirement of debt or the ability to control another enterprise, a company may make long-term investments in another business for other reasons. For example, a company that desires to expand operations to a new product line or geographic area may presently lack adequate liquid resources. The company may discover, however, that it can capitalize on such opportunities immediately by investing in other enterprises that are already involved in those activities. Because the appropriate accounting treatment is affected by management's intent, accountants should understand completely the nature and purpose of the investment.

NONCURRENT INVESTMENTS IN EQUITY SECURITIES

If one company acquires the equity securities of another firm as a noncurrent investment, we must classify the investment as one of the following types:

1. **Passive.** The investment is consummated in order to earn a return (dividends and/or long-term capital increment). Securities may be voting or nonvoting. Securities are reported at the *lower of cost or market.*
2. **Significant influence.** The investment is consummated in order to affect the operating or financial policies of the investee and to earn a return. Securities must convey voting rights to the investor to establish influence. Securities are reported by using the *equity method* in which investee earnings (net income), net of dividends received, are recognized by the investor.

Substance over Form

3. **Control.** The investment is consummated to obtain the ability to mandate operating or financial policies of a subsidiary and to earn a return. Securities must convey voting rights to permit control. The financial statements of the investee are *consolidated* with those of the investor, because in substance only a single economic entity exists.

Determination of whether an investment is passive or designed to obtain significant influence or control of the investee is based primarily on the magnitude of the investment. Accounting and reporting practices differ for each type of equity investment. Exhibit 10–8 displays the nature and objective of each type of investment and describes the general reporting practice for each. The next three subsections of this chapter consider the conceptual differences and accounting practices for each of the three types of equity investments.

Passive Equity Investments

Our previous discussion of marketable equity securities revealed that *SFAS No. 12* specifies accounting and reporting practices for both current and noncurrent portfolios of marketable equity securities. Now we shall consider financial accounting and reporting standards for *noncurrent* portfolios of marketable equity securities.

EXHIBIT 10–8

Summary of Investments in Equity Securities

Issue	Level of Investment		
Ownership of voting stock	Less than 20%	20%–50%	More than 50%
Character of investment	Passive	Significant influence	Control
General reporting practice	Lower of cost or market	Equity method	Consolidation
Primary relevant literature	*SFAS No. 12;* *ARB No. 43,* Ch.3	*APB Opinion No. 18.*	*ARB No. 51;* *APB Opinion Nos. 16* and *17;* *SFAS No. 94*

Conservatism

Revenue
Realization

The noncurrent portfolio, like the current portfolio, is valued at the *lower of aggregate cost or market* at each balance sheet date. Several accounting practices specified for noncurrent marketable equity securities, however, differ from those employed for the current portfolio. Foremost among the differences is the practice of recognizing only *realized* gains and losses in the income statement. Although the carrying amount of the noncurrent marketable equity securities portfolio is reduced from aggregate cost to a lower aggregate market, only *permanent* aggregate market declines are recognized in the income of the period. Aggregate market declines that are *temporary,* while requiring recognition in the asset valuation allowance, do not result in losses reported in the income statement.[8] Rather, we report a temporary aggregate market decline below aggregate cost as a direct reduction of stockholders' equity, thereby avoiding the recognition of a loss in the income statement. The practice of not recording in the income statement the temporary market losses on noncurrent marketable equity securities is different from the treatment accorded the current marketable equity securities portfolio. Although it may appear somewhat unusual, the practice is theoretically correct in that temporary market declines do not cause a company to sustain losses on long-term investments. Such securities are held for an extended period of time and later market recoveries are expected to prevent the realization of the temporary market declines. A temporary market decline in the value of a security is much more likely to cause a company to sustain a loss if the security is to be held for only a short period of time. To illustrate, assume that Stable Company acquires the portfolio of noncurrent marketable equity securities indicated in Exhibit 10–9 during 1992. If we assume that the total market decline is considered to be due to temporary market conditions, the following entry will be necessary at December 31, 1992, to value these noncurrent marketable equity securities (NCMES):

Dec. 31, 1992 Net Unrealized Loss on NCMES	110,000	
Allowance to Reduce NCMES to LCM		110,000
($650,000 − $540,000 = $110,000)		

EXHIBIT 10–9

Lower of Aggregate Cost or Market Valuation—Noncurrent Portfolio
December 31, 1992

Security	(1) Number of Shares	(2) Cost per Share	(3) Market Price per Share	(4) (Col. 1 × Col. 2) Total Cost	(5) (Col. 1 × Col. 3) Total Market Value
Volunteer Corporation, common	10,000	$ 30	$ 20	$300,000	$200,000
Crossville Company, common	2,000	50	95	100,000	190,000
Sunshine Corporation, common	1,000	250	150	250,000	150,000
Aggregate totals				$650,000	$540,000

---

[8]*FASB Statement of Financial Accounting Standards No. 12,* par. 11.

The noncurrent investments and stockholders' equity sections of the Stable Company balance sheet reflect the results of the above entry in the following manner:

Noncurrent investment
    Noncurrent marketable equity securities
      carried at market on December 31, 1992 $540,000
Stockholders' equity
    Net unrealized loss on noncurrent marketable
      equity securities $(110,000)

Disclosure

The negative stockholders' equity account is typically presented as one of the last stockholders' equity items in the balance sheet, immediately before or after retained earnings. Note disclosure of the amount of the valuation allowance and other required information, which is similar to that required for the current portfolio presented earlier, should accompany the financial statements. The valuation allowance amount ($110,000) should be disclosed as part of the asset presentation in the balance sheet or as part of the note.

Since the loss is unrealized and relates to a noncurrent marketable equity security portfolio, net income is not affected. Any subsequent reductions in the valuation allowance arising from an increase in the market value of the long-term portfolio is recorded as a reduction in the Net Unrealized Loss on NCMES (stockholders' equity) account. The reduction in the Net Unrealized Loss on NCMES account can never exceed the balance of the account, and therefore a lower of cost or market valuation is ensured. Since this account is part of the stockholders' equity, and thus a real account, direct credits can be made to the account for subsequent market recoveries.

Continuing the example from Exhibit 10–9, assume that one year later the company holds the same securities, but now they have an aggregate market value of $615,000. The entry to record the $75,000 market value recovery ($615,000 − $540,000) is as follows:

Dec. 31, 1993   Allowance to Reduce NCMES to LCM   75,000
                Net Unrealized Loss on NCMES   75,000

If the market had risen to $660,000, then the market value would *exceed* cost, and both the valuation allowance account and the Net Unrealized Loss on NCMES account would have to be totally eliminated. The same entry as above would be made, except the amounts would be $110,000. Notice that any increase in market value beyond the original cost is not recorded.

The FASB distinguishes between realized and unrealized losses for the noncurrent portfolio by stating that **only realized losses should be recognized in income.** The FASB gives three conditions under which losses on noncurrent investments must be treated as realized losses and recognized in income in the year of the loss: (1) sale or disposal of the security, (2) a **permanent decline** in the market value of an individual security below its cost;[9] or (3) transfer of the security to the current marketable equity security classification, or vice versa.

Conditions 1 and 2 provide convincing evidence that a permanent loss has been sustained by the investing company, which requires income statement recognition of the loss. Transfers of securities between the current and noncurrent portfolios (condition 3) may also give rise to a realized loss on the income statement. The purpose of this condition is to prevent managers from "dressing up" the income statement via

---

[9]*FASB Statement of Financial Accounting Standards No. 12,* pars. 7, 10–11.

classification changes between current and noncurrent investments in equity securities. In the absence of condition 3, a manager could transfer a security with a large unrealized loss position to the noncurrent portfolio. This would effectively remove the recognition of the unrealized loss from the income statement and, hence, arbitrarily improve net income. Condition 3 reduces the incentive for this type of behavior by requiring a loss position to be recognized in income upon portfolio reclassification of a security.

A realized gain or loss resulting from the sale of a security is handled as the sale of any other asset: A debit is made to Cash for the amount received, the investment account is reduced (credited) by the cost of the security, and a realized gain or loss is recognized for the difference between the two. As is the case with the current portfolio of marketable equity securities discussed earlier, the valuation allowance is not adjusted at the time of the sale of the security. Also, with the noncurrent portfolio the Unrealized Loss on NCMES account in stockholders' equity is not adjusted at the time of sale. Both the valuation allowance and the Unrealized Loss on NCMES accounts are adjusted at the end of the accounting period, and the fact that securities were sold during the period may affect the amount of the adjustment to these accounts.

To illustrate changing to the current classification, assume that Stable Company changes its investment intent regarding the Sunshine stock on January 30, 1993, when the stock has a market value of $195 per share. The entry to reclassify the security, including recognition of the loss, is as follows:

Jan. 30, 1993	CMES	195,000	
	Loss on Valuation of Marketable Equity		
	Securities	55,000	
	NCMES		250,000

The recognition of a permanent decline in an individual security in the noncurrent portfolio of marketable equity securities is relatively straightforward. The difference between the cost and the lower market value of the security is debited to a realized loss account and credited to the NCMES investment account. The valuation allowance is unaffected by this procedure. In subsequent aggregate cost and market comparisons made to determine the lower of the two, the revised (lower) cost figure is used rather than the original (higher) cost figure for the security that has been revalued.

Changes in the value of marketable equity securities taking place after the balance sheet date should *not* be reflected in the financial statements, even if such a decline is considered permanent. However, when changes in the market value of securities take place after the balance sheet date, the following considerations apply:[10]

1. For marketable equity securities for which a change in carrying amount is included in stockholders' equity (rather than in net income), in judging whether a decline is other than temporary, a gain or loss realized on subsequent disposition or changes in market prices occurring after the date of the financial statements shall be taken into consideration along with other factors.
2. A recovery in market value after the balance sheet date tends to indicate that a portion or all of the decline at the balance sheet date was temporary. Such recovery should be considered when estimating the amount of decline as of the balance sheet date judged to be permanent.

---

[10]*FASB Interpretation No. 11,* "Changes in Market Value After the Balance Sheet Date," 1976, pars. 3–4.

Thus, information becoming available after the date of the balance sheet guides financial reporting for the year just ended. The amount of gain or loss to be recognized, however, is measured by the market value of the securities at the balance sheet date.

When cash dividends are received on passive investments in marketable equity securities, revenue is recognized in the amount of the dividend. For example, if Stable Company receives a dividend of $3,000 from Volunteer Corporation, the following entry is needed:

Cash	3,000	
Dividend Revenue		3,000
(To record receipt of cash dividend.)		

Occasionally, an investee company declares a dividend that exceeds its existing retained earnings. In such cases the recipient company recognizes the receipt of a *liquidating dividend* and, instead of recognizing dividend revenue, records a recovery of a portion of the original investment. Liquidating dividends are fairly common in mining and petroleum operations. To illustrate, assume that Stable Company receives a $1,000 liquidating dividend from Volunteer Corporation. The following entry should be made:

Cash	1,000	
NCMES		1,000
(To record receipt of liquidating dividend.)		

Exhibit 10–10 includes the stockholders' equity section of the balance sheet and the note disclosure of noncurrent marketable equity securities for Overseas Shipholding Group, Inc., for 1990 and 1989. This company is a large bulk shipping company engaged in ocean transportation of liquid and dry bulk cargo throughout the world. Notice first the negative stockholders' equity element, "net unrealized loss on noncurrent marketable equity securities." This amount is $38,782,000 and $34,339,000 for 1990 and 1989, respectively. These figures correspond to the same amounts in Note F for the "allowance for net unrealized loss on noncurrent marketable equity securities" which reduces the cost of the portfolio of securities to the lower of cost or market. The description which follows the numerical presentation in Note F indicates the change in the amounts of these items for each year.

Passive investments in *nonmarketable* equity securities, such as stock of a closely held corporation, should be carried at cost unless there is clear evidence of an impairment in carrying value. Since no market value exists, such investments are not considered current except in unusual circumstances such as an imminent sale.

A Learning Tool.   The learning summary flowchart in Exhibit 10–11 describes accounting and reporting practices for noncurrent marketable equity securities. These same principles apply for all marketable equity securities in unclassified balance sheets (balance sheets that do not distinguish between current and noncurrent assets and liabilities). The flowchart provides a useful review tool and condenses the preceding illustrations and explanations to facilitate a comprehensive understanding of financial accounting and reporting for noncurrent marketable equity securities.

Equity Investments Representing Significant Influence

Different accounting practices are required if the level of a long-term investment in voting marketable equity securities reaches a point at which **significant influence** is exercised by the investor over the operating and financial policies of the investee. The

EXHIBIT 10-10

Overseas Shipholding Group, Inc.
Disclosure of Noncurrent Marketable Equity Securities

Balance Sheet Excerpt:

	As of December 31, 1990	As of December 31, 1989
Stockholders' Equity—Notes F, H and L:		
Common Stock, par value $1 per share:		
Authorized—60,000,000 shares		
Issued—36,140,759 shares	36,141,000	36,141,000
Paid-in Additional Capital	20,906,000	20,906,000
Retained Earnings	733,349,000	694,724,000
	790,396,000	751,771,000
Less—cost of Treasury Stock—3,102,981 and 1,252,581 shares	44,486,000	16,648,000
	745,910,000	735,123,000
Less—net unrealized loss on noncurrent marketable equity securities	38,782,000	34,339,000
Total Stockholders' Equity	707,128,000	700,784,000

Note F—Investments in Marketable Securities:

Certain information concerning noncurrent marketable equity securities follows:

	Cost at December 31, 1990	Approximate Market at December 31, 1990	Cost at December 31, 1989	Approximate Market at December 31, 1989
Marketable equity securities included in:				
Investments in Marketable Securities	$ 78,807,000	$ 45,621,000	$132,449,000	$ 97,443,000
Capital Construction and Restricted Funds	38,404,000	32,808,000	32,640,000	33,307,000
	117,211,000	$ 78,429,000	165,089,000	$130,750,000
Allowance for net unrealized loss on noncurrent marketable equity securities—also deducted from Stockholders' Equity	38,782,000		34,339,000	
Carrying amount	$ 78,429,000		$130,750,000	

The allowance for net unrealized loss on noncurrent marketable equity securities deducted from stockholders' equity increased $4,443,000 (1990), $13,892,000 (1989) and $65,000 (1988). At December 31, 1990, gross unrealized gains on marketable equity securities were not material.

At February 25, 1991, the approximate aggregate market quotation of the above investments in marketable equity securities was $89,000,000.

SOURCE: Overseas Shipholding Group, Inc., 1990 Annual Report.

EXHIBIT 10–11

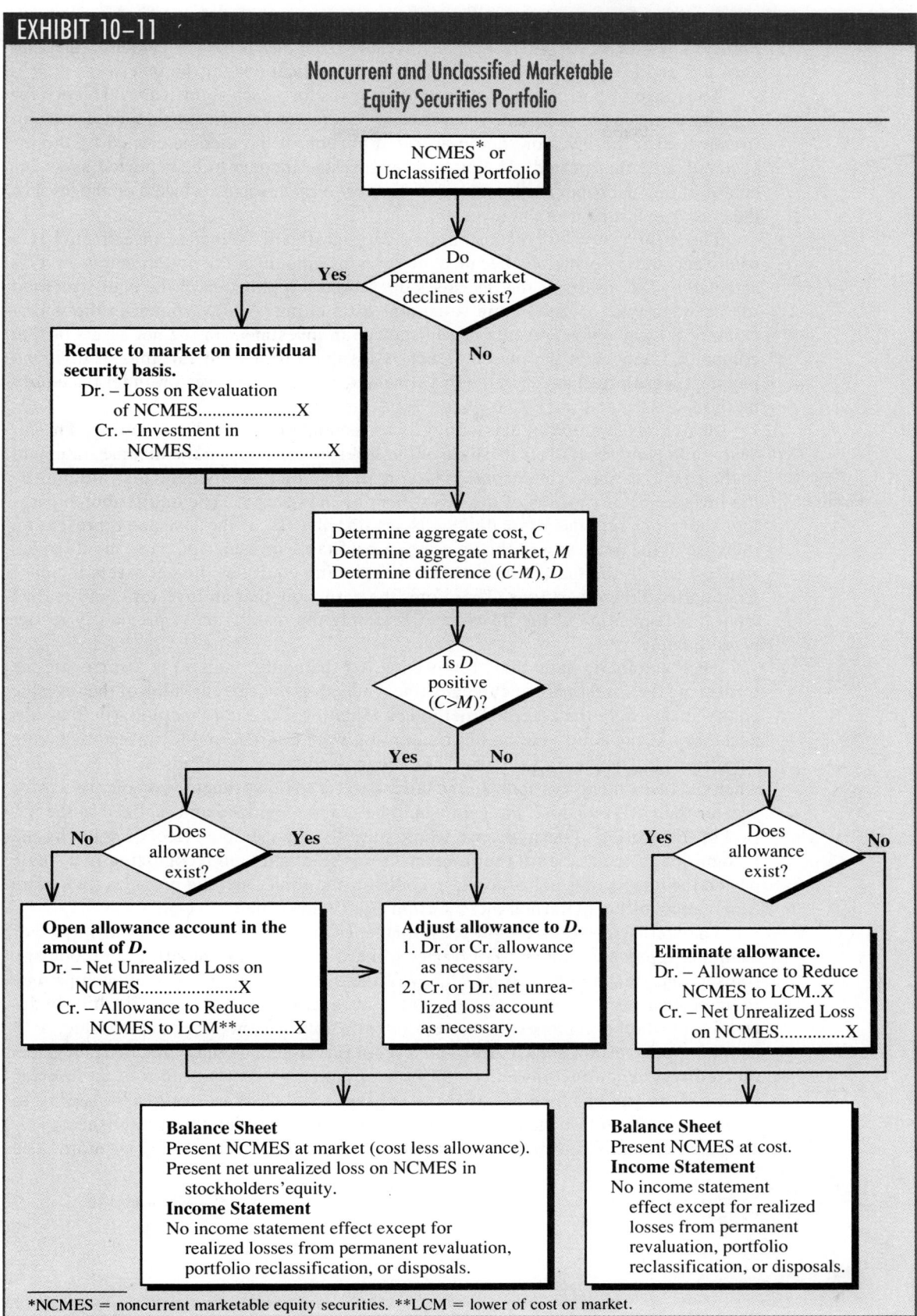

Noncurrent and Unclassified Marketable Equity Securities Portfolio

NCMES* or Unclassified Portfolio

Do permanent market declines exist?

Yes → **Reduce to market on individual security basis.**
Dr. – Loss on Revaluation
    of NCMES......................X
Cr. – Investment in
    NCMES............................X

No

Determine aggregate cost, *C*
Determine aggregate market, *M*
Determine difference (*C-M*), *D*

Is *D* positive (*C>M*)?

Yes

Does allowance exist?

No → **Open allowance account in the amount of *D*.**
Dr. – Net Unrealized Loss on
    NCMES....................X
Cr. – Allowance to Reduce
    NCMES to LCM**............X

Yes → **Adjust allowance to *D*.**
1. Dr. or Cr. allowance as necessary.
2. Cr. or Dr. net unrealized loss account as necessary.

Balance Sheet
Present NCMES at market (cost less allowance).
Present net unrealized loss on NCMES in stockholders'equity.
Income Statement
No income statement effect except for realized losses from permanent revaluation, portfolio reclassification, or disposals.

No

Does allowance exist?

Yes → **Eliminate allowance.**
Dr. – Allowance to Reduce
    NCMES to LCM..X
Cr. – Net Unrealized Loss
    on NCMES..............X

No

Balance Sheet
Present NCMES at cost.
Income Statement
No income statement effect except for realized losses from permanent revaluation, portfolio reclassification, or disposals.

*NCMES = noncurrent marketable equity securities. **LCM = lower of cost or market.

ability to significantly influence an investee company provides evidence that the earnings and losses of the investee have direct implications for the investor.

The range of business activities and purposes for which significant influence investments are made is broad. If an investor exercises significant influence over an investee, then the investor should accrue a portion of the income earned by the investee during that period. The amount of investee income to be reported as an increase in the investment account and as income to the investor is based on the level of the equity investment in the investee.

The **equity method** of accounting for significant influence investments is a sound accounting principle, because the carrying amount of the investment is directly affected by the results of the investee's operations. Application of the equity method represents a type of "automatic valuation" accounting. An investment in the voting stock of a company represents, in substance, an investment in the net assets of that company. Changes in the investee's net assets that result from earnings or dividend payments result in changes in the investment account of the investor under the equity method.

Revenue Realization

The equity method of accounting is an example of accrual accounting. The investor company recognizes its share of the investee earnings on the income statement in the period earned. The income is later realized either via dividend distributions by the investee or disposition of the investment by the investor. The undistributed earnings (earnings retained after dividends are distributed) of the investee represent an increase in the net assets of the investee. A profitable investee company should experience a rise in the market value of its outstanding equity as the net assets increase from undistributed earnings. Therefore, the cash flow that an investor could realize from the disposition of the investment is simply the realization of previously recognized income.

The "automatic valuation" represented by the equity method is a surrogate for measuring the investment at current value. Indeed, if the current value of the investee equity shares were the accepted method of valuation, the equity method would be unnecessary. If the equity method of accounting were *not* required for investors having significant influence, income would be recognized when dividends were received or when the investment was sold. In the latter case, if the investment was sold for a price greater than original cost, the gain would be both recognized and realized in the period of disposition. This approach would have the undesirable effect of delaying the recognition of income until the investment was sold and then recognizing in a single period the lump sum gain (or loss). In contrast, the equity method provides for a more timely recognition of earned income from equity investments.

The ability to exercise significant influence may be evident in several ways. For example, representation on the investee's board of directors, material intercompany transactions, technological dependency of the investee, and other relationships may indicate an ability to exercise significant influence. Because of the difficulties in determining whether an investor exercises significant influence over the investee, *APB Opinion No. 18* established a threshold level of investment to guide practice.[11] It states that a direct or indirect investment of 20% or more in the *voting* stock of an investee indicates, **in the absence of contrary evidence,** that an investor has the ability to exercise significant influence over an investee.[12] The Opinion thus establishes a presumption of significant influence arising at investment levels of 20% or more. The

---

[11]*APB Opinion No. 18,* "The Equity Method of Accounting for Investments in Common Stock," 1971.
[12]*APB Opinion No. 18,* par. 17.

presumption may be rebutted, however, if evidence is available to support alternative practices. Recently, several companies have applied the equity method of accounting to holdings of investee voting stock as small as 5% to 10%, contending that even such small investments create significant influence if the rest of the investee's stock is widely distributed.

An important observation is that *APB Opinion No. 18* does not absolutely require application of the equity method if 20% or more of the voting stock of an investee is held. *FASB Interpretation No. 35* provides guidance as to what types of evidence may overcome the presumption of significant influence arising at investment levels of 20% or more of the voting stock. Specifically, it provides five examples of evidence which tend to rebut the presumption of significant influence, even if 20% or more of the voting stock is held:

> *Opposition by the investee, such as litigation or complaints to governmental regulatory authorities, challenges the investor's ability to exercise significant influence.*

> *The investor and investee sign an agreement under which the investor surrenders significant rights as a shareholder.*

> *Majority ownership of the investee is concentrated among a small group of shareholders who operate the investee without regard to the views of the investor.*

> *The investor needs or wants more financial information to apply the equity method than is available to the investee's other shareholders (for example, the investor wants quarterly financial information from an investee that publicly reports only annually), tries to obtain that information, and fails.*

> *The investor tries and fails to obtain representation on the investee's board of directors.*[13]

Finally, although the test for significant influence is based on voting stock, the equity method is applied only to investments in common stock, whether or not it is voting stock. Thus, the investment level used to assess the existence of significant influence may differ from the investment level used in accounting for the investment.

A Basic Example of the Equity Method.   An investor applying the equity method bases the recognition of income and the accompanying increase in the investment account on the percentage of stock represented by the investment. The receipt of dividends is treated as a reduction of the carrying amount of the investor's investment account. The receipt of dividends represents a partial conversion of the investment to cash from equity in the investee's assets.

The following example illustrates accounting practices appropriate for the equity method. Assume that Stable Company acquires a 25% interest in the voting stock of Thomas Company on January 1, 1993. Also assume that Thomas Company has only one class of common stock, all of which is voting, and that both companies report on a calendar-year basis. If Stable paid $500,000 for the investment, and Thomas reports a net income of $100,000 for 1993 and pays a $20,000 dividend on December 31, 1993, the following entries are necessary:

---

[13]*FASB Interpretation No. 35*, "Criteria for Applying the Equity Method of Accounting for Investments in Common Stock: An Interpretation of APB Opinion No. 18," 1981, par. 4.

Jan. 1, 1993	Investment in Equity Securities	500,000	
	Cash		500,000
	(To record acquisition of 25% voting interest in Thomas Company.)		

Dec. 31, 1993	Investment in Equity Securities	25,000	
	Equity in Investee Income		25,000
	(To record equity in investee net income. $100,000 \times 25\% = \$25,000$.)		

Dec. 31, 1993	Cash	5,000	
	Investment in Equity Securities		5,000
	(To record receipt of dividend. $20,000 \times 25\% = \$5,000$.)		

Excerpts from the 1993 balance sheet and income statement of Stable Company would appear as follows:

Stable Company
PARTIAL BALANCE SHEET
December 31, 1993

Noncurrent assets
   Investment in equity securities $520,000
   ($500,000 + $25,000 − $5,000 = $520,000)

Stable Company
PARTIAL INCOME STATEMENT
For the Year Ended December 31, 1993

Other revenue
   Equity in investee income $25,000

The favorable impact of the investee's earnings are, thus, immediately reflected in the investor's financial statements. The dividends received by the investor are treated as a partial recovery or liquidation of the investment. Financial reporting for investments accounted for under the equity method contain many additional significant issues, and the following paragraphs discuss several of these.

The Existence of Positive and Negative Differential.   One issue arises in applying the equity method if the investor pays more or less for an investment than the book value of the underlying assets. For example, if the earning potential of the investee is abnormally high, the current value of the investee's net assets as represented by the market value of the investee's stock is frequently greater than the carrying amount on the investee's books.

If an excess amount is paid to acquire an equity interest in specifically identifiable undervalued assets, the difference is amortized over the individual lives of those assets. For example, assume that the book value of the net assets (assets minus liabilities) of Thomas Company in the previous example is $1,960,000 and that Stable Company acquires a 25% ownership interest for a cost of $500,000. A 25% ownership in Thomas' net assets, however, equals only $490,000 ($1,960,000 × 25%); therefore, Stable Company paid $10,000 more for the investment than is represented by the book value. If the management of Stable Company concludes that this differential represents an excess of the current value over the book value of Thomas Company's plant assets, which have a 10-year life, the following entry to amortize this differential is necessary at the end of each year.

Equity in Investee Income	1,000	
Investment in Equity Securities		1,000
($10,000 ÷ 10 years = $1,000)		

Combining this entry with those above results in $24,000 being included in the net income of the investor ($25,000 − $1,000) and an investment in the balance sheet of $519,000 [$500,000 + ($25,000 − $1,000) − $5,000]. After $1,000 has been amortized each year for 10 years, the $10,000 excess of cost over book value will have been fully amortized and that adjustment will no longer be necessary.

In practice, accountants frequently find it difficult to determine which specific assets are overvalued or undervalued and how much of the difference relates to general excess earning capacity. If the differential relates to excess earning capacity, rather than to specific assets, the excess is considered **goodwill.** *APB Opinion No. 17* specifies that amounts recorded for goodwill must be amortized over a period not to exceed 40 years.[14] Accountants frequently attribute all of the difference between the cost of an equity-method investment and the book value of the underlying net assets to goodwill because information about the value of specific assets is difficult to obtain.

Materiality   Furthermore, differences caused by this simplifying assumption are normally not material. Therefore, in most situations any excess of cost over the book value of the underlying assets is amortized as goodwill over a period no greater than 40 years. For example, in Stable Company's acquisition of Thomas Company—resulting in a $10,000 difference between cost and book value—if the $10,000 is interpreted as goodwill with a 20-year life, $500 would be amortized against the Equity in Investee Income account each year ($10,000/20 years = $500). Any **negative differential** (excess of book value acquired over investment cost) is usually amortized in a similar fashion; however, the amortization results in *increases,* rather than decreases, in Equity in Investee Income and Investment in Equity Securities.

Investee Operating Losses.   Another significant accounting issue arises if an investee company incurs operating losses to such an extent that application of the equity method reduces the investor's asset account to zero. To illustrate, assume that Thomas Company incurs $50,000 net loss; then Stable Company prepares the following entry:

Equity in Investee Loss	12,500	
Investment in Equity Securities		12,500
($50,000 × 25% = $12,500)		

This entry is appropriate unless it brings the investment account to a credit (negative) balance. Investors ordinarily discontinue applying the equity method if the investment account reaches zero, unless the investor (1) has guaranteed the indebtedness of the investee or (2) is otherwise committed to provide financial support. For example, if the stock of the investee was acquired from the investee at less than par, then the investor may be obligated (in the event of investee dissolution) to contribute amounts that would make the investment equal to the par value of the stock. In such cases the Investment account may properly contain a credit balance and be reported as a liability to the extent of any contingent obligation.

---

[14]*APB Opinion No. 17,* "Intangible Assets," 1970, par. 29. The subject of goodwill and amortization of goodwill are covered in greater depth in Chapter 13.

The investor may suspend the use of the equity method because the recognition of investee net losses reduces the investment balance to zero and therefore the conditions (described earlier) that would require the continued recognition of investee losses do not apply. The investor should resume applying the equity method if the investee becomes profitable again only after its share of the net income equals the net losses that were not recognized during the period of suspension.

Sale of an Investment.   When all or part of an equity-method investment is sold, the seller removes the appropriate percentage of the existing investment balance and determines a gain or loss by comparing the proceeds from the sale with that amount. For example, Stable Company owned 10,000 shares of Alexander, Inc., common stock, representing 40% of Alexander's voting stock. Stable has appropriately applied the equity method, and the investment balance at the time of sale was $125,000, including the original cost and adjusted for Stable's share of Alexander's net incomes and net losses, dividends, and amortization of positive and negative differential. If Stable sells 2,000 of the shares on June 1, 1993, for $35,000, the following entry is required:

June 1, 1993 Cash	35,000	
Investment in Equity Securities		25,000
($\frac{2}{10} \times$ $125,000)		
Gain on Sale of Equity Securities		10,000

The $10,000 gain represents the excess of the $35,000 received over a pro-rata share (2/10 or 20%) of the carrying amount of the investment. Since 2,000 of 10,000 shares are being sold, 2/10 of the carrying value of the investment, or $25,000, is taken out of the investment account. If the entire investment had been sold, the entire investment account would have been eliminated at $125,000 and compared with the cash received to determine the amount of gain or loss.

The equity method is a complicated accounting procedure which involves application principles beyond the scope of this textbook. For example, the two companies involved may have intercompany transactions that require elimination. Also, the percentage of stock held by the investor may change and, as a result, the investor may be required to change to or from the equity method. These procedures are generally given greater attention in advanced accounting texts which provide in-depth coverage of business combinations and consolidated financial statements.

Disclosure   **Equity-Method Disclosures.**   *APB Opinion No. 18* requires the following disclosures for investments in common stock when such investments are significant to the financial position and results of operations of the investor:[15]

1. Name of each investee.
2. Percentage of ownership of common stock.
3. Accounting policies with respect to the investment. (In cases where 20% or more of the voting stock is held and the equity method **is not used** or where less than 20% of the voting stock is held and the equity method **is used,** the following should be disclosed: name of the investee and the reason(s) for departure from the 20% guideline.)
4. Difference between investor's carrying value and the underlying equity in net assets, and the accounting treatment for this difference.
5. Aggregate value, based on quoted market price, of the investment in common stock of each identified investee which is not a subsidiary.

---

[15]*APB Opinion No. 18*, par. 20.

EXHIBIT 10–12

Whirlpool Corporation
Equity Method Disclosures

(5) Affiliated Companies The Company has direct voting interests, ranging from 17% to 49%, in three Brazilian companies (Brastemp S.A., Embraco S.A. and Consul S.A.) engaged in the manufacture and sale of major home appliances and related component parts and in Vitromatic, S.A. de C.V., a Mexican manufacturer of home appliances. Other significant investments include an interest in Brasmotor S.A., a Brazilian holding company that has interests in Brastemp S.A., Embraco S.A. and Consul S.A.

Equity in the net earnings (losses) of affiliated companies is as follows:

(millions of dollars)	1990	1989	1988
Brazilian affiliates	$ (27)	$ 32	$ 16
Mexican affiliate	(3)	8	3
Other	3	2	—
	(27)	42	$ 19
Less foreign withholding and related federal income taxes	(6)	(4)	(4)
	$ (33)	$ 38	$ 15

Brazilian equity losses for 1990 were partially offset by the reversal of litigation and other non-operating reserves that were established in 1989. In 1990, the Company recorded a $12 million charge against equity earnings of its Mexican affiliate as described in Note 9.

Combined financial information for all affiliated foreign operating companies follows:

(millions of dollars)	1990	1989	1988
Current assets	$ 535	$ 541	$ 422
Other assets	706	602	471
	$1,241	$1,143	$ 893
Current liabilities	$ 342	$ 345	$ 246
Other liabilities	185	117	87
Stockholders' equity	714	681	560
	$1,241	$1,143	$ 893
Net sales	$1,823	$1,554	$ 934
Cost of products sold	$1,518	$1,226	$ 770
Net earnings (losses)	$ (74)	$ 126	$ 48
Whirlpool share of foreign currency translation gains (losses) included in operating results	$ 32	$ (46)	$ (11)
Dividends and fees paid to Whirlpool by affiliates	$ 10	$ 13	$ 11

SOURCE: Whirlpool Corporation, 1990 Annual Report.

6. Summarized financial information of investees (either individually or combined).
7. Material effects of the possible exercise of options or warrants, possible conversions, etc.

Exhibit 10–12 includes the equity-method disclosures from the 1990 annual report of Whirlpool Corporation. Whirlpool is a manufacturer and marketer of major home appliances. The company manufactures in 10 countries and markets in over 45 countries under several well-known brand names, including *Whirlpool, KitchenAid,*

Roper and *Kenmore* (through Sears, Roebuck and Co.). Whirlpool's assets in the balance sheet include "Affiliated Companies" under an investments caption totaling $281 million in 1990 and $299 in 1989. These amounts represent the balances resulting from applying the equity method, as described in the financial statement note identifying accounting policies employed in the preparation of the statements. The disclosure in Exhibit 10–12 includes selected balance sheet and income statement information of the affiliated companies which is intended to comply with the disclosure requirements identified above.

Equity Investments Representing Control of Investee

If a company acquires an investment in the voting stock of an investee that exceeds 50%, the investor is presumed to be capable of **controlling** the investee's operating and financial policies. The investor is then called the **parent** and the investee is called the **subsidiary.** In such circumstances accountants prepare **consolidated financial statements** for the two entities rather than separate financial statements for each. This practice is based on the position that the two separate legal entities represent only one *economic* entity as a result of the majority investment. Therefore, financial reporting reflects the economic reality—not the mere legal form of organization—by consolidating the financial statements of the companies. Accounting and reporting practices underlying consolidated financial statements, while similar to the equity method, are discussed at length in advanced accounting texts and are discussed here only briefly.[16]

Substance over Form

Consolidating the financial statements of two or more corporations involves aggregating the adjusted trial balances of each company after eliminating the residual effects of all intercompany transactions. Such transactions may involve buying and selling, lending and borrowing, and investing activities. Furthermore, *consolidated net income* generally remains the same whether the investor applies the equity method to the investee or fully consolidates the investee into a complete set of consolidated financial statements. The difference between the equity method and the **consolidation method** is, one of the degree of detail disclosed and not one of earnings measurement. Under the equity method, only a single asset account and revenue account are presented in the investor's financial statements which represent the investment in the investee. Hence, the equity method is frequently called a **single-line consolidation.** The consolidation approach requires adding the specific individual asset, liability, revenue, and expense accounts of the subsidiary to those of the parent for financial reporting purposes. Any **minority interest**—outstanding stock held by individuals or entities other than the parent company—is usually included as part of the stockholders' equity of the consolidated entity.

The annual reports of many major companies include consolidated financial statements. The 1989 annual report to stockholders of The Dow Chemical Company provides an excellent example. Dow Chemical is a diversified, worldwide supplier of chemicals, plastics, consumer specialties and other products. All of the financial statements are titled with the word "consolidated," such as the consolidated statement of cash flows. The summary of significant accounting policies includes the following statement: "The accompanying consolidated financial statements include the assets, liabilities, revenues and expenses of all majority-owned subsidiaries. Investments in companies 20%–50% owned are carried on the equity basis."

---

[16]For an excellent discussion of financial accounting and reporting for various business combinations, see Arnold J. Pahler and Joseph E. Mori, *Advanced Accounting: Concepts and Practice,* 4th ed. (San Diego: Harcourt Brace Jovanovich, 1991).

NONCURRENT INVESTMENTS IN DEBT SECURITIES

A company may acquire the debt securities of other businesses as long-term invest-ments for such reasons as (1) accumulating liquid resources for some noncurrent pur-pose, and (2) earning an acceptable rate of return on those liquid resources during the accumulation process. These objectives contrast with the purposes of making short-term investments in debt securities; that is, to invest temporarily excess cash for a short period of time. Because of these differing investment objectives, accounting practices for noncurrent debt investments differ from those appropriate for current debt investments.

Recording Bond Investments

When a company acquires the debt securities of another company as a noncurrent in-vestment, the acquisition price frequently differs from the maturity value of the debt instrument. The rate of interest stated on a security, which was established when it was issued, may have become unrealistic as a result of changing economic conditions in money markets, changes in the risk class of the company issuing the bond, or other factors. In such cases, buyers are willing to pay more or less for the security than its stated or face value. If this occurs, the difference between the cash paid to acquire a security and the face value of the security is viewed as an adjustment of the security's stated rate of interest. *Accounting Principles Board Opinion No. 21* deals with this par-ticular phenomenon and many other areas of financial accounting.[17]

In general, investments in bonds and notes receivable are recorded at the fair market value of the consideration given for the security. When debt securities are ac-quired solely for cash, their value is presumed to be the amount of cash paid. If a secu-rity is exchanged for *noncash consideration,* the fair market value of the noncash consideration is presumed to represent the present value of the security. If the fair market value of the noncash consideration is not determinable, however, we must then select an appropriate interest rate and compute the present value of the security by using techniques described in Chapter 6. In such cases, the interest rate to be used in valuing the transaction can be affected by several considerations, such as the credit standing of the issuer, any restrictive covenants in the security, tax consequences, and collateral. Prevailing rates of interest for similar securities of issuers with similar credit ratings also help in the selection of an appropriate interest rate for determining the present value. The objective in selecting an interest rate is to approximate the rate that would have been incurred in an arm's-length transaction involving lending of cash.

In some circumstances, a stated rate of interest may not represent the rate that would exist in an arm's-length transaction. For example, the existence of related parties and related-party transactions may indicate that the stated rate of interest is not reasonable. In such situations, stated or unstated rights and privileges may alter the effective (or actual) rate of interest. If a right to abnormal purchase or sales dis-counts is granted as part of the consideration for a loan, the difference between the present value of the security and the cash loaned is properly regarded as an element of interest and the effective rate of interest implicit in such notes will differ from the stated rate.

Substance over Form

Accounting for Premium and Discount

Any **premium** or **discount** recognized in conjunction with a debt investment is treated as a direct increase (premium) or reduction (discount) in the carrying amount

---

[17]*APB Opinion No. 21,* "Interest on Receivables and Payables," 1971.

of that investment. That is, a debt investment is originally presented in the balance sheet at its present value, its market value when it is acquired. The related premium or discount is then amortized as an adjustment to interest revenue over the life of the security by using the effective rate of interest.[18] The effective rate of interest is represented by the discount rate that equates the purchase price with the two future cash flows (interest payments and maturity amount) obtainable from the investment. We apply the effective rate of interest to the carrying value at the beginning of each period to determine annual interest. In this manner a constant rate of interest is recognized over the life of the investment. The difference between the total interest revenue, determined by applying the effective rate of interest to the carrying amount and the cash received during the period represents the amount of premium or discount to be amortized. This is consistent with amortization practices discussed in Chapter 6.

Materiality   The straight-line method of amortizing premium or discount is not acceptable unless the results of applying that method are not materially different from the **effective interest method** (also called the **compound interest method** or the **interest method**) described above.

A Comprehensive Example

The following example illustrates the provisions of *APB Opinion No. 21* as applied to noncurrent investments in debt securities. Later chapters illustrate applications of this important pronouncement in other circumstances.

Assume that Stable Company acquires ten $1,000 bonds of the Leverage Company on January 1, 1991, as a long-term investment at 89.2 (i.e., at 89.2% of the face amount). The bonds mature in five years and bear a stated rate of interest of 9% payable annually on December 31. The following entry would record the acquisition of the bonds:

Jan. 1, 1991	Investment in Bonds	10,000	
	Discount on Bond Investment		1,080
	Cash		8,920

The computations are as follows:

$1,000 \times 10$	= $10,000	Face amount
$1,000 \times 10 \times 89.2\%$ =	(8,920)	Cash paid
	$ 1,080	Discount

The determination of the interest rate (12%) implicit in this transaction requires trial and error, because it represents a present-value problem involving both an annuity and a single amount. To illustrate, note that when Stable bought the Leverage bonds, rights to two cash flows were acquired:

1. Interest payments of $900 (9% × $1,000 × 10) per year for five years.
2. The maturity value of $10,000 at the end of five years.

Since the Stable Company is willing to pay only $8,920 for both of these rights, there is some interest rate (r) that will equate both future cash flows (interest and principal) with the investment price or present value (PV) of $8,920. The equation may be expressed as follows:

PV of the interest payment annuity for five years at r rate
+ PV of the maturity value in five years at r rate = PV of total investment

---

[18]*APB Opinion No. 21*, par. 15.

In the case of Stable Company, the equation would become:

$900 yearly for five years at r + $10,000 in five years at r = $8,920

Both the present values of an annuity (series of interest payments) and an amount (single principal payment) are involved, so we must estimate the effective rate by using the present-value tables in Chapter 6. Since the bonds were acquired below par value, the effective rate is logically greater than the stated rate of 9%.

Trying 12%, we compute as follows:

($900 × 3.60478*) + ($10,000 × .56743**) ≈ $8,920
$3,244 + $5,674 ≈ $8,920
$8,918 ≈ $8,920

---

*3.60478 is the present value of 5 payments of $1 at 12%. See Table 6–4.
**.56743 is the present value of a single $1 due five years from now at 12%. See Table 6–2.

The effective interest rate of 12% approximately equates both of the future cash flows with the amount paid for the investment and is therefore the effective rate of interest. If a higher or lower rate had been selected originally, then the computation would have failed to equate the two numbers, thereby requiring the testing of different rates until the equation was satisfied.

At the end of the year, the 9% interest payment is received and a portion of the discount on the bonds is amortized:

Dec. 31, 1991	Cash	900	
	Interest Revenue		900
	(9% × $10,000 = $900 interest)		
Dec. 31, 1991	Discount on Bond Investment	170	
	Interest Revenue		170
	(To record amortization of discount.		
	$8,920 × 12% = $1,070;		
	$1,070 − $900 = $170.)		

During the first year of the investment, 12% is earned on the carrying amount of the investment. Since the carrying amount of the investment during the year is $8,920, then $1,070 ($8,920.00 × 12%) total interest revenue is earned. Only $900 ($10,000 × 9%) is received in cash, however, and the difference of $170 ($1,070 − $900) represents the amount of discount to be amortized. Exhibit 10–13 presents an amortization table developed for Stable Company as an aid to accounting for this investment.

At the end of the second year the effective interest rate (12%) is applied to investment's carrying amount at the beginning of the *second* period. Because $170 of discount was amortized at the end of the first year, the carrying amount of the investment increased by that amount as demonstrated in the following computation:

Investment in Bonds	$10,000
Discount at Jan. 1, 1992 ($1,080 − $170)	910
Carrying amount at Jan. 1, 1992	$ 9,090

The carrying amount of the investment is $9,090 at the beginning of the second year. By multiplying the carrying value of the note by the effective interest rate (12%), we compute the total interest revenue for the second year to be $1,091. Again, since $900 of this amount is received in cash, the difference of $191 ($1,091 − $900)

EXHIBIT 10–13

Amortization Table for Investment in Bonds at Discount

Date	Explanation	(1) (12% carrying value [Col. 6]) Total Interest Revenue	(2) (9% × $10,000) Cash Received	(3) (Col. 1– Col. 2) Discount To Be Amortized	(4) Face Amount of Bonds	(5) (Reduced by Col. 3) Remaining Discount	(6) (Col. 4– Col. 5) Carrying Amount
Jan. 1, 1991	Acquisition of bonds	—	—	—	$10,000	$1,080	$8,920
Dec. 31, 1991	Recognition of interest	$1,070	$900	$170	10,000	910	9,090
Dec. 31, 1992	Recognition of interest	1,091	900	191	10,000	719	9,281
Dec. 31, 1993	Recognition of interest	1,114	900	214	10,000	505	9,495
Dec. 31, 1994	Recognition of interest	1,139	900	239	10,000	266	9,734
Dec. 31, 1995	Recognition of interest	1,166*	900	266	10,000	—	10,000

*Minor rounding adjustment in 1995 figures to eliminate remaining discount.

represents the amount of discount to be amortized as additional interest revenue. This process continues each year until all of the discount has been amortized and the bonds mature with the discount fully amortized, no gain or loss is recognized at the maturity of the bonds as reflected in Exhibit 10–13. The carrying value of the investment at the maturity date is $10,000.

If the straight-line method of amortization had been used in this example, the amount of amortization would be $216 ($1,080/5) per year. As in the effective interest method, the carrying amount of the bond investment would increase to $10,000, except the increase would accumulate in equal increments of $216. Compared to the effective interest method, the straight-line method is conceptually inferior. The interest revenue is overstated in the earlier years and understated in the latter years for a bond purchased at a discount. The opposite pattern would hold for bonds purchased at a premium. As a result, the straight-line amortization method is not generally acceptable unless the periodic difference between it and the effective interest method is

Materiality   immaterial.

How would these procedures differ if the bonds had been acquired at a **price greater than par value?** The effective interest rate would be less than the stated rate. This rate is applied to the carrying amount of the investment to determine interest revenue for the period, which would be an amount less than the cash received. The difference between the interest revenue and the cash received is amortized as a *reduction* in the carrying amount of the investment. As in the case of an investment acquired at a discount, the straight-line method of amortization is appropriate only if it

Materiality   renders amounts that do not vary materially from those obtained from the effective interest method.

To illustrate, assume that Stable Company acquired the $10,000 par value bonds at $10,400, which results in an approximate effective interest rate of 8%. The journal entries to record the acquisition of the bonds on January 1, 1991, and to recognize interest revenue at December 31, 1991, are as follows:

Jan. 1, 1991	Investment in Bonds	10,000	
	Premium on Bond Investment	400	
	Cash		10,400
Dec. 31, 1991	Cash	900	
	Interest Revenue ($10,400 × 8%)		832
	Premium on Bond Investment		68

The December 31, 1991, entry reduces the Premium on Bond Investment to $332 ($400 − $68), and interest revenue for 1992 is computed as $827 ($10,332 × 8%). If straight-line amortization were applied, annual amortization of the premium would be $80 ($400/5 years).

In both the discount and premium examples illustrated above we have debited the Investment in Bonds account for the par value of the bonds and used a separate Discount or Premium on Bond Investment account for the difference between the acquisition price of the investment and the par value of the bonds. The Investment in Bonds account and the Discount or Premium on Investment account are usually combined for presentation in the balance sheet and may be combined in the company's records as well. If the investment is carried in a single investment account rather than in separate accounts as illustrated here, amortization of any discount or premium is made directly to the Investment account. In the previous example, if a single investment account were used rather than one account for the face value and another for the premium (or discount), the following entries would have been appropriate:

Jan. 1, 1991	Investment in Bonds	10,400	
	Cash		10,400
Dec. 31, 1991	Cash	900	
	Interest Revenue		832
	Investment in Bonds		68

In this text and in the problem material at the end of this chapter, we assume that a separate Discount or Premium account is used **unless otherwise indicated.** The separate Discount or Premium account is then combined with the Investment account into a single amount for balance sheet presentation.

Sale of Debt Investments

If the bonds are sold before their maturity date, a gain or loss may arise. Because any premium or discount recognized at the acquisition of the bond has been subject to amortization since acquisition, the amount of gain or loss depends in part on the remaining unamortized premium or discount. Returning to the previous example where Stable purchased bonds for $8,920, including a $1,080 discount, assume that Stable sells the Leverage bonds on June 30, 1993, for $10,200 plus accrued interest. The following entries would be necessary to update the accounts:

June 30, 1993	Interest Receivable	450	
	Interest Revenue		450
	(To accrue interest for January 1–June 30, 1993.		
	$10,000 × 9% × $6/12$ = $450.)		
June 30, 1993	Discount on Bond Investment	107	
	Interest Revenue		107
	(To amortize discount on bonds for the period		
	Jan. 1, 1993 through June 30, 1993.)		

Calculations for the discount are as follows:

$$\$9,281 \times 12\% \times \text{^{6}/\textsubscript{12}} = \$557$$
$$\text{Less: Amount to be received in cash} \quad (450)$$
$$\text{Discount to be amortized} \quad \underline{\$107}$$

This amount may also be determined as ½ of the 1993 amortization in Exhibit 10–13 (½ × $214). A third entry would be required to record the sale:

June 30, 1993	Cash	10,650	
	Discount on Bond Investment	612	
	Gain on Sale of Bonds		812
	Investment in Bonds		10,000
	Interest Receivable		450

(To record receipt of cash, $10,200 + $450 = $10,650; elimination of remaining discount, $719 − $107 = $612; elimination of investment in bonds; and recognition of gain.)

The gain of $812 can be verified as follows:

Cash received, excluding interest		$10,200
Carrying amount of investment at June 30, 1993:		
Face value	$10,000	
Unamortized discount ($719 − $107)	(612)	(9,388)
Gain on sale of investment		$ 812

In this illustration we have assumed that the entire investment in the bonds held by Stable Company was sold. If only part of the bonds had been sold, the entries to record interest receivable, amortization of discount, and the sale would be made for only that part of the investment that was sold. For example, if 4 of the 10 bonds had been sold, only $180 of interest revenue would be recognized ($450 × 40%); only $43 of bond discount amortization would be recognized ($107 × 40%); and a gain of only $325 would be recognized ($812 × 40%).

In the above illustration, the bond investment was sold at a gain because the cash received was *greater than* the carrying amount (face value, less the unamortized discount). Had the cash received been *less than* the carrying amount, a loss would have been recognized on the sale equal to the difference between the cash received and the carrying amount.

ADDITIONAL INVESTMENT CONSIDERATIONS

Several additional investment instruments may be held by companies and classified as marketable equity securities. Specifically, stock purchase warrants and stock rights may be held by an investing company and included in the current or noncurrent marketable equity securities portfolio. Also, an investor may receive shares of stock through the issuance of stock dividends and stock splits by the investee, adding to the number of shares held by the investor. In this section, we introduce these situations briefly and consider them from the perspective of the investor. In Chapters 15, 16 and

17, we cover these topics in greater depth when we consider them from the perspective of the issuing company. In this section, we also introduce accounting for the cash surrender value of life insurance and the accumulation of cash in a fund for a specified future purpose, such as retirement of long-term debt.

STOCK PURCHASE WARRANTS

Stock purchase warrants convey to the holder the ability to buy a given number of shares of stock at a stated price for a specified period of time. These warrants are often issued when a company sells bonds or stock to make the primary securities more attractive.

When an investor acquires a stock purchase warrant along with another security such as a bond or share of preferred stock, we must allocate the price paid between the two securities. This is accomplished by using the relative market values of the two securities as indicated in the following formula:

$$\begin{array}{c}\text{Allocated cost} \\ \text{of stock} \\ \text{warrants}\end{array} = \frac{\text{Fair market value of warrants}}{\left(\begin{array}{c}\text{Fair market} \\ \text{value of} \\ \text{warrants}\end{array}\right) + \left(\begin{array}{c}\text{Fair market} \\ \text{value of} \\ \text{other security}\end{array}\right)} \times \begin{array}{c}\text{Total cost} \\ \text{of} \\ \text{investment}\end{array}$$

For example, assume that Stable Company purchases ten $1,000 bonds for $1,050 each and receives with every bond 10 detachable stock purchase warrants, each of which may be used to acquire one additional share of common stock. Immediately after the securities are acquired, separate markets arise for the warrants and the bonds because the warrants are detachable and the two securities can sell separately. The fair market value of each bond is $1,025, while the fair market value of each warrant is $5. The following calculation is necessary to allocate the total cost:

$$\text{Cost of warrants} = \frac{\$5 \times 100 \text{ warrants}}{\left[\begin{array}{c}(\$5 \times 100 \text{ warrants}) \\ + \\ (\$1,025 \times 10 \text{ bonds})\end{array}\right]} \times (\$1,050 \times 10 \text{ bonds})$$

$$= \$488.37$$

The following entry records the acquisition of the two securities:

Investment in Bonds	10,012	
Stock Purchase Warrants	488	
Cash		10,500
(To record acquisition of bonds with stock purchase warrants.)		

Each warrant has an allocated cost of $4.88 ($488 ÷ 100). Since the life of most warrants is limited, they must be exercised or sold, or else they become worthless.

To illustrate the accounting for stock warrants subsequent to purchase, assume that the bond investor exercises half of the warrants (50 warrants). Further assume that the investor can exercise each warrant by paying $50 for one share of common stock. The journal entry would appear as follows:

Marketable Equity Securities	2,744	
Stock Purchase Warrants (50 × $4.88)		244
Cash ($50 × 50)		2,500
(To exercise 50 stock purchase warrants.)		

The market price of the stock when the warrants are exercised does not determine the cost of the stock acquired. Rather, the cost is determined by the $4.88 allocated cost of the warrant, plus the $50 cash paid when the warrant was exercised. If the remaining 50 warrants are sold for $6 each, a gain is recognized as follows:

Cash (50 × $6)	300	
Stock Purchase Warrants (50 × $4.88)		244
Gain on Sale of Warrants		56
(To record the sale of the remaining warrants.)		

Warrants that expire unexercised or unsold are eliminated from the accounting records by recognizing a loss equal to the allocated cost of the expired warrants. To illustrate, assume that the investor allowed the 50 warrants that were not exercised in the previous example to expire rather than selling them. A loss is recognized as follows:

Loss on Expiration of Stock Purchase Warrants	244	
Stock Purchase Warrants		244
(To record expiration of warrants.)		

STOCK RIGHTS

Stock rights are distributed by a corporation to employees or shareholders on a pro rata basis to permit them to maintain their proportionate interest in the corporation pursuant to a new stock issue. Although one right is usually issued for each share held, the number of rights required to purchase an additional share depends on the terms of the offering. Rather than exercise the right to purchase additional shares, the stockholder may choose instead to sell the rights on the open market.

When stock rights are received, the accountant for the investor allocates the cost of the original stock investment between (1) the original investment and (2) the rights just received. This allocation should be based on the relative fair market values of the rights and the stock at the time the rights are received. When separate stock rights are issued, a market price will exist for them as well as for the related stock because the two securities can be traded separately. The following formula should be used to determine the amount to be assigned to the rights:

$$\text{Allocated cost of rights} = \frac{\text{Fair market value of rights}}{\left(\begin{array}{c}\text{Fair market}\\ \text{value of}\\ \text{rights}\end{array}\right) + \left(\begin{array}{c}\text{Fair market}\\ \text{value of}\\ \text{stock}\end{array}\right)} \times \text{Total cost of investment}$$

For example, assume that Stable Company acquires 100 shares of Cypress Company's common stock for $75 per share and later receives a stock right for each share of stock held. If the market value of the rights is $5 per right and the value of the stock is $88¾ per share at the time the rights are received, the following calculation is necessary:

$$\text{Allocated cost of rights} = \frac{(100 \times \$5)}{(100 \times \$5) + (100 \times \$88.75)} \times (100 \times \$75) = \$400$$

A journal entry is then made to reflect the allocation of cost to the new investment:

Investment in Stock Rights	400	
Investment in Common Stock		400
(To record receipt of stock rights.)		

If the rights are sold, a gain or loss is recognized if the proceeds from the sale differ from the allocated cost of $4 per right ($400/100 = $4). If the rights are exercised and new shares are acquired, the cost of the new shares is calculated as the $4 allocated cost of the rights plus the additional amount paid for the shares. If the rights expire and become worthless, then the Investment in Stock Rights account is eliminated with a loss recognized equal to the allocated cost. The loss represents the dilution of the ownership interest experienced by the investor because of nonexercise of the rights. The journal entries to account for the disposition of stock rights whether they are exercised, sold or allowed to expire are similar to those for stock purchase warrants presented in the previous section.

STOCK DIVIDENDS AND STOCK SPLITS

Occasionally a company may receive shares of stock of the investee company by issuance of a *stock dividend* or *stock split.* In such cases, the recipient (investor) of the additional stock makes no accounting entry. Rather, a memorandum is written to indicate that the original investment cost must now be allocated over the greater number of shares, thereby *lowering the cost per share.*

To illustrate, assume that Stable Company holds 200 shares of Hill Company's common stock that were purchased for $11,000 ($55 a share) when Hill declares a 10% stock dividend. Stable will receive an additional 20 shares (200 × 10%) of Hill stock. Subsequent to the dividend, Stable holds 220 shares of stock at a cost of $11,000, or $50 per share ($11,000/220 = $50). If 50 shares are then sold for $60 per share, the following entry is appropriate:

Cash (50 × $60)	3,000	
Investment in Common Stock (50 × $50)		2,500
Gain on Sale of Stock		500
(To record sale of 50 shares of Hill Company's common		
stock.)		

The remaining 170 shares (220 − 50) of Hill stock are carried on Stable's books at $8,500 ($11,000 − $2,500), or $50 per share ($8,500/170 = $50).

If Hill Company had issued a stock split rather than a stock dividend, the same procedure would be followed. However, the increase in shares would have been much greater than 10%; for example, it could have been 100% or 200%.

CASH SURRENDER VALUE OF LIFE INSURANCE

A company may insure the lives of key executives and name the company as beneficiary. The purpose of this arrangement is to compensate the company for the loss of services arising from the untimely death of important members of management.

Two forms of insurance are commonly used: term and whole life insurance. With **term life insurance,** the company is simply buying protection for the loss of the insured individual. The insurance does not represent an investment and the premiums are ordinarily expensed as paid. **Whole life,** on the other hand, has the unique feature of accumulating cash surrender value in addition to providing insurance protection. The cash surrender value represents an investment to the company in that it can borrow the accumulated cash value from the insurance company or terminate the policy and receive the cash surrender value outright.

When a company pays an annual premium on whole life insurance, part of the premium is recognized as Insurance Expense. The remaining portion represents an increase in cash surrender value and should, therefore, be recognized as an increase in an investment asset. The amount of the annual premium reflecting an increase in the cash surrender value is specified by the insurance contract. The insurance contract will frequently include a schedule of cash surrender values listed by the number of years the policy has been in effect. On the financial statements of the investing company, the cash surrender value should be disclosed as a noncurrent asset, because corporations do not usually intend to terminate insurance policies within the operating cycle.

To illustrate the accounting for cash surrender values, assume Stable Company takes out a whole life policy, naming the company as beneficiary. The insurance contract calls for coverage of $200,000 on the life of Stable's chief executive officer (CEO) in return for premiums of $3,500 per year. The cash surrender value schedule indicates the cash value increases for the first three years as follows:

End of Coverage Year	Cash Surrender Value
1	–0–
2	$ 500
3	1,100

Because the first year's premium does not result in an increased cash surrender value, the entire $3,500 premium is debited to Insurance Expense when paid. The following journal entries record the second and third years' premiums:

Insurance Expense	3,000	
Cash Surrender Value of Life Insurance	500	
Cash		3,500
Insurance Expense	2,900	
Cash Surrender Value of Life Insurance ($1,100 − $500)	600	
Cash		3,500

Notice that the increase in the cash surrender value is debited to an investment account, Cash Surrender Value of Life Insurance, and the remainder of the $3,500 premium is debited to Insurance Expense.

If Stable's CEO died at the end of the fifth year of coverage when the cash surrender value was $3,700, the following journal entry would be necessary to record the receipt of the death benefit:

Cash	200,000	
Cash Surrender Value of Life Insurance		3,700
Gain from Life Insurance Settlement		196,300

A corporation may also establish life insurance coverage for the benefit of employees and their named beneficiaries. Since this type of insurance is for the benefit of the employee, not the company, all of the premium is considered a form of compensation expense. Any accumulation of cash surrender value belongs to the employee and should not be identified as a company asset.

FUNDS

Business enterprises establish special funds for a variety of purposes, including bond or other debt redemption, future plant expansion, and pension commitments. When such funds are established, several significant accounting and reporting issues arise.

Fund assets may be held and managed by corporate personnel, or fund resources may be transferred to a **fiscal agent** or **trustee,** such as a bank, for administration. Although many long-term special funds are created in compliance with such things as contractual provisions, bond indentures, or covenants in debt instruments or pension plans, others are the result of internal management decisions.

To illustrate, assume that Stable Company management decides to create a bond-retirement fund in the amount of $10,000; the following entry would be necessary:

Bond-Retirement Fund Cash	10,000	
Cash		10,000
(To establish bond-retirement fund.)		

If the Stable Company management decides to acquire treasury bills so that the fund will earn interest, the investment is recorded at cost:

Bond-Retirement Fund Investment	10,000	
Bond-Retirement Fund Cash		10,000
(To record acquisition of treasury bills by bond-retirement fund.)		

Subsequent accounting for investments made by such a fund follow the principles previously described and depend on the nature, extent, and investment objectives of the fund. Dividends and interest earned on fund investments are debited to the Bond-Retirement Fund Investment account.

When fund assets are transferred to a fiscal agent, the fund assets and related liabilities may be excluded from the financial statements. Liabilities are excluded only to the extent that the company's obligations have been discharged. Pension-fund assets and liabilities are frequently accounted for in this manner. Bond sinking funds and related bonds payable are normally reported in corporate financial statements, however, even if sinking-fund assets have been transferred to a fiscal agent. Although a fund may consist of a variety of assets, such as cash and investments in several types of securities, all these assets normally are aggregated into a single account for balance sheet presentation.

A fund is usually created by an original contribution and augmented by additional contributions and the earnings of the fund itself. If a company desires to accumulate a certain amount in the fund by some specific date, it will need estimates of the earning power of the assets in the fund in order to ascertain the specific amount of the contributions. The company may then use present-value techniques to determine the future contribution necessary to accumulate the desired amount. The accountant should monitor the performance of the fund in terms of earnings and contributions to ascertain whether the fund is accumulating resources at the level anticipated in the

THE BANKERS' NEW HEADACHE

How's this for bizarre accounting? Suppose you're carrying wide neckties in inventory at cost, $4 million. Suddenly skinny ties become fashionable and the value of your wide tie inventory drops to $1 million. You keep the old ties on the books at $4 million, arguing to your accountants that wide ties will be fashionable again someday, and you'll be able to realize their historical value then—all the time selling off wide ties for less than their carrying value.

Something similar to this has been common practice among banks, savings and loans and other financial institutions for years. The game isn't played with neckties, of course. It's played with their huge portfolios of fixed-income securities. Here's how:

When a financial institution buys debt securities, it generally allocates them to either a long-term "investment" account, or a short-term "trading" account. The accountants let the institution keep "investment" securities on the books at historical cost, on the theory that the company plans to hold them until maturity, when they can be redeemed at par.

By contrast, "trading" securities have to be carried at current market value. If interest rates fall and the values of the securities rise, earnings and capital surplus are credited. But if rates rise and the securities' values fall, the drop must be charged against earnings and surplus. Reported earnings can thus fluctuate violently, even if no securities are sold.

In the past, banks and thrifts have protected themselves against writing up and down their portfolios by putting most of their securities into "investment" accounts. But then they buy and sell the securities anyway. This stabilizes reported earnings—but at a cost of misstating the value of the bonds on the balance sheet. If interest rates rise and bond prices plunge, a bank's or a thrift's assets look as strong as ever—though they're not. It's akin to carrying those wide ties in inventory at pre-skinny-tie prices.

Worse, financial institutions can (and do) easily bury investment losses by "cherry picking"—selling the securities that have appreciated, while quietly sitting on those that are worth less than the balance sheet says.

Consider Columbia Savings & Loan, whose chairman, Thomas Spiegel, just resigned under attack for investing too much of its portfolio in risky junk bonds. At the end of 1988 Columbia had $8.7 billion of fixed-income securities. Of that, only $320 million, or 4%, was carried at market values. The rest, deemed investment securities, was carried at cost.

Was Columbia holding its investments until they matured? Hardly. In 1988 the thrift sold over $5 billion of fixed-income securities—more than half its portfolio. Gains from selling the securities amounted to almost two-thirds of pretax earnings, $83 million. Recently, Columbia got a taste of how much market valuation can hurt. In August Congress required thrifts to divest themselves of their junk bonds within five years. Under generally accepted accounting principles, assets held for sale have to be valued at the lower of cost or market. On Sept. 30 Columbia marked its junk bond portfolio down to market value, taking a $351 million writeoff.

Columbia is not an isolated case. Virtually all of the thrift industry's profits over the last five years came from selling investment securities. Yet at the end of 1988 the top 30 thrifts had only 2% of their assets in trading or held-for-sale accounts.

What of the big commercial banks? They, too, allot most of their securities to "investment" accounts. For

---

original present-value calculation. If fund assets earn at a level higher than anticipated, the remaining contributions may be reduced. Conversely, if the fund performs more poorly than planned, the company must increase its contributions to meet its goals for the fund. The techniques incident to evaluating the earnings performance of a fund involve the compound interest concepts discussed in Chapter 6.

MARKET VALUE: AN ALTERNATIVE TO PRACTICE

Many accounting theorists have advocated accounting for marketable securities at market value, without regard to the relationship of that value to historical cost. The primary virtue of accounting for marketable securities at market value is to provide decision makers with current and useful information that reports the economic consequences of holding investments during an accounting period. This method would require revaluation of investments at the end of each accounting period, based on market example, at the end of 1988, Citicorp had $15.2 billion of investment assets, and $3.9 billion of trading assets.

Finally, under pressure from the Securities & Exchange Commission, the accounting rulemakers appear ready to make financial institutions carry more of their securities at market values. In mid-January the American Institute of Certified Public Accountants' standard-setting committee is scheduled to vote on new rules. If they are passed, as seems likely, the new rules say that banks, savings and loan associations, finance companies and credit unions may classify their debt securities as "investments," and value them at cost, under only two conditions. The financial institution must have (a) the financial ability to hold the securities to maturity, and (b) the intention—barring unforeseen events—to hold them long enough to recover their book value. Otherwise the securities must be put in a trading account—carried at market value—or in a "held for sale" account, carried at the lower of cost or market value.

What if a bank sells lots of "investment" securities, saying there were "unforeseen events"? The new rules will probably provide that any institution that sells, for virtually any reason, over 10% of its investment securities in a year must mark its entire portfolio to the lower of cost or market.

Under the new rules, earnings are likely to be much more volatile. The American Bankers Association (which is lobbying hard against the new rules) recently released a study of the effect of market value accounting on bank earnings at a time of volatile interest rates. In spring 1981, national banks with over $1 billion in assets would have earned $1 billion in aggregate. Six months later the group would have lost $1.5 billion. Three months after, earnings would have

rebounded to $4 billion, and then dropped back to $1.5 billion. Over the same period, using the historical cost method, earnings would have been constant at about $1 billion.

Does this volatility matter? After all, if banks really hold their securities until maturity, the ups and downs will average out. But this doesn't mollify Jerry Von Rohr, chairman of little Mega Bancshares, Inc., a three-bank holding company in St. Ann, Mo. "We're sitting here earning better than 1% on assets," he says. "Now suddenly [under the proposed rules], Mega pops up in the *St. Louis Post Dispatch* with a loss. What will public perception be? What will our customers think?"

As part of their lobbying effort, the bankers contend that forcing them to mark their "investment" securities to market will discourage purchases of long-term securities—which fluctuate more in price than short-term ones—making it hard for business and the Treasury to issue long-term debt.

"That's a real red herring," says John Kreischer of the accounting firm Kreischer, Miller, and head of the accountants' committee developing the new proposal. "Banks don't invest in long-term securities to begin with. They buy two-year securities, maybe three. And if the investment made economic sense before, it will still."

In any case, says Timothy Lucas of the Financial Accounting Standards Board, "It is not appropriate for us to encourage people to buy long-term debt by setting up accounting standards that mislead them." It's hard to argue with that.

SOURCE: Dana Wechsler, "The Bankers' New Headache," *Forbes*, January 8, 1990, pp. 76, 80. Reprinted by permission of *Forbes* magazine. © Forbes Inc., 1990.

value at that time. It is not widely employed in financial reporting at the present time, except for certain specialized industry situations.

The market value method raises an interesting question of revenue recognition. Some argue that the periodic adjustment in value should be recognized in the determination of income, much like the current portfolio unrealized loss and loss recovery examples in this chapter, but with the use of market value not limited to historical

Realization   cost. Others prefer unrealized gains and losses be accumulated in stockholders' equity, much like the noncurrent portfolio adjustment presented earlier, but with use of market value not limited to historical cost.

Accounting theorists have advocated the use of current value for asset accounting and balance sheet presentation for many years. These include Moonitz and Sprouse,[19]

---

[19]Robert T. Sprouse and Maurice Moonitz, *Accounting Research Study No. 3*, "A Tentative Set of Broad Accounting Principles for Business Enterprise" (New York: AICPA, 1962).

Edwards and Bell,[20] Chambers,[21] Sterling,[22] and Beaver.[23] Marketable securities have often been used by these authors to illustrate their particular approach for the valuation of assets at current or market value. After decades of research in this area, Sterling concludes: "In research different people from different schools of thought using different postulates and different research methods have drawn the same conclusion: Marketable securities ought to be valued at market. That conclusion has not been challenged in the research literature."[24] In practice, however, the predominant method of measuring and reporting marketable securities remains historical cost or some variation of cost, such as the lower of cost or market or the equity method.

Asset/Liability Measurement

More recently, Foran and Foran attempt to evaluate marketable equity security accounting in light of the FASB's conceptual framework. They correctly state that one purpose of the framework is to be a standard of comparison by which current practice can be evaluated. These authors carefully analyze market value and lower of cost or market procedures with the individual parts of the conceptual framework, concluding that it is unnecessary to delay recognition until a cash-to-cash cycle is complete. They recommend that the FASB implement its conceptual framework by revising accounting for marketable securities so that it will be consistent with the current objectives, qualitative characteristics, elements, and recognition and measurement standards of financial reporting.[25]

CONCLUDING REMARKS

In this chapter, we have considered accounting practices and theory related to accounting for investments in equity and debt securities and been introduced to several other investment accounting issues. Accounting procedures currently employed in practice to measure investment assets are heavily based in historical cost, as the following summary indicates:

Asset/Liability Measurement

Investment Type	Current Accounting Practice
Equity—Current	Lower of cost or market (LCM), applied on an aggregate portfolio basis*
Noncurrent Passive	LCM applied on an aggregate portfolio basis**
Significant Influence	Equity method
Control	Consolidated financial statements
Debt—Current	Cost or LCM, applied on an aggregate portfolio basis or to individual securities
Noncurrent	Historical cost, adjusted for portion of premium or discount already recognized as adjustment to interest revenue

*Unrealized losses and loss recoveries included in income.
**Unrealized losses accumulated in stockholders' equity.

[20]E.O. Edwards and P. W. Bell, *The Theory of Measurement of Business Income* (Berkeley: University of California Press, 1964).
[21]R. J. Chambers, *Accounting Evaluation and Economic Behavior* (Englewood Cliffs, N.J.: Prentice-Hall, 1966).
[22]Robert R. Sterling, *The Theory of the Measurement of Enterprise Income* (Lawrence: The University Press of Kansas, 1970).
[23]William H. Beaver, "Reporting Rules for Marketable Equity Securities," *Journal of Accountancy,* October 1971, pp. 57–61.
[24]Robert R. Sterling, "Accounting Research, Education and Practice," *Journal of Accountancy,* September 1973, pp. 43–50.
[25]Nancy J. Foran and Michael F. Foran, "SFAS No. 12 and the Conceptual Framework," *Accounting Horizons,* December 1987, pp. 43–50.

The variations to historical cost found in these accounting procedures represent the unique attributes of the markets in which these securities exist and purposes for which they are held by the investing company.

You have also been introduced to the criticisms of market value accounting for marketable securities. Current value accounting, of which market value is one example, is sometimes criticized for its lack of objectivity in that the company holding the asset (e.g., investment) has not participated in the market which would be used to establish the accounting valuation. Others observe that we use market value in accounting for current and noncurrent marketable equity securities, as well as selected other assets, when the market declines by requiring a lower of cost or market approach. If market is sufficiently objective when it is below cost to permit its use, is it not equally objective when market is above cost? Some argue that the lower of cost or market method lacks internal consistency in that assets valued in this manner may be carried at either cost or market value.

Consistency

The use of current value, including market value, will undoubtedly continue to receive significant attention as it is evaluated in light of the conceptual framework. In the authors' opinion, accounting research should play an increasingly important role in this evaluation.

KEY POINTS

1. Companies invest in a variety of securities for many business reasons. (Objective 1)

2. Investments in voting equity securities must be classified as either passive, significant influence, or control in nature. (Objective 2)

3. Classification of securities between current and noncurrent categories involves assessing management intent, marketability and maturity dates of the security, and other corroborative evidence. (Objective 2)

4. Marketable securities representing passive investments should be valued at the lower of cost or market for financial reporting purposes. (Objective 3)

5. Unrealized losses and unrealized loss recoveries on the current marketable equity securities portfolio are recognized in the income statement of the period of the change. (Objective 4)

6. Unrealized losses on noncurrent marketable equity securities portfolios are recognized as a direct reduction of stockholders' equity rather than in the income statement for the period of the decline. (Objective 4)

7. Investments in voting stock which provide the investor significant influence over the investee are accounted for by using the equity method. (Objective 4)

8. A proportionate amount of the investee's net income is accrued by an investor using the equity method, whereas dividends are reported as reductions of the Investment account. (Objective 4)

9. Investment of more than 50% in the voting stock of an investee results in control of the investee by the investor, and consolidated financial statements are appropriate. (Objective 4)

10. Business enterprises frequently establish funds for a variety of reasons, such as meeting bond maturities or pension commitments and expanding plant operations. (Objective 4)

11. Extensive financial-statement disclosures are required for material investments. (Objective 5)

12. Accounting for marketable securities at market value, while not widely used at the present time, has conceptual merit and has been suggested by accounting researchers as an alternative to current practice. (Objective 6)

QUESTIONS

10–1 What methods of cost identification are most commonly used for securities which have been sold?

10–2 In accounting for temporary investments in bonds, how should one treat discounts or premiums for financial reporting purposes?

10–3 Distinguish between temporary and noncurrent investments. Is it possible for purchases of a specific company's stock to be a current investment for one company and a long-term investment for another? Why?

10–4 Explain the difference in the cost and equity methods of accounting for a long-term investment in common stock.

10–5 How should the excess of investment cost over the proportionate share of the investee's book value at the date of acquisition be recognized in the investor's balance sheet? Discuss the implications of this excess for the income statement.

10–6 How is a stock dividend that is received by an investor company recognized?

10–7 Give three circumstances under which an investment that is accounted for by the cost method will be written down.

10–8 What are "current assets" as the term is used to classify amounts on a balance sheet? How may marketable securities qualify as current assets?

10–9 With regard to marketable equity securities, when should realized gains be recognized?

10–10 With marketable equity securities, in what circumstances should realized losses be recognized?

10–11 *APB Opinion No. 18* specifies that a direct or indirect investment of 20% or more of the voting stock of an investee company leads to a *presumption* that, in the absence of evidence to the contrary, an investor has an ability to exercise significant influence over an investee. What are some examples of "contrary evidence" that might tend to refute this presumption?

10–12 What is a stock right? What three events can transpire after receiving a stock right? How are they accounted for?

10–13 In accounting for long-term investments in bonds, what causes premiums and discounts? How are these items accounted for while the investment is held?

10–14 How are investee operating losses accounted for under the equity method?

10–15 Distinguish between the accounting for temporary investments in marketable equity securities and noncurrent investments in marketable equity securities when the investor owns less than 20% of the investee's stock.

10–16 What is the cash surrender value of a life insurance policy? How should the cash surrender value be presented in the balance sheet?

10–17 What is a fund? What are the significant issues related to accounting for a fund?

10–18 Describe the market value method of accounting for marketable securities. Why is it advocated by some accounting theorists over those methods currently used to account for marketable securities?

10–19 A company may acquire a stock purchase warrant in conjunction with another investment. What procedure is required to place a value on the warrant?

10–20 A company which holds an investment in the common stock of another company may receive additional shares when the investee distributes a stock dividend or a stock split. Describe the appropriate accounting for the newly acquired shares in these circumstances.

EXERCISES   **10–21** CURRENT MARKETABLE EQUITY SECURITIES Murphy Manufacturing Company had the following securities in its current marketable equity securities portfolio on December 31, 1992:

	Cost	Market
Horton Company	$ 25,000	$ 28,000
Austin Company	50,000	47,000
Myrna Company	30,000	25,000
Lawton, Inc.	15,000	4,000
Total	$120,000	$104,000

All the securities were purchased during December 1992. The following events took place during 1993:

Mar. 15   Lawton, Inc., filed for protection under the federal bankruptcy laws. The market value of Murphy's holdings in Lawton stock fell to $500. Lawton's situation was apparently permanent.

June   5   One thousand shares of Orbit Electronics were purchased at $28 per share as a temporary investment. The brokerage commission on this purchase was $140.

July 17   Half of the Austin Company holdings were sold for $31,000, net of commissions.

Nov. 10   Murphy's management decided to begin developing a controlling interest in Myrna Company, and the Myrna shares were transferred to a noncurrent equity investment status. The Myrna stock had a market value of $29,000 on the transfer date.

On December 31, 1993, the market value of Murphy's holdings in marketable equity securities appeared as follows:

	Market Value
Horton Company	$19,000
Austin Company	30,000
Orbit Electronics	24,000
Lawton, Inc.	400
Myrna Company	30,000

Instructions

Provide the appropriate journal entries relating to the marketable securities. (Beginning with the December 31, 1992, adjusting entry, list the entries in chronological order.)

10–22   CURRENT DEBT INVESTMENTS   During 1993, Richfield Company made several transactions in current marketable debt instruments. Richfield uses the lower of cost or market method, applied on an aggregate basis, for valuation of these investments.

Jan. 31   Richfield purchased $10,000 face amount, 11% bonds at 103 plus accrued interest. Interest is payable on July 1 and January 1.

Feb. 28   Richfield purchased $20,000 face value, 10% bonds at 97 plus accrued interest. Interest is payable on July 1 and January 1.

July   1   Interest on both bond investments was received.

Aug. 31   Richfield sold half of the 11% bonds at 95 plus accrued interest.

Oct.   1   Richfield sold half of the 10% bonds at 101 plus accrued interest.

Dec. 31   Interest was accrued.

   31   The market prices of the bonds were as follows:

11% bonds	102
10% bonds	95

Instructions

Provide the appropriate journal entries for the above transactions. Round all amounts to the nearest dollar.

10–23   CURRENT AND NONCURRENT MARKETABLE EQUITY SECURITIES   Nifty Thrifty Supermarkets invests in marketable equity securities for long-term funding purposes. On February 15, 1992, Nifty Thrifty made the following purchases:

	Market Price Per Share (including commissions)
900 shares Alberts	$99
500 shares Browns	42
300 shares Carsons	33

During 1992, the following transactions took place:

June 30   Nifty Thrifty received dividends of $3,700 on the three investments.

Aug. 1   150 shares of Browns were sold for $45 per share. Commissions on the transaction were $120.

Sept. 15   200 shares of Alberts were sold for $98 per share. Commissions on the transaction were $180.

Nov. 11   The remaining Alberts shares were transferred to a temporary investment status when the Alberts stock was trading for $94 per share.

On December 31, 1992, the per-share market values of Nifty Thrifty's holdings were as follows:

Alberts	$90
Browns	41
Carsons	30

On December 31, 1993, the market values of Nifty Thrifty's holdings were as follows:

Alberts	$85
Browns	43
Carsons	29

Instructions

[a]   Provide the appropriate journal entries for Nifty Thrifty's transactions and adjustments.

[b]   In the balance sheet and income statement, what reporting distinctions are made in accounting for *temporary* versus *noncurrent* investment portfolios? Outline your answer by utilizing the December 31, 1992, information on Nifty Thrifty Supermarkets.

10–24   CURRENT DEBT AND EQUITY INVESTMENTS   At the beginning of 1993, Dennis Company held in its current investments account the following:

[1] $150,000 face amount, 8% bonds purchased at a cost of $137,000.

[2]   1,200 shares of $50 par value, 7% preferred stock purchased at a cost of $66,000.

Interest on the bonds is payable on March 31 and September 30, and the preferred dividend is paid quarterly on a calendar-year basis. On October 31, 1993, half the bonds were sold for $77,000 (including accrued interest) and 500 shares of stock were sold for $24,000.

Instructions

Prepare the necessary journal entries for 1993. (Assume all dividends declared were received by December 31, 1993 and round all amounts to the nearest dollar.)

10–25   NONCURRENT DEBT INVESTMENTS   Mouser Co. purchased $20,000 face value, 10-year, zero coupon bonds (bonds with a zero nominal interest rate) for 38.55 on January 1, 1993, for long-term funding purposes. On the same date Mouser purchased $30,000 face value, 5-year, 12% bonds that were priced to yield 8%, with interest payable annually on December 31. Mouser utilizes the effective interest method of amortization and carries the investment and any related discount or premium in separate accounts.

Instructions

Round all amounts to the nearest dollar:

[a]   List the journal entries needed to record the purchase of the bond investments.

[b]   List the necessary journal entries related to the interest on the bond investments for December 31, 1993.

[c]   Why are bond investments sometimes purchased at prices that differ from the face value?

10–26   NONCURRENT DEBT INVESTMENTS   The following is a partial effective interest amortization table for a bond investment due in eight years:

Date	Interest Revenue	Cash Received	Amortization	Present (Carrying) Value
Jan. 1, 1992				$11,000
July 1, 1992	$440	$600	$160	?
Jan. 1, 1993				

Instructions

[a] Is the effective rate less than or greater than the nominal rate?
[b] Is the carrying value less than or greater than the face value?
[c] What is the nominal rate?
[d] What is the effective rate?
[e] What is the carrying value on July 1, 1993?
[f] What is the face amount of bond investment?
[g] What will be the sum of the amortization column for the eight years?
[h] At the end of eight years, what will be the final carrying value?

10–27 NONCURRENT DEBT INVESTMENTS On September 1, 1992, Adams Company purchased $300,000 face value, 8% bonds, which would mature in eight years. The bonds were purchased as a long-term investment at a price to yield 12% compounded semiannually. Interest is payable on August 31 and February 28.

Instructions

Round amounts to the nearest dollar:

[a] Using the appropriate present-value table, compute the purchase price of the bonds and prepare the journal entry to record their purchase with any premium or discount in a separate account from the par value.
[b] Prepare the December 31, 1992, adjusting entry.
[c] Prepare the February 28, 1993, journal entry.

10–28 COST AND EQUITY METHODS Phillips, Inc., owns exactly 20% of the voting common stock (10,000 shares) of Rand Company. The investment cost $250,000 and was purchased on January 1, 1993 when Rand's common stock was selling at $25 per share and the total recorded amount of stockholders' equity was $900,000. During 1993 Rand Company reported net income of $85,000 and paid $50,000 in cash dividends. At December 31, 1993, Rand Company had recorded stockholders' equity of $935,000 and the common was selling at $22 per share. Rand has no preferred stock in its capital structure and Phillips' investment in Rand is considered to be a noncurrent investment with any excess of cost over book value attributable to goodwill with an expected 20-year life.

Instructions

Consider each of the following cases *independently:*

[a] Assuming Phillips, Inc., has significant influence over Rand Company, prepare the general journal entries to record the above and indicate the balance sheet and income statement amounts that will be presented by Phillips for 1993 concerning this investment.
[b] Assuming Phillips, Inc., does **not** have significant influence over Rand Company, prepare the general journal entries to record the above and indicate the balance sheet and income statement amounts that will be presented by Phillips for 1993 concerning this investment.

10–29 EQUITY METHOD On January 1, 1993, Qualls Company purchased 20% of Green Company's outstanding common stock for $1,000,000 when the underlying book value of the company was $4,500,000. Forty percent of the excess is attributable to assets with a remaining life of 8 years, and the remainder to unrecorded goodwill to be amortized over 40 years. Green Company reported net income of $280,000 in 1993 and declared dividends of $.90 per share on all 200,000 outstanding shares.

Instructions

Prepare Qualls's journal entries, relative to the Green investment, that are required on December 31, 1993.

10–30 EQUITY METHOD WITH LOSSES On January 1, 1989, Kids Stuff Toy Company purchased a 40% influential interest in Clothes for Tots, Inc., for $110,000. The subsequent earnings and dividend distributions of Clothes for Tots were as follows:

Year	Net Income (loss)	Dividends
1989	$ 50,000	$60,000
1990	(160,000)	$40,000
1991	(150,000)	10,000
1992	20,000	–0–
1993	140,000	10,000

Instructions

For each of the five years determine Kids Stuff's reported income (loss) from the investment in Clothes for Tots. Determine the balance of the investment account at the end of 1993.

10–31 SINKING FUND   Krippin Manufacturing Company established a sinking fund on January 1, 1992, for the retirement to a bond issue. The following transactions occurred:

Jan. 1, 1992	Established a sinking fund with $270,000 cash.
Jan. 18	Purchased marketable equity securities for $250,000.
July 15	Paid fund expenses of $10,000.
Sept. 9	Sold marketable equity securities having an original cost of $60,000 for $53,000.
Dec. 20	Received dividends on marketable equity securities of $15,000.
Feb. 12, 1993	Purchased certificate of deposit for $50,000.
Dec. 31	Interest and dividends of $27,000 were received.
Dec. 31	Sold all securities in the fund for $275,000 and retired an outstanding bond issue of $300,000. The remaining fund balance was transferred back to the corporate Cash account.

Instructions

Provide the appropriate journal entries for the above transactions.

10–32 CASH SURRENDER VALUE   On January 2, 1991, Lambert Company insured its president with a $100,000 face value life insurance policy with Lambert as the beneficiary. Premiums are $1,900 per year and are payable each January 2, beginning in 1991. The cash surrender value after each payment is made for the first three payments is as follows:

Cash Surrender Value	
Jan. 2, 1991	–0–
Jan. 2, 1992	$300
Jan. 2, 1993	$650

Lambert records each payment in a prepaid expense account, appropriately adjusting that account each December 31, the end of its financial reporting period.

Instructions

Prepare all general journal entries required for this insurance policy from January 2, 1991 through December 31, 1993.

10–33 STOCK RIGHTS   Stout Company owns 1,200 shares of stock purchased for $75 per share. One right is received for each share of stock outstanding; the market values of the stock and rights at the issuance date of the rights are $90 and $4, respectively. Two rights are required to purchase one share of stock at $80.

Stout exercises 500 rights one month later, sells 400 rights at $5.30 per right toward the end of the year, and allows the remaining rights to expire.

Instructions

Round all amounts to the nearest dollar:

[a]   Provide the appropriate journal entry for:

    [1]   The receipt of the rights.
    [2]   The exercise of 500 rights.
    [3]   The sale of 400 rights.
    [4]   The expiration of the remaining rights.

[b] Is the account carrying the original investment in stock reduced when stock rights are received? Why? Could the receipt of the stock rights be recorded as a memorandum entry similar to that for stock dividends? Explain your answer.

10–34 EQUITY METHOD On January 1, 1993, Holland Shipbuilders, Inc., purchased a 35% interest in Vernon Iron Works at $20 per share. As a result, Holland was able to appoint two members of the board of directors. The balance sheet of Vernon Iron Works appeared as follows on January 1, 1993:

Vernon Iron Works
BALANCE SHEET
January 1, 1993

Assets

Current assets		$ 20,000
Land		40,000
Fixed assets	$ 160,000	
Accumulated depreciation	(50,000)	110,000
Total assets		$170,000

Liabilities and Owners' Equity

Current liabilities	$ 15,000
Long-term liabilities	75,000
Common stock (no par; 6,000 shares authorized, issued, and outstanding)	50,000
Retained earnings	30,000
Total liabilities and owners' equity	$170,000

Vernon had a net income of $25,000 and declared dividends of $10,000 during 1993. The depreciable assets of Vernon are undervalued by $30,000. The average remaining life of the depreciable assets is 6 years. Holland Shipbuilders amortize goodwill over a 20-year period.

Instructions

Round all amounts to the nearest dollar:

[a] Provide Holland's journal entry to record the acquisition of 35% of Vernon Iron Works.
[b] Provide the journal entry to record Holland's share in the income and dividends of Vernon Iron Works.
[c] Provide the journal entry to amortize the excess of investment cost over equity. (*Hint:* Remember that Holland is purchasing only 35% of the $30,000 amount by which the depreciable assets are undervalued.)

10–35 LCM AND EQUITY METHOD On January 1, 1991, Overland Railroad Company established significant influence over K&K Railroad by acquiring 60,000 shares of common stock, a 30% interest, for $570,000. The book value of K&K was $1,300,000 on January 1, 1991. Since this purchase K&K earned income and paid dividends as follows:

Year	Net Income	Dividends
1991	$180,000	$100,000
1992	310,000	140,000

The market value per share on K&K common stock on December 31, 1991 and 1992, was $8 and $9, respectively. The Overland Railroad incorrectly accounted for this investment as if significant influence had **not** been established.

Instructions

[a] As a result of incorrectly applying accounting principles, the financial statements of the Overland Railroad Company are incorrect. At December 31, 1991 and 1992, were the following accounts overstated, understated, or correct? If incorrect, by what amount? Show supporting computations. Assume that any excess of cost over book value should be amortized over 30 years.

[1]   Net Investment in K&K Railroad.

[2]   Net Income.

[b]   If the K&K investment were sold on January 1, 1993, would a greater gain be reported under the incorrect approach or the equity method? Which method better assigns income to periods? Discuss your reasoning.

10–36 CURRENT MARKETABLE EQUITY SECURITY SALE   The temporary marketable equity security portfolio of Fowler Company is as follows on December 31, 1992:

	Cost	Market
Thayer Company	$16,000	$14,000
Webber, Inc.	21,000	20,000
Lincoln Company	32,000	25,000
Totals	$69,000	$59,000

On December 31, 1992, Fowler's accountant established a lower of cost or market (LCM) valuation for the current marketable equity securities (CMES) by the following adjusting journal entry:

Dec. 31, 1992   Loss on Valuation of Current MES   10,000

      Allowance to Reduce CMES to LCM   10,000

      (To adjust MES to LCM valuation.)

Prior to this journal entry no allowance account existed.

On January 2, 1993, Fowler sold all of its holdings in Lincoln for the market price of $25,000. Fowler's accountant has proposed the following entry to record this sale:

Jan. 2, 1993   Cash   25,000

      Allowance to Reduce

        CMES to LCM   7,000

        CMES   32,000

Instructions

[a]   Do you agree with the accountant's entry? Why or why not?

[b]   According to FASB standards, what entry would be required on Jan. 2, 1993, to record the sale of the Lincoln stock?

[c]   Referring to your answer in [b] above, how would you respond to the criticism of the Fowler accountant when she says that the loss is being recognized in income twice—once in 1992 when the market declined below cost and once in 1993 when the securities were actually sold?

10–37 STOCK PURCHASE WARRANTS   Esau Company purchased 10 units of a bond and three stock purchase warrants in Frank, Inc., at $1,050 per unit. Immediately thereafter, the bonds were selling for $1,040 and the warrants were selling for $12 each.

Instructions

Determine the cost that should be associated with each individual security involved in the purchase.

PROBLEMS   10–38 CURRENT MARKETABLE EQUITY SECURITIES   Synthetic Fuels Company has invested its idle cash in temporary marketable equity securities. Synthetic Fuels uses the FIFO method of assigning cost to security investments. On January 31, 1991, the following investments were made:

	Market Price per Share (including commissions)
500 shares of West	$ 47
1,000 shares of IBX	100
700 shares of Macs	70

On March 31, 1991, IBX issued a 20% stock dividend. Cash dividends of $12,000 were declared and paid by the three investments.

On September 7, 1991, Synthetic Fuels Company invested additional idle cash in the following temporary investments:

	Market Price per Share (including commissions)
200 shares of West	$51
400 shares of IBX	86

On December 20, 1991, Synthetic Fuels sold 1,100 shares of IBX for $90 per share.

The market values per share of Synthetic Fuels' temporary investment holdings on December 31, 1991, were:

West	$48
IBX	88
Macs	55

On February 28, 1992, Synthetic Fuels Company sold 300 shares of West at $45 per share. Dividends of $7,000 were earned by Synthetic Fuels on March 31, 1992. The Company purchased 200 additional shares of IBX at $85 per share on August 31, 1992.

The market values of Synthetic Fuels' temporary investment holdings on December 31, 1992, were:

West	$49
IBX	83
Macs	65

On December 31, 1993, the market values for the Synthetic Fuels' holdings were:

West	$48
IBX	87
Macs	78

Instructions

[a] Provide the appropriate journal entries for the transactions and adjustments from January 31, 1991, to December 31, 1993.

[b] Comment briefly on the impact that the periodic valuation of these securities at the lower of cost or market has on Synthetic Fuels' net income.

10–39 STOCK RIGHTS Elliott, Inc., engaged in the following transactions during 1993.

Jan.   6   Purchase of 500 shares of Kann Company common stock at $87 per share. Brokerage commissions were $390. The Kann stock is to be held for long-term funding purposes.

May 24   Kann issued a 10% stock dividend, followed by a cash dividend of $2.70 per share.

Aug.   1   Elliott, Inc., received one stock right from Kann for every share of Kann common held. Four stock rights entitled the owner to purchase one share of Kann common at $50 per share. Each right had a market value of $11, while Kann common was trading ex-rights (without rights) at $80 per share. The stock rights expire on August 1, 1994.

Sept. 21   Elliott sold 200 Kann stocks rights for $13.50 per right.

Sept. 30   300 stock rights were exercised for the acquisition of Kann common.

Dec. 31   The market value for Kann stock rights was $16.50 per right. Kann common closed at $68 per share.

Instructions

Provide the appropriate journal entries and year-end adjustments for the Elliott, Inc., transactions, rounding all amounts to the nearest dollar.

10–40 CURRENT MARKETABLE EQUITY SECURITIES Wampler Company used idle cash to invest in current marketable equity securities. The following table summarizes relevant information related to the CMES portfolio for the years 1991–1993.

Marketable Equity Securities

	Date Purchased	Shares Purchased	Purchase Price	Market Price per Share		
				12/31/91	12/31/92	12/31/93
Sax	1/15/91	700	$45	$44	$46	$47
Xon	3/1/91	400	47	50	45	49
Citco	9/21/91	1,000	56	50	51	53
STL	2/2/92	500	31	29	25	26

In 1992 Wampler sold 200 shares of Sax for $28 per share and 400 shares of Citco for $52 per share.

Instructions

Provide all the appropriate journal entries relating to the current marketable equity securities portfolio for 1991–1993.

10–41   LONG-TERM BOND INVESTMENT   Pillar, Inc., decided to invest in bonds to achieve long-term funding objectives. On January 2, 1991, Pillar purchased $100,000 face amount, 6% bonds due in 3 years. The bonds were priced to yield an effective interest rate of 10%. Interest is payable semiannually on June 30 and December 31. Pillar utilizes the effective interest method of amortization and adjusts the carrying value of the bonds on interest payment dates. On June 30, 1992, Pillar sold half the bond investment at 99.

Instructions

Round all amounts to the nearest dollar.

[a]   Compute the price paid for the investment and provide the appropriate journal entry for the acquisition on January 2, 1991, assuming Pillar uses a separate discount or premium account on bond investments.

[b]   Provide the appropriate journal entries related to the bond investment through December 31, 1993. Construct a table similar to Exhibit 10–13 to determine the proper amortization, adjusted for the June 30, 1992, sale.

10–42   LONG-TERM BOND INVESTMENT   On June 1, 1992, Warner, Inc., purchased as a long-term investment 800 of the $1,000 face value, 8% bonds of Universal Corporation for $738,300. The bonds were purchased to yield 10% interest. Interest is payable semiannually on December 1 and June 1. The bonds mature on June 1, 1997. Warner uses the effective interest method of amortization. On November 1, 1993, Warner sold the bonds for $795,000. This amount includes the appropriate accrued interest.

Instructions

Round all amounts to nearest dollar:

[a]   Prepare a schedule of interest revenue and bond discount amortization for the original bond investment from June 1, 1992, to June 1, 1997.

[b]   Prepare a schedule showing the income or loss before income taxes from the bond investment that Warner should record for the years ended December 31, 1992 and 1993. Show supporting computations in good form.   (AICPA adapted)

10–43   LONG-TERM BOND INVESTMENT   On May 1, 1992, Pope Company purchased for long-term funding purposes $20,000 face amount, 12% bonds, due in three years, at 105.076. The bonds pay interest on May 1 and November 1. Pope utilizes the effective interest method of amortization on interest dates and at calendar year-end. Pope sold $5,000 face amount bonds for 101.5 plus accrued interest on August 1, 1993.

Instructions

Round all amounts to the nearest dollar:

[a]   Provide the appropriate journal entries for the bond investment from the date of original purchase through December 31, 1993, assuming Pope Company does *not* use a separate discount or premium account on bond investments. Construct an effective interest amortization table to

support your journal entries based on the $20,000 investment without regard to the August 1, 1993, sale. (*Hint:* You must first determine the effective interest rate by trial and error.)

[b] Write a brief explanation of how your answer to [a] would differ had Pope Company carried the investment account at par value with any premium or discount in a separate account. Illustrate your explanation by preparing again the journal entries for the purchase of the investment on May 1, 1992, and the November 1, 1992, interest received.

[c] Might a rational business person ever purchase bonds with a $20,000 face value for an amount greater than this? Why?

10-44 SINKING FUND   For purposes of redeeming a bond issue, Whisper Company has established a sinking fund. The following transactions relate to this fund for 1993:

Jan. 1   Dividends of $6,500 received on North Company stock held in the fund.
Jan. 14 Expenses of $365 paid by the fund.
Feb. 23 Annual company contribution of $77,500 transferred to the fund.
Apr. 1   Purchased at par, $120,000 of 8% bonds plus accrued interest. Interest payable June 30 and December 31.
May 31   Sold bonds purchased on April 1 at 102 plus accrued interest.
Aug. 17 Sold $450,000 of sinking-fund assets for $432,700.
Nov. 30 Received dividends of $8,200 on Wood Company stock.
Dec. 22 Sold remaining fund assets for 105% of carrying value for $680,400.
Dec. 23 Fund cash now totals $1,247,515, of which $1,200,000 is used to retire bond issue.
Dec. 31 Remaining fund cash returned to the general Cash account.

Instructions

Prepare journal entries for the above transactions.

10-45 EQUITY METHOD   On June 30, 1991, Miller Company purchased 30% of the outstanding common voting stock of Rex Company for $1,300,000. At that time, the net assets of Rex Company amounted to $4,000,000. The level of investment is sufficient to provide Miller significant influence over the activities of Rex. Any difference between the purchase price and the underlying book value of Rex Company's net assets is due to the following:

[1] Land is undervalued by $25,000.
[2] Depreciable assets with a 10-year remaining life are worth $30,000 more than the book value.
[3] Goodwill is determined to exist for any remaining difference between cost and book value. Goodwill is estimated to have a useful life of 25 years from the date of the stock purchase described above. The following relates to Rex Company:

Year	Net Income	Dividends Declared and Paid on December 31
1991	$100,000	$25,000
1992	120,000	40,000
1993	75,000	-0-

Instructions

[a] Prepare all necessary journal entries for the transactions described above on the books of Miller Company through 1993.

[b] Compute the investment account balance on December 31, 1991, 1992, and 1993. (*Hint:* By purchasing 30% of the outstanding common stock of Rex Company, Miller Company has purchased only 30% of the undervalued amount of land ($25,000) and depreciable assets ($30,000). Also, recall that land is **not** subject to amortization.)

10-46 EQUITY METHOD   Porter Company has made substantial dollar investments in several companies over the past several years to diversify and to reduce Porter's dependence on the high quality steel market. Porter has manufactured high quality steel for over 50 years. The company policy has been to acquire a substantial portion, but not a majority, of the equity issues of specialty product companies that have been identified as good performers in growth industries. Porter exercises significant influence over the managements of these companies because Porter has at least a 25% representation on each of the boards of directors of these companies.

The following schedule presents the companies in which Porter has invested, the percentage of ownership in each company, and the carrying amount of the investment as of December 31, 1992.

Company	Percentage Ownership	Carrying Amount of Investment as of Dec. 31, 1992
Specialty Alloy	15%	$72,000,000
Aerospace, Inc.	40	10,000,000
Temper, Inc.	30	8,000,000
Air Flow, Inc.	30	100,000

Investment performance varied greatly among the companies during 1993. Presented below is a schedule of the income and dividend performance of each company and the market value of its outstanding stock. An interpretation of the information follows.

1993 Performance

Company	Income (Loss)	Dividends Paid	Market Value of Outstanding Stock as of Dec. 31, 1993
Specialty Alloy	$50,000,000	$8,000,000	$540,000,000
Aerospace, Inc.	8,000,000	2,000,000	35,000,000
Temper, Inc.	(6,000,000)	500,000	10,000,000
Air Flow, Inc.	(800,000)	none	1,400,000

Temper, Inc., lost a substantial portion of the market for one of its product lines because a competitor introduced a lower-priced model based upon technology not available to Temper. This was the cause of the current year's loss. Management has restructured the company so that it will be profitable in the future, although the level of dollar profits will be reduced from those experienced in the past. Consequently, the market value of the Temper stock is not expected to return to the levels experienced when it was purchased. The $10 million market value reflects this restructuring.

Air Flow, Inc., expects to be profitable from now on. The current year's loss contains the final expenditures incurred in the redevelopment of its product lines. A substantial number of orders for future deliveries have been received.

Instructions

Porter Company reports on a calendar year basis and is preparing its 1993 financial statements in accordance with generally accepted accounting principles.

[a] Determine the amount that each of the investments Porter holds in the four companies contributes to the total investment that should be reported on the December 31, 1993, Statement of Financial Position.

[b] Calculate the amount of income each investment contributes to Porter's income for 1993.

(CMA adapted)

10–47 GENERAL EQUITY INVESTMENTS On December 31, 1992, ABM, Inc., reported as long-term investments the following marketable equity securities:

Danner Corp., 5,000 shares of common stock (a 1% interest)	$125,000
Ewing Corp., 10,000 shares of common stock (a 2% interest)	160,000
Fox Corp., 25,000 shares of common stock (a 10% interest)	700,000
Marketable equity securities at cost	985,000
Less valuation allowance to reduce long-term investments in marketable equity securities to market value	50,000
Marketable equity securities at market	$935,000

Additional Information

On May 1, 1993, Danner issued a 10% stock dividend, when the market price of its stock was $24 per share.

On November 1, 1993, Danner paid a cash dividend of $0.75 per share.

On August 5, 1993, Ewing issued, to all shareholders, stock rights on the basis of one right per share. Market prices at date of issue were $13.50 per share (ex-rights) of stock and $1.50 per right. ABM sold all rights on December 16, 1993, for net proceeds of $18,800.

On July 1, 1993, ABM paid $1,520,000 for 50,000 additional shares of Fox Corp.'s common stock which represented a 20% investment in Fox. The fair value of all of Fox's identifiable assets net of liabilities was equal to their carrying amount of $6,350,000. As a result of this transaction, ABM owns 30% of Fox and can exercise significant influence over Fox's operating and financial policies. ABM amortizes goodwill over a 40-year period.

ABM's initial 10% interest of 25,000 shares of Fox's common stock was acquired on January 2, 1992, for $700,000. At that date the net assets of Fox totaled $5,800,000 and the fair value of Fox's identifiable assets net of liabilities was equal to their carrying amount.

Market prices per share of the marketable equity securities, all listed on a national securities exchange, were as follows:

	December 31, 1992	1993
Danner Corp.—common	$22	$23
Ewing Corp.— common	15	14
Fox Corp.—common	27	29

Fox reported net income and paid dividends of:

	Net Income	Dividends per Share
Year ended 12/31/92	$350,000	None
Six months ended 6/30/93	200,000	None
Six months ended 12/31/93	370,000	$1.30
(Dividend was paid 10/1/93)		

There were no other intercompany transactions between ABM and Fox.

Instructions

[a] Prepare a schedule setting forth for each investment the transactions and computations necessary to determine the ending balance in ABM's December 31, 1993, balance sheet:

[1] For investments carried at the lower of cost or market.
[2] For investments carried under the equity method of accounting.

[b] Prepare a schedule showing all revenue, gains, and losses relating to ABM's long-term investments for the year ended December 31, 1993.   (AICPA adapted)

10–48   CORRECTION OF ERRORS   The following asset side of the balance sheet was provided by the Krause Corporation on December 31, 1993.

Krause Corporation
December 31, 1993

Assets

Cash	$ 20,000
Temporary marketable equity securities (market: $16,000)	22,000
Inventory	30,000
Current assets	72,000
Noncurrent investment in 8%, 10-year bonds (at face value; cost: $87,711)	100,000
Noncurrent marketable equity securities (at market; cost: $62,000)	75,000
Plant assets	100,000
Less: Accumulated depreciation	(25,000)
Total assets	$322,000

The long-term investment in bonds was purchased on January 1, 1993. The difference between cost and face value was recognized on the 1993 income statement as an unrealized gain on the acquisition date. The interest on the bonds is payable annually on January 1. The noncurrent marketable equity securities include a 30% interest in the Alomar Company. This investment (with a $45,000 market value on December 31, 1993) was purchased on January 2, 1993, for $40,000 and represents a significant influence. Alomar had net income of $50,000 and dividends of $20,000 in 1993. Krause reported 1993 net income of $57,000. The books for Krause Corporation have not been closed for 1993. Assume that all items are material.

Instructions

[a]   Provide correcting and adjusting journal entries for Krause Corporation in light of the information given. Any discount or premium on the bond investment is to be carried in a separate account from the face value.

[b]   What is Krause's correct net income for 1993? Show your computations.

[c]   Recast the asset side of the December 31, 1993, balance sheet for Krause Corporation according to generally accepted accounting principles.

10–49   COMPREHENSIVE INVESTMENT ANALYSIS   The following correct balance sheet was provided by Chakos, Inc., on December 31, 1992:

Chakos, Inc.
BALANCE SHEET
December 31, 1992

Assets

Current marketable equity securities	$ 12,000	
Less: Allowance to reduce CMES to LCM	(1,500)	$ 10,500.00
Other current assets		40,000.00
Total current assets		50,500.00
Investment in bonds		94,793.25
Noncurrent investment in marketable equity securities	75,000	
Less: Allowance to reduce NCMES to LCM	(25,000)	50,000.00
Investment in Baxter		
Company (accounted for by the equity method)*		75,000.00
Land		74,500.00
Total assets		$344,793.25

Liabilities and Owners' Equity

Current liabilities	$ 35,000.00
Bonds payable (issued at face value)	100,000.00
Common stock (no par, 40,000 shares authorized, issued, and	
outstanding)	100,000.00
Unrealized loss on NCMES	(25,000.00)
Retained earnings	134,793.25
Total liabilities and owners' equity	$344,793.25

---

*The investment in Baxter Company is a 25% interest and represents significant influence.

The market values of the investments held by Chakos, Inc., on December 31, 1993, were:

Current marketable equity securities	$ 11,000
Noncurrent marketable equity securities	45,000
Investment in bonds	100,000
Investment in Baxter Company	70,000

Chakos did not have any significant financing or investing transactions during 1993. The bond investment was an $80,000 face amount, 10-year, 12% bond purchased on December 31, 1988. Interest is received annually on December 31. Chakos uses the effective interest method of amortization. Baxter Company reported income for 1993 of $100,000 and declared dividends of $80,000. The operating income of Chakos, Inc., for 1993 was $15,000. Current liabilities on December 31, 1993, were $35,000. Assume no taxes.

Instructions

Prepare the December 31, 1993, balance sheet for Chakos, Inc. Provide a supporting schedule to derive the balances for retained earnings and other current assets.

CASES

10–50 BOND INVESTMENT Wilson Company purchased $ 1,000,000 of face amount, 5%, six-year bonds at 71.22 on January 1, 1990. Calendar year 1993 was a poor year for Wilson because of declining revenues and tighter operating margins. The company had an operating income of only $100,000 on revenues of $2,000,000 (or 5%). The treasurer decided to remedy the situation by selling the $1,000,000 face amount, 5% bonds on December 31, 1993, at 90 and recognizing a gain for that period. The following calculation determined the gain on the sale:

Proceeds	$900,000
Carrying value	712,200
Gain	$187,800

As a result of this transaction, Wilson Company's net income totaled $287,800, or 14.4% of sales. The treasurer was very pleased. The company was now above the industry-wide profitability average for 1993, the stockholders would be satisfied, and the treasurer's year-end bonus, which is based on net income, would be almost triple what it would have been before the transaction. As the treasurer's assistant, you are not comfortable with his remedy. You confront the treasurer and tell him, "I have good news, and I have bad news."

Instructions

[a] What is the "good news"?
[b] What is the "bad news"?

10–51 EQUITY METHOD On the following page is a reprint from the *Forbes* "Numbers Game" column. The article is critical of the use of the equity method.

Instructions

Read the article carefully. Do you agree with the conclusions of this article? Why? How would you respond to the allegations presented in this article?

JUDGMENT CASES

10–52 CURRENT AND NONCURRENT CLASSIFICATION ISSUES Your client, Come Clean, Inc., specializes in the removal and treatment of a hazardous waste that is created by other companies in their productive processes. This particular toxic waste was only identified 5 years ago. Because little was known about some of its toxic properties, liability insurance was not available prior to the most recent year. In prior years the company was required by a state regulatory agency to perpetually maintain a large fund in lieu of liability insurance to compensate anyone injured by the activities of the company in disposing of the waste. To date no claims have been made and none are known to exist. Further, the company was successful last year in acquiring liability insurance and the state has agreed that the fund no longer needs to be maintained.

The assets in the fund are marketable equity securities of a wide range of large corporations. At the end of the preceding year the aggregate market value of the fund had declined below the aggregate cost due primarily to a broad and sudden decline in the stock market shortly before year end. At that time you believed that the decline in the market value was temporary in light of the broad market decline and the requirement that the fund be maintained in perpetuity. The aggregate decline, therefore, was reported as a direct charge to the stockholders' equity of Come Clean, Inc. rather than as a realized loss.

Since that time, the value of the portfolio has gradually risen and you believe that it will eventually equal or exceed their cost. However, the fund is no longer required, and the company has been selling the securities to expand capacity or replace obsolete equipment. You note that the market value of the securities sold have all exceeded their costs, and realized gains have been appropriately recorded. The president of Come Clean, Inc. has informed you that he intends to use the fund to replace outdated plant assets and to increase the disposal capacity of the company. He therefore

EQUITY ACCOUNTING ISN'T EQUITABLE

Under a 1971 Accounting Principles Board [APB] ruling, if company A owns between 20% and 50% of company B, A is required to report a portion of B's earnings—equal to A's percentage of ownership. Nevertheless, B continues to show 100% of its earnings. It's called equity accounting.

There's nothing equitable about equity accounting. It is grossly misleading.

The crux of the problem lies in how you define "earnings." Most investors think of earnings as the money a company has to spend—the dollars left over after all the obligations are taken care of. But that's not how the accountants define it: "Earnings are simply not synonymous with cash or working capital," explains Michael J. Walters, a partner with Peat, Marwick, Mitchell & Co., a big-eight accounting firm. So, earnings aren't necessarily dollars you can spend. They are dollars that can contribute to assets.

Fair enough, but this use of equity accounting brings in alleged earnings, not corresponding revenues. So it can throw off all the common measures of success: profit margin, return on equity, even price/earnings multiples.

Take a modest example of the resulting confusion: Giant Bendix Corp. ($3.8 billion revenues) has a 21% interest in ASARCO, a metals producer. Bendix adds on to its income statement some $25.5 million from ASARCO, driving up its earnings to $163 million. This deflates Bendix' current P/E from 8.2 to 6.9, inflates its profit margin from 3.6% to 4.2% and blows up its return on equity from 15% to a more impressive 18%.

Mark this, however: When ASARCO was losing money, Bendix carefully kept its interest below 20%. But it became apparent that ASARCO was going to make money. So in 1978 Bendix signed an antitakeover agreement with ASARCO—an increasingly common move—then picked up more stock and started to pick up earnings.

Bendix is not doing anything shady. It is simply complying with generally accepted accounting principles (GAAP).

What is happening here is an exercise in *reductio ad absurdum*. Start with a shaky premise and extend the logic further and further until it becomes ridiculous. Before 1971, earnings were generally brought in only when a firm achieved a 51% interest—clear control—in a second company. At that point the two balance sheets were consolidated entirely, with minority interests in earnings subtracted out. This is still the method that is used for companies with more than 50% ownership.

Now that *seems* logical. You run a company, you get the earnings. But that isn't entirely true. Even at 51% you can't simply take those earnings. However, since the statements were totally consolidated, the earnings ratios still have meaning.

But companies liked the idea of being able to report those earnings and wanted to carry it a step further and bring in earnings from minority investments. After all, they said, you can have control over the use of much of a firm's income with less than 51% of its stock. You can elect directors, and those directors mean influence over dividend policy and most other major decisions. That influence, they argued, should give them the right to show a portion of the resulting income on their own income statements. The Accounting Principles Board was compliant, and all that remained was to pick a percentage at which significant influence would be presumed.

Somewhat arbitrarily, the APB set forth 20% as the point at which you could *presume* control. Earnings could be brought in with a smaller investment if you could *prove* control. So now Saul Steinberg is taking in 3% of Reliance Group's profits, claiming that his own Leasco is run by the same group of directors and that this demonstrates control.

Steinberg is not alone. Bangor Punta, with only 7% of the stock of Lone Star Industries, is bringing in 7% of Lone Star's earnings, worth some $3 million of BP's $29 million in earnings.

The alternative to this foolishness would be to use cost accounting for partially owned companies, which allows a firm to show only dividends received as earnings—the pre-1971 method.

During the famous monkey trials, William Jennings Bryan proclaimed: "The Bible states it, it must be so." Well, equity accounting is in the accountant's bible, but that doesn't necessarily make it so.

SOURCE: Richard Greene, "Equity Accounting Isn't Equitable," *Forbes,* March 31, 1980, pp. 104–105. Reprinted by permission of *Forbes* Magazine. © Forbes Inc., 1980.

contends that the decline in the aggregate market value of the portfolio below its cost should continue to be considered temporary and the difference reported as a direct reduction of stockholders' equity. You further predict that the company can hold the securities for the foreseeable future.

Instructions

How should the difference between the aggregate cost and market value of the portfolio be reported in the financial statements for the current year? Support your answer with consideration of the relevant factors and accounting principles.

10–53   EQUITY METHOD   Hi-Flyer Airline, Inc., acquired a 25% interest in the voting stock of a large regional travel agency, We-Book-Em, Inc. Originally, the airline planned to use the travel agency as a "feeder" for a charter business it intended to develop. The airline has since abandoned the charter business program, but it continues to hold stock in the travel agency. Hi-Flyer has appropriately applied the equity method of accounting to its interest in the travel agency, and that investment has been largely profitable.

Now, however, the travel agency has lost three accounts that collectively represent 40% of its revenues. Its cash flow and profitability forecasts reveal anticipated losses through each of the next 5 years. The value of We-Book-Em stock has also been adversely affected and the amount of Hi-Flyer's related investment account substantially exceeds the market value of the shares and any price that might be realized in a unitary sale of the interest. You have just received the latest audited financial statements of the travel agency which discuss the loss of the contracts but do not contain any write-down of assets or loss in the corresponding income statement.

Hi-Flyer does not intend to sell its interest and now plans to acquire even a larger share of the travel agency in order to gain control and finally implement its own charter and reservation service. The president tells you, "We know how to make lemonade out of lemons and that is exactly what we are going to do with We-Book-Em. While our program won't be launched for at least three years and we don't expect it to generate material amounts of revenue for five, we are quite confident that the more distant future is very, very rosey."

You are pondering the implications of the situation when you read that the FASB has initiated a project of accounting for impairments of assets. You become concerned that some kind of a write-down in the carrying amount of the We-Book-Em investment might be necessary. You are also aware that the major lending institution assisting Hi-Flyer has expressed concern about the debt/equity ratio and net income level reported recently by the airline. Any write-down of the investment in We-Book-Em would certainly increase the concerns of Hi-Flyer's lenders and would be resisted strongly by the management of Hi-Flyer.

Instructions

Is a write-down of the investment in We-Book-Em necessary at this time? If you believe that a current write-down of the investment is or may be necessary be sure to describe the amount of the write-off that will be required. Draw on your knowledge of equity method accounting as well as other accounting standards and principles.

CHAPTER 11

Property, Plant, and Equipment: Acquisition and Disposal

OBJECTIVES

1. To describe the roles of tangible and intangible assets in the revenue-producing process.
2. To discuss the basic accounting principles that underlie accounting for tangible and intangible assets.
3. To apply the asset/liability measurement principle to specific plant assets in a variety of circumstances.
4. To discuss the proper accounting treatment of plant-asset expenditures that are incurred after the initial acquisition of the related assets.
5. To discuss transactions that result in the disposal of plant assets, including their sale, abandonment, destruction, or exchange for other plant assets.
6. To identify and discuss those limited situations in which a departure from historical cost is warranted in accounting for plant assets.

468

CLASSIFICATION OF PLANT AND INTANGIBLE ASSETS

Although assets are used in the production or distribution of goods or services in virtually all businesses, they vary in nature because of the differences in the business activities of the enterprises. These assets include both tangible properties, such as equipment and buildings, and intangible assets, such as patents and franchise rights. **Tangible assets** are often called **property, plant,** and **equipment** or simply **plant assets** or **fixed assets. Assets lacking physical substance** are typically referred to as **intangible assets.**

All plant and intangible assets have two primary characteristics in common:

1. **They are acquired as operating assets.** Plant and intangible assets are acquired for use in the production or distribution of goods or services. They are *not* acquired primarily for purposes of resale, even though they may later be sold.
2. **They are relatively long-lived.** Plant and intangible assets are expected to have relatively long lives in terms of their contribution to the production and distribution of goods and services. In most cases, therefore, the cost of these assets is allocated as an expense over their productive lives.

Despite these similarities characteristics of *specific* plant and intangible assets vary considerably. For example, although most are readily transferable between enterprises, others cannot be separated from the original enterprise. Furthermore, some are natural resources while others are man-made properties. Numerous classifications of plant and intangible assets are available. In this text, we use the classification that follows:

Asset Classification	Example Assets	Allocation of Cost
Tangible Plant Assets		
Property, plant, and equipment subject to depreciation	Buildings Equipment Furniture Fixtures	Depreciation
Property not subject to depreciation	Land	—
Natural resources	Oil and gas reserves Mineral deposits	Depletion
Intangible Assets Lack of physical substance		
Separately identifiable	Patents Copyrights Trademarks Franchises Leaseholds	Amortization
Not separately identifiable	Goodwill	Amortization

Chapters 11, 12, and 13 deal with accounting for plant and intangible assets. The balance sheet inside the front cover of the book lists "Properties, Fixtures, and Equipment" as an asset category in the balance sheet of Strawbridge & Clothier. These assets include significant investments in tangible assets that are used in the day-to-day operations of the company. We discuss plant assets in Chapters 11 and 12.

The first part of Chapter 11 presents general principles of accounting for all plant and intangible assets. We then focus on specific issues concerning the acquisition and disposal of various types of plant assets. Chapter 12 covers the depreciation and depletion of plant assets and includes several special accounting problems. In Chapter 13 the accounting principles discussed in Chapters 11 and 12 are applied to intangible assets, and several problems associated with accounting for assets that lack physical substance are identified and discussed. Because a detailed discussion of depreciation is included in Chapter 12, Chapter 11 uses only *straight-line* depreciation.

DEFINITIONS AND BASIC ACCOUNTING PRINCIPLES

Plant assets are acquired primarily for use in the production and distribution of goods and services, are expected to be used over a relatively long period, and have tangible physical properties. Although plant assets are apparent through their physical qualities, their value lies in their **service potential** (i.e., the positive contribution that the asset is capable of making to the revenue-producing process of the enterprise). Service potential can also exist in an intangible asset, where it is manifested in the form of rights and privileges that accrue to the holder of the asset.

Several principles that underlie accounting for all plant and intangible assets are discussed in the following paragraphs. Application of the principles to specific assets, problems encountered in applying the principles, and specified exceptions to the general principles are discussed throughout this and subsequent chapters.

Asset/Liability Measurement

Principle 1. Plant and intangible assets are initially recorded at historical cost.

Plant and intangible assets are *initially* measured and recorded at **historical cost,** which is the cash price or the cash-equivalent value of other consideration. The cash or cash-equivalent price represents the bargained value of the asset at the time of acquisition. From the viewpoint of the acquirer, the cash or cash-equivalent price represents the future value of the service potential expected from the asset.

The method of historical cost that is used in accounting for plant and intangible assets is broader than simply the cash or cash-equivalent price. All costs related to the acquisition and preparation of the asset for its intended use are considered part of the asset's cost. In addition, subsequent costs to extend the useful life of the asset (beyond that originally expected) or to increase either the quantity or quality of service rendered by the asset are considered part of the cost of the asset.

Historical cost, as applied to plant and intangible assets, is best described as a **full-cost concept,** because it includes expenditures related to the acquisition of the asset and the continuing enhancement of the service potential of the asset.

Matching

Principle 2. The cost of plant and intangible assets is allocated as depreciation, depletion, or amortization in a systematic and rational manner to achieve a matching of expenses and revenues during the useful life of the asset.

As plant and intangible assets are used in the production of revenue, their *future* service potential declines. Since these assets are established at historical cost, this decline in service potential is measured by treating a portion of historical cost as an expense in the periods that benefit from the use of the asset. From the accountant's perspective, **depreciation** is the process of allocating the cost of property, plant, and equipment as an expense to those periods during which the asset contributes to the revenue-producing process. The terms **depletion** and **amortization** are used to describe this allocation process for **natural resources** and **intangible assets,** respectively.

Matching

Although expenditures for a plant or intangible asset are typically made when the asset is initially acquired, the cost is allocated as an expense over the useful life of the asset; only *part* of the cost is charged as an expense in the period of acquisition. This procedure is important to the process of matching revenues and expenses in the determination of net income.

Methods to determine depreciation expense must be **systematic** and **rational.** A systematic method calculates the periodic depreciation charge in advance or on the basis of the activity level during a particular period. A rational method identifies the association between the amount of depreciation expense recognized and the decline in the service potential of the asset during the period. Chapter 12 covers in detail a number of systematic methods that are widely practiced. Specific circumstances must be considered in evaluating the rational feature of a particular method.

Principle 3. The establishment of cost and the subsequent allocation of that cost is necessarily based on many estimates and assumptions about the use of the plant or intangible asset.

Estimates and assumptions are an important part of accounting for plant and intangible assets. If cash transactions are not used in acquiring the assets and if costs related to acquisition are incurred, judgments must be made in determining the historical cost. Cost allocation methods (i.e., depreciation, depletion, and amortization) require an estimate of useful life in terms of calendar time, service time, or productive output. Finally, an estimate of residual (or salvage) value is required in applying the various cost allocation methods that are used in practice.

An additional judgment must estimate the pattern of the decline in the service potential of a plant or intangible asset. Since the allocation method must be rational, it should reflect—to the extent possible—the estimated decline in the service potential of the asset on a periodic basis over its estimated useful life.

Principle 4. The unallocated cost of a plant or intangible asset, called "book value," is *not* intended to approximate the current market value of the asset.

Matching

As indicated in Principle 2, the process for allocating the cost for plant and intangible assets to those periods that benefit from their use is important in matching revenues and expenses to determine net income. The historical cost of the asset, less accumulated depreciation, depletion, or amortization, is called **book value.** We can define book value best in terms of the process followed in its calculation: the historical cost reduced by the accumulated depreciation, depletion, or amortization recognized to date. Alternatively, book value can be defined as the *un*allocated portion of the historical cost of the asset.

Given how book value is determined, we cannot *expect* it to equal the current market value of the asset. After an asset is acquired its market value may remain constant, decline, or increase. If the market value declines, it may or may not equal the book value. The term "book value" may be a misnomer, because it seems to imply that the number measures the current worth of the asset. Although "unallocated cost" is more descriptive of the number, "book value" is widely used in practice. While book value does not equal the current value of the asset, depreciation policy should generally be applied so that the book value does not exceed the current value of the asset.

DETERMINING COST OF SPECIFIC ITEMS OF PROPERTY, PLANT, AND EQUIPMENT

Property, plant, and equipment—or simply plant assets—should be established in appropriate accounts at cost. The full cost includes expenditures necessary to acquire the assets and to prepare them for their intended use. The following paragraphs develop and apply the full-cost concept to specific types of plant assets.

LAND

The cost of land includes a variety of expenditures related to the acquisition of the land and its preparation for use as intended by the acquiring enterprise. Several major expenditures should be capitalized as the cost of land:

1. The original bargained acquisition price.
2. Commissions related to acquisition.
3. Legal fees related to acquisition.
4. Cost of surveys.
5. Cost of an option to buy the acquired land.
6. Cost of removing unwanted buildings from the land, less any proceeds from salvage.
7. Unpaid taxes (to date of acquisition) assumed by the purchaser.
8. Cost of permanent improvements (e.g., landscaping) and improvements maintained and replaced by the government (e.g., street lights and sewers).

What happens when some of these costs are incurred but the land is *not* acquired? For example, in deciding whether or not to acquire a parcel of land, a company may pay for surveys, purchase options, and other items related to several parcels of land but eventually buy only one. While a case can be made that costs associated with land not acquired are necessary expenditures for the land acquired, in the authors' opinion such costs should be expensed as incurred. The relationship between such costs and the acquired land is indirect, and care must be taken not to capitalize costs in an amount that exceeds the fair value of the acquired land.

Expenditures for land improvements that have limited lives should be capitalized in accounts other than the Land account and depreciated over their estimated useful lives. Examples are private driveways, sidewalks, fences, parking lots, and easements or rights-of-way of limited duration.

Land and other plant assets that are held for speculative or other investment purposes should be classified as investments rather than as property, plant, and equipment. Taxes and other expenditures required to maintain these assets should be capitalized as part of the cost of the assets if they are not producing revenue while they are considered an investment. If the assets produce revenue (e.g., through rental) *Matching* these expenditures should be treated as expenses and matched against the revenue that the investments generate.

Land is generally considered to have an unlimited life and is not expected to decline in service potential as it is used. Thus, land is usually carried at the original cost figure and not depreciated over the periods during which it is used in the operations of the enterprise.

BUILDINGS

The cost of a building includes all necessary expenditures to acquire or construct and prepare the building for its intended use. The following major expenditures should be capitalized as part of the cost of buildings.

If acquired by purchase:

1. The original bargained purchase price of the building.
2. Cost of renovation necessary to prepare the building for its intended use.

3. Cost of building permits related to renovation.
4. Unpaid taxes (to date of acquisition) assumed by the purchaser.

If acquired by construction:

1. Cost of constructing new building, including material, labor, and overhead.
2. Cost of excavating land in preparation for construction.
3. Cost of plans, blueprints, specifications, and estimates related to construction.
4. Cost of building permits.
5. Architectural and engineering fees.
6. Interest cost when an extended period of time is required for construction.[1]

The cost of a building that is acquired but *immediately* removed to prepare the land for construction of a new building should be treated as part of the cost of the *land* rather than as part of the cost of the new building. As we indicated earlier, the cost of *removal* is also treated as part of the land cost. Also the cost of removing an existing building that the new purchaser actually used for a time should be treated as an adjustment to the gain or loss on the disposal of the old building rather than as part of the cost of the newly constructed building.

Care must be taken to distinguish between building costs and the cost of other assets, such as removable fixtures. The latter represent separate assets that should be recorded in appropriate asset accounts and depreciated over their expected useful lives. This holds even if they were acquired with the building and used in a manner closely related to it.

MACHINERY, EQUIPMENT, FURNITURE, AND FIXTURES

Machinery, equipment, furniture, and fixtures are various types of property, plant, and equipment that are used by enterprises in the production and distribution of goods and services. The following list includes some of the costs that should be capitalized in the appropriate asset account:

1. The original bargained acquisition price.
2. Freight, insurance, handling, storage, and other costs related to acquiring the asset.
3. Cost of installation, including site preparation, assembling, and installing.
4. Cost of trial runs and other tests required before the asset can be put into full operation.
5. Cost of reconditioning equipment acquired in a used state.

Making the proper distinction in the accounting records between the types of property, plant, and equipment is important because the estimated lives of assets and the methods of depreciation may vary among the various asset categories.

NATURAL RESOURCES

Natural resources (e.g., timber, coal, and oil) represent tangible assets that are recorded at cost when they are acquired. These costs are then allocated, usually on a production basis, as depletion to the periods benefiting from the use of the natural resources, as we explain in Chapter 12.

---

[1]The subjects of overhead as part of the cost of internally constructed plant assets and capitalization of interest are covered in later sections of this chapter.

The cost of natural resources includes the original purchase price plus exploration and development costs related to the location and extraction of the resources.[2] Other plant assets, separate from the natural resource, are frequently acquired for use in the development and production of natural resources. Buildings and equipment, for example, are typically used in the successful exploitation of natural resources. These assets are established in separate accounts and depreciated over the shorter of (1) their expected useful lives or (2) the expected useful life of the related natural resource.

OTHER PLANT ASSETS

Types of property, plant, and equipment are as numerous as types of enterprises. Each enterprise must acquire those plant assets required to succeed in its line of business. In addition to the more common plant assets—land, buildings, machinery, equipment, furniture, fixtures, and natural resources—a wide variety of assets is used by some enterprises. Several of these are discussed in the following paragraphs.

Returnable containers are used in certain types of businesses to transfer products between the enterprise and its customers. Such containers may represent a significant asset, particularly when a large number are in circulation at any particular time. In some cases the customer makes no deposit; the container is simply returned by the customer or picked up by the enterprise after it has been used. In these cases the enterprise typically uses an inventory method whereby the asset cost is increased as units are acquired and reduced as a periodic count or estimate reveals the number of units that are no longer in use. The reduction may be due to normal wear and tear, breakage, or other causes. The amounts of deposits that are intended to be returned later represent a liability of the enterprise. This liability is often called **deposits from customers.** Returnable containers that are not returned within a reasonable period should be treated as sales at the deposit amount. To complete the matching process, the cost of unreturned containers should then be charged to an appropriate expense.

Matching

Miscellaneous tools and other small items of equipment are another type of plant asset, despite their relatively low unit cost. The practical limitations of capitalizing and depreciating a large number of inexpensive assets result in the cost of such items being treated as expenses when incurred—or later on an inventory basis similar to that for returnable containers. Materiality is an important consideration in these situations, and a departure from the strict application of the matching principle may be justified if expensing small assets or using an inventory approach does not have a significant impact on the financial statements.

Materiality
Matching

In a manufacturing process various tools and other devices are used to mold, stamp, cut, and shape other materials. Such devices, commonly called *patterns and dies,* should be capitalized in appropriate asset accounts and depreciated over their estimated useful lives. If such devices are useful only in a particular job rather than in a continuous manufacturing process, they should be charged to cost for that particular job.

PROBLEMS OF ESTABLISHING HISTORICAL COST

The concept of full cost, whereby plant assets are established at the cost of acquisition and preparation for intended use, is more easily stated than applied. Numerous problems are encountered in attempting to apply this general principle in specific situa-

---

[2]Unique problems associated with accounting for exploration costs in the oil and gas industry are covered in Chapter 13.

tions. Judgment is required in assessing which expenditures should be classified as part of the cost of assets and which costs should be treated in other ways.

This section discusses several frequently encountered problems: cash discounts; deferred-payment plans; internally constructed assets; capitalization of interest; acquisition by issuing securities; basket purchases; and installation, preparation, and start-up costs. Although these problems and their resolutions can apply to a wide range of plant assets, they are illustrated here in the context of *specific* plant assets.

CASH DISCOUNTS

The bargained purchase price of a plant asset is the cash paid or the cash-equivalent price. If cash discounts are available for early payment, should cost include or exclude the cash discount? A related question is whether the amount of the recorded cost should depend on whether or not the cash discount is taken.

Theoretically, the cash-equivalent price should equal the original price *minus* any cash discount available, **whether or not the discount is taken,** because the net amount is the price at which the asset could be acquired in a cash transaction. If the discount is not taken, a **discount lost** should be recorded and treated as an expense in the current period.

As an illustration, assume that Elmwood Company acquired equipment with a list price of $88,000 with terms 2/10, n/30. The asset should be recorded at the net amount of $86,240 [$88,000 − (.02 × $88,000)]:

Equipment	86,240	
Accounts Payable		86,240

If payment is made within the 10-day period, the $86,240 payment of Accounts Payable is recorded. If payment is made *after* the 10-day period, however, the following entry is appropriate:

Accounts Payable	86,240	
Discount Lost	1,760	
Cash		88,000

Recording the asset at the **net amount** is preferable, because this represents the cash equivalent price. However, some accountants record the asset at the total price paid ($88,000 in the above example) if the discount is not taken. The basis for this treatment is that the total price was the actual amount paid; in some particular circumstances it may not be appropriate or possible for management to take the discount. Materiality may be an important consideration in these decisions, because relatively small discounts may not have a significant impact on the financial statements.

Materiality

DEFERRED-PAYMENT PLANS

Plant assets may be acquired on a long-term financing plan whereby periodic payments are made or a single payment is made at some future date. An asset acquired in this manner should be recorded at the current cash-equivalent price and any interest included in the financing plan recognized as expense in the appropriate period(s). The objective of this practice is to distinguish properly between the portion of payments that represents the historical cost of the asset acquired and that portion representing interest charges for the credit received. Failure to make this distinction results in a misstatement of the cost of the asset, depreciation expense, and interest expense.

If interest is not stated in a deferred-payment contract, if the stated interest is not reasonable in view of current market conditions, or if the face amount of the obligation differs from the current selling price for the same or equivalent asset, interest may need to be *imputed*. The amount of the obligation is assumed to include the **acquisition price** of the asset and **interest charges.** The obligation is recorded at the asset's estimated fair value and the difference between the face amount of the obligation and the estimated fair value of the asset at the date of acquisition is recognized as interest over the life of the obligation. The asset and related obligation should be recorded at an amount equal to (1) the fair value of the asset being acquired, (2) the market value of the obligation, or (3) the present value of the obligation determined by present-value techniques that use an estimated interest rate. The most objectively determinable of the first two measures should generally be used. In some cases, however, these amounts are not available and the value of the asset and related obligation must be estimated by the third method. If either of the first two methods is used to record the transaction, the difference between the **face value of the note** and the **recorded amount of the asset** must be used to compute a rate upon which the recognition of interest will be based. If the third method is used, the borrower's (i.e., the purchaser's) incremental borrowing rate should be used as a basis for computing the recorded amount of the asset, the obligation, and the subsequent recognition of interest. This process is a *specific* application of the general process of imputing interest required by *Accounting Principles Board Opinion No. 21* that we discussed in Chapter 10. Exhibit 11–1 summarizes the processes used in accounting for deferred-payment acquisitions.

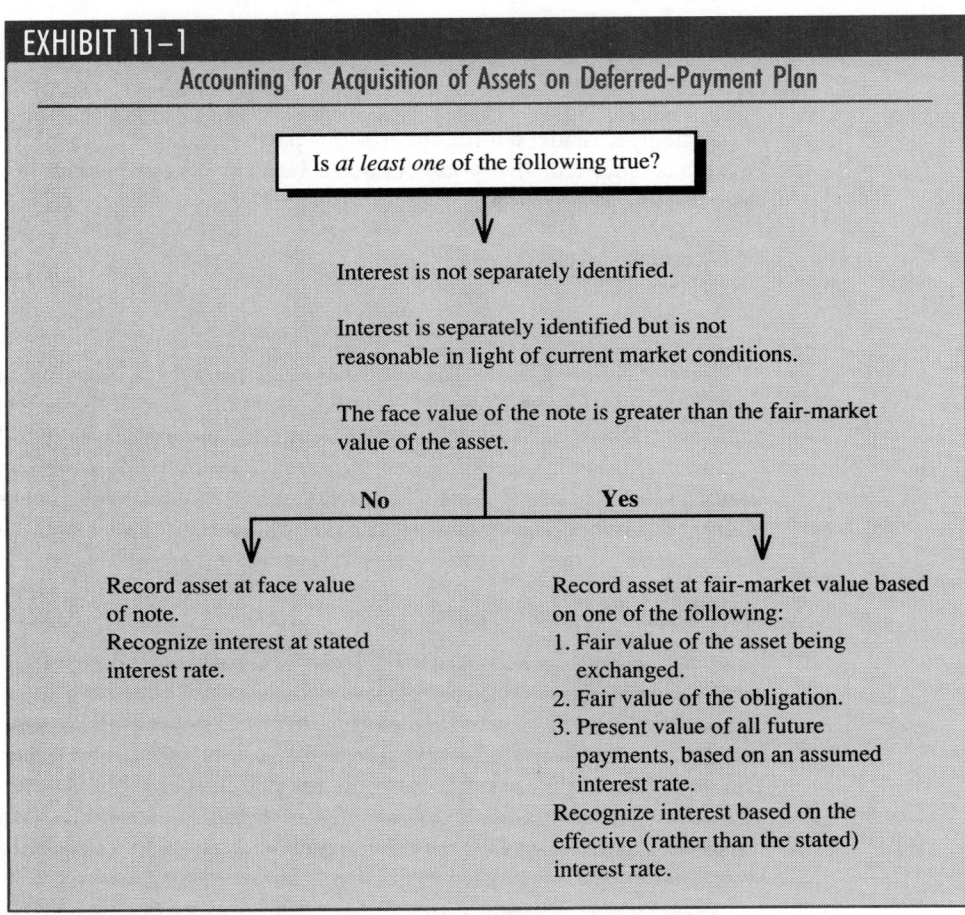

EXHIBIT 11–1

Accounting for Acquisition of Assets on Deferred-Payment Plan

Is *at least one* of the following true?

Interest is not separately identified.

Interest is separately identified but is not reasonable in light of current market conditions.

The face value of the note is greater than the fair-market value of the asset.

No

Record asset at face value of note.
Recognize interest at stated interest rate.

Yes

Record asset at fair-market value based on one of the following:
1. Fair value of the asset being exchanged.
2. Fair value of the obligation.
3. Present value of all future payments, based on an assumed interest rate.
Recognize interest based on the effective (rather than the stated) interest rate.

Two independent examples illustrate the process of imputing interest on such acquisitions.

In the first example, we shall assume that Bryson Production Company acquired a used machine by issuing a $150,000 noninterest-bearing note. The transaction took place on December 31, 1990, and payment is due on December 31, 1993. Neither the market value of the note nor the fair value of the property are determinable. Recently, however, Bryson paid 12% interest on similar transactions.

Since no stated interest rate exists and market values of the note and the asset are unknown, the portion of the note representing interest must be separated by using the 12% interest rate. Using the present value of one factor from Table 6–2, we can determine the present value as follows:

$$\text{Present value of note} = \left[\begin{matrix} \text{Face} \\ \text{value} \end{matrix} \cdot pvf_{\overline{n}|\,i} \right]$$

$$= [\$150,000] \cdot [pvf_{\overline{3}|\,12\%}]$$
$$= (\$150,000)\,(.71178)$$
$$= \$106,767$$

The cost of the machinery is recorded at $106,767 and the note payable, net of a discount to reduce the face value of $150,000 to its present value, is recorded at the same amount. This may be done by using a separate Discount account as follows:

Machinery *Interest on a*	106,767	
Discount on Notes Payable *(Non interest bearing note)*	43,233	
Notes Payable		150,000

The discount of $43,233 is then recognized as interest over the life of the note according to the following schedule:

Date	Interest Computation	Carrying Value of Obligation
		$ 106,767
Dec. 31, 1991		
Interest recognition	(12% × $106,767 = $12,812)	12,812
		119,579
Dec. 31, 1992		
Interest recognition	(12% × $119,579 = $14,349)	14,349
		133,928
Dec. 31, 1993		
Interest recognition	($150,000 − $133,928 = $16,072)	16,072
		150,000
Payment of note		(150,000)
		–0–

Interest at December 31, 1993, can also be determined by applying the 12% rate to the carrying value of the obligation, as was done in 1991 and 1992. The following computation would result: 12% × $133,928 = $16,071. The $1 difference from the amount in the preceding schedule is due to a rounding difference caused by stating the amounts in whole dollars. One way to get around this rounding problem is to adjust for the difference between the face value and carrying value of the note in the last year, as we did in the schedule.

The following entry recognizes the interest at December 31 of each intervening year:

	1991	1992	1993
Interest Expense	12,812	14,349	16,072
Discount on Notes Payable		12,812	14,349	16,072

As each entry recognizing interest is made, the carrying value of the note is increased—as indicated in the schedule. The final payment at December 31, 1993, is made by a debit to the Notes Payable account and a credit to the Cash account for $150,000. The cost of the asset for purposes of depreciation and financial-statement presentation is $106,767.

Plant acquisitions resulting in *multiple* payments may also require interest imputations. To illustrate, Chesney Company acquired a used machine by issuing three $50,000 noninterest-bearing notes, payable one, two, and three years from the transaction date of December 31, 1990. Neither the market value of the notes nor the fair value of the asset is determinable. In recent similar transactions, however, Chesney paid 12% interest.

As in the previous case, no interest rate is stated and the market values of the notes and asset are not determinable. The portion of the notes representing interest must be separated by using the appropriate present-value factor for an ordinary annuity from Table 6–4, as follows:

Face value of notes (representing both principal and interest)	$150,000
Present value of notes [$50,000] · [$pvoaf_{\overline{3}|\,12\%}$] ($50,000) · (2.40183) =	(120,092)
Amount of imputed interest	$ 29,908

The purchase of the asset and the related obligation are then recorded as follows:

Machinery	120,092	
Discount on Notes Payable	29,908	
Notes Payable		150,000

The portion of each $50,000 payment representing interest is separated and recognized periodically over the life of the notes according to the following schedule:

Date	Interest Computation	Carrying Value of Obligation
		$120,092
Dec. 31, 1991		
Interest recognition	12% × $120,092 = $14,411	14,411
Payment		(50,000)
		84,503
Dec. 31, 1992		
Interest recognition	12% × $84,503 = $10,140	10,140
Payment		(50,000)
		44,643
Dec. 31, 1993		
Interest recognition	12% × $44,643 = $5,357	5,357
Payment		(50,000)
		–0–

An entry is made to record the periodic payment and to recognize interest at December 31 of each intervening year, as follows:

	1991		1992		1993	
Notes Payable	50,000		50,000		50,000	
Cash		50,000		50,000		50,000
Interest Expense	14,411		10,140		5,357	
Discount on Notes Payable		14,411		10,140		5,357

This series of entries results in the complete elimination of the obligation of $120,092 recognized at the date of acquisition and the proper recognition of interest expense for the intervening accounting periods. The cost of the asset for purposes of depreciation and financial statement presentation is $120,092.

Asset/Liability Measurement

Substance over Form

Imputing interest for a plant-asset acquisition is required in order to distinguish between the historical cost of the plant asset and interest expense. This, in turn, results in a proper measurement of the asset in the balance sheet and interest expense and depreciation expense in the income statement. It is also an interesting example of the principle of substance over form in that we recognize interest expense on debt obligations that are in form noninterest-bearing. Failure to impute interest in those situations described in Exhibit 11–1 results in improper figures for these important financial-statement items.

INTERNALLY CONSTRUCTED ASSETS

In certain circumstances companies construct their own plant assets rather than acquire them from other enterprises. For some companies this is done routinely and is an expected part of business operations; for others this is done only occasionally. Several frequently cited reasons for constructing assets internally are:

1. To acquire needed productive services at prices lower than those from external sources.
2. To make use of facilities and personnel that would otherwise be idle in slack periods.
3. To produce specialized assets that might not otherwise be available.
4. To ensure the privacy of information concerning future production plans.

Historical cost applies to plant assets that are developed internally as well as acquired from external sources. However, measuring the cost of internally constructed assets poses some unusual problems. Costs of producing inventory are generally identified in terms of material, labor, and overhead costs. This classification also provides the basis for determining the cost of plant assets that are constructed internally.

Accountants generally agree that materials and direct labor should be included in the cost of an internally constructed asset since they represent both tangible material and payment to employees involved in the production of the asset. Overhead costs are more controversial, however, because they are indirect costs of production that are not closely associated with any specific product or any specific constructed asset.

Several positions exist concerning inclusion of manufacturing overhead in the cost of internally constructed assets. One position holds that the costs of such assets should *not* include any overhead charge because of the indirect nature of overhead and the inability to associate overhead charges with the particular asset being constructed. The basis of this assumption is that overhead costs are the same whether or not assets (other than inventory) are being constructed. However, the exclusion of overhead does not appear viable if overhead costs increase as a result of constructing plant assets internally. A second position, thus, requires only *incremental* overhead to be included in the cost of the internally constructed asset. While intuitively logical, isolating the increase in overhead costs that can be specifically identified with constructing a plant asset internally is often difficult.

The concept of full cost supports a third position concerning the amount of overhead, if any, to be capitalized as part of the cost of a plant asset that is constructed internally. This position holds that the asset should be charged overhead on the same basis as inventory that is also being produced. For example, if overhead is charged to the manufacture of inventory at $1.50 per hour of direct labor, the same allocation procedure is used to charge overhead to the plant asset; thus, the cost of the asset includes $1.50 of overhead per hour of direct labor. While this method is widely used in practice, it is difficult to justify if production below capacity is a reason for constructing the asset internally. Absorbing the cost of idle capacity in the cost of the internally constructed asset relieves current income and inventory of charges that would otherwise have been made to them and results in a higher cost of the constructed asset. This process increases income of the current and near-future years (by reducing costs of sales and inventory) and reduces income of distant-future years (by increasing depreciation charges).

Authoritative accounting pronouncements do not resolve the issue. Proper accounting is, thus, a matter of professional judgment in applying the concept of full cost. The authors believe that the full-cost concept should be generally followed and that the total cost of internally developed assets should include material, labor, and overhead prorated in the same manner as for inventory being manufactured. A logical exception to this general policy would arise if the company were operating below capacity and constructing a plant asset internally in order to utilize more efficiently its employees and facilities. In such a case, if it is *practical* to determine the incremental overhead, only the incremental overhead associated with the manufacture of the asset should be included in the cost of the asset.

What amount should be capitalized as the cost of an internally constructed asset when the internal costs total more than the price at which the asset could have been purchased externally? Accountants generally agree that the *maximum* amount at which the asset should be established is its *market value*. Any costs beyond that amount represent inefficiencies of internal construction and should not be included in the cost of the asset. Future periods should not be burdened by the greater depreciation charges that would result from the capitalization of those costs. Any costs beyond the external market price of the internally constructed asset should be treated as expenses in the period in which they are incurred.

CAPITALIZATION OF INTEREST

Our earlier discussion of deferred payment for plant assets emphasizes the importance of distinguishing between expenditures that represent payments for interest on money borrowed and expenditures that are made to acquire the productive services of various types of assets. Controversy has surrounded the determination of the historical cost of assets, however, when interest costs are incurred specifically for the acquisition and preparation of assets for their intended use.

Historically most enterprises have treated all interest as expense when incurred. The **capitalization of interest** as part of the historical cost of assets has been a common practice among public utilities, however, because customers are charged regulated rates based on costs incurred and designed to provide stockholders of the utilities with a fair rate of return on their investments. When interest costs are incurred to construct utility facilities, interest is capitalized as part of the cost of those facilities. Therefore, utility rates on the new facilities are based on higher asset-acquisition costs, and future utility users in those areas will pay rates that cover the interest costs required to finance the facilities that produce the services they consume.

The practice of capitalizing interest has not been limited to public utilities. An increasing number of other enterprises began adopting the policy of capitalizing interest in certain circumstances. Standards of accounting and reporting in this area were subsequently established by the Financial Accounting Standards Board (FASB) in its *Statement of Financial Accounting Standards No. 34.*[3] This pronouncement requires the capitalization of interest by all enterprises in certain circumstances on the premise that the historical cost of acquiring an asset includes all costs necessary to bring the asset to the condition and location required for its intended use. In addition, the capitalization of interest cost in certain circumstances is necessary to achieve a proper matching of revenues and expenses as the asset costs are depreciated in future periods.

Matching

Interest is capitalized as part of the cost of acquiring an asset if an **extended period** is required to prepare the asset for its intended use and **significant expenditures** related to the asset take place during that period. The objectives of capitalizing interest in such cases are (1) to obtain a cost that reflects the enterprise's total investment in the asset and (2) to recognize depreciation expense in future periods that adequately measures the cost of services provided by the asset. Interest should be capitalized *only* if the amounts are material and the benefits of capitalization exceed the costs of accumulating the required information. Within those constraints, capitalization of interest is appropriate in situations such as the following:

Materiality

1. Assets constructed by the enterprise for its own use.
2. Assets constructed for an enterprise by another enterprise if the acquiring enterprise makes deposits or progress payments.
3. Land under development for a particular use.
4. Assets intended for sale or lease that are constructed as discrete projects.

Common characteristics of these assets are (1) they are *not yet* being used in earning activities and (2) they are undergoing preparation for use in earning activities in the *future*. If the production of an asset is complete, if the asset is not being changed in some way, or if obsolescence, excess capacity, or need of repair prevents an asset from being used in earning activities, the asset does not qualify for the capitalization of interest. Also, interest is not capitalized on inventories that are routinely manufactured or otherwise produced in large quantities on a repetitive basis.

Theoretically, capitalized interest is the interest that was actually incurred during a period but that *could have been avoided* if expenditures related to the qualifying asset had not been made. Interest is based on the average accumulated expenditures for the asset during the development period, including interest capitalized in prior periods.

If specific borrowings are associated with an asset for which interest is being capitalized, the interest rates on those borrowings are used. If this direct association cannot be made, a **weighted average interest rate** on all borrowings of the company will determine the amount of interest to be capitalized. Because the interest to be capitalized is based on actual outstanding debt, the amount capitalized cannot exceed the interest incurred during the period. Interest capitalization begins when the initial

[3]*FASB Statement of Financial Accounting Standards No. 34,* "Capitalization of Interest Cost," 1979.

expenditure related to the development of the asset is made and continues as long as the asset is undergoing active development. Interest capitalization ends when the asset is ready for its intended use, whether or not it is placed in service at that time.

To illustrate interest capitalization, assume that Harper Company is constructing a warehouse for use in its own operations. Costs of material, labor, and overhead of $160,000 have been identified and charged to the asset account. Initial expenditures in early January 1993 were $70,000. In early May of that year $50,000 more was invested; in early October, an additional $40,000. On January 2, 1993, the company arranged for a 12%, $100,000 loan to partially finance the construction. In January the company borrowed the full amount of the loan and used it to finance the first $100,000 of expenditures in the warehouse. The remaining investment in the project came from available cash within the company. The company has a substantial amount of additional debt outstanding at an average interest rate of 10%. The amount of interest to be capitalized is as follows:

Period of Time	Investment	No. of Months	(Investment) × (No. of Months)
January–April	$ 70,000	4	$ 280,000
	50,000		
May–September	$120,000	5	600,000
	40,000		
October–December	$160,000	3	480,000
			$1,360,000

Average expenditure for 1993:
$1,360,000/12 months = $113,333

Interest capitalization for 1993:

$100,000 × 12%	=	$12,000
13,333 × 10%	=	1,333
$113,333	=	$13,333

The average accumulated expenditure for the construction of the asset during 1993 is $113,333. This amount is determined by computing the amount of the investment for three periods of time during the year, the end of the first two periods being determined when an additional investment was made in the asset and the end of the last period determined by the end of the financial reporting period. A weighted average investment is then computed and interest is determined in two steps: (1) on the first $100,000 investment in the asset at the 12% rate on the $100,000 loan taken out specifically for this project; and (2) on the remaining $13,333 ($113,333 − $100,000) at the 10% rate on the remaining debt of the company.

If we assume that interest on the $100,000 debt incurred specifically for this asset is charged directly to the asset account as incurred and that other interest is allocated from interest expense previously recognized, the entry to record the capitalization of interest is as follows:

Warehouse	13,333	
Cash (or Interest Payable)		12,000
Interest Expense		1,333

In reality, several entries totaling the amounts in the above entry may be made at different points in time. The $12,000 interest on debt incurred specifically for this asset would be charged to the asset as it was paid or accrued. The transfer of $1,333 interest previously recognized as an expense is most likely made when the asset is complete or at the end of the accounting period if the asset is still in process. This is necessary in order to state properly the asset cost and the interest expense for the period.

When the $13,333 interest is combined with the $160,000 of material, labor, and overhead costs that are capitalized as part of the cost of the asset, the total asset cost is $173,333 ($160,000 + $13,333). This amount is the basis for financial-statement presentation and depreciation calculation.

In this case the investment in the asset for which interest is being capitalized is greater than the debt directly related to that project. In addition, Harper has other debt outstanding that provides the basis for the capitalization of interest on the additional investment of $60,000 ($160,000 investment, less $100,000 of directly related debt). If the company had no debt beyond the $100,000 directly related to the asset under construction, no additional interest could be capitalized, because the amount of capitalized interest is limited to the amount of interest actually incurred during the construction period.

Disclosure   When a company has capitalized a part of interest incurred during an accounting period in accordance with *FASB Statement No. 34*, special disclosure must be made in notes to the financial statements. Exhibit 11–2 presents an example of this disclosure from the 1990 financial statements of The Goodyear Tire & Rubber Company. Goodyear's principle business is the development, manufacture, distribution, and sale of tires throughout the world. In addition, the company produces and sells a broad spectrum of rubber, chemical, and plastic products for the transportation industry and various other industrial and consumer markets.

ACQUISITION BY ISSUING SECURITIES

Plant assets may be acquired by issuing securities (e.g., stock certificates) rather than paying cash or transferring other assets to the seller. In such transactions accountants record the equivalent amount of cash that would have been transferred in a comparable cash transaction. Several problems may obscure the determination of the cash-equivalent amount. Market values of either the securities or the asset(s) exchanged may not be readily available. On the other hand, although a market value of the securities may be readily determinable from a market quotation, such value may be based on a level of market activity substantially different from the number of shares

---

EXHIBIT 11–2

The Goodyear Tire & Rubber Company
Capitalization of Interest Disclosure

Interest Expense

Interest expense includes interest and amortization of debt discount and expense less amounts capitalized as follows:

(In millions)	1990	1989	1988
Interest expense before capitalization	$362.9	$374.2	$358.0
Capitalized interest	34.7	118.9	126.2
	$328.2	$255.3	$231.8

The Company made cash payments for interest in 1990, 1989 and 1988 of $347.9 million, $367.5 million and $345.0 million, respectively.

SOURCE: The Goodyear Tire & Rubber Company, 1990 Annual Report.

involved in the acquisition. In such situations, the market price may not indicate the value of the shares if the number issued in the acquisition had been included in the transactions determining the market price.

When securities are issued in exchange for assets, the market value of the shares issued should normally be used as the basis for recording both the assets acquired and the stock issued. When the market value of the property exchanged is more objectively determinable than the market value of the stock, the value of the property should be used. If the market value of the stock is based on a level of market activity so far below the number of shares included in the transaction that the current market value is not appropriate, the estimated valuation of the property exchanged or an estimate of the value of the stock apart from the original market value should be made by the officers of the issuing corporation. This value is used in recording the transaction. Generally, neither the **par** (or **stated) value** nor the current book value of the stock is an appropriate base for recording transactions in which securities are exchanged for plant assets.

To illustrate, assume that Lyons Company purchases land from another enterprise by issuing 22,000 shares of its $25 par value stock. The market price of the stock is $32 at the time of the transaction. The 22,000 shares do not represent a substantial number of shares in relation to the volume of stock activity in the market. The purchase of the land is recorded by the following entry:

Land	704,000	
Common Stock (22,000 × $25)		550,000
Paid-In Capital in Excess of Par Value		154,000
[22,000 × ($32 − $25)]		

BASKET PURCHASES

Asset/Liability Measurement

Basket purchase is a term that refers to the acquisition of several assets for a single price. The primary accounting problem arising from the basket (lump-sum) purchase is the apportionment of the total price paid to the individual assets acquired. Sometimes several assets can be purchased in a single transaction for less than the individual assets could be acquired separately. In such cases the allocation of the total price paid for the group of assets to the individual assets is based on the relative values of the individual assets acquired. In accordance with the historical cost method of measuring assets, the total cost recorded must not exceed the total price paid, even if the total appraised value exceeds that amount. The individual asset values that are assigned for purposes of allocation may be based on current market prices, appraisal values, the present values of expected future benefits, or other appropriate estimations.

To illustrate, we will assume that Ledford Company acquires several assets in a single transaction from a competitor who is going out of business. The total purchase price is $855,000. The acquired assets and their individually estimated values, based on current market prices and independent appraisals, are as follows:

Inventory	$100,000
Building	500,000
Land	150,000
Fixtures	200,000

The allocation of the $855,000 cost to the individual assets is based on the relative estimated value of the individual assets, as follows:

Asset	Appraisal Value	Cost Allocation
Inventory	$100,000	(100/950) $855,000 = $ 90,000
Building	500,000	(500/950) $855,000 = 450,000
Land	150,000	(150/950) $855,000 = 135,000
Fixtures	200,000	(200/950) $855,000 = 180,000
	$ 950,000	$ 855,000

Alternatively, a percentage of cost to total appraisal value may be computed as follows: $855,000/$950,000 = 90%. This percentage is then applied to the estimated value of each asset to determine the portion of the total cost allocated to that asset. For example, Land would be allocated $135,000, as follows: $150,000 × 90% = $135,000. The entry to record the basket purchase in this example is as follows:

Inventory	90,000	
Building	450,000	
Land	135,000	
Fixtures	180,000	
Cash		855,000

Although this illustration deals with a purchase of several different classes of assets, the same procedure may be used to allocate the cost of several items of the same type to individual items. For example, several inventory items or several pieces of machinery may be purchased for a single price. The cost of each individual inventory or machinery item is determined by allocating the cost of all items on the basis of the relative value of the individual items.

When a company makes a basket purchase of assets, it may also make expenditures that relate to only one of the assets. Accountants must carefully distinguish between the common price paid for several assets and any related expenditures that apply only to a single asset. The former should be allocated among the assets acquired, as illustrated above. Any related expenditures that apply to specific assets should be associated entirely with those assets. For example, a company may acquire inventory, furniture, and land in a single purchase transaction. The price paid should be allocated among these assets based on their individual relative fair values. Legal fees paid to transfer title of the land, however, should be assigned only to the land and should not affect the recorded cost of the inventory and fixtures.

INSTALLATION, PREPARATION, AND START-UP COSTS

Under the full-cost concept plant assets are established at the cost of acquisition. This includes expenditures necessary to bring them to the appropriate location and to prepare them for their intended use. Substantial outlays for transportation, installation, remodeling, and reconditioning may be required to advance the asset to the point of becoming a positive factor in the generation of revenue.

Significant time may lapse between the purchase of the asset and the placement of the asset into service. This is particularly true in the case of buildings undergoing extensive renovation. Costs related to the asset incurred during this period (e.g., insurance, taxes, and supervisory salaries) are capitalized as part of the cost of the asset. For some assets, such as machinery, trial runs and other tests may be necessary before the asset can be put into full service. These tests may require supplies, materials, and other assets. Such costs are also part of the cost of acquiring the asset and preparing it for its intended use.

Depreciation is not recognized on assets until they are placed into service, even if they were acquired at some previous date. No depreciation is recognized during a

Matching

period of remodeling or renovation between the time the asset is acquired and placed into service. In compliance with the matching principle, recognition of depreciation is deferred until the asset becomes a part of the revenue-producing process.

POSTACQUISITION EXPENDITURES

After plant assets are acquired and placed into service, additional costs may be related to the continued use of the assets. An important distinction is that of capital and revenue expenditures. **Capital expenditures** are those expected to benefit *future* periods and, thus, are recorded as assets and depreciated over those periods. **Revenue expenditures** are normal, recurring expenditures designed to sustain the usefulness of the asset through the *current* accounting period and, thus, are charged to expense as incurred.

In distinguishing between capital and revenue expenditures, accountants commonly identify capital expenditures as those expenditures expected to allow the related asset to render greater future benefits to the enterprise. Accordingly, capital expenditures are expected to have one or both of the following positive impacts on future operations:

1. The *quantity* of services received from the asset will be increased. This may take the form of a longer useful life or more units of output.
2. The *quality* of the services from the asset will be increased.

If neither of these conditions is met, the expenditure is intended to maintain the present level and quality of services rendered by the asset. These expenditures are appropriately designated as revenue expenditures and charged to expense as incurred.

Materiality

A common practice to distinguish between capital and revenue expenditures is to establish a dollar amount that represents a materiality threshold. Expenditures that are less than the designated amount are treated as expenses when incurred, even if they are beneficial to future periods. The designated level for this distinction varies with the size of the enterprise. For example, a small company might expense all amounts below $100, and a large company might follow the same practice for amounts below $10,000. While this practice is justifiable only on grounds of materiality, it also eliminates the practical problem of judging the nature of a large number of small dollar amounts.

Expenditures related to plant assets incurred after the original acquisition may be classified in four categories: (1) additions, (2) replacements and betterments, (3) rearrangement and relocation, and (4) repair and maintenance. The following discussion of post-acquisition expenditures in terms of these four categories will help you distinguish between capital and revenue expenditures and identify the period over which the capital expenditures should be allocated.

ADDITIONS

Additions represent major expenditures that, by definition, are capital in nature because they increase the service potential of the related asset. Additions to buildings are common when the size of the asset can be increased by adding a new wing or level to the existing facility.

Two major problems exist in relation to additions. First, the period over which the expenditure is to be depreciated must be determined. If the estimated useful life of the addition is independent of the asset to which it relates, the addition is treated as a *separate* asset and depreciated over its estimated useful life, regardless of the life of the original asset. This is common practice when structures are built as components and the addition would continue to exist even if the original structure were removed. In many cases, however, the addition is not independent of the original structure, and the period of depreciation for the addition must be determined in relation to the original structure. In such cases the cost of the addition is depreciated over the shorter of the estimated life of the addition or the remaining life of the original asset.

The second problem related to additions is the identification of the costs that are appropriately capitalized. Adding to a facility frequently requires alteration of the original structure. For example, the addition of a new wing may involve removing walls or rerouting plumbing. If the original unit was constructed with a plan to expand, costs related to the original asset incurred when the addition takes place are appropriately capitalized as part of the cost of the addition. On the other hand, costs incurred that *could have been avoided* if appropriate planning had taken place at an earlier date should be expensed rather than carried forward as part of the addition. Distinguishing between such costs requires great judgment, and care should be taken to ensure proper classification.

REPLACEMENTS AND BETTERMENTS

Replacements and betterments represent the substitution of a new part of an asset for an existing part. For example, the base of a machine may be replaced with a new base, or the roof of a building may be replaced with a new roof.

If the new part of the asset is similar in nature to the part being eliminated, the substitution is called a **replacement.** If the new part represents an improvement in quality over the part being eliminated, the substitution is called a **betterment.** An important consideration in determining the appropriate accounting treatment of replacements and betterments is whether the original part of the existing asset is separately identifiable. If separate identification is possible, the new expenditure should be substituted for the portion of the book value being replaced or improved. This is possible when the components of the asset have been separately identified and depreciated.

To illustrate, we assume that Fagan Company acquires a building at a cost of $250,000. Separate identification of the cost components indicates that $30,000 of the cost relates to the roof of the building. The building is being depreciated over a 25-year life by the straight-line method, with an estimated salvage value of $20,000. The roof, however, is being depreciated over a 10-year life by the straight-line method, with no estimated salvage value. After nine years the roof is replaced at a cost of $50,000. The replacement is expected to last for the remaining years of the original estimate of the building's life.

The replacement is substituted in the accounts as follows:

Building (new roof)	50,000	
Accumulated Depreciation	27,000	
(90% × $30,000)		
Loss on Replacement of Roof	3,000	
Building (old roof)		30,000
Cash		50,000

[handwritten annotation: Loss is the remaining BV of Old Asset]

The cost of the building, other than that allocated to the roof, should continue to be depreciated over the remaining unchanged useful life. The roof is depreciated at $3,125 per year ($50,000/16) over the remaining 16 years of the life of the building.

While this substitution approach is logical in accounting for replacements and betterments, the separate identification of elements of an asset is frequently not possible due to the lack of separate records of the components of the asset or the integrated nature of the asset. Also, the parts of an asset changed by replacements and betterments during remodeling or renovation are generally difficult to separate in the manner we have described.

If separate identification is not possible or practical, the cost of replacements and betterments are treated as increases in the book value of the asset, thereby increasing the basis for depreciation over the remaining life of the asset. If the replacement or betterment is designed primarily to enhance the **quality** of the service potential of the asset, the cost is charged to the asset account and an appropriate increase in depreciation expense recognized in future years. Although the book value of the replaced or improved portion remains in the asset and accumulated depreciation accounts, the replacement or betterment usually takes place when the original expenditure is nearing the point of full depreciation and book value is a relatively small amount.

If the replacement is designed primarily to **extend the length of the service life** of the asset rather than to enhance the quality of the service rendered, the book value should be increased by charging Accumulated Depreciation. The accountant then depreciates the revised book value, less any salvage value, over the revised useful life.

For an illustration, we assume that Webb, Inc. replaces the electrical system in its building at a cost of $100,000. The building originally cost $800,000 and had $425,000 accumulated depreciation at the time of the replacement. The company has no record of the separate components of the building. Prior to the replacement the asset had a remaining life of 10 years with an expected $50,000 residual value.

If the replacement is made in order to enhance the quality of service potential in the future, the replacement is accounted for as follows:

Building	100,000	
Cash		100,000

This entry increases the book value to $475,000, as follows:

Original cost of building	$ 800,000
Cost of replacement of electrical system	100,000
	900,000
Accumulated depreciation	(425,000)
	$ 475,000

Depreciation expense thereafter is recognized at $42,500 per year [($475,000 − $50,000) ÷ 10 years].

If the replacement is made in order to extend the useful life, the replacement is accounted for as follows:

Accumulated Depreciation—Building	100,000	
Cash		100,000

This entry also increases the book value to $475,000, computed as follows:

Original cost of building		$800,000
Accumulated depreciation prior to replacement	$ 425,000	
Cost of replacement of electrical system	(100,000)	325,000
		$475,000

If we further assume that the replacement adds seven years to the current estimated service period of 10 years and that the estimated residual value is unchanged, the depreciation thereafter is recognized at $25,000 per year [($475,000 − $50,000) ÷ 17].

The distinction between charging the asset account or accumulated depreciation with the cost of the replacement is one of classification, because the impact on book value is identical. Capitalization by debiting the asset (i.e., the Building account) provides recognition of the increased value of the asset to the enterprise in terms of future service potential. Alternatively, capitalization by charging Accumulated Depreciation recognizes that costs extending the asset's life are essentially a recovery of past depreciation charges.

REARRANGEMENTS AND RELOCATIONS

Materiality

Matching

Rearrangements and **relocations** frequently occur to facilitate future operations. If the costs of such activities are material and can be separated from recurring operating expenses, they should be capitalized and recognized as expenses over the periods expected to benefit in accordance with the matching principle. Alternatively, if the costs are *not* material, if they are *inseparable* from recurring operating expenses, or if the future benefits in terms of increased efficiency are *questionable,* they should be expensed in the period in which they are incurred.

The unamortized portion of costs of previously capitalized rearrangement and relocation costs is sometimes presented as an intangible asset, but it is more appropriately described as a **deferred charge** (i.e., an unamortized balance awaiting amortization). Deferred charges are usually presented in the balance sheet as a part of an "other-asset" category. Chapter 13 discusses this balance sheet category in more detail.

REPAIR AND MAINTENANCE

Repair and **maintenance** expenditures are necessary to maintain the current operating capabilities of plant assets. Such expenditures range from custodial care and recurring minor repairs on buildings to periodic inspection and servicing of machinery and equipment. Repair and maintenance expenditures are treated as expenses when incurred since they are designed to ensure continued and dependable service of the asset.

Materiality

Distinguishing between repair or maintenance expenditures and those expenditures that should be capitalized is sometimes difficult. Major repairs that take on the characteristics of replacements and betterments in terms of the expected future use of the asset are capitalized if the impact on future income is judged to be material.

The treatment of repair and maintenance as expenses when incurred is based on the assumption that such expenses are evenly distributed over time and that individual expenditures are relatively small. Expenditures made in one period that provide for the use of the asset in a subsequent period are usually small and/or are offset by similar expenditures incurred during the subsequent period. If financial statements are prepared on a monthly or quarterly basis, the assumptions of immateriality and even distribution over time may be less appropriate. In these cases repair and maintenance expense may be accrued on an estimated basis by establishing an Allowance account, with actual expenditures charged to that allowance when made.

To illustrate the accrual of repair and maintenance, assume that Progolf Company incurs substantial amounts of repair and maintenance related to its equipment. Because of the size of the expenditures, their relative infrequency, and the need to prepare monthly financial statements, the company recognizes the estimated annual cost of $120,000 for 1993 on a monthly basis. Actual costs incurred during January,

February, and March 1993 are $500, $18,500, and $1,200, respectively. Entries to recognize the expenses and related expenditures are as follows:

January			
Various dates	Allowance for Repair and Maintenance	500	
	Cash (or other asset, liability, or expense account, as appropriate)		500
31	Repair and Maintenance Expense ($120,000/12)	10,000	
	Allowance for Repair and Maintenance		10,000
February			
Various dates	Allowance for Repair and Maintenance	18,500	
	Cash (or other appropriate account)		18,500
28	Repair and Maintenance Expense	10,000	
	Allowance for Repair and Maintenance		10,000
March			
Various dates	Allowance for Repair and Maintenance	1,200	
	Cash (or other appropriate account)		1,200
31	Repair and Maintenance Expense	10,000	
	Allowance for Repair and Maintenance		10,000

This method results in equal recognition of repair and maintenance expense of $10,000 each month, even though expenditures vary considerably between periods. A question arises, however, as to the balance in the Allowance for Repair and Maintenance account at the end of a reporting period. For Progolf Company this amount is as follows:

		Balance in Allowance Account
January	Expense recognized	$(10,000)
	Costs charged to allowance	500
	Balance in allowance at January 31	(9,500)
February	Expense recognized	(10,000)
	Costs charged to allowance	18,500
	Balance in allowance at February 28	(1,000)
March	Expense recognized	(10,000)
	Costs charged to allowance	1,200
	Balance in allowance at March 31	$ (9,800)

Diversity in practice exists in the treatment of the Allowance account in balance sheets prepared at the end of each month. The nature of the item, as well as the process giving rise to it, suggests treating the allowance in the same way that accumulated depreciation is treated (i.e., as a deduction in determining the book value of the related asset). An alternative interpretation of treating the allowance as a liability is difficult to justify, because expenditure in the future depends on future events. Also, the notion that the enterprise has a liability to itself for repair and maintenance on its assets is difficult to support. A related question concerns the treatment of any balance in the Allowance account at the end of the **annual** reporting period. If the estimated accrual method is used to spread the expense over the interim periods of the year, the estimated amount should be continually evaluated and adjusted in the final month or quarter so that the Allowance account is eliminated at year-end. This way, the problem of balance-sheet classification in annual financial statements is avoided.

Matching

Consistency

Materiality

Careful judgment is required in accounting for plant-asset-related expenditures made subsequent to original acquisition. The overriding objective is to match properly the cost of the expiration of the service potential with the revenue generated by that effort. Consistency in application is also important, because inconsistent treatment may materially affect the financial position and the results of operation. Accounting policies should reflect the most logical and realistic assumptions available.

Accounting for the various types of capital and revenue expenditures discussed in this section are summarized in Exhibit 11–3. In some cases, companies present their accounting policies concerning repairs, maintenance, and other postacquisition expenditures in notes to the financial statements. Exhibit 11–4 includes a section of the accounting policy statement from the 1990 annual report of H. J. Heinz Company, a worldwide provider of processed food products and nutritional services. The disclosure makes specific reference to the accounting treatment of improvements and repairs and maintenance, as well as other aspects of accounting for plant assets.

DISPOSALS OF PLANT ASSETS

Plant assets are disposed of for a variety of reasons and in a variety of ways. They may be **sold;** or they may be **abandoned** or **converted involuntarily,** as in the case of loss by fire, flood, or other natural disaster. They can also be **exchanged.** Regardless of the cause, two basic steps are followed in accounting for the disposal. First, depreciation is recognized to the date of the disposal. This is necessary in order to reflect properly the cost of operations for that portion of the year in which the asset is used and to correctly establish the book value of the asset at the time of disposal. Second, the cost and accumulated depreciation of the asset are eliminated from the accounts, any cash received is recorded and a gain or loss on the disposal is recognized. In exchanges, other assets are received and cash may be paid, both requiring accounting recognition.

To illustrate, assume that Gatlin Corporation acquired a building in January 1987 at a total cost of $510,000. The building has been depreciated by the straight-line method using a 20-year life with an estimated residual value of $60,000. On June 30, 1993, the building is **sold** for $425,000. The company reports on a calendar-year basis.

Depreciation must be brought up to date prior to recording the sale itself. To account for the half-year depreciation in 1993, the following entry is made:

Depreciation Expense	11,250	
[½ × ($510,000 − $60,000)/20]		
Accumulated Depreciation		11,250

This brings accumulated depreciation on the asset up to $146,250, determined as follows:

Depreciation, 1987–1992	
[($510,000 − $60,000)/20 years](6 years)	$135,000
Depreciation, partial year 1993	
[($510,000 − $60,000)/20 years](½ year)	11,250
	$146,250

EXHIBIT 11-3

Summary of Accounting for Postacquisition Expenditures

Type of Expenditure	Circumstances	Accounting Treatment
Additions	Useful life is *independent* of original asset.	Capitalize expenditure in separate account and depreciate over the estimated useful life.
	Useful life is *limited* to remaining life of original asset.	Capitalize expenditure as part of the original asset and increase the depreciation recognized over the remaining useful life.
Replacement and Betterment	*Separate* identification of portion of asset substituted is possible.	Capitalize expenditure to asset account and depreciate over shorter of the estimated useful life of (1) the replacement/betterment or (2) the original asset. Cost and accumulated depreciation on portion of asset being replaced are removed, and gain or loss is recognized.
	Separate identification of portion of asset substituted is *not* possible; service *potential* of asset is improved.	Charge expenditure to asset account and depreciate over the shorter of the estimated life of (1) the replacement/betterment or (2) the original asset.
	Separate identification of portion substituted is *not* possible; service *life* of asset is extended.	Charge expenditure to Accumulated Depreciation and depreciate book value over revised estimated life.
Rearrangement and Relocation	Costs are *identifiable* and *material* in amount; changes are expected to produce *discernible* future benefits.	Capitalize expenditure and amortize over the period expected to benefit.
	Costs are *not* separately identifiable nor material in amount; future benefits are *not* discernible.	Treat expenditure as expense when incurred.
Repair and Maintenance	Incurrence of costs is *evenly* distributed over the annual period.	Treat expenditures as expenses when incurred.
	Incurrence of costs is *not* evenly distributed over the annual period.	Accrue periodic expense on an estimated basis and charge actual expenditures to Allowance. (No allowance should be carried forward from one annual period to the next.)

EXHIBIT 11-4

H. J. Heinz Company
Plant Asset Policy Disclosure

Property, Plant and Equipment

Land, buildings and equipment are recorded at cost. For financial reporting purposes, depreciation is provided on the straight-line method over the estimated useful lives of the assets. Accelerated depreciation methods are generally used for income tax purposes. Expenditures for new facilities and improvements which substantially extend the capacity or useful life of an asset are capitalized. Ordinary repairs and maintenance are expensed as incurred. When property is retired or otherwise disposed, the cost and related depreciation are removed from the accounts and any related gains or losses are included in income.

SOURCE: H. J. Heinz Company, 1990 Annual Report.

Many companies would defer recording the depreciation of $11,250 until the end of the year, when depreciation on all plant assets is recognized. Regardless of when the entry is made, the accumulated depreciation used in recording the sale of the asset is $146,250.

The entry for the sale of the asset is then recorded as follows:

Cash	425,000	
Accumulated Depreciation—Building	146,250	
Building		510,000
Gain on Sale of Building		61,250

The gain is measured by subtracting the book value from the proceeds of the sale:

$$\text{Gain} = \$425,000 - (\$510,000 - \$146,250) = \$61,250$$

Sometimes assets are **abandoned** without being sold or otherwise disposed. The process of recording a disposal by abandonment is the same as that illustrated above except that no proceeds are received. In this case the loss equals the book value of the asset after depreciation is updated to the date of abandonment.

Sometimes an enterprise loses an asset due to factors other than its own choice, that is, by **involuntary conversion.** Examples are loss by fire, flood, or other disaster. The accounting procedures parallel those for abandonment if *no* insurance proceeds are received; if insurance proceeds *are* received, the accounting procedures are much like those for the sale of plant assets.[4]

To illustrate an exchange transaction, we assume that on June 30, 1993, Gatlin Corporation exchanges the building described above for a building valued at $750,000. Gatlin paid $350,000 in the exchange. Depreciation must first be updated to the date of the transaction, as in previous examples. The exchange is then recorded as follows:

June 30, 1993	Building (new)	750,000	
	Accumulated Depreciation	146,250	
	Building (old)		510,000
	Cash		350,000
	Gain on Exchange of Buildings		36,250

---

[4]Property insurance, including the computation of amounts to be received on insurance policies that include coinsurance requirements, is covered in Chapter 12. In Chapter 11, any situation involving insurance proceeds states the amount to be received from the insurance recovery.

This transaction is a **monetary exchange** because a significant portion of the value Gatlin is giving up is in the form of cash. A **nonmonetary exchange** is one in which little or no cash is involved. Special valuation problems in nonmonetary exchanges arise when fair value of the assets in the exchange cannot be determined or the exchange involves similar assets and, thus, the earning process is considered incomplete. The subject of nonmonetary exchanges is covered in greater depth in Appendix A of this chapter.

Materiality

Gains and losses on plant assets are ordinarily not considered to be extraordinary items in the income statement. Depending on the extent of detail in the income statement, such items may be separately disclosed, however. If a gain or loss of this type is material in amount and is judged to be **either** unusual in nature **or** infrequent in occurrence, separate disclosure should be made. An occasion in which such gains and losses are presented as extraordinary items is found in involuntary conversions. *Accounting Principles Board Opinion No. 30* states that in rare instances an event or transaction may occur that clearly meets the criteria of **unusual in nature** and **infrequent in occurrence** and that results in the disposal of a plant asset.[5] One example is the destruction of a plant asset by an earthquake. Therefore, it is important to consider the underlying cause of a write-down or write-off of a plant asset in judging whether it is an **extraordinary** item or not. While such write-downs or write-offs are usually not presented as extraordinary items, they may be considered such if they result from a major casualty *and* are clearly unusual in nature and infrequent in occurrence.

DEPARTURES FROM HISTORICAL COST

Asset/Liability Measurement

Historical cost is well established as the basis for measuring and reporting property, plant, and equipment and is supported by authoritative pronouncements. As with most accounting principles, however, exceptions exist to the general practice of recording and depreciating assets at cost. Although departures from historical cost are not frequent, this section discusses several situations representing departures from the general concepts developed earlier in this chapter.

DONATED ASSETS

Enterprises may receive assets by donation, such as when land is donated to an enterprise by a city as an inducement to locate a facility in the city. The advantages to the city in the future result from increased property-tax revenues, increased levels of employment, improved reputation, and other positive aspects of increased business activity.

Strict adherence to historical cost in such cases would result in recording the asset acquired at a zero cost or at an amount equal to the relatively minor costs incidental to the acceptance of the land, such as the cost of transferring title. Accounting for donated assets at a zero cost, however, is not generally thought to represent the substance of the transaction in terms of the fair value of the donated asset received by the enterprise.

Substance over Form

Accounting for **nonreciprocal transfers,** which are transfers of assets or services in one direction, either to or from the enterprise, is also discussed in *APB Opinion No. 29,* which concludes that the receipt of an asset in a nonreciprocal transfer should be based on the fair value of the asset received.[6] The APB relied heavily on the modifying convention of substance over form in reaching this conclusion.

---

[5]*APB Opinion No. 30,* "Reporting the Results of Operations," 1973, par. 23.
[6]*APB Opinion No. 29,* "Accounting for Nonmonetary Transactions," 1973, par. 18.

To illustrate the receipt of a donated asset, we assume that Shelby Company receives land appraised at $130,000 as an inducement to locate a manufacturing facility in the city of Manchester. The receipt of the land and the related contribution by the city is recorded as follows:

Land	130,000	
Donated Capital—Plant Site		130,000

Costs incurred relative to the transfer that *would have been incurred* had the asset been purchased are also charged to the asset account. Any other costs are treated as expenses in the current period. The Donated Capital account becomes a part of the stockholders' equity of the enterprise that receives the donated asset.

PERMANENT IMPAIRMENT IN VALUE

The price that an enterprise pays for a plant asset is based on estimates of future use, of future demand for products and services, and of other considerations of future events. When circumstances dramatically change, plant assets may experience a **permanent impairment in value**.

A permanent impairment in value may occur when the demand for products or services significantly declines, when assets become obsolete or inadequate, or when other circumstances change. Depreciation (allocating cost to the periods benefiting from the use of the asset) is designed to facilitate the determination of net income via *Matching* the matching principle. Although depreciation accounting is not designed primarily as a method of asset valuation, generally assets are not carried in the balance sheet at amounts exceeding their value. We have already seen this practice in the rule of applying the lower of cost or market value to inventory and marketable securities.

In the case of plant assets this general rule discourages carrying assets in the accounts or in the balance sheet at amounts exceeding the value of the assets. This sometimes means that the future value of the assets has been reduced from that originally expected, even though the assets will continue to be used. In other cases, the assets have become valueless for their original purpose and are worth only their salvage value.

If a permanent impairment in value has occurred, the book value of the asset is reduced by crediting the accumulated depreciation and recognizing a loss. If the asset is to continue in use, future depreciation charges may require adjustment to account for revised estimates of useful life, salvage value, and other factors.

To illustrate, we shall assume that Fraker Company acquired machinery in 1990 for use in producing a line of toys. The asset cost $100,000 and had an expected $20,000 residual value at the end of an expected eight-year life. At the end of 1992 the machinery had a book value of $70,000, computed as follows:

Asset cost in 1990	$100,000
Accumulated depreciation at December 31, 1992 [($100,000 − $20,000)/8](3 years)	(30,000)
Book value at December 31, 1992	$ 70,000

Because of changes in consumer demand, management determines in early 1993 that the asset is worth substantially less than originally expected. Specifically, it is determined that the book value should be reduced to $20,000; the remaining life, to two years; and the salvage value, to $2,000.

"YOU KNOW IT WHEN YOU SEE IT"

Last winter wasn't a particularly good one for Pillsbury Co., and a footnote in the company's third-quarter report to shareholders showed why: a $113 million loss on the sale or shutdown of several restaurant operations, including its money-losing Godfather's Pizza chain. But precisely how did Pillsbury, which saw its stock jump nearly 10% in value on the day of the announced write-offs, wind up with the $113 million figure? You'll search Pillsbury's financials in vain for an answer, as indeed you would in the case of almost any other company engaged in writing off failed (or failing) assets.

The 1980s are clearly the decade of business restructurings and write-offs. But, ironically, accounting provides few rules to protect shareholders regarding when management can (or must) write off an "impaired asset," and by how much.

Since 1986 the Dow Jones industrials alone have taken at least $10 billion in writedowns, much of it related to impairment questions. A recent study by the National Association of Accountants reports that these impairment writeoffs are one of the fastest-growing categories of all asset writedowns. Further, the study concludes that behind the numbers lurks "a climate of vague accounting standards" that gives companies too much leeway in choosing when and how to write down assets. That feeling was echoed in a survey of accountants by the Financial Accounting Standards Board who ranked impairment at the top of outstanding issues warranting new standards.

Yet many corporations don't seem eager for tightened standards, arguing that management is the best guide for when an asset becomes worthless. Even so, lax accounting standards can lead to abuses. In 1986, for example, the Securities & Exchange Commission took action against Charter Co. for attempting to sell a refinery at well below book value without first writing it down on its balance sheet. Warns Edmund Coulson, chief accountant at the SEC: "There are many other such cases in the pipeline."

What are the rules governing impairment? Under current accounting principles, a long-lived asset (plant, property and so on) should be labeled "impaired" when there is no hope of recovering its book value. Of course, hope, or lack of it, is in the eye of the beholder. Comments Wayne Kolins, partner at accounting firm Seidman & Seidman/BDO: "In these situations, it's often a case of people saying, 'You know it when you see it.'"

Once an asset has been judged impaired, companies also have considerable leeway in determining what balance sheet value to assign to it. Among the acceptable methods: net realizable value (what the asset will bring if sold); a total of projected future cash flows over the life of the asset; and "discounting"—the present value of those future cash flows based on a given rate of return. Since future cash flow is worth less than cash in hand, discounting can result in lower valuations and larger writeoffs.

To complicate matters, businesses have begun announcing partial writedowns based on "probable" impairment. This includes assets whose return no longer meets carrying costs but which might recover their value in the future. Thus in 1986 Squibb Corp. decided that political and economic conditions in South America and Asia had impaired its pharmaceuticals operations there. Squibb took a writedown of $68 million on those assets, declaring them "permanently" impaired. But are they really? Since Squibb concedes that there remains a "small probability" that those assets will recover, it is operating those facilities on a reduced scale.

With writedowns becoming such a common—and costly—feature of a business scene that is complex enough already, such accounting double-speak is hardly to be welcomed. But without a clarification of the rules, there seems little doubt that it will continue.

SOURCE: Penelope Wang, "You Know It When You See It," *Forbes*, July 25, 1988, p. 84. Reprinted by permission of *Forbes* magazine. © Forbes Inc., 1988.

The entry to record this impairment in value is as follows:

Loss—Obsolescence of Machinery ($70,000 − $20,000) 50,000
    Accumulated Depreciation—Machinery 50,000

Materiality   Depreciation recognized in 1993 and 1994 will be $9,000 [($20,000 − $2,000)/2 years]. If material, the loss of $50,000 should be separately disclosed in the income statement on the basis that it is not a typical transaction that reflects normal business operations. However, this type of loss should *not* be treated as extraordinary.

If the book value of an asset is being reduced to the salvage value and no future use of the asset is expected, an entry similar to the one in the previous paragraph is made for the amount that leaves the estimated residual value as the book value. No further depreciation is recognized on the asset after it has been retired from active service.

QUASI REORGANIZATION

A **quasi reorganization** is a specialized situation in which assets are reduced from their book values to lower estimates of future value. To this extent, the quasi reorganization is similar to a permanent impairment in value.

The quasi reorganization, however, is different in that it involves a simultaneous adjustment in the book values of several assets. It represents a general decline in the value of the enterprise rather than the decline in usefulness of one asset or a few specific assets. The quasi reorganization involves adjustments to several stockholders' equity accounts, including Retained Earnings, as part of the process by which the book values of assets are reduced. The circumstances that call for the quasi reorganization process are considered in Chapter 17.

DISCOVERY VALUE

The value of property may increase significantly if a hidden quality is discovered subsequent to acquisition. An example is the discovery of a valuable natural resource on land subsequent to acquisition. Since the existence of the resource was unknown when the land was acquired, the original cost would not reflect the value exchanged.

The accounting treatment of assets discovered subsequent to acquisition varies considerably, ranging from nonrecognition to the complete recognition of the estimated value of the discovered assets. Accountants generally hesitate to record increases in asset values that have not been verified by transactions with other enterprises. Thus, the most common treatment of discovery is nonrecognition. This is consistent with the APB's conclusion:

> The Board is of the opinion that property, plant and equipment should not be written up by an entity to reflect appraisal, market or current values which are above cost to the entity. . . .Whenever appreciation has been recorded on the books, income should be charged with depreciation computed on the written up amounts.[7]

Some increases in value were recorded prior to this APB pronouncement. In addition, some accountants believe that the discovery of assets that were unknown at the time of acquisition is different from the appreciation in asset value that results from changing market conditions, changes in consumer tastes, or other factors occurring after acquisition. Therefore, an accountant may occasionally encounter an increase in the recorded basis of a plant asset that represents the recording of discovery value. As indicated in *APB Opinion No. 6*, depreciation (or depletion) of the asset should reflect the increased cost basis of the asset. Accountants generally agree that when such asset write-ups are appropriate, the credit side of the entry should be to the stockholders' equity rather than to a revenue or gain account.

To illustrate, we shall assume that Royal Mining Company acquired land for $200,000 in 1991. In 1993 mineral deposits in the estimated amount of 75,000 tons and appraised at $4.25 per ton (net of anticipated extraction costs) were discovered on

---

[7]*APB Opinion No. 6*, "Omnibus Opinion," 1965, par. 17.

the land. Management estimates that the land will be worth its original cost of $200,000 after the exploitation of the mineral deposits. The entries to record the above events assume that 15,700 tons were extracted and sold in 1993:

1991	Land	200,000	
	Cash		200,000
1993	Land—Mineral Deposits Discovered	318,750	
	Unrealized Capital Increment—		
	Discovery of Mineral Deposits		318,750
	(75,000 × $4.25 = $318,750)		
	Depletion Expense	66,725	
	Land—Mineral Deposits Discovered		66,725
	[(15,700/75,000) × $318,750 = $66,725]		

The capital account, Unrealized Capital Increment—Discovery of Mineral Deposits, is presented as part of the stockholders' equity section in the balance sheet.

FINANCIAL-STATEMENT DISCLOSURE

At the end of Chapter 12, after completing our study of plant assets and depreciation, we look more carefully at the disclosure requirements for property, plant and equipment. Many companies include only total amounts for property, plant and equipment in their balance sheets and then provide more detailed information in notes to the financial statements. In Exhibit 11–5 we illustrate that type of presentation for

EXHIBIT 11–5

Meredith Corporation
Plant Asset Disclosure

3. Property, Plant and Equipment
A comparative summary of property, plant and equipment follows:

	1990	1989	1988
			(in thousands)
Land and improvements	$ 6,298	$ 6,181	$ 6,306
Buildings and improvements	57,377	56,751	56,859
Machinery and equipment	107,116	100,529	96,539
Leasehold improvements	4,414	4,946	4,595
Construction in progress	949	859	471
Total (at cost)	176,154	169,266	164,770
Less accumulated depreciation	(98,074)	(91,665)	(83,821)
Net	$ 78,080	$ 77,601	$ 80,949
Depreciation expense for the year	$ 11,805	$ 11,759	$ 13,031

For each classification of property, plant and equipment, depreciable life is as follows:

	Depreciable Life
Buildings and improvements	5 to 45 years
Machinery and equipment	3 to 20 years
Leasehold improvements	4 to 15 years

SOURCE: Meredith Corporation, 1990 Annual Report.

Meredith Corporation, a company that describes itself as a magazine and book publisher, television broadcaster, residential real estate franchiser and marketer, and commercial printer.

CONCLUDING REMARKS

Asset/Liability Measurement

Several accounting principles are significant in accounting for plant assets. Chapter 11 has focused primarily on the determination of *historical cost* as the principle means of measuring plant assets. While historical cost may seem to be a relatively simple and straightforward principle, complications may arise in a variety of circumstances, such as the purchase of more than one asset in a single transaction, the treatment of costs related to acquisition, the internal construction of plant assets, the incurrence of interest cost in the construction of plant assets, and postacquisition expenditures that may impact the historical cost of plant assets. Generally accepted accounting principles in all of these situations reflect the considered judgment of accountants in determining historical cost.

Consistency Materiality

In determining historical cost, *objectivity* is important. Accountants base their measurements on objective, verifiable evidence to the extent possible. The *consistency principle* is also important in the treatment of plant assets expenditures since similar expenditures are made from period to period. The *materiality principle* comes into play in accounting for plant assets, as it does in virtually all areas of accounting. The strict application of the principles discussed in this chapter is not required if the results are insignificant and, therefore, not cost effective.

Matching

One of the primary purposes for carefully establishing the correct historical cost of plant assets is to determine the appropriate amount for depreciation in accordance with the matching principle. In the next chapter, we consider depreciation of plant assets in depth, building on the general principles of historical cost determination discussed here.

KEY POINTS

1. Property, plant, and equipment and intangible assets are long-lived assets that are acquired for use in the production and distribution of goods and services. (Objective 1)

2. Several basic accounting principles impact the proper accounting for plant and intangible assets. Most notable are the historical cost method of measuring and reporting and matching principle. (Objective 2)

3. Several unique problems may be encountered in attempting to apply historical cost to specific types of plant assets, such as land, buildings, machinery, equipment, furniture, fixtures, and natural resources. (Objective 3)

4. General problems of establishing historical cost include the treatment of:
   a. Cash discounts.
   b. Deferred-payment plans.
   c. Internally constructed plant assets.
   d. Capitalization of interest.
   e. Acquisition by issuing securities.
   f. Basket purchases.
   g. Installation, preparation, and start-up costs. (Objective 3)

5. An important distinction in accounting for postacquisition expenditures is to separate capital expenditures from revenue expenditures. Capital expenditures are amortized over their estimated useful lives, whereas revenue expenditures are charged to expense as incurred. (Objective 4)

6. Disposals of plant assets may result from sales, abandonments, involuntary conversions, or exchanges. Disposals may result in gains or losses, which are presented as part of net income. (Objective 5)

7. Certain specialized situations dictate a departure from historical cost in accounting for plant assets. These exceptions are found in the cases of donated assets, permanent impairments in value, quasi reorganizations, and discovery value. (Objective 6)

APPENDIX A: ACQUISITIONS AND DISPOSALS BY EXCHANGE

A business enterprise can participate in an **exchange** transaction whereby it simultaneously acquires an asset and disposes of another asset. For example, an enterprise may exchange land that it owns for land held by another enterprise. Also, used machinery may be exchanged for other used machinery. These transactions may include either the *receipt* or *payment* of a small amount of cash, sometimes referred to as **boot,** to adjust for the perceived difference in the value of the assets exchanged. Transactions like this are called **nonmonetary transactions.** The Accounting Principles Board (APB) established the proper accounting for nonmonetary transactions in *Opinion No. 29,* which was cited earlier in this chapter.

Concepts Underlying Exchange Transactions

The general principle governing the recording of a nonmonetary exchange is to record the acquired asset at the **fair value** of the assets involved in the exchange. Accordingly, the fair value of the surrendered asset is used as a measure of the historical cost of the acquired asset, and a gain or loss may be recognized on the exchange. This principle was illustrated earlier in this chapter when we recorded the exchange of buildings. However, if the fair value of the asset received is more clearly evident than the fair value of the asset surrendered, the former amount is used. Fair value of a nonmonetary asset may be established by estimated realizable value in cash transactions of similar assets, quoted market prices, independent appraisals, and other available evidence.

Modification of this fair value concept is required in several circumstances, including instances in which fair value is not determinable or the transaction does not result in the completion of an earning process. In some circumstances the fair value of assets surrendered or received cannot be determined within reasonably objective limits. In these cases the acquired asset is recorded at the book value of the surrendered asset. No gain or loss on the exchange is recorded, because the new asset is simply substituted for the old asset in the accounts.

Two types of nonmonetary exchanges are not considered to result in the completion of an earning process:

1. An exchange of a product or property held for sale in the ordinary course of business for a product or property to be sold in the same line of business to facilitate sales to customers other than parties to the exchange.

2. An exchange of a productive asset not held for sale in the ordinary course of business for a similar productive asset or an equivalent interest in the same or similar productive asset.[8]

In the first case inventory is exchanged for inventory. A subsequent transaction in which the inventory is sold to the ultimate customer must take place before the earning process is considered complete. In the second case productive assets are exchanged for productive assets of the same general type performing essentially the same function. The earning process is not considered complete until these assets are used in the production of goods or services that are sold. These transactions are sometimes referred to as **swaps** of inventory or similar productive assets.

Assets acquired in swaps are generally recorded at the book value of the assets surrendered, and no gain is recognized as a result of the exchange. If boot is received in a transaction in which a gain is apparent (i.e., the fair value received exceeds the book value surrendered), the recipient of the boot has realized a gain to the extent that the cash received exceeds a pro rata share of the book value of the surrendered asset. This gain and the acquired asset should be recorded at a pro rata share of the book value of the surrendered asset.

In certain circumstances the fair value inherent in a swap of inventory or plant assets may indicate that a loss would be recorded if fair value were the basis for recording the transaction. In such cases fair value is used and the loss is recognized in accordance with the modifying convention of conservatism. Methods of accounting for assets acquired through nonmonetary exchanges are summarized in Exhibit 11–6.

Conservatism

In summary, recording nonmonetary transactions represents an interesting application of the accounting principles of revenue realization and asset measurement and of the modifying convention of conservatism. Transactions are generally recorded on the basis of fair value, which is consistent with revenue-

Revenue
Realization

Asset/Liability
Measurement

Conservatism

---

[8]*APB Opinion No. 29*, par. 21.

EXHIBIT 11–6

Recording Bases of Assets Acquired in Nonmonetary Exchanges

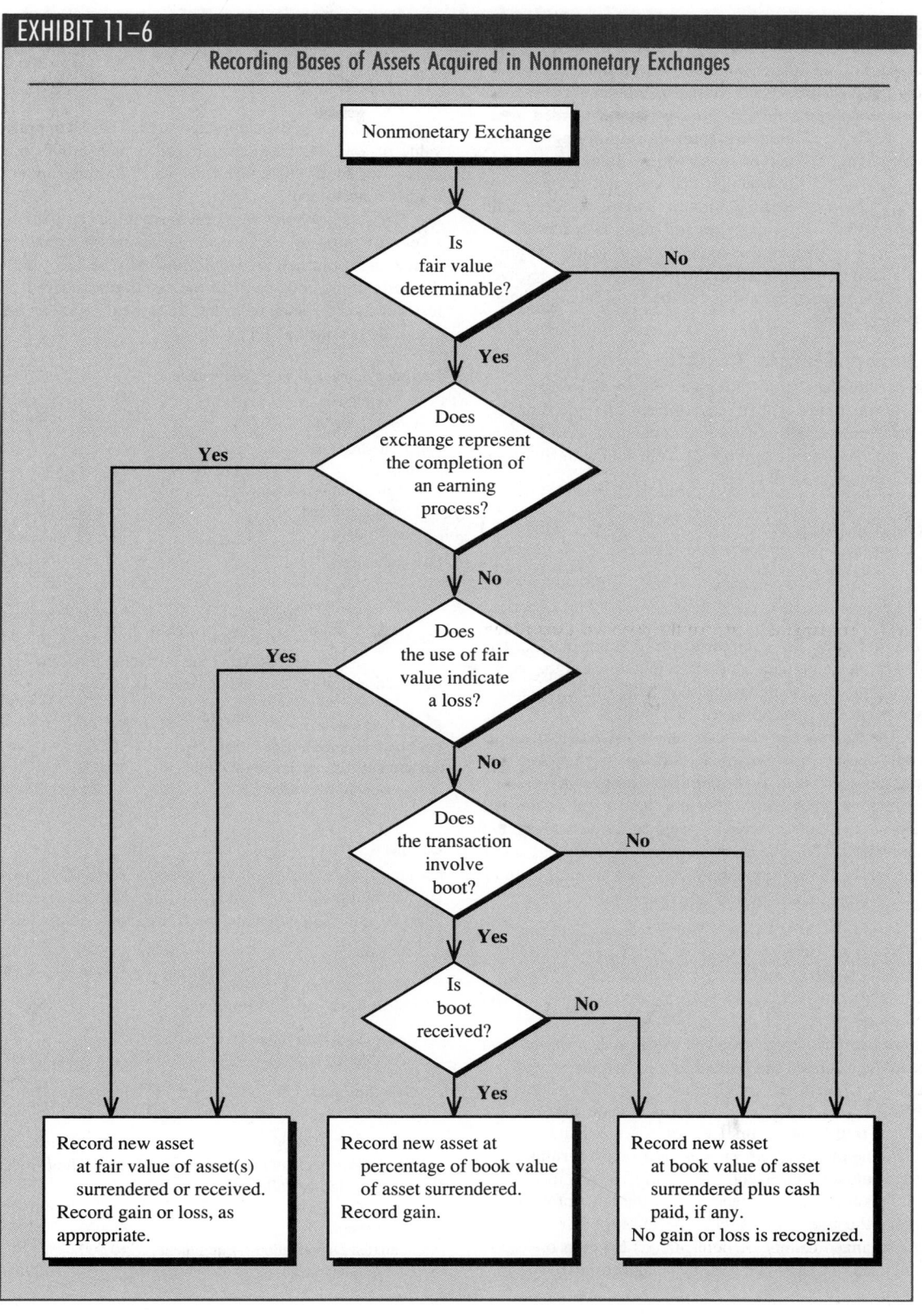

realization and historical cost if the transaction represents the completion of an earning process. If the earning process is not complete, however, the acquired asset is recorded at the book value of the surrendered asset unless a loss is apparent; in that case, the loss is recorded in accordance with the modifying convention of conservatism. In a nonmonetary transaction that does not complete the earning process and in which a gain is apparent and boot is received, the revenue-realization principle requires that a gain be recognized to the extent that boot received exceeds a proportionate share of the book value of the asset surrendered.

Conservatism

Revenue
Realization

Illustrations of Exchange Transactions

This section analyzes a number of transactions, each of which illustrates a different concept in recording exchange transactions. In each independent case Carland Company is trading equipment. The following information is common to all cases:

Cost of equipment traded	$100,000 FV
Accumulated depreciation to date of trade	40,000
Book value of equipment traded	$ 60,000 BV

Example 1   *dissimiliar, earning process complete*

Carland trades the equipment for several trucks. The value of the equipment is not determinable, but the trucks have a total estimated market value of $75,000. No cash is involved in the transaction. *No boot*

This transaction is a nonmonetary exchange that represents the **completion** of an earning process, because the assets exchanged are **not similar in nature.** Since the fair value of the equipment is not determinable, the fair value of the trucks received is used as the value inherent in the transaction. The assets acquired are recorded at fair value, and any resulting gain or loss is recorded, as indicated in the entry at the top of the next page.

Trucks	75,000	
Accumulated Depreciation—Equipment	40,000	
Equipment		100,000
Gain on Exchange of Assets		15,000

If boot had been either received or paid, cash would have been either debited or credited as part of the entry.

Example 2   *dissimiliar, earning proc. complete*

Carland trades the equipment for office furniture. The value of neither the equipment nor the office furniture can be determined objectively.

This transaction is recorded on the basis of the book value of the assets surrendered, because the fair value being exchanged cannot be determined. No gain or loss is recognized. The following entry is appropriate:

Office Furniture	60,000	
Accumulated Depreciation—Equipment	40,000	
Equipment		100,000

Example 3

Carland exchanges the equipment, which has an appraised value of $50,000, and pays an additional $5,000 in exchange for similar equipment for which a value cannot be readily determined.

This transaction does not represent the completion of an earning process, because similar assets are exchanged. While such transactions would normally be recorded on the basis of the book value of the assets surrendered, any loss indicated must be recorded. In this case a loss is indicated, determined as follows:

Recorded amount of assets surrendered		
Equipment	$60,000	
Cash	5,000	$65,000
Fair value inherent in transaction		
Fair value of equipment surrendered	50,000	
Cash paid	5,000	(55,000)
Loss indicated		$10,000

Conservatism

Because a loss is indicated, conservatism dictates that the assets acquired be recorded at the fair value inherent in the transaction and the loss recognized, as follows:

Equipment (new)	55,000	
Loss on Exchange of Equipment	10,000	
Accumulated Depreciation—Equipment	40,000	
Equipment (old)		100,000
Cash		5,000

Example 4

Carland trades the equipment, valued at $67,000 for other similar equipment for which no fair value is determinable. A gain is apparent in the transaction, computed as follows:

Fair value inherent in transaction	
Fair value of asset surrendered	$67,000
Recorded amount of asset surrendered	
Equipment	(60,000)
Gain indicated	$ 7,000

However, the gain is not recorded, because the **earning process has not been completed.** The transaction is recorded as follows:

Equipment (new)	60,000	
Accumulated Depreciation—Equipment	40,000	
Equipment (old)		100,000

Example 5

Carland exchanges the equipment (valued at $65,000) and $5,000 cash for similar equipment for which a market value is not determinable.

This transaction **does not represent the completion of the earning process,** because similar items of equipment are being exchanged. A gain is indicated because the fair value inherent in the transaction exceeds the recorded amounts of assets surrendered.

Fair value inherent in transaction		
Fair value of equipment surrendered	$65,000	
Cash	5,000	$70,000
Recorded amount of assets surrendered		
Equipment	60,000	
Cash	5,000	(65,000)
Gain indicated		$ 5,000

The **gain is not recorded,** and the equipment acquired is recorded at the book value of the equipment surrendered plus the $5,000 cash paid:

Equipment (new)	65,000	
Accumulated Depreciation—Equipment	40,000	
Equipment (old)		100,000
Cash		5,000

Example 6   *not complete*

Carland trades the equipment for similar productive equipment valued at $69,000. In addition, Carland receives $6,000 in cash. *Boot*

Although this is a nonmonetary exchange that does not represent the completion of an earning process, the **receipt of boot in a gain situation** requires recognition of a gain to the extent that the cash received exceeds an appropriate portion of the book value surrendered. The gain inherent in the transaction is computed as follows:

Fair value inherent in transaction		
Cash received	$ 6,000	
Fair value of equipment received	69,000	$75,000
Recorded amount of asset surrendered		
Equipment		(60,000)
Gain indicated		$15,000

The portion of the transaction that represents a sale is determined by dividing the cash received by the total fair value inherent in the transaction:

$$\text{Sale } \% = \frac{\$6,000}{\$75,000} = 8\%$$

The book value of the equipment surrendered must be separated into the portion sold (8%) and the portion traded ($100\% - 8\% = 92\%$):

Book value sold: $60,000 × 8% =	$ 4,800
Book value traded: $60,000 × 92% =	55,200
	$60,000

The gain recognized in the transaction is measured as follows:

Cash received	$6,000
Book value sold	(4,800)
Gain recognized	$1,200

The $1,200 can also be computed by multiplying the total gain on the transaction by the percentage of the transaction representing a sale:

$$\$15,000 \times 8\% = \$1,200.$$

The acquired equipment is recorded at the book value of that portion of the assets surrendered that is considered to have been traded ($60,000 × 92% or $55,200):

Equipment (new)	55,200	
Accumulated Depreciation—Equipment	40,000	
Cash	6,000	
Equipment (old)		100,000
Gain on Exchange of Equipment		1,200

Asset/Liability Measurement Conservatism

These methods reveal the influence of historical cost as a means of measuring plant assets and the modifying convention of conservatism. The nonrecognition of gains in transactions that do not complete the earning process is designed to prevent artificial write-ups of assets and the recording of gains in value from holding assets that result from meaningless transactions in which similar assets are exchanged. One word of caution: The use of fair value in recording exchanges of unlike assets is *not a departure* from historical cost. Rather, it is an *application* of that method, because the historical cost in a noncash transaction (or part-cash transaction) is the fair value of the consideration given up to acquire that asset. If the fair value of the asset received is more clearly determinable, however, we use it as a substitute measure of historical cost.

QUESTIONS

11–1   Identify the two primary characteristics of all plant and intangible assets.

11–2   Distinguish between plant and intangible assets and identify several types of each.

11–3   Identify four principles that underlie accounting for plant and intangible assets within generally accepted accounting principles.

11–4   What is the "full-cost" interpretation of historical cost, as applied to plant assets?

11–5   In determining the full cost of land, what expenditures in addition to the bargained acquisition price might be included?

11–6   Why is it generally desirable for land improvements to be capitalized in a separate account from the Land account?

11–7   How should land which is held for investment or speculative purposes be classified in the balance sheet?

11–8   For items of machinery, equipment, furniture, and fixtures, what expenditures may be included in the cost figure in addition to the original acquisition price?

11–9   What is the preferred treatment of cash discounts in determining the cost of plant assets?

11–10   In what circumstances may it be necessary to *impute* interest included in the payments in a deferred-payment plan for plant assets? What is the purpose of imputing interest?

11–11   What distortions will exist in the financial statements of the buyer of a plant asset if interest is not imputed in an installment contract for which interest should have been imputed?

11–12   As a general rule, a careful distinction is maintained between interest and the cost of plant assets. In certain circumstances, however, it is appropriate to capitalize interest in establishing the correct historical cost of an asset. What are these circumstances?

11–13   When a plant asset is acquired by issuing capital stock, what is the appropriate basis for recording the asset acquired?

11–14   If several assets are acquired in a single transaction for one price, how is the historical cost of the individual assets determined?

11–15   Enterprises may produce their own plant assets for use in future operations. Determining the cost of such assets is complicated by the fact that production activities of plant assets may be mixed with production activities of inventory items. Describe how the cost of internally developed assets should be determined, including an identification of specific costs to be included.

11–16   Distinguish between capital expenditures and revenue expenditures, citing several examples of each.

11–17   Distinguish between the accounting treatment of the following three types of betterments:
   [a] Substitution of part of an asset when separate cost identification is possible.
   [b] Substitution of part of an asset when separate cost identification is not possible and the advantage of the expenditure is improved quality of future services.
   [c] Substitution of part of an asset when separate cost identification is not possible and the advantage of the expenditure is an extension of the useful life of the asset.

11–18   Under what circumstances should the allowance method of recognizing repair and maintenance expense be used as an alternative to recognition as costs are incurred? What is the purpose of the allowance method?

11–19 (Appendix A)   Assets acquired in exchange transactions may be recorded in one of several ways, depending on the circumstances of the exchange. Identify the circumstances in which each of the following bases are appropriate for recording an asset acquired in a nonmonetary exchange:

   [a] Fair value inherent in the exchange.
   [b] Book value of asset(s) surrendered.
   [c] A percentage of the book value of asset(s) surrendered.

11–20   Cardwell Company acquired a three-acre site for the construction of a new branch plant. Which of the following costs (or groups of costs) should *not* be charged to the Land account of the company?

   [a] Title examination fees, recording fees, and surveying fees.
   [b] Costs of grading, clearing, and draining the property.
   [c] Costs of removing the old, unwanted building from the land.
   [d] Property taxes accruing during the period of plant construction.   (AICPA adapted)

11–21 (Appendix A) Horwitz Company received $20,000 in cash and a used computer with a fair value of $180,000 from Harvest Corporation for Horwitz's existing computer having a fair value of $200,000 and an undepreciated cost of $160,000 recorded on its books. Which answer shows, respectively, how much gain Horwitz should recognize on this exchange and at what amount should the acquired computer be recorded?

[a] Zero and $140,000   [c] $20,000 and $160,000
[b] $4,000 and $144,000   [d] $40,000 and $180,000   (AICPA adapted)

11–22 (Appendix A) Sipp Company exchanged inventory items that cost $8,000 and normally sold for $12,000 for a new delivery truck with a list price of $13,000. At which figure should the delivery truck be recorded on Sipp's books?

[a] $8,000   [b] $8,667   [c] $12,000   [d] $13,000   (AICPA adapted)

EXERCISES

11–23 BUILDING AND LAND COST Weber Company acquired land and a building for $275,000 on October 15, 1992. The land was appraised at $125,000 and the building at $175,000. Unpaid property taxes assumed by Weber were $12,000, 40% allocated to the land and 60% to the building. Additional costs incurred were:

[1] Building renovation, $57,500.
[2] Option on alternative land and building which were not acquired, $1,750.
[3] Cost of survey, $210.

Instructions

Determine the cost of the building and the land, identifying the individual elements of cost included in each asset.

11–24 PLANT ASSET ACQUISITION COST Anders Co. recently acquired several items of property, plant, and equipment. The transactions are described as follows:

June 5   Purchased land appraised at $175,000 and machinery appraised at $50,000 for a total of $195,000.
July 16   Purchased a building for $185,000 in cash and 100,000 in shares of the company's $7 par value common stock, which sold for $10 on the transaction date.
Aug. 21   Received a parcel of land from the city of Hillsboro as an inducement to locate a plant in the city. No payment was required. The land was appraised at $65,000.
Sept. 25   Acquired furniture and fixtures by issuing a $75,000, two-year, noninterest-bearing note. In similar transactions the company has paid 12% interest.

Instructions

Prepare the journal entry appropriate in each case to record the acquisition of property, plant, and equipment.

11–25 LAND COST Paulson Company acquired land on June 1, 1993, for $170,000, on which a new building will be immediately constructed. Costs related to the acquisition include:

[1] A commission of 4% of the price for the location of the land and the negotiation of the acquisition price.
[2] $1,700 for legal fees related to the transfer of the title of the land and other matters.
[3] $350 for a survey pursuant to the closing of the transaction.
[4] $2,500 for options acquired at an earlier date: $1,500 for the land acquired, and $1,000 for an alternative parcel of land which was seriously considered but not acquired.
[5] $16,000 for removal of an existing building. $2,750 was received from the salvage of materials.
[6] $2,400 for 1992 property taxes which were delinquent on June 1, 1993. Taxes for 1993 are expected to be $3,000 and will be paid by Paulson before December 31, 1993.

Instructions

Determine the historical cost of the land as it should be presented in the company's balance sheet on December 31, 1993.

11–26   FIXTURES COST   Wexler Company acquired several fixtures for its new building, including display cases, shelves, and hanging racks. The invoice price of the fixtures was $72,500. The company received 2% cash discount by paying within the discount period. Freight and insurance during shipment totaled $352. Costs of assembling and installing the fixtures were $475. While installing a display case, a new employee carelessly broke a glass top. This top was replaced at a cost of $185. —> *expense, not a capitalized cost*

Instructions

Determine the total cost of the fixtures, identifying the individual elements making up the total.

11–27   EQUIPMENT TRANSACTIONS   On January 1, 1993, Prosser Company acquired used equipment by issuing the seller a two-year, noninterest-bearing note for $200,000. The value of the equipment is apparently less than $200,000, but a specific amount cannot be determined. In recent borrowings, Prosser has paid 10% interest.

On January 7 the company installed the equipment. Estimated costs of installation were $1,750 for labor and $670 for materials, both included in the manufacturing accounts. On January 12 the company paid $675 for freight and insurance charges during shipment.

Instructions

[a] Prepare general journal entries for the above transactions and for adjustments required on December 31, 1993. Provide supporting computations. The company plans to depreciate the asset over eight years, with the salvage value being approximately equal to the costs of removal. Straight-line depreciation should be used. Interest is recognized by the effective interest method.

[b] What amount of interest expense will be recognized at December 31, 1994 on the equipment note?

11–28   PLANT ASSET TRANSACTIONS   Clyde Products acquired the following plant assets during 1993:   *Main objective is to record cash or equiv.*

Equipment.   Acquired at an invoice price of $60,000, subject to a 1% cash discount which was not taken. Freight and insurance during shipment cost $350. The equipment has a five-year life expectancy and a salvage value of 10% of the invoice price.

Land.   Acquired by issuing 10,000 shares of $5 par value common stock when the market price of the stock was $11. The stock issued was treasury stock which had been acquired at an earlier date at $9 per share.   *11-15   6   11-9=2*

Machinery.   Acquired at a cost of $27,600. Installation costs were $770. Trial runs and other testing cost $510. These expenses have been included in the Manufacturing Overhead account. The machinery is expected to be useful for ten years, at the end of which it will have a $2,500 salvage value.

Instructions

Prepare all general journal entries needed to record the acquisition and depreciation of the assets for 1993. Straight-line depreciation should be used with a full year recognized.

11–29   INTERNALLY CONSTRUCTED ASSETS   Wicker Company decided to construct its own equipment rather than acquire similar assets from other companies. Management believed that the assets could be built for less than they could be bought. Material and labor costs were determined to be $195,000 and $220,000, respectively. Overhead is normally charged to production at the rate of 85% of the direct labor cost. The actual increment in overhead resulting from the construction was determined to be $162,000.

Instructions

Assuming the company is operating at full capacity and must curtail production operations to construct the equipment, determine the appropriate amounts to be capitalized as the cost of the equipment. Justify your treatment of overhead costs.

11–30   (Appendix A)   NONMONETARY EXCHANGE   Mannis Company recently swapped used machinery for similar used machinery with a competing company. Mannis's previous machinery cost $7,000 and had a book value of $5,500 at the time of the trade. The machinery's estimated value was $6,200 and Mannis paid $500 in cash as part of the transaction. Machinery received in the trade had not been appraised recently. Mannis's accountant recorded the trade as follows:

Machinery (new)	6,700	
Accumulated Depreciation	1,500	
Machinery (old)		7,000
Cash		500
Gain on Exchange of Machinery		700

Instructions

[a] Prepare the general journal entry you would suggest for recording the transaction.

[b] Explain the fallacy, if any, in the accountant's entry and how your entry corrects that problem.

11–31   REPLACEMENT   Bills Enterprise replaced a portion of its building for $675,000. Before the replacement, the Building and Accumulated Depreciation accounts were as follows:

Building	$3,500,000
Accumulated depreciation	(2,250,000)
	$1,250,000

Instructions

Prepare the general journal entry to record the $675,000 expenditure in each of the following *independent* cases:

[a] Separate identification of the portion of the building being replaced is not possible. The replacement was designed to improve the service potential of the total facility for the remainder of its original expected useful life.

[b] The portion of the building being replaced accounts for $1,000,000 and $785,000 of the Building and Accumulated Depreciation accounts, respectively.

[c] Separate identification of the portion of the building being replaced is not possible. The primary purpose of the expenditure is to lengthen the life of the building from that originally estimated.

11–32 MISCELLANEOUS PLANT ASSET ENTRIES   Reese, Inc., engaged in the following transactions involving plant assets during the current year:

[1] A building expansion costing $260,000 is expected to provide service for 20 years, even though the original building will be useful for only ten more years. *Depreciate over 20 yrs.*

[2] The base of a machine was replaced for $9,000. The portion of the original cost allocated to the base was $5,000, and the cost of the asset was 40% depreciated at the time of the replacement. The old base was sold for $800. The new base is expected to serve the machine to the end of its useful life.

[3] A number of improvements were made in a building for $87,400. The cost of items replaced could not be determined. The improvements were made to ensure the original estimated useful life of the building.   *can't use Substitution because cost isn't determined*

[4] The reorganization required to move into the new addition cost $12,500. Management believes that the rearrangement will benefit the company for at least three years.   *Capitalize*

[5] Servicing of machinery on a regular basis resulted in expenditures of $4,200.   *recording expenses to assets*

Instructions

[a] Prepare the general journal entry to record each transaction.

[b] Describe the appropriate period of depreciation or amortization of any items capitalized in each entry.

11–33   IMPAIRMENT IN VALUE   CD, Inc., invested heavily in equipment that was needed to produce a new line of stereophonic equipment. On January 1, 1993, the cost and accumulated depreciation balances on the equipment were as follows:

Equipment	$5,250,000
Accumulated depreciation	(2,700,000)
	$2,550,000

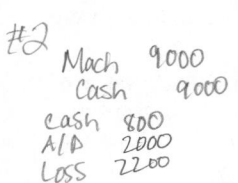

#2
Mach   9000
*   Cash   9000*
Cash   800
A/D   2000
Loss   2200
*   Machinery 5000*

Due to changes in consumer tastes and unexpected advances in electronics, CD's management now believes that the future service potential of the equipment is greatly reduced and the useful life is much shorter than originally estimated. Specifically, management believes the future service potential of the asset is limited to $1,000,000 and the future life extends only through 1994.

Instructions

Determine the amounts which should be presented in the company's balance sheet and income statement relative to the equipment at December 31, 1993.

11–34   CORRECTION OF ERRORS   Fulmer, Inc., carried out a number of transactions involving the acquisition of several assets. All expenditures were recorded in the following single asset account, identified as Fixed Assets:

Fixed Assets

Acquisition price of land and building	$120,000
Options taken out on several pieces of property	2,000
List price of machinery purchased	39,800
Freight on machinery purchased	625
Repair to machinery resulting from damage during shipment	185
Cost of removing old machinery	600
Driveways and sidewalks	12,750
Building remodeling	50,000
Utilities paid since acquisition of building	2,600
	$228,560

Based on property tax assessments, which are believed to fairly represent the relative values involved, the building is worth twice as much as the land. The machinery was subject to a 2% cash discount, which was taken and credited to Purchases Discounts. Of the two options, $750 related to the building and land purchased and $1,250 related to those not purchased. The old machinery was sold at book value.

Instructions

Prepare the general journal entry or entries to correct the Fixed Asset account. Provide supporting calculations for the amounts capitalized in individual plant asset accounts. All expenditures were made in the current year and the books have not been closed.

11–35   BUILDING DISPOSALS   Estes, Incorporated, owns a building with a book value of $85,000 on October 31, 1992, the end of the company's fiscal year.

Building	$180,000
Accumulated depreciation	(95,000)
	$ 85,000

Depreciation is computed by the straight-line method at $1,500 per month.

Instructions

Prepare the general journal entry or entries to record the disposal of the building under each of the following *independent* situations:

[a] The building is sold on June 30, 1993, for $105,000.
[b] The company incurs costs of $15,800 to improve the building in preparation for its sale. The building is sold on August 31, 1993, for $97,000.
[c] The building is destroyed by fire on March 31, 1993. Proceeds from insurance total $67,800.

11–36   CAPITALIZATION OF INTEREST COST   Waco Company entered into a contract with Dallas Company to construct a building for Waco. The contract called for work to begin on June 1, 1992, and for Waco to make an initial payment of $100,000 at that time. Another $50,000 was to be paid by Waco at the end of each three-month period until May 31, 1993, when the building was to be completed, transferred to Waco, and placed into service.

All aspects of the contract were completed on schedule. Waco Company made the payments from existing working capital and did not incur any additional debt for the specific purpose of financing the construction of the building. Throughout the construction period, however, Waco had $750,000 of debt outstanding at an average interest rate of 13%.

Instructions

[a] Determine the appropriate cost of the building on the books of Waco Company.
[b] Explain the rationale for the various components of cost in [a].

11–37 (Appendix A) MACHINERY DISPOSALS Powell Manufacturing Company has a machine which it plans to eliminate. The machine has the following cost and accumulated depreciation at the time of the anticipated transaction:

Machinery	$75,000 *Hist. cost*
Accumulated depreciation	(62,500)
	$12,500 *Book Value*

Instructions

Prepare the general journal entry to record the disposal in each of these *independent* cases:

Different economic — all gain+ loss is recognized Dissimiliar

[a] The machine is appraised at $17,000 and is traded for a patent with an unknown value.
[b] The machine is appraised at $5,000 and is traded for a similar machine with an indeterminate value. In addition, cash of $27,000 is paid. *Same position*
[c] The machine is sold for $13,700 cash. *No exchange only sale*
[d] The machine is traded, along with $700 cash, for a similar machine with an appraisal value of $15,000.
[e] The machine is traded for a similar machine with a value of $15,000. In addition, $1,000 cash is received.

11–38 REPAIR AND MAINTENANCE EXPENSE The controller of Tucker, Inc., asked you to review the Repair and Maintenance Expense account for the year to determine if all of the charges are appropriate. You have identified the following ten transactions for further scrutiny. All of these transactions are considered material in amount.

Date	Amount	Description
Jan. 3	$10,000	Service contract on office equipment.
Mar. 7	10,000	Initial design fee for proposed extension of office building.
Apr. 12	18,500	New condenser for central air conditioning unit located on the roof of office building.
Apr. 20	7,000	Purchase of two executive chairs and desks.
May 12	40,850	Purchase of storm windows and screens and their installation on all office windows.
May 18	38,450	Sealing of roof leaks in production plant.
June 19	28,740	Replacement of large door to production area.
July 3	11,740	Installation of automatic door-opening system on the above door to speed opening.
Sept. 14	38,500	Overhead crane for the assembly department to speed up production.
Oct. 18	11,000	Replacement of broken gear on machine in the machining department.

Instructions

For each of the above transactions, indicate whether the Repair and Maintenance Expense account is properly charged, and if not, indicate the appropriate account to which the transaction should be charged. Explain your reasoning in each case.   (CMA adapted)

PROBLEMS   **11–39 HISTORICAL COST DETERMINATION** The determination of historical cost may be complicated by a number of factors related to the transaction in which the asset is acquired. Chumley Company has been involved in a number of transactions in which plant assets have been acquired.

Instructions

In each of the following *independent* situations, determine the historical cost of the plant assets to Chumley Company:

[a] Land and building are acquired by Chumley for $580,000. The building is destroyed at a cost of $37,000 to make way for a new facility which is to be constructed in the future. Proceeds of $10,000 were received from salvaged materials from the old building.

[b] Land and building are acquired by Chumley for $500,000 and are appraised at $200,000 and $350,000, respectively. Plans call for the renovation of the building, after which it will be used in future operations.

[c] Land is acquired by Chumley at a cost of $125,000. An option had been taken out earlier for $5,000 which guaranteed the purchase price for 90 days. Another option for $5,000 was negotiated on an alternative land site which was not acquired. Legal costs related to the transaction were $650.

[d] Land was purchased by Chumley by issuing 1,300 shares of common stock. The stock has a market value of $16 per share and a par value of $10. No independent appraisal has been made on the land.

[e] Equipment was purchased by Chumley by issuing a $67,000, three-year, noninterest-bearing note. The purchaser's borrowing rate is estimated to be 12%, based on other recent borrowing. Transportation and installation costs incurred by the purchase totaled $2,100.

[f] Equipment was acquired by Chumley at an invoice price of $85,000. A 1% cash discount was taken by payment within the 10-day period required under the terms of the agreement. Damage to the asset during shipment required a $125 payment by the purchaser. The costs of installation were $2,450. Insurance on the equipment for one year ($350) was paid.

[g] Chumley exchanged items of specialized equipment with another company; $50,000 cash was paid by Chumley. The book value of the equipment surrendered was $88,000. Market value approximates book value.

[h] Upon the advice of a management consulting firm, Chumley reorganized its production facilities. Costs of $18,775 were incurred for rearrangement activities. At the same time, equipment costing $47,500 was acquired, on which an available 2% cash discount was not taken due to an oversight by the bookkeeper. The equipment which was being replaced was sold at a price which resulted in a $1,000 loss.

11–40 MISCELLANEOUS PLANT ASSET TRANSACTIONS   Dinville Company recently acquired land and a building in a single transaction.

Instructions

Prepare the journal entry to record the acquired assets in each of the following *independent* situations:

[a] Cash of $285,000 is paid. The land is appraised at $250,000 and an existing building, which will be destroyed to make room for a new one, is appraised at $50,000.

[b] Cash of $275,000 is paid. The land is appraised at $175,000 and an existing building, which will be retained and used, is appraised at $125,000.

[c] Cash of $285,000 is paid. In addition, $15,000 is received from the salvage of an existing building which was destroyed to make room for a new one. The land was appraised at $250,000 and the old building at $35,000.

[d] A $370,000 noninterest-bearing note that requires a single payment at the end of three years is given for the land. No appraisal on the land is available. Dinville Company has recently borrowed money at 10%.

[e] Cash of $500,000 is paid. The land was appraised at $250,000; other assets acquired in the same transaction were appraised as follows:

Equipment	$100,000
Fixtures	115,000
Patent	85,000

11–41 MISCELLANEOUS PLANT ASSET TRANSACTIONS   Barth Company acquired several items of property, plant, and equipment during 1993, its first year of operation:

Jan. 5   The city of Lincoln donated land to the company as an inducement to locate facilities in the city. The land was appraised at $215,000 and resulted in no cash payment by the company.

Jan. 12   Issued 50,000 shares of $20 par value common stock and paid $500,000 cash for assets appraised as follows:

Building	$1,700,000
Land	850,000
Machinery	150,000
Inventory	450,000

31500000

At the time of the transaction the common stock was selling for $51 per share.

Feb. 5   Acquired machinery on account for $145,000, terms 2/10, n/30. Payment was made on Mar. 2.

July 17   Machinery priced at $30,000 was acquired by issuing a 90-day, 10% note. The note was paid at maturity.

Aug. 1   Machinery was purchased by issuing a noninterest-bearing note for $85,000, payable at the end of two years. In similar transactions the company paid an interest rate of 10%.

Instructions

Prepare the journal entries necessary to record the acquisitions of property, plant, and equipment indicated above. Also, prepare any additional entries which would be required during 1993 as a result of the information given. (Do not prepare adjusting entries to recognize depreciation at the end of 1993.)

Good Example

11–42   CORRECTION OF ERRORS   McClain Company recently acquired a building and the surrounding land. The company's accountant established a single Land and Building account and has made the following entries:

1993		Land and Building Account
Jan. 3	Acquisition price	$425,000
3	Prepayment of insurance on building (2 years)	10,500
Feb. 1	Payment of property taxes ($2,400 delinquent for 1992; $3,600 for 1993)	6,000
Mar. 7	Renovation costs on building	42,500
Apr. 1	Cost of open house to familiarize the public with new facility opened that day	2,000
		486,000
Dec. 31	Depreciation for 1993, computed by straight-line method with 20-year life	(24,300)
		$461,700

McClain's accountant has shown the $461,700 Land and Building account in the balance sheet and the $24,300 as Depreciation Expense in the income statement. As a staff member of the independent CPA firm responsible for auditing the financial statements of the company, you must propose any adjustments you consider necessary. Your investigation reveals the following:

[1] Upon acquisition, the land was independently appraised at $115,000 and the building at $325,000.

[2] Company policy calls for depreciation by the straight-line method, computed monthly.

[3] The building is expected to have a residual value of 10% of its cost basis at the end of its 20-year life. The building was placed in service on April 1, 1993.

[4] Property taxes are allocated 74% to the building and 26% to the land.

Instructions

Prepare any adjusting entry or entries which you think are necessary. Provide computations which you would present to your supervisor to support your position. (All amounts may be rounded to the nearest dollar.)

11–43 (Appendix A) NONMONETARY EXCHANGES You have been retained by Jacksboro Metal Products Company to evaluate its accounting procedures in several areas. One area is nonmonetary transactions. Andy Jack, President of Jacksboro Metal, has met with you concerning these transactions and indicated that in his opinion no "sale" has taken place until at least 50% of the transactions is represented in cash. Therefore, in accounting for exchanges of assets that do not meet this 50% test, he has instructed his accountant to simply transfer the book value of the surrendered asset, plus cash (if any), into the new asset account. In Andy's opinion, ". . . this makes a lot of sense and is real easy. In addition, it does not clutter up the income statement with gains and losses that are meaningless in that they have no significant cash consequences."

In evaluating the company's financial records, you discover the following transactions:

[1] Jacksboro Metal traded metal inventory to a competitor for a small strip of land adjacent to Jacksboro's warehouse. The metal had a cost of $10,000; the strip of land had been appraised at $18,000. Jacksboro's accountant had recorded the land at $10,000 as instructed by Andy.

[2] Jacksboro Metal had several unneeded trucks which were traded to a competitor for some metal inventory that was difficult to obtain. The trucks had a book value of $45,000 (cost, $120,000; accumulated depreciation $75,000). While no appraisal value was available for the trucks, the metal was valued at $42,000. Jacksboro paid $3,500 "boot" in addition to the trucks to complete the transaction. Andy instructed the accountant to record the metal inventory at $48,500 ($45,000 + $3,500) since the cash did not constitute 50% of the transaction.

Instructions

[a] React to Andy Jack's rule concerning accounting for nonmonetary exchanges. Do you agree or disagree with it? Why?

[b] Evaluate Jacksboro's accounting treatment of each of the exchanges described above. What changes, if any, would you suggest to bring Jacksboro accounting into conformity with generally accepted accounting principles?

[c] For the two exchanges described above, state briefly the theoretical justification for recording the required asset in the way you have suggested it should be recorded.

11–44 (Appendix A) NONMONETARY EXCHANGES Rothchild, Inc. plans to dispose of certain gymnastics equipment in one of several ways. The equipment originally cost $200,000, and depreciation recognized to date is $70,000. A recent appraisal values the equipment at approximately $150,000 on the used equipment market. Rothchild's owner wants to know the impact of various methods of disposal on the company's financial statements.

Instructions

Prepare the general journal entry or entries for the following *independent* alternative methods of disposal. Following each entry, comment on the impact the alternative would have on the income statement for the year in which the transaction took place.

[a] Rothchild trades the equipment for a vacant lot whose current value is not known.

[b] Rothchild trades the equipment for similar equipment valued at $160,000 and pays $8,000 in the exchange.

[c] Rothchild trades the equipment for similar equipment valued at $140,000 and receives $10,000 cash.

[d] Rothchild sells the equipment for $170,000. The proceeds are combined with an additional $50,000 cash and a $125,000, five-year, 10% note to purchase new equipment. (The 10% interest rate on the note appears fair.)

[e] Rothchild trades the equipment for similar equipment also valued at $150,000. No cash is included in the transaction.

11-45 REPAIR AND MAINTENANCE   Neptune Company uses the allowance method of accounting for equipment repair and maintenance expenditures. A monthly amount of $1,200 is recognized as an expense and credited to the allowance on a quarterly basis. Expenditures for repairs and maintenance are charged to this allowance. Any existing balance in the allowance is adjusted to zero through the expense at the end of the company's fiscal year, March 31. Depreciation on equipment is computed at 2% of the gross asset balance at the end of each quarter. Account balances on April 1, 1992, are as follows:

Equipment	$125,000
Accumulated depreciation	(57,200)
	$ 67,800

Neptune engaged in the following transactions involving equipment from April 1, 1992, through March 31, 1993:

Apr. 18	Repair costs	$ 550
May 17	Equipment acquisition	5,275
July 30	Repair costs	3,620
Oct. 19	Repair costs	5,200
Dec. 17	Equipment acquisition	10,900
Feb. 18	Repair costs	4,990

Instructions

[a] Determine the amounts to be included in the company's balance sheet based on the equipment accounts at the end of each quarter from April 1, 1992, through March 31, 1993. Compute all amounts to the nearest dollar.

[b] What amount of repair and maintenance expense will appear in the annual income statement on March 31, 1993?

[c] Briefly explain the rationale for the allowance method of accounting for repairs and maintenance in this situation, as opposed to simply recognizing repair and maintenance expenditures as expenses when they are incurred.

11-46 CAPITALIZATION OF INTEREST COST   Ritter, Inc., contracted a company to build a storage warehouse in 1993. Construction began on January 2 and Ritter paid $50,000 on that date. Ritter then made additional payments as follows, based on progress made toward completion of the structure:

Apr. 1	$50,000
June 1	75,000
Sept. 1	85,000
Nov. 1	45,000

Ritter arranged for a 13½% loan of $120,000 on January 2 and borrowed the total amount at that time. The proceeds were used to partially finance the construction. Amounts invested in the project in excess of $120,000 were financed from available working capital. During 1993 the company had debt obligations, other than the one related directly to the construction project of $1,000,000 on which interest expense of $120,000 was recognized.

Completion of the project is expected sometime during 1994. Ritter's reporting period ends on December 31.

Instructions

[a] Prepare a schedule to determine the cost of the construction in progress at December 31, 1993.

[b] Prepare general journal entries to record the above events, assuming all interest has been charged to interest expense as incurred. Capitalized interest is to be recognized at year-end.

[c] Prepare the note disclosure that should accompany the financial statements relative to this construction project.

11-47 MISCELLANEOUS PLANT ASSET TRANSACTIONS   Sidler Company presented the following items of property, plant, and equipment in its balance sheet on December 31, 1992:

Property, Plant, and Equipment

Equipment	$ 126,250	*BV*
Accumulated depreciation	(32,500)	$ 93,750 Equip
Buildings	751,000	
Accumulated depreciation	(251,500)	499,500 Bldg
Land	162,720	

During 1993 the company engaged in the following transactions involving property, plant, and equipment:

Jan. 1   Construction of a small office building was begun and a $10,000 initial payment was made. (The project was completed on August 1.)

2   Bonds in the face amount of $200,000 were sold at par value. Annual interest of 12% is to be paid semiannually on June 30 and Dec. 31. Sidler plans to use the proceeds to purchase several property, plant, and equipment items in the near future and to finance construction of the small office building.

Feb. 5   A piece of equipment with a list price of $35,250 was acquired. A 2% cash discount was received by paying on Feb. 10, within the 10-day discount period.

28   The second progress payment ($20,000) on the office building was made.

Apr. 30   The third progress payment ($20,000) on the office building was made.

May 1   A piece of used equipment was acquired in a trade for a similar asset which the company had owned for several years. The newly acquired asset had a market value of $18,000. The asset surrendered had a book value of $15,000 (cost $25,000; accumulated depreciation $10,000). Sidler paid $750 in cash.

(*Hint:* The proper amount for recording the newly acquired asset is the book value of the asset surrendered, plus cash paid. This transaction represents the exchange of similar productive assets in which the earning process is not complete.)

June 30   The fourth progress payment ($20,000) on the office building was made.

July 1   Land was acquired by issuing a $55,000, two-year noninterest-bearing note. The note calls for two payments of $27,500, one and two years after the date of the note. A recent appraisal of the land indicates an estimated value of $46,475.

Aug. 1   The small office building was completed and placed in service. The building had been constructed by another company between Jan. 1 and Aug. 1. Sidler made the final payment of $10,000 on Aug. 1.

Instructions

[a] Prepare all journal entries for the preceding transactions and any additional necessary entries.

[b] Prepare any adjusting entries required on December 31, 1993. Depreciation is computed at 10% of the ending account balance for equipment and 4% of the ending account balance for buildings, approximating straight-line depreciation with 10- and 25-year lives for equipment and buildings, respectively.

[c] Prepare the presentation of property, plant, and equipment to be included in the December 31, 1993, balance sheet.

11–48   CORRECTION OF ERRORS   Foster Company purchased land and a building, demolished the existing building, and immediately constructed a new building. All of this occurred in the first eight months of 1992. In evaluating the company's Building account at year-end, you find the following amounts make up the $954,800 balance:

Jan.	5	Purchase price of land and building	$175,000
	15	Demolition cost of old building, net of $10,000 salvage	54,000
Sept.	1	Cost of new building	630,000
	1	Insurance on new building	12,000
	5	Display fixtures in new building	62,800
Dec.	31	Interest expense on new building	21,000
			$954,800

Upon further analysis, you discover the following explanation for these amounts:

$175,000—The land was appraised at $150,000 and the existing building, $50,000. A combined purchase price of $175,000 was negotiated because the seller was anxious to sell the property as soon as possible.

$ 54,000—The company negotiated a price of $64,000 for demolition of the old building, with the contractor retaining all salvageable materials. The latter were estimated to be worth $10,000.

$630,000—This represents the contract price for the new building, which was placed into service on September 1. No interest was paid directly or indirectly related to this building prior to September 1.

$ 12,000—Insurance was taken out on the building and its contents at $12,000 for a twelve-month period.

$ 62,800—Display fixtures, which are separate from the building itself, were installed.

$ 21,000—A loan was taken out when the building was placed into service to cover the $630,000 contract price. Interest was calculated at $630,000 at the effective 10% interest rate for four months, or $21,000.

Foster Company depreciates all plant assets by the straight-line method. Useful lives are 20 years for buildings and 10 years for all others. Expected salvage values are 25% of cost for buildings and 10% of cost for all others.

Instructions

[a] Prepare individual correcting entries for each item in the Building account which was incorrectly charged to that account. Provide a one-sentence explanation of your reasoning in each case.

[b] Prepare depreciation adjusting entries for all plant assets, assuming depreciation is computed to the nearest whole month.

11–49 (Appendix A) NONMONETARY EXCHANGES Alvarez, Inc. owns Asset A, a used asset for which no current market value is readily determinable. Asset A cost $125,000 several years ago, and has a book value of $65,000 on June 30, 1993. The company is considering alternative opportunities to dispose of Asset A in an exchange transaction which would result in the acquisition of another similar asset.

Instructions

For each of the following independent cases, prepare the general journal entry necessary to record the exchange of Asset A for the appropriate alternative asset. For each alternative, briefly explain the amount at which the new asset is capitalized.

	Asset B	Asset C	Asset D	Asset E	Asset F
Original cost	$145,000	$90,000	$100,000	$ 165,000	$110,000
Accumulated depreciation	(75,000)	–0–	(25,000)	(100,000)	(10,000)
Book value	$ 70,000	$90,000	$ 75,000	$ 65,000	$100,000
Current market value	–*–	$90,000	$ 50,000	$ 90,000	$100,000
Cash paid by (received by) Alvarez, Inc.	–0–	$20,000	$ (3,000)	$ (10,000)	$ 45,000

*Unable to determine.

11–50 (Appendix A) MISCELLANEOUS PLANT ASSET TRANSACTIONS Cronan Manufacturing Company had several transactions during 1992 and 1993 concerning plant assets. Several of these transactions are described below, followed by the entry or entries made by the company's accountant.

Equipment.   Several used items were acquired on February 1, 1992, by issuing a $100,000 noninterest-bearing note. The note is due one year from the date of issuance. No market value of the note or the equipment is available. Cronan's most recent borrowing rate was 8%.

Feb. 1, 1992	Equipment	100,000	
	Notes Payable		100,000
Dec. 31, 1992	Depreciation Expense	10,000	
	Accumulated Depreciation—Equipment		10,000

Buildings.   A building was acquired on June 1, 1992, by issuing 100,000 shares of the company's $5 par value common stock. The common stock is not widely traded, therefore no market price is available. The building was appraised on the transaction date at $650,000.

June 1, 1992	Building	500,000	
	Common Stock (100,000 × $5)		500,000
Dec. 31, 1992	Depreciation Expense	20,000	
	Accumulated Depreciation—Building		20,000

Inventory/Fixtures.   Inventory and display fixtures were acquired for $125,000 cash on April 1, 1993, from a competitor who was liquidating her business. The estimated value of the inventory was $85,000 and the value of the fixtures was $55,000.

Apr. 1, 1993	Inventory	85,000	
	Display Fixtures	55,000	
	Cash		125,000
	Gain on Acquisition of Inventory and Fixtures		15,000

Land.   Land was donated to Cronan by the city of Sandford in September 1993 as an inducement to build a facility there. Plans call for construction at an undetermined future date. The land was appraised at $48,500. No entry was made.

Machinery.   Machinery was acquired in an exchange for similar equipment on October 12, 1993. The assets surrendered had originally cost $52,500, had $16,000 accumulated depreciation, and were appraised at $45,000 on the date of the exchange. Cronan received machinery valued at $40,000 and $5,000 in cash in the transaction.

Oct. 12, 1992	Machinery	40,000	
	Cash	5,000	
	Accumulated Depreciation—Machinery	16,000	
	Machinery		52,500
	Gain on Exchange of Machinery		8,500
Dec. 31, 1992	Depreciation Expense	4,000	
	Accumulated Depreciation—Machinery		4,000

Additional Information

Cronan uses straight-line depreciation, applied to all assets as follows:

[1] A full year's depreciation taken in the year of acquisition and no depreciation taken in the year of disposal.

[2] Estimated life: 25 years for buildings; 10 years on all other assets. (No salvage values are assumed.)

Instructions

For each of the items of property, plant, and equipment above:

[a] Describe the error(s) made in recording the assets and related depreciation, if any.

[b] Prepare journal entries to correct the accounts and to properly record depreciation for 1993. The books for 1993 have not been adjusted or closed.

CASES

11–51 INTERNALLY CONSTRUCTED ASSETS   Five years ago, Martin Manufacturing, Inc., began producing "probos," a new type of instrument it hoped to sell to doctors, dentists, and hospitals. The demand for probos far exceeded initial expectations, and the company was unable to produce enough probos to meet the demand.

The company was manufacturing its product on equipment which it built at the start of its operations. To meet demand more efficient equipment was needed. The company decided to design and build the equipment, since that currently available on the market was unsuitable.

In 1993 a section of the plant was devoted to development of the new equipment and a special staff was hired. Within six months a machine was developed at a cost of $170,000 that successfully increased production and reduced labor costs. Sparked by the success, the company built three more machines at a cost of $80,000 each.

Instructions

[a] In addition to satisfying a need that outsiders cannot meet within the desired time, why might a firm construct plant assets for its own use?
[b] In general, what costs should be capitalized for a self-constructed plant asset?
[c] Discuss the reasonableness of including in the capitalized cost of self-constructed assets:

[1] The increase in overhead caused by the self-construction of plant assets.
[2] A proportionate share of overhead on the same basis as that applied to goods manufactured for sale.

[d] Discuss the proper accounting treatment of the $90,000 difference by which the cost of the first machine exceeded the cost of the subsequent machines.   (AICPA adapted)

11–52 LAND AND BUILDING COST   Travis Company purchased land for use as its corporate headquarters. A small factory that was on the land when it was purchased was torn down before construction of the office building began. Furthermore, a substantial amount of rock blasting and removal had to be done to the site before construction of the building foundation began. Because the office building was set back on the land far from the public road, Travis had the contractor construct a paved road which led from the public road to the parking lot of the office building.

Three years after the office building was occupied, Travis added four stories to the office building. The four stories had an estimated useful life of five years more than the remaining estimated useful life of the original office building.

Ten years later the land and building were sold at an amount more than their net book value and Travis had a new office building constructed in another state for use as its new corporate headquarters.

Instructions

[a] Which of the above expenditures should be capitalized? How should each be depreciated or amortized? Discuss the rationale for your answers.
[b] How would the sale of the land and building be accounted for? Include in your answer how to determine the net book value at the date of sale. Discuss the rationale for your answer.

(AICPA adapted)

JUDGMENT CASES

11–53 REPAIR AND MAINTENANCE   Seaborne Carriers, Inc., is involved in the transport of petroleum by ocean going vessels throughout the world. The company has typically accounted for their major repair and maintenance costs by charging them to expense when related liabilities were incurred. Seaborne has become aware of the generally accepted accounting practice in the airline industry by which the anticipated costs of major repairs and maintenance are charged to operations as an expense over the period that the asset is used prior to the actual repair or maintenance activity being performed. For example, jet engines must be maintained carefully and at precise points of use measured in hours. The costs of the maintenance are charged as an expense while the aircraft is used rather than only at the point that the maintenance must be performed. The propriety of this accounting is well recognized in the airline industry.

Seaborne Carriers now wishes to use the same type of accounting for the regularly scheduled maintenance and repairs that are performed on their vessels. The president says to you, "What is good for the goose is good for the gander and this will more closely match the costs of our operations with the revenues that are generated at the same time. Further, with all present environmental concerns, we can demonstrate our commitment to proper maintenance programs."

You have not thought about this idea before as you are not skilled in airline industry accounting. As a result of a discussion with a staff person at the AICPA, you are now aware that such accounting is considered appropriate for airlines but that other industries typically have not adopted such procedures because no liability has been incurred prior to the performance of the maintenance and no obligation exists to maintain equipment; generally the charge for depreciation expense is thought to measure the cost of using the asset during a period of time. You are aware that airlines do depreciate their equipment in normal fashion.

Instructions

Would you be willing to accept the accounting proposed by Seaborne Carriers for their scheduled maintenance and repair activities? Explain the rationale for your position.

11–54   CAPITALIZATION OF INTEREST   Adaptable, Inc., is a real estate developer that constructs and, on occasion, operates large commercial buildings (e.g., warehouses, office buildings, and apartment complexes). One of the buildings that they recently completed and operated is a medical office building near a large hospital. Interest and other construction costs were appropriately charged to the building during its construction. The original plan was to lease office space to physicians and other professionals associated with the hospital. That plan, however, has not proven successful and occupancy rates have remained relatively low.

Now, Adaptable has decided to convert the building to an apartment complex primarily to rent to hospital employees and to students enrolled in the hospital's nursing school. The company estimates that the conversion will take about a year, and it is wondering whether it will be able to capitalize interest on the entire cost of the asset during its conversion period. That is, will the entire cost of the asset now recorded on the books of the company and the costs incurred on the conversion qualify as expenditures on which interest should be capitalized during the construction period? The president of Adaptable is particularly anxious to capitalize as much interest as possible. He tells you, "We going to have a small bottom line next year anyway, and this would certainly help keep income as high as possible."

Instructions

Should interest be capitalized during the conversion period? If so, what amount of average accumulated expenditures should be used to calculate the amount of interest to be capitalized? That is, should the amount of average accumulated expenditures include the total cost of the asset to Adaptable or be limited to the new expenditures made to accomplish the conversion?

CHAPTER 12

Property, Plant, and Equipment: Depreciation, Depletion, and Special Problems

OBJECTIVES

1. To describe the depreciation process as an application of the matching principle in accounting for property, plant, and equipment.
2. To describe and illustrate depreciation methods that are commonly used in practice, including methods based on time and on activity level.
3. To discuss accounting for natural resources and the related amortization of historical cost through the depletion process.
4. To illustrate typical presentations of plant assets and related disclosures of depreciation in the primary financial statements and related notes.
5. To introduce the accounting treatment of changes in estimates and corrections of errors affecting plant assets.

REVENUE-EXPENSE ASSOCIATION

Matching

Matching principle is a term used to identify the process by which accountants determine net income. It involves the recognition of revenues associated with business activities during a certain period and the identification of expenses related to the generation of those revenues. The difference between these revenues and expenses is the **net income** of the enterprise for that period.

Three principles govern the inclusion of an expenditure (or part of an expenditure) as an expense in the matching process for a particular time period. The principles are (1) associating cause and effect, (2) systematic and rational allocation, and (3) immediate recognition.[1]

Associating cause and effect refers to the fact that some expenditures are directly associated with specific revenues and, thus, are included in determining net income for the period in which those revenues are received. For example, certain manufacturing costs, such as direct materials and direct labor, are directly related to items of inventory produced and help to determine income when those items are sold.

Systematic and rational allocation explains the accounting recognition of those costs that do not have a direct cause-and-effect relationship on the generation of revenue but that are recognized as expenses in an attempt to allocate costs in a systematic and rational manner among several accounting periods. An expenditure that is made in one period but provides benefits to several accounting periods, such as the cost of a plant asset, provides an example of the need for interperiod allocations in the determination of income.

Immediate recognition explains the inclusion of certain costs in determining income because expenditures of the current period (or those carried forward from previous periods) have no discernible future benefits. The recognition of certain expenses, such as research and development, and the expensing of items that do not result in increased revenues, such as the write-off of obsolete equipment, exemplify the immediate recognition of costs in determining income.

THE DEPRECIATION PROCESS

Accounting for property, plant, and equipment when they enter the productive processes of the enterprise is best described by systematic and rational allocation. We have seen in Chapter 11 that plant assets are acquired for the purpose of being used in the production or distribution of other goods or services and are expected to provide service over a relatively long period. With the exception of land, plant assets are believed to possess valuable, but limited, economic usefulness to the enterprise holding the rights to the service potential of the assets.

DEPRECIATION DEFINED

Asset/Liability Measurement

Plant assets are measured and recorded at historical cost, and that cost is allocated to the periods benefiting from the use of the assets on the basis of several estimates concerning the use of the assets. In theory, the accountant prefers to allocate the cost of property, plant, and equipment in a manner that is proportionate to the contribution that the assets make to the generation of revenue each period. In other words, the

---

[1]*APB Statement No. 4*, "Basic Concepts and Accounting Principles Underlying Financial Statements of Business Enterprises," 1970, pars. 156–160.

greater the contribution to revenue for a particular accounting period, the more depreciation expense should be charged for a given asset. However, because of the uncertainties surrounding the precise pattern in which a given asset contributes to revenue, accountants estimate periodic depreciation by methods that include simplifying assumptions and that are both systematic and rational.

Cost allocation via depreciation does not measure the value of an asset; it is intended to recognize a portion of the cost of the asset as an expense each period in determining net income. Accordingly, **depreciation** is defined as the process of allocating the cost of property, plant, and equipment as an expense in a systematic and rational manner to those periods expected to benefit from the use of the asset.

A common misconception is that the depreciation process provides a cash fund that is available for the replacement of the asset at the end of its useful life. Depreciation is a process of cost allocation intended primarily to determine net income during those accounting periods in which the asset is used as part of the revenue-producing process. When **periodic depreciation** is recognized, cash is not affected. The company may set aside cash for the replacement of depreciable assets at the end of their useful lives, but this would be done in addition to the recognition of depreciation expense for purposes of determining income. Setting aside cash to replace plant assets is not a common practice among business enterprises.

The assumption that the economic usefulness or service potential of plant assets declines over time is supported by the realities of the process of producing and distributing goods and services. Declining service potential is caused by changes in both the asset and the environment in which the asset is used.

The changes in property, plant, and equipment that support the notion of declining service potential result from routine wear and tear, deterioration, and other effects of constant use in normal business operations. Over time these **physical factors** result in a decline in the future service potential of the assets and provide support for allocating the acquisition cost of plant assets as an expense. Due to the finite service potential of most plant assets, use of the assets in one period results in a decline in the service potential available for use in future periods.

Changes in the environment in which property, plant, and equipment are used, sometimes called **functional factors,** also influence the amount of future service potential present in an asset at a given time. Business expansion and growth may render a plant asset obsolete. At that time the asset is **inadequate for the intended purpose,** although it may still be suitable for its original purpose and may prove quite useful to another enterprise. For example, adequate buildings acquired at the inception of a business may become limited in their future service potential when unexpected growth requires larger facilities for efficient operation.

Supercession, on the other hand, results when an enterprise acquires improved assets that are capable of providing the same service as present plant assets at an increased level of efficiency or at a significantly reduced cost. **Obsolescence** broadly refers to the decline in future service potential due to the functional factors relating to the environment in which the enterprise operates rather than to a decrease in the asset's physical utility. Functional factors include inadequacy, supercession, and other changes that affect the asset's potential to provide future service.

ESTIMATES REQUIRED IN THE DEPRECIATION PROCESS

Asset/Liability
Measurement

The depreciation process requires several estimates concerning property, plant, and equipment. Measuring plant assets at historical cost involves estimates, assumptions, and allocations, many of which are described in Chapter 11. These include the treatment of acquisition-related costs, the capitalization of interest costs, the treatment of overhead for internally constructed assets, and others. Nevertheless, the historical cost of plant assets is better described as an actual or computed figure than an estimate. However, other figures necessary to apply the depreciation process (i.e., the useful life and salvage value of the asset) are clearly estimates of future events.

Allocating the cost of an asset over future periods requires an estimate of its **useful life,** which may be expressed in **time** (e.g., months or years), **productive output** (e.g., units produced), or **service quantities** (e.g., machine hours operated or miles driven). The logical basis for estimating useful life varies from asset to asset. Accountants attempt to identify the measure of useful life that is most closely associated with the decline in the service potential of the asset to the enterprise. Time is usually the measure used for buildings, furniture, and fixtures. The useful life of machinery that turns out identifiable products may be appropriately stated in terms of a variable measuring productive output. In still other cases service capacity (determined by some physical quantity used or consumed) may be appropriate; for example, miles driven may provide the best estimate of the useful life of a vehicle. Regardless of the nature of the depreciable asset, however, **an estimate of the useful life must be made** in order to identify the period over which the asset will be depreciated. This life may be identified by a number of titles, all of which have common meanings: service life, economic life, estimated useful life, and other similar terms.

In all widely used methods the depreciation amount is the difference between the historical cost of the asset and the estimated salvage value expected to accrue to the asset holder at the end of the useful life. Thus, the residual value of the asset when it is no longer useful to the enterprise must be estimated. In some methods this estimate must be made initially, when the depreciation schedule is established. In other cases this estimate can be deferred until later in the life of the asset.

The amount expected to be available at the end of the service life is identified by a variety of terms with common meanings: residual value, salvage value, and other similar terms. Any anticipated costs of preparing the asset for disposal at the end of its expected useful life should be treated as reductions in the residual value for purposes of determining depreciation. The estimates of useful life and residual value are based on the expected usefulness of the asset to the present owner.

Regardless of the method selected, depreciation is recorded at the end of each accounting period by an adjusting entry in which Depreciation Expense is debited and Accumulated Depreciation is credited, as discussed in Chapter 5. The depreciation expense then becomes a component of income determination for that period and represents an application of the matching principle. The increase in accumulated depreciation further reduces the book value of the asset as presented in the balance sheet.

Matching

DEPRECIATION ESTIMATION METHODS: INDIVIDUAL ASSETS

Several methods have been developed to apply the general concept of depreciation to property, plant, and equipment. These methods combine the historical cost, the estimated useful life, and the estimated residual value of the asset with certain assumptions about the pattern of decline in the asset's service potential.

This section discusses several methods for determining periodic depreciation for individual assets. These methods may be classified as those based on time and those based on activity level.

Depreciation Methods Based on Time
1. Straight line
2. Accelerated
   a. Sum-of-the-years'-digits
   b. Declining balance

Depreciation Methods Based on Activity Level
1. Productive output
2. Service quantity

Several additional depreciation methods are discussed briefly in Appendix A of this chapter. Three of these are infrequently used methods for depreciating individual assets which warrant brief mention: the fixed percentage on book value, the annuity, and the sinking fund methods. The other methods presented in Appendix A are applied to plant assets in groups rather than individually.

Periodic depreciation expense determined by any of the methods based on time can be computed in advance and will be the same regardless of the level of activity during the period. Depreciation determined by any method based on activity level results in the determination of a constant depreciation charge per unit of activity. Depreciation expense for any single period is then computed at the end of that period and is based on the activity level achieved during the period.

To illustrate the depreciation methods in this section, the following asset is assumed:

Asset 147

Cost	$12,000
Estimated salvage value	$ 2,000
Estimated life	
In years	5
In units of output	25,000
In service hours	60,000

It would be unusual to have a depreciable asset for which the useful life could be stated equally well in terms of years, units of output, and service hours. The example here includes all three to facilitate the illustration and comparison of the methods, and we indicate the circumstances most appropriate for applying the individual method, recognizing that all methods would usually not apply to the same asset.

STRAIGHT-LINE METHOD

The **straight-line method** of depreciation is simple and results in the same amount of depreciation expense for each full year in the life of the asset. The depreciation charge is based on the **passage of time** rather than the level of productive activity.

Periodic depreciation under the straight-line method is computed as follows (D = depreciation):

$$D = \frac{(\text{Cost}) - (\text{Salvage value})}{\text{Number of years in asset's life}}$$

Depreciation for the first year (D_1) for Asset 147 is computed as follows:

$$D_1 = \frac{\$12,000 - \$2,000}{5}$$
$$= \$2,000$$

Due to the straightforward nature of the calculation, the absence of complicating assumptions, and the ease of understanding, the straight-line method is widely practiced. The method is conceptually appropriate if the decline in service potential relates primarily to the passage of time rather than to the level of activity and if the decline is thought to be approximately the same amount each period. The straight-line method may also provide a reasonable basis for depreciation when the level of activity is important but the use of the asset is relatively constant from period to period.

Applying the straight-line method to the five-year life of Asset 147, we arrive at the schedule in Exhibit 12–1. The book value at the end of the fifth year is the $2,000

EXHIBIT 12–1

Depreciation Schedule for Asset 147
Straight-Line Method

End of Year	Depreciation Entry: Dr.: Depreciation Expense Cr.: Accumulated Depreciation	Balance: Accumulated Depreciation	Book Value
—	—	—	$12,000
1	$2,000	$ 2,000	10,000
2	2,000	4,000	8,000
3	2,000	6,000	6,000
4	2,000	8,000	4,000
5	2,000	10,000	2,000

salvage value originally used to determine the total depreciation to be charged ($10,000). The book value at the end of each year is the amount presented as an asset in the enterprise's balance sheet. The financial-statement disclosure requirements for plant assets are covered in a later section of this chapter.

ACCELERATED METHODS

Accelerated depreciation methods, sometimes referred to as **reducing-charge methods,** are designed to recognize greater amounts of depreciation in the early years of an asset's life and smaller amounts in the later years. Of the several variations of accelerated depreciation, the most widely used are the declining-balance and the sum-of-the-years'-digits methods. Both are presented in this section. Even though the amount of depreciation varies from year to year with accelerated methods, depreciation is still based on the passage of time; it is computed in advance and is based on estimates of useful life and salvage value.

Accelerated depreciation methods emerged out of income tax law, which allowed companies to take more depreciation in the early years in the asset's life than in later years. As we discuss later in this section, the use of accelerated depreciation for income tax purposes does not necessitate its use for financial reporting purposes. However, accelerated depreciation may be conceptually sound if the declining pattern of expense recognition is consistent with the actual contribution the asset makes to the revenue-generating process.

Accelerated depreciation methods are conceptually attractive when the asset is believed to provide superior performance (i.e., operate with greater efficiency) in the early years of its life. Further support for accelerated depreciation is found in the expected pattern of repair and maintenance. If repair and maintenance costs are expected to increase during the life of the asset, declining depreciation charges coupled with increasing repair and maintenance charges result in a pattern of expense recognition that may relate more closely to the decline in service potential than would result from other depreciation methods. The potential for obsolescence is also cited as a reason for using accelerated depreciation: The greater charges to income in the early years of the asset's life reduce the book value early and reduce the probability that a significant write-off will have to be made later because of a permanent impairment in value due to obsolescence.

Sum-of-the-Years'-Digits Method
The **sum-of-the-years'-digits method** is applied by computing a fraction, the denominator of which equals the **life of the asset in years plus all digits between that**

number and zero. The numerator of the fraction represents the **specific number of the year** in the useful life of the asset, but the numbers are applied in **descending order** throughout the life of the asset; for example, if the useful life is 10 years, the number 10 would be the numerator in D_1, the number 9 in D_2, etc. This fraction is then multiplied by **depreciable cost** (i.e., the cost minus salvage value). Thus, depreciation is computed:

$$D = \left(\frac{\text{Current year digit}}{\text{Sum-of-the-years'-digits}} \right) \times (\text{Cost} - \text{Salvage value})$$

Applying these concepts to Asset 147, we find that the denominator (the sum-of-the-years'-digits, $5 + 4 + 3 + 2 + 1$) equals 15. Depreciation is determined for each year by multiplying the appropriate fraction by the depreciable amount. Remember that the numerator is selected in *reverse (descending)* order, resulting in the following computations:

$$
\begin{aligned}
D_1 &= \tfrac{5}{15} \times (\$12{,}000 - \$2{,}000) = \quad \$\ 3{,}333 \\
D_2 &= \tfrac{4}{15} \times (\$12{,}000 - \$2{,}000) = \quad 2{,}667 \\
D_3 &= \tfrac{3}{15} \times (\$12{,}000 - \$2{,}000) = \quad 2{,}000 \\
D_4 &= \tfrac{2}{15} \times (\$12{,}000 - \$2{,}000) = \quad 1{,}333 \\
D_5 &= \tfrac{1}{15} \times (\$12{,}000 - \$2{,}000) = \quad \underline{667} \\
&\phantom{= \tfrac{1}{15} \times (\$12{,}000 - \$2{,}000) =} \quad \underline{\$10{,}000}
\end{aligned}
$$

These computations result in a schedule for Asset 147 as illustrated in Exhibit 12–2. As with straight-line depreciation, the book value of $2,000 at the end of the five years equals the salvage value anticipated at the beginning of the asset's life.

For assets with relatively long lives, determining the sum of the digits as computed above may be burdensome. In these cases the denominator in the fraction may be determined as follows (n = years in asset's life; SYD = sum-of-the-years'-digits):

$$SYD = n \left(\frac{n + 1}{2} \right)$$

For example, for an asset with a 35-year life, the sum of the digits is computed as follows:

$$SYD = 35 \left(\frac{35 + 1}{2} \right)$$

$$= 630$$

The depreciation rate is 35/630 for the first year, 34/630 for the second year, etc.

Declining-Balance Method

The **declining-balance method** is a second type of accelerated depreciation in which the charge in early years exceeds that of later years. In the sum-of-the-years'-digits method a declining fraction is multiplied by a constant base. In the declining-balance method the opposite is true: a **constant percentage** is multiplied by a **declining base.**

In the declining-balance method a percentage is based on some multiple of the straight-line rate. The most common application of this method is the **double-declining balance,** wherein the percentage is twice the straight-line rate. This fixed percentage is then applied to the declining book value of the asset, giving a depreciation figure that declines throughout the life of the asset. **The book value, however, should never be reduced below the estimated salvage value.**

EXHIBIT 12-2

Depreciation Schedule for Asset 147
Sum-of-the-Years'-Digits Method

End of Year	Depreciation Entry: Dr.: Depreciation Expense Cr.: Accumulated Depreciation	Balance: Accumulated Depreciation	Book Value
—	—	—	$12,000
1	$3,333	$ 3,333	8,667
2	2,667	6,000	6,000
3	2,000	8,000	4,000
4	1,333	9,333	2,667
5	667	10,000	2,000

The double-declining balance rate is computed as twice the straight-line rate, as follows (DDB = double-declining balance):

$$DDB\% = \left(\frac{100\%}{\text{Life in years}}\right) \times (2)$$

For Asset 147 this rate is 40%:

$$DDB\% = \left(\frac{100\%}{5}\right) \times (2)$$

$$= 40\%$$

Applying 40% to the declining book value of Asset 147 and ignoring salvage value until the book value is reduced to salvage value, we compute the depreciation for each year in the asset's life as follows:

$$D_1 = 40\% \, (\$12,000) = \$4,800$$
$$D_2 = 40\% \, (\$12,000 - \$4,800) = \$2,880$$
$$D_3 = 40\% \, [\$12,000 - (\$4,800 + \$2,880)] = \$1,728$$
$$D_4 = \$10,000 - (\$4,800 + \$2,880 + \$1,728) = \$592$$

Depreciation at 40% of the book value cannot be taken in Year 4 because this would reduce book value below the $2,000 salvage value expected. Likewise, no depreciation can be taken in Year 5. Some companies avoid this problem by systematically switching to straight-line at the point where it exceeds declining balance.

Exhibit 12-3 shows a schedule for Asset 147 that results from applying the double-declining balance method.

Accelerated depreciation is an area in which the determination of a company's federal income tax liability has had a significant impact on financial reporting practices. The popularity of the double-declining balance method in past years has resulted, at least in part, from the fact that for many assets the maximum depreciation that could be deducted in computing the income tax liability was an amount equal to twice the straight-line rate in the first year, without regard to salvage value. Because this maximum has not applied to all assets, however, variations of the declining-balance method are found in practice. For example, maximum depreciation on used assets, acquired before 1954, and certain

EXHIBIT 12-3

	Depreciation Schedule for Asset 147 Double-Declining Balance Method		
End of Year	Depreciation Entry: Dr.: Depreciation Expense Cr.: Accumulated Depreciation	Balance: Accumulated Depreciation	Book Value
—	—	—	$12,000
1	$4,800	$ 4,800	7,200
2	2,880	7,680	4,320
3	1,728	9,408	2,592
4	592	10,000	2,000
5	–0–	10,000	2,000

other assets is 1½ times the straight-line amount. Accordingly, the declining-balance method at 150% of the straight-line rate is used in some circumstances. The mechanics of applying the declining-balance method are the same regardless of the multiple of the straight-line rate used. The use of a multiple of less than two, however, results in a less dramatic acceleration of depreciation in the early years of the asset's life.

As we again relate in Chapter 18, which deals with accounting for income taxes in financial reporting, companies may use different accounting methods for financial reporting and for income tax purposes. Regardless of this option many companies use their tax methods for their financial statements to avoid keeping two sets of records. The objective of selecting a depreciation method for financial reporting purposes is to properly

Matching   match revenues and expenses. The inability to directly associate the decline in service potential of plant assets with revenues produced by those assets, however, precludes precise measurements of the amount of cost to treat as depreciation each period. Thus, methods designed primarily for income tax purposes frequently become a part of financial reporting on the basis that the tax methods are consistent with the general principle of matching. Also, the differences in amounts between accounting and income tax methods

Materiality   may be immaterial when placed in the context of a company's financial statements.

In 1981 income tax law was changed to incorporate a new method of deciding which portion of the cost of assets could be deducted when determining a company's income tax liability. That method is called the **Accelerated Cost Recovery System (ACRS)** and permits accelerated recovery of the cost of assets over periods generally shorter than their useful lives. This system remains in effect for assets placed in service between 1981 and 1986 but was modified by the Tax Reform Act of 1986 for assets placed in service after 1986. In the opinion of the authors, the amounts that are written off for income tax purposes under ACRS (or modified ACRS) are generally not appropriate as depreciation expense for financial reporting purposes because they are not based on the estimated useful lives of the assets. This is particularly true for real estate and other property with relatively long lives.

In situations where companies use an acceptable depreciation method, such as straight-line, for financial-statement presentation and ACRS (or modified ACRS) for income tax purposes for the same assets, a temporary difference between financial and taxable income arises. Chapter 18 of this text discusses ACRS in greater detail and considers more carefully the differences between the way the cost of plant assets is recognized in financial statements and the way cost is recognized in preparing tax returns. At this point, simply keep in mind that it is acceptable and, in fact, may even be mandatory for companies to use different methods in preparing financial statements from those used in the preparation of income tax returns. Depreciation is one of those areas where this frequently occurs.

PRODUCTIVE-OUTPUT METHOD

The **productive-output** (or **units-of-output**) **method** uses the output of plant assets as a basis for recognizing periodic depreciation. The rationale is that some assets are capable of producing a determinable number of units of productive output and depreciation should be recognized in relation to the portion of that output that occurs in each accounting period.

A cost factor **per unit of output** is first calculated. This factor is then applied to the actual output for the period to determine the depreciation charge. Depreciation expense cannot be determined in advance, because it is dependent on the level of output during the period. The depreciation computation on the productive-output method is generalized as follows:

$$D = \left(\frac{\text{Cost} - \text{Salvage value}}{\text{Life in units of output}}\right) \times \left(\begin{array}{c}\text{Units of output} \\ \text{for period}\end{array}\right)$$

The first element in the computation may be stated as depreciation rate per unit of output. Applying this concept to Asset 147 results in a cost per unit of $.40:

$$\begin{array}{c}\text{Estimated cost} \\ \text{per unit of} \\ \text{output}\end{array} = \frac{\$12,000 - \$2,000}{25,000 \text{ units}}$$

$$= \$.40$$

We shall assume that units are produced in Years 1–5 in the following pattern: 4,000, 9,000, 8,000, 2,000, and 2,000. Depreciation may then be computed for each year by applying the $.40 cost per unit to the units of output:

$$D_1 = \$.40 \times 4,000 = \$1,600$$
$$D_2 = \$.40 \times 9,000 = \$3,600$$
$$D_3 = \$.40 \times 8,000 = \$3,200$$
$$D_4 = \$.40 \times 2,000 = \$800$$
$$D_5 = \$.40 \times 2,000 = \$800$$

Exhibit 12–4 shows the schedule that results for Asset 147 when the units-of-output method is applied to the five years in the asset's life. As in the other methods, the book value at the end of five years equals the expected salvage value of $2,000, because the total amount of the recognized depreciation expense is $10,000.

The productive-output method is suitable only if the asset provides a separate, identifiable unit of product, as is the case with equipment used to manufacture items of inventory. The productivity of many plant assets, such as buildings and fixtures, however, cannot be measured in terms of a unit of output. In such cases, the productive-output method is *not* appropriate. For those assets whose contribution to operations can best be measured in terms of units of productive output, this method is particularly suitable if the decline in service potential is thought to be more closely tied to the production of units than to the passage of time. If an asset is used very little in a period, depreciation by the units-of-output method will be small; if the level of activity is high, depreciation will be high. If obsolescence or additional factors other than physical output are considered important in determining the pattern of decline in the asset's service potential from period to period, the productive-output method is *not* suitable.

EXHIBIT 12-4

Depreciation Schedule for Asset 147
Productive-Output Method

End of Year	Depreciation Entry: Dr.: Depreciation Expense Cr.: Accumulated Depreciation	Balance: Accumulated Depreciation	Book Value
—	—	—	$12,000
1	$1,600	$ 1,600	10,400
2	3,600	5,200	6,800
3	3,200	8,400	3,600
4	800	9,200	2,800
5	800	10,000	2,000

SERVICE-QUANTITY METHOD

The productivity of some assets is best measured in terms of service quantity; for example, we state the productivity of certain machinery in terms of operating hours and the productivity of vehicles in terms of miles. While the mechanics of applying the service-quantity method are similar to those of the productive-output method, the concepts underlying the methods are somewhat different.

Under the **service-quantity method** the contribution to operations is stated in terms of **productive-input factors** rather than output of the production process. Accordingly, depreciation recognized in any period is dependent on the quantity of the productive-input factor consumed in the use of the asset during that period. The amount of the productive input is limited, and the depreciable amount (cost less salvage value) is recognized as an expense on the basis of the expiration of this limited quantity of productive inputs.

Depreciation under the service-quantity method is generalized as follows:

$$D = \left(\frac{\text{Cost} - \text{Salvage value}}{\text{Total quantity of productive service}} \right) \times \left(\begin{array}{c} \text{Productive} \\ \text{service for} \\ \text{period} \end{array} \right)$$

As in the productive-output method, the first factor may be stated as a depreciation rate per unit of productive service. For Asset 147 the appropriate service quantity is 60,000 service hours, resulting in a cost per hour of $.1667:

$$\frac{\text{Estimated cost per unit}}{\text{of productive service}} = \frac{\$12,000 - \$2,000}{60,000 \text{ hours}}$$
$$= \$.1667$$

The asset is used during Years 1–5 in the following service hours: 14,000, 15,000, 20,000, 4,000, and 7,000. Depreciation is computed for each year as follows:

$$D_1 = \$.1667 \times 14,000 = \$2,334$$
$$D_2 = \$.1667 \times 15,000 = \$2,501$$
$$D_3 = \$.1667 \times 20,000 = \$3,334$$
$$D_4 = \$.1667 \times 4,000 = \$667$$
$$D_5 = \$.1667 \times 7,000 = \$1,164$$

A $3 rounding adjustment is made in the D_5 computation.

EXHIBIT 12–5

Depreciation Schedule for Asset 147
Service-Quantity Method

End of Year	Depreciation Entry: Dr.: Depreciation Expense Cr.: Accumulated Depreciation	Balance: Accumulated Depreciation	Book Value
—	—	—	$12,000
1	$2,334	$ 2,334	9,666
2	2,501	4,835	7,165
3	3,334	8,169	3,831
4	667	8,836	3,164
5	1,164	10,000	2,000

The schedule for Asset 147 that results when we apply the service-quantity method to the five years in the asset's life is illustrated in Exhibit 12–5.

The depreciation varies annually depending on the level of use of the asset during the period. If the decline in service potential relates to the physical use of the asset, the service-quantity method is appropriate. In particular, if the use of the asset varies from period to period, this method more realistically reflects the decline in service potential through depreciation expense than does a method that recognizes depreciation based on the passage of time but disregards the level of activity. If the decline in the service potential relates more to the passage of time or obsolescence, however, the straight-line or an accelerated method is more suitable, even when the contribution of the asset is stated in terms of service quantities.

In our discussion of depreciation methods, we have used the same asset throughout, assuming that we could estimate useful life in terms of time, units of production, and service quantities. This was done for purposes of illustration only. As stated earlier, in practice only one of these would be used for any particular asset. In these illustrations, the fact that the exhaustion of service quantities or the completion of units of product took place precisely over a five-year period is of no particular relevance because depreciation would be based on only one of these variables (service quantities, units of production, or passage of time) for any particular asset.

What is the proper accounting treatment when fully depreciated assets continue to be used by an enterprise? Obviously, the estimate of useful life in terms of either time or activity level proved to be inaccurate, even if it was based on the best information available at the time. The cost and accumulated depreciation of fully depreciated assets should remain in the accounts as long as the assets are actively used, even though these figures effectively cancel each other out in the determination of book value. The use of fully depreciated plant assets in the revenue-producing process presents a theoretical problem, because no portion of the cost of these assets is included among expenses. This violates the matching principle. If fully depreciated assets make significant contributions to revenue, this fact should be disclosed in the financial statements. This is usually not a major problem, because fully depreciated assets still in use are usually not an important part of total assets.

Matching Disclosure

SELECTING AN APPROPRIATE DEPRECIATION METHOD

We have discussed several factors that should be considered when a company selects a depreciation method: physical use, expected obsolescence, the expected pattern of decline in usefulness, the periodic contribution of the asset to the revenue-producing process, and others. These considerations are often difficult, if not impossible, to quantify, and they sometimes offset each other, resulting in some uncertainty about the most appropriate method in a given set of circumstances: The authoritative literature suggests only that the depreciation method be both systematic and rational.

Many times *practical,* rather than conceptual, considerations govern the selection of a depreciation method. For example, the simplicity of the straight-line method explains its frequent use in accounting practice. Companies often adopt ACRS for income tax purposes and straight-line depreciation for financial reporting, thereby reducing taxable income and deferring income tax payments without reducing the net income reported in the early years of the assets' lives. This combination is particularly popular among rapidly expanding companies that are investing additional amounts in plant assets on a continuous basis. In other cases, however, simplicity may influence the choice, and a company will use straight-line depreciation for both income tax reporting and financial reporting to avoid the cost and inconvenience of retaining two sets of depreciation records. In many cases depreciation methods used in the past are applied to new assets without any real consideration of the appropriateness of those methods. In some cases depreciation methods used by other companies with which the enterprise may be compared may influence the choice of depreciation method.

Consistency   **Consistency** is an important accounting principle when considering the depreciation of plant assets. Once a depreciation method is selected for a particular asset or class of assets, that method should be used consistently from period to period so that the net incomes of successive accounting periods are comparable.

In summary, it is difficult to generalize exactly how companies determine the depreciation methods they use. Conceptual as well as practical considerations are important, and consistency over time must also be considered.

FRACTIONAL-YEAR PROBLEMS

In the previous examples, we have assumed that the **depreciation year** and the **financial reporting period** are the same. That is, Asset 147 was acquired at the beginning of a reporting period and a full year's depreciation was taken in that year. However, plant assets are not always acquired at the beginning of a fiscal period. Likewise, assets are not always disposed of at the end of the period. The problem of accounting for depreciation for assets acquired and disposed of at various times during the year is frequently encountered in applying all of the methods that were discussed in the previous section. The computation of depreciation expense differs, however, only for those methods in which depreciation is based on the passage of time. Depreciation for partial years under the activity-based methods is computed in the same way as for full years of use, because the expense is based on productive output or service quantity rather than a time period.

Numerous policies may be adopted in applying depreciation methods in reporting periods when assets have been held only part of the period. This may occur twice in the life of every asset: once in the period the asset is acquired and once in the period of disposal of the asset. Only if acquisition and disposal transactions occur on or very close to the first and last days of the financial reporting period are the problems of depreciation for partial years avoided.

To illustrate several problems and alternative approaches to depreciation for partial years, the example of Asset 286 is used.

Asset 286

Cost	$100,000
Estimated salvage value	None
Estimated life in years	4
Date of acquisition	Aug. 10
Financial reporting period	Jan. 1–Dec. 31

A fractional-year problem exists because the four years in the asset's life do not correspond precisely to four financial reporting years:

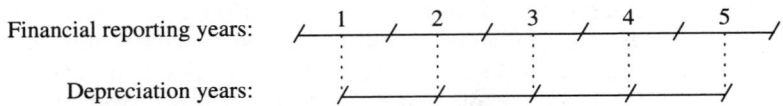

The first depreciation year begins during the first financial reporting year and ends during the second financial reporting year. This sequence continues throughout the life of Asset 286, with the financial reporting periods following a January-through-December pattern and the depreciation years following an August-to-August pattern.

A number of policies may be adopted for the fractional-year problem that exists in the first and last years in the asset's life. Several of these are applied to Asset 286 in Exhibit 12–6 which uses the straight-line method of depreciation.

Several observations are possible concerning these approaches to the fractional-year problem. Policy 1 is widely practiced and results in the most precise recognition of depreciation in terms of time. Because depreciation computations incorporate numerous assumptions and estimates, computations based on a period of time shorter than one month are rarely made. In the case of Asset 286, five months (August–December) of depreciation are recognized in the first financial reporting period, because the asset was acquired in the first half of August. Seven months of depreciation remain to be recognized in the fifth financial reporting period. Under Policy 2 no depreciation is taken in the first year, because the enterprise acquired the asset in the last half of the year. If the asset had been acquired in the first half, a full year's depreciation would have been taken in the first year and none in the last year. In Policy 3 depreciation is recognized to the nearest half year. Thus, if the asset is acquired in the period of January–March, a full year's depreciation is taken in the first year. If the asset is acquired in the period April–September, a half-year's depreciation is taken; and if the asset is acquired in the period October–December, no depreciation is taken. In Policies 1, 2, and 3 the date of the acquisition of the asset influences the amount of depreciation recognized in the first and last years.

Policies 4, 5, and 6 differ from Policies 1, 2, and 3 in that assets are treated the same, regardless of when they are acquired. In Policy 4 a half-year's depreciation is taken in the first year and the same in the last year. In Policy 5 a full year's depreciation is taken in the first year and none in the last year. In Policy 6 no depreciation is taken in the first year and a full year's depreciation is taken in the last year. Policies 5 and 6 resolve the fractional-year problem by forcing the depreciation year and the financial reporting year to coincide.

Applying fractional-year policies where accelerated depreciation methods are used varies only in that the amount of depreciation recognized declines each year. For example, with the sum-of-the-years'-digits method, Asset 286 would be depreciated as follows under Policies 1 and 3:

EXHIBIT 12–6

Alternative Approaches to Fractional-Year Problem for Asset 286 Straight-Line Method

Fractional-Year Policy	Depreciation Recognized in Financial-Reporting Periods				
	1	2	3	4	5
1. Recognize depreciation to nearest full month.	10,417*	25,000**	25,000	25,000	14,583†
2. Recognize depreciation to nearest full year.	–0–	25,000	25,000	25,000	25,000
3. Recognize depreciation to nearest half year.	12,500‡	25,000	25,000	25,000	12,500
4. Recognize one-half year's depreciation in period of acquisition and one-half in period of disposal.	12,500	25,000	25,000	25,000	12,500
5. Recognize full-year's depreciation in period of acquisition and none in period of disposal.	25,000	25,000	25,000	25,000	–0–
6. Recognize no depreciation in period of acquisition and full year in period of disposal.	–0–	25,000	25,000	25,000	25,000

*5/12 (100,000/4)
**(100,000/4)
†7/12 (100,000/4)
‡(25,000 × ½)

	Policy 1 Nearest Full Month	Policy 3 Nearest Half Year

Year 1: $\$100,000 \times \left(\frac{4}{10}\right) \times \left(\frac{5 \text{ mo.}}{12 \text{ mo.}}\right) = \underline{\$16,667}$ $\$100,000 \times \left(\frac{4}{10}\right) \times \left(\frac{1}{2}\right) = \underline{\$20,000}$

Year 2: $\$100,000 \times \left(\frac{4}{10}\right) \times \left(\frac{7 \text{ mo.}}{12 \text{ mo.}}\right) = \$23,333$ $\$100,000 \times \left(\frac{4}{10}\right) \times \left(\frac{1}{2}\right) = \$20,000$

$\$100,000 \times \left(\frac{3}{10}\right) \times \left(\frac{5 \text{ mo.}}{12 \text{ mo.}}\right) = \underline{\ 12,500}$ $\$100,000 \times \left(\frac{3}{10}\right) \times \left(\frac{1}{2}\right) = \underline{\ 15,000}$

$\underline{\$35,833}$ $\underline{\$35,000}$

The same procedure is followed for the declining balance method in that the depreciation expense for each "depreciation year" is allocated between two "financial reporting years." Assuming double-declining balance, we compute the following:

	Policy 1 Nearest Full Month	Policy 3 Nearest Half Year

Year 1: $\$100,000 \times 50\% \times \left(\frac{5 \text{ mo.}}{12 \text{ mo.}}\right) = \underline{\$20,833}$ $\$100,000 \times 50\% \times \left(\frac{1}{2}\right) = \underline{\$25,000}$

Year 2: $\$100,000 \times 50\% \times \left(\frac{7 \text{ mo.}}{12 \text{ mo.}}\right) = \$29,167$ $\$100,000 \times 50\% \times \left(\frac{1}{2}\right) = \$25,000$

$(\$100,000 - \$50,000)$ $(\$100,000 - \$50,000)$

$\times 50\% \times \left(\frac{5 \text{ mo.}}{12 \text{ mo.}}\right) = \underline{\ 10,417}$ $\times 50\% \times \left(\frac{1}{2}\right) = \underline{\ 12,500}$

$\underline{\$39,584}$ $\underline{\$37,500}$

In the case of declining-balance, depreciation for the second and subsequent years can be computed directly by multiplying the percentage times the book value at the beginning of the year. For example, under Policy 1, the second year's depreciation is computed as follows: $(\$100,000 - \$20,833) \times 50\% = \$39,584$ under Policy 3, the second year's depreciation is computed as follows:

$$(\$100,000 - \$25,000) \times 50\% = \$37,500.$$

Consistency

The keys to applying fractional-year policies are practicality, logic, and consistency. If numerous assets are acquired and disposed of frequently and during various times of the year, all of the policies in Exhibit 12–6 are suitable for coping with the fractional-year problem. However, the policy selected must be applied consistently.

Materiality

Infrequent acquisitions and disposals of major assets that individually have a material impact on financial position and results of operations should be depreciated under an appropriate depreciation method to the nearest full month.

NATURAL RESOURCES AND DEPLETION

Business operations frequently use **natural resources,** sometimes referred to as **wasting assets.** Natural resources include coal, oil, ore, precious metals (e.g., silver, gold), and timber and are characterized by their removal and consumption and, thus, the loss of physical characteristics. The replacement of natural resources comes about only by the process of nature and is not subject to human production. **Depletion** is the term used to describe the accounting procedure by which the costs of natural resources are allocated to expense as they contribute to the revenue-producing processes.

Asset/Liability Measurement

Matching

Accounting for natural resources parallels closely accounting for property, plant, and equipment. The measurement of natural resource at historical cost is based on the sacrifice made to acquire the asset. The allocation of this cost over the quantities of the natural resource used to produce revenue (i.e., depletion) is typically computed on a unit basis, much like the units-of-output method of depreciation. This allocation matches revenues with expenses in the determination of periodic income. The book value of the natural resource at any time is that portion of the cost that has not been charged to income. Book value does not necessarily represent the current market value of the natural resource, because the book value is only a portion of the original cost of the asset. The similarity between plant assets and natural resources is further emphasized by the fact that they are usually presented together in the balance sheet, with separate disclosure by major categories.

The **depletion rate**, an estimate of the cost per unit of the natural resource, is based on the historical cost, reduced by any expected residual value after the natural resource has been fully exploited. The depletion rate is then applied to the number of units of the natural resource withdrawn during the period.

To illustrate the depletion process, we shall assume that Universal Mining Company acquired the rights to mineral deposits for $2,250,000. Management expected 500,000 tons of the mineral to be economically removed and sold. If, during 1993, 65,000 tons are removed and sold, the depletion rate and depletion charge for the year are computed as follows:

$$\text{Depletion rate per ton} = \frac{\$2,250,000}{500,000 \text{ tons}} = \$4.50 \text{ per ton}$$

$$\text{Cost of mineral removed in 1993} = (\$4.50 \times 65,000 \text{ tons})$$
$$= \$292,500$$

Depletion is recognized by the following general journal entry:

Depletion Expense	292,500	
Accumulated Depletion		292,500

The natural resource and related depletion are shown in the balance sheet:

Mineral deposits	$2,250,000	
Less: Accumulated depletion	(292,500)	$1,957,500

The depletion expense for the period ($292,500) is presented as a cost of production in the income statement.

If some portion of the natural resource is not sold and remains in inventory, that portion of the depletion will be included in the inventory cost and not charged to income as a cost in the period of production. For example, in the previous case, if 15,000 of the 65,000 tons extracted in 1993 remained in inventory at the end of the year, depletion expense and the cost of the depletable resource held in inventory would be as follows:

$$\text{Depletion expense} = 50,000 \text{ tons} \times \$4.50 = \$225,000$$
$$\text{Inventory} = \underline{15,000} \text{ tons} \times \$4.50 = \underline{\quad 67,500}$$
$$\phantom{\text{Inventory} = }\,65,000 \phantom{\text{ tons} \times \$4.50 = }\,\overline{\$292,500}$$

Although this process appears relatively straightforward and analogous to the depreciation process presented earlier in this chapter, several unique aspects of natural resources are frequently encountered. These aspects are discussed individually in the following paragraphs:

1. The costs of exploration, development, and restoration.
2. The discovery of natural resources subsequent to acquisition.
3. Unique tax aspects of natural resources.
4. The distribution of liquidating dividends.

EXPLORATION, DEVELOPMENT, AND RESTORATION COSTS

The cost of natural resources may include a variety of expenditures after the initial acquisition of the property or the purchase of rights to explore on another's property. **Exploration costs** are frequently incurred in attempts to locate the reserves of the natural resource that can be economically extracted. Sometimes these costs result in the location of reserves that can be economically exploited, and at other times, in the failure to locate reserves that can be economically exploited. This difference has led to two accounting methods for exploration costs. Under the **successful-efforts method** only those exploration costs that can be associated with the discovery of producible reserves are considered to be a part of the depletion base of the natural resource; costs not associated with the discovery of producible reserves are expensed as incurred on the basis that they fail to represent future expected benefits. The alternative, the **full-cost method,** assumes that all exploration costs are necessary expenditures to discover the location of producible reserves and thus are a part of the cost of those producible reserves. Both methods are used in practice and a great deal of controversy has surrounded the use of the two methods, particularly in the oil and gas industry. We discuss this controversy in greater depth in Chapter 13.

Development costs are expenditures that are necessary to exploit reserves of natural resources that have been located through successful exploration activities. Development costs in the form of tangible assets, such as special machinery and equipment, tunnels, shafts, and wells, should be separately classified in appropriate asset accounts and depreciated over their estimated useful lives in accordance with normal depreciation policies. If these assets are limited in their usefulness to the development of a specific natural resource project, however, they should be depreciated over the life of that project by the same method used for the natural resource.

The property containing a natural resource may be sold after extraction activities are complete. The amount expected to be derived from such sale represents the salvage or residual value and reduces the depletion base. To prepare the property for sale, however, **restoration costs** may be necessary to return the property to its natural state. Restoration costs reduce the net amount expected to be received in the form of a salvage value and therefore increase the depletion base.

To illustrate, assume that for $1,750,000 Willow Mines acquires property believed to contain valuable minerals. The company incurs $500,000 in exploration costs and an additional $1,550,000 in tangible developmental costs before the mineral can be successfully extracted. Geological estimates indicate that 75,000 tons of the mineral is a reasonable estimate of the amount that can be economically extracted. Willow Mines expects to sell the property for $500,000 after exploitation. However, restoration costs of $150,000 will be required to prepare the property for sale. The depletion base and depletion rate per ton are computed as follows:

Initial acquisition price	$1,750,000
Exploration costs	500,000
Development costs	1,550,000
Total acquisition cost	$3,800,000

Total acquisition cost (from previous page)		$3,800,000
Less: Estimated residual value	$ 500,000	
Restoration costs	(150,000)	(350,000)
Depletion base		$3,450,000
Depletion rate per ton ($3,450,000/75,000 tons)		$46.00

DISCOVERY SUBSEQUENT TO ACQUISITION

Natural resource reserves may be discovered on previously acquired property. In this case the historical cost of the property does not include a price paid for the natural resource, because that resource was not known to exist at the time of purchase. As noted in Chapter 11, diversity in recording discovery value ranges from the full recognition of the discovered amount to not recording the amount at all. In terms of including a reasonable depletion charge in the determination of income in future years, support exists for the capitalization of discovery value and its inclusion in the depletion base on which the periodic depletion charge is computed. Where the existence of the natural resource was known at the time of acquisition, the historical cost of the asset would reflect that fact and depletion should be based on cost.

TAX ASPECTS OF NATURAL RESOURCES

Under certain provisions of the Internal Revenue Code, the amount of depletion that can be deducted in determining a company's income tax liability may be computed as a percentage of gross income, which is essentially the same as gross margin in financial reporting. This method is called percentage depletion and permits from 5% to 22% of gross income to be deducted for income tax purposes, depending on the particular natural resource involved. Percentage depletion is not available for all natural resources. For example, it cannot be used for timber or large oil and gas holdings. A company would logically deduct percentage depletion instead of depletion based on historical cost for any year in which percentage depletion exceeds cost depletion. If gross income is large, the percentage depletion taken for income tax purposes may exceed depletion for financial reporting in an accounting period or in total over the life of the asset. Tax law allows the deduction in excess of historical cost as an incentive for companies to take the risk of exploring for necessary natural resources.

Asset/Liability Measurement Matching   Despite this unique approach for determining depletion for income tax purposes, the historical cost approach is used in measuring the plant asset and applying the matching principle for financial reporting. Recent changes in the Internal Revenue Code, which have limited considerably the applicability of percentage depletion, have reduced the differences in accounting for depletion between income tax reporting and financial-statement reporting.

DISTRIBUTION OF LIQUIDATING DIVIDENDS

In some cases the major business activity of a company centers around the exploitation of natural resources, and no plans exist for the replacement of the resource upon exhaustion. A common practice is to distribute dividends to stockholders in amounts up to the total of the retained earnings plus accumulated depletion. To the extent that dividends exceed the amount of retained earnings, however, distributions represent **liquidating dividends** or a **return of stockholders' investments** to them rather than a return **on** their investments.

To illustrate, we shall assume that Huffman Company has a retained earnings balance of $1,200,000 at December 31, 1993. Accumulated depletion on natural resources totals $1,000,000. Cash dividends of $2,000,000 are declared. Shares of common stock outstanding total 1,000,000. The entry to record the dividend is as follows, assuming paid-in capital in excess of par of at least $800,000 exists:

Retained Earnings (or Dividends Declared)	1,200,000	
Paid-In Capital in Excess of Par	800,000	
Dividends Payable		2,000,000

Care must be taken to inform stockholders that the $2.00 dividend per share represents a $1.20-per-share return on the investment and an $.80-per-share liquidating dividend.

THE ALLOCATION PROBLEM

Matching

This chapter frequently points out that depreciation and depletion are cost allocation processes. They are an integral part of applying the matching principle to an enterprise's nonmonetary inputs, such as inventories and plant assets, to accounting periods for purposes of determining net income. The costs that have not yet been assigned as expenses to an accounting period are maintained as assets in anticipation of future assignment as expenses. We are attempting to match the various **inputs** (costs) into an enterprise's revenue-producing process with the **outputs** (revenues) of that process.

As Arthur L. Thomas has indicated, however, the outputs of a process are the result of not only a number of inputs but the *interaction* of those inputs:

> *The allocation problem has several dimensions, some of which are subtle. But one is easily described: to match costs with revenues, we must know what the contributions of the firm's individual inputs are. Unfortunately, . . . there is no way to know this.*
>
> *Seeing why this is so requires introducing a final concept, interaction. Inputs to a process interact whenever they generate an output different from the total of what they would yield separately. For instance, labor and equipment interact whenever people and machines working together produce more goods than the total of what people could make with their bare hands and machines could make untended. As this example suggests, interaction is extremely common. Almost all of a firm's inputs interact with each other—their failure to do so would ordinarily signal their uselessness.*
>
> *Surprising as it may seem, it can be proved that whenever inputs interact, calculations of how much total revenue or cash flow has been contributed by any individual input are as meaningless as, say, calculations of the proportion of a worker's services due to any one internal organ: heart, liver or lungs. Thus, despite all textbooks and American Institute of CPAs or FASB releases to the contrary—despite what you have been trained to believe—our attempts to match costs with revenues must almost always fail.*[2]

Matching

Does this interaction mean that the allocation of asset costs is futile and that we should not attempt to apply the matching principle? Not necessarily, but understanding the limitations of matching and cost allocation is important. Thomas further

---

[2]Arthur L. Thomas, "The FASB and the Allocation Fallacy," *Journal of Accountancy* (November 1975), p. 66.

suggests that wherever possible the Financial Accounting Standards Board (FASB) should develop accounting standards that do not rely on arbitrary allocation. Two primary allocation-free alternatives to conventional financial reporting exist: current value accounting and reporting of fund flows based on cash and near-cash assets. Where allocations cannot be eliminated in financial reporting, allocations should be kept simple. Complex cost allocation methods should be avoided, and care should be taken not to extend allocation methods to additional areas of financial reporting wherever possible.[3]

FINANCIAL-STATEMENT PRESENTATION

Property, plant, and equipment have a significant impact on the financial position of business enterprises. For many enterprises the investment in property, plant, and equipment exceeds that of any other asset category. The method of depreciation used may also significantly influence the financial position and results of operations of the reporting enterprise.

Disclosure
The Accounting Principles Board (APB) identified four disclosures related to property, plant, and equipment to be included in the financial statements or in related notes:[4]

1. Depreciation expense for the period.
2. Balances of major classes of depreciable assets, by nature or function, at the balance sheet date.
3. Accumulated depreciation, either by major classes of depreciable assets or in total, at the balance sheet date.
4. A general description in the method or methods used in computing depreciation with respect to major classes of depreciable assets.

Due to differences in assets of various enterprises and the flexibility permitted by the authoritative literature, information about plant assets is presented in numerous ways in financial statements. In Chapter 11 we reviewed the plant asset disclosure of Meredith Corporation in which only total amounts were presented in the balance sheet with detailed amounts for types of plant assets presented in a note to the financial statements (Exhibit 11–5). In Exhibit 12–7, we present the plant asset disclosure from the 1990 annual report of Exxon Corporation. Exxon's principal business is energy, involving exploration for and production of crude oil and natural gas, manufacturing of petroleum products and transportation and sale of crude oil, natural gas and petroleum products. Exxon operates in the United States and 79 other countries. Exhibit 12–7 includes Note 11 from the 1990 annual report and an excerpt from the summary of accounting policies concerning property, plant and equipment, including depreciation. The consolidated balance sheet includes a single asset line, "Property, plant and equipment, at cost, less accumulated depreciation and depletion," at $60,425 million (1989) and $62,688 million (1990). These amounts tie to the totals in the first and last columns in Exhibit 12–7. In the consolidated income statement, depreciation and depletion are presented as one of several expense items at $4,790 million, $5,002 million and $5,545 million in 1988, 1989, and 1990, respectively.

Asset categories that are closely related are frequently combined to avoid unnecessary detail in the balance sheet. For example, land may be combined with land

---

[3]Thomas, p. 68.
[4]*APB Opinion No. 12*, "Omnibus Opinions," 1967, pars. 4–5.

AN EXAMPLE OF THE ALLOCATION PROBLEM

A Prospector manufacturers sourdough bread by a three-stage process:

1 He makes leaven by mixing flour, sugar and water in a crock, then keeps it in a warm place for about a week (until it bubbles).

2 He makes bread by transferring all but a cup of leaven to a large pot, where he mixes it with soda and additional flour, sugar and water, kneads it slightly and then lets it rise. He digs a shallow pit, fills it with coals from his camp fire, covers the pot, places it in the pit, buries it in hot coals and keeps it there until the bread is baked.

3 He replenishes the leaven (for the next baking) by adding enough flour and water to restore the crock to its original level.

Water, airborne yeasts and wood are free goods here. We accountants would be concerned with the following inputs to this process: flour, sugar, soda, labor, the crock, the pot and a shovel. Finally, part of the flour and sugar leaven for one loaf becomes included in the leaven for the next. The output of each baking is one loaf of bread.

Although its manufacture is simple, the moment we try to calculate the contributions of any individual input to this output we face a dilemma. Each input (except, perhaps, the soda and the shovel) is essential. Therefore, we could plausibly assign all of the output to any individual input. For example, we could as-

sign all of the output to the flour, reasoning that were flour withheld from the process there would be no bread. Yet we could equally well assign all of the output to the pot, since without it the loaf would have been incinerated.

Having assigned all output to any one input, we've implicitly assigned zero to each other input. But if either all or zero is appropriate for each input, any intermediate allocation will be equally appropriate—say, half the loaf to the flour and a sixth each to the pot, labor and the crock.

I'm unable to prove which of the infinitely many possible ways of allocating the loaf is correct. Therefore, I can't specify the individual contributions of the inputs; instead, all I'm entitled to say is that they generate the loaf jointly. Research shows that other writers on economics and accounting—even efficient-markets investigators—are equally unable to solve this problem. Perhaps the reader can. But until someone does, any contributions calculated for these inputs must be incorrigible [incapable of being corrected or improved]:

1 One can't verify them, because any other calculation is just as good.

2 One can't refute them, because their calculation is just as good as any other.

Therefore, any attempts at matching based on these contributions (say, depreciation of the pot or

---

improvements or other assets closely related to land. Buildings may be combined with improvements, equipment, or other assets closely related to buildings.

In recent years straight-line depreciation has been the most widely used method in financial reporting. *Accounting Trends and Techniques,* a summary of the financial reporting practices of 600 companies, indicates that from 1986 through 1989 approximately 94% of the companies used straight-line depreciation. During this same four-year period, 22%–23% used an accelerated depreciation method and 8%–9% used units of production. These percentages exceed 100% because some companies use different methods on various classes of assets. For example, 562 companies in 1989 reported using straight-line depreciation, 125 used an accelerated method, 50 used units of production, and 8 used other unidentified methods, a total of 745 companies. Declining-balance depreciation is the most widely used accelerated method.[5]

CHANGES IN ESTIMATES AND CORRECTIONS OF ERRORS

Companies often have to change estimates incorporated in depreciation methods. They may also have to correct errors in past historical cost and depreciation amounts.

---

[5]*Accounting Trends & Techniques* (New York: AICPA, 1990), p. 261.

calculation of a value for the ending leaven inventory) will also be incorrigible. But the sourdough process is so much simpler than the productive processes of business enterprises, that *matching must necessarily be incorrigible for them, too*—unless, again, the reader can show how complications ease the calculations. To generalize, when a company tries to match costs with revenues there's no way either to refute or to verify the results. Instead, all possible ways of matching will be just as good—or bad—as each other.

If it's any consolation, I don't like this conclusion either, and have spent years trying to disprove it. Nor should you accept it without further inquiry. But I urge you at least to suspend disbelief in it (and in what follows) until you've read the detailed research, cited earlier, that backs it up.

And please notice that the difficulty here isn't one of being unable to allocate—there might be some way of getting around that problem. Instead, we're drowned in possible allocations, with no defensible way to choose among them. To be sure, since we must prepare reports, we eventually do pick one set of figures or another. Long before completing our training, we became accustomed to do this with few (if any) pangs. First, we narrow the possibilities by looking to generally accepted accounting principles and then select one of the survivors according to industry custom, apparent advantage to the company, apparent appro-

priateness of the method to the firm's circumstances or some other plausible rationale. But how can the incorrigible results be useful to decision makers?

Unless you (or someone) can suggest ways in which calculations that can neither be verified nor refuted assist decisions, our allocations of the costs of depreciable assets, inventories, labor and other inputs are irrelevant to investor needs. Indeed, although it's painful to say this, they are mere rituals—solemn nonsense—and our beliefs in them are fallacies. This should trouble all of us, because practitioners spend much time conducting such rituals, and theorists much time elaborating on such fallacies.

The Accounting Principles Board was well aware of this, but, underrating its severity, was satisfied to claim that exact measurements are seldom possible and that allocation often requires informed judgment. With all due respect, acknowledging that few allocations are exact is like replying, "Few animals are ever completely healthy," in response to the statement, "Sir, your cow is dead."

SOURCE: Adapted from Arthur L. Thomas, "The FASB and the Allocation Fallacy," *Journal of Accountancy*, November 1975, pp. 65–68. Copyright ©1975 by the American Institute of Certified Public Accountants, Inc.

CHANGES IN ESTIMATES

Matching
Asset/Liability
Measurement

As we have seen in studying depreciation and depletion, matching revenues and expenses requires several estimates. Measuring the asset at historical cost may involve estimates, assumptions, and allocations. Furthermore, estimates of useful life—in terms of either time or service quantities—must be made, as well as estimates of the residual value of the asset.

These estimates are made when the asset is placed into service, and they are based on information available at that time. As conditions change, however, estimates of useful lives may need to be either lengthened or shortened. Likewise, estimates of salvage value may also require revision. Management has a responsibility to continuously monitor its operations and to periodically reevaluate the estimates used in recognizing depreciation and depletion.

A change in estimated life or salvage value is not a correction of an error if the estimate was originally made in good faith and was based on all information available at the time. The change simply verifies the fact that as time passes and more information becomes available, more accurate estimates are possible.

Changes in estimates of useful lives and salvage values should be treated on a **prospective basis,** according to *APB Opinion No. 20*.[6] This means that the effect of

---

[6]*APB Opinion No. 20*, "Accounting Changes," 1971, par. 31.

EXHIBIT 12-7

Exxon Corporation
Disclosure of Plant Assets

11. Investment in property, plant and equipment

| | Investment Dec. 31, 1989 | Additions–1990 | | | Investment Dec. 31, 1990 | |
	Less accumulated depreciation and depletion	United States	Foreign	Total	At cost	Less accumulated depreciation and depletion
			(millions of dollars)			
Petroleum and natural gas						
Exploration and production	$34,706	$1,199	$2,027	$3,226	$ 62,188	$34,938
Refining and marketing	14,526	423	1,342	1,765	27,398	15,754
Total petroleum and natural gas	49,232	1,622	3,369	4,991	89,586	50,692
Chemicals	4,318	360	437	797	8,594	4,950
Other	6,875	249	437	686	9,419	7,046
Total	$60,425	$2,231	$4,243	$6,474	$107,599	$62,688

Accumulated depreciation and depletion totaled $39,131 million at the end of 1989 and $44,911 million at the end of 1990. Interest capitalized in 1988, 1989 and 1990 was $98 million, $113 million and $210 million, respectively.

Summary of Accounting Policies Excerpt

   Property, plant and equipment.   Depreciation, depletion and amortization, based on cost less estimated salvage value of the asset, are primarily determined under either the unit of production method or the straight-line method. Unit of production rates are based on oil, gas and other mineral reserves estimated to be recoverable from existing facilities. The straight-line method of depreciation is based on estimated asset service life taking obsolescence into consideration.

   Maintenance and repairs are expensed as incurred. Major renewals and improvements are capitalized, and the assets replaced are retired.

   The corporation's exploration and production activities are accounted for under the "successful efforts" method. Under this method, costs of productive wells and development dry holes, both tangible and intangible, as well as productive acreage are capitalized and amortized on the unit of production method. Costs of that portion of undeveloped acreage likely to be unproductive, based largely on historical experience, are amortized over the period of exploration. Other exploratory expenditures, including geophysical costs, other dry hole costs and annual lease rentals, are expensed as incurred.

SOURCE: Exxon Corporation, 1990 Annual Report.

the change is recognized in the period in which the change is made and future periods. No recognition is made of the depreciation or depletion that would have been recognized in the past if new estimates had been in effect.

   To illustrate the change in depreciation estimates, we shall assume that Mosteller Company acquired machinery in early 1990 for $275,000. The machinery was expected to have a five-year life and a salvage value of $25,000. Depreciation recognized in 1990, 1991, and 1992 was based on these estimates. In 1993, management determines that the machine can be used four more years, after which it will have an approximate $5,000 salvage value.

Depreciation for 1993 and the remaining years in the asset's life is $30,000:

Cost	$275,000
Depreciation, 1990–1992	
[($275,000 − $25,000)/5 years] × 3 years	(150,000)
Book value at beginning of 1993	125,000
Expected salvage value, end of 1996	(5,000)
Depreciation base, 1993–1996	$120,000
Depreciation expense, 1993–1996	
($120,000/4 years)	$ 30,000

The book value ($125,000) at the time of the change in estimate is used as the cost figure in the revised depreciation computation, and the depreciation method is applied as usual. At the end of 1995 the book value of the asset will be $5,000, the expected salvage value:

$$\$275,000 - [(\$50,000 \times 3 \text{ years}) + (\$30,000 \times 4 \text{ years})] = \$5,000$$

The same basic process is followed with other depreciation methods if either the useful life or the salvage value is changed.

CORRECTIONS OF ERRORS

Corrections of past errors in recording assets, depreciation, and depletion are treated as **prior-period adjustments** in accordance with *FASB Statement of Financial Accounting Standards No. 16*.[7] Errors involving property, plant, and equipment frequently result from the expensing of asset costs that should have been capitalized and from the incorrect application of depreciation methods.

We illustrate the correction of plant-asset and depreciation errors by assuming that Watson Corporation acquired equipment in 1990 that was expected to be used for 10 years. The asset cost $150,000 and was expected to have a $10,000 salvage value at the end of its 10-year life. During the 1993 audit, management discovered that the equipment had been incorrectly expensed in 1990. Correct depreciation policy called for the use of the straight-line method of depreciation with a half-year depreciation taken in the first and last years of the asset's life.

Ignoring any income tax effects of the error, we can determine the appropriate corrections to the accounts and the proper depreciation expense for 1993:

Cost of equipment		$150,000
Depreciation expense		
1990: [($150,000 − $10,000)/10] ½ = $ 7,000		
1991: [($150,000 − $10,000)/10] = $14,000		
1992: [($150,000 − $10,000)/10] = $14,000	(35,000)	
Book value at beginning of 1993		115,000
Depreciation expense		
1993: [($150,000 − $10,000)/10]	(14,000)	
Book value at end of 1993		$101,000

The following entry records the asset and related depreciation of 1990–1992:

---

[7]*FASB Statement of Financial Accounting Standards No. 16,* "Prior Period Adjustments," 1977, par. 11.

Equipment	150,000	
Accumulated Depreciation		35,000
Retained Earnings		
(or Prior Period Adjustment)		115,000

The credit to retained earnings represents the net effect of the $150,000 understatement of income resulting from the expensing of the asset in 1990, less the $35,000 overstatement to income in 1990, 1991, and 1992 resulting from the failure to record depreciation ($7,000 + $14,000 + $14,000).[8] The entry to record depreciation for 1993 is made as if the asset and related depreciation had been properly recorded in the past:

| Depreciation Expense | 14,000 | |
| Accumulated Depreciation | | 14,000 |

The prior period adjustment is presented on the statement of retained earnings as a restatement of the beginning balance, as discussed in Chapter 4. In the Watson case the adjustment of the beginning retained earnings of 1993 would be $115,000, the amount credited to retained earnings in the entry above.

The location of errors and the analysis required to determine the impact of errors on the financial statements may be quite complicated, particularly if comparative financial statements are presented. Companies may also change accounting methods (e.g., depreciation method), a subject not covered at this point. Accounting changes and correction of errors are covered more extensively in Chapter 19.

CONCLUDING REMARKS

Matching

The *matching principle* is the primary accounting principle which explains the process of depreciation. In Chapter 12 we have illustrated several methods of depreciation. We have also discussed problems inherent in applying the matching principle such as partial-year depreciation.

Consistency

The *consistency principle* is particularly important in depreciation inasmuch as consistent application of accounting methods over time is necessary in generating information for successive accounting periods that can be compared in evaluating the

Disclosure

financial progress of the reporting entity. The *disclosure principle* also presents plant assets in the financial statements. Companies typically include important information concerning plant assets in both the financial statements and in related notes.

Asset/Liability
Measurement
Matching
Consistency

We can see the problems inherent in applying the *asset/liability measurement, matching, and consistency principles* in situations where errors of previous periods are discovered and where changes in estimates required to apply these accounting principles are made. These accounting problems are only introduced in Chapter 12 and are addressed and illustrated more completely in Chapter 19.

KEY POINTS

1. Depreciation is the process of allocating the cost of property, plant, and equipment as an expense in a systematic and rational manner to those periods expected to benefit from the use of the asset. (Objective 1)

---

[8]The income tax consequences of the correction are not considered in this illustration. As we have seen in Chapter 4, the correction should be presented in the financial statements on a net-of-tax basis. The subject of corrections of errors, including the income tax implications, is covered more extensively in Chapters 18 and 19 of this text.

2. Depreciation is a necessary part of applying the matching principle to long-lived assets that are used in the production of revenue. (Objective 1)

3. Several accounting methods are used to allocate the historical cost of individual plant assets to the periods that benefit from their use. Those methods can be divided into methods based on time and those based on activity level. (Objective 2)

4. Special accounting policies must be adopted to handle situations in which plant assets are used for less than a complete accounting period. Consistency is an important accounting principle in handling this special accounting problem. (Objective 2)

5. Natural resources are a special type of property, plant, and equipment. The allocation of the historical cost of natural resources is called depletion and is similar to depreciation of other plant assets. (Objective 3)

6. Authoritative accounting pronouncements require several specific items of information to be disclosed in the financial statements concerning plant assets. These include the balances in major classes of depreciable assets, accumulated depreciation, depreciation expense, and a general description of the depreciation methods used. (Objective 4)

7. Changes in estimates required to recognize depreciation and depletion are handled on a prospective basis and, therefore, recognized in the period of the change and in future periods. (Objective 5)

8. Corrections of errors in accounting for plant assets, depreciation, and depletion are treated as prior period adjustments. Previously issued financial statements are restated, and retained earnings are corrected for the past errors. (Objective 5)

APPENDIX A: ALTERNATIVE DEPRECIATION METHODS

ADDITIONAL—INDIVIDUAL ASSET METHODS

Several alternatives to the depreciation methods presented in Chapter 12 are available. While these methods are not as widely used in practice, they do represent alternatives that meet the criteria of being both systematic and rational. Three of these alternatives are presented here: the fixed percentage on book-value method, the annuity method, and the sinking-fund method.

To illustrate these methods, Asset 147 is again used. For your convenience, we repeat the necessary information as follows:

Asset 147

Cost	$12,000
Estimated salvage value	$2,000
Estimated life in years	5

An assumed interest rate of 10% is used for the annuity and sinking-fund methods.

Fixed Percentage on Book-Value Method

The **fixed percentage on book-value method** works much like the declining-balance method, except that the method of computing the rate used to depreciate the asset is different. Under this method the annual depreciation rate is determined as follows:

$$\text{Fixed percentage rate} = 1 - \sqrt[n]{\frac{\text{Salvage value}}{\text{Cost}}}$$

In the calculation, n equals the life of the asset in years. If no expected salvage value exists for the asset, some nominal amount must be used so that a rate can be computed. The computed rate is applied annually to the declining book value of the asset, leaving an unamortized cost at the end of the life of the asset exactly equal to the estimated salvage value.

Applying these concepts to Asset 147, we compute the depreciation rate, which equals 30.12%:

$$\text{Fixed percentage rate, Asset 147} = 1 - \sqrt[5]{2,000/12,000}$$
$$= 30.12\%$$

Annual depreciation expense is computed in the same way as in the declining-balance method, using 30.12% instead of some multiple of the straight-line rate.

The fixed percentage on book-value method is not widely used for several reasons: First, as you can see in the example, the method involves a complex computation of the depreciation rate. Second, prior to 1981 companies preferred to use the double-declining balance method for income tax purposes because it provided the maximum amount of depreciation that could be deducted in determining the company's income tax liability. Since the results of the double-declining balance method and the fixed percentage on book-value method are similar, the former was more widely used. Also, unusually low salvage values relative to the assets' costs result in very large fixed percentage rates and extreme acceleration of the depreciation expense.

Annuity Method

The **annuity method** of depreciation is based on the assumption that in acquiring property, plant, and equipment, an enterprise makes an investment much like an annuity (i.e., an investment yielding a fixed return for a stated period of time). Periodic returns on the investment are separated into two elements: a return of the principal amount and an interest revenue on the investment. Throughout the life of the asset, the interest revenue diminishes as the return of the principal reduces the investment.

Under the annuity method, periodic depreciation is computed by using the equation stated below, where *PV* is equal to the present value of 1 at the assumed rate for the estimated life of the asset and *PVOA* is equal to the present value of an ordinary annuity of 1 at the assumed rate for the estimated life of the asset:

$$D = \frac{\text{Cost} - (\text{Salvage value} \times PV)}{PVOA}$$

Applying this equation to Asset 147 at an assumed 10% interest rate, we determine depreciation as $2,838:

$$D_1 = \frac{\$12,000 - (\$2,000 \times .62092)}{3.79079}$$

$$= \$2,838$$

Depreciation is recognized at the constant amount of $2,838 each year. Interest revenue is recognized each year in an amount equal to the book value of the asset times the appropriate interest rate, and Accumulated Depreciation is credited for the difference between the depreciation expense ($2,838) and the interest revenue. Since interest revenue declines each year, the credit to Accumulated Depreciation increases each year.

The application of these concepts to Asset 147 is illustrated in Exhibit 12–8.

The primary limitation with the annuity method, in addition to judgment involved in selecting an appropriate interest rate, is that total depreciation expense recognized over the life of the asset exceeds the cost of the asset by the amount of the interest revenue recognized. In the case of Asset 147 this relationship is as follows:

Total depreciation expense recognized ($2,838 × 5 years)	$14,190
Total interest revenue recognized ($1,200 + $1,036 + $856 + $658 + $440)	(4,190)
Cost less estimated salvage value of Asset 147	$10,000

EXHIBIT 12–8

Depreciation Schedule for Asset 147
Annuity Method

	Depreciation Entry				
End of Year	Dr.: Depreciation Expense	Cr.: Interest Revenue	Cr.: Accumulated Depreciation	Balance: Accumulated Depreciation	Book Value
—	—	—	—	—	$12,000
1	$2,838	$1,200	$1,638	$1,638	10,362
2	2,838	1,036	1,802	3,440	8,560
3	2,838	856	1,982	5,422	6,578
4	2,838	658	2,180	7,602	4,398
5	2,838	440	2,398	10,000	2,000

Computations:
Interest revenue is the book value of the asset multiplied by the interest rate.

Example—Year 1: $12,000 × 10% = $1,200
        Year 2: ($12,000 − $1,638) × 10% = $1,036

The credit to Accumulated Depreciation is the difference between the Depreciation Expense and the Interest Revenue.

Example—Year 1: $2,838 − $1,200 = $1,638
        Year 2: $2,838 − $1,036 = $1,802

Also, the net effect on income is an *increasing* charge, since depreciation expense is constant while interest revenue declines over time. These problems of the amount and pattern of depreciation recognition raise questions as to the appropriateness of the method under current generally accepted accounting principles which stress matching and historical cost.

Sinking-Fund Method

The **sinking-fund method** is a variation of the annuity method, wherein interest revenue and depreciation expense are not recognized as separate elements in the determination of income during the life of the asset. The computations under the sinking-fund method are the same as those for the annuity method.

Applying the sinking-fund method to Asset 147, we find that the depreciation expense is the difference between the $2,838 depreciation cost and the interest revenue each year. This is the same as the credit to the accumulated depreciation column of Exhibit 12–8 and is not recomputed here.

The concept of establishing a sinking fund to provide for the replacement of property, plant, and equipment is rarely applied in practice. However, the existence of the fund is not a prerequisite to the use of the depreciation method derived from this concept.

The sinking-fund method poses the same questions as does the annuity method in regard to an increasing depreciation charge during the life of the asset and the appropriate interest rate for applying the method.

GROUP-DEPRECIATION SYSTEMS

The depreciation methods discussed earlier apply the concept of depreciation to specific individual assets. In some cases, however, it is impractical or even impossible to apply one of the generally accepted depreciation methods to individual assets or to individual components of a complex asset. Several systems are available to compute depreciation for groups of assets that are treated as a single asset for purposes of determining periodic depreciation expense.

Of the many variations of group-depreciation systems, the following are included in this section: inventory system, retirement and replacement systems, and group and composite-life systems.

Inventory System

The **inventory system** of determining periodic depreciation of plant assets parallels closely the determination of expense and the related asset for supplies. As assets are acquired, an asset account is debited. At the end of the financial reporting period, an inventory count is made of the items on hand. The difference between the asset balance and the cost of the items on hand, possibly adjusted to an amount below cost to reflect wear and tear, represents the depreciation charge for the period.

The inventory system is appropriate if a large number of items with a small unit cost are used in the productive process and if the application of a depreciation method to individual assets is impractical. Examples are machine tools, hand tools, and patterns used in the manufacturing process. The inventory method approximates the depreciation amount that would have resulted from depreciating the assets on an individual basis.

To illustrate, we assume that Tyson Manufacturing Company uses a large number of small hand tools in its manufacturing process. Rather than compute depreciation individually on these relatively inexpensive tools, the company uses the inventory method of depreciating them. The asset account reflects the following activity during 1993:

Small Tools Account	
Balance, January 1, 1993	$12,750
Acquisitions	
March 5, 1993	1,300
August 29, 1993	5,420
October 7, 1993	3,500
	$22,970

An inventory on December 31, 1993 reveals that hand tools costing $17,250 are in use. Management determines that these assets should be reduced by 20% due to wear and tear on them to date. Depreciation expense to be recognized in 1993 is determined as follows:

Balance in Small Tools account	$22,970
Value of ending inventory	
$17,250 − .20($17,250)	13,800
Depreciation for 1993	$ 9,170

The entry to recognize depreciation is as follows:

Depreciation Expense	9,170	
Small Tools		9,170

No accumulated depreciation account is maintained, and Depreciation Expense is debited periodically for the reduction in the asset account necessary to bring it to the appropriate balance.

Cash may be received when assets are sold. In the entry debiting Cash, the asset account is credited. This effectively reduces the difference between the ending balance in the asset account and the value of the inventory of tools on hand, thus reducing the depreciation recognized.

For example, for the Tyson case we will assume that the beginning balance and acquisitions are the same as previously stated but, in addition, that $1,500 was received from the sale of used hand tools at December 31, 1993. The following general journal entries would be required:

Cash	1,500	
Small Tools		1,500
Depreciation Expense	7,670	
Small Tools		7,670

The $1,500 from the cash sale is credited directly into the asset account (Small Tools), reducing the balance from $22,970 to $21,470. Depreciation is then computed as $7,670 ($21,470 − $13,800).

Retirement and Replacement Systems

The retirement and replacement systems may be used in much the same situations as the inventory system. They are suitable depreciation systems if a large number of similar items are employed by the enterprise and the items are being replaced on a relatively constant schedule. Under both systems, no depreciation is recognized until items are replaced.

The retirement and replacement systems are frequently used by public utilities, which have large numbers of virtually identical items that are constantly being installed and retired: utility poles, utility lines, accessories used in utility lines, meters (gas, water, electric), and telephone receivers.

Under the **retirement system** the cost of retired items is debited to Depreciation Expense at the time of retirement, and the asset account is reduced by the same amount. The cost of the new items that replace the existing ones is debited to the asset account, and the process continues. No identification of depreciation by individual unit is kept, no accumulated depreciation account is maintained, and no depreciation is taken until units are replaced.

Assume that Ozark Utility Company uses the retirement system to determine depreciation on a large number of utility poles located throughout the city of Ozark. The balance in the Utility Pole account is $250,000 at the beginning of 1993. During the year poles originally costing $72,500 are replaced with new poles costing $97,000. In addition, new poles that are installed in a new service area cost $19,600.

The following entries are necessary to recognize these events:

Depreciation Expense	72,500	
Utility Poles		72,500
Utility Poles	97,000	
Cash		97,000
Utility Poles	19,600	
Cash		19,600

Any cash received from the salvage of the poles being replaced is treated as a reduction in the $72,500 depreciation expense.

The **replacement system** is similar to the retirement system in terms of the circumstances in which it is appropriate. Under the replacement system, however, the cost of replacing the assets—not the cost of the original assets—is treated as the periodic depreciation. In applying the replacement system to the Ozark situation, we need to record the following entries:

Depreciation Expense	97,000	
Cash		97,000
Utility Poles	19,600	
Cash		19,600

The original cost of the utility poles is left in the asset account and the cost of replacement ($97,000) is the depreciation amount recognized. Normally the asset account would be affected only if new poles were acquired for purposes other than replacement of existing poles (such as those for $19,600 in the Ozark case).

As is the case with the retirement system, in the replacement system no identification or depreciation by individual unit is kept, no accumulated depreciation account is maintained, and depreciation expense is not recognized until existing units are replaced. Also, any cash received from the salvage of individual units is treated as a reduction of depreciation expense.

A criticism of both the retirement and the replacement systems is that they do not present the allocation of historical cost as an expense during the period of time when the assets are being used to produce revenue. The reasonableness of either system as an approximation of the allocation of cost depends on the constancy of retirement and replacement over time on a continuous basis. If this continuous retirement and replacement of a large number of similar assets does not apply, these systems should not be used.

The retirement system is a type of first-in, first-out (FIFO) cost determination, since the oldest costs are charged to expense and the most recent costs are maintained in the asset account. In the case of Ozark Utility Company, the 1993 depreciation expense is $72,500 (made up of the oldest costs), and the balance sheet asset is $294,100 ($250,000 − $72,500 + $97,000 + $19,600), which includes the more recent costs of replacement. On the other hand, the replacement system is a form of last-in, first-out (LIFO) since the most recent costs are charged as an expense and the older costs are retained in the asset account. In the case of Ozark Utility Company, the 1993 depreciation expense is $97,000 (made up of the most recent costs), and the balance sheet asset is $269,600 ($250,000 + $19,600), including the original cost of those items that have now been replaced.

Group and Composite Systems

In some cases individual assets are combined and depreciated at an average depreciation rate for the assets included. When assets are combined in this manner because of their similarity (e.g., a fleet of vehicles), the depreciation system is called a **group system**. Dissimilar assets may be combined for depreciation purposes if they are used in operations as an integrated unit (e.g., components of an integrated manufacturing assembly). In such cases the depreciation system is called a **composite system**.

The group and composite systems differ from the other methods of multiple- asset depreciation that we discussed earlier in that an Accumulated Depreciation account is kept for the **group of assets** involved. However, the accumulated depreciation does not relate to any particular asset within the group. The mechanics of applying the group and composite systems are outlined in the following steps:

1. The cost of individual assets that comprise the group are debited to a single asset account.
2. An average depreciation rate is determined by stating the total of the annual depreciation of the individual assets as a percentage of a total cost of the assets included in the group.
3. Depreciation on the group of assets is charged to the Depreciation Expense account and credited to the Accumulated Depreciation account in an amount equal to the percentage computed in Step 2 multiplied by the cost of the assets.
4. The removal of an individual asset from the group is recorded as a debit to the Accumulated Depreciation account and a credit to the asset account in an amount equal to the cost of the individual asset removed. No gain or loss is recognized. Any proceeds received on the asset removal are debited to Cash and serve to reduce the amount that would otherwise be charged to Accumulated Depreciation.

To illustrate, we shall assume that Time Manufacturing Company has a number of small production processes that operate simultaneously to produce several consumer products. The composite depreciation system is used for the assets employed in each process. Information concerning the components of the integrated production assembly for digital watches is presented in Exhibit 12–9.

The five components have been debited to a single asset account, Digital-Watch Production Assembly. We compute the depreciation per year on each component by using the straight-line method. The average depreciation rate is 9.4%, determined by dividing the total de-

preciation per year of $11,750 by the historical cost of the assets, $125,000. The composite life is 9.7 years ($114,000/$11,750). This indicates that the group of assets will be fully depreciated in approximately 10 years if the 9.4% depreciation rate is applied to the historical cost annually.

A single depreciation entry is made each year for the group of assets, as follows:

```
Depreciation Expense                    11,750
    Accumulated Depreciation—
    Digital-Watch Production
    Assembly                                    11,750
```

The disposal of a component of the group of assets is recorded by charging the Accumulated Depreciation account. No gain or loss is recognized, because the accumulated depreciation cannot be associated with any particular asset or component of the group. For example, if Component P is sold for $1,000 after five years of service, the following entry is made:

```
Cash                                    1,000
Accumulated Depreciation—Digital-
    Watch Production Assembly           11,000
    Digital-Watch Production
    Assembly                                    12,000
```

The cost of replacing removed components is debited into the composite asset account. When the components of a composite asset change significantly, as might be the case after several components have been replaced, the depreciation rate may require revision. Periodically a recalculation of the depreciation amount should be made based on the existing components at that time. The periodic depreciation amount is then updated to reflect the current makeup of the composite asset.

The major advantage of the group and composite method is the clerical cost savings that result from maintaining a single asset account and single accumulated depreciation account for several individual assets. In our example of the Digital-Watch Production Assembly only

EXHIBIT 12–9
Digital-Watch Production Assembly

Component	Historical Cost	Estimated Salvage Value	Estimated Depreciable Amount	Useful Life in Years	Depreciation per Year
L	$ 27,000	$ 3,000	$ 24,000	8	$ 3,000
M	19,000	4,000	15,000	10	1,500
N	5,000	–0–	5,000	5	1,000
O	62,000	2,000	60,000	12	5,000
P	12,000	2,000	10,000	8	1,250
	$125,000	$11,000	$114,000		$11,750

five components exist, so the cost savings would not be very great. This example is intended to illustrate an approach, however, and if the composite asset had many parts, the clerical savings could be significant. A major problem in the case of the composite method is the application of a single depreciation rate, based on a weighted average life, to diverse components whose lives may vary considerably. This variance is illustrated in the Time Manufacturing example, in which the estimated lives of the components range from 5 to 12 years, but the same rate of depreciation is applied to all components. This problem does not arise in the group method, because the basis for combining the assets is their similarity; there-

fore, the life of each asset is similar to that of the other assets in the group.

Another problem with both the group method and the composite method is that no gain or loss is recorded on the disposal of individual assets within the group, because the cost of the individual asset, minus any proceeds from disposal, is charged to the Accumulated Depreciation account. Inaccurate estimates of useful lives and individual assets that are not productive may go unnoticed more easily under the group and composite methods than they would if the assets were depreciated on an individual basis.

APPENDIX B: CASUALTY INSURANCE

To reduce the risk of financial loss due to casualties (e.g., from fires, thefts, floods, or accidents), business enterprises commonly acquire **casualty insurance.** The purpose of this insurance is to shift to an insurance company the burden of a potential loss from such unexpected occurrences. The **face value** of the insurance policy is the largest amount that the insurance company may be required to pay if a loss occurs. Payments made to the insurance company are called **premiums** and are paid in advance of the period of insurance coverage. Thus, payments initially represent prepaid expenses when they are made. Since premiums are typically lower when insurance contracts provide for coverage over longer periods of time (i.e., more than one year) and payment for the entire period may be made in advance, the current portion of the prepayments appears in the balance sheet as a current asset and the remainder as a noncurrent asset (i.e., other asset or deferred charge).

We are accustomed to thinking in terms of historical cost or book value of property, plant, and equipment. For insurance purposes, however, the relevant dollar measurement of these assets is **fair market value.** The amount recoverable from an insurance company is the lesser of the loss based on fair market value or the face value of the insurance policy, unless the policy includes a coinsurance clause, which is discussed in the next section. The recorded basis of the asset—the historical cost or book value—is *not* the basis for determining the insurance reimbursement and is used only to determine the book gain or loss resulting from the asset loss and related insurance reimbursement.

Common complexities in accounting for casualty insurance are coinsurance and coverage by multiple insurance policies. These topics are discussed in the following sections, after which the accounting process for recording an insured casualty loss is illustrated.

COINSURANCE

Casualty insurance policies frequently contain **coinsurance requirements** to encourage companies to insure assets at amounts based on their fair market values. Companies realize that many casualties result in only partial destruction of plant assets. In the absence of coinsurance requirements, companies are inclined to insure assets at less than their fair market values, because they would receive full reimbursement for any losses up to the face amounts of the insurance policies.

The coinsurance requirement is stated as a percentage of fair market value of the insured asset and requires the property to be insured to at least the percentage indicated or the insured must share in any loss that occurs. For example, if an asset with a fair market value of $100,000 is insured under a policy including an 80% coinsurance requirement, the asset must be insured for at least $80,000 ($100,000 × 80%) to collect the full amount of any loss from the insurance company. The amount paid, however, will not exceed the face value of the insurance policy in any case.

The amount recoverable under a coinsurance situation is computed by multiplying the loss incurred (based on fair market value at the time of the casualty) by the percentage of face value of the policy to the coinsurance requirement in dollars. The amount actually reimbursed is the smallest of three amounts: the amount recoverable under the coinsurance requirements, the amount of the loss, or the face value of the policy. These relationships are presented in Exhibit 12–10.

To illustrate, we assume that Stevens Company has insurance for several of its assets under separate insurance policies containing coinsurance requirements. These policies are described below, including losses incurred from casualties on each asset:

EXHIBIT 12–10

Reimbursement Under Coinsurance Requirements

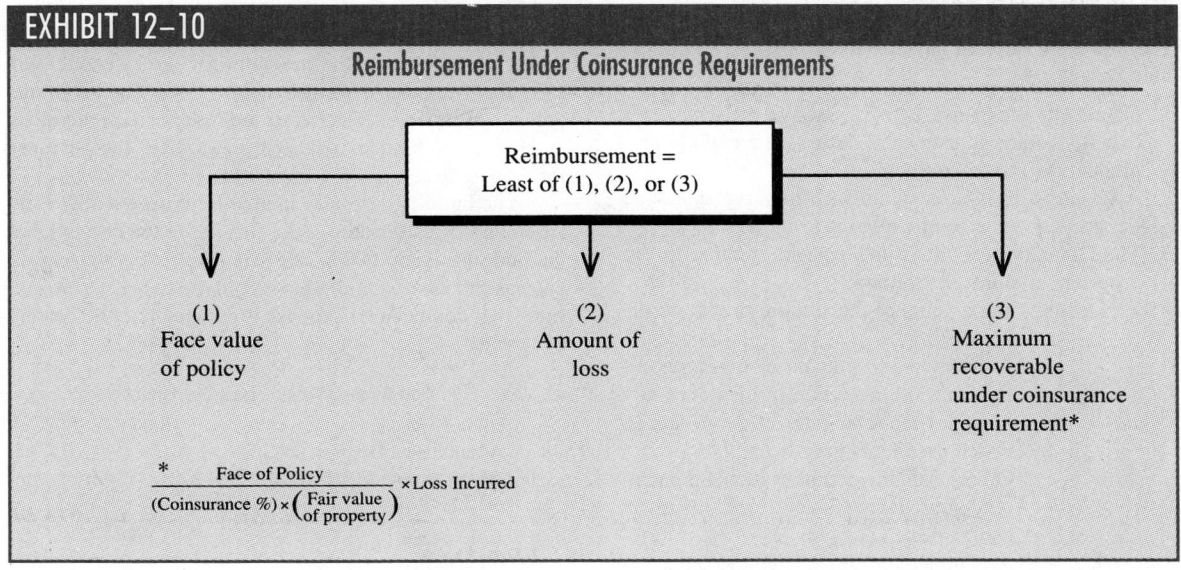

Reimbursement =
Least of (1), (2), or (3)

| (1) Face value of policy | (2) Amount of loss | (3) Maximum recoverable under coinsurance requirement* |

* $$\frac{\text{Face of Policy}}{(\text{Coinsurance \%}) \times \left(\begin{array}{c}\text{Fair value}\\\text{of property}\end{array}\right)} \times \text{Loss Incurred}$$

	Asset A	Asset B	Asset C
Fair market value of asset	$200,000	$250,000	$300,000
Face value of policy	$180,000	$150,000	$250,000
Coinsurance requirement	90%	70%	80%
Amount of loss from casualty (based on fair market value)	$150,000	$120,000	$290,000

For Asset A, the coinsurance requirement is met since the $180,000 face value of the policy is exactly equal to the coinsurance requirement ($200,000 × 90%). Thus, the computation of the amount recoverable under the coinsurance requirement is not necessary and the insurance company will pay $150,000, the smaller of the face value of the policy ($180,000) or the amount of the loss ($150,000).

For Asset B the coinsurance requirement is not met since the $150,000 face value of the policy is less than the coinsurance requirement of $175,000 ($250,000 × 70%). The maximum amount recoverable is computed as follows:

$$\frac{\$150,000}{\$250,000 \times 70\%} \times \$120,000 = \$102,857$$

Since the policy will pay the least of the face value of the policy ($150,000), the amount of the loss ($120,000), or the amount recoverable under the coinsurance requirement ($102,857), only $102,857 will be recovered.

The insured party will share in any loss, with the insurance company paying 85.7% of the loss ($102,857/$120,000) and the insured paying 14.3% of the loss [($120,000 − $102,857)/$120,000].

For Asset C the coinsurance requirement is met, because the $250,000 face value of the policy is greater than the coinsurance requirement of $240,000 ($300,000 × 80%). Thus, the computation of the amount recoverable is not necessary and the insurance company will pay the $250,000 face value of the policy since it is less than the $290,000 loss.

COVERAGE BY MULTIPLE INSURANCE POLICIES

If more than one insurance policy covers the same property, the amount reimbursable under each policy is determined in the same way as described in the previous section. Each policy will pay the *least* of the following: (1) the face value of the policy; (2) an allocated portion of the loss; or (3) the maximum recoverable under a coinsurance requirement.

The allocated portion of the loss is based on the face value of the policies. For example, if a company has a $100,000 policy on a piece of property and another policy of $50,000 on the same property, the first policy would be allocated two-thirds ($100,000/$150,000) of any loss and the second policy would be allocated one-third ($50,000/$150,000) of the loss. The maximum recoverable under a coinsurance requirement is computed as illustrated in the previous section, with the face value of the individual policy used in the numerator of the computation.

ACCOUNTING FOR CASUALTIES

The following steps summarize the process of accounting for a casualty:

1. Depreciation expense is recognized to the date of the casualty; other adjustments, such as the expiration of prepaid insurance, are made.
2. A Casualty account is established to serve as a clearing account for amounts relative to the casualty.
3. The Casualty account is debited and credited for appropriate amounts, as follows:

Debits: Book value of the asset(s) destroyed or damaged.
Adjustments to prepaid insurance resulting from the reduction in insurance coverage for the remainder of the period for which premiums have been paid.
Other costs incidental to the settlement.

Credits: Amounts recoverable from insurance companies.
Amounts recoverable from the salvage of damaged assets.

4. The Casualty account is closed into the Income Summary as a single amount representing the net loss or gain on the casualty and related insurance settlement.

Since the amounts relative to the casualty and related insurance settlement become available over an extended period of time, the Casualty account is used temporarily to house the various components as they become available. A debit balance in the account represents a loss, and a credit balance represents a gain. The latter results when insurance is based on the fair market value of assets and the final settlement from the insurance company exceeds the book value of the lost asset(s) and other costs related to the settlement.

Amounts recoverable from the insurance company are classified as current assets when collection is anticipated in the near future. The loss or gain resulting from the closing of the Casualty account is presented as an extraordinary item in the income statement only if it is both unusual in nature and infrequent in occurrence.

To illustrate the process of recording a casualty, we shall assume that Murray Manufacturing Company, a calendar-year corporation, has a building that was damaged by fire on May 1, 1993. Specific information on the building and the fire loss are as follows:

Cost of building	$450,000	
Accumulated depreciation through December 31, 1992	125,000	$325,000
Fair value of building at May 1, 1993		$700,000
Face value of insurance policy		$500,000
Amount of fire loss (based on fair value)		$350,000
Coinsurance requirement		80%
Prepaid insurance at January 1, 1993		$1,800

Depreciation expense is computed on a monthly basis at an annual rate of $45,000. The prepaid insurance at January 1 represents the premium for the calendar year 1993 that was paid in advance in late 1992. The insurance policy continues in effect after the loss for the remainder of 1993 in an amount adjusted forward for the payment for the fire loss.

The building is determined to have been a 50% loss, based on the relationship of the fire loss to the fair value of the building ($350,000/$700,000). The following general journal entries are required to record the casualty if we assume that depreciation expense is computed to the nearest full month.

To Adjust Accounts to the Date of the Fire Loss

Depreciation Expense	15,000	
Accumulated Depreciation		15,000
[4 months × ($45,000/12) = $15,000]		
Insurance Expense	600	
Prepaid Insurance		600
(4/12 × $1,800 = $600)		

To Close Accounts to Casualty Account

Casualty ($225,000 − $70,000)	155,000	
Accumulated Depreciation	70,000	
[½ ($125,000 + $15,000)]		
Building (½ × $450,000)		225,000
Receivable from Insurance Company	312,500	
Casualty		312,500

$$\left[\frac{\$500,000}{\$700,000 \times 80\%} \times \$350,000 = \$312,500\right]$$

Casualty	750	
Prepaid Insurance		750
[($312,500/$500,000) × $1,200 = $750]		

To Close Casualty to Income Summary

Casualty	156,750	
Income Summary		156,750
($155,000 + $750 − $312,500)		

The entry for $750 to reduce prepaid insurance and adjust the Casualty account is necessary because the insurance in effect after the payment of $312,500 is reduced to $187,500 ($500,000 − $312,500). The Casualty is charged with a pro-rata share of the premium related to the remainder of the year. The balance in the Prepaid Insurance account after this adjustment is $450 ($1,200 − $750), representing the premium related to insurance coverage of $187,500 for the remainder of 1993.

In this situation, the Casualty account had a credit balance, indicating that the company had a gain rather than a loss. This gain is presented in the income statement as "proceeds from insurance in excess of book value of building destroyed by fire" or another appropriate title.

QUESTIONS

12–1   What is the primary theoretical justification for recognizing the cost of property, plant, and equipment as expense over their estimated useful lives?

12–2   Identify the specific elements in the definition of the term "depreciation."

12–3   Under the matching principle, what distortion in income would take place if plant assets were written off as expenses when they were acquired rather than during their estimated useful lives through depreciation?

12–4   Distinguish between "physical" and "functional" factors as they relate to the decline in usefulness of property, plant, and equipment.

12–5   What specific estimates are required to apply the widely used methods of depreciation?

12–6   What is the primary justification for the straight-line depreciation method?

12–7   What are primary justifications for the accelerated depreciation methods?

12–8   For an asset with a relatively long life, computing the denominator base for the sum-of-the-years'-digits depreciation method can be burdensome if done by adding the digits from zero to the number of years in the asset's life. Apply the shortcut method of determining the denominator for an asset with an estimated useful life of 18 years.

12–9   The double-declining balance depreciation rate can be computed by dividing the dollar amount of straight-line depreciation by the cost less the estimated salvage value of the asset and then doubling the resulting rate. How can the same rate be computed without using the dollar amount of depreciation?

12–10   What is the primary impetus behind the use of accelerated depreciation methods?

12–11   What justification exists for the use of depreciation methods based on productive output or service quantities?

12–12   Under all depreciation methods, the book value of a plant asset declines through the life of the asset. What does this declining book value represent?

12–13   When a plant asset is acquired or disposed of at a time other than the beginning or ending of a year, how should depreciation be handled for the first and last financial reporting periods during which the asset is used?

12–14 (Appendix A)   What is the justification for group depreciation systems in which numerous assets are depreciated as a single asset?

12–15 (Appendix A)   Describe the amount that represents the debit to depreciation expense in each of the following group-depreciation methods:

[a] Inventory system   [c] Replacement system
[b] Retirement system   [d] Group and composite systems

12–16   What is depletion and how is it different from or similar to depreciation?

12–17   What is a change in an accounting estimate and how should such changes be treated in the financial statements of the period of change?

12–18   If an accountant determines in 1993 that a depreciable asset with a 10-year life was incorrectly treated as an expense in 1990, what accounting treatment is appropriate in 1993 and future years?

12–19 (Appendix B)   What is coinsurance and how does it affect the amount that a company will receive from the insurer in the event of a loss?

12–20 (Appendix A)   Which of the following depreciation methods does *not* result in decreasing charges?

[a] Double-declining balance.   [c] Sinking fund.
[b] Fixed percentage on book value.   [d] Sum-of-the-years'-digits.

12–21   Property, plant, and equipment are conventionally presented in the balance sheet at which of the following amounts?

[a] Replacement cost less accumulated depreciation.
[b] Historical cost less salvage value.
[c] Original cost adjusted for general price-level changes.
[d] Acquisition cost less depreciation recognized to date.   (AICPA adapted)

12–22   In general accounting usage, which statement(s) applies (apply) to depreciation?

[a] It is a process of asset valuation for balance sheet purposes.
[b] It applies only to long-lived intangible assets.
[c] It is used to indicate a decline in market value of a long-lived asset.
[d] It is an accounting process that allocates long lived asset cost to accounting periods.

(AICPA adapted)

12–23   Which of the following four statements is the assumption on which straight-line depreciation is based?

[a] The operating efficiency of the asset decreases in later years.
[b] Service value declines as a function of time rather than use.
[c] Service value declines as a function of obsolescence rather than time.
[d] Physical wear and tear are more important than economic obsolescence.

(AICPA adapted)

12–24   A graph is set up with "depreciation expense" on the vertical axis and the years listed
along the horizontal axis. Assuming linear relationships, how would the graphs for straight-line and
sum-of-the-years'-digits depreciation, respectively, be drawn?

[a] Vertically and sloping down to the right.
[b] Vertically and sloping up to the right.
[c] Horizontally and sloping down to the right.
[d] Horizontally and sloping up to the right.   (AICPA adapted)

EXERCISES

12–25   DEPRECIATION COMPUTATIONS   Walker Company acquired a new machine costing
$147,500. The machine is expected to have a $20,000 residual value at the end of its six-year life.
The machine is expected to provide 17,000 hours of useful service.

Instructions

Determine the first full year's depreciation, to the nearest dollar, under each of the following methods. The machine was used 2,750 hours during the year.

[a] Straight line
[b] Sum-of-the-years'-digits
[c] Double-declining balance
[d] Service hours

12–26   DEPRECIATION COMPUTATIONS   The Wilmington Daily News acquired a delivery truck
to distribute newspapers throughout the city of Wilmington. The truck cost $12,500 and is expected
to last approximately four years, during which it will be driven approximately 80,000 miles. The
estimated salvage value of the truck is $1,500. The truck was driven 14,500 and 17,600 miles in its
first two years.

Instructions

Determine annual depreciation for the first two years of the truck's life using each of the following
methods:

[a] Straight line
[b] Service miles
[c] Sum-of-the-years'-digits
[d] Double-declining balance

12–27   COST DETERMINATION AND DEPRECIATION   Winfred Products Company purchased
machinery that had a cash selling price of $175,000 by paying $85,000 cash and issuing $108,000
of face-value, noninterest-bearing notes. The company paid an additional $5,000 for delivery and

installation. A service contract was taken out, calling for $2,500 annual payments; the first year's payment was made at the time the machinery was acquired. The machinery is expected to have a useful life of ten years and an estimated salvage value at the end of that time of $20,000.

Instructions

[a] Determine the cost of the machine for purposes of computing depreciation.
[b] Prepare general journal entries to record the above events.
[c] Determine the first-year depreciation expense using each of the following methods:
   [1] Straight-line
   [2] Sum-of-the-years'-digits
   [3] Declining balance at 150% the straight-line rate.

12–28   PARTIAL YEAR DEPRECIATION   Roth Company acquired equipment for $500,000 on April 8, 1992. The asset is expected to have a four-year life and a salvage value of $60,000. Straight-line depreciation is to be used. The company reports on a calendar-year basis.

Instructions

[a] Compute depreciation to be recognized in 1992, 1993, 1994, 1995, and 1996 under each of the following *independent* fractional year policies:
   [1] Depreciation recognized to nearest full month.
   [2] Depreciation recognized to nearest full year.
   [3] Half-year depreciation taken in the year of acquisition and in the year of disposal.
   [4] Full-year depreciation taken in the year of acquisition and none in the year of disposal.
[b] If the asset had been acquired on November 20, 1992, instead of April 8, under which policies would depreciation in 1992 and 1996 differ from that computed in [a]? Why?

12–29   **PARTIAL YEAR DEPRECIATION**   On January 1, 1992, Fenner, Inc., purchased a new machine for $600,000. The machine has an estimated useful life of seven years with an expected salvage value at the end of that time of $25,000. Management of Fenner specifies depreciation of machinery by the sum-of-the-years'-digits method.

Instructions

[a] What amount should be shown on Fenner's balance sheet on December 31, 1993, net of accumulated depreciation, for this asset?
[b] Assume the asset was acquired on August 5, 1992, rather than January 1. Compute the projected book value of the machine on December 31, 1992, 1993, and 1994 under each of the following *independent* fractional-year policies:
   [1] A half-year's depreciation is taken in the year of acquisition and disposal.
   [2] Depreciation is computed to the nearest full month.

12–30   COST DETERMINATION AND DEPRECIATION   The Building account of Cochran Company includes the following items on December 31, 1993:

	Building		
		Gain on sale of	
Contract price	225,000	old building	17,500
Options	7,000		
Repair and maintenance	12,000		

The building was acquired in early 1993 and all entries have been made since the acquisition. The options include $5,000 on the building acquired and $2,000 on a building which was not acquired. Repair and maintenance costs relate to routine activities occurring after the building was occupied.

Instructions

[a] Prepare the entry (or entries) needed to correct the Building account on December 31, 1993, before the books are closed.

[b] Determine depreciation expense for 1993 using each of the following methods, assuming a 20-year life and $80,000 salvage value. A half-year depreciation is taken in the year of acquisition and the year of disposal.

[1] Straight line

[2] Sum-of-the-years'-digits

[3] Double-declining balance

12–31   COST DETERMINATION AND DEPRECIATION   Salem, Inc., a calendar-year company, purchased a machine for $65,000 on January 1, 1991. On that day Salem incurred the following additional costs:

Loss on sale of old machinery	$1,000
Freight-in on new machinery	500
Installation	2,000
Testing before regular operation	300

The estimated salvage value of the new machine was $5,000. Salem estimates that the machine will have a useful life of 20 years, with depreciation being computed on the straight-line method. In January 1993 accessories costing $5,400 were added to the machine to reduce its operating costs. The accessories neither prolonged the machine's life nor provided salvage value.

Betterment— enhanced quality of service potential. Cost is charged to asset Acct.

Instructions *+ an increase in Dep. Exp. is recognized*

[a] Compute depreciation expense for 1991.

[b] Compute depreciation expense for 1993.   (AICPA adapted)

12–32   COST DETERMINATION AND DEPRECIATION   On January 1, 1992, Phillips, Inc., purchased a machine for $50,000. Phillips paid shipping expenses of $500 and installation costs of $1,200. The machine was estimated to have a 10-year life and a salvage value of $3,000. In January 1993, additions costing $3,600 were made to comply with pollution control ordinances. These additions neither prolonged the life of the machine nor provided salvage value.

Betterment— enhanced quality of service potential

Instructions

Prepare a schedule showing the components of book value for the machine at the end of years 1992 through 1995 under the straight-line method of depreciation.   (AICPA adapted)

12–33   ASSET EXCHANGES AND DEPRECIATION   Carter Company acquired a used machine in an exchange for a similar machine from Darter Company. Just before the exchange, the book values of the respective assets were as follows:

	Cost	Accumulated Depreciation	Book Value
Carter Company	$55,000	$25,000	$30,000
Darter Company	47,500	22,500	25,000

Instructions

Prepare the journal entries to record the exchange and the first year's depreciation expense on the books of both companies in the following *independent* situations:

[a] No market value of either asset is available. The Carter Company uses straight-line depreciation with a six-year life for the asset acquired. The Darter Company uses double-declining balance depreciation with a 10-year life for the asset acquired. No salvage value is expected from either asset. (*Hint:* Because no market value information is available, the acquired assets must be recorded at the book value of the assets surrendered.)

[b] The asset relinquished by Carter Company is valued at $22,000. (Both parties are aware of this value.) No value can be determined for the asset relinquished by Darter Company. The Carter Company uses straight-line depreciation with an eight-year life and a $4,000 salvage value on the asset acquired. The Darter Company uses sum-of-the-years'-digits depreciation with a six-year life and no salvage value on the asset acquired. (*Hint:* Because losses are apparent, the acquired assets must be recorded at $22,000 and those losses recognized.)

12–34 (Appendix A) INVENTORY DEPRECIATION METHOD   Stark Co. uses the inventory system to account for numerous small tools used by employees. Under this system depreciation is based on an inventory of tools on hand at the end of the year. Expenditures are charged to a Tools account throughout the year. The balance in the Tools account at the beginning of 1993 was $35,000. The following activity concerning small tools occurred during 1993:

Acquisitions (at cost)	
Mar. 12	$18,750
Aug. 28	6,300
Sale of used tools	
(at salvage value)	
Dec. 19	4,600

An inventory at the end of the year revealed that tools costing $34,800 were on hand and in use.

Instructions

[a] Prepare all general journal entries for activities related to small tools during 1993.
[b] Prepare the balance sheet and income statement for small tools for 1993.

12–35 (Appendix A) RETIREMENT AND REPLACEMENT METHODS   Mack Utility Company has a balance in its Water Meter account of $1,790,000 on January 1, 1993. This balance represents a large number of items, each with a small dollar value. The company is continually replacing the meters as its service employees identify units which are not functioning properly. During 1993 the company installed new meters in three different geographical areas, as follows:

Date of Job Completion	Cost of New Meters Installed	Cost of Old Meters Replaced	Proceeds from Sale of Old Meters
Feb. 17	$265,000	$192,000	$17,000
May 28	350,000	—	—
Oct. 30	160,000	93,000	5,000

The May 28 installation of new meters was in a new service area.

Instructions

[a] Prepare all journal entries for these transactions using the following depreciation methods:
  [1] Retirement method
  [2] Replacement method
[b] Prepare the balance sheet and income statement amounts using both of the above methods for the year ended December 31, 1993.

12–36 (Appendix A) COMPOSITE DEPRECIATION METHOD   A schedule of machinery owned by Remdal Manufacturing Company for its Assembly P is presented below:

	Total Cost	Estimated Salvage Value	Estimated Life in Years
Component P1	$440,000	$40,000	10
Component P2	280,000	20,000	5
Component P3	175,000	—	4

Remdal computes depreciation by the straight-line method.

Instructions

[a] Compute the composite life of the machines (in years) and the average depreciation rate for the machines (as a percentage).
[b] Prepare the general journal entry to record depreciation on the machines as a group for one year.

12–37   CORRECTION OF ERRORS   On January 2, 1992, Denver Company exchanged a used truck with a competitor, receiving a similar truck in the transaction. The original cost of Denver's truck was $7,000. It had accumulated depreciation of $3,800 and a market value of approximately $4,200 at the time of the exchange. Denver paid an additional $4,400 cash for the "new" truck, which was valued at approximately $8,600.

The accountant for Denver Company recorded the truck at $7,600, the total of the cash paid and the book value of the old truck. He recorded depreciation on the basis of miles driven, assuming a total useful life of 50,000 miles, with 12,200 miles driven in 1992. However, he failed to consider the $2,700 expected salvage value after the 50,000-mile life.

Instructions

[a] At what amount should the acquired truck have been recorded by Denver? Why?

[b] Assume that the accountant's errors are found in 1993 before depreciation expense has been recorded for that year. Prepare the journal entries necessary to correct the accounts and to properly recognize depreciation expense for 1993, assuming that 17,200 miles were driven that year.

12–38   COST DETERMINATION AND DEPRECIATION   Melcher Company acquired a used delivery truck for $14,350. The following expenditures were made upon acquisition:

New tires	$425
Body repair and paint	515
Installation of special shelves	375
One-year insurance premium	450

Management expects the truck will be of service for four years and will be driven a total of 60,000 miles. A $3,000 salvage value is expected.

Instructions

[a] Determine the cost of the truck for financial accounting purposes.

[b] Determine the depreciation expense for the first and second years using each of the following methods:

[1] Straight line

[2] Service quantity—miles (The truck was driven 9,760 and 13,950 miles in the first and second years, respectively.)

12–39   CHANGE IN ASSET LIFE   Gatan, Inc., purchased machinery in January of 1991 and applied straight-line depreciation during 1991 and 1992. The machinery cost $128,400, had an estimated six-year life, and was expected to be worth $8,400 at the end of six years. In 1993 management reevaluated its plant assets and determined that this machinery would be useful for seven more years, including 1993. At the end of that period a salvage value of only $2,000 is expected.

Instructions

[a] What amount of depreciation was recorded in 1991 and in 1992?

[b] When the change in estimated useful life is made in 1993, what entry, if any, should be made to account for the difference between annual depreciation taken in previous years and that which will be taken in future years?

[c] Prepare the general journal entry to record depreciation expense for 1993.

12–40   CHANGE IN ASSET LIFE   Wellman Corporation purchased a machine on January 1, 1988, for $160,000. Upon acquisition, the machine had an estimated useful life of ten years with no salvage value. The machine is being depreciated on a straight-line basis. On January 1, 1993, as a result of experience with the machine, management decided that the machine had an estimated useful life of 15 years from the date of purchase.

Instructions

[a] Prepare the general journal entry to record depreciation for 1993.

[b] Independent of your answer to [a], assume that on January 1, 1993, Wellman determines that it can extend the asset's life 10 years beyond that date only by investing an additional $15,000 in the asset. The company anticipates a residual value at the end of the revised life of $5,000.

Prepare the journal entries required in 1993, including the recognition of depreciation for the year.

(AICPA adapted)

12–41 CORRECTION OF ERRORS   In 1991 North Company bought a piece of machinery, the cost of which was erroneously charged to Depreciation Expense in 1991. The company depreciates this class of assets by the double-declining balance method with one-half year's depreciation taken in the year of acquisition and in the year of disposal. This particular machine cost $62,000 and is expected to have an $8,000 residual value at the end of eight years, at which time the company plans to dispose of the asset.

The error indicated above was discovered in 1993 as a result of the periodic evaluation of the estimated useful lives of all plant assets.

Instructions

Prepare the general journal entries to correct the accounts and to properly record Depreciation Expense for 1993.

12–42 DEPLETION   Worsham Company acquired a tract of land containing an extractable natural resource. The purchase contract requires Worsham to restore the land to a condition suitable for recreation after it has extracted the natural resource. Geological surveys estimate recoverable reserves of 4,000,000 tons and a land value of $1,000,000 after restoration. Relevant cost information follows:

Land purchase price	$10,000,000
Estimated restoration costs	1,200,000

Instructions

[a] What is the depletion charge per ton of the recoverable reserves?

[b] If the company extracts 550,000 tons in the first year and sells 525,000 tons, determine the following amounts:

  [1] Depletion expense.

  [2] Inventory cost of the recovered natural resource.

(AICPA adapted)

12–43 DEPLETION   Farr Corporation quarries limestone at two locations, crushes it, and sells it to be used in road building. The Internal Revenue Code provides for 5% depletion on such limestone. Quarry No. 1 is leased, and Farr is paying a royalty of $.01 per ton of limestone quarried. Quarry No. 2 is owned, Farr having paid $100,000 for the site; the Company estimates that the property can be sold for $30,000 after production ceases. Other data follow:

	Quarry No. 1	Quarry No. 2
Estimated total reserves (tons)	30,000,000	100,000,000
Tons quarried through Dec. 31, 1992	2,000,000	40,000,000
Tons quarried, 1993	800,000	1,380,000
Sales, 1993	$600,000	$1,000,000

All of the quarried stone is sold by the end of the year.

Instructions

[a] Determine the 1993 depletion for Quarry No. 1 for financial reporting purposes.

[b] Determine the 1993 depletion for Quarry No. 2 for financial reporting purposes.

[c] Assume the same information except that a new engineering study performed early in 1993 indicated that as of January 1, 1993, 75,000,000 tons of limestone were available in Quarry No. 2. Depletion of Quarry No. 2 in 1993 for financial reporting purposes would be how much?

(AICPA adapted)

12–44 (Appendix B) PROPERTY INSURANCE   Information about four independent cases concerning casualty insurance on equipment is presented below:

	Case A	Case B	Case C	Case D
Fair market value of equipment at date of fire	$75,000	$100,000	$120,000	$150,000
Amount of fire loss	65,000	80,000	70,000	120,000
Face value of insurance policy	50,000	90,000	75,000	110,000
Coinsurance requirement	None	80%	90%	70%

Instructions

[a] For each case, determine the amount which would be recoverable from the insurance company.

[b] Prepare the general journal entry to record the fire loss and insurance recovery for Case B. Assume that the equipment destroyed had originally cost $155,000 and had accumulated depreciation of $86,700. No adjustment to Prepaid Insurance is required.

PROBLEMS

12–45   DEPRECIATION COMPUTATIONS   Fox Machine Company acquired heavy machinery at a cost of $160,000. In addition to the purchase price, $5,000 was paid for delivery of the machinery and $2,000 was paid for training of company personnel to operate the equipment. The machinery was expected to provide 10,000 machine hours of service for five years, after which the machine can be sold for approximately $17,000. Actual machine operating hours during the first five years are as follows: 2,700, 2,200, 2,400, 1,600, and 1,500.

Instructions

[a] Compute depreciation for each of the five years using the following depreciation methods:

[1] Straight line   [3] Sum-of-the-years'-digits
[2] Service quantity—machine hours   [4] Double-declining balance

[b] Comment briefly on the impact on book value that you see when comparing the four methods.

12–46   PLANT ASSET COST AND DEPRECIATION   Information pertaining to Rand Corporation's property, plant and equipment for 1993 is presented below.

Account Balances at January 1, 1993

	Debit	Credit
Land	$ 150,000	
Building	1,200,000	
Accumulated depreciation		$263,100
Machinery and equipment	900,000	
Accumulated depreciation		250,000
Automotive equipment	115,000	
Accumulated depreciation		84,600

Depreciation Method and Useful Life

Building—150% declining balance; 25 years.
Machinery and equipment—Straight-line; 10 years.
Automotive equipment—Sum-of-the-years'-digits; 4 years

The salvage value of the depreciable assets is immaterial. Depreciation is computed to the nearest month.

Transactions during 1993 and Other Information

On January 2, 1993, Rand purchased a new car for $10,000 cash and trade-in of a two-year-old car with a cost of $9,000 and a book value of $2,700. The new car has a cash price of $12,000; the market value of the trade-in is not known.

On April 1, 1993, a machine purchased for $23,000 on April 1, 1988, was destroyed by fire. Rand recovered $15,500 from its insurance company.

On July 1, 1993, machinery and equipment were purchased at a total invoice cost of $280,000; additional costs of $5,000 for freight and $25,000 for installation were incurred.

Rand determined that the automotive equipment comprising the $115,000 balance at January 1, 1993, would have been depreciated at a total amount of $18,000 for the year ended December 31, 1993.

Instructions

[a] For each asset classification prepare schedules showing depreciation expense, and accumulated depreciation that would appear on Rand's income statement for the year ended December 31, 1993, and balance sheet at December 31, 1993, respectively.

[b] Prepare a schedule showing gain or loss from disposal of assets that would appear in Rand's income statement for the year ended December 31, 1993.

[c] Prepare the property, plant, and equipment section of Rand's December 31, 1993, balance sheet.   (AICPA adapted)

12–47   MISCELLANEOUS TRANSACTIONS   Rosman Supply Company entered into a series of transactions involving plant assets during 1992, its first year of operations. These transactions are summarized as follows:

Jan. 10   Machinery was acquired for $10,250 on account, terms 2/10, n/30.

12   Freight-in of $250 on machinery acquired on Jan. 10 was paid. The machine was immediately put into service.

18   The account related to the machinery acquired on Jan. 10 was paid.

Mar. 19   Inventory, fixtures, a building, and land were acquired for a single price of $520,000. The assets were appraised as follows:

Inventory	$150,000
Fixtures	70,000
Building	250,000
Land	100,000

May   1   Renovation costs of $50,000 on the building acquired on Mar. 19 were completed, and the fixtures, building, and land placed into service.

Nov.   1   A truck was acquired and immediately placed into service. The truck had a list price of $9,000 and was purchased by issuing an $8,200, 12%, two-year note. The 12% interest rate was typical for this type of transaction and is payable annually. The truck was driven 2,750 miles in 1992.

Dec. 5   A second machine was acquired, similar to that acquired on Jan. 10. (Both machines will be used.) The machine was acquired on account for $10,700, terms 2/10, n/30. Payment was not made until 1993. Rosman did not incur a freight charge on this machine.

31   The executive group of Rosman Supply Company decided that the following policies should be used to determine the periodic depreciation on plant assets:

Asset	Life	Salvage	Method	Fractional-Year Policy
Machinery	8 yrs.	None	Double-declining balance	Nearest full month
Fixtures	12 yrs.	$10,000	Sum-of-the-years'-digits	Half-year in years of acquisition and disposal
Building	25 yrs.	$60,000	Straight line	Half-year in years of acquisition and disposal
Truck	50,000 miles	$800	Service quantity—miles	None

Instructions

[a] Prepare general journal entries to record the transactions described above.

[b] Prepare all adjusting entries.

[c] Prepare the property, plant, and equipment section of the balance sheet for Rosman Supply Company on December 31, 1992.

[d] Briefly describe the meaning of the book values you included in [c]. Explain their relationship to the current market value of the assets.

12–48   COST AND DEPRECIATION CALCULATIONS   On January 1, 1992, Mock Corporation purchased a tract of land (site number 101) with a building for $650,000. Additionally, Mock paid a real estate brokers' commission of $36,000, legal fees of $6,000, and title guarantee insurance of $18,000. The closing statement indicated that the land value was $500,000 and the building value was $100,000. Shortly after acquisition, the building was razed at a cost of $75,000.

Mock entered into a $3,000,000 fixed-price contract with Smart Builders, Inc., on March 1, 1992, for the construction of an office building on land site number 101. The building was completed and occupied on September 30, 1993. Additional construction costs were incurred as follows:

Plans, specifications and blueprints	$ 17,000
Architects' fees for design and supervision	112,000

The building is estimated to have a forty-year life from date of completion and will be depreciated using the declining balance method at 150% of the straight line rate.

To finance the construction cost, Mock borrowed $3,000,000 on March 1, 1992. The loan is payable in ten annual installments of $300,000 plus interest at the rate of 14%. Mock's average amounts of accumulated building construction expenditures were as follows:

For the period March 1 to December 31, 1992	$ 900,000
For the period January 1 to September 30, 1993	2,300,000

Instructions

[a] Prepare a schedule to determine the individual costs making up the balance in the land account in respect of land site number 101 as of September 30, 1993.

[b] Prepare a schedule which discloses the individual costs that should be capitalized in the office building account as of September 30, 1993. Show supporting computations.

[c] Comment briefly on the rationale for capitalizing interest as part of the building as you have done in (b) above.

[d] Prepare a schedule showing the depreciation expense computation of the office building for the year ended December 31, 1993.   (AICPA adapted)

12–49   MISCELLANEOUS TRANSACTIONS   Swenson Manufacturing Company produces tools which are sold to a variety of manufacturing companies for use in their production operations. Many items of machinery are used to manufacture these tools. Presented below are the Machinery account and the related accumulated depreciation account of Swenson on January 1, 1993, the beginning of the company's fiscal year:

Machinery	$725,400
Accumulated depreciation	(276,100)
	$449,300

The company uses the straight-line method of depreciation. The machinery is expected to have a ten-year life and no salvage value. Each piece of machinery is accounted for individually with a half-year's depreciation taken in the years of acquisition and disposal. Depreciation is recorded on December 31 of each year.

The following transactions involving machinery took place during 1993:

Feb. 1   A machine acquired in 1991 for $10,500 was sold for $4,860.

  15   New machinery costing $15,750 was acquired to replace the machine sold Feb. 1.

Mar. 25   Repair and maintenance costs of $7,500 were incurred.

Nov. 7   A machine costing $25,500, acquired in 1990, was traded for a similar machine. The acquired machine had a fair market value of $20,000. Swenson paid $1,000 as a part of the exchange.

  11   Repair and maintenance costs of $7,260 were incurred.

Dec. 5   A machine acquired in 1990 for $7,250 was sold for $2,500.

  10   New machinery costing $12,500 was acquired.

  31   Depreciation for all machinery for 1993 was recorded.

Instructions

[a] Prepare general journal entries for all machine-related transactions for 1993, including the recognition of depreciation for the year. Provide supporting computations for your entries. (*Hint:* In the Nov. 7 transaction, the machine acquired should be recorded at the book value surrendered, plus cash paid, because a gain is indicated.)

[b] Determine the balances in the Machinery and Accumulated Depreciation accounts for the December 31, 1993, balance sheet.

12–50 MISCELLANEOUS TRANSACTIONS AND CORRECTIONS Parnell Company takes a full year's depreciation in the year of acquisition and no depreciation in the year of disposal for all long-lived assets.

At the beginning of 1993 Parnell had five assets, described below:

	Asset V	Asset W	Asset X	Asset Y	Asset Z
Historical cost	$92,000	$127,500	$27,800	$70,000	$110,000
Year of acquisition	1990	1993	1988	1989	1993
Depreciation method	Straight line	Double-declining balance	Units of production	Straight line	Sum-of-the-years'-digits
Estimated life	10 yrs.	5 yrs.	100,000 units	7 yrs.	5 yrs.
Estimated salvage value	None	$5,000	$3,800	None	$20,000

Additional information about four of the assets has been collected to facilitate making the appropriate journal entries at the end of 1993.

Asset V—Management has determined that the asset will be useful for a total of 17 years rather than the 10 years originally estimated. No salvage value is expected at the end of the asset's life.

Asset X—During 1993, $10,000 was spent to improve the asset, adding 40,000 units of output to its total expected capacity. Before 1993, 65,000 units had been produced; during 1993 the asset produced 20,000 units. The estimated salvage value remained unchanged as a result of the improvement in 1993 which was recorded as a debit to accumulated depreciation.

Asset Y—During 1993 Asset Y was sold for $25,000. The bookkeeper recorded the sale as follows:

Depreciation Expense	10,000	
Cash	25,000	
Asset Y		35,000

Asset Z—Asset Z was acquired in late 1993 to replace Asset Y, which was sold.

Instructions

Prepare general journal entries for each asset on December 31, 1993, the end of Parnell Company's reporting period, to correct any errors made during the year and to properly record depreciation for the year. Show supporting computations.

12–51 CORRECTION OF ERRORS You have been assigned to help audit Mallard for 1992. Part of your responsibility is to evaluate the accounting procedures used to record plant assets and depreciation during 1990 and 1991, the first two years of the company's existence. No audit was made during those years.

The company applies the straight-line method of depreciation to buildings and the double-declining balance method to equipment. A full year's depreciation is taken in the year of acquisition and none is taken in the year of disposal. Balances in these accounts at the end of 1992 (before 1992 depreciation has been recognized) are as follows:

	Building (10-year life)	Equipment (5-year life)
Cost	$400,000	$160,000
Accumulated depreciation	(75,000)	(102,400)
	$325,000	$ 57,600

Your analysis of the company's records reveals the following:

Buildings.   The building was acquired before the beginning of operations on January 1, 1990, for $400,000. Of this amount, $50,000 was allocable to the land on which the building is situated. Transaction costs were an additional $25,000. Another $152,000 in renovation costs were incurred before the building was placed in service. The transaction and renovation costs were charged to expense in 1990. The building was originally expected to have a residual value of $25,000, which appears to have been a reasonable estimate at that time. Recent changes in economic conditions during 1992 indicate that the building will likely be disposable at $100,000 at the end of its 10-year life.

Equipment.   No salvage value was expected from the equipment at the end of its five-year life. It now (1992) appears that the equipment will be worth $40,000 at the end of that period. It is also determined that machinery acquired during 1992 for $40,000 was incorrectly recorded as repair and maintenance expense. This mistake has not been corrected.

Instructions

For the Building and Equipment accounts separately, prepare all general journal entries necessary to correct the accounts and to properly record depreciation for 1992. Present supporting computations with your entries.

12–52   CORRECTION OF ERRORS   Dobson Co. acquired the assets of a competitor in order to establish a branch of Dobson's main store. Dobson paid $500,000 in cash and issued 10,000 shares of common stock which had a $25 par value and a $30 market value at the date of issuance. The market value is based on active trading of the stock in quantities far in excess of the 10,000 shares exchanged in the acquisition. An appraisal of the assets, used by Dobson to negotiate the purchase price, reveals the following values on the transaction date:

Inventory	$200,000
Accounts receivable	100,000
Display fixtures	100,000
Building	300,000
Land	100,000
	$800,000

An inexperienced bookkeeper for Dobson recorded the acquisition as follows:

Inventory	200,000	
Accounts Receivable	100,000	
Fixed Assets	450,000	
Cash		500,000
Common Stock		250,000
(10,000 shares @ $25)		

A further analysis of the Fixed Asset account reveals that the same bookkeeper entered the following items in the account during 1992:

Debit Entries

May 1	Acquisition price	$450,000	
May 1	Insurance on building and fixtures		
	(May 1, 1992, to April 30, 1993)	10,000	$460,000

Credit Entries

May 1	Proceeds from the sale of unneeded		
	display fixtures	17,500	
Dec. 31	Depreciation for 1992	22,125	(39,625)
	Balance, December 31, 1992		$420,375

A computation accompanying the depreciation figure for 1992 is as follows: ($460,000 − $17,500)/20 years = $22,125. You have determined that the unneeded display fixtures that were sold represent 10% of the fixtures acquired from the competitor on May 1.

You have also learned that Dobson depreciates fixtures over a 10-year life by the sum-of-the-years'-digits method and assumes a salvage value of 10% of the cost of items on hand when the depreciation calculation is made. The building is subject to straight-line depreciation over a 20-year life. The building has an estimated $50,000 residual value at the end of the 20 years. All depreciation is computed to the nearest full month. This information was apparently ignored by the bookkeeper.

Instructions

[a] Prepare general journal entries to correct the accounts on December 31, 1992, assuming the books have not been closed. For each entry, explain to the bookkeeper why the entry is necessary and what error(s) were made in the original recording of the item.

[b] Prepare the balance sheet for property, plant, and equipment on December 31, 1992.

[c] Determine the appropriate depreciation expense amounts for the display fixtures and building for 1993.

12–53 DEPLETION AND DEPRECIATION Rim Mine Corporation acquired property in 1993 which is believed to include valuable mineral deposits. The cost of the property was $900,000. Geological estimates indicate that approximately 10,000,000 tons of the mineral may be economically extracted. It is further estimated that the property can be sold for $250,000 to be used for commercial development following mineral extraction. For $80,000, Rim expects to restore the land to a condition appropriate for resale.

After initial acquisition, the following costs were incurred:

Exploration costs—$350,000 (related to expected producible mineral reserves).
Development costs—$325,000 (related to development of tunnels and shafts in the ground);
$460,000 (related to specialized production equipment).

Instructions

[a] Prepare general journal entries necessary to record the above transactions, beginning with the initial acquisition and including depletion and depreciation for 1993 using the following additional information:

[1] 3,720,000 tons of the mineral are extracted and sold during 1993.

[2] The specialized production equipment will be useful in ongoing production operations, and has an eight-year life expectancy and a $35,000 salvage value. Double-declining balance depreciation is to be used, with a full year's depreciation taken in 1993.

[b] How would your entries in [a] differ if the specialized production equipment was acquired exclusively for use in the extraction of the mineral for this project? (The $35,000 salvage value is still a reasonable estimate.)

12–54 INCOME STATEMENT Wilman Mining Company went into business in January 1992 to mine and sell a mineral. Assets were acquired as follows:

Asset	Cost	Estimated Useful Life	Residual Value
Land and mineral deposit	$1,000,000(a)	10,000,000 tons	$200,000(b)
Mine building	75,000	life of mine	5,000
Equipment	650,000	8 years	65,000

(a) Additional costs

Exploration costs (related to minerals discovered)	$ 88,000
Development costs	110,000

(b) Restoration costs (estimated cost of preparing
land for sale at $200,000) 75,000

Depreciation policies of the company are as follows:
Mineral deposits—tons extracted basis
Mine building—same basis as mineral deposits
Equipment—double-declining balance

Operating data for 1992 and 1993 are as follows:

	1992	1993
Tons of mineral extracted	1,500,000	2,500,000
Tons of mineral sold at $4 per ton	1,200,000	2,000,000
Costs of mineral extraction, exclusive of depreciation and depletion (labor, maintenance, etc.)	$1,175,000	$2,260,000
Selling and administrative costs	$985,000	$1,660,000

Inventory of extracted minerals is carried on the first-in, first-out basis. The cost basis for inventory produced during a given period is computed at the average production cost for that period.

Wilman had 500,000 shares of common stock outstanding in 1992 and 1993.

Instructions

Prepare comparative income statements for 1992 and 1993, providing computations to support your entries, and ignoring income taxes. The company's year-end is December 31.

12–55 (Appendix A)   COMPOSITE DEPRECIATION METHOD   Wong Manufacturing Company uses the composite depreciation method for its Production Assembly L35. The individual components in the assembly and their estimated residual values and estimated lives are presented below:

Component	Cost	Estimated Salvage Value	Estimated Useful Life in Years
L35-1	$125,000	$25,000	5
L35-2	36,000	1,000	7
L35-3	117,000	17,000	10
L35-4	42,000	–0–	6
L35-5	19,500	1,500	6
L35-6	211,250	11,250	8
L35-7	82,600	1,600	9

Instructions

[a] Determine the composite life of Assembly L35 and the annual depreciation rate.
[b] Prepare the adjusting entry to record depreciation for the first year of the assembly's life. Depreciation is recorded to the nearest hundred dollars.
[c] During the second year of the asset's life, Component L35-2 is determined to be incompatible with the other components and is sold for $20,000. Record the disposal of Component L35-2.
[d] Component L35-2 is replaced with a new component costing $50,000 and having an estimated nine-year life and a $500 salvage value. Record this replacement and depreciation for the second year.
[e] Disregard the information in [d]. Management determines that Component L35-2 must be replaced with a highly specialized piece of equipment, now in the experimental stage. This component costs $100,000, is expected to be useful for only two years, and will have no salvage value. Record the replacement and depreciation for the second year.

12–56 (Appendix A)   GROUP DEPRECIATION METHODS   Maples Company is considering the use of a group depreciation method for Asset X. The company has many units of Asset X in use at all times and is constantly replacing the units, each of which has a relatively low price. Statistics about Asset X for 1993 have been estimated as follows:

	Units
Beginning balance	100,000
Additions	78,000
Retirements	(62,000)
Ending balance	116,000

Asset X is replaced on a FIFO basis. The beginning balance in Asset X is $250,000, indicating a $2.50 unit cost. Additions were made at a $2.60 unit cost during 1993. Retirements were salvaged for $5,000.

Instructions

[a] Prepare the general journal entries to record additions, retirements, and depreciation for the year using each of the following group depreciation methods:
[1] Inventory system
[2] Replacement system
[3] Retirement system

[b] Determine the depreciation expense and the asset balance to be presented in the 1993 financial statements under each depreciation method in [a].

[c] Why might a company choose to use a group depreciation method rather than treating each asset as an individual unit?

12–57 (Appendix B)   PROPERTY INSURANCE   12–57 contains two *independent* parts.

Part 1.   Blue Company has several assets under separate insurance policies which contain coinsurance requirements. Descriptions of these policies and insurable losses sustained on each asset are as follows:

	Asset W	Asset X	Asset Y
Fair market value			
of asset	$45,000	$25,000	$40,000
Face value of policy	$40,000	$22,500	$25,000
Coinsurance			
requirement	80%	90%	85%
Amount of casualty			
loss	$25,000	$25,000	$30,000

Instructions

Determine the amount to be reimbursed by the insurance company for Assets W, X, and Y.

Part 2.   Red Company has two insurance policies on its building. Policy 1 has a face value of $500,000; Policy 2 has a face value of $300,000. The estimated value of the building is $1,000,000. A loss of $750,000 was recently sustained when a fire destroyed a major portion of the building.

Instructions

Determine the amount to be received from each policy in the following independent cases:

[a] The policies contain no coinsurance requirements.

[b] Both policies have 90% coinsurance requirements.

[c] Policy 1 has a 90% coinsurance requirement and Policy 2 has a 70% coinsurance requirement.

12–58 (Appendix A)   ALTERNATIVE DEPRECIATION METHODS   Wampler Corporation bought a new asset on January 1, 1993. Wampler plans to put the asset into service immediately. The following information is available:

Cost	$100,000
Expected salvage value	$5,000
Estimated life in years	15
Current corporate interest rate	12%

Instructions

[a] Calculate the depreciation for the first two years of the asset's life using each of the following methods:

[1] Fixed percentage on book-value method. (The fifteenth root of 5,000/100,000 is .8189637.)

[2] Annuity method. (Show both the depreciation expense and accumulated depreciation amounts.)

[3] Sinking-fund method.

[b] Explain how an expected salvage value of zero would affect the depreciation calculations using the fixed percentage on book-value method.

12–59   ASSET SECTION OF BALANCE SHEET   Mallory, Inc., manufactures a variety of medical instruments and supplies. The company uses the calendar year for reporting purposes. Information regarding Mallory's assets as of December 31, 1993, before any year-end adjustments, is given below.

Short- and Long-term Investments.   Mallory invests excess funds in short-term marketable securities. The company also has long-term investments in the common stock of other companies. Mallory's holdings of common stock represent less than 5% ownership in those companies. Details are shown below.

Information on Mallory's Holdings of Common Stocks

Investments	Acquisition Date	Purchase Price	Market Values Dec. 31, 1992	Market Values Dec. 31, 1993
Short-term				
PWR, Inc.	Mar. 1, 1993	$ 130,000	—	$ 123,000
Tyra Company	Aug. 15, 1993	80,000	—	75,500
Marank Company	Nov. 20, 1993	50,000	—	51,500
Total short-term investments		260,000	—	250,000
Long-term				
Grabill Corporation	July 1, 1992	117,000	$112,000	113,000
Mikott, Inc.	Mar. 1, 1991	242,000	260,000	252,000
Stanor Company	Dec. 15, 1990	165,000	168,000	170,000
Clarmit, Inc.	Aug. 22, 1989	286,000	272,000	260,000
Total long-term investments		810,000	812,000	795,000
Total investments		$1,070,000	$812,000	$1,045,000

None of the declines in market prices are considered permanent. Dividends which have been declared but have not been received as of December 31, 1993, total $10,300.

Accounts Receivable. The outstanding accounts receivable as of December 31, 1993, total $304,000. The allowance for uncollectible accounts had a credit balance of $16,800 on December 31, 1992. A total of $6,400 in uncollectible accounts was written off during 1993. An aging of the accounts receivable on December 31, 1993, shows a total of $12,400 of the accounts receivable will be uncollectible.

Notes Receivable. Mallory holds two notes from trade customers which are due in 1994. In addition, Mallory holds a note which resulted from the sale of some of its manufacturing equipment. This note is not due until 1996. Interest is due on the anniversary date of the note and has not been accrued as of December 31, 1993. Details are given below, with the two trade notes listed first.

Date of Note	Maturity Date	Face Amount	Annual Interest Rate
Apr. 1, 1993	Mar. 31, 1994	$150,000	8%
July 1, 1993	June 30, 1994	275,000	8%
Jan. 1, 1992	Dec. 31, 1996	450,000	9%
		$875,000	

Inventories. Inventories are valued at the lower of cost or market value. Cost is determined by the FIFO method. Mallory's physical count of inventory reflects that merchandise with a cost of $2,500,000 and market value of $3,200,000 was on hand on December 31, 1993. In addition to this inventory, Mallory had merchandise still out on consignment. The cost of this merchandise was $240,000, the handling and shipping charges to get the merchandise to the consignee totaled $8,000, and the market value was $300,000.

Property, Plant, and Equipment. Mallory states all property at cost. The property and related account balances before the current year's depreciation expense are shown below. The depreciation expense for 1993 is $125,000 for the building and $150,000 for the equipment and furniture.

	Cost	Accumulated Depreciation (before adjustment)
Land	$1,450,000	—
Buildings	3,600,000	$1,425,000
Equipment and furniture	1,750,000	785,000
	$6,800,000	$2,210,000

Included in the amount for land is $250,000 for a parcel of land acquired on December 28, 1993, as a potential building site. As part of the contract to acquire the land, Mallory also had to pay $20,000 in delinquent property taxes; this amount was recorded as an expense.

Additional Information

Cash.   The total in the various bank accounts and imprest petty cash funds amounts to $165,000.

Insurance.   Mallory has purchased insurance to protect its assets and operations. The policies which will be in effect during 1994 are shown below:

Policy No.	Date of Policy	Premium Amount	Coverage in Years
JNA-XY5782	July 1, 1991	$18,000	3
DOME-NX85472	Apr. 1, 1992	30,000	3
FMC-BD287X	Oct. 1, 1993	8,000	1

Patent.   Mallory acquired patent rights on January 2, 1993, for $75,000. At that time, management estimated that the patent would provide economic benefits to the company for the next five years.

Instructions

[a] Prepare a classified asset section of the statement of financial position for Mallory, Inc., on December 31, 1993, as it should appear in the annual report to shareholders.

[b] Describe the information pertaining to Mallory's assets which must be disclosed in the notes to the 1993 financial statements in the annual report to its shareholders.   (CMA adapted)

CASES

12–60   EXPENSING VS. AMORTIZING ASSET COSTS   Constructo Corporation sells and erects "shell houses." These are frame structures that are completely finished on the outside but are unfinished on the inside except for flooring, partition studding, and ceiling joists. Shell houses are sold chiefly to customers who are handy with tools and who have time to do the interior wiring, plumbing, wall finishing, and other work necessary to complete the houses.

Constructo buys shell houses from a manufacturer in unassembled packages consisting of all lumber, roofing, doors, windows, and similar materials. Upon commencing operations in a new area, Constructo buys or leases land for its local warehouse, field office, and display houses. Sample display houses are erected for $6,000 to $10,000. The unassembled packages constitute the majority of the expense; erection is a short, low-cost operation. Sample models are torn down or altered every three to seven years. Sample display houses have little salvage value because dismantling and moving costs amount to nearly as much as the cost of an unassembled package.

Instructions

[a] A choice must be made between (1) expensing the costs of sample display houses in the period in which the expenditure is made and (2) spreading the costs over more than one period. Discuss the advantages of each method.

[b] Would it be preferable to amortize the cost of display houses on the basis of (1) the passage of time or (2) the number of shell houses sold? Explain.   (AICPA adapted)

12–61   DEPRECIATION POLICY   Ron's Manufacturing Company was organized January 1, 1992. During 1992 it has used in its reports to management the straight-line method of depreciating its plant assets.

On November 8 you meet with Ron's officers to discuss the depreciation method to be used for income tax and stockholder reporting. Ron's president has suggested a new method, which he feels is more suitable than the straight-line method for the period of rapid expansion of production and capacity that he foresees. Below, the proposed method is applied to a fixed asset with an original cost of $32,000, and estimated useful life of five years, and an estimated salvage value of $2,000.

Year	Years of Life Used	Fraction Rate	Depreciation Expense	Accumulated Depreciation at Year-End	Book Value at Year-End
1	1	1/15	$ 2,000	$ 2,000	$30,000
2	2	2/15	4,000	6,000	26,000
3	3	3/15	6,000	12,000	20,000
4	4	4/15	8,000	20,000	12,000
5	5	5/15	10,000	30,000	2,000

The president favors the new method because he has heard that

[1] It will increase the funds recovered during the years near the end of the assets' useful lives, when maintenance and replacement disbursements will be high.

[2] It will result in increased write-offs in later years and thereby reduce taxes.

Instructions

[a] What is the purpose of accounting for depreciation?

[b] Is the president's proposal within the scope of generally accepted accounting principles? Discuss the circumstances under which the method would be reasonable and those under which it would not be reasonable.

[c] The president asks your advice:

[1] Do depreciation charges recover or create funds? Explain.

[2] Assume that the IRS will accept the proposed depreciation method in this particular case. If the method were used for stockholder and tax reporting purposes, how would it affect the availability of funds generated by operations?   (AICPA adapted)

12–62 SIGNIFICANCE OF BOOK VALUE When John Severance, President of Severance, Inc., opened his office on Monday, March 8, he discovered that a robbery had occurred over the weekend. Someone had entered the office through a back window and had stolen a computer from one of the office desks. After notifying authorities, John identified the serial number on those computers that were not taken and compared them with the plant asset records that were kept in the company vault. After doing this John said to his employees: "Thank goodness the thief took one of our computers that was almost fully depreciated. That serves him right and certainly eases our situation since the computers are not insured."

Instructions

[a] What is your reaction to John's evaluation of this situation?

[b] Is Severance, Inc., "better off" because a thief stole a computer on which more depreciation has already been taken (as opposed to one with less depreciation taken)? Why?

 **JUDGMENT CASES**

12–63 GAIN RECOGNITION AND DEPLETION White Paper Company owns large holdings of forest lands in the Pacific Northwest that are used to supply the company's mills with various types of pulp. The company has recently received an offer on some of its least productive land and has decided to sell.

Specifically, the company has received an offer to sell a portion of one large forest that they have owned for many decades. The president wants to determine how the sale will be reported in the company's financial statements and the amount of gain to be recognized. The current carrying amount of the forest on the company's books of $8,000,000 represents the cost of the forest, less charges for depletion, plus improvements (such as roads and reforestation) and cultivation costs. The portion to be sold represents about 1/8 of the total forest land and the proposed sales price is $5,000,000. The land subject to the sale is mountainous, near a river, and is in a particularly remote area that does not currently have roads developed on it. Recent geological tests, however, reveal that substantial and valuable mineral deposits exist on the land and the buyer plans to exploit those deposits.

Your assistant has prepared the following proposed accounting for the sale. He has assigned a pro-rata share of the carrying amount of the tract ($8,000,000 × 1/8) or $1,000,000 to the sale and proposes reporting a gain of $4,000,000 on the transaction. You believe the problem is rather simple and are satisfied with this suggestion. You have arranged a meeting with the president to discuss the proposed accounting.

You are surprised when you arrive at the meeting and the president points out a number of considerations that he believes are important to the determination of the proper accounting treatment for the transaction. He states that the land has been virtually worthless to the company up to this point. The president believes that the other factors and considerations as to the newly found minerals should be recognized in accounting for the sale and argues that only a nominal amount, if any, of the carrying amount of the forest should be attributed to the portion sold, resulting in a gain of virtually all of the $5,000,000 sales price. He reasons:

> *The land we are selling has never been of value to us in our productive processes. Indeed, we never would have bought it if we could have avoided doing so when we acquired the large tract from the U.S. Department of Interior many years ago. The fact that mineral deposits have now been found on it is simply fortuitous for us. The productivity of this forest to our company will remain unchanged by the sale and, therefore, the entire sales price of $5,000,000 is simply a windfall gain that we are receiving. Finally, if we allocate the cost as you suggest, this will leave a relatively small amount of original cost for us to allocate to the revenues generated by the timber production that we will sell in the future on other parts of the land. We will report much higher profitability on the sale of timber than we actually achieve and you don't want that, do you?*

Instructions

React to the president's proposal. Do you think that the proposed accounting for the sale is acceptable?

12-64 DEPRECIATING AND VALUING INACTIVE ASSETS High Flyer Aviation has a group of airplanes of various designs and ages. Some of the older planes are not fuel efficient and have lately been used only when all other aircraft are already in use and for charter flights when other more efficient planes are not readily available in the location desired.

Very recently an oil crisis has arisen due to the invasion of one small mid-eastern country by another. One result of this crisis has been a dramatic increase in the cost of petroleum products, including aircraft fuel. In fact, the cost of fuel has become so high that the older, less efficient aircraft are not being used at all because they simply cannot be operated at a positive contribution margin due to the high fuel prices and the effects of intense charter competition. At the time that the company's financial statements are being prepared, the crisis shows no signs of relenting. In fact, the situation appears to be worsening and most oil analysts predict that the price of petroleum products will remain very high for the foreseeable future.

As a result of these factors, High Flyer Aviation has "moth-balled" all of its older, inefficient aircraft and is attempting to sell them. No buyers have been found, however, and prospects look dim for finding a buyer in the near future. You are concerned with whether the carrying amounts in the financial statements of these older aircraft should continue to be depreciated or whether they have been impaired and should be written down to lower figures than their current carrying values. The aircraft have been depreciated by a combination of methods. The engines, controls, and avionics are depreciated over flying hours while the airframes are depreciated over a period of ten years by the straight-line method. The president of the company has indicated to you that if she cannot sell the planes at a gain, she will hold them until fuel prices come back down and things stabilize.

> *At that time we will begin to use these places again profitably. Until then, I don't believe that any aspect of the aircraft should be depreciated or written down to some arbitrary amount that has nothing to do with their value in use. I certainly don't think that the components of the aircraft that are ordinarily depreciated over flying hours should be depreciated when no flying is conducted—that just doesn't make sense.*

Despite the president's assurances, you still have concern about both appropriate depreciation policy and the realizability of the carrying amount of the aircraft. You are aware, for example, that replacing the old engines with new, fuel-efficient ones is one way of making the aircraft more serviceable. You also know that this is a very expensive alternative.

Instructions

Should any (or all) of the components of the inactive aircraft continue to be depreciated while they are not being used? Should the value of the aircraft be written down to an amount lower than their undepreciated cost? If so, describe the conceptual amount at which they should be carried on the financial statements of High Flyer Aviation. If you believe continued depreciation and/or a write-down is appropriate, how will you convince the president to accept this accounting treatment?

12–65   DEPRECIATING A LEASED ASSET   Dryden Petroleum Company has constructed equipment for a large offshore drilling platform that it planned to use in its exploration and production efforts. The company has now decided, however, to lease that equipment to another company because of unanticipated cash flow needs. This lease has a term of five years, and the company expects to be able to lease the equipment to other companies for its entire economic life of approximately 15 years. If fact, management believes that it will be possible to negotiate leases with higher payments through other companies after the initial five-year lease is complete. The total amount of the lease payments that the company expects to receive over the economic life of the equipment exceeds the current carrying amount of the equipment on the financial statements of Dryden by only a small amount. If those anticipated cash receipts were discounted at any reasonable rate of interest, however, the present value of the future cash receipts would be substantially less than the carrying value of the equipment.

The company is in the process of preparing its annual financial statements and you wonder how the equipment that was constructed to be used but that is now being leased should be depreciated and whether it should be considered impaired in value at this time. That is, the net present value of the expected future cash flows from the leases, some of which are yet to be negotiated, are less than the carrying value of the asset.

Instructions

Should the equipment be depreciated in a normal fashion? Should any recognition be given in the selection of a depreciation method to the belief that the leases following the first lease will result in substantially greater lease payments? Should a loss be recognized now in these circumstances? If so, how will this loss affect the amount of depreciation to be recognized on the equipment in the future? If you believe that a loss should be recognized, be sure to describe how the amount of the loss should be measured.

CHAPTER 13

Intangible Assets

OBJECTIVES

1. To distinguish between intangible assets and property, plant, and equipment and to explain how intangible assets contribute to the revenue-producing process.
2. To distinguish between separately identifiable intangible assets and goodwill, an intangible asset relating to the enterprise as a whole.
3. To apply basic accounting principles, such as matching and asset/liability measurement, in accounting for intangible assets.
4. To illustrate the preparation of the financial-statement items and accompanying disclosures for intangible assets.
5. To explain the intangible asset "goodwill," including how it arises, how to estimate its value, and how to determine its cost.
6. To discuss the accounting problems associated with several special areas of accounting that involve intangible assets, including research and development, development-stage enterprises and oil and gas accounting.

DEFINING INTANGIBLE ASSETS

Intangible assets are factors in the production or distribution of goods or services that generate revenue. Most intangible assets have relatively long lives and are subject to amortization over several periods subsequent to their acquisition. They are similar to property, plant, and equipment. However, the distinguishing feature of intangibles is their **lack of physical characteristics.** Additionally, the uncertainty of the amount and timing of future benefits is generally thought to be greater with intangible assets than with other long-lived assets. The value of an intangible asset accrues primarily from the rights or privileges that the intangible provides the owner.

The absence of physical existence alone does not qualify an asset to be presented as an "intangible." Assets that lack physical existence are also found in several balance sheet categories other than intangibles. For example, receivables, short-term investments, and prepaid expenses are presented as current assets; noncurrent receivables and investments in stocks and bonds are classified as investments and funds; and long-term prepayments are presented as other assets or deferred charges. Thus, in addition to the lack of physical existence, assets classified as intangible must be used in the production or distribution of other goods or services and must have relatively long lives, making them subject to amortization.

Intangible assets are frequently divided into those that are separately identifiable and those that lack specific identification. Examples of **separately identifiable intangible assets** are patents, copyrights, franchises, licensing agreements, trade names, trademarks, and organization costs. Intangible assets lacking specific identification are inherent in a continuing business and relate to an enterprise as a whole. While the name given such assets varies from entity to entity, a common name for this type of intangible asset is **goodwill,** the term used in this chapter.

Despite the fact that intangible assets lacking specific identification vary considerably in nature from separately identifiable intangibles, standards that guide the accounting for *all* intangibles have been developed by the accounting profession. The most significant of these standards are in *Accounting Principles Board Opinion No. 17,* which provides the basis for much of the material in this chapter.[1]

ACCOUNTING STANDARDS FOR INTANGIBLE ASSETS

Asset/Liability
Measurement
Matching

Generally accepted standards of accounting for intangible assets incorporate historical cost in applying the asset/liability measurement and matching principles. In much the same way as with property, plant, and equipment, intangible assets are recorded initially at historical cost, determined as the fair value at the time of acquisition. This cost is subsequently amortized over those periods in which the assets are used as factors in the production or distribution of goods and services. Accounting for intangible assets is described below in terms of acquisition, amortization, disposal, and financial-statement presentation.

ACQUISITION OF INTANGIBLE ASSETS

An intangible asset is recorded at cost, which may be described as the sacrifice in assets or the incurrence of liabilities necessary to acquire the asset. Intangible assets may be acquired from other enterprises, in which case cost is normally the fair value of consideration given in the exchange transaction. In unusual circumstances the

---

[1]*APB Opinion No. 17,* "Accounting for Intangible Assets," 1970.

value of the intangible asset received may be more readily determinable than the value of the consideration given, and in these cases the former should be used to record the cost of the intangible asset received.

Intangible assets may also be acquired as part of a group of assets or as part of the acquisition of an entire enterprise. Separately identifiable assets and liabilities, including intangible assets, acquired in such transactions are assigned part of the total cost of the group of assets or enterprise acquired. This assignment is normally based on the fair value of individual assets. The cost of an intangible asset not specifically identifiable that is acquired in this manner is measured by the difference between the total cost of the group of assets and the cost assigned to the other assets, including the separately identifiable intangible assets. This process is developed in greater depth in a subsequent section of this chapter.

Some intangible assets are developed internally. Costs of developing, maintaining, or restoring intangible assets that can be separately identified and have determinate lives are capitalized in appropriate intangible-asset accounts. Similar costs that do not relate to separately identifiable, intangible assets, that have indeterminate lives, or that are inherent in a continuing business should not be capitalized as intangible assets.

We must take care in distinguishing between costs of intangible assets and other expenditures that should be charged to expense when incurred under generally accepted accounting principles (GAAP). Examples of the latter are advertising, research, and development costs. Frequently these expenses are closely related to the development of intangible assets and are sometimes confused with them.

The initial accounting for potential intangible-asset acquisition costs is summarized in Exhibit 13–1. Separately identifiable intangible assets with determinable lives are capitalized in specific intangible-asset accounts, whether they were acquired from another entity, or developed internally. Patents, for example, may be acquired from other enterprises or developed internally. Intangible assets, such as goodwill, that cannot be separately identified but result from transactions with other entities should be established in appropriate intangible-asset accounts. Costs relating to internally developed intangibles that cannot be separately identified are treated as expenses when incurred, even though they may have many of the characteristics of goodwill. For example, a company may develop an outstanding reputation, much like one that it could acquire through a business merger. Costs incurred to develop this reputation internally are normally expensed as incurred. Expenditures that are charged to expense when incurred under generally accepted accounting principles, such as research and development or advertising, are not established as intangible assets, even though they may relate closely to the development, maintenance, or enhancement of certain intangible assets.

AMORTIZATION OF INTANGIBLE ASSETS

Before the Accounting Principles Board (APB) issued *Opinion No. 17,* companies divided intangible assets into those *with* determinable lives and those *without* determinable lives. Those with determinable lives were amortized, whereas those without determinable lives were not amortized. Under *APB Opinion No. 17,* however, intangible assets must be amortized over the periods benefiting from their use.[2] In establishing this requirement, the APB made the following observation:

---

[2]In requiring the amortization of intangible assets, the APB indicated that companies were not required to amortize intangibles acquired before November 1, 1970, the effective date of *APB Opinion No. 17.* Because some companies began amortizing intangibles that previously had not been amortized whereas others continued to carry these intangibles at their historical cost, some intangible assets may still be found on some companies' balance sheets at unamortized historical cost.

EXHIBIT 13-1

Initial Accounting for Potential Intangible-Asset Costs

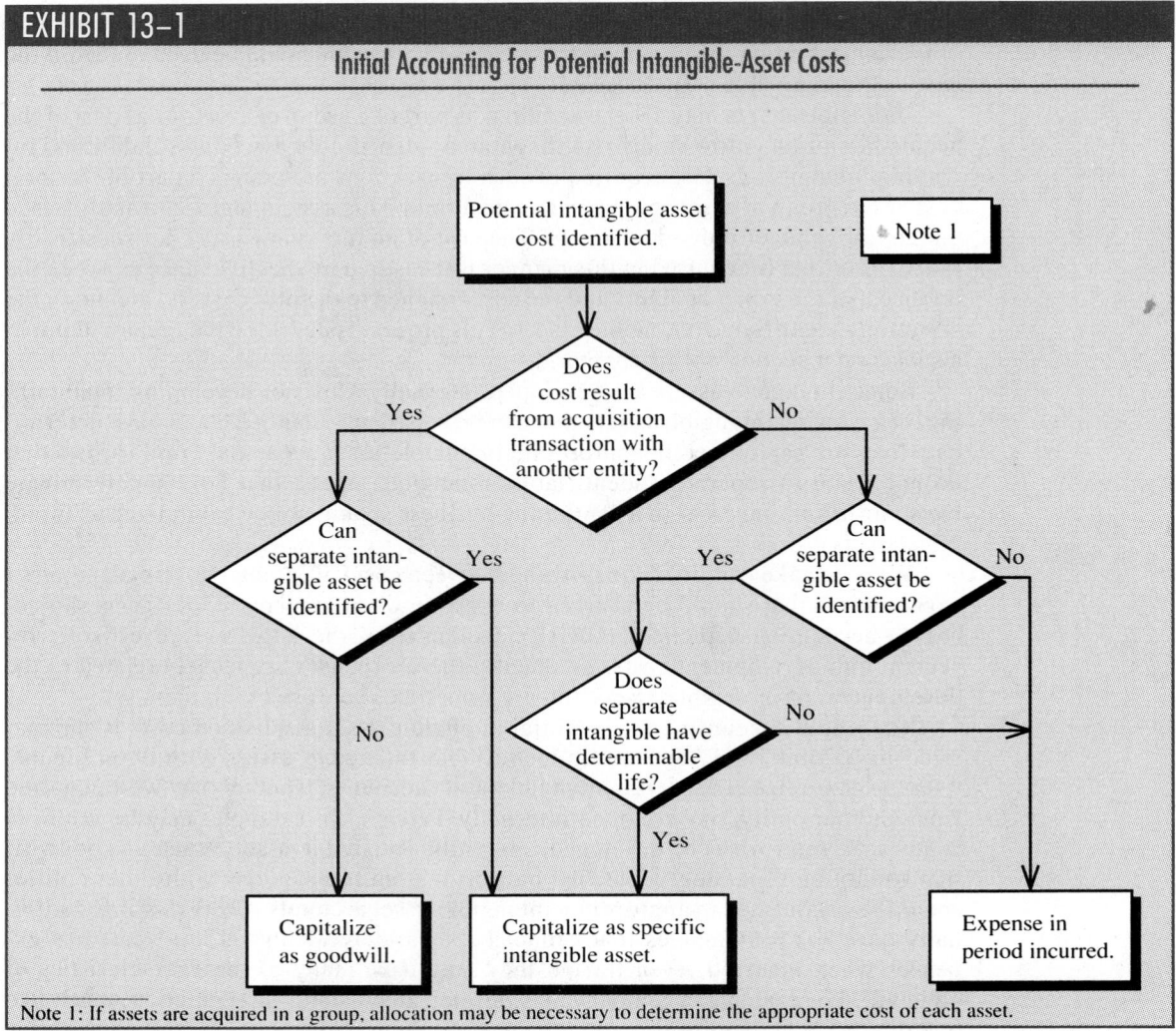

Note 1: If assets are acquired in a group, allocation may be necessary to determine the appropriate cost of each asset.

The value of intangible assets at any one date eventually disappears and . . . the recorded costs of intangible assets should be amortized by systematic charges to income over the periods estimated to be benefited.[3]

A number of pertinent factors must be considered in establishing the periods expected to benefit from intangible assets. These include the following:[4]

1. Legal, regulatory, or contractual provisions may limit the maximum useful life.
2. Provisions for renewal or extension may alter a specified limit on useful life.
3. Obsolescence, demand, competition, and other economic factors may affect useful life.
4. Useful life may parallel the service life expectancies of individuals or groups of employees.

---

[3]*APB Opinion No. 17*, par. 27.
[4]*APB Opinion No. 17*, par. 27.

5. Present competitive advantage may be restricted by expected actions of competitors or others.
6. An apparent unlimited life may in fact be indefinite and benefits cannot be reasonably projected.
7. An intangible may be a composite of any individual factors with varying effective lives.

As a practical matter the APB established a maximum period of 40 years for the amortization of intangible assets. Thus, an intangible asset should be amortized over the shorter of its economic life (which may be influenced by legal or contractual limitations) or 40 years. The APB offered little justification for the 40-year maximum amortization period; however, several explanations appear reasonable.

Intangible assets with indeterminate lives, such as goodwill, are frequently amortized over the maximum period. These assets may relate to individual employees or groups of employees and other conditions that are of limited duration. These same conditions are not likely to continue beyond a period of 40 years. Amortization over a 40-year period, even though this is an arbitrary assignment of cost, prevents any one accounting period from being burdened with such a significant amortization charge that income is materially affected. Also, few intangible assets are useful to an enterprise for more than 40 years. In fact, the makeup of a corporation in terms of asset structure, personnel, production processes, marketing strategy, and many other aspects will generally be significantly different when viewed in 40-year intervals.

Materiality

In summary, although the 40-year maximum amortization period appears somewhat arbitrary, justification exists for amortization over a relatively long period. Also, if the value of intangible assets does in fact diminish over time, the matching principle requires some portion of the cost of such assets to enter into the determination of income in the periods benefited. This is true even if the life of the asset is not precisely determinable when it is acquired.

Matching

An enterprise should continuously evaluate the period over which intangible assets are being amortized. If estimates of useful lives change due to subsequent events and circumstances, the unamortized cost remaining at that point should be allocated to the increased or reduced number of periods in the remaining expected life. The period of amortization should never exceed 40 years from the date of acquisition.

The APB also recommended the straight-line method of amortization unless a company can specifically demonstrate that another method is more appropriate. Accountants typically ignore residual values in applying the straight-line method in the amortization of intangible assets. Policies followed in recognizing amortization for partial years vary, but the alternatives available parallel closely those for property, plant, and equipment as discussed in Chapter 12. Amortization may be computed to the nearest full month, half year, or full year in applying the straight-line method in periods during which the intangible asset is disposed of or acquired. Expenditures during the life of the intangible asset that are considered to increase the cost of the asset should be amortized over the remaining life of the related asset.

To illustrate the process of acquiring and amortizing an intangible asset, we shall assume that Howard Company acquired a patent in 1992 from another enterprise for $10,000. Production personnel of Howard Company estimate that the patent will be used for 10 years and will be worthless at the end of that time. The straight-line method of amortization is used by Howard for amortization of intangibles, with a full year's amortization in the first year.

Entries to record the acquisition of the patent and amortization for 1992 are:

Patent	10,000	
Cash		10,000
Amortization Expense	1,000	
Patent		1,000
($10,000/10 years = $1,000)		

Chapters 11 and 12 explain that accumulated depreciation of property, plant, and equipment must be disclosed in the financial statements. No similar requirement exists, however, for intangible assets, so we usually credit amortization directly to the asset account, as illustrated in the Howard example. Although this approach is commonly practiced, an Accumulated Amortization account for intangible assets is certainly acceptable and is sometimes encountered in business. In fact, if a clear record of the relationship of the historical cost of an intangible asset and its related accumulated amortization is particularly important, such an account is preferable. Unless indicated otherwise this text follows the procedure of crediting amortization directly to the intangible-asset account.

Continuing the example of Howard Company, assume that in 1994 the company incurs $2,000 in legal costs for successfully defending the patent when a competitor charges that Howard Company's patent violates a patent held by the competitor. Entries to record the $2,000 additional cost of the patent and amortization expense for 1994 are as follows:

Patent	2,000	
Cash		2,000
Amortization Expense	1,250	
Patent		1,250
[($8,000 + $2,000)/8 years = $1,250]		

The $8,000 book value of the patent and the $2,000 additional cost are totaled and amortized over the remaining life of eight years. Amortization of 1994 is thus $1,250.

DISPOSAL OF INTANGIBLE ASSETS

Companies may sell separately identified intangible assets in the same way as other assets. When such a transaction occurs the **unamortized cost** of the asset must be removed from the books; the proceeds from the sale or exchange, recorded; and a gain or loss, if any, recognized. The company's amortization policy may require the recording of amortization before the sales transaction is recorded.

The cost of intangible assets should not be written off as a loss in the period of acquisition, as was sometimes done before the issuance of *APB Opinion No. 17*. Estimates of value and future benefits of intangible assets may indicate that the unamortized cost should be reduced significantly by a charge against income at some point in the expected useful life. Unwarranted losses based on temporary conditions or other circumstances that do not support a diminished value of intangible assets are not recorded.

FINANCIAL-STATEMENT PRESENTATION OF INTANGIBLE ASSETS

Financial-statement disclosures include the method and the period of amortization of intangible assets. While balance sheet presentations of intangible assets vary, typical presentations include a general category designated "intangible assets" or "other assets" in which the various specific intangible assets held by the enterprise are listed.

EXHIBIT 13–2

Rockwell International
Intangible Asset Disclosure

Note 5—Intangible Assets

Intangible assets are summarized as follows (in millions):

September 30	1989	1988
Goodwill, less accumulated amortization (1989, $72.2; 1988, $53.6)	$ 583.9	$ 480.8
Patents, product technology and other intangibles, less accumulated amortization (1989, $438.3; 1988, $340.8)	510.7	572.8
Intangible assets	$1,094.6	$1,053.6

Goodwill represents the excess of the cost of purchased businesses over the fair value of their net assets at date of acquisition and generally is being amortized by the straight-line method over periods ranging from 15 to 40 years. The increase in goodwill resulted principally from the purchase of the Baker Perkins printing machinery business in March 1989.

Patents, product technology and other intangibles, relating principally to Allen-Bradley, are being amortized on a straight-line basis over their estimated useful lives, generally ranging from 5 to 20 years.

SOURCE: Rockwell International, 1989 Annual Report.

Exhibit 13–2 presents the disclosure of intangible assets in a note to the financial statements by Rockwell International in the company's 1989 annual report. Rockwell International is recognized as a multi-industry company that applies advanced technology to a wide range of products in electronics, aerospace, automotive, and graphics businesses. A single line appears in the company's 1988–89 comparative balance sheets, labeled "Intangible assets." The note presented in Exhibit 13–2 details the specific intangible assets held by the company and the dollar amounts of each one. The italicized text presents the accounting policy concerning amortization of the intangible assets. Acceptable alternative presentations are to include the detailed information of individual intangible assets in the body of the balance sheet and to present the accounting policy employed in a separate policy statement rather than in an intangibles note.

SEPARATELY IDENTIFIABLE INTANGIBLE ASSETS

Companies may acquire separately identifiable intangible assets from other enterprises or governmental entities, or they may develop them internally. Separately identifiable intangibles that are developed internally and have determinable lives or that are acquired from others should be established in separate intangible-asset accounts that describe the nature of the right or privilege involved.

Several different types of separately identifiable intangible assets are encountered in practice. This section explores some of the most common types of intangibles: patents, copyrights, trade names, trademarks, franchises, licensing agreements, and leaseholds. We also discuss organization costs and deferred charges, assets that are frequently presented with or close to intangible assets in the balance sheet.

PATENTS

A **patent** is a document issued by the U.S. Patent Office that grants the holder the right to exclude others from making, using, or selling the item that is the subject of the patent. Patents are frequently received on new and innovative products for which a market may exist. The legal life of a patent is 17 years. A patent is not renewable, but during the legal life of the original patent the holder can sometimes extend its life effectively by obtaining a new patent that includes slight variations.

Many of the consumer products we use every day are manufactured under patents granted to the producing companies. For example, cameras, household appliances, and hair dryers are frequently produced under patents.

Obtaining a patent does not guarantee that the holder has something of value. The value of a patent stems from its potential for creating competitive advantage, which may include the ability to produce and sell a different or superior product, obtain a higher selling price for the product, produce it at a lower cost, and exclude competition from producing a specific product or utilizing a specific process.

A patent acquired from another enterprise is recorded at the fair value of consideration given in the purchasing transaction unless the fair value of the assets received is more readily determinable. The cost of internally developed patents includes legal and registration fees, including the cost of models and drawings that accompany registration applications. Research and development costs incurred in the generation of patents, however, are charged to expense as incurred. (We will cover this topic later in the chapter.)

Costs of successful legal defenses of patents are capitalized as part of the patent cost, because such action supports the inherent value of the patent. Costs of unsuccessful legal defenses of patents, however, are expensed as incurred. In addition, the unsuccessful defense of a patent raises a question concerning the existence of an asset and usually implies that the unamortized patent cost should be written off as a loss. If a new patent is obtained as a result of refinement, improvement, or other modification of an existing patent, the unamortized cost of the existing patent is considered part of the cost of the new patent if the benefits provided by the two patents are essentially the same.

The cost of a patent is amortized over the shorter of the economic or legal life. Numerous factors tend to reduce the useful life of a patent, including:

1. Technical progress resulting in new and more efficient inventions.
2. Substitute products for current products.
3. Changes in customer demands.
4. Developments by competitors that are sufficiently different to qualify for different patents.

Thus, the economic life of a patent is frequently less than the maximum legal life.

COPYRIGHTS

A **copyright** provides the holder with exclusive rights to the publication, production, and sale of the rights for a literary, dramatic, musical, or artistic work. **Exclusive right** means that the holder can use the work and can **preclude others from using it.** Individuals holding copyrights typically use them to reproduce the work, to sell or otherwise distribute the work, and to perform or record the work.

Prior to 1978 the Copyright Office (a department of The Library of Congress) granted copyrights good for 28 years with a right to renew for another 28 years. Since

1978 the Copyright Office has issued copyrights for the length of the author's life plus 50 years.

The cost of acquired copyrights includes the acquisition price and any related expenditure. The cost of internally developed copyrights includes legal and other registration costs. Generally, the cost is amortized over the economic life of the copyright, which is the period over which the copyright is expected to produce revenue. If the economic life exceeds 40 years, a 40-year period is used for amortization. Due to the limited period of time over which most copyrights are expected to generate revenue, however, the economic life is usually much shorter than the legal life. As a practical matter the cost of copyrights is often amortized over a relatively short period.

TRADE NAMES AND TRADEMARKS

A **trade name** or **trademark** is a symbol, design, word, or phrase that is used by an enterprise to distinguish itself or its product from other enterprises. Trademarks frequently consist of designs or other unique symbols to encourage public identification of products or enterprises. Legal protection for trade names and trademarks is granted by registration with the U.S. Patent Office.

We are all familiar with many trade names, such as Coca-Cola, Polaroid, Ford, and Zenith. These, along with other recognizable trade names, create immediate product identification.

Registration of trade names and trademarks provides continuous protection, subject to periodic renewal. Capitalizable costs of trade names and trademarks include legal fees, registration costs, design costs, acquisition costs, successful legal defense, and other expenditures directly related to the acquisition of the right to use the trade name or trademark. Although advertising expenditures may enhance the value or extend the life of a trade name or trademark, this association is generally believed to be too indirect to warrant the capitalization of such costs as part of the trade name or trademark.

The cost of a trade name or trademark is amortized over the shorter of 40 years or the economic life of the asset. Due to the uncertainties inherent in estimating useful life when factors such as consumer demand are important, the cost of trade names and trademarks is typically amortized over a relatively short period of time.

FRANCHISES

A **franchise** is a contractual agreement that allows the holder to perform certain functions, to sell certain products or services, to use certain trade names or trademarks, or to do other specific things identified in the franchise agreement. Many of the businesses we encounter daily operate under franchises. Examples are Burger King, McDonald's, and Kentucky Fried Chicken restaurants.

Some enterprises enter into franchise agreements with other enterprises to sell products, use trade names, or engage in other activities in exchange for specific payments and the fulfillment of other obligations. In other cases enterprises enter into franchise agreements with governmental units to use public property or to furnish certain types of services, such as water, gas, electric power, public transportation, and waste disposal.

The initial cost of a franchise is recorded as an intangible asset to be amortized over future periods. The franchise cost is then amortized over the shorter of 40 years or the economic life of the franchise. In computing the economic life of the franchise, the holder must consider the time (if any) specified in the franchise contract. If the franchise can be terminated at the option of the entity granting the franchise, the holder should amortize the cost of the franchise over a relatively short period of time. Periodic payments made under a franchise agreement should generally be charged to expense as incurred.

LICENSING AGREEMENTS

Some enterprises obtain licensing agreements to engage in certain lines of business or to use properties or rights owned by other entities. For example, radio and television stations obtain licenses from the Federal Communications Commission. The cost of such licenses represents an intangible asset, the accounting for which parallels closely the accounting for franchises. The cost is amortized over the shorter of the economic life or 40 years.

An interesting example of licensing agreements is found in the trucking industry. Due to deregulation as a result of the Motor Carrier Act of 1980, the Financial Accounting Standards Board (FASB) issued *Statement of Financial Accounting Standards No. 44*, which requires companies to write off as an expense any unamortized costs of interstate operating rights subject to the provisions of that act. The cost of other licensing agreements, such as *intrastate* operating rights in a state that has not deregulated the industry, may still be carried as intangible assets.[5]

LEASEHOLDS

Leasehold costs are frequently found in balance sheets as either property, plant, and equipment or intangible assets. A **lease** is a contract in which the owner of the property **(lessor)** grants another party **(lessee)** the right to use the property for a specified period of time for fixed or determinable payments. The lease typically states other rights and obligations of both the lessor and lessee.

In accounting for leases, some are treated as purchases of the property by the lessee. We follow this accounting treatment if the lease contract is similar to an acquisition of the property by the lessee and includes certain specified characteristics. This is called the **capitalization of the lease** and is a clear example of substance over form, the modifying convention discussed in Chapter 2. In these cases the capitalized cost of the lease, which is usually the present value of the required lease payments, is presented as an asset in the lessee's balance sheet. This is a complex subject, which we treat extensively in Chapter 23 of this text. Leases that are not capitalized are called **operating leases.**

Substance over Form

With both capital and operating leases, lessees may have costs that are presented as intangible assets. Lease contracts frequently call for lessees to prepay lease payments. Such payments must be associated with the appropriate periods and represent intangible assets prior to amortization. Some portion of these prepayments may be appropriately classified as current assets.

Lessees frequently make expenditures that improve the quality of service rendered by leased property. Examples of such leasehold improvements include improvements to building space and improvements to land, such as driveways, shrubbery, and parking lots. Although these expenditures are made in anticipation of benefits to be derived by the lessee, the improvements typically become the property of the lessor at the end of the lease term. Leasehold improvements are capitalized by the lessee in a separate Leasehold Improvement account and amortized over the shorter of the lease term, the life of the property resulting from the improvement, or 40 years.

---

[5]*FASB Statement of Financial Accounting Standards No. 44*, "Accounting for Intangible Assets of Motor Carriers," 1980, pars. 3–7.

ORGANIZATION COSTS

Numerous costs are incurred in organizing a business enterprise, particularly a corporation. Such **organization costs** include the following:

1. Legal fees of drafting the corporate charter and bylaws.
2. Legal fees of corporate registration.
3. Compensation to promoters of the enterprise and other promotional costs.
4. Initial stock-issuance costs.
5. Miscellaneous costs of organization.

Theoretically one can argue that all periods in which the enterprise operates benefit from the incurrence of these costs. In practice, however, the life of the enterprise is usually not known or determinable at the inception of the enterprise, when these costs are incurred. On the other hand, support exists for the position that the early years in the enterprise's life benefit most from organization costs and that such costs lose significance once the enterprise becomes an established operating unit.

Organization costs are frequently treated as an intangible asset and amortized over a relatively short period in the early years of the enterprise's life. The fact that certain organization costs may be amortized for income tax purposes over a period of five years may have encouraged some enterprises to use the same period of amortization for financial reporting purposes.

Distinguishing between organization costs and costs that relate to normal operations is a difficult determination requiring the accountant to use judgment. Costs of normal operations should not be capitalized as organization costs or any other type of intangible asset.

DEFERRED CHARGES

Deferred charges, sometimes called **deferred costs** or **deferred debits**, may be found in balance sheets with or near the intangible assets. As we saw in Chapter 4, deferred charge is a broad term used to identify a number of different items with debit balances that do not fit well in any of the other asset categories of the balance sheet. Organization costs are referred to as deferred charges in some cases. Other costs, such as long-term prepayments, plant rearrangement costs, and deferred income taxes with debit balances, are sometimes referred to as deferred charges.

The presence of deferred charges indicates the problem of attempting to define all costs that have not been amortized in one of the common asset categories. The deferred-charge category is necessary because some debit-balance accounts simply do not fit elsewhere.

Exhibit 13–3 contains the deferred charges and other assets section from the 1989–90 comparative balance sheets of Piedmont Natural Gas Company, Inc. This company is engaged in the transportation and sale of natural gas to residential, commercial, and industrial customers in North Carolina, South Carolina, and Tennessee. The single item that is separately identified is unamortized debt expense representing the cost of issuing debt securities that are outstanding. The unamortized expense represents that portion of the issue costs that are yet to be written off as expense. The remaining assets described as "Other" are not separately disclosed, because of the

Materiality   materiality of the individual amounts.

INTANGIBLE ASSETS NOT SEPARATELY IDENTIFIABLE: GOODWILL

Certain transactions give rise to intangible assets that are not separately identifiable as are patents, copyrights, and other intangibles discussed previously. Intangible

---

EXHIBIT 13-3

Piedmont Natural Gas Company, Inc.
Disclosure of Deferred Charge and Other Assets

Partial balance sheet presentation:

Assets	*1990*	*1989*
	(in thousands)	
Deferred Charges and Other Assets:		
Unamortized debt expense (amortized over life of related debt on a straight-line basis)	**1,106**	1,268
Other	**4,022**	3,372
Total deferred charges and other assets	**5,128**	4,640
Total	**$617,082**	$560,340

SOURCE: Piedmont Natural Gas Company, Inc., 1990 Annual Report.

---

assets that cannot be separately identified relate to the enterprise as a whole. They frequently exist because of the unique combination of separate assets and personnel of the enterprise, and their synergism explains why the value of an enterprise as a whole—measured in terms of its anticipated earning capacity—may be greater than the sum of the values of the individual parts of the enterprise. While such intangible assets are identified with a variety of titles, a commonly used term, goodwill, is used throughout this text.

GOODWILL CONCEPT

Goodwill is the capability of an enterprise to produce earnings in excess of normal. This unique earning capability results from intangible advantages working for the enterprise in conjunction with the separately identifiable tangible and intangible assets. We apply the excess-earning-capacity concept in the various techniques of estimating the dollar amount of goodwill. A closely related notion is that the value of an enterprise as a whole may exceed the value of the sum of the individual assets, less the liabilities, of the enterprise. Such situations result from the existence of intangible qualities, such as an outstanding reputation, superior managerial capability, and ability to operate at an above-normal level of efficiency. Any characteristic or combination of characteristics that gives an enterprise a competitive advantage over other enterprises, thereby allowing a higher level of earnings than would normally be expected, supports the existence of goodwill.

Goodwill has been described as a master valuation account, which indicates that it provides a reconciliation of the difference between the value of an enterprise as a whole and the aggregate value of the individual parts of the enterprise. When viewed in this context, goodwill explains the difference between enterprises that have above-normal earnings and those with normal earnings. The goodwill at work for the former enterprise represents an additional **working asset** that contributes to the enterprise's ability to earn a return on specific individual assets at a level in excess of that normally expected.

Inasmuch as the value of goodwill is identified with an enterprise as a whole, the asset goodwill is inseparable from that enterprise. Thus, goodwill is not exchangeable in the same sense as separately identifiable assets. In certain circumstances, however, goodwill is exchanged when an entire enterprise is acquired. Therefore, when goodwill is evident in the acquisition of an entire enterprise, an appropriate intangible-asset account is established. As depicted in Exhibit 13–1, internally developed qualities similar to acquired goodwill are not recognized as an asset.

When an enterprise contemplates the acquisition of another business, it must determine the value of that business. A starting point is to estimate the current value of all specific assets to be received and liabilities to be assumed. This amount is identified as the fair value of **net assets** received. The seller will desire to include any existing goodwill in determining the exchange price, whether or not the goodwill has previously been recorded as an asset. Once an exchange price is agreed on and a sale takes place, the purchaser acquires the goodwill to the extent that the overall purchase price exceeds the current value of the other net assets received. Goodwill is then recorded by the purchaser. The recorded cost of the goodwill may vary from the valuation of the goodwill estimated to be inherent in the business being acquired, because the goodwill recorded is the amount necessary to reconcile the total purchase price to the current value of the other net assets received.

Conceptually goodwill should be measured by identifying those factors that offer a competitive advantage to an enterprise, such as superior managerial efficiency, an excellent reputation among customers, and ability to operate at a high level of efficiency. By placing a monetary valuation on these features and aggregating these amounts, the value of goodwill could be established.

Realistically, valuing the individual intangible qualities supporting the existence of goodwill involves measurement problems too complex for present accounting practice. Accountants have therefore turned to an indirect method of valuing goodwill, whereby they estimate the total anticipated excess earning capability rather than the individual elements that support the existence of goodwill. This process involves estimating future periodic earnings from an investment in another enterprise, comparing this estimation with what would normally be expected, and aggregating the excess of anticipated earnings over normal earnings. The estimation of excess earning capacity is made for purposes of determining a price to pay for the enterprise rather than for purposes of financial-statement presentation.

For example, assume that Red Company is considering the acquisition of Blue Company. Red Company will take over all the assets and will assume all the liabilities of Blue Company. Red Company estimates the current value of the net assets (assets less liabilities) of Blue Company at $750,000. In addition, Red Company believes it will be able to achieve a level of earnings substantially in excess of normal on its investment due to Blue Company's outstanding reputation. Specifically, the excess earnings are estimated to total $100,000. Red Company is therefore willing to pay up to $850,000 for the net assets of Blue Company. If an amount greater than $750,000 is paid, the excess is identified as the cost of goodwill resulting from the transaction. In this case, goodwill should not exceed $100,000, since that is the value that has been estimated for goodwill. The cost of goodwill is less than $100,000, however, if the final bargained exchange price is less than $850,000. For example, if the agreed-upon purchase price is $780,000, the amount of goodwill is $30,000 ($780,000 − $750,000). On the other hand if the agreed upon price is $840,000, the amount of goodwill is $90,000 ($840,000 − $750,000).

ACCOUNTING FOR GOODWILL

Once acquired, goodwill is accounted for in much the same way as other intangible assets because the general requirements of *APB Opinion No. 17* apply to goodwill. Exhibit 13–1 indicates that goodwill acquired from another enterprise is recorded at cost in an appropriate intangible-asset account. The life of goodwill is not constrained by legal or contractual limitations and therefore may be judged by management to be indeterminate. In such cases we would amortize the goodwill over a 40-year period. In other cases management may decide that the period over which excess earnings can be anticipated is limited to a period shorter than 40 years, and we would amortize the goodwill over the expected period of advantageous operations.

In taking the position that goodwill should be treated as an asset and amortized over its estimated useful life, the APB considered several alternative treatments. These included (1) retaining the cost of goodwill as an asset indefinitely unless a reduction in value becomes evident and (2) deducting the cost of goodwill from stockholders' equity when it is acquired. Supporting the nonamortization approach is the notion that until the future value becomes less than the historical cost, no loss should be recognized. The basis for deducting the cost of goodwill from stockholders' equity at the time of purchase is that the nature of goodwill differs from other assets and warrants special accounting treatment; since goodwill relates to the business as a whole and its value fluctuates widely, estimates of either its value or term of existence are too unreliable for purposes of income determination.[6] These positions were rejected by the APB in favor of the amortization approach we describe in this text.

Many of the advantages of goodwill that can be acquired externally may be developed internally. For example, a company may develop an excellent reputation, superior managerial capability, and the other attributes that allow it to earn at an above normal level without acquiring another enterprise. Despite the similarity between these internally developed characteristics and goodwill acquired from another enterprise, only the latter is capitalized in an intangible-asset account. The cost of internally developed attributes that are similar to acquired goodwill are recognized as expense when incurred.

The reason for not recognizing internally developed goodwill as an asset is primarily the **lack of objective evidence**; in an external acquisition the two enterprises agree on the existence and amount of goodwill. Thus, the difference in accounting for goodwill acquired externally and that developed internally is based primarily on differences in the verifiability of existence of an asset.

GOODWILL EXAMPLE: DIVERSIFIED ENTERPRISES/SINGLE PRODUCT, INC.

In the following paragraphs we use an example involving Diversified Enterprises and Single Product, Inc., to illustrate various computational considerations in accounting for goodwill. Diversified Enterprises is considering the acquisition of Single Product, Inc., a relatively small company that has an excellent reputation. Single Product deals in a product line into which Diversified wants to move. Diversified Enterprises would acquire all the assets and assume all the liabilities of Single Product. The balance sheet of Single Product is presented in Exhibit 13–4. Single Product, Inc., has no cash to be transferred to Diversified Enterprises.

Two questions must be answered by Diversified Enterprises in determining a reasonable price to pay for the net assets of Single Product, Inc. First, to what extent do the balance sheet figures represent the current value of the individual assets and liabilities? Second, is goodwill evident in the past performance of Single Product, Inc.? The price that Diversified is willing to pay should be based on the current value of Single Product's net identifiable assets (assets less liabilities) plus the value of any excess earning capability included in the acquisition. The total of the two elements establishes an amount around which to negotiate an acquisition price.

---

[6]*APB Opinion No. 17*, pars. 17, 19–20.

EXHIBIT 13-4

Single Product, Inc.
BALANCE SHEET
June 30, 1992

Assets			Liabilities	
Marketable securities		$ 5,000	Accounts payable	$ 99,000
Accounts receivable		28,000	Bonds payable	112,000
Inventories		140,000		$211,000
Property, plant, and equipment	$ 275,000		**Stockholders' Equity**	
Accumulated depreciation	(125,000)	150,000	Capital stock	$150,000
Patents		85,000	Retained earnings	47,000
				$197,000
			Total liabilities and stockholders'	
Total assets		$408,000	equity	$408,000

Because the purchase of Single Product, Inc., by Diversified Enterprises represents an acquisition transaction, the recorded amounts of assets on the books of Single Product are of no particular importance to Diversified except as a possible starting point for the establishment of the current value of the acquired assets. Based on appraisals, current market prices, and the application of specific price indexes to historical cost figures, Diversified Enterprises has established the values presented in Exhibit 13–5 for the assets of Single Product. We shall assume that the amounts of liabilities on Single's books fairly reflect the obligations Diversified is assuming.

Asset/Liability Measurement

Why are the recorded amounts of assets in the balance sheet of Single Product, Inc., different from the current value estimates in Exhibit 13–5? The recorded amounts of assets are based on GAAP, which usually do not reflect the current value of the assets. The basis for measuring and recording most assets is historical cost. Adjustments to costs are made to reflect market declines in applying the lower of cost or market method to marketable securities, inventories, and other assets whose realizabilities have been impaired. The balance sheet amounts for many items, however, may be significantly different from their current market values. Also, the accounting method used to account for inventories may cause a difference between recorded amounts and current market values. If the last-in, first-out (LIFO) method is used, for example, the balance sheet amount may be well below the current value, whereas the first-in, first-out (FIFO) method would normally cause the recorded amount and the current value to be closer together. If the inventory to be acquired will be used in a different way by the acquiring enterprise, it may have a greater or lesser value than the amount recorded on the books of the acquired company. Differences in the valuation of receivables most likely reflect differences in the assessment of uncollectible accounts, because the receivables amount reflects the net realizable value of the asset.

Asset/Liability Measurement

Differences between the recorded amounts and the current values of plant assets or of separately identifiable intangible assets are due primarily to the initial measuring and recording of these assets at historical cost and the subsequent depreciation and amortization of the cost figures. The market prices of the assets may remain constant, decline at a different rate from the book value, or actually increase. The book values as presented in the balance sheet are not designed to reflect current value.

EXHIBIT 13-5

Current Value of the Net Assets of Single Product, Inc.

Assets		
Marketable securities	$ 6,000	
Accounts receivable	25,000	
Inventories	125,000	
Property, plant, and equipment	182,000	
Patents	100,000	$438,000
Liabilities		
Accounts payable	99,000	
Bonds payable	112,000	(211,000)
Estimated current value of net assets		$227,000

If Diversified pays a price believed fair in light of the earning potential of the enterprise acquired, goodwill will emerge only if that price exceeds $227,000. For example, if the two enterprises agree on a $250,000 cash purchase price, goodwill is $23,000, computed as follows:

Purchase price	$ 250,000
Less: Estimated current value	
of net assets received	(227,000)
Cost of goodwill	$ 23,000

In this case the journal entry to record the acquisition of the net assets and the assumption of liabilities of Single Product, Inc., by Diversified Enterprises is as follows:

Marketable Securities	6,000	
Accounts Receivable	25,000	
Inventories	125,000	
Property, Plant, and Equipment	182,000	
Patents	100,000	
Goodwill	23,000	
Accounts Payable		99,000
Bonds Payable		112,000
Cash		250,000

If Diversified pays a higher price, the implied goodwill will be more. For example, if $275,000 is paid, the cost of goodwill will be $48,000, determined by the excess of the $275,000 purchase price over the $227,000 estimated value of the net assets received.

Implicit in this transaction is the belief by Diversified Enterprises that the value of goodwill is at least equal to the cost implied in the transaction. Diversified Enterprises should not pay a price in excess of the estimated current value of the identifiable net assets unless its management believes that the earning potential accruing to it in the transaction equals or exceeds the acquisition price.

EXHIBIT 13–6

Anheuser-Busch Companies, Inc.
Purchase of Business Resulting in Goodwill

2. ACQUISITION AND DISPOSITION

On November 2, 1982 the company acquired all of the outstanding common stock of Campbell Taggart, Inc. (Campbell Taggart). Campbell Taggart, through its operating subsidiaries, is engaged in the production and sale of food and food-related products. The cost of the acquisition was $560.0 million, consisting of $275.0 million paid in cash for approximately 50% of Campbell Taggart's outstanding common stock and 7.5 million shares of Anheuser-Busch convertible redeemable preferred stock with an estimated fair value of $285.0 million issued in exchange for the remaining Campbell Taggart common stock.

   The acquisition has been accounted for using the purchase method of accounting. Campbell Taggart's assets and liabilities have been recorded in the company's financial statements at their estimated fair values at the acquisition date. The excess cost of the acquisition over the estimated fair value of the net assets is being amortized on a straight-line basis over 40 years.

   Assuming the acquisition of Campbell Taggart had occurred on January 1, 1982, the pro forma combined net sales would have been $5.6 billion for 1982. The pro forma combined net income and net income per share for 1982 would not have been materially different than that reported in the Consolidated Statement of Income.

   In March 1982, the company sold its corn refining plant in Lafayette, Ind., resulting in a nonrecurring, after-tax gain of $13.3 million or $.28 per share (fully diluted). Sales and income from operations of this plant for the year ended December 31, 1982 were not material.

SOURCE: Anheuser-Busch Companies, Inc., 1984 Annual Report.

The Diversified illustration was hypothetical. Exhibit 13–6, however, discloses an actual purchase transaction involving goodwill. In 1982, Anheuser-Busch Companies purchased Campbell Taggart, Inc., for $560 million. The purchase price was paid in cash ($275 million) and Anheuser-Busch convertible redeemable preferred stock ($285 million). Notice in the second paragraph of the disclosure that the assets and liabilities of Campbell Taggart have been recorded at their estimated fair values at the acquisition date. The excess of cost over the estimated fair value of the net assets, goodwill, is being amortized on a straight-line basis over 40 years.

ESTIMATING THE VALUE OF GOODWILL

For goodwill to exist, evidence of a capability to earn amounts in excess of that which would normally be expected must exist. An evaluation of the existence of goodwill therefore requires a comparison of expected earnings with normal earnings. If the anticipated earnings exceed the norm, evidence of goodwill is present.

   How is the **normal rate of earnings** for an enterprise determined? The normal rate used for goodwill estimation is typically an approximation of the rate required to attract capital into the company that is acquiring another company. The risk associated with the enterprise is a major variable in determining the cost of capital: The higher the risk associated with the company, the higher the cost of capital. Risk, in turn, is assessed by considering the company's line of business, existing debt-equity relationships, past profitability, and other variables. In determining the normal rate,

GOODWILL IS MAKING A LOT OF PEOPLE ANGRY

Write-offs of Intangible Assets Are Giving Service Companies a Big Pain in the Earnings

When Philip Morris Cos. gobbled up Kraft Inc. for $12.9 billion last year, it acquired a passel of prizes that are household names to nearly every shopper in America: Velveeta cheese and Chiffon margarine, to mention just a few. Wall Street has applauded vigorously, sending Philip Morris stock up more than 50%. But according to accountants, Philip Morris was taken to the cleaners. The fair value of the Kraft assets, say the bean counters, was only $1.3 billion. The difference, a staggering $11.6 billion, or 90% of the purchase price, is a wispy, intangible asset known as goodwill.

There are scores of issues on which investors and accountants part company, but few are as contentious—or important—as the treatment of goodwill. And in an era of megadeals, the balance sheets of U.S. companies are piling it up at a torrid pace. Because of the Kraft deal, Philip Morris' goodwill climbed to $15 billion from $4 billion. That's nearly triple its net worth (table). And for many other companies, especially those in consumer products and media, goodwill is becoming an ever larger piece of the balance sheet. At Gannett, Dow Jones, and PepsiCo, goodwill and other intangibles make up more than 80% of net worth.

'Slippery Concept.' All that goodwill is bad news for reported earnings. U.S. corporations must "amortize" or write it off—without the benefit of a tax deduction. That puts American companies at a disadvantage when bidding against foreign buyers for acquisitions. In Britain, companies don't amortize goodwill at the expense of earnings. In Japan, West Germany, and Canada, they do, but the write-off is cushioned by tax breaks. "If there's a more slippery concept [in accounting,] I don't know of it," says Robert Willens, an accounting analyst at Shearson Lehman Hutton Inc.

No one's advocating doing away with goodwill entirely. Indeed, it's a "plug" number that makes a balance sheet balance. When one company buys another, the fair value of the physical assets go into the inventory or plant, property, and equipment accounts. The remainder is called goodwill, also known as "going concern value," and is classified as an intangible asset. In that light, it makes sense. Kraft spent decades building up its food products, and consumer loyalty to the Kraft label is a valuable asset.

But will the value of the Kraft name decline to zero in 40 years? That's how Philip Morris has to treat it, deducting $290 million a year from earnings—about $1.25 a share. While assets such as machines deteriorate visibly, it's not so easy to pinpoint when an intangible is losing value. The write-off is "ludicrous," says Hans G. Storr, Philip Morris' chief financial officer. "It's camouflaging real income."

The goodwill rules also have a vastly different impact on different industries. In capital-intensive businesses, the bulk of the purchase price can be attributed to physical assets. Goodwill is not a major factor, and the write-off does not chew up earnings.

But in consumer products and media, the bulk of the purchase price is goodwill. If Time Inc. succeeds in buying Warner Communications Inc., nearly $11 billion of its $14 billion bid will result in goodwill. The write-off—and it could be more than $300 million annually—will throw Time's reported earnings into the red for several years, even though it takes no cash out of the till. "We have an accounting system that works fine for bricks and mortar," says Lee Seidler, senior managing director at Bear, Stearns & Co. "But it penalizes service companies."

Companies didn't always have to write down their goodwill. Prior to 1970, goodwill was carried at cost and cut only when there was evidence that the asset's value was diminishing. That's essentially what some would like to see today. "If you take care of it, the asset lasts indefinitely," says Roman L. Weil, professor of accounting at the University of Chicago Graduate School of Business. "But bad management can destroy it quickly, too."

Accountants made the write-off of goodwill mandatory because some managers were loath to recognize that the value of intangibles, such as brand

---

a common approach is to consult financial services and other sources for an average cost of capital for other companies in the same industry. Of course, care must be taken that industry figures represent companies that are truly comparable.

Projecting expected future earnings for purposes of comparison with normal earnings involves a careful analysis of past earnings and projected changes in future conditions. Although information about the past may be useful in estimating future earnings, unadjusted past earnings would rarely be an appropriate measure of expected future earnings. Trends in the past, however, may be projected into the future names, had eroded. "The goodwill write-off is only a compromise," says Arthur R. Wyatt, a partner at Arthur Andersen & Co. "But no one's yet come up with a better solution."

Unfair Advantage.   U.S. companies can also be hurt by the goodwill write-off in international deals. Seidler, among others, thinks that goodwill helped two British advertising giants, Saatchi & Saatchi PLC and WPP Group PLC, swallow up U.S. advertising agencies. As service businesses, nearly all the purchase price of the companies wound up as goodwill. The British don't have to charge it off before reporting earnings on their profit-and-loss statement. Instead, they turn directly to the balance sheet and deduct the goodwill from retained earnings. That can make a company look precariously leveraged. To remedy that problem, a few aggressive British companies have begun to shore up their balance sheets by creating an entry called intangible assets, just as it's called in the U.S. But they don't have to amortize it. The bottom line: Since the accounting for acquisitions doesn't penalize earnings, the British can outbid the U.S.

That advantage is under fire in Britain. The British Accounting Standards Committee is weighing a proposed move to a U.S.-style treatment of goodwill. That would coincide with a proposal from the International Accounting Standards Committee, which has proposed a goodwill rule that would write off the asset over five years, though the period could be extended to as much as 20 years if the company could justify it. If adopted in the U.S., that standard would be even more punishing on reported profits.

Of course, some dealmakers say that goodwill's distortion of profits doesn't matter much, because the smart money knows what's going on anyway. "We've never backed off an acquisition because of the goodwill," says Douglas H. McCorkindale, chief financial officer of Gannett Co., the media giant.

Still, McCorkindale says it has taken a long time for Wall Street to realize that goodwill "is an accounting charge without any substance." That could be true for Gannett, Philip Morris, and a few others. But if scores of companies started reporting big losses just because of goodwill, shareholders would surely start screaming.

SOURCE: Jeffrey D. Laderman and Leah J. Nathans, "Goodwill Is Making a Lot of People Angry," *Business Week*, July 31, 1989, pp. 73, 76. Reprinted from July 31, 1989 issue of *Business Week* by special permission. Copyright © 1989 by McGraw-Hill, Inc.

HOW GOODWILL WEIGHS ON THE BALANCE SHEETS

When one company buys another, the difference between the purchase price and the fair value of the physical assets is goodwill. Most companies put it under the heading of intangible assets.

Company	Intangible assets	
	Millions of dollars	Percentage of net worth
VIACOM	$ 2,468	721%
FRUIT OF THE LOOM	908	352
TELE-COMMUNICATIONS	3,143	261
PHILIP MORRIS	15,071	196
COCA-COLA ENTERPRISES	2,935	188
BAXTER INTERNATIONAL	2,705	87
GANNETT	1,526	85
DOW JONES	964	83
PEPSICO	2,582	82
SHEARSON LEHMAN HUTTON	1,758	76
CAPITAL CITIES/ABC	2,217	73
EASTMAN KODAK	4,610	68
McGRAW-HILL	507	55
GENERAL ELECTRIC	8,552	46
WASTE MANAGEMENT	838	38
CHRYSLER	2,688	35
AMERICAN HOME PRODUCTS	643	22
XEROX	1,089	20
GENERAL MOTORS	5,392	15
IBM	717	2

DATA: STANDARD & POOR'S COMPUSTAT SERVICES INC.

and may serve as a reasonable basis for estimating future profitability. Extraordinary items and other infrequently recurring items included in past earnings are usually excluded when using the past to project the future.

Several methods of estimating the goodwill in an acquisition are discussed in this section. The following four steps are common to all methods:

Step 1.   Estimate the periodic earnings that are expected to be achieved on the investment in the current value of the net assets to be received.

Step 2. Estimate the periodic earnings that would normally be expected on the investment in the current value of the net assets to be received.

Step 3. Comparing amounts in Steps 1 and 2, compute the amount of **anticipated periodic excess earnings over normal earnings**

Step 4. Convert the amount computed in Step 3 from a periodic figure to an aggregate figure that represents an estimate of the **total anticipated excess earnings** (i.e., goodwill).

Several methods are available for making the conversion required in Step 4 of the **periodic** anticipated excess earnings to an **aggregate** figure that represents the total value of future anticipated excess earnings.

Estimating Expected Periodic Earnings

A starting point for **estimating expected future earnings** is past performance. However, our intent is to estimate *future* earnings, and in the future the factors influencing earnings may be different from those in the past. When we base assessments of future earnings on past earnings, we should use several periods in an attempt to eliminate the impact of nonrecurring events and to identify significant trends in earnings or components of earnings.

Continuing the Diversified Enterprises example, we shall assume the earnings information for Single Product for the past four years as given in Exhibit 13–7.

The average net income for the four years is $50,000 or a 22% return on the current value of the net assets of Single Product, Inc. These amounts are computed as follows:

$$\frac{\text{Average}}{\text{net income}} = \frac{\$51,000 + \$50,000 + \$43,000 + \$56,000}{4 \text{ years}} = \$50,000$$

$$\frac{\% \text{ Return on current}}{\text{value of net assets}} = \frac{\$50,000}{\$227,000} = 22\%$$

Several factors should be considered in deciding on the appropriateness of using $50,000 as an expected level of earnings in the future. The inclusion of the extraordinary items is questionable, because they are by definition not expected to recur. Also, the accounting policies followed by Diversified to determine net income may be different from those used by Single Products. Such a difference could influence the assessment of future earnings. Other factors could also impact the expected future earnings. For example, in the future depreciation and amortization on property, plant,

EXHIBIT 13–7				
Single Product, Inc. Income Data for Years Ending June 30, 1989–1992				
	1989	*1990*	*1991*	*1992*
Revenues	$ 255,000	$ 262,000	$ 212,000	$ 238,000
Expenses	(204,000)	(224,000)	(160,000)	(182,000)
Income before extraordinary items		38,000	52,000	
Extraordinary gain (loss)		12,000	(9,000)	
Net income	$ 51,000	$ 50,000	$ 43,000	$ 56,000

and equipment and patents will be based on the **new cost basis** (i.e., the estimated fair value), and their estimated lives may be extended or reduced.

Furthermore, trends in the components of earnings may reveal that conditions in 1992, are more indicative of the future than the average of several periods. Considerations that are not apparent in the financial statements and that are discernible only through careful consideration of the operating characteristics of the enterprise being acquired may affect the evaluation of expected earnings. For example, the management of Diversified may believe Single Products could be even more profitable with the incorporation of more efficient production processes.

To continue our example, we shall assume that the average earnings of Single Product during 1989–1992, after the elimination of extraordinary items and the inclusion of an additional charge of $3,850 per year for expected increases in depreciation and amortization, represent a reasonable estimate of future earnings. This amount is computed as follows:

Average annual income before extraordinary items

1989	$ 51,000
1990	38,000
1991	52,000
1992	56,000

$197,000 ÷ 4 years = $49,250

Less: Additional depreciation and amortization (3,850)
Estimated future annual income $45,400

This estimate reflects a rate of return on the estimated current value of the net assets being acquired of 20% ($45,400/$227,000 = 20%). These amounts are used in the continuation of the Diversified Enterprise illustration.

Estimating Normal Periodic Earnings

The selection of a **normal rate of earnings** should reflect an estimate of the rate necessary to attract capital into the business under existing circumstances. As with determining all interest rates, the risk taken in the investment is an important consideration. A related consideration is the industry in which the enterprise operates.

Published rates that represent averages of a number of similar enterprises can usually be obtained from various financial services (e.g., Dun & Bradstreet or Standard & Poor's). However, rates obtained in this manner are based on historical figures and may be different from rates based on current values. Also, the unique features of the enterprise under consideration may make the identification of comparable enterprises difficult. Any valid rate must be based on companies that are similar to the one for which goodwill is being computed.

In continuing the example of Diversified Enterprises, we will assume 12% as a rate that represents a normal cost of attracting capital into enterprises similar to Single Product. Thus, normal annual earnings on the $227,000 investment are $27,240 ($227,000 × 12%).

Computing the Anticipated Annual Excess Earnings

The amounts computed in Steps 1 and 2 are combined to determine the **anticipated annual earnings in excess of normal**. In the case of Single Product, Inc., this computation is made as follows:

Estimated future annual earnings ($227,000 × 20%)	$45,400
Estimated normal annual earnings ($227,000 × 12%)	(27,240)
Estimated excess of expected annual earnings over normal	$18,160

Estimating Total Excess Earnings

Several methods are available to convert the annual amount of anticipated excess earnings to an **estimate of total goodwill** Three methods are illustrated in the following paragraphs.

Method 1. Years Multiple of Excess Earnings.   This method is based on the assumption that the excess earnings will continue for a determinable number of periods. Goodwill is computed by multiplying the excess annual earnings by the number of years the management believes it can sustain the advantages acquired.

For Diversified Enterprises we assume (for this calculation) that management believes it can sustain the anticipated level of excess earnings for six years, after which it will disappear. In this case goodwill is valued as follows:

$$\text{Goodwill} = 6 \text{ years} \times \$18,160 = \$108,960$$

A deficiency in this method is the failure to recognize the difference between the value of the excess earnings of the first year after the acquisition and that of subsequent years (i.e., the time value of money). Also, the difficulty in accurately estimating the number of years over which the excess earnings can be sustained indicates that this method contains an implementation problem.

Method 2. Present Value of Excess Earnings.   Recognition of the time value of the excess earnings is a major advantage of basing the value of goodwill on the **present value** of excess earnings rather than on the total amount as in Method 1. The period over which the excess earnings can be sustained must be estimated. The amount of annual excess earnings is then discounted to its present value by an appropriate interest rate.

Assuming that Diversified estimates that the excess earnings will continue for six years, we discount at the normal rate (i.e., the estimated cost of capital, which—in this case—is 12%), and goodwill is computed as follows:

$$\text{Goodwill} = 4.11141 \times \$18,160 = \$74,663$$

Table 6–4 shows that the present value of an annuity factor for six periods at 12% is 4.11141. That figure is used because the estimated excess earnings of $18,160 per year will accrue to Diversified Enterprises over a six-year period.

The greater risk inherent in the continuation of the excess earnings in the future may encourage the use of a higher interest rate in estimating the total value of goodwill. For example, if the 20% rate is used in estimating the goodwill in the Diversified acquisition of Single Product, goodwill is estimated as follows:

$$\text{Goodwill} = 3.32551 \times \$18,160 = \$60,391$$

We again use an annuity factor (3.32551 from Table 6–4) to estimate the value of goodwill. In this case, however, the factor is for six periods at *20%*.

Conceptually, the present-value method has merit because explicit recognition is given to the limited life of the excess earnings and the time value of money is considered. Practical problems of implementation are the estimations of the number of years and the interest rate. As seen in the Method 2 examples, judgments about these factors can significantly affect the resulting goodwill estimate.

Method 3. Capitalization of Excess Earnings.   The assumption that the excess earnings will continue *indefinitely* leads to estimating goodwill by capitalizing the excess earnings at an appropriate rate. If the normal rate is used in the Diversified example, then

$$\text{Goodwill} = \frac{\$18,160}{12\%} = \$151,333$$

Goodwill computed in this manner represents the amount that would have to be invested to yield a return equal to the **excess earnings in perpetuity.** In other words an investment of $151,333 that yields a 12% return will yield $18,160 annually ($151,333 × 12% per year in perpetuity). The primary flaws in this computation are (1) that the computed goodwill figure is based on the assumption that estimated excess earnings will continue indefinitely and (2) that this perpetual advantage relates entirely to conditions that exist when goodwill is acquired.

The uncertainty concerning the continuity of excess future earnings may encourage the use of a higher interest rate, indicating the higher level of risk. In the Diversified Enterprises case, a 20% rate for capitalizing excess earnings results in the following computation:

$$\text{Goodwill} = \frac{\$18,160}{20\%} = \$90,800$$

We have used two different interest rates in the previous illustrations to point out the difficulty of selecting the appropriate rate for purposes of applying this method. One study on valuing a closely held business suggests that the rate used should represent the expected yield on an investment in the company and can be selected by either the summation or the direct market comparison methods. Under the summation method, the accountant determines the required rate of return and then adjusts that rate for any portion of the expected return that may not be reflected in the earnings stream being capitalized. To illustrate this method, the authors of the study suggest the following approach:

Long-term U.S. government bond rate	10%
Plus: Average premium return on small stocks over U.S. government bonds	8
Expected total rate of return on small publicly held stocks	18
Plus: Premium for greater risk and liquidity	10
Total required expected rate of return for subject company	28
Less: Consensus long-term inflation expectation	6
Capitalization rate to apply to current earnings	22%

The direct market comparison method requires the accountant to develop a rate, or range of rates, based on information from comparable companies. One of the implementation problems associated with this method is the difficulty of getting information about other similar companies, particularly if the company for which goodwill is being estimated is not publicly held.[7]

Asset/Liability Measurement

In summary, the assumptions underlying the various methods of estimating goodwill and the judgments required in the implementation of the methods demonstrate the difficulty of measuring the asset, goodwill. The estimates of goodwill in the Diversified and Single Product illustrations range from $60,391 to $151,333. At best these figures represent a rough approximation of the range in which goodwill falls. An important point to remember is that the amount recorded as goodwill is the actual cost that is implied in the purchase transaction. The estimation procedures we have just illustrated are used to quantify the value of goodwill to assist management in determining an appropriate amount for negotiating a purchase price of another enterprise. Estimates of the value of goodwill may also be useful to auditors in assessing the appropriateness of the recorded amount of goodwill in the balance sheet.

---

[7]Warren Kissin and Ronald Zulli, "Valuation of a Closely Held Business," *The Journal of Accountancy* (June 1988), p. 42. (The illustration presented here differs only in the numbers used from that found in this reference.)

"NEGATIVE GOODWILL"

Asset/Liability
Measurement

In the previous examples we have assumed that the price paid for an enterprise *exceeds* the sum of the current value of the individual identifiable assets, less liabilities. If the sum of the values of the individual assets, less liabilities, is *more* than the price paid, does "negative goodwill" exist? Presumably the answer is no, because this would result in assets being recorded at amounts in excess of the price paid for them, a violation of applying the asset/liability measurement principle using historical cost.

If the price paid for an enterprise is *less* than the sum of the values of the individual identifiable assets, less liabilities, the difference should be allocated as a reduction of the recorded cost of those separately identifiable noncurrent assets other than investments. If, in an unusual case, this allocation reduces noncurrent assets (other than investments) to zero, the difference should be recorded as a deferred credit and amortized as an *addition* to future income over a period not to exceed 40 years. Such a deferred credit would be identified as an "excess of book value over cost of purchased subsidiary" or another appropriate title. (The terms "negative goodwill" or "badwill" are not usually found in published financial statements.) This item is placed in the balance sheet among noncurrent liabilities or in a separate deferred credit section between liabilities and stockholders' equity.

SPECIAL PROBLEM AREAS

Several special problem areas exist in accounting for intangible assets and related costs. Accounting for research and development costs is closely related to accounting for intangible assets, particularly because some intangible assets are developed internally through research and development. Also, intangible assets are often used in research and development activities. Accounting for development-stage enterprises is another area closely related to accounting for intangible assets. Accounting for costs in the oil and gas industry relates to intangible-asset accounting and represents an area of continuing controversy for the accounting profession. Since some understanding of all these areas is necessary to gain an appreciation of proper accounting for intangible assets, these subjects are discussed in the remaining sections of this chapter.

RESEARCH AND DEVELOPMENT COSTS

Research and development (R & D) is an important aspect of business operations for many enterprises. Prior to 1975, R & D costs were frequently capitalized as intangible assets and amortized over several periods. *FASB Statement of Financial Accounting Standards No. 2* was issued in 1974 to establish standards for the accounting and reporting of R & D costs and related tangible and intangible assets.[8] Under this pronouncement many costs that were previously identified as R & D are part of the cost of other tangible and intangible assets. Those costs that are identified as R & D are treated as expenses in the period incurred.

Research and **development** are defined as follows by the FASB:

> *Research is planned search or critical investigation aimed at discovery of new knowledge with the hope that such knowledge will be useful in developing a new product or service . . . or a new process or technique . . . or in bringing about a significant improvement to an existing product or process.*

---

[8]*FASB Statement of Financial Accounting Standards No. 2,* "Accounting for Research and Development Costs," 1974.

Development is the translation of research findings or other knowledge into a plan or design for a new product or process whether intended for sale or use.[9]

The distinction between R & D costs and expenditures that are capitalized in various asset categories requires that the accountant use careful judgment. Identifying R & D costs is facilitated by understanding the activities that lead to R & D costs. Such activities typically occur **prior to the beginning of commercial production and distribution of a product or process.** Various activities can result in R & D costs:[10]

1. Laboratory research aimed at the discovery of new knowledge.
2. Searching for applications of new research findings or other knowledge.
3. Conceptual formulation and design of possible product or process alternatives.
4. Design, construction, and testing of preproduction prototypes and models.
5. Design, construction, and operation of a pilot plant that is not of a scale economically feasible for commercial production.

Activities that relate to commercial production do not result in the incurrence of R & D costs, even though many are similar in nature to activities giving rise to R & D costs.

The following are examples of activities that do **not** result in R & D costs:[11]

1. Engineering follow-through in an early stage of commercial production.
2. Quality control during commercial production, including routine testing of products.
3. Routine, ongoing efforts to refine, enrich, or otherwise improve on the quality of an existing product.
4. Adaptation of an existing capacity to a particular requirement or customer's need as part of a continuing commercial activity.
5. Seasonal or other periodic design changes to existing products.

Several elements of costs identified with R & D activities can be identified: (1) materials, equipment, and facilities; (2) personnel; (3) intangibles purchased from others; (4) contract services; and (5) indirect costs. R & D expense of an enterprise includes some or all of the above costs in a given reporting period. If a cost is considered to be R & D, that cost is charged to expense when incurred.

Materials, Equipment, and Facilities

Materials, equipment, and facilities acquired for use in R & D activities that have alternative future uses—either in other R & D activities or in non-R & D activities—are capitalized in appropriate asset categories when acquired. The cost of materials subsequently used in R & D activities and depreciation on equipment and facilities used in R & D activities are classified as R & D expense when recognized. Costs of materials, equipment, and facilities acquired for particular R & D projects that have no alternative use are expensed as R & D when incurred.

Personnel

Salaries, wages, and other personnel costs of employees involved in R & D activities are charged to R & D expense as incurred.

---

[9]*FASB Statement of Financial Accounting Standards No. 2*, par. 8.
[10]*FASB Statement of Financial Accounting Standards No. 2*, par. 9.
[11]*FASB Statement of Financial Accounting Standards No. 2*, par. 10.

Intangibles Purchased from Others

The costs of **purchased intangible assets** used in R & D activities that have alternative future uses in other R & D activities or non-R & D activities are capitalized in appropriate asset categories. As these intangible assets are amortized, R & D expense is charged. The amortization of the intangibles used in R & D thus becomes part of R & D expense as they are used. The costs of intangible assets that are purchased for use in present R & D projects only and that have no alternative future use are charged to R & D expense as incurred.

Contract Services

Enterprises may engage others to perform R & D activities for them. The costs of such **contract services** are treated as R & D expenses when incurred.

Indirect Costs

A reasonable allocation of **indirect costs** that relate to R & D activities is included in the R & D expense in determining net income. Indirect costs include general and administrative expenses not directly related to R & D activity. To be included in R & D expense, however, general and administrative expenses must have some relationship to R & D activity.

In summary, R & D expense consists of the following elements: costs of materials, equipment, facilities, and intangible assets; personnel costs; costs of contract services; and an allocation of general and administrative expenses. Whether the costs of equipment, facilities, and intangible assets represent R & D in the period acquired or in a subsequent period through amortization depends on whether the items have alternative future uses in ongoing R & D activities or in other activities of the enterprise.

To illustrate the identification of R & D costs, we shall assume that Energy-Efficient Company is involved in the production of high-efficiency home heating and air conditioning equipment. Energy-Efficient incurs a number of expenditures related to its activities that are listed on the left in Exhibit 13–8. The proper accounting for these activities is described in the analysis on the right.

Numerous examples can be cited to illustrate the distinction between R & D costs and other expenditures. Most of the items in the Energy-Efficient example are obvious from the previous discussion. The capitalization of legal costs (item *e*) and the cost of acquiring a competing patent (item *g*) are appropriately capitalized in the Patent account. Because this patent is related to a product that is being produced for sale, the amortization of the cost (item *k*) is treated as a manufacturing cost. If the patent had been used in R & D activities, the amortization would have been classified as R & D expense. The cost of market research (item *f*) on the new product is not included as R & D, because the research relates to the **marketability** of the product, not to its technical development. In summary, those costs incurred prior to the beginning of commercial production are either capitalized in appropriate asset accounts or charged to R & D expense. Amortization of the cost of assets used in R & D activities is included in R & D expense when recognized.

We indicated earlier that prior to the issuance of *Statement No. 2*, companies frequently capitalized R & D costs and amortized them over future periods. Why did the FASB take the position that R & D costs are to be expensed as incurred unless they are for specific assets that have identifiable alternative future uses? The board carefully considered several capitalization alternatives for R & D expenditures: (1) capitalization of all costs when incurred; (2) capitalization of costs when specified conditions are present; and (3) accumulation of all R & D costs in a special category until the existence of future benefits could be determined. Applying the asset/liability measurement principle is particularly difficult because the future benefits of individual R & D projects involve a high degree of uncertainty and estimates of the rates of suc-

Asset/Liability Measurement

EXHIBIT 13-8

Cost Analysis for Energy-Efficient Company

Expenditure	Capitalize as	Expense as
a. Acquisition of equipment and building to be used in ongoing research activity.	Building, equipment	
b. Salaries of research staff responsible for the design of new heating unit.		R & D
c. Material, labor, and overhead of model of new heating unit.		R & D
d. Costs of testing of model of new heating unit.		R & D
e. Legal fees related to patent on new heating unit.	Patent	
f. Costs of research on marketability of new heating unit.		Operating expense
g. Cost of acquiring patent believed to compete with one on new heating unit.	Patent	
h. Costs of engineering activity necessary to advance heating unit to point of commercial production.		R & D
i. Costs of quality control in early stages of commercial production.		Manufacturing cost
j. Depreciation of equipment and building acquired in **a.**		R & D
k. Amortization of patent acquired in **e.**		Manufacturing cost
l. Salaries of salespersons selling new heating unit.		Operating expense
m. Warranty costs on heating units sold.		Operating expense

cess of R & D projects vary considerably. Also, a direct relationship between R & D costs and specific future revenue generally cannot be determined. Even if a relationship between present R & D costs and future revenue can be demonstrated, the problem of measuring the asset still exists. Generally an expenditure is not treated as an asset unless the future economic benefits can be identified and objectively measured at the time it is made.[12] For these and other reasons, the FASB determined that R & D costs should be expensed as incurred. This position is consistent with the modifying

Conservatism convention of conservatism, which indicates that the least favorable alternative presentation should be followed when significant doubt exists about the appropriate accounting principle to be applied.

One area of particular difficulty in accounting for R & D in recent years has been the treatment of the costs of developing computer software. If software is developed in conjunction with activities typically associated with R & D, the cost should be expensed as incurred. For example, if software is developed to create a new or significantly improved product or process without any contractual arrangement for sale or cost reimbursement, the development costs are considered R & D costs. Likewise, costs of developing software that is intended for use in the company's ongoing R & D activities are expensed as R & D as incurred.[13]

---

[12]*FASB Statement of Financial Accounting Standards No. 2*, pars. 37–44.
[13]*FASB Interpretation No. 6*, "Application of FASB Statement No. 2 to Computer Software: An Interpretation of FASB Statement No. 2," 1975, par. 7–8.

In 1985 the FASB specified accounting for the costs of computer software to be sold, leased, or otherwise marketed as a separate product or as part of a product or process. *FASB Statement of Financial Accounting Standards No. 86* specifies that costs incurred internally in creating a computer software product should be charged to expense when incurred as R & D until its technological feasibility has been established. Technological feasibility is established upon completion of a detailed program design or working model. Thereafter, all software production costs are capitalized and subsequently reported at the lower of unamortized cost or net realizable value. Capitalized software development costs are amortized based on current and expected future revenue for each product, subject to a minimum amortization equal to straight-line amortization over the remaining estimated economic life of the product.[14]

Companies may enter into arrangements through which R & D is funded by other parties. The accounting question involved is whether the company simply has a contract to perform R & D for others or whether the company has a liability equivalent to a borrowing. If the company has an obligation to repay any of the funds provided by the other party, regardless of the outcome of the R & D, the company must estimate and recognize this liability.[15]

DEVELOPMENT-STAGE ENTERPRISES

A **development-stage enterprise** is either: (1) an organization that is devoting substantially all of its effort to establishing a new business and that has not begun planned principal operations; or (2) an organization that has begun planned principal operations but that has not yet generated significant revenue from those operations. Prior to 1976 a variety of accounting and financial reporting practices existed for development-stage enterprises, including the deferral of many costs without regard to their recoverability and the offsetting of revenue against deferred costs. The FASB issued *Statement of Financial Accounting Standards No. 7* in 1975 to standardize accounting and reporting practices by newly developed companies.

Development-stage enterprises typically are devoting a substantial amount of effort to activities like the following:[16]

1. Financial planning.
2. Raising capital.
3. Exploring for natural resources.
4. Developing natural resources.
5. Research and development.
6. Establishing sources of supply.
7. Acquiring property, plant, equipment, and other operating assets.
8. Recruiting and training personnel.
9. Starting up production.

Matching   Development-stage enterprises engaged in these activities incur significant costs but generate little or no revenue. Thus, development-stage enterprises typically incur operating losses during the development stage.

FASB Statement No. 7 requires development-stage enterprises to account and report on much the same basis as do established operating enterprises in financial state-

---

[14]*FASB Statement of Financial Accounting Standards No. 86*, "Accounting for the Costs of Computer Software To Be Sold, Leased, or Otherwise Marketed," 1985, pars. 3, 5, 8.
[15]*FASB Statement of Financial Accounting Standards No. 68*, "Accounting for Research and Development Arrangements," 1982, par. 10.
[16]*FASB Statement of Financial Accounting Standards No. 7*, "Accounting and Reporting by Development Stage Enterprises," 1975, par. 9.

ments that purport to present financial position and results of operations. The same generally accepted accounting principles that apply to established enterprises govern the recognition of revenue and expense and the capitalization of costs for development-stage enterprises.

The financial statements issued by a development-stage enterprise should present **financial position**, **results of operations**, and **cash flows** as do those issued by established enterprises. *Additional disclosures* that are necessary because of the unique nature of the development-stage enterprise are summarized in Exhibit 13–9.

The financial statements must clearly indicate that the enterprise is in a development stage and must also include a description of the specific developmental activities in which the enterprise is involved. In the first year that the enterprise is no longer considered to be in the development stage, disclosure should indicate that in previous years it had been a development-stage enterprise.

The reporting requirements of *FASB Statement No. 7* simply apply generally accepted accounting principles of established operating enterprises to development-stage enterprises. Past practices of capitalizing operating losses and nonrecoverable costs as intangible assets are not acceptable. The treatment of a cost should be governed by the nature of the cost rather than the degree of maturity of the company incurring the cost. Under certain circumstances, however, a development-stage company may prepare financial statements on a basis other than generally accepted accounting principles.

In Chapter 1 we discussed the economic impact of accounting principles and raised the question of whether the FASB should be concerned with the economic impact of the standards it sets. This issue is important with respect to financial reporting by development-stage companies. Some accountants have pointed out that applying generally accepted accounting principles to developing enterprises frequently

EXHIBIT 13–9
Financial Reporting Requirements of Development-Stage Enterprises

Financial Statements	Special Disclosure Requirements*
Balance sheet	Cumulative net losses reported with a descriptive title, such as "deficit accumulated during the development stage" in stockholders' equity.
Income statement	Cumulative amounts of revenues and expenses from the enterprise's inception.
Statement of cash flows	Cumulative amounts of sources and uses of cash since the enterprise's inception.
Statement of stockholders' equity	For each issuance of stock, the date, number of shares of stock, warrants, rights, or other equity securities issued.
	For each issuance, the dollar amounts assigned to the consideration received (per share and in total).
	For each issuance involving noncash consideration, the nature of the transaction and the basis for assigning a dollar amount.

*These special disclosures are required in *addition* to those normally required under generally accepted accounting principles.

results in reporting net losses, which may not be fully understood by investors and creditors who could supply capital for these companies. If these reported losses influenced investors and creditors to withhold or delay investments in developing companies, new companies would have an even more difficult time getting started.

In an attempt to consider this issue, the FASB questioned officers of fifteen venture-capital enterprises. The conclusion of this limited research was that the accounting treatment of preoperating losses has little effect, if any, on the amount of capital that would be provided or the terms under which it would be provided to newly developed companies. According to these officers, the venture-capital investor typically relies on an assessment of cash flows based on an investigation of the technological, marketing, management, and financial aspects of the enterprise.[17] Other research in this general area tends to support these conclusions.

The FASB concluded that requiring cumulative figures in the financial statements, as described in Figure 13–9, would be useful in understanding the position of the developing company until it reached the position of being fully operative. The FASB determined, in addition, that the special report forms used in the past were less useful than were the financial-statement forms of established operating enterprises, with which investors were already familiar.

ACCOUNTING BY OIL AND GAS PRODUCING COMPANIES

Oil and gas producing companies incur substantial costs in locating and developing oil and gas reserves. Given the current state of technology, exploration requires many drilling efforts, only some of which locate producible oil and gas reserves. Other such efforts result in "dry holes" that provide no producible oil and gas.

Two methods of accounting for costs incurred in exploration activities are used in the oil and gas industry. The **successful-efforts method** is based on the theory that only the costs of locating producing wells (i.e., those wells from which gas and oil can economically be extracted) should be capitalized and amortized over future periods. In this method costs associated with activities that do not result in the location of producible oil and gas reserves are treated as expenses when they are incurred.

In the alternative method, the **full-cost method,** the costs of *all* efforts are treated as the costs of locating producing wells. Because many unsuccessful efforts are usually necessary to locate reserves that can be successfully exploited, exploration costs that would be treated as expenses when incurred in the successful-efforts method are treated as assets and amortized over future periods in the full-cost method.

Both the successful-efforts and the full-cost methods have been widely used in accounting for the numerous costs incurred in oil and gas explorations. In practice, the successful-efforts method has been widely adopted by larger companies, while smaller companies have favored the full-cost method.

In response to strong encouragement by the Securities and Exchange Commission (SEC), in December 1977 the FASB issued *Statement No. 19.*[18] In this statement, which resulted from a lengthy process of considering many diverse views, the FASB attempted to eliminate the full-cost method and establish successful-efforts as the only acceptable accounting method for oil and gas exploration costs. Costs in oil and gas producing activities fall into several classifications: acquisitions, explorations, development, production, support equipment, and facilities. Under the successful-

---

[17]*FASB Statement of Financial Accounting Standards No. 7,* par. 49.
[18]*FASB Statement of Financial Accounting Standards No. 19,* "Financial Accounting and Reporting by Oil and Gas Producing Companies," 1977.

efforts method, the costs of acquiring oil and gas rights are capitalized when incurred. These costs are amortized as a part of the cost of oil and gas produced. Exploration costs, except for the costs of drilling exploratory wells, are expensed as incurred. The costs of drilling exploratory wells are **temporarily deferred** until a determination is made on whether or not the well is producible. If producible reserves exist, the costs of the exploratory wells are capitalized and amortized as part of the cost of oil and gas produced. If producible reserves do not exist, the costs of the exploratory wells are expensed when this determination is made.

Costs of developing proved reserves are capitalized and depreciated as part of the cost of oil and gas produced. Production costs are treated as part of the cost of oil and gas produced and are expensed as incurred. Costs of support equipment and facilities are capitalized and depreciated as costs of oil and gas produced to the extent that they are used in oil and gas producing activities.

The application of the basic concept underlying the successful-efforts method is apparent in the accounting for exploration costs as previously described. All exploration costs, *except* those for drilling exploratory wells that result in producible oil and gas reserves, are treated as expenses as incurred. Thus, costs that are capitalized and amortized over a long period relate only to recoverable oil and gas reserves, the basic concept underlying the successful-efforts method.

An important issue that emerged in the FASB's consideration of alternative accounting methods used in the oil and gas industry was the potential negative economic impact of requiring companies to expense the costs of unsuccessful explorations. Proponents of the full-cost method argued that the required expensing of the costs of unsuccessful efforts would discourage exploration in the oil and gas industry at a time when exploration was greatly needed. A related argument was that the reduced profitability of companies under the successful-efforts method would discourage investment in oil and gas producing companies. These arguments were stated as being particularly significant for newer, developing companies that had aggressive exploration policies and, therefore, had a greater need for outside capital than established operating enterprises.

Does the accounting method used by a company for exploration activities in the oil and gas industry identify those companies that are aggressive in exploration? One researcher concluded that full-cost companies are *not* more aggressive in exploration than successful-effort companies, although full-cost companies did make a greater use of outside capital.[19] One interpretation of this research is that the method used to account for oil and gas production costs is not necessarily a factor that encourages or discourages exploration in the oil and gas industry.

A more recent study examined the circumstances surrounding voluntary changes from the successful-efforts to the full-cost methods of accounting by oil and gas producing companies. One explanation offered for such changes is that highly levered companies (i.e., those with high levels of debt financing), or those with high drilling risk, prefer full-cost accounting in an attempt to reduce the probability of violating accounting-based debt covenant restrictions. The research conclusions suggest that full-cost adoption is associated not only with high leverage but also with current increases in debt financing and, to a lesser extent, with exploration activities. The researchers conclude that we can expect full-cost method adoptions to occur concurrently with abnormal increases in debt financing and exploration activities.[20]

[19]Edward B. Deakin III, "An Analysis of Differences Between Non-Major Oil Firms Using Successful-Efforts and Full Cost Methods," *Accounting Review* (October 1979), pp. 722–734.
[20]W. Bruce Johnson and Ramachandran Ramanan, "Discretionary Accounting Changes from 'Successful-Efforts' to 'Full-Cost' Methods: 1970–1976," *Accounting Review* (January 1988), p. 108.

Despite the fact that the FASB was cooperating with the SEC in attempting to eliminate the diversity in accounting for oil and gas producing activities, the SEC responded negatively to the position of the FASB. Reacting to numerous pressures, including the strength of the smaller oil and gas producing companies and the fear of discouraging oil and gas exploration activities if the successful-efforts method was required, the SEC took the position that both full-cost and successful-efforts methods were unsatisfactory methods of accounting by oil and gas producing companies.

The SEC indicated its preference for the development of a method of current-value accounting that would eventually replace both existing methods. It further indicated that it would develop such a method and tentatively referred to it as **reserve-recognition accounting.** In the meantime enterprises reporting to the SEC could continue to use either the full-cost or the successful-efforts method.

In light of these developments, the FASB issued *Statement of Financial Accounting Standards No. 25,* "Suspension of Certain Accounting Requirements for Oil and Gas Producing Companies."[21] This statement suspended the effective date of *Statement No. 19,* thereby allowing companies to continue using either the full-cost or the successful-efforts method. Companies that were not required to report to the SEC, as well as those that were required to do so, continued to have the option of reporting under either method. At a later date the SEC abandoned its plan to develop the reserve-recognition accounting method. Its decision was based primarily on the practical problems encountered in attempting to apply a current value approach to oil and gas reserves. Thus, oil and gas producing companies continue to choose either the full-cost method or the successful-efforts method.

In 1987, the SEC again considered the fact that two methods were being used in accounting by oil and gas producing companies and resolved **not to issue** a release concerning the abolishment of the full-cost method. The SEC concluded that the potential harm to struggling oil and gas producing companies of going forward with a proposal to discontinue the full cost method would outweigh the benefits to investors.[22]

This series of events verifies the fact that the SEC has ultimate responsibility for the establishment of standards for reporting by publicly held corporations in the United States. Although the positions of the FASB have generally been supported by the SEC, if the two do not agree, the legal position of the SEC is superior. This series of events concerning oil and gas accounting also indicates that the reporting requirements applicable to those companies that must report to the SEC have significant influence on those enterprises that do not report to the SEC.

CONCEPTUAL CONSIDERATIONS

Asset/Liability Measurement

Accounting for intangible assets is governed primarily by the accounting principles of *asset/liability measurement, matching and consistency,* much like plant assets. In measuring intangible assets, the accountant must exercise significant judgment, particularly in accounting for the intangible asset, goodwill.

As with plant assets, reliable evidence is important in accounting for intangible assets. Recorded assets should be based on verifiable evidence. Also, careful distinctions must be made between the cost of intangible assets and other expenditures, such as research and development, that are expensed as incurred. The *modifying convention of conservatism* is also apparent in accounting for research and development and other costs often associated with intangible assets.

Conservatism

---

[21]*FASB Statement of Financial Accounting Standards No. 25,* "Suspension of Certain Accounting Requirements for Oil and Gas Producing Companies," 1979.
[22]"SEC Votes Against Change in Oil and Gas Accounting," *Journal of Accountancy* (January 1987), p. 50.

Matching

Consistency

The *matching principle* is apparent in the required amortization of intangible assets over the shortest of the asset's useful life, its legal or contractual period, or 40 years. The *consistency principle* requires that intangible assets be treated alike from period to period so that the resulting financial information will be comparable.

CONCLUDING REMARKS

In studying a company's balance sheet, remember that the principles underlying accounting for different types of assets vary. These differing principles are used in recognition of the fact that the values of various assets are realized in several ways. For example, receivables are shown in the balance sheet at their net realizable value (gross amount less an estimate of the portion that will not be collected). Inventories are shown at the lower of cost or market. We have seen, however, that cost can be determined by several different flow assumptions and that variations also exist in the methods of determining the lower of cost or market once the cost has been determined.

Concerning investments, we learned that a number of different methods are applied. These methods vary, depending on whether the investment is in debt or equity securities and whether it is current or noncurrent.

Now that we have studied the major asset categories, it is useful to review the significance of the dollar amounts to the various types of assets included in a company's balance sheet. A review of the primary valuation techniques included within generally accepted accounting principles is presented in Exhibit 13–10.

EXHIBIT 13–10
Review of Asset Valuation Techniques

Type of Asset	Basis of Valuation Generally Found in Balance Sheet
Current Assets	
Cash	Face amount
Marketable securities	
Debt securities	Cost
Equity securities	Lower of aggregate cost or market
Receivables	Net realizable value
Inventories	Lower of cost or market
Prepaid expenses	Unexpired cost
Investments	
Debt securities	Cost, adjusted for unamortized premium or discount
Equity securities	
Investments lacking significant influence	Lower of aggregate cost or market
Investments providing significant influence	Equity method
Plant and Intangible Assets	
Property, plant, and equipment	Portion of cost not yet recognized as depreciation
Natural resources	Portion of cost not yet recognized as depletion
Intangibles	Portion of cost not yet recognized as amortization
Other Assets	Miscellaneous, depending on nature of specific asset

KEY POINTS

1. Intangible assets differ from property, plant, and equipment primarily because the intangibles lack physical substance. Both types of assets have relatively long lives and are used in the production and distribution of goods and services. (Objective 1)

2. Some intangible assets (e.g., patents, copyrights, and franchises) are separately identifiable. Some intangibles, usually identified as goodwill, are associated with an enterprise as a whole and cannot be transferred apart from that enterprise. (Objective 2)

3. Intangible assets (acquired from other enterprises or developed internally) that can be separately identified and have determinable lives are recorded as assets. Other costs related to internally developed intangibles, including those with characteristics similar to those of goodwill, are treated as expenses when they are incurred. (Objective 2)

4. Intangible assets are initially recorded at historical cost and then amortized over their estimated useful lives. The period of amortization cannot exceed 40 years, and the straight-line method is typically used. (Objective 3)

5. Financial-statement disclosure of intangible assets includes the method and period of amortization. Intangibles are typically presented in a separate asset section designated as "intangible assets" or "other assets." (Objective 4)

6. Goodwill is an intangible asset representing anticipated excess earning capacity. It arises when the price paid for another business exceeds the current value of the identifiable net assets acquired. Goodwill is recorded at cost and amortized over its estimated useful life in the same manner as other intangible assets. (Objective 5)

7. The value of goodwill can be estimated by several methods that are based on a comparison between anticipated earnings and normal earnings. (Objective 5)

8. Research and development costs are treated as expenses when they are incurred. Some costs related to R & D activities, however, are capitalized in appropriate asset categories and amortized as R & D expense over their estimated useful lives. (Objective 6)

9. Development-stage enterprises must apply generally accepted accounting principles in preparing financial statements purporting to present financial position and results of operations in much the same way as do established enterprises. In addition, development-stage enterprises must disclose certain cumulative figures that relate to the enterprise since its inception. (Objective 6)

10. Oil and gas producing companies may account for exploration costs under either the successful-efforts or the full-cost method within current GAAP. This is an area of significant controversy in which the FASB attempted to reduce variation in accounting practice by requiring companies to use only the successful-efforts method. Under pressure from the SEC, however, the FASB suspended this requirement. (Objective 6)

QUESTIONS In questions 13–1 through 13–4, circle the letter of the correct answer.

13–1 The following procedure best describes the proper accounting of the cost of intangible assets subsequent to acquisition:

[a] Amortize over the longer of 40 years or the estimated useful life.
[b] Amortize over 40 years.
[c] Amortize over the shorter of the estimated useful life or 40 years.
[d] Amortize over 10 years.

13–2 Assets that should be presented in the intangible-asset category of the balance sheet include all of the following *except:*

[a] Goodwill   [c] Patents
[b] Copyrights   [d] Accounts receivable

13–3 The following characteristic is *not* necessary for an asset to qualify as intangible:

[a] Has a determinable life.
[b] Conveys a right or privilege.

[c] Has a relatively long life.

[d] Is used in the production of other goods or services.

13-4   The following statement best describes proper accounting by development-stage companies:

[a] The same as established operating enterprises except for the capitalization of R & D.

[b] The same as established operating enterprises except for the capitalization of operating losses in early years of operations.

[c] The same as established operating enterprises except for the requirement of additional disclosures in the financial statements and related notes.

[d] The same as established operating enterprises except that the statement of cash flows is not required.

13-5   Briefly identify the key elements in the definition of "intangible asset."

13-6   What basic feature distinguishes intangible assets from tangible plant assets?

13-7   Distinguish between intangible assets that can be separately identified and those that cannot be separately identified, indicating the type(s) of transactions in which each typically arises.

13-8   Identify several types of expenditures that are closely related to intangible assets but that should *not* be capitalized and amortized over periods after their incurrence.

13-9   With regard to *APB Opinion No. 17*, what was the basic rationale for requiring the amortization of intangible assets, even in cases in which the life of the intangible is apparently unlimited?

13-10   Identify several factors that should be considered in estimating the useful life of a separately identifiable intangible asset.

13-11   Indicate the current legal life of the following intangible assets: patents, copyrights, and trademarks.

13-12   Cite several examples of intangible assets whose lives may be limited through contractual arrangements between two enterprises or between an enterprise and a governmental unit.

13-13   What types of individual costs are properly included in organization costs?

13-14   How should organization costs be treated subsequent to the beginning of operations?

13-15   Define goodwill. Identify any specific circumstances that must be met for goodwill to be established as an asset in the balance sheet.

13-16   Outline briefly specific procedures that are followed in accounting for goodwill, including the determination of cost and the recognition of periodic amortization.

13-17   Outline briefly the steps that should be followed in placing an estimate on the value of goodwill existing in a potential acquisition.

13-18   Of the various methods of estimating the value of goodwill presented in this chapter, which appears to have the greatest merit on a conceptual basis? Why?

13-19   Research and development costs are classified in five categories: (1) materials, equipment, and facilities; (2) personnel; (3) intangibles purchased from others; (4) contract services; and (5) indirect costs. Describe the items included in each category and provide one or more example(s) of each.

13-20   Distinguish between the full-cost method and the successful-efforts method of accounting by oil and gas producing companies.

13-21   Define the term "development-stage enterprise" and suggest several activities in which such an enterprise would typically be engaged.

13-22   To what extent do the accounting and reporting standards that are applicable to established operating enterprises apply to development-stage enterprises?

EXERCISES

13-23   FRANCHISE   On January 2, 1992, East Company entered into a franchise agreement to operate a fast food restaurant called Hot Dog Haven. The initial franchise fee was $12,000 and is expected to be revenue-producing as long as the company retains the right to use the designation.

The franchise contract is for a five-year period, at the end of which a new agreement will be negotiated, if desired, by the original parties. The franchise also calls for payment of 5% of gross revenues by East Company each year. Revenues for 1992 and 1993 were $89,500 and $128,600, respectively. Straight-line amortization is used on all intangible assets. East Company reports on a calendar-year basis.

Instructions

[a] Prepare all journal entries for East Company relative to the franchise agreement for 1992 and 1993.
[b] Determine the amounts to be included in the 1993 financial statements relative to the franchise.

13–24   RESEARCH AND DEVELOPMENT   Distinguishing between R & D costs and other related costs is sometimes difficult.

Instructions

Identify the accounts that should be debited in each of the following transactions or adjustments:

[a] Cost of models of products under development.
[b] Cost of patent usable only in a current R & D project.
[c] Legal fees paid to successfully defend a patent used in ongoing R & D activities.
[d] Amortization of a patent on a product currently being manufactured and sold.
[e] Costs of quality control over the production process.
[f] Amortization of a patent used in ongoing R & D activities.
[g] Warranty costs on products sold.
[h] Costs of R & D contract services expected to be of continuing benefit.
[i] Materials expected to be used only in current R & D projects.

13–25   PATENTS   Wells Manufacturing Company acquired three patents in January 1992. The patents have different lives, as indicated in the following schedule:

	Cost	Estimated Useful Life in Years	Remaining Legal Life in Years
Patent X	$12,500	10	17
Patent Y	27,250	5	7
Patent Z	65,620	Indefinite	17

Patent Z is believed to be uniquely useful as long as the company retains the right to use it. In June 1993, the company unsuccessfully attempted to defend its right to Patent Y. Legal fees of $12,700 were incurred in this action.

The company's policy is to amortize intangible assets by the straight-line method to the nearest half year. The company reports on a calendar-year basis.

Instructions

Determine the amount of amortization that should be recognized for 1992, 1993, and 1994.

13–26   PATENT   Lance Company acquired a patent on June 25, 1990, for $13,000. Management expects the patent to be useful to the company for its remaining legal life of 13 years.

On January 12, 1992, the company spent $5,000 to successfully defend the patent against a competing company.

During 1993 management determines that the estimated remaining life of the patent should be reduced to only five remaining years, including the current year. This decision was made after careful consideration of actions of various competing companies.

Instructions

Prepare all journal entries relating to the patent for 1990 through 1993, assuming the company's year-end is December 31. Company policy is to amortize intangible assets by the straight-line method, computed to the nearest full month.

13–27   ORGANIZATION COSTS   Williard Manufacturing Company was organized during 1992. In assisting in the preparation of the financial statements for the year ending December 31, you discover that the following items were debited to the Organization Cost account during early January 1992:

Legal fees of corporate registration	$27,500
Compensation of promoters of corporation	13,800
Salaries of employees before the beginning of operations	5,600
Discount on 10-year bonds issued before the beginning of operations	2,770
	$49,670

Plans call for the amortization of organization costs over a five-year period by the straight-line method. The company's accountant does not plan to begin this amortization until 1993, however, due to the large operating loss which the company sustained in 1992.

No amortization of the discount on the bonds has been made. The straight-line method is considered appropriate.

Instructions

Prepare all correcting and adjusting entries that you would propose on December 31, 1992. Closing entries for the year have *not* been made.

13–28   LEASEHOLD   Prosser Enterprises has leased several items of equipment under a lease that does not qualify for capitalization. The lease was entered into on May 1, 1990. Prosser paid the $150,000 rental for the first year in advance; a similar payment is made each year on May 1. The lease term is 10 years; the equipment is expected to have a useful life of 25 years.

On May 1, 1992, the company spent $36,000 to make certain improvements on the equipment. These improvements are expected to guarantee the maximum usefulness of the equipment for the duration of the lease term.

Leasehold improvements are amortized by the straight-line method, computed to the nearest half year.

Instructions

Determine the balance sheet and income statement amounts related to the equipment lease for the years ending December 31, 1990–1993.

13–29   GOODWILL   Ramsey Company is considering acquisition of the net assets of Fuller Company to expand its operations. The book value and current value of the net assets of Fuller Company are $165,000 and $200,000, respectively. The normal rate of return is believed to be 9%, but Ramsey believes it can earn 12% annually on its investment in Fuller due to the excellent reputation of Fuller.

Instructions

Compute the goodwill that results from applying the following methods to the situation described above:

[a] Years multiple of excess earnings (assuming a 10-year period of excess earnings).
[b] Present value of excess earnings at the expected rate (assuming an 8-year period of excess earnings).
[c] Capitalization of excess earnings at the normal rate.
[d] Capitalization of excess earnings at 12%.

13–30   GOODWILL   Filson Company is considering acquisition of the net assets of Roth Company as part of a diversification program. The management of Filson believes the excellent reputation of Roth provides an opportunity to achieve a level of earnings in excess of the normal rate of 10%. In fact, it expects to earn a rate of return of 16% on its investment.

The following information is available on Roth Company:

	Estimated Current Value
Current assets	$ 175,000
Noncurrent assets	280,000
Total reported assets	455,000
Liabilities	(272,000)
Net assets	$ 183,000

In determining the amount it should bid for Roth Company, the management of Filson is attempting to estimate a value for goodwill.

Instructions

Compute the goodwill resulting from each of the following methods:

[a] Years multiple of excess earnings (assuming a five-year period).
[b] Present value of excess earnings at the expected rate (assuming a five-year period).
[c] Capitalization of excess earnings at the normal rate.
[d] Capitalization of excess earnings at the expected rate.

13–31   GOODWILL   Dover Diversified acquired Simplified Products Company on January 1, 1993. Conditions of the acquisition include the following:

[1] Dover issued $1,200,000 of 20-year bonds to finance the transaction. The $1,200,000 received from the bonds was transferred to Simplified Products Company to complete the acquisition. Interest is payable annually on December 31 at 13%.

[2] Dover is to take over all assets (except cash) and all liabilities of Simplified Products Company. Simplified Products is then to liquidate its assets by distributing cash to stockholders in retirement of their shares of stock.

[3] Dover has established the following current valuations on assets and liabilities to be assumed:

	Book Value on Simplified's Books	Estimated Current Value
Receivables	$ 100,000	$ 90,000
Inventory	550,000	720,000
Property, plant, and equipment	900,000	1,300,000
Current liabilities	(300,000)	(250,000)
Noncurrent liabilities	(1,000,000)	(1,000,000)
Net assets	$ 250,000	$ 860,000

[4] Dover has determined through various estimation techniques that goodwill inherent in the transaction has a value of at least $400,000. Goodwill is to be amortized over a 20-year period by the straight-line method.

Instructions

Prepare all journal entries on the books of Dover Diversified for the year ended December 31, 1993. Include amortization of goodwill for the full year.

13–32   RESEARCH AND DEVELOPMENT   An account for a research project identified as AM423 is included on the trial balance of your client, Buckley Company. The account balance consists of the following charges:

Salaries of research staff	$28,500
Patent acquired solely for use in project AM423	12,000
Patent acquired for use in several research projects, including AM423	16,200
Cost of models	8,950
	$65,650

Intangible assets are amortized by the straight-line method over the shorter of the legal life or estimated useful life. The company's patents have generally been found to be useful for approximately 10 years. You determined that both of the patents were acquired in early 1993 and that the cost of models and salaries were incurred throughout 1993.

Instructions

Determine the items that should be presented in the Buckley's balance sheet and income statement on December 31, 1993.

13–33   COPYRIGHT   Storeytime Company incorrectly charged the $60,000 cost of a copyright acquired in early 1992 to the retained earnings account. The error was discovered as part of the 1993 audit. The company holds several copyrights and follows the policy of amortizing their cost over the period expected to benefit by the straight-line method, computed to the nearest whole year. The $60,000 copyright was expected to be useful in producing revenue for twelve years from the time of acquisition, even though the legal life was 27 years from that date.

Instructions

[a] Prepare the entry necessary in 1993 to correct the error of 1992.
[b] Prepare the entry to record amortization of the copyright for 1993.

13–34   AMORTIZATION OF INTANGIBLES   Borton Company acquired three intangible assets during 1993 from other enterprises: patent, $15,270; leasehold improvement, $18,975; and good-will, $248,000. The patent has a remaining legal life of six years. The leasehold improvement has an expected life of 25 years. The goodwill is expected to provide benefits in the form of high earnings indefinitely. The leasehold improvement is on property that Borton has leased for 15 years; renewal depends on the intent of both parties at that time. No further information on the lives of the various intangible assets is available or determinable.

Instructions

[a] State your recommendation for the useful life to be used for amortization of the three intangible assets. Justify your recommendations.
[b] Assuming that straight-line amortization is used with a full year taken in the year of acquisition, prepare the entry or entries necessary to record the amortization of the intangible assets at the end of 1993, based on your recommendation in [a].

13–35   RESEARCH AND DEVELOPMENT   For several years Martin Manufacturing Company has accounted for R & D costs in accordance with *Statement of Financial Accounting Standards No. 2*. In 1993 research efforts materialize and three patents are acquired. Patent 87–1 will be used in the ongoing R & D activities of the enterprise. Patent 87–2 will be used in one specific research project that is currently underway. Patent 87–3 will be used in the company's manufacturing process.

Company officials suggest that the cost of the patents be established as follows:

Patent	Legal Costs of Obtaining Patents	Costs Previously Charged to R & D	Total Cost
87–1	$ 6,500	$17,625	$24,125
87–2	2,000	–0–	2,000
87–3	4,250	19,000	23,250
	$12,750	$36,625	$49,375

Because legal costs were charged to the Legal Fees account when they were incurred, the company's accountant recommends the following entry:

Patents	49,375	
Legal Fees		12,750
Retained Earnings		36,625

Instructions

[a] Evaluate the suggested entry to record the patents. Justify your position.
[b] Suggest alternative entries for the capitalization of the patents.
[c] How should the amortization of the patent costs be treated in subsequent years?

13–36   TRADEMARK   Fisher, Inc., developed a trademark to distinguish its products from those of its competitors. Through advertising and other means, the company is seeking to establish significant product identification to increase future sales.

The similarity between the trademark costs and other intangible and operating costs has caused some confusion over proper accounting. The following items are being treated as part of the cost of the trademark:

Marketing research to study consumer tastes	$32,500
Design costs of trademark	17,800
Legal fees of registering trademark	850
Advertising to establish recognition of trademark	17,800
Registration fee with U.S. Patent Office	1,200

Through renewals, the trademark is expected to have an unlimited life.

Instructions

[a] Evaluate each of the costs as appropriate for capitalization in the Trademark account.

[b] Recommend the period of amortization for the cost of the trademark. Justify your recommendation.

13–37   OIL AND GAS COSTS   Texas Oil Company is involved in oil and gas production activities. The following costs were incurred during 1993:

Acquiring mineral rights	$13,500,000
Exploration	
Drilling exploratory wells resulting in recoverable reserves	8,400,000
Drilling exploratory wells not resulting in recoverable reserves	5,550,000
Other costs	7,890,000
Developing recoverable oil reserves	9,375,000
Producing oil and gas (after extraction)	10,550,000
Acquiring equipment for use in oil and gas producing activities	17,650,000

Instructions

For each of the above cost categories, indicate the proper accounting treatment within the successful-efforts method by choosing among the following:

[a] Expense as incurred.

[b] Capitalize and amortize as a cost of oil and gas produced.

[c] Treat as a cost of oil and gas produced as incurred.

PROBLEMS

13–38   INTANGIBLE ASSET COST   Superco, Inc., has accumulated a number of costs in a single Intangibles account. As a new employee in the company's accounting department, you have been asked to analyze the account and recommend any corrections you think should be made. The Intangibles account for 1993 is presented to you as follows:

Date	Transaction Description	Intangibles Dr.	Cr.	Balance
Jan. 2	Legal fees related to organization of business	10,500		10,500
Jan. 2	Prepayment of lease on building for one year	18,000		28,500
Feb. 1	Prepayment of insurance for two years	1,800		30,300
Feb. 28	Advertising expenses (radio, television, and newspaper)	8,000		38,300
Apr. 7	Premium on bonds issued		10,500	27,800
Apr. 25	Interest paid on short-term notes	2,500		30,300
May 5	Legal fees in filing for trade name (Superco)	7,200		37,500
June 30	Cash discount on merchandise purchased		175	37,325

The company plans to present financial statements as of June 30, 1993, to a local bank to support a request for additional financing. Company policy is to amortize intangible asset costs over a 10-year period, computed to the nearest full month. The president suggests an amortization on June 30, 1993, of $1,866, computed as follows:

$$(\$37{,}325/10 \text{ years}) \times \tfrac{1}{2} \text{ year} = \$1{,}866$$

Instructions

[a] Prepare an analysis of the entries in the Intangibles account and indicate corrections you would propose in the account, including reclassifications of items.
[b] Based on your response to [a] above, prepare the entries to properly record amortization of intangible assets on June 30, 1993. Assume all amounts are material and that straight-line amortization is to be used.

13–39 MISCELLANEOUS INTANGIBLE ASSETS Sanders Company acquired three intangible assets before 1993. The company is involved in the preparation of financial statements on June 30, 1993. Before that date no formal statements were prepared and the cost of intangible assets had been charged (debited) to retained earnings when acquired.

The following intangible assets were accounted for in this manner:

Asset	Acquisition Date	Estimated Useful Life in Years	Cost
Copyright No. 1	Jan. 2, 1989	25	$30,000
Copyright No. 2	July 15, 1990	15	33,000
Goodwill	Feb. 28, 1991	Indeterminate	32,000

Management has now decided to correct the past accounting treatment and to account for the intangibles as if they had been properly capitalized at the time of acquisition and subsequently amortized. The straight-line method of amortization is to be used, computed to the nearest half-year. The company has selected July 1–June 30 for its financial reporting period.

Instructions

[a] Prepare the entries necessary to reclassify the intangible assets and to record amortization for 1993. Provide adequate support for your entries.
[b] Briefly explain in a written paragraph the process you followed in preparing the entry or entries in [a].

13–40 RESEARCH AND DEVELOPMENT Nashville Sound, Inc., has initiated an extensive research program to develop a more efficient method of recording compact discs. Management expects to be able to lease its production facilities, when completely refined, to the many record-producing companies in the area.

You have been asked to assist in the preparation of financial statements for the year ended December 31, 1993. Costs related to the project have been accumulated in a master account identified simply as "Recording" since the beginning of the project in early 1993, as follows:

Debits

$185,000	Equipment purchased for use in many research projects over a five-year period.
78,000	Salaries of staff working on research project.
17,500	Computer program services purchased through a contract with another enterprise.
24,800	Legal fees related to the patent acquired on the new production process, which is expected to be useful in producing revenue for ten years.

Credits

$ 88,000	Down payments received from other companies that have contracted to use the new production process in the future.

Management has determined that general and administrative expenses of $175,500 were incurred during 1993. Based on the time spent on the various enterprise functions, you estimate that 25% of this amount relates to the research project identified as "recording."

Discussions with corporate officials reveal that all long-lived assets are depreciated with a full year's amortization taken in the year of acquisition and none in the year of disposal. You determine that the process began to generate revenue in 1993 and, therefore, the amortization of the patent should begin this year.

Instructions

[a] Prepare all journal entries you would suggest to correct the Recording account and other accounts related to the company's research and development effort.

[b] Prepare all adjusting entries that should be made on December 31, 1993, to reflect amortization and depreciation for the year.

[c] Identify all items that will appear in the financial statements on December 31, 1993, related to plant and intangible assets and research and development.

[d] Describe in a short paragraph your treatment of items that are comprised in the research and development expense in [c].

13–41   PATENTS   Phoenix Supply Company acquired two patents, several items of equipment, and a parcel of land for a total of $137,500. Appraisal values of the assets on the date of acquisition are as follows:

Patent A	$30,000
Patent B	40,000
Equipment	19,700
Land	62,000

By acquiring the assets in a group, the company was able to get a favorable price. The acquisition took place on April 27, 1991. Patent A has a five-year remaining life and Patent B a 12-year remaining life. Amortization on intangible assets is determined on a straight-line basis, computed in whole dollars to the nearest full month.

During 1992 the company became involved in two lawsuits resulting in the successful defense of Patent B but the unsuccessful defense of Patent A. Total legal fees of $17,600 were incurred. Management estimates that approximately equal effort went into defending each patent. The established date of these settlements was March 7, 1992.

No further transactions affecting the patents occurred through October 31, 1993.

Instructions

[a] Prepare journal entries for the years 1991, 1992, and 1993, related to the intangible asset accounts. The company's reporting year ends on October 31.

[b] Briefly explain any difference in your treatment of the legal costs of the defenses of Patents A and B.

13–42   GOODWILL   Washington Company is negotiating to acquire Jefferson Company. Washington manufactures and sells wood-burning stoves, and Jefferson Company produces parts that are required to manufacture the stoves. Jefferson Company enjoys an exceptional reputation, and the management of Washington believes it can continue the level of income currently experienced by Jefferson Company, and satisfy its own need for parts.

Under the contemplated arrangement, Washington Company will negotiate for the acquisition of the net assets of Jefferson Company. The following information has been developed to determine the appropriate price:

[1] Recorded amounts and estimated current values of assets and liabilities of Jefferson Company are as follows:

	Recorded Amounts	Estimated Current Values
Assets to be received	$1,485,000	$1,925,000
Liabilities to be assumed	510,000	510,000
	$ 975,000	$1,415,000

[2] Earnings of Jefferson Company for the past five years averaged $192,000. This is believed to be a reasonable estimate of future income.

[3] The level of income normally experienced by companies similar to Jefferson Company is 9%.

Instructions

[a] Compute the estimated value of goodwill under each of the following methods and assumptions:

[1] Years multiple of excess earnings, assuming a five-year period of excess earnings.

[2] Present value of excess earnings, assuming a seven-year period of excess earnings and a 10% interest rate.

[3] Capitalization of excess earnings at the normal rate.

[4] Capitalization of excess earnings at twice the normal rate.

[b] If the present-value of excess earnings method is accepted by management as the appropriate value of goodwill for negotiation purposes, what is the maximum price Washington Company should pay for the net assets of Jefferson Company?

13–43   GOODWILL   Trudeau Company is considering the acquisition of Martin Company. A considerable amount of information about Martin Company has been accumulated, including the following.

Net income. Net income figures are:

1988	$78,500	1991	$51,500
1989	59,000	1992	72,000
1990	67,200		

Net income for 1988 included a $12,500 extraordinary gain; 1990 net income included a $14,000 extraordinary gain.

Selected Balance-Sheet Data.   As of the transaction date, recorded amounts and estimated current values of assets are:

	Recorded Amount	Estimated Current Value
Receivables	$125,000	$120,000
Inventories	216,000	415,000
Property, plant, and equipment	300,000	425,000
Patents	10,000	75,000

Liabilities to be assumed are $665,000.

Management of Trudeau Company believes the investment in Martin Company will provide a return in excess of the 10% normal for the industry. Analysis of the components of earnings indicates that average net income for the past five years is a reasonable basis for estimating future income. It is believed, however, that the effect of extraordinary items should be eliminated and that depreciation and amortization can be expected to increase by $12,500 annually.

Instructions

[a] Estimate the amount of goodwill in the Martin Company acquisition by each of the following methods:

[1] Years multiple of estimated excess earnings, assuming a five-year period of excess earnings.

[2] Present value of estimated excess earnings, discounted at the normal rate over a five-year period.

[3] Capitalization of the estimated excess earnings at a 15% rate.

[b] For each category of assets, indicate the probable reason for the difference between the recorded amount and the estimated current value.

[c] After extended negotiations, a price of $400,000 is finally agreed on by the two companies. Prepare the journal entry to record the acquisition by Trudeau Company. You may include all liabilities in a single Liability account. The agreement calls for a cash payment of $175,000 and the issuance of 10,000 shares of $10 par value stock of Trudeau Company. The current market price of the stock is 22½.

13–44   GOODWILL   Johnson Company has negotiated to acquire the net assets of Robbins Company. The companies have agreed that the purchase price should be established at the fair market value of the assets, less liabilities, plus the value of the goodwill of Robbins Company. The value of the goodwill has been agreed upon as the average of the last three years' excess of income from normal operations over 10% of stockholders' equity, at the beginning of the year, discounted to the present at 10% for a five-year period. The last three years are 1990, 1991, and 1992.

The following figures have been taken from the last four years' financial statements of Robbins Company (December 31 year-end):

	1989	1990	1991	1992
Net income	$ 225,000	$ 250,000	$ 350,000	$ 550,000
Stockholders' equity				
Common stock	1,000,000	1,000,000	1,200,000	1,200,000
Additional paid-in capital	500,000	500,000	600,000	600,000
Retained earnings	125,000	250,000	400,000	500,000
	$1,625,000	$1,750,000	$2,200,000	$2,300,000

You have been engaged as an independent CPA to determine the total purchase price which has apparently been agreed upon by both parties. As part of your investigation you discover the following:

[1] The two companies have agreed on the following estimates of the current value of the assets to be transferred (other than goodwill):

Receivables	$150,000	Buildings	$1,400,000
Inventory	400,000	Land	1,600,000
Equipment	500,000	Franchise	150,000

[2] Liabilities to be assumed by Johnson Company total $1,200,000.

[3] Additional shares of stock were sold in May 1991.

[4] The following questionable items have been recorded by year:

1990.   An extraordinary gain of $25,500 was included in net income. This represents the excess of the proceeds over cost of land purchased by the city under condemnation proceedings.

1991.   A franchise agreement was entered into in January and $100,000 paid in advance. The period of the franchise is five years. No amortization has been taken. The $100,000 was debited to an intangible asset account.

1992.   A sum of $15,000 was received from a customer whose account had been erroneously written off as uncollectible in 1991 by a direct charge to bad debts expense. The arrangement with the customer had explicitly called for repayment in 1992. The $15,000 was credited to Miscellaneous Income when received.

An insurance recovery of $125,000 was received on inventory which was totally destroyed by a flood. The $125,000 was presented as an extraordinary gain due to the unusual circumstances surrounding the flood. The cost of the inventory, $75,000, was debited to Retained Earnings. The flood was extremely unusual; a similar event has never occurred in the location of the company this century and is not expected to recur.

An additional tax assessment of $97,000 was paid. Of this amount, $25,000 related to 1989, $35,000 to 1990, and $37,000 to 1991. Retained Earnings was debited for the total of $97,000, since this adjustment resulted from an accounting error.

Instructions

[a] Prepare a schedule which includes:
   [1] The corrected net income for 1989, 1990, 1991, and 1992.
   [2] The amount to be used for computing goodwill for 1990, 1991, and 1992. A conference with officials of the two companies reveals that the phrase "income from normal operations" appears to have meant income before extraordinary items.
[b] Prepare a schedule restating retained earnings for 1989, 1990, 1991, and 1992 at year-end.
[c] Based on information from your schedules in [1] and [2], compute goodwill as agreed upon by the two companies.

[d] Prepare the journal entry to record the net assets of Robbins Company acquired by Johnson Company, assuming payment is made by issuing 100,000 shares of Johnson Company common stock and the remainder in cash. The common stock has a $20 par value and a $25 market price. The transaction was finalized on January 5, 1993.

[e] Prepare the adjusting entry one year after the acquisition to record amortization on the intangible assets acquired. The franchise is expected to have a six-year life, and the goodwill is to be amortized over a period consistent with the method by which it was computed.

13–45 MISCELLANEOUS INTANGIBLE ASSETS   Information concerning Roach Corporation's intangible assets is as follows:

[1] On January 1, 1992, Roach signed an agreement to operate as a franchisee of Rapid Copy Service, Inc., for an initial franchise fee of $85,000. Of this amount, $25,000 was paid when the agreement was signed and the balance is payable in four annual payments of $15,000 each beginning January 1, 1993. The agreement provides that the down payment is not refundable and no future services are required of the franchisor. The present value at January 1, 1992, of the four annual payments discounted at 14% (the implicit rate for a loan of this type) is $43,700. The agreement also provides that 5% of the revenue from the franchise must be paid to the franchisor annually. Roach's revenue from the franchise for 1992 was $900,000. Roach estimates the useful life of the franchise to be ten years.

[2] Roach incurred $78,000 of experimental and development costs in its laboratory to develop a patent which was granted on January 2, 1992. Legal fees and other costs associated with registration of the patent totaled $16,400. Management estimates that the useful life of the patent will be eight years.

[3] A trademark was purchased from Sampson Company for $40,000 on July 1, 1989. Expenditures for successful litigation in defense of the trademark totaling $10,000 were paid on July 1, 1992. Management estimates that the useful life of the trademark will be 20 years from the date of acquisition.

Instructions

[a] Prepare a schedule showing the intangibles section of Roach's balance sheet at December 31, 1992. Show supporting computations in good form.

[b] Prepare a schedule showing all expenses resulting from the transactions that would appear on Roach's income statement for the year ended December 31, 1992. Show supporting computations in good form.   (AICPA adapted)

13–46 MISCELLANEOUS INTANGIBLE ASSETS   Barber, Inc., was organized and began operations in 1993. Selected transactions for the first year of operation are listed below:

Jan. 5   Paid $5,000 to the attorneys who assisted in preparing the corporate bylaws, obtaining the corporate charter, and generally advising the company on several legal matters.

Jan. 10   Issued 1,000 shares of the company's common stock to promoters of the corporation. In another recent transaction stock sold at $12 per share. The par value of the stock is $10.

Feb. 5   Paid $10,000 to develop and acquire the exclusive right to use the company's trademark.

Mar. 21   Paid $8,500 to an advertising firm to promote the company and its products, emphasizing the new trademark recently developed. A second installment is to be paid in six months.

Apr. 1   A license to operate a shop in the local airport was obtained for $12,000 from the city on April 1. The license covers a five-year period, at the end of which the company must pay $12,000 for renewal for five years. In addition, the company must pay 5% of gross revenues to the city to cover utilities, maintenance, and other operating expenses. As an estimate of this amount for April 1–December 31, $15,000 was paid on April 15. In subsequent years this payment will be made at the end of the calendar year.

July 25   A marketing research firm was hired to help survey potential customers and assess ways to capitalize more on consumer demand. An initial payment of $3,250 was made to the firm.

Sept. 30   A second payment of $8,500 was made to the advertising firm for promotional services rendered. The advertising is expected to enhance the value of the trademark and to generally benefit the company for several years.

Oct. 5   Another company, Malott Enterprises, was acquired. In the transaction, $265,000 cash was paid to acquire assets valued as follows: inventory, $97,500; property, plant, and equipment, $180,000; franchise rights, $42,500. Noncurrent liabilities assumed totaled $96,000. Management has placed an estimated value of $80,000 on goodwill, based on the present value of excess future earnings over a 10-year period. The franchise has a 5-year remaining life.

Nov. 7   Paid $2,500 in legal fees to successfully defend the trademark against a competitor who had begun using an identical diagram of a different color to market similar products.

Instructions

[a] Prepare general journal entries to record the above transactions.
[b] Prepare any adjusting entries necessary for intangible assets on December 31, 1993, in anticipation of the preparation of financial statements. Consider the following information:
   [1] Revenues for 1993 were $336,000.
   [2] Intangible assets are to be amortized by the straight-line method, computed to the nearest full month. Intangibles are to be amortized over the contractual period, if any. Other intangibles, including goodwill, are to be amortized over a 10-year period.
   [3] Amortization should be rounded to the nearest dollar.
[c] Indicate items and amounts relative to intangible assets that should be presented in the company's balance sheet and income statement on December 31, 1993.

13–47   RESEARCH AND DEVELOPMENT   Loszynski Corporation was founded in 1980 and experienced only moderate growth during its first ten years. However, Loszynski was able to attract several scientists and researchers with technical experience and ability and became a pioneer in the field of robotics.

Loszynski experienced a 30% annual growth in revenue for the years 1990–1992 due to the increased demand for its products and consulting services. The company, assured of sufficient financing, planned several expenditures in 1992 that would enable it to meet increased demand and continue its excellent growth rate through the rest of the decade.

Ron Griffin of Loszynski's General Accounting Department is experiencing difficulty in understanding several transactions made during the first quarter of 1993, some of which include expenditures that were planned in 1992. Griffin has asked the controller for assistance in determining how to record the six transactions listed below, and how they will affect the financial statements of Loszynski Corporation in both current and future periods. All amounts are considered material.

[1] Loszynski paid $260,000 for land upon which to build a new research facility. The cost to raze and remove an old building on the site of the newly proposed research facility was $50,000. Lumber, copper tubing, and a few remaining usable fixtures from the old building were salvaged and sold for $10,000. Loszynski paid $4,000 to the architect that designed the new building, $30,000 for excavation of the basement, and $420,000 to a contractor for construction of the building. Due to the foundation, construction, and materials used, the new building is expected to last for at least 60 years. Loszynski's research director, however, believes the building will not be appropriate for the needs of the company after 20 years.

[2] Loszynski gave a one-year noninterest-bearing note for $165,000 to Roberts Industries in exchange for a conveyor to be installed in the new research facility and a temperature monitoring system (TMS). The imputed interest rate on the note is 10% per year. At the date of the exchange, the remaining life of both items on the books of Roberts Industries was seven years. The conveyor had an estimated value of $60,000 at the date of the exchange, is expected to last 30 years, and will be needed as long as the new research facility is used by the company. The TMS had an estimated value of $100,000 at the date of the exchange and is expected to last five years.

[3] Loszynski incurred the following costs in securing a trademark.

Design costs	$2,000
Registration fees	300
Attorney's fees	700

Loszynski's attorney informed the company that the trademark registration system provides for an initial registration term of 20 years and an indefinite number of renewals for periods of 20 years each. Loszynski's marketing manager believes the trademark will be of value to the company for 50 years.

[4] Loszynski incurred $9,000 of legal fees in defending the rights to a patent. The patent was purchased in the first quarter of 1991 at a cost of $15,000 and is being amortized over a period of 12 years.

[5] Loszynski made improvements to a building it has occupied since the first quarter of 1989 under the terms of a 20-year lease. Carpeting installed at a cost of $2,800 is expected to last 10 years and shelving installed at a cost of $4,200 is expected to last 30 years.

[6] Loszynski spent $37,000 searching for practical applications of new research findings that are believed to be of use to the company for the next 20 years.

Instructions

As controller for Loszynski Corporation, review the six transactions brought to your attention by Ron Griffin. For each of the six transactions:

[a] Identify whether the item is to be expensed in 1993 or capitalized.

[b] Identify the amount to be capitalized or expensed (other than depreciation or amortization).

[c] Identify the number of years to be used to write-off the items that are capitalized.

[d] Justify your answers by reference to underlying accounting theory or to authoritative accounting pronouncements. You need not cite accounting pronouncements by name, number, or by promulgating body.

Income tax implications and calculation of annual depreciation or amortization charges for capitalized items are to be ignored. Use the following format to present your answer.

Item Number	Amount to Be Expensed (if any)	Capitalized Items (if any)		Justification of Treatment and/or Life
		Amount	Life	

(CMA adapted)

13–48 PATENTS Malik, Inc., is involved in the development, manufacture, and sale of burglar alarm systems, ranging from relatively simple units for private residences to sophisticated units for large office buildings. The company's operations depend largely on an ongoing research and development program, resulting in the internal development of patents. Also, the company occasionally acquires patents from other companies.

As the accountant for Malik, Inc., you are responsible for the proper accounting of many transactions relative to research and operating activities. The following activities have taken place over several years:

1989

Continuous	Research to develop improved alarm systems	$179,000
May 31	Acquisition of Patent A, with a 12-year remaining legal life, from a competitor	72,000

1990

Feb. 28	Costs of models of new alarm system	32,250
Oct. 31	Legal fees for acquisition of Patent B on new alarm system	38,000

1991

Continuous	Development to advance new alarm system to commercial production	38,000
June 30	Initiation of advertising campaign to promote new alarm system, enhancing the value of Patents A and B	42,000
Oct. 25	Legal expenses for the successful defense of Patent B	18,000

1992

Mar. 19	Legal expenses for the unsuccessful defense of Patent A	8,500
May 24	Acquisition of Patent C, with a six-year remaining legal life, from a competitor in anticipation that it will replace Patent A	43,500

1993

Continuous	Research on improved alarm system to replace Patent B	82,650

In 1993 management determined that the remaining life of Patent B was only three years, including the current year. Research was begun in that year to prepare for the replacement of Patent B with a new patent—presumably Patent D—at some future date.

Instructions

Prepare the Patent account for 1989 through December 1993—the end of Malik's current reporting year—following these guidelines:

[a] Amortization is to be made by the straight-line method, with no assumed residual value.

[b] Amortization is to be based on the shorter of the legal life or 10 years, unless indicated otherwise, computed to the nearest half year from acquisition or to disposal.

[c] The book value to be presented in the balance sheet on December 31 of each year should be indicated.

13–49   MISCELLANEOUS INTANGIBLE ASSETS   Memphis Diversified Enterprises has been in business for several years. A trial balance prepared by the company's staff accountant for December 31, 1993, is presented below:

Memphis Diversified Enterprises
UNADJUSTED TRIAL BALANCE
December 31, 1993
(in thousands of dollars)

	Dr.	Cr.
Cash	$ 20	
Accounts receivable	50	
Inventory	120	
Equipment	800	
Accumulated depreciation—Equipment		$ 250
Buildings	1,200	
Accumulated depreciation—Buildings		400
Patents	550	
Franchise agreement	95	
Organization costs	102	
Goodwill	345	
Accounts payable		12
Accrued wages payable		5
Accrued taxes payable		60
Bonds payable		500
Premium on bonds payable		35
Preferred stock ($100 par value)		100
Common stock ($25 par value)		1,100
Additional paid-in capital		220
Retained earnings (as of January 1)		400
Sales revenue		900
Cost of goods sold	400	
Selling and administrative expenses	300	
	$3,982	$3,982

Before 1993, Memphis Diversified Enterprises prepared financial statements internally. The company has not been audited because the ownership is held completely by one family and is not actively sold. As of 1993, however, in anticipation of bank loans and a possible public offering of common stock, the company needs audited financial statements prepared in conformity with generally accepted accounting principles.

As a member of the team of independent auditors responsible for Memphis Diversified Enterprises, you have been assigned the intangible assets. You have observed that four intangible asset accounts appear on the unadjusted trial balance. Additional investigation reveals the following:

Patents.   All patents were purchased from another company when Memphis Diversified Enterprises began operations on January 2, 1986. These patents are being amortized over an expected useful life of 14 years. Improvements made to equipment covered by the patents costing

$75,000 were debited to the account in January 1990. Amortization in 1990–1992 included amortization on the $75,000 for the remaining life of the relevant patent. It is determined that the $75,000 should have been expensed in 1990. It is further determined on December 31, 1993, that one of the patents has a remaining life of only 2 years. This patent was originally assigned a cost of $210,000.

Franchise Agreement. A franchise agreement was signed on January 1, 1993. A $50,000 fee was paid, covering a 5-year period, at the end of which the company may renew the agreement by paying $50,000. A decision on renewal has not been made as of December 31, 1993. The agreement calls for an annual payment of 5% of revenue. An entry debiting the account for $45,000 was made at the time of the cash payment for 1993.

Organization Costs. Organization costs include the unamortized portion of amounts paid to promoters for services rendered at the inception of the corporation. These fees have been amortized, since inception, over an estimated 40-year life. The decision is made, as of December 31, 1993, to reduce the total period of amortization of organization costs to 12 years.

Goodwill. The Goodwill account includes three items:

$ 45,000—Legal expenses relative to incorporation. These were assigned to the account in January 1986.

   200,000—Excess of cost over assigned net asset values of an enterprise acquired in early 1991, expected to be of value for an indefinite period.

   100,000—Paid to an advertising consulting firm in early 1992 for a major advertising effort expected to be beneficial for an indefinite period.

No amortization has been taken on any amount in the Goodwill account.

Instructions

[a] Prepare an analysis of each intangible asset, indicating (1) the changes needed to restate each intangible account on a corrected basis for determining the amount of amortization for 1993, and (2) the proper amount of amortization for 1993.

[b] Prepare two compound journal entries (1) to correct the intangible asset account balances before the recording of 1993 amortization, and (2) to record 1993 amortization.

CASES

13–50   INTANGIBLE COSTS   Honeyall, Inc., is a large publicly held corporation. Listed below are six selected expenditures made by the company during the current fiscal year ended April 30, 1992. The proper accounting treatment of these transactions must be determined in order that Honeyall's annual financial statements will be prepared in accordance with generally accepted accounting principles.

[1] Honeyall Inc. spent $2 million on a program designed to improve relations with its dealers. This project was favorably received by the dealers and Honeyall's management believes that significant future benefits should be received from this program. The program was conducted during the fourth quarter of the current fiscal year.

[2] A pilot plant was constructed during 1991–1992 at a cost of $4 million to test a new production process. The plant will be operated for approximately five years. At that time, the company will make a decision regarding the economic value of the process. The pilot plant is too small for commercial production, so it will be dismantled when the test is over.

[3] A new product will be introduced next year. The company spent $3 million during the current year for design of tools, jigs, molds, and dies for this product.

[4] Honeyall Inc. purchased Merit Company for $5 million in cash in early August 1991. The fair market value of the identifiable assets of Merit was $4 million.

[5] A large advertising campaign was conducted during April 1992 to introduce a new product to be released during the first quarter of the 1992–1993 fiscal year. The advertising campaign cost $2.5 million.

[6] During the first six months of the 1991–1992 fiscal year, $500,000 was expended for legal work in connection with a successful patent application. The patent became effective November 1, 1991. The legal life of the patent is 17 years while the economic life of the patent is expected to be approximately 10 years.

Instructions

For each of the six transactions described above, determine the amount that should be included on Honeyall's April 30, 1992, Balance Sheet and in Honeyall's Income Statement for the year ended April 30, 1992.   (CMA adapted)

13–51   RESEARCH AND DEVELOPMENT   Burke Company is in the process of developing a revolutionary new product. A division of the company was formed to develop, manufacture, and market this product. As of year end (December 31, 1993) the new product has not been manufactured for resale; however, a prototype unit is in operation.

Throughout 1993 the new division incurred certain costs. These costs include design and engineering studies, prototype manufacturing costs, administrative expenses (including salaries of administrative personnel), and market research costs. In addition, approximately $800,000 in equipment (estimated useful life, 10 years) was purchased for use in developing and manufacturing the new product. Approximately $300,000 of this equipment was built specifically for the design development of the new product. The remaining $500,000 of equipment was used to manufacture the preproduction prototype and will be used to manufacture the new product once it is in commercial production.

Instructions

[a] What are the definitions of "research" and of "development" as defined in *Statement of Financial Accounting Standards No. 2?*
[b] Briefly indicate the practical and conceptual reasons for the conclusion reached by the FASB on accounting and reporting practices for research and development costs.
[c] In accordance with *Statement of Financial Accounting Standards No. 2,* how should the various costs described above be recorded on the financial statements for the year ended December 31, 1993?   (AICPA adapted)

13–52   DEVELOPMENT-STAGE ENTERPRISE   The president of New Company, Thomas P. New, has engaged you to assist in the preparation of financial statements to be used in conjunction with a proposed bank loan. Officials of the bank have requested financial statements which are "based on good accounting."

New Company was organized during 1993. The company has been raising capital, acquiring assets, developing personnel, and developing products which it plans to market in the future. Only insignificant amounts of revenue have been generated to date.

Mr. New has prepared the following balance sheet which he considers adequate for purposes of the proposed bank loan. He also offers the information which accompanies the balance sheet as an explanation of some of the activities of the enterprise to date.

New Company
BALANCE SHEET
October 31, 1993

Assets	
Cash	$ 17,650
Machinery (at cost)	59,350
Land (at cost)	15,000
Intangibles	41,400
	$133,400
Liabilities	
Accrued expenses	$ 11,975
Notes payable (90-day)	21,425
	33,400
Stockholders' Equity	
Common stock	100,000
	$133,400

Notes:

[1] Intangible assets consist of the following:

Research and development	$15,400
Marketing research	3,400
Personnel recruitment and training	12,600
Legal fees relative to organization of corporation	4,750
Operating expenses incurred through October 31, 1993	5,250
	$41,400

[2] Common stock has been issued as follows:

[a] Thomas P. New, President, acquired 8,000 shares at the $10 par value.

[b] George M. New, brother of Thomas, received 2,000 shares in exchange for land which he had purchased five years earlier for $15,000.

[c] One thousand shares were issued to John X. New, a cousin of both Thomas and George, for managerial services rendered in operating the enterprise to date. John will become the general manager at some future date when he quits his current position with another company.

Thomas asks you to verify the authenticity of his balance sheet and transfer it to the bank as soon as possible so that he may proceed with his application for the much needed bank loan.

Instructions

[a] Identify deficiencies in Mr. New's balance sheet, considering both his draft of the statement and the additional information which he has provided. Indicate the proper treatment of each item you have listed as a deficiency.

[b] In addition to the changes you propose in [a], what items must be included to provide the bank with financial statements that are prepared in conformity with generally accepted accounting principles?

13–53 ORGANIZATION COSTS Big Time Co., Inc., was formed during the previous year and you, the newly appointed controller of the company, have encountered a thorny issue involving a large series of payments to the founder and chief executive officer (CEO) for his work in establishing the company and attracting investors. The CEO has directed you to treat all the amounts paid to him as "organization costs" and to amortize them over a five year period. He stated, "Without my strenuous efforts this company wouldn't even exist. I worked night and day to find investors and put these deals together. I developed corporate bylaws, obtained the corporate charter, and simply got the wheels rolling. When we start generating revenue next year, I want to match it with these costs in an appropriate manner. If any costs were necessary to form and organize this business, the amounts paid to me are it."

You are more than a little concerned because the amounts paid to the CEO constitute 10% of the total stockholders' equity of $6,000,000 contributed by the other investors. Indeed, this is the manner by which the amounts paid to the CEO were determined. He has consistently had checks written to himself in the amount of 10% of all payments received for the issuance of capital stock. The corporate charter and bylaws do not specifically prohibit such withdrawals and, in fact, provide that the CEO and other officers shall be compensated adequately for the services rendered to the company.

Instructions

How should you account for these amounts? If you believe that they cannot be considered organization costs and reported as assets, what treatment do you recommend? Be sure to address the theoretical as well as the practical issues inherent in the case.

13–54 CAPITALIZATION VS. EXPENSE Fast Change, Inc., has just undergone substantial personnel changes in its executive leadership. The board of directors has replaced the chief executive officer (CEO), the vice presidents for production, marketing, and finance, and a number of other high-level positions. The executive search (headhunter) costs involved in the transition, as well as severance pay (parachutes) to those whose contracts were prematurely terminated, are each individually material to the company. The changes were made because the company's poor performance in recent years has come close to violating several of its lending covenants relating to debt-equity ratios and the rate of return on assets employed (net income divided by total assets).

The new CEO would like the company to stop perceiving itself as a "loser" and wants to avoid issuing financial statements that reveal the violations of lending covenants and the attendant negotiations with the banks that will follow. He observes that if the personnel costs involved in changing the management team were capitalized rather than charged to expense, the company's financial statements would not depict a violation of the lending covenants. He has called you, the new chief accounting officer, to his office and instructs you to research the possibility of appropriately capitalizing these costs. He tells you, "All of these costs were incurred by the company to remedy a bad management situation. The result of incurring these costs is the excellent management team that is now in place and those costs will continue to benefit the company throughout our tenure. I personally believe that these costs should be reported as an intangible asset and amortized over the next five years (the length of his contract). As you know, however, I'm not an accountant by any means, and I don't want to do anything wrong by issuing financial statements that contain departures from GAAP. However, I also want to put our best foot forward as we move to improve the operating performance of this business. We're all new here, and I know you want to get off on the right foot. Because of the importance of this matter to me, I know I can count on you, as a valuable member of our team, to leave no stone unturned in justifying our position in treating these costs as intangible assets."

Instructions

Perform the research requested by the CEO. Be sure to consider the appropriate technical and conceptual issues that underly the preparation of financial statements in accordance with GAAP. Also, consider any ethical issues that come to mind as you consider the wishes of your new boss.

PART 4

LIABILITY AND STOCKHOLDERS' EQUITY ACCOUNTING

CHAPTER 14

Current and Contingent Liabilities

OBJECTIVES

1. To discuss the conceptual characteristics of liabilities of business enterprises.
2. To present the meaning and nature of current liabilities.
3. To describe the characteristics distinguishing among determinable, estimated, and contingent liabilities.
4. To understand the many complex and often ambiguous and subjective determinations necessary in accounting for loss contingencies.
5. To apply acceptable accounting measurement and disclosure practices to a variety of current liabilities.
6. To describe the various types of obligations arising from employee compensation.
7. To classify liabilities as current or long-term, including short-term obligations expected to be refinanced.
8. To apply acceptable accounting measurement and disclosure practices to a variety of contingent and estimated liabilities.

CHARACTERISTICS OF LIABILITIES

Companies often acquire goods and services that are to be paid for at a later date. Examples include the purchase of supplies, items of inventory, and other services and assets on account. Events and actions of organizations and individuals external to a company can also give rise to various liabilities that eventually must be paid. Examples include obligations to taxing authorities, lawsuits that are initiated against the firm, and claims resulting from warranties and guarantees. Not all potential obligations of a firm are necessarily reportable liabilities, however, because certain criteria must be met before an accounting liability is recognized.

As we discussed in Chapter 3, the Financial Accounting Standards Board (FASB) has defined the term **liability** as:

> *probable future sacrifices of economic benefits arising from present obligations of a particular entity to transfer assets or provide services to other entities in the future as a result of past transactions or events.*[1]

To provide more guidance, the FASB established three characteristics of a liability:

> *1.   A liability embodies a present duty or responsibility to one or more other entities that entails settlement (of the obligation) by probable future transfer or use of assets at a specified or determinable date, on occurrence of a specified event, or on demand.*
>
> *2.   The duty or responsibility obligates a particular entity, leaving it little or no discretion to avoid the future sacrifice.*
>
> *3.   The transaction or other event obligating the entity has already happened.*[2]

The focus of liability recognition then is to provide information about likely future cash outflows that the reporting entity is currently obliged to pay. Financial information users such as present and prospective creditors and investors are greatly interested in the expected future cash flows of an organization. Information about present obligations that will require future cash payments is an important aspect of understanding *total* future expected cash flows. Furthermore, the amounts reported as liabilities generally require payments that the reporting entity can neither influence in amount or timing nor avoid. Such obligations differ from other expected future cash payments in that they already exist and cannot be avoided readily by management decisions or actions.

Not all liabilities represent obligations that must be paid in cash. Some, such as customer order deposits and warranties, will be satisfied by providing goods or services for those to whom the obligations are owed. Nevertheless, the amounts reported on the balance sheet for all liabilities should approximate the cash that will be required to discharge whatever obligation exists. In this manner, liabilities provide information about one type of future cash outflow: presently existing obligations that will be satisfied at some future time.

This chapter discusses a company's obligations that represent accounting liabilities classified as **current**. We first examine current liabilities that are known to exist and whose amounts are readily determinable. Next we discuss accounting and report-

---

[1]*FASB Statement of Financial Accounting Concepts No. 6,* "Elements of Financial Statements," 1985, par. 35.
[2]*FASB Statement of Financial Accounting Concepts No. 6,* par. 36.

ing for liabilities that are contingent. **Contingent liabilities** are uncertain obligations; that is, their existence and, in many cases, their related amounts are not known precisely. Contingent liabilities include—among other things—lawsuits, claims, and assessments in progress against the firm, warranties, and guarantees.

CURRENT LIABILITIES

Accounting Research Bulletin No. 43 provides the basic definition of **current liabilities:**

> *The term is used principally to designate obligations whose liquidation is reasonably expected to require the use of existing resources properly classified as current assets, or the creation of other current liabilities.*[3]

More recently, the FASB has provided additional guidance as to how that basic definition should be applied in practice. Specifically, *SFAS No. 78* indicates that current liabilities should include obligations that are due on demand or that will become due on demand within one year (or one operating cycle, if longer) from the balance sheet date. Additionally, in some cases debt with a long-term maturity date should also be considered a current liability.

Debt agreements frequently contain a variety of clauses and requirements to which a debtor must adhere. Examples include covenants made at the outset of a loan by the debtor to maintain a certain level of cash, working capital, or stockholders' equity. A violation of such covenants usually provides certain additional rights to the creditor and among those rights is frequently an option to call the debt and demand repayment immediately. Not all loan covenants contain clear and objective criteria for determining compliance. For example, a covenant may provide that the debtor must maintain ". . . adequate liquidity to service the debt for six months in the absence of operating profits." Determining compliance with such a provision would require much analysis, careful estimates, and seasoned judgments on the part of the company and its accountants. If it is determined that a covenant has been violated, the creditor may demand repayment in the near future. The debt should be reclassified as a current liability by the debtor unless the creditor has waived the violation or has lost the right to demand repayment. A creditor may lose the right to call the debt if, for example, the violation has been cured *before* the right is exercised.

Additionally, long-term debt should not be reclassified as current if it is *probable* that the violation will be cured within a grace period provided by the agreement. Such determinations require particular care because they involve direct estimates of future activities and conditions. Again, considerable judgment is required on the part of accountants making such estimates. Generally, positive events or conditions that are expected to resolve a particular violation should be specifically identifiable and should demonstrate a high probability of occurance. Examples include a commitment from a willing and capable third party buyer to purchase large amounts of goods immediately in the following period or a strong recovery of an investment portfolio subsequent to the balance sheet date that may have cured the condition of default by the time financial statements are issued. The notes to the financial statements should disclose cases in which it is believed that violations of covenants will be cured within a grace period.

The underlying theme of *SFAS No. 78* is consistent with the general provisions of *Accounting Research Bulletin No. 43*. The FASB pronouncement is simply more direct

---

[3]*Accounting Research Bulletin No. 43*, "Restatement and Revision of Accounting Research Bulletins," 1953, Sec. A, Ch. 3, par. 7.

and describes specific circumstances in which debt with a noncurrent maturity is considered likely to require the use of existing working capital. In such circumstances, accountants should classify the debt as a current liability regardless of its original maturity date.[4] Therefore, current liabilities are defined in terms of claims on the working capital of a company and in terms of their due date. That is, if the satisfaction of a liability is expected to require the use of existing working capital, then the obligation is considered current regardless of its maturity date.

VALUATION OF CURRENT LIABILITIES

In theory, liabilities should originally be stated at the present value of the future cash payments necessary to extinguish or satisfy the obligation. We apply present-value techniques to many liabilities in order to present them at their present value. In practice, however, current liabilities are frequently recorded and presented in the financial statements at their full maturity amounts. Although this practice may result in a slight theoretical overstatement of certain current liabilities, clerical simplicity,

Materiality
Conservatism

immateriality, and conservatism support such a minor overstatement of current liabilities. Generally, the time until maturity is short for current liabilities, and the amount of any overstatement inherent in the face amount of the liability is relatively small. Furthermore, recording current liabilities at their full amounts results in a larger charge to the goods or services acquired and thereby typically results in a more conservative measure of income. The Accounting Principles Board (APB), in its *Opinion No. 21*, requires the presentation of most liabilities at their net present value then adds:

> *This Opinion is not intended to apply to . . . receivables and payables arising from transactions with customers or suppliers in the normal course of business which are due in customary trade terms not exceeding approximately one year.*[5]

Businesses, therefore, are not required to apply present-value techniques to the valuation of most current liabilities. Current liabilities, however, may be (and, in many cases, are) presented at their net present value.

Before reading the following discussion on financial accounting and reporting for different types of liabilities, refer to the balance sheet of Strawbridge & Clothier presented on the inside back cover of the text. Notice that several types of current liabilities are presented, including the current portion of long-term debt and capital leases as well as a variety of current items and other payables. The importance of current liabilities can be seen in this balance sheet, because they make up approximately 31% of total liabilities and approximately 19% of total liabilities and stockholders' equity.

SPECIFIC TYPES OF CURRENT LIABILITIES

Accounts Payable

As previously indicated, there are a great many types of current liabilities; however, the most common is probably represented by trade accounts payable. **Accounts payable** are those liabilities that arise in the acquisition of goods and services in the normal course of business. Many of the accounting and reporting issues related to ac-

---

[4]*FASB Statement of Financial Accounting Standards No. 78*, "Classification of Obligations That Are Callable by the Creditor," 1983.
[5]*APB Opinion No. 21*, "Interest on Receivables and Payables," 1971, par. 3.

counts payable have counterparts in **accounts receivable,** as discussed in Chapter 7, and we will review many of them in this section.

Trade accounts payable are recognized when the acquisition of goods or services results in a liability. If Artesia Company acquires $1,000 worth of supplies on account, the following journal entry should be made at the point of acquisition:

Supplies on Hand	1,000	
Accounts Payable		1,000
(To record the acquisition of supplies.)		

If the invoice amount is $1,000 and a purchase discount is allowed for early payment, then other problems arise. If Artesia acquired the same supplies on terms of 2/10, n/30, the journal entry would be as follows:[6]

Supplies on Hand	980	
Accounts Payable		980
(To record acquisition of supplies for invoice		
amount of $1,000, terms 2/10, n/30.)		

If the invoice is paid prior to the expiration of the 10-day discount period, accounts payable is charged and cash credited for $980. If the invoice is not paid within the discount period, however, the payment of the invoice should be recorded as follows:

Accounts Payable	980	
Purchase Discounts Lost	20	
Cash		1,000
(To record payment of invoice and lost discount.)		

The Purchase Discounts Lost account is treated as an element of financial or interest expense on the income statement. Further, unpaid invoices existing at the year-end should be evaluated to determine if any discounts have been lost at that time. If, for example, it is determined at year-end that purchase discounts in the amount of $15 have already been lost on unpaid invoices, the following adjusting entry is necessary:

Purchase Discounts Lost	15	
Accounts Payable		15

Materiality

As discussed in Chapter 8, "Inventories: Basic Valuation Methods," we may encounter a variety of methods of accounting for purchase discounts in practice. Generally, such amounts are immaterial and therefore the issue is relatively unimportant. The differences in these methods may accumulate to a material amount, however, and the following considerations should take precedence:

1. The good or service acquired should be recorded at its cash-equivalent price at the point of acquisition.
2. Any difference between the cash-equivalent price at acquisition (in 1) and the payment required to settle the account should generally be treated as a financial expense.

---

[6]This entry seems theoretically preferable because $980 represents the cash-equivalent price and present value of the liability at the point of acquisition. Furthermore, the presentation of the liability at the net amount reflects management's intent to take the discount.

Current Notes Payable

Current notes payable generally arise from three types of transactions:

1. **Trade notes payable** that result from the acquisition of goods or services (usually equipment or other large items).
2. **Loan notes payable** that result from cash-borrowing activities.
3. **Current maturities** of long-term notes and bonds payable that represent amounts payable from current assets. Such current maturities have typically been previously classified as noncurrent liabilities.

Trade notes payable generally do not present significant accounting and reporting problems. The maturity date, the amount necessary to satisfy the note, and the interest rate are usually available; the major calculation required is determining the amount of interest to be accrued at the end of an accounting period.

For example, if we assume that Heyman Company reports on a calendar year and that on November 1, 1992, it acquires machinery with a value of $1,000 by issuing a $1,000 note bearing interest at 20%, due in six months, the following entries computed to the nearest dollar are necessary:

Nov. 1, 1992	Machinery	1,000	
	Trade Notes Payable		1,000
	(To record the acquisition of machinery by issuing a six-month 20%, $1,000 note.)		
Dec. 31, 1992	Interest Expense	33	
	Interest Payable		33
	(To record accrued interest at year-end. $1,000 × 20% × ⅙ = $33.)		
May 1, 1993	Trade Notes Payable	1,000	
	Interest Payable	33	
	Interest Expense	67	
	Cash		1,100
	(To record payment of note and related interest at maturity.)		

The May 1 entry assumes no reversing entry was made at the beginning of 1993.

Interest-Bearing Notes.   Notes payable that arise from cash-borrowing activities are generally of two types: **interest-bearing notes** and so-called **noninterest-bearing notes.** Accounting and reporting for interest-bearing notes requires the accountant to accrue interest and report a liability in the amount of the accrued interest payable plus the face value of the note. The accounting practices for such interest-bearing notes are similar to those previously described for the acquisition of equipment and, therefore, contain no additional accounting complications.

Noninterest-Bearing Notes.   Certain notes do not pay any stated rate of interest in addition to the face amount of the note. This type of liability is frequently referred to as **noninterest-bearing.** Interest on such notes, however, is deducted by the lender in advance and the notes are issued at discount; that is, the borrower (the maker of the note) receives an amount that is less than the face value of the note.

To illustrate, assume that on November 1, 1992, Century Company issues a one-year note payable with a face amount of $10,000 to a bank and in return receives $8,800 in cash. This note was discounted by the bank at 12% ($10,000 × .12 = $1,200; $10,000 − $1,200 = $8,800). The effective rate of interest in the note exceeds 12%, however, as indicated below:

$$\frac{\text{Interest}}{\text{Amount Received}} = \frac{\$1,200}{\$8,800} = 13.64\% \text{ (For a one-year note)}$$

Therefore, $1,200 of interest was paid for a loan of $8,800 for a one-year period. The journal entry to record the loan, the discount representing future interest, and the amount to be repaid on November 1, 1993, is as follows:

Nov. 1, 1992	Cash	8,800	
	Discount on Notes Payable	1,200	
	Notes Payable		10,000
	(To record issuance of note and receipt of cash.)		

The Notes Payable account could have been credited with the $8,800 instead of the $10,000. In that case no figure would be entered in the Discount on Notes Payable account. If a Discount on Notes Payable account is used, it appears on the balance sheet as a **contra account** (reduction) to the Notes Payable account. In any case the note is reported in the balance sheet at its present value ($8,800) at the date of issuance, rather than its maturity value ($10,000).

The adjusting entry at December 31, 1992 appears below:

Dec. 31, 1992	Interest Expense	200	
	Discount on Notes Payable		200
	(To record accrued interest on note payable. $1,200 \times \frac{2}{12} = \$200$.)		

As a result of this adjusting entry, the note is reported in the balance sheet as a $9,000 ($10,000 − $1,000) current liability at December 31, 1992. We have amortized $200 of the original discount of $1,200 and, therefore, the remaining discount is $1,000.

When the note matures and is paid during 1993, the following entry is made:

Nov. 1, 1993	Notes Payable	10,000	
	Interest Expense	1,000	
	Discount on Notes Payable		1,000
	Cash		10,000
	(To record payment of note payable and recognize interest expense.)		

This entry assumes no reversing entry was made January 1, 1993.

Some companies may amortize the discount or premium during the year to facilitate the preparation of interim financial statements. Adjustments at the end of the year are thereby confined to the amount necessary to complete the annual amortization.

Current Maturities.   Current maturities of long-term notes payable must frequently be reported as current liabilities to the extent they must be paid during the next year or operating cycle, whichever is longer. A sinking fund may exist to service such liabilities, and, if so, the current maturities of long-term debt should be excluded from current liabilities. Such obligations are classified as noncurrent liabilities in a manner consistent with the sinking fund. Chapter 10 discusses sinking funds in dealing with a variety of investments and funds; consequently, Chapter 14 does not discuss these issues further. Occasionally, a company plans to refinance current debt on a noncurrent basis; such anticipated action produces some additional accounting and reporting problems, which we discuss in the following section.

Short-Term Obligations Expected to Be Refinanced

In certain circumstances a company may wish to **refinance a short-term obligation** on a noncurrent basis. Examples include the current maturity of a previously noncurrent debt or a line of credit with a bank that a company wishes to extend. Furthermore, a short-term obligation may be refinanced on a long-term basis after the date of the balance sheet but before financial statements are issued. Because those debts may not require the use of working capital, questions arise about the proper classification at the balance sheet date.

To guide such liability classification issues, the FASB issued *Statement of Financial Accounting Standards No. 6,*[7] which calls for the following evidence whenever a company excludes a short-term obligation from current liabilities:

1. An indication of the *intent* to refinance the note on a noncurrent basis, and
2. A demonstration of the *ability* to accomplish the long-term refinancing.

Management's **intent** to refinance a short-term obligation is usually evidenced by express representation or action. The **ability** to refinance a short-term obligation on a long-term basis, however, is frequently more difficult to establish. *SFAS No. 6* provides two ways for a company to demonstrate the ability to refinance a short-term obligation:

1. Subsequent to the balance sheet date but prior to the issuance of the balance sheet, the firm must issue long-term debt or equity securities to refinance the obligation; *or*
2. Prior to the issuance of the balance sheet, the firm must secure a noncancelable, long-term (the longer of one year or one operating cycle from the balance sheet date) financing agreement that clearly allows the firm to refinance the short-term liability on a long-term basis.

Obviously, if a company actually accomplishes such a refinancing transaction, then both the ability and the intent criteria are met. However, if the debt is still outstanding when the financial statements are issued, the accountant should obtain a formal declaration of intent from management and carefully read the details of the refinancing agreement. The accountant must also exercise great care in analyzing the terms of refinancing agreements to assure proper interpretation and application.

If refinancing is accomplished, accountants use information that became available after the balance sheet date to alter accounting measurements and classification on the financial statements of the period already ended. This use of hindsight is appropriate because the newly acquired information relates to a condition that existed at the balance sheet date rather than to a new condition.

If both the intent and ability criteria are met, the accountant *must* exclude the short-term obligation from current liabilities. In this fashion the *timing* of future cash flows is better reflected in the balance sheet classifications of liabilities. The amount of short-term debt to be excluded from current liabilities should not exceed:

1. The amount available for refinancing under the agreement; *or*
2. A reasonable estimate of the minimum amount expected to be available, if the amount available for refinancing will fluctuate.

---

[7]*FASB Statement of Financial Accounting Standards No. 6,* "Classification of Short-Term Obligations Expected To Be Refinanced," 1975.

The accountant must adjust the amount to be excluded from current liabilities to reflect any financing-agreement limitations or restrictions that indicate that a portion of the amount in the agreement may not be available. For example, a limitation dealing with working capital may provide "the amounts to be refinanced will not exceed 50% of the company's working capital at the time of refinancing."

Short-term liabilities arising from transactions in the ordinary course of business and due in customary terms are not subject to these reclassification tests. Such short-term liabilities should be routinely classified as current. Examples of those liabilities include accounts payable incurred in the acquisition of inventory and supplies, collections received in advance of rendering services or providing goods, and other debts resulting from normal operating transactions.

Another question arises when a short-term obligation is repaid after the balance sheet date and the cash used to pay the debt is subsequently replenished through long-term borrowing. In its *Interpretation No. 8,*[8] the FASB observed that repayment of a short-term obligation before funds are obtained through long-term borrowing requires the use of current assets. Therefore, a short-term obligation repaid after the balance sheet date should be classified as current. This is true even if long-term debt or equity securities are subsequently issued and the proceeds are used to replenish current assets, because working capital was employed temporarily to retire the short-term debt making the debt a current liability.

Disclosure **Disclosure of Short-Term Obligations Classified as Long-Term Liabilities.** *SFAS No. 6* requires total current liabilities to be presented in a classified balance sheet, regardless of whether a short-term obligation has been excluded. If a short-term obligation is classified as a noncurrent liability, the amount of and reasons for the classification should also be disclosed in the notes to the financial statements. Other required disclosures include a general description of any financing agreements, the terms of any new obligations incurred or expected to be incurred, and the terms of any equity securities issued or expected to be issued. Those disclosure requirements are illustrated in Exhibit 14–1 for Calico, Inc., and Darnell, Inc.

Dividends Payable

The topic of dividends is treated more fully in Chapter 17, "Stockholders' Equity: Operations, Earnings, Dividends, and Other Issues." Since many types of dividends result in current liabilities, however, the matter is discussed briefly at this time. When the board of directors of a company declares a cash or property dividend, then the amount to be paid to stockholders becomes a liability of the company. Once declared, dividends are usually paid within a few months. Therefore, dividends payable are usually classified as current liabilities. For example, if on December 26, 1992, Arnold Company declares a $1.50 per share dividend to be paid on January 31, 1993, to shareholders of record as of January 5, 1993, and if 10,000 shares of common stock are outstanding, the accountant should make the following entries:

Dec. 26, 1992	Dividends (or Retained Earnings)	15,000	
	Dividends Payable		15,000
	(To record declaration of cash dividend.)		
Jan. 31, 1993	Dividends Payable	15,000	
	Cash		15,000
	(To record payment of dividend.)		

---

[8]*FASB Interpretation No. 8,* "Classification of a Short-Term Obligation Repaid Prior to Being Replaced by a Long-Term Security: An Interpretation of FASB Statement No. 6," 1976.

EXHIBIT 14-1

Illustrations of Debt Refinancings

Illustration No. 1: Actual Refinancing
Excerpt from Balance Sheet of Calico, Inc.

	Dec. 31, 1992
Current Liabilities	
Accounts payable	$ 2,000,000
Accrued expenses	3,000,000
Income taxes payable	1,000,000
Current maturities of long-term debt	1,000,000
Total current liabilities	$ 7,000,000
Long-Term Debt	
Notes payable refinanced in January 1993	
[Note 8]	$ 4,000,000
Other long-term debt	10,000,000
	$14,000,000

Note 8: On January 20, 1993, the Company issued 100,000 shares of common stock and received proceeds totaling $4,500,000 of which $4,000,000 was used to liquidate notes payable that matured on January 31, 1993. Accordingly, such notes payable have been excluded from current liabilities at December 31, 1992.

Illustration No. 2: Financing Agreement
Excerpt from Balance Sheet of Darnell, Inc.

	Dec. 31, 1992
Current Liabilities	
Accounts payable	$1,000,000
Accrued expenses	1,500,000
Income taxes payable	500,000
Total current liabilities	$3,000,000
Long-Term Debt	
8% Notes payable [Note 9]	$2,000,000

Note 9: The Company has entered into a financing agreement with a bank to borrow up to $3,000,000 at any time through 1994. Amounts borrowed under the agreement mature three years from the date of the loan and bear interest at one percent above the bank's prime interest rate. The agreement requires the Company to maintain working capital of at least $8,000,000 and prohibits the payment of dividends and reacquisition of the Company's common stock without prior approval of the bank. Because the Company intends to borrow $2,000,000 under the agreement to pay its 8% notes payable that mature on April 1, 1993, the notes have been classified as long-term debt.

The accountant should not record a liability for a dividend until it is declared by a company's board of directors, because no liability exists for undeclared dividends, regardless of how profitable the company has been.

Advances from Customers

In many circumstances a company may require its customers to make deposits that are either refundable or applicable to future purchases. Such payments are usually designed to provide security for the company receiving the deposit. For example, a business may require a customer to make a substantial payment before the business will accept and manufacture an order designed specifically for that customer.

Revenue
Realization

In transactions such as these, we do not recognize revenue at the time cash is received, because it has not been earned. The recipient company must perform some service or provide some good to earn the revenue. Therefore, the amount of the deposit should be treated as a liability until the obligation to produce the good or service has been discharged. Such liabilities do not require cash repayment but, rather, will be satisfied by providing goods or services. To illustrate, assume that Thin Spread Company, a mill manufacturer of cloth, receives a $500,000 order to manufacture a type of cloth with an unusual design. Prior to beginning the mill run, Thin Spread requests a deposit of $50,000 (10% of total order price) from the customer. The entry to record the receipt of the deposit appears as follows:

Cash	50,000	
Advances from Customers		50,000
(To record receipt of deposit.)		

Advances from Customers is a liability to deliver goods or services in the future. When the mill run is complete and shipped, the following entry is necessary:

Accounts Receivable	450,000	
Advances from Customers	50,000	
Sales Revenue		500,000
(To record sale of cloth and		
recognition of revenue.)		

A company may receive advance payments in a variety of other circumstances as well. Examples include magazine subscriptions, construction deposits, gift certificates, airline and other travel tickets, and promotions such as ticket-book sales by restaurants or theaters. Such deposits will not be refunded in the normal course of business, but will be applied to the total sales price of the goods or services. Those advances should be accounted for as liabilities until the good or service is provided and the revenue earned. This is another place in which estimates of expected future events and conditions are required to prepare *historic* financial statements. In some situations, such as the advance sale of subway tokens or restaurant and theater gift certificates, the expected future utilization rates must be estimated in order to properly account for the revenue to be realized from the transaction. Expiration dates, if they exist for such items, may be helpful in assessing the completion of the earnings process.

Returnable containers and refundable deposits should also be recorded as liabilities. Many states have recently enacted returnable container laws to encourage environmental cleanliness. For example, manufacturers may be required to offer a price for returned cans or bottles that exceeds the worth of the container. In such cases, the company that is obligated to return the reward should accrue a liability for the estimated amount of the returns at the time that product sales are made. Management and the accountant must make estimates of future events and conditions to prepare historic financial statements. Experience in prior periods may help to assess the likely amount of returns in the future, but because many of these programs are relatively new and changes in existing ones occur rather frequently, the accountant may be faced with unusual uncertainties relating to potentially large amounts. In such cases, disclosure of the uncertain conditions is of particular importance to help financial statement users make informed decisions.

Companies also receive refundable deposits in a number of situations. For example, warehouse and space rental agreements often require the renter to make security, repair, and cleaning deposits. At the time such amounts are paid, a liability should be recorded by the party receiving the deposit. The liability is then reduced when the deposit is refunded. If deposits are forfeited, however, the liability should be removed and the amount recognized as revenue. If the deposit was securing an asset of the company, such a rental security deposit on equipment that is not returned, then

Matching the asset should be written off as a loss and matched with the revenue from the forfeited deposit.

Tax Liabilities Other Than Income Taxes

Sales Taxes.   In many governmental jurisdictions, sales tax laws require merchants to collect and remit sales taxes to a government authority. The tax is usually added to the invoice or sales receipt, and merchants collect the sales tax along with the sales price of the good. To illustrate, if Huntington Company sells $1,000 of merchandise that is subject to a 5% sales tax, the following entry is necessary:

Cash	1,050	
Sales Revenue		1,000
Sales Tax Payable		50
(To record the sale of merchandise.)		

When the sales taxes that have been collected are remitted to the taxing authority, the following entry is made:

Sales Tax Payable	50	
Cash		50
(To record remittance of sales taxes collected.)		

Note that sales taxes are expenses of the customer rather than the business collecting the tax. When a company collects sales taxes, the business incurs a liability to the extent of the sales taxes collected. Similarly, when the sales taxes are paid, the liability is merely removed. Neither revenue nor expense should be reported in the financial statements of the tax-collecting enterprise.

In practice, however, many businesses merely record sales taxes collected as additions to revenue and the remittance of the collected taxes as reductions in revenue. In such cases, if financial statements are prepared after sales are made but before the sales taxes are remitted, an adjusting entry is necessary to report the liability to the taxing authority and the related reduction of revenue. This simple clerical procedure facilitates recording cash sales. In the previous example, the entries would appear as follows:

Cash	1,050	
Revenue		1,050
(To record sale and related sales tax.)		

Because liability accounts are not credited, the amount of the sales tax liability is unclear. Therefore, the following calculation is required:

$$X = \text{Taxable sales (cash price of goods alone)}$$
$$X + .05X = \$1,050$$
$$1.05X = \$1,050$$
$$X = \frac{\$1,050}{1.05}$$
$$X = \$1,000 \text{ (cash price of goods alone)}$$

The sales tax payable may then be determined by multiplying the tax rate (5%) times the net sales amount ($1,000). An overpayment of the sales tax occurs if one merely multiplies the tax rate times the unadjusted balance in the sales account ($1,050 × .05 = $52.50). The adjusting entry to reduce revenue and record the liability for sales taxes collected is a charge to revenue and a credit to sales tax payable.

Another problem in accounting for sales taxes arises if the taxing jurisdiction allows collecting merchants a fee to cover the cost of collecting and remitting the tax. Continuing with the previous example, if the taxing authority allows merchants a 2% fee for collecting sales taxes, then we find that the $1 fee (.02 × $50) should be recorded as additional revenue at the time the taxes are remitted by charging sales tax payable for the full $50, crediting cash for $49, and crediting a revenue account for $1.

This illustration may appear to indicate that sales tax is recorded on each individual sale. In practice, many sales might be combined and sales tax recorded for the group of sales. For example, sales tax might be recorded at one time for all sales occurring during a day or week. Some customers—for example, churches or governments—may be exempt from sales taxes. In these cases the company does not collect taxes on sales made to such customers and must take care to ensure that sales taxes are not inadvertently collected or paid to taxing authorities. Separate records of sales made to tax-exempt organizations should be kept to avoid this type of error.

Property Taxes.   Property taxes are usually based on the **assessed value** of various real and personal properties and represent a substantial source of revenue for state and local governments. Such taxes generally become a liability of the paying company at the time they become obligations to the government. This date is usually called the **lien date.** Two accounting questions arise in regard to property taxes:

1. When should the liability be recognized?
2. When should the expense be recognized?

In essence, the liability comes into existence at the lien date, whereas the expense is generally considered to be incurred throughout the period covered by the lien. Property taxes represent expenses associated with the right to use the property subject to the taxes during the tax year of the government. Two commonly encountered accounting methods are illustrated in the example that follows.

Assume that Braunegg Corporation, which uses a calendar year for financial reporting, owns some real estate which is subject to city property taxes of $24,000 per year. The taxes are levied on October 1, 1992, for the forthcoming tax year of the city government and are payable on February 1, 1993. The two methods of accounting for property taxes are illustrated in Exhibit 14–2.

Matching   Under each method the income statement reports the same expense. That is, property taxes are charged to expense during the periods benefited. Because the FASB has stated that the primary purpose of financial reporting is to provide information about an enterprise's earnings, either method seems consistent with the overall goals of financial accounting.[9] The differences between the two methods are confined solely to the balance sheet. The differences, advantages, and disadvantages of each method are summarized below:

[9]*FASB Statement of Financial Accounting Concepts No. 1,* "Objectives of Financial Reporting by Business Enterprises," 1978, par. 43.

EXHIBIT 14-2					
Property Tax Accounting Methods Compared					
Explanation	Immediate Liability-Recognition Method		Accruing Liability-Recognition Method		
Oct. 1, 1992 City levies property tax for coming fiscal year, 10/1/92 to 9/30/93.	Deferred Property Taxes Property Taxes Payable	24,000 24,000	No entry		
Dec. 31, 1992 Company records adjusted by accruing property-tax expenses for financial reporting purposes.	Property Tax Expense Deferred Property Taxes	6,000 6,000	Property Tax Expense Property Tax Payable	6,000 6,000	
Feb. 1, 1993 Payment of property tax recorded.	Property Taxes Payable Cash	24,000 24,000	Property Tax Payable Deferred Property Taxes Cash	6,000 18,000	 24,000
Dec. 31, 1993 Remaining 1992-1993 levied taxes are charged to expense.	Property Tax Expense Deferred Property Taxes	18,000 18,000	Property Tax Expense Deferred Property Taxes	18,000 18,000	

	Immediate Liability-Recognition Method	Accruing Liability-Recognition Method
Difference	Liability and deferred charge are recognized in total at lien date.	Liability is accrued at same amount and time as expense is recognized.
Advantage	Liability is recognized in full as legal obligation of company at time it is incurred.	Assets are not overstated as a result of recognizing a deferred charge for unpaid property taxes.
Disadvantage	An "asset" is recognized for unpaid property taxes.	Legal liability of company not recognized at time it is incurred.

The American Institute of Certified Public Accountants (AICPA) has taken the position that the accruing liability-recognition method is preferable,[10] and the authors concur with this position. A liability exists at the time the taxes are levied; however, if the property is sold, the buyer is generally required to pay the seller for property taxes related to the remaining portion of the year. From an economic perspective the liability is thus prospective and not final at the lien date. Furthermore, the accruing liability-recognition method avoids the problem of overstated assets, because it does not recognize an asset for unpaid property taxes.

Liabilities Related to Payroll Taxes.   Another type of tax liability frequently encountered in practice relates to a company's payroll. Employers are required by law to withhold certain amounts from the salaries and wages of employees and to remit these amounts to the appropriate taxing authorities. Furthermore, the law places additional

---

[10]*Accounting Research Bulletin No. 43*, "Restatement and Revision of Accounting Research Bulletins," 1953, Sec. A, Ch. 10, par. 14.

payroll taxes directly on employers. Accountants must be well acquainted with the various types of **payroll taxes** and **payroll withholdings.** Amounts typically withheld from the pay of employees include federal, state and city income taxes, and the employees' share of social security taxes. Amounts withheld to be paid directly to various government agencies are recorded as part of the salary expense of the employer and as liabilities to the appropriate government agency rather than as payable to the particular employee. These amounts are subsequently paid to the appropriate government agency on behalf of the employer. Payroll related taxes charged to the employer generally include federal and state unemployment taxes and the employers' share of social security taxes. Taxes levied directly on the employer that are not withheld from the pay of employees are reported as additional payroll tax expenses and as related liabilities to the appropriate government agencies. As such, these latter taxes represent payroll expenses to the employer in addition to the basic salary of the employee. A variety of payroll related taxes and the associated financial accounting and reporting issues are discussed in more detail in Appendix A of this chapter.

Bonus and Profit-Sharing Plans

Companies often compensate key employees for superior profits made by the enterprise or for those profits attributed to the segment of the enterprise managed by the particular employee. Although there are many variations of such plans, the central theme is to motivate employees by directly relating their well-being to the success of the company. These types of compensation plans give rise to liabilities and expenses that must be measured and reported in the financial statements. To illustrate three commonly employed formulas for computing bonuses, we shall assume that Mark Company reports a net income before deducting income taxes and bonuses of $100,000. Any bonus accrued at the end of the year is deductible for income tax purposes in the year accrued, and the company's income tax rate is 40%.

Example 1.   The bonus to be paid is expressed as 5% of net income over $60,000. The computation will be made before bonus and income tax expenses are deducted. Therefore, the following computations and entries are necessary to determine and record the bonus and income taxes:

Bonus:

$$\text{Bonus} = .05(\$100,000 - \$60,000)$$
$$\text{Bonus} = .05(\$40,000)$$
$$\text{Bonus} = \$2,000$$

Income taxes:

$$\text{Taxes} = .40(\$100,000 - \text{Bonus})$$
$$\text{Taxes} = .40(\$100,000 - \$2,000)$$
$$\text{Taxes} = .40(\$98,000)$$
$$\text{Taxes} = \$39,200$$

Example 2.   Assume now that the bonus is to be paid in the amount of 5% of net income in excess of $60,000 *after* deducting the bonus but *before* considering income taxes.

Bonus:

$$\text{Bonus} = .05(\$100,000 - \$60,000 - \text{Bonus})$$
$$\text{Bonus} = .05(\$40,000 - \text{Bonus})$$
$$\text{Bonus} = \$2,000 - .05 \text{ Bonus}$$
$$1.05 \text{ Bonus} = \$2,000$$
$$\text{Bonus} = \$2,000/1.05$$
$$\text{Bonus} = \$1,905$$

Income taxes:

$$\text{Taxes} = .40(\$100,000 - \text{Bonus})$$
$$\text{Taxes} = .40(\$100,000 - \$1,905)$$
$$\text{Taxes} = .40(\$98,095)$$
$$\text{Taxes} = \$39,238$$

Example 3.   Assume now that the bonus is to be paid in the amount of 5% of net income after deducting *both* bonus and taxes. In this case, the amount of the bonus depends on taxes and the amount of taxes depends on the bonus. Two equations, each containing two unknowns (bonus and income taxes), are required to determine the individual amounts of bonus and income taxes:

$$\text{Bonus} = .05(\$100,000 - \text{Bonus} - \text{Income taxes}) \qquad (14\text{--}1)$$
$$\text{Taxes} = .40(\$100,000 - \text{Bonus}) \qquad (14\text{--}2)$$

Substitute Equation (14–2) in Equation (14–1):

$$\text{Bonus} = .05[\$100,000 - \text{Bonus} - .40(\$100,000 - \text{Bonus})]$$
$$\text{Bonus} = .05(\$100,000 - \text{Bonus} - \$40,000 + .40\ \text{Bonus})$$
$$\text{Bonus} = \$5,000 - .05\ \text{Bonus} - \$2,000 + .02\ \text{Bonus}$$
$$1.03\ \text{Bonus} = \$3,000$$
$$\text{Bonus} = \frac{\$3,000}{1.03}$$
$$\text{Bonus} = \$2,913$$
$$\text{Taxes} = .4(\$100,000 - \text{Bonus})$$
$$\text{Taxes} = .4(\$100,000 - \$2,913)$$
$$\text{Taxes} = .4(\$97,087)$$
$$\text{Taxes} = \$38,835$$

Proof:

$$\text{Bonus} = .05(\$100,000 - \text{Bonus} - \text{Taxes})$$
$$\$2,913 = .05(\$100,000) - \$2,913 - \$38,835)$$
$$\$2,913 = .05(\$100,000 - \$41,748)$$
$$\$2,913 = .05(\$58,252)$$
$$\$2,913 = \$2,913$$

Compensation expense and a related liability should be recorded in the amount of the bonus calculated. For the many other types and variations of bonus plans and profit-sharing arrangements accountants are guided by the provisions of those agreements concerning the timing and amount of liabilities and related expenses. Careful study of such agreements is necessary to assure comprehension and proper accounting.

CONTINGENT LIABILITIES

The term **contingent liability** is used to describe a circumstance in which the existence of a liability is uncertain. In many cases, the amount of a contingent liability, if any, also may not be known with precision. A contingent liability is thus distinguishable from an estimated liability. In sum, a contingent liability is uncertain as to its existence and usually its amount. An **estimated liability,** on the other hand, is known to exist but its exact amount is unknown. If an enterprise is relatively certain that a contingent liability exists and if the amount can be reasonably estimated, the contingent liability should be recorded in the financial statements. As such, contingent liabilities represent another area in which estimates of future events are necessary to prepare current financial statements. In fact, the estimates involved in accounting for loss contingencies in accordance with SFAS No. 5 are among the most complex and pervasive in financial accounting. The range of events to which these contingencies relate is extremely broad and may involve matters about which the accountant is largely uninformed. Examples include contingent losses related to environmental pollution, wrongful discharge of employees, the effects of drought on the growth rate and size of plants, and other events far from the accounting and financial reporting issues typically confronted. In a number of these circumstances the accountant will wish to consult experts on the particular issue being considered.

The FASB considered the accounting and reporting issues for many types of contingencies and issued *SFAS No. 5,* which defines a contingency as

> *An existing condition, situation, or set of circumstances involving uncertainty as to possible gain or loss to an enterprise that will ultimately be resolved when one or more future events occur or fail to occur.* [11]

An unsettled lawsuit provides an example of both a **gain contingency** and a **loss contingency.** For the plaintiff (the party that brings suit against another), the possibility of gain exists if the suit is won. To the defendant (the party charged by the plaintiff of some wrongdoing), the suit represents a loss contingency because payment must be made if the plaintiff prevails. Uncertainty exists for both parties until the suit is resolved either in the courts or through a negotiated settlement.

Revenue Realization

Conservatism

Although *SFAS No. 5* recognizes that contingencies may involve either gain or loss, it is concerned exclusively with loss contingencies and simply carries forward the conclusions of *Accounting Research Bulletin No. 50,* which states that "gain contingencies should not be accrued since to do so might recognize revenue prior to its realization."[12] In this chapter we consider loss contingencies. Revenue recognition, including contingent gains, is treated more fully in Chapter 20 (which deals with many unusual problems of determining the timing and amount of revenue to be reported in financial statements). Nevertheless, the role of conservatism is clearly evident in the different accounting treatments accorded gain and loss contingencies. In the following discussion, consider how the modifying convention of conservatism is applied in the specific accounting standards used by our profession in reporting loss contingencies. Also, consider the complex judgments and estimates of future events that underly historic financial statements.

CRITERIA FOR ACCRUING LOSS CONTINGENCIES

Conservatism

Loss contingencies involving either the impairment of an asset or the incurrence of a liability require accrual on the basis of less evidence than is required for recognizing gain contingencies. This practice is consistent with the modifying convention of conservatism found throughout the financial accounting process. The FASB set forth three conditions that, if met, require the accrual of a loss contingency:[13]

1. The likelihood of the future event or events confirming the loss must be **probable;**
2. The amount of the loss must be **reasonably estimable;** and
3. The event giving rise to the loss must have **taken place** by the balance-sheet date.

Thus, a loss must be *probable* of being ultimately sustained, *estimable,* and *timely* to require accrual in the financial statements. A loss contingency that meets each of

---

[11]*FASB Statement of Financial Accounting Standards No. 5,* "Accounting for Contingencies," 1975, par. 1.
[12]*FASB Statement of Financial Accounting Standards No. 5,* par. 17.
[13]*FASB Statement of Financial Accounting Standards No. 5,* par. 8.

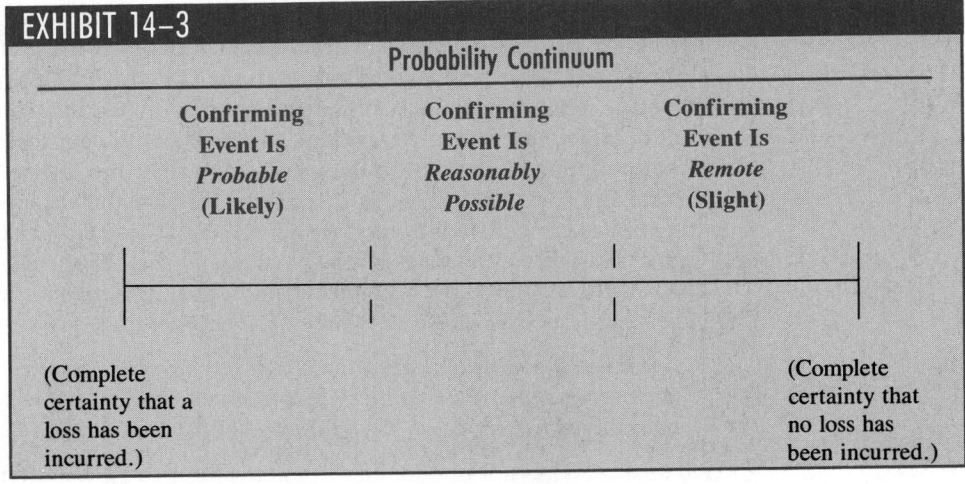

those criteria will also satisfy the conceptual requirements contained in *SFAC No. 6,* "Elements of Financial Statements." According to that concepts statement, liabilities are probable future sacrifices of economic resources arising from present obligations of an enterprise due to past events or transactions. Therefore, when the criteria for accruing a loss contingency according to *SFAS No. 5* are met, then the concepts in *SFAC No. 6* defining a liability are also satisfied.

Probability of Contingent Losses

To help accountants evaluate the likelihood of a future event occurring and, thereby confirming a loss, the FASB defined three conditions of **probability.** These categories represent a continuum ranging from an extreme of almost complete certainty that a loss has been incurred to an extreme of almost complete certainty that no loss has been incurred. Exhibit 14–3 illustrates such a continuum.

The three categories of probability established by *SFAS No. 5* are [14]

1. **Probable.** The future event or events are *likely* to occur.
2. **Reasonably possible.** The chance of the future event or events occurring is *more than remote* but *less than likely.*
3. **Remote.** The chance of the future event or events occurring is *slight.*

The FASB did not assign probability percentages to those categories but relies on the professional judgment of accountants to assess the category of probability in which a particular loss contingency should be placed. Assessing the probability of the outcome of many future events is one of the most demanding aspects of professional accounting.

Estimability of Contingent Losses

SFAS No. 5 also requires accountants to estimate the amount of contingent losses. An FASB interpretation[15] provides that if the estimated amount of a loss contingency is a range of amounts, then the condition of reasonable estimability is met. Therefore, if a loss is probable, if the event giving rise to the loss has occurred by the balance sheet date, and if a range of loss can be estimated, then a loss should be accrued. If one

---

[14] *FASB Statement of Financial Accounting Standards No. 5,* par. 3.
[15] *FASB Interpretation No. 14,* "Reasonable Estimation of the Amount of a Loss: An Interpretation of FASB Statement No. 5," 1976, par. 3.

particular amount in the range represents a superior estimate of the loss ultimately to be incurred, then *that* amount should be accrued. If no specific amount in the range appears to be a better estimate, however, then the *minimum* amount of the range should be selected. This practice represents the least conservative method of applying a fundamentally conservative policy. The amount of the range and the nature of the contingency should both be disclosed in such circumstances.

Conservatism

If the estimability, probability, and timeliness conditions are met then the estimated amount of the loss should be charged against income in the current period and the related asset written down or the related liability recognized. Generally, disclosures of the nature of the contingency and the amount of the loss accrued are necessary.

Disclosure

DISCLOSURE OF LOSS CONTINGENCIES NOT ACCRUED

Disclosure

A loss contingency that is possible, but not probable, must be disclosed even if the loss is not reasonably estimable or if the event giving rise to the loss occurred after the balance sheet date. The disclosure should include the nature of the contingency and an estimate of the loss or a statement that such an estimate is not possible.

Remote Loss Contingencies

The FASB generally does not require the disclosure of remote loss contingencies. Disclosure is not prohibited, however, and if an unusually large potential loss is remotely possible, disclosure of the nature and amount of loss may be desirable. Furthermore, certain types of loss contingencies, including the following, must be disclosed even if the probability of loss is remote: (1) guarantees of the indebtedness of others; (2) guarantees to repurchase receivables; and (3) obligations of commercial banks under certain letters of credit.

General or unspecified business risks, such as a practice of self-insurance for fire or other catastrophe, do not meet the criteria for accrual and no disclosure about them is *required* by *SFAS No. 5*. Two documents issued by the AICPA call into question the rather passive provisions of *SFAS No. 5* in regard to the disclosure of exposure to business risks. *Disclosure Concerning Insurance Coverage* and *Report of the Task Force on Risks and Uncertainties* each recommend that the FASB adopt new standards of disclosure.[16] The recommendations would improve and require certain disclosures when an entity is exposed to various types of risks. According to these AICPA documents, publicly held entities and entities with public accountability such as state and local governments are encouraged but not required to disclose uninsured or underinsured exposure to the following types of risks:

1. *Torts [civil wrongs that may be judicially remedied],*
2. *Theft of, damage to, expropriation of, or destruction of assets,*
3. *Business interruption,*
4. *Errors or omissions,*
5. *Injuries to employees*
6. *Acts of God.*

In addition to the disclosures suggested above, the AICPA documents also recommend that additional disclosure be made about the following aspects and uncertainties of a business enterprise:

---

[16]Task Force on Disclosure of Insurance, *Disclosure Concerning Insurance Coverage* (New York: AICPA, July 1987), pp. 14 and 15. Task Force on Risks and Uncertainties, *Report of the Task Force on Risks and Uncertainties* (New York: AICPA, July 1987), p. 29.

1. *Nature of Operations.* *A description of the kinds of products or services the enterprise sells, its principal markets, and the locations of those markets.*

2. *Basis of Financial Statement Preparation.* *An explanation that the preparation of historical financial information requires the use of management's estimates.*

3. *Certain Significant Estimates.* *A discussion of significant, change-sensitive estimates used by management to measure assets and liabilities at the reporting date. Disclosure would be required for any significant estimate used in the determination of the carrying amount of an asset or a liability at the current reporting date that, based on facts and circumstances existing at that date, is particularly susceptible to changes that could result in material effects on near-term results of operations.*

4. *Current Vulnerability Due to Concentrations.* *Information about current vulnerability to risk due to concentrations—for example, in the enterprise's assets, customers, or suppliers—other than those generally known to be associated with the industry or trade in which the entity operates, would be required in the following circumstances: (a) concentrations existing at the report date make the enterprise vulnerable to the risk of severe impact on near-term cash flows or results of operations and (b) it is at least reasonably possible that the events that could cause the severe impact will occur.* [17]

More recently, the FASB has issued SFAS No. 105, "Disclosure of Information about Financial Instruments with Off-Balance Sheet Risk and Financial Instruments with Concentrations of Credit Risk," which, among other requirements, calls for disclosing concentrations of credit risk. The standard, which is discussed more fully in Chapter 25, requires disclosure of receivables and other financial instruments aggregated according to geographic and industry classifications of debtors. This new FASB standard addresses only a small part of the risks described in the two AICPA documents. Nevertheless, it is significant that information about the risks confronted by reporting entities is beginning to be required as part of the financial statement disclosures.

These two AICPA documents represent the best thoughts of a leading technical group of accountants in the profession. As such, many companies may be expected to follow the recommendations even before the FASB issues additional new standards in the area. In fact, many companies already provide such types of disclosures in their financial statements. A good example of such a disclosure is provided in Exhibit 14–4.

Exhibit 14–5 displays the normal accounting practices for a variety of loss contingencies. While much of the table is easily understood and applied, the problems of accounting for litigation, claims, and assessments in items 7 and 8 are more complex.

Litigation, Claims, and Assessments

Litigation has become an all too common problem for many companies, and when a company is sued certain accounting and reporting implications are evident. If a lawsuit or other claim is lodged against a company and the final outcome is not known when financial statements are issued, then a contingent liability exists and the probability of an unfavorable outcome as well as the amount of the loss, including attor-

---

[17]*Disclosure Concerning Insurance Coverage,* p. 14.

EXHIBIT 14-4

Squibb, Inc.
Disclosure of Insurance Coverage

The Corporation's comprehensive general liability insurance coverage (which includes product liability insurance coverage) with respect to insured events occurring after December 31, 1985, is substantially less than the amount of that insurance available in the recent past. Consequently, the Corporation is now predominantly self-insured. The reduction in insurance coverage reflects trends in the liability insurance field generally and is not unique to the Corporation.

SOURCE: Squibb, Inc., 1985 Annual Report.

ney's fees, must be estimated. Lawyers usually assist in making these estimates. However, the general criteria for accounting and reporting loss contingencies should be applied and, therefore, accountants must also be acquainted with the facts of the litigation.

One special type of loss contingency, referred to as an **unasserted claim,** requires additional analysis. An unasserted claim is a situation involving a **potential claim** or assessment in which the **potential claimant** has not indicated an awareness of a right to proceed with the claim. Examples include violations of tax or customs regulations, pollution of the environment, and a variety of torts (social wrongs) involving possible lawsuits.

Unasserted claims do not require disclosure in the financial statements unless (1) assertion is probable, even if no disclosures are made in those financial statements; and (2) a related loss is at least reasonably possible should the claim be asserted. The rationale underlying these additional criteria for disclosure of unasserted claims is the idea that a company need not "tell on itself." That is, no disclosure regarding an unasserted claim is required unless the claim will *probably* be asserted even if the disclosures were not made in the financial statements. Unasserted claims that are probable of assertion and meet the other criteria for accruing loss contingencies should be recorded as liabilities and related losses.

To illustrate proper accounting and reporting for loss contingencies over a relatively long period of time, a single circumstance covering several years is taken from practice. Exhibit 14-6 is a note that appeared in the annual report of Tony Lama Company. The authors' believe that the accounting illustrated in the following two exhibits provides a classic example of the process by which accountants make these difficult, complex, and uncertain determinations. The "fact" that the amount accrued at the time of the event was later determined to be approximately $2,000,000 less than the actual resulting loss in no way calls into question the propriety of the original accounting. No one can predict the future with great accuracy and accountants are simply charged with exerting professional care when faced with such difficult exercises.

Note that the loss was estimated to be probable, the event giving rise to the loss had occurred, and an estimate of a range of loss was possible. Although the range was extremely large ($510,000–$36,000,000), the company, nevertheless, properly accrued the lower end of the range. Much later, Exhibit 14-7 appeared in *The Wall Street Journal*.

The difference between the amount originally accrued ($510,000) and the total liability ($2,549,487) was properly reflected as an expense at the time of the settlement.

EXHIBIT 14–5

Loss Contingencies

Loss Related To	Usually Should Be Accrued	Should Not Be Accrued	Accrual Depends on Circumstances*
1. Collectibility of receivables.	X		
2. Obligations related to product warranties and product defects.	X		
3. Risk of loss or damage of enterprise property by fire, explosion, or other hazards.		X	
4. General or unspecified business risks.		X	
5. Risk of loss from catastrophes assumed by property and casualty insurance companies, including reinsurance companies.		X	
6. Threat of expropriation of assets.			X
7. Pending or threatened litigation.			X
8. Actual or possible claims and assessments.**			X
9. Guarantees of indebtedness of others.			X
10. Obligations of commercial banks under "standby letters of credit."			X
11. Agreements to repurchase receivables (or the related properties) that have been sold.			X

*Should be accrued when both criteria are met (probable and reasonably estimable).
**Estimated amounts of losses incurred prior to the balance sheet date but settled subsequent thereto should be accrued as of the balance sheet date.

SOURCE: Ernst & Whinney, *Financial Reporting Developments*, "Accounting for Contingencies," August 1975, p. 4.

Evidence About Litigation, Claims, and Assessments

Accountants must collect sufficient competent evidence to support accounting entries. In litigation, claims, and assessments, accountants frequently rely on attorneys to study and evaluate the merits and prospects of individual lawsuits. In fact, lengthy written representations from lawyers are usually requested by accountants attempting to apply *SFAS No. 5* to loss contingencies arising from litigation, claims, and assessments. Lawyers can analzye each lawsuit and comment on the probability of an unfavorable outcome, amount of possible loss, the defendant's proposed course of action, and any other relevant issues. Accountants typically do not have the requisite legal expertise to make such determinations alone and therefore frequently rely on the knowledge and experience of members of the legal profession.

The skill and expertise of accountants is limited to the education, training, and experience they have obtained. Therefore, in many cases, including accounting for a variety of loss contingencies, accountants rely on the judgment and expertise of specialists to provide the basis for financial reporting practices. The use of specialists is

EXHIBIT 14-6

Contingency Disclosure

(10) Contingency

During the year ended July 31, 1976 the U.S. Customs Service instituted an investigation of the duty declarations made by the Company in connection with the importation of footwear parts from Mexico during the period from October 1969 to May 1976. Upon completion of its internal investigation of the customs matter in accordance with guidelines suggested by the Customs Service, the Company, on November 1, 1976, filed with the Service a schedule of applicable costs which reflected unpaid duties aggregating approximately $365,000 and provision was made for this amount in the 1976 consolidated financial statements.

During fiscal 1977 the Customs Service completed its investigation of the Company's duty declarations and the Company was assessed an additional $145,000 for duties lost. This additional deficiency was charged to operations during fiscal 1977 and the aggregate amount of duties lost as determined by the Customs Service was paid by the Company during the year.

In August 1977 the Company pleaded guilty to criminal charges in connection with the duty declarations and subsequently paid a fine of $15,000. In addition, the Customs Service assessed the Company a civil penalty of approximately $36 million, which represents the forfeiture value of the goods imported during the period in question. The Company is preparing its petition for mitigation of the penalty, and normally such penalties are mitigated to a multiple (generally from one to eight) of the alleged loss of revenue ($510,000). The Company has made provision in its 1977 consolidated financial statements for $510,000, the minimum penalty it expects to incur in connection with the customs matter; however, the penalty ultimately assessed may be substantially in excess of this amount. The total ultimate liability to the Company which may result from the customs matter is not presently determinable. Customs penalties normally may be repaid with interest over a period of five years from the date of final adjudication. Such penalties are not deductible for Federal income tax purposes.

thus rather common as accountants attempt to gather evidence to support the many complex and subjective assertions made in the financial statements. Examples of other accounting issues that may be resolved by relying on specialists include the valuation of gems, the assessment of recoverable oil and gas reserves, and estimates of the obsolescence of technologically complex equipment and items of inventory. The key point to remember is that each financial-statement account makes several assertions related to such items as existence, ownership, and valuation. The accountant must be sure that each assertion made by the financial statements is supported by adequate evidence, and sometimes expert opinions of specialists must be obtained.

WARRANTIES AND GUARANTEES

Many companies offer their customers warranties and guarantees of product performance or capability that extend well beyond the time of the sale. Reasonable estimates of the selling company's contingent liability for such commitments are usually possible. The estimated warranty expense and the related liability under the warranty should be recognized at the time of the original sale of the product. If the amount of the liability under the warranty cannot be reasonably estimated, then no expense or liability should be recognized. Revenue from the sale of the item, however, should usually be deferred in such cases until the actual amount of the warranty expense becomes known. In this manner, the matching of revenue and expense is accomplished even if warranty expense is not currently estimable.

Matching

EXHIBIT 14-7

Resolution of Contingency

Tony Lama Co. Agrees To Settle Duties Case By Paying $2,549.487

By a WALL STREET JOURNAL *Staff Reporter*

EL PASO, Texas—Tony Lama Co. said it agreed to settle with the U.S. Customs Service for $2,549,487, instead of the $36 million asked in the case involving duties on leather imported from Mexico.

The company had set up an allowance of $510,000 for a possible penalty in the case, so the agreed payment will cause a $2,039,487 charge against earnings for the fourth quarter. This will cause a deficit in the last quarter but won't cause a loss for the year, a spokesman said. For the nine months, the bootmaker earned $1.7 million, or 96 cents a share.

The payment won't be tax deductible. It will be made over three years, in monthly installments of $81,074 at 9% interest, starting in March.

SOURCE: *Wall Street Journal*, December 20, 1979, p. 31. Reprinted by permission of *Wall Street Journal*, © Dow Jones & Company, Inc., 1979. All rights reserved.

To illustrate, assume that Andrews, Inc., a manufacturer of high-quality kitchen appliances, warrants its products to be "oven safe." Engineering estimates and historical analysis, however, indicate that 1% of all products sold will fail within the warranty period and about one-half of those products will be returned. If sales for Andrews, Inc., are $5,000,000 for 1992 and the company's gross margin on sales is 40%, the following entry is needed to record the estimated warranty expense for 1992:

Dec. 31, 1992 Warranty Expense	15,000	
Estimated Liability		
for Warranties		15,000

The calculations to arrive at that figure are as follows:

$$\text{Amount originally received for returned products} = \$5,000,000 \times .01 \times .5 = \$25,000$$

$$\text{Sales} - \text{Gross margin} = \text{Cost of goods sold}$$

$$\$25,000 - .4(\$25,000) = \text{Cost of goods expected to be returned}$$

Therefore, $15,000 ($25,000 − $10,000) is the amount estimated to be necessary to honor warranties.

If goods costing $2,000 are drawn from inventory on January 15, 1993, to honor warranties, the following entry is appropriate:

Jan. 15, 1993 Estimated Liability for Warranties	2,000	
Inventory		2,000

Even if some of the warranties to sales made in 1992 were honored during 1992, a similar entry is appropriate. Honoring a warranty discharges a liability of the company. The entry to adjust the Warranty Expense account at the end of the year is based on prior experience and estimated remaining warranties to be honored.

In some cases extended warranties are available at added cost when products are purchased. Examples include automobile and appliance warranties that extend

ACCOUNTANTS' MOVE FAVORS AIRLINES

After years of debate, an accounting group yesterday abandoned its plan to propose a new way for airlines to treat frequent-flier miles when calculating their profits. The move is likely to please airline executives, who can report higher earnings under current accounting methods.

The decision came in an 8-to-5 vote, with 2 abstentions, by a committee of the American Institute of Certified Public Accountants.

The development may well be the first piece of good news that the airline industry has received since tensions in the Persian Gulf touched off sharp increases in fuel costs and put a chill on discretionary travel.

"Fantastic," William M. Hawkins, the vice president for finance and taxation for the Air Transport Association, said when reached at home last night. "Of all the things that could have happened, that is one I did not count on."

He predicted that the leading carriers, which his association represents, would welcome the development. "The industry believes its current accounting is correct and is within the parameters of the guidance that exists within good accounting," he said.

By terminating the project, the committee, which is known as the Accounting Standards Executive Committee, not only throws a bone to the airlines, but also averts a showdown with the Financial Accounting Standards Board, a seven-member group that sets standards for the profession and has historically had to approve any of the committee's pronouncements.

The board had indicated that it was unhappy with many of the committee's proposals, which in many cases would have allowed the airlines to continue using the "incremental cost method." That method requires an airline to take a small charge each time it sells a ticket to a frequent flier. The charge, generally no more than a few dollars, represents what the airline would theoretically have to spend on food, fuel and other incidentals to carry the extra passenger.

The board had argued that the incremental cost method might understate the true cost of transporting frequent fliers—especially if they displaced large numbers of paying customers. Though the airlines contend that they have taken steps, like restricting travel on certain flights and dates, to limit their losses, the risk of displacement has grown along with the programs' popularity.

An Alternative Method

For that reason, the board had favored a far more conservative alternative known as the deferred revenue method, which calls for an airline to defer some portion of the revenues it collects from frequent fliers until the travelers claim their free trips.

Although the committee members approved in principle a compromise plan proposed yesterday, the committee apparently felt that the support was too thin to explore it and moved to abandon the whole project.

"I couldn't have predicted what happened, but I think it was probably the right answer under the current circumstances," John L. Kreischer, the committee's chairman, said in an interview shortly after the meeting concluded in Seattle.

Mr. Kreischer said he was alluding to the departure in October of two committee members who supported the compromise as well as to the lingering dispute with the Financial Accounting Standards Board.

Talk of a Showdown

"It's not that we were concerned about facing a showdown and we'd lose," he said. "We felt a showdown would gain nothing for anybody."

He disputed that the committee's decision could be seen as a setback for investors by taking pressure off the airlines to alter their accounting.

"I wouldn't characterize what we did as trying to accommodate industry," he said. "They may be happier short term but they may not like the long-term result if the F.A.S.B. determines it will take some action of its own which it certainly has the right to do."

The institute's committee could reexamine the question on a narrower basis next year, or the standards board could take it up if there is pressure from the Securities and Exchange Commission, which has expressed concern about frequent flier accounting.

J. T. Ball, a representative for the standards board who observes the committee's meetings, said he did not know what action the board would take since the vote was so unexpected.

SOURCE: Alison Leigh Cowan, "Accountants' Move Favors Airlines," *New York Times* (September 13, 1990). Copyright © 1990 by The New York Times Company. Reprinted by permission.

beyond the basic warranty that comes with the product. When extended warranties are sold in connection with products that already have limited warranties, revenues from the sale of the extended warranties generally should be deferred, reported as a liability, and recognized as revenue during the additional expected warranty period.

PREMIUMS

Premiums often are used to enhance product sales. Usually a company acquires an inventory of premium items and offers to "give" them away to customers upon proof that the customer has acquired a certain quantity of the primary product. Accounting for premiums of this nature is illustrated in the following example.

Assume that Suds City Soap Company initiated a premium program whereby the company will sell customers a kitchen utensil at a reduced price upon presentation of ten box tops from its soap product. During the first year of the program Suds acquired 10,000 kitchen utensils at $1 each and sold 750,000 boxes of the soap product at $2.50 per box. The company estimated that 10% of all sales would result in the return of box tops for the utensil. By the end of the year Suds City had received 50,000 box tops and had sent the kitchen utensils to the customers. Assume that customers must send $.60 with each 10 box tops as a reduced purchased price and that shipping and handling costs are $.20 per utensil. The following entries reflect proper accounting for these events.

Inventory of Premiums (10,000 × $1.00)	10,000	
Cash		10,000
(To record acquisition of kitchen utensils.)		
Cash (750,000 × $2.50)	1,875,000	
Sales		1,875,000
(To record sale of soap.)		
Cash (5,000 × $.60)	3,000	
Premium Expense [5,000 × ($1.00 − $.60)]	2,000	
Inventory of Premiums (5,000 × $1.00)		5,000
(To record premiums sent to customers based on box tops received. 50,000 ÷ 10 = 5,000)		
Premium Expense (5,000 × $.20)	1,000	
Cash		1,000
(To record postage expense on premiums mailed.)		
Premium Expense	1,500	
Estimated Liability Under Premium Plan		1,500
(To accrue the estimated premium liability at year end.)		

Calculations for the fifth entry are as follows:

Total sales (in boxes)	750,000
Percent expected to claim premiums	× .10
Total box tops to be received	75,000
Less: Box tops received	(50,000)
Estimated remaining box tops to be received	25,000
	÷ 10
Estimated premiums to be sent	2,500
Cost per premium ($.40 + $.20)	× .60
Remaining liability and expense related to annual sales	$ 1,500

As the 25,000 box tops are subsequently received and utensils shipped, the following entry is necessary:

Cash (2,500 × $.60)	1,500	
Estimated Liability Under Premium Plan (2,500 × $.40)	1,000	
Inventory (2,500 × $1.00)		2,500
(To record premiums sent to customers based on box tops		
received.)		
Estimated Liability Under Premium Plan	500	
Cash (2,500 × $.20)		500
(To record postage expense on premiums mailed.)		

If the original estimate of the liability under the premium plan differs from actual experience, the difference is charged or credited to income during the period in which this fact becomes evident.

COMPENSATED ABSENCES

The compensation of employees often exceeds the amount they are immediately paid for services rendered. For example, companies frequently provide retirement benefits, paid vacations, and sick leave for their employees. Sabbatical leaves are granted to employees such as physicians and college professors. Employees usually earn the right to such **compensated absences** in periods prior to the absence. If conditions described in the following paragraph are met, compensation expense for each accounting period should include the cost to the employer of future absences earned by employees during that period. Because accounting for pension plans and other postretirement benefits is more complex and controversial, Chapter 24 is devoted to that topic. Other types of deferred payments for employee services, however, are clearly in the nature of contingent liabilities, and we discuss some of them in the following paragraphs.

FASB Statement of Financial Accounting Standards No. 43 [18] addresses financial reporting for various programs of employee benefits. According to that pronouncement compensated absences represent a type of contingency, and the recognition criteria contained in *SFAS No. 5* are expanded to encompass the special aspects of those costs. In accordance with *SFAS No. 43,* employers must accrue a liability for employees' compensation for future absences when four separate conditions exist:

1. The employer's obligation is attributable to services **already rendered** by the balance sheet date;
2. The obligation relates to **vested rights** that are not contingent on continued employment or to rights that **accumulate** from period to period even if not taken;
3. Payment of the compensation is **probable;** and
4. The amount is **reasonably estimable.**

Disclosure Disclosure of such contingencies is required when the first three conditions exist but the amount is not reasonably estimable. *SFAS No. 5* requires disclosure of loss contingencies when there is at least a reasonable possibility of loss, regardless of whether the amount of the loss is reasonably estimable. Therefore, we should consider the desirability of disclosing unaccrued compensated-absence obligations for which payment is deemed reasonably possible, whether or not the amount is estimable. That logic parallels the disclosure requirements of *SFAS No. 5.*

---

[18]*FASB Statement of Financial Accounting Standards No. 43,* "Accounting for Compensated Absences," 1980.

The FASB does not require the accrual of sick leave prior to a spell of illness unless the leave is *vested* in the employee. The payment of unvested but accumulated sick leave is contingent on a future illness; because the illness is not a condition existing at the balance sheet date, accrual is not required. However, the wording of this provision regarding sick leave is "permissive," and the accrual of accumulating but nonvesting sick leave for which payment is probable is acceptable. The authors of this text recommend disclosure of the particular accounting policy followed for material amounts of accumulating, but nonvesting, sick leave.

Materiality

Occasionally, a company desires to reorganize its affairs and in doing so encourages various groups of employees to voluntarily leave the firm. The reasons for providing inducements to terminate employment may relate to declining or changing markets, financial failures, or other operating difficulties. Regardless of the reasons, however, accounting issues are evident whenever management offers special termination benefits to encourage employees to leave the company. *SFAS No. 88,* "Employers' Accounting for Settlements and Curtailments of Defined Benefit Pension Plans and for Termination Benefits," provides guidance in such circumstances.

Generally, if an employer offers, for a short-period of time, special termination benefits to employees, an expense and a related liability should be recognized when two conditions are met. Those conditions are

1. It is probable that the employees will accept the offer; and
2. The amount can be reasonably estimated.

If both conditions are met, accountants should record an expense and a related liability in the amount of the present value of the estimated costs. Sometimes, the special termination plan may affect additional benefit programs to which the employees would otherwise be entitled, such as pension benefits and other compensated absence rights. In such cases, the effects of the special termination plan on those other benefit programs should be considered when determining the effects of the termination benefits. In this fashion likely future cash outflows resulting from past events are appropriately estimated and reported in the balance sheet. This assists financial statement users to assess risks and probable future flows of cash.

This book focuses on financial accounting and reporting for businesses operated for profit. Standards of financial accounting and reporting, however, also apply to nonbusiness enterprises. New pronouncements can substantially affect both profit-seeking and not-for-profit organizations. For example, cities frequently adopt very liberal policies on compensated absences to alleviate budget constraints while still providing attractive overall compensation packages. Accruing compensated absences can have a much more significant effect on governmental organizations than on business enterprises.

CONCEPTUAL CONSIDERATIONS

Accounting for many of the current liabilities discussed in this chapter is rather straightforward. Conceptual issues exist, however, that complicate considerably accounting for a number of liabilities. Perhaps the most difficult of these lies in determining proper classification when loan covenants of long-term debt have or may have been violated. In such circumstances, the issues are of exceptional importance and determining whether covenants have been violated may required complex judgments. Further, determining whether a company may be able to cure such violations within a

Conservatism

grace period may involve estimates of future events. Remember that conservatism is an important part of financial accounting especially as related to uncertainties. Conservatism is not, however, an objective of financial accounting and care should be taken not to understate financial statements as well.

Accounting for contingent losses is even more complex. Accountants must identify events, sometimes far afield from accounting processes, that may have impaired assets or caused liabilities to have been incurred and then estimate the outcome of other future events affecting the existence and amount of the contingent losses. It is obvious that considerable knowledge of the business, its exposures to risks of various types, keen intellect, and seasoned judgment are all necessary to work effectively in this perilous area of professional accounting. Due professional care is of utmost importance in these challenging and difficult circumstances.

CONCLUDING REMARKS

Accounting for current and contingent liabilities is an important part of the preparation of financial statements in accordance with generally accepted accounting

Disclosure   principles. The authors' believe that in the future additional disclosures will almost certainly be required about a variety of risks faced by particular business enterprises. We believe these disclosures will be made prior to actual events of loss and will thereby expand considerably the responsibility of professional accountants. The authoritative standards will be involved in these matters for many years and accountants should be prepared to accept these changes when they occur. Indeed, consider how you can increase your awareness of deliberations such as these as your career expands and your own responsibilities increase.

KEY POINTS

1. Financial accounting and reporting for current and contingent liabilities require a good understanding of both the concepts underlying recognition and valuation of liabilities as well as the specific practices required by authoritative bodies. (All objectives)

2. As in other areas of financial reporting, broad and relatively abstract concepts guide accounting practice in the area of liabilities. (Objective 1)

3. An obligation must exhibit three characteristics in order to represent a reportable liability: (1) It must entail a probable future economic sacrifice; (2) it must require a transfer of resources; and (3) it must be the result of a past transaction or event. Not all obligations and commitments of an enterprise are considered reportable liabilities. (Objective 1)

4. A current liability is a liability that will be satisfied with current assets or through the creation of a new current liability, or one due on demand or that will become due on demand during the next period. (Objective 2)

5. Several major categories of current liabilities exist, including:
   a. Trade accounts payable
   b. Notes payable
   c. Dividends payable
   d. Advances from customers
   e. Various liabilities for taxes (e.g., payroll, sales, property, income)
   f. Contingent liabilities
   (Objectives 3 and 5)

6. To exclude a short-term obligation from current liabilities an enterprise must *intend* to refinance the obligation on a noncurrent basis and *demonstrate the ability* to accomplish the refinancing. (Objective 6)

7. A contingent liability is uncertain as to existence and, usually, as to amount. (Objectives 3 and 7)

8. Examples of contingent liabilities include the following:
   a. litigation
   b. inventory obsolescence
   c. collectibility of receivables
   d. warranties
   e. guarantees
   f. compensated absences (Objective 7)

9. For a loss contingency to require accrual it must be probable that a liability has been incurred or an asset impaired by the balance sheet date and the amount of the loss must be reasonably estimable. (Objectives 4 and 7)

10. Loss contingencies that are at least reasonably possible must be disclosed even if the other conditions for accrual are not met. (Objectives 4 and 7)

11. The concept of conservatism suggests that liabilities and loss contingencies be accrued and reported in the financial statements on the basis of less evidence than is required for receivables and gain contingencies. (Objectives 4 and 7)

12. Complex estimates and determinations requiring seasoned professional judgment and great care are frequently encountered in accounting for contingent liabilities.
    (Objectives 1, 2, 3, 4, 5, 7, and 8)

APPENDIX A: LIABILITIES RELATED TO PAYROLL TAXES

The liabilities of various taxes related to payroll are a significant matter for most companies. These taxes are sometimes levied on the employee, and the employer merely withholds amounts from the employees pay and remits those amounts to the appropriate government authority. In other cases, payroll taxes are levied on the employing company based on its payroll. In the following paragraphs we describe the most common and significant payroll-related taxes and the accounting practices for each.

Income tax withholding laws require an employer to withhold an amount from an employee's salary that approximates the federal (and if applicable, state and local) income tax due on those earnings. The withholding requirements pertain only to **employer/employee relationships.** Payments to independent contractors, such as CPAs or attorneys in public practice who prepare tax returns and render other services to businesses, are not subject to the withholding laws since no employer/employee relationship exists.

The amount to be withheld from employee salaries is determined by the government. Employers use tables or formulas supplied by the government to determine the specific amounts to be withheld from individual employees. Withholding amounts vary according to several factors, such as the amount of earnings, the length of the pay period, and the employee's marital status and number of dependents. The employer must remit income tax withholdings at regular intervals, the frequency of which is determined by the total amounts withheld. Income tax withholdings are taxes levied on the employee rather than the employer.

Social Security taxes—also called **Federal Insurance Contribution Act (FICA)** taxes—provide for

old-age and survivor benefits for qualified people and hospitalization insurance through the Medicare program. Social Security taxes are levied on both the employer and the employee. Social Security taxes are stated as a percentage rate to be applied to the "base earnings" of each employee (e.g., 8% of earnings up to $50,000 per year). As a result of the rising costs of operating the Social Security system, the rates and base earnings amounts have been raised frequently in the past; future upward changes are also assured by law. For purposes of this text, we assume Social Security taxes of 8% for both employer and employee on the first $50,000 per year of the employee's base earnings. The increase is determined through the use of a formula that is based primarily on the consumer price index. Employers are required to make periodic remittances of Social Security taxes to the federal government.

The federal unemployment tax (FUTA), instituted by the **Federal Unemployment Tax Act,** is paid by employers to provide for unemployment benefits to individuals who have lost their jobs through no fault of their own. This tax, like Social Security taxes, is expressed as a percentage (e.g., 6.2%) of a base wage (e.g., $7,000) per year. Unlike Social Security taxes, however, FUTA are levied on employers only. A credit of up to 5.4% of the total tax is allowed, however, for contributions made to a qualified state plan. Employers who pay an amount less than 5.4% to a state plan as a reward for low unemployment-compensation claims are, nevertheless, allowed the full 5.4% credit against the total federal tax. As with other employment-related taxes, employers are required to make periodic remittances of FUTA.

A **state unemployment tax (SUTA)** is usually levied only on employers; however, in a few states the tax is levied on employees as well. The greatest distinction between state plans is that most of them allow a merit reduction in the tax rate for favorable employment histories. Under these merit plans enterprises whose former employees have made only a few unemployment claims are rewarded with reduced tax rates for stable employment. Therefore, a company may be paying a rate of only 1% or less while continuing to receive the full 5.4% credit against FUTA.

To illustrate the accounting entries necessary to record various types of payroll taxes, assume that Warder Company payroll for the month ending January 31 is $10,000; Social Security taxes, 8% of the first $50,000 earned by each employee; and unemployment taxes, 6.2% of the first $7,000 of each employee's wages with 5.4% of the total being due to the state and the balance due to the federal government. Federal withholding tax tables reveal that $1,750 is to be withheld for employee income taxes. We should prepare the following entry to record the January payroll:

Jan. 31	Salary Expense	10,000	
	Payroll Tax Expense	1,420	
	Income Tax Withholding Payable		1,750
	FICA (Social Security) Taxes Payable		1,600
	FUTA Payable		80
	SUTA Payable		540
	Cash		7,450
	(To record payment of January payroll.)		

The calculations are as follows:

Taxes Paid by Employer:

FICA $10,000 × .08 = $	800
FUTA $10,000 × .008 =	80
SUTA $10,000 × .054 =	540
(.008 + .054 = .062)	
$ 1,420	

Withheld from Employee:

FICA $10,000 × .08 $	800
Federal income tax (from tables)	1,750
$ 2,550	

Cash Required:

Total payroll	$10,000
Less withholding	2,550
$ 7,450	

Note that FICA taxes are levied on both employer and employee in the same amount ($800) for a total of $1,600. Therefore, $800 of this amount is withheld from employees and the additional $800 represents a payroll tax expense of the employer. FUTA and SUTA are both taxes on the employer in this example and as such represent increases in payroll tax expense. Federal income taxes withheld, however, are not additional payroll tax expenses of employers. They are simply amounts that are withheld from employees' salaries.

Although for simplicity we assumed that only taxes were withheld, **other payroll withholdings** would be recorded as liabilities in a similar fashion. Companies frequently agree to withhold health insurance premiums, union dues, savings-plan deductions, and other amounts from employees' salaries as a convenience to the employee. Such amounts should be accounted for in a fashion similar to any payroll withholding and reported as a liability until remitted to the appropriate agency. Of course, those items are reflected as part of salary expense and do not represent incremental expenses to the employer. In other cases, employers provide "fringe" benefits, such as life and hospitalization insurance; such costs are expenses in addition to the employees' basic salary.

QUESTIONS

14–1 Define the term "liability" and list its three essential characteristics.

14–2 What characteristics distinguish a current from a noncurrent liability?

14–3 What are some of the problems that arise in attempting to value current liabilities? Describe what, in your opinion, is the theoretically preferable valuation amount of liabilities. Do not consider implementation problems in your answer.

14–4 How would each of the following be reported on the balance sheet?
[a] Bank overdraft.
[b] Cash dividend declared.
[c] Dividends in arrears on preferred stock.
[d] Estimates of income taxes payable.
[e] Personal-injury claim pending.
[f] Customer accounts with credit balances.
[g] Deposits received by a public utility for meter installations.
[h] Current portion of a serial bond issue.

[i] Interest on note payable that is deducted from the face amount of the note in determining the net proceeds.

[j] Strike settlement calling for retroactive wage payments.

[k] The obligation at the balance sheet date for vacation time to be taken (and paid) during the coming year.

14–5 In what situations should a short-term note payable be reported on the balance sheet at an amount less than face (maturity) value?

14–6 When, if ever, is it proper to report a short-term obligation as a noncurrent liability?

14–7 If a company pays off a short-term obligation immediately after the balance sheet date and then replenishes the funds used through long-term borrowing, should that short-term debt be classified as a noncurrent liability on the balance sheet? Why?

14–8 Advances from customers are considered to be liabilities, even though they typically will not require a cash payment to customers in the future. Explain how this is consistent with the definition of the term "liability."

14–9 Describe the two methods of accounting for sales tax collection.

14–10 Real estate taxes become a lien on the property owned by Thacker Company on the assessment date in May. Yet the company does not begin to accrue taxes on its books until August, which begins the city's fiscal year. Comment on this practice.

14–11 (Appendix A) What types of liabilities commonly arise in connection with a payroll? Discuss each type briefly, indicating whether the item typically represents an expense of the employer, the employee, or both.

14–12 The sales manager for Acme Company is entitled to a bonus of "10% of company profits." What problems could arise in interpreting this agreement?

14–13 Define the term "contingent liability."

14–14 A company's working capital position can be affected by the existence and evaluation of contingent claims. Explain this statement.

14–15 Give five examples of contingent liabilities. For each type, discuss the desirability and usual practice of disclosure or accrual accorded it in the current period.

14–16 Discuss the reporting methods and techniques frequently employed to disclose contingent liabilities.

14–17 What are unasserted claims and how should they be presented in the financial statements?

14–18 Warranties and premiums may require the recognition of an estimated liability for services or products to be provided in the future. What basic accounting principle explains these accounting procedures? Discuss briefly.

14–19 Under what conditions should compensated absences be recognized as an expense in the period in which the employer earns the right to the future absence?

14–20 If sick leave does not vest in employees, a company is not required to record a liability at the time the employee earns the right to be paid during an absence in the future. Why are compensated absences for sick-pay benefits treated differently from compensated absences for vacations?

14–21 The FASB set forth three conditions that, if met, require the accrual of a loss contingency. Discuss each of them.

EXERCISES

14–22 CASH DISCOUNTS Marina Company purchased equipment on September 5, 1992, with a list price of $150,000 on terms of 2/10, n/30. The company paid the account in full on September 13, 1992.

Instructions

[a] Prepare the general journal entry to record the purchase and the final payment, assuming accounts payable are recorded at their gross amount.

[b] Prepare the general journal entry to record the purchases and the final payment, assuming accounts payable are recorded at an amount net of cash discounts.

14–23 NOTES PAYABLE Hammond Company borrowed $25,000 from the bank in the form of a noninterest-bearing note on August 15, 1992. The note was discounted at 15% and matures in one year. On November 30, 1992, Hammond borrowed $15,000 with interest payable of 12½% per annum, due in six months.

Instructions

Prepare the journal entries to record the above transactions and any December 31, 1992, year-end adjustments.

14–24 NOTES PAYABLE—ALTERNATIVES Willie Manufacturing Company is considering a one-year loan from the Lincoln State Bank. Two alternatives are available: (1) a $17,500, 15% note, issued at face value; and (2) a $17,500, noninterest-bearing note, discounted at 15%. Willie plans to borrow the money on November 1. The end of the company's financial reporting year is December 31.

Instructions

For each alternative, complete the following requirements:

[a] Prepare the general journal entries for the note issued on November 1 and any required adjustment at December 31.
[b] Prepare the financial-statement presentation at December 31.

14–25 DEBT CLASSIFICATION On May 31, 1992, Dryden Company had the following liabilities:

Account	Amount	Description
Accounts Payable	$10,500	Payable in 10–60 days.
Accrued Expenses	7,250	Payable in 10–30 days.
Notes Payable	17,800	$7,800 note payable on July 7, 1992; $10,000 note payable on Aug. 17, 1992.
Bonds Payable	65,000	Payable on May 31, 1999.

On July 7, before the 1992 financial statements were issued, the $7,800 note payable was replaced by an 18-month note for the same amount. The company is considering similar action on the $10,000 note due on August 17, 1992. The 1992 financial statements were issued on July 19, 1992.

Instructions

Prepare the liability presentation for Dryden Company's May 31, 1992, balance sheet, including any required notes.

14–26 DIVIDENDS PAYABLE Priest Company has the following capital stock outstanding at October 31, 1992, the end of the company's fiscal year:

[1] 8% preferred stock, $100 par value, 100,000 shares issued and outstanding.
[2] Common stock, $50 par value, 520,000 shares issued and outstanding.

On October 31, 1992, the board of directors declared the specified preferred dividend and a $2.75 dividend per share on the common stock. These dividends were paid on November 30, 1992.

Instructions

[a] Prepare the general journal entries to record the declaration and payment of these dividends. Use separate liability accounts for the two classes of stock.
[b] Describe the presentation of the dividend liabilities in the October 31, 1992, balance sheets.

14–27 CUSTOMER ADVANCES Laguna Printers produces printed materials to its customers' specifications for orders of $50,000 or more. A 12% advance is required when the order is placed. The balance is due 30 days after delivery of the printed materials.

On May 13, 1992, Laguna Printers received an order totaling $178,500, including the 12% advance. The company delivered the finished products on June 3, 1992, and received final payment, including 4% sales tax, on June 30, 1992.

Instructions

[a] Prepare the general journal entries to record the above events.

[b] Describe briefly the impact of these events on the current liabilities of Laguna Printers.

14–28   SALES TAX   Total amounts received or receivable from sales by Colyer Manufacturing Company in January 1992 were $120,460, including sales tax. Seventy-five percent of the sales are normally on account.

Instructions

Prepare the journal entry to record these data (in whole dollars) for 1992 if the sales tax rate is 4%.

14–29   SALES TAX   Rainbow Company records sales at amounts which include any state and local sales taxes. During April 1992, Rainbow recorded sales of $107,100.

[1] Fifty percent of sales were subject to both 7% state sales tax and a 4% city sales tax.

[2] Forty percent of sales were subject to a 4% city sales tax only.

[3] Ten percent of sales were labor and not subject to any tax.

Instructions

Prepare the entry to record the sales for April 1992.

14–30   PROPERTY TAX   The real estate property taxes paid by Gazette Company for 1991–1992 were $25,000. The city's fiscal year is July 1–June 30 and the company accrues property taxes quarterly over the fiscal period of the city. Gazette makes property improvements during 1992 and the real estate tax bill increases to $30,000. The company protests the increase but pays half of the $30,000 when it receives the tax bill on October 15, 1992. The company is confident it will prevail in its appeal. On March 15, 1993, Gazette is notified that the assessment has been reduced to $28,500. The balance due is paid on April 1, 1993. Annual financial statements are prepared on June 30, 1993.

Instructions

Prepare any journal entries necessary to record the real estate taxes for July 1, 1992, to June 30, 1993. The company prepares quarterly financial statements and makes property tax accruals only when interim or annual financial statements are prepared.

14–31   (Appendix A)   PAYROLL TAX   Stephen Carlson, CPA, has five employees, each paid $300 weekly. The employer is responsible for remitting 16% of the salaries quarterly for Social Security taxes—8% for each of the employee's and employer's contribution. One percent of the base salary, $8,000, is remitted quarterly for federal unemployment insurance. Two and seven-tenths percent of the base salary is remitted quarterly for state unemployment insurance. Weekly federal income tax withholding per person is $70, and weekly state income tax withholding per person is $10.

Instructions

Prepare the entries to record the payment of a weekly salary and the quarterly remittance to the appropriate agencies. Base quarterly computations on 13 weeks, and assume that your computations are for the first quarter of a year.

14–32   BONUS COMPUTATION   Pamela Company provides an incentive compensation plan under which the company president receives a bonus equal to 10% of the company's income in excess of $100,000 before income taxes are deducted but after the bonus is deducted.

Instructions

If income before tax and bonus is $320,000 and the effective tax rate is 40%, what amount should the bonus be?

14-33   BONUS COMPUTATION   Sterling Company's bonus agreement provides that each branch manager receives an annual bonus of 10% of the branch's net income after taxes and bonus. The income tax rate is 40%. Branch manager A received $5,660.

Instructions

Determine the amount of Branch A's income before bonus and income tax.

14–34 BONUS COMPUTATION   Forman Company has an agreement to pay its sales manager a bonus of 6% of the company's earnings. Company income for the year before the bonus and taxes is $110,000. Income taxes are 40% of income after bonus.

Instructions

Compute the bonus in the following independent situations:

[a] Bonus is computed on income before bonus and income tax deductions.
[b] Bonus is computed on income after deduction for bonus but before deduction for income taxes.
[c] Bonus is computed on income before deduction for bonus but after deduction for income taxes.
[d] Bonus is computed on net income after deductions for both bonus and income taxes.

14–35 WARRANTY   Sherman Corporation grants a one-year warranty with each machine it sells. Expenses during the warranty period average $2,500. Sherman sells a machine for $110,000 cash on July 1, 1992. The Product Warranty Expense account is debited at the time of sale.

Instructions

Prepare the entries to record the sale and subsequent payment of $1,870 on October 17, 1992, for service covered by the warranty.

14–36 WARRANTY   In 1992 Pacific Corporation began selling a new line of products with a two-year warranty against defects. Based on past experience, the estimated warranty costs related to dollar sales are first year of warranty, 2%; second year of warranty, 5%. Sales and actual warranty expenditures for 1992 and 1993 are presented below.

	1992	1993
Sales	$500,000	$700,000
Actual warranty expenditures	10,000	30,000

Instructions

Determine the estimated warranty liability at the end of 1992 and 1993.

14–37 PREMIUM LIABILITY   Anaheim Company includes two coupons in each box of corn flakes. Fifteen coupons are needed to receive a free kitchen utensil. In 1992 Anaheim Company purchased 6,500 kitchen utensils at $1.10 each and sold 115,000 boxes of corn flakes. In 1992, 47,325 coupons were redeemed. Management estimates 65% of the coupons will be sent in for redemption.

Instructions

Prepare the general journal entries to record the premium plan for 1992.

14–38 CONTINGENT LIABILITY   Grover Company was named the defendant in a legal action. The plaintiff is asking for $500,000 in damages. The initial judgment called for $220,000 in favor of the plaintiff. Grover attorneys have appealed the case as of December 31, 1992, and expect a reversal due to errors in law and fact in the original judgment.

Instructions

Describe how, if at all, the financial claim resulting from this suit should be recorded on the books and disclosed in the financial statements at the end of 1992.

14–39 CONTINGENT LIABILITY   Riker Company sells football helmets. In 1992 Riker discovered a defect in the helmets which has led to lawsuits that are reasonably estimated to result in losses of $750,000. Based on its own experience and that of similar enterprises, Riker believes that additional lawsuits reasonably estimated to result in losses of $1,500,000 will probably occur, even though the parties that will bring suit are not identifiable at this time.

Instructions

Determine the amount of expense, if any, that should be charged to income in 1992 as a result of this situation.

14–40   GENERAL CURRENT LIABILITIES   The following items represent common liabilities recorded on the books of an ordinary business corporation.

[1] Dividends
[2] Purchase commitments
[3] Purchase of goods on credit

[4] Officers' salaries
[5] Special bonus to employees

Instructions

[a] When should each item be recorded as a liability?
[b] Prepare *pro forma* entries (accounts only) to record these items as liabilities.

14–41   CURRENT PORTION OF LONG-TERM DEBT   Powell Corporation purchased a new home office building on August 1, 1992. To pay for the building, the company secured a $430,000, 12% mortgage to be repaid over 25 years with monthly payments of $4,528.90, payable on the first of each month. Each payment includes interest for the previous month.

Instructions

Determine how this mortgage should be shown in Powell's December 31, 1992, balance sheet, assuming the first payment is made on September 1, 1992.

PROBLEMS

14–42   BALANCE SHEET PRESENTATION   The following information about Millard Company is available at December 31, 1992:

[1] Employee income taxes withheld, $900.
[2] Cash balance at First Federal Bank, $2,500.
[3] Cash overdraft at Farmers Bank, $1,350.
[4] Accounts receivable with credit balance, $2,850.
[5] Estimated expenses of meeting warranties on merchandise previously sold, $3,200.
[6] Estimated damages as a result of unsatisfactory performance on a contract, $1,250.
[7] Accounts payable, $29,750.
[8] Dividends in arrears on preferred stock, $25,000.
[9] Deferred serial bonds of $500,000, issued at par and bearing interest at 10%, payable in semi-annual installments of $50,000, due April 1 and October 1 of each year; the last bond to be paid on October 1, 1999. Interest is also paid semiannually.
[10] Par value of capital stock to be distributed as a result of a stock dividend, $40,000.

Instructions

[a] Prepare the current liability section of the balance sheet for Millard Company on December 31, 1992.
[b] Briefly explain those items that you have *not* included among the current liabilities, citing reasons for their exclusion.

14–43   GENERAL CURRENT LIABILITIES   The following information is available for Lake Company for 1992:

Sales on Account. The total for the year is $201,400 (including sales tax of 6%). Accounts receivable totaling $35,800 remain uncollected at the end of the year. Seventy percent of the sales tax has been remitted by the end of 1992.

Cash Dividend. The sum of $15,000 is declared on December 1, 1992, to be paid in January 1993. Lake's accounting period ends on December 31.

Machinery Purchased. A noninterest-bearing, $34,200 note was issued on December 31, 1992, payable in one year to acquire machinery. (An appropriate interest rate for the note is 14%.)

Note Payable. A $7,500, one-year note was discounted at the bank at 10% on November 2, 1992, to provide cash for current operations.

Instructions

[a] Prepare all general journal entries required to record the information presented above.

[b] Prepare the current liability section of the 1992 balance sheet for the Lake Company, assuming that additional current liabilities are as follows:

Accounts payable	$15,200
Wages payable	10,600
Payroll taxes payable	2,150

14–44 GENERAL CURRENT LIABILITIES Harbor Company, a calendar-year company, was involved in several transactions during 1992 that potentially involved current liabilities. These are described below.

[1] Two purchases of merchandise were made in the last half of December. The first, for $15,500, was made on December 15, subject to terms 2/10, n/30. It has not been paid at year-end. The second, for $18,800, was made on December 28, subject to terms 1/10, n/20. It has not been paid by year-end, but management intends to pay the invoice within the discount period. The company maintains a periodic inventory system and records purchases at the net amount.

[2] On October 16 the company borrowed $10,000 from Ocean State Bank by issuing a $10,000, 14% note, due one year from the date of issuance.

[3] Accrued wages for the last three days of December totaled $12,500 before the following withholdings:

Income tax	$1,560
FICA tax	875

The company must match the amount withheld from employees for FICA tax and remit both portions to the IRS.

[4] Dividends declared on December 31, 1992, payable on January 31, 1993, were $1 per share. The company has 54,250 shares of stock outstanding.

[5] On November 8, 1992, a customer signed an agreement for Harbor to produce certain specialty items to the customer's specifications. The items are currently under construction and are expected to be delivered in January 1993. The total amount of the order is $17,500. The customer paid Harbor a 15% advance on November 8, when the agreement was reached.

Instructions

[a] Prepare the general journal entries to record the transactions described in items 1–5 above through the end of 1992. Include any adjustments that would be necessary at December 31, 1992.

[b] Indicate the impact of each item on the current liability section of the December 31, 1992, balance sheet of Harbor Company.

14–45 MISCELLANEOUS LIABILITIES Arrow, Inc., a publishing company, is preparing its December 31, 1992, financial statements and must determine the proper accounting treatment for each of the following situations:

[1] Arrow sells subscriptions to several magazines for a one-year, two-year, or three-year period. Cash receipts from subscribers are credited to Magazine Subscriptions Collected in Advance. This account had a balance of $2,400,000 at December 31, 1992. Outstanding subscriptions at December 31, 1992, expire as follows:

During 1993	$600,000
During 1994	900,000
During 1995	400,000

[2] On January 2, 1992, Arrow, a large publicly held company, discontinued collision, fire, and theft coverage on its delivery vehicles and became self-insured for these risks. Actual losses of $45,000 during 1992 were charged to delivery expense. The 1991 premium for the discontinued coverage amounted to $100,000. The controller wants to set up a reserve for self-insurance by a debit to delivery expense of $55,000 and a credit to the reserve for self-insurance of $55,000.

[3] A suit for breach of contract seeking damages of $1,500,000 was filed by an author against Arrow on July 1, 1992. The company's legal counsel believes that an unfavorable outcome is probable. A reasonable estimate of the court's award to the plaintiff is between $250,000 and $500,000. No amount within this range is a better estimate of potential damages than any other amount.

[4] During December 1992, a competitor filed suit against Arrow for industrial espionage, claiming $2,000,000 in damages. Management and company counsel believe it is reasonably possible that damages will be awarded to the plaintiff, although the amount cannot be reasonably estimated.

Instructions

Prepare the journal entries for 1–4 at December 31, 1992. If you think that no entry is required, explain your reasoning. Show supporting computations in good form.

14–46 GENERAL CURRENT LIABILITIES Included in Newport Corporation's liability account balances at December 31, 1991 is the following:

Note payable, bank $2,800,000

Transactions during 1992 and other information relating to Newport's liabilities are as follows:

[1] The principal amount of the note payable above is $2,800,000 and bears interest at 15%. The note is dated April 1, 1991 and is payable in four equal annual installments of $700,000 beginning April 1, 1992. The first principal and interest payment was made on April 1, 1992.

[2] On July 1, 1992, Newport issued for $1,774,000 a $2,000,000 face amount note to a wealthy stockholder. The note was dated July 1, 1992 and matures on July 1, 1993. No explicit interest is stated in the note and the entire face amount of the note is payable at the maturity date. Newport uses the straight-line method of amortizing discount on this note because of its short life.

Instructions

[a] Prepare the current liabilities section of Newport's balance sheet at December 31, 1992.

[b] Determine the interest expense to be reported during 1992.   (AICPA adapted)

14–47 WARRANTY LIABILITY Ventana Company, a manufacturer of heavy machinery, grants a four-year warranty on its products. The Estimated Liability for Product Warranty account shows the following transactions for the year:

Opening balance	$ 45,000
Provision (made at interim dates)	20,000
	65,000
Cost of servicing claims	(12,000)
Ending balance (before adjustment)	$ 53,000

A review of unsettled claims and the company's experience indicates that claims have averaged 2% of net sales per year.

The following additional information is available from the company's records at the end of the current year:

Gross sales	$2,040,000
Sales returns and allowances	40,000
Cost of goods sold	1,350,000

Instructions

[a] Prepare any necessary adjusting journal entries, giving effect to the proper accounting treatment of product warranties. Support any entries with clearly detailed computations. The books have not been closed.

[b] Identify the amount of the expense included in the determination of net income and the amount of the liability presented in the balance sheet for warranties.

14–48 WARRANTY LIABILITY   Excel Tube Company manufactures television tubes and sells them with a six-month guarantee under which defective tubes are replaced free of charge. On June 30, 1992, the Liability for Product Warranty account had a balance of $450,000. By December 31, 1992, this amount had been reduced to $50,000 by charges for tubes returned.

Excel has operated for many years and has consistently experienced an 8% return rate. Due to the introduction of new models, the rate increased to 10% on October 1, 1992. It is assumed that no tubes sold during a given month are returned in that month. Each tube is stamped with a date at the time of sale so that the warranty indicates the likely pattern of returns during the six-month period, starting with the month following the sale.

Month Following Sale	Percent of Total Returns Expected During That Month
First	20
Second	30
Third	20
Fourth	10
Fifth	10
Sixth	10
Total	100

For example, for January sales, 20% of the returns are expected in February, 30% in March, and so on.

Gross sales of tubes for the second half of 1992 were

Month	Amount	Month	Amount
July	$3,600,000	October	$2,850,000
August	3,300,000	November	2,000,000
September	4,100,000	December	1,800,000

The company's warranty also covers the payment of freight cost on defective tubes returned and on new tubes sent as replacements. This freight cost is 10% of the sales price of the tubes returned. The manufacturing cost of the tube is roughly 75% of the sales price, and the salvage value of the returned tubes averages 25% of their sales price.

Instructions

[a] Compute the Product Warranty Liability account balance as of December 31, 1992.
[b] Prepare any adjusting entries necessary.

14–49 COUPON LIABILITY   This problem consists of two *independent* parts.

Part 1.   The Nature Food Company distributed coupons to consumers which can be presented to grocers for discounts on some of its products. The grocers are reimbursed when they send Nature the coupons. In Nature's experience, 40% of such coupons are redeemed, and generally, one month elapses between the date a grocer receives a coupon from a consumer and the date Nature receives it. During 1992 Nature issued two separate series of coupons as follows:

Date Issued	Total Value	Amount Disbursed on Redemption as of December 31, 1992
Jan. 1, 1992	$78,000	$22,700
July 1, 1992	93,000	29,900

Instructions

Determine the amount that should appear in the December 31, 1992, balance sheet as a liability for unredeemed coupons. Show all computations.

Part 2.   Harvest Cereals distributes coupons to consumers which can be presented to grocers for discounts on certain cereals, on or before a stated expiration date. The grocers are reimbursed when they send the coupons to Harvest. In the company's experience, 30% of such coupons are redeemed, and on the average, one month elapses between the date a grocer receives a coupon from the buyer and the date Harvest receives it. On May 1, 1992, Harvest issued coupons with a total value of $15,000 and an expiration date of December 31, 1992. As of December 31, 1992, Harvest has disbursed $3,000 to grocers for these coupons.

Instructions

[a] Prepare the general journal entries to record the above transactions.
[b] Briefly explain the error(s) that would exist in the financial statements if Harvest recognized the coupon expense only at the time they disbursed cash to grocers.

14-50 COUPON LIABILITY Aunt Mabel Company manufactures a packaged pancake mix. A free spatula is offered to customers who send in three proofs of purchase. The following data have been accumulated:

	1992	1993
Pancake mix sales ($1.25 per box)	$600,000	$500,000
Number of spatula purchases ($.85 per spatula)	17,000	15,000
Number of spatulas distributed as premiums	16,500	12,750
Spatulas estimated to be distributed in subsequent periods	4,000	2,500
Mailing costs are $.30 per spatula.		

Instructions

[a] Prepare the general journal entries necessary to record sales, premium purchases, redemptions, and year-end adjustments.
[b] Give the account balances that would appear in the income statements and balance sheets for 1992 and 1993.

14-51 TOKEN LIABILITY The Rapid Transit Authority sells tokens good for one bus ride at $.50 each. Sales for 1992 are as follows:

Month	Tokens Sold	Month	Tokens Sold
January	19,500	July	18,000
February	20,000	August	20,500
March	21,000	September	30,000
April	23,000	October	28,000
May	22,000	November	25,000
June	26,000	December	23,500

Past experience has shown that 70% of the tokens are used in the month of sale, 15% in the following month, and 10% in the next. Five percent of tokens are unused and void after six months.

Instructions

[a] Prepare the entries for 1992, assuming a liability account is credited when the tokens are sold.
[b] Prepare the entries for 1992, assuming a revenue account is credited when the tokens are sold.

14-52 GENERAL CURRENT LIABILITIES Little People, Inc., has produced quality children's apparel for over 25 years. The company's fiscal year is from April 1 to March 31. The following information relates to the obligations of Little People as of March 31, 1992:

   Bonds Payable.   The company issued $4,000,000 of 7% bonds on July 1, 1986, at 98, which yielded proceeds of $3,920,000. The bonds will mature on July 1, 1996. Interest is paid semi-annually on July 1 and January 1. Little People uses the straight-line method to amortize the bond discount.

   Notes Payable.   Little People has signed several long-term notes with financial institutions and insurance companies. The maturities of these notes are given below. The total unpaid interest for all of these notes amounts to $90,000 on March 31, 1992.

Due Date	Amount Due
Apr. 1, 1992	$ 100,000
July 1, 1992	200,000
Oct. 1, 1992	100,000
Jan. 1, 1993	200,000
Apr. 1, 1993–Mar. 31, 1994	600,000
Apr. 1, 1994–Mar. 31, 1995	400,000
Apr. 1, 1995–Mar. 31, 1996	400,000
Apr. 1, 1996–Mar. 31, 1997	500,000
Apr. 1, 1997–Mar. 31, 1998	500,000
	$3,000,000

Estimated Warranties. Little People has a one-year product warranty on selected items. The estimated warranty liability on sales made during the 1990–1991 fiscal year and still outstanding as of March 31, 1991, amounted to $55,000. The warranty costs on sales made from April 1, 1991, through March 31, 1992, are estimated at $145,000. The actual warranty costs incurred during the current 1991–1992 fiscal year are as follows:

Warranty claims honored on 1990–1991 sales	$ 55,000
Warranty claims honored on 1991–1992 sales	75,000
	$130,000

Additional Information

[1] **Trade payables.** Accounts payable for supplies, goods, and services purchased on open account amount to $325,000 as of March 31, 1992.

[2] **Payroll related items.** The following outstanding obligations relate to Little People's payroll as of March 31, 1992.

Accrued salaries and wages	$145,000
FICA taxes	15,000
State and federal income taxes withheld from employees	30,000
Other payroll deductions	3,000

[3] **Taxes.** The following taxes are incurred but not due until the next fiscal year:

State and federal income taxes	$250,000
Property taxes	100,000
Sales and use taxes	185,000

[4] **Miscellaneous accruals.** Other accruals not separately classified amount to $50,000 as of March 31, 1992.

[5] **Dividends.** On March 15, 1992, the company's board of directors declared a cash dividend of $.40 per common share and a 10% common stock dividend. Both dividends were to be distributed on April 12, 1992, to the common stockholders of record at the close of business on March 31, 1992. Data regarding Little People's common stock are as follows:

Par value	$5 per share
Number of shares issued and outstanding	2,500,000 shares
Market value of common stock	
Mar. 15, 1992	$22.00 per share
Mar. 31, 1992	$21.50 per share
Apr. 12, 1992	$22.50 per share

Instructions

[a] Prepare the current liability section of the balance sheet for Little People, Inc., as of March 31, 1992, as it should appear in the annual report to stockholders.

[b] If you have excluded any items from the presentation of current liabilities, explain why you have done so.

(CMA adapted)

14–53 CURRENT LIABILITIES—CLASSIFICATION Katella, Inc., is planning to refinance certain short-term obligations on a long-term basis. The company has a December 31 year-end; 1992 financial statements will be published on March 15, 1993. At December 31, 1992, before the reclassification of short-term debt, the liabilities and stockholders' equity sections of the company's balance sheet appear as follows.

Liabilities and Stockholders' Equity

	1992	*1991*
Current liabilities		
Accounts payable	$ 7,000,000	$ 5,000,000
Notes payable to banks	12,000,000	4,000,000
Accrued liabilities	4,000,000	4,500,000
Total current liabilities	23,000,000	13,500,000
Long-term debt	4,000,000	3,000,000
Total liabilities	27,000,000	16,500,000
Stockholders' equity		
Common stock ($1 par value; authorized 4,000,000 shares; issued 2,000,000 shares in 1992 and 1991)	2,000,000	2,000,000
Additional paid-in capital	1,000,000	1,000,000
Retained earnings	6,000,000	5,000,000
Total stockholders' equity	9,000,000	8,000,000
Total liabilities and stockholders' equity	$36,000,000	$24,500,000

The company intends to refinance $9,000,000 of the $12,000,000 notes payable on a long-term basis. Although the entire $12,000,000 is due on June 30, 1993, the bank has informally agreed to extend the maturity date for up to $6,000,000 of this amount to June 30, 1994, if necessary. On January 31, 1993, the company issues 1,000,000 additional shares of the $1 par value common stock for $4,000,000 ($4 per share). After issue costs and underwriting fees, the company's net proceeds from the stock issuance were $3,500,000. On February 15, 1993, the company entered a financing agreement with a financially capable commercial bank, permitting the company to borrow up to $3,000,000 at the bank's prime interest rate. Borrowings, available at the company's options after April 1, 1993, will mature five years after the loan date. The lender can cancel the agreement only if the company's retained earnings drop below $750,000. The company must also maintain compensating balances equal to 10% of the amount borrowed.

Katella, Inc., uses the entire proceeds of the sale of the common stock to retire part of the current notes payable and now intends to draw down the entire available commitment of five-year debt on April 1, 1993. The company plans to refinance the rest of the notes before June 30, 1993, and is currently negotiating with various lenders.

Instructions

[a] Prepare the liabilities and stockholders' equity sections of Katella's comparative balance sheet as of December 31, 1992 and 1991, after any necessary reclassifications based on the above information. The statements are issued on March 15, 1993.

[b] Describe any financial statement disclosures that would be desirable based on the above information.

CASES

14–54 CLASSIFICATION OF LIABILITIES The following items are listed under "liabilities" on the balance sheet of Huntington Industrial Company on December 31, 1992:

Accounts payable	$ 300,000
Notes payable	400,000
Bonds payable	1,040,000

Accounts payable represent obligations to suppliers which were due in January 1993. Notes payable mature during 1993. However, the company expects to refinance the notes. Bonds payable mature on July 1, 1993.

These liabilities must be reported on the balance sheet in accordance with GAAP governing the classification of liabilities as current and noncurrent.

Instructions

[a] What is the general rule for determining whether a liability is classified as current or noncurrent?

[b] Under what conditions may any of Huntington Industrial Company's liabilities be classified as noncurrent? Explain your answer.   (CMA adapted)

14–55   CONTINGENT LIABILITIES—LITIGATION   In May 1992 Burns Company became involved in litigation. As a result, Burns will probably have to pay $1,400,000. In July 1992 a competitor commenced a suit against Burns, alleging violation of antitrust laws and seeking damages of $2,200,000. Burns denies the allegations, and the likelihood of Burns paying or sustaining any damages is remote. In September 1992 Mitchell County brought action against Burns for $1,800,000 for polluting Lake Amboy. It is reasonably possible that Mitchell County will be successful in its vigorous suit; however, the amount of damages Burns will have to pay is not reasonably estimable.

Instructions

[a] What amount, if any, should be accrued by a charge to income in 1992?

[b] Prepare any disclosures that Burns Company should make with respect to the pollution suit.

14–56   CONTINGENT LIABILITIES—LITIGATION   The sole operations of Lawler, Inc., consist of the manufacture and sale of water skis. Several uncertainties surround certain aspects of Lawlers operations for the year ended December 31, 1992. As head of Lawler's accounting department, you must determine the effect of each of these uncertainties on the company's annual financial statements. Of primary concern are the following situations.

[1] During tight turns, the skeg (keel) of the company's top-line slalom ski has a tendency to pop off and skim across the water. In the past year ten people are known to have been hospitalized with head injuries as a result of this defect. Legal counsel believes that while no claims have been made yet, a class action suit will probably be filed soon, and although successful prosecution is unlikely, the company will probably sustain losses of $250,000.

[2] In October 1992 a worker was injured in the manufacturing plant in an accident partially the result of his own negligence. The worker has sued Lawler for $1,000,000. Counsel believes it is reasonably possible that the outcome of the action will be unfavorable and that the settlement would cost the company from $125,000 to $500,000.

Instructions

Discuss the appropriate accounting treatment, including any required disclosures in each circumstance. Provide the basis and logic of your conclusions.

14–57   RECLASSIFICATION OF DEBT   Ebony Corporation has notes payable of $1,500,000 among its liabilities at December 31, 1992. These notes are due as follows:

Due Date	Amount
May 1, 1993	$250,000
Oct. 1, 1993	650,000
Nov. 1, 1993	600,000

The company is considering the appropriate balance sheet classification of the liabilities at December 31, 1992, and has asked your advice.

Instructions

[a] Discuss briefly the conditions that must be met for short-term obligations to be excluded from the current liabilities in the balance sheet.

[b] Under each of the following independent situations, indicate your recommendation for the proper balance-sheet classification of the notes payable.

[1] At March 15, 1993, before the 1992 financial statements are issued, the company is actively seeking opportunities to refinance the total $1,500,000 on a long-term basis.

[2] On March 1, 1993, before the 1992 financial statements are issued, a bank formally commits to refinance the $250,000 short-term note due on May 1, 1993. The bank has indicated its plans to consider Ebony's request to refinance the remainder of its short-term debt on a long-term basis as those obligations come due. The final decision will depend on Ebony's financial situation at the due dates of the short-term obligations.

[3] On February 1, 1993, before the 1992 financial statements are issued, the company issues 500,000 shares of capital stock at $1.25 per share. The funds are to be used to refinance the short-term debt as it comes due during 1993. The company plans another issue of stock before November 1, 1993.

[4] On February 1, 1993, before the 1992 financial statements are issued, the company enters into a long-term agreement with a local bank to refinance its short-term debt on a long-term basis. The agreement provides for refinancing of up to $2,000,000 and requires the company to maintain a $50,000 cash balance with the bank.

[c] Give the definition of a current liability. Why is it logical, in light of this definition, to exclude certain short-term obligations from current liabilities, even though they may come due very soon after the date of the financial statements?

14–58   CONTINGENT LIABILITIES—WARRANTIES   Allison Company sells two types of merchandise, collars and dog house kits. Each carries a one-year warranty. The following is known about each warranty:

[1] Collars—Product warranty costs, based on past experience, will normally be 1% of sales.

[2] Dog house kits—Product warranty costs cannot be reasonably estimated because this is a new product line. However, the chief engineer believes that product warranty costs are likely to be incurred.

Instructions

How should Allison report the estimated product warranty costs for each of the two types of merchandise above? Explain your answer. Do not discuss disclosures that should be made in Allison's financial statements or notes. Be sure to discuss any issues related to revenue recognition in light of the information provided about the warranty programs.   (AICPA adapted)

14–59   CONTINGENT LIABILITIES—VARIOUS   Molly Company is a manufacturer of toys. During the year, the following situations arose:

1. A safety hazard related to one of its toy products was discovered. It is considered probable that liabilities have been incurred. Based on past experience, a reasonable estimate of the amount of loss can be made.

2. One of its small warehouses is located on the bank of a river and could no longer be insured against flood losses. No flood losses have occurred after the date that the insurance became unavailable; however, such losses are highly probable.

3. This year, Molly began promoting a new toy by including a coupon, redeemable for a movie ticket, in each toy's carton. The movie ticket, which cost Molly $2, is purchased in advance and then mailed to the customer when the coupon is received by Molly. Molly estimated, based on past experience, that 60% of the coupons would be redeemed. Forty percent of the coupons were actually redeemed this year, and the remaining 20% of the coupons are expected to be redeemed next year.

Instructions

[a] How should Molly report the safety hazard? Why?

[b] How should Molly report the noninsurable flood risk? Why?

[c] How should Molly account for the toy promotion campaign in this year?

(AICPA adapted)

14–60   CONTINGENT LIABILITIES—LITIGATION   Tamara Company is being sued for $2,000,000 for an injury caused to a visitor as a result of alleged negligence while the individual was touring the Tamara Company plant in March 1993. The suit was filed in July 1993. Tamara's lawyer states that it is probable that Tamara will lose the suit and be found liable for a judgment costing anywhere from $200,000 to $900,000. However, the lawyer states that the most probable judgment is $400,000.

Instructions

[a] How should Tamara report the suit in its 1993 financial statements? Discuss the rationale for your answer. Include in your answer disclosures, if any, that should be made in Tamara's financial statements or notes.

[b] Assume that Tamara Company is a large public company and has decided to allow its insurance coverage to expire for personal injuries to employees, customers, and others such as the visitor in the case. What disclosures, if any, would you recommend in the financial statements of Tamara Company to inform readers of this decision? (AICPA adapted)

JUDGMENT CASES

14–61 ESTIMATING A CONTINGENT LIABILITY American Health Maintenance Organization (AHMO) provides a full range of prepaid health care services to its subscribers. AHMO has approximately 1,000,000 subscribers who are generally enrolled through group plans. In exchange for enrollment fees, usually paid by employers, members and their dependents are entitled to almost unlimited medical care at no additional charge, except for a nominal fee charged for medications.

Although AHMO offers a wide range of health services through its wide network of clinics and hospitals, members must sometimes be referred to other health care providers. In addition, it may be necessary for some outside providers to render extended programs of care for critically ill patients for whom AHMO is not equipped to render care. These outside referrals are often necessary when a member has a specialized medical need which his local AHMO clinic is not equipped to provide. A referral may also be necessary in an emergency situation when a member cannot reach an AHMO clinic on a timely basis. In such cases, the outside provider must verify the referral by calling a 24-hour telephone line to receive a billing code. Granting such a billing code provides authorization for the outside provider to treat the AHMO member and bill the AHMO for its services.

AHMO keeps a record of billing codes granted, including the date of initial care provided by the outsider, membership account number, type of provider and identity of the provider. Billing codes on statements received from outside providers are matched against this record to verify that authorization for service was granted. However, no system exists for identifying billing codes for which services may have been provided and unbilled at any point in time. The amounts corresponding to the unbilled services may be quite significant in relation to the financial statements of AHMO.

Outside providers have varied systems for billing AHMO. Large providers may have reciprocal arrangements with AHMO or they may provide services on a fixed fee basis. Smaller providers may bill secondary health insurance or Medicare initially and then bill AHMO for any remaining amounts unpaid by the other insurers. Some providers may bill AHMO at the same time they bill other insurers and later refund any duplicate or overpayments to AHMO. Some providers may require the patient to pay prior to treatment and reimburse the patient upon receipt of AHMO's payment.

As the controller of AHMO you must determine the appropriate accounting treatment for these incurred but not reported (IBNR) claims against AHMO at the time the year-end financial statements are issued, generally within 45 days after close of the calendar year.

Instructions

Discuss the problems associated with accounting for the IBNR liability at year-end. Develop a method for estimating the liability for IBNR claims, if any, which should be accrued as of year-end. Discuss any contingent liability associated with injuries sustained prior to year end for services which may be performed after year-end by outside providers.

14–62 DISCLOSING UNASSERTED CLAIMS Small Time Company, a limited partnership formed last year, has just realized that the process of its formation violated certain laws and regulations of the Securities and Exchange Commission (SEC). Specifically, interests in the partnership were offered to too many individuals thereby requiring the sale of partnership interests to come under the registration requirements of the SEC. The top management of Small Time was unaware of the limitation on the number of investors contained in the law at the time the partnership was formed and has just been informed of the violation by their legal counsel. They had requested legal counsel to research the propriety of some planned distributions to the limited partners and, in so doing, the attorneys then realized the problems in the formation of the partnership. The primary result of this finding is that it provides the investors in the limited partnership a right of recission; that is, the right to get their investments back from the partnership. In addition, according to the law the partnership is required to file an offering document under the securities laws and to get Small Time registered appropriately.

The president and you, the controller, are attempting to determine the effects of this matter, if any, on the annual financial statements of Small Time. The president, a former practicing CPA, suggests, "This seems like an unasserted claim to me. That is, the investors have not manifested an awareness of their rights to proceed in making a claim for recision of their investment. According to my recollection of *FASB Statement No. 5*, we are not required to disclose such events unless it is already probable that the investors will find out about their rights to proceed notwithstanding any disclosures in our financial statements. Therefore, I say, "Mum's the word!" We'll straighten all this out next year in any event. I was already thinking about forming a new corporation, getting it registered with the SEC, and having all the limited partners contribute their interests in exchange for stock. That way, we can accomplish the same thing as we would with a recision offer without all the alarming aspects of making a recision offer for no real reason but some little legal technicalities. So, I expect you to go ahead with the annual financial statements on a 'business as usual basis' without sounding any unnecessary alarms."

Instructions

What should you do? Be sure to consider the guidance about the disclosure of unasserted claims that is contained in *FASB Statement No. 5*, "Accounting for Contingencies."

14–63 ESTIMATING RETURNS Wall-Nut Manufacturing, Inc., a manufacturer of office equipment, has adopted a program to boost sales by sponsoring a number of limited partnerships that will acquire its equipment and lease that equipment to companies on a temporary basis. Wall-Nut acts as the general partner for the limited partnerships and has the responsibility for marketing the equipment leases to customers. According to the terms of the partnership agreement, Wall-Nut has agreed to repurchase the equipment from the limited partnerships at the end of three years at its then fair value at the option of the individual partners unless Wall-Nut communicates to the partners in writing within 6 months of the original investment that it will not continue to act as the general partner. The president of Wall-Nut has indicated that he expects to act as the general partner throughout the three-year period covered by the agreement.

Although the equipment will be in used condition at the end of three years, Wall-Nut has stated in the offering documents that because the equipment is expected to be "out on rental" at the end of three years, thus providing an income stream, its fair value may well exceed its original cost. A sample calculation was provided that indicated a present value of future rentals at the end of three years that would indeed exceed the original cost of the equipment. The offering document further stated that "fair value is to be determined by independent appraisal." During the past year several of these partnerships have been funded and the equipment "sold" to the partnerships. Most of the individual partners are physicians and other skilled health care professionals.

You are the accountant for Wall-Nut and are attempting to account for the sales of equipment to the partnerships. In particular you are wondering how you should account for the repurchase provision (put option) available to the individual limited partners.

Instructions

Assess the provisions of the investment contracts and the offering documents and develop a method of accounting for the right of the individual partners to return the equipment to Wall-Nut. Be sure to describe all of the factors that you considered in developing your suggested solution.

CHAPTER 15

Long-Term Debt

Most companies rely, at least to some extent, on long-term debt as a method of financing operations. Of course, equity investments contributed by owners are also important sources of long-term financing. The decision to support long-term operational needs, such as the acquisition of property, plant, and equipment, by issuing debt rather than raising funds through equity financing is a complex one and receives substantial attention in finance courses. Generally, companies attempt to secure resources at the lowest possible cost. Thus many combinations of debt and equity financing are commonly encountered in practice.

Here we focus primarily on financial accounting and reporting for several types of long-term debt rather than on the decision to incur debt. The following section considers, among other things, the characteristics that distinguish current liabilities from long-term debt and those that separate debt from equity securities.

As we begin our study of long-term debt, turn to the balance sheet of Strawbridge & Clothier inside the back cover of your text. Notice the large amounts of noncurrent liabilities, particularly long-term debt, included in the liability section. Many of the details of the individual debt issues making up those total amounts are presented in note C to the financial statements included in the appendix at the end of this book. Also, briefly review the statement of earnings inside the front cover of your text and notice the relatively large amount of interest expense included in the determination of net income. Those items are the end result of the accounting process for long-term debt that is described in this chapter.

THE NATURE AND CHARACTERISTICS OF DEBT

DEBT/EQUITY DISTINCTIONS

Although the distinction between debt and equity financing is sometimes hazy, certain distinguishing characteristics are evident. Generally, **debt instruments** contain a maturity date that establishes the time at which the face value of the debt must be repaid to the lender. Financial statement users are thereby informed of future cash outflows that will be necessary without regard to the results of operations or management discretion. Furthermore, debt usually bears interest that must be paid periodically, regardless of the profitability of the borrowing company.

Equity securities, conversely, usually do not have maturity dates and therefore do not require redemption by the issuing company. Dividends are not paid on equity securities except at the discretion of the issuing company's board of directors.

During the last 20 years several "hybrid" securities have been introduced. Corporations have turned to creative financing to secure long-term resources at the lowest possible cost. Many hybrid securities have characteristics of both debt and equity; examples include convertible bonds that are exchangeable for stock at the option of the bondholder, income bonds requiring the payment of interest only if income is earned, and redeemable stock that may require reacquisition at the discretion of the investor.

Substance over Form
As is the case in all areas of accounting, the determination of whether a given financing instrument represents debt or equity is based on substance rather than form. In practice most companies account for a security as debt if it (1) requires the periodic payment of interest, and (2) contains a fixed maturity date (or allows redemption at the discretion of the investor [lender]). Conversely, a security containing neither of these characteristics is generally classified as some type of corporate stockholders' equity. The determination of whether a particular security is debt or equity to the issuing enterprise can, nevertheless, be complex and require substantial judg-

ment. In recognition of the difficulties faced by practitioners in accounting for a variety of financial instruments, the FASB has initiated a project to provide much needed guidance. One part of that project deals with distinguishing between debt and equity instruments. At the time of this writing the FASB has progressed only to the stage of issuing a discussion memorandum.[1] While this project is now only in its infancy, much progress can be expected in the coming years.

Once we have classified a particular security as some type of debt, we must then further classify the item as either current or long-term.

CURRENT AND LONG-TERM DEBT

Although Chapter 14 discussed the characteristics that distinguish between **current liabilities** and **long-term debt,** a brief review is useful. The accounting profession has defined the characteristics of current liabilities while all other debt not containing those attributes is classified as long-term.

Generally, if the satisfaction of a liability is expected to require presently existing working capital, or if a liability is due on demand within one year from the date of the balance sheet, then a current classification is appropriate. Other liabilities not expected to require presently existing working capital for repayment are classified as long-term. Remember that a primary objective of reporting and classifying liabilities is to provide information about the magnitude and timing of future cash outflows. Classifying liabilities as either current or long-term contributes to both reporting objectives. Not all liabilities that mature within one year, however, are expected to require the use of cash that is currently on hand or that is expected to become available through successful operations. Thus, even if a liability matures in the near future, we may consider it noncurrent if resources other than current assets are used to extinguish the debt. For example, a company may have established a sinking fund to retire a bond issue. You will recall that special funds, such as bond-redemption sinking funds, are classified as noncurrent investments. The bonds that will be redeemed with the assets in the sinking fund are classified in a manner consistent with the sinking fund. Therefore, bonds to be retired with sinking fund assets classified as noncurrent are considered noncurrent liabilities, even if the bonds mature in the very near future. Some noncancelable financing agreements may also cause accountants to classify a liability with a current maturity date as a long-term debt.

Certain types of long-term liabilities are considered elsewhere in this book. Specifically, accounting and reporting for lease and pension liabilities are discussed in Chapters 23 and 24, respectively. Contingent liabilities, some of which may be noncurrent, are discussed in Chapter 14. Nevertheless, this chapter discusses a variety of long-term bonds and notes payable. Because accounting and reporting problems associated with bonds and notes are similar, the discussion centers primarily on bonds. Remember, however, that the underlying ideas apply to both notes and bonds payable.

THE NATURE OF BONDS

Bonds represent contracts of debt whereby one party, an **issuer,** borrows funds from an **investor** or lender. Usually many individual bonds, each evidenced by a certificate, are issued and the contractual agreement between the issuer and investors is

---

[1]FASB Discussion Memorandum, "Distinguishing between Liability and Equity Instruments and Accounting for Instruments with Characteristics of Both," 1990.

BAD HANGOVER

Many Firms Find Debt They Piled On in 1980s Is a Cruel Taskmaster

They Now Yearn for Equity As They Slash Expenses, Plead With Bondholders

Little Sympathy From Banks

Even before a recession hits, the financial screws are tightening on many heavily indebted companies. Facing huge interest and principal obligations, they have fallen captive to debt, changing priorities to make ends meet and, increasingly, pressing banks and bondholders for relief.

Western Union, for example, is selling the telex and electronic-mail unit it once counted on as an engine for growth. And Foster Grant filed for Chapter 11 protection against creditors before it could market a new line of fancy sunglasses.

"They bet on the come," says R. Daniel Evans, president of Fitch Investors Service, the bond-rating agency. But, as cash flow slows and financing alternatives evaporate, "One by one we are watching them get in trouble."

Other companies, such as Harcourt Brace Jovanovich, are tightening their belts and considering tougher measures. But they are doing so not because of any immediate problems but because they could face serious difficulties with debt sometime down the road.

Many companies that borrowed heavily during the 1980s, such as Gillette, Kroger and Coca-Cola, remain prosperous, of course—showing that big leverage can be beneficial if all goes according to plan.

But legions of executives who piled on debt in the 1980s, whether to buy out shareholders, pay special dividends to thwart a takeover, or acquire other companies, are realizing their chances of repaying it are slipping away—and could dwindle further in a recession. Already, corporate interest expenses as a percentage of total costs are higher than during any expansion in the past 50 years, says John Lonski, an economist at Moody's Investors Service.

"Companies don't have the luxury in a downturn to hold on to as many workers and undertake as much capital expenditure as before," he adds. The belt tightening "will deepen the unfolding slump" in the economy, he predicts.

Already this year, more than 25 companies, including Southland, Interco, Insilco and Great American Communications, have floated exchange offers to replace nearly $13 billion of high-yield junk bonds, according to Salomon Brothers.

And that's just the beginning. "What's going on now behind the scenes is a lot of companies approaching bondholders at an informal level, horse trading over an eventual restructuring," says Garrett Moran, head of high-yield bonds at Donaldson, Lufkin & Jenrette.

As many as 150 companies will have trouble making interest payments in the next few years, estimates C. Richard Lehmann, president of the Bond Investors Association. Until a few months ago, he was expecting defaults on about $15 billion of junk bonds this year. Now, after a surge in defaults this summer, he anticipates more than $20 billion of junk-bond defaults in 1990 and as much as $69 billion over three years ending in 1992. A default is usually the prelude to an exchange offer for new debt that leaves bondholders with less than they had expected.

The debt crisis at many companies is the impending bill for junk-bond financing in the mid-to-late 1980s that carried deferred or low-interest payments until 1991 and beyond. Called split coupon, zero coupon or payment-in-kind, these securities were designed to give companies several years to get their leveraged houses in order. Forbes magazine recently reported that 200 companies issued about $40 billion of these so-called trigger bonds in the late 1980s. Also looming are so-called sinking-fund principal payments on seven- to 10-year bonds, issued in the mid-1980s and specifying that repayments begin two years before maturity.

Terms of the new exchange offers can indicate the seriousness of the debt problem. The deal offered by Forstmann & Co., for instance, isn't as radical as most. Forstmann, the largest domestic manufacturer of woolen and worsted fabrics for suits, "is a classic example of a good company trapped with too much

contained in another document called a **bond indenture.** Companies generally issue bonds to borrow significant amounts while providing a large number of relatively small debt instruments. For example, a company may borrow $10,000,000 by issuing 10,000 separate $1,000 bonds covered by a single bond indenture. This way the issuing company obtains a large amount of needed capital while allowing many different investors to provide the funds. This system also allows investors (1) to make smaller leverage," says Wilbur Ross, a senior managing director of Rothschild Inc., which is representing the bondholders.

Forstmann took on heavy debt when an investment group acquired the company in December 1988. Soon afterward, higher suit prices caused men and career women to put off purchases. Now, Forstmann's cash flow is barely covering the nearly $15 million annual interest on a $100 million bond issue. So, Forstmann is asking bondholders to accept new securities that will pay no cash but will accrue interest at a higher rate for three years. In addition, the company has cut its payroll to 2,700 from 3,300 and its working-capital needs through tighter inventory control.

Western Union, in contrast, has put on the table an exchange offer smacking of a do-or-die situation. Saying it "cannot bear" the interest burden on more than $500 million of 19¼% and 16% notes, Western Union is asking the note holders to accept a package that includes cash, stock and new bonds with interest rates far lower and deferred for several years. The cash may console note holders dubious about the company's future because it would put nearly a third of the face value of the securities in their pockets now.

Western Union, which has been struggling for years as it got out of one business after another, is now pinning its hopes on growth in its last remaining business, consumer financial services. When Brooke Partners, run by financier Bennett LeBow, took control of Western Union at the end of 1987, the game plan was to revive the company through growth in electronic messaging and financial services. But shortly after Western Union bought ITT's telex operation, telex revenues, which were a big part of electronic messaging, nose-dived.

"The fax business exploded, and we did not foresee the very dramatic falloff in telex revenues this would cause," says Robert J. Amman, Western Union's president.

Western Union revamped its telex communications lines, slashed costs and forged new strategies. But it needed fresh cash to carry out the exchange offer. American Telephone & Telegraph, a budding competitor in electronic messaging, has agreed to pay a hefty $180 million for Western Union's telex operation and EasyLink, its electronic-mail service.

A Future Problem

A third variety of the too-much-leverage problem is illustrated by Harcourt Brace Jovanovich, one of the largest textbook publishers. Although debt payments aren't a problem now, they will be in a few years when the clock runs out and interest on $800 million of deferred-payment bonds has to be paid in cash.

Bondholders began to worry when the sale of the company's theme parks last fall yielded only $1.1 billion, about $500 million less than analysts expected. And three of its five series of bonds are trading at less than 50 cents on the dollar.

John S. Herrington, Harcourt's chairman, says his board is considering its options, including an exchange offer or sale of assets, because "we recognize that unless we do something, it will be impossible to meet those payments." He adds, "There's an advantage to solving your problems early when you are not in a defensive position." If all else fails, cuts in capital spending, amounting to tens of millions of dollars, are "also on the table."

In Harcourt's latest financial report to the government, it said, "The consequences of being highly leveraged are palpable . . . higher interest costs result in a lower investment in products." It added that the debt "could impinge on the company's ability to withstand adverse economic or business conditions."

Beating the wolf to the door is many a company's strategy as it scrambles to raise funds or use whatever cash is available to buy back as many "underwater" bonds as it can. That's what RJR Nabisco plans to do, using new bank loans and extra equity from Kohlberg Kravis Roberts. R. H. Macy also is considering ways to finance a repurchase of bonds now trading at 50 cents on the dollar and less.

SOURCE: Fred R. Bleakley, "Bad Hangover," *Wall Street Journal,* October 9, 1990. Reprinted by permission of the *Wall Street Journal.* © Dow Jones & Company, Inc., 1990. All rights reserved.

investments in a variety of companies, thereby avoiding some risk by diversifying their investments, and (2) to buy or sell additional bonds in the capital market while retaining some or all of their original holdings.

The bond indenture usually requires that an independent fiscal agent, called a **trustee,** protect the interests of both the issuer and the investors. Bond indentures also specify other terms, such as the maturity date, bond amounts (e.g., $1,000 and

$10,000 denominations), any conversion or call features, sinking-fund requirements, other repayment terms, and any other special provisions or restrictions.

TYPES OF BONDS

The goal of the issuing company is to acquire long-term funds at the lowest cost. Because investment policies differ from time to time and from company to company, various provisions are found in bond issues. The following paragraphs discuss some of the most common distinguishing characteristics and types of bonds.

Bonds may be **serial bonds** or **term bonds.** All of the term bonds in a single issue mature on the same date, whereas groups of individual serial bonds mature at various scheduled times in the future. Serial bonds allow the issuing company to retire an entire bond issue in installments. Term bonds, however, normally require the issuing company to establish a sinking or bond-redemption fund to provide adequate money to retire the entire bond issue at one time. We discuss term bonds throughout this chapter and serial bonds in Appendix B.

Bonds may be **registered bonds** or **coupon bonds.** Interest and principal payments on registered bonds are paid only to the owner of the bonds as recorded in the trustee's records. Interest on coupon bonds, also called **bearer bonds,** is paid to the person submitting a detachable interest coupon. In the case of coupon bonds, the company does not maintain a record of who owns the individual bonds at any point in time.

Senior bonds are those with higher claims on a company's assets; **subordinated bonds** or **second-mortgage bonds** are those whose claim on assets is secondary. **Callable bonds** may be retired (reacquired) prior to maturity if the issuing company opts to pay a call premium to bondholders in addition to accrued interest and the face amount of the bond. **Convertible bonds,** on the other hand, may be exchanged for equity securities of the issuing company at the option of the investor.

State and local governments as well as other nonprofit organizations also frequently issue many types of bonds. For example, **revenue bonds** are those whose interest and principal are payable from resources generated by a particular government operation, such as an airport or a public utility. **General obligation bonds,** on the other hand, are secured by the full faith and credit of the issuing unit of government.

More recently, several other types of debt instruments have emerged. For example, "deep-discount" and "zero coupon" interest rate bonds bear little or no stated rate of interest in addition to their face amount. The bonds sell initially at a very great discount so as to provide the investor a competitive rate of return. Investors buy the bonds by paying only a fraction of the maturity amount and buy only the right to the maturity value of the bonds at some distant date. The difference between the amount paid for the bonds and the maturity amount received represents interest expense to the issuing company and interest revenue to the investor. Correctly structured, income taxes may be deferred until the maturity date of the bonds, when the amount invested and related interest are received by the investor in the form of the face amount. The corporation issuing the bonds does not have to make periodic interest payments and that may also be attractive. So called "Junk Bonds" are issued at relatively high rates of interest due to the high credit risk they represent. These bonds were used to effect high risk corporate buyouts during the 1980s and defaults have resulted in much adverse publicity.

Corporations issue many types of bonds and other debt instruments and, consequently, the long-term debt section of the balance sheet is frequently complex. Exhibit 15–1 presents a footnote taken from a recent annual report of Bethlehem Steel Corporation, a leading integrated steel producer in the United States. The total long-term debt amounts of $415,800,000 and $446,600,000 for 1990 and 1989, respectively, reflect a substantial rise in one year and correspond to the long-term debt figures reported on the face of the balance sheet. The Financial Accounting Standards Board (FASB), in its *Statement of Financial Accounting Standards No. 47,* requires certain

Disclosure disclosures concerning long-term debt in the company's financial statements.[2] Those disclosures include the amount of long-term debt maturing in each of the next five years, as presented in the Bethlehem Steel Corporation example in Exhibit 15–1. Such disclosures are particularly helpful to financial statement users attempting to assess a company's expected future cash flows.

ACCOUNTING FOR BONDS PAYABLE

Substantial time is required to plan and execute most bond issues, and many of the terms in a bond indenture are established well in advance of the sale of the bonds. Between the time that bond terms are established and the point of sale, many economic and market conditions—as well as the financial status of the issuing company—may change substantially. Changes in conditions normally affect the desirability of the bonds as investments and cause the market value of the bonds to change.

Investors view bond purchasing as an investment that requires present-value techniques. Basically, a bond may be viewed as a set of future cash flows consisting of (1) the series of interest payments to be received representing an annuity, and (2) a single repayment of principal at the maturity date. The cash received as interest is determined by multiplying the rate of interest stated on the bond times the face or maturity value of the bonds. Once the aggregate amount of both future cash flows has been determined, an investor then calculates the present value of those flows. The investor selects a discount rate that provides a satisfactory return on an investment with the risk characteristics of the company issuing the bonds. The resulting number, which represents the present value of the two types of cash flows provided by the bond, is the price that the investor is willing to pay for the bond.

If the discount rate employed by the investor differs from the rate of interest stated on the bond, then the present value of the bond determined by the investors' discount rate will differ from the face amount of the bond. Of course, in a normal bond issue, the final price to be received for the bonds is set by the market for all bonds rather than merely a single buyer's appropriate discount rate. The market price for all bonds, however, is based on a consideration of alternative investment opportunities as well as the specific characteristics of the issuing company. If the issuer of the bonds receives cash in an amount less than the face amount of the bonds, the bonds are said to be issued at a **discount.** If the issuer receives more than the face amount of the bonds, the bonds are issued at a **premium.** The difference between the selling price and the face amount of the bonds is the premium or discount.

To illustrate a discount, assume the Baycraft Corporation decides to issue bonds with terms as described in Exhibit 15–2. If subsequent to printing the bond indenture but prior to issuance, Baycraft suffers serious financial or operating problems or if the market interest rate for similar investments rises, then the market value of Baycraft bonds will fall as they become a less desirable investment.

Exhibit 15–2 shows that interest will be paid five times in the amount of $900 each time. If we know the rate of interest demanded by investors as an adequate

---

[2]*FASB Statement of Financial Accounting Standards No. 47,* "Disclosure of Long-Term Obligations," 1981.

EXHIBIT 15-1

Bethlehem Steel Corporation
Long-Term Debt Disclosure

Long-term Debt

(dollars in millions)	December 31 1990	1989
Debentures:		
5.40% Due 1992	$ 30.0	$ 36.0
6⅞% Due 1999	18.8	18.8
9% Due 2000	41.3	41.3
8⅜% Due 2001	41.6	41.6
8.45% Due 2005	90.8	90.7
9⅝% Note Due 1991–1997	15.5	17.3
Pollution control and industrial revenue bonds:		
5¼%–8.8%, Due 1991–2002	112.1	124.0
Variable interest at 50%–70% of prime rate, Due 1991–1996	70.3	82.3
Notes of consolidated subsidiaries:		
10%–12.75%, Due 1991–1995	27.0	31.0
Revolving credit agreements	10.0	—
Unamortized debt discount	(2.6)	(2.8)
Amounts due within one year	(39.0)	(33.6)
Total long-term, debt	$415.8	$446.6

Maturities and sinking fund requirements at December 31, 1990 for the next five years were $39.0 million in 1991, $77.3 million in 1992, $20.3 million in 1993, $20.9 million in 1994 and $23.7 million in 1995.

In December 1990, we entered into an agreement with a consortium of Japanese trading companies to provide up to $270 million to finance a major portion of the costs to construct hot-dip coating lines at our Sparrows Point and Burns Harbor plants. We have entered into major equipment supply contracts for these projects and will begin borrowing under this financing in the first quarter of 1991. These loans will be repaid in equal semiannual installments over a seven-year period after construction is complete. Borrowings will be collateralized by the coating lines and incur interest based on the London Interbank Offered Rate. We may elect to convert the interest rate to a fixed rate after construction is completed. A 1/2 of 1% per annum commitment fee is charged on the unused loan commitment. No borrowings were outstanding at December 31, 1990.

return on the bonds, we can then determine the issuance price. The present-value formula (shown below) illustrates how to calculate the issuance price of the bonds in order to yield a 12% rate of interest. Figures are rounded to the nearest dollar.

$$
\begin{aligned}
\text{Present value (PV) of the bonds} &= \text{(PV of interest payments)} + \text{(PV of maturity amount)} \\
&= \text{(PV of 5 payments of \$900 at an annual rate of 12\%)} + \text{(1 payment of \$10,000 at the end of 5 years at an annual rate of 12\%)} \\
&= (3.60478 \times \$900) + (.56743 \times \$10,000) \\
&= \$3,244 + \$5,674 \\
&= \$8,918
\end{aligned}
$$

In September 1990, we entered into a two-year, $100 million unsecured revolving credit agreement with a group of Japanese banks. Borrowings under this agreement are expected to be used primarily in conjunction with the trading companies financing to fund costs to construct the two hot-dip coating lines, but can be used for general corporate purposes. Borrowings outstanding at December 31, 1990 were $10 million, used to fund the capital costs of the coating lines, and incur interest based on the London Interbank Offered Rate. We pay a 3/8 of 1% commitment fee on the unused available credit.

Under our 1987 revolving credit agreement, we may borrow a total of $500 million subject to collateral coverage requirements. The maximum loan amount under this credit agreement will be reduced by one-sixteenth quarterly over four years beginning March 15, 1992. Our accounts receivable and inventories are pledged as collateral for any borrowings and letters of credit under this credit agreement and for certain other debt obligations to participating banks. No borrowings were outstanding at December 31, 1990. Any borrowings would incur interest based on the prime rate, certificate of deposit rates, or London Interbank Offered Rate. We pay a 1/4 of 1% per annum facility fee on the available credit and a 1/8 of 1% commitment fee on the unused available credit.

Bethlehem's revolving credit and trading company loan agreements contain restrictive covenants which require Bethlehem to maintain a minimum tangible net worth. At December 31, 1990 our tangible net worth exceeded the requirement by approximately $1,700 million.

Bethlehem has entered into interest rate swap agreements to fix interest rates on a portion of its floating rate debt. At December 31, 1990, Bethlehem had three interest rate swap agreements outstanding, each having a notional principal amount of $25 million. Two of these agreements were entered into in 1985 at a fixed rate of 11.95%, and mature in February 1992 and January 1995. The third agreement was entered into during 1990 at a fixed rate of 8.69% and matures in 2000 unless the counterparty elects to terminate the agreement in 1995.

During 1988, we retired debt early which resulted in extraordinary gains of $11.4 million.

The investors are willing to pay $8,918 for the Baycraft bonds in order to earn a return of 12% rather than the 9% rate of interest stated on the face of the bonds. The buyers of the bonds will receive repayment of $10,000 on the maturity date in addition to $900 interest per year for the years 1992–1996.

If we assume the interest payment is to be paid semiannually rather than annually, the conversion is not difficult. In this case the annual rate (12%) must be expressed as a semiannual rate (6%), and the five annual compounding periods are changed to ten semiannual compounding periods. The interest annuity is one-half year's interest, $450, rather than $900. The present value of the bonds (rounded to the nearest dollar) can now be determined by the same technique we illustrated:

$$\text{PV of bonds} = (7.36009 \times \$450) + (.55839 \times \$10,000)$$
$$= \$3,312 + \$5,584$$
$$= \$8,896$$

EXHIBIT 15–2

Baycraft Corporation
Bond Terms

Face amount ($1,000 each)	$10,000
Stated interest rate	9%
Annual interest payment date	January 1
Date of bonds	January 1, 1992
Date of maturity	December 31, 1996 1/1/97
Issue costs	$500

In this case interest is assumed to compound more frequently, resulting in a slightly greater amount of interest than in the annual-interest case and, therefore, a slightly smaller present value ($8,896 compared to $8,918).

In this illustration we calculated the price of a bond for which the stated interest rate is less than the rate of return required by investors (market rate), resulting in sale of the bond issue below its face amount (at a discount). If the stated interest rate had been greater than the rate of interest required by investors (market rate), the bond issue would sell at a premium rather than a discount. We illustrate that situation later in the chapter.

Once the selling price of a particular bond issue has been established, that price is typically stated as a percentage of the par or face value of the bonds, such as 98 or 103. For example, if a $10,000,000 face value bond issue sells for 98, the issuer of the bonds receives $9,800,000 ($10,000,000 × 98%), and the bonds are sold at a discount of $200,000. If the $10,000,000 bonds sell for 103, the issuer of the bonds receives $10,300,000 ($10,000,000 × 103%), and the bonds are sold at a premium of $300,000.

ISSUANCE OF BONDS

Issue Costs

Costs are usually incurred in preparing and marketing a bond issue such as legal and accounting fees, broker commissions, printing and engraving costs, registration fees, and promotional costs. Such issue costs are recorded as deferred charges, reported in the assets section of the balance sheet, and amortized over the life of the related debt. Issue costs are recorded as separate assets, because they are not related to the market rate of interest implicit in the bond issue. As discussed both here and earlier in Chapter 10, premium or discount results from differences between the rate of interest stated on the bonds and the effective rate of interest that exists when the bonds are sold. We discuss the conceptual and practical accounting issues related to premium and discount more extensively later in this chapter. Accountants usually amortize issue costs by the straight-line method, although other methods are satisfactory and are occasionally encountered in practice.

A Simplified Example

The terms of bond issues generally provide (1) a long period to maturity, (2) an interest rate to be paid, and (3) other terms of the issue. The amount of consideration received when the bonds are issued provides the basis for accounting entries. To illustrate accounting for bonds payable, we continue the example of the Baycraft Corporation. Assume, however, that interest is payable semiannually on January 1 and July 1.

If Baycraft sells its bonds on January 1, 1992, at their face amount, the following entries are necessary during 1992 and at the beginning of 1993.

Jan. 1, 1992	Cash	10,000	
	Bonds Payable		10,000
	(To record sale of bonds at face amount.)		
Jan. 1, 1992	Deferred Bond-Issue Costs	500	
	Cash		500
	(To record issue costs.)		
July 1, 1992	Interest Expense	450	
	Cash		450
	(To record semiannual payment of interest. $10,000 \times .09 \times \frac{1}{2} = \$450$.)		
Dec. 31, 1992	Interest Expense	450	
	Interest Payable		450
	(To accrue interest for second half of 1992, payable on January 1, 1993.)		
Dec. 31, 1992	Issue Cost Expense	100	
	Deferred Bond-Issue Costs		100
	(To amortize issue costs. $\$500 \div 5 = \$100$.)		
Jan. 1, 1993	Interest Payable	450	
	Cash		450
	(To pay interest accrued on December 31, 1992.)		

In this case the process of recognizing interest expense and the amortization of issue costs continues each year until maturity when the retirement of the bonds is accounted for by the following entry:

Dec. 31, 1996	Bonds Payable	10,000	
	Cash		10,000
	(To account for retirement of bonds.)		

COMPLICATING FACTORS IN ACCOUNTING FOR BONDS

The previous example reflects accounting under simplified conditions. The following section illustrates several realistic circumstances that complicate financial accounting and reporting for bonds payable. Many of those problems have counterparts in Chapter 10 with respect to investments in the bonds of other corporations. A brief review is provided, however, because there are some differences between accounting for investment in bonds and accounting for the issuance of bonds. Also, certain aspects of accounting for bonds relate exclusively to the liability of issuing companies.

Issuance Between Interest-Payment Dates

Bonds are frequently issued at a point after the date printed on the bonds and between interest-payment dates. Interest begins to accrue on the date of the bonds, however, even if the bonds have not been issued. Of course, if the bonds are never issued no accounting entries or interest payments are made. For example, assume that the Baycraft Corporation issues the bonds described in Exhibit 15–2 on May 1, 1992, at

"100" (100% of face amount) plus accrued interest. We continue our assumption that interest is paid semiannually on January 1 and July 1.

The following entry and supporting calculations are required:

May 1, 1992	Cash	10,300	
	Interest Expense		300
	Bonds Payable		10,000

(To record issuance of bonds @ 100 plus accrued interest. $10,000 issuance price of bonds + $300: [$10,000 × .09 × 4/12 = accrued interest].)

Interest Expense is credited for the amount of accrued interest *received* by the *issuer* at the issuance of the bonds. Although Interest Payable could just as easily have been credited, the entry as made is logical, because on July 1, 1992, when the first semiannual interest payment is made, interest for only two months (May and June) will be reflected as an expense of the Baycraft Corporation. The following entry and T-account analysis illustrates this procedure:

July 1, 1992	Interest Expense	450	
	Cash		450

(To pay semiannual interest. $10,000 × .09 × 1/2 = $450.)

Interest Expense

1992			1992		
July 1	Payment of interest	450	May 1	Receipt of accrued interest upon issuance of bonds	300
July 1	Interest expense for six months ended July 1, 1992	150			

If the $300 for accrued interest is credited to Interest Payable at the date of issuance, Interest Payable must be debited for $300 and Interest Expense must be debited for $150 when the $450 interest is paid on July 1, 1992.

Recognition of Accrued Interest

Another complication arises if the interest-payment date does not coincide with the company's year-end. Interest payable and interest expense must be accrued in order Matching to apply the matching principle. The entry to record the accrued but unpaid interest expense at December 31, 1992, and related calculation appears below:

Dec. 31, 1992	Interest Expense	450	
	Interest Payable		450

(To accrue interest expense payable on January 1, 1993. $10,000 × .09 × 1/2 = $450.)

Because interest for the entire six months is payable on the following day (January 1), that entire amount is accrued. Lesser amounts are accrued if the payment date is more distant than the following day. For example, if interest is payable on February 1 and August 1, then only five months of interest would be accrued at December 31.

Accounting Subsequent to Issuance

Chapter 10 notes that premium or discount on bonds is treated, respectively, as a direct addition to or deduction from the face amount of the bonds. In the Baycraft Corporation example in which bonds payable are issued at an effective interest rate of 12%, the issue price is $8,918 with a related discount of $1,082 ($10,000 − $8,918). This illustration is based on the original assumption of annual interest payments. Thus, immediately following the bond issuance on January 1, 1992, the liability for the bonds is presented in the Baycraft balance sheet at $8,918. Because that amount represents the present value of the future cash flows—both interest and principal—on the date of issuance, the requirements of *Accounting Principles Board Opinion No. 21* are satisfied.[3] That pronouncement requires most receivables and payables to be recorded at their present value when issued. The amounts so reported and maturity

Disclosure disclosures provide investors and creditors with useful information about future cash outflows required by the bonds and the present value of those amounts.

Amortization: The Effective Interest Method. The discount that emerges as a result of a difference between the rate of interest stated on the bonds (9%) and the market rate of interest (12%) is amortized as an increase of reported interest expense over the life of the bonds. For example, during 1992 the following entries are required:

Jan. 1, 1992	Cash	8,918	
	Discount on Bonds Payable	1,082	
	Bonds Payable		10,000
	(To record issuance of Bonds.)		
Dec. 31, 1992	Interest Expense	900	
	Interest Payable		900
	(To accrue annual interest payable at Dec. 31, 1992.)		
Dec. 31, 1992	Interest Expense	170	
	Discount on Bonds Payable		170
	(To record amortization of discount.)		

The discount is computed as follows:

Carrying amount of bonds @ Jan. 1, 1992	$8,918
Effective rate of interest expense	.12
Total annual interest expense (rounded)	1,070
Less: Interest expense recognized with Dec. 31, 1992, interest accrual	900
Amortization—1992	$ 170

The calculation demonstrates the manner in which we can determine the amount of discount or premium to be amortized. In practice accountants, usually aided by a computer, prepare amortization tables to facilitate recording the amortization of any premium or discount related to the bonds. Such a table is presented in Exhibit 15–3 for the Baycraft Corporation.

This process of amortization continues each year until the Discount on Bonds Payable account is fully amortized at the maturity date of the bonds. If the bonds are issued subsequent to the original date printed on the face of the bonds (as discussed earlier), any premium or discount is amortized over the remaining life of the bonds *beginning at the date of issuance and continuing to the maturity date*. The

---

[3]*APB Opinion No. 21*, "Interest on Receivables and Payables," 1971.

EXHIBIT 15-3

Baycraft Corporation
Amortization of Bond Discount
Effective Interest Method
(amounts rounded to the nearest dollar)

Date	(1) Interest Expense	(2) Cash Paid	(3) Discount Amortization	(4) Par Value Outstanding	(5) Unamortized Discount	(6) Carrying Value
Jan. 1, 1992	—	—	—	$10,000	$1,082	$ 8,918
Dec. 31, 1992	$1,070	$ 900	$ 170	10,000	912	9,088
Dec. 31, 1993	1,091	900	191	10,000	721	9,279
Dec. 31, 1994	1,113	900	213	10,000	508	9,492
Dec. 31, 1995	1,139	900	239	10,000	269	9,731
Dec. 31, 1996	1,169*	900	269	10,000	—	10,000
	$5,582	$4,500	$1,082			

(1) (Previous year Column 6) × 12%
(2) ($10,000 par value) × 9%
(3) (Column 1) − (Column 2)
(4) $10,000 par value
(5) (Previous year Column 5) − (Current year Column 3)
(6) (Column 4) − (Column 5)

*Adjusted for rounding difference.

amortization of premium or discount in such situations does not present any significant additional problems and is treated routinely. That is, the premium or discount is amortized over the life of the debt by the **effective interest method** (also called **compound interest method** or simply **interest method**) of amortization.

The total interest expense each year is computed by multiplying the effective rate of interest (12% in the Baycraft example) by the carrying amount of the liability at the beginning of each year. The total interest expense computed in that manner is then compared to the interest that has been paid or accrued on the bonds in accordance with the bond indenture. The difference between the amount of interest paid or payable during the year and the total interest expense to be recognized represents the discount or premium to be amortized. Remaining unamortized discount continues to be classified as a reduction from the par value of the bonds payable to determine their carrying amount in the company's balance sheet.

The carrying amount of the bonds increases each year as the discount is amortized to interest expense until, at the maturity date of the bonds, the discount is fully amortized. At that time the carrying amount of the bonds is their face amount. Therefore, when the bonds are retired at maturity no gain or loss arises, because the cash required to retire the bonds is equal to the carrying amount of the bonds at that time.

Amortization: The Straight-Line Method.   Although the effective interest method of discount amortization is required by *APB Opinion No. 21* because it recognizes a constant rate of interest on the bonds payable over the life of the bonds, other methods of amortization are occasionally encountered in practice. These alternative procedures are acceptable only if their results do not differ materially from the results of the effective interest method. Because the differences resulting from each method of amortization are frequently immaterial, the **straight-line method** of amortization is

Materiality

sometimes used in practice. The amount of discount or premium recognized at the issuance of the bonds is divided by the number of years the bonds are outstanding. The resulting amount is amortized each year in the same fashion as described here.

Bonds Issued at a Premium. Companies frequently issue bonds at amounts exceeding the face value of the bonds. We refer to the excess of the price received over the face amount of the bonds as **premium.** Premium, like discount, also represents an adjustment to the stated rate of interest expense on the bonds. In essence, premium exists if the interest rate stated on the bonds is *higher* than the interest rate required by the market for similar securities. Investors are, thus, willing to pay more than the face amount of the bonds. Accounting for premium mirrors the procedures we employed in reporting discount.

To illustrate premium, assume that the Baycraft bonds sell on January 1, 1992, at an effective interest rate of 6% with interest being paid semiannually at January 1 and July 1 each year. The total amount received for the bonds is $11,280 (rounded to the nearest dollar), determined as follows:

$$
\begin{aligned}
\text{PV of bonds} &= \text{(PV of interest payments)} + \\
&\quad \text{(PV of maturity)} \\
&= (\$450 \text{ for 10 six-month periods} \\
&\quad \text{at 6\% annual interest}) + (\$10,000 \\
&\quad \text{at 6\% annual interest}) \\
&= (\$450 \times 8.53020) + (\$10,000 \times .74409) \\
&= \$3,839 + \$7,441 \\
&= \$11,280
\end{aligned}
$$

The present-value factor for the interest payments, 8.53020, is the present value of an annuity at *3% for 10 periods,* because interest is paid semiannually. The present-value factor for the maturity value of the bonds, .74409, is the present value of one at 3% for 10 periods. These values are taken from Table 6–4 and Table 6–2, respectively.

The entry to record the issuance follows:

Jan. 1, 1992	Cash	11,280	
	Bonds Payable		10,000
	Premium on Bonds Payable		1,280

The following entry records the first interest payment and amortizes six months of premium (rounded to the nearest dollar) by using the effective interest method:

July 1, 1992	Interest Expense	450	
	Cash		450
	($10,000 × .09 × ½ = $450)		
July 1, 1992	Premium on Bonds Payable	112	
	Interest Expense		112
	($11,280 × .06 × ½ = $338;		
	$450 − $338 = $112)		

The credit to interest expense resulting from amortizing the premium reduces reported interest expense to 6% (the effective rate) of the carrying value of the bonds ($11,280). The carrying value of the bonds during the second six-month period declines from $11,280 by the amount of the premium amortized ($112) to $11,168. Total interest expense for the second six-month period becomes $335

($11,168 × .06 × ½). The premium amortized during the last half of 1992 is the difference between the cash paid ($450) and the total interest expense to be reported ($335), or $115.

The process of amortization continues each six-month period until the bonds mature and the premium has been fully amortized. An amortization table similar to the one presented for discount in Exhibit 15–3 may be useful in accounting for the premium over the entire life of the bonds. Such a table is presented in Exhibit 15–4. The amortization of the premium *reduces* interest expense below the $450 *cash paid* rather than increasing interest expense, as was the case in the discount example.

Materiality   As in the discount case, practitioners frequently use the straight-line method of amortizing premium rather than the more complex, but theoretically superior, effective interest method. As before, if material differences do not result from the straight-line method, there is little objection to its use. But *APB Opinion No. 21* requires the use of the effective interest method if material differences result from other methods.

Retirement of Bonds.   Normally, bonds are retired at maturity, and any premium or discount is amortized over the life of the bonds. Therefore, because the carrying amount of the bonds at their maturity represents the amount of cash required to retire them, no gain or loss on the retirement of bonds at maturity is usually recognized.

If the bonds are retired early, however, recognition of gain or loss is frequently necessary because the carrying amount of the debt, including unamortized premium

---

EXHIBIT 15–4

Baycraft Corporation
Amortization of Bond Premium
Effective Interest Method
(amounts rounded to the nearest dollar)

Date	(1) Interest Expense	(2) Cash Paid	(3) Premium Amortization	(4) Par Value Outstanding	(5) Unamortized Premium	(6) Carrying Value
Jan. 1, 1992	—	—	—	$10,000	$1,280	$11,280
July 1, 1992	$ 338	450	$ (112)	10,000	1,168	11,168
Dec. 31, 1992	335	450	(115)	10,000	1,053	11,053
July 1, 1993	332	450	(118)	10,000	935	10,935
Dec. 31, 1993	328	450	(122)	10,000	813	10,813
July 1, 1994	324	450	(126)	10,000	687	10,687
Dec. 31, 1994	321	450	(129)	10,000	558	10,558
July 1, 1995	317	450	(133)	10,000	425	10,425
Dec. 31, 1995	313	450	(137)	10,000	288	10,288
July 1, 1996	309	450	(141)	10,000	147	10,147
Dec. 31, 1996	303*	450	(147)	10,000	—	10,000
	$3,220	$4,500	$(1,280)			

(1) (Previous period Column 6) × (6% × ½)
(2) ($10,000 par value) × (9% × ½)
(3) (Column 1) − (Column 2)
(4) $10,000 par value
(5) (Previous period Column 5) − (Current period Column 3)
(6) (Column 4) + (Column 5)

*Adjusted for rounding difference.

or discount and issue costs, differs from the amount paid to accomplish the early retirement. The reasons that a company might reacquire its own debt prior to maturity are numerous. For instance, if management thinks interest rates are likely to drop in the near future, the reacquisition of bonds paying a relatively high rate of interest might be prudent. Once the interest rates drop, the market would place a premium on existing instruments bearing higher interest rates and the company would be required to pay the premium to reacquire its own bonds in an open-market purchase.

There are several ways for a company to retire its debt without actually repaying it. *SFAS No. 76,* "Extinguishment of Debt," provides that debt should be considered extinguished in two circumstances other than those in which the debtor repays the creditor and is relieved of all obligations under the debt. The first situation arises when the debtor is legally released from being the primary obligor under the debt, and it is probable that the debtor will not make future cash payments under the debt. For example, property that is subject to a mortgage may be sold and the related debt may be assumed by the buyer, thereby relieving the original debtor of all responsibilities under the debt instrument. This situation arises in real estate lending because mortgages are sometimes nonrecourse other than to the property securing the loan.

Another way that debt may be extinguished requires the debtor to establish an irrevocable trust for the retirement of the debt. The assets in the trust must be U.S. government securities or securities backed by the U.S. government. Such monetary securities are virtually risk free as to the amount and timing of repayment. The future cash flows from the securities must be adequate and timely to service the debt for which the trust was created. When such a trust exists, the related debt is considered "retired," and the debt is removed from the balance sheet along with the assets in the trust fund. This type of arrangement is called an **in-substance defeasance** of debt.

The accounting profession has considered the problems with reporting extinguishments of debt and issued a series of related pronouncements. The first of these pronouncements, *APB Opinion No. 26,*[4] evaluates how any difference (differential) between the retirement cost of a debt and the carrying amount of the debt at the time of the extinguishment should be treated. Prior to *Opinion No. 26* several methods of accounting for this difference were used. For example, the differential arising from the extinguishment of debt was frequently amortized over the life of the new debt. Some companies amortized the differential over the original life of the debt just extinguished; they maintained that a difference between the carrying amount of the debt and the reacquisition price of the debt was a cost (or benefit) that was incurred to avoid future interest costs. Those companies contended that the differential should be allocated to the future periods affected by the decision to retire the debt. Such alternatives are now unacceptable. Specifically, *Opinion No. 26* states:

> *A difference between the reacquisition price (of the debt) and the net carrying amount of the extinguished debt should be recognized currently in income of the period of the extinguishment as losses or gains.*[5]

Some accountants disagreed strongly with the position of the APB. Others felt that the rule could, in some circumstances, cause the financial statements to appear misleading. As presented in Exhibit 15–5, Aeronca, Inc. (manufacturers of aircraft

---

[4]*APB Opinion No. 26,* "[Early] Extinguishment of Debt," 1972. ("Early" is in brackets because FASB amendments increased the scope of *APB Opinion No. 26* to include extinguishments other than those taking place before the scheduled maturity of the debt.)
[5]*APB Opinion No. 26,* par. 20.

EXHIBIT 15–5

Aeronca, Inc.
Extinguishment of Debt

Notes to Financial Statements
Note 1–Summary of Accounting Policies:

• • • •

Extinguishment of Debt: In October, 1973, the Company issued 50,000 shares of 6% Prior Preferred Shares, par value $100, in exchange for the outstanding $5,000,000 of 6% Senior Subordinated Notes. It also issued 18,040 shares of convertible $6 Serial Preference Shares, Series A, stated value $100 a share, in exchange for $1,300,000 and $504,000 of outstanding 6% convertible subordinated debentures and 5¾% convertible subordinated debentures, respectively. The Company expensed the unamortized balance (approximately $148,000) of the deferred financing costs associated with the issuance of each of the three classes of subordinated debt to the extent that such unamortized balances were allocable to the debt so extinguished.

Opinion No. 26 of the Accounting Principles Board of the American Institute of CPA's states that the excess of the carrying amount of the extinguished debt over the present value of the new securities issued should be recognized as a gain in the statement of operations of the period in which the extinguishment occurred. While it is not practicable to determine the present value of the new equity securities issued, such value is at least $2,000,000 less than the face amount of the debt extinguished. However, the terms and provisions of these new equity securities are substantially similar to those of the debt securities extinguished, both on the basis of the Company's continuing operations and in the event of liquidation. It is the opinion of the management, therefore, that no gain as a result of this exchange has been realized or should be recognized in the financial statements.

SOURCE: Aeronca, Inc., 1973 Annual Report.

and aerospace structures, jet aircraft, engine components, and environmental and air-control systems) departed from the requirements of *APB Opinion No. 26*. Aeronca, Inc., elected to record the difference between the carrying amount of the extinguished bonds and the value of the preferred stock issued to reacquire the bonds as additional paid-in capital rather than as a gain recognized in income. The company contended that reporting a gain in the circumstances described would have caused their financial statements to be misleading.

Following the issuance of *APB Opinion No. 26,* gains or losses from the extinguishment of debt were included in income *before* extraordinary items during the period of the extinguishment, because such items generally were not considered both unusual in nature and infrequent in occurrence. The potential materiality of those gains and losses in addition to the ability of a company to control the timing of their recognition caused concern in the business community. In essence, company managements could directly, and frequently in an arbitrary fashion, influence reported earnings through debt-retirement activities. In extreme cases (such as described in Exhibit 15–5) the results reported for a debt extinguishment seemed to defy economic realities.

Materiality

Responding to those criticisms, the FASB issued *Statement of Financial Accounting Standards No. 4,* which specified precisely the reporting requirements for such items:

Materiality

Gains and losses from extinguishment of debt that are included in the determination of net income shall be aggregated and, if material, classified as an extraordinary item.[6]

One exception to the FASB rule relates to cash purchases of debt made within one year of a sinking-fund requirement that an enterprise must meet.[7] For example, a typical bond indenture may specify that at December 31, 1992, a sinking fund to retire an issue of bonds must represent at least 50% of the face amount of the bonds outstanding. If a company retires some of its bonds within one year prior to December 31, 1992, to comply with that indenture requirement, gains or losses may arise. Because such gains or losses result from well-planned contractual requirements, the FASB concluded that they should *not be classified as extraordinary items.*

Remember that an extraordinary item represents a special type of gain or loss to be reported separately in the income statement. Extraordinary items are presented net of any related tax effects, and reported after income from operations. Financial statement users are thereby put on notice not to expect such unusual and infrequent items of gain or loss to recur in the foreseeable future. While many debt extinguishments may not satisfy both of the criteria for treatment as an extraordinary item (unusual in nature and infrequent in occurrence), *SFAS No. 4* requires that gains or losses from extinguishing debt be treated as extraordinary. The rationale for this treatment, in part, is to avoid some of the problems of management manipulation previously discussed. By excluding gains or losses on debt extinguishments from operating income, financial statement users are made aware of their special nature.

To illustrate accounting for an extinguishment of debt, we shall again modify the example of the Baycraft Corporation. Assume that after amortizing discount for 1992, the company—in anticipation of lower interest rates—reacquires the bonds presented in Exhibit 15–3 for $9,800 on January 4, 1993. The following entry reflects the reacquisition and recognition of the related extraordinary loss:

Loss on Retirement on Bonds—Extraordinary	1,112	
Bonds Payable	10,000	
Cash		9,800
Discount on Bonds Payable		912
Deferred Bond-Issue Costs		400
(To reflect the reacquisition of debt at an early date preceding maturity.)		

The remaining discount of $912 at the date of extinguishment is merely the original discount ($1,082) less the amount amortized at December 31, 1992 ($170). The $400 remaining issue costs related to those bonds are also removed from the accounting records, thereby affecting the amount of gain or loss reported.

What would be the proper accounting treatment if only part of the outstanding bonds were reacquired? The percentage of the issue reacquired would be applied to the par value, the unexpired discount or premium, and the deferred bond-issue costs to determine the portion of each to be removed. Cash is then credited for the price paid and an extraordinary gain or loss recognized.

[6]*FASB Statement of Financial Accounting Standards No. 4,* "Reporting Gains and Losses from the Extinguishment of Debt," 1975, par. 8.
[7]*FASB Statement of Financial Accounting Standards No. 64,* "Extinguishments of Debt Made to Satisfy Sinking-Fund Requirements," 1982, par. 3.

To illustrate, we assume the same facts as in the previous illustration except that only 50% of the bond issue is extinguished for $4,900. The entry to record the retirement, including a loss of $556, is presented as follows:

Loss on Retirement of Bonds—Extraordinary	556	
Bonds Payable ($10,000 × 50%)	5,000	
Cash		4,900
Discount on Bonds Payable ($912 × 50%)		456
Deferred Bond-Issue Costs ($400 × 50%)		200

A company may reacquire its own bonds but not retire them. Rather, the company intends to sell the bonds at a later time. Such bonds are called **treasury bonds** and a Treasury Bonds account may be debited when the bonds are acquired rather than the liability account (Bonds Payable). An extraordinary gain or loss should still be recognized on the reacquisition, however, and the Treasury Bonds account should be deducted from the liability Bonds Payable in the balance sheet. Treasury Bonds should not be reported as an asset. Furthermore, interest on treasury bonds should not be paid, accrued, or otherwise recognized in the financial statements.

Companies experiencing financial and operating difficulties occasionally reach agreements with creditors to restructure liabilities or retire debts for less than their maturity amounts. Restructurings of debt occurring because of financial difficulties of the debtor present a number of accounting issues. A comprehensive discussion of troubled-debt restructurings from the perspective of both creditors and debtors appears in Appendix A of this chapter.

OTHER LONG-TERM DEBT ACCOUNTING PROBLEMS

Other types of bonds and long-term debt instruments exist. The following section considers unusual accounting issues posed by several of those types of liabilities.

DEBT COMMINGLED WITH EQUITY RIGHTS

Companies have developed various hybrid debt instruments in their efforts to obtain external financing at the lowest cost. This is obvious in accounting and reporting for debt instruments containing provisions that allow bondholders the opportunity to become common stockholders under specified conditions. When such obligations are issued, we must resolve several additional accounting and reporting problems.

We may generally classify debt instruments containing equity-acquisition features as either (1) bonds issued with detachable stock-purchase warrants or (2) bonds that may be converted into equity securities. The following discussion describes general accounting theory and reporting practices for each type of debt security.

Accounting Theory and Equity-Acquisition Features

The accounting profession has addressed the issue of accounting for debt with **equity-acquisition features** on several occasions, the most recent of which resulted in the issuance of *APB Opinion No. 14*.[8]

Theoretically, whenever an investor acquires a debt security that in some way facilitates the acquisition of equity securities, some amount of the purchase price is paid for the right to acquire the equity security in a potentially advantageous manner. The

---

[8]*APB Opinion No. 14*, "Accounting for Convertible Debt and Debt Issued with Stock Purchase Warrants," 1969.

remaining amount of the purchase price relates to the liability aspects of the security. Stated alternatively, if the same bond were issued without the equity-acquisition feature, it would normally sell for less. The equity-acquisition feature has a value and serves to enhance the market value of the composite security. Furthermore, to the extent purchasers pay for the equity-conversion right or feature, such payment represents a permanent contribution to equity not requiring repayment. Indeed, only the principal at maturity and related interest when earned must be paid to the investor. Therefore, in theory, some portion of the total consideration received for convertible debt and debt with detachable stock rights should be considered a contribution to equity and the remainder as the incurrence of a liability. The following discussion considers both types of securities, presents the accounting profession's position on each, and illustrates appropriate accounting and reporting techniques.

Accounting for Debt with Detachable Stock-Purchase Rights

When debt is issued with **detachable stock-purchase warrants,** the repayment of the debt at maturity is generally expected, regardless of whether or not the stock-purchase warrants are exercised. Because the stock purchase warrants are detachable and may be exercised separately from the debt, a market for the warrants will normally be established and will provide information on the relative value of the warrants. Furthermore, because a market for the separate debt instrument will also be established, we can easily determine the value of the debt portion of the composite security in an objective manner. Thus, the equity and debt instruments do not represent mutually exclusive investment alternatives, and separate values for each element exist independent of the other and should be so recorded in the accounting records.

If active markets for the two securities exist immediately after issuance, the allocation of the total proceeds of the sale is based on the relative fair market values of the two securities. The portion of the total consideration to be allocated to debt is represented by the ratio of the fair market value of the debt to the total fair market value of the debt and warrants. The remaining portion of the consideration received is associated with the warrants. To understand this concept consider the following example.

Bradfield, Inc., issues 1,000 bonds with a maturity value of $1,000 each. A detachable stock warrant, attached to each bond, may be exchanged for a share of stock with a payment of $25 per share. Bradfield, Inc., sells the bonds with the warrants attached at 102. Shortly after issuance the bonds are traded in the market at 103 and the warrants are traded at $5 each. The following calculation presents the basis for an entry to record the issuance:

$$\text{Total consideration to be treated as debt} = \left[\frac{\text{Market value of bonds without warrants}}{\text{Market value of bonds without warrants} + \text{Market value of warrants}}\right] \times \$1,020,000$$

$$= \frac{\$1,030}{\$1,030 + \$5} \times \$1,020,000$$

$$= \frac{\$1,030}{\$1,035} \times \$1,020,000$$

$$= \$1,015,072$$

The remaining proceeds of $4,928 ($1,020,000 − $1,015,072) represent the amount included in the total price that is allocated to the detachable stock-purchase warrants.

The following entry records the issuance of the bonds and warrants, based on the preceding calculation:

Cash	1,020,000	
Bonds Payable		1,000,000
Premium on Bonds Payable		15,072
Stock-Purchase Warrants		4,928

(To record issuance of bonds and detachable warrants.)

For purposes of financial reporting, immediately after issuance the bonds are presented in the balance sheet with the premium added, as follows:

Long-Term Liabilities

Bonds payable	$1,000,000	
Add: Premium on bonds payable	15,072	$1,015,072

The stock warrants appear in the stockholders' equity section of the balance sheet as a separate element of paid-in capital.

From this point forward we account for the bonds in the manner illustrated earlier in this chapter. The premium is amortized over the life of the bonds as a reduction of interest expense. Again, the effective interest method of amortization should be used unless other amortization methods approximate the results of the effective interest method.

If market values of the bonds and attached warrants are not available, other allocation techniques must be used. For example, we may select an estimated interest rate that appears reasonable for the debt security alone. In doing so we should consider the risk class of the issuing company as well as other economic conditions. Factors such as the prime rate of interest and government security rates provide useful guides for selecting an appropriate rate. Using the estimated interest rate, we can determine the present value of the liability. The difference between the present value of the debt and the total consideration received may be appropriately attributed to the detachable warrants and reported as contributed capital. This approach should be used only when fair market values of the bonds and the stock warrants are not available. Another possibility is that a market value would be available for either the bonds or the warrants but not both. In this case we would either estimate the unknown value and allocate the total proceeds as before or assign the known value to the one security and allocate the remaining proceeds to the other security.

The amount initially attributed to the warrants is recognized as part of paid-in capital and is classified as such until the warrants are exercised or expire. Accounting for stock-purchase warrants subsequent to issuance is considered in Chapter 16, which deals with a variety of issues involving stockholders' equity.

Accounting for Convertible Debt

Different problems arise if a company issues debt containing a feature allowing conversion of that debt into some type of the company's capital stock. In considering the accounting problems of such securities, the APB stated:

> *A convertible debt security is a complex hybrid instrument bearing an option, the alternative choices of which cannot exist independently of one another. The holder ordinarily does not sell one right and retain the other. Furthermore, the two choices are mutually exclusive; they cannot both be consummated. Thus the security will either be converted into common stock or will be redeemed for cash. The holder cannot*

exercise the option to convert unless he foregoes the right to redemption, and vice versa.[9]

Substance over Form

While the APB ultimately selected the logic implicit in that statement for guiding financial accounting and reporting, an alternative argument is based on the idea of substance over form. Specifically the APB acknowledged:

> *The contrary view is that convertible debt possesses characteristics of both debt and equity and that separate accounting recognition should be given to the debt characteristics and to the conversion option at the time of issuance. This view is based upon the premise that there is an economic value inherent in the conversion feature or call on the stock and that the nature and value of this feature should be recognized for accounting purposes by the issuer. . . . Similar separate accounting recognition for disparate features of single instruments is reflected in, for example . . . the allocation of the purchase cost in a bulk acquisition between goodwill and other assets.*[10]

As indicated, the first position was ultimately adopted and consequently **no portion of the proceeds from the issuance of convertible debt should be attributed to the conversion feature.** In reaching this conclusion, the APB attributed much significance to the inseparability of the debt and conversion option of such instruments. Therefore, all the proceeds from the issuance of convertible debt are attributed to the liability. Stockholders' equity of the issuing company remains

Disclosure

unaffected by the issuance of convertible debt. Disclosure of the conversion feature in the notes is necessary, however, to inform financial statement users of the possible changes in the financial structure of the company.

The APB did, however, provide for an exception to the general rule cited above. Recognizing that in unusual cases, an extremely high value may be placed on the conversion feature of a convertible debt instrument, the APB concluded that "when convertible debt is issued at a substantial premium, there is a presumption that such premium represents paid-in capital."[11] Thus, if a convertible debt instrument is issued at an extremely high rate of interest, the accountant may well conclude that a portion of the premium on that issuance should be classified as paid-in capital. In that way the effective yield on the debt portion of the instrument will become more reasonable as the amount of premium on the debt is reduced.

To illustrate the application of the general provisions in which there is not a "substantial premium," consider the previous example of Bradfield, Inc., but assume that convertible bonds are issued instead of bonds with detachable warrants. If convertible bonds with a face amount of $1,000,000 are issued for $1,115,000 and if each bond is convertible into 10 shares of common stock, the following entry is necessary:

Cash	1,115,000	
Bonds Payable		1,000,000
Premium on Bonds Payable		115,000
(To record issuance of convertible bonds.)		

---

[9]*APB Opinion No. 14*, par. 7.
[10]*APB Opinion No. 14*, par. 9.
[11]*APB Opinion No. 14*, par. 18.

The entire amount received is related to the bonds, and no proceeds are considered to be an addition to stockholders' equity. The liabilities section of the balance sheet at the date of issuance appears as follows:

Long-Term Liabilities
Convertible bonds payable	$1,000,000	
Premium on bonds payable	115,000	$1,115,000

If a "substantial premium" was judged to exist, then a portion of the proceeds should be allocated to stockholders' equity. One way of accomplishing the allocation would involve determining the present value of the debt by discounting it using a rate appropriate for similar debt not containing the conversion feature. The difference between the present value of the debt portion, so determined and the total consideration received would be attributed to stockholders' equity. Chapter 16 discusses the exchange of convertible bonds for common stock and deals with a variety of other issues involving stockholders' equity.

OTHER LONG-TERM LIABILITIES

One encounters several other types of long-term liabilities in practice. For example, companies frequently issue **serial bonds,** which mature in several scheduled maturity dates rather than at a single maturity date as in the case of term bonds. Although financial accounting and reporting for serial bonds does not differ conceptually from the practices illustrated for term bonds, several complicating factors arise. Appendix B of this chapter illustrates the accounting practices unique to serial-bond issues. Furthermore, lease and pension obligations are frequently reported as liabilities in the financial statements of business enterprises. Because accounting classification, measurement, and reporting standards for those liabilities are complex, Chapters 23 and 24, respectively, are devoted to these topics. Chapter 18, which deals with financial reporting of income taxes, discusses noncurrent deferred tax credits. Also, certain loss contingencies, discussed in Chapter 14, may represent long-term liabilities of an enterprise. Lawsuits and other claims provide examples of contingent liabilities that may require noncurrent classification.

The present chapter discusses only a limited number of noncurrent liabilities. Although notes and bonds payable frequently represent most of a company's noncurrent liabilities, the other important items mentioned in the preceding paragraph are considered elsewhere in this book.

CREATIVE FINANCING INSTRUMENTS

One of the most significant business developments of the last several decades has been the evolution of creative financing instruments. Companies have sought to lower the cost of the resources obtained from creditors and investors, to hedge risks, to increase returns on assets employed, and to achieve a variety of other objectives through alternative, complex, and creative means of financing. In many cases, accountants are closely involved in designing and developing such arrangements. Indeed, one principal reason for developing such innovative financing instruments is to structure transactions in such a manner as to obtain a desired accounting result. For example, many companies wish to avoid reporting liabilities on their balance sheets and attempt to accomplish "off-balance-sheet" financing.

Some of the securities that have been developed recently include **shared appreciation or participating mortgages,** in which the lender benefits from increases in the value of the asset used to secure a loan; **zero coupon convertible bonds,** for which interest will be paid only if the security is held to maturity; **preferred** or **common stock** with "put" options that allow the investor to "sell" the security back to the issuer; and debt payable in the common stock of the issuing entity. The accounting questions that arise for such instruments relate to their classification (i.e., debt or stockholders' equity); their valuation (e.g., the amount at which the item should be recorded); and the amount, timing, and classification of the return paid on the instrument (e.g., interest expense or dividends).

Consider, for example, shared appreciation or "participating" mortgage, which generally allows the lender to share in any increases in the value of the property securing the debt. To illustrate, a clause in such an instrument might provide that after five years the property is to be appraised and 50% of any increase in the fair value of the property over its worth at the time of the loan is to become due to the lender. If the amount of the liability to the borrower increases, then the property's fair value rises. Such terms are found in real estate financing because real estate commonly increases in value over time. Participating loans generally bear interest at rates less than equivalent notes that do not contain the participation feature. The lower interest compensates the borrower for relinquishing some of the rights to the property's appreciation.

The accounting questions that surround such agreements are complex and numerous. For example, at what rate should interest be recognized during the period between the inception of the loan and the appraisal date? Should annual appraisals be performed and any increase in the fair value of the property be used as a basis for increasing the liability? Should the offsetting charge resulting from any increase in the liability of the participation feature be reported as an increase in the related asset, as interest expense, or in some other way?

There are currently no authoritative answers to these questions, and students should realize that the creativity of lenders and borrowers is almost unlimited. New and different financing instruments will continue to be developed in response to events and circumstances not now foreseen. *SFAS No. 105,* "Disclosure of Information about Financial Instruments with Off-Balance-Sheet Risk and Financial Instruments with Concentrations of Credit Risk" represents a recent action of the FASB to assure financial statement users receive information necessary to understand terms, conditions, and risks involved in a wide variety of financial instruments. This new standard is, however, limited to disclosure and no guidance on accounting measurements or recognition is provided. Organizations that set accounting standards tend to trail practice in such circumstances and accountants are frequently required to develop acceptable accounting solutions for complex financial instruments without precise authoritative guidance. Substantial seasoned judgment and analysis are necessary to appropriately address and resolve such complex accounting problems. The rights and risks that are created and assigned to the parties involved in the agreement must be well understood to successfully account for the underlying transactions. Consultation with other professional accountants is common when such problems are encountered. Indeed, the intellectual challenges implicit in circumstances such as these represent extremely interesting and important aspects of professional practice.

Disclosure (margin note)

CONCEPTUAL CONSIDERATIONS

Asset/Liability Measurement (margin note)

Matching (margin note)

Accounting for debt is governed primarily by the accounting principles of asset/liability measurement, matching, and disclosure. Liabilities are recorded at their historic amounts and adjusted for the accrual and payment of interest and the amortization of premium or discount, if any. Interest expense is measured by matching the cost

Disclosure

incurred with time periods in which the debt is outstanding. Changes in the value of debt, such as bonds, caused by the financial markets are not recognized in the accounting records of the issuing company. The principle of disclosure is also important in the information about debt terms and maturities that is provided in the notes to the financial statements.

CONCLUDING REMARKS

Accounting for long-term debt is generally rather straightforward and not unduly complex. Recording debt when incurred and recognizing periodic interest expense, including determining the effective interest rate and amortizing any discount or premium, do not pose major problems for accountants. There are, however, a number of complex conceptual issues that accountants must resolve in preparing financial statements and that accounting standards-setting organizations are only now beginning to address. Examples include distinguishing between debt and equity instruments for purposes of balance sheet classification, accounting for participating loans, and the valuation of liabilities subsequent to issuance or incurrence.

Students can expect to see significant changes in the professional accounting standards that may require major revisions in the manner in which we currently account for liabilities. In addition, we can expect the financial markets to continue to develop new financial instruments that contain complex rights and risks. Accountants must understand and report these changes in accordance with acceptable professional concepts and standards.

KEY POINTS

1. Long-term debts are those reportable obligations of an enterprise that do not require the use of current assets or the creation of new current liabilities for repayment and those with due dates more than one year (or operating cycle, if longer) in the future. (Objectives 1 and 7)

2. Long-term debt should usually be recorded at the present value of the future cash obligations. (Objective 3)

3. Premium and discount arise when the market rate of interest for an obligation differs from the rate of interest stated on the face of that security. (Objective 4)

4. Premium or discount should be amortized over the life of the related debt by applying a constant interest rate to the carrying amount of the liability (effective interest method). The straight-line method of amortization is acceptable only if the results do not differ materially from the effective interest method. (Objective 5)

5. When debt is extinguished, any difference between its carrying amount and its reacquisition price is treated as an extraordinary gain or loss. (Objective 3)

6. When a company sells a debt instrument with detachable stock-purchase warrants, an increase in stockholders' equity is recognized as well as an increase in liabilities. The proceeds from the sale of the hybrid security must be allocated between the debt and equity components based on the relative fair values of the two. (Objectives 2 and 6)

7. When a company sells a convertible debt security, the value that can be attributed to the equity-acquisition feature is usually not recognized in the accounts. The liability for the debt security is normally recorded in the accounting records as if the conversion feature did not exist. (Objective 6)

8. Some financial instruments issued by a company may contain provisions that complicate classification and accounting. Such instruments must be carefully analyzed to assure appropriate treatment in the financial statements. (Objectives 1, 2, 3 and 7)

APPENDIX A: TROUBLED-DEBT RESTRUCTURINGS

A company with financial difficulties may have trouble repaying its debt on a timely basis. Furthermore, most debt instruments contain covenants requiring a company to maintain certain financial characteristics as evidenced by the financial statements. For example, a debt covenant may require the maintenance of a given debt/equity ratio, current ratio, or working capital amount. A company experiencing operating and financial difficulty may at some time violate some or all of its debt covenants. When covenant violations occur, a common practice is for creditors and debtors to renegotiate and restructure the troubled debt.

As a result of the variety and complexity of **troubled-debt restructurings,** the FASB issued *Statement of Financial Accounting Standards No. 15,* which discusses the accounting and reporting by both debtors and creditors.[12] Because there is considerable similarity between debtor and creditor accounting for such restructurings, we consider both in this appendix. First, however, we shall explore the steps necessary to *identify* troubled-debt restructurings.

IDENTIFYING TROUBLED-DEBT RESTRUCTURINGS

Not all debt restructurings represent troubled debt restructurings; we must therefore exercise care in determining whether a particular debt restructuring is in fact, a *troubled*-debt restructuring. For example, a troubled-debt restructuring is not involved if a creditor, experiencing financial difficulty, makes concessions in debt terms to induce a debtor to pay the debt at a point *earlier* than the scheduled maturity date.

In a troubled-debt restructuring, the *debtor* must be experiencing financial difficulty and the creditor, attempting to make the best of a bad situation, grants a concession to the debtor that would not be granted in a normal business relationship. Thus, creditors sustain accounting losses on troubled-debt restructurings while debtors realize accounting gains. Examples of restructurings include a modification of debt terms, such as interest-rate reductions or maturity-date extensions, settlement of the debt for less than its face amount, and the granting to creditors of equity interests in the debtor. Once a troubled-debt restructuring has occurred and been identified, appropriate accounting measurements and disclosures must be accorded the restructuring.

---

[12]*FASB Statement of Financial Accounting Standards No. 15,* "Accounting by Debtors and Creditors for Troubled Debt Restructuring," 1977.

ACCOUNTING BY DEBTORS

Four types of troubled-debt restructurings are recognized for accounting purposes. The first two involve full settlement of the debt as a result of a debtor (1) transferring assets to the creditor or (2) granting an equity interest to the creditor; the third type involves a modification of debt terms (e.g., extension of maturities, reduction of interest); and the fourth, some combination of the first three types. We shall discuss each type in the following pages.

Transfer of Assets

In a troubled-debt restructuring creditors are sometimes willing to accept various debtor assets in immediate settlement of the debt. In a **transfer of assets** debtors must consider how much of any resulting gain or loss is related to the disposition of the assets and how much is related to the extinguishment of debt.

For example, assume that Covina Company has been experiencing poor sales of its latest real estate project and is near default on its loan from Pomona National Bank. Recognizing that if Covina defaults on its loan other creditors may file suit, Pomona has agreed to accept Covina Company's land, which has a fair value of $40,000, in full settlement of a Covina Company debt. If the land has a book value of $35,000 and the liability is reflected on the books at its maturity value of $50,000, then the following entries are necessary on Covina's books:

Land	5,000	
Gain on Disposal of		
Land—Ordinary		5,000
(To adjust land to its fair value		
at the time of disposal.)		
Note Payable	50,000	
Land		40,000
Gain from Restructuring		
of Debt—Extraordinary		10,000
(To recognize gain on the		
extinguishment of debt.)		

These entries demonstrate that two steps may be required when assets are transferred in settlement of a debt. We first adjust the carrying amount of the asset to be transferred from its current book value to its fair value at the time of transfer with a resulting gain or loss recognized on the disposal of the asset. Such gains or losses are *not* extraordinary because gains or losses on asset disposals occur frequently and are not unusual.

After the asset has been adjusted to its fair value, we next recognize any difference between the fair value of the asset and the carrying amount of the extinguished debt as an *extraordinary gain.* This is consistent with the nature of troubled-debt restructurings wherein creditors grant concessions to debtors so as to provide at least some recovery of a loan.

Remember, gains on the extinguishment of debt should be reflected as extraordinary items according to *SFAS No. 4* and *SFAS No. 15*.

Grant of Equity Interest

A second method by which troubled debt may be restructured occurs when a debtor **grants an equity interest** to the creditor in consideration for the debt extinguishment. Debtors should record the fair value of the equity securities granted and recognize an extraordinary gain for any difference between the carrying amount of the debt extinguished and the fair value of the equity grant.

To illustrate, assume that instead of transferring land to Pomona National Bank, the Covina Company grants 1,000 shares of $25 preferred stock to Pomona in consideration for the extinguishment of the $50,000 note. If the preferred stock has a fair value of $45,000, the following entry is necessary to reflect the transaction:

Note Payable	50,000	
Preferred Stock (1,000		
shares @ $25)		25,000
Paid-in Capital in Excess of Par		20,000
Gain from Restructuring		
of Debt—Extraordinary		5,000
(To record extinguishment		
of note as a result of		
equity grant with a fair		
value of $45,000.)		

We may observe several important points: Only gains (not losses) are recognized on this type of troubled-debt restructuring, because the fair market value of the equity grant will not be greater than the carrying amount of the extinguished debt. Also, the gain is treated as extraordinary in accordance with *SFAS No. 15*.

From a practical perspective it is frequently difficult to determine the fair value of the equity interest that is granted, because the market value of the securities of a troubled company may be highly volatile or even nonexistent. This is especially true for companies whose securities are not actively traded in a public market. Therefore, accountants must exercise considerable judgment to develop reasonable estimates of fair value when debt is extinguished through an equity grant.

Modification of Terms

The third type of restructuring transaction involves a **modification of the terms** of the debt. Although the terms of a debt may be modified in many ways, accounting for all such debt alterations involves the same underlying principles. When the terms of a debt are adjusted in a troubled-debt restructuring, the *total amount* of the future cash payments should be determined. This total should include all payments for both principal and interest required in the future without using present-value tech-

niques. In other words, the gross future cash payments for principal and interest after the modification of terms should be calculated. This number is then compared with the current carrying amount of the debt on the books of the debtor. If the carrying value of the debt is less than the aggregate future cash payments required by the debt, we amortize the difference over the life of the debt as interest expense by using the effective interest method specified in *APB Opinion No. 21* (see footnote 2). No gain is recognized in the period of the extinguishment if the future cash flows exceed the carrying amount of the debt.

On the other hand, if the carrying amount of the debt is greater than the aggregate total future cash payments required under the modified debt agreement, we adjust the carrying value of the debt to the aggregate total future cash flows and recognize an extraordinary gain for the difference. Furthermore, in such circumstances no interest expense is recognized on the debt following such a write-down. All payments in satisfaction of the debt are considered payments of principal even if some portion of the payments is designated as interest in the revised debt agreement.

To illustrate, assume that the note payable to Pomona National Bank bears interest at 12% and, as before, is carried as a liability on Covina's books at $50,000. Instead of the previous restructuring examples, however, assume now that Pomona agrees to reduce the principal amount of the note by $10,000 but continues to require interest to be paid at 12% on the remaining $40,000. If the note is due in one year, the following entry is necessary:

Note Payable	5,200	
Gain from Restructuring of		
Debt—Extraordinary		5,200

The calculations are as follows:

$40,000 × .12 =	$ 4,800	Interest to be paid on new principal amount
+	40,000	Remaining principal
	$44,800	Aggregate future cash payments
	$50,000	Current carrying amount of liability
−	44,800	Aggregate payments required after restructuring
	$ 5,200	Gain on restructuring

The carrying value of the liability is now $44,800 as a result of the foregoing entry. Consequently, all cash payments now made in satisfaction of the note are considered payments of principal, even though a portion ($4,800) has been designated in the restructuring agreement as interest. Covina recognizes no interest expense on the note subsequent to restructuring.

Combination of Methods

The final manner in which a troubled-debt restructuring may occur involves some combination of the first three methods: transfer of assets, grant of equity interest, or modification of terms. In such a **combination restructuring** if an asset is transferred to the creditor in partial settlement of the debt, the asset is adjusted from its carrying value to its fair value and a gain or loss is recognized on the disposal of the asset. Next, the fair value of the asset transferred is credited and the debt is reduced by a similar amount. In a combination restructuring in which some debt remains on the books after these adjustments, no extraordinary gain on the extinguishment is recognized.

An equity interest might also have been granted to the creditor. The debtor should record the fair value of the equity interest with a corresponding charge to the carrying amount of the debt. If the extinguishment is completed as a result of the asset transfer and equity grant, then an extraordinary gain should normally be recognized. The amount of the gain is the difference between the carrying value of the debt prior to extinguishment and the fair values of the asset transferred and the equity grant.

If the debtor still has a residual liability on the restructured debt following a transfer of assets or grant of equity interest, or both, then the provisions governing a modification of terms should be applied. That is, the gross future payments for both interest and principal still required following the asset transfer and/or grant of equity should be compared to the adjusted carrying value of the debt. If the gross future cash payments exceed the adjusted carrying amount of the debt, the difference is recognized as interest expense over the life of the debt. However, if the gross future cash payments are less than the adjusted amount of the debt, then the debt should be written down to the total of the gross future cash flows with an extraordinary gain recognized to the extent of the difference.

To illustrate accounting for combination restructuring, assume that a debtor in a troubled-debt restructuring agrees to the following terms: (1) Covina will transfer land with a carrying value of $15,000 and a fair value of $12,000 to Pomona; (2) Covina will grant to creditor 100 shares of its $10 par value stock, which has a current fair value of $6 per share; and (3) in consideration of the asset transfer and equity grant, Pomona will reduce the principal balance of the note from $30,000 to $10,000 and will reduce the interest rate on the note from 12% to 10%, compounded annually. Assume those transactions occur on January 1, 1992, when the note payable has a carrying value of $29,000. Under the restructuring the note matures on December 31, 1993, at which time both accrued interest (compounded annually) and principal are due. Exhibit 15–6 illustrates the necessary calculations and en-

tries to analyze and record this restructuring on the books of Covina Company.

ACCOUNTING BY CREDITORS

Accounting and reporting practices for troubled-debt-restructurings by creditors parallel those of debtors; however, certain differences exist. In a troubled-debt restructuring creditors grant concessions to debtors because of debtors' impaired ability to fulfill the original terms of the obligation. Since creditors are attempting to recoup as much of a receivable as possible, losses on the settlement of such receivables are likely to be sustained.

Asset Receipts

A troubled-debt restructuring may occur in several ways. From the creditor's perspective, however, there is no conceptual difference between the receipt of a debtor's asset such as inventory and the receipt of an equity interest in the debtor. Both transfers result in the **receipt of an asset** by the creditor.

When assets are received by a creditor in satisfaction of a receivable in a troubled-debt restructuring, the assets received should be recorded at their fair value on the date of receipt. If an allowance for uncollectible accounts has been established specifically for the receivable in question, the allowance account as well as the receivable should be removed from the books of the company with a loss recognized for any remaining difference.

To illustrate, assume that Pomona National Bank accepts land with a fair value of $40,000 in satisfaction of a note receivable with a carrying amount of $50,000, but for which a $6,000 allowance for uncollectible accounts has been established. The following entry is necessary:

Land (Real Estate Owned)	40,000	
Allowance for Loan Losses	6,000	
Loss on Settlement of Receivable	4,000	
Note Receivable		50,000
(To record receipt of land in satisfaction of note receivable.)		

We can make several observations in regard to this entry. First, a loss of $10,000 has been sustained in the settlement of this receivable; $6,000 was recognized in an earlier period as a result of the use of the allowance method of recognizing bad debts; and the additional $4,000 loss is recognized in the period of the settlement. Second, these losses are not considered to be extraordinary, because—from the creditor's perspective—they are losses on the collection of receivables and not on the extinguishment of debt. Furthermore, if the assets received are equity securities of the debtor (equity grant), the accounting and reporting techniques are not changed; that is, the equity securities received should be recorded as an asset at their fair market value on the date received.

EXHIBIT 15–6

Comprehensive Illustration of a Combination Troubled-Debt Restructuring

Journal entries:

Jan. 1, 1992	Loss on Disposal of Land	3,000	
	Land		3,000
	(To recognize loss on disposal of land.)		
Jan. 1, 1992	Note Payable	12,600	
	Discount on Common Stock	400	
	Inventory		12,000
	Common Stock (100 shares @ $10)		1,000
	(To attribute fair value of inventory transferred and equity granted to an equivalent portion of debt.)		

Calculation for consideration:

Land (written down from $15,000 value)	$12,000
Equity grant (par $1,000)	600
Total fair value of consideration	$12,600

On January 1, 1992, the following test is made to determine if further accounting entries are necessary:

Debt carrying value:	
Original carrying amount of debt	$29,000
Less: Write-down from above	12,600
Carrying value of debt	$16,400
Future cash flows:	
Maturity cash requirement	$10,000
Interest	
Dec. 31, 1992 ($10,000 × .10)	1,000
Dec. 31, 1993 ($11,000 × .10)	1,100
Total aggregate future payments required	$12,100

Since the adjusted carrying amount of the debt ($16,400) exceeds the future cash requirements ($12,100), an entry is necessary for the difference ($4,300):

Jan. 1, 1992	Note Payable	4,300	
	Gain from Restructuring of Debt—Extraordinary		4,300
	(To reduce carrying amount of note to aggregate of future cash payments.)		

On December 31, 1992, no entry is required; all payments represent principal following restructuring; thus, no interest should be accrued.

Dec. 31, 1993	Note Payable	12,100	
	Cash		12,100
	(To record retirement of debt at maturity; no interest expense recognized.)		

Modification of Terms

If the terms of a receivable are changed pursuant to a troubled-debt restructuring, creditors must determine the total amount of cash to be received in the future. This amount is then compared with the carrying amount of the receivable, net of any related allowance account. If the total aggregate cash to be received in the future exceeds the carrying amount of the receivable, the difference should be amortized as interest revenue over the life of the receivable by using the effective interest method.

If the total aggregate payments to be received in the future, however, are less than the carrying amount of the receivable, then an ordinary loss should be recognized for the difference. All remaining collections are then treated as direct reductions of the receivable, and no interest revenue is recognized even if the revised agreement specifies a portion of the amount received as interest.

Combination of Methods

If the restructuring is a combination of a partial settlement by receipt of assets and a modification of terms, the fair market value of the asset received should be used to reduce an equivalent amount of the receivable. If the cash to be received in the future exceeds the net adjusted carrying amount of the receivable, the difference should be amortized as interest revenue over the life of the receivable. Conversely, if the aggregate of the cash to be received in the future is less than the net adjusted carrying amount of the receivable, the receivable should be written down to the total of the aggregate future cash receipts and a loss recognized. Again, no interest revenue should be recognized on future cash receipts in the latter circumstances. Furthermore, the future cash flows should not be subjected to any present-value calculations.

COMPARING AND CONTRASTING DEBTOR AND CREDITOR ACCOUNTING

While there are many similarities between debtor and creditor accounting for troubled-debt restructurings, several differences are also apparent. In essence, the differences relate primarily to timing and classification. Gains on the extinguishment of debt should be classified as extraordinary by the debtor, whereas losses on the collections of receivables should not be classified as extraordinary items by the creditor.

Creditors may recognize the impairment of a receivable and a related loss by using the allowance method of bad-debt recognition at an earlier time than debtors recognize gains from the consequences of an actual restructuring. This is consistent with the accrual of loss and gain contingencies discussed in Chapter 14; that is, gain contingencies should not be accrued prior to realization, because revenue might be recognized prematurely, but loss contingencies should be recognized when it is probable that a loss has been incurred and the amount of the loss is reasonably estimable. Furthermore, these practices are themselves in harmony with the modifying convention of conservatism, which requires that accounting and reporting properly recognize inherent uncertainties in the commercial process.

Conservatism

Different estimates of the fair value of the consideration exchanged can cause other inconsistencies in accounting treatment between debtors and creditors. Existing differences in the recorded values of receivables and payables may also result in nonsymmetrical accounting treatments.

DISCLOSURE OF TROUBLED-DEBT RESTRUCTURINGS

Exhibit 15–7 provides a summary of the disclosure requirements for troubled-debt restructurings. Substantial disclosures are required to assure adequate comprehension of the underlying transactions by financial statement users.

DEBT EXTINGUISHMENTS: FINAL NOTES

Although *SFAS No. 15* is specifically limited to *troubled-debt restructurings*, we can reflect on the accounting practices to be accorded restructurings that are not related to troubled debt. The authors believe that the accounting practices described by *SFAS No. 15* for troubled-debt restructurings, with the exception of certain of the disclosures enumerated in Exhibit 15–7, are desirable and would represent GAAP when applied to any debt restructuring. For a restructuring not related to troubled debt, judgment should be applied in deciding the nature and extent of any disclosure considered necessary. Of course, *SFAS No. 4*, "Reporting Gains and Losses from Extinguishment of Debt," stipulates certain disclosures that are necessary for *all* debt extinguishments.

EXHIBIT 15–7
Disclosure of Troubled-Debt Restructurings

Debtor Disclosures	Creditor Disclosures
1. Description of changes in terms.	1. Aggregate recorded investment.
2. Aggregate gain and tax effects of restructuring.	2. Gross interest revenue that *would* have been recognized without the troubled-debt restructuring.
3. Aggregate gain or loss on asset transfers.	3. Interest revenue recognized
4. Per share amount of gain or loss on debt extinguishment	4. Commitments to lend additional funds.
5. Extent of a contingent amount payable in the total liability.	

The events leading to the issuance of *FASB Statement No. 15* are interesting and worth noting. If the FASB had required the use of present value techniques to account for troubled-debt restructurings, creditors would generally have been required to report substantially greater losses in troubled-debt restructurings than under the provisions of *FASB Statement No. 15*. Banks that renegotiate loan maturities and other terms on less favorable terms due to debtor difficulties generally do not wish to recognize losses on those restructurings. To do so would result in reporting smaller earnings and possibly impairing the minimum capital required by government regulators. Further, banks have suggested that they would be much less likely to engage in troubled-debt restructurings if greater losses were required to be recognized and that public confidence in financial institutions could be impaired. Accordingly, financial institutions applied considerable pressure on the FASB to provide for the type of accounting contained in *FASB Statement No. 15* for troubled-debt restructurings.

Remember, in compliance with *FASB Statement No. 15* a loss is recognized only if the future cash to be received after the restructuring is less than the balance of the receivable. No discounting of those future expected cash receipts is allowed even though interest rates may have been reduced and maturity dates extended. Accounting for troubled-debt restructurings provides a good example of how the FASB is influenced by the perceived economic consequences of a proposed accounting standard. Such considerations commonly occur in the accounting standards-setting process and help explain some of the provisions of individual accounting pronouncements.

APPENDIX B: ACCOUNTING FOR SERIAL BONDS

Serial bonds allow an issuing company to repay the principal portion of the bonds in a series of installments. Several maturity dates are established for portions of an entire bond issue. When serial bonds are issued, groups of individual bonds within that issue have maturity dates different from those of the other groups. A series of maturity dates allows the issuer to retire the bonds gradually. Serial bonds may eliminate the need for a sinking fund or reduce the financial stress of meeting the maturity requirements of an entire bond issue at a single date.

Serial bonds are also attractive to state and local governments that rely on tax revenues to service debt. For example, if voters approve a bond issue and a related tax to fund a road-building project, the government may choose to issue serial bonds. The governmental unit then constructs the road with the proceeds of the bond issue and, as tax revenues are received, retires the debt in a series of maturities rather than in a single maturity.

Several accounting and reporting problems arise when a company issues serial bonds. Generally, these problems relate to the timing of premium or discount amortization and classification of the liability for the bonds payable.

The entry to record the issuance of the bonds in Exhibit 15–8 is relatively simple and parallels the entries discussed earlier in regard to term bonds. The proceeds of

EXHIBIT 15–8

Facts to Illustrate
Accounting for Serial Bonds

Issuing company	Staging	
Total bond issue	$1,000,000	
Date of bonds and date of issue	Jan. 1, 1992	
Maturity dates as shown:		

Group	Amount	Maturity Date
A	$ 250,000	Dec. 31, 1993
B	250,000	Dec. 31, 1994
C	500,000	Dec. 31, 1995
	$1,000,000	

Interest rate stated	10%	
Interest payment terms	Annually on Dec. 31	
Proceeds of issue	$949,200	

Note: Bond issues usually involve much larger amounts and longer periods of time between issuance and maturity. However, for illustrative purposes a smaller amount and shorter period of time are assumed.

the issue are debited to cash with a credit to bonds payable for the face amount of the entire issue. Any difference is treated as premium or discount on the bonds. As we mentioned earlier, premium or discount represents the difference, if any, between the interest rate stated on the bonds and the effective market rate of interest for those bonds on the date of issuance. The following entry is required to record the issuance of the bonds:

Jan. 1, 1992

Cash	949,200	
Discount on Bonds Payable	50,800	
Bonds Payable		1,000,000
(To record issuance of serial bonds.)		

We must next determine the effective rate of interest implicit in the bond issue. While this problem is not conceptually different from that encountered for term bonds, there are complicating factors. The several maturity dates cause uneven cash flows throughout the life of the bonds, not only for principal repayments but for interest payments as well. Cash flow patterns for term-bond interest payments are constant over the life of the bonds, and there is only a single maturity date. While the application of present-value techniques to serial bonds is more difficult, the objective remains the same. Specifically, we are seeking to determine the rate of interest (effective rate) that equates the present value of the liability (cash proceeds of the issue) with the future cash flows (various principal maturities and interest payments) required under the bond indenture. We make this calculation in order to meet the reporting requirements of *APB Opinion No. 21*, "Interest on Receivables and Payables," which requires the effective interest method for amortizing premium or discount over the life of the debt unless other methods do not cause material differences. Remember that even the simpler straight-line method of premium or discount amortization is not acceptable unless the results are close to those obtained by using the effective interest method. Therefore, we will use only the effective interest method to illustrate accounting for serial bonds.

When a combination of annuity (series of payments) and single amounts of cash flows are involved, we must select a rate of interest that equates the future cash flows with the issue price of the debt. The rate should appear reasonable and can be tested by determining if the future cash flows, discounted at that rate, approximate the present value of the liability (proceeds of the issue).

In Exhibit 15–8, because the bonds sold at a discount we know that the effective or market rate of interest demanded must be higher than the stated interest rate of 10%. In other words, if the stated rate of interest on the bonds provided a rate of return equal to that required by the market, then the bonds would have sold at their par value. Because the bonds were sold at a discount we can conclude that the market required a higher rate of return than was stated on the bonds. Therefore, in attempting to select the appropriate rate we should test a higher rate than the stated rate (10%). We shall select 12% to test, and the calculations on this page and the next demonstrate how the effective rate of interest implicit in a serial-bond issue can be determined.

General formula:

Proceeds of bond (present value [PV]) = PV of Group-A cash flows

+

PV of Group-B cash flows

+

PV of Group-C cash flows

Application:

Group A = PV of $250,000 due in 2 years +
  PV of 2 ordinary annuities of $25,000

+

Group B = PV of $250,000 due in 3 years +
  PV of 3 ordinary annuities of $25,000

+

Group C = PV of $500,000 due in 4 years +
  PV of 4 ordinary annuities of $50,000

Using a 12% effective interest rate:

Price of Bonds   **Present Value at 12%**

Group A

$949,200 = (.79719 × $250,000) + (1.69005 × $25,000)

Group B

+ (.71178 × $250,000) + (2.40183 × $25,000)

Group C

+ (.63552 × $500,000) + (3.03735 × $50,000)

Accumulating:

Group A

$949,200 = $199,298 + $42,251

Group B

$+ $177,945 + $60,046

Group C

$+ $317,760 + $151,868

$949,200 ≈ $949,168 (Approximate equality; therefore the 12% interest rate is a reasonable approximation.)

Note: The annuity amounts are merely the interest payments required under the terms of the bond. $250,000 × .10 = $25,000; $500,000 × .10 = $50,000.

Because these two amounts are virtually equal, we select 12% as an adequate approximation of the effective rate of interest. If such an approximation does not result from applying the test rate of interest, then another rate is selected for testing. This process continues until a rate is found that satisfactorily equates the present and future values of the cash flows.

In practice, computer routines search for and find the appropriate discount rate. Computers also develop amortization tables assisting further in properly accounting for the bonds payable. Nevertheless, accountants must understand the logic and techniques underlying the determination of implicit effective rates in such circumstances.

Once the effective interest rate is established (in this case, 12%), we can compute and recognize interest expense and amortize the premium or discount on the bonds. The amortization table in Exhibit 15–9 facilitates this process and illustrates how the serial maturities affect interest-expense recognition.

The entries to be made at December 31 of each year are based on the table in Exhibit 15–9. Discount is amortized over the life of the serial bonds in much the same manner as is the case for term bonds. That is, a constant rate of interest (12%) is recognized on the carrying value of the liability. The entries are as follows:

Jan. 1, 1992	Cash	949,200	
	Discount on Bonds Payable	50,800	
	Bonds Payable		1,000,000
	(To record issuance of bonds.)		
Dec. 31, 1992	Interest Expense	113,904	
	Discount on Bonds Payable		13,904
	Cash		100,000
	(To pay interest and amortize discount.)		
Dec. 31, 1993	Interest Expense	115,572	
	Discount on Bonds Payable		15,572
	Cash		100,000
	(To pay interest and amortize discount.)		
	Bonds Payable	250,000	
	Cash		250,000
	(To retire Group-A serial bonds.)		
Dec. 31, 1994	Interest Expense	87,441	
	Discount on Bonds Payable		12,441
	Cash		75,000
	(To pay interest and amortize discount.)		
	Bonds Payable	250,000	
	Cash		250,000
	(To retire Group-B bonds.)		
Dec. 31, 1995	Interest Expense	58,883	
	Discount on Bonds Payable		8,883
	Cash		50,000
	(To pay interest and amortize discount.)		
	Bonds Payable	500,000	
	Cash		500,000
	(To retire Group-C serial bonds.)		

EXHIBIT 15-9

Serial Bonds Amortization Table

Date	(1) Interest Expense	(2) Cash Paid	(3) Discount Amortization	(4) Par Value Outstanding	(5) Unamortized Discount	(6) Carrying Value
Jan. 1, 1992	—	—	—	$1,000,000	$50,800	$949,200
Dec. 31, 1992	$113,904	$100,000	$13,904	1,000,000	36,896	963,104
Dec. 31, 1993	115,572	100,000	15,572	750,000	21,324	728,676
Dec. 31, 1994	87,441	75,000	12,441	500,000	8,883	491,117
Dec. 31, 1995	58,883*	50,000	8,883	–0–	–0–	–0–
	$375,800	$325,000	$50,800			

(1) (Previous year Column 6) × 12%
(2) (Outstanding par value) × 10%
(3) (Column 1) − (Column 2)
(4) Outstanding par value
(5) (Previous year Column 5) − (Current year Column 3)
(6) (Column 4) − (Column 5)

*Adjusted for rounding difference.

QUESTIONS

15-1 What principal characteristics distinguish long-term debt and equity financing?

15-2 Why is it usually desirable for firms to issue large numbers of relatively small long-term debt instruments?

15-3 Define and describe the following types of bonds:
- [a] serial bonds
- [b] term bonds
- [c] registered bonds
- [d] coupon bonds
- [e] zero coupon bonds

15-4 What are "issue costs" associated with a bond issue? How should such costs be accounted for throughout the term of the bond issue?

15-5 What factors may cause the price of a bond to differ from its face amount at the date of sale?

15-6 If a company has several bond issues outstanding, each with different interest rates, due dates, and other provisions, how might the company disclose this information in the financial statements without burdening the balance sheet with undue detail?

15-7 Describe the various ways in which a debt may be extinguished. Include in your answer a discussion of qualified defeasance transactions.

15-8 How are discounts and premiums on bonds payable accounted for at the following times?
- [a] At issuance.
- [b] During the term of the debt.
- [c] At the time of the debt retirement.

15-9 How is the amount of the discount or premium computed for a bond issue?

15-10 Describe two methods of amortizing premiums or discounts on bonds payable. Which method is required? Why?

15-11 The treasurer of Older Company proposes that treasury bonds be recorded as assets in the investments section of the balance sheet. Do you agree? Why or why not?

15-12 Describe two different types of securities representing a combination of debt and equity instruments. How does financial accounting and reporting differ for each type?

15-13 What are the primary reasons for not recognizing a separate value for the equity element in a convertible bond at the time of issuance?

15–14   How is the equity element valued in the case of debt issued with detachable stock purchase warrants?

15–15 (Appendix A)   What characteristics must a debt restructuring possess before it should be considered a troubled-debt restructuring?

15–16 (Appendix A)   What are the four types of troubled-debt restructurings?

15–17 (Appendix A)   What disclosures should be made in the financial statements about a troubled-debt restructuring?

15–18 (Appendix A)   *Statement of Financial Accounting Standards No. 15,* "Accounting for Troubled Debt Restructurings," should bring accounting for common events by debtors and creditors closer together. Discuss the symmetry of accounting by debtors and creditors for the same transaction and discuss how differences might arise.

15–19 (Appendix B)   Briefly describe the accounting procedures employed for serial bonds.

EXERCISES

15–20   BOND ENTRIES   Hemingway, Inc., issued $1,000,000 of 20-year, 10% term bonds on January 1, 1992, at 101. Interest is payable semiannually on June 30 and December 31.

Instructions

Prepare general journal entries to record:
[a] The issuance of the bonds.
[b] The payment of the interest for the first two six-month periods.
[c] The amortization of premium for the year. (For simplicity, use the straight-line method of premium amortization.)

15–21   BOND RETIREMENT   Stanford, Inc., called an outstanding bond issue seven years before its maturity date. At the time the bonds were called, they had a carrying value of $55,000. Furthermore, Stanford was required to pay $72,000 to reacquire the bonds.

Instructions

[a] What amount of gain or loss, if any, should Stanford report during the year the call provision was exercised?
[b] How should the gain or loss in [a] be classified?

15–22   BOND RETIREMENT   Turner Corporation reports long-term debt of $1,000,000, less unamortized discount of $50,000 at December 31, 1992. While the bonds bear a stated interest rate of 10%, they were issued at an effective yield of 12%. Interest is payable on January 1 of each year. On June 30, 1993, Turner retires the bonds for 103 plus accrued interest. Turner amortizes bond discount by the effective interest method.

Instructions

[a] What gain or loss, if any, should Turner report from the bond retirement on its 1993 income statement?
[b] How should this gain or loss be classified?

15–23   BOND DISCOUNT—ISSUE PRICE   Hillman Company sold 1,000, $100 par value bonds, that had a coupon rate of interest of 14% when the market rate of interest was 16%. The bonds mature 10 years from their date of issuance.

Instructions

[a] Compute the price at which the bonds sold if interest is paid annually, and identify any premium or discount to be recognized.
[b] Compute the price at which the bonds sold if interest is paid semiannually, and identify any premium or discount to be recognized.

15–24   BOND PREMIUM—ISSUE PRICE   Avery Company sold 11% bonds at a time when the market rate of interest for comparable securities was 10%. The company sold 10,000, $1,000 par value bonds. The bonds pay interest semiannually and mature 20 years from the date they were issued.

Instructions

[a] Compute the price at which the bonds sold.
[b] Prepare the general journal entry to record the sale of the bonds.

15–25 AMORTIZATION OF DISCOUNT Weston Enterprises sold 100, $1,000 par value bonds that bear interest at 12%, at a price to yield an effective 16%. Interest is paid annually on the bonds, which mature eight years from their date of issuance. –

Instructions

[a] Compute the issue price of the bonds.
[b] Prepare the general journal entry to record the sale of the bonds.
[c] Determine interest expense and the discount or premium amortization for the first year of the bond issue by the effective interest method.
[d] Determine interest expense and the discount or premium amortization for the first year of the bond issue by the straight-line method.

15–26 AMORTIZATION OF PREMIUM Wilmington, Inc., issued 10,000, $100 par value bonds that bear interest at 12% when bonds of comparable quality were paying only 10% interest. Wilmington's bonds pay interest semiannually and mature 10 years from their date of issuance. n=20 i=.05

Instructions

[a] Determine the price at which the bonds sold.
[b] Compute interest expense and the amortization of premium or discount for the first two six-month periods under both the effective interest and straight-line methods.

15–27 SALE OF BONDS BETWEEN INTEREST DATES Bixby, Inc., issued $1,000,000, 12%, 20-year bonds at 102 plus accrued interest on February 1, 1992. The bonds are dated January 1, 1992, and pay interest semiannually on June 30 and December 31. The premium is to be amortized by the straight-line method over the period during which the bonds are outstanding. Bond issue costs totaled $50,000.

Instructions

Prepare all general journal entries for the bonds for 1992, assuming that amortizations are recorded annually on December 31, the end of the company's financial reporting period.

15–28 RETIRING PART OF A BOND ISSUE Potter Manufacturing Company had the following bonds outstanding at December 31, 1992:

Bonds payable	$1,000,000
Less: Discount	(80,000)
	$ 920,000 CV

The bond discount was being amortized over the 10-year life of the bonds (8 years remaining after December 31, 1992) by the straight-line method. 8000 pr yr.
At June 30, 1993 (a semiannual interest payment date), the company retired $600,000 of the bonds at 101% of par value. 60%

Instructions

[a] Determine the appropriate carrying value of the bonds at June 30, 1993.
[b] Prepare the general journal entry to record the retirement of the bonds at June 30, 1993.
[c] Prepare the balance sheet presentation of the remaining bonds at December 31, 1993.

15–29 BOND ENTRIES On July 1, 1989, Kinter Company issued 1000, $1,000 par value bonds at 99. The bonds pay interest annually on June 30, at 13% and mature eight years from their date of issuance. Discount is amortized by the straight-line method.
On June 30, 1992, the company retired the bonds at 102 after interest had been paid.

Instructions

Prepare the entries to record the final interest payment and the retirement of the bonds. Provide computations for each entry.

15–30   AMORTIZATION OF DISCOUNT   Cramer Company issued $100,000 par value, 12% bonds on January 1, 1992. The bonds mature in 10 years and pay interest semiannually on June 30 and December 31. The bonds were sold for $89,406, which yields an effective annual interest rate of 14%.

Instructions

[a] Determine the amount of interest expense to be recognized in 1992 using the effective interest method of discount amortization.

[b] What amount of the interest expense is represented by the amortization of the discount?

15–31   BONDS WITH DETACHABLE WARRANTS   On July 1, 1992, Pinder Corporation issued $2,000,000 of 7% bonds payable in 10 years. The bonds pay interest semiannually. The bonds include detachable warrants giving the bondholder the right to purchase for $30 one share of $1 par value common stock at any time during the next 10 years. The bonds and warrants were sold for $2,000,000. The value of the warrants at the time of issuance was $100,000. No valuation of the bonds, separate from the warrants, is available.

Instructions

[a] Prepare in general journal form the entry to record the issuance of the bonds.

[b] Explain the basis of your valuation of the warrants.   (AICPA adapted)

15–32   BONDS WITH DETACHABLE WARRANTS   Lane Corporation issued 100 bonds, each with a $1,000 face amount, on May 31, 1992. The bonds are due in 10 years and pay interest annually at 10%. A detachable stock-purchase warrant was attached to each bond that allows the holder of each warrant to acquire a share of the company's $25 par preferred stock for $15. Each bond with the detachable warrant sold at 102. Immediately after the issuance, the stock-purchase warrants were traded in the market at $40 while the market value of the bonds (without the warrants) was 101.

Instructions

Prepare the entry to record the issuance of the bonds and detachable stock-purchase warrants and the later exercise of half of the warrants.

15–33   CONVERTIBLE BONDS   Herman Corporation issued 100, $1,000 par value bonds that pay 12% interest on par value at a price to yield 10%. Each bond is convertible to 10 shares of Herman Corporation common stock on any interest-payment date. Interest is paid semiannually on January 1 and July 1, and the bonds mature 10 years from the date of issuance.

Instructions

[a] Prepare the general journal entry to record the issuance of the bonds.

[b] Explain briefly your treatment of the equity element included in the bond issue.

15–34   BONDS WITH DETACHABLE WARRANTS   Falkland Corporation sold a $1,000,000 20-year, 8% bond issue for $1,030,000. Each $1,000 bond has a detachable warrant that permits the purchase of one share of the corporation's common stock for $30. The stock has a par value of $25 per share. Immediately after the sale of the bonds, the corporation's securities had the following market values:

8% bond without warrants	$1,020
Warrants	10
Common stock	28

Instructions

What entry should the corporation make to record the sale of the bonds?

15–35   BONDS WITH DETACHABLE WARRANTS   Sunset Development, Inc., issued $2,000,000 of $1,000 face amount, 7% bonds on January 1, 1992, for $1,920,000. Two detachable stock-purchase warrants were attached to each $1,000 bond. Each warrant conveys the right to purchase one share of $100 par value common stock at $110 per share before July 1, 1992.

When the bonds were issued, Sunset's common stock was selling exactly at par and the market value of the warrants was $15 each.

Instructions

Prepare the entry that Sunset Development should make at the date the bonds were issued.

15–36 BOND ACCOUNTING On January 1, 1992, Kallis Company issued $100,000 of 10% bonds, due December 31, 2011 (20 years). Interest is to be paid annually on December 31. At the time the bonds were issued, the market rate of interest was 8%.

Instructions

[a] Calculate and record the proceeds of the bond issue.
[b] Prepare a schedule to calculate the interest expense and amortization of the premium or discount for the first four years (through December 31, 1995) using the effective interest method.
[c] Prepare the entry to retire the bonds on January 1, 1996, at 101.

15–37 BOND RETIREMENT Harrison, Inc., reports the following liability on its December 31, 1992, balance sheet:

Bonds payable (9%, due Dec. 31, 2001)	$400,000
Premium on bonds—	10,800
	$410,800

The bonds were issued on December 31, 1991, at 103, with interest payable on June 30 and December 31 of each year. On March 1, 1993, Harrison retired $200,000 of the bonds at 98 plus accrued interest.

Instructions

[a] Is Harrison amortizing the premium by the effective interest or the straight-line method?
[b] Prepare the general journal entry to record the retirement of the bonds on March 1, 1993, including the payment of interest for the period January 1 through March 1, 1993.

(AICPA adapted)

15–38 (Appendix A) TROUBLED-DEBT RESTRUCTURING Silverton Company is experiencing financial difficulty and is renegotiating debt restructurings with its creditors to relieve its financial stress. Silverton has a $125,000 note payable to Sun State Bank. The bank is considering two alternatives:

Alternative 1. Acceptance of land owned by Silverton Company, valued at $100,000 and carried on the books of Silverton at its historical cost of $70,000.

Alternative 2. Acceptance of an equity interest in Silverton Company in the form of 11,000 shares of common stock valued at $10 per share. (The common stock has an $8 par value.)

Instructions

Prepare the general journal entry that Silverton Company would make under each alternative. Identify any extraordinary items that would be recognized.

15–39 (Appendix A) TROUBLED-DEBT RESTRUCTURING Due to adverse economic circumstances and poor management, Barrington, Inc., has negotiated a restructuring of its $85,000 note payable to Lincoln Bank. Lincoln Bank has agreed to reduce the face value of the note from $85,000 to $60,000, reduce the interest rate from 14% to 10%, and extend the due date one year from the date of restructuring. The restructuring will occur on August 31, 1992, the last day of Barrington, Inc.'s annual reporting period. There is no unpaid interest on the restructured loan at this time.

Instructions

[a] Prepare the general journal entry to record the restructuring on August 31, 1992. Include computations to support your figures.
[b] Prepare the general journal entry one year later to record the final payment of the note, assuming that no interest was paid during the year.

PROBLEMS

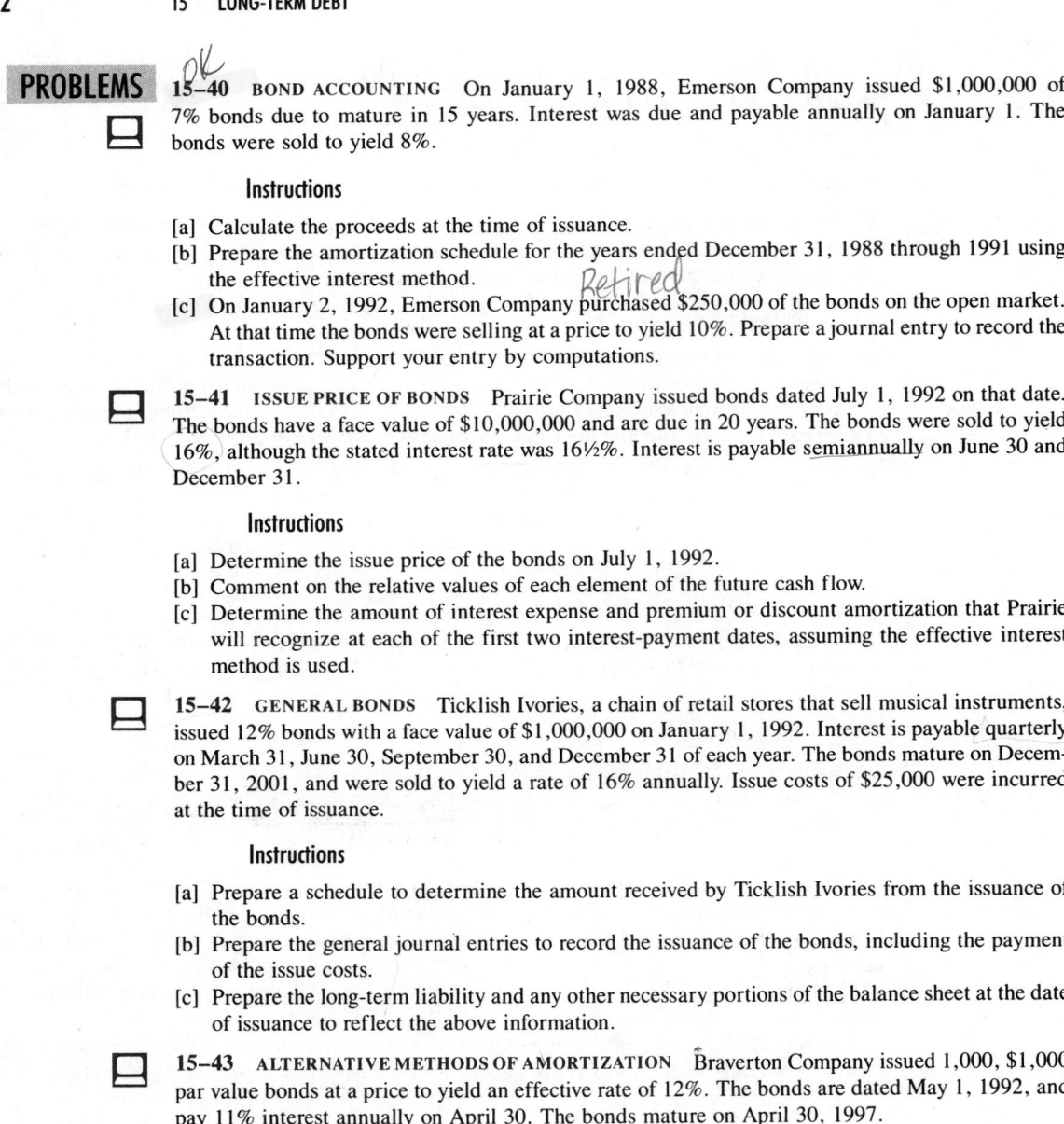

15–40   BOND ACCOUNTING   On January 1, 1988, Emerson Company issued $1,000,000 of 7% bonds due to mature in 15 years. Interest was due and payable annually on January 1. The bonds were sold to yield 8%.

Instructions

[a] Calculate the proceeds at the time of issuance.
[b] Prepare the amortization schedule for the years ended December 31, 1988 through 1991 using the effective interest method.
[c] On January 2, 1992, Emerson Company purchased $250,000 of the bonds on the open market. At that time the bonds were selling at a price to yield 10%. Prepare a journal entry to record the transaction. Support your entry by computations.

15–41   ISSUE PRICE OF BONDS   Prairie Company issued bonds dated July 1, 1992 on that date. The bonds have a face value of $10,000,000 and are due in 20 years. The bonds were sold to yield 16%, although the stated interest rate was 16½%. Interest is payable semiannually on June 30 and December 31.

Instructions

[a] Determine the issue price of the bonds on July 1, 1992.
[b] Comment on the relative values of each element of the future cash flow.
[c] Determine the amount of interest expense and premium or discount amortization that Prairie will recognize at each of the first two interest-payment dates, assuming the effective interest method is used.

15–42   GENERAL BONDS   Ticklish Ivories, a chain of retail stores that sell musical instruments, issued 12% bonds with a face value of $1,000,000 on January 1, 1992. Interest is payable quarterly on March 31, June 30, September 30, and December 31 of each year. The bonds mature on December 31, 2001, and were sold to yield a rate of 16% annually. Issue costs of $25,000 were incurred at the time of issuance.

Instructions

[a] Prepare a schedule to determine the amount received by Ticklish Ivories from the issuance of the bonds.
[b] Prepare the general journal entries to record the issuance of the bonds, including the payment of the issue costs.
[c] Prepare the long-term liability and any other necessary portions of the balance sheet at the date of issuance to reflect the above information.

15–43   ALTERNATIVE METHODS OF AMORTIZATION   Braverton Company issued 1,000, $1,000 par value bonds at a price to yield an effective rate of 12%. The bonds are dated May 1, 1992, and pay 11% interest annually on April 30. The bonds mature on April 30, 1997.

Instructions

[a] Prepare an amortization table showing the amount of interest expense and amortization of the discount or premium for each year of the bond issue by the effective interest method.
[b] Prepare an amortization table showing the amount of interest expense and the amortization of the discount or premium for each year of the bond issue by the straight-line method.
[c] Explain why the amortization of the discount or premium by the straight-line method exceeds that by the effective interest method in some years but not in other years.

15–44   GENERAL BONDS   Sounds Stereo Company issued 10%, $3,000,000 face value bonds on October 1, 1989. Sounds received $3,250,000, plus accrued interest. Interest is payable twice a year on January 1 and July 1. On December 31, 1991, the book value of the bonds, including the unamortized premium, was $3,142,000. On March 1, 1992, Super purchased the bonds on the open market at 97 plus accrued interest. Sounds used the straight-line method of premium amortization because the results did not differ materially from the effective interest method.

Instructions

Prepare general journal entries to record the following:

[a] The issuance of the bonds.

[b] Any adjusting entry necessary at December 31, 1989.

[c] Any entries necessary during 1992.

15–45 CONVERTIBLE BONDS/BONDS WITH WARRANTS Broward, Inc., issued $40,000,000 of *40000 bond issued* $1,000 bonds payable maturing in 20 years and bearing interest at a stated rate of 14%. The interest is payable semiannually and each bond includes a detachable warrant enabling the holder to purchase one share of $50 par value common stock at any time prior to 1997 for $30. The bonds were dated and issued on January 1, 1992, for $40,500,000. The total market value of the warrants immediately after issuance was $1,000,000, and each bond (without the warrant) sold at 99.

Instructions

Warrant 25

[a] Prepare a journal entry to record the issuance of these securities at January 1, 1992.

[b] Prepare the journal entry to record the subsequent exercise of the warrants.

[c] How, if at all, would your answer differ if the bonds were convertible rather than attached to a stock warrant? Assume each bond is convertible into 10 shares of stock with no additional charge for conversion. Answer both [a] and [b] and assume the bonds are converted shortly after issuance.

15–46 GENERAL BONDS Trawlins issued bonds as follows:

Two thousand $1,000 par value bonds. *2 million*

Ten percent stated annual interest, payable on Feb. 28 (or 29) and Aug. 31 of each year. *semiannually*

Selling price, 103% of par value (plus accrued interest which is credited to interest expense).

Date of bonds, March 1, 1992.

Date of sale, May 1, 1992.

Due date of bonds, Feb. 28, 2002.

The company will amortize (by the straight-line method) any premium or discount at year-end (December 31) for the entire year. (Amortization is rounded to the nearest dollar.) No reversing entries are made on January 1.

Instructions

[a] Prepare all general journal entries required for the years 1992 and 1993.

[b] Prepare the balance sheet and income statement presentations of the bond and interest expense accounts for 1992 and 1993.

15–47 GENERAL BONDS Old Ranch, Inc., issued $800,000 par value bonds on July 1, 1990. *Retire 400000* The bonds mature eight years from the date of issuance and pay interest semiannually on December 31 and June 30. Issue costs of the bonds were $12,000 and are amortized by the straight-line method over the life of the bond issue.

The following partial amortization table accounts for the bonds and the related interest:

Date	Cash Interest Paid	Interest Expense Recognized	Amortization	Carrying Value of Bonds
July 1, 1990	—	—	—	$846,611
Dec. 31, 1990	$36,000	$33,864	$2,136	844,475
June 30, 1991	36,000	33,779	2,221	842,254
Dec. 31, 1991	36,000	33,690	2,310	839,944
6/30/92	*36,000*	*33598*	*2402*	*837542*

4.5% Face *4 Mkt*

The bonds are callable at 110 on any interest payment date after December 31, 1991.

Instructions

[a] Determine the nominal or stated interest rate on the bond issue.

[b] Determine the effective (annual) interest rate on the bond issue.

[c] Prepare all journal entries required for 1990 and 1991 concerning the bond issue.

[d] Prepare the general journal entries to record the June 30, 1992, interest payment and the reacquisition of $400,000 of the bonds at that date.

15–48   CONVERTIBLE BONDS/BONDS WITH WARRANTS   Two comparable companies issued bonds on January 1, 1991, as described below:

Anchor Company.   Issued $1,000,000, 10% 10-year bonds, at 102. Each $1,000 bond is convertible into 100 shares of the company's $5 par value common stock on any interest payment date after January 1, 1991. Immediately after the sale, the bonds were selling at 102 and the common stock at $11.

Helm Company.   Issued $1,000,000, 10% bonds, at 103. Each $1,000 bond is accompanied by two detachable warrants to purchase one share each of the company's $50 par value common stock at $100 per share. Immediately after the sale, the bonds were selling at 102, the warrants at $20, and the common stock at $112.

Instructions

For each company, complete the following:

[a] Prepare the general journal entry to record the sale of the bonds.

[b] Explain your treatment of the equity portion of the hybrid security that was recorded in [a].

[c] Prepare the relevant portion(s) of the balance sheet immediately following the sale of the bonds.

[d] Prepare the entry to record the conversion on July 1, 1991 of the entire debt of Anchor Company and the exercise of all Helm Company warrants. Use straight-line amortization for simplicity where applicable.

15–49   GENERAL BONDS   On March 1, 1991, Keystone Company sold its 100 5-year, $1,000 face value, 8% bonds dated March 1, 1991 at an effective annual interest rate (yield) of 10%. Interest is payable annually and the first interest payment date is February 28, 1992. Keystone uses the interest method of amortization. Bond issue costs were incurred in preparing and selling the bond issue. The bonds can be called by Keystone at 101 at any time on or after March 1, 1992.

Instructions

[a] [1] Determine the selling price of the bonds.

　　[2] Specify how all items related to the bonds would be presented in a balance sheet prepared immediately after the bond issue was sold.

[b] What items related to the bond issue would be included in Keystone's 1991 income statement, and how would each be determined? What amount of interest would be reported at December 31, 1991?

[c] Would the amount of bond discount amortization using the interest method of amortization be lower in the second or third year of the life of the bond issue? Why?

[d] Assuming that the bonds were called in and retired on March 1, 1992, how should Keystone report the retirement of the bonds on the 1992 income statement?   (AICPA adapted)

15–50   GENERAL BONDS   On July 1, 1991, Andrews Manufacturing Company sold $2,500,000 of bonds dated July 1, 1991, paying interest at 10% and issued to yield 12%. Bond issue costs totaled $28,000.

The bonds mature on June 30, 2001. They pay interest annually at June 30. The company's policy is to amortize bond premium and discount by the effective interest method and bond issue costs by the straight-line method on a monthly basis.

Instructions

[a] Compute the price at which the bonds sold.

[b] Prepare an amortization table for the first four years of the bond issue.

[c] Prepare all general journal entries to record bond-related events for 1991 and 1992. (No reversing entries are made on January 1.)

[d] Prepare the financial-statement presentation of all bond-related items for the company's 1991 and 1992 financial statements. (Andrews' accounting period ends on December 31.)

15–51 DEBT RETIREMENT   Your client, Warner Manufacturing, Inc., is planning to issue new bonds at a lower interest rate in order to extinguish bonds currently outstanding. You have been asked to assist with some calculations regarding these transactions.

After reviewing the data, you realize that the decision to redeem bonds and issue new ones can be viewed as a capital-budgeting decision. When using capital-budgeting techniques, Warner has adopted the following cutoff points: maximum payback period is eight years, and minimum desired rate of return is 16%.

The following data relate to the original (outstanding) bonds and the new bonds to be issued:

	Original Bond Issue	New Bond Issue
Face value	$20,000,000	$20,000,000
Coupon rate	6%	5%
Call premium	4%	4½%
Expired life	5 years	—
Remaining life to maturity	15 years	15 years
Issued at	98½	100
Total issue costs	$120,000	$135,000

The new issue is to be sold, then one month later the original issue is to be redeemed. The overlapping month's interest on the original issue is *not* to be considered a miscellaneous cost of reacquisition.

All discounts and issue cost are amortized on a straight-line basis because that method is not materially different from the effective interest method of amortization. Interest is paid annually. All cash flows are assumed to occur at year-end. The federal income tax rate is 40%.

Instructions

[a] Compute Warner's accounting gain or loss on the early extinguishment of the original (outstanding) bonds.
[b] Compute the net cash investment based on the difference between the net cash outflow to redeem the original issue and the amount raised by the new issue.
[c] Compute the net cash benefit per year based on the difference between the annual net cash outlay required on the original issue and that required on the new issue.
[d] Independent of your answers to [b] and [c], assume that the net cash investment was $550,000 and that the net cash benefit per year was $120,000. Evaluate this "investment" by using the following capital-budgeting methods: (1) payback and (2) present value.   (AICPA adapted)

15–52 (Appendix A) TROUBLED-DEBT RESTRUCTURING   In connection with a debt restructuring on December 31, 1992, Pacific Corporation, experiencing cash flow problems stemming from poor operations, transferred real estate to the First International Bank of Monterey in full settlement of a debt of $1,700,000. However, the real estate was carried on the books of Pacific Corporation at $1,200,000. The current fair market value for similar real estate is $1,350,000.

Instructions

[a] Is the restructuring a troubled-debt restructuring? Why?
[b] Should the debtor recognize a gain or loss on the transfer of the real estate? If your answer is yes, indicate how the amount would be presented in the income statement.
[c] Should the debtor recognize a gain or loss in the restructuring? If your answer is yes, indicate the amount and how it would be treated in the income statement.
[d] What is the proper accounting treatment of this debt restructuring by the creditor?

15–53 (Appendix A) TROUBLED-DEBT RESTRUCTURING   On December 31, 1992, a $100,000 note is restructured by modifying the terms of the debt. The modifications, which are due to debtor financial difficulties, include the following:
[1] Forgiving $10,000 of principal and $6,969 of accrued interest.
[2] Extending the maturity date by five years.
[3] Reducing the interest rate from 10% to 6%.

Interest at 6% is to be paid annually on the new principal amount under the new terms. Therefore, the aggregate future cash payments under the new term total $117,000. This total represents $90,000 of principal and $27,000 of interest (6% × $90,000 × 5).

Instructions

[a] Is the restructuring a troubled-debt restructuring? Why?

[b] Will interest expense be recognized by the debtor in the future? If so, what is the effective interest rate under the new terms?

[c] A partial amortization schedule is provided below. Complete the schedule for the restructured debt presented in this case.

Date	(.06 × 90,000) Stated Interest Payment	Principal Payment	Reported Effective Interest Expense	Balance
12/31/92				$106,969
12/31/93	$5,400			
12/31/94	5,400			
12/31/95	5,400			
12/31/96	5,400			
12/31/97	5,400			

[d] How should the debtor record the payment made on December 31, 1993?

[e] How should the creditor record the payment made on December 31, 1993?

15–54 (Appendix B) SERIAL BONDS On December 31, 1984, Metro Company issued 1,000,000 of 8% serial bonds when the market rate was 10%. The bonds pay interest annually and will be retired according to the following schedule:

1984 issue

12/31/92	$ 400,000
12/31/93	300,000
12/31/94	200,000
12/31/95	100,000
Total	$1,000,000

On December 31, 1992, Metro Company had excess cash and decided to retire the $100,000 of the bonds due December 31, 1995, on the open market. At that time the market interest rate was 8% per annum. In accordance with GAAP, Metro uses the effective interest method.

sold at face

Instructions

Answer the following questions and provide supporting computations. Formal schedules are *not* necessary unless otherwise noted.

[a] Calculate the proceeds from the issuance.

[b] Prepare an amortization schedule for 1985 and 1986.

[c] Show the balance sheet presentation for the bonds at December 31, 1985 and 1986.

[d] How much did it cost to buy back the December 31, 1995, bonds at December 31, 1992?

[e] What was the gain or loss on the retirement of the December 31, 1995, bonds?

Amt of carrying value is on B/S or ammor. table

CASES **15–55 AMORTIZATION/EXTINGUISHMENT** This case consists of two *independent* parts.

Part 1. The effective interest method is appropriate for amortizing a premium or discount arising on the issuance of bonds.

Instructions

[a] Describe the effective interest method of amortization and how it compares with the straight-line method of amortization.

[b] How is amortization computed using the effective interest method? How do the results differ from those computed under the straight-line method, and why?

Part 2. Gains or losses from the early extinguishment of debt that is refunded can theoretically be accounted for in three ways:

[1] Amortized over remaining life of old debt.

[2] Amortized over the life of the new debt issue.

[3] Recognized in the period of extinguishment.

Instructions

[a] Provide supporting arguments for each of the three methods.

[b] Which method is generally accepted, and how should the appropriate amount of gain or loss be recorded in a company's financial statements?   (AICPA adapted)

15–56   CONVERTIBLE DEBT   Cahan Company recently issued $1,000,000 face value, 5%, 30-year subordinated debentures at 97. The debentures are redeemable at 103 on demand by the issuer and at any date on 30 days' notice 10 years after the issue. The debentures are convertible into $10 par value common stock of the company at the conversion price of $12.50 per share for each $500 or multiple thereof of the principal amount of the debentures.

Instructions

[a] Explain how the conversion feature of convertible debt is valuable to (1) the issuer and (2) the purchaser.

[b] Management of Cahan Company has suggested that in recording the issuance of the debentures, a portion of the proceeds should be assigned to the conversion feature.

 [1] What are the arguments for according separate accounting recognition to the conversion feature of the debentures?

 [2] What are the arguments in favor of accounting for the convertible debentures as a single element?

[c] Assume that no value is assigned to the conversion feature upon issue of the debentures. Assume further that five years after issue, debentures with a face value of $100,000 and book value of $97,500 are tendered for conversion on an interest payment date when the market price of the debentures is 104 and the common stock is selling at $14 per share. The company records the conversion as follows:

Bonds Payable	100,000	
Bond Discount		2,500
Common Stock		80,000
Paid-in Capital in Excess of Par		17,500

Discuss the propriety of the above accounting treatment.   (AICPA adapted)

15–57   CONVERTIBLE DEBT/DEBT WITH WARRANTS   Incurring long-term debt with an arrangement whereby lenders receive an option to buy common stock during all or a portion of the time the debt is outstanding is a frequently used corporate financing practice. In some situations the result is achieved through the issuance of convertible bonds; in others the debt instruments and the warrants to buy stock are separate.

Instructions

[a] Describe the differences that exist in current accounting for original proceeds of the issuance of convertible bonds and of debt instruments with separate warrants to purchase common stock.

[b] Discuss the rationale for the differences described in [a].

[c] Summarize the arguments that support the alternative accounting treatment.

          (AICPA adapted)

15–58   GENERAL DEBT ACCOUNTING   One way for a corporation to accomplish long-term financing is through the issuance of long-term debt instruments in the form of bonds.

Instructions

[a] Describe how to account for the proceeds from bonds issued with detachable stock-purchase warrants.

[b] Contrast a serial bond with a term (straight) bond.

[c] For a five-year term bond issued at a premium, why would the amortization in the first year of the life of the bond differ using the effective interest method of amortization instead of the straight-line method? Indicate whether the amount of amortization in the first year of the life of the bond would be higher or lower using the effective interest method instead of the straight-line method.

[d] When a bond issue is sold between interest dates at a discount, what journal entry is made and how is the subsequent amortization of the discount affected? Include an explanation of how the amounts of each debit and credit are determined.

[e] Describe how to account for and classify the gain or loss from the reacquisition of a long-term bond before its maturity.   (AICPA adapted)

15–59   CONVERTIBLE DEBT/DEBT WITH WARRANTS   The equityholders of a business entity usually include both creditors and owners. These two classes of equityholders share some characteristics, and sometimes it is difficult to distinguish between them. Examples of this problem include (1) convertible debt and (2) debt issued with stockpurchase warrants. While both examples represent debts of a corporation, there is a question as to whether there is an ownership interest in each case which requires accounting recognition.

Instructions

[a] Define convertible debt and debt issued with stock-purchase warrants.
[b] Discuss the similarities and differences of convertible debt and debt issued with stock-purchase warrants.
[c] Describe the alternative accounting treatments for the proceeds from convertible debt. Explain which treatment is preferable.
[d] Describe the alternative accounting treatments for the proceeds from debt issued with stock-purchase warrants. Explain which treatment is preferable.   (AICPA adapted)

15–60   DEBT REFINANCING   Fallbrook Vineyards, Inc., suffered a crop failure during the summer of 1992. As the end of their reporting year nears, the controller of Fallbrook is searching for ways to increase reported earnings. Among other alternatives, the controller is considering refinancing the company's long-term borrowing. Fallbrook issued $500,000 of 6% notes payable to a bank at 100 several years ago when interest rates were much lower. The bank has since approached Fallbrook with the following proposal. The old note matures at December 31, 2012.

In exchange for the $500,000 note now owed, the bank will allow Fallbrook to issue a new note for only $475,000 maturing in 20 years at the current rate of 20%. Under each alternative, interest is paid annually on the liability.

Instructions

[a] Prepare a *pro forma* journal entry that would be made if Fallbrook accepts the proposal.
[b] Describe the theoretical support for this treatment. Also, comment on any problems you see in this treatment.
[c] Suggest a way to overcome the problem(s) discussed in [b]. Do not limit your discussion to contemporary generally accepted accounting principles.
[d] Comment on the controller's decision. Should Fallbrook refinance the debt? Consider present value concepts in your answer, but do not attempt any present-value calculations.

15–61   DEBT FINANCING VS. LEASING   The president of Tots Toy Company has decided to expand the manufacturing capacity of his company in order to meet increased demand for certain low-cost toys. Betty Stone, vice-president for production, has located two similar plant sites on which comparable industrial buildings already exist. Betty has approached the president to decide which site should be selected.

The first site could be purchased for $200,000. The toy company's banker, C. Jenkins, indicates that an 80% loan of $160,000 for 20 years could be arranged at an interest rate of 15% to allow Tots to buy the facility. Equal annual payments of $25,562 will be made to the bank under the terms of the proposed loan. The second site is available only through a long-term lease which requires a 20-year term with payments of $25,000 to be made at the end of each year.

In evaluating the two alternatives, Ms. Stone points out that under the lease, no down payment is required, the annual payments are virtually equal, and best of all, the company will not be required to record any liability for the lease on its financial statements. In this manner the debt to equity and return on assets ratios will be maintained. Under the purchase arrangement, however, both ratios mentioned above will become weaker.

Instructions

[a] If you were president of Tots Toy Company, would you accept Ms. Stone's advice? If not, what additional information would you request?

[b] Discuss the propriety of not recording the lease as a liability. Do not consider current authoritative pronouncements in your answer. Rather, discuss the conceptual meaning and characteristics of liabilities in general.

15-62 FINANCIAL STATEMENT PRESENTATION   On January 1, 1992, Hanford Corporation issued $1,106,775 in 20-year bonds which have a maturity value of $1,000,000 and pay interest semiannually on January 1 and July 1. Bond issue costs were not material in amount. The following three presentations of the long-term liability section of the balance sheet might be used for these bonds at the issue date:

[1] Bonds payable (maturing Jan. 1, 2012)	$1,000,000
Unamortized premium on bonds payable	106,775
Total bond liability	$1,106,775
[2] Bonds payable, principal (face value $1,000,000, maturing Jan. 1, 2012)	$ 252,572*
Bonds payable, interest (semiannual payment $40,000)	854,203**
Total bond liability	$1,106,775
[3] Bonds payable, principal (maturing Jan. 1, 2012)	$1,000,000
Bonds payable, interest ($40,000 per period for 40 periods)	1,600,000
Total bond liability	$2,600,000

*The present value of $1,000,000 due at the end of 40 (six-month) periods at the yield rate of 3½% per period.
**The present value of $40,000 per period for 40 (six-month) periods at the yield rate of 3½% per period.

Instructions

[a] Discuss the conceptual merit(s) of each of the date-of-issue balance sheet presentations shown above for these bonds.

[b] Explain why investors would pay $1,106,775 for bonds with a maturity value of only $1,000,000.

[c] Assuming that a discount rate is needed to compute the carrying value of the obligations arising from a bond issue at any date during the life of the bonds, discuss the conceptual merit(s) of using for this purpose:
  [1] The coupon or nominal rate.
  [2] The effective or yield rate at date of issue.

[d] If the obligations arising from these bonds are to be carried at their present value, computed by means of the current market rate of interest, how would the bond valuation after the date of issue be affected by an increase or a decrease in the market rate of interest? (AICPA adapted)

15-63 (Appendix A) TROUBLED-DEBT RESTRUCTURING   While discussing troubled-debt restructurings, a CPA commented: "The determination of whether or not a debt restructuring is a troubled-debt restructuring is simplified because the economic results of any restructuring clearly indicate what type of transaction has occurred. Little judgment is required, other than the possible determination of fair market value of assets or equity interests transferred."

Instructions

Describe other areas, if any, requiring interpretation and judgment in identifying and accounting for debt restructurings.

JUDGMENT CASES

15–64   CLASSIFYING FINANCIAL INSTRUMENTS   You are the controller of Soltalt, Inc., and are in the process of preparing its annual financial statements. During the year the company borrowed $10,000,000 by issuing "income bonds." The bonds mature in 20 years but require the payment of interest only if income is earned in an amount sufficient to pay the interest in each year.

You have just received a memo from the president of Soltalt stating his belief that the bonds should not be reported in the balance sheet caption as "liabilities" due to the unusual interest-paying feature. While he does not suggest that the bonds be reported as a part of stockholders' equity, it is clear that he does not want them included in the company's liabilities on the balance sheet. He also points out that the present value of the maturity amount of the bonds is just a small portion of the present value of the maturity and interest payments. That is, the present value of the interest payments represents most of the present value of the total future cash outflows of the bonds, and that amount is contingent on the ability of Soltalt to earn sufficient income in each year.

Instructions

Develop a method of presenting the bonds that you believe meets professional standards but that also satisfies the wishes of your boss. If both can not be achieved, develop a solution that meets professional standards and comes as close as possible to meeting the wishes of the president.

15–65   RELATED PARTY OBLIGATIONS   During the past year your client, Young Win, Inc., borrowed $250,000 from its president and sole owner. It is now January 25 and you are preparing the December 31 financial statements for the year just ended. There is no note to support the loan and Mr. Win has told you that the terms were never well developed. He stated, "The company needed the money to pay one of its notes that had come due, and I had to make sure that the company didn't default. The company will pay me back when it can afford to." Now you must consider whether the borrowing should be reported as current or a long-term liability, and you have approached Mr. Win to resolve the issue. In response to your question he states, "if anything, the amount is a long-term liability. It is certainly not current. Wow, reporting that amount as a current liability will result in violations of working capital maintenance covenants on one of my bank loans, and that will be bad news. In fact, why don't we just consider the amount as a permanent contribution to the capital of the company? Yeah. That's it. Then the bank will be even more impressed by my debt/equity ratio. Just report the amount as an addition to the stockholders' equity of the company. I'll be happy to write you up something to that effect, if it will make you feel better." At that point he prepares a memo that asserts that the amounts provided by him to the company are permanent contributions to the equity of the company.

You leave this meeting with mixed emotions. While the terms and conditions of the transaction are clearly within Mr. Win's authority to define, you remember a discussion you had with him about his personal tax situation in which he spoke of withdrawing funds from his company to facilitate a payment to the Internal Revenue Service. When you call to remind of this conversation, he responds, "I can get that money from a lot of places, and you need not worry about where or if I can pay my taxes. Just prepare the financial statements for my company along the lines we discussed and everything will be O.K." You now wonder what to make of all this information.

Instructions

Determine how the $250,000 amount should be reported. If you believe that additional disclosures are necessary be sure to describe what information should be included.

15–66   EXISTENCE OF A LIABILITY   You are auditing the financial statements of Real World, Inc., a real estate developer located and operating exclusively in the Chicago area and have just stumbled across a 5-year nonrecourse note payable that was incurred during the past year. The note, which has not been recorded in the general ledger, was incurred in the acquisition of a parcel of land in Wyoming. However, you are not aware of any plans to begin development activities away from the Chicago area and when you ask management about the note, the president responds as follows:

> *We didn't want to sign that note; however, that was the only way that our local bank would give us a construction loan for the shopping center project out in the Cicero suburb. The note is without recourse except for the Wyoming property which*

serves as the only collateral. The interest payable on the $5,000,000 note was to come from the proceeds of our large shopping center loan. So we had to sign our shopping center loan for $21,000,000 rather than the $20,000,000 that we wanted just to allow them to withhold the extra $1,000,000 as interest on the $5,000,000 nonrecourse note.

> *The lending officer assured us that when the note matured in five years we could default on it and they would take back the property at that time in accordance with the nonrecourse provisions without any prejudice to us. In fact the president of the bank personally assured me of the acceptability of this arrangement. Since that was the only way we could get our loan, we agreed. That's all there is to this deal. We do not intend to repay the loan at its maturity. Indeed, one of our people who is familiar with land in that area told us that the property is probably worth only about $500,000. We view this deal as a way for the bank to increase the effective rate of interest on our big construction loan. We now have to repay and pay interest on an extra $1,000,000 which, of course, is reported appropriately. We don't think that we have acquired land or incurred additional debt in the amount of $5,000,000.*

When you suggest that it might be necessary to record the loan and related property the president of Real World responds, "No, we are not going to do that. The substance of the transaction is not the acquisition of land and the incurrance of debt. We are never going to pay that debt. At maturity, we are simply going to let the property revert to our lender. To report a liability in this circumstance would cause the financial statements to be misleading."

You have since confirmed the essence of the transaction with officials at the bank. They also stated that they acquired the land through foreclosure proceedings that resulted from a default on a loan they had made to a party completely unrelated and unknown to Real World, Inc. They added that the current deal was structured to accomplish certain financial reporting objectives of theirs, and that in no way should any of this reflect adversely on Real World, Inc.

Instructions

Determine how you should respond to this situation. Should you insist on recording the loan and related debt? If so, at what amount should the debt and land be recorded?

CHAPTER 16

Stockholders' Equity: Corporate Formation and Contributed Capital

OBJECTIVES

1. To discuss characteristics, advantages, and disadvantages of the corporate form of business enterprise.
2. To explain various stockholders' rights and different types of equity securities.
3. To identify the characteristics of common and preferred stock.
4. To explain the judgments necessary in distinguishing between debt and equity securities and among various types of equity instruments.
5. To describe and illustrate acceptable accounting and reporting practices for the issuance of capital stock for both cash and noncash consideration.
6. To describe and illustrate acceptable accounting and reporting practices for the issuance of capital stock through subscription.
7. To describe and illustrate methods of accounting for treasury stock.
8. To describe and illustrate acceptable accounting and reporting practices for the retirement of capital stock including treasury stock.
9. To describe and illustrate acceptable accounting and reporting practices for property and treasury stock donations.

T he substantial growth in the corporate form of business during the industrial revolution was, in part, a response to the demands of commerce. As capital was substituted for labor and as mass production economies replaced individual craft shops, the need for larger accumulations of capital became more intense. Few individuals possessed the resources necessary to build factories, hire employees, and sustain operations until an adequate level of profitability and accumulated earnings was generated. As a result of these and related factors, the modern corporate form of business was developed, expanded, and refined.

THE CORPORATE ENVIRONMENT

Corporations offer important advantages over other forms of business, such as sole proprietorships and partnerships. For example, the corporate organization (1) facilitates the accumulation of large amounts of capital; (2) provides for economies of scale in production due to the potential large size of corporate organizations; and (3) facilitates a capital market in which resources are easily allocated to more efficient producers. Other advantages include **limited liability,** in that stockholders have no personal liability for the debts of the corporation and risk only their capital investments; and **unlimited life of the corporation,** in that the death of a stockholder does not cause the termination of the corporation, as in the case of the death of a partner in a partnership.

Unfortunately, the advantages of limited liability and unlimited life do not come without some cost to the stockholders. One cost is in the form of **double taxation.** A corporation, unlike a partnership or a sole proprietorship, is generally subject to taxation on net income. Furthermore, individual stockholders are subject to taxation on the distributions of that corporate net income as they receive dividends. Therefore, income is taxed at the corporate level and again at the individual level.

The corporation stockholders often are not involved in the custody and management of corporate assets. Financial accounting and reporting therefore provides valuable communication between the owners and the managers of a corporation. The custodians of resources report on the efficiency and effectiveness of their performance to the providers of those resources. Resource providers of corporations are either (1) owners, or stockholders; or (2) creditors. Chapters 14 and 15 discuss accounting and reporting for the liabilities of the corporation. This chapter and the following one are concerned with financial accounting and reporting for stockholders' equity.

THE CORPORATE STRUCTURE

A corporation is established under the authority of state law. In most cases a state official, frequently the Secretary of State, responds to a request for a corporate charter made by **incorporators,** who will become **stockholders** of the corporation. A corporate charter and related **articles of incorporation** describe the nature of the business, the classes and types of corporate stock to be issued, and other pertinent information. After a corporate charter is granted, the **common stockholders** elect a **board of directors** which, in turn, appoints members of corporate management, such as the president, several vice-presidents, and other executives. The board of directors also approves the corporate **bylaws** under which the company operates.

TYPES OF CORPORATIONS

Corporations are usually stock-ownership companies that are organized for profit. There are, however, other types of corporate organizations. For example, **public corporations** may be established and owned by a unit of government to meet a social need. Examples include the Federal Deposit Insurance Corporation, which insures deposits in certain commercial banks, and the Off Track Betting Corporation, which provides revenue to the City of New York from pari-mutuel horse race betting.

Mutual companies are cooperative organizations designed to benefit consumer groups. Shares are distributed to customers of the organization. Many life insurance companies and savings and loan associations are mutual companies. Policyholders of mutual life insurance companies and depositors of savings and loan associations are given the rights and privileges usually afforded owners in a stock company. Corporate profits can be distributed to the customers in the form of lower prices or as dividends. Because mutual companies do not have stockholders, their balance sheets have no owner contributions or stockholders' equity section.

In contrast to public corporations and mutual companies, **private corporations** are owned by individuals or institutions and may be publicly held or closely held. **Publicly held corporations** register stock and other securities with the Securities and Exchange Commission (SEC) and are usually actively traded in an organized securities market such as the New York or American Stock Exchange. Ownership of publicly held companies is usually widespread and may include thousands of shareholders. **Closely held corporations** issue stock to a limited and well-defined group. Ownership is generally closed to prospective stockholders.

Two types of closely held corporations are the **professional corporation** and the **S corporation.** Professional corporations are established by members of a legally recognized profession, such as medicine, law, and accountancy. Ownership shares are usually available only to members of the profession. This limitation is intended to ensure the integrity of the profession by minimizing conflict of interest and professional compromise. S corporations (named for subchapter S of the Internal Revenue Code) have many advantages of the corporate form, without the negative element of double taxation. To maintain this favorable tax status, S corporations can have no more than 35 stockholders.[1]

Exhibit 16–1 summarizes the types of corporations introduced here.

EXHIBIT 16–1
Types of Corporations

Corporation Type	Nature of Ownership
1. Public corporations	Government owned
2. Mutual companies	Consumer controlled
3. Private corporations	Stockholder owned
(a) Publicly held corporations	Widely distributed ownership by institutions and/or individuals; shares typically traded on organized exchanges
(b) Closely held corporations	Limited distribution of ownership
(1) Professional corporations	Shares restricted to members of a legally recognized profession
(2) S corporations	Designed to avoid double taxation
(3) Other closely held corporations	Limited ownership by institutions and/or individuals; shares not traded on organized exchanges

---

[1]This limit may be increased to 70 if spouses are included as shareholders.

STOCKHOLDERS' RIGHTS AND TYPES OF STOCKHOLDERS' EQUITY

Because the rights and risks of the various resource providers differ greatly, accountants must clearly understand stockholders' rights and responsibilities. The basic rights of the shareholder fall into three major categories: (1) rights to management; (2) rights to corporate property; and (3) rights to pass on changes in the original contract.[2] **Rights to management** include the right to elect directors, based on the pro rata ownership share in the firm, and the right to receive financial statements. **Rights to corporate property** include the right to declared dividends and the right to a proportionate share of corporate property at dissolution. **Rights to pass on changes in the original contract** include the right to vote on changes in the corporate bylaws and the right to maintain the pro rata ownership share based on the level of the original investment. The right to maintain the pro rata ownership share is called a **preemptive right,** and it enables a stockholder to purchase additional securities from a new stock offering up to the percentage that the individual owned prior to the new issuance. Accordingly, a stockholder's percentage of ownership cannot be reduced as a result of a corporation issuing additional shares of stock to different investors, unless the stockholder declines the opportunity to acquire additional shares.

Not all stockholders receive all of the rights mentioned above. For example, the preemptive right has often been eliminated in recent elections passing on changes in the corporate bylaws. Furthermore, all stockholders of a corporation may not be entitled to the same rights. Many large corporations issue several classes of stock, with different characteristics and rights (e.g., dividend preferences, dividend amounts, and voting privileges). For example, Giant Food, Inc., which operates almost 150 supermarkets, has authorized three classes of stock. Exhibit 16–2 is the footnote description of these classes of stock in the company's annual report. Each class of stock has distinct characteristics and confers certain rights. Class AC and AL common stock, for example, provide voting privileges. In this way, control of the corporation can be maintained by a select group of stockholders, while capital can be accumulated from a widespread distribution of Class A common stock.

Accountants classify stockholders' equity as either **contributed equity** or **earned equity.** Distinguishing between these types of equity in financial reports is important, because such information enables investors to determine how much a company relies on owner contributions versus profitable operations to sustain its financial base. Earned equity, called **retained earnings,** is discussed in the following chapter. Stockholders' contributed equity, the subject of this chapter, is usually classified for accounting and reporting purposes as **preferred stock** or **common stock.** We will now discuss the major characteristics of common stock and preferred stock.

CHARACTERISTICS OF CAPITAL STOCK

The term **capital stock** identifies shareholder contributions to the enterprise. It can also be used to discuss classes of common stock or preferred stock. Two of the most significant features of capital stock are the following: (1) capital stock does *not* generally have a maturity date on which the principal portion of the security must be repaid; and (2) dividends are *not* required to be paid on capital stock.

These characteristics of capital stock are also the most important factors distinguishing debt financing from stockholders' contributed equity. Most debt instruments require the payment of interest on a regular basis and specify a maturity date. In

---

[2]For more detailed discussion, see Richard A. Scott, "Owners' Equity, the Anachronistic Element," *Accounting Review* (October 1979), pp. 750–763.

EXHIBIT 16-2

Giant Food, Inc.
Note Disclosure of Classes of Stock

6. Common Stock, Capital in Excess of Par and Treasury Stock

Common stock, $1 par:

		Outstanding		
Class	Authorized	1990	1989	1988
"A", non-voting	75,000,000	59,507,182	59,913,473	29,825,975
"AC", voting	125,000	125,000	125,000	125,000
"AL", voting	125,000	125,000	125,000	125,000
	75,250,000	59,757,182	60,163,473	30,075,975

The Class "A" stock has all of the rights and privileges pertaining to common stock except the right to vote. No dividends may be declared on any class of common stock without declaring at least an equal dividend on Class "A" stock; however, dividends may be declared on Class "A" stock without declaring dividends on any other class of common stock.

Changes in issued common stock, capital in excess of par and treasury stock for the three years ended February 24, 1990 were as follows:

	Common stock, all classes		Capital in excess of par	Treasury stock (Class "A")	
	Shares	Amount		Shares	Amount
Balance, March 1, 1987	30,128,310	$30,128	$ 3,183	83,550	$ 2,076
Purchase of treasury shares				92,000	2,665
Issuance of shares under employee benefit plans			(667)	(123,215)	(3,250)
Balance, February 27, 1988	30,128,310	30,128	2,516	52,335	1,491
Capitalization of retained earnings			30,000		
Issuance of shares pursuant to two-for-one stock split	30,128,310	30,129	(30,129)	35,038	
Purchase of treasury shares				189,000	3,838
Issuance of shares under employee benefit plans			(1,329)	(183,226)	(3,364)
Balance, February 25, 1989	60,256,620	60,257	1,058	93,147	1,965
Purchase of treasury shares				646,800	16,424
Issuance of shares under employee benefit plans			(1,058)	(240,509)	(5,559)
Balance, February 24, 1990	60,256,620	$60,257		499,438	$12,830

SOURCE: Giant Food, Inc., 1990 Annual Report.

contrast, equity securities generally require neither dividends nor repayment of the principal amount of the investment. Distinguishing between debt and equity instruments is not, however, as simple as it may first appear. A number of securities that are in relatively common use contain elements of both. For example, some options sold by a company may require that entity to issue shares of its own capital stock at a certain price. Does such an obligation represent a liability or part of stockholders' equity?

The question may be particularly significant if the price at which the stock must be issued is substantially less than the market price of the shares.

We discuss some of these questions in the following pages of this chapter. However, these and many other questions are currently being considered as part of a major FASB agenda project. A discussion memorandum of the FASB, "Distinguishing Between Liability and Equity Instruments and Accounting for Instruments with Characteristics of Both" was issued in 1990 and identifies many of the important issues that need to be resolved in this area of financial reporting. Further progress on this project is expected during the next several years and students should be alert for any developments that take place. In the interim, professional accountants must use great judgment in classifying and accounting for such hybrid instruments. In complex situations financial statement disclosures should include a description of the instrument and the related accounting policies accorded it.

Minimum Legal Capital

In the event of dissolution of a corporation, creditors receive assets to satisfy their claims before assets are distributed to stockholders. Therefore, the greater the assets contributed to the enterprise by stockholders, the greater the security of creditors. In order to protect creditors from an excessive or unwarranted distribution of assets to stockholders, states have enacted laws requiring corporations to maintain certain minimum levels of stockholders' equity. Through these laws enterprises are prohibited from distributing assets to shareholders to such an extent that the minimum legal capital is impaired. Creditors are thus assured of at least a minimum continuing economic commitment of stockholders in the enterprise.

To assure an adequate measure of minimum legal capital, many state laws require corporations to issue stock with a **par value**. State laws frequently require corporations: (1) to assign a formal par value to stock; (2) to ensure that the stock not be sold **at discount** (i.e., at an amount less than par); and (3) to maintain a minimum amount of legal capital. Accordingly, companies frequently assign a relatively low par value to their stock and issue enough shares to meet the legal requirements. For example, if a company is required to maintain minimum legal capital of $5,000 and issues $10 par value stock, then at least 500 shares should be issued at an amount no less than par to comply with this provision of state law.

In some jurisdictions common stock may be issued at a discount. Under those circumstances the amount of the discount is considered a contingent liability of the owners to the creditors of the corporation. In the event of liquidation of corporate assets, the creditors may recover unsatisfied obligations by assessing the owners for additional contributions up to the amount of the original discount. Although most stock is nonassessable, accountants should be alert to the possibility of such a problem, especially if stock has been issued at a discount on par.

A corporation may also issue **no-par stock**. State law usually requires the company to **assign** or **state a value** for no-par stock in order to comply with the corporate charter and minimum legal capital requirements. The use of stated or assigned value is usually legally acceptable and poses no significant accounting problems. Some jurisdictions allow the issuance of **true no-par stock**, which has no par, stated, or assigned value. In addition, true no-par stock cannot be issued at a discount and thus involves no contingent liability of the stockholders to corporate creditors.

Par, stated, or assigned value on common stock must not be confused with either market value or book value per share. The **market value per share of stock** is the price at which both buyer and seller would agree to transact a sale. Market values for common stock are quoted for most publicly held companies in publications such as the *Wall Street Journal*. The **book value per share of stock** is the total stockholders' equity divided by the total number of shares outstanding. The book value per share is the dollar amount per share an owner would receive if assets were liquidated and obligations were satisfied at the amounts reported on the financial statements. Both the market value and the book value per share are generally much larger than the par, stated, or assigned value. The market value of stock is influenced by a variety of factors including analysts' and others' expectations about a company's future profits and cash flows. The par value of a stock is not a measure of the value or worth of a company. Par value is simply a legal device frequently used by states to protect creditors. Many persons would call the concept of par or stated value an anachronism in the context of the modern corporation.

States grant corporate charters to enterprises in their jurisdictions and enforce laws governing corporate conduct. Because these laws differ, the American Bar Association (ABA) has tried to establish a unified system of law for all states. Specifically, the ABA's Committee on Corporate Laws has suggested a Model Business Corporation Act. However, not all states have adopted the provisions of the model act. Furthermore, the act contains terminology that can be interpreted differently, and certain provisions have become obsolete. Accountants must be aware of the state corporation laws affecting their employers or clients in order to adequately account for the rights and protections of the various resource providers.

CLASSES OF CAPITAL STOCK

Common Stock

Common stock represents the most fundamental type of equity and generally gives the owner the right to vote, to share in residual profits, and, in the event of dissolution, to share in all assets remaining after creditors' and preferred stockholders' claims have been satisfied. If there is only one class of stock, it is common stock.

Common stockholders have a residual interest in the corporation, because they receive economic benefit *only if* the corporation successfully meets its obligations to creditors and preferred stockholders. Therefore, common stockholders tend to assume more risk than other groups associated with the enterprise. Consistent with the relatively high level of risk, however, is the potential for great financial reward. Common stockholders have no upper limit on their economic rewards from profitable operations. Creditors receive only interest and principal repayment, while preferred stockholders, with certain exceptions, receive a fixed or limited return on their investment regardless of profitability. Therefore, if a company is exceptionally profitable in its operation, the holdings of common stockholders will become more valuable. Conversely, if a company suffers losses, the value of the common stockholders' equity will be reduced as fewer assets are available to satisfy residual claims.

Preferred Stock

Preferred stock represents equity securities that receive a preference over the claims of common stockholders in terms of dividends from earnings and assets in the event of dissolution. Therefore, preferred stock usually represents a somewhat less risky investment than common stock. Although the board of directors of a corporation is not required to declare dividends on either stock, any dividend declared must go first to preferred stockholders to the extent of their preference claims. The amount of the dividend to be paid on preferred stock is generally stated as a percentage of the par or stated value of the stock. For example, a holder of $100 par value 12% preferred stock has the right to receive a dividend, if declared, each year of $12 ($100 × .12). Furthermore, in the event of bankruptcy or other dissolution, preferred stockholders receive the par or stated value of their investment before any distribution is made to common stockholders. Occasionally, no-par preferred stock is issued, with the dividend stated as a fixed dollar amount rather than as a percentage of par. An amount to be distributed upon dissolution is also stated in the event of the termination of the business. Preferred stock, which usually conveys no voting rights, often carries other types of preference claims.

Cumulative Preferred Stock. A **cumulative clause** on preferred stock means that all dividends, including dividends that were not declared and paid in prior years, must be updated and paid before any dividends can be paid to common stockholders. Although stockholders cannot directly require the payment of dividends, a cumulative clause protects preferred stockholders from situations in which no dividends are paid on preferred or common shares for several years and then an exceptionally large dividend is declared. If preferred stock is not cumulative, preferred stockholders receive only the dividends attributable to the current year. If, however, preferred is cumulative, the current year's dividend and all **dividends in arrears** must be paid to preferred stockholders before the common stockholders share in a distribution. The application of the cumulative feature is illustrated in Chapter 17, where we discuss dividends in detail.

Participating Preferred Stock. A **participation right** allows preferred stockholders not only to receive the preference dividend but also to share with common stockholders in any further dividends that are declared. Participating preferred stock may be either fully or partially participating. If the stock is **fully participating,** the preferred stockholders share dividend distributions with common stockholders without limit. With **partially participating** preferred stock, the preferred stockholders share dividends in excess of the stated rate in only a limited way. Participation features are illustrated in Chapter 17.

Callable Preferred Stock. Some preferred stock issues are **callable,** which means the shares may be redeemed at the option of the corporation. Although the individual shareholder cannot demand the exercise of a call provision (as at the maturity date of a bond issue), the corporation can terminate the life of a callable preferred stock issue. When such a feature is present, the stock certificate states a **call price,** which is usually a few percentage points higher than the issuance price. Such a call premium is generally necessary to make the callable stock attractive to investors.

Corporations may favor a call provision, because it allows them to use the money generated from the stock issue for only as long as needed and then to call the stock and return the money to the stockholders. Excess resources are thus divested, allowing the corporation to retain only needed productive assets. Moreover, the call provision provides an escape mechanism for the corporation in the event of a market decline. Specifically, if the market cost of capital decreases significantly from the preferred stock's dividend rate, a call provision allows the corporation to redeem the preferred stock and issue a new offering at the lower financing rate. Of course, from the investor's perspective, a call provision is a negative characteristic that may cause the involuntary divestiture of an investment that is generating above-market returns. As a result, investors frequently demand a dividend rate on callable preferred stock above the market rate for similar noncallable preferred stock.

Convertible Preferred Stock. With this type of stock, stockholders can exchange preferred stock for common stock at a predetermined ratio or price. Convertible preferred stock may be quite attractive to investors, because it provides them with preferred claims on dividends and enables them to become common shareholders and participate without limitation in the earnings of the business.

The outstanding feature of convertible preferred stock is the opportunity for the preferred stock investor to participate in potential gains in the price of common shares. For example, assume the Hydrophonics Corporation (a producer of underwater amplifiers) issues $100 par, 10% preferred stock at par that is convertible into four common shares. If the market value per common share is $20, the preferred shareholder would not find the conversion feature attractive. Conversion would imply a trade of $100 preferred stock for common stock worth $80. However, if the price of the common stock increased to $35 per share, the conversion feature would accumulate explicit value. A preferred stockholder could trade $100 of preferred stock for common shares worth $140 (4 × $35).

The preferred stockholder could realize this benefit not only through conversion but also by selling the preferred stock to someone who would be willing to pay $140 per share. Because of the attractiveness of the convertibility feature to investors, corporate issuers can frequently offer a dividend rate on convertible preferred stock that is less than the rate on similar nonconvertible shares.

Redeemable Preferred Stock.   Corporations have found redeemable preferred stock an attractive means of obtaining capital contributions. Redeemable preferred stock has the unique feature of mandatory redemption at a specified date or, less frequently, redemption at the stockholder's discretion. This feature is not to be confused with callability. Callable preferred stock is redeemable at the issuer's discretion, whereas redeemable preferred stock must be retired at a specified date according to the provisions of the preferred stock contract.

A question arises as to whether this type of preferred stock possesses more of the characteristics of debt than of equity. Redeemable preferred stock is not a form of permanent capitalization and must be retired or refunded at a specified date, much the same as debt. However, redeemable preferred stock does not guarantee a return on the investment, as does debt. The omission of a preferred stock dividend payment does not initiate grounds for default, as does the omission of a debt interest payment. Furthermore, redeemable preferred stock is subordinate to debt in the event of final liquidation of assets. Therefore, redeemable preferred stock has the characteristics of *both* debt and equity. If, however, we assume a viable business, the return guarantee and subordination characteristics would not seem critical to the investor. The dominant characteristic would appear to be the mandatory redemption requirement. As a result,

Substance
over
Form

many people believe that redeemable preferred stock is in substance a type of pseudo-debt.[3] Indeed, the SEC requires companies subject to its jurisdiction to report redeemable preferred stock outside of the stockholders' equity section of the balance sheet. As previously discussed, this subject and many other related topics are under active consideration by the FASB at this time.

Exhibit 16–3 illustrates the financial statement disclosure of redeemable preferred stock for the hypothetical enterprise, Suburban Paper Company. The note disclosure included in the exhibit presents the details of the redeemable preferred stock which is included in the company's balance sheet.

If redeemable preferred stock is in substance a form of debt, why doesn't the corporate issuer just issue straight debt? This question is especially intriguing because preferred stock dividends are not deductible for tax purposes, whereas debt interest payments are deductible. The answer may lie in the corporate manager's desire to avoid the violation of restrictive bond covenants prohibiting the issuance of further debt. An inspection of corporate lending agreements of publicly held companies reveals the expression of restrictive covenants in terms of generally accepted accounting principles (GAAP). As a result, a corporate borrower could circumvent a restrictive covenant on the issuance of additional debt by issuing redeemable preferred stock,

---

[3]See R. D. Nair, Larry E. R. Henberg, and Jerry J. Weygandt, "Accounting For Redeemable Preferred Stock: Unresolved Issues," *Accounting Horizons* (June, 1990), pp. 33–41, for a further discussion of these issues.

EXHIBIT 16–3

Suburban Paper Company
Financial Statement Disclosure of Redeemable Preferred Stock

(in thousands)	1992
Liabilities and Stockholders' Equity	
Current liabilities	
Accounts payable	$ 41,250
Income taxes (Note 3)	13,400
Accrued expenses	82,950
Current portion of long-term debt and redeemable preferred stock (Note 4)	6,790
	$144,390
Long-term debt (Note 5)	217,050
Deferred income taxes (Note 6)	42,700
$10 cumulative preferred stock, $1 par value; stated at $100 redemption value, less $1,500,000 included in current liabilities; 90,000 shares authorized and issued (Note 4)	9,000
Common stock, $5 par value; 5,000,000 shares authorized, 2,700,000 shares issued and outstanding	13,500
Paid-in capital in excess of par	181,000
Retained earnings	195,000
Total liabilities and stockholders' equity	$802,640

Note 4—$10 cumulative preferred stock

The $10 cumulative preferred stock is redeemable at $100 per share. Fifteen thousand shares are required to be redeemed on June 30 annually through 1999. The company has the option of redeeming the stock entirely, or in part, at any time through 1999. Fifteen thousand shares were redeemed in 1992. The cumulative preferred stockholders are not entitled to voting rights.

which has the main characteristics of debt but is not technically debt according to GAAP. In this way the corporate borrower could obtain "near debt" financing without violating existing contracts. Furthermore, if the corporation issues the redeemable preferred stock to other corporations, a below-market dividend rate can be offered. Corporate investors may agree to accept a below-market return, because corporations can exclude most of their dividend income from federal income taxation.[4]

ACCOUNTING FOR CAPITAL STOCK

The issuance of capital stock is a fairly infrequent but highly significant event in the operation of a corporation. As an example, in late 1982 CBS, Inc., the second largest broadcaster in the United States, brought a new equity offering to the market for the

---

[4]The **exclusion rule** was established to prevent corporate profits distributed to an investor corporation from being taxed more than twice. To illustrate, assume Corporation B has an investment in Corporation A common stock. Without the exclusion rule, Corporation A profits that were distributed to Corporation B would be taxed three times: as net income to Corporation A, as dividend income to Corporation B, and as dividend income to individual equity investors in Corporation B. The exclusion rule eliminates most of the second stage of taxation, so that corporate profits are taxed only twice: once at the corporate level, and once at the individual investor level.

first time in 45 years. Likewise, RCA, the consumer electronics company, issued new equity shares in 1982 for the first time since the company's inception in 1919.

The issuance of capital stock should not be confused with transactions in the **secondary market,** such as the New York or American Stock Exchange. The secondary market is represented by transactions between owners of previously issued shares of stock. The corporation is not a party to transactions involving its own stock in the secondary market, except in the case of treasury stock transactions, which are discussed later in this chapter. New issues are sold through an intermediary, called an **underwriter.** The underwriter, or more frequently an underwriting syndicate, makes the new offering available to investors, much like a retail store for new common stock offerings. Exhibit 16–4 illustrates a new issue announcement by an underwriting syndicate. These announcements are called "tombstones" (they resemble tombstones) and are placed in financial publications such as the *Wall Street Journal*.

Issuances of capital stock require the approval of a company's board of directors and also must result in a total number of outstanding shares that is within the number authorized in the corporate charter granted by the state. A great deal of planning and research generally precedes a stock issue in order to make it attractive to investors. Although stock is usually issued for cash, other consideration may be accepted as payment. Also, subscriptions for future stock are frequently sold before the stock is issued.

STOCK ISSUED FOR CASH

Par or Stated Value Capital Stock

When capital stock is issued for cash, an entry is made to debit Cash, credit either Common Stock or Preferred Stock for the par or stated value, and recognize any Discount on Par or Paid-in Capital in Excess of Par on the issuance. To illustrate, if Haller Company issues 500 shares of $10 par value common stock at $15 per share on October 31, 1992, the following journal entry is necessary:

Oct. 31, 1992	Cash	7,500	
	Common Stock		5,000
	Paid-in Capital in Excess of Par		2,500
	(To record issuance of stock.)		

Note that no gain or loss is recognized on the issuance of stock. Indeed, gains and losses are not recognized on any investment transactions with owners. Such increases and decreases in equity do not result from revenue-generating activities and are therefore excluded from the income statement. Changes in net assets resulting from investment transactions with owners are treated as direct changes in the appropriate contributed stockholders' equity accounts.

Paid-in capital in excess of par represents an increase in contributed capital above the par amount, while a discount on par represents owner contributions in an amount less than the total par value. Neither discount on par nor paid-in capital in excess of par affects retained earnings. Again, in many states it is illegal to issue stock at a discount because of laws establishing minimum legal capital. Therefore, the par value of stock is generally set at a low enough level to ensure the stock will sell at an amount above or at least equal to par. Accountants seldom encounter discount on par and we do not discuss discount extensively here.

Paid-in Capital in Excess of Par or Discount on Capital Stock, as an element of contributed capital, remains as an account during the entire time the stock is outstanding. Thus, paid-in capital in excess of par or discount on par is reported in the balance sheet from the time the stock is issued until it is reacquired and retired. Nor

EXHIBIT 16–4

Northrim Bank
New Issue Announcement

This announcement is neither an offer to sell nor a solicitation to buy any of these securities.
This offer is made only by the Offering Circular.

New Issue   November 6, 1990

1,087,500 Shares

Northrim Bank
(In Organization)

Common Stock

Price $8.00 Per Share

Copies of the Offering Circular may be obtained in any State only from the undersigned
as may lawfully offer these securities in such State.

Wedbush Morgan Securities

Bateman Eichler, Hill Richards
a division of Kemper Securities Group, Inc.

Boettcher & Company, Inc.
a division of Kemper Securities Group, Inc.

Dain Bosworth
Incorporated

Piper, Jaffray & Hopwood
Incorporated

Ragen MacKenzie Incorporated   **Raymond James & Associates, Inc.**

Seidler Amdec Securities Inc.

do the amounts in these accounts vary with changes in the market value of the company's stock. At the time of retirement all accounts related to the issuance of the stock are removed from the contributed stockholders' equity section of the balance sheet.

Costs incurred in issuing stock are appropriately treated as reductions of the related proceeds, and only the net amount of cash received is capitalized. Preferably, such issue costs are charged directly to the Capital Stock or Paid-in Capital in Excess of Par account. Law sometimes prohibits this treatment, however, and Retained Earnings may be charged. We discuss the few exceptions to these rules later in this chapter.

True No-Par Capital Stock

Occasionally a corporation may issue true no-par stock. Accounting for this type of stock issuance is simple. To illustrate, assume that Haller Company issued 500 shares of no-par common stock at $15 per share on October 31, 1992. The following journal entry is appropriate:

Oct. 31, 1992	Cash	7,500	
	Common Stock		7,500
	(To record issuance of no-par stock.)		

In contrast to the journal entry for the par value stock, there is no credit to a Paid-in Capital in Excess of Par account. Indeed, the issuance of true no-par stock never results in the recording of a separate Paid-in Capital in Excess of Par or a Discount on Par account. The total proceeds of the issuance should be credited to the appropriate capital stock account (either common or preferred).

Lump Sum Issuances

A corporation may issue multiple classes of capital stock and/or debt for a lump sum consideration. The accounting problem is to assign the lump sum purchase price to the various classes of securities. The solution is to allocate to each security in the package an issue price proportional to the fair market value of the security relative to the total fair market value of the package. To illustrate, assume that Haller Company issues the following securities for a lump sum consideration of $800,000:

Security	Number of Shares	Par Value	Market Price per Share	Total Value
Common—Class A	1,000 shares	$ 1.00	$ 30	$ 30,000
Common—Class B	10,000 shares	.50	36	360,000
$10 Preferred	5,000 shares	90.00	102	510,000
				$900,000

The $800,000 issue price is allocated to each security on the basis of relative market values, calculated as follows:

Security	Proportion	×	Lump Sum Price	=	Security Allocation	=	Par Value	+	Paid-in Capital in Excess of Par Value
Common—Class A	$ 30,000 / $900,000		$800,000		$ 26,667		$ 1,000		$ 25,667
Common—Class B	$360,000 / $900,000		800,000		320,000		5,000		315,000
$10 Preferred	$510,000 / $900,000		800,000		453,333		450,000		3,333
					$800,000	=	$456,000	+	$344,000

Haller Company makes the following journal entry for the $800,000 multiple security issuance:

Cash	800,000	
Common Stock—Class A		1,000
Common Stock—Class B		5,000
$10 Preferred Stock		450,000
Paid-in Capital in Excess of Par, Common Stock—Class A		25,667
Paid-in Capital in Excess of Par, Common Stock—Class B		315,000
Paid-in Capital in Excess of Par, $10 Preferred Stock		3,333

STOCK ISSUED FOR CONSIDERATION OTHER THAN CASH

In general, if a company's stock is issued for consideration other than cash, the transaction should be based on the *fair market value of the consideration received or the market value of the stock issued, whichever is more clearly discernible.* To illustrate, assume that Haller Company issues 1,000 shares of its $10 par value common stock for an automobile with a fair market value of $12,500. The following journal entry is required to properly record the transaction for consideration in the form of stock:

Equipment—Transportation	12,500	
Common Stock (1,000 shares at $10)		10,000
Paid-in Capital in Excess of Par		2,500
(To record acquisition of automobile and issuance of stock.)		

The automobile is subsequently depreciated in normal fashion, but the contributed stockholders' equity accounts are unchanged on successive balance sheets. Retained earnings will, of course, decrease through the recognition of depreciation expense over the life of the asset.

Occasionally, companies issue stock for services received that have no future benefit and do not qualify as assets. To illustrate, assume that an attorney agrees to accept 100 shares of Haller's $10 par value common stock in satisfaction of the legal fee of $1,370. The following entry records these transactions:

Professional Fees Expense	1,370	
Common Stock		1,000
Paid-in Capital in Excess of Par		370
(To record legal fee expense and issuance of common stock.)		

In this case Haller's net assets are unaffected, even though an expense is reported and net income is decreased. The balance sheet effect of this transaction is confined to the stockholders' equity section. Specifically, as retained earnings decrease through the recognition of the expense, contributed stockholders' equity accounts increase. There are no changes in the company's assets or liabilities as a result of this event.

STOCK ISSUED IN THE ABSENCE OF MARKET VALUES

A company may issue stock for noncash consideration, and neither the stock nor the consideration has an established market value. This situation most commonly occurs with development-stage companies. Recall from Chapter 13 that a development-stage company devotes substantial effort to establishing a new business, and either planned principal operating activities have not commenced, or, if such activities have begun, no significant revenues have been generated.

Because developing corporations frequently lack the resources to acquire the skills or rights necessary to achieve success, they often issue stock in exchange for noncash consideration. For example, a development-stage high-technology firm may need highly specialized engineering skills and product patent rights in order to begin operations. If these costs are prohibitive, new stock may have to be offered to the engineers and patent holders in return for their cooperation. An accounting problem arises if the noncash consideration received in exchange for the stock has no objectively determinable value. The lack of objectively determinable values is not uncommon in the case of legal rights, such as patents or copyrights, or with the acquisition of specialized skills. In addition, the stock may not have an established market value, because the development-stage corporation generally will not have traded stock in an organized market.

How then does the accountant assign a dollar amount to the stock issuance if neither the stock nor the related consideration has an objective market value? The Financial Accounting Standards Board (FASB) has required that a dollar amount be assigned to any noncash consideration received in exchange for equity securities. In the case of a noncash consideration without an objectively determinable market value, the FASB has given the accountant wide latitude in assigning dollar amounts to both the stock and the consideration received. For example, an estimate may be made by analyzing other stocks or considerations that are similar to those being exchanged and for which objective determination of market value is possible. In addition, the financial statements of the corporation must disclose the basis for assigning dollar amounts.[5]

STOCK SUBSCRIPTIONS

Corporations often sell rights to the shares in an initial stock issue before the stock is actually issued. Such rights are called **stock subscriptions.** Stock subscriptions are a useful way for development-stage corporations to market equity securities to public investors in an orderly manner. Stock subscriptions are generally sold to investors at a fraction of the total cost of the stock. The remaining portion of the stock price is paid by the subscriber at the time the shares are issued. Questions frequently arise as to how to record stock subscriptions if cash is received prior to the issuance of stock. Further, if the subscription down payment is forfeited because the subscription is not exercised and lapses, how should that circumstance be reported?

When a stock subscription contract is initiated, the company records the cash received and a "subscription receivable" for the unpaid balance of the stock price; credits are made to reflect an increase in the par value and the paid-in capital in excess of par value. Although the corporation is required to issue the stock after the subscription receivable has been fully paid, a liability does not exist as a result of the subscription contract. There are no claims on the corporation's assets but rather an obligation to issue capital stock when the subscription has been fully received. As such, the credit portion of the entry represents a direct increase in the equity of the company.

Another question related to stock subscriptions is whether a subscription receivable is an asset. The unpaid portion of the stock subscription represents a mutual promise of the corporation and the subscriber. The corporation promises to deliver stock in the future, and the subscriber promises to pay the balance of the subscription price. Accountants do not generally consider such *mutual promises* (executory con-

[5]*FASB Statement of Financial Accounting Standards No. 7,* "Accounting and Reporting by Development Stage Enterprises," 1975, par. 11. Under SEC rules, a dollar amount may *not* be assigned to noncash consideration lacking objectively determinable market value for issuances by development-stage corporations.

tracts) an accounting event, which generally results from the *partial performance* of a contract by one of the contracting parties. As an example, accounts receivable are recorded when one party to the contract delivers goods or services but remains unpaid. The delivering of goods or services on account is a partial performance of the agreement by the seller to the buyer and is considered a recordable event. The subscription receivable does not have this characteristic, because neither party has partially performed the agreement with respect to the unpaid portion of the subscription.

As a result, some have favored treating the subscription receivable as a reduction in stockholders' equity rather than as an asset. The stockholders' equity section would then reflect an increase only for the actual cash consideration. Presently, either an asset or a contra-equity presentation of the subscription receivable is acceptable. If little uncertainty exists as to the collectibility of the subscription receivable, many accountants would prefer recording the item as an asset. Conversely, the subscription receivable should be treated as a reduction of stockholders' equity if collection is uncertain. The preferred presentation also depends on the state laws applicable to stock subscriptions. For example, some state laws grant the subscriber all rights of stock ownership, including dividends and voting rights, for the complete subscription; others grant such rights only for the prepaid portion of the subscription. Under the former legal arrangement, the whole subscription should be disclosed as an increase in stockholders' equity; in the latter case a net equity presentation (subscriptions receivable as contra equity) would be more appropriate.

To illustrate the accounting for a subscription contract, assume that Nesor Corporation issues stock subscriptions for 1,000 shares of its $10 par value common stock at a subscribed price of $125. Further assume that investors must make a 50% down payment for all subscribed stock. The following journal entry is appropriate:

Cash	62,500	
Stock Subscriptions Receivable	62,500	
Common Stock Subscribed		10,000
Paid-in Capital in Excess of Par		115,000
(To record receipt of stock subscriptions.)		

The increase in the stockholders' equity account originates from stock subscriptions rather than the outright sale of stock; the common stock account is therefore identified as subscribed. When Nesor receives additional cash that pays the subscription receivable in full, the following entry is recorded:

Cash	62,500	
Stock Subscriptions Receivable		62,500
(To record receipt of cash for full payment of subscribed stock.)		
Common Stock Subscribed	10,000	
Common Stock		10,000
(To record issuance of 1,000 shares of subscribed stock.)		

If the subscription is defaulted because payment is not made in the prescribed time period, the remaining Stock Subscriptions Receivable and Common Stock Subscribed are removed from the books. Three common alternatives exist to properly dispose of down payments on the forfeited shares:[6]

---

[6]A fourth alternative requires an amendment to the original contract, such that a pro rata distribution of shares equal to the partial payment is made.

1. Refund the partial payment on the forfeited shares to the subscriber.
2. Retain the partial payment on the forfeited shares until the subscription is sold to another investor. (Refund the remaining cash to the original subscriber after deducting expenses of the reissue and any reductions in selling price below the subscription price.)
3. Retain the cash advance as a default penalty.

The subscription contract and applicable state laws will guide the contracting parties to the appropriate solution in the event of default.

To illustrate the first alternative, assume that 100 shares of the Nesor Corporation subscription are defaulted after the cash advance is made. The entry necessary to record the default and the refund to the subscriber is as follows:

Common Stock Subscribed ($10 × 100)	1,000	
Paid-in Capital in Excess of Par	11,500	
Cash ($62.50 × 100)		6,250
Stock Subscriptions Receivable		6,250
(To record defaulted stock subscription and return of cash		
to subscriber.)		

If the subscription contract contains the third alternative and Nesor retained the cash advance, the journal entry would be identical to the one above, except that cash would not be credited and the paid-in capital in excess of par value account would be debited for only $5,250. Under the second alternative, Nesor's retention of part of the cash down payment would be credited to the paid-in capital account, and the remaining refund would be credited to Cash. As these entries indicate, if the corporation retains any cash advanced under a defaulted stock subscription, the amount should be reported as an increase in contributed capital. No gain or loss is recognized on such transactions, because their effects are totally associated with contributed equity.

Retaining the cash advance may first appear to be an unreasonably harsh penalty to the defaulting subscriber. However, the purpose of such a provision is to give the subscriber an incentive to purchase shares. Without this incentive the subscriber could treat the stock subscription as a risk-free stock option. To illustrate, if Nesor Corporation already had stock outstanding and trading in an organized market, the investor could subscribe stock at $125 per share and exercise the subscription if the market value of the shares exceeded $125 or default if the market value of the shares was less than $125. If the investor does not stand to lose the down payment, the subscription provides a no-loss investment opportunity. Because this is not the purpose of a stock subscription, provisions for the partial or full forfeiture of the down payment are not unreasonable when previously issued shares are already trading in the secondary market.

TREASURY STOCK

Companies frequently acquire shares of their own stock through market purchases without intending to retire the stock. A company's stock that has been issued and then acquired by the company for some future purpose is referred to as **treasury stock**. Some of the reasons that a company acquires shares of its own stock include:

1. Buying out a stockholder or retiring executive.
2. Meeting provisions of stock option plans for employees.
3. Meeting the requirements of a proposed merger in which large amounts of stock are to be exchanged.
4. Preparing to meet the requirements of a stock dividend.
5. Reducing stockholder pressure for an increased dividend rate.

When treasury stock is purchased, the acquisition must be recorded in the accounting records. Questions persist as to whether treasury stock is an asset or a reduction of stockholders' equity. On rare occasions, annual reports present small amounts of treasury stock as assets. This practice, however, is generally undesirable and discouraged. A company has equity in its assets and does not have an asset in its own equity. A company cannot own itself via stock purchases. The characteristics of treasury stock are not similar to those of other types of investments, such as plant assets. To illustrate, unlike plant asset investments, common stock purchases reduce the size (capitalization) of the firm. Furthermore, the retirement of treasury stock cannot be considered the liquidation of productive property, as would, for example, the leveling of a corporate plant. Therefore, treasury stock should be presented as a reduction of shareholders' equity and not as an asset.

TWO METHODS OF ACCOUNTING FOR TREASURY STOCK

There are two acceptable methods of recording the reduction in stockholders' equity that occurs when treasury stock is acquired: (1) the **cost method,** which is more frequently encountered in practice, and (2) the **par value method.** To illustrate, consider the stockholders' equity section of the balance sheet of Bender, Inc., as presented in Exhibit 16–5. Not all of Bender's authorized common stock has been issued. The 50,000 authorized but unissued shares are not presented in the financial Disclosure statements. A note in the balance sheet discloses the authorization of those shares.

Cost Method

The **cost method** of accounting for treasury stock assumes the eventual reissuance of the stock. Therefore, the cost method is preferred when management intends to hold the treasury shares temporarily for later reissuance, rather than for later retirement. To illustrate, assume that Bender, Inc., acquires 2,000 shares of its common stock at $145 per share. The company purchases these shares to provide for a stock option plan and intends to reissue the shares at a later time. The following entry is necessary to record the transaction using the cost method:

Treasury Stock (2,000 shares × $145)	290,000	
Cash		290,000
(To record acquisition of treasury stock.)		

EXHIBIT 16–5

Bender, Inc.
Partial Balance Sheet

Stockholders' Equity [Note 1]	
Preferred stock ($100 par, 7% cumulative; 100,000 shares authorized, issued, and outstanding)	$10,000,000
Common stock ($100 par; 200,000 shares authorized, 150,000 shares issued and outstanding)	15,000,000
Paid-in capital in excess of par (common)	750,000
Contributed equity	25,750,000
Retained earnings	42,500,000
Total stockholders' equity	$68,250,000

Note 1: The 7% cumulative preferred stock was issued at par value and is callable at any time at 103. Fifty thousand of the 200,000 shares were reserved by the board of directors and are intended to be issued to employees as part of a recently introduced employee stock option plan.

JUNK-BOND HOLDERS RELISHING STOCK-FOR-DEBT BONANZAS

Now that **RJR Nabisco's** new shares are a big hit, investors are expecting other debt-heavy companies to start cleaning up their financial acts by issuing shares and retiring junk bonds.

Such maneuvers could produce a bonanza for junk-bond holders, and they may even leave many shareholders feeling pleased, after an initial jolt.

A popular game among junk-bond investors now is to bet which companies will swap new stock for old high-cost debt, making themselves financially healthier. The goal is to find the next **McCaw Cellular Communications,** a company whose bonds soared after it divulged plans to offer new stock in exchange for as much as $600 million face amount of junk.

In the short run, of course, such swaps tend to be better for bondholders than for current shareholders, whose stake in a company shrinks when extra shares are issued. But stock investors lately have seemed willing to overlook the dilution in some cases where a big reduction in debt can be achieved. McCaw's shares initially fell when the company recently announced plans to swap stock for its 12.95% junk bonds, representing about 17% of total debt. But the stock soon rebounded.

"When you've got bonds trading at a discount and a strong stock, like McCaw, it's a real good play" for all investors, says money manager Gerald Unterman, who runs Cypress Capital Management in New York. Recently, he has been buying bonds of companies "that have the flexibility" to do swaps or stock sales.

Such companies have plenty of incentive. With the stock market booming, companies that piled up debt and slashed their equity in the 1980s now can partly reverse past excesses. They can retire securities having high interest rates or short maturities—often at discounts to face value. And instead of paying cash for their bonds, they can offer bondholders common

shares that don't have to be redeemed and needn't pay any dividends. In the long run, everybody gains, because companies with less debt can cope better with any setbacks.

"During the 1980s, people made money buying stocks before companies levered up. In the 1990s, they're making superb returns by buying debt of companies before they de-lever," says Robert Long, who runs First Boston's junk bond research.

Speculators are bidding up bond prices among seeming candidates for swaps, bond buy-backs or stock offerings, including **Dr Pepper, Duracell Holdings, Storer Communications, Stone Container** and **Time Warner** (which has a lot of high-cost preferred shares.) Currently, **Kroger** Co. is soliciting investors in the private placement market for some convertible securities. Duracell recently said it expects to get permission from its bankers to buy back junk; some investors expect that company to go public in a year or so.

RJR Nabisco's recent swap offer for $1.18 billion of costly 17% bonds has sent some of the company's junk rocketing 50% since December. The swap offer was heavily oversubscribed; the company accepted 43% of the bonds tendered in the offer, which expired Friday. Meanwhile RJR's newly issued stock, trading in recent weeks on a "when issued" basis, has climbed to 9¾ from 5½.

"RJR is the classic 'everybody's a winner' situation," says New York money manager John Gordon of Deltec Securities. He owns some RJR bonds that aren't involved in the swap, and even those have climbed about 35%.

So far this year, junk bonds have already racked up returns of around 12%, according to First Boston's High Yield Index. Much of the profit has come from RJR's bonds, a large part of the index, and from an-

---

The Treasury Stock account is classified as a reduction in the stockholders' equity of the company. Exhibit 16–6 presents the stockholders' equity section of Bender's balance sheet following this transaction.

The Common Stock and Paid-in Capital in Excess of Par accounts are not affected by the treasury stock transaction if the cost method is used. It is also acceptable to report the acquired stock as a reduction of Retained Earnings or Contributed Equity. However, the treatment demonstrated in Exhibit 16–6 is commonly applied in practice and adequately demonstrates the nature of the item.

When treasury stock is reissued, the cost of the treasury stock is removed from the books. To illustrate, assume that Bender, Inc., sells the treasury stock listed in Exhibit 16–6 for $275,000 cash. The following entry records this transaction:

nounced or rumored bond swaps or purchases involving other debt-ridden companies, says First Boston's Mr. Long.

Some swap candidates already have shares trading in the public market. Others, including **Container Corp. of America** and Duracell, are wholly owned by leveraged-buyout firms and private investors who might want to cash in some shares through a public stock sale. The likeliest candidates for a swap or stock sale are companies that badly want or need to cut debt. But a company also should have enough pizzazz to tempt people to take the shares. Bulls envision dizzying growth for McCaw's cellular-telephone service. And the company's operations should be improving; Duracell's batteries are doing well.

Although the rising stock market has certainly smoothed the way for stock-for-debt swaps, it has at the same time restrained the bondholders' potential profit. The higher a company's stock soars, the fewer shares it must issue to retire each bond. (Many companies are trying to do swaps in bankruptcy court; investors' profits there can be very elusive.)

Debt-for-stock swaps may prove more popular with investors than outright stock sales, especially if a company is partly owned by an LBO firm. Says Deltec's Mr. Gordon: "There's always been a slight suspicion that a [stock sale] for an LBO was bailing out the LBO group at a high price and foisting the securities on the public."

He thinks RJR's swap was "ingenious" because the company's big shareholders at Kohlberg Kravis Roberts "are not explicitly asking people to pony up any money to buy shares." Mr. Gordon says he "would just as soon not make Henry Kravis any richer" by paying high cash prices for RJR shares.

Some swap candidates could disappoint investors. Top executives who own big stakes in Stone

More Stock Coming?

Here are some companies that traders believe are candidates to issue stock and retire high-yield junk bonds.

COMPANY	INDUSTRY
Arkansas Best	Trucking
Container Corp. of America	Packaging
Fort Howard	Forest Products
Dr Pepper	Soft Drinks
Duracell Holdings	Batteries
Storer Communications (SCI Holdings)	Cable Television
Stone Container	Paper Products
Stop & Shop Cos.	Supermarkets
Time Warner	Entertainment
TW Services	Food Services

Container, **Golden Nuggett** and **Viacom** Inc. might resist having their ownership diluted if they can find another way to cut debt, traders speculate.

Moreover, many companies that badly need to cut debt aren't faring well, and might find takers for their stock only by twisting people's arms, in or out of bankruptcy court. In this class, investors put **Itel** Corp., which has been buying back some of its own shares; **Federated Department Stores,** and **Grand Union.**

"For some companies, it would be a stretch" to do a swap, says Mr. Long. "But bull markets do amazing things."

SOURCE: Linda Sandler, "Junk-Bond Holders Relishing Stock-for-Debt Bonanzas," *Wall Street Journal*, March 5, 1991, pp. c1, c2. Reprinted by permission of *Wall Street Journal*, © Dow Jones & Company, Inc., 1990. All rights reserved.

Cash	275,000	
Paid-in Capital in Excess of Par	15,000	
Treasury Stock		290,000
(To record reissuance of treasury stock at $15,000 below cost.)		

In this case the treasury stock was sold below its cost and Paid-in Capital in Excess of Par was reduced by $15,000. State law may require other treatments, such as charging Retained Earnings for the difference, but the entry presented here is acceptable in most circumstances. If the company's stockholders' equity did not include any paid-in capital in excess of par, the $15,000 difference between the acquisition and resale price of the treasury stock would have been charged to the Retained Earnings

EXHIBIT 16–6

Bender, Inc.
Partial Balance Sheet with Treasury Stock-Cost Method

Stockholders' Equity

Preferred stock ($100 par, 7% cumulative; 100,000 shares authorized, issued, and outstanding)	$10,000,000
Common stock ($100 par; 200,000 shares authorized, 150,000 shares issued, 148,000 shares outstanding, 2,000 shares held in treasury)	15,000,000
Paid-in capital in excess of par (common)	750,000
Contributed equity	25,750,000
Retained earnings	42,500,000
Total contributed equity and retained earnings	68,250,000
Less: Cost of treasury shares	(290,000)
Total stockholders' equity	$67,960,000

account. If the stock was sold for more than its cost, an additional amount of paid-in capital in excess of par would be recognized.[7] In any event, no losses or gains are recognized on treasury stock transactions because they represent transactions in a company's own capital stock. Because the permanent contributed capital accounts were not adjusted when the treasury stock was purchased, no further entry is needed to reestablish the status of the stock as outstanding.

Another complication in the cost method of accounting for treasury stock arises if treasury shares are acquired at different times and at different prices. Companies typically follow either a first-in, first-out (FIFO) or a weighted average cost flow assumption, similar to that used in accounting for inventories. As with the case of inventory

Consistency

accounting, consistent application of the method selected is important. To illustrate, assume that a company first acquired 100 shares of treasury stock at $10 per share and then acquired 100 more shares at $12 per share. Later the company sold 50 shares at $13 per share. What is the cost of the treasury shares that have been sold? The cost flow assumption made by the accountant clearly becomes important in cases such as this. If the FIFO method is used, the 50 shares are considered to cost $10 per share, the first price paid. If the weighted average method is used, the shares are considered to cost $11 per share, because that is the average price paid for the 200 shares of treasury stock the company has when the 50 shares are sold [(100 × $10) + (100 × $12)/ 200 shares = $11 per share]. The entries to record the sale of the treasury stock under each method are as follows:

	FIFO Method	Weighted Average Method
Cash (50 × $13)	650	650
Treasury Stock	500*	550*
Paid-in Capital in Excess of Par	150**	100**

*Cost of treasury shares sold: FIFO: 50 × $10 = $500; Weighted average: 50 × $11 = $550
**Additional Paid-in Capital: FIFO: 50 shares ($13 − $10) = $150;
  Weighted average: 50 shares ($13 − $11) = $100

---

[7]Contributed capital arising from treasury stock transactions may be carried in a separate account, such as Paid-in Capital from Treasury Stock Transactions.

Par Value Method

The second acceptable method of accounting for treasury stock is the **par** or **stated value method.** In substance, this method is consistent with an assumption that common stock may be retired. Under this method, treasury stock is recorded at the par (or stated) value of common stock, while the paid-in capital in excess of par from the original common stock issuance is eliminated.

We illustrate the par value method using Bender, Inc., and the acquisition and reissuance data from the previous example. Recall that Bender acquired 2,000 shares of its $100 par value common stock at $145 per share. The following entry records the acquisition of the treasury stock for $290,000, using the par value method:

Treasury Stock	200,000	
Paid-in Capital in Excess of Par	10,000	
Retained Earnings	80,000	
Cash (2,000 × $145)		290,000
(To record purchase of treasury shares.)		

Using this method, the treasury shares are reported at par value (2,000 shares × $100 par). The difference between the cost of the shares ($290,000) and their par value ($200,000) is treated as a reduction in paid-in capital in excess of par on a pro rata basis and next as a reduction in retained earnings. In this case, Bender's 150,000 shares of common stock were originally issued at an average price per share of $105, determined as follows (see Exhibit 16–5):

Par value	$15,000,000
Paid-in capital in excess of par	750,000
	$15,750,000

$$\frac{\$15,750,000}{150,000} = \$105 \text{ per share}$$

Therefore, the pro rata portion of paid-in capital in excess of par on the acquired treasury shares equals 2,000 × ($105 − $100), or $10,000. If the pro rata paid-in capital in excess of par is eliminated, any remainder is treated as a reduction of retained earnings. Because the 2,000 shares were purchased at $145 per share, the excess $40 per share is treated as a direct reduction of retained earnings.

Exhibit 16–7 illustrates the stockholders' equity section of Bender's balance sheet after the acquisition of shares for $290,000 under the par value method. Notice that the total stockholders' equity is the same in Exhibits 16–6 and 16–7, but that the disclosure of the treasury stock differs according to the method applied.

Disclosure

If treasury stock is reissued under the par value method, accounting is again different. Continuing the example of Bender, Inc., the reissuance is treated as if the stock were being issued for the first time at par value, except that the credit is to the Treasury Stock account. The entry under the par value method for reissuance of the stock for $275,000 is presented below.

Cash	275,000	
Paid-in Capital in Excess of Par		75,000
Treasury Stock		200,000
(To record reissuance of treasury stock.)		

EXHIBIT 16-7

Bender, Inc.
Partial Balance Sheet
with Treasury Stock-Par Value Method

Stockholders' Equity

Preferred stock ($100 par, 7% cumulative; 100,000 shares authorized, issued, and outstanding)	$10,000,000
Common stock ($100 par; 200,000 shares authorized, 150,000 shares issued, 148,000 shares outstanding, 2,000 shares held in treasury)	14,800,000
Paid-in capital in excess of par (common)	740,000
Contributed equity	25,540,000
Retained earnings	42,420,000
Total stockholders' equity	$67,960,000

The difference between the carrying amount of the Treasury Stock, in this case its par value, and the consideration received is treated as an increase in Paid-in Capital in Excess of Par.

Treasury Stock Acquired in Takeover Attempts

An exception to the methods previously described involves corporate takeover attempts. In a **corporate takeover,** one company attempts to acquire another by buying a controlling interest in its stock. Companies that are the subject of takeover attempts often take defensive action; one common defense is to purchase large amounts of treasury stock—often at prices that exceed both those offered by the party attempting to accomplish the takeover and the market price of the stock. The exception to the cost and par value methods comes up if the treasury stock is acquired at a price that exceeds the market price of the stock.

The FASB has determined that only the fair value of the treasury stock should be accounted for as the cost of acquiring the stock. Amounts paid in excess of the market price to acquire shares of treasury stock should generally be treated as a loss in the income statement rather than as a reduction in the paid-in capital in excess of par. Amounts paid to stockholders to preclude their purchase of additional shares should be charged to expense as incurred. Further, costs incurred in defending against takeovers should not be classified as extraordinary items.[8]

SUMMARY OF TREASURY STOCK ACCOUNTING

Regardless of whether the cost method or the par value method is used for treasury stock accounting, several points are important:

1. Treasury stock should not be classified as an asset.
2. Dividends are not recorded as paid or received on treasury stock (the company cannot distribute dividends to itself).
3. Retained earnings are not increased as a result of treasury stock transactions, although decreases in retained earnings are possible when applying the par value method or if shares are sold below cost when applying the cost method and no paid-in capital in excess of par exists.

[8]*FASB Technical Bulletin No. 85-6*, "Accounting for a Purchase of Treasury Shares at a Price Significantly in Excess of the Current Market Price of the Shares and the Income Statement Classification of Costs Incurred in Defending Against a Takeover Attempt," 1985.

4. Gains or losses are not recognized on treasury stock transactions.
5. Regardless of which method is used, total stockholders' equity remains the same, although the individual components may differ.
6. Legal minimum capital must be preserved.

RETIREMENT OF STOCK

COMMON STOCK RETIREMENT

If a company acquires stock which is to be retired, accounting is similar to the par value method of accounting for treasury stock. Instead of charging the Treasury Stock account for the par value of the securities, however, the original Capital Stock account is charged. Such an entry effectively removes the stock from the company's accounts, which, of course, is consistent with the nature of the transaction.

For example, if Bender, Inc., acquires and retires 2,000 shares of $100 par value stock, which was originally issued for $105 per share, at $145 per share, the following entry is necessary:

Common Stock	200,000	
Paid-in Capital in Excess of Par	10,000	
Retained Earnings	80,000	
Cash		290,000
(To record acquisition and retirement of 2,000 shares of common stock at $145 per share, originally issued at $105 per share.)		

The disclosures of stock authorized, issued, and outstanding are adjusted to reflect the retirement of the acquired stock. The rationale, previously discussed, for the direct charge to Retained Earnings under the par value method of accounting for treasury stock is also valid here. A permanent distribution of $80,000 of earned equity has taken place as a result of the transaction.

If a company acquires and retires stock at a price below the original selling price, additional paid-in capital results from the retirement. To illustrate, assume that Bender, Inc., acquired and retired 2,000 shares of its common stock at $85 per share. In this case the following entry would be appropriate:

Common Stock	200,000	
Cash (2,000 × $85)		170,000
Paid-in Capital in Excess of Par		30,000
(To record acquisition and retirement of 2,000 shares of common stock at $85 per share, originally issued at $105 per share.)		

The paid-in capital from the retirement arises because the company was able to retire stock that originally sold for $105 per share for only $85 per share, resulting in a permanent increase in the company's contributed equity of $20 per share ($5 recognized when the stock was sold and $15 when it was retired), even though those shares are no longer outstanding.

PREFERRED STOCK RETIREMENT

Preferred stock can be redeemed through either a call provision or a mandatory redemption provision. Other than this, the principles underlying the redemption of preferred stock are similar to those for the retirement of common stock. When preferred stock is redeemed, the Preferred Stock account and associated Paid-in Capital in Excess of Par on the preferred stock are eliminated. Any difference between the sum of these accounts and the cash redemption price will be either charged to Retained Earnings or credited to Paid-in Capital in Excess of Par.

To illustrate the accounting, refer to the $10,000,000 preferred stock issue of Bender, Inc., in Exhibit 16–5. Assume that Bender elects to call the preferred stock at 103 according to the provisions of the preferred stock contract (Note 1, Exhibit 16–5). Bender records the following entry for the redemption:

Preferred Stock	10,000,000	
Retained Earnings	300,000	
Cash ($10,000,000 × 1.03)		10,300,000
(To redeem the preferred stock at 103.)		

The Preferred Stock account is eliminated. Because the preferred stock was issued at par, there is no Paid-in Capital in Excess of Par account to eliminate. The $300,000 charge to Retained Earnings represents the distribution of earned equity to the preferred shareholders upon redemption of their shares. If the call provisions specified a call price of 97, the journal entry would appear as follows:

Preferred Stock	10,000,000	
Paid-in Capital in Excess of Par		300,000
Cash		9,700,000
(To redeem the preferred stock at 97.)		

The credit to the Paid-in Capital in Excess of Par account represents a contribution to the remaining stockholders' equity as a result of retiring the preferred stock at an amount less than book value.

TREASURY STOCK RETIREMENT

A firm may eventually decide to retire treasury stock if there are no plans for reissuance. Retired treasury stock becomes authorized but unissued common stock. Accounting for treasury stock retirement involves removing the Treasury Stock and Common Stock from the accounting records. Because the Treasury Stock is recorded differently under the cost and par value methods, accounting for its retirement also differs under the two approaches.

Recall the Bender situation in which 2,000 shares of $100 par value common stock are purchased for the treasury at $145 a share. Assuming the treasury stock was recorded at cost, the Treasury Stock account balance is $290,000 and the journal entry to retire these shares is as follows:

Common Stock	200,000	
Paid-in Capital in Excess of Par	10,000	
Retained Earnings	80,000	
Treasury Stock		290,000
(To retire treasury stock.)		

The Common Stock, related Paid-in Capital in Excess of Par, and Treasury Stock are eliminated from the accounting records. The $80,000 charge to Retained Earnings can be evaluated in the same manner as discussed previously for the par value method. The Treasury Stock account is, of course, eliminated at cost.

Under the par value method, Paid-in Capital in Excess of Par and Retained Earnings have already been reduced in the appropriate amounts at the time the treasury stock was acquired. The Treasury Stock account has a $200,000 balance, representing the par value of the treasury stock. All that remains is eliminating the treasury shares and outstanding common stock at their par values. The journal entry is

Common Stock	200,000	
Treasury Stock		200,000
(To retire treasury stock.)		

As expected, both the cost and par value methods produce the same results when the treasury stock purchase and treasury stock retirement transactions are combined.

PROPERTY AND TREASURY STOCK DONATIONS

In this chapter we have discussed obtaining corporate capital through owner contributions. In Chapter 17 we will discuss earnings as a source of corporate capital. A third and less common source of corporate capital is the donation of either property or stock, frequently called donated capital. Donated capital should not be confused with contributed capital; the terms "donated" and "contributed" have entirely different meanings in this context. **Donated capital** represents a nonreciprocal transfer of property from an outsider to the company. **Contributed capital** is cash, property, or services received by the company in exchange for ownership shares and accompanying rights.

PROPERTY DONATIONS

Cities and counties often attract new businesses and thereby stimulate their economies by donating land or property to particular enterprises. This is not a normal exchange transaction but a unilateral transfer of assets to the corporation. Because the donation is a gift, the firm does not release assets in the acquisition. Consequently, the asset acquired by the enterprise has no cost to that entity. Recall that assets given or received in unilateral transfers are recorded at their estimated fair market values. In arm's-length exchange transactions, the cost of acquiring an asset is a measure of its fair market value, and that amount is used to record the acquisition of the item. Therefore, because cost is a good measure of the fair market value of an asset at the time of purchase, recording *donated* assets at their estimated fair market values is consistent with recording other assets acquired in exchange transactions at their cost.

To account for a donated asset, accountants charge the specific asset account for the estimated fair market value of the donated item and make an offsetting credit to an account called "Donated Capital." The use of a separate account, Donated Capital, is preferable to crediting Paid-in Capital in Excess of Par to recognize the nature of the stockholders' equity. Donated assets are not capital contributions by stockholders but capital donations from outsiders. They should therefore be given distinctive recognition.

To illustrate, consider the donation of a warehouse and adjoining land by the city of Ramsey to Valley Electric Company. If the land is appraised at $15,000 and the warehouse at $75,000, Valley Electric should record the donation as

Land	15,000	
Building	75,000	
Donated Capital		90,000
(To record asset donations.)		

Disclosure   Donated capital is presented separately in the stockholders' equity section of the balance sheet.

TREASURY STOCK DONATIONS

Stockholders, or a stockholder's estate, may sometimes donate capital stock back to the company. This transfer is treated somewhat differently from property transfers, because the company should not consider the donated shares as assets. The donated shares are treasury shares to the corporation and are therefore subject to either the cost or the par value method of accounting.

Under the cost method, donated treasury shares are usually not formally entered in the records, because the firm incurred no cost in acquiring the treasury stock. The number of shares outstanding is reduced by the donated shares via a memorandum to the accounting records. Subsequent reissue of donated treasury shares requires a credit to Donated Capital for the total reissue price.

Under the par value method, donated treasury shares are recorded at par value with an offsetting credit to Donated Capital. If the donated shares are reissued at a price greater (lesser) than the par value, the difference is disclosed by increasing (decreasing) the Donated Capital account.

Donated treasury stock gives a business an opportunity to issue the same shares twice—first to the initial owner, then as donated treasury stock. The second issuance benefits the firm by generating additional capital. This additional capital results only because the original owner voluntarily forfeited the rights to the shares. Therefore, under both accounting methods, the increase in stockholders' equity from issuance of donated treasury shares is labeled "Donated Capital."

CONCLUDING REMARKS

In this chapter we have reviewed the basic elements of corporate organization and contributed capital. Corporate ownership capital is provided through the issuance of capital stock to acquiring individuals and institutions (e.g., banks, pension funds, and investment mutual funds). Capital stock offers owners a variety of rights and preferences, as specified by the company's board of directors.

Disclosure   The stockholders' equity section of the balance sheet should disclose not only the main classifications of ownership, but also information about the rights and preferences of each class of stock. As an example, the dividend preference rate and provisions should be disclosed for preferred stock. In this way, the various classes of shareholders will understand the basic rights and preferences of each ownership class in relation to other ownership classes. Furthermore, the shares authorized, issued, and outstanding should be disclosed for each class of stock.

Exhibit 16–8 illustrates the share status relationships. Authorized shares can be either issued or unissued. The unissued shares can be further divided into subscribed and unsubscribed stock. Recall that subscribed stock is authorized but unissued. Issued stock can be classified as issued and outstanding or issued and not outstanding. Shares that are issued but not outstanding result from treasury stock purchases or donations.

Exhibit 16–8 includes hypothetical share amounts to aid in understanding the relationships. To illustrate how the various categories of stockholders' equity change as transactions occur, assume that the 50,000 subscribed shares are issued. In this case the total unissued stock would decrease to 350,000, the total issued stock would increase to 650,000, and the total stock outstanding would increase to 630,000 shares. The unsubscribed and treasury amounts are unchanged by the issuance of the 50,000 shares of subscribed stock. Other adjustments in share status may be evaluated in this way.

EXHIBIT 16–8

Share Status Relationships

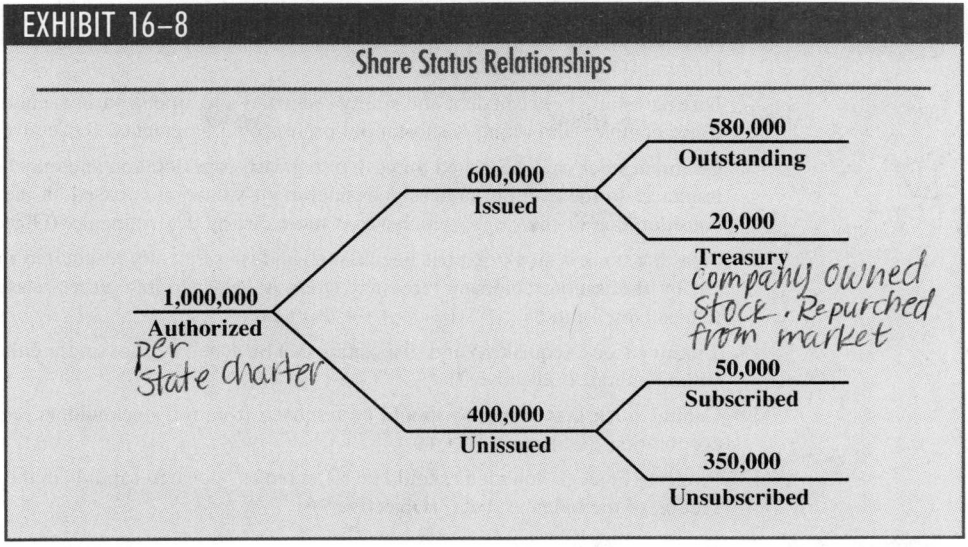

Handwritten annotations: "per State charter" (near Authorized); "company owned stock. Repurched from market" (near Treasury)

1,000,000 Authorized

600,000 Issued

400,000 Unissued

580,000 Outstanding

20,000 Treasury

50,000 Subscribed

350,000 Unsubscribed

To illustrate a financial statement presentation of the stockholders' equity section of the balance sheet, refer to the 1990 Strawbridge & Clothier balance sheet, reproduced on the front endpapers of this book. Notice that Strawbridge & Clothier had redeemable preferred stock outstanding at February 3, 1990. The company reported this item between liabilities and stockholders' equity. Note E to the company's financial statements states that these shares are redeemable at $105 per share, an amount in excess of the stock's $100 par value. The redeemable preferred stock accrued dividends at a rate of $5 per share. The company charged these dividends to retained earnings, which reflects the equity aspects of the redeemable preferred stock. Notice also that the company had outstanding two series of common stock with $1 par values. These items are clearly elements of stockholders' equity. Finally, note that additional paid-in capital is reported as a single amount and that retained earnings are separately disclosed. In the next chapter we will discuss in greater detail the accounting issues pertaining to retained earnings and other specialized topics in the context of stockholders' equity.

KEY POINTS

1. The corporate form of business organization has certain advantages over the sole proprietorship and partnership forms, particularly in terms of allowing the accumulation of large amounts of capital from many diverse owners. (Objective 1)

2. Corporations provide limited liability to shareholders, facilitate the generation of additional equity capital, and continue in existence despite the death of one or more shareholders. (Objective 1)

3. A primary disadvantage of the corporate form of business organization is the double taxation of income, first at the corporate level and again as corporate profits are distributed to stockholders. (Objective 1)

4. Preferred stock contains a preference claim over common stock in dividend distributions and in the distribution of assets upon liquidation. Preferred stock may be fully or partially participating, cumulative, or both. (Objectives 2 and 3)

5. Preferred stock may be callable, convertible, or redeemable. (Objectives 2 and 3)

6. Common stock is considered the residual equity of a corporation because the claims of other investors and creditors must be satisfied before distributions may be made to common stockholders. (Objectives 2 and 3)

7. Distinguishing between debt and equity securities and among various equity securities is sometimes complex and requires substantial professional judgments. (Objective 4)

8. Common stock may be issued for cash or noncash consideration and may be subscribed prior to issuance. In the event of noncash consideration, valuation is based on the market value of the consideration or the stock, whichever is more clearly determinable. (Objectives 5, 6, and 9)

9. Treasury stock is stock that has been issued and subsequently reacquired in the secondary market by the issuing company. Treasury stock is held pending either reissuance or retirement. (Objectives 7 and 8)

10. Treasury stock acquisition and disposition can be accounted for under either the cost or the par value method. (Objective 7)

11. Capital stock that is retired should be removed from the stockholders' equity accounts of the corporation. (Objective 8)

12. Property or stock donations should be reflected as "donated capital" in the stockholders' equity section of the balance sheet. (Objective 9)

QUESTIONS

16–1 Describe some of the operating and financing advantages of a corporation compared to a partnership or a sole proprietorship.

16–2 What is the difference between publicly held and closely held corporations?

16–3 Why do corporations frequently issue more than one class or type of stock?

16–4 Define cumulative preferred stock and participating preferred stock.

16–5 How should cumulative dividends in arrears on preferred stock be presented (if at all) in a corporation's financial statements?

16–6 Describe redeemable preferred stock. How should redeemable preferred stock be presented on the financial statements?

16–7 Describe the most important distinction between accounting for corporations and accounting for other forms of business organizations.

16–8 In what way should the term "reserve" be used, if at all, in financial accounting?

16–9 How does a company account for stock issuances in which there are no established market values for either the stock or the consideration received?

16–10 Explain subscribed common stock. How should common stock subscriptions be presented on the balance sheet?

16–11 What are some accounting alternatives related to the cash advanced on a defaulted stock subscription?

16–12 How does a company account for the difference between proceeds and cost when the company transacts in its own stock?

16–13 Describe treasury stock. How is treasury stock presented in the balance sheet?

16–14 Describe appropriate accounting practices for the acquisition of shares of a company's own stock.

16–15 What is minimum legal capital and why does state law usually require corporations to maintain a certain amount of stockholders' equity?

16–16 If a company issues shares of its own stock in consideration for property or services, at what amount should the transaction generally be recorded?

16–17 Describe the acceptable accounting considerations and procedures for the receipt of (1) property donations and (2) donations of the company's stock.

16–18 Why isn't the stockholders' equity of a corporation valued at the aggregate *market* value of the outstanding stock?

EXERCISES   **16–19** STOCKHOLDERS' EQUITY SECTION PRESENTATION Edwards Corporation was organized on January 1, 1990. On that date it issued 100,000 shares of $10 par value common stock at $12 per share (200,000 shares were authorized). During the period January 1, 1990, through December 31, 1992, Edwards earned net income of $400,000 and declared and paid cash dividends of $150,000. On January 10, 1992, Edwards purchased 5,000 shares of its common stock at $10 per share. On December 29, 1992, Edwards subscribed an additional 50,000 shares for 40% down at $14 per share. On December 31, 1992, 3,000 treasury shares were sold at $15 per share. Edwards used the cost method in accounting for treasury stock.

Instructions

Prepare the stockholders' equity section of the Edwards Corporation balance sheet as it should appear on December 31, 1992.   (AICPA adapted)

16–20 COMMON STOCK TRANSACTIONS Diamond Corporation was organized on January 1, 1992, with an authorization of 500,000 shares of common stock with a par value of $5 per share. The company uses the cost method of accounting for treasury stock transactions. During 1992 Diamond had the following capital transactions:

Jan. 5   Issued 100,000 shares at $5 per share.
Apr. 6   Issued 50,000 shares at $7 per share.
June 8   Issued 15,000 shares at $10 per share.
July 28   Purchased 25,000 shares at $4 per share.
Dec. 31   Sold 25,000 shares held as treasury stock at $8 per share.

Instructions

Provide the appropriate journal entries for each of the above transactions.   (AICPA adapted)

16–21 LUMP SUM CONSIDERATION FOR CAPITAL STOCK Able Corporation incorporated on January 1, 1992, with an authorization of 100,000 shares of no-par common stock and 15,000 shares of $100 par preferred stock. The corporation issued 60,000 shares of common stock and 10,000 shares of preferred stock on January 7, 1992, for a lump sum price of $2,700,000.

Instructions

Provide the appropriate journal entry for the capital stock issuance of January 7, 1992, under each of the following *independent* assumptions:

[a] The common stock and preferred stock traded in the secondary market at $35 and $105 per share, respectively, immediately after the issuance.

[b] The common stock traded immediately in the secondary market at $25 per share. Because the preferred stock was closely held, a market price was not established for the preferred shares.

[c] At the issuance of common stock, the board of directors established a stated value of $25 per share. Both the common and preferred stock issuances became closely held. Therefore, a market price was not established for either issue. (*Hint:* Base the allocation on par and stated values.)

16–22 TREASURY STOCK TRANSACTIONS Cameron Company exchanged 100 shares of treasury stock (its $50 par common stock) for some land to be used in its business. The treasury stock had cost $60 per share, and on the exchange date, it had a fair market value of $65 per share. Cameron received $1,200 for scrap when an existing building was immediately removed from this land.

Instructions

Provide the appropriate journal entry to record the acquisition of the land, assuming the treasury shares were originally recorded under:

[a] The cost method
[b] The par value method   1:3 ratio   (AICPA adapted)

16–23 CONVERSION OF PREFERRED STOCK TO COMMON STOCK In 1992 Carver, Inc., issued 8,000 shares of $100 par value convertible preferred stock for $105 per share. One share of preferred stock can be converted into three shares of Carver's $25 par value common stock at the option of the preferred shareholder. In August 1992, all of the preferred stock was converted into common stock. The market value of the common stock at the date of the conversion was $30 per share.

Instructions

[a] What is the appropriate journal entry for the issuance of the preferred stock?
[b] Record the journal entry required to convert preferred shares to common shares.
[c] Why would a company issue convertible preferred stock instead of just placing common stock directly? Why would an investor be willing to accept the conversion feature?

(AICPA adapted)

16–24   TREASURY STOCK ACQUISITION AND DONATION   Gamble Corporation has 25,000 shares of $5 par value stock authorized, issued, and outstanding. All of these shares were issued at a price of $11 per share. The company had retained earnings of $75,000.

Instructions

Identify the changes in the stockholders' equity section of the balance sheet for each of the following *independent* situations:

[a] Twenty-five hundred shares were acquired at $21 per share (assume the use of the par value method of accounting).
[b] Twenty-five hundred shares were acquired by a stockholder donation (assume the use of the cost method of accounting).
[c] Twenty-five hundred shares were acquired at $21 per share, then reissued at $18 per share (assume the use of the cost method of accounting).

16–25   STOCK SUBSCRIPTION TRANSACTIONS   On January 1, 1992, Armand Corporation subscribed 60,000 shares of their $10 par common stock. The subscription contract required a down payment equal to 40% of the total purchase price of the securities, with the remainder due in two months. The contract specified a subscription price of $22 per share. On March 2, 1992, all but 4,000 shares were issued. These shares were not issued because a subscriber defaulted. On March 2, Armand issued these 4,000 shares to another party for $18 per share.

Instructions

[a] Provide the appropriate January 1, 1992, journal entry to reflect the subscribing of common stock.
[b] Provide the appropriate journal entry on March 2, 1992, to reflect the issuance of common stock.
[c] Provide the appropriate journal entry to record the default on 4,000 shares, assuming each of the following *independent* contract terms:
  [1] The partial payment is refunded.
  [2] The partial payment is refunded, less any expenses or reductions in issue price from the resale of the stock.
  [3] The partial payment is forfeited.
[d] Why would an issuing company insist on provision [c–2] or [c–3] above in a subscription contract?

16–26   TREASURY STOCK TRANSACTIONS—COST METHOD   An analysis of the stockholders' equity of Ramon Corporation as of January 1, 1992, is as follows:

Common stock ($20 par value; 100,000 shares authorized, 60,000 shares issued and outstanding)	$1,200,000
Paid-in capital in excess of par	140,000
Retained earnings	760,000
Total stockholders' equity	$2,100,000

Ramon acquired 1,000 shares of its stock for $35,000, and during 1992 it entered into the following transactions:

Sold 600 treasury shares at $38 per share.
Sold 200 treasury shares at $31 per share.
Retired the remaining treasury shares.

Instructions

[a] Provide the appropriate journal entries to reflect the treasury transactions indicated above. Assume the use of the cost method of accounting.

[b] How should treasury stock be presented on the financial statements? Why? (AICPA adapted)

16–27 TREASURY STOCK TRANSACTIONS—COST AND PAR VALUE METHODS Gregory Corporation acquired 2,000 shares of its own $5 par value stock at $21 per share on February 10, 1992. Gregory sold 1,200 of these shares at $27 per share on May 1, 1992, and an additional 600 shares on August 17, 1992, for $14 per share. Gregory Corporation's common stock was originally issued at $16 per share.

Instructions

[a] Provide the journal entries to record the initial purchase of treasury shares under:
  [1] The cost method
  [2] The par value method
[b] Provide the journal entries to record the reissuances of treasury stock under:
  [1] The cost method
  [2] The par value method

16–28 TREASURY STOCK TRANSACTIONS The stockholders' equity section of Byron, Inc.'s balance sheet on December 31, 1991, was as follows:

Common stock ($5 par value; 1,200,000 shares authorized, 800,000 shares issued, 700,000 shares outstanding)	$ 4,000,000
Paid-in capital in excess of par	3,250,000
Retained earnings	5,240,000
	12,490,000
Less: Treasury stock, at cost, 100,000 shares $8 per share	800,000
Total stockholders' equity	$11,690,000

During 1992, Byron, Inc., reissued 50,000 shares of the treasury stock at $14 per share. No other similar transactions occured during 1992.

Instructions

[a] Provide the appropriate journal entry to record the reissuance of the treasury shares.
[b] Revise the stockholders' equity section of Byron, Inc.'s balance sheet for December 31, 1992, assuming the par value method was used for all treasury stock transactions. Net income was $300,000. (*Hint:* Restate the December 31, 1991, stockholders' equity, assuming the 100,000 shares of treasury stock had been accounted for by the par value method. Then record the reissue of the 50,000 shares. Treat the treasury stock as a reduction in common stock in stockholders' equity.) (AICPA adapted)

16–29 VARIOUS CAPITAL STOCK RETIREMENT TRANSACTIONS The stockholders' equity section of the balance sheet for Zebra, Inc., appeared as follows on December 31, 1991:

$4 Preferred stock ($40 par value; 5,000 shares authorized, issued, and outstanding, callable at 102%)	$ 200,000
Common stock ($5 stated value; 100,000 shares authorized, 60,000 shares issued and outstanding)	300,000
Paid-in capital in excess of par (common)	600,000
Retained earnings	1,000,000
Total stockholders' equity	$2,100,000

On February 2, 1992, Zebra purchased and retired 5,000 shares of common stock at $18 per share. On March 2, 3,000 shares of common stock were acquired as treasury stock at $14 per share (use the cost method). On April 2 the shares acquired on March 2 were retired. On August 10, Zebra called 3,000 shares of preferred stock.

Instructions

[a] Provide the appropriate journal entries for the transactions indicated in 1992.

[b] How would total stockholders' equity be affected if the par value method was used for the treasury stock acquisition of March 2 and the April 2 retirement?

16–30   STOCKHOLDERS' EQUITY REPORTING   Grunion Corporation was incorporated on January 1, 1992, with an authorization of 200,000 shares of $5 par value common stock and 20,000 shares of 10%, nonparticipating, cumulative, $30 par preferred stock. On February 2, 1992, Grunion issued 100,000 shares of common stock at $24 per share and 15,000 shares of preferred stock at $29 per share. Subscriptions were taken for 40,000 common shares at a contracted price of $25 per share. The subscription contract required a 60% cash advance. The stock will be issued when the subscription price is paid in full on January 31, 1993. In 1992 Grunion received land from the City of Oakhurst for future plant expansion at no cost. The land had a cost to Oakhurst of $12,000 and a market value on the transfer date of $25,000. In 1992 Grunion purchased 15,000 shares of its own common stock for $30 per share (assume the cost method). Grunion declared dividends for preferred and common stock only once during 1992. The common stock dividend was $10,000. Net income for 1992 was $65,000.

Instructions

Prepare in good form the stockholders' equity section of the balance sheet on December 31, 1992, for Grunion Corporation.

16–31   STOCK SUBSCRIPTIONS AND ISSUANCES   The stockholders' equity section of the balance sheet for Francis Corporation appeared as follows on December 31, 1992:

Preferred stock ($20 par value; 20,000 shares authorized, issued, and outstanding)	$ 400,000
Common stock ($2 par value; 100,000 shares authorized, 60,000 shares issued, and 50,000 shares outstanding)	120,000
Paid-in capital in excess of par (common)	1,150,000
Paid-in capital from defaulted subscriptions	150,000
Retained earnings	70,000
Treasury stock (at par)	(20,000)
Total stockholders' equity	$1,870,000

Francis Corporation was formed on January 1, 1992, with the issuance of 20,000 preferred shares and 10,000 common shares. The common shares were issued for $25 per share. Francis issued an additional 50,000 common shares on a subscription basis. The original subscription contract was for 70,000 shares at a subscription price of $25 per share, with a required cash down payment equal to 30% of the purchase price. The subscription contract requires the cash advance on all defaulted shares to be forfeited. Francis earned $100,000 in 1992 but declared no dividends.

Instructions

Provide the journal entries that must have been made in 1992, as determined from the December 31, 1992, stockholders' equity balances and related information.

16–32   STOCKHOLDERS' EQUITY—TRANSACTION EFFECTS   Consider the following statement of stockholders' equity for Comtech, Inc.:

Comtech, Inc.
STOCKHOLDERS' EQUITY
December 31, 1992

Common stock, $1 par value; authorized 3,000,000 shares; issued 1,500,000 shares; outstanding 1,400,000 shares	$ 1,400,000
Additional paid-in capital:	
In excess of par	20,000,000
From treasury stock	200,000
Total paid-in capital	21,600,000
Unappropriated retained earnings	8,100,000
Total stockholders' equity	$29,700,000

All of the outstanding common stock and treasury stock were originally issued in 1986 for $11 per share. The treasury stock is common stock reacquired on March 31, 1992. Comtech uses the par value method of accounting for treasury stock.

During 1993 the following events or transactions occurred relating to Comtech's stockholders' equity:

[1] February 12, 1993—Issued 400,000 shares of unissued common stock for $12.50 per share.

[2] September 20, 1993—Comtech's president retired. Comtech purchased from the retiring president 100,000 shares of Comtech's common stock for $13 per share, which was equal to market value on this date. This stock was canceled.

[3] At December 31, 1993, Comtech is being sued by two separate parties for patent infringements. Comtech's management and outside legal counsel share the following opinions regarding these suits:

Suit	Likelihood of Losing the Suit	Estimated Loss
1	Reasonably possible	$600,000
2	Probable	400,000

Instructions

[a] Determine the amount by which Comtech's paid-in capital in excess of par will increase as a result of the February 12, 1993, transaction.

[b] Determine the amount by which Comtech's paid-in capital in excess of par will decrease as a result of the September 20, 1993, transaction.

[c] Comtech wishes to appropriate retained earnings for all loss contingencies that are not properly accruable by a charge to earnings. What amount of retained earnings should be appropriated?

(AICPA adapted)

PROBLEMS

16–33 RECORDING STOCK TRANSACTIONS The stockholders' equity section of the January 1, 1992, balance sheet for Pentel Corporation is as follows:

12% Callable preferred stock ($100 par value; 1,000 shares issued and outstanding)	$ 100,000
Common stock ($10 par value; 40,000 shares authorized, 25,000 shares issued and outstanding)	250,000
Paid-in capital in excess of par (preferred)	1,000
Paid-in capital in excess of par (common)	1,200,000
Retained earnings	900,000
Total stockholders' equity	$2,451,000

The following transactions occurred in 1992:

Jan. 16 Issued 15,000 shares of common stock for $63 per share.

Feb. 18 Purchased 20,000 shares of common stock for the treasury at $54 per share (assume the cost method).

Mar. 10 The city of Kerryville donated land with an appraised value of $300,000 for use as a future plant site.

Apr. 1 Retired 10,000 shares of the treasury stock purchased in February. The market price of common shares was $57 per share at the time.

July 29 Called 250 preferred shares at a call price of $103 per share.

Aug. 17 Reissued the remaining treasury shares from February at $66 per share.

Sept. 9 Acquired land and building by issuing 10,000 common shares when the common was selling for $48 per share. Appraised value of the land was $200,000, and the building $350,000. Consider the market value of the stock as the basis for determining the value of the acquired assets.

Oct. 9 A shareholder donated 6,000 common shares to the corporation (assume the cost method).

Dec. 7 Sold the donated shares for $80 per share.

Instructions

Provide the appropriate journal entries for the above transactions.

16–34 STOCKHOLDER EQUITY TRANSACTIONS   Guardian Corporation began operations on January 1, 1992, by issuing the following shares:

5,000 shares of 12% redeemable preferred stock, $100 par value	$ 500,000
60,000 common shares, $2 par value, 100,000 shares authorized	1,080,000

In addition, the following transactions took place during the year:

Jan. 9   An additional 20,000 shares were subscribed at $20 per share. Subscribers were required to put down 40% of the purchase price, with the remainder due in six months.

Feb. 2   Paid legal fees with respect to the stock offering by issuing 1,000 common shares when the market price was $22 per common share.

Mar. 19   Purchased 10,000 common shares for the treasury at $16 per share (assume the par value method).

July 1   Purchased and retired 5,000 common shares at $20 per share.

July 10   The remaining amount due on 19,000 shares of the stock subscription was paid. The remaining 1,000 shares were defaulted. The down payment was refunded to the defaulting party. At this time the market price per share was $24.

Aug. 21   Retired 3,000 treasury shares.

Sept. 30   Reissued 7,000 treasury shares at $25 per share.

Nov. 12   The estate of a deceased stockholder donated 1,000 common shares to the company (assume the par value method).

Nov. 23   Sold the donated shares for $30 per share.

Instructions

Provide the appropriate journal entries for each transaction above.

16–35 STOCKHOLDERS' EQUITY JOURNAL ENTRIES AND FINANCIAL REPORTING   Ming Corporation's stockholders' equity section of the balance sheet appears as follows on January 1, 1992:

11% Callable preferred stock ($100 par value; 60,000 shares authorized, issued, and outstanding)	$ 6,000,000
Common stock ($10 par value; 400,000 shares authorized, issued, and outstanding)	4,000,000
Paid-in capital in excess of par (common)	12,000,000
Retained earnings	15,000,000
Total stockholders' equity	$37,000,000

Common and preferred stock were issued at the corporation's inception. There were no capital stock transactions from the inception of the corporation through January 1, 1992. In 1992 the following transactions took place:

Jan. 16   Purchased 30,000 treasury shares of common stock at $52 per share (assume the cost method).

Feb. 3   Retired 10,000 treasury shares when the market price was $48 per share.

Mar. 6   Called 10,000 preferred shares at $102 per share.

May 22   Received 15,000 shares as a donation from a stockholder when the market price was $41 per share.

Sept. 30   Purchased 10,000 common shares at $38 per share for immediate retirement.

Oct. 16   Reissued 10,000 of the treasury shares purchased in January at $47 per share.

Nov. 17   Reissued 10,000 donated common shares at $51 per share.

Dec. 1   Retired the remaining donated shares.

Net income for 1992 was $1,000,000.

Instructions

[a] Provide the appropriate journal entries for each of the above transactions.

[b] Prepare the stockholders' equity section of the balance sheet for Ming as it should appear on December 31, 1992.

16–36 COMPREHENSIVE STOCKHOLDERS' EQUITY TRANSACTIONS Hampton Manufacturing Company initiated operations on January 1, 1992. On December 31, 1992, the company's stockholders' equity section of the balance sheet appeared as follows:

Common stock ($30 par value; 60,000 shares authorized, 50,000 shares issued, and 35,000 shares outstanding)	$1,500,000
Common stock subscribed (5,000 shares)	150,000
Paid-in capital in excess of par value	1,375,000
Retained earnings	800,000
Treasury stock (at cost)	(780,000)
Total stockholders' equity	$3,045,000

During 1993 40% of the purchase price of the subscribed shares was remitted by subscribers. All but 500 of the subscribed shares were issued, because the original subscriber defaulted on the shares. These shares were issued at $50 per share to a new owner, and the remaining cash advance was returned to the original subscriber (less any price loss). The common stock subscriptions were subscribed at the same price as the original issue of 50,000 shares. Furthermore, in 1993 Hampton resold 5,000 treasury shares at $56 per share. Later in the year another 5,000 treasury shares were sold at $25 per share after a sharp drop in the company's stock price. Towards the end of the year, 3,000 treasury shares were retired.

Instructions

Provide the appropriate journal entries for Hampton Manufacturing Company for 1993 based on the discussion above.

16–37 TREASURY STOCK TRANSACTIONS The stockholders' equity section of Colyer Furniture Company's balance sheet appeared as follows on January 1, 1993:

Common stock ($5 par value; 80,000 shares authorized, issued, and outstanding)	$ 400,000 *Donated −5000*
Paid-in capital in excess of par value	1,000,000
Retained earnings	800,000
Total shareholders' equity	$2,200,000

The following events occurred in sequence during 1993:

[1] Ten thousand common shares were purchased for the treasury at $20 per share.
[2] An additional 10,000 shares were purchased for the treasury at $30 per share.
[3] Twelve thousand treasury shares were resold at a market price of $27 per share.
[4] Five thousand Colyer common shares were donated to the company by a stockholder's estate.
[5] Eleven thousand treasury shares were reissued at a market price of $23 per share.
[6] The remaining shares were retired.

Instructions

[a] Provide the appropriate journal entries assuming the cost method of accounting for treasury stock, and treasury stock reissuance on a first-in, first-out basis.
[b] Provide the appropriate journal entries assuming the cost method of accounting for treasury stock, and treasury stock reissuance under an average-cost assumption.
[c] Provide the appropriate journal entries assuming the par value method of accounting for treasury stock.

16–38 COMPARATIVE STOCKHOLDERS' EQUITY ANALYSIS AND JOURNAL ENTRIES The following are comparative stockholders' equity sections of the balance sheets for Brighton Corporation. Some items that require disclosure are not included.

	Dec. 31, 1992	Dec. 31, 1993
10% Preferred stock ($20 par value; 90,000 shares authorized)	$ 100,000	$ 120,000
Common stock ($5 par value; 150,000 shares authorized)	300,000	400,000
Common stock subscribed (10,000 shares)	–0–	50,000
Paid-in capital in excess of par (common)	360,000	410,000
Donated capital (10,000 shares Brighton common)	–0–	50,000
Retained earnings	400,000	660,000
Treasury stock (10,000 shares of common)	–0–	(50,000)
Total stockholders' equity	$1,160,000	$1,640,000

Net income for 1993 was $300,000. The subscribed stock sold at $7.

Instructions

[a] Provide the appropriate journal entries to account for the changes in the stockholders' equity account balances for Brighton Corporation.

[b] How many shares were issued and outstanding of the preferred and common stock at December 31, 1992 and 1993?

16–39   CORRECTION OF IMPROPER STOCKHOLDERS' EQUITY PRESENTATION   Limon Corporation presented the following balance sheet for December 31, 1992:

Assets

Current assets	$ 30,000
Treasury stock (at market; cost = $15,000)	14,000
Fixed assets	56,000
Total assets	$100,000

Liabilities and Stockholders' Equity

Current liabilities	$ 20,000
Common stock subscribed (500 shares)	10,000
Long-term debt	8,000
Total liabilities	38,000
Stockholders' equity	
Common stock (4,000 shares issued)	18,000
10% Preferred stock (1,000 shares issued)	12,000
Less: Stock subscriptions receivable	(4,000)
Reserve for depreciation	16,000
Earned surplus	20,000
Total liabilities and stockholders' equity	$100,000

Your investigation of Limon Corporation's financial records indicates that all authorized shares have been either issued or subscribed. In addition, the par values for the common and preferred stock are $2 and $10, respectively. The treasury stock was originally purchased when the market price was $20 per share. During 1992, 250 treasury shares were resold for $25 per share. A "gain on treasury stock transactions" was credited for the difference between the original cost and the selling price. Furthermore, the excess of cost over market of the treasury shares at the end of the period was recognized as an unrealized loss on the 1992 income statement. You also discovered that the City of Bingham donated land with a market value of $9,000 to Limon during 1992.

Instructions

Revise the December 31, 1992, balance sheet for Limon Corporation as it should be presented according to generally accepted accounting principles.

16–40   TREASURY STOCK—COST FLOW ASSUMPTIONS   Mandel Company has 30,000 shares of $10 par value common stock authorized and 20,000 shares issued and outstanding. On August 15, 1992, Mandel purchased 1,000 shares of treasury stock at $12 per share. Mandel uses the cost method to account for treasury stock. On September 14, 1992, the company sold 500 shares of the treasury stock for $14 per share.

On October 20, 1992, Mandel acquired another 1,000 shares of common stock for the treasury, paying $9 per share and on November 24, 1992, reissued 750 shares of treasury stock receiving $10.50 per share.

Instructions

[a] Prepare the journal entries to record the above transactions using:
  [1] The average cost method of accounting, and
  [2] the FIFO method of accounting.
[b] Determine the balance to be reported in the Treasury Stock account under each method of accounting.   (AICPA adapted)

16–41 OWNERSHIP RESTRUCTURING Tamara Company is a small, closely held corporation with three stockholders. C. Bradway plans to retire leaving S. Harris and J. Brown to manage the business. The owners agreed to alter the capitalization of the firm to reflect this event. Bradway will redeem his capital stock in return for nonvoting preferred stock. Before the agreement, the stockholders' equity section of Tamara's balance sheet appeared as follows:

Common stock ($20 par value; 10,000 shares authorized and issued, 9,000 shares outstanding)	$200,000
Paid-in capital in excess of par	50,000
Retained earnings	140,000
Treasury stock (cost method)	(30,000)
Total stockholders' equity	$360,000

The three owners presently have the following ownership interests: Bradway, 20%; Harris, 40%; and Brown, 40%. The corporation will be reorganized according to the following agreement:

[1] The treasury stock will be canceled.
[2] Two new stock issues will be authorized: $10 par value common stock, and 12% cumulative nonvoting preferred stock ($100 par value).
[3] The stockholders will surrender their shares for cancellation and will receive the newly authorized shares as follows:
  [a] Bradway will receive only preferred stock.
  [b] Harris will receive 40% of the common stock.
  [c] Brown will receive 60% of the common stock and the remainder of the preferred stock.
[4] The total number of shares for the preferred stock and common stock issue is 19,000.

Instructions

[a] Prepare the journal entry to cancel the treasury stock account on the company's books.
[b] Prepare a schedule computing the amount of each stockholder's equity in the company before the recapitalization.
[c] Compute the number of new common stock and new preferred stock shares to be issued, given that they total 19,000 shares.
[d] Prepare a schedule computing the number of shares of each type of newly issued stock that each stockholder will receive under the agreement described above.

16–42 PREPARATION OF STOCKHOLDERS' EQUITY SECTION Ryner, Inc., a manufacturer of restaurant and kitchen equipment, was incorporated in 1958. Its stock is publicly held. The stockholders' equity section of the balance sheet at September 30, 1992, follows.

$2 Cumulative redeemable preferred stock ($15 par value; 500,000 shares authorized, 4,000 shares issued and outstanding)	$ 60,000
Common stock ($10 par value; 1,000,000 shares authorized, 110,000 shares issued and outstanding)	1,100,000
Retained earnings	622,000
Total stockholders' equity	$1,782,000

Ryner's capital stock transactions during fiscal 1993 were as follows:

[1] On January 2, 8,000 preferred shares were issued in exchange for land with an appraised value of $100,000. Six months ago 1,000 shares of Ryner preferred were exchanged "over the counter" for $14 per share.

[2] On January 17, 4,500 shares of common stock were sold to Tom Stoddard at $25 per share.

[3] On September 14, Ryner purchased dissident stockholder Stoddard's 4,500 shares at $27 per share. The shares are to be held as treasury shares and accounted for at cost. (Stoddard violently opposed Ryner's business strategy and Ryner management decided to eliminate his interest.)

[4] On September 28, Ryner contracted with Kathryn Reynolds for the sale of 10,000 previously unissued shares at $25 per share to be issued when the purchase price is fully paid. At September 30, only $195,000 had been paid. Reynolds agreed to pay the balance on or before November 3, 1993.

[5] On September 30, Ryner redeemed 4,000 preferred shares according to the issue agreement. The shares were redeemed at $18 per share.

[6] A cash dividend of $2 was declared on the preferred shares on March 11, and paid on March 30.

[7] A cash dividend of $1.50 per share was declared on September 15, and payable October 11.

[8] Ryner's net income for fiscal year 1993 was $250,000.

Instructions

Prepare the stockholders' equity section of the balance sheet for the year ended September 30, 1993. This statement should be supported by the following schedules, presented in the order given:

[a] Changes in preferred stock account.
[b] Changes in common stock account.
[c] Calculation of paid-in capital in excess of par.
[d] Changes in retained earnings.   (AICPA adapted)

16–43   ANALYZING CHANGES IN STOCKHOLDERS' EQUITY   On January 1, 1992, the stockholders' equity section of Triton Electronics Company's balance sheet revealed the following information:

$5 Convertible preferred stock ($40 par value; 50,000 shares authorized, 20,000 shares issued and outstanding)	$ 800,000
Common stock ($5 stated value; 200,000 shares authorized, 120,000 shares issued and outstanding)	600,000
Paid-in capital in excess of par	3,000,000
Retained earnings	4,500,000
Total stockholders' equity	$8,900,000

In addition, the following information is known:

[1] On February 2, 1992, 15,000 common shares were acquired by the company for $33 per share (assume the cost method).

[2] On September 30, 1992, 5,000 preferred shares were converted to common shares. One share of preferred stock is convertible into one share of common stock. At the time of conversion, the common stock had a market value of $42 per share.

[3] On December 21, 1992, the company placed a stock subscription of 10,000 common shares at a subscription price of $33 per share. The subscription contract required a cash down payment equal to 60% of the subscription price, with the balance due on February 1, 1993.

[4] On February 1, 1993, 8,500 common shares were issued according to the subscription contract. Because of default by a subscriber, 1,500 shares were not issued. The subscription contract requires the subscriber to forfeit all cash advances.

[5] On April 15, 1993, 10,000 shares held in treasury were reissued at $50 per share.

[6] On May 16, 1993, a special dividend of preferred stock was distributed to common stockholders. One hundred shares of common stock entitled a shareholder to one share of preferred stock. The market price of preferred stock was $40 per share at the time. (*Hint:* Record this dividend at the market price of the preferred shares.)

[7] Cash dividends are declared for preferred and common shares on October 31 and April 30 of each year. Semiannual cash dividends for common shares are $0.50 per share.

[8] Net income for 1992 was $660,000, and for 1993, $890,000.

Instructions

Analyze the changes in Triton Electronics stockholders' equity accounts for 1992 and 1993. Create column headings for the stockholders' equity accounts. Enter under each column heading the beginning balances and the changes in the accounts due to transactions in 1992 and 1993. Draw balances for each account for December 31, 1992, and December 31, 1993. Provide in good form a schedule supporting computations for dividend calculations.

CASES

16–44   CHARACTERISTICS OF CAPITAL STOCK   Capital stock is an important part of corporate equity. The term "capital stock" generally includes common and preferred stock issued by a corporation.

Instructions

[a] What are the basic rights of ownership of common stock? How are they exercised?
[b] What is preferred stock? Discuss the various preferences that may be afforded preferred stock.

(AICPA adapted)

16–45   PRESENTATION OF STOCKHOLDERS' EQUITY SECTION   The stockholders' equity section of the balance sheet reports the ownership interest in the corporation. This interest is usually separated into contributed capital and earned capital.

Instructions

[a] Why is the distinction made between these two components of stockholders' equity?
[b] The contributed capital section is frequently divided into legal (or stated) capital and paid-in capital in excess of par. What is the reason for this disclosure method?

16–46   PRESENTATION OF STOCK SUBSCRIPTIONS   Johnson Corporation presented its balance sheet to the bank prior to negotiating a loan. The balance sheet included among its current assets $300,000 in stock subscriptions receivable. The loan officer took exception to this presentation and suggested that this amount should be reported as a reduction of the stockholders' equity.

Instructions

[a] What arguments could the bank loan officer use for his position?
[b] What arguments could Johnson Corporation use in support of their presentation method?

16–47   CHARACTERISTICS OF REDEEMABLE PREFERRED STOCK   The right side of Carson Corporation's balance sheet at December 31, 1992, appears as follows:

Current liabilities	$ 200,000
10% Bond payable (due in 2003)	2,000,000
$5 Redeemable preferred stock ($50 par value; cumulative and nonvoting, to be redeemed in 2001 at par)	1,000,000
Common stock ($5 par value; 600,000 shares authorized, issued, and outstanding)	3,000,000
Total liabilities and stockholders' equity	$6,200,000

Instructions

[a] In what ways is the redeemable preferred stock similar to the 10% bond payable?
[b] In what ways is the redeemable preferred stock similar to the common stock?
[c] Is the redeemable preferred stock more like an equity or a debt?
[d] How should redeemable preferred stock be presented in the financial statements?

16–48   ELIMINATING PREFERRED STOCK   Preferred stock may be eliminated from a corporation's capital structure in several ways:

[1] The corporation may call the preferred stock.
[2] The corporation may redeem the preferred stock according to a mandatory redemption provision.
[3] The corporation may purchase the preferred stock as treasury stock and retire it at a later date.
[4] The corporation may purchase the preferred stock directly off the market for immediate retirement.
[5] The preferred stockholders may convert the preferred stock to common stock according to a conversion provision.

Instructions

Identify the characteristics of each of the above elimination methods.

16–49 TREASURY STOCK Canon Company recently entered into an agreement with Sue Simon, a common stockholder, in which the company reacquired the stock held by that individual. The stock is to be held as treasury stock and reissued to others at a later time. Because Canon is short of cash, however, they issued a note payable to Simon for $100,000 payable in 18 equal monthly payments plus interest at 15%, a reasonable rate. As security for the note, Canon agreed to allow Simon to retain possession of the shares, receive dividends, and to vote the shares at stockholder meetings until the note has been completely paid.

The controller of Canon has called you, its external accountant, for your advice on how to report this transaction. Specifically, he asks a question with two aspects: "Should I record this stock as if it has been reacquired and is now treasury stock, or, if not, how should I report the note that has been issued to Ms. Simon?"

Instructions

Prepare a brief report to the controller describing how you believe the transactions described should be reported in Canon's financial statements for the year ending next week.

JUDGMENT CASES

16–50 INDUCED CONVERSION OF CONVERTIBLE DEBT The management of Leveraged, Inc., issued convertible bonds two years ago. The terms of the bonds allowed the bondholders, at their option, to convert each bond into four shares of the company's common stock. The bonds have a current market value that exceeds their carrying amount and the market value of the stock for which they could be exchanged. Therefore, few bondholders have exercised their rights to conversion. Further, Leveraged has an adequate number of authorized but unissued shares to effect the conversion without making any open market purchases.

Leveraged has decided to induce a conversion of its convertible bonds by adding a sweetner to the conversion terms and conditions. Leveraged hopes that this move will help the company obtain a better debt/equity ratio in order to meet certain lending covenants in its other debt instruments. The sweetner provides that a cash premium will be paid to each bondholder who elects to exercise the conversion option. The premium will be sufficient to provide the bondholders with stock and cash that has a fair value equivalent to the current market value of the bonds. While no time limit has been set for the sweetened conversion period, the company has reserved the right to cancel the sweetner at any time after an initial eight-month period.

Subsequently a large number of the convertible bonds have been converted and the company is now considering how to account for the conversion transactions.

Instructions

Determine how the bond conversion should be accounted for and reported in the financial statements of Leveraged, Inc.

16–51 DISTINGUISHING BETWEEN DEBT AND EQUITY INSTRUMENTS Quirky Company, Inc., a manufacturer of electronic products that prepares a classified balance sheet, would like your assistance with an unusual problem. Quirky has issued preferred stock that allows holders to redeem it after an initial five-year period for its par value. The company controller tells you that he is completely aware that the Securities and Exchange Commission requires merely that such securities be reported outside of stockholders' equity section of the balance sheet. The controller's boss wants to create and report a third section of the balance sheet between liabilities and stockholders' equity called "Other Sources of Financing." According to the controller, the balance sheet would contain totals for "Liabilities," "Other Sources of Financing," and "Stockholders' Equity." In this fashion, the company believes that the balance sheet more appropriately displays the various methods the company has used and the extent to which each has financed the business.

Instructions

Respond to the controller. Would you be willing to accept a balance sheet that is classified in the manner described? If not, what presentation that incorporates the desires of the company would you be willing to accept?

16–52 ACCOUNTING FOR CALL OPTIONS PAYABLE IN AN ENTERPRISE'S OWN STOCK Coronado Company, Inc., has issued a number of call option contracts that require the company to sell shares of the company's common stock to the optionholder for $50 per share. Each option allows the holder to acquire 100 shares of the stock through December 31, 1995, at which time the options expire. The company sold 1,000 of the options for $5,000 each. If the options are not exercised, the holders may redeem them for 50% of the purchase price. While the value of the stock currently is above the exercise price of the options (and the cost of the option contract), the holders have not yet chosen to exercise them and they remain outstanding.

The president of Coronado wishes to classify the options as equity securities rather than debt. In developing her arguments she states:

> "Of course, no one has yet exercised the option. If the stock goes up, they will exercise near the end of the expiration period due to the present value of the dollars they will have to pay when they exercise. If the stock goes way down, which, by the way, is inconceivable, then they will simply redeem the option at the 50% amount. Either way we win. If we have to issue stock, it costs us nothing. Even in the extremely unlikely case that we have to honor the redemption clause, the amount we have to pay is only one-half of what we received originally. It is clear to me that this instrument is a classic equity call option and should be so classified."

Instructions

Comment on the president's position. Do you believe that the options can be acceptably classified as an equity instrument? Provide supporting arguments for your position.

CHAPTER 17

Stockholders' Equity: Operations, Earnings, Dividends, and Other Issues

OBJECTIVES

1. To demonstrate acceptable accounting for several types of dividends on different classes of stock.

2. To explain appropriate accounting and reporting standards for a variety of stock option and compensation plans, stock warrants, and stock rights.

3. To convey a number of the important judgments necessary in accounting for stock based compensation plans.

4. To describe the circumstances in which a quasi reorganization is appropriate and to demonstrate the accounting procedures that are applied.

5. To describe the events directly affecting retained earnings.

6. To describe what an appropriation of retained earnings accomplishes and how it should be reported.

7. To discuss the judgments necessary in identifying accounting errors.

T he preceding chapter is primarily concerned with the initial incorporation of a business and the issuance and reacquisition of capital stock. In this chapter we consider accounting and reporting problems involving earned equity—specifically, dividends, stock options, stock warrants, stock rights, appropriations of earned equity, and quasi reorganizations.

Recall that corporations maintain a reporting distinction between earned and contributed stockholders' equity. If the owners and managers of a business are different groups of people, as in many corporations, the owners as well as creditors and other financial statement users are commonly interested in the extent to which the company is financed by retained earnings versus contributed equity. The earned equity portion of total stockholders' equity, called **retained earnings,** generally provides a cumulative measure of the extent of that success, net of any dividend declarations and distributions.

In addition to representing a source of financing for a corporation, retained earnings also reflect equity in assets which are subject to distribution to shareholders as dividends. Dividends are normally paid with resources generated from the earnings of a corporation and therefore represent a distribution of profits (a return *on* invested capital rather than a return *of* invested capital).

Occasionally a company uses the term "earned surplus" in financial statements to describe retained earnings. However, the practice is rare and is discouraged by the accounting profession. The Committee on Terminology of the American Institute of Certified Public Accountants recommended that accountants stop using the term "surplus", which connotes excess or unneeded equity.[1] However, "surplus" is often used in legal instruments and in statutes regulating commerce, and accountants may thus occasionally encounter the term. As used in financial statements, "surplus" connotes "the amount that remains when use or need is satisfied" (Webster)—a definition that is incompatible with the meaning of retained earnings. Accordingly, we emphasize the preferred term "retained earnings."

RETAINED EARNINGS

Two financial statements are necessary to broadly report the results of operations: an income statement and a statement of changes in retained earnings. These two statements are often combined. In some cases, the statement of retained earnings is presented in a statement summarizing changes in all stockholders' equity accounts, including retained earnings. Both the income and retained earnings statements present activity for a *period of time,* in contrast to the balance sheet, which provides information about economic resources and obligations at a *point in time.* During the closing process, an accountant transfers the amount of a company's net income or loss to retained earnings.

The accounting profession has adopted standards that carefully specify the types of activities and events which affect income and should therefore appear initially on the income statement rather than the statement of retained earnings. Briefly, revenues, expenses, gains, and losses determine income and should always appear on the income statement. It would therefore be improper to directly charge or credit retained earnings for a revenue, expense, gain, or loss.

The statement of retained earnings is affected by a limited and carefully defined set of events. This practice provides financial statement users with assurance that net income is determined in a comparable fashion by all reporting entities engaging in

---

[1]*Accounting Terminology Bulletin No. 2*, "Review and Résumé," 1953, par. 65.

similar transactions or encountering similar events. Specifically, the items presented in Exhibit 17–1 are the most common economic events that are charged or credited directly to the Retained Earnings account. As explained in Chapter 16, certain treasury stock transactions cause adjustments to retained earnings. In addition, the adoption of certain accounting principles sometimes results in a retroactive adjustment through retained earnings. The Financial Accounting Standards Board (FASB) often requires a retroactive adjustment through retained earnings for the transition to a new accounting standard, as when *FASB Statement of Financial Accounting Standards No. 2*, "Accounting for Research and Development Costs" (1974) became effective. Retroactive adjustment through retained earnings is also appropriate when certain existing standards are adopted, such as the initial application of the equity method by an investor establishing significant influence over an investee (see Chapter 10). Furthermore, when a company is reorganized due to financial difficulty, retained earnings may also be affected. We discuss reorganizations and the other items in Exhibit 17–1 more fully later in this chapter.

THE INCOME STATEMENT AND RETAINED EARNINGS

Earlier in this text we developed various concepts of income. We also discuss income determination and presentation in greater detail in Chapter 20. At the present time the accounting profession supports a modified all-inclusive determination of net income in which items of revenue, expense, gain, and loss are included in the determination of net income. Thus, in applying the matching principle to determine an enterprise's net income, only selected, well-defined items are excluded and treated as direct charges or credits to the Retained Earnings account.

Matching

Procedurally, all income statement accounts are closed to an Income Summary account, which, in turn, is closed to the Retained Earnings account. Therefore, the net income earned or loss sustained during the period is reported as a single number on the statement of retained earnings. Individual revenues, expenses, gains, and losses comprising net income are displayed on the income statement. Accountants should not bypass the income statement by recording revenues, expenses, gains, and losses directly in the Retained Earnings account.

PRIOR PERIOD ADJUSTMENTS

Prior period adjustments are recorded as direct charges or credits to the Retained Earnings account and do not affect net income. **Prior period adjustments,** although quite rare, usually result from accounting errors made in previous years that have been detected and corrected in the current year. Management has a strong incentive to provide fairly stated financial information initially and, thereby, to minimize public disclosure of prior period mistakes in later reports. A prior period adjustment informs financial information users that decisions made in prior years may have been based on flawed information provided by management.

Accounting Principles Board Opinion No. 20 defines errors in financial statements as "mathematical mistakes, mistakes in the application of accounting principles, oversights or misuses of facts that existed at the time the [previous] financial statements were prepared."[2] The Accounting Principles Board (APB) also defined changes from unacceptable accounting principles to generally accepted accounting principles (GAAP) as corrections of errors. Normal recurring changes in accounting estimates, however, do not constitute corrections of errors. For example, the useful

---

[2]*APB Opinion No. 20*, "Accounting Changes," 1971, par. 13.

EXHIBIT 17-1

Primary Items Directly Affecting Retained Earnings*

Nature of Event	Debits to Retained Earnings	Credits to Retained Earnings
Income Summary account closed to Retained Earnings	Net Loss	Net Income
Distributions to stockholders (cash, property, or stock)	Dividends Declared	—
Initial adoption of certain accounting principles	Retroactive Negative Adjustment (loss, expense)	Retroactive Positive Adjustment (gain, revenue)
Corrections of accounting errors made in prior years	Prior Period Adjustment (loss, expense)	Prior Period Adjustment (gain, revenue)
Reservation of earned equity for a specific purpose (e.g., plant expansion, debt service)	Appropriation	Cancellation of Existing Appropriation
Treasury stock transactions	Negative adjustments from treasury stock transactions	
Quasi reorganization	Write-down of assets to fair value	Establishment of a zero balance by charging contributed capital

[handwritten annotations: "Available now for Dividends", "Approp. RE", "Reallocation of assets", "RE", "Approp. For Plant Expansion", "Reissue TS under cost method. Not enough in PIC", "Happens when there's a Net Loss (Debit). Legal Proceeding."]

*This list is not intended to be comprehensive. For example, other items that can affect retained earnings are changes in certain accounting principles and changes in the accounting entity (see Chapter 19).

---

lives and salvage values of depreciable assets must be estimated in advance in order to calculate depreciation expense. Revisions in such estimates as a result of new or better information are not considered corrections of errors whose effects are recorded directly in retained earnings. Rather, changes in estimates affect net income of the current and, possibly, future periods. Other examples of circumstances which require accounting estimates include the recognition of bad debts and the evaluation of loss contingencies.

In sum, if available information is misused or intentional misestimates are made, an error occurs. If new information becomes available that provides for a better estimate, a change in accounting estimate results. Accountants must evaluate whether original estimates are wrong as a result of intentional action or honest misestimates. Financial accounting and reporting for each type of event differs greatly. We discuss accounting changes more fully in Chapter 19.

Matching
The presentation of prior period adjustments in the retained earnings statement is made net of any related income tax effects. For example, assume that a $3,000 advertising commission that had been incurred and should have been charged to expense in a prior period is paid and charged to expense during the current period. To facilitate proper matching, the correction of this error is properly treated as a prior period adjustment. The advertising expense may also be deductible for federal income taxes.

Thus, a tax benefit may be associated with the prior period adjustment, and the effect on retained earnings of the correction of the error should be shown net of the related income tax effect. We discuss the techniques for calculating the tax effects of prior period adjustments in Chapters 18 and 19.

DIVIDEND DISTRIBUTIONS OF CORPORATE ASSETS

Dividends involve the unilateral transfer of items of value from a corporation to its stockholders. Corporate assets are usually the items transferred, although, in some cases, additional stock of the corporation is transferred as a stock dividend. In any event, dividends represent a reduction of retained earnings, unless the dividend is a liquidating dividend. Liquidating dividends are presumed to be paid from resources which were originally contributed by stockholders rather than earned by the enterprise. As such, contributed capital accounts are charged when liquidating dividends are declared and paid. The various classes, types, and amounts of dividends and the related accounting and reporting practices are considered next; liquidating dividends are discussed later.

The board of directors of a corporation must **declare** a dividend before a liability to pay dividends is incurred by the corporation. The day the board of directors decides that a dividend should be distributed is called the **date of declaration.** Usually, the declaration provides for a **date of record** and a **date of payment.** Exhibit 17–2 summarizes the accounting and reporting implications of each of these important dates.

The board of directors declares a dividend via a news release to the financial press and shareholders. A typical dividend announcement is provided in Exhibit 17–3 for the Walt Disney Company, an entertainment and leisure-oriented company.

Although the phrase "dividends are paid out of retained earnings" is frequently used, we should clearly recognize that dividends are paid with cash or other assets: Retained earnings merely represents the funding source or equity for the reduction of assets used to pay the dividend. For example, a company may have retained earnings far in excess of cash available for supporting operations and dividend payments. Cash generated by operations may be invested in plant assets or used to retire debt and thus not be available for distribution as dividends.

EXHIBIT 17–2
Summary of Dividend Paying Events

Event	Explanation	Accounting Entry		
Date of declaration	Board of directors declares dividend and corporation incurs liability to pay dividend.	Retained Earnings Dividends Payable	XX	XX
Date of record	Declaration specifies that ownership of stock on record date determines the specific dividend recipient.	No journal entry required; however, a memo entry is made to specific stockholder accounts in subsidiary records.		
Date of payment	Cash (or other assets) is disbursed to appropriate stockholders of record.	Dividends Payable Cash	XX	XX

EXHIBIT 17-3

The Walt Disney Company
Dividend Announcement

The Walt Disney Company®

News Release

For Further Information

Erwin Okun
Senior Vice President
818-560-5400

FOR IMMEDIATE RELEASE

November 26, 1990

DISNEY DECLARES DIVIDEND

Burbank, Calif.--Directors of The Walt Disney Company today declared a quarterly cash dividend of 14.5 cents per share. The dividend is payable February 20, 1991, to shareholders of record January 18, 1991.

# # #

SOURCE: The Walt Disney Company, 1990.

Cash Dividends

When a corporation's board of directors declares a **cash dividend**, the total amount to be disbursed as well as the per share amount of the dividend is usually stated explicitly, and accounting is consistent with that described in Exhibit 17–2. When there is more than one class of stock, allocating dividends among the classes of stock can become complex. We discuss several of these complexities in the following pages.

Dividends on Cumulative Preferred Stock. A cumulation clause requires a company to pay all dividends to preferred stockholders, including unpaid dividends from prior years called **dividend in arrears**, before any dividends are paid to common stockholders. **Dividends in arrears** are not a liability until a dividend is declared by a corporation's board of directors. Accountants must be aware of such clauses to properly calculate the dividends due each stockholder class.

Exhibit 17–4, the stockholders' equity section of Sundeen Corporation's balance sheet at December 31, 1992, illustrates the difficulties that can arise and the related computations necessary to appropriately distribute dividends. Assume that on December 31, 1992, Sundeen's board of directors declares a dividend of $600,000 to be paid on January 31, 1993, to stockholders of record at January 15, 1993. Further

EXHIBIT 17–4

Sundeen Corporation
Partial Balance Sheet

December 31, 1992

Stockholders' Equity

Preferred stock ($100 par, 7% cumulative, nonvoting; 10,000 shares authorized, issued, and outstanding)	$1,000,000
Common stock ($25 par; 100,000 shares authorized, 60,000 shares issued and outstanding)	1,500,000
Paid-in capital in excess of par value	750,000
Total paid-in capital	3,250,000
Retained earnings	2,500,000
Total stockholders' equity	$5,750,000

assume that no dividends have been paid for the previous three years. The following computation demonstrates how the $600,000 dividend will be distributed if Sundeen's preferred stock outstanding was unchanged for the periods in question.

Par value of preferred stock outstanding	$1,000,000
Dividend percentage	× .07
Annual dividend to preferred stockholders	70,000
X number of years in arrears (3) + current year's dividend	× 4
Total dividend to preferred stockholders	$ 280,000

Because the preferred stock is cumulative, the three years' dividends in arrears and the current year's dividend are paid before the common stockholders receive any dividend. Therefore, of the total dividend declared ($600,000), the preferred stockholders receive $280,000 while the common stockholders receive only $320,000. The total dividends declared result in the following dividends per share:

Preferred stock	
In arrears ($210,000/100,000 shares)	$21.00
Current ($70,000/10,000 shares)	7.00
Total dividends per share (preferred)	$28.00
Common stock	
Current ($320,000/60,000 shares)	$ 5.33

The following entries to record the declaration and payment of the dividend:

Dec. 31, 1992	Retained Earnings	600,000	
	Dividends Payable (Preferred)		280,000
	Dividends Payable (Common)		320,000
	(To record declaration of dividend.		
	Preferred 3 years in arrears.)		
Jan. 31, 1993	Dividends Payable (Preferred)	280,000	
	Dividends Payable (Common)	320,000	
	Cash		600,000
	(To record payment of dividends.)		

No formal accounting entry is necessary on the date of record, when the stockholders who will receive the dividends are determined.

Dividends on Noncumulative Preferred Stock.   Now assume the same facts except that the preferred stock is *not* cumulative. The following calculation reflects the distribution of the dividend under this condition:

Par value of preferred stock outstanding	$1,000,000
Dividend percentage	× .07
Total dividend to preferred stockholders	$ 70,000

Because the preferred stock is noncumulative, only the current year's dividend is paid to the preferred stockholders. This is the case even though the preferred stockholders have received no dividends for the last three years. The common stockholders will, of course, receive the remaining $530,000. Dividends per share are

Preferred stock ($70,000/10,000 shares)	$7.00
Common stock ($530,000/60,000 shares)	8.83

The cumulative feature of preferred stock affects the value of common stock and preferred stock. When preferred stock is cumulative, dividends for common shareholders may be reduced if dividends on preferred stock fall in arrears. As a result, common stock investors will likely discount the market value of the common shares. In contrast, preferred stockholders perceive the cumulative feature as an attractive characteristic that provides some protection against omitted dividends. As a result, the market price of preferred stock will likely be higher than it would be without the cumulation clause.

Dividends on Participating Preferred Stock.   Preferred stock may be fully participating, partially participating, or nonparticipating. Participation features may also be combined with cumulation clauses. (For simplicity we illustrate each separately.) Participating preferred stockholders share additional dividends with common stockholders after each has received an initial dividend. The initial dividend distribution is based on the preference percentage of the preferred stock. The extent of the sharing depends on whether the preferred stock is fully or partially participating.

To illustrate, consider again the stockholders' equity of Sundeen Corporation presented in Exhibit 17–4. For simplicity, however, assume that there are no dividends in arrears and that the preferred stock is fully participating. The following calculation demonstrates the manner in which the $600,000 dividend is distributed:

Step 1. Preference Distribution to Preferred Stockholders

Total preferred par value		$1,000,000
Preference rate		× .07
Initial distribution amount		$ 70,000

Step 2. Equivalency Distribution to Common Stockholders

Total common par value		$1,500,000
Equivalency rate (based on preferred rate)		× .07
Initial distribution amount		$ 105,000

Step 3. Participation Distribution

Total dividend declared		$ 600,000
Preference to preferred stockholders	$ 70,000	
Equivalency to common stockholders	105,000	
Total distributed prior to participation		175,000
Remaining participation dividend		$ 425,000

Step 4. Distribution of Remaining Dividend Based on Ratio of Total Par Values

Remaining participation dividend (Step 3)		$425,000
Ratio of total par values		
Preferred par	$1,000,000	40%
Common par	1,500,000	60%
Total combined par values	$2,500,000	100.0%
Portion of remainder to preferred stockholders		
(.40 × $425,000)		$170,000
Portion of remainder to common stockholders		
(.60 × $425,000)		255,000
Total remainder distributed		$425,000

Step 5. Summary of Total Dividend Allocation

Preferred stock		
Preference amount (Step 1)	$ 70,000	
Participation amount (Step 4)	170,000	
Total preferred dividend		$240,000
Common stock		
Preference equivalency amount (Step 2)	105,000	
Participation amount (Step 4)	255,000	
Total common dividend		360,000
Total dividend		$600,000

When preferred stock is **fully participating,** both common and preferred shareholders usually receive an equal percentage dividend on the par value of their holdings. An exception occurs if the dividend declared is too small to pay common stockholders the preference rate. In the example above, in which the preference rate is 7%, the percentage to be paid is calculated in the following manner:

Preferred stock ($240,000/$1,000,000) 24%
Common stock ($360,000/$1,500,000) 24%
Total (dividend/total par value of both classes)
($600,000/$2,500,000) 24%

The percentage paid to each class, as computed in Step 5 above, is 24%. Since the percentage in our example (24%) exceeds the preferred rate (7%), we conclude that each class of stockholder shares the dividend equally on a pro rata basis.

Several other points are significant in the calculations above. First, a participation clause in preferred stock does not apply until the preferred stockholders receive the preference amount and the common stockholders receive dividends equivalent (on a weighted average) to those received by the preferred stockholders. Therefore, if a dividend fails to meet both requirements, the preferred stockholders receive only the preference amount. The participation clause applies only to dividends in excess of the original preference dividend paid on preferred stock and an equivalent dividend on common stock. Of course, if a dividend is too small to meet even the preference amount of the preferred stock, the preferred shareholders receive the entire dividend.

Once a participation clause is in effect, the number of shares outstanding must be multiplied by the related par values of each class of stock as a basis for allocating the remaining dividend. The total dividend to be received by each class of stockholder may comprise a base dividend computed on the preference clause in the preferred stock and the participating amount. Finally, if the preferred stock is both cumulative and participating, *any dividends in arrears are paid first and are not considered part of the current distribution to preferred shareholders.*

The example presented previously is based on a fully participating clause in the preferred stock issue. In such situations preferred stockholders continue to share dividends with common stockholders regardless of the total dividend declared.

Some participating preferred stock issues are partially rather than fully participating. **Partial participation** means that preferred stockholders share to a limited extent in any dividends declared above the preference rate. The participation rate establishes an upper limit, not a preference.

To illustrate, assume that the participation clause of Sundeen Corporation's preferred stock specifies only partial participation. Also assume that preferred stockholders receive a 7% preference dividend and participate with common stockholders up to a maximum of 10%, including the preference amount. In this case the first three steps are those of the previous analysis; the next two steps involve modifications.

Step 1. Preference Distribution to Preferred Stockholders

Same as fully participating ($70,000 to preferred stockholders).

Step 2. Equivalency Distribution to Common Stockholders*

Same as fully participating ($105,000 to common stockholders).

Step 3. Participation Distribution

Same as fully participating ($425,000 remaining dividend).

Step 4. Distribution of Remaining Dividend**

Total combined par value of stockholders' equity (preferred and common)	$2,500,000
Partial participation percentage	× .03
Participating dividend	$ 75,000
Preferred share (.03 × $1,000,000)	$ 30,000
Common share (.03 × $1,500,000)	45,000
	$ 75,000

---

*Had the undistributed dividend at this point been $105,000 or less, it would all go to the common stockholders and no further calculation would be necessary.

**Had the undistributed dividend at this point been less than $75,000, it would be allocated between common and preferred in proportion to their total par value, 40% and 60%, respectively.

Step 5. Summary of Total Dividend Allocation

Preferred stock		
Preferred amount (Step 1)	$ 70,000	
Participation amount (Step 4)	30,000	
Total preferred dividend		$100,000
Common stock		
Initial common equivalency amount (Step 2)	105,000	
Participation amount (Step 4)	45,000	
Remaining dividend ($600,000 − $250,000)*	350,000	
Total common dividend		500,000
Total dividend		$600,000

---

*The total dividend is reduced by the preference and participation amounts previously determined: $100,000 + $105,000 + $45,000 = $250,000.

Several observations are possible. The participation amount of 3% is applied to both common and preferred stock to determine if any nonparticipating additional dividend is available exclusively to common stockholders. In this case, $350,000 of the total dividend is available to common stockholders only. The largest dividend preferred stockholders can ever receive is 10% of the total par value of the outstanding preferred stock, or $100,000 (.10 × $1,000,000), in addition to any dividends in arrears.

If preferred stock is cumulative or participating (or both) accountants must be particularly careful in computing dividends. Note that the overall financial statements are not affected by cumulation or participation clauses. Rather, the total dividend declared is charged to retained earnings regardless of which stockholder class receives a particular amount. The question of which stockholder groups receive what amount of dividends is very important, however, and complicated calculations may be required to determine the correct distribution.

The decision to declare and pay dividends is also highly complex and generally involves careful planning of both the total amount of the dividends as well as the amount to be paid on each share and class of stock. For simplicity we have assumed the total amount of a dividend and illustrated the calculations necessary to allocate the total dividend to various classes of stockholder. In practice, however, most companies attempt to select the per share amount of dividends to be paid to each class of stockholder, then calculate the total dividend necessary. Many companies strive to maintain consistent dividend policies from year to year, because management generally believes that a consistent dividend policy communicates stability and strength to the investment community. If the total dividend is too great, the per share amounts are revised to reduce the total dividend to a more reasonable amount that is consistent with management goals and corporate capabilities.

Property Dividends

While most corporations routinely declare and pay cash dividends, other assets such as marketable securities may be distributed to stockholders as **property dividends.** If a corporation distributes noncash assets as dividends, accounting is based on the fair value of the property transferred. Such noncash dividends, sometimes referred to as **nonreciprocal transfers of nonmonetary assets,** may require the recognition of a gain or loss on the disposal of the asset.

To illustrate, assume that Drand, Inc., elects to declare a dividend whereby inventory with a recorded book value of $10,000 and a fair market value of $16,000 is to be distributed to stockholders. The entry to record the dividend declaration and distribution appears below:

Retained Earnings	16,000	
Inventory		10,000
Gain on Disposal of Inventory		6,000
(To record declaration and distribution of property dividend.)		

A gain is recognized only on the inventory to be distributed. Remaining amounts of inventory continue to be carried at the lower of cost or market. An exception to the general practice of recognizing gains or losses occurs if the fair value of the asset to be distributed is not determinable. In such cases the dividend declaration and payment should be based on the recorded book values. These practices reflect the provisions of *APB Opinion No. 29,*[3] which is discussed in Chapter 11. In essence, fair values are used to record most nonmonetary transactions, including nonreciprocal transfers such as the declaration and payment of property dividends. The extent of a property divi-

---

[3]*APB Opinion No. 29,* "Accounting for Nonmonetary Transactions," 1973, par. 26.

dend is best represented by the fair value of the property distributed rather than its historical cost.

An additional accounting and reporting problem arises if a property dividend is declared in one period and is to be paid in the following period. If a property dividend is declared near the end of an accounting period and is to be distributed in the next year, when should any gain or loss on the disposal of the asset be recognized? Further, should changes in the value of the asset between the date of declaration and the date of distribution be recognized and, if so, in what manner?

Although these issues are not explicitly addressed in the authoritative literature, the authors support the recognition of gain or loss when a property dividend is declared. No further adjustments should be made to the asset for later changes in its fair value prior to distribution. In the authors' judgment, the amount of the dividend to be paid is usually established at the declaration date. The board of directors' action to declare a dividend creates a liability, and the amount of the liability to be recognized should be measured by the fair value of the consideration to be given. Of course, adequate disclosure of the timing and valuation basis employed is necessary in such circumstances.

Disclosure

As an example, assume that Drand, Inc., declares a property dividend on December 31, 1992, to be paid on January 15, 1993. On December 31, the equipment has a book value of $25,000 and a fair market value of $35,000. The following entries are necessary on December 31, 1992, to record the dividend declaration and the revision in the carrying value of the asset:

Dec. 31, 1992	Retained Earnings	35,000	
	Dividend Payable		35,000
Dec. 31, 1992	Equipment	10,000	
	Gain on Disposition Commitment		
	of Equipment		10,000
	(To record declaration of dividend and to		
	record gain on disposal of property.)		

Note that the liability and related asset to be used in satisfying the liability are now carried on Drand's books at the same amount ($25,000 + $10,000 = $35,000). Net income rises as a result of the recognized gain, which causes a related increase in retained earnings. However, the direct charge to Retained Earnings in the first entry shown above reduces Retained Earnings by an amount equal to the sum of the gain and the carrying amount of the equipment. Thus, the direct effect of the $10,000 *gain* on retained earnings is offset by $10,000 of the $35,000 debit to retained earnings in the first entry.

The entry to record the payment of the dividend on January 15, 1993, is:

Jan. 15, 1993	Dividends Payable	35,000	
	Equipment		35,000
	(To record distribution on property subject		
	to the dividend.)		

If changes in the equipment's fair value occur following the declaration of the dividend and related revaluation of the property, the authors suggest nonrecognition of the change for the following reasons. First, any change in the value of the asset results in a related change in the liability, because the former is to be used to satisfy the latter. Therefore, any gains or losses on revaluing the asset would be directly offset by losses and gains on revaluing the related liability. Second, once the commitment to the assets disposition has been made and the asset is revalued, no further gain or loss is sustained by the enterprise. This, of course, assumes that no specific event, such as fire or theft, changes the underlying circumstances and requires the dividend to be paid with other assets.

Scrip Dividends

On rare occasions a company may be short of cash and yet still wish to declare a dividend. In such cases a company may issue **scrip dividends** in the form of written promises to pay cash in the future. Such promises are considered similar to notes payable and are accounted for as a liability. Scrip dividends may bear interest and may be traded, sold, or otherwise disposed of by the shareholder or other owner of the scrip.

Scrip dividends are usually declared only by companies which are quite profitable but for some reason are temporarily short of cash. For example, a construction company may have generated substantial net income during a period but may have only limited cash available if the other party to a contract retains a large amount of cash pending completion of the project. In such a situation, the company may elect to declare a scrip dividend.

Scrip dividends are rare in practice. Most companies which are short of cash are unwilling to incur additional claims on cash through their own unilateral action. Further, most companies that have the profitability to declare dividends either have cash available or can arrange short-term financing for such purposes.

Liquidating Dividends

Liquidating dividends represent distributions of corporate assets which are a return of contributed equity rather than a distribution of earned equity resulting from profitable operations. Such dividends are commonly encountered in the extractive industries and in situations involving corporate dissolution. If a corporation elects to dissolve, creditor claims take precedence over the claims of stockholder groups. Even prior to the repayment of all corporate debt, however, it may be possible to pay a liquidating dividend to the extent that creditors are adequately protected and legal minimum stated capital is not impaired.

Accountants recognize liquidating dividends only after retained earnings have been exhausted by prior operating losses or previous dividend distributions. Once retained earnings is completely exhausted, further distributions of assets to stockholders are charged to paid-in capital in excess of par rather than capital stock accounts. Finally, in a complete dissolution, remaining assets distributed to residual equity holders result in the total elimination of both assets and corporate equity, thereby closing corporate records.

STOCK DIVIDENDS AND SPLITS

Stock dividends and stock splits are two types of stock distributions that are frequently encountered in practice. **Stock dividends** are dividend declarations to be satisfied in the form of additional shares of the declaring company's stock. Because each shareholder receives additional shares based on the extent of present holdings, no problems are encountered in regard to stockholders' preemptive rights.

A **stock split** occurs when a corporation exchanges a different number of shares of stock for the shares currently held by stockholders. Thus, a shareholder owns more shares after the split than before. Conversely, in a **reverse stock split,** a shareholder owns fewer shares after the split.

A primary reason for a company declaring a stock split is to influence the market for its shares of stock. When a company operates successfully, the market value of its stock may rise to a level that limits active trading. Some investors may be reluctant or unable to acquire shares with a high individual value and trading in the stock may be limited. In such circumstances the company may decide to "split" the number of shares to reduce the market price of each share and thereby encourage active trading.

Stock dividends are frequently distributed by companies that, while successful, have operating or financing needs for all available cash. For example, a highly successful company may want to build new factories and expand operations as quickly as possible. Management may therefore wish to retain all available cash. The corporation, however, may also want to distribute dividends to shareholders in recognition of the successful operating results. Stock dividends are a solution to this dilemma.

Stock Dividends

The nature of stock dividends has been discussed by the accounting profession for a long time, yet the subject remains controversial. The central question about the declaration and distribution of stock dividends is whether a significant accountable event has transpired. The company neither disposes of assets nor acquires cash or other assets through the issuance of additional shares. The declaration of a stock dividend does not give rise to a claim on the assets of a corporation, because *additional* shares of the corporation's own stock are to be issued. The recognition of a liability is thus inappropriate. Rather, the declaration of a stock dividend generally requires a charge to retained earnings with a corresponding credit to "stock dividends distributable," also a stockholders' equity account. When the dividend is distributed, the stock dividend distributable account is eliminated and the newly outstanding commmon stock is recorded.

When a corporation's board of directors declares a stock dividend, a permanent capitalization of a portion of retained earnings takes place. That is, a stock dividend causes a portion of retained earnings which were previously available for dividends to be permanently capitalized as additional shares of stock.

Small Stock Dividends. If a stock dividend represents an increase of less than 20% to 25% of the previously outstanding shares of similar stock, it is called a **small stock dividend.** Such dividends are so small that the market value of each outstanding

Materiality
share is not expected to change materially. This perception is best expressed by *Accounting Research Bulletin 43*, which states:

> As has been previously stated, a stock dividend does not, in fact, give rise to any change whatsoever in either the corporation's assets or its respective shareholders' proportionate interests therein. However, it cannot fail to be recognized that, merely as a consequence of the expressed purpose of the transaction and its characterization as a dividend in related notices to shareholders and the public at large, many recipients of stock dividends look upon them as distributions of corporate earnings and usually in an amount equivalent to the fair value of the additional shares received. . . . The committee therefore believes that where these circumstances exist [small stock dividends] the corporation should in the public interest account for the transaction by transferring from earned surplus [retained earnings] to the category of permanent capitalization . . . an amount equal to the fair value of the additional shares issued. Unless this is done, the amount of earnings which the shareholder may believe to have been distributed to him will be left . . . in earned surplus [retained earnings] subject to possible further similar stock issuances or cash distributions. [4] [Emphasis added.]

---

[4]*Accounting Research Bulletin No. 43*, Ch. 7, Sec. B, par. 10.

Accounting principles require accountants to record the declaration of small stock dividends by transferring from retained earnings to contributed capital an amount equal to the market value of the shares issued. The rationale for this approach is that stockholders believe they are receiving something of value, even when in reality each stockholder's proportionate interest in the company remains unchanged. Accounting policy makers were concerned that unless stock dividends were accounted for in this manner, investors would be misled into believing the potential for total dividends was greater than was really the case due to the unchanged balance of retained earnings that would remain. Recent research into stock prices indicates that the market prices of securities will fall in proportion to stock dividend distributions and that the resulting market prices will properly reflect the underlying value of the total ownership. As a result, the rationale for recording small stock dividends at market value rests on tenuous, possibly incorrect, assumptions. Regardless, the procedure of transferring an amount equal to the market value of the shares issued from retained earnings to contributed capital remains a part of current accounting practice.

In sum, the market value of the stock subject to the dividend is permanently capitalized and is no longer treated as part of retained earnings, because the amount is represented by shares of stock. Again, the theory of accounting for small stock dividends is that the issuance of stock is so small that there will be little, if any, effect on the market value of the company's stock. Therefore, the best measure of the earned equity which has been converted to contributed equity through the stock dividend is the market value of the shares issued.

Large Stock Dividends. When a stock dividend increases the number of outstanding shares by more than 20% to 25%, the value of each share in the market is expected to decline. Such declarations are known as **large stock dividends.** The difference between accounting for a small stock dividend and a large stock dividend involves the amount of equity reclassified as the par or stated value of the newly issued shares. While the market value of the stock is used in small stock dividends to change retained earnings and credit contributed capital, the amount to be reclassified in large stock dividends from retained earnings is limited to the par or stated value of the stock.

The theory underlying large stock dividends recognizes that if the number of shares of stock outstanding substantially increases and no changes occur in total assets or liabilities, the value of each share of stock declines. As indicated previously, the same case can be made for accounting for small stock dividends, although current accounting practice does not reflect this similarity.

Stock Splits

A **stock split,** sometimes called a **stock split-up,** is a distribution of a company's own capital stock to existing stockholders with the intent of reducing the market price of the stock. For example, in a 2-to-1 stock split, stockholders receive two shares for each share they owned before the split.

As previously stated, the primary purpose of a stock split is to reduce the market price of the stock to a level that will encourage investment in the company. If a company has been operating successfully, the market price of its stock may have risen so high that active trading, particularly by individual investors, is discouraged. For example, the most expensive New York Stock Exchange issue in 1983 was Metromedia, which sold at more than $400 per share. An investor would need $40,000 to purchase a round lot of 100 shares. Subsequently, the price of Metromedia's stock rose to over $550 per share. Shortly thereafter, several officers of the company gained control through the acquisition of stock in a leveraged buyout. When the number of shares of a company's stock is increased through a stock split, the price of each share in the market declines. The assets and liabilities of the company remain constant while the number of ownership shares increases. Consequently, each share after the stock split represents a smaller interest in the same total ownership than existed before the stock split. By exchanging a larger number of shares for a smaller number of shares, management may restore the market price of its company's stock to a more desirable level. Most companies try to maintain their stock price in a certain range to encourage trading and wide ownership.

Some believe that the prices of securities will not adjust to the full extent of a stock split but will adjust to a price that reflects a premium after the stock split. To illustrate, they would expect a stock selling at $200 which is split 4 to 1 to sell at more than $50 ($200/4) after the split. The suggestion is that the stock split action increases the value of each shareholder's holdings, even though the theoretical value should remain unchanged. An argument in favor of this position suggests that the stock split (or large stock dividend) significantly increases the potential breadth of ownership. Advocates of this position argue that a decrease in the price of the stock increases the number of individuals able to purchase the stock and thus increases the actual demand (price) for the stock.

Some have also argued that if enough people believe a stock split will increase the total value of stockholder holdings, it will become a self-fulfilling prophecy. Empirical evidence on the adjustment of stock prices to stock splits indicates that stock prices adjust fully for the dilutive effect of stock splits. As A. Wilfred May cogently states, "a pie does not grow through its slicing."[5] The empirical evidence supports the proposition that there is no intrinsic value in stock splits, but that stock prices may reflect a post-split premium because the stock split signals information to market participants about managements' positive expectations for future performance.[6]

When a stock split is issued, the par or stated value of the stock is adjusted in proportion to the size of the stock split. For example, a $100 par value stock that is split 2:1 will have a $50 par value after the split; a $50 par value stock that is split 5:1 will have a $10 par value after the split.

The accounting procedure for recording a stock split is to simply prepare a memorandum entry that indicates the change in the number of shares and the par value of those shares. No formal general journal entry is required since there is no change in the balance of the capital stock accounts, only a change in the number of shares and the par value of those shares. Recall again the outstanding common stock of Sundeen Corporation presented in Exhibit 17–4 (60,000 shares of $25 par value stock). If the company declared a 2:1 stock split, the company would have 200,000 shares of common stock authorized, 120,000 of which were outstanding at a $12.50 par value. The total amount in the Common Stock account, $1,500,000, is unchanged. No amount of retained earnings is transferred to contributed capital as was done in the case of a stock dividend discussed earlier.

In a **reverse stock split** or **stock split-down,** shareholders own fewer shares after the split. An example of a stock split-down is a 1-for-2 split in which a stockholder who holds 50 shares of stock before the split owns only 25 shares after the exchange. The objective of a reverse stock split is the opposite of a stock split. That is, a reverse stock split is designed to increase the price of the stock in the market.

---

[5]A. Wilfred May, "Current Popular Delusions About the Stock Split and Stock Dividend," *The Commercial and Financial Chronicle* (November 15, 1956), p. 5.

[6]Eugene Fama, Lawrence Fisher, Michael Jensen, and Richard Roll, "The Adjustment of Stock Prices to New Information," *International Economic Review* (February 1969), pp. 1–21. Also Guy Charest, "Split Information, Stock Returns, and Market Efficiency—I," *Journal of Financial Economics* (June/September 1978), pp. 265–296.

The distinction between a large stock dividend and a stock split is a fine one at best. Basically, a *large stock dividend* is the issuance of stock with the same par (or stated) value as the shares outstanding; hence the increase in legal capital (credit to common stock). A *stock split* is simply the exchange of existing shares for new shares with a different par (or stated) value per share; the total par (or stated) value of the outstanding shares is maintained. The end result of the two approaches is similar: more shares are outstanding, and the total stockholders' equity remains unchanged. With large stock dividends, however, the components of stockholders' equity are altered, since an amount equal to the par (or stated) value of the shares issued has been transferred from retained earnings to contributed capital.

TREASURY STOCK AND DIVIDENDS

Substance over Form

As mentioned previously, cash dividends are not declared on treasury stock. To do so would imply that the corporation is an owner of itself and is able to earn income from a common stock investment in itself. If such dividends were declared, the company would essentially be reducing retained earnings and simultaneously recording dividend revenue (increasing retained earnings through income) with no corresponding change in resources. Although the economic substance of the corporation remains unchanged, the transfer of retained earnings to dividend revenue may be misleading to financial statement users. As a result, most states do not allow cash dividends to be declared on treasury shares.

Stock dividends and stock splits on treasury shares are appropriate because they involve only a rearrangement within the stockholders' equity accounts and do not affect the income statement. As a result, stock dividends and stock splits may be declared on treasury shares in some states, although a few states prohibit stock dividends on treasury shares. A stock split on treasury shares has the same effect as on outstanding shares. The par value of the treasury shares is adjusted so that the total par value of all treasury shares remains unchanged after the split. Naturally, the total cost of the treasury shares is also unaffected.

APPROPRIATION OF RETAINED EARNINGS

Occasionally the management of a company decides to commit corporate resources to some project or purpose and wishes to communicate that fact through the financial statements. For example, management may wish to retain resources to expand plant assets or repay debt rather than pay dividends to stockholders. In such situations retained earnings may be appropriated to notify financial statement users about the intended use of the company's resources. To illustrate, if Montclair Company management decides to build a new factory at an estimated cost of $2,500,000, the following appropriation of retained earnings is acceptable:

Retained Earnings	2,500,000	
Retained Earnings Appropriated		
for Plant Expansion		2,500,000
(To appropriate retained earnings		
according to company plans.)		

The account Retained Earnings Appropriated for Plant Expansion is reported as part of stockholders' equity rather than as a liability or a contra asset account. The appropriation provides financial statement users with information on corporate plans and may also help explain a reduction in dividends as resources are held to finance construction.

LATEST CASUALTY OF EXCESSIVE '80s—STOCK DIVIDENDS

Another of the corporate excesses of the 1980s is being reversed in executive suites across the country.

The common stock dividend, the venerable piece of the capitalist system's pie that grew robustly at many companies in the last decade, is being sliced.

Profits are shrinking as the recession digs in, leaving the nation's auto, aerospace, appliance and other companies with little extra cash to pay to shareholders.

General Motors Corp., the nation's largest car maker, cut its quarterly payout Monday nearly by half—a step that Robert C. Stempel, GM's chairman, called "an extremely difficult decision."

Ford Motor Co., which put off its dividend decision for a few months, and Chrysler Corp. are expected to follow GM's lead.

On Tuesday, McDonnell Douglas Corp., the aerospace and defense company, trimmed its regular payment to shareholders.

And yesterday, Maytag Corp., the giant appliance maker, and Goodyear Tire & Rubber Co. decreased their dividends sharply.

Until now, the beleaguered banking industry was the most notable dividend-cutter, as bankers searched for ways to conserve cash and raise capital.

Citicorp, Chase Manhattan, Manufacturers Hanover and others lowered their payouts in the past couple of months, saving funds to offset problems with bad loans.

"There is a tremendous squeeze these days," said Arnold Kaufman, editor of Standard & Poor's Outlook newsletter, which tracks dividend trends.

"Profits are no longer high enough to pay for dividends at many companies," he added.

Dividend costs at many companies are high these days, thanks to a run-up in profits and an outpouring of corporate largesse in the 1980s.

The generous payments were partly to buy the loyalty of shareholders and thus discourage corporate raiders. Such was the ethos of the 1980s that even companies facing no imminent threat were under pressure from shareholders to pass out cash.

The Commerce Department estimates that American corporations paid out 44 percent of their pretax profits in dividends last year, up from 23 percent in 1980. Strong business conditions often made those decisions easier. But in many cases, corporations loaded up on debt while dividends were rising.

This brought a decline in retained earnings as companies doled out more to shareholders while making higher interest payments.

Thus, an increasing share of profit was diverted from reinvestment in factories, training or research on new products.

At a time when international competition is intensifying and some of America's leading rivals, notably the Japanese, pay meager dividends and invest heavily, many analysts find this trend disturbing and a threat to the nation's economic growth.

"We should be running American companies for the long term," said Joseph L. Bower, a professor and director of research at the Harvard Business School.

"Companies should be creating opportunities for growth and investment rather than paying out their funds as dividends."

Dividend policy is a matter of lively dispute, both in boardrooms and academia.

One camp contends that dividends should be modest-sized and flexible, if they are paid at all.

Exponents of this view point to growing high-technology companies, which often pay no dividends and spend heavily on research and investment.

Intel Corp., for example, a $3.9-billion-a-year maker of semiconductors, has never paid a dividend.

The company, whose stock trades over the counter, considered a dividend last year, but decided against it, choosing to bolster its share-price instead by purchasing some of its own shares.

Intel recently announced that it would spend up to $1 billion this year on new plants and equipment.

SOURCE: Steve Lohr, "Latest Casualty of Excessive '80s—Stock Dividends," *New York Times* as printed in the *San Francisco Chronicle*, February 8, 1991, p. E12. Adapted from "Companies Cut Stock Dividends as Profits Drop." Copyright © 1991 by The New York Times Company. Reprinted by permission.

Appropriating retained earnings does *not* necessarily imply that resources have been set aside for the purpose indicated. The appropriation is simply a reclassification of retained earnings, which signals owners about possible reductions in dividends.

State law occasionally requires an appropriation of retained earnings in the case of treasury stock. Law sometimes requires companies to record an appropriation of retained earnings equal to the cost of any treasury stock. Such regulations are designed to protect the creditors of a company from a substantial reduction of stockholders' equity through treasury stock acquisitions.

Management may also record an appropriation of retained earnings as a reporting response to loss contingencies, as discussed in Chapter 14. An appropriation of retained earnings, however, is not considered an alternative to recording loss contingencies in accordance with *Statement of Financial Accounting Standards No. 5*.[7] Rather, accountants consider an appropriation of retained earnings as a supplement to other practices required by generally accepted accounting principles, such as note

Disclosure   disclosure.

Finally, when the reason for the appropriation no longer exists, the appropriated retained earnings should be returned directly to unappropriated retained earnings. Losses or gains should be presented in the income statement and never charged or credited to appropriated retained earnings. Similarly, the Appropriated Retained Earnings account should never be included in the determination of net income.

STATEMENT OF CHANGES IN STOCKHOLDERS' EQUITY

Disclosure   The foregoing issues complicate the presentation of the statement of retained earnings as well as the disclosure of changes in other stockholders' equity accounts. Although a separate statement of retained earnings is frequently presented, it is also common to combine the changes in retained earnings with a statement presenting changes in other stockholders' equity accounts. The resulting statement of stockholders' equity reflects the activity that has taken place in all equity accounts during the accounting period. An illustrative comprehensive disclosure of changes in stockholders' equity is presented in Exhibit 17–5 for DEP Corporation, a developer, manufacturer, and marketer of personal care products.

Although not all possible changes in equity accounts are contained in the report of DEP Corporation, the statement is representative of presentations commonly encountered in practice. Several stock transactions are evident: the issuance of stock under option plans in each year and the purchases of treasury stock in 1988 and 1989. In each year the retained earnings column reflects additions for annual net income although no dividends are reported.

CAPITAL STOCK AND EMPLOYEE COMPENSATION

Corporate management and the board of directors exercise great control over stockholders' equity. The stock of a company may be used to provide part of the remuneration of employees as well as to provide funds for capital expenditures and to finance ongoing business operations. Stock option plans and stock appreciation rights are frequently used as important incentives for employees. The primary purposes of these plans are to motivate employees, reward high performance, and reduce employee attrition. If employees own stock in their company, the success of the company becomes even more important to them. If the company operates profitably and the value of the stock increases, employees who own stock become better off.

STOCK OPTION PLANS

An **employee stock option** is a temporary right granted by the company that permits an employee to purchase a limited amount of corporate stock at a specified price,

---

[7]*FASB Statement of Financial Accounting Standards No. 5*, "Accounting for Contingencies," 1975, par. 15.

EXHIBIT 17-5

DEP Corporation
Changes in Stockholders' Equity

Years ended July 31, 1990, 1989, and 1988 DEP Corporation and Subsidiaries	Common stock, at cost		Additional paid-in capital	Retained earnings	Foreign currency translation adjustment	Treasury stock, at cost	
	Shares	Amount				Shares	Amount
Balance, July 31, 1987	5,724,816	$57,000	$6,029,000	$10,800,000	$(30,000)		
Stock issued under option plan	72,534	1,000	119,000				
Cumulative translation adjustment					42,000		
Net income for the year				4,588,000			
Balance, July 31, 1988	5,797,350	58,000	6,148,000	15,388,000	12,000		
Stock issued under option plan	70,911	1,000	191,000				
Purchase of treasury stock						(43,500)	$(348,000)
Cumulative translation adjustment					(74,000)		
Net income for the year				1,521,000			
Balance, July 31, 1989	5,868,261	59,000	6,339,000	16,909,000	(62,000)	(43,500)	(348,000)
Stock issued under option plan	49,074		21,000				
Purchase of treasury stock						(88,000)	(372,000)
Cumulative translation adjustment					(16,000)		
Net income for the year				1,882,000			
Balance, July 31, 1990	5,917,335	$59,000	$6,360,000	$18,791,000	$(78,000)	(131,500)	$(720,000)

SOURCE: DEP Corporation, 1990 Annual Report.

called the **exercise price.** An employee can exercise the option by purchasing the stock at the exercise price, then resell those shares at the market price to realize a gain or hold the shares for other investment purposes. Employee stock options are not transferable, so only the employee can realize the potential benefits. In addition, companies frequently prohibit the exercise of an option until the end of a prespecified **service (holding) period.** This restriction ensures a degree of employee loyalty and tenure. The stock option agreement typically establishes an exercise period and an expiration date. Exhibit 17–6 shows a typical and stock option plan.

Stock option plans may be compensatory or noncompensatory, depending on whether employee compensation is intended in the specific plan.

Noncompensatory Stock Option Plans

Stock option plans for employees are **noncompensatory** and result in no recognition of salary expense if four characteristics are *each* present. To be noncompensatory, a plan must:[8]

1. Involve substantially all full-time employees (executives may be excluded);
2. Be offered to eligible employees equally or on the basis of a uniform percentage of salary;
3. Limit the time permitted for exercise of an option right to a reasonable period; and
4. Provide for a discount from the market price no greater than would be available to others.

Accounting for noncompensatory stock option plans is relatively simple and straightforward. If an employee exercises an option to acquire shares of stock, the corporation simply records the cash received and the related issuance of the stock. Only the cash received is treated as consideration for the stock issued in a noncompensatory plan. The difference between the market price and the exercise price on the exercise date is a benefit to the employee that is disregarded in the corporate accounting records. The rationale for this treatment is that management does not intend to compensate employees for past or future services but to raise additional capital or to improve loyalty in the work force.

Compensatory Stock Option Plans

Compensatory stock option plans do not meet all four characteristics of noncompensatory plans. **Compensatory** plans convey a right to selected employees in return for either past or future services to the company. Many large corporations compensate their corporate officers with both salaries and stock options. In compensatory stock option plans, the consideration a corporation receives for stock issued from exercised options consists of the option price and the value of services rendered by employees above their salary levels. A major accounting difficulty is measuring the incremental value of services arising from the stock option plan. These services must be valued in order to correctly assign compensation expense equal to the total value of services rendered by employees.

Accountants objectively measure the compensatory portion of employee stock options as the excess of the market price of the stock over the exercise price. This spread is computed on the date that *both* (1) the number of shares an individual employee is entitled to receive and (2) the option or purchase price of the shares first become known.[9] This date, called the **measurement date,** is used to determine the amount of compensation to be recognized in conjunction with the plan.

---

[8]*APB Opinion No. 25,* "Accounting for Stock Issued to Employees," 1972, par. 7.
[9]*APB Opinion No. 25,* par. 10.

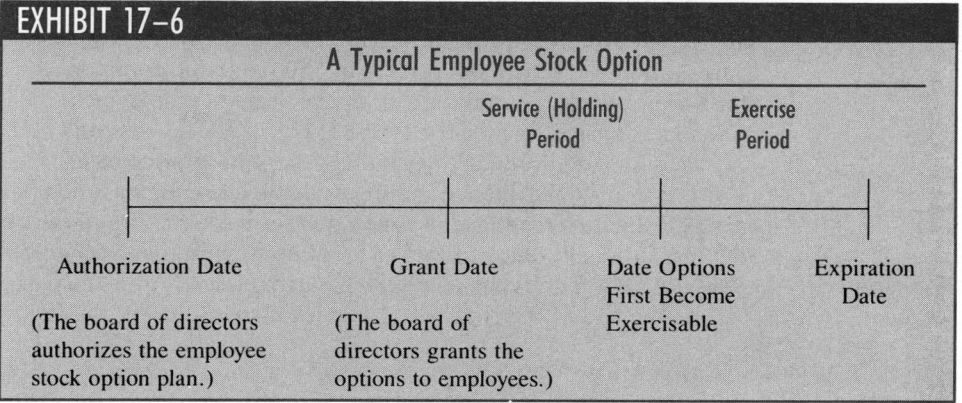

EXHIBIT 17–6

A Typical Employee Stock Option

	Service (Holding) Period	Exercise Period

Authorization Date

(The board of directors authorizes the employee stock option plan.)

Grant Date

(The board of directors grants the options to employees.)

Date Options First Become Exercisable

Expiration Date

As a result of the two criteria for determining the measurement date, the measurement date often coincides with the grant date. Therefore, the compensatory portion of the option is usually determined as the excess of the market value of the stock over the exercise price of the option on the grant date.

Compensation expense is recorded only as the services giving rise to the stock options are rendered. Thus, if an employee must perform services for several periods after the option is granted and before the stock is issued, the employer recognizes salary expense in each period in which services are performed. This principle is applied even if the total amount of compensation was known at the grant date. The procedure is simply an application of the matching principle, whereby the compensation expense is allocated to the periods in which services are performed.

Matching

One of the problems with the present method of accounting for compensatory stock options is the measurement of the compensation expense. Compensatory stock options are often granted with the exercise price equal to the market price of the stock at the measurement date. As such, generally accepted accounting principles require no compensation expense to be recorded. This treatment clearly biases financial reporting towards understating compensation expense, because the options have obvious value. An employee who was granted a stock option with the exercise price equal to the market price would not be willing to give the options away. The options are valuable because the employee cannot lose money if the stock price decreases but can realize a substantial gain if the stock price increases.[10]

Another complication arises if the measurement date occurs after the grant date. In such cases compensation expense should be recorded in each period from the grant date to the measurement date based on the quoted market price of the stock at the end of each period. The difference between the option price and the market value of the stock at the end of each period represents the total compensation to be recognized. Amounts previously recognized as compensation under the option plan in prior periods are subtracted from the total compensation to determine the compensation for the current period.

---

[10]Several methods have been suggested for the valuation of stock options. See, for example, Fischer Black and Myron Scholes, "The Pricing of Options and Corporate Liabilities," *Journal of Political Economy* (May/June 1973), pp. 158–162. The Black and Scholes valuation model was tested for accuracy against a set of publicly traded warrants similar to executive stock options. The valuation model was found to perform admirably. See Eric Noreen and Mark Wolfson, "Equilibrium Warrant Pricing Models and Accounting for Executive Stock Options," *Journal of Accounting Research* (Autumn 1981), pp. 384–398.

To illustrate the accounting for compensatory stock options, assume that on January 1, 1989, Value Corporation provides a stock option plan to the president of the corporation whereby 1,000 shares of $50 par value common stock may be purchased for $40 per share immediately after five years of employment on December 31, 1993. The market price on January 1, 1989, is $75. Because both (1) the number of shares that may be acquired (1,000) and (2) the option price ($40) are known, January 1, 1989, is considered the measurement date. The compensation per share to be recognized is the difference between the market price ($75) and the option price ($40) on the measurement date. In this case Value Corporation recognizes compensation expense of $35 per share as the services are rendered over the 5-year period.

At the end of the first year, on December 31, 1989, the following entry is made:

Dec. 31, 1989	Salary Expense	7,000	
	Stock Options Exercisable		7,000
	(To record portion of compensatory stock option plan earned at 12/31/89. 1,000 shares × $35 = $35,000 × ⅕ = $7,000.)		

This entry is repeated each year until the options become exercisable.[11] Market price changes in the stock *after* the measurement date are not recognized as additional compensation from the perspective of the employing corporation. The account Stock Options Exercisable is a contributed stockholders' equity account that remains open until the final exercise date on December 31, 1993. When the options are exercised and the employee remits the $40 per share option price, the following entry is necessary:

Dec. 31, 1993	Cash	40,000	
	Stock Options Exercisable	35,000	
	Common Stock		50,000
	Paid-in Capital in Excess of Par		25,000
	(To record issuance of stock under compensatory option plan: 1,000 × $40 = $40,000; 7,000 × $5 = $35,000; 1,000 × $50 = $50,000; $75,000 − $50,000 = $25,000)		

If the options are not exercised, the Stock Options Exercisable account is reclassified as part of Paid-in Capital in Excess of Par. The entry to record the expiration of the options is

Jan. 1, 1994	Stock Options Exercisable	35,000	
	Paid-in Capital in Excess of Par		35,000
	(To record expiration of options.)		

---

[11]An alternative approach is to record the total future compensation expense on the measurement date as follows:

Jan. 1, 1989	Deferred Compensation Expense	35,000	
	Stock Options Exercisable		35,000

The Deferred Compensation Expense account is disclosed in stockholders' equity in the balance sheet as a contra account to the Stock Options Exercisable account. The Deferred Compensation Expense account is amortized over the five-year period of intended compensation as follows:

Dec. 31, 1989	Salary Expense	7,000	
	Deferred Compensation Expense		7,000

A similar entry is made at the end of each year until the Deferred Compensation Expense account is fully amortized on December 31, 1993.

Substance over Form

This treatment is acceptable even though the stock option is not exercised. The corporation, as of the grant date, transferred an item of value to the employee. The employee can then choose to exercise the option in order to realize its value or hold the option in an attempt to realize further price appreciation on the security. If the employee allowed the option to lapse because the price of the stock decreased during the holding period, the speculative behavior should not affect the valuation of the option by the corporation. The paid-in capital in excess of par from nonexercise of the option is theoretically justified as the value of services contributed by the employee. In addition, this treatment is similar to that for detachable warrants issued with certain debt instruments which lapse. We discussed this topic in Chapter 15.

Measurement Date Controversy

The choice of the measurement date for determining the total compensation has been an issue of considerable controversy in the accounting profession. As we have already stated, *APB Opinion No. 25* defines the measurement date as the time when (1) the number of shares an employee is entitled to receive *and* (2) the option price (exercise price) are known. As mentioned, those criteria are frequently satisfied on the *grant date*. The grant date is justified as the measurement date on the basis of the opportunity foregone by the corporation. On the grant date the corporation restricts shares of stock that could otherwise be issued on the market at a fair market price. Furthermore, on the grant date the corporation must decide the number of options to grant and the exercise price of each option. These decisions are based on the corporation's estimate of the value of services to be received from the employee. The option compensation is determined as the value of services to be received above the value of salary-compensated services. Advocates of this approach believe that a corporation's intended additional compensation is determined at the grant date and should therefore provide the basis for future expense allocation.

Alternatively, some have supported measuring the total compensation as the excess of the market price of the stock over the exercise price on the *date the option first becomes exercisable*. The rationale for this approach is that the increase in the market value of the stock from the grant date to the earliest exercisable date may be an accurate proxy for the value of services provided by employees who benefit from the stock option plan. In addition, because the employees cannot exercise the option during the service period, some question remains about whether the value of the option to the employee can actually be known until the right to exercise exists. Finally, the date on which options first become exercisable is preferable to subsequent dates because exercise decisions during the exercise period are made by the executives themselves and not by the corporation. Critics contend that such decisions are speculative and should not affect the valuation of services received.

The excess of the market value of the stock over the exercise price has been suggested as the proper measure of the compensation expense on the *exercise date*. Advocates of this position point out that the exercise date is when the true value of the option is realized by the employee. Any valuation prior to exercise is simply an estimate of the final worth of the option contract and, presumably, an estimate of the final value of the incremental employee services associated with these options. The exercise date is the date the employee actually receives an ownership interest and, correspondingly, the date the corporation releases ownership shares at a price below what alternative market sources would provide.

Despite the conceptual merit of these alternatives, *APB Opinion No. 25* requires the recognition of compensation expense based on the difference between the exercise price and the market price at the measurement date. This practice is therefore well established in the accounting literature.

STOCK APPRECIATION RIGHTS

Compensatory stock options have two major disadvantages to the employee. First, the employee must make a cash outlay equal to the exercise price times the number of shares acquired. The size of the cash outlay could be burdensome to the employee acquiring a large number of optioned shares. Second, optioned shares are taxable for the difference between the market price and the exercise price (on the date of exercise). An employee is thus immediately liable for taxes on optioned shares, even though the employee may want to hold the shares beyond the date of exercise. Therefore, an employee experiences an immediate cash outflow for the exercise price coupled with a tax on the increment of market price over exercise price.

To eliminate the negative characteristics of compensatory stock options, companies may grant **stock appreciation rights (SARs)**. A SAR entitles an employee to either cash or corporate stock in an amount equal to the excess of the market value of the company's stock over a predetermined price for a stated number of shares. This right awards the employee participation in price appreciation for a stated number of shares of the company's stock without actually requiring the employee to remit cash, as in the case of stock options.

The FASB has provided guidance in accounting for stock appreciation rights.[12] SARs fall in the category of variable award plans, in which, according to the FASB, the number of shares of stock or the amount of cash that may be awarded to an employee is unspecified on the grant date. As a result, the criteria for determining the measurement date, as discussed earlier, remain unsatisfied on the grant date. The number of shares or amount of cash an employee is entitled to receive becomes known only on the date the employee exercises the SAR. The number of shares of stock or cash awarded is a function of the appreciation of share price over the predetermined price at the date of exercise. Therefore, the measurement date, used for determining the total compensation, is the exercise date rather than the earlier grant date.

Because the total compensation to be recognized in conjunction with the SAR is unknown until the exercise date, a question remains about how to accrue compensation expense. Total compensation to be allocated is estimated by the excess of the market value over the predetermined price. This amount is then allocated over the service period (or vesting period). During the period until exercise, subsequent increases or decreases in the market price of the shares require adjustments to the compensation accrued.

To illustrate, consider Pueblo Corporation, which granted an SAR to the chief executive officer (CEO) on January 1, 1990. After the three-year holding period, the SAR entitled the CEO to the appreciation in share price over the market value of the stock, as determined at the grant date. The SAR had the following terms:

> Service (holding) period: Jan. 1, 1990–Dec. 31, 1992
> Number of shares: 1,000
> Exercise date: Jan. 1, 1993
> Form of compensation: Cash or common stock at CEO's discretion

The quoted market prices of Pueblo's shares were as follows:

Jan. 1, 1990	$20
Dec. 31, 1990	28
Dec. 31, 1991	26
Dec. 31, 1992	32

---

[12]*FASB Interpretation No. 28*, "Accounting for Stock Appreciation Rights and Other Variable Stock Option or Award Plans," 1978.

The SAR was exercised on January 1, 1993. Exhibit 17–7 summarizes the accounting for Pueblo Corporation.

The Compensation Expense is adjusted annually to reflect the accrued compensation to date. As of December 31, 1990, the total compensation to be allocated is the difference between the excess of the market price ($28) over the predetermined price ($20) times the number of shares specified by the SAR. However, only one-third (33⅓%) of this amount was earned by the CEO as of December 31, 1990. The employee must provide services over a three-year period before the right can be exercised. Therefore, the total compensation should be allocated over this period. The total compensation to be allocated is readjusted annually to reflect the new market price of the company's stock. The journal entry would be recorded on December 31, 1990, as follows:

Dec. 31, 1990	Compensation Expense	2,667	
	Compensation Payable		2,667
	(To record accrual of compensation from SAR plan.)		

Similar entries are made in 1991 and 1992 for $1,333 and $8,000, respectively. The credit to Compensation Payable assumes that the appreciation will be paid in cash by the employer. If the plan called for the appreciation to be paid only in the company's common stock, a credit to a stockholders' equity account, such as Stock Appreciation Rights Exercisable, would be appropriate. In this case the employee has the option of receiving either cash or shares of stock, so the liability account is appropriate.

In 1991 the market price of the shares exceeded the option price by $6 per share. This represents a total compensation of $6,000 ($6 × 1,000 shares) to be allocated. Through December 31, 1991, two-thirds (66⅔%) of the service period elapsed; therefore, 66⅔% of the compensation was earned by the CEO. The compensation accrued to date was $4,000 ($6,000 × 66⅔%), of which $2,667 has already been recognized for 1990. The remaining $1,333 is the compensation expense to be recognized in 1991. The $1,333 reflects a "catch-up" adjustment for changes in market value in 1991, as required by *FASB Interpretation No. 28*.

Notice that the market price fell between the end of 1990 and 1991. Because the market price fell below the previous period's market price, the total compensation to be allocated decreased. In the example, the total compensation to be allocated fell to $6,000 [($26 − $20) × 1,000 shares] from the previous amount of $8,000. As of the

EXHIBIT 17–7

Pueblo Corporation
Accrued Compensation Expense Under an SAR Plan

Date	Market Price	Predetermined Price	Compensation to be Allocated	Service Period Allocation	Compensation Accrued to Date	Annual Compensation Expense
1/1/90	$20	$20	–0–	0%	–0–	–0–
12/31/90	28	20	$ 8,000	33⅓%	$ 2,667	$ 2,667
					1,333	
12/31/91	26	20	6,000	66⅔%	4,000	1,333
					8,000	
12/31/92	32	20	12,000	100%	$12,000	$ 8,000

end of 1992 the employee has completely satisfied the service obligation so that the rights are now 100% earned. Therefore, $8,000 of Compensation Expense is recognized in 1992, determined in the same manner as 1991.[13]

On January 1, 1993, the SAR was exercised by the CEO. If the CEO chose to receive cash, the following journal entry would be appropriate:

Jan. 1, 1993	Compensation Payable	12,000	
	Cash		12,000
	(To record exercise of SAR for cash.)		

If the CEO chose to receive stock, the following journal entry would be appropriate, assuming the stock has a par value of $20:

Jan. 1, 1993	Compensation Payable	12,000	
	Common Stock (375 shares @ $20)		7,500
	Paid-in Capital in Excess of Par		4,500
	(To record exercise of SAR for common stock.)		

Notice in the last entry that the CEO does not receive 1,000 shares of common stock. The 1,000 shares included in the SAR agreement are simply a mechanism for determining the amount that the CEO will receive in either cash or common stock. In this case, if the CEO chooses to receive stock, he or she will receive 375 shares, determined by dividing the stock appreciation on 1,000 shares by the market price of the stock on the exercise date: ($12,000/$32 = 375 shares).

STOCK OPTION PLAN DISCLOSURE

Disclosure   The specific characteristics of a stock option plan are typically disclosed in a note to the financial statements. The reference should include information about the number of options outstanding, granted, and exercised during the period, as well as the option price. The stock option plan disclosure of Triton Energy Corporation, a petroleum exploration and production company, presented in Exhibit 17–8, illustrates the type of information normally provided.

STOCK RIGHTS, STOCK WARRANTS, AND CONVERTIBLE SECURITIES

STOCK RIGHTS

Companies frequently issue **stock rights** conveying the right to acquire stock in the future. The terms of the rights specify the price per share of the stock (usually an amount below the market price), the number of shares subject to the rights, the expiration date of the rights, and other relevant information. Stock rights are usually valuable because they allow a person to acquire stock below the market price.

---

[13]A decline in the market price of the stock could result in a negative Compensation Expense, although this did not occur in the case of Pueblo Corporation. To illustrate, assume that the market price of Pueblo's stock at the end of 1991 was $22 instead of $26. Total compensation to be allocated would be $2,000 ($2 × 1,000 shares). Since $2,667 compensation expense was recognized during 1990, negative compensation of $1,334 [($2,000 × 66⅔%) − 2,667 = − $1,334] should be recognized in 1991, as follows:

Dec. 31, 1991	Compensation Payable	1,334	
	Compensation Expense		1,334

If this occurs, the amount eliminated should never exceed the total amount accrued to date, even if the market price of the stock is less than the predetermined price.

EXHIBIT 17–8

Triton Energy Corporation
Employee Stock Option Disclosure

(6)   (c) Stock Options

Options to purchase the Company's common stock have been granted to officers and employees under various stock option plans. Grants generally become exercisable in 25% cumulative annual increments beginning one year from the date of issuance and expire at the end of ten years. At May 31, 1990, 571,500 shares were available for grant under the 1989 plan and 812,425 shares were exercisable under the four plans. A summary of option transactions follows:

	Number of shares	Option price per share
Outstanding at May 31, 1989	1,449,474	$ 9.95–21.22
Granted.	5,000	16.25–16.50
Exercised	(71,927)	9.95–15.18
Outstanding at May 31, 1990	1,382,547	10.16–21.22

SOURCE: Triton Energy Corporation, 1990 Annual Report.

Rights are issued for various reasons. For example, if a stock dividend is declared, some stockholders may have the right to receive fractional shares, and rights may be issued to meet the obligation. Rights may also be used to protect the preemptive rights of present stockholders if a new stock issue is forthcoming. The rights allow present stockholders to maintain their existing percentage of ownership.

STOCK WARRANTS

Stock warrants are issued by a company in exchange for cash and provide the owner the right to acquire shares of stock at a specific price. At the time of issuance, the market price of the stock is usually greater than the sum of the price of the warrant and the additional cash required to exercise the warrant. When a company sells warrants in the market, a journal entry is required. For example, assume that Rosewell Corporation sells warrants that allow the holders to acquire 100,000 shares of $10 par value common stock for $25 per share. If the warrants are sold for $100,000, the journal entry necessary to record the issuance of those warrants is

Cash	100,000	
Common Stock Warrants Exercisable		100,000
(To record issuance of warrants.)		

The Common Stock Warrants Exercisable account is presented in the stockholders' equity section of the balance sheet.

At the time the warrants are exercised the following journal entry is required:

Cash (100,000 × $25)	2,500,000	
Common Stock Warrants Exercisable	100,000	
Common Stock (100,000 × $10)		1,000,000
Paid-in Capital in Excess of Par		1,600,000
(To record exercise of warrants.		
100,000 shares at $25 per share plus		
the amount paid for the warrants.)		

If the owners of the warrants allow them to lapse without exercising them, however, then the necessary entry becomes

Common Stock Warrants Exercisable	100,000	
Paid-in Capital in Excess of Par		100,000
(To record the expiration of stock warrants)		

The amount paid for the warrants becomes part of paid-in capital in excess of par if the warrants are not exercised.

Warrants may also be used as a "sweetener" to improve the market for other securities, such as debt, issued by the company. If debt is issued with detachable stock warrants or options, some of the consideration received for the composite security (debt and equity) is allocated to stockholders' equity. The method usually employed to accomplish the allocation is based on the relative fair market values of bonds and warrants considered individually. We discussed and illustrated accounting for detachable warrants in Chapter 15.

Recall that the Stock Warrants Exercisable account appears in the contributed capital section of stockholders' equity until the warrants either are exercised or expire. In the event of exercise, additional consideration is received and the Stock Warrants Exercisable account is removed from the records. The stock issued is recorded at the sum of the carrying amount of the warrants, if any, and the exercise price received.

To illustrate, assume that Harmon Corporation originally issued 1,000 bonds, including one detachable warrant per bond. Also assume that after the proceeds of the issue had been allocated, the Stock Warrants Exercisable account had a credit balance of $15,000 (or $15 per warrant). Each warrant, upon exercise, grants the holder one share of $10 par value common stock at a cash price of $35 per share. Further assume that half of the warrants were exercised when the market price of the common stock was $60 per share. The following journal entry would reflect the exercise:

Cash ($35 × 500)	17,500	
Stock Warrants Exercisable ($15 × 500)	7,500	
Common Stock ($10 × 500)		5,000
Paid-in Capital in Excess of Par		20,000
(To record exercise of 500 stock warrants.)		

The $60 market value of the stock when the warrant is issued is not used to record the issuance of the stock. Rather, the stock is recorded at an amount equal to the total of the cash received ($35 per share), plus the amount allocated to the warrant when it was originally issued ($15), for a total per share of $50.

If a warrant expires or lapses, the Stock Warrants Exercisable account is reclassified as Paid-in Capital in Excess of Par, unless a portion of the warrant is refunded; in which case the warrant account is removed to the extent of the refund and reclassified as a liability. Any residual balance in the warrant account is then reclassified as Paid-in Capital in Excess of Par Value. To illustrate, if the remaining warrants of Harmon Corporation were allowed to expire, the following journal entry would be made:

Stock Warrants Exercisable ($15 × 500)	7,500	
Paid-in Capital in Excess of Par		7,500
(To record expiration of 500 stock warrants.)		

CONVERTIBLE SECURITIES

If the owner of a convertible security, such as a bond or preferred stock, exercises the conversion feature, certain accounting issues emerge. The carrying amount of the convertible security (par value, plus any premium or less any discount) may differ from the market value of the stock issued at the time the conversion takes place.

To illustrate, assume that Rag Top, Inc., issues convertible bonds which have a maturity value of $1,000,000 and are carried in the corporate books net of a $25,000 discount. Further assume that each $1,000 bond is convertible into 10 shares of $75 par value common stock. The current market value of the common stock is $104 per share. If all 1,000 bonds are converted on January 1, 1993, the following entry is necessary:

Jan. 1, 1993	Bonds Payable	1,000,000	
	Discount on Bonds Payable		25,000
	Common Stock (1,000 × $10 × 75)		750,000
	Paid-in Capital in Excess of Par		225,000
	(To record the conversion of bonds and issuance of stock.)		

Recording the conversion in this manner results in reporting the stock at the book value of the converted debt ($975,000) rather than the $1,040,000 market value of the stock ($104 per share × 10,000 shares).

The rationale for this position is provided by the treatment accorded the convertible debt when originally issued. Remember that some of the proceeds of convertible debt may be considered a permanent contribution to stockholders' equity. Due to the inseparability of the debt and equity components of a convertible security, however, the proceeds from the issuance of convertible debt are classified as debt. Therefore, when a conversion takes place, an apparent gain or loss on the extinguishing of the debt may result from the accounting treatment at the issuance of the convertible security. The difference between the carrying amount of converted debt and the fair value

Substance over Form of the stock issued upon conversion is properly treated as an adjustment to stockholders' equity rather than as a gain or loss on the debt retirement. Underlying theory suggests that if the debt is converted to stock, the security represents a permanent increase in stockholders' equity at issuance, and no gain or loss is recognized when the form of the instrument is converted.

The key concept to remember in accounting for convertible securities is that the carrying amount of the security being converted is merely reclassified as the carrying amount of the new security being issued. This is the case regardless of whether the convertible security is debt or preferred stock. The conversion of one form of financing to another does not give rise to accounting gains or losses.

MISCELLANEOUS STOCKHOLDERS' EQUITY CONSIDERATIONS

EARNINGS PER SHARE

Disclosure A required disclosure for publicly held corporations is the earnings per share. Basically, the **earnings per share (EPS)** of a corporation results from the division of the accounting net income available to common shareholders for a particular period by the number of *common* shares outstanding during the period. The EPS figure is a measure of the amount of net income attributable to each share of common stock. This measure can be useful to the common stockholder because the market price per share of stock is to some degree dependent upon the EPS of that stock. In addition, with EPS figures the common stock investor can more readily evaluate the dividend policy of the company, because dividends are frequently expressed in per share terms.

Minor complications arise if the corporation changes the number of shares outstanding during the year or has preferred stock outstanding. If the corporation changes the number of shares outstanding during the period, either through new stock issues or purchases of treasury shares, the denominator of the EPS calculation should be adjusted to reflect a weighted average of the number of common shares outstanding during the period. If preferred stock is outstanding during the period, the numerator of the EPS calculation should be adjusted by subtracting all preferred dividends declared during the period or which accumulate under a cumulative feature. In this way the numerator measures the net income available to common shareholders after dividend preferences for preferred stock are satisfied.

To illustrate, assume that Tyler Chemical Company reported a net income of $1,000,000 for 1992. In addition, Tyler declared preferred dividends on their preferred stock of $200,000 for 1992. Tyler had 400,000 common shares outstanding at the beginning of the year and issued an additional 400,000 shares halfway through the year, on June 30, 1992. There were no other stock transactions during the year.

The weighted average number of common shares outstanding during 1992 is calculated as follows:

(1)	(2)	(3)	(4)
			Weighted
Outstanding	Period	Share-months	Average
Shares	Outstanding	(Col. 1 × Col. 2)	(Col. 3) ÷ (Col. 2)
400,000	6 mos.	2,400,000	
800,000	6 mos.	4,800,000	
	12 mos.	7,200,000	600,000

The EPS calculation for Tyler Chemical would be:

$$\frac{\$1,000,000 - \$200,000}{600,000 \text{ shares}} = \$1.33 \text{ per share}$$

The common stockholders have $1.33 in earnings for each share of stock.

The EPS calculation is complicated considerably by the introduction of stock dividends and stock splits. Furthermore, securities such as stock warrants, employee stock options, and securities convertible to common stock represent potential common shares (dilution) that must be considered when attempting to determine EPS. These considerations are rather involved and are therefore discussed separately and in greater detail in Chapter 21.

APPRAISAL CAPITAL

Conservatism

As discussed in Chapter 2, contemporary accounting theory recognizes the desirability of valuing assets held for exchange, such as inventories or marketable securities, at the lower of cost or market. Plant assets are valued at historical cost less accumulated depreciation and are not revalued upward in the normal course of financial accounting and reporting. The modifying convention of conservatism influences financial accounting extensively. At present there is little support for valuing many assets at amounts *exceeding* their original cost, because to do so might recognize gains or revenues before they are realized. During the past decade, however, increased professional interest in adjusting the carrying amounts of assets upward has been evident. The theoretical arguments favoring this change usually are based on recognizing the effects of inflation, changing replacement costs, or changing values.

Notwithstanding the controversy of valuing assets above their cost, accountants generally agree that if such asset write-ups occur, a direct increase in a separate section of stockholders' equity is also appropriate. Accountants consider the direct adjustment of stockholders' equity preferable to recognizing gains in the income statement with resultant increases in retained earnings. An account title to recognize such an asset write-up might be "Appreciation Capital" or "Appraisal Capital." This type of stockholders' equity is not frequently encountered in practice and generally would represent a departure from GAAP.

QUASI REORGANIZATION

Occasionally a corporation finds that it simply cannot operate profitably given its operating situation and asset and liability structure. In such circumstances a possible solution is a quasi reorganization. The term "quasi" means "the same as," and accounting for a quasi reorganization is similar to that required in a complete reorganization of a business enterprise. A quasi reorganization, however, costs far less than a complete legal reorganization. In a **quasi reorganization** the assets of a company are generally revalued at their net realizable values, and the net revaluation loss is reflected in retained earnings. For example, a company may have forecasted an expanding demand for its products and invested in major plant expansion. If the forecast is not realized, excess plant assets may result. Idle or partially productive plant assets may cause the company to be unable to operate profitably. Debt repayment may become impossible under original lending terms. In such cases, the plant assets may be written down to an amount approximating their net realizable value, and debt may be restructured to allow additional time for repayment. In extreme cases creditors may also agree to accept reduced amounts in satisfaction of corporate debts to maximize the partial recovery of loaned funds. Quasi reorganization, which is permitted under many state laws, requires the approval of the corporate board of directors and stockholders, and care must be exercised to ensure the maintenance of minimum legal corporate capital.

Four general conditions usually indicate the desirability of a quasi reorganization:

1. Various assets of the company are overvalued.
2. Retained Earnings contains a deficit.
3. The future of the company from an operating perspective appears favorable if adjustments to the assets and liabilities are made.
4. A change in control of the entity takes place.

In most quasi reorganizations, common stockholders sacrifice in terms of reduced reported equity. Preferred stockholders may sacrifice through a lack of dividends, and creditors may decide to forego some of their legal rights to require timely payment. Those shareholders may also relinquish control of the organization to additional shareholders who are granted ownership rights in consideration for forgiving debts owed by the entity. The resource providers of the company are thus attempting to make the best of a bad situation and take action to facilitate the survival of the company.

As the carrying value of assets is reduced to a level facilitating future profitable operations, Retained Earnings is charged directly for the amount of the write-down.

The Retained Earnings account will have a debit balance (i.e., a deficit) due to operating losses and the asset write-down. Therefore, other entries are frequently necessary to adjust Retained Earnings to a zero balance. To remove a deficit from Retained Earnings, we credit Retained Earnings and charge Paid-in Capital in Excess of Par. If insufficient Paid-in Capital in Excess of Par is available to absorb the entire deficit in Retained Earnings, the par or stated value of the common stock is usually reduced. A reduction of the par value of the stock gives rise to additional Paid-in Capital in Excess of Par, which in turn is credited to the remaining debit balance in Retained Earnings.

Profitable operations following a quasi reorganization may facilitate new stock issues and other financing sources for the troubled enterprise. Dividends may be paid from resources generated by profitable operations after a quasi reorganization.

Following a quasi reorganization, the Retained Earnings account is dated in a manner such as "Retained Earnings from January 1, 1992." In this way financial statement users can assess the degree of operating success attained by a company after a quasi reorganization.

To illustrate accounting for a quasi reorganization, the following example is provided. Exhibit 17–9 presents an abbreviated balance sheet of Static Company prior to a quasi reorganization. Note that Static's Retained Earnings account contains a deficit even before the quasi reorganization. This condition is typical in that operating losses usually precede the need to reorganize. Because Static has been unable to operate profitably and has experienced difficulty servicing its debt, and because profitable operations appear possible in the future if a reorganization is effected, the board of directors authorizes a quasi reorganization.

A review of Static's property reveals that various assets should be adjusted to net realizable values as follows:

Assets	Current Carrying Amount	Net Realizable Value
Inventory	$ 30,000	$ 25,000
Machinery	50,000	40,000
Building	250,000	250,000
Land	100,000	90,000
	$430,000	$405,000

In this case a total assets write-down of $25,000 takes place, which increases the deficit in Retained Earnings as indicated in the entry below:

Dec. 31, 1992	Retained Earnings	25,000	
	Inventory		5,000
	Machinery		10,000
	Land		10,000

(To reduce the carrying amounts of various assets to net realizable value in accordance with quasi reorganization.)

Following this entry, the deficit in retained earnings is $83,500 ($58,500 + $25,000). Because the Paid-in Capital in Excess of Par of $75,000 is not sufficient to absorb the $83,500 deficit in retained earnings, the par value of the common stock must be reduced. We shall assume a reduction in par value to $7.50 per share, which is reflected by the following entry:

EXHIBIT 17-9

Static Company
Abbreviated Balance Sheet
Prior to Quasi Reorganization

December 31, 1992
Assets

Current Assets		
Cash	$ 1,500	
Accounts receivable (net of allowance for doubtful accounts of 7,000)	10,000	
Inventory at FIFO cost	30,000	
Total current assets		$ 41,500
Property, Plant, and Equipment		
Machinery (net of accumulated depreciation of $25,000)	50,000	
Building (net of accumulated depreciation of $75,000)	250,000	
Land	100,000	
Total property, plant, and equipment		400,000
Total assets		$441,500

Liabilities and Stockholders' Equity

Liabilities		
Current liabilities		$ 75,000
Long-term bonds payable		250,000
Total liabilities		$325,000
Stockholders' Equity		
Common stock ($10 par; 10,000 shares authorized, issued, and outstanding)		100,000
Paid-in capital in excess of par		75,000
Total contributed equity		175,000
Retained earnings (deficit)		(58,500)
Total stockholders' equity		116,500
Total liabilities and stockholders' equity		$441,500

Dec. 31, 1992	Common Stock	25,000	
	Paid-in Capital in Excess of Par		25,000
	(To reflect change in par value to accomplish quasi reorganization. $2.50 × 10,000 shares.)		

Permission of the stockholders, regulatory agencies, and usually the creditors is necessary before the par value of stock is changed. The final step in completing the quasi reorganization is elimination of the deficit in Retained Earnings of $83,500:

Dec. 31, 1992	Paid-in Capital in Excess of Par	83,500	
	Retained Earnings		83,500
	(To eliminate deficit balance in Retained Earnings pursuant to quasi reorganization.)		

EXHIBIT 17-10

Static Company
Partial Balance Sheet
One Year After Quasi Reorganization

December 31, 1993

Stockholders' Equity

Common stock ($7.50 par; 10,000 shares authorized, issued, and outstanding	$ 75,000
Paid-in capital in excess of par	16,500
Total contributed capital	91,500
Retained earnings (since Jan. 1, 1993)	20,000
Total stockholders' equity	$111,500

Following the quasi reorganization and a year in which operations generate net income of $20,000, the stockholders' equity section of Static's balance sheet appears as presented in Exhibit 17-10. Note that retained earnings is dated and that the company reflects a reduced equity structure.

In practice, a quasi reorganization is infrequently encountered, because it is an extreme measure in a company's fight for survival. The "fresh-start" provided by a quasi reorganization does not change the underlying economic difficulties; cash flow and profitability problems usually remain. Therefore, a quasi reorganization is generally not effective unless new management or improved products or conditions tend to support favorable future operating prospects. A quasi reorganization does give a company the opportunity to organize in a way that allows operations to be conducted in a more realistic and orderly fashion. In this way management may be able to generate adequate revenues to sustain the enterprise.

CONCLUDING REMARKS

Transactions affecting stockholders' equity accounts involve a wide range of activities throughout the life of an enterprise. The first economic events affecting a company upon its formation and the final acts of dissolution involve equity accounts. Furthermore, most events directly affecting stockholders' equity are usually material and require careful study to assure acceptable practices.

Materiality

Creditors and stockholders share many characteristics. For example, both provide resources to the organization, and both accept risk in attempting to make profitable investments. As discussed in Chapter 16, the dividing line between debt and equity is sometimes difficult to discern. This is especially true when dealing with hybrid instruments such as convertible securities and redeemable preferred stock. The importance of distinguishing between debt and equity, however, is significant. Many restrictive bond covenants, for example, require the maintenance of specified debt/equity ratios, and the classification of hybrid securities may represent the difference between contract compliance and violation.

The equity sections of the balance sheets of most large corporations usually contain many different classes and types of stock which have been issued over a long period of time. Therefore, careful review of each issue is necessary to ensure proper accounting for dividends, new stock issues, and other activities affecting individual stockholders. In summary, the stockholders' equity section of a company's balance sheet must be considered and treated as carefully as any other element of a corporation's financial position.

KEY POINTS

1. The major items affecting retained earnings of a company are earnings and dividends. Less frequent items are corrections of errors, certain treasury stock transactions, appropriations, initial adoption of certain accounting principles, and quasi reorganizations. (Objectives 5 and 6)

2. Dividends are a liability of a company only when declared by the board of directors. (Objective 1)

3. Property dividends, like other dividends, should be accounted for at fair market value, with gains and losses recognized upon disposal of the property. (Objective 1)

4. If outstanding preferred stock is cumulative or fully or partially participating, careful analysis is required to properly allocate dividends between common and preferred stockholders. (Objective 1)

5. Small stock dividends are accounted for on the basis of fair market value, while large stock dividends are recorded on the basis of par or stated value. (Objective 1)

6. Stock splits require no formal accounting treatment, just a memorandum noting the new par or stated value per share and the number of shares authorized, issued, and outstanding. (Objective 1)

7. Employee stock options can be considered compensatory or noncompensatory. Compensatory stock options require the recognition of compensation expense. The total compensation is measured as the excess of the market value over the option price on the measurement date, which is usually the grant date. (Objectives 2 and 3)

8. Stock appreciation rights (SARs) entitle certain employees to stock appreciation over some specified price multiplied by a specified number of shares. SARs are compensatory and therefore require compensation recognition in the accounting records. Because the measurement date is the exercise date, accounting recognition is based on estimates until final exercise. (Objectives 2 and 3)

9. Assets should generally not be written up above cost based on appraisals; consequently, the use of appraisal capital is rare. (Objective 4)

10. Quasi reorganizations are appropriate only when a company is faced with severe financial or operating problems which appear to be manageable if adjustments to assets, liabilities, and stockholders' equity accounts are made. (Objective 4)

11. A number of significant judgments are frequently necessary to distinguish accounting errors from changes in accounting estimates and other events. (Objectives 5 and 6)

QUESTIONS

17–1   What is meant by the term "retained earnings"? Comment on the propriety of using the term "earned surplus."

17–2   Briefly describe some of the items that affect retained earnings.

17–3   Three dates are important in evaluating dividend status: date of declaration, date of record, and date of payment. Describe the accounting implications of each date.

17–4   Preferred stock may have a cumulation clause and/or a participation clause. What does each term imply to the preferred stockholder?

17–5   Can an investor unambiguously state that, for a particular investment, receiving a dividend is preferable to receiving no dividend? Why or why not?

17–6   What is a property dividend, and what are the significant accounting issues related to this kind of dividend?

17–7   What is a scrip dividend, and what are the significant accounting issues related to this kind of dividend?

17–8   What are liquidating dividends, and what are the significant accounting issues related to this kind of dividend?

17–9   What is a stock dividend? What is the economic result of a stock dividend?

17–10   Accounting authoritative pronouncements distinguish between small and large stock dividends. How is this distinction defined, what are the accounting implications, and how is this distinction justified?

17–11   What is the distinction between a large stock dividend and a stock split? What are the accounting implications of this distinction?

17–12   What is the purpose of a large stock dividend or stock split? What is the purpose of a reverse stock split?

17–13   Why aren't cash and property dividends paid on treasury stock?

17–14   Why does a company appropriate retained earnings? What does a retained earnings appropriation communicate to financial statement users?

17–15   What is an employee stock option? What is the distinction between a compensatory and noncompensatory employee stock option?

17–16   What significant accounting issues are related to compensatory employee stock options?

17–17   What is a stock appreciation right? Why is the measurement date for stock appreciation rights usually different from that for employee stock options? What are the major accounting considerations for stock appreciation rights?

17–18   What is "appraisal capital," and how is it recognized in the accounting records?

17–19   What is a quasi reorganization? What is the economic impact of a quasi reorganization? How is a quasi reorganization effected in the accounting records?

17–20   Explain why corporate executives might wish to receive stock options or stock appreciation rights rather than cash for part of their compensation.

EXERCISES

17–21   DIVIDENDS ON COMMON AND PREFERRED STOCK   Sheridan Corporation was organized on January 1, 1991. On that date 10,000 shares of $4 preferred stock ($40 par) were issued. The preferred stock is cumulative and participating up to a <u>maximum</u> amount of 15%, including the preference amount. In addition, 150,000 shares of Sheridan common ($10 par) were issued. No dividends were declared or paid in 1991. On July 1, 1992, Sheridan declared a 5% common stock dividend to common stockholders of record on July 20, 1992, distributable on August 1, 1992. The market price of Sheridan common was $28 a share on July 1, 1992, and $30 a share on August 1, 1992. On December 1, 1992, Sheridan declared a $300,000 cash dividend to stockholders of record on December 10, 1992, payable on December 31, 1992.

Instructions

[a] Provide all journal entries relating to dividends by Sheridan Corporation for 1992. Separately identify the dividends to the common and preferred shares.
[b] Briefly discuss how the cumulation feature on the preferred stock affects the market value of common stock.

17–22   DIVIDEND CALCULATION AND JOURNAL ENTRIES   Gibson Corporation has experienced a highly profitable year, and the board of directors has decided to bring all dividends in arrears up to date. The preferred stock of the company is fully participating as well as cumulative. The board wishes to accomplish three objectives with the dividend:

[1] Pay all dividends in arrears.
[2] Pay the current year's preference amount.
[3] Pay the maximum possible amount of dividend to the common stockholders without invoking the participation clause of the preferred stock.

The stockholders' equity section of Gibson Corporation's balance sheet is summarized as follows:

Preferred stock ($100 par, 15% cumulative, fully participating; 4 years'
  dividends in arrears; 10,000 shares authorized, 8,000 shares issued of
  which 3,000 shares are held in treasury) $ 500,000

Common stock ($10 par; 500,000 shares authorized, 300,000 shares issued of which 50,000 shares are held in treasury)	2,500,000
Paid-in capital in excess of par	350,000
Retained earnings	1,150,000
Total stockholders' equity	$4,500,000

The company uses the par value method of accounting for treasury stock.

Instructions

[a] Prepare the calculations necessary to determine the maximum dividend consistent with the three objectives of the board of directors.

[b] If such a dividend was declared, prepare the entry or entries necessary to record the declaration.

17–23 PROPERTY DIVIDEND   Environ, Inc., owned 100,000 shares of marketable common stock of Brooks Corporation on December 31, 1992. At that time the Environ account Investment in Marketable Equity Securities had a carrying value of $7 per share, which was the cost of the securities. The market value of the investment on that date was $8 per share. On that same date, Environ's board of directors declared a property dividend in which the shares of Brooks Corporation were to be distributed to Environ stockholders on January 17, 1993. At the time the shares were distributed, the market value of the Brooks Corporation stock had dropped to $5 per share.

Instructions

[a] Prepare the entries necessary to record the declaration and distribution of this property dividend.

[b] What is the proper accounting treatment, if any, of the $3 drop in market value from the declaration to the distribution date?

17–24 DIVIDEND CALCULATION—TOTAL AMOUNT   The board of directors of Lorber, Inc., wishes to declare a dividend whereby common stockholders are to receive a total per share dividend of $4. Lorber's stockholders' equity section appears as follows:

Preferred stock ($100 par, 7%, participating to 10%, noncumulative; 100,000 shares authorized, 25,000 shares issued and outstanding)	$ 2,500,000
Common stock ($25 par; 250,000 shares authorized, issued, and outstanding)	6,250,000
Paid-in capital in excess of par	1,250,000
Retained earnings	5,000,000
Total stockholders' equity	$15,000,000

Instructions

Determine the total amount of the dividend that must be declared to meet the per share goals of the board of directors.

17–25 LARGE STOCK DIVIDENDS AND RETAINED EARNINGS APPROPRIATION   Murray Company has had an agreement with its bondholders that required the company to make payments to a sinking fund and to maintain a related appropriation of retained earnings to retire the bonds. The company has been required to make sinking fund contributions of $500,000 for each of the last 5 years. At the beginning of 1990 the bonds are repaid, the retained earnings appropriation is canceled, and a 40% common stock dividend is declared and distributed. Immediately before the declaration of the dividend the company had 1,250,000 shares of $10 par value common stock outstanding with a per share market value of $12.50. Immediately before repaying the bonds at their carrying amount, the company's unappropriated retained earnings balance was $4,000,000.

Instructions

Prepare the journal entries to record the removal of the appropriated retained earnings and the declaration and distribution of the stock dividend. Then compute the remaining amount of unappropriated retained earnings.

17–26 SMALL STOCK DIVIDEND   On February 1, 1992, the board of directors of Macoris, Inc., declared a 5% common stock dividend distributable to common stockholders of record on February 15, 1992. Distribution of the dividend took place on February 28, 1992.

Market prices of the stock were as follows:

Feb. 1, 1992	$75 per share
Feb. 15, 1992	80 per share
Feb. 28, 1992	76 per share

There were 100,000 shares of $50 par value stock authorized and 75,000 of the shares were issued and outstanding prior to the stock dividend.

Instructions

[a] Prepare the journal entries to record the stock dividend.

[b] If prior to the stock dividend the retained earnings was $1,000,000, additional paid-in capital was $250,000, and there were no other issues of stock outstanding, prepare the stockholders' equity section of the balance sheet as of:

[1] February 1, 1992   [2] February 28, 1992

17–27 PREFERRED STOCK DIVIDEND   Ranger Corporation has 20,000 shares of $10 par value common stock and 1,000 shares of $100 par value, 7% preferred stock outstanding. A total dividend of $25,000 is declared by the corporation. No dividends were paid in the prior year.

Instructions

[a] If the preferred stock is neither participating nor cumulative, determine the amount of dividends payable to each class of stock.

[b] Assume that the preferred stock is fully participating but noncumulative. What dividends are payable to each class of stock?

[c] Assume that the preferred stock is cumulative but not participating. What dividends are payable to each class of stock?

[d] Assume that the preferred stock is both cumulative and fully participating. Compute the dividends for each class of stock.

17–28 STATEMENT OF RETAINED EARNINGS   As the accountant responsible for preparing the financial statements for Heartland, Inc., you have assembled the following general ledger information related to retained earnings for the year ended December 31, 1992.

Retained Earnings

Date	Item	Dr.	Cr.
1/1/92	Beginning balance		$1,500,000
4/15/92	1st quarterly dividend for 1992 in cash	$12,000	
7/12/92	2nd quarterly dividend for 1992 in cash	10,000	
8/12/92	Small stock dividend	25,000	
10/12/92	3rd quarterly dividend for 1992 in cash	15,000	
11/15/92	Completed litigation—appropriation closed		100,000
11/29/92	Correction of error in inventory pricing of prior year		72,000
12/31/92	Net income for the year		155,000
12/31/92	Totals	$62,000	$1,827,000

While reading the minutes of the December 26, 1992, meeting of the board of directors, you learn that a dividend of $13,000 was declared, which is to be paid on January 5, 1993.

Instructions

Prepare a retained earnings statement in good form for Heartland, Inc., for 1992.

17–29 MAXIMUM DIVIDEND DECLARATION   Javier, Inc., began operations in January 1988 and had the following reported net income or loss for each of its five years of operations:

1988	$ 150,000 loss
1989	130,000 loss
1990	120,000 loss
1991	250,000 income
1992	1,000,000 income

At December 31, 1992, the Javier capital accounts were as follows:

Preferred stock, ($100 par value; 8% fully participating, cumulative; 10,000 shares authorized, issued, and outstanding)	$1,000,000
Preferred stock ($100 par value; 4% nonparticipating, noncumulative; 1,000 shares authorized, issued, and outstanding)	100,000
Common stock ($10 par value; 100,000 shares authorized, 50,000 shares issued and outstanding)	500,000

Javier has never paid a cash or stock dividend. The capital accounts have not changed since Javier began operations. The appropriate state law permits dividends only from retained earnings.

Instructions

Prepare a worksheet showing the *maximum* amount available for cash dividends on December 31, 1992, and how it would be distributable to holders of the common shares and each type of the preferred shares. Show supporting computations in good form.   (AICPA adapted)

17–30 SCRIP, PROPERTY, AND STOCK DIVIDENDS   The balance sheet of Take Care Products Company appeared as follows on December 31, 1992:

Assets

Cash	$ 10,000
Marketable equity securities (market value = $60,000)	50,000
Inventory	70,000
Plant assets	200,000
Less: Accumulated depreciation	(50,000)
Total assets	$280,000

Liabilities and Stockholders' Equity

Current liabilities	$ 10,000
Long-term debt	100,000
Common stock ($2 par; 20,000 shares authorized, 10,000 shares issued, and outstanding)	20,000
Paid-in capital in excess of par	100,000
Retained earnings	50,000
Total liabilities and stockholders' equity	$280,000

The market value of the outstanding common shares on December 31, 1992, was $25 per share.

Instructions

[a] Provide the appropriate journal entries for each of the following *independent* situations:

    [1] On January 1, 1993, Take Care declared a property dividend of all holdings of marketable equity securities.

    [2] On January 1, 1993, Take Care declared a scrip dividend of $35,000.

    [3] On January 1, 1993, Take Care declared a cash dividend of $80,000.

    [4] On January 1, 1993, Take Care declared a 10% stock dividend.

    [5] On January 1, 1993, Take Care declared a 40% stock dividend.

[b] How do the applications of accounting principles differ for [4] and [5] above? What is the rationale for the difference in procedure?

17–31 EMPLOYEE STOCK OPTIONS   As president of Bush Company, Brenda Vance received options to buy 1,000 shares of his employer's $10 par stock on June 30, 1992. The options call for a price of $18 per share and are exercisable for 5 years following the grant date. Vance exercised his option on August 1, 1992, and sold the shares on November 1, 1992. The market prices of the stock on selected dates were as follows:

June 30, 1992	$18 per share
Aug. 1, 1992	25 per share
Nov. 1, 1992	28 per share

Instructions

[a] Provide the appropriate journal entries for Bush Company with respect to the stock options.

[b] Provide the appropriate journal entries for Bush Company with respect to the stock options, assuming the option prices to Vance were:

[1] $15 per share
[2] $21 per share

[c] Provide the appropriate journal entry for the exercise of the option on August 1, 1992, under the original assumptions.

[d] What is the distinction between a compensatory and a noncompensatory stock option? How does the accounting for these types of stock options differ?

17–32   APPROPRIATION OF RETAINED EARNINGS   The board of directors of Cavanaugh, Inc., has decided to embark on substantial plant expansion. In order to demonstrate the need to retain assets in the company, the board agrees on December 31, 1991, to authorize an appropriation of retained earnings in the amount of $2,500,000, the anticipated cost of the plant expansion. The plant was partially constructed on December 31, 1992, and the board decided to reduce the appropriation by $800,000, the cost incurred to date. Finally, in September 1993 the plant was completed and the remaining portion of the appropriation was removed.

Instructions

[a] Prepare the entries to record, reduce, and finally remove the appropriation.

[b] Describe where the Appropriated Retained Earnings account should appear on the 1991 and 1992 financial statements of Cavanaugh, Inc.

[c] What does the Appropriated Retained Earnings account communicate to the financial statement user?

17–33   WARRANT EXERCISE   Garden Company issues a series of bonds along with detachable stock warrants. Each warrant conveys the right to buy one share of $10 par value common stock for $50 per share. Ten thousand bonds were issued (each with one detachable warrant attached), and $80,000 was correctly recorded as Stock Warrants Exercisable. Eighty percent of the warrants are exercised at a time when the market value of the stock is $65 per share.

Instructions

Record the appropriate journal entry for the exercise of the warrants.

17–34   STOCK APPRECIATION RIGHTS   On December 31, 1989, Harnett Textile Company offered its top management share appreciation rights with the following terms:

Option price (predetermined)	$50 per share
Number of shares	7,000
Holding period	3 years
Expiration date	Dec. 31, 1992

The share appreciation is to be paid upon exercise in Harnett common stock ($20 stated value). The market value of Harnett common was as follows:

Dec. 31, 1989	$50 per share
Dec. 31, 1990	48 per share
Dec. 31, 1991	57 per share
Dec. 31, 1992	56 per share

The stock appreciation rights were exercised on December 31, 1992.

Instructions

Provide the correct journal entries to accrue compensation expense for 1990, 1991, and 1992. Record the proper journal entry for the exercise of the stock appreciation rights.

17–35 DIVIDENDS AND EARNINGS PER SHARE   Purser Company presented the following comparative stockholders' equity sections of the balance sheet:

Purser Company
PARTIAL BALANCE SHEET
For the Years Ended December 31

	1991	1992
Stockholders' Equity		
9% Preferred stock ($90 par value; 1,000 shares authorized, issued, and outstanding)	$ 90,000	$ 90,000
Common stock ($5 par; 100,000 shares authorized, 50,000 shares issued and outstanding on December 31, 1991, and 70,000 shares issued and outstanding on December 31, 1992)	250,000	350,000
Paid-in capital in excess of par	250,000	450,000
Retained earnings	200,000	350,000
Total stockholders' equity	$790,000	$1,240,000

Quarterly common stock dividends of $.25 were declared on March 31, June 30, September 30, and December 31, 1992. Semiannual preferred stock dividends were declared on June 30 and December 31, 1992. On May 1, 1992, and September 1, 1992, 10,000 common shares were issued. The retained earnings were affected by only dividends and earnings for 1992.

Instructions

Compute the earnings per share for Purser Company for 1992.

PROBLEMS

17–36 JOURNAL ENTRIES—RETAINED EARNINGS   The following transactions and events of Perry, Inc., occurred during 1992:

[1] A former employee sued Perry for injuries sustained in the company's parking lot. Although legal counsel considered it highly unlikely that the former employee would win the case, Perry's management decided to appropriate retained earnings of $200,000 (10% of the amount sought by the former employee) on January 31, 1992.

[2] A 40% stock dividend was declared on February 10, 1992, when the market price of the stock was $25. On March 1, 1992, 4,000 shares of $10 par value common stock were issued in distributing the stock dividend. The market value of the stock on March 1, 1992 was $18.

[3] On April 15, 1992, a plant expansion fund was created by acquiring certificates of deposit in the amount of $300,000. Retained earnings in the same amount were appropriated.

[4] On June 30, 1992, a second stock dividend of 1,000 shares of $10 par value common stock was declared. The dividend was distributed on July 15, 1992. The market values of a share of common on June 30 and July 15, 1992, were $16.00 and $16.50, respectively.

[5] The lawsuit described in item [1] above was dropped by the former employee on September 1, 1992, with no cost to the company except attorney's fees, which have been paid and properly recorded.

[6] A cash dividend of $.25 per common share was declared on September 30, 1992, and paid on October 15, 1992.

[7] On December 20, 1992, an expenditure of $45,000 was made from the plant expansion fund using a certificate of deposit which matured earlier that month. The certificate cost $40,000 and matured with interest at $48,000 on December 15, 1992.

Instructions

Prepare necessary entries for the above information. You may assume that adequate paid-in capital in excess of par and retained earnings exist to account for these transactions.

17–37   QUASI REORGANIZATION   Astro, Inc., has suffered substantial operating losses for several years. The ability of the company to service its debts and pay operating expenses has been impaired. Consequently, Astro's owners, managers, and creditors have decided to execute a quasi reorganization. An abbreviated balance sheet of Astro prior to the quasi reorganization is presented below.

Astro, Inc.
BALANCE SHEET
December 31, 1992

Assets

Current Assets

Cash	$ 10,000
Accounts receivable (less allowance of $5,000)	15,000
Inventory	25,000
Total current assets	50,000

Noncurrent Assets

Plant and equipment (net of accumulated depreciation of $155,000)	340,000
Goodwill *Assets worth more in total than in parts*	60,000
Total noncurrent assets *Not possible in Quasi*	400,000
Total assets	$450,000

Liabilities and Stockholders' Equity

Current Liabilities

Accounts payable	$ 55,000
Notes payable	25,000
Total current liabilities	80,000

Long-term Liabilities

Mortgage payable	210,000

Stockholders' Equity

Common stock ($10 par value; 25,000 shares authorized, issued, and outstanding)	250,000
Paid-in capital in excess of par	50,000
Retained earnings	(140,000)
Total stockholders' equity	160,000
Total stockholders' equity and liabilities	$450,000

The following information may bear on accounting for the quasi reorganization. The owners of Astro, Inc., decides to reduce plant assets to a more reasonable level to increase utilization of remaining assets. He has decided to sell certain equipment which originally cost $100,000 and which has been depreciated to $40,000 by the end of 1992. The expected selling price for the equipment is $15,000, although no sale has been made yet.

An independent appraisal of the company's inventory reveals goods with a carrying value of $8,000 to be obsolete and worthless. The holder of a $25,000 note agrees to accept the proceeds from the sale of the idle equipment mentioned above in full satisfaction of the note.

The mortgage holder agrees to accept 2,000 shares of new $100 par value voting preferred stock in satisfaction of the liability. In addition, the par value of the common stock is reduced to $1 per share and suspends voting rights for 10 years in order to effect the quasi reorganization.

Instructions

[a] Prepare the necessary entries to record the above events.

[b] Prepare a balance sheet for Astro as of January 1, 1993, following the quasi reorganization.

17–38   COMPREHENSIVE DIVIDEND CALCULATION   Foothill, Inc., has three classes of stock outstanding at December 31, 1992:

Preferred stock (Class A) ($100 par value, 12%, cumulative and fully participating; 2 years' dividends in arrears; 10,000 shares authorized, issued, and outstanding)	$1,000,000
Preferred stock (Class B) ($100 par value, 10%, noncumulative, participating to 12%; 10,000 shares authorized, 5,000 shares issued and outstanding)	500,000
Common stock ($50 par value; 100,000 shares authorized, 50,000 shares issued, and 40,000 shares outstanding)	2,500,000
Paid-in capital in excess of par	750,000
Treasury stock (10,000 shares of $50 par value common)	(600,000)
Retained earnings	3,250,000
Total stockholders' equity	$7,400,000

The board of directors of Foothill, Inc., is deliberating about the amount of dividend to pay. Because no dividends have been paid for three years, determining how a dividend should be divided is somewhat complex. *2 yr. arrear, 1 CY DIV*

Instructions

The chairman of the board of directors of Foothill, Inc., has asked you to compute the amount of dividend payable to each class of stock under each of the following assumptions:

[a] The total dividend is $600,000.
[b] The total dividend is $650,000.
[c] The total dividend is $750,000.

17–39 QUASI REORGANIZATION Adverse financial and operating circumstances warrant that Foster Company undergo a quasi reorganization at December 31, 1993. The following information may be relevant in accounting for the quasi reorganization.

[1] Inventory with a cost of $215,000 is currently recorded in the accounts at its market value of $200,000.
[2] Plant assets with a fair market value of $700,000 are currently recorded at $875,000 net of accumulated depreciation.
[3] A creditor agrees to extend the maturity date of a loan for five years, although interest as originally stated must continue to be paid.
[4] Individual stockholders contribute $600,000 to create additional paid-in capital to facilitate the reorganization. No new shares of stock are issued, although control of a majority of the company's outstanding stock passes to the company's creditors.
[5] The par value of the common stock is reduced from $25 to $15.
[6] Immediately before the events described above, the stockholders' equity section appears as follows:

Common stock ($25 par value; 100,000 shares authorized and outstanding)	$2,500,000
Paid-in capital in excess of par	1,750,000
Retained earnings (deficit)	(750,000)
Total stockholders' equity	$3,500,000

Instructions

Prepare the stockholders' equity section of Foster Company's balance sheet after the quasi reorganization.

17–40 EMPLOYEE STOCK OPTIONS On January 2, 1991, the stockholders of Gulf Company authorized a stock option plan which provided key employees with options to purchase an aggregate of 20,000 shares of the company's $10 par value common stock at $14 per share. The market value of the stock was $16 on this date.

The next day, January 3, 1991, options to purchase 3,000 shares were granted to the president: 1,000 shares for services to be rendered in 1991; 1,000 shares for services to be rendered in 1992; and 1,000 shares for services to be rendered in 1993. The options are exercisable during the six months following the year in which the services were rendered. The market value of the stock was $17 on January 3, 1991.

The president exercised his option for 1,000 shares on April 1, 1992, when the market price was $20 per share. Subsequently he sold the stock on September 1, 1992, at $18 per share.

The president did not exercise his options in 1993. When the options lapsed on June 30, 1993, the market value of the stock was $12 per share.

Instructions

[a] Give the journal entries required in 1991–1993 under the plan, and to record lapsing of the option in 1993 (if necessary).

[b] Explain fully the reasons or principles underlying the entries.   (AICPA adapted)

17–41   COMPREHENSIVE CHANGES IN STOCKHOLDERS' EQUITY   Tustin, Inc., began operations in 1989 in a state which defines minimum legal capital as $1,000 or the par value of outstanding common stock less 10% to provide for treasury stock transactions, whichever is larger. Stock dividends, once declared, become part of minimum legal capital. The company employes a calendar year for purposes of financial reporting.

Immediately after Tustin was organized, the stockholders' equity section of its balance sheet appeared as below:

Common stock ($25 par value; 100,000 shares authorized, 25,000 shares issued and outstanding)	$625,000
Paid-in capital in excess of par	20,000
Retained earnings	–0–
Total stockholders' equity	$645,000

Net income (loss) for the period 1989–1993 appears below:

1989	$30,000
1990	40,000
1991	8,000
1992	(10,000)
1993	30,000

Activities related to the various types of dividends are described below:

1989   A cash dividend of $.75 per share was declared on December 31, 1989. The dividend was paid on January 15, 1990.

1990   A 5% stock dividend was declared on December 31, 1990, when the stock was selling for $26 per share. The dividend was distributed on January 20, 1991.

1991   A dividend was declared on December 31, 1991, in the amount of $.60 per share to be paid with marketable equity securities held by Tustin as a temporary investment. The cost of each share of the marketable equity security held by Tustin was $45 and the market value at December 31, 1991, was $50. The dividend was paid on January 10, 1992, when the marketable equity security was selling for $56 per share. (Hint: The gain on the dividend shares should be recorded and included in 1991 income.)

1992   Despite the loss reported for the current year, Tustin declared a cash dividend on December 20, 1992, of $.50 per share. The dividend was paid on January 5, 1993.

1993   On June 30, 1993, the company declared a 2-for-1 stock split and changed the par value of the stock to $12.50. On December 26, 1993, the company declared a 2% stock dividend, at which time the company's stock was selling for $17.50 per share.

Instructions

[a] Prepare the entries necessary to record the above events through December 31, 1993.

[b] Prepare an analysis of the changes in stockholders' equity accounts as a result of the above events.

17–42   COMPREHENSIVE STOCKHOLDERS' EQUITY EMPHASIZING RETAINED EARNINGS PRESENTATION   Norris Company was formed on July 1, 1990. It was authorized to issue 200,000 shares of $5 par value common stock and 50,000 shares of 6%, $10 par value, cumulative and nonparticipating preferred stock. Norris has a July 1–June 30 fiscal year.

The following information relates to Norris's stockholders' equity accounts.

Common Stock.   Prior to the 1992–1993 fiscal year, Norris had 105,000 shares of outstanding common stock issued as follows:

[1] On July 1, 1990, 95,000 shares were issued for cash at $20 per share.

[2] On July 24, 1990, 5,000 shares were exchanged for a plot of land which cost the seller $70,000 in 1993 and had an estimated market value of $130,000 on July 24, 1990.

[3] On March 1, 1992, 5,000 shares were issued. The shares had been subscribed for $32 per share on October 31, 1991.

During the 1992–1993 fiscal year, the following transactions involving common stock took place:

Oct. 1, 1992   Subscriptions were received for 10,000 shares at $40 per share. Cash of $80,000 was received in full payment for 2,000 shares and stock certificates were issued. The remaining subscriptions for 8,000 shares were to be paid in full by September 30, 1993, at which time the certificates were to be issued.

Nov. 30, 1992   Norris purchased 2,000 shares of its own stock on the open market at $38 per share. Norris uses the cost method for treasury stock.

Dec. 15, 1992   Norris declared a 2% stock dividend for stockholders of record on January 15, 1993, to be issued on January 31, 1993. Norris was having a liquidity problem and could not afford a cash dividend at the time. Norris's common stock was selling at $43 per share on December 15, 1992. (The stock dividend was not distributed on treasury or subscribed shares.)

June 20, 1993   Norris sold 500 shares of its own common stock that it had purchased on November 30, 1992, for $21,000.

Preferred Stock.   Norris issued 30,000 shares of preferred stock at $15 per share on July 1, 1991.

Cash Dividends.   Norris has followed a schedule of declaring cash dividends in December and June and paying stockholders of record the following month. The cash dividends which have been declared since inception of the company through June 30, 1993, are shown below.

Declaration Date	Common Stock	Preferred Stock
Dec. 15, 1991	$.10 per share	$.30 per share
June 15, 1992	$.10 per share	$.30 per share
Dec. 15, 1992	—	$.30 per share

No cash dividends were declared during June 1993 due to the company's liquidity problems.

Retained Earnings.   As of June 30, 1992, Norris's Retained Earnings account had a balance of $370,000. For the fiscal year ending June 30, 1993, Norris reported net income of $20,000.

In March 1992, Norris received a term loan from Guardian National Bank. The bank requires Norris to establish a sinking fund and restrict retained earnings for an amount equal to the sinking fund deposit. The annual sinking fund payment of $40,000 is due on April 30 each year; the first payment was made on schedule on April 30, 1993.

Instructions

Prepare the stockholders' equity section of the statement of financial position (balance sheet), including appropriate notes, for Norris Company as of June 30, 1993, as it should appear in the annual report to shareholders.   (CMA adapted)

17–43   COMPREHENSIVE DIVIDENDS   For the first time, Durham Products, Inc., is including a five-year summary of earnings and dividends per share in its 1993 annual report to stockholders. At January 1 1989, the corporation had issued 7,000 shares of 4% cumulative, nonparticipating, $100 par value preferred stock and 40,000 shares of $10 par value common stock, of which 108 shares of preferred and 4,000 shares of common stock were held in treasury.

Dividends were declared and paid semiannually on the last day of June and December. Cash dividends paid per share of common stock and net income (loss) for each year were:

	1989	1990	1991	1992	1993
Net income (loss)	$126,568	$(11,812)	$47,148	$115,824	$193,210
Dividend on common					
June 30	.40	.11	.10	.40	.60
Dec. 31	.48	.11	.30	.40	.40

In addition, a 10% stock dividend was declared and distributed on all common stock (including treasury shares) on April 1, 1991, and common stock was split 5 for 1 on October 1, 1993. The corporation has met a sinking fund requirement to purchase and retire 140 shares of its preferred stock on October 1 of each year, beginning in 1992, using any available treasury stock. On July 1, 1990, the corporation purchased 400 shares of its common stock and placed them in the treasury and on April 1, 1992, issued 5,000 shares of common stock to officers, using treasury stock to the extent available.

Instructions

[a] Prepare a schedule showing the computation of preferred stock dividends paid semiannually and annually for the five years. Use the following column headings:

		Number of Shares		Dividends Paid	
Year	Half (1st or 2nd)	Purchased and Retired	Outstanding	Semiannually	Annually

[b] Prepare a schedule which shows for each of the five years the cash dividends paid to common stockholders and the average number of shares of common stock outstanding after adjustment for the stock dividend and split. Use the following format:

	Shares of Common Stock		Dividends Paid		Common Stock Adjusted for:	
Dividend Date	In Treasury	Outstanding	Per Share	Total	10% Stock Dividend	5-for-1 Stock Split
6/30/89						
12/31/89						
		Total for year				
		Average for year				

(Continue this format for the next four years.) (AICPA adapted)

17–44 COMPREHENSIVE STOCKHOLDERS' EQUITY EMPHASIZING RETAINED EARNINGS During May 1991, Gennaro, Inc., was organized with 3,000,000 authorized shares of $10 par value common stock, and 300,000 shares of its common stock were issued for $3,300,000. Net income through December 31, 1991, was $125,000.

On July 3, 1992, Gennaro issued 500,000 shares of its common stock for $6,250,000. A 5% stock dividend was declared on October 2, 1992, and issued on November 6, 1992, to stockholders of record on October 23, 1992. The market value of the common stock was $11 per share on the declaration date. Gennaro's net income for the year ended December 31, 1992, was $350,000.

During 1993 Gennaro had the following transactions:

[1] In February Gennaro reacquired 30,000 shares of its common stock for $9 per share. Gennaro uses the cost method to account for treasury stock.
[2] In June Gennaro sold 15,000 shares of its treasury stock for $12 per share.
[3] In September each stockholder was issued (for each share held) one stock right to purchase two additional shares of common stock for $13 per share. The rights expire on December 31, 1993.
[4] In October 250,000 stock rights were exercised when the market value of the common stock was $14 per share.
[5] In November 400,000 stock rights were exercised when the market value of the common stock was $15 per share.

[6] On December 15, Gennaro declared its first cash dividend to stockholders of $.30 per share, payable on January 10, 1994, to stockholders of record on December 31, 1993.

[7] On December 21, in accordance with the applicable state law, Gennaro formally retired 10,000 shares of its treasury stock and had them revert to an unissued basis. The market value of the common stock was $16 per share on this date.

[8] Net income for 1993 was $800,000.

Instructions

Prepare a schedule of all transactions affecting the capital stock (shares and dollar amounts), additional paid-in capital, retained earnings, and the treasury stock (shares and dollar amounts) and the amounts that would be included in Gennaro's balance sheet at December 31, 1991, 1992, 1993, as a result of the above transactions. Show supporting computations in good form.

(AICPA adapted)

17–45 COMPREHENSIVE STOCKHOLDERS' EQUITY WORKSHEET Rainville Corporation is a publicly owned company whose shares are traded on a national stock exchange. At December 31, 1993, Rainville had 25,000,000 shares of $10 par value common stock authorized, of which 15,000,000 shares were issued and 14,000,000 shares were outstanding.

The stockholders' equity accounts at December 31, 1992, had the following balances:

Common stock	$150,000,000
Paid-in capital in excess of par	80,000,000
Retained earnings	50,000,000
Treasury stock	18,000,000

During 1993, Rainville had the following transactions:

[1] On February 1, a secondary distribution of 2,000,000 shares of $10 par value common stock was completed. The stock was sold to the public at $18 per share, net of offering costs.

[2] On February 15, Rainville issued at $110 per share, 100,000 shares of $100 par value, 8% cumulative preferred stock with 100,000 detachable warrants. Each warrant contained one right which with $20 could be exchanged for one share of $10 par value common stock. On February 15, the market price for one stock right was $1.

[3] On March 1, Rainville reacquired 20,000 shares of its common stock for $18.50 per share. Rainville uses the cost method to account for treasury stock.

[4] On March 15, when the common stock was trading for $21 per share, a major stockholder donated 10,000 shares.

[5] On March 31, Rainville declared a semiannual cash dividend on common stock of $.10 per share, payable on April 10, 1993.

[6] On April 15, when the market price of the stock rights was $2 each and the market price of the common stock was $22 per share, 30,000 stock rights were exercised. Rainville issued new shares to complete the transaction.

[7] On April 30, employees exercised 100,000 options that were granted in 1990 under a noncompensatory stock option plan. When the options were granted, each option had a preemptive right and entitled the employee to purchase one share of common stock for $20 per share. On April 30, the market price of the common stock was $23 per share. Rainville issued new shares to settle the transaction.

[8] On May 31, when the market price of the common stock was $20 per share, Rainville declared a 5% stock dividend distributable on July 1, 1993, to stockholders of record on June 1, 1993. The appropriate state law prohibits stock dividends on treasury shares.

[9] On June 30, Rainville sold the 20,000 treasury shares reacquired on March 1 and an additional 280,000 treasury shares costing $5,600,000 that were on hand at the beginning of the year. The selling price was $25 per share.

[10] On September 30, Rainville declared a semiannual cash dividend on common stock of $.10 per share and the yearly dividend on preferred stock, both payable on October 30, 1993, to stockholders of record on October 10, 1993.

[11] On December 31, the remaining outstanding rights expired.

[12] Net income for 1993 was $25,000,000.

Instructions

Prepare a worksheet that summarizes, for each transaction, the changes in Rainville's stockholders' equity accounts for 1993. The columns on this worksheet should have the following headings:

> Date of transaction (or beginning date)
> Common stock—number of shares
> Common stock—amount
> Preferred stock—number of shares
> Preferred stock—amount
> Common stock warrants—number of rights
> Common stock warrants—amount
> Paid-in capital in excess of par
> Retained earnings
> Treasury stock—number of shares
> Treasury stock—amount   (AICPA adapted)

17–46   COMPREHENSIVE STOCKHOLDERS' EQUITY   At December 31, 1991, Ryan, Inc., had 6,000,000 authorized shares of $20 par value common stock, of which 1,000,000 shares were issued and outstanding. The stockholders' equity accounts at December 31, 1991, had the following balances:

Common stock	$20,000,000
Additional paid-in capital	6,000,000
Retained earnings	5,000,000

Transactions during 1992 and other information relating to the stockholders' equity accounts were as follows:

[1] On January 5, 1992, Ryan issued at $54 per share, 100,000 shares of $50 par value, 9% cumulative convertible preferred stock. Each share of preferred stock is convertible, at the option of the holder, into two shares of common stock. Ryan had 600,000 authorized shares of preferred stock. The preferred stock has a liquidation value equal to its par value.

[2] On February 1, 1992, Ryan reacquired 10,000 shares of its common stock for $32 per share. Ryan uses the cost method to account for treasury stock.

[3] On April 30, 1992, Ryan sold 250,000 shares (previously unissued) of $20 par value common stock to the public at $34 per share.

[4] On June 18, 1992, Ryan declared a cash dividend of $2 per share of common stock, payable on July 12, 1992, to stockholders of record on July 1, 1992.

[5] On November 10, 1992, Ryan sold 5,000 shares of treasury stock for $42 per share.

[6] On December 14, 1992, Ryan declared the yearly cash dividend on preferred stock, payable on January 14, 1993, to stockholders of record on December 31, 1992.

[7] On January 20, 1993, before the books were closed for 1992, Ryan became aware that the ending inventories at December 31, 1991, were understated by $300,000 (after tax effect on 1991 net income was $180,000). The appropriate correcting entry was recorded the same day.

[8] After correcting the beginning inventory, net income for 1992 was $3,500,000.

Instructions

[a] Prepare a statement of retained earnings for the year ended December 31, 1992. Assume that only single-period financial statements for 1992 are presented.

[b] Prepare the stockholders' equity section of Ryan's balance sheet at December 31, 1992.

                                                         (AICPA adapted)

CASES   **17–47   RELATIONSHIP BETWEEN DIVIDENDS AND RETAINED EARNINGS**   Bixby Corporation has been in business for four years. The corporation has never paid a dividend but has accumulated earnings over the past four years of $600,000. The balance sheet on December 31, 1992, appears as follows:

Assets

Current assets	$ 50,000
Land	300,000
Plant assets	500,000
Less: Accumulated depreciation	(100,000)
Patents	400,000
Total assets	$1,150,000

Liabilities and Stockholders' Equity

Current liabilities	$ 50,000
Long-term debt	100,000
Common stock (no par; 10,000 shares authorized, issued, and outstanding)	400,000
Retained earnings	600,000
Total liabilities and stockholders' equity	$1,150,000

Net income for 1992 was $150,000. The statement of retained earnings indicates that $200,000 of retained earnings is appropriated for future plant expansion. John Wolf, a stockholder with a 20% holding, is concerned about the lack of dividends over the last four years. Specifically, he notices that retained earnings are $600,000, and he is therefore thinking about pressuring the company to pay some of this amount in dividends. Wolf believes 40%, or $240,000 of retained earnings, could be paid in dividends, leaving $200,000 for plant expansion and $160,000 as a cushion against economic downturns.

Instructions

Mr. Wolf has come to you for advice on how best to proceed against the company.

[a] What is your advice to Mr. Wolf?

[b] How would you alleviate Mr. Wolf's concern about the lack of dividends? In other words, show Mr. Wolf that the lack of dividends may not be as bad as he thinks.

17–48 ALTERNATIVE DIVIDEND PLANS   The board of directors of Western Fixtures Company is considering several strategies for the upcoming annual dividend. Alice Hemming, the treasurer of the company, has been asked to explain to the board of directors the advantages and disadvantages of each strategy. The four strategies are:

[1] Declare the normal cash dividend of $1.00 per share.

[2] Declare a 2% stock dividend on the outstanding common stock.

[3] Declare a 40% stock dividend on the outstanding common stock.

[4] Split the stock, 2 for 1, and declare a $.50 per share dividend on the new outstanding shares.

Western has 100,000 shares of $2.50 par value common stock outstanding. The market price of the common stock is $50 per share.

Instructions

[a] Provide the information needed by the board of directors. Be sure to identify the amount to be charged to retained earnings for each method.

[b] The chair of the board discovers that the amount charged to retained earnings is the same under each alternative and therefore concludes that the methods are identical in terms of economic effect on the firm. Respond to this observation.

17–49 STOCK-BASED COMPENSATION PLANS   IBR Company is considering an employee incentive plan for certain key employees. The compensation committee of the board of directors is considering either a stock option plan or a stock appreciation right plan. The compensation committee wants a brief report on the advantages and disadvantages of each type of plan for both employer and employee. In addition, the compensation committee wishes to know the financial statement reporting principles for each method.

Instructions

Provide the information requested by the compensation committee of the board of directors.

17–50 STOCK OPTIONS MEASUREMENT DATE   On December 14, 1990, the board of directors of Park Company authorized a grant of nontransferable (restricted) options to company executives for the purchase of 10,000 shares of $50 par value common stock at $52½ any time during 1993 if the executives were still employed by the company. The closing price of Park common stock was $55 on December 14, 1990, $52 on January 2, 1993, and $49⅛ on December 31, 1993. None of the options was exercised.

Instructions

[a] Prepare a schedule computing the compensation expense attributable to the stock options that should be recognized by Park Company. Prepare any entries for 1990 through 1993.

[b] Assume that the market price of Park common stock rose to $57 (instead of declining to $52) on January 2, 1993, and that all options were exercised on that date. What cost would the company incur for executive compensation? Why? Prepare any additional entries necessary in these circumstances.

[c] Discuss the arguments for measuring compensation from executive stock options in terms of the spread between:

   [1] Market price and option price when the grant is made.
   [2] Market price and option price when the options are first exercisable.
   [3] Market price and option price when the options are exercised.
   [4] Cash value of the executives' services estimated at the grant date and the amount of their salaries.   (AICPA adapted)

17–51 CONVERTIBLE BONDS   On February 1, 1989, Newman Company sold its 5-year, $1,000 par value, 8% bonds which were convertible at the option of the investor into Newman Company common stock at a ratio of 10 shares of common stock for each bond. The convertible bonds were sold by Newman Company at a discount. Interest is payable annually each February 1. On February 1, 1992, Karr Company, an investor in the Newman Company convertible bonds, tendered 1,000 bonds for conversion into 10,000 shares of Newman Company common stock which had a market value of $110 per share at the date of the conversion.

Instructions

How should Newman Company account for the conversion of the convertible bonds into common stock under both the book value and market value methods? Discuss the rationale for each method and indicate which method Newman should use.   (AICPA adapted)

17–52 DISTINGUISHING ERRORS FROM CHANGES IN ESTIMATES   Your new client, Rapid Fire Change Artists, Inc., fired their former chief executive officer and immediately appointed a new president. Shortly after the end of the year and following the issuance of financial statements, the company also discharged its independent auditors.

You were pleased when the new president requested your accounting firm to perform the current year's audit. In discussing the engagement with the old auditors and the new president you have learned that a number of assets were written off shortly after the new president was appointed and the estimated lives of most of the company's assets were shortened. In fact, the company now reports few assets on its balance sheet and the charges for depreciation are extremely small. You have also determined that the old auditors had initially disagreed with those actions although they agreed with the new management in the end. That disagreement, however, was the source of the action taken to discharge the prior audit firm.

During this year's work, you have learned that one of the company's factories that was written down to its salvage value is continuing to operate at full capacity. When you ask the president about the seeming inconsistency between the write-off of the plant last year and its continued operation, the president simply smiles and states:

When we wrote off that plant, I thought we would almost immediately abandon it. The more I thought about it, however, the more I realized that my earlier estimates needed to be revised and that we could still operate the plant and make a profit. Therefore, I changed my mind shortly after the financial statements for last year were issued and decided to continue operating it. I realize that given the write-off there won't be any depreciation expense to recognize on that facility. However, I need to report a lot of profit anyway to demonstrate the turnaround I was hired to engineer. But given the accounting for changes in estimate, I don't see any other way to report the results of our operations this year. Anyway, its an ill wind that blows no good, right?"

Instructions

Is the president correct in his analysis of this situation? Prepare a response to the president's position. If you believe that you need additional information, describe what else you would like to determine in order to provide acceptable accounting in this set of circumstances.

17–53 ACCOUNTING FOR REDEEMABLE PREFERRED STOCK   You are the controller for Leveraged, Inc., a private company not subject to the registration requirements of the Securities and Exchange Commission, which issued redeemable preferred stock during the current year. The stockholders have the option of redeeming the stock five years after its issuance at a stated redemption value. If redeemed, any dividends in arrears must be paid in addition to the redemption value.

The company has decided to report the stock outside the stockholders' equity section of the balance sheet as it would be required to do if the company were a public registrant. Other accounting issues have arisen, however, and you are attempting to determine acceptable financial reporting practices. The principal issue relates to the difference between the issuance price and the redemption value of the stock. The stock was issued at a substantial discount from the redemption value and you are wondering whether this difference should be amortized as would be the case if the stock was clearly a debt instrument. Further, if the difference is to be amortized, you wonder how the annual amount should be recognized. If the instrument was a note or bond payable, any such amortization would be an adjustment to interest expense recognized on the debt. In this case, however, the stock may not even be redeemed by the stockholders.

Instructions

How should the difference between the issuance price and the redemption value of the stock be accounted for and reported in the company's financial statements?

PART 5

ADDITIONAL FINANCIAL REPORTING ISSUES

CHAPTER 18

Financial Reporting of Income Taxes

OBJECTIVES

1. To explain differences in the determination of net income for financial reporting purposes (financial income) and income for purposes of determining a company's income tax liability to the government (taxable income).

2. To illustrate the impact that income tax laws have on the elements of the financial statements related to income taxes.

3. To explain and illustrate accounting for operating loss carrybacks and carryforwards.

4. To explain the conceptual justification for recognizing deferred tax assets and liabilities and demonstrate accounting for permanent and temporary differences between financial and taxable income in a variety of circumstances.

5. To evaluate the recognition of deferred taxes on all temporary differences and introduce alternatives to current practices of accounting for income taxes.

6. To explain and illustrate intraperiod income tax allocation, whereby the income tax expense of an accounting period is divided into components for financial-statement presentation.

INTRODUCTION TO INCOME TAX REPORTING

Income taxes represent a major expense for many businesses. While income taxes are comparable in many respects to other expenses, there are several unusual and complicating features of accounting for income taxes and the presentation of those taxes in the financial statements. These complications result from the fact that the amount of income taxes to be paid must be in accordance with legal requirements of the Internal Revenue Code. This requires complex determinations of the amounts of income taxes to be paid that then become the basis for several items that appear in the financial statements and accompanying notes of the enterprise.

As you begin this chapter, turn to the Strawbridge & Clothier financial statements on the inside front and back covers of this text or in the text appendix. These statements contain several references to income taxes. The income statement includes an expense labeled "income taxes," which follows a line labeled "earnings before income taxes." Several income tax items appear in the balance sheet. First, among current liabilities are "federal, state and local taxes" and "deferred income taxes." Also, the single item described under the category of "Other Liabilities" is deferred income taxes. Notes to the financial statements include an explanation of income taxes in the description of significant accounting policies. More extensive information about income taxes is presented in Note G. At this point, you probably do not understand all of these items, but we will study them in this and subsequent chapters.

Going Concern

Matching

Several underlying accounting principles are important in forming specific accounting practices relating to the financial reporting of income taxes. The going-concern assumption is important because we assume that the enterprise will remain in existence in the foreseeable future and will continue to pay income taxes as profits are earned. The determination of income is heavily influenced by the matching principle, in that expenses associated with revenues being recognized are included in the income statement as a part of the determination of the net income figure. While some people view income taxes as a *distribution* of income of the enterprise, the generally accepted interpretation is that income taxes are appropriately viewed as a **determinant** of income of the enterprise. Thus **income taxes are an expense** and are subject to accrual accounting methods in the same manner as other expenses. Accordingly, the income tax effects of revenue and expense transactions must be recognized in the income statement in the same accounting period in which those revenues and expenses affect net income, even if the items appear in the income tax return in a different accounting period. Thus, a direct association exists between income tax expense in a given accounting period and the revenues and other expenses recognized in that same period.

The objectives of financial reporting and the accounting principles that underlie financial reporting were given due consideration in developing the rules that govern presentation of income taxes in the financial statements. The basic objective of financial reporting is to provide useful information to investors, creditors, and other financial statement users for making financial decisions. Income tax laws, on the other hand, have been developed through government action to reach quite different ends, such as the generation of income for the government, the redistribution of wealth within the economy, and the encouragement of the long-run growth of the economy. Given the different objectives of financial reporting and the income tax laws, it is not surprising that the recognition of revenue and expense items sometimes varies between income tax law and GAAP.

Corporations are subject to federal income tax rates that vary from time to time as changes are made in income tax laws. The Tax Reform Act of 1986 significantly reduced the corporate income tax rates from those in effect in earlier years. Income tax rates for most corporations beginning July 1, 1987, are as follows:

Income Tax Rate	Income Subject to This Rate
15%	First $50,000 of taxable income
25%	Next $25,000 of taxable income
34%	Next $25,000 of taxable income
39%	Next $235,000 of taxable income
34%	All remaining taxable income

Once taxable income reaches $100,000, the rate is 39%. The five-percentage-point adjustment at that point (39% − 34%) is designed to increase the tax to the amount that it would be had a flat 34% rate been applied to all income up to the $335,000 level. Therefore, once taxable income reaches $335,000, all income is effectively taxed at 34%.

As you are probably aware from reading newspapers and listening to radio and television news, tax laws change from time to time. The authors expect that many students studying this chapter will not yet have taken a course in corporate income taxation. Accordingly, in this chapter we focus on basic principles of reporting income tax information in financial statements and do not attempt to explain every financial reporting and income tax problem that can occur. We simplify certain income tax procedures in order to facilitate our study of financial reporting. For example, we generally assume simplified single income tax rates, such as 34%, 36%, and 40%, as a basis for the determination of income tax amounts, rather than using the graduated income tax rate schedule mentioned above. We also limit our coverage of income taxation to the federal level and do not cover, for example, accounting for state income taxes.

Matching

Through the years, several important authoritative accounting pronouncements have been issued that deal with accounting and reporting income taxes in the financial statements. From 1967 to 1987, guidance was provided by *APB Opinion No. 11,*[1] which emphasized the matching process. That pronouncement was replaced by *FASB Statement of Financial Accounting Standards No. 96,*[2] which requires an asset/liability valuation approach to determining the elements of financial statements concerning income taxes. The FASB encountered great resistance in practice in its attempts to implement *SFAS No. 96,* however, and the effective date of that pronouncement was delayed three times. While *SFAS No. 96* remains in effect through 1992 for those companies choosing to adopt it early, *FASB Statement No. 109*[3] was issued in early 1992 to replace *SFAS No. 96,* effective in 1993. In addition to these primary authoritative pronouncements, several other pronouncements on specialized areas of accounting for income taxes have been issued since *APB Opinion No. 11* was issued in 1967.

In this chapter, we discuss several important aspects of the subject of accounting for income taxes. The material is generally consistent with current authoritative literature, but has been simplified to permit us to focus on basic principles of financial reporting rather than on detailed application of income tax procedures.

---

[1]*APB Opinion No. 11,* "Accounting for Income Taxes," 1967.
[2]*FASB Statement of Financial Accounting Standards No. 96,* "Accounting for Income Taxes," 1987.
[3]*FASB Statement of Financial Accounting Standards No. 109,* "Accounting for Income Taxes," 1992.

The remainder of this chapter is presented in three major sections. First, we explore the area of loss carrybacks and carryforwards, a unique feature of income tax law that permits a company to move losses from one year back or forward in time to offset income of other years, thereby reducing the amount of income taxes that would otherwise have to be paid. Second, we consider the subject of deferred income taxes brought about by temporary differences in the way certain items are treated in determining pretax financial income and taxable income. Finally, we discuss intraperiod income tax allocation and the presentation of income tax expense in the various sections of the income and, possibly, the retained earnings statement. Appendix A deals with implementing the general principles of this chapter under current authoritative pronouncements; Appendix B discusses another unique feature of income tax law, the investment tax credit.

OPERATING LOSS CARRYBACKS AND CARRYFORWARDS

Certain provisions of income tax law allow companies to offset losses of one year against income of other years to reduce the total income tax burden of the company. Thus, while the company must report its taxable income to the government periodically for the purpose of paying income taxes, those payments are subject to refund, as the amount of income taxes ultimately paid is based on the long-run profitability of the enterprise.

Operating loss carrybacks result when the loss of a particular year is taken back in time and used to reduce income taxes of past years. The effect of the carryback is that the enterprise has a right to a refund of income taxes that have already been paid. **Operating loss carryforwards** result when the loss of a particular year is taken forward in time and used to reduce income taxes of future years. The effect of the carryforward is an **anticipated** reduction of income taxes that would otherwise have to be paid if operations of future years result in income subject to income taxes. Since carrybacks are based on past income and related income taxes that have already been paid and carryforwards are based on expected future income and related income taxes that *may* have to be paid, the value of carryforwards to an enterprise is more speculative or uncertain than carrybacks.

THE ALTERNATIVES: CARRYBACK/CARRYFORWARD OR CARRYFORWARD-ONLY

A loss of a particular year can be carried *back* if the enterprise has reported income and paid income taxes within a specified period (three years under present tax law). If the enterprise has not had income and therefore has not paid income taxes within the specified carryback period, the loss of a particular year can be carried *forward* and offset against income of future periods for a specified period of time (fifteen years under present tax law). Additionally, if the loss of the current period exceeds the income reported during the carryback period, the portion that cannot be carried back can be carried forward. Finally, the enterprise has the option of carrying the entire loss of a particular period forward instead of back. This election must be made in the loss year and cannot be changed once an option has been selected. However, a company may use one option for one loss year and the other option for another loss year. Once the option is selected, the income of the earliest year possible is reduced by the loss of the year in question. These alternatives are illustrated in Exhibit 18–1.

Under the *carryback/carryforward option,* the loss of 1992 in Exhibit 18–1 would be used to reduce income and income taxes of 1989, 1990, and 1991, in that order. Income taxes paid in those years would be refundable to the enterprise to the extent that the 1992 loss offset part or all of the incomes reported in those years. If the

EXHIBIT 18–1

Operating Loss Carrybacks and Carryforwards

Option	Carryback Period (Reduction in Taxes Determinable)			Current Period	Carryforward Period (Reduction in Taxes Speculative)							
	1989	1990	1991	1992	1993	1994	1995	1996	1997	. . .	2007
Carryback/ carryforward	← Carry back 3 years			Loss Reported	Carry forward 15 years →							
Carryforward only	Not applicable				Carry forward 15 years →							

1992 loss were so great that it more than offset the incomes of 1989, 1990, and 1991, the remainder would be carried forward to offset income in 1993, 1994, and so on. The refund of past income taxes for which the company is eligible is based on actual income taxes paid in those years. Any reduction in future income taxes is uncertain, however, since it is to be based on future income not yet earned.

Under the *carryforward-only* option, Exhibit 18–1 indicates that the loss of 1992 is not carried back but is carried forward and applied in consecutive order to the carryforward years beginning with 1993. You may wonder why a company would choose the speculative carryforward option if it could carry back the loss of a particular period and have the certainty of the refund of past income taxes. The answer lies in the *anticipation* that future income will be taxed at *higher* income tax rates than in the past. Since the amount of refund (if the loss is carried back) or the reduction in future income taxes (if the loss is carried forward) is based on actual taxes paid in the carryback year or to be paid in the carryforward year, the income tax rates in effect in the year(s) for which income is reduced by the loss are very important. Income taxes in the future may be greater than in the past because (1) enacted income tax rates may increase or (2) a higher level of future income may place the company in a higher income tax bracket. If either of these is expected to take place, the company that sustains a loss in a given year might logically select the option of carrying forward the entire loss and forfeiting the certainty of the carryback option.

Another consideration in choosing between the carryback/carryforward option or the carryforward-only option is the timing of the receipt of the tax refund (carryback) compared to the reduction in future income taxes (carryforward). If the loss is carried back, the company can expect to receive the tax refund in the near future, whereas if the loss is carried forward, the company forfeits the right to the cash until some future time—after the company has earned future taxable income. If the company needs immediate cash, the carryback option may be attractive, even if income tax rates are expected to increase in the future. Throughout this chapter, including the assignment material at the end, we assume that companies choose the carryback/carryforward option unless specifically indicated otherwise.

This discussion has focused on the provisions of income tax law that govern the actual payment of income taxes to the government. Our primary interest, however, is on the reporting of loss carrybacks and carryforwards in the financial statements of the enterprise. The reduction in income taxes resulting from loss carrybacks is recognized in the determination of the net loss in the loss year. That is, the loss is reduced by the income taxes of past years that will be refunded because of the carryback and

**Revenue
Realization**

a receivable for past taxes is included in the balance sheet. This accounting treatment is logical, because the refund of past income taxes is both realizable and measurable.

The subject of loss carryforwards, on the other hand, represents a more difficult conceptual problem and has been a subject of debate in the accounting profession in recent years. One alternative is to recognize carryforwards in the same manner as carrybacks with the realizability of the asset subject to the condition that future taxable

Conservatism

income will be present within the carryforward period. A more conservative approach is to delay the recognition of the carryforward until realization is assured, meaning that taxable income against which the carryforward can be used has already been reported. In the example which follows, we develop these alternatives further, because both alternatives are found in practice through 1992.

AN ILLUSTRATION OF CARRYBACKS AND CARRYFORWARDS

To illustrate the way operating loss carrybacks and carryforwards work, we will assume that Dimick Company has pretax financial income (loss) and income tax rates for 1990 through 1993 as follows:

	1990	1991	1992	1993
Pretax financial income (loss)	$75,000	$80,000	$55,000	$(165,000)
Income tax rate	40%	36%	35%	38%

Dimick selects the carryback/carryforward option for purposes of applying the 1993 loss to reduce income taxes. Accordingly, the amount of refund to which the company is immediately entitled as a result of the 1993 loss is $ 62,300, computed as follows:

Year	Income		Income Tax Rate		Refund
1990	$ 75,000	×	40%	=	$30,000
1991	80,000	×	36%	=	28,800
1992	10,000	×	35%	=	3,500
	$165,000				$62,300

Only $10,000 of 1992 income is included in the refund to reach the level of $165,000 to offset the 1993 loss of that amount. The remaining $45,000 of 1992 income ($55,000 − $10,000) may be used as a basis for the refund of income taxes in the future if additional losses in 1994 or 1995 are carried back. The journal entry to record income tax for 1993 is as follows:

Receivable for Past Income Taxes	62,300	
Tax Benefit of Net Operating Loss		62,300

The receivable of past income taxes is presented in the balance sheet as a current asset because it represents a refund that will be received in the near future. The credit entry, "Tax Benefit of Net Operating Loss," is presented in the income statement in lieu of income tax expense, resulting in the following presentation:

Loss before income tax	$(165,000)
Tax benefit of net operating loss	62,300
Net loss	$(102,700)

As long as the amount of 1993 loss is $210,000 or less, accounting for the income tax effects of the loss is essentially the same with only the numbers differing for losses other than $165,000. ($210,000 is the total of the pretax financial incomes of the three years prior to the loss year: $75,000 + $80,000 + $55,000 = $210,000.) Had Dimick Company's loss in 1993 exceeded $210,000, however, the portion in excess of $210,000 is available for carryforward to offset future income which is yet to be earned. As indicated earlier, recognizing loss carryforwards in the year of loss, rather than deferring their recognition until future taxable income is earned has been a controversial issue in financial reporting. In the past, most companies have **not**

Revenue Realization recognized loss carryforwards on the basis that to do so was a violation of the revenue realization principle. Current thinking, however, is that this may be too restrictive and, considering the relatively long 15-year carryforward period during which the benefit of the carryforward can be realized, recognition is appropriate. The profession's current position on this issue is developed in Appendix A.

In the Dimick example, let's assume that the 1993 loss is $250,000, $210,000 of which is carried back and $40,000 of which is available for carryforward purposes. If we recognized the carryforward in 1993, the journal entry to recognize income taxes would appear as follows:

Receivable for Past Income Taxes	78,050	
Deferred Income Tax (Asset)	15,200	
Tax Benefit of Net Operating Loss		93,250

The $78,050 receivable is calculated the same as in the previous example:

Year	Income		Income Tax Rate		Refund
1990	$ 75,000	×	40%	=	$30,000
1991	80,000	×	36%	=	28,800
1992	55,000	×	35%	=	19,250
	$210,000				$78,050

The deferred tax account of $15,200 is computed by multiplying the $40,000 carryforward amount ($250,000 − $210,000) by the current (1993) income tax rate: $40,000 × 38% = $15,200. The net loss reported in 1993 would be $156,750 ($250,000 − $93,250). As you can see, we have assumed that the enacted 1993 income tax rate of 38% also applies to future years and that rate was used in computing the tax benefit of the $40,000 loss carryforward.

If the $40,000 amount of the 1993 loss that is available for carryforward had not been recognized in 1993, it would have been used to reduce taxable income in the first year possible in the future. The $15,200 part of the tax accrual recorded above would be eliminated, resulting in a larger net loss in 1993 by $15,200, but a lower income tax expense in one or more future years. The amount of unused carryforward avail-

Disclosure able to reduce future income should be disclosed in notes to the financial statements.

TEMPORARY DIFFERENCES AND DEFERRED INCOME TAXES

Earlier in this chapter, you were introduced to the idea that certain transactions affect financial income and taxable income in different accounting periods. An important objective of accrual accounting for income taxes is to recognize the appropriate amount of current and deferred income taxes payable or refundable in the balance sheet for these differences.

Differences between the amount of income for financial reporting purposes and taxable income are caused by temporary and permanent differences. Both relate to differences in the way certain items are treated in determining financial income and taxable income; both are important in understanding financial reporting of income taxes. A discussion of each of these follows, including an explanation of how they affect the determination of deferred tax assets and liabilities.

TEMPORARY DIFFERENCES

The tax consequences of most events recognized in a company's financial statements are included in determining income taxes payable in the same period. Despite this general similarity in treatment, tax laws and GAAP sometimes differ in their recognition and measurement of assets, liabilities, owners' equity, revenues, expenses, gains, and losses. As a result, differences may arise in the amounts of taxable income and pretax financial income and in the tax bases of assets or liabilities and their reported amounts in financial statements. Differences that will result in taxable or deductible amounts in the future are called **temporary differences.** A difference is a *taxable temporary difference* when the item causes financial income to exceed taxable income, with the expectation that the difference will be offset in future periods. Likewise, a difference is a *deductible temporary difference* when it causes taxable income to exceed financial income, with the expectation that the difference will be offset in future periods.

An important assumption inherent in an enterprise's balance sheet prepared in accordance with GAAP is that assets will be recovered at their reported amounts and liabilities will be settled at their reported amounts. Building on that assumption, we further assume that a difference between the income tax basis of an asset or a liability and its reported amount in the balance sheet will result in taxable or deductible amounts in determining taxable income in some future year.

Temporary differences result from differences in the pattern or timing of recognition of certain items in reporting financial income and taxable income. For every temporary difference, eventually that item's treatment will be the same in financial and taxable income. Temporary differences are said to **originate** in one accounting period (the period in which the difference is first determined) and **reverse** in a later accounting period (the later period in which the difference is offset.)

The most frequently encountered temporary difference is the difference in plant asset write-off for tax purposes and depreciation for financial-reporting purposes. The Economic Recovery Act of 1981 made significant changes in the manner in which companies write off the cost of plant assets in determining their income tax liability. That law introduced a system called the **Accelerated Cost Recovery System (ACRS),** which permitted rapid write-off of asset costs over predetermined periods that were generally shorter than the estimated useful lives of the property.

Those procedures were modified in the Tax Reform Act of 1986, but the system remains essentially the same. Under the **Modified Accelerated Cost Recovery System (MACRS),** the cost of eligible property is recovered over a 3-, 5-, 7-, 10-, 15-, 20-, 27.5-, or 31.5-year period, depending on the type of property, at preestablished percentage rates for each year. For example, the 5-year category includes such assets as cars, light general-purpose trucks, and computer equipment. The 7-year category includes office furniture and fixtures. The 20-year and longer periods are generally reserved for various types of real estate.

Accelerated cost recovery is an area of difference between income tax law and generally accepted accounting principles that illustrates clearly the nature of temporary differences. The periods of write-off for tax purposes are often not consistent with the useful lives of the assets and, as a result, accelerated cost recovery is usually not acceptable for financial reporting purposes. When the company uses a different method in determining financial income, such as straight-line, temporary differences occur.

We separate temporary differences into those that result in financial income that exceeds taxable income and those that result in taxable income that exceeds financial income. First, types of temporary differences that result in financial income greater than taxable income at the time of the origination of the temporary differences include the following:

1. Revenues or gains that are taxable after they are recognized in financial income. An example is an installment sale that is recognized as revenue in financial income at the time of the sale and included in taxable income when cash is later collected.
2. Expenses or losses that are deductible for income tax purposes before they are recognized in financial income. An example is the write-off of plant assets on an accelerated basis for income tax purposes with straight-line depreciation being used in the financial statements.

These result in what we defined earlier as **taxable temporary differences.**

Other temporary differences have the opposite effect when they originate, in that taxable income exceeds financial income. Examples include the following:

1. Revenues and gains that are taxable before they are recognized in financial income. An example is a cash advance received for services to be provided in the future that is taxable when received but is recognized in financial income when later earned.
2. Expenses and losses that are deductible for income tax purposes after they are recognized in financial income. An example is a litigation loss that is recognized in financial income when it is probable and measurable but deducted for income tax purposes when the litigation is settled.

These result in what we defined earlier as **deductible temporary differences.**

In practice, a number of other temporary differences exist. These are generally beyond the scope of this text and, accordingly, in the examples that follow, as well as in the assignment material at the end of the chapter, we limit our consideration to these four temporary differences. This means you do not need an in-depth knowledge of income tax laws and advanced financial accounting topics in order to understand the financial reporting implications of income taxes.

PERMANENT DIFFERENCES

Permanent differences result from differences in the definitions of financial and taxable income. Certain items of revenue and expense are included in either financial or taxable income, but will *never* be included in the other. Permanent differences do not originate and reverse as do temporary differences. Thus, permanent differences do not give rise to deferred tax assets or liabilities because they have no future tax consequences.

In this text we limit permanent differences included in the illustrations and end-of-chapter materials to two specific items:

1. Interest received on investments in securities issued by a municipal government. This type of interest is included in financial income, as is interest on all types of investments, but is not included in taxable income.
2. Amortization of goodwill. This is a required expense in the determination of financial income, but it is not deductible in determining taxable income.

PRINCIPLES OF ACCOUNTING FOR DEFERRED INCOME TAXES

In this chapter we discuss a general approach to recognizing deferred income taxes called the *asset/liability method* (sometimes simply called the liability method). The FASB has worked extensively to implement the asset/liability method in practice. Coverage of those attempts, including a description of the current status of accounting for income taxes, is presented in Appendix A of this chapter. The approach used in the following sections is generally consistent with the FASB's approach, but is simplified to focus on basic principles of recognizing income tax assets, liabilities and expense. Our primary focus is on developing analytical and conceptual thinking rather than memorizing an ever-expanding set of professional standards.

Recall from our discussion of accounting theory in Chapter 3 that the asset/liability view of earnings defines revenues, expenses, gains and losses in terms of certain changes that occur in assets and liabilities. The asset/liability method of determining deferred income taxes and income tax expense is consistent with the asset/liability view of earnings.

In contrast, another method called the *deferred method* was widely used in the past under *APB Opinion No. 11*. That method represents an excellent example of the revenue/expense view of earnings, also discussed in Chapter 3. Under the deferred method of accounting for income taxes, primary emphasis is placed on the amount of income tax expense. That is, the accountant computed the amount of income tax expense directly, by multiplying the pretax accounting income subject to tax by the income tax rate. If this amount differed from the current tax liability owed to the government (i.e., taxable income multiplied by the tax rate), the difference was recognized as deferred income taxes. Under that approach, deferred income taxes represent the residual effects of recognizing the amount of income tax expense. In computing income tax expense, only the current period's income tax rate is used; future rates are ignored even when they have already been enacted. While the deferred method was prominent in the past, it is rapidly disappearing from practice because it is inconsistent with the current emphasis being placed on measuring and reporting assets and liabilities in the balance sheet. For that reason, we do not cover that method extensively in this chapter.

Following are several broad principles that are important to keep in mind as we consider in more detail proper accounting for deferred tax assets and liabilities under the generalized asset/liability approach illustrated in the next section.

1. A deferred tax asset or liability is recognized for the income tax consequences of *all temporary differences* that have been recognized in either financial income or taxable income.
2. Deferred tax assets and liabilities are determined on the basis of *enacted income tax rates*. No attempt is made to estimate future income tax rates that are not yet enacted.

3. When enacted future tax rates change, deferred taxes are remeasured at the end of the next accounting period to incorporate the new rates.

EXAMPLES OF DEFERRED TAX ASSETS AND LIABILITIES

In this section, we illustrate accounting for permanent and temporary differences, focusing our attention on the determination of deferred tax assets and liabilities. We shall see that the related income tax expense is determined by combining the amount of income tax currently payable and the *change* in the amount of deferred tax assets or liabilities. Using the asset/liability method, we directly measure the assets and liabilities related to income taxes and then determine income tax expense residually.

Example 1: First Year of Operations

Pinson Company has determined its pretax financial income for 1992, its first year of operations, to be $130,000. Included in that amount are the following permanent and temporary differences from taxable income:

> **Permanent difference:** Interest received on investments in municipal bonds, $5,000.
> **Temporary differences:** (1) Excess of accelerated asset write-off for income tax purposes over straight-line depreciation in determining financial income, $25,000; (2) Recognition of loss from litigation against the company in financial income that will not be tax deductible until settled in the future, $10,000.

For purposes of recognizing current income taxes payable, as well as deferred tax assets and liabilities, we assume that the 1992 income tax rate is 35% and the enacted rate for all future years is 38%. The following analysis facilitates our preparation of the appropriate year-end tax accrual:

	1992	Future Years
Pretax financial income	$130,000	—
Permanent difference:		
Municipal interest	(5,000)	—
Pretax financial income subject to income tax	$125,000	—
Temporary differences:		
Depreciation	(25,000)	$25,000
Litigation	10,000	(10,000)
Taxable income	$110,000	$15,000
Income tax rate	35%	38%
Income tax payable (receivable)		
Current	$ 38,500	
Deferred		$ 5,700

The depreciation temporary difference is a future taxable amount; the litigation temporary difference is a future deductible amount. You can tell this by the manner in which they are presented in the "Future Years" column. Based on this analysis, we can now prepare the 1992 year-end income tax accrual for Pinson, as follows:

Dec. 31, 1992	Income Tax Expense ($38,500 + $5,700)	44,200	
	Income Tax Payable		38,500
	Deferred Income Tax		5,700

Several observations are important concerning this accrual. First, notice that we have assumed no future income beyond the year 1992, other than that which we can determine from the reversal of temporary differences. Also, we have not attempted to predict future income tax rates but, rather, have based the figures on enacted rates at the time of the accrual. Notice that the permanent difference is eliminated from consideration (i.e., not included in the amount of "pretax financial income subject to income tax") and has no impact on the amount of deferred income taxes. Finally, as a result of this accrual, we have two tax liabilities: the current income tax payable of $38,500 and the deferred income tax of $5,700. The amount of income tax expense is determined by simply combining these two liabilities.

Example 2: Second Year of Operations/No Tax Rate Change

We now extend Example 1 to add the complication of dealing with accounting for deferred taxes where a beginning balance exists and temporary differences reverse, as well as originate. Recall that an assumption of Example 1 was that 1992 was Pinson Company's first year of operations and, thus, no deferred tax assets or liabilities existed at the beginning of the year. We now consider 1993, the company's second year of operations, keeping in mind that the year begins with a credit balance of $5,700 in deferred income taxes.

New information for 1993 follows:

Permanent difference: Interest on investments in securities issued by municipalities totals $6,000.

Temporary differences: (1) Accelerated write-off for income tax purposes exceeds straight-line depreciation by $30,000; in addition, $12,000 of the temporary difference from depreciation from 1992 reverses in 1993. (2) The litigation loss from 1992 is settled at the $10,000 estimated amount.

Pretax financial income for 1993 is $156,000, and for this illustration, we maintain our assumption that all years beginning with 1993 are subject to a 38% income tax rate. We are now ready to analyze 1993 in a manner similar to that of 1992:

	1993	Future Years
Pretax financial income	$156,000	—
Permanent difference:		
Municipal interest	(6,000)	—
Pretax financial income subject to income tax	$150,000	—
Temporary differences:		
Depreciation:		
1993 originating	(30,000)	$30,000
1992 reversing	12,000	13,000*
Litigation:		
1992 reversing	(10,000)	—
Taxable income	$122,000	$43,000
Income tax rate	38%	38%
Income tax payable (receivable)		
Current	$ 46,360	
Deferred		$16,340

*$25,000 originating in 1992, less $12,000 reversing in 1993.

The amount of deferred income tax indicated at the end of 1993 is $16,340, representing a liability for income taxes on temporary differences that are taxable amounts in the future. The *increase* in deferred income taxes for 1993 is $10,640, however, because the 1992 balance was $5,700: $16,340 − $5,700 = $10,640. The accrual for income taxes for 1993, to record the current payable and the **net increase in deferred income taxes,** is as follows:

Dec. 31, 1993	Income Tax Expense ($46,360 + $10,640)	57,000	
	Income Tax Payable		46,360
	Deferred Income Tax		10,640

Example 3: Second Year of Operations/Tax Rate Change

In Example 3, we add one more complication to accounting for deferred tax assets and liabilities—a change in the enacted future income tax rate. All information from Example 2 is repeated in Example 3 except we now assume that during 1993 the enacted income tax rate for all future years is changed to 40%. Applying this rate to the accumulated temporary differences, we determine that the net change in deferred income taxes for 1993 is $11,500:

Accumulated net temporary differences	$43,000
(see analysis from Example 2)	
Income tax rate	40%
Ending balance in deferred income taxes	$17,200
Beginning balance of deferred taxes	(5,700)
Increase for 1993	$11,500

Alternatively, the $11,500 change in deferred taxes can be computed as follows:

Origination of 1993 excess depreciation: $30,000 × 40%	$ 12,000
Reversal of 1992 excess depreciation: $12,000 × 38%	(4,560)
Reversal of 1992 litigation: ($10,000) × 38%	3,800
Change in tax rate on temporary difference carried forward	
from prior year: $13,000 × (40% − 38%)	260
	$ 11,500

The 1993 accrual under this new tax-rate assumption is as follows:

Dec. 31, 1993	Income Tax Expense ($46,360 + $11,500)	57,860	
	Income Tax Payable		46,360
	Deferred Income Taxes		11,500

The use of currently enacted income tax rates and the procedure followed when the enacted rate changes represent an interesting example of accounting for a change in accounting estimate. Changes in estimate were introduced in Chapter 12 when we considered changes in the estimated useful lives of plant assets; the subject is considered again in Chapter 19. In the case of accounting for income taxes, the change in income tax rate is incorporated into the determination of income tax expense by simply adjusting the amount of expense that would otherwise have been recognized. The increase in deferred income taxes in Example 3 compared to Example 2, due to the increase in the income tax rate, is $860:

Deferred income taxes, Example 3 (40%)	$ 17,200
Deferred income taxes, Example 2 (38%)	(16,340)
Increase [$43,000 × (40% − 38%)]	$ 860

Of this amount, $600 is due to 1993 originating differences ($30,000 × 2%); $260 is attributable to the increased income tax rate applicable to temporary differences originating in 1992 but not reversing in 1993 ($13,000 × 2%). The $260 amount, while not recognized as a separate component in determining 1993 net income, is an adjustment to income tax expense for the change in income tax rate and, thus, represents a change in accounting estimate. Had the enacted income tax rate been *reduced,* this would have resulted in a *decrease* in income tax expense recognized on the accumulated temporary differences, as well as a lower current payable on the taxable income of 1993.

The examples of deferred income taxes arising from temporary differences in this section have focused on deferred tax credits or liabilities. Where tax law gives companies the latitude of selecting methods that defer taxable income, prudent management will naturally elect to do that. For that reason, the typical position for a company relative to deferred income taxes is a net liability position, indicating that it has deferred or delayed the payment of income taxes on some transactions that have already been included in pretax financial income. Inasmuch as the most common temporary difference, and frequently the largest one, arises from the use of accelerated write-off of plant assets in taxable income and the straight-line depreciation of those same assets in pretax financial income, we would expect many companies to reflect a net liability deferred income tax position in their balance sheets. In the year-end analysis to establish the amount of deferred income taxes, a situation could arise in which taxable income exceeds pretax accounting income. For example, that situation would result from a taxable amount entering taxable income from the reversal of an earlier temporary difference which caused financial income to exceed taxable income. If this is the case, an existing deferred tax liability would be debited. Another possibility is that an originating temporary difference results in a future deductible amount and, thus, taxable income exceeds financial income. In this case, a deferred tax asset would be debited in the income tax accrual.

In illustrating the application of the asset/liability method of accounting for deferred income taxes, we have carefully avoided two complications in order to permit us to focus on basic underlying principles. One simplifying assumption we have made is that once the enacted future income tax rate is changed, the new rate applies to all future years. That assumption would not always hold true, because a series of rate changes could be enacted, resulting in different income tax rates in effect in different future years.

Secondly, we have treated the subjects of loss carrybacks/carryforwards and deferred income taxes as discrete or separate subjects. In practice, they are frequently encountered simultaneously, adding complexity to the determination of the elements of financial statements related to income taxes. As indicated earlier, the FASB has done extensive work in this area and the results of their efforts are described in Appendix A of this chapter.

DEFERRED TAXES: INTERPRETATIONS AND ALTERNATIVES

Are deferred income taxes significant items in corporate balance sheets? While the answer to this question varies from company to company, on average the response is yes. Exhibit 18–2 indicates the noncurrent deferred income tax credits, where most deferred taxes reside, for selected companies for 1990 in dollars and as a percentage of total equities (liabilities plus stockholders' equity).

The dollar amounts and relative sizes of the noncurrent deferred income tax accounts vary, but Exhibit 18–2 indicates that they may be significant balance sheet

EXHIBIT 18-2

Deferred Income Taxes of Selected Companies

Company	Noncurrent Deferred Income Tax Credits	
	Millions of Dollars	As Percent of Liabilities Plus Stockholders' Equity
Union Pacific Corporation	$ 2,257.0	17.3
Shell Oil Company	4,355.0	15.3
Exxon Corporation	12,353.0	14.8
Kellogg Company	347.0	9.3
Delta Airlines, Inc.	506.0	7.0
The Procter and Gamble Company	1,258.0	6.8
Texaco, Inc.	1,169.0	6.4
General Mills, Inc.	203.4	6.2
Minnesota Mining and Manufacturing (3M)	160.0	1.4

SOURCE: 1990 Annual Reports.

items. Of the companies presented, Union Pacific Corporation has the highest percentage of deferred taxes included in total equities—17.3%. The smallest percentage is 1.4% for 3M. The large noncurrent deferred income tax credit balances are due primarily to temporary differences caused by accelerated write-off of plant asset cost for income tax purposes, coupled with the use of straight-line depreciation for financial reporting purposes.

Accounting for deferred income tax assets and liabilities arising from temporary differences has been a controversial subject in the accounting profession for many years. Procedures resulting in the recognition of deferred tax assets and liabilities were initiated several decades ago when relatively simple temporary differences (related primarily to alternative depreciation methods) emerged.[4] As the concept expanded and was applied to a wide variety of differences between financial income and taxable income, numerous questions arose. Several authoritative pronouncements commenting on specific aspects of deferred income taxes have been issued since the basic concept was initially developed.

The Accounting Principles Board favored *comprehensive interperiod income tax allocation,* meaning that deferred taxes are recognized on all temporary differences, regardless of whether they are recurring or nonrecurring in nature. That decision was based on several general concepts and assumptions relative to the nature of income taxes and their relationship to the determination of net income. These concepts and assumptions are summarized as follows:[5]

Going Concern

1. The operations of an entity subject to income taxes are expected to continue on a going-concern basis, in the absence of evidence to the contrary. Accordingly, income taxes are expected to continue to be assessed in the future.

2. Income taxes are an expense of business enterprises earning income subject to income taxes.

---

[4]Homer A. Black, *Accounting Research Study No. 9,* "Interperiod Allocation of Corporate Income Taxes" (New York: AICPA, 1966), pp. 12, 64.

[5]*APB Opinion No. 11,* par. 14.

Periodicity

3. Accounting for income tax expense requires measurement and identification with the appropriate time period. Accruals, deferrals, and estimations are involved in the same manner as these concepts are applied in the measurement and time-period identification of other expenses.

Matching

4. Matching—perhaps the most basic principle of income determination—involves the association of specific costs with specific revenues or time periods. Expenses of the current period consist of those costs that are identified with revenue of the current period and those costs that are identified with the current period on some basis other than revenues.

As we stated earlier, the APB stressed an approach called the **deferred method,** which emphasized the determination of income tax expense. Under that approach, deferred income tax accounts were residual amounts that resulted from the determination of income tax expense and were not directly determined by measuring the assets and liabilities that resulted from individual temporary differences. Income tax expense under the deferred method was based only on the income tax rate of the period of the origination of the underlying temporary differences. This poses a particular problem in situations where temporary differences originate when one tax rate is in effect and reverse when another tax rate is in effect.

Going
Concern

The FASB has recently changed the orientation of accounting for deferred income taxes to the *asset/liability method,* as described earlier in this chapter. While the FASB would agree with the APB in terms of the general conclusion that income taxes are an expense and that operations are expected to continue on a going-concern basis, the FASB's emphasis is on *asset and liability determination* as a means of determining income tax expense. In this approach, income tax expense is the amount obtained when the current income tax payable is combined with the change in deferred income taxes. Thus the expense is a residual amount that results from the measurement of the income tax assets and liabilities. Heavy emphasis is placed on the reversal of temporary differences and the currently enacted future income tax rates.

Alternative Methods to Comprehensive Allocation

Generally accepted accounting principles require that deferred income tax accounts include the tax effects of *all* temporary differences between financial and taxable income. This procedure, often referred to as *comprehensive income tax allocation,* is a well-established accounting practice. Several alternatives have been suggested, however, that warrant at least brief mention before we leave the subject of deferred taxes arising from temporary differences.

One alternative to comprehensive allocation is **partial allocation.** Partial allocation assumes that for a particular period income tax expense should be the same as income tax payable except for the impact of *nonrecurring* temporary differences. Proponents of partial allocation reason that recurring differences between financial income and taxable income, such as those resulting from depreciation, give rise to the *indefinite* postponement of income taxes, and thus the recognition of the tax effects of such recurring temporary differences should *not* be required. For example, a company may engage in a continuous investment policy in plant assets, coupled with the use of accelerated write-off for income tax purposes, and straight-line depreciation for financial reporting purposes. The reversal of temporary differences (when the tax write-off falls below straight-line depreciation on older assets) is offset by the origination of temporary differences (when the tax write-off exceeds straight-line depreciation on newer assets). The net effect is that income taxes on temporary differences

"TRY IT, YOU'LL LIKE IT"

It's a little-understood peculiarity of U.S. business that the books corporations keep for the taxmen are different from the books the same corporations present to investors. Out of this fact comes the concept of the deferred tax liability, which is the amount a company tells investors it owes in taxes. The amount it actually hands the IRS, however, is different. Since capital investments can allow a company to put off a good hunk of its taxes, the deferred tax item can amount to a tidy sum. These liabilities are shown in every annual report, and they are highly controversial.

Accountants point out that although deferred tax liabilities are supposed to represent taxes a company may owe in the future, in practice these taxes are often never paid. What happens is that as businesses grow and make more tax-credit-generating capital investments, deferred taxes mount accordingly. IBM, for example, has some $212 million in deferred taxes, General Motors has $146 million and General Electric $79 million.

Companies grumble because one effect of the current system is to put money into deferred tax accounts that really should flow through earnings and be added to stockholders' equity. And the Financial Accounting Standards Board says the current method of accounting for deferred tax liabilities doesn't square with its general concept of what liabilities are. As a result, it is working on a new way of dealing with the subject—something that experts say is among its most important projects of the decade.

It just might be possible to get a glimpse at the future. Immense deferred tax liabilities may be relatively new in the U.S., but British corporations have long had massive deferred tax accounts. "Sometimes the whole of a company's net equity was no larger than its deferred tax balance," says Michael Carey, a British partner with Ernst & Whinney. "Everyone knew that the vast bulk of those deferred tax balances would never be payable, and people began to say that the system didn't make sense because these deferred taxes being booked as liabilities were not real liabilities."

So, about five years ago, when the U.K. reached the point the U.S. is reaching today, accountants decided to change the way of dealing with taxes that may never actually be paid. Under the new British system, if a company can demonstrate with reasonable assurance that its deferred taxes will be deferred indefinitely, it doesn't have to provide for them in its financial reports.

Whether or not a deferred tax will ever be paid can be difficult to prove, but the British have allowed companies to use their capital spending budgets and conservative profit projections to provide an assurance that these bills will be deferred forever. What happens then? "Substantial chunks of deferred taxes on balance sheets were released into shareholder equity," says Carey. "And deferred tax balances came down to a much more realistic figure."

For a hint at how U.S. financial reports could change with a new method for figuring deferred taxation, look at Grand Metropolitan Ltd., the London-based brewery, liquor and food corporation that, in 1980, acquired Liggett Group. That deal carried with it $5.7 million in deferred taxes that showed up on Liggett's U.S. books. But Grand Met on consolidation got to put nearly all of this amount into shareholders' equity. According to British rules, "It wasn't foreseeable that Liggett would have to pay any of that tax to the U.S. government," says Robert Mitchell, Grand Met's controller.

Naturally, this is a less conservative system than one that assumes all deferred taxes will have to be paid. And under it some companies may not report deferred taxes that eventually turn into real liabilities. Nonetheless, the U.K. approach is still clearly more accurate than the current U.S. treatment, which soberly maintains that every last cent of these taxes will eventually be paid.

The result, of course, is that under British rules Grand Met and Liggett look like far healthier companies than they would if they were based in the U.S.

Depressing. First *Masterpiece Theatre*, and now this.

SOURCE: Janet Bamford, "Try It, You'll Like It," *Forbes*, June 6, 1983, p. 162. Reprinted by permission of *Forbes* magazine, June 6, 1983. © Forbes Inc., 1983.

are continuously deferred and effectively never paid. Temporary differences from depreciation then take on the characteristics of permanent differences.

Proponents of partial allocation believe that only **nonrecurring** temporary differences between financial income and taxable income should give rise to deferred income taxes. Because the reversal of a nonrecurring difference is not expected to be offset by the origination of another difference (due to the nonrecurring nature of the revenue or expense), income tax expense may be materially misstated if the tax effects of the temporary difference are ignored. Under partial allocation the income tax expense of the period is increased or decreased by income taxes on nonrecurring temporary differences that can reasonably be expected to affect taxable income in the foreseeable future. A five-year period has been suggested as an appropriate time frame for the application of this concept.[6]

Materiality

Another alternative is **nonallocation** of income tax. Within this relatively simple method, the total of income tax paid during the period and payable at the end of the period would constitute income tax expense, regardless of differences in methods of recognizing revenues and expenses in the financial statements as compared with the tax return. Because this approach omits deferred income tax assets and liabilities from the balance sheet, some accountants question its appropriateness. On the other hand, historically the methods of determining income for financial reporting and income tax purposes were quite similar. Some accountants feel that the two have gradually drifted so far apart that attempting to link them together via the recognition of deferred tax assets and liabilities is no longer appropriate.

One final issue concerning interperiod income tax allocation is whether deferred income taxes should be *discounted* and reported in the balance sheet at their present value. We have not discounted deferred income taxes in the illustrations in this chapter. Present authoritative accounting pronouncements indicate that deferred income taxes should *not* be discounted to their present value in measuring the elements of financial statements.[7] The FASB is currently studying the broad issue of discounting in the financial statements, including discounting deferred income taxes. We may see change in this area when that study is completed. If discounting were required, it would likely have a material effect on the financial statements of those companies that carefully manage their income taxes so that significant amounts are indefinitely deferred to future periods.

Materiality

INTRAPERIOD INCOME TAX ALLOCATION

Intraperiod income tax allocation refers to the allocation of the total income tax expense recognized in an accounting period among the various components of income and changes in stockholders' equity recognized during that same period. Earlier chapters explain that certain items are granted special treatment in financial reporting, including presentation on a net-of-tax basis. These include, but are not limited to, the following items:

1. **Extraordinary items.** Presented in a separate income statement category immediately preceding the income statement amount, "net income."
2. **Prior period adjustments.** Presented as adjustments to beginning retained earnings of the period in which the correction or other adjustment is made.

---

[6]*APB Opinion No. 11*, par. 27.
[7]*APB Opinion No. 10*, "Omnibus Opinion—1966," 1966, par. 6.

In discussing intraperiod income tax allocation, we refer to these as "special items."[8] Intraperiod income tax allocation is a problem of **financial-statement presentation**. It does not affect the total *amount* of income tax expense recognized during a period; rather, it involves the manner of presentation of income tax expense in the various sections of the income statement and the retained earnings statement.

Intraperiod income tax allocation requires the presentation of special items on a **net-of-tax basis**. The rationale underlying this requirement is that for disclosure of special items to be complete, separate presentation requires that they be on a net-of-tax basis in order to maintain the appropriate relationship between the various elements of income and stockholders' equity. The income tax effect of special items are computed by determining the amount of income tax expense that would be recognized **with and without the special item**. The difference **between** these two tax amounts is the tax effect of the special item.

EXAMPLES OF INTRAPERIOD ALLOCATION

Several situations involving the application of intraperiod income tax allocation procedures may be encountered. These involve situations of income or loss before income tax, combined with one or both of the special items described earlier. In the following examples, three representative situations are illustrated.

Three companies, Red, White, and Blue, are currently determining the appropriate financial-statement presentation of income tax expense for 1992. During the year the companies reported the following information:

	Income (Loss) Before Income Tax and Special Item	Special Items	Basis for Computing Total Tax
Red Company	$ 20,000	$27,000 extra-ordinary gain	$47,000
White Company	35,000	$(15,000) extra-ordinary loss	20,000
Blue Company	(30,000)	$42,000 positive correction of error	12,000

The appropriate income tax rate on all items is assumed to be 35%.

The amount presented as income tax expense is based on income before income tax and special items. For example, in the case of Red Company, the income before income tax and special item is $20,000; the extraordinary gain is $27,000, resulting in $47,000 as the basis for computing total income tax expense. The total income tax is separated into two components for presentation in the financial statements: (1) the portion associated with income before the special item and (2) the portion associated with the special item. The line-item "income tax expense" in the income statement represents the aggregate income tax effect of all items included in income (loss) before income tax and the special item and is determined as if the special item did not exist; the special item is then presented on a net-of-tax basis. This process is illustrated for the three companies in Exhibit 18–3.

---

[8]In later chapters additional items are covered that also require separate presentation in the financial statements on a net-of-tax basis. These include (1) discontinued operations when a business has disposed of one of its segments, and (2) the cumulative effect of a change in an accounting principle. The application of intraperiod income tax allocation to those items is similar to the application to extraordinary items and prior period adjustments illustrated in this chapter.

EXHIBIT 18–3

Examples of Intraperiod Income Tax Allocation

Red Company—Extraordinary Gain

Total income tax to be recognized ($47,000 × 35%)	$ 16,450
Less: Income tax expense associated with income before extraordinary gain ($20,000 × 35%)	7,000
Additional income tax associated with extraordinary gain	$ 9,450

Red Company
PARTIAL INCOME STATEMENT
For the Year Ended December 31, 1992

Income before income taxes and extraordinary item	$ 20,000
Income tax expense	7,000
Income before extraordinary gain	13,000
Extraordinary gain, net of $9,450 income tax expense	17,550
Net income	$ 30,550

White Company—Extraordinary Loss

Total income tax to be recognized ($20,000 × 35%)	$ 7,000
Less: Income tax expense associated with income before extraordinary loss ($35,000 × 35%)	12,250
Reduction in income tax associated with extraordinary loss	$ (5,250)

White Company
PARTIAL INCOME STATEMENT
For the Year Ended December 31, 1992

Income before income taxes and extraordinary item	$ 35,000
Income tax expense	12,250
Income before extraordinary loss	22,750
Extraordinary loss, net of $5,250 income tax savings	(9,750)
Net income	$ 13,000

Blue Company—Prior Period Adjustment

Total income tax to be recognized ($12,000 × 35%)	$ 4,200
Plus: Income tax savings associated with loss before considering prior period adjustment ($30,000 × 35%)	10,500
Additional income tax associated with correction of error	$ 14,700

Blue Company
PARTIAL INCOME STATEMENT
For the Year Ended December 31, 1992

Loss before income taxes	$(30,000)
Income tax savings	10,500
Net loss	$(19,500)

The correction of error is presented in the retained earnings statement as a positive adjustment to the beginning balance. The amount of this adjustment is $27,300, which represents the $42,000 positive adjustment, net of $14,700 income tax associated with that item.

In all three cases, we see that the income tax effect of the special item is computed by comparing the income tax to be recognized with and without the special item and allocating the difference to the special item. If a single income tax rate applies to all items subject to income tax, this computation is simplified, because the income tax associated with each item can be computed directly, as follows for Red, White, and Blue Companies:

Red Company:	$27,000 × 35% = $9,450	Additional income taxes associated with extraordinary gain.
White Company:	$15,000 × 35% = $5,250	Reduction in income taxes associated with extraordinary loss.
Blue Company:	$42,000 × 35% = $14,700	Additional income taxes associated with prior period adjustment.

COMPLICATIONS IN APPLYING INTRAPERIOD ALLOCATION

Several complications may be encountered in applying the principles of intraperiod income tax allocation. We will next look at the determination of the tax effect of a special item with differential tax rates.

Green Company determines its income to be $20,000 before an extraordinary gain of $16,000 and before income taxes. Appropriate income tax rates are 25% on the first $25,000 of income and 38% on all income in excess of $25,000. The determination of the income tax expense, the income tax associated with the extraordinary gain, and the related income statement presentation at December 31, 1992 are presented in Exhibit 18–4. The direct computation of the income tax associated with the extraordinary gain is more complex in this case, because all income is not taxed at the same rate. We determine the income tax effect of the extraordinary item by applying

---

EXHIBIT 18–4

Example of Intraperiod Income Tax Allocation: Differential Income Tax Rates

Green Company

Total income tax expense		
$25,000 × 25%	$6,250	
11,000 × 38%	4,180	$ 10,430
$36,000		
Income tax expense associated with income before extraordinary item		
($20,000 × 25%)		(5,000)
Additional income tax expense associated with extraordinary gain		$ 5,430

Green Company
PARTIAL INCOME STATEMENT
For the Year Ended December 31, 1992

Income before income taxes and extraordinary item	$ 20,000
Income tax expense	5,000
Income before extraordinary gain	15,000
Extraordinary gain, net of $5,430 income tax expense	10,570
Net income	$ 25,570

the **marginal tax rate(s)**. This simply means that the extraordinary gain is considered to come *after* the income before extraordinary items and, therefore, is subject to the marginal income tax rates applicable. For Green Company the income tax effect of the extraordinary gain can be computed by applying the marginal income tax rates as follows:

Taxable at 38%

$36,000 − $25,000 = $11,000

$11,000 × 38%   = $4,180

Taxable at 25%

$16,000 − $11,000 = $ 5,000

$5,000 × 25%   =   1,250

Income tax applicable to special item $5,430

As we stated earlier and as you can see in the preceding examples, intraperiod income tax allocation deals with the presentation of income tax expense in the financial statements, not the measurement of the total amount of that expense. If distinctively different types of income items (e.g., normal operations, extraordinary items, and prior period adjustments) are presented in the financial statements, the total income tax expense must also be separated into parts for presentation in those statements.

The existence of more than one special item in the same accounting period presents another complication in determining the tax related to special items. For example, a company might have both an extraordinary item and a prior period adjustment. In this situation the income tax effect of the two or more special items is determined as a single amount by computing the amount of income tax without *any* of the special items and comparing it with the amount of income tax including *all* of the special items. The difference between these two amounts, representing the tax effect of all special items in the aggregate, is then allocated among the individual items. This allocation is based on the ratio of the amount of each special item to the total of all special items.

CONCLUDING REMARKS

Income taxes have a significant impact on the financial position and results of operations of business enterprises. Accounting for income taxes represents a unique blend of accounting principles and legal compliance.

The presentation of income taxes in this chapter has intentionally simplified certain aspects of income tax law and omitted others in order to focus on the *financial reporting of income taxes*. Moreover, the income tax implications of certain financial reporting topics that are beyond the scope of intermediate accounting (e.g., business combinations and foreign currency translation) have not been presented. Current GAAP require that we carefully measure the amount of income tax assets and liabil-

Going
Concern

ities that a company has within the framework of the going-concern assumption and accrual accounting principles. Based on the amounts of those assets and liabilities, we may determine the amount of the company's income tax expense. This emphasis on the balance sheet represents a change from the income statement orientation of earlier authoritative pronouncements issued by the APB.

The specific standards of accounting for income taxes will undoubtedly continue to evolve as income tax laws change, new situations emerge that give rise to temporary differences, and the conceptual basis for financial statements becomes more clearly determined by the FASB through interpretation of its conceptual framework. The authors believe it is reasonable to expect continuing change and refinement in this important and pervasive area of financial reporting as managers, corporate accountants, and auditors learn more about the implementation problems of accounting for income taxes under current and future authoritative accounting pronouncements.

KEY POINTS

1. The elements of financial statements related to income taxes are unlike other elements in the financial statements because their recognition and measurement are strongly affected by income tax law. (Objective 1)

2. Two areas in which income tax law has a particularly important impact on the elements of the financial statements are operating loss carrybacks and carryforwards and temporary differences between financial and taxable income. (Objective 2)

3. Operating loss carrybacks and carryforwards allow the loss of one year to be used to reduce income taxes that have already been paid (carrybacks) or that will otherwise have to be paid in the future (carryforwards). The benefits of carrybacks are recognized in the loss year because they give rise to immediate refund claims from the government. Accounting for loss carryforwards is a matter of current debate in the accounting profession. (Objective 3)

4. Temporary differences between pretax financial income and taxable income give rise to deferred tax assets and liabilities. The going-concern assumption is important in justifying the inclusion of certain future income tax events in the financial statements. (Objective 4)

5. The tax effects of temporary differences are projected into the future and income taxes payable or receivable are calculated based on enacted tax rates. No assumption is made about other revenue and expense transactions of the future which may affect income taxes payable. (Objective 4)

6. Current GAAP require the recognition of deferred tax assets and liabilities for all temporary differences. Several alternative methods exist, including partial allocation and non-allocation. (Objective 5)

7. Intraperiod income tax allocation is required in order to report special income-related transactions, such as extraordinary items and prior period adjustments, in the financial statements on a net-of-tax basis. (Objective 6)

APPENDIX A: CURRENT FASB STANDARDS

In 1987, the FASB issued *Statement of Financial Accounting Standards No. 96*, "Accounting for Income Taxes." This pronouncement was intended to make sweeping changes in how income taxes are accounted for in the financial statements. For reasons explained later, *SFAS No. 96* was replaced before it was ever required to be implemented by *SFAS No. 109*, also titled "Accounting for Income Taxes." The principles of accounting for income taxes explained earlier in this chapter are generally consistent with *SFAS No. 96* and *SFAS No. 109*. We have, however, simplified aspects of accounting for income taxes and avoided certain complexities in order to focus on fundamental principles. The purpose of this appendix is to give more in-depth insight into current FASB standards in this important area.

The FASB originally intended for *SFAS No. 96* to become effective for fiscal years beginning after December 15, 1988. Reaction from business and public accounting

was so strong, however, that the effective date of *SFAS No. 96* was delayed three times.[9] *SFAS No. 96* was subsequently replaced by *SFAS No. 109*, effective for fiscal years beginning after December 15, 1992. Criticisms of *SFAS No. 96* focused on complexity in applying the standard and conceptual flaws related to overly restrictive criteria for recognizing deferred tax assets. Because both *SFAS No. 96* and *SFAS No. 109* are important for an understanding of accounting for income taxes and will be applied in practice during the life of this textbook edition, we cover both in this appendix.

---

[9]*SFAS No. 100*, "Accounting for Income Taxes—Deferral of the Effective Date of FASB Statement No. 96," 1988; *SFAS No. 103*, "Accounting for Income Taxes—Deferral of the Effective Date of FASB Statement No. 96," 1989; *SFAS No. 108*, "Accounting for Income Taxes—Deferral of the Effective Date of FASB Statement No. 96," 1991.

SFAS NO. 96

SFAS No. 96 requires an approach called "scheduling" in which each future year is individually considered in valuing deferred tax assets and liabilities. This is more complex than the approach taken earlier in this chapter in which all future years were combined and treated as a single time period. The reversal of taxable and deductible temporary differences are projected by year, and taxable income or loss from those items is computed for each year. Enacted tax rates and other aspects of tax law, such as recognition of loss carryback and carryforward rules, are applied. Amounts of deferred taxes are then aggregated for all future years to determine the total amounts of deferred tax assets and liabilities. An important requirement of *SFAS No. 96* is that no future income is assumed, other than that projected from the reversal of temporary differences that already exist.

SFAS No. 96 requires the amount of deferred income to be adjusted when changes in income tax rates are enacted:

> *This statement requires that a deferred tax liability or asset be adjusted in the period of enactment for the effect of an enacted change in tax laws or rates. A change in tax laws or rates is an event that has economic consequences for an enterprise. An enterprise's financial condition improves if it owes a smaller amount of taxes or if it would receive a larger refund. Its financial condition weakens if the enterprise owes more taxes or would receive a smaller refund.*[10]

The tax effects of temporary differences are established in the accounts when the differences originate by using enacted tax rates that are expected to be in effect when the amounts are expected to enter taxable income. If different income tax rates are enacted between the time a temporary difference originates and later reverses, an adjustment to the amount of deferred income taxes is required.

Example: Applying *SFAS No. 96*

We now consider the case of Rothchild, Inc., a company that has two temporary differences: depreciation and litigation. Depreciation of $10,000 is a taxable temporary difference; that amount is expected to reverse over the next five years at $2,000 per year. In 1992, a litigation loss of $5,500 was recognized on an estimated basis in determining financial income; this is a deductible temporary difference that will result in a tax deduction when the litigation is complete, which is expected to be in 1996. Enacted income tax rates are 35% for 1992 and 1993, 33% for 1994 and 1995, and 32% for all years after 1995.

Exhibit 18–5 demonstrates the scheduling requirement of *SFAS No. 96*. For purposes of this illustration, we assume that pretax financial income for 1992 is $25,000. Each year's activity is projected and an amount of annual "net taxable income" is determined. The enacted tax rate is applied for each year to determine the amount of current (1992) or deferred (1993–1997) income tax payable.

Observe that in 1996 the difference between the two temporary differences is a *negative* $3,500, indicating a net deductible rather than a net taxable amount. Recall that under *SFAS No. 96* we are assuming that the temporary differences are the only income items for the future years; we are making no assumptions about other revenues and expenses that will enter taxable income. Taking the $5,500 litigation loss into taxable income in 1996 results in a *loss* of $3,500 after offset by the $2,000 temporary difference for depreciation. *SFAS No. 96* requires that we carry back this assumed $3,500 loss, as we did a net

EXHIBIT 18–5

Rothchild, Inc.
Analysis of Current and Deferred Income Taxes

	1992	1993	1994	1995	1996	1997
Pretax financial income	$ 25,000	—	—	—	—	—
Temporary differences:						
Depreciation	(10,000)	$ 2,000	$ 2,000	$ 2,000	$ 2,000	$2,000
Litigation loss	5,500	—	—	—	(5,500)	—
Net taxable (deductible)						
amount before carryback	$ 20,500	$ 2,000	$ 2,000	$ 2,000	$(3,500)	$2,000
Carryback	—	(2,000)	(1,500)	—	3,500	—
Net taxable income	$ 20,500	—	$ 500	$ 2,000	—	$2,000
Income tax rate	35%	35%	33%	33%	32%	32%
Income tax payable:						
Current	$ 7,175					
Deferred			$ 165	$ 660		$ 640

---

[10]*Statement of Financial Accounting Standards No. 96*, Summary.

operating loss in the earlier discussion of loss carrybacks and carryforwards. The amount is carried back three years and applied to the earliest year first; $2,000 is offset against the taxable amount in 1993 and $1,500 against the taxable amount in 1994 ($3,500 − $2,000 = $1,500). This eliminates the projected deductible amount in 1996 and offsets all of the projected income in 1993 and $1,500 of the projected income in 1994. The remaining taxable income in 1994 and income taxable in 1995 and 1997 are then calculated and multiplied by applicable income tax rates to determine the amount of deferred income tax at the end of 1992. The year-end accrual for income tax is as follows:

Dec. 31, 1992	Income Tax Expense	8,640	
	($7,175 + $1,465)		
	Income Tax Payable		7,175
	($20,500 × 35%)		
	Deferred Income Tax		1,465
	($165 + $660 + $640)		

In this example, we have seen the interaction of two temporary differences and the technique of carrying back the deductible amount to offset taxes that would otherwise be payable in earlier years.

In the authors' opinion, one of the significant problems of implementing the asset/liability method under *SFAS No. 96* is the difficulty of anticipating the expected reversal of temporary differences. The timing of the reversal of temporary differences, as well as the dollar amount of those differences, may be difficult to anticipate in practice, but they have a very significant impact on the elements of the financial statements under *SFAS No. 96*. A significant question also arises about the nature of deferred taxes over long periods of time. Empirical research into the behavior of deferred tax credits appears to support the argument that deferred taxes arising from recurring temporary differences, namely depreciation, tend to increase over time rather than decrease as those differences reverse. Davidson, Skelton, and Weil studied 3,108 companies for a 19-year period (1954–1955 through 1972–1973). In their study 18,184 changes in the deferred tax credit accounts were identified, 14,288 (79%) of which were increases and only 3,896 (21%) of which were decreases. Furthermore, the increases amounted to $39.5 billion while the decreases amounted to only $5.9 billion.[11] Studies such as this lend support for the notion that recurring differences between pretax financial income and taxable income give rise to the *indefinite postponement* of income taxes rather than temporary postponement that will reverse in the foreseeable future.

The scheduling requirement of *SFAS No. 96,* which is illustrated in the example we have just covered, was one

of the major criticisms of that pronouncement. Companies that adopted *SFAS No. 96* early, as well as those that experimented with its implementation without adopting it, reported that individual-year projections were difficult and costly to make. In addition, the restrictive rules concerning the recognition of deferred tax assets could result in financial statement distortions. Let's return to the example in Exhibit 18–5 to better understand the nature of the restrictive deferred tax asset recognition criteria of *SFAS No. 96*. Had the litigation loss been $9,000 instead of $5,500, the taxable income (loss) before carryback would have been $(7,000) and the entire taxable income during the three-year carryback period would have been eliminated ($2,000 each for 1993, 1994, and 1995). In addition, $1,000 would have been available for carryforward recognition in the scheduling process. This would reduce net taxable income of 1997 to $1,000 and the only deferred taxes would be $320: $1,000 × 32% = $320. What if the litigation loss had been $13,000? The taxable income (loss) before carryback would have been $11,000, $6,000 of which could be carried back against the reversal of the taxable temporary difference (depreciation) at $2,000 per year for 1993, 1994, and 1995. An additional $2,000 would then be carried forward against the reversal of the depreciation temporary difference in 1997, but the tax benefit of the remaining $3,000 ($11,000 − $8,000) could not be recognized under *SFAS No. 96*. That pronouncement limits the recognition of deferred tax assets on deductible temporary differences, like the litigation loss, to the amount of taxable temporary differences expected to reverse in the same accounting period. In the situation just described, because there are no known taxable temporary differences available, the last $3,000 of the deductible temporary difference for litigation could not be recognized.

When *SFAS No. 96* was first issued, some companies adopted it early. As the effective date of *SFAS No. 96* was delayed three times, and it became apparent that the FASB would replace the pronouncement in time, the number of companies adopting it slowed. The 1991 edition of *Accounting Trends & Techniques* reports accounting changes for 600 companies for the four-year period from 1987–1990. A total of 182 changes classified as "income taxes" were reported:[12]

1987	37
1988	98
1989	31
1990	16
	182

While these changes are not identified solely as relating to the adoption of *SFAS No. 96*, it is reasonable to assume

[11]Sidney Davidson, Lisa Skelton, and Roman L. Weil, "A Controversy Over the Expected Behavior of Deferred Tax Credits," *Journal of Accountancy* (April 1977), p. 53.

[12]*Accounting Trends & Techniques* (New York: AICPA, 1991), p. 43.

that most, if not all, of the changes are for that reason. The following conclusions can be drawn from this information: (1) approximately 30% (182/600 = 30.3%) of the reporting companies adopted *SFAS No. 96* early during this four-year period; (2) the pace of companies changing to *SFAS No. 96* slowed as its effective date continued to be delayed and it became clear that the statement would eventually be replaced.

SFAS NO. 109

In *SFAS No. 109*, the FASB attempts to respond to the criticisms of *SFAS No. 96* and simplify the procedures required to account for income taxes. *SFAS No. 96* and *SFAS No. 109* have much in common, primarily that each requires the asset/liability method of accounting. *SFAS No. 109*, however, reduces the need to schedule each future year individually, and it relaxes the recognition criteria for deferred tax assets in comparison with *SFAS No. 96*.

SFAS No. 109 clearly places priority on the balance sheet when it indicates the following two objectives of accounting for income taxes:

1. To recognize the amount of *taxes payable or refundable* for the current year.
2. To recognize *deferred tax liabilities and assets* for the future tax consequences of events that have been recognized in the financial statements or tax returns.[13]

To implement these objectives, four basic principles are applied in accounting for income taxes under *SFAS No. 109*:

1. A tax liability or asset is recognized for the amount of taxes currently payable or receivable on the current year's tax returns.
2. A deferred tax liability or asset is recognized for the estimated future tax effects attributed to temporary differences and carryforwards.
3. The measurement of tax liabilities and assets is based on provisions of enacted tax law. The effects of future anticipated changes in tax law are not considered.
4. The measurement of deferred tax assets is reduced, if necessary, by the amount of any tax benefits that are not expected to be realized.[14]

Two important differences exist in these basic principles from those underlying *SFAS No. 96*. First, principle 2 *requires* the recognition of a deferred tax asset for all deductible temporary differences and carryforwards. This is a significant departure from the restrictive criteria for recognizing deferred tax assets in *SFAS No. 96* and reduces the need to schedule individual future years as required by *SFAS No. 96*. Second, principle 4 requires a reduction in the recorded amount of deferred tax assets

via valuation allowance to their lower, realizable value if it appears that some portion of those assets will not be realized. This procedure is similar to ones we have studied earlier in this text for reductions in receivables to net realizable value (i.e., allowance for uncollectible accounts), and reductions in inventories or marketable securities to an amount less than cost (i.e., allowance to reduce inventories [marketable securities] to the lower of cost or market).

At the end of each accounting period, the enterprise must calculate the amount of deferred tax liabilities and assets on the basis of cumulative temporary differences and carryforwards. This process involves completing the following steps:

1. Identify the types and amounts of all temporary differences and the amounts and remaining periods of all carryforwards.
2. Measure the total deferred tax liabilities based on taxable temporary differences, applying enacted tax law.
3. Measure the total deferred tax assets based on deductible temporary differences and carryforwards, applying enacted tax law.
4. Reduce the deferred tax assets by a valuation allowance if it is *more likely than not* that some portion of all of the deferred tax assets will not be realized.[15]

Applying the first three steps is similar to the examples we studied earlier in this chapter. The valuation allowance procedure of *SFAS No. 109* is a new requirement, which we will discuss later in this appendix.

Comprehensive Illustration

In the following comprehensive example, we illustrate many of the important aspects of *SFAS No. 109* by considering three consecutive years of Zorc Company with the assignment to prepare the year-end income tax accrual and income tax information for the company's financial statements. Zorc Company's first year of operations is 1992. During that year, the company reported $160,000 of pretax accounting income. Permanent and temporary differences are combined with pretax financial income to derive taxable income, as follows:

Pretax financial income	$160,000
Permanent differences:	
Interest on municipal securities	(5,000)
Pretax financial income subject to tax	$155,000
Temporary differences:	
Depreciation	(28,000)
Warranties	10,000
Revenue received in advance	7,000
Taxable income	$144,000

---

[13]*SFAS No. 109*, par. 6.
[14]*SFAS No. 109*, par. 8.

[15]*SFAS No. 109*, par. 17.

The $5,000 interest on municipal securities represents nontaxable income and the $28,000 depreciation temporary difference represents the excess of accelerated write-off for tax purposes over straight-line depreciation for financial reporting purposes. Warranties are expensed at the time of sale on an estimated basis, but deductible for income tax purposes only when paid. In 1992, $10,000 more was accrued than paid. Revenue received in advance is taxable at the time received, but deferred for financial reporting purposes until earned. In 1992, $7,000 was received that was not earned by year-end. Depreciation is a *taxable temporary difference* that reduces current tax payable and gives rise to a deferred tax liability. The warranties and revenue received in advance are *deductible temporary differences* that increase current tax payable and give rise to deferred tax assets (i.e., prepaid taxes).

Exhibit 18–6 presents analyses that facilitate the preparation of the year-end tax accrual, as well as information for the financial statements. We will use similar analyses for each of the three years in this example. The top analysis in Exhibit 18–6 simply "rolls forward" the amount of the temporary differences from the beginning to the end of the year. Since 1992 is the first year for Zorc Company, the beginning balances are all zero. The change column includes the amounts used in the previous calculation to determine taxable income from pretax accounting income. The numbers without brackets are deductible temporary differences; those in brackets are taxable temporary differences. The company is in a net taxable temporary difference position at the end of the year because the net amount of temporary differences is $(11,000), due to the relatively large amount of the depreciation difference.

The lower portion of Exhibit 18–6 converts the temporary differences in the top analysis to amounts of deferred income taxes based on those differences. Again, the beginning balances are zeroes and the ending balances are computed at 34%, the assumed income tax rate for 1992 in this illustration. Each ending balance is computed by multiplying the tax rate by the ending amount of the temporary difference (e.g., for depreciation, $28,000 \times 34\% = \$9,520$). The bracketed numbers are deferred tax liabilities, based on taxable temporary differences. The amounts without brackets are deferred tax assets, based on deductible temporary differences.

EXHIBIT 18–6

Zorc Company
ANALYSIS OF CUMULATIVE TEMPORARY DIFFERENCES AND DEFERRED TAXES
1992

Cumulative Temporary Differences (TD)

	Beginning Balance 1992	Change	Ending Balance 1992
Deductible TD			
Warranties	—0—	$ 10,000	$ 10,000
Revenue received in advance	—0—	7,000	7,000
(Taxable) TD			
Depreciation	—0—	(28,000)	(28,000)
	—0—	$(11,000)	$(11,000)

Deferred Income Taxes

	Beginning Balance @—%	Change	Ending Balance @34%	Classification Current	Classification Noncurrent
Assets					
Warranties	—0—	$3,400	$ 3,400		$ 3,400
Revenue received in advance	—0—	2,380	2,380	$2,380	
(Liabilities)					
Depreciation	—0—	(9,520)	(9,520)		(9,520)
	—0—	$(3,740)	$(3,740)	$2,380	$(6,120)

The classification columns on the right side of the lower analysis separate the ending balances into current and noncurrent for balance sheet classification purposes. This distinction is based on the asset or liability underlying the temporary difference. In this case, we assume that the warranty period is five years, so the related temporary difference is considered noncurrent, as is depreciation, because of the noncurrent classification of the underlying plant assets. We further assume that the revenue received in advance is expected to be earned in the coming period and, thus, is a current liability.

The December 31, 1992 entry to record the income tax accrual for Zorc Company is as follows:

Dec. 31, 1992	Income Tax Expense		
	($48,960 + $3,740)	52,700	
	Deferred Income		
	Tax—Current	2,380	
	Income Tax Payable		
	($144,000 × 34%)		48,960
	Deferred Income Tax—		
	Noncurrent		6,120

Notice that the amounts of Deferred Income Tax—Current and Noncurrent are taken from the lower analysis in Exhibit 18–6. The Income Tax Payable is determined by multiplying the $144,000 taxable income by the 34% tax rate. An important point to understand is the way Income Tax Expense is determined—it is the net of the other three numbers and can only be computed after the remaining elements of the entry have been determined. Referring again to the analysis of deferred income taxes in the lower section of Exhibit 18–6, the change in deferred taxes is a $3,740 increase in the net liability (total of the change column). That is the net of the increases in the noncurrent liability and the current asset for deferred taxes: $(6,120) − $2,380 = $(3,740).

An important step to complete before moving to 1993 is a proof of our numbers that is commonly referred to as a "statutory rate reconciliation." In this procedure, the product of the pretax financial income and the statutory tax rate is reconciled to the income tax expense for the period. For Zorc Company for 1992, this calculation is as follows:

Pretax financial income @ statutory rate	
($160,000 × 34%)	$54,400
Less: Permanent differences	
($5,000 × 34%)	(1,700)
Income tax expense	$52,700

The tax effect of the permanent differences is the only reconciling item for 1992. Even though the interest is included in pretax accounting income, it is not subject to tax and that alone accounts for the difference between $54,400 and the income tax expense of $52,700.

We will look at how the balance sheet and income statement are affected by these calculations after we have completed all three years of analysis.

Zorc Company's second year of operations is 1993, in which pretax financial income is $150,000. Municipal interest is $12,000 and temporary differences for depreciation and warranties are $(35,000) and $12,000, respectively. Of the revenue received in advance in 1992, $5,000 is earned and an additional $9,000 is received in 1993 that is expected to be earned in 1994. A new temporary difference is the litigation loss that results from the $10,000 accrual on an estimated basis for accounting purposes. This loss will be deductible for tax purposes when the suit is settled, which is expected in 1994.

Taxable income is determined as follows for 1993:

Pretax financial income	$150,000
Permanent difference:	
Interest on municipal securities	(12,000)
Pretax financial income subject to tax	$138,000
Temporary differences:	
Depreciation *—total difference*	($35,000)
Warranties	12,000
Revenue received in advance	
($9,000 − $5,000)	4,000
Litigation loss	10,000
Taxable income	$129,000

Exhibit 18–7 includes an analysis for 1993 similar to the 1992 analysis in Exhibit 18–6 for Zorc Company. Notice that the ending balances of both cumulative temporary differences and deferred income taxes from 1992 become the beginning balances for 1993. We also assume that during 1993, new tax legislation increases the income tax rate for 1993 and all future years to 40%. The amounts in Exhibit 18–7 are simply moved forward for one additional year. In both analyses in Exhibit 18–7, the columns identified as "Change" are forced or "plugged" by determining the amount of change required to move the beginning balance to the desired ending balance. The litigation loss is classified as current because of its expected settlement in 1994.

The entry to record income taxes at the end of 1993 is as follows:

Dec. 31, 1993	Income Tax Expense		
	($51,600 + $4,260)	55,860	
	Deferred Income		
	Tax—Current		
	($8,400 − $2,380)	6,020	
	Income Tax Payable		
	($129,000 × 40%)		51,600
	Deferred Income		
	Tax—Noncurrent		
	($16,400 − $6,120)		10,280

Notice that the debits and credits to Deferred Income Tax—Current and Noncurrent, respectively, are calculated as the changes in those accounts. We did not have to deal with that consideration in 1992 because it was the

EXHIBIT 18–7

Zorc Company
ANALYSIS OF CUMULATIVE TEMPORARY DIFFERENCES
AND DEFERRED TAXES
1993

Cumulative Temporary Differences (TD)

	Beginning Balance 1993	Change	Ending Balance 1993
Deductible TD			
Warranties	$ 10,000	$ 12,000	$22,000
Revenue received in advance	7,000	4,000	11,000
Litigation	—0—	10,000	10,000
(Taxable) TD			
Depreciation	(28,000)	(35,000)	(63,000)
	$(11,000)	$ (9,000)	$(20,000)

Deferred Income Taxes

	Beginning Balance @34%	Change	Ending Balance @40%	Classification Current	Noncurrent
Assets					
Warranties	$ 3,400	$ 5,400	$ 8,800		$8,800
Revenue received in advance	2,380	2,020	4,400	$4,400	
Litigation loss	—0—	4,000	4,000	$4,000	
(Liabilities)					
Depreciation	(9,520)	(15,680)	(25,200)		(25,200)
	$(3,740)	$(4,260)	$(8,000)	$8,400	$(16,400)

(handwritten notes): New Balances; Journal Entry → 2380 6020 ↑Asset; 6120 Old; 102800 ↑Liability

company's first year. The desired ending balances of current and noncurrent deferred income taxes from Exhibit 18–7 are compared with the balances from Exhibit 18–6 and the differences debited or credited into the deferred tax accounts, as appropriate, to produce the desired ending balances. For example, Deferred Income Tax—Noncurrent must have a credit (liability) balance of $16,400 at the end of 1993. The account began with a credit balance of $6,120, requiring a credit of $10,280 in the year-end tax accrual. Similarly, the required debit (asset) balance for Deferred Income Taxes—Current is $8,400; with a debit balance of $2,380 at the end of 1992, the adjustment is $6,020 ($8,400 – $2,380). This illustrates the basic approach of the asset/liability method of accounting for income taxes—the desired balance sheet figures are first determined and the expense is recognized in the amount required to meet the balance sheet objective.

The statutory reconciliation has an additional component in 1993, due to the tax rate change from 34% to 40%. This change has the effect of increasing deferred taxes and, therefore, tax expense, as indicated in the following reconciliation:

Pretax financial income @ statutory rate ($150,000 × 40%)	$60,000
Less: Permanent differences ($12,000 × 40%)	(4,800)
Plus: Tax increase on beginning cumulative temporary differences [$11,000 × (40% – 34%)]	660
Income tax expense	$55,860

Notice that the adjustment for the tax increase is calculated only for the beginning balance of cumulative temporary differences. The temporary differences originating in 1993 have already been taxed at 40%. As we indicated earlier, we will consider the balance sheet and income statement presentation of deferred tax information when we have completed our analysis of 1994.

We now turn our attention to the third year of our illustration of Zorc Company by considering 1994, a year in which the company's activities took a significant downturn. Due to negative economic trends and a loss of several important contracts, the company reported a pretax financial loss of $275,000. Interest earned on municipal securities was $15,000. Temporary differences consisted of the following: (1) write-off of plant assets for tax purposes exceeded depreciation expense by $40,000;

(2) warranty expense by the accrual method for accounting purposes exceeded amounts paid to honor warranty commitments by $18,000; (3) revenue of $10,000 received in advance that was previously taxed was recognized in accounting income and an additional $15,000 was received that was deferred for accounting purposes, but taxed currently; and (4) the litigation of 1993 was completed and the $10,000 loss was deducted for tax purposes.

An analysis of the pretax financial loss, permanent and temporary differences, and the amount of loss for tax purposes are analyzed as follows:

Pretax financial (loss)	$(275,000)
Permanent difference:	
Interest on municipal securities	(15,000)
Pretax financial (loss) subject to tax	$(290,000)
Temporary differences:	
Depreciation	(40,000)
Warranties	18,000
Revenue received in advance ($15,000 − $10,000)	5,000
Litigation loss	(10,000)
Taxable (loss)	$(317,000)

This analysis is similar to those for 1992 and 1993, except for the negative amount entered as pretax financial loss.

Notice that the loss for tax purposes is $317,000. We shall assume that Zorc Company decides to carry back the loss, to the extent possible and receives a refund for income taxes paid in the carryback period. From our discussion in this chapter, we know that a loss can be carried back three years. In this case, the company has only existed for two years, however, so the loss can only be carried back to 1992 and 1993. Remember, also, that in determining the amount of the refund, the tax rate in effect in the year to which the loss is carried back is used to calculate the amount of the refund. For Zorc Company for 1994, the amount of the refund to be received is $100,560:

1992	$144,000 × 34% =	$ 48,960
1993	$129,000 × 40% =	51,600
		$100,560

The determination of deferred tax balances in Exhibit 18–8 is similar to those in the two previous exhibits with those modifications necessary to include the loss carryforward of $44,000, which is determined by subtracting the amount of loss that is carried back from the total loss for tax purposes for 1994:

$$317,000 − (\$144,000 + \$129,000) = \$44,000$$

Notice in Exhibit 18–8 that a category for the loss carryforward has been added to the analysis at the top of the exhibit and the $44,000 1994 loss carryforward has been included. This item should be identified by year because other years may result in loss carryforwards and each year will have a different expiration year. The loss carryforward gives rise to a deferred tax asset, as indicated in the analysis at the bottom of Exhibit 18–8. We have classified this item as noncurrent on the assumption that, given the large loss encountered by Zorc Company in 1994, it will be several years before the company returns to profitable operations and is able to recognize the benefit of the loss carryforward. That item is treated in the same manner as a deductible temporary differences for purposes of determining deferred tax assets and liabilities.

The journal entry to record income taxes at the end of 1994 is as follows:

Dec. 31, 1994		
Receivable for Past Income Taxes		
[($144,000 × 34%) +		
($129,000 × 40%)]	100,560	
Deferred Income Tax—Noncurrent		
($16,400 − $7,600)	8,800	
Deferred Income Tax—Current		
($8,400 − $6,400)		2,000
Income Tax Benefit		
($100,560 + $6,800)		107,360

Comparing the two right columns in Exhibits 18–7 and 18–8, we see that the balances of both Deferred Income Taxes—Current (debit) and Deferred Income Taxes—Noncurrent (credit) declined from 1993 to 1994. The two most significant differences are the reversal of the temporary difference from the litigation loss and the inclusion of the loss carryforward, both of which are relatively large amounts.

Notice in the journal entry above that Income Tax Expense has been replaced by the account, Income Tax Benefit, which indicates the positive impact (loss reduction) resulting from using the 1994 loss to receive the refund of 1992 and 1993 income taxes and to offset income taxes that would otherwise have to be paid after 1994.

We can now prepare the statutory rate reconciliation, as follows:

Pretax financial (loss) at statutory rate [$(275,000) × 40%]	$(110,000)
Less: Permanent differences ($15,000 × 40%)	(6,000)
Plus: Loss carryback at 34% [$144,000 × (40% − 34%)]	8,640
Income tax (benefit)	$(107,360)

The last item in the reconciliation, identified as "Loss carryback at 34%," is required because the 1992 part of the carryback was determined at 34%, the 1992 income tax rate, rather than the current (1994) rate of 40%.

Now that we have completed our three-year analysis of cumulative temporary differences and the loss carryforward, the related deferred tax assets and liabilities, and

EXHIBIT 18-8

Zorc Company
ANALYSIS OF CUMULATIVE TEMPORARY DIFFERENCES
AND DEFERRED TAXES
1994

Cumulative Temporary Differences (TD) and Loss Carryforward

	Beginning Balance 1994	Change	Ending Balance 1994
Deductible TD			
Warranties	$ 22,000	$ 18,000	$ 40,000
Revenue received in advance	11,000	5,000	16,000
Litigation	10,000	(10,000)	—0—
(Taxable) TD			
Depreciation	(63,000)	(40,000)	(103,000)
Loss Carryforward			
1994 Loss*	—0—	44,000	44,000
	$(20,000)	$ 17,000	$ (3,000)

Deferred Income Taxes

	Beginning Balance @40%	Change	Ending Balance @40%	Classification Current	Classification Noncurrent
Assets					
Warranties	$ 8,800	$ 7,200	$16,000		$16,000
Revenue received in advance	4,400	2,000	6,400	$6,400	
Litigation	4,000	(4,000)	—0—		
Loss Carryforward	—0—	17,600	17,600		17,600
(Liabilities)					
Depreciation	(25,200)	(16,000)	(41,200)	_____	(41,200)
	$(8,000)	$ 6,800	$(1,200)	$6,400	$ (7,600)

*[$317,000 − ($144,000 + $129,000)]

the year-end journal entries to record income taxes, we can focus attention on the amounts that will be presented in the balance sheet and income statement. That information is presented in Exhibit 18-9. For each year, a portion of deferred taxes appears in the current asset section of the balance sheet. This amount represents the net amount of deferred taxes on temporary differences that are classified as current assets and liabilities in the balance sheet. In addition, in 1994, a current asset is presented for the $100,560 receivable of 1992 and 1993 taxes resulting from the 1994 carryback. For 1992 and 1993, a current liability is presented for income taxes payable—$48,960 and $51,600 in 1992 and 1993, respectively.

Among noncurrent liabilities, each year is a deferred tax amount that represents deferred taxes resulting from temporary differences classified as noncurrent and from the loss carryforward. The decline in the amount of noncurrent deferred taxes between 1993 and 1994 is due to the loss carryforward, which partially offsets the large deferred tax liability related to the depreciation temporary difference for the first time in 1994.

The income statement presentation each year displays pretax financial income (loss), followed by income tax expense (benefit), separated into current and deferred components. In 1992 and 1993, income tax expense reduces the amount of net income reported, as we would expect given the profitability reported by the company in those years. In 1994, however, the benefit of the carryback and carryforward results in a reduction in the amount of loss that would otherwise have been reported because of the refund of past taxes and the anticipation of reduced taxes in the future when the carryforward is realized.

EXHIBIT 18-9

Zorc Company
FINANCIAL STATEMENT PRESENTATION OF INCOME TAXES
1992–1994

Balance Sheet

	1992	1993	1994
Current Assets			
Receivable for Past Income Taxes	—	—	$100,560
Deferred Income Taxes	$ 2,380	$ 8,400	6,400
Current Liabilities			
Income Taxes Payable	48,960	51,600	—
Noncurrent Liabilities			
Deferred Income Taxes	6,120	16,400	7,600

Income Statement

	1992	1993	1994
Income (Loss) Before Income Tax	$160,000	$150,000	$(275,000)
Income Tax Expense (Benefit):			
Current	48,960	51,600	(100,560)
Deferred	3,740	4,260	6,800
	52,700	55,860	(107,360)
Net Income (Loss)	$107,300	$ 94,140	$(167,640)

Valuation Allowance

Earlier we identified one additional step in determining the items and amounts that are presented in the financial statements relative to income taxes: to determine if it is more likely than not that some or all of the deferred tax assets will not be realized and, if so, to recognize that decline in value via a valuation allowance. This is an important step in applying *SFAS No. 109* and requires a great deal of judgment on the part of the accountant.

Under *SFAS No. 109*, deferred tax assets are recorded for all deductible temporary differences and loss carryforwards. For these assets to be realized, future income, against which the deductible temporary differences and loss carryforwards can be offset, must exist. The decision concerning the need for and amount of a valuation allowance is, therefore, based on the evidence that there will or will not be sufficient income in the future to permit the recognition of the deferred tax assets.

Sources of future income, against which deductible temporary differences and loss carryforwards can be recognized, are as follows:[16]

1. Future reversals of existing taxable temporary differences.
2. Future taxable income from sources other than the reversals of existing temporary differences.
3. Tax-planning strategies.

Tax planning strategies are actions that could be taken for the specific purpose of recognizing the benefits of deferred tax assets. These actions must be prudent and feasible and, while management might not ordinarily take them, it would take them to prevent the loss of a deferred tax asset, such as the expiration of an unused loss carryforward. Examples are to accelerate the reversal of taxable temporary differences to offset a loss carryforward and to transfer dollars invested in tax-exempt investments into taxable investments for the same purpose.

Negative evidence may exist that implies a great deal of doubt concerning future income and, thus, the realizability of deferred tax assets. Examples include the following:[17]

- A series of net loss years
- A history of loss carryforwards expiring unused
- Losses projected in near future years
- Unsettled circumstances, such as lawsuits, which would adversely affect future operations and profitability if unfavorably resolved.
- A change in tax law resulting in a shortened carryforward period

On the other hand, evidence may exist that projects a much more positive picture and may lead to the decision that realization of deferred tax assets is likely and that a valuation allowance is not required:[18]

- A strong historical earnings history
- Existing contracts or other revenue-generating transactions that will produce future taxable income in

---

[16]*SFAS No. 109*, par. 21.

[17]*SFAS No. 109*, par 23.
[18]*SFAS No. 109*, par. 24.

sufficient quantities to permit realization of deferred tax assets
- Assets whose value exceeds their tax basis which, when realized, will result in significant future income

Management must use considered, professional judgment in determining the need for and amount of the valuation allowance. Because the decision is based on the predictability of future income, the decision is of necessity highly judgmental. Both positive and negative factors, such as those described above, must be carefully analyzed in making this important judgment.

To illustrate the accounting procedures required when a valuation allowance is established for deferred tax assets, we return to the Zorc Company illustration for 1994. We assume that, after careful consideration, management determines that it is more likely than not that 25% of the deferred tax assets will not be realized. This requires a valuation allowance of $10,000, determined as follows, based on information obtained from Exhibit 18–8:

Current Deferred Tax Assets		
Revenue received in advance		$ 6,400
Noncurrent Deferred Tax Assets		
Warranties	$16,000	
Loss carryforward	17,600	33,600
		$40,000
Valuation allowance:		
25% × $40,000		$10,000
Allocation to Current/Noncurrent:		
Current: ($6,400/$40,000) × $10,000		$ 1,600
Noncurrent: ($33,600/$40,000) × $10,000		8,400
		$10,000

This allocation results in a $1,600 *reduction* in the current deferred tax asset and a $8,400 *addition* to the net noncurrent deferred tax liability. In the following comparative analysis, the impact of the valuation allowance is determined as indicated in the right columns and is compared with the figures presented earlier without a valuation allowance in the left columns.

	Without Valuation Allowance	With Valuation Allowance
Current Deferred		
Tax Asset	$ 6,400	$ 6,400
Less: Allowance	—0—	(1,600)
	$ 6,400	$ 4,800
Noncurrent Deferred		
Tax Liability		
Asset component	$33,600	$ 33,600
Less: Allowance	—0—	(8,400)
	$33,600	$ 25,200
Liability component	(41,200)	(41,200)
Net noncurrent	$(7,600)	$(16,000)
Total deferred tax	$(1,200)	$(11,200)

Notice that the difference between the totals in the two columns is $10,000, exactly the amount of the valuation allowance.

The journal entry to record income taxes at the end of 1994 under these revised assumptions and including the valuation allowance, is as follows:

Dec. 31, 1994

Receivable for Past Income Taxes		
[($144,000 × 34%) +		
($129,000 × 40%)]	100,560	
Deferred Income Tax—Noncurrent		
($16,400 − $7,600)	8,800	
Allowance to Reduce Deferred Tax		
Assets to Lower Recoverable Value		10,000
Deferred Income Tax—Current		
($8,400 − $6,400)		2,000
Income Tax Benefit		
($100,560 + $6,800 − $10,000)		97,360

The statutory rate reconciliation for 1994, including the recognition of the valuation allowance, is as follows:

Pretax financial income (loss) at	
statutory rate [($275,000) × 40%]	$(110,000)
Less: Permanent differences	
($15,000 × 40%)	(6,000)
Plus: Loss carryback at 34%	
[$144,000 × (40% − 34%)]	8,640
Increase in valuation allowance	10,000
Income tax (benefit)	$ (97,360)

The valuation allowance will be evaluated at the end of each year, as is done with valuation allowances on other assets. At the end of 1995, for example, a determination will be made concerning the continuing need for the $10,000 valuation allowance and, if needed, the amount required to reduce deferred tax assets from their recorded amounts to their lower realizable value. At that time, the allowance will either be increased or reduced; reduction could result in the complete elimination of the allowance if positive evidence indicates that the value of the deferred tax assets are no longer impaired and the allowance is no longer required.

THE CURRENT SITUATION

The accounting profession currently finds itself in a very interesting situation relative to accounting for income taxes. *SFAS No. 96* was issued in 1987, but its effective date was delayed until the fiscal years beginning after December 15, 1992. The effective date of an FASB statement, however, is the *latest* date by which companies must have adopted the statement. Earlier adoption is encouraged and, in fact, many companies adopted *SFAS No. 96* early. Now the FASB has issued *SFAS No. 109,* also effective for fiscal years beginning after December 15, 1992, to replace *SFAS No. 96.* Companies that adopted *SFAS No. 96* early are changing from that pronouncement to *SFAS No. 109;* companies that did not adopt *SFAS No. 96* early are changing directly from *APB Opinion 11,* the authoritative pronouncement on accounting for income taxes before *SFAS No. 96,* to *SFAS No. 109.*

This series of events is unprecedented in standard setting in the United States. In 1992, we are in the unique position of having three sets of accounting standards in use at the same time: most companies reporting under *APB Opinion 11,* with some companies adopting *SFAS No. 96* or *SFAS No. 109* early. In 1993, practice is standardized because all companies are required to report under the new standards of *SFAS No. 109.*

This long and difficult process of changing accounting for income taxes demonstrates the significance of financial reporting standards and the seriousness with which management, CPAs, government bodies and other interested parties approach standard setting. Clearly, acceptance of FASB standards by these important groups is a significant part of the standard setting process. The phrase "generally accepted accounting principles" implies an acceptance of promulgated standards; if that acceptance does not exist, standard-setters find it difficult, if not impossible, to set standards that are then applied in practice.

FINANCIAL STATEMENT PRESENTATION

Disclosure

Throughout this textbook, we have identified disclosure requirements and illustrated the presentation of information in published financial statements of U.S. corporations. Because the disclosure requirements in both *SFAS No. 96* and *109* are quite long and include items that are beyond the scope of this text, we do not list all of them here. We complete our study, however, with Exhibit 18–10, which includes the 1990 note disclosure of Parker Hannifen Corporation relative to income taxes. The company adopted *SFAS No. 96* in 1988, so 1990 is the third year of reporting under that standard. This disclosure is typical of those found in the financial statements of companies that adopted *SFAS No. 96* and it is similar to disclosures required in *SFAS No. 109.* It includes a reconciliation of the statutory rate (34%) and the effective rate as well as a description of the temporary differences giving rise to deferred income taxes. Deferred income taxes, included among noncurrent liabilities in the balance sheet, total $53,424,000 in 1990, representing 2.6% of total liabilities and stockholders' equity.

EXHIBIT 18-10

Example Disclosure of Income Taxes

3. Income Taxes

Income taxes of continuing operations before extraordinary item and cumulative effect of changes in accounting principles include the following:

	1990	1989	1988
Federal	$22,151	$ 37,885	$ 49,913
Foreign	30,961	28,812	23,379
State and local	6,928	7,134	8,827
Deferred	12,787	(8,534)	(26,486)
	$72,827	$ 65,297	$ 55,633

A reconciliation of the Company's effective income tax rate to the statutory Federal income tax rate follows:

	1990	1989	1988
Statutory Federal income tax rate	34.0%	34.0%	34.0%
State and local income taxes	2.5	2.9	3.7
Tax rate differential*	—	—	(3.7)
FSC income not taxed	(3.0)	(2.7)	(1.8)
Foreign tax rate difference	5.0	4.2	2.9
Other	1.2	1.5	(.1)
Effective income tax rate	39.7%	39.9%	35.0%

*Resulting from reversal of taxes on prefunded employee health benefits and installment sales previously deferred at higher tax rates in the financial statements.

The deferred provision for federal income taxes results from timing differences in the recognition of revenues and expenses for tax and financial reporting purposes. The tax effects of significant timing differences include the following:

Deferred tax items:	1990	1989	1988
Accelerated depreciation	$ 3,790	$ 6,073	$ 6,455
Prefunded employee health benefits	—	—	(16,086)
Installment sales	—	—	(5,549)
Long-term contracts	9,779	(20,716)	(182)
Capitalized overhead	(3,954)	32,535	(11,339)
Other net deferred charges and credits	3,172	(5,786)	215
Total deferred tax	$12,787	$ 12,106	$(26,486)
Cumulative effect of changes in accounting principles	$ —	$ 20,640	$ —
Current deferred tax	3,295	(14,896)	(29,974)
Noncurrent deferred tax	9,492	6,362	3,488
Total deferred tax	$12,787	$ 12,106	$(26,486)

SOURCE: Parker Hannifen Corporation, 1990 Annual Report.

APPENDIX B: INVESTMENT TAX CREDIT

Income tax policy is frequently used to accomplish certain economic and social objectives, as well as to serve as a source of governmental revenue and meet various other objectives. Since 1962, Congress has occasionally attempted to stimulate investment in capital assets by allowing a reduction in income taxes equal to a specified percentage of the cost of qualifying assets. Since its inception, the **investment tax credit (ITC)** has been suspended and restored several times in order to accomplish various objectives. The Revenue Act of 1978 established the ITC at 10% of the cost of qualifying assets. Additionally, limitations were placed on the amount of the ITC that could be used in any one year to offset income taxes that would otherwise be paid that year. These limitations changed from time to time. Any ITC resulting from the acquisition of assets in one year, but that cannot be used to reduce taxes in that particular year due to these limitations, could be carried forward to future years. This works much like the operating loss carryforward provisions of the tax law, which were covered earlier in this chapter.

The Tax Reform Act of 1986 repealed the ITC from the tax law. Despite this development, we cover the ITC in this appendix for several reasons. It has been suspended and restored several times in the past and it is reasonable to assume that the same may occur in the future. As we will see in the following examples, the ITC may be accounted for by the deferred method, in which the effect of the credit is spread over the life of the asset. Even though the ITC may not be a part of the income tax law in a given year, amortization of previously recognized ITC may be an important factor for financial reporting. Finally, the ITC symbolizes the nature of political influences on the formation of financial reporting standards. The series of events leading up to the current accounting procedures for the ITC are explained in the latter part of this appendix to help you appreciate how politics may affect the determination of generally accepted accounting principles.

ALTERNATIVE ACCOUNTING METHODS

Two methods of accounting for the impact of the ITC on the income tax *expense* are used in practice: the **deferred method** and the **flow-through method**. The impact on the income tax liability is the same, regardless of the method of expense recognition used, because the ITC reduces taxes payable, within specified limitations, in the period in which the qualifying asset is acquired. In determining the appropriate amount of income tax expense for the income statement, the deferred and the flow-through methods differ. With the deferred method, the benefit of the ITC is recognized as a reduction in income tax expense throughout the life of the asset. With the flow-

through method, however, the entire reduction in income tax expense is recognized in the year the asset qualifying for the ITC is acquired.

To illustrate these two methods, we will assume that Kapp Company acquired an item of equipment costing $200,000 in 1985. This asset qualified for the 10% ITC and had an expected useful life of eight years. During 1985 Kapp Company earned $182,000 before income tax, and the appropriate income tax rate was 46%. Entries to account for the ITC under the two alternative methods are illustrated in Exhibit 18–11.

The initial acquisition of the equipment (first entry) and the payment of income taxes (fourth entry) are identical under the two methods. The difference is found in the treatment of the impact of the ITC on the income tax expense in the second and third entries. The reduced income taxes are treated as a reduction in tax expense of $20,000 in 1985 under the flow-through method but deferred and allocated over the asset's life under the deferred method. Thus only one-eighth, or $2,500, of the benefit is recognized as a reduction in income tax expense in 1985.

Continuing the example of Kapp Company, we find that the income statement and balance sheet amounts for 1985 relative to the investment tax credit are as follows:

	Deferred Method	Flow-Through Method
Income Statement		
Income tax expense	$81,220	$63,720
Balance Sheet		
Deferred investment tax credit	17,500	NONE

Under the deferred method, the income tax expense of each year in the asset's life is reduced by the allocation of the deferred investment tax credit. For 1985, this results in an income tax expense of $81,220 ($83,720 − $2,500). The declining balance in the Deferred Investment Tax Credit account is presented in the balance sheet as a deferred income tax credit until it is fully amortized. Under the flow-through method, the full impact of the ITC is reflected in 1985, the year of the acquisition of the asset. Thus no deferred investment tax credit appears in the balance sheet under this method.

THE CONTROVERSY OVER ACCOUNTING METHODS

The origin of the investment tax credit, the emergence of two methods of accounting for it, and the response of the Accounting Principles Board to this new feature of financial reporting resulted in a significant controversy. Both accounting methods that emerged for the ITC—deferred and flow-through—have merit and thus were attractive to

EXHIBIT 18–11

Example of Alternative Methods: Investment Tax Credit

Journal Entries: Deferred Method		Transaction Description	Journal Entries: Flow-Through Method	
Equipment 200,000		Acquisition of	Equipment 200,000	
Cash	200,000	equipment	Cash	200,000
Tax Expense 83,720		Income tax	Tax Expense 63,720	
Deferred ITC	20,000	accrual for	Tax Payable	63,720
Tax Payable	63,720	1985		
Computation			*Computation*	
Tax on $182,000			Tax expense	
$182,000 × .46 =	$83,720		$83,720 − $20,000 =	$63,720
Deferred ITC				
$200,000 × .10 =	$20,000			
Tax payable				
$83,720 − $20,000 = $63,720				
Deferred ITC 2,500		Amortization	None	
Tax Expense	2,500	of ITC		
Computation				
$20,000/8 years =	$2,500			
Tax Payable 63,720		Payment of	Tax Payable 63,720	
Cash	63,720	tax liability	Cash	63,720

individual accountants. Advocates of the deferred method held that the credit should be considered a reduction in the cost of the asset, because management was aware of the availability of the credit, considering it in deciding to acquire the asset. Continuing this line of reasoning, they argued that income is generated through the *use,* not the acquisition, of assets. Spreading the credit over the life of the asset was logical and consistent with allocating the asset's cost over its useful life in a systematic and rational manner, much like the method for depreciation. Matching is a major part of the justification for this method. Furthermore, this treatment was consistent with the recapture feature of the income tax law that required the company to repay some or all of the ITC if the asset were not held and used for a specified period of time.

Matching

Other accountants advocated the tax reduction or flow-through method primarily on the basis that the ITC represented a selective income tax reduction that was available only to those who met certain specified conditions. They argued that the ITC was a feature of income tax law that did not alter the inherent value of the related asset, but was more like a permanent difference between pretax-accounting income and taxable income than a reduction in the depreciation on the asset.

Professional accounting standards for the investment tax credit were originally developed in *APB Opinion No. 2*

in 1962 and subsequently modified in *APB Opinion No. 4* in 1964.[19] These opinions were issued when the APB was attempting to establish itself as the major authoritative body responsible for guiding the development of financial accounting standards in the United States. The general acceptance of its pronouncements was an important element in establishing this authority.

Initially the APB advocated the deferred or cost reduction method. Many corporate managers and practicing CPAs, however, favored the flow-through or tax reduction method. The flow-through method has an advantage in terms of the early recognition of income in the financial statements, because the full effect of the reduction in income tax expense is recognized in the initial year.

Two significant developments during this period had a negative impact on the authoritative position of the APB and resulted in the board's subsequent acceptance of *either* method of accounting for the investment tax credit. First, the American Institute of Certified Public Accountants (AICPA) made an urgent plea to members to issue an unqualified audit opinion *only* if clients used the deferred method, because the flow-through method was not consistent with *APB Opinion No. 2*. Despite this plea, many many unqualified opinions were issued for financial

[19]*APB Opinions Nos. 2 and 4,* "Accounting for the Investment Tax Credit," 1962 and 1964.

statements in which the flow-through method was used. Second, the Securities and Exchange Commission (SEC) took a position that allowed either method. In light of these setbacks, the APB issued *Opinion No. 4,* in which it voiced its acceptance of the flow-through method, even though it continued to maintain a *preference* for the deferred method.

In a reconsideration of the two methods in 1971, when Congress reinstated the ITC, the APB again attempted to limit accounting to the deferred method. A great deal of political pressure emerged as influential businessmen were successful in lobbying Congress to stipulate in the income tax law that no specific method of accounting for the ITC could be required by a standard-setting body such as the APB.

This history of accounting for the investment tax credit is of considerable concern to the accounting profession. The lack of general acceptance of the deferred method under *APB Opinion No. 2* and the subsequent changes in *APB Opinion No. 4,* in which the board adjusted its position to parallel accounting practice, had a detrimental impact on the credibility of the APB. In the opinion of many, this action reduced the effectiveness of the board on many fronts. The imposition of political pressure and the intervention of Congress in allowing alternative accounting procedures in this one area of accounting caused considerable concern. Historically, accounting principles have developed within the private sector under the careful observation of the SEC. The precedent set by the situation surrounding the ITC is of concern to those who feel strongly that the future development of financial reporting standards should continue in the private sector to the maximum extent possible.

In reflecting on the events of late 1971, when the second series of episodes concerning the investment tax credit took place, an APB member suggested that the board should perhaps have been renamed the "Accounting Principles—Political Action Board." The following statements summarize his feelings:

Will lobbying become the modus operandi *for generating or blocking the accounting pronouncements of the 1970's? . . . Congress has no monopoly on obtaining "correct" answers. The long-run implications for external financial reporting of the increasing tendencies to contact Congress on every issue are frightening.*

This may be a sad story but it illustrates why some members of the APB are supersensitive to industry reaction. We live in a democracy, and setting accounting principles is indeed subject to popularity testing. That is why we will continue to see an evolution of accounting principles. A natural resistance to change seems widespread. Radical changes may occur occasionally, but only when there is no widespread hostility among the reporting companies. [20]

---

[20]Charles T. Horngren, "Accounting Principles: Private or Public Sector?" *Journal of Accountancy* (May 1972), pp. 40–41.

QUESTIONS

18–1   Explain the significance of the conclusion that income taxes are an expense rather than a distribution of income.

18–2   Briefly explain the following two features of income tax law which significantly influence financial reporting of income tax information:

[a] Operating loss carrybacks and carryforwards.

[b] Temporary differences.

18–3   Give three examples of temporary differences between financial income and taxable income and explain how they give rise to deferred income taxes.

18–4   After a projection of the tax effect of temporary differences has been completed, describe the process by which the accountant properly records the year-end income tax accrual.

18–5   What impact, if any, does an enacted change in the tax rate have on the elements of the balance sheet and income statement?

18–6   Why might a company forego the certainty of a loss carryback in favor of carrying a current-year loss forward to reduce future taxable income?

18–7   If the item "deferred income taxes" appears in a company's balance sheet as a noncurrent liability, what does this indicate about past relationships between pretax financial income and taxable income?

18–8   Contrast permanent differences with temporary differences, giving two examples of permanent differences. Why do permanent differences not give rise to deferred income tax assets and liabilities?

18–9   Distinguish between taxable and deductible temporary differences and give an example of each.

18–10   Contrast accounting for deferred income taxes under the asset/liability method and the deferred method.

18–11   Using installment sales as an example, explain what is meant by the "origination" and "reversal" of temporary differences.

18–12   Are deferred tax amounts significant balance sheet items for U.S. corporations? Justify your response.

18–13   Briefly describe the alternatives that have been considered to the current methods of accounting for deferred taxes on temporary differences.

18–14   In what circumstances might the Deferred Income Tax Liability account be debited rather than credited as part of the year-end accrual yet still appear in the company's balance sheet?

18–15   What is the basic objective of intraperiod income tax allocation? Why is this procedure needed and how does it affect the content of financial statements?

18–16 (Appendix A)   Why must individual future years' taxable income be projected under *SFAS No. 96* rather than treating all future years in the aggregate?

18–17 (Appendix A)   How may temporary differences that are projected into the future under *SFAS No. 96* result in loss carrybacks and carryforwards? What accounting treatment is required in this situation?

18–18 (Appendix A)   What is the financial statement impact of recognizing loss carryforwards in the loss year when applying *SFAS No. 109*?

18–19 (Appendix B)   Explain the differences in concept underlying the deferred (cost reduction) method and the flow-through (tax reduction) methods of accounting for the investment tax credit.

18–20 (Appendix B)   What impact do the deferred (cost reduction) and flow-through (tax reduction) methods of accounting for the investment tax credit have on the recognition of the elements of financial statements?

EXERCISES

18–21   LOSS CARRYBACK   Ross Company reported the following figures for the years 1990, 1991, and 1992.

	1990	1991	1992
Income (loss) before income tax	$100,000	$130,000	$(160,000)
Income tax rate	32%	34%	36%

The entire loss of 1992 is available to offset income taxes paid or becoming payable. No permanent or temporary differences exist in any of the three years.

Instructions

Prepare the income statement for each year, beginning with "income (loss) before income tax." Assume the carryback/carryforward option is employed.

18–22   LOSS CARRYBACK   Hamilton Company reported the following for 1991 and 1992:

	1991	1992
Income (loss) before income tax	$257,000	$(163,000)
Income tax rate	40%	35%

The entire 1992 loss is available to offset income taxes paid or becoming payable. No permanent or temporary differences exist for either year.

Instructions

Prepare the income statement for each year, beginning with "income (loss) before income tax," applying the carryback/carryforward option.

18–23 LOSS CARRYBACK AND CARRYFORWARD Income and loss figures, accompanied by income tax rates, for Elder, Inc., for the first four years of operations are as follows:

	1990	1991	1992	1993
Income (loss) before income tax	$175,000	$182,000	$(405,000)	$121,000
Income tax rate	36%	32%	38%	36%

The entire loss in 1992 is available to reduce income taxes paid or that would otherwise be paid. No permanent or temporary differences exist in any of the years.

Instructions

Prepare the income statement for each year, beginning with "income (loss) before income tax," applying the carryback/carryforward option. Carryforward of the 1992 loss is not recognized until 1993.

18–24 LOSS CARRYBACK AND CARRYFORWARD Wolfe, Inc., had taxable income (loss) figures as follows for 1990, 1991, and 1992, respectively: $100,000, $78,000, and ($25,000). Income tax rates are 35% for 1990 and 1991 and 32% for 1992. No permanent or temporary differences existed in any of the years.

Instructions

[a] Prepare the year-end income tax accrual for 1992, assuming the company selects the option to carry back losses, if possible.
[b] Assume that for 1993, taxable income was $80,000 and the income tax rate is further reduced to 30%. Prepare the year-end income tax accrual for 1993 under each of the independent assumptions which follow:

 [1] In 1992 the company selected the option to carry back losses, as indicated in your response to [a].
 [2] In 1992 the company selected the option to carry losses forward only but did not recognize the carryforward at that time.

18–25 LOSS CARRYFORWARD Thronebary Company had a loss of $100,000 in 1991, its first year of operation. In 1992, the company had pretax financial income of $28,500, followed by $155,000 in 1993. The appropriate income tax rates are 34% for 1991 and 1992 and 35% for 1993.

Instructions

The carryforward value of the 1991 loss was not recognized in that year but deferred until future taxable income was certain.

[a] What income tax information, if any, will appear in the company's 1991 financial statements?
[b] Prepare the general journal entries, if any, required at the end of 1992 and 1993 to properly account for income taxes.

18–26 PERMANENT AND TEMPORARY DIFFERENCES Waller Company includes the following items in pretax accounting income for 1993:

[1] Litigation loss of $25,000 (estimated), which will become tax deductible when settled in the future.
[2] Amortization of goodwill of $35,000, which will never be deductible for income tax purposes.
[3] Revenue from an installment sale of $45,000, which will be recognized in taxable income as received over the next three years.

Pretax financial income is $175,000.

Instructions

[a] Determine the amount of pretax financial income subject to income tax and the amount of taxable income for 1993.

[b] Briefly explain the difference in the way you have treated the three items listed above and justify that difference.

18–27 CALCULATING FINANCIAL INCOME FROM TAXABLE INCOME   The controller of Rouder, Inc., is attempting to determine the amount of pretax financial income for 1993 by making adjustments to taxable income from the company's 1993 income tax return. The tax return indicates taxable income of $190,000, on which a tax liability of $66,500 has been recognized ($190,000 × 35% = $66,500).

The controller has prepared the following list of items that may be required to determine pretax financial income from the amount of taxable income:

[1] Accelerated write-off for income tax purposes was $67,000; straight-line depreciation on the same assets is $40,000.

[2] Goodwill amortization was not included as a deduction in the tax return, but may be required in the income statement. The appropriate amount, if required, is $22,500.

[3] Several expenses were included in the income tax return on an estimated basis. These items will be in the income statement at these same amounts, but they are subject to change if new information in the future indicates that the original estimates were inaccurate.

[4] Interest on municipal securities was not included in the tax return. During the year, $12,350 was received on these investments.

Instructions

Determine the amount of pretax financial income and pretax financial income subject to tax, working from the amount of taxable income. Carefully explain each adjustment to taxable income to determine the required figures.

18–28 INCOME TAX ACCRUAL WITH TEMPORARY DIFFERENCES   Foster, Inc., reports pretax financial income for 1993 of $85,000. Included are the following items:

[1] Depreciation on plant assets, determined by the straight-line method, of $38,000. Accelerated cost recovery, taken for income tax purposes, totaled $55,000.

[2] Goodwill amortization of $15,000, which is not deductible for income tax purposes.

[3] A litigation loss, recognized on an estimated basis, of $12,000. This item will not be deductible for income tax purposes until final settlement is reached in a future year.

Enacted income tax rates are 30% for 1993 and 35% for all future years.

Instructions

Analyze the company's income for financial and tax purposes in a manner which facilitates the preparation of the 1993 income tax accrual, and prepare that accrual in general journal form.

18–29 INCOME TAX ACCRUAL WITH TEMPORARY DIFFERENCES   Saunders Company has correctly determined its 1993 pretax financial income to be $750,000. Included in that figure are two items that do not have tax consequences: amortization of goodwill at $25,000 and interest received on investments in municipal bonds, $10,000.

In addition, the company has two temporary differences: accelerated write-off for income tax purposes exceeds straight-line depreciation on the same plant assets by $135,000, and $50,000 cash received in advance for an order of merchandise is taxable in 1993 but will be recognized in accounting income in 1994.

The income tax rate for 1993 is 35%; the enacted rate for years after 1993 is 38%.

Instructions

[a] Prepare an analysis of Saunders' financial and taxable income for 1993, which provides the amount of the current income tax payable and the balance needed in deferred income taxes at the end of the year.

[b] Prepare the income tax accrual for 1993.

18-30 REVERSING TEMPORARY DIFFERENCE WITH INCOME TAX RATE CHANGE   Sprouse, Inc., had $20,000 of deferred income taxes (credit balance) at the beginning of 1993. During that year, pretax financial income and taxable income were determined by the company's accountant to be as follows:

Pretax financial income	$ 255,000
Temporary difference:	
Depreciation:	
1993 originating	(75,000)
Pre-1993 reversing	48,500
Taxable income	$ 228,500

The enacted income tax rate for 1993 was 30%. During 1993 the enacted rate for all years after 1993 was increased to 36%. Depreciation temporary differences arising prior to 1993 that will reverse after 1993 totaled $60,000.

Instructions

[a] Prepare the income tax accrual at December 31, 1993, the end of the company's financial reporting period.

[b] Calculate the impact of the income tax rate change for years after 1993 on the amount of income tax expense recognized in 1993.

18-31 (Appendix A) SCHEDULING WITH SINGLE TEMPORARY DIFFERENCE (SFAS NO. 96) Riviera, Inc., determines its pretax financial income to be $88,500 for 1992. During the year the company purchased assets which it plans to write off for income tax purposes on an accelerated basis while using straight-line for financial reporting purposes. The difference between the two is $25,000 in 1992, and that amount is expected to reverse over the next five years at an equal amount per year. The currently enacted income tax rate for all years is 35%.

Instructions

[a] Prepare a six-year summary, including 1992, to assist in determining the company's 1992 income tax liability and its deferred income taxes in accordance with *SFAS No. 96*.

[b] Prepare the general journal entry required to record income taxes for 1992.

18-32 (Appendix A) SCHEDULING WITH SINGLE TEMPORARY DIFFERENCE (SFAS NO. 96) During 1992, Ramsey Company had pretax financial income of $52,850. This amount included an installment sale of $22,000 that is expected to be collected during 1993, 1994, and 1995 at the following percentages for each year, respectively: 40%, 40%, 20%. The enacted income tax rate for all years is 30% at the present time, although an increase to 32% is currently under consideration by appropriate governmental bodies. Ramsey accounts for income taxes in accordance with *SFAS No. 96*.

Instructions

[a] Prepare a four-year analysis of income taxes for Ramsey that will assist in determining the appropriate income tax information for the 1992 financial statements.

[b] Prepare the income tax accrual at the end of 1992.

18-33 (Appendix A) ACCOUNTING FOR INCOME TAXES BY SFAS NO. 109 Hill, Inc., has determined its 1993 pretax financial income to be $150,000. The following differences between accounting income and taxable income have also been identified: (1) Goodwill amortization in accounting income of $12,000; (2) Excess of tax write-off of plant assets over depreciation in financial income of $40,000; (3) Revenue received in advance that is taxed currently but deferred for purposes of financial income of $10,000. This revenue will be earned in 1994. The income tax rate is 40% and no previous temporary differences exist.

Instructions

Prepare the income tax accrual entry for 1993.

18–34 (Appendix A) ACCOUNTING FOR INCOME TAXES BY SFAS NO. 109   Fosteur Company's pretax financial income for 1993 is $790,000. Temporary differences have been identified as follows:

Depreciation:	Tax write-off exceeds financial depreciation by $100,000
Litigation:	Loss taken for financial reporting purposes of $45,000 will be deducted for tax purposes in the <u>distant future</u>
Warranty:	Amount expensed for financial reporting purposes exceeds amount currently deductible for tax purposes by $25,000

The warranty liability is classified as a current liability in the company's balance sheet. The income tax rate is 35% and this is Fosteur's first year of operations.

Instructions

[a] Prepare the income tax accrual entry for 1993.
[b] Identify the income tax elements, including dollar amounts, for the 1993 balance sheet and income statement.

18–35 (Appendix A) TEMPORARY DIFFERENCES AND STATUTORY RECONCILIATION (SFAS NO. 109)   Welsch, Inc. determines its pretax financial income to be $550,000 for 1993. The only temporary difference is for depreciation, where the amount written off for tax purposes exceeds straight-line depreciation recognized for financial reporting purposes by $70,000. At the beginning of 1993, the cumulative temporary difference for depreciation was $250,000, for which a $75,000 deferred tax liability has been recognized. The income tax rate is 40%.

Instructions

[a] Identify the income statement elements relative to income taxes for 1993.
[b] Prepare a statutory rate reconciliation for 1993, carefully labeling each item.

18–36 INTRAPERIOD ALLOCATION   Robin, Inc., has properly determined its taxable income for 1992 to be $650,500. There are no permanent or temporary differences between taxable and financial income. Included in taxable income is a gain of $110,000 resulting from a transaction that will be presented as "extraordinary" in the 1992 income statement. The appropriate income tax rate for all items is 36%.

Instructions

[a] Determine the income tax expense to be included in the 1992 income statement.
[b] Describe the disclosure of the extraordinary gain to be included in the 1992 income statement.

18–37 INTRAPERIOD ALLOCATION   Mowery Company has determined the following items for 1992:

Pretax financial income	$158,500
Income (loss) items not included in pretax financial income:	
Correction of error in 1991 financial statements	7,500
Extraordinary loss	(16,250)
Retained earnings, Jan. 1, 1992, as previously stated	400,000
Dividends declared during 1992	50,000
Income tax rate	30%

There are no permanent or temporary differences between taxable and financial income. The company's reporting period is January 1–December 31.

Instructions

[a] Prepare the income statement, beginning with "income before income tax," for 1992, giving proper recognition to intraperiod income tax allocation requirements.

[b] Prepare the retained earnings statement for 1992, giving proper recognition to intraperiod income tax allocation requirements.

18–38   INTRAPERIOD ALLOCATION WITH TEMPORARY DIFFERENCE   Walker, Inc., correctly determines its 1992 pretax financial income as $80,000. This amount includes an extraordinary gain of $20,000 before income taxes.

During the year, the company made an installment sale for $25,000 that is included in the financial income figure stated above but will not be taxed until payment is received in 1993.

The enacted income tax rates are 30% for 1992 and 35% for 1993.

Instructions

[a] Prepare the income tax accrual at December 31, 1992, the end of the company's financial reporting period.

[b] Prepare a partial income statement applying appropriate intraperiod income tax allocation procedures for the extraordinary gain.

18–39 (Appendix B) INVESTMENT TAX CREDIT   Orpha Manufacturing Company acquired several items of machinery costing a total of $175,000 during 1985. The machinery is expected to be used by the company for 10 years. The machinery qualifies for the 10% investment tax credit, reducing taxes paid in 1985 by $17,500. Pretax financial income for 1985 and 1986 is $98,500 and $125,600, respectively. The income tax rate for both years was 30%.

Instructions

Determine the amount of income tax expense to be presented in the income statement in 1985 and 1986 under the following methods of accounting for the investment tax credit:

[a] Flow-through (tax reduction) method.

[b] Deferred (cost reduction) method.

18–40 (Appendix B) INVESTMENT TAX CREDIT   Dataquick Company acquired a computer for $262,000 in early 1985. The computer is expected to be useful for 20 years. It is subject to a 10% investment tax credit, reducing taxes which would otherwise have been paid in 1985. Income before income taxes in 1985 totaled $192,500, which is subject to a 40% income tax rate. The company intends to depreciate the computer by the straight-line method with no salvage value for both book and tax purposes.

Instructions

Prepare general journal entries under both the deferred and the flow-through methods for all transactions and events relating to the computer, including the impact of the acquisition on income tax expense.

PROBLEMS

18–41   LOSS CARRYBACK AND CARRYFORWARD   Dexter, Inc., experienced a $550,000 pretax financial loss in 1992, a year in which the income tax rate was 34%. The following data pertain to the period 1990–1992:

Year	Income (Loss) Before Income Taxes	Income Tax Rate
1990	$192,000	30%
1991	465,000	32%
1992	(550,000)	34%

Management estimates that the income tax rate beyond 1992 will be approximately 36%. The end of Dexter's financial reporting period is December 31.

Instructions

[a] Prepare the 1992 general journal entries to account for income taxes and the income statement presentation of income taxes in each of the following *independent* situations:

[1] Dexter intends to carry forward the 1992 loss, deferring recognition until taxable income is earned.

[2] Dexter intends to carry back the 1992 loss.

[b] Explain how your answer to [a] [1] would be different if the benefit of the carryforward had been recognized in 1992. (Do not prepare a revised journal entry.)

18-42 LOSS CARRYBACK AND CARRYFORWARD Smothers, Inc., is trying to decide whether to exercise the carryback/carryforward option or the carryforward-only option in recognizing the income tax refundable as a result of its 1992 loss (before income taxes) of $85,000. The company began operations in 1991 and reported an income before income taxes of $28,000 that year.

An important consideration is the impact of the two options on the income statement and the balance sheet for 1992 and 1993. While the company is optimistic about future operations, income is *not* believed to be assured. The company does expect, however, to report an income of approximately $75,000 in 1993 and anticipates profitable operations in future years.

The appropriate income tax rate for 1991 and 1992 was 35%. No change is expected in the income tax rate for the foreseeable future. The end of the company's financial reporting period is December 31.

Instructions

[a] Explain the difference between the carryback/carryforward option and the carryforward only option. Indicate why each might be a desirable alternative for Smothers, Inc.

[b] Determine the balance sheet and income statement presentation for 1992 (based on actual data) and for 1993 (based on projected data), assuming that management decides to exercise the carryback/carryforward option and that carryforward recognition is deferred until income is earned. The latter stipulation is assumed because the company is in its infancy and has not established a record of profitability. *Journal Entries*

18-43 TEMPORARY DIFFERENCES AND DEFERRED INCOME TAXES Frisbee, Inc., has correctly determined its 1992 pretax financial income as $500,000. Included in that amount is a litigation loss of $45,000 that will not be resolved in the courts until sometime in the future, at which time it will be deductible for income tax purposes. Also, during 1992 the company purchased equipment that is being written off on an accelerated basis for income tax purposes. The $100,000 temporary difference will reverse over the useful life of the asset. No deferred income taxes existed prior to 1992. The enacted income tax rate for all years is 40%.

Instructions

[a] Prepare a summary to assist Frisbee, Inc., in determining the amounts of its current income tax liability and any deferred income taxes, omitting any consideration of potential loss carryback provisions.

[b] Prepare the year-end income tax accrual at December 31, 1992, including supporting computations for the amounts in your entry.

[c] What impact, if any, would an enacted change in income tax rate for 1993 and future years have on your answers to previous questions? (Provide a discussion answer but do not recompute the amounts in the previous parts.)

18-44 TEMPORARY AND PERMANENT DIFFERENCES Herring, Inc., reports pretax financial income of $750,000 for 1993. The following differences between financial income and taxable income have been correctly identified:

[1] A $25,000 deposit received in 1993 is taxable immediately, but will be reported in financial income in the future.

[2] Goodwill amortization of $50,000 is deducted in financial income but not in taxable income.

✓[3] Accelerated write-off of plant assets for tax purposes exceeds straight-line depreciation for financial reporting purposes by $175,000. This difference will reverse over the estimated useful lives of the assets.

✓[4] A litigation loss of $65,000 was recognized on an estimated basis in financial income, but will become tax deductible only after final settlement in the future.

Instructions

[a] Prepare an analysis that results in a computation of income taxes currently payable and deferred income taxes, assuming an enacted 34% income tax rate for all years.

[b] Prepare the income tax accrual for 1993, assuming no deferred income taxes are carried forward from 1992.

[c] Prepare the income tax accrual for 1993, assuming a credit (liability) balance of $13,500 is carried forward from 1992.

[d] Explain the difference between permanent and temporary differences in pretax financial and taxable income, using your answer to [a] above to illustrate your point(s).

18–45 TEMPORARY AND PERMANENT DIFFERENCES   Marcus, Inc., has determined the following information concerning pretax financial income and taxable income:

1992:

Pretax financial income is $175,000.

Interest revenue on municipal securities is $5,500.

Depreciation temporary differences of $50,000 originate during the year.

Installment sale temporary differences of $10,000 originate during the year.

The enacted income tax rate for 1992 is 30% and for all future years is 35%.

1993:

Pretax financial income is $190,000.

Interest revenue on municipal securities is $7,200.

Depreciation temporary differences of $70,000 originate during the year; 25% of the 1992 originating differences reverse during the year.

Installment sales temporary differences of $12,000 originate during the year; 50% of the 1992 originating differences reverse during the year.

The enacted income tax rate for all years after 1993 is changed to 38% during the year.

Instructions

[a] Prepare an analysis for 1992 to determine the amount of current and deferred income taxes payable. (Hint: Keep in mind that at the end of 1992, you are not aware of the 1993 information given in the problem.)

[b] Prepare an analysis for 1993 to determine the amount of current income taxes payable and deferred income taxes.

[c] Prepare the journal entries to record income taxes for 1992 and 1993, assuming no balance exists in deferred income taxes prior to 1992.

18–46 INTRAPERIOD ALLOCATION   Dyson Company is preparing its income and retained earnings statements for 1992 and 1993. The following selected information has been developed to date:

	Fiscal Year 1992	Fiscal Year 1993
Retained earnings, Nov. 1	$575,000	?
Pretax financial income	162,000	$135,000
Dividends declared	40,000	42,000
Extraordinary gain	18,700	—
Correction of prior periods—correction of error in 1991 financial statements (loss)	—	(24,000)
Effective income tax rate	38%	36%

There are no permanent or temporary differences in 1992 or 1993. Dyson Company's fiscal year-end is October 31. The company had 100,000 shares of common stock outstanding throughout 1992 and 1993. The 1991 income tax rate was 38%. The items in the preceding schedule are included at their total amounts, before income tax consideration.

Instructions

[a] Prepare comparative statements of income and retained earnings for 1992 and 1993.

[b] Briefly explain the rationale for intraperiod income tax allocation.

18–47 (Appendix A) SCHEDULING AND DEFERRED INCOME TAXES (SFAS NO. 96) Fallon, Inc., has correctly determined its 1992 pretax financial income to be $180,000. This year is the first year of operations and four temporary differences between financial and taxable income originated during the year. They are described below:

[1] An installment sale of $15,000 was recognized in financial income, although it will not be taxable until it is collected. The company anticipates collection in 1994.

[2] Revenue received in advance amounted to $8,000 during the year. While this is taxable in 1992, it will be recognized for financial reporting purposes when it is earned, which is expected to be 1995.

[3] Depreciation for income tax purposes exceeded that for financial reporting by $40,000. This difference is expected to reverse $20,000 in 1993 and $10,000 in each of 1994 and 1995.

[4] The company became involved in litigation that resulted in a $30,000 loss recognized in financial income. That amount will not be deductible for income tax purposes, however, until the litigation is completed, which is expected to be 1994.

The enacted income tax rates are 34% for 1992 and 1993 and 36% for 1994 and 1995. Pretax financial income for 1992 also includes $5,000 of interest revenue on municipal securities which is not taxable. Fallon, Inc., accounts for income taxes in accordance with *SFAS No. 96*.

Instructions

[a] Prepare a schedule determining taxable income for 1992, beginning with the $180,000 of pretax financial income. Identify the adjustments you make to reach taxable income.

[b] Prepare a four-year schedule for 1992–1995 for computing the amount of 1992 income tax payable, deferred taxes at the end of 1992, and the income tax expense for 1992.

[c] Prepare the income tax accrual at December 31, 1992, the end of Fallon, Inc.'s reporting year.

18–48 (Appendix A) ACCOUNTING FOR INCOME TAXES BY SFAS NO. 109 Business Analysts, Inc., has determined its 1992 pretax financial income to be $50,000 for 1992 and $85,000 for 1993, its first two years of operations. Temporary differences are as follows:

1992: 34%

[1] An installment sale for $15,000 is included in financial income but will <u>not</u> be included in taxable income until <u>1993</u> when it is collected. *No cash rec'd – no tax now*

[2] Revenue received in advance of $7,000 will not be included in financial income until it is earned in 1995 but is taxable in 1992. *Cash rec'd – tax*

1993: 40%

[3] Assets purchased in 1993 are being written off for income tax purposes on an accelerated basis, resulting in an excess of write-off for income tax purposes over financial statement depreciation by $30,000. That amount will reverse over the period 1994–1996.

[4] A litigation loss, recognized in financial income in 1993, will not be <u>deductible for income tax</u> purposes until the litigation is complete, which is expected in 1996. The amount is $12,000.

In 1992, the income tax rate enacted for 1992 and all future years is 34%. During 1993, new rates were enacted which increased the percentages for 1993 and future years to 40%. The company ends its reporting year on December 31. There are no permanent differences between pretax financial and taxable income. Business Analysts, Inc., accounts for income taxes in accordance with *SFAS No. 109*.

Instructions

[a] Compute the amount of taxable income for 1992 and 1993, beginning with pretax financial income and adjusting for temporary differences.

[b] Prepare an analysis of cumulative temporary differences and deferred taxes (similar to Exhibit 18–6) to support the year-end income tax accrual for 1992, assuming that you know only the information that would be available at the end of 1992 (i.e., you are not aware of actual events pertaining to 1993 because those events have not yet occurred.) Prepare the income tax accrual and statutory reconciliation at December 31, 1992, using the information in your analysis.

[c] Repeat requirement [b] for 1993, incorporating the additional information that is now available.

[d] Prepare in comparative columns the elements of the income statement and balance sheet that would appear in the 1992 and 1993 financial statements relative to income taxes.

18–49 (Appendix A)   ACCOUNTING FOR INCOME TAXES BY SFAS NO. 109   Grant Company applies *SFAS No. 109* in accounting for income taxes. At the end of 1992, the following balances of temporary differences and deferred taxes exist:

	Cumulative Temporary Differences	Deferred Tax Assets (Liabilities)	Classification
Depreciation	$(125,000)	$(47,500)	Noncurrent
Installment sales	(75,000)	(28,500)	Current
Litigation loss	60,000	22,800	Noncurrent
	$(140,000)	$(53,200)	

For 1993, pretax financial income is $400,000, including municipal interest of $25,000. Additional temporary difference activity during the year is as follows:

Depreciation—Originating $35,000 from use of accelerated write-off for tax purposes and straight-line depreciation for financial reporting.

Installment sales—$65,000 of the amount included in the temporary difference was collected and included in taxable income; $90,000 of new installment sales were recognized for accounting purposes and deferred for tax purposes.

Warranty expense—Short-term warranties were offered for the first time on products sold. The amount expensed in the income statement exceeded the amount deductible currently for income tax purposes by $10,000.

Instructions

[a] Prepare the 1993 income tax accrual entry and statutory reconciliation, including detailed documentation of all calculations. The enacted income tax rate for 1993 and future years is 34%.

[b] During 1994, Grant Company determines its pretax financial loss to be $100,000, including municipal interest of $20,000 and temporary differences, as follows:

Depreciation—Additional originating difference of $45,000.

Installment sales—$75,000 of previous balance collected; 1994 sales amounts uncollected at year end of $98,000.

Warranty—Additional originating difference of $15,000.

The loss for income tax purposes is carried back to 1992 when the income tax rate was $38%. (Assume that 1991 was a break-even year.)

Using this additional information, repeat requirement [a] for 1994.

[c] For this requirement, repeat requirement [b] for 1994 with the following changes in information: The pretax financial loss is $620,000, rather than $100,000. Taxable income in 1992 was $250,000 which was subject to income taxes at 38%. The deferred tax asset arising from the operating loss carryforward is classified as noncurrent.

(*Hint:* This problem does not require analyses for each year like the one included in Exhibit 18–8 of Appendix A. You may find that useful, however, in completing the above requirements.)

18–50 (Appendix B)   INVESTMENT TAX CREDIT   Torenson, Inc., acquired heavy construction equipment in 1985 for $880,000, which qualified for a 10% investment tax credit. The equipment is expected to be useful for 10 years, and straight-line depreciation will be used. Operating information for 1985 and 1986 is as follows:

	1985	1986
Pretax financial income	$982,500	$1,050,000
Income tax rate	48%	46%

Instructions

[a] Prepare all journal entries for 1985 and 1986 to account for equipment, depreciation, and income taxes. The flow-through (tax reduction) method is to be used in accounting for the investment tax credit.

[b] Prepare the journal entries in [a] that would be different if the deferred (cost reduction) method were used in accounting for the investment tax credit instead of the flow-through method.

[c] Compute the amount of net income that would be recognized in 1985 and 1986 under the flow-through method and the deferred method.

18–51 (Appendix B)   INVESTMENT TAX CREDIT   Pepper Company, which began operations in 1983, continuously invests in equipment for use in its manufacturing process. This equipment qualifies for the investment tax credit (ITC), thereby reducing income taxes paid by 10% of the cost of qualifying assets in the year of acquisition.

Information related to the company during its first three years of operation is shown below:

	1983	1984	1985
Pretax financial income	$500,000	$528,000	$617,000
Income tax rate	48%	46%	46%
Equipment acquisitions eligible for ITC	$424,000	$370,000	$360,000
Estimated life of equipment acquisitions	8 years	10 years	9 years

Pretax financial income includes $18,000 amortization of goodwill in each year. In addition, 1984 pretax income includes $5,000 of interest received by Pepper on investments in municipal securities.

Instructions

[a] Prepare a detailed calculation of income tax expense for each year, assuming the deferred method of accounting for the ITC is used.

[b] The president of Pepper Company has asked you to determine the impact of the flow-through method on net income by preparing *pro forma* calculations for 1983, 1984, and 1985 under that method.

[1] Prepare *pro forma* calculations showing what net income would have been in 1983, 1984, and 1985 if the flow-through method had been used.

[2] Outline the items you would include in an explanation of the impact of the two alternative methods on the company's financial statements.

CASES

18–52   RELATIONSHIP OF FINANCIAL AND TAXABLE INCOME   Jack Frost, the president of a company that is one of your clients, has confronted you with something in the company's financial statements he does not understand. You have correctly prepared the income statement from information provided by the company's accountant. That statement shows pretax income of $100,000 and income tax expense of only $20,400. The income tax payable in the balance sheet is also $20,400, despite the fact that the enacted income tax rate is 34%. The company has been profitable in the past and no loss carrybacks or carryforwards exist to explain this relationship.

Frost's reaction is mixed. On the one hand, he is glad that you have computed the income tax the company must pay to be only $20,400 because of the benefit of the reduced cash outflow from what he had expected. On the other hand, he is concerned whether you have correctly determined the amount of income tax expense and payable and, also, that users of the company's financial statements may be confused by this unusual-looking relationship in the income statement.

Instructions

[a] What is the most likely explanation for the relationship Frost sees in the income statement and how will you explain this "problem" to him?

[b] What financial reporting requirement would be useful in explaining to readers of the financial statements why the income tax expense recognized may not equal the enacted income tax rate multiplied by the pretax financial income in the income statement?

18–53   JUSTIFICATION FOR DEFERRED INCOME TAXES   Mr. Gordo, the president of Greekline, Inc., your client, has come to you with questions concerning amounts in the financial statements concerning income taxes. Mr. Gordo is particularly interested in how the amount of the income tax expense could possibly be greater than the liability for income taxes currently payable to the government for income of 1992, the current year.

In expressing his concern, he notes that he has seen an amount for deferred income taxes in the balance sheet. He further points out that you would certainly not include in this year's financial statements amounts that do not come due until future years, and thus he sees no justification for those amounts.

You are having a conference with Mr. Gordo tomorrow and are reasonably certain that the matter will come up, as the purpose of the meeting is to finalize amounts in the financial statements prior to their distribution to the company's investors and creditors.

Instructions

How will you explain the financial statement elements related to income taxes to Mr. Gordo?

18–54 (Appendix A)   USING FUTURE TAX RATES   You have recently been engaged by Hart, Inc., as auditor for the company's annual financial statements. As you were at the client's office familiarizing yourself with the accounting system and making preliminary plans for the upcoming audit, Sylvia Hart, President of Hart, Inc., stopped by for a brief conversation.

You quickly learned that although Hart is not an accountant, she is an astute reader of financial statements and takes pride in being relatively well informed about important financial reporting issues. She quickly moves the conversation toward income tax reporting and the complexities of *FASB Statements of Financial Accounting Standards No. 96* and *109*. While she has not read the statements, she has read in the *Wall Street Journal* about them and their likely impact on financial statements.

Hart is concerned about the incorporation of enacted income tax rates, other than the present rate, in the numbers that affect the financial statements. Her position is that enacted tax rates may change frequently and to base important financial statement numbers on future income tax rates seems to be counter to the accounting objective of recording items on the basis of reliable information. Also, she feels that to incorporate income tax rates that do not go into effect until some future date into current financial statements is not consistent with the historical orientation of the financial statements.

Instructions

How would you respond to Hart's conclusions?

18–55 (Appendix A)   YEAR-END INCOME TAX ACCRUAL (SFAS NO. 96)   You have just been engaged by Newly, Inc., a company whose first year of operations (1992) has just been completed. The company was profitable, reporting $100,000 in pretax financial income. The company's accountant has prepared the summary to support his income tax accrual for the year which appears below.

Newly, Inc.
1992 Income Tax Accrual Information

	1992	1993	1994	1995	1996
Pretax financial income	$ 100,000	—	—	—	—
Temporary differences:					
Litigation loss	16,000	—	$(16,000)	—	—
Depreciation	(40,000)	$10,000	10,000	$10,000	$10,000
Taxable income (loss)	$ 76,000	$10,000	$ (6,000)	$10,000	$10,000
Income tax rate	40%	40%	N/A	40%	40%
Income tax liability	$ 30,400	$ 4,000	–0–	$ 4,000	$ 4,000

N/A = Not applicable (no income taxes due in 1994)

You determine that taxable income is determined as pretax financial income of $100,000, reduced by a $40,000 temporary difference for depreciation which will reverse equally over the next four years, and increased by $16,000 of litigation expense recognized in financial income that will not be deductible until the litigation is settled in 1994. Enacted income tax rates are 40% for 1992, 35% for 1993 and 1994, and 30% for 1995 and 1996. The company applies *SFAS No. 96*.

The accountant has provided you with this information to review in advance of your conference with him tomorrow concerning his proposed year-end income tax accrual, which is as follows:

Dec. 31, 1992	Income Tax Expense	42,400	
	Income Tax Payable		30,400
	Noncurrent Liability—Deferred Income Tax		12,000

Instructions

[a] What errors, if any, do you find in the accountant's calculations supporting the income tax accrual for 1992? List and discuss those items which you feel have been handled incorrectly.

[b] Prepare a revised income tax accrual for 1992 that corrects those items you listed in [a] above.

[c] Identify the amounts and classification of the income tax items that will appear in the company's December 31, 1992, balance sheet.

18–56 MATERIALITY OF DEFERRED INCOME TAXES Laid-back, Inc., has been your employer for a number of years and your boss, the company president, is not too enthusiastic about the preparation of financial statements in conformity with GAAP. The company's bank, however, requires two-year comparative financial statements as a condition of a relatively large loan.

In prior years, the company's president has not wished to go to the trouble to determine the proper amount of deferred income taxes and you have acquiesed because the amounts have not seemed material. While you have not computed the exact tax effects of temporary differences, you have roughly estimated them and, although they have increased in recent years, you have never believed that the total amount could be material to the financial statements taken as a whole.

During the current year, however, the company has acquired a large amount of new equipment and due to originating temporary differences you are convinced that the determination of deferred income taxes and the inclusion of them in the financial statements will be necessary this year. In fact, your preliminary calculations indicate that the amount of deferred income taxes are a material amount. To your dismay, you also observe that the amount of deferred income taxes that would have been classified as a current liability last year would have reduced the company's working capital and current ratio to a level that would have caused the company to be in violation of one of its lending covenants with the bank. You wonder whether the deferred income tax amounts that existed at the end of the preceding year should be restated as a correction of an error. The effect of the omitted deferred income taxes on last year's financial statements taken as a whole is negligible, other than the impact on the current liabilities, working capital and the current ratio. As the two of you discuss this matter, your boss states:

> Look, this thing just wasn't material to last year's income or to the balance sheet taken as a whole. Furthermore, the change from last year to this year is merely a change in accounting estimate in any event. Last year we estimated deferred income taxes were immaterial and this year they are material. The entire effect of that change should be picked up in the year of the change, right? Regardless of what some theoretical analysis might suggest, we are not going to restate our financial statements over some trivial event and unduly alarm the bank. Last year's statements are just ancient history and we aren't going to rewrite them now.

Instructions

Respond to the position taken by the president. Be sure to include in your answer what you believe the appropriate accounting for this matter should be. Assuming that your solution differs from that of your boss, what course of action do you believe you should take?

18–57 (Appendix A) TIMING OF TEMPORARY DIFFERENCES (SFAS NO. 96)   You are nearing the end of your audit of Good News, Inc., and have just finished calculating the amount of deferred income taxes. While presenting the results to the president and chief financial officer of the company, you observe that a very large "expected taxable income" arises in three years due to the reversal of temporary differences related to the use of completed contract revenue recognition for income tax purposes. The project in question is by far the most significant activity of the company and the amounts involved are clearly material. In addition, the future income expected to be recognized will be taxed at a higher income tax rate than is currently effective due to enacted changes in the tax law that will take effect two years in the future.

The president says with a sigh that she wishes the deferred income taxes could be based on this year's income tax rate, as it is lower than that enacted for future years. The chief financial officer then makes the following suggestion:

> *Well, why don't we just revise our estimates as to when the project will be completed. That way, the temporary difference can be assumed to enter taxable income in an earlier year and the related income taxes will be based on the lower income tax rate. Of course, we will not want to estimate that the difference will reverse next year because that will give rise to an increase in the current liability for deferred income taxes. Our estimate should be that the project will be completed year after next. That way, the deferred income tax liability will be noncurrent and will still be measured at the current, lower income tax rate.*

The president grins broadly and states: "Ideas like that explain why you are my CEO and have such a great future with this company. Just redo your calculations to reflect our change in estimate and our statements will look much better."

Instructions

Describe the course of action you believe is appropriate for you, the auditor, in these circumstances. Be specific in evaluating the alternative courses of action you identify.

18–58 (Appendix A) VALUATION ALLOWANCE FOR DEFERRED TAX ASSETS   Your client, Value-Add Company, has just completed its financial statements for 1993, the first year in which they have applied *SFAS No. 109* in accounting for income taxes. As you begin your audit of those financial statements, you immediately notice a significantly smaller balance in the noncurrent liability balance for deferred income taxes than in previous years.

You approach Sharon Vorner, controller for Value-Add Company, in search of an explanation. Sharon responds with the following statement:

> *Applying* SFAS No. 109 *has really improved our financial position. That statement changes accounting for income taxes in two important ways that help us. First, it requires that we recompute deferred taxes at the end of each accounting period on the basis of newly enacted income tax rates. Since our deferred tax balances have been growing for many years and were initially recorded when corporate tax rates were in the 46%–50% range, we benefited a great deal by being able to reduce our liability balance when we recomputed these items at the current 34%. Secondly,* SFAS No. 109 *requires the recognition of deferred tax assets for all deductible temporary differences and for operating loss carryforwards. We have had significant operating losses that were so large that we could not carry them back because of the short carryback period. We do intend, however, to use them sometime in the next 15 years as our fortunes improve and we become profitable.*

Instructions

You are impressed with Sharon's knowledge of *SFAS No. 109* and realize that much of what she has said is, in fact, correct. On the other hand, you are concerned about the "too favorable" impact that *SFAS No. 109* may have had on the company's financial statements and wonder if she and you are missing something in applying *SFAS No. 109*? What will you do to alleviate this uneasy feeling you have? If you believe changes are required in the financial statements to make them conform to the standards of *SFAS No. 109*, how will you convince Sharon and other representatives of the company?

CHAPTER 19

Accounting Changes and Corrections of Errors

OBJECTIVES

1. To describe the nature of accounting changes and errors.
2. To develop the theoretical and practical aspects of financial reporting for accounting changes and corrections of errors.
3. To demonstrate financial accounting and reporting practices for each type of change and corrections of errors.
4. To discuss the calculations necessary to restate financial statements, including comparative statements of income and retained earnings.
5. To illustrate the analysis and correction of common errors that are made when recording transactions and year-end adjustments.

Will Rogers claimed that the only thing certain about weather was that "it's bound to change." The same might be said for financial accounting and reporting. Indeed, accounting changes may occur frequently and may be caused by a variety of factors. Examples include the effects of new authoritative pronouncements, new business transactions or forms, changes in the environment, changes in estimates, and changes in the reporting entity. Occasionally mistakes are found in financial statements and correction is required.

In Chapter 19 we discuss the nature of accounting changes, distinguish among the various types of accounting changes, discuss relevant issues and concepts, and explain the appropriate accounting practices for each type of change. We also examine various types of errors and describe how corrections to financial statements that have already been issued are made. Earlier chapters occasionally mention accounting for certain types of changes and errors; for example, Chapter 12, in dealing with depreciation of plant assets, discusses changes in the useful life of a plant asset. Each of these previous illustrations was introduced in accordance with practices to be covered in greater depth in this chapter.

ACCOUNTING CHANGES AND CORRECTIONS OF ERRORS: A CONCEPTUAL ANALYSIS

In *Opinion No. 20,* the Accounting Principles Board (APB) classified the effects of all accounting-related changes in three categories:[1]

1. Changes in accounting principle.
2. Changes in accounting estimate.
3. Changes in the reporting entity.

A similar type of event requiring accounting recognition is the correction of an error. Although not considered an accounting change, the correction of an error requires analysis and accounting similar to that accorded accounting changes. Therefore, this chapter discusses each of the four events.

We must carefully classify all accounting changes by type and carefully distinguish accounting changes from corrections of errors because different accounting and reporting practices are required for each.

CHANGES IN ACCOUNTING PRINCIPLE

A **change in accounting principle** occurs when a company selects a different generally accepted accounting principle (GAAP) from the one used in prior reporting periods. Examples include a change from the specific identification method to the first-in, first-out method of inventory pricing or a change from the sum-of-the-years'-digits to the straight-line method of depreciating plant assets. The term **accounting principle** as used here is broad and includes not only specific practices and procedures, but also the methods of applying them. For example, a company may continue to base its inventory valuation on the lower of cost or market value but change the *application* of the method from the inventory as a whole to individual inventory items. Although the lower of cost or market principle is still used, the method of applying the principle has changed. Such changes are considered to be changes in accounting principle.

---

[1]*APB Opinion No. 20,* "Accounting Changes," 1971, par. 6.

Materiality

Consistency

If we initially adopt an accounting principle for items that were previously immaterial or because of new transactions or events, a change in accounting principle does not occur. Furthermore, some changes in accounting methods that are *initially planned* as part of an overall accounting policy do not represent changes in accounting principle. For example, a change from an accelerated depreciation method to the straight-line method at some specific point in an asset's life may be planned at the time the asset is acquired. Consistent application of this policy does not represent a change in accounting principle when the straight-line method is applied.

CHANGES IN ACCOUNTING ESTIMATE

Changes in accounting estimate arise because the preparation of financial statements requires accountants to estimate the outcome of many future events. Those estimates may require accounting adjustments as new information is gained or as different conditions arise. For example, estimates of the useful life and salvage value of plant assets, collectibility of receivables, and the outcome of current or pending litigation represent situations in which management and accountants must forecast the outcome of future events in order to prepare financial statements at a point in time. If differences arise between early estimates and the later outcome of the events being estimated, we must recognize the effects of those differences in the accounting records.

Although estimates of future events require substantial judgment, most estimates are quite accurate. As more experience is acquired and as new information becomes available, however, revisions of some estimates may be necessary.

Occasionally the effects of a change in estimate are commingled with a change in accounting principle. For example, a company may decide to begin expensing certain costs associated with self-constructed assets when they are incurred rather than capitalizing and depreciating the costs. Such a change may be made partially in recognition of more doubtful future benefits (change in estimate) of the asset being constructed and partially as a result of a different philosophy about the measurement of periodic earnings and related cost of the asset (change in principle). Accountants consider the effects of such mixed-type changes to be changes in estimate rather than changes in accounting principle.[2] These changes are frequently caused by the acquisition of new information or changing circumstances and are closely associated with the continuing evolution of existing practices. In effect, changes like the one described above arise in complete or partial recognition of changes in estimated future events.

CHANGES IN THE REPORTING ENTITY

A change in the reporting entity occurs when the financial statements of the current year are those of a new, or at least substantially different, operating enterprise from the one reporting in previous years. Changes of this type arise if the individual companies included in a set of consolidated or combined financial statements are changed or if consolidated statements are presented for a group of companies that previously reported individually. Our coverage of changes in entity will be brief, as we will leave more extensive treatment of this subject to advanced accounting courses.[3]

---

[2]*APB Opinion No. 20*, par. 11.

[3]The subject of business combinations and changes in the reporting entity are considered extensively in advanced accounting courses. For an excellent discussion of the theoretical issues, concepts, and financial accounting and reporting standards in this area, see Arnold J. Pahler and Joseph E. Mori, *Advanced Accounting: Concepts and Practice*, 4th ed. (San Diego: Harcourt Brace Jovanovich, 1991).

CORRECTIONS OF ERRORS

Errors in financial statements result from mistakes or omissions in the financial accounting process. Examples of errors include "mathematical mistakes, mistakes in the application of accounting principles, or oversight or misuse of facts" existing at the time the financial statements were prepared.[4] A change from an accounting principle that is *unacceptable* to a generally *acceptable* accounting principle is also considered to be a correction of an error. Likewise a *misuse* of available facts results in an error, whereas *newly available* information or the acquisition of *new* facts results in a change of estimate. This distinction is important because substantially different accounting practices are required for changes in estimates and corrections of errors.

REPORTING ALTERNATIVES FOR CHANGES AND CORRECTIONS

Three fundamental alternatives exist to account for the effects of accounting changes and corrections of errors: the restatement method, the cumulative effect method, and the current and prospective method. In current practice, however, only one of the alternatives is acceptable for each type of change or correction. In this section, we discuss the three methods in terms of their general description and their strengths and weaknesses, and we identify those types of changes or corrections associated with each alternative. Later in the chapter, we will illustrate the specific accounting application of each alternative.

Users of financial statements are able to gain better insights and make more informed decisions if comparative statements for several accounting periods are presented. Comparative statements may reveal trends and relationships that would not be detected from single-year statements. Although generally accepted accounting principles do not specifically require comparative financial statements, such comparisons are strongly recommended in *Accounting Research Bulletin No. 43:*

> *The presentation of comparative financial statements in annual and other reports enhances the usefulness of such reports and brings out more clearly the nature and trends (of events affecting the enterprise). . . . Such presentation emphasizes the fact that statements for a series of periods are far more significant than those for a single period and that the accounts for one period are but an installment of what is essentially a continuous history.*[5]

Most annual reports of business enterprises contain comparative financial statements. Managements recognize that financial statement users need comparative information. The Securities and Exchange Commission (SEC) also requires comparative financial statements of registrants, as do most banks as a condition of loan agreements. Consequently, most companies routinely prepare annual reports containing financial statements for two or more periods. This is a particularly important point to keep in mind as we consider alternative methods of treating accounting changes and corrections of errors. An important difference in the restatement, cumulative effect, and current and prospective methods is the extent to which previously issued financial statements, which are now being presented as comparative information, are altered from the way they were initially presented.

---

[4]*APB Opinion No. 20,* par. 13.
[5]*Accounting Research Bulletin No. 43,* "Restatement and Revision of Accounting Research Bulletins," 1953, Ch. 2, Sec. A, par. 1.

RESTATEMENT METHOD

One way to account for the effects of changes involves the retroactive restatement method. When the restatement approach is used, previously issued financial statements that are being presented for comparative purposes are revised to show the figures that would have appeared in them if the change had been in effect at the time of their original issuance. For example, if a company changes its method of accounting for inventory from last-in, first-out (LIFO) to first-in, first-out (FIFO), the difference between the figures for beginning inventory as computed under each method is treated as an adjustment to prior years' reported earnings. The effect of the change on past years does not alter the current year's income. The effect of the change at the beginning of the current year is treated as an adjustment of the beginning balance of retained earnings for the current year rather than recorded as a component of income of the current year.

Advantages of the Restatement Method

The restatement alternative possesses several advantages. For example, previously issued financial statements, when reissued after restatement, are "better" than they originally were. Since the prior financial statements are changed for events subsequent to their issuance, more complete or accurate information underlies the reissued statements, thereby resulting in an improved presentation.

Another advantage is that the current year's financial statements contain no trace of events not actually affecting those statements. Under the restatement approach a "clean slate" is assumed each time an event occurs which would have altered the original statements if the information had been available at the date they were issued. The effects of events relating to a prior period are confined to the prior period only; therefore, the current income statement excludes any of the effects of the past event. Since the restatement method results in the retroactive revision of previously issued financial statements, those statements issued for comparative purposes are presented in conformity with the accounting principle of consistency. In the earlier example of changing from the LIFO method to the FIFO method, if this change were made in 1993 then the comparative statements for 1991 and 1992 would be restated and prepared on the FIFO basis, thereby making the three periods that are presented comparable.

Consistency

Disadvantages of the Restatement Method

A major problem of the restatement method is the possible loss of credibility in published financial statements. If an individual relies on information contained in financial statements while making decisions and then observes the restatement of that information in comparative financial statements in a later year, the reliability and validity of the entire financial accounting and reporting process may be questioned.

Another problem attributed to the restatement method is the possibility that items of revenue and expense affecting the enterprise may never be reported as a determinant of *any* year's net income. To illustrate, assume that a company fails to report a material liability and related expense resulting from losing a lawsuit and discovers the error only after financial statements for the year have been issued. Unless comparative financial statements are presented, the loss from the lawsuit is never reported as an expense and related reduction in the net income of any year. The restatement approach causes the loss, in these circumstances, to be reported as an adjustment of the beginning balance of retained earnings. Management might intentionally ignore unfavorable events in the year they arise and instead, report the effects of the events as adjustments to beginning retained earnings in later years. Net income for each year in question is unburdened by the unfavorable event.

CUMULATIVE EFFECT METHOD

An alternative to the restatement method involves recording the **cumulative effect** of the event as an adjustment to the current year's income. Under this approach, the cumulative effect of the change is determined as of the beginning of the year of change, and that effect is presented in the current year's income statement in a special nonoperating category, much like an extraordinary item. The new method of accounting or new information is applied at the beginning of that year in which the event takes place. For example, if a company changes from the straight-line depreciation method to an accelerated method, an accountant determines what the accumulated depreciation would have been at the beginning of the year if the company had been using the accelerated method in the past. The accountant then compares the balance in the Accumulated Depreciation account at the beginning of the year with the amount that would have been in Accumulated Depreciation if the new method had been used. The difference between the two balances, stated on a net-of-tax basis, represents the cumulative effect of the change and is reported as a separate component of current net income. Depreciation expense for the year in which the change occurs is based on the new method and reported in normal fashion.

Advantages of the Cumulative Effect Method

Advantages of the cumulative effect method include the fact that the effects of the event are completely accounted for in the year of the change. That is, the accountant prepares entries which adjust the affected accounts and bring them up to date as if the new method had been used in the past. Future reported earnings and financial position are determined as if the new (and presumably preferable) accounting method had been consistently employed. Future financial-statement amounts are unaffected by changes taking place in prior periods. Advocates of the cumulative effect method contend that financial statement users are more likely to notice and comprehend the nature and significance of the change if its effects are included as a special item in the current year's income. Such a treatment spotlights the change and assures that readers of the statements are adequately informed.

Disadvantages of the Cumulative Effect Method

Consistency

A disadvantage of the cumulative effect method is that financial statements of years prior to the change are presented in their old form for comparative purposes. The old methods or assumptions on which prior financial statements were based have been discontinued or updated in the current year's statements. Thus, the financial position and results of operations reported after the event are not presented on a basis consistent with the information presented for periods prior to the change because previous years are not restated as they are in the restatement method.

CURRENT AND PROSPECTIVE METHOD

A third approach of accounting for the effects of accounting changes spreads the cumulative effect of the change over current and future reporting periods. For example, a company may decide that a plant asset will have a longer life than originally estimated. Using the **current and prospective approach**, the company bases depreciation for the *current* and *future* years on the remaining undepreciated cost of the asset and the revised estimate of the asset's life. No attempt is made to apply the new estimate to past statements nor to adjust the existing balances accordingly.

Advantages of the Current and Prospective Method

Supporters of the current and prospective approach observe that many accounting changes are inevitable and as such should be reported in a normal fashion without focusing on the effect of the change as do the two previously discussed methods. When changes are due to new or recently available information, one can make a strong case that only the current and future periods are actually affected.

The current and prospective approach assures that each event that normally affects net income is included in the income of *some* particular period or periods. Thus, this method also overcomes one of the objections to the restatement method.

Disadvantages of the Current and Prospective Method

Others note that if new information indicates that previous estimates or accounting methods were deficient, it should be used to adjust the statements completely, including any cumulative or retroactive effect. Effects of informational deficiencies on past financial statements can affect current and future financial statements if no adjustment is made to bring the statements up to date with regard to the new information. Another criticism of the current and prospective method is that the nature and effect of the event may be overlooked by financial statement users because no special financial-statement category or presentation is employed. The items that are normally presented in the financial statements are simply presented in dollar amounts that are different from those that would have been shown had the change not been made.

COMPARING AND EVALUATING THE ALTERNATIVES

The three methods of reporting accounting changes and corrections of errors differ substantially in terms of financial-statement measurement and presentation. Each method possesses advantages and disadvantages. A summary of the restatement, cumulative effect, and current and prospective methods is presented in Exhibit 19–1.

The accounting profession has carefully considered these three alternatives and concluded that *each is appropriate in certain circumstances*. The accounting situations where each method is applied are identified at the bottom of Exhibit 19–1. The restatement method is used for corrections of errors, certain specified changes in accounting principle, and changes in entity. The cumulative effect method is the general rule for most changes in accounting principle. The current and prospective method is used for changes in estimates.

THE RESTATEMENT METHOD: EXPANSION AND ILLUSTRATION

The distinguishing characteristic of the restatement method is that when it is applied, financial statements of previous accounting periods that are presented for comparative purposes are restated. Elements of those statements that would have been different if the new accounting assumption had been made earlier are changed to reflect that new assumption. The primary advantage of the restatement method over the alternatives is *consistency* in that all financial statements presented are prepared by the same accounting assumption. Their elements are not affected by artificial differences that do not represent real economic phenomena.

Consistency

The reader of the financial statements is made aware of the restatement by a special item presented in the statement of retained earnings, or in the retained earnings column of the statement of stockholders' equity, which restates the beginning retained earnings of each period presented for the impact of the changed assumption on all previous periods. The journal entry to record an event by the restatement method includes an adjustment to Retained Earnings. That account is credited (increased) if

EXHIBIT 19–1

Analysis of Alternatives of Accounting for Changes and Errors

Issue	Restatement Method	Cumulative Effect Method	Current and Prospective Method
Description of Method	The effect of the change is used to restate any prior period financial statements presented. Any remaining effect is charged or credited to beginning retained earnings of the earliest period presented.	The effect of the change is reported as a component of the current year's income. A special category of gain or loss is used to bring the statements up to date.	The effect of the change is spread over the current and future years' income. No special categories of gain or loss are used in reporting the effect of change, and no catch-up entry is made.
Current Year Nominal Accounts Affected	None. (Effects adjusted directly to Retained Earnings.)	Special nonoperating income statement account charged or credited.	Normal income statement account charged or credited.
Major Advantages	Statements are ultimately presented "correctly." Items affecting prior years are associated individually with those years.	Financial statements are brought up to date, and future amounts are computed as if the new method had been used consistently. Users may easily focus on and understand the effects of the change.	Many changes are normal and recur frequently; such events do not justify catch-up entries or separate presentation. Many changes are due to new information, and only current and future periods should be adjusted.
Major Disadvantages	May erode the credibility of the accounting process. Decisions are made by users of financial statements, and later changes in those statements may cause a lack of faith in financial reporting.	Current and prior financial statements lack comparability. Events affecting prior years are reflected in current income.	The effect of previous "deficiencies" are allowed to affect current and prospective financial position and income. The nature and effects of the changes are obscure because no special category or presentation of the event is required.
Applicable Situations	Corrections of errors. Changes in principle (special cases). Changes in entity.	Changes in principle (general rule).	Changes in estimate.

net incomes of earlier periods would have been higher under the new assumption; it is debited (decreased) if net incomes of earlier periods would have been lower.

The following items are accounted for by the restatement method:

1. Corrections of errors in financial statements of previous periods.
2. Selected special changes in accounting principle.
3. Changes in accounting entity.

The second item in this listing refers to the fact that the authoritative accounting literature specifies a small number of changes in accounting principle whose impact is believed to be so significant that only the restatement method results in acceptable financial statement information. These include changes *away from* the LIFO method of accounting for inventory and changes in the revenue recognition methods used in accounting for long-term construction projects. (The latter subject is covered in greater depth in Chapter 20 of this text.) Other changes in accounting principle that require the restatement method are beyond the scope of this text and are not identified or covered here.

Another type of accounting event that may require the restatement method is the first-time adoption of a new FASB Statement of Financial Accounting Standards. In each new SFAS, the FASB identifies the transition method to be followed in changing from the current accounting practice to that specified in the new SFAS. Frequently this involves application of the restatement method, although in some instances the FASB requires other methods of implementation or gives the company a choice of transition method.

THE RESTATEMENT METHOD ILLUSTRATED

To illustrate accounting by the restatement method, we assume that Murphy Company has never accounted for uncollectible receivables by the estimation method, opting instead to simply write off accounts directly as they are deemed uncollectible by management. This has not been a problem for the company in the past, as financial statements have been distributed on a very limited basis, primarily to management and to a bank that provides financial services for the company. In 1992, however, the company decides to apply for a loan that requires audited financial statements and must now fully comply with generally accepted accounting principles. Remember that one type of event that is considered a correction of an error is a change from an unacceptable accounting method to an acceptable method. Changing from the direct write-off method of accounting for uncollectibles to a method that estimates uncollectibles, matches that expense against revenue and measures receivables at net realizable value is one example of such a change.

Matching Asset/Liability Measurement

A study of historical records of Murphy indicates that uncollectible accounts constitute approximately 5% of sales. The following analysis compares the difference between the accrual of estimated uncollectibles and the direct write-off of uncollectible accounts for years prior to 1992, the year in which the change is being made.

Year(s)	Accrual based on 5% estimate	Direct Write-off	Difference
Before 1990	$50,000*	$43,750	$ 6,250
1990	7,500**	4,500	3,000
1991	8,750***	6,000	2,750
	$66,250	$54,250	$12,000

```
  *$1,000,000 sales × 5% = $50,000
 **  $150,000 sales × 5% = $ 7,500
***  $175,000 sales × 5% = $ 8,750
```

This analysis reveals that an allowance for doubtful accounts of $12,000 is required to state receivables at net realizable value. Had the estimated amount of uncollectibles been properly recognized in the past, additional expenses of $6,250 would have been recognized before 1990, $3,000 in 1990, and $2,750 in 1991. We will assume that all amounts are material.

Because the change is being made in 1992 and 1990 and 1991 will be presented separately for comparative purposes, the impact of the change must be separately identified for those years. All years prior to the earliest year presented may be combined, as is done in the line identified above as "Before 1990."

In addition to the above information, we shall assume that the retained earnings statements presented in Exhibit 19–2 were included in the previously-issued financial statements of Murphy Company for 1991.

Now we are ready to record the correction. First we shall ignore income tax effects and record the change as follows:

Retained Earnings	12,000	
Allowance for Doubtful Accounts		12,000

Observe in this entry that Retained Earnings is reduced with the debit entry, representing the additional expense that would have been recognized in previous years had the estimation method been used. The account, Allowance for Doubtful Accounts, is a contra-account to Accounts Receivable and serves to reduce the amount at which that account is presented in the balance sheet from the face value of the receivables to their net realizable value.

Now let's add income tax considerations to this situation by assuming a 35% income tax rate. Also, we shall assume that a $25,000 deferred tax liability exists from other temporary differences and that the direct write-off method of accounting for uncollectibles will continue to be used for income tax purposes. The entry to record the correction under these revised assumptions is as follows:

Retained Earnings	7,800	
Deferred Income Taxes	4,200	
Allowance for Doubtful Accounts		12,000

The deferred tax amount of $4,200 is computed as the $12,000 adjustment to the Allowance for Doubtful Accounts times the income tax rate: $12,000 × 35% = $4,200. The debit to Retained Earnings is the net-of-tax amount of that adjustment: $12,000 × (1 − .35) = $7,800. We stated earlier that a Deferred Income Tax balance of $25,000 existed, so the debit to that account of $4,200 simply reduces that balance to $20,800 ($25,000 − $4,200). This adjustment is required because restated financial income exceeds taxable income for past years by $12,000 due to the temporary difference between the estimation and direct write-off methods of accounting for uncollectible accounts.

We are now ready to prepare a revised statement of retained earnings for 1991 and 1990. The change in method of accounting for uncollectible accounts, which we have recorded as a correction of an error, results in a restatement of beginning retained earnings of *each year at a different amount.* Also, net income for each year is

EXHIBIT 19–2

Murphy Company
STATEMENT OF RETAINED EARNINGS
(as previously reported)

	1991	1990
Retained earnings, beginning balance	$110,000	$100,000
Net income	40,000	25,000
Dividends declared	(25,000)	(15,000)
Retained earnings, ending balance	$125,000	$110,000

restated to reflect the reduction that results from the additional expense recognized by the estimation method of accounting for uncollectible accounts. The revised statement is presented in Exhibit 19–3.

Observe that for each year, the restatement for correction of error is limited to the impact of the change on income of previous years on a net-of-tax basis. For 1990, restatement is based on previous years' incomes of $6,250; for 1991, restatement is based on previous years' incomes of $9,250 ($6,250 + $3,000). Also, observe that the ending retained earnings of 1990 ($103,987) reconciles with the *restated* beginning retained earnings of 1991 rather than the beginning retained earnings as previously stated. The net income figures of each year are also restated to reflect the additional expense, on a net-of-tax basis, that is required under the estimation method of accounting for uncollectible accounts.

As stated at the beginning of this illustration, figures from all years are restated for the new accounting assumption, the impact of the correction is adjusted to the Retained Earnings account and presented as restatements to the beginning retained earnings figures in the statement of retained earnings, and all amounts presented are consistently determined by the newly-adopted method or assumption. While the circumstances in which the restatement method is applied vary considerably, these conclusions are true whenever the method is used. Net income for 1992 will be computed based on the allowance method of accounting for uncollectible accounts.

A PRACTICE EXAMPLE OF THE RESTATEMENT METHOD

Restatements of beginning retained earnings in published financial statements are relatively rare in practice. In the authors' opinion, this is because companies prefer to not restate financial statements and are particularly careful to avoid those situations that require restatement unless they are unavoidable, as when a new FASB Statement requires that transition approach. Also, many error corrections may be judged

Materiality   immaterial to the financial statements taken as a whole.

Exhibit 19–4 includes a restatement from the 1987 financial statements of Matrix Science Corporation, taken from the AICPA's *Accounting Trends & Techniques*. The accounting method in question involves recording sales prior to shipment and has been accounted for as a correction of an error. Notice the last sentence in the

---

EXHIBIT 19–3

Murphy Company
STATEMENT OF RETAINED EARNINGS
(Restated)

	1991	1990
Retained earnings, beginning as previously stated	$110,000	$100,000
Restatement for correction of error*	(6,013)	(4,063)
Retained earnings, restated	$103,987	$ 95,937
Net income**	38,212	23,050
Dividends	(25,000)	(15,000)
Retained earnings, ending	$117,199	$103,987

*1990: $6,250 × (1 − .35) = $4,063
  1991: ($6,250 + $3,000) × (1 − .35) = $6,013
**1990: $25,000 − [$3,000 × (1 − .35)] = $23,050
  1991: $40,000 − [$2,750 × (1 − .35)] = $38,212

EXHIBIT 19-4

Matrix Science Corporation
Example Correction of Error

Consolidated Statements of Shareholders' Equity

	Number of shares	Amount	Additional paid-in capital	Retained earnings
	Common stock			
Balance at June 30, 1984 (Note 2)	3,946,010	$39,500	$5,015,400	$27,326,800
Cash dividends	—	—	—	(394,600)
Net income	—	—	—	7,802,100
Balance at June 30, 1985 (Note 2)	3,946,010	39,500	5,015,400	34,734,300
Cash dividends	—	—	—	(394,600)
Net income	—	—	—	7,853,200
Balance at June 30, 1986 (Note 2)	3,946,010	39,500	5,015,400	42,192,900
Cash dividends	—	—	—	(631,400)
Shares issued under stock option plan	550	—	14,400	—
Stock split, 2 for 1.................................	3,946,560	39,400	(39,400)	—
Net income	—	—	—	1,883,700
Balance at June 30, 1987	7,893,120	$78,900	$4,990,400	$43,445,200

Notes to Consolidated Financial Statements

2. Special Investigation and Accounting Practices

In August 1987, it became known that the Company had followed a practice of recording sales prior to the shipment of goods. In connection therewith, the Board of Directors engaged special legal counsel and the Company's auditors to conduct an investigation of the Company's accounting practices. Additionally, in September 1987, it was determined that substantial amounts of credit memorandums, primarily for customer returns, had not been processed in a timely manner.

The above practices involved certain senior officers and other employees of the Company. In October 1987, the former president, executive vice president and chief financial officer resigned their positions and entered into consulting agreements as of the date of their resignations with the Company. The consulting agreement with the former president ended on January 8, 1988 and the other two agreements are on a month-to-month basis.

The results of the investigation concluded that the sales recording and credit memo practices discussed above resulted in the incorrect recording of sales. While the Company does not believe the resulting adjustments were material to its financial statements, when taken as a whole in any prior year, the Company has determined that a restatement of prior years' financial statements is appropriate. Accordingly, the financial statements for 1982 through 1986 have been restated. A summary of the impact of restatement for fiscal 1986 and 1985 is shown below:

	1986		1985	
	Reported	*Restated*	*Reported*	*Restated*
Net Sales	$75,094,500	$74,676,500	$67,134,200	$64,809,200
Net Income	8,271,100	7,853,200	8,056,200	7,802,100
Working Capital	45,198,500	43,319,000	37,370,100	35,908,600
Total Assets.................	59,294,100	56,918,400	52,828,000	50,732,900
Shareholders' Equity..........	49,127,300	47,247,800	41,250,800	39,789,200
Earnings Per Share	1.05	1.00	1.02	.99

At June 30, 1984, retained earnings as previously reported, was $28,534,300. Retained earnings, as restated, is $27,326,800.

SOURCE: AICPA, *Accounting Trends & Techniques,* 1988, p. 312.

explanation states that retained earnings has been restated to $27,326,800 and that figure appears as the June 30, 1984, balance in the retained earnings column of the Consolidated Statement of Shareholders' Equity.

THE CUMULATIVE EFFECT METHOD: EXPANSION AND ILLUSTRATION

Changes in accounting principle are the only events that are accounted for and reported in financial statements by the cumulative effect method. Except for those few special changes in principle that require the restatement method, all changes in accounting principle are accounted for as described in this section.

Recall that changes in accounting principle are changes from one generally accepted accounting principle to another, including methods of applying principles. Common examples are changes in methods of accounting for inventories (e.g., FIFO to LIFO) and change in methods of depreciation (e.g., straight-line to units of production) and other similar changes. A change from LIFO to another accepted inventory method is one of the exceptions that requires the restatement method. As we saw in Exhibit 19–3, a change from an accounting method that is not generally accepted to one that is in accordance with GAAP is considered a correction of error and requires the restatement method.

The following steps outline proper accounting for changes in accounting principle by the cumulative effect method:

1. The cumulative effect of the change on all previous years' income is computed. That amount, net of income taxes, if applicable, is presented in the income statement of the year of change as a special gain or loss, immediately following extraordinary items, if any. This special income statement item is computed as if the change occurred at the beginning of the year, regardless of when the decision to change was made within the year.
2. Items in the income statement that are affected by the change (e.g., cost of goods sold for an inventory method change or depreciation expense for a depreciation method change) are computed by the new method in the year of the change.
3. Comparative financial statements of previous periods are *not restated* to apply the new method retroactively, as would be done in the restatement method. This results in the income statement items affected by the change being presented by different methods in the current year's statement, as compared with comparative years' statements.
4. Required disclosures include the retroactive restatement of income and earnings per share for all years presented on a *pro-forma basis* at the bottom of the income statement to supplement information presented in the body of that statement. Also, notes to the financial statements report the reason and justification for change and the impact of the change on income and earnings per share for the year of the change.

Justifications for changes in accounting principle vary considerably. Some focus on the idea that the change brings the reporting entity in conformity with standard industry practices. Other justifications make reference to preference for the newly-adopted method on the basis that it produces better information with regard to an underlying accounting principle (e.g., matching principle).

Matching

The FASB has provided some additional guidance for accountants attempting to justify changes in accounting principle. *SFAS No. 32* indicates that justification for a change in principle on the basis of preferability is satisfied if a company elects to change to a standard recommended by a variety of AICPA documents. *SFAS No. 32* has, thus, enhanced the stature of the AICPA industry audit guides, accounting guides and statements of position.[6]

Statement of Auditing Standards No. 52 affirms *SFAS No. 32* by defining the types of documents listed above, as well as AICPA Interpretations and FASB Technical Bulletins, as "established accounting principles."[7] *SAS No. 52* also requires auditors to justify any departure from established accounting principles, thereby further enhancing the preferability of these additional AICPA and FASB documents.

GENERAL CHANGE IN ACCOUNTING PRINCIPLE ILLUSTRATED

To illustrate accounting for a general change in accounting principle, assume that during 1992, Northern Company elects to change from the straight-line method of computing the depreciation on an important machine to the service quantity/machine hours method. The company uses accelerated write-off for income tax purposes and will continue to do so in the future. The change is justified on the basis that the straight-line method depreciates the asset at too rapid a rate and that the service potential declines more closely in relation to the actual usage of the machine which varies significantly from year to year. The machine cost $140,000 in 1989 and has been depreciated through 1991 by the straight-line method, assuming an 8-year life with no salvage value. Management believes that the machine's total life in machine hours is 20,000, and plant records indicate that the machine was used 1,000, 2,600, and 1,300 hours in 1989, 1990, and 1991, respectively. Northern's income for 1992, before depreciation and income taxes, is $75,000. To simplify the calculations, let us assume that applying a 35% income tax rate produces amounts that are consistent with current GAAP. We also assume that the percentages presented in the explanation of the ACRS write-off amounts in Exhibit 19–5 are appropriate in light of income tax law in effect when the asset was placed in service. The machine was used 1,600 hours in 1992.

Exhibit 19–5 includes information necessary to prepare the journal entries required to implement this change in accounting principle. The $7 per machine-hour rate is determined as follows: $140,000/20,000 hours = $7 per hour.

For a moment, let's ignore income taxes and record the accounting change and the 1992 depreciation expense:

Accumulated Depreciation ($52,500 − $34,300)	18,200	
Cumulative Effect of Change in Accounting Principle		18,200
Depreciation Expense	11,200	
Accumulated Depreciation		11,200

Notice that the first entry includes the difference between the two methods *up to the beginning of the year of change*, regardless of when the change was made in that year. The $18,200 is the difference between Accumulated Depreciation under the straight-line and machine hours methods for 1989–1991: $52,500 − $34,300 = $18,200. The debit to Accumulated Depreciation reduces that account balance and the Cumulative Effect of Change in Accounting Principle represents a *gain* due to the reversal of past depreciation charges. The 1992 depreciation expense is recorded at $11,200 on the basis of the new depreciation method. Observe also that the Accumulated Depre-

---

[6]*FASB Statement of Financial Accounting Standards No. 32*, "The Preferability of Accounting Principles and Practices Contained in Certain AICPA Audit Guides, Accounting Guides, and Statements of Position," 1981.
[7]*Statement on Auditing Standards No. 52*, "Omnibus Statement on Auditing Standards—1987," 1988.

EXHIBIT 19-5

Accounting for a Change in Accounting Principle
(Based on Northern Company Illustration)

Year	ACRS Write-off*	Straight-Line Depreciation**	Machine Hours Depreciation†
1989	$ 21,000	$17,500	$ 7,000
1990	30,800	17,500	18,200
1991	29,400	17,500	9,100
	$ 81,200	$52,500	$34,300
1992	29,400	17,500	11,200
	$110,600	$70,000	$45,500

*1989 $140,000 × 15% = $21,000	†1989 1,000 hrs. × $7 = $ 7,000
1990 $140,000 × 22% = 30,800	1990 2,600 hrs. × $7 = 18,200
1991 $140,000 × 21% = 29,400	1991 1,300 hrs. × $7 = 9,100
1992 $140,000 × 21% = 29,400	1992 1,600 hrs. × $7 = 11,200
**1989–1991: $140,000/8 years = $17,500	

ciation balance is now exactly what it would have been had the company been on the machine hours method from the time the machine was acquired:

Depreciation recorded 1989–1991	$ 52,500
Adjustment for accounting change	(18,200)
Depreciation recorded 1992	11,200
Accumulated Depreciation balance, 1992	$ 45,500

How does the incorporation of income taxes alter this recording of the change in accounting principle? Remember that Northern Company uses ACRS for income tax purposes and will continue to do so. Because temporary differences have existed between taxable income and pretax financial income for 1989–1991, deferred income taxes of $10,045 have already been recorded [($81,200 − $52,500) × .35 = $10,045]. Had the company been on the machine hours depreciation method since 1989, however, deferred income taxes would have been even greater because of the larger temporary differences resulting from the fact that the machine hours depreciation amounts are less than straight-line. In fact, deferred income taxes through 1991 would have been $16,415, determined as follows: [($81,200 − $34,300)] × .35 = $16,415. These additional deferred income taxes must be recorded at the time the change in principle is recorded and the cumulative effect presented on a net-of-tax basis, as follows:

Accumulated Depreciation	18,200	
Deferred Income Taxes [($52,500 − $34,300) × .35]		6,370
Cumulative Effect of Change in Accounting Principle		11,830

Deferred income taxes are now $16,415, as follows:

Deferred income tax balance before change [($81,200 − $52,500) × .35]	$10,045
Adjustment recorded as part of accounting change	6,370
Deferred income tax balance after change [($81,200 − $34,300) × .35]	$16,415

The purpose of this adjustment to the deferred income tax account is to place the accounting records precisely where they would have been, had the newly adopted method been used from the beginning, and had such indirect effects as income taxes been included. Note that the additional consideration of income taxes does not change the entry to record depreciation expense for 1992 at $11,200.

Exhibit 19–6 includes partial comparative income statements for Northern Company for 1991 and 1992, with the assumption that net income was properly reported in 1991 at $30,000. Income before income taxes and the cumulative effect was $46,154 [$30,000/(1 − .35)] and income tax expense was $16,154 ($46,154 × .35). This amount includes depreciation expense determined by the straight-line method. The *pro forma* amounts at the bottom of the statement show what net income would have been had the new (machine hours) method been used in

EXHIBIT 19–6

Northern Company
Partial Income Statements

	1992	1991
Income before income tax and cumulative effect of change in accounting principle	$63,800*	$46,154
Income tax expense (35%)	22,330	16,154
Income before cumulative effect of change in accounting principle	41,470	30,000
Cumulative effect of change in accounting principle, net of $6,370 income tax	11,830	—
Net income	$53,300	$30,000
Earnings per share		
Income before cumulative effect of change in accounting principle	$.41	$.30
Cumulative effect of change in accounting principle	.12	—
Net income	$.53	$.30
Pro forma restatement of income and earnings per share, applying machine-hour depreciation retroactively		
Net income	$41,470**	$35,460†
Earnings per share	$.41	$.35

*Computed as follows:

1992 income before deducting depreciation	$ 75,000
Machine hours depreciation	(11,200)
	$ 63,800

**Same as income before cumulative effect of change in accounting principle.
†Computed as follows:

1991 net income	$30,000
1991 difference between straight-line depreciation and machine hours depreciation, net of 35% income tax [($17,500 − $9,100) × (1 − .35)]	5,460
	$35,460

both years. The earnings per share are based on 100,000 shares of common stock out-standing and no preferred stock.

The 1992 income is determined by using the newly adopted machine hours method. The cumulative effect gain of $11,830 is presented on a net-of-tax basis, and income is presented before and after that item. For 1992 the *pro forma* restated income simply consists of income before the effect of the change in accounting princi-ple. The 1991 *pro forma* restated income is computed by restating the 1991 income for the difference between the two depreciation methods on a net-of-tax basis. In the body of the financial statement the inconsistency resulting from the use of straight-line depreciation in 1991 and machine hours depreciation in 1992 remains because the 1991 statement is not restated under the cumulative effect method. However, the effect of restatement is included in the *pro forma* figures.

In addition to the financial-statement disclosure presented above, a note to the financial statements will explain and justify the change and indicate the impact of the change on 1992 income. The impact of the change on 1992 income is twofold: (1) the impact on depreciation expense and the related difference this causes in income tax expense and (2) the inclusion of the cumulative effect "gain" in 1992 net income. Specifically, depreciation expense for 1992 is $11,200 rather than $17,500, causing income tax expense to be $2,205 higher [($17,500 − $11,200) × .35 = $2,205], combined this causes net income to be $4,095 higher [($17,500 − $11,200) × (1 − .35) = $4,095]. Also, the cumulative effect increases net income by a net-of-tax amount of $11,830. Combining the two positive effects on 1992 net income means that the change in accounting principle raised 1992 net income by $15,925 ($4,095 + $11,830).

Cumulative Effect Not Determinable

In some circumstances we may be unable to determine the cumulative effect of certain accounting changes. Perhaps the best example of such a circumstance involves a change *to* the LIFO method of inventory pricing. If we attempt to change from another method of inventory pricing to the LIFO method, we may find it difficult or even impossible to establish what the amount of inventory at the beginning of the year would have been if the LIFO method had previously been used. Remember that the LIFO method treats the cost of the last inventory items acquired as the cost of the first items sold. The cost of the earliest items of inventory acquired are considered to remain in ending inventory. Therefore, LIFO inventory costs may include inventory cost layers that are several decades old. Determining the cost of exceptionally old LIFO cost layers is difficult or even impossible unless the accounting system was specifically designed to capture that information.

If the cumulative effect of a change in accounting principles is not determinable, we simply apply the new method to the existing account balances and no cumulative effect of the change is reported. In our example of a change from FIFO to LIFO, the ending inventory of the previous year under the FIFO pricing method is treated as if it were the beginning inventory under the LIFO pricing method. Disclosures in the notes to the financial statements must point out that no cumulative effect or *pro forma* amounts can be determined.

Disclosure

A PRACTICE EXAMPLE OF A GENERAL CHANGE IN ACCOUNTING PRINCIPLE

An example of the reporting of a change in accounting principle from the 1990 annual report of The Sun Company is presented in Exhibit 19–7. Sun Company explores for, develops, produces and markets crude oil and natural gas outside the U.S., primarily

EXHIBIT 19-7

The Sun Company
Example Change in Accounting Principle

Partial Income Statement and Note

Consolidated Statements of Income
Sun Company, Inc. and Subsidiaries

For the Years Ended December 31 (millions of dollars except per share amounts)	1990	1989	1998
Income (loss) before provision (credit) for income taxes and cumulative effect of change in accounting principle	390	211	(43)
Provision (credit) for income taxes (Note 5)	191	113	(50)
Income before cumulative effect of change in accounting principle	199	98	7
Cumulative effect of change in accounting principle (Note 6)	30	—	—
Net Income	$ 229	$ 98	$ 7
Earnings per share of common stock:*			
Income before cumulative effect of change in accounting principle	$1.86	$.92	$.06
Cumulative effect of change in accounting principle	.28	—	—
Net Income	$2.14	$.92	$.06
Pro forma amounts assuming the accounting change had been retroactively applied (Note 6):			
Net income	$199	$113	$13
Net income per share of common stock*	$1.86	$1.06	$.12
Cash dividends paid on common stock	$192	$192	$286
Cash dividends per share of common stock	$1.80	$1.80	$2.70

*Based on the weighted average number of shares outstanding (in thousands) of 106,848 in 1990, 106,870 in 1989 and 106,139 in 1988.

6. Change in Accounting Principle

Effective January 1, 1990, Sun changed its method of accounting for the cost of maintenance and repairs incurred in connection with major maintenance shutdowns at its refineries (turnaround costs). Turnaround costs are comprised principally of amounts paid to third parties for materials, contract services and other related items. Under the new method, turnaround costs on projects exceeding $500 thousand are capitalized when incurred and then charged against income over the period benefitted by the major maintenance shutdown (usually 3 to 4 years). Prior to this change in accounting, turnaround costs were charged against income as incurred. Sun believes that the new method of accounting is preferable in that it provides for a better matching of turnaround costs with future refined product revenues. Decisions regarding major maintenance shutdowns are generally based on engineering studies and economic analyses (such as discounted cash flow techniques) performed in connection with the capital budgeting process. As a result, management of Sun believes that the investment in turnaround costs enhances the reliability and performance of the refinery unit and therefore economically benefits future periods.

The cumulative effect of this accounting change for years prior to 1990, which is shown separately in the consolidated statement of income for 1990, resulted in a benefit of $30 million (after related income taxes of $15 million), or $.28 per share of common stock. Excluding the cumulative effect, this change increased net income for 1990 by $16 million or $.15 per share of common stock. The pro forma amounts shown on the consolidated statements of income reflect net income and net income per share of common stock as if the accounting change had been retroactively applied.

SOURCE: The Sun Company, 1990 Annual Report.

in Canada and the North Sea. Sun also mines coal in the U.S., refines crude oil and markets a full range of petroleum products. The company is also involved in real estate development. The change in accounting principle involves the method of accounting for the cost of maintenance and repairs incurred in connection with major maintenance shutdowns at its refineries. The cumulative effect gain is included in the 1990 income statement at $30 million, which is $.28 per share. The note disclosure and the pro-forma disclosures that are included in the income statement clearly explain the impact of the change on net income.

THE CURRENT AND PROSPECTIVE METHOD: EXPANSION AND ILLUSTRATION

Changes in accounting estimate result from uncertainties in forecasting future events and their effects. Many financial-statement elements require current estimates of future events for presentation in financial statements. Examples include the collectibility of receivables, obsolescence of inventory, and useful lives and salvage values of plant and intangible assets. After financial statements are issued, if new or additional evidence indicates previous estimates should be revised, changes affecting the financial statements must be recorded. Changes in accounting estimates are accounted for in the current period if the changes affect only that period. If they also affect the future, they are accounted for in the period of change and applicable future periods.[8] As mentioned earlier this treatment is called the **current and prospective method**. Changes in estimate are the only accounting events that are normally accounted for by this method.

CHANGES IN ESTIMATE ILLUSTRATED

To illustrate, assume that Simmons Company has consistently estimated its bad-debt expense to be 2% of credit sales. During 1992, however, the company recognizes that the estimate for the last two years has been too low and that an additional amount of $100,000 should be recognized to present the accounts receivable at net realizable value. The entry at December 31, 1992, to record the additional provision is as follows:

Bad Debt Expense	100,000	
Allowance for Uncollectible Accounts		100,000

The entire amount of the changed estimate is included in income during 1992 because no future periods are affected by the change. Also, no special account is established to record the change. If the change in estimate affects future periods, however, the analysis is more complex.

Assume that Simmons Company also determines during 1992 that one of its buildings will have a useful life greater than originally expected. The building, acquired in early 1982 at a cost of $300,000, was originally estimated to have a 25-year useful life and a salvage value of $50,000. Simmons Company, which uses the straight-line depreciation method, now estimates that the building will be used for a total of 40 years and that a salvage value of $20,000 appears reasonable. The depreciation expense to be recorded in 1992 is computed as follows:

---

[8]*APB Opinion No. 20*, par. 31.

Depreciation Recognized on Building Prior to 1992

Original cost	$300,000
Less: Salvage value	50,000
Depreciable cost	250,000
÷ Original estimate of useful life in years	÷ 25
Depreciation expense per year	10,000
× Number of years depreciated (1982–1991)	× 10
Total depreciation expense through 1991	$100,000

Remaining Depreciable Cost at Beginning of 1992

Original cost	$300,000
Less: Depreciation taken 1982–1991	100,000
Remaining cost	$200,000
Less: Salvage value (revised)	20,000
Remaining depreciable cost	$180,000
÷ Number of years of useful life remaining at Jan. 1, 1992	÷ 30
Revised depreciation expense per year (1992–2021)	$ 6,000

In 1992 Simmons Company records the Depreciation Expense by using the revised estimated life as follows:

Depreciation Expense	6,000	
Accumulated Depreciation		6,000

Each year thereafter Simmons records depreciation in the amount and manner indicated above. Critics of the current and prospective method observe that the straight-line depreciation of a building with an original depreciable cost of $280,000 ($300,000 − $20,000) and a useful life of 40 years is $7,000 per year ($280,000 ÷ 40). This amount of depreciation expense, however, is never presented on any of the income statements of Simmons Company. Application of generally accepted accounting principles in accounting for the effects of this change in estimate results in depreciation expense of $10,000 per year for the first 10 years and $6,000 per year for the next 30 years.

In contrast to the restatement and cumulative effect methods, no special financial-statement item exists to account for the effect of a change in an accounting estimate. The accounts affected by the change in an accounting estimate, such as bad-debt expense and depreciation expense, are simply recorded at different amounts from those that would have been used had the change in estimate not been made.

We have seen in the previous section that a change in accounting principle may result in an adjustment to deferred income tax. The same is true for changes in accounting estimates. For example, a company that uses straight-line depreciation for plant assets in its financial statements but ACRS for income tax purposes will have temporary differences between pretax-accounting income and taxable income in the early years of the assets' lives. These differences reverse as the asset continues to be depreciated for financial reporting purposes and after the cost has been completely written off for income tax purposes. If the company, for financial reporting purposes, extends the life of the asset from its original estimate (as illustrated in the previous example), it will probably continue to write off the asset's cost for income tax purposes in accordance with the percentages prescribed by ACRS. With an extended asset life, resulting in reduced income-statement depreciation charges and fixed ACRS percentages for income tax purposes, deferred income taxes will increase more rapidly than before the change in estimate was made—until the ACRS writeoff is complete. Then deferred income taxes will decline as the asset continues to be depreciated for financial reporting purposes and after its cost has been completely written off for tax purposes.

A PRACTICE EXAMPLE OF A CHANGE IN ESTIMATE

An example of the disclosure of a change in accounting estimate is shown in Exhibit 19–8 for Delta Air Lines, Inc. Delta is a major air carrier providing scheduled air transportation for passengers, freight and mail over a network of routes throughout the United States and abroad. The nature of the change is the lengthening of the estimated useful lives of flight equipment from ten to fifteen years. As the note indicates, the impact of the change was a $130 million decrease in depreciation expense and a $69 million increase in net income for the year ended June 30, 1987.

ERROR ANALYSIS AND CORRECTION

Errors in the financial statements include "mathematical mistakes, mistakes in the application of accounting principles, or oversight or misuse of facts that existed at the time the financial statements were prepared."[9] Changes from unacceptable accounting principles to generally accepted accounting principles are also defined as corrections of errors.

Materiality   Accountants frequently discover minor errors that occur in the accounting process. If an error is immaterial and is not expected to have any impact on the decisions made by financial statement users, the error does not necessarily require correction. Several small errors can, nevertheless, amount to a material misstatement of the financial statements. Accountants, therefore, keep track of all the errors they detect in order to determine which, if any, should be corrected. Effects of errors that are individually material must be accounted for and reported. Errors in the financial statements are corrected by retroactively reporting the effect of the error as a prior period adjustment, net of any income tax effect. Thus, any previously issued financial statements that are presented with the current year's statements for comparative purposes are restated to remove the effects of material errors.

EXHIBIT 19–8

Delta Air Lines, Inc.
Disclosure of Change in Accounting Estimate

Depreciation and Amortization—Prior to July 1, 1986, substantially all of the Company's flight equipment was being depreciated on a straight-line basis to residual values (10% of cost) over a 10-year period from dates placed in service. As a result of a comprehensive review of its fleet plan, effective July 1, 1986, the Company increased the estimated useful lives of substantially all of its flight equipment. Flight equipment that was not already fully depreciated is now depreciated on a straight-line basis to residual values (10% of cost) over a 15-year period from dates placed in service. The effect of this change was a $130 million decrease in depreciation expense, and a $69 million ($1.54 per share) increase in net income, for the year ended June 30, 1987. Ground property and equipment are depreciated on a straight-line basis over their estimated service lives, which range from three to 30 years.

SOURCE: Delta Air Lines, Inc., 1989 Annual Report.

---

[9]*APB Opinion No. 20*, par. 13.

Important considerations in the process of correcting errors are the timing of the error and the timing of the correction of the error. We frequently refer in this chapter to the correction of errors "in previously issued financial statements." Errors that are made and discovered within an accounting period can ordinarily be corrected easily by adjusting the financial-statement elements affected by the error, including revenue and expense accounts, because they have not been closed to Retained Earnings. Errors in *previously issued financial statements,* on the other hand, are generally more complex and require an adjustment to Retained Earnings, because the nominal accounts (revenues and expenses) of the period in which the error was made have been closed to Retained Earnings. Care must be taken in analyzing errors to determine the period in which the error was made so that the appropriate accounts can be properly corrected.

GENERAL TYPES OF ERRORS

Certain errors affect only one financial statement, whereas others affect two or more financial statements. Errors that affect only a single financial statement are frequently called classification errors. Another important distinction is whether an error is self-correcting or permanent.

Classification Errors

Classification errors may occur on any financial statement and corrections of this type of error are usually straightforward and relatively simple. For example, a particular note payable in 10 years might have been classified improperly in previously issued financial statements as a current liability. To correct this error, an accountant merely reclassifies the note as a noncurrent liability in both the current year's balance sheet and any previously issued balance sheets that are presented for comparative purposes with the current financial statements.

Since this type of error does not affect income for either the current year or prior years, no adjustments to prior years' income statements or the statement of retained earnings are required.

Self-Correcting Errors

The correction of certain other errors is also fairly straightforward. In fact, many errors are self-correcting over a two-year period. For example, if the ending inventory for 1992 is overstated, cost of goods sold is understated and net income is overstated for 1992. Because 1992's ending inventory becomes 1993's beginning inventory, the error affects 1993 as well. In 1993, however, the beginning inventory is overstated, causing the goods available for sale and the related cost of goods sold to be overstated. Net income for 1993 is consequently understated. The effect of this self-correcting error is to overstate net income for 1992 and understate net income for 1993 by the same amount. Even if the error is never detected, net income for 1994 and later years will be properly stated.

Most errors eventually correct themselves. Consider an extreme example: If an item of equipment is acquired in 1992 and is inadvertently charged to an expense account, net income for 1992 is understated. Net income in later years, however, is overstated, because no depreciation expense on the equipment is recognized. Assuming no salvage value, we find that the effect of the error made in 1992 will be self-corrected over the life of the asset. Eventually the effects of the error are eliminated from the financial statements, even though the financial statements for all intervening years contain the error.

Permanent Errors

Not all errors are self-correcting. For example, if a parcel of land is acquired and inadvertently charged to expense, the effect of this error is not self-correcting. Since land is *not* a depreciable asset, the Land and Retained Earnings accounts on the balance sheet will be understated indefinitely unless the error is corrected.

ANALYSIS OF SELECTED ERRORS

Many types of errors may exist in the accounting records. In this section we discuss three specific types of errors that are frequently encountered: (1) errors in recording deferrals and accruals; (2) errors in inventories; and (3) errors in plant assets and depreciation. These discussions are followed by a series of illustrations of recording error corrections.

Failure to Record Deferrals and Accruals

Matching

Financial statements prepared according to GAAP apply the accrual concept as required by the matching principle. **Accrual accounting** refers to the process whereby revenues are recognized in income determination when they are earned rather than when cash is received. Likewise, expenses are recognized in the determination of income when their benefit is received, not necessarily when cash is paid out.

Four types of **deferrals and accruals** exist: (1) accrued revenues; (2) unearned revenues; (3) accrued expenses; and (4) prepaid expenses. The purpose of recognizing these items is to adjust the recognition of revenues and expenses from the period in which cash is received or paid to the period in which the item should be recognized in the determination of income. If the accrual or deferral is not recognized properly, the related revenue or expense will be recognized when the cash is received or paid, but it will be recognized in the wrong accounting period.

The accruals (accrued revenues and accrued expenses) and deferrals (unearned revenues and prepaid expenses) are described as follows:

Accrued revenues. Revenues for which earning is complete but cash has not been received (e.g., interest receivable).

Unearned revenues. Revenues for which cash has been received but earning is incomplete (e.g., rent collected in advance).

Accrued expenses. Expenses for which benefit has been received but cash has not been paid (e.g., wages payable).

Prepaid expenses. Expenses for which cash has been paid but benefit has not been received (e.g., prepaid insurance).

Exhibit 19–9 includes a summary of the impact on the financial statements from the *failure* to recognize the four types of deferrals and accruals and of the adjustments required to correct for the omitted deferral or accrual, assuming the error is detected *before* the books for that accounting period are closed.

Inventory Errors

Inventory errors usually result from miscounting inventory, incorrectly pricing inventory by the inventory method being applied, or miscalculating the dollar amount of inventory as physical amounts and dollar prices are combined to determine the total dollar amount of inventory.

Inventory errors affect *ending* inventory first and, if not corrected, *become errors in the beginning inventory of the next accounting period*. An understanding of inventory errors rests on an understanding of the process by which we determine cost of goods sold within a periodic inventory system. Recall from our earlier discussion of

EXHIBIT 19-9

Analysis of Deferrals and Accruals

Error—Failure to Record	Income Statement Errors*	Balance Sheet Errors*	Journal Entry Needed to Correct Error	
Accrued Revenue				
Example: Accrued interest receivable	− Interest Revenue − Net Income	− Interest Receivable − Retained Earnings	Interest Receivable X Interest Revenue	X
Unearned Revenue*				

Example: Rent received in advance	+ Rent Revenue
	+ Net Income
		− Unearned Rent Revenue
		+ Retained Earnings
			Rent Revenue X
			  Unearned Rent
			  Revenue
				X

Accrued Expenses				
Example: Accrued wages payable	− Wages Expense + Net Income	− Wages Payable + Retained Earnings	Wages Expense X Wages Payable	X
Prepaid Expenses†				
Example: prepaid insurance	+ Insurance Expense − Net Income	− Prepaid Insurance − Retained Earnings	Prepaid Insurance X Insurance Expense	X

* + = overstatement; − = understatement.

**This analysis assumes that the total unearned rent revenue was credited to Rent Revenue when received. Alternatively, the amount could have been credited to Unearned Rent Revenue, in which case the adjusting entry would be

        Unearned Rent Revenue   X
          Rent Revenue   X

The failure to make this adjustment would cause an understatement of net income, an overstatement of Unearned Rent Revenue, and an understatement of Retained Earnings.

†This analysis assumes that the total expense paid was debited to Insurance Expense. Alternatively, the amount could have been debited to Prepaid Insurance, in which case the adjusting entry would be

        Insurance Expense   X
          Prepaid Insurance   X

The failure to make this adjustment would cause overstatements of net income, Prepaid Insurance, and Retained Earnings.

inventory that beginning inventory plus the net cost of purchases equals goods available for sale. At the end of the accounting period these goods have either been sold or they are still in inventory. We see these relationships in the following abbreviated calculation of gross margin, where assumed dollar amounts are used:

Sales		$1,000
Cost of goods sold		
Beginning inventory	$ 150	
Net cost of purchases	700	
Goods available for sale	850	
Ending inventory	(320)	530
Gross margin		$ 470

Notice that the *ending inventory is deducted* and *beginning inventory is added* in determining cost of goods sold. Thus, an error in ending inventory has the opposite effect on cost of goods sold as the same error in beginning inventory. This helps explain why an error in inventory that is not corrected will be offset in the next accounting period as the error moves from the ending inventory of the first period to the beginning inventory of the next period.

EXHIBIT 19–10

Analysis of Inventory Errors

Errors	Income Statement Errors*	Balance Sheet Errors*
Ending Inventory		
Overstatement	− Cost of Goods Sold + Net Income	+ Inventory + Retained Earnings
Understatement	+ Cost of Goods Sold − Net Income	− Inventory − Retained Earnings
Beginning Inventory		
Overstatement	+ Cost of Goods Sold − Net Income	None**
Understatement	− Cost of Goods Sold + Net Income	None**

* + = overstatement; − = understatement.
**This assumes that the error in beginning inventory is the reversal of an error in ending inventory of the previous period.

Exhibit 19–10 summarizes the impact of inventory errors, beginning with ending inventory errors and continuing to beginning inventory errors.

Errors in Recording Depreciation

Errors in recording depreciation are generally of three types: (1) recording depreciation at an incorrect amount; (2) failing to record depreciation; and (3) expensing plant assets at acquisition. We consider each of these in the following paragraphs.

Recording Depreciation at an Incorrect Amount.   When depreciation is recorded at an incorrect amount, the financial statement amounts affected are Depreciation Expense and net income in the income statement and Accumulated Depreciation and Retained Earnings in the balance sheet. An understatement of Depreciation Expense results in an overstatement of net income, an understatement of Accumulated Depreciation, and an overstatement of Retained Earnings. An overstatement of Depreciation Expense results in an understatement of net income, an overstatement of Accumulated Depreciation, and an understatement of Retained Earnings.

Failing to Record Depreciation.   Failure to record depreciation has the same impact on the financial statements as an understatement of Depreciation Expense: an overstatement of net income, an understatement of Accumulated Depreciation, and an overstatement of Retained Earnings.

If depreciation is not recorded for a series of accounting periods, the effect of the errors accumulate in the balance sheet while only the amount of depreciation expense omitted each year affects the income statement. For example, if $10,000 of Depreciation Expense is ignored in 1992 and $9,000 in 1993, net income will be overstated by $10,000 and $9,000 in 1992 and 1993, respectively. The impact of the errors accumulates in the balance sheet, however, and Accumulated Depreciation will be understated and Retained Earnings will be overstated by $10,000 and $19,000 ($10,000 + $9,000) in 1992 and 1993, respectively.

Expensing Plant Assets at Acquisition.   The erroneous expensing of a plant asset at acquisition results in an understatement of net income of that period and an offsetting overstatement of net income throughout the asset's life as Depreciation Expense is not recorded.

To illustrate, assume that a $10,000 asset with a five-year life and no salvage value was erroneously treated as an expense when it was acquired. If straight-line depreciation is appropriate and a full year's depreciation would have been taken in 1989, the year of acquisition, the impact of the series of errors on the five years is as presented in Exhibit 19–11.

RECORDING CORRECTIONS OF ERRORS

In this section we illustrate the correction of multiple errors for Everett Company, which began operations on January 1, 1991. The company reports on a calendar-year basis. In reviewing the financial records of the company in early 1993, we discover the following errors and omissions:

1. Merchandise inventory at December 31, 1991 was *overstated* by $10,000.
2. Merchandise inventory at December 31, 1992 was *understated* by $8,000.
3. Accrued wages payable of $4,200 at December 31, 1992, were not recorded.
4. Interest receivable of $2,750 was overlooked at December 31, 1991.
5. A machine purchased in 1991 for $45,000 was incorrectly expensed in that year rather than being capitalized and depreciated over its estimated 10-year life. Straight-line depreciation is appropriate, with a full-year's depreciation taken in the year of acquisition.

Everett Company's accountant has determined that 1991 net income was $75,000 and 1992 net income was $87,500, but these figures include the above-listed errors.

First, we shall analyze each error to determine its impact on 1991 and 1993 net income and compute a corrected net income figure for each year.

	1991	1992
Net income as previously determined	$ 75,000	$87,500
1. Overstatement of 12/31/91 inventory	(10,000)	10,000
2. Understatement of 12/31/92 inventory	—	8,000
3. Accrued wages payable at 12/31/92	—	(4,200)
4. Interest receivable at 12/31/91	2,750	(2,750)
5. Machinery errors		
Cost incorrectly expensed	45,000	—
Depreciation expense omitted	(4,500)	(4,500)
Corrected net income	$108,250	$94,050

Notice in this analysis that the $10,000 overstatement of merchandise inventory in 1991 is offset by an opposite adjustment in 1992. The same is true for the 1991 interest receivable adjustment because the interest receivable that was not recorded at the end of 1991 would have been recorded as interest revenue when received in 1992.

Recording Assuming 1992 Books Are Closed

We shall first record these corrections, assuming that the 1992 books are closed and ignoring income tax considerations. The compound general journal entry to record the corrections is as follows:

Merchandise Inventory	8,000	
Machine	45,000	
Accrued Wages Payable		4,200
Accumulated Depreciation ($4,500 × 2)		9,000
Retained Earnings		39,800

EXHIBIT 19-11					
Example Analysis of Plant-Asset Error					
	1989	1990	1991	1992	1993
Overstatement of expense and understatement of income from original error—expensing $10,000 plant asset	$10,000	—	—	—	—
Reversal of error via understatement of depreciation expense ($10,000/5 years)	(2,000)	$(2,000)	$(2,000)	$(2,000)	$(2,000)
Accumulated understatement of net plant assets and retained earnings:					
1989	$ 8,000	8,000			
1990		$ 6,000	6,000		
1991			$ 4,000	4,000	
1992				$ 2,000	2,000
1993					–0–

The $8,000 debit to Merchandise Inventory corrects the inventory currently carried on the company's books by increasing that account by $8,000. The machine is established in the accounts with the $45,000 debit, and the Accumulated Depreciation for two years is established with the $9,000 credit. The credit to Accrued Wages Payable establishes the liability for accrued wages. The $39,800 credit to Retained Earnings is verified as follows:

Corrected net income figures:	1991	$108,250	
	1992	94,050	$202,300
Incorrect net income figures:	1991	75,000	
	1992	87,500	(162,500)
Required Retained Earning adjustment			$ 39,800

To incorporate income taxes into this analysis, we first assume that the previously reported net income figures ($75,000 for 1991 and $87,500 for 1992) are after-tax figures. Assuming that Everett will file amended income tax returns to correct the errors and that no temporary differences exist, corrected net income figures are as follows, applying a 30% income tax rate:

	1991	1992
Corrected net income (previous analysis)	$108,250	$ 94,050
Incremental income tax expense		
($108,250 − $75,000) × .30	(9,975)	
($94,050 − $87,500) × .30		(1,965)
	$ 98,275	$ 92,085

The compound general journal entry to record the correction of these errors, including the impact on income taxes, is as follows:

Merchandise Inventory	8,000	
Machine	45,000	
Accrued Wages Payable		4,200
Accumulated Depreciation		9,000
Income Taxes Payable ($9,975 + $1,965)		11,940
Retained Earnings		27,860

Again, the credit to Retained Earnings of $23,880 can be verified by subtracting the incorrect net income totals of 1991 and 1992 from the revised figures: [($98,275 + $92,085) − ($75,000 + $87,500) = $27,860].

Recording Assuming 1992 Books Are Open

Again, we will ignore income taxes but assume that the 1992 books are open, meaning that adjustments to 1992 revenue and expense accounts can be made rather than adjusting them through retained earnings as we did in the previous illustration. Remember, however, that revenues and expenses for 1991 are closed and cannot be adjusted.

The compound general journal entry to record the corrections is as follows:

Merchandise Inventory	8,000	
Machine	45,000	
Depreciation Expense	4,500	
Wages Expense	4,200	
Interest Revenue	2,750	
Cost of Goods Sold ($10,000 + $8,000)		18,000
Accumulated Depreciation ($4,500 × 2)		9,000
Accrued Wages Payable		4,200
Retained Earnings ($108,250 − $75,000)		33,250

Notice that the adjustment to Retained Earnings is limited to the correction of income for 1991 only, $33,250.

Now let's impose income taxes on the situation, again assuming that income is taxed at a rate of 30%, that Everett will file amended income tax returns to correct the errors, and that no temporary differences exist. The compound general journal entry to record the corrections, including income taxes, is as follows:

Merchandise Inventory	8,000	
Machine	45,000	
Depreciation Expense	4,500	
Wages Expense	4,200	
Interest Revenue	2,750	
Income Tax Expense	1,965	
Cost of Goods Sold ($10,000 + $8,000)		18,000
Accumulated Depreciation		9,000
Accrued Wages Payable		4,200
Income Taxes Payable ($9,975 + $1,965)		11,940
Retained Earnings ($98,275 − $75,000)		23,275

The income tax expense recognized in 1992 is only $1,965, the adjustment related to that year. The income tax expense adjustment for 1991 is incorporated into the retained earnings adjustment of $23,275, which is the difference between corrected 1991 net income and the amount of income for 1991 as previously determined.

These illustrations all include adjustments to retained earnings to correct the errors discovered in 1993. This procedure is consistent with the discussion earlier in the chapter concerning the use of the restatement method for corrections of errors.

SOLUTIONS, ANYONE?

I f as an investor you're not confused by corporate earnings statements, you ought to be. Consider the 1987 results reported by General Electric, certainly one of our more conservative and straightforward companies:

GE reported net earnings of $2.9 billion, a nice increase over 1986's $2.5 billion. But look above the bottom line. Before various credits from accounting changes, GE's net income fell nearly 15%, to $2.1 billion. Was GE cooking its books? No. Here's what happened:

By recalculating its deferred-tax provision at the new 34% corporate tax rate, GE created a gain of $577 million, thus more than offsetting the drop in operating income. Nothing nefarious here: The company was simply taking some reserves against taxes that were no longer needed as reserves, and swinging them into the profit column. GE also changed its inventory accounting method, thus adding another $281 million to net earnings.

It would be easy to jump to the conclusion that GE was trying to make its operating profits look better than they really were. But that would be a false conclusion. As against these substantial noncash credits to income, there were even larger debits to income—more than $1 billion—for restructuring.

Add it all up and one can only conclude that General Electric did indeed probably make more money from continuing operations in 1987 than in the year before.

The point here is, How is the average investor to make sense out of all these changes? The answers are anything but clear.

In recent years the Financial Accounting Standards Board has issued a bumper crop of accounting changes, each one with a different method of adoption and also a different effective date. "They [the changes] make for confusing financial reporting," frets Coopers & Lybrand partner Clark Chandler.

Consider GE's aforementioned income tax change. It resulted from the FASB's recently introduced Statement of Financial Accounting Standards 96. SFAS 96 can be adopted either in 1987, 1988 or 1989. Moreover, companies have the option to restate past income figures, or post a cumulative catch-up adjustment in the year of adoption.

General Electric decided to adopt SFAS 96 immediately, in 1987, and not restate prior years' results. But many companies—including Du Pont and Citicorp—say they may wait until 1989 to adopt SFAS 96, and will restate prior years' earnings.

Inevitably, the comparability of financial statements suffers. Grumbles Thornton O'glove, publisher of the *Quality of Earnings Report:* "One of the FASB's original missions was to foster more comparability, and they've just made it worse. Nowadays, unless you're a sophisticated portfolio manager, you can just forget about having comparability."

By no means is SFAS 96 the only problem here. The accounting board has also issued such calculator-breaking changes as SFAS 91 on loan origination fees; SFAS 94 on consolidated subsidiaries; and SFAS 95 on cash flow statements.

Some companies have adopted these rules, while others are still weighing the impact of the changes on their bottom line.

Restating prior years' results can really set investors' minds spinning. In 1986, for instance, Tenneco rewrote its past numbers to reflect a change in the accounting method used for oil and gas operations. As a result, Tenneco's 1985 income from continuing operations was cut by $173 million and in 1984 by $262 million. But the company's 1986 net income was boosted by a hefty $1.7 billion.

Herein is a problem that is both easy to describe and difficult to redress. You can't really blame the companies—the accountants, after all, make the rules. And you can't blame the accountants, either, unless you think accountants should stop trying to discover more accurate ways of describing the financial health of a company.

Should the accounting board insist that companies adopt new rules uniformly—all at the same time, all in the same way? That would make financial statements more like apples and apples, but at a cost of imposing rigid rules on a reality that is too complex for straightforward yes or no answers.

Says Peat Marwick Main & Co. partner Walter Schuetze: "We go through a handwringing and soul-searching discussion, and we very seldom come up with two transition and effective dates that are similar."

Comparability of financial statement: a serious problem in search of a solution.

SOURCE: Penelope Wang, "Solutions, Anyone?" *Forbes*, April 18, 1988, p. 72. Reprinted by permission of *Forbes* magazine. Copyright © 1988 Forbes, Inc.

CONCLUDING REMARKS

Many new pronouncements of the FASB require the implementation of accounting changes. Most of these pronouncements also describe the manner in which such changes should be reported. In many cases the methods of transition contained in a new pronouncement differ from the requirements of *APB Opinion No. 20*. In such circumstances the provisions of the new pronouncement govern and should be followed. If the new pronouncement does not specify how to account for the transition to the new practices, however, then the general provisions of *APB Opinion No. 20* that we have discussed in this chapter should be followed.

Financial accounting and reporting for various types of accounting changes and corrections of errors is complex. While logic and reason underlie the standards of accounting and reporting for changes and errors, many rules must be applied to comply successfully with generally accepted accounting principles. Most knowledgeable accountants refer frequently to the technical literature for guidance if changes or errors are encountered. To help you understand and apply the standards of financial accounting and reporting in this area, Exhibit 19–12 presents a useful summary. Study the summary and refer to the part of the chapter that deals with issues about which you may desire further study.

KEY POINTS

1. There are three types of accounting changes: (1) changes in accounting principle; (2) changes in accounting estimate; and (3) changes in the reporting entity. (Objective 1)

2. Errors result from mathematical mistakes, mistakes in the application of accounting principles, oversight or misuse of facts that existed at the time the financial statements were prepared, and using an unaccepted accounting principle. (Objective 1)

3. Three approaches are available for integrating an accounting change into the financial records: (1) the restatement method; (2) the cumulative effect method; and (3) the current and prospective method. (Objective 2)

4. The cumulative effect of *general* types of changes in accounting principle is reported in a separate special category of the income statement in the year of the change. (Objective 3)

5. The cumulative effect of *special* changes in accounting principle is retroactively reported by restating previously issued financial statements. (Objective 3)

6. The nature and justification of each change in accounting principle must be disclosed as well as the monetary effects of the change. (Objective 5)

7. Changes in accounting estimate are reported currently if only the current period is affected, or currently and prospectively if both the current and future periods are affected. (Objective 3)

8. Changes in reporting entity are reported by restating previously issued financial statements. (Objective 3)

9. The effects of errors in financial statements are reported by restating previously issued financial statements. (Objective 3)

10. The restatement method requires that previous years' financial statements be restated and is appropriate for certain "special" changes in accounting principle, changes in entity and corrections of errors. (Objective 4)

11. Errors must be carefully analyzed and the appropriate accounts corrected to establish the accounts at amounts that would have existed if the errors had not been made. (Objective 5)

QUESTIONS

19–1 Describe a change in accounting principle and give one example of such a change.

19–2 Describe a change in accounting estimate and give one example of such a change.

19–3 Describe a change in reporting entity and give one example of such a change.

19–4 Identify several situations that result in accounting errors.

EXHIBIT 19-12

Summary of Accounting Changes and Corrections of Errors

Type	Basic Accounting Treatment	Summary Accounting and Disclosure Requirements
Changes in Principle:		
General	Cumulative effect method	1. Cumulative effect in income, immediately following extraordinary items, if any. 2. Disclosure of impact on income and EPS. 3. *Pro forma* restatement of prior years' income and EPS.
Special*	Restatement method	1. Previous years' statements restated. 2. Disclosure of effect on income and EPS for all years presented.
Changes in Estimate	Current and Prospective method	1. Disclosure of effect on income and EPS.
Changes in Entity	Restatement method	1. Previous years' statements restated. 2. Disclosure of effect on income and EPS for all years presented.
Corrections of Errors	Restatement method	1. Previous years' statements restated. 2. Disclosure of effect on income and EPS for year of error.

_____
*The FASB has designated certain changes in accounting principle "special" changes, requiring the restatement method rather than the cumulative effect method. Examples are a change from LIFO to another inventory method and a change in the method of accounting for long-term construction contracts.

19–5   Describe the restatement method of handling accounting changes and corrections.

19–6   What types of accounting events are incorporated into the financial records by the restatement method in accordance with generally accepted accounting principles?

19–7   Describe the cumulative effect method of handling accounting changes.

19–8   What types of accounting changes are incorporated into the financial records by the cumulative effect method?

19–9   Describe the current and prospective method of handling accounting changes.

19–10   What types of accounting changes are incorporated into the financial records by the current and prospective method?

19–11   In comparative financial statements, which of the three methods of incorporating accounting changes into the financial records is most compatible with the accounting principle of consistency? Justify your answer.

19–12   In applying the cumulative effect method of incorporating an accounting change into the accounting records, how does the accountant determine the cumulative effect and how is this item presented in the income statement?

19–13   What is the purpose of the *pro forma* disclosure that is presented in the cumulative effect method?

19–14   What procedure is followed when the cumulative effect of a change in accounting principle cannot be determined? What financial statement disclosure is appropriate in these circumstances?

19–15   If a company—after depreciating a plant asset for several years—determines that the asset's life should be shortened, how is depreciation expense for each year after the change determined?

19–16   What is meant by "self-correcting" errors? Cite an example of a self-correcting error.

19–17   What is meant by "permanent" errors? Cite an example of a permanent error.

19–18   Assume that an error in previously issued financial statements is detected in 1993, after the books have been closed for 1992. In the comparative statements for 1992 and 1993, how should this item be presented? (Assume that the error correction results in a decrease of net income in both 1993 and 1992 and in the beginning retained earnings of 1992.)

19–19   Briefly explain the impact that each of the following errors has on the financial statements of the period of the error:

[a] Failure to record accrued wages payable at the end of the year.
[b] Failure to adjust the prepaid insurance account for the portion of the prepaid insurance premiums that have expired.
[c] An overstatement of ending merchandise inventory.
[d] Failure to record depreciation expense for the year.

19–20   If a company inadvertently expensed the cost of a plant asset that should have been capitalized, what impact will this error have on the financial statements in the year of the error and the next year? (You may assume that the company's policy calls for recording a half-year's depreciation in the year of acquisition.)

EXERCISES   **19–21**   CHANGE IN DEPRECIATION ESTIMATE   Wampler Corporation purchased a machine for $300,000 on January 1, 1990. The machine had an estimated useful life of 8 years with no expected salvage value and Wampler depreciates the machine by the straight-line method. As a result of experience using the machine, on January 1, 1993, management determines that the machine will have a total useful life of 12 years from the time of acquisition rather than the eight years originally expected.

Instructions

Compute the amount of depreciation expense on this machine to be recognized in 1993.

19–22   CHANGE IN DEPRECIATION METHOD   On January 1, 1990, Sanders Company purchased machinery at a cost of $175,000. The machine was depreciated by the double-declining balance method, assuming a ten-year life and no salvage value, from 1990 through 1992. During 1993, management decided to change depreciation methods to straight-line.

Instructions

[a] Ignoring income tax considerations, compute the amount of the cumulative effect of the accounting change to be recognized during 1993.
[b] Prepare the general journal entries required to record the cumulative effect of the change and depreciation expense for 1993.

19–23   CHANGE IN DEPRECIATION ESTIMATE   Maxwell Company purchased a machine for $3,000,000 on January 1, 1990, when the machine had an estimated useful life of six years with no salvage value. The machine is being depreciated on a straight-line basis. On January 1, 1993, Maxwell determined, as a result of additional information, that the machine had an estimated useful life of eight years from the date of acquisition with no salvage value. An accounting change was made in 1993 to reflect this additional information.

Instructions

[a] Assume that the direct effects of this change are limited to the effect on depreciation and the related income tax provision. For simplicity, we will assume that applying a 35% income tax rate produces appropriate income tax amounts under current GAAP. Show what should be reported in Maxwell's income statement for the year ended December 31, 1993, as the cumulative effect on prior years of changing the estimated useful life of the machine. Explain your answer.
[b] What amount of depreciation expense on this machine should be recognized in Maxwell's income statement for the year ended December 31, 1993?   (AICPA adapted)

19–24 CHANGE IN INVENTORY METHOD On January 1, 1993, Belmont Company changed its inventory cost-flow method to the FIFO cost method from the LIFO cost method. Belmont can justify the change, which was made for both financial-statement and income tax reporting purposes. Inventories totaled $4,000,000 on the LIFO basis at December 31, 1992. Supplementary records showed that the inventories would have totaled $4,950,000 at December 31, 1992, on the FIFO basis.

Instructions

[a] Ignoring income taxes, compute the 1993 adjustment for the effect of changing to FIFO.
[b] Prepare the journal entry to record this inventory change in January 1993. (AICPA adapted)

19–25 CORRECTION OF ERRORS Hennon Company has (incorrectly) determined its 1992 and 1993 net income figures to be $115,000 and $110,000, respectively. In a first-time audit of the company's financial statements, you determine the following errors:

[1] Merchandise inventory was incorrectly determined: $5,000 overstatement for 1992 and $15,000 overstatement for 1993.
[2] Revenue received in advance in 1992 of $25,000 was credited to a revenue account when received. Of the $25,000, $5,000 was earned in 1992, $12,000 was earned in 1993 and the remainder will be earned in 1994.
[3] A $12,000 gain on the sale of plant assets in 1993 was erroneously credited to the retained earnings account.

Instructions

[a] Determine the correct net income for 1992 and 1993.
[b] Prepare the correcting entry in early 1994, assuming the 1993 books are closed.
[c] Prepare the journal entry in early 1994 to correct the books, assuming the 1993 books are not closed.

19–26 CHANGE IN DEPRECIATION ESTIMATE Hunt Company acquired machinery on January 1, 1990, for $75,000. For three years the company depreciated the asset by the straight-line method over an eight-year life with a $5,000 salvage value. Then Hunt determines that the asset's useful life will be a total of only five years rather than eight years, with no salvage value.

Instructions

Prepare the general journal entry to record depreciation in the fourth year of the asset's life and provide computations to support the depreciation amount.

19–27 CHANGE IN UNCOLLECTIBLE ESTIMATE Maxey Company estimated uncollectible accounts at 2% of credit sales for several years, including 1992—when credit sales totaled $135,000. During 1993 management decided the percentage estimate should be changed to 3%. Credit sales for 1993 totaled $250,000.

Instructions

[a] The company's accountant recommends a prior period adjustment of $1,350 to apply the new 3% estimate retroactively to 1992 sales, some of which have not been collected by the end of 1993. (The $1,350 was determined by applying an additional 1% to the $135,000 credit sales for 1992.) Do you agree with the accountant's recommendation? Why?
[b] Prepare the journal entry to record uncollectible accounts for 1993.

19–28 CHANGE IN WARRANTY ESTIMATE KUB Company sells appliances with a two-year warranty. Historically the company established a liability for product warranties of 2% of sales at the time of the sale to provide for the warranty. (This amount has been debited to an expense and credited to a liability account. Payments have been charged to the liability account.) The company's controller is concerned that 2% of sales does not provide an adequate amount for warranties because of the rapidly increasing warranty costs.

In evaluating the adequacy of this estimate, the following information has been accumulated in early 1992.

Year	Sales	Warranty Payments Through Dec. 31, 1991	Revised Estimated Warranty Payments After Dec. 31, 1991
1988	$185,000	$3,800	—
1989	198,500	4,550	—
1990	251,000	5,000	$1,025
1991	262,800	3,000	3,800

Instructions

[a] Compute to the nearest half percentage of sales the amount of warranty expense you would provide for 1992 sales, which totaled $288,700.

[b] Prepare the journal entry to record the warranty expense and year-end liability for 1992.

[c] What adjustment, if any, would you make for years prior to 1992?

19–29 CHANGE IN INCOME RECOGNITION METHOD The following information represents a comparison of net income computed by the percentage-of-completion and completed contract method for Elam Company's long-term contracts for the years 1988–1992.

	Net Income	
	Percentage-of-Completion Method	Completed Contract Method
1988	$100,000	$ 80,000
1989	150,000	135,000
1990	195,000	206,000
1991	190,000	175,000
1992	205,000	192,000

At the end of 1992, management decided to change from the completed contracts to the percentage-of-completion method on its long-term contracts because of new engineering estimates of the degree of completion.

Instructions

[a] Ignoring income taxes, show the retroactive adjustments that should be made to beginning retained earnings figures for 1991 and 1992.

[b] The company presented retained earnings for 1991 as follows:

Beginning balance	$ 400,000
Net income	175,000
	575,000
Dividends	(75,000)
Ending balance	$ 500,000

Assuming dividends for 1992 were $100,000, prepare comparative retained earnings statements for 1991 and 1992.

19–30 CHANGE IN INVENTORY OVERHEAD METHOD Weeks, Inc., changed its procedure for associating manufacturing overhead with inventory items. The previous procedure for allocating overhead to inventory was based on a percentage of direct labor dollars. The company will now allocate overhead at a predetermined rate based on a fixed amount per direct labor hour.

The change is being implemented in 1993. Comparisons of amounts related to ending inventory for 1990–1993 are as follows:

	Inventory Costs Other Than Overhead	Overhead by Previous Method	Overhead by New Method
1990	$100,000	$ 50,000	$ 45,000
1991	150,000	75,000	80,000
1992	200,000	100,000	125,000
1993	250,000	125,000	130,000

Instructions

[a] What kind of accounting change is Weeks, Inc., making?

[b] Ignoring income taxes, compute the cumulative effect of this change in 1993. Prepare the journal entry to recognize the change.

[c] What amount should be used for the ending inventory in computing the cost of goods sold for the 1993 income statement?

19–31 CORRECTION OF ERROR On May 1, 1992, Iver Company prepaid an insurance policy to cover the year beginning on that date. The bookkeeper debited Insurance Expense and credited Cash for the $3,600 payment. No adjustment was made at October 31, the end of Iver's fiscal year. For the year ending October 31, the company reported net income of $27,800.

Instructions

Ignore income taxes.

[a] Compute the correct net income for the year ended October 31, 1992.

[b] Assuming the 1992 books have not yet been closed, prepare the entry to adjust the accounts for the correction of the error.

[c] Assuming the 1992 books have been closed, prepare the entry to adjust the accounts for the correction of the error.

19–32 CORRECTION OF ERROR Lemon Company included in manufactured inventory only direct materials and direct labor and treated all manufacturing overhead as an expense of the period in which it was incurred. On advice of the company's auditors, the company changed in 1993 to full absorption costing in order to be in conformity with generally accepted accounting principles.

Beginning inventory for 1993 was $152,000, made up of $100,000 of material and $52,000 of labor. Ending inventory was $247,500, made up of $125,000 of material, $70,000 of labor, and $52,500 of overhead. Overhead applied to finished goods is 75% of the direct labor cost. The ending inventory for 1993 was properly determined, but it has not been recorded because adjusting and closing entries have not been made.

Instructions

[a] Ignoring income taxes, prepare the general journal entry to implement this change in accounting policy for determining the cost of manufactured inventory during 1993.

[b] Briefly explain your adjustment to the beginning inventory.

19–33 IMPACT OF ERRORS While examining the December 31, 1993, financial statements of Hickey Company, a new client, you discover the following:

[1] Inventory at January 1, 1993, had been overstated by $3,000.

[2] Inventory at December 31, 1993, was understated by $5,000.

[3] A three-year insurance policy had been purchased on January 2, 1992, for $1,500. The entire amount was charged as an expense in 1992.

[4] During 1993 Hickey received a $1,000 cash advance from a customer for merchandise to be manufactured and shipped during 1994. The $1,000 was credited to sales revenue. Hickey's gross profit on sales is 50%.

[5] Net income reported on the 1993 income statement (before reflecting any adjustments for the above items) is $21,500.

Instructions

Determine the proper net income for 1993 and label any adjustments to the reported net income.

(AICPA adapted)

19–34 IMPACT OF ERRORS Wallon Corporation began operations on January 1, 1992. Financial statements for the years ended December 31, 1992 and 1993, contained the following errors:

	1992	1993
Ending inventory	$16,000 understated	$15,000 overstated
Depreciation expense	$6,000 understated	—
Insurance expense	$10,000 overstated	$10,000 understated
Prepaid insurance	$10,000 understated	—

In addition, on December 31, 1993, fully depreciated machinery was sold for $10,500 cash, but the sale was not recorded until 1994. There were no other errors during 1992 or 1993, and no corrections have been made for any of the errors.

Instructions

[a] Ignoring income taxes, determine the total effect of the errors on 1993 net income.
[b] Ignoring income taxes, determine the total effect of the errors on the amount of working capital (i.e., excess of current assets over current liabilities) at December 31, 1993.

(AICPA adapted)

19–35 IMPACT OF ERRORS Sharp Company received $8,000 of inventory items on the last day of its fiscal year, May 31, 1992. The company employs a periodic inventory system.

Instructions

Determine the impact of the error(s) on the company's 1992 net income in each of the following independent cases:

[a] The items were included in inventory at May 31, but the purchase was not recorded until June 3.
[b] The items were excluded from the May 31 inventory, but the purchase was recorded on May 31.
[c] The items were excluded from the May 31 inventory; the purchase was not recorded until June 3.

19–36 IMPACT OF ERRORS Welsley, Inc., acquired a machine in 1992 for $400,000 and erroneously charged the cost to an expense account. Correct accounting treatment would have called for the depreciation of the asset over its estimated useful life of five years with a 10% salvage value by the straight-line method. Welsley's policy is to take one-half year's depreciation in the year of acquisition and one-half in the year of disposal.

Instructions

Ignoring income taxes, determine the impact of this error on 1992 and 1993 net income.

19–37 CORRECTION OF ERRORS Potts Company's bookkeeper is not familiar with accrual accounting concepts. He determined net income for 1993 to be $79,800. In your audit of the company you determine the following:

[1] Accrued, but unpaid, wages at the end of 1993 amounted to $4,575 and have not been recorded.
[2] Insurance premiums paid in 1993 totaled $18,000, only one-third of which relate to coverage for 1993. The other two-thirds relates to coverage in future years. (The complete amount was expensed when paid.)
[3] Accounts receivable of $50,000, which have been properly recorded, are expected to result in losses from uncollectibility of $3,000. (No specific accounts have been written off as of the end of the year.)
[4] Cash of $11,500, received in late 1993, was recorded as revenue, although the work to be performed under the related contract will take place in 1994.

Instructions

[a] Prepare a revised net income figure for 1993.
[b] Assuming that the 1993 books have *not* been closed, prepare separate general journal entries to correct each of the four items.
[c] How will these adjustments affect the 1993 balance sheet?

19–38 IMPACT OF ERRORS The bookkeeper of Manners Company, which has an accounting year ending December 31, made the following errors:

[1] A $1,000 collection from a customer on account was received on December 29, 1992, but not recorded until the date of its deposit in the bank, January 4, 1993.
[2] A supplier's $1,600 invoice for inventory items received in December 1992 was not recorded until January 1993. (Inventories at December 31, 1992 and 1993, were based on physical count and stated correctly.)
[3] Depreciation for 1992 was understated by $900.

[4] In September 1992 a $200 invoice for office supplies was charged to the Utilities Expense account. Office supplies are expensed as purchased.

[5] Sales on account of $3,500 for December 31, 1992, were recorded in January 1993.

Instructions

Determine the effect of these errors on each of the following financial statement items and provide your explanations.

[a] Net income for 1992.

[b] Working capital at December 31, 1992.

[c] Total assets at December 31, 1992.   (AICPA adapted)

19–39 CONVERTING CASH TO ACCRUAL Atkins Company has cash receipts and disbursement records that are summarized as follows for 1993, its first year of operations:

Cash receipts	$ 128,000
Cash disbursements	(82,500)
	$ 45,500

Management wants you to compute its income by accrual accounting principles.

You have identified the following items that may impact your computation:

[1] Depreciation of plant assets for 1993 computed by the straight-line method is $10,500.

[2] Prepaid insurance of $1,800, two-thirds of which relates to 1994, is included in the 1993 cash disbursement figure. This amount was recognized as insurance expense when it was paid.

[3] Atkins received $12,000 in advance rent for space in its building. The entire amount is included in the cash receipts figure and was recognized as rent revenue when received. However, $7,000 of it was for space that will be provided in 1994.

[4] Employees are due $2,800 at the end of 1993.

[5] Interest amounting to $3,170 from investments is receivable at the end of 1993.

[6] You estimate that your 1993 fee for accounting services that have not been billed will be $500.

Instructions

[a] Compute the correct income before income tax for 1993 by accrual accounting concepts.

[b] Prepare a journal entry to record the items that have not been properly recorded, assuming that the 1993 books are open.

19–40 IMPACT OF ERRORS Hoping to understand the impact of errors on the financial statement, your client has prepared a schedule with the following column headings:

Error 1992	Error 1993
Net Income	Net Income
Assets	Assets
Liabilities	Liabilities
Stockholders' Equity	Stockholders' Equity

Instructions

For each of the following errors, indicate whether the item at the head of each column is overstated (+), understated (−), or not affected (0) by the error:

[a] Omission of wages payable at the end of 1992.

[b] Failure to record depreciation expense for 1992.

[c] Failure to adjust insurance expense recognized in 1992 for amounts representing prepaid insurance for 1993.

[d] Overstatement of ending 1992 inventory.

[e] Understatement of ending 1993 inventory.

[f] Failure to record interest receivable at the end of 1992.

[g] Failure to adjust earned portion of amounts credited to unearned rent in 1992.

[h] Mathematical error in which $10,000 of amortization on an intangible asset was recorded at $1,000 at the end of 1992.

PROBLEMS   **19–41**   CHANGE IN ACCOUNTING PRINCIPLE   Starnes, Inc., began operations in 1991 and used straight-line depreciation on its single piece of machinery, which cost $500,000 in early 1991. The machine was being depreciated over a 10-year period with no expected salvage value. For income tax purposes, the machinery was subject to write-off under the Accelerated Cost Recovery System at the rates of 15%, 22% and 21% of cost in the first three years, respectively.

Income information for 1991–1993, assuming straight-line depreciation, is as follows:

	1991	1992	1993 (preliminary)
Income before depreciation and taxes	$ 250,000	$ 365,000	$ 280,000
Depreciation expense—straight-line	(50,000)	(50,000)	(50,000)
Income before income tax	200,000	315,000	230,000
Income tax expense at 35%	(70,000)	(110,250)	(80,500)
Net income	$ 130,000	$204,750	$ 149,500

In 1993 the company decided to switch to the units of production method, due to the high variability of use of the machine. The machine is expected to produce 500,000 units of output and have no material residual value. Units produced in 1991, 1992, and 1993 were 15,000, 65,000, and 25,000, respectively.

Since Starnes, Inc., is a nonpublic company, no earnings-per-share figures are presented.

Instructions

[a] Prepare an analysis similar to Exhibit 19–5, identifying the amount of depreciation expense under the units of production and straight-line methods and showing the amount of ACRS write-off taken in 1991–1993.

[b] Prepare the journal entries required to record the accounting change in 1993 and depreciation expense for 1993. You may assume that the 35% income tax rate produces income tax amounts that are consistent with accepted accounting standards.

[c] Prepare the income statement for 1993, with comparative year 1992, including the *pro forma* disclosures required by *APB Opinion No. 20*.

[d] Describe the difference in the entry in [b] above to record this change if the units of production for 1991, 1992, and 1993 had been 75,000, 55,000, and 85,000, respectively.

19–42   IMPACT OF ERRORS   Wang, Inc., is a calendar-year corporation. Its financial statements for the years 1993 and 1992 contained errors as follows:

	1993	1992
Ending inventory	$1,000 understated	$4,000 overstated
Depreciation expense	$700 understated	$2,500 overstated

Instructions

[a] Assume that the proper correcting entries were made at December 31, 1992. Determine the amount that 1993 income will be overstated or understated and provide computations. (Ignore income taxes.)

[b] Assume that no correcting entries were made at December 31, 1992. Ignoring income taxes, compute the amount by which Retained Earnings will be overstated or understated at December 31, 1993. (Provide supporting computations.)

[c] Assume that no correcting entries were made at December 31, 1992, nor at December 31, 1993, and that no additional errors occurred in 1994. Ignoring income taxes, compute the amount by which December 31, 1994, working capital will be overstated or understated and provide supporting computations or explanation.   (AICPA adapted)

19–43   ACCOUNTING CHANGES AND CORRECTION OF ERRORS   This problem consists of four *independent* parts, but each company's accounting period ends on December 31. Ignore income taxes except where they are mentioned.

Part 1.   At the beginning of 1990 Orange Company acquired, for $250,000, equipment that is being depreciated over an 8-year life with a salvage value of 10% of historical cost. In 1993 the decision was made to extend the useful life to 12 years with no salvage value.

Instructions

Prepare the journal entry, if any, to record this change and the 1993 depreciation expense.

Part 2.   Red Company has consistently expensed warranty costs as they were incurred rather than recognize them on an estimated basis in the period in which the products were sold. During 1993 management decided to change to the accrual basis in which estimates of warranty expense are made annually on the basis of sales and past warranty experience. Red Company officials estimate that the liability for warranty at the beginning of 1993 was $35,600. Warranty costs for 1993 are estimated at 2% of sales of $1,500,000. During 1993, $18,000 of warranty costs were paid, $14,500 of which relate to pre-1993 sales. Warranty Expense was debited with $18,000. The company's income tax rate has consistently been 34%, and you may assume that use of that rate produces appropriate income tax amounts. Red will continue to deduct warranty costs for income tax purposes as actual cash payments are made. ⁊S/6 35%

Instructions

Prepare the general journal entry, if any, to record this change and warranty expense for 1993.

Part 3.   Blue Company determined in 1993 that repair and maintenance expense of 1991 included the cost of a $80,000 machine that had a five-year estimated useful life with no expected salvage value. If the asset had been properly accounted for in 1991, a half-year's depreciation would have been taken in that year by the straight-line method.

Instructions

Prepare the general journal entry, if any, to correct this oversight and to record depreciation expense in 1993.

Part 4.   White Company changed inventory methods from FIFO to LIFO in 1993. Inventory figures are as follows:

	FIFO	LIFO
Beginning 1993	$86,500	—
Ending 1993	92,800	$79,800

The beginning 1993 inventory under the LIFO method cannot be determined.

Instructions

Prepare the general journal entry, if any, to record the change and the 1993 ending inventory.

19–44   CHANGE IN ACCOUNTING PRINCIPLE   Bill Jones, accountant for Reynolds, Inc., has contacted you concerning a financial reporting situation in a subsidiary company. Bill describes the situation as follows:

The subsidiary company changed from the weighted average to the FIFO method during 1993. Inventory amounts under each method are as follows:

	Weighted Average	FIFO
Beginning 1993 inventory	$88,800	$82,600
Ending 1993 inventory	97,600	84,700

The subsidiary's accountant has recorded the change as follows:

Retained Earnings ($88,800 − $82,600)	6,200	
Inventory		6,200
(To restate the 1993 beginning inventory.)		

The accountant has then computed the 1993 cost of goods sold as follows:

Beginning FIFO inventory	$ 82,600
Net cost of purchases	200,000
	282,600
Ending FIFO inventory	84,700
Cost of goods sold	$197,900

The subsidiary's income tax rate is 35% and you may assume that use of that rate produces acceptable amounts. The weighted average method has been used for income tax purposes in the past, and this practice will be continued in the future.

Instructions

[a] Identify the type of accounting change that has taken place and briefly describe the proper accounting treatment for that change (without regard to the approach taken by the subsidiary's accountant).

[b] List the errors you can identify in the accountant's recording of the accounting change.

[c] Prepare a revised entry to record the accounting change in 1993.

[d] Has the accountant properly computed cost of goods sold? Give reasons for your answer.

[e] How should the effect of this change in inventory method be presented in the company's 1993 income statement?

19–45 IMPACT OF ERRORS Warm-Glow Company manufactures kerosene heaters for home use. The company's December 31 year-end financial statements contained the following errors:

	Dec. 31, 1992	Dec. 31, 1993
Ending inventory	$2,000 understated	$1,800 overstated
Depreciation expense	$400 understated	—

An insurance premium of $1,500 was prepaid in 1992 to cover 1992, 1993, and 1994. The entire amount was charged to expense in 1992. On December 31, 1993, fully depreciated machinery was sold for $3,200 cash, but the sale was not recorded until 1994. There were no other errors during 1992 or 1993, and no corrections have been made for any of the errors. Ignore income tax considerations.

Before any of the above errors were corrected, the company's 1992 and 1993 net income figures were determined to be $13,600 and $24,700, respectively.

Instructions

[a] Compute revised net income figures for 1992 and 1993 and label any adjustments to the previously determined figures.

[b] What is the effect of these errors on the amount of Warm-Glow's working capital at December 31, 1993? (Working capital is defined as the excess of current assets over current liabilities.)

[c] What is the effect of these errors on the amount of Warm-Glow's retained earnings at December 31, 1993?   (AICPA adapted)

19–46 CORRECTION OF ERRORS LED Corporation is negotiating a loan for expansion. Its books had never been audited and the bank requested an audit. LED then prepared the following comparative financial statements for the years ended December 31, 1993 and 1992:

LED Corporation
BALANCE SHEET
As of December 31

	1993	1992
Assets		
Current Assets		
Cash	$163,000	$ 82,000
Accounts receivable	392,000	296,000
Allowance for uncollectible accounts	(37,000)	(18,000)
Marketable securities, at cost	78,000	78,000
Merchandise inventory	207,000	202,000
Total current assets	803,000	640,000
Fixed Assets		
Property, plant, and equipment	167,000	169,500
Accumulated depreciation	(121,600)	(106,400)
Total fixed assets	45,400	63,100
Total assets	$ 848,400	$ 703,100

Liabilities and Stockholders' Equity

Liabilities

Accounts payable	$121,400	$196,100

Stockholders' Equity

Common stock ($10 par value; 50,000 shares authorized, 20,000 shares issued and outstanding)	260,000	260,000
Retained earnings	467,000	247,000
Total stockholders' equity	727,000	507,000
Total liabilities and stockholders' equity	$ 848,400	$ 703,100

(handwritten: 7 $\times$ slb 200000)

LED Corporation
STATEMENT OF INCOME
For the Years Ended December 31

	1993	1992
Sales	$1,000,000	$900,000
Cost of sales	430,000	395,000
Gross profit	570,000	505,000
Operating expenses	210,000	205,000
Administrative expenses	140,000	105,000
	350,000	310,000
Net income	$ 220,000	$195,000

Additional Information

After auditing LED's books and records, the auditor wrote down the following information:

[1] An analysis of collections and losses on accounts receivable during the past two years indicates a drop in anticipated losses due to bad debts. After consultation with management it was agreed that the loss experience rate on sales should be reduced from the recorded 2% to 1%, beginning with the year ended December 31, 1993. *(handwritten: Change in Est. Current + Prospective)*

[2] An analysis of marketable securities revealed that this investment portfolio consisted entirely of short-term investments in marketable equity securities that were acquired in 1992. The total market valuation for these investments as of the end of each year was as follows:

Dec. 31, 1992	$81,000
Dec. 31, 1993	$62,000

(handwritten: record at LCM)

[3] The merchandise inventory at December 31, 1992, was overstated by $4,000, and the merchandise inventory at December 31, 1993, was overstated by $6,100.

[4] On January 2, 1992, equipment costing $12,000 (estimated useful life of ten years and residual value of $1,000) was incorrectly charged to operating expenses. LED records depreciation on the straight-line method. In 1993 fully depreciated equipment (with no residual value) that originally cost $17,500 was sold as scrap for $2,500. LED credited the proceeds of $2,500 to property and equipment.

[5] An analysis of 1992 operating expenses revealed that LED charged to expense a three-year insurance premium of $2,700 on January 15, 1992. *(handwritten: 1993 1992)*

Instructions

(handwritten: new 212400 203700)

[a] Prepare the journal entries to correct the books at December 31, 1993. The books for 1993 have not been closed. (Ignore income taxes.)

[b] Assuming that any adjustments will be reported on comparative statements for the two years, prepare a schedule showing the corrected net income for the years ended December 31, 1993 and 1992. The first item on your schedule should be reported income for each year. (Ignore income taxes.)

(AICPA adapted)

19–47 CORRECTION OF ERRORS During 1993, Harris, Inc., discovered that a plant asset acquired in 1989 had been erroneously charged to expense rather than capitalized and depreciated over its estimated useful life. The specifics of the asset are as follows:

[1] Machine cost, $75,000.
[2] Estimated residual value, $5,000.
[3] Estimated useful life, 7 years.
[4] Intended method of depreciation, straight-line (full year taken in year of acquisition).

Harris's retained earnings statements for 1991–1992 are summarized as follows:

	1991	1992
Retained earnings, beginning	$140,500	$ 165,500
Net income	40,000	38,500
	180,500	204,000
Dividends declared	(15,000)	(15,000)
Ending balance	$ 165,500	$ 189,000

Instructions

[a] Prepare an analysis showing the impact of this error on the retained earnings balance for each year from 1989 through 1992.

[b] Ignoring income taxes, prepare a 1993 general journal entry to correct this error.

[c] Prepare comparative retained earnings statements for 1992 and 1993. The company declared dividends of $12,000 in 1993 and has determined that its 1993 income, before correction of the error described above, is $50,000.

[d] How would you respond to [b] and [c] if Harris determined that it must file corrected income tax returns for 1989–1992 and its income tax rate was 35%? You may assume that use of that rate produces amounts consistent with GAAP.

19–48   CHANGE IN ACCOUNTING PRINCIPLE   To save money and keep the nature of its plant assets from being widely known, Smalley, Inc., has constructed many of its plant assets. During 1993 the company changed the way it determined the cost of these assets by including in the cost those amounts that were previously treated as expenses when incurred. Both the previous method and the newly adopted method are generally accepted. Management believes the new method more closely approximates the company's investment in the assets, and the depreciation on the new cost method provides a superior matching of revenues and expenses. The previous method had been used since 1991, when the company began operations.

Information for 1990–1993 has been accumulated as follows:

	1993	1992	1991
Income information			
Net income (by old method)	—	$175,000	$180,000
Income before cumulative effect of accounting change (by new method)	$200,000	—	—
Depreciation expense (including depreciation on additional capitalized costs in 1990 figure)	60,000	40,000	35,000
Expenditures incorporated in accounting change			
Expensed in 1991 and 1992	—	45,000	50,000
Capitalized in 1993	40,000	—	—

The plant assets affected by the change in accounting principle are depreciated over a five-year life with no salvage value. A full year's depreciation is taken in the year the assets are constructed. The impact of the change in accounting principle is limited to the capitalization of expenditures and the related impact on depreciation expense. The company had 210,000 shares of common stock outstanding throughout the 1991–1993 period.

The company's effective income tax rate for purposes of recognizing income tax expense and deferred income taxes is 35%. The previous method of determining the cost of its assets will continue to be used for purposes of determining the income tax liability.

Instructions

[a] Compute the cumulative effect of the change in accounting principle that should be included in 1993 net income.

[b] Prepare comparative income statements, beginning with income before the cumulative effect of the accounting change, for 1992 and 1993. Include earnings-per-share figures and the *pro forma* disclosures required by *APB Opinion No. 20*.

[c] Briefly identify the problems in comparing the information in the body of the comparative income statements. Explain how the *pro forma* disclosures remedy these problems.

19–49 ACCOUNTING CHANGES   Mentor Company decided in the preparation of its 1993 financial statements to make two changes from the procedures used in previous years:

Inventory—Mentor has always used the weighted-average method but management has now decided to change to the FIFO method. Comparative inventory figures for 1991, 1992, and 1993 are as follows:

	1991	1992	1993
Ending inventories:			
Weighted-average method	$138,000	$150,000	$180,000
FIFO method	$152,000	$162,500	$187,800

Uncollectible accounts—Mentor has recognized expense for uncollectible accounts at 2% of sales, virtually all of which are on credit. Based on past records and the anticipation of relaxed credit-granting standards, Mentor has decided that the percentage should be increased to 3%.

Mentor Company's bookkeeper was unaware of these decisions made by management and has prepared the following preliminary income statements, based on the previous methods and assumptions:

Mentor Company
INCOME STATEMENTS
For the Years Ended December 31, 1992 and 1993

	1993	1992
Sales	$ 800,000	$ 750,000
Cost of goods sold	(500,000)	(485,000)
Gross margin	300,000	265,000
Operating expenses	(235,000)	(212,000)
Income before income tax	65,000	53,000
Income tax expense (40%)	(26,000)	(21,200)
Net income	$ 39,000	$ 31,800
Earnings per share	$.78	$.64

The expense for uncollectible accounts is included in the operating expense figure, and earnings-per-share figures are based on the 50,000 shares of common stock that were outstanding throughout the two-year period. For simplicity, you may assume that the 40% income tax rate may be used to determine the tax effects of the change in accounting principle, in accordance with GAAP.

Mentor plans to continue to use the weighted-average method of inventory valuation for income tax purposes, as it has done in the past. The change in percentage used to estimate uncollectible receivables will be applied for both income tax and financial reporting purposes.

Instructions

[a] Prepare revised income statements for 1992 and 1993, incorporating the impact of the change in inventory valuation and bad-debt estimation. Include the *pro forma* disclosures required by *APB Opinion No. 20*.

[b] Explain the difference in approach you have applied for the two types of accounting changes.

[c] Describe the lack of comparability in these statements and explain how the *pro forma* disclosures improve comparability.

19–50 CORRECTION OF ERRORS   Miller Manufacturing Company has an inexperienced bookkeeper who has maintained records on the basis of cash transactions. She recognizes expenses when cash is paid and revenues when cash is received. Operating results, recorded on this basis, are summarized for 1993 as follows:

Revenues		$88,000
Expenses		
Salaries	$18,000	
Equipment	60,000	
Insurance	15,000	93,000
Net loss		$ (5,000)

You have accumulated the following information concerning these revenue and expense items:

Revenues. Of the $85,000 cash received in 1993, $18,500 was related to sales transactions in 1992 and $10,000 was a one-year loan from a bank on December 1, 1993. The interest rate for this loan is 15%. Additional 1993 revenues for which cash has not yet been received amount to $25,000.

Salaries. Of the $18,000 paid in 1993, $1,850 represents salaries for the last four days of 1992. The company owes salaries of $2,200 at the end of 1993 that will be paid in early 1994.

Equipment. The $60,000 cash paid represents the price of a new machine purchased in 1993. This machine should be depreciated over a five-year period with a full year's depreciation taken in 1993 and no salvage value. Pre-1993 acquisitions amounted to $110,000. If the appropriate depreciation policies had been followed, depreciation prior to 1993 would have been $45,000 and 1993 depreciation would have been $22,000 on pre-1993 acquisitions.

Insurance. Of the $15,000 paid in 1993, $10,000 represents prepaid insurance for 1994. Also, $4,000 of $8,000 paid for insurance in 1992 represented prepaid insurance for 1993.

Instructions

[a] Compute a correct income figure for 1993, applying appropriate accrual accounting procedures and ignoring income taxes.

[b] Assuming the 1993 books are not closed, prepare the general journal entries for 1993 to correct the accounts and place them on an accrual basis.

19–51   IMPACT OF ERRORS You have been engaged to examine the financial statements of Lon Corporation for the year ended December 31, 1993. In the course of your examination you have ascertained the following information:

[1] A check for $1,500 representing the repayment of an employee advance was received on December 29, 1993, but was not recorded until January 2, 1994.

[2] Lon uses the allowance method of accounting for uncollectible trade accounts receivable. The allowance is based on 3% of past due accounts (over 120 days) and 1% of current accounts as of the close of each month. Due to a changing economic climate, the amount of past due accounts has increased significantly, and management has decided to make a one-time adjustment to eliminate the negative allowance balance and to increase the percentage based on past due accounts to 5%. The following balances are available:

	As of Nov. 30, 1993 Dr. (Cr.)	As of Dec. 31, 1993 Dr. (Cr.)
Accounts receivable	$390,000	$430,000
Past due accounts (included in accounts receivable)	12,000	30,000
Allowance for uncollectible accounts	(28,000)	9,000

[3] The merchandise inventory on December 31, 1992, did *not* include merchandise (having a cost of $7,000) which was stored in a public warehouse. Merchandise having a cost of $3,000 was erroneously counted twice and included twice in the merchandise inventory on December 31, 1993. Lon uses a periodic inventory system.

[4] On January 2, 1993, a new machine was installed in Lon's main factory. The cost of this machine was $97,000, and the machine is being depreciated on the straight-line method over an estimated useful life of 10 years. When the new machine was installed, Lon paid for the following items which were not included in the cost of the machine, but were charged to repairs and maintenance:

Delivery expense	$ 2,500
Installation costs	8,000
Rearrangement of related equipment	4,000
	$14,500

[5] On January 1, 1992, Lon leased a building for 10 years at a monthly rental of $12,000. On that date, Lon paid the landlord the following amounts:

Rent deposit	$ 6,000
First month's rent	12,000
Last month's rent	12,000
Installation of new walls and offices	80,000
	$110,000

The entire amount was charged to rent expense in 1992.

[6] In January 1992 Lon issued $200,000 of 8%, 10-year bonds at 97. The discount was charged to interest expense in 1992. Interest on the bonds is payable on December 31 of each year. Lon has recorded interest expense of $22,000 for 1992 and $16,000 for 1993.

[7] On May 3, 1993, Lon exchanged 500 shares of treasury stock (its $50 par value common stock) for a parcel of land to be used as a site for a new factory. The treasury stock had cost $70 per share when it was acquired, and on May 3, 1993, it had a fair market value of $80 per share. Lon received $2,000 when an existing building on the land was sold for scrap. The land was capitalized at $40,000, and Lon recorded a gain of $5,000 on the sale of its treasury stock.

[8] The Advertising and Promotion account included $75,000, which represented the cost of printing sales catalogs for a special promotional campaign in January 1994.

[9] Lon was named as a defendant in a law suit by a former customer. Lon's counsel advised management that Lon has a good defense and that counsel does *not* anticipate that there will be any impairment of Lon's assets or that any significant liabilities will be incurred as a result of this litigation. Management, however, has conservatively established a $100,000 loss contingency.

Instructions

Prepare a schedule showing the effect of errors upon the financial statements for 1993. The items in the schedule should be presented in the same order as the facts are given, with corresponding numbers 1 through 9. Use the following columnar headings for your schedule:

		Income Statement		Balance Sheet Dec. 31, 1993		
No.	Explanation	Dr.	(Cr.)	Dr.	(Cr.)	Account

(AICPA adapted)

CASES

19–52 ACCOUNTING CHANGES AND ERROR CORRECTIONS Engler Manufacturing is preparing its year-end financial statements. The controller is confronted with several decisions about statement presentation with regard to the following items:

[1] Upon making the year-end physical inventory adjustment for the current year, the prior year's physical inventory sheets for an entire warehouse were discovered to have been mislaid and excluded from last year's count.

[2] The method of accounting used for financial reporting purposes for certain receivables has been approved for tax purposes during the current tax year by the Internal Revenue Service. This change for tax purposes will cause both deferred and current taxes payable to change substantially.

[3] Management has decided to switch from the FIFO inventory valuation method to the LIFO inventory valuation method for all inventories.

[4] Engler's Custom Division manufactures large-scale, custom designed machinery on a contract basis. Management decided to switch from the completed-contract method to the percentage-of-completion method of accounting for long-term contracts.

[5] The vice-president of sales has indicated that one product line has lost its customer appeal and will be phased out over the next three years. Therefore, a decision has been made to lower the estimated lives on related production equipment from the remaining five years to three years.

[6] Estimating the lives of new products in the Leisure Products Division has become very difficult due to the highly competitive conditions in this market. Therefore, the practice of deferring and amortizing preproduction costs has been abandoned in favor of expensing such costs as they are incurred.

[7] The Miller Building was converted from a sales office to offices for the Accounting Department at the beginning of this year. Therefore, the expense related to this building will now appear as an administrative expense rather than a selling expense on the current year's income statement.

Instructions

[a] *APB Opinion No. 20*, "Accounting Changes," identifies three types of accounting changes—changes in accounting principle, changes in estimates, and changes in entity. Corrections of errors—which are not in themselves accounting changes—make up a fourth type of event accountants may have to deal with. For each of these four categories:

[1] Describe the change or correction.

[2] Explain the general accounting treatment required according to *APB Opinion No. 20* with respect to the current year and prior years' financial statements.

[b] For each of the seven situations described for Engler Manufacturing, identify and explain whether the event is a correction of an error or the result of a change in accounting principle, in estimate, or in entity. If one of these four categories does not accurately describe the situation, explain why.

(CMA adapted)

19–53   ACCOUNTING CHANGES   Riggs Company has made two accounting changes during 1992 that affect its 1992 income statement. These changes are described below:

Change in Life of Machinery.   During 1992 the decision was made to depreciate all machinery over a 10-year life rather than over the 8-year life used in the past for both book and income tax purposes. The company's bookkeeper determined that accumulated depreciation would have been $37,800 less under the 10-year life than under the 8-year life as of the beginning of 1992. The bookkeeper, therefore, made the following entry during 1992:

Accumulated Depreciation	37,800	
Cumulative Effect of Change in Accounting Estimate		37,800

Depreciation expense of $12,200 (assuming a 10-year life from acquisition) has been recorded during 1992.

Change in Inventory Method.   During 1992 a change was made from the FIFO to the weighted average method of costing merchandise inventory. The ending 1991 inventory was $61,750 under FIFO. When management decided to change to the weighted average method in mid-1992, the beginning inventory was recalculated as $67,510, and the bookkeeper made the following entry:

Inventory ($67,510 − $61,750)	5,760	
Retained Earnings		5,760

Instructions

[a] What type of accounting change is the change in the life of the machinery? Do you agree with the bookkeeper's entry? Why? How would you have recorded this accounting change?

[b] What type of accounting change is the change in inventory methods? Do you agree with the bookkeeper's entry? Why? How would you have recorded this accounting change?

19–54   ACCOUNTING CHANGES   A change in the method of accounting may be classified as a change in accounting principle, a change in accounting estimate, or a change in reporting entity. Listed below are three independent situations relating to accounting changes:

Situation 1.   Ramsey Company determined that the depreciable lives of its plant assets were too long to fairly match the cost of the assets with the revenue they generated. The company decided at the beginning of the current year to reduce the depreciable lives of all of its existing plant assets by five years.

Situation 2.   On December 31, 1992, Gary Company owned 70% of Allen Company. At that time Gary used the cost method to report its investment because of political uncertainties in the country in which Allen was located. On January 2, 1993, the management of Gary Company was satisfied that the political uncertainties were resolved and that the assets of the company were no longer in danger of nationalization. Accordingly, Gary plans to prepare consolidated financial statements for Gary and Allen Companies for the year ended December 31, 1993.

Situation 3.   Pepper Company decides in January 1993 to adopt the straight-line method of depreciation for plant assets. The straight-line method will be used for new acquisitions as well as for previously acquired assets for which depreciation has been recorded on an accelerated basis.

Instructions

For each of those situations provide the information indicated below. Complete [a] through [d] for each situation before going to the next situation.

[a] Type of accounting change.
[b] Manner of reporting the change under current generally accepted accounting principles, including a discussion, where applicable, of how amounts are computed.
[c] Effect of the change on the statement of financial position (balance sheet) and income statement.
[d] Any necessary note disclosure.   (AICPA adapted)

19–55   ACCOUNTING CHANGE CONCEPTS   Connie Post, President of Post, Inc., has contacted you recently concerning several things that have occurred in her company during the current year. Specifically, the company has made several accounting changes and has corrected several errors that were identified during the year. Now the company is attempting to prepare its financial statements and is in need of assistance.

Connie has always prepared financial statements for her company based on procedures that she thought were appropriate. Since the statements were primarily for her own use, along with management personnel, she saw no particular reason to prepare statements in accordance with generally accepted accounting principles. To quote Connie, "I have always prepared statements in accordance with good common sense and have simply tried to handle transactions in the most logical way possible." In a recent phone conversation, Connie revealed to you that in anticipation of a bank loan she needs to be sure that she understands certain accounting procedures and that this year's statements follow acceptable accounting procedures.

Specifically, she made the following statements to you:

[1] Changes in accounting estimates and corrections of errors are essentially the same things and, therefore, should be accounted for in the same manner.
[2] Once financial statements have been prepared and distributed outside the company, they should never be altered when they are presented in a later financial report for comparative purposes.
[3] All changes of a particular type—for example, changes in accounting principle—should be accounted for in the same way so that persons studying the financial statements will not be confused by different accounting methods for similar changes.

Instructions

In anticipation of your upcoming meeting with Connie Post in which you will be required to explain generally accepted accounting principles for several accounting changes and corrections that the company has made during the year, write a brief paragraph in reaction to each of Connie's statements.

JUDGMENT CASES

19–56   INVENTORY ACCOUNTING AND REVENUE RECOGNITION   You have just been appointed the new controller for Just-Rite Machine, Inc. Your predecessor only worked for the company for two months before being discharged; however, he had replaced another individual who had retired after serving as the company's chief financial officer for twenty years. During the two months that your predecessor served as controller, the company issued year-end financial statements that were distributed to its primary lender, The Last National Bank. To familiarize yourself with the company you decided to carefully review the just issued financial statements prepared by the prior controller.

Now, you are beginning to wish that you had not done so. You have found a number of deficiencies and changes from accounting principles that the company had previously used.

Specifically, Just-Rite has changed the method used to value ending inventory. The company had used FIFO for the last ten years but the new controller prepared the financial statements on a weighted average basis applied to purchases during the year and the beginning inventory. He left a memo stating that change was made to increase reported earnings for the year. Worse, the previous controller recognized revenue on a special order of machine parts that had not yet been produced by year-end. You have found a memo of his that explained:

> *The manufacture of the machine is routine, and management has tried to get this order for a number of months. Therefore, obtaining the order represents the critical event in earning this revenue, and I consider it appropriate to record the revenue immediately. Of course, the estimated cost of goods sold will also be recorded to achieve a proper matching.*

Neither of these matters is disclosed in the financial statements beyond the summary of significant policies that indicates that the company uses the average cost method of determining ending inventory.

You note that the effect of each of these two items is to increase income by a material amount for the year just ended. You are also aware that Just-Rite greatly values its relationship with the bank and doesn't wish to do anything that could cause the bank to question its operations or financial statements.

Instructions

[a] Without regard to part [b], which follows, describe how the matters mentioned above should be resolved. Be specific. If, for example, you believe that the bank should be notified about either of these matters, prepare the necessary communication. Be sure to address all relevant accounting considerations.

[b] Now assume that you have brought the matter to the attention of the president along with your suggested solution to the problems. With regard to your answer to part [a], assume that you believe that the bank should be informed of the two matters. The president, however, states:

> *"Your concern about these matters shows me that you are a very thorough person, and I like that in a controller. In fact, that's why the last guy is no longer here. I just had a bad feeling about him from the start. However, there is no way that we are going to now tell the bank that the financial statements it just received are wrong. I can't imagine a worse course of action. To do so would destroy the credibility of this company. The bank would never be able to accept information from us without questioning whether it was right or wrong. No, we'll just let sleeping dogs lie on this one. You just go back to your office and worry about things that have happened since you got here."*

What do you do now?

19–57 ORGANIZATION COSTS At the end of the current year the limited partnership for which you are the controller is "converted" to a corporation when the limited partners transfer their interests in the partnership for shares of stock in the corporation. In such a transaction, the corporation generally records its assets and liabilities at amounts that are the same as the amounts on the partnership's books. You have prepared the entries necessary to effect the change in the form of the business and have presented them to the president of the corporation (previously the general partner) who responds to your proposal by stating:

> *This all looks pretty good except for the organization costs that were on the books of the partnership. I don't want them carried forward on the books of the corporation because they don't have any future benefit. They probably should not have been capitalized even on the books of the partnership because they represented commissions to our sales people for finding investors. Let's get rid of them now while we are forming a new entity and not carry forward the same mistake.*

You are aware that the last financial statements for the limited partnership have not been issued yet but are due in the near future. As they are now prepared, they will report the commissions as organization costs. You have only been the controller of the partnership for the last two years and are surprised to hear about the origin of those costs. You wonder whether the last financial statements of the partnership should continue to show the organization costs as assets given what you now know about their composition.

Instructions

Decide what you should do, if anything, to account for the organization costs on the final financial statements of the limited partnership. Should this information have any effect on the financial statements of the new corporation?

CHAPTER 20

Revenue Measurement and Income Presentation

OBJECTIVES

1. To discuss the theory and concepts underlying contemporary revenue-recognition practices.

2. To identify and describe acceptable methods of revenue recognition for long-term contracts and to describe the circumstances under which each is appropriate.

3. To describe circumstances in which the installment sales and cost recovery methods of revenue recognition are acceptable.

4. To describe the circumstances in which revenue should be recognized when the right of return exists.

5. To discuss the purposes and objectives of income determination.

6. To review the proper method of presenting a variety of irregular income statement items.

COMPLEXITIES IN INCOME DETERMINATION

**Revenue
Realization
Matching**

The determination and reporting of income is one of the most important topics in contemporary financial reporting. Crucial in determining net income is the timing of the recognition of revenue and related expenses. Applying the revenue realization principle, accountants must make many decisions about the timing and extent to which revenue is recognized. In applying the matching principle, we must also identify the expenses to be included in the determination of income. Finally, we must establish the appropriate form, organization, and content of the income statement.

The appropriate practices governing the recognition of revenue can be complicated. Consider, for example, accounting and reporting problems of aerospace companies (such as Boeing, Lockheed, and McDonnell Douglas) which agree—under a variety of long-term contracts—to provide research and development services and to produce aircraft, missiles, space vehicles, and the support systems. Determining when and in what amount to recognize revenue and identifying the related expenses to be matched against the revenue are especially difficult problems.

After accountants decide how to recognize revenue and identify expense, they must prepare income statements to reflect the earning performance of their enterprises. In earlier chapters you learned several alternative methods of income presentation and how some transactions complicate the presentation of income. Accountants must often exercise seasoned judgment to choose the most appropriate format and the extent of detail in presenting income.

This chapter begins by developing concepts of accounting theory underlying the recognition of revenue and by illustrating their application in several practical situations. Then the chapter looks more closely at theoretical questions underlying the determination and presentation of income and introduces some considerations that complicate the presentation of income. Finally, a comprehensive model income statement summarizes our knowledge of income presentation.

REVENUE RECOGNITION: A CONCEPTUAL ANALYSIS

**Revenue
Realization**

Before beginning our discussion, you need to have a good understanding of the term **revenue**. Historically, the word is derived from the French word *revenir*, which means "to return" or "to come again." Thus, "revenue" has its roots in a return-on-investment concept; that is, the business invests resources in a particular project or endeavor in the hope of earning a return on that effort.

Many attempts have been made to define the conceptual meaning of revenue. The Financial Accounting Standards Board (FASB) gives a particularly useful definition in its *Statement of Financial Accounting Concepts No. 6:* "Revenues are inflows or other enhancements of assets of an entity, or settlements of its liabilities (or a combination of both) from delivering or producing goods, rendering services, or other activities that constitute the entity's ongoing major or central operations."[1] Careful study of this definition reveals several important characteristics that an event must possess to qualify for accounting recognition as an element of revenue.

**Revenue
Realization**

Accountants generally believe that revenue results from productive activity and therefore is earned or realized in a continuous fashion. For revenue to qualify for accounting recognition, however, at least three essential criteria must be met. The revenue must be: (1) earned; (2) measurable; and (3) collectible. Revenue should be

---

[1]*FASB Statement of Financial Accounting Concepts No. 6,* "Elements of Financial Statements," 1985, par. 78.

recognized for accounting purposes at the earliest point at which all three of these critical tests are met. Often the earliest point is the time of sale. Thus, in many situations, the recognition of revenue at the point of sale most closely follows the principles underlying the accrual basis of accounting.

Chapter 2 states that revenue is typically recognized at the point of sale, because the sale signifies the completion of the earning process and the sale transaction establishes the amount of revenue to be recognized. Only collectibility remains in question, and most sales are not made unless collectibility is reasonably certain. At a minimum, companies can make reasonably accurate estimates of the extent to which credit sales will not be collected, and they establish credit and collection policies that tend to minimize the collectibility problem. Thus, revenue recognition at the point of sale is an established practice that works well in most situations.

Revenue Realization

To illustrate, consider a company that manufactures and sells television sets to retail customers. From an economic perspective the manufacturer combines raw materials and component parts with labor and overhead to construct a functioning television set, thereby enhancing value. Stated simply, the productive process creates wealth and enhances value. The end product—a functioning television set—is worth more than the sum of the value of its parts. This process alone, however, does not provide sufficient evidence of the realization of revenue to support accounting recognition. Specifically, until an external event (sale) takes place, there is inadequate evidence as to how much (measurable) revenue was earned in the manufacturing process and whether the enhancement in value will ever be realized (collected).

This description of revenue realization is similar to that presented in *SFAC No. 5*. Specifically, the FASB indicates that for recognition, revenue must be realized (or realizable) and earned. Revenue is realized when products, merchandise, or other assets are exchanged for cash or claims to cash; they are realizable when related assets received are readily convertible into cash or claims to cash. Revenue is earned when the entity has substantially accomplished what it must do to be entitled to the benefits represented by the revenues.[2]

Consider the evidence supporting revenue recognition provided by a sale to an external party:

1. Few or no continuing obligations are retained by the seller (earned).
2. The relative value of the product sold is established by a market transaction between independent parties (measurability).
3. The buying party, who is deemed capable of paying the agreed-upon price, either pays or promises to pay the contract price (collectibility).

For sales situations in which one or more of the above criteria are not met, the recognition of revenue should be deferred.

Substance over Form

Sometimes sales are made to relatively poor credit risks with a condition for the seller to regain control of the property if the buyer defaults. Such practices are common, for example, in the real estate industry. Repossession of the property pursuant to a loan default is not difficult, because real estate cannot be transported or hidden. Thus, certain types of real estate are frequently sold to relatively poor credit risks. Such sales are similar to short-term leases in terms of their economic substance. In these cases the real estate sale completes the earning process and provides a measure of the profit to be recognized, but the collectibility of that revenue is not deemed adequately predictable. Recognition of revenue is therefore deferred until collectibility is more assured.

---

[2]*FASB Statement of Financial Accounting Concepts No. 5*, "Recognition and Measurement in Financial Statements of Business Enterprises," 1984, par. 83.

For another example, magazine, book, and encyclopedia companies frequently sell annual or even longer subscriptions, collecting the full fee in advance. The amount of revenue to be recognized ultimately is both collected and measurable; however, it remains unearned until the materials have been provided to the customers. Therefore, recognition is deferred until the revenue has been earned. In this situation the earning process follows the point of sale.

Accountants must carefully analyze specific transactions to avoid recognizing revenue prematurely. They should accumulate and analyze objective evidence in light of the three critical criteria to assure compliance with GAAP. While many businesses conduct operations in a fashion compatible with recording revenue at the point of sale, many others require unique or unusual revenue-recognition practices.

SPECIAL REVENUE-RECOGNITION PROBLEMS

Industries and businesses with special revenue-recognition requirements frequently depend on complex, lengthy, or unusual earnings processes or contractual relationships between buyers and sellers. In this section we deal with several circumstances in which revenue is not recognized at the point of sale. Specifically, we consider the revenue recognition problems inherent in long-term construction contracts, installment sales, and sales transactions involving the right of return. The Appendix to this chapter discusses revenue recognition in specialized situations involving real estate sales, retail land sales, and franchises.

LONG-TERM CONSTRUCTION CONTRACTS

In many industries, such as shipbuilding, aircraft design and production, and building construction, the earning activities of an enterprise are related to a number of large projects extending through several accounting periods. Accounting and reporting problems of such activities relate primarily to the timing and extent of revenue to be recognized and the treatment of costs incurred in the productive process. Because of the variety of circumstances and contractual relationships in construction projects, alternative financial accounting methods have been developed. We now turn to those methods and the circumstances in which each is appropriate.

ACCOUNTING AND REPORTING ISSUES

The various methods developed to account for long-term contracting activity should not be viewed as equally acceptable in the same circumstances. Rather, each method is appropriate only when certain conditions are present.

When a large construction project is contemplated, the buyer and the builder usually draw up a contract prior to beginning the construction. When such contracts are signed, a portion of the criteria necessary to recognize revenue is usually met. The construction company usually will not sign the contract if it has significant doubt about the buyer's ability to pay. For example, when an airplane manufacturer signs a contract with the U.S. Department of Defense to develop and produce a new type of aircraft, the collectibility of the contract amount is virtually assured. Although not all long-term contracts involve government buyers, construction companies usually accept only customers with an assured ability to pay the contract amount. The earning process is obviously not complete, however, and the amount of earnings to be ultimately realized in excess of costs incurred may still not be determinable. Therefore, *Revenue Realization* the recognition of revenue must wait until both the earnings and measurability criteria are met. As previously stated, the principle that revenue is realized through the productive process is widely accepted in practice. Therefore, as development and production of the contract item proceed, revenue is said to be "earned." The final criterion of measurability, however, may still remain uncertain, and revenue should not be recognized in the accounting records until all three criteria are met.

Measuring the amount of revenue earned is particularly difficult in the area of long-term construction contracts. Even if the revenue is collectible and earned through production, the amount that has been earned and the related costs associated with the earning process may still not be determinable. The amount of revenue and expenses recognized during the production process relate to the **degree of completion** of the project and to the remaining costs and effort to be incurred in finishing the project.

Routine projects lend themselves to reliable predictions of costs and productive efforts. Other developmental projects may involve many uncertainties. Furthermore, some contracts specify how final sales prices will be determined. For example, a contract may guarantee the contractor with reimbursement of all costs incurred plus some amount of profit. The profit portion may be stated as a certain number of dollars, a percentage above costs incurred, or an amount based on some other variable, such as days or hours of direct labor expended on the project. On the other hand, a contract may specify a total fixed amount to be received regardless of costs incurred. All these factors are considered in determining the appropriate accounting treatment for any specific situation.

Two basic methods are used in accounting for long-term construction contracts: the percentage-of-completion method and the completed-contract method. The **percentage-of-completion method** provides for the recognition of gross profit as production takes place. The **completed-contract method** defers recognition of gross profit until all production is complete and the customer's acceptance of the project is finalized.

Under the percentage-of-completion method, revenue and expenses are recognized to the extent that production has progressed. Therefore, estimates of costs and effort to complete the project are necessary to determine the amount of profit that should be recognized at interim points during construction. Specifically, *Accounting Research Bulletin No. 45* states:

> When estimates of costs to complete and extent of progress toward completion of long-term contracts are reasonably dependable, the percentage-of-completion method is preferable. When lack of dependable estimates or inherent hazards cause forecasts to be doubtful, the completed-contract method is preferable. Disclosure of the method followed should be made.[3]

Disclosure

According to this statement, the selection of the method requires analysis of the *quality* of available evidence, primarily regarding the measurability of revenue earned. When effort has been expended on a long-term construction contract, we generally agree that both the earning process and the collectibility criteria have been satisfactorily met. Therefore, the measurability of the revenue earned is the last critical prerequisite for the recognition of revenue. If the construction company can satisfactorily estimate the amount of revenue earned, it should employ the percentage-of-completion method.

A more recent pronouncement confirms this position. Specifically, *FASB Statement of Financial Accounting Standards No. 56* states, "The percentage-of-completion and completed-contract methods are not intended to be free choice alternatives for

---

[3]*Accounting Research Bulletin No. 45*, "Long-Term Construction-Type Contracts," 1955, par. 15.

the same circumstances."[4] A Statement of Position (SOP) of the American Institute of Certified Public Accountants (AICPA) provides important guidance about the circumstances in which each method should be selected and the manner of applying each method. A company should use the percentage-of-completion method of accounting if estimates are reasonably dependable and three other conditions exist:[5]

1. The contract specifies the enforceable rights of each party, the amount of consideration to be exchanged, and the manner and terms of settlement.
2. The buyer can be expected to honor the obligations of the contract.
3. The contractor can be expected to perform according to the terms of the contract.

Contractors are usually able to make the necessary reliable estimates and consequently should report most contracting activities by the percentage-of-completion method. This presumption is based on the notion that contractors would refuse contracts if reasonable estimates were impossible. However, if the construction company cannot meet the criteria for the percentage-of-completion method, then the completed-contract method is appropriate.

Percentage-of-Completion Method

In practice, contractors use two basic methods to measure the progress of the construction:

1. **Input measures** (e.g., ratio of costs incurred to total estimated costs).
2. **Output measures** (e.g., units of delivery).

A common input measure bases the progress on the ratio of the costs *already* incurred to the total *estimated* costs. In using costs incurred as a measure of degree of completion, the accountant must be cautious, because the costs may not be spread evenly over the contract period. For example, if a disproportionate amount of the costs were required in the early part of the contract period, costs incurred might not be a suitable measure of the degree of completion.

Output measures base the progress on the results achieved. One common output measure, the units of delivery approach, recognizes revenue when specific, discrete components of the project are completed and accepted by the buyer. The units of delivery approach to applying the percentage-of-completion method is most useful in contracts which require several large, but individual, components of production. For example, the construction of several condominium units or a group of similar ships or aircraft may be accounted for on a units of delivery basis. Revenue is recognized when a particular discrete component of the entire project is completed and delivered to or accepted by the customer. For example, if a construction company signs a contract to provide ten condominium units and completes four of the units—which are accepted by the buyer—at the end of the first year, then 40% of the total revenue provided under the contract should be recognized. The treatment of costs incurred under the contract, however, is not so obvious. In many contracts, certain costs incurred at the beginning of a contract relate to all the units to be constructed. In the preceding example, the contractor should prorate such costs among the ten units rather than charge them immediately to expense. Costs of planning and design are especially significant in state-of-the-art production, such as the design and construction of defense or scientific projects that have never before been attempted. In the early stages, such projects

---

[4]*FASB Statement of Financial Accounting Standards No. 56*, "Designation of AICPA Guide and Statement of Position (SOP) 81–1 on Contractor Accounting and SOP 81–2 Concerning Hospital-Related Organizations as Preferable for Purposes of Applying APB Opinion No. 20," 1982, par. 6.

[5]*AICPA Statement of Position 81–1*, "Accounting for Performance of Construction-Type and Certain Production-Type Contracts," 1981, par. 23.

frequently incur many **learning curve costs** (i.e., expenditures necessary to learn how to do a particular construction project). Once learned, the productive process may be replicated more easily and efficiently. Careful analysis and allocation of learning curve costs to appropriate accounting periods are necessary to ensure a proper matching of revenues and expenses.

Matching

Completed-Contract Method

When reasonable estimates of the degree of completion are not possible, the completed-contract method of accounting for long-term contracts is applied. Under completed-contract accounting, no gross profit is recognized until the contract is complete and the products or services have been accepted by the buyer. At that time all gross profit earned on the contract is recorded. Prior to the recognition of profit, contract costs are presented on the balance sheet as Construction in Progress, an inventory account.

When costs are incurred under a contract and charged to an inventory account, such as Construction in Progress, we must ascertain that the amount reported as an asset does not exceed the net realizable value of the contract. Recall from Chapter 8 that the **net realizable value** of an item of inventory is defined as the sales (contract) value of the item less any costs still to be incurred to complete and sell the product. Thus, even under completed-contract accounting, estimates of the remaining costs are necessary to ensure that the Construction in Progress account is not overvalued. If we determine that the costs included as an asset under a particular contract exceed the net realizable value of the contract, we should write down the asset to its net realizable value and recognize a loss at that time.

A Long-Term Contract Example

To illustrate the appropriate accounting procedures for the percentage-of-completion and completed-contract methods, we shall consider the following example. Dryden Construction Company agrees to build a large apartment building for Cozy Homes, Inc., for a total contract price of $5,000,000. Cozy Homes will make annual payments to Dryden, but the amounts of these payments cannot exceed the direct costs incurred by Dryden. The contract is signed on October 1, 1991, and Dryden's year-end is December 31. The contract provides Cozy with a final inspection right to ensure compliance with the contract terms prior to accepting the completed project. Exhibit 20–1 provides further information about the contract.

EXHIBIT 20–1

Long-Term Contracts—Illustrative Information

	Total contract price	$5,000,000		
	Total anticipated costs (at 10/1/91)	4,000,000		
Item	1991	1992	1993	Total
Costs incurred each year	$ 500,000	$2,500,000	$1,400,000	$4,400,000
Estimated costs to complete (at year-end)	3,500,000	1,250,000	–0–	–0–
Progress billings each year	400,000	2,000,000	2,600,000	5,000,000
Progress payments received each year	275,000	2,100,000	2,625,000*	5,000,000

*Since the contract was completed and accepted during 1993, the buyer paid the remaining balance of the total contract amount, computed as follows:

Contract amount		$5,000,000
Prior progress payments		
1991	$ 275,000	
1992	2,100,000	2,375,000
Remaining amount		$2,625,000

Dryden based its percentage-of-completion method on costs incurred rather than units delivered, because the contract calls for one large project rather than several separate projects. Dryden assumes that costs incurred will accurately measure the progress. Exhibit 20–2 presents the current year's gross profit calculations for the percentage-of-completion method. To illustrate the difference in the methods, Exhibit 20–3 shows the accounting entries for each contract year for both the percentage-of-completion and completed-contract methods. The resulting financial-statement presentations for both methods are summarized in Exhibit 20–4.

These exhibits reveal that the only difference between the two methods is the timing of the recognition of gross profit on the contract. Both methods ultimately result in the recognition of the same total amount of gross profit ($600,000). The only balance sheet differences between the two methods relate to the carrying value of the Construction in Progress (inventory) account and Retained Earnings. Under the percentage-of-completion method, the amount of gross profit recognized is reflected as an increase in Construction in Progress and as an increase in Retained Earnings after being reported as an increase in net income in the income statement.

Under the percentage-of-completion method, we calculate the amount of revenue to be recognized by determining the gross profit to be recognized during the current year and adding that figure to the actual costs incurred during the year. As Exhibit 20–2 shows, a revised estimate of the cumulative percentage of completion is computed each year. This percentage is applied to the expected gross profit (which will also vary as revised estimates of expected costs to be incurred are made). The difference between the cumulative gross profit and the gross profit recognized in the previous year(s) is the current year's gross profit. The final entry in Exhibit 20–3 for each year under the percentage-of-completion method records revenues, costs, and the increase in Construction in Progress for the gross profit recognized.

Under the completed-contract method, we defer the recognition of revenue until the project is completed. In the case of Dryden Construction Company, the $5,000,000 of revenue and the $4,400,000 of costs are recognized in 1993 when the contract is complete and the uncertainties that preclude the use of the percentage-of-completion method are

EXHIBIT 20–2

Revenue Recognized by Percentage-of-Completion Method

	1991	1992	1993
Total contract price	$5,000,000	$5,000,000	$5,000,000
Costs incurred to date	500,000	3,000,000	4,400,000
Anticipated costs to complete	3,500,000	1,250,000	–0–
Total estimated costs	4,000,000	4,250,000	4,400,000
Expected gross profit	$1,000,000	$ 750,000	$ 600,000
Percentage of completion			
$500,000/$4,000,000	12.5%		
$3,000,000/$4,250,000		70.6%	
$4,400,000/$4,400,000			100%
Gross profit earned to date			
$1,000,000 × 12.5%	$ 125,000		
$750,000 × 70.6%		$ 529,500	
$600,000 × 100%			$ 600,000
Less: Gross profit previously recognized	—	(125,000)	(529,500)
Current year gross profit	$ 125,000	$ 404,500	$ 70,500

KNOW

EXHIBIT 20–3

Comparison of Completed-Contract and Percentage-of-Completion Journal Entries

Date	Event	Accounts	Completed-Contract Dr.	Completed-Contract Cr.	Percentage-of-Completion Dr.	Percentage-of-Completion Cr.
1991	Contract signed	(No entry necessary to record contract commitment.)				
	Costs incurred	Construction in Progress *Inventory Acct*	500,000		500,000	
		Cash		500,000		500,000
	Progress billings	Accounts Receivable	400,000		400,000	
		Contract Billings *contra acct to CIP*		400,000		400,000
	Billing collections	Cash	275,000		275,000	
		Accounts Receivable		275,000		275,000
	Revenue recognition	Construction in Progress *CP*			125,000	
		Cost of Earned Revenue	—		500,000	
		Construction Revenue		—		625,000
1992	Costs incurred	Construction in Progress	2,500,000		2,500,000	
		Cash		2,500,000		2,500,000
	Progress billings	Accounts Receivable	2,000,000		2,000,000	
		Contract Billings		2,000,000		2,000,000
	Billing collections	Cash	2,100,000		2,100,000	
		Accounts Receivable		2,100,000		2,100,000
	Revenue recognition	Construction in Progress *GP*			404,500	
		Cost of Earned Revenue	—		2,500,000 = *3 million as reported*	
		Construction Revenue		—		2,904,500
1993	Costs incurred	Construction in Progress	1,400,000		1,400,000	
		Cash		1,400,000		1,400,000
	Progress billings	Accounts Receivable	2,600,000		2,600,000	
		Contract Billings		2,600,000		2,600,000
	Billing collections	Cash	2,625,000		2,625,000	
		Accounts Receivable		2,625,000		2,625,000
	Revenue recognition	Construction in Progress *GP*	—		70,500	
		Cost of Earned Revenue	—		1,400,000	
		Construction Revenue		—		1,470,500
	Elimination of inventory	Contract Billings	—		5,000,000	
		Construction in Progress		—		5,000,000
	Recognition of costs and revenues on entire contract	Contract Billings	5,000,000		—	
		Cost of Earned Revenue	4,400,000		—	
		Construction Revenue		5,000,000		—
		Construction in Progress		4,400,000		—

EXHIBIT 20–4

Comparison of Completed-Contract and Percentage-of-Completion Financial-Statement Presentations

	Dec. 31, 1991		Dec. 31, 1992		Dec. 31, 1993	
	Completed Contract	Percentage of Completion	Completed Contract	Percentage of Completion	Completed Contract	Percentage of Completion
Balance Sheet						
Current assets						
Accounts receivable	$ 125,000	$ 125,000	$ 25,000	$ 25,000	–0–	–0–
Inventory						
Construction in						
progress	500,000	625,000	3,000,000	3,529,500	–0–	–0–
Less:						
Contract billings	(400,000)	(400,000)	(2,400,000)	(2,400,000)	–0–	–0–
Construction in						
progress in						
excess of billings	100,000	225,000	600,000	1,129,500	–0–	–0–
Income Statement						
Construction revenue	—	$ 625,000	—	$ 2,904,500	$ 5,000,000	$ 1,470,500
Cost of earned revenue	—	(500,000)	—	(2,500,000)	(4,400,000)	(1,400,000)
Gross margin	—	$ 125,000	—	$ 404,500	$ 600,000	$ 70,500

resolved. Actual companies may employ different account titles and certain other minor variations, but the procedures illustrated here are representative of the two methods.

Exhibit 20–4 shows the difference between the inventory account, Construction in Progress, and the Contract Billings as a *current* asset. The "current" classification of this item is based on the operating cycle definition. An asset is current if it is expected to be sold, consumed, or converted to cash within the next year (or operating cycle if the cycle exceeds one year). The period of the accounting cycle for long-term contracts—which frequently exceeds one year—is typically used to identify current assets.

If the contract provided for billings in excess of costs incurred, the Construction in Progress account could be less than the Contract Billings account. In this case, the difference is presented as a *current liability* labeled "Excess of Contract Billings over Construction in Progress" or another appropriate title.

Although the comparison of the percentage-of-completion and completed-contracts methods in the Dryden example demonstrated the similarities and differences, *the methods are not equally acceptable in the same circumstances.* We must consider the circumstances and available evidence and select the *appropriate* method. We use the completed-contract method only when reliable estimates of effort and resources to complete the project are not available. The percentage-of-completion method is preferable when reasonably dependable estimates of the degree of completion can be made, because it presents the economic substance of the company's transactions and events more clearly and in a more timely fashion than does the completed-contract method. The percentage-of-completion method informs financial statement users of the volume of the economic activity of the company.[6] While the

Substance over Form

---

[6]*AICPA Statement of Position 81–1*, par. 22.

completed-contract method is based on results as finally determined rather than on estimates, it does not reflect current performance when contract periods extend beyond one accounting period and it may result in irregular recognition of income.[7]

A Hybrid Method

In certain types of contracts (e.g., cost-plus contracts in which the revenue will be the costs incurred plus a specified percentage) the contractor is assured of no loss. If the contractor is protected in this manner but is unable to make reasonable estimates of the percentage of completion, *SOP 81–1* recommends a **hybrid method** described as the percentage-of-completion method based on a **zero profit margin**.[8] Under this method, revenue is recognized in an amount exactly equal to costs incurred until reasonably objective estimates of the percentage of completion can be made. In the earlier example, if Dryden Construction Company had used this method, revenue and costs would be recognized in 1991 and 1992 for $500,000 and $2,500,000 (the amount of costs incurred), respectively:

1991	Cost of Earned Revenue	500,000	
	Construction Revenue		500,000
1992	Cost of Earned Revenue	2,500,000	
	Construction Revenue		2,500,000

In 1993, the year in which the contract is complete, the entire gross profit is recognized, much as in the completed-contract method:

1993	Construction in Progress	600,000	
	Cost of Earned Revenue	1,400,000	
	Construction Revenue		2,000,000
	Contract Billings	5,000,000	
	Construction in Progress		5,000,000

The first three entries in Exhibit 20–3 for each year would also apply to the hybrid method. The significant difference between the hybrid method and the completed-contract method is that the hybrid method requires the inclusion of both revenues and costs in the income statement for 1991 and 1992. Performance during the period would be included in the income statement, although the method would not impact net income since revenue and costs recognized would be equal. The zero profit margin approach gives financial statement users an indication of the volume of the company's business while deferring the recognition of gross profit until more reliable estimates of the degree of completion can be made.

Anticipated Losses on Contracts

During the contract period the fact that a loss will be incurred on the contract may become apparent. Under all the methods presented above, a projected loss on a contract must be recognized immediately in conformity with the modifying convention of conservatism.

Conservatism

To illustrate, assume that Johnson Construction Company is using the completed-contract method on a project. At the end of 1993 the balance in the Construction in Progress account is $2,500,000, representing the costs incurred to date. If the company now projects a $350,000 loss on the contract because of unexpected increases in materials, labor, and overhead, the following entry is appropriate:

---

[7]*AICPA Statement of Position 81–1*, par. 30.
[8]*AICPA Statement of Position 81–1*, par. 33.

| 1993 | Loss on Construction Contract | 350,000 | |
| | Construction in Progress | | 350,000 |

From this point forward, construction costs will be charged to the Construction in Progress account, and the balance in that account at the end of the contract will equal the contract revenue if the loss estimate is accurate. If the loss estimate is not accurate, an adjustment is made when the appropriate amounts are determinable.

Assume that on another contract, Johnson is using the percentage-of-completion method. The Construction in Progress account at the end of 1993 has a balance of $6,500,000:

Construction costs incurred through 1993	$5,700,000
Gross profit recognized in previous years	800,000
Construction in Progress balance	$6,500,000

At the end of 1993 the company expects a $300,000 loss on the contract. The following entry should be made:

| 1993 | Loss on Construction Contract | 1,100,000 | |
| | Construction in Progress | | 1,100,000 |

The $1,100,000 loss represents a reversal of the $800,000 gross profit recognized in previous years, plus the $300,000 loss we now expect on the contract. From this point forward, construction costs will be charged to the Construction in Progress account, and the balance in that account at the end of the contract will equal the contract revenue if the loss estimate is accurate. As in the completed-contract method, if the loss estimate is inaccurate, further adjustment must be made in the future as the appropriate amounts are determinable.

INSTALLMENT SALES

The collectibility of credit sales is usually predictable and reasonably assured as a result of credit approval, collection procedures, and historical evidence. In these cases, revenue is appropriately recognized at the point of sale. However, if a company makes credit sales to customers of relatively poor credit risk, recognition of revenue at the point of sale may be inappropriate. While such revenue may be deemed to have been earned and measurable, collectibility remains uncertain. Therefore, the creditor should ordinarily defer the recognition of revenue until collecting the amount due. This practice is supported by the professional literature:

> There are exceptional cases where receivables are collectible over an extended period of time, and because of the terms of the transactions or other conditions, there is no reasonable basis for estimating the degree of collectibility. When such circumstances exist, and as long as they exist, either the installment method or the cost recovery method of accounting may be used. (Under the cost recovery method, equal amounts of revenue and expense are recognized as collections are made until all costs have been recovered, postponing any recognition of profit until that time.)[9]

[9]APB Opinion No. 10, "Omnibus Opinion—1966," 1966, par. 12.

The **installment sales method** recognizes a portion of each cash collection as revenue and the remaining amount of cash collected as a recovery of cost. The **cost recovery method** treats all cash collected as a recovery of cost of the item sold until the full cost of the item sold is collected. Subsequent collections are treated entirely as

Conservatism

revenue. The cost recovery method is even more conservative than the installment method, and application of the cost recovery technique is most desirable when the collectibility of receivables is extremely uncertain.

Under the installment sales method, revenue is recognized on a pro rata basis as each installment is received. To illustrate, assume that EZ Credit Auto Sales Company sells a $6,000 automobile to a customer on November 1, 1993, with the following terms: The customer will pay $600 down and $150 per month for 36 months plus interest at 15%. Since EZ Credit paid $4,200 for the automobile, it will make a gross profit of $1,800 on the sale. For simplicity, we shall ignore the interest revenue, because it is not related to the recognition of profit on the sale.

Because of the significant uncertainty of collection resulting from granting credit to relatively poor credit risks, EZ Credit Company uses the installment sales method of revenue recognition. Exhibit 20–5 presents the entries necessary to record the sale, collection of cash, and recognition of revenue. The gross profit percentage, which indicates the gross profit included in each payment received, is 30%, computed by dividing the gross profit by the sales price [($6,000 − $4,200)/$6,000 = 30%].

The Deferred Gross Profit account established at the point of sale is treated either as a contra account to Notes Receivable or as a deferred revenue (liability) account. The entry on December 31, 1993, which reflects the portion of cash collected that is recognized as revenue, may be made as each cash receipt occurs. If this practice is selected, each cash receipt of $150 (ignoring interest) is recorded in the following manner:

Cash	150	
Deferred Gross Profit	45	
Notes Receivable		150
Realized Gross Profit ($150 × 30% = $45)		45

If different sales transactions result in different gross profit percentages, separate gross profit records must be kept for each sale. For example, if installment sales in 1992 result in a gross profit percentage of 32% and installment sales in 1993 result in a gross profit percentage of 34%, the receivables and deferred gross profit amounts related to 1992 sales must be kept separate from the 1993 sales so that a proper accounting may be made of the gross profit recognized as receivables are collected.

Considering the uncertainty of collection for installment sales, it is not surprising that sellers typically retain a right of repossession (the right to take the property and resell it) if the buyer defaults. When inventory is thus acquired, the installment receivable and any deferred gross profit on the original sale must be eliminated. If the resale value of the repossessed property is greater or less than the carrying amount of the receivable (face amount, less the deferred gross profit), a gain or loss is recognized.

To illustrate, assume that Careyville Appliance Company sells a refrigerator for $500 on an installment contract calling for 25 monthly payments of $20, plus interest. The refrigerator cost Careyville $420, resulting in a gross profit percentage of 16% [($500 − $420)/$500]. After 10 payments the customer discontinued paying and Careyville repossessed the refrigerator. The carrying amount of the receivable is as follows:

EXHIBIT 20-5

Installment Sales Accounting—Illustrative Entries

Date	Accounts	Dr.	Cr.
Nov. 1, 1993	Cash	600	
	Notes Receivable	5,400	
	Inventory		4,200
	Realized Gross Profit* ($600 × 30%)		180
	Deferred Gross Profit ($5,400 × 30%)		1,620
	(To record sale of automobile under installment sales method.)		
Nov. 30, 1993	Cash	150	
	Notes Receivable		150
	(To record receipt of payment.)		
Dec. 31, 1993	Cash	150	
	Notes Receivable		150
	(To record receipt of payment.)		
Dec. 31, 1993	Deferred Gross Profit ($300 × 30%)	90	
	Realized Gross Profit*		90
	(To record revenue for the year based on cash received.)		

*For income statement presentation purposes, the components of Realized Gross Profit may be presented rather than the net amount of $270 ($180 + $90). In this situation, sales of $900 ($600 + $150 + $150) would be included in sales revenue and $630 ($900 × 70%) would be included in Cost of Goods Sold.

Receivable balance [$500 − 10 ($20)]	$300
Deferred gross profit balance {$80 − [10($20) × 16%]}	48
Carrying amount of installment receivable	$252

If the estimated resale value of the refrigerator is $200, the entry to record the repossession is as follows:

Repossessed Inventory	200	
Deferred Gross Profit	48	
Loss on Repossession	52	
Installment Receivables		300

If the estimated resale value of the refrigerator had been greater than $252, a Gain on Repossession would have been recorded.

REVENUE RECOGNITION WHERE THE RIGHT OF RETURN EXISTS

A company may sell an item with a provision for the customer to return it under certain circumstances. For example, a manufacturer may sell its products to a retailer with the **right to return** products that are unsatisfactory to the consumer. In such circumstances the manufacturer should not recognize revenue until six conditions are met:

1. The seller's price to the buyer is substantially fixed or determinable at the date of sale.

2. *The buyer has paid the seller, or the buyer is obligated to pay the seller and the obligation is not contingent on resale of the product.*
3. *The buyer's obligation to the seller would not be changed in the event of theft or physical destruction or damage of the product.*
4. *The buyer acquiring the product for resale has economic substance apart from that provided by the seller. [That is, a separate, arm's-length relationship between the parties is evident.]*
5. *The seller does not have significant obligations for future performance to directly bring about resale of the product by the buyer.*
6. *The amount of future returns can be reasonably estimated.*[10]

Disclosure

Sales revenue and related expenses which are deferred because at least one of these six conditions does not exist are recognized when all the conditions are met. Disclosure of the circumstances and the enterprise's accounting policies are necessary to adequately inform the users of the financial statements.

To illustrate the recognition of revenue where the right of return exists, we shall assume the following information about the Rockford Corporation for 1993:

Sales	$500,000
Cost of goods sold	$325,000
Expected returns	2% of sales
Actual returns during year (at selling price)	$6,000
Cash collected on receivables	$285,000

Since Rockford is able to make a reasonable estimate of returns, we shall assume that all of the conditions for revenue recognition are met in the entries required to record sales and related transactions for 1993.

To record sales and cost of goods sold:

Accounts Receivable	500,000	
Cost of Goods Sold	325,000	
Sales		500,000
Inventory		325,000

To record estimated sales returns:

Sales Returns ($500,000 × .02)	10,000	
Inventory—Estimated Returns ($10,000 × 65%)	6,500	
Allowance for Sales Returns		10,000
Cost of Goods Sold		6,500

(The 65% represents the cost-to-sales percentage in the sales: $325,000/$500,000 = 65%.)

To record collection of receivables:

Cash	285,000	
Accounts Receivable		285,000

To record sales returns and reclassification of inventory:

Allowance for Sales Returns	6,000	
Inventory ($6,000 × 65%)	3,900	
Accounts Receivable		6,000
Inventory—Estimated Returns		3,900

---

[10]*FASB Statement of Financial Accounting Standards No. 48*, "Revenue Recognition When Right of Return Exists," 1981, par. 6.

As a result of the recording of these transactions, net sales and cost of goods sold will be presented at $490,000 and $318,500, respectively, maintaining the 65% cost-to-sales ratio—as shown in the following computations:

Sales	$500,000	
Sales returns	(10,000)	$490,000
Cost of goods sold ($325,000 − $6,500)		318,500
Gross margin		$171,500

Matching This treatment is consistent with the matching principle. Accounts Receivable are presented at a net amount of $205,000, after considering $6,000 of returns received, $285,000 of collections, and $4,000 of estimated future returns:

Accounts receivable ($500,000 − $285,000 − $6,000)	$209,000	
Allowance for estimated returns ($10,000 − $6,000)	(4,000)	$205,000

The cost of inventory expected to be returned is presented in a special inventory classification, Inventory—Estimated Returns, at $2,600 ($4,000 × 65%).

In this illustration we assumed that the conditions for revenue recognition were met and the question then became one of estimating returns and appropriately adjusting cost of goods sold so that the 65% cost-to-sales relationship is maintained in the income statement. Had the conditions for revenue recognition not been met, the sales and cost of goods sold amounts recognized in the first entry would have been deferred and recorded only when the conditions for revenue recognition were met.

OTHER UNUSUAL REVENUE-RECOGNITION CIRCUMSTANCES

The timing and magnitude of revenue recognition remain areas of complexity and controversy for the accounting profession. Judgments are frequently required in determining when revenue should be recognized and in what amount. These circumstances raise the possibility of manipulation and the "managing" of earnings. Because of the central importance of revenue in the financial statements and the susceptibility to *abuse,* accountants must remain alert to the possibility of misstatement.

In our study of revenue recognition, we have emphasized situations involving physical products. Service industries, such as insurance, medical services, legal services, accounting services, management consulting, moving and storage, and banking, also encounter revenue-recognition problems. The questions of income determination for service industries are similar to those for product-related industries: When is revenue earned, measurable and collectible? How should costs related to the generation of service revenue be treated? Few authoritative accounting pronouncements presently exist to help accountants answer these important questions. Theoretically, service revenue should be recognized when services are performed (earned), amounts can be objectively determined (measurable), and collection is reasonably assured (collectible). Expenses should be recognized as the revenues they helped to cre-

Matching ate are recognized, in accordance with the matching principle. Accountants must apply judgment in this important area of business activity. Undoubtedly, as the FASB continues to refine accounting practices, particularly in specialized industries, more guidance concerning the recognition of revenue and the determination of income in service industries will be forthcoming.

As previously mentioned, many industries engage in transactions and business relationships that require unusual accounting and reporting practices. The Appendix to this chapter discusses financial accounting and reporting for several additional situations involving unique revenue-recognition problems.

The first part of this chapter has dealt with the criteria and circumstances influencing the recognition of revenue. Accounting and reporting standards have also been established in regard to the presentation of various items of revenue and expense in the income statement. The following section considers theories, standards, and practices relevant to the format, organization, and content of the income statement.

INCOME PRESENTATION

A major objective of financial reporting is to provide information to investors and creditors about **financial performance** during the reporting period. Although **performance** may refer to numerous aspects of an enterprise's operations, the FASB has clearly designated **earnings** as a focal point for financial reporting:

> *The primary focus of financial reporting is information about an enterprise's performance provided by measures of* earnings *and its* components. *Investors, creditors, and others who are concerned with assessing the prospects of net cash flows are especially interested in that information. Their interest in an enterprise's future cash flows and its ability to generate favorable cash flows leads primarily to an interest in information about its* earnings *rather than information about its cash flows.*[11] *[Emphasis added.]*

Revenue
Realization

Matching

Current accounting practice uses a transactions approach to income measurement. Under this approach, positive and negative asset and liability changes are measured and recognized in conformity with accounting principles, such as revenue realization and matching. The combined results of these changes is the determination of net income, one of the most prominent figures in financial reporting.

OBJECTIVES OF REPORTING EARNINGS

We could cite many objectives of reporting earnings. In Chapter 3 we examined the usefulness of accounting income figures and discussed net income as a measure of operating efficiency and a predictor of future cash flows.

The ability of management is a major factor in the success of a business enterprise, and income is the primary measure of business performance. Therefore, one objective of earnings is to *evaluate management efficiency* by comparing the results of management effort with some standard or goal. The objectives of business activity vary from enterprise to enterprise. A profit-oriented enterprise attempts to achieve some desired level of earnings as the basis for providing a desired level of cash flow to investors and creditors. Net income is a valuable measure of progress toward that goal. Periodic measures of earnings are useful in evaluating how well management has employed the resources at its disposal to achieve the desired level of earnings. The desired level of earnings may be determined in several ways, including management-established goals, industry averages, or individual investor expectations.

The basic objective of financial reporting is to provide useful information for making decisions about investment, credit, and other important matters. The primary focus of financial reporting is information about the enterprise's earnings and its components. *Information about earnings is generally more useful in predicting and evaluating future cash flow potentials than is information about the enterprise's past cash flows.* Therefore, support for the presentation of earnings and its components is

---

[11]*FASB Statement of Financial Accounting Concepts No. 1,* "Objectives of Financial Reporting by Business Enterprises," 1978, par. 43.

based primarily on the need for this information in assessing the enterprise's future activities, particularly those that have cash flow prospects.

Inherent in the presentation of net income is the distinction between investment and income. **Investment** refers to the accumulated resources which the enterprise has as a result of contributions by investors. **Income** is the net result of the inflow of resources resulting from the employment of that investment. Another objective of reporting earnings is *to distinguish between the accumulation of investments and the accumulation of additional resources that result from the employment of investments.* These additional resources are either retained by the enterprise or distributed as dividends to the owners of the enterprise.

ALTERNATIVE INCOME CONCEPTS

We shall now consider several alternative definitions of income that have been suggested by accounting theorists. The primary differences among these definitions are found in the treatment of wages, income taxes, interest, and preferred dividends.

Net Income to Stockholders

The current concept of income is founded on the notion that the amount identified as net income is that amount which accrues to *all* stockholders. **Determinants** of income are those revenues, gains, expenses, and losses which are included in the computation of net income, such as sales revenue, cost of goods sold, operating expenses, interest expense, and income tax expense. **Distributions** of income are transfers of assets to owners of the enterprise, including both common and preferred stockholders. This concept of income, which is strongly emphasized in traditional accounting thought, is often identified as **net income to stockholders.** All expenses incurred in the generation of revenue are deducted in determining income, but no distributions to owners are deducted. Several alternative approaches to this concept are explained in the following paragraphs.

Value Added Income

Under the value added concept of income, a variety of interested parties are identified as the **recipients** of the income of the enterprise. The **value added** is the sales price of the enterprise's products or services minus the cost of the goods and services paid to other enterprises that produced those goods and services. Other groups who receive the advantages of enterprise operations—employees, creditors, government, and owners—are recipients of the income of the enterprise. Whereas the cost of goods sold is a determinant of income, expenditures such as income taxes, interest, and dividends are considered distributions of that income to the various recipients.

Enterprise Net Income

Under the concept of **enterprise net income,** income taxes and interest expense, as well as dividends, are considered distributions of income. Thus, the recipients of the income of the enterprise are the government, creditors, and owners. The resulting income is much like the operating income figure commonly appearing in income statements today, because taxes and interest are frequently presented after that amount.

Net Income to Investors

Another variation of net income is **net income to investors.** Within this concept all interest payments to creditors and dividend payments to stockholders are considered distributions of the enterprise's income, and all other distributions are considered determinants of income. This interpretation of income varies from current reporting practice only in that interest paid to creditors is treated as a distribution, rather than a determinant, of income.

Net Income to Residual Stockholders

The **residual** (or **common**) **stockholders** are typically thought of as the ultimate owners of the enterprise. Although the claim represented by preferred stock is legally that of an owner, there is some support for income to be regarded as the amount which accrues to the residual stockholders. This concept is reflected in the computation of earnings per share in which the net income (to all stockholders), as reported in the income statement, is reduced by the preferred dividend to derive an income figure accruing to the common stockholders. The resulting amount then becomes the basis for computing earnings per share. This view of income is consistent with the theory that common stockholders are the ultimate riskbearers and the group to whom the long-run profitability of the enterprise ultimately accrues.

Exhibit 20–6 summarizes the concepts of income and shows whether wages (return to employees), income taxes (return to government), interest (return to creditors), and preferred dividends (return to preferred stockholders) are treated as determinants or distributions of income under each concept. The concept of income reflected in current income presentation, **net income to stockholders,** is included in the fourth column.

CURRENT OPERATING PERFORMANCE VERSUS ALL-INCLUSIVE INCOME

A continuing question about the presentation of income concerns which specific transactions, if any, should be *excluded* from income determination because of their unique nature. Accountants agree that sales, cost of goods sold, and other similar revenue and expense items should be *included* in the determination of net income. They also agree that the results of capital transactions, such as dividends and stock transactions, should be *excluded* in determining net income. Opinions differ, however, on the proper treatment of items that differ in nature from normal revenues and expenses, that do not recur in any established pattern, or that represent adjustments of the income of some past accounting period. Suppose, for example, that a company sustains a loss from an earthquake. Such a loss is unusual and will not recur in any predictable pattern. If an objective of reporting earnings is to provide information for predicting future events, should the company include this loss in the measurement of income? Assume that in 1993 the company finds an error in the determination of 1991 net income. Should it include the gain or loss necessary to correct this error in the determination of 1993 net income? Special or irregular events like these are clearly part of the history of the enterprise's earnings, but their unique characteristics have led to disagreement on the most appropriate way to present them in the financial statements. The presentation of items such as those described above has produced two opposing schools of thought: the **current operating performance** view and the **all-inclusive** view.

Proponents of the current operating performance view believe that a company's income should be based on its normal, recurring operations. That is, unusual items, nonrecurring items, and items relating to other accounting periods should be *excluded* from the current year's measurement of income and reported as direct increases or decreases in retained earnings. These types of items would appear in the statement of retained earnings rather than the income statement. Proponents of this view believe that financial statement users rely heavily on reported measurements of *net income* but that they lack the knowledge necessary to understand the detailed components of an income statement. They also believe that financial statement users can make more accurate predictions and more meaningful evaluations of management performance if net income reflects only the normal, recurring activities of the business.

The opposite perspective is the all-inclusive view. Proponents of this position believe that net income for a period should equal the change in owners' equity during the

EXHIBIT 20-6

Comparative Income Presentations
(in thousands of dollars)

	(1) Value Added Income	(2) Enterprise Net Income	(3) Net Income to Investors	(4) Net Income to Stockholders	(5) Net Income to Residual Stockholders
Sales	$2,000	$2,000	$2,000	$2,000	$2,000
Determinants of income					
Cost of goods sold	1,000	1,000	1,000	1,000	1,000
Wages	—	400	400	400	400
Income taxes	—	—	150	150	150
Interest	—	—	—	200	200
Preferred dividends	—	—	—	—	50
	1,000	1,400	1,550	1,750	1,800
Income	$1,000	$ 600	$ 450	$ 250	$ 200
Distributions of income					
Wages	$400	—	—	—	—
Income taxes	150	$150	—	—	—
Interest	200	200	$200	—	—
Preferred dividends	50	50	50	$ 50	—
Common dividends	100	100	100	100	$100
Total distributions of income	$900	$500	$350	$150	$100
Groups to whom income accrues					
Employees	X				
Government	X	X			
Creditors	X	X	X		
Preferred stockholders	X	X	X	X	
Common stockholders	X	X	X	X	X

period, except for dividends and capital stock transactions. They contend that unusual items, events not recurring frequently, and items related to other accounting periods should be reported in the current income statement. Advocates of this view assume that financial statement users will not focus excessively on the bottom-line net income figure and that they will appropriately consider the components of net income when they interpret the enterprise's performance. All-inclusive advocates claim that irregular items tend to be unnoticed when not reported in the income statement. Considerable judgment is required to determine which items should be included under the current operating performance approach, which—according to all-inclusive proponents—allows management to manipulate reported income by including or excluding items as desired.

A careful analysis of authoritative accounting pronouncements reveals an evolution[12] in thought from a strong all-inclusive position in 1941 (*Accounting Research Bulletin No. 8*[13]) to an equally strong current operating performance position in 1948 (*Accounting Research Bulletin No. 35*[14]). By 1953, the pendulum had begun to swing away from the current operating performance position. A strong step in the direction

---

[12]For a discussion of the evolutionary process of income presentation, see Jack E. Kiger and Jan R. Williams, "An Emerging Concept of Income Presentation," *Accounting Historians Journal* (Fall 1977), pp. 63–77.
[13]*ARB No. 8*, "Combined Statement of Income and Earned Surplus," 1941.
[14]*ARB No. 35*, "Presentation of Income and Earned Surplus," 1948.

of the all-inclusive approach came in 1966 when the Accounting Principles Board, in *Opinion No. 9*, concluded that "net income should reflect all items of profit and loss recognized during the period with the sole exception of prior period adjustments."[15] The APB opinion further stated that extraordinary items should be shown separately from the results of ordinary operations in the income statement and that prior period adjustments should be reported as adjustments to the beginning balance of retained earnings. Finally, it listed criteria for identifying both extraordinary items and prior period adjustments. These criteria have subsequently been changed, however, by other authoritative pronouncements.

In 1977, the FASB moved a step closer to an all-inclusive income statement when it issued *Statement of Financial Accounting Standards No. 16*.[16] Previously, companies were allowed to treat a variety of items as prior period adjustments. Under *Statement No. 16* the number of items properly treated as adjustments to retained earnings was reduced considerably. In view of all these events we can conclude that current accounting practice supports a *modified* all-inclusive view within which all income items except limited prior period adjustments are included in the determination of net income.

COMPREHENSIVE INCOME

In 1984 the FASB issued *Statement of Financial Accounting Concepts No. 5*, "Recognition and Measurement in Financial Statements of Business Enterprises." In this statement, the concept of "comprehensive income" is introduced and a distinction is drawn between comprehensive income and earnings.

Comprehensive income is defined as follows:

> *A broad measure of the effects of transactions and other events of an entity, comprising all recognized changes in equity (net assets) of the entity during a period from transactions and other events and circumstances except those resulting from investments by owners and distributions to owners.*[17]

The concept of "earnings," on the other hand, is similar to net income in current practice. **Earnings** is a measure of performance for a period and to the extent feasible *excludes* items that are extraneous to that period. One example of an item that is included in present net income but excluded from this definition of earnings is the cumulative effect of a change in accounting principle.[18] While the FASB expects net income, profit, net loss and other equivalent terms will continue to be used in financial statements as names for "earnings," we can reasonably expect some future changes in income-statement content and display as the FASB implements in practice the concepts of comprehensive income and earnings as described in *SFAC No. 5*. One possible outcome of this distinction is a movement back toward a current operating performance approach as extraneous transactions are identified as part of comprehensive income but not part of earnings.

CONTEMPORARY INCOME PRESENTATION

Contemporary income presentation practices are based on the concept of income to stockholders (see Column 4, Exhibit 20–6). Emphasis is placed on the all-inclusive

---

[15]*APB Opinion No. 9*, "Reporting the Results of Operations," 1966, par. 17.
[16]*FASB Statement of Financial Accounting Standards No. 16*, "Prior Period Adjustments," 1977.
[17]*Statement of Financial Accounting Concepts No. 5*, "Recognition and Measurement in Financial Statements of Business Enterprises," 1984, par. 39.
[18]*SFAC No. 5*, pars. 33–34.

concept of income with limited exceptions. Concern for the presentation of the results of current operations, however, is apparent in the many separate classifications and subtotals required in the statement if certain types of events have taken place.

Throughout this text, various aspects of income statement presentation have been discussed and illustrated. In the following paragraphs, several important features of the income statement which have been considered earlier are briefly reviewed. That discussion is followed by a discussion of the disposal of a segment of an enterprise, and an explanation of how the discontinued operations are reported in the income statement.

Single- and Multiple-Step Income Statements

A **single-step income statement** is a relatively simple presentation in which all revenues and gains included in pretax income are grouped together at the top of the statement. Next, all expenses and losses included in pretax income are grouped together and subtracted from the total of revenues and gains. This subtotal, reduced by income tax expense, is net income. In a **multiple-step income statement,** revenues from sales are presented first. From this amount, cost of goods sold is deducted to determine gross margin. Operating expenses, which may be classified into specific categories such as selling and administrative expenses, are deducted from the gross margin to obtain income from operations. Other income and expense items are added to or deducted from the income from operations to obtain net income. The resulting net income figure is the same for both statements, and the difference lies in the format and extent of detail. Both types of presentations are acceptable and each is frequently encountered. You may wish to refresh your memory about these two forms of income statement presentation by reviewing Exhibits 4–1 and 4–2.

Individually Identified Gains and Losses

Gains and losses which are unusual in nature *or* infrequent in occurrence are individually identified in the income statement. Under the multiple-step format, these items are usually displayed among other gains and losses, following income from operations. Examples of this type of item are gains and losses from the sale of plant assets or investment securities. Care should be taken not to present these items in a way that implies that they are extraordinary items. They are *not* presented on a net-of-tax basis, and earnings-per-share figures are not presented on these items.

Intraperiod Income Tax Allocation

Gains and losses presented in the financial statements in separate categories, such as extraordinary items and prior period adjustments, are presented on a net-of-tax basis. **Intraperiod income tax allocation** procedures require the determination of the income tax effect of these items and the direct association of the tax with the related gain or loss. A gain is reduced by the additional income tax resulting from that gain. A loss is reduced by the income tax benefit resulting from the reduction in income due to the inclusion of that loss. The income tax expense which relates to all revenues and expenses not separately classified is computed as if any separately classified item(s) did not exist.

Extraordinary Gains and Losses

Gains and losses which are judged to be *both* unusual in nature *and* infrequent in occurrence are defined as **extraordinary** and are presented in a separate income statement category on a net-of-tax basis. This presentation is required in both single- and multiple-step income statements. An income subtotal immediately preceding extraordinary items entitled "income before extraordinary items" must be included in the income statement. This caption is followed by the extraordinary gain or loss, presented net of its tax effect, and then by the net income amount.

To illustrate the presentation of an extraordinary item, Exhibit 20–7 includes the income statement and a related note to the financial statements from the 1990 annual report of Phillips Petroleum Company. Phillips is engaged in petroleum exploration and production on a worldwide scale, petroleum refining and marketing primarily in the United States, and chemicals production and distribution worldwide. Note 1 of the financial statements, which is presented at the bottom of Exhibit 20–7, explains the nature of the extraordinary item, specifically the settlement of litigation with the government of Iran over 1979 exploration activities. Observe also that the income statement includes the cumulative effect of a change in accounting principle which follows the extraordinary item and immediately precedes the net income figure.

Cumulative Effect of a Change in Accounting Principle

When an enterprise changes from one generally accepted accounting principle (or method of applying a principle) to another, the **cumulative effect** of that change on

---

EXHIBIT 20–7

PHILLIPS PETROLEUM COMPANY
Example Extraordinary Item

Partial Income Statement

Years Ended December 31	Millions of Dollars		
	1990	1989	1988
Income before income taxes, extraordinary item and cumulative effect of change in accounting principle	1,187	536	1,115
Provision for income taxes	646	317	465
Income before Extraordinary Item and Cumulative Effect of Change in Accounting Principle	541	219	650
Extraordinary gain	101	—	—
Cumulative effect of change in accounting for income taxes	137	—	—
Net Income	$ 779	219	650
Net Income Applicable to Common Stock	$ 779	219	639
Per Share of Common Stock			
Income before extraordinary item and cumulative effect of change in accounting principle	$2.18	.90	2.72
Extraordinary gain	.40	—	—
Cumulative effect of change in accounting for income taxes	.55	—	—
Net income	$3.13	.90	2.72

Notes to Financial Statements

Note 1—Extraordinary Item and Accounting Change   In January 1990, the company recorded a $101 million gain ($.40 per share) from the settlement of litigation with the Government of Iran and the National Iranian Oil Company. The dispute was over the 1979 expropriation of Phillips' interest in two producing offshore Iranian oil fields and concludes all claims and counterclaims.

Effective January 1, 1990, the company adopted *FASB Statement No. 96*, "Accounting for Income Taxes," which requires an asset and liability approach in accounting for income taxes. Under the new method, the amount of deferred tax liabilities or assets is calculated by applying the provisions of enacted tax law to determine the amount of taxes payable or refundable currently or in future years. The effect of the change was to increase income before extraordinary item and cumulative effect of a change in accounting principle by $130 million ($.52 per share) for the year. In addition, the cumulative effect of the change on prior years increased net income by $137 million ($.55 per share). Prior years' financial statements have not been restated.

SOURCE: Phillips Petroleum Company, 1990 Annual Report.

retained earnings at the beginning of the period of change is usually included in income of the period of the change.[19] The cumulative effect may be a gain or loss, depending on the nature of the specific change. The cumulative effect immediately follows extraordinary items, if any, and is presented on a net-of-tax basis.

Prior Period Adjustments

Corrections of errors in previously issued financial statements and certain other adjustments are *not* included in the determination of net income. Primarily because they do not relate to the period in which they are recorded, these items (presented on a net-of-tax basis) belong in the retained earnings statement as adjustments to the beginning balance of the period—even though they are part of the enterprise's total earnings history.

Several types of events and transactions that are presented as prior period adjustments are discussed in Chapter 19. These include corrections of errors, and certain retroactive adjustments resulting from the application of authoritative accounting pronouncements.

Earnings Per Share

Earnings-per-share figures are included in the income statement of all publicly held companies. Other companies may choose to present earnings-per-share data, and several authoritative pronouncements require the presentation of earnings-per-share figures for certain income statement items.

When presented, earnings-per-share figures appear on the face of the income statement and may also be explained in related notes. A common practice is to present an earnings-per-share schedule (which parallels the income statement presentation) at the bottom of the income statement.

Exhibit 20–8 illustrates this method of presentation with the hypothetical Foster Company's 1992–1993 comparative income statement, which includes a typical

EXHIBIT 20–8

Foster Company
PARTIAL INCOME STATEMENT
For the Fiscal Years Ended October 31, 1992 and 1993

	1992	1993
Income before extraordinary item and cumulative effect of change in accounting principle	$870,000	$ 740,000
Extraordinary loss—Major casualty loss, net of $70,000 income tax benefit	—	(130,000)
Cumulative effect of change in depreciation method, net of $28,000 income taxes	52,000	—
Net income	$922,000	$ 610,000
Earnings per common share		
Income before extraordinary item and cumulative effect of change in accounting principle	$8.70	$7.40
Extraordinary loss	—	(1.30)
Cumulative effect of change in accounting principle	.52	—
Net income	$9.22	$6.10

[19]As seen in Chapter 19, the effects of certain *special types of changes in an accounting principle* are presented by retroactively restating previous financial statements rather than by including the cumulative effect of the change in the income of the period of change. Also, in rare circumstances it may not be possible to compute the cumulative effect of a change in accounting principle for inclusion in the income statement.

DICTIONARY, PLEASE

You don't have to be a philologist to be an accountant. But an appreciation of the subtle meanings of words can be a real asset, especially for those interested in minimizing the impact of unexpected events on operating earnings.

Consider Primerica Corp., the big (1987 revenues, $3.8 billion) financial services supplier put together in recent years by Gerald Tsai Jr. In June, shortly before the stock market peaked and not long after Tsai bought his new 120-foot yacht *Longitude Zero,* Primerica bought the brokerage firm Smith Barney.

Came then Oct. 19. Wall Street, Smith Barney included, got creamed. But you'd never know that from the unaudited results for 1987 Primerica just released. Net income for the year was down, but only slightly, to $199 million—and the year-to-year comparison is owed to big gains on discontinued operations the year before. Primerica's 1987 net income on continuing operations, by contrast, was up 43%, to $183 million.

But what of that well-publicized $61 million bath Smith Barney took on its arbitrage business during the October crash? Primerica buried that little embarrassment in a footnote on "nonrecurring items."

Confused? Think of it this way: Had the $61 million arb loss not been filtered through the nonrecurring items account, earnings from continuing operations would have been $61 million ($43 million aftertax) lower than reported for last year.

Still confused? You're in good company. "The rules [governing the use of terms like nonrecurring] are not that clear," warns Robert Wilkins, project

manager at the Financial Accounting Standards Board. "It all comes down to a judgment."

Ted O'glove, publisher of the *Quality of Earnings Report,* isn't confused. He's outraged. "Arbitrage losses are part and parcel of the brokerage business," he blasts. "It is no more nonrecurring than previous periods' gains were nonrecurring. Who are they trying to kid?"

The disclosure was an unkind warning to Smith Barney's arbitragers. On Feb. 1, after the statement came out, Tsai closed down the firm's arbitrage unit, sacking its five highly paid traders. *Voilà!* By definition, whatever the arbitration desk made or lost was no longer part of continuing operations.

Ah, but what was it? Here's where the philology comes in.

Primerica might well have wanted to report the arbitrage loss as an "extraordinary" loss. Extraordinary items are reported separately—after income from continuing operations. Both Standard & Poor's and Value Line, in reporting earnings from continuing operations, relegate extraordinary items to a footnote.

There was one problem. Back in 1973 the Accounting Principles Board decreed that to be "extraordinary," an item must be both unusual in nature and infrequent in occurrence. A loss from a lawsuit, for example, would be an extraordinary item. But a securities firm's loss on arbitrage would not necessarily satisfy the definition.

"An arbitrage loss by a brokerage firm may be infrequent but it is usual in nature in that kind of business," explains Leopold A. Bernstein, professor of

earnings-per-share presentation at the bottom. The exhibit assumes that 100,000 shares of common stock were outstanding throughout 1992 and 1993.

The computation of earnings per share is complicated by the presence of convertible securities, stock options, warrants and rights, and other arrangements which include the possibility of changing the number of common shares outstanding. An in-depth discussion of this subject is found in Chapter 21 of this text.

DISCONTINUED OPERATIONS

When an enterprise has disposed of a major portion of its operations, the results of *continuing operations* should be separated from the operating results of the *discontinued segment.* Any gain or loss on the disposal of the discontinued part of the business is also shown separately. Prior to the development of this income statement presentation technique, the most frequent extraordinary items in financial reports were gains and losses from the disposal of portions of business enterprises.[20] The frequency of

---

[20]Leopold A. Bernstein, "Reporting the Results of Operations—A Reassessment of APB Opinion No. 9," *Journal of Accountancy* (July 1970), pp. 57–58.

accounting at Baruch College. "Primerica calls the loss 'nonrecurring' because it knows the loss is usual and does not fit the definition of extraordinary."

"Nonrecurring" is not the only fudge word accountants have come up with to get around the definition of "extraordinary." Other choices are "one-time" and "special." Many of these words—"nonrecurring" among them—don't have a technical meaning in the accounting glossary. But the clients use them anyway.

Why did Primerica judge its arb losses to be "nonrecurring"? The real advantage to Primerica, notes Baruch's Bernstein, is the effect of aggregating the different "nonrecurring" items in a footnote, more than canceling out losses with gains. Besides the arb loss, the footnote includes a handsome gain from the sale of Primerica's Looart Press. Net nonrecurring items: $16 million, aftertax. Again, it seems that Black Monday never happened—unless, of course, you parse the footnote.

Primerica's is not the only way to treat nonrecurring items. Consider the way Baltimore brokerage firm Alex. Brown & Sons accounted for last year's reorganization of its taxable fixed-income business and cancelation of a data processing project. The loss on the activity came to $1.3 million. Alex. Brown labeled the loss a "one-time charge"—but included it as part of operating expenses.

Salomon Inc., too, listed several "special" items in its unaudited 1987 financials. These include a charge for its abandoned New York City Coliseum project and a gain from the sale of its mortgage securities business. Together, the "special" items amount to a $107 million loss. Unlike Primerica, Salomon deducted its special losses from operating earnings.

Why didn't Primerica report the arb disaster as a "loss from discontinued operations"? That's what computer lessor Comdisco did when it closed its arbitrage operation and booked an $80 million (aftertax) loss in its most recent quarter. Like "extraordinary items," "discontinued operations" receive aftertax, below-the-line exposure. But they are defined as the sale or disposal of a division or subsidiary that can be clearly distinguished from other assets. Smith Barney was not likely to convince anyone that arbitrage is a separate business segment.

Primerica declined to discuss its accounting of the $61 million arb loss with *Forbes*. But in a statement the company insisted that treating the loss as "nonrecurring" was "an informative disclosure to the public and is entirely consistent with our practice of highlighting significant events."

The next day, a company spokesman called to assure us that when Primerica releases its audited figures this spring, the "nonrecurring" loss will indeed be included as an element of income from continuing operations. The investing public may grumble about such obfuscation, but accounting's philologists will have a field day.

SOURCE: Penelope Wang, "Dictionary, Please," *Forbes*, March 7, 1988, pp. 88–89. Reprinted by permission of *Forbes* Magazine. © Forbes Inc., 1988.

these items, combined with their tendency to represent large dollar amounts, prompted the APB to establish the reporting standards for discontinued operations as a part of *APB Opinion No. 30*.[21]

Income or loss from the operations of a segment prior to its disposal and any gain or loss on the disposal are *not* extraordinary items under current accounting standards. These items are combined in a section of the income statement identified as **discontinued operations.** This section is *preceded* by an income subtotal, **income from continuing operations.** The income or loss from the operations of the disposed segment and the gain or loss from the actual disposal are presented separately on a net-of-tax basis. This section is followed by "net income" or "income before extraordinary item and/or cumulative effect of change in accounting principles," as appropriate.

Earnings-per-share figures for income from continuing operations and net income are presented on the face of the income statement for publicly held companies. In practice, earnings-per-share figures are also frequently presented for the two

---

[21]*APB Opinion No. 30*, "Reporting the Results of Operations," 1973, par. 13–18.

components of discontinued operations or for the discontinued operations section as a single figure.

What constitutes a *segment* disposal (which, in turn, requires the company to present discontinued operations as described above)? A **segment** is a component of an enterprise whose activities represent a separate major line of business or a separate class of customer. A segment may be a subsidiary or other investee, a division, or a department; and the disposal may be accomplished by sale or abandonment. A major criterion distinguishing the disposal of a segment from other transactions requires that the assets and results of operations of the discontinued part of the business can be clearly distinguished physically, operationally, and for financial accounting purposes from other assets, results of operations, and activities of the enterprise. The inability to identify separately the results of operations of the discontinued unit suggests that the transaction is not a disposal of a *segment* of the business.

To illustrate the accounting and reporting for the disposal of a segment, assume that Ball Company has determined its preliminary aggregate operating figures for 1993 as follows:

Revenue from sales	$8,000,000
Cost of goods sold	3,500,000
Operating expenses	2,000,000
	5,500,000
Income before income tax	$2,500,000

At the end of the year the company disposed of its nuts-and-bolts division, which was operationally separate from the rest of the business. Operating results of this division, which are included in the above aggregate figures, are as follows:

Revenue from sales	$1,500,000
Cost of goods sold	1,400,000
Operating expenses	800,000
	2,200,000
Loss before income tax	$ (700,000)

In addition, the actual disposal of the nuts-and-bolts division resulted in a $450,000 non-operating loss before income tax, which is *not* included in the above figures:

Proceeds from the sale of nuts-and-bolts division	$ 6,500,000
Net book value of assets of nuts-and-bolts division	(6,950,000)
Loss on sale before income tax	$ (450,000)

The appropriate income tax rate for all items is 40%.

The presentation of discontinued operations for Ball Company is illustrated in the income statement in Exhibit 20–9. The revenue and expense amounts for continuing operations are determined by removing the figures for the discontinued division. The earnings-per-share figures are computed on the basis of 1,000,000 shares of common stock outstanding with no preferred stock.

The disposal of a major segment of a business enterprise frequently takes place over an extended period of time. It is not unusual for such a disposal to begin in one accounting period and extend into one or more future accounting periods. In this situation, two dates are particularly important:

EXHIBIT 20-9

Ball Company
INCOME STATEMENT
For the Year Ended December 31, 1993

Revenue from sales		$6,500,000
Cost of goods sold	$2,100,000	
Operating expenses	1,200,000	3,300,000
Income from continuing operations before income tax		3,200,000
Income tax expense (at 40%)		1,280,000
Income from continuing operations		1,920,000
Discontinued operations		
Loss from operations of discontinued nuts-and-bolts division, less applicable income taxes of $280,000	(420,000)	
Loss on disposal of nuts-and-bolts division, less applicable income taxes of $180,000	(270,000)	(690,000)
Net income		$1,230,000
Earnings per share		
Income from continuing operations		$1.92
Discontinued operations		
Loss from operations of nuts-and-bolts division	$(.42)	
Loss on disposal of nuts-and-bolts division	(.27)	(.69)
Net income		$1.23

Measurement Date—The date on which the management having the authority to approve the action commits itself to a formal plan to dispose of a segment of the business, whether by sale or abandonment. The plan of disposal should include, as a minimum, identification of the major assets to be disposed of, the expected manner of disposal, the period expected to be required for completion of the disposal, an active program to find a buyer if disposal is to be by sale, the estimated results of operations of the segment from the measurement date to the disposal date, and the estimated proceeds or salvage to be realized by disposal.

Disposal Date—The date of closing the sale if the disposal is by sale or the date that operations cease if the disposal is by abandonment.[22]

If the **measurement date** is in one accounting period and the **disposal date** is in a subsequent accounting period, accounting for the disposal of the segment is more complex.

In presenting discontinued operations, any operating results after the measurement date are included in the gain or loss from *disposal* of the discontinued segment, rather than as the results of operations. At the measurement date, if a loss is expected from the planned disposal, the estimated loss is recognized immediately. On the other hand, an anticipated gain from the disposal is not recognized until the gain is realized, which is usually at the disposal date. This procedure results in a *conservative* presentation of income, since an estimated loss is recognized immediately and an estimated gain is deferred until the later disposal date when it is fully realized.

Conservatism

In estimating whether a gain or loss will result from the disposal of the segment, the net amount expected to be received from the disposal includes any estimated costs

[22]*APB Opinion No. 30*, par. 14.

and expenses directly associated with the disposal. Additionally, if the disposal will take time and if continued operations of the segment are planned during the period of disposal, any estimated income or loss from operations is included in the estimated gain or loss on the disposal. Amounts of income or loss from operations included in the gain or loss on disposal are limited to amounts which can be reasonably projected. Normally such projections should not exceed a one-year period.

Disclosure   In addition to the information presented in the discontinued operations section of the income statement, the notes to the financial statements must disclose the following information:[23]

1. The identity of the segment of the business that has been or will be discontinued.
2. The expected disposal date, if known.
3. The expected manner of disposal.
4. A description of the remaining assets and liabilities of the segments at the financial-statement date.
5. The income or loss from operations and any proceeds from disposal of the segment during the period from the measurement date to the financial-statement date.

Many of the items which must be disclosed are also necessary to establish the measurement-date. Such information is frequently made available only through management action and estimates. Accountants, therefore, should attempt to gather additional objective evidence to support the assertions and disclosures contained in the financial statements.

When discontinued operations are presented in comparative financial statements, the operating results of the discontinued part of the business must be reclassified for the comparative year(s) for purposes of comparability and an amount of income from continuing operations presented for all years that are included in the statement.

Exhibit 20–10 presents the disclosure of discontinued operations from the income statement of Armstrong World Industries, Inc., for 1987–1989. Armstrong World Industries, Inc., is primarily a manufacturer and marketer of interior furnishings. It produces floor coverings, building products, and furniture. During 1989, the company disposed of a subsidiary company, Applied Color Systems, at a gain of $21.7 million, net of $8.0 million income taxes. Net earnings for the discontinued part of the business were $12.2 million in 1989; comparable amounts for 1988 ($11.7 million) and for 1987 ($10.4 million) have been reclassified in the income statement for purposes of comparability.

COMPREHENSIVE MODEL INCOME STATEMENT

The income statement in Exhibit 20–11 incorporates many of the revenue, expense, gain, and loss items discussed in this chapter and in previous chapters. The influence of the all-inclusive philosophy can be seen in the inclusion of the discontinued operations, extraordinary gain, cumulative effect of change in depreciation method, and other revenues and expenses not directly related to operations. On the other hand, the influence of the current operating performance philosophy can be seen in the separation of these items from normal, recurring transactions and the resulting subtotals, such as "income from operations," "income from continuing operations," and "income before extraordinary item and cumulative effect of change in accounting principle."

---

[23]*APB Opinion No. 30*, par. 18.

EXHIBIT 20–10

Armstrong World Industries, Inc.
Presentation of Discontinued Operations

Consolidated Statements of Earnings

Years ended December 31 (millions except for per-share data)	1989	1988*	1987*
Current earnings			
Net sales	$2,512.5	$2,289.5	$1,999.4
Cost of goods sold	1,782.4	1,631.7	1,404.1
Gross profit	730.1	657.8	595.3
Selling and administrative expense	450.7	402.3	349.1
Earnings from continuing businesses before other income (expense) and income taxes	279.4	255.5	246.2
Other income (expense):			
Interest expense	(41.2)	(26.4)	(11.9)
Miscellaneous, net	(.6)	13.0	2.5
	(41.8)	(13.4)	(9.4)
Earnings from continuing businesses before income taxes	237.6	242.1	236.8
Income taxes	83.9	91.1	96.8
Earnings from continuing businesses	153.7	151.0	140.0
Discontinued businesses:			
Earnings, net of income taxes of $8.2 in 1989, $7.9 in 1988, and $9.1 in 1987	12.2	11.7	10.4
Gain on sale, net of income taxes of $8.0 million	21.7	—	—
Net earnings	$ 187.6	$ 162.7	$ 150.4
Per share of common stock:			
Primary:			
Earnings from continuing businesses	$ 3.17	$ 3.26	$ 2.96
Earnings from discontinued businesses	.27	.25	.22
Gain on sale of discontinued businesses	.48	—	—
Net earnings	$ 3.92	$ 3.51	$ 3.18
Fully diluted:			
Earnings from continuing businesses	$ 3.03	$ 3.26	$ 2.96
Earnings from discontinued businesses	.24	.25	.22
Gain on sale of discontinued businesses	.45	—	—
Net earnings	$ 3.72	$ 3.51	$ 3.18

Discontinued businesses included in the financial statements reflect the fourth-quarter sale of certain assets (primarily inventory and property, plant, and equipment) of the company's carpet business and of the company's subsidiary, Applied Color Systems, Inc.

Net sales in 1989, through the measurement date of November 30 for carpet and October 31 for Applied Color Systems, Inc., totaled $344.7 million, and for the years 1988 and 1987 were $390.8 million and $365.6 million, respectively.

Operating statement categories, except where otherwise indicated, have been restated to exclude the effects of these discontinued businesses.

*Restated for the results of discontinued businesses.
SOURCE: Armstrong World Industries, Inc., 1989 Annual Report.

EXHIBIT 20-11

Morrow Company
INCOME STATEMENTS
For the Years Ended December 31, 1992 and 1993
(in thousands of dollars except earnings-per-share figures)

	1993	1992
Sales	$5,525	$5,108
Cost of goods sold	2,100	1,950
Gross margin	3,425	3,158
Selling and administrative expenses	1,250	1,200
Income from operations	2,175	1,958
Other income		
Gain on sale of plant assets	—	100
Dividend income	75	80
Other expenses		
Interest on long-term debt	(255)	(307)
Unrealized loss on valuations of current marketable equity securities	(92)	—
Income before income tax	1,903	1,831
Provision for income tax	761	732
Income from continuing operations	1,142	1,099
Discontinued operations		
Loss from operations of business segment, net of applicable income tax savings of $44 in 1993 and $48 in 1992	(66)	(72)
Loss on disposal of business segment, net of applicable income tax savings of $80	(120)	—
Income before extraordinary item and cumulative effect of change in accounting principle	956	1,027
Extraordinary item—gain on forced sale of assets to state municipality, net of applicable income taxes of $210	—	525
Cumulative effect of change in method of depreciation, net of applicable income taxes of $68	(102)	—
Net income	$ 854	$1,552
Earnings per common share		
Income from continuing operations	$11.42	$10.99
Discontinued operations	(1.86)	(.72)
Income before extraordinary item and cumulative effect of accounting change	9.56	10.27
Extraordinary gain	—	5.25
Cumulative effect of change in accounting principle	(1.02)	—
Net income	$ 8.54	$15.52
Pro forma amounts assuming retroactive application of new depreciation method		
Income before extraordinary item	$ 956	$ 967
Earnings per common share	$ 9.56	$ 9.67
Net income	$ 956	$1,492
Earnings per common share	$ 9.56	$14.92

The following aspects of this statement are particularly worthy of attention and provide a review of several concepts covered earlier:

1. The provision for income tax incorporates the income tax effects of all transactions presented above that item in the income statement. All items in the statement below this item are presented on a net-of-tax basis.

2. The major types of irregular items are presented in the following order: discontinued operations, extraordinary item, cumulative effect of a change in accounting principle. Appropriate titles are assigned to the income figures that *precede* each of these items.

3. The discontinued segment is presented immediately before the extraordinary item and is divided into the results of *operations* of the discontinued segment and the loss on the *disposal* of the discontinued segment. This section is preceded by the caption, "income from continuing operations." All items in this section are presented on a net-of-tax basis.

4. The extraordinary gain is separately disclosed after the discontinued operations section and is presented on a net-of-tax basis.

5. The cumulative effect of the change in depreciation method follows the extraordinary item and is presented on a net-of-tax basis.

6. The earnings per share and *pro forma* effects of the retroactive application of the newly adopted accounting principle are presented at the bottom of the income statement, following net income.

While it is unlikely that a single income statement would contain all the irregular items in Exhibit 20–11, it is important to understand the relation of each item to the others and to the income statement as a whole. The fictitious Morrow Company statement is presented to facilitate this understanding.

CONCEPTUAL CONSIDERATIONS

Revenue Realization

Matching

Conservatism

Substance over Form

Disclosure

A great deal of the first part of Chapter 20 centered on the accounting principles of *revenue realization* and *matching.* We determined that revenue is recognized when it is earned, measurable and collectible. The *matching principle* is the basis for the income statement and requires a careful association of expenses with revenues. Frequently this means that expenses are recognized in a different accounting period from the one in which they are actually incurred or paid.

We have also seen that the modifying conventions of *conservativism* and *substance over form* are influential in the recognition of revenue and in the application of the matching principle.

Income statement presentation is an application of the *disclosure principle.* Many authoritative accounting pronouncements have been issued which deal with the content of the income statement and the placement of items within the statement. At the present time, the income statement is prepared on a modified all-inclusive basis, with only prior period adjustments and selected other items excluded. As the FASB implements its concept of comprehensive income, however, we can expect further refinement in income presentation.

CONCLUDING REMARKS

Income presentation is one of the central themes of corporate financial reporting. In meeting the objectives of financial reporting, the income statement and information derived from that statement are particularly important. In this chapter, we have discussed revenue realization at the point of sale as the norm and we have also discussed and illustrated several situations where revenue is logically recognized at other times and in somewhat unusual ways. We have also seen that careful preparation of the income statement and the proper ordering and wording of items within that statement are important in meeting the objectives of financial reporting. While there is some evidence in recent years that the FASB is placing increased emphasis on the balance sheet in developing financial reporting standards, the income statement remains a vital part of financial reporting. Careful recognition of revenue and preparation of the income statement will undoubtedly continue to be a major responsibility of accountants in the future.

KEY POINTS

1. Revenue is not recognized until it is earned, measurable, and collectible. In many situations these conditions are met at the point of sale, although departures from revenue recognition at the point of sale are found in certain circumstances. (Objective 1)

2. The percentage-of-completion and completed-contract methods of accounting for long-term contracts are acceptable in different circumstances. Within the percentage-of-completion method, revenue is recognized throughout the construction period as objective evidence indicates the proper amount to be recognized. Within the completed-contract method, all revenue is deferred and recognized at the completion of the contract. (Objective 2)

3. The installment sales method defers the recognition of revenue until cash is collected, and this method is acceptable in financial reporting only when collectibility is highly uncertain. (Objective 3)

4. When customers have the right to return products, six conditions must be met before the revenue can be recognized. These conditions relate to the transfer of the risks and rewards of ownership from the seller to the buyer and the ability of the seller to make a reasonably objective estimate of the amount of returns. (Objective 4)

5. A major objective of financial reporting is to present information to investors and creditors concerning an enterprise's financial performance. The primary focus is information concerning earnings and its components. (Objective 5)

6. The presentation of income is carefully defined and structured in the authoritative literature. At the present time, income is presented in a manner consistent with a modified all-inclusive concept in that all items of profit and loss, except prior period adjustments, are included in the income statement. (Objective 6)

7. "Discontinued operations"—which follows the caption "income from continuing operations"—is a separate section of the income statement and includes both the gain or loss from the disposal of a discontinued segment of the business and the operating income or loss of that segment. These items are separated from the income or loss from ongoing business activities. (Objective 6)

8. Discontinued operations, extraordinary items, and the cumulative effect of a general change in accounting principle are presented in separate income statement categories on a net-of-tax basis. (Objective 6)

APPENDIX A: SPECIAL REVENUE-RECOGNITION PRACTICES

This appendix deals with the unique circumstances and business practices in several industries which require unusual or complex revenue-recognition practices. The general criteria for revenue recognition developed in the body of this chapter apply equally to special industries and routine situations. Therefore, when studying the appendix, consider carefully how each of the practices specified by the accounting profession is consistent with general or fundamental concepts of revenue recognition. Although specific practices are discussed, the purpose of this appendix is to develop a conceptual understanding of these special industry circumstances rather than detailed knowledge of the accounting procedures that are applied.

REAL ESTATE TRANSACTIONS

A unique aspect of real estate transactions is that risk of uncollectible receivables is reduced by the nature of the asset sold. Land and other real property is relatively easily repossessed if the purchasing party fails to comply with the terms of the sales agreement. Real property is not readily transportable, does not generally depreciate in value, and is frequently not susceptible to damage and destruction. While the foregoing characteristics are usually associated with land, many structural improvements and buildings possess similar characteristics.

Since sellers of real estate recognize these characteristics of real estate, a greater credit risk may be assumed without creating an unacceptable risk of loss to the selling enterprise. Although the recovery of the investment in real estate may be assured to a greater degree than in other types of sales, the recognition of additional sales revenue should be carefully considered when the buyer is a poor credit risk.

The American Institute of Certified Public Accountants (AICPA) considered these circumstances and issued an Industry Accounting Guide,[24] which subsequently

Substance over Form

became part of *FASB Statement of Financial Accounting Standards No. 66.* In addition to the issues already mentioned, the guide recognized that many real estate transactions are exceptionally complex and that the legal form of the transaction may often obscure the real economic substance of an event.

The accounting guide and the subsequent *SFAS No. 66* establish general criteria for the timing of recognition of revenue and provide modifying conventions for use when the conceptual criteria for revenue recognition are not met at the time of the sale.

> *[Revenue should be recognized] in full when real estate is sold, provided (a) the profit is measurable, that is, the collectibility of the sales price is reasonably assured or the amount that will not be collectible can be estimated, and (b) the earning process is virtually complete, that is, the seller is not obliged to perform significant activities after the sale to earn the profit. Unless both conditions exist, recognition of all or part of the profit shall be postponed.*[25]

If the collectibility of the sales price is uncertain, as is the case in many real estate transactions, then the installment sales method of revenue recognition or the even more conservative cost recovery method should be used. In certain circumstances involving the collectibility of the sales price, the seller should use "deposit accounting," wherein no sale is presumed to have occurred and all cash received is treated as deferred revenue (liability) in the balance sheet. Furthermore, if the earning process is incomplete, recognition of revenue moves from the time of sale to the time of the seller's performance of the earning process. Finally, no profit is recognized until a sale is actually consummated.

Certain requirements must be met in order to recognize revenue when the receivables are material after the sale and completion of the earning process. These criteria relate to: (1) the amount of the down payment; (2) the composition of the down payment; and (3) the terms regarding the receivable portion of the consideration.

In regard to the amount of the initial payment, a range from 5% to 25% of the purchase price, depending on the nature of the property sold, has been established for purposes of profit recognition.[26]

Even if a down payment is large enough to qualify for the recognition of profit, the composition of the payment and terms of collection must also be considered. Generally, the down payment must consist of cash or notes supported by irrevocable letters of credit from established lending institutions to support the immediate recognition of revenue. Buyers must also maintain a continuing financial commitment in that the payments being made must be sufficient to pay the total indebtedness, including interest, within 20 years for land and within normal first mortgage terms of financial institutions for other real estate.

If a buyer's down payment amount or quality or the buyer's continuing investment is not adequate, then the installment sales method should normally be used to recognize revenue on the sale. However, if there is uncertainty as to whether cost will be recovered if a buyer defaults or if cost has already been recovered through down payment but future collections are uncertain, then the cost recovery method of revenue recognition is employed.

ACCOUNTING FOR RETAIL LAND SALES

Land developers frequently acquire a large parcel of land, develop a master plan for subdivision and improvement, obtain construction approval, perform necessary improvements, and sell lots. Furthermore, certain characteristics inherent in retail land sales create special problems concerning the recognition of revenue and related expenses. Examples are small down payments,

---

[24]*AICPA Industry Accounting Guide,* "Accounting for Profit Recognition on Sales of Real Estate," 1973.

[25]*FASB Statement of Financial Accounting Standards No. 66,* "Accounting for Sales of Real Estate," 1982, par. 3.

[26]*FASB Statement of Financial Accounting Standards No. 66,* par. 54.

unenforceable sales contracts, and cancellation periods during which buyers can obtain refunds.

Consideration of the foregoing problems encouraged the AICPA to develop another Industry Accounting Guide; this one pertains to the timing and magnitude of revenue recognition.[27] This guide also became part of *SFAS No. 66*. In essence, *SFAS No. 66* contains the following requirements for recording a sale:[28]

1. The buyer must make a down payment and regular subsequent payments throughout the period covered by any cancellation with refund right.
2. The aggregate payments, including interest, must at least equal 10% of the contract sales price.
3. Collection experience on similar sales must indicate that collection of the receivable is reasonably assured.
4. Generally, the receivable from the sale must not be subject to subordination to new loans on the property.
5. The seller must not be obligated to complete improvements of lots sold nor to construct facilities applicable to lots sold.

For transactions in which the first four criteria are met and substantial progress has been made toward the completion of improvements and facilities (mentioned in requirement 5), the percentage-of-completion method is applicable.

ACCOUNTING FOR FRANCHISE ACTIVITIES

The growth of franchising as a means of commerce began intense acceleration during the 1960s and continues today. Many contentious accounting and reporting issues are posed by such activities, and these problems are resolved in *FASB Statement of Financial Accounting Standards No. 45*.[29] **Franchises** generally involve the creation or extension of a business in which two parties join together in a continuing contract with a joint public identity. Each party normally contributes resources. The **franchisor** frequently contributes products, processes, equipment, company reputation, and trademarks. The **franchisee** generally provides operating capital and managerial and operational resources. Franchise activities are extremely broad; they cut across industry lines and are radically different in terms of organization, concept, and philosophy. For example, some franchise agreements provide for a relatively passive franchisor role after establishment, while others require extensive participation or

the supply of products and skill on a continuing basis. Therefore, precise accounting and reporting standards are not possible. Certain broad guidelines, however, are provided by *FASB Statement No. 45*.

The general bases for accounting and reporting practices are contained in the franchise agreement. Most such agreements require the franchisee to make a substantial initial payment, called a franchise fee, to the franchisor in consideration for the reputation, skill, products, and processes contributed by the franchisor. Financial accounting for the franchise fee in terms of revenue recognition is most controversial, and careful study of the franchise agreement is necessary.

FASB Statement No. 45 notes that the problem of recognizing revenue in regard to franchise fees generally results from two issues: (1) the point at which the fee is to be considered earned, and (2) the assessment of collectibility of any unpaid portion of the fee. Initial fees are generally quite specific and, therefore, the amount of the initial fee is usually known. Most franchise agreements also call for continuing payments related to the level of franchisee business. For example, continuing payments to franchisors are usually based on the sales of products to franchisees or on a percentage of the franchisee's sales or profits.

The three revenue-recognition practices that are used with franchisees are summarized as follows:

1. **Cash basis.** This method calls for recording revenue when cash is received. Proponents cite the simplicity of application, the complexity of franchise agreements, and collection problems as support for this practice.
2. **Spread over life of agreement.** This method treats the initial fee as a prepayment for the privilege of using franchise rights. Accordingly, the prepayment should be recognized ratably over the life of the franchise agreement. Franchisors agree that the franchise fee is payment for a confirmation of initial and continuing services and transfers of rights.
3. **Inception of the franchise agreement.** This method treats the sale of a franchise in a manner similar to the sale of any other commercial property, tangible or intangible. The sale represents the transfer of specified rights in exchange for specified consideration and thus supports the recognition of revenue at the point of sale.

FASB Statement No. 45 finds merit in each argument under certain separate circumstances and indirectly supports each in specific individual situations. In essence, revenue should be recognized when a franchise sale occurs *and* when all material obligations of the franchisor have been *substantially performed*. Substantial performance may take place at different points in time under

---

[27]*AICPA Industry Accounting Guide*, "Accounting for Retail Land Sales," 1973.
[28]*FASB Statement of Financial Accounting Standards No. 66*, par. 45.
[29]*FASB Statement of Financial Accounting Standards No. 45*, "Accounting for Franchise Fee Revenue," 1981.

different franchise agreements. Even if the franchise agreement requires no further franchisor services, revenue is not recognized if business conditions or informal policy indicates that substantial voluntary services are likely to be rendered by the franchisor.

Any unpaid franchise fees must also be assessed as to collectibility prior to the recognition of revenue. If collection of the franchise fee is uncertain, the installment method or cost recovery method may be necessary to avoid a premature recognition of revenue.

QUESTIONS

20–1 What three conditions must be met for revenue to be recognized?

20–2 Why is the point of sale frequently used as the point of revenue recognition?

20–3 Why do long-term contracts pose a difficult revenue-recognition problem?

20–4 Under what circumstances should the percentage-of-completion method of recognizing revenue on long-term contracts be used?

20–5 Under what circumstances should the completed-contract method of recognizing revenue on long-term contracts be used?

20–6 What is the difference in accounting treatment of contract revenues and costs under the percentage-of-completion and completed-contract methods?

20–7 Assuming a contract is started in 1991 and completed in 1993, explain the procedure for estimating the amount of gross profit in each year if the percentage of completion is determined based on costs incurred to date as a percentage of total expected costs.

20–8 Under what circumstances is the installment sales method appropriate for financial reporting purposes? How does this method differ from recognizing revenue at the point of sale?

20–9 State briefly the six criteria that must be met for revenue to be recognized if the customer has the right to return the purchased products. If one or more of these conditions are not met, what accounting procedures are appropriate?

20–10 Explain how the presentation of income contributes to meeting the primary objectives of financial reporting.

20–11 How does the presentation of income assist in judging management efficiency?

20–12 Explain the concept of "value added income." How does it differ from the concept of income underlying the income statement as currently prepared?

20–13 What is the difference between "income to stockholders" and "income to residual stockholders"?

20–14 Distinguish between the all-inclusive and current operating performance definitions of income in terms of the meaning of the final income figure resulting from each.

20–15 Distinguish between the FASB's concepts of "comprehensive income" and "earnings."

20–16 What determines a "segment" in deciding whether the disposal of a portion of a business qualifies for separate disclosure in a discontinued operations section of the income statement?

20–17 Explain the meaning of the income subtotal "income from continuing operations."

20–18 Distinguish between the "measurement date" and the "disposal date." Explain their significance in reporting discontinued operations in the income statement.

20–19 State a rule for identifying those revenues, expenses, gains, and losses which must be presented on a net-of-tax basis in the income statement.

20–20 Which of the following is an example of an extraordinary item in reporting results of operations?

[a] A loss incurred because of a strike by employees.

[b] The write-off of deferred research and development costs believed to have no future benefit.

[c] A gain resulting from the devaluation of the U.S. dollar.

[d] A gain resulting from the state exercising its right of eminent domain on a piece of land used as a parking lot.   (AICPA adapted)

20–21 Which of the following is *not* a generally practiced method of presenting the income statement?

[a] Including prior period adjustments in determining net income.
[b] The single-step income statement.
[c] The consolidated statement of income.
[d] Including gains and losses from discontinued operations of a segment of a business in determining net income.   (AICPA adapted)

20–22 Which of the following shows how the gain or loss from an event or transaction that meets the criteria for infrequent occurrence but not unusual nature should be disclosed?

[a] Separately in the earnings statement immediately after earnings from continuing operations.
[b] On a net-of-tax basis in the earnings statement immediately after earnings from continuing operations.
[c] As an extraordinary item and treated accordingly in the earnings statement.
[d] Separately in the earnings statement as a component of earnings from continuing operations.
                                                                 (AICPA adapted)

20–23 When a company discontinues an operation and disposes of the discontinued operation (segment), the transaction should be included in the earnings statement as a gain or loss on disposal reported as which of the following?

[a] A prior period adjustment.
[b] An extraordinary item.
[c] An amount after continuing operations and before extraordinary items.
[d] A bulk sale of fixed assets included in earnings from continuing operations.

                                                                 (AICPA adapted)

EXERCISES   **20–24** LONG-TERM CONTRACT   Matthews Construction Company began work on a contract in 1992 and completed the contract in 1993. The total contract price was $4,200,000.
     Information concerning the contract for 1992 and 1993 is as follows:

	1992	1993
Costs incurred during year	$ 600,000	$3,150,000
Estimated costs to complete at end of year	2,400,000	–0–
Billings during year	720,000	3,280,000
Collections during year	400,000	3,000,000

Instructions

[a] Determine the amount of the $4,200,000 contract price to be recognized each year under the completed-contract method.
[b] Determine the amount of the $4,200,000 contract price to be recognized each year under the percentage-of-completion method.

20–25 LONG-TERM CONTRACT   Quick-Build Construction Company contracted to construct a building for $450,000. Quick-Build began construction in 1992 and completed the project in 1993. Cost information for the project is as follows:

	1992	1993
Costs incurred	$200,000	$120,000
Estimated costs to complete	100,000	—

Quick-Build uses the percentage-of-completion method for recognizing income on the contract.

Instructions

[a] Determine the amount of income that the company should recognize in 1992 and 1993.
[b] Prove the amount of income you have computed in [a] by computing the total income on the contract and comparing it with the incomes you have computed for 1992 and 1993.
[c] Prepare the journal entry required at the end of each year to recognize that year's income.

20–26 INSTALLMENT SALES   Mall Company, which began business on January 1, 1992, appropriately uses the installment sales method of recognizing revenue because of the uncertainty of the collection of its receivables. The following data pertain to 1992 and 1993:

	1992	1993
Installment sales	$350,000	$420,000
Cost of installment sales	280,000	315,000
General and administrative expenses	35,000	42,000
Cash collections on installment sales of:		
1992	150,000	135,000
1993	—	220,000

Instructions

[a] Determine the balance in the Deferred Gross Profit account at December 31, 1993.

[b] A 1992 sale resulted in a default in 1993. At the date of default, the balance of the installment receivable was $6,400, and the repossessed merchandise had a fair value of $4,750. Assuming the repossessed merchandise is recorded at fair value, determine the amount of gain or loss on the repossession.   (AICPA adapted)

20–27 INSTALLMENT SALES   Ratner Company sells appliances through installment contracts. Because of the uncertainty of collection and the relatively high potential for repossession, the company appropriately recognizes revenue on an installment basis, deferring revenue recognition until cash is collected.

During 1992, Ratner determined that its gross profit percentage was 40%; during 1993 this percentage increased to 42%. Of $150,000 sales in 1992, Ratner collected $70,000 in 1992 and $50,000 in 1993. Of $170,000 sales in 1993, Ratner had collected $97,000 by year-end.

Instructions

For 1992 and 1993, compute the amounts of gross profit to be recognized and the amounts to be deferred at the end of the year.

20–28 RENT COLLECTED IN ADVANCE   On August 1, 1993, Wilcox Company received $90,000 for one year's advance rent on space that it leases to another company. Wilcox Company's fiscal year ends on October 31.

Instructions

[a] Determine the portion of the $90,000 that should be recognized as revenue for the fiscal year ending October 31, 1993.

[b] Prepare the adjusting journal entry Wilcox should make on October 31, 1993, if the $90,000 was credited to Unearned Rent Revenue when it was received.

[c] Prepare the adjusting journal entry the company should make on October 31, 1993, if the $90,000 was credited to Rent Revenue when it was received.

20–29 RIGHT OF RETURN   Clark Company sold $225,000 of merchandise on credit to its customers during 1993. The cost of this merchandise was $153,000 and Clark uses a perpetual inventory system. Based on past trends, Clark expects returns of 2.5% of sales within 90 days of the sales transaction. During 1993, cash collections of receivables were $174,200, and the selling price of merchandise returned totaled $4,050.

Instructions

[a] Prepare journal entries for all transactions and events mentioned above for Clark Company for 1993, the company's first year of operations.

[b] Indicate the items and dollar amounts that will appear in the 1993 income statement as a result of these events.

20–30 EXTRAORDINARY ITEM   Massey Production Company determines its pretax financial income for 1993 to be $1,420,000. The appropriate income tax rate for all income items is 35%, and no permanent or temporary differences are involved. The company's reporting period ends on December 31. Included in pretax financial income are the following items:

[1] A loss of $335,000 on the destruction of a plant facility from a natural disaster. This item is considered both unusual in nature and infrequent in occurrence.

[2] A gain of $16,700 on the sale of stock owned in another company. Although Massey does not buy and sell stock investments often, this type of transaction is common for companies of this type.

Instructions

Prepare the income statement to the extent possible from the information given, beginning with the caption "income before income tax."

20–31 SPECIAL INCOME ITEMS   Fairfield Fashions, Inc., has correctly determined the following information related to operations for 1993:

Revenue from sales	$650,000
Expenses	415,000
Income before income tax	$235,000

In reviewing the company's records, you discover the following items:

because of error
Dep exp ↑
NI ↑
RE↑

[1] During 1993, the company discovered an error in the amount of depreciation recognized in 1991 and 1992. The correction of this error, which has not been recorded, will result in an increase in depreciation for 1991 of $42,000 and for 1992 of $37,000. *Prior Period Adj*

[2] During 1993, an inventory loss of $37,800 was due to a government ban on certain highly flammable fabrics. This loss was considered both unusual and infrequent and has not been recorded.

During 1993 dividends of $62,500 were paid on 62,500 shares of common stock, which were outstanding throughout 1993. Income taxes are to be recognized at 30% on all income items.

Instructions

Assuming that retained earnings at January 1, 1993, were previously reported as $590,000, prepare a partial income statement and a retained earnings statement for Fairfield Fashions, Inc., for calendar year 1993.

20–32 DISCONTINUED OPERATIONS   Wilbur Company, a holding company, has two operating subsidiaries: one manufacturing wheelbarrows and the other manufacturing toothbrushes. The wheelbarrow subsidiary has been unprofitable, and in late December 1992, Wilbur's management contracted to sell that subsidiary to another company for $60,000. The sale will be effective on April 1, 1993. Wilbur will operate the wheelbarrow subsidiary during the first three months of 1993, even though those operations are expected to result in a $10,000 loss (before income taxes).

At December 31, 1992, the carrying amount of Wilbur's investment in the wheelbarrow subsidiary is $100,000. Both the $40,000 loss on the sale of the investment and the $10,000 operating loss will be deductible on Wilbur's 1993 income tax return, resulting in an anticipated tax savings at an assumed 30% tax rate.

Instructions

Determine the amount of the "loss on disposal of wheelbarrow subsidiary, net of applicable income tax benefit" which should be presented in Wilbur's income statement for the year ended December 31, 1992.   (AICPA adapted)

20–33 EXTRAORDINARY ITEMS   The December 31, 1993 financial statements of Waller Corporation reported a total of $325,000 under the caption "extraordinary losses." An analysis further revealed that the $325,000 in losses was comprised of the following items:

[1] Waller recorded a loss of $75,000 in the abandonment of equipment formerly used in the business.

[2] In an unusual and infrequent occurrence, a loss of $90,000 was sustained as a result of hurricane damage to a warehouse.

[3] During 1993 several factories were shut down during a major strike by employees. Shutdown expenses totaled $140,000.

[4] Accounts receivable of $20,000 were written off as uncollectible.

Instructions

[a] Ignoring income taxes, compute the amount of loss that Waller should report as extraordinary on its 1993 statement of income.

[b] Explain the proper disclosure, if any, for any of the four items that should not be reported as extraordinary items. (AICPA adapted)

20–34 DISCONTINUED OPERATIONS The following condensed statement of income of Banner Corporation, a diversified company, is presented for the two years ended December 31, 1993 and 1992.

	1993	1992
Net sales	$5,000,000	$4,800,000
Cost of sales	3,100,000	3,000,000
Gross profit	1,900,000	1,800,000
Operating expenses	1,100,000	1,200,000
Operating income	800,000	600,000
Gain on sale of division	450,000	–0–
Income before income taxes	1,250,000	600,000
Provision for income taxes	437,500	210,000
Net income	$ 812,500	$ 390,000

On January 1, 1993, Banner entered into an agreement to sell for $1,600,000 the assets and product line of one of its separate operating divisions. The sale was consummated on December 31, 1993, and resulted in a pretax gain on disposition of $450,000. This division's contribution to reported operating income before income taxes for each year was as follows:

| 1993 | $(320,000) loss |
| 1992 | (250,000) loss |

Assume an income tax rate of 35%.

Instructions

[a] In the preparation of a revised comparative statement of income, what amounts should Banner present for "Income from continuing operations" for 1992 and 1993?

[b] In the preparation of a revised comparative statement of income, what amounts should Banner present for "Discontinued operations" for 1992 and 1993? (AICPA adapted)

20–35 SPECIAL INCOME ITEMS Winter Company reports income before income tax of $952,000 for 1993. This figure *includes* the following items which may require adjustment and/or reclassification before the formal income statement can be prepared:

[1] A change in depreciation method from the straight-line to the accelerated method resulted in a $40,000 loss that was due to the cumulative effect on previous years. Depreciation for 1993 was computed on the accelerated method.

[2] A gain of $127,500 on the excess of insurance recovery over the book value of a plant destroyed by a hurricane. This was the first hurricane in the county in over a century.

[3] A gain of $18,700 on the sale of noncurrent marketable equity securities.

All items are subject to 38% income tax except the gain on insurance recovery and the gain on the sale of securities. These are subject to 25% income tax. The end of the fiscal year is November 30, 1993.

Instructions

Prepare the income statement, beginning with "income before income tax," and provide computations. You may ignore earnings-per-share figures.

20–36 INCOME STATEMENT PRESENTATION Pinson Company has accumulated information to be used in the preparation of its income statement for the year ended December 31, 1993. All items are on a pretax basis.

Sales	$7,750,000
Cost of goods sold	4,200,000
Operating expenses	1,600,000
Interest revenue	125,000
Extraordinary loss from major casualty	55,000
Cumulative effect (gain) of change in accounting principle	138,000
Number of outstanding shares of common stock throughout 1993	120,000
Income tax rate applicable to all items	35%

Instructions

Prepare a multiple-step income statement for 1993 to conform with GAAP.

20–37   CORRECTION OF INCOME STATEMENT   Friends, Inc., has prepared a preliminary income statement for 1993 as follows:

Friends, Inc.
INCOME STATEMENT
For the Year Ended December 31, 1993

Sales		$520,000
Cost of goods sold		221,000
Gross profit		299,000
Operating expenses		105,000
Income before special items		194,000
Special items		
Gain on the sale of land	$ 60,000	
Interest expense	(12,500)	
Cumulative effect of change in method of overhead recognition	(35,800)	11,700
Income before income tax		205,700
Income tax expense		73,280
Net income		$132,420

You have been engaged to review this statement and revise it as appropriate. You determine that the gain on the sale of land should be presented as an extraordinary item because it resulted from the forced sale caused by newly enacted legislation. All items are subject to a 40% income tax except this gain, which is subject to a special 25% rate.

Instructions

Prepare a revised income statement based on generally accepted accounting principles. (You may ignore earnings-per-share calculations.)

20–38   FINANCIAL-STATEMENT CLASSIFICATION   The following classification codes are to be used in completing this exercise:

Income Statement Categories/Items
  1. Revenue.
  2. Cost of goods sold.
  3. Operating expenses.
  4. Other revenues, expenses, gains, losses.
  5. Discontinued operations.
  6. Extraordinary items.
  7. Cumulative effect of change in accounting principle.

Items Omitted from the Income Statement
  8. Included in balance sheet.
  9. Included in retained earnings statement.
  10. Included in notes to the financial statements.
  11. Omitted from the financial statements.

Instructions

Indicate the preferred code number for each of the following items. If an explanation is necessary, state it briefly. If more than one classification is needed, list all appropriate code numbers.

[a]   Accumulated depreciation—buildings.
[b]   Interest revenue.
[c]   Loss of plant from hurricane.
[d]   Revenues and expenses from segment disposed of during current year.
[e]   Dividends declared.
[f]   Gain on the sale of plant assets.
[g]   Loss on expropriation of assets by foreign government.
[h]   Annual bonus paid store manager.
[i]   Impact on previous years' earnings of changing depreciation method.
[j]   Correction of error in inventory that was carried forward from previous year.
[k]   Depreciation expense on manufacturing equipment.
[l]   Loss on disposal of a segment of the business.
[m]   Interest paid on outstanding debt.
[n]   Loss on sale of temporary marketable securities.
[o]   Accounting policies.
[p]   Adjustment for change from unacceptable to acceptable accounting method.
[q]   Details of outstanding debt issues.
[r]   Revenue received in advance (to be earned in next accounting period).

PROBLEMS

20–39   LONG-TERM CONTRACTS   Buildco Construction Company began operations January 1, 1993. During the year Buildco entered into a contract with Pepperdine Company to construct a manufacturing facility. At that time Buildco estimated that it would take five years to complete the facility at a total cost of $4,800,000. The total contract price for construction of the facility is $5,800,000.

During 1993, Buildco incurred $1,250,000 in construction costs related to the project. Because of rising material and labor costs, the estimated cost to complete the contract at the end of 1993 is $3,750,000. Pepperdine was billed for and paid 30% of the contract price in accordance with the contract agreement.

Instructions

Prepare schedules to compute the amount of gross profit to be recognized for the year ended December 31, 1993, and the amount to be shown as "cost of uncompleted contract in excess of related billings" or "billings on uncompleted contracts in excess of related costs" at December 31, 1993, under each of the following methods:

[a]   Completed-contract method.
[b]   Percentage-of-completion method.

Provide supporting computations in good form.   (AICPA adapted)

20–40   INSTALLMENT SALES   Warren Corporation sells farm machinery on the installment plan. On July 1, 1993, Warren entered into an installment sale contract with Agriculture, Inc., for an eight-year period. Equal annual payments under the installment sale are $100,000 and are due on July 1. The first payment was made on July 1, 1993.

Additional information is as follows:

[1]   The amount to be realized on an outright sale of similar farm machinery is $556,000.
[2]   The cost of the farm machinery sold to Agriculture is $417,000.
[3]   The finance charges relating to the installment period are $244,000 based on a stated interest rate of 12%, which is appropriate.
[4]   The collection of installments due under the contract is reasonably assured.

Instructions

What income or loss before income taxes should Warren record for the year ended December 31, 1993, as a result of the above transaction? Show supporting computations in good form.

(AICPA adapted)

20–41   LONG-TERM CONTRACTS   Fara Construction Company recognizes income under the percentage-of-completion method on its long-term contracts. During 1991 the company entered into a fixed-price contract to construct a bridge for $15,000,000. Contract costs incurred and estimated costs to complete the bridge were:

	Cumulative Contract Costs Incurred	Estimated Costs to Complete
At Dec. 31, 1991	$ 1,000,000	$8,000,000
At Dec. 31, 1992	5,500,000	5,500,000
At Dec. 31, 1993	10,000,000	2,000,000

Instructions

[a] Prepare a schedule and determine the estimated percentage of completion at the end of each year. (Round percentage to nearest two decimal points.)

[b] Prepare a schedule and determine the amount of revenue to be recognized each year. (Round dollars to the nearest thousand.)

[c] Prepare a schedule and determine the amount of income to be recognized each year.

[d] Prepare journal entries to record transactions for 1991 using the percentage-of-completion method, assuming that Fara billed its client $1,325,000 in 1991, of which $1,200,000 has been collected by the end of the year.   (AICPA adapted)

20–42   INSTALLMENT SALES   Mann Company sells computers. On January 1, 1993, Mann entered into an installment sale contract with the Banner Company for a seven-year period expiring December 31, 1999. Equal annual payments under the installment sale are $1,000,000 and are due on January 1. The first payment was made on January 1, 1993.

Additional information is as follows:

[1] The cash selling price of the computer (i.e., the amount that would be realized on an outright sale) is $5,355,000.

[2] The cost of sales relating to the computer is $4,284,000.

[3] The finance charges relating to the installment period are $1,645,000—based on a stated interest rate of 10%, which is appropriate. For tax purposes, Mann appropriately uses the accrual basis for recording finance charges.

[4] Circumstances indicate that the collection of the installment sale is reasonably assured.

[5] The installment sale qualifies for the installment method of reporting for tax purposes.

[6] Assume that the income tax rate is 30%.

Instructions

[a] What income (loss) before income taxes should Mann record as a result of this transaction for the year ended December 31, 1993? Show supporting computations in good form.

[b] What provision for deferred income taxes, if any, should Mann record as a result of this transaction for the year ended December 31, 1993? Show supporting computations in good form.

(AICPA adapted)

20–43   LONG-TERM CONTRACTS   The directors of Myer Construction Company are meeting to determine which method of accounting for long-term construction contracts should be used in the company's financial statements: completed-contract or percentage-of-completion. You have been engaged to assist Myer's controller in preparing a presentation for the meeting.

The controller provides you with the following information:

[1] Myer commenced business on January 1, 1992.

[2] Construction activities for the year ended December 31, 1992 are summarized as follows:

Project	Total Contract Price	Billings Through Dec. 31, 1992	Cash Collections Through Dec. 31, 1992	Contract Costs Incurred Through Dec. 31, 1992	Estimated Additional Costs to Complete Contracts
A	$ 520,000	$ 350,000	$ 310,000	$ 424,000	$106,000
B	670,000	210,000	210,000	126,000	504,000
C	475,000	475,000	395,000	315,000	—
D	200,000	70,000	50,000	112,750	92,250
E	460,000	400,000	400,000	370,000	30,000
	$2,325,000	$1,505,000	$1,365,000	$1,347,750	$732,250

[3] All contracts are with different customers.

[4] Any work remaining to be done on the contracts is expected to be completed in 1993.

Instructions

[a] Prepare a schedule by project to compute the amount of revenue and income (or loss) before selling, and general and administrative expenses for the year ended December 31, 1992, that would be reported under:

  [1] The completed-contract method.

  [2] The percentage-of-completion method (based on estimated costs).

[b] Following is a balance sheet which compares balances resulting from the use of the two methods of accounting for long-term contracts. For each numbered blank space on the statement, supply the correct balance [indicating Dr. (Cr.) as appropriate]. Disregard income taxes.

Myer Construction Company
BALANCE SHEET
December 31, 1992

Assets	Completed-Contract Method	Percentage-of-Completion Method
Cash	$XXXX	$XXXX
Accounts receivable		
Due on contracts	(1)	(5)
Cost of uncompleted contracts in excess of billings	(2)	—
Costs and estimated earnings in excess of billings on uncompleted contracts	—	(6)
Property, plant, and equipment, net	XXXX	XXXX
Other assets	XXXX	XXXX
	$XXXX	$XXXX

Liabilities and Stockholders' Equity

	Completed-Contract Method	Percentage-of-Completion Method
Accounts payable and accrued liabilities	$XXXX	$XXXX
Billings on uncompleted contracts in excess of costs	(3)	—
Billings in excess of costs and estimated earnings	—	(7)
Estimated losses on uncompleted contracts	(4)	—
Notes payable	XXXX	XXXX
Common stock	XXXX	XXXX
Retained earnings	XXXX	XXXX
	$XXXX	$XXXX

(AICPA adapted)

20–44 INCOME STATEMENT Waddell, Inc., has prepared an income statement for the year ended June 30, 1993. This statement is presented for your evaluation as follows:

Waddell, Inc.
INCOME STATEMENT
For the Fiscal Year Ended June 30, 1993

Sales		$765,000
Cost of goods sold	$400,000	
Operating expenses	250,000	
Income tax expense	46,000	696,000
Income before extraordinary item		69,000
Extraordinary loss		24,000
Net income		$ 45,000

In reviewing the statement, you determine the following:

[1] The extraordinary loss resulted from the sale of a division of the company at $24,000 less than its book value. The division had been operating at a loss for several years, including a $15,000 operating loss included in the sales and expense figures in the company's income statement. The income tax benefit of the operating loss has been considered in computing the $46,000 income tax expense. The accountant who prepared the statement was not aware, however, that the loss on disposal would result in a 40% income tax benefit and has included the entire $24,000 loss as an extraordinary item.

[2] The company sold 40,000 shares of common stock on December 31, 1992, resulting in a total of 120,000 shares outstanding. The company has no preferred stock. The accountant was unaware of the need to present earnings per share figures.

[3] All income items are subject to a 40% income tax rate.

Instructions

[a] Prepare a revised income statement beginning with "income before income tax" for the year ended June 30, 1993. Provide computations to support your figures.

[b] Comment on why the operating results of a discontinued segment is presented as part of "discontinued operations."

20–45 INCOME AND RETAINED EARNINGS STATEMENTS Mills Corporation is accumulating the last portions of financial data needed to prepare the financial statements for the year ended December 31, 1992. The retained earnings totaled $1,700,000 at January 1, 1992. Cash dividends of $39,000 were declared during 1992 but only $30,000 of these were paid in 1992. The 1992 estimated income before income taxes without considering the five activities described below is $920,000. The information regarding the following activities has been taken from the company's records:

[1] A lawsuit arising from a 1990 claim was settled by the company during 1992 for $70,000. The loss has not been accrued and is due for payment in March 1993.

[2] The company sold one of several buildings in its Finishing Division at a gain of $20,000.

[3] Mills experienced a $200,000 loss of timber in 1992 due to a flood resulting from the eruption of a volcano that had been inactive for over 50 years. The loss was not covered by insurance.

[4] The company changed its method for depreciating its buildings in 1992 from an accelerated method to straight-line. Total depreciation on the buildings through the end of 1991 would have been $260,000 lower by using the straight-line method. The change was made for both book and tax purposes.

[5] Office equipment purchased in January 1991 for $45,000 was incorrectly debited to office supplies expense. The straight-line method is used to depreciate office equipment for book and tax purposes. The office equipment was estimated to have a three-year life with no expected scrap value. This error has not been corrected.

Assume Mills Corporation is subject to a 40% income tax rate on all transactions.

Instructions

[a] [1] Calculate the 1992 income from operations before income taxes for Mills Corporation identifying adjustments, if any, that need to be made to the estimated income of $920,000.

[2] Prepare a partial Statement of Income for Mills Corporation for the year ended December 31, 1992, beginning with the amount for adjusted income from operations before income taxes as calculated above.

[b] Prepare a Statement of Retained Earnings for Mills Corporation for the year ended December 31, 1992.   (CMA adapted)

20–46 INCOME STATEMENT   Presented below is information concerning the results of operations of Lewis Corporation for the calendar year 1993:

Cost of goods sold	$2,985,000
Administrative expenses	1,300,000
Gain on the sale of marketable securities	15,000
Loss on sale of discontinued segment of business	95,000
Interest expense	65,000
Selling expenses	1,500,000
Sales	8,650,000
Loss on sale of plant assets	25,500
Cumulative effect (gain) resulting from change in depreciation method from double-declining balance to straight-line method	157,000
Correction of error (loss) in previous year's income, due to capitalization of research and development costs	76,000

The following additional information is available:

[1] All income items are subject to a 35% income tax rate except the loss on disposal of a segment of the company's operations, which is subject to a 20% income tax rate.

[2] The company had 1,000,000 shares of common stock outstanding from January 1 to June 30, when an additional 200,000 shares were sold. There was no other stock activity during 1993.

[3] The following amounts related to the disposed segment are included in the appropriate revenue and cost figures:

Sales	$750,000
Cost of goods sold	600,000
Selling expenses	100,000
Administrative expenses	350,000
Interest expense	10,000

Instructions

[a] Prepare an income statement for Lewis Corporation for the year ended December 31, 1993.

[b] Comment on why income items, such as the cumulative effect of an accounting change and components of discontinued operations, are presented in the income statement on a net-of-tax basis.

20–47 DISCONTINUED OPERATIONS   Barth Company, a diversified manufacturing company, had four separate operating divisions engaged in the manufacture of products in each of the following areas: food products, health aids, textiles, and office equipment.

Financial data for the two years ended December 31, 1992 and 1993, are as follows:

	Net Sales		Cost of Sales		Operating Expenses	
	1993	1992	1993	1992	1993	1992
Food products	$3,500,000	$3,000,000	$2,400,000	$1,800,000	$ 550,000	$ 275,000
Health aids	2,000,000	1,270,000	1,100,000	700,000	300,000	125,000
Textiles	1,580,000	1,400,000	500,000	900,000	200,000	150,000
Office equipment	920,000	1,330,000	800,000	1,000,000	650,000	750,000
	$8,000,000	$7,000,000	$4,800,000	$4,400,000	$1,700,000	$1,300,000

On January 1, 1993, Barth adopted a plan to sell the assets and product line of the office equipment division and expected to realize a gain on this disposal. On September 1, 1993, the division's assets and product line were sold for $2,100,000 cash, resulting in a gain of $640,000 (exclusive of operations during the phase-out period).

The company's textiles division had six manufacturing plants, which produced a variety of textile products. In April 1993, the company sold one of these plants and realized a gain of $130,000. After the sale, the operations at the plant that was sold were transferred to the remaining five textile plants, which the company continued to operate.

In August 1993, the main warehouse of the food products division, located on the banks of the Maas River, was flooded when the river overflowed. The resulting damage of $420,000 is not included in the financial data given above. Historical records indicate that the Maas River normally overflows every four to five years causing flood damage to adjacent property.

For the two years ended December 31, 1993 and 1992, the company had interest revenue of $70,000 and $40,000, respectively, which was earned on investments.

The provision for income tax expense for each of the two years should be computed at a rate of 35%.

Instructions

Prepare in proper form a comparative statement of income of Barth Company for the two years ended December 31, 1993 and 1992.   (AICPA adapted)

20–48   INCOME STATEMENT   Perry Company has always prepared its income statement on the current operating performance basis. Because the statements have been used strictly for internal purposes, adherence to GAAP has not been a major consideration.

In early 1993 the company's accountant contacts you for advice in preparing income and retained earnings statements for 1992 in accordance with generally accepted accounting principles for use with a bank loan application. The accountant presents you with the following statements, which had been prepared for internal use:

Perry Company
INCOME STATEMENT
For the Year Ended December 31, 1992

Sales revenue	$851,000
Cost of goods sold	415,000
Gross profit	436,000
Operating expenses	305,000
Income before income tax	131,000
Income tax expense	55,020
Net income	$ 75,980

Perry Company
RETAINED EARNINGS STATEMENT
For the Year Ended December 31, 1992

Retained earnings, January 1, 1992		$1,405,000
Additions		
Gain on the sale of investments*	$157,000	
Correction of error—income earned in 1991 but erroneously omitted*	120,000	
Net income for 1992	75,980	352,980
		1,757,980
Deductions		
Extraordinary loss—major casualty*	72,500	
Cumulative effect of change in accounting principle in 1992*	67,000	
Cash dividends, 1992	75,000	
Stock dividends, 1992	50,000	(264,500)
Retained earnings, December 31, 1992		$1,493,480

---

*Presented on net-of-tax basis.

You determine that all items are appropriately described and that all items subject to income tax appropriately reflect a 42% income tax rate and that the company had 75,000 shares of common stock outstanding throughout 1992.

Instructions

Prepare income and retained earnings statements for 1992 in accordance with generally accepted accounting principles, including all relevant disclosures which can be determined from the given data. Provide computations to support your financial-statement items.

20–49 INCOME STATEMENT   The following trial balance of Garr Corporation at December 31, 1992, has been adjusted except for income tax expense.

Garr Corporation
TRIAL BALANCE
December 31, 1992

	Dr.	Cr.
Cash	$ 675,000	
Accounts receivable (net)	1,695,000	
Inventory	2,185,000	
Property, plant and equipment (net)	8,660,000	
Accounts payable and accrued liabilities		$ 1,895,000
Income tax payable		360,000
Deferred income tax		285,000
Common stock		2,300,000
Additional paid-in capital		3,675,000
Retained earnings, 1/1/92		3,350,000
Net sales—Regular		10,750,000
—Plastics Division		2,200,000
Cost of sales—Regular	5,920,000	
—Plastics Division	1,650,000	
Selling and administrative expenses—Regular	2,600,000	
—Plastics Division	660,000	
Interest income—Regular		65,000
Gain on litigation settlement—Regular		200,000
Depreciation adjustment from accounting change—Regular	350,000	
Gain on disposal of Plastics Division		150,000
Income tax expense	835,000	
	$25,230,000	$25,230,000

Other financial data for the year ended December 31, 1992:

Income tax expense

Estimated tax payments	$475,000
Accrued	360,000
Total charged to income tax expense (estimated)	$835,000
Tax rate on all types of income	40%

Gain from litigation settlement is a taxable gain and is not considered infrequent.

The $835,000 does not properly reflect current or deferred income tax expense or intraperiod income tax allocation for financial statement purposes.

Temporary difference (not related to Plastics Division)

Depreciation per tax return	$750,000
Depreciation per financial statements (excluding cumulative effect of accounting change)	575,000

Discontinued operations

On October 31, 1992, Garr sold its Plastics Division for $2,950,000 when the carrying amount was $2,800,000. For financial statement reporting, this sale was considered a disposal of a segment of a business. Since there was no phase-out period, the measurement date was October 31, 1992.

Change in depreciation method

On January 1, 1992, Garr changed to the 150% declining balance method from the straight-line method of depreciation for certain of its plant assets. The pretax cumulative effect of this accounting change was determined to be a charge of $350,000. There was no change in depreciation method for income tax purposes.

Capital structure

Common stock, $10 par, traded on a national exchange:

	Shares
Outstanding at 1/1/92	200,000
Issued on 7/1/92 as a 15% stock dividend	30,000
	230,000

Instructions

Using the multiple-step format, prepare a formal income statement for Garr for the year ended December 31, 1992. All components of income tax expense should be appropriately shown.

(**Hint:** The 15% stock dividend should be treated as outstanding for the entire year in computing earnings per share figures.)   (AICPA adapted)

CASES   20–50 METHODS OF REVENUE RECOGNITION AMB Industries has three operating divisions— Queenswood Construction Division, Paperback Publishing Division, and Protection Securities Division. Each division maintains its own accounting system and method of revenue recognition.

Queenswood Construction Division. During the fiscal year ended November 30, 1993, Queenswood Construction Division had one construction project in process. A $24,000,000 contract for construction of a civic center was granted on June 19, 1993, and construction began on August 1, 1993. Estimated costs of completion at the contract date were $20,000,000 over a two-year time period from the date of the contract. On November 30, 1993, construction costs of $6,000,000 had been incurred, and progress billings of $6,600,000 had been made. The construction costs to complete the remainder of the project were reviewed on November 30, 1993, and were estimated to amount to only $12,000,000 due to an expected decline in raw materials costs. Revenue recognition is based upon a percentage of completion method.

Paperback Publishing Division. The Paperback Publishing Division sells large volumes of novels to a few book distributors which in turn sell to several national chains of bookstores. Paperback allows distributors to return up to 30% of sales, and distributors give the same terms to bookstores. While returns from individual titles fluctuate greatly, the returns from distributors have averaged 20% in each of the past five years. A total of $8,000,000 of paperback novel sales were made to distributors during fiscal 1993. On November 30, 1993, $3,000,000 of fiscal 1993 sales were still subject to return privileges over the next six months. The remaining $5,000,000 of fiscal 1993 sales had actual returns of 21%. Sales from fiscal 1992 totaling $2,000,000 were collected in fiscal 1993 less 18% returns. This division records revenue according to the method referred to as revenue recognition when the right of return exists.

Protection Securities Division. Protection Securities Division works through manufacturers' agents in various cities. Orders for alarm systems and down payments are forwarded from agents, and the Division ships the goods f.o.b. factory directly to customers (usually police departments and security guard companies). Customers are billed directly for the balance due plus actual shipping costs. The firm received orders for $6,000,000 of goods during the fiscal year ended November 30, 1993. Down payments of $600,000 were received and $5,000,000 of goods were billed and shipped. Actual freight costs of $100,000 were also billed. Commissions of 10% on product price are paid manufacturing agents after goods are shipped to customers. Such goods are warranted for 90 days after shipment, and warranty returns have been about one percent of sales. Revenue is recognized at the point of sale by this Division.

Instructions

[a] There are a variety of methods for revenue recognition. Define and describe each of the following methods and indicate whether each is in accordance with GAAP.

[1] Point of sale.   [3] Percentage of completion.
[2] Completed contracts.   [4] Installment contract.

[b] Compute the revenue to be recognized in fiscal year 1993 for each of the three operating divisions of AMB Industries in accordance with generally accepted accounting principles.

(CMA adapted)

20–51 INCOME STATEMENT PRESENTATION   Phillips Company is a major manufacturer of foodstuffs whose products are sold in grocery and convenience stores throughout the United States. The company's name is well known and respected because its products have been marketed nationally for over 50 years.

In April 1993 the company was forced to recall one of its major products. A total of 35 persons in Phoenix were treated for severe intestinal pain, and eventually three people died from complications. All of the people had consumed Phillips' product.

The product causing the problem was traced to one specific lot. Phillips keeps samples from all lots of foodstuffs. After thorough testing, company management and the legal authorities confirmed that the product had been tampered with after it had left the company's plant and was no longer under the company's control.

All of the product was recalled from the market—the only time a Phillips product has been recalled nationally and the only time for tampering. Persons who still had the product in their homes, even though it was not from the affected lot, were encouraged to return the product for credit or refund. A media campaign was designed and implemented by the company to explain what had happened and what the company was doing to minimize any chance for recurrence. Phillips decided to continue the product with the same trade name and same wholesale price. However, the packaging was redesigned completely to be tamper resistant and safety sealed. This required the purchase and installation of new equipment.

The corporate accounting staff recommended that the costs associated with the tampered product be treated as an extraordinary charge on the 1993 financial statements. Corporate accounting was asked to identify the various costs that could be associated with the tampered product and related recall. These costs ($000 omitted) are as follows.

[1]	Credits and refunds to stores and consumers	$20,000
[2]	Insurance to cover lost sales and idle plant costs for possible future recalls	4,000
[3]	Transportation costs and off-site warehousing of returned product	4,000
[4]	Future security measures for other Phillips products	6,000
[5]	Testing of returned product and inventory	800
[6]	Destroying returned product and inventory	2,400
[7]	Public relations program to re-establish brand credibility	1,800
[8]	Communication program to inform customers, answer inquiries, prepare press releases, etc.	1,600
[9]	Higher cost arising from new packaging	700
[10]	Investigation of possible involvement of employees, former employees, competitors, etc.	500
[11]	Packaging redesign and testing	2,000
[12]	Purchase and installation of new packaging equipment	5,000
[13]	Legal costs for defense against liability suits	600
[14]	Lost sales revenue due to recall	22,000

Phillips' estimated earnings before income taxes and before consideration of any of the above items for the year ending December 31, 1993, are $200 million.

Instructions

[a] Phillips Company plans to recognize the costs associated with the product tampering and recall as an extraordinary charge.

[1] Explain why Phillips could classify this occurrence as an extraordinary charge.
[2] Describe the placement and terminology used to present the extraordinary charge in the 1993 income statement.

[b] Refer to the 14 cost items identified by Phillips' corporate accounting staff.

[1] Identify the cost items by number that should be included in the extraordinary charge for 1993.

[2] For any item that is not included in the extraordinary charge, explain why it would not be included in the extraordinary charge.   (CMA adapted)

20–52   INCOME STATEMENT CLASSIFICATION   Willis Company, a publicly held regional manufacturer of western-style clothing, uses a calendar year for financial reporting. During 1991 Willis purchased a small chain of retail specialty clothing stores which were privately owned and which had been a good customer of Willis for a number of years.

Susan Helms was hired as controller of Willis Company in May 1992. In preparation for the 1993 budget, she completed a detailed comparison of the 1992 performance with the 1991 figures as reported. This analysis revealed the following items which affected the reported figures for 1991:

[1] The accounts receivable at December 31, 1991, were understated by $63,000. A subsidiary ledger had a balance with a transposed number. The Accounts Receivable control account was reduced by this amount in the adjusting entries of 1991.

[2] In May 1992, $60,000 was received in settlement for a $130,000 claim against a vendor for defective merchandise. The claim was filed in March 1991, but no receivable was recorded by Willis because the vendor's financial condition was very weak.

[3] In 1992 Willis paid $48,000 for additional federal income tax that was determined to be due for 1988 by an IRS audit.

[4] Willis paid $75,000 in August 1992 to settle an employee discrimination suit filed in September 1991 by a labor union who charged bias in promotion practices. No liability had been recorded in 1991, but the suit had been disclosed in the notes to the 1991 financial statements.

[5] The retail chain Willis acquired in 1991 recorded its bad debts on the direct write-off basis even though the chain had significant credit sales and bad-debt losses. The chain was included in the consolidated earnings of Willis for 1991. Susan Helms estimated that the chain would have had an allowance for doubtful accounts of $50,000 if an allowance system had been used.

Instructions

Discuss how Susan should handle each of the five situations in preparing the 1992 financial statements, paying particular attention to whether the items should be treated as prior period adjustments or as part of 1992 income.   (CMA adapted)

JUDGMENT CASES

20–53   BAD DEBT ACCOUNTING AND REVENUE RECOGNITION   Foreign Ideas, Inc., is a wholesaler of electronic products such as television sets, stereo equipment, and microwave ovens. The company, located in south Texas, wishes to discuss an accounting and financial reporting issue with you because your firm is the company's auditor. The company sells many of its products to retail outlets located in Mexico. The receivables that arise from these sales are denominated in U.S. dollars. That is, although the Mexican retailers will sell the products to Mexican nationals for pesos, those retailers will have to convert the pesos into U.S. dollars in order to pay Foreign Ideas the amounts owed.

Near the end of the past year, the exchange rate between the two currencies changed abruptly and significantly. From a relatively stable ratio of about 2 to 1, the exchange rate is now about 4 to 1. This change adversely affects the ability of the Mexican retailers to pay Foreign Ideas the amounts due. Before, when pesos were exchanged for dollars, an individual would receive one dollar for two pesos; now it takes four pesos to acquire one dollar. To illustrate, suppose Foreign Ideas sold a Mexican retailer a television set for $400. If the Mexican retailer sold the product to one of its customers for 1,600 pesos, those pesos could be converted to $800 dollars and the obligation to Foreign Ideas could easily be settled. Now, however, 1,600 pesos will bring only $400 dollars when converted by the Mexican retailer. The loss in the conversion rate limits the ability of the Mexican retailers to sell U.S. products, convert their proceeds, and pay for the products.

The chief financial officer of your client describes the above conditions and acknowledges that estimating the amount of bad debts expected from the Mexican receivables has proved difficult. He then states the company's intentions, as follows:

> *What we propose to do is to follow* FASB Statement No. 5, *"Accounting for Contingencies," very carefully. We are also mindful of* FASB Interpretation No. 14, *"Reasonable Estimation of the Amount of a Loss," which provides that the amount of a loss that should be reported is the best estimate of the expected loss within the range when only a range of loss can be estimated. If no amount of loss within the range appears to be a better estimate than any other, however, then the low end of the range should be accrued. That is what we propose to do.*
>
> *The range of loss that we face this year extends from the total amount of our Mexican receivables to the amount that proved uncollectible in past years. Because the change in the exchange rate was so recent, abrupt, and significant, we are unable to identify any amount within the range that appears to be more likely than any other amount. We just don't have enough experience with a situation like this. By the way, we have stopped anything other than C.O.D. shipments to most of our international customers. So, it is only the receivables that existed at the end of the year that are in question. Therefore, in accordance with* FASB Interpretation No. 14, *we are going to accrue the same amount we did last year. That is the low end of the range that seems to us to meet the requirements of the authoritative accounting literature.*
>
> *We need to know if you agree with our analysis because we are going to inform our banker of our preliminary operating results later this week and don't want to struggle with this issue when the audit begins.*

Instructions

Do you agree with this analysis and resolution? (Address this issue without regard to the fact that accounting for loss contingencies is discussed primarily in Chapter 14 of this textbook.)

20–54 INCOME STATEMENT PRESENTATION   Paper Tiger, a manufacturer of a wide variety of paper products, owns and operates forest lands in several locations in the western United States. Recently, a volcano erupted and destroyed a large forest owned by the company in Oregon. That forest is the only timber that the company owned near the volcano. The loss of the forest is very large relative to the company's financial statements and the company is concerned about the preparation of its income statement for the year and the manner in which the loss should be reported.

The president of Paper Tiger maintains that the loss has never happened before and it is clearly unusual. Furthermore, the president believes that the mere size of the item suggests that it should be presented as an extraordinary loss.

You are the engagement partner of the company's auditor and have been consulted as to whether the loss can be considered an extraordinary item. As you are reviewing the relevant authoritative accounting literature, you happen to hear a newscast that states that eruptions of the volcano are expected to continue into the foreseeable future. You have directed your assistant to consult the U.S. Geological Survey and that research confirms that eruptions are, in fact, expected to continue indefinitely.

Instructions

Determine whether you believe the loss can be reported as an extraordinary item in Paper Tiger's income statement and justify your position. Be sure to cite the appropriate authoritative accounting literature in your answer and provide your reasoning as to how that literature should be applied in this particular situation.

CHAPTER 21

Earnings per Share

OBJECTIVES

1. To explain the significance of earnings per share (EPS) figures, particularly for publicly held companies.
2. To explain the various situations that present the potential for dilution (reduction) in earnings per share.
3. To distinguish between companies with simple capital structures and complex capital structures and to identify the EPS requirements of each.
4. To demonstrate the computation of EPS for companies with simple capital structures and primary and fully diluted EPS for companies with complex capital structures.
5. To prepare the appropriate financial statement presentation of EPS, based on the specific circumstances of the reporting company.
6. To discuss how certain modifying conventions explain the need to incorporate potential dilution in EPS calculations.

BASIC EARNINGS PER SHARE CONCEPTS

F inancial analysts, individual investors, and other financial statement users often use indexes, ratios, and percentages to relate various financial statement items to one another. Many of the commonly used measures will be discussed in Chapter 25. Although these measures are not usually included in the financial statements, the numbers needed for their computation are.

Earnings per share (EPS) figures represent an exception, because they are computed by the accountant and become an integral part of the income statement when required. This is a result of the many complexities that may exist in the computations, the specific implications of which are generally not available to an external user of the financial statements.

In its simplest form, EPS is computed by dividing the net income by the number of shares of common stock outstanding:

$$EPS = \frac{\text{Net income}}{\text{Number of shares of common stock outstanding}}$$

The concept of EPS relates only to an enterprise's common stock and is best thought of as "earnings per *common* share." The concept of EPS does not apply to preferred stock, because preferred stock typically receives a fixed return and is not the ownership interest to which residual earnings accrue.

HISTORICAL DEVELOPMENT OF EPS

The development of EPS over the last several decades demonstrates an interesting reversal of position by the authoritative accounting organizations in reaction to the ways financial statements are used and the needs of their users. Before 1966 presentation of EPS figures was a matter of management discretion, and many years ago accountants were actually *discouraged* from being associated with EPS figures.

In 1966 the Accounting Principles Board (APB), in *APB Opinion No. 9,* "Reporting the Results of Operations," strongly *encouraged* companies to disclose EPS. In 1969 *APB Opinion No. 15 required* the disclosure of EPS and set up the relatively complicated structure of computation and presentation that now exists.[1] This pronouncement provides the basis for most of the material in this chapter.

In 1978, the Financial Accounting Standards Board (FASB) concluded in *Statement of Financial Accounting Standard No. 21*[2] that EPS figures should *not* be required in the financial statements of **nonpublic enterprises.**[3] At the present time, therefore, EPS figures are *required* only in the financial statements of public enterprises.

In no longer requiring nonpublic companies to present EPS in their income statements, the FASB apparently gave careful consideration to both the cost burden of preparing and presenting EPS figures and the usefulness of the information to financial statement users. A growing concern is the excessive burden placed on small or nonpublic companies when they are subject to the same financial reporting requirements as large, publicly held companies. The FASB lightened this burden somewhat

---

[1] *APB Opinion No. 15,* "Earnings Per Share," 1968.

[2] *FASB Statement of Financial Accounting Standards No. 21,* "Suspension of the Reporting of Earnings Per Share and Segment Information by Nonpublic Enterprises," 1978.

[3] A **nonpublic enterprise** is one whose debt or equity securities do not trade in a public market on a foreign or domestic stock exchange or in the over-the-counter market, or that is not required to file financial statements with the Securities and Exchange Commission.

by excluding the EPS requirement for nonpublic companies. As we shall see in the following section, the significance of EPS is frequently interpreted in relation to stock market prices. The lack of active trading of stock in the case of nonpublic companies supports the position that EPS figures are generally not of great usefulness to users of their financial statements. Even though nonpublic companies are not required to present EPS figures in their income statements, if management decides to present the figures, the reporting standards for public companies presented in this chapter must be followed.

SIGNIFICANCE OF EPS FIGURES

EPS is regarded by many as the most important single number in the financial statements. EPS figures are frequently cited in corporate annual reports, press releases, investment service publications, financial periodicals, and elsewhere as measures of an enterprise's success in achieving its profit objective. Many financial statement users believe EPS figures are useful indicators of an enterprise's management effectiveness, earnings potential, and future dividends.

Several studies support the usefulness of EPS figures in financial analysis. For example, one researcher gathered data from Chartered Financial Analysts (CFAs) concerning the importance of items in the financial statements. He concluded:

> *Security analysts are more interested in information items that concern the income statement and affect the amount of income earned by a corporation than in balance sheet information items.* Earnings per share continues to lead the list as the most important item.[4] *[Emphasis added.]*

Net income is an **aggregate earnings calculation,** reflecting the return on all of the enterprise's resources derived from many sources, such as creditors, preferred and common stockholders, and past operations. However, the extent to which creditors and investors other than common stockholders share in earnings is normally fixed in amount due to their contractual arrangements with the enterprise. For example, preferred stocks and bonds have stated dividend and interest rates that establish the return that investors expect to receive. Common stock, on the other hand, represents the **residual equity** that is the first to lose if earnings decrease and is in a position to benefit if earnings increase. Thus, EPS may have relevance to current and prospective common stockholders as income increases and decreases, if the return to creditors and preferred stockholders is recognized first.

Since EPS is actually a measure of **earnings per common share,** we must deduct the required return to all senior securities, such as bonds and preferred stock, to derive the earnings attributable to common stock. Interest to debt holders has already been deducted (as an expense) in determining net income. One of the first adjustments we must make in computing EPS is to subtract the dividend on preferred stock from net income to determine the amount of income that should be associated with common stock. We can now modify our general notion of EPS as follows:

$$EPS = \frac{\text{Net income} - \text{Preferred dividend}}{\text{Number of shares of common stock outstanding}}$$

Comparing the relative desirability of common stock of different companies is particularly difficult if the analysis is based on net income and dollars invested in the company's common stock, as is the case in computing such ratios as return on stock-

---

[4]Gyan Chandra, "Information Needs of Security Analysts," *Journal of Accountancy* (December 1975), p. 70.

holders' equity. Because of differences in asset structure, dollars invested by various classes of creditors and investors, rates of change in these variables over time, and other considerations, comparing companies on an aggregate basis is difficult for certain types of investment decisions. Since market prices of common stock are quoted per share, users of financial statements want a per share measure of income to facilitate comparisons among companies. This desire has resulted in the emphasis on EPS in addition to net income.

EPS figures are frequently quoted in direct comparisons between companies. For example, one company may report EPS of $1.75 ($175,000 net income divided by 100,000 common shares outstanding), and another company may report EPS of $1.25 ($10,625,000 net income divided by 8,500,000 common shares outstanding). Because a number of differences in the enterprises might explain such a difference in EPS, a reader of financial statements should not necessarily conclude that the first company is more profitable or a more desirable investment than the second company. One important difference may be the number of shares of common stock in the common stockholders' equities and the relative number of dollars representing those equities. Also, differences in accounting principles used in determining net income can cause significant differences in EPS.

EPS figures are frequently used in conjunction with other per-share measures of an enterprise. The price/earnings ratio, for example, is computed by dividing the per-share market price of the stock by EPS. To illustrate, assume that a company has common stock with a market price of $25 and has EPS of $4.50. The related price/earnings ratio is 5.6 ($25.00/$4.50), indicating that the stock is selling at 5.6 times EPS. The price/earnings ratio must be interpreted carefully. If the price/earnings ratio is judged to be low relative to other stocks, at least two alternative explanations exist. The stock may be considered an excellent investment opportunity because of the low price at which it can be acquired in relation to earnings. Alternatively, a declining trend in the price/earnings ratio may reflect a negative attitude on the part of the investors in the enterprise's growth potential.

Another frequently cited measure is dividend payout, in which the dividend paid on a per-share basis is divided by the EPS for the same time period. For example, if a company with EPS of $4.50 pays $2.00 in dividends, the dividend payout is 44% ($2.00/$4.50), indicating that cash in an amount equal to 44% of net income was paid out as dividends to common stockholders. As a general rule, if the investor's primary objective is the periodic cash return that can be expected on the dollars invested, a company with a high dividend payout is considered a superior stock investment to a company that retains a higher portion of earnings and has a lower dividend payout. Of course, many factors affect the relationship between a company's net income and its cash dividends paid to stockholders for the same period of time. Normally, dividends paid are less than net income as companies retain assets generated by income activities for other uses. In fact, too high a dividend payout ratio may raise significant questions about the future of the enterprise.

These illustrations express the need for per-share measures that enhance the value of comparisons among enterprises. Although the examples are not comprehensive, they show how EPS figures may be used in comparing enterprises. Caution should be taken when attempting to simplify the results of complex events and transactions into a single figure that is then used as a comparative tool. Many transactions and events influence the determination of net income and other items that appear in financial statements. Many judgments and estimates must be made when reporting these transactions and events. Finally, differences in business enterprises and the economic circumstances surrounding them must also be considered.

In summary, while figures may provide important input into an investment or other decision about an enterprise, they should be interpreted in light of the circumstances of the enterprise and the decision maker. This is true for EPS as well as many other measures that are commonly used to evaluate and compare business enterprises.

POTENTIAL DILUTION IN EPS

The general concept of allocating income to shares of common stock is relatively simple. In certain situations, however, the existence of convertible securities, rights to acquire stock, and obligations to distribute shares of stock under various arrangements may complicate the calculation of EPS. These situations create the *potential for a decline* in EPS if certain actions are taken. This **potential dilution** is of particular concern because it may result from actions over which the enterprise has no control. For example, if outstanding stock options allow the option holders to acquire shares of common stock at a fixed or determinable price, the potential for reduced EPS exists because the number of shares of common stock outstanding may increase if the options are exercised. Arrangements such as stock options and convertible bonds are identified as **potentially dilutive securities,** or simply **potential diluters,** for purposes of computing EPS.

The capital structures of some corporations include potential diluters, while others do not. For purposes of computing EPS, a **simple capital structure** is one that includes no potential diluters; a **complex capital structure** includes one or more potential diluters. The capital structures of large corporations often include several types of potential diluters. Some large corporations, however, have no potential diluters. The distinction between a simple and a complex capital structure is based not on the size of the enterprise but on whether or not the capital structure includes arrangements that potentially dilute EPS.

The computation of EPS for companies with simple capital structures requires understanding the treatment of the claim on income of those securities that are senior to common stock, such as preferred stock, and understanding the number of shares of common stock necessary to compute EPS. These concepts are equally important for computing EPS figures for companies with complex capital structures. EPS of companies with complex capital structures are further complicated by potential diluters. These considerations are the subjects of the following sections. In all illustrations in the text and in the cases, exercises, and problems at the end of the chapter, the enterprises for which information is presented are assumed to be public companies that are required to present EPS figures in their financial statements.

EPS COMPUTATIONS FOR SIMPLE CAPITAL STRUCTURES

The computation of EPS in a simple capital structure is not affected by potential diluters. Two factors, however, may complicate this computation. First, the number of shares of common stock outstanding during the reporting period may change as a result of the sale of stock, treasury stock transactions, stock splits, stock dividends, and other stock transactions. The EPS computation must be based on the **weighted average number of common shares outstanding during the period.** Second, the existence of preferred stock with a prior claim on income must be considered in determining the income allocable to common stock.

WEIGHTED AVERAGE NUMBER OF COMMON SHARES

The **weighted average number of common shares,** as used in computing EPS, is the number of shares of common stock outstanding during the accounting period, giving consideration to the length of time specific numbers of shares were actually outstanding. The most frequently encountered activities that change the number of outstanding shares are the sale of additional shares of common stock and treasury stock transactions. The sale of new shares of stock increases the number of outstanding shares; the acquisition of treasury stock decreases the number of outstanding shares; and the resale of treasury stock increases the number of outstanding shares.

To illustrate the determination of a weighted average, assume that Diamond Company reports a net income of $178,000 and has the following common stock activity during 1992:

		Number of Shares
	Stock Activity	Outstanding
Jan. 1	Common stock outstanding	100,000
Mar. 1	Sale of common stock	20,000
		120,000
July 1	Purchase of treasury stock	(5,000)
		115,000
Nov. 1	Sale of treasury stock	3,000
Dec. 31	Common stock outstanding	118,000

The weighted average number of common shares outstanding is computed by preparing a schedule in which the number of months is multiplied by the number of shares outstanding.[5] The "months × shares" figures are totaled and divided by 12 to determine the weighted average, as follows:

Period	Months	×	Shares Outstanding	=	Months × Shares
Jan. 1–Feb. 28	2		100,000		200,000
Mar. 1–June 30	4		120,000		480,000
July 1–Oct. 31	4		115,000		460,000
Nov. 1–Dec. 31	2		118,000		236,000
	12				1,376,000

$$1,376,000/12 = 114,667$$

EPS for 1992 is then computed as follows:

$$\text{EPS} = \frac{\$178,000}{114,667} = \$1.55$$

When the enterprise issues a stock dividend or a stock split during the accounting period, the number of shares outstanding during the different parts of the period must be *restated to retroactively apply* the stock dividend or stock split. Remember that stock splits and stock dividends do *not* increase the total stockholders' investment in the corporation. They simply represent a *reallocation of the common stock investment over a larger number of shares of common stock*. Treating the stock dividend or stock

---

[5]An alternative method may be used that weights the various numbers of shares outstanding by multiplying each number by the length of time outstanding, with 12 months as the denominator of the fraction. For Diamond Company in 1992, this computation is as follows:

Number of Shares	Fraction of Year Outstanding	Weighted Average
100,000	$^{12}/_{12}$	100,000
20,000	$^{10}/_{12}$	16,667
(5,000)	$^{6}/_{12}$	(2,500)
3,000	$^{2}/_{12}$	500
		114,667

split retroactively restates the common stock activity during the year in terms of the stock at the end of the year, *after* the stock dividend or stock split.

Continuing the example of Diamond Company, assume that in 1993 a net income of $220,000 is reported and the following common stock activity took place:

	Stock Activity	Number of Shares Outstanding
Jan. 1	Common stock outstanding	118,000
Mar. 1	Sale of common stock	10,000
		128,000
July 1	Purchase of treasury stock	(5,000)
		123,000
Oct. 1	Distribution of 2:1 stock split	123,000
		246,000
Nov. 1	Purchase of treasury stock	(6,000)
Dec. 31	Common stock outstanding	240,000

The weighted average number of common shares outstanding is computed much like that in the previous example, except that the number of shares outstanding prior to the 2:1 stock split must be converted to the basis of the shares at the end of the year. This is done by multiplying the number of shares by 2, as illustrated below:

| | | | | | | Months × Shares | | |
| | | | | | | | Stock Split | |
Period	Months	×	Shares Outstanding	=	Original	×	Conversion	=	Restated
Jan. 1–Feb. 28	2		118,000		236,000		2		472,000
Mar. 1–June 30	4		128,000		512,000		2		1,024,000
July 1–Sept. 30	3		123,000		369,000		2		738,000
Oct. 1–Oct. 31	1		246,000						246,000
Nov. 1–Dec. 31	2		240,000						480,000
	12								2,960,000

2,960,000/12 = 246,667

EPS for 1993 is then computed as follows:

$$\text{EPS} = \frac{\$220,000}{246,667} = \$.89$$

In this illustration, the stock split conversion factor, 2, is used because the increase in shares in a 2:1 split results in twice as many shares outstanding after the split as before. This factor is based on the specific distribution made. For example, if a 3:1 split is distributed, the factor is 3; if a 10% stock dividend is distributed, a stock dividend conversion factor of 1.10 is used. This adjustment is made only to those shares outstanding prior to the stock split or stock dividend because the share activity after that event is stated on an after-split or after-dividend basis.

PREFERRED STOCK

Certain securities have claims that must be satisfied before dividends may be paid on common stock. These securities are called **senior securities,** indicating their preferential rights over common stock.

Debt instruments are examples of senior securities, and the return to debt holders is deducted in determining net income. Preferred stock is also a senior security, but since net income is the income accruing to *all* owners (stockholders) of the enterprise, dividends on preferred stock are *not* deducted in determining net income. Because EPS is a concept relating only to common stock, however, the income figure in the computation must be reduced by the return on all senior securities. Accordingly, net income as reported in the income statement must be reduced by the dividends on preferred stock to obtain a "residual" income figure that represents the amount allocable only to common stockholders.

To illustrate, Walls Company reports net income of $2,700,000 for 1992 and has 2,300,000 weighted average number of shares of common stock outstanding for the year. In addition, the company has preferred stock outstanding throughout 1992 as follows: 1,000,000 shares, $12 par, 7% dividend rate. The preferred dividend of $840,000 (1,000,000 × $12 × 7%) must be deducted from the reported net income in determining EPS, as follows:

$$\text{EPS} = \frac{\$2,700,000 - \$840,000}{2,300,000} = \$.81$$

If the company reports a net loss rather than a net income, the preferred dividend is subtracted from the net loss in computing a loss per share on common stock. To illustrate, Walls Company reports a net loss of $1,700,000 in 1993 and still has 2,300,000 outstanding shares of common stock and an $840,000 preferred dividend requirement. The 1993 *loss per share* is computed as follows:

$$\text{Loss per share} = \frac{\$(1,700,000) - \$840,000}{2,300,000}$$

$$= \frac{\$(2,540,000)}{2,300,000}$$

$$= \$(1.10)$$

Observe the following guidelines when adjusting the reported net income for preferred dividends. If the preferred stock is *cumulative,* the dividends are deducted from net income or net loss whether or not they were declared. If preferred dividends are *not cumulative,* only dividends actually declared are deducted from net income or net loss in computing EPS. Any dividends in arrears on cumulative preferred stock are not subtracted in determining the income that accrues to the common stockholders.

FINANCIAL STATEMENT PRESENTATION

Investors attach a great deal of importance to EPS figures and frequently evaluate them in conjunction with other information contained in the financial statements. Accordingly, EPS figures are prominently presented on the face of the income statement, and the presentation should be consistent with the income statement presentation in which the EPS figures are included.

To illustrate the income statement presentation of EPS, consider Longwood Company, which had 110,000 shares of common stock outstanding throughout 1993 and 95,000 shares throughout 1992. Dividends on the company's cumulative preferred stock amounted to $50,000 each year. The company's income statement shows net income of $230,500 in 1993 and $208,000 in 1992, with a $44,500 gain (net of $23,000 income tax) on the refunding of long-term debt in 1993. The income and EPS figures are presented in Exhibit 21–1.

EPS figures must be presented for each of the following income figures if they appear in the income statement: income from continuing operations; income before

EXHIBIT 21-1

Longwood Company
Partial Income Statement

	1993	1992
Income before extraordinary items	$186,000	$208,000
Extraordinary item—Gain on refunding of long-term debt, net of $23,000 income tax	44,500	—
Net income	$230,500	$208,000
Earnings per common share:		
Income before extraordinary items	$1.24*	$1.66‡
Extraordinary item	.40**	—
Net income	$1.64†	$1.66

*($186,000 − $50,000)/110,000 shares = $1.24.
**$44,500/110,000 shares = $.40.
†($230,500 − $50,000)/110,000 shares = $1.64.
‡($208,000 − $50,000)/95,000 shares = $1.66.

extraordinary items; and net income. Additionally, various authoritative accounting pronouncements require disclosure of EPS either in the body of the income statement or in related notes for specific types of items. For example, EPS must be presented for the cumulative effect of a change in accounting principle and for an extraordinary gain or loss that results from extinguishment of debt.

Exhibit 21–2 is an example of the EPS presentation for a simple capital structure from the 1990 income statement of Phillips Petroleum Company, a company dedicated primarily to petroleum exploration, production, refining, and marketing. This exhibit includes only the lower portion of the income statement and the brief explanation of Income Per Share of Common Stock, which is included in the Summary of Significant Accounting Policies that follows the financial statements in the 1990 annual report. Notice that the EPS information follows the structure of the income statement with EPS figures presented for income before extraordinary gain and cumulative effect of accounting change, extraordinary gain, cumulative effect, and net income.

EPS COMPUTATIONS FOR COMPLEX CAPITAL STRUCTURES

In complex capital structures, EPS may be reduced because of one or more potential diluters. Although the arrangements that could result in the dilution of EPS are numerous, the following three classifications are commonly encountered:

1. **Stock options, warrants, and rights.** Arrangements whereby the holder has the right to purchase common stock in accordance with the terms of the agreement or instrument upon payment of a specified amount.
2. **Convertible securities.** Senior securities that, by their terms, allow the holders to receive shares of common stock in exchange for the senior securities. Convertible preferred stock and convertible bonds are examples of convertible securities.
3. **Other contingent issuances.** Potential future issuances of common stock that may depend on the satisfaction of certain future conditions. Shares of common stock that a company may be required to issue in the future as a result of a past transaction or contractual agreement are an example of other contingent issuances.

In all of these cases, the potential exists for additional shares of common stock to be issued and EPS to be reduced as the net income is distributed over a larger number of common shares.

EXHIBIT 21–2

PHILLIPS PETROLEUM COMPANY
EPS Disclosure—Simple Capital Structure

Years Ended December 31	Millions of Dollars		
	1990	1989	1988
Income before Extraordinary Item and Cumulative Effect of Change in Accounting Principle	**541**	219	650
Extraordinary gain	**101**	—	—
Cumulative effect of change in accounting for income taxes	**137**	—	—
Net Income	**$779**	219	650
Net Income Applicable to Common Stock	**$779**	219	639
Per Share of Common Stock			
Income before extraordinary item and cumulative effect of change in accounting principle	**$2.18**	.90	2.72
Extraordinary gain	**.40**	—	—
Cumulative effect of change in accounting for income taxes	**.55**	—	—
Net Income	**$3.13**	.90	2.72

Income Per Share of Common Stock

Income per share of common stock is calculated based upon the daily weighted average number of common shares outstanding during the year.

SOURCE: Phillips Petroleum Company, 1990 Annual Report.

DUAL EPS PRESENTATION

For public companies with complex capital structures, dual EPS may be necessary, incorporating the potentially dilutive impact of securities and arrangements such as stock options, warrants and rights, convertible securities, and other contingent issuances. The first EPS figure, commonly referred to as **primary EPS,** is based on the outstanding common stock and securities that are determined to be equivalent to common stock, known as **common stock equivalents.** The second presentation, called **fully diluted EPS,** reflects the dilution of EPS that would have taken place if the common stock represented by *all* potential diluters had been issued. Common stock equivalents and other potential diluters are ordinarily included in the calculation of EPS only if they reduce EPS (i.e., their effect is **dilutive**). If the effect of the assumed issuance of a potential diluter is **antidilutive** (i.e., results in an increase in EPS or a reduction in loss per share) in a particular accounting period, the shares are **not included in the EPS computations of that period.** Also, as we shall see later in this

Materiality   chapter, immaterial amounts of dilution are not presented.

Potential diluters, therefore, are of two types: common stock equivalents and others. The relationship of this distinction to the dual presentation of EPS is depicted in Exhibit 21–3. The distinction between potential diluters that are common stock equivalents and those that are not is extremely important, because it determines which securities are treated as common stock when computing primary EPS.

At this point, we can define more precisely several terms introduced previously.

1. **Potential diluters.** Arrangements under which an enterprise *may be* required to issue shares of common stock in the future.

2. **Common stock equivalents.** Potential diluters which, because of the terms of
Substance   their issuance, are treated substantially *the same as* common stock. Although a
over   common stock equivalent is not common stock in form, it derives a large portion of
Form   its value from its common stock characteristics.

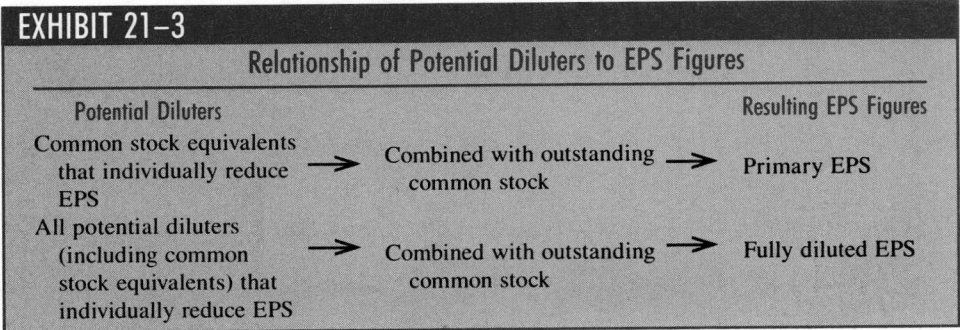

EXHIBIT 21–3

Relationship of Potential Diluters to EPS Figures

Potential Diluters		Resulting EPS Figures
Common stock equivalents that individually reduce EPS →	Combined with outstanding common stock →	Primary EPS
All potential diluters (including common stock equivalents) that individually reduce EPS →	Combined with outstanding common stock →	Fully diluted EPS

3. **Primary EPS.** The amount of income attributable to each share of common stock outstanding and common stock equivalent.

4. **Fully diluted EPS.** The amount of income per common share, reflecting the maximum dilution that would result from conversions, exercises, and other contingent issuances of common stock that would have individually decreased earnings per share.

Substance over Form

In Chapter 2 we discussed the modifying convention of substance over form. We stated that when an apparent difference exists between the economic substance of an item and its legal form, accountants emphasize the economic substance. The application of this concept is evident in computing EPS where potential dilution is included. In legal form, potential diluters are not outstanding common stock. They are convertible bonds, stock options, and other arrangements which *may* result in additional shares of outstanding common stock in the future. In substance, however, management in such cases usually expects to eventually increase the number of shares of common stock outstanding. Assuming certain conditions are met, we anticipate that

Conservatism

increase in outstanding shares by conservatively stating EPS at the lower figure that would have resulted if the outstanding shares had already been increased.

The treatment of the potential diluters and the resulting dual EPS presentation are summarized in Exhibit 21–4.[6]

Two major decisions must be made about each potential diluter. First, we must decide whether the potential diluter is a common stock equivalent. This decision determines whether the potential diluter will be considered in computing both primary and fully diluted EPS or only in fully diluted EPS. Second, we must decide whether the potential diluter is, in fact, dilutive in the current accounting period. This decision must be made periodically (i.e., each time a company computes EPS), in the context of the income or loss and the outstanding shares for that accounting period. **A potential diluter may be dilutive in one period but not in another.** The outcome of this second decision determines whether the potential diluter will be used in the EPS computations for the specific accounting period under consideration.

BASIC EPS COMPUTATIONS

The treatment of preferred dividends and the computation of the weighted average number of common shares presented in the section on computing EPS for simple capital structures also apply to the determination of primary and fully diluted EPS in the

---

[6]The model in Exhibit 21–4 presents an overview of the decision-making process required to develop the primary and fully diluted EPS figures. In certain circumstances exceptions to this general process exist. Several of these exceptions are covered later in this chapter.

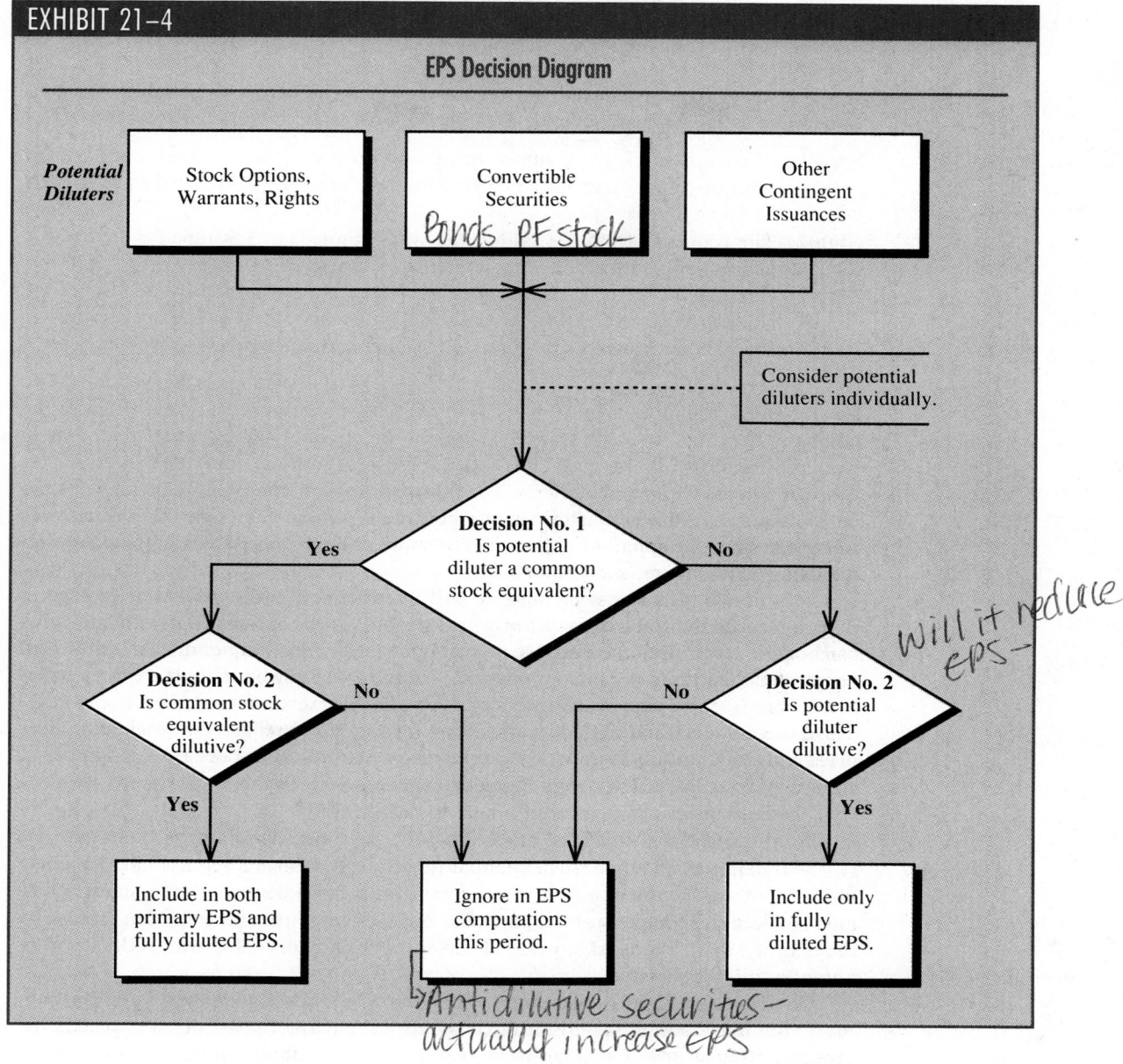

EXHIBIT 21–4

EPS Decision Diagram

Potential Diluters

Stock Options, Warrants, Rights

Convertible Securities

Bonds PF stock

Other Contingent Issuances

Consider potential diluters individually.

Decision No. 1 Is potential diluter a common stock equivalent?

Yes — No

will it reduce EPS–

Decision No. 2 Is common stock equivalent dilutive?   No

No   **Decision No. 2** Is potential diluter dilutive?

Yes

Yes

Include in both primary EPS and fully diluted EPS.

Ignore in EPS computations this period.

Include only in fully diluted EPS.

Antidilutive securities– actually increase EPS

dual presentation. Because these EPS computations include activities that have not actually occurred, additional adjustments must be made in the numbers reported. The EPS calculations in a complex capital structure are referred to as *pro forma* because they incorporate dilution that *might* take place.

   The potential diluters identified earlier are discussed individually below. In this section we limit our discussion to basic computations, ignoring certain complications which are explained later in the chapter and in the Appendix.

Stock Options, Warrants, Rights

Stock options, warrants, and rights are, by definition, *always* identified as common stock equivalents. They usually have no cash yield, and they derive their value from the right to obtain common stock at specified prices for a specified period of time.

Because such arrangements are always considered common stock equivalents, they are elements in the computation of both primary and fully diluted EPS if they are dilutive.

The **treasury stock method** determines the dilutive effect of stock options, warrants, and rights. The treasury stock method involves the following three steps:

Step 1. Shares of stock are assumed to be sold according to the stock option, warrant, or right agreement. The amount to be received from these sales is identified as the **proceeds.**

Step 2. The proceeds from the sale of the stock (Step 1) are assumed to be used to acquire common stock at the existing market price.

Step 3. The net increase in the number of shares is determined by deducting the shares reacquired (Step 2) from the shares sold (Step 1): The *net increase* in the number of shares is added to the outstanding common shares.

This series of computations deals with **hypothetical** (assumed) transactions. The sale-of-stock assumption in Step 1 is followed by an assumption about the way the company uses the proceeds from the sale. In Step 2 we assume that shares of stock were reacquired from the market. The assumed *net* increase, computed in Step 3, is then used in the EPS computations. The treasury stock method gets its name from the basic assumption that underlies the method, namely, that the company will acquire relatively small numbers of shares of common stock to meet stock option requirements by acquiring *treasury stock*.

The number of shares outstanding will increase only if the market price used in Step 2 exceeds the price in Step 1 at which the holders of options, warrants, or rights can acquire stock (i.e., the exercise price). In this case, the number of shares sold will be greater than the number repurchased. If the opposite were true (i.e., the market price were *less than* the exercise price), the assumed exercise would be illogical, because the holder of the option, warrant, or right could purchase the stock at a lower price from the market. Moreover, it would also be antidilutive, because the number of shares sold would be fewer than the number reacquired. In this case, the outstanding shares would be reduced, resulting in an increased EPS.

To illustrate the treasury stock method, assume that Palmer Company has 600,000 shares of common stock outstanding through 1993 and reported a net income of $282,500 for the year. In 1992 the company issued 100,000 options to acquire common stock in the company at the par value of $50. No options have been exercised by the end of 1993. The market price of the stock throughout 1993 was $60. No other potential diluters exist.

Remember that the stock options are common stock equivalents by definition. Also note that the options are dilutive because the market price of $60 exceeds the exercise price of $50. Thus, when the treasury stock method is applied, more shares will be sold (at $50) than can be repurchased (at $60). In addition, since options are the only potential diluter and they are common stock equivalents, primary and fully diluted EPS will be the same.

The application of the treasury stock method in this situation indicates a net increase of 16,667 in the number of common shares:[7]

---

[7] A short-cut method for computing the number of shares that results from the application of the treasury stock method uses the following formula:

$$I = \left[\frac{M - E}{M} \right] N$$

Step 1. One hundred thousand shares assumed sold at $50 = $5,000,000.

Step 2. Five million dollars used to buy stock at $60, resulting in the reacquisition of 83,333 shares ($5,000,000/$60).

Step 3. Number of shares sold (100,000) exceeds the number of shares repurchased (83,333) by 16,667.

Primary and fully diluted EPS are computed as follows:

$$\text{Primary and fully diluted EPS} = \frac{\$282{,}500}{600{,}000 + 16{,}667} = \$.46$$

If options, warrants, and rights are outstanding for only part of the financial reporting period, the incremental number of shares identified by the treasury stock method is weighted for the length of time they were outstanding. For example, in the above illustration, if the options had been issued on May 1, 1993, and Palmer Company reported on a calendar-year basis, the equivalent number of shares would be 11,111, because the common stock equivalents were outstanding for only $\frac{8}{12}$ of the year:

$$\text{Common equivalent shares} = 16{,}667 \times \frac{8}{12} = 11{,}111$$

What market price is used in applying the treasury stock method where the price changes during the financial reporting period? In the previous illustration, we assumed a single market price of $60. Now we will assume that $60 is the average market price for the year 1993 but that the ending market price is a different figure. In computing primary EPS, we use the average market price in applying the treasury stock method to determine the dilutive effect of stock options, warrants, and rights. If the market price at the end of the accounting period is *higher than the average*, however, we use the higher (ending) figure for computing fully diluted EPS.

To understand the impact of this difference, recall the assumptions that underlie the treasury stock method. First, we assume that shares are sold to holders of stock options, warrants, and rights at the prices established by those agreements. Next, we assume that the company used the proceeds from this sale to acquire treasury stock. Keep in mind that the higher the market price, the fewer shares we would be able to obtain with the fixed amount of money acquired from the assumed sale of shares. Finally, we determine the net increase in the number of shares of common stock outstanding that results from the sale of shares and the subsequent reacquisition of treasury shares. The higher the market price used to determine the number of shares that can be reacquired, the fewer shares will be bought. Likewise, the fewer shares bought, the greater the net increase in the number of outstanding shares and the greater the dilution in EPS when those shares are incorporated into the EPS calculations.

---

where I = incremental number of shares
M = market price per share
E = exercise price per share
N = number of shares obtainable

Applying this formula to the information presented for Palmer Company, the incremental number of shares obtained from the treasury stock method is computed as follows:

$$I = \left[\frac{\$60 - \$50}{\$60}\right] 100{,}000$$
$$I = 16{,}667$$

For example, in the illustration of Palmer Company above, we will assume that the average market price was $60 but the market price at the end of the accounting period was $95. Also, we will return to the assumption that the options were issued in 1992 and were therefore outstanding throughout 1993. Primary EPS is $.46 as computed earlier. Fully diluted EPS is $.44, however, because the use of the $95 ending market price results in a greater assumed dilution:

Step 1. One hundred thousand shares assumed sold at $50 = $5,000,000.

Step 2. Five million dollars used to buy stock at $95, resulting in the reacquisition of 52,632 shares ($5,000,000/$95).

Step 3. Number of shares sold (100,000) exceeds the number of shares repurchased (52,632) by 47,368.

$$\text{Fully diluted EPS} = \frac{\$282,500}{600,000 + 47,368} = \$.44$$

Conservatism

If the ending market price of the stock is less than the average for the period, the average price is used to compute both primary and fully diluted EPS. In this procedure the emphasis is on conservatism in computing EPS figures, because EPS will always be the lowest possible figure, given the assumptions of the treasury stock method.

In the illustrations of the treasury stock method above, we used the average market price in computing EPS, except where the higher ending market price was used in computing fully diluted EPS. The average market price might exceed the exercise price of stock options, warrants, or rights, but the market price *at the end of the period* might be below the exercise price. In this situation, the assumption that the options, warrants, and rights are exercised is not logical, because the holders could acquire shares at a lower price without the option, warrant, and right. To cover this situation, the APB determined that the assumption that stock options, warrants, and rights have been exercised should not be reflected in EPS calculations until the market price of the stock has been above the exercise price for substantially all of the last three months of the period for which EPS is being computed.[8]

The application of the treasury stock method, as we have used it here, is limited to situations where no more than 20% of the outstanding common stock can be reacquired with the assumed proceeds of the exercise of stock options, warrants, and rights. Where the proceeds are so great that more than 20% of the outstanding stock can be acquired, a modification must be made in the application of the method. This procedure is covered in the Appendix to this chapter.

Convertible Securities

Convertible securities are considered common stock equivalents if the return to the holder at the time of issuance is significantly less than the return on a comparable security without the conversion privilege. As we discussed in Chapter 15, convertible securities are complex hybrid securities that incorporate elements of more than one type of debt or ownership interest. The logic behind the treatment of convertible securities as common stock equivalents when there is a significant reduction in return is that investors' willingness to accept the reduced return to obtain the conversion privilege signifies that the conversion privilege has substantial value and, therefore, the value of the convertible security depends to a large extent on the value of common stock.

---

[8]*APB Opinion No. 15,* par. 36. If stock options, warrants, and rights are issued during the last three months of the accounting period, this stipulation is usually interpreted to mean the last three months of the period or the length of time outstanding, if shorter.

How could we determine that an investor was sacrificing a significant amount of return in order to acquire a security with a conversion feature? Ideally, we would compare the return on the convertible security with the return on an identical security in all respects *except* that it was not convertible. This is impractical, however, since the convertible security would not also be available without the conversion feature.

In its *Opinion No. 15*, the APB sought to achieve a degree of uniformity in making this important decision by stating that a convertible security was a common stock equivalent if its **cash yield**[9] at the date of issuance was **less than two-thirds of the bank prime interest rate at that date.** If this test was met, the convertible security would be treated as if conversion had already taken place for purposes of computing both primary and fully diluted EPS. If this test was not met, the convertible security would be treated as if conversion had taken place only in computing fully diluted EPS. An important feature of this test is that the classification of a convertible security is made only once—when the security is issued. This classification remains with the convertible security as long as it is outstanding and is not changed as market conditions change that might affect the desirability of the conversion feature.

Several aspects of this classification method were criticized by accountants, especially the use of the bank prime interest rate (a measure of the short-term borrowing cost of financially strong companies) for classifying long-term securities for purposes of computing EPS. In 1982 the FASB issued its *Statement of Financial Accounting Standards No. 55*,[10] which changed the standard for this evaluation from the bank prime interest rate to the average Aa corporate bond yield. The FASB noted that since *APB Opinion No. 15* was issued in 1968, the bank prime interest rate has become more volatile and the high degree of correlation between the bank prime interest rate and the rates of return on long-term debt and preferred stock no longer existed. In a subsequent change, the FASB replaced the "cash yield" test with an "effective yield" test.[11] This change was made in response to problems encountered in applying the cash yield test to zero coupon convertible bonds, instruments which do not pay any interest until maturity. Under the previous cash yield test, these instruments would always be common stock equivalents due to the lack of any periodic cash yield.

Summarizing the previous discussion, under current accounting standards a convertible security is a common stock equivalent if its *effective yield* is less than two thirds of the *Aa corporate bond yield* at the date of issuance. This relationship is depicted in Exhibit 21–5, using a 12% Aa corporate bond yield as an example.

In selecting the average Aa corporate bond yield over the bank prime interest rate for purposes of applying this test, the FASB was influenced by the relationship of the bank prime interest rate to short-term securities and the Aa corporate bond yield to long-term securities. For example, the board cites the fact that in recent years the United States and some other countries have experienced an inverted yield curve in which short-term interest rates have exceeded long-term rates.[12] In applying the two-thirds test, the FASB intends Aa to refer to bonds of equal quality to those rated Aa by either Moody's or Standard & Poor's. Aa bonds are defined by those organizations as bonds of high quality, issued by companies with a strong capacity to pay interest and

---

[9]The **cash yield** on a convertible bond is the effective interest rate, determined by adjusting the nominal interest rate for any premium or discount resulting from sale of the bond. This is computed by dividing the annual interest by the market price of the bond at the date of issuance. The cash yield on a preferred stock is the effective return, determined by dividing the stated dividend amount by the selling price of the stock.

[10]*FASB Statement of Financial Accounting Standards No. 55*, "Determining Whether a Convertible Security Is a Common Stock Equivalent," 1982.

[11]*FASB Statement of Financial Accounting Standards No. 85*, "Yield Test for Determining Whether a Convertible Security Is a Common Stock Equivalent," 1985.

[12]*FASB Statement of Financial Accounting Standards No. 55*, par. 5.

EXHIBIT 21-5

Aa Corporate Bond Yield Rule

Aa corporate bond yield	12%		Convertible securities with an effective yield in this range *are not common stock equivalents.*
⅔ × 12%	8%	↑	
Less than 8%		↓	Convertible securities with an effective yield in this range *are common stock equivalents.*

repay principal. The average Aa bond yield should be based on bond yields for a brief period of time, such as one week preceding the date of issuance of the security being tested.

The changes in the two-thirds rule as a result of *FASB Statements Nos. 55 and 85* do not change any other aspect of the procedure. The classification is still made at the date of issuance and is not changed thereafter. In applying the two-thirds test in this text, including the cases, exercises, and problems at the end of the chapter, we use figures for the Aa corporate bond yield that do not necessarily reflect actual yield rates for the year specified. Also, we typically assume that the security's nominal interest rate is its effective yield.

Convertible Bonds.   To incorporate convertible securities into the EPS computations, the **"if converted" method** is applied. Under this method, convertible securities are assumed to have been converted at the beginning of the accounting period or at their date of issuance, if later. The interest (after income taxes) that would not have been paid if the security had been converted must be taken into consideration in addition to the increased number of shares of common stock that would have been outstanding. This procedure recognizes that the holders of senior securities cannot share in distributions of earnings that apply to common stock without first relinquishing their rights to the senior securities.

Because the "if converted" method results in an adjustment to both the numerator and the denominator of the EPS computation, it may not be immediately obvious whether the assumed conversion is dilutive. In such cases, EPS must be computed with and without the assumed conversion to determine whether the conversion will reduce EPS. This procedure is illustrated in the following example.

Martin Company calculates EPS for 1993, without considering any potential dilution, as $2.50. This was correctly determined by dividing the $10,000,000 net income for 1993 by the weighted average number of common shares outstanding, 4,000,000. However, the company has $5,000,000 par value of convertible bonds that were sold in 1992 at par and yield an 8% interest rate. The bonds are convertible into 50 shares of common stock per $1,000 bond. The Aa corporate bond yield when the bonds were issued was 11%; the company's income tax rate is 35%.

The first step is to determine whether the potential diluter is a common stock equivalent. Because the yield (8%) is greater than two-thirds of the Aa corporate bond yield at the date of issuance (11% × ⅔ = 7.3%), we conclude that the security is *not a common stock equivalent.* Therefore, the assumed dilution will be incorporated only into the fully diluted EPS computation.

Next, the numbers to incorporate the effect of the conversion into the EPS figures are accumulated as follows:

Numerator Adjustment

Reduction in interest expense ($5,000,000 × 8%)	$ 400,000
Increase in income tax expense ($400,000 × 35%)	(140,000)
Increase in net income	$ 260,000

Denominator Adjustment

Number of shares of common stock (5,000 bonds × 50 shares of common stock per bond)	250,000

The bonds are convertible into 250,000 shares of common stock. If converted, Martin would incur $400,000 less interest expense, but because the interest is income tax deductible, it would incur $140,000 in additional income taxes. The *net* savings is $260,000. This can be computed directly by multiplying the interest savings by one minus the income tax rate:

$$\begin{aligned} \text{Increase in income} &= (\text{Interest savings}) \times (1 - \text{Income tax rate}) \\ &= (\$5,000,000 \times 8\%) \times (1 - .35) \\ &= (\$400,000) \times (.65) \\ &= \$260,000 \end{aligned}$$

Because the convertible bond is not a common stock equivalent, the EPS as originally computed by the company represents primary EPS:

$$\text{Primary EPS} = \frac{\$10,000,000}{4,000,000} = \$2.50$$

Fully diluted EPS is computed by incorporating the assumed conversion of the convertible bond into the above computation:

$$\text{Fully diluted EPS} = \frac{\$10,000,000 + \$260,000}{4,000,000 + 250,000} = \$2.41$$

The assumed conversion of the bond is dilutive in this case, because it reduces EPS from $2.50 to $2.41.

A useful shortcut for testing dilution is to compute a **dilution index** by dividing the adjustment to the numerator by the adjustment to the denominator. In this case the dilution index is $1.04 ($260,000/250,000). If this index is *less than EPS without considering dilution*, as it is in this case, the potential diluter is dilutive because its inclusion will reduce EPS. The dilution index is compared with EPS assuming no dilution each time EPS is computed, because the numbers representing both the net income and the weighted average number of common shares outstanding may change from period to period. The dilution index may be used in all cases in which potential diluters result in adjustments to both the numerator and the denominator in EPS calculations.

If convertible securities are outstanding only part of the period for which EPS figures are being calculated, the adjustments to both the numerator and denominator must be weighted for the length of time the securities were actually outstanding. For example, if the convertible bonds in the previous example had been issued on March 1, 1993 and we assume that Martin reports on a calendar-year basis, the bonds were outstanding only $^{10}/_{12}$ of the year. Both the numerator and denominator must be weighted accordingly and fully diluted EPS is calculated as follows:

$$\text{Fully diluted EPS} = \frac{\$10,000,000 + \$216,667^*}{4,000,000 + 208,333^{**}} = \$2.43$$

*$260,000 \times {}^{10}/_{12} = \$216,667$
**250,000 \times {}^{10}/_{12} = 208,333$ shares

In the example in this section we have assumed that only one convertible security was present and we used a simplified dilution index to test for dilution. In situations where multiple convertible securities are present, an additional complexity is introduced that requires a modification of the dilution index approach discussed earlier. This complexity is briefly discussed and illustrated in the Appendix of this chapter.

Convertible Preferred Stock.   Preferred stock plays a dual role in EPS computations when it is a potential diluter. On the one hand, preferred stock is a senior security for purposes of computing EPS. On the other hand, preferred stock that is convertible into common stock is a potential diluter that must be treated like a convertible security in computing primary EPS and fully diluted EPS.

In computing EPS without dilution, net income is reduced by the dividend on preferred stock, as described earlier. If the preferred stock is convertible, however, the dividend must be added back to net income, and the equivalent number of common shares must be added to the weighted average number of common shares outstanding. This procedure is identical to the way we treated convertible bonds, with one exception. Interest on the bonds is income tax deductible, and the exclusion of interest expense results in increased income taxes. This is why we adjusted net income for the reduced interest expense, net of the income tax effects. Dividends that a company pays on its preferred stock are *not tax deductible*. Therefore, when the numerator in the EPS computation is adjusted for preferred dividends, the adjustment is for the full amount of those dividends and is not reduced by an income tax adjustment.

To illustrate the "if converted" method for convertible preferred stock, we will use the case of Amsler Company, which reports a $5,000,000 net income for 1993 and has 500,000 shares of common stock outstanding the entire year. In addition, 100,000 shares of $100 par value, 9%, cumulative preferred stock are outstanding. Each share of preferred stock may be converted into two shares of common stock. The preferred stock was sold in 1986 at par value when the Aa corporate bond yield was 10%.

In this situation the preferred stock is *not* a common stock equivalent, because its yield of 9% (the same as the nominal dividend rate since the stock sold at par) is greater than two-thirds of the Aa corporate bond yield at issuance ($10\% \times \frac{2}{3} = 6.7\%$). EPS without assuming dilution, also primary EPS in this case, is computed by subtracting the preferred dividend in the numerator and dividing by the 500,000 shares of common stock outstanding:

$$\begin{array}{c}\text{Primary EPS}\\ \text{(also EPS without} \\ \text{dilution)}\end{array} = \frac{\$5,000,000 - (9\% \times \$100 \times 100,000)}{500,000} = \$8.20$$

Fully diluted EPS is computed by adding back the preferred dividend in the numerator and adding the increased number of common shares to the figures in the primary EPS computation. Since the preferred dividend is the $900,000 subtracted above ($9\% \times \$100 \times 100,000$), we are simply returning to the $5,000,000 net income figure. The increased number of common shares that would result from the conversion of the preferred is 200,000 (100,000 shares of preferred $\times$ 2). Fully diluted EPS is computed as follows:

$$\text{Fully diluted EPS} = \frac{\$5,000,000}{500,000 + 200,000} = \$7.14$$

As with convertible bonds, the dilution index can be computed to determine if the conversion is dilutive. Here the index is \$4.50 (\$900,000/200,000). Since this is less than EPS without considering dilution (\$8.20), the conversion is dilutive.

Other Contingent Issuances

Other contingent issuances represent potential future distributions of common stock that may or may not depend on the satisfaction of certain future conditions. If the shares to be issued depend on merely the passage of time, or are issuable upon the attainment of certain conditions and those conditions are already met, the shares are included in computing both primary and fully diluted EPS. Shares awaiting issuance in a stock dividend are an example of a contingent issuance that would be included in both primary and fully diluted EPS because the distribution would depend on only the passage of time.

Other contingent issuances may occur only when certain future conditions are met, such as attaining a specified level of income. Such issuances are sometimes encountered in business combinations. If attaining a stated level of income is a condition for issuance and that condition is not currently met, the contingent shares are not common stock equivalents and, therefore, are included only in fully diluted EPS. For this computation, earnings are adjusted to include the higher level of income specified in the agreement. As in the case of all potential diluters, shares in a contingent issuance should not be included in fully diluted EPS unless their effect is dilutive. Also, if the contingent issuance arose during the accounting period for which EPS is being computed, the figures should be weighted for the appropriate length of time.

To illustrate, Sarasota, Inc., had 1,000,000 shares of common stock outstanding throughout 1993, a year in which the company reported a net income of \$3,250,000. Dividends of \$92,500 on noncumulative preferred stock were declared and paid during the year. Under the terms of a business combination of a previous year, the company is required to issue 500,000 additional shares of common stock if the net income reaches \$4,000,000 and is maintained at that level between the year of the business combination and the end of 1997. This condition has not been met through 1993.

Primary EPS is computed without considering the contingent issuance resulting from the business combination, because the condition for issuance has not been met. Primary EPS is thus computed by reducing net income by the preferred dividend and dividing by the number of shares of common stock.

$$\text{Primary EPS} = \frac{\$3,250,000 - \$92,500}{1,000,000} = \$3.16$$

The computation of fully diluted EPS must consider the impact of the contingent issuance, including the increase in income that must be achieved, if the contingent issuance is dilutive. In this case dilution would result, because the increase in the numerator and the increase in the denominator result in an index below \$3.16:

Increase in Income

Required income for distribution	\$4,000,000
1993 income	3,250,000
Incremental income required	\$ 750,000
Increased number of shares	500,000
Dilution index (\$750,000/500,000)	\$1.50

Fully diluted EPS is computed as follows:

$$\text{Fully diluted EPS} = \frac{\$3,250,000 - \$92,500 + \$750,000}{1,000,000 + 500,000} = \$2.61$$

We have now seen how the questions of whether a security is a common stock equivalent and whether it is dilutive are answered for three types of potential diluters. A summary of these important decisions is found in Exhibit 21–6.

THREE PERCENT MINIMUM DILUTION PRESENTED

Companies with complex capital structures usually make the dual presentation of primary and fully diluted EPS in their income statements. As a practical matter, the dual presentation is required only if the aggregate dilution of all potential diluters is at least 3%. To assess whether aggregate dilution is 3% or greater, *EPS assuming no dilution* is compared with *EPS assuming full dilution*. If the latter is 97% or less of the former, the test is met and primary and fully diluted EPS are required. The impact of the 3% test on the type of EPS presentation required is illustrated in Exhibit 21–7.

To illustrate this test, EPS assuming no dilution for Pepper Company is $1.85 for 1993. To report dual EPS, fully diluted EPS must be $1.79 (97% × $1.85) or less. For example, if the company's fully diluted EPS is $1.54, the dual presentation is required. On the other hand, if fully diluted EPS is computed to be $1.82, the 3% dilution test is not met and the dual presentation need not be made. In the latter case EPS might be presented as follows:

Earnings per common share (no material potential dilution) $1.85

Materiality   The 3% minimum dilution test is a practical application of the modifying convention of materiality. We do not further complicate the financial statements with the dual EPS figures unless the dollar impact is significant. The 3% materiality standard

EXHIBIT 21–6

Summary of EPS Decisions

Potential Diluters	Decision No. 1: Is Potential Diluter a Common Stock Equivalent (CSE)?	Decision No. 2: Does Potential Diluter Reduce EPS?
Stock options, warrants, rights	Always CSE. *if exercisable within 5yrs.*	Application of the treasury stock method results in dilution if the market price of the stock exceeds the exercise price.
Convertible securities	CSE if the effective yield is less than two-thirds of the Aa corporate bond yield at the date of issuance. (If yield is equal to or exceeds this level, not CSE.)	Must be tested by computing EPS with and without assumed conversion. *Trial + error*
Other contingent issuances	CSE if issuance depends only on passage of time or if conditions necessary for issuance are currently being met. (Not CSE if conditions necessary for issuance are not being met.)	Must be tested by computing EPS with and without assumed issuance of stock.

used here is solely for purposes of presenting EPS. A similar standard for materiality in other situations is not implied by the use of 3% in the case of EPS.

FINANCIAL STATEMENT PRESENTATION

Primary and fully diluted EPS are terms used for computational purposes to determine the numbers to be presented in the income statement. The APB did not specify titles to identify EPS figures in the income statement. As you review financial statements, you will find that some companies use these terms and other companies use terms such as the following:

Situation	Primary EPS Concept	Fully Diluted EPS Concept
No common stock equivalents	Earnings per common share—assuming no dilution	Earnings per common share—assuming full dilution
With common stock equivalents	Earnings per common and common equivalent share	Earnings per common share—assuming full dilution

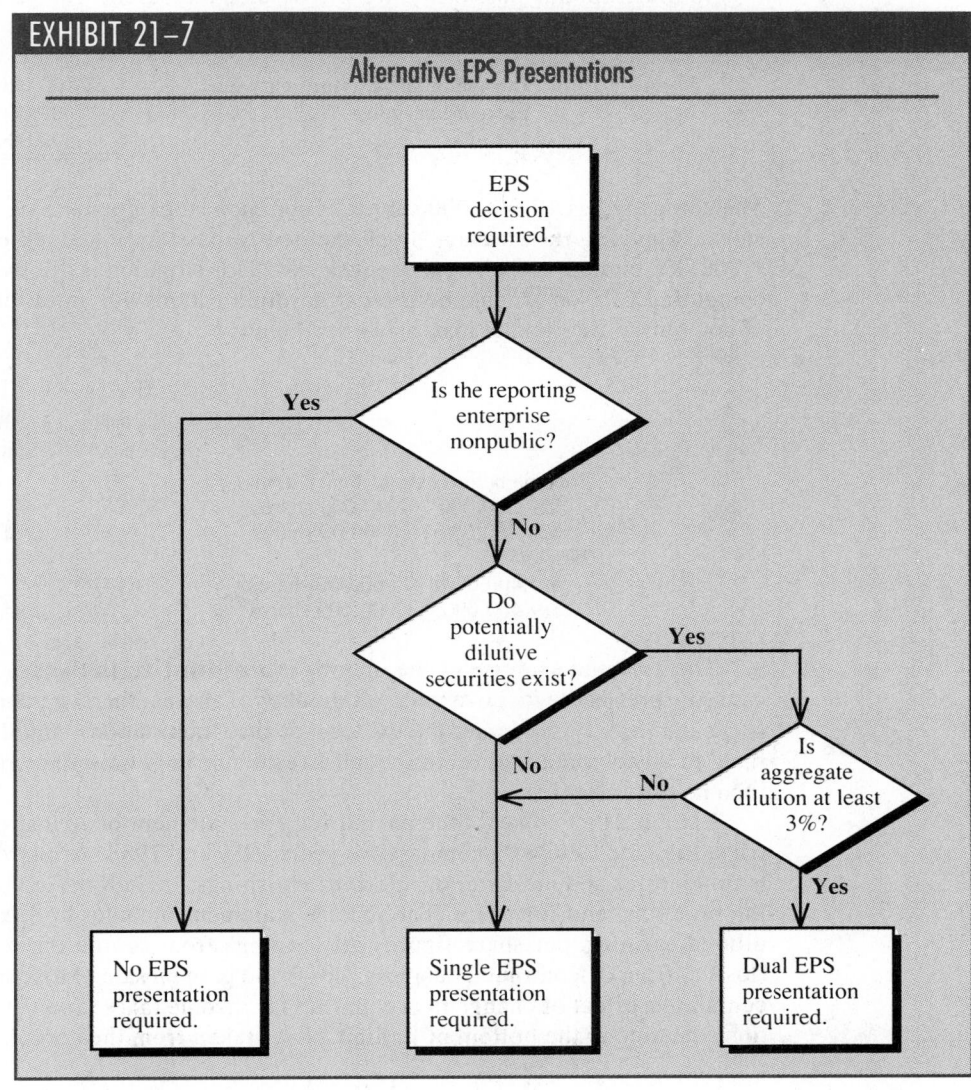

EXHIBIT 21–7

Alternative EPS Presentations

EPS decision required.

Is the reporting enterprise nonpublic?

Yes

No

Do potentially dilutive securities exist?

Yes

No

Is aggregate dilution at least 3%?

No

Yes

No EPS presentation required.

Single EPS presentation required.

Dual EPS presentation required.

Note that the designations above vary, depending on whether or not the capital structure of the company includes common stock equivalents.

Disclosure   In addition to disclosure in the income statement, disclosure in the notes to the financial statements is made to explain the rights and privileges of the holders of potentially dilutive securities, the bases on which primary and fully diluted EPS are computed, and other information necessary for an understanding of the EPS figures. Such information includes dividend and liquidation preferences, participating rights, call prices and dates, conversion or exercise prices or rates and dates, sinking fund requirements, and unusual voting rights.

In discussing the financial statement presentation of EPS for companies with simple capital structures, we stated that EPS figures are presented on income from continuing operations, income before extraordinary items, and net income, if these figures appear in the income statement. For complex capital structures, potential diluters are included in the EPS computations on all of these income figures if they are dilutive in any one of the income figures. This is true even if they are **antidilutive** in one or both of the other income figures.

To illustrate this possibility, we will assume that Arens Company reports the following items in its 1993 income statement:

Income before extraordinary item	$ 28,500,000
Extraordinary loss	(37,900,000)
Net loss	$ (9,400,000)

The company has 10,000,000 shares of common stock outstanding and no preferred stock. Applying the treasury stock method to outstanding stock options results in 1,000,000 common stock equivalent shares. This situation is dilutive for purposes of computing EPS on income before extraordinary items but antidilutive for purposes of computing EPS on net loss, as we see below:

	EPS Without Dilution	EPS With Dilution
Income before extraordinary items		
$28,500,000/10,000,000 shares	$2.85	
$28,500,000/11,000,000 shares		$2.59
Net loss		
$(9,400,000)/10,000,000 shares	$ (.94)	
$(9,400,000)/11,000,000 shares		$ (.85)

The assumed exercise of the options is **antidilutive** in the net loss situation because it spreads the loss over a larger number of shares, thereby resulting in a *smaller loss per share*. In this case, the exercise of the stock options would still be incorporated in all computations, even though it results in an antidilutive effect for one of the income (loss) figures.

Exhibit 21–8 presents the partial income statement of Armstrong World Industries, Inc., for 1990 with comparative years 1989 and 1988. Armstrong is primarily a manufacturer and marketer of interior furnishings, including floor coverings, building products, and furniture. The income statement includes both primary and fully diluted earnings per share figures for earnings from continuing business, earnings (losses) from discontinued business, (loss) and gain on sale of discontinued business, cumulative effect of change in accounting for income taxes, and net income. In addition, the note at the bottom of Exhibit 21–8, taken from the accounting policy state-

EXHIBIT 21-8

Armstrong World Industries, Inc.
EPS Disclosure—Complex Capital Structure

Consolidated Statements of Earnings

Years ended December 31 (millions except for per-share data)	1990	1989*	1988*
Current earnings			
Earnings from continuing businesses	**143.2**	154.9	151.6
Discontinued businesses:			
Earnings (losses), net of income taxes benefit of $.7 in 1990, and tax expense of $7.6 in 1989, and $7.7 in 1988	(1.1)	11.0	11.1
Provision for (loss) gain on disposition of discontinued businesses, net of income tax benefit of $3.8 in 1990 and tax expense of $8.0 in 1989	(9.1)	21.7	—
Cumulative effect of change in accounting for income taxes	8.0	—	—
Net earnings	$141.0	$187.6	$162.7
Dividends paid on $3.75 preferred stock	$ —	$ .2	$ .4
Dividends paid on Series A convertible preferred stock	19.5	9.5	—
Net earnings applicable to common stock	$121.5	$177.9	$162.3
Per share of common stock:			
Primary:			
Earnings from continuing businesses	$ 3.18	$ 3.20	$ 3.27
Earnings (losses) from discontinued businesses	(.03)	.24	.24
Provision for (loss) gain on disposition of discontinued businesses	(.23)	.48	—
Cumulative effect of change in accounting for income taxes	.20	—	—
Net earnings	$ 3.12	$ 3.92	$ 3.51
Fully diluted:			
Earnings from continuing businesses	$ 2.91	$ 3.04	$ 3.27
Earnings (losses) from discontinued businesses	(.03)	.23	.24
Provision for (loss) gain on disposition of discontinued businesses	(.20)	.45	—
Cumulative effect of change in accounting for income taxes	.18	—	—
Net earnings	$ 2.86	$ 3.72	$ 3.51

Earnings per common share are presented on the consolidated statements of earnings.

During 1990, 1989, and 1988, the company purchased 5,205,626 shares, 4,101,118 shares, and 80,534 shares, respectively, of its common stock on the open market and in negotiated transactions. In 1989 the company sold 5,654,450 shares of Series A convertible preferred stock to the leveraged Employee Stock Ownership Plan described on page 22.

The reduction in average common shares outstanding resulting from the purchases had the effect of increasing the earnings per share in 1990 (primary $.25 and fully diluted $.20) and 1989 (primary $.09 and fully diluted $.07).

Primary earnings per share for "earnings from continuing businesses" amd "net earnings" are determined by dividing the earnings, after deducting preferred dividends, by the average number of common shares outstanding and shares issuable under stock options.

Fully diluted earnings per share include the shares of common stock outstanding, as calculated above, and the adjustments to common shares snd earnings required to portray the convertible preferred shares on an "if converted" basis.

*Restated for the results of discontinued businesses and to conform to 1990 expense classifications.

SOURCE: Armstrong World Industries, Inc., 1990 Annual Report.

ment in the annual report, explains capital stock transactions engaged in by the company during the three-year period and also explains generally how primary and fully diluted EPS figures were computed.

EXAMPLE EPS COMPUTATIONS

This section presents a step-by-step approach to the computation of EPS for a company with a complex capital structure. We illustrate this approach by preparing the EPS presentation for Express Company for 1993. Excerpts from the balance sheet of Express Company and other relevant information are presented as follows:

Partial Balance Sheet at December 31, 1993

Stockholders' Equity

Convertible preferred stock ($50 par, 7% cumulative; 100,000 shares authorized, 65,000 shares issued and outstanding, each share convertible into three shares of common stock)	$ 3,250,000
Common stock ($10 par; 4,000,000 shares authorized, 1,700,000 shares issued)	17,000,000
Paid-in capital in excess of par value on common stock	4,685,000
Retained earnings	12,755,000
	$37,690,000
Less: Treasury stock (75,000 shares of common at $17 cost)	(1,275,000)
	$36,415,000

Common Stock Activity in 1993		Number of Common Shares
Jan. 1	Number of shares outstanding	1,100,000
Apr. 1	Distribution of 10% stock dividend	110,000
May 1	Sale of previously unissued stock	490,000
Oct. 1	Acquisition of treasury stock	(300,000)
Dec. 1	Sale of treasury stock	225,000
Dec. 31	Number of shares outstanding	1,625,000

Other Information

1. Express Company had 100,000 stock options outstanding throughout 1993; each option allowed the acquisition of one share of common stock at $15. The market price of the common averaged $24 during 1993. The market price at the end of 1993 was $30.
2. Express Company had 75,000 stock purchase warrants outstanding throughout 1993; each warrant allowed the acquisition of one share of common stock at $32.
3. As the result of a business combination in 1991, Express Company is required to issue 300,000 shares of common stock if income reaches the $5,000,000 level in any year through 1995. This level of income has not been reached before 1993.
4. The convertible preferred stock was originally sold at par value in 1991 and may be converted into three shares of common stock per share of preferred stock at the discretion of the preferred stock holders at any time. Through 1993, no conversions have taken place.
5. Express Company has outstanding $10,000,000 of convertible bonds that were issued at par in 1989 and yield 7%. Each $1,000 bond may be converted into 40 shares of common stock. The Aa corporate bond yields since the year of issuance have been as follows:

1989	12%	1991	10%	1993	11%
1990	11%	1992	10½%		

6. Net income reported by Express Company for 1993 is $4,750,000.

7. The income tax rate for Express Company is 35%.

Step 1.   Determine Weighted Average Number of Common Shares Outstanding

The weighted average number of common shares outstanding is determined by considering the amount of time various numbers of shares of common stock were outstanding during the year. The 10% stock dividend of March 31, is applied retro-actively.

Period	Number of Months	×	Number of Shares Outstanding	=	Months × Shares Original	×	Stock Dividend Conversion	=	Restated
Jan. 1–Mar. 31	3		1,100,000		3,300,000		1.10		3,630,000
Apr. 1–Apr. 30	1		1,210,000						1,210,000
May 1–Sept. 30	5		1,700,000						8,500,000
Oct. 1–Nov. 30	2		1,400,000						2,800,000
Dec. 1–Dec. 31	1		1,625,000						1,625,000
	12								17,765,000

$$\text{Weighted average} = 17,765,000/12 = 1,480,417$$

Step 2.   Compute Base EPS (EPS assuming no dilution)

Base EPS is computed by reducing the net income of $4,750,000 by the preferred dividend and dividing by the weighted average common shares. The preferred dividend is $227,500 (65,000 shares × $50 par × 7%).

$$\text{Base EPS} = \frac{\$4,750,000 - \$227,500}{1,480,417} = \$3.05$$

Notice that the conversion feature of the preferred stock does not affect this computation.

Base EPS provides the basis for comparing potential diluters to determine whether they dilute EPS if included in the computations.

Step 3.   Evaluate Potential Diluters for Common Stock Equivalency Status

Each potential diluter must be evaluated to determine if it is a common stock equivalent and therefore included in primary EPS (if dilutive). The five potential diluters of Express Company are evaluated as follows:

Potential Diluter	Evaluation
Stock options	Common stock equivalent (by definition).
Stock purchase warrants	Common stock equivalent (by definition).
Contingent issuance resulting from business combination	Not a common stock equivalent since the conditions required for the stock to be issued have not been met (i.e., the $5,000,000 level of income has not been attained).
Convertible preferred stock	Not a common stock equivalent since the effective yield (7%) is more than two-thirds of the Aa corporate bond yield when the stock was issued (2/3 × 10% = 6.7%).
Convertible bonds	Common stock equivalent since the effective yield (7%) is less than two-thirds of the Aa corporate bond yield when the bonds were issued (⅔ × 12% = 8%).

Step 4.   Determine Whether Potential Diluters Are Dilutive in This Accounting Period

Because potential diluters are included in EPS computations only when they are individually dilutive, each must be evaluated to determine if it will be included in the EPS computations in the current period. This evaluation is made as follows:

Potential Diluter	Evaluation	
Stock options	Dilutive—Both the average and ending market prices ($24 and $30) exceed the exercise price ($15).	
Stock purchase warrants	Antidilutive—Both the average and ending market prices ($24 and $30) are less than the exercise price ($32).	
Contingent issuance resulting from business combination	Dilutive—The dilution index is less than base EPS:	
	Addition to numerator ($5,000,000 − $4,750,000)	$250,000
	Addition to denominator	300,000
	Dilution index ($250,000/300,000)	.83
Convertible preferred stock	Dilutive—The dilution index is less than base EPS:	
	Addition to numerator	$227,500
	Addition to denominator (65,000 × 3)	195,000
	Dilution index ($227,500/195,000)	1.17
Convertible bonds	Dilutive—The dilution index is less than base EPS:	
	Addition to numerator ($10,000,000 × 7%)(1 − .40)	$420,000
	Addition to denominator (10,000 bonds × 40 shares)	400,000
	Dilution index ($420,000/400,000)	1.05

Step 5.   Summarize Potential Diluters

The potential diluters can now be summarized to determine how they will affect the computation of primary and fully diluted EPS. This is done for Express Company as follows:

Potential Diluter	Use in Computing	
	Primary EPS	Fully Diluted EPS
Stock options (common stock equivalent, dilutive)	Yes	Yes
Stock purchase warrants (common stock equivalent, antidilutive)	No	No
Contingent issuance (not common stock equivalent, dilutive)	No	Yes
Convertible preferred stock (not common stock equivalent, dilutive)	No	Yes
Convertible bonds (common stock equivalent, dilutive)	Yes	Yes

From this summary we see that primary EPS will include the elements of base EPS, plus the dilutive effect of the *stock options* and the *convertible bonds*. Fully diluted EPS will include the dilutive effect of these same items *plus* the contingent issuance and the convertible preferred stock. Also, the dilutive effect of the options will be greater in fully diluted EPS than in primary EPS, because the year-end market price of the stock exceeds the average price for the year.

Step 6. Compute Primary and Fully Diluted EPS and Apply 3% Test

The elements for computing primary and fully diluted EPS are calculated as follows:

Numerator

Net income	$4,750,000
Less: Preferred dividend (see Step 2)	(227,500)
Plus: Interest (after tax) on convertible debt (see Step 4)	420,000
For primary EPS	$4,942,500
Plus: Income increase for contingent issuance (see Step 4)	250,000
Preferred dividend (see Step 2)	227,500
For fully diluted EPS	$5,420,000

Denominator

Weighted average common shares outstanding (see Step 1)	1,480,417
Plus: Application of treasury stock method to stock options (at the average market prices)	
Proceeds from sale: 100,000 × $15 = $1,500,000	
Shares acquired: $1,500,000/$24 = 62,500	
Net increase: 100,000 − 62,500 =	37,500
Plus: Equivalent shares for convertible debt (see Step 4)	400,000
For primary EPS	1,917,917
Plus: Shares increase from contingent issuance (see Step 4)	300,000
Equivalent shares for convertible preferred stock	195,000
Application of treasury stock method to stock options (at the ending market price)	
Proceeds from sale: 100,000 × $15 = $1,500,000	
Shares acquired: $1,500,000/$30 = 50,000	
Net increase: 100,000 − 50,000 = 50,000	
Excess of increase for fully diluted over primary:	
50,000 − 37,500 =	12,500
For fully diluted EPS	2,425,417

Primary and fully diluted EPS are then computed using the appropriate numbers:

$$\text{Primary EPS} = \$4,942,500/1,917,917 = \$2.58$$
$$\text{Fully diluted EPS} = \$5,420,000/2,425,417 = \$2.23$$

For the dual presentation of EPS to be required, fully diluted EPS must be 97% or less of base EPS as computed in Step 2 above. Because base EPS is $3.05, the dual presentation is required if fully diluted EPS is $2.96 or less ($3.05 × 97%). This condition is clearly met in this case since fully diluted EPS is $2.23.

Step 7. Prepare the Income Statement Presentation of EPS

The dual presentation of EPS is reported after the net income figure at the bottom of the income statement. Appropriate wording depends on the circumstances of the presentation. The presentation for Express Company for 1993 might appear as follows:

Net income	$4,750,000
Earnings per share	
Earnings per common and common equivalent share	$2.58
Earnings per common share, assuming full dilution	$2.23

INVISIBLE DILUTION

Introduced with great fanfare a few weeks ago by Shearson Lehman Hutton Inc., "unbundled stock units" are being marketed as a way to lessen the threat of takeover, cut taxes and improve earnings per share. If this gimmick is approved by the Securities & Exchange Commission, American Express Co., Pfizer Inc., Sara Lee Corp. and Dow Chemical Co. say they will offer them to their shareholders as a swap for existing common shares of up to 20% of their capitalization.

If a shareholder takes the bait, what does he get? A package of three separate securities. One is a 30-year, deep-discount bond that will provide guaranteed interest payments equal to the current dividend on the common. The second is a preferred stock that will pay dividends equal to any dividend increases on the common. The third is a 30-year common stock warrant with a strike price equal to the maturity value of the bond—meaning that after 30 years the investor can swap the bond back to the company for a share of common stock.

So the old stockholder gets about what he started with, but in three separate pieces. Presumably, the stockholder can then decide to sell off part of the package and keep the rest. By selling the warrant, for example, he keeps the dividend but loses some future appreciation. If he sells the bond and preferred, he gives up income and some capital appreciation but gains big if the stock takes off. To institutional holders, the package is worth slightly more than the original share, because of its built-in downside protection. If 30 years from now the stock is worth less than the maturity value of the bond, the warrant expires worthless, but a holder of the units still gets the full bond maturity value. To individuals, the package has a serious downside: higher trading costs if they want to sell.

What's in it for the company? A tax saving. As FORBES has repeatedly pointed out, our tax laws subsidize debt and penalize common equity. By paying deductible interest rather than nondeductible dividends, the unbundled stock units will provide a nice tax saving for the company. Will Internal Revenue disallow this tax ploy? That remains to be seen. If the IRS goes along, there will be tangible gains to the companies involved—and a corresponding loss for the Treasury.

The final supposed advantage of the unbundling is, in our view, an illusion. By replacing common stock with a package of securities, the recapitalization would reduce the number of common shares outstanding and thus the divisor that determines earnings per share. If earnings remain the same, reduction of the divisor makes earnings per share seem larger.

We say "appear" for good reason. In fact, the company is incurring a potential dilution that will eventually offset much of this apparent gain.

Here's why: Years and perhaps even decades later, as rising stock prices induce holders to exercise their warrants, the warrants will be exercised and the canceled stock will reappear, reducing earnings per share.

Argues Norman Weinger, accounting analyst at Oppenheimer & Co., "There's a hidden dilution effect in these units." Abraham Briloff, accounting professor emeritus at Baruch College, agrees: "The unbundled stock unit is the equivalent of a share of common stock, period. The sum of its parts should be equal to a common share and have no earnings impact."

These accounting experts are simply saying that— not counting the hoped-for subsidy from the U.S. Treasury—two and two equals four and cannot equal five.

In the best of all worlds, issuing companies would be required to recognize the potential dilution in the common stock, which would probably cancel any gains in earnings per share. In devising the unbundled stock units, the Shearson Lehman people got around this problem. Under current accounting rules, warrants are considered "common stock equivalents" and therefore dilutive only when the exercise price of the warrant is lower than the stock price. When the situation is reversed and the warrant is "out of the money," that is, at a price above the current market—as with unbundled stock units—existing accounting rules do not require that the potential dilution be recognized. When initially issued, the 30-year USU warrants are expected to be priced far above the current stock price and thus out of the money.

But here's the rub: If they were certain to stay forever out of the money, the warrants would have no value. But presumably they will have a value. Thus the market recognizes a liability for the company even if the accounting rules don't. Calculating a warrant's value is no simple matter, but that doesn't seem to stop the options boys in Chicago with their sophisticated computers.

If unbundled stock units take hold, the accounting profession will have to address the accounting problems posed by them—in particular, how to evaluate out-of-the-money warrants. It took the accountants a long time to figure out how to deal with the more obvious kind of dilution—in-the-money warrants and convertibles. Our guess is they will be a little slow catching on to this latest trick, too.

SOURCE: Penelope Wang, "Invisible Dilution," *Forbes*, February 6, 1989. Reprinted by permission of *Forbes* magazine, February 6, 1989. © Forbes Inc., 1989.

CONCLUDING REMARKS

Earnings per share is an area of accounting where many types of situations may be encountered. Several aspects of EPS that are beyond the scope of this text have been omitted in an attempt to focus our attention on basic concepts and methods of computation. Several additional considerations in the computation of EPS are covered in the Appendix to this chapter.

Substance over Form

The requirements of *APB Opinion No. 15* regarding EPS computations represent an interesting combination of the modifying conventions of substance over form and conservatism. *Substance over form* refers to emphasizing in financial reporting the economic implications of events rather than the legal form when the two are different. This concept is applied in an attempt to provide information in financial statements that better reflects the economic impact of activities being presented. Applying substance over form in computing EPS requires that we incorporate events and activities that have not actually occurred. This is different from traditional accounting. The adjustments to net income and to the number of shares of common stock outstanding are only for the purposes of computing diluted EPS figures. These adjustments are not entered in the accounting records except as a memorandum in conjunction with the documentation of EPS calculations.

Conservatism

Conservatism refers to the financial reporting practice of using the accounting alternative that results in the least favorable impact on net income when reporting in a context of significant uncertainty. Uncertainties about EPS computations center primarily on the ultimate issuance of additional shares of common stock that may reduce EPS (i.e., potential dilution). Procedures for computing EPS are designed to state EPS on a diluted basis, thereby reflecting the potential decline expected from these potential increases in the number of common shares outstanding.

KEY POINTS

1. EPS is frequently cited by users of financial statements as one of the most important figures on which they base financial decisions. (Objective 1)

2. The term "dilution" refers to a reduction in EPS resulting from the issuance of additional shares of common stock. "Potential dilution" refers to possible future reductions in EPS. (Objective 2)

3. The potential for dilution of EPS exists in situations such as stock options, warrants, and rights; convertible securities; and other contingent issuances of common stock. (Objective 2)

4. A company with a simple capital structure has no potential diluters. A company with a complex capital structure has one or more potential diluters. (Objective 3)

5. A publicly held company with a simple capital structure must present EPS in the income statement, based on the outstanding common stock for that period. (Objective 3)

6. A publicly held company with a complex capital structure must present EPS in the income statement based on both the outstanding common stock for that period and the potential diluters in its capital structure. (If the potential dilution is not material, however, the potential dilution is not required to be presented.) (Objective 3)

7. EPS figures are based on the weighted average number of shares of common stock outstanding. Securities whose claim on income precedes the claim of the common stockholders, such as preferred stock, must be deducted before computing EPS. (Objective 4)

8. Primary EPS is based on the outstanding common stock, plus potential diluters identified as *common stock equivalents*. Fully diluted EPS is based on the outstanding common stock plus *all potential diluters*. (Objective 4)

9. In preparing the EPS figures for complex capital structures, events that have not actually taken place are incorporated, resulting in *pro forma* figures. Methods used to incorporate these

assumed events include the treasury stock method for stock options, rights, and warrants, and the "if converted" method for convertible securities. (Objective 4)

10. EPS figures are presented on the face of the income statement. The precise wording and disclosure varies, depending on the circumstances of each company. (Objective 5)

11. The modifying conventions of substance over form and conservatism explain the incorporation of potential dilution in EPS figures. We attempt to reflect the economic substance of events rather than simply their legal form. We incorporate only those events that reduce EPS. (Objective 6)

APPENDIX A: ADDITIONAL EPS CONSIDERATIONS

In practice, many variations are encountered in computing EPS, particularly in the case of companies with complex capital structures. The model for computing EPS presented in this chapter is designed to cover major problem areas.

This appendix discusses several additional considerations in computing EPS. Some relate to circumstances that were intentionally avoided in the previous discussion. Others concern points that must be understood for a more complete knowledge of EPS but that the authors consider less important than material covered earlier.

MODIFICATION OF THE TREASURY STOCK METHOD

In developing the methods for computing EPS, the Accounting Principles Board concluded that the treasury stock method should be modified when the number of shares involved with stock options and warrants exceeded 20% of the number of shares outstanding. To put that modification into practice, a company must first apply a test to determine whether or not the number of shares that might be sold by stock option and similar plans exceeds 20% of the outstanding shares at the end of the accounting period. If that test is met, then a 20% limitation is in effect on the assumed stock buyback that is part of the treasury stock method. In other words, the assumption that a company will use the proceeds to buy back treasury stock is limited to 20% of the outstanding shares at the end of the accounting period.

When this situation exists, the proceeds from the assumed sale are distributed as follows:

1. As if the funds were first applied to the repurchase of common stock, up to 20% of the shares outstanding at the end of the period.
2. As if the remaining funds were used to reduce short-term or long-term borrowing and any remaining funds were invested in U.S. government securities or commercial paper.

If the net effect of these assumptions is dilutive, the results of these two steps are combined and included in EPS computations.

To illustrate, assume Montvale Company had 200,000 shares of outstanding common stock throughout 1993; the company also had outstanding stock options allowing the purchase of 100,000 shares of common stock at $20 per share. The market price of the common stock throughout 1993 was $37. The 20% test is met since the company stock option plan permits the purchase of stock by option holders in excess of 20% of the outstanding shares (100,000 shares exceeds 20% of 200,000 shares). The 20% limitation is also in effect since the proceeds from the sale of 100,000 shares at $20 would permit the buyback of more than 40,000 shares (20% × 200,000): [(100,000 × $20)/$37 = 54,054]. Assuming Montvale Company has at least $520,000 of outstanding debt at a 15% interest rate, that the company's income tax rate is 35%, and that net income for 1993 was $450,000, we determine the dilutive effect of the stock options as follows:

Proceeds from assumed exercise of options (100,000 × $20)		$2,000,000
20% limitation, 20% × 200,000 = 40,000		
Reacquisition of treasury shares (40,000 × $37)		1,480,000
Proceeds available for debt reduction		$ 520,000
Interest savings, after tax ($520,000 × 15%)(1 − .35)		$50,700
Increase in outstanding shares		
Shares sold	100,000	
Shares repurchased	(40,000)	60,000

Primary EPS, incorporating the dilution caused by the assumed exercise of the options, is computed as follows:

$$\text{Primary EPS} = \frac{\$450,000 + \$50,700}{200,000 + 60,000} = \$1.93$$

APB Opinion No. 15 does not indicate the order in which the company's debt should be assumed to have been retired. Also, if the proceeds available for debt reduction

($520,000 in the above example) exceed the amount of outstanding debt, the remaining amounts are assumed to have been invested in U.S. government securities or commercial paper. This has a similar impact on income as debt reduction, because the interest, after income tax, is added to income.

In applying this modification in the treasury stock method, all options and warrants are combined, including those that are antidilutive (i.e., ones for which the exercise price exceeds the market price). The aggregate results are included in the EPS calculations, however, only if the net effect of the assumed exercise of all options and warrants is dilutive.

RETROACTIVE APPLICATION OF STOCK SPLITS AND STOCK DIVIDENDS

In computing the weighted average number of common shares outstanding, stock splits and stock dividends are applied retroactively to restate stock outstanding prior to the split or dividend on the basis of the stock at the end of the accounting period. Financial statements are typically presented on a comparative basis, with the current period set in the context of one or more additional (historical) accounting periods.

If a stock split or stock dividend takes place in the current year, the split or dividend is applied retroactively to the comparative year figures, as well as within the current period, as we studied earlier.

To illustrate this point, assume that EPS for Pioneer Company for 1992 was originally reported in that year as $3.26, determined by dividing the $326,000 net income by 100,000 shares of outstanding common stock. Assume further that in 1993 the company reported a net income of $350,000, distributed a 2:1 stock dividend during the year, and had no other common stock activity. EPS for 1993 is $1.75, determined by dividing the $350,000 net income by 200,000 shares of common stock. Remember that the stock dividend is applied retroactively and, thus, the 200,000 shares are considered outstanding for the entire period, even though 100,000 shares were issued in a stock split during the year. For comparative purposes, the 1992 EPS figure of $3.26 must be restated on a basis consistent with that of 1993, as follows:

$$\$326,000/(100,000 \text{ shares} \times 2) = \$1.63$$

Comparative EPS figures in the 1993–1992 comparative income statements are $1.75 and $1.63, respectively.

MULTIPLE CONVERTIBLE SECURITIES

In the text we illustrated a simplified method for determining whether a convertible security is dilutive, a method that involves the calculation of a dilution index which is compared with base EPS. If the dilution index is less than base EPS, the convertible security is dilutive. A

refinement is required where the dilution index is close to the base EPS amount and multiple dilutive securities exist.

To illustrate this situation, assume that Mintz Company had a net income of $9,500 with 2,000 shares of common stock outstanding.[13] Assume further that the two classes of convertible preferred stock are outstanding as follows:

Class A—1,000 shares convertible into common on a 1:1 ratio; $2.50 dividend paid per share.
Class B—1,500 shares convertible into common on a 1:1 ratio; $1.00 dividend paid per share.

Base EPS is $2.75, computed as follows:

$$\frac{\$9,500 - (\$2,500 + \$1,500)}{2,000 \text{ shares}} = \$2.75$$

Computing a dilution index as discussed earlier, both issues of preferred stock appear to be dilutive:

Class A dilution index: $\frac{1,000 \text{ shares} \times \$2.50}{1,000 \text{ shares}} = \$2.50$

Class B dilution index: $\frac{1,500 \text{ shares} \times \$1.00}{1,500 \text{ shares}} = \$1.00$

Notice that the dilution index for the Class A preferred is $2.50, relatively close to the base EPS figure of $2.75. Rather than automatically assuming that each is dilutive, we must compute a series of EPS figures that incorporates the potential diluters, **starting with the most dilutive security.** In this example, the Class B convertible preferred stock is more dilutive than the Class A convertible preferred stock because the Class B dilution index is $1.00, compared to $2.50 for the Class A. EPS, including the dilutive effect of the Class B preferred, is determined as follows:

$$\frac{\$9,500 - \$2,500}{2,000 + 1,500 \text{ shares}} = \$2.00$$

Including the Class B preferred stock reduces EPS from $2.75 to $2.00. Now we must compare the dilution index of the Class A convertible preferred stock to determine if it will further dilute the EPS calculation. In this case it will not because the dilution index of the Class A convertible preferred is $2.50 which exceeds $2.00. Thus, the Class A convertible preferred is not included and diluted EPS is stated at $2.00, the maximum potential dilution. Had the dilution index of the Class A convertible preferred been less than $2.00, both classes of convertible preferred stock would have been included in the calculation.

This example illustrates a refinement in the procedure covered in the chapter text in which multiple convert

---

[13]This illustration is based on a similar illustration adapted from *AICPA Accounting Interpretation,* "Computing Earnings Per Share," sec. 43, "Conversion Assumed for Primary Only" (New York: AICPA, 1970).

ible securities are entered in the EPS calculation in order of their dilutive effect. Each resulting EPS calculation becomes the basis for determining the dilutive status of the next convertible security. Applying this refinement to the Express Company comprehensive illustration in this chapter would have no effect on the resulting EPS figures because of the strong dilutive effect of each individual potential diluter. In this illustration, no distinction has been made between computing primary and fully diluted EPS. If the two (or more) convertible securities are common stock equivalents, the above procedure must be applied in computing both primary and fully diluted EPS. If they are not common stock equivalents, the procedure is applied only in computing fully diluted EPS.

DELAYED EFFECTIVENESS AND CHANGING RATES OR PRICES

Some convertible securities are not convertible until a future date, and in some cases conversion rates vary over time. Similarly, some options or warrants are not exercisable until a future date, and in some cases exercise prices vary over time. Conversion rates on convertible securities and exercise prices on stock options and warrants are important in applying the "if converted" and treasury stock methods to compute primary and fully diluted EPS.

In computing *primary EPS*, the conversion rate or price in effect for the period of computation is used. If the conversion or exercise privilege is delayed, the earliest rate or price in the *next five years* is used. If conversion or exercise is not available within the five-year period, the potential diluter is not used to compute primary EPS.

In computing *fully diluted EPS*, the most advantageous conversion rate or exercise price to the holder that becomes effective in the *next ten years* is used. If conversion or exercise is not available within the 10-year period, the potential diluter is not used in computing fully diluted EPS.

QUESTIONS

21–1 What is meant by the term "dilution" as it relates to EPS?

21–2 Describe three types of potential diluters and indicate how each may reduce EPS.

21–3 What is meant by the term "senior security" when computing EPS? How does the existence of senior securities affect EPS?

21–4 Describe the difference between companies with simple capital structures and those with complex capital structures, and indicate the type of EPS presentation that each must make.

21–5 In computing EPS, a weighted average number of common shares outstanding is used. Indicate the impact, if any, of each of the following common stock transactions on the weighted average computation.

[a] Sale of additional shares.
[b] Acquisition of treasury stock.
[c] Distribution of a stock dividend.
[d] Resale of treasury stock.
[e] Distribution of a cash dividend.
[f] Distribution of a stock split.

21–6 In what circumstances is the dividend on preferred stock subtracted from net income in computing EPS? In what circumstances is this subtraction not made?

21–7 Describe the difference between the two EPS figures in each pair below and indicate under what circumstances the two would be the same:

[a] Base EPS and primary EPS.
[b] Primary EPS and fully diluted EPS.

21–8 Distinguish between common stock equivalents and other potentially dilutive securities. Explain when each of the following would be considered common stock equivalents:

[a] Convertible securities.
[b] Stock options, warrants, and rights.
[c] Other contingent issuances.

21–9 How could a common stock equivalent be included in the determination of EPS in one year but not in another year, even though it existed throughout both years?

21–10 When incorporating the dilutive impact of some potential diluters in EPS, the numerator in the computation is adjusted. In other cases, the numerator is not adjusted. Explain the reason for this difference and indicate when an adjustment is necessary.

21-11 Explain the distinction between companies that are publicly held and those that are not publicly held and the importance of this distinction in determining the appropriateness of presenting EPS.

21-12 The treasury stock method is used to determine the dilutive effect of the exercise of stock options, warrants, and rights. Explain how it is possible to determine whether the application of the method will result in a reduction in EPS prior to actually making the computations to determine the amount of the dilution.

In questions 21-13 through 21-22, select the correct answers.

21-13 The presentation of EPS is best described as:

[a] Required in the financial statements of all companies.
[b] Required in the financial statements of companies whose stock is publicly held.
[c] Required in the financial statements of companies whose stock is not publicly held.
[d] Not required in the financial statements of any company.

21-14 When EPS figures are presented, they should be located:

[a] In the income statement following net income.
[b] In the stockholders' equity section of the balance sheet.
[c] In the notes to the financial statements.
[d] In any of the three places suggested in [a], [b], and [c].

21-15 Potential diluters of EPS include all of the following except:

[a] Stock options, warrants, and rights to acquire common stock.
[b] Contingent issuances of common stock.
[c] Debt that is convertible into common stock.
[d] Preferred stock that is cumulative and nonconvertible.

21-16 Primary EPS is based on the shares of common stock described as:

[a] The number outstanding at the end of the accounting period.
[b] The weighted average number of shares outstanding plus common stock equivalents.
[c] The weighted average number of shares outstanding plus all potential diluters.
[d] The simple average of common shares outstanding.

21-17 Fully diluted EPS is best described as:

[a] EPS assuming the dilutive effect of events judged by management as most likely to occur.
[b] EPS based on historical income and outstanding shares.
[c] EPS incorporating the negative effect of all possible extraordinary losses that could occur in the future.
[d] EPS based on the assumption of full dilution of all potential diluters.

21-18 (Appendix A) To what extent is treasury stock assumed to be acquired by a corporation applying the treasury stock method in EPS calculations?

[a] To the maximum extent possible.
[b] Up to 20% of earnings for the period being reported on.
[c] None until all long-term debt has been retired, then to the maximum extent possible.
[d] Up to 20% of outstanding common stock. (AICPA adapted)

21-19 Which of the following statements best describes the impact of effective yield at issuance of convertible securities on calculating EPS?

[a] If less than two-thirds of the then current Aa corporate bond yield, these securities are used to calculate primary EPS but not fully diluted EPS.
[b] If less than two-thirds of the then current Aa corporate bond yield, these securities are used to calculate fully diluted EPS but not primary EPS.
[c] If greater than two-thirds of the then current Aa corporate bond yield, these securities are used to calculate primary EPS and fully diluted EPS.
[d] If greater than two-thirds of the then current Aa corporate bond yield, these securities are used to calculate fully diluted EPS but not primary EPS. (AICPA adapted)

21–20   In computing EPS, the equivalent number of shares of convertible preferred stock (cumulative) is added as an adjustment to the denominator (number of shares outstanding). If the preferred stock is preferred as to dividends, which amount should be added as an adjustment to the numerator (net earnings)?

[a] Annual preferred dividend.
[b] Annual preferred dividend $\times$ (1 − income tax rate).
[c] Annual preferred dividend $\times$ income tax rate.
[d] Annual preferred dividend $\div$ income tax rate.   (AICPA adapted)

21–21   A company issued a new class of convertible preferred stock during the year. At the date of issuance, the yield on the stock was 60% of the Aa corporate bond yield; by the end of the year, the cash yield was 90% of the Aa corporate bond yield. At the end of the year, what type of classification should this security receive for computation of EPS?

[a] Long-term debt equivalent.   [c] Convertible preferred stock.
[b] Other potentially dilutive security.   [d] Common stock equivalent security.

(AICPA adapted)

21–22   The computation of EPS in accordance with generally accepted accounting principles may involve the consideration of securities deemed common stock equivalents. Common stock equivalents are an example of:

[a] Form over substance.   [c] Form over accounting principle.
[b] Substance over form.   [d] Substance over accounting principle.

(AICPA adapted)

EXERCISES

21–23   SIMPLE EPS   Randall Company had 145,000 shares of common stock outstanding throughout 1993. The income statement for the year includes the following:

Income before extraordinary item	$195,000
Extraordinary loss	27,500
Net income	$167,500

The company had 70,000 shares of $12 par value, 7% cumulative preferred stock outstanding throughout 1993.

Instructions

Prepare the EPS presentation for Randall's income statement for 1993.

21–24   SIMPLE EPS   Sims Company had 100,000 shares of common stock outstanding on January 1, 1993. During the year the company sold and subsequently repurchased stock as follows:

July 1, 1993   Sold 70,000 shares of common stock.
Dec. 1, 1993   Purchased 25,000 shares of common treasury stock.

The company reported a net income for 1993 of $856,000.

Instructions

Compute EPS for the company for 1993.

21–25   CONVERTIBLE BONDS   Wilkes Company had 100,000 shares of common stock outstanding throughout 1993, a year in which the company reported a $150,000 net income. In addition to common stock, the company had the following securities in its capital structure, as shown in the following:

Cumulative preferred stock—9,000 shares, 7%, $100 par value.
Long-term debt—$1,000,000, 6%, convertible into 60 shares of common stock per $1,000 bond. These bonds were issued when the average Aa corporate bond yield was 8%.

The company's income tax rate is 35%.

Instructions

Compute primary and fully diluted EPS for 1993 for Wilkes Company.

21–26 TREASURY STOCK METHOD   Aaron Company had 157,000 shares of common stock outstanding at December 31, 1993. There were 150,000 shares outstanding at January 1, 1993, and 7,000 shares were sold on August 1, 1993. Net income for the year was reported as $250,000.

Outstanding throughout the year were stock options allowing the holders to acquire 30,000 shares of common stock at $25 per share. The market price of the stock averaged $35 in 1993, was $48 at December 31, 1993, and did not fall below $25 during the year.

Instructions

Compute primary and fully diluted EPS for 1993 for Aaron Company.

21–27 CONVERTIBLE PREFERRED   Wesley Company has two classes of capital stock:

Cumulative preferred stock—1,000,000 shares authorized, $10 par value, 500,000 shares outstanding, 7% dividend rate, each share convertible into 5 shares of common stock.

Common stock—9,000,000 shares authorized, $6 par value, 7,000,000 shares outstanding.

In 1993, net income of $10,000,000 was reported. No capital stock activity took place during the year. The company's income tax rate is 35%.

The preferred stock was issued in 1991 at par value when the average Aa corporate bond yield was 10%.

Instructions

Compute primary and fully diluted EPS for 1993.

21–28 WEIGHTED AVERAGE CALCULATION   Saffell Company had 745,000 shares of common stock outstanding at the beginning of 1993. During the year the company had the following common stock activity:

Jan. 31   Sold 100,000 additional shares.
May 31   Acquired 10,000 shares of treasury stock.
Aug. 31   Resold 1,000 shares of treasury stock.
Oct. 31   Resold 6,000 shares of treasury stock.

Instructions

Compute the weighted average common shares outstanding for 1993 to be used in computing EPS.

21–29 WEIGHTED AVERAGE CALCULATION   Farrell Company had 1,475,000 shares outstanding at December 31, 1993, the end of the company's fiscal year. On March 31, 1993, the company had sold 150,000 additional shares of stock; a 2:1 stock split was declared on August 1, 1993, and distributed on September 1, 1993.

Instructions

Compute the weighted average common shares outstanding for 1993 to be used in computing EPS.

21–30 DENOMINATOR CALCULATION   At December 31, 1992, AMT, Inc., had 500,000 shares of common stock outstanding. On October 1, 1993, an additional 150,000 shares of common stock were issued for cash. AMT also had $4,000,000 of 8% convertible bonds outstanding at December 31, 1993, which are convertible into 135,000 shares of common stock. The bonds were considered common stock equivalents at the time of issuance and are dilutive in the 1993 EPS computations. No bonds were issued or converted into common stock during 1993.

Instructions

Determine the number of shares that should be used in computing AMT's primary EPS for the year ended December 31, 1993.   (AICPA adapted)

21–31 TEST FOR DILUTION   Meller, Inc., has asked you to help compute EPS figures for its 1993 income statement. Net income for the year is $10,000,000 and the company had 2,600,000 shares of common stock outstanding the entire year. The company has no preferred stock in its capital structure.

Meller officials are attempting to determine whether the following securities will have a dilutive effect on EPS if they are assumed to have been converted or exercised:

Convertible bonds—$10,000,000 par value, 12%, each $1,000 bond convertible into 30 shares of common stock.

Stock options—1,000,000 options to acquire one share each at $16.

Meller's income tax rate is 35% and its common stock sold for $12 throughout 1993. Both the convertible bonds and the stock options were issued in 1991.

Instructions

Test the convertible bonds and the stock options for dilution and indicate your results.

21-32 TEST FOR DILUTION   Haskins Co. has 100,000 shares of common stock outstanding throughout 1993. The reported net income for the year is $125,000, after an income tax rate of 35%.

Instructions

Determine whether the potential diluters below are dilutive in 1993. Treat each item *independently*.

[a] Convertible bonds are outstanding as follows: $100,000 par value, 6%, convertible into 60 shares of common stock per $1,000 bond.

[b] Convertible bonds are outstanding as follows: $200,000 par value, 7%, convertible into 10 shares of common stock per $1,000 bond.

[c] Fifty thousand stock options are outstanding that allow the holders to purchase one share per option for $10. The stock sold for $12 throughout the year.

[d] Preferred stock (20,000 shares with a par value of $10) is outstanding. The preferred has a 7% dividend rate and is convertible into two shares of common per preferred share.

21-33 TREASURY STOCK METHOD   PBM Company had stock options outstanding throughout the year that allow the acquisition of 75,000 shares of common stock from the company at $10 per share. There are 1,000,000 shares of common stock outstanding in the current capital structure.

Instructions

Determine the number of common shares which will be used in computing both primary and fully diluted EPS resulting from the options in each of the following *independent* situations:

[a] The average market price of the common stock was $15, and the year-end price was $15.

[b] The average market price of the common stock was $16, and the year-end price was $18.

[c] The average market price of the common stock was $14, and the year-end price was $10½.

[d] The average market price of the common stock was $9, and the year-end price was $12.

21-34 (Appendix A) TREASURY STOCK METHOD   Falco, Inc., had stock options outstanding throughout 1993, allowing the holders to acquire 100,000 shares of common stock from the company at the $50 par value per share. The market price of the stock was $75 throughout the year and at year-end.

The company has a 35% income tax rate and pays 8% interest on its $5,000,000 debt. Net income for 1993 was $275,000.

Instructions

Compute primary and fully diluted EPS for 1993 in each of the following *independent* situations:

[a] The weighted average number of outstanding shares of common stock was 600,000 during 1993, with 610,000 outstanding at December 31.

[b] The weighted average number of outstanding shares of common stock was 300,000 during 1993, with 325,000 outstanding at December 31.

21-35 "IF CONVERTED" METHOD   Kemp Manufacturing Company began operation in 1992 and in that year issued the following securities:

Preferred stock—175,000 shares, $100 par value, 7½%, issued at $110, convertible into 3 shares of common stock per preferred share.

Bonds—$10,000,000 par value, 6½%, issued at par value and convertible into 5 shares per $100 bond.

In 1993 the preferred stock and bonds just described are still outstanding, none having been converted or retired. Kemp Manufacturing Company's income tax rate is 35%.

Instructions

For both the preferred stock and the bonds, determine the adjustments that would have to be made to the 1993 EPS calculations, assuming each has a dilutive effect.

21–36 ANALYSIS OF POTENTIAL DILUTERS Hendee Company has two potentially dilutive securities, as follows: *8% cash yield* *stated* *Par = 100* *Not issued at PAR!!*

8.00 Dividend / 140 = 5.7% → effective yield

Cumulative preferred stock (8%)—50,000 shares authorized and outstanding, $100 par value, *issued at $140* in 1990, convertible into two shares of common per preferred share.

Convertible debt (6%)—$2,000,000 par value, issued at par in 1989, convertible into 15 shares of common stock per $1,000 bond. *Stated % = mkt % = issued at par*

Hendee's management is attempting to compute EPS for 1993 and has correctly determined that EPS, without considering potential dilution, is $3.25. The Aa corporate bond yield from 1989 to 1991 was 10½% and in 1992 and 1993 was 9%. The company's income tax rate is 35%.

Instructions

[a] Determine whether the potential diluters are common stock equivalents.

[b] Determine whether the potential diluters are dilutive in 1993.

21–37 3% MINIMUM DILUTION TEST Beverly, Inc., is attempting to determine whether the potential dilution in its capital structure is sufficient to warrant a dual EPS presentation in 1993. The company has not had to present primary and fully diluted EPS in the past.

The company reported a $500,000 net income and has 300,000 shares of common stock outstanding. The company's income tax rate is 35%. The following potentially dilutive securities exist:

CSE **Stock options**—50,000 outstanding, allowing the purchase of one share each of common stock at $100. The market price of common stock throughout 1993 was $105.

Convertible debt—$500,000 par value, 6%, convertible to 20 shares of common stock per $1,000 bond.

Instructions

[a] Determine whether Beverly, Inc., must make a dual presentation of EPS by applying the 3% guideline.

[b] Would your answer to [a] be different if the bonds were convertible into 60 shares per $1,000 bond?

21–38 OPTIONS OUTSTANDING PART OF YEAR The fiscal year of Spectra Company ends June 30. On September 30, 1992, the company issued 50,000 stock options to its employees, allowing them to acquire one share of common stock for each option at the $10 par value of the stock.

9/12

During fiscal year 1993, Spectra Company had a weighted average of 286,500 shares outstanding and reported a net income of $575,500. The stock of the company sold at $17 throughout the year.

Instructions

Compute primary EPS for 1993.

21–39 CONVERTIBLE BONDS OUTSTANDING PART OF YEAR On May 31 of the last calendar year, Rolf Company issued $1,000,000 of 12% bonds at par value. Each $1,000 bond may be converted into 80 shares of common stock. *interest saved 1A* *7/12*

Rolf Company reports $147,000 of net income for the year ended December 31. The weighted average number of shares of common stock outstanding was 100,000 and the company's income tax rate is 35%.

Instructions

Assuming that the convertible debt is not a common stock equivalent, compute primary and fully diluted EPS for Rolf Company for the last calendar year.

21–40 (Appendix A)   STOCK SPLIT   The 1992 income statement of Phillip, Inc., a calendar-year company, included earnings per share of $2.29. This figure was determined as follows:

1992 net income	$1,700,000
Less: Preferred dividend	(100,000)
	$1,600,000
Divided by: Number of common shares outstanding entire year	700,000
Earnings per share	$2.29

During 1993 Phillip issued a 2:1 stock split on March 1, reported a net income of $2,750,000, and had no other capital transactions. A $100,000 preferred dividend was paid on December 31, 1993.

Instructions

[a] Determine EPS for 1993.

[b] Apply the stock split of 1993 retroactively to 1992 and restate the EPS for that year.

21–41 (Appendix A)   STOCK DIVIDEND   Parton, Inc., a company with a simple capital structure, reported EPS of $1.57 for the calendar year 1992, computed as follows:

Net income	$18,800,000
Divided by: Weighted average common shares outstanding	12,000,000
Earnings per share	$1.57

At January 1, 1993, Parton, Inc., declared a 10% stock dividend on the 12,500,000 shares of common stock outstanding at that time. The dividend shares were issued on February 28, 1993.

Instructions

[a] Determine EPS for 1993, assuming that the Parton, Inc., reports a $25,000,000 net income.

[b] Determine EPS for 1992 that should be presented for comparative purposes in the 1992–1993 comparative income statement.

21–42 (Appendix A)   DELAYED STOCK OPTIONS   Arnold Company has 150,000 options outstanding to acquire one share of common stock each. These options can be exercised at any time after December 31, 2000, at $50 per share.

During 1993 Arnold Company reports a net income of $6,500,000; has 1,000,000 shares of common stock outstanding; and has 500,000 shares of 9%, $100 par value, cumulative preferred stock outstanding. The average and year-end market price of the company's common stock was $65 during 1993.

Instructions

Compute primary and fully diluted EPS for Arnold Company for 1993.

PROBLEMS

21–43   SIMPLE EPS   Potter Company had the following common stock activity in 1993:

	Number of Shares
Outstanding, Jan. 1	150,000
New shares issued, May 1	25,000
Treasury shares acquired, July 1	10,000
Treasury shares resold, Dec. 1	7,500
Outstanding, Dec. 31	172,500

Potter had 100,000 shares of cumulative preferred stock outstanding during 1993. The preferred stock has a $10 par value and an 8% dividend rate.

Instructions

[a] Prepare the EPS presentation for 1993, assuming income before extraordinary items is $600,000 and net income is $675,000. There is one extraordinary item in 1993.

[b] Independent of [a], prepare the earnings (loss) per share presentations for 1993, assuming the company sustained a $420,000 net loss for 1993, with no extraordinary item.

21-44 SIMPLE EPS Row Company had the following common stock activity in 1992:

	Number of Shares
Outstanding, Jan. 1	500,000
New shares issued, Mar. 1	50,000
Stock issued in 2:1 split, June 1	550,000
Treasury shares acquired, Nov. 1	40,000
Outstanding, Dec. 31	1,060,000

Row had 200,000 shares of $25 par value cumulative preferred stock outstanding throughout 1992. The dividend rate of this stock is 8%. The company reports a net income of $1,750,000 for 1992 with no extraordinary items.

The accountant for Row indicates that EPS should be reported as $1.65, determined by dividing the reported net income by 1,060,000 shares of common stock.

Instructions

[a] Do you agree with the accountant's computation? What specific items have not been considered by the accountant?

[b] Recompute EPS for Row Company for 1992. Provide supporting schedules for the amounts used in your computation.

21-45 SEVEN-STEP EPS CALCULATION Powell Company had 175,000 shares of common stock outstanding at July 1, 1992, the beginning of its fiscal year. On September 30, 1992, the company sold an additional 25,000 shares. On May 31, 1993, 15,000 shares of treasury stock were acquired off the market.

The company had 48,000 shares of preferred stock outstanding throughout the year ended June 30, 1993. The preferred stock has a $10 par value and a 8% dividend rate and is cumulative and nonconvertible.

In addition to the common and preferred stock, Powell has the following securities outstanding:

[1] Ten percent short-term notes payable of $35,000 due in varying amounts in 30, 60, and 90 days.

[2] Stock options which allow employees to purchase 35,000 shares of common stock at $25 per share. The stock sold for $32.50 throughout the 1993 fiscal year. The options were originally issued in 1989.

[3] Convertible bonds, issued at the par amount of $500,000 in 1990. The bonds yield 10% interest, payable semiannually, and each $100 bond is convertible into 15 shares of common stock on any interest payment date (December 31 and June 30). semiannually

For the year ended June 30, 1993, the following items have been determined to be appropriate for inclusion in Powell's income statement:

Income before tax	$320,000	35% Tax rate
Income tax expense	112,000	
Net income	$208,000	

The Aa corporate bond yield was 8% in 1989 and increased 1% each year from 1990-1993.

1990 9%   1992 11%
1991 10%   1993 12%

Instructions

Following the seven-step process outlined in the chapter, prepare the financial statement presentation of EPS for Powell Company for the year ended June 30, 1993.

21-46 EPS—ALTERNATIVE FINANCING PLANS Toyex Corporation is considering several methods of increasing its long-term capitalization to provide funds for an expansion of facilities. One consideration is the impact of the method on EPS.

Toyex Corporation reported an EPS of $2.25 for the most recent fiscal year, determined on the basis of $1,687,500 net income and 750,000 shares of common stock outstanding.

The plans under consideration for obtaining approximately $1,000,000 include the following alternatives:

[1] Sell 200,000 additional shares of common stock at approximately $5 per share.

[2] Sell $1,000,000 of 9% bonds approximately at par value.

[3] Sell 100,000 shares of 8% preferred stock approximately at $10 par value, each share convertible into 2 shares of common stock.

[4] Sell $1,000,000 of 7½% convertible bonds approximately at par value, each $1,000 bond convertible into 50 shares of common stock.

Toyex management expects to earn 15% (before income tax) on the increased funds available. The 35% income tax rate for the company is expected to continue. The Aa corporate bond yield throughout the period is expected to be 11%.

Instructions

[a] Determine the EPS which Toyex may be expected to present in the income statement under each of the four alternative plans.

[b] Identify factors which Toyex should consider in addition to the specific figures in [a] above.

[c] From the viewpoint of a current common stockholder, which alternative method of financing the $1,000,000 is preferable? Why?

21–47 (Appendix A)   SIMPLE EPS   Weber Corporation is preparing the comparative financial statements to be included in the annual report to stockholders. Weber employs a fiscal year ending May 31.

Income from operations before income taxes for Weber was $1,600,000 and $785,000 respectively for fiscal years ended May 31, 1993 and 1992. Weber experienced an extraordinary loss of $600,000 due to an earthquake on March 3, 1993. A 40% combined income tax rate pertains to any and all of Weber Corporation's profits, gains, and losses.

Weber's capital structure consists of preferred stock and common stock. The company has not issued any convertible securities or warrants and there are no outstanding stock options.

Weber issued 50,000 shares of $100 par value, 6% cumulative preferred stock in 1979. All of this stock is outstanding, and no preferred dividends are in arrears.

There were 2,000,000 shares of $1 par common stock outstanding on June 1, 1991. On September 1, 1991, Weber sold an additional 500,000 shares of the common stock at $17 per share. Weber distributed a 20% stock dividend on the common shares outstanding on December 1, 1992. These were the only common stock transactions during the past two fiscal years.

Instructions

[a] Determine the weighted average number of common shares to be used in computing earnings per share on the current comparative income statement for:

[1] the year ended May 31, 1992.

[2] the year ended May 31, 1993.

[b] Starting with income from operations before income taxes, prepare a comparative income statement for the years ended May 31, 1993 and 1992. The statement will be part of Weber's annual report to stockholders and should include appropriate earnings per share presentation.

[c] The capital structure of a corporation is the result of its past financing decisions. Furthermore, the earnings per share data presented on a corporation's financial statements is dependent upon the capital structure.

[1] Explain why Weber Corporation is considered to have a simple capital structure.

[2] Describe how earnings per share data would be presented for a corporation that has a complex capital structure.   (CMA adapted)

21–48   COMPLEX CAPITAL STRUCTURE   Pfitzer Company is attempting to determine its primary and fully diluted EPS for 1993. The controller believes that it may be necessary to consider some or all of the following securities, all of which were issued prior to 1993.

Security	Number or Par Value (in dollars)	Interest/Dividend Rate	Aa Corporate Bond Yield at Issuance	Convertibility (in total) or Purchase Option
Bonds A	$100,000	10%	12%	10,000 shares
Bonds B	$200,000	9%	9½%	None
Bonds C	$500,000	7%	11%	15,000 shares
Preferred stock	$500,000	7½%	10%	50,000 shares
Options	45,000	—	12½%	1 share per option at $30

The controller has correctly determined that the net income for 1993 is $595,000 and the weighted average number of outstanding shares is 475,000. The company's income tax rate is 35% and the Aa corporate bond yield in 1993 was 11½%. The common stock sold for $47 throughout 1993. The preferred stock is cumulative.

Instructions

[a] Prepare a schedule indicating the common stock equivalency status of each security listed and whether each security is dilutive in 1993.

[b] Compute primary and fully diluted EPS for 1993.

[c] Discuss briefly your reason for omitting any of the securities in the above table that you did not use in computing EPS.

21–49 COMPREHENSIVE EPS CALCULATIONS   Morgan Corporation's capital structure is as follows:

	Dec. 31, 1993	Dec. 31, 1992
Outstanding shares of:		
Common stock	336,000	300,000
Nonconvertible preferred stock	10,000	10,000
8% convertible bonds	$1,000,000	$1,000,000

Additional Information

[1] On September 1, 1993, Morgan sold 36,000 additional shares of common stock.

[2] Net income for the year ended December 31, 1993, was $750,000.

[3] During 1993 Morgan paid dividends of $3 per share on its nonconvertible preferred stock.

[4] The 8% convertible bonds are convertible into 40 shares of common stock for each $1,000 bond and were not considered common stock equivalents at the date of issuance.

[5] Unexercised stock options to purchase 30,000 shares of common stock at $22.50 per share were outstanding throughout 1993. The average market price of Morgan's common stock was $36 per share during 1993. The market price was $33 per share at December 31, 1993.

[6] Warrants to purchase 20,000 shares of common stock at $38 per share were attached to the preferred stock at the time of issuance. The warrants, which expire on December 31, 1998, were outstanding at December 31, 1993.

[7] Morgan's effective income tax rate was 40% for 1992 and 1993.

Instructions

[a] Determine the number of shares that should be used to compute Morgan Corporation's primary EPS for the year ended December 31, 1993.

[b] Compute the primary EPS for the year ended December 31, 1993.

[c] Determine the number of shares that should be used to compute fully diluted EPS for the year ended December 31, 1993.

[d] Compute the fully diluted EPS for the year ended December 31, 1993.   (AICPA adapted)

21–50 COMPREHENSIVE EPS CALCULATIONS   The statement of income and the stockholders' equity section of the statement of financial position for the fiscal year ended September 30, 1993, are presented for Dobson Company as follows:

Dobson Company
STATEMENT OF INCOME
For the Fiscal Year Ended September 30, 1993
(in thousands)

Sales		$1,000,000
Cost of goods sold		750,000
Gross margin		250,000
Operating expenses (including interest expense of $6,000)		50,000
Income before income taxes		200,000
Income taxes (40%)		
Current	$60,000	
Deferred	20,000	80,000
Income before extraordinary item		120,000
Extraordinary gain, net of income taxes of $20,000		30,000
Net income		$ 150,000

Dobson Company
Stockholders' Equity Section of the
Statement of Financial Position
September 30, 1993
(in thousands)

Preferred stock ($50 par value, 6%; 10,000,000 shares authorized, 5,000,000 shares issued and outstanding)	$250,000
Common stock ($1 par value; 100,000,000 shares authorized with 54,250,000 issued and 53,250,000 shares outstanding)	54,250
Paid-in capital in excess of par value	275,000
Retained earnings	200,000
Total equity	$779,250
Less: Treasury stock—at cost (1,000,000 shares)	40,000
Total stockholders' equity	$739,250

Additional Information

[1] Dobson issued 6% convertible debentures during the 1989–1990 fiscal year at par value of $1,000 each. Each debenture is convertible into 30 shares of common stock. No conversions were made during the fiscal year ended September 30, 1993, and the value of the outstanding debentures is $100,000,000.

[2] A 5% common stock dividend was declared in January 1993 and issued during February 1993 to all stockholders of record; 2,250,000 shares were issued.

[3] Dobson's management has the following options to purchase shares of the company's common stock, adjusted for all dividends declared to date:

Option	Number of Shares	Option Price	Expiration Date
A	2,000,000	$25	Sept. 30, 1995
B	3,000,000	45	Sept. 30, 1996

[4] Market price information for Dobson Company common stock and data on the Aa corporate bond yield are as follows:

	For the Year Ended Sept. 30			
	1990	1991	1992	1993
Average price of common stock	$28	$35	$38	$40
Year-end market price of common stock	$25	$38	$35	$40
Average Aa corporate bond yield	8%	9%	10%	10%

[5] Changes in the number of common shares outstanding during the current fiscal year are summarized below:

Date	Shares Outstanding	Explanation
Oct. 1, 1992	45,000,000	Shares outstanding at the beginning of the year.
Feb. 1, 1993	47,250,000	Shares after a 5% stock dividend was issued.
June 1, 1993	53,250,000	Shares after 6,000,000 new shares were issued for $42.

[6] The outstanding preferred stock is noncumulative and no preferred dividend was declared or paid during 1993. Don't include in ANI

Instructions

[a] Calculate the weighted average number of common shares outstanding for Dobson Company for the fiscal year ended September 30, 1993.

[b] Prepare an analysis of the potentially dilutive securities included in Dobson Company's capital structure. Indicate whether they are included in only primary EPS or in both primary and fully diluted EPS, or excluded from EPS computations.

[c] Compute primary and fully diluted EPS for the year ended September 30, 1993.
Hint: When a stock dividend is distributed, the number of shares into which the convertible debentures may be converted should be adjusted to an after-dividend basis. (CMA adapted)

21–51 COMPREHENSIVE EPS CALCULATIONS The controller of LXT, Inc., has asked you to help to determine both primary and fully diluted EPS for presentation in the company's income statement for the year ended September 30, 1993.

Your working papers disclose the following opening balances and transactions in the company's capital stock accounts during the year:

[1] Common stock (at October 1, 1992, stated value $10, authorized 300,000 shares; effective December 1, 1992, stated value $5, authorized 600,000 shares):

Balance, Oct. 1, 1992—issued and outstanding 60,000 shares.
Dec. 1, 1992—60,000 shares issued in a 2-for-1 stock split.
Dec. 1, 1992—280,000 shares (stated value $5) issued at $39 per share.

[2] Treasury stock—common:

Mar. 1, 1993—purchased 40,000 shares at $38 per share.
Apr. 1, 1993—sold 40,000 shares at $40 per share.

[3] Stock purchase warrants, Series A (initially each warrant was exchangeable with $60 for one common share; effective December 1, 1992, each warrant became exchangeable for two common shares at $30 per share):

Oct. 1, 1992—25,000 warrants issued at $6 each.

[4] Stock purchase warrants, Series B (each warrant is exchangeable with $45 for one common share):

Apr. 1, 1993—20,000 warrants authorized and issued at $10 each.

[5] First mortgage bonds, 5½%, due 2000 (nonconvertible; priced to yield 5% when issued):

Balance, Oct. 1, 1992—authorized, issued, and outstanding at $1,400,000 face value.

[6] Convertible debentures, 7%, due 2012 (initially each $1,000 bond was convertible at any time until maturity into 12½ common shares; effective December 1, 1992, the conversion rate became 25 shares for each bond):

Oct. 1, 1992—authorized and issued at their face value (no premium or discount) of $2,400,000.

The following table shows market prices for the company's securities and the assumed Aa corporate bond yield during 1992–1993.

	Price (or Rate)			Average for Year Ended
	Oct. 1, 1992	Apr. 1, 1993	Sept. 30, 1993	Sept. 30, 1993
Common stock	66	40*	42*	37½*
First mortgage bonds	88½	87	86	87
Convertible debentures	100	120	119	115
Series A warrants	6	22	19½	15
Series B warrants	—	10	9	9½
Aa corporate bond yield	8%	7¾%	7½%	7¾%

*Adjusted for stock split.

Instructions

Assuming that net income for the year was $850,000 and that the income tax rate was 35%, prepare computations of primary and fully diluted EPS. Provide schedules and analyses which support your conclusions on each of the following:

[a] Common stock equivalency status of all potential diluters.
[b] Dilutive status of all potential diluters.
[c] Consideration of the minimum materiality standard for a dual presentation of EPS.

(AICPA adapted)

CASES

21–52 CONCEPT OF SUBSTANCE OVER FORM   Financial accounting usually emphasizes the economic substance of events, even though the legal form may differ and suggest different treatment. For example, under accrual accounting, expenses are recognized when they are incurred (substance) rather than when cash is disbursed (form).

Although substance over form dominates most generally accepted accounting principles and practices, form sometimes prevails over substance.

Instructions

Discuss EPS for a complex capital structure, identifying specific instances where substance or form prevails.   (AICPA adapted)

21–53 STOCKHOLDERS' EQUITY AND EPS   Winfield Company had the following account titles on its December 31, 1992, trial balance:

> 6% cumulative convertible preferred stock, $100 par value
> Premium on preferred stock
> Common stock, $1 stated value
> Premium on common stock
> Retained earnings

The following additional information is available for the year ended December 31, 1992:

[1] Two million shares of preferred stock were authorized, of which 1,000,000 were outstanding. All shares outstanding were issued on January 2, 1989, for $120 a share. The Aa corporate bond yield was 8.5% on January 2, 1989, and 10% on December 31, 1992. The preferred stock is convertible into common stock on a one-for-one basis until December 31, 1998, after which the preferred stock ceases to be convertible and is callable at par value by the company. No preferred stock has been converted into common stock, and there were no dividends in arrears at December 31, 1992.

[2] The common stock has been issued at amounts above stated value per share since Winfield's incorporation in 1974. Of the 5,000,000 shares authorized, 3,500,000 shares were outstanding at January 1, 1992. The market price of the outstanding common stock has increased slowly, but consistently, for the last five years.

[3] The company has an employee stock option plan whereby certain key employees and officers may purchase shares of common stock at 100% of the market price at the date of the option grant. All options are exercisable in installments of one-third each year, beginning one year

after the date of the grant, and expire if not exercised within four years of the grant date. On January 1, 1992, options for 70,000 shares were outstanding at prices ranging from $47 to $83 a share. Options for 20,000 shares were exercised at $47 to $79 a share during 1992. No options expired during 1992 and additional options for 15,000 shares were granted at $86 a share during the year. The 65,000 options outstanding at December 31, 1992, were exercisable at $54 to $86 a share; of these, 30,000 were exercisable at that date at prices ranging from $54 to $79 a share.

[4] The company also has an employee stock purchase plan whereby the company pays one half and the employee pays the other half of the market price of the stock at the date of the subscription. During 1992, employees subscribed to 60,000 shares at an average price of $87 a share. All 60,000 shares were paid for and issued late in September 1992.

[5] On December 31, 1992, a total of 355,000 shares of common stock was set aside for the granting of future stock options and for future purchases under the employee stock purchase plan. The only changes in the stockholders' equity for 1992 were those described above, 1992 net income, and cash dividends paid.

Instructions

[a] Prepare the stockholders' equity section of Winfield Company's balance sheet at December 31, 1992. Substitute Xs, where appropriate, for unknown dollar amounts. Use good form and provide full disclosure. Write appropriate footnotes as they should appear in the published financial statements.

[b] Explain how the denominator should be determined to compute *primary* EPS for presentation in the financial statements. Be specific about the handling of each item. If additional information is needed to determine whether an item should be included and to what extent, identify the information needed and how the item would be handled if the information were known. Assume Winfield Company had substantial net income for the year ended December 31, 1992.

(AICPA adapted)

21–54 (Appendix A) ADVANCED EPS CONCEPTS EPS is one of the most frequently featured financial statistics of modern corporations. Daily quotations of stock prices have recently been expanded to include a "times earnings" figure for many securities which is based on EPS. Analysts often focus their discussions on the EPS of corporations in which they are interested.

Instructions

[a] Explain how dividends or dividend requirements on any class of preferred stock that may be outstanding affect the computation of EPS.

[b] One of the technical procedures used in computing EPS is the treasury stock method.
  [1] Briefly describe the circumstances in which the treasury stock method should be applied.
  [2] There is a limit to the applicability of the treasury stock method. Identify this limit and briefly indicate the procedures that should be followed beyond the limit of the treasury stock method.

[c] Under some circumstances convertible debentures are considered common stock equivalents.
  [1] When should convertible debentures be treated as common stock equivalents? In such cases what is the effect on the computation of EPS?
  [2] When convertible debentures are not considered common stock equivalents, how are they handled in EPS computations? (AICPA adapted)

JUDGMENT CASES

21–55 MANAGING EPS You are the controller of Litigious, Inc., which last year won and collected a large judgment from a competitor for unfair market infringement. The company is a small publicly-held corporation with approximately 10 major stockholders and a large number of additional shares outstanding that are widely held. The financial statements for the preceding year appropriately reported the large gain from the litigation as part of income from continuing operations and before extraordinary items. The effects on the company's reported earnings per share of that gain were also large and favorable. Now the president of Litigious wishes to continue to report a high earnings per share number in the current year; however, operating results have been disappointing and it is expected that the rest of the current year will not show much improvement.

The large cash fund resulting from the judgment described above is still held in short term investments; however, there are a number of highly desirable long term projects available to the company that would probably result in highly profitable results in approximately three years. Notwithstanding these desirable potential uses of the resources, the president has tentatively decided to use the funds to reacquire a large block of the company's outstanding stock. He states:

> *Why don't we simply reacquire a lot of our stock off the market with the proceeds from the litigation. That way we will be able to report a high earnings per share for the current year as well. That is particularly desirable from my personal perspective because my compensation and retirement agreements are based, in large measure, on the company's reported earnings per share. Further, I am scheduled to retire at the end of next year, my retirement formula is highly weighted to the last three years of the company's performance as indicated by its earnings per share. I know there are potentially a large number of very attractive long-term projects available for the company, but I simply don't have the time to wait for them to bear fruit. I am, therefore, going to begin the stock reacquisition program immediately because, as you know, the calculation is based on outstanding shares.*

Instructions

What, if anything, should you do? Can you ethically participate in the plan to reacquire the shares as the president intends? What considerations should affect your course of action?

21–56   INFORMATION CONTENT OF EPS   A friend of yours, Roger Jones, is a financial analyst for a national brokerage firm with offices in the same building as your public accounting firm. Ocassionally, he calls to ask you "accounting type" questions that usually require only a simple, brief answer. Today, however, he has called to discuss the concept of fully diluted earnings per share. He states:

> *I am considering investing in a company whose fully diluted earnings per share is much less than the number it reports for primary earnings per share. The difference between the two, as best as I can tell, relates to a large number of bonds that can be converted into common stock. Because the company is currently troubled, its stock is trading a low amount and the bondholders clearly won't be converting their bonds any time soon. Therefore, I think that the acquisition of common stock today makes a lot of sense because there is no way that the fully diluted earnings per share number is realistic. That is, the value of the shares may be depressed by the possible conversion of the bonds, but I just don't think that will happen. Therefore, the shares are very likely undervalued. What do you think of my analysis?*

You are aware that your friend does not have a strong accounting background having majored in general business in college and worked for the brokerage firm for the past two years. He sometimes feels insecure in his position because he does not understand much about the assumptions and practices under which financial statements are prepared in conformity with generally accepted accounting principles.

Instructions

Respond to the views of your friend. Remember, you have your own work to do and cannot spend a lot of time coaching him at work.

CHAPTER 22

Reporting Cash Flow Information

OBJECTIVES

1. To identify the role that cash flow information plays in meeting the objectives of financial reporting.

2. To discuss the importance of cash flow information to users of financial statements.

3. To define the three categories of cash flows of business enterprises—operating, investing, and financing—and explain how they are presented in a statement of cash flows.

4. To explain the nature of those investing and financing transactions that do not affect cash flows directly and to explain the manner of reporting such events.

5. To present procedures for preparing a statement of cash flows in a relatively complex situation.

OBJECTIVES OF FINANCIAL REPORTING AND CASH FLOW INFORMATION

When the FASB specified the objectives of financial reporting in *SFAC No. 1*, information useful in assessing cash flow prospects was identified as being particularly important. Subsequently, cash flow information was specified as a requirement for a full set of financial statements in *SFAC No. 5* and the statement of cash flows became a reporting requirement in *SFAS No. 95*. In this chapter, we study the background of the current reporting requirements associated with the statement of cash flows and illustrate the preparation of that statement at two levels of complexity.

The FASB identified three broad types of information as necessary to meet the objectives of financial reporting:

1. *Information useful in investment and credit decisions.* Financial reporting should assist present and potential investors and creditors and other users in making rational investment, credit, and similar decisions.[1]
2. *Information useful in assessing cash flow prospects.* Financial reporting should provide information to help present and potential investors and creditors and other users in assessing the amounts, timing and uncertainty of prospective cash receipts to them from dividends or interest and the proceeds from the sale, redemption, or maturity of securities or loans.[2]
3. *Information about enterprise resources, claims to those resources, and changes in them.* Financial reporting should provide information about an enterprise's economic resources, obligations, and owners' equity. That information helps users identify the enterprise's financial strengths and weaknesses and assess its liquidity and solvency.[3]

An enterprise's ability to generate enough cash to meet its financial obligations and other cash operating needs, to reinvest in operations, and to pay cash dividends may affect the market prices of the enterprise's securities. Thus, financial reporting should provide information to help investors, creditors and other users to assess the amounts, timing and uncertainty of prospective cash flows to the enterprise in which they have an economic interest.[4] In other words, cash flow information about the reporting entity is believed to help investors, creditors and other users of financial information to assess cash flow prospects from the entity to them.

In *SFAC No. 5*, the FASB indicates that the amount and variety of information that financial reporting should provide about an entity requires several financial statements. Specifically, a full set of financial statements should show the following:

1. Financial position at the end of the period.
2. Earnings (net income) for the period.
3. Comprehensive income (total nonowner changes in equity) for the period.
4. *Cash flows for the period.*
5. Investments by and distributions to owners during the period.[5]

---

[1]*FASB Statement of Financial Accounting Concepts No. 1*, "Objectives of Financial Reporting by Business Enterprises," 1978, par. 34.
[2]*SFAC No. 1*, par. 37.
[3]*SFAC No. 1*, par. 41.
[4]*SFAC No. 1*, par. 37.
[5]*Statement of Financial Accounting Concepts No. 5*, "Recognition and Measurement in Financial Statements of Business Enterprises," 1984, par. 13.

Earlier we stated that the FASB's concepts statements, which constitute the conceptual framework for financial reporting, is partially normative in that it does not necessarily describe specific accounting practices at the time the concept statements were issued. Subsequent to *Statements of Financial Accounting Concepts Nos. 1* and *5*, which have been cited above, the FASB issued *Statement of Financial Accounting Standards No. 95*, "Statement of Cash Flows."[6] This pronouncement established the statement of cash flows as a requirement, thereby bringing accounting practice into closer conformity with the conceptual framework. Much of this chapter is based on this important and recent authoritative accounting pronouncement.

Before we consider more carefully the specific objectives and reporting requirements of the statement of cash flows, let's refresh our memory of the basic structure of the statement. Exhibit 22–1 repeats the statement of cash flows from the review of

EXHIBIT 22–1

Sunrise Corporation
STATEMENT OF CASH FLOWS
For the Year Ended December 31, 1993

Indirect

Cash Flows from Operating Activities		
Cash received from customers	$538,700	
Interest received	2,100	
Dividends received	5,200	
Rent received	8,400	
Cash provided by operating activities		$554,400
Cash paid to suppliers and employees	455,900	
Interest paid	14,200	
Taxes paid	47,300	
Cash disbursed for operating activities		517,400
Net cash flow from operating activities		37,000
Cash Flows from Investing Activities		
Short-term loans made	(18,000)	
Collections on short-term loans	8,000	
Purchases of long-term investments	(14,000)	
Proceeds from sale of long-term investments	10,900	
Purchases of property, plant and equipment	(38,800)	
Proceeds from disposals of property, plant, and equipment	76,400	
Net cash provided by investing activities		24,500
Cash Flows from Financing Activities		
Proceeds of short-term debt	23,000	
Payments to settle short-term debt	(25,000)	
Proceeds of long-term debt	50,000	
Payments to settle long-term note	(110,000)	
Proceeds from issuing common stock	55,000	
Dividends paid	(16,000)	
Net cash used by financing activities		(23,000)
Net increase in cash and cash equivalents		38,500
Cash and cash equivalents, Jan. 1, 1993		24,000
Cash and cash equivalents, Dec. 31, 1993		$ 62,500

---

[6]*Statement of Financial Accounting Standards No. 95*, "Statement of Cash Flows," 1987.

financial statements in Chapter 4. Notice that it is prepared in three major sections: cash flows from operating, investing, and financing activities. Also, at the bottom of the statement the change in cash is used to reconcile the beginning and ending cash balances for the period. This example is simplified in several ways, including the fact that it does not present all of the required disclosures that must accompany a statement of cash flows in conformity with *SFAS No. 95*. We shall consider those details in greater depth later in this chapter.

The primary purpose of the statement of cash flows is stated very simply in *SFAS No. 95* — to provide relevant information about the cash receipts and payments of an enterprise during a period of time. The information included in the statement, when used in conjunction with related disclosures and information in the other financial statements, should help investors, creditors and others to

1. Assess the enterprise's ability to generate positive future net cash flows;
2. Assess the enterprise's ability to meet its obligations and pay dividends and its needs for external financing;
3. Assess the reasons for differences between net income and associated cash receipts and payments; and
4. Assess the effects on the enterprise's financial position of its investing and financing transactions during the period.[7]

Keep in mind as we study the statement of cash flows that it is designed to report a process that is continuously taking place in a business enterprise. Cash is continuously flowing through operating, financing, and investing activities. Although we tie the reporting of this process to the cash balance at a point in time (i.e., the end of the accounting period), the major thrust of the statement is to explain a continuous flow of transactions over time within the enterprise. The statement of cash flows is closely tied to the other major financial statements, but it presents information prepared on a cash, rather than an accrual, basis. It should be viewed as presenting equally important, instead of competing, information when compared with that presented in the other major financial statements.

HISTORICAL DEVELOPMENT OF THE STATEMENT OF CASH FLOWS

For many years the income statement, the balance sheet, and the retained earnings statement constituted a complete set of financial statements when accompanied by disclosures in the form of notes and supplementary schedules. "Funds flow" information was primarily a tool of financial statement users to assist them in understanding how an enterprise's balance sheet changed between two points in time. Recognizing that important information is not disclosed when only these three statements are presented, the American Institute of Certified Public Accountants (AICPA) published *Accounting Research Study No. 2* in 1961.[8] This research study explored many of the financial reporting issues that led to the requirement of a statement of changes in financial position and later a statement of cash flows. That study was followed in 1963 by *Accounting Principles Board Opinion No. 3*, which discussed the need for a statement to complete the disclosure of changes in financial position and encouraged publication of such a "funds" statement.[9] This voluntary disclosure gained popularity between 1963 and 1971, when the Accounting Principles Board (APB) issued *Opin-*

---

[7]*SFAS No. 95*, pars. 4–5.
[8]Perry Mason, *Accounting Research Study No. 2*, "Cash Flow Analysis and the Funds Statement" (New York: AICPA, 1961).
[9]*APB Opinion No. 3*, "The Statement of Sources and Application of Funds," 1963.

Disclosure   *ion No. 19,* which *required* that a financial statement be presented to fill the disclosure gap existing when only a balance sheet, income statement, and statement of retained earnings are presented.[10] The suggested title of the statement was "Statement of Changes in Financial Position."

In the late 1970s and early 1980s a great deal of interest emerged about the statement of changes in financial position. This interest centered on the importance of funds-flow information to users of the financial statements and the concern that attempting to provide funds-flow information *and* describe all changes in financial position in the same financial statement might reduce the clarity and usefulness of the information. Concern was also expressed about the comparability of statements of changes in financial position due to the different definitions of the term "funds." Some companies prepared statements that reported changes in cash while others reported changes in working capital, net "quick" assets, or cash and short-term investments.

In a 1980 *Discussion Memorandum* the FASB emphasized the importance of information concerning cash flows, liquidity, and financial flexibility. The memorandum was prepared to serve as a basis for the discussion of these types of information in anticipation of changing reporting requirements. The importance of information on cash flows, liquidity, and financial flexibility is summarized in statements from the 1980 *Discussion Memorandum:*

Funds Flows

Information about past cash flows or other funds flows may help users of financial statements improve their understanding of the activities of an enterprise, understand the effects on funds flows of income-generating activities, and evaluate the investing and financing activities of an enterprise. In those and other ways the information may be used as a basis for making assessments of future cash flows associated with operating, investing and financing activities.

Liquidity

Liquidity is an indication of the "nearness to cash" of the assets and liabilities of an enterprise. Nearness to cash can be regarded as the time that must elapse before assets and liabilities result in cash receipts and payments through normal operations. Information about liquidity may help to identify the relationship between income-generating activities and the related receipts and payments of cash. It also may help to identify the pay-back period on investments in operating assets. A short pay-back period may indicate a high level of financial flexibility.

Financial Flexibility

Financial flexibility is the capacity to adapt to favorable and unfavorable changes in operating conditions. For example, financial flexibility may enable an enterprise to undertake a new investment or to introduce a new product line. Equity investors may be particularly interested in this aspect of financial flexibility. When change has an adverse effect, financial flexibility may be critical to the survival of an enterprise. Declining funds flows from operations and reduced liquidity may signal an impending cash flow problem. The solvency of an enterprise may depend on its financial flexibility. . . . Sources of financial flexibility include the ability to generate additional cash flows by

---

[10]*APB Opinion No. 19,* "Reporting Changes in Financial Position," 1971, par. 7.

*financing, by liquidating assets, and by modifying operations. Informa-
tion about past funds flows and the liquidity of assets and liabilities
may be useful in assessing financial flexibility.*[11]

The lack of comparability among the financial statements of various companies, concern about the basic purpose of the statement of changes in financial position, and increased recognition of the importance of cash flow information led the Financial Accounting Standards Board (FASB) to issue *Statement of Financial Accounting Standards No. 95,* "Statement of Cash Flows," in 1987. This statement replaced *APB Opinion No. 19* and requires a statement of cash flows.

While the statement of cash flows may be viewed as the result of the evolutionary process just described, it represents a significant change from past financial reporting practices. It shifts the focus from information prepared on an accrual basis, as found in the other major financial statements, to information prepared on a cash basis. It also takes an important step away from the disclosure objective of the previous statement of changes in financial position as a means of reconciling all balance sheet changes. Finally, it significantly narrows areas of difference in practice by establishing specific reporting requirements and carefully defining operating, investing, and financing cash flow categories.

Disclosure

In the opinion of the authors, the renewed emphasis on cash flow reporting represents one of the most exciting and constructive developments in the accounting profession in many decades. In the past, an extreme emphasis on accrual accounting has limited efforts to improve the quality of financial reporting. We view the renewed emphasis on cash flow information *in conjunction with accrual accounting information* as a positive move that will enhance the presentation of information that is useful to investors, creditors, and other users in making economic decisions.

THE STATEMENT OF CASH FLOWS

Businesses continuously convert assets into goods and services or into other assets and obligations. In a simplified situation, this conversion process can be viewed as a series of short-term conversions and a series of long-term conversions. In the short-term conversion cycle, cash is converted into inventory that is subsequently converted into receivables and then back into cash. Typically, several of these cycles take place during a single reporting period. The long-term conversion cycle involves investments of cash in machinery, equipment, furniture, fixtures, buildings, land, and other operating assets. These assets contribute to the operations of the enterprise over several accounting periods, but they subsequently are converted back into cash through successful generation of goods and services that are provided for customers. These long-lived assets may eventually be sold for cash when they are no longer useful to the company, but the amounts may be nominal. Both cycles are continuous, and at any point in time the enterprise will be involved in several short- and long-term cycles simultaneously. Financing these short- and long-term cycles may involve external debt and equity in addition to the use of cash provided by operations.

Exhibit 22–2 demonstrates the major categories of transactions that affect the amount of cash held by a company. Many decisions are made by business enterprises on the basis of availability of cash. For example, credit policies and dividend distributions are influenced by the availability of cash. Thus, in attempting to judge prospective cash flows, investors and creditors are particularly interested in the impact

---

[11]*FASB Discussion Memorandum,* "Reporting Funds Flow, Liquidity, and Financial Flexibility," 1980, pp. 2, 4.

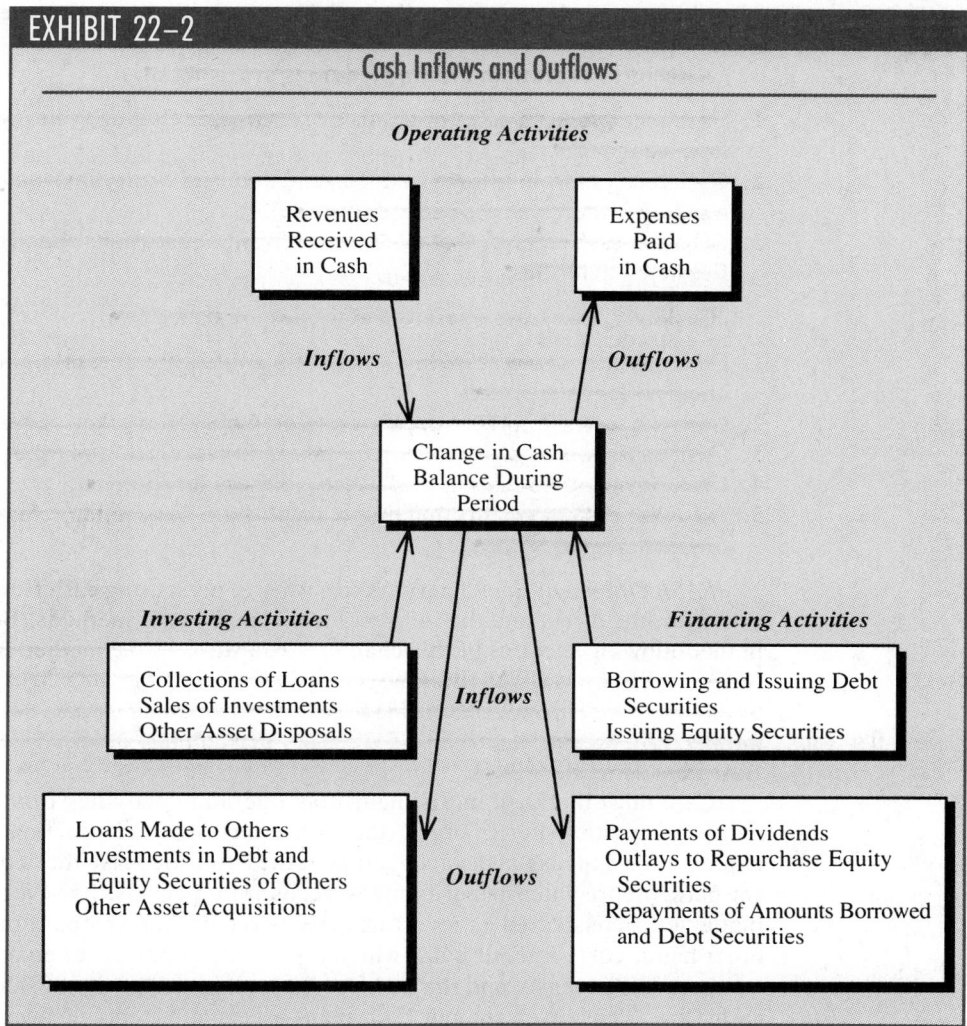

EXHIBIT 22-2

Cash Inflows and Outflows

Operating Activities

Revenues Received in Cash

Expenses Paid in Cash

Inflows

Outflows

Change in Cash Balance During Period

Investing Activities

Financing Activities

Collections of Loans
Sales of Investments
Other Asset Disposals

Borrowing and Issuing Debt
　Securities
Issuing Equity Securities

Inflows

Loans Made to Others
Investments in Debt and
　Equity Securities of Others
Other Asset Acquisitions

Outflows

Payments of Dividends
Outlays to Repurchase Equity
　Securities
Repayments of Amounts Borrowed
　and Debt Securities

of financing and investing activities on the flow of cash in and out of the business enterprise.

In *SFAS No. 95*, the FASB established the categories of operating, investing, and financing activities for presentation of cash flows. This presentation was used in Exhibit 22–1 and is also the basis for describing the types of cash flows in Exhibit 22–2. In the paragraphs that follow, we explore each of these major categories in greater depth and introduce several other reporting requirements of *SFAS No. 95*.

OPERATING ACTIVITIES

All transactions affecting cash that are **not considered investing or financing activities** are included in the operating activities category of the statement of cash flows. Generally, these transactions represent the cash flow effects of transactions affecting net income. Another way of looking at the types of transactions classified as operating activities is to think of them as revenues collected in cash and expenses paid in cash. While the terms "revenues" and "expenses" should be used only when describing accrual accounting, the cash flow equivalents of those items typically represent operating activities in the statement of cash flows.

Cash inflows from operating activities are as follows:

1. Cash receipts from sales of goods or services, including collections of receivables from customers.
2. Cash receipts from returns on loans and debt and equity instruments of other entities (e.g., interest and dividend revenue).
3. All other cash receipts that do not result from transactions classified as investing or financing activities.

Cash outflows from operating activities are as follows:

1. Cash payments to acquire materials for manufacture or resale, including payments on payables to suppliers.
2. Cash payments to other suppliers and employees for other goods or services.
3. Cash payments to governments for taxes, duties, fines, and other fees or penalties.
4. Cash payments to lenders and other creditors for interest.
5. All other cash payments that do not result from transactions classified as investing or financing activities.[12]

FASB Statement No. 95 permits two ways of presenting cash flows from operating activities, the direct and the indirect (or reconciliation) methods. Both are discussed in the following sections of this chapter. Regardless of the method of presenting cash flows from operating activities, a *schedule reconciling net income to net cash provided by or used in operating activities* is required. Also, *interest paid* (net of amounts capi-

Disclosure   talized) and *income taxes paid* during the period *must be disclosed* in the financial statement or related notes.

Care must be taken in distinguishing operating activities from investing and financing activities. For example, the cash effect of the transaction that gives rise to depreciation expense is the acquisition of the asset. Because the acquisition of the asset being depreciated benefits many accounting periods, however, the purchase of that asset is considered an investing activity rather than an operating activity. On the other hand, cost of goods sold, which represents goods acquired and disposed of, is an operating expense, and the cash purchase of inventory is considered an operating cash flow. Thus, even though both plant assets and items of inventory may be acquired and paid for during one period and be charged to expense in a future period or periods, the acquisition of plant assets is considered an investing activity, while the acquisition of inventory is considered an operating activity. Different reporting treatments are required even though the economic phenomena they represent are somewhat similar. The key to understanding this distinction is that inventory is acquired to be sold while plant assets are acquired as an investment to be used internally by the company for a relatively long period of time.

Notice that operating activities include interest paid to creditors or received from borrowers—and dividends received from companies in whose stock the reporting entity has invested. Refer once more to Exhibit 22–1 and study the operating activities category of the Sunrise Corporation's statement of cash flows. Notice that the company reports a positive net cash flow from operating activities of $37,000. That amount compares to the net income of $74,400 reported by Sunrise for the same period. (The income statement of Sunrise Corporation is presented in Chapter 4 in Exhibits 4–1 and 4–2.) Remember that while both numbers are important, they address different economic phenomena and the differences between the two can be sub-

---

[12]*FASB Statement of Financial Accounting Standards No. 95*, pars. 22–23.

stantial. The principal reasons for the difference can be determined by a careful analysis of the income statement and the statement of cash flows.

INVESTING ACTIVITIES

The investing activities of a company are presented in a separate category of the statement of cash flows following operating activities. These activities focus on asset transactions and involve cash inflows and outflows resulting from those transactions. Cash inflows from investing activities are as follows:

1. Receipts from collections or sales of loans made by the enterprise and of other entities' debt instruments that were purchased by the enterprise.
2. Receipts from sales of equity instruments of other enterprises and from returns of investments in those instruments.
3. Receipts from sales of property, plant, and equipment and other productive assets.

Cash outflows from investing activities are described in the following categories:

1. Disbursements for loans made by the enterprise and payments to acquire debt instruments of other entities.
2. Payments to acquire equity instruments of other enterprises.
3. Payments to acquire property, plant, and equipment and other productive assets.[13]

When a company pays cash for a plant asset, that transaction is reported as a use of cash in the investing activities category of the statement of cash flows. Similarly, when that asset is later sold in a used condition, the amount of cash received is reported as a source of cash from investing activities. Remember, any gain or loss on the disposal of the asset is reported in the income statement. The actual proceeds from the disposal are reported in the investing activities category of the statement of cash flows, and any gain or loss on the sale is removed from net income in the operating section of the statement (discussed below). If a company makes a loan to another company, including the purchase of that other company's debt securities, the money lent is reported as a use of cash in the investing activities category of the statement of cash flows. When the loan is collected, cash received (other than interest) is reported as a source of cash in the investing activities category of the statement.

Dividends received in cash from investments in equity securities of another company—and cash collected as interest revenue on loans made to another company—are **not** considered investing activities. Rather, amounts received as dividend revenue or collected as interest revenue are reported in the operating activities category of the statement of cash flows.

At this time you may wish to refer back to Exhibit 22–1 and review the presentation of the investing activities category for Sunrise Corporation. Notice that Sunrise made short-term loans and collected amounts on those types of loans, purchased long-term investments and sold some of them, and purchased and disposed of certain items of plant assets. The net cash provided by all of these activities was $24,500. Notice that in the investing activities category, both increases and decreases in cash from the various types of transactions are reported.

FINANCING ACTIVITIES

Cash flow effects of financing activities should be presented in a separate category of the statement of cash flows, much as are investing activities. Cash inflows from financing activities are as follows:

---

[13]*FASB Statement of Financial Accounting Standards No. 95*, pars. 16–17.

1. Proceeds from issuing equity instruments.
2. Proceeds from issuing bonds, mortgages, notes, and other short-term or long-term borrowings.

Cash outflows from financing activities are as follows:

1. Payments of dividends or other distributions to owners, including outlays to reacquire the enterprise's equity instruments (e.g., purchases of treasury stock).
2. Repayments of amounts borrowed.
3. Other principal payments to creditors who have extended long-term credit (e.g., seller-financed debt related to the purchase of plant assets).[14]

Notice that while interest paid to creditors is not considered to be a financing activity of the company, dividends paid to equity investors are. The difference in treatment here is related to the basic concept discussed in Chapter 20—that dividends are a *distribution* of net income, while the interest cost of borrowed funds is a *determinant* of income. Therefore, interest costs paid in cash are defined as part of operating activities rather than as a financing activity based primarily on the fact that interest expense is a determinant of net income.

Another review of Exhibit 22–1 shows that Sunrise Corporation reports a net negative cash flow of $23,000 as a result of financing activities taking place during the year. Observe that Sunrise obtained cash from short-term borrowing and also made payments to settle short-term debts. In addition, the company repaid a rather large long-term loan ($110,000) but also borrowed additional amounts by issuing new long term debt ($50,000). The company also issued common stock in the amount of $55,000. The payment of dividends of $16,000 also contributed to the net use of cash reported in the financing activities category of the statement.

CASH AND CASH EQUIVALENTS

The FASB indicates that when presenting cash flow information, the term "cash" should actually be interpreted as "cash and cash equivalents." **Cash equivalents** are short-term, highly liquid investments having the following characteristics:

1. They are readily convertible to known amounts of cash.
2. They are so near their maturity that they present insignificant risk of changes in value because of changes in interest rates.

Examples of securities that meet these criteria are Treasury bills, commercial paper, money market funds, and similar investments whose original maturities are three months or less. Longer-term securities that are purchased within 90 days of their maturity also qualify as cash equivalents. Transactions involving the purchase and sale of these securities are generally considered part of the enterprise's cash management activities rather than part of its operating, investing, and financing activities.

Not all investments that meet the above criteria are required to be treated as cash equivalents in the preparation of the statement of cash flows. The enterprise must establish a policy concerning short-term, highly liquid investments and treat them

Consistency   consistently as either cash equivalents or part of the enterprise's investing activities. Any change in that policy is a change in accounting principle that requires restatement of financial statements of previous years presented for comparative purposes.[15]

---

[14]*FASB Statement of Financial Accounting Standards No. 95*, pars. 19–20.
[15]*FASB Statement of Financial Accounting Standards No. 95*, pars 8–10.

NONCASH TRANSACTIONS

Disclosure

Certain financing and investing activities do not involve the payment or receipt of cash. Even though these transactions do not affect cash flows directly, their disclosure is necessary to provide supplemental information about all financing and investing activities. An example of such transactions is financing the acquisition of a plant asset, directly from the seller rather than from an external source, such as a bank. The acquisition of the asset is an investing activity and the loan from the seller is a financing activity. Transactions such as these are disclosed in a separate schedule accompanying the statement of cash flows. Other examples of transactions that require disclosure are the conversion of debt securities into common stock and the issuance of stock in exchange for plant assets. While the FASB does not specifically require the disclosure of stock dividends and stock splits, the authors suggest that their disclosure as noncash activities is desirable.

PREPARING THE STATEMENT OF CASH FLOWS: A SIMPLIFIED EXAMPLE

Preparing the statement of cash flows involves three basic steps:

1. Determine the net change in cash by comparing the beginning and ending amounts of cash.
2. Identify all transactions that resulted in increases or decreases in cash and all noncash financing and investing activities.
3. Use the information from steps 1 and 2 to prepare a formal financial statement that conforms with the presentation and disclosure requirements of the FASB.

Information to complete these steps is found in the other basic financial statements and in the underlying accounting records of the reporting enterprise. Because this information is accumulated primarily for purposes of preparing balance sheets and income statements on an accrual basis, adjustments may be necessary to prepare the information needed for the statement of cash flows. In a sense we begin with the ending balance sheet and work backwards to determine the causes of the changes in cash during the period.

To illustrate the preparation of a simplified statement of cash flows, we assume that Hamilton Company has prepared comparative balance sheets and a condensed income statement for 1992 and 1993 along with selected additional information, all as presented in Exhibit 22–3. The following paragraphs apply the three steps identified earlier to produce the required statement of cash flows.

DETERMINATION OF THE CHANGE IN CASH

We determine the change in cash by comparing the 1993 cash balance of $50,000 with the $100,000 balance for 1992. Cash decreased $50,000, so cash paid out must have exceeded cash received by $50,000. The decline in cash of $50,000 provides an important check figure as we identify the underlying causes of the net change.

TRANSACTION ANALYSIS

Next we analyze the changes in all balance sheet accounts other than cash to determine the causes of the changes in cash. Exhibit 22–4 illustrates one way to identify the individual changes that in the aggregate caused cash to decline by $50,000. This approach involves a simple worksheet that analyzes the change in each account in terms of its impact on the three categories of activities presented in the statement of

EXHIBIT 22-3

Financial Information for Hamilton Company

Hamilton Company
COMPARATIVE BALANCE SHEETS
December 31, 1992 and 1993
(in thousands of dollars)

	1992	1993
Assets		
Cash	$ 100	$ 50
Accounts receivable	400	300
Plant assets	1,000	1,700
Accumulated depreciation	(100)	(200)
	$1,400	$1,850
Equities		
Accrued expenses	$ 150	$ 200
Bonds payable	650	800
Capital stock	500	600
Retained earnings	100	250
	$1,400	$1,850

Hamilton Company
INCOME STATEMENT
For the Year Ended December 31, 1993
(in thousands of dollars)

Revenue		$1,500
Expenses		
Depreciation	$ 100	
Other	1,100	1,200
Net income		$ 300

Additional Information

Capital stock was sold at par value for $100,000.

Bonds of $100,000 were retired, and $250,000 of new bonds were issued.

Machinery of $800,000 was acquired.

Land with a book value of $100,000 was sold for $100,000.

Cash dividends of $150,000 were declared and paid.

cash flows. An alternative approach, which some people prefer, is identified as the T-Account approach and is presented for the Hamilton Company in Appendix A.

First, we shall consider current assets and current liabilities other than cash. The $100,000 decrease in accounts receivable is shown as a positive adjustment to operating activities (revenues) as a source of cash. To understand this treatment, we must look beyond the balance sheet account and consider the income statement implications of that account. Accounts receivable are tied directly to sales when they increase and to cash when they decrease. If accounts receivable decreased during the period ($100,000 in this case), the cash received on accounts exceeds the amount of sales included in the income statement by that amount. We must add $100,000 to revenues in determining cash provided by selling activities to include the collection of cash on accounts that were recognized from sales in a previous accounting period. Here we see a fundamental difference between information prepared on an accrual basis and a cash flow basis.

The $50,000 increase in accrued expenses requires a similar analysis. If accrued expenses increased during the period ($50,000 in this case), the cash paid for expenses is less than the amount of expenses recognized in the income statement. Again we see a difference between accrual and cash flow information. The increase in accrued expenses requires a subtraction from expenses (addition to net income) to determine cash used in operating activities.

We now turn our attention to the analysis of nonworking capital accounts that changed during the period. The changes in plant assets, bonds payable, and capital stock accounts indicate that investing and financing transactions have taken place during the year.

Capital stock was sold for $100,000 (an increase in cash) which we know from the additional information and can check by computing the change in the Capital Stock account balance from $500,000 to $600,000. In a like manner, we also know and can check that the company issued bonds payable in the amount of $250,000 (a cash increase) and retired bonds payable in the amount of $100,000 (a cash decrease). Cash was paid out for dividends of $150,000. These transactions are financing activities that, in the aggregate, provided cash of $350,000 ($100,000 + $250,000) and used cash of $250,000 ($100,000 + $150,000).

We also know from the additional information that the company paid $800,000 to acquire machinery (a cash decrease) and sold land for $100,000 (a cash increase) during the year. These transactions are investing activities, identified as such in Exhibit 22–4.

The change in the accumulated depreciation account and the related amount of depreciation expense during the year do not affect cash and, therefore, do not affect the cash flows from operating activities. Recall, however, that depreciation expense has been deducted in determining net income. We complete the worksheet in Exhibit 22–4 by adjusting the change in accumulated depreciation against depreciation

EXHIBIT 22–4

Hamilton Company
Cash Analysis by Worksheet
(in thousands of dollars)

	Trial Balance		Increase (Decrease)	Cash Increase (Decrease)	Sources and (Uses) of Cash		
	1992	1993			Operating	Investing	Financing
Assets							
Cash	$ 100	$ 50	$ (50)	$(50)	—	—	—
Accounts receivable	400	300	(100)		$100		
Plant assets	1,000	1,700	700[a]			$ 100	
						(800)	
Accumulated depreciation	(100)	(200)	100		100		
	$1,400	$1,850					
Equities							
Accrued expenses	$ 150	$ 200	50		50		
Bonds payable	650	800	150[b]				(100)
							250
Capital stock	500	600	100				100
Retained earnings	100	250	150		300		(150)
	$1,400	$1,850					
Decrease in cash				$ (50) =	$550	(700)	100

[a]Offsetting investing transactions: acquisition of machinery ($800 decrease in cash), less sale of land ($100 increase in cash).
[b]Offsetting financing transactions: sale of bonds ($250 increase in cash), less retirement of bonds ($100 decrease in cash).

expense, effectively removing that expense as a reduction from revenues in computing cash from operations. Also, net income (the excess of revenues over expenses) is carried over into the operating column to complete our analysis of the change in retained earnings. In determining cash from operating activities, net income will be adjusted for the other operating source and use amounts—decrease in receivables, increase in accrued expenses and depreciation expense—all of which represent differences between accrual accounting amounts and the cash-flow consequences of the same items.

PREPARATION OF THE STATEMENT OF CASH FLOWS

Our statement of cash flows is presented in Exhibit 22–5. Notice that the statement is presented in the three required sections. Operating activities provided $550,000 in cash, which differs substantially from the reported net income of $300,000 as explained in the reconciliation at the bottom of the statement; Investing activities used $700,000; financing activities provided $100,000. Disclosure is not presented for noncash transactions, interest paid, or income taxes paid because we have no information concerning these activities.

EXHIBIT 22–5

Hamilton Company
STATEMENT OF CASH FLOWS
For the Year Ended December 31, 1993
(amounts in thousands)

Cash Flows from Operating Activities		
Cash received from customers	$1,600	
Cash disbursed for operating activities	1,050	
Net Cash provided by operating activities		550
Cash Flows from Investing Activities		
Purchases of plant assets	(800)	
Proceeds from sale of land	100	
Net cash used by investing activities		(700)
Cash Flows from Financing Activities		
Proceeds of bond issuance	250	
Payments to retire bonds	(100)	
Proceeds from issuing capital stock	100	
Dividends paid	(150)	
Net cash provided by financing activities		100
Net decrease in cash		$ (50)
Cash, January 1, 1993		100
Cash, December 31, 1993		$ 50
Reconciliation of net income to net cash provided by operating activities:		
Net income		$ 300
Adjustments to reconcile net income to net cash provided by operating activities:		
Depreciation expense		100
Decrease in accounts receivable		100
Increase in accrued expenses		50
Net cash provided by operating activities		$ 550

The conversion of information maintained on an accrual basis to a cash basis is sometimes difficult to understand. The following analysis will help illustrate these important relationships for Hamilton Company's 1993 financial statements.

	Accrual Amounts	Accrual-to-Cash Adjustments	Cash Flows
Revenues	$1,500	+ $100*	$1,600
Expenses			
Depreciation	100	− 100**	–0–
Other	1,100	− 50†	1,050
	1,200	− $150	1,050
Net income	$ 300		
Cash flows from operating activities			$ 550

*Increased positive cash flows from collection of receivables.
**Reduced negative cash flows from depreciation expense.
†Reduced negative cash flows from increase in accrued expenses.

COMPREHENSIVE ILLUSTRATION: STATEMENT OF CASH FLOWS

This section provides a comprehensive illustration of the preparation of the statement of cash flows in a relatively complex situation. Several items not covered in the previous example of the Hamilton Company are included. Financial-statement information for Hudson, Inc., presented in Exhibit 22–6 for 1992 and 1993, includes balance sheets for both years, an income statement for 1993, and additional information required to prepare the statement of cash flows.

In some situations, the analysis of transactions becomes quite complicated. This is particularly true in cases, such as Hudson, Inc., that include extraordinary items, deferred income taxes, bond discounts and premiums, and gains and losses on the sales of assets. A useful tool for accumulating the necessary information for the statement of cash flows is a four-column worksheet, which we use in this section. The worksheet is used here primarily as a device for learning the material. It may also be used in solving some of the more comprehensive problems at the end of the chapter, or for preparing a statement of cash flows in relatively complex situations in practice.

DETERMINATION OF THE CHANGE IN CASH

The comparative balance sheets for 1992 and 1993 for Hudson, Inc., reveal that cash decreased by $2,600 during 1993 ($70,000 − $67,400). This **net change** is caused by many operating, investing, and financing activities. The statement of cash flows that we will prepare in this section separates those changes into the three basic categories and presents the cash inflows and outflows from each. We know in advance, however, that the increases in cash from all activities must be less than the decreases by $2,600.

TRANSACTION ANALYSIS

The worksheet for Hudson's 1993 statement of cash flows is presented in Exhibit 22–7. The purposes of this worksheet are (1) to identify the specific operating, investing, and financing cash flows that took place during the year, and (2) to identify any noncash financing and investing activities that require disclosure. The worksheet is simply a device to facilitate the accumulation of information needed to prepare the statement of cash flows. Entries made on the worksheet are **not recorded** in the

EXHIBIT 22–6

Financial Information for Hudson, Inc.

Hudson, Inc.
COMPARATIVE BALANCE SHEETS
December 31, 1992 and 1993

	1993	1992
Assets		
Cash	*(2600)* $ 67,400	$ 70,000
Accounts receivable, net	*(5000)* 60,000	65,000
Inventory	*√32600* 94,600	62,000
Total current assets	222,000	197,000
Property, plant, and equipment	*(10000)* 190,000	200,000
Accumulated depreciation	*√3000* (33,000)	(30,000)
Patents	*√(1000)* 9,000	10,000
Total noncurrent assets	166,000	180,000
Total assets	$388,000	$377,000
Liabilities	*√7000*	
Dividends payable	$ 17,000	$ 10,000
Accounts payable *- relate to COGS*	*(14700)* 35,300	50,000
Income taxes payable	*(2000)* 40,000	42,000
Notes payable *- LT, Financing*	–0–	20,000
Total current liabilities	92,300	122,000
Deferred income taxes *- Oper. Activity*	*1400 √* 11,400	10,000
Convertible bonds payable	60,000	100,000
Unamortized bond discount	*(4700)* (5,300)	(10,000)
Total noncurrent liabilities	66,100	100,000
Stockholders' Equity		
Preferred stock	10,000	10,000
Common stock	75,000	60,000
Additional paid-in capital	18,000	15,000
Retained earnings	*(56600)* 126,600	70,000
Total stockholders' equity	229,600	155,000
Total liabilities and stockholders' equity	$388,000	$377,000

[Handwritten margin annotations:]
Operating Activity (brackets Cash, Accounts receivable, Inventory)
Investing (brackets Property, plant, and equipment; Accumulated depreciation; Patents)
Financing / Operating (brackets Dividends payable, Accounts payable, Income taxes payable, Notes payable)
Financing (brackets Convertible bonds payable, Unamortized bond discount)
Financing (brackets Stockholders' Equity section)

Notes Payable - to be Act, considered for Oper. Act, have to be directly tied to Operations (such as borrowing to buy inventory)

company's formal accounting records. That is, they are neither journalized nor posted to ledger accounts.

The worksheet in Exhibit 22–7 is organized as follows:

1. The extreme left and right columns are trial balances of the real (balance sheet) accounts as of the beginning of the period (left) and the end of the period (right).
2. Debit and credit columns are placed in the center columns and are used to enter transactions and changes that took place during the accounting period.
3. The nominal (income statement) accounts are listed below the real accounts in the middle two columns with the amount of net income flowing into retained earnings (see arrow).

Hudson, Inc.
STATEMENT OF INCOME
For the Year Ended December 31, 1993

Revenues		$1,200,000
Expenses		
Cost of goods sold	$500,000	
Selling expenses	300,000	
General and administrative expenses	250,000	
Interest expense	40,000	1,090,000
Income before income tax		110,000
Income tax expense		
Current	38,200	
Deferred	1,400	39,600
Income before extraordinary item		70,400
Extraordinary gain—retirement of		
long-term debt, net of $1,800		
applicable income tax		3,200
Net income		$ 73,600

Handwritten annotations: From AR; +5000 = 120,5000; +32600+14700 = 547300; 295000; 243000; 39200; −2000−3000 =; −6000−1000 =; 40,000 − 800; (1124500); −1400+2000 +1800; (42000); 3200+1800=5000 GAIN; 38500; payable; Current –payable

Additional Information

[1] Income before income tax includes the following items:

Depreciation expense ($2,000 in selling expenses and $6,000 in general and administrative expenses)	$8,000
Amortization of patents (included in general and administrative expenses)	1,000
Amortization of bond discount (included in interest expense)	800
Loss on sale of plant assets (included in selling expenses)	3,000

[2] Plant assets were purchased for $10,000 during 1993.

[3] Plant assets with a historical cost of $20,000 and a book value of $15,000 were sold at a $3,000 loss during 1993.

[4] Bonds with a $20,000 face value and a book value of $18,100 were retired with a cash outlay of $13,100 during 1993.

[5] Bonds with a $20,000 face value and a book value of $18,000 were converted into 1,500 shares of $10 par value common stock during 1993.

[6] Notes payable represent bank loans of short-term duration.

[7] The dividend liability of $10,000 at December 31, 1992 was paid in early 1993. Dividends of $17,000, which were declared in late 1993, are to be paid in early 1994. *(handwritten: Not paid)*

[8] Accounts payable all relate to merchandise purchased for resale.

4. At the bottom of the worksheet, the basic categories included in the statement of cash flows are identified, with space left below each:

    Operating activities   Financing activities

    Investing activities   Noncash financing and/or investing activities

5. Mechanical checks provided by the worksheet are:

    a. The trial-balance debit total must equal the trial-balance credit total; this is true for both the beginning (left) and ending (right) trial balance amounts.

    b. In the changes (middle) columns, the debit total must equal the credit total after all transactions have been identified and correctly entered on the worksheet. This is true for categories (real accounts, nominal accounts, and statement of cash flows categories) and for the two columns in total.

EXHIBIT 22–7

Hudson, Inc.
WORKSHEET FOR STATEMENT OF CASH FLOWS

Real Accounts	Balances Dec. 31, 1992	Changes Debits		Changes Credits		Balances Dec. 31, 1993
Debits						
Cash	70,000			(o)	2,600	67,400
Accounts receivable, net	65,000			(a)	5,000	60,000
Inventory	62,000	(b)	32,600			94,600
Property, plant, and equipment	200,000	(k)	10,000	(c)	20,000	190,000
Patents	10,000			(f)	1,000	9,000
Unamortized bond discount	10,000			(h)	800	
				(j)	1,900	
				(l₁)	2,000	5,300
	417,000					426,300
Credits						
Accumulated depreciation	30,000	(c)	5,000	(d)	2,000	
				(f)	6,000	33,000
Dividends payable	10,000	(m₁)	10,000	(m₃)	17,000	17,000
Accounts payable	50,000	(b)	14,700			35,300
Income taxes payable	42,000	(i)	2,000			40,000
Notes payable	20,000	(n)	20,000			–0–
Deferred income taxes	10,000			(i)	1,400	11,400
Convertible bonds payable	100,000	(j)	20,000			
		(l₁)	20,000			60,000
Preferred stock	10,000					10,000
Common stock	60,000			(l₂)	15,000	75,000
Additional paid-in capital	15,000			(l₂)	3,000	18,000
Retained earnings	70,000	(m₂)	17,000		73,600 ←	126,600
	417,000		151,300		151,300	426,300
Nominal Accounts						
Revenues				(a)	1,200,000	
Cost of goods sold		(b)	500,000			
Selling expenses		(c)	3,000			
		(d)	2,000			
		(e)	295,000			
General and administrative expenses		(f)	7,000			
		(g)	243,000			
Interest expense		(h)	40,000			
Income tax expense, before extraordinary item		(i)	39,600			
Extraordinary gain on debt extinguishment (net of tax)		(i)	1,800	(j)	5,000	
			1,131,400		1,205,000	
			73,600 ←			
			1,205,000		1,205,000	

Cash Flow Categories		Changes		
Operating Activities		Debits		Credits
Cash collected from customers	(a)	1,205,000		
Cash paid for goods to be resold			(b)	547,300
Cash paid for selling expenses			(e)	295,000
Cash paid for general and				
administrative expenses			(g)	243,000
Cash paid for interest expense			(h)	39,200
Cash paid for income taxes			(i)	42,000
Investing Activities				
Cash received from sale of property,				
plant, and equipment	(c)	12,000		
Cash paid to acquire plant assets			(k)	10,000
Financing Activities				
Cash paid to retire bonds payable			(j)	13,100
Cash paid for dividends			(m_1)	10,000
Cash paid to retire notes payable			(n)	20,000
Noncash Financing and/or Investing Activities				
Retirement of bonds by conversion			(l_1)	18,000
Issuance of common stock for bonds	(l_2)	18,000		
Declaration of dividends			(m_2)	17,000
Dividends to be paid	(m_3)	17,000		
		1,252,000		1,254,600
Decrease in cash	(o)	2,600		
		1,254,600		1,254,600

c. Each real account must "crossfoot" (i.e., the beginning balance, plus and minus changes, must equal the ending balance) after all transactions are identified and recorded.

The process by which transactions are analyzed and entered on the worksheet is illustrated in the following section by letters corresponding to the entries in the changes columns of the worksheet in Exhibit 22–7.

Operating Activities

We begin our analysis with operating activities. To identify all cash flows from operating activities, we must analyze each of the revenue and expense accounts, keeping in mind that each account increased from a zero balance at the beginning of the year to the balance that the account contained at the end of the year.

The increases in revenue and expense accounts occurring during the year are usually not explained completely by corresponding changes in cash. For example, the amount of revenue reported in the income statement of Hudson, Inc., is not necessarily equal to the amount of cash collected from customers during the period. Some sales may have been made on account and remain uncollected at the end of the year. On the other hand, some sales made in the previous year may have been collected during the current year. Some expenses may be recognized that did not require current cash payment, and some current cash payments may have been made for expenses reported earlier (e.g., accrued expenses) or later (e.g., prepaid expenses). Therefore, we must adjust the amount of individual revenue or expense accounts from an accrual basis, as presented in the income statement, to the amount of cash flowing in or out during the year. To accomplish this logically and systematically, we will analyze revenue and expense accounts in the order in which they appear on the worksheet to determine their cash flow consequences.

Revenues

(a)	Operating Activities—Cash Collected from Customers	1,205,000	
	Revenues		1,200,000
	Accounts Receivable		5,000

This worksheet entry adjusts the Revenue account for the collection of cash, as indicated by the decrease in accounts receivable, to determine cash collected from customers during the year. Hudson, Inc., reported revenue for 1993 of $1,200,000 in the income statement. However, because accounts receivable decreased by $5,000 during the year, we know that the actual cash collected from customers was greater than the revenue recognized in the income statement. Analytically, we can assume that the company collected cash equal to all of the sales made during the current year (revenue for the year), plus the amount of the decline in accounts receivable.

Cost of Goods Sold

(b)	Cost of Goods Sold	500,000	
	Inventory	32,600	
	Accounts Payable	14,700	
	Operating Activities—Cash Paid for Goods to be Resold		547,300

The amount of cost of goods sold for the year is $500,000. That amount, however, is not equal to the cash disbursed to acquire merchandise to be sold. Two other balance sheet accounts affect the cash paid during the year for goods held for resale—Inventory and Accounts Payable.

The increase in inventory indicates that cash was paid for the acquisition of inventory in a greater amount than the cost of goods sold included in net income. The increase in inventory indicates that more goods were acquired than were sold during the year. This conclusion is made independently of the change in accounts payable which we consider in the following paragraph.

The decrease in accounts payable signifies that the cost-of-goods-sold figure is less than the cash paid out for inventory purchases. In addition to the cost of goods sold, cash was also used to reduce accounts payable. This conclusion is made without regard to any change in the inventory level which we considered above and included in the worksheet entry.

Our analysis and the worksheet entry above reveals that cash disbursed to acquire items to be resold is the sum of the following: the increase in inventory ($32,600), the decrease in accounts payable ($14,700), and the cost of goods sold ($500,000). These items total $547,300.

Selling Expenses

The analysis of selling expenses is more complex because either certain transactions have caused that expense account to increase without consuming cash, or the transactions represent activities other than operating activities. We consider each of these types of transactions separately as we determine the cash consumed by selling expenses.

(c)	Investing Activities—Cash Received from Sale of		
	Property, Plant, and Equipment	12,000	
	Selling Expenses (Loss on Sale of Equipment)	3,000	
	Accumulated Depreciation	5,000	
	Property, Plant, and Equipment		20,000

This entry removes the loss recognized on the sale of equipment from the cash flows associated with the selling expenses. Recall that *sales of equipment are classified as investing activities* rather than operating activities, even though any resulting gain or loss is included in net income. Notice that entry (c) above does not make any adjustment for the income tax effects of the loss on the sale of equipment. The income tax effects of gains and losses such as this one are included in the income tax expense figure in the income statement. The FASB reasoned that all income taxes should be presented in the operating activities section of the statement of cash flows, including the income tax effects of transactions presented in the statement of cash flows as financing or investing activities. (We discuss this unique classification requirement later in this chapter when we prepare the worksheet entry for the extraordinary gain from the extinguishment of debt.)

(d)	Selling Expenses (Depreciation Expense)	2,000	
	Accumulated Depreciation		2,000

The recognition of depreciation expense does not require or provide cash. Therefore, the effects of this noncash transaction must be identified to determine cash disbursed for selling activities. Entry (d) simply identifies the noncash depreciation expense included in selling expenses and adjusts accumulated depreciation for the change.

(e)	Selling Expenses	295,000	
	Operating Activities—Cash Paid for Selling		
	Expenses		295,000

This entry establishes the amount of cash used to pay selling expenses. The amount is determined by subtracting the selling expenses that did not require cash (depreciation of $2,000) and the loss on the sale of equipment ($3,000) from the total selling expenses. The difference represents those selling expenses that required the use of cash.

General and Administrative Expenses

General and administrative expenses, like selling expenses, contain noncash components, and we must identify the amounts of those items before we can determine the cash consumed in paying the expenses. From the additional information, we find that there are two types of noncash expenses included in general and administrative expenses: depreciation of plant assets and amortization of patents.

(f)	General and Administrative Expenses	7,000	
	Patents		1,000
	Accumulated Depreciation		6,000

This entry is similar to (d) above and represents the noncash expenses included in general and administrative expenses. We may conclude that the remaining amount of general and administrative expenses required the disbursement of cash because there is nothing in the additional information that indicates otherwise.

(g) General and Administrative Expenses	243,000	
Operating Activities—Cash Paid for General and		
Administrative Expenses		243,000

This entry establishes the amount of general and administrative expenses that required the payment of cash. This amount is determined by subtracting the expenses that did not require cash from the total general and administrative expenses: $250,000 - $7,000 = $243,000.

Interest Expense

(h) Interest Expense	40,000	
Unamortized Bond Discount		800
Operating Activities—Cash Paid for Interest		
Expense		39,200

The next account appearing in the income statement is Interest Expense. If bonds are sold at a discount or premium, the interest expense for the period is not the same as the amount of cash paid for interest costs. If a *discount* is being amortized, interest expense exceeds interest paid and the worksheet entry must recognize the amortization to determine the amount of cash actually paid. The preceding worksheet entry therefore includes a credit to Unamortized Bond Discount, the appropriate balance sheet account. As in the case of depreciation and amortization recognized in previous entries, the amortization of bond discount does not require the use of cash. Rather, the discount amortized is an adjustment to the amount of cash paid for interest.

If a premium were being amortized, the interest expense included in the determination of net income is not as large as the interest paid during the period. In that case, the worksheet entry would reveal that the amount of cash paid for interest *exceeds* interest expense. The following *pro forma* worksheet entry shows how amortization of a premium would be handled:

Interest Expense	XXX	
Unamortized Bond Premium	XXX	
Operating Activities—Cash Paid for Interest Expense		XXX

The credit to Operating Activities—Cash Paid for Interest Expense is the sum of the interest expense and the premium amortized for the period.

Income Tax Expense

(i) Income Tax Expense	39,600	
Extraordinary gain on debt extinguishment	1,800	
Income Taxes Payable	2,000	
Operating Activities—Cash Paid for Income Taxes		42,000
Deferred Income Taxes		1,400

The next account appearing in the income statement section of the trial balances is Income Tax Expense. Four accounts affect the amount of cash paid for income taxes: Income Tax Expense, the extraordinary gain on debt extinguishment, Income Taxes Payable, and Deferred Income Taxes. The changes in Deferred Income Taxes and Income Taxes Payable cause the amount of income tax expense to differ from the amount of cash paid for income taxes during the current period. We will consider the changes in Deferred Income Taxes and Income Taxes Payable independently in the following paragraphs.

The decrease in the Income Taxes Payable account indicates that more cash was paid for income taxes than the income tax expense included in determining net income. Thus, cash used to pay income taxes is more than the combined $39,600 of income tax expense and $1,800 of tax on the extraordinary gain.

The change in the Deferred Income Taxes account also operates in a similar fashion. Because that account increased, we conclude that tax expense is *more than* the amount paid to taxing authorities in the amount of $1,400. Temporary differences cause the Deferred Income Taxes account to increase by $1,400.

For Hudson in 1993, the actual cash paid for income taxes was $42,000, detailed as follows:

Income tax expense	$39,600
Income tax on extraordinary gain	1,800
Reduction in income tax payable	2,000
Increase in deferred income taxes	(1,400)
	$42,000

Extraordinary Gain on Debt Extinguishment

The extraordinary gain on the debt extinguishment, although included in the determination of net income, is excluded from the operating activities category of the statement of cash flows. Rather, the amount of cash paid to retire the bonds is reported in the *financing activities* category of the statement. The worksheet entry below accomplishes these purposes.

(j) Convertible Bonds Payable	20,000	
Unamortized Bond Discount		1,900
Extraordinary Gain on Debt Extinguishment		5,000
Financing Activities—Cash Paid to Retire Bonds Payable		13,100

Recall from entry (i) that we have already included the income tax effects of the debt extinguishment in the amount paid for income taxes and classified that amount as an operating cash flow. The FASB requires that all income taxes be classified as operating activities, even though some portion of the total taxes may have resulted from investing or financing activities. In reaching this decision, the FASB concluded that allocation of income taxes paid to operating, investing, and financing activities would be so complex and arbitrary that the benefits, if any, would not justify the costs involved.[16]

To summarize the procedures followed in implementing this unusual classification decision, if a gain or loss is presented in the income statement at the gross amount, the item is removed from net income and reclassified at that amount and no adjustment is made to income tax expense. If the gain or loss is presented in the income statement at a net-of-tax amount, the item is removed from net income and reclassified at the gross amount and cash paid for income taxes in the operating activities section is adjusted for the related amount of income taxes paid (gain) or saved (loss).

This completes the analysis of the income statement accounts and we may conclude that we have identified all cash provided or consumed in operating activities. We have also identified two other transactions included in income that represent investing and financing activities. Specifically, we have reclassified the loss on sale of

---

[16]*FASB Statement of Financial Accounting Standards No. 95*, par. 92.

equipment as an investing activity and the gain on the extinguishment of debt as a financing activity.

Financing and Investing Activities

Our next step is to proceed through the balance sheet accounts of the trial balance and determine the cash flow implications of any remaining changes that have not been fully explained by our analysis to this point. We will begin our work by analyzing changes in balance sheet accounts other than cash. The first accounts following cash on the trial balance in Exhibit 22–7 are Accounts Receivable and Inventory. Because of our earlier work in determining cash provided by operating activities, we have completely explained the changes in those two accounts. We know this because they "crossfoot." For example, Accounts Receivable started the period with a $65,000 debit balance, was credited for $5,000, and ended with a $60,000 debit balance. Similarly, Inventory started with a $62,000 debit balance, was debited $32,600, and ended with a $94,600 debit balance.

Purchase of Property, Plant, and Equipment

The next account on the trial balance is Property, Plant, and Equipment. Our analysis of the income statement accounts has explained only a portion of the changes in that account. Therefore, we conclude that additional analysis will be necessary to determine whether these additional changes represent investing activities affecting cash.

(k) Property, Plant, and Equipment	10,000	
Investing Activities—Cash Paid to Acquire Plant Assets		10,000

For the additional information, we can determine that Hudson, Inc., purchased plant assets of $10,000 during the year. That purchase represents a cash payment related to investing activities. Once this entry is recorded, we have completed our analysis of Property, Plant, and Equipment because that account now crossfoots on the worksheet ($200,000 + $10,000 − $20,000 = $190,000).

The next account in the trial balance is Patents. The change in that account has already been fully explained through our analysis of income statement accounts. Recall that the amortization expense related to patents was treated as a noncash transaction in determining cash used to pay general and administrative expenses.

Unamortized Bond Discount

The change in the unamortized bond discount account has been only partially explained as a result of our analysis to this point. Additional work is therefore necessary.

From the additional information, we learn that $20,000 of Hudson, Inc., bonds were converted into common stock. The additional information also provides other data that allow us to prepare the worksheet entries presented below. For example, the additional information indicates that 1,500 shares of stock were issued with a par value of $10. That allows us to determine that the proper credit to Common Stock is $15,000 (1,500 shares @ $10). Because the carrying value of the bonds is $18,000 ($20,000 − $2,000), we also are able to determine that Additional Paid-in Capital of $3,000 must be recognized ($18,000 − $15,000). The conversion of bonds payable to

Disclosure   common stock is an example of a noncash financing transaction that must be disclosed in a separate schedule accompanying the statement of cash flows.

To illustrate the two aspects of this type of financing activity—issuance of common stock and retirement of bonds payable —we divide entry (1) into two parts as follows:

(l₁)	Convertible Bonds Payable	20,000	
	Unamortized Bond Discount		2,000
	Noncash Financing Activities—Retirement of		
	Bonds By Conversion		18,000
(l₂)	Noncash Financing Activities—Issuance of Common		
	Stock for Bonds	18,000	
	Common Stock		15,000
	Additional Paid-In Capital		3,000

This permits us to see clearly the dual aspects of this noncash financing activity which must be disclosed with the statement of cash flows. In the formal statement which follows, you will see precisely how this transaction is disclosed. Notice that we have now fully accounted for the change in the Unamortized Bond Discount account.

We have now completed our analysis of the balance-sheet accounts with debit balances and can turn our attention to those with credit balances. The change in Accumulated Depreciation has been completely reconciled by our previous work. Note that the change in Accumulated Depreciation is caused by both depreciation expense and the depreciation adjustment related to the asset that was sold.

Dividends

The next account, Dividends Payable, has increased during 1993 by a net amount of $7,000. From the additional information, we determine that the change was caused by two different transactions. First, the $10,000 dividends declared during the previous year were paid during the current year. Second, dividends of $17,000 were declared during 1993 and are to be paid during 1994, the next year.

(m₁)	Dividends Payable	10,000	
	Financing Activities—Cash Paid for Dividends		10,000

This entry records the payment of the 1992 dividend, representing a negative cash flow during 1993.

The declaration of the dividend during 1993 to be paid in 1994 is somewhat more difficult to understand on the worksheet for the statement of cash flows. The declaration of a dividend represents a transfer from stockholders' equity to debt inasmuch as Retained Earnings is reduced and Dividends Payable is increased. The declaration of a dividend is a significant financing activity, despite the fact that it does not require a cash flow until payment is made. We enter the dividend declaration as follows:

(m₂)	Retained Earnings	17,000	
	Noncash Financing Activities—Declaration of		
	Dividends		17,000
(m₃)	Noncash Financing Activities—Dividends to Be Paid	17,000	
	Dividends Payable		17,000

The first of these two entries recognizes the declaration of the dividend as a reduction in stockholders' equity. The second recognizes the liability the company assumes with the declaration of the dividend. In the formal statement of cash flows that we prepare at the end of this illustration, you will see how this noncash financing activity is disclosed.

Notes Payable

| (n) | Notes Payable | 20,000 | |
| | Financing Activities—Cash Paid to Retire Note | | 20,000 |

The change in notes payable is caused by the repayment of the note. The use of cash to repay the notes is also a financing activity that consumes cash.

All of the changes in the remaining accounts presented in the trial balances have now been fully explained with the exception of cash itself. By providing the worksheet entry for the change in cash, we will complete the analysis necessary to prepare the statement of cash flows.

Cash

The final worksheet entry is one that we must make to determine the net change in cash. That amount is then included in the accounts used to prepare the statement of cash flows.

| (o) | Decrease in Cash | 2,600 | |
| | Cash | | 2,600 |

This entry completes the worksheet and provides us with the information necessary to prepare the statement of cash flows. Cash is credited for $2,600, representing the net decrease in cash during the year, and Decrease in Cash is debited at the bottom of the worksheet to balance the statement.

PREPARATION OF THE STATEMENT OF CASH FLOWS

Our next step is to prepare the statement of cash flows. Exhibit 22–8 presents Hudson's 1993 statement in three major categories of activities—operating, investing, and financing. Information to prepare the statement is taken from the bottom of the worksheet in Exhibit 22–7.

The operating activities section shows the cash provided by revenues and used by the various expense classifications, resulting in $38,500 positive cash flows (excess of cash receipts over cash payments). This method of determining cash flows from operating activities, where positive cash flows from revenues are reduced by negative cash flows from expenses, is identified as the **direct method.** We have used this method in the Hudson, Inc., example because it is the method favored by the authors and encouraged by the FASB. Notice that we have complied with the requirement that the **amounts paid for taxes and interest be separately disclosed.**

The next section of the statement of cash flows presents the investing activities of Hudson during 1993. As you can see, the company both purchased and sold plant assets during the year, and those activities provided the company with a net amount of $2,000 cash.

The financing activities section of the statement shows that Hudson paid dividends, repaid notes payable, and retired bonds payable, all resulting in negative cash flows. The combined effect of these events was a cash decrease during the year of $43,100.

As we expected, the total decrease in cash of $2,600 (resulting from the combined operating, investing, and financing activities) corresponds to the decrease in cash we determined by comparing the beginning and ending cash balances.

Disclosure   Two important disclosures accompany the statement of cash flows in Exhibit 22–8. First is the reconciliation of net income to cash flows from operating activities.

EXHIBIT 22-8

Hudson, Inc.
STATEMENT OF CASH FLOWS
For the Year Ended December 31, 1993

Cash Flows from Operating Activities

Cash received from customers		$1,205,000
Less: Cash paid for goods to be sold	$547,300	
Cash paid for selling expenses	295,000	
Cash paid for general and administrative expenses	243,000	
Cash paid for interest	39,200	
Cash paid for taxes	42,000	
Cash disbursed for operating activities		1,166,500
Net cash provided by operating activities		38,500

Cash Flows from Investing Activities

Sale of property, plant and equipment	12,000	
Purchase of property, plant and equipment	(10,000)	
Net cash provided by investing activities		2,000

Cash Flows from Financing Activities

Payment of dividends	(10,000)	
Repayment of notes payable	(20,000)	
Repayment of convertible bonds payable	(13,100)	
Net cash used by financing activities		(43,100)
Net decrease in cash		(2,600)
Cash, January 1, 1993		70,000
Cash, December 31, 1993		$67,400

Reconciliation of Net Income to Net Cash Provided by Operating Activities

Net Income	$ 73,600

Adjustments to Reconcile Net Income to Net Cash
Provided by Operating Activities

Depreciation expense	8,000
Amortization expense	1,000
Amortization of bond discount	800
Loss on sale of equipment	3,000
Increase in deferred income taxes	1,400
Decrease in accounts receivable	5,000
Increase in inventory	(32,600)
Decrease in accounts payable	(14,700)
Decrease in income taxes payable	(2,000)
Extraordinary gain—retirement of long-term debt	(5,000)
Net cash provided by operating activities	$ 38,500

Supplemental Schedule of Noncash Investing and Financing Activities

Declaration of dividend in 1993 to be paid in 1994	$ 17,000
Conversion of bonds payable into common stock	$ 18,000

[Handwritten annotations: "Indirect" next to Reconciliation heading; "Adj to NI 1. Dep + Amor 2. Δ in CA + CL 3. Δ in Def Tax 4. Gains/Losses" in right margin]

In this presentation, net income is adjusted for noncash items that are included in the determination of income following the guidelines in Exhibit 22–9. As you can see from the disclosure, this calculation results in $38,500, which is exactly the amount of cash from operating activities in the statement of cash flows determined by the direct approach.

The second disclosure accompanying the statement of cash flows is the presentation of noncash financing and investing activities. In this illustration, the declaration of a cash dividend to be paid in the following accounting period and the conversion of debt securities into common stock are examples.

The FASB permits an alternative to the direct method, identified as the **indirect method,** in presenting cash flows from operating activities. The indirect method of determining cash flows from operating activities is the approach followed in the supplemental disclosure in Exhibit 22–8, wherein net income is adjusted for noncash items included in its determination. If the indirect method is followed in the preparation of the statement of cash flows, the supplemental disclosure simply becomes the operating activities part of the statement. The indirect method is widely used in practice, despite the FASB's preference for the direct method, because it was widely used before *SFAS No. 95* was issued. When the indirect method is used, supplemental disclosure of noncash investing and financing activities is still required. Also, the amount of interest and taxes paid is usually made by note because that information is not apparent from the indirect (reconciliation) presentation.

EXHIBIT 22–9
Adjustments to Net Income in Determining Net Cash Flows from Operating Activities

	Additions to net income	Deductions from net income
Noncash expenses:	Asset depreciation Asset depletion Asset amortization Bond discount amortization Deferred income tax increase	Bond premium amortization Deferred income tax decrease
Reclassifications:	Loss-plant asset sale Loss-investment sale Loss-debt extinguishment	Gain-plant asset sale Gain-investment sale Gain-debt extinguishment
Accrual-to-cash adjustments:	Decrease in operating current assets (e.g., accounts receivable, inventory, prepaid expenses) Increase in operating current liabilities (e.g., accounts payable, accrued expenses)	Increase in operating current assets (e.g., accounts receivable, inventory, prepaid expenses) Decrease in operating current liabilities (e.g., accounts payable, accrued expenses)
Other:	Equity method loss recognized	Equity method income recognized

AN EXAMPLE FROM PRACTICE

Throughout this text, we have provided examples from published financial statements of major corporations to illustrate actual reporting practices. Exhibit 22–10 presents the statement of cash flows of Eastman Kodak Company for 1989 with comparative years of 1988 and 1987. Eastman Kodak, probably best known for its photographic products, operates in four primary areas: imaging, chemicals, health, and information systems.

Notice that the statement of cash flows is presented in three major sections, paralleling the requirements of *FASB Statement No. 95*: cash flow from operating activities, cash flow from investing activities, and cash flow from financing activities. The operations section is presented by the indirect method. Cash flows from investing activities include both positive and negative flows from various asset transactions. Cash flows from financing activities include both positive and negative flows from various financing transactions, including borrowing and repaying loans, as well as transactions with stockholders (e.g., dividends and treasury stock transactions).

The note at the bottom of the statement is from the accounting policy disclosure and indicates the amounts of interest and income taxes paid, as well as a noncash transaction in which the company acquired Sterling Drug, Inc.

CASH FLOW CLASSIFICATION ISSUES

Several interesting classification issues exist in preparing a statement of cash flows. The FASB dealt with these issues in the preparation of *Statement of Financial Accounting Standards No. 95* and reached a position on how the items of controversy should be handled. In this section, we briefly explore some of these areas of controversy in order to indicate the complexity that underlies the statement of cash flows and the articulation of that financial statement with the other primary statements.

We have learned that dividends paid by a company to its stockholders are presented as negative cash flows in the **financing** activities section. Interest paid on debt obligations is presented, however, as a negative **operating** cash flow, despite the similarity of interest and dividends. The primary reason for this treatment is that interest expense is a component in the determination of net income while dividends paid are treated as a distribution rather than a determinant of net income.

Cash inflows from interest and dividend revenues are presented in the statement of cash flows as operating activities because these items help to determine net income. Other transactions involving the debt and equity investments to which the interest and dividends relate are presented as investing activities; some would argue that cash inflows from interest and dividend revenues should be classified as investing as well. Apparently, the fact that these items enter into the determination of net income was a strong incentive for the FASB to require that they be included as operating cash flows.

We briefly discussed earlier the tax consequences of certain gains and losses that are included in the determination of net income, pointing out that the total income tax paid is considered an operating cash flow. This is true, even if some portion of the tax results from transactions that are classified as financing or investing activities. This is a questionable treatment, in the minds of the authors, because the financial effects of gains and losses are overstated and cash flows from operations are distorted when the gains and losses and their related tax effects are separated. The FASB relied heavily on the cost-benefit argument to support its decision not to allocate income taxes

EXHIBIT 22–10

Eastman Kodak Company
Statement of Cash Flows

Consolidated Statement of Cash Flows

Indirect Method

	1989	1988	1987
		(in millions)	
Cash flows from operating activities:			
Net earnings	$ 529	$ 1,397	$ 1,178
Adjustments to reconcile net earnings to net cash provided by operating activities:			
Depreciation and amortization	1,326	1,183	995
Provision for deferred taxes	—	160	193
Retirement of properties	322	265	303
Increase in receivables	(174)	(503)	(535)
Decrease (increase) in inventories	518	(507)	(106)
Increase in liabilities excluding borrowings	334	10	606
Other items, net	(236)	(694)	(350)
Total adjustments	2,090	(86)	1,106
Net cash provided by operating activities	2,619	1,311	2,284
Cash flows from investing activities:			
Additions to properties	(2,118)	(1,914)	(1,652)
Acquisitions—net of cash acquired	—	(4,781)	—
Marketable securities—purchases	(356)	(329)	(394)
Marketable securities—sales	406	684	288
Other items, net	10	16	22
Net cash used in investing activities	(2,058)	(6,324)	(1,736)
Cash flows from financing activities:			
Net increase (decrease) in short-term borrowings	482	413	(178)
Proceeds from long-term borrowings	762	5,432	1,537
Repayment of long-term borrowings	(878)	(71)	(132)
Dividends to shareowners	(649)	(600)	(568)
Treasury stock purchases	—	—	(978)
Other items, net	5	2	(3)
Net cash provided by (used in) financing activities	(278)	5,176	(322)
Effect of exchange rate changes on cash	(36)	(17)	40
Net increase in cash and cash equivalents	247	146	266
Cash and cash equivalents, beginning of year	848	702	436
Cash and cash equivalents, end of year	$ 1,095	$ 848	$ 702

Cash Flow Information

For purposes of the Consolidated Statement of Cash Flows, the Company considers marketable securities with maturities of three months or less at the time of purchase to be cash equivalents.

Cash paid for interest and income taxes is as follows:

(in millions)	1989	1988	1987
Interest, net of portion capitalized	$910	$581	$157
Income taxes	346	621	248

In 1988, the Company paid $5.1 billion to acquire substantially all of the outstanding common stock of Sterling Drug Inc. The Company acquired assets with a fair market value of $2.3 billion and assumed liabilities of $1.6 billion in connection with the acquisition.

SOURCE: Eastman Kodak Company, 1989 Annual Report.

among the categories in the statement of cash flows; it also weighed in its decision the complexity of the calculations that would be involved if allocation were required. Tax considerations may also have been factors in the FASB's decision to include interest expense, dividend revenue, and interest revenue in operations; including them avoids the distortion that might result if these items were presented as financing and investing activities with their tax effects presented in operations.

In the authors' opinion, these classification problems point out the complexity of financial statement classification and the fact that the terminology used in the income statement does not correspond precisely with the more recent terminology that has been developed for the statement of cash flows. Undoubtedly, as we gain additional experience in the preparation of statements of cash flows, we will refine our definitions and classifications of items over time.

CONTINUING REFINEMENTS OF *SFAS NO. 95*

After *SFAS No. 95* had been in effect only a short time, the FASB issued two pronouncements which amended it in special circumstances. While a detailed coverage of these specialized situations are beyond the scope of this text, they provide an opportunity to understand the difficulty the FASB faces in its attempts to anticipate problems of implementing new financial reporting requirements. The fact that the Board must amend and refine its earlier pronouncements after some experience from practice is not unusual.

Briefly, the following changes have been implemented since *SFAS No. 95* was originally issued:

1. A statement of cash flows is not required to be presented by defined benefit pension plans that present information in accordance with *SFAS No. 35*. Also, if certain specified conditions are met, investment companies are not required to present a statement of cash flows.[17]

2. Cash receipts and payments resulting from purchases and sales of securities and other assets of banks, brokers, and dealers in securities shall be classified as operating cash flows if those assets were acquired specifically for resale and are carried at market value in a trading account.[18]

3. While gross cash flow information is generally preferred over net cash flow information, banks, savings institutions, and credit unions are not required to report gross amounts of cash receipts and payments for specified deposits and loans.[19]

4. Cash flows resulting from futures contracts, forward contracts, option contracts, or swap contracts that are accounted for as hedges of identifiable transactions or events may be classified in the same category as the cash flows from the items being hedged, provided that accounting policy is disclosed.[20]

Throughout this chapter, we have emphasized the direct method of presentation for cash provided by or used in operating activities. Briefly, the direct method presents both positive and negative cash flows by category of operating activities in a manner similar to that used for investing and financing activities. The indirect method, on the other hand, begins with net income and reconciles that figure to the

---

[17]*FASB Statement of Financial Accounting Standards No. 102*, "Statement of Cash Flows—Exemption of Certain Enterprises and Classification of Cash Flows from Certain Securities Acquired for Resale," 1989, par. 5–7.
[18]*SFAS No. 102*, par. 8.
[19]*FASB Statement of Financial Accounting Standards No. 104*, "Statement of Cash Flows—Net Reporting of Certain Cash Receipts and Cash Payments and Classification of Cash Flows from Hedging Transactions," 1989, par. 7.
[20]*SFAS No. 104*, par. 7.

EARNINGS, SCHMERNINGS—LOOK AT THE CASH

These days, more investors are saying it's cash flow that counts

In coming weeks, Wall Streeters will be glued to their video terminals as companies start to report second-quarter earnings. It's a tense time, especially for securities analysts who pride themselves on the ability to forecast profits. But some savvy investors say the singular focus on net income is foolhardy. The bottom line isn't an end in itself but just the beginning of the more difficult, and more rewarding, process of tracking a company's cash flow.

Looking past earnings to invest in companies for their cash flow isn't new, but it's finding new popularity. It represents a return to one of the most basic rules in economics: The value of an investment is derived from cash flow. More than anything else, it's the boom in takeovers and leveraged buyouts that has turned investor attention toward cash flow. And scrutinizing it is more feasible now that the accountants require public companies to publish more of the statistical building blocks. Some big companies are going further, talking up cash flow in their annual reports or asking Wall Street to look beyond their meager earnings and marvel at their bounteous streams of green.

The problem with cash flow is that not all investors see it quite the same way. Cash flow, in its simplest form, is net income plus items such as depreciation—bookkeeping charges that have cut into net income even though they don't take any cash out of the corporate coffers. Simple cash flow isn't a particularly useful figure by itself—it's just an accountant's way station (box).

Free Ride. Takeover artists and LBO operators hunt for "operating cash flow." That's the money generated by the company before the cost of financing and taxes come into play. LBO specialists will take on as much debt as their operating cash flow (OCF) can support—just as home buyers may borrow as much as a lender will approve for their level of income. When the OCF is dedicated to debt payments, there isn't anything left over for taxes. But that's all right. Since there's no profit to declare, there won't be taxes to pay.

You don't have to be a raider to like OCF. In recent years, investing in companies based on their price-to-OCF multiples has been one of the best strategies around, says Robert C. Jones, an analyst at Goldman, Sachs & Co. In 1988, a portfolio comprised of the stocks that were cheapest in OCF terms would have gained about 30.5%—nearly double the return of the Standard & Poor's 500-stock index. For the first half of 1989, OCF stocks again beat the market, though only by one percentage point.

While OCF is the broadest measure of a company's funds, some prefer to zero in on the narrower "free cash flow." That measures truly discretionary funds—company money that an owner could pocket without harming the business. Companies with free cash flow, and not all public companies have any, are golden. They can use it to boost dividends, buy back shares, or pay down debt. And businesses that look pricey based on earnings may be bargains when measured by the yardstick of free cash flow (table).

"I will not invest in a company that has no free cash flow," says Kenneth S. Hackel, whose Systematic Financial Management Inc. picks stocks for their cash-flow characteristics. That choice immediately cuts out many hot-growth companies that consume more cash than they generate and thus depend on external financing. The constraint hasn't cost Hackel much in performance: Since 1980, his portfolio has recorded annual average returns of more than 20%. It was up 29% in 1988 and 17% in the first half of 1989.

Consumer Loyalty. A few industries, including real estate and energy, have long been viewed through a cash-flow prism. In real estate, depreciation usually wipes out "profits"—even though the property is actually appreciating. For oil and gas, depletion knocks the wind out of earnings. But increasingly, the cash-flow standard is applied to companies with valuable "franchises" in their markets. Tobacco, food, and media companies are among those where tangible assets matter a lot less than the consumer loyalty they command.

That's what Time Inc. Chairman J. Richard Munro told shareholders at the recent annual meeting: "When it comes to valuing media and entertainment companies like ours, what matters is not profits but cash flow." Munro had good reason for his conversion to the cult of cash flow. If Time succeeds in its bid to acquire Warner Communications Inc. for $70 a share, earnings will disappear for several years to come. Likewise, executives at Paramount Communications Inc. have asked Wall Street to look at it as a company driven by cash flow, rather than by earnings. If Paramount prevails in its quest to buy Time for $200 a share, its profits will vanish.

Are the media moguls trying to deflect investor concern that earnings are going to the dogs? Not really. "Reported earnings are a complete fiction," says Robert L. Wiley III, who follows media companies for brokers Furman Selz Mager Dietz & Birney Inc. "Earnings have nothing to do with what cash flows the company has available to it." In fact, Wiley argues that either deal involving Time would allow ample cash to service debt immediately and would generate enough free cash flow to start paying down the principal by 1991.

The best reason for judging a "franchise" company by its cash flow is that it usually has a lot of goodwill on the balance sheet. That's the difference between what the business paid for an acquisition and the target's lower book value. Accounting rules make companies amortize the goodwill, which reduces reported profit. And since the write-off is not tax deductible, there's no tax savings. Even though the write-off may be spread over as many as 40 years, the impact on reported profits can be substantial. Wiley estimates that annual goodwill write-offs for Paramount could be as much as $257 million, or $2.20 per share, and $313 million, or $5.53 per share, for Time.

The case for cash flow doesn't mean that profits are passé. For most investors, net income will remain the handiest snapshot of a company. Even so, following the cash as it flows through a company, says Stuart Crane, an analyst with Gruntal & Co., "gives you insight into the quality of earnings." Indeed, if profits are soaring, but the cash flow isn't, a company's good fortunes may prove to be short-lived.

SOURCE: Jeffrey M. Laderman, "Earnings, Schmernings—Look at the Cash," *Business Week*, July 24, 1989, pp. 56–57. Reprinted from July 24, 1989 issue of *Business Week* by special permission, copyright © 1989 by McGraw-Hill, Inc.

CASH FLOW? WHAT DO YOU MEAN BY THAT?

CASH FLOW = NET INCOME + DEPRECIATION + DEPLETION + AMORTIZATION

Net Income   It's the bottom line but just the starting point when figuring out a company's cash flow

Depreciation   An accounting charge that writes down the cost of an asset, such as a factory or a machine tool, over its useful life. This charge is made for shareholder and tax reporting, but it does not require cash outlays

Depletion   When the asset being used is a natural resource, such as oil, gas, coal, or minerals, the write-off is called depletion

Amortization   A write-down of limited-term or intangible assets is called amortization. Acquisitive companies often have an entry on the books called goodwill, the difference between what they paid for a company and the lower book value. Goodwill is amortized over a long period, usually 40 years, and requires no cash outlay

OPERATING CASH FLOW = CASH FLOW + INTEREST EXPENSE + INCOME TAX EXPENSE

Interest Expense   Add back the interest expense to get the broadest measure of cash flow. If you're a raider, you'll reorder the whole debt scene anyway

Income Tax Expense   Add back the taxes because they won't have to be paid after a new owner adds so much debt that there is no book profit and hence no tax due

FREE CASH FLOW = CASH FLOW − CAPITAL EXPENDITURES − DIVIDENDS

Capital Expenditures   Subtract only the capital expenditures necessary to maintain plant and equipment and keep the company competitive but not optional ones such as a costly new headquarters

Dividends   If the company deems the dividend sacrosanct, deduct it here. But if a major recapitalization is under way, the dividend will probably be scratched anyway and need not be deducted

WHERE CASH FLOW TELLS A DIFFERENT STORY

Based on the widely used yardstick of price-earnings ratios, all of these stocks appear pricey. Each has a p-e of at least 19, vs. 13.7 for the Standard & Poor's industrials. For free cash flow, the average multiple is 25.5; on that basis, all these companies look cheap

Company	Price-earnings ratio	Price-free cash flow ratio	Company	Price-earnings ratio	Price-free cash flow ratio
Belo (A.H.)	60.7	16.3	Meredith	21.0	10.0
Bowne & Co.	24.5	17.3	Multimedia	39.5	14.4
Campbell Soup	23.5	18.6	Network Systems	23.9	15.9
Cordis	33.9	8.7	Occidental Petroleum	25.9	10.8
General Signal	44.5	11.1	Santa Fe Southern Pacific	29.3	9.7
Halliburton	47.5	9.2	TGI Friday's	20.7	12.1
Huffy	26.1	18.8	United Asset Management	21.2	11.9
Itel	38.1	16.6	Volt Information Sciences	49.3	9.3
Knight-Ridder	20.9	18.6	Weingarten Realty Trust	25.8	12.4
Lotus Development	23.4	13.9	Wiley (john) & Sons	60.0	12.1

DATA: Systematic Financial Management Inc.

amount of cash provided by or used in operating activities by adjusting noncash items and reclassifying items as investing or financing, as required by *SFAS No. 95*. We also stated that the FASB preferred the direct method but permitted the indirect method.

The debate over whether to require the direct method or permit both methods was an important part of the standard-setting process from which *SFAS No. 95* emerged. The FASB apparently believed the direct method has considerable merit in that it shows operating cash receipts and payments by category, information which may be useful in estimating future operating cash flows.[21] Interestingly, a majority of respondents to the exposure draft for *SFAS No. 95* expressed a preference for the direct method and asked that the FASB make it mandatory.[22] Many financial statement preparers cited the difficulty and cost of accumulating the information required for the direct method as reasons for permitting either the direct or the indirect method. They said that they do not presently collect information in a manner that allows the determination of gross cash flows by operating categories and that to do so would require costly changes in their accounting systems.

In the final analysis, the FASB did permit either the direct or indirect method to be used. The authors are strong advocates of the direct method, both from the perspective of investors and creditors who seek to understand a company's activities and from the perspective of students attempting to learn about the statement of cash flows and its relationship to the other financial statements. While the FASB has not yet amended *SFAS No. 95* in this important area, we see this as fertile ground for continuing consideration and experimentation as both preparers and users of financial statements gain experience with the statement of cash flows, particularly the direct method of presenting cash flows from operating activities.

CONCLUDING REMARKS

The emergence of the statement of cash flows as one of the primary financial statements is a major event for the accounting profession. Rarely do reporting requirements in an area change as dramatically as was the case when *SFAS No. 95* was issued, replacing the statement of changes in financial position with the statement of cash flows.

Throughout this chapter, we have emphasized the preparation of the statement of cash flows by making appropriate adjustment to accrual accounting information. A logical question is why would we not simply open a company's cash disbursement records and prepare the statement directly from that source. Logically, one might argue that this should be the most direct and easiest manner in which to prepare the statement.

As we have mentioned, the other financial statements are prepared on the basis of accrual concepts. Procedures to implement accrual accounting have been a part of practice for many years. The emergence of the statement of cash flows, which represents a break from a strict accrual orientation in financial reporting, is relatively new. At the present time, the authors believe that most accounting systems produce information designed first to produce the other major financial statements. Statements of cash flow are then prepared by adjusting accrual accounting information.

In the future, as we gain experience with cash flow information, we may design accounting systems specifically intended to produce information to prepare the statement of cash flows. For example, cash disbursement journals might require classifica-

---

[21]*SFAS No. 95*, par. 107.
[22]*SFAS No. 95*, par. 111.

tion of all payments into operating, investing, and financing categories at the time of initial recording. An even more dramatic change might be for accounting systems to move toward cash-based recording with financial statements based on accrual concepts being prepared "outside the system," without formal recording, as we have done in this chapter in preparing the statement of cash flows. In short, we see the changing orientation toward cash flow information as a very important development that will have long-term and far-reaching implications for financial reporting.

KEY POINTS

1. The statement of cash flows has one primary objective: to provide information about a company's liquidity in terms of its cash receipts and cash payments. (Objective 1)

2. Cash flow information is generally thought to be important to users of financial statements— particularly investors and creditors—in assessing the company's cash flow, liquidity, and financial flexibility. (Objective 2)

3. The statement of cash flows is presented in three major categories which parallel the major types of cash flows for a company: operating activities, investing activities, and financing activities. (Objective 3)

4. Some investing and financing activities do not affect cash but are still important in explaining changes in financial position. Such transactions must be disclosed in a schedule accompanying the statement of cash flows. (Objective 4)

5. Three essential steps for preparing a statement of cash flows are: (1) Determining the change in cash for the period; (2) transaction analysis in which cash receipts and payments are identified and classified, as are noncash financing and investing activities; and (3) preparation of a formal statement in accordance with standards promulgated by the FASB. For relatively complex situations, a worksheet is a valuable tool in analyzing transactions and accumulating the information necessary to prepare a statement of cash flows. (Objective 5)

APPENDIX A: T-ACCOUNT APPROACH OF CASH FLOW TRANSACTION ANALYSIS

An alternative to using a worksheet to identify the causes of changes in cash during an accounting period is the T-Account approach. This relatively simple procedure calls for establishing a T-Account for each real and nominal account and identifying changes in those accounts in terms of their impact on operating, investing, and financing activities.

Exhibit 22–11 demonstrates the application of this approach for the information presented in the chapter for Hamilton Company. Notice that for each real and nominal account, the net change for the period is identified beside the account title [e.g., Accounts Receivable includes (−100), which means that the account went down by $100 during the year].

Entries to identify all changes in real and nominal accounts in terms of their impact on the three cash flow classifications and then to reclassify the net income and the change in cash are described as follows (SCF = statement of cash flows):

(a) SCF/Operating   1,600
        Revenues   1,500
        Accounts Receivable   100
  To identify cash receipts from sales and collections of receivables as positive operating cash flow.

(b) Plant Assets   800
        SCF/Investing   800
  To record purchase of plant assets as investing negative cash flow.

(c) SCF/Investing   100
        Plant Assets   100
  To record sale of plant assets as investing positive cash flow.

(d) Expense (Depreciation)   100
        Accumulated Depreciation   100
  To record depreciation expense. (No impact on cash flows.)

EXHIBIT 22–11

Hamilton Company
Cash Analysis of T-Accounts
(in thousands of dollars)

REAL ACCOUNTS		NOMINAL ACCOUNTS

REAL ACCOUNTS

Cash (−50)

	(k)	50

Plant Assets (+ 700)

(b)	800	(c)	100
	(100)		
	700		

Accrued Expenses (+ 50)

	(e)	50

Capital Stock (+ 100)

	(h)	100

Accounts Receivable (− 100)

(a)	100		

Accumulated Depreciation (+ 100)

	(d)	100

Bonds Payable (+ 150)

(g)	100	(f)	250
			(100)
			150

Retained Earnings (+ 150)

(i)	150	(j)	300
			(150)
			150

NOMINAL ACCOUNTS

Revenues (+ 1,500)

	(a)	1,500

Expenses (depreciation) (+ 100)

(d)	100	

Expenses (other) (+ 1,100)

(e)	1,100	

Summary:

Revenues		1,500
Expenses:		
Depreciation		(100)
Other		(1,100)
Net income		300
Reclassification (j)		(300)
		−0−

CASH FLOW CLASSIFICATIONS

Operating

(a)	1,600	(e)	1,050
	(1,050)		
	550		

Investing

(c)	100	(b)	800
			(100)
			700

Financing

(f)	250	(g)	100
(h)	100	(i)	150
	350		250
	(250)		
	100		

Summary:

Operating	550
Investing	(700)
Financing	100
Net decrease in cash	(50)
Reclassification (k)	50
	−0−

(e) Expenses (other)   1,100
      Accrued Expenses   50
      SCF/Operating   1,050
    To record operating expenses and increase in
    accrued expenses as negative operating
    cash flow.

(f) SCF/Financing   250
      Bonds Payable   250
    To record issuance of bonds as positive
    financing cash flow.

(g) Bonds Payable   100
      SCF/Financing   100
    To record the retirement of bonds as negative
    financing cash flow.

(h) SCF/Financing   100
      Capital Stock   100
    To record the sale of capital stock as positive
    financing cash flow.

(i) Retained Earnings   150
      SCF/Financing   150
    To record the cash dividend as negative
    financing cash flow.

(j) Income Summary   300
      Retained Earnings   300
    To transfer net income to real account, retained
    earnings.

(k) SCF Summary   50
      Cash   50
    To transfer the net effect of operating,
    investing, and financing activities to the real
    account, cash.

The entries account for the entire change in the balance of each real and nominal account (e.g., Bonds Payable increased by $250 from one transaction, decreased by $100 from another transaction, netting to an increase of $150 as indicated at the top of the T-Account). The analysis is complete when all changes in real and nominal accounts have been accounted for, the amount of net income reconciles the change in retained earnings (entry **(j)** above), and the net amount of all cash changes reconciles the change in cash (entry **(k)** above).

QUESTIONS

22–1 The FASB has recently identified several reasons why information concerning cash flows is useful to financial statement users. List these reasons briefly.

22–2 What are the objectives of a statement of cash flows?

22–3 What information is included in a statement of cash flows that is not available in comparative income statements, balance sheets, and retained earnings statements for the same reporting period?

22–4 Why must adjustments be made to net income to determine "cash provided by or used in operating activities"?

22–5 Identify three major categories of transactions that may result in increases in cash, and state a general conclusion about the circumstances in which an increase in cash would actually result.

22–6 Identify three major categories of transactions that may result in decreases in cash, and state a general conclusion about the circumstances in which a decrease in cash would actually result.

22–7 Explain briefly how gross and net cash flows from investing and financing activities should be presented in a statement of cash flows.

22–8 Define "noncash investing and financing transactions." How are they presented in the statement of cash flows?

22–9 Explain briefly how net income may be a source of cash and how a net loss may be a use of cash.

22–10 Is it possible for a net loss for a period to result in a source of cash for that same period? Explain.

22–11 A plant asset was sold at a loss during the current year. The loss was included in income before extraordinary item on the enterprise's income statement. Explain the proper presentation of this transaction in the statement of cash flows.

22–12 A plant asset was sold in a condemnation proceeding, resulting in a substantial gain. The gain was appropriately presented as an extraordinary item in the enterprise's income statement. Explain the proper presentation of this transaction in the statement of cash flows.

22–13 What is the relationship between the change in cash during a period and the three types of cash flows—operating, investing and financing?

22–14 What is the definition of "cash" as that term is used in a statement of cash flows?

22–15 Explain the treatment of the following transactions in a statement of cash flows:

[a] Declaration of a cash dividend to be paid in the next period.

[b] Declaration and payment of a cash dividend in the current period.

22–16 The controller of Lammers Company, your audit client, argues that the refunding of outstanding 10% debt by issuing 8% debt does not materially affect the company's financial position, because the difference between the net amount of debt outstanding is not great (i.e., not material in relation to the other balance sheet items). The controller argues, therefore, that the transaction does not need to be included in the statement of cash flows, particularly since cash is not affected. Do you agree or disagree with the controller? Why?

22–17 Select the correct answer.

Which of the following financial statements has as its primary function the presentation of information about cash receipts and payments and financing and investing aspects of all significant transactions?

[a] Retained earnings statement.   [c] Statement of cash flows.

[b] Income statement.   [d] Statement of financial position.   (AICPA adapted)

22–18 Select the correct answer.

In 1993, Wilkes Company retired convertible bonds for which stock was issued pursuant to a conversion option. The exchange took place on an interest payment date and except for the interest payment no cash changed hands. In preparing a statement of cash flows, the exchange in securities should be treated in which of the following ways?

[a] Ignored because the "book-value" method was used to record the exchange.

[b] Added to net income to arrive at cash provided by operating activities.

[c] Subtracted from net income to arrive at cash provided by operating activities.

[d] Disclosed separately as a noncash financing activity.   (AICPA adapted)

22–19 Select the correct answer.

Which of the following items represents a potential decrease in cash?

[a] Goodwill amortization.

[b] Sale of plant assets at a loss.

[c] Net loss from operations.

[d] Declaration of a stock dividend.   (AICPA adapted)

22–20 Select the correct answer.

When preparing a statement of cash flows, an increase in ending inventory over beginning inventory results in an adjustment to reported net income in computing cash flows from operating activities by the indirect method because:

[a] Cash was increased since inventory is a current asset.

[b] The net increase in inventory reduced cost of goods sold but represents an assumed use of cash.

[c] Inventory is not an expense deducted in computing net income, but is not a use of cash.

[d] All changes in noncash accounts must be disclosed.   (AICPA adapted)

22–21 Wilmer, Inc.'s income statement includes income tax expense of $150,000, of which $112,500 was paid by year-end and $37,500 was deferred because of the use of accelerated cost recovery for income tax purposes and straight-line depreciation for financial reporting. How will these facts affect the presentation of "cash provided by operating activities" in the statement of cash flows?

EXERCISES   **22–22** CASH FLOW FROM OPERATING ACTIVITIES   Fancher Company reported $175,000 of net income in 1993. Expenses reported in the determination of this income included the following: salaries, $200,000; cost of sales, $400,000; interest, $50,000; depreciation and amortization, $127,000; and income taxes, $400,000 (none of which was deferred). All sales are made for cash, expenses (other than depreciation and amortization) were paid in cash, the balance of inventory was unchanged during the year.

Instructions

Using only the above information, compute cash provided by operating activities during 1993 by the indirect method.

22–23 CASH FLOW FROM OPERATING ACTIVITIES   Brown Company's income statement for the year ended December 31, 1993, is as follows:

Brown Company
INCOME STATEMENT
For the Year Ended December 31, 1993

Revenue		
Sales	$110,000	
Services	75,000	$185,000
Expenses		
Cost of goods sold	$ 96,000	
Selling and administrative expenses	45,000	
Depreciation expense	25,000	
Amortization of intangibles	7,000	173,000
Income before income taxes		12,000
Income tax expense		4,200
Net income		$ 7,800
Earnings per common share		$.78

(handwritten: Non cash { Depreciation expense / Amortization of intangibles; 2940 pd; 1260 Deferred)

Instructions

Compute the amount of cash from operating activities for the year by the direct method, assuming the following:

(handwritten: operating activity; LT Asset)

[a] A sale of $15,000 resulted in the acceptance of a three-year, 8% note receivable. All other sales were for cash.

[b] The $4,200 provision for income taxes is distributed as follows:

Paid during 1993	$2,940
Deferred	1,260
	$4,200

(handwritten: Tax Exp; Tax Exp 4200 / Tax Pay 2940 / DT 1260)

The deferral relates to the temporary difference resulting from the use of accelerated cost recovery for tax purposes and straight-line for income statement reporting purposes.

[c] All current assets (other than cash) and current liabilities remained constant during 1993.

22–24 CASH FLOW FROM OPERATING ACTIVITIES   Telecom Company reports the following summarized income statement data for 1993:

Revenue	$1,950,000
Expenses	1,500,000
Net income	$ 450,000

Accounts receivable resulting from revenue-producing transactions increased by $56,000 from January 1 to December 31, 1993. Depreciation expense amounted to $172,000.

Instructions

Using only the information explicitly given above, compute cash provided by operating activities during 1993, applying the direct method.

22–25 CASH FLOW FROM OPERATING ACTIVITIES   Net income of the Wall Company for 1993 was reported as $162,000. The following related information is available:

	At Dec. 31, 1992	At Dec. 31, 1993
Accrued interest payable recognized	$10,000	$12,500 + 2500
Depreciation expense recognized	18,200 Dep G&P =	18,900 + 700 = AD
CA Prepaid expenses recognized	775	1,235 + 460

Instructions

Using the above information, determine the cash provided by operating activities during 1993 by the indirect method.

22–26 CASH FLOW FROM OPERATING ACTIVITIES Abbott Company's income statement for 1993 is presented below with explanatory information for selected items:

Abbott Company
INCOME STATEMENT
For the Year Ended December 31, 1993

Revenue from sales [1]		$5,432,000
Cost of goods sold		3,150,000
Gross profit		2,282,000
Expenses		
Selling	$246,000	
Depreciation	235,000	
Amortization of intangibles	52,000	
Salaries and wages [2]	400,000	
Interest [3]	72,000	
Miscellaneous operating G&P	5,000	1,010,000
Income before income taxes		1,272,000
Income tax expense [4]		445,000
Net income		$ 827,000
Earnings per common share		$.19

Additional Information

[1] All sales were for cash except a $120,000 sale resulting in the acceptance of a three-year, 9% note receivable and a $75,000 sale resulting in the acceptance of a tract of land valued at $75,000.   ↳ NC T-action

[2] Accrued salaries and wages at December 31, 1992 and 1993 were $40,000 and $45,600, respectively. ↑5600

[3] Interest expense includes $6,800 of amortization of bond discount. All interest, other than the discount amortization, was paid during 1993.

[4] Income tax expense includes $110,000 of taxes deferred due to the use of accelerated cost recovery for tax purposes and straight-line for reporting purposes. All other tax expense was paid during the year.

Instructions

Compute the cash provided by operating activities for 1993 by the direct method.

22–27 STATEMENT OF CASH FLOWS PREPARATION (INDIRECT) Maxwell Company reported net income of $188,200 for 1993 with no extraordinary items. The following information is available:

[1] Current assets other than cash increased by $27,500 and current liabilities increased by $12,250 during the year—all related to operating activities and affected net income.

[2] Dividends of $37,500 were declared and paid to stockholders.

[3] Depreciation expense recognized was $25,600.

[4] Treasury stock was acquired for $10,000.

[5] Long-term debt was retired at $59,150.

[6] New items of property, plant, and equipment were acquired for $20,000.

[7] Cash increased by $71,900, from $110,000 to $181,900.

Instructions

Prepare a statement of cash flows for 1993. The company's fiscal year ends on December 31. Use the indirect method of presenting cash flows from operating activities.

22–28 STATEMENT OF CASH FLOWS PREPARATION (DIRECT) Comparative data taken from the balance sheets of Franklin Company at December 31, 1992 and 1993, are as follows:

	1992	1993
Assets		
Cash	$ 10,000	$ 15,000 +5000
Receivables, short-term	35,000	26,700 -8300
Inventory	60,000	85,000 +25000
Property, plant, and equipment, net	75,000	70,000 -5000 in AD } 7000 A Dep
Intangibles	12,000	10,000 -2000
	$192,000	$206,700
Equities		
Current liabilities	$ 6,500	$ 6,200 -300
Noncurrent liabilities	60,000	40,000 -20000
Capital stock	100,000	125,000 +25000
Retained earnings	25,500	35,500 +10000
	$192,000	$206,700

During 1993 capital stock was sold, noncurrent debt was retired, and dividends of $5,000 were declared and paid. The income statement showed $7,000 of depreciation and amortization combined.

Dep Exp 7000
AD 7000

Instructions

[a] Determine the net change in cash during 1993.

[b] Assuming that revenues for 1993 totaled $100,000 and operating expenses totaled $85,000, prepare the 1993 statement of cash flows, applying the direct method of determining cash flows from operating activities. Accompanying disclosures are not required.

22–29 STATEMENT OF CASH FLOWS PREPARATION (DIRECT AND INDIRECT) Arrington Company's balance sheets at December 31, 1992 and 1993, are as follows:

	1992	1993
Assets		
Cash	$ 17,000	$ 2,300 -14700
Accounts receivable, net	45,000	42,000 -3000
Inventory	23,000	36,200 +13,200
Property, plant, and equipment, net	165,000	147,000 -18000
Intangibles	—	17,500 +17500
	$250,000	$245,000
Equities		
Current liabilities	$ 40,000	$ 50,000 +10000
Noncurrent liabilities	90,000	95,000 +5000
Capital stock	100,000	120,000 +20000
Additional paid-in capital	40,000	40,000
Retained earnings	(20,000)	(60,000) -40000
	$250,000	$245,000

The following additional information has been accumulated about 1993 activities:

[1] Patents were acquired by issuing a $5,000 long-term note payable and paying the remainder in cash; however, no amortization was taken since the acquisition took place at year-end.

[2] The only entries to property, plant, and equipment accounts were for depreciation and the acquisition of a $10,000 machine.

[3] No dividends were declared.
[4] Capital stock of $20,000 was issued at par.
[5] Revenues were $150,000; expenses totaled $190,000.

Instructions

[a] Prepare a statement of cash flows for 1993, applying the direct method of determining cash flows from operating activities. The net cash flows from operating activities to net income reconciliation disclosure is not required.

[b] Prepare a statement of cash flows for 1993, applying the indirect method of determining cash flows from operating activities.

22–30   STATEMENT OF CASH FLOWS—NONCASH TRANSACTIONS (DIRECT)   Information from Rogoff Company's balance sheets at December 31, 1992 and 1993 indicate the following:

	Dollar Change Dec. 31, 1992- Dec. 31, 1993
Assets	
Cash	+ 15,000
Accounts receivable	− 5,000
Inventory	+ 17,000
Property, plant, and equipment, net	+ 25,000
	+ 52,000
Equities	
Current liabilities	− 7,000
Bonds payable	+ 16,000
Capital stock	+ 20,000
Additional paid-in capital	+ 2,000
Retained earnings	+ 21,000
	+ 52,000

Depreciation of $7,000 was recognized in the income statement. Additional bonds were sold during the year. Land valued at $22,000 (included in property, plant, and equipment) was acquired by the issuance of stock. No dividends were declared. Revenues for 1993 were $125,000 and operating expenses were $104,000. The cash balance at the beginning of 1993 was $37,500.

Instructions

Prepare a statement of cash flows for 1993, using the direct method for operating activities, including all required disclosures.

22–31   STATEMENT OF CASH FLOWS CLASSIFICATIONS   The following items may appear in the statement of cash flows:

[1] Revenues and operating expenses.
[2] Depreciation expense.
[3] Acquisition of treasury stock.
[4] Exchange of common stock for land.
[5] Declaration and payment of cash dividend.
[6] Payment of cash dividend declared in previous period.
[7] Acquisition of property, plant, and equipment.
[8] Retirement of long-term debt.
[9] Conversion of bonds into common stock.
[10] Amortization of intangible assets.
[11] Increase in inventory from previous year-end.
[12] Decrease in accounts receivable from previous year-end.
[13] Sale of property, plant, and equipment.
[14] Sale of capital stock.
[15] Declaration and distribution of stock dividend.

Instructions

For each item indicate the proper classification in a statement of cash flows, using the following code. Where an item is treated differently by the direct and indirect methods of determining cash flows from operating activities, indicate the answers for both.

	Code
Operating activities	A
Investing activities	B
Financing activities	C
Separate schedule	D
Not required to be included in the statement of cash flows	E

22–32 STATEMENT OF CASH FLOWS PREPARATION (INDIRECT)   The beginning and ending balances for Smedley Company for 1993 are as follows:

	Jan. 1, 1993	Dec. 31, 1993
Cash	$10,000	$15,000
Other current assets	20,000	26,000 +6000
Fixed assets	20,000	20,000
Accumulated depreciation	(4,000)	(5,000) 1000 Dep Exp
Investments	10,000	10,000
Intangible assets	5,000	4,000 1000 Amor Exp
	$61,000	$70,000
Current liabilities	$10,000	$13,000 + 3000
Long-term liabilities	13,000	12,000 −1000
Capital stock	25,000	25,000
Retained earnings	13,000	20,000 +7000
	$61,000	$70,000

RE + DIV / NI

An analysis of the company's records reveals the following additional information.

[1] Depreciation and amortization of intangibles included in the determination of net income were $1,000 each.

[2] $1,500 of dividends were declared and paid during the year.

[3] $1,000 of long-term liabilities were retired during the year.

Instructions

Prepare a statement of cash flows, applying the indirect method of determining cash flows from operating activities.

22–33 STATEMENT OF CASH FLOWS PREPARATION (INDIRECT)   The beginning and ending balances for Kimball Company for 1993 are as follows:

	Jan. 1, 1993	Dec. 31, 1993
Current assets	$25,000	$28,500 +3500
Fixed assets	20,000	25,000
Accumulated depreciation	(5,000)	(6,500) 1500
Investments	10,000	10,000
Intangible assets	4,000	3,000
	$54,000	$60,000
Current liabilities	$13,000	$16,000 +3000
Long-term liabilities	12,000	8,000 −4000
Capital stock	25,000	30,000
Retained earnings	4,000	6,000 +2000
	$54,000	$60,000

RE + DIV / NI

1500 DIV

An analysis of the company's records reveals the following additional information.

√[1] Depreciation and amortization of intangibles included in the determination of net income were $1,500 and $1,000, respectively.

√[2] $1,500 of dividends were declared and paid during the year.

√[3] $5,000 of capital stock was sold, $4,000 of which was subsequently used to retire long-term liabilities.

√[4] Fixed assets of $5,000 were acquired.

[5] Cash, included in the current asset figures, increased $2,500 during 1993. The ending balance was $10,000.

Instructions

[a] Prepare a statement of cash flows for 1993, applying the indirect method of determining cash from operating activities.

[b] What information that is not available would be required to be able to calculate cash flows from operating activities by the direct method?

22–34   STATEMENT OF CASH FLOWS PREPARATION (DIRECT)   During 1993, Friar Company reported revenues of $150,000 and expenses of $127,500. The following information is available:

[1] Current assets changed as follows:

Accounts receivable	+ $12,500
Inventory	− $ 7,500
Prepaid expenses	+ $ 2,000

Current liabilities changed as follows:

Accounts payable	+ $ 8,200
Accrued expenses	− $ 5,300

[2] Nonoperating activities are reported as follows:

[a] Bonds Payable with a book value of $10,000 were retired for cash.

[b] Land was acquired by issuing common stock. The value attributed to the transaction was $25,000.

√[c] Machinery was sold at book value of $7,500.

Instructions

Prepare a statement of cash flows for the year, applying the direct method for operating activities. The reconciliation of net income to net cash flows from operating activities may be omitted. The beginning cash balance was $42,600.

22–35   CASH FLOW FROM OPERATING ACTIVITIES   Samuelson Company reported the following information in its income statement for 1993:

Revenues		$305,000
Cost of goods sold	$185,000	
Operating expenses	50,000	(235,000)
Income from operations		70,000
Loss from sale of equipment		(7,000)
Net income		$ 63,000

During the year, accounts receivable declined by $12,000, inventory increased by $16,000, accounts payable increased by $8,000, and accrued expenses declined by $6,250. The loss on the sale of equipment resulted from the sale of equipment with a $27,000 book value for $20,000 cash.

Instructions

Compute cash from operating activities by the direct method, including calculations to support the numbers that would appear in the statement of cash flows for cash provided by revenues and used for expenses.

22–36 STATEMENT OF CASH FLOWS PREPARATION Telecom, Inc., has determined its cash flows from operating activities as $53,500. During 1993, the company had the following investing and financing activities:

[a] Cash dividends of $35,000 were declared and paid. An additional $17,000 of cash dividends were declared but remained unpaid at the end of the year.

[b] Machinery with a book value of $17,500 was sold for that amount. Additional machinery of $26,000 was acquired to replace that sold.

[c] Notes payable of $38,000 were taken out at the local bank early in the year. By the end of the year, $12,000 of this amount had been repaid.

[d] Bonds payable with a book value of $25,000 were converted into common stock.

Instructions

Prepare a statement of cash flows for the year, including only a single amount for cash flows from operating activities. (You do not have the information to determine the components of this number.) Assume the beginning cash balance was $65,000.

PROBLEMS

22–37 STATEMENT OF CASH FLOWS PREPARATION (DIRECT) Information taken from the detailed trial balance sheet of Hunt Company is as follows:

	Dr. (Cr.) Balances At December 31	
	1992	1993
Cash	$ 20,000	$ 30,000
Accounts receivable	45,000	78,000
Investments	15,000	–0–
Property, plant, and equipment	92,600	118,100
Accumulated depreciation	(27,100)	(33,600)
Intangible assets	17,000	16,000
Accrued expenses	(7,500)	(7,000)
Bonds payable	(25,500)	(25,500)
Common stock, $10 par	(75,000)	(100,000)
Additional paid-in capital	(40,000)	(55,000)
Retained earnings	(14,500)	(21,000)
	–0–	–0–

Other information relating to various financing and investing activities of the company is as follows:

[1] Investments were sold at their carrying value.

[2] Items of equipment costing $27,500 and having $18,000 accumulated depreciation were sold at book value. New equipment was acquired to replace the outdated models that were sold.

[3] During the year, 2,500 shares of common stock were sold for cash.

[4] Dividends of $8,500 were declared and paid during the year. No other entries were made to the Retained Earnings account except the recognition of net income which included revenues of $107,000 and operating expenses of $92,000.

Instructions

[a] Prepare a statement of cash flows for 1993. Use the direct method to determine cash flows from operating activities and include all required disclosures for which you have information.

[b] Why is the reconciliation of net income to net cash provided by or used in operating activities a required disclosure when the direct method is used?

22–38 STATEMENT OF CASH FLOWS PREPARATION (DIRECT) Kelley Company is preparing a statement of cash flows for 1993. Information has been accumulated concerning changes in account balances during 1993 as follows:

	Change in Dr. (Cr.) 1993
Cash	$ (5,500)
Accounts receivable, net	12,000
Inventory	60,500
Property, plant, and equipment	17,650
Accumulated depreciation	(7,300)
Intangible assets	10,000
Accrued expenses	(1,600)
Accounts payable	(10,750)
Notes payable, 90-day	(31,150)
Bonds payable	(10,000)
Common stock	(10,000)
Additional paid-in capital	(2,000)
Retained earnings	(21,850)
	–0–

The following explanations of account changes are available:

Property, Plant, and Equipment.   Fully depreciated equipment with a cost of $7,500 was discarded. Equipment with a cost of $6,250 and accumulated depreciation of $4,000 was sold for $2,250. Depreciation expense was $18,800. Additional items of new equipment were acquired during the year.

Intangible Assets.   A patent was acquired during the year in exchange for 1,000 shares of the company's $10 par value common stock. The market value of the shares on the date of the exchange was $12. Amortization of existing intangible assets was recognized during the year.

Bonds Payable. $100,000 of 10% bonds payable were retired at book value and $110,000 of 8% bonds were issued.

Retained Earnings.   The only entries during the year were to recognize net income and dividends declared of $25,000. Revenues for 1993 totaled $285,000 and expenses totaled $238,150.

Instructions

Prepare a statement of cash flows for 1993, including all required disclosures for which you have information. Use the direct approach for determining cash from operating activities and assume that the beginning cash balance was $14,285.

22–39   ANALYSIS OF CASH FLOW TRANSACTIONS   Friar Company recorded the items listed below during 1993. The controller believes that some or all of the items may have an impact on the company's statement of cash flows.

[1] Net income is $145,000. This amount includes a $15,000 extraordinary loss resulting from the condemnation of land by the city. The company received $165,000 for land carried on the books at $180,000. (Assume no income tax effect of the extraordinary loss.)

[2] Intangible assets increased by $28,000 during the year, representing the acquisition of a patent for $34,000 and amortization of intangibles of $6,000.

[3] Cash dividends of $12,500 were declared and paid.

[4] Treasury stock with a par value of $17,000 was acquired for $31,000 and recorded by the cost method. None of the treasury shares has been resold as of the end of the year.

[5] An analysis of the Accumulated Depreciation account reveals the following:

Balance, end of year	$210,000
Balance, beginning of year	175,000
Increase	$ 35,000
Accumulated depreciation on fully depreciated assets retired during year	$ 11,250

[6] Convertible bonds issued at $100,000 par value in 1991 were converted into common stock during the year. The par value of the stock issued was $50,000; additional paid-in capital was increased by $50,000.

[7] The balance of various noncurrent asset accounts changed during the year as follows (assume no gains or losses, other than the extraordinary loss in [1] above):

Land	decrease	$ 50,000	
Equipment	increase	60,000	
Building	increase	100,000	

(handwritten: Land Buy 130000 | 180000 Sold (50000))

√[8] An analysis of working capital accounts reveals that working capital increased by $9,750 during the year. *(handwritten: only cash)*

(handwritten: CA−CL)

Instructions

In preparing your responses to the following questions, assume that the amounts all current assets and current liabilities, other than cash, were unchanged during the year.

[a] Describe how each of the eight items above should be presented in Friar's statement of cash flows for 1993.

[b] Compute the following items:

[1] Net cash provided (used) by operating activities.
[2] Net cash provided (used) by investing activities.
[3] Net cash provided (used) by financing activities.

22–40 STATEMENT OF CASH FLOWS PREPARATION (INDIRECT) Trial balances at December 31, 1992 and 1993, for Cain Company are presented below, along with additional information necessary for the preparation of a statement of cash flows.

	1992	1993
Debits		
Cash	$ 19,235	$ 25,471 *(6236)*
Accounts receivable, net	42,515	41,760
Inventory	55,600	59,255 *(3655)*
Prepaid expenses	1,200	1,100
Property, plant, and equipment	125,450	200,450 *(75000)*
Intangible assets	57,200	55,000 *(2200)*
Treasury stock	–0–	12,000 *(12000)*
	$301,200	$395,036
Credits		
Accrued expenses	$ 5,400	$ 6,200
Accounts payable	29,800	27,119
Note payable, 60-day	43,350	23,350
Accumulated depreciation	47,100	44,600
Note payable, 5-year	–0–	10,000
Common stock	125,000	160,000
Additional paid-in capital	10,000	25,000
Retained earnings	40,550	98,767
	$301,200	$395,036

(handwritten right margin: Δ RE + DIV NI)

(handwritten: 98767 −40550 58217 RE + 10000 DIV 68217 NI)

During 1993 a building with a cost of $75,000 and $30,000 of accumulated depreciation was completely destroyed by a fire resulting from an electrical storm. Insurance proceeds of $60,000 *(handwritten: ⟶ Extraordinary)* were received. The event was considered both unusual in nature and infrequent in occurrence. The building was replaced by a new facility at a cost of $100,000. In addition, 3,500 shares of $10 par value stock were exchanged for equipment during the year. The stock was not actively traded; the equipment had a listed selling price of $50,000.

Dividends of $10,000 were declared and paid during 1993. All notes payable represent bank loans.

Instructions

Prepare a statement of cash flows for 1993, including all required disclosures for which you have information, under the following assumptions:

[a] The 60-day note payable represents a bank loan that the company does not consider part of cash provided by or used in operations.

[b] The indirect method is used to compute cash from operating activities.

22-41 REVISED STATEMENT OF CASH FLOWS PREPARATION (INDIRECT) The accountant for Max Enterprises has drafted the following financial statement for 1993. The accountant was unaware of the FASB's statement concerning the statement of cash flows in cash flow reporting. He was also unfamiliar with the detailed reporting requirements under *APB Opinion No. 19*.

Max Enterprises
WORKING CAPITAL STATEMENT
December 31, 1993

Source of Working Capital

Net income	$762,750	
Depreciation	19,775	
Issuance of preferred stock	50,000	
Book value of fixed asset sold	35,000	$867,525

Uses of Working Capital

Acquisition of fixed assets	375,000	
Acquisition of patents	50,000	
Purchase of treasury stock	75,250	
Retirement of bonds	150,000	
Dividends on preferred stock	5,000	
Dividends on common stock	72,000	727,250
Increase in working capital		$140,275

The company's accountant accepted a position as a ski instructor at a Canadian ski resort and left town on short notice. The president of Max Enterprises has engaged you to evaluate the above statement and to revise it, if necessary, in accordance with current FASB standards. You have found the items included in the above statement to be accurate. Additional information that was apparently not incorporated into this statement, however, includes the following:

[1] In addition to the bonds retired for $150,000, bonds of $350,000 were converted into common stock during the year. Non cash

[2] An analysis of changes in current assets and current liabilities reveals the following:

	Dollar Change in Account Balance During 1993
Cash	− 53,650
Marketable securities	+ 15,750
Accounts receivable, net	+ 85,623
Inventory	+ 97,245
Accounts payable	− 4,762
Income taxes payable	+ 9,455

[3] The fixed asset sold during the year resulted in a $15,000 gain that was included in net income. No extraordinary items were recognized during 1993.

[4] The patent account increased $50,000 during the year. This change included the acquisition of one patent for $37,500, the successful defense of an existing patent for $19,250, and amortization for the year.

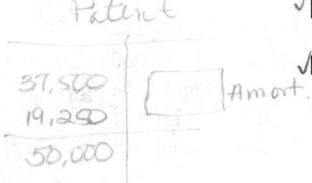

Instructions

[a] Identify all errors and omissions in the financial statement prepared by the previous accountant for Max Enterprises.

[b] Prepare a revised statement of cash flows for 1993, applying the indirect method for determining cash from operating activities. You may assume a beginning cash balance of $105,000. Include all required disclosures for which you have information.

22-42 STATEMENT OF CASH FLOWS PREPARATION WITH WORKSHEET (DIRECT) Piper Company has not yet prepared a formal statement of cash flows for 1993. Comparative statements of financial position as of December 31, 1992 and 1993, and a statement of income and retained earnings for the year ended December 31, 1993, are presented below:

Piper Company
STATEMENT OF FINANCIAL POSITION
December 31, 1992 and 1993
(in thousands)

	1992	1993
Assets		
Current Assets		
Cash	$ 100	$ 60 (40000) > (90000)
U.S. treasury notes *CE*	50	–0– (50000)
✓Accounts receivable	500	610 110 000
✓Inventory	600	720 +20000
Total current assets	1,250	1,390
Long-Term Assets		
Land	70	80 +10000
Buildings and equipment	600	710 110000
Accumulated depreciation	(120)	(180) –60000
Patents (less amortization)	130	105 –25000
Total long-term assets	680	715
Total assets	$1,930	$2,105
Liabilities and Ownership		
Current Liabilities		
✓Accounts payable	$ 300	$ 360 60000
Income taxes payable	20	25 5000
Notes payable	400	400 0
Total current liabilities	720	785
Term Notes Payable, Due 1992	200	200 0
Total liabilities	920	985
Owners' Equity		
Common stock outstanding	700	830 130000 → Increase due to stock dividend
Retained earnings	310	290
Total owners' equity	1,010	1,120
Total liabilities and equity	$1,930	$2,105

Piper Company
STATEMENT OF INCOME AND RETAINED EARNINGS
For the Year Ended December 31, 1993
(in thousands)

Sales		$2,408
Less expenses and interest		
Cost of goods sold ✓	$1,100	
Salaries and benefits ✓	850	
Heat, light, and power ✓	75	
Depreciation ✓	60	
Property taxes ✓	18	
Patent amortization	25	
Miscellaneous expense ✓	10	
Interest ✓	55	2,193
Income before income taxes		215
Income taxes		105 –5000 ↑ in Tax Payable
Net income		110
Retained earnings, Jan. 1, 1993		310
		420
Stock dividend		(130)
Retained earnings, Dec. 31, 1993		$ 290

Instructions

[a] Prepare a worksheet using the format of Exhibit 22–7 to facilitate the preparation of a statement of cash flows for 1993.

[b] Prepare a statement of cash flows for 1993, using the direct method for determining cash from operating activities. Treat the U.S. treasury notes as a cash equivalent. You may omit the schedule reconciling net income to cash flows from operating activities, but include all other required disclosures for which you have information.   (CMA adapted)

22–43 WORKSHEET ENTRIES The following information is to be used in developing worksheet entries for the preparation of a statement of cash flows. Each item should be treated *independently* in complying with the problem requirements as stated. In all cases the year is 1993.

Company 1.   Net income for the year includes the effect of the following transactions involving the sale of fixed assets:

Sales Price	Cost	Accumulated Depreciation	Gain (Loss)
$15,000	$75,000	$70,000	$10,000
42,500	92,000	40,000	(9,500)

Company 2. Income taxes are presented in the income statement as follows:

Income before income taxes		$XXX,XXX
Provision for income taxes		
Payable currently	$147,623	
Deferred	56,557	204,180
Net income		$XXX,XXX

Company 3.   Equipment and the related depreciation accounts for 1993 are as follows:

	Debit	Credit	Balance Dr. (Cr.)
Equipment			
Balance, Jan. 1			$472,000
Cost of equipment sold for $72,800		$126,000	346,000
Cost of equipment purchased	$266,000		612,000
Cost of fully depreciated equipment discarded		27,850	584,150
Accumulated Depreciation			
Balance, Jan. 1			(255,000)
Depreciation on equipment sold	102,000		(153,000)
Depreciation on fully depreciated equipment discarded	27,850		(125,150)
Depreciation expense for 1993		86,000	(211,150)

Company 4.   Interest expense was recorded during 1993 with the following entry:

Interest Expense	105,000	
Cash		100,000
Unamortized Bond Discount		5,000

Company 5.   Interest expense was recorded during 1993 with the following entry:

Interest Expense	388,000	
Unamortized Bond Premium	12,000	
Interest Payable		400,000

Company 6.   Income statement data for the company for 1993 are as follows:

Income before extraordinary items	$150,000
Extraordinary loss—retirement of bonds, net of $8,750 income tax	16,250
Net income	$133,750

The extraordinary loss resulted from the retirement of bonds payable with a face value of $300,000 and a related unamortized discount of $2,000 at a cost of $323,000. The tax rate relative to the transaction is 35%.

Company 7. Land was acquired by issuing preferred stock with $100,000 par value. The preferred stock is not actively traded. The land had a current appraisal value of $117,500.

Instructions

Analyze the information given for each company and prepare the entry in general journal form to account for the item on a worksheet similar to that in Exhibit 22–7. Treat each item independently and provide a brief explanation for each entry.

22–44 STATEMENT OF CASH FLOWS PREPARATION (INDIRECT) Endsley Company has requested your assistance in the preparation of a statement of cash flows for the year ended June 30, 1993. Comparative trial balances as of June 30, 1992 and 1993, are presented below:

	Dr. (Cr.)	
	June 30, 1992	June 30, 1993
Cash	$ 2,825	$ 3,612
Accounts receivable, net	25,600	17,401
Inventory	42,700	33,250
Equipment	126,000	120,750
Accumulated depreciation, equipment	(42,700)	(52,700)
Building	122,000	207,000
Accumulated depreciation, building	(25,000)	(43,500)
Land	90,000	67,500
Patent	–0–	34,500
Accrued expenses	(2,453)	(1,100)
Accounts payable	(12,462)	(11,400)
Notes payable	(50,000)	(40,000)
Deferred income taxes	(5,430)	(6,550)
Bonds payable	(75,000)	(75,000)
Premium on bonds payable	(2,000)	(1,750)
Common stock ($10 par)	(125,000)	(150,000)
Additional paid-in capital	(25,000)	(35,000)
Retained earnings	(44,080)	(67,013)
	–0–	–0–

The following information also pertains to the fiscal year ending June 30, 1993:

Income/Dividends. Net income for the year ended June 30, 1993, was $42,933. No extraordinary items were reported in the income statement. Dividends of $20,000 were declared and paid to common stockholders.

Property, Plant, and Equipment. Equipment costing $25,000 with accumulated depreciation of $20,000 was sold at book value. Depreciation of $30,000 was recognized during the year. Additional equipment of $19,750 was acquired.

An addition to the building was made during the year at a cost of $85,000. Depreciation of $18,500 was recognized during the year.

Land with a cost of $57,500 was sold for $97,800. Additional land was acquired by issuing 2,500 shares of common stock that had a total value of $35,000. A recent appraisal value of the land was not available.

Patent. A patent was acquired for $34,500 during the year.

Notes Payable. A series of short-term loans was taken out under a revolving line of credit with a local bank. These loans are for [nonoperating purposes.]

Instructions

[a] Prepare a statement of cash flows for 1993, applying the indirect method of determining cash from operating activities. Include all required disclosures for which you have information.

[b] In determining net cash provided by operating activities, explain your treatment of the $1,120 increase in deferred income taxes and the $250 decrease in premium on bonds payable.

22–45 STATEMENT OF CASH FLOWS PREPARATION (INDIRECT) Dove Company's statement of cash flows has not yet been prepared for the year ended December 31, 1993. The schedule below compares the net change in the balance sheet accounts between December 31, 1993 and 1992.

	Net Change Increase (Decrease)
Debit Balance Accounts	
Cash	$ (340,000)
Accounts receivable, net	440,000
Inventories	580,000
Property, plant, and equipment	1,800,000
Total	$2,480,000
Credit Balance Accounts	
Accumulated depreciation	$ 950,000
Accounts payable	1,250,000
Notes payable, current	(150,000)
Serial bonds payable	(2,000,000)
Common stock, $10 par value	9,000,000
Capital contributed in excess of par value	1,300,000
Retained earnings	(7,870,000)
Total	$2,480,000

Additional Information

[1] Dove incurred a net after-tax loss from regular operations of $500,000 for the year ended December 31, 1993. It also had an extraordinary gain from the sale of condemned land in the amount of $1,400,000 net of income tax of $600,000. The condemned land had a book value of $2,500,000.

[2] Accounts receivable of $650,000 were written off during 1993, by charging Allowance for Doubtful Accounts. The provision for bad debts during 1993 was $1,250,000.

[3] Machinery acquired in 1988 at a cost of $2,000,000 was sold for $550,000. The machinery had a net book value of $350,000 at the date of sale.

[4] A new parcel of land was purchased during April 1993. The market value of the land was $6,300,000. Cash of $1,500,000 and 400,000 shares of Dove's common stock were given in exchange for the land.

[5] The serial bonds mature at a rate of $2,000,000 each year. The bonds were sold at par value.

[6] A 5% stock dividend was declared January 15, 1993, on 10,000,000 shares of Dove's common stock. The stock dividend was issued on February 10, 1993, to all stockholders of record as of January 31, 1993. The market value of the stock at these three dates was as follows:

Jan. 15, 1993	$11.00 per share
Jan. 31, 1993	$10.45 per share
Feb. 10, 1993	$10.60 per share

[7] A cash dividend of $.30 per share of common stock was declared on June 30, 1993, to all stockholders of record as of July 15, 1993. The dividend was paid on July 31, 1993.

[8] The notes payable resulted from extended terms granted by one of Dove Company's major suppliers of inventory.

[9] Dove's cash balance at the beginning of 1993 was $978,000.

Instructions

Prepare a statement of cash flows for the year ended December 31, 1993. Dove Company uses the indirect method in determining cash from operating activities. Include all required disclosures permitted by the information you have. (CMA adapted)

22–46 STATEMENT OF CASH FLOWS PREPARATION WITH WORKSHEET (DIRECT) Webster Company has prepared its financial statements for the year ended December 31, 1992, and for the three months ended March 31, 1993. The company's balance sheet at December 31, 1992, and

March 31, 1993, and its income statement data for the three months ended March 31 are presented below. You are satisfied that the amounts presented are correct.

BALANCE SHEET

	Dec. 31, 1992	Mar. 31, 1993	
Cash	$ 25,300	$ 87,400	+62100
Marketable investments	16,500	7,300	−9200
Accounts receivable, net ✓	24,320	49,320	+25000
Inventory ✓	31,090	48,590	+17500
Total current assets	97,210	192,610	
Land ✓	40,000	18,700	−21300
Building	250,000	250,000	0
Equipment	—	81,500	+81500
Accumulated depreciation	(15,000)	(16,250)	+1250
Investment in 30%-owned company	61,220	67,100	+5880
Other assets	15,100	15,100	0
Total	$448,530	$608,760	
Accounts payable ✓	$ 21,220	$ 17,330	−3890
Dividend payable ✓	—	8,000	+8000
Income taxes payable ✓	—	34,616	+34616
Total current liabilities	21,220	59,946	
Other liabilities	186,000	186,000	0
Bonds payable ✓	50,000	115,000	+65000
Discount on bonds payable ✓	(2,300)	(2,150)	−150
Deferred income taxes ✓	510	846	+336
Preferred stock	30,000	—	−30000
Common stock	80,000	110,000	+30000
Dividends declared	—	(8,000)	−8000
Retained earnings	83,100	147,118	64018
Total	$448,530	$608,760	

(handwritten right margin: RE + DIV NI)

INCOME STATEMENT

check reconciliation

	For the Three Months Ended Mar. 31, 1993
Sales	$242,807
Gain on sale of marketable investments ✓	2,400
Equity in earnings of 30%-owned company	5,880
Gain on condemnation of land ✓	10,700
	261,787
Cost of sales ✓	138,407
General and administrative expenses ✓	22,010
Depreciation ✓	1,250
Interest expense ✓	1,150
Income taxes	34,952 −336 = 34616
	197,769
Net income	$ 64,018

(handwritten right margin: No cash effect, only expensed it. Tax pay. on Books for 34616. Tax Exp 34952 − Tax Pay 34616 DT 336)

Your discussion with the company's controller and a review of the financial records have revealed the following information:

[1] On January 8, 1993, the company sold marketable securities for cash of $11,600. These securities had been held for more than six months.

[2] The company's preferred stock is convertible into common stock at a rate of one share of preferred for two shares of common. The preferred stock and common stock have par values of $2 and $1, respectively.

√[3] On January 17, 1993, three acres of land were condemned. An award of $32,000 in cash was received on March 22, 1993. Purchase of additional land as a replacement is not anticipated.

√[4] On March 25, 1993, the company purchased equipment for cash.

[5] On March 29, 1993, bonds payable were issued by the company at par for cash.

[6] The investment in 30%-owned company included $3,220 attributable to goodwill at December 31, 1992. Goodwill is being amortized at an annual rate of $480.

Instructions

[a] Prepare a worksheet similar to Exhibit 22–7 to be used in preparing a statement of cash flows for the three months ended March 31, 1993.

[b] Prepare a statement of cash flows, based on your worksheet from part [a]. Use the direct method of determining cash from operating activities and include all required disclosures.

(AICPA adapted)

22–47   STATEMENT OF CASH FLOWS PREPARATION WITH WORKSHEET (DIRECT)   Presented below are the comparative statements of position of Filson Corporation as of December 31, 1993 and 1992, together with the income statement for the year ended December 31, 1993.

Filson Corporation
STATEMENTS OF FINANCIAL POSITION

	December 31, 1993	December 31, 1992	Increase (Decrease)
Assets			
Current assets			
Cash	$ 100,000	$ 90,000	$ 10,000
Accounts receivable (net of allowance for uncollectible accounts of $10,000 and $8,000, respectively)	210,000	140,000	70,000
Inventories	260,000	220,000	40,000
Total current assets	570,000	450,000	120,000
Land	325,000	200,000	125,000
Plant and equipment	580,000	633,000	(53,000)
Less: Accumulated depreciation	(90,000)	(100,000)	10,000
Patents	30,000	33,000	(3,000)
Total assets	$1,415,000	$1,216,000	$199,000

Liabilities and Shareholders' Equity

Liabilities			
Current liabilities			
Accounts payable	$ 260,000	$ 200,000	$ 60,000
Accrued salaries and wages	200,000	210,000	(10,000)
Total current liabilities	460,000	410,000	50,000
Deferred income taxes	140,000	100,000	40,000
Long-term bonds (due Dec. 15, 1995)	130,000	180,000	(50,000)
Total liabilities	730,000	690,000	40,000
Shareholders' equity			
Common stock, par value $5; authorized 100,000 shares; issued and outstanding 50,000 and 42,000 shares, respectively	250,000	210,000	40,000
Additional paid-in capital	233,000	170,000	63,000
Retained earnings	202,000	146,000	56,000
Total shareholders' equity	685,000	526,000	159,000
Total liabilities and shareholders' equity	$1,415,000	$1,216,000	$199,000

Filson Corporation
INCOME STATEMENT
For the Year Ended December 31, 1993

Sales	$1,000,000
Expenses	
Cost of sales	560,000
Salary and wages	190,000
Depreciation	20,000
Amortization	3,000
Loss on sale of equipment	4,000
Interest	16,000
Miscellaneous	8,000
Total expenses	801,000
Income before income taxes and extraordinary item	199,000
Income taxes	
Current	50,000
Deferred	40,000
Provision for income taxes	90,000
Income before extraordinary item	109,000
Extraordinary item—gain on repurchase of long-term bonds (net of $10,000 income tax)	12,000
Net income	$ 121,000
Earnings per share	
Income before extraordinary item	$2.21
Extraordinary item	.24
Net income	$2.45

Additional Information

[1] On February 2, 1993, Filson issued a 10% stock dividend to shareholders of record on January 15, 1993. The market price per share of the common stock on February 2, 1993, was $15.
[2] On March 1, 1993, Filson issued 3,800 shares of common stock for land. The common stock and land had current market values of approximately $40,000 on March 1, 1993.
[3] On April 15, 1993, Filson repurchased long-term bonds with a face value of $50,000. The gain of $22,000 was reported as an extraordinary item on the income statement.
[4] On June 30, 1993, Filson sold equipment costing $53,000, with a book value of $23,000, for $19,000 cash.
[5] On September 30, 1993, Filson declared and paid a $.04 per share cash dividend to shareholders of record August 1, 1993.
[6] On October 10, 1993, Filson purchased land for $85,000 cash.
[7] Deferred income taxes represent temporary differences relating to the use of accelerated cost recovery for income tax reporting and straight-line depreciation for financial reporting.

Instructions

[a] Analyze Filson's transactions and prepare a worksheet similar to Exhibit 22–7 for use in preparing a statement of cash flows for 1993.
[b] Prepare a statement of cash flows for Filson Corporation for 1993, applying the direct method for determining cash flows from operations. You may omit the schedule reconciling net income to net cash provided by operating activities, but include all other required disclosures.

(AICPA adapted)

22–48 STATEMENT OF CASH FLOWS PREPARATION (INDIRECT) The management of Romper Co., concerned over a decrease in working capital, has provided you with the following comparative analysis of changes in account balances at December 31, 1992 and 1993:

| | December 31, | | Increase |
	1993	1992	(Decrease)
Debit Balances			
Cash	$ 145,000	$ 186,000	$ (41,000)
Accounts receivable	253,000	273,000	(20,000)
Inventories	483,000	538,000	(55,000)
Securities held for plant expansion purposes	150,000	—	150,000
Machinery and equipment	927,000	647,000	280,000
Leasehold improvements	87,000	87,000	—
Patents	27,800	30,000	(2,200)
Totals	$2,072,800	$1,761,000	$311,800

| | December 31, | | Increase |
	1993	1992	(Decrease)
Credit Balances			
Allowance for uncollectible accounts receivable	$ 14,000	$ 17,000	$ (3,000)
Accumulated depreciation of machinery and equipment	416,000	372,000	44,000
Allowance for amortization of leasehold improvements	58,000	49,000	9,000
Accounts payable	232,800	105,000	127,800
Cash dividends payable	40,000	—	40,000
Current portion of 6% serial bonds payable	50,000	50,000	—
6% serial bonds payable	250,000	300,000	(50,000)
Preferred stock	90,000	100,000	(10,000)
Common stock	500,000	500,000	—
Retained earnings	422,000	268,000	154,000
Totals	$2,072,800	$1,761,000	$311,800

Additional Information

During 1993 the following transactions occurred:

[1] New machinery was purchased for $386,000, and obsolete machinery, with a book value of $61,000, was sold for $48,000. No other entries were recorded in Machinery and Equipment or related accounts other than provisions for depreciation.

[2] The company paid $2,000 legal costs in the successful defense of a new patent. Amortization of patents amounting to $4,200 was recorded.

[3] Preferred stock, par value $100, was purchased at 110 and subsequently canceled. The premium was charged to retained earnings.

[4] On December 10, 1993, the board of directors declared a cash dividend of $.20 per share payable to holders of common stock on January 10, 1994.

[5] A comparative analysis of retained earnings as of December 31, 1993 and 1992, is presented below:

| | December 31, | |
	1993	1992
Balance, Jan. 1	$268,000	$131,000
Net income	195,000	172,000
	463,000	303,000
Dividends declared	(40,000)	(35,000)
Premium on preferred stock repurchased	(1,000)	—
	$422,000	$268,000

Instructions

[a] Prepare a statement of cash flows for Romper Co. for the year ended December 31, 1993. Use the indirect method of presenting cash from operating activities and include all required disclosures for which you have information.

[b] Explain your treatment of the $13,000 loss on the sale of obsolete equipment ($61,000–$48,000) in computing net cash flows from both operating and investing activities.

(AICPA adapted)

CASES

22–49   SOURCES AND USES OF CASH   Clinton Electronics Corp. (CEC) is a young and growing producer of electronic measuring instruments and technical equipment. You have been asked to help prepare a statement of cash flows for the fiscal year ended October 31, 1992. You have obtained the following information concerning certain events and transactions:

[1] The amount of reported earnings for the fiscal year was $800,000, which included a deduction for an extraordinary loss of $93,000 (See item [5]).

[2] Depreciation expense of $265,000 was included in the earnings statement.

[3] Uncollectible accounts receivable of $40,000 were written off against the allowance for uncollectible accounts. Also, $47,000 of bad debts expense was included in determining earnings for the fiscal year, and the same amount was added to the allowance for uncollectible accounts.

[4] A gain of $4,700 was realized on the cash sale of a machine; it originally cost $75,000, of which $25,000 was undepreciated on the date of sale.

[5] On April 1, 1992, a freak lightning storm caused an uninsured building loss of $93,000 ($180,000 loss, less reduction in income taxes of $87,000). This extraordinary loss was included in determining earnings, as indicated in item [1].

[6] On July 3, 1992, building and land were purchased for $600,000. CEC paid $100,000 cash and issued $200,000 market value of its unissued common stock and a $300,000 purchase-money mortgage.

[7] On August 3, 1992, $700,000 face value of CEC's 6% convertible debentures were converted into $140,000 par value of its common stock. The bonds were originally issued at face value.

[8] The board of directors declared a $265,000 cash dividend on October 20, 1992, payable on November 15, 1992, to stockholders of record on November 5, 1992.

Instructions

For each of the eight items above, explain whether the item is a source or use of cash. Describe how the item should be disclosed in CEC's statement of cash flows for the fiscal year ended October 31, 1992. If the item is neither a source nor a use of cash, explain why, and indicate the disclosure, if any, that should be made.

(AICPA adapted)

22–50   INTERPRETATION OF STATEMENT OF CASH FLOWS   Black and Blue companies operate in the same industry and are similar in size, in terms of investment in assets and sales volume. The ratio of current assets to current liabilities at the 1993 balance sheet date is the same for both companies, approximately 2.4 to 1. This is very close to the average for all companies in the industry.

Selected data from the statements of cash flows of the two companies are presented as follows:

Black Company	1990	1991	1992	1993
	(amounts in thousands)			
Net Cash Provided				
Operating activities	$ 100	$ 125	$ 115	$ 128
Investing activities				
Sale of assets	15	12	50	25
Financing activities				
Long-term borrowing	10	—	—	15
Issuance of capital stock	—	25	—	—
	125	162	165	168
Net Cash Used (Various)	(115)	(150)	(170)	(164)
Net increase (decrease) in cash	$ 10	$ 12	$ (5)	$ 4

Blue Company	1990	1991	1992	1993
		(amounts in thousands)		
Net Cash Provided				
Operating activities	$ 50	$ 30	$ (60)	$ 10
Investing activities				
Sale of assets	10	25	50	50
Financing activities				
Long-term borrowing	75	15	70	—
Issuance of capital stock	—	75	100	75
	135	145	160	135
Net Cash Used (Various)	(125)	(133)	(165)	(131)
Net increase (decrease) in cash	$ 10	$ 12	$ (5)	$ 4

Instructions

[a] Identify similarities in the two companies.

[b] Identify differences between the two companies.

[c] Which company appears to be in a stronger position from the viewpoint of potential investors in the company's stock and major creditors? Why?

22–51 DEFICIENCIES IN STATEMENT OF CASH FLOWS   The following financial statement was prepared by Mex Company's accountant:

Mex Company
STATEMENT OF SOURCE AND APPLICATION OF CASH
For the Year Ended September 30, 1992

Source of Funds

Net income	$ 52,000
Depreciation and depletion	59,000
Increase in long-term debt	178,000
Common stock issued under employee option plans	5,000
Changes in current receivables and inventories, less current liabilities (excluding current maturities of long-term debt)	3,000
	$297,000

Application of Funds

Cash dividends	$ 33,000
Expenditures for property, plant, and equipment	202,000
Investments and other uses	9,000
Change in cash	53,000
	$297,000

The following additional information is available for the year ended September 30, 1992:

[1] The balance sheet of Mex Company distinguishes between current and noncurrent assets and liabilities.

[2]

Depreciation expense	$ 56,000
Depletion expense	3,000
	$ 59,000

[3]

Increase in long-term debt	$620,000
Retirement of debt	442,000
Net increase	$178,000

[4] Mex Company received $5,000 in cash from its employees on its employee stock option plans, and wage and salary expense attributable to the plan (which has not been recorded) was an additional $22,000.

[5]

Expenditures for property, plant, and equipment	$240,000
Proceeds from retirements of property, plant, and equipment	38,000
Net expenditures	$202,000

[6] A stock dividend of 10,000 shares of Mex Company's common stock was distributed to common stockholders on April 1, 1992, when the per share market price was $6 and par value was $1.

[7] On July 1, 1992, when its market price was $5 per share, 16,000 shares of Mex Company common stock were issued in exchange for 4,000 shares of preferred stock.

Instructions

[a] Explain the objectives of a statement of the type shown above.

[b] Identify the weaknesses in the form and format of Mex Company's statement, without reference to the additional information.

[c] For each item of additional information above, indicate the preferable treatment and explain why it is preferable.   (AICPA adapted)

JUDGMENT CASES

22–52   CASH EQUIVALENTS   The president of Prudent, Inc., has directed that a plant replacement and improvement fund be created to finance needed improvements in the manufacturing processes for the company's principal product in the coming years. The current processes are rather obsolete and have caused some of the company's oldest customers to place orders with competitors.

Specifically, the president wants to set aside $250,000 a year for the next 5 years at which time the company will obtain a loan for approximately $5,000,000 to rebuild and improve the efficiency of several machines and to acquire several new ones. The board of directors (which the president dominates) agreed to the idea during its December board meeting and on December 31, 1992, the company established a fund in the amount of $250,000. The fund is currently composed of short term treasury bills that mature in 60 days. Upon maturity of these amounts, the president plans to invest the proceeds in a forthcoming municipal bond issue as a gesture of support to the small town in which the company is located.

The company's accountant, Roger Readytick, is compiling the company's general purpose financial statements and is in the midst of preparing the statement of cash flows. He is unsure about how the recently created plant replacement fund should be reported on that statement. He has discussed the issue with the company president who has responded:

> *Roger, I just don't see the problem. The fund is clearly a cash equivalent at this time. The investments are even specifically mentioned in the FASB Statement as a cash equivalent. As for the purpose of the fund, we created it and we can discontinue it at any time we wish. We can use these assets for any purpose we want. It isn't as if we were dealing with a sinking fund that some lender required as a condition of a loan. I want the fund treated as part of our cash and cash equivalents at the end of the year. Besides, we need to show a high liquidity anyway, because one of our banks is making noises about not renewing our annual line of credit.*

Instructions

Help Roger resolve this reporting issue. How should the fund be reported in the statement of cash flows? Also, be sure to consider how the fund should be presented in the balance sheet of the company.

22–53   REPORTING FINANCING AND OPERATING ACTIVITIES   On January 1, 1992, Deep Vee, Inc., borrowed $5,000,000 by issuing a "noninterest bearing" note with a face (maturity) amount of $7,500,000. The entire face amount of the note is due on January 1, 1997. Assume, for purposes of simplicity, that the discount is being amortized on a straight line basis over the 5-year term of the note. (*APB Opinion No. 21* requires use of the effective rate method rather than the straight line method if the differences are material.)

Instructions

[a] How should Deep Vee report the $5,000,000 received in 1992 and the $7,500,000 cash payment in 1997 on its statements of cash flows?

[b] Assume that Deep Vee pays the note off early for $5,400,000 on January 1, 1993. How should the company report the cash payment on its statement of cash flows for the year ending December 31, 1993?

22–54 INVESTING AND OPERATING ACTIVITIES Classic Video Rentals, a nonpublic company, acquires video tapes of older classic movies at a variety of locations throughout the Southwest. While the tapes are rented for short periods of time, the company has found that many of the customers that choose to rent the tapes are occasionally motivated to buy them. Although the company does not advertise the tapes for sale and had not originally intended to sell tapes, it does not object to selling them when approached and has developed pricing policies for that purpose. The company depreciates the tapes in its rental collection and considers the rentals to be operating rather than capital leases.

Instructions

How should the purchases of the tapes be presented on the company's statement of cash flows? Also, how should the proceeds from the sales of the tapes be presented on the statement of cash flows? Explain your conclusions.

CHAPTER 23

Accounting for Leases

OBJECTIVES

1. To discuss why many businesses use leasing to acquire service rights to assets.
2. To describe the controversial financial accounting and reporting issues that underlie leasing.
3. To discuss the conditions that cause the economic substance of a lease to change from the mere rental of property to a presumed sale and purchase.
4. To classify leases for accounting purposes from the perspectives of both lessees and lessors.
5. To demonstrate the application of appropriate accounting recognition, measurement, and disclosure principles to various types of leases.

LEASING AS A BUSINESS TRANSACTION

A lease is an agreement in which the owner of property, identified as the **lessor,** allows another party, identified as the **lessee,** to use the property in exchange for periodic payments. The lease agreement usually specifies responsibilities of each party to the lease, such as coverage of maintenance costs, taxes, and insurance, and specifies the period of time during which the agreement is in effect.

Leasing has become a very important mechanism by which companies acquire the resources needed to effectively operate their businesses. Many companies gain access to machinery, equipment, and other needed plant assets by means of leasing rather than outright purchase of the assets. The dollar magnitude of assets that are the subject of leases, as well as the significance of leasing as a method of financing important business transactions, justifies our study of this important topic in reasonable depth.

A variety of changes in our economy explain the increased popularity of leasing during the last few decades. One of the most beneficial aspects of leasing is the flexibility it provides the contracting parties to divide the risks and rights of ownership. In most purchase transactions the principal rights and risks of ownership are transferred from the seller to the buyer—although certain risks, such as product guarantees or warranties, may be retained by the seller. Leasing provides the parties to the agreement much greater flexibility than is possible in an outright sale and purchase.

For example, the rapid rate of technological advance in the computer industry has caused many potential buyers to lease rather than purchase equipment to avoid the risk of obsolescence. If the equipment becomes obsolete, and more modern capabilities become available, the lessee can allow the lease to expire and acquire or lease new equipment. The lessee is not limited by a long-term purchase obligation and old, out-of-date equipment. In such cases the risk of obsolescence is retained by the lessor. The lessor, who may also be the manufacturer of the product, may be better able to assess the possibility of obsolescence and, therefore, be willing to accept greater risk in order to more effectively market the product. Also, after an initial lease period, the lessor may be able to lease the property to a second lessee who does not require the latest technology. Some of the rights of ownership, such as the salvage value of the equipment at the end of the lease, may be retained by the lessor as compensation for accepting the increased risks of leasing. Rental rates are usually set at levels that recognize the relative distribution of the risks and rights of ownership to the two parties to the lease.

The income tax implications of leasing may also prove attractive; for example, lease payments may be deductible long before the same amounts of depreciation could be deducted if the asset had been purchased. Lessors may be able to depreciate assets that are leased to others and report only the lease payments received as revenue. If those assets had been sold, gross profit on the sale would have been recognized and taxed immediately. While the subject of structuring transactions for favorable tax results is beyond the scope of this text, we should nevertheless recognize the significant role income taxes play in influencing the manner in which business affairs are conducted.

Another reason that companies may choose to lease assets, rather than buy them, relates to avoiding the need to disburse large amounts of cash in acquiring needed assets. Cash preserved in that manner may then be used for other profitable projects. Companies may also enter into leases to avoid reporting large liabilities incurred in the purchase of an asset. Companies often attempt to lease assets to avoid reporting the liability and the related asset that would have resulted from a purchase. This practice is referred to as **off-balance-sheet financing** and is advantageous from a financial reporting perspective because of its effect on the company's reported financial position and results of operations. For example, the debt/equity ratio and the rate of return on assets employed each improves if the company leases assets in a manner which permits it to avoid reporting the assets and related liabilities in its balance sheet. Furthermore, if some of the liabilities would have been current, leasing may improve reported working capital and the current ratio. The accounting profession has recognized the possibility of abusive accounting practices in this area and has acted to eliminate some of the ability to achieve off-balance-sheet financing as we shall see later in this chapter.

The decision to lease, rather than purchase, is a complex business decision that requires careful analysis on the part of the lessee. The following are suggestive of the types of questions that must be answered before an informed decision can be made:

1. Are the rates firm or subject to interest rate change?
2. Is the lease noncancellable?
3. Does the acquiring company pay maintenance and taxes?
4. Are the monthly payments made at the beginning or end of the month?
5. Is casualty insurance included?
6. Are equipment upgrades guaranteed, and what is the cost?
7. What flexibility does the acquiring company have at the end of the lease?[1]

THE PRIMARY ACCOUNTING ISSUES

To properly account for and report leasing activities in financial statements, accountants must understand both the economics of these transactions and the motivations of the individuals who design and enter into them. The accounting profession has studied carefully the issue of leasing and has attempted to design standards that distinguish among various types of leases.

Substance over Form The primary goal in accounting for all types of leases is to recognize the economic substance of a particular lease rather than its mere legal form. When a lease contains provisions that change the substance of a transaction from merely the periodic payment of money for the use of property (rent) to an installment acquisition of substantial economic rights or benefits (purchase), the lease should be treated by the lessee as the purchase of an asset and the incurrence of a liability. According to the Financial Accounting Standards Board (FASB),

> *A lease that transfers substantially all of the benefits and risks incident to the ownership of property should be accounted for as the acquisition of an asset and the incurrence of an obligation by the lessee.*[2]

In such leases the lessor should record a sale of the property and recognize a receivable for the future rent, in recognition of the economic substance of the transaction. Likewise, the lessee should record the purchase of an asset and the incurrence of a liability for the obligation assumed. The concept of substance over form in regard to leases has been long established, well understood, and generally accepted. However, the specific circumstances in which leases should be treated as sales by lessors and purchases by lessees have been the subject of debate for many years.

---

[1]Ralph L. Benke, Jr., and Charles P. Baril, "The Lease vs. Purchase Decision," *Management Accounting* (March 1990), p. 46.
[2]*FASB Statement of Financial Accounting Standards No. 13,* "Accounting for Leases," 1976, par. 91.

A long history of problems is associated with accounting for leases. The Accounting Principles Board (APB) issued four separate major opinions dealing with different aspects of the subject. More recently, the FASB issued *Statement of Financial Accounting Standards No. 13*, which superseded all four of the APB Opinions and established comprehensive financial accounting and reporting requirements for both lessees and lessors. However, further demonstrating the complexity of this area of accounting, *SFAS No. 13* has been amended and interpreted many times by the FASB.

Financial reporting for complex lease agreements is a technical challenge and current authoritative pronouncements contain many subtle provisions and implications. Before accountants can resolve the many practical and conceptual leasing problems, they must acquire an understanding of basic leasing terms and concepts employed in the FASB pronouncements. Therefore, before proceeding to a discussion of lease classification, accounting, and financial statement presentation, we shall establish a common ground and understanding in regard to some important leasing terms and concepts.

IMPORTANT LEASING TERMS

We begin our discussion by considering the basic types of leases and how they are distinguished from each other. Other concepts and terms, less central to the overall theories underlying lease accounting, are introduced throughout the chapter when necessary and relevant to the particular issues being discussed.

LESSEES

In financial accounting, lessees initially classify leases as either operating or capital.

An **operating lease** is a rental agreement requiring periodic payments for the use of an asset. An operating lease, in substance, does *not* represent the purchase of an asset; consequently, the lease itself is not recorded and no new assets or liabilities are included in the accounting records of the lessee. Instead, rent expense is recognized as the leased asset is used by the lessee.

Substance over Form

A **capital lease** is a rental agreement that **represents, in substance, the purchase of an asset and incurrence of a liability.** In concept, when most of the rights and risks of ownership of a particular asset are transferred from a lessor to a lessee in a lease transaction, the lease is considered a capital lease and is a recordable transaction. To illustrate, assume that Maddox Company enters into a capital lease properly valued at $10,000. At the beginning of the lease term, Maddox will make the following entry to record the acquisition of the asset and incurrence of the liability.

Equipment	10,000	
Lease Liability		10,000

This asset and liability are subject to accounting requirements that are identical to other long-lived assets and liabilities we have studied. Whether a lease is treated as an operating or a capital lease may have important implications on the financial statements of the lessee. Therefore, the classification of the lease requires careful analysis and consideration of many factors. Several specific criteria in *SFAS No. 13* are used to make the distinction between operating and capital leases and are discussed in a later section of this chapter.

LESSORS

Lessors are required to classify a lease agreement into one of four possible types: operating, sales-type, direct-financing, and leveraged leases.

An **operating lease** is the direct counterpart of a lessee's operating lease. From the perspective of the lessor an operating lease merely represents an agreement in which rent is received for the use of property owned by the lessor. **The property is not presumed to have been sold** by the lessor to the lessee. The lessor recognizes rent revenue during the time the leased asset is used by the lessee. Furthermore, the lessor depreciates the leased asset in a normal fashion because the asset has not been sold to the lessee.

The three remaining lease types represent leasing circumstances which, in substance, indicate that the lessor has "sold" the property (or most of the property rights) and obtained a receivable from the lessee. Once a lessor concludes that a particular lease is one of the three types of **capital leases,** rather than an operating lease, further classification as a sales-type, direct-financing, or leveraged lease is necessary.

A **sales-type lease** is a form of capital lease that gives rise to manufacturer's or dealer's gross profit (or loss) to the lessor. That is, the fair value of the leased property at the inception of the lease is greater (or less) than its cost or carrying value on the books of the lessor. When the lease takes effect, the property is considered to be sold. The difference between the cost of the property on the books of the lessor and the fair value of the property is recorded as gross profit (loss) on the sale at that time. Normally a sales-type lease occurs when manufacturers or dealers use leasing as a means of marketing their products. In sales-type leases, the lessor earns profit both from the sale of the property and as interest revenue from financing the sale. To illustrate, assume that Luper Company, a lessor, enters into a sales-type lease properly valued at $16,000. The cost of the leased asset to Luper was $12,500. The entry to record the lease (i.e., sale), remove the leased equipment from the books, and recognize the manufacturer or dealer profit on the sale appears below:

Lease Receivable	16,000	
Cost of Goods Sold	12,500	
Equipment		12,500
Sales		16,000

The difference between the cost of goods sold ($12,500) and the sales revenue ($16,000) is the gross profit ($3,500) resulting from the sales-type lease. The entry to record a sales-type lease is similar to the recording of the sale of merchandise in a perpetual inventory system, as explained in Chapter 8 of this textbook.

A **direct-financing lease** is a form of capital lease which does *not* give rise to manufacturer's or dealer's gross profit (or loss), on the assumed sale of the property to the lessee. In a direct-financing lease, the cost or carrying amount of the property on the lessor's books and the fair value of the leased property at the inception of the lease are not materially different. The revenue to the lessor in a direct-financing lease consists solely of *interest* revenue from the *financing function* the lessor provides. To illustrate, assume that a lessor, Reese Company, enters into a direct-financing lease properly valued at $15,500. The entry to record the lease receivable and remove the leased equipment appears below:

Materiality

Lease Receivable	15,500	
Equipment		15,500

A **leveraged lease** is a three-party lease agreement involving a lessee, a long-term creditor (such as a bank), and a lessor, in which the long-term creditor provides financing to the lessor. For example, if a shipyard agrees to build a supertanker and lease it to an oil company, construction financing may be needed. In such circumstances, a bank may lend money to the shipbuilder (lessor) but require repayment from the oil company (lessee). The lessor constructs the tanker with a relatively small amount of its own cash and the money provided by the bank. Once the asset is constructed, the oil company operates the ship under a long-term lease, repays the bank, and makes an additional payment to the shipbuilder. Leveraged leases are complex financing arrangements that are beyond the scope of this text. However, a brief explanation is offered in the final section of this chapter.

Exhibit 23–1 summarizes the lease categories that are acceptable for financial accounting and reporting. While the foregoing discussion relates to the basic issues of lease classification, several other terms are also important for a general understanding of accounting for leases.

The **fair value** of the leased property is the price for which the leased property could be sold in an arm's-length transaction. If the lessor is a manufacturer or dealer, fair value is ordinarily the asset's normal selling price less any applicable volume or trade discounts. If the lessor is not a manufacturer or dealer, fair value is ordinarily its cost or carrying amount. Fair value is determined in light of prevailing market conditions at the inception of the lease.

The **estimated residual value** is the expected fair value of the property at the end of the lease term. The estimated residual value, like estimated salvage value for purposes of depreciating plant assets, encompasses consideration of both diminished productivity and obsolescence.

Accountants use several methods of estimating the residual value of a leased asset. For example, appraisals, dealer quotations, engineering estimates, and previous experience in regard to similar assets may prove helpful in formulating residual value estimates. In making such estimates, one should not attempt to anticipate increases in value or changes in price level. Amortization of leased assets, like depreciation of plant assets, is a cost allocation process that is required to apply the matching principle rather than an asset valuation process.

Matching

Residual value may be **guaranteed** to the lessor, in which case the lessee or a third party ensures a specified amount will be realized by the lessor at the end of the lease term. If the leased asset's value is not as great as the guaranteed residual value at the end of the lease, the guarantor must make up the difference in cash. An **unguaranteed residual value** represents a residual value that has not been guaranteed by the lessee or other third party.

LEASE CLASSIFICATION

A lease meeting **any one** of the following four criteria is treated as a **capital lease** by lessees and **tentatively** classified as a type of capital lease by lessors:

1. **The lease transfers ownership of the property to the lessee by the end of the lease term.** When a lease contains a transfer of title clause, the lease is presumed to be a sale by the lessor and a purchase by the lessee. Such leases are clearly installment sales/purchases of assets.
2. **The lease contains a bargain purchase option.** A bargain purchase option is a lease provision that allows the lessee to purchase the property at a price substantially lower than the expected fair value of the property at the time the option becomes exercisable. Because determining whether a particular purchase option represents a *bargain* purchase option is important to both lease classification and financial accounting, the economic substance of all purchase clauses must be carefully assessed.

Substance over Form

3. **The lease term is equal to 75% or more of the estimated economic life of the property at the beginning of the lease term.** When a lessee acquires the use of a leased asset for most of its useful life, accountants conclude that, in substance, a sale has taken place.

EXHIBIT 23-1

Lease Classification Summary

General Lease Type	Lessor	Lessee
Noncapitalized (no sale and purchase of asset presumed)	Operating lease	Operating lease
Capitalized (sale and purchase of asset presumed)	Sales-type lease Direct-financing lease Leveraged lease	Capital lease

4. **The present value of the minimum lease payments at the inception of the lease is 90% or more of the fair market value of the leased asset.** When the value of the lease is great enough that it represents most of the fair value of the property, the lease is considered, in substance, a sale/purchase transaction. In applying this criterion, minimum lease payments are reduced by any executory costs to be paid by the lessee to the lessor, and fair market value is reduced for any investment tax credit retained and expected to be realized by the lessor. **Executory costs** are expenses necessary to operate and maintain the leased property, such as taxes, insurance, and maintenance. A lease agreement may require the lessee to pay such costs directly to taxing authorities or insurance companies. In other cases, the lease may provide that the lessor is to retain formal responsibility for paying executory costs while the property is being used by the lessee. In that way the lessor is assured that taxes are being paid and that the asset is adequately insured. In such circumstances, lease payments made by the lessee are presumed to include both a lease payment for the use of the property and a reimbursement to the lessor of executory expenses.

In the sections which follow, we refer to these four criteria by the following abbreviated titles: (1) The **transfer-of-title** criterion; (2) the **bargain-purchase-option** criterion; (3) the **length-of-lease-term** criterion; and (4) the **amount-of-lease-payment** criterion.

To illustrate these capitalization criteria, we consider the case of Waller Corporation, a lessor, that enters into a lease with Sacramento Company, a lessee. The 10-year lease has minimum lease payments with a present value of $150,000. The lease involves the use of machinery that has a 12-year estimated useful life and is valued at $160,000. The lease contains no transfer of ownership clause and no purchase or renewal options. We draw the following conclusions when we consider each capitalization criterion:

Lease Criteria	Conclusions
1. Transfer of title	This criterion is *not* met because no clause transferring title to the lessee is included in the lease.
2. Bargain purchase option	This criterion is *not* met because no purchase option is included in the lease.
3. Length of lease term	This criterion is *met*, because the lease term of 10 years exceeds 75% of the asset's expected life (75% × 12 years = 9 years).
4. Amount of lease payment	This criterion is *met*, because the amount of the lease, $150,000, exceeds 90% of the value of the leased asset (90% × $160,000 = $144,000).

This is a **capital lease** because at least one capitalization criterion is met.

FOR SALE OR RENT, NO MONEY DOWN

Three years ago Henry A. Goudreau was presented with a dilemma of sorts. His construction company, which specializes in marine projects such as bridges and piers, needed new machinery and computer equipment. But the Goudreau Corp., Danvers, Mass., also had an especially good reason to conserve cash.

Government contracts, which require builders to have surety bonding, account for about 90% of the company's business. And in 1986 the bonding company that guarantees Goudreau's contracts got tough on clients. For every dollar a client had in the bank, it would approve no more than $10 in bonding. In short, the more cash Goudreau had in the bank, the more jobs he could bid on.

So how could Goudreau purchase the necessary equipment for his company, which had reached sales of $2 million in eight years? Bank financing wasn't the answer because it would tie up his line of credit. Instead, he turned to another type of lender, an equipment leasing company, and negotiated 36-month capital leases at interest rates of 11% to 14%. Today Goudreau Corp. uses nearly $200,000 worth of leased goods, including trucks, machinery, a computer system, and office furniture. The company's sales hit $5 million in 1988, with earnings of about 12%, and Goudreau is securing all the bonding he needs.

"Leasing helps us satisfy our bonding company without getting too tied up at the bank," says Goudreau. "Because our relationships with the [lessor and the bank] are autonomous, we can still go to the bank if we need working capital."

Leasing deals have become a popular financing option for many companies as equipment lessors increasingly compete with banks for their business. The U.S. Dept. of Commerce estimates that $104.2 billion in new equipment was leased in 1988, up 15% from $90.6 billion a year earlier. Independent leasing companies do most of the deals, but original equipment manufacturers and some banks have leasing operations as well.

For young companies short on cash, leasing is a trade-off. While interest rates on leased equipment can run one to two points higher than bank debt, the deals require no down payments. The leased equipment is the only collateral needed, and lessors typically offer a three- to five-year term. There is an obvious catch: Just

as with banks, lessees must prove their creditworthiness. To evaluate prospective clients, equipment leasing companies typically want to see three years of historical financial statements and a cash flow statement projected out at least three years.

When negotiating a leasing agreement, entrepreneurs can opt for an operating lease or a capital lease. The latter is used to purchase equipment outright through the lessor. With an operating lease, on the other hand, the company never takes title to the equipment. At the end of the lease term, it is returned to the lessor, who then resells the equipment for its residual value. In general, interest rates tend to be higher on a capital lease because the lessor has no chance to profit from a resale.

An operating lease is treated as an expense rather than as a liability on the balance sheet, in effect freeing up a company to increase its bank borrowings. "It's like off-balance-sheet financing. This can allow a company to expand its capital base, especially if they're dealing with a small or regional bank," says Terry A. Isom, a principal of Bettinger Isom & Associates, a Midvale, Utah, leasing company.

Another advantage to operating leases is that a company doesn't have to purchase equipment that may become obsolete after the term ends. EPI Technologies Inc., a semiconductor testing company founded by Phillip M. Drayer in 1980, has 18-month and 36-month operating leases on about $2.2 million worth of high-technology testing equipment and machinery. Operating leases work well for EPI, says Larry Kern, chief financial officer of the Richardson, Tex., company, since the equipment could become obsolete or, based on the type of work needed by customers, apply to a relatively small amount of future business. Though he won't reveal interest rates, Kern does say that EPI will pay about 75% of the equipment's market price over the life of the operating leases.

With a capital lease, entrepreneurs have the option of buying equipment outright at the end of the lease term, often at a very low buyout price. "My philosophy is that I've literally paid for that equipment with my lease payments, so I'm not going to give the lessor too much money just so I can own it," says Goudreau. "One of my leases has a $1 buyout, the others are between 5% and 10% of the original price." These deals are handy when financing costly equipment because the company can claim ownership without making a hefty down payment. A capital lease is treated as a loan by accountants so that it does show up on the balance sheet. Depreciation expense is then claimed against it.

For companies in an expansion phase, leasing's low down payments can help enhance their rate of growth. Formtek Inc., a Pittsburgh company that makes software for engineering-document management, saw sales jump from $6 million in 1987 to $8 million last year. To accommodate such rapid growth, the six-year-old company, founded by Sam Leinhardt and Charles Eastman, has hired 35 engineers, all of whom need computer workstations that cost $20,000 to $30,000 each on average. Formtek has conserved cash initially by acquiring about $1 million in computers and related equipment through capital leases.

"Funneling out large chunks of cash for equipment isn't necessarily how you want to spend your resources as a start-up," says Vincent F. Zumbo, controller at Formtek, which has received $20 million in venture capital. "If you're venture-backed and rely on cash generated from operations, you want to spend that cash on your day-to-day operations."

Unlike Goudreau, Zumbo doesn't negotiate a buyout price up front on Formtek's leases, which typically carry three-year terms and interest rates of three to four points over prime. Instead, the company agrees to pay fair market value for any equipment it keeps. That way, says Zumbo, monthly payments are lower because the equipment lessor is not running the risk that the agreed-upon buyout price will be much lower than the residual, or fair market, value three years later when the lease ends.

Equipment leasing companies tend to be quite willing to negotiate the specific terms of a deal. Lessees can make payments monthly, quarterly, semiannually, or annually. Sometimes the payments are a fixed amount; other times they vary. Step-up payments, for instance, increase as the term progresses, while step-down payments decrease. Some lessors will even authorize skipped payments, so that no money is due during seasonal periods when a company's cash needs peak. "Leasing companies got their start by providing flexibility not always available at the time from traditional lending institutions," says Floyd S. Robinson, president of Denrich Leasing Inc., Miami. "Today the increased competition among leasing companies demands that you provide that same flexibility."

Companies on an especially tight budget may want to opt for a fixed interest rate. John F. Krumme and three partners, for instance, launched Beta Phase Inc., Menlo Park, Calif., in 1984. But they didn't launch their product, an electronic connector used by computer makers and military aerospace companies, until last October. Beta Phase, whose sales had reached about $240,000 by the end of 1988, has received about $6.5 million in venture capital, which also made it a candidate for leasing deals that include equity kickers.

Robert Y. Newell, a cofounder and chief financial officer, has negotiated fixed rates on the $350,000 in various high-tech equipment that the company has leased. As an equity kicker, the leasing company got stock warrants in Beta Phase for 12.5% of the lease value. The company pays an interest rate of 11.5%, so that each monthly payment is about 2.5% of the value of the equipment. "Monthly payments are good for us because we don't have too big a hit at any one time," he says. "And I wanted fixed payments because the financial markets are still very volatile."

Leasing companies also bargain on so-called "bundled services" such as maintenance, product warranties, and consulting time. Of course, the more service a company wants, the higher its payments are likely to be. But companies can push for a few throw-ins at the start. When Goudreau leased his computers, the lessor provided six days of on-site training for his employees at no extra cost.

Entrepreneurs who have secured lease financing say the benefits offset the somewhat higher cost as compared with bank debt. If nothing else, holding on to cash can help a company build goodwill with all the right contacts. "I'd prefer to pay for everything lock, stock, and barrel and not owe anybody anything," says Goudreau. "Unfortunately, when you're running a business you can't always do that. Cash looks good to banks and bonding companies."

SOURCE: Don Nichols, "For Sale or Rent, No Money Down," *Venture*, April, 1989, pp. 54, 56–57. Reprinted by permission of *Venture Magazine*.

Now that we have an understanding of some lease terminology and the lease capitalization criteria of *SFAS No. 13,* let us consider the rationale that underlies these concepts. The primary financial reporting problem that the lease capitalization criteria are attempting to resolve is that of off-balance-sheet financing by lessees. If the lessee enters into a lease that is in substance the equivalent of a purchase and that obligates the lessee in a manner equivalent to that of debt financing, the obligation must be included among the liabilities in the lessee's balance sheet. Of course, if the liability is included, then the asset acquired must also be included. The ability to incur obligations equivalent to debt and not present those obligations as liabilities in the balance sheet is what we mean when we refer to "off-balance-sheet financing." Prior to *SFAS No. 13,* this was a prevalent practice and, in fact, was a very attractive feature of leasing. The four capitalization criteria previously presented attempt to identify those conditions in leases which strongly suggest that the lease is so similar to the purchase of the asset and the incurrence of related debt that the entire transaction should be treated as a purchase by the lessee rather than as a lease. If none of the capitalization criteria are met, the lease is *not* considered equivalent to a purchase and the related asset and liability are not included in the lessee's balance sheet.

While we emphasize the lessee and the issue of off-balance-sheet financing, we should not overlook the importance of the lease criteria to the lessor. From the lessor's viewpoint, the criteria are important in resolving revenue realization issues concerning the timing of lease revenue recognition in the income statement. For the lessor, the lease capitalization criteria govern the pattern of the amounts recognized and whether revenue from leases is recognized at the beginning of the lease or over the life of the lease. For example, in an operating lease, rent revenue is recognized by the lessor in a straight-line pattern, usually based on the receipt of payments from the lessee. In a direct-financing lease, the lessor recognizes no profit from the sale of the property; however, the lessor recognizes interest (based on the investment in the lease and the rate of interest implicit in the lease) over the lease term. In a sales-type lease, the lessor recognizes a gross profit or loss in the period of the inception of the lease and then recognizes interest revenue (based on the investment in the lease and the rate of interest implicit in the lease) over the lease term. Therefore, *whether* a lease is capitalized, and if it is, *how* it is capitalized, are important factors in the recognition of revenue by the lessor. Later sections of this chapter illustrate the specific accounting procedures for these various kinds of leases.

In addition to being concerned about the off-balance-sheet financing dimensions of lessee accounting and the revenue recognition dimensions of lessor accounting, we are also interested in compatible accounting treatment of the same lease by both parties. "Symmetry" is a word that is sometimes used to describe the desirable situation where a lease that is treated as a capital lease by the lessor is also treated as a capital lease by the lessee. The same is true for operating leases. Symmetrical treatment of leases is a desired goal of financial reporting and the authoritative accounting literature has been written to encourage symmetry.

CLASSIFICATION-RELATED TERMS

Additional definitions which are important in understanding the lease capitalization criteria presented earlier are as follows:

1. The **lease term** is the fixed noncancelable[3] term of the lease plus all of the following periods:
    a. Those covered by bargain renewal options. A **bargain renewal option** allows the lessee to renew the lease for an amount substantially lower than the fair rental of the property at the date the option becomes exercisable. Determining whether a particular renewal option is a bargain renewal option requires substantial judgment and is important because lease classification and related accounting treatments are influenced directly.
    b. Periods for which failure to renew the lease imposes a penalty on the lessee in an amount such that renewal appears, at the inception of the lease, to be reasonably assured.
    c. Periods covered by ordinary renewal options during which a guarantee by the lessee of the lessor's debt related to the leased property is expected to be in effect.
    d. Periods covered by ordinary renewal options preceding the date a bargain purchase option is exercisable.
    e. Periods representing renewals or extensions of the lease at the lessor's option. Accountants always consider the lease term to end at the date a bargain purchase option becomes exercisable.
2. The **estimated economic life** of leased property is the remaining period the property is expected to be economically usable in its intended function without limitation by the lease term.
3. **Minimum lease payments** are the payments that the lessee is obligated to make in connection with the leased property. If the lease contains a bargain purchase option, only the **minimum rental payments** over the lease term preceding that option and the payment called for by the option are minimum lease payments. If the lease does *not* contain a bargain purchase option, *minimum lease payments include* all of the following:
    a. The **minimum rental payments** over the lease term.
    b. Any **guarantee of the residual value** of the leased property at the expiration of the lease term.
    c. Any **payment that the lessee must make** or can be required to make upon failure to renew or extend the lease at the expiration of the lease term.

An appendix to *SFAS No. 13* provides, "The period covered by a bargain renewal option is included in the lease term . . . and the option rentals [required under a bargain renewal option] are included in the minimum lease payments."[4]

From the standpoint of lessors, minimum lease payments are the same as those described from the standpoint of the lessee, plus any guarantee of residual value or rental payments beyond the lease term by a third party unrelated to either the lessee or the lessor.

---

[3]*A noncancelable lease* is a lease that is cancelable only under one or more of the following conditions:

1. Upon the occurrence of some remote contingency.
2. With the permission of the lessor.
3. If the lessee enters into a new lease with the same lessor.
4. Upon payment by the lessee of a large penalty so that continuation of the lease appears reasonably assured.

Even if a lessor has the ability to permit the lease to be canceled, the lease is still considered noncancelable by both the lessee and lessor. This treatment is consistent with accounting practices in other areas, such as convertible debt, and is proper because the lessor can compel the lessee to pay the lease payments and meet the other terms of the lease.
[4]*FASB Statement of Financial Accounting Standards No. 13*, par. 88.

OTHER LEASE CLASSIFICATION ISSUES

The transfer-of-title and bargain-purchase-option criteria are applied to all leases; however, the length-of-lease-term and amount-of-lease-payment criteria are *not* applied if the lease term begins within the last 25% of the total estimated life of the property. This exception is present in the authoritative literature in recognition of the fact that the criteria using percentages are subject to distortion and may result in leases that begin late in the asset's life being treated as capital leases, whereas identical leases earlier in the asset's life were treated as operating leases.

We stated earlier that a lease meeting one (or more) of the four basic capitalization criteria was **tentatively** classified by the lessor as a capital lease. Lessors must apply two additional criteria to permanently classify a lease as a capital lease. These criteria concern the evidence necessary to record a receivable and the ability to predict any future expenses associated with the leased property. When a lease is classified as a capital lease, lessees record additional assets and liabilities and begin to reflect expenses such as depreciation and interest. When lessors record capital leases, assets are reclassified from plant or inventory to receivables and gross profit may be recognized. Interest revenue also begins to be earned and recognized in the income statement.

Conservativism   Consistent with the modifying convention of conservatism, generally accepted accounting principles require more evidence to record receivables than to record payables, and the same relationship exists between revenues and expenses. Therefore, lessors are required to assess the **collectibility of rent** *and* future **predictability of costs** prior to recording a capital lease. Unless future rental collections are reasonably assured *and* future costs to be incurred under the lease are reasonably predictable, even a lease meeting one of the initial four criteria, will be accounted for as an operating lease by the lessor. The collectibility of rent and predictability of costs criteria must be met prior to recording a receivable and recognizing gross profit or interest revenue, considerations that only have relevance to the lessor.

If a lease meets *one* or more of the four initial classification criteria and *both* the rental collectibility and cost predictability criteria, then the lease is classified as a capital lease by the lessor. Remaining lessor classification criteria in *SFAS No. 13* relate to what type of capital lease a given lease is, not whether the lease is an operating or capital lease.

To summarize, both the lessor and lessee must consider the four primary capitalization criteria in classifying a lease as either capital or operating. If one or more of those criteria are met, the lessor must further consider the two revenue-recognition criteria before making a final classification decision. Exhibit 23–2 serves as a learning aid to summarize the classification process (excluding leveraged leases) for both the lessor and lessee.

ACCOUNTING AND REPORTING STANDARDS FOR LESSEES

We now turn to financial accounting and reporting practices for various types of leases. First we consider how lessees account for and report operating and capital leases.

OPERATING LEASES

From the perspective of lessees, operating leases are relatively simple to account for and pose few financial reporting problems. Rent expense is usually recognized as lease payments are made. The lease itself is not considered a recordable transaction

EXHIBIT 23–2

Criteria for Lease Classification

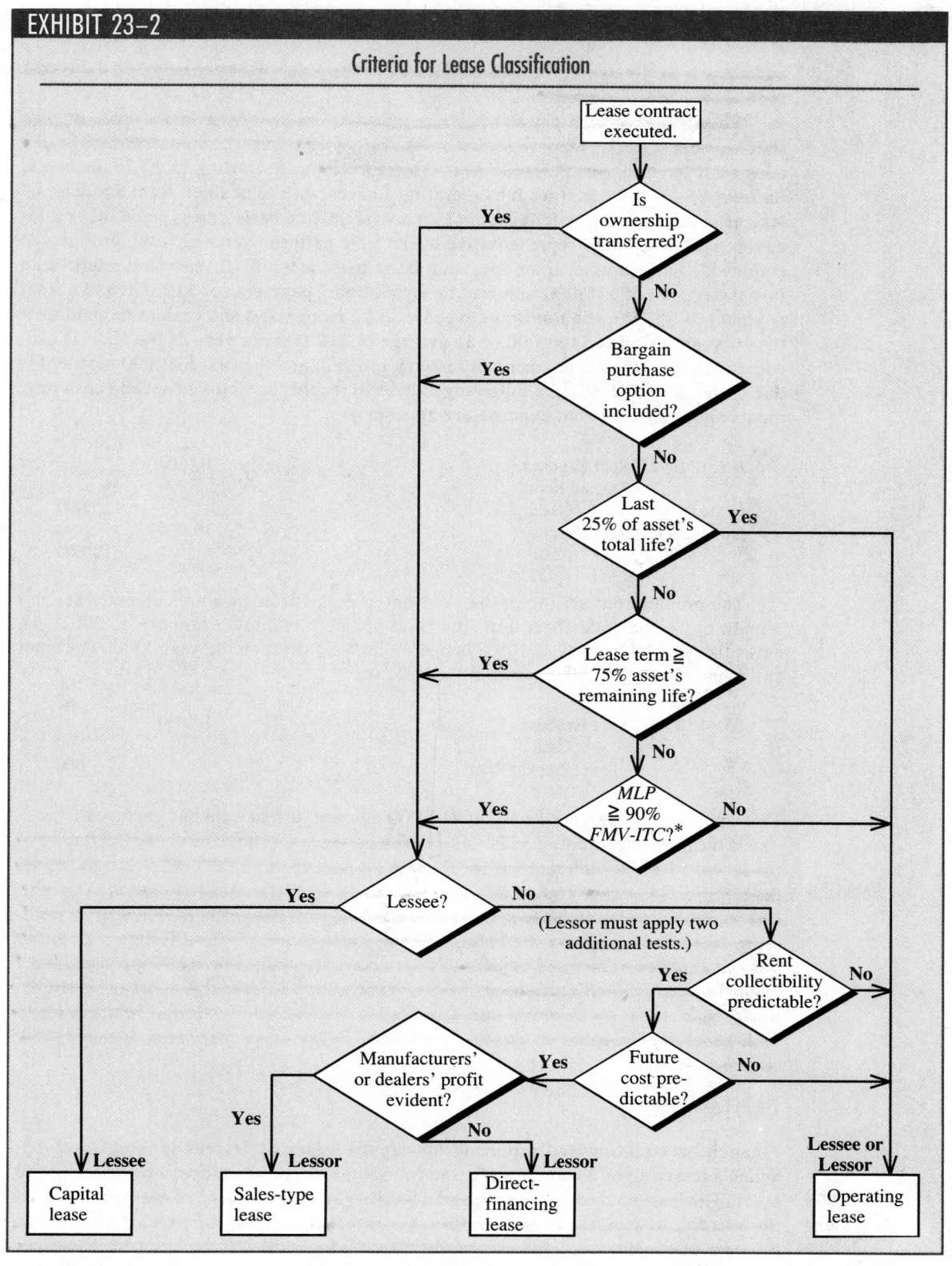

MLP = present value of minimum lease payments; *FV* = fair value; *ITC* = investment credit retained by lessor.
SOURCE: Adapted from Raymond J. Clay and William W. Holder, "A Practitioner's Guide to Accounting for Leases," *Journal of Accountancy,* August, 1977, p. 63. Copyright © 1977 by the American Institute of Certified Public Accountants, Inc.

and no new assets or liabilities are reflected in the financial statements of the lessee at the inception of the lease.

When unequal cash payments are required by an operating lease, rent expense should, nevertheless, be recognized on a straight-line basis and determined by the total cash payments to be made over the lease term. According to *FASB Technical Bulletin 85–3,* "Accounting for Operating Leases with Scheduled Rent Increases," lessees should recognize rent expense on a straight-line basis unless some other allocation method is more representative of the time pattern over which the property is employed. For example, if an operating lease has a term of 10 years and requires an initial payment of $15,000 followed by eight annual payments of $10,000 and a final payment of $5,000, the total rent expense to be recognized and cash to be paid over the 10-year period is $100,000 or an average of $10,000 per year. If the lease is executed with the $15,000 payment on January 1, 1992, and the first $10,000 payment is due on January 1, 1993, the following entries to record the first and second cash payments and recognize rent expense are appropriate:

Jan. 1, 1992	Rent Expense		10,000	
	Prepaid Rent		5,000	
	Cash			15,000
Jan. 1, 1993	Rent Expense		10,000	
	Cash			10,000

The prepaid rent arising in the 1992 entry is classified as a noncurrent asset and remain on the balance sheet until the final payment is due on January 1, 2001. An entry like that of January 1, 1993, is made each year through the year 2000. The final entry on January 1, 2001, would be as follows:

Jan. 1, 2001	Rent Expense		10,000	
	Cash			5,000
	Prepaid Rent			5,000

This approach recognizes an equal $10,000 amount of rent expense each year.

If the opposite situation exists and cash payments are deferred at the beginning of the lease, a liability is recorded for the unpaid portion of the expense recognized on the straight-line basis. Thus, when there is a material difference between the straight-line recognition of rent expense and the individual cash payments required by an operating lease, we recognize the balance sheet implications of the difference as either prepaid expense or accrued payable. Present-value techniques are not appropriate for operating leases. Executory costs, such as insurance and property taxes incurred directly by lessees, are accrued and allocated to the periods benefited in accordance with generally accepted accounting principles in the same manner as other similar expenses.

Materiality

CAPITAL LEASES

Substance over Form

Financial accounting and reporting for capital leases by lessees is more involved. When a lessee signs a capital lease, the transaction is, in substance, a purchase of the asset. The lessee records the asset and a liability at the beginning of the lease term, at the present value of the minimum lease payments. However, the amount assigned as the cost of the asset cannot exceed the fair market value of the asset at that time. Therefore, it is possible for the carrying amounts of the asset and liability to be the fair market value of the asset rather than the present value of the lease payments.

Accounting for Lease Assets

Lessees must address several other issues of significance in accounting for capital leases. For example, the amortization of the asset and interest relating to the lease obligation pose substantial accounting problems. The general principles that govern the systematic depreciation of other assets also apply to assets recorded under capital leases. If either the transfer of title or bargain purchase option classification tests are met, the lessee has, in substance, acquired all of the property rights inherent in the asset and the asset is properly classified as a plant asset. The lessee is acquiring not only the right to use the asset for the lease term but also is expected to become legal owner and, thus, control use of the asset after the lease term. If the transfer-of-title or bargain-purchase-option tests are not met, and the lease meets either the length-of-lease-term or amount-of-lease-payment test, the lease is still classified as a capital lease. The lessee's capitalized rights to the use of the property during the lease term, however, are properly considered an intangible asset and identified as "leasehold rights" or other similar designation.

In applying the matching principle, a company depreciates and amortizes leased assets in the same manner that it does other assets it owns. However, certain modifications may be necessary in the case of a capitalized leased asset. If either the transfer-of-title or bargain-purchase-option criterion is met, the leased asset is depreciated over the estimated useful life of the asset without regard to the lease term. Also, the asset should not be depreciated below its estimated salvage value. In these circumstances the entire asset, including the residual value, has been acquired by the lessee. The lease term is relevant only to accounting for the liability aspects of the lease. On the other hand, if the lease is capitalized because it meets either the length-of-lease-term or amount-of-lease-payment criterion, the asset is amortized over the shorter of the lease term or the life of the asset. While it may seem illogical to enter into a lease for a longer period than the life of the asset, such transactions do occur in some operations. For example, in fast food and other similar industries, lessees sometimes intend to refurbish leased facilities several times during a single, relatively long, lease term.

Substance over Form

Matching

Accounting for Lease Liabilities

Accounting for the liability in a capital lease presents several accounting issues. Foremost among these is the determination of interest on the lease obligation. We record a liability for capital leases at the **present value of the minimum lease payments**. The difference between the sum of the minimum lease payments and their present value is the interest to be recognized over the lease term. The lease obligation is usually recorded at the net present value of the future cash payments. During the term of the lease, the difference between the total lease payments and their present value is recognized as interest expense. The effective interest method is used so that a constant rate of interest is recognized each period throughout the lease term. This treatment is consistent with that required by *APB Opinion No. 21*[5] and discussed in Chapters 10 and 15.

The interest rate applied by the lessee to determine the present value of the future minimum lease payments is the lower of the lessee's incremental borrowing rate or the rate implicit in the lease, assuming the lessee has knowledge of the rate used by the lessor in establishing the lease payments. The **lessee's incremental borrowing rate** is the rate that the lessee would have incurred if the funds to purchase the asset had been borrowed from a bank or other financial institution. The **interest rate implicit**

---

[5]*APB Opinion No. 21*, "Interest on Receivables and Payables," 1971.

in the lease is the rate that causes the gross future minimum lease payments to equal the fair value of the leased asset. Any residual value that the lessee guarantees to the lessor is included in the minimum lease payments. Executory costs that are included in the lease payments are subtracted in determining the minimum lease payments. If the rate implicit in the lease is not known by the lessee, the incremental borrowing rate must be used without regard to the rate implicit in the lease.

ILLUSTRATION OF ACCOUNTING FOR A CAPITAL LEASE

In this section we illustrate lessee accounting for a capital lease by considering a contract entered into by King Company for a machine. The first $10,000 lease payment was made on December 31, 1991, and a similar payment will be made at the end of each of the following five years to compensate the lessor for use of the machine during the year following payment. The lease does not contain a purchase option or a transfer of title to the lessee at the end of the lease. The fair market value of the machine at December 31, 1991, is $55,000, its estimated useful life is nine years, and its residual value at the end of the lease is expected to be $7,800. In fact, the lessee has guaranteed that value to the lessor at the end of the six-year lease term. Both King Company's incremental borrowing rate and the lessor's rate implicit in the lease are 10%.

We must first evaluate the lease in terms of the four capitalization criteria. The transfer-of-title and bargain-purchase-option criteria are not applicable in this lease. In testing for the length-of-lease-term criterion, we find that the lease represents $66\frac{2}{3}\%$ of the asset's estimated useful life ($6/9 = 66\frac{2}{3}\%$) and, therefore, the 75% standard is not met. Finally, to determine whether the amount-of-lease-payment criterion is met, we must compute the present value of the lease payments and determine whether that amount equals or exceeds 90% of the $55,000 fair value of the asset. Thus, the "benchmark" figure for that determination will be $49,500 ($55,000 × 90%).

The present value of the lease is computed as follows:

Present value of six $10,000 payments:		
$10,000 × (1.00000 + 3.79079)	=	$47,908
Present value of $7,800 residual value:		
$7,800 × .56447	=	4,403
Present value of lease		$52,311

Comparing the $52,311 present value of the lease with the benchmark figure of $49,500, we determine that the 90% criterion is met and **the lease is a capital lease.** In calculating the present value of the lease, the first $10,000 payment is assigned a present value of 1.00000 because it represents a down payment and includes no interest. The second through sixth payments are represented by the annuity of 3.79079 ($pvoaf_{\overline{5}|10\%}$). In other words, the six $10,000 payments represent an annuity due, as explained in Chapter 6. The residual value guarantee is a single payment at the end of the sixth year, so the appropriate factor (.56447) is the present value of one, six years later ($pvf_{\overline{6}|10\%}$). These present value factors are taken from Tables 6–4 (present value of an annuity) and 6–2 (present value of one).

Exhibit 23–3 is a table that separates each payment into the portion that is interest and the portion that is a reduction in the outstanding debt represented by the lease. Notice that the first $10,000 payment has no interest because it is made at the beginning of the lease and no interest has yet accrued. In all subsequent payments, the amount of interest is 10% of the net liability for the period since the last payment

EXHIBIT 23-3

King Company
Lease Amortization Table

Date	Payment	Interest	Decline in Net Liability	Net Liability
—	—	—	—	$52,311
	$10,000	—	$10,000	42,311
Dec. 31, 1992	10,000	$ 4,231	5,769	36,542
Dec. 31, 1993	10,000	3,654	6,346	30,196
Dec. 31, 1994	10,000	3,020	6,980	23,216
Dec. 31, 1995	10,000	2,322	7,678	15,538
Dec. 31, 1996	10,000	1,554	8,446	7,092
Dec. 31, 1997	7,800	708*	7,092	–0–
	$67,800	$15,489		

*Rounding difference included in this number to clear accounts.

was made. For example, the payment at December 31, 1992, includes $4,231 of interest, which is 10% times the $42,311 net liability for that period. The net liability of the lease at the beginning is its present value of $52,311; the total amount of the payments is $67,800 (six $10,000 payments, plus the $7,800 residual value); the total amount of interest recognized is the difference between these two figures: $67,800 − $52,311 = $15,489.

The following entries are required for the year 1991:

Dec. 31, 1991	Leasehold Rights	52,311	
	Lease Liability		52,311
	(To record capital lease.)		
	Lease Liability	10,000	
	Cash		10,000
	(To record first lease payment.)		

At the end of the first year of the lease, entries are required to amortize the asset purchased by lease, recognize interest expense, and record the second lease payment.

Dec. 31, 1992	Amortization Expense	7,419	
	Leasehold Rights		7,419
	(To record amortization on asset acquired by capital lease.)		
	Interest Expense	4,231	
	Lease Liability		4,231
	(To recognize interest expense for 1992 on capital lease.)		
	Lease Liability	10,000	
	Cash		10,000
	(To record second lease payment.)		

The amount of amortization is the $52,311 cost of the asset (i.e., the present value of the lease), less the $7,800 residual value, divided by the number of years in the lease term: ($52,311 − $7,800)/6 years = $7,419. The $4,231 amount of interest expense recognized is taken from the Dec. 31, 1992, line from Exhibit 23–3.

Identical entries are made each year except that the dollar amount of interest expense declines, as indicated in the "Interest" column of Exhibit 23–3.

At the end of the lease term, after recording amortization and interest expense but before settlement of the residual value, the asset Leasehold Rights will have a $7,800 balance, the same as the Lease Liability. Assuming that the asset is valued at $7,800 or more and is returned to the lessor, the lessee will make the following entry:

Dec. 31, 1997	Lease Liability	7,800	
	Leasehold Rights		7,800
	(To record settlement of residual value		
	of capital lease.)		

Alternatively, if the asset is appraised at only $5,000, the lessee must pay $2,800 ($7,800 − $5,000) and the appropriate entry is:

Dec. 31, 1997	Lease Liability	7,800	
	Loss on Transfer of Residual Value	2,800	
	Cash		2,800
	Leasehold Rights		7,800
	(To record settlement of residual value on		
	capital lease.)		

The lessee would not record a gain on the settlement of the residual value unless the lease contained a provision that returned to the lessee a refund of lease payments equal to any excess of the appraised residual value over the guaranteed amount. For example, if the King Company lease contained this provision and the appraisal resulted in a value of $9,000 for the machine at the end of the lease term, the following entry would be appropriate:

Dec. 31, 1997	Lease Liability	7,800	
	Cash ($9,000 − $7,800)	1,200	
	Leasehold Rights		7,800
	Gain on Transfer of Residual Value		1,200
	(To record settlement of residual value on		
	capital lease.)		

The lease may permit the lessee to pay the residual value in cash and retain the asset. In this case, the guaranteed residual value is essentially a purchase option. If this alternative is chosen, the lessee must eliminate the Lease Liability and Leasehold Rights balances, record the cash payment and establish the acquired asset in an appropriate account, as follows:

Dec. 31, 1997	Lease Liability	7,800	
	Machinery	7,800	
	Leasehold Rights		7,800
	Cash		7,800
	(To record purchase of leased asset.)		

Balance sheet presentation for the lessee involves determining the amount and classification of the asset acquired by the lease and the liability represented by the lease. The asset is classified as an intangible asset because the basis for capitalization is the amount-of-lease-payment criterion (i.e., the present value of the lease equals or exceeds 90% of the fair value of the asset). The liability is subject to current and non-current classification, like any other liability which will be retired in installments.

The intangible asset, "Leasehold Rights," is presented in the balance sheet at its net amount each year. At December 31, 1991, this amount is $52,311 because no amortization will have been recognized yet. At December 31, 1992 and 1993, the net asset balances are determined as follows:

$$1992: \$52,311 - \$7,419 = \$44,892$$
$$1993: \$52,311 - (\$7,419 \times 2) = \$37,473$$

Similar calculations are required each year, with an additional year's amortization recognized each time.

Separating the liability into current and noncurrent portions is more complicated. The preferred method for determining the current portion of the liability is to compute the present value of the next payment, as follows:

$$\$10,000 \times .90909 \ (pvf_{\overline{1}|10\%} = \$9,091$$

This is the amount that will be presented as current each year, with the remainder of the liability classified as noncurrent. For example, at December 31, 1991, the current liability is $9,091 and the noncurrent portion is $33,220 ($42,311 − $9,091). A year later at December 31, 1992, the current liability would be $9,091 and the noncurrent portion is $27,451 ($36,542 − $9,091). The total liability figures, which are reduced by $9,091 each year to determine the noncurrent portion, are taken from the net liability column of Exhibit 23–3.

A second method of separating the liability into current and noncurrent portions is to associate with the current portion all interest to be included in the next payment. Once the current portion has been determined in this way, the remainder is presented as noncurrent. For example, at December 31, 1991, we would determine the current and noncurrent portions as follows:

$$
\begin{aligned}
\text{Current: } \$10,000 - \$4,231 \ &= \$ 5,769 \\
\text{Noncurrent: } \$42,311 - \$5,769 &= \underline{\$36,542} \\
& \ \$42,311
\end{aligned}
$$

The $4,231 subtracted from $10,000 to determine the current portion is the interest amount from the December 31, 1992, line in Exhibit 23–3. The $42,311 amount, which is the basis for determining the noncurrent amount, is the total liability from the December 31, 1991, line. Notice that the total liability of $42,311, presented as $5,769 current and $36,542 noncurrent, reconciles with the net liability column at the date of presentation, December 31, 1991.

In evaluating the two methods of separating the liability into current and noncurrent portions, the authors prefer the first method because it consistently places the same value on the current liability, the present value of $10,000 payable one year later. Applying the second method in successive years, the current liability increases in amount as the interest portion of future $10,000 payments declines because the carrying amount of the obligation declines. In solving exercises and problems at the end of this chapter, the authors have chosen the first approach unless specifically indicated otherwise.

Income statement presentation of this capital lease by King Company involves recognition of amortization expense on the leasehold rights and interest expense, as reflected in the year-end journal entries recorded earlier. Notice that the $10,000 payments are not recorded as an expense as they would be in an operating lease. Rather, they represent reductions in the liability balance. The payments are presented as a negative cash flow from financing activities in the statement of cash flows.

Accounting for capital leases has been illustrated here using a simplified approach in which the liability is presented at a net amount. Alternatively, the lease liability may be recorded at its total dollar or gross amount and the interest portion recorded in a separate discount account. Interest expense is then recognized by amortizing that discount, much as we did when we discussed bond accounting in Chapter 15. For the King Company illustration, we would record the lease at December 31, 1991, and the recognition of interest at the end of the first year of the lease as follows:

Dec. 31, 1991	Leasehold Rights	52,311	
	Discount on Lease Liability	15,489	
	Lease Liability		67,800
	(To record capital lease.)		
Dec. 31, 1992	Interest Expense	4,231	
	Discount on Lease Liability		4,231
	(To recognize interest for 1992 on capital lease.)		

All other 1991 and 1992 entries are the same as presented earlier. The Discount on Lease Liability account is a contra-account to the Lease Liability, so the net liability balances are the same whether the accounts are combined, as in the earlier presentation, or separated as done here.

MISCELLANEOUS LESSEE CONSIDERATIONS

The capital lease example presented above was based on a lease which met the amount-of-lease-payment criterion. As such, the amortization period for the leasehold rights was logically the lease term because the use of the asset reverts to the lessor at the end of the lease. If the lease had been capitalized because of either the transfer-of-title or bargain-purchase-option criteria, the lessee would classify the leased asset as a plant asset (e.g., machinery) and depreciate it over its estimated useful life by the same depreciation method used for other similar assets. Notice that if either of these latter criteria is met, the lessee is acquiring not only the right to use the asset for the lease term, but is also expected to have legal ownership in the future and, thereby, control the use of the asset after the end of the lease term until the end of its useful life.

The earlier example did not make specific reference to executory costs, such as insurance, property taxes, and maintenance. The implicit assumption we made was that the lessee was responsible for these costs and paid them directly, recognizing appropriate expenses at that time. Alternatively, the lease may require the lessee to make payment directly to the lessor for these costs with the lessor having responsibility for payment to the appropriate outside parties.

If the amount of the lease payments is adjusted for a reimbursement to the lessor for executory costs, that amount is excluded in calculating the present value of the lease. As each lease payment is made, executory expenses are recognized by the lessee. Assume, for example, that the $10,000 payments in the King Company example we covered earlier had been $11,500, with $1,500 designated for the coverage of executory costs. The present value of the lease would be calculated and the asset and liability recorded exactly as we did before. Each payment, however, would be separated into that portion representing a reduction in the liability and that portion representing executory costs. For example, each payment would be recorded as follows:

Lease Liability	10,000	
Executory Expenses on Capital Lease	1,500	
Cash		11,500
(To record first lease payment.)		

In the King Company example, we have dealt with a single lease. In practice, lessees often acquire the services of many assets by leasing and the amounts described here in the balance sheet, the income statement and the statement of cash flows represent aggregate amounts for many leases. In these more complex situations, computer programs are particularly helpful in determining lease amortization figures, such as those in Exhibit 23–3, as well as current and noncurrent portions of payables, asset amortization amounts, and other important information. In addition to the lease-related items included in the financial statements, the authoritative accounting literature requires a significant amount of additional disclosure which is typically done in notes to the financial statements.

Exhibit 23–4 presents the lease disclosure from the 1990 annual report of Control Data Corporation, a company which applies computer technology to meet its customers' specialized computing and information management needs. The relatively small amount of capital leases ($8,000,000) ties to that amount in the liability section of the company's balance sheet. The large amount of operating leases ($327,200,000) is not included among the balance-sheet liabilities and is, thus, an example of off-balance-sheet financing.

ACCOUNTING AND REPORTING STANDARDS FOR LESSORS

Ideally, accounting for operating and capital leases by lessors should mirror accounting by lessees. Lease revenue for the lessor in operating leases replaces the lessee's lease expense. In capital leases, sales and/or interest revenue recognition by the lessor replaces the purchase of assets and interest expense recognition by the lessee.

In the following sections we discuss lessor accounting, considering first operating leases and then two types of capital leases: direct financing and sales-type. We build on the examples presented earlier when we considered lessee accounting, looking now at the lessor side of the transaction.

OPERATING LEASES

In an operating lease, lessors usually recognize rent revenue on a straight-line basis over the lease term, even if the cash received under the terms of the lease varies from a straight-line pattern. In such cases, a deferred revenue account is established on the balance sheet if the cash received exceeds straight-line recognition of revenue. If the cash received is less than the rent revenue recognized on a straight-line basis, a receivable is established.

The asset leased to the lessee is usually classified as part of the plant assets section of the balance sheet of the lessor and depreciated in normal fashion. Because an operating lease does not presume that a sale has taken place, the asset is depreciated over its useful life rather than over the lease term. Revenue under an operating lease is rent revenue, and expenses incurred under such leases include depreciation expense on the leased asset. Any initial direct-costs incurred by a lessor are

EXHIBIT 23–4

Control Data Corporation

Lessee Disclosure

(dollars in millions, except per share data)

L. Leasing Arrangements as Lessee

Control Data conducts a substantial portion of its operations from leased facilities. Most of such leases contain renewal options and require payments for taxes, insurance, and maintenance. Although in most cases management expects that leases will be renewed or replaced by other leases in the normal course of business, downsizing activities in recent years have resulted in a diminished need for such renewals and replacements, and increased subletting of leased facilities.

    Most leasing arrangements for equipment and facilities are operating leases and are not included in the consolidated balance sheets. The rental payments under these leases are charged to operations as incurred. The amounts of rental expense, net of sublease income, for each of the three years ended December 31, were $94.9 for 1990, $135.1 for 1989, and $129.2 for 1988.

    Minimum noncancelable lease payments, net of $65.0 of sublease income, on both capital and operating leases existing at December 31, 1990 which have an initial term of more than one year, are described in the accompanying table. These amounts do not include obligations which have been recorded as liabilities in the consolidated balance sheet as the result of restructuring actions.

Minimum Future Lease Payments

Fiscal Years Ending	Capital Leases	Operating Leases
1991	$ 2.9	$ 74.6
1992	8.8	65.4
1993	.4	47.1
1994	.1	27.2
1995	—	23.7
Thereafter	—	89.2
Total minimum lease payments	12.2	$327.2
Less amount representing interest	2.8	
Present value of net minimum lease payments	9.4	
Less current portion of obligations under capital leases	1.4	
Long-term obligations under capital leases, less current portion	$ 8.0	

SOURCE: Control Data Corporation, 1990 Annual Report.

Matching   capitalized and amortized over the term of the operating lease as an expense to be matched against the rental revenue. **Initial direct costs** are those costs incurred by lessors that are essential in and directly related to originating a lease and that were incurred only because the particular leasing transaction occurred. Activities giving rise to initial direct costs include evaluating the prospective lessee's financial condition, evaluating and securing guarantees and other collateral, negotiating lease terms, preparing and processing lease documents, and closing the transactions. Initial direct costs do not include amounts expended for advertising, soliciting potential lessees, servicing existing leases, rent, depreciation, and supervisory and administrative functions.[6]

    To illustrate lessor accounting for an operating lease, consider again the earlier example in which the lessee paid $15,000 in the first year of a ten-year operating

---

[6]*FASB Statement of Financial Accounting Standards No. 91*, "Accounting for Nonrefundable Fees and Costs Associated with Originating or Acquiring Loans and Initial Direct Costs of Leases," 1986, par. 24.

lease, $10,000 per year for the second through the ninth years, and $5,000 in the tenth year. We also assume that on January 1, 1992, the first year of the lease, the lessor incurs $6,000 of initial direct costs that are to be amortized by the straight-line method over the ten-year lease term. Selected journal entries to record these transactions are as follows:

Jan. 1, 1992	Cash	15,000	
	Rent Revenue		10,000
	Deferred Rent Revenue		5,000
	Prepaid Initial Direct Costs	6,000	
	Cash		6,000
Dec. 31, 1992	Lease Expense	600	
	Prepaid Initial Direct Costs		600
Jan. 1, 1993	Cash	10,000	
	Rent Revenue		10,000

In the first entry, the $15,000 is separated into the $10,000 that is revenue for 1992 and the $5,000 that is deferred and will be recognized in the tenth year of the lease. The Deferred Rent Revenue account is a noncurrent liability until the ninth year when it is a current liability. The initial direct costs are capitalized as prepaid expenses and $600 ($6,000/10 years) is recognized each year. The prepaid amount of initial direct costs is an asset that declines each year as amortization is recognized.

Materiality Assuming the amounts are material, $600 is appropriately classified as a current asset and the remainder as a noncurrent asset in each year's balance sheet. For the second through the ninth years, an entry like the one at January 1, 1993 will be made to record receipt of each $10,000 rent amount and $600 of prepaid initial direct costs will be amortized as was done on December 31, 1992.

Notice that the lease transaction is not recorded. Rather, only the cash payments (initial direct costs) and the cash receipts (rent revenue) are recorded, with adjustment to result in recognition over the lease term by the straight-line method.

CAPITAL LEASES

Capital leases from the viewpoint of the lessor are those leases that are treated as if the asset that is the subject of the lease had been sold to the lessee. The asset on the books of the lessor that emerges from the recording of a capital lease is a lease receivable, which mirrors the lease liability recorded by the lessee for a capital lease.

Before we delve into the details of recording capital leases and presenting them in the financial statements of lessors, let's review briefly the criteria that must first be met for a lease to be subject to this treatment. A capital lease for a lessor must meet one or more of the four basic capitalization criteria: transfer of title to the lessee, bargain purchase option, lease term that equals or exceeds 75% of the asset's expected useful life, or the present value of lease equals or exceeds 90% of the fair value of the asset. If one or more of these criteria are met, the lessor must consider two additional revenue recognition criteria, the costs related to the lease are known or reasonably estimable and collection of the lease payments is reasonably assured. Once these conditions are met, the lessor must further classify the lease as a sales-type or a direct-financing lease.

Lessors may earn two types of revenue from capital leases: gross profit and interest revenue. In a sales-type lease, the lessor earns both types of revenue; in a direct-financing lease, the lessor earns only interest revenue. To determine what type of capital lease the lessor is engaged in requires a consideration of the role the lessor plays in the leasing transaction and the relationship of the present value of the lease to the carrying amount of the leased assets on the lessor's books. That carrying amount is usually the cost of the asset to the lessor.

If the lessor is the manufacturer of the asset, the lease is most likely a sales-type capital lease. The lessor/manufacturer may offer its customers the opportunity to purchase the asset outright or, alternatively, to lease the asset from the lessor. In this situation, the lessor will establish a lease-payment schedule so that the present value of the lease approximates the amount at which the customer (lessee) could have purchased the asset. Had the property been sold outright rather than leased, a gross profit would have been earned equal to the difference between the sales price and the manufactured cost of the asset to the lessor. In a sales-type lease, approximately the same thing takes place with the present value of the lease payments substituting for the sales price of the asset. The lessor earns a gross profit equal to the difference between the present value of the lease payments and the manufactured cost of the asset.

In addition to the gross profit on the sales-type lease, the lessor is also providing a financing function for the lessee inasmuch as credit is extended in the form of the deferred lease payment schedule. The difference between the total lease payments that are required and the present value of those payments represents interest revenue to the lessor, mirroring the interest expense recognized by the lessee.

In a direct-financing lease, the lessor has usually purchased the asset rather than having manufactured it. The function of the lessor is that of providing financing to the lessee. The lease payment schedule is established so that the present value of the lease payments approximates the carrying amount or cost of the asset and, therefore, there is no gross profit on the transaction. Rather, the lessor simply recognizes interest revenue over the lease term equal to the difference between the total lease payments and the present value of the lease.

Recall the specifics of the King Company lease in which that company agreed to make six annual $10,000 payments, beginning on December 31, 1991, for the use of a machine that is expected to have a nine-year useful life. A residual value of $7,800 at the end of the sixth year was guaranteed by the lessee. Finally, both the interest rate implicit in the lease and the lessee's incremental borrowing rate were 10%. We shall now assume that the lessor is Queen Company and that the lease amortization schedule presented in Exhibit 23–5 correctly separates each lease payment into interest revenue and the portion representing a reduction in the receivable. Information in Exhibit 23–5 is identical to that in Exhibit 23–3, except for the columnar headings, which reflect lessor terminology (i.e., receivable) rather than lessee terminology (i.e., payable). The lessor will receive $67,800 in total payments, of which $15,489 is interest revenue, resulting in a net receivable (i.e., the present value of the lease) at December 31, 1991, the inception of the lease, of $52,311. We shall use this information to illustrate both the sales-type and the direct financing lease.

Sales-Type Lease

For this illustration, we assume that Queen Company is a manufacturer of the machinery which is the subject of the lease. Queen Company incurred a cost of $30,000 to manufacture the asset and offers it to customers at $55,000. Customers have the alternative of leasing the machine from Queen Company and when this alternative is chosen, a lease payment schedule is negotiated that results in a present value amount approximately equal to the normal selling price, subject to good-customer discounts of up to 5%. Recall from our earlier example that the present value of this lease, including the six $10,000 payments and the guaranteed residual value of $7,800 at the end of the sixth year, was $52,311. Because this amount exceeds 90% of the fair value of the asset, we treated this lease as a capital lease for King Company, the lessee. We

EXHIBIT 23-5

Queen Company
Lease Amortization Table

Date	Payment	Interest	Decline in Net Receivable	Net Receivable
Dec. 31, 1991	—	—	—	$52,311
	$10,000	—	$10,000	42,311
Dec. 31, 1992	10,000	$ 4,231	5,769	36,542
Dec. 31, 1993	10,000	3,654	6,346	30,196
Dec. 31, 1994	10,000	3,020	6,980	23,216
Dec. 31, 1995	10,000	2,322	7,678	15,538
Dec. 31, 1996	10,000	1,554	8,446	7,092
Dec. 31, 1997	7,800	708*	7,092	–0–
	$67,800	$15,489		

*Rounding difference included in this number to clear accounts.

shall further assume here that the lessor is confident of collection of the lease payments and has determined all costs relative to the lease. Therefore, this is also a capital lease for the lessor and we can further classify it as a sales-type lease because the present value of the lease ($52,311) differs considerably from the cost to manufacture the asset ($30,000).

This sales-type lease is recorded by the lessor as follows:

Dec. 31, 1991	Lease Receivable	52,311	
	Cost of Goods Sold	30,000	
	Sales		52,311
	Machinery Inventory		30,000
	(To record sales-type lease.)		
	Cash	10,000	
	Lease Receivable		10,000
	(To record receipt of first lease payment.)		
Dec. 31, 1992	Lease Receivable	4,231	
	Interest Revenue		4,231
	(To record interest revenue on sales-type lease for 1992.)		
	Cash	10,000	
	Lease Receivable		10,000
	(To record receipt of second lease payment.)		

When the sales figure and the cost of goods sold from the December 31, 1991, entry are carried into the lessor's income statement, a gross profit of $22,311 is recognized as follows:

Sales	$52,311
Cost of Goods Sold	(30,000)
Gross Profit on Sale	$22,311

Interest revenue for 1992 is $4,231; entries similar to those of December 31, 1992, will be made at the end of each year, with the amount of interest revenue declining as indicated in the "Interest" column of Exhibit 23–5. The lessor is recognizing two forms of revenue in this sales-type lease: gross profit on the sale in 1991 only and interest revenue over the lease term as the financing function is fulfilled. Notice that the asset is removed from the records of the lessor and no depreciation is recorded.

In Queen Company's balance sheet, the net receivable is subject to current and noncurrent classifications, much like the net payable was for the lessee. In fact, those considerations are identical and are not repeated here. (You may want to refer to the earlier discussion of separating the lease payable into current and noncurrent portions.) Following the method preferred by the authors for making this distinction, $9,091 is presented as a current receivable in each balance sheet and the remainder of the net receivable is presented as a noncurrent receivable.

At the end of the six-year lease, the lessor will receive asset(s) valued at $7,800 in some combination of the machine and cash. If the machine's value is $7,800 or greater, the following entry is appropriate:

```
Dec. 31, 1997   Machinery Inventory              7,800
                    Lease Receivable                      7,800
                (To record return of machine at end of
                 lease term.)
```

Recall that when we considered this lease from the lessee's perspective, in one case we assumed that the machine was valued at $5,000 and the lessee was required to pay $2,800 in cash ($7,800 − $5,000) in addition to returning the machine. In that situation, the lessor would record receipt of the machine and cash, as follows:

```
Dec. 31, 1997   Machinery Inventory              5,000
                Cash                             2,800
                    Lease Receivable                      7,800
                (To record return of machine and cash
                 at end of lease term.)
```

Direct-Financing Lease

Accounting for a direct-financing lease can be easily illustrated by changing a few assumptions. We shall assume that Queen Company purchases assets for lease as contracts are negotiated with lessees, rather than manufacturing those assets as indicated earlier. Queen Company establishes the lease payment schedules so that the present value of the lease equals the cost of the asset. We shall assume that the cost of the machine to the lessor is $52,311.

The lease amortization schedule in Exhibit 23–5 can again be used in accounting for this lease. The major difference is in the first entry to record the lease transaction, in which the Machinery Inventory is reclassified as a receivable and no sales or cost of goods sold is recorded.

```
Dec. 31, 1991   Lease Receivable                52,311
                    Machinery Inventory                  52,311
                (To record direct-financing lease.)
                Cash                            10,000
                    Lease Receivable                     10,000
                (To record receipt of first lease payment.)
Dec. 31, 1992   Lease Receivable                 4,231
                    Interest Revenue                      4,231
                (To record interest revenue on
                 direct-financing lease for 1992.)
                Cash                            10,000
                    Lease Receivable                     10,000
                (To record receipt of second lease payment.)
```

Thereafter, all entries are identical to those appropriate for recording the sales-type lease as presented earlier. The only form of revenue recognized by the lessor is interest revenue, following the schedule of the "Interest" column in Exhibit 23–5. As with the sales-type lease, no depreciation is recorded by the lessor inasmuch as the asset is assumed to have been transferred to the lessee.

ADDITIONAL LESSOR CONSIDERATIONS

In the Queen Company illustration of both the sales-type and the direct-financing leases, we have recorded the receivable at the net amount which represents the present value of the lease. An alternative procedure is to record the receivable at the gross amount, equal to the total future payments, and record the amount included in that figure which represents interest in a separate contra-account identified as "Unearned Income." Assuming a sales-type lease, the entry to record the lease by this approach is as follows:

Dec. 31, 1991	Lease Receivable	67,800	
	Cost of Goods Sold	30,000	
	Sales		52,311
	Unearned Income		15,489
	Machinery Inventory		30,000

If the lease is a direct-financing lease, the entry to record the lease by this approach is as follows:

Dec. 31, 1991	Lease Receivable	67,800	
	Machinery Inventory		52,311
	Unearned Income		15,489

In either case, the net amount of the receivable is $52,311 ($67,800 − $15,489) and as interest revenue is recognized each period, the Unearned Income account is debited rather than the Lease Receivable account. In all other respects, the entries for the "net receivable" approach presented earlier apply.

For operating leases, we discussed accounting for initial direct costs. Those same costs arise for capital leases and require special treatment. Initial direct costs related to sales-type leases are charged to expense at the beginning of the lease term and, thereby, reduce the amount of gross profit recognized on the lease. In the case of direct-financing leases, initial direct costs are debited to the amount of unearned income (gross method of recording) or the net receivable (net method of recording). In either case, the impact is to reduce the amount of interest included in the net receivable and, accordingly, the amount of interest revenue that will be recognized over the lease term. The lessor must then impute a new (lower) interest rate that will be used to amortize the interest over the lease term at a constant rate. This indirectly results in the amortization of initial direct costs in a pattern which parallels the recognition of interest revenue.

Matching Initial direct costs are treated differently in each type of lease by the lessor. The objective of matching revenues and expenses explains each treatment in light of different leasing circumstances. For operating leases, these costs are deferred and amortized over the lease term, thereby matching the costs with the lease revenue as it is recognized. For sales-type leases, initial direct costs are taken directly into income and reduce the amount of gross profit recognized on the lease. For direct-financing leases, initial direct costs reduce the amount of future interest revenue that will be recognized.

Like lessees, lessors are required to disclose significant information about leases in their financial statements and related notes. Exhibit 23–6 presents the note

EXHIBIT 23-6

Ford Motor Company
Lessor Disclosure

**Note 8. Receivables and Lease Investments,
    net—Financial Services**

Included in receivables and lease investments, net at December 31 are: (a) net finance receivables, as well as (b) investment in direct financing leases and (c) investment in operating leases. The investments in direct financing and operating leases relate to the leasing of motor vehicles and various types of transportation and other equipment and facilities as follows:

(in millions)	1990	1989
(a) Net finance receivables		
Automotive	$ 55,719.1	$56,205.1
Real estate	27,568.3	24,574.8
Other	19,953.3	18,577.9
Total finance receivables	**103,240.7**	99,357.8
Plus		
Loan origination costs	**133.6**	85.5
Less		
Unearned income	**8,027.2**	7,774.2
Allowance for credit losses	**1,573.3**	1,410.7
Unearned insurance premiums and unpaid insurance		
claims related to finance receivables	**412.3**	465.9
Net finance receivables	**$ 93,361.5**	$89,792.5

Other finance receivables consist primarily of commercial and consumer loans, collateralized loans, credit card receivables, general corporate obligations and accrued interest. Also included in other finance receivables at December 31, 1990 and 1989 were $2,315 million and $1,541 million, respectively, of accounts receivable purchased by the Financial Services segment from the Automotive segment. Contractual maturities of automotive and other finance receivables are as follows (in millions): 1991—$37,463; 1992—$15,323; 1993—$10,317; thereafter—$12,569. Experience indicates that a substantial portion of the loan portfolio generally is repaid before contractual maturity dates.

disclosure of Ford Motor Company for 1990 for those leasing transactions for which Ford is the lessor. Ford Motor Company, known primarily as a manufacturer of cars and trucks, also does business in electronics, glass, plastics, castings, climate-control systems, service and replacement parts, vehicle leasing and rental, space technology, satellite communications, defense systems and land development.

Information about capital leases is included in a broader note identified as "Receivables and Lease Investments, net—Financial Services." The (b) part of the note includes information about the company's direct-financing leases, which ties to information presented in the asset sections of the balance sheet. The (c) part of the note includes information about operating leases in which the company serves as lessor.

ADVANCED LEASING TOPICS

Leasing is a very important and complex business activity. For the lessee, leasing is a primary source of financing assets needed to support ongoing business op-

Financial Services periodically sells finance receivables. As a result of such sales, Financial Services net income increased by $31 million in 1990, $153 million in 1989 and $46 million in 1988. Anticipated credit losses have been provided for where limited guarantee provisions of the sales contracts exist.

(in millions)	1990	1989
(b) Investment in direct financing leases		
Minimum lease rentals	**$7,573.5**	$5,893.1
Estimated residual values	**2,732.9**	2,915.4
Lease origination costs	**39.7**	34.0
Less		
Unearned income	**2,086.0**	1,786.8
Allowance for credit losses	**207.9**	188.0
Net investment in direct financing leases	**$8,052.2**	$6,867.7

Minimum direct financing lease rentals (including executory costs of $157 million) for each of the five succeeding years are as follows (in millions): 1991—$2,314; 1992—$1,836; 1993—$1,147; 1994—$506; 1995—$194.

(in millions)	1990	1989
(c) Investment in operating leases		
Vehicles and other equipment, at cost	**$5,284.3**	$3,376.9
Lease origination costs	**6.4**	5.3
Less		
Accumulated depreciation	**1,122.6**	817.4
Allowance for credit losses	**66.3**	33.8
Net investment in operating leases	**$4,101.8**	$2,531.0

Future minimum rentals on operating leases for each of the five succeeding years are as follows (in millions): 1991—$1,668; 1992—$443; 1993—$187; 1994—$19; 1995—$9.

Depreciation expense on operating leases is provided for primarily on a straight-line basis over the term of the leases and was as follows (in millions): 1990—$882; 1989—$610; 1988—$496.

SOURCE: Ford Motor Company, 1990 Annual Report.

erations. For the lessor, leasing is a primary source of revenue generation and may be an essential mechanism through which the sale of assets to customers is accomplished.

To this point in our study of leases, we have attempted to focus attention on important underlying principles. Perhaps the most compelling principle in explaining

Substance over Form

accounting for leases is the notion of substance over form. Accountants attempt to understand the true substance or intent of the business transaction being carried out via lease and account for it accordingly, rather than allowing the legal form of the transaction to dictate the accounting treatment.

Situations involving leases may become very complex. Many authoritative accounting pronouncements have been issued and are currently in effect that attempt to explain these complexities and address the accounting issues inherent in them. While our intent here is not to provide comprehensive coverage of all dimensions of accounting for leases, in this section we briefly introduce some of the more common complexities that may be encountered in applying accounting standards for leases.

UNGUARANTEED RESIDUAL VALUE

Our earlier example of lessee/lessor accounting included a residual value guarantee. Recall the lease in which the lessee, King Company, guaranteed a value of $7,800 to the lessor, Queen Company, at the end of the six-year lease term. Inasmuch the content of leases is typically governed by the lessor, the inclusion of a guarantee of the residual value is common because of the protection it offers the lessor from unexpected obsolescence, excess usage, unexpected market changes and other factors that might affect the value of the used asset that will be returned to the lessor at the end of the lease term.

If the residual value is guaranteed, it is included in the determination of the present value of the lease and in the lease amortization schedule as a final payment, as we saw in the earlier examples. If the residual value is not guaranteed, however, procedures must be altered to reflect this difference for both the lessee and lessor.

The most obvious difference in accounting for a capital lease with an unguaranteed residual value is the fact that no final amount to cover the residual value is included in the computation of the lease liability for the lessee. The lessor computes the present value of the lease to include the residual value because the asset will be returned to the lessor at the end of the lease term. Assuming a sales-type lease, if the residual value is not guaranteed, the present value of the residual is not included in the sales figure recorded by the lessor. To offset the reduction in the sales amount caused by the omission of the present value of the residual, the lessor must also reduce cost of goods sold by the present value of the residual.

The following example illustrates accounting for an unguaranteed residual value and contrasts it with that for a guaranteed residual value. Topper Company (lessor) leases equipment under a standard leasing arrangement that calls for $5,000 payments at the beginning of each year for five years. The interest rate implicit in the lease is 12% and the asset is expected to be worth $3,000 at the end of the five-year term. In Case A, we assume that the residual value is guaranteed; in Case B we assume that the residual value is not guaranteed.

The present value of the lease under both circumstances is computed as follows:

$$
\begin{aligned}
&\text{Present value of five \$5,000 payments:}\\
&\quad \$5,000 \times (1.00000 + 3.03735^*) = \$20,187\\
&\text{Present value of \$3,000 residual:}\\
&\quad \$3,000 \times .56743^{**} \qquad\qquad = \underline{1,702}\\
&\text{Present value of lease} \qquad\qquad\qquad \$21,889
\end{aligned}
$$

$^*pvoaf_{\overline{4}|12\%}$
$^{**}pvf_{\overline{5}|12\%}$

The lease is amortized according to the amounts indicated in Exhibit 23–7. Whether the residual value is guaranteed or not, the lessor includes the residual value in the recorded asset because that value accrues to the lessor in either case.

We shall assume that Topper manufactured the equipment at a cost of $15,000. When the residual value is guaranteed, the lessor's asset is appropriately labeled "receivable"; when the residual value is not guaranteed, the authors prefer the label "investment" because it includes two diverse elements: a receivable plus the lessor's interest in the used asset to be returned at the end of the lease term. That terminology is used in following selected entries regarding this lease:

EXHIBIT 23-7

Topper Company
Lease Amortization Schedule (Lessor)

Date	Payment	Interest	Decline in Net Receivable	Net Receivable
Dec. 31, 1992	—	—	—	$21,889
	$ 5,000	—	$5,000	16,889
Dec. 31, 1993	5,000	$2,027	2,973	13,916
Dec. 31, 1994	5,000	1,670	3,330	10,586
Dec. 31, 1995	5,000	1,270	3,730	6,856
Dec. 31, 1996	5,000	823	4,177	2,679
Dec. 31, 1997	3,000	321	2,679	–0–
	$28,000	$6,111		

		Case A—Guaranteed Residual	
Dec. 31, 1992	Lease Receivable	21,889	
	Cost of Goods Sold	15,000	
	Sales		21,889
	Equipment Inventory		15,000
	(To record sales-type lease with guaranteed residual value.)		
	Cash	5,000	
	Lease Receivable		5,000
	(To record first lease payment.)		
Dec. 31, 1997	Lease Receivable	321	
	Interest Revenue		321
	(To recognize interest revenue for last year of lease.)		
	Cash/Equipment Inventory	3,000	
	Lease Receivable		3,000
	(To record final settlement of lease residual value.)		

On December 31 of 1993–1996, an interest revenue accrual (DR–Lease Receivable; CR–Interest Revenue) is made according to the amounts reflected in Exhibit 23–7. Also, a cash receipt (DR–Cash; CR–Lease Receivable) of $5,000 is recorded each December 31.

The final entry shows a debit to "Cash/Equipment Inventory" to indicate that some combination of cash and used equipment will be returned to the lessor at a total of $3,000. The precise amount of each is dependent on the appraised value of the used asset, as discussed in our earlier example.

The entries at the top of page 1110 are appropriate for the same lease if the **residual value is not guaranteed.** Entries to accrue interest revenue and the receipt of cash are made each December 31. The amounts of sales and cost of goods sold in Case B are based on the same amounts included in Case A, except each is reduced by the present value of the residual, as follows:

Sales: $21,889 − $1,702 = $20,187
Cost of Goods Sold: $15,000 − $1,702 = $13,298

		Case B—Unguaranteed Residual	
Dec. 31, 1992	Investment in Lease	21,889	
	Cost of Goods Sold	13,298	
	Sales		20,187
	Equipment Inventory		15,000
	(To record sales-type lease with unguaranteed residual value.)		
	Cash	5,000	
	Investment in Lease		5,000
	(To record first lease payment.)		
Dec. 31, 1997	Investment in Lease	321	
	Investment Revenue		321
	(To recognize interest revenue for last year of lease.)		
	Equipment Inventory	3,000	
	Investment in Lease		3,000
	(To record final settlement of lease residual value.)		

Comparing the accounting treatment of the sales-type lease with and without the residual value guarantee, we find that the amount of gross profit and interest revenue recognized are the same, as indicated below:

	Case A Guaranteed	Case B Unguaranteed
Gross profit		
Sales	$21,889	$20,187
Cost of Goods Sold	(15,000)	(13,298)
Gross Profit	$ 6,889	$ 6,889
Interest Revenue		
Receivable (gross)	$28,000	—
Investment (gross)	—	$28,000
Present value of lease	(21,889)	(21,889)
Interest Revenue	$ 6,111	$ 6,111

DIFFERENT INTEREST RATES

In the primary illustrations in this chapter, we have made the simplifying assumption that the lessor's rate implicit in the lease and the lessee's incremental borrowing interest rate were the same. This would certainly not be the case in every instance. We further stated that the general policy to be followed is that the lessor accounts for the lease using the interest rate implicit in the lease without regard to the lessee's incremental borrowing rate. The lessee, however, is required to use the lower of the two rates if the lessor's rate is known to the lessee. If the rate implicit in the lease is not known to the lessee, the lessee's incremental borrowing rate is used by the lessee.

An important observation is that the use of different rates results in different present value amounts and potentially important differences in the way leases are treated by the two parties to the lease. In our earlier examples, we were able to use the same amortization figures to separate payments into interest and receivable/payable reduction because the two parties were using the same interest rate. If different interest rates are used, however, the lessor and lessee will have different amounts recorded for the lease receivable and payable and the amounts of interest revenue and expense recognized will differ.

Recall that the fourth capitalization criterion indicates that a lease is classified as a capital lease if the present value of the lease equals or exceeds 90% of the fair value of the asset. The use of different interest rates could result in a difference in lease capitalization if, for example, one party's present value calculation fell on or above the 90% of fair value standard; the other party's present value calculation fell below that amount; and none of the other recapitalization criteria are met.

To illustrate these differences in treatment with varying interest rates, assume that Franklin Company, a lessor, leases equipment to Jefferson Company, a lessee, for $7,000 annually, with payments due on the first day of each of the next seven years. Franklin establishes the lease payment schedule based on an assumed rate of return (interest rate) of 16%; Jefferson Company's incremental borrowing rate is 10%. In this case, whether or not Jefferson Company is aware of the rate implicit in the lease, a 10% rate is used for the lessee, and the two present value calculations are as follows:

	10%	16%
$7,000 \times (1.00000 + 4.35526*)$	$37,487	—
$7,000 \times (1.00000 + 3.68474**)$	—	$32,793

$*pvoaf_{\overline{6}|10\%}$
$**pvoaf_{\overline{6}|16\%}$

Assuming that 90% of the fair value of the asset is $32,793 or less, this lease will be treated as a capital lease by both parties. The amounts of the receivable/payable and interest revenue/expense will be different, however, because of the differences in present value calculation and interest rates used to amortize the lease. If 90% of the fair value of the asset is an amount between the two figures, the lease would be interpreted as an operating lease by the lessor (using the 16% rate) and as a capital lease by the lessee (using the 10% rate). For example, if the fair value of the asset is $40,000, the cutoff for capital lease evaluation is $36,000 ($40,000 × 90%) and the outcome described above will exist. This is one situation in which the accounting treatment of the lease lacks symmetry in that the lessee treats the lease as a purchase but the lessor does not treat the same lease as a sale.

LEVERAGED LEASES—LESSOR ACCOUNTING

Leveraged leases, which apply only to lessors, have been used more and more in recent years. This growth is a response to the increasing burden of income taxes and to a desire by lessors to avoid reporting the large liabilities that result from the acquisition of property that, in turn, is leased to others under long-term leases. From the standpoint of the lessee, leveraged leases are accounted for in the same manner as nonleveraged leases. To the lessor, leveraged leases are **direct-financing leases** that meet the following four additional criteria:

1. The lease involves three parties: a lessee, a long-term creditor, and a lessor.
2. The financing provided by the long-term creditor must be nonrecourse as to the general credit of the lessor. (The leased property may, however, be subject to a mortgage.)

3. The lessor's net investment in the lease must decline in the early years of the lease and rise during the later years before final elimination.

4. The lessor's investment tax credit must be deferred and allocated to income over the life of the lease. (The investment tax credit was eliminated from law in the Tax Reform Act of 1986; therefore, this criterion is generally inoperative for leases subsequent to 1985.)

If any of these criteria are not met, the lease is considered a direct-financing lease rather than a leveraged lease. Before proceeding to a technical discussion of the financial accounting and reporting aspects of leveraged leases, we need a firm conceptual understanding of the economic sense and meaning of this form of leasing. We should understand why a leveraged lease is desirable from the lessor's perspective, because an appreciation of the benefits will aid the comprehension of the related accounting and reporting practices. The following list enumerates some of the benefits that accrue to the lessor in a leveraged lease:

1. Most funds necessary to purchase the leased asset are supplied by a long-term creditor.

2. The loan from the long-term creditor provides for no recourse against the lessor (other than a possible mortgage on the leased property).

3. The lessor receives the benefit of the investment tax credit related to the leased asset.

4. During the early years of the lease arrangement, the tax deductions for depreciation on the leased asset and interest on the nonrecourse long-term debt exceed the annual lease rental revenue. This provides the lessor with excess deductions to be applied against other taxable income.

5. At the conclusion of a leveraged lease agreement, the equipment is returned to the lessor. This benefit may also exist in a direct financing lease but *must* be present in a leveraged lease.

For these reasons, many lessors desire a leveraged lease rather than a direct financing and structure the transaction to achieve a leveraged lease classification. We now turn our attention to recording a leveraged lease. To illustrate, we assume that the present value of the minimum lease payments and the unguaranteed residual value accruing to Frost, Inc., a lessor, at the end of the lease is $50,000 ($60,000 gross payments + $7,800 residual value − $17,800 unearned income) and that the equipment cost Frost, Inc., $50,000. Further, assume that the lease now qualifies as a leveraged lease because the equipment was acquired by Frost, Inc., recently with a nonrecourse loan of $46,000. The entry to record the acquisition of the equipment at the inception of the lease appears as follows:

Investment in Lease*	21,800	
Unearned Revenue		17,800
Cash		4,000
(To record the inception of leveraged lease.)		

*The investment in lease account is determined as follows:

Gross lease payments	$60,000
Unguaranteed residual value accruing to the lessor	7,800
Total investment	$67,800
Less:	
Nonrecourse note	46,000
Investment in Lease	$21,800

The Investment in Lease Account is charged for the gross amount of lease rentals *net* of the total amount of the nonrecourse debt. The estimated residual value is the fair value of the leased property at the end of the lease term. This amount accrues to the benefit of the lessor in a leveraged lease.

The Unearned Revenue account consists of the estimated pretax deferred revenue after deductions for the initial direct costs remaining to be allocated to income over the lease term. The credit to cash in the transaction represents the investment made by the lessor in the leased property and is the difference between the cost of the leased property and the nonrecourse debt secured from the long-term creditor ($50,000 − $46,000 = $4,000).

The long-term debt is offset against the lease receivable. From the lessor's perspective, this treatment is desirable, because it improves the debt/equity ratio and rate of return on assets employed. Such an offsetting of receivable and payable is appropriate only because the creditor financing is nonrecourse to the lessor.

Subsequent to this entry, for income tax purposes the leased asset is depreciated and interest expense on the nonrecourse liability to the creditor is recognized. Rent revenue is recognized as cash is received. From an income tax perspective, therefore, the lease is treated much like an operating lease. As a result, temporary differences emerge, because in the early years of the leveraged lease the tax expense computed on the accounting income exceeds the taxes payable, which are based on the tax return. The resulting deferred credits serve to reduce the investment balance. This aspect of leveraged leasing causes a fluctuating investment balance. The *tax effects* of accelerated depreciation, along with interest expense on the third-party creditor loan, contribute to a declining investment account as a result of tax losses and emerging deferred tax credits in the early years of the lease. Later—when depreciation charges and interest expense become less than the gross lease payments being received—taxable income is recognized, thereby causing the deferred tax credits to reverse, and the Investment account rises.

Perhaps the most difficult aspect of leveraged leases to apply involves the calculation of the appropriate rate of interest for use in allocating total cash flow between the recovery of the investment and interest revenue. The amortizing rate represents that rate of interest which, when applied to the investment account balance in the years that the net investment is positive, will fully amortize the unearned revenue as interest revenue over the life of the lease. This process usually involves considerable trial and error, because: (1) the annuity amounts (cash flow after taxes) are uneven; (2) during some years the investment account may be zero or negative (so the annuity series is broken); and (3) the residual value represents a single amount at the conclusion of the lease. In complex situations computers are frequently used to ascertain the appropriate amortizing rate for leveraged leases.

SALE-LEASEBACK

A **sale-leaseback transaction** involves property that is simultaneously sold and leased back by the seller. Many times such arrangements are desirable because a large amount of liquid resources are provided to the seller while the *use* of the asset sold is still retained by the seller-lessee. Standards of accounting for sales with leasebacks are established in *FASB Statement of Financial Accounting Standards No. 28.*[7]

Generally a seller-lessee classifies leases arising in sale-leaseback transactions in accordance with the four classification criteria previously discussed. For a capital lease, any profit on the sale is deferred and amortized in proportion to the amortization of the leased asset; for an operating lease, profit on the sale is recognized in proportion to the related gross rent expense recognized over the lease term. If the fair

---

[7]*FASB Statement of Financial Accounting Standards No. 28,* "Accounting for Sales with Leasebacks," 1979.

market value of the asset sold is less than its cost or carrying amount, however, a loss on the sale should be recognized in the period of the sale and leaseback. Other types of losses on the transaction should generally be deferred and amortized over the lease term. If only a minor portion of the property is leased back, then profit or loss on the sale is generally recognized in a normal fashion at the time of the transaction.

SUBLEASES

The central concept establishing subleases as a special type of lease is that a lessee, now acting as a sublessor, cannot transfer to a sublessee more rights than were obtained in the original lease. For example, if a lessee treats an original lease as an operating lease, then any sublease of that property granted by the original lessee (now a sublessor) can be considered only as an operating lease.

If the original lease contains either a transfer of ownership or a bargain purchase option, then the original lessee (now a sublessor) is presumed to have acquired all of the rights associated with the property. The original lessee is therefore capable of completely disposing of those rights. In determining the proper classification of a sublease, the lessor should apply all four of the normal classification criteria and the two additional criteria of rent collectibility and cost predictability.

If the original lease does not transfer title to the lessee, a sublease of the property from that lessee cannot contain a transfer of title to a sublessee. If either the length of lease term or the amount of lease payment criterion is met in the original lease but neither a transfer of title nor a bargain purchase option is provided, then the sublease should be subjected only to new length of lease term and amount of lease payment criteria. Of course, the new rent collectibility and cost predictability tests must also be met.

Sublessees incur no problems in accounting for subleases that are not encountered in any other leasing arrangements, and, therefore, they apply normal classification procedures.

RELATED-PARTY LEASES

Substance over Form

SFAS No. 13 states that economic substance, rather than mere form, governs accounting for all leases, including those between related parties. **Related parties** include a parent company and its subsidiaries, joint ventures, partnerships and partners, and investors and investees, provided that the parent company, owner, or investor has the ability to exercise **significant influence** over the operating and financial policies of the other party. The test for significant influence is also consistent with the concept of significant influence discussed in Chapter 10 and contained in *APB Opinion No. 18.*[8] Other situations and circumstances may also create related-party conditions. Examples include the extension of credit, guarantees of indebtedness, and other relationships and economic dependencies. Accountants should gain an understanding of the business purpose and the economics of related-party leases in order to report properly the substance of those transactions. This is especially true when the form of the agreement is unusual or is not representative of normal business practice.

REAL ESTATE LEASES

The unusual characteristics of the asset land cause most of the differences underlying financial accounting and reporting for real estate leases. Basically, the problem stems from the fact that land is considered to have an unlimited life for purposes of financial

---

[8]*APB Opinion No. 18,* "The Equity Method of Accounting for Investments in Common Stock," 1971.

accounting. It is not logical, therefore, to consider a lease of land to be a sale unless either the transfer-of-title or bargain-purchase-option criterion has been met. In other words, it is impossible for a lease of land to meet the lease term criterion of 75% of useful life, because land is presumed to have an unlimited life. Furthermore, the fact that the present value of the minimum lease payments exceeds 90% of the fair market value of the leased land does not indicate that the lease is in substance a sale of the land. Indeed, the land does not expire; it reverts to the lessor at the end of the lease; and it may be worth a great deal more at the conclusion of a lease than at the beginning. Given a conceptual understanding of the unusual aspects of real estate leases, we now consider the technical requirements of *SFAS No. 13* that are related to a variety of real estate leases.

Leases of Land Only

In order to account for real estate leases, accountants must carefully consider the types of real estate being leased. For a lease of land to be considered a capital lease by lessees and lessors, the lease agreement must contain a transfer of title or a bargain purchase option. Furthermore, lessors must also meet the rent collectibility and cost predictability tests. Because real estate lease terms frequently extend for periods of time in excess of 20 years, the assessment of the collectibility of rent is unusually complex. Accordingly, a lease of real estate should not be classified as a sales-type lease with manufacturer's or dealer's profit recognized unless specific criteria are met.[9] The criteria, related to predicting the collectibility of rent, require a certain amount of down payment, which must consist of cash or marketable securities readily convertible to cash. The amount of the required down payment ranges from 5% to 25% of the total purchase price for different types of real estate. Because few leases contain initial balloon payments, in which large amounts of the total lease payable must be paid at the beginning of the lease term, most real estate leases that otherwise qualify as sales-type leases are properly accounted for as operating leases because of a failure to meet the down-payment quantity and quality criteria.

Leases of Land and Buildings

When a lease involves both land and a building, accountants must assess the magnitude of the portion of the assets represented by the land. If the fair market value of the land portion of the leased assets equals or exceeds 25% of the total fair market value of the leased assets, the land is considered separately in accordance with the provisions for leases of land only. In order to determine the portion of the minimum lease payments associated with the land, the incremental borrowing rate is multiplied by the estimated fair market value of the land. This is done because the land is assumed to have an unlimited life and is, therefore, capable of earning that rate of return perpetually. The amount of the rental payment attributable to the land is considered to represent an operating lease unless the lease contains a transfer of title or a bargain purchase option. The remaining amount of the lease payment is related to the building and that portion of the lease is classified using the same criteria as are applied to any other leased asset.

If the fair market value of the land portion of the leased assets is less than 25% of the total fair market value of both the land and building, however, the land portion can be ignored for purposes of lease classification. Therefore, if land represents less than 25% of the fair market value of the package of real estate assets leased and if the lease

---

[9]*FASB Statement of Financial Accounting Standards No. 26*, "Profit Recognition in Sales Type Leases of Real Estate," 1979, states that the criteria for recognizing profit contained in the AICPA *Industry Accounting Guide*, "Accounting for Profit Recognition on Sales of Real Estate," should be applied to leases of real estate.

contains neither a transfer of title nor a bargain purchase option, the lease may still be classified as a capital lease if one of the two remaining classification criteria is met. In that case the land is considered sold, and the lessee would amortize the leased assets *(including land)* over the life of the lease or the life of the building, whichever is shorter. However, the asset would not be the land but a right to *use* the land. The 25% land-portion limitation ensures that the amount of the intangible asset represented by land is relatively small. In such situations lessors remove the leased asset (including land) from the plant assets section of the balance sheet and record an investment in the lease. The residual value of the assets should be added to the investment by the lessor because the residual value of the leased asset is presumed to revert to the lessor when a transfer of title and a bargain purchase option are absent from the lease.

Leases of Portions of a Building

Another complex issue arises if the leased asset is a *part* of a building. Such situations are common in leases involving shopping centers or high-rise office buildings and occur frequently in practice.

When only a part of a building is leased, the cost and fair market value amounts required to apply the fourth classification test (amount of lease payment) are often difficult to estimate. For example, what is the cost of the fortieth floor of a high-rise office building? Without such estimates, application of the amount-of-lease-payment test, which relies on estimates of fair market value, is impossible. Furthermore, without cost estimates a lessor may have trouble determining whether a given capital lease is a sales-type or direct-financing lease. Because gross profit (or loss) and interest revenue are recognized on sales-type leases whereas only interest revenue is recognized on direct-financing leases, the cost of the property subject to the lease has a direct bearing on the classification of a lease and the nature and timing of the revenue to be recognized.

FASB Interpretation No. 24 provides guidance on how to estimate the cost and fair market value when only a portion of a building is leased.[10] It states that estimates of cost and fair market value are usually possible and suggests that appraisals and replacement cost estimates may be appropriate in determining the fair market value and cost of portions of a building. Therefore, although precise figures may be impossible to obtain, accountants must attempt to develop reasonable estimates of value and cost.

CONCLUDING REMARKS

In this chapter, we have focused attention on lease capitalization because this is where the primary controversy concerning lease accounting exists. The FASB, in *SFAS No. 13* and the large body of authoritative pronouncements that have resulted since its issuance, took the position that leases with certain characteristics require capitalization. These characteristics are described in the four basic capitalization criteria that we have discussed in this chapter. Some have suggested that to specify criteria to this extent simply invites companies to negotiate leases that fail all four criteria, thereby preserving a major advantage of leasing, off-balance-sheet financing. In fact, the large dollar amounts of operating leases that can be discovered only by a careful reading of the notes to the financial statements provides some support for this assertion.

Assuming that lease capitalization is believed to be appropriate, what alternatives to current practice exist to correct the situation described in the previous paragraph? Some have argued in favor of capitalizing all leases that have certain characteristics

---

[10]*FASB Interpretation No. 24*, "Leases Involving a Part of a Building," 1978.

(e.g., are noncancelable and have terms of at least one year), thereby removing most, if not all, of the judgment factor in classifying a lease as capital or operating.[11] Another alternative is to permit the legal form of the transaction to govern and to treat all leases as we currently treat operating leases, with expanded note disclosure as a means of communicating the nature of obligations to users of financial statements.

The complexity of lease accounting has also been the source of much criticism, prompting one practitioner to make the following observations about applying current lease pronouncements:

> *"Clearly, from a practitioner's viewpoint,* Statement 13 *has created practice problems and difficulties by forcing one to rummage through rules, amendments and interpretations when analyzing a lease. Conclusions on lease accounting seem to reach the lowest common denominator in practice, so that most practitioners have concluded that the objectives of* Statement 13 *and substance over form give way to a literal interpretation of the rules of* Statement 13. *No white knights are appearing to invoke the Board's objectives, since the Board itself, through its amendments and interpretations, has opted, for the most part, to apply the arbitrary rules and percentages literally."* [12]

Earlier we identified "symmetry" as a desirable objective of lease accounting, referring to the compatible treatment by the two parties to the lease. One situation was cited that might result in the lack of symmetry—the use of different interest rates in computing the present value of the lease by the lessor and the lessee. Recall, also, that the lessor has two revenue realization criteria to apply that are not applied by the lessee—the ability to determine or estimate costs associated with the lease and the predictability of lease payments. A lease could meet one of the four basic criteria, but fail one or more of these additional lessor criteria, and be treated as a capital lease by the lessee and as an operating lease by the lessor. Finally, the four capitalization criteria certainly leave some room for judgment when they base lease capitalization on such determinations as "bargain" purchase option, "estimated" useful life of the leased asset, and "fair value" of the leased asset. Differences in applying the judgment required to make these assessments could result in differences in classification between the two parties to the lease.

While FASB has developed a sizeable body of literature concerning lease accounting, all questions have not been answered and all accountants do not agree with the answers that are currently offered. This important subject will undoubtedly continue to be a source of interest and controversy to practitioners and standard-setters in the future.

KEY POINTS

1. The first step in accounting for leases requires lessees and lessors to classify leases according to the substance of the transaction. (Objectives 1, 2, and 3)
2. Lessees classify leases as either operating leases or capital leases. Operating leases result in the recognition of only rent expense. Capital leases require the recognition of the asset acquired, liability incurred, amortization or depreciation expense on the asset, and interest expense on the liability. (Objectives 3 and 4)

---

[11]For an excellent discussion of this recommendation, see Arthur R. Wyatt, "Leases Should Be Capitalized," *CPA Journal* (September 1974), pp. 35–38.
[12]Richard Dieter, "Is Lessee Accounting Working?" *CPA Journal* (August 1979), p. 19.

3. Lessors classify leases as either operating leases or one of three types of capital leases (direct-financing, sale-type, and leveraged leases). (Objectives 3 and 4)

4. A capital lease must meet at least one of four separate criteria: (1) It contains a transfer of title; (2) it contains a bargain purchase option; (3) the lease term is equal to or greater than 75% of the asset's remaining life; or (4) the present value of the minimum lease payments exceeds 90% of the asset's fair market value. (Objectives 3 and 4)

5. In addition to meeting one of the four initial classification tests, lessors must apply two additional criteria to classify a lease as a capital lease: (1) Rent collectibility must be reasonably certain, and (2) future costs must be reasonably predictable. (Objectives 3 and 4)

6. Lessees recognize rent expense on operating leases on a straight-line basis over the lease term. (Objective 5)

7. Lessees recognize depreciation or amortization expense, interest expense, and executory costs on capital leases over the lease term. The capitalized lease liability is separated into current and noncurrent components in the balance sheet. (Objective 5)

8. Lessors recognize rental revenue on a straight-line basis and continue to depreciate assets subject to operating leases. (Objective 5)

9. Lessors recognize only interest revenue on direct-financing and leveraged leases, whereas gross profit and interest revenue are recognized on sales-type leases. Investments in capital leases (or lease receivables) are subject to current and noncurrent balance sheet classifications. (Objective 5)

10. Many other unusual circumstances in regard to leasing activities require careful consideration and analysis in order to properly report such transactions. (Objective 5)

QUESTIONS

23–1   The issue of "substance over form" is central in financial accounting and reporting for leases. Discuss the issue of substance and form as it relates to lease accounting.

23–2   Name the usual two parties to a lease and describe their roles.

23–3   What is a capital lease? Under what circumstances do lessees classify leases as capital leases? If a lease fails to meet the requirements for a capital lease, what type of lease is it?

23–4   Under what circumstances is a lease classified as a sales-type lease by a lessor?

23–5   How should a lessee account for and report a capital lease?

23–6   How should lessors account for and report sales-type leases?

23–7   What happens in a sale-leaseback transaction? Discuss the event from the perspective of both parties to the lease.

23–8   Mark Company is a major automobile dealer and is required to lease large parking lots to house its inventory of automobiles. The owner, Mark William, has approached you about the accounting problems he faces in regard to these leases. You ascertain that several of the leases contain bargain purchase options while several others do not. Discuss the classification and accounting problems presented by these real estate leases.

23–9   Application of *FASB Statement of Financial Accounting Standards No. 13,* "Accounting for Leases," will generally result in symmetrical treatment of the same lease by both lessee and lessor (i.e., both will treat the same lease as an operating lease or as some form of capital lease). Give two examples of circumstances and situations in which a departure from this general rule may arise.

23–10   An estimate of residual value is sometimes necessary when applying *SFAS No. 13.* Under what circumstances is it necessary for a lessor and lessee to estimate residual value?

23–11   What are initial direct costs? When is it important to determine initial direct costs under a lease? Explain your answer.

23–12   Are the following statements true (T) or false (F) in regard to leases?

[a] The unguaranteed residual value accrues to the lessor only if the lease contains a bargain purchase option.

[b] For a capital lease, initial direct costs incurred by lessees are deferred and allocated over the lease term in proportion to depreciation recognized on the leased asset.

[c] Leveraged leases require third-party creditor involvement unless the lessee guarantees the residual value of the asset.

[d] Salespersons' compensation should never be included in initial direct costs, because it represents a selling expense and is not related to the initial direct costs of executing the lease.

[e] For a sales-type lease, the lessor uses the incremental borrowing rate of the lessee, if known, to compute the present value of the lease.

[f] From the lessor's perspective, minimum lease payments include the residual value guarantee of the lessee.

[g] From the lessee's perspective, a lease of land will not result in a capital lease even when the lease contains a bargain purchase option.

23–13 Indicate whether the following statements are true (T) or false (F) in regard to leases.

[a] Under a leasing arrangement, it is possible for lessees to amortize as an expense the full cost of a leased asset, including land and residual values.

[b] If the original lessee enters into a sublease or if the original lease agreement is sold or transferred by the original lessee to a third party, the original lessor must reevaluate his accounting treatment of the lease and make adjustments as required by the sublease arrangement.

[c] If a lease involving real estate also includes equipment, the portion of the minimum lease payments applicable to the equipment element of the lease shall be estimated by whatever means are appropriate in the circumstances.

[d] From the standpoint of the lessee, leveraged leases shall be classified and accounted for in the same manner as nonleveraged leases.

[e] During the term of a capital lease, each minimum lease payment is allocated between a reduction of the obligation and interest expense in order to produce a constant periodic rate of interest on the remaining balance of the obligation.

[f] The lessee usually records a capital lease as an asset and an obligation at an amount equal to the current cost of the leased property.

[g] Any profit or loss experienced by the seller-lessee in a sale-leaseback transaction must be included in income at the date of the lease agreement.

[h] In a sales-type lease, the lessor realizes a profit (or loss) at the beginning of the lease.

[i] In an operating lease, the lessee assigns rent expense to the periods benefiting from the use of the asset and does not record the commitment to make future payments.

23–14 Skyscraper Corporation owns a large building complex and leases portions of the complex for offices, retail stores, and a bank. Skyscraper substantially alters the physical layout of a part of the complex to induce Carolyn's Clothing, a high-fashion retailer, to sign a five-year lease. How should the costs of altering the building be treated if the following conditions are true?

[a] Tenants subsequent to Carolyn's Clothing will probably find the alterations desirable.

[b] Tenants subsequent to Carolyn's Clothing will not be able to use the facility until the modifications are removed.

23–15 Leasing activity has been increasing in our economy for some time. What are three reasons that help explain the popularity of leasing as a means of acquiring the service rights of an asset?

23–16 *SFAS No. 13* explicitly defines a "leveraged lease" and prescribes the accounting practice for this type of lease. Describe the criteria that must be met for a lease to be classified as a leveraged lease.

23–17 What are the primary economic differences that distinguish between sales-type leases and direct-financing leases?

23–18 What circumstances in an original lease would preclude a sublease from being accounted for as a capital lease by the sub-lessor?

23–19 What two methods may be used to separate the amount of a lease liability into current and noncurrent elements? Which method is theoretically preferable? Why?

23–20 What are executory costs and what impact, if any, do they have on the calculation of the present value of the minimum lease payments?

EXERCISES

23–21   LESSEE AND LESSOR—OPERATING LEASE   Miller Company agreed to lease a building from Light Company on January 1, 1992, for three years. There is no renewal option, and no purchase option is exercisable. The building, with a book value of $300,000, has a remaining useful life of ten years and no salvage value. Miller's incremental borrowing rate is 10%, and the company has no knowledge of Light's implicit rate. Payments of $85,000 per year are due on December 31 of each year. Miller and Light both use straight-line depreciation.

Instructions

Record this transaction for 1992 on Miller's books and Light's books.

23–22   LEASE PAYMENT COMPUTATION   Kiko Corporation leased machinery, which had a sales price of $400,000. Kiko's interest rate was 10% and the lease was for eight years with payments due at the end of each year for the life of the lease. Title is transferred to Kiko at the end of the lease.

Instructions

Compute the annual payment required by the lease.

23–23   LESSEE AND LESSOR—OPERATING LEASE   On July 1, 1992, King Company leased a new building valued at $4,500,000 to Prince Company for five years. Five equal payments of $250,000 are due on December 31 of each year starting in 1992. Depreciation is calculated on a straight-line basis by both parties, and the building has an expected useful life of 25 years. Both companies recognize a full year's depreciation in the year a new asset is acquired.

Instructions

Prepare journal entries to record all aspects of this transaction for 1992 on Prince Company's books and King Company's books.

23–24   LESSOR—OPERATING LEASE   On April 1, 1992, Jackson Corporation leased assets with a book value of $1,000,000 to Long Corporation for three years for an annual lease payment of $180,000 due each March 31. The equipment has a useful life of 16 remaining years. At the end of the lease term the equipment returns to Jackson. Long Corporation has an incremental borrowing rate of 10% but has no knowledge of Jackson Corporation's implicit rate. Depreciation is recorded on a straight-line basis by both companies, and both companies report on a calendar-year basis.

Instructions

Record this transaction for Jackson for 1992 and 1993.

23–25   DIRECT-FINANCING LEASE   On January 1, 1992, Frost Company, the lessee, signs a six-year lease with Pawn Company for equipment with annual payments $43,263 due on December 31 of each year. The fair value of the equipment and the carrying amount on Pawn's books is $200,000. Frost's incremental borrowing rate is 9%. The lease is a direct-financing lease; Pawn's implicit interest rate is 8%. Don't recognize profit, sales, COGS

Instructions

Record all lease-related transactions on Pawn's books for 1992 and 1993. (Round all amounts to the nearest dollar.)

23–26   LESSEE-LEASE AMORTIZATION   Expo Corporation leased equipment from Show Company on January 1, 1992, for four years on a noncancelable lease. The equipment cost $1,000,000, which is its fair value at the inception of the lease. All maintenance costs are paid by Expo, and at the end of the lease the equipment reverts to Show. The incremental borrowing rate for the lessee is 12%, and the useful life of the equipment is five years. Annual lease payments are $329,234.54, payable December 31 each year.

Instructions

Prepare a schedule showing the amortization of the lease by Expo over the four-year lease term.

23–27   LESSOR—CAPITAL LEASE   Brad Corporation leased equipment costing $150,000 to White Company for an implied profit of $30,000. Brad's implied interest rate is 10% and the lease

profit = sales type
need => profit, sales, COGS

is for 10 years, which equals the economic life of the equipment. The lease is noncancelable, costs are predictable, and payment is reasonably assured at the end of each lease year.

Instructions

[a] Determine the annual payment Brad will collect from White Company.
[b] What is the total amount of the lease payments and the amount of interest included in those payments?
[c] Prepare the journal entry to record the lease on Brad's books.

23–28 **DIRECT-FINANCING LEASE** On January 1, 1992, O'Hara Company leased a machine to McClure Company. The lease was for 10 years, which approximated the useful life of the machine. O'Hara purchased the machine for $80,000 and expects to earn a 10% return on its investment, based on an annual rental of $11,836 payable in advance each January 1. *Annuity Due*

Instructions

Assuming this is a direct-financing lease, prepare the entry that should be made on December 31, 1992, to recognize interest revenue.

23–29 **LESSEE AND LESSOR—OPERATING LEASE** Hinkle Corporation leases from Gray Company a building with a book value of $350,000. The building has a five-year useful life remaining. The lease calls for annual payments of $90,000, to be paid at the beginning of the year. The lease has a three-year term and is considered an operating lease. Gray Company spends $15,000 a year on maintenance and uses straight-line depreciation.

Instructions

Record journal entries for Gray Company and Hinkle Corporation on January 1 and December 31 of the first year of the lease.

23–30 **IMPLICIT INTEREST RATE** Wild Company buys equipment for $100,000 cash and leases it to Quigley Corporation for three years. Lease payments of $25,000 are to be made at the beginning of each year. At the end of the third year, the equipment is to be returned to Wild, when its value is estimated to be $46,000.

Instructions

Approximate the interest rate implicit in the Wild Company lease. (Round computations to the nearest dollar.)

23–31 **LESSEE AND LESSOR—OPERATING LEASE** On February 20, 1992, Barnes, Inc., purchased a machine for $1,200,000 for the purpose of leasing it to others. The machine is expected to have a 10-year life and no residual value; it will be depreciated on the straight-line basis, computed to the nearest month. The machine was leased to Rally Company on March 1, 1992, for four years, at a monthly rental of $18,000. There is no provision for the renewal of the lease or purchase of the machine by the lessee upon expiration of the lease. Barnes paid $60,000 in commissions associated with negotiating the lease in February 1992.

Instructions

[a] What expense will Rally record for the year ended December 31, 1992? Show supporting computations.
[b] What income or loss before income taxes will Barnes record for the year ended December 31, 1992? Show supporting computations. (AICPA) adapted)

23–32 **LESSEE—CAPITAL LEASE** On January 1, 1992, Alan Corporation signed a 10-year noncancelable lease for certain machinery. The terms of the lease call for annual payments of $30,000 for ten years, with the title to pass to Alan at the end of this period. The machinery has an estimated remaining useful life of 15 years and no salvage value. Alan uses straight-line depreciation for all of its fixed assets, and it accounted for this capital lease in a similar manner. The lease payments have a present value of $201,302 and an effective interest rate of 8%. Payments are made each December 31.

Instructions

With respect to this lease, what entries will Alan make for 1992? (Round all entries to the nearest dollar and record the lease liability in a single account, net of any discount.)   (AICPA adapted)

23–33   LESSEE—CAPITAL LEASE ACCOUNTING AND CLASSIFICATION   The trial balance of Rogers, Inc., for the year ended December 31, 1992, includes the following liability:

Lease Liability $456,376

The minimum lease term is for a period of ten years and began on December 31, 1990. Equal annual payments of $100,000 are due on December 31 of each year, and the interest rate implicit in this lease is 12%. The present value of the seven lease payments remaining on December 31, 1992 is the $456,376 reported above.

Instructions

[a] Determine the amount of interest expense that would appear in the Rogers, Inc., income statement for the year ended December 31, 1993.
[b] Prepare the current and long-term liability sections of the balance sheet of Rogers, Inc., related to this lease at December 31, 1993. The current portion of the lease liability should be computed as the present value of the December 31, 1994, payment.

23–34   SALES-TYPE LEASE   Wofford Company leased equipment from Burnette Company on July 1, 1992, for an eight-year period expiring June 30, 2000. Equal annual payments of $500,000 are due on July 1. The first payment was made on July 1, 1992. The rate of interest contemplated by both parties is 10%. The cash selling price of the equipment is $2,934,000, and the cost of the equipment on Burnette's accounting records was $2,500,000. The lease is properly accounted for as a sale by Burnette Company.

Instructions

Determine the amount of profit on the sale and the interest revenue that Burnette Company will recognize for the year ended December 31, 1992.   (AICPA adapted)

23–35   SALES-TYPE LEASE   Mize Company leased equipment to Murray, Inc., on January 1, 1992. The lease is for an eight-year period expiring December 31, 1999. The first of eight equal annual payments of $600,000 was made on January 1, 1992. Mize had purchased the equipment on December 29, 1991, for $3,200,000. The lease is appropriately accounted for as a sales-type lease by Mize. Assume that the present value at January 1, 1992, of all rent payments over the lease term, discounted at a 10% interest rate, is $3,520,000.

Instructions

Determine the amount of interest revenue that Mize will record for 1993, the second year of the lease period.   (AICPA adapted)

23–36   LESSEE—CAPITAL LEASE   On January 2, 1992, Walker, Inc., signed a 10-year noncancelable lease for a heavy-duty drill press. Annual payments of $15,000 are made at the end of each year, with title passing to Walker at the expiration of the lease. Walker treated this transaction as a capital lease. The drill press has an estimated useful life of 15 years and no salvage value. Walker uses straight-line depreciation for all of its fixed assets. Aggregate lease payments were determined to have a present value of $92,170, based on implicit interest of 10%.

Instructions

For 1992 and 1993, determine the amount Walker will recognize as interest expense and depreciation expense. (Round all computations to the nearest dollar.)   (AICPA adapted)

PROBLEMS

23–37   LEASEHOLD IMPROVEMENTS   On January 1, 1993, Uptown Clothes leased a warehouse in which large amounts of clothing inventory are to be stored. Because the warehouse is located in a high crime area, Uptown Clothes installs bars on windows and an expensive silent alarm system.

The improvements acquired on March 1, 1993, which will not be removed when the lease expires, cost $100,000 and have a useful life of 10 years. The lease on the warehouse is for one year, although the lease contains a renewal option for additional one-year periods, up to a maximum of four renewals. The lease payments under each renewal are to be renegotiated but cannot rise more than 20% each year. Consequently, the option is clearly not a *bargain* renewal option. Uptown Clothes intends to lease the property throughout the renewal periods. The salvage value of the improvements is $90,000 at the end of one year, $20,000 at the end of five years, and $1,000 at the end of 10 years.

Instructions

In your answers to the following, round amounts to the nearest dollar.

[a] Prepare the entry to record the acquisition of the security devices on March 1, 1993.

[b] Prepare the entry at December 31, 1993, if any is necessary, for the security devices. Explain your answer.

23–38 LESSEE-CAPITAL LEASE   Furnace Equipment Company signed a six-year lease in which it agreed to pay $12,000 per year for the use of a piece of equipment. At the end of the lease term, the equipment becomes the property of Furnace Equipment Company. The equipment is expected to be useful to the company for eight years.

Lease payments are due each May 1, beginning in 1992. The company's fiscal year is from May 1 to April 30. Management estimates that $700 of each lease payment is designated for executory costs that the lessor pays. The lease was executed on May 1, 1992.

Furnace recently acquired financing at 12% for other equipment it was acquiring.

Instructions

In your answers to the following, round amounts to the nearest dollar.

[a] At what amount should Furnace Equipment capitalize this lease in its balance sheet?

[b] Prepare an amortization table for the recognition of interest expense for the six-year lease term.

[c] Prepare the balance sheet presentation of this lease for Furnace Equipment Company as of April 30, 1994.

23–39   LESSEE AND LESSOR—CAPITAL LEASE   Ace Trucking Company manufactures diesel trucks for interstate transportation and leases a number of them to All-the-Way Trucking. The trucks have an estimated life of 16 years and the leases are for 14 years. The normal selling price of each truck is $195,000 and the estimated residual value at the end of the lease is $20,000. All-the-Way pays all maintenance costs, insurance, and taxes in connection with these trucks. Ace Trucking paid $170,000 to manufacture each truck. Ace Trucking also requires an implicit rate of 10%, based on the normal selling price and ignoring any salvage value to the lessor. Payments are assumed to be collectible and are paid at the end of each year. The lease is initiated on January 1, 1992.

Instructions

In your answers to the following, round amounts to the nearest dollar.

[a] What type of lease is this from the viewpoint of Ace Trucking Company and All-the-Way Trucking? Explain your answer.

[b] Calculate the amount of the annual lease payment.

[c] Prepare the entry to record the lease on Ace's books.

[d] Prepare All-the-Way's initial entry for this lease.

23–40   LESSEE AND LESSOR—INCOME EFFECT OF CAPITAL LEASES   Tulip Company leased equipment from Rose Company on October 1, 1992. The lease is appropriately accounted for as a purchase by Tulip and as a sale by Rose. The lease is for eight years and expires on September 30, 2000. Equal annual payments under the lease are $600,000, due on October 1. The first payment was made on October 1, 1992. The cost of the equipment on Rose's accounting records was $3,000,000. It has an estimated useful life of eight years with no residual value. A full year's depreciation is taken in the year assets are acquired by Tulip Company. The appropriate rate of interest for both Tulip and Rose is 10%.

Instructions

[a] What expenses should Tulip appropriately record for the year ended December 31, 1992? Show supporting computations in good form and round amounts to the nearest dollar.

[b] What income or loss before income taxes should Rose appropriately record for the year ended December 31, 1992? Show supporting computations in good form and round amounts to the nearest dollar.   (AICPA adapted)

23–41   LESSOR AND LESSEE—CAPITAL LEASE   Katie Company leases equipment to Baker Company for four years. The equipment, valued at $1,000 (which is also the cost of the equipment to Katie Company), is to be transferred to Baker on January 1, 1992, and lease payments are to be made on December 31, 1992, 1993, 1994, and 1995 in the amount of $330 per year. Salvage value at the end of the four years is negligible and the property may be bought at the end of the lease by Baker for $1.

Instructions

In your answers to the following, round all amounts to the nearest dollar.

[a] Determine the appropriate interest rate implicit in this lease.

[b] Prepare necessary entries for Katie's books on January 1, 1992, December 31, 1992, and December 31, 1993. Assume Katie records the gross receivables and unearned income in separate accounts.

[c] Prepare the relevant portion of Katie's balance sheet and income statement at December 31, 1993 and 1994.

[d] Prepare the necessary entries for Baker's books on January 1, 1992, December 31, 1992, and December 31, 1993. Assume that the lease is treated as an intangible asset. Baker Company records the lease liability and the related discount in separate accounts.

[e] Prepare the relevant portion of Baker's balance sheet and income statement on December 31, 1993 and 1994.

23–42   LESSOR—CAPITAL LEASE   On January 1, 1992, Katie Company leased equipment costing $700 to Baker Company. The sales price of the equipment is $1,000. Annual lease payments of $330 are made on December 31 for the next four years. There is no salvage value and the equipment may be purchased after the four years for $1.

Instructions

[a] Prepare the necessary entries for Katie's books at January 1, 1992, December 31, 1992, and December 31, 1993.

[b] Prepare the relevant portion of Katie's balance sheet and income statement at December 31, 1992 and 1993. Assume Katie records the gross receivables and unearned income in separate accounts.

[c] Discuss any differences in accounting and reporting that the change in circumstances from P23–41 will cause for Katie Company and Baker Company.

23–43   LESSEE—CAPITAL LEASE   In 1992 Seidel Food Company signed a long-term lease for new warehousing equipment, including conveyors and lifts. The equipment was installed according to Seidel's specifications and was placed in operation on October 1, 1992.

Seidel could have purchased the equipment for $1.5 million but instead decided on a noncancelable lease with the option to purchase the equipment at the end of the lease. The equipment has an estimated useful life of 20 years.

The terms of the lease are as follows:

[1] Lease period 10 years, October 1, 1992, through September 30, 2002.

[2] Rental payments of $300,000 payable to the lessor on October 1 of each of the first five years of the lease.

[3] Rental payments of $120,000 payable to the lessor on October 1 of each of the last five years of the lease.

[4] All payments for property taxes, insurance, and maintenance are the direct responsibility of the lessee. (Seidel estimates that the total amount will be $30,000 annually.)

[5] Upon termination of the lease, the lessee has the option to purchase the equipment for $41,250.

Seidel's independent auditor has established that the leased equipment and related obligation should be accounted for as an installment purchase. Seidel uses double-declining balance depreciation for plant assets. The lease yields a 12% rate of return to the lessor. Seidel's incremental borrowing rate exceeds 12%.

Use the following present-value factors in making the necessary computations:

Discount Factors for 12% (rounded)

Period	Present Value of $1.00	Present Value of $1.00 per Period Received at End of Period
1	.89	.89
2	.80	1.69
3	.71	2.40
4	.64	3.04
5	.57	3.60
6	.51	4.11
7	.45	4.56
8	.40	4.97
9	.36	5.33
10	.32	5.65

Instructions

[a] Prepare Seidel's balance sheet presentation of this lease on September 30, 1993. Provide supporting computations in good form.

[b] Prepare Seidel's income statement presentation of this lease for the year ended September 30, 1993. Provide supporting computations in good form.   (CMA adapted)

23-44 LESSEE AND LESSOR—CLASSIFICATION AND ACCOUNTING   Oil-Patch, Inc., leases a truck to Rogers Company for petroleum exploration. Such trucks normally last 10 years, but because of the intense use and primitive conditions in oil exploration, the expected useful life is no more than six years. The terms of the lease and other information are as follows: *sales type*

6 yrs × 75% = 4.5 yrs

Beginning of the lease term	May 1, 1992
Lease term	5 years
Lease payments	$4,000/year, beginning May 1, 1992
Cost of truck to Oil-Patch	$14,000
Fair value of truck on May 1, 1992	$16,800
Interest rate implicit in the lease	12%
Residual value of asset at Apr. 30, 1997 (estimated)	$1,000

— No transfer of title
— No BOP
✓ PV 16150 ≥ 15120
✓ lease term
  ≥ 75% of useful life
$16,800 ⇒ 90% = 15120

There is no bargain purchase option or transfer of title in the lease. No significant uncertainties exist about the collectibility of lease payments or any future costs to be incurred by Oil-Patch.

Rogers Company has an incremental borrowing rate of 18%. Rogers can compute the interest rate implicit in the lease and normally depreciates and amortizes assets on a straight-line basis to the nearest month.

Instructions

[a] From the viewpoint of Oil-Patch, Inc.:

[1] What type of lease is this? Why?

[2] Prepare the entries to record the lease at May 1, 1992, and December 31, 1992, and any other entries required during 1992. (Round amounts to the nearest dollar.) Oil-Patch records the lease in a single investment account, net of any unearned income.

[b] From the viewpoint of Rogers Company:

[1] What type of lease is this? Why?

[2] Prepare the entries to record the lease at May 1, 1992, and December 31, 1992, and any other entries necessary during 1992. Rogers records the lease liability in a single account, net of any discount. (Round amounts to the nearest dollar.)

Residual value?

23–45 LESSEE AND LESSOR—CAPITAL LEASE Stapleton Company leased an asset to Allbright Company on January 1, 1992. Conditions of the lease and other information include the following:

Lease term	6 years
Annual payments made on Jan. 1 of each year, including	
$1,000 of executory costs	$11,000
Estimated residual value at the end of lease term	$5,000
Initial direct costs	$1,500
Estimated life of property	10 years
Selling price of comparable assets	$53,500
Interest rate implicit in lease	8%
Incremental borrowing rate of lessee	10%
Cost of the asset to lessor	$37,500
Fiscal year of lessor	Jan. 1–Dec. 31
Fiscal year of lessee	Oct. 1–Sept. 30

Allbright is aware of the 8% interest rate implicit in the lease.

Instructions

In your answers to the following, round amounts to the nearest dollar.

[a] Stapleton's accounting:
   [1] Prepare all journal entries during 1992, assuming the lessee guarantees the residual value of the leased property.
   [2] Prepare all journal entries during 1992, assuming the residual value is not guaranteed by the lessee or otherwise.
[b] Allbright's accounting:
   [1] Prepare all journal entries during 1992, assuming the lessee guarantees the residual value of the leased asset.
   [2] Prepare the asset and liability presentations for Allbright's September 30, 1992, balance sheet. Assume for this problem only that the discount related to the current portion of the liability is the amount of interest to be recognized in the next payment.
[c] Discuss briefly how your answer in [b] would differ, if at all, if the lessee's incremental borrowing rate had been 7% instead of 10%.

23–46 LESSEE AND LESSOR—CAPITAL LEASE Goggans Corporation, a lessor of office machines, purchased a new machine for $450,000 on December 31, 1992. The machine was delivered the same day to Krull Company, the lessee. The following information relating to the lease transaction is available:

[1] The asset has an estimated useful life of seven years, which coincides with the lease term.
[2] At the end of the lease term, the machine will revert to Goggans, at which time it is expected to have a residual value of $60,000 (none of which is guaranteed by Krull).
[3] Krull is aware of the 12% implicit interest rate on Goggan's net investment.
[4] Krull's incremental borrowing rate is 14% at December 31, 1992.
[5] Lease rentals consist of seven equal annual payments, the first of which was paid on December 31, 1992.
[6] The lease is appropriately accounted for as a direct-financing lease by Goggans and as a capital lease by Krull. Both lessor and lessee are calendar-year corporations and depreciate all fixed assets on the straight-line basis.

Instructions

Compute the following to the nearest dollar and show supporting computations in good form.

[a] The annual rental under the lease. (*Hint:* Determine the *net amount* that must be recovered by Goggans, then divide by the appropriate present-value factor.)
[b] The amounts of the gross lease rentals receivable and the unearned interest revenue for Goggans on December 31, 1992.
[c] What expense should Krull record for the year ended December 31, 1993? (AICPA adapted)

23–47   LESSEE AND LESSOR—CAPITAL LEASE   On January 1, 1992, Overton Company entered into a five-year lease with Weeter Company. Overton transferred a machine to Weeter on that date, and Weeter agreed to make annual payments on January 1 of $10,000. The first payment was made on January 1, 1992. Approximately $1,000 of each payment is designated for taxes, insurance, and other costs related to the machine that are to be paid by the lessor. *Exec. costs*

Overton sells as well as leases machines. The following information relates to Overton's operations: *Usually sales-type*

Normal selling price of machine	$39,710 *) profit*
Costs to manufacture machine	$26,000 - *COGS*
Initial direct cost-sales commission	$2,000
Interest rate implicit in lease	10%

Weeter expects the machine to be useful for six years. Weeter has an incremental borrowing rate of 12% and is aware that the rate implicit in the lease is 10%. In addition to the annual $10,000 payments, Weeter has guaranteed the residual value at the end of the five-year lease at $3,500. The lease contains no purchase or renewal options.

Instructions

In your answers to the following, round amounts to the nearest dollar. Assume both companies report on a calendar-year basis.

[a] What is the present value of the lease for both the lessor and the lessee?
[b] What is the proper classification of this lease by the lessee? By the lessor?
[c] Prepare an amortization table appropriate for both the lessor and lessee for the five-year lease term.
[d] Prepare the journal entries for the lessee through January 1, 1993. Weeter records the lease liability, net of discount, in a single account.
[e] Prepare the journal entries for the lessor through January 1, 1993.

23–48   SALES-TYPE AND OPERATING LEASE (LESSOR)   Bingham Company, which started operating in 1991, leases medical equipment to hospitals. All its leases are appropriately accounted for as operating leases, except for a major lease entered into on January 1, 1993, which is appropriately accounted for as a sale.

For the year ended December 31, 1993, the following information is available:
Operating Leases.   Revenues from operating leases were $800,000. The cost of the related leased equipment is $3,700,000, which is being depreciated on a straight-line basis over a five-year period. The estimated residual value of the leased equipment after five years is $200,000. No leased equipment was acquired or constructed in 1993. Maintenance and other related costs and the costs of any other services rendered under the provisions of the leases were $70,000 in 1993.
Lease Recorded as a Sale.   The January 1, 1993, lease recorded as a sale is for a six-year period expiring December 31, 1998. The cost of this leased equipment is $3,500,000. The equipment is estimated to have no residual value at the end of the lease. Maintenance and other related costs and the costs of any other services rendered under the provisions of this lease, all of which were paid by the lessee, were $120,000 in 1993. Equal annual payments of $750,000 are due on January 1. The first payment was made on January 1, 1993. The present value of an annuity of $1 in advance at 10% is as follows:

Number of Periods	Present Value
5	4.170
6	4.791
7	5.355

Selling, general, and administrative expenses exclusive of amounts specified above earlier, were $600,000 in 1993.

Other revenue, exclusive of amounts specified above, was $50,000 in 1993.

Instructions

Prepare an income statement for Bingham Company for the year ended December 31, 1993, stopping at income (loss) before income taxes. Show supporting computations in good form. (Ignore income tax and deferred tax considerations. Use the rounded present-value factors presented in the problem to make necessary computations.)   (AICPA adapted)

CASES   **23–49   ADVANTAGES OF LEASING**   The controller of Ocean Repair Service, in discussing various financing alternatives, made the following statement:

> *Leasing is consistently the most attractive method of financing. Not only does it normally provide 100% financing with no down payment or compensating balance requirements, it also allows us to acquire only the particular asset rights we want. For example, we may not wish to buy an asset because we have no wish to own it when it becomes obsolete. The lessor is better able to dispose of such an asset at the end of a lease than we would be if we had bought it outright. Furthermore, we avoid tying up our cash unnecessarily. Therefore, the asset we lease, as well as the cash we conserve, can both be used productively. Finally, our balance sheet appears more favorable, because we do not record additional liabilities or lose liquidity when we lease assets.*

Instructions

Evaluate the controller's comments.

23–50   GENERAL LEASES—LESSOR AND LESSEE   Estes Corporation entered into a lease arrangement with Bayless Leasing Corporation for a certain machine. Bayless's primary business is leasing; it is not a manufacturer or dealer. Estes will lease the machine for three years, which is 50% of the machine's economic life. Bayless will take possession of the machine at the end of the initial three-year lease and lease it to a smaller company that does not need the most current version of the machine. Estes does not guarantee any residual value for the machine and will not purchase the machine at the end of the lease term.

Este's incremental borrowing rate is 10%, and the implicit rate in the lease is 8.5%. Estes has no way of knowing the implicit rate used by Bayless. Using either rate, the present value of the minimum lease payments is between 90% and 100% of the fair value of the machine at the date of the lease agreement.

Estes has agreed to pay all executory costs directly. No allowance for these costs is included in the lease payments.

Bayless is reasonably certain that Estes will meet all lease payments, and because Estes has agreed to pay all executory costs, there are no important uncertainties regarding costs to be incurred by Bayless.

Instructions

[a] With respect to Estes, answer the following:
   [1] What type of lease has been entered into? Explain the reason for your answer.
   [2] How should Estes compute the appropriate amount to be recorded for the lease or asset acquired?
   [3] What accounts will be created or affected by this transaction? How will the lease or asset and other costs related to the transaction be matched with earnings?
   [4] What disclosures must Estes make regarding this lease or asset?
[b] With respect to Bayless, answer the following:
   [1] What type of lease has been entered into? Explain the reason for your answer.
   [2] How should this lease be recorded by Bayless? How are the appropriate amounts determined?
   [3] How should Bayless determine the appropriate amount of earnings to be recognized from each lease payment?
   [4] What disclosures must Bayless make regarding this lease?   (AICPA adapted)

23-51 LESSEE ACCOUNTING   Paulsen Corporation is a diversified company with nationwide interests in commercial real estate developments, banking, copper mining, and metal fabrication. The company has offices and operating locations in major cities throughout the United States. The corporate headquarters for Paulsen are located in a metropolitan area of a midwestern state, and executives connected with various phases of company operations travel extensively. Corporate management is presently evaluating the feasibility of acquiring a business aircraft that can be used by company executives to expedite business travel to areas not adequately served by commercial airlines. Proposals for either leasing or purchasing a suitable aircraft have been analyzed, and the leasing proposal was considered to be more desirable.

The proposed lease agreement involves a twin-engine turboprop Viking that has a fair market value of $900,000. This plane would be leased for a period of 10 years beginning January 1, 1992. The lease agreement is cancelable only upon accidental destruction of the plane. An annual lease payment of $127,600 is due on January 1 of each year; the first payment is to be made on January 1, 1992. Maintenance operations are strictly scheduled by the lessor, and Paulsen Corporation will pay for these services as they are performed. Estimated annual maintenance costs are $6,200. The lessor will pay all insurance premiums and local property taxes, which amount to $3,600 annually and are included in the annual lease payment of $127,600. Upon expiration of the 10-year lease, Paulsen Corporation can purchase the Viking for $40,000. The estimated useful life of the plane is 15 years, and its salvage value in the used-plane market is estimated to be $100,000 after 10 years. The salvage value probably will never be less than $75,000 if the engines are overhauled and maintained as prescribed by the manufacturer. If the purchase option is not exercised, possession of the plane will revert to the lessor, and there is no provision for renewing the lease agreement beyond its termination on December 31, 2001.

Paulsen Corporation can borrow $900,000 under a 10-year term loan agreement at an annual interest rate of 12%. The lessor's implicit interest rate is not expressly stated in the lease agreement, but this rate appears to be approximately 8% based on 10 net rental payments of $124,000 per year and the initial market value of $900,000 for the plane. On January 1, 1992, the present value of all net rental payments and the purchase option of $40,000 is $800,000 if the 12% interest rate is used. The present value of all net rental payments and the $40,000 purchase option on January 1, 1992, is $920,000 if one uses the 8% interest rate implicit in the lease agreement. The financial vice-president of Paulsen Corporation has established that this lease agreement is a capital lease as defined in *Statement of Financial Accounting Standards No. 13,* "Accounting for Leases."

Instructions

[a] What is the appropriate amount that Paulsen should recognize for the leased aircraft on its statement of financial position after the lease is signed?

[b] Without prejudice to your answer in [a], assume that the annual lease payment is $127,600 (as stated in the preceding information), that the appropriate capitalized amount for the leased aircraft is $1,000,000 on January 1, 1992, and that the interest rate is 9%. How will the lease be reported in the December 31, 1992, statement of financial position and related income statement? (Ignore income tax implications.)

[c] Explain the four factors which differentiate a capital lease from an operating lease.

(CMA adapted)

23-52 THEORETICAL CONSTRUCTS OF LEASING   On January 1, 1992, Thacker Company entered into a noncancelable lease for a machine to be used in its manufacturing operations. The lease transfers ownership of the machine to Thacker at the end of the lease term. The term of the lease is eight years. The minimum lease payment made by Thacker on January 1, 1992, was one of eight equal annual payments. At the inception of the lease, the criteria established for classification as a capital lease by the lessee were met.

Instructions

[a] What is the theoretical basis for the accounting standard which requires certain long-term leases to be capitalized by the lessee? Do not discuss the specific criteria for classifying a specific lease as a capital lease.

[b] How should Thacker account for this lease at its inception and how should management determine the amount to be recorded?

[c] What expenses related to this lease will Thacker incur during the first year of the lease, and how will they be determined?

[d] How should Thacker report the lease transaction on its December 31, 1992, balance sheet?

(AICPA adapted)

JUDGMENT CASES

23-53   CONSIDERATION OF LEASE PROVISIONS   Your client is a chain of fast food restaurants known as Slick Chick, which specializes in the preparation of sauteed chicken dishes. During a recent expansion of operations, the company executed a number of real estate leases to serve as sites for new restaurants. The lessor has constructed the buildings as part of the lease agreement.

These leases all contain the same basic terms. None of the leases contain a transfer of title or a bargain purchase option. The fair value of the land portion of the lease is considered greater than 25% of the total fair value of the leased property. Each of the leases contains a 20-year term with a right to renew the lease for an additional 20 years. You have satisfied yourself that the renewal options are not "bargain renewal options" as defined by *SFAS No. 13* and that the life of the buildings is approximately 40 years. The present value of the lease payments attributable to the building portion of the leases during the minimum lease terms represent only about 80% of the fair value of those portions of the assets being leased.

During lunch you have informed the president of the company that your preliminary determination is that none of the leases require treatment as capital leases. He responds:

> *"Well, that is good news. If there is one thing we can't have, its cluttering up our balance sheet with a lot of liabilities and assets that are just leased items. We are really excited about these new locations. We expect to open them within a month and predict great results from this expansion. We are planning to operate them for 15 years and then to renovate the buildings entirely in anticipation of renewing the leases at the end of the first lease term. That way, when we exercise the renewal option, the facilities will be ready to go and we won't miss a beat. We have tied up 40 years of access to these locations, and will be able to use them productively during that entire period.*

Instructions

The president's statement has made you lose interest in your dessert! Why? Do the comments made by the president have any implications for the classification of the leases? If so, why?

23-54   REVISING TRANSACTIONS   Your client, Hot Boats, Inc., a manufacturer of traditional family watercraft, has decided to begin producing small personal watercraft, called jet skis, in addition to their existing product line. The company has decided to use a contract source for the fiberglass hulls of the new watercraft since it does not have the ability or desire to produce them. The contractor Hot Boats approached to produce the hulls has indicated that additional advanced computers will be necessary to assure appropriate design. The computers are rather expensive and will be useful only to produce the hulls for Hot Boats.

As a result of these considerations, Hot Boats originally considered an agreement with the contractor to lease the computers on a long-term basis and place them in the facilities of the contractor. The controller of Hot Boats approached you, the auditor for the company, to determine the accounting treatment for the proposed lease agreement. You determined that because the lease required the lessee to guarantee the residual value of the computers, the lease would have to be treated as a capital lease. The controller was clearly disappointed and subsequently approached you concerning another lease that differed from the first one in that it had a longer lease term.

Careful analysis of the revised lease proposal revealed that the new length term clearly exceeded 75% of the life of the computer and, therefore, would also be considered a capital lease. The controller was quite concerned and indicated that Hot Boats wished to avoid recording a large liability and related asset for the acquisition of the computers. She has then appeared with a third agreement in hand and wants your opinion.

The new agreement has the contractor leasing the equipment from the computer manufacturer with Hot Boats entering into an unconditional and noncancelable purchase obligation with the contractor for a specified number of watercraft hulls to be produced over the next ten years. The controller is quite excited and states:

> *Because this is not a lease, we are confident that we won't have to record the commitment as a liability and the related asset. This is nothing more than an executory contract much like a construction contract and, as you know, generally accepted accounting principles do not require recording such executory contracts in the accounting records.*

In analyzing the three alternatives, you become aware that the purchase commitment will result in Hot Boats paying the greatest amount of the three agreements to acquire the hulls. When told this, the controller responds:

> *Yes, we determined that in our analysis, as well. The way we look at it is that the excess is just the cost of achieving the accounting result we prefer. Sometimes you just have to pay a price for the financial position you want and this is one of those times.*

Instructions

Should the unconditional and noncancelable purchase obligation be recorded and included in the balance sheet of Hot Boats? How would you respond to the comments of the controller? Would your answer to the above questions differ if Hot Boats had originally proposed the purchase obligation and you were not aware of the previous lease proposals and the company's desire to avoid reporting the liability that would have resulted from the lease agreements?

CHAPTER 24

Accounting for Retirement Benefits

OBJECTIVES

1. To describe the nature of modern pensions and other retirement benefits.
2. To explain the complexities in determining the cost of retirement benefits to employers.
3. To identify and compute the primary components of net periodic pension cost and net postretirement benefit cost.
4. To specify and illustrate situations which require the balance-sheet recognition of assets and liabilities related to retirement plans.
5. To explain the information about retirement plans that must be maintained by employers that does not appear in the employer's financial statements.
6. To introduce several other aspects of accounting and financial statement disclosure for pension and other retirement benefit plans.

THE EVOLUTION AND SIGNIFICANCE OF RETIREMENT PLANS

R etirement commitments made by employers to employees are a common characteristic of modern employment agreements. A pension commitment represents an agreement in which an employer promises payments to employees after they retire. Pension plans range from relatively simple employer commitments to make specific periodic payments to a retirement fund, to promises to provide a certain level of income to employees after retirement based on a variety of factors. For example, the pension benefits a person receives may be a function of the years of service rendered to the employer, earnings levels prior to retirement, changes in the general price level, and the life span of the retired employee. In addition to pension plans, many employers provide other types of retirement benefits for former employees, including health care, life insurance and other similar benefits. Retirement benefits are best thought of as **deferred compensation arrangements** in which employees receive a portion of their previously-earned compensation during their retirement years. Retirement benefits are **not** gratuities from the employer to the employee, but are part of the cost of compensation for employment services rendered.

Retirement plans have become increasingly significant in our economy during the last 50 years. Before then the responsibility for one's welfare after retirement was generally considered a function of individual savings and family duty. Events such as the industrial revolution and the great depression, as well as changing social perceptions of governmental and business responsibilities, have increased social awareness of the need to provide relatively comfortable and secure retirement for long-term employees. Today it is common for an individual's largest asset to be the value of a retirement plan. Employers contribute resources to the plan on behalf of employees. These resources are then available for investment, and investment earnings increase the amounts available for retirement benefits.

The assets controlled and invested by pension plans are substantial, and they represent a significant part of the available investment capital in the United States. For this reason, the activities of corporate sponsors of pension plans are of interest to businesses and employees, as well as to governments and other institutional and individual investors.

Exhibit 24–1 illustrates the magnitude of pension plans. Information for five corporations is listed in the order of the dollar value of pension plan assets as disclosed in the 1990 financial statements. The fair value of plan assets measures the worth of the stocks, bonds, and other investments and, stated as a percentage of total assets, ranges from 4.3% to 18.6% for these five companies. The projected benefit obligation is one measure of the pension obligation of the company to present and retired employees for benefits already earned. Stated as a percentage of total stockholders' equity, these range from 11.9% to 118% for the five companies described. Clearly we

Materiality can conclude that pension plans involve material amounts for these five companies, which are typical of many other companies.

Accounting standards for pensions have been in existence for many years, but the FASB has recently revised these standards and provided authoritative guidance on accounting and reporting for other types of retirement benefits. Our primary emphasis in this chapter is on pension accounting as the primary example of retirement benefit plans. We briefly examine accounting for other retirement benefits at the end of this chapter.

EXHIBIT 24-1

Selected Pension Information
(Dollar Figures in Millions)

	Fair Value of Plan Assets	% of Total Assets	Projected Benefit Obligation	% of Stockholders' Equity
General Electric Company	$22,237	14.4	$16,751	77.3
Xerox Corporation	$ 3,504	11.1	$ 3,579	57.7
Exxon Corporation (U.S. plans)	$ 3,785	4.3	$ 3,942	11.9
The Dow Company (U.S. plans)	$ 3,447	14.4	$ 3,315	38.0
Ralston Purina Company	$ 816	18.6	$ 691	118.0

SOURCE: 1990 Annual Reports.

THE NATURE OF PENSION PLANS

The relationships and responsibilities of the various parties in a typical employer-sponsored pension plan are illustrated in Exhibit 24–2. The employer frequently has primary responsibility to the employee for the capacity of the pension plan to meet contracted payments. The employer ensures the plan's solvency by making periodic contributions to it. The pension plan is usually administered by a trustee, such as an insurance company or bank, which is independent of the sponsor and responsible for stewardship of the plan's assets. In addition, the trustee determines the contributions that are needed to maintain the plan.

Pension plans may be broadly classified as either defined contribution plans or defined benefit plans. Financial accounting and reporting is usually much more simple and straightforward for defined contribution plans. Defined benefit plans, on the other hand, are more complicated and involve additional considerations in administering and accounting for the plan.

DEFINED CONTRIBUTION PLANS

Defined contribution plans contain provisions which allow employers to determine the resources that must be contributed to a pension plan each year. Defined contribution plans usually require employers to contribute a percentage of company income or employee salaries to a pension fund. Once the defined contribution is paid, the sponsor has no additional liability to provide pension benefits. Pension expense for the period is the amount of the required contribution. Pension benefits are distributed in the future from the assets accumulated in the trust fund. If the defined contribution for the period has not been paid at the balance sheet date, a liability is accrued in that amount. The liability is normally classified as current, because the defined contribution must be paid promptly.

In defined contribution plans the *employees accept the risk* of the plan's investment performance. In a sense, the accumulated contributions plus earnings belong to the employees. Therefore, if the plan provides exceptional investment performance, employees share in the gains in the form of increased pension benefits. Likewise, if the plan does poorly, employees share in the losses by receiving smaller pension bene-

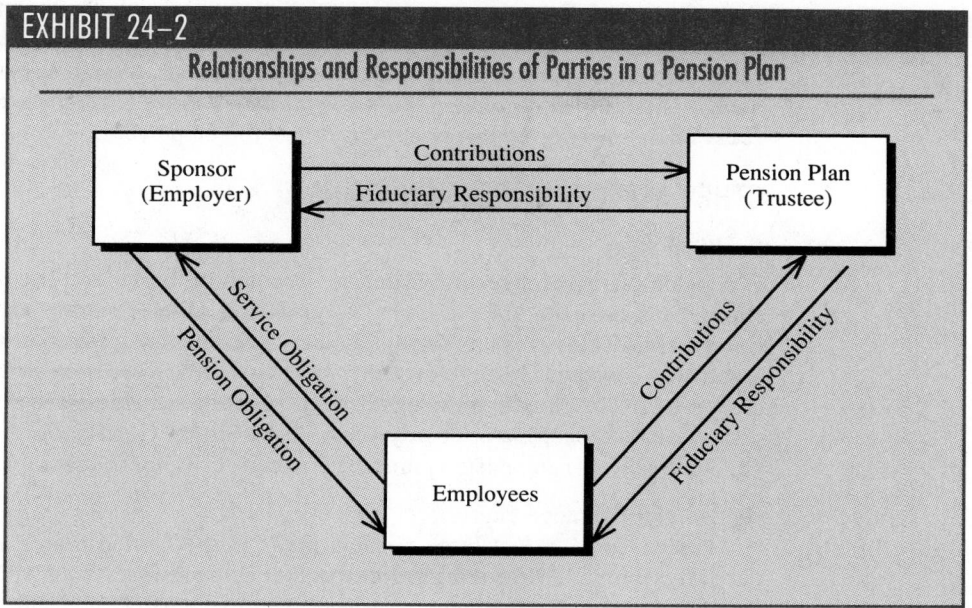

EXHIBIT 24-2

Relationships and Responsibilities of Parties in a Pension Plan

fits. The benefits that are ultimately paid to retirees in a defined contribution plan are based on the amounts available, given the defined level of employer contribution and the earnings performance of the plan's portfolio of investments.

DEFINED BENEFIT PLANS

Many pension plans are referred to as **defined benefit plans** because they specify the benefits to be received by retirees in terms of factors such as employee age, years of service, and salary levels. The benefits are usually expressed in terms of a formula that incorporates the above factors and other factors specified in the employment agreement. For example, the formula may calculate the annual pension cost as a percentage rate times the number of years of service times the final salary (or average of several years' salary) before retirement. As an example, a pension that credited an employee with 2% of final salary for each year worked would grant a pension of 60% of final salary for an employee with 30 years of service.

Defined benefit pension plans describe the benefits employees are to receive, and the related pension expense of the sponsor is based on estimates of the cost of providing those benefits. Employer and employee contributions to the plan, plus earnings on investments made with plan assets, are designed to provide the benefits promised. Because the liability and related pension expense for defined benefit plans usually depend on final compensation levels and years of service, the accounting issues become more complex than under a defined contribution plan. Many variables must be estimated to determine the periodic pension contribution required and the pension expense to recognize in the determination of net income. These estimates are commonly referred to as **actuarial assumptions**. They are important considerations in applying the **actuarial cost method** to determine amounts employers must fund and recognize as pension expense in the determination of net income.

In contrast to defined contribution plans, in defined benefit plans the *employer accepts the investment risk* of the plan. The employee does not own an accumulated fund, but is promised a contractual pension based on a formula. If the investment performance of the plan is good enough to exceed the actuarially determined pension obligation according to the formula, the employer may reduce further contributions. Likewise, if the plan's investment performance is poor, the employer must make additional contributions to ensure that formula benefits are funded. In effect, *investment gains and losses accrue to the employer,* not the employees.

OTHER ASPECTS OF PENSION PLANS

Qualified Plans

If pension plans meet certain criteria contained in the federal income tax laws, substantial tax benefits are available. A **qualified plan** (i.e., one meeting the tax law criteria) has features that allow employees to avoid paying taxes on benefits until they are actually received by employees. Employers are allowed a tax deduction at the time contributions are made to the fund. Earnings on fund assets are also not taxed until distributed to beneficiaries many years in the future. Clearly, our national tax policy encourages well-run pension plans, as you can see in these favorable tax alternatives.

Funded and Unfunded Plans

Funded Plans.   Most large pension plans in the United States are either fully or partially funded. A **funded plan** means that the resources from which future pension benefits are to be paid have been transferred to a trustee or fiscal agent. If the complete amount that has been recognized as an expense has been transferred to a trustee or fiscal agent, the plan is called **fully funded.** If only part of the expense recognized has been transferred, the plan is considered **partially funded.**

Most private pension plans are subject to the provisions of the **Employee Retirement Income Security Act of 1974 (ERISA).** This law requires companies to establish certain minimum funding, participation, and vesting policies. Employers make annual contributions to pension plans that are sufficient to fully fund the plan in accordance with an acceptable actuarial cost method. If funding in a reasonable fashion does not occur, sponsoring companies are subject to substantial fines and penalties. The sponsoring company usually pays cash to the funding agent, who then invests the moneys and pays beneficiaries as retirement or separations occur.

One way of funding a plan is to purchase annuity contracts from an insurance company. The sponsoring company then requires the insurance company to pay the defined benefits as they come due. The sponsoring company pays a premium to the insurance company and, in many cases, effectively transfers the risk of honoring the pension commitments to the insurance company. Such plans are called **insured plans.**

Unfunded Plans.   Pension plans that do not require sponsoring companies to transfer funds to a trustee are considered to be **unfunded.** Unfunded plans are frequently referred to as **pay-as-you-go plans,** because funding takes place when pension benefits are paid to retirees rather than when pension expense was recognized during the period of active employment. Although such plans are rare today, they are still occasionally found in certain industries, such as certain nonbusiness organizations. If the assets set aside to pay the pension plan are retained and controlled by the plan sponsor (employing company), the plan is generally considered *nonfunded.*

Financial Reporting by Employers and by Pension Plans

Issues of financial reporting exist for employers (sponsors) who maintain pension plans and for pension plans themselves. In this chapter we confine our discussion to financial accounting and reporting for pensions by employers that sponsor pension plans. Thus, we emphasize the recognition of pension assets and liabilities, pension expense, and funding procedures for employer-companies. Pension plans, on the other hand, prepare financial statements that are available for employee-participants in the plans and other interested parties. Accounting standards governing the financial reporting of pension plans as separate reporting entities are beyond the scope of this textbook.

PRINCIPLES UNDERLYING PENSION PLANS

A pension plan is merely an arrangement whereby an employer provides a mechanism for employees to receive a portion of their compensation after retirement. In most pension plans, the amounts an employee will receive are not precisely known before retirement. Financial accounting and reporting issues parallel those for similar economic circumstances, such as compensated absences for vacation and illness, which we discussed in Chapter 14.

Matching

An employee renders services for many years prior to retirement, but some of the remuneration for those services is paid only *after retirement.* The cost of those services to the employer, however, must be recognized as an obligation to pay retirement benefits as the employee renders services that qualify for those benefits. In this way, the financial reporting principle of matching is achieved. Stated differently, the cost to a company of an employee's labor includes not only the direct salaries and benefits currently paid but also an amount representing the right to a pension earned by the employee during the year. As an employee works, pension benefits increase each year. The expense and related liability of the company to the employee for these pension benefits requires accounting recognition in the employer's records *at the time the benefits are earned* in order to properly state the elements of the financial statements, particularly expenses and liabilities.

The nature of the pension liability, however, remains controversial. Does the employer's liability extend merely to making adequate contributions to the plan, or does the liability extend to the employees directly? In the former case, a pension liability would arise only for the excess of the actuarially determined obligation over the actual assets available in the plan. In the latter case, the pension liability would remain with the employer until actual cash payments were made **to the employee after retirement.** Historically, generally accepted accounting principles (GAAP) have embraced the notion of the liability arising only from contribution shortfalls to the plan. Since many corporations fund their pension plans to avoid contribution shortfalls, many corporate balance sheets do not include pension assets and liabilities. Critics of this approach assert that the employer has an obligation to the employees and not to the plan itself and that to exclude that obligation from the balance sheet is a form of "off-balance-sheet financing," much like operating leases. In their view, the present value of outstanding pension commitments, as well as the pension assets, should be included in the employer's balance sheet. The pension obligation would then be satisfied only as pension payments from the accumulated pension assets were made to the employees.

A CONCEPTUAL ILLUSTRATION

As a simple illustration of the concepts underlying a pension plan, consider the highly simplified pension plan of Burr Corporation, which adopted a pension plan for its single employee, A. Burr, 10 years before A. Burr retires at age 65. When Burr retires, the plan will provide for 10 equal annual payments of $10,000. The first pension payment begins one year after Burr retires. If we assume that the pension plan accumulated interest at 10% compounded annually, the present value (*PV*) of the pension agreement *as of the retirement date* is computed as follows:

$$PV = \$10,000 \times [pvoaf_{\overline{10}|10\%}]$$
$$= \$10,000 \ (6.14457)$$
$$= \$61,446$$

Because A. Burr will receive $10,000 each year, we are dealing with an annuity computation. Because we want to know the value of that annuity at A. Burr's retirement date (after which the payments to him will begin), we compute the present value of the annuity. The appropriate present value factor, 6.14457, is taken from the 10% column, 10-period row of Table 6–4. To simplify this example, we assume that the payments are to be made annually, at the end of each year.

The amount of $61,446 must be accumulated in the pension plan by the retirement date in order for the plan to be fully funded at the employee's retirement. Burr Corporation has 10 years in which to accumulate this amount. If the corporation wants to make 10 equal annual contributions to the plan, with the first contribution beginning one year from today, the following equation will solve for the amount of the equal contributions (*R* = required annual contribution):

$$AOA = (R)[aoaf_{\overline{n}|i}]$$

$$R = \frac{\$61,446}{aoaf_{\overline{10}|10\%}}$$

$$R = \frac{\$61,446}{15.93742}$$

$$R = \$3,855.45$$

The amount of an ordinary annuity factor for 10 periods at 10% (15.93742) is taken from Table 6–3.

Burr Corporation can accumulate $61,446 in 10 years by making equal annual contributions of $3,855.45 into a fund that earns interest at 10% compounded annually. Exhibit 24–3 illustrates the accumulation and payment phases of the pension plan. The plan can pay out much more than the amount of the contributions because of the interest earned.

Notice in this example the uncertainties that are assumed away but that would have to be estimated in a real-life situation. We assumed that retirement would begin in 10 years, whereas retirements actually vary among employees and is usually not known until much closer to the retirement date. We assumed an exact payment ($10,000 per year) for an exact period of time (10 years). In reality, pension payments may be based on employees' incomes between the time benefits are earned and the time of retirement. Also, payments ordinarily continue until the employee's death rather than being limited to a specific number of years. Another uncertainty we assumed away was the interest rate on assets invested in the pension fund (10%). This rate varies, depending on investment policy, economic conditions, and other factors. In practice, actuarial assumptions must be made to deal with these uncertainties that are inherent in pension plans.

MEASUREMENT OF PENSION EXPENSE

Recall from the discussion in Chapter 2 on financial accounting theory and in Chapter 20 on revenue measurement and income presentation that an objective of financial reporting by enterprises is to provide information about earnings and its components.

EXHIBIT 24–3

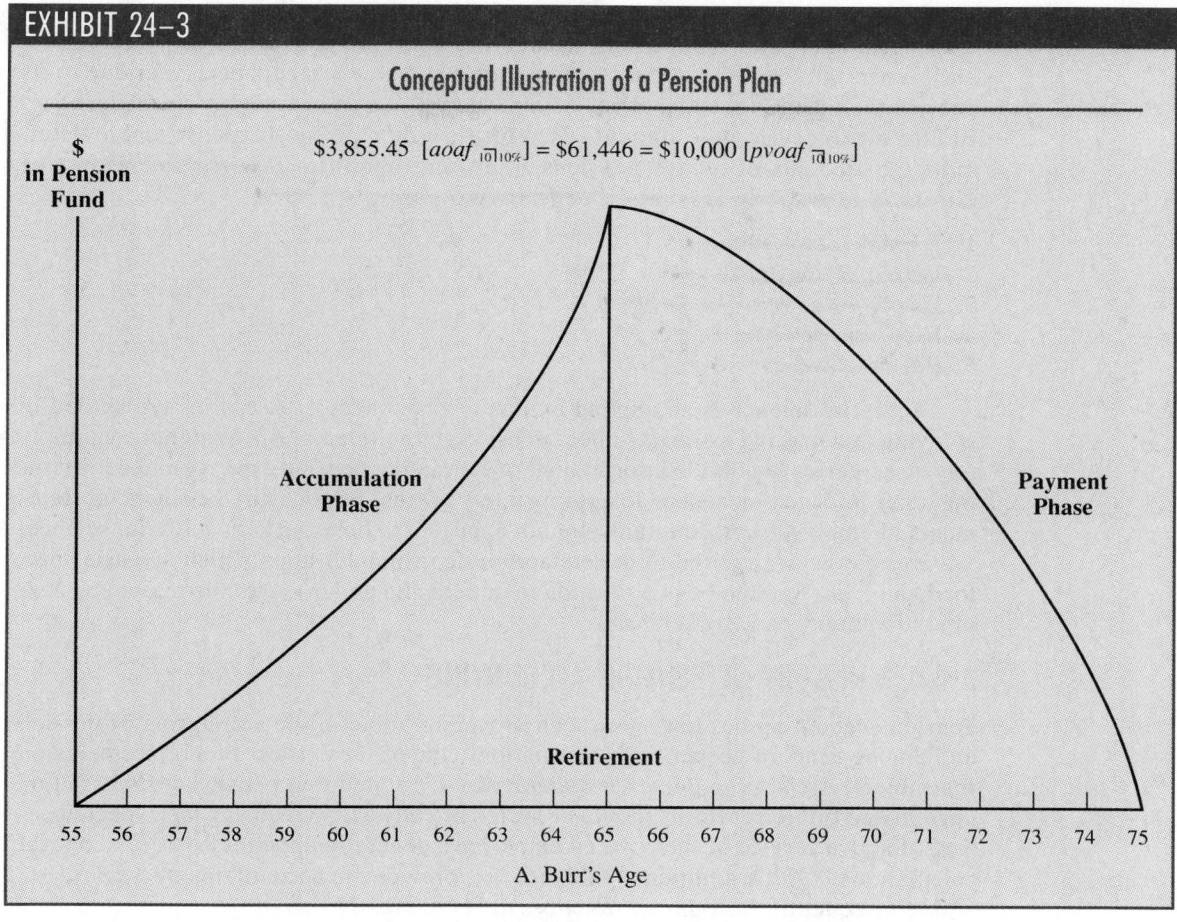

Conceptual Illustration of a Pension Plan

$\$3,855.45 \ [aoaf_{\,\overline{10}|10\%}] = \$61,446 = \$10,000 \ [pvoaf_{\,\overline{10}|10\%}]$

$

Earnings are composed of revenues, expenses, gains, and losses. The cost incurred by a business each year for its pension commitments represents a type of operating expense. Recall further that **expenses** are defined in *Statement of Financial Accounting Concepts No. 6* as "outflows or other using up of assets or *incurrences of liabilities . . . during a period . . .* [and] represent actual or *expected* cash outflows that have occurred or *will eventuate* as a result of the enterprise's . . . operations."[1] (Emphasis added.)

Pension expense meets this definition and is considered a component of income during each accounting period, even though the person earning the pension may not receive benefits for many years. Most accountants agree on these conceptual issues; however, determining the *amount of pension expense* to be recognized during a period in applying the matching principle has created substantial controversy.

Matching

That an employee earns the right to a pension in the current period but may not receive the payment for many years causes uncertainties. A formal pension agreement may exist setting forth criteria for receiving a pension (e.g., years of service) and the basis on which pension benefits are computed (e.g., salary at date of retirement). Pension plans vary extensively, however, and reflect a "complex array of social concepts

---

[1]*FASB Statement of Financial Accounting Concepts No. 6,* "Elements of Financial Statements," 1985, pars. 80–81.

and pressures, legal considerations, actuarial techniques, income tax laws and regulations, business philosophies, and accounting concepts and practices."[2] Therefore, many uncertainties exist about the actual cost a business incurs each year due to its pension plan. Consequently, many estimates are required in applying a pension benefit formula to develop the amounts used for recording pension expense and to determine the amounts of related pensions assets and liabilities. Various items must be estimated to properly account for pension commitments, such as

1. Employee turnover rates
2. Employee mortality ages
3. Employee compensation levels
4. Employee retirement ages
5. Pension fund earnings

Actuarial science is an applied branch of mathematics. Actuaries are skilled in studying and making estimates about pension commitments. Accountants commonly rely on actuaries to provide information for estimating pension expense and determining other information needed to appropriately present pensions in the financial statements of employers. Accountants are not expected to be experts in actuarial science. We are, however, required to understand basic principles upon which actuaries perform their work and to be in a position to understand and evaluate the reasonableness of assumptions made by actuaries.

A BRIEF HISTORY OF PENSION ACCOUNTING

Pension accounting has long been a controversial topic in the accounting profession and among users of accounting information. One of the earliest pronouncements on the subject, *Accounting Research Bulletin No. 47,* stated that pension costs based on current and future services "should be systematically accrued during the expected period of active service of the covered employees, generally upon the basis of actuarial calculations."[3] Little additional guidance was provided to accountants by *ARB No. 47* and, consequently, accounting practices differed greatly.

In an attempt to clarify accounting principles and narrow the practices applicable to pension plans, the Accounting Principles Board (APB) issued *Opinion No. 8,* which superseded *ARB No. 47* and provided more precise guidance for practitioners. *APB Opinion No. 8* provided for a range of acceptable amounts which could be charged as pension expense. All APB members agreed that "the entire cost of benefit payments ultimately to be made should be charged against income subsequent to the adoption or amendment of a plan and that no portion of such costs should be charged directly against retained earnings."[4] Individual board members differed substantially, however, on how best to measure the annual cost of a pension plan. While there was little controversy over the conceptual aspects of accounting for pensions, disagreement arose in putting the concepts into practice. To account for this divergence, the APB

Matching   allowed wide latitude in how the cost of a particular pension plan should be measured and matched with revenue.

In the 1970s concern arose in the accounting and investment communities over suspected deficiencies in financial accounting and reporting under *APB Opinion No. 8.* Specifically, the wide latitude allowed in the determination of pension expense and the potential for companies to have an unrecorded pension obligation were of primary

---

[2]*APB Opinion No. 8,* "Accounting for the Cost of Pension Plans," 1966, par. 1.
[3]*Accounting Research Bulletin No. 47,* "Accounting for Costs of Pension Plans," 1956, par. 5.
[4]*APB Opinion No. 8,* par. 17.

Disclosure   concern. In 1980 the FASB issued *SFAS No. 36*, "Disclosure of Pension Information," to temporarily alleviate the pressure for improved financial reporting by requiring additional information in notes to the financial statements.[5] At that time no changes were made in the accounting procedures used in measuring and recording the elements of the financial statements. The FASB determined, however, that a major effort should be made to reevaluate pension accounting under *APB Opinion No. 8*.

After a great deal of effort and debate, the FASB issued *SFAS No. 87*, "Employers' Accounting for Pensions," in 1985.[6] This pronouncement substantially changed the financial accounting and reporting procedures for defined benefit pension plans by employers in ways that were intended to address the problems noted in the previous paragraph. The remainder of this chapter is based primarily on *SFAS No. 87* and, as such, deals with accounting procedures and reporting requirements that are relatively new to accounting practice.

AN OVERVIEW OF PENSION ACCOUNTING

Financial accounting and reporting of pension obligations involves a complicated process of determining the cost of offering pension benefits to employees and associating that cost with specific accounting periods. In addition, the presentation of financial position is very important, and a minimum pension liability and related intangible pension asset may be required. At this point, we discuss these requirements briefly and then develop them more completely in the remainder of this chapter.

The pension expense of an accounting period, referred to as **net periodic pension cost** in *SFAS No. 87*, is made up of several components that reflect different aspects of the employers' pension plan. The primary components of net periodic pension cost are identified as follows:

1. Service cost.
2. Interest cost.
3. Return on plan assets.
4. Recognition of gain or loss.
5. Amortization of unrecognized prior service cost.

In a defined benefit pension plan, the employer's estimate of its pension obligation results from many actuarial assumptions. Net periodic pension cost is computed on the basis of the present value of the pension obligation as of a particular date, including all benefits attributed by the pension benefit formula to employee services rendered prior to that date. According to *SFAS No. 87*, this obligation, referred to as the **projected benefit obligation,** is measured using assumptions concerning future compensation levels if the pension benefits are to be based on those future levels.

Another important factor in calculating net periodic pension cost is the **fair value of plan assets.** Plan assets are investments—usually stocks and bonds—that have been purchased with the funds contributed into the pension plan. The fair value of the assets is the amount that the pension plan could reasonably expect to receive in the sale of its investments and, therefore, represents a measure of funds available to satisfy pension benefit requirements. Increases in the value of the plan assets represent reductions in the amounts that otherwise have to be contributed so that sufficient funds are available to satisfy pension demands. The projected benefit obligation, the fair value of plan assets, and other factors discussed later in this chapter interact to

---

[5]*FASB Statement of Financial Accounting Standards No. 36*, "Disclosure of Pension Information," 1980.
[6]*FASB Statement of Financial Accounting Standards No. 87*, "Employers' Accounting for Pensions," 1985.

determine the net periodic pension cost to be recognized in the determination of net income for each accounting period.

When must a company recognize pension assets and liabilities in its financial statements? First, when the pension funding differs from the amount of pension expense recognized, an accrued pension cost (a liability representing underfunding) or a prepaid pension cost (an asset representing overfunding) is recognized. Second, if the amount of the pension obligation exceeds the fair value of the plan's assets, a minimum pension liability and a related intangible asset must be recognized. The **accumulated benefit obligation** is used to calculate pension liability, however, rather than the projected benefit obligation that is used to compute net periodic pension cost. The accumulated benefit obligation calculation differs from the projected benefit obligation in that the former does *not* take future salary levels into consideration.

Disclosure   In the following sections, we discuss the nature and illustrate the determination of the components of net periodic pension cost and illustrate the pension liabilities and assets resulting from the application of *SFAS No. 87* and the related financial statement disclosures. Our intent is to gain a conceptual understanding of pension accounting rather than a comprehensive understanding of all the technical aspects of *SFAS No. 87*. As you study the following material, the authors suggest that you pay particular attention to the definitions of important terms that are introduced throughout the discussion and the basic accounting principles that are being applied.

ACCOUNTING FOR PENSIONS: BASIC PRINCIPLES

In this section, we use a simplified example to introduce the determination of important financial statement elements concerning pensions. We will limit our discussion to three of the components of net periodic pension cost—service, interest, and return on assets—deferring consideration of the other components and the recognition of the additional pension liability until a more advanced illustration is presented in a later section.

In approaching the study of pension accounting, a helpful frame of reference is to view the employer's interest in a pension plan as a subentity within a primary entity. The subentity is the pension plan; the primary entity is the employer company. Information is maintained about the subentity that does not appear in the financial statements of the primary entity. We refer to the specialized records of the subentity or interest in the pension plan as "memorandum" records because they are maintained outside the general ledger accounts of the primary company. As we will see, the memorandum records articulate directly with the financial statement elements of the primary entity and are very important even though they are labeled "memorandum." The idea of the interest in a pension plan as a subentity of the primary entity is analogous to an equity-method investment that we covered in Chapter 10.

Note the relationships in the following illustration:

Memorandum Records		Financial Statement Element
Fair value of plan assets [FVPA]	− Projected benefit obligation [PBO]	= Prepaid/Accrued Pension Cost [P/APC]

In this simplified example, the relationship indicates that the fair value of the plan assets, less the company's projected benefit obligation, equals the prepaid/accrued pension cost that appears in the employer's financial statements. The first two items—fair value of plan assets and pension obligation—are memorandum records that do not appear in the financial statements of the employer. The FVPA is analogous to an off-balance-sheet asset with a debit balance; the PBO is analogous to an off-balance sheet liability with a credit balance. They are offset and only the difference in the form of the prepaid/accrued pension cost is shown in the employer's balance sheet.

To develop these concepts further, we assume that Bean Company has a pension plan in which the fair value of plan assets is $15,000, the projected benefit obligation is $18,500, and thus the accrued pension cost (a liability) is $3,500. This is logical because even though the value of the assets and the pension obligation are both omitted from the employer's balance sheet, the employer has an unsatisfied obligation to the extent that the assets are insufficient to meet the obligation. The assumption is made that by transferring $15,000 of assets to a plan which will be used to satisfy pension benefits in the future, the employer has effectively provided for (already paid) $15,000 of the pension obligation and only $3,500 remains to be included among the employer's liabilities as a shortfall in funding of the pension plan.

We now assume that during the following year service cost of $3,750 is incurred, interest cost at 10% is recognized, a return on plan assets of 10% is earned, and the employer contributes (funds) $3,000 to the pension plan. An analysis to accumulate information for the memorandum records and the financial statement elements appears in Exhibit 24–4.

Observe the relationship of the three components of net periodic pension cost in this illustration. Service and interest cost are combined and *reduced* by the return on the assets to determine net periodic pension cost. The following general journal entry records the pension plan transactions for the year, including the $3,000 funding:

Pension Expense ($3,750 + $1,850 − $1,500)	4,100	
Cash		3,000
Prepaid/Accrued Pension Cost ($4,600 − $3,500)		1,100

A liability increase of $1,100 is required because the pension expense of $4,100 was not completely funded. Combining the $3,500 liability balance at the beginning of the period with the $1,100 increase during the period, the prepaid/accrued pension cost appears in the balance sheet as a liability of $4,600 at the end of the period.

Let's look more closely at the three components of net periodic pension cost illustrated in this example. **Service cost** is the actuarial present value of benefits attributed by the pension benefit formula to employee services rendered during the period.[7] Determining the service cost for a period requires actuarial assumptions that reflect the time value of money (such as the discount or interest rate) and assumptions reflecting the probability of payment (such as mortality rates, turnover, attrition, and retirement age). This involves a complicated set of actuarial calculations for which accountants typically rely on actuaries. In the analysis in Exhibit 24–4, entry (a) recognizes service cost for the period as a component of pension expense (debit) and as an increase in the company's pension obligation (credit).

The **interest cost** component of net periodic pension cost is determined as the increase in the projected benefit obligation due to the passage of time. At any given time, the **projected benefit obligation** is the present value of all future retirement payments attributed by the pension benefit formula to employee services rendered

---

[7]*SFAS No. 87*, par. 21.

EXHIBIT 24–4

Analysis of Pension Accounting Information
Simplified Case

Memorandum Records	Beginning Balance†	Adjustments Debit	Adjustments Credit	Ending Balance†
Fair value of plan assets	$ 15,000	(c) 1,500 (d) 3,000		$ 19,500
Projected benefit obligation	(18,500)		(a) 3,750 (b) 1,850	(24,100)
Financial Statement Elements				
Prepaid/Accrued Pension Cost	($3,500)	4,500	5,600	($4,600)

Pension Expense:		
Service	(a) 3,750	
Interest*	(b) 1,850	
Return on Assets**		(c) 1,500

Cash		(d) 3,000
	$10,100	$10,100

Pension Expense:	
Service	$ 3,750
Interest	1,850
Return on assets	(1,500)
	$ 4,100

*Interest cost: $18,500 (PBO) × 10%
**Return on plan assets: $15,000 (FVPA) × 10%
†Debit (Credit)

prior to that date.[8] If the pension benefit formula specifies retirement benefits in terms of future salary levels, expected salaries are incorporated into the present value calculations. Notice that no assumption is made about future employee services that have not yet been rendered. Rather, the assumption is only concerning future compensation levels upon which benefits already earned will be based. Determination of the interest cost component requires accrual of interest at the rates equal to the assumed discount rates used in determining the service component of net periodic pension cost. Referring again to the analysis in Exhibit 24–4, entry (b) recognizes the interest cost component of pension expense (debit) and the related increase in the pension obligation (credit).

Plan assets are stocks, bonds, and other investments that have been transferred to the pension fund or have been acquired with cash that has been transferred to the fund. To qualify as a plan asset, the investment must have been segregated in a pension fund and not be available for use by management except for the payment of pen-

---
[8]*SFAS No. 87*, par. 264.

sion benefits. The **return on plan assets** is a reduction in the amount of net periodic pension cost; it is subtracted from the service and interest components because the return reduces the employer's net cash outflow required to satisfy the pension obligation. In Exhibit 24–4, the return is recognized in entry (c) as a reduction in pension expense (credit), indicating the offset against the service and interest components; also the fair value of plan assets is increased (debit) to indicate the enhanced value of the assets based on earnings during the year.

Entry (d) in Exhibit 24–4 records the cash payment into the pension plan which increases the fair value of the assets (debit) and reduces cash (credit).

In this simple illustration, we have assumed that the obligation exceeded the value of the assets and that the pension expense for the period was not fully funded. We could have made alternate assumptions. For example, we could have assumed that the value of the assets in the plan exceeded the obligation and that the company included a prepaid pension cost (asset) in its balance sheet rather than an accrued pension cost (liability). We could have assumed over-funding of the pension expense rather than underfunding. These changes would not alter the basic principles illustrated in the example, however. Records of the value of the plan assets and the pension obligation are maintained on a memorandum basis and only the prepaid/accrued pension cost item appears in the employer's balance sheet. The net periodic pension cost, or pension expense, appears in the employer's income statement.

We have omitted two important components of net periodic pension cost in this illustration—recognition of gain or loss, and amortization of unrecognized prior service cost—and we have not yet encountered the recording of the additional pension liability introduced earlier. We explain these complexities in the more advanced discussion and examples that appear in the following section.

ADDITIONAL PENSION ACCOUNTING CONSIDERATIONS

In the illustration in the previous section, we discussed the interaction of the service, interest, and return on assets components of net periodic pension cost. In this section, we identify two more components and illustrate their application: recognition of gain or loss, and amortization of unrecognized prior service cost. At that point we will have completed our discussion of the five components of net periodic pension cost and we will summarize the calculation of this important financial statement element, after which we discuss and illustrate the recording of an additional pension liability.

RECOGNITION OF GAIN OR LOSS

Gains and losses represent changes in the amount of the projected benefit obligation and/or the value of plan assets which result from experience that differs from projections. They include amounts that have been realized (for example, by sale of a security) as well as amounts that have not been realized (for example, market-value changes in a security that has not yet been sold).

Recognition of gain or loss is required as a component of net periodic pension cost for a year if, *at the beginning of the year,* the absolute value of the net unrecognized gain or loss exceeds 10% of the greater of the projected benefit obligation or the value of the plan assets. This 10% amount is referred to as the **corridor** in *SFAS No. 87* and Materiality represents a materiality threshold for determining when gains and losses are sufficiently large to require recognition. If accumulated gains or losses are less than the amount of the corridor, they are not recognized in net periodic pension cost for that particular accounting period. The rationale for this procedure is that gains and losses associated with pension plans offset over time and ordinarily should not be included in net periodic pension cost due to the amount of volatility they would introduce. Only when the unrecognized amount of gain or loss reaches a high level does this element of net periodic pension cost come into play.

If recognition of gain or loss is required, the amount is the excess of the accumulated unrecognized gain or loss over the corridor amount divided by the average remaining service period of active employees expected to receive benefits under the plan.[9] If a *gain* is being recognized, net periodic pension cost is *reduced* by the amount; if a *loss* is being recognized, net periodic pension cost is *increased* by the amount.

A common instance of gain or loss occurs when a change in the value of plan assets differs from the expected return on those assets.[10] The expected return on plan assets gives rise to the return-on-plan-assets component of net periodic pension cost. But when changes in the value of the plan assets are other than the expected return, then the recognition-of-gain-or-loss component of net periodic pension cost is called for if the corridor test is met. In the same manner, assumptions upon which the projected benefit obligation are based may prove inaccurate and may require adjustment. As a result of these adjustments to the value of plan assets and to the projected benefit obligation, an accumulated net gain or loss will be continuously carried forward from one accounting period to the next, with recognition of part of that amount as a compo-

Materiality   nent of net periodic pension cost only if the corridor (materiality) test is met.

To illustrate the recognition of gain or loss in determining net periodic pension cost, we assume the projected benefit obligation and fair value of plan assets amounts in Exhibit 24–5 for Lancaster, Inc., *at the beginning of* 1991, 1992, and 1993. For simplicity, we also assume that prior to 1991 no accumulated gain or loss existed.

For 1991, the actual amount of the projected benefit obligation (PBO) exceeds the expected amount by $10,000 ($175,000 − $165,000). Because the actual obligation is greater than expected, this represents a loss in the accumulated gain/loss column. Conversely, the fair value of plan assets ($185,000) exceeds their expected value ($165,000) by $20,000, a gain. Netting the gain and loss results in an accumulated $10,000 gain. Referring to the recognition calculation at the bottom of Exhibit 24–5, no amortization is required in 1991 because the $10,000 accumulated gain is not as great as the corridor. In this year, the corridor is determined as 10% of the fair value of plan assets because their amount exceeds the projected benefit obligation. In other

Materiality   words, applying the corridor test, the accumulated gain is not a sufficiently material amount to require recognition.

Moving to 1992, the $10,000 gain is carried forward from 1991 and combined with a $5,000 loss on the projected benefit obligation and a $30,000 gain on the fair value of plan assets for a net gain of $35,000. In 1992, the corridor is determined as 10% of the fair value of plan assets, as that amount ($225,000) exceeds the projected

Materiality   benefit obligation ($195,000). In this case, the accumulated gain is material and the difference between that accumulated gain and the corridor is recognized over the estimated remaining service life of active employees. We use an assumed 10 years in this illustration. The $1,250 amount requiring recognition will reduce net periodic pension cost because it represents a gain.

---

[9]*SFAS No. 87*, par. 32.

[10]Specifically, *SFAS No. 87* indicates that the expected return on plan assets shall be computed on the basis of the expected long-term rate of return on plan assets and the *market-related value of plan assets*. The market-related value of plan assets may be either the fair value or a calculated value that recognizes changes in fair value in a systematic and rational manner over not more than five years (*SFAS No. 87*, par. 30). In this text, we assume for illustration purposes that the expected long-term rate of return is based on the fair value of the plan assets.

EXHIBIT 24–5

Lancaster, Inc.
Gain/Loss Recognition

	1991			1992			1993		
	Expected	Actual	Accumulated Gain/Loss	Expected	Actual	Accumulated Gain/Loss	Expected	Actual	Accumulated Gain/Loss
Projected Benefit Obligation	$165,000	$175,000	$10,000 L						
Fair Value of Plan Assets	$165,000	$185,000	20,000 G						
			$10,000 G						
Recognition*			-0-						
Projected Benefit Obligation				$190,000	$195,000	$10,000 G			
Fair Value of Plan Assets				$195,000	$225,000	5,000 L			
						30,000 G			
						$35,000 G			
Recognition*						(1,250)			
Projected Benefit Obligation							$215,000	$200,000	$ 33,750 G
Fair Value of Plan Assets							$240,000	$150,000	15,000 G
									90,000 L
									$ 41,250 L
Recognition*									(2,125)
Unrecognized Loss to 1994									$ 39,125 L

*Recognition calculations:

Year	Corridor	Accumulated Gain/Loss	Excess of Gain/Loss Over Corridor	Recognition[x]
1991	10% × $185,000 = $18,500	$10,000 G	-0-	-0-
1992	10% × $225,000 = $22,500	$35,000 G	$12,500	$1,250
1993	10% × $200,000 = $20,000	$41,250 L	$21,250	2,125

[x](Excess of Gain/Loss over corridor)/10

Continuing to 1993, a similar process is followed. The unrecognized gain of $33,750 is carried forward and combined with the $15,000 gain on the projected benefit obligation and the $90,000 loss on the fair value of plan assets to render an accumulated unrecognized loss of $41,250. Notice that in 1993 the corridor is defined as 10% of the projected benefit obligation (rather than the fair value of plan assets as in 1991 and 1992) because of its larger dollar amount. Because a loss is being recognized, the $2,125 calculated amount results in an increase in net periodic pension cost.

To summarize the impact of these calculations, gains and losses are an expected part of pension accounting because of the inherent uncertainty of the variables that make up the fair value of plan assets and the projected benefit obligation. In addition, over time gains and losses tend to offset and, effectively, cancel out. Only when the accumulated unrecognized amount reaches a size that is considered material is a part of the gain or loss included as a component in net periodic pension cost. The corridor test is used to make this materiality assessment. If gain recognition is appropriate, net periodic pension cost is reduced; if loss recognition is appropriate, net periodic pension cost is increased. Whether gain or loss is recognized, the unrecognized amount is carried forward to the following accounting period.

Materiality

AMORTIZATION OF UNRECOGNIZED PRIOR SERVICE COST

New or amended pension plans often include provisions that grant increased benefits to employees based on services rendered before the change. The cost of such amendments to employers is referred to as **prior service cost**.[11] Despite their association with past services, such retroactive adjustments are granted with the expectation that the employer will realize benefits in the future. For example, in union contract negotiations, management may agree to a specified increase in employee compensation and allow the union to decide how it should be applied. Granting increased benefits with a plan amendment on the basis of past services is logical because the employer expects increased employee loyalty and quality of performance in the future.

The amount of prior service cost associated with a new plan or a plan amendment is the increase in the projected benefit obligation resulting from the change. Rather than include the entire amount of prior service cost in the net periodic pension cost in the period of the change, the FASB specifies that it is to be **amortized over certain periods after the change.** Specifically, prior service cost is amortized by assigning an equal amount to each future period of service of each employee active at the date of the change who is expected to receive plan benefits.

While this amortization approach may involve a complicated set of calculations, the following example serves to illustrate an amortization scheme consistent with the above requirement. We shall assume that Lumpkin, Inc., amends its pension plan such that a prior service cost of $165,000 is incurred (i.e., the amendment increases the projected benefit obligation by $165,000). This amendment was made on January 1, 1991. The company has 10 employees and one will retire at the end of each year beginning in 1991. The calculations described in Exhibit 24–6 satisfy the amortization requirements of *SFAS No. 87*.

Applying a procedure similar to the sum-of-the-years'-digits method of depreciation, the $165,000 of prior service cost is amortized by a fraction, the numerator of which is the columnar total indicating the number of employees active in that particular year and the denominator of which is the total of the column of "future service

---

[11]*SFAS No. 87*, par. 264.

EXHIBIT 24-6

Amortization of Prior Service Cost

Employee	Future Service Years Remaining	Years									
		1	2	3	4	5	6	7	8	9	10
A	1	1									
B	2	1	1								
C	3	1	1	1							
D	4	1	1	1	1						
E	5	1	1	1	1	1					
F	6	1	1	1	1	1	1				
G	7	1	1	1	1	1	1	1			
H	8	1	1	1	1	1	1	1	1		
I	9	1	1	1	1	1	1	1	1	1	
J	$\underline{10}$	$\underline{1}$	$\underline{1}$	$\underline{1}$	$\underline{1}$	$\underline{1}$	$\underline{1}$	$\underline{1}$	$\underline{1}$	$\underline{1}$	$\underline{1}$
	55	10	9	8	7	6	5	4	3	2	1

Amortization fractions:

Year 1   10/55

Year 2   9/55

. . .

Year 10   1/55

years remaining." For this example, prior service cost amortization for 1991 (Year 1) would be:

$$10/55 \times \$165{,}000 = \$30{,}000$$

For 1992 (Year 2), amortization would be:

$$9/55 \times \$165{,}000 = \$27{,}000$$

This procedure is continued until the $165,000 is completely amortized at the end of the tenth year in which 1/55 of the $165,000, or $3,000, is amortized.

Consistency . To simplify the computation, the FASB allows the consistent use of alternative amortization plans—*if they more rapidly reduce* the unrecognized cost of retroactive amendments. In the previous example, Lumpkin, Inc., might choose to amortize the $165,000 prior service cost over a five-year period at the rate of $33,000 per year ($165,000/5 years = $33,000) rather than use the procedure outlined in Exhibit 24–6. For simplicity, in this text and in the problem material at the end of the chapter, we assume a simplified average service life unless otherwise indicated.

SUMMARY OF COMPONENTS OF NET PERIODIC PENSION COST

Now that we have completed our discussion of recognition of gains and losses and amortization of prior service cost, we are able to summarize the five components of net periodic pension cost as follows:

Component	Probable Impact on Net Periodic Pension Cost
Service	Increase
Interest	Increase
Return on assets	Decrease
Recognition of gain or loss	Decrease (if gain)
	Increase (if loss)
Amortization of prior service cost	Increase

After we consider the recording of an additional pension liability in the following section, we end the chapter with a comprehensive multiple-year example that demonstrates the interaction of these five components in arriving at the annual pension expense (i.e., net periodic pension cost) and in updating the memorandum pension records that must be maintained by companies sponsoring pension plans for their employees.

RECOGNITION OF PENSION ASSETS AND LIABILITIES

Management may decide to fund the pension plan at the same rate as net periodic pension cost is recognized. Alternatively, the plan may be funded more rapidly or less rapidly than the recognition of the net periodic pension cost. If the expense recognized exceeds the amount funded, a liability arises; if the expense recognized is less than the amount funded, an asset arises.

To illustrate, assume that Wallen Company determines its net periodic pension cost for 1992 to be $200,000; the company's policy is to fund the amount of expense that is recognized. The general journal entry to record the expense and funding is as follows:

Pension Expense	200,000	
Cash		200,000

Rather than fully funding the amount of expense recognized, let's assume that Wallen funds only $175,000 of the expense. The entry to record the recognition of pension expense, the funding, and the resulting liability is as follows:

Pension Expense	200,000	
Cash		175,000
Prepaid/Accrued Pension Cost		25,000

On the other hand, if the company had funded $225,000, the entry would be as follows:

Pension Expense	200,000	
Prepaid/Accrued Pension Cost	25,000	
Cash		225,000

In addition to the prepaid/accrued pension cost which may be recognized because the expense is over- or underfunded, an **additional liability** may also be required. If, at the end of the accounting period, the *accumulated benefit obligation* exceeds the fair value of the plan assets, the employer must include a liability equal to the unfunded accumulated benefit obligation in the balance sheet. The amount of the liability recorded because of this situation is adjusted by the amount of the prepaid/accrued pension cost that has already been recorded as a result of the over- or underfunding of the net periodic pension cost. If this additional liability is required, an equal amount is usually recorded as an intangible asset. The amount of the intangible asset, however, is limited to the amount of unrecognized prior service cost. If the amount of liability that must be recorded exceeds the amount of the intangible asset, the excess is charged to a special stockholders' equity account with a negative balance.[12]

---

[12]*SFAS No. 87*, par. 36–37.

The **accumulated benefit obligation**referred to in the previous paragraph is the actuarial present value of benefits attributed by the pension benefit formula to employee services rendered before a specified date and based on employee services and compensation prior to that date. It differs from the projected benefit obligation, referred to earlier while discussing net periodic pension cost, in that the accumulated benefit obligation includes *no assumption about future compensation levels.* [13]

In the following illustration, we demonstrate the recognition of pension assets and liabilities as described above.[14] Turpen Manufacturing Company maintains a defined benefit pension plan for its employees. The company has accumulated the following information concerning that plan as of December 31, 1991, 1992, and 1993, the end of the company's financial reporting period.

	At December 31		
	1991	1992	1993
	(amounts in thousands)		
Plan assets at fair value	$1,200	$1,304	$1,450
Accumulated benefit obligation	1,320	1,395	1,480
Net periodic pension cost	141	144	151
Contribution made by company	125	186	120
Unrecognized prior service cost	92	86	80

First, we record the net periodic pension cost (pension expense) and the company's contribution to the plan for 1991:

Dec. 31, 1991	Pension Expense	141	
	Cash		125
	Prepaid/Accrued Pension Cost		16

Neither the assets invested in the pension fund ($1,200) nor the employer's obligation to employees ($1,320) will appear on the employer's balance sheet. The funding of net periodic pension cost is recorded *as if the employer's responsibility to employees has been satisfied,* except to the extent that funding of the expense has not taken place ($16). This is referred to as the *offsetting* feature of accounting for pensions and is criticized by some as understating both the employer's assets (amounts in the pension fund) and liabilities (obligation for future pension benefits).

Next, we determine whether the situation requires the recording of an additional liability. We do this by comparing the accumulated benefit obligation with the fair value of the plan assets:

Accumulated benefit obligation	$ 1,320
Plan assets at fair value	1,200
Required liability	$ 120

Remember that we already have a liability balance (Prepaid/Accrued Pension Cost) of $16. To include the required liability of $120, we must record $104 as an *additional liability* ($120 − $16 = $104). As stated earlier, when we record this liability we establish an intangible asset; that intangible asset, however, is limited to the amount of the unrecognized prior service cost ($92). Any excess amount of the liability is recorded in a negative stockholders' account, as follows:

---

[13]*SFAS No. 87,* par. 264.
[14]This example is a modified version of Illustration 4 of Appendix B of *SFAS No. 87.*

Dec. 31, 1991	Intangible Pension Asset	92	
	Excess of Additional Pension Liability		
	Over Unrecognized Prior Service Cost	12	
	($104 − $92)		
	Additional Pension Liability		104

This entry is required because the accumulated benefit obligation exceeds the fair value of the plan assets by more than $16. If the fair value of the plan assets had been greater than the accumulated benefit obligations, or if the accumulated benefit obligation had exceeded the fair value of plan assets by $16 or less, no additional liability would be required.

The direct charge (debit) to stockholders' equity represents a reduction in the equity of owners that is not recognized as part of net income. Recall that in Chapter 10 we discussed a similar adjustment when the aggregate market value of noncurrent marketable equity securities fell below their aggregate cost. We reduced stockholders' equity directly and established an allowance (contra-asset) that reduced the portfolio cost to the lower market value. The adjustment described here for pensions is similar to that for noncurrent marketable equity securities. The recognition of the additional liability is strictly a balance sheet procedure. If the amount of the additional liability is equal to or less than the amount of unrecognized prior service cost, no adjustment to stockholders' equity is required.

As a result of these entries, we will include pension expense of $141 in the income statement. In the balance sheet, we will have the following items:

Assets	
Intangible pension asset	$92
Liabilities	
Net pension liability	120
Stockholders' equity	
Excess of additional pension liability over unrecognized	
prior service cost	(12)

The net pension liability is the total of the accrued pension cost and the additional pension liability ($16 + $104 = $120). This liability will ordinarily be noncurrent; if the company intends to fund a portion of it during the next year, that portion is current.

Now, let's continue our example by recording the pension information for 1992. Again we must record pension expense and funding:

Dec. 31, 1992	Pension Expense	144	
	Prepaid/Accrued Pension Cost	42	
	Cash		186

Observe that the Prepaid/Accrued Pension Cost now has a debit balance of $26, resulting from the combination of the $42 debit of 1992 and the $16 credit of 1991 ($42 − $16 = $26). This represents a change from a net liability position in 1991 to a net asset position in 1992.

Again we determine whether an additional liability is required and, if so, the amount of that liability. We do that by comparing the accumulated benefit obligation with the fair value of plan assets.

Accumulated benefit obligation	$ 1,395	
Plan assets at fair value	1,304	
Required liability	$ 91	

Remember that we have a $26 *debit balance* in Prepaid/Accrued Pension Cost, representing a **net asset** position. To include a net liability of $91, we must combine the additional liability and the Prepaid/Accrued Pension Cost, and then apply the resulting subtotal to the net liability; the result is that we must increase the additional pension liability by $13 in 1992.

Net liability required		$91
Existing balances		
Additional pension liability	$104	
Prepaid/accrued pension cost	(26)	78
1992 *increase* in additional liability		$13

Because the intangible asset, which has a balance of $92, cannot exceed the amount of unrecognized prior pension cost, it must be reduced by $6 ($92 − $86 = $6). The entry to record these items is as follows:

Dec. 31, 1992 Excess of Additional Pension Liability Over		
Unrecognized Prior Service Cost	19	
Intangible Pension Asset		6
Additional Pension Liability		13

In the 1992 income statement we will include pension expense of $144. The balance sheet will include the following pension items:

Assets	
Intangible pension asset	$ 86*
Liabilities	
Net pension liability	91**
Stockholders' equity	
Excess of additional pension liability over unrecognized prior service cost	(31)†

*$92 − $6 = $86	**[($104 + $13) − $26] = $91	†$(12) + $(19) = $(31)

We will now complete our example of recording pension assets and liabilities by recording the appropriate journal entries for 1993. Again, we record the recognition of pension expense and the related funding, as follows:

Dec. 31, 1993 Pension Expense	151	
Cash		120
Prepaid/Accrued Pension Cost		31

Prepaid/Accrued Pension Cost now has a $5 credit (liability) balance: $31 − $26 = $5. As before we determine the need for an additional liability by comparing the accumulated benefit obligation with the fair value of plan assets:

Accumulated benefit obligation	$ 1,480	
Plan assets at fair value	1,450	
Required liability	$ 30	

In 1993 the liability must be *reduced* by $92, determined as follows:

Net liability required		$ 30
Existing balances		
Additional pension liability	$117	
Prepaid/accrued pension cost	5	(122)
1993 *decrease* in additional liability		$ 92

We reduce the liability by $92, eliminate the negative stockholders' equity account, and reduce the intangible pension asset simultaneously as follows:

Dec. 31, 1993 Additional Pension Liability	92	
Excess of Additional Pension Liability Over		
Unrecognized Prior Service Cost		31
Intangible Pension Asset		61

With this adjustment, the intangible pension asset balance is $25 ($86 − $61 = $25), less than the amount of unrecognized prior service cost of $80.

In the 1993 income statement we include $151 of pension expense and the balance sheet will include the following:

Assets	
Intangible pension asset	$25*
Liabilities	
Net pension liability	30**

*$86 − $61 = $25
**[($117 − $92) + $5] = $30

To summarize, the Prepaid/Accrued Pension Cost account is a cumulative difference between the expense recognized and the amount funded. The account has a debit balance, representing an asset, when pension expense has been overfunded; it has a credit balance, representing a liability, when pension expense has been underfunded. An additional liability is recognized when, at the end of the accounting period, the accumulated benefit obligation exceeds the fair value of the plan assets by more than the total of existing recorded pension liabilities. In recognizing an additional pension liability, we establish or increase an intangible pension asset that is limited in amount to the unrecognized prior service cost. Any reconciling difference is adjusted to the negative stockholders' equity valuation account.

What is the logic behind the recording of an intangible pension asset when an additional pension liability is required? Recall that companies grant retroactive credit when a pension plan is amended because of the expectation of future services from employees. By granting the plan amendment retroactively the company is purchasing something of future value in terms of employee motivation, morale, and other factors (i.e., "employee goodwill"). The intangible asset is a measure of that value, but it is limited to the amount of prior service cost which is an actuarial computation of the cost of that asset.

The intangible pension asset is not amortized directly as we would amortize other intangible assets. The amount of the intangible pension asset may vary considerably from year to year as we compare the accumulated benefit obligation and the fair value of plan assets at the end of each year and adjust for the amount of prepaid/accrued pension cost. As in the previous example, the amount may go up or down. Remember, however, that the intangible pension asset balance cannot exceed the unamortized balance of prior service cost. The intangible pension asset will eventually be eliminated as the prior service cost is amortized as part of net periodic pension cost over the remaining service period of employees expected to benefit from the plan amendment. In any one period, however, the change in the intangible pension asset and the amortization of prior service cost component of net periodic pension cost will not necessarily be the same.

EXPANDED PENSION RELATIONSHIPS

Now that we have covered the five primary components of net periodic pension cost and we have discussed prior service costs and the recognition of gains and losses, we can expand the relationships introduced earlier. Remember that pension expense is the result of the netting of several diverse components. Also, the difference between the fair value of the plan assets and the projected benefit obligation equals the balance sheet item, prepaid/accrued pension cost. These conclusions were reached, however, before we added prior service costs and the recognition of gains and losses to our body of knowledge. Remember also that where there are prior service costs, an *unamortized balance exists,* and where there are gains and losses, an *unrecognized balance exists.* These become part of the memorandum records that are maintained by the employer but do not appear in the employer's financial statements.

We expand our definition of net periodic pension cost or pension expense as follows:

$$\begin{matrix} \text{Net Periodic Pension Cost} \\ \text{(Pension Expense)} \end{matrix} = \left[\begin{matrix} \text{Service Cost} + \text{Interest Cost} - \text{Return on Plan Assets} \pm \\ \text{Loss or Gain Recognition} + \text{Prior Service Cost Amortization} \end{matrix} \right]$$

The relationship of the memorandum records that must be kept for the pension plan and the accounts on the employer's financial statements can be expanded:

Memorandum Records				Financial Statement Element
Fair Value of Plan Assets	$-$	$\left[\begin{matrix}\text{Projected Benefit} \\ \text{Obligation}\end{matrix} - \begin{matrix}\text{Unamortized Prior} \\ \text{Service Cost}\end{matrix}\right]$	$\pm \begin{matrix}\text{Unrecognized} \\ \text{Loss or Gain}\end{matrix}$	$= \begin{matrix}\text{Prepaid/Accrued} \\ \text{Pension Cost}\end{matrix}$

This relationship indicates that in the memorandum records, the fair value of plan assets, less the projected benefit obligation reduced by the unamortized prior service cost, adjusted up or down for the unrecognized loss or gain, equals the balance sheet element, prepaid/accrued pension cost. The amount representing unamortized prior service cost is included in the projected benefit obligation, but it has not yet been recognized in net periodic pension cost. The projected benefit obligation must be reduced by the unamortized balance to reconcile the memorandum records with the prepaid/accrued pension cost account. The same is true for the unrecognized loss or gain, which represents an adjustment to either the fair value of plan assets, the projected benefit obligation, or both.

Analytically, the fair value of plan assets can be viewed as an unrecorded (off-balance-sheet) asset with a debit balance and the projected benefit obligation as an unrecorded (off-balance-sheet) liability with a credit balance. Similarly, unamortized prior service cost can be viewed as a contra-liability to the projected benefit obligation that is awaiting amortization and, thus, has a debit balance. Unrecognized loss or gain represents either a debit balance (unrecognized loss) or credit balance (unrecognized gain) that awaits recognition in a manner similar to unamortized prior service cost. Making these analogies of the memorandum records with similar financial statement elements, including the assumption of normal debit and credit balances, helps explain the mechanics underlying the relationship of the memorandum records and the financial statement element, prepaid/accrued pension cost.

A COMPREHENSIVE PENSION ACCOUNTING ILLUSTRATION

In this section, we work through a comprehensive two-year illustration for the Roberts Company that summarizes many of the principles in this chapter. The illustration demonstrates the relationship of the five primary components of net periodic pension cost and the articulation of the memorandum records with the financial statement elements related to the employer's pension plan.

We will again use a worksheet approach that is an expanded version of the one found in Exhibit 24–4. The authors suggest that you study the worksheets in Exhibits 24–7 and 24–8 in conjunction with the related text discussion, which provides the numbers in the worksheet as well as the underlying explanation. Each worksheet begins with a beginning balance. Notice that the column starts with the fair value of plan assets, subtracts the projected benefit obligation, adds unamortized prior service cost and adds or subtracts unrecognized losses or gains, respectively.

We will now work through the adjustments in the worksheet, following the key letters indicated in Exhibit 24–7.

YEAR 1 ANALYSIS

(a) Recognition of Service Cost
Service cost of $12,000 (assumed) is recorded by debiting pension expense and crediting the projected benefit obligation to recognize the increased obligation of the employer for employee services rendered in the current period.

(b) Recognition of Interest Cost
Interest cost is recognized at 10% (assumed) on the projected benefit obligation at the beginning of the year: $75,000 \times 10\% = $7,500$. Pension expense is debited and the projected benefit obligation is credited.

(c) Recognition of Return on Assets
Recall that the return on asset component of net periodic pension cost is the expected return. We assume in this example that the expected return on the assets is 10% and the actual return was only $2,000 for the year:

Expected return ($50,000 \times 10\%$)	$ 5,000
Actual return	(2,000)
Unexpected loss	$ 3,000

We record the return by debiting the assets for the $2,000 increase in value, debiting the unrecognized loss (gain) item for the $3,000 loss and crediting pension expense for the $5,000 expected return.

(d) Amortization of Prior Service Cost
Prior service cost is being amortized over the remaining service period of active employees who will benefit from the plan amendment, 15 years in this case (assumed). Amortization is $1,000, determined as follows: $15,000/15 = $1,000$. Pension expense is debited and unamortized prior service cost is credited.

(e) Recognition of Gain
Recall that gain or loss is recognized only if the unrecognized amount *at the beginning of the year* exceeds the corridor, which is 10% of the greater of the fair value of the plan assets or the projected benefit obligation. In this case, the corridor is defined by the projected benefit obligation and we will recognize over 15 years (assumed):

EXHIBIT 24–7

Analysis of Roberts Company Pension Accounting Information
Advanced Case—Year 1

Memorandum Records	Beginning Balance*	Adjustments Debit	Adjustments Credit	Ending Balance*
Fair value of plan assets	$ 50,000	(c)$ 2,000 (f) 20,000	(h)$17,500	$54,500
Projected benefit obligation	(75,000)	(h) 17,500	(a) 12,000 (b) 7,500 (g) 15,000	(92,000)
Unamortized prior service cost	15,000		(d) 1,000	14,000
Unrecognized loss (gain)	(9,000) Gain	(c) 3,000 (e) 100 (g) 15,000		9,100
Financial Statement Elements				
Prepaid/Accrued Pension Cost	($19,000)	57,600	53,000	($14,400)

Pension Expense:
Service	(a) 12,000	
Interest	(b) 7,500	
Return on assets		(c) 5,000
Prior service cost	(d) 1,000	
Gain		(e) 100

Cash		(f) 20,000
	$78,100	$78,100

Key (see text pp. 1156–1158):
(a) Service cost recognition
(b) Interest cost recognition
(c) Return on asset recognition
(d) Amortization of prior service cost
(e) Recognition of gain
(f) Funding of pension plan
(g) Adjustment of projected benefit obligation
(h) Payment of benefits

Pension Expense:
Service	$ 12,000
Interest	7,500
Return on assets	(5,000)
Prior service cost	1,000
Gain	(100)
	$15,400

*Debit (Credit)

Unrecognized gain	$9,000
Corridor ($75,000 × 10%)	(7,500)
Gain subject to recognition	$1,500
Recognized in current year ($1,500/15)	$ 100

The partial gain is recognized by debiting the unrecognized gain and crediting pension expense.

(f) Funding of Pension Plan

We make the assumption that the company funds $20,000 by transferring cash to the pension fund trustee. The entry is a debit to the fair value of plan assets and a credit to cash.

(g) Adjustment to Projected Benefit Obligation

Adjustment to the projected benefit obligation is required when assumptions made do not parallel actual experience. In this case, we assume that the company's obligation increased $15,000 because of revisions in the actuarial assumptions used to compute the projected benefit obligation. The adjustment is recorded by debiting the unrecognized loss (gain) and crediting the projected benefit obligation.

(h) Payment of Benefits

When retirees receive benefits, the memorandum accounts are adjusted but the financial statements of the employer are unaffected. When $17,500 (assumed) of benefits are paid, for example, the projected benefit obligation is debited (reduced) and the fair value of plan assets is credited (reduced).

YEAR 1 SUMMARY

We are now ready to summarize our worksheet information in the form of a journal entry to record pension expense for the year. Combining the components of net periodic pension cost, we see that the expense is $15,400, cash paid is $20,000, and the entry to record the pension plan for the year is as follows:

Pension Expense	15,400	
Prepaid/Accrued Pension Cost	4,600	
Cash		20,000

Observe that $4,600 is exactly the amount required to reconcile the beginning and ending balance of the Prepaid/Accrued Pension Cost in Exhibit 24–7: $19,000 − $14,400 = $4,600.

When we began this illustration we did not consider the issue of the additional pension liability. Assuming that the accumulated benefit obligation at the beginning of the year was $65,000 (logically less than the projected benefit obligation), we determine the liability status at that time as follows:

Fair value of plan assets	$50,000
Accumulated benefit obligation	(65,000)
Required total pension liability	($15,500)
Prepaid/accrued pension cost	($19,000)

On the basis of these numbers, no additional liability was required at the end of the previous year because a sufficient amount of liability was already in the balance sheet.

We will now assume that at the end of the year the accumulated benefit obligation is $80,000. An analysis similar to the one just given is as follows:

Fair value of plan assets	$54,500
Accumulated benefit obligation	(80,000)
Required total pension liability	($25,500)
Prepaid/Accrued Pension Cost	$14,400
Required additional liability	($11,100)

The amount of the intangible asset that can be established is limited to the amount of unamortized prior service cost of $14,000. Inasmuch as we must record an additional liability of only $11,100, that does not present a problem and we can record the additional liability as follows:

Intangible Pension Asset	11,100	
Additional Pension Liability		11,100

When this liability is combined with the $14,400 Prepaid/Accrued Pension Cost already in the balance sheet, the total liability is the difference between the accumulated benefit obligation and the fair value of plan assets: $14,400 + $11,100 = $25,500.

YEAR 2 ANALYSIS

For the second year of the Roberts Company example, we turn our attention to the pension information analysis in Exhibit 24–8. Observe that the beginning balances are identical to the ending balances in Exhibit 24–7. Several of the adjustments are identical to year 1, except for different assumed amounts: (a) service cost of $25,000; (b) interest on the projected benefit obligation at 10%, or $9,200; (d) amortization of prior service cost at $1,000; (f) funding of the pension plan at $25,000; and (h) payment of pension benefits at $21,750.

We will now focus our attention on the worksheet adjustments that differ from those in the first year of the Roberts Company example.

(c) Return on Plan Assets
In this year, we assume that the return on plan assets was $7,000 while the expected return was 10% of $54,500, or $5,450. This means that the company had an unanticipated gain rather than a loss as in the first year. The worksheet adjustment debits the fair value of plan assets for the increase of $7,000. The unrecognized loss (gain) item is credited for the unexpected part of that return is ($1,550) and the expected return of $5,450 is credited to pension expense, reducing the amount that would otherwise be recognized.

(e) Recognition of Loss
In the second year, Roberts Company begins in a loss position rather than a gain position as in the first year. The amount is not sufficient, however, to require recognition because the accumulated unrecognized loss of $9,100 is less than 10% of the projected benefit obligation ($92,000 × 10% = $9,200). Notice that the corridor is again established by the projected benefit obligation rather than the fair value of plan assets because of its larger size. The entry "–0–" in the worksheet is simply there to indicate the nature of the adjustment that would be made had one been required.

(g) Adjustment of Projected Benefit Obligation
Again we assume that the projected benefit obligation requires adjustment for experience differences from the assumptions made. This adjustment, however, is a gain of $2,000 (assumed) in that the projected benefit obligation is reduced. For example, salary increases may not have been as great as expected or turnover may have accelerated, resulting in more individuals leaving the company's work force before qualifying for pension benefits. The adjustment is recorded as a debit to the projected benefit obligation and a credit to the unrecognized loss (gain).

EXHIBIT 24-8

Analysis of Roberts Company Pension Accounting Information
Advanced Case—Year 2

Memorandum Records	Beginning Balance*	Adjustments Debit	Adjustments Credit	Ending Balance*
Fair value of plan assets	$ 54,500	(c)$ 7,000	(h)$21,750	$ 64,750
		(f) 25,000		
Projected benefit obligation	(92,000)	(g) 2,000	(a) 25,000	
		(h) 21,750	(b) 9,200	(102,450)
Unamortized prior service cost	14,000		(d) 1,000	13,000
Unrecognized loss (gain)	9,100		(c) 1,550	5,550
			(e) –0–	
			(g) 2,000	
Financial Statement Elements				
Prepaid/Accrued Pension Cost	($14,400)	55,750	60,500	($19,150)

Pension Expense:
Service   (a) 25,000
Interest   (b) 9,200
Return on assets   (c) 5,450
Prior service cost   (d) 1,000
Loss   (e) –0–

Cash   (f) 25,000
                               $90,950 $90,950

Key (see text p. 1159):
(a) Service cost recognition
(b) Interest cost recognition
(c) Return on asset recognition
(d) Amortization of prior service cost
(e) Recognition of loss
(f) Funding of pension plan
(g) Adjustment of projected benefit obligation
(h) Payment of benefits

Pension Expense:	
Service	$25,000
Interest	9,200
Return on assets	(5,450)
Prior service cost	1,000
Loss	–0–
	$29,750

*Debit (Credit)

YEAR 2 SUMMARY

To complete this example, we must again recognize pension expense and determine the need to adjust the additional pension liability. The pension expense is recorded as follows:

Pension Expense	29,750	
Prepaid/Accrued Pension Cost		4,750
Cash		25,000

Assuming that the accumulated benefit obligation is now $91,000, the required liability position of the company is as follows:

Fair value of plan assets		$ 64,750
Accumulated benefit obligation		(91,000)
Required total pension liability		($ 26,250)
Present liability position:		
Additional pension liability from year 1	($11,100)	
Prepaid/accrued pension cost (credit)	(19,150)	(30,250)
Required *reduction* in additional pension liability		$ 4,000

We record this reduction as follows:

| Additional Pension Liability | 4,000 | |
| Intangible Pension Asset | | 4,000 |

Notice that the balance in the intangible asset is now $7,100 ($11,100 − 4,000), which is within the constraint of the unamortized prior service cost balance of $13,000.

Summarizing for the two-year period for Roberts Company, the following financial statement elements will appear in the income statement and balance sheet:

	First Year	Second Year
Income statement:		
Pension Expense	$15,400	$29,750
Balance sheet:		
Asset: Intangible Pension Asset	$11,100	$ 7,100
Liabilities: Net Pension Liability	$25,500*	$26,250**

*$14,400 + $11,100 = $25,500   **$19,150 + $7,100 = $26,250

MISCELLANEOUS PENSION ACCOUNTING CONSIDERATIONS

We have thus far centered our efforts on the basics of pension accounting, focusing primarily on the computation of net periodic pension cost and the assets and liabilities related to pensions that may appear in the employers' financial statements. We complete our study by considering several miscellaneous aspects of accounting for pensions that have not been covered earlier.

FINANCIAL STATEMENT DISCLOSURE

Disclosure An employer's financial statements shall include the following information concerning defined benefit pension plans:[15]

1. A description of the plan, including:
   a. Employee groups covered.
   b. Type of benefit formula.
   c. Funding policy.
   d. Types of assets held.
   e. Significant nonbenefit liabilities.
   f. Effect of significant matters affecting comparability of information for all periods presented.
2. The amount of net periodic pension cost for the period, showing separately the service cost component, the interest cost component, the return on plan assets for the period, and the net total of all other components.

---

[15]*SFAS No. 87*, par. 54.

3. A schedule reconciling the funded status of the plan with amounts reported in the employer's statement of financial position, showing separately:
   a. The fair value of plan assets.
   b. The projected benefit obligation, the accumulated benefit obligation, and the vested benefit obligation.[16]
   c. The amount of unrecognized prior service cost.
   d. The amount of unrecognized net gain or loss.
   e. The amount of any remaining unrecognized net obligation or net asset existing at the date of initial application of *SFAS No. 87*. (This item is discussed briefly in a later section of this chapter.)
   f. The amount of any additional liability recognized.
   g. The amount of net pension asset (prepaid pension cost) or liability (unfunded accrued pension cost) recognized in the statement of financial position.

Disclosure

Exhibit 24–9 presents the 1990 pension information disclosure for Paramount Communications, a world leader in producing and distributing entertainment, with operations in motion pictures, television programming, cable and broadcasting television, home video, theatres, and sports. The company is also a leading book publisher, serving education, consumer and professional markets in the United States and internationally. The first table shows the components of net periodic pension cost. The second table reconciles the accumulated benefit obligation with the projected benefit obligation, the plan assets, and, finally, the net pension (liability) asset. The remainder of the disclosure provides additional information about assumptions and other details underlying the accounting procedures employed.

PROCEDURES TO REDUCE VOLATILITY IN NET PERIODIC PENSION COST

A concern of the FASB and others in accounting for the cost of pension plans by employers is the volatility in earnings that might take place in certain circumstances. For example, the determination of net periodic pension cost requires many actuarial assumptions about future events that are subject to change over time—employee turnover, life expectancies, interest rates, future salary levels, and so on. Pension expense would be particularly susceptible to volatility when a change in actuarial assumption results in a gain in one period and a loss in another period, if both were required to be recognized in full in the determination of pension expense.

The FASB was sensitive to this problem and permits certain procedures that are designed to **reduce volatility.** While some of these are beyond the scope of this text, we have studied two specific procedures intended to reduce volatility—the recognition of gain or loss and the amortization of prior service cost.

Materiality

The FASB requires that gains or losses are to be incorporated into net periodic pension expense *only when they exceed a defined materiality threshold* (i.e., the corridor). Even if the accountant determines that this materiality threshold has been met, the entire gain or loss is not recognized. Rather, the *excess* of the gain or loss over the corridor is recognized over the remaining service period of the employees to receive benefits under the plan. This **limited recognition** requirement has the effect of spreading fluctuations out over time, permitting gains and losses to offset each other, rather than being fully recognized as they occur.

The second example of a procedure to reduce volatility is the amortization of prior service costs. These costs are amortized over the remaining service period of

---

[16]Vested benefits are benefits for which the employee's right to receive present or future pension benefits is not contingent on remaining in the service of the employer. (*SFAS No. 87,* par. 264)

EXHIBIT 24–9

Paramount Communications, Inc.
Pension Disclosure

Note 1—Commitments and Contingencies

Employee Benefit Plans

The cost of retirement benefits for eligible employees, measured by length of service, compensation and other factors, is currently being funded through trusts established under the plans. In general, the Company's funding policy is to make annual contributions to the plans as necessary to meet minimum funding requirements.

The Company adopted the provisions of Statement of Financial Accounting Standards ("SFAS") No. 87 on pension accounting for its domestic plan in fiscal 1988 and its non-U.S. plans in fiscal 1990. The components of net periodic pension cost from continuing operations for the Company's plans were as follows *(in millions)*:

Year Ended October 31	1990	1989	1988
Service cost-benefits earned	$ 15.8	$ 13.5	$ 9.9
Interest cost on projected benefit obligation	30.6	26.9	27.9
Less return on plan assets	(36.0)	(28.8)	(26.1)
Net amortization and deferral	(3.4)	0.4	0.4
Net periodic pension cost	$ 7.0	$ 12.0	$ 12.1

Pension expense from continuing operations computed under previous standards for the Company's non-U.S. pension plans was $0.8 million and $1.0 million for the years ended October 31, 1989 and 1988, respectively.

In addition, the Company had other pension expense for the years ended October 31, 1990, 1989 and 1988 of $10.6, $9.5 and $8.6 million, respectively, primarily related to multiemployer pension plans.

The following table [see column at right] sets forth the funded status and amounts recognized in the Company's consolidated balance sheets for its domestic and non-U.S. plans for fiscal 1990 and its domestic plan for fiscal 1989 *(in millions)*.

Plan assets consist primarily of marketable equity and fixed income securities and the Company's Common Stock. At October 31, 1990

and 1989, the Company's plans owned 1,000,076 shares of the Company's Common Stock with an aggregate market value of $35.3 and $55.9 million, respectively.

October 31	1990	1989
Actuarial present value of benefit obligation		
Vested	$294.1	$261.8
Nonvested	15.0	17.4
Accumulated benefit obligation	309.1	279.2
Effect of projected future salary increases	42.8	35.5
Projected benefit obligation	351.9	314.7
Plan assets at fair value ...	384.2	335.0
Plan assets in excess of projected benefit obligation	32.3	20.3
Unrecognized net gain	(11.4)	(24.3)
Unrecognized prior service cost	(9.8)	
Unrecognized net (asset) obligation at date of adoption of SFAS No. 87	(13.5)	5.7
Net pension (liability) asset	$ (2.4)	$ 1.7

In fiscal 1990 and 1989, the weighted average discount rate and rate of increase in future compensation levels used in determining the actuarial present value of the projected benefit obligation for the Company's plans were 8.5% and 6.0%, respectively. The expected long-term rate of return on assets used for the majority of the Company's plans was 10.0% in fiscal 1990, 1989 and 1988.

In addition to providing pension benefits, the Company provides certain health care and life insurance benefits for retired employees. Substantially all of the Company's employees may become eligible for those benefits when they reach normal retirement age while working for the Company. The cost of health care and life insurance benefits is recognized as insurance premiums are paid or as claims are paid for those uninsured benefits. Such costs were not material.

SOURCE: Paramount Communications, Inc. 1990 Annual Report

employees expected to receive benefits from the plan amendment, thereby preventing the total cost of the plan amendment from impacting income in any one accounting period.

FINANCIAL STATEMENT ARTICULATION

We learned in Chapter 4 that the basic financial statements articulate. They are fundamentally related and are based on the same underlying accounting information. Changes in one financial statement may affect changes in other financial statements.

In the case of pension accounting under *SFAS No. 87,* we see an interesting—and perhaps even confusing—example of articulation. Rarely do we find the determination of an expense which requires the combining of five distinct components as we do in the case of pension expense. Once that expense is determined, however, the articulation of balance sheet and income statement works much as we would expect. If the expense is paid (i.e., funded), cash is reduced; if the expense is not funded, a liability is established. The recognition of the additional liability, however, where the accumulated benefit obligation exceeds the fair value of plan assets, is unique in terms of asset/liability recognition. We would not typically recognize an intangible asset while simultaneously recognizing a liability. In this instance, the intangible asset is not amortized through the income statement as would ordinarily be the case, but rather is *adjusted again* at the end of the next accounting period based on a subsequent comparison of the accumulated benefit obligation and the fair value of plan assets. As we saw in an earlier example, prior service cost is amortized, but that amortization is not based on a reportable asset.

Remember that net periodic pension cost is determined in part by the *projected* benefit obligation—which itself takes into consideration expected future salary levels. The recording of the additional liability, however, is based on the *accumulated* benefit obligation which does not consider expected future salary levels. Again, we have a unique aspect of this accounting model, in that ordinarily both the income statement and balance sheet implications of a particular event or transaction are computed on the basis of the same underlying methods and assumptions. The recording of the additional liability and the related intangible asset is strictly a balance sheet **Disclosure** disclosure, inasmuch as the pension expense (net periodic pension cost) is computed separately, by applying different underlying assumptions. In addition, the desire to include among liabilities any excess of the accumulated benefit obligation over the fair value of plan assets may result in an adjustment to stockholders' equity that is not taken through the income statement as an expense or loss. This apparent anomaly results from the limit on the intangible asset to an amount no greater than the unrecognized prior service cost.

TRANSITION TO *SFAS NO. 87*

In this chapter we have focused attention almost entirely on *SFAS No. 87* and have said little about the previous accounting requirements under *APB Opinion No. 8*. The procedures described in this chapter represent dramatic change from the past and have been a subject of considerable debate for many years.

Under *APB Opinion No. 8*, the projected benefit obligation and the fair value of plan assets did not enter into the determination of balance sheet assets and liabilities as they do under *SFAS No. 87*. As a result, an additional component of net periodic pension cost will be included for several years as part of the transition process. Under *APB Opinion No. 8,* a Prepaid Pension Cost or an Accrued Pension Cost account existed if the amount funded was either more or less than the amount of pension expense recognized. During the transition period, that amount is combined with the difference between the projected benefit obligation and the fair value of plan assets at the time *SFAS No. 87* was adopted and the total (or net) amount amortized over the average remaining service period of employees expected to receive benefits under the plan. If that period is less than 15 years, however, the company may amortize the balance over a 15-year period.[17] This transition adjustment was included among the many disclosure requirements described earlier in the chapter. Again, you can see in this procedure the interest of the FASB in reducing volatility in the amount of pension expense recognized in any one accounting period.

SETTLEMENT AND CURTAILMENT OF PENSION PLANS

At the same time that the FASB issued *SFAS No. 87*, the Board also issued *SFAS No. 88*, which deals with the settlement and curtailment of pension plans.[18] A **settlement** of a pension plan is defined as an irrevocable action that relieves the employer (or the plan) of primary responsibility for an obligation and eliminates significant risks related to the obligation and the assets used to effect the settlement. A **curtailment** of a pension plan is defined as a significant reduction in, or elimination of, defined benefit accruals for present employees' future services.[19]

While an underlying philosophy of *SFAS No. 87* is to delay the recognition in determining net periodic pension cost of certain gains and losses, the effects of changes in assumptions, and the cost of retroactive plan amendments, *SFAS No. 88* requires immediate recognition of certain gains and losses related to the settlement and curtailment of pension plans. The maximum gain or loss subject to recognition in earnings when a pension obligation is settled is the unrecognized net gain or loss, plus any remaining unrecognized net asset existing at the date of initial application of *SFAS No. 87*. The maximum amount is recognized in earnings if the entire projected benefit obligation is settled. If only part of the projected benefit obligation is settled, a pro rata portion of the maximum amount is recognized equal to the percentage reduction in the projected benefit obligation.[20]

SFAS No. 88 also deals with **special termination benefits** offered as an inducement for employees to terminate their employment (e.g., take early retirement). An employer that offers such benefits recognizes a liability and a loss when it is *probable* that employees will be entitled to benefits and the amount can be *reasonably estimated*. The amount of liability and related loss that are recognized is the amount of any lump-sum payments and the present value of any expected future payments.[21]

RETIREMENT BENEFITS OTHER THAN PENSIONS

In this chapter we have focused our attention primarily on accounting and reporting for pension plans. While pension plans are perhaps the most significant retirement plans offered by employers, they are by no means the only such plans. In addition to pension benefits, employers often offer other benefits to employees upon their retirement, such as health care, life insurance, tuition assistance, day care, legal services, and housing subsidies. The FASB has issued its *Statement of Financial Accounting*

---

[17]*SFAS No. 87*, par. 77.
[18]*FASB Statement of Financial Accounting Standards No. 88*, "Employers' Accounting for Settlements and Curtailments of Defined Benefit Pension Plans and for Termination Benefits," 1985.
[19]*SFAS No. 88*, pars. 3, 6.
[20]*SFAS No. 88*, par. 9.
[21]*SFAS No. 88*, par. 15.

FASB ISSUES RULE CHANGE ON BENEFITS

The Financial Accounting Standards Board, in one of the most significant changes to accounting ever, issued a rule on post-retirement health benefits that could cut corporate profits by hundreds of billions of dollars.

The controversial new rule, approved unanimously by the FASB's seven members, requires companies beginning in 1993 to accrue, or set up a reserve for, future medical benefits of retirees rather than deduct them from reported profits each year when paid, as is current practice. Government officials estimate that the rule may reduce total corporate profits by at least $200 billion—and maybe by as much as $1 trillion—over a period of years.

"It's the most significant accounting change since the adoption of depreciation about 80 years ago," says Eugene H. Flegm, assistant controller of General Motors Corp.

Like most corporate executives, Mr. Flegm agrees with the basic principle of accruing such benefits because they are a real and rapidly growing obligation. But he is unhappy that the FASB wasn't able to do more damage control in framing the rule. "We're not thrilled by this new FASB statement [rule] because we're not sure it will produce accurate enough data worthy of the annual financial statement," he said.

For some time, it has been clear that the rule would sharply reduce reported corporate profits. But now that companies and their benefit consultants are crunching more definite numbers, they are discovering exactly how great the damage will be—even with recent FASB changes to accommodate corporate gripes.

Companies with long-standing union contracts guaranteeing health benefits are particularly concerned. For examples, financial analysts and actuaries estimate the rule could reduce General Motors Corp.'s annual reported profits by more than $600 million, or about $1 a share. For 1989, GM reported after-tax profit of $4.2 billion, or $6.33 a share.

Asked about this estimate, Mr. Flegm said it is too early to gauge the FASB rule's effect on GM profits "but there's no question it will be a significant number."

For some big industrial companies, the rule could wipe out retained earnings or possibly stockholder's equity, depending on how they apply it, say financial analysts and accountants.

Financial analysts, for example, point to Chrysler Corp., whose actual "pay-as-you-go" retiree health costs amounted to $260 million in 1989, or $47% of pretax profits. Actuaries and health-benefit consultants say the FASB rule could boost annual health-care costs on an accrual basis for Chrysler by as much as six times.

And the huge amount that Chrysler would have to book to catch up on health-care retiree costs for its current employees could wipe out its retained earnings of $5.2 billion reported last Dec. 31, say financial analysts, actuaries and accountants. Chrysler declines to confirm or deny this estimate. "We aren't in a position to estimate the potential impact [of the FASB rule] . . . due to the flexibility that the company will have in implementing it," a Chrysler spokesman said.

Under the final version of the FASB rule, however, Chrysler has an out. It can spread that catch-up accrual costs over the next 20 years, avoiding the major damage to its financial results. All companies, in fact, may amortize such costs over the two decades or take the big hit immediately over one of the next three years.

But the dual choice will make it tough for financial analysts to compare corporate financial results.

Standards No. 106 to provide accounting standards for retirement benefits other than pensions.[22]

SFAS No. 106 parallels closely accounting for pensions under *SFAS No. 87* in most important respects. For that reason, and in an effort to limit the technical complexity of our coverage of accounting for retirement benefits, we provide only an overview of accounting for other retirement benefits.

A defined benefit postretirement plan is one that defines the postretirement benefits in terms of monetary amounts (e.g., a fixed dollar amount of life insurance) or benefits covered (e.g., a maximum dollar per day of hospitalization). Such agreements represent an exchange between the employer and the employee. The employee

---

[22]*FASB Statement of Financial Accounting Standards No. 106,* "Employers' Accounting for Postretirement Benefits Other Than Pensions," 1990.

"It's an analyst's nightmare," said Pat McConnell, a managing director with Bear Stearns & Co. . . .

The new FASB rule also creates tricky new problems for business in designing health-plan changes. "The new FASB statement [rule] contains a lot of minefields that will trigger damage to the bottom line for unwary companies making such changes," warns Harold Dankner, a benefits-consulting partner in Washington, D.C., with Coopers & Lybrand, a major accounting firm based in New York. For example, the rule immediately penalizes reported profits if new health-plan changes aren't consistent with past practice, says Mr. Dankner.

Timothy Lucas, research director for FASB, the chief rule-making body for accountants, based in Norwalk, Conn., concedes that the new rule "does have a downside for financial analysis." Mr. Lucas says the dual accounting treatment "was in response to some corporate requests for relief" from the huge catch-up charge for the current work force.

But many companies are still riled at the FASB for not providing more relief from the rule. Currently, companies only deduct health-care benefits from profits as they are paid each year because, unlike pension benefits, such costs aren't tax-deductible.

Paul Lukens, chairman of a subcommittee on health-benefit accounting of the 13,500-member Financial Executives Institute, asked the FASB to ease the rule even further but was rejected.

Mr. Lukens asked the FASB to calculate benefits from the date of hire until actual retirement rather than the date of eligibility for benefits, which would have reduced the profit decline by as much as 15%. He asked the FASB to permit companies to deduct the accrual costs from retained earnings—where the reduction is less damaging to a company's stock-market performance and debt-raising—rather than profits. And he asked that a less-punitive index be used to measure such costs.

Many companies haven't yet decided whether to implement the rule now or over 20 years. "We're tilting toward a one-time hit but we still haven't made up our minds," said Earl Timmons, vice president and controller of Du Pont Co. in Wilmington, Del. "Why choose to hemorrhage your earnings over 20 years when you can get the entire hemorrhage behind you?" he says.

Some companies are reducing their health-care costs for retirees to ease the effect of the FASB rule, which has been under study for years. For example, American Telephone & Telegraph Co., for example, last year negotiated with its union to pay health-care benefits to retirees to a maximum fixed amount, based on years of service.

This dollar-denominated cap—in contrast to open-ended medical benefits that many companies offer retirees—will help reduce health costs from 30% to 50% in the future when retirees begin sharing premium costs in mid-1995, AT&T said.

And Grand Metropolitan PLC's Pillsbury subsidiary in Minneapolis is giving employees dollar credits for years of service to be applied to retiree health care.

Coopers & Lybrand's Mr. Dankner said that with the FASB rule, companies will have to be very careful to avoid immediate impact on their profits. "Its very tricky," he adds.

SOURCE: Lee Berton, "FASB Issues Rule Change on Benefits," *Wall Street Journal,* December 20, 1990, pp. A1, A4. Reprinted by permission.

provides services currently and the employer promises to provide certain retirement benefits in addition to current wages. Retirement benefits are appropriately viewed as a form of deferred compensation, the cost of which is logically recognized by the employer during the period of active employment of the individual who will receive benefits or whose beneficiaries or dependents will receive benefits.

The **expected postretirement benefit obligation** for an employer is the actuarial present value as of a particular date of the postretirement benefits expected to be paid to the employee, the employee's beneficiaries, and any covered dependents. This measurement is based on the expected amount and timing of future benefits, taking into consideration the expected future cost of providing the benefits and the extent to which those costs are shared by the employer, the employee, and others. The **accumulated postretirement benefit obligation** is the present value of all future benefits attributed to an employee's service rendered to the date of the evaluation.

Prior to the time that an employee attains full eligibility for the benefits in the plan, the accumulated obligation is a portion of the expected obligation. Once full eligibility is reached by the employee, the two are the same.

Net postretirement benefit cost, the name assigned the periodic expense associated with providing retirement benefits other than pensions, is made up of five diverse and offsetting components which parallel those we have already studied in accounting for pensions. These are summarized as follows:

Cost component	Impact on Net Postretirement Benefit Cost
Service cost	Increase
The portion of the expected postretirement benefit obligation attributed to employee services during that period.	
Interest cost	Increase
The increase in the accumulated postretirement benefit obligation to recognize the effects of the passage of time.	
Return on Plan Assets	Decrease
The change in the value of the plan assets, adjusted for contributions and benefit payments.	
Prior Service Cost	
The effects of plan amendments which increase or reduce benefits to employees.	
If benefits are increased	Increase
If benefits are reduced	Decrease
Gains and Losses	
Changes in the amount of the accumulated postretirement benefit obligation or plan assets resulting from experience different from that assumed or from changes in assumptions.	
If loss is recognized	Increase
If gain is recognized	Decrease

A sixth element of net periodic postretirement benefit cost may be required as part of the transition to the reporting requirements of *SFAS No. 106*. In the past, most companies accounted for postretirement benefits other than pensions on a cash basis. That is, they expensed benefits as they were paid rather than as they were earned by employees, provided no funding in advance of the time benefits were paid and recognized no obligation for the provision of benefits. One alternative for implementing *SFAS No. 106* is to recognize the previously-unrecognized obligation for retirement benefits gradually over time as an increase in the amount of net periodic postretirement cost. When this is done, the addition to the amount of expense recognized is the sixth component.

As is the case in accounting for pensions, detailed disclosures are required for other retirement benefits. These focus on the components of the periodic expense recognized in the determination of income and the funded status of the plan.

CONCLUDING REMARKS

Three distinct features of accounting under *SFAS No. 87 and No. 106* warrant noting as we complete our study of accounting for retirement benefits—the delayed recognition feature, the net cost feature, and the offsetting feature.

The *delayed recognition* feature means that changes in the retirement obligation and changes in the value of plan assets are not recognized in the employer's financial statements as they occur but are recognized systematically and gradually over subsequent periods. All changes are eventually recognized except to the extent that they are offset by subsequent changes, but at any point changes that have been identified and quantified await subsequent accounting recognition as net cost components and as liabilities and assets.

The *net cost* feature means that the recognition consequences of events and transactions affecting a retirement plan are reported as a single net amount in the employer's income statement. This approach results in the aggregation of at least three items that might be reported separately for any other part of an employer's operations: the compensation (service) cost, the interest cost related to deferred payment of benefits, and the results of investing what are often significant amounts of assets (return on plan assets).

Finally, the *offsetting* feature means that values of assets contributed to a plan, and obligations for pensions and other benefits are shown net in the employer's statement of financial position (balance sheet), even though the liability has not been settled and the assets may be controlled, and substantial risks and rewards associated with both are clearly borne by the employer.[23]

KEY POINTS

1. Retirement plans are complex arrangements whereby employers provide pension payments and other benefits to retired employees for services rendered during their periods of active employment. (Objective 1)

2. For employers with defined benefit pension plans, determining the cost of such plans involves a series of complex actuarial calculations that rely to a significant degree on actuarial assumptions, such as mortality rates, employee turnover, interest rates, future compensation levels, and so on. (Objective 2)

3. Net periodic pension cost is determined by combining five distinct components—service cost, interest cost, return on plan assets, recognition of gain or loss, and amortization of prior service cost. Determining pension expense is necessary because of the matching principle. (Objective 3)

4. Prepaid/accrued pension cost is recognized for the difference between pension expense and the amount of assets funded into the pension plan to satisfy the pension obligation. (Objective 4)

5. An additional liability may be required if the amount of accumulated benefit obligation at the end of the accounting period exceeds the fair value of the plan assets. To offset that liability, an intangible asset is recorded, but that asset is limited to the amount of unrecognized prior service cost. To the extent that the required liability exceeds the amount of unrecognized prior service cost, stockholders' equity is reduced. (Objective 4)

6. Employers must maintain records of the value of plan assets, projected benefit obligation, unrecognized gain or loss and unamortized prior service cost in order to properly account for pension plans, even though these items do not appear in the employer's financial statements. (Objective 5)

7. Several financial statement disclosures are required for defined benefit pension plans. These disclosures focus on the components of net periodic pension cost and the funded status of the plan. (Objective 6)

8. Accounting for retirement benefits other than pensions parallels closely accounting for pension benefits. (Objective 6)

---

[23]*SFAS No. 87*, Summary.

QUESTIONS

24–1   Discuss the nature of the relationship among the employer, employee, and pension plan.

24–2   What is a defined **contribution** pension plan? What are the major characteristics of such a plan?

24–3   What is a defined **benefit** pension plan? How do the major characteristics of a defined benefit plan differ from those of a defined contribution plan?

24–4   List and describe some of the uncertainties in estimating the employer's future pension commitment for a defined benefit pension plan.

24–5   Why is accrual accounting appropriate for pension plans?

24–6   What is the "service cost" of a pension plan?

24–7   For financial reporting purposes under *SFAS No. 87,* when is it appropriate to recognize a pension liability?

24–8   List the five primary components of net periodic pension cost. Briefly describe each.

24–9   Under what circumstances must a component of net periodic pension cost be included for the recognition of gain or loss?

24–10   How are prior service costs accounted for?

24–11   Why does the FASB provide for the amortization of prior service cost over future periods rather than by immediate recognition?

24–12   How does the accountant determine whether an additional pension liability is required (i.e., a liability in addition to the difference between the expense recognized and the cash paid into the pension fund)?

24–13   What is the rationale for recognizing an intangible pension asset when an additional pension liability is established?

24–14   How do interest rate assumptions affect the pension expense recognized for the period?

24–15   What is the relationship between the two following components of net periodic pension cost: *return on plan assets* and *gain or loss.*

24–16   Two of the components of net periodic pension cost may be negative costs (i.e., reductions in pension expense). Which components are these, and why do they reduce pension expense?

24–17   What procedures included in *SFAS No. 87* are specifically designed to reduce volatility in the recognition of pension expense from year to year?

24–18   Briefly explain the net cost feature of *SFAS No. 87.*

24–19   Briefly explain the offsetting feature of *SFAS No. 87.*

24–20   Explain the nature of retirement benefits other than pensions and briefly outline the accounting procedures for these benefits as indicated in *SFAS No. 106.*

EXERCISES

24–21   EXPENSE AND FUNDING ENTRIES   Rosser, Inc., has correctly determined its net periodic pension cost as $125,000 for the current year.

Instructions

Prepare the general journal entries to record pension expense and funding under each of the following *independent* situations:

[a] Rosser, Inc., funds the same amount as the expense.
[b] Rosser, Inc., funds $145,000.
[c] Rosser, Inc., funds $117,000.

24–22   EXPENSE AND FUNDING ENTRIES   R&B Company determines its net periodic pension cost to be $175,000 in 1992 and $185,000 in 1993.

Instructions

[a] If the company funds $162,000 in 1992 and $175,000 in 1993, prepare the appropriate general journal entries and determine the amount of any prepaid or accrued expense to be reported in the balance sheet for each year.

[b] If the company funds $195,000 in 1992 and $200,000 in 1993, prepare the appropriate general journal entries and determine the amount of any prepaid or accrued expense to be reported in the balance sheet for each year.

24–23   FINANCIAL STATEMENT ELEMENTS   Barlow, Inc., has the following balances in pension-related accounts as of January 1, 1992.

Fair value of plan assets	$100,000
Projected benefit obligation	(80,000)
Prepaid/accrued pension cost	$ 20,000

During the year, the company's accountant determines that service cost is $25,000. Interest cost is to be recognized as 10% on the projected benefit obligation and the estimated and actual return on plan assets is also 10%.

Instructions

[a] Determine pension expense for the year, identifying the individual components.

[b] Determine the amount of prepaid/accrued pension cost that will appear in the balance sheet at the end of 1992 under each of the following independent situations:

[1] The company funds $30,000 into the pension plan at the end of the year.

[2] The company funds $15,000 into the pension plan at the end of the year.

24–24   FINANCIAL STATEMENT ELEMENTS   Stoudt, Inc., has the following balances in pension-related items on June 1, the first day of its 1992 fiscal year:

Fair value of plan assets	$ 575,000
Projected benefit obligation	(628,000)
Prepaid/accrued pension cost	$(53,000)

The company's actuary has determined service cost for the year beginning June 1, 1992, as $65,800. He also informs Stoudt's accountant that the interest cost and return-on-asset components of net periodic pension cost should be calculated at 10%.

Instructions

[a] Determine the amount of pension expense that will be recognized during the year beginning June 1, 1992, identifying the amounts of the individual components.

[b] Determine the amount of prepaid/accrued pension cost that will appear in the balance sheet at May 31, 1993, under each of the following independent assumptions:

[1] Stoudt funds $50,000 into the pension fund at the end of the year.

[2] Stoudt funds $90,000 into the pension fund at the end of the year.

24–25   SERVICE AND INTEREST COST   On January 1, 1992, Delta Company agrees to pay a lump-sum pension to George Parker, the company's only employee, equal to 5% of his final year's pay times the number of years worked after January 1, 1992. You estimate that George's salary for 2000, his last year with the company, will be $75,000.

Instructions

Determine the service and interest portions of net periodic pension cost for 1992 and 1993, assuming an appropriate interest rate of 12%.

24–26   EXPECTED RETURN ON PLAN ASSETS   Disc, Inc., has a defined benefit pension plan with plan assets having a fair value of $100,000 at January 1, 1992. The company expects a 12% return on plan assets and the expected value of those assets at January 1, 1992 is also $100,000. The fair value of the plan assets increased to $135,000 at January 1, 1993.

Instructions

[a] Determine the expected return on plan assets component of net periodic pension cost for 1992 and 1993.

[b] Will the computation of net periodic pension cost include a component for recognition of gain or loss in either 1992 or 1993? Explain your answer for both years.

24–27   RECOGNITION OF GAIN AND LOSS   Ray, Inc., has a defined benefit pension plan with an expected value of plan assets and a projected benefit obligation of $2,000,000 at the beginning of 1992. The company has determined that its average remaining service period of active employees at that date is 10 years.

Instructions

Determine the amount of gain or loss to be recognized, if any, in each of the following *independent* situations:

[a] The fair value of plan assets at January 1, 1992, is $1,500,000.

[b] The fair value of plan assets at January 1, 1992, is $2,400,000.

24–28   PRIOR SERVICE COST AMORTIZATION   Bradley, Inc., amends its pension plan, resulting in a prior service cost of $110,000. The company has three employees who are expected to retire as follows:

Employee	Expected retirement
Jones	Two years from plan amendment
Rogers	Four years from plan amendment
Wallace	Five years from plan amendment

Instructions

Prepare an amortization schedule for the prior service cost, assuming amortization over the future service period of the three employees.

24–29   BALANCE SHEET PRESENTATION OF PENSION LIABILITY   Berton Company has a defined benefit pension plan which has been in existence for several years. As of the end of 1992, a total of $125,000 of net periodic pension cost has been recognized in previous years, of which $115,000 has been funded.

At the end of 1992, the accumulated benefit obligation totals $165,000 and the fair value of plan assets is $180,000.

Instructions

Determine the item(s) and amount(s) that will appear in the company's balance sheet at the end of 1992, relative to the pension plan. Briefly explain your answer.

24–30   EXPECTED RETURN AND GAIN/LOSS   At January 1, 1992, Whitt, Inc., has a defined benefit pension plan with plan assets as follows:

Fair value	$275,000
Expected value	200,000

Other relevant information is as follows:

[1] The projected benefit obligation is less than the fair value of the plan assets.

[2] Administrators of the plan expect an 8% return on plan assets.

[3] Service cost and interest components of net periodic pension expense for 1992 have been computed as $70,000 and $35,000, respectively.

[4] The average service period of employees benefitting from the plan is 15 years.

[5] No prior service costs exist.

Instructions

Determine net periodic pension cost for 1992, identifying each component separately.

24–31 PRIOR SERVICE COST AMORTIZATION   MBZ Corporation amends its defined benefit pension plan, resulting in a significant amount of prior service cost due to the retroactive application of certain plan amendments that increased employee benefits.

The employees affected by the plan amendments are described as follows:

Group	Number of employees	Remaining years of service
A	2	5
B	5	7
C	6	9

Instructions

[a] Prepare a schedule that identifies the amortization fraction to be used, assuming the company decides to amortize the prior service cost over the remaining service period of those employees expected to benefit from the plan amendment. Specifically indicate the amortization fraction for the first, sixth, and ninth years.

[b] If management indicates a preference for the straight-line amortization method, what would you propose as the maximum appropriate number of years? Justify your answer.

24–32 RECOGNITION OF LOSS   Four independent companies have determined their projected benefit obligation and fair value of plan assets for 1992 as follows:

Company	Projected Benefit Obligation	Fair Value of Plan Assets	Remaining Service Period of Affected Employees
A	$1,000,000	$ 800,000	10
B	1,300,000	1,070,000	6
C	1,550,000	1,600,000	5
D	1,600,000	1,900,000	7

The amount of unrecognized loss for companies A, B, C, and D, respectively, is $70,000, $180,000, $185,000, and $150,000.

Instructions

Prepare a table determining the amount of recognition of loss that is required, if any, for each company. Include in your table the following columnar headings: projected benefit obligation, fair value of plan assets, corridor, unrecognized loss, and amount recognized.

24–33 ADDITIONAL LIABILITY ENTRIES   Mills, Inc., has had a defined benefit pension plan for several years. In the past, the company has funded the amount of net periodic pension cost recognized. Also, the accumulated benefit obligation had always been less than the fair value of the plan assets.

In 1992, however, these variables changed. Net periodic pension cost was computed at $255,000, but the company funded only $200,000 due to a cash shortage. Also, at the end of the year the accumulated benefit obligation was $1,488,000, but the fair value of plan assets was only $1,400,000. The unrecognized prior service cost at the end of 1992 totaled $50,000.

Instructions

Prepare the general journal entries necessary to record pension expense and funding and the pension liabilities at the end of 1992.

24–34 ADDITIONAL LIABILITY ENTRIES   Winston, Inc., has always funded the amount of its net periodic pension cost each year in the past, and the amount of its accumulated benefit obligation has consistently been less than the fair value of the pension plan's assets. In 1992, however, the company placed $340,000 in its pension plan, even though the expense for the year was only $325,000.

In preparing the adjusting entries at the end of the year, the following additional information has been accumulated:

Fair value of plan assets at December 31	$1,415,000
Amount of unrecognized prior service cost at December 31	65,000
Accumulated benefit obligation at December 31	1,500,000

Instructions

Prepare the general journal entries required to record pension expense and funding and the pension liabilities at the end of 1992.

24–35   PENSION EXPENSE DETERMINATION WITH ENTRY   Missoula, Inc., is preparing its entries to record pension expense and funding for 1992 and has determined the following information:

[1] Service cost for the year is $119,000.

[2] Both interest cost and the return on plan assets are $12,500 for the year.

[3] An unrecognized loss of $48,000 exists at the beginning of 1992. The corridor has been computed as $25,000 and the recognition is to be over an eight-year period.

[4] Unrecognized prior service cost totals $30,000, and the amortization fraction for 1992 is 4/20.

[5] The company plans to fund $100,000 for the year.

Instructions

[a] Determine the amount of net periodic pension cost for 1992, indicating the amount of each component and including required calculations.

[b] Prepare the general journal entry to record the expense and funding for 1992.

24–36   PENSION EXPENSE DETERMINATION WITH ENTRY   Frank Company has determined the following concerning its defined benefit pension plan as of June 30, 1992, the end of its fiscal year:

Service cost component of pension expense for 1992	$525,000
Interest cost component of pension expense for 1992	60,000
Expected return on plan assets for 1992	80,000
Recognition of gain or loss for 1992 (see instructions)	10,000
Amortization of unrecognized prior service cost for 1992	15,000

Instructions

Identify the components of pension expense and prepare the general journal entry to record the pension expense and funding for 1992 in each of the following independent situations:

[a] The recognition of gain or loss represents a *gain* and the company pays $475,000 into the pension plan.

[b] The recognition of gain or loss represents a *loss* and the company pays $550,000 into the pension plan.

PROBLEMS

24–37   FINANCIAL STATEMENT ELEMENTS   Ashland, Inc., has the following pension-related account balances on January 1, 1992:

Fair value of plan assets	$ 157,500
Projected benefit obligation	(174,200)
Prepaid/accrued pension cost	($16,700)

During 1992, the service cost as measured by the pension plan's actuary was $28,500 and the appropriate interest-rate assumption for determining interest cost is 12%. In addition, the return on plan assets (both expected and actual) was 12%. Ashland funded $25,000 into the pension plan during the year.

Instructions

[a] Prepare the general journal entry to record pension expense and funding for 1992. Provide supporting computations for the amounts in your entry.

[b] Determine the financial statement elements related to pensions for the 1992 statements.

[c] Why did the accrued pension expense increase during the year? (Explain briefly.)

[d] Reconcile the balance in the Prepaid/Accrued Pension Cost account with the memorandum record amounts of fair value of plan assets and projected benefit obligation.

24–38   FINANCIAL STATEMENT ELEMENTS   Ojo, Inc., has pension-related accounts in its memorandum records as follows:

Fair value of plan assets	$ 580,000
Projected benefit obligation	(475,000)
Prepaid/accrued pension cost	$ 105,000

During 1992, service cost was $75,500, interest cost is to be recognized at 10%, and the return on assets is also 10%. The company has no prior service cost or accumulated unrecognized gain or loss.

Instructions

[a] Determine the amount of pension expense, carefully identifying each component and providing computations where appropriate.

[b] Prepare the general journal entry to record pension expense and funding, assuming $75,000 was deposited in the pension fund at the end of the year. Provide a reconciliation of the memorandum records for the projected benefit obligation and the fair value of plan assets and the amount of the prepaid/accrued pension cost at the end of 1992.

[c] Repeat instruction [b], assuming that the company funded only $60,000 at the end of 1992.

[d] Briefly explain the difference in the impact on the financial statements in [b] and [c].

24–39 COMPONENTS OF NET PERIODIC PENSION COST The management of Baltic, Inc., makes a pension commitment to an employee to pay 10% of her terminal salary per year for each year of service. The commitment is made at the beginning of 1992; the employee is expected to retire at the end of 1998. A single payment is to be made at retirement.

Actuarial estimates indicate that 12% is the appropriate rate to use in determining the interest component of net periodic pension cost. The expected salary for the employee for 1998 is $78,000. A 15% rate of return is expected on plan assets.

Each year the net periodic pension cost is fully funded. The fair value of the plan assets is as follows:

Year-end	Fair Value of Plan Assets
1992	$ 3,952
1993	9,500
1994	15,000

The fair value of plan assets listed above includes the amount funded on the last day of each year, as well as the accumulation of amounts, plus earnings, from previous years.

Instructions

Determine the amount of net periodic pension cost for Baltic, Inc., for 1992, 1993, and 1994. Carefully detail your computations, including appropriate explanations for components that are not included in any year.

24–40 PRIOR SERVICE COST AMORTIZATION On May 1, 1992, Wynn Company established a pension plan for its seven employees. An actuary engaged by the company has calculated the past service cost to be a total of $108,000. The employees are expected to work the following numbers of years to retirement:

Employee	Years to Retirement
A, B	2
C, D, E	3
F	6
G	8

Instructions

[a] Prepare the schedule needed to compute the amortization fraction for each year over which the prior service cost will be amortized. Assume amortization is to be over the expected remaining period of active employment of the seven employees.

[b] Determine the dollar amount of amortization of prior service cost for each fiscal year, assuming the company's financial reporting period is May 1–April 30.

[c] What is the longest period over which prior service costs could be amortized if Wynn chose to use the straight-line method?

[d] Briefly explain how the amortization of prior service costs results in less volatility in net periodic pension cost when compared with alternative accounting treatments.

24–41   EXPECTED RETURN/GAIN AND LOSS RECOGNITION   Nunn, Inc., has a defined benefit pension plan for its employees. At the beginning of 1992, both the actual and expected amounts of the projected benefit obligation were $100,000. Both amounts grew at a rate of 12% per year through 1993 and 1994.

At the beginning of 1992, the fair value of the plan assets was $120,000, while the expected value was only $100,000. The company expects a return of 15% on the beginning fair value of plan assets for each year. The actual values of the plan assets at the end of 1992 and 1993 were $200,000 and $260,000, respectively.

During 1992–1994, actuaries expect employees who worked during each year to remain active for approximately six more years.

Instructions

[a] Prepare a schedule comparing the expected and actual amounts of the projected benefit obligation and the value of plan assets. Include in your schedule an amount representing the under- or overperformance of the plan assets at the beginning of each year, 1992–1994.

[b] Determine the amount of the gain or loss that should be recognized, if any, for each year as part of net periodic pension cost. If none should be recognized, explain why. Specifically identify the corridor for each year.

[c] Prepare a schedule indicating the amounts of the following components of net periodic pension cost for each year: Return on plan assets, interest, and gain or loss recognition. (For purposes of this problem, you may ignore the service and prior service cost amortization components.)

[d] Briefly explain how the procedure you have applied for recognizing gain or loss reduces the volatility in the amount of pension expense recognized each year.

24–42   PENSION COMPONENT ANALYSIS   Onker, Inc., has a balance in its prepaid/accrued pension cost of ($116,000) at the beginning of 1992, a liability position. The fair value of plan assets totals $785,000 and the projected benefit obligation totals $901,000.

During 1992 service cost of $120,000 is determined by the company's actuary. The interest cost component of net periodic pension cost is determined at 12% on the projected benefit obligation and the return on assets is also determined at 12%. (Expected and actual return are the same, no prior service cost exists, and no unrecognized gain or loss exists.)

At the end of 1992, management decides to fund $120,000 into the pension plan even though this is not the precise amount of the expense to be recognized for the year.

Instructions

[a] Prepare a worksheet analysis of the pension accounts similar to that in Exhibit 24–4 in the text. Provide an explanation for the entries in your worksheet and for the calculations that are required to determine the components of net periodic pension cost.

[b] Prepare the general journal entry to record pension expense for 1992.

[c] Reconcile the difference between the pension expense recognized and the pension funding with the change in the prepaid/accrued pension cost during the period.

24–43   ADDITIONAL PENSION LIABILITY   Boatman, Inc., has a defined benefit pension plan that covers all of its salaried employees. At the beginning of 1993, the Prepaid/Accrued Pension Cost account had a $10,000 credit balance. Management has accurately determined the following information for 1993 and 1994:

	1993	1994
Net periodic pension cost for year	$124,500	$128,000
Funding into pension plan at end of year	115,000	120,000
Accumulated benefit obligation at end of year	560,000	625,000
Fair value of plan assets at end of year	528,000	530,000
Unrecognized prior service cost at end of year	40,000	35,000

Instructions

[a] Record the recognition of pension expense and the funding into the pension plan for each year, as well as the recognition of the additional pension liability, if required. Provide details of your computations.

[b] In comparative columns for 1993 and 1994, indicate the amounts that will appear in the income statements and balance sheets at the end of each year that relate directly to the pension plan.

24–44 CORRECTION OF PENSION ERROR/ADDITIONAL LIABILITY You have been selected as auditor for Metz, Inc., as of 1993. The company has a defined benefit pension plan for its employees that has been in operation for several years. Prior to 1992, the company's accountant had properly accounted for the recognition of net periodic pension cost. In 1992, however, due to a change in personnel an inexperienced bookkeeper had simply recorded the pension expense as the amount of cash funded into the plan—$8,000. The proper amount of expense for the year was $10,000. You also determine that the amount of accumulated benefit obligation was less than the fair value of plan assets. (The inexperienced bookkeeper had not recorded an additional liability.) A credit balance of $1,000 is carried forward from previous years in the account, Prepaid/Accrued Pension Cost.

You have accumulated the following information for 1993:

Net periodic pension cost	$12,000
Funding into pension plan	9,000
Accumulated benefit obligation	91,000
Fair value of plan assets	82,500
Unrecognized prior service cost	26,000

Instructions

[a] Prepare the general journal entries required to correct for the 1992 error in recording the pension and to record the 1993 pension expense and funding and the additional liability.

[b] Assume the following information for 1994:

Net periodic pension cost	$ 13,000
Funding into pension plan	10,500
Accumulated benefit obligation	100,000
Fair value of plan assets	101,000
Unrecognized prior service cost	24,000

Prepare the general journal entries required to record the pension for 1994.

[c] Describe how your answer to part [b] would have been different if the fair value of plan assets had been only $91,000, rather than $101,000.

24–45 ADDITIONAL PENSION LIABILITY Vester Manufacturing Company has a defined benefit pension plan that has been in operation for several years. At the end of 1992, the company's balance sheet includes the following items related to this pension plan:

Prepaid/Accrued pension cost (debit balance)	$25,700
Additional pension liability (credit balance)	72,000
Intangible pension asset (debit balance)	72,000

Management has correctly determined the following information for 1993 and 1994:

	1993	*1994*
Net periodic pension cost for year	$150,000	$162,500
Funding into pension plan for year	150,000	150,000
Accumulated benefit obligation at end of year	751,000	865,000
Fair value of plan assets at end of year	655,000	835,000
Unrecognized prior service cost at end of year	67,000	60,000

Instructions

[a] For 1993, prepare the general journal entries required to record the annual expense and funding and the adjustment to the additional liability. Indicate the financial statement amounts that relate to the pension plan, including detailed calculations.

[b] Repeat requirement [a] for 1994.

24–46 COMPONENTS OF NET PERIODIC PENSION COST   Skadden, Inc., initiated a pension plan for its president, George S. Skadden, on January 1, 1992. Skadden is expected to work through the end of 2002. Terms of the pension plan and other information concerning the plan are as follows:

[1] The plan was originally planned to pay Skadden 4% per year of service, times his terminal salary in a single lump-sum on his retirement date. At the beginning of 1994 the company decided to increase the percentage to 6%, with all other aspects of the pension remaining the same. This amendment is to be applied retroactively.

[2] Management expects Skadden's salary in the year 2002 to be $150,000.

[3] An interest rate of 10% is determined to be appropriate for purposes of calculating the interest component of net periodic pension cost.

[4] A 12% return is expected on assets invested in the pension plan. The amount invested in the plan each year and the fair value of the plan assets at the end of each year are as follows:

Year-end	Amount Invested	Accumulated Fair Value
1992	$2,000	$2,000
1993	2,000	5,500
1994	3,000	8,800

Instructions

[a] For each year, 1992–1994, determine the five components of net periodic pension cost: service, interest, prior service amortization, return on plan assets, and gain or loss recognition. If no amount exists for one or more component(s) in any year, indicate that fact.

[b] Prepare the general journal entries to record the pension expense and funding for each year.

24–47 PENSION COMPONENT ANALYSIS   Jollay, Inc., began 1992 with the following balances in pension-related accounts: fair value of plan assets, $95,000 debit; projected benefit obligation, $110,000 credit; unamortized prior service cost, $25,000 debit; unrecognized gain, $17,000 credit; prepaid/accrued pension cost, $7,000 credit.

During 1992, the following events and transactions take place:

[a] Service cost is $18,500, as determined by the company's actuary.

[b] Interest cost on the projected benefit obligation is to be determined at 12%.

[c] Return on assets is 12% (both expected and actual).

[d] Prior service cost is to be amortized over a 10-year period.

[e] Gain and loss recognition, if required, is to be over a 10-year period.

[f] The company funds $25,000 into the pension plan at year-end.

[g] The projected benefit obligation is reevaluated at the end of the year, resulting in a $2,800 loss (i.e., the projected benefit obligation requires a $2,800 increase due to unexpected changes in various actuarial assumptions).

[h] Pension benefits are paid in the amount of $19,900.

Instructions

[a] Prepare a pension information analysis, similar to that in Exhibits 24–7 and 24–8, for Jollay, Inc., for 1992. Key your entries to the items of information presented in the problem above.

[b] Prepare the general journal entry to record the pension plan for the year, indicating the detailed computation of the components of net periodic pension cost (i.e., pension expense).

[c] Assume that no additional pension liability was required at the beginning of 1992 and that the accumulated benefit obligation at the end of 1992 is $119,000. Prepare the general journal entry, if any, required to record the additional pension liability.

[d] Determine the financial statement elements that will appear in the company's 1992 balance sheet and income statement.

24–48 PENSION COMPONENT ANALYSIS   Fowler, Inc., has the following pension-related items in its memorandum records at the beginning of 1992.

	Balances	
	Debit	Credit
Fair value of plan assets	$425,000	
Projected benefit obligation		$375,000
Unamortized prior service cost	17,000	
Unrecognized loss	50,000	

During the year, the company determined that its service cost was $50,000 and that interest cost should be recognized at 10% on the projected benefit obligation. The expected return on plan assets was 10% but the actual return during the year was 12%. Prior service cost and any gain or loss is to be recognized over eight years.

Additional information is as follows:

Pension funding at the end of 1992	$60,000
Reevaluation of projected benefit obligation for experience differences (gain)	$10,000
Benefits paid during 1992	$20,000

Instructions

[a] Prepare an analysis of pension information for Fowler, Inc., for 1992 similar to that in Exhibits 24–7 and 24–8. Prepare details of the computed amounts included in the worksheet and identify your entries with an appropriate letter with description.

[b] Prepare the journal entry to recognize pension expense and funding for 1992.

[c] Identify the elements of the financial statements related to the pension plan for 1992.

[d] Describe the circumstances in which Fowler would be required to record an additional pension liability. Is this likely to be required for Fowler for 1992?

CASES

24–49 MISCELLANEOUS PENSION CONCEPTS   Jack Murphy, a young CPA who recently joined the accounting firm of Johnson, Smith and Jones, PC, has been asked to speak to the local chapter of a professional banking organization. Jack was an outstanding student at the local university, graduated two years ago with high honors, and received a commendation for high achievement on the CPA examination.

In asking Jack to speak to the group, the president asked him to address the pension accounting requirements of *FASB Statement of Financial Accounting Standards No. 87*. The president indicated that many companies encountered by the bankers have defined benefit pension plans that may significantly affect their financial statements.

Specifically, Jack determines that the following should be covered:

[1] Why accrual accounting is appropriate, rather than simply charging to expense the amount funded into the plan for the accounting period or the benefits paid employees during the period.

[2] A brief discussion of the components of net periodic pension cost.

[3] The major financial statement items that could appear in the financial statements that the bankers will encounter.

Instructions

[a] Help Jack prepare his response to these areas of pension accounting.

[b] Identify other areas of concern that you think the bankers should understand.

24–50 FINANCIAL-STATEMENT PRESENTATION   You are the auditor for High Fashion Company. The company's president, Gail West, has approached you with some questions concerning pension accounting. West is not an accountant, but she is an astute reader of financial statements and has obviously been doing her "homework" before your conversation. Her comments to you are as follows:

I observe what seems to me to be some inconsistency in reporting pensions by different companies. For example, some show prepaid/accrued pension expense as an asset and others show it as a liability. Surely it can't be both! Also, I notice that some

*companies have the following accounts in their balance sheets and others do not—
Intangible Pension Asset, Additional Pension Liability, and Excess of Additional
Pension Liability over Unrecognized Prior Service Cost. The accounting profession
must be in some degree of turmoil over pension accounting since companies are apparently using different systems of accounting for their pension plans.*

You have a meeting scheduled with West tomorrow and you are certain that some of these issues
will come up. Since you are uncertain which topics she will bring up, you feel it necessary to be
prepared on all fronts.

Instructions

How will you respond to the specific criticisms West has leveled at the accounting profession?

24–51   UNIQUE FEATURES OF PENSION ACCOUNTING   As an experienced professional, Mar-
garet Fowler, CPA is frequently called upon by members of her firm to present authoritative accounting pronouncements to staff personnel as part of the firm's continuing professional education
program.

Soon after the FASB issued its new pension pronouncements, a seminar was scheduled. Fowler
prepared her presentation, wrote an outline of *FASB Statements of Financial Accounting Standards
Nos. 87 and 88* and scheduled a half-day seminar on the subject. After an overview lecture by
Fowler, a young staff accountant asked the following questions:

*Hasn't the FASB incorporated some rather revolutionary approaches in these pro-
nouncements? For example, it seems to me that the periodic pension expense is a
conglomerate of several distinctly different items, some of which actually offset the
others. Also, there seems to be a conscious attempt on the part of the FASB to avoid
the recognition of certain items that took place during the accounting period by requiring that they be deferred and recognized over a long period of time. Is this correct? Finally, the FASB seems to encourage offsetting of assets and liabilities. Isn't it
true that assets and liabilities are usually presented separately rather than being
offset against each other?*

Instructions

If you were in Fowler's position as instructor for this seminar, how would you respond to these
assertions?

JUDGMENT CASES

24–52   UNUSUAL OPERATING CONDITIONS AND PENSION REPORTING   Hi-Tech, Inc., has a
highly skilled work force of scientists and engineers that are young, highly motivated, and well
compensated. Little turnover or attrition in this group is expected. These factors result in an actuarial determination that recognizes a relatively small pension expense in the early years of the plan but
will rise dramatically in later years as this work force nears retirement. This expense pattern results
generally from the FASB mandated actuarial benefit method that is used to attribute pension costs
to accounting periods.

The president and the board of directors of Hi-Tech have decided to fund amounts for the pension in excess of the amounts attributed by the benefit formula. This is being done for what you
consider sound business purposes. That is, the company wishes to use a cost-based actuarial
method for funding rather than the benefit-based method that, according to the FASB, must be used
for financial reporting purposes. This will allow the company to fund relatively similar amounts
over the life of the work force rather than small amounts in the early years and rapidly increasing
amounts in later years.

The president, however, does not wish to report the large prepaid cost that will result from the
company's funding policy. He would prefer to recognize the larger of the attribution amounts or the
amount funded each year as net periodic pension cost. The president has recently stated,

*Aren't you guys supposed to be conservative? What could warm the accountant's
heart more than stating expenses at a higher amount than you absolutely have to?*

Further, I think it might be misleading to report such a large prepaid pension cost because it will be many years before we really know what the actual obligation will be. Won't it be acceptable to recognize a larger expense in this case?

Instructions

Respond to the president's questions. Is his suggestion permissible? What ideas can you identify that might help the president in his desire to recognize a larger pension expense, if any?

24–53   RELYING ON ACTUARIES   As controller of Ocean Topics, Inc., you are interested in and responsible for seeing that the company's financial statements are presented fairly in conformity with GAAP. In the current period, the company's operations have not lived up to expectations and promises made by the president. While the company was still profitable, the president asserted in a speech made to the shareholders at the beginning of the year that higher operating profits would be achieved than now appear possible.

Against this background, the president has recently fired the firm of actuaries that performed the actuarial valuation of the company's defined benefit pension plan each year. She also sent you a new actuarial valuation of the plan conducted by other actuaries with whom you are not familiar. The new study reports a substantially lower net periodic pension cost than the study by the previous actuaries. The president has directed you to record the pension cost for the year on the basis of the new actuarial report without consideration of the old report. Out of concern for the change, you phone the old actuarial firm and talk with the actuary with whom you had previously worked. He states,

We were fired because the president did not like our numbers. She suggested that we were being overly conservative in a number of our assumptions about several actuarial factors. When we indicated that the amounts we had used were and continued to be our best estimates of the factors in question, she stated that unless we were willing to reconsider our position she would have to obtain the opinion of other, more reasonable, actuarial experts. My boss told her that our position was final and we immediately received a letter informing us that our services were no longer needed.

When you question the previous actuary about the new firm of actuaries, he responds,

Those guys have been around for a couple of years, but I don't know much about them. They don't seem interested in participating in the profession much. I certainly don't suggest that they are incompetent or dishonest. We have lost a couple of other clients to them. They seem to be willing to be quite aggressive in their assumptions. I certainly could not support some of the things they have come up with, but I am not aware of your specific situation.

Instructions

What course of action should you take at this time? Can you accept the work of the new actuaries without reservation or question? What responsibility does the accountant have when relying on specialists who have knowledge of matters that affect accounting measurements?

CHAPTER 25

Additional Disclosure Issues and Financial Analysis

OBJECTIVES

1. To explain interim reporting of financial information.
2. To explain the reporting of financial information for segments of a business enterprise.
3. To explore the nature of related-party transactions and the disclosures required by GAAP.
4. To explore the nature of financial instruments and the disclosures required by GAAP.
5. To explain the analysis of financial statements.

R ecall from Chapter 1 that the **objectives** of financial reporting are (1) to provide useful information in investment, credit, and similar decisions, (2) to provide information helpful in assessing cash flow prospects, and (3) to provide information about enterprise resources, claims to those resources, and changes in them. In Chapter 2, we discussed the disclosure principle, which calls for revealing information that will be useful in the decision-making processes of reasonably informed users. We also explained that complying with the disclosure principle requires a knowledge of GAAP, a knowledge of the circumstances involved, and professional judgment. As a part of most chapters that followed Chapter 2, we covered specific disclosure requirements related to such topics as inventories, depreciation, leases, pensions, and so forth.[1]

This chapter has two primary objectives: (1) to discuss and illustrate several important disclosure issues that we have not yet presented, and (2) to explain the analysis of financial statements. These objectives are related in that information disclosed by accountants comprises an important part of the information that investors, creditors, and others use to assess the financial health and prospects of particular enterprises. In this chapter we cover the disclosure of interim information, financial reporting for segments of a business enterprise, related-party transactions, disclosures about financial instruments, and analysis of financial statements.

INTERIM REPORTING

Annual financial statements are often not **timely** enough for investors and creditors, who make decisions throughout a year. Interim reporting means the presentation of financial information for periods of less than one year. Interim reports may be presented for semiannual, quarterly, or monthly periods. Quarterly periods are the most common. Although quarterly reports are usually much more condensed than annual reports, empirical research indicates that quarterly information is useful in decision making.[2]

As explained in Chapter 1, the SEC requires certain companies to file a Form 10–Q report, which includes quarterly financial information that has been reviewed but not audited by an independent CPA. These companies also typically distribute interim reports to their shareholders. The SEC also requires these companies to disclose certain quarterly information in the notes to their *annual* financial statements.

In 1973 the APB issued *Opinion No. 28*, which deals with interim financial reports.[3] This pronouncement provides accounting principles for companies to use when preparing interim reports. It also provides a list of the minimum information that publicly held companies must disclose in their interim reports.[4]

ALTERNATIVE INTERIM PERIOD VIEWS

Determining the results of business operations for intervals of less than a year is difficult. Wide fluctuations in revenue that are due to seasonal business patterns, for example, or substantial fixed costs incurred in a single interim period for the benefit of

---

[1]The nature of required disclosures is so extensive that most accountants use a **disclosure checklist** to ensure that all important disclosures have been made in a set of financial statements. Such a checklist summarizes the disclosures required by GAAP.

[2]For example, see George J. Foster, "Quarterly Accounting Data: Time Series Properties and Predictive-Ability Results," *The Accounting Review* (January 1977), pp. 1–21.

[3]*APB Opinion No. 28*, "Interim Financial Reporting," 1973.

[4]A publicly held company is one whose securities trade in a public market, either a stock exchange or the over-the-counter market. The minimum disclosures are discussed later in this chapter.

several periods complicate the determination of earnings on a short-term basis. Although the same problems may exist in annual reporting, the longer period allows the business cycle to more nearly complete its course, thereby offsetting some of the fluctuations.

The unique features of interim reporting have resulted in two basic positions concerning the nature of interim financial statements. These positions are the **discrete** or **independent view** and the **integral** or **dependent view.** Advocates of the discrete view of interim reporting regard each interim period as a basic accounting period, regardless of the length of time involved. The results of operations for each interim period would be determined in essentially the same way as for an annual period. In the determination of income, those accruals, deferrals, and estimations that would normally be applied for annual periods are also applied for interim periods.

Advocates of the integral view see each interim period as an important part of the annual period and emphasize this feature in reporting results of operations. Accruals, deferrals, and estimates required at the end of each interim period are applied in the context of expected annual results of operations. Allocations among interim periods are sometimes made to reflect the relationship of the interim period to the annual period, whereas the same allocation between annual periods would not be appropriate.

To illustrate the difference between the discrete and integral views, assume that a company launches a major advertising campaign in January. Although the costs are incurred entirely in the first quarter, the company expects results throughout the year. Applying the discrete view of interim reporting, the entire cost of the advertising campaign should be expensed in the first quarter because advertising would ordinarily not be carried forward as a prepaid expense at the end of an accounting period. Within the integral view of interim reporting, however, an expense such as advertising might be allocated among four quarters in order to more clearly reflect the relationship of each quarter's results of operations to the annual period.

The APB took the position that the usefulness of interim financial information depends on the **relationship that it has to annual results of operations.** Therefore, the board concluded that each interim period should be viewed as an **integral part** of the corresponding annual period. In general, financial information presented in interim reports should be based on the accounting principles used by the enterprise in its annual reporting unless an accounting change has occurred. However, because of the unique nature of the interim period as a part of a longer period, certain modifications in accounting principles may be necessary for the interim information to better relate to annual results of operations.

BASIC ACCOUNTING PRINCIPLES FOR INTERIM REPORTING

Revenues from products sold or services rendered are generally recognized for interim periods on the same basis as for the annual period. Methods of revenue recognition that are used in annual reporting, such as the percentage-of-completion method on long-term contracts, should be followed in interim reports as well.

The recognition of expenses in interim periods is more complex. Expenses for interim reporting purposes are classified in two categories: (1) those associated directly with revenue, and (2) all other expenses.

Matching   Expenses associated directly with revenue are matched against revenue in those interim periods in which the related revenue is recognized. Examples of expenses associated directly with revenue are costs of materials; wages, salaries, and related fringe benefits; manufacturing overhead; and warranties.

The application of traditional inventory methods in determining the inventory and cost of goods sold at the end of interim periods raises some interesting questions. The practical problems are significant. Also, the application of annual inventory procedures for interim periods may produce interim figures that would not, when added together, equal the annual figures. As a result, practices vary in determining the cost of inventory at the end of interim periods. While essentially the same procedures used for annual reporting should also be used at interim dates, several exceptions are appropriate at interim dates:[5]

1. Some companies use estimated gross margin rates to determine the cost of goods sold during interim periods or use other methods different from those used at annual inventory dates. (We discussed this method of inventory estimation in Chapter 9.) These companies should disclose the method used at the interim date and any significant adjustments that result from reconciliations with the annual physical inventory.

2. Companies that use LIFO may encounter a liquidation of base period inventories at an interim date that is expected to be replaced by the end of the annual period. In such cases the inventory at the interim reporting date should not give effect to the LIFO liquidation, and cost of sales for the interim reporting period should include the *expected cost of replacing* the liquidated LIFO base.

3. Inventory losses from market declines should not be deferred beyond the interim period in which the decline occurs. Recoveries of such losses on the same inventory in later interim periods of the same fiscal year through market price recoveries should be recognized as gains in the later interim period. Such gains should not exceed losses recognized in previous interim periods. Some market declines at interim dates, however, can reasonably be expected to be restored in the fiscal year. Such *temporary* market declines need not be recognized at the interim date because no loss is expected for the fiscal year.

4. Companies that use standard cost accounting systems for determining inventory and product costs should generally follow the same procedures in reporting purchase price, wage rate, usage or efficiency variances from standard cost at the end of an interim period as followed at the end of a fiscal year. Purchase price variances or volume or capacity cost variances that are planned and expected to be absorbed by the end of the annual period, should ordinarily be deferred at interim reporting dates. The effect of unplanned or unanticipated purchase price or volume variances, however, should be reported at the end of an interim period following the same procedures used at the end of a fiscal year.

The influence of the integral view of financial reporting is evident in these procedures. For example, in the case of the last-in, first-out (LIFO) liquidation (item 2 of the preceding list) the procedure to be followed in the interim period is based on the desire to apply LIFO on an annual basis. Therefore, any LIFO liquidation that takes place in an interim period but which is expected to be replaced by the end of the annual period is not treated as a LIFO liquidation in the interim period. Similarly, if market declines in inventory at interim dates are temporary and are expected to be recovered by the end of the annual period (item 3 of the preceding list), no loss is recognized in the interim period. In these cases the interim report should present figures that are most indicative of expected annual results rather than those obtained by

---

[5]*APB Opinion No. 28*, par. 14.

strictly applying GAAP in each interim period as they would be applied in an annual period.

All other expenses (i.e., those not directly associated with revenue) should be recognized in interim periods as incurred or be allocated among interim periods on the basis of an estimate of time expired, benefit received, or activity associated with the period. The objective of recognizing expenses is to achieve a fair measure of **results of operations for the annual period** and to present fairly the **financial position at the end of the annual period.** To meet this objective, procedures may be followed at the end of an interim period that would normally not be followed at the end of an annual period. Assume, for example, that a cost (such as repair and maintenance) usually expensed for annual reporting purposes is incurred in one interim period but clearly benefits two or more interim periods. Accruals or deferrals should then be used to charge an appropriate portion of the annual cost to each interim period. However, if no discernible benefits exist, arbitrary amounts should not be allocated among interim periods.

The amounts of certain expenses that can be reasonably estimated at interim dates are subject to year-end adjustments. Examples are inventory shrinkage, uncollectible receivables, and discretionary year-end bonuses. As the year progresses, more reliable estimates of annual amounts are usually possible. Estimates should be made at interim dates, with consideration given to all available information that is expected to influence the amount of expense to be recognized for annual reporting purposes. Whenever possible, estimated expenses should be assigned to interim periods so that the interim periods bear a reasonable portion of the anticipated annual amount.

At this point you may want to refer to Appendix A of Chapter 5, where we discussed using a worksheet to prepare interim financial statements.

SPECIAL PRINCIPLES OF INTERIM REPORTING

The general principles just described apply to the recognition of a wide range of revenues and expenses in interim reports, but a number of unique problems are encountered when accounting principles that were originally designed for annual reporting are applied to interim reports. Several of these problems are discussed below.

Seasonal Revenues and Expenses

Revenues and expenses of certain businesses are subject to material seasonal variations. In these circumstances, to avoid the possible misinterpretation that interim results indicate estimated annual results, companies should disclose the seasonal nature of their business activities.

Disclosure

To further emphasize the relationship of interim information to information relating to the annual period, *APB Opinion No. 28* requires that companies present information either for year to date or for the last twelve months to date along with quarterly information. We discuss these and other specific disclosure requirements later in this chapter.

Income Taxes

Interim period income tax expense should reflect interperiod and intraperiod income tax allocation applicable in annual reporting. At the end of each interim period an estimate is made of the effective income tax rate expected for the annual period. This rate is then applied to income earned to date for that year. Any income tax recognized in previous interim periods is subtracted from the amount resulting from the above computation, and the difference is recognized as income tax expense in the current interim period. The estimate of the annual effective income tax rate should reflect anticipated investment tax credits, capital gains rates, and other information available from tax planning techniques. In arriving at this rate, no effect should be included for the income tax related to extraordinary or other items that will be reported on a net-of-tax basis when they are recognized.

For example, assume that during the first quarter of 1993 Atkins Company estimated its effective annual income tax rate to be 34%. Income before income tax for the first quarter was $485,000. During the second quarter of 1993, the estimate of the effective annual income tax rate was reduced to 32% because of revised plans to take advantage of certain income tax credits. Pretax financial income for the second quarter of 1993 was $650,000. The income tax expense for the first two quarters is determined in the schedule below:

First Quarter

Pretax financial income for first quarter of 1993	$485,000
Estimated annual income tax rate	34%
Income tax expense for first quarter	$164,900

Second Quarter

Pretax financial income for first quarter of 1993	$485,000	
Pretax financial income for second quarter of 1993	650,000	$1,135,000
Estimated annual income tax rate		32%
Income tax for first and second quarters of 1993		$ 363,200
Income tax expense recognized in first quarter		(164,900)
Income tax expense for second quarter		$ 198,300

The same process is followed for subsequent quarters as additional information on pretax financial income and the annual effective income tax rate becomes available.

Operating losses recognized in interim periods are subject to carryback and carryforward treatment similar to that discussed in Chapter 18 for annual periods. Operating losses of an interim period may be carried back to an earlier annual period or an earlier interim period of the year of the interim period loss. If carryback is not possible, interim period operating losses may be carried forward and recognized when the interim period loss is recognized *if realization is assured beyond a reasonable doubt* within the current annual period. An established pattern of losses in early interim periods offset by income in later interim periods may constitute this evidence if it appears that this pattern will continue in the current year. This accounting treatment is consistent with the integral interpretation of interim reporting, which emphasizes the relationship of amounts recognized in interim periods to related amounts recognized in annual periods.

Disclosure of Irregular Income Items

Materiality

Disclosure

Extraordinary items should be separately disclosed in the interim period in which they occur. The materiality of extraordinary items should be judged in relation to estimated income for the entire year. Gains and losses on disposal of a segment of a business and unusual or infrequently occurring transactions that are material with respect to the operating results of the interim period should be separately disclosed. Extraordinary items, gains and losses from segment disposals, and unusual or infrequently occurring items should *not be allocated* over several interim periods of the year in which they occur. Irregular income items that would be presented on a net-of-tax basis in an enterprise's annual financial statements, such as extraordinary items, are presented in the same manner in its interim financial statements.

Accounting Changes

The Accounting Principles Board recommended that accounting changes be made in the first interim period of a fiscal year. This recommendation is supported by the APB's belief that changes in accounting principles and methods made in later interim periods of a fiscal year tend to obscure operating results and complicate disclosure in interim periods. Accounting changes in interim periods should generally be accounted for in the same way as they would be in annual reporting. Chapter 19 discussed the proper procedures for accounting changes.

An exception is a change in accounting principle for which there is a cumulative effect that must be recognized in income in the period of change. If the change is made in the first interim period, accounting for the change is the same as in annual reporting, because the cumulative effect to the beginning of the first interim period is the same as the cumulative effect to the beginning of the annual period in which the change is made. However, a problem arises if a change in accounting principle is made in a subsequent interim period, because the cumulative effect to the beginning of the interim period of change is not the same as the cumulative effect to the beginning of the annual period. This difference is due to the additional time encompassed by the interim periods prior to the interim period of change. *FASB Statement of Financial Accounting Standards No. 3* gave special consideration to this problem and concluded that a cumulative effect type accounting change made in other than the first interim period should be accounted for **as if the change had been made in the first interim period.**[6] Income of previous interim periods of the fiscal year in which such a change is made should be restated, with consideration given to the impact of the change in the first interim period. This procedure is consistent with the **integral view** of interim reporting, because it makes the amount of the cumulative effect included in interim income the same as the amount to be included in the determination of annual income.

Adjustments of Previous Interim Periods

An item of profit or loss that occurs in an interim period may relate to previous annual periods or previous interim periods of the same year or both. Examples are settlements of litigation and adjustments of income taxes. If this type of event is recorded in an interim period other than the first interim period, the following guidelines should be followed:[7]

1. The portion of the item that is directly related to business activities of the current interim period should be included in the determination of net income for that period.
2. The portion of the item that relates to previous interim periods of the same annual period should be included in restated income of those periods.
3. The portion of the item that relates to previous annual periods should be included in the determination of net income of the first interim period of the year of the change.

DISCLOSURE REQUIREMENTS FOR INTERIM REPORTS

Disclosure   Most companies disclose interim financial information in considerably less detail than that provided in annual financial statements. When a company reports sum-

---

[6]*FASB Statement of Financial Accounting Standards No. 3,* "Reporting Accounting Changes in Interim Financial Statements," 1974, par. 10.
[7]*FASB Statement of Financial Accounting Standards No. 16,* "Prior Period Adjustments," 1977, par. 14.

marized financial information at interim dates, *at least* the following should be presented:[8]

1. Selected income statement items, as applicable:
    a. Sales or gross revenues.
    b. Provision for income taxes.
    c. Unusual or infrequently occurring items.
    d. Disposal of a segment of a business.
    e. Extraordinary items, including related income tax effects.
    f. Cumulative effect of an accounting change.
    g. Net income.
    h. Earnings per share.
2. Seasonal revenues, costs, or expenses.
3. Contingent items.
4. Changes in accounting principles or estimates, including significant changes in estimates or provision for income taxes.
5. Significant changes in financial position.

The above listing shows the *minimum* information that *APB Opinion No. 28* requires of publicly traded companies that report quarterly information on a regular basis. The APB encouraged such companies to publish condensed balance sheet and cash-flow information at interim dates because such information is often helpful to users of interim financial information in understanding and interpreting the income data that are reported.

When summarized financial information is regularly reported on a quarterly basis, information for the current quarter and the current year to date or last twelve months to date should be presented. In addition, similar information for the preceding year should be presented on a comparative basis. These disclosures are designed to facilitate **comparison** of the current quarter with a longer period of time (year to date or last twelve months) and with the comparable quarter of the previous year.

Disclosure   Many companies that report on a quarterly basis do not provide a separate fourth quarter statement, because the end of the fourth quarter coincides with the end of the annual reporting period. Where a separate fourth quarter report is not issued, significant events occurring in the fourth quarter should be separately disclosed in the notes to the annual financial statements.

The interim report for Fuqua Industries for the third quarter of 1990 is presented in Exhibit 25–1. Fuqua Industries is a consumer products and services company with four areas of business: lawn and garden, photo finishing, financial services and sporting goods. Their third quarter is for the period July 1 through September 30. The information presented is an abbreviated income statement for the comparative 1990 and 1989 third quarters and for the nine months through the third quarters for the two years. Also, an abbreviated balance sheet as of September 30, 1990, is presented.

SEGMENT REPORTING

In financial analysis, an important consideration is the industry in which the enterprise operates. The markets in which an enterprise buys and sells vary by industry. The risks and potential rewards of business operation vary considerably by industry. If an enterprise operates in a single industry, consideration of industry factors

---

[8]*APB Opinion No. 28*, par. 30.

EXHIBIT 25-1

Fuqua Industries
Interim Reporting Example

SUMMARY OF EARNINGS

In thousands except per share amounts	Three Months Ended September 30, 1990	Three Months Ended September 30, 1989	Nine Months Ended September 30, 1990	Nine Months Ended September 30, 1989
Net sales	$ 239,281	$ 233,674	$ 736,075	$ 712,222
Operating costs and expenses	(215,268)	(218,341)	(678,210)	(677,647)
Operating profit	24,013	15,333	57,865	34,575
Interest expense and other	(3,743)	(2,514)	(9,518)	(6,164)
Income before income taxes and minority interest	20,270	12,819	48,347	28,411
Provision for income taxes	11,821	8,969 [a]	23,156	14,584 [a]
Income before minority interest	8,449	3,850	25,191	13,827
Minority interest	(6,801)	(2,976)	(11,761)	(4,861)
Income from continuing operations	1,648	874	13,430	8,966
Discontinued operations	—	—	—	(805)
Income before extraordinary item	1,648	874	13,430	8,161
Extraordinary item[b]	977	—	977	—
Net income	$ 2,625	$ 874	$ 14,407	$ 8,161
Earnings Per Share of Common Stock—Primary				
Continuing operations	$.10	$.04	$.74	$ .42
Discontinued operations	—	—	—	(.04)
Extraordinary item[b]	.05	—	.05	—
Net Income	$.15	$.04	$.79	$ .38
Earnings Per Share of Common Stock—Fully Diluted				
Continuing operations	$.10	$.04	$.74	$ .42
Discontinued operations	—	—	—	(.04)
Extraordinary item[b]	.05	—	.05	—
Net Income	$.15	$.04	$.79	$ .38
Average common and common equivalent shares	16,865	21,540	18,239	21,504

is relatively straightforward; if an enterprise operates in more than one industry, the consideration of industry factors in financial analysis is more complex.

During the 1960s a significant trend toward diversification developed, and many **diversified companies** (i.e., companies operating in several different industries) emerged. Many companies that previously operated in a single industry moved into additional industries as a result of natural growth or by acquiring other companies. These companies diversified their operations for several reasons, including the desire of corporate managements to spread the risks of investment over a number of industries and product lines to reduce dependence on any one set of suppliers and customers.

For over a decade the APB, and then the FASB, considered whether special information relative to operations in different industries should be required. This type of disclosure was called **segment reporting.** The authoritative boards identified many

CONDENSED CONSOLIDATED BALANCE SHEET

In thousands	September 30, 1990
Assets	
Cash	$ 4,027
Short-term investments	175,323
Receivables	212,998
Inventories	78,686
Prepaid expenses	15,751
Future income tax benefits	22,035
Current Assets	**508,820**
Property, plant and equipment—net	176,918
Notes receivable & other assets	31,436
Intangibles	295,334
Total Assets	**$1,012,508**
Liabilities and Equity	
Accounts payable & other liabilities	$ 184,777
Current portion of long-term debt	9,161
Current Liabilities	**193,938**
Deferred income taxes	61,224
Long-term debt	48,478
Subordinated debt	200,037
Minority interest	201,613
Stockholders' equity	307,218
Total Liabilities and Stockholders' Equity	**$1,012,508**

(a) During the year Fuqua provides for income taxes using anticipated effective annual tax rates. The rates are based on expected operating results and estimated permanent differences between book and tax income. Adjustments are made each quarter for changes in the anticipated rates used in previous quarters. If the actual annual effective tax rates for 1989 had been used in each of the first three quarters of 1989, net income would have been $3,497,000 and $7,849,000 for the three months and nine months ended September 30, 1989.
(b) Represents gain on the repurchase of a portion of Fuqua's 6% Senior Subordinated Swiss Franc Bonds due in 1996.

SOURCE: Fuqua Industries, 1990 Third Quarter Report.

advantages and disadvantages of segment reporting and carefully considered the problems of separating aggregate financial information into components.

In 1976 the FASB issued *Statement of Financial Accounting Standards No. 14*. While the major consideration centered around information along industry or product lines, the separation of information on other bases was also considered. *SFAS No. 14* resulted in disclosure requirements in three different areas:[9]

1. The enterprise's **operations in different industries.**
2. The enterprise's **foreign operations and export sales.**
3. The enterprise's **dependence on major customers.**

---

[9]*FASB Statement of Financial Accounting Standards No. 14*, "Financial Reporting for Segments of a Business Enterprise," 1976, par. 3.

In subsequent pronouncements, the applicability of these requirements has been limited in several ways. A major limitation was the suspension of segment reporting requirements for nonpublic enterprises, as indicated in *SFAS No. 21*.[10] As a result of this pronouncement, the disclosure requirements discussed here were limited to publicly held companies. Another limitation states that segment disclosures are not required in interim financial presentations.[11]

Empirical research has shown that segment information is useful in decision making.[12] In deciding to require segment reporting for selected companies, the FASB determined that disaggregated information along industry or product lines, by geographic area, and by major customers is useful for purposes of assessing the risk and return inherent in investment and credit decisions. Therefore, these three areas of

Disclosure   disclosure specified in *SFAS No. 14* are discussed in the following sections of this chapter. While specific disclosure requirements are identified by the FASB, considerable flexibility exists in the manner of accumulating the necessary information that underlies these disclosures. This fact, coupled with the fact that each enterprise has unique operating characteristics, led the FASB to conclude that segment information may be of limited usefulness in attempting to compare the information of one enterprise with similar information of other enterprises.

INFORMATION ABOUT DIFFERENT INDUSTRIES

Information about industry segments is required if the enterprise has significant operations in more than one industry. An **industry segment** is a component of an enterprise that tries to earn a profit by providing a product or service or a group of related products or services primarily to customers outside the enterprise. Industry segments are determined by identifying the products and services of an enterprise and grouping those products and services by industry lines. Those industry seg-

Materiality   ments that meet the materiality guidelines described below are then identified as **reportable segments.**

Several standardized systems exist for classifying business activities. These include the **Standard Industrial Classification (SIC)** and the **Enterprise Standard Industrial Classification (ESIC),** both of which are used by the U.S. government. The SIC is a system of classifying business enterprises by the type of economic activity in which they engage. The ESIC system is based on the form of business organization. The FASB has indicated that these systems may help an enterprise to identify its industry segments and reportable segments. Because no single system of classification is universally applicable for determining the industry segments of all enterprises, identification of an enterprise's industry segments depends largely on **managerial judgment.** In determining whether products and services are related or unrelated for purposes of identifying reportable segments, factors such as the following should be considered: the nature of the products and services, the nature of the production process, and markets and marketing methods for the distribution of the products and services.

Management's primary responsibility in identifying industry segments is to separate the enterprise's operations into those components that will be most meaningful to

---

[10]*FASB Statement of Financial Accounting Standards No. 21,* "Suspension of the Reporting of Earnings per Share and Segment Information by Nonpublic Companies," 1978, par. 12.

[11]*FASB Statement of Financial Accounting Standards No. 18,* "Financial Reporting for Segments of a Business Enterprise—Interim Financial Statements," 1977, par. 7.

[12]See, for example, Bruce A. Baldwin, "Segment Earnings Disclosure and the Ability of Security Analysts to Forecast Earnings Per Share," *The Accounting Review* (July 1984), pp. 376–89.

the users of the financial statements. As examples of the kinds of industry segments, Anheuser-Busch Companies has beer and beer-related products, food products, and entertainment; Georgia-Pacific Corporation has building products, pulp and paper, and other operations; and The Procter & Gamble Company has laundry and cleaning, personal care, food and beverage, and pulp and chemicals.

In identifying reportable segments and preparing the information to be presented, the terms **revenue, operating profit or loss,** and **identifiable assets** are important:

1. **Revenue.** The revenue of an industry segment includes both sales to unaffiliated customers and intersegment sales or transfers of products or services similar to those sold to unaffiliated customers.
2. **Operating profit or loss.** The operating profit or loss of an industry segment is its revenue less all operating expenses. Operating expenses include expenses that relate to revenues as defined above. Operating expenses which are not directly traceable to an industry segment are allocated on a reasonable basis among the segments benefiting from the expense. Revenues and expenses of a general corporate nature and not associated with the operations of specific industry segments are not included in the determination of operating profit or loss of industry segments.
3. **Identifiable assets.** The identifiable assets of an industry segment are the assets used by the segment, including those assets used exclusively by the segment and an allocated portion of assets used jointly by two or more industry segments. Assets used for general corporate purposes and not used in the operation of any industry segment are not allocated to industry segments.

The criteria for translating **industry segments** into **reportable segments** are based on the revenues, operating profits or losses, and identifiable assets of the industry segments. An industry segment constitutes a reportable segment (i.e., a segment for which information must be disclosed separately) if *any one* of the following criteria is met:

1. Revenue of the segment is 10% or more of the combined revenue of all industry segments.
2. The absolute amount of the operating profit or loss of the segment is 10% or more of the greater (in absolute amount) of the following:
   a. The combined operating profit of all industry segments with an operating profit.
   b. The combined operating loss of all industry segments with an operating loss.
3. The identifiable assets of the segment are 10% or more of the combined identifiable assets of all industry segments.

Let's consider an example in which we apply these criteria to identify reportable segments. Assume that Diversity, Inc., has identified five industry segments in which it operates. Revenue, operating profit (loss), and identifiable assets in millions of dollars for each industry are as follows:

Industry	Revenue	Operating Profit (Loss)	Identifiable Assets
Food products	$150	$ 17	$250
Publishing	125	5	108
Metal products	62	(10)	38
Lumber	30	2	18
Electrical machinery	18	(1)	40
	$385	$ 13	$454

Any one of the three criteria of 10% revenue, operating profit or loss, and identifiable assets is sufficient for an industry segment to qualify as a reportable segment. In this example all three criteria apply to the process of identifying reportable segments.

Based on revenue alone, food products, publishing, and metal products are reportable segments, because revenue associated with each of these exceeds $38.5 million ($385 million × 10%). Based on identifiable assets, food products and publishing are reportable segments, because identifiable assets associated with each of these exceed $45.4 million ($454 million × 10%).

Applying the criterion of 10% of operating profit or loss is somewhat more complicated, because some segments have an operating profit and others have an operating loss. The operating profits must be combined and the operating losses must be combined to determine which is greater (based on the absolute amounts of the two). For Diversity, Inc., total operating profits are $24 million and total operating losses are $11 million, determined as follows (in millions of dollars):

Industry Segment	Absolute Amount of Operating	
	Profit	Loss
Food products	$17	
Publishing	5	
Metal products		$10
Lumber	2	
Electrical machinery		1
	$24	$11

Because the total profit figure exceeds the total loss figure, $24 million is the basis for identifying the reportable segment. Any industry with an **operating profit or loss** of $2.4 million or greater ($24 million × 10%) qualifies as a reportable segment. Therefore food products, publishing, and metal products are reportable segments.

Summarizing for Diversity, Inc., we have identified the industry segments of food products, publishing, and metal products as reportable segments. The other two industries (lumber and electrical machinery) may be combined, because they do not

Materiality   meet any one of the materiality criteria for identification as reportable segments.

Judgment is needed to identify reportable segments. Comparability between periods is important. Accordingly, an industry segment that does not meet any of the above criteria in a particular year but that has been significant in the past and is expected to be significant in the future might be considered a reportable segment. Also, an industry that is significant by these criteria in one year but has not been significant in the past and is not expected to be significant in the future may be excluded as a reportable segment. We can see the elusive nature of the materiality decision and the

Materiality   significance of applying judgment in making important materiality decisions.

SFAS No. 14 requires that **reportable segments account for 75% or more of the combined revenue from sales to unaffiliated customers of all industry segments.** If this criterion is not met, industry segments should be redefined to include additional industries as reportable segments so that the amount of revenue from sales to unaffiliated customers accounted for by reportable segments equals at least 75% of the combined total. This requirement exists to ensure that the reportable segments account for the major portion of business activity of the enterprise as a whole.

For example, assume that Newton Company has identified three reportable segments by applying the criteria of 10% of revenue, operating profit or loss, and identifiable assets. These segments are tobacco, chemicals, and rubber. ("Miscellaneous other" includes amounts from several smaller segments.) Revenue information (in millions of dollars) for these segments is as follows:

Segment	Sales to Unaffiliated Companies	Intersegment Sales	Total Revenue
Tobacco	$ 812	$ 38	$ 850
Chemicals	311	114	425
Rubber	128	125	253
Miscellaneous other	140	8	148
	$1,391	$285	$1,676

To determine if the reportable segments represent a sufficient portion of enterprise operations, 75% of the sales to unaffiliated companies must be accounted for by the reportable segments. This criterion is met in the case of the Newton Company, because sales to unaffiliated companies of the reportable segments total $1,251 ($812 + $311 + $128) and this exceeds 75% of the total of all sales to unaffiliated companies ($1,251/$1,391 = 89.9%). If this condition had not been met, some industry segments included in "miscellaneous other" would need to be combined with each other or with the previously identified reportable segments until the reportable segments accounted for 75% or more of sales to unaffiliated companies.

Once the reportable segments are identified, **the following information must be presented for each reportable segment and for other segments in the aggregate:**

1. Revenue.
2. Operating profit or loss.
3. Identifiable assets.
4. Depreciation, depletion, and amortization expense.
5. Expenditures for property, plant, and equipment.
6. Equity in the net income and net assets of vertically integrated investees that are either unconsolidated subsidiaries or accounted for by the equity method.
7. Effects of changes in accounting principle.

Disclosure   Companies may disclose this information in the body of the primary financial statements, in accompanying notes, or in separate supplemental schedules. If the latter approaches are used, the information should be related to consolidated information in the primary financial statements.

As a practical matter the number of industry segments presented should not be so great that it causes information overload. The FASB indicates a preference for **no more than *10* segments.** If the number of industry segments exceeds 10, closely related segments may be combined to reduce the number of reportable segments.

A company that operates in several industries may be dominated by operations in a single industry. A single industry segment is considered dominant if it accounts for more than 90% of revenue, operating profit or loss, *and* identifiable assets and if no other industry segment meets any of the 10% tests discussed earlier. When an enterprise operates predominantly in a single industry, this industry should be identified in the financial statements. While the reporting requirements of *SFAS No. 14* are limited to publicly held companies, a desirable financial reporting practice is for *all* companies to clearly identify the industry in which they operate. Many small companies do this as part of their Summary of Significant Accounting Policies.

INFORMATION ON FOREIGN OPERATIONS AND EXPORT SALES

In the current global economic environment, many companies derive significant revenue from operations in foreign countries and from exporting goods and services from the United States to foreign countries. **Foreign operations** refers to the presence of production and distribution facilities in countries other than the United States. **Export sales** refers to the operation of facilities in the United States from which goods and services are distributed to foreign countries.

Due to differences in the economic and political environments in foreign countries, significant uncertainty may be associated with foreign operations and export sales. For example, companies with operations in certain Middle-Eastern and South American countries have found their operations in jeopardy because of political unrest. *SFAS No. 14* establishes certain disclosure requirements that apply even if the industry segment disclosures and major customer disclosures do not. A publicly held company is required to present information concerning foreign operations if *either* of the following conditions is met:[13]

Disclosure

1. Revenue generated by foreign operations from sales to unaffiliated customers is 10% or more of consolidated revenue as reported in the enterprise's income statement.
2. Identifiable assets of the enterprise's foreign operations are 10% or more of consolidated total assets as reported in the enterprise's balance sheet.

If a significant portion of foreign operations is conducted in two or more geographic areas, the information should be presented for each area separately. A geographic area is considered significant if its revenue from sales to unaffiliated customers or its identifiable assets are 10% or more of related consolidated amounts. The determination of what constitutes a **geographic area** is a management decision and should reflect such factors as proximity, economic relationship, similarity of business environment, and the nature and interrelationship of business activities in various foreign locations.

Information concerning foreign operations that should be presented (by geographic area, if appropriate) includes: (1) revenues; (2) operating profit or loss or some other measure of profitability; and (3) identifiable assets.

If products and services exported from a company's domestic operations to foreign countries make up 10% or more of the total revenue from sales to unaffiliated customers, that amount of revenue must be separately disclosed. If significant exports are made into different geographic areas, separate disclosure by geographic area should be made as considered appropriate in the circumstances.

For example, assume that Proffitt Company is a publicly held U.S. company with both foreign operations and export sales. The total revenue of $230,000,000 for 1993, all of which is to unaffiliated customers, is distributed over various components of the company's operations as follows:

	Revenue (in millions of dollars)
Domestic operations	
Sales in United States	$105
Export sales	45
	$150

---

[13]*FASB Statement of Financial Accounting Standards No. 14*, par. 32.

Foreign operations	
France	25
Germany	30
Miscellaneous other countries	25
	80
Total revenue	$230

Assume further that the $45 million of export sales is made in a single geographic area and that the $25 million of revenues from "miscellaneous other countries" represents sales in five countries, none of which exceed $7 million. In addition, none of the foreign operations from which these sales are derived represent an investment in 10% or more of identifiable assets.

The Proffitt Company should make the following separate disclosures:

Segment	Information Disclosed	Justification
Export portion of domestic operations	Revenue	Exports make up more than 10% of total revenue ($45/$230 = 19.6%)
Foreign operations in France and Germany	Revenue Operating profit Identifiable assets	Revenues in France and Germany exceed 10% of total revenues (France: $25/$230 = 10.9%; Germany: $30/$230 = 13.0%)

Because all export sales are made to a single geographic area, no further separation of this revenue amount is necessary. Because foreign operations in countries other than France and Germany do not meet the significance tests of 10% of revenues ($7/$230 = 3%) or identifiable assets, no further separation of the amounts attributable to operations in these countries is necessary.

Disclosure   As with industry segment disclosure, information concerning foreign operations and export sales may be presented in the body of the primary financial statements or in the notes or supplementary schedules that accompany the financial statements.

MAJOR CUSTOMER INFORMATION

Disclosure   If an enterprise derives 10% or more of its revenue from sales to a single customer, that fact and the amount of revenue from each customer meeting this criterion must be disclosed. The purpose of this disclosure is to make the users of the financial statements aware of the extent of reliance of the enterprise on a small number of customers. The identity of the customer is not required.

To illustrate, suppose a company produces seat belts, which it sells to a major automobile manufacturer and to independent automobile-parts suppliers throughout the United States. If 10% or more of sales are made to a single customer, such as the manufacturer, this fact may be important to users of the company's financial statements, because future sales are linked to the success of the automobile manufacturer.

The disclosure of reliance on **major customers** is required even if the other segment reporting requirements do not apply. If industry segment information is presented and major customer disclosure is also required, the industry segment making the sales should be disclosed.

For purposes of applying the major customer disclosure, a group of entities under common control is considered a single customer. In dealings with domestic governments, the federal government, an individual state government, or an individual local

---

EXHIBIT 25-2

Simpson Industries, Inc.
Example Major Customer Disclosure

Note 1-Major Customers

The Company's operations are conducted within one business segment and revenues attributable to foreign customers are not material.

Net sales to major customers:

(In thousands)	1989	1988	1987
General Motors Corporation	$66,600	$74,300	$64,500
Ford Motor Company	42,900	36,100	24,000
Chrysler Corporation	31,100	20,600	21,500
Consolidated Diesel Corporation	25,100	19,700	12,800
Caterpillar Inc.	12,300	13,500	11,100

SOURCE: Simpson Industries, Inc., 1989 Annual Report.

---

government is considered a single customer. The governments of individual foreign countries are considered single customers. The major customer disclosure usually appears in the footnotes to the financial statements. The disclosure of major customers is a desirable practice for all companies, even though the specific requirements of *SFAS No. 14* are limited to publicly held companies. Exhibit 25–2 shows a major customer disclosure of Simpson Industries, a company that produces machined parts, assemblies, and modules for manufacturers of automobiles, trucks, diesel engines, and heavy equipment.

EXAMPLE OF SEGMENT DISCLOSURE

The segment reporting disclosures of Bristol-Myers Squibb Company for 1990 with comparative years 1989 and 1988 are shown in Exhibit 25–3. The information presented for each of the company's four industry segments includes net sales, profit, year-end assets, capital expenditures, and depreciation. Bristol-Myers Squibb also reports its net sales, profit, and year-end assets in different geographic areas, as shown in Exhibit 25–3.

RELATED-PARTY TRANSACTIONS

Materiality Many companies engage in transactions with related parties; such transactions, if material, must be disclosed. **Related parties** include "affiliates of the enterprise; entities for which investments are accounted for by the equity method by the enterprise; trusts for the benefit of employees, such as pension and profit-sharing trusts that are managed by or under the trusteeship of management; principal owners of the enterprise; its management; members of the immediate families of principal owners of the enterprise and its management; and other parties . . . which control or can significantly influence the management or operating policies of the other."[14]

Of course, all entities have related parties; however, not all entities engage in related-party transactions. The management of a company should establish procedures to identify related parties and enumerate any material related-party transactions.

---

[14]*FASB Statement of Financial Accounting Standards No. 57*, "Related Party Disclosures," 1982, par. 24.

Although types of related-party transactions are almost limitless, several examples occur frequently in practice: Related parties commonly lend money to and borrow money from each other; they may sell products to and buy products from each other; and services may be provided by one related party to another without charge. When such related-party transactions are material, several accounting issues arise.

Substance over Form

As a general rule, **accountants attempt to recognize the substance of a related-party transaction rather than its mere form.** Many transactions between related parties differ in substance and purpose from normal transactions merely because the participants in the transaction are related. Accountants must understand the business purposes of such transactions to account for and disclose the events properly.

For example, one party may lend money to a related second party without specifying the timing and amount of repayment. In such a case the proper classification (current or noncurrent) and valuation (imputation of interest) are uncertain. To understand the underlying purpose of the event, an accountant may need to have extensive discussions with the related parties.

Substance over Form

Another common related-party transaction arises when an asset is sold at an amount that differs substantially from its market value. When such transactions occur, accountants emphasize the *substance* of the event, which is sometimes highly unusual. For example, a major shareholder may sell an asset to a closely held corporation at a price substantially lower than the market value of the property. The shareholder may be providing assistance to a financially troubled business; if so, that fact may need to be disclosed.

Disclosure

Once a related-party transaction is identified and an understanding of the transaction is gained, the accountant should disclose the following aspects of the event.[15]

1. The nature of the relationship between the transacting parties.
2. The nature and description of the transaction.
3. The amount of the transaction and any changes in terms and effects from the preceding period.
4. Any amounts due from or to the related parties.

In addition, the disclosure of common control may be necessary even if no related-party transactions occur, because common control of several entities can itself cause the operating results and financial position of each controlled entity to differ.[16] For example, assume that Rhonda Rich owns two clothing stores that operate as separate corporate entities. Rhonda also has a contract to provide all uniforms to a city's street maintenance, police, and fire departments. In some years, she decides, one of the clothing stores will fulfill the contract, whereas in other years the other store fulfills the contract. The contract is large enough to materially affect the financial statements of either company. Thus, even though neither company transacts business with the other, the existence of common control clearly affects each of them. Disclosure of the common control and other details of these circumstances is necessary.

Economic dependency may create higher risk if one enterprise relies on another for a material amount of financing or operational support. For example, if much of the output of a small factory is purchased by a large retail department-store chain, the chain can probably exert significant influence over the management and operating

---

[15]*FASB Statement of Financial Accounting Standards No. 57*, par. 2.
[16]*FASB Statement of Financial Accounting Standards No. 57*, par. 4.

EXHIBIT 25-3

Bristol-Myers Squibb Company
Segment Reporting Example

Note 12   Segment Information

The company's products are reported in four industry segments as follows:

Pharmaceutical Products—prescription medicines, mainly cardiovascular drugs and antibiotics, which comprise about forty percent and twenty-five percent, respectively, of the segment's sales, anti-cancer and central nervous system drugs, diagnostic agents and other pharmaceutical products.

Medical Devices—orthopaedic implants, which comprise about forty percent of the segment's sales, ostomy care and wound management products, surgical instruments and other medical devices.

Nonprescription Health Products—infant formulas and other nutritional products, which comprise about sixty-five percent of the segment's sales, analgesics, vitamins, cough/cold remedies and skin care products.

Toiletries, Beauty Aids and Household Products—haircoloring and hair care preparations, which comprise about forty-five percent of the segment's sales, deodorants and anti-perspirants, beauty appliances, household cleansing and specialty products.

Unallocated expenses consist principally of general administrative expenses and net interest income, and in 1989 include a portion of the charge for integrating operations. Other assets are principally cash and cash equivalents, time deposits and marketable securities. Inter-area sales by geographic area for each of the three years ended December 31, 1990, 1989 and 1988, respectively, were: United States—$741 million, $638 million and $558 million; Europe, Mid-East and Africa—$360 million, $302 million and $306 million; Other Western Hemisphere—$34 million, $30 million and $31 million; and Pacific—$3 million, $4 million and $8 million. These sales are usually billed at or above manufacturing costs.

Net assets relating to operations outside the United States amounted to approximately $1,186 million, $957 million and $1,563 million at December 31, 1990, 1989 and 1988, respectively.

Industry Segments (in millions of dollars)	Net Sales			Profit[a]			Year-End Assets		
	1990	1989	1988	1990	1989	1988	1990	1989	1988
Pharmaceutical Products	$ 5,261	$4,442	$3,987	$1,548	$ 703	$ 949	$3,972	$3,474	$3,132
Medical Devices	1,436	1,227	1,102	346	282	246	906	817	737
Nonprescription Health Products	1,773	1,662	1,638	390	349	443	727	651	620
Toiletries, Beauty Aids and Household Products	1,830	1,858	1,831	326	215	303	686	710	714
Net sales, operating profit and assets	$10,300	$9,189	$8,558	$2,610	$1,549	$1,941	$6,291	$5,652	$5,203

Geographic Areas (in millions of dollars)	Net Sales			Profit[b]			Year-End Assets		
	1990	1989	1988	1990	1989	1988	1990	1989	1988
United States	$ 7,017	$6,478	$6,013	$1,747	$1,259	$1,462	$4,251	$3,943	$3,484
Europe, Mid-East and Africa	2,682	2,127	1,992	633	228	372	1,590	1,272	1,172
Other Western Hemisphere	906	769	672	198	119	130	382	336	330
Pacific	833	789	784	80	40	71	550	496	505
Inter-area eliminations	(1,138)	(974)	(903)	(48)	(97)	(94)	(482)	(395)	(288)
Net sales, operating profit and assets	$10,300	$9,189	$8,558	2,610	1,549	1,941	6,291	5,652	5,203
Unallocated expenses and other assets				(86)	(272)	(52)	2,924	2,845	3,070
Earnings before income taxes and total assets				$2,524	$1,277	$1,889	$9,215	$8,497	$8,273

Industry Segments (in millions of dollars)	Capital Expenditures			Depreciation		
	1990	1989	1988	1990	1989	1988
Pharmaceutical Products	$360	$417	$295	$144	$111	$103
Medical Devices	51	50	56	26	21	16
Nonprescription Health Products	43	37	29	29	27	26
Toiletries, Beauty Aids and Household Products	38	36	37	31	25	26
Identifiable industry totals	492	540	417	230	184	171
Other	34	22	54	14	12	14
Consolidated totals	$526	$562	$471	$244	$196	$185

[a]The 1989 operating profit of the company's industry segments includes the charge for integrating businesses as follows: Pharmaceutical Products—$500 million; Medical Devices—$16 million; Nonprescription Health Products—$22 million; and Toiletries, Beauty Aids and Household Products—$108 million.
[b]The 1989 earnings before income taxes include the charge for integrating businesses as follows: United States—$350 million; Europe, Mid-East and Africa—$208 million; Other Western Hemisphere—$47 million; Pacific—$41 million; and unallocated expenses—$209 million.

SOURCE: Bristol-Myers Squibb Company 1990 Annual Report.

"AN INNATE FEAR OF DISCLOSURE"

JESSICA REIF, an industrious media securities analyst at First Boston Corp., explains what she does for a living: "I spend a good part of my time trying to get numbers that aren't reported."

In this day of information overload, aren't people like Reif drowning in numbers? In numbers, yes. But in useful numbers, not necessarily—especially when analysts and other investors try to disaggregate a large corporation to see how each of its important segments is doing.

Consider IBM. As befits its size, the $63 billion (estimated 1989 sales) computer company is in several lines of business, including personal computers, mainframes, electronic mail systems and semiconductors (IBM'S semiconductor facilities rank among the world's largest). How is each of these segments doing? That's hard to say. IBM reports figures for a grand total of one segment, called "information-processing systems, software, communications systems and other products and services."

At first glance, $17 billion (sales) Eastman Kodak is more forthcoming. Kodak lists three segments in its annual report: imaging, chemicals and health. But don't expect much enlightenment. With an aggregate $11 billion of revenues, the "imaging" segment includes everything from cameras to batteries to a giant copier business. The group as a whole earns $1.7 billion, 60% of Kodak's operating earnings. How much of that comes from copiers or other businesses, nobody outside Kodak knows for sure.

Does anybody care? They should. Says Eugene Glazer, technology analyst at Dean Witter Reynolds:

"Investors need to know how a company is doing in each major business. Maybe one business is so dominant and earning such huge profits that it's masking errors in other businesses."

In theory, companies are supposed to report line-of-business financial information. Segment reporting came into being after a vicious battle waged between the Federal Trade Commission and big corporations in the mid-1970s. The corporations fought the FTC's demands for income statements and balance sheets on each of their different lines of business all the way to the Supreme Court, and they lost.

In 1976 the Financial Accounting Standards Board decreed that all companies must break out the industry segments that constitute more than 10% of sales, and must report revenues, profits, assets, depreciation expenses and capital expenditures for each. But no sooner was the rule printed than companies began blurring distinctions among segments.

CBS is a good case in point. A lot of people are poring over CBS' financial statements these days, trying to understand why the company's operating profits dropped by $173 million between 1984 and 1988. Most important, they want to know just how badly the company's television network—traditionally CBS' bread and butter—is doing. But CBS, which operates the television network, 5 television stations, 2 radio networks and 20 radio stations, reports only two segments: broadcasting and other. All the networks and stations are lumped together under broadcasting.

"We know that the network has done badly," says Salomon Brothers media analyst Edward Atorino, "but

---

Disclosure policies of the small factory. Even if significant influence is not exerted, disclosure of economic dependency may be desirable to adequately inform financial statement users of the risk of relying on a limited number of customers or suppliers.

Materiality   Information about material related-party transactions is sometimes quite sensitive; however, such information is also vital to an intelligent use of the financial statements. An accountant's responsibility to external users of financial statements cannot be subordinated to management's desire for privacy. Indeed, in extreme cases the lack of adequate disclosure of related-party transactions and their effects has harmed independent CPAs in later litigation.[17]

---

[17]For example, in the case of Continental Vending Company, Inc., independent CPAs were held guilty of criminal fraud. Material loans made by a company to another commonly controlled company were not repaid. The court held that disclosure of more facts and circumstances regarding the loan and its questionable collectibility was necessary, and the findings of the court contributed to the issuance of *Statement on Auditing Standards No. 6*, "Related Party Transactions."

we don't know how badly." Instead, Atorino and his peers must deduce what they can from such annual report phrases as "Network sales declined slightly" and "Television stations sales rose modestly," plus management's hints and industry research.

Will CBS consider increasing the number of segments it reports? "Historically, we have always reported this way," bristles CBS spokeswoman Ann Morfogen. "We are an integrated company, and we don't plan to start doing it any other way."

Typically, companies voice two objections to providing information on their separate lines of business. First, they say, it would give an advantage to their competitors. Second, it would cost too much. But neither objection holds much water.

"I'm not aware of anyone who ever lost a nickel giving this kind of information to their competitors," says Sidney Spencer, a finance executive at General Electric. "Nevertheless, there's an innate fear of disclosure."

Some executives are less fearful than others. For an example of more useful reporting, look at Knight-Ridder's latest annual report. The $2 billion (sales) company reports two segments, newspapers and financial information products, and lists each of its major newspapers' contributions to revenues. And Lin Broadcasting, which still derives most of its sales and earnings from television and publishing assets, early on disclosed how its rapidly growing cellular telephone division was doing. It was this segment that attracted McCaw Cellular, which recently agreed to pay $3.4 billion for about 40% of Lin (McCaw already owned 10%), giving investors who understood the disclosures a huge profit.

How should a company determine how many segments to report? Wayne Kolins, a partner of the accounting firm BDO Seidman, has a sound idea: If a company has businesses that respond differently to changes in the economy, or if they face different kinds of competitors, or earn different levels of profits, then the company probably should report the businesses separately.

"It really comes down to the risks and the rewards," says Kolins. "Ask yourself: Are the risks different? Are the rewards different? If either answer is a significant yes, then you've got two segments."

Securities & Exchange Commission officials say their agency is certainly interested in good segment reporting. The SEC has required several companies—including Amfac and Duty Free International—to split their segments more narrowly. "It's a key component of financial reports," says SEC chief accountant Edmund Coulson. "Auditors ought to challenge the companies, and if investors believe a company is doing inappropriate segment reporting, they ought to write to us." Coulson's address: Office of the Chief Accountant, Securities & Exchange Commission, 450 Fifth St. N.W., Washington, D.C. 20549.

SOURCE: Dana Wechsler and Katarzyna Wandycz, "An Innate Fear of Disclosure," *Forbes*, February 5, 1990, pp. 126, 128. Reprinted by permission of *Forbes* magazine.

DISCLOSURES ABOUT FINANCIAL INSTRUMENTS

In recent years Wall Street innovators have developed many new types of financial instruments in response to market volatility, deregulation, tax law changes, and other stimuli. These innovative financial instruments, which bear such clever names as carrot and stick bonds, ZEBRAs, butterfly spreads, and OPPOSSMS, have raised many interesting accounting and reporting questions.[18] Among these questions are concerns about off-balance-sheet financing (i.e., borrowing money without fully reporting the liability), unjustified deferral of losses, premature recognition of gains, and inadequate disclosure about a company's risks. Moreover, many questions have been raised about the adequacy

---

[18]The number of innovative financial instruments seems to increase every day, and this book will not catalog the many types. Readers who want more details about some of the new instruments should see "Glossary of Selected Financial Instruments," *Journal of Accountancy*, November 1989, pp. 59–60. The November 1989 issue of the *Journal of Accountancy* contains several other good articles on financial instruments.

of current accounting standards for *traditional* financial instruments such as bonds and common stock. Accordingly, the FASB is currently working on a major project dealing with financial instruments.

A **financial instrument** is cash, evidence of an ownership interest in an entity, or a contract that has *both* of the following characteristics:

1. The contract imposes on one entity a contractual obligation (a) to deliver cash or another financial instrument to a second entity *or* (b) to exchange financial instruments on potentially unfavorable terms with the second entity.
2. The contract conveys to the second entity a contractual right (a) to receive cash or another financial instrument from the first entity *or* (b) to exchange other financial instruments on potentially favorable terms with the first entity.[19]

The definition emphasizes the future receipt, payment or exchange of cash or other financial instrument that ultimately results in cash.

The broad term "financial instrument" includes traditional financial instruments such as cash, receivables, payables, debt and equity securities, and investments in debt or equity securities, as well as the more innovative financial instruments such as financial guarantees and interest rate swaps. Examples of items that are *not* financial instruments are inventory, prepaid expenses, advances to or from suppliers, warranty obligations, plant assets, intangible assets, and deferred revenue.

The FASB has divided its financial instruments project into three major phases: disclosure, recognition and measurement, and distinguishing between liabilities and owners' equity. *SFAS No. 105* is the FASB's initial pronouncement in this area of accounting. It requires **disclosure of information about financial instruments that have off-balance-sheet risk and about financial instruments with concentrations of credit risk.** *SFAS No. 105* does not contain new standards for the recognition, measurement, or classification of financial instruments. These new standards are expected to come from future FASB work on financial instruments.

The disclosures required by *SFAS No. 105* are designed to help users assess a company's *risks*. One risk is the **risk of accounting loss,** which has three components: **credit risk,** or the risk that the other party will not perform according to the contract, **market risk,** or the risk that future changes in market prices could make a financial asset less valuable or a financial liability more burdensome, and the **risk of theft or physical loss.** *SFAS No. 105* addresses credit and market risk only.

Risk of accounting loss differs from the risk of economic loss. Suppose, for example, that a company has an investment in common stock. The historical cost (book value) is $14,000, and the current market value is $20,000. If the stock becomes worthless, the accounting loss is $14,000 while the economic loss is $20,000. *SFAS No. 105* deals only with the accounting loss.

Another type of risk that sometimes pertains to a financial instrument is **off-balance-sheet (OBS) risk.** OBS risk exposes a company to a risk of accounting loss that exceeds the amount recognized for the instrument in the balance sheet. For example, if the ultimate obligation under a financial guarantee exceeds the amount that the company has recognized as a liability, the company has OBS risk.

SFAS No. 105 requires disclosures in three major areas.[20] First, the pronouncement requires that for those financial instruments with OBS risk, a company should disclose

Disclosure (margin)

---

[19]*Statement of Financial Accounting Standards No. 105*, "Disclosure of Information about Financial Instruments with Off-Balance-Sheet Risk and Financial Instruments with Concentrations of Credit Risk," 1990, par. 6.
[20]Certain financial instruments that are subject to the disclosure requirements of other FASB pronouncements are excluded from the disclosure requirements of *SFAS No. 105*. These include certain insurance contracts, unconditional purchase obligations, pensions and other forms of deferred compensation, and extinguished debt

(1) the face or contract amount (or notional principal amount if there is no face or contract amount), and (2) the nature and terms. In disclosing the nature and terms of financial instruments with OBS risk, a company should disclose, at a minimum, the credit and market risk, the cash requirements, and accounting policies used for those instruments.

Second, *SFAS No. 105* requires that for those financial instruments with OBS credit risk, a company should disclose the *maximum* accounting loss that the company could incur and information about the collateral that supports the financial instruments.

Finally, *SFAS No. 105* requires all companies to disclose concentrations of credit risk for all financial instruments. Specifically, a company should disclose information about the (shared) activity, region, or economic characteristic that identifies the concentration of credit risk, the maximum accounting loss that the company could incur, and information about the collateral that supports the financial instruments. Concentrations of credit risk can exist in even the smallest of companies. For example, a small retailer that has granted credit exclusively to customers who are local residents or a local bank that has granted loans only to companies in a particular industry clearly have concentrations of credit risk.

A company should disclose the information summarized above, by class of financial instrument, either in the body of the financial statements or the footnotes.

On December 31, 1990, the FASB issued an **exposure draft** of a proposed Statement of Financial Accounting Standards that would require all entities to disclose, either in the body of the statements or the notes, information about the **market value** of those financial instruments for which it is practicable to estimate market value.[21] The proposed statement would apply to both assets and liabilities on and off a company's balance sheet. The exposure draft says that quoted market prices are generally the best evidence of the market value of financial instruments. However, in those cases where quoted market prices are not available, a company may use other ways (e.g., present value techniques) to estimate market value.

ANALYSIS OF FINANCIAL STATEMENTS

Basic financial statements, which include the related notes, provide information that is **useful** in decision making by financial analysts, stockholders, bondholders, bank lending officers, and others. Although they are responsible for *preparing* financial statements, corporate managers also *use* them to make planning and control decisions. Moreover, accountants and auditors not only prepare and attest to financial statements, but also *interpret* those statements. Thus, accountants and auditors must understand financial-statement analysis. For convenience, all parties who analyze financial statements will be called *analysts* in the rest of this chapter.

Financial-statement analysis provides insights about a company's financial position and performance. These insights can help an analyst to make predictions, assess risk, and evaluate profitability, solvency, and management's performance.

An analyst studies current and past information in an attempt to gain insight into the future. Nowhere does the old adage that "those who are ignorant of the past are condemned to repeat it" seem more appropriate than in the analysis of financial

---

and related assets held in trust. For certain other financial instruments, companies are not required to disclose information about OBS risk but must disclose information about concentrations of credit risk. These instruments include lease contracts and certain payables that result in amounts recorded in foreign currencies. The items excluded are described more fully in *SFAS No. 105*, pars. 14–15.

[21]FASB Proposed Statement of Financial Accounting Standards, "Disclosures about Market Value of Financial Instruments," 1990.

statements. A basic premise is that "relationships among data may reasonably be expected to exist and continue in the absence of known conditions to the contrary."[22] This section of the chapter provides an overview of the most widely used techniques of financial-statement analysis.

FUNDAMENTAL ANALYSIS OF FINANCIAL STATEMENTS

An analyst who simply focused on single amounts reported in financial statements would likely have difficulty forming rational judgments about a company. Imagine, for example, the difficulty of trying to evaluate a company's profitability by focusing only on the company's current net income. An analyst can evaluate profitability much more meaningfully by *relating* net income to such other measures as stockholders' equity, total assets, and shares of common stock. Financial-statement analysis, which requires considerable judgment, seeks to clarify relationships between items of financial information.

Financial-statement analysis often identifies major **changes,** or **turning points,** in amounts, trends, and relationships. The analyst then investigates the reasons for these changes because they may provide important clues about the company's future prospects. Unusual relationships indicate "red flags" that the analyst should investigate further to understand the **underlying causes.**

Financial-statement analysis can take many forms. In this textbook we discuss and illustrate **ratio analysis,** the most widely-used form. Ratios are computed by dividing an item in the financial statements by another related item. Most ratios are expressed as percentages or as times per period. In this chapter, we discuss only some of the more commonly-used ratios. Any number of ratios could conceivably be computed from financial statements.

Considered alone, a single ratio may not mean much. **Interpreting a ratio** therefore requires **comparing the ratio with certain benchmarks,** such as (1) the corresponding ratio for the same company in previous periods, (2) the corresponding ratio that was planned for the same company in the current period, (3) the corresponding ratio for a similar company in the current period, and (4) the average corresponding ratio of all companies in the same industry in the current period. A popular source for obtaining industry averages is *Robert Morris Associates Annual Statement Studies.* Even after comparing a given ratio with these four benchmarks, the analysis usually does not provide conclusive evidence of good or bad performance. It simply suggests an area that may need further investigation.

Analysts use financial ratios to gain insight about a company's *return* and the *risk* associated with that return. An analyst ordinarily accepts a higher risk only in exchange for a higher expected return.

One way to classify financial ratios is based on whether a ratio focuses primarily on **short-term solvency, long-term solvency,** or **profitability.** Solvency relates to risk, while profitability relates to return. As explained in Chapter 1, profitability and solvency are two company attributes that analysts ordinarily evaluate. That is, an analyst usually wants to know about a company's ability to generate earnings (profitability) and its ability to pay debts when due (solvency). A company can remain viable over the long run only if it is sufficiently profitable and able to remain solvent. Of course profitability and solvency are interrelated and therefore the three categories of ratios *are not completely independent.*

Exhibit 25–4 shows the basic financial statements of Ventura, Inc. The information needed to compute each ratio is found in this exhibit. In the following discussion, we focus on ratios for 1993, the latest year in Ventura's financial statements.

---

[22]*Statement on Auditing Standards No. 56,* "Analytical Procedures," (New York: AICPA, 1988), par. 2.

Short-Term Solvency Ratios

The ratios in this category help the analyst to assess a company's short-term debt paying ability, and therefore the company's chances of remaining solvent in the short run.

Current Ratio.   As discussed in Chapter 4, a company's **working capital** is the *difference* between its current assets and current liabilities. While working capital represents a dollar amount, an analyst may compute a **current ratio** to provide a **relative measure of short-term solvency,** as shown below for Ventura:

$$\text{Current ratio} = \frac{\text{Current assets}}{\text{Current liabilities}} = \frac{\$185,680}{\$85,200} = 2.18$$

The current ratio, sometimes called the **working capital ratio,** provides a relative measure of the extent to which a company's current assets cover its current liabilities. Although widely used in financial analysis, especially by short-term creditors, the current ratio is a static measure that only considers whether existing current assets are sufficient to pay existing current liabilities. It implies that current assets will be liquidated and the proceeds used to pay current liabilities, which is highly unlikely in a going concern. To maintain its short-term solvency, a company must generate *future* cash inflows that are sufficient to cover its *future* cash outflows.

Quick (Acid-Test) Ratio.   The quick ratio, also called the **acid-test ratio,** is a more conservative measure of short-term solvency than the current ratio. Of a company's current assets, only cash, temporary investments, and current receivables are considered "quick" assets. The quick ratio recognizes that inventory may contain some slow-moving goods that will require considerable time to convert to cash. Moreover, although prepaid expenses benefit current operations, they will not be converted directly into cash. Thus, the quick ratio *excludes* inventory and prepaid expenses. Ventura's quick ratio is shown below:

$$\text{Quick ratio} = \frac{\text{Cash} + \begin{matrix}\text{Temporary}\\\text{investments}\end{matrix} + \begin{matrix}\text{Short-term}\\\text{receivables}\end{matrix}}{\text{Current liabilities}} = \frac{\$52,000 + \$10,000 + \$48,000}{\$85,200}$$
$$= 1.29$$

The quick ratio indicates a company's ability to cover its current liabilities with cash and assets that can be converted quickly to cash. A limitation of this ratio is that some short-term receivables may require a lengthy collection period and may have to be factored at less than their carrying amount to obtain cash. Another limitation is that fluctuating market conditions may adversely affect the market prices of temporary investments.

Ratio of Net Cash Flow from Operating Activities to Current Liabilities.   The current and quick ratios are based on amounts that existed on the balance sheet date. Both ratios are distorted if the amounts on that date do not reflect normal conditions. A ratio that avoids this limitation is the **ratio of net cash flow from operating activities to current liabilities,** which is computed below:[23]

$$\begin{matrix}\text{Ratio of net cash flow}\\\text{from operating activities}\\\text{to current liabilities}\end{matrix} = \frac{\begin{matrix}\text{Net cash flow from}\\\text{operating activities}\end{matrix}}{\text{Average current liabilities}} = \frac{\$28,880}{(\$85,200 + \$97,600)/2}$$

$$= .32$$

---

[23]In those ratios that rely on an annual average, we compute the average by using the beginning and ending balances. In practice, an average using monthly balances may be computed when the beginning and ending balances are not considered representative of the entire year.

EXHIBIT 25-4

Ventura, Inc.
Basic Financial Statements

Ventura, Inc.
COMPARATIVE BALANCE SHEETS
December 31, 1993 and 1992

	1993	1992
Assets		
Cash	$ 52,000	$ 56,000
Marketable securities	10,000	10,000
Accounts receivable, net	48,000	52,000
Inventory	75,680	49,600
Total current assets	185,680	167,600
Property, plant, and equipment	152,000	160,000
Accumulated depreciation	(26,400)	(24,000)
Patents	7,200	8,000
Total noncurrent assets	132,800	144,000
Total assets	$318,480	$311,600
Liabilities		
Dividends payable	$ 13,600	$ 8,000
Accounts payable	28,240	40,000
Income taxes payable	43,360	33,600
Notes payable	–0–	16,000
Total current liabilities	85,200	97,600
Deferred income taxes	6,880	8,000
Convertible bonds payable	–0–	32,000
Bonds payable	48,000	48,000
Unamortized bond discount	(4,240)	(8,000)
Total noncurrent liabilities	50,640	80,000
Total Liabilities	135,840	177,600
Stockholders' Equity		
Common stock ($10 par, Notes 1 and 2)	60,000	48,000
Additional paid-in capital	14,400	12,000
Retained earnings	108,240	74,000
Total stockholders' equity	182,640	134,000
Total liabilities and stockholders' equity	$318,480	$311,600

Ventura, Inc.
INCOME STATEMENT
For the Year Ended December 31, 1993

Sales		$960,000
Expenses		
Cost of goods sold	$400,000	
Selling expenses	240,000	
General and administrative expenses	200,000	
Interest expense	32,000	872,000
Income before income tax		88,000
Income tax expense		42,240
Income before extraordinary item		45,760
Extraordinary gain—retirement of long-term debt, net of $1,920 applicable income tax		2,080
Net income		$ 47,840
Earnings per share:		
Income before extraordinary item		$7.62
Extraordinary gain, net of tax		.35
Net income		$7.97

Ventura, Inc.
STATEMENT OF RETAINED EARNINGS
For the Year Ended December 31, 1993

Retained earnings, Jan. 1, 1993	$ 74,000
Add: Net income	47,840
	121,840
Less: Dividends declared ($2.27 per share)	13,600
Retained earnings, Dec. 31, 1993	$108,240

Ventura, Inc.
STATEMENT OF CASH FLOWS
For the Year Ended December 31, 1993

Cash Flows from Operating Activities		
Cash received from customers		$964,000
Less: Cash paid for goods to be sold	$437,840	
Cash paid for selling expenses	236,000	
Cash paid for general and administrative		
expenses	194,400	
Cash paid for interest	31,360	
Cash paid for taxes	35,520	
Cash disbursed for operating activities		935,120
Net cash flow from operating activities		28,880
Cash Flows from Investing Activities		
Sale of property, plant, and equipment	9,600	
Purchase of property, plant, and equipment	(8,000)	
Net cash provided by investing activities		1,600
Cash Flows from Financing Activities		
Payment of dividends	(8,000)	
Repayment of notes payable	(16,000)	
Repayment of convertible bonds payable	(10,480)	
Net cash used by financing activities		(34,480)
Net decrease in cash		(4,000)
Cash, January 1, 1993		56,000
Cash, December 31, 1993		$ 52,000

Reconciliation of Net Income to Net Cash Provided by Operating Activities

Net income	$47,840
Adjustments to Reconcile Net Income to Net Cash	
Provided by Operating Activities	
Depreciation expense	6,400
Amortization	1,440
Loss on sale of equipment	2,400
Decrease in deferred income taxes	(1,120)
Decrease in accounts receivable	4,000
Increase in inventory	(26,080)
Decrease in accounts payable	(11,760)
Increase in income taxes payable	9,760
Extraordinary gain	(4,000)
Net cash provided by operating activities	$28,880

Supplemental Schedule of Noncash Investing and Financing Activities

Declaration of dividend in 1993 to be paid in 1994	$13,600
Conversion of bonds payable into common stock on January 2, 1993	$14,400

NOTES

1. The market price per share of common stock on December 31, 1993, was $87.67.
2. On January 2, 1993, 1,200 shares of common stock were issued when certain convertible bondholders exercised their conversion privilege.

Observe that the numerator pertains to the entire year and comes from the statement of cash flows. To be consistent with the numerator, the denominator also pertains to the entire year by reflecting an annual average that is based on the ending and beginning amounts of current liabilities.

This ratio shows the extent to which a company has been able to cover its current liabilities by generating cash through its operating activities. A limitation is that net cash provided by operations in the past may not be a good predictor of the future amount of this variable.

Long-Term Solvency Ratios

By indicating a company's long-term debt paying ability, the ratios in this category help the analyst to assess the risk that the company will become insolvent in the long run.

Debt to Total Assets.   Analysts use certain ratios to assess a company's relative reliance on debt and equity financing. The debt to total assets ratio relates a company's total liabilities to its total assets, as shown below for Ventura:

$$\text{Debt to total assets} = \frac{\text{Total liabilities}}{\text{Total assets}} = \frac{\$135,840}{\$318,480} = .43, \text{ or } 43\%$$

The ratio shows that 43% of Ventura's assets has come from creditors, implying that 57% was provided by owners. The debt to total assets ratio indicates creditor protection in the event of a corporate liquidation. A high ratio suggests that while the company tries to secure benefits from financial leverage, it also faces increased risk of becoming insolvent. Companies with low debt to assets ratios are generally better able to pay their liabilities at maturity, but they may miss out on good opportunities to use financial leverage favorably. The optimal mix of debt and equity financing depends on many factors, such as the stability of a company's income and the company's consistency in generating net cash inflows from operating activities.

A similar ratio frequently encountered in practice is the **debt to equity ratio,** which equals total liabilities divided by total stockholders' equity. Ventura's debt to equity ratio is 74% ($135,840/$182,640 = .74, or 74%).

Times Interest Earned.   Interest charges are fixed and must be paid when due. A company's ability to pay interest from the assets generated by its earnings process is therefore very important. The times interest earned ratio reveals the number of times that a company's annual earnings before interest and taxes cover its annual interest expense. The higher the ratio, the lower the risk that the company cannot make its interest payments. We illustrate this ratio below:

$$\text{Times interest earned} = \frac{\text{Income before interest and taxes}}{\text{Interest expense}}$$

$$= \frac{\$47,840 + \$32,000 + \$42,240 + \$1,920}{\$32,000} = 3.88 \text{ times}$$

Observe that the numerator is income before interest and taxes because this is the amount of earnings that can cover interest charges. A company does not owe income taxes unless interest charges are met.

Cash Flow Interest Coverage.   This ratio, which is based on information reported in the statement of cash flows, indicates the number of times per year that a company can cover interest payments from the net cash flow from operating activities. In essence, it is the cash flow counterpart of the times interest earned ratio. The cash flow interest coverage is potentially more useful than the times interest earned ratio because it recognizes that a company pays interest with *cash,* not earnings. The ratio for Ventura follows:

$$\begin{array}{l}\text{Cash flow}\\ \text{interest}\\ \text{coverage}\end{array} = \frac{\text{Net cash flow from operating activities} + \text{Interest paid} + \text{Taxes paid}}{\text{Interest paid}}$$

$$= \frac{\$28,880 + \$31,360 + \$35,520}{\$31,360} = 3.05 \text{ times}$$

In this case, the ratio shows that, when the relevant variables are expressed on a cash flow basis, Ventura could cover its interest payments somewhat fewer times than indicated by the accrual-based, times interest earned ratio.

Ratio of Cash Provided by Operating Activities to Sales.   This ratio indicates the percentage of sales that is available for spending. In other words, it reveals the cash flow effects of a company's sales. The ratio, shown below, reflects the company's success in making sales, collecting cash from operating sources, and using cash for operating purposes.

$$\begin{array}{l}\text{Ratio of net}\\ \text{cash flow}\\ \text{from}\\ \text{operating}\\ \text{activities}\\ \text{to sales}\end{array} = \frac{\text{Net cash flow from operating activities}}{\text{Net sales}} = \frac{\$28,880}{\$960,000} = .03, \text{ or } 3\%$$

Ratio of Net Cash Flow from Operating Activities to Net Income.   This ratio shows how much operating cash flow is represented by each dollar of net income. Generally, the cash flows from operating activities represent the cash effects of transactions that are reflected in net income. Thus the numerator of this ratio is a cash-basis number and the denominator is a closely-related measurement on the accrual basis, as shown below:

$$\begin{array}{l}\text{Ratio of net}\\ \text{cash flow from}\\ \text{operating}\\ \text{activities to}\\ \text{net income}\end{array} = \frac{\text{Net cash flow from operating activities}}{\text{Net income}} = \frac{\$28,880}{\$47,840} = .60, \text{ or } 60\%$$

The fact that this ratio is less than 1 indicates that Ventura had more success earning income than in generating cash from its operating activities. In general, the higher this ratio, the higher the perceived quality of a company's earnings in a given year.

Profitability Ratios

The ratios in this category provide information about the success of the company's earnings activities. For a company to be profitable, management must use the company's assets (i.e., receivables, inventories, and other assets) productively to generate revenue. Moreover, management must control expenses to ensure a reasonable net income.

Receivables Turnover Ratio.   The receivables turnover ratio is computed by dividing net credit sales by the average accounts receivable. Frequently only the net sales figure (instead of net *credit* sales) is available in published financial statements. Nevertheless, if an analyst consistently uses net sales and no material changes occur in the mix of cash and credit sales, the ratio using net sales is still useful. The receivables turnover ratio indicates the number of times a year the company collects its accounts receivable.

A low receivables turnover ratio may indicate such factors as large amounts of uncollectible accounts, a weak collections policy, or credit terms that are too lenient. On the other hand, a high ratio could be the result of overly restrictive credit terms that are reducing profitability by causing the company to lose sales. The receivables turnover ratio for Ventura is shown below:

$$\text{Receivables turnover} = \frac{\text{Net credit sales}}{\text{Average accounts receivable (net)}}$$

$$= \frac{\$960,000}{(\$48,000 + \$52,000)/2} = 19.2 \text{ times per year}$$

Observe that Ventura collects its accounts receivable about 19.2 times per year. A similar measure is the **number of days' sales in receivables,** which equals 365 divided by the receivables turnover ratio. For Ventura, this ratio equals $365/19.2 = 19.01$ days. In other words, Ventura takes, on average, about 19 days to collect its accounts receivable.[24]

Inventory Turnover.   A company's **inventory turnover** is computed by dividing cost of goods sold by the average inventory. This ratio indicates the average number of times the company sells its inventory in a year.

A low inventory turnover may suggest such factors as poor inventory management, ineffective marketing programs, or a weakening economy. Although a high turnover may suggest the opposite factors, it could also mean that the company does not carry enough inventory and is missing opportunities to sell goods. Moreover, inventory cost-flow methods directly affect this ratio. Suppose that an analyst wants to compare a LIFO company with a FIFO company. The analyst would likely use the LIFO company's *footnote disclosures* of FIFO inventory to estimate the inventory turnover of the LIFO company on a FIFO basis. This would make the two ratios more comparable. Remember that ratios provide important clues to ask further questions, but alone do not provide conclusive answers.

Ventura's inventory turnover ratio is computed below:

$$\text{Inventory turnover} = \frac{\text{Cost of goods sold}}{\text{Average inventory}} = \frac{\$400,000}{(\$75,680 + \$49,600)/2}$$

$$= 6.39 \text{ times per year}$$

Note that the numerator is the cost of goods sold, not sales, because inventory is ordinarily measured at cost, not selling price.

A measure similar to inventory turnover is the **number of days' sales in inventory,** which equals 365 divided by the inventory turnover ratio. For Ventura, this ratio equals $365/6.39 = 57.12$ days.

Asset Turnover.   Receivables and inventories are two of a typical company's most important assets. Managers use receivables, inventories, and other assets to generate revenues. Asset turnover, computed by dividing net sales by average total assets, shows how efficiently a company has used its assets to generate revenues. Ventura's asset turnover ratio is computed below:

$$\text{Asset turnover} = \frac{\text{Net sales}}{\text{Average total assets}} = \frac{\$960,000}{(\$318,480 + \$311,600)/2}$$

$$= 3.05 \text{ times per year}$$

---

[24]In computing the number of days' sales in accounts receivable (and other ratios that are expressed as a number of days), we use calendar days in this book. Some analysts prefer a numerator of 360 while others prefer 300, which is the approximate number of *business days* in a year. *Consistency in calculating comparative figures* is particularly important in these types of measurements.

A low asset turnover suggests an inefficient use of assets; therefore a reduction in assets may be warranted. On the other hand, an important limitation of this ratio is that net sales are measured at recent prices, while certain assets may be measured at costs incurred many years ago. Thus a high asset turnover may occur simply because a company has acquired certain assets long ago when prices were considerably below current replacement costs.

Profit Margin on Sales.   An analyst computes the profit margin on sales by dividing net income by net sales, as shown below:

$$\text{Profit margin on sales} = \frac{\text{Net income}}{\text{Net sales}} = \frac{\$\ 47,840}{\$960,000} = .05, \text{ or } 5\%$$

This ratio shows the percentage of each sales dollar earned as net income. It therefore provides an approximate measure of management's efficiency. When a company's profit margin on sales is too low, the company should try to increase sales, reduce expenses, or both. A detailed analysis of each expense can help identify those expenses to target for reduction.

Observe that in computing Ventura's profit margin on sales, our numerator is "all-inclusive" in the sense that it includes an extraordinary gain from retirement of long-term debt. This is really a *special type of extraordinary item*. As discussed in Chapter 15, *SFAS No. 4* requires that a gain or loss from debt extinguishment be classified as an extraordinary item, even though the gain or loss may *not* be unusual and nonrecurring. Some analysts prefer an income numerator that ignores all kinds of extraordinary gains and losses, while others go even further and ignore *any* income statement item believed to be nonrecurring. **Whenever you are comparing ratios, remember to make sure they have been computed in a comparable manner.**

The profit margin on sales ratio is similar to the ratio of net cash flow from operating activities to net income, except that the numerator is computed on an accrual rather than a cash-flow basis. Note that for Ventura, the profit margin on sales is 5%, while the ratio of net cash flow from operating activities to sales is only 3%. During 1993, the company had more success earning net income than it did in generating cash from operating activities.

Rate of Return on Assets.   This ratio, computed by dividing net income by average total assets, relates the amount of return achieved to the assets used in the earnings process.[25] Ventura's rate of return on assets is computed below:

$$\frac{\text{Rate of return}}{\text{on assets}} = \frac{\text{Net income}}{\text{Average total assets}} = \frac{\$47,840}{(\$318,480 + \$311,600)/2} = .15, \text{ or } 15\%$$

If a company's rate of return on assets is considered too low, the company should try to find ways to (1) increase net income without increasing the asset base, and/or (2) reduce the asset base without reducing net income. An analyst may gain additional insight into this ratio by separating it into components, as shown below:

Rate of return on assets		Profit margin on sales		Asset turnover
	=	on sales	×	turnover
	=	.05	×	3.05
	=	.15, or 15%		

In other words, a company's rate of return on assets depends on the amount of net income the company earns on each sales dollar and on the company's efficiency in

---

[25]Some analysts prefer a numerator equal to net income plus interest expense (net of tax savings because of the interest expense). Their rationale is that because the denominator is assets that creditors and owners have provided, the numerator should show the return on both debt and equity capital.

using its assets to generate sales. Some companies (e.g., discount stores, variety stores, large grocers) have low profit margins and high asset turnovers, while others (e.g., expensive jewelry stores, fine furniture stores, furriers) have high profit margins and low asset turnovers.

For some companies, the rate of return on assets may be somewhat high merely because the company acquired certain assets long ago when prices were considerably below current replacement costs. Moreover, net income may be "too high" in the sense that depreciation is based on historical costs, rather than higher replacement costs.

Return on Common Stockholders' Equity.   The rate of return on common stockholders' equity reveals the profitability of the common shareholders' investment in the company. It is computed by dividing the net income minus preferred dividends, by the average common stockholders' equity, as shown below:

$$\frac{\text{Return on common}}{\text{stockholders' equity}} = \frac{\text{Net income} - \text{Preferred dividends}}{\text{Average common stockholders' equity}}$$

$$= \frac{\$47,840 - \$0}{(\$182,640 + \$134,000)/2} = .30, \text{ or } 30\%$$

A company finances its assets using debt and shareholder investments (Assets = Liabilities + Stockholders' equity). Debt and preferred stock ordinarily require fixed interest or dividend payments. **Financial leverage** or **trading on the equity** mean using debt and preferred stock financing to increase the return to common stockholders. **Favorable financial leverage** occurs when a company earns more on the assets acquired with the funds than the fixed cost of obtaining the funds. **Unfavorable financial leverage** occurs when the company earns less than the fixed cost of the funds. In the case of Ventura, the return on common stockholders' equity is 30%, while the return on assets is 15%. The company is therefore using debt capital wisely to generate additional returns for common stockholders.

Earnings per share (EPS).   One measure of profitability, EPS, is already shown on the face of Ventura's income statement (see Exhibit 25–4). When a company has no potentially dilutive securities outstanding, EPS is computed by dividing net income minus preferred dividends, by the weighted average number of common shares outstanding. When potentially dilutive securities exist, EPS calculations may become considerably more complex, as discussed in Chapter 21. Note in Exhibit 25–4 that because Ventura had an extraordinary gain, the company's income statement shows *three* EPS amounts. For brevity, only the final EPS amount is shown below:[26]

$$\text{Earnings per share} = \frac{\text{Net income} - \text{Preferred dividends}}{\text{Weighted average common shares outstanding}}$$

$$= \frac{\$47,840 - \$0}{6,000} = \$7.97$$

A limitation of EPS as a measure of profitability is that it ignores the amount invested in the firm. Two companies may have identical net incomes and earnings per share and therefore appear equally profitable. Yet if one company has twice the asset base as the other, the smaller company is really the more profitable in the sense that it earned the same amount on a smaller investment.

Another EPS limitation involves the denominator. Two companies may be alike in all major respects. Yet if one company has fewer shares outstanding than the other,

---

[26]Ventura had 6,000 common shares outstanding during 1993.

perhaps because the shares were arbitrarily assigned a higher par value, then the first company will have a higher EPS. Moreover, EPS can be increased merely by purchasing treasury stock and thereby reducing the denominator.

Users of financial statements perceive EPS as extremely important. Large increases (decreases) in the price of a company's stock frequently occur when the company reports EPS that are significantly above (below) financial analysts' previous estimates. Despite its importance, the analyst should understand the limitations of EPS and avoid focusing only on this single measure of a company's performance.

Price/Earnings Ratio.   Analysts frequently compare a company's market price per common share with the company's earnings per share by computing a price/earnings (P/E) ratio, as shown below:

$$\text{Price/Earnings ratio} = \frac{\text{Market price per share}}{\text{Earnings per share}} = \frac{\$87.67}{\$7.97} = 11$$

Analysts use the P/E ratio as an indication of the future earning power of the company. Companies believed to have high growth potential usually have high P/E ratios, while those believed to have low growth potential generally have low P/E ratios. Of course, market prices change, sometimes very quickly. If a company has a low P/E ratio and the analyst believes that the company's growth prospects are much better than the P/E ratio suggests, the analyst may wish to buy the company's stock. P/E ratios are published in the *Wall Street Journal* on each business day. On May 30, 1990, for example, the P/E ratios for some well known companies were Goodyear, 16; Exxon, 20; IBM, 18; Phillips Van Heusen, 12; Shoneys, 30; and Union Carbide, 6.

Book Value per Share.   The common stockholders' equity of a profitable enterprise ordinarily increases over time. An analyst may compute the book (accounting) value of each common share by dividing the stockholders' equity attributable to common stockholders by the number of shares of common stock outstanding, as shown below:

$$\text{Book value per share} = \frac{\text{Common stockholders' equity}}{\text{Number of common shares outstanding}}$$

$$= \frac{\$182,640}{6,000} = \$30.44$$

Book value per share shows the value of each common share *assuming* that assets are liquidated and liabilities settled at their recorded amounts (book values). Because accounting valuations rely largely on historical costs, the book value of a company's stock seldom equals its current market value. Book values reflect historical valuations, while market values reflect future prospects. When the market price of a company's common stock is less than book value, this suggests that investors are relatively pessimistic about the company's prospects. Of course, investor pessimism is not always justified, and stocks selling below book values are sometimes good buys.

Dividend Payout Ratio.   The dividend payout ratio shows the percentage relationship between cash dividends declared on common stock and net income attributable to common stockholders, as shown below for Ventura:

$$\text{Dividend payout ratio} = \frac{\text{Cash dividends declared on common stock}}{\text{Net income} - \text{Preferred dividends}}$$

$$= \frac{\$13,600}{\$47,840 - \$0} = .28, \text{ or } 28\%$$

Common stock investors who seek high current income may prefer companies that pay dividends equal to a relatively high percentage of net income. Investors who seek long-term growth tend to favor companies that retain a relatively high percentage of net income to finance continued growth and expansion.

A closely-related ratio is **dividend yield,** computed by dividing the dividend per common share by the market price per common share. For Ventura, the dividend yield is 2.6% ($2.27/$87.67 = .026, or 2.6%). A company that reinvests most of the assets generated by its earnings process will have a relatively low dividend yield.

Exhibit 25–5 summarizes the financial ratios presented in this chapter.

LIMITATIONS OF FINANCIAL-STATEMENT ANALYSIS

The analysis of financial statements has several important limitations, the most important of which are the following:

EXHIBIT 25–5

Summary of Financial Ratios

Ratio	Formula	Computation
Short-Term Solvency Ratios		
1. Current ratio	$\dfrac{\text{Current assets}}{\text{Current liabilities}}$	$\dfrac{\$185,680}{\$85,200} = 2.18$
2. Quick ratio	$\dfrac{\text{Cash} + \dfrac{\text{Temporary}}{\text{investments}} + \dfrac{\text{Short-term}}{\text{receivables}}}{\text{Current liabilities}}$	$\dfrac{\$52,000 + \$10,000 + \$48,000}{\$85,200} = 1.29$
3. Ratio of net cash flow from operating activities to current liabilities	$\dfrac{\text{Net cash flow from operating activities}}{\text{Average current liabilities}}$	$\dfrac{\$28,880}{(\$85,200 + \$97,600)/2} = .32$
Long-Term Solvency Ratios		
4. Debt to total assets	$\dfrac{\text{Total liabilities}}{\text{Total assets}}$	$\dfrac{\$135,840}{\$318,480} = .43, \text{ or } 43\%$
5. Times interest earned	$\dfrac{\text{Income before interest and taxes}}{\text{Interest expense}}$	$\dfrac{\$47,840 + \$32,000 + \$42,240 + \$1,920}{\$32,000} = 3.88 \text{ times}$
6. Cash flow interest coverage	$\dfrac{\text{Net cash flow from operating activities} + \text{Interest paid} + \text{Taxes paid}}{\text{Interest paid}}$	$\dfrac{\$28,880 + \$31,360 + \$35,520}{\$31,360} = 3.05 \text{ times}$
7. Ratio of net cash flow from operating activities to sales	$\dfrac{\text{Net cash flow from operating activities}}{\text{Net sales}}$	$\dfrac{\$28,880}{\$960,000} = .03, \text{ or } 3\%$
8. Ratio of net cash flow from operating activities to net income	$\dfrac{\text{Net cash flow from operating activities}}{\text{Net income}}$	$\dfrac{\$28,880}{\$47,840} = .60, \text{ or } 60\%$

1. The analysis ignores the effects of changing prices. When a company has operated for many years, these effects can be very important, as will be explained in Chapter 26.
2. Corporate managers can sometimes manipulate financial ratios. A manager can increase the current ratio, for example, merely by accelerating the payment of some current liabilities at year-end. Although such an action would not affect working capital, the current ratio increases.
3. The use of different accounting principles may reduce the comparability of financial ratios between two companies. For example, if one company uses FIFO for its inventories while another has used LIFO for many years, many ratios will not likely be comparable.

Profitability Ratios

9. Receivables turnover	$\dfrac{\text{Net credit sales}}{\text{Average accounts receivable (net)}}$	$\dfrac{\$960,000}{(\$48,000 + \$52,000)/2} = 19.2 \text{ times per year}$
10. Inventory turnover	$\dfrac{\text{Cost of goods sold}}{\text{Average inventory}}$	$\dfrac{\$400,000}{(\$75,680 + \$49,600)/2} = 6.39 \text{ times per year}$
11. Asset turnover	$\dfrac{\text{Net sales}}{\text{Average total assets}}$	$\dfrac{\$960,000}{(\$318,480 + \$311,600)/2} = 3.05 \text{ times per year}$
12. Profit margin on sales	$\dfrac{\text{Net income}}{\text{Net sales}}$	$\dfrac{\$47,840}{\$960,000} = .05, \text{ or } 5\%$
13. Rate of return on assets	$\dfrac{\text{Net income}}{\text{Average total assets}}$	$\dfrac{\$47,840}{(\$318,480 + \$311,600)/2} = .15, \text{ or } 15\%$
14. Return on common stockholders' equity	$\dfrac{\text{Net income} - \text{Preferred dividends}}{\text{Average common stockholders' equity}}$	$\dfrac{\$47,840 - \$0}{(\$182,640 + \$134,000)/2} = .30, \text{ or } 30\%$
15. Earnings per share	$\dfrac{\text{Net income} - \text{Preferred dividends}}{\text{Weighted average common shares outstanding}}$	$\dfrac{\$47,840 - \$0}{6,000} = \$7.97$
16. Price/Earnings ratio	$\dfrac{\text{Market price per share}}{\text{Earnings per share}}$	$\dfrac{\$87.67}{\$7.97} = 11$
17. Book value per share	$\dfrac{\text{Common stockholders' equity}}{\text{Number of common shares outstanding}}$	$\dfrac{\$182,640}{6,000} = \$30.44$
18. Dividend payout ratio	$\dfrac{\text{Cash dividends declared on common stock}}{\text{Net income} - \text{Preferred dividends}}$	$\dfrac{\$13,600}{\$47,840 - \$0} = .28, \text{ or } 28\%$

4. Comparing financial ratios of a single company over time can be misleading because of underlying changes in the company (e.g., new products).
5. Comparing financial ratios of a company with another similar company can be misleading because, although the companies may appear similar, certain underlying differences may exist between them (e.g., somewhat different product lines).
6. Comparing financial ratios of one company with industry averages can be misleading because many companies operate in more than one industry.

These limitations underscore the fact that analysis of financial statements is more an art than a science. Interpreting the results of financial-statement analysis requires a sound understanding of the **company,** the **industry** in which it operates, and the general **economic environment.** The analyst frequently acquires this understanding by studying information obtained from sources other than financial statements.

OTHER SOURCES OF FINANCIAL INFORMATION

An analyst may obtain information from many sources. **Published corporate information** includes such materials as annual and interim reports sent to stockholders, various reports filed with the SEC, corporate prospectuses, company news letters and bulletins, and financial advertising. Information may also be obtained by **personal contact with corporate officials,** such as conversations, speeches, corporate tours, correspondence with companies, and attending stockholders' meetings. Various **noncompany sources of information** may also be helpful, including financial services (e.g., *Moody's* or *Standard & Poor's*), business and industry journals, investment advisory services, newspapers, analysts' reports, and economic statistics. Basic financial statements, although important, are only one source of information for analysts.

FINANCIAL-STATEMENT ANALYSIS IN AN EFFICIENT CAPITAL MARKET

As explained in Chapter 1, extensive empirical research in accounting and finance suggests that the stock market (especially the New York Stock Exchange) is highly efficient. In such an environment, stock prices behave as if they fully reflect *publicly available information,* including information in basic financial statements. If this information is quickly reflected in a company's stock price, as efficient-market theory suggests, is financial-statement analysis still useful? The answer is yes, for the following major reasons:

1. Not everyone believes that the stock market is highly efficient. First, many believe that the evidence which points to a high degree of market efficiency is inconclusive. Second, even if the market is highly efficient, its efficiency implies that sophisticated analysts consistently try to gain a market advantage, partly by applying techniques of financial-statement analysis soon after the statements are published. Paradoxically, for the stock market to *be* highly efficient, investors *must behave* as though it is not.
2. The stocks of many companies are not traded in large, well-defined markets. Efficient-market research does not apply to these companies.
3. Efficient-market research pertains only to the stock market. It does not apply to the numerous nonstock market users of financial statements (e.g., bank lending officers, or labor unions).

CONCLUDING REMARKS

Consistent with present GAAP, the financial information presented in this chapter and previous chapters has emphasized the historical cost measurement attribute denominated in nominal dollars. We have not extensively discussed the effects on financial statements of changing specific and general prices, although these concepts were introduced in Chapter 3. In Chapter 26 we discuss accounting for changing prices, one of the most important and pervasive topics in financial accounting. Although the general kinds of information in the next chapter are only encouraged and not required by the FASB at this time, this study will help you to better understand the nature and limitations of conventional financial statements as well as important changes in GAAP that could occur in the future.

KEY POINTS

1. Interim reporting means presenting financial information for periods of less than one year. (Objective 1)

2. Current accounting standards reflect the integral view of interim reporting, in which the interim period is viewed as an important part of the annual period. Accounting and reporting requirements are designed to help the user of the interim information to assess progress of the enterprise toward the annual results. (Objective 1)

3. Although certain minimum disclosures are required in interim reports, these reports tend to be much less detailed than annual reports. (Objective 1)

4. Publicly held companies must provide disaggregated information about several important aspects of their operations: operations in different industries, operations in different geographic areas, and reliance on major customers. (Objective 2)

5. Industry segment information must be reported if a material part of a company's operations extends over more than one industry segment or product line. (Objective 2)

6. Geographic area information must be presented if a material part of a company's operations is carried out in more than one geographic area. (Objective 2)

7. Major customer disclosure is required if a company generates a substantial portion of its sales revenue from a single customer. (Objective 2)

8. Material related party transactions, such as transactions between a company and its management, require special disclosures in the financial statements. (Objective 3)

9. Current accounting standards require disclosure of information about financial instruments that have off-balance-sheet risk and about financial instruments with concentrations of credit risk. (Objective 4)

10. Financial-statement analysis is designed to reveal important relationships between items of financial information and thereby provide insights about a company's short-term solvency, long-term solvency, and profitability. (Objective 5)

11. Financial-statement analysis requires considerable judgment and has several limitations. (Objective 5)

12. Published financial statements are only one source of financial information about a company. (Objective 5)

13. Financial-statement analysis is useful even in an efficient-market environment. (Objective 5)

QUESTIONS

25–1 What is meant by the term, "interim reporting"?

25–2 Explain the difference between the discrete (independent) and integral (dependent) views of interim financial reporting periods.

25–3 Which of the two concepts of interim reporting—the discrete or the integral—appears to be supported by the authoritative accounting pronouncements? Support your position by references to specific interim reporting practices.

25–4 Describe the process by which income tax expense should be determined in interim periods.

25–5 Should separately classified income statement items, such as extraordinary items, be prorated over several interim periods or recognized in a single interim period? Explain.

25–6 *APB Opinion No. 28* identifies several items of information that must be presented when publicly traded companies provide interim information to security holders on a regular basis. In addition to current-period information, for what additional time periods must information be presented? What is the purpose of this additional information?

25–7 In considering interim financial reporting, the APB concluded that such reporting should be viewed in which of the following ways?

[a] As a special type of reporting that need *not* follow GAAP.
[b] As useful only *if* activity is evenly spread throughout the year so that estimates are unnecessary.
[c] As reporting for a basic accounting period.
[d] As reporting for an integral part of an annual period.   (AICPA adapted)

25–8 Which of the following is an inherent difficulty in the determination of the results of operations on an interim basis?

[a] Cost of sales reflects only the amount of product expense allocable to revenue recognized as of the interim date.
[b] Depreciation on an interim basis is a partial estimate of the actual annual amount.
[c] Costs expensed in one interim period may benefit other periods.
[d] Revenues from long-term construction contracts accounted for by the percentage-of-completion method are based on annual completion, and interim estimates may be incorrect.   (AICPA adapted)

25–9 Which of the following reporting practices is permissible for interim financial reporting?

[a] Use of the gross-profit method for interim inventory pricing.
[b] Use of the direct-costing method for determining manufacturing inventories.
[c] Deferral of unplanned variances under a standard-cost system until year-end.
[d] Deferral of inventory market declines until the end of the year.   (AICPA adapted)

25–10 Discuss the basic rationale underlying the need of financial statement users for information by industry for an enterprise that operates in several industries at the same time.

25–11 The FASB outlines disclosure requirements in three different areas: industry operations, foreign operations and export sales, and major customers. Are these requirements independent of each other?

25–12 Which of the following is the primary purpose of segment reporting information?

[a] Interperiod comparisons of the particular enterprise.
[b] Comparisons between different enterprises.

25–13 What is the distinction between the terms "industry segment" and "reportable segment"? How is each determined?

25–14 What guidelines exist to ensure that industry segment information conforms with each of the following:

[a] It incorporates the majority of total enterprise operations.
[b] It does not become overly detailed by the presentation of an excessive number of industries?

25–15 What is the basic rationale underlying the requirement for disclosure of foreign operations and export sales?

25–16 Define major customer. What is the purpose of major customer disclosure?

25–17   What is a related-party transaction? What disclosures does GAAP require about related-party transactions?

25–18   What is a financial instrument?

25–19   What special disclosures about financial instruments are required by *SFAS No. 105?*

25–20   What is the main purpose of financial-statement analysis?

25–21   How should an analyst determine whether a financial ratio computed for a given company is "good" or "bad"?

25–22   Explain the meaning and computation of each of the following ratios: current, quick, and net cash flow from operating activities to current liabilities.

25–23   Explain the meaning and computation of each of the following ratios: debt to total assets, times interest earned, cash flow interest coverage, net cash flow from operating activities to sales, and net cash flow from operating activities to net income.

25–24   Explain the meaning and computation of each of the following ratios: receivables turnover, inventory turnover, asset turnover, profit margin on sales, rate of return on assets, return on common stockholders' equity, earnings per share, price/earnings ratio, book value per share, and dividend payout ratio.

25–25   What are the most important limitations of financial-statement analysis?

25–26   What major sources of information are potentially available to a person who wants to perform a financial analysis?

25–27   Assuming that the stock market is highly efficient, is it still worthwhile to learn about financial-statement analysis? Explain your answer.

EXERCISES

25–28   INTERIM REPORTING   In January 1993 Rongo, Inc., estimated that its year-end bonus to executives would be $240,000 for 1993. The amount paid for the year-end bonus for 1992 was $224,000. The estimate for 1993 is subject to year-end adjustment.

Instructions

Determine the amount of bonus expense that should be reflected in Rongo's quarterly income statement for the three months ended March 31, 1993, and justify your answer.   (AICPA adapted)

25–29   INTERIM REPORTING   In August 1992 Fizz Company spent $120,000 on an advertising campaign for subscriptions to its magazine on preparing for the skiing season. There are only two issues: one in October and one in November. The magazine is sold only on a subscription basis, and the subscriptions started in October 1992. Fizz's fiscal year ends on March 31, 1993.

Instructions

Determine the amount of expense that should be included in Fizz's quarterly income statement for the three months ended December 31, 1992, as a result of this expenditure. Justify your answer.

(AICPA adapted)

25–30   INTERIM REPORTING   In May 1993 an inventory loss of $500,000 occurred from a market decline. Box Company recorded this loss in May 1993 after its March 31, 1993, quarterly report was issued. None of this loss was recovered by the end of the year.

Instructions

Explain the general treatment of market declines in inventory in interim reports. How should the $500,000 loss be recognized in Box's 1993 quarterly financial statements?   (AICPA adapted)

25–31   INTERIM REPORTING   In May 1993 Brady Company spent $300,000 on an advertising campaign for subscriptions to the school magazine it sells. The subscriptions do not start until September 1993, and the magazine is sold only on a yearly subscription basis.

Instructions

How would you recognize the $300,000 advertising expense in the interim periods of 1993? Determine the amount of the advertising expense that should be included in Brady's quarterly income statement for the three months ended June 30, 1993, and justify your answer.   (AICPA adapted)

25–32 INTERIM REPORTING   Brandenberger Company reported income before income tax of $85,000 and $124,000 for the first two quarters of 1993. The company's estimate of the annual effective income tax rate was 36% at the end of the first quarter and 34% at the end of the second quarter.

Instructions

Determine the income tax expense for the first two quarters of 1993.

25–33 INTERIM REPORTING   Hallyburton Company's revenue, standard cost of goods sold, and variance information for the four quarters of 1993 are as follows:

	Quarter Ending			
	Mar. 31, 1993	*June 30, 1993*	*Sept. 30, 1993*	*Dec. 31, 1993*
Revenue	$445,000	$480,000	$510,000	$505,000
Standard cost of goods sold	200,000	220,000	240,000	250,000
Variance from standard*				
Planned	10,000	(15,000)	20,000	—
Unplanned	12,000	(7,000)	5,000	8,000

*Amounts in parentheses represent favorable variances or cost reductions. Other amounts represent unfavorable variances or additions to cost.

Instructions

Determine the amount of gross margin to be recognized in each quarter's income statement.

25–34 MAJOR CUSTOMER DISCLOSURE   Black Company made sales in 1993 to customers as follows:

Blue Company	$ 8,300,000
White Company	4,200,000
Brown Company	2,500,000
Red Company	1,850,000
Domestic governments	9,500,000
Foreign governments	7,260,000
Other	19,890,000
	$53,500,000

The following additional information is available:

[1] "Other" sales include sales to many customers, none of which exceed $1,000,000.
[2] Red and White Companies are both subsidiaries of Purple Company. Sales made to Purple Company amounted to $850,000 and are included in the "other" amount.
[3] Sales to domestic governments include $7,150,000 to federal governmental agencies, $1,100,000 to state governmental agencies, and $1,250,000 to local governmental agencies.
[4] Sales to foreign governments consisted of $4,200,000 to the government of Country Yellow and $3,060,000 to the government of Country Maroon.

Instructions

Identify the customers for which major customer disclosure must be made, justifying each.

25–35 INDUSTRY DISCLOSURE   Mid-America Company operates in three industries. Information on industry operations for 1993 is as follows:

	Identifiable Assets	Revenue	Operating Profit
Industry A	$620,000	$695,000	$49,500
Industry B	50,000	55,000	2,750
Industry C	12,000	15,000	975
	$682,000	$765,000	$53,225

Instructions

Identify the reporting requirements for the company in terms of industry segments in accordance with *SFAS No. 14*.

25–36 INDUSTRY DISCLOSURE Micro Shield Company operates in four industries. Operating statistics (in millions of dollars) for the four industries are as follows for 1993:

Industry	Revenue	Operating Profit	Identifiable Assets
Plastics	$112	$27	$120
Metals	75	24	75
Tobacco	18	4	20
Glass	7	1	10

There were no sales between segments in 1993.

Instructions

Determine the reportable industry segments for Micro Shield for 1993, applying all relevant criteria from *SFAS No. 14*. Present figures to support your conclusions.

25–37 FOREIGN OPERATIONS DISCLOSURE Northwest, Inc., is a publicly held company with domestic (U.S.) operations as well as several operating units in foreign countries. Information (in millions of dollars) concerning these operations is summarized below:

	Revenue	Operating Profit	Identifiable Assets
Domestic operations	$545	$ 60	$508
Foreign operations			
Country A	160	20	250
Country B	80	8	106
Country C	45	24	50
Country D	30	(5)	71
Consolidated totals	$860	$107	$985

Instructions

[a] Identify the separate disclosures related to foreign operations which must be presented in accordance with *SFAS No. 14*, justifying each item requiring disclosure.

[b] Prepare the disclosure of information concerning foreign operations for Northwest, Inc., based on the limited information given, in a format of your choice.

25–38 EXPORT SALES DISCLOSURE In its U.S. production facility International Technology Company produces a single product, which it sells in several domestic and foreign markets. In 1993 sales totaled $12,000,000, of which $5,500,000 were export sales in the following geographic areas:

European Common Market countries	$2,000,000
South American countries	1,700,000
Miscellaneous other countries	800,000
	$4,500,000

Instructions

Determine the specific information concerning domestic and export sales which must be presented with the 1993 financial statements to comply with the reporting requirements of *SFAS No. 14*.

25–39   INDUSTRY DISCLOSURE   Fidelity Company is subject to industry segment reporting requirements. Operating figures for 1993 are as follows:

Industry	Revenue	Operating Profit	Identifiable Assets
Metal containers	$ 850,000	$177,000	$ 628,000
Recording	700,000	5,000	919,000
Stereophonic equipment	200,000	22,000	275,000
Lawn equipment	172,000	32,000	250,000
Household appliances	658,000	90,000	400,000
Electronic calculators	230,000	11,000	198,000
	$2,810,000	$337,000	$2,670,000

Interindustry sales are as follows: metal containers to household appliances, $80,000; recording to stereophonic equipment, $35,000.

Instructions

Determine the industries which require separate disclosure in the 1993 financial statements. Present computations to support your conclusions.

25–40   INDUSTRY DISCLOSURE   Operating profit and loss figures for the seven industries in which the Kell Company operates are as follows:

	1993 Operating Profit (Loss)
Industry 1	$1,100,000
Industry 2	100,000
Industry 3	650,000
Industry 4	(208,000)
Industry 5	(28,000)
Industry 6	5,000
Industry 7	(2,000)
	$1,617,000

Instructions

Identify those industries which meet the criterion of 10% or more of operating profit or loss for Kell Company for 1993.

25–41   SHORT-TERM SOLVENCY RATIOS   The following information was extracted from the financial statements of Subway Corporation.

	1993	1992
Cash	$ 55,142	$ 61,543
Current assets	163,240	178,456
Current liabilities	64,173	71,227
Net cash flow from operating activities	36,250	48,342
Short-term receivables	15,125	18,158
Temporary investments	38,546	42,590

Instructions

Compute each of the following ratios for 1993:

[a] Current
[b] Quick
[c] Net cash flow from operating activities to current liabilities

25–42   LONG-TERM SOLVENCY RATIOS   The following information was taken from the 1993 financial statements of Endero Enterprises.

Cash paid for income taxes	$ 45,960
Cash paid for interest	35,050
Income tax expense	43,150
Interest expense	31,940
Net cash flow from operating activities	76,242
Net income	63,490
Net sales	989,000
Total assets	351,142
Total liabilities	145,310

Instructions

Compute each of the following ratios for 1993:

[a] debt to total assets
[b] times interest earned
[c] cash flow interest coverage
[d] net cash flow from operating activities to sales
[e] net cash flow from operating activities to net income

25–43 PROFITABILITY RATIOS The following information was obtained from the financial statements of Beefeaters, Inc.

	1993	1992
Accounts receivable (net)	$ 37,000	$ 43,000
Cash dividends on common stock	3,000	3,000
Common stockholders' equity	115,000	107,000
Cost of goods sold	516,200	464,550
Merchandise inventory	58,000	62,000
Net income	55,960	52,125
Net sales (all on credit)	890,000	815,000
Preferred dividends	5,000	5,000
Total assets	215,000	207,000

Beefeaters had 10,000 shares of common stock outstanding throughout 1992 and 1993. The market price of the company's common stock was $73.60 at the end of 1993.

Instructions

Compute each of the following ratios for 1993:

[a] receivables turnover
[b] inventory turnover
[c] asset turnover
[d] profit margin on sales
[e] rate of return on assets
[f] return on common stockholders' equity
[g] earnings per share
[h] price/earnings ratio
[i] book value per share
[j] dividend payout ratio

25–44 MISCELLANEOUS RATIOS Financial information for Kelso Company for 1993 and 1992 is shown below:

	December 31	
	1993	1992
Cash	$ 10,000	$ 80,000
Accounts receivable (net)	50,000	150,000
Merchandise inventory	90,000	150,000
Short-term marketable securities	30,000	10,000
Land and buildings (net)	340,000	360,000
Mortgage payable (no current portion)	270,000	280,000
Accounts payable (trade)	70,000	110,000
Short-term notes payable	20,000	40,000

| | Year ended December 31 | |
	1993	1992
Cash sales	$1,800,000	$1,600,000
Credit sales	500,000	800,000
Cost of goods sold	1,000,000	1,400,000

Instructions

Compute the following ratios for 1993 from the information given:

[a] Acid test   [c] Inventory turnover

[b] Receivables turnover   [d] Current   (AICPA adapted)

25–45 IMPACT OF INVENTORY METHODS ON RATIOS The controller of Hadnot, Inc., is analyzing her company's inventory accounting policy and asks you to perform certain calculations. She is particularly concerned with the effects a proposed change to LIFO may have on certain key ratios. The following information is available to you.

| | December 31 | |
	1993	1992
Inventory using present FIFO method	$ 500,000	$ 450,000
Inventory using proposed LIFO method	400,000	375,000
Current assets (using FIFO)	1,000,000	800,000
Current liabilities	500,000	425,000
Cost of goods sold (using FIFO)	2,100,000	1,900,000

Instructions

[a] Compute the following items for the year ended December 31, 1993, by using the current inventory method and the proposed method:

    [1] Current ratio   [2] Working capital   [3] Inventory turnover

[b] Comment on the analysis you have performed.

25–46 MISCELLANEOUS RATIOS The following is information from the financial records of the Loma Company:

Net accounts receivable at Dec. 31, 1992	$1,500,000
Net accounts receivable at Dec. 31, 1993	1,800,000
Inventories at Dec. 31, 1992	2,200,000
Inventories at Dec. 31, 1993	2,500,000
Accounts receivable turnover	10
Inventory turnover	4

Instructions

[a] How much were sales during 1993? (Assume all sales were on credit.)

[b] How much was cost of goods sold for 1993?

[c] Assuming a 365-day year, compute the number of days' sales in average receivables for 1993.

[d] Assuming a 365-day year, compute the number of days' sales in average inventory for 1993.

25–47 MISCELLANEOUS COMPUTATIONS BASED ON RATIOS The December 31, 1993, balance sheet of Dobyns Company is presented below. These are the only accounts in the company's balance sheet. Amounts indicated by a question mark (?) can be calculated from the additional information given.

Assets	
Cash	$ 25,000
Accounts receivable (net)	?
Inventory	?
Property, plant, and equipment (net)	294,000
	$432,000

Liabilities and Stockholders' Equity

Accounts payable (trade)	$?
Income taxes payable (current)	25,000
Long-term debt	?
Common stock	300,000
Retained earnings	?
	$?

Additional information that pertains to 1993

Current ratio	1.5 to 1
Total liabilities divided by total stockholders' equity	.8
Inventory turnover based on sales and ending inventory	15 times
Inventory turnover based on cost of goods sold and ending inventory	10.5 times
Gross margin	$315,000

Instructions

Compute the following items for Dobyns Company:

[a] Balance in trade accounts payable.

[b] Balance in retained earnings.

[c] Balance in inventory.   (AICPA adapted)

25–48   TEST OF REASONABLENESS AND DISCLOSURE   Apple Company had interest-bearing debt of $1,000,000 on its balance sheet at December 31, 1993, which represented an increase of $500,000 over interest-bearing debt at December 31, 1992. The company had interest expense of $50,000 for the year ended December 31, 1993. The market rate of interest for 1993 was 12%.

Instructions

[a] Comment on the reasonableness of Apple's interest expense to debt ratio. Give possible explanations for any unreasonable relationships that exist.

[b] Assume the same information except that the market rate of interest was 10% and the $500,000 additional debt represented an interest-free loan from Peach Company, a major customer of Apple. The two-year Peach loan was granted on January 1, 1993, in exchange for Apple's agreement to sell its special production equipment to Peach at a 5% discount during 1993 and 1994. Peach is expected to purchase from Apple equipment with a fair value of $2,000,000 over the two-year period.

   Prepare the entry that Apple should have made at the end of 1993.

[c] Prepare any footnote disclosure that should be included in Apple's financial statements as a result of the situation in [b].

25–49   MISCELLANEOUS COMPUTATIONS BASED ON RATIOS   Dockendorff, Inc., generated sales revenue of $5,000,000 during 1993. Dockendorff's statistical summary indicates the following ratios for the year ended December 31, 1993.

Rate of return on year-end stockholders' equity	15%
Rate of return on year-end assets	10%
Net income/sales	8%
Debt/equity	50%

Instructions

Based on this information, compute the following:

[a] Total assets   [d] Total debt

[b] Stockholders' equity [e] Total expenses

[c] Net income

PROBLEMS   **25–50   INTERIM PERIOD INCOME**   Hibler Company reports quarterly to its stockholders. Condensed financial information is presented, emphasizing quarterly results of operations. The company reports on a calendar-year basis with quarterly reports provided on March 31, June 30, September 30, and December 31.

Selected information for the four quarters of 1993 is shown below. All "other costs and expenses" are to be recognized in the period incurred except the following:

[1] $90,000 of machinery repairs incurred in the first quarter are expected to benefit each quarter equally.

[2] Advertising costs are allocated among the remaining quarters of the annual period, including the quarter in which the costs are incurred, on the basis of the historical pattern of sales: 20%, 30%, 15%, and 35% in the first through fourth quarters, respectively. Advertising expense amounted to $120,000 of the other costs and expenses incurred in the second quarter.

| | Quarter | | | |
	1	2	3	4
Revenue	$560,000	$675,000	$352,000	$875,000
Costs associated directly with revenue	265,000	308,000	176,000	490,000
Other costs and expenses (indicated in the period incurred)	110,000	165,000	45,000	162,000

Instructions

Determine income before income taxes for each quarter of 1993.

25–51 INTERIM PERIOD INCOME TAX Rios Company makes a quarterly estimate of the annual income tax rate and recognizes income tax expense on a cumulative year-to-date basis in the interim reports at the end of each quarter. For 1993, the expected income tax rate gradually declined as the company took advantage of certain tax credits and other methods of reducing income taxes which had not previously been anticipated.

Figures for the four quarters of 1993 are as follows:

End of Quarter	Anticipated Annual Income Tax Rate at This Date	Income for Quarter Ending on this Date
Mar. 31, 1993	46%	$150,000
June 30, 1993	44	182,000
Sept. 30, 1993	42	127,000
Dec. 31, 1993	40	185,000

Instructions

Determine the amount of income tax expense which should be recognized in determining net income for each quarter of 1993.

25–52 INTERIM PERIOD INCOME Silverberg Corporation is preparing information for its 1993 second quarter interim report that is provided to stockholders. The company is on a calendar-year basis. Information which has been accumulated to date includes the following:

[1] Revenue for the second quarter totaled $2,894,000, including a reduction for a loss on the sale of securities of $28,000, which is considered infrequent but not unusual.

[2] Expenses directly related to revenues are $1,600,000. During the first quarter of 1993, a loss of $125,000 on inventory declines below cost was recognized. During the second quarter inventory market values increased to a level in excess of cost. This increase in market is not reflected in the revenue or expense figures described above.

[3] Other costs and expenses incurred during the second quarter totaled $285,000. None of these are allocable to other quarters. In the first quarter, however, other costs and expenses of $40,000 were allocated to the second quarter.

[4] Income tax expense of $86,250 was recognized in the first quarter report. This was determined in the following way:

Income before income tax to Mar. 31, 1993	$187,500
Estimated annual income tax rate	46%
	$ 86,250

At June 30, 1993, the estimate of the annual effective income tax rate was revised to 42%.

Instructions

Determine net income for the quarter ended June 30, 1993.

25-53 INTERIM PERIOD INCOME STATEMENT   Tavassoli Company is publicly held and provides stockholders with quarterly financial information prepared in accordance with GAAP.

Selected data for the four quarters of 1993 are presented in the following schedule:

| | Quarter Ended | | | |
	Mar. 31	June 30	Sept. 30	Dec. 31
Revenue	$1,150,000	$1,068,000	$875,000	$1,245,000
Expenses				
Directly associated with revenue	$655,000	$548,000	$389,000	$625,000
Other	50,000	180,000	125,000	258,000
Expenses other than tax	$705,000	$728,000	$514,000	$883,000

You determine the following information concerning these data and other items of importance to Tavassoli's interim reporting.

[1] Included in third quarter revenue is an extraordinary gain of $212,000 (before income tax), which resulted from the involuntary conversion of a plant asset. The gain is subject to a 25% income tax rate.

[2] Included among other expenses of the second quarter are annual machinery repair costs of $120,000, which are expected to benefit all periods equally.

[3] Estimates of the annual effective income tax rate made at the end of each quarter are as follows: March 31, 46%; June 30, 40%; September 30, 44%; December 31, 42%.

[4] 100,000 shares of common stock were outstanding throughout 1993. The company has no preferred stock.

[5] Sales and costs directly associated with sales in 1993 followed a relatively normal seasonal pattern based on the past performance of Tavassoli Company.

Instructions

[a] Prepare condensed income statements for each quarter of 1993, including schedules to support your figures.

[b] Based on the limited information given in this problem, prepare a schedule for the quarter ending September 30, 1993, which includes the minimum disclosures required to be presented to stockholders.

25-54 INDUSTRY SEGMENT DISCLOSURE   Finelli Inc., is a publicly held corporation which is subject to the reporting requirements of *SFAS No. 14*. The company's controller has asked your assistance in determining whether industry segment information is necessary in the 1993 financial statements. The controller presents you with the following information:

Industry	Identifiable Assets	Revenues	Expenses Directly Allocable to Industry
Wholesale	$ 9,500,000	$8,300,000	$6,850,000
Retail trade	400,000	265,000	180,000
Manufacturing	300,000	420,000	263,800
Construction	300,000	197,000	125,200
	$10,500,000	$9,182,000	$7,419,000

General expenses are as follows:

Operating expenses associated with all industry segments	$ 762,000
General corporate expenses associated with corporate office	1,225,000
	$1,987,000

Further investigation reveals that all figures are accurate and that the operating expenses associated with all industry segments are allocable as follows: 70% to wholesale trade and 10% to each of the other industries.

Instructions

[a] Prepare a recommendation concerning the need to present industry segment information. Provide computations to support your opinion.
[b] Identify the financial-statement disclosures, if any, which are needed in relation to the company's operations in different industries.

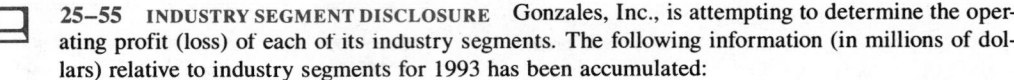 **25–55 INDUSTRY SEGMENT DISCLOSURE**   Gonzales, Inc., is attempting to determine the operating profit (loss) of each of its industry segments. The following information (in millions of dollars) relative to industry segments for 1993 has been accumulated:

Industry Segment	Revenue	Expense Directly Associated with Industry
Transportation equipment	$108	$ 67
Rubber products	80	60
Apparel	22	17
Lumber and wood products	7	5
Paper products	13	12
	$230	$161

The following additional revenue and expense information has been accumulated:

Revenue earned at the corporate level	$10,500,000
General corporate expenses	7,850,000
Operating expenses allocable to industry segments	22,000,000

The operating expenses allocable to industry segments relate to the rubber products, lumber and wood products, and paper products industries. Allocation is to be based on the relative amounts of revenue generated by each industry.

Instructions

[a] Determine the operating profit or loss of each segment for purposes of segment reporting requirements.
[b] Apply the 10% of revenue and operating profit tests to determine the reportable segments for Gonzales, Inc., for 1993. (For purposes of this problem, ignore the 10% of identifiable assets test.)
[c] Assuming that no intersegment sales were made, does your identification of reportable segments in [b] comply with the requirements of *SFAS No. 14?* You may assume that there are no comparability problems with previous years.

25–56 FOREIGN OPERATIONS AND EXPORT SALES   Billings Corporation has significant domestic and foreign operations. Revenues from the domestic operations result from sales within the United States and export sales.

You have been asked to help identify disclosure requirements in conformity with GAAP. As a part of your work you determine the following:

[1] Billings Corporation is a publicly held company whose stock is traded in the over-the-counter market.
[2] Revenue from sales for the year 1993 totaled $138,000,000 ($85,000,000 from domestic operations and $53,000,000 from foreign operations).
[3] Seventy percent of the domestic revenues were derived from sales within the United States. The remaining 30% resulted from export sales distributed as follows:

England	$16,000,000
Sweden	1,800,000
Canada	4,600,000
Mexico	3,100,000
	$25,500,000

[4] Activities from foreign operations are summarized in the following schedule:

	Revenue	Operating Profit	Identifiable Assets
South American operations	$44,000,000	$7,000,000	$52,000,000
African operations	5,000,000	100,000	4,000,000
Australian operations	4,000,000	(500,000)	4,500,000
	$53,000,000	$6,600,000	$60,500,000

[5] Summary figures from Billings' 1993 consolidated income statement and other company records are as follows:

Revenues (including $2,000,000 general corporate revenues)		$140,000,000
Expenses		
Operating expenses—Domestic operations	$65,000,000	
Operating expenses—Foreign operations	46,400,000	
General corporate expenses	13,600,000	125,000,000
Income before income tax		$ 15,000,000

Assets are as follows:

Identified with domestic operations	$ 78,000,000
Identified with foreign operations	60,500,000
Identified with corporate headquarters	10,500,000
	$149,000,000

Instructions

[a] Identify the information, if any, which must be presented concerning export sales.

[b] Identify the information, if any, which must be presented concerning foreign operations.

[c] Prepare a supplementary schedule incorporating the information you have identified in [a] and [b]. Design the schedule so that the disclosure of export sales and foreign operations relate to aggregate amounts taken from the company's financial statements.

25–57   INDUSTRY SEGMENT DISCLOSURE   In the early 1970s Armour Company (a publicly held corporation), entered a diversification program which resulted in its involvement in six different industries. In attempting to apply appropriate accounting and disclosure requirements in the 1993 financial statements, accountants have accumulated the data (in millions of dollars) on Armour's industry operations as shown:

Industry	Total Revenue	Expenses Directly Incurred by Industry	Assets Used Directly by Industry
Agriculture	$110	$ 60	$120
Mining	80	55	140
Construction	70	60	80
Transportation	20	21	17
Wholesale trade	5	2	4
Retail trade	3	2	2
	$288	$200	$363

Additional operating expenses allocable to industry operations total $45,000,000. You determine that these expenses should be allocated as follows: 40% to agriculture, 20% each to mining and construction, 10% to transportation, and 5% each to wholesale trade and retail trade.

General corporate expenses total $12,500,000. Interest income at the corporate level was $1,780,000. Equity in earnings of an investment in an affiliated company was $2,450,000.

An analysis of Armour's assets reveals that $38,500,000 of assets are used at the corporate level. This includes the $18,000,000 equity accounting basis in the affiliated company. Also, assets of $27,000,000 are used jointly by three industries and are allocable to them as follows: agriculture, 60%; mining, 30%; and wholesale trade, 10%.

Interindustry sales during 1993 are as follows: mining industry to construction industry, $7,000,000; transportation industry to agriculture industry, $15,500,000.

Instructions

[a] Identify the reportable segments for 1993 for Armour Company, applying all relevant tests of significance included in *SFAS No. 14*.

[b] Prepare a supplementary schedule, based on the information presented in the problem and your response in [a], to be used to present industry segment information in the 1993 financial statements.

[c] What additional information, not available in this problem, would be required to complete the industry segment disclosure requirements of *SFAS No. 14?*

25–58 RELATED-PARTY TRANSACTION DISCLOSURES The Moss, Inc., annual report dated December 31, 1993, contained the following consolidated statements of changes in stockholders' equity along with a footnote on related-party transactions:

Moss, Inc.
CONSOLIDATED STATEMENTS OF CHANGES IN STOCKHOLDERS' EQUITY

| | Preferred Stock | | Common Stock | | Paid-in | Retained | |
	Shares	Value	Shares	Value	Capital	Earnings	Total
Balances at Jan. 1, 1993	29,058	$290,580	63,660	$318,300	$92,410	$ 740,457	$1,441,747
Issuance of common stock for services	—	—	—	—	—	—	—
Redemption of preferred stock in exchange for property	(29,058)	(290,580)	—	—	—	(67,400)	(357,980)
Issuance of common stock	—	—	—	—	—	—	—
Net earnings	—	—	—	—	—	1,179,742	1,179,742
Balances at Dec. 31, 1993	—	—	63,660	$318,300	$92,410	$1,852,799	$2,263,509

Related-Party Transactions

In August 1992 the company issued 1,518 shares of common stock to an officer in exchange for a proven oil and gas property valued at $100,000, the property's approximate cost. The company incurred costs of approximately $61,000 to further develop the oil and gas property. In April 1993 the company entered into an agreement with the officer whereby the company exchanged the proven oil and gas property (which then had an estimated fair market value of $300,000) for a drilling rig and related equipment. The transaction resulted in a gain for the company of approximately $139,000 and is included in gain on sale of property and equipment in the consolidated statements of earnings.

In February 1992 the company issued 29,058 shares of preferred stock to an officer and forgave him for an indebtedness of an $88,000 note receivable in exchange for a drilling rig and related equipment having a fair market value of $378,580. In January 1993 the company redeemed all of the outstanding preferred stock for $11 per share and paid accrued dividends aggregating $38,342 in exchange for certain proven oil and gas properties carried on the books at $105,140, their approximate current value. This transaction resulted in a gain of approximately $253,000 and is included as a gain on the sale of property and equipment in the consolidated statements of earnings.

Instructions

[a] Prepare the entries to record the transactions that are described in the footnote.

[b] Discuss the propriety of the treatment accorded these events. Be sure to include a discussion of the basic theoretical issues involved.

25–59 RATIO COMPUTATIONS Comparative balance sheets, income and retained earnings statements, and additional information pertaining to the Kitkat Company appear below.

Kitkat Company
BALANCE SHEET
December 31, 1993 and 1992

Assets

Current Assets	1993	1992
Cash	$ 3,500,000	$ 3,600,000
Marketable securities, at cost which approximates market	13,000,000	11,000,000
Accounts receivable, net of allowance for doubtful accounts	105,000,000	95,000,000
Inventories, lower of cost or market	126,000,000	154,000,000
Prepaid expenses	2,500,000	2,400,000
Total current assets	250,000,000	266,000,000
Noncurrent Assets		
Property, plant, and equipment, net of accumulated depreciation	311,000,000	308,000,000
Investments, at equity	2,000,000	3,000,000
Long-term receivables	14,000,000	16,000,000
Goodwill and patents, net of accumulated amortization	6,000,000	6,500,000
Other assets	7,000,000	8,500,000
Total assets	$590,000,000	$608,000,000

Liabilities and Stockholders' Equity

Current Liabilities	1993	1992
Notes payable	$ 5,000,000	$15,000,000
Accounts payable	38,000,000	48,000,000
Accrued expenses	24,500,000	27,000,000
Income taxes payable	1,000,000	1,000,000
Payments due within one year on long-term debt	6,500,000	7,000,000
Total current liabilities	75,000,000	98,000,000
Noncurrent Liabilities		
Long-term debt	169,000,000	180,000,000
Deferred income taxes	74,000,000	67,000,000
Other liabilities	9,000,000	8,000,000
Total liabilities	327,000,000	353,000,000
Stockholders' Equity		
Common stock, par value $1 per share; authorized 20,000,000 shares; issued and outstanding 10,000,000 shares	10,000,000	10,000,000
5% cumulative preferred stock, par value $100 per share; $100 liquidating value; authorized 50,000 shares; issued and outstanding 40,000 shares	4,000,000	4,000,000
Additional paid-in capital	107,000,000	107,000,000
Retained earnings	142,000,000	134,000,000
Total stockholders' equity	263,000,000	255,000,000
Total liabilities and stockholders' equity	$590,000,000	$608,000,000

Kitkat Company
STATEMENT OF INCOME AND RETAINED EARNINGS
For the Years Ended December 31, 1993 and 1992

	1993	1992
Net sales	$600,000,000	$500,000,000
Cost and expenses		
Cost of goods sold	490,000,000	400,000,000
Selling, general, and administrative expenses	66,000,000	60,000,000
Other, net	7,000,000	6,000,000
Total costs and expenses	563,000,000	466,000,000

Income before income taxes	37,000,000	34,000,000
Income taxes	16,800,000	15,800,000
Net income	20,200,000	18,200,000
Retained earnings at beginning of period	134,000,000	126,000,000
Dividends on common stock	12,000,000	10,000,000
Dividends on preferred stock	200,000	200,000
Retained earnings at the end of period	$142,000,000	$134,000,000

Additional Information

1. Market price per share of Kitkat's common stock on 12-31-93 $10.00
2. Interest expense for 1993 (included among the costs and expenses on the income statement) $19,500,000
3. Net cash flow from operating activities during 1993 $48,000,000
4. Cash paid for interest during 1993 $19,500,000
5. Cash paid for income taxes during 1993 $16,800,000

Instructions

Compute the following ratios for 1993 and show supporting computations in good form:

[a] Current
[b] Quick
[c] Net cash flow from operating activities to current liabilities
[d] Debt to total assets
[e] Debt to equity
[f] Times interest earned
[g] Cash flow interest coverage
[h] Net cash flow from operating activities to sales
[i] Net cash flow from operating activities to net income
[j] Receivables turnover
[k] Number of days' sales in receivables (assume 365 days in a year)
[l] Inventory turnover
[m] Number of days' sales in inventory (assume 365 days in a year)
[n] Asset turnover
[o] Profit margin on sales
[p] Rate of return on assets
[q] Return on common stockholders' equity
[r] Earnings per share
[s] Price/earnings ratio
[t] Book value per share
[u] Dividend payout ratio
[v] Dividend yield.

25–60   RATIO COMPUTATIONS AND REVISED FINANCIAL STATEMENTS   Peyton Company manufactures and sells children's plastic toys. The company has experienced continued growth over the past three years and has forecast sales of $3,000,000 for 1994. Peyton applied to Anderson State Bank for a short-term loan of $50,000 to cover expanding working capital needs. This is the first loan application Anderson State Bank has ever received from Peyton, and the bank is anxious to develop a lasting relationship.

The following financial and other information has been supplied by Peyton at the bank's request or developed by bank personnel.

Peyton Company
BALANCE SHEET
December 31, 1992 and 1993
(in thousands)
(unaudited)

Assets	1992	1993
Current assets		
Cash	$ 85	$ 60
Marketable securities (cost)	20	20
Accounts receivable (net)	520	600
Inventories	365	475
Prepaid items	40	45
Total current assets	1,030	1,200
Investments (cost)	80	80
Property, plant, and equipment (net)	590	520
Total assets	$1,700	$1,800

Equities

Current liabilities		
Notes payable (trade)	$ 90	$ 80
Notes payable (officers)	100	100
Accounts payable	190	280
Accrued expenses and taxes	50	40
Total current liabilities	$ 430	$ 500
Long-term debt, 7%	420	400
Total liabilities	$ 850	$ 900
Stockholders' equity	850	900
Total equities	$1,700	$1,800

Peyton Company
INCOME STATEMENT
For the Year Ended December 31, 1992 and 1993
(in thousands)
(unaudited)

	1992	1993
Net sales	$2,500	$2,800
Cost of goods sold	1,750	2,100
Gross margin	750	700
Operating expenses		
Advertising	145	155
Bad debts estimate	25	28
Depreciation	70	70
Insurance	35	36
Lease payment	—	8
Salaries	185	190
Supplies	13	8
Taxes (nonincome)	25	25
Interest	42	40
Total operating expenses	540	560
Earnings before income taxes	210	140
Income taxes	105	70
Net income	$ 105	$ 70

Additional Information

[1] **Accounts receivable.** Sales are highly seasonal, with most sales occurring in the summer and fall for the upcoming Christmas season. Peyton allows many customers to wait until January or February to settle their accounts (a common practice in the industry).

The allowance for uncollectible accounts had a balance of $30,000 on December 31, 1992, and $40,000 on December 31, 1993.

The aged accounts receivable balance on December 31, 1993, is shown as follows:

Days Past Due	Amount	Industry Collection Experience
Not due	$340,000	99% collected
1–60	120,000	97% collected
61–120	40,000	90% collected
121–180	70,000	80% collected
Over 181	70,000	50% collected
	$640,000	

[2] **Inventory.**

	1992	1993
Raw materials (LIFO)	$100,000	$100,000
Work in process (FIFO)	50,000	300,000
Finished goods (FIFO)	215,000	75,000

The raw materials consist primarily of plastic. Plastic prices rose approximately 10% in 1992 and by the same amount in 1993. Peyton began its LIFO program on January 1, 1992.

[3] **Employment contract.**   The company president has a five-year contract at $45,000 per year with three years remaining.

[4] **Insurance.**   The company has purchased ordinary life insurance on its key officers. The policies have accrued a total of $5,000 cash surrender value.

[5] **Marketable securities.**   The marketable securities were worth $21,000 at December 31, 1993.

[6] **Investments.**   The investments of $80,000 consist of 800 shares of Fisher Company, which is owned in part by several of Peyton's directors. Fisher discontinued one of its major products as a result of a legal suit concerning product safety standards. The stock declined to $60 per share following this action.

[7] **Property, plant, and equipment.**   The company uses the same depreciation methods for book and tax purposes. The straight-line method is used on the plant, and the double-declining balance method is used on all equipment.

A purchase agreement for a parcel of land was signed in September 1993. Payment was to be made on January 10, 1994. The check for $10,000 was written on December 27, 1993, and delivered to the seller. The transaction was not recorded in December.

In January 1993 a noncancellable lease for equipment was signed by Peyton. The lease calls for Peyton to make annual payments of $8,000 for five years. The equipment can be purchased at the end of the lease for $10,000. The purchase price of the equipment was $40,000. At the date the lease was signed the value of the lease payments and option price was $40,000 (using a 10% rate), and the present value of the remaining lease payments and option price at December 31, 1993 is $35,000.

[8] **Notes payable (officers).**   The officers loaned the company $100,000 early in 1991. The notes have been renewed each year, and it is expected they will be renewed annually for the next three years. The notes are subordinated to other notes outstanding.

[9] **Dividends.**   The company paid dividends of $20,000 to its stockholders during 1993.

Instructions

[a] Calculate the following ratios for 1993 by using the preceding financial information:

    [1] Return on total assets.
    [2] Acid-test ratio.
    [3] Average collection period for receivables.
    [4] Inventory turnover.
    [5] Times interest earned.

[b] Revise the balance sheet on a *pro forma* basis as of December 31, 1993, to make it more useful for the bank's needs.

[c] Prepare a summary of estimated cash flows for 1993.   (CMA adapted)

25–61   FINANCIAL STATEMENTS DERIVED FROM RATIOS   Ratio analysis is often applied to test the reasonableness of the relationships among current financial data against those of prior financial data. Given prior financial relationships and a few key amounts, an accountant can prepare estimates of current financial data to test the reasonableness of current financial information.

Mayo Company has in recent years maintained the following relationships among the data in its financial statements:

Gross profit rate on net sales	40%
Net profit rate on net sales	10%
Rate of selling expenses to net sales	20%
Accounts receivable turnover	8 per year
Inventory turnover	6 per year
Acid-test ratio	2 to 1
Current ratio	3 to 1

Quick-asset composition:
    8% cash
    32% marketable securities
    60% accounts receivable

Asset turnover	2 per year
Ratio of total assets to intangible assets	20 to 1
Ratio of accumulated depreciation to cost of fixed assets	1 to 3
Ratio of accounts receivable to accounts payable	1.5 to 1
Ratio of working capital to stockholders' equity	1 to 1.6
Ratio of total debt to stockholders' equity	1 to 2

The corporation had a net income of $120,000 for 1993, which resulted in earnings of $5.20 per share of common stock.

Additional Information

[1] Capital stock authorized, issued (all in 1985), and outstanding: common, $10 per share par value, issued at 10% premium; preferred, 6% nonparticipating, $100 per share par value, issued at 10% premium.
[2] Market value per share of common stock at December 31, 1993: $78.
[3] Preferred dividends paid in 1993: $3,000.
[4] Times interest earned in 1993: 33.
[5] The amounts of the following were the same at December 31, 1993, as at January 1, 1993: inventory, accounts receivable, 5% bonds payable—due in 1998—and total stockholders' equity.
[6] All purchases and sales were "on account."

Instructions

[a] Prepare in good form the condensed balance sheet and income statement for the year ended December 31, 1993, presenting the amounts you would expect to find in Mayo's financial statements based on the ratios and other information provided.

    Major captions appearing on Mayo's balance sheet are: Current Assets, Fixed Assets, Intangible Assets, Current Liabilities, Long-Term Liabilities, and Stockholders' Equity. In addition to the accounts divulged in the problem, you should include accounts for Prepaid Expenses, Accrued Expenses, and Administrative Expenses. Supporting calculations should be in good form. You may ignore income taxes.

[b] Compute the following ratios for 1993 and show your computations:

    [1] Rate of return on stockholders' equity.
    [2] Price/earnings ratio for common stock.
    [3] Dividends paid per share of common stock.
    [4] Dividends paid per share of preferred stock.
    [5] Yield on common stock.

(AICPA adapted)

CASES

25-62 INTERIM REPORTING Roth Manufacturing Company, a California corporation listed on the Pacific Coast Stock Exchange, budgeted activities for 1993 as follows:

	Amount	Units
Net sales	$6,000,000	1,000,000
Cost of goods sold	3,600,000	1,000,000
Gross margin	2,400,000	
Selling, general, and administrative expenses	1,400,000	
Operating earnings	1,000,000	
Nonoperating revenues and expenses	–0–	
Earnings before income taxes	1,000,000	
Estimated income taxes (current and deferred)	550,000	
Net earnings	$ 450,000	
Earnings per share of common stock	$4.50	

Roth has operated profitably for many years and has experienced a seasonal pattern of sales volume and production similar to the following amounts forecasted for 1993. Sales volume is expected to follow a quarterly pattern of 10%, 20%, 35%, and 35%, respectively, because of the seasonality of the industry. Because of production and storage limitations, production is expected to follow a pattern of 20%, 25%, 30%, and 25%, per quarter, respectively.

At the end of the first quarter of 1993, the controller of Roth prepared and issued the following interim report for public release:

	Amount	Units
Net sales	$ 600,000	100,000
Cost of goods sold	360,000	100,000
Gross margin	240,000	
Selling, general and administrative expenses	275,000	
Operating loss	(35,000)	
Loss from warehouse fire	(175,000)	
Loss before income taxes	(210,000)	
Estimated income taxes	–0–	
Net loss	$(210,000)	
Loss per share of common stock	$(2.10)	

The following additional information is available for the first quarter just completed, but was not included in the public information released:

[1] The company uses a standard cost system in which standards are set at currently attainable levels on an annual basis. At the end of the first quarter there was underapplied fixed factory overhead (volume variance) of $50,000 that was treated as an asset at the end of the quarter. Production during the quarter was 200,000 units, of which 100,000 were sold.

[2] The selling, general, and administrative expenses were budgeted on a basis of $900,000 fixed expenses for the year plus $.50 variable expenses per unit of sales.

[3] The warehouse fire loss met the conditions of an extraordinary loss. The warehouse had an undepreciated cost of $320,000; $145,000 was recovered from insurance on the warehouse. No other gains or losses are anticipated this year from similar events or transactions, nor has Roth had any similar losses in preceding years; thus, the full loss will be deductible as an ordinary loss for income tax purposes.

[4] The effective income tax rate, for federal and state taxes combined, is expected to average 55% of earnings before income taxes during 1993. There are no permanent differences between pretax financial earnings and taxable income.

[5] Earnings per share were computed on the basis of 100,000 shares of capital stock outstanding. Roth has only one class of stock issued, no long-term debt outstanding, and no stock option plan.

Instructions

[a] Without reference to the specific situation described above, what are the standards of disclosure for interim financial data (published interim financial reports) for publicly traded companies? Explain.

[b] Identify the weakness in form and content of Roth's interim report without reference to the additional information.

[c] For each of the five items of additional information, indicate the preferable treatment for each item for interim reporting purposes and explain why that treatment is preferable.

(AICPA adapted)

25–63   SEGMENT REPORTING   Kearns, Inc., manufactures a wide variety of pharmaceuticals, medical instruments, and other related medical supplies. Eighteen months ago the company developed and began to market a new product line of antihistamine drugs under various trade names. Sales and profitability of this product line during the current fiscal year greatly exceeded management's expectations. The new product line will account for 10% of the company's total sales and

12% of the company's operating income for the fiscal year ending June 30, 1993. Management believes sales and profits will be significant for several years.

Kearns fears that disclosure in its annual financial statements about the volume and profitability of its new product line will adversely affect its market position in relation to its competitors. Management is not sure how *FASB Statement of Financial Accounting Standards No. 14*, "Financial Reporting for Segments of a Business Enterprise," applies in this case.

Instructions

[a] Why should segment information be disclosed in financial statements?

[b] Explain the factors that should be considered when attempting to decide how products should be grouped to determine a single business segment.

[c] What options, if any, does Kearns, Inc., have regarding the disclosure of its new antihistamine product line? Explain your answer.   (CMA adapted)

25–64   MEANING AND LIMITATIONS OF RATIOS   As the CPA responsible for the audit engagement of a small client, you are requested by the client to provide him at the earliest possible date with some key ratios based on the final audited figures appearing on the comparative financial statements. The information is to be used to convince creditors that the client's business is solvent and to justify a request for continued financial support. The client wishes to save time by concentrating on only these key data.

The requested data and the computations taken from the financial statements follow:

	Last Year	*This Year*
Current ratio	2.0:1	2.5:1
Quick (acid-test) ratio	1.2:1	.7:1
Ratio of property, plant, and equipment to owners' equity	2.3:1	2.6:1
Ratio of sales to owners' equity	2.8:1	2.5:1
Net income	Down 10%	Up 30%
Earnings per common share	$2.40	$3.12
Book value per common share	Up 8%	Up 5%

Instructions

[a] The client asks that you prepare a list of brief comments stating how each of these items supports the solvency and going-concern potential of his business. He wishes to use these comments to support his presentation of data to his creditors. Prepare the comments by listing the implications and the limitations of each item separately. Then explain the collective inference that one may draw from them about the client's solvency and going-concern potential.

[b] Prepare a brief list of additional ratio-analysis-type data that you think this client's creditors will request to supplement the data provided in [a]. Explain why the additional data will be helpful to these creditors in evaluating this client's solvency.

[c] What warnings should you offer these creditors about the limitations of ratio analysis for the purpose stated here?   (AICPA adapted)

25–65   USE OF RATIOS IN FINANCIAL DECISION   Fast Track Corporation was formed in 1988 through a public subscription of common stock. Ann Downing, who owns 15% of the common stock, was one of the organizers of Fast Track and is its current president. The company has been successful, but currently it is experiencing a shortage of funds. On June 10, 1993, Downing asked First National Bank for a 24-month extension of two $30,000 notes, which were due on June 30, 1993, and September 30, 1993. Another note of $7,000 is due on December 31, 1993, but she expects no difficulty in meeting that due date. Downing explained that Fast Track's cash flow problems are due primarily to the company's desire to finance a $300,000 plant expansion over the next two fiscal years through internally generated funds.

The commercial loan officer of First National requested financial reports for the last two years. These reports were provided, as follows:

Fast Track Corporation
STATEMENT OF FINANCIAL POSITION
For the Fiscal Years Ended March 31, 1992 and 1993

Assets	1992	1993
Cash	$ 12,500	$ 16,400
Notes receivable	104,000	112,000
Accounts receivable (net)	68,500	81,600
Inventories (at cost)	50,000	80,000
Plant and equipment (net of depreciation)	646,000	680,000
Total assets	$881,000	$970,000
Liabilities and Owners' Equity		
Accounts payable	$ 72,000	$ 69,000
Notes payable	54,500	67,000
Accrued liabilities	6,000	9,000
Common stock (60,000 shares, $10 par)	600,000	600,000
Retained earnings*	148,500	225,000
Total liabilities and owners' equity	$881,000	$970,000

*Cash dividends were paid at the rate of $1.00 per share in fiscal year 1992 and $1.25 per share in fiscal year 1993.

Fast Track Corporation
INCOME STATEMENT
For the Fiscal Years Ended March 31, 1992 and 1993

	1992	1993
Sales	$2,700,000	$3,000,000
Cost of goods sold**	1,720,000	1,902,500
Gross margin	980,000	1,097,500
Operating expenses	780,000	845,000
Income before taxes	200,000	252,500
Income taxes (40%)	80,000	101,000
Net income	$ 120,000	$ 151,500

**Depreciation charges of $100,000 and $102,500 on the plant and equipment for fiscal years ended March 31, 1992 and 1993, respectively, are included in cost of goods sold.

Instructions

[a] Calculate the following items for Fast Track Corporation:

[1] Current ratio for fiscal years 1992 and 1993.
[2] Acid test (quick) ratio for fiscal years 1992 and 1993.
[3] Inventory turnover for fiscal year 1993.
[4] Return on year-end assets for fiscal years 1992 and 1993.
[5] Percentage change in sales, cost of goods sold, gross margin, and net income from fiscal year 1992 to 1993.

[b] Identify and explain what other financial reports and/or financial analyses might be helpful to the commercial loan officer of First National Bank in evaluating Downing's request for a time extension on Fast Track's notes.

[c] Assume that the percentage changes (when comparing fiscal year 1993 with fiscal year 1992) for sales, cost of goods sold, gross margin, and net income will be repeated in each of the next two years. Is Fast Track's desire to finance the plant expansion from internally generated funds realistic? Explain your answer.

[d] Should First National Bank grant the extension on Fast Track's notes, in light of Downing's statement about financing the plant expansion through internally generated funds? Explain your answer.

(CMA adapted)

25–66 FINANCIAL DECISION BASED ON RATIOS   Wall Company is considering extending credit to Mart Company. It is estimated that sales to Mart would amount to $2,000,000 annually. Wall wholesales throughout the midwest, and Mart (a retail chain) has a number of stores in the midwest. Wall has had a gross margin of approximately 60% in recent years and expects to have a similar gross margin on the Mart order, which would be approximately 15% of Wall Company's present sales.

Information derived from Mart's financial statements for 1991–1993 is as follows:

	1991	1992	1993
Rate of return on total assets	1.96%	1.12%	(.87)%
Return to sales	1.69%	.99%	(.69)%
Acid test ratio	1.73/1	1.36/1	1.19/1
Current ratio	2.39/1	1.92/1	1.67/1
Inventory turnover (times)	4.41	4.32	4.52
Equity relationships			
Current liabilities	36.0%	43.0%	48.0%
Long-term liabilities	16.0	10.5	5.0
Shareholders' equity	48.0	46.5	47.0
	100.0%	100.0%	100.0%
Asset relationships			
Current assets	77.0%	72.5%	69.5%
Property, plant, and equipment	23.0%	27.5%	30.5%
	100.0%	100.0%	100.0%

Instructions

[a] For each of the first five items of information given, indicate whether the statistic is favorable, unfavorable, or neutral in the decision to grant credit to Mart.

[b] Based on the information provided, would you grant credit to Mart? Support your answer with facts given for the case.

[c] What additional information, if any, would you want before making a final decision?

(CMA adapted)

JUDGMENT CASES

25–67 INTERIM REPORTING   Fast-Set, Inc., a hazardous waste disposal company, holds a large portfolio of noncurrent marketable equity securities. The company acquired the securities several years ago to provide a surety bond because insurance for the company's activities was not available at the time. The state had required the portfolio as a condition of granting the company's corporate charter. In the first quarter of the current year, insurance coverage became available, and the company obtained the coverage required by the state. This means that the portfolio is no longer required and can be used for other corporate purposes.

The portfolio now has a market value significantly below its cost due to a widespread decline in the market values of securities in a variety of industries subsequent to year-end. Most analysts believe the broad market decline will last for about 12 to 18 months.

Management has tentatively decided to accelerate a much needed plant modernization with the resources now available. Competitors have recently begun to take business away from Fast-Set, and it is clear that state-of-the-art technology is necessary if the company is to remain successful.

Most of the securities are expected to be sold beginning in the third quarter of the current year and continuing ratably for approximately 6 more months. As the accountant for Fast-Set, you recommend that the securities that will be sold within the next 12 months should be reclassified as current. You also suggest that the losses on the aggregate current portfolio should be reported as losses in the current (first) quarter's income statement. The president of the company simply smiles and states:

> *You just don't know how to manage generally accepted accounting principles. First, our plans are tentative and we might not begin the plant modernization. Second, we will never sell securities below their original cost to us. We are not in the business of taking such losses. We will just hold those securities until their values*

rise. You know that the recent decline is just a temporary overall market correction. We will take great care to select for sale this year only those securities whose market values are equal to or in excess of their current carrying amount in the accounting records. In this fashion, the cost of the securities reclassified as a current portfolio will be greater than or equal to their market values.

Third, if the value of securities doesn't rise, then we will borrow the money to finance the plant expansion and use the securities as collateral. Fourth, this is just an interim determination and we can treat the decline in value similar to a temporary LIFO layer liquidation that will be restored before year-end.

Now, what's the problem? Nothing that I can see and I don't think you can find any reasons not to go for it either, can you? If this was an annual reporting situation, I would probably agree with you, but in interim statements, you can defer these drastic accounting decisions until the end of the year. And that is what I plan to do. As luck would have it, we only issue an income statement at interim reporting dates. Thus we don't even have to report the decline in the noncurrent portfolio, which is confined to the balance sheet.

Instructions

Prepare an appropriate response to the accounting that Fast-Set's president has proposed.

25–68   RELATED-PARTY TRANSACTION   Hy Lee Optimistic serves as the general partner for a number of real estate limited partnerships. You are the accountant for one of those partnerships, Builders LTD., which is a real estate development company. At the previous annual partners' meeting, Mr. Optimistic asserted that the partnership's principal project, a small office building named Commerce Center, would soon be completed and sold, with profit distributions to the limited partners to follow quickly.

Builders, LTD., completed the construction of the complex early in the past year as anticipated and has attempted to sell it for the last eight months. Until the last week of December those efforts were unsuccessful, due primarily to factors beyond the control of the general partner. Rapid, significant, and unforeseen rises in interest rates and the closure of a major local corporation which produced a large office vacancy rate have adversely affected commercial real estate generally.

You are aware that Optimistic has felt considerable pressure to sell the building at the price anticipated and to provide the promised distributions to the limited partners. Only a single offer on the building for $265,000 (an amount that was $10,000 less than the building's cost) had been received recently, and it was declined. During the last week of December, Optimistic sold the building to another limited partnership for which he acts as the general partner. That partnership, which was organized to acquire and operate troubled commercial real estate projects, paid $575,000 in cash for the building, an amount that was $25,000 less than the anticipated sales price.

You have pointed out to Optimistic that the transaction will have to be disclosed as a related-party transaction in accordance with *FASB Statement No. 57*, "Related Party Disclosures" and Optimistic agrees. Accordingly, you have drafted the following proposed note to the financial statements:

> *During the year the company sold its principal asset, Commerce Center, to a limited partnership operated by the same general partner as Builders LTD. The sales price of $575,000 resulted in a reported profit to Builders of $300,000. The transaction was consummated for cash and no amounts receivable or payable remain at year-end. The only offer received on the property from an unrelated third party was for $265,000, which probably represents the fair value of the property. The sale took place between two entities that are under the common control of a single general partner, and accordingly, the transaction cannot be considered to have occurred at arm's length.*

When you present Optimistic with the proposed language of the disclosure he takes exception to your presentation and asserts:

This goes far beyond anything that FASB Statement No. 57 *requires. The description of that other lowball offer just confuses the issue. I know what this property is worth, and I know how to operate it at a profit to all involved. I paid a fair price for it and I am confident that I will be able to operate it profitably for the new owners. Anyway, why do the partners of Builders care about any of this? They got their money and are quite happy even though the amount was less than anticipated. In fact, almost all of them have just agreed to contribute to a second Builders partnership that will construct a sister complex to Commerce Center. If you insist on this adverse disclosure, they may have second thoughts and try to back out of the deal. There is simply no way that I will accept the disclosure that you have suggested.*

Instructions

What should you do? If you believe that it would be appropriate to revise your disclosure, prepare a new note in its entirety. If you believe that the information contained in the note presented in the case is all necessary, respond to the beliefs and assertions of Mr. Optimistic.

CHAPTER 26

Financial Reporting and Changing Prices

OBJECTIVES

1. To discuss the nature and measurement of price changes.
2. To explain the difference between a general price-level change and a specific price change.
3. To discuss and illustrate constant dollar accounting.
4. To explain the major forms of current value accounting.
5. To discuss and illustrate current cost accounting.
6. To discuss and illustrate current cost/constant dollar accounting.
7. To present an overview of the current recommendations of the Financial Accounting Standards Board in the area of accounting for changing prices.

C onventional financial statements often are criticized because they do not reflect current values and are not reported in dollars of the same purchasing power. These criticisms are particularly strong because of the magnitudes of price changes that have occurred in the United States and elsewhere. In this chapter we discuss the nature of price changes and illustrate how financial statements can be adjusted for them. We also discuss the current recommendations of the Financial Accounting Standards Board in the area of accounting for changing prices.

This book does not cover all the FASB's requirements, nor is it limited to those requirements. Today the FASB merely *encourages,* but does not require, companies to disclose supplementary information on the effects of changing prices. In this chapter we explain and illustrate comprehensive financial statements adjusted for changing prices. An understanding of these comprehensive statements will help you to better understand the nature and limitations of conventional financial statements as well as the FASB's current disclosure recommendations concerning the effects of changing prices. It will also help you to more easily understand the kinds of information that may be required in the future, especially if the inflation rate should increase from its present, relatively low level. As you study this chapter, keep in mind how pervasive the subject matter is. That is, it applies to the entire set of financial statements, not merely to a few selected accounts. Accounting for changing prices has probably been the most widely discussed topic in financial accounting during the twentieth century.

NATURE AND MEASUREMENT OF PRICE CHANGES

A **price change** is an increase or decrease in the price of a good or service in a given market, such as a wholesale market or a retail market. Two major types of price changes are general price-level changes and specific price changes. Some of the concepts relating to these price changes were initially explained in Chapter 3.

GENERAL PRICE-LEVEL CHANGES

A **general price-level change** is an increase or decrease in the overall level of prices of goods and services throughout the economy. An increase in the general price-level means that money's **purchasing power** (its ability to buy goods and services) has decreased; this is known as **inflation.** A decrease in the general price-level, known as **deflation,** means that money's purchasing power has increased. During most of the twentieth century, inflation has occurred much more frequently than deflation in the United States and in most other countries. For this reason most of the illustrations and problem assignments in this chapter assume the existence of inflation. Recognize, however, that the same general principles apply when deflation occurs.

General price-level changes are measured by using a **general price-level index** constructed by the federal government. Such an index is designed to show how much the overall level of prices in the economy has changed over time. Theoretically, a general price-level index should be constructed by monitoring changes in the prices of *all* goods and services in the economy. For practical reasons, however, the federal government derives a general price-level index by considering price changes in only a sample of goods and services. The government derives several different indexes, and each one is calculated in relation to a predetermined "market basket" of goods and services.

In constructing an index, a base period is selected and assigned an index number of 100. All other periods in the index are then assigned index numbers that relate to the base. Suppose, for example, that 1980 is selected as the base period of a particular index and that prices in the "market basket" comprising the index rise by an average of 25% during 1981. Under these circumstances, 1980 and 1981 would be assigned index numbers of 100 and 125, respectively. Dividing 125 by 100 indicates that prices have risen by 25% during 1981 (125 ÷ 100 = 1.25). The reciprocal of this ratio (100 ÷ 125 = .80) indicates that a dollar in 1981 could buy only 80% of what a dollar in 1980 could buy. General price-level indexes in use today provide only rough approximations of general price-level changes, because they are not based on all prices in the economy. Furthermore, these indexes do not accurately reflect changes in the quality of products over time.

The most comprehensive general price-level index in the United States is the **Gross National Product Implicit Price Deflator (GNP Deflator),** which is published quarterly by the U.S. Department of Commerce. Perhaps the most widely publicized index of general prices is the **Consumer Price Index for all Urban Consumers (CPI-U),** published monthly by the U.S. Department of Labor. Generally, the inflation rates measured by the GNP Deflator and the CPI-U are similar over the long run. For this reason and because the CPI-U is calculated more frequently and is more widely publicized than the GNP Deflator, the FASB required companies to use the CPI-U when disclosing information under *SFAS No. 33.* Exhibit 26-1 shows the average annual level of the CPI-U during each year since 1961. The Department of Labor currently uses 1982–84 as the base for deriving the CPI-U. To simplify the calculations involved, we will merely assume certain values of the CPI-U in the illustrations and assignment material in this chapter.

SPECIFIC PRICE CHANGES

A second type of price change is known as a **specific price change.** A specific price change is an increase or decrease in the price of a specific good or service, such as food or entertainment. Specific price changes occur primarily because of changes in the demand for or supply of particular goods or services. An increase in the demand for Buick Skylarks, for example, tends to increase the automobile's price. On the other

EXHIBIT 26-1

Average Consumer Price Index for All Urban Consumers

1961	29.9	1976	56.9
1962	30.2	1977	60.6
1963	30.6	1978	65.2
1964	31.0	1979	72.6
1965	31.5	1980	82.4
1966	32.4	1981	90.9
1967	33.4	1982	96.5
1968	34.8	1983	99.6
1969	36.7	1984	103.9
1970	38.8	1985	107.6
1971	40.5	1986	109.6
1972	41.8	1987	113.6
1973	44.4	1988	118.3
1974	49.3	1989	124.0
1975	53.8	1990	130.6

SOURCE: U.S. Department of Labor.

hand, an increase in the supply of Buick Skylarks tends to decrease the price. Forces of supply and demand interact to determine the specific price of each good and service in the economy.

Distinguishing clearly between a general price-level change and a specific price change is important. The price of a specific good or service may change at a different rate and even in the opposite direction from the overall level of prices in the economy. In a particular year, for example, the general price-level might increase by 10% while the price of medical care rises by 16%, the price of new cars rises by 7%, the price of fuel oil remains stable, and the price of home video games falls by 20%. To assume that the price of a particular product will increase by 10% during a given year merely because the inflation rate is 10% in that year is incorrect.

Specific price changes may be measured by using the following methods of determining an asset's current cost:

1. **Direct pricing.**   This method requires the use of current market prices to calculate an asset's current cost. Current market prices may be obtained by referring to current invoice prices, vendors' price lists, current standard manufacturing costs, and appraisals. Suppose, for example, that a company acquired an inventory item for $100 at the beginning of the current year and that a seller's price list shows that the same item would cost $130 if purchased at year-end. Under these circumstances, the specific price increase for the inventory item is $30 ($130 − $100).
2. **Indexing.**   This method requires an appropriate specific price index to restate an asset's historical cost to a current cost basis. A company may obtain the index internally or externally. Specific price indexes for many different kinds of assets are available from a variety of government and industry sources. Unlike a general price-level index, which measures changes in the overall level of prices in the economy, a specific price index applies only to a particular good or service. Suppose that a company purchased a building at the beginning of a year for $100,000 and that an appropriate specific price index indicates that the cost of similar buildings increased by 20% during the year. Under these circumstances, a specific price increase of $20,000 [($100,000 × 1.20) − $100,000] has occurred.

FOUR BASES OF ACCOUNTING

ATTRIBUTE MEASURED AND MEASURING UNIT

Asset/Liability
Measurement

Monetary
Unit

To prepare financial statements according to GAAP, accountants must ordinarily measure nonmonetary assets, such as inventories, plant assets, and intangible assets, at **historical cost** until the assets are sold. Moreover, the monetary unit principle requires accountants to use the **nominal dollar** (a dollar that has not been adjusted for inflation) measuring unit. The combined effect of emphasizing historical costs and measuring those costs in nominal dollars is that neither specific price changes nor general price-level changes are recognized separately in conventional financial statements. Critics of the conventional accounting model contend that financial statements would be more **useful** for decision-making purposes if the statements were adapted to reflect specific price changes, general price-level changes, or both types of price changes.

The approaches to accounting under conditions of changing prices are shown in Exhibit 26–2.[1] The exhibit shows that either the historical cost attribute or the current

---

[1]Paul Rosenfield, "The Confusion Between General Price-Level Restatement and Current Value Accounting," *Journal of Accountancy* (October 1972), pp. 63–68.

EXHIBIT 26-2

Four Bases of Accounting

Measuring Unit Used in Financial Statements	Attribute Measured in Financial Statements	
	Historical Cost (HC)	Current Value (CV)
Nominal Dollars (ND)	1	2
Constant Dollars (CD)	3	4

---

value attribute of the elements of financial statements may be measured and reported. The exhibit also indicates that either nominal dollars or **constant dollars** (dollars that have been adjusted for inflation) may be used as the measuring unit.

Cell 1 of the matrix shown in Exhibit 26-2 represents the intersection of historical cost and nominal dollars (HC/ND). HC/ND financial statements are the type that accountants presently produce under GAAP. These financial statements are not adjusted for either specific price changes or general price-level changes. HC/ND financial statements were discussed in previous chapters of this textbook and are therefore not covered extensively in this chapter.

Cell 2 of the matrix depicts current value/nominal dollar (CV/ND) accounting. CV/ND financial statements are adjusted to reflect specific price changes, because current values are used instead of historical costs. Because nominal dollars are the measuring unit, however, CV/ND financial statements are not adjusted for general price-level changes.

Cell 3 presents the intersection of historical cost and constant dollars (HC/CD). HC/CD financial statements are adjusted for general price-level changes, because constant dollars are used. But these statements are not adjusted for specific price changes, because the attribute measured is historical cost, not current value.

Cell 4 of the matrix shows the current value/constant dollar (CV/CD) basis of accounting. CV/CD financial statements include adjustments for both specific price changes (because current values are used) *and* general price-level changes (because constant dollars are used).

A SIMPLIFIED EXAMPLE

To illustrate the income statement results that would occur under each of the four bases of accounting shown in Exhibit 26-2, assume the following facts about Carter Company:[2]

1. The company was organized on January 1, 1992. On that date the company sold common stock for $10,000 and immediately invested the proceeds in land costing $10,000.
2. On December 31, 1992, the land held by Carter Company was estimated to have a market value of $12,000.

---

[2]The idea for this example is based on Rosenfield, pp. 67-68.

3. On December 31, 1993, Carter Company sold the land for $15,000 and used the proceeds to retire all the common stock. The company terminated its operations at that time.
4. The inflation rate was zero in 1992 and 10% in 1993.

Based on these facts, the income statement results that Carter Company would report in 1992 and 1993 under each of the four bases of accounting are shown in Exhibit 26–3. Under HC/ND accounting (the conventional accounting model), Carter Company reports no gain or loss in 1992, because the company did not sell the land in that year. In 1993 the company reports a $5,000 gain ($15,000 − $10,000), because it sold the land.

Under CV/ND accounting, Carter Company reports a $2,000 gain in 1992. This amount equals the $12,000 market price at the end of 1992 minus the historical cost of $10,000. In 1993 the company reports a $3,000 gain, because it sold the land for $15,000, which is $3,000 more than the land's market price at the beginning of 1993. Observe that when we sum Carter Company's income statement results for *both* 1992 and 1993 under either HC/ND accounting or CV/ND accounting, we derive a *total gain* of $5,000.

The key to understanding the results under HC/CD accounting and CV/CD accounting is to recognize that these results are not measured in nominal dollars but in *1993 constant dollars*. Under HC/CD accounting, Carter Company reports no gain or loss in 1992, because no sale occurred in that year. In 1993, when the land is sold, the company reports a $4,000 gain. This amount equals the $15,000 selling price minus the $10,000 historical cost adjusted for the 10% inflation that has occurred since the land was acquired [$15,000 − ($10,000 × 1.10) = $4,000].

Under CV/CD accounting, Carter Company reports a $2,200 gain for 1992. This amount equals the $12,000 market price at the end of 1992 minus the historical cost of $10,000, adjusted for the 10% inflation that occurred during *1993*

EXHIBIT 26–3

Carter Company
Income Statement Results
Under Four Bases of Accounting

	(1) Results Under HC/ND Accounting		(2) Results Under CV/ND Accounting
1992	–0–	1992	$2,000 gain
1993	$5,000 gain	1993	$3,000 gain
Total	$5,000 gain	Total	$5,000 gain

	(3) Results Under HC/CD Accounting, Measured in 1993 Constant Dollars		(4) Results Under CV/CD Accounting, Measured in 1993 Constant Dollars
1992	–0–	1992	$2,200 gain
1993	$4,000 gain	1993	$1,800 gain
Total	$4,000 gain	Total	$4,000 gain

[($12,000 − $10,000) × 1.10 = $2,200]. Remember that we are measuring the 1992 results in *1993 constant dollars;* of course we can do this only at the end of 1993, *after* we know the 1993 inflation rate. In 1993 Carter Company reports a gain of $1,800 under the CV/CD approach. This amount equals the selling price of $15,000 minus the market price at the beginning of 1993 adjusted for the 1993 inflation of 10% [$15,000 − ($12,000 × 1.10) = $1,800]. Observe carefully that when we sum Carter Company's income statement results for *both* 1992 and 1993 under either HC/CD accounting or CV/CD accounting, we calculate a $4,000 *total gain.*

The Carter Company example is highly simplified, but it allows us to see more clearly the following major differences between the four bases of accounting:

1. Changing from historical cost accounting to current value accounting *changes the timing but not the total amount of income recognized over the life of a firm.* When the measuring unit is nominal dollars, Carter Company's *total gain* is $5,000, but it is allocated differently between 1992 and 1993, depending on whether historical cost (HC/ND) or current value (CV/ND) measurement is used. Measured in constant dollars, Carter Company's total gain is $4,000, but once again the manner in which the total gain is allocated between years depends on whether historical cost (HC/CD) or current value (CV/CD) measurement is used. The reason that current value accounting produces a timing change is because under historical cost accounting, we generally recognize income only when a sale occurs, whereas under current value accounting, we recognize income when specific prices change. The timing of income recognition can make a big difference to investors and creditors when they evaluate the amount, timing, and uncertainty of the cash flows they expect to receive from their investments.

2. Changing from nominal dollar measurement to constant dollar measurement *changes the total amount of income recognized over the life of a firm.* Carter Company's total gain is $5,000 when expressed in nominal dollars (HC/ND and CV/ND) and $4,000 when measured in 1993 constant dollars (HC/CD and CV/CD). The reason for the difference is that the measuring unit itself has changed.

Later in this chapter, we illustrate complete financial statements prepared under the HC/CD, CV/ND, and CV/CD bases of accounting. In practice, these statements may be prepared by using the conventional HC/ND financial statements and certain additional information. Journal entries to record adjustments for general price-level changes or specific price changes are unnecessary.

MAJOR FASB ACTIVITIES IN ACCOUNTING FOR CHANGING PRICES

Spurred on by the SEC, the FASB in 1979 issued *SFAS No. 33,* "Financial Reporting and Changing Prices." *SFAS No. 33* applied only to certain large companies, specifically "to public enterprises that have either (1) inventories and property, plant, and equipment (before deducting accumulated depreciation) amounting to more than $125 million or (2) total assets amounting to more than $1 billion (after deducting accumulated depreciation)."[3] *SFAS No. 33* applied to about 1,300 publicly held U.S. corporations. It did *not* change the primary financial statements, which are based on historical cost/nominal dollar accounting. Instead, the pronouncement required the disclosure of selected items of **supplementary information** in published annual reports. When it was originally issued, *SFAS No. 33* required that most of the supplementary items be prepared in accordance with the historical cost/constant dollar basis

---

[3]*FASB Statement of Financial Accounting Standards No. 33,* "Financial Reporting and Changing Prices," 1979, Summary.

and the current value/constant dollar basis of accounting. As we explain later in the chapter, there are really three forms of current value accounting, and the FASB decided on the *current cost* form.

When *SFAS No. 33* was issued, the FASB stated that the supplementary information required was experimental and that the pronouncement would be reviewed extensively within five years. The idea was to require certain companies to report the supplementary information adjusted for changing prices and then assess the usefulness of the information from the perspectives of preparers and users of financial statements. Only large companies were affected because many people regularly use these companies' financial statements and because these companies are more capable than smaller companies of bearing the costs of producing the information. The FASB provided assistance for several research studies about *SFAS No. 33* information, and in mid-1983, a task force was formed to help the board decide whether to continue the *SFAS No. 33* experiment beyond the initial five-year period. As a result of numerous studies of the usefulness of *SFAS No. 33* information, the FASB concluded that historical cost/constant dollar information is generally less useful than information about current costs. Accordingly, the board in 1984 issued *SFAS No. 82,* an amendment to *SFAS No. 33* which eliminated the requirements to report certain information on a historical cost/constant dollar basis.[4] The FASB continued to study the usefulness of accounting information adjusted for changing prices, and near the end of 1986, concluded in *SFAS No. 89* that companies should be *encouraged,* but *not required,* to disclose supplementary information about the effects of changing prices.[5] *SFAS No. 89* was a controversial pronouncement that only received the assenting votes of four of the seven members of the FASB. The three FASB members who were outvoted felt that supplementary accounting information adjusted for changing prices should continue to be required.

In a later section of this chapter, we explain the disclosures that the FASB encourages. In the meantime, we discuss and illustrate comprehensive financial statements adjusted for changing prices. The primary goal of this chapter is to explain the most important models that have been seriously considered by the accounting profession for dealing with the issue of accounting for changing prices. The FASB has encouraged but has never required comprehensive statements such as those we are about to discuss. Nevertheless, in order to adequately understand the topic of accounting for changing prices and the specific disclosures currently encouraged by the FASB, you should understand the complete process of adjusting financial statements for changing prices. With this understanding, you will be able to quickly grasp not only the present disclosure recommendations of the FASB but also the requirements of professional pronouncements that may be issued in the future.

CONSTANT DOLLAR ACCOUNTING

NATURE AND OBJECTIVE

Historical cost/constant dollar accounting, represented by Cell 3 of the matrix in Exhibit 26–2, is commonly called **constant dollar accounting.** It is sometimes referred to as **general price-level accounting** or **general purchasing-power accounting.** Under constant dollar accounting, the attribute measured in financial statements is historical cost, and the measuring unit is the constant dollar.

---

[4]*FASB Statement of Financial Accounting Standards No. 82,* "Financial Reporting and Changing Prices: Elimination of Certain Disclosures," 1984.
[5]*FASB Statement of Financial Accounting Standards No. 89,* "Financial Reporting and Changing Prices," 1986.

TACKLING ACCOUNTING, SEC PUSHES CHANGES WITH BROAD IMPACT

The Securities and Exchange Commission is shaking up the world of accounting.

The overhaul, so far, is a sedate one in a notoriously sedate field. But it could radically change companies' financial reports, and so the way companies are evaluated by investors. Even small variations in accounting can translate into big changes in stock prices, and some of the contemplated rule changes aren't small.

"This isn't evolutionary, it's revolutionary," comments Christopher J. Steffen, chief financial officer at Honeywell Inc.

Right now, the SEC is focusing solely on debt securities and certain types of loans held by banks and other financial institutions. Next to be affected will probably be other companies with significant financial assets. Finally, much of corporate America, ranging from General Motors to a Silicon Valley startup, may feel pressure to revise the way it accounts for assets.

No Complete Overhaul

Although no one is suggesting that the SEC will revamp financial statements altogether, it wants to force companies to go a long way toward putting up-to-date values on assets currently on their books at historical cost—the original purchase price. It has launched an aggressive campaign in Congress and with the accounting profession to get fast action.

"If accounting standards aren't adequate to give an accurate picture of a firm's condition, they're not doing the job they need to do," says SEC Chairman Richard C. Breeden.

The agency's focus on accounting is another indication of its renewed scrutiny of corporate America, and its shift away from targeting Wall Street stock-trading abuses. The SEC recently adopted rules making it easier for companies to sell debt directly to large institutions and is awaiting congressional approval to toughen enforcement against wrongdoing by corporate officials.

Sweeping changes in corporate accounting won't come easily. Many companies oppose, and are lobbying against, any change that could raise costs, skew numbers or reduce reported profits. Banks especially are leery of any change that could make their balance sheets look worse. And SEC officials themselves are wary of doing anything that might make U.S. companies less competitive with foreign rivals, or trigger, through accounting advantages, foreign takeovers of U.S. companies.

SEC's Own Uncertainty

The SEC's chiefs aren't unanimous about how far they want to go. "I'd be happy just to have small changes," says Commissioner Philip Lochner Jr., who heads the agency's accounting project. But Mr. Breeden, who increasingly dominates the commission, seems determined to go forward with significant changes.

Although most of this work of revision has been going on behind closed doors, Mr. Breeden recently went public with his first target. Testifying before the Senate Banking Committee, he said he wants to force banks and other financial companies to alter the way they account for bonds and other securities held for investment.

Under federal law, the SEC has the mandate to determine accounting principles for publicly traded companies. But it has generally ceded that authority to private-sector accounting bodies such as the Financial Accounting Standards Board.

Should the SEC decide to change the rules, it has a lot of weapons at its disposal besides just pressuring accounting bodies. For example, it has the power simply to change accounting rules by voting a rule proposal at an open meeting. After a period for public comment, the commission could pass a final rule. Alternatively, the agency can issue interpretative releases, telling public companies and the accounting

The objective of constant dollar accounting is to report the elements of financial statements in dollars that have the same purchasing power. To accomplish this objective, the amounts reported in the conventional historical cost/nominal dollar financial statements are restated in constant dollars by using a general price-level index, such as the CPI-U. The financial statement amounts are converted to constant dollars by using the following general formula:

$$\text{Constant dollar amount} \atop (\text{HC/CD amount}) = {\text{Nominal dollar amount} \atop (\text{HC/ND amount})}$$

$$\times \frac{\text{General price-level index adjusting to}}{\text{General price-level index adjusting from}}$$

industry how it reads a specific rule and that they should abide by that reading.

'A Statement of History'

Under today's standards, financial companies—banks, thrifts and insurance concerns—holding stacks of investment securities can make their own judgments on whether to use historical accounting or current, "market" standards. "Financial-institution balance sheets should have the words 'once upon a time' on top of them," Mr. Breeden says scornfully. "They are a statement of history." Under the SEC plan, recently rejected by an industry accounting panel, only current values of a financial company's securities would be listed on the balance sheet and reflected in quarterly profit-and-loss statements.

Some financial concerns already are sharpening their pencils to current accounting and stepping away from historical levels. Rouse Co., a real-estate developer based in Columbia, Md., which began the switch in 1976, shows the differences on the balance sheet in its annual report. At year-end 1989, for example, the company's assets, largely land and buildings, totaled $4.13 billion, nearly $2 billion more than the assets would reflect on a cost basis. (The company does the same on the liabilities side of the ledger.)

"Initially, it came about as a result of the SEC requesting that companies do replacement cost accounting," says David Tripp, Rouse's director of investor relations. Rather than trying to estimate what it would cost to build a new project, Rouse values its assets on what it would cost to replace the income stream from them.

Not surprisingly, Mr. Tripp notes, the company's stock has tended to trade much closer to the value achieved by the current cost model. At the end of 1989, based on historical cost, Rouse had shareholder equity of $52.9 million, or roughly $1.11 a share, Mr. Tripp says. But under the current-value model, shareholder equity was $1.73 billion, or about $34.80 a share. Only recently, with the real-estate slump, has the stock been trading at a deep discount to current value, Mr. Tripp says.

But James W. Otto, chief financial officer of Ameritrust Corp., a Cleveland-based banking company, says marking assets to current value "would be a very significant and costly effort that wouldn't be useful. . . . It's an estimation of the liquidation value of a company that is totally irrelevant to a going concern."

No Ready Market

Moreover, Mr. Otto adds, "A majority of the assets and liabilities don't have a ready market." Therefore, he argues, "some very subjective assumptions" would be needed to arrive at current values for those assets and liabilities.

At the root of SEC's new zeal are lessons drawn from the thrift crisis. Mr. Breeden cites 1978 numbers that show the thrift industry with a positive net worth. But a harder look—using current instead of historical accounting—shows that the industry was already ailing, with a negative net worth of as much as $118 billion.

The SEC worries that the banking industry could slip into a similar situation, with trouble disguised by accounting anomalies. Many accounting-industry officials agree. "We need to get accounting changes that reflect what has happened," says Arthur R. Wyatt, a principal of Arthur Andersen and the head of the International Accounting Standards Committee. "It's real, and it should be reported."

SOURCE: Kevin G. Salwen and Robin Goldwyn Blumenthal, "Tackling Accounting, SEC Pushes Changes with Broad Impact," *Wall Street Journal*, September 27, 1990, pp. A1, A12. Reprinted by permission of *Wall Street Journal*, © Dow Jones & Company, Inc., 1990. All rights reserved.

The quotient obtained by dividing the general price-level index we are adjusting *to* by the one we are adjusting *from* is called a **conversion factor** because it is used to convert nominal-dollar amounts to constant-dollar amounts. The general price-level index to adjust *from* is the one that existed at the time of origination of the financial statement amount being converted. The general price-level index to adjust *to* could be an index as of any date, although the dates most commonly suggested are the base period of the CPI-U (currently 1982–84), the average CPI-U for the current accounting period, and the ending CPI-U for the current period. In an effort to focus on the underlying concepts and avoid needless confusion, we will convert to the year-end CPI-U in the examples and problem assignments in this chapter.

To illustrate the basic idea behind constant dollar conversion, suppose that Rupp Company acquired a parcel of land on January 1, 1993, for $10,000. On that date the CPI-U was 100. Here is how Rupp Company would express the acquisition price of the land in year-end constant dollars, assuming that the CPI-U is 115 on December 31, 1993:

$$\$10,000 \times \frac{115}{100} = \$11,500$$

Rupp Company would report the land at $10,000 on a conventional (HC/ND) balance sheet dated December 31, 1993, and at $11,500 on a constant dollar balance sheet with the same date. Be careful to interpret the $11,500 correctly. This amount represents the land's **historical cost** expressed in 1993 year-end constant dollars. In effect, we are saying that because the inflation rate during 1993 was 15% (115 ÷ 100 = 1.15), $11,500 would be needed at the end of 1993 to buy the same quantity of goods and services that $10,000 could buy at the beginning of the year.

How much would Rupp Company have to pay at the end of 1993 if the company had to replace the land? How much could Rupp Company sell the land for on December 31, 1993? What is the present value on December 31, 1993, of the net cash receipts that the land will generate for Rupp Company in the future? These are interesting questions that cannot be answered by constant-dollar information, because the answers depend on what has happened to the specific price of Rupp Company's land during the year. Remember that constant dollar accounting adjusts for general price-level changes but not for specific price changes. Constant dollar accounting is not a departure from historical cost accounting but merely a system for reporting historical cost financial statements in units that have the same purchasing power.

MONETARY AND NONMONETARY ITEMS

When preparing constant dollar financial statements, monetary and nonmonetary items must be distinguished. A **monetary item** is cash, assets that represent a fixed number of dollars to be received, or obligations that represent a fixed number of dollars to be paid. Examples of monetary assets include cash, accounts receivable, and notes receivable; examples of monetary liabilities include accounts payable, notes payable, and bonds payable.

Simply stated, a **nonmonetary item** is any financial statement item that is not monetary in nature. Examples of nonmonetary assets include inventories, plant assets, and intangible assets; examples of nonmonetary equities include obligations under product warranties and common stock. Although they are liabilities, obligations under product warranties are nonmonetary because they do not require settlement in a fixed number of dollars but rather in goods and services (or a price that reflects the value of the goods or services).

The distinction between monetary and nonmonetary assets and liabilities is *not* the same as the distinction between current assets and current liabilities. Inventories, for example, are nonmonetary assets even though classified as current, while a 10-year note payable is monetary even though classified as a long-term liability.

Monetary items are automatically stated in current purchasing power and therefore do not require restatement when preparing constant dollar financial statements. Cash, for example, is always stated in current dollars. Consequently, if an enterprise has cash of $5,000 on December 31, 1993, the amount represents $5,000 of general purchasing power at that time, and the correct amount of cash to report on a constant dollar balance sheet dated December 31, 1993, is $5,000. The same rationale applies to other monetary items.

In contrast with monetary items, nonmonetary items are not automatically stated in current purchasing power and therefore must be restated when preparing constant dollar financial statements. Each nonmonetary item is restated to reflect the total change in the general price-level that has occurred since the time of origin of the item being restated. The restatement of nonmonetary items does not produce any gains or losses. Instead, the restatement merely alters the measuring unit from nominal dollars to constant dollars.

PURCHASING POWER GAINS AND LOSSES

Purchasing power gains and losses occur as a result of holding monetary items during periods of inflation or deflation. These gains and losses occur because monetary items are receivable or payable in a *fixed number of dollars* whose *purchasing power* changes when inflation or deflation occurs. Purchasing power gains and losses are measured and reported in the income statement when the measuring unit is constant dollars, but not when it is nominal dollars.

To illustrate, suppose that Brown Company keeps its cash of $10,000 in a checking account throughout a year in which the CPI-U increases from 105 to 210. The actual number of dollars of cash remains constant at 10,000, while the prices of goods and services steadily rise. Clearly, the company has lost purchasing power by holding the cash during the period. With an inflation rate of 100%, Brown Company would need $20,000 at the end of the year to be able to buy the same quantity of goods and services that the company could buy with $10,000 at the beginning of the year. Because the company has only $10,000 at year-end, the purchasing power *loss* expressed in terms of the year-end price level is $10,000 [($10,000 × 210/105) − $10,000].

To generalize, maintaining a positive monetary position (in which monetary assets exceed monetary liabilities) results in a purchasing power loss during periods of inflation and a purchasing power gain during periods of deflation. On the other hand, maintaining a negative monetary position (in which monetary liabilities exceed monetary assets) results in a purchasing power gain when inflation occurs and a purchasing power loss when deflation occurs. These outcomes are shown in Exhibit 26–4.

PREPARATION OF CONSTANT DOLLAR FINANCIAL STATEMENTS

Now that the general principles underlying constant dollar accounting have been explained, the process of preparing a set of comprehensive constant dollar financial statements will be illustrated. The information shown in Exhibits 26–5, 26–6, and 26–7 pertains to Craig Company and is used for the illustration.

EXHIBIT 26–4

Purchasing Power Gains and Losses Under Different Circumstances

Monetary Position	Economic Condition	
	Inflation	Deflation
Positive (monetary assets > monetary liabilities)	Loss	Gain
Negative (monetary liabilities > monetary assets)	Gain	Loss

EXHIBIT 26–5

Basic Information about Craig Company

1. Craig Company was organized and began operations on January 1, 1993.
2. The company's comparative balance sheets on January 1 and December 31, 1993, are shown in Exhibit 26–6.
3. The company's combined statement of income and retained earnings for 1993 is shown in Exhibit 26–7.
4. Selected values of the CPI-U during 1993 are shown below:

Jan. 1	130.0
Average for 1993	143.0
Dec. 31	157.3

5. Conversion factors required to restate financial statement amounts to year-end constant dollars are computed below:

Conversion factors to restate from

Jan. 1 index	157.3/130.0 = 1.21
Average index for 1993	157.3/143.0 = 1.10
Dec. 31 index	157.3/157.3 = 1.00

6. Sales and purchases were made evenly throughout 1993.
7. Operating expenses and income tax expense were incurred evenly throughout 1993.
8. The company declared and paid dividends on December 31, 1993.
9. The company acquired the beginning inventory, land, and equipment on January 1, 1993.
10. The company uses the first-in, first-out (FIFO) method of determining inventory cost. The ending inventory was acquired when the CPI-U was 143.
11. The company uses the straight-line method to depreciate the equipment. A 10-year useful life and no salvage value are assumed.

A Constant Dollar Combined Statement of Income and Retained Earnings

Based on the facts presented for Craig Company, a combined statement of income and retained earnings restated in 1993 year-end constant dollars would be reported as shown in Exhibit 26–8. The following sections explain the calculation of each constant-dollar amount shown in the exhibit.

Sales.   As indicated in Exhibit 26–5, Craig Company's sales were made evenly throughout 1993. The nominal dollar sales of $400,000 are therefore stated in terms of the average price index for 1993. To restate the nominal-dollar amount of sales in year-end constant dollars, we must multiply by the conversion factor 1.10. This conversion factor restates sales from the average index (143) to the December 31 index (157.3).

Of course sales are generally made on each business day. To be precise, each day's sales should be restated separately in year-end constant dollars. But general price-level indexes are not published daily, and even if they were, the benefits of using daily indexes would probably not outweigh the costs. Therefore, companies usually assume that sales are made evenly throughout the year when preparing their constant dollar financial statements. This assumption, which is also typically made in regard to costs incurred throughout the year (such as purchases, salaries, and taxes), simplifies the constant dollar restatement process by permitting a conversion from the average price index for the year.

EXHIBIT 26-6

Craig Company
COMPARATIVE BALANCE SHEETS
Historical Cost/Nominal Dollar Basis
January 1 and December 31, 1993

Assets

	Jan. 1	Dec. 31
Cash	$ 10,000	$ 40,000
Accounts receivable	–0–	67,000
Inventory	100,000	90,000
Land	70,000	70,000
Equipment	120,000	120,000
Less: Accumulated depreciation	–0–	(12,000)
Total assets	$300,000	$375,000

Liabilities and Stockholders' Equity

	Jan. 1	Dec. 31
Accounts payable	–0–	$ 35,000
Long-term note payable	$ 90,000	90,000
Total liabilities	90,000	125,000
Common stock	210,000	210,000
Retained earnings	–0–	40,000
Total stockholders' equity	210,000	250,000
Total liabilities and stockholders' equity	$300,000	$375,000

EXHIBIT 26-7

Craig Company
COMBINED STATEMENT OF INCOME AND RETAINED EARNINGS
Historical Cost/Nominal Dollar Basis
For 1993

Sales		$400,000
Cost of goods sold		
Beginning inventory	$100,000	
Purchases	210,000	
Goods available	310,000	
Ending inventory	90,000	220,000
Gross margin on sales		180,000
Operating expenses	68,000	
Depreciation expense	12,000	80,000
Income before taxes		100,000
Income tax expense		40,000
Net income		60,000
Retained earnings, Jan. 1		–0–
Less: Dividends		20,000
Retained earnings, Dec. 31		$ 40,000

EXHIBIT 26-8

Craig Company
COMBINED STATEMENT OF INCOME AND RETAINED EARNINGS
Historical Cost/Constant Dollar Basis
For 1993

Sales ($400,000 × 1.10)		$440,000
Cost of goods sold		
Beginning inventory ($100,000 × 1.21)	$121,000	
Purchases ($210,000 × 1.10)	231,000	
Goods available	352,000	
Ending inventory ($90,000 × 1.10)	99,000	253,000
Gross margin on sales		187,000
Operating expenses ($68,000 × 1.10)	74,800	
Depreciation expense ($12,000 × 1.21)	14,520	89,320
Income before taxes		97,680
Income tax expense ($40,000 × 1.10)		44,000
Income before purchasing power gain		53,680
Purchasing power gain (see Exhibit 26–9)		8,600
Net income		62,280
Retained earnings, Jan. 1		–0–
Less: Dividends ($20,000 × 1.00)		20,000
Retained earnings, Dec. 31		$ 42,280

Cost of Goods Sold.   The beginning inventory was acquired on January 1, 1993, when the CPI-U was 130. Therefore, to restate the nominal-dollar amount of the beginning inventory in year-end constant dollars, we multiply by the conversion factor 1.21. This conversion factor equals the December 31 index of 157.3 divided by the January 1 index of 130.

When preparing constant dollar financial statements, purchases are generally assumed to have occurred evenly throughout the year. Because Craig Company's purchases were made evenly, the company would restate its purchases by multiplying by the conversion factor of 1.10 (the December 31 index of 157.3 divided by the average index of 143).

Craig Company uses the first-in, first-out (FIFO) inventory costing method, and the company's ending inventory was acquired when the CPI-U was 143. Therefore, to restate the ending inventory in year-end constant dollars, we multiply by the conversion factor 1.10 (the December 31 index of 157.3 divided by the average index of 143).

The calculation of cost of goods sold and ending inventory on a constant-dollar basis is affected by the inventory costing method that a company uses. If, for example, Craig Company had used last-in, first-out (LIFO) instead of FIFO, the company would restate its ending inventory of $90,000 by using the conversion factor 1.21 (the December 31 index of 157.3 divided by the January 1 index of 130), instead of 1.10. Under the LIFO assumption, the ending inventory of $90,000 would be assumed to be part of the $100,000 of inventory that was on hand on January 1.

Operating Expenses.   Operating expenses were incurred evenly throughout 1993 and are therefore restated by multiplying by the 1.10 conversion factor used to restate from the average index for the year.

Depreciation Expense.   The historical cost/nominal dollar depreciation expense of $12,000 represents an allocation of a cost ($120,000) incurred on January 1, 1993. To restate the nominal dollar amount in year-end constant dollars, we multiply by the 1.21 conversion factor used to restate from the January 1 index.

Observe that to restate depreciation expense, we use a conversion factor that adjusts from the acquisition date of the asset being depreciated. Most businesses have many depreciable assets acquired at various dates. Under these circumstances, we must multiply the historical cost/nominal dollar depreciation expense for each asset by a conversion factor that adjusts from the price index in existence when the asset was purchased. This process results in several layers of constant-dollar depreciation amounts that must be summed to derive the total constant-dollar amount of depreciation expense.

Income Tax Expense.   Income tax expense was incurred evenly throughout the year and is restated by multiplying by the 1.10 conversion factor used to restate from the average index. Observe that income tax expense in constant dollar financial statements is derived in relation to the amount shown in the conventional historical cost/nominal dollar income statement. It is not based directly on the amount of the pretax constant-dollar income, because general price-level adjustments are not allowed for income tax purposes.

Purchasing Power Gain.   Earlier in the chapter we explained the nature of purchasing power gains and losses and gave a simple example of a purchasing power loss sustained by a company that held cash during a period of inflation. In reality, all monetary assets, monetary liabilities, and the changes in them that occur during an accounting period must be considered when calculating purchasing power gains and losses. To facilitate the calculation, an accountant prepares a separate schedule or working paper that is not usually published.

A schedule showing the computation of Craig Company's purchasing power gain is shown in Exhibit 26–9. The preparation of a schedule showing the calculation of purchasing power gains and losses requires three major steps that are explained as follows:

1. On a conventional nominal-dollar basis, start with the net monetary items (monetary assets minus monetary liabilities) on hand at the beginning of the period; then add the sources and deduct the uses of net monetary items during the period to derive the net monetary items on hand at the end of the period.

   As shown in Exhibit 26–9, Craig Company's monetary liabilities exceed its monetary assets by $80,000 on January 1. The company's only source of net monetary items during the period was sales. When sales occur, either cash or accounts receivable increases; thus an increase in net monetary items occurs. Other frequently encountered sources of net monetary items are the sale of nonmonetary assets, such as land or equipment, and the issuance of capital stock.

   Craig Company's uses of net monetary items during the period consisted of purchases, operating expenses, income tax expense, and dividends. Notice that each of these uses represents either a decrease in monetary assets or an increase in monetary liabilities (and therefore a decrease in *net* monetary items). A purchase, for example, either decreases cash (a monetary asset) or increases accounts payable (a monetary liability); in either case a decrease in net monetary items occurs. In addition to the uses listed by Craig Company, other frequently encountered uses of net monetary items are the acquisition of nonmonetary assets and the purchase of treasury stock. Depreciation expense does not represent a use of net monetary items, because the credit side of the depreciation entry (i.e., accumulated depreciation) does not affect either monetary assets or monetary liabilities.

EXHIBIT 26-9

Craig Company
SCHEDULE SHOWING COMPUTATION OF PURCHASING POWER GAIN
For 1993

	Nominal-Dollar Basis	Conversion Factor	Constant-Dollar Basis
Net monetary items, Jan. 1	$ (80,000)*	1.21	$ (96,800)
Add: Sources of net monetary items			
Sales	400,000	1.10	440,000
Deduct: Uses of net monetary items			
Purchases	(210,000)	1.10	(231,000)
Operating expenses	(68,000)	1.10	(74,800)
Income tax expense	(40,000)	1.10	(44,000)
Dividends	(20,000)	1.00	(20,000)
Net monetary items, Dec. 31, actually on hand	$ (18,000)**		
Net monetary items, Dec. 31, that should be on hand if no purchasing power gain or loss exists			$ (26,600)
Purchasing power gain ($26,600 − $18,000)			$ 8,600

*Net monetary items, Jan. 1 (amounts obtained from Exhibit 26–6):

Cash	$ 10,000
Long-term note payable	(90,000)
Net monetary items, Jan. 1	$(80,000)

**Net monetary items, Dec. 31 (amounts obtained from Exhibit 26–6):

Cash	$ 40,000
Accounts receivable	67,000
Accounts payable	(35,000)
Long-term note payable	(90,000)
Net monetary items, Dec. 31	$(18,000)

After adding the sources and deducting the uses of Craig Company's net monetary items, the company's monetary liabilities exceed its monetary assets by $18,000 on December 31. The accuracy of this amount should be verified by determining the net monetary items that appear on the historical cost/nominal dollar balance sheet dated December 31; this verification is shown in the second footnote to Exhibit 26–9. If the two amounts are not equal, an error must have been made in preparing the schedule.

2. Restated in terms of year-end constant dollars, start with the net monetary items on hand at the beginning of the period; then add the sources and deduct the uses of net monetary items during the period to derive the net monetary items that should be on hand at the end of the period if no purchasing power gain or loss has occurred. To comply with this step, we multiply each of the nominal-dollar amounts listed in Step 1 by a conversion factor that adjusts from the time that the measurement of the amount was made.

For Craig Company, net monetary assets on January 1 are multiplied by 1.21 (the December 31 index of 157.3 divided by the January 1 index of 130). Sales, purchases, operating expenses, and income tax expense are each multiplied by 1.10 because this is the conversion factor that adjusts from the average price index for the year. Finally, the dividends are multiplied by 1.00 (157.3 ÷ 157.3) because they were declared and paid on December 31 and therefore are already stated in terms of year-end constant dollars. After converting to year-end constant dollars, then adding the sources and deducting the uses of Craig Company's net monetary items, we find that Craig Company's monetary liabilities *would exceed* its monetary assets by $26,600 on December 31 *if no purchasing power gain or loss occurred during the year.*

3. The final step is to compare (1) the net monetary items actually on hand at the end of the period with (2) the net monetary items that should be on hand if no purchasing power gain or loss exists. If (1) exceeds (2), a purchasing power gain has occurred; if (2) exceeds (1), a purchasing power loss has occurred.

   In the case of Craig Company, (1) exceeds (2), because a negative $18,000 is larger than a negative $26,600. A purchasing power gain of $8,600 therefore exists, as shown in Exhibit 26–9. An important factor contributing to this gain was Craig Company's indebtedness (the long-term note payable of $90,000) throughout a period of inflation. The company can now pay the debt with dollars that have less purchasing power than the dollars received when the debt was incurred.

Including the $8,600 purchasing power gain in the constant-dollar income statement results in a constant-dollar net income of $62,280 for Craig Company. In this example, the purchasing power gain is the major reason that the constant-dollar net income ($62,280) exceeds the conventional nominal-dollar net income ($60,000).

Dividends. In this example, the nominal-dollar dividends of $20,000 are also stated in year-end constant dollars, because the dividends were declared on December 31. Consequently, we simply multiply the nominal-dollar amount by the conversion factor 1.00 (157.3 ÷ 157.3) to obtain the year-end constant-dollar amount shown in Exhibit 26–8. Dividends are always restated in constant dollars by using a conversion factor that adjusts from the date on which they were declared. Thus, if Craig Company had declared dividends on a date other than December 31, we would have used a conversion factor that adjusts from the date of declaration.

Craig Company's constant-dollar retained earnings balance on December 31, 1993, may now be computed by adding the constant-dollar net income to the constant-dollar retained earnings balance on January 1 and deducting the constant-dollar dividends. As shown in Exhibit 26–8, the December 31 balance is $42,280. This is the correct amount of retained earnings to report in a constant dollar balance sheet dated December 31, 1993.

Craig Company had no retained earnings on January 1, 1993, because the company began operations on that date. If the company had been operating for several years and had retained earnings on January 1, the constant-dollar retained earnings balance on January 1 to include in Exhibit 26–8 would be the December 31, *1992*, constant-dollar retained earnings balance multiplied by 1.21 (157.3 ÷ 130).

A Constant Dollar Balance Sheet

A constant dollar balance sheet for Craig Company on December 31, 1993, is shown in Exhibit 26–10. The following sections explain the calculation of each balance sheet amount.

EXHIBIT 26-10

Craig Company
BALANCE SHEET
Historical Cost/Constant Dollar Basis
December 31, 1993

Assets

Cash		$ 40,000
Accounts receivable		67,000
Inventory ($90,000 × 1.10)		99,000
Land ($70,000 × 1.21)		84,700
Equipment ($120,000 × 1.21)	$145,200	
Less: Accumulated depreciation ($12,000 × 1.21)	(14,520)	130,680
Total assets		$421,380

Liabilities and Stockholders' Equity

Accounts payable	$ 35,000
Long-term note payable	90,000
Total liabilities	125,000
Common stock ($210,000 × 1.21)	254,100
Retained earnings (see Exhibit 26-8)	42,280
Total stockholders' equity	296,380
Total liabilities and stockholders' equity	$421,380

Monetary Items.   The monetary items (cash, accounts receivable, accounts payable, and long-term note payable) are already stated in year-end constant dollars and therefore do not require restatement for the constant dollar balance sheet. The amounts reported for these items on a constant dollar balance sheet (Exhibit 26-10) are the same as on a nominal dollar balance sheet (Exhibit 26-6).

Inventory.   Craig Company uses the FIFO costing method, and the ending inventory was acquired when the CPI-U was 143. The nominal-dollar amount of $90,000 is therefore restated in year-end constant dollars by multiplying by 1.10 (157.3 ÷ 143). As we pointed out earlier when discussing the calculation of cost of goods sold, we would restate Craig Company's inventory using the conversion factor of 1.21 instead of 1.10 if the company had used LIFO instead of FIFO.

Land.   Craig Company acquired the land on January 1, 1993. The constant-dollar amount to report for the land therefore equals the nominal-dollar amount of $70,000 multiplied by the conversion factor 1.21 (157.3 ÷ 130) that adjusts from the price index on January 1.

Equipment and Accumulated Depreciation.   The equipment costing $120,000 was acquired on January 1, 1993, and the $12,000 of accumulated depreciation has resulted from charging one-tenth of the equipment's cost to expense during 1993. Accordingly, both amounts are restated to constant dollars by multiplying by the 1.21 (157.3 ÷ 130) conversion factor that adjusts from the price index on January 1.

Common Stock.   The common stock of $210,000 was issued on January 1 and is therefore multiplied by 1.21 (157.3 ÷ 130) to convert the nominal-dollar measurement to year-end constant dollars. Again we use a conversion factor that adjusts from the price index on January 1, which is when Craig Company issued the common stock.

Retained Earnings.   The ending balance of retained earnings is obtained directly from the constant dollar statement of income and retained earnings shown in Exhibit 26-8. Recall that in Chapter 5 we used the same general approach to derive the ending retained earnings balance in a conventional nominal dollar balance sheet (i.e., we added net income to the beginning retained earnings balance and deducted dividends). The ending balance of retained earnings shown on the combined statement of income and retained earnings should cause total assets to equal total liabilities and stockholders' equity; if this equality does not exist, an error must have been made.

Subsequent Years

When preparing constant dollar financial statements in subsequent years, Craig Company should follow the same general approach illustrated thus far. If the company prepares *comparative financial statements* at the end of 1994, the individual amounts shown in the constant dollar financial statements prepared at the end of 1993 would simply be **rolled forward** (adjusted) for comparative purposes to the price index that exists at the end of 1994. This would be done to permit a meaningful comparison of the 1993 and 1994 financial statements expressed in terms of the same 1994 constant dollar measuring unit. To roll forward the 1993 constant dollar financial statements to 1994 year-end constant dollars, each amount shown in Exhibits 26–8 and 26–10 (including the monetary items) would simply be multiplied by a conversion factor, the numerator of which is the price index at the end of 1994 and denominator of which is the price index at the end of 1993 (157.3).

ARGUMENTS FOR AND AGAINST CONSTANT DOLLAR ACCOUNTING

Accountants have actively debated the pros and cons of constant dollar accounting during most of the twentieth century. The following arguments are used to support constant dollar accounting:

1. Constant dollar accounting provides measurements that can be added and subtracted logically, because a uniform measuring unit is used. In contrast, nominal dollar measurements reflect dollars of mixed purchasing power; adding and subtracting nominal dollars in financial statements is similar to adding and subtracting apples and oranges.
2. Constant dollar accounting enables users of financial statements to make more meaningful comparisons between different companies. Under constant dollar accounting, each company would report a set of financial statements expressed in the same measuring unit.
3. Constant dollar accounting permits users to make more meaningful comparisons of a given company's performance over time, because each year's financial statements are expressed in the same measuring unit.
4. Constant dollar accounting does not depart from historical cost accounting. Historical cost information has been used for many years, is widely understood in the financial community, and is generally perceived as highly reliable.

   On the other hand, opponents of constant dollar accounting use the following arguments against it:

1. Constant dollar accounting does not reflect adjustments for specific price changes. The general price-level index used in constant dollar accounting may bear little relation to the changes in the specific prices of the goods and services that a particular company actually purchases or manufactures.
2. Constant dollar accounting may confuse users of financial statements. These users may erroneously believe that constant dollar financial statements present current values instead of historical costs.
3. Purchasing power gains and losses, which are included in constant-dollar net income, are never received or paid in cash. Unlike purchasing power gains and

losses, other income statement elements are associated with past, present, or expected future cash receipts or disbursements.

Materiality

4. Inflation in the United States has not been severe enough to warrant constant dollar accounting. Nominal dollar financial statements are not materially distorted unless the inflation rate is sufficiently high over a sustained period.

CURRENT VALUE ACCOUNTING

NATURE AND OBJECTIVE

Suppose that a company buys some land for $50,000 at the beginning of a year and sells it 10 years later for $150,000. Assume further that the land's market value increased by $10,000 during each of the 10 years it was held. Under these circumstances, the land would be reported on a conventional historical cost balance sheet at $50,000 during the entire time it was held, and a $100,000 gain ($150,000 − $50,000) would be reported on the income statement prepared at the end of the tenth year. The reason for reporting these amounts is that historical cost accounting is based on completed transactions. Increases that occur in the market values of a company's assets are ignored until the time the assets are sold.

Proponents of current value accounting believe that ignoring changes in market values when they occur is misleading. In the example cited in the previous paragraph, current value proponents would argue that the company is actually *better off* by $10,000 each year the land is held. Consequently, the usefulness of year-end balance sheets would be enhanced by increasing the carrying value of the land by $10,000 each year it is held. Moreover, periodic income statements would be more useful if they reflected $10,000 of income each year. Why postpone the recognition of all the income until the tenth year merely because the land was sold at that time? Although current value accounting may be somewhat less reliable than historical cost accounting, advocates argue that it is much more relevant, and more useful, to users of financial statements.

Current value/nominal dollar accounting is represented by Cell 2 of the matrix presented earlier in Exhibit 26–2. Under this system of accounting, the attribute measured in financial statements is current value; the measuring unit is the nominal dollar. Because the nominal dollar is the conventional measuring unit used in financial statements, current value/nominal dollar accounting is often simply called **current value accounting.**

The objective of current value accounting is to report financial statements that reflect the effects of specific price changes. In a set of current value financial statements, assets and liabilities are reported at their current values (instead of their historical costs) on the balance sheet date, and holding gains and losses (discussed below) are reported as the specific prices of a company's assets and liabilities change.[6] As explained earlier, specific price changes are commonly measured by direct pricing or indexing methods.

Fundamentally, the **current value** of an item refers to the item's value at the present time. But the term "value" can have many different meanings, and the term "current value accounting" therefore can mean different things to different people. In the accounting literature, "current value accounting" refers to three major forms or types of accounting: (1) present value accounting, (2) exit value accounting, and

---

[6]In this chapter we cover current value accounting primarily from the standpoint of assets. Current value accounting for liabilities has not been widely discussed in the accounting literature and has never been required by the FASB.

(3) current cost accounting. Just as historical cost accounting is based primarily (but not exclusively) on the historical cost attribute, each form of current value accounting is based primarily (but not exclusively) on an attribute other than historical cost.

PRESENT VALUE ACCOUNTING

In **present value accounting,** an asset is measured at the present discounted amount of the net cash inflows that the asset is expected to generate in the future. Income consists of three components: (1) an amount determined when an asset is acquired by subtracting the asset's cost from its present value; (2) interest revenue that is earned on the asset over time; and (3) holding gains and losses that are based on changes that occur in the asset's present value while it is held.

Determining an asset's present value requires that we discount all the net cash inflows that the asset is expected to generate in the future. The discounting process requires estimates of the amount of the net cash inflows, the timing of those flows, and the discount rate to use in computing the present value.

A strong theoretical case can be made that present value accounting information would be extremely relevant to users of financial statements. The existence of expected future economic benefits is the essence of an asset, and the asset's present value is a measure of how much those benefits currently are worth. A major weakness of present value accounting is that the information generally lacks reliability. Because of uncertainty about the future and because it is usually impossible to determine exactly how much cash inflows are associated with each one of a company's many interacting assets, accountants cannot reliably measure present values for most types of nonmonetary assets, such as equipment, buildings, and patents.

EXIT VALUE ACCOUNTING

Under **exit value accounting,** an asset is measured at the amount of cash it could be sold for in an orderly liquidation. Income consists of two components: (1) an amount determined when an asset is acquired by subtracting the asset's cost from its exit value, and (2) holding gains and losses that are based on changes that occur in the asset's exit value while it is held.

The exit value of an asset indicates the opportunity cost that a company incurs by holding rather than selling the asset. Proponents argue that exit values are relevant because they indicate the ability of a company to adapt to its changing environment by selling assets and investing the money elsewhere. Exit values are also considered more objective and reliable than present values.

Opponents of exit value accounting believe that exit values lack relevance for assets, such as equipment, that a company intends to use rather than sell. Opponents also point out that many assets, such as goodwill, work-in-process inventory, and specialized plant assets, do not usually have readily determinable exit values.

CURRENT COST ACCOUNTING

In **current cost accounting,** an asset is measured at the amount of cash (or cash equivalent) that a company would currently have to pay to acquire the same asset in its existing condition. Income consists of two components: (1) holding gains and losses based on changes that occur in the asset's current cost while it is held, and (2) an amount determined when an asset is sold by subtracting the asset's current cost on the date of sale from its selling price.

Proponents argue that current cost information is relevant because it helps users to make more accurate predictions of future cash flows and more meaningful evaluations of a company's financial position and performance. Opponents tend to question the reliability of current cost measurements in relation to those based on historical costs.

Although all forms of current value accounting are highly controversial and still in the early stages of their development, current cost accounting appears to be the most widely supported form of current value accounting today. The FASB opted for current cost measurements in *SFAS No. 33*. Many people prefer current cost accounting because they see current costs as more reliable than other types of current value measurements. Moreover, although current costs are used instead of historical costs, current cost accounting still represents an approach based on costs rather than selling prices. Conventional historical cost accounting is also, of course, a cost-based approach. Finally, present value accounting and exit value accounting systems allow income to be recognized when goods are purchased or manufactured. Thus, under these systems, all of the income associated with an asset such as inventory may be recognized before the time of sale. In contrast, when current cost accounting is used, holding gains and losses are recognized before the time of sale, but additional income is also recognized when a sale occurs based on the difference between the selling price and the current cost of the asset sold. The current cost approach therefore requires a less radical departure from the age-old general rule in accounting that income should be recognized only at the time of sale.

We will emphasize current cost accounting in the rest of this chapter because of the support it has received and because it may be even more widely accepted in the future.

HOLDING GAINS AND LOSSES UNDER CURRENT COST ACCOUNTING

Holding gains and losses in current cost accounting result from changes in the current cost of an asset while it is held over time. Suppose, for example, that a company invests in land costing $10,000 on January 1, 1991. Assume further that the company holds the land on December 31, 1991, when the land's current cost is $14,000, and on December 31, 1992, when the land's current cost is $19,000. On December 31, 1993, the land is determined to have a current cost of $25,000, and the company sells it for that amount. Under current cost accounting, the company would report a holding gain of $4,000 in 1991 ($14,000 − $10,000), $5,000 in 1992 ($19,000 − $14,000), and $6,000 in 1993 ($25,000 − $19,000). The rationale for reporting these amounts as gains is that the company's management has been smart enough or lucky enough to achieve a cost saving by purchasing the land before its price increased. Holding gains sometimes are called **cost savings**. The *total* holding gain reported during the three-year period would be $15,000 ($4,000 + $5,000 + $6,000). In conventional historical cost accounting, all of the $15,000 gain would be reported in 1993, the year in which the land was sold. The amount of the gain, of course, would be determined in 1993 by subtracting the land's cost of $10,000 from its selling price of $25,000.

Holding gains and losses may be either unrealized or realized. **Unrealized holding gains and losses** pertain to assets still on hand at the end of a period. The adjective "unrealized" is appropriate because the assets have not yet been sold or used in operations. The *total* unrealized holding gain or loss equals the difference between the current cost and the historical cost of the asset on hand. However, the amount of unrealized holding gain or loss to recognize in a current cost income statement in any year is the *increase or decrease* in the *total* unrealized holding gain or loss during the year. This increase or decrease is computed by subtracting the total unrealized holding gain or loss at the beginning of the period from the total unrealized holding gain or loss at the end of the period.

To illustrate, suppose that a company buys an inventory item costing $100 on January 1, 1991, and that the company continues to hold the item on December 31, 1991, when the current cost is $120, and on December 31, 1992, when the current cost is $150. Under these circumstances, the *total* unrealized holding gain is $0 on January 1, 1991 ($100 − $100), $20 on December 31, 1991 ($120 − $100), and $50 on December 31, 1992 ($150 − $100). The correct amount of unrealized holding gain to report in a current cost income statement is $20 for 1991 ($20 − $0) and $30 for 1992 ($50 − $20). Notice carefully that $50 is *not* the correct amount of unrealized holding gain to report in 1992, because $20 of that amount pertains to an increase in current cost during 1991.

Realized holding gains and losses pertain to assets sold or consumed in operations during a period. The adjective "realized" applies because the assets to which the gains or losses pertain have been sold or consumed. The amount of realized holding gain or loss to report in a current cost income statement is the difference between the current cost and the historical cost of the asset sold or consumed. If the inventory item described in the previous paragraph is sold in 1993 for $200 at a time when the current cost is $170, the realized holding gain to report in 1993 will be $70 (the current cost on the date of sale of $170 minus the historical cost of $100).

CURRENT COST VERSUS HISTORICAL COST INCOME STATEMENTS

To illustrate the major elements of a current cost income statement and to compare the statement with a historical cost income statement, assume that Miles Company acquires an inventory item on January 1, 1992, for $300. The item has a current cost of $500 on December 31, 1992; Miles Company sells the item for $1,000 on December 31, 1993, at which time the item's current cost is $900. A comparison of the income statement results under historical cost accounting and current cost accounting is shown in Exhibit 26–11. For simplicity, we will assume that cost of goods sold is the only expense.

Under historical cost accounting, Miles Company reports no income in 1992 because the company did not sell the inventory in that year. In 1993 the company sells

EXHIBIT 26-11

Miles Company
Historical Cost and Current Cost Income Statements

Historical Cost Basis

	For 1992	For 1993
Sales	–0–	$1,000
Cost of goods sold	–0–	300
Net income	–0–	$ 700

Current Cost Basis

	For 1992	For 1993
Sales	–0–	$1,000
Cost of goods sold	–0–	900
Current operating income	–0–	100
Realized holding gain	–0–	600
Conventional income	–0–	700
Unrealized holding gain (loss)	$200	(200)
Net income	$200	$ 500

the inventory and reports net income of $700, which equals the inventory's selling price of $1,000 minus the historical cost of $300.

Observe the major components of the current cost income statement in Exhibit 26–11. Under current cost accounting, cost of goods sold is measured at the current cost on the date of sale and is deducted from sales revenue to derive **current operating income**. Realized holding gains and losses are then added and subtracted to derive **conventional income** (often called **realized income**). Note that Miles Company had a realized holding gain of $600 in 1993. This amount was calculated by subtracting the historical cost of the inventory item ($300) from its current cost ($900) on the date of sale. Unrealized holding gains and losses are then added and subtracted to derive **current cost net income**. Miles Company reported an unrealized holding gain of $200 in 1992; this amount equals the total unrealized holding gain of $200 at the end of 1992 minus the total unrealized holding gain of $0 at the beginning of 1992. In 1993 the company reported an unrealized holding loss of $200. This amount was calculated by subtracting the total unrealized holding gain of $200 at the end of 1992 from the total unrealized holding gain of $0 at the end of 1993. (The total unrealized holding gain was $0 at the end of 1993 because the inventory was sold in 1993 and is therefore not on hand at year-end.)

Several observations about current cost income statements can now be made:

1. Current operating income is measured by matching current costs (not historical costs) with current revenues. Proponents of current cost accounting believe that requests from labor organizations for higher wages, from governments for additional taxes, and from stockholders for greater dividends should be based on current operating income and not on historical cost net income. In our example, $600 of Miles Company's historical cost net income resulted from specific price changes; only $100 was due to operations. If Miles Company distributed the $700 of historical cost income to employees, governments, and stockholders, the company could not replace the inventory item that was sold. The company's physical capacity would therefore contract. In a broader sense, any company that pays out cash equal to its historical cost net income during periods in which the current costs of inventories and plant assets increase will not be able to maintain its physical capacity without obtaining outside financing.

   Proponents of current cost accounting also believe that current operating income is a better measure for predictive purposes than is historical cost net income. They believe that current operating income more accurately reflects an amount that the company can expect to earn from future operations.

2. Conventional income in a current cost income statement always equals historical cost net income. Observe in Exhibit 26–11 that these amounts equal $0 in 1992 and $700 in 1993. The equality exists because historical cost net income actually consists of income from operations and realized holding gains. But these two components are not separately identified in a historical cost income statement, which means that users of the statement cannot determine how much of the historical cost net income was due to operations and how much was due to specific price changes.

3. Realized and unrealized holding gains and losses are reported separately on a current cost income statement. Current cost advocates believe this is desirable because holding gains and losses are generally less predictable than current operating income and are not caused by the same factors.

4. Unrealized holding gains and losses are included in the calculation of current cost net income, but not historical cost net income. Proponents believe that current cost

net income provides a better measure than historical cost net income of how much better or worse off a company is each period.

5. The total amount of net income reported over the life of a company is the same under current cost accounting as under historical cost accounting, but the timing differs. Note in Exhibit 26–11 that if we add Miles Company's net incomes for 1992 and 1993, we obtain the same total under either historical cost accounting or current cost accounting ($0 + $700 = $700; $200 + $500 = $700).

PREPARATION OF CURRENT COST FINANCIAL STATEMENTS

We will now illustrate the process of preparing a set of comprehensive current cost financial statements. The illustration is based on the information presented earlier in the chapter for Craig Company (see Exhibits 26–5, 26–6, and 26–7) and on the *current cost* amounts in Exhibit 26–12.

We will assume that the current cost amounts of financial statement items not shown in Exhibit 26–12 are the same as their historical cost amounts. The methods used to obtain current cost measurements such as the ones shown in Exhibit 26–12 were explained earlier in the chapter. When solving the assignment materials at the end of this chapter, you will be given current cost amounts.

A Current Cost Combined Statement of Income and Retained Earnings

A combined statement of income and retained earnings presented on a current cost basis for Craig Company is shown in Exhibit 26–13. In the following sections we explain the current cost amounts shown in the exhibit.

Sales. Sales are made at current selling prices throughout the period. Craig Company's historical cost/nominal dollar sales of $400,000 are therefore not restated when preparing a current cost income statement.

Cost of Goods Sold. In current cost accounting, cost of goods sold equals the current costs of the units sold at the time of sale. In practice, cost of goods sold is usually based on the average current costs of the units sold during the period. An average is considered appropriate because sales generally are made fairly evenly throughout a period. Craig Company's current cost of goods sold is $260,000.

Operating Expenses. The historical cost/nominal dollar operating expenses of $68,000 are measured at current costs when incurred. Accordingly, these expenses are already stated on a current cost basis.

Matching **Depreciation Expense.** Recall that depreciation expense is recorded because of the matching principle. Because sales are made at current selling prices throughout the period, we measure depreciation expense based on the average current cost of the service potential of the assets used during the period. For Craig Company, the 1993 current cost depreciation expense is calculated as follows:

EXHIBIT 26–12

Craig Company
Current Cost Information

	Current Cost
Cost of goods sold for 1993	$260,000
Inventory, Dec. 31, 1993	102,000
Land, Dec. 31, 1993	160,000
Equipment (gross), Dec. 31, 1993	140,000

EXHIBIT 26-13

Craig Company
COMBINED STATEMENT OF INCOME AND RETAINED EARNINGS
Current Cost/Nominal Dollar Basis
For 1993

Sales		$400,000
Cost of goods sold		260,000
Gross margin on sales		140,000
Operating expenses	$68,000	
Depreciation expense	13,000	81,000
Income before taxes		59,000
Income tax expense		40,000
Current operating income		19,000
Realized holding gain*		41,000
Conventional income		60,000
Unrealized holding gain**		120,000
Net income		180,000
Retained earnings, Jan. 1		–0–
Less: Dividends		20,000
Retained earnings, Dec. 31		$160,000

*Realized holding gain for 1993:

Inventory sold ($260,000 – $220,000)	$ 40,000
Equipment used ($13,000 – $12,000)	1,000
Total	$ 41,000

**Unrealized holding gain for 1993:

Inventory on hand ($102,000 – $90,000)	$ 12,000
Land on hand ($160,000 – $70,000)	90,000
Equipment on hand—net ($126,000 – $108,000)	18,000
Total on Dec. 31	120,000
Less: Unrealized holding gain, Jan. 1	–0–
Amount to recognize in 1993	$120,000

$$\frac{\$120,000 + \$140,000}{2} = \$130,000 \text{ average current cost of equipment during 1993}$$

$$\$130,000 \div 10 \text{ years} = \$13,000 \text{ current cost depreciation expense for 1993}$$

Income Tax Expense.   Income tax expense on a current cost basis is computed in relation to pretax historical cost/nominal dollar income. Accordingly, Craig Company's income tax expense is shown at $40,000 in Exhibit 26–13.

Realized Holding Gain.   As explained earlier, realized holding gains and losses pertain to assets sold or consumed during a period and equal the difference between the current cost and the historical cost of the assets sold or consumed. As shown in the first footnote of Exhibit 26–13, Craig Company has a realized holding gain of $40,000 on the inventory sold (the current cost of goods sold of $260,000 minus the historical cost of goods sold of $220,000) and a realized holding gain of $1,000 on the equipment used in operations (the current cost depreciation expense of $13,000 minus the historical cost depreciation expense of $12,000). The total realized holding gain is $41,000.

Unrealized Holding Gain.   Earlier we explained that unrealized holding gains and losses pertain to assets still on hand at the end of a period and that the correct amount to report in a given year equals the increase or decrease in the total unrealized holding gain or loss during the year. As shown in the second footnote of Exhibit 26–13, Craig Company's unrealized holding gain for 1993 is attributable to the inventory, land, and equipment on hand at year-end. The unexpired historical cost of each asset on December 31, 1993, is subtracted from the unexpired current cost on that date in order to derive the total unrealized holding gain for each asset. These totals are then summed to derive the total unrealized holding gain of $120,000 on December 31, 1993. Because no unrealized holding gains or losses existed on January 1, 1993 (when the company began operations), $120,000 is the correct amount of unrealized holding gain to report for 1993.

The calculation of the unrealized holding gain of $18,000 on the equipment deserves additional explanation. Note that we derived the $18,000 amount by subtracting the historical cost book value of $108,000 from the current cost book value of $126,000 on December 31, 1993. But remember that the current cost of the equipment before accumulated depreciation is $140,000 and the current cost depreciation expense is $13,000. Why then is the current cost book value *$126,000* instead of *$127,000* ($140,000 − $13,000 = $127,000)? The answer is that the depreciation expense of $13,000 is based on an *average* of beginning and ending current cost amounts, while the accumulated depreciation to report at year-end is based only on the *ending* current cost amount and equals $14,000 ($140,000 × 10% = $14,000). The year-end accumulated depreciation ($14,000) must be based on the year-end current cost ($140,000) so that the ending balance sheet will correctly show the current cost of the asset's remaining service potential of $126,000 ($140,000 − $14,000 = $126,000; $140,000 × 90% = $126,000).

Dividends. The historical cost/nominal dollar dividends of $20,000 were declared at year-end and are already stated in terms of year-end current costs.

A Current Cost Balance Sheet

A current cost balance sheet for Craig Company on December 31, 1993, is shown in Exhibit 26–14. The amounts are explained in the following sections.

Cash and Accounts Receivable. These items are normally reported on a current value basis in conventional financial statements and are therefore not restated when preparing a current cost balance sheet.

Inventory and Land. These items are reported at their respective current cost amounts determined at year-end.

Equipment and Accumulated Depreciation. The equipment is shown at the current cost amount of $140,000 determined at year-end. Accumulated depreciation of $14,000 ($140,000 ÷ 10 years = $14,000) is subtracted so that the equipment's remaining service potential is reported at a current cost book value of $126,000 on December 31, 1993.

Accounts Payable and Long-Term Note Payable. Accounts payable are conventionally reported on a current value basis and therefore do not require restatement in a current cost balance sheet. We shall assume that the market rate of interest on the long-term note payable has not changed during the year; therefore, the current cost amount to report for the note is the same as the amount shown in a historical cost/nominal dollar balance sheet. Current cost accounting for liabilities has not been widely discussed in the accounting literature and has never been required by the FASB. We do not discuss this topic in detail in this chapter.

Common Stock. This item is reported on a current cost balance sheet at the amount originally paid in by the stockholders. This is the same amount reported on a historical cost/nominal dollar balance sheet.

EXHIBIT 26–14

Craig Company
BALANCE SHEET
Current Cost/Nominal Dollar Basis
December 31, 1993

Assets

Cash		$ 40,000
Accounts receivable		67,000
Inventory		102,000
Land		160,000
Equipment	$140,000	
Less: Accumulated depreciation	(14,000)	126,000
Total assets		$495,000

Liabilities and Stockholders' Equity

Accounts payable	$ 35,000
Long-term note payable	90,000
Total liabilities	125,000
Common stock	210,000
Retained earnings (see Exhibit 26–13)	160,000
Total stockholders' equity	370,000
Total liabilities and stockholders' equity	$495,000

Retained Earnings.   The amount of this item is obtained directly from the current cost combined statement of income and retained earnings shown in Exhibit 26–13. For Craig Company, the amount is determined as follows:

Current cost retained earnings, Jan. 1	–0–
Add: Current cost net income	$180,000
Subtotal	180,000
Less: Current cost dividends	20,000
Current cost retained earnings, Dec. 31	$160,000

The ending balance of retained earnings shown on the combined statement of income and retained earnings should be the amount that causes total assets to equal total liabilities and stockholders' equity on the current cost balance sheet. If these totals are not equal after including retained earnings, an error has been made.

ARGUMENTS FOR AND AGAINST CURRENT COST ACCOUNTING

Current cost accounting has been widely discussed in the financial community in recent years. Here are the major arguments in favor of current cost accounting:

1. Current cost accounting leads to income statements that are useful for predictive purposes. Current operating income is more predictable than holding gains and losses; these two kinds of income are reported separately on a current cost income statement.
2. Current cost accounting leads to income statements that are useful for evaluating management's performance. The separation of current operating income from holding gains and losses allows users of financial statements to evaluate management's **operating activities** (activities directly related to producing and selling

products) separate from **holding activities** (holding assets while specific prices change).

3. Current cost accounting can help a company to maintain its physical capacity. During periods of rising costs, current operating income indicates the maximum amount that a company can distribute and still maintain its capacity to produce and sell products without obtaining new debt or equity capital.
4. Current cost balance sheets are relevant because they reflect current valuations of a company's resources and equities.

Here are the major arguments against current cost accounting:

1. Current cost measurements are too subjective and unreliable. This argument is particularly strong in the case of specialized assets that do not have a ready market.
2. Current cost financial statements are denominated in dollars of mixed purchasing power. Holding gains and losses are therefore not adjusted for inflation, and purchasing power gains and losses are not even reported. Suppose that a company buys land for $10,000 on January 1, 1993, and holds the land on December 31, 1993, when the current cost is $11,000. The company is better off by $1,000 on December 31 only if no inflation occurred during the year. If, in fact, the inflation rate for the year was 20%, the company is actually $1,000 *worse off* at year-end [$11,000 − ($10,000 × 1.20) = ($1,000)].

CURRENT COST/CONSTANT DOLLAR ACCOUNTING

NATURE AND OBJECTIVE

We have discussed constant dollar accounting, in which the attribute measured is historical cost and the measuring unit is the constant dollar. We have also discussed current cost accounting, in which the attribute measured is current cost and the measuring unit is the nominal dollar. In this section we shall see that it is possible to combine current cost and constant dollar accounting in a single set of financial statements. Current cost accounting and constant dollar accounting are not mutually exclusive but are highly compatible with one another.

Current cost/constant dollar accounting is represented by Cell 4 of the matrix presented earlier in Exhibit 26–2. The objective of this system of accounting is to measure the current cost attribute of the elements of financial statements using dollars that have the same purchasing power. Current cost/constant dollar financial statements reflect adjustments for general price-level changes and for specific price changes. These statements therefore contain complete adjustments for the effects of changing prices and are regarded as theoretically sound.

PURCHASING POWER GAINS AND LOSSES AND HOLDING GAINS AND LOSSES ADJUSTED FOR INFLATION

Purchasing power gains and losses are measured and reported under constant dollar accounting, and holding gains and losses are measured and reported under current cost accounting. Both types of gains and losses are measured and reported under current cost/constant dollar accounting. Purchasing power gains and losses are measured in the same manner as in constant dollar accounting. Holding gains and losses in current cost/constant dollar accounting are reported net of inflation. To illustrate, suppose that a company buys an inventory item for $100 on January 1, 1993. Assume further that the 1993 inflation rate is 8% and that the company holds the inventory item on December 31, 1993, when the item's current cost is $120. In current cost accounting, a holding gain of $20 ($120 − $100) would be reported for 1993. But in current cost/constant dollar accounting, the holding gain would be adjusted for inflation and reported at $12 [$120 − ($100 × 1.08)]. Under current cost/constant dollar accounting, we say that only $12 of the $20 nominal dollar holding gain is a *real holding gain*. The other $8 is merely a *fictional holding gain* due to inflation.

PREPARATION OF CURRENT COST/CONSTANT DOLLAR FINANCIAL STATEMENTS

Using the same information given earlier for Craig Company (see Exhibits 26–5, 26–6, 26–7, and 26–12), we will now illustrate how to prepare a set of current cost/constant dollar financial statements.

A Current Cost/Constant Dollar Combined Statement of Income and Retained Earnings

A combined statement of income and retained earnings reported on a current cost/constant dollar basis for Craig Company is shown in Exhibit 26–15. The amounts shown in the exhibit are explained as follows:

Sales.   Craig Company's sales of $400,000 were made at current selling prices throughout the year and are adjusted to year-end constant dollars by multiplying by 1.10. Recall that 1.10 (157.3 ÷ 143) is the conversion factor used to restate amounts *from* the average price-level index of 143 *to* the December 31 index of 157.3.

Cost of Goods Sold.   Cost of goods sold expense was incurred throughout the year. Therefore, the current cost amount of $260,000 is adjusted to year-end constant dollars by multiplying by 1.10.

Operating Expenses.   The operating expenses were incurred throughout the year; the current cost amount is restated in year-end constant dollars by multiplying by 1.10.

Depreciation Expense.   The current cost depreciation expense is based on the average current cost of the equipment during the year. Accordingly, this amount is multiplied by 1.10 in order to adjust to year-end constant dollars.

Income Tax Expense.   Income tax expense is incurred throughout the year. Therefore, the current cost amount of $40,000 is restated in year-end constant dollars by multiplying by 1.10.

Purchasing Power Gain.   As indicated earlier, purchasing power gains and losses under current cost/constant dollar accounting are calculated in the same manner as under constant dollar accounting. The $8,600 amount shown in Exhibit 26–15 is calculated exactly as shown in Exhibit 26–9.

Realized Holding Gain, Adjusted for Inflation.   Recall that realized holding gains and losses pertain to assets sold or consumed during a period. In a current cost/constant dollar system, these gains and losses are reported net of inflation.

As shown in the first footnote of Exhibit 26–15, Craig Company has a realized holding gain, adjusted for inflation, of $33,000 on the inventory sold. The $33,000 amount equals the current cost/constant dollar cost of goods sold of $286,000 (as shown in Exhibit 26–15) minus the historical cost/constant dollar cost of goods sold of $253,000 (as shown in Exhibit 26–8). Observe that both cost of goods sold amounts are expressed in *constant dollars;* therefore, the difference between them equals a realized holding gain *adjusted for inflation*. Craig Company also has a realized holding loss, adjusted for inflation, of $220 on the equipment used in operations. The $220 amount equals the current cost/constant dollar depreciation expense of $14,300 (as shown in Exhibit 26–15) minus the historical cost/constant dollar depreciation expense of $14,520 (as shown in Exhibit 26–8). The difference between the

EXHIBIT 26-15

Craig Company
COMBINED STATEMENT OF INCOME AND RETAINED EARNINGS
Current Cost/Constant Dollar Basis
For 1993

Sales ($400,000 × 1.10)		$440,000
Cost of goods sold ($260,000 × 1.10)		286,000
Gross margin on sales		154,000
Operating expenses ($68,000 × 1.10)	$74,800	
Depreciation expense ($13,000 × 1.10)	14,300	89,100
Income before taxes		64,900
Income tax expense ($40,000 × 1.10)		44,000
Current operating income		20,900
Purchasing power gain (see Exhibit 26-9)		8,600
Current operating income after purchasing power gain		29,500
Realized holding gain, adjusted for inflation*		32,780
Conventional income, adjusted for inflation		62,280
Unrealized holding gain, adjusted for inflation**		73,620
Net income		135,900
Retained earnings, Jan. 1		–0–
Less: Dividends ($20,000 × 1.00)		20,000
Retained earnings, Dec. 31		$115,900

*Realized holding gain, adjusted for inflation, for 1993:

	CC/CD	HC/CD	Difference
Inventory sold	$286,000	$253,000	$33,000
Equipment used	14,300	14,520	(220)
Total			$32,780

**Unrealized holding gain, adjusted for inflation, for 1993:

	CC/CD	HC/CD	Difference
Inventory on hand	$102,000	$ 99,000	$ 3,000
Land on hand	160,000	84,700	75,300
Equipment on hand—net	126,000	130,680	(4,680)
Total on Dec. 31			73,620
Less: Unrealized holding gain, adjusted for inflation, Jan. 1			–0–
Amount to recognize in 1993			$73,620

two depreciation amounts represents a realized holding loss *adjusted for inflation,* because both amounts are expressed in *constant dollars.* The total realized holding gain, adjusted for inflation, is $32,780.

Notice that after including the $32,780 amount in the combined statement of income and retained earnings, we derive a conventional income adjusted for inflation of $62,280. Through no coincidence, this amount equals the net income shown in Craig Company's constant dollar combined statement of income and retained earnings (as shown in Exhibit 26-8).

Unrealized Holding Gain, Adjusted for Inflation. Unrealized holding gains and losses are also reported net of inflation in current cost/constant dollar financial statements. Remember that unrealized holding gains and losses pertain to assets still on hand at the end of a period.

As shown in the second footnote of Exhibit 26-15, Craig Company has a total unrealized holding gain, adjusted for inflation, of $73,620 at the end of 1993. This amount is associated with the inventory, land, and equipment on hand at year-end.

Notice that for each asset, we subtracted the historical cost/constant dollar amount (as shown in Exhibit 26–10) from the current cost/constant dollar amount (as shown in Exhibit 26–16). Because the two amounts for each asset are expressed in *constant dollars,* the differences between them represent holding gains (or losses) *adjusted for inflation.* The total holding gain, adjusted for inflation, of $73,620 is also the correct amount to report for 1993, because Craig Company began operations on January 1, 1993, and no unrealized holding gains or losses adjusted for inflation existed at that time.

Dividends.   Craig Company's dividends were declared at year-end and are already stated in terms of year-end constant dollars. We therefore simply multiply by a conversion factor of 1.00 (157.3 ÷ 157.3), as shown in Exhibit 26–15.

A Current Cost/Constant Dollar Balance Sheet

A current cost/constant dollar balance sheet for Craig Company is shown in Exhibit 26–16. Notice the similarity between this balance sheet and the current cost balance sheet in Exhibit 26–14. Each asset and liability is reported at the same amount on a current cost/constant dollar balance sheet as on a current cost balance sheet. The reason for this is because the current cost measurements of the assets and liabilities are obtained *at year-end* and are therefore automatically expressed in year-end constant dollars.

The differences between a current cost balance sheet and a current cost/constant dollar balance sheet are in the stockholders' equity section. As shown in Exhibit 26–16, Craig Company's common stock balance of $210,000 is adjusted to year-end constant dollars by multiplying by 1.21. Recall that this conversion factor is the one used to restate amounts *from* the January 1 price-level index of 130 *to* the December

---

EXHIBIT 26–16

Craig Company
BALANCE SHEET
Current Cost/Constant Dollar Basis
December 31, 1993

Assets

Cash		$ 40,000
Accounts receivable		67,000
Inventory		102,000
Land		160,000
Equipment	$140,000	
Less: Accumulated depreciation	(14,000)	126,000
Total assets		$495,000

Liabilities and Stockholders' Equity

Accounts payable	$ 35,000
Long-term note payable	90,000
Total liabilities	125,000
Common stock ($210,000 × 1.21)	254,100
Retained earnings (see Exhibit 26–15)	115,900
Total stockholders' equity	370,000
Total liabilities and stockholders' equity	$495,000

31 price-level index of 157.3 (157.3/130 = 1.21). The 1.21 conversion factor is appropriate to use because the common stock balance originated on January 1.

The ending balance of retained earnings for a current cost/constant dollar balance sheet is obtained, as usual, directly from the combined statement of income and retained earnings. The amount for Craig Company is calculated as follows:

Current cost/constant dollar retained earnings, Jan. 1	–0–
Add: Current cost/constant dollar net income	$135,900
Subtotal	135,900
Less: Current cost/constant dollar dividends	20,000
Current cost/constant dollar retained earnings, Dec. 31	$115,900

ARGUMENTS FOR AND AGAINST CURRENT COST/CONSTANT DOLLAR ACCOUNTING

The major argument in favor of current cost/constant dollar accounting is that it combines the most desirable features of the current cost and constant dollar approaches. The use of current costs enhances the relevance of financial statements; the use of constant dollars provides a stable measuring unit that helps users make better comparisons over time and between companies.

Opponents of current cost/constant dollar accounting argue that the measurements are unreliable, relatively costly to derive, and likely to confuse most users.

THE FASB'S DISCLOSURE RECOMMENDATIONS

Earlier in the chapter we explained that *SFAS No. 33* applied only to certain large companies, did not change the primary financial statements, and required the disclosure of selected items of supplementary information in published annual reports. We also indicated that the FASB has encouraged but never required the reporting of comprehensive statements such as those we have discussed and illustrated in this chapter. Although comprehensive statements have never been required, the FASB *may decide* to require them in the future. But even if comprehensive statements are never required, an understanding of them helps a person to appreciate the issues involved in accounting for changing prices. Moreover, a knowledge of comprehensive statements can help a person to more easily grasp the current disclosure recommendations of the FASB.

RESULTS OF THE *SFAS NO. 33* EXPERIMENT

The original disclosure requirements of *SFAS No. 33* called for the supplementary disclosure of both historical cost/constant dollar and current cost/constant dollar information. The FASB's rationale for requiring both approaches was to allow preparers and users of financial statements to experiment with both kinds of information. After a reasonable period (not to exceed five years), the FASB felt that it would be better able to evaluate the benefits and costs of these major approaches to accounting for changing prices.

After *SFAS No. 33* information became available, many research studies were conducted to determine whether the information is useful. The results generally suggested that (1) basic historical cost information as required by GAAP is more useful than either current cost/constant dollar or historical cost/constant dollar information, and (2) current cost/constant dollar information is more useful than historical cost/constant dollar information.[7] Accordingly, in 1984 the FASB eliminated the original *SFAS No. 33* requirement to report historical cost/constant dollar information. Late in 1986, the FASB decided that companies should be *encouraged,* but *not required,* to disclose supplementary information on the effects of changing prices.

Here are some reasons that may explain why accounting information adjusted for changing prices was not considered more useful than it was during the early years of the *SFAS No. 33* experiment:

1. Users may simply have needed more time to become familiar with the relatively new types of measurements.
2. The FASB's initial approach of requiring both historical cost/constant dollar and current cost/constant dollar information may have been too complex and may have caused users of financial statements to become confused.
3. The U.S. inflation rate declined after *SFAS No. 33* was issued. User interest in accounting information adjusted for changing prices may increase if inflation increases significantly.
4. Many users make their own evaluations of the impact of changing prices on a business and are not convinced *SFAS No. 33* measurements are better than their own.
5. A longer time series of *SFAS No. 33* measurements may be needed if the information is to become more useful. Information is more useful for assessing trends when several periods are presented.
6. The initial *SFAS No. 33* disclosures may have contained measurement errors that can be reduced if preparers are encouraged to continue reporting the information.[8]

After experimenting with accounting information adjusted for changing prices for several years, the FASB decided that the benefits of the information were not greater than the costs of providing it. Accordingly, the FASB's present position is merely to *encourage* companies to present the information. In the following paragraphs, we explain the general measurement and disclosure guidelines that the FASB advises. Because the information is merely encouraged and is still considered experimental in nature, the FASB's guidelines are reasonably flexible. Companies are not discouraged from experimenting with other forms of disclosure.

DISCLOSURE RECOMMENDATIONS

The FASB encourages companies to report the following *major* items of supplementary information:[9]

1. The purchasing power gain or loss on net monetary items for the current fiscal year.

---

[7]Examples of research that questions the usefulness of *SFAS No. 33* information are William H. Beaver and Wayne R. Landsman, *Incremental Information Content of Statement 33 Disclosures* (Stamford, Conn.: FASB, 1983); Mostafa M. Maksy, "The Use of Inflation-adjusted Accounting Data by U.S. Banks," *Accounting and Business Research* (Winter 1984), pp. 37–43; and Thomas E. McCaslin and Keith G. Stanga, "Accounting Information Adjusted for Changing Prices: How Do Users React?" *Journal of Commercial Bank Lending* (July 1983), pp. 50–60. Most, but not all, research has found that accounting information adjusted for changing prices lacks usefulness. For examples of studies that suggest that this information may be useful, see Bruce Bublitz, Thomas J. Frecka, and James C. McKeown, "Market Association Tests and FASB Statement No. 33 Disclosures: A Reexamination," *Journal of Accounting Research* (Supplement 1985), pp. 1–23; and Jon W. Bartley and Calvin M. Boardman, "The Relevance of Inflation Adjusted Accounting Data to the Prediction of Corporate Takeovers," *Journal of Business Finance and Accounting* (Spring 1990), pp. 53–72.
[8]For an interesting study of the nature and sources of measurement error that may occur when using specific price indexes to estimate the current cost of machinery and equipment, see Keith A. Shriver, "An Empirical Examination of the Potential Measurement Error in Current Cost Data," *The Accounting Review* (January 1987), pp. 79–96.
[9]*FASB Statement of Financial Accounting Standards No. 89,* pars. 7–13.

2. Income from continuing operations for the current fiscal year on a current cost/constant dollar basis.

3. The current cost/constant dollar amounts of inventory and property, plant, and equipment at the end of the current fiscal year.

4. Increases or decreases for the current fiscal year in the current cost amounts of inventory and property, plant, and equipment, net of inflation. (These are essentially the total holding gains or losses adjusted for inflation, as measured in a current cost/constant dollar system. Realized and unrealized amounts are simply combined and reported as a single amount.)

5. A summary for each of the five most recent years of:
   a. Net sales and other operating revenues.
   b. Income from continuing operations on a current cost/constant dollar basis.
   c. Income per common share from continuing operations on a current cost/constant dollar basis.
   d. Net assets at fiscal year-end on a current cost/constant dollar basis.
   e. Increases or decreases in the current cost amounts of inventory and property, plant, and equipment, net of inflation (the total of the realized and unrealized holding gains or losses adjusted for inflation, as measured under current cost/constant dollar accounting).
   f. Purchasing power gain or loss on net monetary items.
   g. Cash dividends declared per common share.
   h. Market price per common share at fiscal year-end.

In essence, the above items are those that had been required by the FASB immediately before the FASB decided late in 1986 to make the information optional.

Materiality

The SEC also encourages its registrants to voluntarily present quantified disclosures about the impact of inflation. Moreover, the SEC requires registrants to discuss the impact of inflation, when the impact is material, in the section of the annual report that presents management's discussion and analysis of financial condition and the results of operations. This discussion, however, need not include quantified information about the impact of inflation.

MEANING OF CURRENT COST

According to the FASB, the current cost of inventory is the current cost of purchasing or producing the goods owned by the company. The current cost of property, plant, and equipment is the current cost of acquiring the same service potential as embodied in the asset owned.

MEASUREMENT OF CURRENT-COST AMOUNTS

As stated earlier in the chapter, the current cost of an asset is the amount a company would have to pay currently to acquire the same asset *in its existing condition*. A company may measure the current cost of a used asset that it owns by:

1. *Measuring the current cost of a new asset that has the same service potential as the used asset had when it was new and deducting an allowance for depreciation.*

2. *Measuring the current cost of a used asset of the same age and in the same condition as the asset owned.*

3. *Measuring the current cost of a new asset with a different service potential and adjusting that cost for the value of the difference in service potential*

due to differences in life, output capacity, nature of service, and operating costs. [10]

The FASB specifies that a company may measure current costs by using the direct pricing method or the indexing method (or both). These methods were explained earlier in the chapter.

MEASUREMENT OF AMOUNTS IN CONSTANT DOLLARS

As explained earlier, *SFAS No. 33* required companies to use the CPI-U when calculating any amounts in constant dollars. Companies that choose to report comprehensive financial statements in constant dollars may measure the elements of those statements in either average-for-the-year constant dollars or year-end constant dollars (as illustrated in this chapter). Those companies that report only selected items of information measured in constant dollars, as opposed to comprehensive statements, should calculate amounts in average-for-the-year constant dollars. The use of average-for-the-year constant dollars simplifies the constant dollar measurement process by eliminating the need to restate revenues and expenses that are spread evenly throughout a year. In the five-year summary of selected financial information, companies should report the constant-dollar measurements in average-for-the-year constant dollars (year-end constant dollars if used in comprehensive statements) or in dollars having a purchasing power equal to that of dollars of the base period of the CPI-U (currently 1982–84).

CONCLUDING REMARKS

Accounting for changing prices has been one of the most widely debated financial accounting topics during the twentieth century. The topic deals with fundamental issues of accounting measurement and has far-reaching implications concerning the types of information that companies may be required to report in the future. Should the FASB require companies to report comprehensive financial statements adjusted for changing prices? If so, should these statements replace or merely supplement the conventional financial statements? Also, should the financial statements reflect adjustments for general price-level changes, specific price changes, or both? Ultimately, the answers to these and similar questions will depend on the relevance and reliability of the information and on whether the benefits of information exceed the costs of providing it. Although current value accounting would likely cause companies to report more volatile earnings, the current SEC chairman believes that "if you are in a volatile business, then your balance sheet and income statement should reflect that volatility." [11] Your textbook authors agree with the SEC chairman on this point.

After conducting an experiment from 1979 through 1985 in which certain large companies were required to make supplementary disclosures of accounting information adjusted for changing prices, the FASB has decided that companies should be encouraged, but not required, to disclose this kind of information. Since *SFAS No. 89* was issued, the vast majority of companies have elected *not* to report the information about changing prices that the FASB encourages. Recently, however, "there has been a growing interest by companies that invest in and operate real estate properties in presenting supplementary current value information." [12]

---

[10]*FASB Statement of Financial Accounting Standards No. 89,* par. 18.
[11]Dana Wechler Linden, "If Life is Volatile, Account for It," *Forbes,* November 12, 1990, p. 114.
[12]Gerald Searfoss and Judith Fellner Weiss, "Current Value Reporting for Real Estate," *Journal of Accountancy,* October 1990, p. 69.

In the future, as the FASB continues to learn more about the uses, limitations, and costs of accounting information adjusted for changing prices, the FASB could decide to make the information mandatory once again, perhaps even in the primary financial statements. Considerable research on the usefulness of accounting information adjusted for changing prices is still in progress, despite the fact that the information is no longer mandatory. If the inflation rate should increase from its present, relatively low level, this would probably increase the chances of the FASB deciding to make the information mandatory. Readers of this textbook should be prepared to actively participate in the debate about accounting for changing prices and to understand the additional changes that could occur in this area.

KEY POINTS

1. A price change is an increase or decrease in the price of a good or service that occurs in a given market. (Objective 1)

2. A general price-level change is an increase or decrease in the overall level of prices of goods and services throughout the economy. It is measured by using a general price-level index, such as the CPI-U, constructed by the federal government. (Objective 2)

3. A specific price change is an increase or decrease in the price of a good or service. It may be measured by applying direct pricing or indexing methods. (Objective 2)

4. Constant dollar accounting calls for historical cost measurements in dollars having the same purchasing power. Adjustments are made for general price-level changes, but not for specific price changes. (Objective 3)

5. Purchasing power gains and losses are measured and reported when constant dollars are used as the measuring unit in financial statements. They occur as a result of holding monetary items during periods of inflation or deflation. (Objective 3)

6. Current value accounting calls for current value measurements in dollars that are not adjusted for inflation or deflation. Adjustments are made for specific price changes, but not for general price-level changes. (Objective 4)

7. The three major forms of current value accounting are
   [a] Present value accounting, in which an asset is measured at the present discounted amount of the net cash inflows that the asset is expected to generate in the future.
   [b] Exit value accounting, in which an asset is measured at the amount of cash it could be sold for in an orderly liquidation.
   [c] Current cost accounting, in which an asset is measured at the amount of cash that a company would currently have to pay to acquire the same asset in its existing condition. (Objective 4)

8. The disclosure requirements of *SFAS No. 33* reflected the current cost version of current value accounting. (Objectives 5 and 7)

9. Holding gains and losses are measured and reported when current costs are used in financial statements. They occur as a result of changes in the current cost of an asset held over time. (Objective 5)

10. Unrealized holding gains and losses pertain to assets still on hand at the end of a period; realized holding gains and losses pertain to assets sold or consumed in operations during a period. (Objective 5)

11. Current cost/constant dollar accounting calls for current cost measurements in dollars having the same purchasing power. Adjustments are made for general price-level changes and specific price changes. (Objective 6)

12. Current cost/constant dollar accounting requires the reporting of purchasing power gains or losses *and* holding gains or losses adjusted for inflation. (Objective 6)

13. *SFAS No. 33* applied only to large public companies, did not change the primary financial statements, and requires certain supplemental disclosures. (Objective 7)

14. The supplemental disclosures required by *SFAS No. 33* originally reflected both the historical cost/constant dollar and current cost/constant dollar approaches. Later only the current cost/constant dollar approach was emphasized. (Objective 7)

15. Today the FASB *encourages,* but does *not require,* companies to disclose supplementary information on the effects of changing prices. (Objective 7)

QUESTIONS

26–1   Distinguish between a general price-level change and a specific price change.

26–2   What is the basic nature of a general price-level index?

26–3   Explain the methods that may be used to determine an asset's current cost.

26–4   What is constant dollar accounting?

26–5   Explain the difference between a monetary item and a nonmonetary item. Include four examples of each type of item in your explanation.

26–6   What are purchasing power gains and losses?

26–7   Discuss the major arguments for and against constant dollar accounting.

26–8   What is current value accounting?

26–9   Explain current cost accounting.

26–10   What are holding gains and losses in current cost accounting?

26–11   Distinguish between realized and unrealized holding gains and losses in current cost accounting.

26–12   Why does conventional income for any given year under current cost accounting always equal net income for that year under historical cost accounting?

26–13   Discuss the major arguments for and against current cost accounting.

26–14   What is current cost/constant dollar accounting?

26–15   What are holding gains and losses, adjusted for inflation, in current cost/constant dollar accounting?

26–16   Discuss major arguments for and against current cost/constant dollar accounting.

26–17   What was the nature and purpose of *SFAS No. 33?*

26–18   Summarize the major disclosure recommendations of the FASB in the area of accounting for changing prices.

EXERCISES

26–19   CONVERSION FACTORS   Listed below are selected accounts that pertain to Cate Company on December 31, 1993.

[1] Land acquired on July 31, 1976.
[2] Purchases made evenly throughout 1993.
[3] Common stock issued on April 30, 1973.
[4] Accounts receivable resulting from credit sales made on November 30, 1993.
[5] Bonus expense incurred on March 31, 1993.
[6] Twenty-year bonds payable issued on August 31, 1989.
[7] Interest expense applicable to the 20-year bonds payable issued on August 31, 1989.
[8] Cash in bank.
[9] Depreciation expense applicable to equipment purchased on January 31, 1986.
[10] Investment in common stock acquired on May 31, 1991.
[11] Sales made evenly throughout 1993.
[12] Income tax expense for 1993.
[13] Cash dividends declared on June 30, 1993.
[14] Inventory acquired evenly throughout 1993.
[15] Note receivable acquired on October 31, 1992.

Selected values of the CPI-U are given below:

Apr. 30, 1973	64	Mar. 31, 1993	192
July 31, 1976	80	June 30, 1993	194
Jan. 31, 1986	112	Nov. 30, 1993	199
Aug. 31, 1989	147	Dec. 31, 1993	200
May 31, 1991	167	Average for 1993	195
Oct. 31, 1992	187		

Instructions

Indicate the numerator and the denominator of the conversion factor that should be used to restate each of the accounts listed above to 1993 year-end constant dollars.

26–20 CONSTANT DOLLAR COST OF LAND Pyles Company acquired land on April 30, 1984, for $400,000. The CPI-U was 110 on April 30, 1984, and 176 on December 31, 1993.

Instructions

[a] At what amount would the land be reported in a December 31, 1993, balance sheet prepared in constant end-of-year dollars?
[b] Explain the meaning of your answer to [a].
[c] Based only on the information presented above, can you calculate how much Pyles Company could sell the land for on December 31, 1993? Explain your answer.

26–21 FIFO—CONSTANT DOLLAR BASIS Himell Company began operations on January 1, 1993. Information about the company's inventory during 1993 appears below:

	Number of Units	Unit Cost
Inventory, Jan. 1, 1993	300	$10
Purchases made evenly during 1993	900	12
Sales made evenly during 1993	800	
Inventory, Dec. 31, 1993	400	

The CPI-U during 1993 was as follows:

Jan. 1, 1993	90
Average for 1993	120
Dec. 31, 1993	135

Instructions

Compute the ending inventory and cost of goods sold for Himell Company in 1993 year-end constant dollars, assuming the company uses the FIFO method of inventory pricing.

26–22 LIFO—CONSTANT DOLLAR BASIS Refer to the information presented for Himell Company in 26–21.

Instructions

Compute the ending inventory and cost of goods sold for Himell Company in 1993 year-end constant dollars, assuming the company uses the LIFO method of inventory pricing.

26–23 EQUIPMENT—CONSTANT DOLLAR BASIS Fogarty Company wants to prepare constant dollar financial statements on December 31, 1993. An analysis of the company's Equipment and related Accumulated Depreciation accounts on December 31, 1993, after adjusting entries have been made, reveals the following information:

Item	Equipment Cost	When Acquired	Accumulated Depreciation
A	$100,000	Dec. 1986	$ 80,000
B	50,000	Dec. 1988	30,000
C	175,000	Dec. 1989	87,500
	$325,000		$197,500

Selected values of the CPI-U at the end of the years appear below:

Year	CPI-U
1986	100
1987	106
1988	120
1989	132
1990	141
1991	149
1992	156
1993	165

Instructions

Compute the 1993 year-end constant-dollar amount to report for (1) equipment and (2) accumulated depreciation.

26–24   PURCHASING POWER GAIN OR LOSS   The following information pertains to Boyd Company for 1993:

[1] The company had net monetary items of $80,000 on January 1.

[2] Sales of $300,000 and purchases of $120,000 were made evenly throughout the year.

[3] Operating expenses of $90,000 and income tax expense of $60,000 were incurred evenly throughout the year.

[4] Cash dividends of $20,000 were declared on December 31. Selected values of the CPI-U during 1993 appear below:

Jan. 1	110.0
Average for year	121.0
Dec. 31	133.1

Instructions

Prepare a schedule showing the computation of Boyd Company's purchasing power gain or loss for 1993 expressed in constant end-of-year dollars.

26–25   PURCHASING POWER GAIN OR LOSS   Khan Company's financial position, shown below, did not change during January 1993. The CPI-U was 90 on January 1, 1993, and 99 on January 31, 1993.

Khan Company
BALANCE SHEET
January 1 and January 31, 1993

Assets

Cash	$ 5,000
Accounts receivable	10,000
Short-term investment in common stock	8,000
Inventory	50,000
Land	27,000
Total assets	$100,000

Equities

Accounts payable	$ 40,000
Common stock	50,000
Retained earnings	10,000
Total equities	$100,000

Instructions

[a] Compute the purchasing power gain or loss in constant January 31 dollars.

[b] Explain why Khan Company had a purchasing power gain (or loss) during January.

26–26 CONSTANT DOLLAR COMBINED STATEMENT OF INCOME AND RETAINED EARNINGS At the end of its first year in business, Flippo Company prepared the combined statement of income and retained earnings shown below:

Flippo Company
COMBINED STATEMENT OF INCOME AND RETAINED EARNINGS
Historical Cost/Nominal Dollar Basis For 1993

Sales		$180,000
Cost of goods sold		
Beginning inventory	$10,000	
Purchases	88,000	
Goods available	98,000	
Ending inventory	8,000	90,000
Gross margin on sales		90,000
Operating expenses	15,000	
Depreciation expense	25,000	40,000
Income before taxes		50,000
Income tax expense		20,000
Net income		30,000
Retained earnings, Jan. 1		–0–
Less: Dividends		5,000
Retained earnings, Dec. 31		$ 25,000

Additional Information

[1] Sales, purchases, operating expenses, and income tax expense occurred evenly throughout 1993.

[2] Flippo Company uses the LIFO method of inventory pricing. The company acquired the beginning inventory on January 1, 1993.

[3] Depreciation expense relates to machinery acquired on March 1, 1993.

[4] Dividends were declared on November 1, 1993.

[5] Flippo Company had a purchasing power gain of $1,800 during 1993.

[6] The CPI-U on various dates during 1993 appears below.

Jan. 1	100
Mar. 1	150
Nov. 1	250
Dec. 31	300
Average for year	200

Instructions

Prepare a combined statement of income and retained earnings in constant end-of-year dollars for 1993.

26–27 CONSTANT DOLLAR BALANCE SHEET Ingley Company prepared the balance sheet shown below in accordance with GAAP.

Ingley Company
BALANCE SHEET
December 31, 1993

Assets

Cash	$ 24,000
Receivables	28,000
Inventory	34,000
Plant assets (net)	67,000
Total assets	$153,000

Equities

Payables	$ 58,000
Common stock	60,000
Retained earnings	35,000
Total equities	$153,000

Additional Information

[1] The cash, receivables, and payables originated when the CPI-U was 105.
[2] The inventory and plant assets were acquired when the CPI-U was 99.
[3] The common stock was issued when the CPI-U was 90.
[4] The average CPI-U for 1993 was 100, and the ending CPI-U was 108.9.

Instructions

Prepare a balance sheet on December 31. 1993. in constant end-of-year dollars.

26–28   ROLL FORWARD PROCEDURE—CONSTANT DOLLAR BASIS   Stair Company has prepared constant dollar financial statements for five years and is currently preparing the statements for 1993. The company's balance sheet prepared at the end of 1991, and expressed in 1992 year-end constant dollars, appears below:

Stair Company
CONSTANT DOLLAR BALANCE SHEET
December 31, 1992

Assets

Cash	$ 6,000
Accounts receivable	33,000
Temporary investments	15,000
Inventory	60,000
Equipment (net)	55,000
Total assets	$169,000

Equities

Accounts payable	$ 19,000
Bonds payable	55,000
Common stock	80,000
Retained earnings	15,000
Total equities	$169,000

The CPI-U increased from 100 on December 31, 1992, to 200 on December 31, 1993.

Instructions

[a] Prepare a balance sheet, dated December 31, 1992, expressed in terms of 1993 year-end constant dollars.
[b] Assuming that Stair Company prepares a constant dollar balance sheet as of December 31, 1993, why would the balance sheet you prepared in [a] be useful to the company at the end of 1993?

26–29   HOLDING GAINS AND LOSSES   Longmire Company purchased land costing $10,000 on January 1, 1991. The current cost of the land was $15,000 on December 31, 1991, and $25,000 on December 31, 1992. The company sold the land on December 31, 1993, for $40,000, an amount equal to the land's current cost on that date.

Instructions

Compute the unrealized and realized holding gains or losses to report for 1991, 1992, and 1993.

26–30   HISTORICAL COST AND CURRENT COST INCOME STATEMENTS   Tanolli Company purchased inventory costing $5,000 on January 1, 1991. The company sold the inventory for $15,000 on December 31, 1993. By examining the prices quoted in suppliers' catalogs, Tanolli Company determined that the current cost of the inventory was $6,000 on December 31, 1991, $8,000 on December 31, 1992, and $11,000 on December 31, 1993.

Instructions

Prepare income statements for 1991, 1992, and 1993 under the accounting bases listed below. You may assume that cost of goods sold is Tanolli Company's only expense.

[a] Historical cost/nominal dollar basis.
[b] Current cost/nominal dollar basis.

26–31 HOLDING GAINS AND LOSSES—UNADJUSTED AND ADJUSTED Ledet Company acquired land costing $100,000 on January 1, 1993. The company continued to hold the land on December 31, 1993, and on that date an independent appraisal indicated that the land's current cost was $120,000. The CPI-U was 110 on January 1, 1993, and 121 on December 31, 1993.

Instructions

[a] Compute the amount of holding gain or loss for 1993 under current cost accounting.
[b] Compute the amount of holding gain or loss, adjusted for inflation, for 1993 under current cost/ constant dollar accounting.
[c] Explain your answers to [a] and [b].

26–32 GAIN OR LOSS—HISTORICAL COST AND CURRENT COST The Jack and Mack Partnership was formed on January 1, 1992. On that date, Jack and Mack each contributed $20,000 to their partnership, and the partnership immediately invested the $40,000 in a parcel of land. The partnership continued to hold the land on December 31, 1992, at which time the land was appraised at $45,000. On December 31, 1993, the partnership sold the land for $60,000, distributed the proceeds to the partners, and ended operations.

Instructions

Compute the gain or loss attributable to the land for 1992 and for 1993 under (1) historical cost accounting and (2) current cost accounting.

26–33 GAIN OR LOSS—CONSTANT DOLLAR AND CURRENT COST/CONSTANT DOLLAR Refer to the information presented in 26–32 for the Jack and Mack Partnership. Assume that the CPI-U was as follows:

Jan. 1, 1992	100
Dec. 31, 1992	100
Dec. 31, 1993	132

Instructions

Expressed in terms of December 31, 1993, constant dollars, compute the gain or loss attributable to the land for 1992 and for 1993 under (1) constant dollar and (2) current cost/constant dollar accounting.

26–34 CURRENT COST INCOME STATEMENT On January 1, 1993, Lavert Company acquired inventory for $20,000. The inventory consisted of 10,000 identical units. The current cost of the inventory was $30,000 on July 1, 1993; on that date Lavert Company sold three-fourths of the inventory for $28,000. On December 31, 1993, the current cost of the inventory on hand was $7,500.

Instructions

Prepare a current cost income statement for 1993. Assume that cost of goods sold is Lavert Company's only expense.

26–35 CURRENT COST/CONSTANT DOLLAR INCOME STATEMENT Refer to the information presented for Lavert Company in 26–34. The CPI-U on various dates is as follows:

Jan. 1, 1993	110.0
July 1, 1993	121.0
Dec. 31, 1993	133.1

Instructions

Prepare a current cost/constant dollar income statement for 1993. Assume that cost of goods sold is Lavert Company's only expense and that no purchasing power gain or loss exists.

26–36 DEPRECIATION EXPENSE UNDER FOUR BASES Hughes Company acquired a machine on January 1, 1993, for $50,000. Depreciation will be computed using the straight-line method, assuming a five-year useful life and no salvage value. A specific price index applicable to the machine was 150 on January 1, 1993, and 225 on December 31, 1993. The CPI-U was 100 on January 1, 1993, and 121 on December 31, 1993. The average CPI-U for 1993 was 110.

Instructions

Compute the amount of depreciation expense for 1993 under each basis of accounting listed below:

[a] Historical cost/nominal dollar basis.
[b] Historical cost/constant dollar basis.
[c] Current cost/nominal dollar basis.
[d] Current cost/constant dollar basis.

PROBLEMS

26–37 PURCHASING POWER GAIN OR LOSS The following information pertains to Gomez Company:

Sales (all on account) made evenly throughout 1993	$220,000
Equipment purchased for cash on May 1, 1993	50,000
Purchases (all on account) made evenly throughout 1993	80,000
Cash received evenly throughout 1993 from customers on account	190,000
Cash dividends declared on Sept. 1, 1993, and paid on Oct. 1, 1993	20,000
Land acquired for cash on June 1, 1993	30,000
Depreciation expense for 1993	10,000
Common stock issued for cash on Mar. 1, 1993	60,000
Operating expenses paid evenly throughout 1993	40,000
Income tax expense paid evenly throughout 1993	25,000
Purchase of treasury stock for cash on Nov. 1, 1993	17,000
Sale of investment in common stock on Aug. 1, 1993, for cash (cost = $5,000; selling price = $8,000)	8,000
Cash paid evenly throughout 1993 on accounts payable	60,000
Monetary assets	
Jan. 1, 1993	25,000
Dec. 31, 1993	71,000
Monetary liabilities	
Jan. 1, 1993	10,000
Dec. 31, 1993	30,000

The following values of the CPI-U for 1993 are available:

1/1	100	8/1	114
2/1	102	9/1	116
3/1	104	10/1	118
4/1	106	11/1	120
5/1	108	12/1	122
6/1	110	12/31	124
7/1	112	Average for year	112

Instructions

Prepare a schedule showing the computation of Gomez Company's purchasing power gain or loss for 1993 in end-of-year dollars.

26–38 CURRENT COST FINANCIAL STATEMENTS Bart Company was formed on January 1, 1993. Financial statements pertaining to the company's first year of operations are shown below:

Bart Company
COMPARATIVE BALANCE SHEETS
Historical Cost/Nominal Dollar Basis
January 1 and December 31, 1993

	Jan. 1	Dec. 31
Assets		
Cash	$ 22,000	$112,000
Accounts receivable	–0–	147,400
Inventory	220,000	198,000
Land	154,000	154,000
Equipment	264,000	264,000
Less:		
Accumulated depreciation	–0–	(26,400)
Total assets	$660,000	$849,000
Liabilities and Stockholders' Equity		
Accounts payable	–0–	$ 77,000
Note payable	$198,000	198,000
Total liabilities	198,000	275,000
Common stock	462,000	462,000
Retained earnings	–0–	112,000
Total stockholders' equity	462,000	574,000
Total liabilities and stockholders' equity	$660,000	$849,000

Bart Company
COMBINED STATEMENT OF INCOME AND RETAINED EARNINGS
Historical Cost/Nominal Dollar Basis
For 1993

Sales		$920,000
Cost of goods sold		
Beginning inventory	$220,000	
Purchases	462,000	
Goods available	682,000	
Ending inventory	198,000	484,000
Gross margin on sales		436,000
Operating expenses	149,600	
Depreciation expense	26,400	176,000
Income before taxes		260,000
Income tax expense		104,000
Net income		156,000
Retained earnings, Jan. 1		–0–
Less: Dividends		44,000
Retained earnings, Dec. 31		$112,000

The following current cost information pertains to Bart Company:

[1] The current cost of the equipment (before deducting accumulated depreciation) on December 31, 1993, was $308,000.

[2] The current cost of the land on December 31, 1993, was $352,000.

[3] The current cost of the inventory on December 31, 1993, was $224,400.

[4] Cost of goods sold on a current-cost basis at the time of sale for 1993 was $572,000.

Additional information pertaining to Bart Company is as follows:

[1] Sales, purchases, operating expenses, and income tax expense occurred evenly throughout 1993.

[2] The beginning inventory, land, and equipment were purchased on January 1, 1993.

[3] The LIFO method of inventory pricing is used.

[4] The equipment is being depreciated over a 10-year life using the straight-line method. No salvage value is assumed.

[5] Dividends were declared when the CPI-U was 132. Selected values of the CPI-U during 1993 are shown below:

Jan. 1	110.0
Average for 1993	132.0
Dec. 31	158.4

Instructions

[a] Prepare a combined statement of income and retained earnings for 1993 under the current cost/nominal dollar basis of accounting.

[b] Prepare a balance sheet as of December 31, 1993, under the current cost/nominal dollar basis of accounting.

26–39 CONSTANT DOLLAR FINANCIAL STATEMENTS   Refer to the information presented in 26–38 for Bart Company.

Instructions

[a] Prepare a schedule showing the computation of Bart Company's purchasing power gain or loss for 1993. The gain or loss should be expressed in constant end-of-year dollars.

[b] Prepare a constant dollar combined statement of income and retained earnings for 1993 in end-of-year dollars.

[c] Prepare a constant dollar balance sheet as of December 31, 1993, in end-of-year dollars.

26–40 CURRENT COST/CONSTANT DOLLAR FINANCIAL STATEMENTS   Refer to the information presented in 26–38 for Bart Company.

Instructions

[a] Prepare a current cost/constant dollar combined statement of income and retained earnings for 1993 in end-of-year dollars.

[b] Prepare a current cost/constant dollar balance sheet as of December 31, 1993, in end-of-year dollars.

26–41 HISTORICAL COST AND CURRENT COST FINANCIAL STATEMENTS   Pueblo Company began operations on January 1, 1993. A balance sheet prepared on the opening day of business appears below:

Pueblo Company
BALANCE SHEET
Historical Cost/Nominal Dollar Basis
January 1, 1993

Assets		Equities	
Cash	$ 10,000	Common stock	$170,000
Inventory	30,000		
Land	50,000		
Equipment	80,000		
Total assets	$170,000		

Additional information pertaining to Pueblo Company is as follows:

[1] Sales (all on account) of $300,000 were made evenly throughout 1993. Seventy-five percent of the credit sales were collected during 1993; the remaining 25% is expected to be collected in 1994.

[2] Purchases (all on account) of $150,000 were made evenly throughout 1993. Eighty percent of the credit purchases were paid during 1993; the remaining 20% will be paid in 1994.

[3] Operating expenses of $40,000 and income tax expense at a rate of 40% of pretax income were incurred and paid in cash evenly throughout 1993.

[4] Cash dividends of $14,000 were declared and paid on December 31, 1993.

[5] The company uses the FIFO method of inventory pricing. The 1993 ending inventory of $20,000 was acquired when the CPI-U was 210.

[6] The company uses the straight-line method of depreciation for the equipment. An eight-year useful life and no salvage value are assumed.

The following *current-cost* information pertains to Pueblo Company:

Cost of goods sold for 1993	$190,000
Inventory, Dec. 31, 1993	24,000
Land, Dec. 31, 1993	65,000
Equipment (before deducting accumulated depreciation), Dec. 31, 1993	96,000

Selected values of the CPI-U during 1993 appear below:

Jan. 1   200.0   Average for year   210.0   Dec. 31   220.5

Instructions

[a] Prepare a combined statement of income and retained earnings for 1993 under the historical cost/nominal dollar basis of accounting.

[b] Prepare a balance sheet on December 31, 1993, under the historical cost/nominal dollar basis of accounting.

[c] Prepare a combined statement of income and retained earnings for 1993 under the current cost/nominal dollar basis of accounting.

[d] Prepare a balance sheet on December 31, 1993, under the current cost/nominal dollar basis of accounting.

[e] Briefly describe the major conceptual differences between the historical cost/nominal dollar financial statements and the current cost/nominal dollar statements. (You need not refer to dollar amounts.)

26–42 CONSTANT DOLLAR FINANCIAL STATEMENTS   Refer to the information presented for Pueblo Company in 26–41.

Instructions

[a] Prepare a schedule showing the computation of Pueblo Company's purchasing power gain or loss for 1993 in end-of-year dollars.

[b] Prepare a historical cost/constant dollar combined statement of income and retained earnings for 1993 in end-of-year dollars.

[c] Prepare a historical cost/constant dollar balance sheet on December 31, 1993, in end-of-year dollars.

[d] Briefly describe the major conceptual differences between the historical cost/nominal dollar financial statements for Pueblo Company and the historical cost/constant dollar statements. (You need not refer to dollar amounts.)

26–43 CURRENT COST/CONSTANT DOLLAR FINANCIAL STATEMENTS   Refer to the information presented for Pueblo Company in 26–41.

Instructions

[a] Prepare a current cost/constant dollar combined statement of income and retained earnings for 1993 in end-of-year dollars.

[b] Prepare a current cost/constant dollar balance sheet on December 31, 1993, in end-of-year dollars.

[c] Briefly describe the major conceptual differences between the historical cost/nominal dollar financial statements and the current cost/constant dollar statements. (You need not refer to dollar amounts.)

26–44 FINANCIAL-STATEMENT AMOUNTS UNDER FOUR BASES   Several transactions concerning one asset of a calendar-year company are summarized as follows:

1991   Purchased land for $80,000 cash on Dec. 31. Current cost at year-end was $80,000.
1992   Held the land all year. Current cost at year-end was $104,000.
1993   Dec. 31—sold the land for $142,000.

Selected values of the CPI-U appear below:

Dec. 31, 1991   100   Dec. 31, 1992   110   Dec. 31, 1993   125

Instructions

[a] Determine the balance sheet valuation that should be assigned to the land *at the end of 1991, 1992, and 1993* under (1) the historical cost basis, (2) the constant dollar basis, (3) the current cost basis, and (4) the current cost/constant dollar basis of accounting.

[b] Determine the amount of net income that should be reported *at the end of 1991, 1992, and 1993* under (1) the historical cost basis, (2) the constant-dollar basis, (3) the current-cost basis, and (4) the current cost/constant dollar basis of accounting.

[c] Why is the timing of income recognition for the land under current cost accounting different from the timing under constant dollar accounting?   (AICPA adapted)

26–45 CONSTANT DOLLAR FINANCIAL STATEMENTS Seago Company (a retailer) was organized on December 15, 1992. The company's initial statement of financial position is presented below:

Seago Company
STATEMENT OF FINANCIAL POSITION
December 31, 1992

Assets

Cash	$250,000
Inventory (at historical cost, which equals market value; FIFO; periodic)	400,000
Furniture and fixtures	200,000
Land (held for future store site)	100,000
Total assets	$950,000

Liabilities and Stockholders' Equity

Accounts payable	$300,000
Capital stock ($5 par, 200,000 shares authorized; 130,000 issued and outstanding)	650,000
Total liabilities and stockholders' equity	$950,000

The statement of income and the statement of financial position prepared at the close of business on December 31, 1993, are shown as follows:

Seago Company
STATEMENT OF INCOME
For the Year Ended December 31, 1993

Sales		$1,100,000
Cost of goods sold		
Inventory 1/1/93	$ 400,000	
Purchases	1,000,000	
Goods available	1,400,000	
Inventory 12/31/93	600,000	
		800,000
Gross profit		300,000
Operating expenses		
Rent	36,000	
Depreciation	20,000	
Other (all required cash expenditures)	44,000	
		100,000
Income before taxes		200,000
Income tax expense		80,000
Net income		$ 120,000
Earnings per share		$1.00

Seago Company
STATEMENT OF FINANCIAL POSITION
December 31, 1993

Assets

Cash	$ 290,000
Accounts receivable	400,000
Inventory (at historical cost; FIFO; periodic)	600,000
Furniture and fixtures (net)	180,000
Land (held for future store site)	100,000
Total assets	$1,570,000

Liabilities and Stockholders' Equity

Accounts payable	$ 800,000
Capital stock ($5 par, 200,000 shares authorized; 130,000 issued and outstanding)	650,000
Retained earnings	120,000
Total liabilities and stockholders' equity	$1,570,000

Seago Company rents its showroom facilities on an operating lease basis at a cost of $3,000 per month. The rent would be $5,000 per month if it were based on the current cost of the facility. All sales and cash outlays for costs and expenses occur uniformly throughout the year.

The following information is indicative of the changing prices since Seago Company began its operations.

[1] The CPI-U for the following times is

Dec. 31, 1992	200
Oct. 1, 1993	216
Dec. 31, 1993	220
Average for 1993	212

[2] The ending inventory was acquired on October 1, 1993.
[3] Inventory at current cost on December 31, 1993, is $700,000.
[4] Cost of goods sold at current cost as of date of sale is $875,000.
[5] Current cost of the land on December 31, 1993, is $150,000.
[6] The sales and purchases occurred uniformly throughout 1993.

Instructions

[a] Calculate Seago Company's purchasing power gain or loss for 1993 in terms of December 31, 1993, dollars. Round all computations to the nearest $100.
[b] Prepare a constant dollar income statement for 1993 for Seago Company in terms of December 31, 1993, dollars. Round all computations to the nearest $100.
[c] Identify and explain the advantages and disadvantages of constant dollar financial statements.

(CMA adapted)

26–46 CONSTANT DOLLAR ADJUSTMENTS   Rabun, Inc., a retailer, was organized during 1990. Rabun's management has decided to supplement its December 31, 1993, nominal dollar financial statements with constant dollar financial statements. The following general ledger trial balance (nominal dollar) and additional information have been furnished:

Rabun, Inc.
TRIAL BALANCE
December 31, 1993

	Dr.	Cr.
Cash and receivables (net)	$ 540,000	
Marketable securities (common stock)	400,000	
Inventory	485,000	
Equipment	650,000	
Equipment—Accumulated depreciation		$ 164,000
Accounts payable		345,000
6% First mortgage bonds, due 2008		500,000
Common stock, $10 par		1,000,000
Retained earnings, Dec. 31, 1992	46,000	
Sales		1,900,000
Cost of sales	1,508,000	
Depreciation	65,000	
Other operating expenses and interest	215,000	
	$3,909,000	$3,909,000

[1] Monetary assets (cash and receivables) exceeded monetary liabilities (accounts payable and bonds payable) by $400,000 at December 31, 1992.

[2] Purchases ($1,840,000 in 1993) and sales are made uniformly throughout the year.

[3] Depreciation is computed on a straight-line basis, with a full year's depreciation being taken in the year of acquisition and none in the year of retirement. The depreciation rate is 10% and no salvage value is anticipated. Acquisitions and retirements have been made fairly evenly over each year, and the retirements in 1993 consisted of assets purchased during 1991 that were scrapped. An analysis of the equipment account reveals the following:

Year	Beginning Balance	Additions	Retirements	Ending Balance
1991	—	$550,000	—	$550,000
1992	$550,000	10,000	—	560,000
1993	560,000	150,000	$60,000	650,000

[4] The bonds were issued in 1991 and the marketable securities were purchased fairly evenly over 1993. Other operating expenses and interest are assumed to be incurred evenly throughout the year.

[5] Assume that values of the CPI-U were as follows:

Annual Averages	Index	Conversion Factors (1993 4th Qtr. = 1.000)
1990	113.9	1.128
1991	116.8	1.100
1992	121.8	1.055
1993	126.7	1.014
End-of-Quarter		
1992 4th	123.5	1.040
1993 1st	124.9	1.029
2nd	126.1	1.019
3rd	127.3	1.009
4th	128.5	1.000

Instructions

[a] Prepare a schedule to convert the Equipment account balance at December 31, 1993, from nominal dollars to 1993 year-end constant dollars.

[b] Prepare a schedule to analyze in nominal dollars the Equipment—Accumulated Depreciation account for 1993.

[c] Prepare a schedule to analyze in 1993 year-end constant dollars the Equipment—Accumulated Depreciation account for 1993.

[d] Prepare a schedule to compute Rabun's purchasing power gain or loss on its net holdings of monetary assets for 1993 (ignore income tax implications). The schedule should consider appropriate items on or related to the balance sheet and the income statement.

(AICPA adapted)

26–47 CONSTANT DOLLAR ADJUSTMENTS   To obtain a more realistic appraisal of her investment, Karen Mabry, your client, has asked you to adjust certain financial data of Thacher Company for price-level changes. On January 1, 1991, she invested $50,000 in Thacher Company in return for 10,000 shares of common stock. Immediately after her investment, the trial balance appeared as follows:

	Dr.	Cr.
Cash and receivables	$ 65,200	
Merchandise inventory	4,000	
Building	50,000	
Accumulated depreciation—building		$ 8,000
Equipment	36,000	
Accumulated depreciation—equipment		7,200
Land	10,000	
Current liabilities		50,000
Capital stock, $5 par		100,000
	$165,200	$165,200

Balances in certain selected accounts as of December 31 of each of the next three years were as follows:

	1991	1992	1993
Sales	$39,650	$39,000	$54,450
Inventory	4,500	5,600	5,347
Purchases	14,475	16,350	18,150
Operating expenses (excluding depreciation)	10,050	9,050	9,075

Assume the 1991 price level as the base year and that all changes in the price level take place at the beginning of each year. Further assume that the 1992 price level is 10% above the 1991 price level and that the 1993 price level is 10% above the 1992 level.

The building was constructed in 1987 at a cost of $50,000, with an estimated life of 25 years. The price level at that time was 80% of the 1991 price level.

The equipment was purchased in 1989 at a cost of $36,000, with an estimated life of 10 years. The price level at that time was 90% of the 1991 price level.

The LIFO method of inventory valuation is used. The original inventory was acquired in the same year the building was constructed and was maintained at a constant $4,000 until 1991. In 1991 a gradual buildup of the inventory was begun in anticipation of an increase in the volume of business.

Mabry considers the return on her investment as the dividend she actually receives. In 1991 and again in 1993, Thacher Company paid cash dividends in the amount of $10,000.

On July 1, 1992, there was a reverse stock split-up of the company's stock in the ratio of one-for-ten.

Instructions

[a] Compute the 1993 earnings per share of common stock in terms of 1991 dollars.

[b] Compute the percentage return on investment for 1991 and 1993 in terms of 1991 dollars.

(AICPA adapted)

26–48 CONSTANT DOLLAR ADJUSTMENTS   Aucoin Company purchased a tract of land as an investment in 1990 for $100,000. Late that year the company decided to construct a shopping center on the site. Construction began in 1991 and was completed in 1993; one-third of the construction was completed each year. Aucoin originally estimated the costs of the project would be $1,200,000 for materials, $750,000 for labor, $150,000 for variable overhead, and $600,000 for depreciation. Actual costs (excluding depreciation) incurred for construction were as follows:

	1991	1992	1993
Materials	$418,950	$434,560	$462,000
Labor	236,250	274,400	282,000
Variable overhead	47,250	54,208	61,200

Shortly after construction began, Aucoin sold the shopping center for $3,000,000, with payment to be made in full on completion in December 1993. One hundred and fifty thousand dollars of the sales price was allocated for the land.

The transaction was completed as scheduled and now a controversy has developed between the two major stockholders of the company. One thinks that the company should have invested in land, because a high rate of return was earned on the land. The other believes that the original decision was sound and that unanticipated changes in the price level affected the original cost estimates.

You were engaged to furnish guidance to these stockholders in resolving their controversy. As an aid, you obtained the following information:

[1] Using 1990 as the base year, price-level indexes for relevant years are as follows:

1987	90
1988	93
1989	96
1990	100
1991	105
1992	112
1993	120

[2] The company allocated $200,000 per year for depreciation of fixed assets allocated to this construction project. Of that amount, $25,000 was for a building purchased in 1987 and $175,000 was for equipment purchased in 1989.

Instructions

[a] Prepare a schedule to restate in base-year (1990) costs the actual costs, including depreciation, incurred each year. Disregard income taxes and assume that each price-level index was valid for the entire year.

[b] Prepare a schedule comparing the originally estimated costs of the project with the total actual costs for each element of cost (materials, labor, variable overhead, and depreciation) adjusted to the 1990 price level.

[c] Prepare a schedule to restate the amount received on the sale in terms of base year (1990) purchasing power. The gain or loss should be determined separately for the land and the building in terms of base-year purchasing power and should exclude depreciation.   (AICPA adapted)

CASES

26–49   CONSTANT DOLLAR FINANCIAL STATEMENTS   *Two independent parts follow.*

Part 1.   Constant dollar financial statements are prepared in an effort to eliminate the effects of inflation or deflation. An integral part of determining restated amounts and applicable gain or loss from restatement is the segregation of all assets and liabilities into monetary and nonmonetary classifications. One reason for this classification is that purchasing power gains and losses for monetary items are currently matched against earnings.

Instructions

What factors determine whether an asset or a liability is classified as monetary or nonmonetary? Include in your response the justification for recognizing gains and losses from monetary items and *not* for nonmonetary items.

Part 2.   Proponents of price-level restatement maintain that a basic weakness of financial statements not adjusted for price-level changes is that they are made up of "mixed dollars."

Instructions

[a] Define "mixed dollars" and explain why is this a weakness of unadjusted financial statements.

[b] Explain how financial statements restated for price-level changes eliminate this weakness. Use property, plant, and equipment as your example in this discussion.   (AICPA adapted)

26–50 CONSTANT DOLLAR FINANCIAL STATEMENTS Published financial statements of U.S. companies are currently prepared on a stable-dollar assumption, even though the general purchasing power of the dollar has declined considerably because of inflation in recent years. To account for this changing value of the dollar, many accountants suggest that financial statements should be adjusted for general price-level changes. Three *independent* statements about general price-level adjusted financial statements follow. Each statement contains some fallacious reasoning.

Statement 1.   The accounting profession has not seriously considered price-level adjusted financial statements before because the rate of inflation usually has been so low from year to year that the adjustments would have been immaterial in amount. Price-level adjusted financial statements represent a departure from historical cost accounting. Financial statements should be prepared from facts, not estimates.

Statement 2.   If financial statements were adjusted for general price-level changes, depreciation charges in the earnings statement would permit the recovery of dollars of current purchasing power and thereby equal the cost of new assets to replace the old ones. General price-level adjusted data would yield statement-of-financial-position amounts closely approximating current values. Furthermore, management can make better decisions if general price-level adjusted financial statements are published.

Statement 3.   When adjusting financial data for general price-level changes, a distinction must be made between monetary and nonmonetary assets and liabilities, which, under historical cost accounting, have been identified as "current" and "noncurrent." When using historical cost accounting, no purchasing power gain or loss is recognized in the accounting process, but when financial statements are adjusted for general price-level changes, a purchasing power gain or loss will be recognized on monetary and nonmonetary items.

Instructions

Evaluate each of the independent statements. Identify the areas of fallacious reasoning in each, and explain why the reasoning is incorrect. Complete your discussion of each statement before proceeding to the next statement.   (AICPA adapted)

26–51 CONSTANT DOLLAR AND CURRENT VALUE STATEMENTS Kershaw Corporation, a manufacturer with large investments in plant and equipment, began operations in 1950. The company's history has been one of expansion in sales, production, and physical facilities. Recently, some concern has been expressed that the conventional financial statements do not provide sufficient information for decisions by investors. After consideration of proposals for various types of supplementary financial statements to be included in the 1993 annual report, management has decided to present a balance sheet as of December 31, 1993, and a statement of income and retained earnings for 1993, both restated for changes in the general price level.

Instructions

[a] On what basis can it be contended that Kershaw's conventional statements should be restated for changes in the general price level?

[b] Distinguish between financial statements restated for general price-level changes and current value financial statements.

[c] Distinguish between monetary and nonmonetary assets and liabilities, as the terms are used in general price-level accounting. Give examples of each.

[d] Outline the procedures Kershaw should follow in preparing the proposed restatements.

[e] Indicate the major similarities and differences between the proposed supplementary statements and the corresponding conventional statements.

[f] Assuming that in the future Kershaw will want to present comparative supplementary statements, can the 1993 supplementary statements be presented in 1994 without adjustment? Explain.   (AICPA adapted)

26–52   FOUR BASES OF ACCOUNTING   This case consists of two *independent* parts.

Part 1.   Advocates of current value accounting propose several methods for determining the valuation of assets to approximate current values. Two of the methods proposed are replacement cost and present value of future cash flows.

Instructions

Describe each method cited above and discuss the pros and cons of the various procedures used to arrive at the valuation of each method.

Part 2.   The financial statements of a business entity could be prepared on the basis of historical cost or current value. In addition, the basis could be stated in terms of unadjusted dollars or dollars restated for changes in purchasing power. The variations of these two distinct areas are shown in the following matrix:

	Unadjusted Dollars	Dollars Restated for Changes in Purchasing Power
Historical cost	1	2
Current value	3	4

Cell 1 of the matrix represents the traditional method of accounting for transactions; the absolute (unadjusted) amount of dollars given up or received is recorded for the asset or liability obtained (**relationship between resources**). Amounts recorded in the method represented by Cell 1 reflect the original cost of the asset or liability and do not give effect to any change in value of the unit of measure (**standard of comparison**). This method assumes the validity of the accounting concepts of going concern and stable monetary unit. Any gain or loss (including holding and purchasing power gains or losses) resulting from the sale or satisfaction of amounts recorded under this method is deferred in its entirety until sale or satisfaction.

Instructions

For each of the remaining cells (2, 3, and 4), respond to the following questions. *Limit your discussion to nonmonetary assets only.* Complete your discussion of *each cell* before proceeding to the next one.

[a] How will this method of recording assets affect the relationship between resources and the standard of comparison?

[b] What is the theoretical justification for using this method?

[c] How will this method of asset valuation affect the recognition of gain or loss during the life of the asset and ultimately from the sale or abandonment of the asset? Your response should include a discussion of the timing and magnitude of the gain or loss and conceptual reasons for any difference from the gain or loss computed using the traditional method.

(AICPA adapted)

26–53   FAIR VALUE IN FINANCIAL STATEMENTS   As the controller of a highly successful real estate holding company, you are now preparing the financial information needed by the company's bank to facilitate a large loan that would allow the company to acquire additional property and refinance certain current holdings. The bank loan officer has requested that the financial statements of the company measure the real estate holdings at fair value (that is, the amount the assets could be sold for in an orderly liquidation). In this case, fair value clearly exceeds historical cost less accumulated depreciation. Your boss, the president of the company, also wants the real estate valued at its fair value so as to "better communicate the realities and strength of our financial position" and to "avoid presenting old and stale numbers that have no validity or usefulness today to anyone who might use our financial reports."

You wonder whether it would be acceptable to measure the real estate of the company at fair value. It seems that everyone that wishes to use the financial statements wants the real estate measured at its fair value rather than its historical cost.

Instructions

Would it be acceptable to measure the real estate at its fair value in the company's financial statements prepared in conformity with GAAP? If your answer is yes, explain why. If it is no, explain the financial reporting alternatives that are available to the company.

26–54   MARKET VALUATION OF AN INVESTMENT PORTFOLIO   A processor of radioactive materials, Glowing Employees, Inc., has been required to maintain a large portfolio of securities as a surety bond in case of a catastrophic accident. Now the company has finally been able to insure for those risks and the need for the surety bond no longer exists. The company's president has decided to retain the portfolio but to begin trading it actively in an attempt to earn superior returns. A group of individuals has been trained to manage the portfolio and considerable trading has occurred with satisfactory results. The president is anxious to report the results to the shareholders in the company's annual report and has asked the corporate controller whether the portfolio could be valued at market value rather than the lower of cost or market as has been the case in the past. When the controller suggests that generally accepted accounting principles would not allow such a treatment, the president is not happy and states:

> *I just don't understand your position. If we were a broker or dealer trading our own portfolio, or a savings and loan with a trading portfolio, or a number of other businesses, we could value the securities at market and you wouldn't have any objections. [Those industries have specific accounting standards that call for or allow such valuations.] To make you happy, perhaps I will just create a subsidiary to manage the portfolio as a broker or dealer. That would involve a lot of costs, but if that's what it takes I just might do it. Of course, another alternative is to find a controller that isn't so uptight about these highly theoretical aspects of our operations.*

Instructions

Prepare a detailed response that you believe the controller should make to the president. Do you think that the entity's operations in managing the investment portfolio are sufficiently distinct to allow the company to value the portfolio at market without regard to cost?

Appendix: Strawbridge & Clothier 1989 Financial Report

Strawbridge & Clothier
Consolidated Balance Sheets
(in thousands, except number of shares and per share data)

The Company operates 37 retail stores, including department and self-service stores, which sell general merchandise in Philadelphia, the surrounding Delaware Valley area of Southeastern Pennsylvania, Southern New Jersey, and Northern Delaware.

Assets	February 3 1990	January 28 1989
Current Assets		
Cash and equivalents	$ 1,932	$ 3,444
Accounts receivable	163,822	169,093
Allowance for doubtful accounts	(4,000)	(4,000)
	159,822	165,093
Merchandise inventories—Note B	139,149	130,434
Prepaid expenses and other	6,632	6,458
Total Current Assets	307,535	305,429
Property, Fixtures and Equipment—on the basis of cost—Notes C and H		
Land	19,538	19,459
Buildings and improvements	276,064	251,966
Store fixtures, furniture and equipment	181,228	166,383
Allowance for depreciation (deduction)	(184,152)	(163,247)
	292,678	274,561
Construction in progress	8,550	4,776
	301,228	279,337
Other Assets	9,783	8,512
	$618,546	$593,278

1301

Strawbridge & Clothier
Consolidated Balance Sheets
(in thousands, except number of shares and per share data)

Liabilities, Preferred Stock and Common Shareholders' Equity

	February 3 1990	January 28 1989
Current Liabilities		
Notes payable to banks—Note C	$ 12,000	$ 34,000
Accounts payable	65,008	52,959
Accrued expenses	13,015	13,710
Federal, state, and local taxes	14,130	10,172
Deferred income taxes	5,204	7,711
Long-term debt and capital lease obligations due within one year	9,767	7,971
Total Current Liabilities	119,124	126,523
Long-Term Debt—due after one year—Note C	167,188	154,267
Capital Lease Obligations—due after one year—Note H	59,179	63,773
Other Liabilities—principally deferred income taxes	37,256	36,755
Preferred Stock—Note E		
$5 Cumulative Preferred Stock, $100 par value, redeemable at $105 a share: authorized 1989—10,230 shares; outstanding—10,217 shares (1988—11,985 shares outstanding)	1,022	1,199
Series Preferred Stock—no par value: authorized—2,000,000 shares; none issued	–0–	–0–
Common Shareholders' Equity—Notes C and F		
Series A Common Stock—par value $1 a share: authorized—20,000,000 shares; issued 1989—5,427,211 shares, 1988—4,966,551 shares	5,427	4,967
Series B Common Stock—par value $1 a share, convertible: authorized—20,000,000 shares; issued 1989—3,051,428 shares, 1988—2,893,347 shares	3,051	2,893
Capital in addition to par value of shares	118,729	97,106
Earnings retained for use in the business	107,570	105,795
Total Common Shareholders' Equity	234,777	210,761
	$618,546	$593,278

See notes to consolidated financial statements.

Strawbridge & Clothier
Consolidated Statements of Operations
(in thousands, except number of shares and per share data)

The Company operates 37 retail stores, including department and self-service stores, which sell general merchandise in Philadelphia, the surrounding Delaware Valley area of Southeastern Pennsylvania, Southern New Jersey, and Northern Delaware.

	Year Ended		
	February 3 1990 (53 Weeks)	January 28 1989 (52 Weeks)	January 30 1988 (52 Weeks)
Net sales, including leased department sales	$950,306	$904,196	$814,313
Other income, net of other deductions	654	591	852
	950,960	904,787	815,165
Deduct:			
Cost of sales, including occupancy and buying costs—Note B	687,713	660,412	592,309
Selling and administrative expenses, net of finance charges	155,436	150,177	130,499
Depreciation	24,565	21,904	18,812
Interest	25,386	22,112	17,694
Provision for doubtful accounts	4,396	3,443	5,232
Pension cost—Note D	1,738	1,713	1,880
	899,234	859,761	766,426
Earnings Before Income Taxes	51,726	45,026	48,739
Income taxes—Note G	20,567	17,756	21,725
Net Earnings	$ 31,159	$ 27,270	$ 27,014
Earnings per share—Note A	$3.41	$3.02	$3.01
Average shares outstanding—Note A	9,119,330	9,000,529	8,949,638

See notes to consolidated financial statements.

Strawbridge & Clothier
Consolidated Statements of Cash Flows
(in thousands)

	Year Ended		
	February 3 1990 (53 Weeks)	January 28 1989 (52 Weeks)	January 30 1988 (52 Weeks)
Cash Flows from Operating Activities			
Net earnings	$ 31,159	$ 27,270	$ 27,014
Adjustments to reconcile net earnings to cash flows from operating activities:			
Provision for depreciation	24,565	21,904	18,812
Provision for deferred income taxes	(4,061)	(2,991)	(2,067)
Changes in:			
Accounts receivable	5,271	(11,815)	(3,868)
Merchandise inventories	(8,715)	(15,412)	(10,949)
Accounts payable and accrued expenses	11,354	801	8,034
Federal, state, and local taxes	3,958	(4,504)	(916)
Other	1,626	(1,254)	884
Total	65,157	13,999	36,944
Net Cash Used for Investing Activities			
Acquisition of property, fixtures and equipment	(46,813)	(62,107)	(46,857)
Changes in other assets	(439)	(633)	(70)
Total	(47,252)	(62,740)	(46,927)
Net Cash Provided by (used for) Financing Activities			
Additional long-term debt	50,000	31,500	18,500
Payment of long-term debt and capital lease obligations	(39,944)	(8,389)	(7,301)
(Decrease) increase in short-term notes payable	(22,000)	34,000	–0–
Purchase of preferred stock and treasury stock	(253)	(204)	(41)
Proceeds from issuance of common stock	1,670	1,635	1,458
Cash dividends	(8,890)	(8,240)	(6,434)
Total	(19,417)	50,302	6,182
Change in Cash and Equivalents	(1,512)	1,561	(3,801)
Cash and equivalents at beginning of year	3,444	1,883	5,684
Cash and Equivalents at End of Year	$ 1,932	$ 3,444	$ 1,883

See notes to consolidated financial statements.

Strawbridge & Clothier
Consolidated Statements of Common Shareholders' Equity
(in thousands, except number of shares and per share data)

	Year Ended		
	February 3 1990 (53 Weeks)	January 28 1989 (52 Weeks)	January 30 1988 (52 Weeks)
Series A Common Stock—Note F			
Balance at beginning of year	$ 4,967	$ 4,351	$ 3,964
Stock dividend	349	307	279
Converted from Series B	51	282	104
Issued for employee stock purchases and upon exercise of stock options	60	27	4
	5,427	4,967	4,351
Series B Common Stock—Note F			
Balance at beginning of year	2,893	2,970	2,868
Stock dividend	201	205	199
Converted to Series A	(51)	(282)	(104)
Issued upon exercise of stock options	8	–0–	7
	3,051	2,893	2,970
Capital in Addition to Par Value of Shares			
Balance at beginning of year	97,106	79,921	57,588
Stock dividend	19,944	16,526	22,134
Credits related to employee stock purchases and exercise of stock options	1,679	659	199
	118,729	97,106	79,921
Earnings Retained for Use in the Business			
Balance at beginning of year	105,795	103,803	105,835
Net earnings	31,159	27,270	27,014
	136,954	131,073	132,849
Less:			
Stock dividends (seven percent)— Series A shares—1989—349,016; 1988—306,718; 1987—279,191 Series B shares—1989—201,176; 1988—205,707; 1987—199,393	20,494	17,038	22,612
Cash dividends on common shares— Series A per share—1989—$1.02; 1988—$.94; 1987—$.74 Series B per share—1989—$.91; 1988—$.87; 1987—$.66	8,837	8,178	6,365
Cash dividends on Preferred Stock— $5 per share	53	62	69
	29,384	25,278	29,046
	107,570	105,795	103,803
Treasury Stock—deduction—Note F			
Balance at beginning of year	–0–	995	2,333
Issued for employee stock purchase plan— Series A shares—1989—1,933; 1988—42,846; 1987—55,238	(68)	(1,006)	(1,379)
Purchases (at cost)—Series A shares— 1989—1,933; 1988—348; 1987—1,072	68	11	41
Stock dividend—Series A shares—1989—0; 1988—2,779; 1987—6,142	–0–	–0–	–0–
	–0–	–0–	995
Total Common Shareholders' Equity	$234,777	$210,761	$190,050

See notes to consolidated financial statements.

The Company operates 37 retail stores, including department and self-service stores, which sell general merchandise in Philadelphia, the surrounding Delaware Valley area of Southeastern Pennsylvania, Southern New Jersey, and Northern Delaware.

NOTE A—SIGNIFICANT ACCOUNTING POLICIES

Principles of Consolidation: The consolidated financial statements include the accounts of the Company and its wholly-owned real estate subsidiaries. All intercompany transactions have been eliminated.

Inventories: Merchandise inventories are priced at cost on the last-in, first-out method.

Store Preopening Costs: Such costs are charged to expense in the year incurred.

Property, Fixtures and Equipment: Property, fixtures and equipment are recorded at cost, which is depreciated by the straight-line method over the estimated useful lives of the assets. Interest capitalized as part of the cost of assets was: 1989—$213,000; 1988—$1,058,000; 1987—$603,000.

Cash Equivalents: For purposes of the statement of cash flows, the Company considers all highly liquid investments with maturities of three months or less when purchased to be cash equivalents.

Per Share Data: Per share amounts for all periods give effect to the seven percent stock dividend declared March 28, 1990, to be paid May 17, 1990. Earnings per share amounts are based on the weighted average number of shares of common stock and common stock equivalents (employee stock options) outstanding during each fiscal year, after recognition of Preferred Stock dividends.

Income Taxes: The Financial Accounting Standards Board issued Statement No. 96, "Accounting for Income Taxes", in December 1987. The Company is required to adopt the new method of accounting for income taxes no later than fiscal 1992. No determination has been made as to whether the new rules will be applied before 1992 or if prior-year financial statements will be restated to reflect the new rules upon adoption. However, the Company estimates that deferred income tax liabilities would be reduced by approximately $10,000,000 if the Statement were applied at February 3, 1990.

NOTE B—INVENTORIES

If the first-in, first-out method of determining inventory cost had been used, inventories would have been $27,850,000 and $28,200,000 higher than reported at February 3, 1990 and January 28, 1989, respectively.

NOTE C—LONG-TERM DEBT AND SHORT-TERM BORROWINGS

Long-term debt—due after one year consists of the following (in thousands):

	February 3 1990	January 28 1989
8¾% notes due November 15, 1996	$ 50,000	$ 50,000
Series A Senior Notes, maturing in equal annual installments from 1994 to 2004 with interest at 9.2%	30,000	–0–
Series B Senior Notes, due September 30, 1999, with interest at 9.0%	20,000	–0–

Term notes payable, secured by mortgages (8½%, 11⅞%, 12¾% and 14⅜%) due in installments of $6,401 annually, including principal and interest, maturing from 5 to 14 years	25,023	30,206
Mortgage notes payable (8¾% and 8⅞%) at $1,313 annually, including principal and interest, maturing from 9 to 14 years	8,529	9,061
Notes payable to bank under revolving credit agreement with interest at 8.6% at February 3, 1990 and 9.7% at January 28, 1989	20,000	20,000
Senior Notes maturing in equal annual installments from 1990 to 2000 with interest at 11.5%	13,636	15,000
Term note, prepaid in 1989	–0–	30,000
	$167,188	$154,267

Among other things, certain loan agreements require that the Company maintain a ratio of current assets to current liabilities of not less than 1.5.

Certain agreements restrict transactions reducing shareholders' equity and the amount available for such transactions at February 3, 1990 is $43,700,000. Fixed assets with a net book value of $52,673,000 are mortgaged by certain agreements.

Under the revolving credit agreement, the Company may borrow from the bank up to $20,000,000 through October 31, 1992. Borrowings may be made at various interest rate options. The Company pays a commitment fee equal to ¼% per annum on the unused portion of the total commitment.

The Company has unused short-term bank credit lines which are subject to annual confirmation and which aggregated $29,000,000 at February 3, 1990.

There are no compensating balance arrangements in connection with debt or credit lines.

Maturities of long-term debt for the next five fiscal years are as follows: 1990—$5,420,000; 1991—$5,598,000; 1992—$25,698,000; 1993—$6,657,000; 1994—$8,641,000.

Interest paid, net of amounts capitalized, was: 1989—$24,465,000; 1988—$21,852,000; 1987—$17,613,000.

NOTE D—RETIREMENT BENEFITS

The Company provides pension benefits for substantially all regular employees under noncontributory defined benefit pension plans. Benefits are determined based on average compensation or years of service. The Company's funding policy is to contribute amounts consistent with the minimum funding standards of the Employee Retirement Income Security Act of 1974.

Net pension cost included the following components (in thousands):

	1989	1988	1987
Service cost—benefits earned during the period	$ 1,636	$ 1,455	$ 1,754
Interest cost on projected benefit obligation	5,356	4,944	4,472
Actual return on plan assets	(10,072)	(8,260)	(1,029)
Net amortization and deferral	4,818	3,574	(3,317)
Net pension cost	$ 1,738	$ 1,713	$ 1,880

The expected long-term rate of return on plan assets used in determining net pension cost was 9.25 percent for 1989 and 1988 and 8.5 percent for 1987.

The following table sets forth the funded status and amounts recognized in the Company's consolidated balance sheets for the Strawbridge & Clothier Employees Retirement Benefit Plan (in thousands):

	1989	1988
Actuarial present value of benefit obligations:		
Vested	$45,614	$41,126
Accumulated	$47,317	$42,662
Projected	$61,167	$54,665
Plan assets at fair value, primarily common equity funds	67,222	60,472
Plan assets in excess of projected benefit obligation	6,055	5,807
Items not yet recognized:		
Net gain	(6,441)	(4,762)
Net obligation at transition	618	675
Unrecognized prior service cost	378	411
Prepaid pension cost included in consolidated balance sheets	$ 610	$ 2,131

The following assumptions were used in determining the actuarial present value of the projected benefit obligation:

	1989	1988
Weighted average discount rate	8.5%	9%
Rate of increase in compensation levels	7%	7%

The Company also sponsors an unfunded Deferred Compensation Plan, which is a non-qualified plan that provides retirement benefits for certain key executive officers. At December 31, 1989, the projected benefit obligation for this plan, which is included in other liabilities in the accompanying balance sheet, totalled $5,869,000.

The Company pays medical insurance premiums on behalf of pensioners. These benefits are accounted for as the costs are paid. The expense for such benefits was: 1989—$2,862,000; 1988—$1,847,000; 1987—$1,329,000.

NOTE E—PREFERRED STOCK

The Preferred Stock ($100 par value) provides for $5 cumulative dividends and redemption at $105 per share (1989—$1,073,000; 1988—$1,258,000). Sinking fund provisions require that on April 1 of each year, the Company shall redeem shares of at least $179,900 in par value. Par value of shares redeemed and retired was as follows: 1989—$180,900; 1988—$179,900; 1987—$216,200. Outstanding shares at fiscal year ends were: 1989—10,217; 1988—11,985; 1987—13,838.

NOTE F—COMMON STOCK

Series A and Series B shares are entitled to one and ten votes per share, respectively. Series B shares are convertible on a share-for-share basis into Series A shares. Series A shares are freely transferable while Series B shares are only transferable to certain permitted transferees. Series A Common Stock is entitled to cash dividends at least 10% higher than any cash dividend declared on Series B Common Stock.

The Company has an Employee Stock Purchase Plan whereby the Company has offered an aggregate of 580,000 shares of Series A Common Stock to employees for purchase through payroll deductions. The purchase price is to be 85% of the closing market price on the offering date or the purchase date, whichever is lower. As of February 3,

1990, 126,852 shares of Series A Common Stock were available for use under the Plan. 58,943, 68,677 and 55,238 shares were issued under the Plan at average prices of $28.11, $23.80 and $25.20 during fiscal 1989, 1988, and 1987, respectively.

The Company also has a Stock Option Plan, which provides for granting to key employees qualified and nonqualified options to purchase a maximum of 447,927 shares of the stock of the Company. Options granted generally are for a term of ten years and become exercisable 180 days after the date of grant. 11,540, 1,274 and 10,032 shares were issued upon exercise of options at average prices of $25.73, $27.76, and $30.65 during fiscal 1989, 1988, and 1987, respectively. Options to purchase 149,694 shares of Series A Common Stock and 169,407 shares of Series B Common Stock at an average exercise price of $27.36 were outstanding at February 3, 1990, of which 148,194 and 169,407 options, respectively, were exercisable.

NOTE G—INCOME TAXES

Income tax expense consists of the following components (in thousands):

	Fiscal Year		
	1989	1988	1987
Current:			
Federal	$19,370	$16,182	$19,193
State	5,258	4,565	4,599
	24,628	20,747	23,792
Deferred:			
Federal	(3,184)	(2,159)	(1,603)
State	(877)	(832)	(464)
	(4,061)	(2,991)	(2,067)
	$20,567	$17,756	$21,725

The components of deferred income tax expense are as follows (in thousands):

	Fiscal Year		
	1989	1988	1987
Installment sales	($4,999)	($3,831)	($2,806)
Depreciation	2,484	2,210	1,100
Other	(1,546)	(1,370)	(361)
	($4,061)	($2,991)	($2,067)

A reconciliation of the effective income tax rate with the statutory federal income tax rate is as follows:

	Fiscal Year		
	1989	1988	1987
Federal tax rate	34.0%	34.0%	39.0%
State taxes, net of federal tax benefit	5.6	5.5	5.2
Other	.2	(.1)	.4
	39.8%	39.4%	44.6%

Income taxes paid were as follows: 1989—$20,728,000; 1988—$23,981,000; 1987—$25,502,000.

NOTE H—COMMITMENTS

Leases:

Capital lease assets, which are included in property, fixtures and equipment, are as follows (in thousands):

	February 3 1990	January 28 1989
Land	$ 2,926	$ 2,926
Buildings	73,723	73,723
Store fixtures and equipment	10,102	11,102
Allowance for amortization (deduction)	(29,827)	(26,816)
	$56,924	$60,935

Amortization of capital lease assets is included in depreciation expense.

Future minimum rental commitments as of February 3, 1990, for all noncancelable leases are as follows (in thousands):

Fiscal Year	Capital Leases*	Operating Leases*
1990	$ 10,238	$ 3,916
1991	9,982	3,021
1992	8,894	2,653
1993	8,040	2,613
1994	7,770	2,621
Thereafter	71,915	27,769
Total minimum rental commitments	116,839	$42,593
Estimated executory costs	(1,668)	
Imputed interest	(51,645)	
Present value of net minimum lease payments	$ 63,526	

*These amounts have not been reduced by future noncancelable sublease rentals of $3,457.

During 1988, the Company incurred a capital lease obligation of $4,814,000 for equipment. During 1987, the Company incurred a capital lease obligation of $7,386,000 in connection with a lease agreement for additional space within an existing distribution facility.

All real estate leases include renewal options for periods ranging from 5 to 100 years. Most of these leases include options to purchase at specified times. In most instances, the Company pays real estate taxes, insurance, and maintenance costs. There are no guarantees, related obligations, or restrictions in connection with the lease agreements.

Total net rental expense amounted to (in thousands):

	Fiscal Year		
	1989	1988	1987
Minimum rentals	$ 4,158	$ 4,261	$ 3,420
Contingent rentals, based on sales	1,307	1,174	1,072
Sublease rentals	(1,377)	(1,206)	(788)
	$ 4,088	$ 4,229	$ 3,704

Other:

Cost to complete construction in progress at February 3, 1990 is approximately $12,300,000.

Report of Ernst & Young Independent Auditors

To the Shareholders of Strawbridge & Clothier

We have audited the accompanying consolidated balance sheets of Strawbridge & Clothier and subsidiaries as of February 3, 1990 and January 28, 1989, and the related consolidated statements of operations, common shareholders' equity, and cash flows for each of the three fiscal years in the period ended February 3, 1990. These financial statements are the responsibility of the Company's management. Our responsibility is to express an opinion on these financial statements based on our audits.

We conducted our audits in accordance with generally accepted auditing standards. Those standards require that we plan and perform the audit to obtain reasonable assurance about whether the financial statements are free of material misstatement. An audit includes examining, on a test basis, evidence supporting the amounts and disclosures in the financial statements. An audit also includes assessing the accounting principles used and significant estimates made by management, as well as evaluating the overall financial statement presentation. We believe that our audits provide a reasonable basis for our opinion.

In our opinion, the financial statements referred to above present fairly, in all material respects, the consolidated financial position of Strawbridge & Clothier and subsidiaries at February 3, 1990 and January 28, 1989, and the consolidated results of their operations and their cash flows for each of the three fiscal years in the period ended February 3, 1990, in conformity with generally accepted accounting principles.

Philadelphia, Pennsylvania
March 28, 1990

Ernst & Young

Annual Meeting

The Annual Meeting of shareholders will be held on Wednesday, May 30, 1990, at 10:30 AM in the auditorium on the eighth floor of the Company's Main Store at 801 Market Street, Philadelphia, PA. All shareholders are cordially invited to attend.

Corporate Headquarters
801 Market Street
Philadelphia, PA 19107-3199
Phone (215) 629-6000

Independent Auditors
Ernst & Young

General Counsel
Morgan, Lewis & Bockius

Transfer Agents

For the Common Stock:
Mellon Securities Trust Company
% Mellon Securities Transfer Services
One Executive Drive
Fort Lee, NJ 07024

For the Preferred Stock:
Mellon Bank (East) N.A.
P.O. Box 444
Pittsburgh, PA 15230

Financial Summary—the Decade of the 1980's
(amounts in thousands, except per share data)

Net Sales (In Millions)

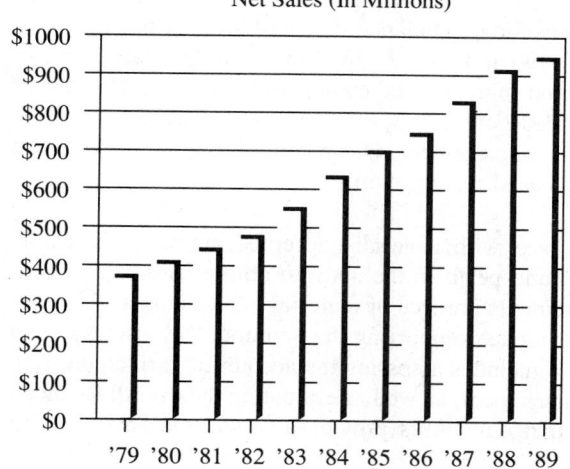

Net Earnings (In Millions)

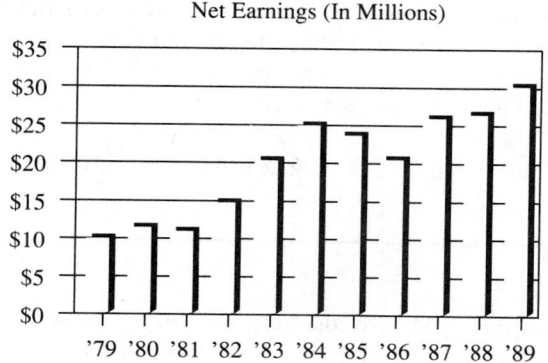

Cash Dividend Payout

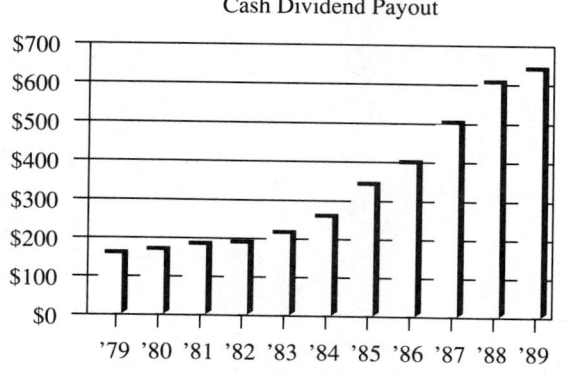

A shareholder owning 100 shares of Strawbridge & Clothier common stock during 1979 would have received $145 in cash dividends. The chart depicts the annual increase in cash dividends on the initial 100 share investment, augmented by stock dividends, a stock split, a stock distribution, and increases in cash dividends, culminating in cash dividends in 1989 of $631.

	1989[1]	1988
OPERATING RESULTS		
Net Sales	$950,306	$904,196
Cost of Sales	687,713	660,412
Interest Expense	25,386	22,112
Earnings Before Income Taxes	51,726	45,026
Income Taxes	20,567	17,756
Net Earnings	31,159	27,270
OTHER OPERATING DATA		
Depreciation	$ 24,565	$ 21,904
Rent	4,088	4,229
Taxes Other Than Income Taxes	23,777	21,965
Cash Dividends:		
Preferred Stock	53	62
Common Stock	8,837	8,178
Stock Dividends on Common Stock	7%	7%
PER SHARE OF COMMON STOCK[2]		
Net Earnings	$ 3.41	$ 3.02
Cash Dividends on Series A Common Stock	1.02	.94
Cash Dividends on Series B Common Stock	.91	.87
Cash Dividends on Common Stock	—	—
Book Value	25.88	23.42
FINANCIAL DATA		
Working Capital	$188,411	$178,906
Property, Fixtures & Equipment—Net	301,228	279,337
Total Assets	618,546	593,278
Long-Term Debt	167,188	154,267
Capital Lease Obligations	59,179	63,773
Redeemable Preferred Stock	1,022	1,199
Common Shareholders' Equity	234,777	210,761
Number of Common Shares Outstanding	8,478	7,860
Square Feet of Store Space	5,591	5,487

Financial Summary—the Decade of the 1980's
(amounts in thousands, except per share data)

1987	1986	1985	1984[1]	1983	1982	1981	1980	1979
$814,313	$739,117	$686,929	$630,497	$545,490	$471,933	$425,606	$390,174	$367,227
592,309	536,932	494,936	452,954	388,869	340,125	307,497	280,181	264,307
17,694	17,066	18,258	15,114	11,523	10,605	8,484	6,955	7,659
48,739	41,734	46,755	49,286	41,463	25,988	22,503	24,841	20,228
21,725	21,042	22,669	24,611	20,606	11,892	10,414	11,990	9,500
27,014	20,692	24,086	24,675	20,857	14,096	12,089	12,851	10,728
$ 18,812	$ 16,911	$ 14,815	$ 13,396	$ 12,446	$ 10,911	$ 8,979	$ 8,106	$ 7,487
3,704	3,183	2,596	2,254	2,056	1,936	1,834	1,905	1,828
20,581	18,896	17,691	16,818	15,172	13,062	12,157	10,436	9,749
69	70	72	77	78	81	92	112	123
6,365	5,631	4,662	4,106	3,379	2,935	2,808	2,711	2,608
7%	7%	7%	7%	7%	5%	7%	5%	5%
$ 3.01	$ 2.31	$ 2.74	$ 2.36	$ 1.89	$ 1.28	$ 1.08	$ 1.12	$ .93
.74	.36	—	—	—	—	—	—	—
.66	.32	—	—	—	—	—	—	—
—	.30	.53	.39	.31	.28	.26	.24	.22
21.31	19.00	17.26	15.02	14.43	12.89	11.94	10.86	9.96
$186,028	$165,418	$148,973	$126,201	$112,782	$ 87,523	$ 95,976	$ 80,695	$ 79,065
233,508	197,801	188,468	184,922	177,577	172,883	151,254	127,376	123,842
518,289	472,639	454,811	430,633	391,283	347,413	310,670	267,575	255,073
128,685	115,271	105,790	101,032	54,119	45,102	46,235	27,383	36,408
63,351	58,780	61,565	65,551	70,805	65,486	62,346	47,554	44,567
1,384	1,384	1,431	1,444	1,558	1,599	1,640	2,203	2,372
190,050	167,922	151,504	130,982	159,734	141,544	130,107	122,904	112,984
7,281	6,744	6,259	3,873	2,298	2,130	2,013	1,955	1,867
5,088	5,088	5,007	4,922	4,893	4,790	4,435	4,267	4,267

[1] 53-week fiscal year.
[2] Shares used adjusted to give effect to 2-for-1 stock split distributed May 14, 1984, 3-for-2 stock distribution paid May 16, 1985 and stock dividends on Common Stock including dividend declared March 28, 1990 to be paid May 17, 1990. Weighted average shares outstanding as adjusted were: 1989—9,119,330; 1988—9,000,529; 1987—8,949,638; 1986—8,917,074; 1985—8,756,904; 1984—10,420,623; 1983—11,016,782; 1982—10,908,074; 1981—11,077,155; 1980—11,350,757; 1979—11,444,635. Net earnings give effect to dividend requirements of the preferred stock.

Quarterly Results of Operations

The following is a summary of quarterly results of operations for the 1989 and 1988 fiscal years. Earnings per share give effect to the 7% stock dividend on Series A and Series B Common Stock declared on March 28, 1990 to be paid May 17, 1990.

Fiscal Quarter	Net Sales 1989	Net Sales 1988	Gross Profit 1989	Gross Profit 1988	Net Earnings 1989	Net Earnings 1988	Net Earnings Per Common Share 1989	Net Earnings Per Common Share 1988
			(amounts in thousands, except per share data)					
First	$190,530	$182,892	$48,720	$47,601	$ 1,559	$ 2,099	$ .17	$ .23
Second ...	202,171	192,930	50,423	46,585	1,735	611	.19	.07
Third	206,727	205,724	56,212	57,100	2,239	3,608	.24	.40
Fourth ...	350,878	322,650	107,238	92,498	25,626	20,952	2.81	2.32

Market and Dividend Information

The Company's Series A Common Stock is traded on the over-the-counter market. There is no trading market for Series B Common Stock but it is readily convertible at any time into Series A Common Stock on a share-for-share basis. The number of shareholders of record as of January 2, 1990, was 4,885 for Series A and 266 for Series B. The following table indicates the range of high and low price quotations for the Series A Common Stock by quarter during the last two fiscal years. This information was obtained through NASDAQ. Cash dividends paid by quarter are adjusted for the 7% stock dividend declared on March 28, 1990 to be paid on May 17, 1990.

Fiscal Quarter	Range of High and Low Price Quotations 1989		Range of High and Low Price Quotations 1988		Cash Dividends Per Share Series A 1989	Cash Dividends Per Share Series A 1988	Cash Dividends Per Share Series B 1989	Cash Dividends Per Share Series B 1988
First	$34⅛	$39¾	$28	$36½	$.24	$.22	$.22	$.21
Second	35	40¼	31½	35¼	.26	.24	.23	.22
Third	36	40	32¼	34¾	.26	.24	.23	.22
Fourth	31½	37½	30½	35¼	.26	.24	.23	.22

APPENDIX: MANAGEMENT'S DISCUSSION AND ANALYSIS OF FINANCIAL CONDITION AND RESULTS OF OPERATIONS

OPERATIONS

Sales for fiscal 1989 were $950,306,000, an increase of 5.1% over the prior year. The opening of a new Clover store in November 1989, a full year of sales from three stores opened in 1988 and an extra week of sales in this 53-week fiscal year were primarily responsible for the increase in sales. Sales in 1988 were 11.0% over 1987, largely due to impressive sales volume from three new stores. Retail price increases were relatively minor during the three-year period.

Net earnings for fiscal 1989 of $31,159,000 were 14.3% above 1988 earnings of $27,270,000 and 15.3% above 1987 earnings of $27,014,000. The record results in 1989 were primarily due to the increase in sales volume, a favorable LIFO adjustment, continued expense control efforts, reduced preopening expenses and careful control of inventory levels during the year. Earnings for 1988 were 1.0% over 1987 earnings. The positive effects of reduced bad debts and a lower federal income tax rate during 1988 when compared with 1987, were offset by higher inflationary cost increases reflected by the LIFO method of accounting for inventories and cost of sales, significant expenses incurred in opening three stores and closing one, and higher interest expense.

Cost of sales, including occupancy and buying costs, was 72.4% of sales in 1989, compared to 73.0% in 1988 and 72.7% in 1987. The decrease in 1989 from 1988 and 1987 is largely attributable to a LIFO benefit of $356,000 in 1989 compared with a $4,278,000 charge in 1988. Also contributing to the improvement in gross margin was a strong emphasis on inventory control which resulted in reduced markdowns. Selling and administrative expenses, net of finance charges, were 16.4% of sales in 1989, compared to 16.6% in 1988 and 16.0% in 1987. Tight control of operating expenses, planned reductions in advertising expenditures and reduced preopening expenses contributed to the decrease in 1989 from 1988. 1988 selling and administrative expenses increased from 1987 due to preopening costs associated with the opening of three new stores and increased selling costs. The increase in depreciation expense to 2.6% of sales in 1989 from 2.4% in 1988 and 2.3% in 1987 is the result of a full year of depreciation for stores opened in 1988. Interest expense was 2.7% of sales in 1989 compared with 2.4% in 1988 and 2.2% in 1987. The increases in 1989 and 1988 reflect higher borrowings as a result of new store openings and higher interest rates. The provision for doubtful accounts increased by $953,000 in 1989 compared to 1988. The 1988 expense reflected the positive effects of an automated credit system installed in February 1986 which helped to reduce risks involved in the credit authorization process. The effective tax rates in 1989 and 1988 were less than 1987 mainly as a result of the reduced federal income tax rate.

FINANCIAL CONDITION

Cash provided by operating activities for 1989 was $65.2 million compared to $14.0 million in 1988. This increase is attributable in part to decreased accounts receivable levels resulting from a reduction in the percentage of sales charged to the Company's credit card as well as improved collections on outstanding balances. Careful control of inventory levels and higher earnings also contributed to the increase. Cash provided by operating activities for 1988 reflected unusually large cash expenditures to stock merchandise inventories in three new stores and increased accounts receivable as a result of increased credit sales.

The Company's capital expenditures in fiscal 1989 were $46.8 million, which includes costs of our new Shore Mall Clover store, the first phase of the expansion and renovation of our Cherry Hill department store and the renovation of our Cinnaminson and Bucks Mall Clover stores. The expenditures were financed through cash flows from operating activities.

In 1988, $50.3 million was provided by financing activities, primarily from borrowings to finance new store openings. Cash used for financing activities was $19.4 million during 1989. On September 14, 1989, the Company borrowed $30.0 million at 9.2%, maturing in equal annual installments from 1994 to 2004, and $20.0 million at 9.0% due September 30, 1999. The proceeds were used to pay off a $30.0 million Term Loan due June 7, 1990 and to reduce short-term borrowings. On November 1, 1989, the Company renewed its $20.0 million Revolving Credit Agreement for three years. The Company has $40.0 million in confirmed bank credit lines. At February 3, 1990, $11.0 million of these lines were in use, in addition to $1.0 million of unconfirmed lines. Long-term debt and capital lease obligations were 49.0% of capitalization at the end of 1989, compared to 50.7% at the end of the prior year.

Anticipated capital expenditures for 1990 of $39.0 million include the final phase of the expansion and renovation of our Cherry Hill department store, the renovation of our Cottman Avenue Clover store and the opening of a new Clover store in the Kirkwood

Plaza, New Castle County, Delaware. An additional $41.0 million is planned for capital expenditures in 1991, including the expansion of our ready to wear merchandise handling facility, the renovation of two Clover stores and the opening of two new Clover stores. The funding for these capital expenditures is expected to be generated from operations and through additional long-term financing. The Company continually investigates potential sites for new stores, and capital expenditure plans may change as opportunities for new stores develop.

The Company believes its relations with banks and other credit sources are good and that it has considerable flexibility in deciding how to fund future capital expenditures and maturities of long-term debt.

Index of Financial Statement Excerpts

Index